D1573367

McGraw Hill's

Taxation of Individuals and Business Entities

Brian C. Spilker
Brigham Young University
Editor

Benjamin C. Ayers
The University of Georgia

Troy K. Lewis
Brigham Young University

Connie D. Weaver
Texas A&M University

John A. Barrick
Brigham Young University

John R. Robinson
Texas A&M University

Ron G. Worsham
Brigham Young University

Mc Graw Hill

McGRAW HILL'S TAXATION OF INDIVIDUALS AND BUSINESS ENTITIES, 2023 EDITION, FOURTEENTH EDITION

Published by McGraw Hill LLC, 1325 Avenue of the Americas, New York, NY 10019. Copyright ©2023 by McGraw Hill LLC. All rights reserved. Printed in the United States of America. Previous editions ©2022, 2021, and 2020. No part of this publication may be reproduced or distributed in any form or by any means, or stored in a database or retrieval system, without the prior written consent of McGraw Hill LLC, including, but not limited to, in any network or other electronic storage or transmission, or broadcast for distance learning.

Some ancillaries, including electronic and print components, may not be available to customers outside the United States.

This book is printed on acid-free paper.

1 2 3 4 5 6 7 8 9 LWI 26 25 24 23 22

ISBN 978-1-265-79029-5 (bound edition)
MHID 1-265-79029-9 (bound edition)
ISBN 978-1-265-61066-1 (loose-leaf edition)
MHID 1-265-61066-5 (loose-leaf edition)
ISSN 1946-7745

Executive Portfolio Manager: *Kathleen Klehr*
Product Developers: *Sarah Wood, Katie Ward*
Marketing Manager: *Clare McLemore*
Content Project Managers: *Jill Eccher, Brian Nacik*
Buyer: *Susan K. Culbertson*
Designer: *Beth Blech*
Content Licensing Specialist: *Melissa Homer*
Cover Image: *Joseph De Sciose/Pixtal/age fotostock*
Compositor: *Aptara®, Inc.*

All credits appearing on page or at the end of the book are considered to be an extension of the copyright page.

The Internet addresses listed in the text were accurate at the time of publication. The inclusion of a website does not indicate an endorsement by the authors or McGraw Hill LLC, and McGraw Hill LLC does not guarantee the accuracy of the information presented at these sites.

mheducation.com/highered

Dedications

We dedicate this book to:

My family and to Professor Dave Stewart for his great example and friendship.

Brian Spilker

My wife Marilyn, daughters Margaret Lindley and Georgia, son Benjamin, and parents Bill and Linda.

Ben Ayers

My wife Jill and my children Annika, Corinne, Lina, Mitch, and Connor.

John Barrick

My wife Mindy; sons Tyler, Braden, and Connor; and parents Kent and Wendy.

Troy Lewis

JES, Tommy, and Laura.

John Robinson

My family: Dan, Travis, Alix, Alan, Anna, and Avery.

Connie Weaver

My wife Anne, sons Matthew and Daniel, and daughters Whitney and Hayley.

Ron Worsham

About the Authors

Brian C. Spilker (PhD, University of Texas at Austin, 1993) is the Robert Call/Deloitte Professor in the School of Accountancy at Brigham Young University. He teaches taxation at Brigham Young University. He received both BS (Summa Cum Laude) and MAcc (tax emphasis) degrees from Brigham Young University before working as a tax consultant for Arthur Young & Co. (now Ernst & Young). After his professional work experience, Brian earned his PhD at the University of Texas at Austin. He received the Price Waterhouse Fellowship in Tax Award and the American Taxation Association and Arthur Andersen Teaching Innovation Award for his work in the classroom. Brian has also been awarded for his use of technology in the classroom at Brigham Young University. Brian researches issues relating to tax information search and professional tax judgment. His research has been published in journals such as *The Accounting Review, Organizational Behavior and Human Decision Processes, Journal of the American Taxation Association, Behavioral Research in Accounting, Issues in Accounting Education, Accounting Horizons, Journal of Accounting Education, Journal of Corporate Taxation, Journal of Accountancy,* and *The Tax Adviser*.

Courtesy of Brian Spilker

Ben Ayers (PhD, University of Texas at Austin, 1996) holds the Earl Davis Chair in Taxation and is the dean of the Terry College of Business at the University of Georgia. He received a PhD from the University of Texas at Austin and an MTA and BS from the University of Alabama. Prior to entering the PhD program at the University of Texas, Ben was a tax manager at KPMG in Tampa, Florida, and a contract manager with Complete Health, Inc., in Birmingham, Alabama. He is the recipient of 11 teaching awards at the school, college, and university levels, including the Richard B. Russell Undergraduate Teaching Award, the highest teaching honor for University of Georgia junior faculty members. His research interests include the effects of taxation on firm structure, mergers and acquisitions, and capital markets and the effects of accounting information on security returns. He has published articles in journals such as *The Accounting Review, Journal of Finance, Journal of Accounting and Economics, Contemporary Accounting Research, Review of Accounting Studies, Journal of Law and Economics, Journal of the American Taxation Association,* and *National Tax Journal*. Ben was the 1997 recipient of the American Accounting Association's Competitive Manuscript Award, the 2003 and 2008 recipient of the American Taxation Association's Outstanding Manuscript Award, and the 2016 recipient of the American Taxation Association's Ray M. Sommerfeld Outstanding Tax Educator Award.

Courtesy of Ben Ayers

John Barrick (PhD, University of Nebraska at Lincoln, 1998) is currently an associate professor in the Marriott School at Brigham Young University. He served as an accountant at the U.S. Congress Joint Committee on Taxation during the 110th and 111th Congresses. He teaches taxation in the graduate and undergraduate programs at Brigham Young University. He received both BS and MAcc (tax emphasis) degrees from Brigham Young University before working as a tax consultant for Price Waterhouse (now PricewaterhouseCoopers). After his professional work experience, John earned his PhD at the University of Nebraska at Lincoln. He was the 1998 recipient of the American Accounting Association, Accounting, Behavior, and Organization Section's Outstanding Dissertation Award. John researches issues relating to tax corporate political activity. His research has been published in journals such as *Organizational Behavior and Human Decision Processes, Contemporary Accounting Research,* and *Journal of the American Taxation Association*.

Courtesy of John Barrick

Courtesy of Troy K Lewis

Troy K. Lewis (CPA, CGMA, MAcc, Brigham Young University, 1995) is an associate teaching professor in the School of Accountancy at Brigham Young University—Marriott School of Business. He teaches graduate and undergraduate courses in introductory taxation, property transactions, pass-through entity taxation, advanced individual taxation, and accounting for income taxes. He is the past chair of the Tax Executive Committee of the American Institute of CPAs (AICPA) in Washington, D.C., as well as the president of the Utah Association of CPAs (UACPA). He has testified six times before the U.S. Senate Finance Committee and the House Committee on Small Business. Prior to joining the faculty at BYU, he was a tax manager at Arthur Andersen and KPMG in Salt Lake City, Utah. In addition, he was employed for over a decade as the CERMO and Tax Director of Heritage Bank in St. George, Utah. He is the recipient of the AICPA Tax Section Distinguished Service Award, the BYU Marriott Ethics Teaching Award, and the UACPA Distinguished Service Award. Troy researches and publishes in professional tax journals in the areas of individual and pass-through taxation, qualified business income deduction, and property transactions as well as professional tax practice standards. His work has been published in journals such as *Practical Tax Strategies, Journal of Accountancy, Issues in Accounting Education,* and *The Tax Adviser.*

Courtesy of John Robinson

John Robinson (PhD, University of Michigan, 1981) is the Patricia '77 and Grant E. Sims '77 Eminent Scholar Chair in Business. Prior to joining the faculty at Texas A&M, John was the C. Aubrey Smith Professor of Accounting at the University of Texas at Austin, Texas, and he taught at the University of Kansas, where he was the Arthur Young Faculty Scholar. In 2009–2010 John served as the Academic Fellow in the Division of Corporation Finance at the Securities and Exchange Commission. He has been the recipient of the Henry A. Bubb Award for outstanding teaching, the Texas Blazer's Faculty Excellence Award, and the MPA Council Outstanding Professor Award. John also received the 2012 Outstanding Service Award from the American Taxation Association (ATA) and in 2017 was named the Ernst & Young and ATA Ray Sommerfeld Outstanding Educator. John served as the 2015–2016 president of the ATA. John conducts research in a broad variety of topics involving financial accounting, mergers and acquisitions, and the influence of taxes on financial structures and performance. His scholarly articles have appeared in *The Accounting Review, The Journal of Accounting and Economics, Journal of Finance, National Tax Journal, Journal of Law and Economics, Journal of the American Taxation Association, The Journal of the American Bar Association,* and *The Journal of Taxation.* John's research was honored with the 2003 and 2008 ATA Outstanding Manuscript Awards. In addition, John was the editor of *The Journal of the American Taxation Association* from 2002–2005. Professor Robinson received his JD (*Cum Laude*) from the University of Michigan in 1979, and he teaches courses on individual and corporate taxation and advanced accounting.

Courtesy of Connie Weaver

Connie Weaver (PhD, Arizona State University, 1997) is the KPMG Professor of Accounting at Texas A&M University. She received a PhD from Arizona State University, an MPA from the University of Texas at Arlington, and a BS (chemical engineering) from the University of Texas at Austin. Prior to entering the PhD program, Connie was a tax manager at Ernst & Young in Dallas, Texas, where she became licensed to practice as a CPA. She teaches taxation in the Professional Program in Accounting and the Executive MBA program at Texas A&M University. She has also taught undergraduate and graduate students at the University of Wisconsin–Madison and the University of Texas at Austin. She is the recipient of several teaching awards, including the American Taxation Association/Deloitte Teaching Innovations award, the David and Denise Baggett Teaching award, and the college and university level Association of Former Students Distinguished Achievement award in teaching. Connie's current research interests include the effects of tax and financial incentives on corporate decisions and reporting. She has published articles in journals such as *The Accounting Review, Contemporary Accounting Research, Journal of the American Taxation Association, National Tax Journal, Accounting Horizons, Journal of Corporate Finance,* and *Tax Notes*. Connie is an editor of *The Accounting Review* and has served as the senior editor of *The Journal of the American Taxation Association* and on the editorial board of *Contemporary Accounting Research.*

Ron Worsham (PhD, University of Florida, 1994) is an associate professor in the School of Accountancy at Brigham Young University. He teaches taxation in the graduate program at Brigham Young University. He has also taught as a visiting professor at the University of Chicago. He received both BS and MAcc (tax emphasis) degrees from Brigham Young University before working as a tax consultant for Arthur Young & Co. (now Ernst & Young) in Dallas, Texas. While in Texas, he became licensed to practice as a CPA. After his professional work experience, Ron earned his PhD at the University of Florida. He has been honored for outstanding innovation in the classroom at Brigham Young University. Ron has published academic research in the areas of taxpayer compliance and professional tax judgment. He has also published legal research in a variety of areas. His work has been published in journals such as *Journal of the American Taxation Association, The Journal of International Taxation, The Tax Executive, Tax Notes, The Journal of Accountancy,* and *Practical Tax Strategies.*

Courtesy of Ron Worsham

In Memoriam

On May 20, 2019, we lost one of our beloved authors, Edmund (Ed) Outslay, aged 67. During his tenure at Michigan State University from 1980 to 2019, Ed was known as a passionate academic, impactful mentor, and devoted community volunteer.

Over the course of his long and distinguished career, Ed gathered a remarkable list of accomplishments. He coauthored three tax textbooks, testified before the U.S. Senate Finance Committee, and presented to the Treasury, the IRS, and the Office of Tax Analysis. He won numerous awards from the Eli Broad College of Business at MSU, including the Distinguished Faculty Award, the Presidential Award for Outstanding Community Service, the Withrow Teacher-Scholar Award, and the Curricular Service-Learning and Civic Engagement Award, in addition to numerous departmental teaching and research awards.

Ed enjoyed volunteering his time and was involved in many community programs, such as Lansing's Meals on Wheels program and MSU's Volunteer Income Tax Assistance (VITA) program. He was also an assistant baseball coach at East Lansing High School.

Ed was an avid reader and enjoyed visiting baseball parks and the zoo; he enjoyed coaching baseball and celebrating Halloween.

He earned his bachelor's degree from Furman University in Greenville, South Carolina, and his MBA and PhD from the University of Michigan.

Ed's guidance, energy, and contributions will be deeply missed.

Courtesy Ed Outslay

TEACHING THE CODE IN CONTEXT

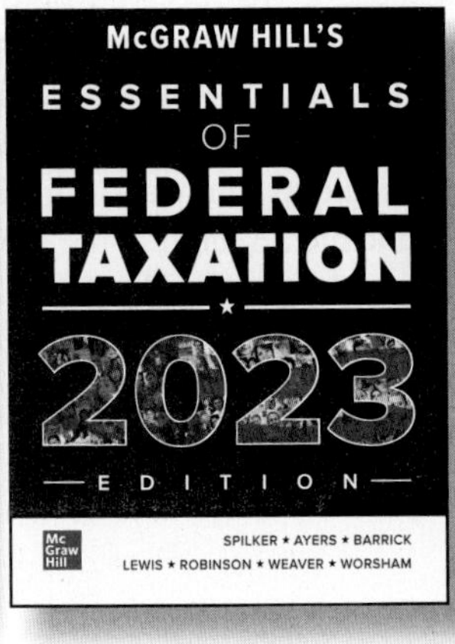

The bold, innovative approach used by McGraw Hill's Taxation *series has become the most popular choice of course materials among instructors and students—a remarkable achievement in just over 10 years since first publishing. It's apparent why the clear, organized, and engaging delivery of content, paired with the most current and robust tax code updates, has been adopted by more than 650 schools across the country.*

McGraw Hill's Taxation is designed to provide a unique, innovative, and engaging learning experience for students studying taxation. The breadth of the topical coverage, **the storyline approach to presenting the material,** the emphasis on the tax and nontax consequences of multiple parties involved in transactions, and the integration of financial and tax accounting topics make this book ideal for the modern tax curriculum.

"Do you want the best tax text? This is the one to use. It has a storyline in each chapter that can relate to real life issues."

Leslie A. Mostow
– University of Maryland—College Park

"This text provides broad coverage of important topics and does so in a manner that is easy for students to understand. The material is very accessible for students."

Kyle Post
–Tarleton State University

Since the first manuscript was written in 2005, 450 professors have contributed 500 book reviews, in addition to 30 focus groups and symposia. Throughout this preface, their comments on the book's organization, pedagogy, and unique features are a testament to the **market-driven nature of *Taxation*'s development.**

"I think this is the best book available for introductory and intermediate courses in taxation."

Shane Stinson
– University of Alabama

A MODERN APPROACH FOR TODAY'S STUDENT

McGraw Hill's Taxation series was built around the following five core precepts:

1. **Storyline Approach:** Each chapter begins with a storyline that introduces a set of characters or a business entity facing specific tax-related situations. Each chapter's examples are related to the storyline, providing students with opportunities to **learn the code in context.**

2. **Integrated Examples:** In addition to providing examples in context, we provide **"What if"** scenarios within many examples to **illustrate how variations in the facts might or might not change the answers.**

3. **Conversational Writing Style:** The authors took special care to write *McGraw Hill's Taxation* in a way that fosters a friendly dialogue between the content and each individual student. The tone of the presentation is intentionally conversational—creating the impression of ***speaking with* the student,** as opposed to *lecturing to* the student.

4. **Superior Organization of Related Topics:** *McGraw Hill's Taxation* provides two alternative topic sequences. In the *McGraw Hill's Taxation of Individuals and Business Entities* volume, the individual topics generally follow the tax form sequence, with an individual overview chapter and then chapters on income, deductions, investment-related issues, and the tax liability computation. The topics then transition into business-related topics that apply to individuals. This volume then provides a group of specialty chapters dealing with topics of particular interest to individuals (including students), including separate chapters on home ownership, compensation, and retirement savings and deferred compensation. Alternatively, in the *Essentials of Federal Taxation* volume, the topics follow a more traditional sequence, with topics streamlined (no specialty chapters) and presented in more of a life-cycle approach.

5. **Real-World Focus:** Students learn best when they see how concepts are applied in the real world. For that reason, real-world examples and articles are included in **Taxes in the Real World** boxes throughout the book. These vignettes demonstrate current issues in taxation and show the relevance of tax issues in all areas of business.

A STORYLINE APPROACH THAT RESONATES WITH STUDENTS

Michaeljung/Shutterstock

Storyline Summary

Taxpayers:	Bill (he/him/his) and Mercedes (she/her/hers)
Family description:	Bill and Mercedes are married with one daughter, Margaret (she/her/hers), and live in Tampa, Florida.
Employment status:	Bill is an economics professor; Mercedes is a small business owner.
Filing status:	Married, filing jointly
Current situation:	Bill and Mercedes face an IRS audit involving a previous year's interest deductions.

Bill and Mercedes received a notice from the Internal Revenue Service (IRS) that their tax return is under audit for certain interest deductions. As you might expect, they are quite concerned, especially because it has been several years since they claimed the deductions and they worry that all their supporting documentation may not be in place. Several questions run through their minds. How could the IRS audit a tax return that was filed so long ago? Why was their tax return selected, and what should they expect during the audit? The interest deductions they reported were based on advice from their CPA. What would cause the IRS and a CPA to interpret the law differently? What is their financial exposure if the deductions are ultimately disallowed? Will they have to pay interest and penalties in addition to the tax they might owe? ■

Each chapter begins with a storyline that introduces a set of characters facing specific tax-related situations. This revolutionary approach to teaching tax emphasizes real people facing real tax dilemmas. Students learn to apply practical tax information to specific business and personal situations. As their situations evolve, the characters are brought further to life.

Examples

Examples are the cornerstone of any textbook covering taxation. For this reason, *McGraw Hill's Taxation* authors took special care to create clear and helpful examples that relate to the storyline of the chapter. Students learn to refer to the facts presented in the storyline and apply them to other scenarios—in this way, they build a greater base of knowledge through application. Many examples also include "What if" scenarios that add more complexity to the example or explore related tax concepts.

Example 2-1

Bill and Mercedes file their 2018 federal tax return on September 6, 2019, after receiving an automatic extension to file their return by October 15, 2019. In 2022, the IRS selects their 2018 tax return for audit. When does the statute of limitations end for Bill and Mercedes's 2018 tax return?

Answer: Assuming the six-year and "unlimited" statute of limitation rules do not apply, the statute of limitations ends on September 6, 2022 (three years after the later of the actual filing date and the *original* due date).

What if: When would the statute of limitations end for Bill and Mercedes for their 2018 tax return if the couple filed the return on March 22, 2019 (before the original due date of April 15, 2019)?

Answer: In this scenario, the statute of limitations would end on April 15, 2022, because the later of the actual filing date and the original due date is April 15, 2019.

THE PEDAGOGY YOUR STUDENTS NEED TO PUT THE CODE IN CONTEXT

Taxes in the Real World

Taxes in the Real World are short boxes used throughout the book to demonstrate the real-world use of tax concepts. Current articles on tax issues, the real-world application of chapter-specific tax rules, and short vignettes on popular news about tax are some of the issues covered in Taxes in the Real World boxes.

TAXES IN THE REAL WORLD Is It a Deductible State Tax Payment or Charitable Contribution?

In recent years, it has become popular for state and local governments to provide state or local tax credits for contributions to certain qualified charities (for example, local hospitals, certain scholarship funds, etc.). While there was no "official" IRS guidance on the federal tax treatment of these contributions, in "unofficial" guidance, the IRS Office of Chief Counsel (see Chief Counsel Advice Memorandum (CCA) 201105010) advised that a payment to a state agency or charitable organization in return for a tax credit might be characterized as either a deductible charitable contribution or a deductible state tax payment. The 2011 CCA advised that taxpayers could take a charitable deduction for the full amount of the contribution without subtracting that otherwise was used to reduce the taxpayer's state tax liability. Because individuals deduct both state taxes and charitable contributions as itemized deductions, the IRS was not too concerned with these types of state tax credit programs.

The IRS's stance changed in 2018 with the enactment of the $10,000 limit on the itemized deduction for state and local taxes. Specifically, the IRS revisited the federal tax consequences of state and local tax credit programs out of concern that taxpayers may use these programs to bypass the $10,000 limit on state and local tax deductions. After further review, the news was not favorable for taxpayers. In Reg. §1.170A-1(h)(3), the IRS states that, effective for contributions after August 27, 2018, taxpayers making

The Key Facts

The Key Facts provide quick synopses of the critical pieces of information presented throughout each chapter.

The **tax base** defines what is actually taxed and is usually expressed in monetary terms, whereas the **tax rate** determines the level of taxes imposed on the tax base and is usually expressed as a percentage. For example, a taxable purchase of $30 times a sales tax rate of 6 percent yields a tax of $1.80 ($1.80 = $30 × .06).

Federal, state, and local jurisdictions use a large variety of tax bases to collect tax. Some common tax bases (and related taxes) include taxable income (federal and state income taxes), purchases (sales tax), real estate values (real estate tax), and personal property values (personal property tax).

Different portions of a tax base may be taxed at different rates. A single tax applied

THE KEY FACTS

How to Calculate a Tax

- Tax = Tax base × Tax rate
- The tax base defines what is actually taxed and is usually expressed in monetary terms.
- The tax rate determines the level of taxes imposed

Exhibits

Today's students are visual learners, and *McGraw Hill's Taxation* understands this student need by making use of clear and engaging charts, diagrams, and tabular demonstrations of key material.

EXHIBIT 2-2 IRS Appeals/Litigation Process

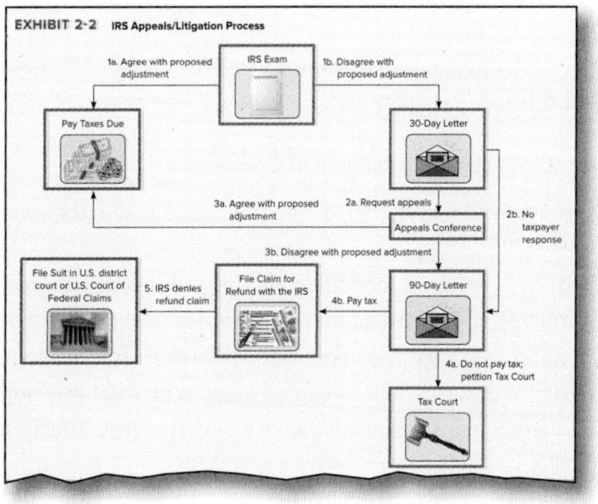

Top: Imageroller/Alamy Stock Photo; Bottom left: Jill Braaten/McGraw Hill

"This is the best text I have found for both my students and myself. Easier to read than other textbooks I have looked at, good examples, and, as mentioned before, I appreciate the instructor resources."

Esther Ehrlich, CPA
– The University of Texas at El Paso

PRACTICE MAKES PERFECT WITH A WIDE VARIETY OF ASSIGNMENT MATERIAL

Summary

LO 5-1 Apply the concept of realization.

- Income is typically realized with a transaction that allows economic benefit to be identified and measured.
- Unless realized income is deferred or excluded, it is included in gross income in the period dictated by the taxpayer's accounting method.
- The accrual method of accounting recognizes income in the period it is earned, and this method is typically used by large corporations.
- The cash method of accounting recognizes income in the period received, and this method offers a simple and flexible method of accounting typically used by individuals.
- The return of capital principle, constructive receipt doctrine, and assignment of income doctrine affect how much income is recognized, when income is recognized, and who recognizes income, respectively.

LO 5-2 Discuss the distinctions between the various sources of income, including income from services and property.

- Income from services is called earned income, whereas income from property is called unearned income...

Summary

A unique feature of *McGraw Hill's Taxation* is the end-of-chapter summary organized around learning objectives. Each objective has a brief, bullet-point summary that covers the major topics and concepts for that chapter, including references to critical exhibits and examples. All end-of-chapter material is tied to learning objectives.

Learning Objectives

Upon completing this chapter, you should be able to:

LO 2-1 Identify the filing requirements for income tax returns and the statute of limitations for assessment.

LO 2-2 Outline the IRS audit process, how returns are selected, the different types of audits, and what happens after the audit.

LO 2-3 Evaluate the relative weights of the various tax law sources.

LO 2-4 Describe the legislative process as it pertains to taxation.

LO 2-5 Perform the basic steps in tax research.

LO 2-6 Describe tax professional responsibilities in providing tax advice.

LO 2-7 Identify taxpayer and tax return preparer penalties.

DISCUSSION QUESTIONS

Discussion Questions are available in Connect®. connect

LO 4-1 1. How are realized income, gross income, and taxable income similar, and how are they different?

LO 4-1 2. Are taxpayers required to include all realized income in gross income? Explain.

LO 4-1 3. All else being equal, should taxpayers prefer to exclude income or to defer it? Why?

LO 4-1 4. Why should a taxpayer be interested in the character of income received?

LO 4-1 5. Is it easier to describe what a capital asset is or what it is not? Explain.

LO 4-1 6. Are all capital gains (gains on the sale or disposition of capital assets) taxed at the same rate? Explain.

LO 4-1 7. Are taxpayers allowed to deduct net capital losses (either net long-term capital loss in excess of net short-term capital gain or net short-term capital loss in excess of net

Discussion Questions

Discussion questions, available in Connect, are provided for each of the major concepts in each chapter, providing students with an opportunity to review key parts of the chapter and answer evocative questions about what they have learned.

Problems

Problems are designed to test the comprehension of more complex topics. Each problem at the end of the chapter is tied to one of that chapter's learning objectives, with multiple problems for critical topics.

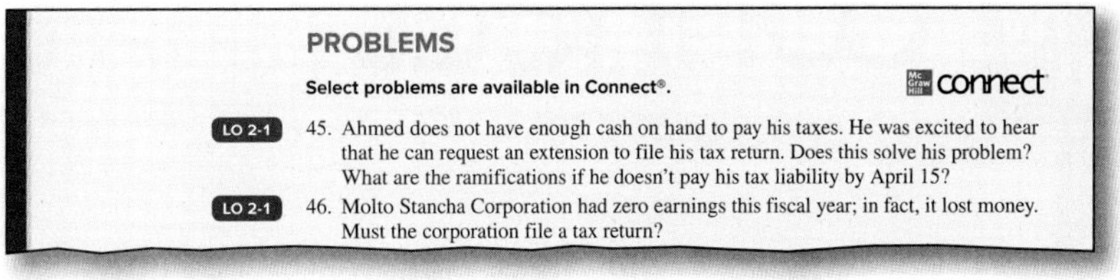
PROBLEMS

Select problems are available in Connect®.

LO 2-1 45. Ahmed does not have enough cash on hand to pay his taxes. He was excited to hear that he can request an extension to file his tax return. Does this solve his problem? What are the ramifications if he doesn't pay his tax liability by April 15?

LO 2-1 46. Molto Stancha Corporation had zero earnings this fiscal year; in fact, it lost money. Must the corporation file a tax return?

Tax Form Problems

Tax form problems are a set of requirements included in the end-of-chapter material of the 2023 edition. These problems require students to complete a tax form (or part of a tax form), providing students with valuable experience and practice with filling out these forms. These requirements—and their relevant forms—are also included in Connect, with select problems available in both static and algorithmic format. Each tax form problem includes an icon to differentiate it from regular problems.

Research Problems

Research problems are special problems throughout the end-of-chapter assignment material. These require students to do both basic and more complex research on topics outside of the scope of the book. Each research problem includes an icon to differentiate it from regular problems.

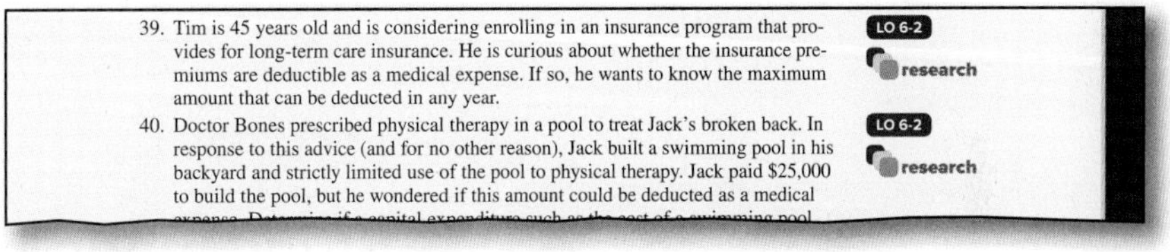
39. Tim is 45 years old and is considering enrolling in an insurance program that provides for long-term care insurance. He is curious about whether the insurance premiums are deductible as a medical expense. If so, he wants to know the maximum amount that can be deducted in any year. LO 6-2 research

40. Doctor Bones prescribed physical therapy in a pool to treat Jack's broken back. In response to this advice (and for no other reason), Jack built a swimming pool in his backyard and strictly limited use of the pool to physical therapy. Jack paid $25,000 to build the pool, but he wondered if this amount could be deducted as a medical LO 6-2 research

Planning Problems

Planning problems are another unique set of problems included in the end-of-chapter assignment material. These require students to test their tax planning skills after covering the chapter topics. Each planning problem includes an icon to differentiate it from regular problems.

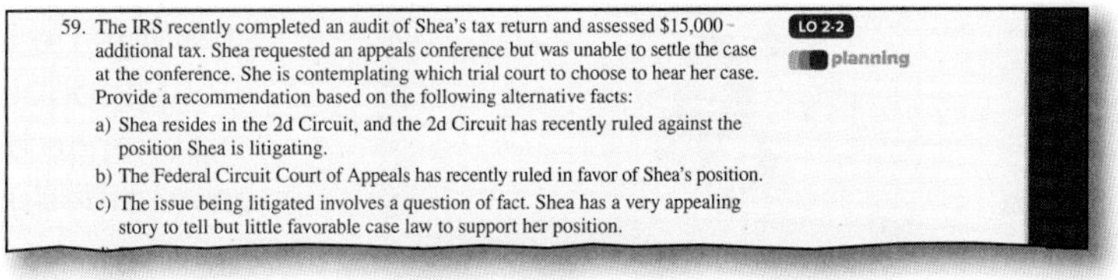
59. The IRS recently completed an audit of Shea's tax return and assessed $15,000 additional tax. Shea requested an appeals conference but was unable to settle the case at the conference. She is contemplating which trial court to choose to hear her case. Provide a recommendation based on the following alternative facts: LO 2-2 planning

a) Shea resides in the 2d Circuit, and the 2d Circuit has recently ruled against the position Shea is litigating.

b) The Federal Circuit Court of Appeals has recently ruled in favor of Shea's position.

c) The issue being litigated involves a question of fact. Shea has a very appealing story to tell but little favorable case law to support her position.

Comprehensive and Tax Return Problems

Comprehensive and tax return problems address multiple concepts in a single problem. Comprehensive problems are ideal for cumulative topics; for this reason, they are located at the end of all chapters. **Tax return problems are also available in *Connect* and *Instructor Resource Center.* These problems range from simple to complex and cover individual taxation, corporate taxation, partnership taxation, and S corporation taxation.**

McGraw Hill connect®

Instructors: Student Success Starts with You

Tools to enhance your unique voice

Want to build your own course? No problem. Prefer to use an OLC-aligned, prebuilt course? Easy. Want to make changes throughout the semester? Sure. And you'll save time with Connect's auto-grading too.

65%
Less Time Grading

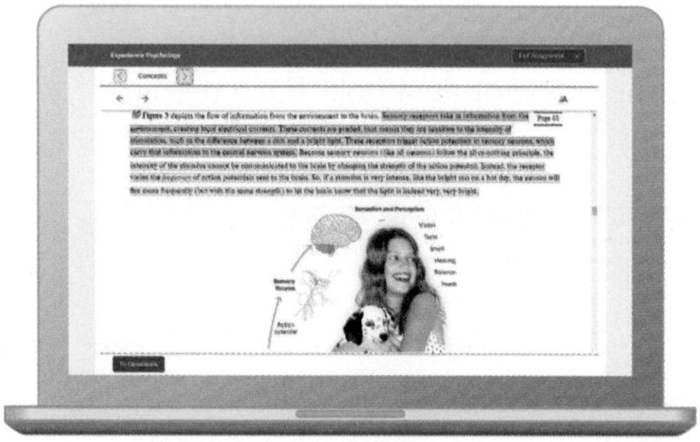

Laptop: McGraw Hill; Woman/dog: George Doyle/Getty Images

Study made personal

Incorporate adaptive study resources like SmartBook® 2.0 into your course and help your students be better prepared in less time. Learn more about the powerful personalized learning experience available in SmartBook 2.0 at **www.mheducation.com/highered/connect/smartbook**

Affordable solutions, added value

Make technology work for you with LMS integration for single sign-on access, mobile access to the digital textbook, and reports to quickly show you how each of your students is doing. And with our Inclusive Access program you can provide all these tools at a discount to your students. Ask your McGraw Hill representative for more information.

Padlock: Jobalou/Getty Images

Solutions for your challenges

A product isn't a solution. Real solutions are affordable, reliable, and come with training and ongoing support when you need it and how you want it. Visit **www.supportateverystep.com** for videos and resources both you and your students can use throughout the semester.

Checkmark: Jobalou/Getty Images

SUPPORT AT every step

Students: Get Learning that Fits You

Effective tools for efficient studying

Connect is designed to help you be more productive with simple, flexible, intuitive tools that maximize your study time and meet your individual learning needs. Get learning that works for you with Connect.

Study anytime, anywhere

Download the free ReadAnywhere app and access your online eBook, SmartBook 2.0, or Adaptive Learning Assignments when it's convenient, even if you're offline. And since the app automatically syncs with your Connect account, all of your work is available every time you open it. Find out more at **www.mheducation.com/readanywhere**

"I really liked this app—it made it easy to study when you don't have your textbook in front of you."

- Jordan Cunningham,
Eastern Washington University

Calendar: owattaphotos/Getty Images

Everything you need in one place

Your Connect course has everything you need—whether reading on your digital eBook or completing assignments for class, Connect makes it easy to get your work done.

Learning for everyone

McGraw Hill works directly with Accessibility Services Departments and faculty to meet the learning needs of all students. Please contact your Accessibility Services Office and ask them to email accessibility@mheducation.com, or visit **www.mheducation.com/about/accessibility** for more information.

Top: Jenner Images/Getty Images, Left: Hero Images/Getty Images, Right: Hero Images/Getty Images

DIGITAL LEARNING ASSETS TO IMPROVE STUDENT OUTCOMES

> "The quality of the online materials in Connect and Learnsmart are market-leading and unmatched in the tax arena."
>
> Jason W. Stanfield
> – Ball State University

Connect helps students learn more efficiently by providing feedback and practice material when they need it, where they need it. Connect grades homework automatically and gives immediate feedback on any questions students may have missed. The extensive assignable, gradable end-of-chapter content includes problems, comprehensive problems (available as auto-graded tax forms), and discussion questions. Also, select questions have been redesigned to test students' knowledge more fully. They now include tables for students to work through rather than requiring that all calculations be done offline.

Auto-Graded Tax Forms

The auto-graded **Tax Forms,** also called the Comprehensive Problems—Static (Tax Form) in Connect, provide a much-improved student experience when solving the tax form–based problems. The tax form simulation allows students to apply tax concepts by completing the actual tax forms online with automatic feedback and grading for both students and instructors.

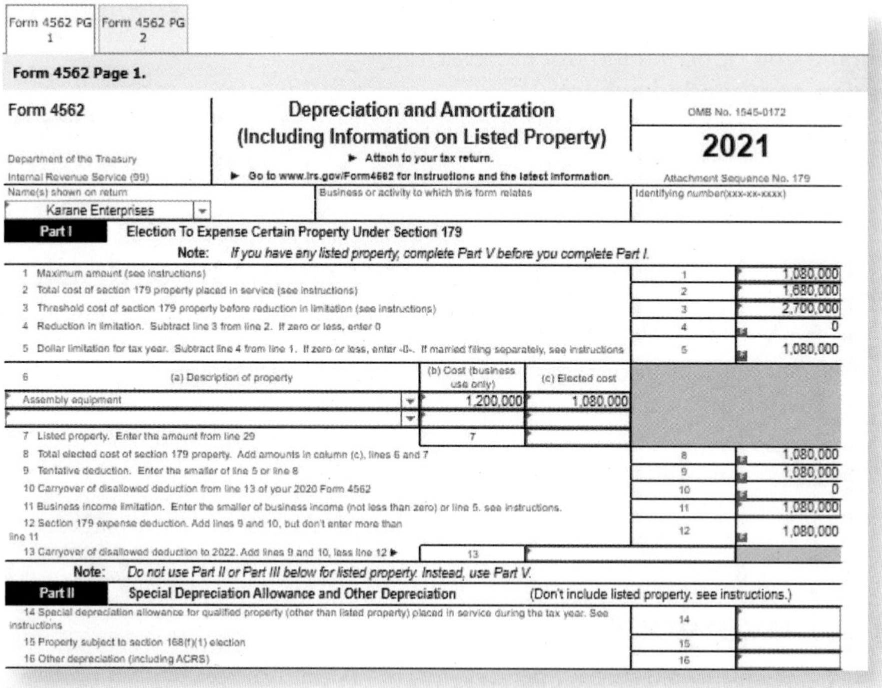
Form 4562 PG 1 | Form 4562 PG 2

Form 4562 Page 1.

Form 4562 — **Depreciation and Amortization (Including Information on Listed Property)** — OMB No. 1545-0172 — **2021**

Department of the Treasury
Internal Revenue Service (99)
► Attach to your tax return.
► Go to www.irs.gov/Form4562 for instructions and the latest information.
Attachment Sequence No. 179

Name(s) shown on return	Business or activity to which this form relates	Identifying number(xxx-xx-xxxx)
Karane Enterprises		

Part I Election To Expense Certain Property Under Section 179

Note: *If you have any listed property, complete Part V before you complete Part I.*

1 Maximum amount (see instructions)	1	1,080,000
2 Total cost of section 179 property placed in service (see instructions)	2	1,680,000
3 Threshold cost of section 179 property before reduction in limitation (see instructions)	3	2,700,000
4 Reduction in limitation. Subtract line 3 from line 2. If zero or less, enter 0	4	0
5 Dollar limitation for tax year. Subtract line 4 from line 1. If zero or less, enter -0-. If married filing separately, see instructions	5	1,080,000

6 (a) Description of property	(b) Cost (business use only)	(c) Elected cost
Assembly equipment	1,200,000	1,080,000
7 Listed property. Enter the amount from line 29	7	

8 Total elected cost of section 179 property. Add amounts in column (c), lines 6 and 7	8	1,080,000
9 Tentative deduction. Enter the smaller of line 5 or line 8	9	1,080,000
10 Carryover of disallowed deduction from line 13 of your 2020 Form 4562	10	0
11 Business income limitation. Enter the smaller of business income (not less than zero) or line 5. see instructions.	11	1,080,000
12 Section 179 expense deduction. Add lines 9 and 10, but don't enter more than line 11	12	1,080,000
13 Carryover of disallowed deduction to 2022. Add lines 9 and 10, less line 12 ► 13		

Note: *Do not use Part II or Part III below for listed property. Instead, use Part V.*

Part II Special Depreciation Allowance and Other Depreciation (Don't include listed property. see instructions.)

14 Special depreciation allowance for qualified property (other than listed property) placed in service during the tax year. See instructions	14	
15 Property subject to section 168(f)(1) election	15	
16 Other depreciation (including ACRS)	16	

Source: irs.gov.

Guided Examples

The **Guided Examples,** or "hint" videos, in Connect provide a narrated, animated, step-by-step walk-through of select problems similar to those assigned. These short presentations can be turned on or off by instructors and provide reinforcement when students need it most.

Tableau Dashboard Activities

Tableau Dashboard Activities allow students to explore live Tableau dashboards directly integrated into Connect through interactive filters and menus as well as auto-graded questions focused on both calculations and analysis. Students can check their understanding and apply what they are learning within the framework of analytics and critical thinking.

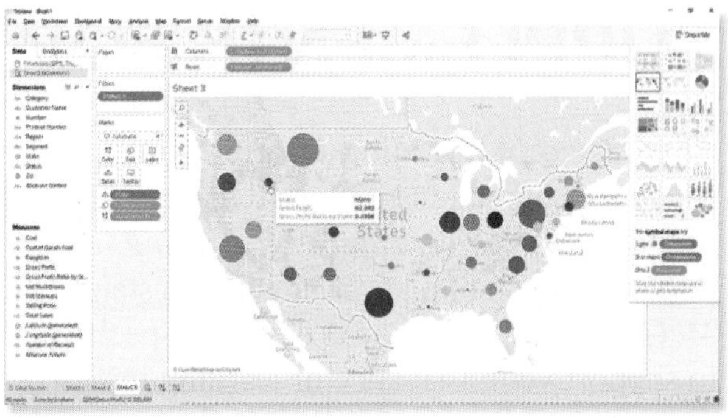

TaxACT®

TaxAct Professional *McGraw Hill's Taxation* features an integrated software package from TaxAct, one of the leading preparation software companies in the market today. TaxAct features in-depth form instructions that supplement *Individuals* and *Business Entities,* making it easier than ever to integrate software into the classroom. Students are provided with the latest tax forms via the Check for Updates from the Online tab in the program so that at the start of the semester, each student will be prepared to work with the most up-to-date information available. With over 120 tax forms, schedules, and worksheets, TaxAct is sure to have the course materials you will need throughout the semester.

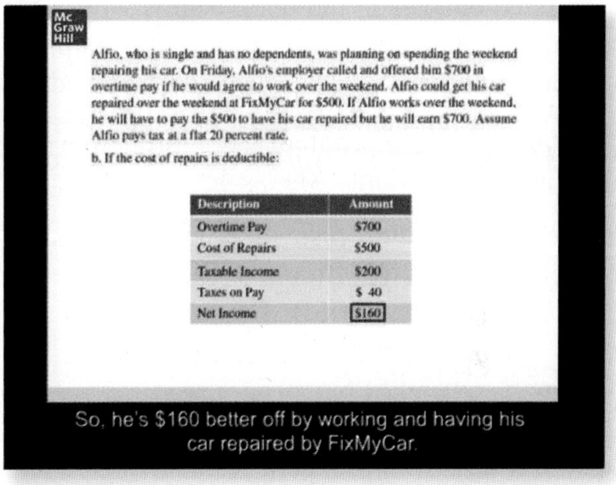

Please note, TaxAct is only compatible with PCs and not Macs. However, we offer easy-to-complete licensing agreement templates that are accessible within Connect and the Instructor Resources Center to enable school computer labs to download the software onto campus hardware for free.

Roger CPA

UWorld | ROGER CPA Review McGraw Hill has partnered with Roger CPA Review (Powered by UWorld), a global leader in CPA Exam preparation, to provide students a smooth transition from the accounting classroom to successful completion of the CPA Exam. While many aspiring accountants wait until they have completed their academic studies to begin preparing for the CPA Exam, research shows that those who become familiar with exam content earlier in the process have a stronger chance of successfully passing the CPA Exam. Accordingly, students using these McGraw Hill materials will have access to Roger CPA Review multiple choice questions supported by explanations written by CPAs focused on exam preparation. McGraw Hill and Roger CPA Review are dedicated to supporting every accounting student along their journey, ultimately helping them achieve career success in the accounting profession. For more information about the full Roger CPA Review program, exam requirements, and exam content, visit www.rogercpareview.com.

McGraw Hill Customer Experience Group Contact Information

At McGraw Hill, we understand that getting the most from new technology can be challenging. That's why our services don't stop after you purchase our products. You can contact our Product Specialists 24 hours a day to get product training online. Or you can search the knowledge bank of Frequently Asked Questions on our support website. For Customer Support, call **800-331-5094,** or visit www.mhhe.com/support. One of our Technical Support Analysts will be able to assist you in a timely fashion.

SUPPLEMENTS FOR INSTRUCTORS

Assurance of Learning Ready

Many educational institutions today are focused on the notion of *assurance of learning,* an important element of many accreditation standards. *McGraw Hill's Taxation* is designed specifically to support your assurance of learning initiatives with a simple, yet powerful, solution.

Each chapter in the book begins with a list of numbered learning objectives, which appear throughout the chapter as well as in the end-of-chapter assignments. Every test bank question for *McGraw Hill's Taxation* maps to a specific chapter learning objective in the textbook. Each test bank question also identifies topic area, level of difficulty, Bloom's Taxonomy level, and AICPA and AACSB skill area.

AACSB Statement

McGraw Hill Education is a proud corporate member of AACSB International. Understanding the importance and value of AACSB accreditation, *McGraw Hill's Taxation* recognizes the curriculum guidelines detailed in the AACSB standards for business accreditation by connecting selected questions in the text and the test bank to the general knowledge and skill guidelines in the revised AACSB standards.

The statements contained in *McGraw Hill's Taxation* are provided only as a guide for the users of this textbook. The AACSB leaves content coverage and assessment within the purview of individual schools, the mission of the school, and the faculty. While *McGraw Hill's Taxation* and the teaching package make no claim of any specific AACSB qualification or evaluation, we have, within the text and test bank, labeled selected questions according to the eight general knowledge and skill areas.

Tegrity: Lectures 24/7

Tegrity in Connect is a tool that makes class time available 24/7 by automatically capturing every lecture. With a simple one-click start-and-stop process, you capture all computer screens and corresponding audio in a format that is easy to search, frame by frame. Students can replay any part of any class with easy-to-use, browser-based viewing on a PC, Mac, iPod, or other mobile device.

Educators know that the more students can see, hear, and experience class resources, the better they learn. In fact, studies prove it. Tegrity's unique search feature helps students efficiently find what they need, when they need it, across an entire semester of class recordings. Help turn your students' study time into learning moments immediately supported by your lecture. With Tegrity, you also increase intent listening and class participation by easing students' concerns about note-taking. Using Tegrity in Connect will make it more likely you will see students' faces, not the tops of their heads.

Test Builder in Connect

Available within Connect, Test Builder is a cloud-based tool that enables instructors to format tests that can be printed or administered within an LMS. Test Builder offers a modern, streamlined interface for easy content configuration that matches course needs, without requiring a download.

Test Builder allows you to:

- access all test bank content from a particular title.
- easily pinpoint the most relevant content through robust filtering options.
- manipulate the order of questions or scramble questions and/or answers.
- pin questions to a specific location within a test.
- determine your preferred treatment of algorithmic questions.
- choose the layout and spacing.
- add instructions and configure default settings.

Test Builder provides a secure interface for better protection of content and allows for just-in-time updates to flow directly into assessments.

Four Volumes to Fit Four Course Approaches

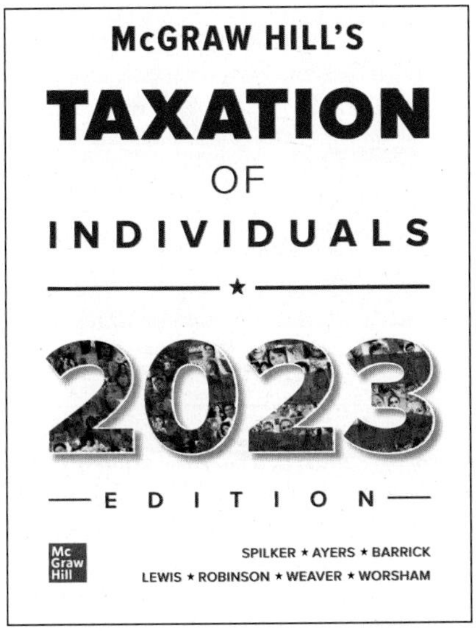

McGraw Hill's Taxation of Individuals is organized to emphasize topics that are most important to undergraduates taking their first tax course. The first three chapters provide an introduction to taxation and then carefully guide students through tax research and tax planning. Part II discusses the fundamental elements of individual income tax, starting with the tax formula in Chapter 4 and then proceeding to more discussion on income, deductions, investments, and computing tax liabilities in Chapters 5–8. Part III then discusses tax issues associated with business-related activities. Specifically, this part addresses business income and deductions, accounting methods, and tax consequences associated with purchasing assets and property dispositions (sales, trades, or other dispositions). Part IV is unique among tax textbooks; this section combines related tax issues for compensation, retirement savings, and home ownership.

Part I: Introduction to Taxation
1. An Introduction to Tax
2. Tax Compliance, the IRS, and Tax Authorities
3. Tax Planning Strategies and Related Limitations

Part II: Basic Individual Taxation
4. Individual Income Tax Overview, Dependents, and Filing Status
5. Gross Income and Exclusions
6. Individual Deductions
7. Investments
8. Individual Income Tax Computation and Tax Credits

Part III: Business-Related Transactions
9. Business Income, Deductions, and Accounting Methods
10. Property Acquisition and Cost Recovery
11. Property Dispositions

Part IV: Specialized Topics
12. Compensation
13. Retirement Savings and Deferred Compensation
14. Tax Consequences of Home Ownership

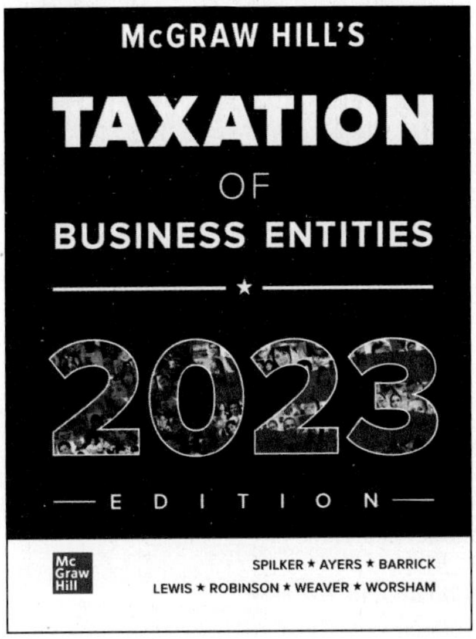

McGraw Hill's Taxation of Business Entities begins with the process for determining gross income and deductions for businesses, and the tax consequences associated with purchasing assets and property dispositions (sales, trades, or other dispositions). Part II provides a comprehensive overview of entities and the formation, reorganization, and liquidation of corporations. Unique to this series is a complete chapter on accounting for income taxes, which provides a primer on the basics of calculating the income tax provision. Included in the narrative is a discussion of temporary and permanent differences and their impact on a company's book "effective tax rate." Part III provides a detailed discussion of partnerships and S corporations. The last part of the book covers state and local taxation, multinational taxation, and transfer taxes and wealth planning.

Part I: Business-Related Transactions
1. Business Income, Deductions, and Accounting Methods
2. Property Acquisition and Cost Recovery
3. Property Dispositions

Part II: Entity Overview and Taxation of C Corporations
4. Business Entities Overview
5. Corporate Operations
6. Accounting for Income Taxes
7. Corporate Taxation: Nonliquidating Distributions
8. Corporate Formation, Reorganization, and Liquidation

Part III: Taxation of Flow-Through Entities
9. Forming and Operating Partnerships
10. Dispositions of Partnership Interests and Partnership Distributions
11. S Corporations

Part IV: Multijurisdictional Taxation and Transfer Taxes
12. State and Local Taxes
13. The U.S. Taxation of Multinational Transactions
14. Transfer Taxes and Wealth Planning

McGraw Hill's Taxation of Individuals and Business Entities covers all chapters included in the two split volumes in one convenient volume. See Table of Contents.

Part I: Introduction to Taxation
1. An Introduction to Tax
2. Tax Compliance, the IRS, and Tax Authorities
3. Tax Planning Strategies and Related Limitations

Part II: Basic Individual Taxation
4. Individual Income Tax Overview, Dependents, and Filing Status
5. Gross Income and Exclusions
6. Individual Deductions
7. Investments
8. Individual Income Tax Computation and Tax Credits

Part III: Business-Related Transactions
9. Business Income, Deductions, and Accounting Methods
10. Property Acquisition and Cost Recovery
11. Property Dispositions

Part IV: Specialized Topics
12. Compensation
13. Retirement Savings and Deferred Compensation
14. Tax Consequences of Home Ownership

Part V: Entity Overview and Taxation of C Corporations
15. Business Entities Overview
16. Corporate Operations
17. Accounting for Income Taxes
18. Corporate Taxation: Nonliquidating Distributions
19. Corporate Formation, Reorganization, and Liquidation

Part VI: Taxation of Flow-Through Entities
20. Forming and Operating Partnerships
21. Dispositions of Partnership Interests and Partnership Distributions
22. S Corporations

Part VII: Multijurisdictional Taxation and Transfer Taxes
23. State and Local Taxes
24. The U.S. Taxation of Multinational Transactions
25. Transfer Taxes and Wealth Planning

McGraw Hill's Essentials of Federal Taxation is designed for a one-semester course, covering the basics of taxation of individuals and business entities. To facilitate a one-semester course, *McGraw Hill's Essentials of Federal Taxation* folds the key topics from the investments, compensation, retirement savings, and home ownership chapters in *Taxation of Individuals* into three individual taxation chapters that discuss gross income and exclusions, for AGI deductions, and from AGI deductions, respectively. The essentials volume also includes a two-chapter C corporation sequence that uses a life-cycle approach covering corporate formations and then corporate operations in the first chapter and nonliquidating and liquidating corporate distributions in the second chapter. This volume is perfect for those teaching a one-semester course and for those who struggle to get through the 25-chapter comprehensive volume.

Part I: Introduction to Taxation
1. An Introduction to Tax
2. Tax Compliance, the IRS, and Tax Authorities
3. Tax Planning Strategies and Related Limitations

Part II: Individual Taxation
4. Individual Income Tax Overview, Dependents, and Filing Status
5. Gross Income and Exclusions
6. Individual For AGI Deductions
7. Individual From AGI Deductions
8. Individual Income Tax Computation and Tax Credits

Part III: Business-Related Transactions
9. Business Income, Deductions, and Accounting Methods
10. Property Acquisition and Cost Recovery
11. Property Dispositions

Part IV: Entity Overview and Taxation of C Corporations
12. Business Entities Overview
13. Corporate Formations and Operations
14. Corporate Nonliquidating and Liquidating Distributions

Part V: Taxation of Flow-Through Entities
15. Forming and Operating Partnerships
16. Dispositions of Partnership Interests and Partnership Distributions
17. S Corporations

A HEARTFELT THANKS TO THE MANY COLLEAGUES WHO SHAPED THIS BOOK

The version of the book you are reading would not be the same book without the valuable suggestions, keen insights, and constructive criticisms of the reviewers below. Each professor listed here contributed in substantive ways to the organization of chapters, coverage of topics, and use of pedagogy. We are grateful to them for taking the time to read chapters or attend reviewer conferences, focus groups, and symposia in support of the development for the book:

Previous Edition Reviewers

Donna Abelli, *Mount Ida College*
Joseph Assalone, *Rowan College at Gloucester County*
Dr. Valeriya Avdeev, *William Paterson University*
Victoria Badura, *Metropolitan Community College*
Robyn Barrett, *St. Louis Community College*
Kevin Baugess, *ICDC College*
Christopher Becker, *Coastal Carolina University*
Jeanne Bedell, *Keiser University*
Marcia Behrens, *Nichols College*
Michael Belleman, *St. Clair County Community College*
David Berman, *Community College of Philadelphia*
Tim Biggart, *Berry College*
Cynthia Bird, *Tidewater Community College*
Lisa Blum, *University of Louisville*
Rick Blumenfeld, *Sierra College*
Cindy Bortman Boggess, *Babson College*
William A. Bottiglieri, *Iona College*
Cathalene Bowler, *University of Northern Iowa*
Justin Breidenbach, *Ohio Wesleyan University*
Suzon Bridges, *Houston Community College*
Stephen Bukowy, *UNC Pembroke*
Esther Bunn, *Stephen F. Austin State University*
Megan Burke, *Texas Woman's University*
Holly Caldwell, *Bridgewater College*
James Campbell, *Thomas College*
Alisa Carini, *University of California San Diego Extension*
Ronald Carter, *Patrick Henry Community College*
Cynthia Caruso, *Endicott College*
Al Case, *Southern Oregon University*
Paul Caselton, *University of Illinois–Springfield*
Machiavelli (Max) Chao, *University of California–Irvine*
Amy Chataginer, *Mississippi Gulf Coast Community College*
Christine Cheng, *Louisiana State University*
Lisa Church, *Rhode Island College*
Marilyn Ciolino, *Delgado Community College*
Wayne Clark, *Southwest Baptist University*
Ann Cohen, *University at Buffalo, SUNY*
Sharon Cox, *University of Illinois–Urbana-Champaign*
Terry Crain, *University of Oklahoma–Norman*
Roger Crane, *Indiana University East*
Cheryl Crespi, *Central Connecticut State University*
Brad Cripe, *Northern Illinois University*
Curtis J. Crocker, *Southern Crescent Technical College*
Richard Cummings, *University of Wisconsin–Whitewater*
Joshua Cutler, *University of Houston*
William Dams, *Lenoir Community College*
Nichole Dauenhauer, *Lakeland Community College*
Susan Snow Davis, *Green River College*
Ginger DeLatte, *Texas A&M—Corpus Christi*
Jim Desimpelare, *University of Michigan–Ann Arbor*
Julie Dilling, *Moraine Park Technical College*
Steve Dombrock, *Carroll University*
Dr. Vicky C. Dominguez, *College of Southern Nevada*
Keith Donnelly, *SUNY Brockport*
Michael P. Donohoe, *University of Illinois–Urbana-Champaign*
John Dorocak, *California State University–San Bernardino*
Katharine Drake, *University of Arizona*
Amy Dunbar, *University of Connecticut–Storrs*
Bob Duquette, *Lehigh University*
John Eagan, *Morehouse College*
Reed Easton, *Seton Hall University*
Esther Ehrlich, CPA, *The University of Texas at El Paso*
Elizabeth Ekmekjian, *William Paterson University*
Ann Esarco, *Columbia College Columbia*
Frank Faber, *St. Joseph's College*
Michael Fagan, *Raritan Valley Community College*
Frank Farina, *Catawba College*
Andrew Finley, *Claremont McKenna*
Tim Fogarty, *Case Western Reserve University*
Wilhelmina Ford, *Middle Georgia State University*
Michele Frank, *Miami University*
George Frankel, *San Francisco State University*
Lawrence Friedken, *Penn State University*
Stephen Gara, *Drake University*
Lauren Garrett, *Shippensburg University*
Robert Gary, *University of New Mexico*
Sheri Geddes, *Hope College*
Greg Geisler, *Indiana University*
Alex Gialanella, *Fordham University*
Earl Godfrey, *Gardner Webb University*
Thomas Godwin, *Purdue University*
David Golub, *Northeastern University*
Marina Grau, *Houston Community College*
Brian Greenstein, *University of Delaware*
Patrick Griffin, *Lewis University*
Lillian Grose, *University of Holy Cross*
Thomas Guarino, *Plymouth State University*
Rosie Hagen, *Virginia Western Community College*
Joni Hammond, *Georgia Southwestern State University*
Marcye Hampton, *University of Central Florida*
Connie Hardgrove, *College of Central Florida*
Cass Hausserman, *Portland State University*
Rebecca Helms, *Ivy Tech Community College*
Melanie Hicks, *Liberty University*
Mary Ann Hofmann, *Appalachian State University*
Robert Joseph Holdren, *Muskingum University*
Bambi Hora, *University of Central Oklahoma*
David Horn, *Metropolitan State University*
Carol Hughes, *Asheville Buncombe Technical Community College*
Helen Hurwitz, *Saint Louis University*
Rik Ichiho, *Dixie State University*

Kerry Inger, *Auburn University*
Paul Johnson, *Mississippi Gulf Coast CC–JD Campus*
Athena Jones, *University of Maryland Global Campus*
Andrew Junikiewicz, *Temple University*
Susan Jurney, *University of Arkansas–Fayetteville*
Beth R. Kane, *Northwestern University and Johnson Wales University*
Sandra Kemper, *Regis University*
Jon Kerr, *Baruch College–CUNY*
Lara Kessler, *Grand Valley State University*
Janice Klimek, *University of Central Missouri*
Pamela Knight, *Columbus Technical College*
Satoshi Kojima, *East Los Angeles College*
Dawn Konicek, *Idaho State University*
Jack Lachman, *Brooklyn College*
Brandon Lanciloti, *Freed-Hardeman University*
Stacie Laplante, *University of Wisconsin–Madison*
Suzanne Laudadio, *Durham Tech*
Stephanie Lewis, *Ohio State University–Columbus*
Teresa Lightner, *University of North Texas*
Robert Lin, *California State University–East Bay*
Chris Loiselle, *Cornerstone University*
Bruce Lubich, *Penn State–Harrisburg*
Elizabeth Lyon, *California State University–Sacramento*
Narelle Mackenzie, *San Diego State University, National University*
Michael Malmfeldt, *Shenandoah University*
Kate Mantzke, *Northern Illinois University*
Robert Martin, *Kennesaw State University*
Anthony Masino, *East Tennessee State University*
Paul Mason, *Baylor University*
Lisa McKinney, *University of Alabama at Birmingham*
Allison McLeod, *University of North Texas*
Lois McWhorter, *Somerset Community College*
Janet Meade, *University of Houston*
Michele Meckfessel, *University of Missouri–St. Louis*
Frank Messina, *University of Alabama at Birmingham*
R. Miedaner, *Lee University*
Ken Milani, *University of Notre Dame*
Syed M Moiz, *University of Wisconsin, Platteville*
Karen Morris, *Northeast Iowa Community College*
Stephanie Morris, *Mercer University*
Michelle Moshier, *University at Albany*
Leslie Mostow, *University of Maryland–College Park*
James Motter, *Indiana University–Purdue University Indianapolis*
Jackie Myers, *Sinclair Community College*
Michael Nee, *Cape Cod Community College*
Liz Ott, *Casper College*
Sandra Owen, *Indiana University–Bloomington*
Edwin Pagan, *Passaic County Community College*
Jeff Paterson, *Florida State University*
Ronald Pearson, *Bay College*
Martina Peng, *Franklin University*
Michael Wayne Penn Jr., *University of Illinois–Urbana-Champaign*
Dr. Theresa Phipps, *Slippery Rock University*
James Pierson, *Franklin University*
Sonja Pippin, *University of Nevada–Reno*
Jonathan David Pittard, *University of California–Riverside*
Anthony Pochesci, *Rutgers University*
Kyle Post, *Tarleton State University*
Christopher Proschko, *Texas State University*
Joshua Racca, *University of Alabama*
Nirmalee Raddatz, *University of Memphis*
Francisco Rangel, *Riverside City College*
Pauline Ash Ray, *Thomas University*
Luke Richardson, *University of South Florida*
Rodney Ridenour, *Montana State University Northern*
John Robertson, *Arkansas State University*
Jennifer Robinson, *Trident Technical College*
Nicholas Robinson, *Eastern Illinois University*
Susan Robinson, *Georgia Southwestern State University*
Morgan Rockett, *Moberly Area Community College*
Miles Romney, *Michigan State University*
Abbie Sadler, *University of Richmond*
Ananth Seetharaman, *Saint Louis University*
Alisa Shapiro, *Raritan Valley Community College*
Deanna Sharpe, *University of Missouri*
Wayne Shaw, *Southern Methodist University*
Sonia Singh, *University of Florida*
Georgi Smatrakalev, *Florida Atlantic University*
Lucia Smeal, *Georgia State University*
Pamela Smith, *University of Texas at San Antonio*
Adam Spoolstra, *Johnson County Community College*
Joe Standridge, *Sonoma State*
Jason Stanfield, *Ball State University*
George Starbuck, *McMurry University*
James Stekelberg, *University of Arizona*
Teresa Stephenson, *University of Alaska Anchorage*
Shane Stinson, *University of Alabama*
Terrie Stolte, *Columbus State Community College*
Pamela J. Strickland, *Campbell University*
Gloria Jean Stuart, *Georgia Southern University*
Kenton Swift, *University of Montana*
MaryBeth Tobin, *Bridgewater State University*
Erin Towery, *University of Georgia*
Ronald Unger, *Temple University*
Glenn Walberg, *University of Vermont*
Karen Wallace, *Ramapo College*
Stephanie Walton, *Louisiana State University*
Natasha Ware, *Southeastern University*
Luke Watson, *University of Florida*
Sarah Webber, *University of Dayton*
Cassandra Weitzenkamp, *Peru State College*
Marvin Williams, *University of Houston–Downtown*
Chris Woehrle, *American College*
Jennifer Wright, *Drexel University*
Massood Yahya-Zadeh, *George Mason University*
James Yang, *Montclair State University*
Scott Yetmar, *Cleveland State University*
Xiaoli (Charlie) Yuan, *Elizabeth City State University*
Zhen Zhang, *Towson University*
Mingjun Zhou, *DePaul University*

Acknowledgments

We would like to thank the many talented people who made valuable contributions to the creation of this fourteenth edition. William A. Padley of Madison Area Technical College, Deanna Sharpe of the University of Missouri–Columbia, and Troy Lewis of Brigham Young University checked the page proofs and solutions manual for accuracy; we greatly appreciate the hours they spent checking tax forms and double-checking our calculations throughout the book. Troy Lewis, Deanna Sharpe, and Teressa Farough accuracy checked the test bank. Thank you to Troy Lewis, Matt Lowenkron, and Jason Stanfield for your contributions to the Smartbook revision for this edition. Special thanks to Troy Lewis for his sharp eye and valuable feedback throughout the revision process. Finally, Deanna Sharpe, Troy Lewis, Nancy Osborne of University of Massachusetts Dartmouth, and Vivian Paige of Christopher Newport University greatly contributed to the accuracy of McGraw Hill's Connect for the 2023 edition.

We are especially grateful to J. T. Eagan for his contributions to the Tableau Dashboard Activities and Guided Examples, as well as Temple University instructors Wayne Williams, David Jones, and Ronald Unger for their assistance developing the Data Analytics Problems.

We also appreciate the expert attention given to this project by the staff at McGraw Hill Education, especially Tim Vertovec, Managing Director; Kathleen Klehr, Executive Portfolio Manager; Sarah Wood and Katie Ward, Freelance Product Developers; Brian Nacik and Jill Eccher, Content Project Managers; Beth Blech, Designer; Natalie King, Marketing Director; Claire McLemore, Marketing Manager; and Sue Culbertson, Senior Buyer.

Changes in *Taxation of Individuals and Business Entities*, 2023 Edition

For the 2023 edition of McGraw Hill's *Taxation of Individuals and Business Entities,* many changes were made in response to feedback from reviewers and focus group participants:

- All tax forms have been **updated for the latest available tax form as of 2022.** In addition, **chapter content** throughout the text has been **updated to reflect tax law changes through February 8, 2022.**

Other notable changes in the 2023 edition include:

Chapter 1

- Updated tax rates for 2022 and Examples 1-3 through 1-7.
- Updated Social Security wage base for 2022.
- Updated unified tax credit for 2022.
- Updated Taxes in the Real World: National Debt for current debt limit.

Chapter 2

- Updated gross income thresholds by filing status for 2022.
- Added Taxes in the Real World: Where Can You Get a 4 to 1 Return on Investment?
- Expanded discussion on questions of fact and questions of law.
- Added discussion of common law under tax professional responsibilities.
- Added discussion of definition of tax return preparer.
- Updated and clarified penalty amounts for failure to file a tax return and failure to pay tax owed.

Chapter 3

- Updated tax rates to 2022 tax rates.
- Updated Exhibit 3-3 for 2022 tax rates.
- Updated Example 3-8 for 2022 tax brackets.
- Added new Taxes in the Real World: Timing Is Everything.

Chapter 4

- Significantly revised the section dealing with taxation of net capital gains and deduction for net capital losses.
- Added problem on netting capital gains and losses.
- Revised discussion on qualifying person for head of household to highlight special rules.
- Reorganized the placement of the discussion on married taxpayers who are treated as unmarried to follow the discussion of married taxpayers filing jointly or separately.
- Updated tax rates to 2022 rates.
- Updated tax forms to 2021 tax forms.
- Edited discussion of Form 1040 to match up with revised tax forms for 2021.
- Updated Exhibit 4-7 to reflect standard deduction amounts for 2022.
- Added new Taxes in the Real World discussion dealing with the definition of married couple and associated terminology.

Chapter 5

- Updated for 2022 dependent care benefit exclusion amount.
- Updated for 2022 amounts for qualified transportation benefits.
- Updated for 2022 flexible spending account contributions and carryover amounts.
- Added discussion of health savings accounts.
- Updated for 2022 foreign income exclusion amounts.
- Updated for annual gift tax exclusion and unified tax credit for 2022.
- Updated U.S. Series EE bond interest income exclusion for 2022.
- Updated tax forms to 2021.

Chapter 6

- Updated excess business loss limitation for 2022.
- Added discussion of deductions for health savings accounts.
- Updated discussion of deduction for interest on qualified education loan for 2022.
- Updated mileage rate for medical expense itemized deduction for 2022.
- Revised discussion of charitable contribution limits.
- Updated standard deduction amounts for 2022 amounts.
- Updated discussion for deduction for qualified business income for 2022.
- Updated tax forms to 2021.

Chapter 7

- Updated tax rates in all examples and problems for 2022.
- Revised discussion of the tax treatment of qualified small business stock.
- Updated Exhibit 7-3 for 2022 capital gains tax brackets.

- Revised and streamlined the discussion of the capital gains netting process.
- Revised examples of capital gains netting process.
- Updated examples for changes in capital gains tax rate thresholds.
- Added new Exhibit 7-6 to provide Form 1099-B for investment income.
- Updated tax forms to 2021.
- Added additional references to cryptocurrency.
- Added new discussion of the treatment of cryptocurrency under the wash sale rules.
- Added new appendix for more detailed step-by-step for the capital gains netting process with all categories of long-term capital gains.
- Added new Taxes in the Real World: The Times They Are A-Changin'.
- Added new Taxes in the Real World: The Next Big Thing?

Chapter 8

- Updated tax rate schedules for 2022.
- Updated discussion of kiddie tax for 2022.
- Updated AMT exemption and tax rate schedule for 2022.
- Updated Social Security tax wage base and self-employment tax base for 2022.
- Revised discussion of 2022 child tax credit.
- Updated for 2022 revised child and dependent care credit.
- Updated discussion of earned income credit for 2022.
- Revised discussion of late filing and late payment penalties when both apply.
- Updated tax forms to 2021.

Chapter 9

- Updated tax forms from 2020 to 2021.
- Updated examples and problems for changes in inflation limit on gross receipts test.
- Added new Taxes in the Real World on whether cost of goods sold is subject to the test for economic performance.
- Clarified exception for prohibition of expense deduction by cannabis businesses.
- Explained and illustrated new small business accounting regulations.
- Integrated gross receipts test into accounting limitations.
- Added explanations of new regulations limiting entertainment and travel deductions including revised examples.
- Described and illustrated accounting for nonincidental material.
- Updated mileage deductions for travel in 2022.
- Added new Taxes in the Real World on Cryptocurrency and Income from a Hard Fork.

Chapter 10

- Updated Exhibit 10-2 for Weyerhaueser's 2020 assets.
- Updated tax rates to 2022 rates.
- Revised section on §179 amounts to reflect the inflation adjustments for 2022.
- Updated examples for 2022 §179 amounts.
- Updated discussion and Exhibit 10-10 relating to automobile depreciation limits.
- Updated §179 amount for SUVs for 2022 inflation amount changes.
- Updated tax forms to 2021.
- Updated and revised end-of-chapter problems for §179 amounts and bonus depreciation rules.
- Revised discussion of research and experimentation expenditures to reflect disallowance of the immediate expensing option in 2022.
- Added new Taxes in the Real World: The Case of How Sports Owners Pay Lower Tax Rates Than the Stadium Beer Server.

Chapter 11

- Updated tax rates for 2022.
- Updated tax forms from 2020 to 2021 forms.
- Added new Taxes in the Real World: Buyer Beware.

Chapter 12

- Updated fringe benefits Exhibit 12-10 for CARES Act.
- Updated qualified transportation fringe benefit amounts for 2022.
- Updated tax forms to 2021.
- Updated Taxes in the Real World for 2021 proxy statement information.

Chapter 13

- Revised introduction to discuss all types of retirement plans discussed in the chapter.
- Revised discussion about compensation limits for purposes of computing retirement benefit from defined benefit plans.
- Added new discussion question and new problem on defined benefit plans.
- Added new discussion question on backdoor Roth IRA contributions.
- Updated footnote 1 to reflect the 2021 OASDI Trustees report.
- Updated inflation-adjusted contribution limits for defined benefit plans, defined contribution plans, and individually managed plans.
- Added new Taxes in the Real World about accumulating wealth in Roth IRAs.
- Updated life expectancy and distribution tables for tables applicable beginning to distribution years beginning on or after January 1, 2022.

- Added basic rules to compute self-employment tax deduction for purposes of determining SEP IRA and individual 401(k) limits.
- Added discussion about Roth option for individual 401(k)s (but not SEPs).
- Added discussion on contributing to SEP and converting to Roth IRA.
- Reorganized Contribution and Distribution sections for traditional IRAs.
- Added discussion of "backdoor" Roth IRA contributions.
- Updated modified AGI phase-out thresholds for deductible contributions to traditional IRAs and contributions to Roth IRAs.
- Updated calculations for limits on self-employed retirement accounts to reflect updated 2022 Social Security wage base limitation.
- Updated saver's credit information for 2022.

Chapter 14

- Revised problems 43, 44, 45, 49, 58, 59, 63, and 69.
- Updated solutions to reflect 2022 inflation-adjusted numbers.
- Updated tax forms to 2021.
- Updated settlement statement in Appendix B to reflect 2022 information.
- Included a discussion and new example explaining how costs are allocated when less than a full dwelling unit is rented (such as a bedroom or a basement).
- Included a Form 1098 with explanation on how to interpret the document.

Chapter 15

- Added discussion and new example illustrating double taxation of C corporations and single taxation of flow-through entities (including basis in ownership interest in entity).
- Added discussion on the qualified business income (QBI) deduction, including two new examples.
- Enhanced QBI-related problems to include limitations.
- Added discussion and new example on self-employment tax.
- Added discussion relating to tax-exempt organizations.
- Added new discussion question dealing with tax-exempt organizations.
- Added new exhibit comparing tax characteristics by tax entity type.
- Added discussion and new example on owner compensation when owners provide services.
- Added new Taxes in the Real World dealing with unreasonable compensation paid to S corporation shareholder/employees.
- Updated Social Security wage base limitation for 2022, including related calculations.
- Updated inflation-adjusted numbers for excess business loss threshold and gross receipts test to reflect 2022 numbers.
- Added and/or revised several discussion questions and problems, including adding a new comprehensive problem.
- Updated tax forms to 2021 in problem solutions.

Chapter 16

- Revised section dealing with book–tax difference on an investment held for trading.
- Added summary of temporary book–tax differences for installment sales and like-kind exchanges.
- Added example on the book-tax differences associated with organizational expenditures.
- Revised net operating loss discussion.
- Added new Taxes in the Real World about whether large corporations are paying enough taxes.
- Added note to Exhibit 16-6 to mention that NOL deductions may be limited when there is an ownership change.
- Revised charitable deduction limitation discussion and example to reflect differences in charitable contribution limit between 2021 and 2022.
- Updated the gross receipts test for the cash method to reflect the inflation-adjusted threshold for 2022.
- Updated dates in examples and problems from 2021 to 2021.
- Updated tax forms to 2022.

Chapter 17

- Added new discussion of ASC 740 objectives.
- Added new Examples 17-1 and 17-2 to illustrate the importance of ASC 740 and its objectives.
- Revised net operating loss discussion in the valuation allowance section to describe tax law changes relating to net operating losses under the CARES Act.
- Updated text discussion for tax law changes introduced by the Consolidated Appropriations Act (CAA), 2021, signed on December 27, 2020. This includes updating the deductibility of the cost of meals purchased at a restaurant and updating the income percentage limitation for qualified charitable contributions.
- Updated examples and problems to reflect the tax law changes introduced by the CAA.
- Revised and streamlined the Tax Provision Process to five steps.
- Added new Exhibit 17-6 for the current tax expense formula.

- Revised discussion of the calculation of the current income tax expense.
- Revised discussion of the determination of the deferred tax assets and liabilities.
- Added new Exhibit 17-7 to illustrate taxable and deductible temporary differences.
- Added new Exhibit 17-8 to provide PCC's tax basis balance sheet.
- Added new discussion of tax basis liabilities and the balance sheet method of determining the deferred tax assets and liabilities.
- Revised Examples 17-7 through 17-13 to illustrate the balance sheet approach.
- Added formula for the total tax expense.
- Revised the discussion of the required journal entries to book the current and deferred income tax expense or benefit.
- Expanded the discussion of the journal entries related to the valuation allowance.
- Added discussion of journal entries related to uncertain tax positions.
- Updated dates in examples and problems from 2021 to 2022.
- Updated the Subsequent Events discussion for uncertain tax benefits.
- Updated Exhibit 17-9 for Microsoft uncertain tax benefit footnote disclosure.
- Added new Taxes in the Real World: Material Weaknesses in Tax Reporting.

Chapter 18

- Modified examples and discussion to clarify distinction between calculating accumulated and current earnings and profits.
- Added new Taxes in the Real World describing the importance of record keeping in calculating the tax basis of shares of corporate stock.
- Clarified examples of stock attribution from entities to owners or beneficiaries.
- Added new Taxes in the Real World illustrating the substance-over-form doctrine.
- Clarified homework problems on calculation of current earnings and profits.

Chapter 19

- Clarified discussion and example of receipt of stock for services in §351.
- Modified version of ethics question on accommodation transfers.
- Revised explanation of corporate basis calculation when shareholders receive boot in a §351 transaction.
- Clarified that merger negotiations must simultaneously consider both the form and the price of a corporate acquisition.
- Added new Taxes in the Real World on reverse Special Purpose Acquisition Company (SPAC) mergers.
- Added new alternatives to corporate liquidation problems.

Chapter 20

- Updated discussion on excess business loss limitation to reflect inflation adjustments of threshold amounts.
- Updated discussion on the availability of the cash method to partnerships with corporate partners to reflect inflation adjustments to the average annual gross receipts test.
- Updated discussion on the applicability of the limitation on business interest expense to partners and partnerships to reflect inflation adjustments to the average annual gross receipts test.
- Added new discussion of forms K-2 and K-3 filed by partnerships.
- Added a new discussion of how passive activity losses carried forward are used when a partner sells their interest in a partnership.
- Updated tax forms to 2021.
- Revised end-of-chapter problems to reflect inflation adjustments.

Chapter 21

- Updated Form 1065 late filing penalty amounts.
- Added a new Taxes in the Real World item describing how owners of sports franchises utilize special basis adjustments available to partners to deduct a substantial amount of their purchase price.
- Added a new discussion of partnership terminations and their implications.

Chapter 22

- Updated excess business loss limitation for 2022.
- Added a new Taxes in the Real World on S corporation elections and venture capital.
- Updated Social Security tax wage base for 2022.
- Updated tax forms to 2021.

Chapter 23

- Updated economic sales tax nexus for updates related to *South Dakota v. Wayfair, Inc.*
- Updated nexus discussion to reflect sales tax nexus and income tax nexus being different.

Chapter 24

- Updated the discussion on the OECD base erosion and profit-shifting project to reflect the recent adoption by OECD countries of a worldwide minimum tax rate.
- Updated the discussion on the level of foreign investment in the U.S and the level of U.S. investment in foreign countries.
- Updated tax forms to 2021.

Chapter 25

- Revised text and Exhibit 25-2 for changes in the applicable exclusion amount.
- Revised for inflation adjustment for annual gift tax exclusion.
- Explained and illustrated calculation of applicable credit in event that the applicable exclusion amount is reduced in the future.
- Explained and illustrated calculation of deceased spousal unused exclusion (DSUE) for changes in the applicable exclusion amount at the death of the surviving spouse.
- Added new homework problem on use of the DSUE portability election.
- Modified homework problem on calculation of estate tax in a contemplation of death transfer.
- Clarified and illustrated shortcut method to calculate transfer taxes.
- Updated 2020 tax forms with 2021 forms.

As We Go to Press

The 2023 Edition includes tax law enacted as part of the Consolidated Appropriations Act, 2021 (CAA), signed into law on December 27, 2020, and the American Rescue Plan Act of 2021 (ARP), signed into law on March 11, 2021. The 2023 Edition is current through February 8, 2022. You can visit the *Connect Library* for updates that occur after this date.

Table of Contents

1 An Introduction to Tax

Who Cares about Taxes and Why? 1-2
What Qualifies as a Tax? 1-4
How to Calculate a Tax 1-5
Different Ways to Measure Tax Rates 1-5
Tax Rate Structures 1-8
  Proportional Tax Rate Structure 1-9
  Progressive Tax Rate Structure 1-9
  Regressive Tax Rate Structure 1-10
Types of Taxes 1-11
  Federal Taxes 1-11
    Income Tax 1-12
    Employment and Unemployment Taxes 1-12
    Excise Taxes 1-13
    Transfer Taxes 1-13
  State and Local Taxes 1-14
    Income Taxes 1-14
    Sales and Use Taxes 1-14
    Property Taxes 1-15
    Excise Taxes 1-15
  Implicit Taxes 1-16
Evaluating Alternative Tax Systems 1-17
  Sufficiency 1-18
    Static versus Dynamic Forecasting 1-18
    Income versus Substitution Effects 1-19
  Equity 1-20
    Horizontal versus Vertical Equity 1-21
  Certainty 1-22
  Convenience 1-22
  Economy 1-22
  Evaluating Tax Systems—The Trade-Offs 1-23
Conclusion 1-23

2 Tax Compliance, the IRS, and Tax Authorities

Taxpayer Filing Requirements 2-2
  Tax Return Due Date and Extensions 2-3
  Statute of Limitations 2-3
IRS Audit Selection 2-4
  Types of Audits 2-6
    After the Audit 2-6
Tax Law Sources 2-9
  Legislative Sources: Congress and the Constitution 2-11
    Internal Revenue Code 2-11
    The Legislative Process for Tax Laws 2-12
    Basic Organization of the Code 2-13
    Tax Treaties 2-14
  Judicial Sources: The Courts 2-14
  Administrative Sources: The U.S. Treasury 2-15
    Regulations, Revenue Rulings, and Revenue Procedures 2-15
    Letter Rulings 2-16
Tax Research 2-17
  Step 1: Understand Facts 2-17
  Step 2: Identify Issues 2-17
  Step 3: Locate Relevant Authorities 2-18
  Step 4: Analyze Tax Authorities 2-19
  Step 5: Document and Communicate the Results 2-21
    Facts 2-21
    Issues 2-21
    Authorities 2-22
    Conclusion 2-22
    Analysis 2-22
    Client Letters 2-22
Tax Professional Responsibilities 2-23
Taxpayer and Tax Return Preparer Penalties 2-26
Conclusion 2-28

3 Tax Planning Strategies and Related Limitations

Basic Tax Planning Overview 3-2
Timing Strategies 3-2
  Present Value of Money 3-3
  The Timing Strategy When Tax Rates Are Constant 3-4
  The Timing Strategy When Tax Rates Change 3-7
    Limitations to Timing Strategies 3-10
Income-Shifting Strategies 3-11
  Transactions between Family Members and Limitations 3-12

Transactions between Owners and Their Businesses and Limitations 3-12
Income Shifting across Jurisdictions and Limitations 3-15
Conversion Strategies 3-15
Limitations of Conversion Strategies 3-18
Additional Limitations to Tax Planning Strategies: Judicially Based Doctrines 3-18
Tax Avoidance versus Tax Evasion 3-19
Conclusion 3-21

4 Individual Income Tax Overview, Dependents, and Filing Status

The Individual Income Tax Formula 4-2
Gross Income 4-2
Character of Income 4-5
Deductions 4-8
For AGI Deductions 4-9
From AGI Deductions 4-9
Income Tax Calculation 4-11
Other Taxes 4-11
Tax Credits 4-12
Tax Prepayments 4-12
Dependents of the Taxpayer 4-13
Dependency Requirements 4-13
Qualifying Child 4-13
Qualifying Relative 4-15
Filing Status 4-19
Married Filing Jointly and Married Filing Separately 4-19
Married Individuals Treated as Unmarried (Abandoned Spouse) 4-21
Qualifying Widow or Widower (Surviving Spouse) 4-22
Single 4-22
Head of Household 4-22
Summary of Income Tax Formula 4-25
Conclusion 4-28

5 Gross Income and Exclusions

Realization and Recognition of Income 5-2
What Is Included in Gross Income? 5-2
Economic Benefit 5-3
Realization Principle 5-3
Recognition 5-4
Other Income Concepts 5-4
Form of Receipt 5-4
Return of Capital Principle 5-4
Recovery of Amounts Previously Deducted 5-5
When Do Taxpayers Recognize Income? 5-6
Accounting Methods 5-7
Constructive Receipt 5-7
Claim of Right 5-7
Who Recognizes the Income? 5-8
Assignment of Income 5-8
Community Property Systems 5-8
Types of Income 5-10
Income from Services 5-10
Income from Property 5-10
Annuities 5-11
Property Dispositions 5-13
Other Sources of Gross Income 5-14
Income from Flow-Through Entities 5-14
Alimony 5-14
Prizes, Awards, and Gambling Winnings 5-16
Social Security Benefits 5-17
Imputed Income 5-19
Discharge of Indebtedness 5-20
Exclusion Provisions 5-21
Common Exclusions 5-21
Municipal Bond Interest 5-21
Gains on the Sale of Personal Residence 5-22
Fringe Benefits 5-23
Education-Related Exclusions 5-25
Scholarships 5-25
Other Educational Subsidies 5-25
U.S. Series EE Bonds 5-26
Exclusions That Mitigate Double Taxation 5-26
Gifts and Inheritances 5-27
Life Insurance Proceeds 5-27
Foreign-Earned Income 5-28
Sickness and Injury-Related Exclusions 5-29
Workers' Compensation 5-29
Payments Associated with Personal Injury 5-29
Health Care Reimbursement 5-30
Disability Insurance 5-30
Deferral Provisions 5-31
Income Summary 5-31
Conclusion 5-32

6 Individual Deductions

Deductions *for* AGI 6-2
Deductions Directly Related to Business Activities 6-2
Trade or Business Expenses 6-3
Rental and Royalty Expenses 6-5

Losses on Dispositions 6-6
Flow-Through Entities 6-6
Excess Business Loss Limitation 6-6
Deductions Indirectly Related to Business Activities 6-7
Moving Expenses 6-7
Health Insurance Deduction by Self-Employed Taxpayers 6-7
Self-Employment Tax Deduction 6-8
Deductions for Individual Retirement Accounts (IRAs) 6-8
Deductions for Health Savings Accounts 6-8
Penalty for Early Withdrawal of Savings 6-9
Deductions Subsidizing Specific Activities 6-10
Deduction for Interest on Qualified Education Loans 6-10
Summary: Deductions for AGI 6-11
Deductions from AGI: Itemized Deductions 6-14
Medical Expenses 6-14
Transportation and Travel for Medical Purposes 6-15
Hospitals and Long-Term Care Facilities 6-15
Medical Expense Deduction Limitation 6-16
Taxes 6-16
Interest 6-18
Charitable Contributions 6-19
Contributions of Money 6-19
Contributions of Property Other Than Money 6-20
Charitable Contribution Deduction Limitations 6-22
Special 2021 from AGI Charitable Contribution Deduction for Taxpayers Not Itemizing Deductions 6-24
Casualty and Theft Losses on Personal-Use Assets 6-25
Other Itemized Deductions 6-25
Summary of Itemized Deductions 6-25
The Standard Deduction 6-27
Standard Deduction 6-27
Bunching Itemized Deductions 6-29
Deduction for Qualified Business Income 6-29
Deduction for Qualified Business Income 6-29
Limitations 6-32
Taxable Income Summary 6-33
Conclusion 6-34

7 Investments

Investments Overview 7-2
Portfolio Income: Interest and Dividends 7-2
Interest 7-3
Corporate and U.S. Treasury Bonds 7-3
U.S. Savings Bonds 7-4
Dividends 7-6
Portfolio Income: Capital Gains and Losses 7-7
Types of Capital Gains and Losses 7-10
25 Percent Gains 7-11
28 Percent Gains 7-12
Netting Process for Gains and Losses 7-13
Calculating Tax Liability on Net Capital Gains 7-17
Limits for Capital Loss Deductions 7-23
Losses on the Sale of Personal-Use Assets 7-23
Capital Losses on Sales to Related Persons 7-23
Wash Sales 7-23
Balancing Tax Planning Strategies for Capital Assets with Other Goals 7-25
Portfolio Income Summary 7-26
Investment Interest Expense and Net Investment Income Tax 7-26
Net Investment Income Tax 7-28
Passive Activity Income and Losses 7-29
Passive Activity Definition 7-30
Income and Loss Categories 7-31
Rental Real Estate Exception to the Passive Activity Loss Rules 7-33
Net Investment Income Tax on Net Passive Income 7-33
Conclusion 7-34

8 Individual Income Tax Computation and Tax Credits

Regular Federal Income Tax Computation 8-2
Tax Rate Schedules 8-2
Marriage Penalty or Benefit 8-3
Exceptions to the Basic Tax Computation 8-3
Preferential Tax Rates for Capital Gains and Dividends 8-4
Kiddie Tax 8-5
Alternative Minimum Tax 8-7
Alternative Minimum Tax Formula 8-7
Alternative Minimum Taxable Income 8-8
AMT Exemption 8-11
Tentative Minimum Tax and AMT Computation 8-12

Additional Taxes 8-13
Net Investment Income Tax 8-13
Employment and Self-Employment Taxes 8-14
Employee FICA Taxes Payable 8-14
Self-Employment Taxes 8-16
Employee vs. Self-Employed (Independent Contractor) 8-21
Tax Credits 8-23
Nonrefundable Personal Credits 8-24
Child Tax Credit 8-24
Additional Child Tax Credit for 2021 Only 8-25
Child and Dependent Care Credit 8-26
Education Credits 8-28
Refundable Personal Credits 8-30
Earned Income Credit 8-30
Special Tax Credit For 2021 8-32
Other Refundable Personal Credits 8-33
Business Tax Credits 8-33
Foreign Tax Credit 8-33
Tax Credit Summary 8-34
Credit Application Sequence 8-35
Taxpayer Prepayments and Filing Requirements 8-36
Prepayments 8-36
Underpayment Penalties 8-36
Filing Requirements 8-38
Late Filing Penalty 8-39
Late Payment Penalty 8-39
Tax Summary 8-39
Conclusion 8-40

9 Business Income, Deductions, and Accounting Methods

Business Gross Income 9-2
Gross Receipts Test for Determining Small Businesses 9-2
Business Deductions 9-3
Ordinary and Necessary 9-4
Reasonable in Amount 9-5
Limitations on Business Deductions 9-6
Expenditures against Public Policy 9-6
Political Contributions and Lobbying Costs 9-6
Capital Expenditures 9-7
Expenses Associated with the Production of Tax-Exempt Income 9-7
Personal Expenditures 9-7
Mixed-Motive Expenditures 9-8
Travel and Transportation 9-9
Property Use 9-11
Record Keeping and Other Requirements 9-12
Limitation on Business Interest Deductions 9-12
Calculating the Interest Limitation 9-12
Losses on Dispositions of Business Property 9-13
Business Casualty Losses 9-13
Accounting Periods 9-14
Accounting Methods 9-15
Financial and Tax Accounting Methods 9-15
Overall Accounting Method 9-16
Cash Method 9-16
Accrual Method 9-17
Accrual Income 9-18
All-Events Test for Income 9-18
Taxation of Advance Payments of Income (Unearned Income) 9-18
Inventories 9-19
Uniform Capitalization 9-20
Inventory Cost-Flow Methods 9-21
Accrual Deductions 9-22
Economic Performance 9-23
Bad Debt Expense 9-27
Limitations on Accruals 9-27
Comparison of Accrual and Cash Methods 9-28
Adopting an Accounting Method 9-29
Changing Accounting Methods 9-30
Tax Consequences of Changing Accounting Methods 9-32
Conclusion 9-33

10 Property Acquisition and Cost Recovery

Cost Recovery and Tax Basis for Cost Recovery 10-2
Basis for Cost Recovery 10-3
Depreciation 10-6
Personal Property Depreciation 10-7
Depreciation Method 10-7
Depreciation Recovery Period 10-8
Depreciation Conventions 10-9
Calculating Depreciation for Personal Property 10-10
Applying the Half-Year Convention 10-11
Applying the Mid-Quarter Convention 10-13
Real Property 10-14
Applicable Method 10-15
Applicable Convention 10-15
Depreciation Tables 10-15

Special Rules Relating to Cost Recovery 10-17
Immediate Expensing (§179) 10-17
Bonus Depreciation 10-21
Listed Property 10-22
Luxury Automobiles 10-25
Depreciation for the Alternative Minimum Tax 10-29
Depreciation Summary 10-29
Amortization 10-31
Section 197 Intangibles 10-31
Organizational Expenditures and Start-Up Costs 10-32
Research and Experimentation Expenditures 10-35
Patents and Copyrights 10-36
Amortizable Intangible Asset Summary 10-36
Depletion 10-37
Conclusion 10-40

11 Property Dispositions

Dispositions 11-2
Amount Realized 11-2
Determination of Adjusted Basis 11-3
Gifts 11-3
Inherited Property 11-3
Property Converted from Personal Use to Business Use 11-3
Realized Gain or Loss on Disposition 11-5
Recognized Gain or Loss on Disposition 11-6
Character of Gain or Loss 11-7
Ordinary Assets 11-7
Capital Assets 11-8
Section 1231 Assets 11-8
Depreciation Recapture 11-10
Section 1245 Property 11-10
Scenario 1: Gain Created Solely through Cost Recovery Deductions 11-11
Scenario 2: Gain Due to Both Cost Recovery Deductions and Asset Appreciation 11-12
Scenario 3: Asset Sold at a Loss 11-12
Section 1250 Depreciation Recapture for Real Property 11-14
Other Provisions Affecting the Rate at Which Gains Are Taxed 11-15
Unrecaptured §1250 Gain for Individuals 11-15
Characterizing Gains on the Sale of Depreciable Property to Related Persons 11-16
Calculating Net §1231 Gains or Losses 11-17
Section 1231 Look-Back Rule 11-17
Gain or Loss Summary 11-20
Tax-Deferred Transactions 11-24
Like-Kind Exchanges 11-24
Definition of Like-Kind Property 11-24
Property Use 11-25
Timing Requirements for a Like-Kind Exchange 11-25
Tax Consequences When Like-Kind Property Is Exchanged Solely for Like-Kind Property 11-26
Tax Consequences of Transfers Involving Like-Kind and Non-Like-Kind Property (Boot) 11-27
Reporting Like-Kind Exchanges 11-29
Involuntary Conversions 11-29
Installment Sales 11-31
Gains Ineligible for Installment Reporting 11-33
Other Tax-Deferred Provisions 11-34
Related-Person Loss Disallowance Rules 11-34
Conclusion 11-35

12 Compensation

Salary and Wages 12-2
Employee Considerations for Salary and Wages 12-2
Tax Withholding 12-2
Employer Considerations for Salary and Wages 12-2
Deductibility of Salary and Wage Payments 12-2
Equity-Based Compensation 12-7
Stock Options 12-9
Employee Tax Considerations for Stock Options 12-10
Employer Tax Considerations for Stock Options 12-14
Restricted Stock 12-16
Employee Tax Considerations for Restricted Stock 12-17
Employer Tax Considerations for Restricted Stock 12-19
Qualified Equity Grants 12-20
Equity-Based Compensation Summary 12-20
Fringe Benefits 12-21
Taxable Fringe Benefits 12-21
Employee Considerations for Taxable Fringe Benefits 12-22
Employer Considerations for Taxable Fringe Benefits 12-24
Nontaxable Fringe Benefits 12-25

Group-Term Life Insurance 12-26
Health and Accident Insurance and Benefits 12-27
Meals and Lodging for the Convenience of the Employer 12-27
Employee Educational Assistance 12-28
Dependent-Care Benefits 12-28
No-Additional-Cost Services 12-28
Qualified Employee Discounts 12-29
Working Condition Fringe Benefits 12-30
De Minimis Fringe Benefits 12-30
Qualified Transportation Fringe Benefits 12-30
Cafeteria Plans and Flexible Spending Accounts 12-31
Employee and Employer Considerations for Nontaxable Fringe Benefits 12-31
Tax Planning with Fringe Benefits 12-31
Fringe Benefits Summary 12-33
Conclusion 12-34

13 Retirement Savings and Deferred Compensation

Employer-Provided Qualified Plans 13-3
Defined Benefit Plans 13-3
Vesting 13-4
Distributions 13-5
Nontax Considerations 13-5
Defined Contribution Plans 13-6
Employer Matching 13-7
Contribution Limits 13-7
Vesting 13-8
After-Tax Cost of Contributions to Traditional (non-Roth) Defined Contribution Plans 13-9
Distributions from Traditional Defined Contribution Plans 13-10
After-Tax Rates of Return for Traditional Defined Contribution Plans 13-12
Roth 401(k) Plans 13-12
Comparing Traditional Defined Contribution Plans and Roth 401(k) Plans 13-15
Nonqualified Deferred Compensation Plans 13-16
Nonqualified Plans versus Qualified Defined Contribution Plans 13-16
Employee Considerations 13-17
Employer Considerations 13-19
Individually Managed Qualified Retirement Plans 13-20
Individual Retirement Accounts 13-20
Traditional IRAs 13-20
Deductible Contributions 13-20
Nondeductible Contributions 13-23
Distributions 13-23
Roth IRAs 13-24
Contributions 13-24
Distributions 13-25
Converting a Traditional IRA to a Roth IRA 13-26
Comparing Traditional and Roth IRAs 13-28
Self-Employed Retirement Accounts 13-29
Simplified Employee Pension (SEP) IRA 13-30
Nontax Considerations 13-31
Individual 401(k) Plans 13-31
Nontax Considerations 13-31
Saver's Credit 13-33
Conclusion 13-34

14 Tax Consequences of Home Ownership

Is a Dwelling Unit a Principal Residence, Residence, or Nonresidence? 14-2
Personal Use of the Home 14-4
Exclusion of Gain on Sale of Personal Residence 14-4
Requirements 14-5
Home Mortgage Interest Deduction 14-8
Acquisition Indebtedness 14-9
Limitation on Acquisition Indebtedness 14-10
Mortgage Insurance 14-13
Points 14-13
Real Property Taxes 14-15
Rental Use of the Home 14-16
Residence with Minimal Rental Use 14-17
Residence with Significant Rental Use (Vacation Home) 14-18
Deducting Rental Expenses of Vacation Home 14-19
Nonresidence (Rental Property) 14-24
Losses on Rental Property 14-24
Business Use of the Home 14-26
Direct versus Indirect Expenses 14-28
Limitations on Deductibility of Expenses 14-29
Conclusion 14-32

15 Business Entities Overview

Business Entity Legal Classification and Nontax Characteristics 15-2
Legal Classification 15-2
Nontax Characteristics 15-2

Responsibility for Liabilities 15-3
Rights, Responsibilities, and Legal Arrangements among Owners 15-3
Business Entity Tax Classification 15-5
Business Entity Tax Characteristics 15-7
Taxation of Business Entity Income 15-7
The Taxation of Flow-Through Entity Business Income 15-8
Overall Tax Rate of C Corporation Income 15-18
Owner Compensation 15-22
Deductibility of Entity Losses 15-26
Other Tax Characteristics 15-31
Converting to Other Business Entity Types 15-31
Conclusion 15-35

16 Corporate Operations

Corporate Taxable Income Formula 16-2
Accounting Periods and Methods 16-2
Computing Corporate Taxable Income 16-3
Book–Tax Differences 16-3
Common Permanent Book–Tax Differences 16-4
Common Temporary Book–Tax Differences 16-5
Corporate-Specific Deductions and Associated Book–Tax Differences 16-10
Stock Options 16-10
Net Capital Losses 16-13
Net Operating Losses 16-14
Charitable Contributions 16-16
Dividends-Received Deduction 16-19
Taxable Income Summary 16-22
Corporate Income Tax Liability 16-23
Compliance 16-23
Consolidated Tax Returns 16-26
Corporate Tax Return Due Dates and Estimated Taxes 16-26
Conclusion 16-30

17 Accounting for Income Taxes

Accounting for Income Taxes and the Income Tax Provision Process 17-2
Why Is Accounting for Income Taxes So Complex? 17-3
Objectives of ASC 740 17-3
The Income Tax Provision Process 17-5
Calculating a Company's Income Tax Provision 17-7
Step 1: Identify All Permanent and Temporary Differences and Tax Carryover Amounts and Calculate the Current Income Tax Provision (ASC 740 objective 1) 17-7
Permanent Differences 17-7
Temporary Differences and Tax Carryover Amounts 17-9
Calculate the Current Income Tax Expense or (Benefit) (ASC 740 Objective 1) 17-10
Step 2: Determine the Ending Balances in the Balance Sheet Deferred Tax Asset and Liability Accounts (ASC 740 Objective 2) 17-12
Identifying Taxable and Deductible Temporary Differences 17-12
Taxable Temporary Difference 17-12
Deductible Temporary Difference 17-13
Step 3: Calculate the Deferred Income Tax Provision and the Total Income Tax Provision 17-17
Deferred Income Tax Provision 17-17
Total Income Tax Provision 17-18
Journal Entries 17-19
Determining Whether a Valuation Allowance Is Needed 17-20
Step 4: Evaluate the Need for a Valuation Allowance for Gross Deferred Tax Assets 17-20
Determining the Need for a Valuation Allowance 17-20
Future Reversals of Existing Taxable Temporary Differences 17-20
Taxable Income in Prior Carryback Year(s) 17-21
Expected Future Taxable Income Exclusive of Reversing Temporary Differences and Carryovers 17-21
Tax Planning Strategies 17-21
Negative Evidence That a Valuation Allowance Is Needed 17-21
Valuation Allowance Journal Entries 17-21
Accounting for Uncertainty in Income Tax Positions 17-24
Step 5: Evaluate the Need for an Uncertain Tax Benefit Reserve 17-24
Application of ASC Topic 740 to Uncertain Tax Positions 17-25
Step 1: Recognition 17-25
Step 2: Measurement 17-25
Uncertain Tax Benefit Reserve Journal Entries 17-26
Subsequent Events 17-27
Interest and Penalties 17-28
Disclosures of Uncertain Tax Positions 17-28
Schedule UTP (Uncertain Tax Position) Statement 17-29

Financial Statement Disclosure and Computing a Corporation's Effective Tax Rate 17-29
Balance Sheet Classification 17-29
Income Tax Footnote Disclosure 17-29
Computation and Reconciliation of the Income Tax Provision with a Company's Hypothetical Tax Provision (Effective Tax Rate Reconciliation) 17-31
Importance of a Corporation's Effective Tax Rate 17-32
Interim Period Effective Tax Rates 17-33
FASB Projects Related to Accounting for Income Taxes 17-33
Conclusion 17-33

18 Corporate Taxation: Nonliquidating Distributions

Taxation of Property Distributions 18-2
Determining the Dividend Amount from Earnings and Profits 18-2
Overview 18-2
Dividends Defined 18-2
Computing Earnings and Profits 18-4
Nontaxable Income Included in Current E&P 18-4
Deductible Expenses That Do Not Reduce Current E&P 18-5
Nondeductible Expenses That Reduce Current E&P 18-5
Items Requiring Separate Accounting Methods for E&P Purposes 18-5
Ordering of E&P Distributions 18-8
Positive Current E&P and Positive Accumulated E&P 18-8
Positive Current E&P and Negative Accumulated E&P 18-10
Negative Current E&P and Positive Accumulated E&P 18-10
Negative Current E&P and Negative Accumulated E&P 18-11
Distributions of Noncash Property to Shareholders 18-12
Effect of Noncash Property Distributions on Taxable Income 18-13
Liabilities 18-13
Effect of Noncash Property Distributions on E&P 18-14
Stock Distributions 18-16
Tax Consequences to Shareholders Receiving a Stock Distribution 18-16
Nontaxable Stock Distributions 18-16
Taxable Stock Distributions 18-17
Stock Redemptions 18-17
The Form of a Stock Redemption 18-18
Redemptions That Reduce a Shareholder's Ownership Interest 18-19
Redemptions That Are Substantially Disproportionate 18-19
Complete Redemption of the Stock Owned by a Shareholder 18-22
Redemptions That Are Not Essentially Equivalent to a Dividend 18-23
Tax Consequences to the Distributing Corporation 18-25
Partial Liquidations 18-25
Conclusion 18-26

19 Corporate Formation, Reorganization, and Liquidation

Review of the Taxation of Property Dispositions 19-2
Tax-Deferred Transfers of Property to a Corporation 19-3
Transactions Subject to Tax Deferral 19-4
Meeting the Section 351 Tax Deferral Requirements 19-4
Section 351 Applies Only to the Transfer of Property to the Corporation 19-4
The Property Transferred to the Corporation Must Be Exchanged for Stock of the Corporation 19-5
The Transferor(s) of Property to the Corporation Must Be in Control of the Corporation, in the Aggregate, Immediately after the Transfer 19-5
Tax Consequences When a Shareholder Receives No Boot 19-7
Tax Consequences When a Shareholder Receives Boot 19-9
Assumption of Shareholder Liabilities by the Corporation 19-11
Tax-Avoidance Transactions 19-11
Liabilities in Excess of Basis 19-11
Tax Consequences to the Transferee Corporation 19-13
Other Issues Related to Incorporating an Ongoing Business 19-17
Depreciable Assets Transferred to a Corporation 19-17
Contributions to Capital 19-18
Section 1244 Stock 19-19
Taxable and Tax-Deferred Corporate Acquisitions 19-19
The Acquisition Tax Model 19-20

Tax Consequences to a Corporate Acquisition 19-22
Taxable Acquisitions 19-22
Tax-Deferred Acquisitions 19-25
Judicial Doctrines That Underlie All Tax-Deferred Reorganizations 19-25
Continuity of Interest 19-25
Continuity of Business Enterprise 19-25
Business Purpose Test 19-25
Type A Asset Acquisitions 19-26
Forward Triangular Merger 19-28
Reverse Triangular Merger 19-29
Type B Stock-for-Stock Reorganizations 19-29
Complete Liquidation of a Corporation 19-32
Tax Consequences to the Shareholders in a Complete Liquidation 19-33
Tax Consequences to the Liquidating Corporation in a Complete Liquidation 19-34
Taxable Liquidating Distributions 19-34
Tax Deferred Liquidating Distributions 19-37
Conclusion 19-37

20 Forming and Operating Partnerships

Flow-Through Entities Overview 20-2
Aggregate and Entity Concepts 20-3
Partnership Formations and Acquisitions of Partnership Interests 20-3
Acquiring Partnership Interests When Partnerships Are Formed 20-3
Contributions of Property 20-3
Contribution of Services 20-9
Organizational Expenditures, Start-Up Costs, and Syndication Costs 20-12
Acquisitions of Partnership Interests after Formation 20-13
Partnership Accounting: Tax Elections, Accounting Periods, and Accounting Methods 20-13
Tax Elections 20-14
Accounting Periods 20-14
Required Year-Ends 20-14
Accounting Methods 20-16
Reporting the Results of Partnership Operations 20-17
Ordinary Business Income (Loss) and Separately Stated Items 20-17
Guaranteed Payments 20-19
Self-Employment Tax 20-20
Limitation on Business Interest Expense 20-22
Deduction for Qualified Business Income 20-22
Net Investment Income Tax 20-23
Allocating Partners' Shares of Income and Loss 20-23
Partnership Compliance Issues 20-24
Adjusting a Partner's Tax Basis in Partnership Interest 20-28
Cash Distributions in Operating Partnerships 20-30
Loss Limitations 20-30
Tax-Basis Limitation 20-30
At-Risk Amount Limitation 20-31
Passive Activity Loss Limitation 20-32
Passive Activity Defined 20-32
Income and Loss Baskets 20-33
Excess Business Loss Limitation 20-35
Conclusion 20-36

21 Dispositions of Partnership Interests and Partnership Distributions

Basics of Sales of Partnership Interests 21-2
Seller Issues 21-2
Hot Assets 21-3
Buyer and Partnership Issues 21-7
Varying Interest Rule 21-8
Basics of Partnership Distributions 21-9
Operating Distributions 21-9
Operating Distributions of Money Only 21-9
Operating Distributions That Include Property Other Than Money 21-10
Liquidating Distributions 21-12
Gain or Loss Recognition in Liquidating Distributions 21-13
Basis in Distributed Property 21-13
Partner's Outside Basis in an Interest Is Greater Than Inside Bases of Distributed Assets 21-14
Partner's Outside Basis in an Interest Is Less Than Inside Bases of Distributed Assets 21-17
Character and Holding Period of Distributed Assets 21-21
Disproportionate Distributions 21-24
Special Basis Adjustments 21-26
Special Basis Adjustments for Dispositions 21-27
Special Basis Adjustments for Distributions 21-29
Conclusion 21-30

22 S Corporations

S Corporation Elections 22-2
- Formations 22-2
- S Corporation Qualification Requirements 22-2
- S Corporation Election 22-3

S Corporation Terminations 22-5
- Voluntary Terminations 22-5
- Involuntary Terminations 22-6
  - *Failure to Meet Requirements 22-6*
  - *Excess of Passive Investment Income 22-6*
- Short Tax Years 22-7
- S Corporation Reelections 22-8

Operating Issues 22-8
- Accounting Methods and Periods 22-8
- Income and Loss Allocations 22-9
- Separately Stated Items 22-10

Shareholder's Basis 22-12
  - *Initial Basis 22-12*
  - *Annual Basis Adjustments 22-13*
- Loss Limitations 22-14
  - *Tax-Basis Limitation 22-14*
  - *At-Risk Amount Limitation 22-15*
  - *Post-Termination Transition Period Loss Limitation 22-15*
  - *Passive Activity Loss Limitation 22-16*
  - *Excess Business Loss Limitation 22-17*
- Self-Employment Income 22-17
- Net Investment Income Tax 22-18
- Fringe Benefits 22-18

Distributions 22-19
- Operating Distributions 22-19
  - *S Corporation with No C Corporation Accumulated Earnings and Profits 22-19*
  - *S Corporation with C Corporation Accumulated Earnings and Profits 22-20*
  - *Property Distributions 22-22*
  - *Post-Termination Transition Period Distributions 22-22*
- Liquidating Distributions 22-23

S Corporation Taxes and Filing Requirements 22-24
- Built-in Gains Tax 22-24
- Excess Net Passive Income Tax 22-26
- LIFO Recapture Tax 22-27
- Estimated Taxes 22-28
- Filing Requirements 22-28

Comparing C and S Corporations and Partnerships 22-30

Conclusion 22-32

23 State and Local Taxes

State and Local Taxes 23-2

Sales and Use Taxes 23-5
- Sales Tax Nexus 23-5
- Sales Tax Liability 23-7

Income Taxes 23-9
- Income Tax Nexus 23-10
  - *Economic Presence 23-11*
  - *Protection under Public Law 86-272 23-11*
- Entities Included on Income Tax Return 23-15
  - *Separate Tax Returns 23-15*
  - *Unitary Tax Returns 23-15*
- State Taxable Income 23-16
- Dividing State Tax Base among States 23-18
  - *Business Income 23-18*
  - *Nonbusiness Income 23-24*
- State Income Tax Liability 23-24
- Nonincome-Based Taxes 23-25

Conclusion 23-26

24 The U.S. Taxation of Multinational Transactions

The U.S. Framework for Taxing Multinational Transactions 24-2
- U.S. Taxation of a Nonresident 24-3
- Definition of a Resident for U.S. Tax Purposes 24-4
- Overview of the U.S. Foreign Tax Credit System 24-5

U.S. Source Rules for Gross Income and Deductions 24-6
- Source-of-Income Rules 24-7
  - *Interest 24-7*
  - *Dividends 24-8*
  - *Compensation for Services 24-8*
  - *Rents and Royalties 24-9*
  - *Gain or Loss from Sale of Real Property 24-10*
  - *Gain or Loss from Sale of Purchased Personal Property 24-10*
  - *Gain or Loss from Sale of Manufactured Inventory 24-11*
- Source-of-Deduction Rules 24-11
  - *General Principles of Allocation and Apportionment 24-11*
  - *Special Apportionment Rules 24-12*

Operating Abroad through a Foreign Corporation 24-16
  - *Foreign-Derived Intangible Income 24-17*

Treaties 24-17

Foreign Tax Credits 24-20

FTC Limitation Categories of Taxable Income 24-20

Passive Category Income 24-20

General Category Income 24-20

Foreign Branch Income 24-20

GILTI Income 24-20

Creditable Foreign Taxes 24-21

Direct Taxes 24-21

In Lieu of Taxes 24-21

Planning for International Operations 24-22

Check-the-Box Hybrid Entities 24-22

U.S. Anti-Deferral Rules 24-24

Definition of a Controlled Foreign Corporation 24-25

Definition of Subpart F Income 24-26

Planning to Avoid Subpart F Income 24-28

Global Intangible Low-Taxed Income 24-29

Base Erosion and Profit-Shifting Initiatives around the World 24-30

Conclusion 24-31

25 Transfer Taxes and Wealth Planning

Introduction to Federal Transfer Taxes 25-2

Beginnings 25-2

Common Features of Integrated Transfer Taxes 25-2

The Federal Gift Tax 25-4

Transfers Subject to Gift Tax 25-5

Valuation 25-7

The Annual Exclusion 25-9

Taxable Gifts 25-10

Gift-Splitting Election 25-10

Marital Deduction 25-10

Charitable Deduction 25-12

Computation of the Gift Tax 25-12

Tax on Current Taxable Gifts 25-13

Applicable Credit 25-14

The Federal Estate Tax 25-17

The Gross Estate 25-17

Specific Inclusions 25-19

Valuation 25-21

Gross Estate Summary 25-22

The Taxable Estate 25-23

Administrative Expenses, Debts, Losses, and State Death Taxes 25-23

Marital and Charitable Deductions 25-24

Computation of the Estate Tax 25-25

Adjusted Taxable Gifts 25-25

Applicable Credit 25-27

Wealth Planning Concepts 25-30

The Generation-Skipping Tax 25-30

Income Tax Considerations 25-30

Transfer Tax Planning Techniques 25-31

Serial Gifts 25-31

Step-Up in Tax Basis 25-31

Integrated Wealth Plans 25-33

Conclusion 25-34

Appendix A Tax Forms A

Appendix B Tax Terms Glossary B-1

Appendix C Tax Rates C-1

Code Index CI-1

Subject Index SI

chapter

1 An Introduction to Tax

Learning Objectives

Upon completing this chapter, you should be able to:

LO 1-1 Demonstrate how taxes influence basic business, investment, personal, and political decisions.

LO 1-2 Discuss what constitutes a tax and the general objectives of taxation.

LO 1-3 Describe the three basic tax rate structures and calculate a tax.

LO 1-4 Identify the various federal, state, and local taxes.

LO 1-5 Apply appropriate criteria to evaluate alternative tax systems.

Pixelheadphoto Digitalskillet/Shutterstock

Storyline Summary

Taxpayer:	Margaret (she/her/hers)
Employment status:	Margaret is a full-time student at the University of Georgia.
Current situation:	She is beginning her first tax class.

Margaret (she/her/hers) is a junior beginning her first tax course. She is excited about her career prospects as an accounting major but hasn't had much exposure to taxes. On her way to campus she runs into an old friend, Eddy (he/his), who is going to Washington, D.C., to protest recent proposed changes to the U.S. tax system. Eddy is convinced the IRS is evil and that the current tax system is blatantly unfair and corrupt. He advocates for a simpler, fairer method of taxation. Margaret is intrigued by Eddy's passion but questions whether he has a complete understanding of the U.S. tax system. She decides to withhold all judgments about it (or about pursuing a career in taxation) until the end of her tax course. ■

LO 1-1 WHO CARES ABOUT TAXES AND WHY?

A clear understanding of the role of taxes in everyday decisions will help you make an informed decision about the value of studying taxation or pursuing a career in taxation. One view of taxation is that it represents an inconvenience every April 15th (the annual due date for filing federal individual tax returns without extensions). However, the role of taxation is much more pervasive than this view suggests. Your study of this subject will provide you a unique opportunity to develop an informed opinion about taxation. As a business student, you can overcome the mystery that encompasses popular impressions of the tax system and perhaps, one day, share your expertise with friends or clients.

What are some common decisions you face that taxes may influence? In this course, we alert you to situations in which you can increase your return on investments by up to one-third! Even the best lessons in finance courses can't approach the increase in risk-adjusted return that smart tax planning provides. Would you like to own your home someday? Tax deductions for home mortgage interest and real estate taxes can reduce the after-tax costs of owning a home relative to renting. Thus, when you face the decision to buy or rent, you can make an informed choice if you understand the relative tax advantages of home ownership. Would you like to retire someday? Understanding the tax-advantaged methods of saving for retirement can increase the after-tax value of your retirement nest egg—and thus increase the likelihood that you can afford to retire, and do so in style. Other common personal financial decisions that taxes influence include choosing investments, evaluating alternative job offers, saving for education expenses, and performing gift or estate planning. Indeed, taxes are a part of everyday life and have a significant effect on many of the personal financial decisions all of us face.

The role of taxes is not limited to personal finance. Taxes play an equally important role in fundamental business decisions such as the following:

- What organizational form should a business use?
- Where should the business be located?
- How should business acquisitions be structured?
- How should the business compensate employees?
- What is the appropriate mix of debt and equity for the business?
- Should the business rent or own its equipment and property?
- How should the business distribute profits to its owners?

Savvy business decisions require owners and managers to consider all costs and benefits in order to evaluate the merits of a transaction. Although taxes don't necessarily dominate these decisions, they do represent large transaction costs that businesses should factor into the financial decision-making process.

Taxes also play a major part in the political process. U.S. presidential candidates often distinguish themselves from their opponents based upon their tax rhetoric. Indeed, the major political parties generally have very diverse views of the appropriate way to tax the public.[1] Determining who is taxed, what is taxed, and how much is taxed are tough questions with nontrivial answers. Voters must have a basic understanding of taxes to evaluate the merits of alternative tax proposals. Later in this chapter, we'll introduce criteria you can use to evaluate alternative tax proposals.

[1]The U.S. Department of the Treasury provides a "history of taxation" on its website (www.treasury.gov/resource-center/faqs/Taxes/Pages/historyrooseveltmessage.aspx). You may find it interesting to read this history in light of the various political parties in office at the time.

TAXES IN THE REAL WORLD Tax Policy: Republicans versus Democrats

Both Democrats and Republicans desire the same things: a civilized society and a healthy economy. However, neither party can agree on what defines a civilized society or which path best leads to a healthy economy. As of August 2021 the national debt was $28.6 trillion, up from $26.8 trillion the year before, and growing, yet the only thing we might agree on is that something has gone wrong. Regardless of which party or candidate you support, each party's agenda will affect your income and taxes in various ways.

To explore the divide, let's examine excerpts from each party's National Platform from our most recent presidential election (2020).

Republicans

"We are the party of a growing economy that gives everyone a chance in life, an opportunity to learn, work, and realize the prosperity freedom makes possible."

"Government cannot create prosperity, though government can limit or destroy it. Prosperity is the product of self-discipline, enterprise, saving and investment by individuals, but it is not an end in itself. Prosperity provides the means by which citizens and their families can maintain their independence from government, raise their children by their own values, practice their faith, and build communities of cooperation and mutual respect."

"Republicans consider the establishment of a pro-growth tax code a moral imperative. More than any other public policy, the way government raises revenue—how much, at what rates, under what circumstances, from whom, and for whom—has the greatest impact on our economy's performance. It powerfully influences the level of economic growth and job creation, which translates into the level of opportunity for those who would otherwise be left behind."

"A strong economy is one key to debt reduction, but spending restraint is a necessary component that must be vigorously pursued."* www.gop.com/platform/restoring-the-american-dream/.

Democrats

"Our tax system has been rigged against the American people by big corporations and their lobbyists, and by Republican politicians who dole out tax cuts to their biggest donors while leaving working families to struggle."

"Democrats will take action to reverse the Trump Administration's tax cuts benefiting the wealthiest Americans and rewarding corporations for shipping American jobs overseas. We will crack down on overseas tax havens and close loopholes that are exploited by the wealthiest Americans and biggest corporations. We will make sure the wealthy pay their fair share in taxes. We will make sure investors pay the same tax rates as workers and bring an end to expensive and unproductive tax loopholes, including the carried interest loophole. Corporate tax rates, which were cut sharply by the 2017 Republican tax cut, must be raised, and 'trickle-down' tax cuts must be rejected. Estate taxes should also be raised back to the historical norm."

"Democrats will reform the tax code to be more progressive and equitable, and reduce barriers for working families to benefit from targeted tax breaks, including the Earned Income Tax Credit and the Child Tax Credit. Our program of reform will provide immediate, marked relief for working families, including more generous, refundable tax credits to benefit low- and middle-income families, and easier and more equitable access to tax provisions that help working families build wealth, including by equalizing tax benefits for retirement contributions and providing more accessible tax breaks for homeownership."† www.democrats.org/where-we-stand/party-platform/.

Conclusion

Each party fundamentally believes the government should create/maintain cities and states that form a civilized society, and that government should foster a healthy economy. However, they choose very different paths to reach this objective. Democrats want to raise taxes on the wealthy and create government programs that cost more money, while Republicans wish to lower taxes and decrease government size and spending. Both motives are authentic; however, current and cumulative deficits indicate that current revenue is insufficient to meet government spending. Solving these problems will require civil discourse, education, and research/information in order to find realistic, effective solutions.

*GOP, "Restoring the American Dream," www.gop.com/platform/restoring-the-american-dream/.

†Democratic Platform Committee, "The 2020 Democratic Party Platform," www.democrats.org/where-we-stand/party-platform/.

In summary, taxes affect many aspects of personal, business, and political decisions. Developing a solid understanding of taxation should allow you to make informed decisions in these areas. Thus, Margaret can take comfort that her semester will likely prove useful to her personally. Who knows? Depending on her interest in business, investment, retirement planning, and the like, she may ultimately decide to pursue a career in taxation.

LO 1-2

WHAT QUALIFIES AS A TAX?

"Taxes are the price we pay for a civilized society." —Oliver Wendell Holmes Jr.

Taxes have been described in many terms: some positive, some negative, some printable, some not. Let's go directly to a formal definition of a tax, which should prove useful in identifying alternative taxes and discussing alternative tax systems.

A **tax** *is a payment required by a government that is unrelated to any specific benefit or service received from the government.* The general purpose of a tax is to fund the operations of the government (to raise revenue). Taxes differ from fines and penalties in that taxes are not intended to punish or prevent illegal behavior. Nevertheless, by allowing deductions from income, our federal tax system encourages certain behaviors like charitable contributions, retirement savings, and research and development. Thus, we can view it as discouraging other legal behavior. For example, **sin taxes** impose relatively high surcharges on alcohol and tobacco products.[2] Cigarette taxes include a $1.01 per pack federal tax, a state tax in all 50 states, and also a few municipal taxes as well.[3]

Key components of the definition of a tax are that the payment is:

- Required (it is not voluntary);
- Imposed by a government agency (federal, state, or local); and
- Not tied directly to the benefit received by the taxpayer.

THE KEY FACTS

What Qualifies as a Tax?

- The general purpose of taxes is to fund government agencies.
- Unlike fines or penalties, taxes are not meant to punish or prevent illegal behavior; however, "sin taxes" are meant to discourage certain behaviors.
- To qualify as a tax, three criteria must be met. The payment must be:
  - Required;
  - Imposed by a government agency; and
  - Not tied directly to the benefit received by the taxpayer.

This last point is not to say that taxpayers receive no benefits from the taxes they pay. They benefit from national defense, a judicial system, law enforcement, government-sponsored social programs, an interstate highway system, public schools, and many other government-provided programs and services. The distinction is that taxes paid are not *directly* related to any specific benefit received by the taxpayer. For example, the price of admission to Yellowstone National Park is a fee rather than a tax because a specific benefit is received.

Can taxes be assessed for special purposes, such as a 1 percent sales tax for education? Yes. Why is an **earmarked tax,** a tax that *is* assessed for a specific purpose, still considered a tax? Because the payment made by the taxpayer does not directly relate to the specific benefit *received by the taxpayer.*

Example 1-1

Margaret travels to Birmingham, Alabama, where she rents a hotel room and dines at several restaurants. The price she pays for her hotel room and meals includes an additional 2 percent city surcharge to fund roadway construction in Birmingham. Is this a tax?

Answer: Yes. The payment is required by a local government and does not directly relate to a specific benefit that Margaret receives.

Example 1-2

Margaret's parents, Bill and Mercedes, recently built a house and were assessed $1,000 by their county government to connect to the county sewer system. Is this a tax?

Answer: No. The assessment was mandatory and it was paid to a local government. However, the third criterion was not met because the payment directly relates to a specific benefit (sewer service) received by the payees. For the same reason, tolls, parking meter fees, and annual licensing fees are also not considered taxes.

[2]Sin taxes represent an interesting confluence of incentives. On the one hand, demand for such products as alcohol, tobacco, and gambling is often relatively inelastic because of their addictive quality. Thus, taxing such a product can raise substantial revenues. On the other hand, one of the arguments for sin taxes is frequently the social goal of *reducing* demand for such products.

[3]Federal excise taxes on cigarettes are found in §5701(b). State taxes are as much as $4.35 per pack in Connecticut and New York. The District of Columbia imposes a tax of $4.50 per pack. Anchorage, New York City, and Chicago impose municipal taxes on cigarettes as well. The taxes on a pack of cigarettes in Chicago are $8.26 ($1.01 federal, $2.98 state, $3.00 county, and $1.98 city).

HOW TO CALCULATE A TAX

LO 1-3

In its simplest form, the amount of tax equals the tax base multiplied by the tax rate:

Eq. 1-1 $$\text{Tax} = \text{Tax Base} \times \text{Tax Rate}$$

The **tax base** defines what is actually taxed and is usually expressed in monetary terms, whereas the **tax rate** determines the level of taxes imposed on the tax base and is usually expressed as a percentage. For example, a taxable purchase of $30 times a sales tax rate of 6 percent yields a tax of $1.80 ($1.80 = $30 × .06).

Federal, state, and local jurisdictions use a large variety of tax bases to collect tax. Some common tax bases (and related taxes) include taxable income (federal and state income taxes), purchases (sales tax), real estate values (real estate tax), and personal property values (personal property tax).

Different portions of a tax base may be taxed at different rates. A single tax applied to an entire base constitutes a **flat tax.** In the case of **graduated taxes,** the base is divided into a series of monetary amounts, or **brackets,** and each successive bracket is taxed at a different (gradually higher or gradually lower) percentage rate.

Calculating some taxes—income taxes for individuals, for example—can be quite complex. Advocates of flat taxes argue that the process should be simpler. But as we'll see throughout the text, most of the difficulty in calculating a tax rests in determining the tax *base,* not the tax rate. Indeed, there are only three basic tax rate structures (proportional, progressive, and regressive), and each can be mastered without much difficulty.

THE KEY FACTS

How to Calculate a Tax

- Tax = Tax base × Tax rate
- The tax base defines what is actually taxed and is usually expressed in monetary terms.
- The tax rate determines the level of taxes imposed on the tax base and is usually expressed as a percentage.
- Different portions of a tax base may be taxed at different rates.

DIFFERENT WAYS TO MEASURE TAX RATES

Before we discuss the alternative tax rate structures, let's first define three different tax rates that will be useful in contrasting the different tax rate structures: the marginal, average, and effective tax rates.

Tax is computed on a tax base, which is generally taxable income. Taxable income is gross income minus deductions (see the Individual Income Tax Overview, Dependents, and Filing Status chapter for a detailed discussion of the individual income tax formula). The **marginal tax rate** is the incremental tax paid on an incremental amount of additional income or deductions.

Eq. 1-2

$$\text{Marginal Tax Rate} = \frac{\Delta\text{Tax}^*}{\Delta\text{Taxable Income}} = \frac{(\text{New Total Tax} - \text{Old Total Tax})}{(\text{New Taxable Income} - \text{Old Taxable Income})}$$

*Δ means *change in.*

Specifically, "old" refers to the current tax and "new" refers to the revised tax after incorporating the additional income (or deductions) in question. In graduated income tax systems, additional income (deductions) can push a taxpayer into a higher (lower) tax bracket, thus changing the marginal tax rate.

Example 1-3

Margaret's parents, Bill and Mercedes, file a joint tax return. They have $160,000 of taxable income this year (gross income minus deductions). Assuming the following federal tax rate schedule applies, how much federal income tax will they owe this year?[4]

(continued on page 1-6)

[4]The tax rate schedules for single, married filing jointly, married filing separately, and head of household are included in Appendix C.

Married Filing Jointly (and Surviving Spouses)	
Not over $20,550	10% of taxable income
Over $20,550 but not over $83,550	$2,055 + 12% of taxable income in excess of $20,550
Over $83,550 but not over $178,150	$9,615 + 22% of taxable income in excess of $83,550
Over $178,150 but not over $340,100	$30,427 + 24% of taxable income in excess of $178,150
Over $340,100 but not over $431,900	$69,295 + 32% of taxable income in excess of $340,100
Over $431,900 but not over $647,850	$98,671 + 35% of taxable income in excess of $431,900
Over $647,850	$174,253.50 + 37% of taxable income in excess of $647,850

Answer: Bill and Mercedes will owe $26,434, computed as follows:

$26,434 = $9,615 + 22% × $76,450 ($160,000 − $83,550)

Note that in this graduated tax rate structure, the first $20,550 of taxable income is taxed at 10 percent, the next $63,000 of taxable income (between $20,550 and $83,550) is taxed at 12 percent, and Bill and Mercedes's last $76,450 of taxable income (between $83,550 and $160,000) is taxed at 22 percent.

Many taxpayers incorrectly believe that all their income is taxed at their marginal rate. This mistake leads people to say, "I don't want to earn any additional money because it will put me in a higher tax bracket." Bill and Mercedes are currently in the 22 percent marginal tax rate bracket, but notice that not all their income is taxed at this rate. Their *marginal* tax rate is 22 percent. This means that small increases in income will be taxed at 22 percent, and small increases in deductions will generate tax *savings* of 22 percent. If Bill and Mercedes receive a large increase in income (or in deductions) such that they change tax rate brackets, we could not identify their marginal tax rate simply by knowing their current tax bracket.

Example 1-4

What if: Bill, a well-known economics professor, signs a publishing contract with an $80,000 royalty advance. Using the rate schedule from Example 1-3, what would Bill and Mercedes's marginal tax rate be on this $80,000 of additional income?

Answer: 23.55 percent, computed as follows:

Description	Amount	Explanation
(1) Taxable income with $80,000 of additional income	$240,000	$80,000 of additional income plus $160,000 taxable income (Example 1-3)
(2) Tax on $240,000 taxable income	$ 45,271	Using the rate schedule in Example 1-3, $45,271 = $30,427 + 24% × ($240,000 − $178,150)
(3) Taxable income before $80,000 of additional income	$160,000	Example 1-3
(4) Tax on $160,000 taxable income	$ 26,434	Example 1-3
Marginal tax rate on $80,000 of additional income	**23.55%**	$\frac{\Delta \text{Tax}}{\Delta \text{Taxable income}} = [(2) - (4)]/[(1) - (3)]$

Note that Bill and Mercedes's marginal tax rate on the $80,000 of additional income rests *between* the 22 percent and 24 percent bracket rates because a portion of the additional income ($178,150 − $160,000 = $18,150) is taxed at 22 percent, with the remaining income ($240,000 − $178,150 = $61,850) taxed at 24 percent.

Example 1-5

What if: Assume now that, instead of receiving a book advance, Bill and Mercedes start a new business that *loses* $90,000 this year (it results in $90,000 of additional deductions). What would be their marginal tax rate for these additional deductions?

Answer: 20.49 percent, computed as follows:

Description	Amount	Explanation
(1) Taxable income with $90,000 of additional deductions	$ 70,000	$160,000 taxable income (Example 1-3) less $90,000 of additional deductions
(2) Tax on $70,000 taxable income	$ 7,989	Using the rate schedule in Example 1-3, $7,989 = $2,055 + 12% × ($70,000 – $20,550)
(3) Taxable income before $90,000 of additional deductions	$160,000	Example 1-3
(4) Tax on $160,000 taxable income	$ 26,434	Example 1-3
Marginal tax rate on $90,000 of additional deductions	**20.49%**	$\frac{\Delta \text{Tax}}{\Delta \text{Taxable income}} = [(2) - (4)]/[(1) - (3)]$

Bill and Mercedes's marginal tax rate on $90,000 of additional deductions (20.49 percent) differs from their marginal tax rate on $80,000 of additional income (23.55 percent) in these scenarios because the relatively large increase in deductions in this example causes some of their income to be taxed in a lower tax rate bracket, while the relatively large increase in income in Example 1-4 causes some of their income to be taxed in a higher tax rate bracket. Taxpayers often will face the same marginal tax rates for small changes in income and deductions.

THE KEY FACTS

Different Ways to Measure Tax Rates

- Marginal tax rate
  - The tax that applies to the next increment of income or deduction.

    $= \frac{\Delta \text{Tax}}{\Delta \text{Taxable income}}$
  - Useful in tax planning.
- Average tax rate
  - A taxpayer's average level of taxation on each dollar of *taxable* income.

    $= \frac{\text{Total tax}}{\text{Taxable income}}$
  - Useful in budgeting tax expense.
- Effective tax rate
  - A taxpayer's average rate of taxation on each dollar of *total* income (taxable *and* nontaxable income).

    $= \frac{\text{Total tax}}{\text{Total income}}$
  - Useful in comparing the relative tax burdens of taxpayers.

The marginal tax rate is particularly useful in tax planning because it represents the rate of taxation or savings that would apply to additional income (or deductions). In the Tax Planning Strategies and Related Limitations chapter, we discuss basic tax planning strategies that use the marginal tax rate.

The **average tax rate** represents a taxpayer's average level of taxation on each dollar of taxable income. Specifically,

Eq. 1-3

$$\text{Average Tax Rate} = \frac{\text{Total Tax}}{\text{Taxable Income}}$$

The average tax rate is often used in budgeting tax expense as a portion of income (i.e., determining what percent of taxable income earned is paid in tax).

Example 1-6

Assuming Bill and Mercedes have $160,000 of taxable income and $10,000 of nontaxable income, what is their average tax rate?

Answer: 16.52 percent, computed as follows:

Description	Amount	Explanation
(1) Taxable income	$160,000	
(2) Tax on $160,000 taxable income	$ 26,434	Example 1-3
Average tax rate	**16.52%**	$\frac{\text{Total tax}}{\text{Taxable income}} = (2)/(1)$

We should not be surprised that Bill and Mercedes's average tax rate is lower than their marginal tax rate because, although they are currently in the 22 percent tax rate bracket, not all of their taxable income is subject to tax at 22 percent. The first $20,550 of their taxable income is taxed at 10 percent, their next $63,000 is taxed at 12 percent, and only their last $76,450 of taxable income is taxed at 22 percent. Thus, their average tax rate is considerably lower than their marginal tax rate.

The **effective tax rate** represents the taxpayer's average rate of taxation on each dollar of total income (sometimes referred to as economic income), including taxable *and* nontaxable income. Specifically,

Eq. 1-4

$$\text{Effective Tax Rate} = \frac{\text{Total Tax}}{\text{Total Income}}$$

Relative to the average tax rate, the effective tax rate provides a better depiction of a taxpayer's tax burden because it gives the taxpayer's total tax paid as a ratio of the sum of both taxable and nontaxable income.

Example 1-7

Again, given the same income figures as in Example 1-6 ($160,000 of taxable income and $10,000 of nontaxable income), what is Bill and Mercedes's effective tax rate?

Answer: 15.55 percent, computed as follows:

Description	Amount	Explanation
(1) Total income	$170,000	$160,000 taxable income plus $10,000 in nontaxable income (Example 1-6)
(2) Tax on $160,000 taxable income	$ 26,434	Example 1-3
Effective tax rate	**15.55%**	$\frac{\text{Total tax}}{\text{Total income}} = (2)/(1)$

Should we be surprised that the effective tax rate is lower than the *average* tax rate? No, the effective tax rate will always be equal to or less than the average tax rate. When a taxpayer has no nontaxable income, the effective and average tax rates will be equal, but anytime a taxpayer has nontaxable income, the effective tax rate will be less than the average tax rate.

TAX RATE STRUCTURES

There are three basic tax rate structures used to determine a tax: proportional, progressive, and regressive.

Proportional Tax Rate Structure

A **proportional tax rate structure,** also known as a flat tax, imposes a constant tax rate throughout the tax base. As the tax base increases, the taxes paid increase proportionally. Because this rate stays the same throughout all levels of the tax base, the marginal tax rate remains constant and, in fact, equals the average tax rate (see Exhibit 1-1). The 21 percent corporate tax rate is an example of a flat tax. Sales tax is another example of a flat tax.

EXHIBIT 1-1 **Proportional Tax Rate**

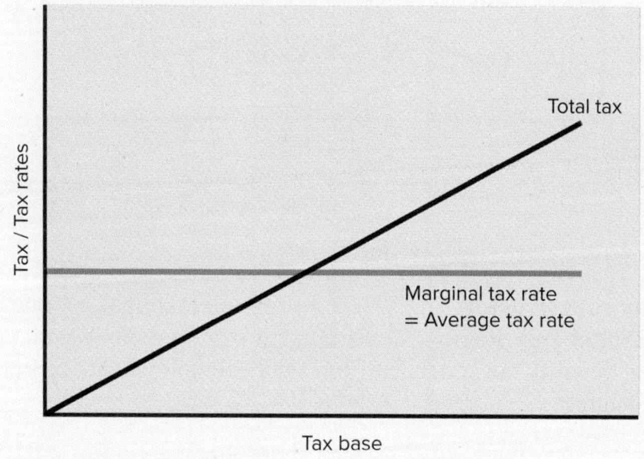

To calculate the tax owed for a proportional tax, simply use Equation 1-1 to multiply the tax base by the tax rate. Specifically,

Eq. 1-5 Proportional Tax = Tax Base × Tax Rate

Example 1-8

Knowing her dad is a serious Georgia Bulldog fan, Margaret buys a $100 sweatshirt in downtown Athens. The city of Athens imposes a sales tax rate of 7 percent. How much tax does Margaret pay on the purchase?

Answer: $100 purchase (tax base) × 7% (tax rate) = $7

Progressive Tax Rate Structure

A **progressive tax rate structure** imposes an increasing marginal tax rate as the tax base increases. Common examples of progressive tax rate structures include federal and most state income taxes. The tax rate schedule in Example 1-3 is a progressive tax rate structure. As illustrated in Exhibit 1-2, the average tax rate in a progressive tax rate structure will always be less than or equal to the marginal tax rate.

EXHIBIT 1-2 Progressive Tax Rate

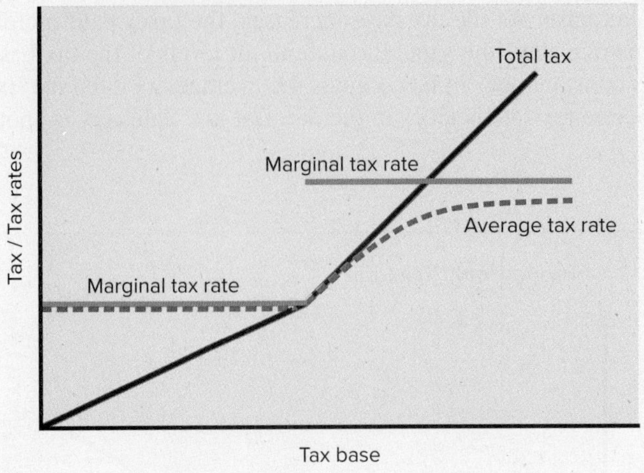

Regressive Tax Rate Structure

A **regressive tax rate structure** imposes a decreasing marginal tax rate as the tax base increases (see Exhibit 1-3). Regressive tax rate structures are not common. In the United States, the Social Security tax and federal and state unemployment taxes employ a regressive tax rate structure.[5]

EXHIBIT 1-3 Regressive Tax Rate

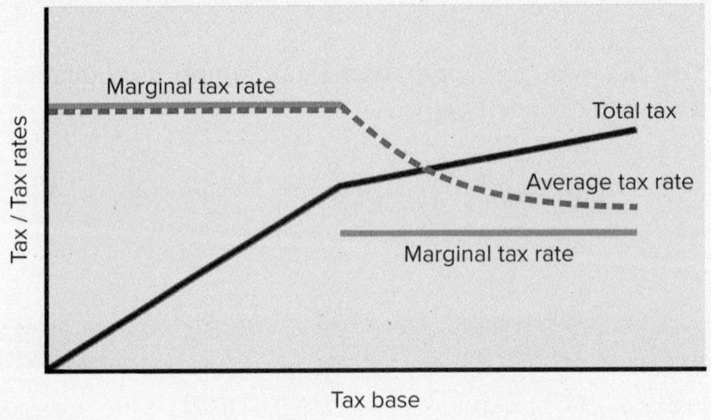

Some taxes are regressive when viewed in terms of effective tax rates. For example, a sales tax is a proportional tax by definition because as taxable purchases increase, the sales tax rate remains constant.[6] Nonetheless, when you consider that the proportion of your total income spent on taxable purchases likely decreases as your total income increases, you can see the sales tax as a regressive tax.

[5]Wages subject to the Social Security tax are capped by an annual limit indexed for inflation. For 2022, the cap is $147,000. Wages in excess of the cap are not subject to the tax. Likewise, the federal and state unemployment tax bases and related unemployment benefits are capped. In contrast, all wages are subject to the Medicare tax, no matter the taxpayer's wages. Thus, the Medicare tax is less regressive.

[6]For example, a destitute taxpayer likely spends all he makes on food and other items subject to the sales tax; thus, all of his income is subject to a sales tax. In contrast, a wealthy taxpayer likely spends only a small fraction of his income on items subject to sales tax (while saving the rest). Thus, less of a wealthy taxpayer's total income is subject to the sales tax, which ultimately results in a lower effective tax rate.

Example 1-9

Bill and Mercedes invite two single friends, Elizabeth and Marc, over for dinner. Elizabeth earns $300,000 annually as CFO of a company and spends $70,000 on purchases subject to the 7 percent sales tax. Marc, who earns $75,000 as a real estate agent, spends $30,000 of his income on taxable purchases. Let's compare their marginal, average, and effective tax rates for the sales tax with those of Bill and Mercedes, who spend $50,000 of their income on taxable purchases:

	Elizabeth	Bill and Mercedes	Marc
(1) Total income	$300,000	$170,000	$75,000
(2) Total purchases subject to 7% sales tax	$ 70,000	$ 50,000	$30,000
(3) Sales tax paid	$ 4,900	$ 3,500	$ 2,100
Marginal tax rate	7.0%	7.0%	7.0%
Average tax rate (3)/(2)	7.0%	7.0%	7.0%
Effective tax rate (3)/(1)	1.6%	2.1%	2.8%

Is the sales tax regressive?

Answer: Yes. In terms of *effective* tax rates, the sales tax is regressive.

THE KEY FACTS

Tax Rate Structures

- A proportional tax rate structure
  - Imposes a constant tax rate throughout the tax base.
  - As a taxpayer's tax base increases, the taxpayer's taxes increase proportionally.
  - The marginal tax rate remains constant and always equals the average tax rate.
- A progressive tax rate structure
  - Imposes an increasing marginal tax rate as the tax base increases.
- A regressive tax rate structure
  - Imposes a decreasing marginal tax rate as the tax base increases.

When we consider the marginal and average tax rates in Example 1-9, the sales tax has a proportional tax rate structure. But when we look at the *effective* tax rates, the sales tax is a regressive tax. Indeed, Marc, who has the smallest total income, bears the highest effective tax rate, despite all three taxpayers being subject to the same marginal and average tax rates. Why do we see such a different picture when considering the effective tax rate? Because unlike the marginal and average tax rates, the effective tax rate captures the *incidence* of taxation, which relates to the ultimate economic burden of a tax. Thus, a comparison of effective tax rates is more informative about taxpayers' relative tax burdens.

TYPES OF TAXES

LO 1-4

"You can't live with 'em. You can't live without 'em." This statement has often been used in reference to bosses, parents, spouses, and significant others. To some degree, it applies equally well to taxes. Although we all benefit in multiple ways from tax revenues, and all civilized nations impose them, it would be hard to find someone who *enjoys* paying them. Most people don't object to the idea of paying taxes. Instead, it's the way taxes are levied that many people, like Margaret's friend Eddy, dislike. Hence, the search for fairness or the "perfect" tax system can be elusive. The following paragraphs describe the major types of taxes currently implemented by federal, state, and local governments. After this discussion, we describe the criteria for evaluating alternative tax systems.

THE KEY FACTS

Federal Taxes

- Income tax
  - The most significant tax assessed by the U.S. government.
  - Represents approximately 60 percent (combined corporate and individual) of all tax revenues collected in the United States.
  - Levied on individuals, corporations, estates, and trusts.
- Employment and unemployment taxes
  - Second-largest group of taxes imposed by the U.S. government.

(continued)

Federal Taxes

The federal government imposes a variety of taxes to fund federal programs such as national defense, Social Security, an interstate highway system, educational programs, and Medicare. Major federal taxes include the individual and corporate income taxes, employment taxes, estate and gift taxes, and excise taxes (each discussed in detail in the following paragraphs). Notably absent from this list are sales tax (a common tax levied by most state and local governments; see the State and Local Taxes chapter) and **value-added tax** (a type of sales tax also referred to as a VAT). Value-added taxes are imposed on the

- Employment taxes consist of the Old Age, Survivors, and Disability Insurance (OASDI) tax, commonly called the Social Security tax, and the Medical Health Insurance (MHI) tax, also known as the Medicare tax.
- Unemployment taxes fund temporary unemployment benefits for individuals terminated from their jobs without cause.
- Excise taxes
  - Third-largest group of taxes imposed by the U.S. government.
  - Levied on the *quantity* of products sold.
- Transfer taxes
  - Levied on the fair-market values of wealth transfers upon death or by gift.

producers of goods and services based on the value added to the goods and services at each stage of production. Most countries in Europe have a VAT.

Income Tax The most significant tax assessed by the U.S. government is the individual **income tax,** representing approximately 50.2 percent of all tax revenues collected in the United States in Fiscal Year 2021. Despite the magnitude and importance of the federal income tax, its history is relatively short. Congress enacted the first U.S. personal income tax in 1861 to help fund the Civil War. This relatively minor tax (with a maximum tax rate of 5 percent) was allowed to expire in 1872. In 1892, Congress resurrected the income tax, but not without dissension among the states. In 1895, the income tax was challenged in *Pollock v. Farmers' Loan and Trust Company,* 157 U.S. 429 (1895). The U.S. Supreme Court ruled that the income tax was unconstitutional because direct taxes were prohibited by the Constitution unless the taxes were apportioned across states based upon their populations. This ruling, however, did not deter Congress. In July 1909, Congress sent a proposed constitutional amendment to the states to remove any doubt as to whether income taxes were allowed by the Constitution—and in February 1913, the 16th Amendment was ratified.

Congress then enacted the Revenue Act of 1913, which included a graduated income tax structure with a maximum rate of 6 percent. The income tax has been an important source of tax revenues for the U.S. government ever since. Today, income taxes are levied on individuals (maximum rate of 37 percent), corporations (flat rate of 21 percent), estates (maximum rate of 37 percent), and trusts (maximum rate of 37 percent). Higher-income taxpayers must also pay a 3.8 percent tax on their net investment income. As Exhibit 1-4 illustrates, the individual income tax and employment taxes represent the largest sources of federal tax revenues. We discuss each of these taxes in greater detail later in the text.

Employment and Unemployment Taxes Employment and unemployment taxes are the second-largest group of taxes imposed by the U.S. government. **Employment taxes** consist of the Old Age, Survivors, and Disability Insurance (OASDI) tax, commonly called the Social Security tax, and the Medical Health Insurance (MHI) tax, known as the Medicare tax. The **Social Security tax** pays the monthly retirement, survivor, and

EXHIBIT 1-4 U.S. Federal Tax Revenues

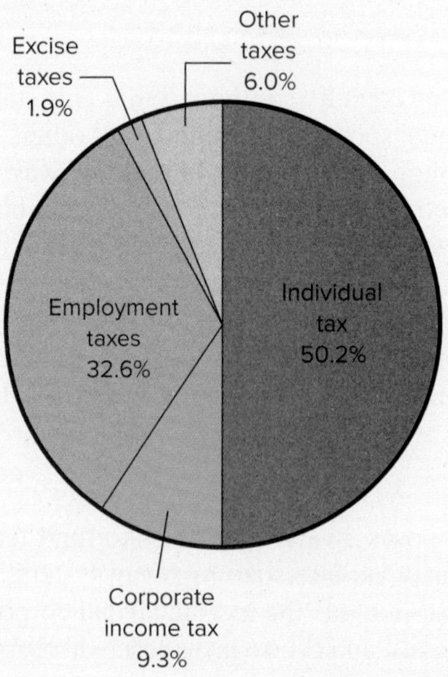

Source: Treasury Department (Fiscal Year 2021).

disability benefits for qualifying individuals, whereas the **Medicare tax** pays for medical insurance for individuals who are elderly or disabled. The tax base for the Social Security and Medicare taxes is wages or salary, and the rates are 12.4 percent and 2.9 percent, respectively. In 2022, the tax base for the Social Security tax is capped at $147,000 (wages over this cap are not subject to the tax). The tax base for the Medicare tax is not capped. Employers and employees split these taxes equally (both pay 6.2 percent Social Security tax and 1.45 percent Medicare tax). Self-employed individuals, however, must pay these taxes in their entirety. In this case, the tax is often referred to as the **self-employment tax.** We discuss these taxes in more depth later in the text. Individual taxpayers with earned income over a threshold amount are also subject to a .9 percent additional Medicare tax (see the Individual Income Tax Computation and Tax Credits chapter for details).

In addition to the Social Security and Medicare taxes, employers are also required to pay federal and state **unemployment taxes,** which fund temporary unemployment benefits for individuals terminated from their jobs without cause. Employers pay federal unemployment tax based on employees' wages or salaries. The Federal Unemployment Tax Act (FUTA) tax is 6.0 percent on only the first $7,000 of income for each employee. Most employers receive a maximum credit of up to 5.4 percent against this FUTA tax for allowable state unemployment tax. Consequently, the effective FUTA rate may be as low as .6 percent (6.0% – 5.4% = .6%).[7]

Excise Taxes **Excise taxes** are taxes levied on the retail sale of particular products. They differ from other taxes in that the tax base for an excise tax typically depends on the *quantity* purchased, rather than a monetary amount. The federal government imposes a number of excise taxes on goods such as alcohol, diesel fuel, gasoline, and tobacco products and on services such as telephone use, air transportation, and the use of tanning beds. In addition, states often impose excise taxes on these same items.

Example 1-10

On the drive home from Florida to Athens, Georgia, Margaret stops at Gasup-n-Go. On each gallon of gasoline she buys, Margaret pays 18.4 cents of federal excise tax and 42.3 cents of state excise tax (plus 4 percent sales tax). Could Margaret have avoided paying excise tax had she stopped in Florida instead?

Answer: No. Had she stopped in Florida instead, Margaret would have paid the same federal excise tax. Additionally, Florida also imposes a state excise tax on gas.

Because the producer of the product pays the excise tax to the government, many people are not even aware that businesses build these taxes into the prices consumers pay. Nevertheless, consumers bear the burden of the taxes because of the higher price.

Transfer Taxes Although they are a relatively minor tax compared to the income tax in terms of revenues collected, federal **transfer taxes**—estate and gift taxes—can be substantial for certain individual taxpayers and have been the subject of much debate in recent years. The **estate tax** (labeled the "death tax" by its opponents) and **gift taxes** are based on the fair market values of wealth transfers made upon death or by gift, respectively. Today, the maximum rate imposed on gifts is 40 percent. Most taxpayers, however, are not subject to estate and gift taxation because of the annual gift exclusion and gift and estate unified tax credits. The annual gift exclusion allows a taxpayer to transfer $16,000 of gifts per donee (gift recipient) each year without being subject to gift taxation. In 2022, the unified tax credit exempts from taxation $12,060,000 in bequests

[7]Although employers pay both federal and state unemployment taxes, all unemployment benefits are actually administered and paid by state governments.

(transfers upon death) and lifetime gifts. Thus, only taxpayers with substantial wealth are subject to the gift and estate taxes.

State and Local Taxes

Like the federal government, state and local governments (such as counties, cities, and school districts) use a variety of taxes to generate revenues for their programs (such as education, highways, and police and fire departments). Some of the more common **state** and **local taxes** include income taxes, sales and use taxes, excise taxes, and property taxes. Typically, as shown in Exhibit 1-5, the largest state tax revenues are generated by individual income taxes and state sales taxes—while federal revenues rely primarily on income and employment taxes. Local tax revenues are predominantly from sales and property taxes.

EXHIBIT 1-5 Average State Tax Revenues

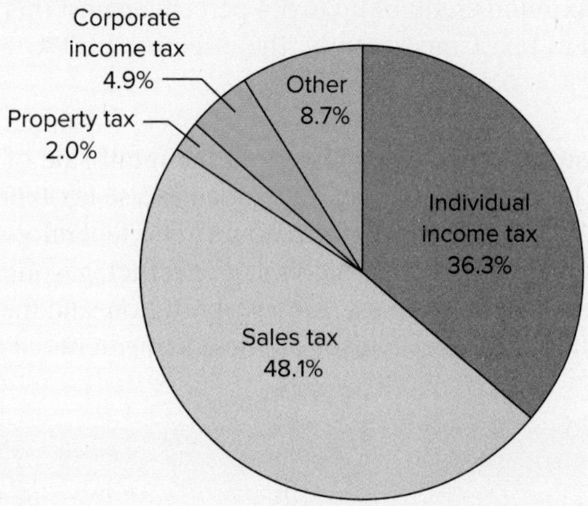

Source: U.S. Bureau of Census. www.census.gov.

THE KEY FACTS

State and Local Taxes

- Income taxes
  - Most state taxable income calculations largely conform to the federal taxable income calculations, with a limited number of modifications.
- Sales and use taxes
  - The tax base for a sales tax is the retail price of goods and some services.
  - The tax base for the use tax is the retail price of goods owned, possessed, or consumed within a state that were *not* purchased within the state.
- Property taxes
  - Property taxes are ad valorem taxes, meaning that the tax base for each property is the fair market value of that property.
  - Real property taxes consist of taxes on land, structures, and improvements permanently attached to land.
  - Personal property taxes include taxes on all other types of property, both tangible and intangible.
- Excise taxes
  - States typically impose excise taxes on items subject to federal excise tax.

Income Taxes Currently, most states and the District of Columbia impose income taxes on individuals and corporations who either reside in or earn income within the state.[8] This requires individuals working in these states to file a state tax return in addition to the federal return they already file. Calculations of individual and corporate taxable income vary with state law. Nonetheless, state taxable income calculations generally conform to the federal taxable income calculations (California is a notable exception because it has numerous modifications). State income tax rates are signficantly less than the federal rates. Certain local governments such as New York City also impose an income tax and, again, the local calculations generally follow the respective state taxable income calculation.

Sales and Use Taxes Most states, the District of Columbia, and local governments impose sales and use taxes. The tax base for a **sales tax** is the retail price of goods and some services, and retailers are responsible for collecting and remitting the tax; typically, sales tax is collected at the point of sale. The tax base for the **use tax** is the retail price of

[8]Currently, Alaska, Florida, Nevada, South Dakota, Texas, Washington, and Wyoming have no personal income tax, and New Hampshire and Tennessee only tax individual dividend and interest income. South Dakota and Wyoming are the only states not imposing either a corporate income or gross receipts tax, although South Dakota does impose a bank franchise tax. Washington imposes a gross receipts tax instead of a corporate income tax. Texas and Ohio have an activity-based tax that is based on net income or gross receipts.

goods owned, possessed, or consumed within a state that were *not* purchased within the state. The purpose of a use tax is to discourage taxpayers from buying goods from retailers without sales tax collection responsibilities in order to avoid or minimize the sales tax in their home state. At the same time, by eliminating the incentive to purchase goods from retailers without sales tax collection responsibilities, a use tax removes any competitive disadvantage a retailer may incur from operating in a state with a high sales tax. To avoid the potential of double-taxing residents on sales taxes, states that impose a sales tax allow residents to take a credit for sales tax paid on goods purchased out of state.

Example 1-11

Margaret buys three new shirts for her dad for $100 from a seller without sales tax collection responsibilities. The seller does not collect Florida sales tax (Margaret's home state). Does Margaret's purchase escape Florida taxation?

Answer: No. Because Florida has a 6 percent use tax, Margaret is liable for $6 in use tax on the purchase ($100 × .06 = $6). Margaret will pay the use tax by filing a Florida use tax return.

Despite the potential importance of the use tax as a source of state tax revenue, states have only recently begun to enforce it. Poor compliance is therefore not surprising; indeed, many individuals have never heard of the use tax. While it is relatively easy to enforce sales tax on goods subject to a registration requirement, such as automobiles, it is quite difficult for states to tax most other untaxed purchases. Recent judicial changes to sales tax collection responsibilities have made the use tax less important. The state of Florida is not likely to search your closet to look for tax-evaded shirts. Note, however, there are several bills before Congress to modernize Internet taxation and to try to subject all Internet sales to sales taxes.

Property Taxes State and local governments commonly use two types of property taxes as sources of revenue: **real property taxes** and **personal property taxes.** Both are **ad valorem taxes,** meaning that the tax base for each is the fair market value of the property, and both are generally collected annually (when imposed).

Real property consists of land, structures, and improvements permanently attached to land, whereas *personal property* includes all other types of property, both tangible and intangible. Common examples of tangible personal property potentially subject to state and local taxation include automobiles, boats, private planes, business inventory, equipment, and furniture. *Intangible personal property* potentially subject to state and local taxation includes stocks, bonds, and intellectual property—although no state currently imposes property taxes on these intangibles.

Of the two types, real property taxes are easier to administer because real property is not movable and purchases often have to be registered with the state, thereby making it easy to identify the tax base and taxpayer. Furthermore, the taxing body can estimate market values for real property without much difficulty. In contrast, personal property is generally mobile (thus easier to hide) and may be more difficult to value; therefore, personal property taxes are difficult to enforce. Accordingly, whereas all states and the District of Columbia provide for a real property tax, only a majority of states currently impose personal property taxes, most of which are assessed at the time of licensing or registration. However, most states do collect personal property taxes on business property.

Excise Taxes We've said that the tax base for excise taxes is typically the quantity of an item or service purchased. States typically impose excise taxes on items subject to federal excise tax. Transactions subject to state excise tax often include the sale of alcohol, diesel fuel, gasoline, tobacco products, and telephone services.

Implicit Taxes

All the taxes discussed above are **explicit taxes;** that is, they are taxes directly imposed by a government and are easily quantified. **Implicit taxes,** on the other hand, are indirect taxes—not paid directly to the government—that result from a tax advantage the government grants to certain transactions to satisfy social, economic, or other objectives. Implicit taxes are defined as the reduced before-tax return that a tax-favored asset produces because of its tax-advantaged status. Let's examine this concept more closely.

First of all, what does it mean to be *tax-favored*? An asset is said to be tax-favored when the income the asset produces is either excluded from the tax base or subject to a lower (preferential) tax rate, or if the asset generates some other tax benefit such as large tax deductions. These tax benefits, *all other things equal,* result in higher after-tax profits (or lower after-tax costs) from investing in the tax-advantaged assets.

Why do tax-advantaged assets bear an implicit tax, or a reduced before-tax rate of return as a result of the tax advantage? The answer is simple economics. The tax benefits associated with the tax-favored asset increase the demand for the asset. Increased demand drives up the price of the asset, which in turn reduces its before-tax rate of return, which is an implicit tax by definition. Consider Example 1-12.

Example 1-12

Consider two bonds, one issued by the Coca-Cola Co. and the other issued by the State of Georgia. Both bonds have similar nontax characteristics (risk, for example), the same face value of $10,000, and the same market interest rate of 10 percent. The only difference between the two bonds is that the interest income from the Coca-Cola Co. bond is subject to a 22 percent income tax rate, whereas the interest income from the State of Georgia bond is tax-exempt with a 0 percent tax rate. Which of the two bonds is a better investment and should therefore have a higher demand?

	Price	Before-Tax Rate of Return*	Interest Income	Income Tax†	After-Tax Income	After-Tax Rate of Return*
Coca-Cola Co. bond	$10,000	10%	$1,000	$220	$ 780	7.8%
State of GA bond	$10,000	10%	$1,000	$ 0	$1,000	10%

*Before-tax rate of return is calculated as the before-tax income divided by the price of the bond. Likewise, after-tax rate of return is calculated as the after-tax income divided by the price of the bond.
†Income tax equals the taxable interest income ($1,000) multiplied by the assumed income marginal tax rate (22 percent).

Answer: Compare the after-tax rate of return on the bonds. Given the difference between the after-tax rate of return (10 percent vs. 7.8 percent), the better investment—again, all other investment features being equal—is the State of Georgia bond because it provides a higher after-tax rate of return. Because all investors in this example should prefer to buy the State of Georgia bond, the demand for the bond will be high, and its price should increase. This increase in price leads to a lower before-tax rate of return due to the bond's tax-favored status (this is an implicit tax).

Example 1-12 is a basic illustration of the need to consider the role of taxes in investment decisions. Without understanding the relative tax effects associated with each bond, we cannot correctly compare their after-tax returns.

At what point in Example 1-12 would you be indifferent between investing in the Coca-Cola Co. bond and the State of Georgia bond? Assuming both bonds have the same nontax characteristics, you would be indifferent between them when they both provide the same after-tax rate of return. This could occur if the State of Georgia raised the price of its bond from $10,000 to $12,820.51 ($1,000 interest/$12,820.51 price = 7.8% return). Or the State of Georgia could lower its bond interest payment from $1,000 to $780 ($780 interest/$10,000 price = 7.8% return). Either way, the State of Georgia benefits from selling the tax-exempt bonds—either at a higher price or at a lower interest rate relative to other bonds. Let's look more closely at this latter option because it is, in fact, what many tax-exempt bond issuers choose to do.

	Price	Before-Tax Rate of Return	Interest Income	Income Tax	After-Tax Income	After-Tax Rate of Return
Coca-Cola Co. bond	$10,000	10%	$1,000	$220	$780	7.8%
State of GA bond	$10,000	7.8%	$ 780	$ 0	$780	7.8%

Assuming each bond has the same nontax characteristics, an investor should be indifferent between the Coca-Cola Co. bond and the State of Georgia bond. What is the tax burden on investors choosing the Coca-Cola Co. bond? Coca-Cola Co. bond investors are paying $220 of income taxes (explicit taxes). What is the tax burden on investors choosing the State of Georgia bond? While it is true they are subject to zero income taxes (explicit taxes), they are subject to implicit taxes in the form of the $220 less in interest income they accept. This $220 of reduced interest income (2.2 percent reduced before-tax rate of return) is an implicit tax. Although the investors in the State of Georgia bond are not paying this tax directly, they are paying it indirectly.

Does this happen in real life? Yes. Municipal bond interest income (interest income paid on bonds issued by state and local governments) generally is not subject to federal income taxation. Because of their tax-advantaged status, municipalities are able to pay a lower interest rate on their bond issuances and investors are willing to accept the lower rate. This type of indirect federal subsidy allows municipalities to raise money at a reduced cost without the need for direct federal subsidy or approval.

Although we were able to quantify the implicit taxes paid in the above example, in reality it is very difficult to estimate the amount of implicit taxes paid. For example, the federal government subsidizes housing by allowing taxpayers to deduct mortgage interest on their principal residence. Does this subsidy result in an implicit tax in the form of higher housing prices? Probably. Nevertheless, it would be difficult to quantify this implicit tax.

Despite the difficulty of quantifying implicit taxes, you should understand the concept of implicit taxes so you can make informed judgments about the attractiveness of alternative investments and the relative total tax burdens of tax-advantaged investments (considering both explicit and implicit taxes).

THE KEY FACTS

Implicit Taxes

- Implicit taxes are indirect taxes that result from a tax advantage the government grants to certain transactions to satisfy social, economic, or other objectives.
- Implicit taxes are defined as the reduced before-tax return that a tax-favored asset produces because of its tax-advantaged status.
- Implicit taxes are difficult to quantify but important to understand in evaluating the relative tax burdens of tax-advantaged investments.

EVALUATING ALTERNATIVE TAX SYSTEMS

LO 1-5

Although it may appear that tax systems are designed without much forethought, in truth lawmakers engage in continuous debate over the basic questions of whom to tax, what to tax, and how much to tax. Margaret's friend Eddy is obviously upset with what he views as an unfair tax system. But fairness, as we will discuss shortly, is often like beauty—it is in the eye of the beholder. What is fair to one may seem blatantly unfair to others. In the following paragraphs, we offer various criteria (sufficiency, equity, certainty, convenience, and economy) you can use to evaluate alternative tax systems.[9] Satisfying everyone at the same time is difficult—hence, the spirited debate on tax fairness and reform, especially leading up to election years when you get to choose between political parties and their platforms.

[9]Adam Smith identified and described the latter four criteria in *The Wealth of Nations*.

THE KEY FACTS

Evaluating Alternative Tax Systems—Sufficiency

- Judging sufficiency requires assessing the aggregate amount of the tax revenues that must be generated and ensuring that the tax system provides these revenues.
- Static forecasting ignores how taxpayers may alter their activities in response to a proposed tax law change and bases projected tax revenues on the existing state of transactions.
- Dynamic forecasting attempts to account for possible taxpayer responses to a proposed tax law change.

Sufficiency

Judging the **sufficiency** of a tax system means assessing the amount of tax revenues it must generate and ensuring that it provides them. For a country's tax system to be successful, it must provide sufficient revenues to pay for governmental expenditures for a defense system, social services, and so on. This sounds easy enough: Estimate the amount of governmental expenditures that will be required, and then design the system to generate enough revenues to pay for these expenses. In reality, however, accurately estimating governmental expenditures and revenues is a rather daunting and imprecise process. Estimating governmental expenditures is difficult because it is impossible to predict the unknown. For example, in recent years governmental expenditures have increased due to the growth of Homeland Security, the Afghanistan and Iraq wars, natural disasters, economic stimulus packages due to COVID-19, and health care. Likewise, estimating governmental revenues is difficult because tax revenues are the result of transactions influenced by these same national events, the economy, and other factors. Thus, precisely estimating and matching governmental expenditures with tax revenues is nearly impossible.

The task of estimating tax revenues becomes even more daunting when the government attempts to make significant changes to the existing tax system or design a new one. Whenever Congress proposes changing who is taxed, what is taxed, or how much is taxed, its members must consider the taxpayer response to the change. That affects the amount of tax collected, and forecasters' prediction of what taxpayers will do affects the amount of revenue they estimate to collect.

Static versus Dynamic Forecasting One option in forecasting revenue is to ignore how taxpayers may alter their activities in response to a tax law change and instead base projected tax revenues on the existing state of transactions, a process referred to as **static forecasting.** However, this type of forecasting may result in a large discrepancy in projected versus actual tax revenues collected if taxpayers do change their behavior.

The other choice is to attempt to account for possible taxpayer responses to the tax law change, a process referred to as **dynamic forecasting.** Dynamic forecasting is ultimately only as good as the assumptions underlying the forecasts and does not guarantee accurate results. Nonetheless, considering how taxpayers may alter their activities in response to a tax law change is a useful exercise to identify the potential ramifications of the change, even if the revenue projections ultimately miss the mark.[10]

Example 1-13

The city of Heflin would like to increase tax revenues by $2,000,000 to pay for needed roadwork. A concerned taxpayer recently proposed increasing the cigarette excise tax from $1.00 per pack of cigarettes to $6.00 per pack to raise the additional needed revenue. Last year, 400,000 packs of cigarettes were sold in the city. Will the proposal be successful in raising the additional $2,000,000 in proposed tax revenue?

Answer: Not likely. The proposed tax increase of $5, and the assumption that 400,000 packs will still be sold, is an example of static forecasting: It ignores that many taxpayers may respond to the tax change by quitting, cutting down, or buying cheaper cigarettes in the next town.

In some cases, static forecasting can lead to a tax consequence that is the opposite of the desired outcome. In Example 1-13, we might estimate that given Heflin's close proximity to other cities with a $1.00 cigarette tax, the number of packs of cigarettes sold within the city would drop significantly to, say, 50,000. In this case, the tax increase would actually *decrease* tax revenues by $100,000 ($400,000 existing tax − $300,000 new tax)—not a good outcome if the goal was to increase tax revenues.

[10]For more information about the congressional revenue estimating process, including dynamic scoring, see the Joint Committee on Taxation explanation at www.jct.gov/publications.html?func=startdown&id=4687.

Income versus Substitution Effects Example 1-13 described proposed changes in an excise tax, which is a proportional tax. In terms of a progressive tax such as an *income* tax, a tax rate increase or an expansion of the tax base can result in one of two taxpayer responses, both of which are important for dynamic forecasting. The **income effect** predicts that when taxpayers are taxed more, they will work harder to generate the same after-tax dollars. The **substitution effect** predicts that when taxpayers are taxed more, rather than working more, they will substitute nontaxable activities like leisure pursuits for taxable ones because the marginal value of taxable activities has decreased. Which view is accurate? The answer depends on the taxpayer. Consider the following examples.

Example 1-14

Margaret's friend George, who earns $40,000 taxable income as a self-employed mechanic, is taxed at an average rate of 10 percent (resulting in $4,000 of tax). If Congress increases the income tax rate such that George's average tax rate increases from 10 percent to 25 percent, how much more income tax will he pay?

Answer: It depends on whether the income effect or the substitution effect is operating. Assuming George is single and cannot afford a net decrease in his after-tax income, he will likely work more (the income effect rules). Prior to the tax rate increase, George had $36,000 of after-tax income ($40,000 taxable income less $4,000 tax). With the increased tax rate, George will have to earn $48,000 of taxable income to keep $36,000 after taxes [$48,000 – ($48,000 × .25) = $36,000]. Thus, if the income effect rules, the government will collect $12,000 of federal income tax from George, or $8,000 more than under the previous lower tax rate. In this scenario, the tax change increases government revenues because of the increased tax rate *and* the increased tax base.

Whether the substitution effect or the income effect will describe any individual taxpayer's reaction to a tax increase is something we can only guess. But some factors—such as having higher disposable income—are likely to correlate with the substitution effect.

Example 1-15

What if: Now let's assume that George is married and has two young children. Both he and his wife work, and they file a tax return jointly with a 10 percent average tax rate. Either of their incomes is sufficient to meet necessities, even after the tax rate increase. But fixed child care costs make the marginal wage rate (the after-tax hourly wage less hourly child care cost) more sensitive to tax rate increases. In this case, the lower-earning spouse may choose to work less. Suppose George quits his full-time job and takes a part-time position that pays $10,000 to spend more time with his kids and to pursue his passion, reading sports novels. What are the taxes on George's income?

Answer: In this case, George will owe $2,500 tax ($10,000 × .25). Here, the substitution effect operates and the government collects much less than it would have if George had maintained his full-time position because the tax rate increase had a negative effect on the tax base.

As Examples 1-14 and 1-15 illustrate, the response to a tax law change can vary by taxpayer and can greatly affect the magnitude of tax revenues generated by the change. Herein lies one of the challenges in significantly changing an existing tax system or designing a new one: If a tax system fails to generate sufficient revenues, the government must seek other sources to pay for governmental expenditures. The most common source of these additional funds for the federal government is the issuance of debt instruments such as Treasury bonds. This, however, is only a short-term solution to a budget deficit. Debt issuances require both interest and principal payments, which require the federal government to identify even more sources of revenue to service the debt issued or to cut governmental spending (both of which may be unpopular choices with voters). A third option is for the government to default on its debt obligations. However, the costs of this option are potentially devastating. If the historical examples of Mexico, Brazil, Argentina, and Greece are any guide, a U.S. government default on its debt obligations would likely devalue the U.S. dollar severely and have extreme negative consequences for the U.S. capital markets.

The best option is for the government to match its revenues with its expenses—that is, to not spend more than it collects. State governments seem to be more successful in this endeavor than the U.S. federal government. Indeed, all states except Vermont require a balanced budget each year, whereas the federal government has had deficit spending for most of the last 40 years.

TAXES IN THE REAL WORLD National Debt

How much debt does the U.S. have? As of August 2021, it was $28.6 trillion. Almost $23.0 trillion of the national debt is held by public investors, including individual bondholders, institutional investors, and foreign governments such as China, Japan, the United Kingdom, and Brazil. The $5.6 trillion remaining amount represents intragovernmental holdings—primarily Social Security.

Is $28.6 trillion too much to handle? The key issue is fiscal sustainability: the ability to pay off a debt in the future. Rising debt also has other negative consequences, such as higher interest payments, a need for higher taxes, restrictions on policy makers' fiscal policy choices, and the increased probability of a sudden fiscal crisis. If nothing is done to change the national debt trajectory, the debt will grow faster than the economy.

Is the national debt sustainable? The federal government has recently been recording budget deficits that are a larger share of the economy than for any year since the end of World War II. With an aging population, Social Security and other benefits will require larger expenditures. By the end of the current decade, barring any significant policy shifts, the vast majority of federal tax revenue will be consumed by just four expenditures: interest on the debt, Medicare, Medicaid, and Social Security. To finance other governmental expenditures, including defense and all other discretionary programs, policy makers will have to borrow the money to pay for them.

Source: www.treasurydirect.gov/govt/reports/pd/mspd/mspd.htm.

Equity

We've looked at the challenges of designing a tax system that provides sufficient revenues to pay for governmental expenditures. An equally challenging issue is how the tax burden should be distributed across taxpayers. At the heart of this issue is the concept of **equity,** or fairness. Fairness is inherently subject to personal interpretation, and informed minds often disagree about what is fair. There is no "one-size-fits-all" definition of equity or fairness. Nevertheless, it is informative to consider in broad terms what makes a fair or equitable tax system.

In general terms, a tax system is considered fair or equitable if the tax is based on the taxpayer's ability to pay. Taxpayers with a greater ability to pay tax pay more tax. In broad terms, each of the federal, state, and local taxes we've discussed satisfies this criterion. For example, those individuals with greater taxable income, purchases, property, and estates (upon death) generally pay higher dollar amounts in federal income tax, sales tax, property tax, and estate tax. If this is the case, why is there so much debate over the fairness of the U.S. income tax system? The answer is that equity is more complex than our first definition suggests. Let's take a closer look.

Horizontal versus Vertical Equity Two basic types of equity are relevant to tax systems. **Horizontal equity** means that two taxpayers in similar situations pay the same tax. In broad terms, each of the federal, state, and local taxes discussed satisfies this definition. Two individual taxpayers with the same taxable income, same purchases, same value of property, and same estate value pay the same federal income tax, sales tax, property tax, and estate tax. However, on closer inspection we might argue that each of these tax systems is *not* horizontally equitable. Here are some examples:

- Two individual taxpayers with the same income will not pay the same federal income tax if one individual's income was earned as salary and the other individual's income was tax-exempt municipal bond interest income, dividend income, or capital gain(s) income, which can be subject to a lower tax rate.
- Two individuals with the same dollar amount of purchases will not pay the same sales tax if one buys a higher proportion of goods that are subject to a lower sales tax rate, such as groceries.
- Two individuals with real estate of the same value will not pay the same property tax if one individual owns farmland, which is generally subject to a lower property tax rate.
- Finally, two individuals with estates of the same value will not pay the same estate tax if one individual bequeaths more of her property to charity or a spouse because these transfers are not subject to estate tax.

These failures of horizontal equity are due to what we call *tax preferences*. Governments provide tax preferences for a variety of reasons, such as to encourage investment or to further social objectives. Whether we view these tax preferences as appropriate greatly influences whether we consider a tax system to be fair in general and horizontally equitable in particular.

The second type of equity to consider in evaluating a tax system is **vertical equity.** Vertical equity is achieved when taxpayers with greater ability to pay tax pay more tax than taxpayers with less ability to pay. We can think of vertical equity in terms of tax dollars paid or in terms of tax rates. Proponents of a flat income tax or of a sales tax—both of which are proportional tax rate structures—are more likely to argue that vertical equity is achieved when taxpayers with a greater ability to pay tax simply pay more in tax *dollars*. Proponents of a progressive tax system are more likely to argue that taxpayers with a greater ability to pay should be subject to a higher tax *rate*. This view is based upon the argument that the *relative* burden of a flat tax rate decreases as a taxpayer's income increases. Which is the correct answer? There is no correct answer. Nevertheless, many feel very strongly regarding one view or the other.

Our discussion has focused on how we can view alternative tax rate structures in terms of vertical equity, ignoring the role that the tax base plays in determining vertical equity. Indeed, focusing on the tax rate structure in evaluating a tax system is appropriate only if the tax base chosen—whether it's taxable income, purchases, property owned, or something else—accurately portrays a taxpayer's ability to pay. This can be a rather strong assumption. Consider the sales tax in Example 1-9. Although taxable purchases in this example increase as the taxpayers' total incomes increase, total incomes increase at a much faster rate than taxable purchases. Thus, the gap between taxable purchases and total income widens as total income increases. The end result is that the effective tax rates for those with a greater ability to pay are *lower* than for those taxpayers with a lesser ability to pay, making this tax regressive. Regressive tax rate structures are generally considered not to satisfy vertical equity, unless you strongly believe that those with a greater ability to pay do so simply by paying more tax dollars, albeit at a lower tax rate. In sum, evaluating vertical equity in terms of effective tax rates may be much more informative than simply evaluating tax rate structures.

THE KEY FACTS

Evaluating Alternative Tax Systems—Equity

- Questions of equity consider how the tax burden should be distributed across taxpayers.
- Horizontal equity means that two taxpayers in similar situations pay the same tax.
- Vertical equity is achieved when taxpayers with greater ability to pay tax pay more tax than taxpayers with a lesser ability to pay tax.

Certainty

Certainty means that taxpayers should be able to determine when to pay the tax, where to pay the tax, and how to determine the tax. Determining when and where to pay each of the taxes previously discussed is relatively easy. For example, individual federal income tax returns and the remaining balance of taxes owed must be filed with the Internal Revenue Service each year on or before April 15th. Likewise, sales taxes, property taxes, and excise taxes are each determined with relative ease: Sales taxes are based on the value of taxable purchases, property taxes are generally based on assessed property values, and excise taxes are based on the number of taxable units purchased. Indeed, these taxes are calculated for the taxpayer and often charged at regular intervals or at the point of purchase; they do not require a tax return.

In contrast, income taxes are often criticized as being too complex. What are taxable versus nontaxable types of income? What are deductible/nondeductible expenses? When should income or expenses be reported? For wage earners with few investments, the answers to these questions are straightforward. For business owners and individuals with a lot of investments, the answers are nontrivial. Yearly tax law changes enacted by Congress can make it more difficult to determine a taxpayer's current tax liability, much less plan for the future.

THE KEY FACTS

Evaluating Alternative Tax Systems—Certainty, Convenience, and Economy

- Certainty
  - Certainty means taxpayers should be able to determine when, where, and how much tax to pay.
  - Determining when and where to pay each of the taxes previously discussed is relatively easy.
  - The income tax has been criticized for the complexity of determining how much to pay.
- Convenience
  - Convenience means a tax system should be designed to facilitate the collection of tax revenues without undue hardship on the taxpayer or the government.
  - Various tax systems meet this criterion by tying the collection of the tax as closely as possible to the transaction that generates it.
- Economy
  - Economy means a tax system should minimize compliance and administration costs.
  - Economy can be viewed from both the taxpayer's and the government's perspectives.

Convenience

Convenience suggests that a tax system should be designed to facilitate the collection of tax revenues without undue hardship on the taxpayer or the government. Various tax systems meet this criterion by tying the collection of the tax as closely as possible to the transaction that generates it (when it is most convenient to pay the tax). For example, retailers collect sales taxes when buyers purchase goods. Thus, it is difficult for the buyer to avoid paying sales tax, assuming she is transacting with an ethical retailer. Likewise, employers withhold federal income and Social Security taxes directly from wage earners' paychecks, which speeds the government's collection of the taxes and makes it difficult for taxpayers to evade taxes. If tax withholdings are not sufficient relative to the taxpayer's anticipated income tax liability, or if the taxpayer is self-employed, he or she is required to make quarterly estimated tax installments. Individual quarterly estimated payments are due on April 15, June 15, September 15, and January 15. Corporate estimated tax payments are due on the 15th day of the third, sixth, ninth, and twelfth months of the corporation's fiscal year.

Economy

Economy requires that a good tax system should minimize the compliance and administration costs associated with the tax system. We can view economy from both the taxpayer's and the government's perspectives. Believe it or not, most tax systems fare well in terms of economy, at least from the government's perspective. For example, the current IRS budget represents approximately one-third of a percent of every tax dollar collected. Compared to the typical costs of a collection agency, this is quite low.

How about from the taxpayer's perspective? Here the picture is a bit different. The sales tax imposes no administrative burden on the taxpayer and only small administrative costs on the local retailer. However, out-of-state sellers argue that collecting and remitting use taxes for thousands of state and city jurisdictions would be a substantial burden. Other taxes such as excise taxes and property taxes also impose minimal administrative costs on the taxpayer. In contrast, as we've seen, the income tax is often criticized for the compliance costs imposed on the taxpayer. Indeed, for certain taxpayers, record-keeping costs, accountant fees, attorney fees, and so on can be substantial. Advocates of alternative tax systems often challenge the income tax on this criterion.

Evaluating Tax Systems—The Trade-Offs

At the heart of any debate about tax reform are fundamental decisions and concessions based on the five criteria we've just discussed. Interestingly enough, much of the debate regarding alternative tax systems can be reduced to a choice between simplicity and fairness. Those taxes that generally are simpler and easier to administer, such as the sales tax, are typically viewed as less fair. Those taxes that can be viewed as more fair, such as the federal income tax, often are more complex to administer. Thus, Margaret's friend Eddy faces a difficult choice about which type of tax system to advocate, as do all taxpayers. An understanding of the evaluative criteria should be helpful to anyone trying to reconcile the trade-offs among alternative tax proposals.

CONCLUSION

In almost any society, taxes are a part of life. They influence decisions about personal finance, investment, business, and politics. In this chapter, we introduced the basic concepts of why one should study tax, what a tax is, and how to calculate a tax. We also discussed various tax rates, tax rate structures, and different types of taxes imposed by federal, state, and local governments. Finally, we discussed the criteria that one might use to evaluate alternative tax rate systems. To make informed personal finance, investment, business, and political decisions, one must have a basic understanding of these items. In the following chapters, we expand the discussion of how taxes influence these decisions while providing a basic understanding of our federal income tax system. Read on and learn more!

Summary

Demonstrate how taxes influence basic business, investment, personal, and political decisions. **LO 1-1**

- Taxes are significant costs that influence many basic business, investment, and personal decisions.
  - *Business decisions* include what organizational form to take; where to locate; how to compensate employees; what should be the appropriate debt mix; whether to own versus rent equipment and property; how to distribute profits; and so forth.
  - *Investment decisions* include alternative methods for saving for education or retirement, and so forth.
  - *Personal finance decisions* include evaluating job offers; gift or estate planning; owning a home versus renting; and so forth.
- Taxes also play a major part in the political process. Major parties typically have very diverse views on whom, what, and how much to tax.

Discuss what constitutes a tax and the general objectives of taxation. **LO 1-2**

- The general purpose of taxes is to fund the government. Unlike fines or penalties, taxes are not meant to punish or prevent illegal behavior, but "sin taxes" (on alcohol, tobacco, tanning beds, etc.) are meant to discourage certain behaviors.
- To qualify as a tax, three criteria are necessary: The payment must be (1) required (it is not voluntary), (2) imposed by a government (federal, state, or local), and (3) not tied directly to the benefit received by the taxpayer.

Describe the three basic tax rate structures and calculate a tax. **LO 1-3**

- Tax = Tax rate × Tax base, where the tax base is what is taxed and the tax rate is the level of taxes imposed on the base. For federal income tax, the tax base is taxable income, or gross income minus deductions. Different portions of a tax base may be taxed at different rates.

- There are three different tax rates that are useful in assessing the different tax rate structures, tax planning alternatives, and/or the tax burden of a taxpayer: the marginal, average, and effective tax rates.
  - The *marginal* tax rate is the tax that applies to the next increment of income or deduction.
  - The *average* tax rate represents a taxpayer's average level of taxation on each dollar of taxable income.
  - The *effective* tax rate represents the taxpayer's average rate of taxation on each dollar of total income (taxable *and* nontaxable income).
- The three basic tax rate structures are proportional, progressive, and regressive.
  - A *proportional* tax rate structure imposes a constant tax rate throughout the tax base. As a taxpayer's tax base increases, the taxpayer's taxes increase proportionally. The marginal tax rate remains constant and always equals the average tax rate. A common example is a sales tax.
  - A *progressive* tax rate imposes an increasing marginal tax rate as the tax base increases. As a taxpayer's tax base increases, both the marginal tax rate and the taxes paid increase. A common example is the U.S. federal income tax.
  - A *regressive* tax rate imposes a decreasing marginal tax rate as the tax base increases. As a taxpayer's tax base increases, the marginal tax rate decreases while the total taxes paid increase.

LO 1-4 Identify the various federal, state, and local taxes.

- Federal taxes include the income tax, employment taxes (Social Security and Medicare taxes), unemployment taxes, excise taxes (levied on quantity purchased), and transfer taxes (estate and gift taxes).
- State and local taxes include the income tax (levied by most states), sales tax (levied on retail sales of goods and some services), use tax (levied on the retail price of goods owned or consumed within a state that were purchased from a seller without sales tax collection responsibility), property taxes (levied on the fair market value of real and personal property), and excise taxes.
- Implicit taxes are indirect taxes that result from a tax advantage the government grants to certain transactions to satisfy social, economic, or other objectives. They are defined as the reduced before-tax return that a tax-favored asset produces because of its tax-advantaged status.

LO 1-5 Apply appropriate criteria to evaluate alternative tax systems.

- Sufficiency involves assessing the aggregate size of the tax revenues that must be generated and ensuring that the tax system provides these revenues. Static forecasting ignores how taxpayers may alter their activities in response to a proposed tax law change and bases projected tax revenues on the existing state of transactions. In contrast, dynamic forecasting attempts to account for possible taxpayer responses to a proposed tax law change.
- Equity considers how the tax burden should be distributed across taxpayers. Generally, a tax system is considered fair or equitable if the tax is based on the taxpayer's ability to pay—that is, taxpayers with a greater ability to pay tax pay more tax. Horizontal equity means that two taxpayers in similar situations pay the same tax. Vertical equity is achieved when taxpayers with greater ability to pay tax pay more tax relative to taxpayers with a lesser ability to pay tax.
- Certainty means taxpayers should be able to determine when, where, and how much tax to pay.
- Convenience means a tax system should be designed to facilitate the collection of tax revenues without undue hardship on the taxpayer or the government.
- Economy means a tax system should minimize its compliance and administration costs.

KEY TERMS

ad valorem taxes (1-15)
average tax rate (1-7)
brackets (1-5)
certainty (1-22)
convenience (1-22)
dynamic forecasting (1-18)
earmarked tax (1-4)
economy (1-22)
effective tax rate (1-8)
employment taxes (1-12)
equity (1-20)
estate tax (1-13)

excise taxes (1-13)
explicit taxes (1-16)
flat tax (1-5)
gift tax (1-13)
graduated taxes (1-5)
horizontal equity (1-21)
implicit taxes (1-16)
income effect (1-19)
income tax (1-12)
local tax (1-14)
marginal tax rate (1-5)
Medicare tax (1-13)
personal property tax (1-15)
progressive tax rate structure (1-9)
proportional tax rate structure (1-9)
real property tax (1-15)
regressive tax rate structure (1-10)
sales tax (1-14)
self-employment tax (1-13)
sin taxes (1-4)
Social Security tax (1-12)
state tax (1-14)
static forecasting (1-18)
substitution effect (1-19)
sufficiency (1-18)
tax (1-4)
tax base (1-5)
tax rate (1-5)
transfer taxes (1-13)
unemployment tax (1-13)
use tax (1-14)
value-added tax (1-11)
vertical equity (1-21)

DISCUSSION QUESTIONS

Discussion Questions are available in Connect®.

1. Jessica's friend Zachary once stated that he couldn't understand why someone would take a tax course. Why is this a rather naïve view? LO 1-1
2. What are some aspects of business that require knowledge of taxation? What are some aspects of personal finance that require knowledge of taxation? LO 1-1
3. Describe some ways in which taxes affect the political process in the United States. LO 1-1
4. Courtney recently received a speeding ticket on her way to the university. Her fine was $200. Is this considered a tax? Why or why not? LO 1-2
5. Marlon and Latoya recently started building a house. They had to pay $300 to the county government for a building permit. Is the $300 payment a tax? Why or why not? LO 1-2
6. To help pay for the city's new stadium, the city of Birmingham recently enacted a 1 percent surcharge on hotel rooms. Is this a tax? Why or why not? LO 1-2
7. As noted in Example 1-2, tolls, parking meter fees, and annual licensing fees are not considered taxes. Can you identify other fees that are similar? LO 1-2
8. If the general objective of our tax system is to raise revenue, why does the income tax allow deductions for charitable contributions and retirement plan contributions? LO 1-2
9. One common argument for imposing so-called sin taxes is the social goal of *reducing* demand for such products. Using cigarettes as an example, is there a segment of the population that might be sensitive to price and for whom high taxes might discourage purchases? LO 1-2
10. Dontae stated that he didn't want to earn any more money because it would "put him in a higher tax bracket." What is wrong with Dontae's reasoning? LO 1-3
11. Describe the three different tax rates discussed in the chapter and how taxpayers might use them. LO 1-3
12. Which is a more appropriate tax rate to use to compare taxpayers' tax burdens—the average or the effective tax rate? Why? LO 1-3
13. Describe the differences between proportional, progressive, and regressive tax rate structures. LO 1-3
14. Arnold and Lilly recently had a discussion about whether a sales tax is a proportional tax or a regressive tax. Arnold argued that a sales tax is regressive. Lilly countered that the sales tax is a flat tax. Who was correct? LO 1-3
15. Which is the largest tax collected by the U.S. government? What types of taxpayers are subject to this tax? LO 1-4

LO 1-4 16. What is the tax base for the Social Security and Medicare taxes for an employee or employer? What is the tax base for Social Security and Medicare taxes for a self-employed individual? Is the self-employment tax in addition to or in lieu of federal income tax?

LO 1-4 17. What are unemployment taxes?

LO 1-4 18. What is the distinguishing feature of an excise tax?

LO 1-4 19. What are some of the taxes that currently are unique to state and local governments? What are some of the taxes that the federal, state, and local governments each utilizes?

LO 1-4 20. The state of Georgia recently increased its tax on a pack of cigarettes by $2. What type of tax is this? Why might Georgia choose this type of tax?

LO 1-4 21. What is the difference between a sales tax and a use tax?

LO 1-4 22. What is an ad valorem tax? Name an example of this type of tax.

LO 1-4 23. What are the differences between an explicit and an implicit tax?

LO 1-4 24. When we calculate average and effective tax rates, do we consider implicit taxes? What effect does this have on taxpayers' perception of equity?

LO 1-4 25. Benjamin recently bought a truck in Alabama for his business in Georgia. What different types of federal and state taxes may affect this transaction?

LO 1-5 26. Kobe strongly dislikes SUVs and is appalled that so many are on the road. He proposes to eliminate the federal income tax and replace it with a $50,000 annual tax per SUV. Based on the number of SUVs currently owned in the United States, he estimates the tax will generate exactly the amount of tax revenue currently collected from the income tax. What is wrong with Kobe's proposal? What type of forecasting is Kobe likely using?

LO 1-5 27. What is the difference between the income and substitution effects? For which types of taxpayers is the income effect more likely descriptive? For which types of taxpayers is the substitution effect more likely descriptive?

LO 1-5 28. What is the difference between horizontal and vertical equity? How do tax preferences affect people's view of horizontal equity?

LO 1-3 LO 1-5 29. Montel argues that a flat income tax rate system is vertically equitable. Oprah argues that a progressive tax rate structure is vertically equitable. How do their arguments differ? Who is correct?

LO 1-3 LO 1-5 30. Discuss why evaluating vertical equity simply based on tax rate structure may be less than optimal.

LO 1-4 LO 1-5 31. Compare the federal income tax to sales taxes using the "certainty" criterion.

LO 1-5 32. Many years ago, a famous member of Congress proposed eliminating federal income tax withholding. What criterion for evaluating tax systems did this proposal violate? What would likely have been the result of eliminating withholding?

LO 1-5 33. "The federal income tax scores very high on the economy criterion because the current IRS budget is relatively low compared to the costs of a typical collection agency." Explain why this statement may be considered wrong.

PROBLEMS

Select problems are available in Connect®.

LO 1-3 34. Chuck, a single taxpayer, earns $75,000 in taxable income and $10,000 in interest from an investment in City of Heflin bonds. Using the U.S. tax rate schedule (see Appendix C), how much federal tax will he owe? What is his average tax rate? What is his effective tax rate? What is his current marginal tax rate?

35. Using the facts in problem 34, if Chuck earns an additional $40,000 of taxable income, what is his marginal tax rate on this income? What is his marginal rate if, instead, he had $40,000 of additional deductions? LO 1-3

36. Campbell, a single taxpayer, earns $400,000 in taxable income and $2,000 in interest from an investment in State of New York bonds. Using the U.S. tax rate schedule (see Appendix C), how much federal tax will she owe? What is her average tax rate? What is her effective tax rate? What is her current marginal tax rate? LO 1-3

37. Using the facts in problem 36, if Campbell earns an additional $15,000 of taxable income, what is her marginal tax rate on this income? What is her marginal rate if, instead, she had $15,000 of additional deductions? LO 1-3

38. Jorge and Anita, married taxpayers, earn $150,000 in taxable income and $40,000 in interest from an investment in City of Heflin bonds. Using the U.S. tax rate schedule for married filing jointly (see Example 1-3), how much federal tax will they owe? What is their average tax rate? What is their effective tax rate? What is their current marginal tax rate? LO 1-3

39. Using the facts in problem 38, if Jorge and Anita earn an additional $100,000 of taxable income, what is their marginal tax rate on this income? What is their marginal rate if, instead, they report an additional $100,000 in deductions? LO 1-3

40. Scot and Vidia, married taxpayers, earn $240,000 in taxable income and $5,000 in interest from an investment in City of Tampa bonds. Using the U.S. tax rate schedule for married filing jointly (see Example 1-3), how much federal tax will they owe? What is their average tax rate? What is their effective tax rate? What is their current marginal tax rate? LO 1-3

41. Using the facts in problem 40, if Scot and Vidia earn an additional $80,000 of taxable income, what is their marginal tax rate on this income? How would your answer differ if they, instead, had $80,000 of additional deductions? LO 1-3

42. Melinda invests $200,000 in a City of Heflin bond that pays 6 percent interest. Alternatively, Melinda could have invested the $200,000 in a bond recently issued by Surething Inc. that pays 8 percent interest and has risk and other nontax characteristics similar to the City of Heflin bond. Assume Melinda's marginal tax rate is 25 percent. LO 1-3 LO 1-4

    a) What is her after-tax rate of return for the City of Heflin bond?
    b) How much explicit tax does Melinda pay on the City of Heflin bond?
    c) How much implicit tax does she pay on the City of Heflin bond?
    d) How much explicit tax would she have paid on the Surething Inc. bond?
    e) What is her after-tax rate of return on the Surething Inc. bond?

43. Hugh has the choice between investing in a City of Heflin bond at 6 percent or investing in a Surething Inc. bond at 9 percent. Assuming that both bonds have the same nontax characteristics and that Hugh has a 40 percent marginal tax rate, in which bond should he invest? LO 1-3 LO 1-4 planning

44. Using the facts in problem 43, what interest rate does Surething Inc. need to offer to make Hugh indifferent between investing in the two bonds? LO 1-3 LO 1-4 planning

45. Fergie has the choice between investing in a State of New York bond at 5 percent and a Surething Inc. bond at 8 percent. Assuming that both bonds have the same nontax characteristics and that Fergie has a 30 percent marginal tax rate, in which bond should she invest? LO 1-3 LO 1-4 planning

46. Using the facts in problem 45, what interest rate does the State of New York bond need to offer to make Fergie indifferent between investing in the two bonds? LO 1-3 LO 1-4 planning

LO 1-3 47. Given the following tax structure, what minimum tax would need to be assessed on Shameika to make the tax progressive with respect to average tax rates?

Taxpayer	Salary	Muni-Bond Interest	Total Tax
Mihwah	$10,000	$10,000	$600
Shameika	$50,000	$30,000	$???

LO 1-3 48. Using the facts in problem 47, what minimum tax would need to be assessed on Shameika to make the tax progressive with respect to effective tax rates?

LO 1-3 LO 1-5 49. Song earns $100,000 taxable income as an interior designer and is taxed at an average rate of 20 percent (i.e., $20,000 of tax). If Congress increases the income tax rate such that Song's average tax rate increases from 20 percent to 25 percent, how much more income tax will she pay assuming that the income effect is descriptive? What effect will this tax rate change have on the tax base and tax collected?

LO 1-3 LO 1-5 50. Using the facts in problem 49, what will happen to the government's tax revenues if Song chooses to spend more time pursuing her other passions besides work in response to the tax rate change and therefore earns only $75,000 in taxable income? What is the term that describes this type of reaction to a tax rate increase? What types of taxpayers are likely to respond in this manner?

LO 1-5 51. Given the following tax structure, what tax would need to be assessed on Venita to make the tax horizontally equitable?

Taxpayer	Salary	Total Tax
Mae	$10,000	$ 600
Pedro	$20,000	$1,500
Venita	$10,000	$???

LO 1-5 52. Using the facts in problem 51, what is the minimum tax that Pedro should pay to make the tax structure vertically equitable based on the tax rate paid? This would result in what type of tax rate structure?

LO 1-5 53. Using the facts in problem 51, what is the minimum tax that Pedro should pay to make the tax structure vertically equitable with respect to the amount of tax paid? This would result in what type of tax rate structure?

LO 1-5 54. Consider the following tax rate structure. Is it horizontally equitable? Why or why not? Is it vertically equitable? Why or why not?

Taxpayer	Salary	Total Tax
Rajiv	$10,000	$600
LaMarcus	$20,000	$600
Dory	$10,000	$600

LO 1-5 55. Consider the following tax rate structure. Is it horizontally equitable? Why or why not? Is it vertically equitable? Why or why not?

Taxpayer	Salary	Total Tax
Marilyn	$10,000	$ 600
Kobe	$20,000	$3,000
Alfonso	$30,000	$6,000

LO 1-5 56. Consider the following tax rate structure. Is it horizontally equitable? Why or why not? Is it vertically equitable? Why or why not?

Taxpayer	Salary	Total Tax
Rodney	$10,000	$600
Keisha	$10,000	$600

57. Lorenzo is considering starting a trucking company in either Texas or Oklahoma. He will relocate his family, which includes his wife, children, and parents, to reside in the same state as his business. What types of taxes may influence his decision of where to locate his business?

LO 1-1 LO 1-4 planning

58. Congress would like to increase tax revenues by 10 percent. Assume that the average taxpayer in the United States earns $65,000 and pays an average tax rate of 15 percent. If the income effect is in effect for all taxpayers, what average tax rate will result in a 10 percent increase in tax revenues? This is an example of what type of forecasting?

LO 1-3 LO 1-5 planning

59. Locate the IRS website at www.irs.gov/. For every $100 the IRS collected, how much was spent on the IRS's collection efforts? What tax system criterion does this information help you to evaluate with respect to the current U.S. tax system?

LO 1-5 research

60. Using the Internet, find a comparison of income tax rates across states. What state currently has the highest income tax rate? In considering individual tax burdens across states, what other taxes should you consider?

LO 1-4 research

UWorld Roger CPA Review

Sample CPA Exam questions from Roger CPA Review are available in Connect as support for the topics in this text. These Multiple Choice Questions and Task-Based Simulations include expert-written explanations and solutions and provide a starting point for students to become familiar with the content and functionality of the actual CPA Exam.

chapter

2 Tax Compliance, the IRS, and Tax Authorities

Learning Objectives

Upon completing this chapter, you should be able to:

LO 2-1 Identify the filing requirements for income tax returns and the statute of limitations for assessment.

LO 2-2 Outline the IRS audit process, how returns are selected, the different types of audits, and what happens after the audit.

LO 2-3 Evaluate the relative weights of the various tax law sources.

LO 2-4 Describe the legislative process as it pertains to taxation.

LO 2-5 Perform the basic steps in tax research.

LO 2-6 Describe tax professional responsibilities in providing tax advice.

LO 2-7 Identify taxpayer and tax return preparer penalties.

Michaeljung/Shutterstock

Storyline Summary

Taxpayers:	Bill (he/him/his) and Mercedes (she/her/hers)
Family description:	Bill and Mercedes are married with one daughter, Margaret (she/her/hers), and live in Tampa, Florida.
Employment status:	Bill is an economics professor; Mercedes is a small business owner.
Filing status:	Married, filing jointly
Current situation:	Bill and Mercedes face an IRS audit involving a previous year's interest deductions.

Bill and Mercedes received a notice from the Internal Revenue Service (IRS) that their tax return is under audit for certain interest deductions. As you might expect, they are quite concerned, especially because it has been several years since they claimed the deductions and they worry that all their supporting documentation may not be in place. Several questions run through their minds. How could the IRS audit a tax return that was filed so long ago? Why was their tax return selected, and what should they expect during the audit? The interest deductions they reported were based on advice from their CPA. What would cause the IRS and a CPA to interpret the law differently? What is their financial exposure if the deductions are ultimately disallowed? Will they have to pay interest and penalties in addition to the tax they might owe? ■

Even the most conservative taxpayer is likely to feel anxiety after receiving an IRS notice. This chapter will help answer Bill and Mercedes's questions and provide an overview of the audit process and tax research. While all taxpayers should understand these basics of our tax system, aspiring accountants should be especially familiar with them.

LO 2-1

TAXPAYER FILING REQUIREMENTS

To file or not to file? Unlike Hamlet's "to be or not to be," this question has a pretty straightforward answer. Filing requirements are specified by law for each type of taxpayer. All corporations must file a tax return annually regardless of their taxable income. Estates and trusts are required to file annual income tax returns if their gross income exceeds $600.[1]

The filing requirements for individual taxpayers are a little more complex. Specifically, they depend on the taxpayer's filing status (single, married filing jointly, and so on, discussed in more detail in the Individual Income Tax Overview, Dependents, and Filing Status chapter), age, and gross income (income before deductions). Exhibit 2-1 lists the 2022 gross income thresholds for taxpayers based on their filing status, gross income, and age. As detailed in Exhibit 2-1, the gross income thresholds are calculated as the sum of the standard deduction and additional deductions for taxpayers age 65 or older.[2] These amounts are indexed for inflation and thus change each year. For certain taxpayers, such as the self-employed and those claimed as dependents by another taxpayer, lower gross income thresholds apply.

EXHIBIT 2-1 2022 Gross Income Thresholds by Filing Status

Filing Status and Age (in 2022)	2022 Gross Income	Explanation
Single	$12,950	$12,950 standard deduction
Single, 65 or older	$14,700	$12,950 standard deduction + $1,750 additional deduction
Married, filing a joint return	$25,900	$25,900 standard deduction
Married, filing a joint return, one spouse 65 or older	$27,300	$25,900 standard deduction + $1,400 additional deduction
Married, filing a joint return, both spouses 65 or older	$28,700	$25,900 standard deduction + $2,800 additional deductions (2 × $1,400)
Married, filing a separate return	$ 5	IRS Publication 501
Head of household	$19,400	$19,400 standard deduction
Head of household, 65 or older	$21,150	$19,400 standard deduction + $1,750 additional deduction
Surviving spouse with a dependent child	$25,900	$25,900 standard deduction
Surviving spouse, 65 or older, with a dependent child	$27,300	$25,900 standard deduction + $1,400 additional deduction

Source: irs.gov.

Whether a taxpayer is due a refund (which occurs when taxes paid exceed tax liability) does *not* determine whether a taxpayer must file a tax return. Gross income determines whether a tax return is required. Further, note that even a taxpayer whose gross income falls below the respective threshold is not precluded from filing a tax return. Indeed, taxpayers due a refund *should* file a tax return to receive the refund (or claim a refundable tax credit), even if they are not required to file a tax return.

[1]Estates file income tax returns during the administration period (i.e., before all of the estate assets are distributed).

[2]§6012. We describe the standard deduction in detail later in the text. A married taxpayer is required to file a tax return (regardless of gross income) if (i) such individual and their spouse, at the close of the taxable year, did not have the same household as their home; (ii) the individual has gross income of $5 or more and their spouse files a separate return; or (iii) the individual or their spouse is a dependent of another taxpayer who has income (other than earned income) in excess of the standard deduction for a dependent taxpayer (see discussion later in the text regarding standard deduction for dependent taxpayers).

Tax Return Due Date and Extensions

Like the filing requirements, due dates for tax returns vary based on the type of taxpayer. Individual tax returns are due on the fifteenth day of the fourth month following year-end—that is, April 15 for calendar-year individuals. (Due dates that fall on a Saturday, Sunday, or holiday are automatically extended to the next day that is not a Saturday, Sunday, or holiday.) Similarly, tax returns for C corporations (taxable corporations) are generally due on the fifteenth day of the fourth month following the corporation's year-end. The exception is for tax returns for C corporations with a June 30 year-end, which are due on the fifteenth day of the third month (September 15). For both partnerships and S corporations (generally nontaxable corporations), tax returns must be filed by the fifteenth day of the third month following the entity's year-end (March 15 for calendar-year partnerships or S corporations). Any individual, partnership, or S corporation unable to file a tax return by the original due date can, by that same deadline, request a six-month extension to file, which is granted automatically by the IRS. Similarly, C corporations may request an automatic six- or seven-month extension to file depending on the corporation's year-end.[3]

An extension allows the taxpayer to delay filing a tax return but does *not* extend the due date for tax payments. Thus, when a taxpayer files an extension, they must estimate how much tax will be owed. If a taxpayer fails to pay the entire balance of tax owed by the original due date of the tax return, the IRS charges the taxpayer interest on the underpayment from the due date of the return until the taxpayer pays the tax.[4] The interest rate charged depends on taxpayer type (individual or corporation) and varies quarterly with the federal short-term interest rate.[5] For example, the interest rate for tax underpayments for individuals equals the federal short-term rate plus 3 percentage points.[6]

What happens if the taxpayer does not file a tax return by the time required, whether April 15 or an extended deadline? As you might guess, the IRS imposes penalties on taxpayers failing to comply with the tax law. In many cases, the penalties can be quite substantial (see later discussion in this chapter). In the case of failure to file a tax return, the penalty equals 5 percent of the tax due for each month (or partial month) that the return is late. However, the maximum penalty is generally 25 percent of the tax owed, and the failure-to-file penalty does not apply if the taxpayer owes no tax.

THE KEY FACTS

Filing Requirements and Due Dates

- Filing requirements
  - Filing requirements are specified by law for each type of taxpayer.
  - For individuals, filing requirements vary by filing status, gross income, and age.
  - Gross income thresholds are indexed each year for inflation.
- Due dates
  - The due date for tax returns varies based on the type of taxpayer.
  - Individual tax returns are due on April 15 for calendar-year individuals.
  - Due dates that fall on a Saturday, Sunday, or holiday are automatically extended to the next day that is not a Saturday, Sunday, or holiday.
  - Any taxpayer unable to file a tax return by the original due date can request an extension to file.
  - An extension allows the taxpayer to delay filing a tax return but does *not* extend the due date for tax payments.

Statute of Limitations

Despite the diligent efforts of taxpayers and tax professionals, it is quite common for tax returns to contain mistakes. Some may be to the taxpayer's advantage, and others may be to the government's advantage. Regardless of the nature of the mistake, the taxpayer is obligated to file an amended return to correct the error (and request a refund or pay a deficiency) if the statute of limitations has not expired for the tax return. Likewise, the IRS can propose adjustments to the taxpayer's return if the statute of limitations for the return has not expired.

By law, the **statute of limitations** defines the period in which the taxpayer can file an amended tax return or the IRS can assess a tax deficiency for a specific tax year. For both amended tax returns filed by a taxpayer and proposed tax assessments by the IRS, the statute of limitations generally ends three years from the *later* of (1) the date the tax return was actually filed or (2) the tax return's original due date.

[3]June 30 year-end C corporations may request a seven-month extension. All other C corporations may request a six-month extension.

[4]The tax law also imposes a penalty for late payment in addition to the interest charged on the underpayment. We briefly discuss this penalty later in the chapter and in the Individual Income Tax Computation and Tax Credits chapter.

[5]The federal short-term rate is determined from a one-month average of the market yields from marketable obligations of the United States with maturities of three years or less. The IRS issues revenue rulings quarterly to announce the applicable interest rates for tax underpayments and tax overpayments. For example, see Rev. Rul. 2021-17.

[6]This same interest rate applies to individuals who overpay their taxes (i.e., receive a tax refund and interest payment as a result of an IRS audit or from filing an amended tax return).

The statute of limitations for IRS assessment can be extended in certain circumstances. For example, the original three-year statute of limitations for IRS assessments is extended to six years if the taxpayer omits items of gross income that exceed 25 percent of the gross income reported on the tax return. For fraudulent returns, or if the taxpayer fails to file a tax return, the news is understandably worse. The statute of limitations remains open indefinitely in these cases. The statute of limitations can also be voluntarily extended by the taxpayer at the request of the IRS to allow both sides sufficient time to resolve issues.

Example 2-1

Bill and Mercedes file their 2018 federal tax return on September 6, 2019, after receiving an automatic extension to file their return by October 15, 2019. In 2022, the IRS selects their 2018 tax return for audit. When does the statute of limitations end for Bill and Mercedes's 2018 tax return?

Answer: Assuming the six-year and "unlimited" statute of limitation rules do not apply, the statute of limitations ends on September 6, 2022 (three years after the later of the actual filing date and the *original* due date).

What if: When would the statute of limitations end for Bill and Mercedes for their 2018 tax return if the couple filed the return on March 22, 2019 (before the original due date of April 15, 2019)?

Answer: In this scenario, the statute of limitations would end on April 15, 2022, because the later of the actual filing date and the original due date is April 15, 2019.

Taxpayers should prepare for the possibility of an audit by retaining all supporting documents (receipts, cancelled checks, etc.) for a tax return until the statute of limitations expires. After the statute of limitations expires, taxpayers can discard the majority of supporting documents but should still keep a copy of the tax return itself, as well as any documents that may have ongoing significance, such as those establishing the taxpayer's *basis* or original investment in existing assets like personal residences and long-term investments.

LO 2-2

IRS AUDIT SELECTION

Why me? This is a recurring question in life and definitely a common taxpayer question after receiving an IRS audit notice. The answer, in general, is that a taxpayer's return is selected for audit because the IRS has data suggesting the taxpayer's tax return has a high probability of a significant understated tax liability. Budget constraints limit the IRS's ability to audit a majority or even a large minority of tax returns. Currently, fewer than 1 percent of all tax returns are audited. Thus, the IRS must be strategic in selecting returns for audit in an effort to promote the highest level of voluntary taxpayer compliance and increase tax revenues.

Specifically, how does the IRS select tax returns for audit? The IRS uses a number of computer programs and outside data sources (newspapers, financial statement disclosures, informants, and other public and private sources) to identify tax returns that may have an understated tax liability. Common computer initiatives include the **DIF (Discriminant Function) system,** the **document perfection program,** and the **information matching program.** The most important of these initiatives is the DIF system. The DIF system assigns a score to each tax return that represents the probability the tax liability on the return has been underreported (a higher score = a higher likelihood of underreporting). The IRS derives the weights assigned to specific tax return attributes from historical IRS audit adjustment data from the National Research Program.[7] The DIF system then uses these (undisclosed) weights to score each tax return based on

[7]Similar to its predecessor, the Taxpayer Compliance Measurement Program, the National Research Program (NRP) analyzes a large sample of tax returns that are randomly selected for audit. From these randomly selected returns, the IRS identifies tax return characteristics (e.g., deductions for a home office, unusually high tax deductions relative to a taxpayer's income) associated with underreported liabilities, weights these characteristics, and then incorporates them into the DIF system. The NRP analyzes randomly selected returns to ensure that the DIF scorings are representative of the population of tax returns.

the tax return's characteristics. Returns with higher DIF scores are reviewed to determine whether an audit is the best course of action.

All returns are checked for mathematical and tax calculation errors, a process referred to as the document perfection program. Individual returns are also subject to the information matching program. This program compares the taxpayer's tax return to information submitted to the IRS from other taxpayers like banks, employers, mutual funds, brokerage companies, and mortgage companies. Information matched includes items such as wages (Form W-2 submitted by employers), interest income (Form 1099-INT submitted by banks), and dividend income (Form 1099-DIV submitted by brokerage companies). For tax returns identified as incorrect via the document perfection and information matching programs, the IRS recalculates the taxpayer's tax liability and sends a notice explaining the adjustment. If the taxpayer owes tax, the IRS will request payment of the tax due. If the taxpayer overpaid tax, the IRS will send the taxpayer a refund of the overpayment.

In addition to computer-based methods for identifying tax returns for audit, the IRS may use a number of other audit initiatives that target taxpayers working in certain industries, engaging in certain transactions like the acquisition of other companies, or having specific attributes like home office deductions. Taxpayers of a given size and complexity, such as large publicly traded companies, may be audited every year.

THE KEY FACTS

IRS Audit Selection

- The IRS uses a number of computer programs and outside data sources to identify tax returns that may have an understated tax liability.
- Common computer initiatives include the DIF (Discriminant Function) system, the document perfection program, and the information matching program.
- The DIF system assigns a score to each tax return that represents the probability the tax liability on the return has been underreported.
- The document perfection program checks all returns for mathematical and tax calculation errors.
- The information matching program compares the taxpayer's tax return to information submitted to the IRS from other taxpayers.

TAXES IN THE REAL WORLD Where Can You Get a 4 to 1 Return on Investment?

The possible answer for the U.S. federal government is the IRS. In a June 2021 testimony before the Select Revenue Measures Subcommittee and the Oversight Subcommittee of the House Ways and Means Committee, IRS Acting Assistant Secretary of the Office of Tax Policy Mark Mazur laid out the case for more IRS funding. In his testimony, Mazur highlighted the growing measure of tax noncompliance, called the "tax gap," due to taxpayers who do not file returns (about 9 percent of the gross tax gap), who underreport income or overclaim deductions or credits on tax returns (about 80 percent of the gross tax gap), and who underpay taxes despite reporting them in a timely manner (about 11 percent of the gross tax gap). Over the next decade, the gross tax gap is projected to total $7 trillion, approximately 15 percent of all taxes owed.

Mazur presented a proposal for $80 billion of additional IRS funding, which is estimated to raise $320 billion of gross revenue over 10 years, a 4 to 1 return on investment. The additional funding would provide the IRS resources and staffing to address tax noncompliance and better serve taxpayers, invest in better IRS technology systems to help identify noncompliance and improve customer service, improve information reporting to give the IRS better information on less transparent sources of taxpayer income, and, more broadly, improve tax administration. If successful, additional benefits of IRS funding include higher tax revenues to fund the nation's fiscal priorities, lower budget deficits and smaller amounts of federal debt, and potentially more confidence in the fairness of the tax system.

Source: Based on "Testimony of Mark J. Mazur, Acting Assistant Secretary, Office of Tax Policy, U.S. Department of the Treasury, Before the Select Revenue Measures Subcommittee and the Oversight Subcommittee of the House Ways and Means Committee," June 10, 2021. https://home.treasury.gov/news/press-releases/jy0220.

How was Bill and Mercedes's tax return selected for audit? Given the audit focus on certain deductions, the IRS likely selected their return for audit because the amount or type of the deductions resulted in a high DIF score. IRS personnel then determined that the deductions warranted further review and, thus, selected the tax return for audit.

ETHICS

After Bill and Mercedes's tax return was selected for audit, Bill read on the Internet speculation that filing a paper tax return (instead of filing electronically) and extending a tax return deadline decrease the chance of IRS audit. Bill has convinced Mercedes that they need to use these strategies in the future and look for other ways to avoid audit. Has Bill crossed an ethical boundary?

Types of Audits

The three types of IRS audits are correspondence, office, and field examinations. **Correspondence examinations** are the most common. These audits, as the name suggests, are conducted by mail and generally are limited to one or two items on the taxpayer's return. Of the three types of audits, correspondence audits are generally the narrowest in scope and the least complex. The IRS typically requests supporting documentation for one or more items on the taxpayer's return, like charitable contributions deducted, for example. When appropriate documentation is promptly supplied, these audits typically can be concluded relatively quickly. Of course, they can also be expanded to address other issues that arise as a result of the IRS's inspection of taxpayer documents.

Office examinations are the second most common audit. As the name suggests, the IRS conducts them at its local office. These audits are typically broader in scope and more complex than correspondence examinations. Small businesses, taxpayers operating sole proprietorships, and middle- to high-income individual taxpayers are more likely, if audited, to have office examinations. In these examinations, the taxpayer receives a notice that identifies the items subject to audit, requests substantiation for these items as necessary, and notifies the taxpayer of the date, time, and location of the exam. Taxpayers may attend the examination alone or with representation, such as their tax adviser or attorney, or simply let their tax adviser or attorney attend on their behalf.

Field examinations are the least common audit. The IRS conducts these at the taxpayer's place of business or the location where the taxpayer's books, records, and source documents are maintained. Field examinations are generally the broadest in scope and the most complex of the three audit types. They can last months to years and generally are limited to business returns and the most complex individual returns.

What type of exam do you think Bill and Mercedes will have? Because their return is an individual tax return and the audit is restricted to a relatively narrow set of deductions, their return will likely be subject to a correspondence audit. If the audit were broader in scope, an office examination would be more likely.

After the Audit After the examination, the IRS agent provides a list of proposed adjustments (if any) to the taxpayer for review. If they agree to the proposed changes, the taxpayer signs an agreement form (Form 870, Waiver of Restrictions on Assessment and Collection of Deficiency in Tax and Acceptance of Overassessment) and pays the additional tax owed or receives the proposed refund. If the taxpayer disputes the proposed changes, the taxpayer will receive a **30-day letter** giving them 30 days to either (1) request a conference with an appeals officer, who is independent and resides in a separate IRS division from the examining agent, or (2) agree to the proposed adjustment. An appeals officer would consider the merits of the unresolved issues as well as the "hazards of litigation"—that is, the probability that the IRS will lose if the case is brought to court and the resulting costs of a taxpayer-favorable ruling. If the taxpayer chooses the appeals conference and reaches an agreement with the IRS there, the taxpayer can then sign Form 870, which signifies that the taxpayer agrees to the immediate assessment and collection of the agreed-upon tax and penalties, if any. If the taxpayer and IRS still do not agree on the proposed adjustment at the appeals conference, or the taxpayer chooses not to request an appeals conference, the IRS will send the taxpayer a **90-day letter.** See Exhibit 2-2.

The 90-day letter (also known as a *statutory notice of deficiency*) explains that the taxpayer has 90 days to either (1) pay the proposed deficiency or (2) file a petition in the U.S. Tax Court to hear the case.[8] The **U.S. Tax Court** is a national court whose judges are tax experts who hear only tax cases. If the taxpayer would like to litigate the case but prefers it to be heard in the local **U.S. district court** or the **U.S. Court of Federal Claims,** the taxpayer must pay the tax deficiency first, then request a refund from the IRS, and then sue the IRS for refund in the court after the IRS denies the refund claim.

[8]If the taxpayer lacks the funds to pay the assessed tax, there is legitimate doubt as to whether the taxpayer owes part or all of the assessed tax, or collection of the tax would cause the taxpayer economic hardship or be unfair or inequitable, the taxpayer can request an offer in compromise with the IRS to settle the tax liability for less than the full amount assessed by completing Form 656, Offer in Compromise.

EXHIBIT 2-2 IRS Appeals/Litigation Process

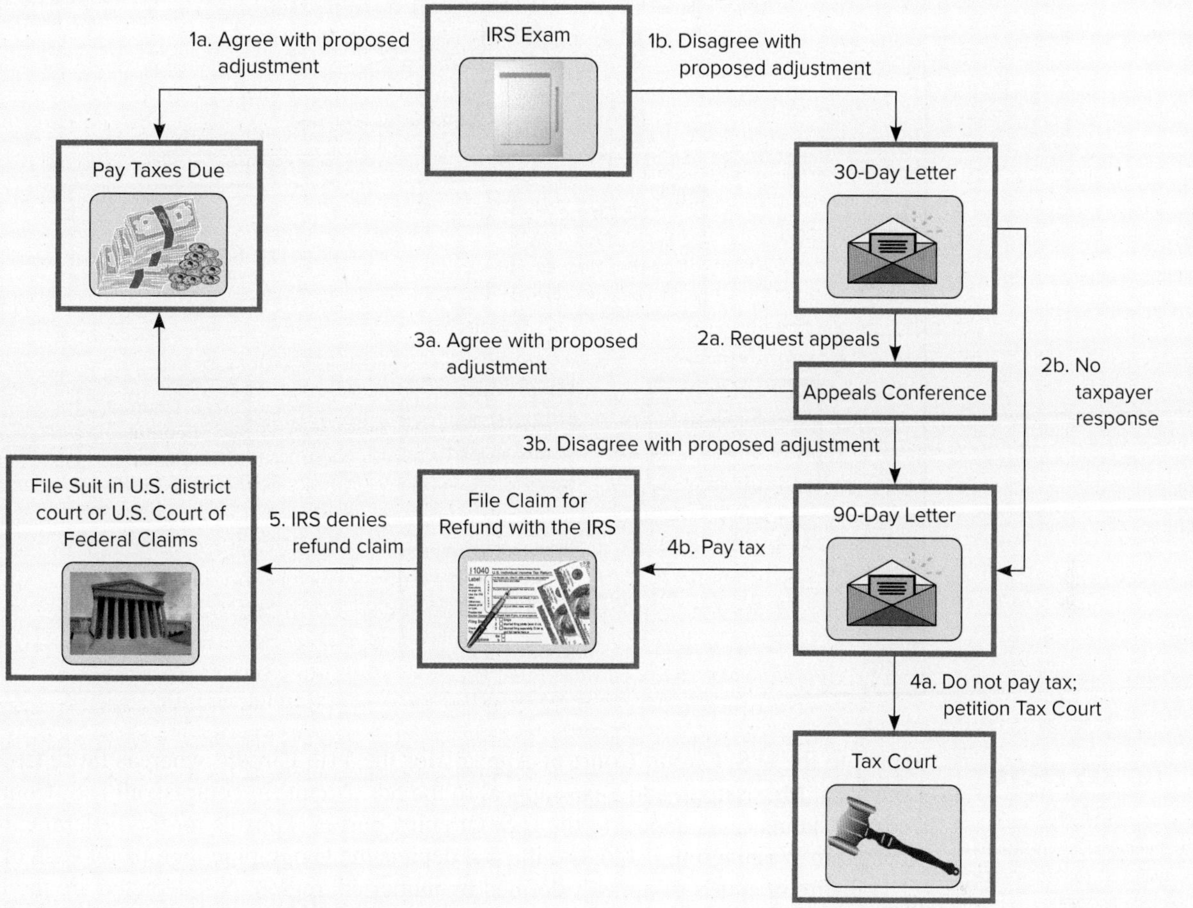

Top: Imageroller/Alamy Stock Photo; Bottom left: Jill Braaten/McGraw Hill

Why would a taxpayer prefer one trial court over others? To understand this, we must appreciate the basic distinguishing factors of each. First and foremost, it is relatively common for the U.S. Tax Court, local U.S. district court, or the U.S. Court of Federal Claims to interpret and rule differently on the same basic tax issue. Given a choice of courts, the taxpayer should prefer the court most likely to rule favorably on their particular issues. The courts also differ in other ways. For example, the U.S. district court is the only court that provides for a jury trial; the U.S. Tax Court is the only court that allows tax cases to be heard *before* the taxpayer pays the disputed liability and the only court with a small claims division (hearing claims involving disputed liabilities of $50,000 or less); and the U.S. Tax Court judges are tax experts, whereas the U.S. district court and U.S. Court of Federal Claims judges are generalists. The taxpayer should consider each of these factors in choosing a trial court. For example, if the taxpayer feels very confident in their tax return position but does not have sufficient funds to pay the disputed liability, they will prefer the U.S. Tax Court. If, instead, the taxpayer is litigating a tax return position that is low on technical merit but high on emotional appeal, a jury trial in the local U.S. district court may be the best option.

What happens after the taxpayer's case has been decided in a trial court? The process may not be quite finished. After the trial court's verdict, the losing party has the right to request one of the 13 **U.S. circuit courts of appeals** to hear the case. Exhibit 2-3 depicts the specific appellant courts for each lower-level court. Both the U.S. Tax Court and local U.S. district court cases are appealed to the specific U.S. circuit court of appeals based on the taxpayer's residence.[9] Cases litigated in Alabama, Florida, and Georgia, for example,

[9]Decisions rendered by the U.S. Tax Court Small Claims Division cannot be appealed by the taxpayer or the IRS.

EXHIBIT 2-3 Federal Judicial System

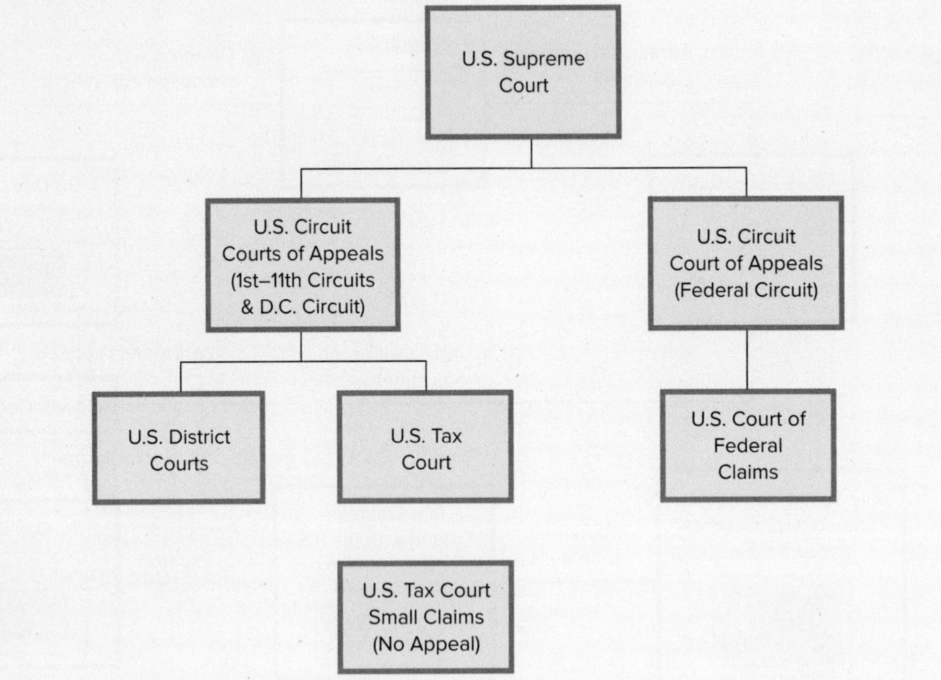

appeal to the U.S. Circuit Court of Appeals for the 11th Circuit, whereas those tried in Louisiana, Mississippi, and Texas appeal to the 5th Circuit. In contrast, all U.S. Court of Federal Claims cases appeal to the U.S. Circuit Court of Appeals for the Federal Circuit (located in Washington, D.C.). Exhibit 2-4 depicts the geographic regions for each of the 11 U.S. circuit courts of appeals defined by numerical region. Not depicted are the U.S. Circuit Court of Appeals for the District of Columbia and the U.S. Circuit Court of Appeals for the Federal Circuit.

Through the initial selection of a trial court—U.S. district court, U.S. Tax Court, or U.S. Court of Federal Claims—the taxpayer has the ability to determine which circuit court would hear an appeal of the case (the U.S. circuit court of appeals based on residence or the U.S. Circuit Court of Appeals for the Federal Circuit). Alternative circuit courts may interpret the law differently, and, therefore, in choosing a trial-level court, the taxpayer should consider the relevant circuit courts' judicial histories to determine which circuit court (and, thus, which trial court) would be more likely to rule in their favor.

After an appeals court hears a case, the losing party has one last option to receive a favorable ruling: a petition to the **U.S. Supreme Court** to hear the case. However, given the quantity of other cases appealed to the U.S. Supreme Court that are of national importance, the Supreme Court agrees to hear only a few tax cases a year—cases with great significance to a broad cross-section of taxpayers or cases litigating issues in which there has been disagreement among the circuit courts. For most tax cases, the Supreme Court refuses to hear the case (denies the ***writ of certiorari***) and litigation ends with the circuit court of appeals decision.

Although litigation of tax disputes is quite common, taxpayers should carefully consider the pros and cons. Litigation can be very costly financially and emotionally, and, thus, it is more appropriately used as an option of last resort, after all other appeal efforts have been exhausted.

What is the likely course of action for Bill and Mercedes's audit? It is too soon to tell. Before you can assess the likely outcome of their audit, you need a better understanding of both the audit issue and the relevant tax laws that apply to the issue. The next section

THE KEY FACTS

IRS Audits

- The three types of IRS audits are correspondence, office, and field examinations.
- After the audit, the IRS will send the taxpayer a 30-day letter, which provides the taxpayer the opportunity to pay the proposed assessment or request an appeals conference.
- If an agreement is not reached at appeals or the taxpayer does not pay the proposed assessment, the IRS will send the taxpayer a 90-day letter.
- After receiving the 90-day letter, the taxpayer may pay the tax or petition the U.S. Tax Court to hear the case.
- If the taxpayer chooses to pay the tax, the taxpayer may then request a refund of the tax and eventually sue the IRS for refund in the U.S. district court or the U.S. Court of Federal Claims.

EXHIBIT 2-4 Geographic Boundaries for the U.S. Circuit Courts of Appeals

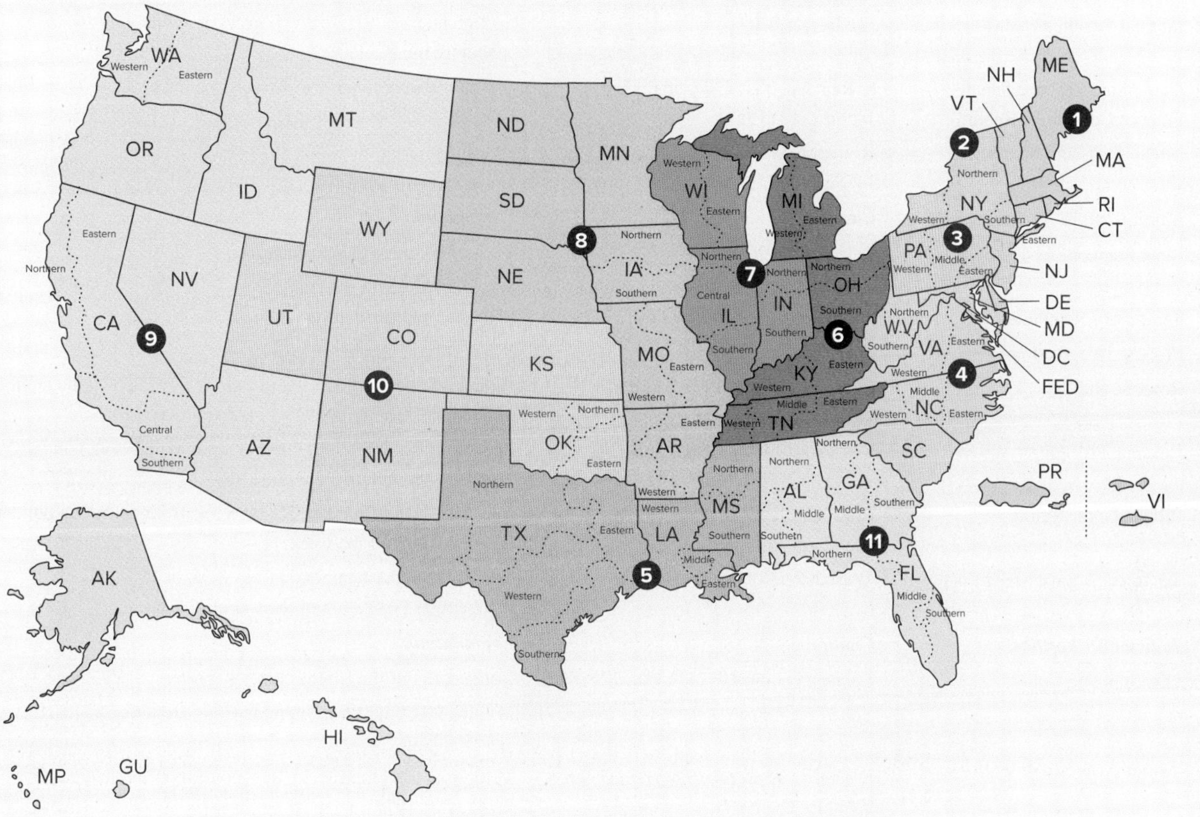

Source: United States Courts. www.uscourts.gov.

explains alternative tax law sources. After we discuss the various sources of our tax laws, we'll describe how Bill and Mercedes (or their CPA) can research the sources to identify the best possible course of action.[10]

TAX LAW SOURCES

LO 2-3 LO 2-4

There are two broad categories of tax authorities: primary authorities and secondary authorities. **Primary authorities** are official sources of the tax law generated by the legislative branch (statutory authority issued by Congress), judicial branch (rulings by the U.S. district courts, U.S. Tax Court, U.S. Court of Federal Claims, U.S. circuit courts of appeals, or U.S. Supreme Court), and executive/administrative branch (Treasury and IRS pronouncements). Exhibit 2-5 displays the most common primary sources, their respective citations, and related explanations. We'll discuss each of these authorities below.

Secondary authorities are unofficial tax authorities that interpret and explain the primary authorities, such as tax research services (discussed below), tax articles from professional journals and law reviews, newsletters, and textbooks. For quick questions, practitioners often use the *CCH Master Tax Guide* or *RIA Federal Tax Handbook*.

[10]Accountants should be mindful to not engage in the unauthorized practice of law. In years past, several court cases have addressed this issue without providing a clear understanding between practicing tax accounting and the unauthorized practice of law. At present, tax accountants are not likely to overstep their responsibilities if they limit their advice to tax issues and leave the general legal advice and drafting of legal documents to attorneys.

EXHIBIT 2-5 Citations to Common Primary Authorities*

Statutory Authorities:	*Citation:*	*Explanation:*
Internal Revenue Code	§162(e)(4)(B)(i)	Section number 162, subsection e, paragraph 4, subparagraph B, clause i
Committee Reports: Senate Finance Committee Report	S. Rep. No. 353, 82d Cong., 1st Sess. 14 (1951)	Senate report number 353, Congress number 82, Congressional session 1, page number 14, year 1951
House Ways and Means Committee Report	H. Rep. No. 242, 82d Cong., 1st Sess. 40 (1951)	House report number 242, Congress number 82, Congressional session 1, page number 40, year 1951
Administrative Authorities:	***Citation:***	***Explanation:***
Final Regulation	Reg. §1.217-2(c)(1)	Type of regulation (1 = income tax), code section 217, regulation number 2, paragraph c, subparagraph number 1
Temporary Regulation	Temp. Reg. §1.217-2(c)(1)	Same as final regulation
Proposed Regulation	Prop. Reg. §1.217-2(c)(1)	Same as final regulation
Revenue Ruling	Rev. Rul. 77-262, 1977-2 C.B. 41	Ruling number 77-262 (262nd ruling of 1977), volume number of cumulative bulletin 1977-2, page number 41
Revenue Procedure	Rev. Proc. 99-10, 1999-1 C.B. 272	Procedure number 99-10 (10th procedure of 1999), volume number of cumulative bulletin 1999-1, page number 272
Private Letter Ruling	PLR 200601001	Year 2006, week number 01 (1st week of 2006), ruling number 001 (1st ruling of the week)
Technical Advice Memorandum	TAM 200402001	Year 2004, week number 02 (2nd week of 2004), ruling number 001 (1st ruling of the week)
Judicial Authorities:	***Citation:***	***Explanation:***
U.S. Supreme Court	*Comm'r v. Kowalski,* 434 U.S. 77 (1977)	Volume 434 of the United States Reporter, page 77, year 1977
	Comm'r v. Kowalski, 98 S. Ct. 315 (1977)	Volume 98 of the West Supreme Court Reporter, page 315, year 1977
	Comm'r v. Kowalski, 77-2 USTC par. 9,748 (S. Ct. 1977)	Volume 77-2 of the CCH USTC court reporter, paragraph 9,748, year 1977
	Comm'r v. Kowalski, 40 AFTR2d 77-6128 (S. Ct. 1977)	Volume 40 of the RIA AFTR2d court reporter, paragraph 77-6128, year 1977
U.S. Circuit Court of Appeals	*Azar Nut Co. v. Comm'r,* 931 F.2d 314 (5th Cir. 1991)	Volume 931 of the West F.2d court reporter, page 314, circuit 5th, year 1991
	Azar Nut Co. v. Comm'r, 91-1 USTC par. 50,257 (5th Cir. 1991)	Volume 91-1 of the CCH USTC court reporter, paragraph 50,257, circuit 5th, year 1991
	Azar Nut Co. v. Comm'r, 67 AFTR2d 91-987 (5th Cir. 1991)	Volume 67 of the RIA AFTR2d court reporter, paragraph 91-987, circuit 5th, year 1991
U.S. Tax Court—Regular decision	*L.A. Beeghly,* 36 TC 154 (1962)	Volume 36 of the Tax Court reporter, page 154, year 1962
U.S. Tax Court—Memorandum decision	*Robert Rodriguez,* RIA TC Memo 2005-012	Paragraph number 2005-012 of the RIA Tax Court Memorandum reporter
	Robert Rodriguez, 85 TCM 1162 (2005)	Volume 85 of the CCH Tax Court Memorandum reporter, page 1162, year 2005
U.S. Court of Federal Claims	*J.R. Cohen v. United States,* 510 F. Supp. 297 (Fed. Cl. 1993)	Volume 510 of the West F. Supp. court reporter, page 297, year 1993
	J.R. Cohen v. United States, 72 AFTR2d 93-5124 (Fed. Cl. 1993)	Volume 72 of the RIA AFTR2d court reporter, paragraph 93-5124, year 1993
	J.R. Cohen v. United States, 93-1 USTC par. 50,354 (Fed. Cl. 1993)	Volume 93-1 of the CCH USTC court reporter, paragraph 50,354, year 1993
U.S. District Court	*Waxler Towing Co., Inc. v. United States,* 510 F. Supp. 297 (W.D. Tenn. 1981)	Volume 510 of the West F. Supp. court reporter, page 297, Western District (W.D.), state Tennessee, year 1981
	Waxler Towing Co., Inc. v. United States, 81-2 USTC par. 9,541 (W.D. Tenn. 1981)	Volume 81-2 of the CCH USTC court reporter, paragraph 9,541, Western District (W.D.), state Tennessee, year 1981
	Waxler Towing Co., Inc. v. United States, 48 AFTR2d 81-5274 (W.D. Tenn. 1981)	Volume 48 of the RIA AFTR2d court reporter, paragraph 81-5274, Western District (W.D.), state Tennessee, year 1981

*It is acceptable to substitute Sec. for § when referring to a code or regulation section.

EXHIBIT 2-6 **Common Secondary Tax Authorities**

Tax Research Services:	*Professional Journals:*
BNA Tax Management Portfolios	*Journal of Accountancy*
CCH Standard Federal Tax Reporter	*Journal of Taxation*
CCH Tax Research Consultant	*Practical Tax Strategies*
RIA Federal Tax Coordinator	*Taxes*
RIA United States Tax Reporter	*Tax Adviser*
Newsletters:	***Quick Reference Sources:***
Daily Tax Report	*IRS Publications*
Federal Tax Weekly Alert	*CCH Master Tax Guide*
Tax Notes	*RIA Federal Tax Handbook*
Law Reviews:	***Textbooks:***
Tax Law Review (New York University School of Law)	*McGraw Hill's Taxation of Individuals and Business Entities*
Virginia Tax Review (University of Virginia School of Law)	*McGraw Hill's Essentials of Federal Taxation*

Secondary authorities may be very helpful in understanding a tax issue, but they hold little weight in a tax dispute (hence their "unofficial" status). Thus, tax advisers should always be careful to verify their understanding of tax law by examining primary authorities directly and to *never* cite secondary authority in a research memo. Exhibit 2-6 lists some of the common sources of secondary authority.

TAXES IN THE REAL WORLD Google: Not Authoritative on Tax Matters

While Internet super giant Google may be the king of all cyberspace knowledge, the Tax Court ruled in *Woodard v. Comm'r,* TC Summary Opinion 2009-150, that a Google search does not constitute reasonable cause to excuse a Harvard MBA/CPA from taking an incorrect tax return position. The Tax Court noted that although the taxpayer had not worked as an accountant for years before filing his tax return, "his accounting degree, MBA, and CPA training, no matter how stale, undoubtedly taught him what sources could be relied upon as definitive; such as, for example, the Internal Revenue Code and the income tax regulations, both of which are readily available on the Internet."

Legislative Sources: Congress and the Constitution

The three legislative or statutory tax authorities are the U.S. Constitution, the Internal Revenue Code, and tax treaties. The **U.S. Constitution** is the highest authority in the United States, but it provides very little in the way of tax law because it contains no discussion of tax rates, taxable income, or other details. Instead, the 16th Amendment provides Congress the ability to tax income directly, from whatever source derived, without apportionment across the states.

Various attempts to amend the U.S. Constitution with regard to taxation—for example, one effort to repeal the 16th Amendment entirely and one to require a two-thirds majority in both houses to raise taxes—have so far met with failure.

Internal Revenue Code The second (and main) statutory authority is the **Internal Revenue Code of 1986,** as amended, known as the Code. The Internal Revenue Code has the same authoritative weight as tax treaties and Supreme Court rulings. Thus, a taxpayer should feel very confident in a tax return position, such as taking a deduction, that is specifically allowed by the Code. The Internal Revenue Code is unique in that all federal tax authorities—all administrative and judicial authorities except tax treaties and the Constitution—can be seen as an interpretation of it. Hence, understanding the relevant code section(s) is critical to being an efficient and effective tax professional.

Congress enacts tax legislation virtually every year that changes the Code; 1986 was simply the last major overhaul. Prior to 1986, tax law changes were incorporated into the Internal Revenue Code of 1954, the year a new numbering system and other significant changes were introduced. Before that, tax law changes were incorporated into the Internal Revenue Code of 1939, which was the year the tax law was first codified.

The Legislative Process for Tax Laws Exhibit 2-7 illustrates the legislative process for enacting tax laws. As required by the U.S. Constitution (Article 1, Section 7), "All Bills for raising Revenue shall originate in the House of Representatives." The Senate may propose tax legislation, but the first to formally consider a bill will be the House, typically within its Ways and Means Committee. After the committee debates the proposed legislation and drafts a bill, the bill goes to the House of Representatives floor for debate and ultimately a vote (either yea or nay without modification). If the bill is approved, it becomes an *act* and is sent to the Senate, which typically refers the act to the

EXHIBIT 2-7 Tax Legislation Process

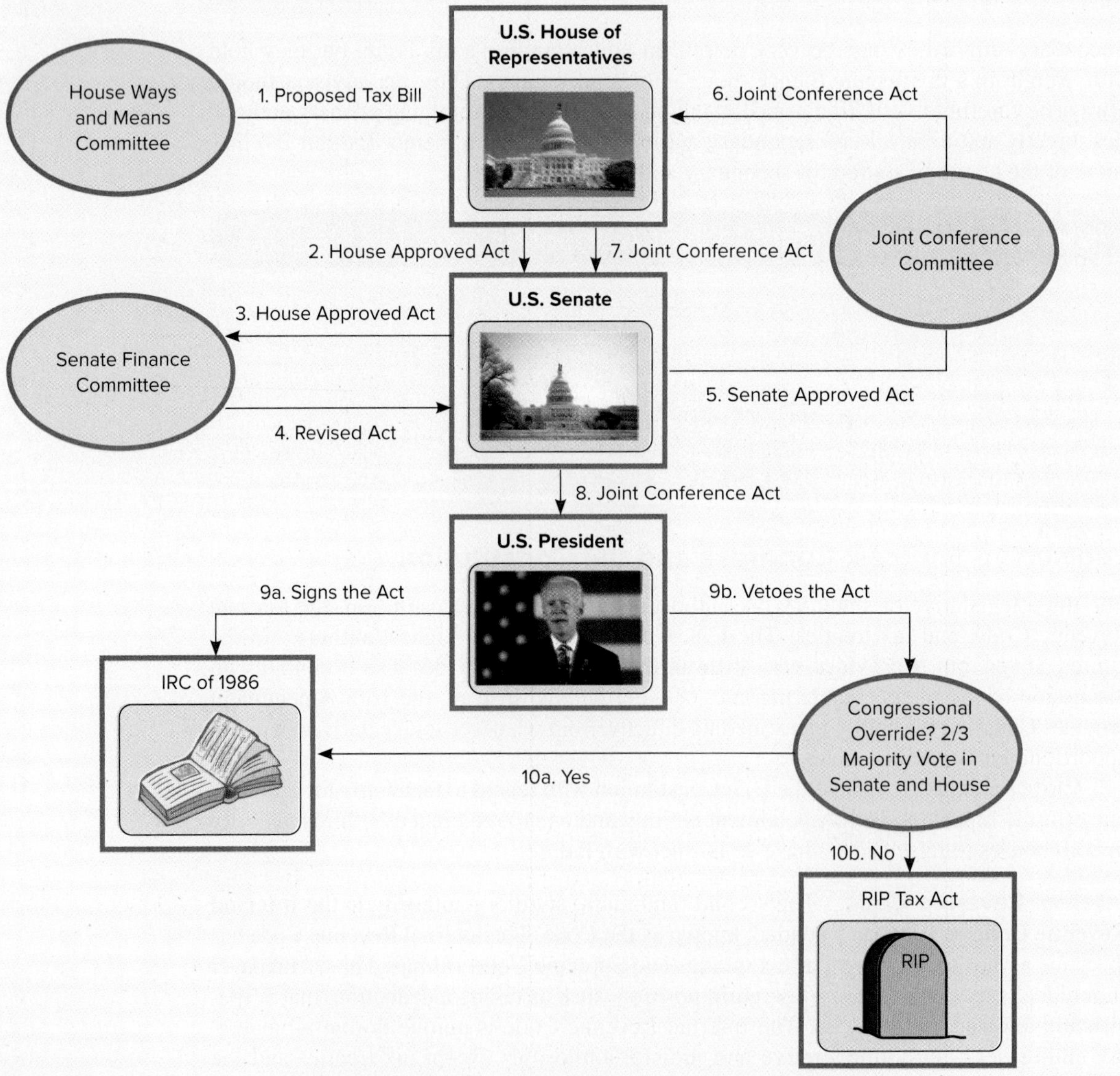

Top: fstockfoto/iStock/Getty Images; middle: Glow Images; bottom: Christos S/Shutterstock

Senate Finance Committee. Not to be outdone by the House, the Senate Finance Committee usually amends the act during its deliberations. After the revised act passes the Senate Finance Committee, it goes to the Senate for debate and vote. Unlike representatives, senators may modify the proposed legislation during their debate.

If the Senate passes the act, both the House and Senate versions of the legislation are sent to the Joint Conference Committee, which consists of members of the House Ways and Means Committee and the Senate Finance Committee. During the Joint Conference Committee deliberations, committee members debate the two versions of the proposed legislation. Possible outcomes for any specific provision in the proposed legislation include adoption of the Senate version, the House version, or some compromise version of the two acts. Likewise, the Joint Conference Committee may simply choose to eliminate specific provisions from the proposed legislation or fail to reach a compromise, thereby terminating the legislation.

After the Joint Conference Committee approves the act, the revised legislation is sent to the House and Senate for vote. If both the House and Senate approve it, the act is sent to the president for their signature. If the president signs the act, it becomes law and is incorporated into the Internal Revenue Code of 1986 (Title 26 of the U.S. Code, which contains *all* codified laws of the United States). If the president vetoes the legislation, Congress may override the veto with a two-thirds positive vote in both the House and the Senate.

The House Ways and Means Committee, Senate Finance Committee, and Joint Conference Committee each produces a committee report that explains the current tax law, proposed change in the law, and reasons for the change. These committee reports are considered statutory sources of the tax law and may be very useful in interpreting tax law changes and understanding congressional intent. These committee reports are especially important after new legislation has been enacted because, with the exception of the Code, there will be very little authority interpreting the new law (i.e., no judicial or administrative authorities because of the time it takes for the new law to be litigated or for the IRS to issue interpretative guidance).

THE KEY FACTS

Statutory Authorities

- U.S. Constitution
  - The 16th Amendment provides Congress the ability to tax income directly, from whatever source derived, without apportionment across the states.
- Internal Revenue Code
  - The main statutory authority is the Internal Revenue Code of 1986.
  - The Internal Revenue Code has the same authoritative weight as tax treaties and Supreme Court rulings.
  - Changes to the Code are passed by the House of Representatives and Senate and signed into law by the president.
  - The House Ways and Means Committee and Senate Finance Committee oversee tax legislation in the House of Representatives and Senate, respectively.
  - When referencing a tax law, the researcher generally refers to the law by its code section.
- Treaties
  - Tax treaties are agreements negotiated between countries that describe the tax treatment of entities subject to tax in both countries.

Basic Organization of the Code The Internal Revenue Code is divided into subtitles, chapters, subchapters, parts, subparts, and sections. All existing and any new tax laws are placed in the Code within a specific subtitle, chapter, subchapter, part, subpart, and section. When referencing a tax law, the researcher generally refers to the law simply by its code section. Code sections are numbered from 1 to 9834, with gaps in the section numbers to allow new code sections to be added to the appropriate parts of the Code as needed. If necessary to create space for new code sections, capital letters may be added to section numbers to create new code sections (e.g., 280A). Each code section is further divided into subsections, paragraphs, subparagraphs, and clauses to allow more specific reference or citation. See Exhibit 2-5 for an example code citation and explanation.

Memorizing the various subtitles and chapters of the Code has limited value (except to impress your friends at parties). However, understanding the *organization* of the Code is important, especially for the aspiring tax accountant. (See Exhibit 2-8.) First, you must understand the organization of a code section, its subsections, paragraphs, subparagraphs, and clauses to be able to cite the respective law correctly as, for example, §162(b)(4). Second, note that many provisions in the Code apply only to specific segments of the Code. For example, it is quite common for a code section to include the phrase "for purposes of this chapter, . . ." If you do not understand what laws are encompassed in the chapter, it will be very difficult for you to interpret the code section and determine its applicability to a research question.

Finally, remember that code sections addressing similar transactions, such as deductions, or topics, such as C corporations, are grouped together. Consider a researcher faced with the question of whether an item of income is taxable. If the researcher understands the organization of the Code, they can quickly focus their research on code sections 61–140, which provide a broad definition of gross income, list items specifically included in gross income, and identify items specifically excluded from gross income.

EXHIBIT 2-8 Example of Code Organization

Subtitle A—Income Taxes
- Chapter 1—Income Taxes
  - **Subchapter A—Determination of Tax Liability**
    - Part I—Definition of Gross Income, Adjusted Gross Income, Taxable Income, etc. (Secs. 61–68)
      - **Sec. 61—Gross Income Defined**
      - **Sec. 62—Adjusted Gross Income Defined**
      - **Sec. 63—Taxable Income Defined**
        - Subsection 63(c)—Standard Deduction
          - **Paragraph 63(c)(2)—Basic Standard Deduction**
            - Subparagraph 63(c)(2)(A)
              - **Clause 63(c)(2)(A)(i)**
    - Part II—Items Specifically Included in Gross Income (Secs. 71–90)
      - **Sec. 71—Alimony**
      - **Sec. 72—Annuities**
      - **Sec. 73—Services of Child**
      - **Sec. 74—Prizes & Awards**
    - Part III—Items Specifically Excluded from Gross Income (Secs. 101–140)
      - **Sec. 101—Certain Death Benefits**
      - **Sec. 102—Gifts and Inheritances**
      - **Sec. 103—Interest on State & Local Bonds**

Tax Treaties **Tax treaties** are negotiated agreements between countries that describe the tax treatment of entities subject to tax in both countries, such as U.S. citizens earning investment income in Spain. The U.S. president has the authority to enter into a tax treaty with another country after receiving the Senate's advice. If you are a U.S. citizen earning income abroad or an accountant with international clients, you need knowledge of U.S. tax laws, the foreign country's tax laws, and the respective tax treaty between the United States and the foreign country for efficient tax planning. Because the focus in this text is on U.S. tax laws, we only briefly mention the importance of tax treaties as a statutory authority.

Example 2-2

Bill recently spent a summer in Milan, Italy, teaching a graduate-level economics course. While in Italy he earned a $20,000 stipend from Bocconi University and some interest in a temporary banking account that he established for the trip. What tax laws must Bill consider to understand any tax liability from his $20,000 stipend?

Answer: U.S. tax laws, Italian tax laws, and the U.S.–Italy tax treaty will determine the tax consequences of the amounts Bill earned in Italy.

THE KEY FACTS

Judicial Authorities

- Our judicial system has the ultimate authority to interpret the Internal Revenue Code and settle disputes between taxpayers and the IRS.
- The Supreme Court is the highest judicial authority.
- Beneath the Supreme Court, the 13 circuit courts of appeals represent the next highest judicial authority.

(continued)

Judicial Sources: The Courts

Our judicial system has the ultimate authority to interpret the Internal Revenue Code and settle disputes between the IRS and taxpayers. As Exhibit 2-3 illustrates, there are five basic sources of judicial authority (three trial-level courts, 13 U.S. circuit courts of appeals, and the Supreme Court). We've noted that the Supreme Court, along with the Code, represents the highest tax-specific authority. An important distinction between the two, however, is that the Supreme Court does not establish law but instead simply interprets and applies the Code (along with other authorities). Thus, the Code and the Supreme Court should never be in conflict.[11]

[11]The Supreme Court has the authority to declare a Code provision unconstitutional.

Below the Supreme Court, the 13 U.S. circuit courts of appeals represent the next highest judicial authority. The lowest level of judicial authority consists of three different types of trial-level courts (94 U.S. district courts that hear cases involving taxpayers that reside within their respective districts, the U.S. Court of Federal Claims, and the U.S. Tax Court). Given that the U.S. Tax Court hears only tax cases and that its judges are "tax experts," its decisions typically have more weight than those rendered by a district court or the U.S. Court of Federal Claims.[12] Likewise, because the U.S. Court of Federal Claims hears a much narrower set of issues than U.S. district courts (only monetary claims against the U.S. government), its decisions have more weight than district court decisions.

In rendering court decisions, all courts apply the judicial doctrine of ***stare decisis.*** This doctrine means that a court will rule consistently with (a) its previous rulings (unless, due to evolving interpretations of the tax law over time, the court decides to overturn an earlier decision) and (b) the rulings of higher courts with appellate jurisdiction (the courts its cases are appealed to). The implication of *stare decisis* is that a circuit court will abide by Supreme Court rulings and its own rulings, whereas a trial-level court will abide by Supreme Court rulings, its respective circuit court's rulings, and its own rulings. For example, a district court in California would follow U.S. 9th Circuit and Supreme Court rulings as well as the court's own rulings.

The doctrine of *stare decisis* presents a special problem for the U.S. Tax Court because it appeals to different circuit courts based on the taxpayer's residence. To implement the doctrine of *stare decisis,* the tax court applies the ***Golsen* rule.**[13] The *Golsen* rule simply states that the Tax Court will abide by rulings of the circuit court that has appellate jurisdiction for a case.

- The lowest level of judicial authority consists of three different types of trial-level courts (U.S. district courts, the U.S. Court of Federal Claims, and the U.S. Tax Court).
- U.S. Tax Court decisions typically are considered to have more authoritative weight than decisions rendered by a district court or the U.S. Court of Federal Claims.
- All courts apply the judicial doctrine of *stare decisis,* which means that a court will rule consistently with its previous rulings and the rulings of higher courts with appellate jurisdiction.

Example 2-3

What if: If Bill and Mercedes opt to litigate their case in the U.S. Tax Court, by which circuit court's rulings will the court abide?

Answer: Because Bill and Mercedes live in Florida, the U.S. Tax Court will abide by the circuit court with appellate jurisdiction in Florida, which happens to be the U.S. 11th Circuit Court.

Administrative Sources: The U.S. Treasury

Regulations, Revenue Rulings, and Revenue Procedures The Treasury Department, of which the IRS is a bureau, is charged with administering and interpreting the tax laws of the United States, among other duties such as printing money and advising the president on economic issues. **Regulations** are the Treasury Department's official interpretation of the Internal Revenue Code, have the highest authoritative weight, and often contain examples of the application of the Code that may be particularly helpful to the tax researcher. Regulations are issued in three different forms: final, temporary, and proposed. The names are very descriptive. **Final regulations** are regulations that have been issued in final form, and, thus, unless or until revoked, they represent the Treasury's interpretation of the Code. **Temporary regulations** have a limited life (three years for regulations issued after November 20, 1988). Nonetheless, during their life, they carry the same authoritative weight as final regulations. Finally, all regulations are issued in the form of **proposed regulations** first, to allow public comment on them. Proposed regulations do not carry the same authoritative weight as temporary or final regulations.

In addition to being issued in three different forms (proposed, temporary, and final), regulations also serve three basic purposes: interpretative, procedural, and legislative.

THE KEY FACTS

Administrative Authorities

- The Treasury Department is charged with administering and interpreting the tax laws.
- Regulations
  - Regulations are the Treasury Department's official interpretation of the Internal Revenue Code and have the highest authoritative weight.
  - Regulations are issued in three different forms (proposed, temporary, and final) and serve three basic purposes (interpretative, procedural, and legislative).

(continued)

[12]The Tax Court renders both "regular" and "memorandum" decisions. Regular decisions involve new or unusual points of law, whereas memorandum decisions involve questions of fact or the application of existing law. Both decisions have similar authoritative weight. Decisions issued by the Tax Court's Small Claims division may not be cited as precedent.

[13]*Golsen v. Comm'r,* 54 TC 742 (1970).

- Revenue rulings and revenue procedures
  - Revenue rulings and revenue procedures are second in administrative authoritative weight after regulations.
  - Revenue rulings address the application of the Code and regulations to a specific factual situation.
  - Revenue procedures explain in greater detail IRS practice and procedures in administering the tax law.
- Letter rulings
  - Letter rulings are less authoritative but more specific than revenue rulings and regulations.
  - Private letter rulings represent the IRS's application of the Code and other tax authorities to a specific transaction and taxpayer.

Most regulations, regardless of whether they are issued in proposed, temporary, or final form, are interpretative or procedural regulations. As the names suggest, **interpretative regulations** represent the Treasury's interpretation of the Code. In Bill and Mercedes's case, these might be the regulations issued under §163, which discuss interest deductions. **Procedural regulations** explain Treasury Department procedures as they relate to administering the Code. Again, for Bill and Mercedes's case, these might be the regulations issued under §6501 regarding the statute of limitations for IRS assessment and collection. **Legislative regulations,** the rarest type, are issued when Congress specifically directs the Treasury Department to create regulations to address an issue in an area of law. In these instances, the Treasury is actually writing the law instead of interpreting the Code. Because legislative regulations represent tax law instead of an interpretation of tax law, legislative regulations generally have been viewed to have more authoritative weight than interpretative and procedural regulations. However, in *Mayo Foundation for Medical Education & Research v. United States,* 562 U.S. 44 (2011), the Supreme Court held (subject to specific conditions) that all Treasury regulations warrant deference. It is thus a very difficult process to challenge any regulation, and taxpayers are cautioned not to take tax return positions inconsistent with regulations.

Revenue rulings and revenue procedures are second in administrative authoritative weight after regulations. But unlike regulations, revenue rulings address the application of the Code and regulations to a specific factual situation. Thus, while **revenue rulings** have less authoritative weight, they provide a much more detailed interpretation of the Code as it applies to a specific transaction and fact pattern. For example, Rev. Rul. 87-22 discusses the deductions of prepaid interest (points) a taxpayer may claim when refinancing the mortgage for a principal residence, whereas the Code and regulations do not specifically address this issue. Although revenue rulings are binding on the IRS (until revoked, superseded, or modified), courts may agree or disagree with a revenue ruling. Thus, while revenue rulings should be carefully evaluated because they represent the IRS's interpretation, courts may provide a different interpretation of the tax law that a taxpayer might choose to follow. **Revenue procedures** are also much more detailed than regulations. They explain in greater detail IRS practice and procedures in administering the tax law. For example, Rev. Proc. 87-56 provides the specific depreciation lives for depreciable assets (discussed in the Property Acquisition and Cost Recovery chapter). As with revenue rulings, revenue procedures are binding on the IRS until revoked, modified, or superseded.

Letter Rulings Below revenue rulings and revenue procedures in authoritative weight rest letter rulings. As you might guess, letter rulings are less authoritative but more specific than revenue rulings and regulations. Letter rulings generally may not be used as precedent by taxpayers. However, they may be cited as authority to avoid the substantial understatement of tax penalty under §6662 imposed on taxpayers and the related tax practitioner penalty under §6694 (discussed later in this chapter). **Private letter rulings** represent the IRS's application of the Code and other tax authorities to a specific transaction and taxpayer. Private letter rulings are issued in response to a taxpayer request and are common for proposed transactions with potentially large tax implications. For example, companies commonly request a private letter ruling to ensure that a proposed corporate acquisition meets the definition of a tax-free exchange. However, the IRS also maintains a list of certain issues on which it refuses to rule, such as the tax consequences of proposed federal tax legislation. Each year, the IRS publishes an updated list of these transactions in a revenue procedure.

Other types of letter rulings include determination letters and technical advice memorandums. **Determination letters,** issued by local IRS directors, are generally not controversial. An example of a determination letter is the request by an employer for the IRS to rule that the taxpayer's retirement plan is a "qualified plan." **Technical advice memorandums** differ from private letter rulings in that they are generated for completed transactions and usually are requested by an IRS agent during an IRS audit.

Is this a comprehensive list of IRS pronouncements? No. In addition to the pronouncements listed above, the IRS issues several less common types, which are beyond the scope of this text. A couple of other pronouncements, however, warrant some discussion.

As we mentioned above, the IRS and taxpayers litigate tax cases in a number of courts and jurisdictions. Obviously, the IRS wins some of these cases and loses others. Except for Supreme Court cases, whenever the IRS loses, it may issue an **acquiescence** or **nonacquiescence** as guidance for how the IRS intends to respond to the loss. Although an acquiescence indicates that the IRS has decided to *follow* the court's adverse ruling in the future, it does not mean that the IRS *agrees* with it. Instead, it simply means that the IRS will no longer litigate this issue.

A nonacquiescence has the exact opposite implications and alerts taxpayers that the IRS does plan to continue to litigate this issue. Finally, the IRS also issues **actions on decisions,** which explain the background reasoning behind an IRS acquiescence or nonacquiescence.[14] What are noticeably absent from the list of administrative authorities? IRS publications and tax return form instructions. *Neither are considered primary authorities and should not be cited as precedent. Likewise, it is not advisable to rely on either to avoid taxpayer or tax practitioner penalties.*

TAX RESEARCH

LO 2-5

Now that you have a basic understanding of the different types of tax authority, why do you think that the IRS and taxpayers disagree with respect to the tax treatment of a transaction? In other words, why would the IRS and Bill and Mercedes's CPA reach different conclusions regarding the deductibility of certain expenses? The answer is that, because the Code does not specifically address the tax consequences of each transaction type or every possible variation of a particular transaction, the application of the tax law is subject to debate and differing interpretations by the IRS, courts, tax professionals, taxpayers, and so on. Tax research, therefore, plays a vital role in allowing us to identify and understand the varying authorities that provide guidance on an issue; assess the relative weights of differing authorities; understand the risks associated with different tax return positions; and, ultimately, draw an appropriate conclusion regarding the application of the tax law to the issue. The following paragraphs describe the basic process of tax research that tax professionals use to identify and analyze tax authorities to answer tax questions. We will then revisit Bill and Mercedes's issue and view the research memo prepared by their CPA.

THE KEY FACTS

Tax Research

- The five steps in tax research are (1) understand the facts, (2) identify issues, (3) locate relevant authorities, (4) analyze the tax authorities, and (5) document and communicate research results.
- The two types of tax services that tax professionals use in tax research are annotated tax services, arranged by code section, and topical services, arranged by topic.
- Research questions often consist of questions of fact or questions of law.
  - The answer to a question of fact hinges upon the facts and circumstances of the taxpayer's transaction.
  - The answer to a question of law hinges upon the interpretation of the law, such as interpreting a particular phrase in a code section.
- When the researcher identifies that different authorities have conflicting views, they should evaluate the "hierarchy," jurisdiction, and age of the authorities.
- Once the tax researcher has identified relevant authorities, they must make sure that the authorities are still valid and up to date.

(continued)

Step 1: Understand Facts

To answer a tax question, you must understand it. To understand the question, you must know the facts. There are two basic types of facts: open facts and closed facts. *Open facts* have not yet occurred, such as the facts associated with a proposed transaction. *Closed facts* have already occurred. The distinction between open and closed facts is important because, unlike closed facts, open facts can be altered, and different facts may result in very different tax consequences. Open facts allow the taxpayer to arrange a transaction to achieve the most advantageous outcome. Thus, they are especially important in tax planning.

How do you establish the facts for a research question? Interview clients, speak with third parties such as attorneys and brokers, and review client documents such as contracts, prior tax returns, wills, trust documents, deeds, and corporate minutes. When interviewing clients, remember that not many are tax experts. Thus, it is up to the tax professional to ask the correct initial and follow-up questions to obtain all the relevant facts. Also consider nontax factors, such as a client's personal values or objectives, because these often put constraints on tax-planning strategies.

Step 2: Identify Issues

A tax professional's ability to identify issues is largely a function of their type of tax expertise. A tax expert in a particular area will typically be able to identify quickly the

[14]Actions on decisions have no precedential value but may be cited as authority to avoid the substantial understatement of tax penalty under §6662 imposed on taxpayers and the related tax practitioner penalty under §6694 (discussed later in this chapter).

- The most common end product of a research question is a research memo, which has five basic parts: (1) facts, (2) issues, (3) authority list, (4) conclusion, and (5) analysis.

specific tax issues that relate to transactions in that area. For example, an expert in corporate acquisitions would quickly identify the tax consequences and specific issues of alternative acquisition types. A novice, on the other hand, would likely identify broader issues first and then more specific issues as they researched the relevant tax law.

What's the best method to identify tax issues? First of all, get a good understanding of the client's facts. Then, combine your understanding of the facts with your knowledge of the tax law. Let's consider the example of Bill and Mercedes's interest deduction. For an expert in this particular area, the issues will be immediately evident. For a novice, the initial response may take the form of a series of general questions: (1) Is this item of expense deductible? (2) Is that item of income taxable? (3) In what year should the expense be deducted? (4) In what year should the item of income be taxed? After you identify these types of general issues, your research will enable you to identify the more specific issues that ultimately determine the tax ramifications of the transaction.

Example 2-4

Elizabeth, Bill and Mercedes's friend who is a shareholder and the CFO of a company, loaned money to her company to help it avoid declaring bankruptcy. Despite Elizabeth's loan, the company did file for bankruptcy, and Elizabeth was not repaid the loan. What issues would a researcher consider?

Answer: The first questions to ask are whether Elizabeth can deduct the bad debt expense and, if so, as what type of deduction? As the researcher delves more into the general issue, he would learn that the type of deduction depends on whether Elizabeth's debt is considered a business or nonbusiness bad debt. This more specific issue depends on whether Elizabeth loaned the money to the company to protect her job (business bad debt) or to protect her stock investment in the company (nonbusiness bad debt). Bad-debt expenses incurred for nonbusiness debts (investment-related debts) are deducted as short-term capital losses but subject to limitations. In contrast, bad-debt expenses for business debts (business-related debts) are generally ordinary deductions and not limited. The exception (potentially applicable to Elizabeth) is that a business bad debt incurred related to an employee loan to an employer is considered a nondeductible unreimbursed employee business expense. Thus, the potential outcomes for Elizabeth are either a deductible short-term capital loss, subject to limitations, or a nondeductible unreimbursed employee business expense.

Why might this case be a good one to litigate in U.S. district court?

Answer: Because a jury might be more likely to be convinced to assess Elizabeth's motives favorably.

Step 3: Locate Relevant Authorities

Step three in the research process is to locate the relevant authorities (code sections, regulations, court cases, revenue rulings) that address the tax issue. Luckily, tax services can aid the researcher in identifying relevant authorities. Most, if not all, of these services are available on the Internet (with a subscription) and thus offer the flexibility to conduct research almost anywhere.[15]

There are two basic types of tax services: annotated and topical. **Annotated tax services** are arranged by Internal Revenue Code section. That is, for each code section, an annotated service includes the code section; a listing of the code section history; copies of congressional committee reports that explain changes to the code section; a copy of all the regulations issued for the specific code section; the service's unofficial explanation of the code section; and brief summaries (called annotations) of relevant court cases, revenue rulings, revenue procedures, and letter rulings that address issues specific to the code section. Two examples of annotated tax services are Commerce Clearing House's (CCH) Standard Federal Tax Reporter and Research Institute of America's (RIA) United States Tax Reporter.

[15]www.irs.gov contains a lot of information (tax forms, IRS publications, etc.) that may be especially useful for answering basic tax questions. In addition, tax publishers, such as CCH and RIA, produce quick reference tax guides (e.g., the *CCH Master Tax Guide* or the *RIA Federal Tax Handbook*) that may be used to answer basic tax questions.

Topical tax services are arranged by topic, such as taxable forms of income, tax-exempt income, and trade or business expenses. For each topic, the services identify tax issues that relate to each topic and then explain and cite authorities relevant to the issue (code sections, regulations, court cases, revenue rulings, etc.). Beginning tax researchers often prefer topical services because they generally are easier to read. Some examples of topical federal tax services include BNA's Tax Management Portfolios, CCH's Tax Research Consultant, and RIA's Federal Tax Coordinator.

How does a researcher use these services? An expert would probably go directly to the relevant portions of an annotated or topical service. A novice may conduct a keyword search in the service, use the tax service's topical index, or browse the tax service to identify the relevant portions. To identify keywords, the researcher should try to describe the transaction in three to five words. An ideal keyword search typically includes (1) the relevant area of law and (2) a fact or two that describes the transaction. Try to avoid keywords that are too broad (income, deduction, taxable) or too narrow ("United Way charitable contribution deduction limit").

Example 2-5

Bill and Mercedes refinanced the mortgage on their principal residence a couple of years ago when their original mortgage's four-year balloon payment came due. Their mortgage institution charged Bill and Mercedes $3,000 of points (prepaid interest) upon the refinancing in order to give them a reduced interest rate. On their CPA's advice, Bill and Mercedes deducted the $3,000 in the year they paid it, but upon audit, the IRS disallowed the deduction. What is the research issue?

Answer: The issue is, should Bill and Mercedes have deducted the $3,000 of points in the year they paid it?

What are some keywords that could identify the relevant tax authority?

Answer: Points (area of law), interest (area of law), refinancing (fact that describes the transaction).

Keyword searching is more an art than an exact science. As you gain a better understanding of different areas of the tax law, you'll become much more efficient at using keywords. If keyword searching is not proving beneficial, check your spelling, make sure you're searching within the correct database, rethink your keywords, use another research method, use another tax service, or, as a last resort, take a break.

While utilizing keyword searches or other research methods to identify potentially relevant areas of law and tax authorities, constantly ask yourself whether you are indeed in the correct area of law. Once the answer to this question is an authoritative yes, you can delve deeper into the area of law and related authorities to answer the question.

Step 4: Analyze Tax Authorities

Once a researcher identifies relevant authorities, they must read carefully to ensure they fully understand them, as well as their application to the research problem. Two basic types of issues researchers will encounter are questions of fact and questions of law.

The answer to a **question of fact** hinges upon the facts and circumstances of the taxpayer's transaction. For example, whether a trade or business expense is "ordinary," "necessary," "reasonable," and, thus, deductible is a question of fact. Specifically, the deductibility of the expense depends upon the underlying facts related to the expense. If you're researching a question of fact, understand *which* facts impact the answer—in this case, which facts make an expense "ordinary," "necessary," and "reasonable" and which do not. In this type of question, the researcher will focus on understanding how various facts affect the research answer and identifying authorities with fact patterns similar to those of their client.

The answer to a **question of law** hinges upon the interpretation of the law, such as a particular phrase in a code section (see the sample research memo in Exhibit 2-9 for an example of a question of law). A researcher faced with this type of question will spend much of their time researching the various interpretations of the code section, taking note of which authorities interpret the code differently and why.

EXHIBIT 2-9 Sample Internal Research Memo

Below is the memo Bill and Mercedes's CPA drafted after researching their issue.

Date: July 8, 2022

Preparer: Joe Staff

Reviewer: Cassandra Miller

Subject: Deductibility of Points Paid in Refinancing

Facts: Four years ago Bill and Mercedes's credit union provided them a $250,000 mortgage loan for their new home. The mortgage loan was a four-year interest-only note with a balloon payment at the end of four years. Bill and Mercedes (Floridians residing in the 11th Circuit) chose this type of loan to allow them to minimize their mortgage payment until their other house was sold. After 18 months, Bill and Mercedes sold their other house and refinanced their original short-term loan with a 15-year conventional mortgage. The credit union charged Bill and Mercedes $3,000 in points (prepaid interest) upon the refinancing.

Issue: Can Bill and Mercedes deduct the points in the year they paid them?

Authorities: §461(g).

Rev. Rul. 87-22, 1987-1 C.B. 146.

J.R. Huntsman v. Comm'r, 90-2 USTC par. 50,340 (8th Cir. 1990), *rev'g* 91 TC 917 (1988).

AOD 1991-002.

P.G. Cao v. Comm'r, 96-1 USTC par. 50,167 (9th Cir. 1996), *aff'g* 67 TCM 2171 (1994).

Conclusion: Because Bill and Mercedes's refinancing represents an integrated step in securing permanent financing for their home, substantial authority supports their deduction of the $3,000 in points this year.

Analysis: §461(g)(1) provides that cash-method taxpayers (Bill and Mercedes) must amortize prepaid interest (points) over the life of the loan instead of receiving a current deduction. §461(g)(2) provides an exception to the general rule of §461(g)(1). Specifically, §461(g)(2) allows cash-method taxpayers to deduct points in the year paid if the related debt was incurred "in connection with the purchase or improvement of," and secured by, the taxpayer's principal residence. The question whether Bill and Mercedes should amortize or currently deduct the points paid to refinance the mortgage on their principal residence depends upon the interpretation of "in connection with the purchase or improvement of" found in §461(g)(2).

There are two basic interpretations of "in connection with the purchase or improvement of." In Revenue Ruling 87-22, the IRS rules that points incurred in refinancing a mortgage on a taxpayer's residence are deductible in the year paid to the extent that the taxpayer uses the loan proceeds to improve the taxpayer's residence. Thus, points paid to simply refinance an existing mortgage without improving the residence must be amortized over the life of the loan.

In contrast, in *J.R. Huntsman v. Comm'r,* the 8th Circuit Court interpreted the phrase "in connection with the purchase or improvement of" much more broadly and held that points incurred to refinance a mortgage on the taxpayer's principal residence are currently deductible if the refinancing represents an *integrated step to secure permanent financing* for the taxpayer's residence. The facts in *J.R. Huntsman v. Comm'r* are very similar to Bill and Mercedes's facts. Like Bill and Mercedes, the taxpayers in *J.R. Huntsman v. Comm'r* also purchased their principal residence using a short-term loan with a "balloon" payment. When the balloon payment came due, the taxpayers obtained a permanent mortgage on their home (a 30-year conventional mortgage). The 8th Circuit Court held that in this case the permanent mortgage was acquired to extinguish the short-term financing and finalize the purchase of the home. "Thus, where taxpayers purchase a principal residence with a short-term three-year loan secured by a mortgage on the residence, and replace the loan with permanent financing . . . , the permanent mortgage obtained is sufficiently in connection with the purchase of the home to fall within the exception provided for by section 461(g)(2)."

In Action on Decision 1991-002, the IRS has indicated that it will not follow the *J.R. Huntsman v. Comm'r* decision outside the 8th Circuit (in the 11th Circuit where Bill and Mercedes live). Nonetheless, other courts (the 9th Circuit in *P.G. Cao v. Comm'r*) have indicated a willingness to apply the 8th Circuit's interpretation of §461(g)(2). That is, they have allowed deductibility of points incurred in refinancing if the refinancing occurred to secure permanent financing, instead of for some other reason such as to secure a lower interest rate.

Given the similarity in facts between Bill and Mercedes's refinancing and those in *J.R. Huntsman v. Comm'r* (refinancing of a short-term note to secure permanent financing), substantial authority supports a current deduction of the points paid.

Identifying whether a research question is a question of fact or question of law is primarily helpful when there is some uncertainty in the application of tax law. Distinguishing between these two types of research questions helps the tax researcher focus their efforts appropriately. For many tax questions, the answer is quite clear (e.g., the question is answered definitively in the Internal Revenue Code, regulations, etc.). In these situations, there is no need to attempt to distinguish the research question as a question of fact or question of law.

For many tax questions, the answer is clear with no opposing interpretations or contrary authorities. For other questions, the researcher may identify that different authorities have conflicting views. In this situation, the tax researcher should evaluate the hierarchical level, jurisdiction, and age of the authorities, placing more weight on higher and newer authorities that have jurisdiction over the taxpayer. A tax researcher will become more adept at this process as they gain experience.

Once the tax researcher has identified relevant authorities, they must make sure the authorities are still valid and up to date. For court cases, a **citator**—a research tool that allows you to check the status of several types of tax authorities—can be used to review the history of a case to find out, for example, whether it was subsequently appealed and overturned and to identify subsequent cases that cite it. Favorable citations (e.g., a citation of the case by another authority in support of its ruling) strengthen a case. In contrast, unfavorable citations weaken it (e.g., a citation of the case by another authority that questions or limits the case's decision). Citators can also check the status of revenue rulings, revenue procedures, and other IRS pronouncements. Checking the status of the Code is fairly simple: Just locate the current version. Checking the status of regulations is a little more complicated. Most tax services alert researchers if a regulation has not been updated for certain changes in the Code. If this is the case, the researcher should evaluate whether the changes in the Code make the regulation obsolete.

As detailed in the analysis section of the sample research memo drafted by Bill and Mercedes's CPA (see Exhibit 2-9), whether they should amortize (deduct over the life of the loan) or currently deduct the points paid to refinance the mortgage on their principal residence is a question of law that ultimately depends upon the interpretation of a particular phrase: "in connection with the purchase or improvement of" found in §461(g)(2). Is there a correct answer to this question? No. There is no clear-cut answer. Rather, this is a situation where the tax professional must use professional judgment. Because there is substantial authority supporting the current deduction of the points (discussed in detail in the sample memo), Bill and Mercedes should be able to deduct the points currently without risk of penalty. However, they should be aware that the IRS has clearly stated in an action on decision that it will fight this issue outside the 8th Circuit—for example, in the 11th Circuit, where Bill and Mercedes live.

Step 5: Document and Communicate the Results

After a researcher finishes their research, the final step of the process is to document and communicate the results. The most common end product of a research question is the internal research memo the researcher drafts for their supervisor's attention. The memo has five basic parts: (1) facts, (2) issues, (3) authority list, (4) conclusion, and (5) analysis. The purpose of the memo is to inform the reader of the answer to a research question, and, thus, it should be written in an objective manner by discussing all relevant authorities to the research question, including those authorities that support, as well as those that conflict with, the answer. Below are some suggestions for each part of the memo. Compare these to the execution within the sample internal research memo presented in Exhibit 2-9.

Facts Discuss facts relevant to the question presented—that is, facts that provide necessary background information related to the transaction (generally, who, what, when, where, and how much) and those facts that may influence the research answer. Keeping the fact discussion relatively brief will focus the reader's attention on the relevant characteristics of the transaction.

Issues State the specific issues that the memo addresses. This section confirms that you understand the research question, reminds the reader of the question being analyzed, and allows future researchers to determine whether the analysis in the memo is relevant. Issues should be written as specifically as possible and limited to one or two sentences per issue.

Authorities In this section, cite the relevant tax authorities that apply to the issue, such as the IRC, court cases, and revenue rulings. How many authorities should you cite? Enough to provide a clear understanding of the issue and interpretation of the law. Remember, in order to reach an accurate assessment of the strength of your conclusion, you should consider authorities that may support your desired conclusion, as well as those that may go against it.

Conclusion There should be one conclusion per issue. Each conclusion should answer the question as briefly as possible and, preferably, indicate why the answer is what it is.

Analysis The goal of the analysis is to provide the reader a clear understanding of the area of law and specific authorities that apply. Typically, you will organize an analysis to discuss first the general area(s) of law (the code section), and then the specific authorities (court cases, revenue rulings) that apply to the research question. How many authorities should you discuss? As many as necessary to provide the reader an understanding of the issue and relevant authorities. After you discuss the relevant authorities, apply the authorities to your client's transaction and explain how the authorities result in your conclusion.

Client Letters In addition to internal research memos, tax professionals often send their clients letters that summarize their research and recommendations. Basic components of the client letter include (1) research question and limitations, (2) facts, (3) analysis, and (4) closing. Below are some suggestions for each part of the client letter. Compare these to the execution within the sample client letter presented in Exhibit 2-10.

Research question and limitations. After the salutation (Dear Bill and Mercedes) and social graces (I enjoyed seeing you last week . . .), clearly state the research question addressed and any disclaimers related to the work performed. This portion of the letter ensures that the tax professional and client have a mutual understanding of the question researched and any limitations on the research performed. As in a memo, issues should be written as specifically as possible and be limited to one or two sentences. Most accounting firms have standard boilerplate language regarding the limitations on work performed that is included in every client letter.

Facts. Briefly summarize the facts relevant to the question presented—that is, facts that provide necessary background of the transaction and those facts that may influence the research answer. Keeping the fact discussion relatively brief will focus the client's attention on the relevant characteristics of the transaction.

Analysis. Summarize the relevant authorities (including citations in most situations) and their implications for the client's research question using precise language appropriate for the client's level of tax expertise. The length of this portion of the letter will vary with the complexity of the research question and the client's interest in understanding the specific research details.

Closing. In this section, summarize the key outcome(s) of the research conducted and any recommended client action, thank the client for requesting your service, and remind the client to contact you with additional questions or for further assistance.

In the case of Bill and Mercedes's interest deduction, their CPA recommended a tax return position that the IRS disallowed upon audit. Did their CPA violate their professional responsibilities by recommending a position the IRS disallowed? Good question. Let's take a look at the rules governing tax professional responsibilities.

EXHIBIT 2-10 Sample Client Letter

Below is the client letter that Bill and Mercedes's CPA sent to them.

July 8, 2022

Dear Bill and Mercedes,

I enjoyed seeing you last week at the Tampa Bay Boys and Girls Clubs charity auction. What a great event for such a worthy cause!

Thank you for requesting my advice concerning the tax treatment of the points paid when refinancing your mortgage.

My research is based upon the federal income tax laws that apply as of the date of this letter and the facts that you have provided as follows: Four years ago your credit union provided you a $250,000 interest-only note on your home that required a balloon payment at the end of four years. You chose this type of loan to minimize your mortgage payment until your previous house sold. After 18 months, you sold your previous house and refinanced the original short-term loan with a 15-year conventional mortgage. The credit union charged you $3,000 in points upon the refinancing.

After a thorough review of the applicable tax authority, I found there is substantial authority supporting a current deduction of the $3,000 in points paid. §461(g)(2) allows cash-method taxpayers to deduct points in the year paid if the related debt was incurred "in connection with the purchase or improvement of," and secured by, the taxpayer's principal residence. There are two basic interpretations of "in connection with the purchase or improvement of." The IRS has ruled (Revenue Ruling 87-22) that points paid to simply refinance an existing mortgage without improving the residence must be amortized over the life of the loan. In contrast, in *J.R. Huntsman v. Comm'r*, the 8th Circuit Court held that points incurred to refinance a mortgage on the taxpayer's principal residence are currently deductible if the refinancing represents an *integrated step to secure permanent financing* for the taxpayer's residence.

The facts in *J.R. Huntsman v. Comm'r* are very similar to your facts. Like you, the taxpayers in *J.R. Huntsman v. Comm'r* purchased their principal residence using a short-term loan with a balloon payment. When the balloon payment came due, the taxpayers obtained a permanent mortgage on their home. The 8th Circuit Court held that in this case the permanent mortgage was acquired to finalize the purchase of the home and allowed the current deduction of the points.

J.R. Huntsman v. Comm'r provides substantial authority to support a current deduction of the $3,000 in points paid to refinance your initial short-term mortgage. In addition, other courts have applied the 8th Circuit's interpretation of §461(g)(2), which adds "strength" to the 8th Circuit decision. However, the IRS has indicated that it will not follow the *J.R. Huntsman v. Comm'r* decision outside the 8th Circuit (in the 11th Circuit where you live). Accordingly, the IRS would likely disallow the $3,000 deduction upon audit, and, thus, while you have substantial authority to deduct the points currently, there is risk in doing so.

I would be happy to discuss this issue with you in more depth because these types of issues are always difficult. Likewise, if you have any other questions or issues with which I may assist you, please do not hesitate to contact me. Thank you again for requesting my advice.

Sincerely,

Cassandra Miller, CPA

TAX PROFESSIONAL RESPONSIBILITIES

LO 2-6

Tax practitioners are subject to a variety of statutes, rules, and codes of professional conduct. Some examples include the American Institute of CPA's (AICPA) Code of Professional Conduct, the AICPA's **Statements on Standards for Tax Services (SSTS),** the IRS's Circular 230, and statutes enacted by a CPA's specific state board of accountancy. Tax practitioners should absolutely have a working knowledge of these statutes, rules, and guidelines because (1) they establish the professional standards for the practitioner and (2) failure to comply with the standards could result in adverse consequences for the tax professional, such as being admonished, suspended, or barred from practicing before the IRS; being admonished, suspended, or expelled from the AICPA; or suffering suspension or revocation of the CPA license. Given the voluminous nature of applicable statutes, rules, and codes, we will simply provide a brief overview of the major common sources of tax professional standards.

CPAs who are members of the AICPA are bound by the AICPA Code of Professional Conduct and SSTS. Other tax professionals use these provisions as guidance of professional standards. The AICPA Code of Professional Conduct is not specific to tax practice and provides broader professional standards that are especially relevant for auditors—that is, for those independent CPAs charged with examining an entity's financial statements. Provisions included in the Code of Professional Conduct address the importance of a CPA maintaining independence from the client and using due professional care in carrying out responsibilities. Additional provisions limit the acceptance of contingent fees, preclude discreditable acts such as signing a false return, and prohibit false advertising and charging commissions. Most of these provisions rightly fall under the heading of common sense. Nonetheless, a regular review should prove useful to the practicing CPA.

THE KEY FACTS

Tax Professional Responsibilities

- Tax practitioners are subject to a variety of statutes, rules, and codes of professional conduct.
- The AICPA's seven Statements on Standards for Tax Services (SSTS) recommend appropriate standards of practice for tax professionals.
  - Many state boards of accountancy have adopted standards similar to the SSTS standards.
- Circular 230 provides regulations governing tax practice and applies to all persons practicing before the IRS.
  - There is a good bit of overlap between Circular 230 and the AICPA SSTS.

The AICPA's SSTS recommend appropriate standards of practice for tax professionals and are intended to complement other provisions that govern tax practice (e.g., Circular 230, discussed below). One objective of these standards is to encourage increased understanding by the Treasury, IRS, and the public of a CPA's professional standards. Many state boards of accountancy have adopted similar standards, thus making the SSTS especially important. Currently, seven SSTS describe the tax professional standards when recommending a tax return position, answering questions on a tax return, preparing a tax return using data supplied by a client, using estimates on a tax return, taking a tax return position inconsistent with a previous year's tax return, discovering a tax return error, and giving tax advice to taxpayers. Exhibit 2-11 provides a brief summary of each SSTS. Most important from a research perspective, SSTS No. 1 provides that a tax professional must comply with the standards imposed by the applicable tax authority when recommending a tax return position or preparing or signing a tax return. §6694 provides these standards for federal tax purposes.

Section 6694 imposes a penalty on a *tax practitioner* for any position that is not supported by **substantial authority.** A good tax professional evaluates whether supporting authority is substantial based upon the supporting and opposing authorities' weight and relevance. Substantial authority suggests the probability that the taxpayer's position will be sustained upon audit or litigation is in the 35 to 40 percent range or above. The tax practitioner can also avoid penalty under §6694 if the tax return position has at least a reasonable basis (is supported by one or more tax authorities) and the position is disclosed on the taxpayer's return (using Form 8275, Disclosure Statement).[16]

Example 2-6

Did Bill and Mercedes's CPA meet her professional standards as provided by SSTS No. 1?

Answer: Yes. Based on *J.R. Huntsman v. Comm'r*, it is safe to conclude that there is a 35 to 40 percent or greater probability that the current points deduction will be sustained upon judicial review. Specifically, Bill and Mercedes's facts are very similar to those in *J.R. Huntsman v. Comm'r*, and subsequent courts have interpreted the phrase "in connection with" consistently with *J.R. Huntsman v. Comm'r*.

Circular 230, issued by the IRS, provides regulations governing tax practice and applies to all persons practicing before the IRS. There are five parts of Circular 230. Subpart A describes who may practice before the IRS (CPAs, attorneys, enrolled agents) and what practicing before the IRS means (tax return preparation, representing clients before the IRS, and so on).[17] Subpart B describes the duties and restrictions that apply to

[16]A "more likely than not" standard, defined as a greater than 50 percent chance of a position being sustained on its merits, applies to tax shelters and other reportable transactions specified by the IRS.

[17]Similar to attorneys and CPAs, enrolled agents and registered tax return preparers can represent taxpayers before the IRS. To become an enrolled agent, you must have either worked for the IRS for five years or passed a comprehensive examination.

EXHIBIT 2-11 Summary of the AICPA Statements on Standards for Tax Services

SSTS No. 1: Tax Return Positions
A tax professional should comply with the standards, if any, imposed by the applicable tax authority for recommending a tax return position, or preparing or signing a tax return. If the tax authority has no written standards (or if they are lower than the following standard), the tax professional may recommend a tax return position or prepare or sign a return when they have a good-faith belief that the position has a realistic possibility of being sustained if challenged, or if there is a reasonable basis for the position and it is *adequately disclosed* on the tax return.
SSTS No. 2: Answers to Questions on Returns
A tax professional should make a reasonable effort to obtain from the taxpayer the information necessary to answer all questions on a tax return.
SSTS No. 3: Certain Procedural Aspects of Preparing Returns
In preparing or signing a tax return, a tax professional may rely without verification on information that a taxpayer or a third party has provided, unless the information appears to be incorrect, incomplete, or inconsistent.
SSTS No. 4: Use of Estimates
Unless prohibited by statute or rule, a tax professional may use taxpayer estimates in preparing a tax return if it is impractical to obtain exact data and if the estimated amounts appear reasonable based on the facts and circumstances known by the professional.
SSTS No. 5: Departure from a Position Previously Concluded in an Administrative Proceeding or Court Decision
A tax professional may sign a tax return that contains a departure from a position previously concluded in an administrative or court proceeding if the tax professional adheres to the standards of SSTS No. 1. This rule does not apply if the taxpayer is bound to a specific tax treatment in the later year, such as by a formal closing agreement with the IRS.
SSTS No. 6: Knowledge of Error: Return Preparation and Administrative Proceedings
A tax professional must advise the taxpayer promptly of an error and its potential consequences when they learn of an error in a previously filed tax return, an administrative hearing (such as an audit), or the taxpayer's failure to file a required return. The tax professional should include a recommendation for appropriate measures the taxpayer should take. The professional is not obligated to inform the IRS of the error, nor may they do so without the taxpayer's permission, except when required by law. However, in an administrative proceeding only, the tax professional should request the taxpayer's agreement to disclose the error to the IRS. If the taxpayer refuses to disclose the error to the IRS, the professional may consider terminating the professional relationship with the taxpayer.
SSTS No. 7: Form and Content of Advice to Taxpayers
In providing advice to taxpayers, tax professionals must use judgment that reflects professional competence and serves the taxpayer's needs. The professional should ensure that the standards under SSTS No. 1 are satisfied for all advice rendered. The professional is not obligated to communicate with a taxpayer when subsequent events affect advice previously provided except when implementing plans associated with the advice provided or when the professional is obligated to do so by specific agreement.

Source: AICPA Statements.

individuals governed by Circular 230. Included in Subpart B are provisions discussing the submission of records to the IRS, guidelines when a practitioner discovers a tax return error, restrictions on charging contingency fees, prohibition of sharing employment with someone suspended from practicing before the IRS, stringent rules relating to providing advice for tax shelters, and standards for when a practitioner can recommend a tax return position.[18] Subparts C and D explain sanctions and disciplinary proceedings for practitioners violating the Circular 230 provisions. Subpart E concludes with a few miscellaneous provisions (such as the Circular 230 effective date). There is a good bit of overlap between Circular 230 and the AICPA SSTS.

[18]Circular 230 imposes the same tax practitioner standards as in §6694 for when a tax practitioner generally may recommend a tax return position (substantial authority and no disclosure or reasonable basis with disclosure).

Although Circular 230 provides many rules governing tax practice, the Internal Revenue Code and other Treasury regulations often contain requirements specific to tax professionals. Thus, it is important for tax professionals to keep abreast of all applicable guidance, regardless of the specific authoritative source. A good example of this is the tax-preparer registration requirement in Reg. §1.6109-2, which requires that all paid tax-return preparers apply for and receive a preparer tax identification number (PTIN). Although not a particularly daunting registration requirement, it is important nonetheless as failure to include the tax-return preparer's PTIN on tax returns is subject to a $50 penalty per violation.

Are there other provisions that govern tax practice? You bet! Tax practitioners are also legally governed by common law. Issues that may arise include breach of contract (e.g., tax practitioner failing to complete a tax return for a client, client providing tax data timely but tax practitioner filing a return late, tax practitioner filing incomplete or incorrect returns), negligence (e.g., tax practitioner's careless actions in filing returns or giving tax advice), or fraud (e.g., tax practitioner intentionally committing reckless action in tax return filing or advice). In each case, the client may sue the tax practitioner for compensation for damages incurred, and in some cases a third party can do so (e.g., intended beneficiary of a trust or estate). Best advice for a tax practitioner to avoid these issues: Use appropriate due care to execute their professional responsibilities in a timely and complete manner.

LO 2-7

TAXPAYER AND TAX RETURN PREPARER PENALTIES

THE KEY FACTS

Taxpayer and Tax Return Preparer Penalties

- The IRS can impose both criminal and civil penalties to encourage tax compliance by both tax return preparers and taxpayers.
- The standard of conviction is higher in a criminal trial, but the penalties are also much higher.
- A taxpayer will not be subject to an underpayment penalty if there is substantial authority that supports the tax return position.
- A tax return preparer will also not be subject to penalty for recommending a tax return position if there is substantial authority that supports the position.

In addition to motivating good behavior via tax professional standards, the IRS can impose both criminal and civil penalties to encourage tax compliance by both **tax return preparers** and taxpayers. A tax return preparer is any person or entity who prepares for compensation, or who employs one or more persons to prepare for compensation, all or a substantial portion of any tax return or any claim for refund. Tax return preparers may be signing or nonsigning preparers. For example, someone who for compensation renders tax advice on a position that is directly relevant to the determination of the existence, characterization, or amount of an entry on a tax return or claim for refund is treated as having prepared that entry, even if they did not sign the tax return. Determining what is a substantial portion of a tax return depends upon the facts and circumstances. Factors considered in determining what is a substantial portion include the size and complexity of an item relative to the taxpayer's gross income, the size of the understatement attributable to the item compared to the taxpayer's reported liability, and whether the tax advisor knows or reasonably should know that the item is a substantial portion of the tax required to be shown on the tax return or refund claim.[19]

Civil penalties are much more common, generally come in the form of monetary penalties, and may be imposed when tax return preparers or taxpayers violate tax statutes without reasonable cause—say, as the result of negligence, intentional disregard of pertinent rules, willful disobedience, or outright fraud. Some common examples of civil penalties are listed in Exhibit 2-12.[20]

Criminal penalties are much less common than civil penalties, although they have been used to incarcerate some notorious criminals who escaped conviction for other crimes. (Prohibition-era mobster Al Capone was convicted and put in prison for tax

[19]For nonsigning preparers, the portion of a return prepared is not substantial if, aggregating all schedules, etc., they prepared, the portion that involves gross income, deductions, or amounts on which credits are based is (1) less than $10,000 or (2) less than $400,000 and less than 20% of the gross income (AGI, for individuals) as shown on the return.

[20]Tax practitioners and clients have the same common law protections of confidentiality that apply to attorney and client communications if the communication would be considered privileged between a taxpayer and an attorney. The privilege only applies to federally authorized tax practitioners (attorneys, CPAs, enrolled agents, and enrolled actuaries) and is not extended to written communications regarding tax shelters (§7525).

EXHIBIT 2-12 Civil Penalties Imposed for Tax Violations

Taxpayers		Tax Return Preparers	
Failure to file a tax return	5% of tax due per month (or partial month). Maximum penalty is 25% of net tax due (penalty applies up to 5 months). If the .5% failure to pay tax owed penalty also applies, the failure to file a tax return penalty is reduced to 4.5% per month (or partial month) and the maximum failure to file a tax return penalty is reduced to 22.5% of net tax due. If the tax return is not filed within 60 days of the due date (including extensions), the minimum penalty is the smaller of $450 or 100% of the unpaid tax.	Failure to provide a copy of the tax return to a taxpayer	$50 per violation
Failure to pay tax owed	.5% of tax due per month (or partial month). Reduces the failure to file a tax return penalty, if applicable. Maximum failure to file penalty is 25% of net tax due (penalty applies up to 50 months). Minimum combined penalty if the tax return is not filed within 60 days of the due date (including extensions) is the smaller of $450 or 100% of the unpaid tax.	Failure to sign a tax return	$50 per violation
Failure to make estimated payments	Penalty varies with federal short-term interest rate and underpayment.	Failure to include the tax return preparer's ID number on the tax return	$50 per violation
Substantial understatement of tax	20% of understatement	Failure to keep a listing of taxpayers or tax returns	$50 per violation
Underpayment of tax due to transactions lacking economic substance	20% of understatement (if position is disclosed on the tax return) or 40% of understatement (if position is not disclosed)	Failure to keep a listing of employees	$50 per violation
Providing false withholding information	$500	Understatement due to unreasonable position	Greater of $1,000 or 50% of income derived from preparing the taxpayer's tax return
Fraud	75% of liability attributable to fraud	Willful understatement of tax	Greater of $5,000 or 75% of income derived from preparing the taxpayer's tax return
		Organizing, promoting, etc. an abusive tax shelter	Lesser of $1,000 or 100% of gross income derived from tax shelter. If activity is based on fraudulent statements, the penalty equals 50% of gross income derived from tax shelter.
		Aiding and abetting the understatement of a tax liability	$1,000 ($10,000 if related to corporate taxes)

evasion.) Criminal penalties are commonly charged in tax evasion cases, which include willful intent to defraud the government, but are imposed only after normal due process, including a trial. Compared to civil cases, the standard of conviction is higher in a criminal trial; guilt must be proven beyond a reasonable doubt (versus the "clear and convincing evidence" standard for civil tax fraud). However, the penalties are also much higher, such as fines up to $100,000 for individuals plus a prison sentence.

Assuming the IRS assesses additional tax upon audit, will the taxpayer always be subject to penalty? No. While the taxpayer will have to pay interest on the underpayment, they will *not* be subject to an underpayment penalty *if there is substantial authority that supports the tax return position.*[21] As discussed above, "substantial authority" suggests that the probability the taxpayer's position will be sustained upon audit or litigation is in the 35 to 40 percent range or higher.

Example 2-7

What is Bill and Mercedes's exposure to penalties in their IRS audit?

Answer: None. Why? Because "substantial tax authority" supports their tax return position and the disputed tax liability is relatively small (the tax savings on a $3,000 tax deduction), Bill and Mercedes have no penalty exposure. Nonetheless, Bill and Mercedes will owe interest on the disputed tax liability unless the IRS recants its position in the audit or appeals process (or if the case is litigated and Bill and Mercedes win).

As we explained in Example 2-6, Bill and Mercedes's CPA met her professional standards (as defined currently in SSTS No. 1) by recommending a tax return position that meets the "substantial authority" standard. Likewise, because substantial tax authority supports the tax return position, Bill and Mercedes's CPA should also not have penalty exposure under §6694.

CONCLUSION

Now that we have a full understanding of the issue under audit for Bill and Mercedes, what is their likely outcome? Another good question. The IRS has stated that it will continue to disallow a current deduction for points incurred for refinanced mortgages. Nonetheless, the courts appear to follow *J.R. Huntsman v. Comm'r,* and, therefore, the IRS stands a strong possibility of losing this case if litigated. In an IRS appeals conference, the appeals officer may consider the hazards of litigation. Accordingly, Bill and Mercedes have a good likelihood of a favorable resolution at the appeals conference.

In this chapter, we discussed several of the fundamentals of tax practice and procedure: taxpayer filing requirements, the statute of limitations, the IRS audit process, the primary tax authorities, tax research, tax professional standards, and taxpayer and tax practitioner penalties. For the tax accountant, these fundamentals form the basis for much of their work. Likewise, tax research forms the basis of much of a tax professional's compliance and planning services. Even for the accountant who doesn't specialize in tax accounting, gaining a basic understanding of tax practice and procedure is important. Assisting clients with the IRS audit process is a valued service that accountants provide, and clients expect all accountants to understand basic tax procedure issues and how to research basic tax issues.

[21]The taxpayer can also avoid penalty if the tax return position has at least a reasonable basis (i.e., supported by one or more tax authorities) and the position is disclosed on the taxpayer's return (§6662).

Summary

Identify the filing requirements for income tax returns and the statute of limitations for assessment. **LO 2-1**

- All corporations must file a tax return annually regardless of their taxable income. Estates and trusts are required to file annual income tax returns if their gross income exceeds $600. The filing requirements for individual taxpayers depend on the taxpayer's filing status, age, and gross income.
- Individual and C corporation tax returns (except for C corporations with a June 30 year-end) are due on the fifteenth day of the fourth month following year-end. For C corporations with a June 30 year-end, partnerships, and S corporations, tax returns must be filed by the fifteenth day of the third month following the entity's fiscal year-end. Any taxpayer unable to file a tax return by the original due date can request an extension to file.
- For both amended tax returns filed by a taxpayer and proposed tax assessments by the IRS, the statute of limitations generally ends three years from the *later* of (1) the date the tax return was actually filed or (2) the tax return's original due date.

Outline the IRS audit process, how returns are selected, the different types of audits, and what happens after the audit. **LO 2-2**

- The IRS uses a number of computer programs and outside data sources to identify tax returns that may have an understated tax liability. Common computer initiatives include the DIF (Discriminant Function) system, the document perfection program, and the information matching program.
- The three types of IRS audits consist of correspondence, office, and field examinations.
- After the audit, the IRS will send the taxpayer a 30-day letter, which provides the taxpayer the opportunity to pay the proposed assessment or request an appeals conference. If an agreement is not reached at appeals or the taxpayer does not pay the proposed assessment, the IRS will send the taxpayer a 90-day letter. At this time, the taxpayer may pay the tax or petition the U.S. Tax Court to hear the case. If the taxpayer chooses to pay the tax, the taxpayer may then request a refund of the tax and eventually sue the IRS for a refund in the U.S. district court or the U.S. Court of Federal Claims.

Evaluate the relative weights of the various tax law sources. **LO 2-3**

- Primary authorities are official sources of the tax law generated by the legislative branch (statutory authority issued by Congress), judicial branch (rulings by the U.S. district court, U.S. Tax Court, U.S. Court of Federal Claims, U.S. circuit courts of appeals, or U.S. Supreme Court), or executive/administrative branch (Treasury and IRS pronouncements). Secondary authorities are unofficial tax authorities that interpret and explain the primary authorities.

Describe the legislative process as it pertains to taxation. **LO 2-4**

- Exhibit 2-7 illustrates the legislative process for enacting tax law changes. Bills proceed from the House Ways and Means Committee to the House of Representatives. If approved, the act is sent to the Senate Finance Committee, with a revised version then sent to the U.S. Senate. If approved, the Joint Conference Committee considers the acts passed by the House of Representatives and Senate. If a compromise is reached, the revised act is sent to the House of Representatives; if approved, it is then sent to the Senate; and if approved by the Senate, it is then sent to the president. If signed by the president, the act is incorporated into the IRC of 1986. If the president vetoes the legislation, Congress may override the veto with a two-thirds positive vote in both the House of Representatives and Senate.

Perform the basic steps in tax research. **LO 2-5**

- The five basic steps in tax research are (1) understand the facts, (2) identify issues, (3) locate relevant authorities, (4) analyze the tax authorities, and (5) document and communicate research results.
- When the researcher identifies that different authorities have conflicting views, they should evaluate the "hierarchy," jurisdiction, and age of the authorities, placing more weight on higher and newer authorities that have jurisdiction over the taxpayer.

LO 2-6 Describe tax professional responsibilities in providing tax advice.

- Tax practitioners are subject to a variety of statutes, rules, and codes of professional conduct. Some examples include the American Institute of CPA's (AICPA) Code of Professional Conduct, the AICPA's Statements on Standards for Tax Services (SSTS), the IRS's Circular 230, and statutes enacted by a CPA's specific state board of accountancy.
- The AICPA's SSTS recommend appropriate standards of practice for tax professionals. Many state boards of accountancy have adopted similar standards, thus making the SSTS especially important. Currently, there are seven SSTS (summarized in Exhibit 2-11) that describe the tax professional standards.
- Circular 230 provides regulations governing tax practice and applies to all persons practicing before the IRS. There is a good bit of overlap between Circular 230 and the AICPA SSTS.

LO 2-7 Identify taxpayer and tax return preparer penalties.

- The IRS can impose both criminal and civil penalties to encourage tax compliance by both tax return preparers and taxpayers. Civil penalties are much more common, generally come in the form of monetary penalties, and may be imposed when tax return preparers or taxpayers violate tax statutes without reasonable cause. Some common examples of civil penalties are listed in Exhibit 2-12.
- Criminal penalties are much less common than civil penalties and are commonly charged in tax evasion cases. Compared to civil cases, the standard of conviction is higher in a criminal trial, but the penalties are also much higher.
- A taxpayer will not be subject to an underpayment penalty if there is substantial authority that supports the tax return position.
- A tax return preparer will also not be subject to penalty for recommending a tax return position if there is substantial authority that supports the position.

KEY TERMS

30-day letter (2-6)
90-day letter (2-6)
acquiescence (2-17)
action on decisions (2-17)
annotated tax services (2-18)
Circular 230 (2-24)
citator (2-21)
civil penalties (2-26)
correspondence examination (2-6)
criminal penalties (2-26)
determination letters (2-16)
DIF (Discriminant Function) system (2-4)
document perfection program (2-4)
field examinations (2-6)
final regulations (2-15)
***Golsen* rule (2-15)**
information matching program (2-4)
Internal Revenue Code of 1986 (2-11)
interpretative regulations (2-16)
legislative regulations (2-16)
nonacquiescence (2-17)
office examinations (2-6)
primary authorities (2-9)
private letter rulings (2-16)
procedural regulations (2-16)
proposed regulations (2-15)
question of fact (2-19)
question of law (2-19)
regulations (2-15)
revenue procedures (2-16)
revenue rulings (2-16)
secondary authorities (2-9)
***stare decisis* (2-15)**
Statements on Standards for Tax Services (SSTS) (2-23)
statute of limitations (2-3)
substantial authority (2-24)
tax return preparers (2-26)
tax treaties (2-14)
technical advice memorandums (2-16)
temporary regulations (2-15)
topical tax services (2-19)
U.S. circuit courts of appeals (2-7)
U.S. Constitution (2-11)
U.S. Court of Federal Claims (2-6)
U.S. district court (2-6)
U.S. Supreme Court (2-8)
U.S. Tax Court (2-6)
***writ of certiorari* (2-8)**

DISCUSSION QUESTIONS

Discussion Questions are available in Connect®.

LO 2-1 1. Name three factors that determine whether a taxpayer is required to file a tax return.

LO 2-1 2. Benita is concerned that she will not be able to complete her tax return by April 15. Can she request an extension to file her return? By what date must she do so?

Assuming she requests an extension, what is the latest date that she could file her return this year without penalty?

3. Agua Linda Inc. is a calendar-year corporation. What is the original due date for the corporate tax return? What happens if the original due date falls on a Saturday? LO 2-1
4. Approximately what percentage of tax returns does the IRS audit? What are the implications of this number for the IRS's strategy in selecting returns for audit? LO 2-2
5. Explain the difference between the DIF system and the National Research Program. How do they relate to each other? LO 2-2
6. Describe the differences between the three types of audits in terms of their scope and taxpayer type. LO 2-2
7. Simon just received a 30-day letter from the IRS indicating a proposed assessment. Does he have to pay the additional tax? What are his options? LO 2-2
8. Compare and contrast the three trial-level courts. LO 2-2
9. Compare and contrast the three types of tax law sources and give examples of each. LO 2-3
10. The U.S. Constitution is the highest tax authority but provides very little in the way of tax laws. What are the next highest tax authorities beneath the U.S. Constitution? LO 2-3
11. Jackie has just opened her copy of the Code for the first time. She looks at the table of contents and wonders why it is organized the way it is. She questions whether it makes sense to try and understand the Code's organization. What are some reasons why understanding the organization of the Internal Revenue Code may prove useful? LO 2-3
12. Laura Li, a U.S. resident, worked for three months this summer in China. What type of tax authority may be especially useful in determining the tax consequences of her foreign income? LO 2-3
13. What are the basic differences between regulations, revenue rulings, and private letter rulings? LO 2-3
14. Under what circumstance would the IRS issue an acquiescence? A nonacquiescence? An action on decision? LO 2-3
15. Carlos has located a regulation that appears to answer his tax research question. He is concerned because the regulation is a temporary regulation. Evaluate the authoritative weight of this type of regulation. Should he feel more or less confident in his answer if the regulation is a proposed regulation? LO 2-3
16. Tyrone recently read a regulation that Congress specifically requested the IRS to issue. What type of regulation is this? How does this regulation's authoritative weight compare to other regulations? LO 2-3
17. In researching a tax question, you find only one authority (a trial-level court opinion) that is directly on point. Which court would you least prefer to have heard this case, and why? LO 2-3
18. What is *stare decisis,* and how does it relate to the *Golsen* rule? LO 2-3
19. Mason was shocked to learn that the current Code is the Internal Revenue Code of 1986. He thought that U.S. tax laws change more frequently. What is wrong with Mason's perception? LO 2-4
20. Describe in general the process by which new tax legislation is enacted. LO 2-4
21. What are the three committees that debate proposed tax legislation? What documents do these committees generate, and how might they be used? LO 2-4
22. The president recently vetoed a tax act passed by the House and Senate. Is the tax act dead? If not, what will it take for the act to be passed? LO 2-4
23. What are the five basic parts of an internal research memo? LO 2-5
24. What is the difference between primary and secondary authorities? Explain the role of each authority type in conducting tax research. LO 2-5
25. Jorge is puzzled that the IRS and his CPA could legitimately reach different conclusions on a tax issue. Why does this happen? LO 2-5

LO 2-5 26. What is the difference between open and closed facts? How is this distinction important in conducting tax research?

LO 2-5 27. In writing a research memo, what types of facts should be included in the memo?

LO 2-5 28. Aminata is a tax expert, whereas Rob is a tax novice. Explain how their process in identifying tax issues may differ.

LO 2-5 29. Discuss the basic differences between annotated and topical tax services. How are these services used in tax research?

LO 2-5 30. In constructing a keyword search, what should the keyword search include?

LO 2-5 31. Lindsey has become very frustrated in researching a tax issue using keyword searches. What suggestions can you give her?

LO 2-5 32. Nola, a tax novice, has a fairly simple tax question. Besides tax services, what are some sources that she can use to answer her question?

LO 2-5 33. Armando identifies a tax research question as being a question of fact. What types of authorities should he attempt to locate in his research?

LO 2-5 34. How are citators used in tax research?

LO 2-5 35. What is the general rule for how many authorities a research memo should discuss?

LO 2-6 36. Identify some of the sources for tax professional standards. What are the potential ramifications of failing to comply with these standards?

LO 2-6 37. Levi is recommending a tax return position to his client. What standard must he meet to satisfy his professional standards? What is the source of this professional standard?

LO 2-6 38. What is Circular 230?

LO 2-6 39. What are some of the common law issues that a tax practitioner may face with respect to their duties, and how might a tax practitioner avoid these issues?

LO 2-7 40. What determines whether someone is considered a tax return preparer?

LO 2-7 41. What are the basic differences between civil and criminal tax penalties?

LO 2-7 42. What are some of the most common civil penalties imposed on taxpayers?

LO 2-7 43. What are the taxpayer's standards to avoid the substantial understatement of tax penalty?

LO 2-7 44. What are the tax return preparer's standards to avoid a penalty for recommending a tax return position?

PROBLEMS

Select problems are available in Connect®. Mc Graw Hill connect

LO 2-1 45. Ahmed does not have enough cash on hand to pay his taxes. He was excited to hear that he can request an extension to file his tax return. Does this solve his problem? What are the ramifications if he doesn't pay his tax liability by April 15?

LO 2-1 46. Molto Stancha Corporation had zero earnings this fiscal year; in fact, it lost money. Must the corporation file a tax return?

LO 2-1 47. The estate of Monique Chablis earned $450 of income this year. Is the estate required to file an income tax return?

LO 2-1 48. Jamarcus, a full-time student, earned $2,500 this year from a summer job. He had no other income this year and will have zero federal income tax liability this year. His employer withheld $300 of federal income tax from his summer pay. Is Jamarcus required to file a tax return? Should Jamarcus file a tax return?

LO 2-1 49. Shane has never filed a tax return despite earning excessive sums of money as a gambler. When does the statute of limitations expire for the years in which Shane has not filed a tax return?

LO 2-1 50. Latoya filed her tax return on February 10 this year. When will the statute of limitations expire for this tax return?

51. Using the facts from the previous problem, how would your answer change if Latoya understated her income by 40 percent? How would your answer change if Latoya intentionally failed to report as taxable income any cash payments she received from her clients? LO 2-1

52. Paula could not reach an agreement with the IRS at her appeals conference and has just received a 90-day letter. If she wants to litigate the issue but does not have sufficient cash to pay the proposed deficiency, what is her best court choice? LO 2-2

53. In choosing a trial-level court, how should a court's previous rulings influence the choice? How should circuit court rulings influence the taxpayer's choice of a trial-level court? LO 2-2

54. Sophia recently won a tax case litigated in the 7th Circuit. She has just heard that the Supreme Court denied the *writ of certiorari*. Should she be happy or not, and why? LO 2-2

55. Campbell's tax return was audited because they failed to report on their tax return interest they earned. What IRS audit selection method identified their tax return? LO 2-2

56. Yong's tax return was audited because he calculated his tax liability incorrectly. What IRS audit procedure identified his tax return for audit? LO 2-2

57. Randy deducted a high level of itemized deductions two years ago relative to his income level. He recently received an IRS notice requesting documentation for his itemized deductions. What audit procedure likely identified his tax return for audit? LO 2-2

58. Jackie has a corporate client that has recently received a 30-day notice from the IRS with a $100,000 tax assessment. Her client is considering requesting an appeals conference to contest the assessment. What factors should Jackie advise her client to consider before requesting an appeals conference? LO 2-2 planning

59. The IRS recently completed an audit of Shea's tax return and assessed $15,000 additional tax. Shea requested an appeals conference but was unable to settle the case at the conference. She is contemplating which trial court to choose to hear her case. Provide a recommendation based on the following alternative facts: LO 2-2 planning
    a) Shea resides in the 2d Circuit, and the 2d Circuit has recently ruled against the position Shea is litigating.
    b) The Federal Circuit Court of Appeals has recently ruled in favor of Shea's position.
    c) The issue being litigated involves a question of fact. Shea has a very appealing story to tell but little favorable case law to support her position.
    d) The issue being litigated is highly technical, and Shea believes strongly in her interpretation of the law.
    e) Shea is a local elected official and would prefer to minimize any local publicity regarding the case.

60. Juanita, a Texas resident (5th Circuit), is researching a tax question and finds a 5th Circuit case ruling that is favorable and a 9th Circuit case that is unfavorable. Which circuit case has more "authoritative weight" and why? How would your answer change if Juanita were a Kentucky resident (6th Circuit)? LO 2-3

61. Faith, a resident of Florida (11th Circuit), recently found a circuit court case that is favorable to her research question. Which two circuits would she prefer to have issued the opinion? LO 2-3

62. Robert has found a "favorable" authority directly on point for his tax question. If the authority is a court case, which court would he prefer to have issued the opinion? Which court would he least prefer to have issued the opinion? LO 2-3

63. Jamareo has found a "favorable" authority directly on point for his tax question. If the authority is an administrative authority, which specific type of authority would he prefer to answer his question? Which administrative authority would he least prefer to answer his question? LO 2-3

LO 2-3

64. For each of the following citations, identify the type of authority (statutory, administrative, or judicial) and explain the citation.
    a) Reg. §1.111-1(b)
    b) §469(c)(7)(B)(i)
    c) Rev. Rul. 82-204, 1982-2 C.B. 192
    d) *Amdahl Corp.,* 108 TC 507 (1997)
    e) PLR 9727004
    f) *Hills v. Comm'r,* 50 AFTR2d 82-6070 (11th Cir. 1982)

LO 2-3

65. For each of the following citations, identify the type of authority (statutory, administrative, or judicial) and explain the citation.
    a) §280A(c)(5)
    b) Rev. Proc. 2004-34, 2004-1 C.B. 911
    c) *Lakewood Associates,* RIA TC Memo 95-3566
    d) TAM 200427004
    e) *United States v. Muncy,* 2008-2 USTC par. 50,449 (E.D. Ark. 2008)

LO 2-4

66. Justine would like to clarify her understanding of a code section recently enacted by Congress. What tax law sources are available to assist Justine?

LO 2-5

67. Aldina has identified conflicting authorities that address her research question. How should she evaluate these authorities to make a conclusion?

LO 2-5

68. Georgette has identified a 1983 court case that appears to answer her research question. What must she do to determine if the case still represents "current" law?

LO 2-5

69. Sandy has determined that her research question depends upon the interpretation of the phrase "not compensated by insurance." What type of research question is this?

LO 2-5 research

70. J. C. has been a professional gambler for many years. They love this line of work and believe the income is tax-free.
    a) Use an available tax research service to determine whether J. C.'s thinking is correct. Is the answer to this question found in the Internal Revenue Code? If not, what type of authority answers this question?
    b) Write a memo communicating the results of your research.

LO 2-5 research

71. Katie recently won a ceramic dalmatian valued at $800 on a television game show. She questions whether this prize is taxable because it was a "gift" she won on the show.
    a) Use an available tax research service to answer Katie's question.
    b) Write a letter to Katie communicating the results of your research.

LO 2-5 research

72. Pierre recently received a tax penalty for failing to file a tax return. He was upset to receive the penalty, but he was comforted by the thought that he will get a tax deduction for paying the penalty.
    a) Use an available tax research service to determine if Pierre is correct.
    b) Write a memo communicating the results of your research.

LO 2-5 research

73. Paris was happy to provide a contribution to her friend Nicole's campaign for mayor, especially after she learned that charitable contributions are tax deductible.
    a) Use an available tax service to determine whether Paris can deduct this contribution.
    b) Write a memo communicating the results of your research.

LO 2-5 research

74. Janelle and Lori were divorced in 2016. Pursuant to the divorce decree, Janelle receives $10,000 of alimony each month. Use an available tax service to determine if the alimony Janelle receives is taxable. Would your answer change if Janelle and Lori still live together?

LO 2-5 research

75. Omar is a huge college football fan. In the past, he has always bought football tickets on the street from ticket scalpers. This year, he decided to join the university's ticket program, which requires a $2,000 contribution to the university for the "right" to purchase tickets. Omar will then pay $400 per season ticket. Omar understands

that the price paid for the season tickets is not tax deductible as a charitable contribution. However, contributions to a university are typically tax deductible.

a) Use an available tax service to determine how much, if any, of Omar's $2,000 contribution for the right to purchase tickets is tax deductible.

b) Write a letter to Omar communicating the results of your research.

76. Latrell recently used his Delta Skymiles to purchase a free round-trip ticket to Milan, Italy (value $1,200). The frequent flyer miles used to purchase the ticket were generated from Latrell's business travel as a CPA. Latrell's employer paid for his business trips, and he was not taxed on the travel reimbursement. LO 2-5 research

a) Use an available tax research service to determine how much income, if any, Latrell will have to recognize as a result of purchasing an airline ticket with Skymiles earned from business travel.

b) Write a memo communicating the results of your research.

77. Benjamin, a self-employed bookkeeper, takes a CPA review course ($3,000 cost) to help prepare for the CPA exam. LO 2-5 research

a) Use an available tax research service to determine if Benjamin may deduct the cost of the CPA exam course.

b) Write a memo communicating the results of your research.

78. Randy has found conflicting authorities that address a research question for one of his clients. The majority of the authorities provide an unfavorable answer for his client. According to Randy's estimates, if the client takes the more favorable position on its tax return, then there is approximately a 48 percent chance that the position will be sustained upon audit or judicial proceeding. If the client takes this position on its tax return, will Randy be subject to penalty? Will the client potentially be subject to penalty? LO 2-6

79. Using the same facts from the previous problem, how would your answer change if Randy estimates that there is only a 20 percent chance that the position will be sustained upon audit or judicial proceeding? LO 2-6

80. Sasha owes additional tax imposed in a recent audit. In addition to the tax, will they be assessed other amounts? If so, how will these amounts be determined? LO 2-7

81. Maurice has a client that recently asked him about the odds of the IRS detecting cash transactions not reported on a tax return. What are some of the issues that Maurice should discuss with his client? LO 2-7

UWorld | ROGER CPA Review

UWorld Roger CPA Review

Sample CPA Exam questions from Roger CPA Review are available in Connect as support for the topics in this text. These Multiple Choice Questions and Task-Based Simulations include expert-written explanations and solutions and provide a starting point for students to become familiar with the content and functionality of the actual CPA Exam.

chapter

3 Tax Planning Strategies and Related Limitations

Learning Objectives

Upon completing this chapter, you should be able to:

LO 3-1 Identify the objectives of basic tax planning strategies.

LO 3-2 Apply the timing strategy.

LO 3-3 Apply the concept of present value to tax planning.

LO 3-4 Apply the income-shifting strategy.

LO 3-5 Apply the conversion strategy.

LO 3-6 Describe basic judicial doctrines that limit tax planning strategies.

LO 3-7 Contrast tax avoidance and tax evasion.

Michaeljung/Shutterstock

Storyline Summary

Taxpayers:	Bill (he/him/his) and Mercedes (she/her/hers)
Family description:	Bill and Mercedes are married with one daughter, Margaret (she/her/hers).
Employment status:	Bill is an economics professor; Mercedes is a small business owner.
Filing status:	Married, filing jointly
Current situation:	Bill and Mercedes want to engage in low-risk tax planning strategies.

While working with their CPA during their audit, Bill and Mercedes decide to inquire about low-risk tax planning opportunities. Specifically, they would like to gain a better understanding of how to maximize their after-tax income without increasing their potential for another audit. (Although it was fun and educational, one audit is enough!) Mercedes is convinced that, as a small business owner (Lavish Interior Designs Inc.), she pays more than her fair share of taxes. Likewise, Bill, an avid investor, wonders whether he is missing the mark by not considering taxes in his investment decisions. ■

Bill and Mercedes have come to the right place. This chapter describes the basic tax planning concepts that form the basis of the simplest to most complex tax planning transactions. In the process, we also discuss the judicial doctrines that serve as basic limits on tax planning.

LO 3-1

BASIC TAX PLANNING OVERVIEW

Effective tax planning requires a basic understanding of the roles that tax and nontax factors play in structuring business, investment, and personal decisions. Although tax factors may not be the sole or even the primary determinant of a transaction or its structure, taxes can significantly affect the costs or benefits associated with business, investment, and personal transactions. Thus, the tax implications of competing transactions warrant careful consideration. Likewise, nontax factors, such as the taxpayer's financial goals or legal constraints, are an integral part of every transaction.

In general terms, effective tax planning maximizes the taxpayer's after-tax wealth while achieving the taxpayer's nontax goals. Maximizing after-tax wealth is not necessarily the same as minimizing taxes. Specifically, maximizing after-tax wealth requires us to consider both the tax and nontax costs and benefits of alternative transactions, whereas tax minimization focuses solely on a single cost—taxes. Indeed, if the goal of tax planning were simply to minimize taxes, the simplest way to achieve it would be to earn no income at all. Obviously, this strategy has potential limitations—most notably, the unattractive nontax consequence of poverty. Thus, it is necessary to consider the nontax ramifications of any planning strategy.

Virtually every transaction includes three parties: the taxpayer, the other transacting party, and the uninvited silent party that specifies the tax consequences of the transaction—the government. Astute tax planning requires an understanding of the tax and nontax costs from the perspectives of both the taxpayer *and* the other parties. For example, it would be impossible for an employer to develop an effective compensation plan without considering the tax and nontax costs associated with different compensation arrangements from both the employer's and the employees' perspectives. With sound tax planning, the employer can design a compensation package that generates value for employees while reducing costs for the employer. (One way to achieve this goal is through the use of nontaxable fringe benefits, such as health insurance, which are deductible expenses to the employer but not taxable income to employees.) Throughout the text, we highlight situations where this multilateral approach to tax planning is especially important.

THE KEY FACTS

The Basics of Tax Planning

- Effective tax planning maximizes the taxpayer's after-tax wealth while achieving the taxpayer's nontax goals.
- Virtually every transaction includes three parties: the taxpayer, the other transacting party, and the uninvited silent party that specifies the tax consequences of the transaction—the government.
- Astute tax planning requires an understanding of the tax and nontax costs from the perspectives of both the taxpayer *and* the other parties.

In this chapter we discuss three basic tax planning strategies that represent the building blocks of tax planning:

1. *Timing* (deferring or accelerating taxable income and tax deductions).
2. *Income shifting* (shifting income from high- to low-tax-rate taxpayers).
3. *Conversion* (converting income from high- to low-tax-rate activities).

LO 3-2 LO 3-3 LO 3-6

TIMING STRATEGIES

One of the cornerstones of basic tax planning is the idea of *timing*. *When* income is taxed or an expense is deducted affects the associated "real" tax costs or savings. This is true for two reasons. First, the time when income is taxed or an expense is deducted affects the *present value* of the taxes paid on income or the tax savings on deductions. Second, the tax costs of income and tax savings of deductions vary as *tax rates* change. The tax costs on income are higher when tax rates are higher and lower when tax rates are lower. Likewise, the tax savings on deductions are higher when tax rates are higher and lower when tax rates are lower. Let's look at the effects of present value and tax rates on the timing strategy.

Present Value of Money

The concept of **present value**—also known as the time value of money—basically states that $1 received today is worth *more* than $1 received in the future. Is this true, or is this some type of new math?

It's true. Assuming an investor can earn a positive **after-tax rate of return** such as 5 percent, $1 invested today should be worth $1.05 in one year.[1] Specifically,

Eq. 3-1

$$\text{Future Value} = \text{Present Value} \times (1 + r)^n$$
$$= \$1 \times (1 + .05)^1 = \$1.05$$

where $1 is the present value, r is the after-tax rate of return (5 percent), and n is the investment period (1 year). Hence, $1 today is equivalent to $1.05 in one year. The implication of the time value of money for tax planning is that the timing of a cash inflow or a cash outflow affects the present value of the income or expense.

Example 3-1

Bill is given the choice of receiving a $1,000 nontaxable gift today or a $1,000 nontaxable gift in one year. Which would Bill prefer? Assume Bill could invest $1,000 today and earn an 8 percent return after taxes in one year. If he receives the gift today, how much would the $1,000 be worth in one year?

Answer: The $1,000 gift today would be worth $1,080 in one year, and thus Bill should prefer to receive the gift today. Specifically,

$$\text{Future value} = \text{Present value} \times (1 + r)^n$$
$$= \$1{,}000 \times (1 + .08)^1 = \$1{,}080$$

In terms of *future value,* the choice in the above example between receiving $1,000 today and $1,000 in one year simplifies to a choice between $1,080 and $1,000. For even the least materialistic individual, choosing $1,080—that is, $1,000 *today*—should be straightforward.

Often tax planners find it useful to consider sums in terms of present value rather than future value. How would we restate the choice in Example 3-1 in terms of present value? Obviously, the present value of receiving $1,000 today is $1,000, but what is the *present value* of $1,000 received in one year? The answer depends on the **discount factor,** which we derive from the taxpayer's expected after-tax rate of return. The discount factor is very useful for calculating the present value of future inflows or outflows of cash. We can derive the discount factor for a given rate of return simply by rearranging the future value equation (Eq. 3-1) from above:

Eq. 3-2

$$\text{Present Value} = \text{Future Value}/(1 + r)^n$$
$$= \$1/(1 + .08)^1 = \$0.926$$

Therefore, the discount factor = 0.926

THE KEY FACTS

Present Value of Money

- The concept of present value—also known as the time value of money—states that $1 received today is worth *more* than $1 received in the future.
- The implication of the time value of money for tax planning is that the timing of a cash inflow or a cash outflow affects the present value of the income or expense.
- Present value = Future value/$(1 + r)^n$.
- When we are considering cash inflows, higher present values are preferred; when we are considering cash outflows, lower present values are preferred.

[1]Assuming a constant marginal tax rate (t), after-tax rate of return (r) may be calculated as follows: $r = R \times (1 - t)$, where R is the taxpayer's before-tax rate of return.

EXHIBIT 3-1 Present Value of a Single Payment at Various Annual Rates of Return

Year	4%	5%	6%	7%	8%	9%	10%	11%	12%
1	.962	.952	.943	.935	.926	.917	.909	.901	.893
2	.925	.907	.890	.873	.857	.842	.826	.812	.797
3	.889	.864	.840	.816	.794	.772	.751	.731	.712
4	.855	.823	.792	.763	.735	.708	.683	.659	.636
5	.822	.784	.747	.713	.681	.650	.621	.593	.567
6	.790	.746	.705	.666	.630	.596	.564	.535	.507
7	.760	.711	.665	.623	.583	.547	.513	.482	.452
8	.731	.677	.627	.582	.540	.502	.467	.434	.404
9	.703	.645	.592	.544	.500	.460	.424	.391	.361
10	.676	.614	.558	.508	.463	.422	.386	.352	.322
11	.650	.585	.527	.475	.429	.388	.350	.317	.287
12	.625	.557	.497	.444	.397	.356	.319	.286	.257
13	.601	.530	.469	.415	.368	.326	.290	.258	.229
14	.577	.505	.442	.388	.340	.299	.263	.232	.205
15	.555	.481	.417	.362	.315	.275	.239	.209	.183

Applying the discount factor, we can see that $1,000 received in one year is worth $926 in today's dollars. Thus, in terms of present value, Bill's choice in Example 3-1 simplifies to a choice between a cash inflow of $1,000 today and a cash inflow worth $926 today. Again, choosing $1,000 today is pretty straightforward.

Exhibit 3-1 provides the discount factors for a lump sum (single payment) received in *n* periods using various rates of return. Tax planners frequently utilize such tables or financial calculators for quick reference in calculating present value for sums under consideration.

Example 3-2

At a recent holiday sale, Bill and Mercedes purchased $1,000 worth of furniture with "no money down and no payments for one year!" How much money is this deal really worth? (Assume their after-tax rate of return on investments is 10 percent.)

Answer: The discount factor of .909 (Exhibit 3-1, 10% Rate of Return column, Year 1 row) means the present value of $1,000 is $909 ($1,000 × .909 = $909)—so Bill and Mercedes saved $91 ($1,000 − $909 = $91).

While Example 3-1 considers a $1,000 cash inflow, Example 3-2 addresses a $1,000 cash *outflow*. In terms of present value, choosing between paying $1,000 today and paying $1,000 in a year simplifies to choosing a cash outflow of either $1,000 (by paying today) or $909 (by paying $1,000 in one year). Most people would prefer to pay $909. Indeed, financial planners always keep the following general rule of thumb in mind: When considering *cash inflows, prefer higher present values;* when considering *cash outflows, prefer lower present values.*

The Timing Strategy When Tax Rates Are Constant

In terms of tax planning, remember that *taxes paid* represent cash *outflows,* while *tax savings* generated from tax deductions are cash *inflows.* This perspective leads us to two basic tax-related timing strategies when tax rates are constant (not changing):

1. Accelerate tax deductions (deduct in an earlier period).
2. Defer recognizing taxable income (recognize in a later period).

Accelerating tax deductions to an earlier period increases the present value of the tax savings from the deduction. That is, tax savings received now have a higher present value than the same amount received a year from now.

Deferring income to a later period decreases the present value of the tax cost of the income. That is, taxes paid a year from now have a lower present value than taxes paid today. These two strategies are summarized in Exhibit 3-2.

EXHIBIT 3-2 The Timing Tax Strategy When Tax Rates Are Constant

Item	Recommendation	Why?
Tax deductions	Accelerate tax deductions into earlier years.	Maximizes the present value of tax savings from deductions.
Taxable income	Defer taxable income into later tax years.	Minimizes the present value of taxes paid.

Example 3-3

Mercedes, a calendar-year taxpayer, uses the cash method of accounting for her small business.[2] On December 28, she receives a $10,000 bill from her accountant for consulting services related to her small business. She can avoid late payment charges by paying the $10,000 bill before January 10 of next year. Let's assume that Mercedes's marginal tax rate is 32 percent *this year and next* and that she can earn an after-tax rate of return of 10 percent on her investments. When should she pay the $10,000 bill—this year or next?

Answer: If Mercedes pays the bill this year, she will receive a tax deduction on this year's tax return.[3] If she pays the bill in January, she will receive a tax deduction on next year's tax return (one year later). She needs to compare the after-tax costs of the accounting service, using the present value of the tax savings for each scenario:

Present Value Comparison

Description	Option 1: Pay $10,000 bill *this year*	Option 2: Pay $10,000 bill *next year*
Tax deduction	$10,000	$10,000
Marginal tax rate	× 32%	× 32%
Tax savings	$ 3,200	$ 3,200
Discount factor	× 1	× .909
Present value tax savings	$ 3,200	$ 2,909
After-tax cost of accounting services:		
Before-tax cost	$10,000	$10,000
Less: Present value tax savings	– 3,200	– 2,909
After-tax cost of accounting services	$ 6,800	$ 7,091

Because Mercedes would surely rather spend $6,800 than $7,091 for accounting services, paying the bill in December is the clear winner.

[2]In the Business Income, Deductions, and Accounting Methods chapter, we discuss the basic accounting methods (e.g., cash vs. the accrual method), which influence the timing of when income and deductions are recognized for tax purposes.

[3]Accelerating her payment from January 10 to December 31 will increase the present value of the $10,000 cash outflow by 10 days. Thus, there is a minor present value cost associated with accelerating her payment.

In terms of accelerating deductions, the intent of the timing strategy is to accelerate the tax deduction significantly *without* accelerating the actual cash outflow that generates the expense. Indeed, if we assume a marginal rate of 32 percent and an after-tax return of 8 percent, accelerating a $1,000 cash outflow by one year to realize $320 in tax savings actually *increases* the after-tax *cost* of the expense from $630 to $680.

Present Value Comparison

Description	Present value of net cash outflow *today*	Present value of net cash outflow in *one year*
Cash outflow	$1,000	$1,000
Less: Tax savings (outflow × 32% tax rate)	− 320	− 320
Net cash outflow	$ 680	$ 680
Present value factor	× 1	× .926
Present value of net cash outflow today	$ 680	$ 630

Generally speaking, whenever a taxpayer can accelerate a deduction without also substantially accelerating the cash outflow, the timing strategy will be more beneficial.

Is the accelerating deductions strategy utilized in the real world? Yes. While it is particularly effective for cash-method taxpayers, who can often control the year in which they pay their expenses, all taxpayers have *some* latitude in timing deductions. Common examples of the timing strategy include accelerating depreciation deductions for depreciable assets, using LIFO instead of FIFO for inventory, and accelerating the deduction of certain prepaid expenses.[4] For large corporations, the benefits associated with this timing strategy can be quite substantial. Thus, tax planners spend considerable time identifying the proper period in which to recognize expenses and evaluating opportunities to accelerate deductions.

Are there certain taxpayer or transaction attributes that enhance the advantages of accelerating deductions? Absolutely. Higher tax rates, higher rates of return, larger transaction amounts, and the ability to accelerate deductions by two or more years all increase the benefits of accelerating deductions. To demonstrate this for yourself, simply rework Example 3-3 and substitute any of the following: 50 percent tax rate, 12 percent after-tax rate of return, $100,000 expense, or a five-year period difference in the timing of the expense deduction. The benefits of accelerating deductions become much more prominent with these changes.

Deferring income recognition is an equally beneficial timing strategy, especially when the taxpayer can defer the recognition of income significantly without deferring the actual receipt of income by a significant amount. Consider the following example.

Example 3-4

In early December, Bill decides he would like to sell $100,000 of his Dell Inc. stock, which 10 years ago cost $20,000. Assume Bill's tax rate on the $80,000 gain will be 15 percent and his typical after-tax rate of return on investments is 7 percent. What effect would deferring the sale to January have on Bill's after-tax cash flow on the sale?

[4]See the discussion of accounting methods in the Business Income, Deductions, and Accounting Methods chapter.

Answer:

Present Value Comparison

Description	Option 1: Sell the $100,000 stock in *December*[5]	Option 2: Sell the $100,000 stock in *January*[5]
Sales price	$100,000	$100,000
Less: Cost of stock	− 20,000	− 20,000
Gain on sale	$ 80,000	$ 80,000
Marginal tax rate	× 15%	× 15%
Tax on gain	$ 12,000	$ 12,000
Discount factor	× 1	× .935
Present value tax cost	$ 12,000	$ 11,220
After-tax cash flow from sale:		
Sales price	$100,000	$100,000
Less: Present value tax cost	− 12,000	− 11,220
After-tax cash flow from sale	**$ 88,000**	**$ 88,780**

Bill would doubtlessly prefer to earn $88,780 to $88,000, so from a tax perspective, selling the Dell Inc. stock in January is preferable. An important nontax issue for Bill to consider is the possibility that the stock price may fluctuate between December and January.

Income deferral represents an important aspect of investment planning, retirement planning, and certain property transactions. Income-related timing considerations also affect tax planning for everyday business operations, such as determining the appropriate period in which to recognize income (e.g., cash or accrual accounting method for income and deduction recognition, and depreciation methods).

Do certain taxpayer or transaction attributes enhance the advantages of deferring income? Yes. The list is very similar to that for accelerating deductions: Higher tax rates, higher rates of return, larger transaction amounts, and the ability to defer revenue recognition for longer periods of time increase the benefits of deferral. To demonstrate this for yourself, simply rework Example 3-4 using any of the following: 50 percent tax rate, 12 percent after-tax rate of return on investments, or $200,000 gain.[6]

THE KEY FACTS

The Timing Strategy

- The time at which income is taxed or an expense is deducted affects the *present value* of the taxes paid on income or tax savings on deductions.
- The tax costs of income and tax savings of deductions vary as *tax rates* change.
- When tax rates are constant, tax planners prefer to defer income and accelerate deductions.
- When tax rates are increasing, the taxpayer must calculate the optimal tax strategies for deductions and income.
- When tax rates are decreasing, taxpayers should accelerate tax deductions into earlier years and defer taxable income to later years.

The Timing Strategy When Tax Rates Change

When tax rates change, the timing strategy requires a little more consideration because the tax costs of income and the tax savings from deductions will now vary. The higher the tax rate, the higher the tax savings for a tax deduction. The lower the tax rate, the lower

[5]This will require Bill to pay the tax on the gain no later than April 15 of the following year (i.e., 3 months after the sale for option 1 and 15 months after the sale for option 2). If Bill and Mercedes's current-year withholding and estimated payments do not equal or exceed 110 percent of their previous year's tax liability, they will have to make an estimated payment by January 15 to avoid the failure to make estimated tax payment penalty (discussed later in the Individual Income Tax Computation and Tax Credits chapter). This example assumes that Bill and Mercedes can avoid the underpayment of estimated tax penalty discussed in the Individual Income Tax Computation and Tax Credits chapter by paying 110 percent of their previous year's tax liability in both options 1 and 2. Thus, they can defer paying the tax on the gain until April 15 of the year following the sale.

[6]In Example 3-4, increasing the deferral period (e.g., from one to five years) also increases the benefits of tax deferral but requires additional assumptions regarding the expected five-year return of the Dell Inc. stock (assuming he does not sell the stock for five years) and his new investment (assuming he sells the Dell Inc. stock and immediately reinvests the after-tax proceeds).

EXHIBIT 3-3 Historical Maximum Ordinary and Capital Gains Tax Rates for Individuals Since 1983

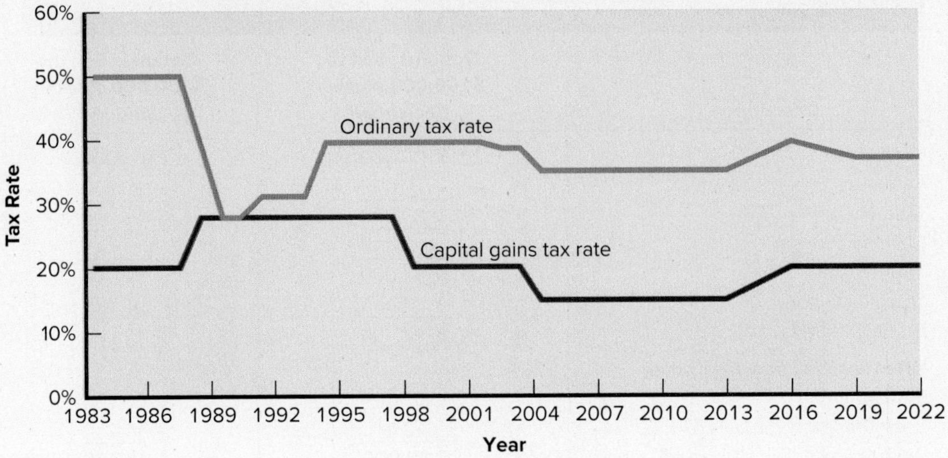

the tax costs for taxable income. *All other things being equal, taxpayers should prefer to recognize deductions during high-tax-rate years and income during low-tax-rate years.* The implication is that before taxpayers implement the timing strategies suggested above (accelerate deductions, defer income), they should consider whether their tax rates are likely to change. In fact, as we discuss below, increasing tax rates may even suggest the taxpayer should *accelerate* income and *defer* deductions.

What would cause a taxpayer's marginal tax rate to change? As we discussed in the introduction chapter, marginal tax rates change as income or deductions change. Consequently, a taxpayer's marginal rate may change as taxable income changes due to changing jobs, retiring, or starting a new business. Also, as we discussed in the Tax Compliance, the IRS, and Tax Authorities chapter, Congress frequently enacts tax legislation because lawmakers use taxes to raise revenue, stimulate the economy, and so on. For example, the Tax Cuts and Jobs Act enacted on December 22, 2017, lowered the top ordinary tax rate from 39.6 percent to 37 percent. In the last 35 years, Congress has changed the maximum statutory tax rates that apply to ordinary income, such as wages and business income, or capital gains, such as gains from the sale of stock, for individual taxpayers no fewer than 11 times (see Exhibit 3-3).

Let's take a look at how changing tax rates affect the timing strategy recommendations. Exhibit 3-4 presents recommendations for when tax rates are increasing. The taxpayer must actually calculate the optimal tax strategies for deductions and income when tax rates are increasing. Specifically, because accelerating deductions causes them to be

EXHIBIT 3-4 The Timing Tax Strategy When Tax Rates Are Increasing

Item	Recommendation	Why?
Tax deductions	Requires calculation to determine optimal strategy.	The taxpayer must calculate whether the benefit of accelerating deductions outweighs the disadvantage of recognizing deductions in a *lower*-tax-rate year.
Taxable income	Requires calculation to determine optimal strategy.	The taxpayer must calculate whether the benefit of deferring income outweighs the disadvantage of recognizing income in a *higher*-tax-rate year.

recognized in a *lower*-tax-rate year, the taxpayer must calculate whether the benefit of accelerating the deduction outweighs the disadvantage. Likewise, because deferring income causes income to be recognized in a *higher*-tax-rate year, the taxpayer must calculate whether the benefit of deferring income outweighs the disadvantage.

Example 3-5

Having decided she needs new equipment for her business, Mercedes is now considering whether to make the purchase and claim a corresponding $10,000 deduction at year-end or next year. Mercedes anticipates that, with the new machinery, her business income will rise such that her marginal rate will increase from 24 percent this year to 32 percent next year. Assuming her after-tax rate of return is 8 percent, what should Mercedes do?

Answer: Given rising tax rates, Mercedes must calculate the after-tax cost of the equipment for *both* options and compare present values.

Present Value Comparison

Description	Option 1: Pay $10,000 bill *this year*	Option 2: Pay $10,000 bill *next year*
Tax deduction	$10,000	$10,000
Marginal tax rate	× 24%	× 32%
Tax savings	$ 2,400	$ 3,200
Discount factor	× 1	× .926
Present value tax savings	$ 2,400	$ 2,963
After-tax cost of equipment:		
Before-tax cost	$10,000	$10,000
Less: Present value tax savings	− 2,400	− 2,963
After-tax cost of equipment	$ 7,600	$ 7,037

Paying the $10,000 next year is the clear winner.

In the above example, if the choice were either to recognize $10,000 of *income* this year or next, the *amounts* would be exactly the same, but the conclusion would be different, and Mercedes would prefer to receive $7,600 of after-tax income this year instead of $7,037. (Remember, when considering cash *inflows,* we prefer the *higher* present value.) Are these always the answers when tax rates are increasing? No, the answer will depend on both the taxpayer's after-tax rate of return and the magnitude of the tax rate increase.

Now let's consider the recommendations when tax rates are *decreasing*—a common scenario when an individual reaches retirement. Exhibit 3-5 presents the timing strategy

EXHIBIT 3-5 The Timing Tax Strategy When Tax Rates Are Decreasing

Item	Recommendation	Why?
Tax deductions	Accelerate tax deductions into earlier years.	Maximizes the present value of tax savings from deductions due to the acceleration of the deductions into earlier years with a *higher* tax rate.
Taxable income	Defer taxable income into later tax years.	Minimizes the present value of taxes paid due to the deferral of the income to later years with a *lower* tax rate.

TAXES IN THE REAL WORLD Timing Is Everything

On April 28, 2021, President Biden announced the American Families Plan, which includes provisions to help families pay for child care, provide family and medical leave, make community college free, establish universal preschool, and recruit more teachers. To pay for these provisions, the plan proposes to increase the top marginal tax rate from 37 percent to 39.6 percent for taxpayers earning more than $1 million, increase the long-term capital gains tax rate to the top ordinary marginal tax rate, tax unrealized capital gains at death, and increase IRS enforcement. These potential changes increase the uncertainty in tax planning and how taxpayers potentially subject to the new provision use the tax planning strategies discussed in this chapter.

How might high-income taxpayers respond to these potential changes in the capital gains tax rates? Options might include (1) keeping income below $1 million, (2) recognizing gains in 2021 before any tax rate increases occur, and (3) continuing the normal tax planning of deferring gains and accelerating tax losses.

The first option—keeping income below $1 million—would mean that capital gains would not be subject to the higher rates. Most taxpayers have income below that threshold and do not have to worry about the increasing tax rates; however, taxpayers around the $1 million may consider deferring income to years when income is below $1 million by contributing to a retirement plan, recognizing losses, accelerating business expenses, or buying and expensing business assets. Although these are common tax planning strategies, the uncertainty from the potential tax rate increase may cause taxpayers to consider whether to defer these strategies until the tax rates increase (if they do).

The second option may come into play when the sale of a capital asset with a large gain may push income above the $1 million amount and into the higher capital gains tax rates. Typically, the timing strategy encourages accelerating deductions and deferring income; however, when tax rates are increasing, taxpayers will need to consider accelerating income into 2021 to take advantage of the current capital gains tax rates.

The third option simply allows taxpayers to continue applying the timing strategy normally to defer capital gains recognition and accelerating tax losses. When taxpayers believe the probability that the American Families Plan will be enacted is low, this option removes the additional uncertainty from their planning and provides the benefits of the timing strategy discussed in this chapter.

Source: Based on The American Families Plan—Fact Sheet, available at www.whitehouse.gov/wp-content/uploads/2021/04/American-Families-Plan-Fact-Sheet-FINAL.pdf.

THE KEY FACTS

Limitations to the Timing Strategy

Timing strategies contain several inherent limitations.

- Whenever a taxpayer is unable to accelerate a deduction without also accelerating the cash outflow, the timing strategy will be less beneficial.
- Tax law generally requires taxpayers to continue their investment in an asset in order to defer income recognition for tax purposes.
- A deferral strategy may not be optimal if the taxpayer has severe cash flow needs, if continuing the investment would generate a low rate of return compared to other investments, if the current investment would subject the taxpayer to unnecessary risk, and so on.
- The constructive receipt doctrine, which provides that a taxpayer must recognize income when it is actually *or* constructively received, also restricts income deferral for cash-method taxpayers.

recommendations in this case. The recommendations are clear. Taxpayers should accelerate tax deductions into earlier years to reap the tax savings from *accelerating* deductions to *higher*-tax-rate years. Likewise, taxpayers should defer taxable income to later years to enjoy the tax benefits of *deferring* taxable income to *lower*-tax-rate years.

Limitations to Timing Strategies Timing strategies contain certain inherent limitations. First, tax laws generally require taxpayers to continue their investment in an asset in order to defer income recognition for tax purposes. In other words, deferral is generally not an option if a taxpayer has "cashed out" of an investment.[7] For example, Bill could not sell his Dell stock in December and thereby choose not to recognize the income until January. A deferral strategy may not be optimal if (1) the taxpayer has severe cash flow needs, (2) continuing the investment would generate a low rate of return compared to other investments, or (3) the current investment would subject the taxpayer to unnecessary risk. For example, the risk that the value of Bill's investment in Dell Inc. will decline from December to January in Example 3-4 may lead Bill to forgo deferring his stock sale until January. Again, the astute taxpayer considers both the tax *and* nontax ramifications of deferring income.

A second limitation results from the **constructive receipt doctrine,** which also restricts income deferral for cash-method taxpayers.[8] Unlike accrual-method taxpayers,

[7]See the discussions of like-kind exchanges in the Property Dispositions chapter.

[8]Later in this chapter we discuss other judicial doctrines that apply to all planning strategies.

cash-method taxpayers report income for tax purposes when the income is *received,* whether it is in the form of cash, property, or services.[9] The cash method affords taxpayers some leeway in determining when to recognize income because such taxpayers can control when they bill their clients. However, the constructive receipt doctrine provides that a taxpayer must recognize income when it is actually *or* constructively received. Constructive receipt is deemed to have occurred if the income has been credited to the taxpayer's account or if the income is unconditionally available to the taxpayer, the taxpayer is aware of the income's availability, and there are no restrictions on the taxpayer's control over the income.

Example 3-6

Mercedes's brother-in-law, Carlos, works for King Acura, which recently instituted a bonus plan that pays year-end bonuses each December to employees rated above average for their customer service. Carlos is expecting a $10,000 bonus this year that will be paid on December 31. Thinking he'd prefer to defer this income until next year, Carlos plans to take a vacation on December 30 so that he will not receive his bonus check until January. Will Carlos's strategy work?

Answer: No, the constructive receipt doctrine applies here. Because Carlos's check was unconditionally available to him on December 31, he was aware of its availability, and there were no restrictions on his control over the income on that date, Carlos must report the income in the current year.

What could taxpayers do to avoid Carlos's problem in the future? They could request that their employer institute a company policy of paying bonuses on January 1, which would allow all employees to report the bonus income in that year. However, if the employer is a cash-method taxpayer, this creates a potential conflict with its employees. Such an employer would most likely prefer to deduct the bonus in the current year, which requires the bonuses to be paid in December. This conflict would not exist if the employer were an accrual-method taxpayer because paying the bonuses in January would not affect its ability to deduct the bonuses in the previous year.[10]

INCOME-SHIFTING STRATEGIES

LO 3-4 LO 3-6

We've seen that the value of a tax deduction, or the tax cost of income, varies with the marginal tax rate. We've also seen that tax rates can vary across time, which leads to basic tax planning strategies regarding when to recognize deductions and income. Tax rates can also vary across *taxpayers* or *jurisdictions* (states, countries), which leads to still other tax planning strategies—for example, shifting income from high-tax-rate taxpayers to low-tax-rate taxpayers or shifting deductions from low-tax-rate taxpayers to high-tax-rate taxpayers.

The type of taxpayers who benefit most from this strategy are (1) related parties, such as family members or businesses and their owners, who have varying marginal tax rates and are willing to shift income for the benefit of the group and (2) taxpayers operating in multiple jurisdictions with different marginal tax rates. In any case, tax planners should seek only legitimate methods of shifting income that will withstand IRS scrutiny. In the following section, we discuss transactions between family members, followed by a discussion of transactions between owners and their businesses, and finally a discussion of income shifting across jurisdictions.

[9]Accrual-method taxpayers report income when it is earned. In general, income is deemed earned when all events have occurred that fix the taxpayer's right to the income and the income can be estimated with reasonable accuracy. Thus, income recognition for accrual-method taxpayers generally is not tied to payment. The constructive receipt doctrine may apply in situations in which no cash, property, or services have been received, but the taxpayer has a right to the income.

[10]§267(a)(2). When an employee/shareholder and an employer/corporation are related (i.e., the employee/shareholder owns more than 50 percent of the value of the employer corporation), the corporation cannot deduct the compensation expense until the employee/shareholder includes the payment in income.

Transactions between Family Members and Limitations

One of the most common examples of income shifting is high-tax-rate parents shifting income to low-tax-rate children. For example, Bill and Mercedes have a 32 percent marginal tax rate, whereas their daughter, Margaret, has a 10 percent marginal tax rate. Assuming their marginal tax rates remain constant with relatively modest changes in income, every $1 of income that Bill and Mercedes shift to Margaret reduces the family's tax liability by 22 cents [$1 × (32% − 10%)]. Thus, if Bill and Mercedes shift $10,000 of taxable income to Margaret, the family's after-tax income will increase by $2,200. Can taxpayers legally do this? Yes and no. As you might expect, there are limitations on this type of income shifting.

The **assignment of income doctrine** requires income to be taxed to the taxpayer who actually earns it.[11] Merely attributing your paycheck or dividend to another taxpayer does not transfer the tax liability associated with the income. The assignment of income doctrine implies that, in order to shift income to a taxpayer, that taxpayer must actually earn the income. For example, if Mercedes would like to shift some of her business income to Margaret, Margaret must actually earn it. One way to accomplish this would be for Mercedes to employ Margaret in her business and pay her a $10,000 salary. The effects of this transaction are to decrease Mercedes's taxable income by $10,000 because of tax-deductible salary expense, and to increase Margaret's income by the $10,000 taxable salary. What if Margaret is paid $10,000 to answer Mercedes's business phone one Saturday afternoon every month? Does this seem reasonable? Not likely. The IRS frowns upon this type of aggressive strategy.

Indeed, the IRS closely scrutinizes such **related-person transactions**—that is, financial activities among family members (also among owners and their businesses, or among businesses owned by the same owners). Unlike **arm's-length transactions,** in which each transacting party negotiates for their own benefit, related-person transactions are useful for taxpayers who are much more willing to negotiate for their own common good to the detriment of the IRS. For example, would Mercedes pay an unrelated person $10,000 to answer the phone once a month? Doubtful.[12]

Are there other ways to shift income to children? For example, could Bill and Mercedes shift some of their investment income to Margaret? Yes, but there's a catch. The assignment of income applies what is referred to as the "fruit and the tree" analogy [*Lucas v. Earl,* 281 U.S. 111 (1930)]. For the owner to avoid being taxed on the fruit from the tree (the income), the owner must transfer the tree. Thus, to shift investment income, Bill and Mercedes would also have to transfer ownership in the underlying investment assets to Margaret.[13] Is there a problem with this requirement? Not for Margaret. However, Bill and Mercedes would likely prefer to maintain their wealth. The nontax disadvantages of transferring wealth to implement the income-shifting strategy often outweigh the tax benefits of the transfer. For example, most parents either could not afford to or would have serious reservations about transferring significant wealth to their children—a prime example of how nontax costs may override tax considerations.

Transactions between Owners and Their Businesses and Limitations

Income shifting is not limited to transactions within a family unit. One of the most common examples occurs between owners and their businesses. Let's consider Mercedes's interior design business. Currently, Mercedes operates her business as a sole proprietorship. A sole proprietorship (unlike a C corporation) is not a separate reporting entity, and, thus, Mercedes reports her business income and deductions on her individual tax return. Shifting income to or from her sole proprietorship offers no benefit because all of her sole

[11]Later in this chapter we discuss other judicial doctrines that apply to all planning strategies.

[12]The Internal Revenue Code also contains specific provisions to curtail benefits from related-person transactions. For example, §267 disallows a tax deduction for losses on sales to related persons (even if the sale was consummated at the asset's fair market value).

[13]Further, the "kiddie tax" may apply when parents shift too much investment income to children. The kiddie tax restricts the amount of a child's investment income that can be taxed at the child's (lower) tax rate and subjects the rest to the parents' (higher) tax rates. For more details on the kiddie tax, see the Individual Income Tax Computation and Tax Credits chapter.

proprietorship income is reported on her tax return, regardless of whether it is attributed to her personally or to her business. On the other hand, if Mercedes operated her interior design business as a C corporation, shifting income to or from the C corporation may make good financial sense because the corporation would be a separate entity with tax rates distinct from Mercedes's individual tax rate. Shifting income to herself from the C corporation may allow Mercedes to decrease the tax on her business profits, thereby increasing her after-tax income. This strategy may become more common under the current tax structure because the corporate tax rate is significantly lower than the top individual rate. Example 3-7 illustrates the savings obtainable from this strategy.

Example 3-7

Mercedes is considering organizing her interior design business as a C corporation. She projects $200,000 of business profit next year. Excluding this profit, Bill and Mercedes expect $70,000 of taxable income next year. If Mercedes would like to minimize her current-year tax liability, should she incorporate her business? (Use the married filing jointly tax rate schedule and the corporate tax rate in Appendix C to answer this question.)

Answer: If Mercedes does not incorporate her business, the first $13,550 of her business profits will be taxed at 12 percent (from $70,000 to $83,550 of taxable income, the marginal tax rate is 12 percent). The next $94,600 (from $83,550 to $178,150 of taxable income) would be taxed at 22 percent. The remaining $91,850 (from $178,150 to $270,000 of taxable income) would be taxed at 24 percent. Upon reviewing the corporate tax rate schedule, you should note that the corporate tax rate is a flat 21 percent, and is lower than Bill and Mercedes's current marginal tax rate of 24 percent. Thus, there appears to be some opportunity for Mercedes to reduce her current-year tax liability by choosing to have her business taxed as a C corporation.[14]

In order to shift income from the corporation to the owner, the corporation must create a tax deduction for itself in the process. Compensation paid to employee–owners is the most common method of shifting income from corporations to their owners. Compensation expense is deductible by the corporation and is generally taxable to the employee. Having the business owner rent property to the corporation or loan money to the corporation are also effective income-shifting methods because both transactions generate tax deductions for the corporation and income for the shareholder. Because corporations don't get a tax deduction for dividends paid, paying dividends is *not* an effective way to shift income. Having a corporation pay dividends actually results in "double taxation"—the profits generating the dividends are taxed first at the corporate level and then at the shareholder level. Depending on the taxpayer's tax rate and dividend tax rate, this strategy may be a good one, though under current tax law it can be quite complicated, and recommending this tax planning strategy without analyzing the taxpayer's situation may not be a good way to keep your job as a tax consultant.

After a taxpayer identifies the opportunity and appropriate method to shift income (compensation paid to a related person), he or she can easily determine the optimal amount to shift depending on the taxpayers' marginal tax rates.

Example 3-8

Assuming Mercedes's goal is to minimize her current-year federal income tax liability by shifting some of the corporate income to Mercedes and Bill, how much of the $200,000 business income should her corporation report?

Answer: It should report $186,450. Comparing the two tax rate schedules reveals how to calculate this number.

(continued on page 3-14)

[14]Note that this is a simplified discussion of one of many tax issues associated with organizing a business as a C corporation and assumes Mercedes's business does not qualify for the deduction for qualified business income discussed in the Individual Deductions chapter. In addition, as discussed later in this chapter, Mercedes must consider the judicial doctrines (economic substance, business purpose, etc.) in making this decision. She also needs to consider further tax planning opportunities described in the following example.

Step 1: Would Mercedes rather have income taxed at 21 percent (the corporation's tax rate) or 12 percent (Bill and Mercedes's marginal tax rate before recognizing any profit from Mercedes's business)? The obvious answer is 12 percent. To take advantage of Bill and Mercedes's 12 percent tax bracket, Mercedes should shift $13,550 of the expected $200,000 in profits to herself and Bill—via a salary paid to Mercedes.

Step 2: Assuming Bill and Mercedes report $83,550 of income, their marginal tax rate will now be 22 percent, and thus Mercedes's choice is to have additional income taxed at 22 percent (Bill and Mercedes's marginal tax rate) or at 21 percent (the corporation's tax rate). The clear answer in this case is 21 percent. To take advantage of the 21 percent corporate tax rate, the corporation should retain the remaining $186,450 of the expected $200,000 in profits.

How much current federal income tax does this strategy save Bill and Mercedes? The corporation's and Bill and Mercedes's combined federal income tax liability will be $48,770 ($39,155 for the corporation plus $9,615 for Bill and Mercedes) compared to $52,471 for Bill and Mercedes if the business is operated as a sole proprietorship. Thus, they will save $3,701.[15]

Are there nontax disadvantages of the income-shifting-via-incorporating strategy? Yes. For example, one nontax disadvantage for Mercedes is that her new corporation now has $147,295 of her after-tax profits ($186,450 profits less $39,155 of corporate tax). If Mercedes has personal cash-flow needs that require use of the $147,295, this is not a viable strategy. Indeed, it's advantageous only if the business owner intends to reinvest the business profits into the business. Furthermore, any subsequent transactions between Mercedes and the corporation would clearly be related-person transactions. Thus, Mercedes should be prepared for IRS scrutiny.[16]

As the above example illustrates, tax-avoiding strategies can be quite beneficial, and as Bill and Mercedes's personal (nonbusiness) income increases (i.e., their tax bracket increases on personal income), the strategies will produce even greater tax savings. With the historically low corporate tax rate, we are likely to see an increasing preference for businesses to operate as corporations. However, tax planning strategies also entail some financial risks if they fail to pass muster with the IRS.

ETHICS

Agnes Meher is the owner of LuPat, a profitable construction company that she operates as a sole proprietorship. As a sole proprietor, Agnes reports the business income from LuPat on her individual tax return. Agnes expects the business to generate $400,000 of taxable income this year. Combined with her other income, this will put her in the top tax bracket (37 percent). Agnes has two children named Ellie Mae and Spencer, ages 9 and 11, respectively, who do not currently have any taxable income. Agnes would like to shift some of her income from LuPat to Ellie Mae and Spencer to reduce the overall tax burden from the business income. To shift the income, Agnes hired Ellie Mae and Spencer to perform some janitorial and clerical services for LuPat, paying each child $20,000. What do you think of Agnes's strategy?

[15]This strategy will result in the eventual double taxation of the income retained in Mercedes's corporation. Specifically, Mercedes will eventually have to pay tax on the income retained by the corporation, either in the form of taxable dividends from the corporation or a taxable gain when she sells or liquidates the corporation. The present value of this additional layer of tax reduces the tax savings from this strategy. The longer that the second layer of tax is deferred, the more advantageous this strategy will be. In addition, the example ignores employment-related taxes. These calculations are beyond the scope of this chapter.

[16]The taxpayer should maintain documentation for related-person transactions (e.g., notes for related-person loans and contemporaneous documentation of reasonable compensation paid to related parties).

Income Shifting across Jurisdictions and Limitations

Taxpayers that operate in multiple jurisdictions (states, countries) also apply the income-shifting strategy. Specifically, income earned in different jurisdictions—whether in the United States or abroad, and for state income tax purposes, income earned in different states—is often taxed very differently. With a proper understanding of the differences in tax laws across jurisdictions, taxpayers can use these differences to maximize their after-tax wealth.

Example 3-9

Carlos's employer, King Acura, has two locations. Its main location is in South Dakota (a state with no corporate tax), with a secondary location in North Dakota (maximum corporate state tax rate of 4.31 percent). What tax planning strategy may save money for King Acura?

Answer: The most obvious strategy is to shift income from the North Dakota location to the South Dakota location, thereby reducing King Acura's state income tax liability by about 4.31 cents for every dollar of income shifted.[17]

A number of possibilities exist to execute a strategy such as King Acura's in Example 3-9. Assuming that the North Dakota and South Dakota locations exchange cars, the firm could shift income via *transfer pricing* (using the price the South Dakota location charges the North Dakota location for cars transferred to North Dakota). Likewise, if the South Dakota location (the corporate headquarters) provides a legitimate support function for the North Dakota location, the firm should allocate a portion of the overhead and administrative expenses from the South Dakota location to the North Dakota location.

What are some of the limitations of income shifting across jurisdictions? First, taxing authorities are fully aware of the tax benefits of strategically structuring transactions across tax borders (across countries or states). Thus, the IRS closely examines transfer pricing on international transactions. Similarly, state tax authorities scrutinize interstate transactions between related taxpayers. Second, when taxpayers locate in low-tax-rate jurisdictions to, in effect, shift income to a tax-advantaged jurisdiction, they may bear **implicit taxes** (i.e., additional costs attributable to the jurisdiction's tax advantage). Implicit taxes occur when the price of tax-advantaged assets like municipal bonds is bid up in competitive markets relative to the price of similar assets, like corporate bonds, without tax advantages. The higher price paid for tax-advantaged assets reduces the rate of return on these assets relative to other similar assets without tax advantages. This difference in rates of return represents an implicit tax on tax-advantaged assets. For example, the demand for workers, services, or property in low-tax-rate jurisdictions, whether a foreign country or a low-tax state, may increase the nontax costs associated with operating a business there enough to offset the tax advantages. Finally, negative publicity from moving operations (and jobs) from the United States to a lower-tax jurisdiction may more than offset any tax benefits associated with these strategies.

THE KEY FACTS

The Income-Shifting Strategy

- Income shifting exploits the differences in tax rates across taxpayers or jurisdictions.
- Common examples of income shifting include high-tax-rate parents shifting income to low-tax-rate children, businesses shifting income to their owners, and taxpayers shifting income from high-tax jurisdictions to low-tax jurisdictions. The assignment of income doctrine requires income to be taxed to the taxpayer who actually earns the income.
- The IRS closely monitors income-shifting strategies that involve related-person transactions.

CONVERSION STRATEGIES

LO 3-5

We've now seen how tax rates can vary across time and taxpayers. They can also vary across different *activities*. For example, ordinary income such as salary, interest income, and business income received by individual taxpayers is taxed at their ordinary marginal tax rates. Long-term capital gains, which are gains from the sale of investment assets held

[17]Because state taxes are deductible for federal tax purposes, every dollar of state taxes reduced with this strategy will increase King Acura's federal income tax liability by its federal marginal tax rate (e.g., 21 percent). Thus, the net tax savings for every dollar of income shifted from North Dakota to South Dakota will be 3.4 percent, which equals the state tax savings (4.31 percent) less the federal tax increase resulting from the lost state tax deduction (4.31% × 21%).

longer than one year, and dividends are taxed at lower tax rates (currently a maximum of 20 percent, generally), and still other forms of income like nontaxable compensation benefits and municipal bond interest are tax-exempt. Expenses from different types of activities may also be treated very differently for tax purposes. Business expenses are generally fully tax deductible, whereas tax deductions for investments may be limited, and tax deductions for personal expenses may be completely disallowed. In sum, the tax law does not treat all types of income or deductions the same. This understanding forms the basis for the conversion strategy—recasting income and expenses to receive the most favorable tax treatment.

To implement the conversion strategy, the taxpayer must be aware of the underlying differences in tax treatment across various types of income, expenses, and activities and have some ability to alter the nature of the income or expense to receive the more advantageous tax treatment. What are some common examples of the conversion strategy? Income and deductions with differing character, investments generating income subject to differing tax rates, expenses with differing deductibility, and compensation resulting in taxable versus nontaxable income are all examples of items to which the conversion strategy can apply.

To analyze the benefits of the conversion strategy, you often compare the after-tax rates of return of alternative investments rather than the **before-tax rates of return.** Given a stationary marginal tax rate, you can calculate an investment's after-tax rate of return as follows:

Eq. 3-3

$$\text{After-Tax Rate of Return} = \text{Before-Tax Rate of Return} - (\text{Before-Tax Rate of Return} \times \text{Marginal Tax Rate})$$

which simplifies to

Eq. 3-4

$$\text{After-Tax Rate of Return} = \text{Before-Tax Rate of Return} \times (1 - \text{Marginal Tax Rate})$$

THE KEY FACTS

The Conversion Strategy

- The conversion strategy is based on the understanding that the tax law does not treat all types of income or deductions the same.
- To implement the conversion strategy, taxpayers should be aware of the underlying differences in tax treatment across various types of income, expenses, and activities and have some ability to alter the nature of the income or expense to receive the more advantageous tax treatment.
- The Internal Revenue Code contains specific provisions that prevent the taxpayer from changing the nature of expenses, income, or activities to a more tax-advantaged status.
- Implicit taxes may reduce or eliminate the advantages of conversion strategies.

Example 3-10

Bill is contemplating three different investments, each with the same amount of risk:

1. A high-dividend stock that pays 8.5 percent dividends annually but has no appreciation potential.
2. Taxable corporate bonds that pay 9.7 percent interest annually.
3. Tax-exempt municipal bonds that pay 6 percent interest annually.

Assuming that dividends are taxed at 20 percent and that Bill's marginal tax rate on ordinary income is 37 percent, which investment should Bill choose?

Answer: To answer this question, we must compute Bill's after-tax rate of return for each investment. The after-tax rates of return for the three investments are:

Investment Choice	Computation	After-Tax Rate of Return
High-dividend stock	8.5% × (1 − 20%) =	6.8%
Corporate bond	9.7% × (1 − 37%) =	6.1
Municipal bond	6% × (1 − 0%) =	6.0

Accordingly, Bill should choose the dividend-yielding stock.

What marginal tax rate on ordinary income would make Bill indifferent between the dividend-yielding stock and the corporate bond?

Answer: The dividend-yielding stock has an after-tax rate of return of 6.8 percent. For Bill to be indifferent between this stock and the corporate bond, the corporate bond would need a 6.8 percent after-tax rate of return. We can use Equation 3-4 to solve for the marginal tax rate.

After-Tax Rate of Return = Before-Tax Rate of Return × (1 − Marginal Tax Rate)
6.8% = 9.7% × (1 − Marginal Tax Rate)
Marginal Tax Rate = 29.90%

Let's check this answer:

After-Tax Rate of Return = 9.7% × (1 − 29.90%) = 6.8%

Example 3-10 shows how taxpayers may compare investments when the investment period is one year. However, when taxpayers hold investments for more than a year, they potentially receive benefits from combining the timing strategy and the conversion strategy. First, they may be able to defer recognizing gains on the assets until they sell them—the longer the deferral period, the lower the present value of the tax when taxpayers ultimately sell the assets. Second, they may pay taxes on the gains at preferential rates. For example, taxpayers who invest in a corporate stock (capital asset) that does not pay dividends will defer gain on any stock appreciation until they sell the stock, and because it is a capital asset held longer than one year, their gains will be taxed at the lower preferential tax rate for long-term capital gains. These tax advantages provide taxpayers with a greater after-tax rate of return on these investments than they would obtain from less tax-favored assets that earn equivalent before-tax rates of return. Investors who quickly sell investments pay taxes on gains at higher, ordinary rates and incur significantly greater transaction costs. Nevertheless, taxpayers should balance the tax benefits available for holding assets with the risk that the asset values will have declined by the time they want to sell the assets.

To compare investments with differing time horizons, taxpayers use the annualized after-tax rate of return. In general, the after-tax rate of return on any investment is $(FV/I)^{1/n} - 1$, where FV is the future value after taxes, I is the investment (in after-tax dollars), and n is the number of investment periods.[18]

Example 3-11

What if: Assume Bill decides to purchase Intel stock for $50,000 and hold the shares for five years. If the Intel stock grows at a constant 8 percent before-tax rate and does not pay any dividends, how much cash will Bill accumulate after taxes after five years, assuming a long-term capital gains tax rate of 20 percent?

Answer: $68,773, computed as follows:

Description	Amount	Explanation
(1) Proceeds from sale	$ 73,466	[$50,000 × (1 + 0.08)^5]
(2) Basis in shares	50,000	This is the investment in the shares.
(3) Gain realized on sale	$ 23,466	(1) − (2)
(4) Tax rate on gain	× 20%	Low rate for long-term capital gains*
(5) Tax on gain	$ 4,693	(3) × (4)
After-tax cash after 5 years	**$68,773**	(1) − (5)

*Assumes Bill doesn't have any capital losses.

What annual after-tax rate of return will Bill earn on the money invested?

Answer: 6.58 percent [($68,773/$50,000)$^{1/5}$ − 1].

(*continued on page 3-18*)

[18]Financial calculators designate this calculation as the IRR, or internal rate of return.

What if: What would be the after-tax rate of return if Bill held the stock for 18 years?

Answer: 7.03 percent, computed as follows:

Description	Amount	Explanation
(1) Proceeds from sale	$199,801	[$50,000 × $(1 + 0.08)^{18}$]
(2) Basis in shares	50,000	This is the investment in the shares.
(3) Gain realized on sale	$149,801	(1) – (2)
(4) Tax rate on gain	× 20%	Low rate for long-term capital gains*
(5) Tax on gain	$ 29,960	(3) × (4)
After-tax cash after 18 years	$169,841	(1) – (5)
After-tax rate of return after 18 years	**7.03%**	[$(\$169,841/\$50,000)^{1/18} - 1$]

*Assumes Bill doesn't have any capital losses.

What if: How does Bill's rate of return on the Intel stock held for five years compare to a taxable corporate bond that pays 9 percent interest annually and is held for five years?

Answer: The annualized rate of return on the stock held for five years is 6.58 percent, as shown above. Because the interest on the taxable corporate bond is taxed annually, the annual after-tax rate of return does not change with the investment horizon and will equal 6.1 percent, as shown in Example 3-10 [9.7% × (1 – 37%)]. In this situation, the combined tax benefits from the timing and conversion strategies cause the stock investment to generate a higher annualized after-tax return than the taxable corporate bond even though its pretax return is lower.

Limitations of Conversion Strategies

Like other tax planning strategies, conversion strategies face potential limitations. The Internal Revenue Code itself also contains several specific provisions that prevent the taxpayer from changing the nature of expenses, income, or activities to a more tax-advantaged status, including (among many others) the depreciation recapture rules discussed in the Property Dispositions chapter and the luxury auto depreciation rules discussed in the Property Acquisition and Cost Recovery chapter. In addition, as discussed in the chapter An Introduction to Tax, implicit taxes may reduce or eliminate the advantages of tax-preferred investments (such as municipal bonds or any investment taxed at preferential tax rates) by decreasing their before-tax rates of return. Thus, implicit taxes may reduce the advantages of the conversion strategy.

LO 3-6

ADDITIONAL LIMITATIONS TO TAX PLANNING STRATEGIES: JUDICIALLY BASED DOCTRINES

THE KEY FACTS

Additional Limitations to Tax Planning Strategies: Judicial Doctrines

- Certain judicial doctrines restrict the common tax planning strategies (timing, income shifting, and conversion).
  - The business purpose doctrine allows the IRS to challenge and disallow business expenses for transactions with no underlying business motivation.

(continued)

The IRS has several other doctrines at its disposal for situations in which it expects taxpayer abuse. These doctrines have developed from court decisions and apply across a wide variety of transactions and planning strategies (timing, income shifting, and conversion). The **business purpose doctrine,** for instance, allows the IRS to challenge and disallow business expenses for transactions with no underlying business motivation, such as the travel cost of a spouse accompanying a taxpayer on a business trip. The **step-transaction doctrine** allows the IRS to collapse a series of related transactions into one transaction to determine the tax consequences of the transaction. The **substance-over-form doctrine** allows the IRS to consider the transaction's substance regardless of its form and, where appropriate, to reclassify the transaction according to its substance. Finally, the **economic substance doctrine** requires transactions to meet two criteria to obtain tax benefits. First, a transaction must meaningfully change a taxpayer's economic position (excluding any federal income tax effects). Second, the taxpayer must have a substantial purpose (other than tax avoidance) for the transaction. Economic substance is clearly related to several other doctrines such as the business purpose, step-transaction, and substance-over-form doctrines; however, the economic substance doctrine was incorporated into the Internal Revenue Code as §7701(o). This codification standardizes the requirement for transactions to meet both tests. None of the other doctrines has yet been codified.

The courts have been inconsistent with the application of the tests, with some requiring the transaction to meet either the business purpose or the economic substance requirement and others requiring that it meet both tests. A key part of the codification of the economic substance doctrine is a stiff penalty of 40 percent of the underpayment for failing to meet the requirements—reduced to 20 percent if the taxpayer makes adequate disclosure. In the Tax Compliance, the IRS, and Tax Authorities chapter, we noted that the Internal Revenue Code is the ultimate tax authority. The business purpose, step-transaction, substance-over-form, and economic substance doctrines allow the IRS to state the tax consequences of transactions that follow only the form of the Internal Revenue Code and not the spirit.

You can often assess whether the business purpose, step-transaction, or substance-over-form doctrine applies by using the "smell test." If the transaction "smells bad," one of these doctrines likely applies. (Transactions usually "smell bad" when the primary purpose is to avoid taxes and not to accomplish an independent business objective.) For example, using the substance-over-form doctrine, the IRS would likely reclassify most of the $10,000 paid to Margaret for answering the phone one Saturday afternoon a month as a gift from Mercedes to Margaret (see the earlier discussion of income shifting and transactions between family members), even though the transaction was structured as compensation and Margaret did do some work for her mother. This recharacterization would unwind the income-shifting benefits for the amount considered to be a gift because gifts to family members are not tax deductible. In sum, the *substance* of the transaction must be justifiable, not just the form.

- The step-transaction doctrine allows the IRS to collapse a series of related transactions into one transaction to determine the tax consequences of the transaction.
- The substance-over-form doctrine allows the IRS to reclassify a transaction according to its substance.
- The economic substance doctrine requires transactions to have both an economic effect (aside from the tax effect) and a substantial purpose (aside from reduction of tax liability).

TAX AVOIDANCE VERSUS TAX EVASION

LO 3-7

Each of the general tax planning strategies discussed in this book falls within the confines of legal **tax avoidance.** Tax avoidance has long been endorsed by the courts and even Congress. Recall, for example, that Congress specifically encourages tax avoidance by excluding municipal bond income from taxation, preferentially taxing dividend and capital gains income, and enacting other provisions. Likewise, the courts have often made it quite clear that taxpayers are under no moral obligation to pay more taxes than required by law. As an example, in *Comm'r v. Newman*, which considered a taxpayer's ability to shift income to his children using trusts, Judge Learned Hand included the following statement in his dissenting opinion:

> Over and over again courts have said that there is nothing sinister in so arranging one's affairs as to keep taxes as low as possible. Everybody does so, rich or poor; and all do right, for nobody owes any public duty to pay more than the law demands: taxes are enforced exactions, not voluntary contributions. To demand more in the name of morals is mere cant.[19]

In contrast to tax avoidance, **tax evasion**—that is, the willful attempt to defraud the government—falls outside the confines of legal tax avoidance and thus may land the perpetrator within the confines of a federal prison. (Recall from the Tax Compliance, the IRS, and Tax Authorities chapter that the rewards of tax evasion include stiff monetary penalties and imprisonment.) When does tax avoidance become tax evasion? Very good question. In many cases, a clear distinction exists between avoidance (such as not paying tax on municipal bond interest) and evasion (not paying tax on a $1,000,000 game show prize). In other cases, the line is less clear. In these situations, professional judgment, the use of a smell test, and consideration of the business purpose, step-transaction, substance-over-form, and economic substance doctrines may prove useful.

THE KEY FACTS

Tax Evasion versus Tax Avoidance

- Tax avoidance is the legal act of arranging your transactions to minimize taxes paid.
- Tax evasion is the willful attempt to defraud the government by not paying taxes legally owed.
- Tax evasion falls outside the confines of legal tax avoidance.

[19]*Comm'r of Internal Revenue v. Newman,* 159 F.2d 848, 850–51 (2d Cir. 1947).

TAXES IN THE REAL WORLD Cheating the IRS

Few people like to pay taxes, but most of us do so. Some, however, try to cheat the IRS, including the rich and famous (among them, Mike "The Situation" Sorrentino, Chris Tucker, and rapper DMX). Folks who are trying to escape the reach of the IRS may fail to file tax returns, claim deductions to which they're not entitled, make up fake business expenses, or otherwise try to disguise how much money they really made. These tax evaders cost the government a lot of money. The IRS recently estimated the "tax gap" for 2019 to be around $600 billion. The tax gap represents the difference between taxes paid and taxes owed by law.

The main cause of the tax gap is underreporting income, accounting for $512 billion of the IRS's missing money. Not filing returns and underpaying taxes owed were two other causes. Some of that money fails to make it into the hands of the government through innocent accounting mistakes or the inability of taxpayers to pay even though they want to. But some of it goes missing due to deliberate fraud.

Source: U.S. Treasury, "The American Families Plan Tax Compliance Agenda" (May 2021), https://home.treasury.gov/system/files/136/The-American-Families-Plan-Tax-Compliance-Agenda.pdf

As you might expect, tax evasion is a major problem for the IRS that vigorous prosecution alone has not been able to solve. Is tax evasion a victimless crime? No. Because the federal government must replace lost tax revenues by imposing higher taxes on others, honest taxpayers are the true victims of tax evasion. Currently, the most recent federal government estimates indicate that tax evasion costs the federal government more than $600 billion annually in lost tax revenues. As citizens and residents of the United States, each of us must recognize our obligation to support our country. As future accountants and business professionals, we also must recognize the inherent value of high ethical standards, which call for us to do the right thing in *all* situations. Business professionals have learned over and over that the costs of doing otherwise far exceed any short-term gains.

TAXES IN THE REAL WORLD Religious Beliefs and Taxation

Taxpayers have refused to pay taxes based on religious beliefs. The IRS website includes a page to debunk those ideas (and other "frivolous tax arguments"), stating that the First Amendment (protecting religious freedom) does not provide an excuse to refuse to pay taxes based on religious beliefs. For example, the Third Circuit held that a taxpayer could not refuse to pay taxes because of his religious belief that payment of taxes to fund the military is against the will of God [*Adams v. Comm'r*, 170 F.3d 173 (3d Cir. 1999)].

Similar concepts apply in other countries as well. In July 2019, the Supreme Court of Tasmania ordered Fanny Alida Beerepoot and her brother, Rembertus Cornelis Beerepoot, to pay $2.3 million after losing their case based on the argument that paying income taxes "goes against God's will." As background, the siblings paid taxes until 2011, when they reasoned that "the Almighty God is the supreme law of the land" and that paying taxes to another authority would be considered "rebelling against God and therefore breaking the first commandment." Associate Justice Stephen Holt disagreed and noted that the Bible does not include a passage claiming that "Thou shalt not pay tax" and subsequently ordered the Beerepoots to pay the tax.

Sources: Based on Phoebe Hosier, "Christian Family Who Argued Taxes 'against God's Will' Ordered to Pay $2.3m Bill," *ABC News Australia* (July 17, 2019), www.abc.net.au/news/2019-07-17/christian-family-ordered-to-pay-2.3-million-tax-bill/11318538. See also IRS, "The Truth About Frivolous Tax Arguments—Section I," www.irs.gov/privacy-disclosure/the-truth-about-frivolous-tax-arguments-section-i-d-to-e#D1.

CONCLUSION

In this chapter we discussed three basic tax planning strategies—timing, income shifting, and conversion—and their related limitations. Each of these strategies exploits the variation in taxation across different dimensions. The timing strategy exploits the variation in taxation across time: The real tax costs of income decrease as taxation is deferred; the real tax savings associated with tax deductions increase as tax deductions are accelerated. However, because tax rates may change over time and the tax costs of income and tax savings of deductions vary with tax rates, tax planning should consider the effects of such changes on the timing strategy. The income-shifting strategy exploits the variation in taxation across taxpayers or jurisdictions. The assignment of income doctrine limits aggressive attempts to shift income across taxpayers. In addition, related-person transactions receive close IRS attention given the increased likelihood of taxpayer abuses in these transactions. Finally, the conversion strategy exploits the variation in taxation rates across activities, although implicit taxes may reduce the advantages of this strategy. In addition to limitations specific to each planning strategy, the judicial doctrines of business purpose, step-transaction, and substance-over-form broadly apply to a wide range of transactions and planning strategies.

The timing, income-shifting, and conversion strategies represent the building blocks for the more sophisticated tax strategies that tax professionals employ on a daily basis. Combining an understanding of these basic tax planning strategies with knowledge of our tax law will provide you with the tools necessary to identify, evaluate, and implement tax planning strategies. Throughout the remainder of the text, we will discuss how these strategies can be applied to different transactions.

Summary

Identify the objectives of basic tax planning strategies. **LO 3-1**

- Effective tax planning maximizes the taxpayer's after-tax wealth while achieving the taxpayer's nontax goals. Maximizing after-tax wealth is not necessarily the same as tax minimization. Maximizing after-tax wealth requires one to consider both the tax and nontax costs and benefits of alternative transactions, whereas tax minimization focuses solely on a single cost (i.e., taxes).
- Virtually every transaction involves three parties: the taxpayer, the other transacting party, and the uninvited silent party that specifies the tax consequences of the transaction (i.e., the government). Astute tax planning requires an understanding of the tax and nontax costs from the taxpayer's *and* the other parties' perspectives.

Apply the timing strategy. **LO 3-2**

- One of the cornerstones of basic tax planning involves the idea of *timing*—that is, *when* income is taxed or an expense is deducted affects the associated "real" tax costs or savings. This is true for two reasons. First, the timing of when income is taxed or an expense is deducted affects the *present value* of the taxes paid on income or the tax savings on deductions. Second, the tax costs of income and the tax savings from deductions vary as *tax rates* change.
- When tax rates are constant, tax planners prefer to defer income (i.e., to reduce the present value of taxes paid) and accelerate deductions (i.e., to increase the present value of tax savings). Higher tax rates, higher rates of return, larger transaction amounts, and the ability to accelerate deductions or defer income by two or more years increase the benefits of the timing strategy.
- When tax rates change, the timing strategy requires a little more consideration because the tax costs of income and the tax savings from deductions vary as *tax rates* change. When tax rates are increasing, the taxpayer must calculate the optimal tax strategies for deductions and income. When tax rates are decreasing, the recommendations are clear. Taxpayers should accelerate tax deductions into earlier years and defer taxable income to later years.

- Timing strategies contain several inherent limitations. Generally speaking, whenever a taxpayer must accelerate a cash outflow to accelerate a deduction, the timing strategy will be less beneficial. Tax law generally requires taxpayers to continue their investment in an asset in order to defer income recognition for tax purposes. A deferral strategy may not be optimal if the taxpayer has severe cash flow needs, if continuing the investment would generate a low rate of return compared to other investments, if the current investment would subject the taxpayer to unnecessary risk, and so on. The constructive receipt doctrine, which provides that a taxpayer must recognize income when it is actually or constructively received, also restricts income deferral for cash-method taxpayers.

LO 3-3 Apply the concept of present value to tax planning.

- The concept of present value—also known as the time value of money—basically states that $1 today is worth *more* than $1 in the future. For example, assuming an investor can earn a positive return (e.g., 5 percent after taxes), $1 invested today should be worth $1.05 in one year. Hence, $1 today is equivalent to $1.05 in one year.
- The implication of the time value of money for tax planning is that the timing of a cash inflow or a cash outflow affects the present value of the income or expense.

LO 3-4 Apply the income-shifting strategy.

- The income-shifting strategy exploits the differences in tax rates across taxpayers or jurisdictions. Three of the most common examples of income shifting are high-tax-rate parents shifting income to low-tax-rate children, businesses shifting income to their owners, and taxpayers shifting income from high-tax jurisdictions to low-tax jurisdictions.
- The assignment of income doctrine requires income to be taxed to the taxpayer who actually earns the income. In addition, the IRS closely monitors such related-person transactions—that is, financial activities among family members, among owners and their businesses, or among businesses owned by the same owners. Implicit taxes may also limit the benefits of income shifting via locating in tax-advantaged jurisdictions.

LO 3-5 Apply the conversion strategy.

- Tax law does not treat all types of income or deductions the same. This understanding forms the basis for the conversion strategy—recasting income and expenses to receive the most favorable tax treatment. To implement the conversion strategy, one must be aware of the underlying differences in tax treatment across various types of income, expenses, and activities and have some ability to alter the nature of the income or expense to receive the more advantageous tax treatment.
- Common examples of the conversion strategy include investment planning to invest in assets that generate preferentially taxed income; compensation planning to restructure employee compensation from currently taxable compensation to nontaxable or tax-deferred forms of compensation; and corporate distribution planning to structure corporate distributions to receive the most advantageous tax treatment.
- The Internal Revenue Code contains specific provisions that prevent the taxpayer from changing the nature of expenses, income, or activities to a more tax-advantaged status. Implicit taxes may also reduce or eliminate the advantages of conversion strategies.

LO 3-6 Describe basic judicial doctrines that limit tax planning strategies.

- The constructive receipt doctrine, which may limit the timing strategy, provides that a taxpayer must recognize income when it is actually *or* constructively received. Constructive receipt is deemed to have occurred if the income has been credited to the taxpayer's account or if the income is unconditionally available to the taxpayer, the taxpayer is aware of the income's availability, and there are no restrictions on the taxpayer's control over the income.
- The assignment of income doctrine requires income to be taxed to the taxpayer who actually earns the income. The assignment of income doctrine implies that, in order to shift income to a taxpayer, that taxpayer must actually earn the income.
- The business purpose, step-transaction, and substance-over-form doctrines apply across a wide variety of transactions and planning strategies (timing, income shifting, and conversion).
- The business purpose doctrine allows the IRS to challenge and disallow business expenses for transactions with no underlying business motivation, such as the travel cost of a spouse accompanying a taxpayer on a business trip.
- The step-transaction doctrine allows the IRS to collapse a series of related transactions into one transaction to determine the tax consequences of the transaction.

- The substance-over-form doctrine allows the IRS to consider the transaction's substance regardless of its form and, where appropriate, reclassify the transaction according to its substance.
- The codified economic substance doctrine requires transactions to have a substantial purpose and to meaningfully change a taxpayer's economic position in order for a taxpayer to obtain tax benefits.

Contrast tax avoidance and tax evasion. LO 3-7

- Tax avoidance is the legal act of arranging one's transactions, and so on, to minimize taxes paid. Tax evasion is the willful attempt to defraud the government (i.e., by not paying taxes legally owed). Tax evasion falls outside the confines of legal tax avoidance.
- In many cases, a clear distinction exists between avoidance (e.g., not paying tax on municipal bond interest) and evasion (e.g., not paying tax on a $1,000,000 game show prize). In other cases, the line between tax avoidance and evasion is less clear. In these situations, professional judgment, the use of a "smell test," and consideration of the business purpose, step-transaction, and substance-over-form doctrines may prove useful.

KEY TERMS

after-tax rate of return (3-3)
arm's-length transactions (3-12)
assignment of income doctrine (3-12)
before-tax rates of return (3-16)
business purpose doctrine (3-18)
constructive receipt doctrine (3-10)
discount factor (3-3)
economic substance doctrine (3-18)
implicit taxes (3-15)
present value (3-3)
related-person transaction (3-12)
step-transaction doctrine (3-18)
substance-over-form doctrine (3-18)
tax avoidance (3-19)
tax evasion (3-19)

DISCUSSION QUESTIONS

Discussion Questions are available in Connect®.

1. "The goal of tax planning is to minimize taxes." Explain why this statement is not true. LO 3-1
2. Describe the three parties engaged in every business transaction and how understanding taxes may aid in structuring transactions. LO 3-1
3. In this chapter, we discussed three basic tax planning strategies. What different features of taxation does each of these strategies exploit? LO 3-1
4. What are the two basic timing strategies? What is the intent of each? LO 3-2
5. Why is the timing strategy particularly effective for cash-method taxpayers? LO 3-2
6. What are some common examples of the timing strategy? LO 3-2
7. What factors increase the benefits of accelerating deductions or deferring income? LO 3-2
8. How do changing tax rates affect the timing strategy? What information do you need to determine the appropriate timing strategy when tax rates change? LO 3-2 LO 3-3
9. Describe the ways in which the timing strategy has limitations. LO 3-2 LO 3-6
10. The concept of the time value of money suggests that $1 today is not equal to $1 in the future. Explain why this is true. LO 3-3
11. Why is understanding the time value of money important for tax planning? LO 3-3
12. What two factors increase the difference between present and future values? LO 3-3
13. What factors have to be present for income shifting to be a viable strategy? LO 3-4
14. Name three common types of income shifting. LO 3-4
15. What are some ways that a parent could effectively shift income to a child? What are some of the disadvantages of these methods? LO 3-4
16. What is the key factor in shifting income from a business to its owners? What are some methods of shifting income in this context? LO 3-4
17. Explain why paying dividends is not an effective way to shift income from a corporation to its owners. LO 3-4

LO 3-5 18. What are some of the common examples of the conversion strategy?

LO 3-5 19. What is needed to implement the conversion strategy?

LO 3-5 20. Explain how implicit taxes may limit the benefits of the conversion strategy.

LO 3-5 LO 3-6 planning 21. Clark owns stock in BCS Corporation that he purchased in January of the current year. The stock has appreciated significantly during the year. It is now December of the current year, and Clark is deciding whether or not he should sell the stock. What tax and nontax factors should Clark consider before making the decision on whether to sell the stock now?

LO 3-5 22. Do after-tax rates of return for investments in either interest- or dividend-paying securities increase with the length of the investment? Why or why not?

LO 3-5 23. Cameron purchases stock in both Corporation X and Corporation Y. Neither corporation pays dividends. The stocks both earn an identical before-tax rate of return. Cameron sells stock in Corporation X after three years, and he sells the stock in Corporation Y after five years. Which investment likely earned a greater after-tax return? Why?

LO 3-5 24. Under what circumstances would you expect the after-tax return from an investment in a capital asset to approach that of tax-exempt assets (assuming equal before-tax rates of return)?

LO 3-5 planning 25. Laurie is thinking about investing in one or several of the following investment options:

- Corporate bonds (ordinary interest paid annually)
- Dividend-paying stock (qualified dividends)
- Life insurance (tax-exempt)
- Savings account
- Growth stock

a) Assuming all of the options earn similar returns before taxes, rank Laurie's investment options from highest to lowest according to their after-tax returns.

b) Which of the investments employ the deferral and/or conversion tax planning strategies?

c) How does the time period of the investment affect the returns from these alternatives?

d) How do these alternative investments differ in terms of their nontax characteristics?

LO 3-5 26. What is an "implicit tax," and how does it affect a taxpayer's decision to purchase municipal bonds?

LO 3-6 27. Several judicial doctrines limit basic tax planning strategies. What are they? Which planning strategies do they limit?

LO 3-6 28. What is the constructive receipt doctrine? What types of taxpayers does this doctrine generally affect? For what tax planning strategy is the constructive receipt doctrine a potential limitation?

LO 3-6 29. Explain the assignment of income doctrine. In what situations would this doctrine potentially apply?

LO 3-6 30. Relative to arm's-length transactions, why do related-person transactions receive more IRS scrutiny?

LO 3-6 31. Describe the business purpose, step-transaction, and substance-over-form doctrines. What types of tax planning strategies may these doctrines inhibit?

LO 3-7 32. What is the difference between tax avoidance and tax evasion?

LO 3-7 33. What are the rewards of tax avoidance? What are the rewards of tax evasion?

LO 3-7 34. "Tax avoidance is discouraged by the courts and Congress." Is this statement true or false? Please explain.

PROBLEMS

Select problems are available in Connect®.

35. Yong recently paid his accountant $10,000 for elaborate tax planning strategies that exploit the timing strategy. Assuming this is an election year and there could be a power shift in the White House and Congress, what is a potential risk associated with Yong's strategies? LO 3-2 planning

36. Billups, a physician and cash-method taxpayer, is new to the concept of tax planning and recently learned of the timing strategy. To implement the timing strategy, Billups plans to establish a new policy that allows all his clients to wait two years to pay their co-pays. Assume that Billups does not expect his marginal tax rates to change. What is wrong with his strategy? LO 3-2 LO 3-3 planning

37. Tesha works for a company that pays a year-end bonus in January of each year (instead of December of the preceding year) to allow employees to defer the bonus income. Assume Congress recently passed tax legislation that decreases individual tax rates as of next year. Does this increase or decrease the benefits of the bonus deferral this year? What if Congress passed legislation that increased tax rates next year? Should Tesha ask the company to change its policy this year? What additional information do you need to answer this question? LO 3-2 LO 3-3 planning

38. Isabel, a calendar-year taxpayer, uses the cash method of accounting for her sole proprietorship. In late December she received a $20,000 bill from her accountant for consulting services related to her small business. Isabel can pay the $20,000 bill anytime before January 30 of next year without penalty. Assume her marginal tax rate is 37 percent this year and next year, and that she can earn an after-tax rate of return of 12 percent on her investments. When should she pay the $20,000 bill—this year or next? LO 3-2 LO 3-3 planning

39. Using the facts from the previous problem, how would your answer change if Isabel's after-tax rate of return were 8 percent? LO 3-2 LO 3-3 planning

40. Manny, a calendar-year taxpayer, uses the cash method of accounting for his sole proprietorship. In late December he performed $20,000 of legal services for a client. Manny typically requires his clients to pay his bills immediately upon receipt. Assume Manny's marginal tax rate is 37 percent this year and next year, and that he can earn an after-tax rate of return of 12 percent on his investments. Should Manny send his client the bill in December or January? LO 3-2 LO 3-3 planning

41. Using the facts from the previous problem, how would your answer change if Manny's after-tax rate of return were 8 percent? LO 3-2 LO 3-3 planning

42. Reese, a calendar-year taxpayer, uses the cash method of accounting for her sole proprietorship. In late December, she received a $20,000 bill from her accountant for consulting services related to her small business. Reese can pay the $20,000 bill anytime before January 30 of next year without penalty. Assume Reese's marginal tax rate is 32 percent this year and will be 37 percent next year, and that she can earn an after-tax rate of return of 12 percent on her investments. When should she pay the $20,000 bill—this year or next? LO 3-2 LO 3-3 planning

43. Using the facts from the previous problem, when should Reese pay the bill if she expects her marginal tax rate to be 35 percent next year? 24 percent next year? LO 3-2 LO 3-3 planning

44. Hank, a calendar-year taxpayer, uses the cash method of accounting for his sole proprietorship. In late December, he performed $20,000 of legal services for a client. Hank typically requires his clients to pay his bills immediately upon receipt. Assume his marginal tax rate is 32 percent this year and will be 37 percent next year, and that he can earn an after-tax rate of return of 12 percent on his investments. Should Hank send his client the bill in December or January? LO 3-2 LO 3-3 planning

LO 3-2 LO 3-3 planning

45. Using the facts from the previous problem, when should Hank send the bill if he expects his marginal tax rate to be 35 percent next year? 24 percent next year?

LO 3-3

46. Geraldo recently won a lottery and chose to receive $100,000 today instead of an equivalent amount in 10 years, computed using an 8 percent rate of return. Today, he learned that interest rates are expected to increase in the future. Is this good news for Geraldo given his decision?

LO 3-3 planning

47. Assume Rafael can earn an 8 percent after-tax rate of return. Would he prefer $1,000 today or $1,500 in five years?

LO 3-3 planning

48. Assume Ellina earns a 10 percent after-tax rate of return and that she owes a friend $1,200. Would she prefer to pay the friend $1,200 today or $1,750 in four years?

LO 3-3 planning

49. Jonah has the choice of paying Rita $10,000 today or $40,000 in 10 years. Assume Jonah can earn a 12 percent after-tax rate of return. Which should he choose?

LO 3-3 planning

50. Bob's Lottery Inc. has decided to offer winners a choice of $100,000 in 10 years or some amount currently. Assume that Bob's Lottery Inc. earns a 10 percent after-tax rate of return. What amount should Bob's offer lottery winners currently in order to be indifferent between the two choices?

LO 3-4 planning

51. Tawana owns and operates a sole proprietorship and has a 37 percent marginal tax rate. She provides her son, Jonathon, $8,000 a year for college expenses. Jonathon works as a pizza delivery person every fall and has a marginal tax rate of 15 percent.
   a) What could Tawana do to reduce her family tax burden?
   b) How much pretax income does it currently take Tawana to generate the $8,000 (after taxes) given to Jonathon?
   c) If Jonathon worked for his mother's sole proprietorship, what salary would she have to pay him to generate $8,000 after taxes (ignoring any Social Security, Medicare, or self-employment tax issues)?
   d) How much money would the strategy in part (c) save?

LO 3-4 planning

52. Moana is a single taxpayer who operates a sole proprietorship. She expects her taxable income next year to be $250,000, of which $200,000 is attributed to her sole proprietorship. Moana is contemplating incorporating her sole proprietorship. Using the single individual tax brackets and the corporate tax rate in Appendix C, find out how much current tax this strategy could save Moana (ignore any Social Security, Medicare, or self-employment tax issues). How much income should be left in the corporation?

LO 3-4 planning

53. Orie and Jane, husband and wife, operate a sole proprietorship. They expect their taxable income next year to be $450,000, of which $250,000 is attributed to the sole proprietorship. Orie and Jane are contemplating incorporating their sole proprietorship. Using the married-joint tax brackets and the corporate tax rate in Appendix C, find out how much current tax this strategy could save Orie and Jane. How much income should be left in the corporation?

LO 3-4 planning

54. Hyundai is considering opening a plant in two neighboring states. One state has a corporate tax rate of 10 percent. If operated in this state, the plant is expected to generate $1,000,000 pretax profit. The other state has a corporate tax rate of 2 percent. If operated in this state, the plant is expected to generate $930,000 of pretax profit. Which state should Hyundai choose? Why do you think the plant in the state with a lower tax rate would produce a lower before-tax income?

LO 3-4 LO 3-6 planning

55. Bendetta, a high-tax-rate taxpayer, owns several rental properties and would like to shift some income to her daughter, Jenine. Bendetta instructs her tenants to send their rent checks to Jenine so Jenine can report the rental income. Will this shift the income from Bendetta to Jenine? Why or why not?

56. Using the facts in the previous problem, what are some ways that Bendetta could shift some of the rental income to Jenine? What are the disadvantages associated with these income-shifting strategies?

LO 3-4 LO 3-6 planning

57. Daniel is considering selling two stocks that have not fared well over recent years. A friend recently informed Daniel that one of his stocks has a special designation, which allows him to treat a loss up to $50,000 on this stock as an ordinary loss rather than the typical capital loss. Daniel figures that he has a loss of $60,000 on each stock. If Daniel's marginal tax rate is 35 percent and he has $120,000 of other capital gains (taxed at 15 percent), what is the tax savings from the special tax treatment?

LO 3-5 planning

58. Hui is currently considering investing in municipal bonds that earn 6 percent interest, or in taxable bonds issued by the Coca-Cola Company that pay 8 percent. If Hui's tax rate is 22 percent, which bond should Hui choose? Which bond should Hui choose if the tax rate is 32 percent? At what tax rate would Hui be indifferent between the bonds? What strategy is this decision based upon?

LO 3-5 planning

59. Helen holds 1,000 shares of Fizbo Inc. stock that she purchased 11 months ago. The stock has done very well and has appreciated $20/share since Helen bought the stock. When sold, the stock will be taxed at capital gains rates (the long-term rate is 15 percent and the short-term rate is the taxpayer's marginal tax rate). If Helen's marginal tax rate is 35 percent, how much would she save by holding the stock an additional month before selling? What might prevent Helen from waiting to sell?

LO 3-5 planning

60. Anne's marginal income tax rate is 32 percent. She purchases a corporate bond for $10,000 and the maturity, or face value, of the bond is $10,000. If the bond pays 5 percent per year before taxes, what is Anne's annual after-tax rate of return from the bond if the bond matures in 1 year? What is her annual after-tax rate of return if the bond matures in 10 years?

LO 3-5

61. Irene is saving for a new car she hopes to purchase either four or six years from now. Irene invests $10,000 in a growth stock that does not pay dividends and expects a 6 percent annual before-tax return (the investment is tax deferred). When she cashes in the investment after either four or six years, she expects the applicable marginal tax rate on long-term capital gains to be 25 percent.

LO 3-5 planning

a) What will be the value of this investment four years from now? Six years from now?
b) When Irene sells the investment, how much cash will she have after taxes to purchase the new car (four and six years from now)?

62. Komiko Tanaka invests $12,000 in LymaBean, Inc. LymaBean does not pay any dividends. Komiko projects that her investment will generate a 10 percent before-tax rate of return. She plans to invest for the long term.

LO 3-5 planning

a) How much cash will Komiko retain, after taxes, if she holds the investment for five years and then sells it when the long-term capital gains rate is 15 percent?
b) What is Komiko's after-tax rate of return on her investment in part (a)?
c) How much cash will Komiko retain, after taxes, if she holds the investment for five years and then sells when the long-term capital gains rate is 25 percent?
d) What is Komiko's after-tax rate of return on her investment in part (c)?
e) How much cash will Komiko retain, after taxes, if she holds the investment for 15 years and then sells when the long-term capital gains rate is 15 percent?
f) What is Komiko's after-tax rate of return on her investment in part (e)?

LO 3-5 planning

63. Alan inherited $100,000 with the stipulation that he "invest it to financially benefit his family." Alan and his wife Alice decided they would invest the inheritance to help them accomplish two financial goals: purchasing a Park City vacation home and saving for their son Cooper's education.

	Vacation Home	Cooper's Education
Initial investment	$50,000	$50,000
Investment horizon	5 years	18 years

Alan and Alice have a marginal income tax rate of 32 percent (capital gains rate of 15 percent) and have decided to investigate the following investment opportunities.

	5 Years	Annual After-Tax Rate of Return	18 Years	Annual After-Tax Rate of Return
Corporate bonds (ordinary interest taxed annually)	5.75%		4.75%	
Dividend-paying stock (no appreciation and dividends are taxed at 15%)	3.50%		3.50%	
Growth stock	*FV* = $65,000		*FV* = $140,000	
Municipal bond (tax-exempt)	3.20%		3.10%	

Complete the two Annual After-Tax Rate of Return columns for each investment and provide investment recommendations for Alan and Alice.

LO 3-7

64. Duff is really interested in decreasing their tax liability and tends to be somewhat tax aggressive. A friend of a friend told Duff that cash transactions are more difficult for the IRS to identify and, thus, tax. Duff is contemplating using this "strategy" of not reporting cash collected in their business to minimize the tax liability. Is this tax planning? What are the risks with this strategy?

LO 3-7

65. Using the facts from the previous problem, how would your answer change if, instead, Duff adopted the cash method of accounting to allow them to better control the timing of their cash receipts and disbursements?

LO 3-2 LO 3-4 LO 3-5 planning research

66. Using an available tax service or the Internet, identify three basic tax planning ideas or tax tips suggested for year-end tax planning. Which basic tax strategy from this chapter does each planning idea employ?

LO 3-7 research

67. Jayanna, an advertising consultant, is contemplating instructing some of her clients to pay her in cash so that she does not have to report the income on her tax return. Use an available tax service to identify the three basic elements of tax evasion and penalties associated with tax evasion. Write a memo to Jayanna explaining tax evasion and the risks associated with her actions.

LO 3-7 research

68. Using the IRS website (www.irs.gov/uac/The-Tax-Gap), how large is the current estimated "tax gap" (i.e., the amount of tax underpaid by taxpayers annually) for years 2011–2013? What group of taxpayers represents the largest "contributors" to the tax gap?

UWorld | ROGER CPA Review

UWorld Roger CPA Review

Sample CPA Exam questions from Roger CPA Review are available in Connect as support for the topics in this text. These Multiple Choice Questions and Task-Based Simulations include expert-written explanations and solutions and provide a starting point for students to become familiar with the content and functionality of the actual CPA Exam.

chapter

4 Individual Income Tax Overview, Dependents, and Filing Status

Learning Objectives

Upon completing this chapter, you should be able to:

LO 4-1 Describe the formula for calculating an individual taxpayer's taxes due or refund.

LO 4-2 Explain the requirements for determining who qualifies as a taxpayer's dependent.

LO 4-3 Determine a taxpayer's filing status.

kate_sept2004/E+/Getty Images

Tara Hall just completed a unit on individual taxation in her undergraduate tax class at South Dakota State University. She was excited to share her knowledge with her parents, Rodney and Anita Hall, as they prepared their tax return. Rodney and Anita have been married for over 25 years, and they have filed a joint tax return each year. The Halls' 12-year-old son Braxton lives at home, but Tara, who is 21, lives nearby in the university dorms. Further, in January of this year, Rodney's younger brother Shawn moved in with the Halls. The Halls expect Shawn to live with them for at least one year and maybe two. Every year Rodney and Anita use tax-preparation software to complete their tax return, but they are not always sure they understand the final result. This year, with Tara's help, they hope that will change. ■

Storyline Summary

Taxpayers:	Rodney (he/him/his) and Anita (she/her/hers) Hall
Other household members:	Tara (she/her/hers), their 21-year-old daughter, and Braxton (he/him/his), their 12-year-old son. Shawn (he/him/his), Rodney's brother, also lives with the Halls.
Location:	Brookings, South Dakota
Employment status:	Rodney is a manager for a regional grocery chain. His annual salary is $74,000. Anita works as a purchasing-card auditor at South Dakota State University. Her annual salary is $56,000.
Current situation:	Determining their tax liability

This chapter provides an overview of individual income taxation. Other chapters provide more depth on individual income tax topics. Here we introduce the individual income tax formula, summarize the formula's components, describe requirements for determining who qualifies as a taxpayer's dependent, and explain how to determine a taxpayer's filing status. Other chapters explain gross income, identify deductions, and explain how to compute an individual's income tax liability.

LO 4-1

THE INDIVIDUAL INCOME TAX FORMULA

Taxable income is the the tax base for the individual income tax. Exhibit 4-1 presents a simplified formula for calculating taxable income.

EXHIBIT 4-1 Individual Income Tax Formula

	Gross income
Minus:	For AGI (above the line) deductions
Equals:	Adjusted gross income (AGI)
Minus:	From AGI (below the line) deductions:
	(1) Greater of
	(a) Standard deduction or
	(b) Itemized deductions
	(2) Charitable contribution deduction for taxpayers who do not itemize deductions*
	(3) Deduction for qualified business income
Equals:	Taxable income
Times:	Tax rates
Equals:	Income tax liability
Plus:	Other taxes
Equals:	Total tax
Minus:	Credits
Minus:	Prepayments
Equals:	Taxes due or (refund)

*Charitable contribution deduction applies for 2021 but had not been extended beyond 2021 at the time we went to press.

Each year, individuals file tax returns to report their taxable income to the Internal Revenue Service.[1] The individual income tax formula is embedded in pages 1 and 2 of the individual income tax return Form 1040, the form individuals generally use to report their taxable income.[2] Exhibit 4-2 presents pages 1, 2, and Schedule 1 of Form 1040. Line 11 on page 1 of Form 1040 is **adjusted gross income (AGI),** an important reference point in the income tax formula, and line 15 on page 1 is taxable income. Let's look at the components of the individual tax formula and provide a brief description of each of the key elements.

Gross Income

The U.S. tax laws are based on the **all-inclusive income concept.** Under this concept, **gross income** generally includes all **realized income** from *whatever source derived.*[3] Realized income is generally income generated in a transaction with a second party in which there is a measurable change in property rights between parties (e.g., appreciation in a stock investment would not represent realized income until the taxpayer sells the stock).

Certain tax provisions allow taxpayers to permanently exclude specific types of realized income from gross income (excluded income items are never taxable), and other provisions allow taxpayers to defer including certain types of realized income items in gross income until a subsequent year (deferred income items are included in gross

[1]See Exhibit 1 in the Tax Compliance, the IRS, and Tax Authorities chapter for a description of who must file a tax return. We use 2021 forms in this text because 2022 forms were unavailable at press time.

[2]To see the 1913 version of the individual tax return form, go to www.irs.gov/pub/irs-utl/1913.pdf.

[3]§61(a).

EXHIBIT 4-2 2021 Form 1040, pages 1, 2, and Schedule 1. The 2022 tax forms were unavailable at press time.

Form **1040** Department of the Treasury—Internal Revenue Service (99) **U.S. Individual Income Tax Return** **2021** OMB No. 1545-0074 IRS Use Only—Do not write or staple in this space.

Filing Status Check only one box. ☐ Single ☐ Married filing jointly ☐ Married filing separately (MFS) ☐ Head of household (HOH) ☐ Qualifying widow(er) (QW)

If you checked the MFS box, enter the name of your spouse. If you checked the HOH or QW box, enter the child's name if the qualifying person is a child but not your dependent ▶

Your first name and middle initial	Last name	Your social security number
If joint return, spouse's first name and middle initial	Last name	Spouse's social security number

Home address (number and street). If you have a P.O. box, see instructions.			Apt. no.
City, town, or post office. If you have a foreign address, also complete spaces below.	State	ZIP code	
Foreign country name	Foreign province/state/county	Foreign postal code	

Presidential Election Campaign Check here if you, or your spouse if filing jointly, want $3 to go to this fund. Checking a box below will not change your tax or refund. ☐ You ☐ Spouse

At any time during 2021, did you receive, sell, exchange, or otherwise dispose of any financial interest in any virtual currency? ☐ Yes ☐ No

Standard Deduction Someone can claim: ☐ You as a dependent ☐ Your spouse as a dependent
☐ Spouse itemizes on a separate return or you were a dual-status alien

Age/Blindness You: ☐ Were born before January 2, 1957 ☐ Are blind **Spouse:** ☐ Was born before January 2, 1957 ☐ Is blind

Dependents (see instructions): If more than four dependents, see instructions and check here ▶ ☐

(1) First name	Last name	(2) Social security number	(3) Relationship to you	(4) ✔ if qualifies for (see instructions): Child tax credit	Credit for other dependents
				☐	☐
				☐	☐
				☐	☐
				☐	☐

Attach Sch. B if required.

Line	Description		Line	Description	Box
1	Wages, salaries, tips, etc. Attach Form(s) W-2				1
2a	Tax-exempt interest	2a	b	Taxable interest	2b
3a	Qualified dividends	3a	b	Ordinary dividends	3b
4a	IRA distributions	4a	b	Taxable amount	4b
5a	Pensions and annuities	5a	b	Taxable amount	5b
6a	Social security benefits	6a	b	Taxable amount	6b
7	Capital gain or (loss). Attach Schedule D if required. If not required, check here ▶ ☐				7
8	Other income from Schedule 1, line 10				8
9	Add lines 1, 2b, 3b, 4b, 5b, 6b, 7, and 8. This is your **total income** ▶				9
10	Adjustments to income from Schedule 1, line 26				10
11	Subtract line 10 from line 9. This is your **adjusted gross income** ▶				11
12a	**Standard deduction or itemized deductions** (from Schedule A)	12a			
b	Charitable contributions if you take the standard deduction (see instructions)	12b			
c	Add lines 12a and 12b				12c
13	Qualified business income deduction from Form 8995 or Form 8995-A				13
14	Add lines 12c and 13				14
15	**Taxable income.** Subtract line 14 from line 11. If zero or less, enter -0-				15

Standard Deduction for—
- Single or Married filing separately, $12,550
- Married filing jointly or Qualifying widow(er), $25,100
- Head of household, $18,800
- If you checked any box under *Standard Deduction,* see instructions.

For Disclosure, Privacy Act, and Paperwork Reduction Act Notice, see separate instructions. Cat. No. 11320B Form **1040** (2021)

Form 1040 (2021) Page **2**

Line	Description		Box
16	**Tax** (see instructions). Check if any from Form(s): 1 ☐ 8814 2 ☐ 4972 3 ☐ ______		16
17	Amount from Schedule 2, line 3		17
18	Add lines 16 and 17		18
19	Nonrefundable child tax credit or credit for other dependents from Schedule 8812		19
20	Amount from Schedule 3, line 8		20
21	Add lines 19 and 20		21
22	Subtract line 21 from line 18. If zero or less, enter -0-		22
23	Other taxes, including self-employment tax, from Schedule 2, line 21		23
24	Add lines 22 and 23. This is your **total tax** ▶		24
25	Federal income tax withheld from:		
a	Form(s) W-2	25a	
b	Form(s) 1099	25b	
c	Other forms (see instructions)	25c	
d	Add lines 25a through 25c		25d
26	2021 estimated tax payments and amount applied from 2020 return		26
27a	Earned income credit (EIC)	27a	
	Check here if you were born after January 1, 1998, and before January 2, 2004, and you satisfy all the other requirements for taxpayers who are at least age 18, to claim the EIC. See instructions ▶ ☐		
b	Nontaxable combat pay election	27b	
c	Prior year (2019) earned income	27c	
28	Refundable child tax credit or additional child tax credit from Schedule 8812	28	
29	American opportunity credit from Form 8863, line 8	29	
30	Recovery rebate credit. See instructions	30	
31	Amount from Schedule 3, line 15	31	
32	Add lines 27a and 28 through 31. These are your **total other payments and refundable credits** ▶		32
33	Add lines 25d, 26, and 32. These are your **total payments** ▶		33

If you have a qualifying child, attach Sch. EIC.

Refund

Line	Description		Box
34	If line 33 is more than line 24, subtract line 24 from line 33. This is the amount you **overpaid**		34
35a	Amount of line 34 you want **refunded to you.** If Form 8888 is attached, check here ▶ ☐		35a
▶b	Routing number ▶c Type: ☐ Checking ☐ Savings		
▶d	Account number		
36	Amount of line 34 you want **applied to your 2022 estimated tax** ▶	36	

Direct deposit? See instructions.

Amount You Owe

Line	Description		Box
37	**Amount you owe.** Subtract line 33 from line 24. For details on how to pay, see instructions ▶		37
38	Estimated tax penalty (see instructions) ▶	38	

Third Party Designee Do you want to allow another person to discuss this return with the IRS? See instructions ▶ ☐ **Yes.** Complete below. ☐ **No**

Designee's name ▶ Phone no. ▶ Personal identification number (PIN) ▶

Sign Here Under penalties of perjury, I declare that I have examined this return and accompanying schedules and statements, and to the best of my knowledge and belief, they are true, correct, and complete. Declaration of preparer (other than taxpayer) is based on all information of which preparer has any knowledge.

Joint return? See instructions. Keep a copy for your records.

Your signature	Date	Your occupation	If the IRS sent you an Identity Protection PIN, enter it here (see inst.) ▶
Spouse's signature. If a joint return, **both** must sign.	Date	Spouse's occupation	If the IRS sent your spouse an Identity Protection PIN, enter it here (see inst.) ▶
Phone no.	Email address		

Paid Preparer Use Only

Preparer's name	Preparer's signature	Date	PTIN	Check if: ☐ Self-employed
Firm's name ▶			Phone no.	
Firm's address ▶			Firm's EIN ▶	

Go to *www.irs.gov/Form1040* for instructions and the latest information. Form **1040** (2021)

EXHIBIT 4-2 2021 Form 1040, pages 1, 2, and Schedule 1 (*continued*)

SCHEDULE 1
(Form 1040)
Department of the Treasury
Internal Revenue Service

Additional Income and Adjustments to Income

▶ Attach to Form 1040, 1040-SR, or 1040-NR.
▶ Go to *www.irs.gov/Form1040* for instructions and the latest information.

OMB No. 1545-0074
2021
Attachment Sequence No. **01**

Name(s) shown on Form 1040, 1040-SR, or 1040-NR | **Your social security number**

Part I Additional Income

1	Taxable refunds, credits, or offsets of state and local income taxes			1	
2a	Alimony received			2a	
b	Date of original divorce or separation agreement (see instructions) ▶				
3	Business income or (loss). Attach Schedule C			3	
4	Other gains or (losses). Attach Form 4797			4	
5	Rental real estate, royalties, partnerships, S corporations, trusts, etc. Attach Schedule E			5	
6	Farm income or (loss). Attach Schedule F			6	
7	Unemployment compensation			7	
8	Other income:				
a	Net operating loss	8a	( )		
b	Gambling income	8b			
c	Cancellation of debt	8c			
d	Foreign earned income exclusion from Form 2555	8d	( )		
e	Taxable Health Savings Account distribution	8e			
f	Alaska Permanent Fund dividends	8f			
g	Jury duty pay	8g			
h	Prizes and awards	8h			
i	Activity not engaged in for profit income	8i			
j	Stock options	8j			
k	Income from the rental of personal property if you engaged in the rental for profit but were not in the business of renting such property	8k			
l	Olympic and Paralympic medals and USOC prize money (see instructions)	8l			
m	Section 951(a) inclusion (see instructions)	8m			
n	Section 951A(a) inclusion (see instructions)	8n			
o	Section 461(l) excess business loss adjustment	8o			
p	Taxable distributions from an ABLE account (see instructions)	8p			
z	Other income. List type and amount ▶	8z			
9	Total other income. Add lines 8a through 8z			9	
10	Combine lines 1 through 7 and 9. Enter here and on Form 1040, 1040-SR, or 1040-NR, line 8			10	

For Paperwork Reduction Act Notice, see your tax return instructions. Cat. No. 71479F **Schedule 1 (Form 1040) 2021**

EXHIBIT 4-2 2021 Form 1040, pages 1, 2, and Schedule 1 (*continued*)

Schedule 1 (Form 1040) 2021 Page 2

Part II Adjustments to Income

11	Educator expenses			11	
12	Certain business expenses of reservists, performing artists, and fee-basis government officials. Attach Form 2106			12	
13	Health savings account deduction. Attach Form 8889			13	
14	Moving expenses for members of the Armed Forces. Attach Form 3903			14	
15	Deductible part of self-employment tax. Attach Schedule SE			15	
16	Self-employed SEP, SIMPLE, and qualified plans			16	
17	Self-employed health insurance deduction			17	
18	Penalty on early withdrawal of savings			18	
19a	Alimony paid			19a	
b	Recipient's SSN ▶				
c	Date of original divorce or separation agreement (see instructions) ▶				
20	IRA deduction			20	
21	Student loan interest deduction			21	
22	Reserved for future use			22	
23	Archer MSA deduction			23	
24	Other adjustments:				
a	Jury duty pay (see instructions)	24a			
b	Deductible expenses related to income reported on line 8k from the rental of personal property engaged in for profit	24b			
c	Nontaxable amount of the value of Olympic and Paralympic medals and USOC prize money reported on line 8l	24c			
d	Reforestation amortization and expenses	24d			
e	Repayment of supplemental unemployment benefits under the Trade Act of 1974	24e			
f	Contributions to section 501(c)(18)(D) pension plans	24f			
g	Contributions by certain chaplains to section 403(b) plans	24g			
h	Attorney fees and court costs for actions involving certain unlawful discrimination claims (see instructions)	24h			
i	Attorney fees and court costs you paid in connection with an award from the IRS for information you provided that helped the IRS detect tax law violations	24i			
j	Housing deduction from Form 2555	24j			
k	Excess deductions of section 67(e) expenses from Schedule K-1 (Form 1041)	24k			
z	Other adjustments. List type and amount ▶	24z			
25	Total other adjustments. Add lines 24a through 24z			25	
26	Add lines 11 through 23 and 25. These are your **adjustments to income.** Enter here and on Form 1040 or 1040-SR, line 10, or Form 1040-NR, line 10a			26	

Schedule 1 (Form 1040) 2021

Source: irs.gov.

income in a later year). Realized income items that taxpayers permanently exclude from taxation are referred to as **exclusions.** Realized income items that taxpayers include in gross income in a subsequent year are called **deferrals.** Exhibit 4-3 provides a partial listing of common income items included in gross income, their character (discussed below), and where in the text we provide more detail on each income item. Exhibit 4-4 provides a partial listing of common exclusions and deferrals and indicates where in the text we discuss each in more detail.

Character of Income

While gross income increases taxable income dollar for dollar, certain types of gross income are treated differently than other types of gross income for purposes of computing a taxpayer's taxable income and income tax liability. For example, one type of income

EXHIBIT 4-3 Partial Listing of Common Income Items

Income Item	Character	Discussed in More Detail in These Chapters
Compensation for services including fringe benefits	Ordinary	Gross Income and Exclusions and Compensation
Business income	Ordinary	Business Income, Deductions, and Accounting Methods
Gains from selling property	Ordinary or capital[4]	Investments and Property Dispositions
Interest and dividends	Ordinary or qualified dividend	Gross Income and Exclusions and Investments
Rents and royalties	Ordinary	Gross Income and Exclusions, Investments, and Tax Consequences of Home Ownership
Alimony received (pre-2019 decree) and annuities	Ordinary	Gross Income and Exclusions
Retirement income	Ordinary	Retirement Savings and Deferred Compensation
Income from the discharge of indebtedness	Ordinary	Gross Income and Exclusions

EXHIBIT 4-4 Partial Listing of Common Exclusions and Deferrals

Exclusion or Deferral Item	Exclusion or Deferral	Discussed in These Chapters
Interest income from municipal bonds	Exclusion	Gross Income and Exclusions
Gifts and inheritance	Exclusion	Gross Income and Exclusions
Alimony received (post-2018 decree)	Exclusion	Gross Income and Exclusions
Gain on sale of personal residence	Exclusion	Gross Income and Exclusions and Tax Consequences of Home Ownership
Life insurance proceeds	Exclusion	Gross Income and Exclusions
Installment sale	Deferral	Property Dispositions
Like-kind exchange	Deferral	Property Dispositions

may be taxed at a different rate than another type of income. The *type* of income is commonly referred to as the **character of income.** The most common characters of income are as follows:

- Ordinary: This is income or loss that is taxed at the ordinary rates provided in the tax rate schedules in Appendix C, or that offsets income taxed at these rates, and is not capital in character.
- Capital: These are gains or losses on the disposition or sale of capital assets. In general, capital assets are all assets *other* than:
  1. Accounts receivable from the sale of goods or services.
  2. Inventory and other assets held for sale in the ordinary course of business.
  3. Assets used in a trade or business, including supplies.[5]

  Thus, capital assets include nonbusiness assets such as personal-use automobiles or personal residences and assets held for investment such as stocks and bonds.

  The tax consequences of recognized capital gains and losses for the year depend on how long the taxpayer has owned the capital assets before selling them and the

[4]Dispositions of assets used in a trade or business for more than a year generate an intermediate character of income called §1231 gain or loss. Ultimately, §1231 gains and losses are treated as either ordinary or capital on the tax return.

[5]§1221(a).

outcome of a specific netting process. The capital gain or loss from the sale of a particular capital asset is long-term when the taxpayer has owned the asset for *more than a year* before selling and it is short-term when the taxpayer has owned the asset for *one year or less* before selling. At the end of the year, taxpayers sort their capital gains from all capital asset sales into long-term and short-term categories. Next, they combine the gains and losses within the long-term and within the short-term groups. This results in a net gain or a net loss in both the long-term and short-term groups.[6] If both the long-term and short-term categories yield gains, the netting process is complete. Otherwise, the taxpayer combines the long-term and short-term outcomes to yield a final net gain or net loss that will be either long-term or short-term, depending on whether the long-term or short-term amount is greater.

With the outcome of the netting process, taxpayers may deduct up to $3,000 of net capital loss for the year ($1,500 for married taxpayers filing separately). Net capital losses are deducted for AGI (see discussion of for AGI deductions in the next section). Net losses in excess of the limitation (i.e., nondeductible losses for the year) carry over and enter the netting process in the next year.[7] Net short-term capital gains are taxed at the same tax rate as ordinary income. Net long-term capital gains (called **net capital gains**) are taxed at rates that are lower than ordinary rates. The rates for net capital gains are provided in Appendix C in the "Tax Rates for Net Capital Gains and Qualified Dividends" rate schedule. As reflected in the schedule, the gain may be taxed at 0, 15, or 20 percent.[8] The specified rate applies to the net capital gains (and qualified dividends—discussed next) that fall within the range of taxable income specified in the rate schedule (net capital gains and qualified dividends are included in taxable income last for this purpose). For example, in 2022, a single taxpayer who reported taxable income of $35,000, including a $5,000 net capital gain, would determine the tax on $30,000 ($35,000 taxable income minus $5,000 net capital gain) at ordinary rates and determine tax on the net capital gain using the net capital gain and qualified dividend rate schedule. In this case, the net capital gain of $5,000 would be taxed a 0% because taxable income plus the net capital gain is below $41,675. If the same taxpayer had $55,000 of taxable income, including a $5,000 net capital gain, the taxpayer would determine tax on $50,000 ($55,000 minus $5,000) using the ordinary rate schedule and would determine tax on the $5,000 net capital gain using the capital gain rate schedule. In this case, the $5,000 gain would be taxed at 15% because the taxable income with and without the net capital gain falls in between where the 15% rate begins (0% rate ends) at $41,676 and where the 20% rate begins (the 15% rate ends) at $459,751.

- Qualified dividend: Shareholders receiving dividends from corporations include the dividend in gross income. If the dividend meets the qualified dividend requirements, it is taxed at the same preferential rate as net capital gains are taxed, as described above.[9] If a dividend does not meet the qualified dividend requirement, it is considered to be ordinary income and is taxed at ordinary rates.[10] While qualified dividends are taxed at the same rate as net capital gains, qualified dividends are a separate and distinct character from capital. Therefore, qualified dividends are not included in the capital gain and loss netting process.

[6]Losses from the sale of personal-use assets are not deductible. Therefore, losses from the sale of personal use property are not included in the netting process, even though they are capital losses.

[7]Net short-term capital losses are deducted before net long-term capital losses in determining the maximum net capital loss deduction for the year.

[8]As we discover in other chapters, certain long-term capital gains may be taxed at a maximum rate of 25 percent and others may be taxed at a maximum rate of 28 percent.

[9]Qualified dividends generally include dividends distributed by U.S. corporations and certain foreign corporations if the shareholder meets certain holding period requirements for the stock. These requirements are discussed in more detail in the Investments chapter.

[10]Higher-income taxpayers may also be subject to a net investment income tax on both qualified and nonqualified dividends (§1411). See the Individual Income Tax Computation and Tax Credits chapter for details relating to the computation of the net investment income tax.

Example 4-1

Rodney earned a salary of $74,000, and Anita earned a salary of $56,000. The Halls also received $600 of interest income from investments in corporate bonds and $300 of interest income from investments in municipal bonds. This was their only realized income during the year. What is the Halls' gross income?

Answer: $130,600, computed as follows:

Description	Amount	Explanation
(1) Rodney's salary	$ 74,000	
(2) Anita's salary	56,000	
(3) Interest from corporate bonds	600	
Gross income	**$130,600***	(1) + (2) + (3)

*The $300 of interest income from municipal bonds is excluded from gross income.

What is the character of the salary, the interest income from the corporate bonds, and the interest income from the investments in municipal bonds?

Answer: The salary and interest income from corporate bonds are ordinary income. The interest income from the municipal bonds is excluded from gross income.

What if: Suppose this year the Halls sold shares of stock in XYZ Corporation at a $4,000 gain (their only transaction involving a capital asset). They purchased the stock three years ago. What would be the character of the gain? At what rate would the gain be taxed?

Answer: This is a long-term capital gain because stock is a capital asset and the Halls owned the stock for more than a year before selling. Given their income level (taxable income without the net capital gain is above the 0/15% breakpoint of $83,350 and taxable income with the net capital gain is not above the 15/20% breakpoint of $517,200—see rate schedule in Appendix C), the $4,000 gain would be taxed at a 15 percent rate.

What if: Suppose this year the Halls sold stock at a $4,000 loss (their only transaction involving a capital asset). They purchased the stock three years ago. What is the character of the loss? How much of the loss may the Halls deduct this year?

Answer: This is a long-term capital loss because the stock is a capital asset and the Halls owned the stock for more than a year before selling. The Halls can deduct $3,000 of the loss as a for AGI deduction this year. The remaining $1,000 loss is carried over to next year as a long-term capital loss.

What if: Suppose this year the Halls sold a personal automobile at a $4,000 loss. They purchased the automobile three years ago. What is the character of the loss? How much of the loss may the Halls deduct in the current year?

Answer: This is a long-term capital loss because the automobile is a capital asset and the Halls owned the auto for more than a year before selling. However, the Halls are not allowed to deduct any of the $4,000 loss this year or any other year because the automobile was a personal-use asset.

THE KEY FACTS

For and From AGI Deductions

- For AGI deductions
  - Reduce AGI.
  - Are referred to as deductions "above the line."
  - Are generally more valuable than from AGI deductions.
- From AGI deductions
  - Deduct from AGI to determine taxable income.
  - Are referred to as deductions "below the line."

Deductions

Deductions reduce a taxpayer's taxable income. However, they are not necessarily easy to come by because, in contrast to the all-inclusive treatment of income, deductions are not allowed unless a specific tax law allows them. Thus, deductions are a matter of **legislative grace.** The tax laws provide for two distinct types of deductions in the individual tax formula: for adjusted gross income (AGI) deductions and from AGI deductions. As indicated in the individual tax formula, gross income minus **for AGI deductions** equals AGI, and AGI minus **from AGI deductions** equals taxable income. Congress identifies whether the deductions are for or from AGI when it enacts legislation that grants deductions. The distinction between the deduction types is particularly important because AGI is a reference point often used in determining the extent to which taxpayers are allowed to claim certain tax benefits. For example, taxpayers with AGI in excess of certain thresholds lose tax benefits from items such as the child tax credit and education credits (we discuss credits later in the chapter).

For AGI Deductions For AGI deductions tend to be deductions associated with business activities and certain investing activities. Because for AGI deductions reduce AGI, they are referred to as **"deductions above the line."** The "line" in this case is AGI, which is line 11 on page 1 of Form 1040 (see Exhibit 4-2). Exhibit 4-5 provides a partial listing of common for AGI deductions and indicates where in the text we discuss them.

EXHIBIT 4-5 **Partial Listing of Common for AGI Deductions**

For AGI Deduction	Discussed in More Detail in These Chapters
Alimony paid (pre-2019 decree)	Individual Deductions
Health insurance deduction for self-employed taxpayers	Individual Deductions
Rental and royalty expenses	Individual Deductions and Tax Consequences of Home Ownership
Net capital losses [limited to $3,000 ($1,500 for married filing separately taxpayers)]	Investments
One-half of self-employment taxes paid	Individual Income Tax Computation and Tax Credits
Business expenses	Business Income, Deductions, and Accounting Methods
Losses on dispositions of assets used in a trade or business	Property Dispositions
Contributions to qualified retirement accounts [e.g., 401(k) plans and traditional individual retirement accounts (IRAs)]	Retirement Savings and Deferred Compensation

Example 4-2

Rodney made a $5,000 deductible (for AGI) contribution to his traditional individual retirement account (IRA). What is the Halls' adjusted gross income?

Answer: $125,600, computed as follows:

Description	Amount	Explanation
(1) Gross income	$ 130,600	Example 4-1
(2) IRA contribution	(5,000)	For AGI deduction (see Exhibit 4-5)
Adjusted gross income	**$125,600**	(1) + (2)

From AGI Deductions From AGI deductions are commonly referred to as **"deductions below the line"** because they are deducted after AGI has been determined. From AGI deductions include **itemized deductions,** the **standard deduction,** and the qualified business income (QBI) deduction, which is generally equal to 20 percent of a taxpayer's QBI. Taxpayers generally deduct the higher of the standard deduction or itemized deductions. In addition, for 2021, taxpayers who claim the standard deduction instead of itemized deductions are allowed to deduct up to $300 ($600 for married filing jointly taxpayers) of cash contributions made to public charities and private operating foundations (except contributions to donor advised funds or supporting organizations) as a from AGI deduction. As of press time, this provision had not been extended to 2022.

Exhibit 4-6 identifies the primary categories of itemized deductions and Exhibit 4-7 presents the basic standard deduction amounts by filing status for 2021 and 2022. The amount of the standard deduction varies by taxpayer filing status (we discuss filing status in more detail later in the chapter) and is indexed for inflation.

EXHIBIT 4-6 Primary Categories of Itemized Deductions

- *Medical and dental expenses:* Deductible to the extent these expenses exceed 7.5 percent of AGI.
- *Taxes:* State and local income taxes, sales taxes, real estate taxes, personal property taxes, and other taxes [the annual aggregate deduction for taxes, other than foreign income taxes, is limited to $10,000 ($5,000 if married filing separately)].
- *Interest expense:* Mortgage and investment interest expense.
- *Gifts to charity (charitable contributions).*
- *Other miscellaneous deductions:* Gambling losses (to the extent of gambling winnings) and certain other deductions.

Note: Itemized deductions are detailed on Schedule A of Form 1040. We discuss itemized deductions in more depth in the Individual Deductions chapter.

EXHIBIT 4-7 Standard Deduction Amounts by Filing Status*

	2021	2022
Married filing jointly	$25,100	$25,900
Qualifying widow or widower	25,100	25,900
Married filing separately	12,550	12,950
Head of household	18,800	19,400
Single	12,550	12,950

*Married taxpayers 65 years of age or over and/or blind are entitled to an additional standard deduction of $1,400 ($1,400 for age and another $1,400 for blindness) for 2022 ($1,350 for 2021); single and head of household taxpayers 65 years of age or over and/or blind are entitled to an additional standard deduction of $1,750 (one for age and another for blindness for 2022 ($1,700 for 2021). (See the Individual Deductions chapter for more detail.) For individuals claimed as a dependent on another tax return, the 2022 standard deduction is the greater of (1) $1,150 or (2) $400 plus earned income not to exceed the standard deduction amount for those who are not dependents (see the Individual Income Tax Computation and Tax Credits chapter for more detail).

Example 4-3

Rodney and Anita Hall annually file a joint tax return. They paid a total of $11,000 for expenditures that qualified as itemized deductions and they had no qualified business income (QBI). What is the total amount of from AGI deductions Rodney and Anita are allowed to deduct on their tax return?

Answer: $25,900, computed as follows:

Description	Amount	Explanation
(1) Standard deduction	$ 25,900	Married filing joint filing status (see Exhibit 4-7).
(2) Itemized deductions	11,000	
(3) Greater of (1) or (2)	25,900	The standard deduction exceeds itemized deductions.
(4) Qualified business income deduction	0	No qualified business income.
Total deductions from AGI	**$25,900**	(3) + (4). (Also referred to as deductions "below the line.")

What if: What would be the amount of the Halls' from AGI deductions if, instead of the original facts, Rodney and Anita had paid a total of $11,000 in expenditures that qualified as itemized deductions, including a $900 charitable donation to the American Red Cross, and they were allowed to claim a $1,000 QBI deduction based on $5,000 of qualified business income they reported? Assume the charitable contribution deduction for nonitemizers is extended to 2022.

Answer: $27,500, computed as follows:

Description	Amount	Explanation
(1) Standard deduction	$ 25,900	Married filing joint filing status (see Exhibit 4-7).
(2) Itemized deductions	11,000	
(3) Greater of (1) or (2)	25,900	The standard deduction exceeds itemized deductions.
(4) Charitable contribution deduction	600	Deduction limited to $600 (assumes charitable deduction provision for nonitemizers is extended to 2022)
(5) QBI deduction	1,000	QBI of $5,000 × 20%
Total deductions from AGI	**$27,500**	(3) + (4) + (5). (Also referred to as deductions "below the line.")

What if: What would be the amount of the Halls' from AGI deductions if, instead of the original facts, Rodney and Anita had paid a total of $28,000 in expenditures that qualified as itemized deductions, including a $900 charitable donation to the American Red Cross? Assume the charitable contribution deduction for nonitemizers is extended to 2022.

Answer: $28,000, computed as follows:

Description	Amount	Explanation
(1) Standard deduction	$ 25,900	Married filing joint filing status (see Exhibit 4-7).
(2) Itemized deductions	28,000	
(3) Greater of (1) or (2)	28,000	The itemized deductions exceed the standard deduction.
(4) Charitable contribution deduction	0	Not eligible because itemizing deductions.
(5) QBI deduction	0	No qualified business income.
Total deductions from AGI	**$28,000**	(3) + (4) + (5). (Also referred to as deductions "below the line.")

Income Tax Calculation

After determining taxable income, taxpayers can generally calculate their regular income tax liability using either a **tax table** or a **tax rate schedule,** depending on their filing status and income level (taxpayers with taxable income under $100,000 generally must use the tax tables).[11] See Appendix C for the ordinary tax rate schedules and the tax rate schedules for net capital gains and qualified dividends. The process for calculating the tax on net capital gains and qualified dividends is described previously in the Character of Income section of this chapter.

Example 4-4

With Tara's help, the Halls have determined their taxable income to be $99,700, computed as follows:

Description	Amount	Explanation
(1) Adjusted gross income	$125,600	Example 4-2
(2) From AGI deductions	(25,900)	Example 4-3
Taxable income	**$ 99,700**	(1) + (2)

They have also determined that all of their income is ordinary income. What is their tax liability?

Answer: $13,168. See the married filing jointly tax rate schedule in Appendix C {$9,615 + $3,553 [22% × ($99,700 – $83,550)]}.

What if: Using the tax rate schedules, what would the Halls' tax liability be if their taxable income were $12,000 (all ordinary income)?

Answer: $1,200 ($12,000 × 10%).

What if: Assume that in addition to the $99,700 of ordinary income, the Halls also reported $5,000 of long-term capital gain and no other capital gains and losses. How much tax would they pay on the additional $5,000 gain?

Answer: $750 ($5,000 × 15%). Because the Halls' net capital gain of $5,000 (long-term capital gain of $5,000 minus short-term capital loss of $0) increases the Halls' taxable income from $99,700 to $104,700 (which is above $83,350 and not above $517,200), the net capital gain is taxed at 15%. The remaining $99,700100,500 is taxed at ordinary rates.

Other Taxes

In addition to the individual income tax, individuals may also be required to pay other taxes such as the **alternative minimum tax (AMT)** or **self-employment taxes.** These taxes are imposed on tax bases other than the individual's taxable income. Furthermore, taxpayers with relatively high AGI are subject to a 3.8 percent net investment income tax

[11]For administrative convenience and to prevent low- and middle-income taxpayers from making mathematical errors using a rate schedule, the IRS provides tax tables that present the gross tax for various amounts of taxable income. For simplicity, we use the tax rate schedule to determine tax liabilities in the examples presented in this text.

on unearned (investment) income and a .9 percent additional Medicare tax on earned income. We discuss these taxes in more detail in the Individual Income Tax Computation and Tax Credits chapter.

Tax Credits

Individual taxpayers may reduce their tax liabilities by **tax credits** to determine their total taxes payable. Like deductions, tax credits are specifically granted by Congress and are narrowly defined. Unlike deductions, which reduce *taxable income,* tax credits *directly reduce taxes payable.* Thus, a $1 deduction reduces taxes payable by $1 times the marginal tax rate, while a $1 credit reduces taxes payable by $1. Common tax credits include the child tax credit, the child and dependent care credit, the earned income credit, the American opportunity credit, and the lifetime learning credit. These credits are subject to full or partial phase-out for higher income taxpayers. The child tax credit is the most common of these tax credits. The basic child tax credit is $2,000 for qualifying children under age 17 (under age 18 for 2021 only). However, for 2021, taxpayers can claim an additional child tax credit of $1,600 for qualifying children who are under age 6 at year-end and an additional $1,000 child tax credit for qualifying children who are at least age 6 but under age 18 at year-end. Thus, in 2021, taxpayers with qualifying children under age 6 at year-end can claim a $3,600 ($2,000 + $1,600) child tax credit for each such child, and taxpayers with qualifying children at least age 6 but under age 18 at year-end can claim a $3,000 ($2,000 + $1,000) child tax credit for each such child. For both 2020 and 2021, taxpayers are allowed to claim a $500 child tax credit for other qualifying dependents who do not meet the requirements for the higher credit amounts. As of press time, the additional child tax credit had not been extended to 2022. We discuss credits in more detail in the Individual Income Tax Computation and Tax Credits chapter.

Tax Prepayments

After calculating the total tax and subtracting their available credits, taxpayers determine their taxes due (or tax refund) by subtracting tax prepayments from the total tax remaining after credits. Tax prepayments include (1) **withholdings,** or income taxes withheld from the taxpayer's salary or wages or from other sources of income (e.g., distributions from retirement plans, social security benefit distributions, and unemployment benefit payments); (2) **estimated tax payments** the taxpayer makes for the year (paid directly to the IRS); and (3) tax that the taxpayer overpaid on the prior-year tax return that the taxpayer elects to apply as an estimated payment for the current tax year instead of receiving as a refund.

If tax prepayments exceed the total tax after subtracting credits, the taxpayer receives a tax refund (or elects to apply the refund as an estimated tax payment) for the difference. If tax prepayments are less than the total tax after credits, the taxpayer owes additional tax and potentially a penalty for the underpayment.

Example 4-5

Based on their calculation in Example 4-4, Rodney and Anita Hall's tax liability is $13,168. The Halls are able to claim a $2,000 child tax credit for their 12-year-old son Braxton and a $500 child tax credit for their 21-year-old daughter Tara. The Halls also had $10,200 of federal income taxes withheld from their paychecks by their employers. What is the Halls' tax due or refund?

Answer: $468 tax due, computed as follows:

Description	Amount	Explanation
(1) Tax liability	$13,168	Example 4-4
(2) Tax credits	(2,500)	Child tax credit: $2,000 for Braxton and $500 for Tara.
(3) Tax prepayments	(10,200)	
Tax due	**$ 468**	(1) + (2) + (3)

Although it is not explicitly stated in the individual tax formula, a taxpayer's filing status affects many parts of the tax formula, including the standard deduction amount and the applicable income tax rate schedule, among others. In the next section, we describe the rules for determining a taxpayer's filing status. However, because a taxpayer's filing status may depend on whether the taxpayer has dependents for tax purposes, we first discuss how to identify who qualifies as a taxpayer's dependent.

DEPENDENTS OF THE TAXPAYER

LO 4-2

Under current tax law, taxpayers are not allowed to claim a deduction for dependents. Nevertheless, as mentioned previously, it is necessary to determine who qualifies as a dependent of the taxpayer for purposes of determining filing status, eligibility for certain tax credits, and other tax-related computations.

Dependency Requirements

To qualify as a dependent of another, an individual:

1. Must be a citizen of the United States or a resident of the United States, Canada, or Mexico.
2. Must *not* file a joint return with their spouse unless there is no tax liability on the couple's joint return and there would not have been any tax liability on either spouse's tax return if they had filed separately.[12]
3. Must be considered either a **qualifying child** *or* a **qualifying relative** of the taxpayer.[13]

While the requirements for determining a qualifying child and a qualifying relative have some similarities, the qualifying relative requirements are broader in scope.

Qualifying Child To be considered a qualifying child of a taxpayer, an individual must satisfy the following four tests: (1) relationship, (2) age, (3) residence, and (4) support.[14]

Relationship test. A qualifying child must be an eligible relative of the taxpayer. Eligible relatives include the taxpayer's:

- Child or descendant of a child. For this purpose, a child includes a taxpayer's adopted child, stepchild, and eligible foster child.
- Sibling or descendant of sibling. For this purpose, a sibling includes a taxpayer's half-brother, half-sister, stepbrother, or stepsister.

Under this definition, the taxpayer's grandchild would qualify as an eligible relative, as would the taxpayer's sister's grandchild.

Age test. A qualifying child must be younger than the taxpayer and *either* (1) under age 19 at the end of the year or (2) under age 24 at the end of the year *and* a full-time student.[15] A person is a full-time student if they were in school full time during any part of each of five calendar months during the calendar year.[16] An individual of any age who is permanently and totally disabled is deemed to have met the age test.[17]

Residence test. A qualifying child must have the same principal residence as the taxpayer for *more* than half the year. Time that a child or the taxpayer is *temporarily* away from the taxpayer's home because the child or taxpayer is ill, is pursuing an education, or has other special circumstances is counted as though the child or taxpayer were living in the taxpayer's home.[18]

[12]Rev. Rul. 54-567.

[13]§152.

[14]Technically, an individual is not eligible to be a qualifying child of another if the individual filed a joint return with their spouse (other than to claim a refund) [see §152(c)(1)(E)]. However, because this is also a requirement to be claimed as a dependent, we do not discuss the requirement separately here.

[15]§152(c)(3)(A).

[16]§152(f)(2).

[17]§152(c)(3)(B).

[18]Reg. §1.152-1(b).

Support test. A qualifying child must *not* have provided more than half of their *own* support (living expenses) for the year. Such support generally includes:

- Food, school lunches, toilet articles, and haircuts.
- Clothing.
- Recreation—including toys, summer camp, horseback riding, entertainment, and vacation expenses.
- Medical and dental care.
- Child care expenses.
- Allowances and gifts.
- Wedding costs.
- Lodging.
- Education—including board, uniforms at military schools, and tuition. When determining who provided the support for a taxpayer's *child* who is a full-time student, scholarships are excluded from the computation.[19]

Example 4-6

Rodney and Anita have two children: Braxton, age 12, who lives at home, and Tara, age 21, who is a full-time student and does not live at home. Tara earned $9,000 from a summer job, but she did *not* provide more than half of her own support during the year. Are Braxton and Tara qualifying dependent children of Rodney and Anita?

Answer: Yes, see analysis of factors below:

Test	Braxton	Tara
Relationship	Yes, son.	Yes, daughter.
Age	Yes, under age 19 at end of year (and younger than his parents).	Yes, under age 24 at year-end *and* full-time student (and younger than her parents).
Residence	Yes, lived at home entire year.	Yes, time away at college is considered as time at home if Tara plans to live in her parents' home again at some point (it is a temporary absence).
Support	Yes, does not provide more than half of own support.	Yes, does not provide more than half of own support.

Because they both meet all the requirements, Braxton and Tara are qualifying children to the Halls. So, both Braxton and Tara are the Halls' dependents.

What if: Suppose Tara provided more than half of her own support. Would she be considered a qualifying child of her parents?

Answer: No. She would fail the support test.

What if: Assume the original facts apply, but now Tara is age 25. Would she be considered a dependent as a qualifying child of her parents?

Answer: No. She would fail the age test. Note, however, that Tara could still qualify as her parents' dependent as a qualifying relative (see Example 4-8 below).

What if: Assume the original facts, except now suppose that Braxton is Anita's stepbrother's son. Would Braxton be considered a qualifying dependent child of Rodney and Anita?

Answer: Yes. Braxton meets the relationship test because he is the descendant of Anita's stepbrother and Anita's stepbrother is considered to be Anita's sibling for this purpose.

Tiebreaking rules. The requirements for determining who is a qualifying child leave open the possibility that one person could be a qualifying child to more than one taxpayer. In these circumstances, the taxpayer who has priority for claiming the person as a dependent is based on the following tiebreaking rules:

1. If the person is a qualifying child of a parent and a nonparent, the parent is entitled to claim the person as a dependent. This situation could arise, for example, when a child lives with a parent *and* grandparents. In this case, the parent has priority for claiming the child as a dependent over the grandparents.

[19]§152(f)(1), (5).

2. If the individual is a qualifying child to more than one parent, the parent with whom the child has resided for the longest period of time during the year has priority for claiming the person as a dependent. This situation may arise in a year when the child lives with both parents for more than half of the year, but the parents separate or divorce in the latter part of the year. Note, however, that for a child of divorced parents, the noncustodial parent (the parent the child does not live with) can claim the child as a dependent qualifying child if the custodial parent signs a form indicating that they will not claim the child as a dependent and the noncustodial parent attaches the form to their tax return.[20] If the child resides with each parent for equal amounts of time during the year, the child is a qualifying child of the parent with the higher AGI.
3. Finally, if the child is a qualifying child of more than one nonparent, the child is the qualifying child of the nonparent with the highest AGI.[21]

Example 4-7

In the previous example, we established that Rodney and Anita's son Braxton is the Halls' qualifying dependent child. Braxton's uncle Shawn—Rodney's brother—has lived in the Halls' home (the same home Braxton lives in) for more than 11 months during the year. Does Braxton meet the requirements to be considered Shawn's qualifying child?

Answer: Yes, see analysis of factors below.

Test	Braxton
Relationship	Yes, son of Shawn's brother.
Age	Yes, under age 19 at end of year (and younger than Shawn).
Residence	Yes, lived in same residence as Shawn for more than half the year.
Support	Yes, does not provide more than half of his own support.

Thus, Braxton is considered to be Rodney's and Anita's qualifying child *and* he is considered to be Shawn's qualifying child. Under the tiebreaking rules, who is allowed to claim Braxton as a dependent for the year?

Answer: Rodney and Anita. Under the first tiebreaking rule, Rodney and Anita are allowed to claim Braxton as a dependent (as a qualifying child) because they are Braxton's parents.

What if: Suppose Shawn is Rodney's cousin. Would Braxton be considered Shawn's qualifying child?

Answer: No, Braxton would not meet the relationship test for Shawn if he is Rodney's cousin. Braxton is not the descendant of Shawn's sibling.

TAXES IN THE REAL WORLD Your Pet May Be Dependent on You, but Your Pet Isn't Your Dependent!

While you may consider your pet as part of your family and your pet may depend on you to take care of it, your pet can't qualify as your dependent. The Tax Code doesn't specifically say your dependent must be human, but you need to report the Social Security number or individual taxpayer identification number of your dependents on your tax return. Unfortunately for pet owners, pets aren't issued Social Security numbers. Even though pets don't qualify as dependents, you still may be eligible for certain pet-related tax benefits (e.g., your pet is a service animal or is used in a business).

Qualifying Relative A qualifying relative is a person who is *not* a qualifying child *and* satisfies (1) a relationship test, (2) a support test, and (3) a gross income test.

Relationship test. As you might expect, the relationship test for a qualifying relative is more inclusive than the relationship test for a qualifying child. To satisfy the qualifying

[20]See §152(e). The custodial parent signs Form 8332, "Release/Revocation of Release of Claim to Exemption for Child by Custodial Parent," and the noncustodial parent attaches it to their tax return.

[21]If the parents may claim the child as a qualifying child, but no parent does so, another taxpayer may claim the individual as a qualifying child but only if the other individual's AGI is higher than the AGI of any parent of the child [§152(c)(4)(C)].

relative relationship test, a person must either (1) have a "qualifying family relationship" with the taxpayer or (2) meet the qualifying relative "member of the household" test. A qualifying family relationship with the taxpayer includes the following:

- A descendant or ancestor of the taxpayer. For this purpose, a child includes a taxpayer's adopted child, stepchild, and eligible foster child, and a parent includes a stepmother and stepfather.
- A sibling of the taxpayer, including a stepbrother or a stepsister.
- A son or daughter of the brother or sister of the taxpayer (cousins do not qualify).
- A sibling of the taxpayer's mother or father.
- An in-law (mother-in-law, father-in-law, sister-in-law, brother-in-law, son-in-law, or daughter-in-law) of the taxpayer.

A person meets the qualifying relative member of the household test if that person has the same principal place of abode as the taxpayer for the entire year. This is true *even if the person does not have a qualifying family relationship with the taxpayer.*[22]

Support test. The support test generally requires that the taxpayer pay more than half the qualifying relative's support/living expenses (note that this is a different support test than the support test for a qualifying child). As we discussed above, support/living expenses include rent, food, medicine, and clothes, among other things. Just as with the qualifying child support test, for children of a taxpayer who are full-time students, scholarships are excluded from the support test.[23] Under a multiple support agreement, taxpayers who don't pay over half of an individual's support may still be allowed to claim the individual as a dependent under the qualifying relative rules if the following apply:[24]

1. No one taxpayer paid over one-half of the individual's support.
2. The taxpayer and at least one other person provided more than half the support of the individual, and the taxpayer and the other person(s) would have been allowed to claim the individual as a dependent except for the fact that they did not provide over half of the support of the individual.
3. The taxpayer contributed *over* 10 percent of the individual's support for the year.
4. Each other person who provided *over* 10 percent of the individual's support [see requirement (3) above] provides a signed statement to the taxpayer agreeing not to claim the individual as a dependent. The taxpayer includes the names, addresses, and Social Security numbers of each other person on Form 2120, "Multiple Support Declaration," which the taxpayer attaches to Form 1040.

Multiple support agreements are commonly used in situations when siblings support elderly parents.

Gross income test. The gross income test requires that a qualifying relative's gross income for the year be *less* than $4,400 in 2022.[25]

Example 4-8

What if: Suppose Tara is age 25, is a full-time student, and does not live with her parents. Tara earned $3,000 from a summer job, and her parents provided more than half her support. Does Tara qualify as her parents' dependent?

Answer: Yes, as their qualifying relative. She is too old to be their qualifying child.

[22]A person is considered to live with the taxpayer for the entire year if they were either born during the year or died during the year and resided with the taxpayer for the remaining part of the year.

[23]§152(f)(1), (5). Just as with a qualifying child, this provision requires that the student be a son, daughter, stepson, stepdaughter, or eligible foster child of the taxpayer.

[24]§152(d)(3).

[25]This is the exemption amount referenced in §152(d)(1)(B) indexed for inflation.

Test	Explanation
Relationship	Yes, Rodney and Anita's daughter.
Support	Yes, the Halls provide more than half of Tara's support.
Gross income	Yes, Tara's gross income for the year is less than $4,400.

Tara's parents may claim her as a dependent. Note that if Tara's gross income were at least $4,400, she would *not* qualify as her parents' dependent.

Example 4-9

In determining who qualified as their dependents, Rodney and Anita evaluated whether Shawn is their *qualifying relative*. Assuming Shawn's gross income for the year is $42,000, the Halls provided food and lodging for Shawn valued at $8,000, and Shawn paid for his other living expenses valued at $14,000, is Shawn a qualifying relative of the Halls?

Answer: No, as analyzed below.

Test	Explanation
Relationship	Yes, Rodney's brother.
Support	No, the Halls provided $8,000 of support to Shawn, but Shawn provided $14,000 of his own support. Because the Halls provided less than half of Shawn's support, Shawn does not pass the support test.
Gross income	No, Shawn's gross income for the year is $42,000, which is not less than $4,400, so Shawn fails the gross income test.

Because Shawn fails the support test and the gross income test, he is not a qualifying relative of the Halls. Consequently, the Halls cannot claim Shawn as a dependent.

What if: Assume that Shawn received $5,000 of tax-exempt interest during the year and that this is his only source of income. Does he meet the gross income test?

Answer: Yes. Because tax-exempt interest is excluded from gross income, Shawn's gross income is $0, so he passes the gross income test. (Note, however, that Shawn would still fail the support test so he would not be a qualifying relative of the Halls no matter the outcome of the gross income test.)

What if: Assume the original facts in the example except now suppose that Shawn paid for his $14,000 of living expenses with interest he had received from tax-exempt bonds. Would Shawn pass the support test?

Answer: No. The Halls would not have provided more than half of Shawn's support. The fact that Shawn received the money he spent on his support from tax-exempt income does not matter. All that matters is that he provided more than half of his own support.

What if: Assume that Anita's 92-year-old grandfather Juan lives in an apartment by himself near the Halls' residence. His gross income for the year is $3,000. Assuming the Halls provide more than half of Juan's living expenses for the year, would Juan be a qualifying relative of the Halls?

Answer: Yes, as analyzed below.

Test	Explanation
Relationship	Yes, Anita's grandfather.
Support	Yes, as assumed in the facts, the Halls provide more than half of Juan's support.
Gross income	Yes, Juan's gross income for the year is $3,000, which is less than $4,400, so Juan passes the gross income test.

What if: Assume that Anita's 92-year-old grandfather Juan lives in an apartment by himself and reports gross income for the year of $3,000. Anita provides 40 percent of Juan's support, Juan provides 25 percent of his own support, Anita's brother Carlos provides 30 percent of the support, and Anita's sister Kamella provides 5 percent of Juan's support. Who is eligible to claim Juan as a dependent under a multiple support agreement?

(*continued on page 4-18*)

Answer: Anita and Carlos. Anita and Carlos are eligible because (1) no one taxpayer provided more than half of Juan's support, (2) Anita and Carlos together provided more than half of Juan's support and Juan would have been both Anita's and Carlos's qualifying relative except for the fact that neither provided over half of Juan's support, and (3) Anita and Carlos each provided over 10 percent of Juan's support (Kamella provided only 5 percent of Juan's support, so she is not eligible). Anita and Carlos will need to agree on who will claim Juan as a dependent. Assuming they agree that Anita will claim Juan as a dependent, she will need to receive a signed statement from Carlos agreeing not to claim Juan as a dependent and she will need to attach Form 2120 to her (and Rodney's) tax return providing Carlos's name, address, and Social Security number.

What if: Assume the facts in the prior what-if scenario in which Anita is allowed to claim Juan as a dependent under a multiple support agreement. What tax benefit does Anita receive from claiming Juan as a dependent?

Answer: Anita is eligible to claim a $500 tax credit for Juan because he is Anita's dependent who is not a qualifying child (he is a qualifying relative).

What if: Assume Juan lives in an apartment by himself and is a friend of the family but is unrelated to either Rodney or Anita. His gross income is $3,000 and the Halls provide over half of his support. Is Juan a qualifying relative of the Halls?

Answer: No, as analyzed below.

Test	Explanation
Relationship	No, not related to the Halls and his principal place of abode is not in the Halls' household for the *entire* year. If the Halls' home were his principal place of abode for the entire year, he would have met the relationship test even though he's not actually related to anyone in the Hall family.
Support	Yes, as assumed in the facts, the Halls provide more than half of Juan's support.
Gross income	Yes, Juan's gross income for the year is $3,000, which is less than $4,400, so Juan passes the gross income test.

The Halls would not be able to claim Juan as a dependent because he fails the qualifying relative relationship test under this set of facts.

The rules for determining who is a qualifying child and who is a qualifying relative for tax purposes overlap to some extent. The primary differences between the two sets of rules are:

1. The relationship requirement is more broadly defined for qualifying relatives than for qualifying children.
2. Qualifying children are subject to age restrictions while qualifying relatives are not.
3. Qualifying relatives are subject to a gross income restriction while qualifying children are not.
4. Taxpayers need not provide more than half a qualifying child's support (though the child cannot provide more than half of their own support), but they must provide more than half of the support of a qualifying relative.
5. Qualifying children are subject to a residence test (they must have the same primary residence as the taxpayer for more than half the year), while qualifying relatives are not.

Exhibit 4-8 summarizes the dependency requirements.

Finally, an individual who is a dependent of another is not allowed to claim any dependents.[26] Appendix A at the end of this chapter provides a flowchart for determining whether an individual qualifies as the taxpayer's dependent.

[26] §152(b)(1).

EXHIBIT 4-8 Summary of Dependency Requirements

Test	Qualifying Child	Qualifying Relative
Relationship	Taxpayer's child, stepchild, foster child, sibling, half-brother or half-sister, stepbrother or stepsister, or a descendant of any of these relatives.	Taxpayer's descendant or ancestor, sibling, stepmother, stepfather, stepbrother or stepsister, son or daughter of taxpayer's sibling, sibling of the taxpayer's mother or father, in-laws, and anyone else who has the same principal place of abode as the taxpayer for the entire year (even if not otherwise related).
Age	Younger than the taxpayer claiming the individual as a qualifying child and under age 19 or a full-time student under age 24. Also anyone totally and permanently disabled.	Not applicable.
Residence	Lives with taxpayer for more than half of the year (includes temporary absences for things such as illness and education).	Not applicable.
Support	The qualifying child must not provide more than half of their own support.	Taxpayer must have provided more than half of the support for the qualifying relative.
Gross income	Not applicable.	Gross income less than $4,400 in 2022.
Other	Not applicable.	Not a qualifying child.

ETHICS

Blake was 21 years of age at the end of the year. During the year, he was a full-time college student. He also worked part time and earned $8,000, which he used to pay all $6,000 of his living expenses. Blake's parents, Troy and Camille, claimed him as a dependent on their joint tax return. After filing the return, Troy and Camille told Blake they owed him $3,001 for his annual living expenses. What do you think of Troy and Camille's strategy to claim Blake as a dependent?

FILING STATUS

LO 4-3

Each year taxpayers determine their **filing status** according to their marital status at year-end and whether they have any dependents. A taxpayer's filing status is important because, as we discussed above, it determines:

- The applicable tax rate schedule for determining the taxpayer's tax liability.
- The taxpayer's standard deduction amount.
- The AGI threshold for the reduction in certain tax benefits including certain tax credits and deductions.

Each year, all taxpayers filing tax returns file under one of the following five filing statuses:

1. Married filing jointly
2. Married filing separately
3. Qualifying widow or widower (surviving spouse)
4. Single
5. Head of household

Married Filing Jointly and Married Filing Separately

Married couples may file tax returns jointly **(married filing jointly)** or separately **(married filing separately).** To be married for filing status purposes, taxpayers must be married on

THE KEY FACTS

Filing Status for Married Taxpayers

- Married filing jointly
  - Taxpayers are legally married as of the last day of the year.
  - When one spouse dies during the year, the surviving spouse is still considered to be married for tax purposes during the year of the spouse's death.
  - Both spouses are ultimately responsible for paying the joint tax.
- Married filing separately
  - Taxpayers are legally married as of the last day of the year.

(continued)

- Generally no tax advantage to filing separately (usually a disadvantage).
- Each spouse is ultimately responsible for paying their own tax.
- Couples may choose to file separately (generally for nontax reasons).

- Qualifying widow or widower
  - When a taxpayer's spouse dies, the surviving spouse can file as a qualifying widow or widower for two years after the year of the spouse's death if the surviving spouse remains unmarried and maintains a household for a dependent child.

the last day of the year. When one spouse dies during the year, the surviving spouse is considered to be *married* at the end of the year to the spouse who died unless the surviving spouse has remarried during the year. Married couples filing joint returns combine their income and deductions and agree to share joint and several liability for the tax liability on the return. Thus, they are both ultimately responsible for seeing that the tax is paid.

When married couples file separately, each spouse reports the income they received during the year and the deductions they are claiming on a tax return separate from that of the other spouse.[27] So that married taxpayers can't file separately to gain more combined tax benefits than they would be entitled to if they were to file jointly, tax-related items for married filing separate (MFS) taxpayers—such as tax rate schedules and standard deduction amounts, among others—are generally one-half what they are for married filing joint (MFJ) taxpayers. Also, if one spouse deducts itemized deductions, the other spouse is required to deduct itemized deductions even if their standard deduction amount is more than the total itemized deductions. Thus, only in unusual circumstances does it make economic sense for *tax* purposes for married couples to file separately.

However, it may be wise for married couples to file separately for *nontax* reasons. For example, a spouse who does not want to be liable for the other spouse's income tax liability, or a spouse who is not in contact with the other spouse, may want to file separately.

Example 4-10

Rodney and Anita Hall are married at the end of the year. What is their filing status?

Answer: Married filing jointly, unless they choose to file separately.

What if: Assume that in 2022 the Halls file a joint return. In 2023, Rodney and Anita divorce and the IRS audits their 2022 tax return and determines that, due to overstating their deductions, the Halls underpaid their taxes by $2,000. Who must pay the tax?

Answer: Both Rodney and Anita are responsible for paying. If the IRS can't locate Rodney, it can require Anita to pay the full $2,000 even though she earned $56,000 and Rodney earned $74,000.

What if: Assume that in 2022 the Halls file separate tax returns. In 2023, Rodney and Anita divorce and the IRS audits Rodney's and Anita's separate tax returns. The IRS determines that by overstating deductions, Rodney understated his tax liability by $1,500 and Anita understated her tax liability by $500. Further, the IRS cannot locate Rodney. What is the maximum amount of taxes Anita is liable for?

Answer: $500. Because she filed a separate return, she is responsible for the tax liability associated with her separate tax return, and she is not responsible for the taxes associated with Rodney's tax return.

TAXES IN THE REAL WORLD If a Marriage Is Lawful, It Counts for Federal Tax Purposes

In 2015 , the U.S. Supreme Court ruled that the 14th Amendment of the Constitution guarantees a right to same-sex marriage. Based on Treasury Regulations effective on September 2, 2016, for federal tax purposes, the terms *spouse*, *husband*, and *wife* mean an individual lawfully married to another individual. However, these terms do not include individuals who have entered into a registered domestic partnership, civil union, or other similar formal relationship that is not recognized as a marriage under the laws of the state, possession, or territory of the United States where they entered the relationship.

If someone gets married outside of the United States, is the marriage recognized for federal tax purposes? It turns out that two individuals who enter into a marriage under the laws of a foreign jurisdiction are recognized as married for U.S. federal tax purposes if the relationship would be recognized as a marriage under the laws of at least *one* state, possession, or territory of the United States.

A taxpayer's marital status is important for determining income tax filing status and has implications for other areas of the tax law (estate and gift tax, for example).

Sources: Treas. Reg. §301.7701-18; *Obergefell v. Hodges*, 576 U.S. 644 (2015).

[27]As we discuss in the Gross Income and Exclusions chapter, under community property laws of certain states, one spouse may be treated as receiving income earned by the other spouse.

Married Individuals Treated as Unmarried (Abandoned Spouse) In certain situations, a couple may be legally married at the end of the year but living apart. Although the couple could technically file a joint tax return, this is often not desirable from a nontax perspective because each spouse would be assuming responsibility for paying tax on income earned by either spouse whether it was reported or not. However, because both spouses are married at the end of the year, generally, their only other option is to file under the tax-unfavorable married filing separately filing status.

To provide tax relief in these situations, the tax laws treat a married taxpayer *as though they were unmarried* at the end of the year if the taxpayer meets the following requirements:

- The taxpayer is married at the end of the year (or is not *legally* separated from the other spouse).
- The taxpayer does not file a joint tax return with the other spouse.
- The taxpayer pays *more than half* the costs of maintaining their home for the entire year, and this home is the principal residence for a child (who qualifies as the taxpayer's dependent[28]) for *more than half* the year (the child must be a child of the taxpayer, including an adopted child, stepchild, or eligible foster child[29]).
- The taxpayer lived apart from the other spouse for the last six months of the year (the other spouse did not live at all in the taxpayer's home during the last six months—temporary absences due to illness, education, business, vacation, or military service count as though the spouse still lived in the taxpayer's home).

Taxpayers who meet these requirements also meet the head of household filing status requirements (discussed later in this section) and may file as head of household for the year. The primary objective of this tax rule is to provide tax relief to one spouse who has been abandoned by or separated from the other spouse and left to care for a dependent child. Thus, a married taxpayer who qualifies as unmarried under this provision is frequently referred to as an **abandoned spouse.** Nevertheless, the provision may still apply even when no spouse has been abandoned. For example, a couple may separate by mutual consent. Further, if both spouses meet the requirements, both spouses may qualify as being unmarried in the same year and, thus, both may qualify for head of household filing status.

Example 4-11

What if: Assume that last year, Rodney and Anita informally separated (they did not *legally* separate). Rodney moved out of the home and into his own apartment. Anita stayed in the Halls' home with Braxton. During the current year, Anita paid more than half the costs of maintaining the home for herself and Braxton. Even though Rodney and Anita were legally married at the end of the year, they filed separate tax returns. Under these circumstances, is Anita considered to be married or unmarried for tax purposes?

Answer: Unmarried. Anita meets the requirements for being treated as unmarried, determined as follows (see requirements above):

- Anita is married to Rodney at the end of the year.
- Anita filed a tax return separate from Rodney's.
- Anita paid more than half the costs of maintaining her home, and her home was the principal residence for Braxton, who is her dependent child.
- Rodney did not live in Anita's home for the last six months of the year (in fact, he didn't live there at any time during the entire year).

What if: Given that Anita meets the requirements for being treated as unmarried, what is her filing status?

Answer: Head of household. Because Anita meets the abandoned spouse requirements, she also meets the head of household filing status requirements. Without the abandoned spouse rule, Anita would have been required to file as married filing separately. Rodney's filing status, however, is married filing separately. Note, however, that if Rodney's new residence becomes Tara's principal residence, Rodney will also be treated as unmarried and will be eligible for head of household filing status.

[28]A taxpayer meets this test if the taxpayer (custodial parent) cannot claim the child as a dependent only because they agreed under a divorce decree to allow the noncustodial parent to claim the child as a dependent.

[29]§152(f).

Qualifying Widow or Widower (Surviving Spouse)

When a taxpayer's spouse dies, the taxpayer is no longer legally married. However, to provide tax relief for widows and widowers *with dependents,* taxpayers who meet certain requirements are eligible for **qualifying widow or widower** filing status, also called surviving spouse status, for up to two years *after* the end of the year in which the other spouse died. Recall that for tax purposes, the couple is still considered to be married at the end of the year of the spouse's death. Taxpayers are eligible for qualifying widow or widower filing status if they (1) remain unmarried and (2) pay over half the cost of maintaining a household where a child who qualifies as the taxpayer's dependent lived for the entire year (except for temporary absences).[30] The dependent child must be a child or stepchild (including an adopted child but not a foster child) of the taxpayer.

Example 4-12

What if: Assume that last year Rodney passed away, and during the current year Anita did not remarry but maintained a household for Braxton and Tara, her dependent children. Under these circumstances, what is Anita's filing status for the current year?

Answer: Qualifying widow. Last year, the year of Rodney's death, Anita qualified to file a joint return with Rodney. This year, she is a qualifying widow because she has not remarried and she has maintained a household for the entire year for her dependent children. She will qualify as a surviving spouse next year (for two years after Rodney's death) if she does not remarry and she continues to maintain a household for Braxton and/or Tara for the entire year.

Single

Unmarried taxpayers who do not qualify for head of household status (discussed below) file as **single** taxpayers. As we discuss below, an unmarried taxpayer generally must have a dependent who is a qualifying person to qualify for head of household filing status.

Example 4-13

Shawn Hall, Rodney's brother, was divorced in January and is unmarried at the end of the year. Shawn does not claim any dependents. What is his filing status?

Answer: Single. Because Shawn is unmarried at the end of the year, and he does not have any dependents, his filing status is single.

Head of Household

In terms of tax rate schedules and standard deduction amounts, the **head of household** filing status is less favorable than the married filing jointly and qualifying widow or widower filing statuses. However, it is more favorable than married filing separately and single filing statuses (see tax rates and standard deduction amounts provided in Appendix C). To qualify for head of household filing status, a taxpayer must:

- Be unmarried (or be considered unmarried under the provisions discussed previously) at the end of the year.
- Not be a qualifying widow or widower.
- Pay more than half the costs of keeping up a home for the year.
- Have a "qualifying person" live in the taxpayer's home for more than half the year (except for temporary absences such as military service, illness, or schooling). However, if the qualifying person is the taxpayer's *dependent* parent, the parent is not required to live with the taxpayer.

[30]§2(a).

There are a few special rules relating to qualifying persons and head of household filing status:

- A qualifying person may not qualify more than one person for head of household filing status.
- If a taxpayer can claim a person as a dependent only because of a multiple support agreement, that person is not a qualifying person.
- If a custodial parent agrees under a divorce decree to allow the noncustodial parent to claim the person as a dependent, the agreement is ignored for purposes of the head of household filing status test. That is, for purposes of determining head of household filing status, the dependent is still considered a qualifying person to the custodial parent and not the noncustodial parent.

Exhibit 4-9 describes who is considered a qualifying person for purposes of head of household filing status.[31]

Example 4-14

What if: Assume Rodney and Anita divorced last year. During the current year, Braxton lives with Anita for the entire year and Anita pays all the costs of maintaining the household for herself and Braxton. Under these circumstances, what is Anita's filing status for the year?

Answer: Head of household. Anita is unmarried at the end of the year, she provides more than half the costs of maintaining her household, Braxton lives with her for more than half of the year, and Braxton is her qualifying child.

What if: Assume Rodney and Anita divorced last year. During the current year, Braxton lives with Anita for the entire year and Anita pays all the costs of maintaining the household for herself and Braxton. Assume that Anita allowed Rodney to claim Braxton as a dependent under the divorce decree. Under these circumstances, what is Anita's filing status for the year?

Answer: Head of household. Braxton is a qualifying person for Anita (the custodial parent) even though Anita is not claiming Braxton as a dependent. Braxton is not a qualifying child of Rodney (he didn't live with Rodney for more than half the year) or a qualifying person for Rodney (the noncustodial parent).

What if: Assume that Rodney and Anita divorced last year. If Braxton is Anita's cousin (rather than her son) and he lives with Anita in her home from June 15 through December 31, what is Anita's filing status for the year?

Answer: Single. Anita does not qualify for head of household filing status because Braxton is not her qualifying child (he fails the relationship test) or her qualifying relative (he fails the relationship test because he did not live in Anita's home for the entire year and he does not have a qualifying family relationship with Anita because he is her cousin).

What if: Assume that Rodney and Anita divorced last year, Braxton is Anita's cousin, and Braxton lives with Anita in her home for the entire year. What is Anita's filing status for the year?

Answer: Single. Even though Braxton is Anita's qualifying relative, Braxton meets the qualifying relative relationship test only because he lived with Anita for the entire year (not because he had a qualifying family relationship with her). Therefore, while Anita may claim Braxton as a dependent, she does not qualify for the head of household filing status.

What if: Assume Rodney's brother Shawn lived with the Halls, but Shawn paid more than half the costs of maintaining a separate apartment that is the principal residence of his mother, Sharon. Sharon's gross income is $1,500. Because Shawn provided more than half of Sharon's support during the year, and because Sharon's gross income was less than $4,400, she qualifies as Shawn's dependent relative. In these circumstances, what is Shawn's filing status?

Answer: Head of household. Shawn paid more than half the costs of maintaining a separate household where his mother resides, and his mother qualifies as his dependent. If Sharon's gross income were at least $4,400, she would fail the dependency gross income test and would not qualify as Shawn's dependent. If she did not qualify as his dependent, she would not be a qualifying person, and Shawn would not qualify for the head of household filing status. Also, if Sharon were Shawn's grandmother rather than his mother, she would not be a qualifying person (no matter the amount of her gross income) and Shawn would not qualify for head of household status. Sharon must be Shawn's parent in order for her to qualify Shawn as a head of household.

[31]§2(b). The tax law imposes due diligence requirements for paid preparers in determining eligibility for a taxpayer to file as head of household and a $560 (for tax returns filed in 2023, including tax returns for the 2022 tax year) penalty each time a paid preparer fails to meet these requirements. See §6695(g).

EXHIBIT 4-9 Who Is a Qualifying Person for Determining Head of Household Filing Status?

IF the person is the taxpayer's . . .	And . . .	THEN, the person is . . .
Qualifying child	the person is single,	a qualifying person, whether or not the taxpayer can claim the person as a dependent (the child is not a citizen of the United States or is not a resident of the United States, Canada, or Mexico).*
	the person is married and the taxpayer may claim the person as a dependent,	a qualifying person.*
	the person is married and the taxpayer may not claim the person as a dependent,	not a qualifying person (unless the only reason the taxpayer cannot claim the person as a dependent is because the taxpayer can be claimed as a dependent on someone else's tax return).
Qualifying relative who is the taxpayer's mother or father	the taxpayer may not claim the taxpayer's mother or father as a dependent,	not a qualifying person.
	the taxpayer may claim the taxpayer's mother or father as a dependent,	a qualifying person even if the taxpayer's mother or father did not live with the taxpayer. However, the taxpayer must have paid more than half the costs to maintain the household of the mother or father.
Qualifying relative other than the taxpayer's mother or father	the person did not live with the taxpayer for more than half the year,	not a qualifying person.
	the taxpayer can claim the person as a dependent, the person lived with the taxpayer for more than half the year, and the person is related to the taxpayer through a qualifying family relationship,	a qualifying person.
	the person is the taxpayer's qualifying relative only because the person lived with the taxpayer as a member of the taxpayer's household for the entire year (the person does not have a qualifying family relationship with the taxpayer),	not a qualifying person.
	the taxpayer cannot claim the person as a dependent or the taxpayer can claim the person as a dependent only because of a multiple support agreement,	not a qualifying person.

Note: Appendix B at the end of this chapter includes a flowchart for determining whether a person is a qualifying person for head of household filing status.

*If a custodial parent allows the noncustodial parent to claim the child as a dependent under a divorce decree, the agreement is ignored for purposes of this test.

Source: Internal Revenue Service, Publication 501, "Dependents, Standard Deduction and Filing Information," www.irs.gov/pub/irs-pdf/p501.pdf.

TAXES IN THE REAL WORLD He's a Head of Household, or Is He?

Mohamed Kaviro first met Abdeia Hassan in Texas around 2006. It is unclear whether they lived together in Texas. When they moved to Maine in 2009, they lived in separate four-bedroom apartments. They did not marry, but by the end of 2009, they had three children together. All three children lived with Mr. Kaviro in his apartment in 2009. The monthly rent on the apartment was about $1,700, but Mohamed's actual payment was about $300 a month because his rent was subsidized under a federal rental assistance program. For the 2009 tax year, Mohamed filed his tax return claiming the head of household filing status. The IRS argued that Mr. Kaviro did not qualify to file as head of household. In ruling on the issue of whether Mr. Kaviro qualified for head of household filing status, the Tax Court determined that Mr. Kaviro met the unmarried at the end-of-year requirement. The Court also determined that the three children were Mr. Kaviro's qualifying children. However, the Court ultimately concluded that Mr. Kaviro did not qualify for head of household status because he "failed to establish that he provided over one-half of the cost of maintaining the apartment in which he and the children resided." The Court further observed that Mr. Kaviro failed to establish the total cost of maintaining the apartment. Specifically, the Court pointed out that Mr. Kaviro's rent was heavily subsidized and that there was no evidence that he actually contributed to other household expenses such as utilities and food consumed on the premises. The facts of the case did not indicate who paid these expenses, but an educated guess would be that the expenses were covered by Ms. Hassan, the mother of the children. This case shows that you can be the only adult living in a residence with children and still not qualify for head of household tax filing status.

Source: *Kaviro v. Comm'r*, T.C. Summary Opinion 2018-57 (USTC Dec. 6, 2018).

Appendix C at the end of this chapter includes a flowchart for determining a taxpayer's filing status.

THE KEY FACTS

Filing Status for Unmarried Taxpayers

- Single
  - Unmarried taxpayers at year-end who do not qualify for head of household.
- Head of household
  - Unmarried taxpayers or taxpayers considered to be unmarried at year-end.
  - Must pay more than half of the costs of maintaining a household in which a qualifying person lives for more than half of the tax year or must pay more than half of the costs for maintaining a separate household for a parent who qualifies as taxpayer's dependent.

SUMMARY OF INCOME TAX FORMULA

Tara put together a summary of her parents' taxable income calculation. She determined that her parents will owe $468 in taxes when they file their tax return. Tara's summary is provided in Exhibit 4-10, and Exhibit 4-11 presents page 1, page 2, and Schedule 1 of the Halls' Form 1040.

EXHIBIT 4-10 Taxable Income and Tax Calculation Summary for Rodney and Anita Hall

Description	Amount	Explanation
(1) Gross income	$130,600	Example 4-1
(2) For AGI deductions	(5,000)	Example 4-2, line (2)
(3) Adjusted gross income	$125,600	(1) + (2)
(4) From AGI deductions	(25,900)	Example 4-3
(5) Taxable income	$ 99,700	(3) + (4)
(6) Income tax liability	$ 13,168	Example 4-4
(7) Credits	(2,500)	Example 4-5, line (2)
(8) Tax prepayments	(10,200)	Example 4-5, line (3)
Tax due	$ 468	(6) + (7) + (8)

EXHIBIT 4-11 Form 1040, pages 1, 2, and Schedule 1, Part II

Form **1040** Department of the Treasury—Internal Revenue Service (99) **U.S. Individual Income Tax Return** **2021** OMB No. 1545-0074 IRS Use Only—Do not write or staple in this space.

Filing Status Check only one box. ☐ Single ☑ Married filing jointly ☐ Married filing separately (MFS) ☐ Head of household (HOH) ☐ Qualifying widow(er) (QW)

If you checked the MFS box, enter the name of your spouse. If you checked the HOH or QW box, enter the child's name if the qualifying person is a child but not your dependent ►

Your first name and middle initial	Last name	Your social security number
Rodney	**Hall**	**224 56 1245**
If joint return, spouse's first name and middle initial	Last name	Spouse's social security number
Anita	**Hall**	**324 43 3478**

Home address (number and street). If you have a P.O. box, see instructions.			Apt. no.
665 Henry Avenue			
City, town, or post office. If you have a foreign address, also complete spaces below.	State	ZIP code	
Brookings	**South Dakota**	**57007**	
Foreign country name	Foreign province/state/county	Foreign postal code	

Presidential Election Campaign Check here if you, or your spouse if filing jointly, want $3 to go to this fund. Checking a box below will not change your tax or refund. ☐ You ☐ Spouse

At any time during 2021, did you receive, sell, exchange, or otherwise dispose of any financial interest in any virtual currency? ☐ Yes ☑ No

Standard Deduction **Someone can claim:** ☐ You as a dependent ☐ Your spouse as a dependent
☐ Spouse itemizes on a separate return or you were a dual-status alien

Age/Blindness **You:** ☐ Were born before January 2, 1957 ☐ Are blind **Spouse:** ☐ Was born before January 2, 1957 ☐ Is blind

Dependents (see instructions): If more than four dependents, see instructions and check here ► ☐

(1) First name Last name	(2) Social security number	(3) Relationship to you	(4) ✔ if qualifies for (see instructions): Child tax credit	Credit for other dependents
Tara Hall	**242 68 9945**	**Daughter**	☐	☑
Braxton Hall	**242 23 7845**	**Son**	☑	☐
			☐	☐
			☐	☐

Attach Sch. B if required.

Standard Deduction for—
- Single or Married filing separately, $12,550
- Married filing jointly or Qualifying widow(er), $25,100
- Head of household, $18,800
- If you checked any box under *Standard Deduction*, see instructions.

Line	Description		Amount	Line	Amount
1	Wages, salaries, tips, etc. Attach Form(s) W-2			1	**130,000**
2a	Tax-exempt interest	2a	**300**	2b b Taxable interest	**600**
3a	Qualified dividends	3a		3b b Ordinary dividends	
4a	IRA distributions	4a		4b b Taxable amount	
5a	Pensions and annuities	5a		5b b Taxable amount	
6a	Social security benefits	6a		6b b Taxable amount	
7	Capital gain or (loss). Attach Schedule D if required. If not required, check here ► ☐			7	
8	Other income from Schedule 1, line 10			8	
9	Add lines 1, 2b, 3b, 4b, 5b, 6b, 7, and 8. This is your **total income** ►			9	**130,600**
10	Adjustments to income from Schedule 1, line 26			10	**5,000**
11	Subtract line 10 from line 9. This is your **adjusted gross income** ►			11	**125,600**
12a	**Standard deduction or itemized deductions** (from Schedule A)	12a	**25,900**		
b	Charitable contributions if you take the standard deduction (see instructions)	12b			
c	Add lines 12a and 12b			12c	**25,900**
13	Qualified business income deduction from Form 8995 or Form 8995-A			13	
14	Add lines 12c and 13			14	**25,900**
15	**Taxable income.** Subtract line 14 from line 11. If zero or less, enter -0-			15	**99,700**

For Disclosure, Privacy Act, and Paperwork Reduction Act Notice, see separate instructions. Cat. No. 11320B Form **1040** (2021)

EXHIBIT 4-11 Form 1040, pages 1, 2, and Schedule 1, Part II *(continued)*

Form 1040 (2021) Page 2

Line	Description			Line	Amount
16	**Tax** (see instructions). Check if any from Form(s): 1 ☐ 8814 2 ☐ 4972 3 ☐ ____			16	13,168
17	Amount from Schedule 2, line 3			17	
18	Add lines 16 and 17			18	13,168
19	Nonrefundable child tax credit or credit for other dependents from Schedule 8812			19	2,500
20	Amount from Schedule 3, line 8			20	
21	Add lines 19 and 20			21	2,500
22	Subtract line 21 from line 18. If zero or less, enter -0-			22	10,668
23	Other taxes, including self-employment tax, from Schedule 2, line 21			23	
24	Add lines 22 and 23. This is your **total tax** ▶			24	10,668
25	Federal income tax withheld from:				
a	Form(s) W-2	25a	10,200		
b	Form(s) 1099	25b			
c	Other forms (see instructions)	25c			
d	Add lines 25a through 25c			25d	10,200
26	2021 estimated tax payments and amount applied from 2020 return			26	
27a	Earned income credit (EIC)	27a			
	Check here if you were born after January 1, 1998, and before January 2, 2004, and you satisfy all the other requirements for taxpayers who are at least age 18, to claim the EIC. See instructions ▶ ☐				
b	Nontaxable combat pay election 27b				
c	Prior year (2019) earned income 27c				
28	Refundable child tax credit or additional child tax credit from Schedule 8812	28			
29	American opportunity credit from Form 8863, line 8	29			
30	Recovery rebate credit. See instructions	30			
31	Amount from Schedule 3, line 15	31			
32	Add lines 27a and 28 through 31. These are your **total other payments and refundable credits** ▶			32	
33	Add lines 25d, 26, and 32. These are your **total payments** ▶			33	10,200

If you have a qualifying child, attach Sch. EIC.

Refund

Line	Description			Line	Amount
34	If line 33 is more than line 24, subtract line 24 from line 33. This is the amount you **overpaid**			34	
35a	Amount of line 34 you want **refunded to you.** If Form 8888 is attached, check here ▶ ☐			35a	
▶b	Routing number ▶ c Type: ☐ Checking ☐ Savings				
▶d	Account number				
36	Amount of line 34 you want **applied to your 2022 estimated tax** ▶	36			

Direct deposit? See instructions.

Amount You Owe

Line	Description			Line	Amount
37	**Amount you owe.** Subtract line 33 from line 24. For details on how to pay, see instructions ▶			37	468
38	Estimated tax penalty (see instructions) ▶	38			

Third Party Designee

Do you want to allow another person to discuss this return with the IRS? See instructions ▶ ☐ **Yes.** Complete below. ☐ **No**

Designee's name ▶ Phone no. ▶ Personal identification number (PIN) ▶

Sign Here

Under penalties of perjury, I declare that I have examined this return and accompanying schedules and statements, and to the best of my knowledge and belief, they are true, correct, and complete. Declaration of preparer (other than taxpayer) is based on all information of which preparer has any knowledge.

Joint return? See instructions. Keep a copy for your records.

Your signature	Date	Your occupation	If the IRS sent you an Identity Protection PIN, enter it here (see inst.) ▶
Spouse's signature. If a joint return, **both** must sign.	Date	Spouse's occupation	If the IRS sent your spouse an Identity Protection PIN, enter it here (see inst.) ▶
Phone no.	Email address		

Paid Preparer Use Only

Preparer's name	Preparer's signature	Date	PTIN	Check if: ☐ Self-employed
Firm's name ▶			Phone no.	
Firm's address ▶			Firm's EIN ▶	

Go to *www.irs.gov/Form1040* for instructions and the latest information. Form **1040** (2021)

EXHIBIT 4-11 Form 1040, pages 1, 2, and Schedule 1, Part II (*continued*)

Schedule 1 (Form 1040) 2021 Page **2**

Part II Adjustments to Income

11	Educator expenses		11	
12	Certain business expenses of reservists, performing artists, and fee-basis government officials. Attach Form 2106		12	
13	Health savings account deduction. Attach Form 8889		13	
14	Moving expenses for members of the Armed Forces. Attach Form 3903		14	
15	Deductible part of self-employment tax. Attach Schedule SE		15	
16	Self-employed SEP, SIMPLE, and qualified plans		16	
17	Self-employed health insurance deduction		17	
18	Penalty on early withdrawal of savings		18	
19a	Alimony paid		19a	
b	Recipient's SSN ▶			
c	Date of original divorce or separation agreement (see instructions) ▶			
20	IRA deduction		20	5,000
21	Student loan interest deduction		21	
22	Reserved for future use		22	
23	Archer MSA deduction		23	
24	Other adjustments:			
a	Jury duty pay (see instructions)	24a		
b	Deductible expenses related to income reported on line 8k from the rental of personal property engaged in for profit	24b		
c	Nontaxable amount of the value of Olympic and Paralympic medals and USOC prize money reported on line 8l	24c		
d	Reforestation amortization and expenses	24d		
e	Repayment of supplemental unemployment benefits under the Trade Act of 1974	24e		
f	Contributions to section 501(c)(18)(D) pension plans	24f		
g	Contributions by certain chaplains to section 403(b) plans	24g		
h	Attorney fees and court costs for actions involving certain unlawful discrimination claims (see instructions)	24h		
i	Attorney fees and court costs you paid in connection with an award from the IRS for information you provided that helped the IRS detect tax law violations	24i		
j	Housing deduction from Form 2555	24j		
k	Excess deductions of section 67(e) expenses from Schedule K-1 (Form 1041)	24k		
z	Other adjustments. List type and amount ▶	24z		
25	Total other adjustments. Add lines 24a through 24z		25	
26	Add lines 11 through 23 and 25. These are your **adjustments to income.** Enter here and on Form 1040 or 1040-SR, line 10, or Form 1040-NR, line 10a		26	5,000

Schedule 1 (Form 1040) 2021

Source: irs.gov.

CONCLUSION

This chapter presents an overview of the individual income tax formula and provides rules for determining who qualifies as a taxpayer's dependents and for determining a taxpayer's filing status. Upcoming chapters address computing gross income, determining individual deductions, computing the individual income tax liability, and calculating a taxpayer's available tax credits.

Appendix A Dependency Exemption Flowchart (Part I)

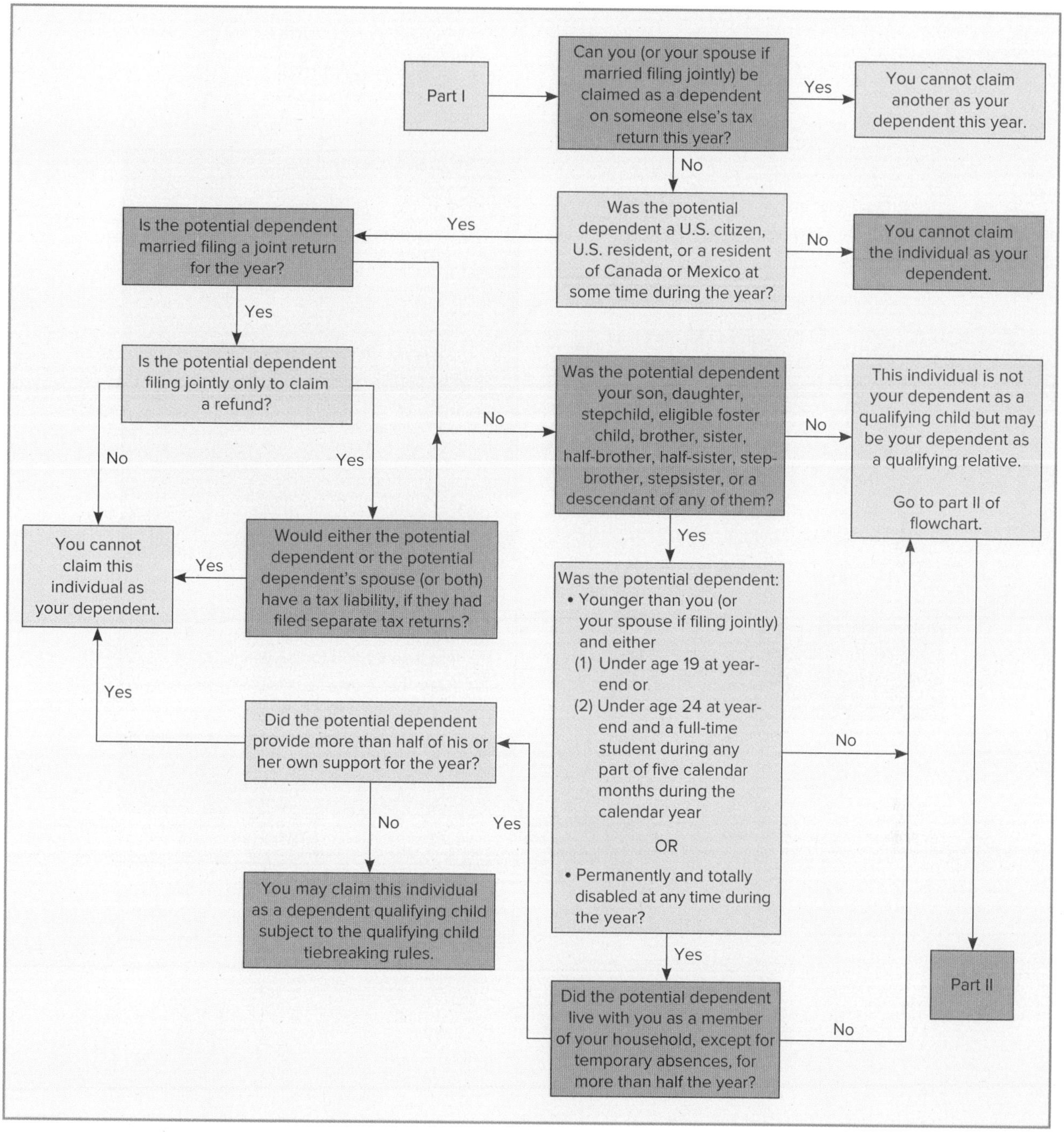

Appendix A (Part II)

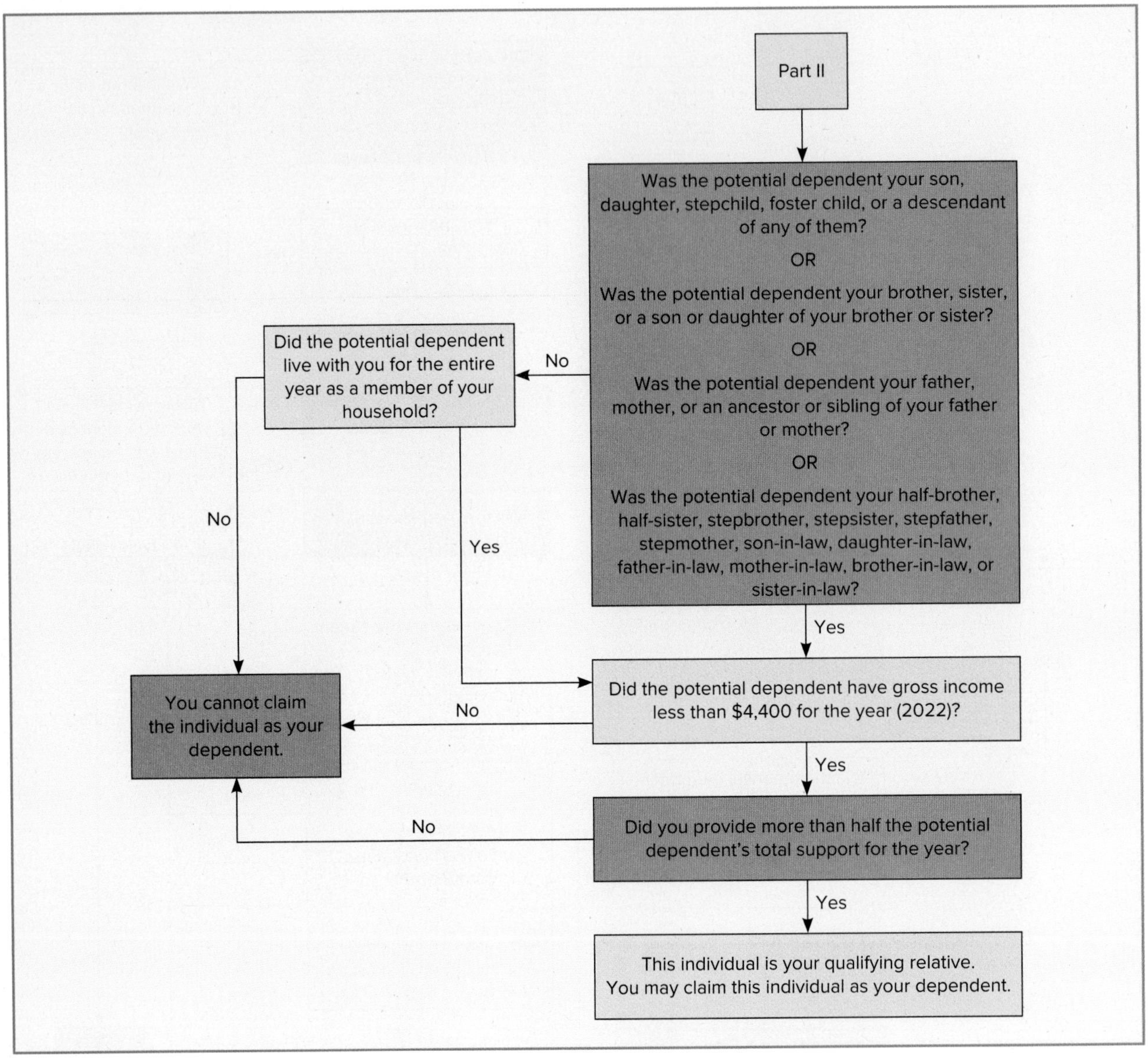

Appendix B Qualifying Person for Head of Household Filing Status Flowchart

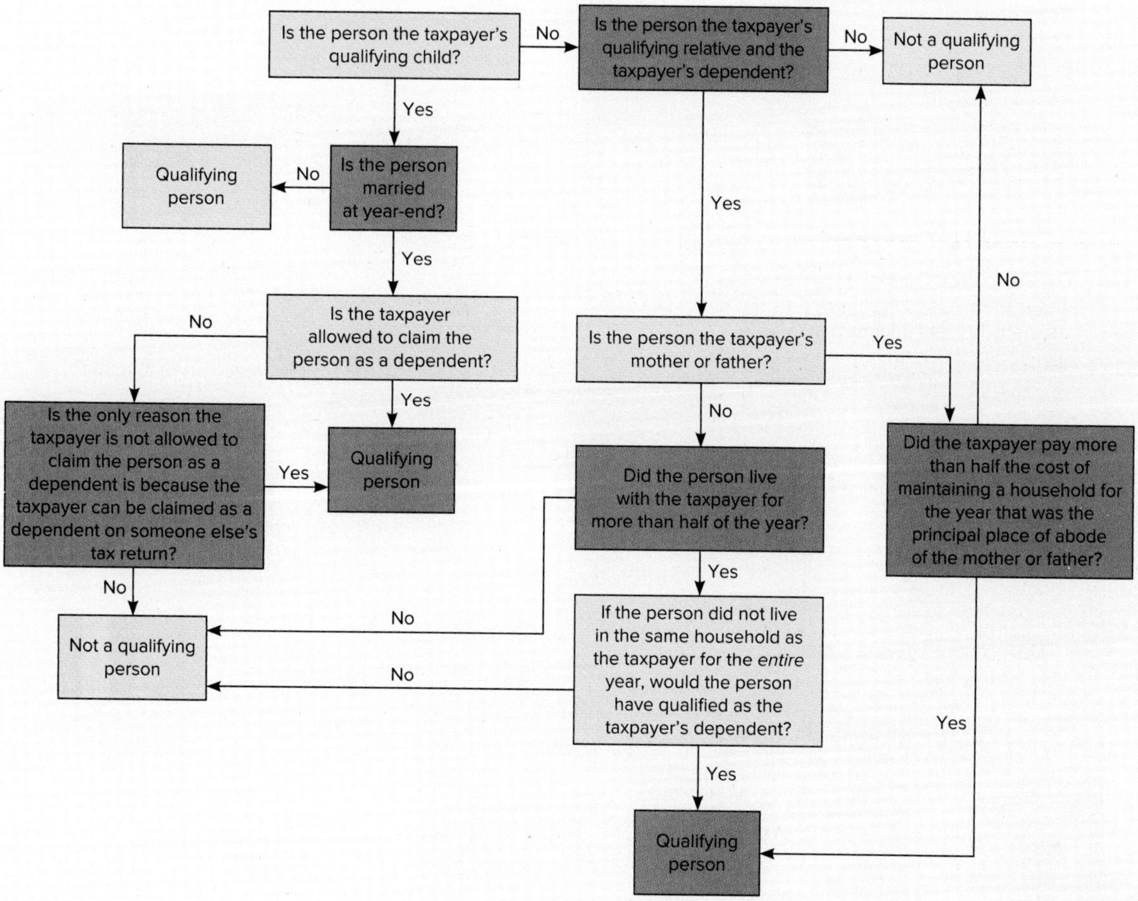

Note:

- If a custodial parent agrees under a divorce decree to allow the noncustodial parent to claim the person as a dependent, the agreement is ignored for purposes of this test.
- If the taxpayer can claim the person as a dependent only because of a multiple support agreement, that person is not a qualifying person.
- One qualifying person may not qualify more than one person for head of household filing status.

Appendix C Determination of Filing Status Flowchart

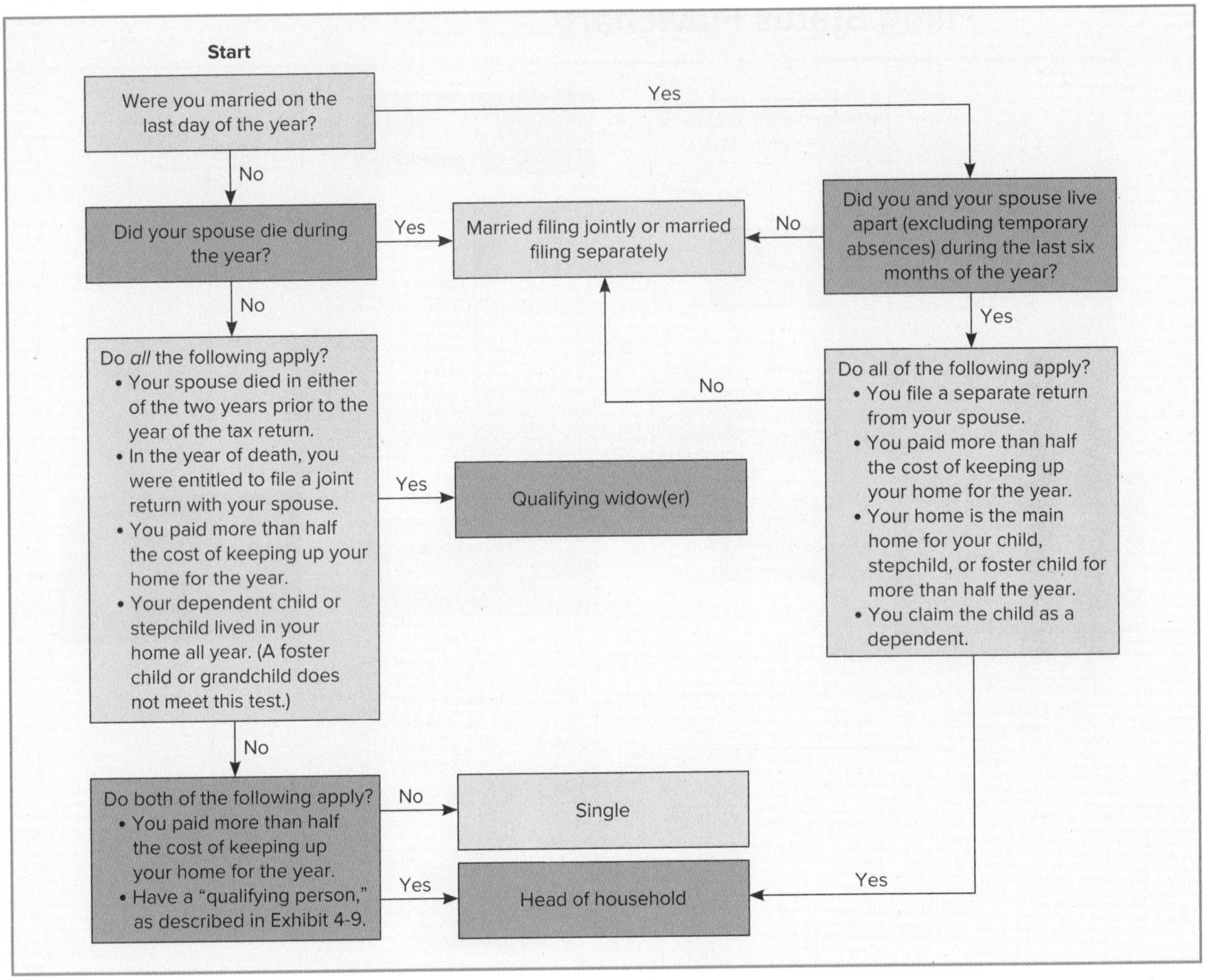

Summary

LO 4-1 Describe the formula for calculating an individual taxpayer's taxes due or refund.

- Generally, taxpayers are taxed on all income they realize during the year, no matter the source. However, the tax laws allow taxpayers to permanently exclude or to defer to a later year certain types of income they realize during the year.
- Income items that taxpayers are allowed to permanently exclude from income are called *exclusions*. Realized income items that taxpayers are not taxed on until a future period are called *deferrals*.
- Taxpayers include gross income on their tax returns.
- The character of the income determines how the income is treated for tax purposes, including, potentially, the rate at which the income is taxed.
- Ordinary income is taxed at the rates provided in the tax rate schedules; net capital gains (net long-term capital gains in excess of net short-term capital losses) and qualified dividends are taxed at 0, 15, or 20 percent, depending on the taxpayer's taxable income as indicated in the net capital gains and qualified dividends tax rate schedule. Higher-income taxpayers may pay an additional 3.8 percent net investment income tax on capital gains and dividends.
- Capital gains and losses arise from the sale or disposition of capital assets. In general, a capital asset is any asset other than accounts receivable from the sale of goods or services,

inventory, and assets used in a trade or business. If a capital asset is owned for more than a year before it is sold, the capital gain or loss is long term. Otherwise, it is short term.

- Taxpayers may deduct up to $3,000 of net capital loss for the year (excess of capital losses over capital gains for the year) against ordinary income as a for AGI deduction ($1,500 limit on deduction for married taxpayers filing separately). The remainder retains its character (either long-term or short-term net capital loss) and is treated as a loss incurred in the subsequent year.
- Even though a personal-use asset meets the capital asset definition, a taxpayer is not allowed to deduct a loss on the sale or disposition of a personal-use asset.
- Deductions reduce a taxpayer's taxable income. The two types of deductions are for AGI deductions and from AGI deductions.
- Gross income minus for AGI deductions equals adjusted gross income (AGI). For AGI deductions are deductions "above the line." The line is line 11 on page 1 of Form 1040, the individual tax return form.
- For AGI deductions tend to relate to business activities and certain investment activities.
- AGI minus from AGI deductions equals taxable income.
- From AGI deductions include the deduction for qualified business income and either the standard deduction or itemized deductions. In addition, for 2021, taxpayers who claim the standard deduction may also deduct up to $300 ($600 for married filing jointly taxpayers) of certain cash donations to charities as a from AGI deduction. From AGI deductions are referred to as "deductions below the line." This deduction has not been extended to 2022 as of the time we went to press.
- AGI is an important reference point in the individual tax formula because it is often used in other tax-related calculations.
- Taxpayers generally deduct itemized deductions when the amount of the itemized deductions exceeds the standard deduction. The standard deduction varies by filing status and is indexed for inflation. Special rules may alter the standard deduction amount for certain taxpayers.
- Taxpayers may deduct the qualified business income deduction as a from AGI deduction whether they claim the standard deduction or itemize deductions.
- Taxpayers generally calculate tax on their taxable income by referring to tax tables or tax rate schedules.
- Taxpayers may be required to pay the alternative minimum tax (AMT), self-employment tax, the net investment income tax on unearned (investment) income, and/or the additional Medicare tax on earned income in addition to their regular income tax.
- Tax credits reduce taxpayers' tax liability dollar for dollar, while deductions decrease taxable income dollar for dollar.
- Taxpayers prepay taxes during the year through withholdings by employers, estimated tax payments, or prior-year overpayments applied toward the current-year tax liability.
- If tax prepayments exceed the taxpayer's total tax after credits, the taxpayer receives a refund. If tax prepayments are less than the total tax after credits, the taxpayer owes additional tax with their tax return.

Explain the requirements for determining who qualifies as a taxpayer's dependent. **LO 4-2**

- Individuals who qualify as the dependent of another are not allowed to claim any dependents.
- Taxpayers may claim as dependents those who (1) are citizens of the United States or residents of the United States, Canada, or Mexico; (2) meet the joint tax return test; and (3) are considered either a qualifying child or a qualifying relative of the taxpayer.
- A child must meet a relationship test, an age test, a residence test, and a support test to qualify as a qualifying child.
- A person who is not a qualifying child may be considered a qualifying relative by meeting a relationship test, a support test, and a gross income test.

Determine a taxpayer's filing status. **LO 4-3**

- Taxpayers may file their tax returns as married filing jointly, married filing separately, qualifying widow or widower (also referred to as surviving spouse), single, or head of household.
- Married taxpayers may file a joint return, or they may file separately. It is generally more advantageous for tax purposes to file jointly. However, for nontax reasons, it may be advantageous to file separately.

- Each spouse is ultimately responsible for paying the tax on a joint return no matter who received the income.
- For two years after the year in which one spouse dies, the surviving spouse may file as a qualifying widow or widower as long as they (1) remain unmarried and (2) maintain a household for a dependent child (child, stepchild, or adopted child).
- Unmarried taxpayers who do not qualify for head of household status file as single taxpayers.
- An unmarried taxpayer who is not a qualifying widow or widower may file as head of household if the person pays more than half the costs of maintaining a household that is, for *more* than half the taxable year, the principal place of abode for a qualifying person (if the qualifying person is a parent, the parent need not reside with the taxpayer). In general, for an individual to be a qualifying person, the taxpayer must be able to claim the person as a dependent and the person must be considered to be related to the taxpayer even if the person does not live with the taxpayer for the entire year. That is, the taxpayer and the person must be related through a qualifying family relationship. See Exhibit 4-9 for a flowchart for determining whether an individual is a qualifying person for purposes of determining head of household filing status.

KEY TERMS

abandoned spouse (4-21)
adjusted gross income (AGI) (4-2)
all-inclusive income concept (4-2)
alternative minimum tax (AMT) (4-11)
character of income (4-6)
deductions (4-8)
deductions above the line (4-9)
deductions below the line (4-9)
deferrals (4-5)
estimated tax payments (4-12)
exclusions (4-5)
filing status (4-19)
for AGI deductions (4-8)
from AGI deductions (4-8)
gross income (4-2)
head of household (4-22)
itemized deductions (4-9)
legislative grace (4-8)
married filing jointly (4-19)
married filing separately (4-19)
net capital gains (4-7)
qualifying child (4-13)
qualifying relative (4-13)
qualifying widow or widower (4-22)
realized income (4-2)
self-employment taxes (4-11)
single (4-22)
standard deduction (4-9)
tax credits (4-12)
tax rate schedule (4-11)
tax tables (4-11)
taxable income (4-2)
withholdings (4-12)

DISCUSSION QUESTIONS

Discussion Questions are available in Connect®.

LO 4-1 1. How are realized income, gross income, and taxable income similar, and how are they different?

LO 4-1 2. Are taxpayers required to include all realized income in gross income? Explain.

LO 4-1 3. All else being equal, should taxpayers prefer to exclude income or to defer it? Why?

LO 4-1 4. Why should a taxpayer be interested in the character of income received?

LO 4-1 5. Is it easier to describe what a capital asset is or what it is not? Explain.

LO 4-1 6. Are all capital gains (gains on the sale or disposition of capital assets) taxed at the same rate? Explain.

LO 4-1 7. Are taxpayers allowed to deduct net capital losses (either net long-term capital loss in excess of net short-term capital gain or net short-term capital loss in excess of net long-term capital gain)? Explain.

LO 4-1 8. Compare and contrast for and from AGI deductions. Why are for AGI deductions likely more valuable to taxpayers than from AGI deductions?

LO 4-1 9. What is the difference between gross income and adjusted gross income, and what is the difference between adjusted gross income and taxable income?

LO 4-1 10. How do taxpayers determine whether they should deduct their itemized deductions or utilize the standard deduction?

LO 4-1 11. Are taxpayers allowed to deduct any from AGI deductions that are not itemized deductions? Explain.

LO 4-1 12. Why are some deductions called "above the line" deductions and others called "below the line" deductions? What is the "line"?

13. If taxpayers are not allowed to claim deductions for dependency exemptions, is it necessary to determine who qualifies as a taxpayer's dependent(s)? Briefly explain. LO 4-1
14. What is the difference between a tax deduction and a tax credit? Is one more beneficial than the other? Explain. LO 4-1
15. What federal income-related taxes are (or might) taxpayers (be) required to pay? In general terms, what is the tax base for each of these other taxes on income? LO 4-1
16. Identify three ways taxpayers can pay their income taxes to the government. LO 4-1
17. If a person meets the qualifying relative tests for a taxpayer, is that person automatically considered to be a dependent of the taxpayer? Explain. LO 4-1
18. Emily and Toni are recently married college students. Can Emily qualify as her parents' dependent? Explain. LO 4-2
19. Compare and contrast the relationship test requirements for a qualifying child with the relationship requirements for a qualifying relative. LO 4-2
20. In general terms, what are the differences in the rules for determining who is a qualifying child and who qualifies as a dependent as a qualifying relative? Is it possible for someone to be a qualifying child and a qualifying relative of the same taxpayer? Why or why not? LO 4-2
21. How do two taxpayers determine who has priority to claim a person as a dependent if the person is a qualifying child of two taxpayers when neither taxpayer is a parent of the child (assume the child does not qualify as a qualifying child for either parent)? LO 4-2
22. How do parents determine who claims the child as a dependent if the child is a qualifying child of both parents when the parents are divorced or file separate tax returns? LO 4-2
23. Isabella provides 30 percent of the support for her father Hastings, who lives in an apartment by himself and has no gross income. Is it possible for Isabella to claim her father as a dependent? Explain. LO 4-2
24. What requirements do an abandoned spouse and a qualifying widow or widower have in common? LO 4-3
25. True or False. For purposes of determining head of household filing status, the taxpayer's mother or father is considered to be a qualifying person of the taxpayer (even if the mother or father does not qualify as the taxpayer's dependent) as long as the taxpayer pays more than half the costs of maintaining the household of the mother or father. Explain. LO 4-3
26. Is a qualifying relative always a qualifying person for purposes of determining head of household filing status? LO 4-3
27. For tax purposes, why is the married filing jointly tax status generally preferable to the married filing separately filing status? Why might a married taxpayer prefer *not* to file a joint return with the taxpayer's spouse? LO 4-3
28. Explain what it means to say that a married couple filing a joint tax return has joint and several liability for the taxes associated with the return. LO 4-3

PROBLEMS

Select problems are available in Connect®. connect

29. Jeremy (unmarried) earned $100,000 in salary and $6,000 in interest income during the year. Jeremy's employer withheld $10,000 of federal income taxes from Jeremy's paychecks during the year. Jeremy has one qualifying dependent child (age 14) who lives with him. Jeremy qualifies to file as head of household and has $23,000 in itemized deductions, including $2,000 of charitable contributions to his church. LO 4-1
    a) Determine Jeremy's tax refund or taxes due.
    b) Assume that in addition to the original facts, Jeremy has a long-term capital gain of $4,000. What is Jeremy's tax refund or tax due including the tax on the capital gain?
    c) Assume the original facts except that Jeremy has only $7,000 in itemized deductions. Assume the charitable contribution deduction for nonitemizers applies to 2022. What is Jeremy's tax refund or tax due?

LO 4-1

30. Aram's taxable income before considering capital gains and losses is $60,000. Determine Aram's taxable income and how much of the income will be taxed at ordinary rates in each of the following alternative scenarios (assume Aram files as a single taxpayer).
   a) Aram sold a capital asset that he owned for more than one year for a $5,000 gain, a capital asset that he owned for more than one year for a $500 loss, a capital asset that he owned for six months for a $1,200 gain, and a capital asset he owned for two months for a $900 loss.
   b) Aram sold a capital asset that he owned for more than one year for a $2,000 gain, a capital asset that he owned for more than one year for a $2,500 loss, a capital asset that he owned for six months for a $200 gain, and a capital asset he owned for two months for a $1,900 loss.
   c) Aram sold a capital asset that he owned for more than one year for a $2,500 loss, a capital asset that he owned for six months for a $4,200 gain, and a capital asset he owned for two months for a $300 loss.
   d) Aram sold a capital asset that he owned for more than one year for a $3,000 gain, a capital asset that he owned for more than one year for a $300 loss, a capital asset that he owned for six months for a $200 gain, and a capital asset he owned for two months for a $1,900 loss.

LO 4-1

31. David and Lilly Fernandez have determined their tax liability on their joint tax return to be $3,100. They have made prepayments of $1,900 and also have a child tax credit of $2,000. What is the amount of their tax refund or taxes due?

LO 4-1 planning

32. Ekiya, who is single, has been offered a position as a city landscape consultant. The position pays $125,000 in wages. Assume Ekiya has no dependents. Ekiya deducts the standard deduction instead of itemized deductions, and she is not eligible for the qualified business income deduction.
   a) What is the amount of Ekiya's after-tax compensation (ignore payroll taxes)?
   b) Suppose Ekiya receives a competing job offer of $120,000 in wages and nontaxable (excluded) benefits worth $5,000. What is the amount of Ekiya's after-tax compensation for the competing offer? Which job should she take if taxes are the only concern?

LO 4-1 planning

33. Through November, Cameron has received gross income of $120,000. For December, Cameron is considering whether to accept one more work engagement for the year. Engagement 1 will generate $7,000 of revenue at a cost to Cameron of $3,000, which is deductible for AGI. In contrast, engagement 2 will generate $5,000 of qualified business income (QBI), which is eligible for the 20 percent QBI deduction. Cameron files as a single taxpayer, and he did not contribute to charity during the year.
   a) Calculate Cameron's taxable income assuming he chooses engagement 1 and assuming he chooses engagement 2. Assume he has no itemized deductions.
   b) Which engagement maximizes Cameron's after-tax cash flow? Explain.

LO 4-1 planning

34. Nitai, who is single and has no dependents, was planning on spending the weekend repairing his car. On Friday, Nitai's employer called and offered him $500 in overtime pay if he would agree to work over the weekend. Nitai could get his car repaired over the weekend at Autofix for $400. If Nitai works over the weekend, he will have to pay the $400 to have his car repaired, but he will earn $500. Assume Nitai's marginal tax rate is 12 percent.
   a) Strictly considering tax factors, should Nitai work or repair his car if the $400 he must pay to have his car fixed is not deductible?
   b) Strictly considering tax factors, should Nitai work or repair his car if the $400 he must pay to have his car fixed is deductible for AGI?

LO 4-1 LO 4-2

35. Rank the following three single taxpayers in order of the magnitude of taxable income (from lowest to highest) and explain your results. Assume none of the taxpayers contributed to charity this year.

	Ahmed	Baker	Chin
Gross income	$90,000	$90,000	$90,000
Deductions for AGI	14,000	7,000	0
Itemized deductions	0	7,000	14,000
Deduction for qualified business income	0	2,000	10,000

36. Aishwarya's husband passed away in 2021. She needs to determine whether Jasmine, her 17-year-old stepdaughter, who is single, qualifies as her dependent in 2022. Jasmine is a resident but not a citizen of the United States. She lived in Aishwarya's home from June 15 through December 31, 2022. Aishwarya provided more than half of Jasmine's support for 2022. LO 4-2
    a) Is Aishwarya allowed to claim Jasmine as a dependent for 2022?
    b) Would Aishwarya be allowed to claim Jasmine as a dependent for 2022 if Aishwarya provided more than half of Jasmine's support in 2022, Jasmine lived in Aishwarya's home from July 15 through December 31 of 2022, and Jasmine reported gross income of $5,000 for the year?
    c) Would Aishwarya be allowed to claim Jasmine as a dependent for 2022 if Aishwarya provided more than half of Jasmine's support in 2022, Jasmine lived in Aishwarya's home from July 15 through December 31 of 2022, and Jasmine reported gross income of $2,500 for the year?
37. The Samsons are trying to determine whether they can claim their 22-year-old adopted son, Jason, as a dependent. Jason is currently a full-time student at an out-of-state university. Jason lived in his parents' home for three months of the year, and he was away at school for the rest of the year. He received $9,500 in scholarships this year for his outstanding academic performance and earned $4,800 of income working a part-time job during the year. The Samsons paid a total of $5,000 to support Jason while he was away at college. Jason used the scholarship, the earnings from the part-time job, and the money from the Samsons as his only sources of support. LO 4-2
    a) Can the Samsons claim Jason as their dependent?
    b) Assume the original facts except that Jason's grandparents, not the Samsons, provided Jason with the $5,000 worth of support. Can the Samsons (Jason's parents) claim Jason as their dependent? Why or why not?
    c) Assume the original facts except substitute Jason's grandparents for his parents. Determine whether Jason's grandparents can claim Jason as a dependent.
    d) Assume the original facts except that Jason earned $5,500 while working part time and used this amount for his support. Can the Samsons claim Jason as their dependent? Why or why not?
38. John and Tara Smith are married and have lived in the same home for over 20 years. John's uncle Tim, who is 64 years old, has lived with the Smiths since March of this year. Tim is searching for employment but has been unable to find any—his gross income for the year is $2,000. Tim used all $2,000 toward his own support. The Smiths provided the rest of Tim's support by providing him with lodging valued at $5,000 and food valued at $2,200. LO 4-2
    a) Are the Smiths able to claim Tim as a dependent?
    b) Assume the original facts except that Tim earned $10,000 and used all the funds for his own support. Are the Smiths able to claim Tim as a dependent?
    c) Assume the original facts except that Tim is a friend of the family and not John's uncle.
    d) Assume the original facts except that Tim is a friend of the family and not John's uncle and Tim lived with the Smiths for the entire year.

LO 4-2

39. Francine's mother Donna and her father Darren separated and divorced in September of this year. Francine lived with both parents until the separation. Francine does *not* provide more than half of her own support. Francine is 15 years old at the end of the year.
    a) Is Francine a qualifying child to Donna?
    b) Is Francine a qualifying child to Darren?
    c) Assume Francine spends more time living with Darren than Donna after the separation. Who may claim Francine as a dependent?
    d) Assume Francine spends an equal number of days with her mother and her father and that Donna has AGI of $52,000 and Darren has AGI of $50,000. Who may claim Francine as a dependent?

LO 4-2

40. Jamel and Jennifer have been married 30 years and have filed a joint return every year of their marriage. Their three daughters, Jade, Lindsay, and Abbi, are ages 12, 17, and 22, respectively, and all live at home. None of the daughters provides more than half of her own support. Abbi is a full-time student at a local university and does not have any gross income.
    a) Which, if any, of the daughters qualify as dependents of Jamel and Jennifer?
    b) Assume the original facts except that Abbi is married. She and her husband live with Jamel and Jennifer while attending school and they file a joint return. Abbi and her husband reported a $1,000 tax liability on their tax return. If all parties are willing, can Jamel and Jennifer claim Abbi as a dependent on their tax return? Why or why not?
    c) Assume the same facts as part (b), except that Abbi and her husband report a $0 tax liability on their joint tax return. Also, if the couple had filed separately, Abbi would not have had a tax liability on her return, but her husband would have had a $250 tax liability on his separate return. Can Jamel and Jennifer claim Abbi as a dependent on their tax return? Why or why not?
    d) Assume the original facts except that Abbi is married. Abbi files a separate tax return. Abbi's husband files a separate tax return and reports a $250 tax liability on the return. Can Jamel and Jennifer claim Abbi as a dependent?

LO 4-2 LO 4-3

41. Dean Kastner is 78 years old and lives by himself in an apartment in Chicago. Dean's gross income for the year is $2,500. Dean's support is provided as follows: himself (5 percent), his daughters Camille (25 percent) and Rachel (30 percent), his son Zander (5 percent), his friend Frankie (15 percent), and his niece Sharon (20 percent).
    a) Absent a multiple support agreement, of the parties mentioned in the problem, who may claim Dean as a dependent?
    b) Under a multiple support agreement, who is eligible to claim Dean as a dependent? Explain.
    c) Assume that Camille is allowed to claim Dean as a dependent under a multiple support agreement. Camille is single, and Dean is her only dependent. What is Camille's filing status?

LO 4-2

research

42. Mel and Cindy Gibson's 12-year-old daughter Rachel was abducted on her way home from school on March 15, 2022. Police reports indicated that a stranger had physically dragged Rachel into a waiting car and sped away. Everyone hoped that the kidnapper and Rachel would be located quickly. However, as of the end of the year, Rachel was still missing. The police were still pursuing several promising leads and had every reason to believe that Rachel was still alive. In 2023, Rachel was returned safely to her parents.
    a) Are the Gibsons allowed to claim Rachel as a dependent for 2022 even though she only lived in the Gibsons' home for two-and-one-half months? Explain and cite your authority.

b) Assume the original facts except that Rachel is unrelated to the Gibsons, but she has been living with them since January 2017. The Gibsons have claimed Rachel as a dependent for the years 2017 through 2021. Are the Gibsons allowed to claim Rachel as a dependent for 2022? Explain and cite your authority.

43. Lacy is divorced and the custodial parent of a three-year-old girl named Bailey. Lacy and Bailey live with Lacy's parents, who pay all the costs of maintaining the household (such as mortgage, property taxes, and food). Lacy pays for Bailey's clothing, entertainment, and health insurance costs. These costs comprised only a small part of the total costs of maintaining the household. Lacy does not qualify as her parents' dependent. LO 4-2 LO 4-3

a) Determine the appropriate filing status for Lacy.

b) What if Lacy lived in her own home and provided all the costs of maintaining the household?

44. Lee is 30 years old and single. Lee paid all the costs of maintaining his household for the entire year. Determine Lee's filing status in each of the following alternative situations: LO 4-2 LO 4-3

a) Lee is Ashton's uncle. Ashton is 15 years old and has gross income of $5,000. Ashton lived in Lee's home from April 1 through the end of the year.

b) Lee is Ashton's uncle. Ashton is 20 years old, not a full-time student, and has gross income of $7,000. Ashton lived in Lee's home from April 1 through the end of the year.

c) Lee is Ashton's uncle. Ashton is 22 years old and was a full-time student from January through April. Ashton's gross income was $5,000. Ashton lived in Lee's home from April 1 through the end of the year.

d) Lee is Ashton's cousin. Ashton is 18 years old, has gross income of $3,000, and is not a full-time student. Ashton lived in Lee's home from April 1 through the end of the year.

e) Lee and Ashton are cousins. Ashton is 18 years old, has gross income of $3,000, and is not a full-time student. Ashton lived in Lee's home for the entire year.

45. Ray Albertson is 72 years old and lives by himself in an apartment in Salt Lake City. Ray's gross income for the year is $3,000. Ray's support is provided as follows: himself (9 percent), his daughters Diane (20 percent) and Karen (15 percent), his sons Mike (20 percent) and Kenneth (10 percent), his friend Milt (14 percent), and his cousin Henry (12 percent). LO 4-2 LO 4-3

a) Absent a multiple support agreement, of the parties mentioned in the problem, who may claim Ray as a dependent?

b) Under a multiple support agreement, who is eligible to claim Ray as a dependent? Explain.

c) Assume that under a multiple support agreement, Diane claims Ray as a dependent. Diane is single with no other dependents. What is her filing status?

46. Juan and Bonita are married and have two dependent children living at home. This year, Juan is killed in an avalanche while skiing. LO 4-3

a) What is Bonita's filing status this year?

b) Assuming Bonita doesn't remarry and still has two dependent children living at home, what will her filing status be next year?

c) Assuming Bonita doesn't remarry and doesn't have any dependents next year, what will her filing status be next year?

47. Gary and Lakesha were married on December 31 last year. They are now preparing their taxes for the April 15 deadline and are unsure of their filing status. LO 4-3

a) What filing status options do Gary and Lakesha have for last year?

b) Assume instead that Gary and Lakesha were married on January 1 of this year. What is their filing status for last year (neither has been married before and neither had any dependents last year)?

LO 4-3

48. Elroy, who is single, has taken over the care of his mother Irene in her old age. Elroy pays the bills relating to Irene's home. He also buys all her groceries and provides the rest of her support. Irene has no gross income.
   a) What is Elroy's filing status?
   b) Assume the original facts except that Elroy has taken over the care of his grandmother, Renae, instead of his mother. What is Elroy's filing status?
   c) Assume the original facts except that Elroy's mother, Irene, lives with him and receives an annual $5,700 taxable distribution from her retirement account. Elroy still pays all the costs to maintain the household. What is his filing status?

LO 4-3

49. Kano and his wife, Hoshi, have been married for 10 years and have two children under the age of 12. The couple has been living apart for the last 2 years and both children live with Kano. Kano has provided all the means necessary to support himself and his children. Kano and Hoshi do not file a joint return.
   a) What is Kano's filing status?
   b) Assume the original facts except that Kano and Hoshi separated in May of the current year. What is Kano's filing status?
   c) Assume the original facts except that Kano and Hoshi separated in November of this year. What is Kano's filing status?
   d) Assume the original facts except that Kano's parents, not Kano, paid more than half of the cost of maintaining the home in which Kano and his children live. What is Kano's filing status?

LO 4-3

50. Horatio and Kelly were divorced at the end of last year. Neither Horatio nor Kelly remarried during the current year and Horatio moved out of state. Determine the filing status of Horatio and Kelly for the current year in the following independent situations:
   a) Horatio and Kelly did not have any children and neither reported any dependents in the current year.
   b) Horatio and Kelly had one child, Amy, who turned 10 years of age in the current year. Amy lived with Kelly for the entire year and Kelly provided all of her support.
   c) Assume the same facts as in part (b), but Kelly allowed Horatio to claim Amy as a dependent under the divorce decree even though Amy did not reside with Horatio at all during the year.
   d) Assume the original facts except that during the current year Madison, a 17-year-old friend of the family, lived with Kelly (for the entire year) and was fully supported by Kelly.
   e) Assume the original facts except that during the current year Kelly's mother, Janet, lived with Kelly. For the current year, Kelly was able to claim Janet as a dependent under a multiple support agreement.

LO 4-2 LO 4-3

51. In each of the following *independent* situations, determine the taxpayer's filing status and the number of dependents the taxpayer is allowed to claim.
   a) Frank is single and supports his 17-year-old brother, Bill. Bill earned $3,000 and did not live with Frank.
   b) Geneva and her spouse reside with their son, Steve, who is a 20-year-old undergraduate student at State University. Steve earned $13,100 at a part-time summer job, but he deposited this money in a savings account for graduate school. Geneva paid the entire $12,000 cost of supporting Steve.
   c) Hamish's spouse died last year and Hamish has not remarried. Hamish supports his father, Reggie, age 78, who lives in a nursing home and had interest income this year of $2,500.
   d) Irene is married but has not seen her spouse since February. She supports her spouse's 18-year-old child, Dolores, who lives with Irene. Dolores earned $5,400 this year.

e) Assume the same facts as in part (d). Also, assume that Craig is Irene's husband. Craig supports his 12-year-old son Ethan, who lives with Craig. Ethan did not earn any income.

52. In each of the following *independent* cases, determine the taxpayer's filing status and the number of dependents the taxpayer is allowed to claim. LO 4-2 LO 4-3

a) Alexandra is a blind widow (her spouse died five years ago) who provides a home for her 18-year-old nephew, Newt. Newt's parents are dead and so Newt supports himself. Newt's gross income is $5,000.

b) Bharati supports and maintains a home for her daughter, Daru, and son-in-law, Sam. Sam earned $15,000 and filed a joint return with Daru, who had no income.

c) Charlie intended to file a joint return with his spouse, Sally. However, Sally died in December. Charlie has not remarried.

d) Deshi cannot convince his spouse to consent to signing a joint return. The couple has not separated.

e) Edith and her spouse support their 35-year-old son, Slim. Slim is a full-time college student who earned $5,500 over the summer in part-time work.

53. Jasper and Crewella Dahvill were married in year 0. They filed joint tax returns in years 1 and 2. In year 3, their relationship was strained and Jasper insisted on filing a separate tax return. In year 4, the couple divorced. Both Jasper and Crewella filed single tax returns in year 4. In year 5, the IRS audited the couple's joint year 2 tax return and each spouse's separate year 3 tax returns. The IRS determined that the year 2 joint return and Crewella's separate year 3 tax return understated Crewella's self-employment income, causing the joint return year 2 tax liability to be understated by $4,000 and Crewella's year 3 separate return tax liability to be understated by $6,000. The IRS also assessed penalties and interest on both of these tax returns. Try as it might, the IRS has not been able to locate Crewella, but they have been able to find Jasper. LO 4-3

a) What is the maximum amount of tax that the IRS can require Jasper to pay for the Dahvills' year 2 joint return? Explain.

b) What is the maximum amount of tax that the IRS can require Jasper to pay for Crewella's year 3 separate tax return? Explain.

54. Janice Traylor is single. She has an 18-year-old son named Marty. Marty is Janice's only child. Marty has lived with Janice his entire life. However, Marty recently joined the Marines and was sent on a special assignment to Australia. During the current year, Marty spent nine months in Australia. Marty was extremely homesick while in Australia because he had never lived away from home. However, Marty knew this assignment was only temporary, and he couldn't wait to come home and find his room just the way he left it. Janice has always filed as head of household, and Marty has always been considered a qualifying child (and he continues to meet all the tests with the possible exception of the residence test due to his stay in Australia). However, this year Janice is unsure whether she qualifies as head of household due to Marty's nine-month absence during the year. Janice has come to you for advice on whether she qualifies for head of household filing status. How would you advise her? LO 4-3 research

55. Dax Jones submitted his 2022 tax return on time and elected to file a joint tax return with his wife, Darlene. Dax and Darlene did not request an extension for their 2022 tax return. Dax and Darlene owed and paid the IRS $124,000 for their 2022 tax liability. Two years later, Dax amended his return and claimed married filing separate status. By changing his filing status, Dax sought a refund for an overpayment for the tax year 2022 (he paid more tax in the original joint return than he owed on a separate return). Is Dax allowed to change his filing status for the 2022 tax year and receive a tax refund with his amended return? LO 4-3 research

COMPREHENSIVE PROBLEMS

Select problems are available in Connect®.

tax forms

56. Marc and Mikkel are married and earned salaries this year of $64,000 and $12,000, respectively. In addition to their salaries, they received interest of $350 from municipal bonds and $500 from corporate bonds. Marc contributed $2,500 to a traditional individual retirement account, and Marc paid alimony to a prior spouse in the amount of $1,500 (under a divorce decree effective June 1, 2006). Marc and Mikkel have a 10-year-old adopted son, Mason, who lived with them throughout the entire year. Thus, Marc and Mikkel are allowed to claim a $2,000 child tax credit for Mason. Marc and Mikkel paid $6,000 of expenditures that qualify as itemized deductions, and they had a total of $2,500 in federal income taxes withheld from their paychecks during the year.
   a) What is Marc and Mikkel's gross income?
   b) What is Marc and Mikkel's adjusted gross income?
   c) What is the total amount of Marc and Mikkel's deductions from AGI?
   d) What is Marc and Mikkel's taxable income?
   e) What is Marc and Mikkel's taxes payable or refund due for the year? (Use the tax rate schedules.)
   f) Complete Marc and Mikkel's Form 1040 pages 1, 2, and Schedule 1 (use the most recent forms available).

tax forms

57. Demarco and Janine Jackson have been married for 20 years and have four children (no children under age 6 at year-end) who qualify as their dependents (Damarcus, Jasmine, Michael, and Candice). The couple received salary income of $105,000 and qualified business income of $10,000 from an investment in a partnership, and they sold their home this year. They initially purchased the home three years ago for $200,000, and they sold it for $250,000. The gain on the sale qualified for the exclusion from the sale of a principal residence. The Jacksons incurred $16,500 of itemized deductions, and they had $4,000 withheld from their paychecks for federal taxes. They are also allowed to claim a child tax credit for each of their children. However, because Candice is 18 years of age at year-end, the Jacksons may claim a child tax credit for other qualifying dependents for Candice.
   a) What is the Jacksons' taxable income, and what is their tax liability or (refund)?
   b) Complete the Jacksons' Form 1040, pages 1, 2, and Schedule 1 (use the most recent form available).
   c) What would their taxable income be if their itemized deductions totaled $28,000 instead of $16,500?
   d) What would their taxable income be if they had $0 itemized deductions and $6,000 of for AGI deductions?
   e) Assume the original facts but now suppose the Jacksons also incurred a loss of $5,000 on the sale of some of their investment assets. What effect does the $5,000 loss have on their *taxable income*?
   f) Assume the original facts but now suppose the Jacksons own investments that appreciated by $10,000 during the year. The Jacksons believe the investments will continue to appreciate, so they did not sell the investments during this year. What is the Jacksons' taxable income?

58. Camille Sikorski was divorced in 2018. She currently provides a home for her 15-year-old daughter Kaly. Kaly lived in Camille's home for the entire year, and Camille paid for all the costs of maintaining the home. Camille received a salary of $105,000 and contributed $6,000 of it to a qualified retirement account (a for AGI deduction). She also received $10,000 of alimony from her former husband

(per divorce decree issued in 2018). Finally, Camille paid $15,000 of expenditures that qualified as itemized deductions.

a) What is Camille's taxable income?

b) What would Camille's taxable income be if she incurred $24,000 of itemized deductions instead of $15,000?

c) Assume the original facts but now suppose Camille's daughter, Kaly, is 25 years old and a full-time student. Kaly's gross income for the year was $5,000. Kaly provided $3,000 of her own support, and Camille provided $5,000 of support. What is Camille's taxable income?

59. Tiffany is unmarried and has a 15-year-old qualifying child. Tiffany has determined her tax liability to be $3,525, and her employer has withheld $1,000 of federal taxes from her paycheck. Tiffany is allowed to claim a $2,000 child tax credit for her qualifying child (this assumes the additional child tax credit was not extended to 2022). What amount of taxes will Tiffany owe (or what amount will she receive as a refund) when she files her tax return?

UWorld ROGER CPA Review

UWorld Roger CPA Review

Sample CPA Exam questions from Roger CPA Review are available in Connect as support for the topics in this text. These Multiple Choice Questions and Task-Based Simulations include expert-written explanations and solutions and provide a starting point for students to become familiar with the content and functionality of the actual CPA Exam.

chapter

5 Gross Income and Exclusions

Learning Objectives

Upon completing this chapter, you should be able to:

LO 5-1 Apply the concept of realization.

LO 5-2 Discuss the distinctions between the various sources of income, including income from services and property.

LO 5-3 Apply basic income exclusion provisions to compute gross income.

Vectorfusionart/Shutterstock

Storyline Summary

Taxpayers:	Courtney Wilson (she/her/hers), age 40 Courtney's mother, Dorothy "Gram" Weiss (she/her/hers), age 70
Family description:	Courtney is divorced with a son, Deron (he/him/his), age 10, and a daughter, Ellen (she/her/hers), age 20. Gram is currently residing with Courtney.
Location:	Kansas City, Missouri
Employment status:	Courtney works as an architect for EWD. Her salary is $138,000. Gram is unemployed.
Current situation:	Determining what income is taxable.

The past year was a year of change for Courtney Wilson. After her divorce from Al Wilson in 2021, Courtney assumed sole custody of their 10-year-old son, Deron. Looking for a fresh start in January, Courtney quit her job as an architect in Cincinnati, Ohio, and moved to Kansas City, Missouri. Courtney wanted to pursue several promising job opportunities in Kansas City and be close to Ellen while she attends the University of Missouri–Kansas City. Courtney's 70-year-old mother "Gram" also lives in Kansas City and is in relatively good health. However, Courtney's father, "Gramps," passed away last December from cancer. At Courtney's insistence, Gram moved in with Courtney and Deron in April.

In late April, Courtney broke her wrist in a mountain biking accident and was unable to work for two weeks. Thankfully, Courtney's disability insurance paid her for lost wages during her time away from work.

While her personal life has been in disarray, Courtney's financial prospects have been improving. Shortly after arriving in Kansas City, Courtney was fortunate to land a job as an architect with Earth Wise Design (EWD). EWD provided Courtney the following compensation and benefits this year:

- Salary $138,000.
- Medical and life insurance premiums.
- Contribution of 10 percent of her base salary to her qualified retirement account.
- No-interest loan with a promise to forgive the loan principal over time if she continues her employment with EWD.
- Performance bonus for her first year on the job.

Courtney also received other payments unrelated to her employment with EWD as follows:

- Alimony from her ex-husband, Al.
- Child support from her ex-husband, Al.
- Consulting income.
- Dividend, interest, and rental income.
- Refund of state taxes she paid last year.

Before Gram moved in with Courtney, she lived alone in an apartment in Kansas City. After Gramps died, Gram was dependent on her Social Security benefits. In early April, Gram received the proceeds from Gramps's life insurance policy. She invested part of the proceeds in an annuity contract that will pay Gram a fixed amount per year. Gram also invested some of the proceeds in the stock of a local corporation. She used the rest of the life insurance proceeds to purchase a certificate of deposit and start a savings account. Gram also spent some of her spare time completing sweepstakes entries. Her hard work paid off when she won a WaveRunner in a sweepstakes contest.

Until their divorce, Courtney's husband, a CPA, always prepared their income tax return. Since EWD hired her, Courtney has become anxious about her income tax and whether her withholding will be sufficient to cover her tax bill. Courtney is also worried about Gram's tax situation because Gram did not make any tax payments this year. ■

In the previous chapter, we presented an overview of individual taxation. In this chapter, we begin to dig deeper into the tax formula to determine a taxpayer's gross income. We focus on whether income is included or excluded from a taxpayer's gross income rather than the rate at which the income is taxed. In the next three chapters, we continue to work through the individual tax formula to determine the tax liabilities for Courtney and Gram. The Individual Deductions chapter describes deductible expenses to determine adjusted gross income and taxable income, the Investments chapter discusses the taxation of investments, and the Individual Income Tax Computation and Tax Credits chapter addresses issues associated with calculating the tax liability, tax credits, and tax return filing concerns.

LO 5-1

REALIZATION AND RECOGNITION OF INCOME

As we learned in the previous chapter, **gross income** is income that taxpayers realize, recognize, and report on their tax returns for the year. In the previous chapter, we discussed gross income in general terms. In this chapter, we explain the requirements for taxpayers to recognize gross income, and we discuss the most common sources of gross income.

What Is Included in Gross Income?

The definition of gross income for tax purposes is provided in §61(a) as follows:

> GENERAL DEFINITION.—Except as otherwise provided in this subtitle, gross income means all income *from whatever source derived* [emphasis added].

In addition to providing this all-inclusive definition of income, §61 includes a list of examples of gross income such as compensation for services, business income, rents, royalties, interest, and dividends. However, it is clear that unless a tax provision says otherwise, gross income includes *all* income. Thus, gross income is *broadly* defined. Reg. §1.61-1(a) provides further insight into the definition of gross income as follows:

> Gross income means all income from whatever source derived, unless excluded by law. Gross income includes income realized in any form, whether in money, property, or services.

Based on §61(a), Reg. §1.61-1(a), and various judicial rulings, taxpayers *recognize* gross income when (1) they receive an economic benefit, (2) they realize the income, *and* (3) no tax provision allows them to exclude or defer the income from gross income for that year.[1] Let's address each of these three requirements for recognizing gross income.

Economic Benefit Taxpayers must receive an economic benefit (i.e., receive an item of value) to have gross income. Common examples of economic benefit include compensation for services (compensation in the form of cash, other property, or even services received), proceeds from property sales (typically cash, property, or debt relief), and income from investments or business activities (such as business income, rents, interest, and dividends). How about when a taxpayer borrows money? Is the economic benefit criterion met? No, because when a taxpayer borrows money, the economic benefit received (the cash received) is completely offset by the liability the taxpayer is required to pay in return for borrowing the funds (the debt amount plus interest).

Realization Principle As indicated in Reg. §1.61-1(a), the tax definition of income adopts the **realization principle.** Under this principle, income is realized when (1) a taxpayer engages in a transaction with another party and (2) the transaction results in a measurable change in property rights. In other words, assets or services are exchanged for cash, claims to cash, or other assets with determinable value.

The concept of realization for tax purposes closely parallels the concept of realization for financial accounting purposes. Requiring a transaction to trigger realization reduces the uncertainty associated with determining the *amount* of income because a change in rights can typically be traced to a specific moment in time and is generally accompanied by legal documentation.

Example 5-1

In April, Gram used part of the life insurance proceeds she received from Gramps's death to purchase 50 shares in Acme Corporation for $30 per share. From April to the end of December, the value of the shares fluctuated between $40 and $25, but on December 31, the shares were worth $35. If Gram does *not* sell the shares, how much income from her stockholdings in Acme Corporation does she *realize* for the year?

Answer: $0. Unless Gram sells the stock, she does not enter into a transaction resulting in a measurable change of property rights with a second party. Thus, she does not realize income even though she experienced an economic benefit from the appreciation of the stock from $30 per share to $35 per share.

Adopting the realization principle for defining gross income provides two major advantages. First, because parties to the transaction must agree to the value of the exchanged property rights, the transaction allows the income to be measured objectively. Second, the transaction often provides the taxpayer with the **wherewithal to pay** taxes (at least when the taxpayer receives cash in the transaction). That is, the transaction itself provides the taxpayer with the funds to pay taxes on income generated by the transaction. Thus, it reduces the possibility that the taxpayer will be required to sell other assets to pay the taxes on the income from the transaction. Note, however, that when taxpayers receive property or services in a transaction (instead of cash), realization has also occurred (despite the absence of wherewithal to pay).

[1]For tax purposes, it does not matter whether income is obtained through legal or illegal activities (e.g., embezzlement). See *Eugene James v. United States,* 366 U.S. 213 (1961).

Recognition Taxpayers who realize an economic benefit must include the benefit in gross income unless a specific provision of the tax code says otherwise. That is, taxpayers are generally required to *recognize* all realized income by reporting it as gross income on their tax returns. However, as we describe later in this chapter, through exclusions Congress allows taxpayers to permanently exclude certain types of income from gross income, and through deferrals it allows taxpayers to postpone recognition of certain types of income from gross income until a subsequent year. Thus, it is important to distinguish between realized and recognized income.

Other Income Concepts

The tax laws, administrative authority, and judicial rulings have established several other concepts important for determining an individual's gross income.

Form of Receipt A common misperception is that taxpayers must receive cash to realize and recognize gross income. However, Reg. §1.61-1(a) indicates that taxpayers realize income whether they receive money, property, *or* services in a transaction. For example, **barter clubs** facilitate the exchange of rights to goods and services between members, many of whom have the mistaken belief that they need not recognize income on the exchanges. However, when members exchange property, they realize and recognize income at the market price, the amount that outsiders are willing to pay for the goods or services. Also, other taxpayers who exchange or trade goods or services with each other must recognize the fair market value of the goods or services as income, even when they do not receive any cash. Indeed, taxpayers have the legal and ethical responsibility to report realized income (assuming no exclusion provision applies) no matter the form of its receipt or whether the IRS knows the taxpayer received the income.

Example 5-2

What if: Suppose during March, Gram paid no rent to her neighbor (also her landlord). Although the neighbor typically charges $550 per month for rent, he allowed Gram to live rent-free in exchange for babysitting his infant son. What income would Gram and Gram's neighbor realize and recognize on this exchange?

Answer: $550. Gram and the neighbor each would recognize $550 of income for March. The neighbor recognizes $550 of rental receipts because this is the value of the babysitting services the neighbor received in lieu of a cash payment for rent from Gram (an economic benefit the neighbor realized through the exchange). Gram recognizes $550 of babysitting income because this is the value of the services provided to her neighbor (an economic benefit was realized because Gram was not required to pay rent).

Return of Capital Principle When taxpayers sell assets, they must determine the extent to which they include the sale proceeds in gross income. Initially, the IRS was convinced that Congress's all-inclusive definition of income required taxpayers to include *all* sale proceeds in gross income. Taxpayers, on the other hand, argued that a portion of proceeds from a sale represented a return of the cost or capital investment in the underlying property, called **tax basis.** The courts determined that when receiving a payment for property, taxpayers are allowed to recover the cost of the property tax-free. Consequently, when taxpayers sell property, they are allowed to reduce the sale proceeds by their unrecovered investment in the property to determine the realized gain from the sale.[2] When the tax basis exceeds the sale proceeds, the **return of capital** principle generally applies to the extent of the sale proceeds. The excess of basis over sale proceeds is generally not

[2]§1001(a).

considered to be a return of capital, but rather a loss that is deductible only if specifically authorized by the tax code. Below, we revisit the return of capital principle when we discuss asset dispositions.

The return of capital principle gets complicated when taxpayers sell assets and collect the sale proceeds over several periods. In these cases, the principle is usually modified by law to provide that the return of capital occurs pro rata as the proceeds are collected over time. We discuss this issue in more detail later in this chapter when we discuss the taxation of annuities and in the Property Dispositions chapter when we discuss installment sales.

Recovery of Amounts Previously Deducted A refund is not typically included in gross income because it usually represents a return of capital or reduction in expense. For example, a rebate of $1,000 on an auto purchased for $12,000 simply reduces the net cost of the vehicle to $11,000. Likewise, a $200 refund of a $700 business expense is not included in gross income but instead reduces the net expense to $500. However, if the refund is made for an expenditure deducted in a *previous* year, then under the **tax benefit rule,** the refund is included in gross income to the extent that the prior deduction produced a tax benefit.[3] For example, suppose an individual paid a $1,000 business expense claimed as a for AGI deduction in 2021, but $250 of the expense was subsequently reimbursed in 2022. Because the $250 business deduction produced a tax benefit in 2021 (reduced taxable income and corresponding tax liability), the $250 refund in 2022 would be included in income.

The application of the tax benefit rule is more complex for individuals who itemize deductions. First, itemized deductions are subject to various limitations (e.g., deductible state and local taxes are limited to $10,000; $5,000 for a taxpayer filing married separate), which may eliminate or reduce their tax benefit. Second, an itemized deduction produces a tax benefit only to the extent that total itemized deductions exceed the standard deduction. For example, suppose an individual's total itemized deductions exceeded the standard deduction by $100. A refund of $150 of itemized deductions would cause the individual's itemized deductions to fall $50 below the standard deduction. If the refund occurred in the same year as the expense, the individual would have elected the standard deduction, and the refund would have caused taxable income to increase by only $100 (because of the difference between claiming the standard deduction and using the total itemized deductions that would have been claimed in the absence of any refund). If the refund occurs the year after the deduction is claimed, then only $100 of the $150 refund would be included in gross income under the tax benefit rule. The $100 is added to taxable income in the year of the refund because this is the increment in taxable income that would have resulted if the refund had been issued in the year the itemized deduction was claimed.

Example 5-3

In 2021 Courtney paid $3,500 in Ohio state income taxes, and she included this payment with her other itemized deductions when she filed her federal income tax return in March of 2022. Courtney filed her 2021 federal return as a head of household and claimed $20,900 of itemized deductions (including $3,500 state income taxes, $2,500 of real estate taxes, $8,000 of mortgage interest expense, and $6,900 of charitable contributions). She also filed an Ohio state income tax return in March of 2022 and discovered she only owed $3,080 in Ohio income tax for 2021. Hence, Courtney received a $420 refund of her Ohio income tax in June of 2022.

Applying the tax benefit rule, how much of the $420 refund, if any, is Courtney required to include in her gross income for 2022 given that the standard deduction for head of household filing status in 2021 was $18,800?

(continued on page 5-6)

[3]§111.

Answer: All $420. Courtney is required to include the entire refund in her 2022 gross income because her itemized deduction for the $420 of state income taxes that she overpaid last year reduced her taxable income by $420. Accordingly, because she received a tax benefit (deduction) for the entire $420 overpayment, she must include it all in gross income for 2022. See the following for the calculation of the amount of tax benefit Courtney received from the $420 overpayment of taxes in 2021.

Deduction	Amount	Explanation
(1) Itemized deductions	$20,900	
(2) 2021 standard deduction	18,800	Head of household filing status
(3) Reduction in taxable income	20,900	Greater of (1) and (2)
(4) Itemized deductions adjusted for the $420 refund	20,480	(1) – $420
(5) Reduction in taxable income after adjustment for the $420 refund	20,480	Greater of (2) and (4)
Tax benefit due to prior deduction or $420 refund	**$ 420**	(3) – (5)

What if: Let's consider *alternative* fact patterns provided in Scenarios A and B to further illustrate the application of the tax benefit rule.

Scenario A: In 2021 Courtney's itemized deductions, including $3,500 in state taxes, were $15,500.

Scenario B: In 2021 Courtney's itemized deductions, including $3,500 in state taxes, were $19,150.

How much of the $420 refund would Courtney include in her 2022 gross income in Scenarios A and B?

Answer Scenario A: $0. As computed below, Courtney received $0 tax benefit from the $420 tax overpayment in 2021, so she need not include any of the refund in her 2022 gross income.

Answer Scenario B: $350. As computed below, Courtney received a $350 tax benefit (reduction in taxable income) from the $420 state tax overpayment in 2021, so she must include $350 of the refund in her 2022 gross income.

Deduction	Scenario A Amount	Scenario B Amount	Explanation
(1) Itemized deductions	$15,500	$19,150	
(2) 2021 standard deduction	18,800	18,800	Head of household filing status
(3) Reduction in taxable income	18,800	19,150	Greater of (1) and (2)
(4) Itemized deductions adjusted for the $420 refund	15,080	18,730	(1) – $420
(5) Reduction in taxable income adjusted for the $420 refund	18,800	18,800	Greater of (2) and (4)
Tax benefit due to prior deduction of $420 refund	**$ 0**	**$ 350**	(3) – (5)

What if: In 2021 Courtney's itemized deductions were $19,150 and included $10,000 of state taxes ($10,500 total state taxes, limited by tax law to $10,000). We discuss the $10,000 state and local tax limitation in the Individual Deductions chapter. How much of the $420 refund would Courtney include in her 2022 gross income?

Answer: $0. Courtney received $0 tax benefit from the $420 tax overpayment in 2021. Her itemized deduction for state taxes adjusted for the $420 refund would still be $10,000 ($10,500 – $420 = $10,080, limited to $10,000) and her total itemized deductions would still be $19,150. So, she need not include any of the refund in her 2022 gross income.[4]

When Do Taxpayers Recognize Income?

Individual taxpayers generally file tax returns reporting their taxable income for a calendar-year period, whereas corporations often use a fiscal year-end. In either case, the taxpayer's method of accounting generally determines the year in which realized income is recognized and included in gross income.

[4]See Rev. Rul. 2019-11.

Accounting Methods Most large corporations are required to use the accrual method of accounting. Under the **accrual method,** income is generally recognized when earned, and expenses are generally deducted in the period when liabilities are incurred. In contrast, most individuals use the **cash method** as their overall method of accounting.[5] Under the cash method, taxpayers recognize income in the period they receive it (in the form of cash, property, or services), no matter when they actually earn it. Likewise, cash-method taxpayers claim deductions when they make expenditures, rather than when they incur liabilities. The cash method greatly simplifies the computation of income for the overwhelming majority of individuals, many of whom have neither the time nor the training to apply the accrual method. Another advantage of the cash method is that taxpayers may have some control over when income is received and expenses are paid. Because of this control, taxpayers can more easily use the timing tax planning strategy (described in the Tax Planning Strategies and Related Limitations chapter) to lower the present value of their tax bill.

> **THE KEY FACTS**
>
> **Income Recognition**
>
> - Cash-method taxpayers recognize income when it is received.
> - Income is realized regardless of whether payments are received in money, property, or services.
> - Income is taxed in the period in which a cash-method taxpayer has a right to receive payment without substantial restrictions.

Constructive Receipt Taxpayers using the cash method of accounting may try to shift income from the current year to the next year when they receive payments near year-end. For instance, taxpayers may merely delay cashing a check or avoid picking up a compensation payment until after year-end. The courts responded to this ploy by devising the **constructive receipt doctrine.**[6] The constructive receipt doctrine states that a cash-method taxpayer realizes and recognizes income when it is actually or *constructively* received. Constructive receipt is deemed to occur when the income has been credited to the taxpayer's account or when the income is unconditionally available to the taxpayer, the taxpayer is aware of the income's availability, and there are no restrictions on the taxpayer's control over the income.

Example 5-4

Courtney is a cash-method taxpayer. Based on her outstanding performance at work, Courtney earned a $4,800 year-end bonus. On December 28, Courtney's supervisor told her that her bonus was issued as a separate check and that Courtney could pick up the check in the accounting office anytime. Courtney did not pick up the check until January 2 of the next year, and she did not cash it until late January. When does Courtney realize and recognize the $4,800 income?

Answer: On December 28 of the tax year in question. Courtney *constructively* received the check that year because it was unconditionally available to her on December 28, she was aware of the check's availability, and there were no restrictions on her control over the check. Courtney must include the $4,800 bonus in gross income for that year, even though she did not actually receive the funds until late January of the next year.[7]

Claim of Right The **claim of right doctrine** is another judicial doctrine created to address the timing of income recognition. Specifically, this doctrine addresses when a taxpayer receives income in one period but is required to return the payment in a subsequent period. The claim of right doctrine states that income has been realized if a taxpayer receives income and there are no restrictions on the taxpayer's use of the income (e.g., the taxpayer does not have an obligation to repay the amount). A common example of the claim of right doctrine is a cash bonus paid to employees based on company earnings. Despite *potentially* having to repay the bonuses (for example, in the case of a "claw-back" provision that requires repayment if the company has an earnings restatement),

[5]Taxpayers involved in a business may use the accrual or hybrid overall method of accounting. We discuss these methods in the Business Income, Deductions, and Accounting Methods chapter.

[6]Justice Holmes summarized this doctrine as follows: "The income that is subject to a man's unfettered command and that he is free to enjoy at his own option may be taxed to him as his income, whether he sees fit to enjoy it or not." See *Corliss v. Bowers,* 281 U.S. 376, 378 (1930).

[7]Note also that Courtney's employer would include her bonus on Courtney's W-2 for the year in which it issued the check.

employees would include the bonuses in gross income in the year received because there are no restrictions on their use of the income.[8]

Who Recognizes the Income?

In addition to determining *when* taxpayers realize and recognize income, we must also consider *who* (which taxpayer) recognizes the income. This question often arises when taxpayers attempt to shift income to other related taxpayers through the income-shifting strategy. For example, a parent (with a high marginal income tax rate) might wish to assign their paycheck to their child (with a low marginal income tax rate) to minimize their collective tax burden.

Assignment of Income The courts developed the **assignment of income doctrine** to prevent taxpayers from arbitrarily transferring the taxation on their income to others. In essence, the assignment of income doctrine holds that the taxpayer who earns income from services must recognize the income. Likewise, income from property, such as dividends and interest, is taxable to the person who actually owns the income-producing property.[9] For example, interest income from a bond is taxable to the person who owns the bond during the time the interest income accrues. Thus, to shift income from property to another person, a taxpayer must also transfer the *ownership* in the property to the other person.

Example 5-5

What if: Courtney would like to begin saving for Deron's college tuition. If Courtney were to direct EWD to deposit part of her salary in Deron's bank account, who would pay tax on the salary income?

Answer: Courtney would be taxed on her entire salary as income because she earned the income.[10] The payment to Deron would be treated as a gift and would not be taxable to him (gifts are excluded from the recipient's income, as discussed later in the chapter).

What if: Suppose Courtney wanted to shift her rental income to Deron. What would she need to do to ensure that her rental income is taxed to Deron?

Answer: Courtney would have to transfer her ownership in the rental property to Deron in order for Deron to be taxed on the rental income.[11]

Community Property Systems While most states use a common law system, nine states (Arizona, California, Idaho, Louisiana, Nevada, New Mexico, Texas, Washington, and Wisconsin) implement **community property systems.**[12] Under community property systems, the income earned from services by one spouse is treated as though it were earned equally by both spouses. Also, property acquired by either spouse during the marriage is usually community property and is treated as though it is owned equally by

[8]§1341 provides relief for a taxpayer who recognizes taxable income because of the claim of right doctrine and in a later year determines that they do not have a claim of right. Specifically, §1341 provides that if a taxpayer recognizes taxable income in an earlier year because they have a "claim of right" (unrestricted right) to the income received, a deduction is then allowable in a later year because they did not have an unrestricted right to the income, and if the related tax deduction exceeds $3,000, then the tax imposed in the later year is the lesser of (1) the tax for the taxable year computed with the deduction or (2) the tax for the taxable year computed without the deduction, less a tax credit for the previous tax paid on the item of income. Individuals who are required to repay compensation previously recognized in a prior year under the claim of right doctrine are not allowed a deduction for the repayment if the amount does not exceed $3,000.

[9]This rule of thumb is also referred to as the "fruit and the tree" doctrine because of the analogy to fruit belonging to the tree upon which it was grown. See *Lucas v. Earl,* 281 U.S. 111 (1930); *Helvering v. Horst,* 311 U.S. 112 (1940).

[10]Note also that EWD has the responsibility of issuing a W-2 to the taxpayer who provided the services—Courtney in this case.

[11]As explained in the Individual Income Tax Computation and Tax Credits chapter, the tax savings from such a transfer would be mitigated in the calculation of Deron's tax by the so-called kiddie tax. Likewise, Courtney should consider the gift tax implications of this transfer before transferring the property to Deron.

[12]Three other states (Alaska, South Dakota, and Tennessee) allow a married couple to opt in to the community property rules through a written agreement signed by both parties.

each spouse.[13] Property that a spouse brings into a marriage is treated as that spouse's separate property. For federal income tax purposes, the community property system has the following consequences:

- Half the income earned from the *services* of one spouse is included in the gross income of the other spouse.
- Half the income from property held as *community* property by the married couple is included in the gross income of each spouse.
- In five community property states (Arizona, California, Nevada, New Mexico, and Washington), all the income from property owned *separately* by one spouse is included in that spouse's gross income.
- In Idaho, Louisiana, Texas, and Wisconsin, half the income from property owned *separately* by one spouse is included in the gross income of each spouse.

In contrast, for federal income tax purposes, the common law system has the following consequences:

- All the income earned from the *services* of one spouse is included in the gross income of the spouse who earned it.
- For property owned *separately,* all the income from the separately owned property is included in that spouse's gross income.
- For property owned *jointly* (i.e., not separately), each co-owner is taxed on the income attributable to their share of the property. For example, suppose that a parcel of property is jointly owned by husband and wife. One-half of income from the property would be included in the gross income of each spouse. Similarly, income from property owned by three or more persons would be included in the gross income of each co-owner based on their respective ownership share.

Example 5-6

In the year prior to their divorce, Courtney and Al Wilson lived in Ohio, a common law state, and filed married filing separately. That year, Al earned $90,000 of annual salary and Courtney earned $70,000. How much of the income earned by Al and by Courtney in the year prior to the divorce did Al report on his individual tax return? How much income did Courtney report on her individual tax return?

Answer: Because they resided in a common law state, Al reports the $90,000 that he earned on his own tax return, and Courtney reports the entire $70,000 she earned on her own tax return.

What if: How much of this income would Al have been required to include on his individual tax return, and how much of this income would Courtney have been required to report on her individual tax return, if they lived in California, a community property state?

Answer: If they resided in a community property state, both Al and Courtney would have included $80,000 of the $160,000 the couple had jointly earned [(Al's $90,000 + Courtney's $70,000)/2] on their respective individual tax returns.

If a couple files a joint tax return, the community property rules do not affect the aggregate taxes payable by the couple because the income of both spouses is aggregated on the return. However, when couples file separate tax returns, their combined tax liability may depend on whether they live in a common law state, a community property state that shares income from separate property equally between spouses, or a community property state that does not split income from separate property between spouses.[14]

[13]Property acquired during the marriage via gift or inheritance or purchased with a spouse's separate property is considered separate property.

[14]§66 provides rules that allow spouses living apart in community property states to be taxed on their individual income from services if (1) the taxpayers live apart for the entire year, (2) they do not file a joint tax return with each other, and (3) they do not transfer any of the income from services between each other.

LO 5-2

TYPES OF INCOME

Now that we have a basic understanding of the general definition of gross income and related concepts, let's turn our attention to specific *types* of income subject to taxation. Our discussion is organized around income from services, income from property, and other sources of income.

Income from Services

Income from labor is one of the most common sources of gross income, and it is rarely exempt from taxation. Payments for services including salary, wages, and fees that a taxpayer earns through services in a nonemployee capacity are all considered income from services, and so is unemployment compensation. Income from services is often referred to as **earned income** because it is generated by the efforts of the taxpayer (this also includes business income earned by a taxpayer even if the taxpayer's business is selling inventory).

Example 5-7

EWD pays Courtney a salary of $138,000. In addition, Courtney earned and received $19,500 in fees from consulting work she did on weekends independent of her employment with EWD. She incurred $1,500 in miscellaneous expenses for supplies and transportation while doing the consulting work. What is Courtney's total *income* from services (earned income) from her employment and from her self-employment activities?

Answer: $156,000, consisting of her $138,000 salary and her $18,000 business income from her consulting activities ($19,500 revenue less $1,500 expenses related to her consulting activities). Note that business deductions are for AGI deductions that taxpayers subtract from their gross business income to derive net business income or loss, reported on Schedule 1 (line 3) of Form 1040. We discuss for AGI deductions in greater detail in the Individual Deductions chapter.

Income from Property

Income from property, often referred to as **unearned income,** may take different forms, such as gains or losses from the sale of property, dividends, interest, rents, royalties, and annuities.[15] The tax treatment of unearned income depends upon the type of income and, in some circumstances, the type of transaction generating the income. For example, as discussed in the Individual Income Tax Overview, Dependents, and Filing Status chapter, qualified dividends and long-term capital gains are taxed at preferential tax rates, whereas other unearned income is generally taxed at ordinary tax rates. Likewise, while gains or losses are typically recognized in the current period, certain types of gains and losses are postponed indefinitely. We discuss annuity income and property dispositions briefly in the following paragraphs. We discuss income from property in more detail in subsequent chapters.

Example 5-8

Courtney owns 1,000 shares of Home Depot stock that she registered in a dividend reinvestment plan. Under this plan, all dividends are automatically used to purchase more shares of the stock. This year, Home Depot declared and paid $700 in dividends on Courtney's stock. Must Courtney include the dividends in her gross income for the year?

Answer: Yes. Courtney includes the $700 of dividends (unearned income) in her gross income. The fact that Courtney chose to reinvest the dividends does not affect their taxability because she received an economic benefit and change in property rights associated with the dividends.

[15]The tax definition of unearned income is different from the financial accounting definition. Unearned income for financial accounting purposes is a liability that represents advance payments for goods or services.

Example 5-9

Gram purchased a $100,000, three-year certificate of deposit (CD) with a portion of the life insurance proceeds she received on Gramps's death. At year-end, her CD account is credited with $4,100 of interest, and her savings account is credited with $650 of interest. Courtney had a total of $271 of interest credited to her savings account and $50 credited to her checking account during the year. How much interest must Gram and Courtney include in their gross income for the year?

Answer: $4,750 ($4,100 + $650) for Gram and $321 ($271 + $50) for Courtney. Gram must include the $4,100 of interest credited to her CD account and the $650 of interest credited to her savings account, regardless of whether she withdraws the interest or not. Courtney must include the $271 of interest credited to her savings account and the $50 credited to her checking account, regardless of whether she withdraws the interest or not.

Example 5-10

Courtney owns a condo in town that she rents to tenants. This year, the condo generated $14,000 of rental revenue. Courtney incurred $4,000 in real estate taxes, $2,500 in utility expenses, $500 in advertising expenses, and $2,000 of depreciation and other expenses associated with the rental. What effect does the rental have on Courtney's *gross income*? What effect does the rental have on Courtney's *taxable income*?

Answer: The rent increases Courtney's *gross income* by $14,000. However, after considering her allowable deductions for the rental, Courtney will report only $5,000 of *taxable income* from rental activities, computed as follows:

Description	Amount	
Rental revenue		$14,000
Less allowable deductions:		
Real estate taxes	(4,000)	
Utilities	(2,500)	
Advertising	(500)	
Depreciation and other expenses	(2,000)	
Total rental expenses		(9,000)
Net (taxable) rental income		**$ 5,000**

Under certain circumstances, the rental income will also generate a "deduction for qualified business income," which would reduce Courtney's taxable income. We discuss the deduction for qualified business income in the Individual Deductions chapter.

Annuities An **annuity** is an investment that pays a stream of equal payments over time. Individuals often purchase annuities as a means of generating a fixed income stream during retirement. There are two basic types of annuities: (1) annuities paid over a fixed period and (2) annuities paid over a person's life (for as long as the person lives). The challenge from a tax perspective is to determine how much of each annuity payment represents gross income (income taxed at ordinary tax rates) and how much represents a nontaxable *return of capital* (return of the original investment). For both types of annuities, the tax law deems a *portion* of each annuity payment as a nontaxable return of capital and the remainder as gross income. Taxpayers use the *annuity exclusion ratio* to determine the portion of each payment that is a nontaxable return of capital.

$$\text{Annuity exclusion ratio} = \frac{\text{Original investment}}{\text{Expected value of annuity}} = \text{Return of capital percentage}$$

For fixed annuities, the expected value is the number of payments times the amount of the payment. In other words, for an annuity payable over a fixed term, the return of capital is simply the original investment divided by the number of payments. The number of payments, however, is uncertain for annuities paid over a person's life. For these annuities, taxpayers must use IRS tables to determine the expected value based upon the taxpayer's life expectancy at the start of the annuity.[16] To calculate the expected value of the annuity, the number of annual payments from the table (referred to as the expected return multiple) is multiplied by the annual payment amount. Taxpayers with an annuity paid over the life of one person (a single-life annuity) use the expected return multiple from the table, a portion of which is presented in Exhibit 5-1.

EXHIBIT 5-1 Table for Expected Return Multiple for Ordinary Single-Life Annuity

Age at Annuity Starting Date	Expected Return Multiple
68	17.6
69	16.8
70	16.0
71	15.3
72	14.6

Source: Reg. §1.72-9.

Some annuities provide payments over the lives of two people. For example, a taxpayer may purchase an annuity that provides an annual payment each year until both the taxpayer *and* the taxpayer's spouse pass away. This type of annuity is called a joint-life annuity. The IRS provides a separate table for determining the expected number of payments from joint-life annuities.

A taxpayer receiving a life annuity who lives longer than their estimated life expectancy will ultimately receive more than the expected number of payments. The entire amount of these "extra" payments is included in the taxpayer's gross income because the taxpayer has completely recovered their investment in the annuity by the time they receive the "extra" payments. If the taxpayer dies *before* receiving the expected number of payments, the amount of the unrecovered investment (the initial investment less the amounts received and treated as a nontaxable return of capital) is deducted on the taxpayer's final income tax return.[17]

Example 5-11

In January of this year, Gram purchased an annuity from UBET Insurance Co. that will pay her $10,000 per year for the next 15 years. Gram received the first $10,000 payment in December. Gram paid $99,000 for the annuity and will receive $150,000 over the life of the annuity (15 years × $10,000 per year). How much of the $10,000 payment received by Gram in December should she include in her gross income?

Answer: $3,400. Because Gram purchased a fixed-payment annuity, the portion of the annuity payment included in gross income is calculated as follows:

Description	Amount	Explanation
(1) Investment in annuity contract	$99,000	
(2) Number of payments	15	
(3) Return of capital per payment	$ 6,600	(1)/(2)
(4) Amount of each payment:	$10,000	
Gross income per payment	**$ 3,400**	(4) – (3)

What if: Assume the annuity Gram purchased pays her $1,000 per month over the remainder of her life. Gram (70 years old) paid $99,000 for the annuity, and she received her first $1,000 payment in December of this year. How much income would she recognize on the $1,000 payment?

[16]See Reg. §1.72-9. Special rules under §72(d) apply to annuities from qualified retirement plans. These rules only apply when a taxpayer makes an after-tax contribution to a qualified employer retirement plan (which is uncommon). In most cases, taxpayers only make pretax contributions to qualified retirement plans, which results in fully taxable annuity distributions.

[17]The unrecovered cost of the annuity is deducted as an itemized deduction. See §§67(b)(10) and 72(b)(3).

Answer: $484.40, computed as follows:

Description	Amount	Explanation
(1) Investment in annuity contract	$ 99,000	
(2) Expected return multiple	16	Exhibit 5-1, 70 years old
(3) Amount of each payment	$ 1,000	
(4) Expected return	$192,000	(2) × (3) × 12 months
(5) Return of capital percentage	51.56%	(1)/(4)
(6) Return of capital per payment	$ 515.60	(3) × (5)
Taxable income per payment	**$ 484.40**	(3) − (6)

After Gram receives her entire $99,000 as a return of capital, each subsequent $1,000 annuity payment would be fully taxable.

Property Dispositions Taxpayers can realize a gain or loss when disposing of an asset. Consistent with the return of capital principle we discussed above, taxpayers are allowed to recover their investment in property (tax basis) before they realize any gain. A loss is realized when the proceeds are less than the tax basis in the property. Because the return of capital principle generally applies only to the extent of the sale proceeds, a loss does not necessarily reduce the taxpayer's taxable income. A loss will reduce the taxpayer's taxable income only if the loss is deductible. Exhibit 5-2 presents a general formula for computing the gain or loss from the sale of an asset.

THE KEY FACTS

Return of Capital

- Taxpayers are allowed to recover the capital invested in property tax-free.
- Payments from purchased annuities are part income and part return of capital.
- When property is sold or disposed of, the realized gain or loss equals the sale proceeds reduced by the tax basis of the property.

EXHIBIT 5-2 Formula for Calculating Gain (Loss) from Sale of an Asset

Sales proceeds
Less: Selling expenses
= Amount realized
Less: Tax basis (investment) in property sold
= Gain (Loss) on sale

The rate at which taxpayers are taxed on *gains* from property dispositions and the extent to which they can deduct *losses* from property dispositions depend on whether they used the asset for business purposes, investment purposes, or personal purposes. For example, as we discussed in the Individual Income Tax Overview, Dependents, and Filing Status chapter, long-term capital gains realized by individuals are taxed at preferential tax rates after a netting process, and deductions for net capital losses realized by individuals are limited to $3,000 per year. In contrast, losses realized on assets used for personal purposes are generally not deductible. We discuss specific rules associated with property dispositions in the Investments and Property Dispositions chapters.

Example 5-12

On December 31, Gram sold her 50 shares of Acme Corporation stock for $40 per share. Gram also paid $150 in broker's commissions on the sale. Gram originally purchased the shares in April of this year for $30 per share. How much gross income does Gram recognize from the stock sale?

Answer: Gram recognizes $350 gross income on the sale, computed as follows:

Sale proceeds ($40 × 50 shares)	$2,000
Less: Selling expenses	−150
= Amount realized	$1,850
Less: Tax basis (investment) in property sold ($30 × 50 shares)	−1,500
Gain (Loss) on sale	**$ 350**

Other Sources of Gross Income

Taxpayers may receive income from sources other than their efforts (earned income from wages or business) and their property (unearned income such as dividends and interest). In this section, we briefly summarize other common types of gross income. If by chance you encounter other types of income that are not specifically discussed here, remember that the tax law is based upon the all-inclusive income concept. That is, unless a specific provision grants exclusion or deferral, economic benefits that are realized generate gross income. This basic understanding of the structure of our tax law (and research skills to investigate the taxability of specific income types) will serve you well as you evaluate whether realized income should be included in gross income.

Income from Flow-Through Entities Individuals may invest in various business entities. For tax purposes, the type of business entity affects how the income generated by the business is taxed. For example, income earned by a corporation (other than an S corporation) is taxed at the entity level as opposed to the owner level. In contrast, the income and deductions from a **flow-through entity,** such as a partnership or S corporation (a corporation electing S corporation status), "flow through" to the owners of the entity (partners or shareholders).[18] That is, the owners report income or deductions as though they operated a portion of the business personally. Specifically, each partner or S corporation shareholder reports their share of the entity's income and deductions, generally in proportion to their ownership percentage, on their individual tax return.[19]

Because different types of income and deductions may be treated differently for tax purposes (e.g., qualified dividends are eligible for a preferential tax rate), each item the partners or shareholders report on their tax returns retains its underlying tax characteristics. That is, the partners are treated as if they personally received their share of each item of the flow-through entity's income. For example, corporate dividend income paid to a partnership is reported and taxed as dividend income on the partners' individual tax returns. Also, it is important to note that owners of flow-through entities are taxed on their share of the entity's income whether or not cash is distributed to them. When owners receive cash distributions from the entity, the distributions are generally treated as a return of capital to the extent of their investment (tax basis) in the entity and, therefore, are not included in the owner's gross income. Distributions in excess of basis are taxable. Partnerships and S corporations report to each partner or shareholder that partner's or shareholder's share of partnership and S corporation income (or loss) on Schedule K-1, which is filed with the partnership and S corporation's annual information returns (Form 1065 and 1120-S, respectively).[20]

Example 5-13

What if: Suppose that Courtney is a 40 percent partner in KJZ partnership. KJZ reported $20,000 of business income and $3,000 of interest income for the year. KJZ also distributed $1,000 of cash to Courtney. What amount of gross income from her ownership in KJZ partnership would Courtney report for the current year assuming her tax basis in KJZ is $15,000 before considering the distribution?

Answer: $9,200, consisting of $8,000 of business income ($20,000 × 40%) and $1,200 of interest income ($3,000 × 40%). Courtney would not include the $1,000 distribution in her gross income because it was a return of her investment.

Alimony When couples legally separate or divorce, one spouse may be required to provide financial support to the other in the form of **alimony.** The tax law defines alimony as (1) a transfer of *cash* made under a written separation agreement or divorce decree and stipulates that (2) the separation or divorce decree does not designate the payment as

[18]The S corporation election is subject to a number of limitations. By electing S corporation status, the corporation is treated as a flow-through entity and generally is not subject to corporate taxes (with a few specific exceptions).

[19]The deduction of losses from partnerships and S corporations is subject to several limitations that we discuss in the Investments chapter.

[20]See Forms 1065 and 1120-S on the IRS website, irs.gov.

something other than alimony; (3) in the case of legally separated (or divorced) taxpayers under a separation or divorce decree, the spouses do not live together when the payment is made; and (4) the payments cannot continue after the death of the recipient.[21]

For tax purposes, a transfer between former spouses represents alimony only if it meets this definition. For any divorce or separation agreement executed before January 1, 2019, if a payment meets the definition of alimony, then the amount of the payment is included in the gross income of the person receiving it and is deductible for AGI by the person paying it. Thus, alimony shifts income from one spouse to the other.[22] In contrast, for any divorce or separation agreement executed after December 31, 2018, alimony payments are not included in the gross income of the person receiving the payments and are not deductible by the person paying alimony.

Example 5-14

In addition to paying child support, under the divorce decree executed in 2021, Al is required to pay Courtney $20,000 cash each year until she or he dies. The decree does not designate this amount as a payment for something other than alimony, and Al and Courtney do not live together. Does this payment qualify as alimony?

Answer: Yes. These payments qualify as alimony for tax purposes because (1) they are cash payments made under a divorce decree, (2) they are not designated as something other than alimony, (3) Al and Courtney do not live together, and (4) the payments cease on Courtney's death. In the current year, Al made a $20,000 alimony payment to Courtney. Because their divorce agreement was executed in 2021, Courtney does not include the $20,000 in her gross income, and Al does not treat the payment as a deduction for AGI.

What if: Suppose that Courtney and Al's divorce agreement was executed in 2018. What amount of the $20,000 payment would Courtney include in her gross income and what amount would Al deduct?

Answer: Because the divorce agreement was executed before January 1, 2019, Courtney would include the $20,000 alimony payment in gross income, and Al would treat the payment as a deduction for AGI.

There may be other types of payments between former spouses that *do not qualify as alimony*. These include (1) property divisions (who gets the car, house, or furniture?) and (2) child support payments fixed by the divorce or separation agreement.[23] In any event, if a transfer of property between spouses does *not* meet the definition of alimony, the *recipient* of the transfer *excludes* the value of the transfer from income, and the person transferring the property is not allowed to deduct the value of the property transferred, regardless of whether the divorce agreement was executed before January 1, 2019, or not.

Example 5-15

As required by the divorce decree, Al made $10,000 in child support payments during the year to Courtney to help her support Deron. Al is required to make child support payments until Deron is 18 years old. Is the current-year payment included in Courtney's gross income and deductible by Al?

Answer: No. The $10,000 of child support payments is not income to Courtney, and Al does not deduct the payments. Child support payments are not includable in gross income by the recipient, and they are not deductible by the payor.

[21] §71(b). In addition, certain payments to third parties on behalf of the spouse, such as mortgage payments, can also qualify as payments in cash.

[22] To minimize tax-avoidance income shifting between a higher-tax-rate payor of alimony and a lower-tax-rate recipient of alimony pursuant to a divorce agreement or separation agreement executed before 2019, Congress enacted a complex set of restrictions called the *anti–front loading* (also known as alimony recapture) rules that make it difficult for taxpayers to disguise property payments as alimony payments.

[23] §71(c).

Example 5-16

As part of the divorce agreement executed in 2021, Al transferred his interest in their joint residence to Courtney. The couple did not have any outstanding debt on the home. At the time of the divorce, the home was valued at $500,000 and Al's share was valued at $250,000. Does the home ownership transfer to Courtney generate taxable income for her and a deduction for Al?

Answer: Property divisions upon divorce are not taxable events. Consequently, Courtney would not have recognized the $250,000 as gross income, and Al would not have deducted the $250,000 transfer.

Prizes, Awards, and Gambling Winnings Prizes, awards, and gambling winnings, such as raffle or sweepstakes prizes or lottery winnings, are included in gross income.

Example 5-17

After devoting much of her free time during the year to filling out sweepstakes entries, Gram hit the jackpot. She won a WaveRunner worth $7,500 in a sweepstakes sponsored by *Reader's Digest*. How much of the prize, if any, must Gram include in her gross income?

Answer: Gram must include the full $7,500 value of the WaveRunner in her gross income. Note that because she must pay taxes on the winnings, she is not really getting the WaveRunner for "free."

There are three specific, narrowly defined exceptions to this rule. First, awards for scientific, literary, or charitable achievement such as the Nobel Prize are excluded from gross income, *but only if* (1) the recipient was selected without any action on their part to enter the contest or proceeding, (2) the recipient is not required to render substantial future services as a condition to receive the prize or award, and (3) the payor of the prize or award transfers the prize or award to a federal, state, or local governmental unit or qualified charity such as a church, school, or charitable organization designated by the taxpayer.[24] The obvious downside of this exception is that the award recipient does not actually get to receive or keep the cash from the award. However, for tax purposes, it is more beneficial for the recipient to exclude the award from income entirely by immediately transferring it to a charitable organization than it is to receive the award, recognize the income, and then contribute funds to a charity for a charitable deduction.

Designating the award for payment to a federal, state, or local governmental unit or qualified charity has the same effect as claiming the transfer as a deduction for AGI. However, by receiving the award, recognizing the income, and then contributing funds to a charity, the taxpayer is deducting the donation as a deduction from AGI. As we discussed in the Individual Income Tax Overview, Dependents, and Filing Status chapter, deductions for AGI are likely more advantageous than deductions from AGI.

The second exception is for employee *awards for length of service or safety achievement*.[25] These nontaxable awards are limited per employee per year to $400 of tangible property other than cash, cash equivalents, gift cards, gift coupons or gift certificates, or vacations, meals, lodging, tickets to theater or sporting events, stocks, bonds, other

[24]§74(b).

[25]Prizes or awards from an employer-sponsored contest are fully taxable.

securities, and other similar items.[26] The award is not excluded from the employee's income if circumstances suggest it is disguised compensation.[27]

The third narrowly defined exception is for the value of any awards (medals) and prize money received by Team USA athletes from the U.S. Olympic Committee on account of competition in the Olympic and Paralympic Games. While there is no limit on the exclusion amount, the exclusion does *not* apply to a taxpayer for any year in which the taxpayer's AGI (after excluding the award) exceeds $1 million ($500,000 for a married individual filing a separate return).[28]

TAXES IN THE REAL WORLD You've Won a Brand New Car!

Who hasn't dreamed of hearing that famous phrase on *The Price Is Right*? Well, while many have dreamed of winning the Showcase Showdown, those who have had the pleasure of doing so have learned that those fabulous prizes come with substantial extras in the form of federal and state income taxes and even sales taxes. Indeed, winners of those fabulous new-model cars get the pleasure of paying sales tax on the cars before they are handed the keys and federal and California income taxes in the year of their big win and 15 minutes of fame. To add a bit of insult to injury, taxes are paid on the manufacturer suggested retail price (MSRP) of the car—not on the value that might be negotiated at the dealer. Nonetheless, a win is a win, even if it is not quite as lucrative as imagined.

Taxpayers must include the *gross* amount of their gambling winnings for the year in gross income.[29] Taxpayers are allowed to deduct their gambling losses and related gambling expenses to the extent of their gambling winnings, but the losses and related expenses are usually deductible as itemized deductions.[30] For professional gamblers, however, the losses and related expenses are deductible (to the extent of gambling winnings) for AGI.

ETHICS

While vacationing you find a $100 bill on the beach. Nobody saw you find it. Assuming the find meets the definition of gross income, would you report it as taxable income? Why or why not? Would your answer differ if you found $100,000 instead of $100?

Social Security Benefits Over the last 40 years, the taxation of Social Security benefits has changed considerably. Forty years ago, Social Security benefits were completely excluded from income. Today, taxpayers may be required to include *up to* 85 percent of the benefits in gross income *depending* on the taxpayer's filing status, the amount of Social Security benefits, and *modified* AGI.[31] Modified AGI is regular AGI (excluding Social Security benefits) plus tax-exempt interest income, excluded foreign income

[26]§74(c).

[27]The $400 limit is increased to $1,600 for qualified award plans (written plans that do not discriminate in favor of highly compensated employees). However, the *average* cost of all qualified plan awards from an employer is limited to $400. Managers, administrators, clerical employees, or professional employees are not eligible for an exclusion for a safety award.

[28]§74(d).

[29]Subject to *de minimis* rules, payers of gambling winnings report winnings to recipients and the IRS on Form W-2G.

[30]See Rev. Rul. 83-130.

[31]§86(d) applies to monthly benefits under Title II of the Social Security Act and tier 1 railroad retirement benefits. The Social Security Administration reports Social Security benefits on Form SSA-1099.

(discussed later in the chapter), and certain other deductions for AGI.[32] The calculation of the amount of Social Security benefits to be included in income is depicted on the IRS worksheet in the appendix at the end of this chapter.[33] The calculation is complex, to say the least. However, the taxability of Social Security benefits can be summarized as follows:

Single taxpayers:

1. If modified AGI + 50 percent of Social Security benefits ≤ $25,000, Social Security benefits are not taxable.
2. If $25,000 < modified AGI + 50 percent of Social Security benefits ≤ $34,000, taxable Social Security benefits are the lesser of (a) 50 percent of the Social Security benefits or (b) 50 percent of (modified AGI + 50 percent of Social Security benefits − $25,000).
3. If modified AGI + 50 percent of Social Security benefits > $34,000, taxable Social Security benefits are the lesser of (a) 85 percent of Social Security benefits or (b) 85 percent of (modified AGI + 50 percent of Social Security benefits − $34,000), plus the lesser of (i) $4,500 or (ii) 50 percent of Social Security benefits.

Taxpayers filing married separate:

Taxable Social Security benefits are the lesser of (a) 85 percent of the Social Security benefits or (b) 85 percent of the taxpayer's modified AGI + 50 percent of Social Security benefits.

Taxpayers filing married joint:

1. If modified AGI + 50 percent of Social Security benefits ≤ $32,000, Social Security benefits are not taxable.
2. If $32,000 < modified AGI + 50 percent of Social Security benefits ≤ $44,000, taxable Social Security benefits are the lesser of (a) 50 percent of the Social Security benefits or (b) 50 percent of (modified AGI + 50 percent of Social Security benefits − $32,000).
3. If modified AGI + 50 percent of Social Security benefits > $44,000, taxable Social Security benefits are the lesser of (a) 85 percent of Social Security benefits or (b) 85 percent of (modified AGI + 50 percent of Social Security benefits − $44,000), plus the lesser of (i) $6,000 or (ii) 50 percent of Social Security benefits.

The implications of the above calculations are that the Social Security benefits of taxpayers with relatively low taxable income are not taxed, and that 85 percent of the Social Security benefits of taxpayers with moderate to high taxable income are taxed. Because the numbers used to determine the taxability of Social Security benefits are not indexed for inflation, more taxpayers over the years have had 85 percent of their Social Security benefits taxed.

Example 5-18

Gram received $7,200 of Social Security benefits this year. Suppose that Gram's modified AGI is $16,000. What amount of the Social Security benefits must Gram include in her gross income?

Answer: $0. Gram's modified AGI plus one-half of her Social Security benefits is $19,600 [$16,000 modified AGI + ($7,200 Social Security benefits × 50%)], which is below $25,000. Hence, Gram may *exclude* the entire $7,200 of Social Security income from gross income.

What if: Assume that Gram received $7,200 of Social Security benefits this year and that her modified AGI is $26,400. What amount of benefits must Gram include in her gross income?

Answer: $2,500. Gram is single and her modified AGI + 50 percent of Social Security benefits falls between $25,000 and $34,000. Her taxable Social Security benefits are the lesser of (a) 50 percent of the Social Security benefits ($7,200 × 50% = $3,600) or (b) 50 percent of [$26,400 modified AGI + $3,600 (50 percent of Social Security benefits) − $25,000] = $2,500. Thus, her taxable Social Security benefits are $2,500.

What if: Assume that Gram received $7,200 of Social Security benefits this year and that her modified AGI is $31,400. What amount of benefits must Gram include in her gross income?

Answer: $4,450. Gram is single and her modified AGI + 50 percent of Social Security benefits exceeds $34,000. Her taxable Social Security benefits are the lesser of (a) 85 percent of Social Security

[32]See §86(b)(2).

[33]Because the 2022 worksheet was not available at press time, we include the 2021 worksheet in the appendix at the end of the chapter. The 2021 worksheet can be used to determine the taxable portion of Social Security benefits received in 2022.

benefits ($7,200 × 85% = $6,120) or (b) 85 percent of [$31,400 modified AGI + $3,600 (50 percent of Social Security benefits) − $34,000] = $850, plus the lesser of (i) $4,500 or (ii) 50 percent of Social Security benefits (50% × $7,200 = $3,600). This calculation simplifies to the lesser of (a) $6,120 or (b) $4,450 [$850 + lesser of (i) $4,500 or (ii) $3,600]. Thus, Gram's taxable Social Security benefits are $4,450.

What if: Assume that Gram received $7,200 of Social Security benefits this year and that her modified AGI is $50,000. What amount of benefits must Gram include in her gross income?

Answer: $6,120 ($7,200 × 85%).

Imputed Income Besides realizing *direct* economic benefits like wages and interest, taxpayers sometimes realize *indirect* economic benefits that they must include in gross income as **imputed income.** Bargain purchases (such as goods sold by an employer to an employee at a discount) and below-market loans (such as a loan from an employer to an employee at a zero or unusually low interest rate) are two common examples of taxable indirect economic benefits. Both bargain purchases and below-market loans generally result in tax consequences (such as gross income or taxable gifts) if the purchase or loan transaction is not an arm's-length transaction (such as transactions between an employer and employee, between an owner and entity, or among family members).

For bargain purchases, the tax consequences vary based on the relationship of the parties. For example, a bargain purchase by an employee from an employer results in taxable compensation income to the employee, a bargain purchase by a shareholder from a corporation results in a taxable dividend to the shareholder, and a bargain purchase between family members is deemed to be a gift from one family member to the other (as discussed later in the chapter, gifts are nontaxable for income tax purposes but are potentially subject to gift tax, to be paid by the person making the gift).

Although the general rule is that bargain purchases by an employee from an employer create taxable compensation income to the employee, the tax law does provide a limited exclusion for employee bargain purchases. Specifically, employees may exclude (a) a discount on employer-provided goods as long as the discount does not exceed the employer's gross profit percentage on all property offered for sale to customers and (b) up to 20 percent employer-provided discounts on services. Discounts in excess of these amounts are taxable as compensation.[34]

Example 5-19

To create more space for Gram, Courtney received EWD architectural design services as part of her compensation package and at a substantial discount. EWD's services were valued at $35,000, but Courtney was charged only $22,000. How much of the discount must Courtney include in gross income?

Answer: $6,000, computed as follows:

Description	Amount	Explanation
(1) Value of services EWD provided to Courtney	$35,000	
(2) Courtney's cost of the services	22,000	
(3) Discount on services	$13,000	(1) − (2)
(4) Excludable discount	7,000	(1) × 20%
Discount in excess of 20% is included in gross income	**$ 6,000**	(3) − (4)

For below-market loans, the indirect economic benefit conveyed to the borrower (such as an employee, shareholder, or family member) is a function of the amount of the loan and the difference in the market interest rate and the rate actually charged by the lender (such as an employer, corporation, or family member). To eliminate any tax

[34]§132(a)(2).

advantages of below-market loans, the tax law generally requires the lender and borrower to treat the transaction as if:

1. The borrower paid the lender the difference between the applicable federal interest rate (compounded semiannually) and the actual interest paid. This difference is called *imputed interest.*
2. The lender then returned the imputed interest to the borrower.

The deemed "payment" of the imputed interest in these transactions is treated as interest income to the lender and interest expense to the borrower. The deductibility of the interest expense for the borrower depends on how they used the loan proceeds (for business, investment, or personal purposes). As we learn in the next chapter, business interest expense is a deduction for AGI, investment interest expense is deductible from AGI subject to limitations, and personal interest is generally not deductible. The tax consequences of the "return" of the imputed interest from the lender to the borrower vary based on the relationship of the parties (similar to the case of a bargain purchase). For example, the return of the imputed interest from an employer lender to an employee borrower is treated by both parties as taxable compensation paid to the employee, the return of the imputed interest from a corporation to a shareholder is considered a dividend, and a return of imputed interest by a family member to another family member is considered a gift. The imputed interest rules generally do not apply to aggregate loans of $10,000 or less between the lender and borrower.[35]

Example 5-20

At the beginning of January, EWD provides Courtney with a $100,000 zero-interest loan. Assume the applicable federal interest rate (compounded semiannually) is 4 percent. Courtney used the loan proceeds to acquire several personal-use assets (an automobile and other items). What amount is Courtney required to include in gross income in the current year?

Answer: $4,000, computed as follows:

Description	Amount	Explanation
(1) Loan principal	$100,000	
(2) Applicable federal interest rate compounded semiannually	4%	
(3) Interest on loan principal at federal rate	$ 4,000	(1) × (2)
(4) Interest paid by Courtney	0	
Imputed interest included in Courtney's gross income	**$ 4,000**	(3) – (4)

Courtney will include the $4,000 imputed interest in gross income as compensation and will also incur an imputed interest expense of $4,000 for the year. EWD will (a) deduct $4,000 of compensation expense and (b) report $4,000 of interest income. In this example, we assume Courtney used the proceeds for personal purposes so she is not allowed to deduct the interest expense.

What if: Assume the same facts except that EWD had loaned Courtney $10,000 at a zero-interest rate. How much imputed interest income would Courtney be required to include in her gross income for the year?

Answer: $0. The imputed interest rules don't apply because the loan did not exceed $10,000.

THE KEY FACTS

Other Sources of Income

- For divorce or separation agreements executed before 2019, alimony is taxable to the recipient when it is paid in cash, it is pursuant to a written agreement or decree, the spouses do not live together, and the payment is contingent on the life of the recipient. For divorce or separation agreements executed after 2018, alimony is not taxable to the recipient.
- Awards are included in gross income unless they meet one of three narrowly defined exceptions.
- A maximum of 85 percent of Social Security benefits is included in gross income depending on level of AGI.
- Discharge of debt is included in gross income unless the taxpayer is insolvent before and after forgiveness.

Discharge of Indebtedness In general, when a taxpayer's debt is forgiven by a lender (the debt is discharged), the taxpayer must include the amount of debt relief in gross income.[36]

[35]§7872. For "gift" loans (loans between individuals), the $10,000 *de minimis* exception is not available for loan proceeds used to purchase or carry income-producing assets. Likewise, the $10,000 *de minimis* exception is not available for compensation-related loans or corporate-shareholder loans where the principal purpose of the loans is to avoid federal tax. For gift loans of $100,000 or less, the imputed interest is limited to the borrower's net investment income (investment income, such as interest income or other investment income not taxed at preferential rates, less related investment expenses). If the borrower's net investment income is $1,000 or less, the imputed interest rules do not apply. The exception for gift loans of $100,000 or less is not available for loans where the principal purpose of the loans is to avoid federal tax.

[36]§61(a)(12). Income from discharge of indebtedness is also realized when debt is forgiven by lenders other than employers, such as banks and credit card companies.

To provide tax relief for insolvent taxpayers—taxpayers with liabilities, including tax liabilities, exceeding their assets—a **discharge of indebtedness** is *not* taxable if the taxpayer is insolvent before *and* after the debt forgiveness.[37] If the discharge of indebtedness makes the taxpayer solvent, the taxpayer recognizes gross income to the extent of their solvency.[38] For example, if a taxpayer is discharged of $30,000 of debt and this causes the taxpayer to be solvent by $10,000 (after the debt relief, the taxpayer's assets exceed their liabilities by $10,000), the taxpayer must include $10,000 in gross income. Taxpayers, regardless of solvency, are also allowed to exclude from gross income most discharges of student loans (loans for post-secondary educational expenses) after 2020 and before 2026. Loan discharges made by an educational institution or private education lender due to services performed to the institution or private education lender are not excludable from gross income.[39]

Example 5-21

In the previous example, Courtney borrowed $100,000 from EWD. Because EWD wants to keep Courtney as an employee, it agreed to forgive $10,000 of loan principal at the end of each year that Courtney stays on board. On December 31 of this year, EWD formally cancels $10,000 of Courtney's indebtedness. How much of this debt relief is Courtney required to include in gross income this year?

Answer: All $10,000 is included in Courtney's gross income.

EXCLUSION PROVISIONS

LO 5-3

So far in this chapter, we've discussed various types of income taxpayers realize and must recognize by reporting it on their tax returns in the current year. However, there are specific types of income that taxpayers realize but are allowed to permanently *exclude* from gross income or temporarily *defer* from gross income until a subsequent period. As we discussed in the previous chapter, exclusions and deferrals are the result of specific congressional action and are narrowly defined. Because taxpayers are not required to recognize income that is excluded or deferred, we refer to tax laws allowing exclusions or deferrals as **nonrecognition provisions.** Nonrecognition provisions result from various policy objectives. In very general terms, Congress allows most exclusions and deferrals for two primary reasons: (1) to subsidize or encourage particular activities or (2) to be fair to taxpayers (such as mitigating the inequity of double taxation). Our discussion in this chapter focuses on exclusions.

Common Exclusions

Because exclusion provisions allow taxpayers to permanently remove certain income items from their tax base, they are particularly taxpayer-friendly. We begin by introducing three common exclusion provisions: the exclusions of municipal bond interest, gain on the sale of a personal residence, and fringe benefits. We continue with a survey of other exclusion provisions based on their underlying purpose: education, double taxation, and sickness and injury.[40]

Municipal Bond Interest The most common example of an exclusion provision is the exclusion of interest on **municipal bonds.** Municipal bonds include bonds issued by state and local governments located in the United States, and this exclusion is generally recognized as a subsidy to state and local governments (the exclusion allows state and

[37]§108(a)(1)(B).

[38]§108(a)(3).

[39]Other circumstances in which taxpayers may exclude a discharge of indebtedness are beyond the scope of this chapter. See §108(f) for discussion of the exclusions of student loan forgiveness and §108(a)(1)(E) for discussion of the exclusion of up to $750,000 of home mortgage forgiveness.

[40]Another common exclusion we discuss in detail elsewhere in the text is the exclusion of earnings on Roth retirement savings accounts.

local governments to offer bonds at a lower before-tax interest rate). In contrast, interest on U.S. government obligations (such as Treasury bills) is taxable for federal tax purposes but is tax-exempt for state and local tax purposes.

Example 5-22

Courtney holds a $10,000 City of Cincinnati municipal bond. The bond pays 5 percent interest annually. Courtney acquired the bond a few years ago. The city used the proceeds from the bond issuance to help pay for renovations on a major league baseball stadium. In late December, Courtney received $500 of interest income from the bond for the year. How much of the $500 interest from the municipal bond may Courtney *exclude* from her gross income?

Answer: All $500 because the interest is from a municipal bond.

Gains on the Sale of Personal Residence The tax law provides several provisions that encourage or subsidize home ownership, and the exclusion of the gain on the sale of a personal residence is a common example of one such provision. Specifically, taxpayers meeting certain home ownership *and* use requirements can permanently exclude up to $250,000 ($500,000 if married filing jointly) of realized gain on the sale of their principal residence.[41] Gain in excess of the excludable amount generally qualifies as long-term capital gain subject to tax at preferential rates after a netting process. To satisfy the ownership test, the taxpayer must have owned the residence (house, condominium, trailer, or houseboat) for a total of two or more years during the five-year period ending on the date of the sale. To satisfy the use test, the taxpayer must have used the property as their principal residence for a total of two or more years (noncontiguous use is permissible) during the five-year period ending on the date of the sale. The tax law limits each taxpayer to one exclusion every two years. Married couples filing joint returns are eligible for the full $500,000 exclusion if *either* spouse meets the ownership test and *both* spouses meet the principal-use test. However, if *either* spouse is ineligible for the exclusion because they personally used the $250,000 exclusion on another home sale during the two years before the date of the current sale, the couple's available exclusion is reduced to $250,000.[42]

Example 5-23

What if: Assume that in October of this year, Courtney sold her home in Cincinnati. Courtney and her ex-husband purchased the home four years ago for $400,000, and Courtney received the house in the divorce settlement and lived there until she moved to Kansas City in January. She sold the home for $550,000. How much taxable gain does she recognize on the sale of the home?

Answer: $0. Because Courtney satisfies the two-year ownership and two-year use tests, she may exclude up to $250,000 of gain from the sale of her home. Thus, Courtney may exclude the entire $150,000 gain that she realized on the sale ($550,000 sales price less $400,000 basis).

What if: Assume the same facts except Courtney sold the home for $700,000. How much taxable gain does she recognize on the sale of the home?

Answer: $50,000. Because Courtney satisfies the two-year ownership and two-year use tests, she may exclude $250,000 of the $300,000 gain from the sale of her home ($700,000 sales price less $400,000 basis). Thus, Courtney recognizes a $50,000 taxable gain on the sale.

[41]§121.

[42]We discuss the rules for sale of principal residence in more detail in the Tax Consequences of Home Ownership chapter, including relief rules for taxpayers who cannot meet the ownership and use test due to unforeseen circumstances and the limitation on the gain exclusion for taxpayers using a home for something other than a principal residence for a period (nonqualified use) before using the home as a principal residence.

Fringe Benefits In addition to paying salary and wages, many employers provide employees with **fringe benefits.** For example, an employer may provide an employee with an automobile to use for personal purposes, pay for an employee to join a health club, pay for an employee's moving expenses, or pay for an employee's home security system. In general, the value of these benefits is *included* in the employee's gross income as compensation for services. However, certain fringe benefits, called "qualified" fringe benefits, are excluded from gross income.[43] Exhibit 5-3 lists some of the most common fringe benefits excluded from an employee's gross income.

In addition to offering excluded fringe benefits, many employers make contributions to retirement plans on behalf of their employees. Subject to specific rules that we discuss in the Retirement Savings and Deferred Compensation chapter, these contributions (as well as employee contributions from salary) are not currently included in the employee's gross income but are deferred until the employee withdraws the contributions and related earnings from the plan. We discuss fringe benefits in more depth in the Compensation chapter.

Example 5-24

EWD paid $6,000 this year for Courtney's health insurance premiums and $150 in premiums for her $40,000 group-term life insurance policy. How much of the $6,150 in benefits can Courtney exclude from her gross income?

Answer: Courtney can exclude all $6,150 in benefits from her gross income. All health insurance premiums paid by an employer on an employee's behalf are excluded from the employee's income. In addition, premiums employers pay on an employee's behalf for group-term life insurance (up to $50,000 of coverage) are also excluded from the employee's gross income.

Example 5-25

In December, Courtney mailed a newsletter to several dozen friends and relatives with a recent picture of her son, daughter, and mother. Courtney printed both the newsletter and the photos on printers at work (with permission of EWD). Courtney would have paid $55 for the duplicate newsletters and photos at a nearby copy center. How much of this $55 benefit that Courtney received from EWD may she *exclude* from her gross income?

Answer: All $55 is excluded. The $55 benefit is considered a nontaxable *de minimis* (so minor as to merit disregard) fringe benefit because it is small in amount and infrequent.

Employee expense reimbursements. As a common fringe benefit, many employees are reimbursed for their employee business expenses by their employers. If an employee is required to submit documentation supporting expenses to receive reimbursement and the employer reimburses only legitimate business expenses, then the employer's reimbursement plan qualifies as an **accountable plan.** Under an accountable plan (which is the most common method for reimbursement), employees *exclude* expense reimbursements from gross income and do *not* deduct the reimbursed expenses. In contrast, if employees receive employer reimbursements for legitimate business expenses but do not have to submit documentation supporting the expenses, the reimbursement is considered taxable compensation, and the employee is *not* allowed to deduct the expenses as employment-related expenses (reimbursed or not). You can imagine that employees really favor accountable plans.

[43]Most nontaxable fringe benefits are listed with "items specifically excluded from gross income" in §§101–140 of the Internal Revenue Code. Employers are generally prohibited from discriminating among employees with respect to nontaxable fringe benefits (i.e., they cannot offer them only to executives). Note that §132 provides an exclusion of qualified moving expense reimbursements for members of the Armed Forces of the United States on active duty who move pursuant to a military order. This exclusion is not available to other individuals.

EXHIBIT 5-3 Common Qualified Fringe Benefits (excluded from employee's gross income)

Item	Description
Medical and dental health insurance coverage [§106]	An employee may exclude from income the cost of medical insurance coverage and dental health insurance premiums the employer pays on an employee's behalf.[44]
Life insurance coverage [§79]	Employees may exclude from income the value of life insurance premiums the employer pays on an employee's behalf for up to $50,000 of group-term life insurance.
De minimis (small) benefits [§132(a)(4)]	As a matter of administrative convenience, Congress allows employees to exclude from income relatively small and infrequent benefits employees receive at work (such as limited use of a business copy machine).
Meals and lodging for the employer's provided convenience [§119]	Employees may exclude employer-provided meals and lodging if (1) they are provided on the employer's business premises to the employee (and spouse and dependents); (2) they are provided for the employer's convenience (such as allowing the employee to be on call 24 hours a day or continue working on-site over lunch); and (3) the employee accepts the lodging as a condition of employment (for lodging only).
Employee educational assistance programs [§127]	Employees may exclude up to $5,250 of employer-provided educational assistance benefits covering tuition, books, and fees for any instruction that improves the taxpayer's capabilities, whether or not job-related or part of a degree program. The $5,250 exclusion also applies to eligible student loan repayments made by an employer on qualified education loans for the education of the employee (but not of the spouse or dependent).
No additional cost services [§132(a)(1)]	Employees may exclude the value of services provided by an employer that generate no substantial costs to the employer (such as free flight benefits for airline employees on a space-available basis or free hotel service for hotel employees).
Qualified employee discounts [§132(a)(2)]	Employees may exclude (a) a discount on employer-provided goods as long as the discount does not exceed the employer's gross profit percentage on all property offered for sale to customers and (b) up to 20 percent employer-provided discount on services. Discounts in excess of these amounts are taxable as compensation. See Example 5-19.
Dependent care benefits [§129]	Employees may exclude up to $5,000 for benefits paid or reimbursed by employers for caring for children under age 13 or dependents or spouses who are physically or mentally unable to care for themselves.
Working condition fringe benefits [§132(a)(3)]	Employees may exclude from income any benefit or reimbursement of a benefit provided by an employer that would be deductible as an ordinary and necessary expense by the employee if the employee had paid the expense.
Qualified transportation benefits [§132(a)(5)]	Employees may exclude up to $280 per month of employer-provided parking and up to $280 per month of the combined value of employer-provided mass transit passes and the value of a carpool vehicle for employee use.
Cafeteria plans [§125]	Cafeteria plans allow employees to choose between various nontaxable fringe benefits (such as health insurance and dental insurance) and cash. These benefits are tax-free to the extent the taxpayer chooses nontaxable fringe benefits and taxable to the extent the employee receives cash.
Flexible spending accounts [§125]	Flexible spending accounts (FSAs) allow employees to set aside a portion of their *before*-tax salary for payment of health and/or dependent-care benefits. These amounts generally must be used by the end of the year or within the first two and a half months of the next plan year, or employees forfeit the unused balance. In lieu of allowing the typical two-and-a-half-month grace period at the beginning of each new year, employers can allow employees to carry over unused amounts to be used anytime during the next year (it is the employer's choice). The carryover is limited annually to 20 percent of the maximum FSA set aside, and the option to carry over amounts does not apply to dependent-care flexible spending accounts.[45] For 2022 the amount of before-tax salary an employee may set aside for medical expenses is limited to $2,850, the carryover limit is $570 ($2,850 × 20%), and the before-tax amount that may be set aside for dependent-care expenses is limited to $5,000.
Health savings accounts [§106; §223]	Health savings accounts (HSAs) allow employees covered by a high deductible health plan to set aside a portion of their before-tax salary for payment of qualified medical and dental expenses for the taxpayer, spouse, and dependents.[46] For 2022, employees can contribute up to $3,650 for self-only coverage ($7,300 for family coverage) to an HSA. Employees age 55 or older at the end of the tax year may contribute an additional $1,000 annually. Employers may also contribute to an employee's HSA, which reduces the employee's maximum contribution. Unlike an FSA, contributions to an HSA remain in the taxpayer's account until used and the funds may earn interest or other investment returns. Distributions from an HSA are nontaxable if they pay for qualified medical and dental expenses of the taxpayer, spouse, and dependents that occurred after the HSA was established (even if the distribution occurs in a year after the expense was incurred or in a year in which the taxpayer is no longer covered under a high deductible health plan). Taxpayers just need to maintain medical receipts to substantiate the previously unreimbursed qualified medical expenses. Otherwise, distributions are taxed as ordinary income (and subject to an additional 20% tax unless the taxpayer is disabled, age 65 or older, or deceased).

[44]The cost of medical coverage paid by an employer and offered through a health insurance exchange is not an excludable benefit unless the employer is a small employer that elects to make all of its full-time employees eligible for plans offered through the small business health options program (SHOP). For this purpose, a small employer is an employer that employs an average of at least 1 but 50 or fewer employees during business days in the prior year, and employs at least 1 employee on the first day of the plan year.

[45]In 2020 and 2021, the 20 percent limit on carryover was suspended.

[46]For 2022, a high deductible health plan must have an annual deductible of at least $1,400 for self-only coverage ($2,800 for family coverage) and the plan's maximum annual deductible and other out-of-pocket expenses cannot exceed $7,050 for self-only coverage ($14,100 for family coverage). To contribute to an HSA, the employee cannot be enrolled in Medicare, be claimed as a dependent on another taxpayer's tax return, or have other health coverage (except worker's compensation, coverage for a specific disease or illness, or for a fixed amount per day or period of hospitalization, accidents, disability, dental care, vision care, long-term care, and in other specific circumstances).

TAXES IN THE REAL WORLD Have Phone, Will Call Tax-Free?

Employee cell phones aid employees in conducting business on behalf of their employer but also benefit the employees to the extent they use the phone for personal use. This use could create quite the record-keeping challenge if the IRS classified employee cell phones issued by employers as a taxable benefit (i.e., taxable compensation). Fortunately, the IRS considers an employer-issued cell phone as an excludable fringe benefit (for both business and personal use) when the phone is provided primarily for noncompensatory business reasons. Even better, the IRS does not require record keeping for employees to receive the tax-free treatment. See Notice 2011-72.

Education-Related Exclusions

As an incentive for taxpayers to participate in higher education (education beyond high school), Congress excludes certain types of income if the funds are used for higher education. In the following paragraphs, we discuss exclusions for scholarships and exclusions for certain types of investment plans used to save for college.[47]

Scholarships College students seeking a degree can exclude from gross income scholarships (including Pell grants) that pay for tuition, fees, books, supplies, and other equipment *required* for the student's courses.[48] Any excess scholarship amounts (such as for room or board) are fully taxable. The scholarship exclusion applies only if the recipient is *not* required to perform services in exchange for receiving the scholarship. "Scholarships" that represent compensation for past, current, or future services are fully taxable. However, tuition waivers or reductions provided by an educational institution for undergraduate courses for student employees or for graduate courses for teaching or research assistants are not taxable.

What about athletic scholarships? Good question. The IRS has ruled that the value of athletic scholarships is excludable from gross income if it (1) is awarded to students by a university that *expects* but *does not require* the students to participate in a particular sport, (2) requires no particular activity in lieu of participation, and (3) is not cancelled if the student cannot participate.[49] Like other scholarships, athletic scholarships are only excludable from gross income to the extent they pay for tuition, fees, books, supplies, and other equipment required for the student's courses. Any excess amount (for example, for room and board) is taxable. Likewise, any compensation received for name, image and likeness (NIL) is taxable.

Example 5-26

Ellen, Courtney's daughter, received a $5,700 scholarship from the University of Missouri–Kansas City that pays $5,400 of her tuition and provides $300 cash for books. Ellen spent $350 on books. How much of the scholarship may she exclude from gross income?

Answer: All $5,700 is excluded. Ellen may exclude all of the scholarship for tuition, and she may exclude the $300 cash she received for books because she spent all $300 purchasing her books for school.

What if: How much is Ellen allowed to exclude if she spent only $250 on books?

Answer: $5,650 is excluded. Ellen excludes all of the scholarship for her tuition and $250 of the $300 in cash payments because she spent $250 on books. She must include the excess cash payment of $50 ($300 – $250) in her gross income.

Other Educational Subsidies Taxpayers are allowed to exclude from gross income earnings on investments in qualified education plans such as 529 plans and Coverdell education savings accounts as long as they use the earnings to pay for qualifying educational expenditures.

[47]A detailed explanation is available in IRS Publication 970, *Tax Benefits for Education,* available on the IRS website at www.irs.gov.

[48]§117(b)(2). Note that exclusion of the scholarship is not required. For example, a taxpayer can elect to treat all or part of the scholarship as taxable income in order to claim the American Opportunity Tax Credit.

[49]Rev. Rul. 77-263.

THE KEY FACTS

Education Exclusions

- Students seeking a college degree can exclude scholarships that pay for required tuition, fees, books, and supplies.
- Taxpayers can elect to exclude interest earned on Series EE savings bonds when the redemption proceeds are used to pay qualified higher-education expenses.
- The exclusion of interest on Series EE savings bonds is restricted to taxpayers with modified AGI below specific limits.

With 529 plans, parents, grandparents, and other individuals are allowed to contribute up to the maximum allowed by state-sponsored 529 plans to fund the qualified educational costs of future *college* students and, subject to limitations, educational costs of students at public, private, or religious elementary or secondary schools.[50] Earnings in 529 plans are distributed tax-free provided they are used for qualified higher-education expenses (no annual limit) or tuition expense attributable to public, private, or religious elementary or secondary schools (subject to a $10,000 limit per beneficiary per year). Qualified higher-education expenses include tuition, books, supplies, required equipment and supplies, computer equipment and software, and reasonable room and board costs attending a higher-education institution. If, on the other hand, distributions are made to the beneficiary for other purposes or exceed the $10,000 limit for tuition expenses attributable to public, private, or religious elementary or secondary schools, the earnings distributed are taxed to the beneficiary at the beneficiary's tax rate and are subject to an additional 10 percent penalty, while distributions of the original investment (contributions) to the beneficiary are treated as gifts.[51] Similarly, distributions to contributors (e.g., parents, grandparents) that represent earnings on their contributions are included in contributors' gross income and are also subject to the 10 percent penalty.

With a Coverdell account, yearly contributions to the account are limited to $2,000 for each beneficiary, and distributions may be used to pay for qualified educational costs of kindergarten through 12th grade and qualified higher-education expenses such as tuition, books, fees, supplies, and reasonable room and board.[52] The $2,000 contribution limit for Coverdell accounts phases out as AGI (modified to include certain types of excluded foreign income) increases from $190,000 to $220,000 for married filing jointly taxpayers, and from $95,000 to $110,000 for all other taxpayers. The AGI limits are not indexed for inflation.

U.S. Series EE Bonds The federal government issues bonds that allow taxpayers to acquire the bonds at a discount and redeem the bonds for a fixed amount over stated time intervals. These bonds don't generate any cash in the form of interest until the taxpayer redeems the bond. At redemption, the amount of the redemption price in excess of the acquisition price is interest included in gross income.[53] U.S. Series EE bonds fall into this category. However, an exclusion is available for interest from Series EE bonds. This exclusion requires that the redemption proceeds be used to pay for higher-education expenses of the taxpayer, the taxpayer's spouse, or a dependent of the taxpayer. Qualified higher-education expenses include the tuition and fees required for enrollment or attendance at an eligible educational institution. Taxpayers may also exclude the interest income if they contribute the proceeds to a qualified tuition program.

The exclusion is partially reduced or eliminated for taxpayers exceeding a fixed level of modified adjusted gross income (adjusted gross income before the educational savings bond exclusion; the foreign-earned income exclusion, discussed below; and certain other deductions).[54] If the taxpayer's modified AGI exceeds the thresholds in the redemption year, the exclusion is phased out (gradually reduced) until all of the interest from the bonds is taxed.[55]

Exclusions That Mitigate Double Taxation

Congress provides certain exclusions that eliminate the potential double tax that may arise for gifts, inheritances, and life insurance proceeds.

[50]Contribution limits vary according to the state administering the 529 plan. In addition, more than half the states offer a state tax deduction or credit to residents contributing to the 529 plan sponsored by the state in which the contributors reside.

[51]Under §529(c)(3), multiple distributions received under these circumstances are treated as annuities. As a result, a portion of each distribution would be treated as a gift, with the remainder treated as income.

[52]§530(b). This definition of qualified higher-education expenses is consistent with the definition used in §221(d)(2) to determine if interest paid on education-related loans is deductible.

[53]Alternatively, taxpayers can elect to include the annual increase in the redemption value in gross income rather than waiting to recognize all the income on redemption. See §454(a).

[54]§135(c)(4).

[55]In 2022, the phase-out range begins at $128,650 of modified adjusted gross income and ends at $158,650 for married taxpayers filing joint returns. For all other taxpayers, the phase-out range begins at $85,800 and ends at $100,800.

Gifts and Inheritances Individuals may transfer property to other taxpayers without receiving or expecting to receive value in return. If the *transferor* is alive at the time of the transfer, the property transfer is called a **gift.** If the property is transferred from the decedent's estate (the transferor is deceased), it is called an **inheritance.** These transfers are generally subject to a federal transfer tax, *not* the income tax. Gifts are typically subject to the federal gift tax and inheritances are typically subject to a federal estate tax.[56] Thus, gift and estate taxes are imposed on *transfer* of the property and *not included in income by the recipient.* The exclusion of gifts and inheritances from income taxation avoids the potential double taxation (transfer and income taxation) on these transfers.

Example 5-27

Ellen graduated from high school last year. As a graduation present, Gram purchased a $1,500 travel package for Ellen so that Ellen could go on a Caribbean cruise. Last year, Ellen also received an inheritance of $2,000 from Gramps's estate. How much gross income does Ellen recognize on the $1,500 gift she received from Gram and the $2,000 inheritance she received from Gramps's estate?

Answer: $0. Ellen is allowed to exclude the entire gift and the entire amount of the inheritance from her gross income. Consequently, she does not recognize any gross income from these transactions.

Life Insurance Proceeds In some ways, life insurance proceeds are similar to inheritances. When the owner of the life insurance policy dies, the beneficiary receives the death benefit proceeds. The decedent (or the decedent's estate) is generally subject to estate taxation on the amount of the insurance proceeds. In order to avoid potential double taxation on the life insurance proceeds, the tax laws allow taxpayers receiving life insurance proceeds to exclude the proceeds from gross income.[57] However, when the insurance proceeds are paid over a period of time rather than in a lump sum, a portion of the payments represents interest and must be included in gross income. In addition, the life insurance proceeds exclusion generally does not apply when a life insurance policy is transferred to another party for valuable consideration. In this case, the eventual life insurance proceeds collected by the purchaser are excluded up to the sum of the purchase price of the policy and any subsequent premiums, with remaining proceeds taxable as ordinary income.[58]

What happens if a taxpayer cashes out a policy before death? The tax treatment varies based on the specific facts. Generally, if a taxpayer simply cancels a life insurance contract and is paid the policy's cash surrender value, they would recognize ordinary income to the extent the proceeds received exceed previous premiums paid. If premiums paid exceed the proceeds received, the loss is not deductible. If, however, the taxpayer is terminally ill (medically certified with an illness expected to cause death within 24 months), early receipt of life insurance proceeds in the form of **accelerated death benefits** is not taxable. If a taxpayer is chronically ill (medically certified to require substantial assistance for daily living activities or due to cognitive impairment), life insurance proceeds are not taxable to the extent they are used to pay for the taxpayer's long-term care.

Example 5-28

What if: Gramps received $200,000 of accelerated death benefits from a life insurance policy last year when he was diagnosed with terminal cancer with an expected life of less than one year. How much gross income would the $200,000 payment generate?

Answer: None, because Gramps was medically certified as terminally ill with an illness expected to cause death within 24 months.

(continued on page 5-28)

[56]As a general rule, for 2022, the federal gift tax does not apply to relatively small gifts ($16,000 or less per person per year), and the federal estate tax only applies to transfers from larger estates (over $12,060,000).

[57]§101. The exclusion does not apply if the insurance policy is sold by the owner.

[58]This exception to the exclusion does not apply if the recipient of the policy is the insured, a partner of the insured, a partnership in which the insured is a partner, or a corporation in which the insured is an officer or shareholder. This exception also does not apply to policies transferred by gift or tax-free exchange.

What if: Due to financial issues, several years ago Gramps transferred a $100,000 life insurance policy on his life to a business associate for $5,000. Since that time, the business associate has continued to pay the annual premiums on the policy (totaling $20,000 before Gramps's death). Upon Gramps's death, the life insurance company paid the business associate the policy's $100,000 face value. How much of the $100,000 payment is taxable?

Answer: $75,000. Because the life insurance policy was purchased from Gramps for valuable consideration, the business associate may exclude the $100,000 proceeds up to the sum of the purchase price of the policy ($5,000) and any subsequent premiums ($20,000), with the remaining proceeds ($100,000 – $5,000 – $20,000 = $75,000) taxable as ordinary income.

THE KEY FACTS

Exclusions to Mitigate Double Taxation

- Gifts and inheritances are subject to federal transfer taxes and are, therefore, excluded from the income of the recipient.
- A maximum of $112,000 (2022) of foreign-earned income can be excluded from gross income for qualifying individuals.
- To be eligible for the foreign-earned income exclusion, the taxpayer must live in the foreign country for 330 days in a consecutive 12-month period.

Foreign-Earned Income U.S. citizens are subject to tax on all income whether it is generated in the United States or in foreign countries. Because most foreign countries also impose tax on income earned within their borders, U.S. citizens could be subject to both U.S. and foreign taxation on income earned abroad. To provide relief from this potential double taxation, Congress allows taxpayers to exclude foreign-earned income (income from foreign sources for personal services performed) up to an annual maximum amount. Income from pensions, annuities, salary paid by the U.S. government, or deferred compensation does not qualify for the exclusion. The maximum exclusion is indexed for inflation, and in 2022 the maximum is $112,000. Rather than claim this exclusion, taxpayers may deduct foreign taxes paid as itemized deductions (not limited to the $10,000 limit on taxes as itemized deductions) or they may claim the foreign tax credit for foreign taxes paid on their foreign-earned income.[59]

To determine whether claiming the annual exclusion, the deduction, or the foreign tax credit is most advantageous, taxpayers should compare the tax effects of each option. To claim the annual exclusion instead of the foreign tax deduction or credit, the taxpayer must elect to do so using Form 2555, Foreign Earned Income. Taxpayers who elect to use the exclusion may revoke the election for later years and use the foreign tax credit or deduct foreign taxes paid. However, once a taxpayer revokes the exclusion election, they may not reelect to use the exclusion before the sixth tax year after the tax year the revocation was made.

As you might expect, individuals must meet certain requirements to qualify for the foreign-earned income exclusion. To be eligible for the annual exclusion, a taxpayer must have their tax home in a foreign country and (1) be considered a resident of the foreign country by living in the country for the entire year (calendar year) or (2) live in the foreign country for 330 days in a consecutive 12-month period, which might occur over two tax years. The *maximum* exclusion is reduced pro rata for each day during the calendar year that is not part of the qualifying 12-month period.

Taxpayers meeting the requirement for the foreign-earned income exclusion may also exclude from income reasonable housing costs (paid by an employer) that exceed 16 percent of the statutory foreign-earned income exclusion amount for the year (exceed 16% × $112,000 = $17,920 in 2022). The exclusion, however, is limited to a maximum of 14 percent of the statutory exclusion amount (14% × $112,000 = $15,680 in 2022). Thus, in 2022, if a taxpayer incurs housing costs (provided by an employer) exceeding $17,920, they may exclude such excess costs up to $15,680 (thus, the first $17,920 of employer-provided housing costs are included in gross income).[60] The housing exclusion limit is also subject to daily proration if the taxpayer's qualifying 12-month period occurs over two tax years.

Example 5-29

What if: Assume Courtney is considering a transfer to EWD's overseas affiliate. If she transfers, she anticipates she will earn approximately $120,000 in salary. How much of her expected $120,000 annual salary will Courtney be allowed to exclude from her gross income, assuming she meets the residency requirements?

[59]See §911(b)(2).

[60]§911(c).

Answer: She is eligible to exclude $112,000 of her $120,000 of compensation from U.S. taxation in 2022. However, her entire $120,000 salary may be subject to the foreign country's income tax.

What if: Assume Courtney decides to transfer, but she expects her 12-month qualifying period to include only 200 days in the first year and 140 days in the second year. How much of her expected $65,000 salary in the first year will she be allowed to exclude from gross income? Assume that there are 365 days in the year.

Answer: $61,370 [$112,000 full exclusion × 200/365 (days in foreign country/days in year)].

What if: Assume that Courtney expects her 12-month qualifying period to include 200 days in the first year and that she expects her salary to be $45,000 during this period. How much of her expected $45,000 salary will she be allowed to exclude from gross income?

Answer: All $45,000. She is eligible to exclude up to $61,370 of salary from income (see above computation).

What if: Assume that if Courtney transfers, EWD's overseas affiliate will also pay for her housing while overseas ($25,000 per year). How much of the $25,000 housing payments may Courtney exclude assuming she lives in the country for the entire year?

Answer: $7,080. Because Courtney meets the requirements for the foreign-earned income exclusion, she may exclude the employer-provided housing costs that exceed $17,920 (16% × $112,000), up to a maximum exclusion of $15,680 (14% × $112,000). Thus, Courtney may exclude $7,080 [the lesser of (a) $7,080 ($25,000 housing cost less $17,920) or (b) $15,680].

Sickness and Injury-Related Exclusions

The tax laws provide several exclusion provisions for taxpayers who are sick or injured. One explanation for these exclusions is that payments for sickness or injury are considered returns of (human) capital.

THE KEY FACTS

Exclusions Related to Sickness and Injury

- Payments from workers' compensation plans are excluded from gross income.
- Payments received as compensation for a *physical* injury are excluded from gross income, but punitive damages are included in gross income.
- Reimbursements by health and accident insurance policies for medical expenses paid by the taxpayer are excluded from gross income.
- Disability benefit payments received from an individually purchased policy (or an employer-purchased policy with the premiums treated as taxable compensation to the employee) are excluded from gross income.

Workers' Compensation The provision for workers' compensation is relatively straightforward. Taxpayers receive workers' compensation benefits when they are unable to work because of a work-related injury. Any payments a taxpayer receives from a state-sponsored workers' compensation plan are excluded from the taxpayer's income.[61] Note that this treatment is *opposite* that of *unemployment* compensation, which is fully taxable.

Payments Associated with Personal Injury Historically, the question of which payments associated with a personal injury were excludable was controversial. Congress settled the matter by deciding that all payments associated with compensating a taxpayer for a *physical* injury (including payments for past, current, and future lost wages) are excluded from gross income. That is, the tax laws specify that any *compensatory damages* on account of a *physical injury* or *physical sickness* are nontaxable. Thus, damages taxpayers receive for emotional distress associated with a physical injury are excluded.

In contrast, *punitive damages* are *fully taxable* because they are intended to punish the harm-doer rather than to compensate the taxpayer for injuries. Likewise, taxpayers receiving damages for emotional distress that are not associated with a physical injury must include those payments in income. In general, all other awards (those that do not relate to physical injury or sickness or are payments for the medical costs of treating emotional distress not associated with physical injury) are included in gross income.

Example 5-30

In February, Courtney's cousin, Kelsey, was struck and injured by a bus while walking in a crosswalk. Because the bus driver was negligent, the bus company settled Kelsey's claim by paying her $1,500 for medical expenses and $500 for emotional distress associated with the accident. How much of the $2,000 Kelsey received from the bus company may she *exclude* from her gross income?

(*continued on page 5-30*)

[61]§104.

Answer: All $2,000. Kelsey may exclude the $1,500 she received for medical expenses and the $500 payment she received for emotional distress because these damages were associated with Kelsey's physical injury.

What if: Assume Kelsey sued the bus company and was awarded $5,000 in punitive damages. How much of the $5,000 would Kelsey be able to exclude from her gross income?

Answer: $0. Payments for punitive damages are not excludable. Kelsey would be required to include the entire $5,000 in her gross income.

Health Care Reimbursement Any reimbursement a taxpayer receives from a health and accident insurance policy for medical expenses paid by the taxpayer during the current year is excluded from gross income. The exclusion applies regardless of whether the taxpayer, their employer, or someone else purchased the health and accident policy for the taxpayer. Of course, the tax benefit rule may require inclusion of reimbursements of medical expenses that were deducted by the taxpayer in a prior year.

Disability Insurance The exclusion provisions for **disability insurance** are more restrictive than those for workers' compensation payments or reimbursements from a health and accident insurance plan. Disability insurance, sometimes called *wage replacement insurance,* pays the insured individual for wages lost when the individual misses work due to injury or disability. If an individual purchases disability insurance directly, the cost of the policy is not deductible, but any disability benefits are excluded from gross income.

Disability insurance may also be purchased on an individual's behalf by an employer. The employer may allow employees to choose whether the premiums paid on their behalf are to be considered taxable compensation or a nontaxable fringe benefit. If the premiums are taxable compensation to the employee, any disability benefits received are excluded from gross income. In contrast, if the premiums paid for by the employer are considered a nontaxable fringe benefit to the employee, the employee must include disability benefits received in gross income.

Example 5-31

Courtney purchased disability insurance last year. In late April of this year, she broke her wrist in a mountain biking accident and could not work for two weeks. Courtney's doctor bills totaled $2,000, of which $1,600 was reimbursed by her health insurance purchased by EWD. How much of the $1,600 health insurance reimbursement for medical expenses is Courtney allowed to *exclude* from her gross income?

Answer: All $1,600 is excluded. All medical expense reimbursements from health insurance are excluded from a taxpayer's gross income.

Courtney also received $6,000 for lost wages due to the accident from her disability insurance policy. How much of the $6,000 is Courtney allowed to exclude from her gross income?

Answer: All $6,000 is excluded. Courtney can exclude the entire amount because she paid the premiums on the policy.

What if: How much of the $6,000 payment for lost wages from the disability insurance policy would Courtney exclude if EWD paid the disability insurance premium on her behalf as a nontaxable fringe benefit?

Answer: $0 would be excluded. Because the disability policy premiums paid by EWD were treated as nontaxable fringe benefits, Courtney would include the payment in gross income and be taxed on the entire $6,000.

What if: How much of the $6,000 payment for lost wages from the disability insurance policy would Courtney be allowed to exclude if she paid half the cost of the policy personally and EWD paid the other half as a taxable fringe benefit?

Answer: All $6,000 would be excluded. Disability benefits received from policies purchased by an individual are excludable. Likewise, disability benefits received from policies purchased by an employer as a taxable fringe benefit are excludable. Thus, the entire $6,000 payment would be excludable. Note that if EWD had paid for half the cost of the policy as a *nontaxable* fringe benefit, Courtney would have been able to exclude $3,000, not $6,000.

Deferral Provisions

We've described exclusion provisions that allow taxpayers to permanently eliminate certain types of income from their tax base. Other code sections, called *deferral provisions,* allow taxpayers to defer (but not permanently exclude) the recognition of certain types of realized income. Transactions generating deferred income include **installment sales,** like-kind exchanges, involuntary conversions, and contributions to non-Roth **qualified retirement accounts.** We "defer" our detailed discussion of these transactions to subsequent chapters.

INCOME SUMMARY

At the end of the year, Courtney calculated her income and Gram's income. Exhibit 5-4 presents Courtney's income calculation, Exhibit 5-5 and Exhibit 5-6 display how this income would be reported on Courtney's tax return (Form 1040, page 1 and Schedule 1, respectively), and Exhibit 5-7 presents Gram's income calculation. We use 2021 forms because 2022 forms were not available at press time. Note that Courtney's actual *gross* income equals her total income on line 9 of page 1 of her Form 1040 plus her $1,500 consulting expenses (see Example 5-7) and her $9,000 deductions for rental expenses (see Example 5-10), which are both for AGI deductions. Because Gram doesn't have any business, rental, or royalty deductions, her gross income is equal to her total income on line 9 of page 1 of her tax return (not included here).

EXHIBIT 5-4 **Courtney's Income**

Description	Amount	Reference
(1) Salary (line 1, page 1, Form 1040)	$138,000	Example 5-7
(2) Employment bonus award (line 1, page 1, Form 1040)	4,800	Example 5-4
(3) Discount architectural design services (line 1, page 1, Form 1040)	6,000	Example 5-19
(4) Compensation on below-market loan from EWD (line 1, page 1, Form 1040)	4,000	Example 5-20
(5) Discharge of indebtedness (line 1, page 1, Form 1040)	10,000	Example 5-21
(6) Interest income (line 2b, page 1, Form 1040)	321	Example 5-9
(7) Dividends (lines 3a and 3b, page 1, Form 1040)	700	Example 5-8
(8) State tax refund (line 8, page 1, Form 1040; line 1, Schedule 1)	420	Example 5-3
(9) Net business income (line 8, page 1, Form 1040; line 3, Schedule 1)	18,000	Example 5-7
(10) Net rental income (line 8, page 1, Form 1040; line 5, Schedule 1)	5,000	Example 5-10
Total income as presented on line 9, page 1 of Form 1040 (see Exhibit 5-5)	**$187,241**	Sum of (1) through (10)

EXHIBIT 5-5 **Courtney's Tax Return**
(total income as reported on Form 1040, page 1, lines 1–9)

	1	Wages, salaries, tips, etc. Attach Form(s) W-2					1	162,800
Attach Sch. B if required.	2a	Tax-exempt interest	2a	500	b	Taxable interest	2b	321
	3a	Qualified dividends	3a	700	b	Ordinary dividends	3b	700
	4a	IRA distributions	4a		b	Taxable amount	4b	
	5a	Pensions and annuities	5a		b	Taxable amount	5b	
	6a	Social security benefits	6a		b	Taxable amount	6b	
	7	Capital gain or (loss). Attach Schedule D if required. If not required, check here ▶ ☐					7	
	8	Other income from Schedule 1, line 10					8	23,420
	9	Add lines 1, 2b, 3b, 4b, 5b, 6b, 7, and 8. This is your **total income** ▶					9	187,241

Source: irs.gov.

EXHIBIT 5-6 Courtney's Income Reported on Schedule 1

SCHEDULE 1 (Form 1040) — **Additional Income and Adjustments to Income** — OMB No. 1545-0074 — **2021**

Department of the Treasury Internal Revenue Service — ▶ Attach to Form 1040, 1040-SR, or 1040-NR. ▶ Go to *www.irs.gov/Form1040* for instructions and the latest information. — Attachment Sequence No. **01**

Name(s) shown on Form 1040, 1040-SR, or 1040-NR: **Courtney Wilson** — **Your social security number**: **111-11-1111**

Part I Additional Income

Line	Description	Sub-line	Sub-amount	Line no.	Amount
1	Taxable refunds, credits, or offsets of state and local income taxes			1	420
2a	Alimony received			2a	
b	Date of original divorce or separation agreement (see instructions) ▶				
3	Business income or (loss). Attach Schedule C			3	18,000
4	Other gains or (losses). Attach Form 4797			4	
5	Rental real estate, royalties, partnerships, S corporations, trusts, etc. Attach Schedule E			5	5,000
6	Farm income or (loss). Attach Schedule F			6	
7	Unemployment compensation			7	
8	Other income:				
a	Net operating loss	8a	( )		
b	Gambling income	8b			
c	Cancellation of debt	8c			
d	Foreign earned income exclusion from Form 2555	8d	( )		
e	Taxable Health Savings Account distribution	8e			
f	Alaska Permanent Fund dividends	8f			
g	Jury duty pay	8g			
h	Prizes and awards	8h			
i	Activity not engaged in for profit income	8i			
j	Stock options	8j			
k	Income from the rental of personal property if you engaged in the rental for profit but were not in the business of renting such property	8k			
l	Olympic and Paralympic medals and USOC prize money (see instructions)	8l			
m	Section 951(a) inclusion (see instructions)	8m			
n	Section 951A(a) inclusion (see instructions)	8n			
o	Section 461(l) excess business loss adjustment	8o			
p	Taxable distributions from an ABLE account (see instructions)	8p			
z	Other income. List type and amount ▶	8z			
9	Total other income. Add lines 8a through 8z			9	
10	Combine lines 1 through 7 and 9. Enter here and on Form 1040, 1040-SR, or 1040-NR, line 8			10	23,420

For Paperwork Reduction Act Notice, see your tax return instructions. — Cat. No. 71479F — Schedule 1 (Form 1040) 2021

Source: irs.gov.

EXHIBIT 5-7 Gram's Income

Deduction	Amount	Reference
Interest income	$ 4,750	Example 5-9
Annuity income	3,400	Example 5-11
Gain on stock sale	350	Example 5-12
Sweepstakes winnings (WaveRunner)	7,500	Example 5-17
Income for current year	$16,000	

CONCLUSION

In this chapter we explained the basic concepts of income realization and recognition, identified and discussed the major types of income, and described the most common income exclusions. We discovered that many exclusions are related to specific congressional objectives, but that absent a specific exclusion, realized income should be included in gross income. In the next chapter, we turn our attention to the deductions available to taxpayers when computing their taxable income. We will continue to follow Courtney and Gram in their quest to determine their taxable income and corresponding tax liability.

Appendix 2021 Social Security Worksheet from Form 1040 Instructions

Social Security Benefits Worksheet—Lines 6a and 6b

Keep for Your Records

Before you begin:

- ✓ Figure any write-in adjustments to be entered on Schedule 1, line 24z (see the instructions for Schedule 1, line 24z).
- ✓ If you are married filing separately and you lived apart from your spouse for all of 2021, enter "D" to the right of the word "benefits" on line 6a. If you don't, you may get a math error notice from the IRS.
- ✓ Be sure you have read the ***Exception*** in the line 6a and 6b instructions to see if you can use this worksheet instead of a publication to find out if any of your benefits are taxable.

1. Enter the total amount from **box 5** of **all** your **Forms SSA-1099** and **RRB-1099.** Also enter this amount on Form 1040 or 1040-SR, line 6a . . . . . **1.** ______

2. Multiply line 1 by 50% (0.50) . . . . . **2.** ______

3. Combine the amounts from Form 1040 or 1040-SR, lines 1, 2b, 3b, 4b, 5b, 7, and 8 . . . . . **3.** ______

4. Enter the amount, if any, from Form 1040 or 1040-SR, line 2a . . . . . **4.** ______

5. Combine lines 2, 3, and 4 . . . . . **5.** ______

6. Enter the total of the amounts from Schedule 1, lines 11 through 20, and 23 and 25 . . . . . **6.** ______

7. Is the amount on line 6 less than the amount on line 5?

☐ **No.** STOP None of your social security benefits are taxable. Enter -0- on Form 1040 or 1040-SR, line 6b.

☐ **Yes.** Subtract line 6 from line 5 . . . . . **7.** ______

8. If you are:
- Married filing jointly, enter $32,000
- Single, head of household, qualifying widow(er), or married filing separately and you **lived apart** from your spouse for all of 2021, enter $25,000
- Married filing separately and you lived with your spouse at any time in 2021, skip lines 8 through 15; multiply line 7 by 85% (0.85) and enter the result on line 16. Then, go to line 17

. . . . . **8.** ______

9. Is the amount on line 8 less than the amount on line 7?

☐ **No.** STOP None of your social security benefits are taxable. Enter -0- on Form 1040 or 1040-SR, line 6b. If you are married filing separately and you **lived apart** from your spouse for all of 2021, be sure you entered "D" to the right of the word "benefits" on line 6a.

☐ **Yes.** Subtract line 8 from line 7 . . . . . **9.** ______

10. Enter $12,000 if married filing jointly; $9,000 if single, head of household, qualifying widow(er), or married filing separately and you **lived apart** from your spouse for all of 2021 . . . . . **10.** ______

11. Subtract line 10 from line 9. If zero or less, enter -0- . . . . . **11.** ______

12. Enter the **smaller** of line 9 or line 10 . . . . . **12.** ______

13. Enter one-half of line 12 . . . . . **13.** ______

14. Enter the **smaller** of line 2 or line 13 . . . . . **14.** ______

15. Multiply line 11 by 85% (0.85). If line 11 is zero, enter -0- . . . . . **15.** ______

16. Add lines 14 and 15 . . . . . **16.** ______

17. Multiply line 1 by 85% (0.85) . . . . . **17.** ______

18. **Taxable social security benefits.** Enter the **smaller** of line 16 or line 17. Also enter this amount on Form 1040 or 1040-SR, line 6b . . . . . **18.** ______

TIP *If any of your benefits are taxable for 2021* ***and*** *they include a lump-sum benefit payment that was for an earlier year, you may be able to reduce the taxable amount. See* Lump-Sum Election *in Pub. 915 for details.*

Source: irs.gov.

Summary

LO 5-1 Apply the concept of realization.

- Income is typically realized with a transaction that allows economic benefit to be identified and measured.
- Unless realized income is deferred or excluded, it is included in gross income in the period dictated by the taxpayer's accounting method.
- The accrual method of accounting recognizes income in the period it is earned, and this method is typically used by large corporations.
- The cash method of accounting recognizes income in the period received, and this method offers a simple and flexible method of accounting typically used by individuals.
- The return of capital principle, constructive receipt doctrine, and assignment of income doctrine affect how much income is recognized, when income is recognized, and who recognizes income, respectively.

LO 5-2 Discuss the distinctions between the various sources of income, including income from services and property.

- Income from services is called earned income, whereas income from property is called unearned income.
- A portion of annuity payments and proceeds from sales of property is a nontaxable return of capital.
- Earned and unearned income generated by flow-through business entities is reported by partners and Subchapter S shareholders.
- Other sources of income include alimony payments, unemployment compensation, Social Security benefits, prizes and awards, bargain purchases, imputed interest on below-market loans, and discharge of indebtedness.

LO 5-3 Apply basic income exclusion provisions to compute gross income.

- Interest received from holding state and local indebtedness (municipal interest) is excluded from gross income.
- A taxpayer satisfying certain home ownership and use requirements can permanently exclude up to $250,000 ($500,000 if married filing jointly) of realized gain on the sale of her principal residence.
- Employment-related nonrecognition provisions include a variety of excludable fringe benefits.
- Gifts, inheritances, life insurance proceeds, and foreign-earned income up to $112,000 are excluded from gross income in order to mitigate the effects of double taxation.
- Common injury-related nonrecognition provisions include the exclusions for workers' compensation, personal injury payments and reimbursements from health insurance policies, and certain payments from disability policies.

KEY TERMS

accelerated death benefits (5-27)
accountable plan (5-23)
accrual method (5-7)
alimony (5-14)
annuity (5-11)
assignment of income doctrine (5-8)
barter clubs (5-4)
cash method (5-7)
claim of right doctrine (5-7)
community property systems (5-8)
constructive receipt doctrine (5-7)
disability insurance (5-30)
discharge of indebtedness (5-21)
earned income (5-10)
flow-through entity (5-14)
fringe benefits (5-23)
gift (5-27)
gross income (5-2)
imputed income (5-19)
inheritance (5-27)
installment sales (5-31)
municipal bonds (5-21)
nonrecognition provisions (5-21)
qualified retirement accounts (5-31)
realization principle (5-3)
return of capital (5-4)
tax basis (5-4)
tax benefit rule (5-5)
unearned income (5-10)
wherewithal to pay (5-3)

DISCUSSION QUESTIONS

Discussion Questions are available in Connect®.

1. Based on the definition of gross income in §61 and related regulations, what is the general presumption regarding the taxability of income realized? LO 5-1
2. Based on the definition of gross income in §61, related regulations, and judicial rulings, what are the three criteria for recognizing taxable income? LO 5-1
3. Describe the concept of realization for tax purposes. LO 5-1
4. Compare and contrast realization of income with recognition of income. LO 5-1
5. Tim is a plumber who joined a barter club. This year Tim exchanged plumbing services for a new roof. The roof is properly valued at $2,500, but Tim would have only billed $2,200 for the plumbing services. What amount of income should Tim recognize on the exchange of his services for a roof? Would your answer change if Tim would have normally billed $3,000 for his services? LO 5-1
6. Andre constructs and installs cabinets in homes. Blair sells and installs carpet in apartments. Andre and Blair worked out an arrangement whereby Andre installed cabinets in Blair's home and Blair installed carpet in Andre's home. Neither Andre nor Blair believes they are required to recognize any gross income on this exchange because neither received cash. Do you agree with them? Explain. LO 5-1
7. What issue precipitated the return of capital principle? Explain. LO 5-1
8. Compare how the return of capital principle applies when (a) a taxpayer sells an asset and collects the sale proceeds immediately and (b) a taxpayer sells an asset and collects the sale proceeds over several periods (an installment sale). If Congress wanted to maximize revenue from installment sales, how would it have applied the return of capital principle for installment sales? LO 5-1
9. This year Jorge received a refund of property taxes that he deducted on his tax return last year. Jorge is not sure whether he should include the refund in his gross income. What would you tell him? LO 5-1
10. Describe in general how the cash method of accounting differs from the accrual method of accounting. LO 5-1
11. Janet is a cash-method, calendar-year taxpayer. She received a check for services provided in the mail during the last week of December. However, rather than cash the check, Janet decided to wait until the following January because she believes that her delay will cause the income to be realized and recognized next year. What would you tell her? Would it matter if she didn't open the envelope? Would it matter if she refused to check her mail during the last week of December? Explain. LO 5-1
12. The cash method of accounting means that taxpayers don't recognize income unless they receive cash or cash equivalents. True or false? Explain. LO 5-1
13. Contrast the constructive receipt doctrine with the claim of right doctrine. LO 5-1
14. Yesenia is a lawyer who uses the cash method of accounting. Last year Yesenia provided a client with legal services worth $55,000, but the client could not pay the fee. This year Yesenia requested that in lieu of paying Yesenia $55,000 for the services, the client could make a $45,000 gift to Yesenia's daughter. Yesenia's daughter received the check for $45,000 and deposited it in her bank account. How much of this income is taxed, if any, to Yesenia? Explain. LO 5-1
15. Bonnie and Clyde were married this year. Bonnie has a steady job that will pay her about $37,000, while Clyde does odd jobs that will produce about $28,000 of income. They also have a joint savings account that will pay about $400 of interest. If Bonnie and Clyde reside in a community property state and file married-separate tax returns, how much gross income will they each report? Is there any difference if they reside in a common-law state? Explain. LO 5-2
16. Distinguish earned income from unearned income, and provide an example of each. LO 5-2

LO 5-2 17. Jim purchased 100 shares of stock this year and elected to participate in a dividend reinvestment program. This program automatically uses dividends to purchase additional shares of stock. This year Jim's shares paid $350 of dividends, and he used these funds to purchase additional shares of stock. These additional shares are worth $375 at year-end. What amount of dividends, if any, should Jim declare as income this year? Explain.

LO 5-2 18. Geri has a certificate of deposit at the local bank. The interest on this certificate was credited to their account on December 31 of last year, but they didn't withdraw the interest until January of this year. When is the interest income taxed?

LO 5-2 19. Conceptually, when taxpayers receive annuity payments, how do they determine the amount of the payment they must include in gross income?

LO 5-2 20. George purchased a life annuity to provide him monthly payments for as long as he lives. Based on IRS tables, George's life expectancy is 100 months. Is George able to recover his cost of the annuity if he dies before he receives 100 monthly payments? Explain. What happens for tax purposes if George receives more than 100 payments?

LO 5-2 21. Brad purchased land for $45,000 this year. At year-end Brad sold the land for $51,700 and paid a sales commission of $450. What effect does this transaction have on Brad's gross income? Explain.

LO 5-2 22. Tomiko is a 50 percent owner (partner) in the Tanaka partnership. During the year, the partnership reported $1,000 of interest income and $2,000 of dividends. How much of this income must Tomiko include in their gross income?

LO 5-2 23. Ida and Clem were married for several years, but in 2018 they finalized their divorce. In the divorce decree, Ida agreed to deed their car to Clem and pay Clem $10,000 per year for twenty years (but not beyond his death). Did these transfers qualify as alimony for tax purposes? Explain.

LO 5-2 24. Larry Bounds has won the Gold Bat Award for hitting the longest home run in Major League Baseball this year. The bat is worth almost $35,000. Under what conditions can Larry exclude the award from his gross income? Explain.

LO 5-2 25. Rory and Nicholi, single taxpayers, each annually receives Social Security benefits of $15,000. Rory's taxable income from sources other than Social Security exceeds $200,000. In contrast, the Social Security benefits are Nicholi's only source of income. What percentage of the Social Security benefits must Rory include in his gross income? What percentage of Social Security benefits is Nicholi required to include in his gross income?

LO 5-2 26. Rolando purchases a golf cart from his employer, E-Z-Go Golf Carts, for a sizable discount. Explain the rules for determining if Rolando's purchase results in taxable income for him.

LO 5-2 27. When an employer makes a below-market loan to an employee, what are the tax consequences to the employer and employee?

LO 5-2 28. Explain why an insolvent taxpayer is allowed to exclude income from the discharge of indebtedness if the taxpayer remains insolvent after receiving the debt relief.

LO 5-3 29. What are the basic requirements to exclude the gain on the sale of a personal residence?

LO 5-3 30. Explain why an employee should be concerned about whether his employer reimburses business expenses using an "accountable" plan.

LO 5-3 31. Cassie works in an office and has access to several professional color printers. Her employer allows Cassie and her fellow employees to use the printers to print color postcards for the holidays. This year Cassie printed out two dozen postcards worth almost $76. Must Cassie include this amount in her gross income this year? Explain your answer.

LO 5-3 32. What are some common examples of taxable and tax-free fringe benefits?

LO 5-3 33. Explain how state and local governments benefit from the provisions that allow taxpayers to exclude interest on state and local bonds from their gross income.

34. Explain why taxpayers are allowed to exclude gifts and inheritances from gross income even though these payments are realized and clearly provide taxpayers with the wherewithal to pay. LO 5-3

35. Describe the kinds of insurance premiums an employer can pay on behalf of an employee without triggering includable compensation to the employee. LO 5-3

36. How are state-sponsored 529 educational savings plans taxed if investment returns are used for educational purposes? Are the returns taxed differently if they are not ultimately used to pay for education costs? LO 5-3

37. Jim was injured in an accident and his surgeon botched the medical procedure. Jim recovered $5,000 from the doctor for pain and suffering and $2,000 for emotional distress. Determine the taxability of these payments and briefly explain to Jim the apparent rationale for including or excluding these payments from gross income. LO 5-3

38. Helaina was just hired by Acme Corporation and has decided to purchase disability insurance. This insurance promises to pay her weekly benefits to replace her salary should she be unable to work because of disability. Disability insurance is also available through Acme as part of its compensation plan. Acme pays these premiums as a nontaxable fringe benefit, but the plan promises to pay about 10 percent less in benefits. If Helaina elects to have Acme pay the premiums, then her compensation will be reduced by an equivalent amount. Should tax considerations play a role in Helaina's choice to buy disability insurance through Acme or on her own? Explain. LO 5-3

PROBLEMS

Select problems are available in Connect®.

39. For the following independent cases, determine whether economic income is present and, if so, whether it must be included in gross income (i.e., is it realized and recognized for tax purposes?). LO 5-1
    a) Asia owns stock that is listed on the New York Stock Exchange, and this year the stock increased in value by $20,000.
    b) Ben sold stock for $10,000 and paid a sales commission of $250. Ben purchased the stock several years ago for $4,000.
    c) Bessie is a partner in SULU Enterprises LLC. This year SULU reported that Bessie's share of rental income was $2,700 and her share of municipal interest was $750.

40. Devon owns 1,000 shares of stock worth $10,000. This year he received 200 additional shares of this stock from a stock dividend. His 1,200 shares are now worth $12,500. Must Devon include the dividend paid in stock in income? LO 5-1 research

41. XYZ declared a $1 per share dividend on August 15. The date of record for the dividend was September 1 (the stock began selling *ex-dividend* on September 2). The dividend was paid on September 10. Ellis is a cash-method taxpayer. Determine if he must include the dividends in gross income under the following independent circumstances: LO 5-1 research
    a) Ellis bought 100 shares of XYZ stock on August 1 for $21 per share. Ellis received a $100 dividend on September 10. Ellis still owns the shares at year-end.
    b) Ellis bought 100 shares of XYZ stock on August 1 for $21 per share. Ellis sold his XYZ shares on September 5 for $23 per share. Ellis received the $100 dividend on September 10 (note that even though Ellis didn't own the stock on September 10, he still received the dividend because he was the shareholder on the record date).
    c) Ellis bought 100 shares of XYZ stock for $22 per share on August 20. Ellis received the $100 dividend on September 10. Ellis still owns the shares at year-end.

LO 5-1
research

42. For the following independent cases, determine whether economic income is present and, if so, whether it must be included in gross income. Identify a tax authority that supports your analysis.
    a) Hermione discovered a gold nugget (valued at $10,000) on her land.
    b) Jay embezzled $20,000 from his employer and has not yet been apprehended.
    c) Keisha found $1,000 inside an old dresser. She purchased the dresser at a discount furniture store at the end of last year and found the money after the beginning of the new year. No one has claimed the money.

LO 5-1

43. Although Hank is retired, he is an excellent handyman and often works part time on small projects for neighbors and friends. Last week his neighbor, Mike, offered to pay Hank $500 for minor repairs to his house. Hank completed the repairs in December of this year. Hank uses the cash method of accounting and is a calendar-year taxpayer. Compute Hank's gross income for this year from each of the following alternative transactions:
    a) Mike paid Hank $200 in cash in December of this year and promised to pay the remaining $300 with interest in three months.
    b) Mike gave Hank tickets in December to the big game in January. The tickets have a face value of $50, but Hank could sell them for $400. Hank went to the game with his son.
    c) Mike bought Hank a new set of snow tires. The tires typically sell for $500, but Mike bought them on sale for $450.

LO 5-1

44. Jim recently joined the Austin Barter Club, an organization that facilitates the exchange of services between its members. This year Jim provided lawn-mowing services to other club members. Jim received the following from the barter club. Determine the amount, if any, Jim should include in his gross income in each of the following situations:
    a) Jim received $275 of car repair services from another member of the club.
    b) Jim received a $550 credit that gave him the option of receiving a season pass at a local ski resort from another member of the club. However, he forgot to request the pass by the end of the ski season and his credit expired.
    c) Jim received a $450 credit that can only be applied for goods or services from club members next year.

LO 5-1
research

45. Last year Acme paid Ralph $15,000 to install a new air-conditioning unit at its headquarters building. The air conditioner did not function properly, and this year Acme requested that Ralph return the payment. Because Ralph could not repair one critical part in the unit, he refunded the cost of the repair, $5,000, to Acme.
    a) Is Ralph required to include the $15,000 payment he received last year in his gross income from last year?
    b) What are the tax implications of the repayment if Ralph was in the 35 percent tax bracket when he received the $15,000 payment from Acme but he was in the 24 percent tax bracket when he refunded $5,000 to Acme?

LO 5-1

46. Louis files as a single taxpayer. In April of this year he received a $900 refund of state income taxes that he paid last year. How much of the refund, if any, must Louis include in gross income under the following independent scenarios? Assume the standard deduction last year was $12,550.
    a) Last year Louis claimed itemized deductions of $12,800. Louis's itemized deductions included state income taxes paid of $1,750 and no other state or local taxes.
    b) Last year Louis had itemized deductions of $10,800 and he chose to claim the standard deduction. Louis's itemized deductions included state income taxes paid of $1,750 and no other state or local taxes.

c) Last year Louis claimed itemized deductions of $13,990. Louis's itemized deductions included state income taxes paid of $2,750 and no other state or local taxes.

47. L. A. and Paula file as married taxpayers. In August of this year, they received a $5,200 refund of state income taxes that they paid last year. How much of the refund, if any, must L. A. and Paula include in gross income under the following independent scenarios? Assume the standard deduction last year was $25,100. LO 5-1

a) Last year L. A. and Paula had itemized deductions of $19,200, and they chose to claim the standard deduction.

b) Last year L. A. and Paula claimed itemized deductions of $31,400. Their itemized deductions included state income taxes paid of $7,500 and no other state or local taxes.

c) Last year L. A. and Paula claimed itemized deductions of $27,600. Their itemized deductions included state income taxes paid of $10,500, which were limited to $10,000 due to the cap on state and local tax deductions.

48. Clyde is a cash-method taxpayer who reports on a calendar-year basis. This year Paylate Corporation has decided to pay Clyde a year-end bonus of $1,000. Determine the amount Clyde should include in his gross income this year under the following circumstances: LO 5-1

a) Paylate Corporation wrote the check and put it in Clyde's office mail slot on December 30 of this year, but Clyde did not bother to stop by the office to pick it up until after year-end.

b) Paylate Corporation mistakenly wrote the check for $100. Clyde received the remaining $900 after year-end.

c) Paylate Corporation mailed the check to Clyde before the end of the year (and it was delivered before year-end). Although Clyde expected the bonus payment, he decided not to collect his mail until after year-end.

d) Clyde picked up the check in December, but the check could not be cashed immediately because it was postdated January 10.

49. Identify the amount, if any, that these individuals must include in gross income in the following independent cases. Assume that the individuals use the cash method of accounting and report income on a calendar-year basis. LO 5-2

a) Elmer was an extremely diligent employee this year, and his employer gave him three additional days off with pay (Elmer's gross pay for the three days totaled $1,200, but his net pay was only $948).

b) Amax purchased new office furniture and allowed each employee to take home old office furniture valued at $250.

50. Ralph owns a building that he is trying to lease. Ralph is a calendar-year, cash-method taxpayer and is trying to evaluate the tax consequences of three different lease arrangements. Under lease 1, the building rents for $500 per month, payable on the first of the next month, and the tenant must make a $500 security deposit that is refunded at the end of the lease. Under lease 2, the building rents for $5,500 per year, payable at the time the lease is signed, but no security deposit is required. Under lease 3, the building rents for $500 per month, payable at the beginning of each month, and the tenant must pay a security deposit of $1,000 that is to be applied toward the rent for the last two months of the lease. LO 5-2 research

a) What amounts are included in Ralph's gross income this year if a tenant signs lease 1 on December 1 and makes timely payments under that lease?

b) What amounts are included in Ralph's gross income this year if the tenant signs lease 2 on December 31 and makes timely payments under that lease?

c) What amounts are included in Ralph's gross income this year if the tenant signs lease 3 on November 30 and makes timely payments under that lease?

LO 5-2 51. Anne purchased an annuity from an insurance company that promised to pay her $20,000 per year for the next 10 years. Anne paid $145,000 for the annuity, and in exchange she will receive $200,000 over the term of the annuity.

a) How much of the first $20,000 payment should Anne include in gross income?

b) How much income will Anne recognize over the term of the annuity?

LO 5-2 52. Larry purchased an annuity from an insurance company that promises to pay him $1,500 per month for the rest of his life. Larry paid $170,820 for the annuity. Larry is in good health and is 72 years old. Larry received the first annuity payment of $1,500 this month. Use the expected number of payments in Exhibit 5-1 for this problem.

a) How much of the first payment should Larry include in gross income?

b) If Larry lives more than 15 years after purchasing the annuity, how much of each additional payment should he include in gross income?

c) What are the tax consequences if Larry dies just after he receives the 100th payment?

LO 5-2 research 53. Gramps purchased a joint survivor annuity that pays $500 monthly over his remaining life and that of his wife, Gram. Gramps is 70 years old and Gram is 65 years old. Gramps paid $97,020 for the contract. How much income will Gramps recognize on the first payment?

LO 5-2 54. Lanny and Shirley divorced in 2018 and do not live together. Shirley has custody of their child, Art, and Lanny pays Shirley $22,000 per year. All property was divided equally.

a) How much should Shirley include in income if Lanny's payments are made in cash but will cease if Shirley dies or remarries?

b) How much should Shirley include in income if $12,000 of Lanny's payments is designated as "nonalimony" in the divorce decree?

c) How much should Shirley include in income if Lanny's payments drop to $15,000 once Art reaches the age of 18?

LO 5-2 55. For each of the following independent situations, indicate the amount the taxpayer must include in gross income and explain your answer:

a) Phil won $500 in the scratch-off state lottery. There is no state income tax.

b) Ted won a compact car worth $17,000 in a TV game show. Ted plans to sell the car next year.

c) Al Bore won the Nobel Peace Prize of $500,000 this year. Rather than take the prize, Al designated that the entire award should go to Weatherhead Charity, a tax-exempt organization.

d) Jerry was awarded $2,500 from his employer, Acme Toons, when he was selected most handsome employee for Valentine's Day this year.

e) Ellen won a $1,000 cash prize in a school essay contest. The school is a tax-exempt entity, and Ellen plans to use the funds for her college education.

f) Gene won $400 in the office March Madness pool.

LO 5-2 56. Grady received $8,200 of Social Security benefits this year. Grady also reported salary and interest income this year. What amount of the benefits must Grady include in his gross income under the following five independent situations?

a) Grady files single and reports salary of $12,100 and interest income of $250.

b) Grady files single and reports salary of $22,000 and interest income of $600.

c) Grady files married joint and reports salary of $75,000 and interest income of $500.

d) Grady files married joint and reports salary of $44,000 and interest income of $700.

e) Grady files married separate and reports salary of $22,000 and interest income of $600.

LO 5-2 57. George and Wanda received $30,200 of Social Security benefits this year ($12,000 for George; $18,200 for Wanda). They also received $5,000 of interest from jointly owned City of Ranburne bonds and dividend income. What amount of the Social

Security benefits must George and Wanda include in their gross income under the following independent situations?

a) George and Wanda file married joint and receive $8,000 of dividend income from stocks owned by George.

b) George and Wanda file married separate and receive $8,000 of dividend income from stocks owned by George.

c) George and Wanda file married joint and receive $30,000 of dividend income from stocks owned by George.

d) George and Wanda file married joint and receive $15,000 of dividend income from stocks owned by George.

58. Priya works for the Shine Company, a retailer of upscale jewelry. How much taxable income does Priya recognize under the following scenarios? LO 5-2

a) Priya buys a diamond ring from Shine Company for $10,000 (normal sales price, $14,000; Shine Company's gross profit percentage is 40 percent).

b) Priya receives a 25 percent discount on jewelry restoration services offered by Shine Company. This year, Priya had Shine Company repair a set of antique earrings (normal repair cost $500; discounted price $375).

59. Wally is employed as an executive with Pay More Incorporated. To entice Wally to work for Pay More, the corporation loaned him $20,000 at the beginning of the year at a simple interest rate of 1 percent. Wally would have paid interest of $2,400 this year if the interest rate on the loan had been set at the prevailing federal interest rate. LO 5-2

a) Wally used the funds as a down payment on a speedboat and repaid the $20,000 loan (including $200 of interest) at year-end. Does this loan result in any income to either party, and if so, how much?

b) Assume instead that Pay More forgave the loan and interest on December 31. What amount of gross income does Wally recognize this year? Explain.

60. Jimmy has fallen on hard times recently. Last year he borrowed $250,000 and added an additional $50,000 of his own funds to purchase $300,000 of undeveloped real estate. This year the value of the real estate dropped dramatically, and Jimmy's lender agreed to reduce the loan amount to $230,000. For each of the following independent situations, indicate the amount Jimmy must include in gross income and explain your answer: LO 5-3

a) The real estate is worth $175,000 and Jimmy has no other assets or liabilities.

b) The real estate is worth $235,000 and Jimmy has no other assets or liabilities.

c) The real estate is worth $200,000 and Jimmy has $45,000 in other assets but no other liabilities.

61. Grady is a 45-year-old employee with AMUCK Garbage Corporation. AMUCK pays group-term life insurance premiums for employees, and Grady chose the maximum face amount of $120,000. What amount, if any, of the premium AMUCK paid on his behalf must Grady include in his gross income for the year? Provide a tax authority to support your answer. LO 5-3 research

62. Fred currently earns $9,000 per month. Fred has been offered the chance to transfer for three to five years to an overseas affiliate. His employer is willing to pay Fred $10,000 per month if he accepts the assignment. Assume that the maximum foreign-earned income exclusion for next year is $112,000. LO 5-3

a) How much U.S. gross income will Fred report if he accepts the assignment abroad on January 1 of next year and works overseas for the entire year? If Fred's employer also provides him free housing abroad (cost of $20,000), how much of the $20,000 is excludable from Fred's income?

b) Suppose that Fred's employer has offered Fred a six-month overseas assignment beginning on January 1 of next year. How much U.S. gross income will Fred report next year if he accepts the six-month assignment abroad and returns home on July 1 of next year?

c) Suppose that Fred's employer offers Fred a permanent overseas assignment beginning on March 1 of next year. How much U.S. gross income will Fred report next year if he accepts the permanent assignment abroad? Assume that Fred will be abroad for 305 days out of 365 days next year. If Fred's employer also provides him free housing abroad (cost of $16,000 next year), how much of the $16,000 is excludable from Fred's income?

LO 5-3

63. For each of the following situations, indicate how much the taxpayer is required to include in gross income and explain your answer:

a) Steve was awarded a $5,000 scholarship to attend State Law School. The scholarship pays Steve's tuition and fees.

b) Hal was awarded a $15,000 scholarship to attend State Hotel School. All scholarship students must work 20 hours per week at the school residency during the term.

LO 5-3

64. Cecil cashed in a Series EE savings bond with a redemption value of $14,000 and an original cost of $9,800. For each of the following independent scenarios, calculate the amount of interest Cecil will include in his gross income assuming he files as a single taxpayer:

a) Cecil plans to spend all of the proceeds to pay his son's tuition at State University. Cecil's son is a full-time student, and Cecil claims his son as a dependent. Cecil estimates his modified adjusted gross income at $63,100.

b) Assume the same facts in part (a), except Cecil plans to spend $4,200 of the proceeds to pay his son's tuition at State University, and Cecil estimates his modified adjusted gross income at $60,600.

LO 5-3

65. Grady is a member of a large family and received the following payments this year. For each payment, determine whether the payment constitutes realized income and determine the amount of each payment Grady must include in his gross income:

a) A gift of $20,000 from Grady's grandfather.

b) One thousand shares of GM stock worth $120 per share inherited from Grady's uncle. The uncle purchased the shares for $25 each, and the shares are worth $125 per share at year-end.

c) A gift of $50,000 of Ford Motor Bonds. Grady received the bonds on October 31, and he received $1,500 of semiannual interest from the bonds on December 31.

d) A loan of $5,000 for school expenses from Grady's aunt.

LO 5-3

66. Bart is the favorite nephew of his aunt Thelma. Thelma transferred several items of value to Bart. For each of the following transactions, determine the effect on Bart's gross income:

a) Thelma gave Bart an auto worth $22,000. Thelma purchased the auto three years ago for $17,000.

b) Thelma elects to cancel a life insurance policy and gives the cash surrender value of $15,000 to Bart.

c) Bart is the beneficiary of a $100,000 whole life insurance policy on the life of Thelma. Thelma died this year, and Bart received $100,000 in cash.

d) Bart inherited 500 shares of stock from Thelma's estate. Thelma purchased the shares many years ago for $1,200, and the shares are worth $45,000 at her death.

LO 5-3

67. Terry was ill for three months and missed work during this period. During the illness, Terry received $4,500 in sick pay from a disability insurance policy. What amounts are included in Terry's gross income under the following independent circumstances?

a) Terry has disability insurance provided by his employer as a nontaxable fringe benefit. Terry's employer paid $2,800 in disability premiums for Terry this year.

b) Terry paid $2,800 in premiums for his disability insurance this year.

c) Terry's employer paid the $2,800 in premiums for Terry, but Terry elected to have his employer include the $2,800 as compensation on Terry's W-2.

d) Terry and his employer share the cost of the disability insurance. Terry's employer paid $1,800 in disability premiums for Terry this year as a nontaxable fringe benefit, and Terry paid the remaining $1,000 of premiums from his after-tax salary.

68. Tim's parents plan to provide him with $50,000 to support him while he establishes a new landscaping business. In exchange for the support, Tim will maintain the landscape at his father's business. Under what conditions will the transfer of $50,000 be included in Tim's gross income? Explain. Do you have a recommendation for Tim and his parents? LO 5-3 planning

69. What amounts are included in gross income for the following taxpayers? Explain your answers. LO 5-3

a) Janus sued Tiny Toys for personal injuries from swallowing a toy. Janus was paid $30,000 for medical costs and $250,000 for punitive damages.

b) Carl was injured in a car accident. Carl's insurance paid him $50,000 to reimburse his medical expenses and an additional $25,000 for the emotional distress Carl suffered as a result of the accident.

c) Ajax published a story about Pete, and as a result Pete sued Ajax for damage to his reputation. Ajax lost in court and paid Pete an award of $20,000.

d) Bevis was laid off from his job last month. This month he drew $800 in unemployment benefits.

70. This year, Janelle received $200,000 in life insurance proceeds. Under the following scenarios, how much of the $200,000 is taxable? LO 5-3

a) Janelle received the proceeds upon the death of her father, Julio.

b) Janelle received the $200,000 proceeds because she was diagnosed with colon cancer (life expectancy of six months), and she needed the proceeds for her care.

c) The proceeds related to a life insurance policy she purchased for $35,000 from a friend in need. After purchase, Janelle paid annual premiums that total $22,000.

71. This year, Leron and Sheena sold their home for $750,000 after all selling costs. Under the following scenarios, how much taxable gain does the home sale generate for Leron and Sheena? LO 5-3

a) Leron and Sheena bought the home three years ago for $150,000 and lived in the home until it sold.

b) Leron and Sheena bought the home one year ago for $600,000 and lived in the home until it sold.

c) Leron and Sheena bought the home five years ago for $500,000. They lived in the home for three years until they decided to buy a smaller home. Their home has been vacant for the past two years.

72. Dontae's employer has offered him the following employment package. What is Dontae's gross income from his employment? LO 5-3

Salary	$400,000
Health insurance	10,000
Dental insurance	1,500
Membership to Heflin Country Club	20,000
Season tickets to Atlanta Braves games	5,000
Tuition reimbursement for graduate courses	4,000
Housing allowance (for a McMansion in his neighborhood of choice)	40,000

COMPREHENSIVE PROBLEMS

Select problems are available in Connect®.

73. Charlie was hired by Ajax this year as a corporate executive and a member of the board of directors. During the current year, Charlie received the following payments or benefits paid on his behalf.

Salary payments	$92,000
Contributions to qualified pension plan	10,200
Qualified health insurance premiums	8,400
Year-end bonus	15,000
Annual director's fee	10,000
Group-term life insurance premiums (face value = $40,000)	750
Whole life insurance premiums (face value = $100,000)	1,420
Disability insurance premiums (no election to treat as taxable benefit)	4,350

a) Charlie uses the cash method and calendar year for tax purposes. Calculate Charlie's gross income for the current year.

b) Suppose that Ajax agrees to pay Charlie an additional $100,000 once Charlie completes five years of employment. Will this agreement alter Charlie's gross income this year relative to your part (a) answer? Explain.

c) Suppose that in exchange for his promise to remain with the firm for the next four years, Ajax paid Charlie four years of director's fees in advance. Will this arrangement alter Charlie's gross income this year relative to your part (a) answer? Explain.

d) Assume that in lieu of a year-end bonus Ajax transferred 500 shares of Bell stock to Charlie as compensation. Further assume that the stock was listed at $35 per share and Charlie would sell the shares by year-end, at which time he expected the price to be $37 per share. Will this arrangement alter Charlie's gross income this year relative to your part (a) answer? Explain.

e) Suppose that in lieu of a year-end bonus Ajax made Charlie's house payments (a total of $23,000). Will this arrangement alter Charlie's gross income this year relative to your part (a) answer? Explain.

74. Irene is disabled and receives payments from a number of sources. The interest payments are from bonds that Irene purchased over past years and a disability insurance policy that Irene purchased herself. Calculate Irene's gross income.

Interest, bonds issued by City of Austin, Texas	$ 2,000
Social Security benefits	8,200
Interest, U.S. Treasury bills	1,300
Interest, bonds issued by Ford Motor Company	1,500
Interest, bonds issued by City of Quebec, Canada	750
Disability insurance benefits	19,500
Distributions from qualified pension plan	5,400

tax forms

75. Ken is 63 years old and unmarried. He retired at age 55 when he sold his business, Understock.com. Though Ken is retired, he is still very active. Ken reported the following financial information this year. Assume Ken files as a single taxpayer. Determine Ken's gross income and complete page 1 of Form 1040 (through line 9) and Schedule 1 for Ken.

a) Ken won $1,200 in an illegal game of poker (the game was played in Utah, where gambling is illegal).

b) Ken sold 1,000 shares of stock for $32 a share. He inherited the stock two years ago. His tax basis (or investment) in the stock was $31 per share.

c) Ken received $25,000 from an annuity he purchased 8 years ago. He purchased the annuity, to be paid annually for 20 years, for $210,000.

d) Ken received $13,000 in disability benefits for the year. He purchased the disability insurance policy last year.

e) Ken decided to go back to school to learn about European history. He received a $500 cash scholarship to attend. He used $300 to pay for his books and tuition, and he applied the rest toward his new car payment.

f) Ken's son, Mike, instructed his employer to make half of his final paycheck of the year payable to Ken as a gift from Mike to Ken. Ken received the check on December 30 in the amount of $1,100.

g) Ken received a $610 refund of the $3,600 in state income taxes his employer withheld from his pay last year. Ken claimed $12,600 in itemized deductions last year (the standard deduction for a single filer was $12,550).

h) Ken received $30,000 of interest from corporate bonds and money market accounts.

76. Consider the following letter and answer Shady's question.

tax forms

To my friendly student tax preparer:

Hello, my name is Shady Slim. I understand you are going to help me figure out my gross income for the year . . . whatever that means. It's been a busy year and I'm a busy person, so let me give you the lowdown on my life and you can do your thing.

I was unemployed at the beginning of the year and got $2,000 in unemployment compensation. I later got a job as a manager for Roca Cola. I earned $55,000 in base salary this year. My boss gave me a $5,000 Christmas bonus check on December 22. I decided to hold on to that check and not cash it until next year, so I won't have to pay taxes on it this year. Pretty smart, huh? My job's pretty cool. I get a lot of fringe benefits like a membership to the gym that costs $400 a year and all the Roca Cola I can drink, although I can't really drink a whole lot—I figure $40 worth this year.

As part of my manager duties, I get to decide on certain things like contracts for the company. My good buddy, Eddie, runs a bottling company. I made sure that he won the bottling contract for Roca Cola for this year (even though his contract wasn't quite the best). Eddie bought me a Corvette this year for being such a good friend. The Corvette cost $50,000, and I'm sure he bought it for me out of the goodness of his heart. What a great friend!

Here's a bit of good luck for the year. Upon leaving my office one day, I found $8,000 lying in the street! Well, one person's bad luck is my good luck, right?

I like to gamble a lot. I won a $27,000 poker tournament in Las Vegas this year. I also won about $5,000 over the year playing the guys at our Friday night poker game. Can you believe that I didn't lose anything this year?

Speaking of the poker games, I got hit by a car one night while leaving a game. I broke my right leg and my left arm. I sued the driver and got $11,000 for my medical expenses and $3,000 to pay my psychotherapist for the emotional problems I had relating to the injuries (I got really depressed!), and I won $12,000 in punitive damages. That'll teach them!

Another bit of bad luck. My uncle Monty died this year. I really liked the guy, but the $200,000 inheritance I received from him made me feel a little better about the loss. I did the smart thing with the money and invested it in stocks and bonds and socked a little into my savings account. As a result, I received $600 in dividends from the stock, $200 in interest from the municipal bonds, and $300 in interest from my savings account.

My ex-wife, Alice, is still paying me alimony. She's a lawyer who divorced me in 2015 because I was "unethical" or something like that. Because she was making so much money and I was unemployed at the time, the judge ruled that she had to pay me alimony. She sent me $3,000 in alimony payments this year. She still kind of likes me, though. She sent me a check for $500 as a Christmas gift this year. I didn't get her anything, though.

So there you go. That's this year in a nutshell. Can you figure out my gross income and complete page 1 of Form 1040 (through line 9) and Schedule 1 for me? And because you're a student, this is free, right? Thanks, I owe you one! Let me know if I can get you a six-pack of Roca Cola or something.

tax forms

77. Diana and Ryan Workman were married on January 1 of last year. Ryan has an eight-year-old son, Jorge, from his previous marriage. Diana works as a computer programmer at Datafile Inc. (DI) earning a salary of $96,000. Ryan is self-employed and runs a day care center. The Workmans reported the following financial information pertaining to their activities during the current year.

a) Diana earned a $96,000 salary for the year.

b) Diana borrowed $12,000 from DI to purchase a car. DI charged her 2 percent interest ($240) on the loan, which Diana paid on December 31. DI would have charged Diana $720 if interest had been calculated at the applicable federal interest rate. Assume that tax avoidance was not a motive for the loan.

c) Ryan received $2,000 in alimony and $4,500 in child support payments from his former spouse. They divorced in 2016.

d) Ryan won a $900 cash prize at his church-sponsored Bingo game.

e) The Workmans received $500 of interest from corporate bonds and $250 of interest from a municipal bond. Ryan owned these bonds before he married Diana.

f) The couple bought 50 shares of ABC Inc. stock for $40 per share on July 2. The stock was worth $47 a share on December 31. The stock paid a dividend of $1.00 per share on December 1.

g) Ryan's father passed away on April 14. He inherited cash of $50,000 from his father and his baseball card collection, valued at $2,000. As the beneficiary of his father's life insurance policy, Ryan also received $150,000.

h) The couple spent a weekend in Atlantic City in November and came home with gross gambling winnings of $1,200.

i) Diana received $400 cash for reaching 10 years of continuous service at DI.

j) Diana was hit and injured by a drunk driver while crossing a street at a crosswalk. She was unable to work for a month. She received $6,000 from her disability insurance. DI paid the premiums for Diana, but it reported the amount of the premiums as compensation to Diana on her year-end W-2.

k) The drunk driver who hit Diana in part (j) was required to pay her $2,000 medical costs, $1,500 for the emotional trauma she suffered from the accident, and $5,000 for punitive damages.

l) For meeting her performance goals this year, Diana was informed on December 27 that she would receive a $5,000 year-end bonus. DI (located in Houston, Texas) mailed Diana's bonus check from its payroll processing center (Tampa, Florida) on December 28. Diana didn't receive the check at home until January 2.

m) Ryan is a 10 percent owner of MNO Inc., a Subchapter S corporation. The company reported ordinary business income for the year of $92,000. Ryan acquired the MNO stock two years ago.

n) Ryan's day care business collected $35,000 in revenues. In addition, customers owed him $3,000 at year-end. During the year, Ryan spent $5,500 for supplies, $1,500 for utilities, $15,000 for rent, and $500 for miscellaneous expenses. One customer gave him use of their vacation home for a week (worth $2,500) in exchange for Ryan allowing their child to attend the day care center free of charge. Ryan accounts for his business activities using the cash method of accounting.

o) Diana's employer pays the couple's annual health insurance premiums of $5,500 for a qualified plan.

Required:

a) Assuming the Workmans file a joint tax return, determine their gross income minus expenses on the day care business (this is called total income on the Form 1040).
b) Using your answer in part (a), complete page 1 of Form 1040 through line 9 and Schedule 1 for the Workmans.
c) Assuming the Workmans live in California, a community property state, and that Diana and Ryan file separately, what is Diana's gross income minus expenses on the day care business?
d) Using your answer in part (c), complete page 1 of Form 1040 through line 9 and Schedule 1 for Diana Workman.

UWorld Roger CPA Review

Sample CPA Exam questions from Roger CPA Review are available in Connect as support for the topics in this text. These Multiple Choice Questions and Task-Based Simulations include expert-written explanations and solutions and provide a starting point for students to become familiar with the content and functionality of the actual CPA Exam.

chapter

6 Individual Deductions

Learning Objectives

Upon completing this chapter, you should be able to:

- **LO 6-1** Identify the common deductions necessary for calculating adjusted gross income (AGI).
- **LO 6-2** Describe the different types of itemized deductions available to individuals.
- **LO 6-3** Determine the standard deduction available to individuals.
- **LO 6-4** Calculate the deduction for qualified business income.

JP Wallet/Shutterstock

Storyline Summary

Taxpayers:	Courtney Wilson (she/her/hers), age 40 Courtney's mother, Dorothy "Gram" Weiss (she/her/hers), age 70
Family description:	Courtney is divorced with a son, Deron (he/him/his), age 10, and a daughter, Ellen (she/her/hers), age 20. Gram is currently residing with Courtney. Ellen is currently a full-time student.
Location:	Kansas City, Missouri
Employment status:	Courtney works as an architect for EWD. Gram is retired.
Filing status:	Courtney files as a head of household. Gram files as a single taxpayer.
Current situation:	Courtney and Gram are trying to determine their allowable deductions and compute taxable income.

Now that Courtney has determined her gross income (see the Gross Income and Exclusions chapter for details), she still must determine her deductions to compute taxable income. Fortunately, Courtney keeps detailed records of all the expenditures she believes to be deductible. Besides expenses associated with her weekend consulting work and rental property, Courtney incurred some significant costs moving from Cincinnati to Kansas City. She also paid self-employment taxes on her consulting income and paid tuition for Ellen to attend summer school. Courtney is confident some of these items are deductible, but she isn't quite sure which items are deductible and how much.

Based on her review of prior-year tax returns, Courtney has a pretty good handle on her itemized deductions. She incurred some extra medical expenses to treat a broken wrist from a mountain biking accident and had additional state income taxes withheld from her paycheck. Courtney paid real estate taxes for her personal residence and investment property and interest expense on loans secured by her new home. She also donated (cash and property) to her favorite charities.

Gram wasn't as busy as Courtney this year. Gram paid a penalty for cashing in her certificate of deposit early. She also paid some medical expenses and donated money to her local church. Gram is a little frustrated because she doesn't incur enough itemized deductions to exceed the standard deduction amount. Gram recently heard that she might be able to save taxes by "bunching" her itemized deductions into one year. She's hoping to learn a little bit more about this technique. In any event, Gram didn't pay any taxes during the year and she wants to learn how much she's going to owe. ■

In the previous chapter, we determined *gross income* for both Courtney and Gram. To compute their taxable income, however, we need to identify their deductions. As emphasized previously, taxpayers are not allowed to deduct expenditures unless there is a specific tax law authorizing the deductions. And as we learn in this chapter, Congress grants many deductions for taxpayers for a variety of reasons.

As we discussed in the Individual Income Tax Overview, Dependents, and Filing Status chapter, deductions appear in one of two places in the individual income tax formula. Deductions "for AGI" are subtracted directly from gross income to arrive at AGI.[1] Next, deductions "from AGI" are subtracted directly from AGI, resulting in taxable income. Deductions for AGI are generally preferred over deductions from AGI because for AGI deductions reduce taxable income dollar-for-dollar. In contrast, deductions from AGI sometimes have no effect on taxable income. Further, because several limitations on tax benefits for higher-income taxpayers are based upon AGI, deductions for AGI often reduce these limitations, thereby increasing potential tax benefits. Thus, it's important to determine both the amount of the deduction and whether it's a deduction for AGI or from AGI. We begin our discussion of deductions by describing deductions for AGI, and we conclude by tackling itemized deductions, the standard deduction, and the deduction for qualified business income.

LO 6-1

DEDUCTIONS *FOR* AGI

Congress allows taxpayers to claim a variety of deductions for AGI.[2] To provide an overview, we select a cross-section of deductions for AGI and classify them into three categories:

1. Deductions *directly* related to **business activities.**
2. Deductions *indirectly* related to business activities.
3. Deductions subsidizing specific activities.

We've organized our discussion around these categories to illustrate the variety of deductions for AGI and explain why Congress provides preferential treatment for certain deductions.

Deductions Directly Related to Business Activities

As a matter of equity, Congress allows taxpayers involved in business activities to deduct expenses incurred to generate business income. That is, because taxpayers include the revenue they receive from doing business in gross income, they should be allowed to deduct against gross income the expenses they incur to generate those revenues.

To begin, we must define "business activities" and, for reasons we discuss below, we must distinguish business activities from **investment activities.** In general, for tax purposes, activities are either *profit-motivated* or motivated by personal objectives. Profit-motivated activities are, in turn, classified as either (1) business activities or (2) investment activities. Business activities are sometimes referred to as a **trade or business,** and these activities require a relatively high level of involvement or effort. For example, if an individual is a full-time employee, the individual is in the business of being an employee. Self-employed individuals are also engaged in business activities.

Unlike business activities, investment activities are profit-motivated activities that *don't* require a high degree of involvement or effort.[3] Instead, investment activities involve investing in property for appreciation or for income payments. An individual who

[1]Most, but not all, deductions for AGI appear on lines 11 through 25 on Schedule 1 of Form 1040.

[2]§62 identifies deductions for AGI.

[3]§162 generally authorizes trade or business expense deductions, while §212 generally authorizes deductions for investment activities. The distinction between these activities is discussed in the Business Income, Deductions, and Accounting Methods chapter.

occasionally buys land or stock in anticipation of appreciation or dividend payments is engaged in an investment activity.

Example 6-1

Suppose that Courtney purchased a parcel of land for its appreciation potential. Would her ownership in the land be considered a business or investment activity?

Answer: Courtney's activity would most likely be considered an investment activity because she acquired the land for its appreciation potential and she does not plan to exercise any special effort to develop the property or to become actively involved in other real estate speculation.

What if: Suppose that Courtney frequently buys and sells land or develops land to sell in small parcels to those wanting to build homes. Would Courtney's activity be considered a business or investment activity?

Answer: Courtney's activity would most likely be considered a business activity because she is actively involved in generating profits from the land by developing it rather than simply holding the land for appreciation.

The distinction between business and investment activities is critical for determining whether a deduction associated with the activity is deductible for AGI or from AGI, or even deductible at all. With one exception, business expenses are deducted for AGI. The lone exception is unreimbursed employee business expenses, which, unfortunately, are not deductible. In contrast, there are only two types of deductible investment expenses. Expenses associated with rental and royalty activities are deductible for AGI regardless of whether the activity qualifies as an investment or a business. Investment interest expense, the second type of deductible investment expense, is deductible from AGI (as an itemized deduction). All other investment expenses are nondeductible. Exhibit 6-1 summarizes the rules for classifying business- and investment-related expenses as for AGI deductions, from AGI deductions, or not deductible.

Trade or Business Expenses Congress limits business deductions to expenses directly related to the business activity and those that are **ordinary and necessary** for the activity.[4] This means that deductible expenses must be appropriate and helpful for generating a profit. Although business deductions are one of the most common deductions for AGI, they are not readily visible on page 1 of Form 1040. Instead, these deductions are reported with business revenues on Schedule C of Form 1040. Schedule C, presented in Exhibit 6-2, is essentially an income statement for the business that identifies typical ordinary and necessary business expenses. Taxpayers transfer the *net* income or loss from Schedule C to Schedule 1, line 3, which is then combined with other items and included on Form 1040 (page 1), line 8 as part of total income.

EXHIBIT 6-1 Individual Business- and Investment-Related Expense Deductions for AGI, from AGI, and Not Deductible

	Deduction Type		
Activity Type	**Deduction for AGI**	**Deduction from AGI (itemized deduction)**	**Not Deductible**
Business activities	Self-employed business expenses	N/A	Unreimbursed employee business expenses
Investment activities	Rental and royalty expenses	Investment interest expense	Other investment expenses

[4]§162. In the Business Income, Deductions, and Accounting Methods chapter, we address the requirements for deductible business expenses in detail.

EXHIBIT 6-2 Parts I and II from Schedule C Profit or Loss from Business

SCHEDULE C
(Form 1040)

Department of the Treasury
Internal Revenue Service (99)

Profit or Loss From Business
(Sole Proprietorship)

▶ Go to *www.irs.gov/ScheduleC* for instructions and the latest information.
▶ Attach to Form 1040, 1040-SR, 1040-NR, or 1041; partnerships must generally file Form 1065.

OMB No. 1545-0074
2021
Attachment Sequence No. **09**

Name of proprietor | **Social security number (SSN)**

A Principal business or profession, including product or service (see instructions) | **B Enter code from instructions** ▶

C Business name. If no separate business name, leave blank. | **D Employer ID number (EIN)** (see instr.)

E Business address (including suite or room no.) ▶
City, town or post office, state, and ZIP code

F Accounting method: (1) ☐ Cash (2) ☐ Accrual (3) ☐ Other (specify) ▶

G Did you "materially participate" in the operation of this business during 2021? If "No," see instructions for limit on losses . ☐ Yes ☐ No

H If you started or acquired this business during 2021, check here ▶ ☐

I Did you make any payments in 2021 that would require you to file Form(s) 1099? See instructions ☐ Yes ☐ No

J If "Yes," did you or will you file required Form(s) 1099? ☐ Yes ☐ No

Part I Income

1	Gross receipts or sales. See instructions for line 1 and check the box if this income was reported to you on Form W-2 and the "Statutory employee" box on that form was checked ▶ ☐	1	
2	Returns and allowances	2	
3	Subtract line 2 from line 1	3	
4	Cost of goods sold (from line 42)	4	
5	**Gross profit.** Subtract line 4 from line 3	5	
6	Other income, including federal and state gasoline or fuel tax credit or refund (see instructions)	6	
7	**Gross income.** Add lines 5 and 6 ▶	7	

Part II Expenses. Enter expenses for business use of your home **only** on line 30.

8	Advertising	8		18	Office expense (see instructions)	18	
9	Car and truck expenses (see instructions)	9		19	Pension and profit-sharing plans	19	
10	Commissions and fees	10		20	Rent or lease (see instructions):		
11	Contract labor (see instructions)	11		a	Vehicles, machinery, and equipment	20a	
12	Depletion	12		b	Other business property	20b	
13	Depreciation and section 179 expense deduction (not included in Part III) (see instructions)	13		21	Repairs and maintenance	21	
				22	Supplies (not included in Part III)	22	
				23	Taxes and licenses	23	
				24	Travel and meals:		
14	Employee benefit programs (other than on line 19)	14		a	Travel	24a	
15	Insurance (other than health)	15		b	Deductible meals (see instructions)	24b	
16	Interest (see instructions):			25	Utilities	25	
a	Mortgage (paid to banks, etc.)	16a		26	Wages (less employment credits)	26	
b	Other	16b		27a	Other expenses (from line 48)	27a	
17	Legal and professional services	17		b	**Reserved for future use**	27b	

28	**Total expenses** before expenses for business use of home. Add lines 8 through 27a ▶	28	
29	Tentative profit or (loss). Subtract line 28 from line 7	29	
30	Expenses for business use of your home. Do not report these expenses elsewhere. Attach Form 8829 unless using the simplified method. See instructions. **Simplified method filers only:** Enter the total square footage of (a) your home: ____ and (b) the part of your home used for business: ____. Use the Simplified Method Worksheet in the instructions to figure the amount to enter on line 30	30	
31	**Net profit or (loss).** Subtract line 30 from line 29. • If a profit, enter on both **Schedule 1 (Form 1040), line 3,** and on **Schedule SE, line 2.** (If you checked the box on line 1, see instructions). Estates and trusts, enter on **Form 1041, line 3.** • If a loss, you **must** go to line 32.	31	
32	If you have a loss, check the box that describes your investment in this activity. See instructions. • If you checked 32a, enter the loss on both **Schedule 1 (Form 1040), line 3,** and on **Schedule SE, line 2.** (If you checked the box on line 1, see the line 31 instructions.) Estates and trusts, enter on **Form 1041, line 3.** • If you checked 32b, you **must** attach **Form 6198.** Your loss may be limited.	32a ☐ All investment is at risk. 32b ☐ Some investment is not at risk.	

For Paperwork Reduction Act Notice, see the separate instructions. Cat. No. 11334P **Schedule C (Form 1040) 2021**

Source: irs.gov.

Example 6-2

Besides being employed by EWD, Courtney is also a self-employed architectural consultant (a business activity). This year her consulting activity generated $19,500 of revenue and incurred $1,500 in expenses (primarily travel and transportation expenses). How does she report the revenue and deductions from the activity?

Answer: Courtney reports the $19,500 of revenue and deducts the $1,500 of business expenses for AGI on her Schedule C. Her net income of $18,000 from her consulting activities is included on Schedule 1, line 3, which is then combined with other items and included on Form 1040 (page 1), line 8.

Rental and Royalty Expenses Taxpayers are allowed to deduct their expenses associated with generating rental or royalty income for AGI.[5] Like business expenses, rental and royalty expenses do not appear directly on page 1 of Form 1040. Instead, rental and royalty deductions are reported with rental and royalty revenues on Schedule E of Form 1040.[6] Schedule E, presented in Exhibit 6-3, is essentially an income statement for the taxpayer's rental or royalty activities. Taxpayers transfer the *net* income or loss from

EXHIBIT 6-3 Page 1 of Schedule E Rental or Royalty Income

SCHEDULE E
(Form 1040)
Department of the Treasury
Internal Revenue Service (99)

Supplemental Income and Loss
(From rental real estate, royalties, partnerships, S corporations, estates, trusts, REMICs, etc.)
▶ Attach to Form 1040, 1040-SR, 1040-NR, or 1041.
▶ Go to *www.irs.gov/ScheduleE* for instructions and the latest information.

OMB No. 1545-0074
2021
Attachment Sequence No. **13**

Name(s) shown on return | **Your social security number**

Part I **Income or Loss From Rental Real Estate and Royalties** **Note:** If you are in the business of renting personal property, use **Schedule C.** See instructions. If you are an individual, report farm rental income or loss from **Form 4835** on page 2, line 40.

A Did you make any payments in 2021 that would require you to file Form(s) 1099? See instructions . . . . . ☐ **Yes** ☐ **No**
B If "Yes," did you or will you file required Form(s) 1099? . . . . . ☐ **Yes** ☐ **No**

1a	Physical address of each property (street, city, state, ZIP code)
A	
B	
C	

1b	Type of Property (from list below)	2 For each rental real estate property listed above, report the number of fair rental and personal use days. Check the **QJV** box only if you meet the requirements to file as a qualified joint venture. See instructions.		Fair Rental Days	Personal Use Days	QJV
A			A			☐
B			B			☐
C			C			☐

Type of Property:
1 Single Family Residence 3 Vacation/Short-Term Rental 5 Land 7 Self-Rental
2 Multi-Family Residence 4 Commercial 6 Royalties 8 Other (describe)

Income:	**Properties:**		**A**	**B**	**C**
3	Rents received	3			
4	Royalties received	4			
Expenses:					
5	Advertising	5			
6	Auto and travel (see instructions)	6			
7	Cleaning and maintenance	7			
8	Commissions.	8			
9	Insurance	9			
10	Legal and other professional fees	10			
11	Management fees	11			
12	Mortgage interest paid to banks, etc. (see instructions)	12			
13	Other interest.	13			
14	Repairs.	14			
15	Supplies	15			
16	Taxes	16			
17	Utilities.	17			
18	Depreciation expense or depletion	18			
19	Other (list) ▶	19			
20	Total expenses. Add lines 5 through 19	20			
21	Subtract line 20 from line 3 (rents) and/or 4 (royalties). If result is a (loss), see instructions to find out if you must file **Form 6198**	21			
22	Deductible rental real estate loss after limitation, if any, on **Form 8582** (see instructions)	22	( )	( )	( )

23a	Total of all amounts reported on line 3 for all rental properties	23a	
b	Total of all amounts reported on line 4 for all royalty properties	23b	
c	Total of all amounts reported on line 12 for all properties	23c	
d	Total of all amounts reported on line 18 for all properties	23d	
e	Total of all amounts reported on line 20 for all properties	23e	
24	**Income.** Add positive amounts shown on line 21. **Do not** include any losses	24	
25	**Losses.** Add royalty losses from line 21 and rental real estate losses from line 22. Enter total losses here .	25	( )
26	**Total rental real estate and royalty income or (loss).** Combine lines 24 and 25. Enter the result here. If Parts II, III, IV, and line 40 on page 2 do not apply to you, also enter this amount on Schedule 1 (Form 1040), line 5. Otherwise, include this amount in the total on line 41 on page 2 .	26	

For Paperwork Reduction Act Notice, see the separate instructions. Cat. No. 11344L **Schedule E (Form 1040) 2021**

Source: irs.gov.

[5]§212.

[6]Rental income and expenses for renting personal property (e.g., equipment, furniture, etc.) instead of real property is generally reported on Schedule C (not Schedule E). If the rental of personal property is not considered a trade or business, the rental income and expenses are reported on lines 8k and 24b, respectively, of Schedule 1 of Form 1040.

Schedule E to Schedule 1, line 5, which is then combined with other items and included on Form 1040 (page 1), line 8 as part of total income.

Rental and royalty endeavors are most commonly considered to be investment activities, but like trade or business expenses, rental and royalty deductions are deductible for AGI.[7] Despite this preferential treatment, the deductibility of rental losses (where expenses exceed income) is subject to limitations (basis, at-risk amount, passive loss, and excess business loss rules). We discuss the excess business loss rules later in this chapter and the basis, at-risk, and passive loss rules in the Investments chapter when we discuss similar limitations that apply to investments in flow-through entities.

Example 6-3

Courtney owns a condominium that she rents to tenants. This year she received $14,000 in rental revenue and incurred $9,000 of expenses associated with the rental, including management fees, maintenance, and depreciation. How does she report the revenue and expenses for tax purposes?

Answer: Courtney reports the $14,000 of rental receipts and deducts the $9,000 of rental expenses for AGI on Schedule E. The net rental income of $5,000 is then reported on Schedule 1 (line 5) and combined with other items on page 1 (line 8) of her Form 1040.

Losses on Dispositions As we discuss in more detail in the Property Dispositions chapter, taxpayers disposing of business assets at a loss are allowed to deduct the losses for AGI. Also, individual taxpayers selling investment (capital) assets at a loss are allowed to deduct the "capital" losses against other capital gains. If the capital losses exceed the capital gains, they can deduct up to $3,000 as a net capital loss in a particular year. Losses in excess of the $3,000 limit are carried forward indefinitely to subsequent years, in which they are deductible subject to the same limitations.

Flow-Through Entities Income from flow-through entities such as partnerships, LLCs, and S corporations passes through to the owners of those entities, with the related net business income reported on Schedule E of the tax returns of the owners. Similarly, any expenses and losses incurred by the entity pass through to the entity owners, with the related net business losses reported on Schedule E, subject to certain restrictions (basis, at-risk amount, and passive loss rules) that we discuss in the Investments chapter and the excess business loss limitation that we discuss next. As with other Schedule E items, taxpayers transfer the net income or loss from flow-through entities from Schedule E (as well as any rental and royalty income or loss) to Schedule 1, line 5, which is then combined with other items and included on Form 1040 (page 1), line 8 as part of total income.[8]

Excess Business Loss Limitation Taxpayers are not allowed to deduct an **excess business loss** for the year. Rather, excess business losses are carried forward to subsequent years. The excess business loss limitation applies to losses that are otherwise deductible under the basis, at-risk, and passive loss rules. An excess business loss for the year is the excess of aggregate business deductions for the year over the sum of aggregate business gross income or gain of the taxpayer plus a threshold amount. The threshold amount for 2022 is $540,000 for married taxpayers filing jointly and $270,000 for other taxpayers. The threshold amounts are indexed for inflation. In the case of partnership or S corporation business losses, the provision applies at the partner or shareholder level.

[7]Royalties are received for allowing others to use property or rights to property. For example, royalties are paid for allowing others to use or sell copyrighted material, such as books or plays, or to extract natural resources from property. The amount of the royalty is often a percentage of total revenues derived from the property or rights to property.

[8] We refer to losses from flow-through entities as for AGI deductions because they reduce a taxpayer's AGI and represent a net excess of business deductions over the entity's gross business income.

Example 6-4

What if: Suppose that Courtney invested in a partnership and that this year her share of business losses from the partnership amounts to $300,000. Assume that the $300,000 loss is deductible under the basis, at-risk amount, and passive loss rules. How much of the loss would be deductible on her tax return?

Answer: $270,000. Deductible net business losses are limited to $270,000 ($540,000 for taxpayers married filing jointly). The $30,000 excess business loss would be carried forward to next year.

Deductions Indirectly Related to Business Activities

Taxpayers can incur expenses in activities that are not directly related to making money but that they would not have incurred if they were not involved in a business activity. Taxpayers are allowed to deduct some of these expenses that are indirectly related to business activities as deductions for AGI. We describe these deductions below.

Moving Expenses Moving expenses, even if incurred to move for a new job, generally are not deductible (and employer reimbursements of moving expenses are taxable). The lone exception is for members of the Armed Forces (or their spouse or dependents) on active duty that move pursuant to a military order and incident to a permanent change of station. Their moving costs are nontaxable if paid by their employer and deductible if the costs are not paid by their employer.[9]

Example 6-5

This year, Courtney moved from Cincinnati to Kansas City, her new place of work with EWD. She incurred considerable expenses associated with the move (none were reimbursed). Can Courtney deduct the expenses of moving her residence to Kansas City?

Answer: No. Because Courtney does not meet the exception for members of the Armed Forces (or their spouse or dependents) on active duty, she cannot deduct the moving costs.

Health Insurance Deduction by Self-Employed Taxpayers The cost of health insurance is essentially a personal expense. However, *employers* often pay a portion of health insurance premiums for employees as a qualified fringe benefit. Employers are allowed to deduct health insurance premiums as compensation expense, while employees are allowed to *exclude* these premiums from gross income. The health insurance fringe benefit does not apply to self-employed taxpayers because they are not "employees." So to provide equitable treatment, Congress allows self-employed taxpayers to claim personal health insurance premiums for the taxpayer, the taxpayer's spouse, the taxpayer's dependents, and the taxpayer's children under age 27 (regardless of whether the child is a dependent of the taxpayer) as deductions for AGI, but only to the extent of the self-employment income derived from the specific trade or business.[10]

This deduction is intended to help self-employed taxpayers who must pay their own insurance premiums. Consequently, self-employed taxpayers are *not* allowed to deduct health care insurance premiums if the taxpayer is eligible to participate in an employer-provided health plan. This restriction applies regardless of whether the health plan is

[9] §217.

[10] §162(l). As we'll explain shortly, health insurance premiums also qualify as itemized deductions as medical expenses, but itemizing these deductions may not produce any tax benefits. To the extent that self-employed taxpayers do not have sufficient self-employment income to deduct all of their health insurance premiums as a for AGI deduction, they may deduct the remaining premiums as an itemized deduction. Finally, subject to certain restrictions, self-employed taxpayers who purchase health insurance through an exchange, have household incomes below 400 percent of the poverty line, and are not eligible for affordable coverage through an employer health plan that provides at least 60 percent of the expected costs for covered services can receive a premium tax credit under §36B. Any premiums offset by the tax credit cannot be deducted as either a for AGI or itemized deduction.

sponsored by either an employer of the taxpayer or an employer of the taxpayer's spouse, and it is irrelevant whether the taxpayer actually participates in the plan.[11,12]

Self-Employment Tax Deduction Employees and employers each pays Social Security and Medicare tax on employee salaries. Employers deduct the Social Security and Medicare taxes they pay on employee salaries. In contrast, because self-employed individuals do not have an employer, these individuals are required to pay self-employment tax. This tax represents both the employee's *and* the employer's share of the Social Security and Medicare taxes. Unfortunately for the self-employed, the self-employment tax is *not* considered a business expense. To put self-employed individuals on somewhat equal footing with other employers who are allowed to deduct the *employer's* share of the Social Security and Medicare taxes, however, self-employed taxpayers are allowed to deduct the employer portion of the self-employment tax they pay.[13]

Example 6-6

As we indicated in Example 6-2, Courtney reported $18,000 of net income from her self-employed consulting activities. She will pay $482 in self-employment taxes on this income, with $241 representing the employer portion of the self-employment tax.[14] What amount of self-employment tax can she deduct this year?

Answer: $241 (the employer portion of the self-employment tax).

Deductions for Individual Retirement Accounts (IRAs) Taxpayers with earned income can contribute to **traditional IRAs.** The deductible amount of the contributions depends on a number of factors (filing status, whether the taxpayer is an active participant in an employer-sponsored retirement plan, and the taxpayer's modified AGI).[15] Deductible contributions to traditional IRAs are for AGI deductions. Distributions from traditional IRAs are taxed as ordinary income to the taxpayer, and early distributions (before age 59½) are generally subject to a 10 percent penalty. Taxpayers with earned income that are not eligible to make deductible contributions can make nondeductible contributions.[16] On distribution, the taxpayer is taxed on the earnings generated by nondeductible contributions but not on the actual nondeductible contributions.[17] We discuss IRAs and related self-employed retirement plans in detail in the Retirement Savings and Deferred Compensation chapter.

Deductions for Health Savings Accounts **Health savings accounts** (HSAs) allow individuals covered by a high-deductible health plan with no other health coverage to set aside amounts for payment of qualified medical and dental expenses for the

[11]§162(l)(2)(B).

[12]Any health insurance deduction for AGI for self-employed taxpayers also reduces the taxpayer's qualified business income for purposes of the deduction for qualified business income (discussed later in the chapter).

[13]Any self-employment tax deduction also reduces the taxpayer's qualified business income for purposes of the deduction for qualified business income (discussed later in the chapter).

[14]In this case, Courtney uses the following equation to determine her total self-employment tax: $18,000 × .9235 × .029 = $482 (Courtney's business income is subject to the Medicare tax but not the Social Security tax due to the level of her salary - See Exhibit 5-4). Of the total self-employment tax, the employer portion is calculated as $18,000 × .9235 × .0145 = $241. We discuss how to compute the self-employment tax in detail in the Individual Income Tax Computation and Tax Credits chapter.

[15]Subject to limitations, taxpayers also can contribute to a Roth IRA. Unlike traditional IRAs, contributions to Roth IRAs are nondeductible and qualified distributions are nontaxable.

[16]The overall annual limit of the sum of both traditional and Roth IRA contributions is the lesser of the taxpayer's earned income or $6,000 ($7,000 if the taxpayer is over 50).

[17]Individually managed retirement plans such as traditional and Roth IRAs are not particularly attractive to self-employed taxpayers due to the relatively low contribution limits on these plans. As such, Congress created a number of retirement savings plans (e.g., SEP IRAs, individual 401(k) plans) with higher contribution limits targeted toward self-employed taxpayers. Contributions to these plans are deducted for AGI, earnings are free from tax until distributed, and distributions from the plans are fully taxable.

taxpayer, spouse, and dependents.[18] For 2022, high-deductible health plans have a minimum annual deductible of $1,400 for self-only coverage ($2,800 for family coverage) and their maximum annual deductible and other out-of-pocket expenses cannot exceed $7,050 for self-only coverage ($14,100 for family coverage). For 2022, individuals can contribute up to $3,650 for self-only coverage ($7,300 for family coverage) to an HSA and deduct these contributions for AGI. Individuals age 55 or older at the end of the tax year may contribute and deduct an additional $1,000 annually.[19] Contributions to an HSA remain in the taxpayer's account until they use them, and the funds may earn interest or other investment returns. Distributions from an HSA are tax-free if they pay for qualified medical expenses of the taxpayer, spouse, and dependents that occurred after the HSA was established (even if the distribution occurs in a year after the expense was incurred or in a year in which the taxpayer is no longer covered under a high deductible health plan). Taxpayers just need to maintain medical receipts to substantiate the previously unreimbursed qualified medical expenses. Otherwise, distributions are taxed as ordinary income (and subject to an additional 20 percent tax unless the taxpayer is disabled, age 65 or older, or deceased).

Example 6-7

What if: Courtney is self-employed and her only health insurance coverage for the entire year is by a family health plan with a $3,000 annual deductible and maximum deductible and out-of-pocket expenses of $8,000. If Courtney contributes $6,300 to an HSA to pay for medical expenses, how much of the HSA contributions could Courtney deduct as a for AGI deduction?

Answer: $6,300. Because Courtney is only covered by a high-deductible plan (minimum annual deductible of $2,800 for family coverage and maximum annual deductible and other out-of-pocket expenses not exceeding $14,100 for family coverage), she may fully deduct her HSA contributions up to $7,300. Hence, she may fully deduct her $6,300 of HSA contributions on Form 8889 and Schedule 1 (line 13).

Penalty for Early Withdrawal of Savings Taxpayers are allowed a deduction for AGI for any interest income an individual forfeits to a bank as a penalty for prematurely withdrawing a certificate of deposit or similar deposit. This deduction reduces the taxpayer's net interest income to the amount they actually received. Otherwise, taxpayers would be required to report the full amount of interest income as taxable income, and, unfortunately, the forfeited interest would be a nondeductible investment expense.

Example 6-8

Gram invested $100,000 in a three-year certificate of deposit (CD). On December 31, she decides to cash out the certificate of deposit after holding it for less than a year. She receives the $4,100 of interest income the CD had generated up to the withdrawal date, less a $410 early withdrawal penalty. How will Gram report the interest and early withdrawal for tax purposes?

Answer: Gram reports $4,100 as interest income this year and deducts the $410 early withdrawal penalty as a deduction for AGI on Schedule 1 (line 18).

[18]To contribute to an HSA, an individual cannot be enrolled in Medicare, be claimed as a dependent on another taxpayer's tax return, or have other health coverage (except worker's compensation; coverage for a specific disease or illness or for a fixed amount per day or period of hospitalization; coverage of accidents, disability, dental care, vision care, and long-term care; and in other specific circumstances). Because employees contributing to an HSA through their employer's cafeteria plan exclude their HSA contributions from their salary income (and do not take a deduction for AGI), taxpayers claiming the HSA deduction are often self-employed. For this reason, we include the discussion of the deduction for HSAs in the section covering deductions indirectly related to business activities. Note, however, that unemployed taxpayers may also claim the HSA deduction for AGI.

[19]The deduction for an HSA is determined on a monthly basis. To take an HSA deduction for a specific month, the taxpayer must be an eligible individual on the first day of the month (i.e., covered by a high-deductible health plan with no other health coverage). However, under the last-month rule, an individual is considered to be eligible for the entire year if (a) they are an eligible individual on the first day of the last month of the tax year and (b) remain so for the following 12 months. For taxpayers who are eligible individuals for the entire year, the deduction for HSA contributions is simply limited to the annual maximum amounts based on their coverage (plus $1,000 if age 55 or older).

Deductions Subsidizing Specific Activities

To address specific policy objectives, Congress provides that certain expenditures are deductible for AGI. For example, alimony payments paid pursuant to divorce or separation agreements executed before 2019 are deductible for AGI to maintain equity given that these payments are taxable to the recipient. In contrast, contributions to retirement savings are deductible for AGI to encourage savings.[20] Further, Congress created an important deduction for AGI to encourage and subsidize higher education. Taxpayers are allowed to deduct for AGI, subject to certain limitations, interest expense on **qualified education loans.**[21] As we discuss throughout the text, Congress has also created a number of related provisions, including education tax credits, to encourage and subsidize higher education.

THE KEY FACTS

Interest on Education Loans

- Up to $2,500 of interest on education loans is deductible for AGI.
- A loan qualifies as an education loan if the proceeds are used to fund qualified education.
- The interest deduction is phased out for taxpayers with AGI exceeding $70,000 ($145,000 if married filing jointly).

Deduction for Interest on Qualified Education Loans Qualified education loans are loans whose proceeds are used to pay qualified education expenses. **Qualified education expenses** encompass expenses paid for the education of the taxpayer, the taxpayer's spouse, or a taxpayer's dependent attending a postsecondary institution of higher education.[22] These expenses include tuition and fees, books and expenses required for enrollment, room and board, and other necessary supplies and expenses, including travel.

The deduction for interest expense on qualified education loans is the amount of interest paid up to $2,500. However, the deduction is reduced (phased out) for taxpayers depending on the taxpayer's filing status and modified AGI. Modified AGI for this purpose is AGI *before* deducting interest expense on the qualified education loans. Married individuals who file separately are not allowed to deduct this expense under any circumstance. The deduction limitations for other taxpayers are summarized in Exhibit 6-4.

EXHIBIT 6-4 Summary of Limitations on Deduction of Interest on Education Loans

Panel A: AGI Limitations	
Modified AGI Level	**Deduction**
Not over $70,000 ($145,000 for married filing jointly)	Amount paid up to $2,500
Above $70,000 ($145,000 for married filing jointly) but below $85,000 ($175,000 for married filing jointly)	Amount paid up to $2,500 reduced by the phase-out amount. The phase-out amount is the amount paid up to $2,500 times the phase-out percentage (see Panel B for the phase-out percentage computation).
Equal to or above $85,000 ($175,000 for married filing jointly)	Zero

Panel B: Phase-Out Percentage*	
Filing Status	**Phase-Out Percentage**
Single or head of household	(Modified AGI – $70,000)/$15,000
Married filing jointly	(Modified AGI – $145,000)/$30,000

*Married taxpayers filing separately are ineligible for the deduction.

[20]See the Gross Income and Exclusions chapter for a detailed discussion of alimony and the Retirement Savings and Deferred Compensation chapter for a detailed discussion of the tax consequences of retirement savings.

[21]See §221.

[22]Postsecondary education includes courses at a university, college, or vocational school, including internship programs leading to a degree or certificate.

Example 6-9

What if: Assume that Courtney's brother Jason paid interest on a qualified education loan that he used to pay the tuition and fees for his three daughters to attend State University. In 2022, Jason was married and filed a joint return, paid $2,000 of interest expense on the loan, and reported modified AGI of $157,000. What amount of interest expense on the education loan is Jason allowed to deduct as a for AGI deduction?

Answer: $1,200, computed as follows:

Description	Amount	Explanation
(1) Modified AGI	$157,000	AGI before higher education deductions
(2) Amount of interest paid up to $2,500	2,000	Lesser of amount paid ($2,000) or $2,500
(3) Phase-out (reduction) percentage	40%	[(1) − $145,000]/$30,000
(4) Phase-out amount (reduction in maximum)	800	(2) × (3)
Deductible interest expense	**$ 1,200**	(2) − (4)

Summary: Deductions for AGI

Business expenses and rental and royalty expenses are two of the most important deductions for AGI. There are other important deductions for AGI that are indirectly related to business or provided to subsidize certain activities. After we have determined the deductions for AGI, we can compute AGI. Exhibits 6-5 and 6-6 summarize the computation of AGI for Courtney and Gram. Exhibit 6-7 and Exhibit 6-8 show Courtney's AGI calculation as presented on page 1 of her Form 1040 and Schedule 1, respectively.

EXHIBIT 6-5 Courtney's Adjusted Gross Income

Description	Amount	Reference
Gross income for current year	$197,741	Exhibit 5-4 and related discussion
Deductions for AGI:		
Business expenses	(1,500)	Example 6-2
Rental expenses	(9,000)	Example 6-3
Employer portion of self-employment taxes	(241)	Example 6-6
Adjusted gross income	**$187,000**	

EXHIBIT 6-6 Gram's Adjusted Gross Income

Description	Amount	Reference
Gross income for current year	$16,000	Exhibit 5-7
Deduction for AGI:		
Penalty for early withdrawal of savings	(410)	Example 6-8
Adjusted gross income	**$15,590**	

EXHIBIT 6-7 Courtney's AGI Computation on Form 1040, Page 1, lines 1–11

	1	Wages, salaries, tips, etc. Attach Form(s) W-2				1	162,800
Attach Sch. B if required.	2a	Tax-exempt interest	2a	500	b Taxable interest	2b	321
	3a	Qualified dividends	3a	700	b Ordinary dividends	3b	700
	4a	IRA distributions	4a		b Taxable amount	4b	
	5a	Pensions and annuities	5a		b Taxable amount	5b	
	6a	Social security benefits	6a		b Taxable amount	6b	
	7	Capital gain or (loss). Attach Schedule D if required. If not required, check here ▶ ☐				7	
	8	Other income from Schedule 1, line 10				8	23,420
	9	Add lines 1, 2b, 3b, 4b, 5b, 6b, 7, and 8. This is your **total income** ▶				9	187,241
	10	Adjustments to income from Schedule 1, line 26				10	241
	11	Subtract line 10 from line 9. This is your **adjusted gross income** ▶				11	187,000

Source: irs.gov.

EXHIBIT 6-8 Courtney's Income and Deductions Reported on Schedule 1

SCHEDULE 1 (Form 1040)
Department of the Treasury Internal Revenue Service

Additional Income and Adjustments to Income
▶ Attach to Form 1040, 1040-SR, or 1040-NR.
▶ Go to *www.irs.gov/Form1040* for instructions and the latest information.

OMB No. 1545-0074
2021
Attachment Sequence No. 01

Name(s) shown on Form 1040, 1040-SR, or 1040-NR: Courtney Wilson
Your social security number: 111-11-1111

Part I Additional Income

1	Taxable refunds, credits, or offsets of state and local income taxes			1	420
2a	Alimony received			2a	
b	Date of original divorce or separation agreement (see instructions) ▶				
3	Business income or (loss). Attach Schedule C			3	18,000
4	Other gains or (losses). Attach Form 4797			4	
5	Rental real estate, royalties, partnerships, S corporations, trusts, etc. Attach Schedule E			5	5,000
6	Farm income or (loss). Attach Schedule F			6	
7	Unemployment compensation			7	
8	Other income:				
a	Net operating loss	8a	( )		
b	Gambling income	8b			
c	Cancellation of debt	8c			
d	Foreign earned income exclusion from Form 2555	8d	( )		
e	Taxable Health Savings Account distribution	8e			
f	Alaska Permanent Fund dividends	8f			
g	Jury duty pay	8g			
h	Prizes and awards	8h			
i	Activity not engaged in for profit income	8i			
j	Stock options	8j			
k	Income from the rental of personal property if you engaged in the rental for profit but were not in the business of renting such property	8k			
l	Olympic and Paralympic medals and USOC prize money (see instructions)	8l			
m	Section 951(a) inclusion (see instructions)	8m			
n	Section 951A(a) inclusion (see instructions)	8n			
o	Section 461(l) excess business loss adjustment	8o			
p	Taxable distributions from an ABLE account (see instructions)	8p			
z	Other income. List type and amount ▶	8z			
9	Total other income. Add lines 8a through 8z			9	
10	Combine lines 1 through 7 and 9. Enter here and on Form 1040, 1040-SR, or 1040-NR, line 8			10	23,420

For Paperwork Reduction Act Notice, see your tax return instructions. Cat. No. 71479F **Schedule 1 (Form 1040) 2021**

EXHIBIT 6-8 Courtney's Income and Deductions Reported on Schedule 1 *(continued)*

Schedule 1 (Form 1040) 2021 Page 2

Part II Adjustments to Income

Line	Description	Sub-line	Sub-amount	Line	Amount
11	Educator expenses			11	
12	Certain business expenses of reservists, performing artists, and fee-basis government officials. Attach Form 2106			12	
13	Health savings account deduction. Attach Form 8889			13	
14	Moving expenses for members of the Armed Forces. Attach Form 3903			14	
15	Deductible part of self-employment tax. Attach Schedule SE			15	241
16	Self-employed SEP, SIMPLE, and qualified plans			16	
17	Self-employed health insurance deduction			17	
18	Penalty on early withdrawal of savings			18	
19a	Alimony paid			19a	
b	Recipient's SSN ▶				
c	Date of original divorce or separation agreement (see instructions) ▶				
20	IRA deduction			20	
21	Student loan interest deduction			21	
22	Reserved for future use			22	
23	Archer MSA deduction			23	
24	Other adjustments:				
a	Jury duty pay (see instructions)	24a			
b	Deductible expenses related to income reported on line 8k from the rental of personal property engaged in for profit	24b			
c	Nontaxable amount of the value of Olympic and Paralympic medals and USOC prize money reported on line 8l	24c			
d	Reforestation amortization and expenses	24d			
e	Repayment of supplemental unemployment benefits under the Trade Act of 1974	24e			
f	Contributions to section 501(c)(18)(D) pension plans	24f			
g	Contributions by certain chaplains to section 403(b) plans	24g			
h	Attorney fees and court costs for actions involving certain unlawful discrimination claims (see instructions)	24h			
i	Attorney fees and court costs you paid in connection with an award from the IRS for information you provided that helped the IRS detect tax law violations	24i			
j	Housing deduction from Form 2555	24j			
k	Excess deductions of section 67(e) expenses from Schedule K-1 (Form 1041)	24k			
z	Other adjustments. List type and amount ▶	24z			
25	Total other adjustments. Add lines 24a through 24z			25	
26	Add lines 11 through 23 and 25. These are your **adjustments to income.** Enter here and on Form 1040 or 1040-SR, line 10, or Form 1040-NR, line 10a			26	241

Schedule 1 (Form 1040) 2021

Source: irs.gov.

Once we have determined AGI, we calculate taxable income by identifying deductions from AGI. These deductions consist of (1) the greater of itemized deductions or the standard deduction, (2) a limited charitable contribution deduction for taxpayers not itemizing their deductions (2021 only), and (3) the deduction for qualified business income.[23] We address these deductions next.

[23]At press time, the limited charitable contribution deduction for taxpayers not itemizing their deduction had not been extended to 2022.

LO 6-2

DEDUCTIONS FROM AGI: ITEMIZED DEDUCTIONS

There are a variety of itemized deductions. Many itemized deductions are personal in nature but are allowed to subsidize desirable activities such as home ownership and charitable giving. Other itemized deductions, such as medical expenses, provide relief for taxpayers whose ability to pay taxes has been involuntarily reduced. We discuss itemized deductions in the order they appear on the individual tax return, Form 1040, Schedule A.

Medical Expenses

The medical expense deduction is designed to provide relief for taxpayers whose ability to pay taxes is seriously hindered by health-related circumstances. Qualified medical expenses include any payments for the care, prevention, diagnosis, or cure of injury, disease, or bodily function that are not reimbursed by health insurance or are not paid for through a "flexible spending account" or "health savings account."[24] Taxpayers may also deduct medical expenses incurred to treat their spouses and their dependents.[25] Common medical expenses include:

- Prescription medication, insulin, and medical aids such as eyeglasses, contact lenses, and wheelchairs. Over-the-counter medicines are generally not deductible.
- Payments to medical care *providers* such as doctors, dentists, and nurses and medical care *facilities* such as hospitals.
- Transportation for medical purposes.
- Long-term care facilities.
- Health insurance premiums (if not deducted for AGI by self-employed taxpayers) and insurance for long-term care services.[26,27]

Example 6-10

In April, Courtney broke her wrist in a mountain biking accident. She paid $2,000 for a visit to the hospital emergency room and follow-up visits with her doctor. While she recuperated, Courtney paid $300 for prescription medicine and $700 to a therapist for rehabilitation. Courtney's insurance reimbursed her $1,840 for these expenses. What is the amount of Courtney's qualified medical expenses?

Answer: $1,160, computed as follows:

Description	Deduction
Emergency room and doctor visits	$ 2,000
Prescription medication	300
Physical therapy	700
Total qualifying medical expenses	$ 3,000
Less insurance reimbursement	−1,840
Qualified medical expenses from the accident	**$1,160**

[24]Taxpayers participating in an employer-sponsored flexible spending account or health savings account are allowed to direct that a fixed amount of their salary be placed in an account to pay for medical expenses. The salary paid into these accounts is excluded from gross income and used to pay for medical expenses. For other health savings accounts, taxpayers deduct their contributions to the health savings account as a for AGI deduction and use the contributions to pay for medical expenses.

[25]For the purpose of deducting medical expenses, a dependent need not meet the gross income test [§213(a)], and a child of divorced parents is considered a dependent of both parents [§213(d)(5)]. We discuss the general requirements for dependency in the Individual Income Tax Overview, Dependents, and Filing Status chapter.

[26]This includes the annual cost of Medicare and prescription insurance withheld from the Social Security recipient's benefits checks.

[27]The portion of any premiums for health insurance purchased through an exchange and offset by a premium tax credit under §36B is not deductible as an itemized deduction.

Medical expenses for cosmetic surgery or other similar procedures are not deductible unless the surgery or procedure is necessary to ameliorate a deformity arising from, or directly related to, a congenital abnormality, a personal injury resulting from an accident or trauma, or a disfiguring disease.[28]

TAXES IN THE REAL WORLD Are Discretionary Medical Expenses Deductible?

While cosmetic surgery is generally not deductible, discretionary medical costs may be deducted where the procedure affects the structure or function of the body. Take, for example, procedures that facilitate pregnancy by overcoming infertility. In IRS Letter Ruling 200318017, the IRS ruled that egg donor fees and expenses related to obtaining a willing donor, paid by a taxpayer who could not conceive using her own eggs, qualified as deductible medical expenses because they were incurred in preparation of the taxpayer's medical procedure (the implantation of a donated egg). Deductible expenses included the donor's fee for her time and expense in following the procedures to ensure successful egg retrieval, the agency's fee for procuring the donor and coordinating the transaction, expenses for medical and psychological testing and assistance of the donor before and after the procedure, and legal fees for preparing a contract between the taxpayer and the donor.

What about the same type of expenses paid by a single male to father a child through a surrogate? Are those expenses deductible? No, because in that situation, the expenses are not related to an underlying medical condition or defect of the taxpayer, nor are they affecting any structure or function of his body. See *William Magdalin*, TC Memo 2008-293.

Source: *William Magdalin*, TC Memo 2008-293 (Dec. 23, 2008).

Transportation and Travel for Medical Purposes Taxpayers traveling for the primary purpose of receiving essential and deductible medical care may deduct the cost of lodging while away from home overnight (with certain restrictions) and transportation.[29] Taxpayers using personal automobiles for medical transportation purposes may deduct a standard mileage allowance in lieu of actual costs. For 2022, the mileage rate is 18 cents per mile.

Example 6-11

Gram drove Courtney, *in Courtney's car,* 100 miles back and forth from the doctor's office and the physical therapist's facility during the period Courtney was being treated for her broken wrist. What is the amount of Courtney's qualifying medical expense for her trips to the doctor's office?

Answer: \$18 (100 × \$0.18).

Hospitals and Long-Term Care Facilities Taxpayers may deduct the cost of meals and lodging at hospitals. However, the cost of meals and lodging at other types of facilities such as nursing homes is deductible only when the principal purpose for the stay is medical care rather than convenience.[30] Of course, taxpayers may deduct the costs of actual medical care whether the care is provided at hospitals or other long-term care facilities.

[28]§213(d)(9)(A).

[29]The cost of travel for and essential to medical care, including lodging (with certain limitations), is also deductible if the expense is not extravagant and the travel has no significant element of personal pleasure. However, under §213(d)(2), the deduction for the cost of lodging is limited to \$50 per night (not indexed for inflation) per individual.

[30]Taxpayers may deduct the cost of long-term care facilities if they are chronically ill under a prescribed plan of care. A taxpayer is deemed to be chronically ill, generally, if they cannot perform at least two daily living tasks (eating, bathing, dressing, toileting, transferring, continence) for 90 days or more. §7702B. Taxpayers may also deduct long-term care insurance premiums, which are limited annually based on the age of the taxpayer.

Example 6-12

Gram considered moving into a long-term care facility before she decided she would move in with Courtney. The facility was not primarily for medical care and would have cost Gram $72,000 a year. During discussions with facility administrators, Gram learned that typically 20 percent of the total cost for the facility is allocable to medical care. If Gram were to stay in the facility for an entire year, what amount of the long-term care costs would qualify as a medical expense for Gram?

Answer: $14,400 ($72,000 × 20% allocable to medical care).

Medical Expense Deduction Limitation The deduction for medical expenses is limited to the amount of unreimbursed qualified medical expenses paid during the year (no matter when the services were provided) *reduced* by 7.5 percent of the taxpayer's AGI. This restriction is called a **floor limitation** because it eliminates any deduction for amounts below the floor. The purpose of a floor limitation is to restrict a deduction to taxpayers with substantial qualified expenses. Because this floor limitation is set at a high percentage of AGI, unreimbursed medical expenses rarely produce tax benefits, especially for high-income taxpayers.

Example 6-13

This year Courtney incurred $2,400 in unreimbursed qualified medical expenses (including the $1,160 of qualifying medical expenses associated with the accident [Example 6-10] and the $18 transportation deduction for mileage [Example 6-11]). Given that Courtney's AGI is $187,000, what is the amount of Courtney's itemized medical expense deduction?

Answer: $0, computed as follows:

Description	Expense
Total unreimbursed qualified medical expenses	$ 2,400
Minus: 7.5% of AGI ($187,000 × 7.5%)	(14,025)
Medical expense itemized deduction	**$ 0**

What if: What amount of medical expenses would Courtney be allowed to deduct if her AGI were $20,000?

Answer: $900, computed as follows:

Description	Expense
Total unreimbursed qualified medical expenses	$2,400
Minus: 7.5% of AGI ($20,000 × 7.5%)	(1,500)
Medical expense itemized deduction	**$ 900**

Taxes

Individuals may deduct as itemized deductions the payments they made during the year for the following taxes:

- State, local, and foreign *income* taxes, including state and local taxes paid during the year through employer withholding, estimated tax payments, and overpayments on the prior-year return that the taxpayer applies to the current year (the taxpayer asks the state to keep the overpayment rather than refund it).
- State and local real estate taxes on property held for personal or investment purposes.
- State and local personal property taxes that are assessed on the *value* of the specific property.[31]

[31]§164.

Taxpayers may elect to deduct state and local sales taxes *instead* of deducting state and local income taxes. This election is particularly advantageous for taxpayers in states that don't have an individual state income tax.[32] The total itemized deduction for state and local taxes is limited to $10,000 ($5,000 for a taxpayer filing married separate). The itemized deduction for foreign income taxes is not subject to this limitation.

Example 6-14

During the year, Courtney paid $6,700 of state income taxes through withholding from her paycheck. She also paid $2,700 of real estate taxes on her personal residence and $980 of real estate taxes on an investment property she owns in Oklahoma. Finally, Courtney paid $180 as a registration fee for her automobile (the fee is based on the year the automobile was manufactured, not its value). What amount of these payments can Courtney deduct as itemized deductions?

Answer: $10,000 ($6,700 state taxes + $2,700 real estate taxes on residence + $980 real estate taxes on investment property, limited to $10,000). Courtney is not allowed to deduct the registration fee for her car because the fee is not based on the value of the automobile.

What if: Suppose that on April 1, 2022, Courtney filed her 2021 state tax return and was due a refund from the state in the amount of $420. However, Courtney elected to have the state keep the overpayment and apply it to her 2022 tax payments. Assume that Courtney also had the $6,700 of state income tax withholding but only had $1,500 of real estate taxes in total. What amount of income taxes is Courtney allowed to deduct as an itemized deduction in 2022?

Answer: $8,620 ($6,700 withholding + $420 overpayment applied to 2022 + $1,500 real estate taxes). The treatment of the overpayment is the same as if Courtney had received the refund in 2022 and then remitted it to the state as payment of 2022 taxes. Because she paid the tax in 2022, she is allowed to deduct the tax in 2022. Recall that under the tax benefit rule (see the Gross Income and Exclusions chapter), Courtney would be required to include the $420 in her 2022 gross income.

TAXES IN THE REAL WORLD Is It a Deductible State Tax Payment or Charitable Contribution?

In recent years, it has become popular for state and local governments to provide state or local tax credits for contributions to certain qualified charities (for example, local hospitals, certain scholarship funds, etc.). While there was no "official" IRS guidance on the federal tax treatment of these contributions, in "unofficial" guidance, the IRS Office of Chief Counsel (see Chief Counsel Advice Memorandum (CCA) 201105010) advised that a payment to a state agency or charitable organization in return for a tax credit might be characterized as either a deductible charitable contribution or a deductible state tax payment. The 2011 CCA advised that taxpayers could take a charitable deduction for the full amount of the contribution without subtracting the value of the state tax credit received. Hence, for federal tax purposes, the taxpayer could take a charitable contribution deduction for an amount that otherwise was used to reduce the taxpayer's state tax liability. Because individuals deduct both state taxes and charitable contributions as itemized deductions, the IRS was not too concerned with these types of state tax credit programs.

The IRS's stance changed in 2018 with the enactment of the $10,000 limit on the itemized deduction for state and local taxes. Specifically, the IRS revisited the federal tax consequences of state and local tax credit programs out of concern that taxpayers may use these programs to bypass the $10,000 limit on state and local tax deductions. After further review, the news was not favorable for taxpayers. In Reg. §1.170A-1(h)(3), the IRS states that, effective for contributions after August 27, 2018, taxpayers making payments or transferring property to an entity eligible to receive tax-deductible contributions will have to reduce their charitable contribution

[32]The deduction can be based upon either the amount paid or the amount published in the IRS tables (see Form 1040, Schedule A instructions or https://www.irs.gov/credits-deductions/individuals/sales-tax-deduction-calculator) based upon the state of residence, income, and number of dependents. The states with no income tax are Alaska, Florida, Nevada, South Dakota, Texas, Washington, and Wyoming. New Hampshire and Tennessee have no state income tax on wages but do impose a tax on unearned income.

deductions by the amount of any state or local tax credit received (or expected to be received). The only exception is that if the state or local tax credit received is 15 percent or less of the taxpayer's charitable contribution, no reduction in charitable contributions is required. Thus, after August 27, 2018, if a taxpayer receives a dollar-for-dollar state tax credit for a contribution to a qualified charity, the charitable contribution deduction is reduced to zero for federal tax purposes.

However, all is not lost. In Reg. §1.164-3(j), the Treasury Department provides a safe harbor for certain individuals who make a payment to a charitable organization in return for a state or local tax credit. Under the safe harbor, an individual who itemized deductions may treat such payment as a payment for state or local tax purposes to the extent the payment is disallowed as a charitable contribution under Reg. §1.170A-1(h)(3). The deduction for the payment would be subject to the $10,000 limit on the itemized deduction for state and local taxes.

Sources: Reg. §§1.170A-1(h)(3) and 1.164-3(j).

Interest

There are two itemized deductions for interest expense.[33] First, subject to limitations described in more detail in the Tax Consequences of Home Ownership chapter, individuals can deduct interest paid on acquisition indebtedness secured by a qualified residence (the taxpayer's principal residence and one other residence).[34] Acquisition indebtedness is any debt secured by a qualified residence that is incurred in acquiring, constructing, or substantially improving the residence.[35] This includes money used for these purposes that was borrowed through what a bank might call a home equity loan.

The home mortgage interest deduction is limited by a cap on acquisition indebtedness that varies based upon when the indebtedness originated. For acquisition indebtedness incurred after December 15, 2017, taxpayers may only deduct mortgage interest on up to $750,000 of acquisition indebtedness ($375,000 if married filing separately). For acquisition indebtedness incurred before December 16, 2017, the limitation on acquisition indebtedness is $1,000,000 ($500,000 if filing married separate), even if the debt is refinanced after December 15, 2017. When a taxpayer has acquisition indebtedness incurred before December 16, 2017, and after December 15, 2017, the $750,000 ($375,000) limit is reduced (not below zero) by the acquisition indebtedness incurred before December 16, 2017.

As we discuss in more detail in the Investments chapter, individuals can also deduct interest paid on loans used to purchase investment assets such as stocks, bonds, or land (investment interest expense). The deduction for investment interest is limited to a taxpayer's net investment income.[36] Any investment interest expenses in excess of the net investment income limitation carries forward to the subsequent year. Taxpayers are not allowed to deduct interest on personal credit card debt or on loans to acquire (and secured by) personal-use automobiles.

[33]Interest paid on loans where the proceeds are used in a trade or business is fully deductible as a business expense deduction for AGI.

[34]Taxpayers can also deduct premiums paid or accrued on mortgage insurance (insurance premiums paid by the borrower to protect the lender against the borrower defaulting on the loan) as qualified residence interest expense. The deduction is subject to phase-out based on the taxpayer's AGI exceeding $100,000 ($50,000 for married taxpayers filing separate) and is completely phased out for taxpayers with AGI exceeding $110,000 ($55,000 for married taxpayers filing separate). At press time, the deduction for mortgage insurance premiums was scheduled to expire after 2021.

[35]Subject to rules discussed in the Tax Consequences of Home Ownership chapter, points paid on indebtedness incurred in acquiring a home are also generally deductible as mortgage interest expense in the year the loan originates and points to refinance a home mortgage are typically amortized and deducted over the life of the loan (but see research memo in the Tax Compliance, the IRS, and Tax Authorities chapter for an exception).

[36]§163(d). Net investment income is defined as investment income minus investment expenses. Because investment expenses are no longer deductible as itemized deductions, the investment interest expense deduction is effectively limited to the taxpayer's investment income.

Example 6-15

Courtney acquired her home in Kansas City in January of this year for $300,000 (also its value throughout the year). She purchased it by paying $40,000 as a down payment and borrowing $260,000 from a credit union. Her home is the collateral for the loan. During the year, Courtney paid $14,848 in interest on the loan. How much of this interest may Courtney deduct?

Answer: $14,848. Because Courtney's home mortgage is secured by her home and is considered acquisition indebtedness, she is allowed to deduct the interest expense on the home as an itemized deduction.

Charitable Contributions

Congress encourages donations to charities by allowing taxpayers to deduct contributions of money and other property to *qualified* domestic charitable organizations as an itemized deduction. Qualified charitable organizations include organizations that engage in educational, religious, scientific, governmental, and other public activities.[37] Political and campaign contributions are not deductible even though they arguably indirectly support the government (contributions to which are generally deductible).

Example 6-16

This year Courtney donated $1,700 to the American Red Cross. She also gave $200 in cash to various homeless people she met on the streets during the year. What amount of these donations is Courtney allowed to deduct as a charitable contribution?

Answer: $1,700. Because the American Red Cross is a public charity recognized by the IRS, Courtney may deduct her $1,700 charitable contribution to it as an itemized deduction. However, despite Courtney's charitable intent, her donations to the homeless are not deductible as charitable contributions because individuals do not qualify as charitable organizations.

What if: Suppose that instead of transferring cash to homeless people on the streets, Courtney donated $200 cash to a local food bank that the IRS Tax Exempt Organization Search identifies as a qualified charity eligible to receive tax-deductible charitable contributions. The food bank provides meals to those in need. Would Courtney be allowed to deduct this contribution?

Answer: Yes, because the food bank is a qualified charity.

The *amount* of the charitable contribution deduction depends on whether the taxpayer contributes money or other property to the charity. Note that in virtually all circumstances, donations are deductible only if the contribution is substantiated by written records.[38]

Contributions of Money Cash contributions are deductible in the year paid, including donations of cash or by check, electronic funds transfers, credit card charges, and payroll deductions.[39] Taxpayers are also considered as making monetary contributions for the cost of transportation and travel for charitable purposes if there is no significant element of

[37]§170(c). The IRS Tax Exempt Organization Search (https://apps.irs.gov/app/eos/) allows you to search an organization to determine if it is a qualified charity eligible to receive tax-deductible charitable contributions.

[38]For example, to deduct monetary donations, taxpayers must keep a bank record or a written communication from the charity showing the name of the charity and the date and amount of the contribution. In addition, to deduct charitable contributions for cash or noncash contributions of $250 or more, a taxpayer must receive a written acknowledgment from the charity that shows the amount of cash and a description of any property contributed. The acknowledgment must also state whether the donee organization provided any goods or services to the donor for the contribution and, if so, either include a description and estimate of the value of the goods or services provided by the donee organization or, if applicable, a statement that the goods or services provided by the donee organization consist entirely of intangible religious benefits. See Publication 526 for more information.

[39]When individual taxpayers mail a contribution, they are allowed to deduct the contribution when they place the payment in the mail. When they pay via credit card, they are allowed to deduct the contribution on the day of the charge. Rev. Rul. 78-38.

pleasure or entertainment in the travel. When taxpayers use their personal vehicles for charitable transportation purposes, they may deduct, as a cash contribution, a standard mileage allowance for each mile driven (14 cents a mile). While taxpayers are allowed to deduct their transportation costs and other out-of-pocket costs of providing services for charities, they are not allowed to deduct the value of the services they provide for charities.

Example 6-17

Once a month, Courtney does volunteer work at a Goodwill Industries outlet about 20 miles from her home. Altogether, Courtney traveled 500 miles during the year driving to and from the Goodwill outlet. Courtney has determined that the services she provided during the year are reasonably valued at $1,500. What amount is Courtney allowed to deduct for her volunteer work with Goodwill Industries?

Answer: $70. Courtney is *not* allowed to deduct the value of the services she provides to Goodwill. However, she is allowed to deduct the $70 cost of her transportation to and from the Goodwill outlet (500 miles × 14 cents per mile).

Taxpayers receiving goods or services from a charity in exchange for a contribution may deduct only the amount of the contribution *in excess of the fair market value of the goods or services they receive* in exchange for their contribution.[40]

Contributions of Property Other Than Money When a taxpayer donates *property* to a charity, the *amount* the taxpayer is allowed to deduct depends on whether the property is **capital gain property** or **ordinary income property.**

Capital gain property. In general, taxpayers are allowed to deduct the *fair market value* of capital gain property on the date of the donation. Capital gain property is any appreciated asset that would have generated a *long-term* capital gain if the taxpayer had sold the property for its fair market value instead of contributing the asset to charity. To qualify as long term, the taxpayer must have held the asset for more than a year. Capital assets include the following:

- Investment assets (stocks, bonds, land held for investment, paintings, etc.).
- Business assets (to the extent that gain on the sale of the business asset would *not* have been considered ordinary income).[41]
- Personal-use assets.

Contributing capital gain property is a particularly tax-efficient way to make charitable contributions because taxpayers are allowed to deduct the fair market value of the property and they are *not* required to include the appreciation on the asset in gross income.

Example 6-18

In December of the current year, Courtney donated 100 shares of stock in JBD Corp. to her church, a qualified charity. Courtney purchased the stock several years ago for $2,600, but the shares were worth $10,600 at the time of the donation. What is the amount of Courtney's charitable deduction for donating the stock?

Answer: $10,600. Because the stock is an appreciated investment asset held for more than a year, it qualifies as capital gain property. Hence, Courtney is allowed to deduct the $10,600 fair market value of the stock, and she is *not* required to recognize any of the $8,000 realized gain ($10,600 – $2,600).

[40]Reg. §1.170A-1(h). To help with this determination, a charity that provides goods or services in return for a contribution of more than $75 must provide contributors with a written statement estimating the value of goods and services that the charity has provided to the donor.

[41]These assets are considered to be §1231(b) assets. We discuss the tax treatment of dispositions of business assets in the Property Dispositions chapter.

Certain contributions of capital gain property do not qualify for a fair market value deduction. The deduction for capital gain property that is *tangible personal property* is limited to the *adjusted basis* of the property if the charity uses the property for a purpose that is *unrelated* to its charitable purpose.[42] That is, this restriction applies to capital gain property that is (1) tangible, (2) personal property (not realty), and (3) unrelated to the charity's operations. The third requirement does not apply if, at the time of the donation, the taxpayer reasonably anticipates that the charity will put the property to a related use.

Example 6-19

What if: Suppose that Courtney donated a religious-themed painting to her church. Courtney purchased the painting several years ago for $2,600, but the painting was worth $10,600 at the time of the donation. When Courtney contributed the painting, she reasonably expected the church to hang the painting in the chapel. What would be the amount of Courtney's charitable contribution deduction?

Answer: $10,600. Because Courtney reasonably expected the church to use the painting in a manner related to its tax-exempt purpose, Courtney is allowed to deduct the full fair market value of the painting without recognizing the $8,000 realized gain.

What if: Suppose that Courtney was told at the time she donated the painting that the church intended to sell it and use the cash to help fund expansion of the church building. What would be Courtney's charitable contribution deduction?

Answer: $2,600, the adjusted basis of the property. Because the church expects to sell it, the painting is being used for a purpose unrelated to the charitable purpose of the church. Thus, Courtney may deduct only the tax basis of the painting.

What if: Suppose that Courtney donated stock to her church ($10,600 current fair market value, originally purchased several years ago for $2,600) and the church informed her that it intended to immediately sell the stock. What would be the amount of Courtney's charitable contribution deduction?

Answer: $10,600. Stock is intangible property, not tangible personal property. Hence, Courtney would deduct the fair market value of the stock.

Ordinary income property. Taxpayers contributing ordinary income property can deduct only the *lesser* of (1) the property's fair market value or (2) the property's adjusted basis. Ordinary income property consists of all assets other than capital gain property. That is, ordinary income property is property that if sold would generate income taxed at ordinary rates. This includes the following types of assets:

- Assets the taxpayer has held for a year or less.
- Inventory the taxpayer sells in a trade or business.
- Business assets held for more than a year to the extent the taxpayer would recognize ordinary income under the depreciation recapture rules if the taxpayer had sold the property.[43]
- Assets, including investment assets and personal-use assets, with a value *less than* the taxpayer's basis in the assets (assets that have declined in value).

[42]Reg. §1.170A-4(b)(2). The taxpayer's deduction for donating capital gain property is also limited to basis if the taxpayer contributes capital gain property other than publicly traded stock to a private nonoperating foundation. There are also other exceptions in which capital gain property might not otherwise qualify for deduction at fair market value, such as the subsequent sale of donated property by the charity. These exceptions are beyond the scope of this text.

[43]We discuss depreciation recapture in the Property Dispositions chapter.

Example 6-20

Before her move from Cincinnati, Courtney decided to donate her excess possessions to Goodwill Industries. Courtney estimated that she paid over $900 for these items, including clothing, a table, and a couch. However, although the items were in excellent condition, they were worth only $160. What amount can Courtney deduct for her donation of these items?

Answer: $160. Because Courtney's possessions have declined in value, they are considered to be ordinary income property. Consequently, Courtney may deduct the lesser of (1) the fair market value of $160 or (2) her tax basis in the property of $900.

Charitable Contribution Deduction Limitations The amount of a taxpayer's charitable contribution deduction for the year is limited to a **ceiling,** or maximum deduction. The ceiling depends upon the type of property the taxpayer donates and the nature of the charity receiving the donation; donations to public charities (charities that are publicly supported such as churches and schools) and **private operating foundations** (privately sponsored foundations that actually fund and conduct charitable activities) are subject to less stringent restrictions than other charities. In general, cash donations to public charities and private operating foundations are limited to 60 percent of the taxpayer's AGI, whereas property donations to public charities and private operating foundations are limited to 50 percent of the taxpayer's AGI.[44] Deductions for contributions of capital gain property to public charities and private operating foundations are generally limited to 30 percent of the taxpayer's AGI.[45] Deductions for cash and property contributions to **private nonoperating foundations** (privately sponsored foundations that disburse funds to other charities, such as the Bill and Melinda Gates Foundation) are limited to 30 percent of the taxpayer's AGI. Finally, deductions for contributions of capital gain property to private nonoperating foundations are limited to 20 percent of the taxpayer's AGI. Exhibit 6-9 summarizes the charitable contribution limitation rules for individual taxpayers.

EXHIBIT 6-9 Summary of Charitable Contribution Limitation Rules

Contribution Type	Public Charity and Private Operating Foundation	Private Nonoperating Foundation
Cash:		
Amount	Cash amount	Cash amount
AGI limit	60%	30%
Capital gain property:		
Amount	FMV	Basis*
AGI limit	30%	20%
Ordinary income property:		
Amount	Lesser of basis or FMV	Lesser of basis or FMV
AGI limit	50%	30%

*FMV if the stock is publicly traded [§170(e)(5)].

When taxpayers make contributions that are subject to different percentage limitations, they apply the AGI limitations in the following sequence:

Step 1: Determine the limitation for the 60 percent contributions, if applicable.

Step 2: Apply the limitations to the 50 percent contributions. The 50 percent contribution limit is AGI × 50% minus the contributions subject to the 60 percent limit.

[44]For 2020 and 2021, cash contributions to public charities and private operating foundations (except contributions to donor advised funds or supporting organizations) were not subject to the 60 percent limit on cash contributions.

[45]If a taxpayer chooses to deduct the basis of capital gain property (instead of its higher fair market value), the deduction is limited to 50 percent of the taxpayer's AGI (30 percent for contributions to private nonoperating foundations).

Step 3: Apply the limitations to the 30 percent contributions. The 30 percent contribution limit is the *lesser* of (a) AGI × 30% or (b) AGI × 50% minus the contributions subject to the 50 percent limit and the contributions subject to the 60 percent limit.

Step 4: Apply the limitations to the 20 percent contributions. The 20 percent contribution limit is the lesser of (a) AGI × 20%, (b) AGI × 30% minus contributions subject to the 30 percent limit, or (c) AGI × 50% minus the contributions subject to the 50 percent limit, the contributions subject to the 60 percent limit, and the contributions subject to the 30 percent limit.

When a taxpayer's contributions exceed the AGI ceiling limitation for the year, the excess contribution is treated as though it were made in the subsequent tax year and is subject to the same AGI limitations in the next year. The excess contribution can be carried forward for five years before it expires. If a charitable contribution deduction is carried forward, the current-year contributions must first be used when applying the AGI percentage limitations. However, because the ceiling limitations are fairly generous, taxpayers exceed the ceiling limitations only in unusual circumstances.

Example 6-21

This year Courtney made the following contributions to qualified charities:

Organization	Amount	Type	AGI Limitation	Reference
Red Cross	$ 1,700	Cash	60%	Example 6-16
Goodwill Industries	70	Cash-mileage	60	Example 6-17
Goodwill Industries	160	Ordinary income property	50	Example 6-20
Church	10,600	Capital gain property	30	Example 6-18
Total contributions	**$12,530**			

After applying the AGI limitations, how much of the $12,530 in contributions is Courtney allowed to deduct if she itemizes her deductions?

Answer: $12,530, computed as follows:

Description	Amount	Explanation
(1) AGI	$187,000	Exhibit 6-5
(2) 60% contributions	1,770	($1,700 + 70)
(3) 60% AGI contribution limit	112,200	(1) × 60%
(4) Allowable 60% deductions	**1,770**	Lesser of (2) or (3)
(5) 50% contributions	160	
(6) 50% AGI contribution limit	91,730	[(1) × 50%] – (4)
(7) Allowable 50% deductions	**160**	Lesser of (5) or (6)
(8) 30% contributions	10,600	
(9) 30% AGI contribution limit	56,100	(1) × 30%
(10) Remaining 50% AGI contribution limit	91,570	(6) – (7)
(11) Allowable 30% deductions	**10,600**	Least of (8), (9), or (10)
Deductible charitable contributions	**$ 12,530**	(4) + (7) + (11)

What if: Suppose that Courtney's AGI was $30,000. After applying the AGI limitations, how much of the $12,530 in contributions would Courtney be allowed to deduct if she itemizes her deductions?

(continued on page 6-24)

Answer: $10,930, computed as follows:

Description	Amount	Explanation
(1) AGI	$ 30,000	
(2) 60% contributions	1,770	($1,700 + 70)
(3) 60% AGI contribution limit	18,000	(1) × 60%
(4) Allowable 60% deductions	**1,770**	Lesser of (2) or (3)
(5) 50% contributions	160	
(6) 50% AGI contribution limit	13,230	[(1) × 50%] – (4)
(7) Allowable 50% deductions	**160**	Lesser of (5) or (6)
(8) 30% contributions	10,600	
(9) 30% AGI contribution limit	9,000	(1) × 30%
(10) Remaining 50% AGI contribution limit	13,070	(6) – (7)
(11) Allowable 30% deductions	**9,000**	Least of (8), (9), or (10)
Deductible charitable contributions	**$10,930**	(4) + (7) + (11)

This year, Courtney would not be allowed to deduct $1,600 of her $10,600 capital gain property contribution to her church. However, she would carry forward the $1,600 to next year (and up to four years after that, if necessary) and treat it as though she made a $1,600 contribution next year subject to the 30 percent of AGI limitation.

Special 2021 From AGI Charitable Contribution Deduction for Taxpayers Not Itemizing Deductions

To provide taxpayer relief associated with hardship surrounding COVID-19, Congress enacted a provision that allowed taxpayers who do *not* itemize deductions to claim up to $300 of cash charitable contributions ($600 for married taxpayers filing jointly) to qualified charitable organizations as a from AGI deduction in 2021. Donations to donor advised funds or supporting organizations were not eligible for this deduction. The deduction was separate and distinct from the standard deduction (discussed below) and only available in 2021.[46]

Example 6-22

In 2021, Gram made charitable contributions of $6,000 to a local church. However, because her itemized deductions did not exceed her standard deduction, Gram did not itemize her deductions in 2021. How much of her $6,000 charitable contribution was Gram able to deduct in 2021 as a separate from AGI deduction?

Answer: $300. Because she did not itemize her deductions, Gram was able to deduct her charitable contributions up to $300 as a separate from AGI deduction.

ETHICS

Sabrina loves the latest fashions, but she is also very charitable. Every year she donates her previous year's clothing to Goodwill to make room in her closet for this year's fashions. Sabrina estimates the value of her donation to be approximately $6,000. Sabrina recently learned that because her donation exceeds $5,000, she must support her donation with an appraisal and a signed statement by the appraiser on page 2 of Form 8283. Sabrina decides to claim a charitable deduction of $4,900 to avoid the appraisal requirement. What do you think of Sabrina's decision? Do you think that nationally there are an abnormally large number of charitable contributions valued just under $5,000?

[46]At press time, this provision had not been extended to 2022.

Casualty and Theft Losses on Personal-Use Assets

Individuals cannot deduct losses they realize when they sell or dispose of assets used for personal purposes (personal-use assets, as opposed to business or investment assets). Taxpayers also generally cannot deduct casualty losses (losses arising from a sudden, unexpected, or unusual event such as a "fire, storm, or shipwreck" or from theft) on personal-use assets unless the losses are attributable to a federally declared disaster. For federally declared disasters, the casualty losses are deductible subject to a $100 floor for each casualty and a 10 percent of AGI floor for all casualties in a year).[47]

Other Itemized Deductions

Prior to 2018, there were a number of expenses, including unreimbursed employee business expenses, tax preparation fees, investment expenses (other than investment interest expense), and hobby expenses (limited to hobby income), among others, that were deductible subject to a 2 percent of AGI floor.[48] After 2017, these expenses are no longer deductible. The nondeductibility of these expenses is especially painful for taxpayers with hobbies, as hobby revenues are included in gross income, but hobby expenses are no longer deductible (unless they are deductible as real estate taxes or mortgage interest expense).

There are a few expenses that remain deductible as other itemized deductions not subject to the 2 percent of AGI floor. Perhaps because gambling includes a significant element of personal enjoyment (losers may think otherwise), individuals include all gambling winnings for the year in gross income, but they may also deduct gambling expenses and gambling losses *to the extent of gambling winnings* for the year.[49] The deductible gambling losses are itemized deductions; therefore, *losses don't directly offset winnings*.[50] Casualty and theft losses on property held for investment (not personal-use property) and the unrecovered cost of a life annuity (if the taxpayer died before recovering the full cost of the annuity) also are deductible as other itemized deductions.

THE KEY FACTS

Other Itemized Deductions

- Employee business expenses, tax preparation fees, investment expenses (other than investment interest expense), and hobby expenses are no longer deductible.
- Gambling expenses and gambling losses are deductible to the extent of gambling winnings for the year.

Summary of Itemized Deductions

This part of the chapter examined the various itemized deductions. Some of these deductions are subject to limitations in the form of floor limitations or caps. All require good records and a good understanding to support and maximize your deductions.

Example 6-23

Given Courtney's current-year AGI of $187,000, what is the amount of her total itemized deductions she may claim on her tax return?

Answer: Courtney's itemized deductions for the year are $37,378, calculated as follows:

Description	Amount	Reference
Taxes	$ 10,000	Example 6-14
Home mortgage interest	14,848	Example 6-15
Charitable contributions	12,530	Example 6-21
Total itemized deductions	**$37,378**	

[47]§165. As we discuss in more detail in the Business Income, Deductions, and Accounting Methods chapter, businesses may deduct casualty and theft losses of business property as a deduction for AGI. Further, casualty or theft losses on investment assets are deductible as an other itemized deduction.

[48]Hobbies are revenue-generating activities for primarily personal enjoyment rather than profit. The IRS considers a list of factors (taxpayer's history of income or losses with the activity, taxpayer's expertise or advisers, taxpayer's time and effort expended in the activity, the activity's elements of personal pleasure or recreation, etc.) in determining whether an activity is a hobby or for profit. See https://www.irs.gov/faqs/small-business-self-employed-other-business/income-expenses/income-expenses.

[49]§165(d).

[50]If gambling is deemed to be a business activity (see *Linda M. Myers*, TC Summary Opinion 2007-194), then the taxpayer reports gambling winnings, expenses, and losses on Schedule C (not as an itemized deduction). However, gambling expenses and losses remain only deductible to the extent of gambling winnings.

Exhibit 6-10 presents Courtney's itemized deductions on Form 1040, Schedule A. As with other forms, we use the 2021 form because the 2022 form was not available at press time.

EXHIBIT 6-10 Courtney's Form 1040, Schedule A

SCHEDULE A (Form 1040)
Department of the Treasury Internal Revenue Service (99)

Itemized Deductions

▶ Go to *www.irs.gov/ScheduleA* for instructions and the latest information.
▶ Attach to Form 1040 or 1040-SR.
Caution: If you are claiming a net qualified disaster loss on Form 4684, see the instructions for line 16.

OMB No. 1545-0074
2021
Attachment Sequence No. **07**

Name(s) shown on Form 1040 or 1040-SR: **Courtney Wilson**
Your social security number: 111-11-1111

Section	Line	Description	Box	Amount	Line	Amount
Medical and Dental Expenses		**Caution:** Do not include expenses reimbursed or paid by others.				
	1	Medical and dental expenses (see instructions)	1	2,400		
	2	Enter amount from Form 1040 or 1040-SR, line 11 [2] 187,000				
	3	Multiply line 2 by 7.5% (0.075)	3	14,025		
	4	Subtract line 3 from line 1. If line 3 is more than line 1, enter -0-			4	0
Taxes You Paid	5	State and local taxes.				
	a	State and local income taxes or general sales taxes. You may include either income taxes or general sales taxes on line 5a, but not both. If you elect to include general sales taxes instead of income taxes, check this box ▶ ☐	5a	6,700		
	b	State and local real estate taxes (see instructions)	5b	3,680		
	c	State and local personal property taxes	5c			
	d	Add lines 5a through 5c	5d	10,380		
	e	Enter the smaller of line 5d or $10,000 ($5,000 if married filing separately)	5e	10,000		
	6	Other taxes. List type and amount ▶	6			
	7	Add lines 5e and 6			7	10,000
Interest You Paid Caution: Your mortgage interest deduction may be limited (see instructions).	8	Home mortgage interest and points. If you didn't use all of your home mortgage loan(s) to buy, build, or improve your home, see instructions and check this box ▶ ☐				
	a	Home mortgage interest and points reported to you on Form 1098. See instructions if limited	8a	14,848		
	b	Home mortgage interest not reported to you on Form 1098. See instructions if limited. If paid to the person from whom you bought the home, see instructions and show that person's name, identifying no., and address ▶	8b			
	c	Points not reported to you on Form 1098. See instructions for special rules	8c			
	d	Mortgage insurance premiums (see instructions)	8d			
	e	Add lines 8a through 8d	8e			
	9	Investment interest. Attach Form 4952 if required. See instructions	9			
	10	Add lines 8e and 9			10	14,848
Gifts to Charity Caution: If you made a gift and got a benefit for it, see instructions.	11	Gifts by cash or check. If you made any gift of $250 or more, see instructions	11	1,770		
	12	Other than by cash or check. If you made any gift of $250 or more, see instructions. You **must** attach Form 8283 if over $500	12	10,760		
	13	Carryover from prior year	13			
	14	Add lines 11 through 13			14	12,530
Casualty and Theft Losses	15	Casualty and theft loss(es) from a federally declared disaster (other than net qualified disaster losses). Attach Form 4684 and enter the amount from line 18 of that form. See instructions			15	
Other Itemized Deductions	16	Other—from list in instructions. List type and amount ▶			16	
Total Itemized Deductions	17	Add the amounts in the far right column for lines 4 through 16. Also, enter this amount on Form 1040 or 1040-SR, line 12a			17	37,378
	18	If you elect to itemize deductions even though they are less than your standard deduction, check this box ▶ ☐				

For Paperwork Reduction Act Notice, see the Instructions for Forms 1040 and 1040-SR. Cat. No. 17145C **Schedule A (Form 1040) 2021**

Source: irs.gov.

THE STANDARD DEDUCTION

LO 6-3

Standard Deduction

The **standard deduction** is a flat amount that most individuals can elect to deduct *instead of* deducting their itemized deductions (if any). That is, taxpayers generally deduct *the greater of their standard deduction or their itemized deductions.*

The amount of the standard deduction varies according to the taxpayer's filing status, age, and eyesight. The basic standard deduction is greater for married taxpayers filing jointly and those supporting a family (head of household) than it is for married taxpayers filing separately and unmarried taxpayers not supporting a family. Taxpayers who are at least 65 years of age on the last day of the year or are blind are entitled to additional standard deduction amounts above and beyond their basic standard deduction.[51] Exhibit 6-11 summarizes the standard deduction amounts.[52] With significantly large standard deduction amounts, many taxpayers deduct the standard deduction instead of deducting itemized deductions.

EXHIBIT 6-11 Standard Deduction Amounts*

2021 Amounts		
Filing Status	**Basic Standard Deduction**	**Additional Standard Deduction for Age and/or Blindness at End of Year**
Married filing jointly	$25,100	$1,350
Head of household	18,800	1,700
Single	12,550	1,700
Married filing separately	12,550	1,350

2022 Amounts		
Filing Status	**Basic Standard Deduction**	**Additional Standard Deduction for Age and/or Blindness at End of Year**
Married filing jointly	$25,900	$1,400
Head of household	19,400	1,750
Single	12,950	1,750
Married filing separately	12,950	1,400

*For individuals claimed as a dependent on another return, the 2022 standard deduction is the greater of (1) $1,150 or (2) $400 plus earned income not to exceed the standard deduction amount of those who are not dependents.

For 2022, the additional standard deduction for either age and/or blindness is $1,400 for married taxpayers and $1,750 for taxpayers who are not married. Thus, a blind individual who is 65 years old and single is entitled to a standard deduction of $16,450 ($12,950 + $1,750 + $1,750). A married couple filing a joint return with one spouse over age 65 and one spouse considered legally blind is entitled to a standard deduction of $28,700 ($25,900 + $1,400 + $1,400). Finally, for an individual who is eligible to be claimed as a dependent on another's return, the standard deduction is the greater of (1) $1,150 or (2) $400 plus the individual's earned income limited to the regular standard deduction. The additional standard deduction amounts for age and blindness, if any, are not impacted by the preceding limitation for eligible dependents.

[51]Taxpayers are considered 65 on the day before their 65th birthday. Taxpayers are considered to be blind if they have a certified statement from their eye doctor or registered optometrist that the corrected vision of their better eye is no better than 20/200 or their field of vision is 20 degrees or less.

[52]The standard deduction amount is indexed for inflation.

Example 6-24

What is Courtney's standard deduction for the year?

Answer: $19,400. Because Courtney is unmarried at the end of the year and she maintains a household for more than six months for Deron and Ellen, who both qualify as her dependents (as qualifying children), Courtney's filing status is head of household, which allows her to claim a standard deduction of $19,400.

Given that Courtney's itemized deductions are $37,378 (see Example 6-23), will Courtney deduct her itemized deductions or her standard deduction?

Answer: She will deduct her itemized deductions because they exceed her standard deduction.

What if: Suppose that Courtney's 10-year-old son, Deron, earned $600 this summer by mowing lawns for neighbors. If Deron is Courtney's dependent, what amount of standard deduction can Deron claim on his individual return?

Answer: Deron will claim a minimum standard deduction of $1,150 because he is Courtney's dependent. Hence, Deron will not pay any income tax because his taxable income is reduced to zero by the standard deduction.[53]

What if: Would there be any difference in the amount of the standard deduction if Deron earned $2,100?

Answer: Because of the amount of his earnings, Deron would claim a standard deduction in the amount of his earned income plus $400. Hence, Deron would claim a standard deduction of $2,500 and he would not pay any income tax.

What if: Suppose Deron earned $14,000.

Answer: Again, Deron would claim a standard deduction in the amount of his earned income plus $400. However, Deron's standard deduction is limited to $12,950, the maximum allowable standard deduction for a taxpayer filing single.

From the government's standpoint, the standard deduction serves two purposes. First, to help taxpayers with lower income, it automatically provides a minimum amount of income that is not subject to taxation. Second, it eliminates the need for the IRS to verify and audit itemized deductions for those taxpayers who choose to deduct the standard deduction. From the taxpayers' perspective, the standard deduction allows them to avoid taxation on a portion of their income, and for those not planning to itemize deductions, it eliminates the need to substantiate and collect information about them.

The standard deduction, however, is a double-edged sword. While it reduces taxes by offsetting income with an automatic deduction, it eliminates the tax benefits of itemized deductions up to the amount of the standard deduction. This is a very important point to consider when evaluating the tax benefits of itemized deductions.

Example 6-25

In Example 6-23, we determined that Courtney is entitled to deduct $37,378 of itemized deductions this year. How much do Courtney's itemized deductions reduce her taxable income relative to a situation in which she has $0 itemized deductions?

Answer: $17,978. Because Courtney files as a head of household, she would have been able to deduct $19,400 as a standard deduction even if she had not incurred *any* itemized deductions. Consequently, her itemized deductions reduce her taxable income by only $17,978 ($37,378 − $19,400) beyond what her taxable income would have been if she did not itemize deductions.

[53]Deron will need to file a tax return because his net self-employment income exceeds $433 and, as explained in the Individual Income Tax Computation and Tax Credits chapter, he will likely owe self-employment tax.

Bunching Itemized Deductions Some taxpayers may deduct the standard deduction every year because their itemized deductions always fall just short of the standard deduction amount and thus never produce any tax benefit. They may gain some tax benefit from their itemized deductions by implementing a simple tax planning strategy called **bunching itemized deductions.** The basic strategy consists of shifting itemized deductions into one year such that the amount of itemized deductions exceeds the standard deduction for the year, and then deducting the standard deduction in the next year (or vice versa).

Because individuals are cash-method taxpayers, they may shift certain itemized deductions by accelerating payment into the current year. For example, a taxpayer could make charitable contributions at the end of December rather than at the beginning of January in the following year. Taxpayers' ability to shift itemized deductions is limited because the timing of these payments is not completely discretionary. For example, real estate taxes have due dates, state taxes are generally paid throughout the year via withholding, and employees may incur and be required to pay business expenses throughout the year. However, taxpayers who annually make a certain amount of charitable contributions, for example, may consider lumping contributions for two years into one year and not contributing in the next year.[54]

Example 6-26

What if: Gram is 70 years old and files as a single taxpayer. This year Gram paid deductible medical expenses (after the AGI floor limitation) of $4,000. She also contributed $7,500 to her local church. This year her total itemized deductions were $11,500 ($4,000 medical + $7,500 charitable). Assuming Gram will have similar expenditures next year, what amount of additional deductions would Gram have been able to deduct this year if she had bunched her deductions by making her 2022 and 2023 charitable contributions in 2022? Use the 2022 standard deduction amounts for both 2022 and 2023.

Answer: $4,300, computed as follows:

	No Bunching		Bunching	
	2022	**2023**	**2022**	**2023**
(1) Standard deduction*	$14,700	$14,700	$14,700	$14,700
(2) Itemized deductions	11,500	11,500	19,000	4,000
Greater of (1) and (2)	$14,700	$14,700	$19,000	$14,700
Total deductions (combined years)	$29,400 ($14,700 + $14,700)		$33,700 ($19,000 + $14,700)	
Deductions gained through bunching	**$4,300 ($33,700 bunching deductions – $29,400 nonbunching deductions)**			

*For 2022, her standard deduction is the $12,950 standard deduction for single taxpayers plus an additional $1,750 standard deduction amount for age. (See Exhibit 6-11.) For 2023, we assume she has the same standard deduction as 2022.

DEDUCTION FOR QUALIFIED BUSINESS INCOME

LO 6-4

Deduction for Qualified Business Income

The last from AGI deduction that we will cover is the **deduction for qualified business income.** If applicable, this deduction is allowed as a from AGI deduction in addition to the taxpayer's itemized deductions or standard deduction and limited charitable

[54]Of course, as we discussed in the Tax Planning Strategies and Related Limitations chapter, taxpayers adopting this strategy must also consider the time value of money for the contribution amounts they pay in advance to determine whether a tax planning strategy designed to save taxes makes economic sense.

THE KEY FACTS

Deduction for Qualified Business Income

- The deduction for qualified business income is a from AGI deduction in addition to the taxpayer's itemized deduction or standard deduction.
- The deduction is limited to qualified trades or businesses and is subject to a number of limitations.

contribution deduction for taxpayers claiming the standard deduction (in 2021 only). The deduction applies to taxpayers with qualified business income from a partnership, S corporation, or sole proprietorship. Specifically, a taxpayer may deduct the lesser of:

(a) 20 percent of the taxpayer's **qualified business income** from a **qualified trade or business** (after application of the wage limit), plus 20 percent of the taxpayer's qualified real estate investment trust dividends and qualified publicly traded partnership income, if any, or

(b) 20 percent of the excess, if any, of taxable income over the taxpayer's net capital gains (including qualified dividends).[55]

If the taxpayer has more than one qualified trade or business, the preceding taxable income limitation is applied to the taxpayer's combined qualified business income (after application of the wage limit to *each* qualified trade or business).

A qualified trade or business is any trade or business other than a **specified service trade or business** and other than the trade or business of being an employee. A specified service trade or business is any trade or business involving the performance of services in the fields of health, law, consulting, accounting, actuarial science, performing arts, athletics, financial services, brokerage services, or any trade or business where the principal asset of such trade or business is the reputation or skill of one or more of its employees or owners, or which involves the performance of services that consist of investing and investment management trading, or dealing in securities, partnership interests, or commodities. Architecture and engineering services are specifically excluded from the definition of specified service trade or business. Rental activities are eligible for the deduction for qualified business income if the rental activity, based upon its facts and circumstances, is considered a trade or business.[56]

For any year in which the taxpayer's taxable income (before the deduction for qualified business income) is less than $170,050 ($340,100 if married filing jointly; $170,050 if married filing separate), the exclusion for specified service trades or businesses will not apply (the business will be deemed a qualified trade or business).[57] This means that a taxpayer operating a business that is not a qualified trade or business still gets the deduction for qualified business income if their taxable income is low enough. For taxpayers with taxable income above $170,050 ($340,100 if married filing jointly; $170,050 if married filing separate), the exclusion from the definition of a qualified business for specified service trades or businesses phases in (the deduction for qualified business income phases out) over a $50,000 range ($100,000, in the case of a joint return). The exclusion from the definition of a qualified business for specified service trades or businesses is fully phased in for taxpayers with taxable income in excess of $220,050 ($440,100 in the case of a joint return; $220,050 if married filing separate).

[55]§199A(a).

[56]Rev. Proc. 2019-38 provides a safe harbor under which a rental real estate enterprise will be considered a trade or business for purposes of the deduction for qualified business income. Under the safe harbor, the enterprise will be considered a trade or business if (a) separate books and records are maintained for the enterprise; (b) for rental real estate enterprises in existence less than four years, 250 or more hours of rental services are performed per year with respect to the enterprise; for real estate enterprises in existence at least four years, 250 or more hours of rental services are performed in three of the last five consecutive years ending with the current year; (c) the taxpayer maintains contemporaneous records, including time reports, logs, or similar documents, regarding the (i) hours of all services performed, (ii) description of all services performed, (iii) dates on which such services were performed, and (iv) who performed the services; and (d) the taxpayer attaches a statement to the timely filed original tax return for each year the taxpayer relies on the safe harbor. The statement must include a description of all real estate properties included in the enterprise (including address and rental category), a description of properties acquired and disposed of during the tax year, and a representation that the requirements of the revenue procedure have been satisfied.

[57]These thresholds (and those listed below) apply in 2022 and are indexed annually for inflation.

Example 6-27

As described in Example 5-7 and Example 5-10, Courtney performs architectural consulting services outside of her employment with EWD and also generates rental income from a condo she owns. Will her income from the architectural services and condo rental be considered qualified business income?

Answer: Yes for the architectural services and possibly for the condo rental. Architectural services are not a specified service trade or business. Thus, her income from the architectural services would be qualified trade or business income. Income from the condo rental would be considered qualified business income if the activity is deemed a trade or business based upon the specific facts and circumstances. If not, income from the condo rental would not be considered qualified business income.

What if: Assume Courtney decides to establish a sole proprietorship to perform investment advising services. This year, Courtney reports $250,000 of taxable income before the deduction for qualified business income. Will her income from investment advisory services be considered qualified business income?

Answer: No. Investment advisory services fall within the definition of a specified service trade or business. Because her taxable income exceeds $220,050 ($170,050 + $50,000 phase-in range), the exclusion from the specified service trade or business rules based on taxable income does not apply. Thus, her investment advisory service income would not be considered qualified trade or business income. Consequently, she is not eligible for the deduction for qualified business income on that income.

What if: Assume Courtney decides to establish a sole proprietorship to perform investment advising services. This year, Courtney reports $100,000 of taxable income before the deduction for qualified business income. Will her income from investment advisory services be considered qualified business income?

Answer: Yes. Because her taxable income falls below $170,050, the exclusion for specified service trades or businesses will not apply (the business will be deemed a qualified trade or business). Consequently, she is eligible for the deduction for qualified business income on that income.

What if: Assume Courtney decides to establish a sole proprietorship to perform investment advising services. This year, Courtney reports $200,050 of taxable income before the deduction for qualified business income. Will her income from advisory services be considered qualified business income?

Answer: If Courtney had $200,050 of taxable income (before the deduction for qualified business income), 60 percent of her investment advising income would not be considered qualified business income [{($200,050 taxable income − $170,050)/($50,000 phase-out range)} = 60%]. The remaining 40 percent of her investment advising income (net of the associated for AGI self-employment tax deduction) would be considered qualified business income.

Qualified business income is the net amount of qualified items of income, gain, deduction, and loss with respect to the taxpayer's qualified trade or business conducted within the United States. Qualified items do not include specified investment-related income, deductions, or losses (e.g., capital gains or losses, dividends, interest income not allocable to a trade or business, etc.).[58] For self-employed taxpayers, qualified business income is generally reduced by the deductible portion of self-employment taxes, the self-employed health insurance deduction, and the deduction for contributions to qualified self-employed retirement plans. If the net amount of qualified business income from all qualified trades or businesses during the taxable year is a loss, it is carried forward as a loss from a qualified trade or business in the next taxable year.[59]

[58]Qualified business income does not include any amount paid by an S corporation that is treated as reasonable compensation of the taxpayer or any guaranteed payment for services rendered with respect to the trade or business.

[59]Any deduction allowed in a subsequent year is reduced (but not below zero) by 20 percent of any carryover qualified business loss. If a taxpayer has more than one trade or business and at least one of the trades or businesses has negative qualified business income, the negative qualified business income for the year is allocated to each trade or business with positive qualified trade or business in proportion to the relative amounts of net qualified business income for those trades or businesses with positive qualified business income. This same process is used to allocate carryover qualified business loss to those qualified trades or businesses in the next year with positive qualified business income.

Limitations

The deduction for qualified business income cannot exceed the greater of:

(i) 50 percent of the wages paid with respect to the qualified trade or business or

(ii) the sum of 25 percent of the wages with respect to the qualified trade or business plus 2.5 percent of the unadjusted basis, immediately after acquisition, of all qualified property in the qualified trade or business.[60]

The preceding wage-based limitation is applied separately to each qualified trade or business.[61] For purposes of the wage-based limit, each partner or S corporation shareholder is treated as having wages for the year equal to their allocable share from the partnership or S corporation. The wage-based limits only apply to taxpayers with taxable income in excess of $170,050 ($340,100 in the case of a joint return; $170,050 for married filing separate). The wage limit is phased in ratably over $50,000 ($100,000 for married filing joint returns) so that it fully applies to taxpayers with taxable income in excess of $220,050 ($440,100 for married filing joint return; $220,050 for married filing separate).

Example 6-28

Courtney reports taxable income this year of $149,622 ($187,000 AGI less $37,378 itemized deductions; see Example 6-23) before the deduction for qualified business income, and she has no capital gains and $700 of qualified dividends included in her taxable income (see Exhibit 5-4). Her architectural consulting services generate $17,759 of qualified business income ($18,000 of consulting profit per Example 5-7, less her $241 deduction for self-employment taxes per Example 6-6), and she paid no wages in this business. Let's also assume that Courtney's condo rental is considered a trade or business, which generates $5,000 of qualified business income. What is Courtney's deduction for qualified business income?

Answer: $4,552. Because her taxable income before the deduction for qualified business income is less than $170,050, the wage limitation does not apply. Likewise, Courtney is not limited by the taxable income limitation because 20 percent of her qualified business income [($17,759 × 20%) + ($5,000 × 20%) = $4,552] is less than 20 percent of her taxable income in excess of her qualified dividends and before the deduction [($149,622 taxable income − $700 qualified dividends) × 20% = $29,784]. Thus, Courtney's deduction for qualified business income is $4,552.

What if: Assume Courtney reports taxable income this year of $300,000 (before the deduction for qualified business income), she has no qualified dividends or capital gains, and her architectural consulting business generates $75,000 of qualified business income (net of the associated for AGI self-employment tax deduction), has no qualified property, and pays $20,000 of wages. Assume that Courtney has no other qualified business income. What is Courtney's deduction for qualified business income?

Answer: $10,000. Before limitation, 20 percent of Courtney's qualified business income is $15,000 ($75,000 × 20%), and the greater of:

1. 50 percent of the wages paid by the qualified business ($20,000 × 50% = $10,000) or
2. 25 percent of the wages paid by the qualified business ($20,000 × 25% = $5,000) plus 2.5 percent of the unadjusted basis of qualified property ($0 × 2.5% = $0)

is $10,000. Because her taxable income of $300,000 exceeds the $170,050 phase-in threshold by more than $50,000, the wage limit fully applies. Thus, Courtney's deduction for qualified business income is limited to $10,000. Courtney is not limited by the taxable income limitation because 20 percent of her qualified business income after application of the wage limitation ($10,000) is less than 20 percent of her taxable income before the deduction ($300,000 × 20% = $60,000).

[60]Qualified property is tangible, depreciable property held and available for use at the end of the tax year, used in the production of qualified business income during the year, for which the depreciable period has not ended by the end of the tax year. The depreciable period with respect to qualified property of a taxpayer means the period beginning on the date the property is first placed in service by the taxpayer and ending on the later of (a) the date 10 years after that date or (b) the last day of the last full year in the applicable recovery period that would apply to the property under §168 [without regard to §168(g)].

[61]Subject to specific restrictions (e.g., common ownership, common relation among the trades or businesses, etc.), a taxpayer may elect to aggregate trades or businesses. Once aggregated, the taxpayer must continue to do so until the businesses no longer qualify for aggregation. See Reg. §1.199A-4.

What if: Assume that Courtney reports taxable income this year of $190,050 (before the deduction for qualified business income), she has no qualified dividends or capital gains, and her architectural consulting business generates $75,000 of qualified business income (net of the associated for AGI self-employment tax deduction), has no qualified property, and has $20,000 of wages. Assume that Courtney has no other qualified business income. What is Courtney's deduction for qualified business income?

Answer: $13,000. Before limitation, 20 percent of Courtney's qualified business income is $15,000 ($75,000 × 20 percent), and the greater of:

1. 50 percent of the wages paid by the qualified business ($20,000 × 50% = $10,000) or
2. 25 percent of the wages paid by the qualified business ($20,000 × 25% = $5,000) plus 2.5 percent of the unadjusted basis of qualified property ($0 × 2.5% = $0)

is $10,000. Because her taxable income of $190,050 exceeds the $170,050 phase-in threshold by $20,000, the wage limit is phased in by 40 percent [[($190,050 – $170,050)/$50,000] phase-in range = 40 percent]. Courtney's wage limit of $5,000 (the excess of (a) 20 percent of business income of $15,000 over (b) 50 percent of wages, $10,000 [$20,000 × 50%]) is phased in by 40 percent. Thus, her deduction for qualified business income is limited to $13,000 [$15,000 – ($5,000 × 40%)]. Courtney is not limited by the taxable income limitation because 20 percent of her qualified business income after application of the wage limitation ($13,000) is less than 20 percent of her taxable income before the deduction ($190,050 × 20% = $38,010).

Taxable Income Summary

We now have enough information to calculate Courtney's and Gram's taxable incomes. Exhibit 6-12 shows Courtney's taxable income calculation and Exhibit 6-13 illustrates how this information would be displayed on page 1 of Courtney's Form 1040.

EXHIBIT 6-12 Courtney's Taxable Income

Description	Amount	Reference
AGI	$187,000	Exhibit 6-5
Less: Greater of (1) itemized deductions ($37,378) or (2) standard deduction ($19,400)	(37,378)	Example 6-23
Less: Deduction for qualified business income	(4,552)	Example 6-28
Taxable income	$145,070	

EXHIBIT 6-13 Courtney's Taxable Income Computation as Presented on Form 1040, Page 1

Side note	Line	Description	Box	Amount	Description	Line	Amount
Attach Sch. B if required.	1	Wages, salaries, tips, etc. Attach Form(s) W-2				1	162,800
	2a	Tax-exempt interest	2a	500	b Taxable interest	2b	321
	3a	Qualified dividends	3a	700	b Ordinary dividends	3b	700
	4a	IRA distributions	4a		b Taxable amount	4b	
	5a	Pensions and annuities	5a		b Taxable amount	5b	
Standard Deduction for—	6a	Social security benefits	6a		b Taxable amount	6b	
• Single or Married filing separately, $12,550	7	Capital gain or (loss). Attach Schedule D if required. If not required, check here ▶ ☐				7	
• Married filing jointly or Qualifying widow(er), $25,100	8	Other income from Schedule 1, line 10				8	23,420
• Head of household, $18,800	9	Add lines 1, 2b, 3b, 4b, 5b, 6b, 7, and 8. This is your **total income** ▶				9	187,241
• If you checked any box under *Standard Deduction*, see instructions.	10	Adjustments to income from Schedule 1, line 26				10	241
	11	Subtract line 10 from line 9. This is your **adjusted gross income** ▶				11	187,000
	12a	**Standard deduction or itemized deductions** (from Schedule A)	12a	37,378			
	b	Charitable contributions if you take the standard deduction (see instructions)	12b				
	c	Add lines 12a and 12b				12c	37,378
	13	Qualified business income deduction from Form 8995 or Form 8995-A				13	4,552
	14	Add lines 12c and 13				14	41,930
	15	**Taxable income.** Subtract line 14 from line 11. If zero or less, enter -0-				15	145,070

For Disclosure, Privacy Act, and Paperwork Reduction Act Notice, see separate instructions. Cat. No. 11320B Form **1040** (2021)

Source: irs.gov.

Exhibit 6-14 provides Gram's taxable income calculation.

EXHIBIT 6-14 Gram's Taxable Income

Description	Amount	Reference
(1) AGI	$ 15,590	Exhibit 6-6
(2) Greater of (a) itemized deductions ($11,500) or (b) standard deduction ($14,700)	(14,700)	Example 6-26
Taxable income	$ 890	(1) + (2)

Note that because Gram's gross income of $16,000 (Exhibit 5-7) is more than her basic standard deduction amount ($14,700), she is required to file a tax return.

CONCLUSION

We started this chapter with Courtney's and Gram's gross incomes. In this chapter, we first identified the duo's separate deductions for AGI and computed their AGI. We then determined their from AGI deductions. Courtney deducted her itemized deductions because they exceeded her standard deduction. Gram, on the other hand, deducted her standard deduction. Finally, Courtney was able to take advantage of the deduction for qualified business income, while Gram did not have any qualified business income. By subtracting their from AGI deductions from their AGI, we determined taxable income for both Courtney and Gram. With this knowledge, we proceed to the next two chapters and address issues relating to investments and determining the amount of tax Courtney and Gram are required to pay on their taxable income.

Summary

LO 6-1 Identify the common deductions necessary for calculating adjusted gross income (AGI).

- Deductions for AGI may be categorized into those that are directly or indirectly business-related and those that address specific policy issues.
- The business-related deductions for AGI include business expenses, rent and royalty expenses, self-employment taxes, medical and health insurance by self-employed taxpayers, health savings accounts, and forfeited interest.
- Other common deductions for AGI include the deductions for interest on student loans and for early withdrawal penalties.

LO 6-2 Describe the different types of itemized deductions available to individuals.

- The medical expense deduction is designed to provide tax benefits to needy individuals but is subject to a significant floor limitation.
- The itemized deduction for interest is limited to home mortgage interest and investment interest, and the latter is limited by net investment income.
- The deduction for charitable contributions extends to contributions of money and property to qualifying charities. The charitable deduction is subject to ceiling limitations, which are more restrictive for donations of property.
- In 2021 only, taxpayers who did not itemize deductions could claim up to $300 of cash charitable contributions ($600 for married taxpayers filing jointly) to qualified charitable organizations as a from AGI deduction in addition to the standard deduction.
- The deduction for state and local taxes is subject to a cap and includes state income and property taxes. Sales taxes can be deducted in lieu of deducting state and local income taxes. The deduction for foreign income taxes is not subject to the cap.

Determine the standard deduction available to individuals. LO 6-3

- Taxpayers generally deduct the greater of their standard deduction or their itemized deductions.
- The amount of the standard deduction varies according to the taxpayer's filing status, age, and eyesight.

Calculate the deduction for qualified business income. LO 6-4

- The deduction for qualified business income is a from AGI deduction in addition to the taxpayer's itemized deduction or standard deduction.
- The deduction is limited to qualified trades or businesses and is subject to a number of limitations.

KEY TERMS

bunching itemized deductions (6-29)
business activities (6-2)
capital gain property (6-20)
ceiling (6-22)
deduction for qualified business income (6-29)
excess business loss (6-6)
floor limitation (6-16)
health savings accounts (6-8)
investment activities (6-2)
ordinary and necessary (6-3)
ordinary income property (6-20)
private nonoperating foundations (6-22)
private operating foundations (6-22)
qualified business income (6-30)
qualified education expenses (6-10)
qualified education loans (6-10)
qualified trade or business (6-30)
specified service trade or business (6-30)
standard deduction (6-27)
trade or business (6-2)
traditional IRAs (6-8)

DISCUSSION QUESTIONS

Discussion Questions are available in Connect®.

1. It has been suggested that tax policy favors deductions for AGI compared to itemized deductions. Describe two ways in which deductions for AGI are treated more favorably than itemized deductions. LO 6-1
2. How is a business activity distinguished from an investment activity? Why is this distinction important for the purpose of calculating federal income taxes? LO 6-1
3. Explain why Congress allows self-employed taxpayers to deduct the cost of health insurance as a for AGI deduction when employees can only itemize this cost as a medical expense. Would a self-employed taxpayer ever prefer to claim health insurance premiums as an itemized deduction rather than as a deduction for AGI? Explain. LO 6-1
4. Explain why Congress allows self-employed taxpayers to deduct the employer portion of their self-employment tax. LO 6-1
5. What are the requirements to contribute to a health savings account? What limits are imposed on the contributions and deductions? LO 6-1
6. Using the Internal Revenue Code, describe two deductions for AGI that are not discussed in this chapter. LO 6-1 research
7. Explain why Congress allows taxpayers to deduct interest forfeited as a penalty on the premature withdrawal from a certificate of deposit. LO 6-1
8. Describe the mechanical limitation on the deduction for interest on qualified education loans. LO 6-1
9. Explain why the medical expense provisions are sometimes referred to as "wherewithal" deductions and how this rationale is reflected in the limit on these deductions. LO 6-2
10. Describe the type of medical expenditures that qualify for the medical expense deduction. Does the cost of meals consumed while hospitalized qualify for the deduction? Do over-the-counter drugs and medicines qualify for the deduction? LO 6-2
11. Under what circumstances can a taxpayer deduct medical expenses paid for a member of their family? Does it matter if the family member reports significant amounts of gross income and cannot be claimed as a dependent? LO 6-2

LO 6-2 12. What types of taxes qualify to be deducted as itemized deductions? Would a vehicle registration fee qualify as a deductible tax?

LO 6-2 13. Explain the argument that the deductions for charitable contributions and home mortgage interest represent indirect subsidies for these activities.

LO 6-2 research 14. Cash donations to a charity are subject to a number of very specific substantiation requirements. Describe these requirements and how charitable gifts can be substantiated. Describe the substantiation requirements for property donations.

LO 6-2 15. Describe the conditions in which a donation of property to a charity will result in a charitable contribution deduction of fair market value and when it will result in a deduction of the tax basis of the property.

LO 6-2 16. Jake is a retired jockey who takes monthly trips to Las Vegas to gamble on horse races. Jake also trains racehorses part time at his Louisville ranch. So far this year, Jake has won almost $47,500 during his trips to Las Vegas while spending $27,250 on travel expenses and incurring $62,400 of gambling losses. Explain how Jake's gambling winnings and related costs will be treated for tax purposes.

LO 6-2 research 17. Frank paid $3,700 in fees for an accountant to tabulate business information (Frank operates as a self-employed contractor and files a Schedule C). The accountant also spent time tabulating Frank's income from his investments and determining Frank's personal itemized deductions. Explain to Frank whether or not he can deduct the $3,700 as a business expense or as an itemized deduction, and provide a citation to an authority that supports your conclusion.

LO 6-2 18. Contrast ceiling and floor limitations, and provide an example of each.

LO 6-2 19. Identify which itemized deductions are subject to floor limitations, ceiling limitations, or some combination of these limits.

LO 6-3 20. Describe the tax benefits from "bunching" itemized deductions in one year. Describe the characteristics of the taxpayers who are most likely to benefit from using bunching and explain why this is so.

LO 6-3 21. Explain how the standard deduction is rationalized and why the standard deduction might be viewed as a floor limit on itemized deductions.

research LO 6-3 22. Determine whether a taxpayer can change their election to itemize deductions once a return is filed. (*Hint:* Read about itemization under Reg. §1.63-1.)

LO 6-3 research 23. Determine whether a taxpayer who is claimed as a dependent on another return is entitled to an addition to the standard deduction for age or blindness. (*Hint:* Read the calculation of the standard deduction under §63.)

LO 6-4 24. Describe what is meant by qualified business income for purposes of the deduction for qualified business income.

LO 6-4 25. Under what circumstances would business income from an accounting practice qualify for the deduction for qualified business income?

LO 6-4 26. For purposes of the deduction for qualified business income, what is a specified service trade or business, and why is it important?

PROBLEMS

Select problems are available in Connect®.

LO 6-1 27. Clem is married and is a skilled carpenter. Clem's wife, Wanda, works part time as a substitute grade school teacher. Determine the amount of Clem's expenses that are deductible for AGI this year (if any) under the following independent circumstances:

a) Clem is self-employed, and this year he incurred $525 in expenses for tools and supplies related to his job. Because neither was covered by a qualified health plan, Clem paid health insurance premiums of $3,600 to provide coverage for himself and Wanda (not through an exchange).

b) Clem and Wanda own a garage downtown that they rent to a local business for storage. This year they incurred expenses of $1,250 in utilities and $780 in depreciation.

c) Clem paid self-employment tax of $15,300 (the employer portion is $7,650), and Wanda had $3,000 of Social Security taxes withheld from her pay.

d) Clem paid $45 to rent a safety deposit box to store his coin collection. Clem has collected coins intermittently since he was a child, and he expects to sell his collection when he retires.

28. Don Juan, a single taxpayer, is the sole owner of DJ's Inc., an S corporation. In 2022, DJ's Inc. incurred a massive $600,000 business loss, all of which is allocable to Don Juan as the sole shareholder. Assume that the $600,000 loss is not limited by the basis, at-risk, or passive loss rules and that Don Juan has no other business income or business losses. How much of the $600,000 loss will Don Juan be able to deduct this year? What happens to any loss not deducted this year? LO 6-1

29. Smithers is a self-employed individual who earns $30,000 per year in self-employment income. Smithers pays $2,200 in annual health insurance premiums (not through an exchange) for his own medical care. In each of the following situations, determine the amount of the deductible health insurance premium for Smithers before any AGI limitation. LO 6-1

a) Smithers is single and the self-employment income is his only source of income.

b) Smithers is single, but besides being self-employed, Smithers is also employed part time by SF Power Corporation. This year Smithers elected not to participate in SF's health plan.

c) Smithers is self-employed and is also married. Smithers's spouse, Samantha, is employed full time by SF Power Corporation and is covered by SF's health plan. Smithers is not eligible to participate in SF's health plan.

d) Smithers is self-employed and is also married. Smithers's spouse, Samantha, is employed full time by SF Power Corporation and is covered by SF's health plan. Smithers elected not to participate in SF's health plan.

30. Hardaway earned $100,000 of compensation this year. He also paid (or had paid for him) $3,000 of health insurance (not through an exchange). What is Hardaway's AGI in each of the following situations? (Ignore the effects of Social Security and self-employment taxes.) LO 6-1

a) Hardaway is an employee, and his employer paid Hardaway's $3,000 of health insurance for him as a nontaxable fringe benefit. Consequently, Hardaway received $97,000 of taxable compensation and $3,000 of nontaxable compensation.

b) Hardaway is a self-employed taxpayer, and he paid $3,000 of health insurance himself. He is not eligible to participate in an employer-sponsored plan.

31. Rocco operates a beauty salon as a sole proprietorship. Rocco also owns and rents an apartment building. In 2022, Rocco had the following income and expenses. Determine Rocco's AGI and complete page 1 (through line 11) and Schedule 1 of Form 1040 for Rocco. You may assume that Rocco will owe $2,502 in self-employment tax on his salon income, with $1,251 representing the employer portion of the self-employment tax. You may also assume that his divorce from Svetlana was finalized in 2016. LO 6-1 tax forms

Interest income	$11,255
Salon sales and revenue	86,360
Salaries paid to beauticians	45,250
Beauty salon supplies	23,400
Alimony paid to his ex-wife, Svetlana	6,000
Rental revenue from apartment building	31,220
Depreciation on apartment building	12,900
Real estate taxes paid on apartment building	11,100
Real estate taxes paid on personal residence	6,241
Contributions to charity	4,237

LO 6-1

32. Jada (age 53) and Elijah (age 60) are married, and both are self-employed. In 2022, they participate in a health insurance plan with a $3,000 annual deductible and out-of-pocket maximum of $9,000. The only other health plan they have is a vision insurance plan. Are they eligible to contribute to a health savings account? Why or why not? If so, what are their maximum HSA contribution and deduction?

LO 6-1

33. This year Diane intends to file a married-joint return. Diane received $177,500 of salary and paid $5,000 of interest on loans used to pay qualified tuition costs for her dependent daughter, Deb. This year Diane has also paid moving expenses of $4,300 and $28,300 of alimony to her ex-spouse, Jack, who she divorced in 2012.
   a) What is Diane's adjusted gross income?
   b) Suppose that Diane also reported income of $8,800 from a half share of profits from a partnership. Disregard any potential self-employment taxes on this income. What AGI would Diane report under these circumstances?

LO 6-1

34. Lionel is an unmarried law student at State University Law School, a qualified educational institution. This year Lionel borrowed $24,000 from County Bank and paid interest of $1,440. Lionel used the loan proceeds to pay his law school tuition. Calculate the amounts Lionel can deduct for interest on higher-education loans under the following circumstances:
   a) Lionel's AGI before deducting interest on higher-education loans is $50,000.
   b) Lionel's AGI before deducting interest on higher-education loans is $79,000.
   c) Lionel's AGI before deducting interest on higher-education loans is $90,000.

LO 6-2 LO 6-1

35. In each of the following independent cases, indicate the amount (1) deductible for AGI, (2) deductible from AGI, and (3) deductible neither for nor from AGI before considering income limitations or the standard deduction.
   a) Ted paid $50 rent on a safety deposit box at the bank. In this box he kept the few shares of stock that he owned.
   b) Tyler paid $85 for minor repairs to the fence at a rental house he owned.
   c) Timmy paid $545 for health insurance premiums this year (not through an exchange and not with pretax dollars). Timmy is employed full time and his employer paid the remaining premiums as a qualified fringe benefit.
   d) Tess paid $1,150 of state income taxes on her consulting income.

LO 6-2 LO 6-1

36. In each of the following independent cases, indicate the amount (1) deductible for AGI, (2) deductible from AGI, and (3) deductible neither for nor from AGI before considering income limitations or the standard deduction.
   a) Fran spent $90 for uniforms for use on her job. Her employer reimbursed her for $75 of this amount under an accountable plan (and did not report the reimbursement as wages).
   b) Timothy, a plumber employed by ACE Plumbing, spent $65 for small tools to be used on his job, but he was not reimbursed by ACE.
   c) Jake is a perfume salesperson. Because of his high pay, he receives no allowance or reimbursement from his employer for advertising expenses even though his position requires him to advertise frequently. During the year, he spent $2,200 on legitimate business advertisements.
   d) Trey is a self-employed, special-duty nurse. He spent $120 for uniforms.
   e) Mary, a professor at a community college, spent $340 for magazine subscriptions. The magazines were helpful for her research activities, but she was not reimbursed for the expenditures.
   f) Wayne lost $325 on the bets he made at the race track, but he won $57 playing slot machines.

LO 6-2

37. Penny, a full-time biochemist, loves stock car racing. To feed her passion, she bought a used dirt-track car and has started entering some local dirt-track races.

The prize money is pretty small ($1,000 for the winner), but she really is not in it for the money. Penny reported the following income and expenses from her nights at the track:

Prize money	$2,500
Expenses:	
Transportation from her home to the races	1,000
Depreciation on the dirt-track car	4,000
Entry fees	3,500
Oil, gas, supplies, repairs for the dirt-track car	2,050

What are the tax effects of Penny's racing income and expenses assuming that the racing activity is a hobby for Penny?

38. Simpson, age 45, is a single individual who is employed full time by Duff Corporation. This year Simpson reports AGI of $50,000 and has incurred the following medical expenses: LO 6-2

Dentist charges	$ 900
Physician charges	1,800
Optical charges	500
Cost of eyeglasses	300
Hospital charges	2,100
Prescription drugs	250
Over-the-counter drugs	450
Medical insurance premiums (not through an exchange)	775

a) Calculate the amount of medical expenses that will be included with Simpson's itemized deductions after any applicable limitations.

b) Suppose that Simpson was reimbursed for $250 of the physician's charges and $1,200 for the hospital costs. Calculate the amount of medical expenses that will be included with Simpson's itemized deductions after any applicable limitations.

39. Tim is 45 years old and is considering enrolling in an insurance program that provides for long-term care insurance. He is curious about whether the insurance premiums are deductible as a medical expense. If so, he wants to know the maximum amount that can be deducted in any year. LO 6-2 research

40. Doctor Bones prescribed physical therapy in a pool to treat Jack's broken back. In response to this advice (and for no other reason), Jack built a swimming pool in his backyard and strictly limited use of the pool to physical therapy. Jack paid $25,000 to build the pool, but he wondered if this amount could be deducted as a medical expense. Determine if a capital expenditure such as the cost of a swimming pool qualifies for the medical expense deduction. LO 6-2 research

41. Charles has AGI of $50,000 and has made the following payments related to (1) land he inherited from his deceased aunt and (2) a personal vacation taken last year. Calculate the amount of taxes Charles may include in his itemized deductions for the year under the following circumstances: LO 6-2 LO 6-1

State inheritance tax on the land	$1,200
County real estate tax on the land	1,500
School district tax on the land	690
City special assessment on the land (new curbs and gutters)	700
State tax on airline tickets (paid on vacation)	125
Local hotel tax (paid during vacation)	195

a) Suppose that Charles holds the land for appreciation.

b) Suppose that Charles holds the land for rent.

c) Suppose that Charles holds the land for appreciation and that the vacation was actually a business trip.

LO 6-2

42. Dan has AGI of $50,000 and paid the following taxes during this tax year. Calculate how much Dan can deduct for taxes as an itemized deduction this year.

State income tax withholding	$1,400
State income tax estimated payments	750
Federal income tax withholding	3,000
Social Security tax withheld from wages	2,100
State excise tax on liquor	400
Automobile license (based on the car's weight)	300
State sales tax paid	475

LO 6-2 LO 6-1

43. Tim is a single, cash-method taxpayer with an AGI of $50,000. In April of this year, Tim paid $1,020 with his state income tax return for the previous year. During the year, Tim had $5,400 of state income tax and $18,250 of federal income tax withheld from his salary. In addition, Tim made estimated payments of $1,360 and $1,900 for state and federal income taxes, respectively. Finally, Tim expects to receive a refund of $500 for state income taxes when he files his state tax return for this year in April next year. What is the amount of taxes that Tim can deduct as an itemized deduction?

LO 6-2

44. This year Randy paid $28,000 of interest on his residence. (Randy borrowed $450,000 to buy his residence, which is currently worth $500,000.) Randy also paid $2,500 of interest on his car loan and $4,200 of margin interest to his stockbroker (investment interest expense). How much of this interest expense can Randy deduct as an itemized deduction under the following circumstances?

a) Randy received $2,200 of interest this year and no other investment income or expenses. His AGI is $75,000.

b) Randy had no investment income this year, and his AGI is $75,000.

LO 6-2

45. Janyce, a single taxpayer, has AGI of $125,000 and paid the following taxes this year. Calculate how much Janyce can deduct for taxes as an itemized deduction this year.

State income tax withholding	$7,200
State income tax estimated payments	600
State income tax refund (applied to this year's tax)	800
State automobile tax (based on car's value)	1,900

LO 6-2

46. This year, Major Healy paid $40,000 of interest on a mortgage on his home (he borrowed $800,000 to buy the residence in 2015; $900,000 original purchase price and value at purchase), $6,000 of interest on a $120,000 home equity loan on his home (loan proceeds were used to buy antique cars), and $10,000 of interest on a mortgage on his vacation home (borrowed $200,000 to purchase the home in 2010; home purchased for $500,000). Major Healy's AGI is $220,000. How much interest expense can Major Healy deduct as an itemized deduction?

LO 6-2

47. Jack, who files married separate, has AGI of $45,000 and paid the following taxes this year. Calculate how much Jack can deduct for taxes as an itemized deduction this year.

State income tax withholding	$6,200
State income tax estimated payments	500
State income tax refund (applied to this year's tax)	1,000
State automobile tax (based on car's weight)	800

LO 6-2

48. Ray Ray made the following contributions in 2022.

Charity	Property	Cost	FMV
Athens Academy School	Cash	$ 5,000	$ 5,000
United Way	Cash	4,000	4,000
American Heart Association	Antique painting	15,000	75,000
First Methodist Church	Coca-Cola stock	12,000	20,000

Determine the maximum amount of charitable deduction for each of these contributions *ignoring* the AGI ceiling on charitable contributions and assuming that the

American Heart Association plans to sell the antique painting to fund its operations. Ray Ray has owned the painting and Coca-Cola stock since 1990.

49. Juanita paid $50,000 of interest on a mortgage on her home (loan of $1,000,000 at 5% interest rate to buy the residence in 2018; $1,200,000 original purchase price and value at purchase) and $6,500 of interest on a $100,000 home-equity loan on her home (loan proceeds were used to buy furniture). Juanita's AGI is $600,000. How much interest expense can Juanita deduct as an itemized deduction? LO 6-2

50. Calvin reviewed his canceled checks and receipts this year (2022) for charitable contributions, which included an antique painting and IBM stock. He has owned the IBM stock and the painting since 2005. LO 6-2

Donee	Item	Cost	FMV
Hobbs Medical Center	IBM stock	$5,000	$22,000
State Museum	Antique painting	5,000	3,000
A needy family	Food and clothes	400	250
United Way	Cash	8,000	8,000

Calculate Calvin's charitable contribution deduction and carryover (if any) under the following circumstances.

a) Calvin's AGI is $100,000.

b) Calvin's AGI is $100,000, but the State Museum told Calvin that it plans to sell the painting.

c) Calvin's AGI is $50,000.

d) Calvin's AGI is $100,000, and Hobbs is a private nonoperating foundation.

e) Calvin's AGI is $100,000, but the painting is worth $10,000.

51. In addition to cash contributions to charity, Dean decided to donate shares of stock and a portrait painted during the earlier part of the last century. Dean purchased the stock and the portrait many years ago as investments. Dean reported the following recipients in 2022: LO 6-2

Charity	Property	Cost	FMV
State University	Cash	$15,000	$15,000
Red Cross	Cash	14,500	14,500
State History Museum	Painting	5,000	82,000
City Medical Center	Dell stock	28,000	17,000

a) Determine the maximum amount of charitable deduction for each of these contributions *ignoring* the AGI ceiling on charitable contributions.

b) Assume that Dean's AGI this year is $150,000. Determine Dean's itemized deduction for his charitable contributions this year and any carryover.

c) Suppose Dean is a dealer in antique paintings and had held the painting for sale before the contribution. What is Dean's charitable contribution deduction for the painting in this situation (ignoring AGI limitations)?

d) Suppose that Dean's objective with the donation to the museum was to finance expansion of the historical collection. Hence, Dean was not surprised when the museum announced the sale of the painting because of its limited historical value. What is Dean's charitable contribution deduction for the painting in this situation (ignoring AGI limitations)?

52. Trevor is a single individual who is a cash-method, calendar-year taxpayer. For each of the next two years (2022 and 2023), Trevor expects to report salary of $80,000, contribute $8,000 to charity, and pay $2,800 in state income taxes. LO 6-2 **planning**

a) Estimate Trevor's taxable income for 2022 and 2023 using the 2022 amounts for the standard deduction for both years.

b) Now assume that Trevor combines his anticipated charitable contributions for the next two years and makes the combined contribution in December of 2022. Estimate

Trevor's taxable income for each of the next two years using the 2022 amounts for the standard deduction. Reconcile the total taxable income to your solution to part (a).

c) Trevor plans to purchase a residence next year, and he estimates that additional property taxes and residential interest will cost $2,000 and $10,000, respectively, each year. Estimate Trevor's taxable income for each of the next two years (2022 and 2023) using the 2022 amounts for the standard deduction and also assuming Trevor makes the charitable contribution of $8,000 and state tax payments of $2,800 in each year.

d) Assume the facts in part (c) but that Trevor makes the charitable contribution for 2023 in December of 2022. Estimate Trevor's taxable income for 2022 and 2023 using the 2022 amounts for the standard deduction. Reconcile the total taxable income to your solution to part (c).

e) Explain the conditions in which the bunching strategy in part (d) will generate tax savings for Trevor.

LO 6-2

53. Simon lost $5,000 gambling this year on a trip to Las Vegas. In addition, he paid $2,000 to his broker for managing his $200,000 portfolio and $1,500 to his accountant for preparing his tax return. In addition, Simon incurred $2,500 in transportation costs commuting back and forth from his home to his employer's office, which were not reimbursed. Calculate the amount of these expenses that Simon is able to deduct (assuming he itemizes his deductions).

LO 6-2 LO 6-1

research

54. Jian teaches elementary school history for the Metro School District. In 2022 they incurred the following expenses associated with their job:

Noncredit correspondence course on history	$ 900
Teaching cases for classroom use	1,800

Jian's employer does not provide any funding for the correspondence course or teaching cases. Identify the amount and type (for AGI or from AGI) of deductible expenses.

LO 6-3

55. Stephanie is 12 years old and often assists neighbors on weekends by babysitting their children. Calculate the 2022 standard deduction Stephanie will claim under the following independent circumstances (assume that Stephanie's parents will claim her as a dependent).

a) Stephanie reported $850 of earnings from her babysitting.

b) Stephanie reported $1,500 of earnings from her babysitting.

c) Stephanie reported $18,000 of earnings from her babysitting.

LO 6-3

56. Jackson is 18 years old and has a dog-sitting business. Calculate the 2022 standard deduction Jackson will claim under the following independent circumstances.

a) Jackson reported $2,000 of earnings from his dog sitting and $300 in interest income from his savings account. Jackson's parents claim him as a dependent.

b) Jackson reported $500 of earnings from his dog sitting and $2,000 in interest income from his savings account. Jackson's parents claim him as a dependent.

c) Jackson reported $8,000 of earnings from his dog sitting and $3,000 in interest income. Jackson's parents do not claim him as a dependent.

LO 6-3

57. Amelie, a retired physician, is 66 years old. Determine her standard deduction in 2022 under the following scenarios.

a) Amelie is married to Roget, age 52, and they file married joint.

b) Amelie is single.

c) Amelie is single and her 10-year-old granddaughter, Emma, lives with her. Amelie supports Emma and claims her as a dependent.

LO 6-4

58. Roquan, a single taxpayer, is an attorney and practices as a sole proprietor. This year, Roquan had net business income of $90,000 from his law practice (net of the associated for AGI self-employment tax deduction). Assume that Roquan pays $40,000 in wages to his employees, has $10,000 of property (unadjusted basis of equipment he purchased last year), and has no capital gains or qualified

dividends. His taxable income before the deduction for qualified business income is $100,000.

a) Calculate Roquan's deduction for qualified business income.

b) Assume the same facts provided above, except Roquan's taxable income before the deduction for qualified business income is $300,000.

59. Katie, a single taxpayer, is a shareholder in Engineers One, a civil engineering company. This year, Katie's share of net business income from Engineers One is $200,000 (net of the associated for AGI self-employment tax deduction). Assume that Katie's allocation of wages paid by Engineers One to its employees is $300,000 and her allocation of Engineers One's qualified property is $150,000 (unadjusted basis of equipment, all purchased within the past three years). Assume Katie has no other business income and no capital gains or qualified dividends. Her taxable income before the deduction for qualified business income is $400,000. LO 6-4

a) Calculate Katie's deduction for qualified business income.

b) Assume the same facts provided above, except Katie's net business income from Engineers One is $400,000 (net of the associated for AGI self-employment tax deduction), and her taxable income before the deduction for qualified business income is $350,000.

60. Felipe, a single taxpayer, is a technology consultant who operates as a sole proprietorship. Felipe's net business income is $600,000 (net of the associated for AGI self-employment tax deduction), he pays wages of $100,000 to his employees, and he has $200,000 of qualified property (unadjusted basis). Felipe's taxable income before the deduction for qualified business income is $500,000. Assume he has no capital gains or qualified dividends. LO 6-4

a) Calculate Felipe's deduction for qualified business income.

b) How would your answer to (a) change if Felipe was an investment broker?

COMPREHENSIVE PROBLEMS

Select problems are available in Connect®.

61. This year (2022) Evan graduated from college and took a job as a deliveryman in the city. Evan was paid a salary of $72,300, and he received $700 in hourly pay for part-time work over the weekends. Evan summarized his expenses as follows:

Cost of moving his possessions to the city (125 miles away)	$1,200
Interest paid on accumulated student loans	2,800
Cost of purchasing a delivery uniform	1,400
Contribution to State University deliveryman program	1,300

Calculate Evan's AGI and taxable income if he files single. Assume that interest payments were initially required on Evan's student loans this year.

62. Read the following letter and help Shady Slim with his tax situation. Please assume that his gross income is $172,900 (which consists only of salary) for purposes of this problem. tax forms

December 31, 2022

To the friendly student tax preparer:

Hi, it's Shady Slim again. I just got back from my 55th birthday party, and I'm told that you need some more information from me in order to complete my tax return. I'm an open book! I'll tell you whatever I think you need to know.

Let me tell you a few more things about my life. As you may recall, I am divorced from my wife, Alice. I know that it's unusual, but I have custody of my son, Shady Jr. The judge owed me a few favors and I really love the kid. He lives with me full time and my wife gets him every other weekend. I pay the vast majority of my son's expenses. I think Alice should have to pay some child support, but she doesn't have to pay a dime. The judge didn't owe me that much, I guess.

I had to move this year after getting my job at Roca Cola. We moved on February 3 of this year, and I worked my job at Roca Cola for the rest of the year. I still live in the same state, but I moved 500 miles away from my old house. I hired a moving company to move our stuff at a cost of $2,300, and I drove Junior in my car. Junior and I got a hotel room along the way that cost us $65 (I love Super 8!).

Can you believe I'm still paying off my student loans, even after 15 years? I paid a total of $900 in interest on my old student loans this year.

Remember when I told you about that guy that hit me with his car? I had a bunch of medical expenses that were not reimbursed by the lawsuit or by my insurance. I incurred a total of $20,000 in medical expenses, and I was only reimbursed for $11,000. Good thing I can write off medical expenses, right?

I contributed a lot of money to charity this year (and have receipt documentation for all contributions). I'm such a nice guy! I gave $1,000 in cash to the March of Dimes. I contributed some of my old furniture to the church. It was some good stuff! I contributed a red velvet couch and my old recliner. The furniture is considered vintage and is worth $5,000 today (the appraiser surprised me!), even though I only paid $1,000 for it back in the day. When I contributed the furniture, the pastor said he didn't like the fabric and was going to sell the furniture to pay for some more pews in the church. Oh well, some people just have no taste, right? Roca Cola had a charity drive for the United Way this year and I contributed $90. Turns out, I don't even miss it because Roca Cola takes it right off my paycheck every month . . . $15 a month starting in July. My pay stub verifies that I contributed the $90 to the United Way. Oh, one other bit of charity from me this year. An old buddy of mine was down on his luck. He lost his job and his house. I gave him $500 to help him out.

I paid a lot of money in interest this year. I paid a total of $950 in personal credit card interest. I also paid $18,000 in interest on my $500,000 home mortgage that helped me buy my dream home. I also paid $2,000 in real estate taxes for my new house.

A few other things I want to tell you about this year. Someone broke into my house and stole my kid's brand new bicycle and my set of golf clubs. The total loss from theft was $900. I paid $125 in union dues this year. I had to pay $1,200 for new suits for my job. Roca Cola requires its managers to wear suits every day on the job. I spent a total of $1,300 to pay for gas to commute to my job this year.

Oh, this is pretty cool. I've always wanted to be a firefighter. I spent $1,400 in tuition to go to the local firefighter's school. I did this because someone told me that I can deduct the tuition as an itemized deduction, so the money would be coming back to me.

That should be all the information you need right now. Please calculate my taxable income and complete page 1 of Form 1040 (through taxable income, line 15) and Schedule A. You're still doing this for free, right?

63. Jeremy and Alyssa Johnson have been married for five years and do not have any children. Jeremy was married previously and has one child from the prior marriage. He is self-employed and operates his own computer repair store. For the first two months of the year, Alyssa worked for Office Depot as an employee. In March, Alyssa accepted a new job with Super Toys Inc. (ST), where she worked for the remainder of the year. This year, the Johnsons received $255,000 of gross income. Determine the Johnsons' AGI for 2022 given the following information:

a) Expenses associated with Jeremy's store include $40,000 in salary (and employment taxes) to employees, $45,000 of supplies, and $18,000 in rent and other administrative expenses.

b) As a salesperson, Alyssa incurred $2,000 in travel expenses related to her employment that were not reimbursed by her employer.

c) The Johnsons own a piece of raw land held as an investment. They paid $500 of real property taxes on the property and they incurred $200 of expenses in travel costs to see the property and to evaluate other similar potential investment properties.

d) The Johnsons own a rental home. They incurred $8,500 of expenses associated with the property.
e) Jeremy paid $4,500 for health insurance coverage for himself (not through an exchange). Alyssa was covered by health plans provided by her employer, but Jeremy is not eligible for the plan until next year.
f) Jeremy paid $2,500 in self-employment taxes ($1,250 represents the employer portion of the self-employment taxes).
g) Jeremy paid $5,000 in alimony and $3,000 in child support from his prior marriage (divorce decree executed in 2018).
h) The Johnsons donated $2,000 to their favorite charity.

64. Shauna Coleman is single. She is employed as an architectural designer for Streamline Design (SD). Shauna wanted to determine her taxable income for this year. She correctly calculated her AGI. However, she wasn't sure how to compute the rest of her taxable income. She provided the following information with hopes that you could use it to determine her taxable income for 2022.

tax forms

a) Shauna paid $4,680 for medical expenses for care from a broken ankle. Also, Shauna's boyfriend, Blake, drove Shauna (in her car) a total of 115 miles to the doctor's office so she could receive care for her broken ankle.
b) Shauna paid a total of $3,400 in health insurance premiums during the year (not through an exchange). SD did not reimburse any of this expense. Besides the health insurance premiums and the medical expenses for her broken ankle, Shauna had Lasik eye surgery last year and paid $3,000 for the surgery (she received no insurance reimbursement). She also incurred $450 of other medical expenses for the year.
c) SD withheld $1,800 of state income tax, $7,495 of Social Security tax, and $14,500 of federal income tax from Shauna's paychecks throughout the year.
d) In 2022, Shauna was due a refund of $250 for overpaying her 2021 state taxes. On her 2021 state tax return that she filed in April 2022, she applied the overpayment toward her 2022 state tax liability. She estimated that her state tax liability for 2022 will be $2,300.
e) Shauna paid $3,200 of property taxes on her personal residence. She also paid $500 to the developer of her subdivision because he had to replace the sidewalk in certain areas of the subdivision.
f) Shauna paid a $200 property tax based on the state's estimate of the value of her car.
g) Shauna has a home mortgage loan in the amount of $220,000 that she secured when she purchased her home. The home is worth about $400,000. Shauna paid interest of $12,300 on the loan this year.
h) Shauna made several charitable contributions throughout the year. She contributed stock in ZYX Corp. to the Red Cross. On the date of the contribution, the fair market value of the donated shares was $1,000 and her basis in the shares was $400. Shauna originally bought the ZYX Corp. stock in 2009. Shauna also contributed $300 cash to State University and religious artifacts she has held for several years to her church. The artifacts were valued at $500 and Shauna's basis in the items was $300. Shauna had every reason to believe the church would keep them on display indefinitely. Shauna also drove 200 miles doing church-related errands for her minister. Finally, Shauna contributed $1,200 of services to her church last year.
i) Shauna paid $250 in investment advisory fees and another $150 to have her tax return prepared (that is, she paid $150 in 2022 to have her 2021 tax return prepared).
j) Shauna is involved in horse racing as a hobby. During the year, she won $2,500 in prize money and incurred $10,000 in expenses. She has never had a profitable year with her horse-racing activities, so she acknowledges that this is a hobby for federal income tax purposes.
k) Shauna sustained $2,000 in gambling losses over the year (mostly horse-racing bets) and had only $200 in winnings.

Required:

a) Determine Shauna's taxable income and complete page 1 of Form 1040 (through taxable income, line 15) and Schedule A assuming her AGI is $107,000.

b) Determine Shauna's taxable income and complete page 1 of Form 1040 (through taxable income, line 15) and Schedule A assuming her AGI is $207,000.

65. Joe and Jessie are married and have one dependent child, Lizzie. Lizzie is currently in college at State University. Joe works as a design engineer for a manufacturing firm, while Jessie runs a craft business from their home. Jessie's craft business consists of making craft items for sale at craft shows that are held periodically at various locations. Jessie spends considerable time and effort on her craft business, and it has been consistently profitable over the years. Joe and Jessie own a home and pay interest on their home loan (balance of $220,000) and a personal loan to pay for Lizzie's college expenses (balance of $35,000). Neither Joe nor Jessie is blind or over age 65, and they plan to file as married joint.

    Based on their estimates, determine Joe and Jessie's AGI and taxable income for the year and complete page 1 of Form 1040 (through taxable income, line 15), Schedule 1, and Schedule A. Assume that the employer portion of the self-employment tax on Jessie's income is $831. Joe and Jessie have summarized the income and expenses they expect to report this year as follows:

Income:	
Joe's salary	$134,100
Jessie's craft sales	18,400
Interest from certificate of deposit	1,650
Interest from Treasury bond funds	716
Interest from municipal bond funds	920
Expenditures:	
Federal income tax withheld from Joe's wages	$13,700
State income tax withheld from Joe's wages	6,400
Social Security tax withheld from Joe's wages	7,482
Real estate taxes on residence	6,200
Automobile licenses (based on weight)	310
State sales tax paid	1,150
Home mortgage interest	16,000
Interest on Masterdebt credit card	2,300
Medical expenses (unreimbursed)	1,690
Joe's employee expenses (unreimbursed)	2,400
Cost of Jessie's craft supplies	4,260
Postage for mailing crafts	145
Travel and lodging for craft shows	2,230
Self-employment tax on Jessie's craft income	1,662
College tuition paid for Lizzie	5,780
Interest on loans to pay Lizzie's tuition	3,200
Lizzie's room and board at college	12,620
Cash contributions to the Red Cross	525

UWorld ROGER CPA Review

UWorld Roger CPA Review

Sample CPA Exam questions from Roger CPA Review are available in Connect as support for the topics in this text. These Multiple Choice Questions and Task-Based Simulations include expert-written explanations and solutions and provide a starting point for students to become familiar with the content and functionality of the actual CPA Exam.

chapter

7 Investments

Learning Objectives

Upon completing this chapter, you should be able to:

LO 7-1 Explain how interest income and dividend income are taxed.

LO 7-2 Compute the tax consequences associated with the disposition of capital assets, including the netting process for calculating gains and losses.

LO 7-3 Calculate the deduction for investment interest expense.

LO 7-4 Apply tax-basis, at-risk amount, and passive activity loss limits to losses from passive investments.

Echo/Juice Images/Getty Images

Storyline Summary

Taxpayers:	Courtney Wilson (she/her/hers), age 40 Courtney's uncle, Jeb Landers (he/him/his), age 65
Family description:	Courtney is divorced with a son, Deron (he/him/his), age 10, and a daughter, Ellen (she/her/hers), age 20. Jeb is single with no children.
Location:	Kansas City, Missouri
Employment status:	Courtney works as an architect for EWD. Her salary is $118,000. Jeb is recently retired.
Current situation:	Courtney is deciding how to invest her inheritance. Jeb is concerned about the tax effects of selling investment assets.

Courtney has settled into her new Kansas City location and is now focusing on her investment portfolio. When her father, "Gramps," passed away last December, he left Courtney an inheritance of $100,000 with the stipulation that she "invest it to financially benefit her family." After considerable thought, Courtney decided to invest the inheritance to accomplish two financial goals. First, she wants to save for her son Deron's college education. She figures that if she immediately invests $50,000 of the inheritance for his college education, she should have a significant sum accumulated when Deron starts college in eight years. Second, she decided that she will immediately invest the remaining $50,000 for five years and use the accumulation to make a significant down payment on a vacation home in Park City, Utah, a town she fell in love with during a college ski trip. Courtney is concerned about how different investment choices will be taxed and how this might affect her ability to meet her financial goals.

Jeb, Courtney's uncle, is single and has sold several investment assets during the year. He hopes to use the proceeds to fulfill his lifelong dream of owning a sailboat. He is uncertain about how much tax he will owe after selling the assets. ■

THE KEY FACTS

Investments Overview

- After-tax rate of return on investment depends on
  - Before-tax rate of return.
  - When investment income and gains are taxed.
    - Taxed annually
    - Tax deferred
    - Tax-exempt
  - When investment losses are deducted.
    - Deduction annually
    - Deduction deferred
  - Rate at which investment income or gains/expenses or losses are taxed/deducted.
    - Ordinary tax rates
    - Preferential tax rates
    - Zero tax rate

INVESTMENTS OVERVIEW

Investors are attracted to certain investments according to their investment philosophy and their appetite for risk, among other things. Some prefer investments that provide a consistent income stream. Others prefer investments that have significant appreciation potential but provide no current cash flows. These investment attributes affect the before-tax rates of return on investments. However, taxes are levied on **investment income,** and, thus, it would be unwise to make an investment without considering the tax cost.

For example, it is possible that two investments with identical before-tax rates of return will generate different after-tax rates of return because the investments are taxed differently. Indeed, it is possible that an investment with a lower before-tax rate of return compared to an alternative investment will have a higher after-tax rate of return because income from the investment is taxed at a later date or at a lower rate than the alternative investment.

Two key tax characteristics that affect after-tax rates of return from investments are (1) the timing of tax payments or tax benefits and (2) the rate at which investment income or gains are taxed or deductible expenses or losses generate tax savings. Not surprisingly, these variables are directly related to the timing and conversion tax planning strategies introduced in the Tax Planning Strategies and Related Limitations chapter.

Income from **portfolio investments,** which are investments producing **dividends,** interest, royalties, annuities, or capital gains, may be taxed at ordinary or preferential rates, or they may be exempt from taxation. Further, depending on the type of investment, tax on income from a portfolio investment may be imposed annually or may be deferred until the taxpayer sells the investment. Losses from portfolio investments are deferred until the investment is sold and are typically subject to limitations.

In contrast to portfolio investments, **passive investments** generate **operating income** and **operating losses.** Operating income is always taxed annually at ordinary rates, while operating losses are either deducted annually at ordinary rates or deferred and deducted later at ordinary rates, depending on the investor's circumstances. Losses from passive investments are also subject to limitations.

This chapter explores several common portfolio and passive investments, discusses important tax and nontax considerations relevant for those investments, and compares investment rates of return on an after-tax basis.

LO 7-1

PORTFOLIO INCOME: INTEREST AND DIVIDENDS

Taxpayers who desire current cash flows from their investments may choose investments that generate interest or regular dividends. Investments generating interest income include **certificates of deposit (CDs),** savings accounts, corporate **bonds,** and governmental bonds. Investments generating dividend income include direct equity investments in corporate stocks and investments in **mutual funds** and **exchange traded funds (ETFs)** that invest in corporate stock.[1] Although all these investments generate current cash flows, they differ significantly in terms of their economic and tax consequences.

By lending money to banks, governmental entities, or corporations, investors essentially become debt holders. As such, they are legally entitled to receive periodic interest payments *and* to recover the amount of principal loaned. In the case of bonds, the principal is the **maturity value** or **face value** of the bonds. Interest payments and the time and manner of repayment of the loan principal are defined either contractually for CDs and savings accounts or by bond covenants for loans made to either governments or corporations.

[1]In contrast to mutual funds that are actively managed and are priced once a day after trading hours, ETF share prices fluctuate throughout the trading day as investors trade. Income (e.g., dividends) from the fund's underlying assets flows through to the ETF investors. ETF investors have some control over the tax from ETF gains and losses because they are recognized and subject to tax when the investor trades the ETF shares. This treatment differs from mutual fund investors, who may be subject to tax when any investor sells their shares (not just when the individual investor does so).

In contrast, investors who purchase stocks become shareholders (also called equity holders) of a corporation. As shareholders, they are entitled to receive dividends if the company declares dividends and to *indirectly* share in either the future appreciation or depreciation in the value of a corporation through stock ownership. Unlike debt holders, shareholders are not legally entitled to receive dividend payments or to recover their initial investment. Thus, from an investor's perspective, debt tends to be less risky than equity.

For tax purposes, individual investors typically are taxed on both interest and dividend income when they receive it. However, interest income is taxed at ordinary rates, while dividend income is generally taxed at lower capital gains rates.

Interest

In general, taxpayers recognize interest income from investments when they receive the interest payments.[2] Taxpayers investing in savings accounts, money market accounts, CDs, and most bonds receive interest payments based on a stated annual rate of return at yearly or more frequent intervals.

Special rules apply for determining the timing and amount of interest from bonds when there is a **bond discount**—that is, when bonds are issued at an amount below the maturity value—or a **bond premium**—that is, when bonds are issued at an amount above the maturity value. Below we discuss these rules as they apply to corporate bonds, U.S. Treasury bonds, and **U.S. savings bonds.**

Corporate and U.S. Treasury Bonds Both corporations and the U.S. Treasury raise money from debt markets by issuing bonds.[3] Corporate bonds, **Treasury bonds,** and **Treasury notes** are issued at maturity value, at a discount, or at a premium, depending on prevailing interest rates.[4] Treasury bonds and Treasury notes pay a stated rate of interest semiannually.[5] However, corporate bonds may pay interest at a stated "coupon" rate, or they may not provide any periodic interest payments. Corporate bonds that do not pay periodic interest are called **zero-coupon bonds.** Overall, the consequences of holding corporate or Treasury bonds are very similar. The two primary differences are that (1) interest from Treasury bonds is exempt from *state* taxation while interest from corporate bonds is not and (2) Treasury bonds always pay interest periodically while corporate bonds may or may not. The tax rules for determining the timing and amount of interest income from corporate and U.S. Treasury bonds are as follows:

- Taxpayers include the actual interest payments they receive in gross income.
- If the bond was issued at a discount, special **original issue discount (OID)** rules apply. Taxpayers are required to amortize the discount and include the amount of the current year **amortization** in gross income in addition to any interest payments the taxpayer actually receives.[6] In the case of zero-coupon bonds, this means taxpayers must report and pay taxes on income related to the bonds even though they did not receive *any* payments from the bonds. Bond issuers or brokers are responsible for calculating the yearly amortization of the original issue discount and providing this information to investors using Form 1099-OID.

[2]Interest income is reported on Part I of Schedule B filed with taxpayers' Form 1040.

[3]Investors in corporate bonds assume more risk than investors in Treasury securities because they are relying on the creditworthiness of the corporation issuing the bonds. To compensate bondholders for this additional risk, corporate bonds usually yield higher before-tax rates of return than Treasury securities.

[4]The bonds are issued at a discount (premium) if the market interest rate is higher (lower) than the stated rate on the bonds.

[5]Treasury notes and bonds differ in terms of their maturities. Treasury notes are issued with 2-, 5-, and 10-year maturities. In contrast, Treasury bonds are issued with maturities greater than 10 years. From this point forward, we use the term Treasury bonds to refer to both Treasury notes and Treasury bonds.

[6]§1272. Original issue discounts are amortized semiannually under the constant yield method, which is consistent with the approach used to amortize bond discount under GAAP.

- If the bond was issued at a premium, taxpayers may *elect* to amortize the premium.[7] Taxpayers or their advisers are responsible for determining the yearly amortization of the bond premium if the election to amortize the premium has been made. The amount of the current-year amortization offsets a portion of the actual interest payments that taxpayers must include in gross income. The original tax basis of the bond includes the premium and is reduced by any amortization of the bond premium over the life of the bond.
- If the bond is purchased in the secondary bond market at a discount, the taxpayer treats all or some of the **market discount** as interest income *when she sells the bond or the bond matures*.[8] If the bond is sold prior to **maturity,** a ratable amount of the market discount (based on the number of days the bond is held over the number of days until maturity when the bond is purchased), called the **accrued market discount,** is treated as interest income on the date of sale.[9] If the bond is held to maturity, the entire bond discount is treated as interest income at maturity.
- If the bond is purchased in the secondary bond market at a premium, the premium is treated exactly like original issue bond premiums. As a result, the taxpayer may elect to amortize the **market premium** to reduce the annual interest income received from the bond. Otherwise, the premium remains as part of the tax basis of the bond and affects the capital gain or loss the taxpayer recognizes when the taxpayer sells or redeems the bond.

U.S. Savings Bonds U.S. savings bonds such as Series EE or Series I bonds are issued either at face value or at a discount. These bonds do not pay periodic interest; rather, interest accumulates over the term of the bonds and is paid when investors redeem them at maturity or earlier.[10] That is, the amount of interest income taxpayers recognize *when they redeem* the bonds is the excess of the bond proceeds over the taxpayer's **basis** in the bonds, meaning its purchase price. Taxpayers may elect to include the increase in the bond redemption value in their income each year, but this is generally not advisable because it accelerates the income from the bond without providing any cash to pay the taxes.[11] Finally, interest from Series EE and Series I bonds may be excluded from gross income to the extent the bond proceeds are used to pay qualifying educational expenses. However, this exclusion benefit is subject to phase-out based on the taxpayer's AGI.

Example 7-1

What if: Assume that Courtney was deciding whether to invest the $50,000 earmarked for the Park City vacation home in (1) Series EE savings bonds that mature in exactly five years, (2) original issue AMD Corporation *zero-coupon* bonds that mature in exactly five years, or (3) U.S. Treasury bonds that pay $46,250 at maturity in five years trading in the secondary bond market with a stated annual

[7]§171. Like an original issue discount, a bond premium is amortized semiannually under the constant yield method—the same method used to amortize bond premiums under GAAP. Unlike premiums on taxable bonds, premiums on tax-exempt bonds must always be amortized.

[8]§1276(a). Under §1278(b)(1), taxpayers may elect to include the amortization of market discounts in their income annually. However, this election accelerates the recognition of income from the market discounts and is therefore usually not advisable.

[9]§1276(b).

[10]Series EE savings bonds are issued at a discount and Series I savings bonds are issued at maturity value. Series EE bonds provide a constant rate of return, while Series I bonds provide a return that is indexed for inflation and thus increases over time.

[11]§454(a). Investors that make this election report the annual increase in the redemption value of their savings bonds using savings bond redemption tables published by the Treasury Department.

interest rate of 10 percent. Further, assume that all bonds yield 8 percent annual before-tax rates of return compounded semiannually. At the end of the first year, (1) the redemption value of the EE savings bonds would be $54,080, or (2) Courtney would receive a Form 1099-OID from AMD reporting $4,080 of OID amortization for the year, or (3) she would receive two semiannual interest payments of $2,312.50 from the Treasury bonds. Under the general rules, how much interest income from each bond would Courtney report at the end of the first year?

Answer: $0 from the Series EE savings bonds, $4,080 from the AMD bonds, and $4,625 (two semiannual payments of $2,312.50) from the Treasury bonds. Note, however, that Courtney could *elect* to include the $4,080 increase in redemption value of the Series EE bonds in interest income even though she did not receive any interest payments on the bonds (probably not optimal). She also could *elect* to amortize $637.50 of the $3,750 premium ($50,000 purchase price less the $46,250 maturity value) on the Treasury bonds to offset the $4,625 in actual interest payments she received on the bonds (probably a good idea). The calculations required to amortize the premium on the Treasury bonds for the first year are reflected in the following table:

Semiannual Period	(A) Adjusted Basis of Bonds at Beginning of Semiannual Period	(B) Interest Received and Reported ($46,250 × 10% × .5)	(C) Interest Earned (A) × 8% × .5	Premium Amortization (B) – (C)
1	$50,000.00	$2,312.50	$2,000.00	$312.50
2	49,687.50	2,312.50	1,987.50	325.00
Yearly Total		4,625.00	3,987.50	637.50

Intuitively, would Courtney be better or worse off purchasing the Series EE savings bonds rather than a corporate bond to save for the Park City home?

Answer: Courtney would be better off purchasing the Series EE savings bonds in two respects. First, she wouldn't have to pay state income taxes on the interest earned from the savings bonds. Second, she would be able to defer paying taxes on the accumulated interest from the savings bonds until the savings bonds are cashed in at maturity.

Intuitively, would Courtney be better or worse off purchasing the AMD zero-coupon bonds rather than a corporate bond to save for the Park City home?

Answer: She would be worse off because she would have to pay taxes currently from the OID amortization on the AMD bonds without receiving any cash flow from the bonds to pay the taxes due.

Example 7-2

What if: Assume that on January 1, Courtney used the $50,000 earmarked for the Park City vacation home to purchase AMD zero-coupon bonds in the *secondary bond market* almost immediately after the bonds were originally issued. If they mature in exactly five years and have a maturity value of $74,000, how much interest income will Courtney report at the end of the first year and in the year the bonds mature?

Answer: $0 in the first year and $24,000 in the year the bonds mature. Because the AMD zero-coupon bonds were not purchased at original issue, the entire $24,000 market discount on the bonds will be reported as interest income when the bonds mature. Thus, Courtney will not report any income related to the AMD bonds until the year the bonds mature.

What if: Assume the same facts as above, except Courtney purchased U.S. Series EE bonds instead of AMD zero-coupon bonds to fund the Park City vacation home in five years. How much interest income will she report at the end of the first year and in the year the bonds mature?

Answer: $0 in the first year and $24,000 in the year the EE savings bonds mature. This is exactly the same outcome as the investment in the AMD zero-coupon bonds (ignoring possible state income tax effects).

EXHIBIT 7-1 Timing of Interest Payments and Taxes

General Rule	Exception	Exception
Interest Received Annually and Taxed Annually	**Interest Received at Sale or Maturity and Taxed at Sale or Maturity**	**Interest Received at Sale or Maturity but Taxed Annually**
• Savings accounts • CDs • Money market accounts • Bond interest payments actually received in the year	• Accrued market discount on bonds • Interest earned on U.S. savings bonds	• Original issue discount (OID) on corporate and Treasury bonds

As our discussion suggests, for certain types of investments such as savings accounts, money market accounts, and CDs, computing the annual taxable interest income is relatively straightforward. However, for investments in bonds, the process is much more involved. Exhibit 7-1 summarizes the general rule and exceptions for the timing of interest payments and related tax payments.

Dividends

Consistent with the general rule for taxing interest income, dividend payments (including reinvested dividends) are taxed annually.[12] However, as we discuss in the Individual Income Tax Computation and Tax Credits chapter, **qualified dividends** are taxed at a preferential rate: 0, 15, or 20 percent, depending on the taxpayer's filing status and amount of taxable income.[13] Qualified dividends are those paid by domestic or certain qualified foreign corporations provided investors hold the dividend-paying stock for *more than* 60 days during the 121-day period that begins 60 days before the **ex-dividend date,** the first day on which purchasers of the stock would not be entitled to receive a declared dividend on the stock.[14] Exhibit 7-2 illustrates the 121-day period surrounding the ex-dividend date.

EXHIBIT 7-2 Holding Period for Qualified Dividends

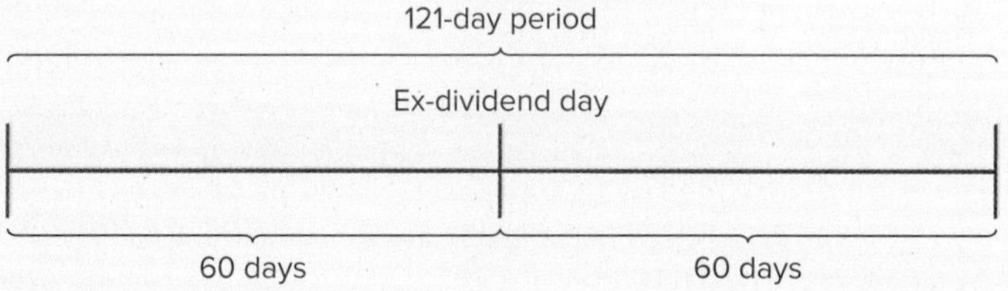

Nonqualified dividends are not eligible for the reduced rate and are therefore taxed at ordinary rates. Corporations distributing dividends report the amounts of the dividends and indicate whether the dividends are potentially eligible for the preferential rate when they send Form 1099-DIV to shareholders after year-end. However, shareholders ultimately must determine whether they qualify for the preferential rate by confirming they held the stock for the required number of days around the ex-dividend date.

[12]Dividends are reported on Part II of Schedule B filed with taxpayers' Form 1040.

[13]The tax rate for qualified dividends follows the capital gains tax rates as discussed later in this chapter. Dividends are taxed at these preferential rates to mitigate the double tax on dividend income.

[14]Qualified foreign corporations are those incorporated in a U.S. possession (e.g., Puerto Rico, U.S. Virgin Islands), those eligible for the benefits of a comprehensive income tax treaty with the United States, or those whose shares are readily traded on an established U.S. securities market.

Example 7-3

What if: Assume Courtney (head of household filing status) decides to purchase dividend-paying stocks to achieve her financial objectives. She invests $50,000 in Xerox stock, which she intends to hold for five years and then sell to fund the Park City home down payment. She invests another $50,000 in Coca-Cola stock (KO), which she intends to hold for eight years and then sell to fund her son's education. How much dividend income will Courtney report at the end of the first year if the dividend payments provide an 8 percent rate of return on her investments?[15]

Answer: At the end of the first year, Courtney will report $4,000 ($50,000 × .08) of dividend income from her investment in the Xerox stock and $4,000 ($50,000 × .08) of dividend income from her investment in the Coca-Cola stock, for a total of $8,000 of dividend income.

What if: Assume Courtney's ordinary marginal tax rate is 32 percent. How much tax will Courtney owe on her dividend income if the dividends are nonqualified?

Answer: Courtney will owe $2,560 ($8,000 × 32%) of tax if the dividends are nonqualified because the income will be taxed at her ordinary income tax rate.

What if: What amount of tax will Courtney owe if the dividends are qualified? Assume Courtney's tax rate on qualified dividends is 15 percent.

Answer: Courtney will owe $1,200 ($8,000 × 15%) of tax if the dividends are qualified because qualified dividends are taxed at preferential rates.

Because dividend income is generally taxed at lower rates than interest income, it appears that taxpayers seeking current cash flows from their investments should favor dividend-paying investments over interest-paying investments. This raises the question why anyone would ever prefer investments paying interest over those paying dividends. Remember, though, that savvy investors also should consider nontax factors, such as before-tax rates of return, risk, and liquidity needs when choosing among investments. These fundamental differences explain why investors may continue to seek out interest income in spite of the associated tax disadvantages.

THE KEY FACTS

Interest and Dividend Income

- Interest
  - Interest is taxed at ordinary rates.
  - Cash interest payments are taxed annually.
  - Accrued market discount is taxed at sale or maturity.
  - Savings bonds are taxed at sale or maturity.
  - Original issue discount is taxed annually.
- Dividends
  - Dividends are taxed annually.
  - Qualified dividends are taxed at preferential rates.

PORTFOLIO INCOME: CAPITAL GAINS AND LOSSES

LO 7-2

Investors who don't need annual cash flows from their investments may prefer to invest in assets with the expectation that the investments will appreciate in value over time, providing cash at some point in the future when they sell the assets. Investors also may be willing to assume greater risk in exchange for greater returns than those provided by interest or dividend-paying investments. For example, they might purchase raw land, fine art, rare coins, precious gems or metals, growth stocks (i.e., stock in corporations that reinvest their earnings to grow the company as opposed to distributing them to shareholders in the form of dividends), mutual fund shares, cryptocurrencies (e.g., Bitcoin, Ethereum, Dogecoin) or even vintage automobiles. Purchasing any such asset is not without risk. Indeed, investments held solely for appreciation potential *may* actually decline in value.

When taxpayers buy and hold assets with appreciation potential, they typically are investing in **capital assets.** As we discuss in the Individual Income Tax Overview, Dependents, and Filing Status chapter, capital assets are typically investment-type assets and personal-use assets.[16] Thus, artwork, corporate stock, bonds, your personal residence, and even your iPhone are capital assets.

[15]Annual rates of return from dividend-paying stocks are typically lower than the rates of return from taxable bonds. However, it is assumed here that the rates of return are equal for the sake of comparability.

[16]§1221 defines capital assets in the negative. This code section excludes the following from the definition of a capital asset: inventory, depreciable property or real property used in a trade or business, certain self-created intangibles, accounts or notes receivable, U.S. government publications, certain commodities, derivative financial instruments, certain hedging transactions, and supplies. Self-created patents, inventions, models or designs (whether or not patented), and secret formulas or processes are among the intangibles excluded from the definition of a capital asset.

TAXES IN THE REAL WORLD So You Want to Invest in Bitcoin?

Since 2014, Bitcoin usage has increased dramatically, averaging over 320,000 transactions per day over the last year (https://blockchain.info/charts/n-transactions?timespan=1year&daysAverageString=7). But what does it mean to invest in Bitcoin, and what effect does it have on a taxpayer's income? Although not the only way, the most common way to invest in Bitcoin is to use a buy-and-hold strategy (called "hodling" where hodl stands for hold on for dear life). This strategy is profitable when the investor buys low and sells high. The appreciation represents the profit from the investment. Bitcoin is a form of virtual currency, which is a "digital representation of value that functions as a medium of exchange, a unit of account, and/or a store of value."[17] Interestingly, the IRS says virtual currency is "property" and not currency. Therefore, taxpayers follow the tax principles that apply to property transactions when determining the income or loss from Bitcoin investments rather than treating such income or loss as currency subject to potential foreign currency gains and losses. For taxpayers holding Bitcoin as an investment, any gains or losses are treated as capital. The IRS includes a question on the front page of Form 1040 asking taxpayers if they sold, sent, exchanged, or acquired any financial interest in any virtual currency at any time during the year.

Keeping in mind that Bitcoin is property and not currency for tax purposes is important, especially when Bitcoin is spent. Bitcoin users have a taxable event each time they purchase goods or services with Bitcoin. Each transaction requires the investor to calculate the gain or loss on the disposition of the Bitcoin investment, report these gains and losses on Form 8949 and Schedule D (for capital asset transactions), and apply the appropriate tax rate depending on the holding period and the investor's tax bracket. If the transaction results in a loss from the Bitcoin, the loss will be subject to the capital loss limitations discussed later in the chapter. And remember . . . taxes are paid in dollars, not Bitcoin (at least for now)!

Source: IRS Notice 2014-21, www.irs.gov/pub/irs-drop/n-14-21.pdf.

While it may be enjoyable to view collectible fine art in your home or watch a stock portfolio grow in value in brokerage accounts, from a tax perspective the real advantages of investing in capital assets are that (1) gains are deferred for tax purposes until the taxpayer sells or otherwise disposes of the assets[18] and (2) gains generally are taxed at preferential rates relative to ordinary income.[19] Why the favorable treatment? One reason is that taxpayers may not have the wherewithal (cash) to pay the tax on their gains until they sell the investment. Another is that the preferential tax rate provides an incentive for taxpayers to invest in assets that may stimulate the economy. Investors can capture these tax benefits when they sell capital assets at a gain. However, when they sell capital assets at a loss, their ability to deduct the loss may be limited.

When a taxpayer sells a capital asset, the difference between the **amount realized** from the sale and the **tax basis** determines whether the taxpayer will realize a gain or a loss. If the amount realized by the seller is greater than the tax basis, the taxpayer recognizes a capital gain. If a taxpayer sells a capital asset for less than its tax basis, he or she recognizes a capital loss (to the extent the loss is deductible).[20] The amount realized or the selling price of a capital asset includes the cash and fair market value of other property received, less broker's fees and other selling costs. The tax basis (discussed in greater detail in the Property Dispositions chapter) of any asset, including a capital asset, is generally the taxpayer's cost of acquiring the asset, including the initial purchase price and other

[17]Notice 2014-21.

[18]Similarly, interest related to the market discount on bonds and the original issue discount on U.S. EE savings bonds accumulates free of tax until the bonds mature or are sold. However, ordinary rather than capital gains rates apply when the tax must finally be paid.

[19]Mutual funds that generate current income by regularly selling capital assets or by holding income-producing securities are an exception to this general rule. However, tax-efficient mutual funds that only buy and hold growth stocks are treated more like other capital assets for tax purposes (capital gains are deferred until mutual fund shares are sold).

[20]As discussed below, losses on personal assets are not deductible for tax purposes.

costs incurred to purchase or improve the asset.[21] Thus, the tax basis of corporate stock purchased from a stockbroker includes the cost of the stock and any additional brokerage fees paid by the taxpayer to acquire the stock. Also, the tax basis in a personal residence includes the initial purchase price plus the cost of subsequent improvements to the home.

TAXES IN THE REAL WORLD The Times They Are A-Changin'

What do Bob Dylan, Imagine Dragons, Shakira, The Killers, Fleetwood Mac, Neil Young, 50 Cent, and Dire Straits have in common? They are all musicians that have recently sold their music catalogs. This trend has picked up since 2020 and is likely driven by many factors. Touring income was down for musicians during 2020 due to COVID-19 restrictions, and many artists are looking for replacement income. Although taxes are not likely the primary reason for the sales, there are tax benefits for the selling artists that may have prompted them to sell. Musicians have a distinct advantage over other artists (e.g., painters and filmmakers) of being able to sell self-created works as capital assets subject to the lower capital gains tax rate rather than ordinary tax rates.[22] In addition, songwriters are not subject to the additional 3.8 percent net investment income tax of other investments because they are active participants in their business. Thus, selling these assets uses the conversion tax strategy to convert royalty income taxed at ordinary rates to capital gains. Timing is also important. With some proposals for new tax legislation increasing the capital gains tax to as high as 39.6 percent, musicians may realize the window of opportunity may be closing.

What about the buyers? There may be tax advantages for them as well. Corporate buyers have a 21 percent tax rate (although there have been some proposals to increase the corporate tax rate), which is much lower than the individual ordinary rate of up to 37 percent. This lower tax rate means that the royalty income is worth more on an after-tax basis to a corporation than a wealthy individual. In addition, buyers can often amortize the cost of the catalog using the cost recovery techniques discussed in the Property Acquisition and Cost Recovery chapter. All in all, the time is ripe for musicians to cash in!

Source: Based on Richard Rubin and Laura Saunders, "Bob Dylan's Catalog Sale Highlights a Tax Advantage for Songwriters," *The Wall Street Journal* (December 11, 2020), www.wsj.com/articles/bob-dylans-catalog-sale-highlights-a-tax-advantage-for-songwriters-11607682604.

Because taxpayers cannot accurately compute the gain or loss on the sale of a capital asset without knowing its tax basis, it is important to maintain accurate records to track the tax basis in capital assets. This process is relatively straightforward for unique assets such as a personal residence or individual jewels in a taxpayer's jewelry collection. However, capital assets such as shares of stock and units of cryptocurrency are much more homogeneous and difficult to track.

For example, a taxpayer may purchase blocks of stock in a given corporation at different times over a period of several years, paying a different price per share for each block of stock acquired. When selling shares of this stock in subsequent years, what tax basis does the taxpayer use to compute gain or loss? By default, taxpayers are required to use the **first-in, first-out (FIFO) method** of determining the tax basis of the shares they sell.[23] However, if they (or their broker) track the tax basis of their stock, taxpayers can sell (or instruct their broker to sell) specific shares using the **specific identification method** to determine the tax basis of the shares they sell.[24] Taxpayers using the specific identification method can choose to sell their high tax basis stock first, minimizing their gains or increasing their losses on stock dispositions. Alternatively, for brokerage accounts, taxpayers can elect LIFO as their default method.

[21]Brokers are required to report to the IRS the cost basis of securities their customers sell if the securities were purchased on or after January 1, 2013.

[22]§1221(b)(3).

[23]Reg. §1.1012-1(c)(1).

[24]Brokerage firms are required to report cost basis and type of capital gain (short-term or long-term) on Form 1099-B provided to investors. These requirements have phased in over several years, and currently, brokerage firms and other financial institutions are required to provide this information for equity securities (including ETFs and RICs) as well as for debt securities.

Example 7-4

After Courtney's car broke down, she decided to buy a new one. To fund the down payment, she sold 200 shares of Cisco stock at the current market price of $40 per share for a total amount realized of $8,000. Courtney held the following blocks of Cisco stock at the time of the sale:

Cisco Corporation Stock Ownership

Holding Period	(1) Cost per Share	(2) Shares	(1) × (2) Basis	Basis of 200 Shares Sold	Explanation
5 years	$25	250	$6,250	$5,000	FIFO basis ($25 × 200)
2 years	$32	250	$8,000	$6,400	Specific ID basis ($32 × 200)

How much capital gain will Courtney recognize if she uses the FIFO method of computing the basis in the Cisco shares sold?

Answer: $3,000. $8,000 amount realized ($40 × 200) minus $5,000 FIFO basis ($25 × 200). As indicated in the table above, under the FIFO (oldest first) method, the shares sold have a holding period of five years.

What if: How much capital gain will Courtney recognize if she uses the specific identification method of computing the basis in the shares sold to minimize the taxable gain on the sale?

Answer: $1,600. $8,000 amount realized ($40 × 200) minus $6,400 ($32 × 200). To minimize her gain on the sale under the specific identification method, Courtney would choose to sell the 200 shares with the highest basis. As indicated in the table above, the shares with the higher basis are those acquired and held two years for $32 per share.

Note in the above example that Courtney receives $8,000 from the stock sale ($40 per share × 200 shares sold) regardless of the method she uses to compute the basis of the shares she sells. The difference between the FIFO and specific identification methods lies in the amount of taxable gain on the *current* sale. Over time, as taxpayers sell all their stock, both methods will ultimately allow them to fully recover their cost in the investments. However, applying the specific identification method will result in lower capital gains taxes currently and thereby minimize the present value of the taxes paid on stock sales.

Types of Capital Gains and Losses

Taxpayers selling capital assets they have held for a year or less recognize **short-term capital gains or losses.**[25] Taxpayers selling capital assets they have held for more than a year recognize **long-term capital gains or losses.** To determine the holding period, taxpayers begin counting with the day after acquisition and include the day of disposition. Short-term capital gains are taxed at ordinary rather than preferential rates. In contrast, long-term capital gains are taxed at preferential rates. However, not all long-term capital gains are taxed equally. Just like dividends, most long-term capital gains are taxed at either 0 percent, 15 percent, or 20 percent, depending on the taxpayer's filing status and taxable income, as shown in Exhibit 7-3. The **maximum zero percent rate amount** defines the threshold for the zero percent rate to apply to long-term capital gains. When

[25]Nonbusiness bad debt is treated as a short-term capital loss no matter how long the debt was outstanding before it became worthless. Whether a bad debt is considered to be a business or nonbusiness bad debt for individuals depends on the facts and circumstances. In general, if the taxpayer experiencing the loss is in the business of loaning money, the bad debt should be considered to be business bad debt; otherwise, the bad debt will likely be considered nonbusiness bad debt.

EXHIBIT 7-3

	Taxable Income by Filing Status†			
Preferential Tax Rates	Married Filing Joint	Married Filing Separate	Single	Head of Household
0%*	$0–$83,350	$0–$41,675	$0–$41,675	$0–$55,800
15%**	$83,351–$517,200	$41,676–$258,600	$41,676–$459,750	$55,801–$488,500
20%	$517,201+	$258,601+	$459,751+	$488,501+

†When determining which capital gains tax rate applies, capital gains and qualified dividends that fall within the range of taxable income specified in the table are included in taxable income last.
*The highest income amount in this range for each filing status is referred to as the maximum zero percent rate amount.
**The highest income amount in this range for each filing status is referred to as the maximum 15 percent amount.

taxable income is between the maximum zero percent and the **maximum 15 percent rate amount,** long-term capital gains are taxed at 15 percent. These maximum rate amounts are often referred to as breakpoints. When taxable income is above the 15 percent rate breakpoint, long-term capital gains are taxed at 20 percent. However, certain long-term capital gains are taxed at a maximum rate of 25 percent, also known as **unrecaptured §1250 gain,** while others are taxed at a maximum rate of 28 percent, specifically gain from **collectibles** and gain from **qualified small business stock,** for tax policy reasons.

25 Percent Gains When individuals sell depreciable real property held more than one year at a gain, a portion (or even all) of the gain may be taxed at a maximum rate of 25 percent (the unrecaptured §1250 gain portion), and a portion may be taxed as a 0/15/20 percent gain. In the Property Dispositions chapter, we discuss the details of how to compute the amount of 25 percent gain and the amount of 0/15/20 percent gain when an individual sells depreciable real property; however, we include a brief discussion in this chapter because the amount of 25 percent gain affects the capital gain and loss netting process we discuss in this chapter.

Example 7-5

What if: Assume Jeb Landers (single), Courtney's uncle, recently sold a rental condo for $160,000. He originally acquired the condo many years ago for $100,000, and he has fully depreciated it for tax purposes. Assume that $100,000 of the gain (the unrecaptured §1250 gain portion) is taxed at a maximum rate of 25 percent. If Jeb's taxable income (before considering this gain) is $210,000, what tax does he owe on the gain if he did not sell any other property during the year?

Answer: $34,000. Because Jeb's tax basis in the condo is $0 (he has fully depreciated it), his gain on the sale is $160,000. Jeb first determines the tax on the portion of the gain taxed at a maximum of 25 percent. Jeb owes 25 percent tax on the $100,000, resulting in $25,000 of tax on this portion of the gain ($100,000 × 25%) because his marginal tax rate on $210,000 is 35 percent, which is higher than the maximum tax rate of 25 percent for this type of gain. Jeb's taxable income after including the 25 percent gain is now $310,000 ($210,000 + $100,000). To determine the capital gains tax rate for the remaining $60,000 gain, Jeb must determine how much of the gain falls within the 15 percent range. Jeb's 15 percent range is $41,676 to $459,750. With a starting point of $310,000, adding the $60,000 gain makes his taxable income $370,000. Because the entire $60,000 gain is within the 15 percent range, Jeb owes $9,000 of tax on this portion ($60,000 × 15%). In total, he owes $34,000 of tax on the gain ($25,000 + $9,000).

What if: Suppose Jeb's taxable income is $475,000 rather than $210,000 before considering the gain on the sale of the rental condo. What tax does he owe on the gain?

Answer: $37,000. The $100,000 is taxed at 25 percent for a tax of $25,000. The remaining $60,000 of gain is taxed at 20 percent because Jeb's taxable income including the 25 percent gain ($575,000) places him in the 20 percent rate for long-term capital gains ($459,750+). Consequently, he owes $12,000 of tax on this portion ($60,000 × 20%). In total, Jeb owes $37,000 of tax on the gain ($25,000 + $12,000).

28 Percent Gains Gains from two types of capital assets are taxable at a maximum 28 percent rate. The first type, collectibles, consists of works of art, rugs or antiques, metals or gems, stamps or coins, alcoholic beverages, or other similar items held for more than one year.[26] The second type is qualified small business stock held for *more than five years*.[27] In general, §1202 defines qualified small business stock as stock received at *original issue* from a C corporation with a gross tax basis in its assets both before and after the issuance of no more than $50,000,000 and with at least 80 percent of the value of its assets used in the active conduct of certain qualified trades or businesses. Under this definition, many investors and employees who hold stock in closely held corporations are likely to hold qualified small business stock. When taxpayers sell qualified small business stock after holding it for more than five years, they may exclude a portion of the gain on the sale from regular taxation. Exhibit 7-4 shows the excluded portion of the gain based on the date the taxpayer acquired the stock.

EXHIBIT 7-4 Exclusion for §1202 Stock Held More Than Five Years

Acquisition Date	Exclusion	Effective Capital Gains Tax Rate on Exclusion Amount
After September 27, 2010	100%	0%
After February 17, 2009, and before September 28, 2010	75	7
After August 10, 1993, and before February 18, 2009	50	14

Source: §1202(a).

For example, using the minimum exclusion percentage of 50 percent, the effective capital gains tax rate is 14 percent on the exclusion amount.[28] Capital gains exceeding the exclusion amount are taxed as 0/15/20 percent gains.

Example 7-6

What if: Assume that Jeb (single) sold his stock in Gangbusters Inc., a qualified small business stock, for $200,000 on December 12, 2022. He acquired the stock on November 8, 2014, and his basis in the stock is $50,000. How much tax will he owe on the sale if his ordinary marginal rate is 32 percent?

Answer: $0. Because Jeb held the qualified small business stock for more than five years and because he acquired the stock when the exclusion percentage was 100 percent, he will exclude the entire $150,000 gain from income.

What if: Assume instead that Jeb sold his Gangbusters stock on December 12, 2022, but had acquired it on February 17, 2019. How much tax will he owe on the sale?

Answer: $22,500. Because Jeb didn't hold the stock for more than five years, he must recognize all $150,000 of long-term capital gain. This gain is taxed at 15 percent, yielding a total tax due of $22,500.

[26]§408(m).

[27]§1(h)(7).

[28]The maximum exclusion is the greater of $10,000,000 ($5,000,000 for married taxpayers filing separately) or 10 times the adjusted basis of the stock [see §1202(b)(1)]. The Protecting Americans from Tax Hikes Act of 2015 (PATH Act) made permanent the exclusion of 100 percent of the gain on the sale or exchange of qualified small business stock acquired after September 27, 2010, and held for more than five years. However, for alternative minimum tax (AMT) purposes, taxpayers must add back 7 percent of the excluded gain as a tax preference. Lastly, the excluded gain is not subject to the net investment income tax of 3.8 percent imposed on capital gains (and other investment income) for high-income taxpayers.

Exhibit 7-5 presents the maximum tax rates applicable to capital gains.

EXHIBIT 7-5 Classification of Capital Gains by Maximum Applicable Tax Rates

Short-Term or Long-Term	Type	Maximum Rate
Short-term	All	37%*
Long-term	Collectibles	28*
Held > 5 years	Qualified small business stock	14**
Long-term	Unrecaptured §1250 gain from depreciable realty	25*
Long-term	All remaining capital gains (and §1231 gains) not included elsewhere	20†,‡

*Lower rates will apply when the taxpayer's ordinary rate is less than the rates reflected in this exhibit.
**The maximum rate of 14 percent applies when the lowest exclusion percentage of 50 percent is in effect.
†This gain is taxed at 0 percent to the extent the taxpayer's income is below the maximum zero rate breakpoint, taxed at 20 percent to the extent the taxpayer's income is above the maximum 15 percent rate breakpoint, and taxed at 15 percent otherwise. When determining which capital gains tax rate applies, capital gains and qualified dividends that fall within the range of taxable income specified in the table are included in taxable income last. For the maximum zero and 15 percent rate breakpoints, see Exhibit 7-3.
‡High-income taxpayers may also be subject to an additional 3.8 percent net investment income tax on capital gains.

TAXES IN THE REAL WORLD The Next Big Thing?

NFTs, or non-fungible tokens, are collectible digital assets. They can represent items like images, GIFs, videos, or basically anything that exists online. NFTs are traded on various platforms such as Top Shot, OpenSea, or SuperRare and are typically bought using cryptocurrencies. Their ownership is recorded and tracked on the blockchain.

Although the IRS has not provided guidance yet on the taxation of NFTs, some basic rules are likely to apply. NFTs are likely considered collectibles, and the tax treatment will depend on whether the taxpayer is the creator of or an investor in the NFT. For creators, NFTs are treated similar to inventory in that sales will result in ordinary income taxed at ordinary tax rates and subject to self-employment taxes.

NFT investors buy and sell NFTs for investment purposes, and most taxpayers would fall into this category. NFTs are often acquired using cryptocurrencies, so purchasing an NFT would trigger a taxable event because the disposal of a cryptocurrency is treated as the sale of property. Upon the sale of the NFT, the taxpayer would have either a short- or long-term capital gain depending on how long the NFT was held. However, because NFTs are likely to be classified as collectibles, the maximum long-term capital gain tax rate on these gains will be 28 percent, with an additional 3.8 percent net investment tax for high-income taxpayers. The sale of NFTs can be reported on Form 8949 and Schedule D like other capital gains.

The IRS is increasing scrutiny of cryptocurrency and digital asset transactions and requires taxpayers to answer the question "At any time during 202X, did you receive, sell, exchange, or otherwise acquire any financial interest in any virtual currency?" on the front page of Form 1040. Because most NFT transactions involve cryptocurrency, taxpayers will need to respond "Yes" to this question.

Source: Based on Shehan Chandrasekera, "How Are Non-Fungible Tokens (NFTs) Taxed?," *Bloomberg Tax* (May 26, 2021), https://news.bloombergtax.com/daily-tax-report/how-are-non-fungible-tokens-nfts-taxed.

Netting Process for Gains and Losses To this point, our discussion of applicable tax rates for capital gains hasn't considered situations in which taxpayers recognize both capital gains and capital losses in the same year. To determine the appropriate tax treatment for the capital gains and losses recognized during the year, the taxpayer must complete a netting process. This netting process can be complex when taxpayers recognize capital losses and long-term capital gains subject to different maximum tax rates. Fortunately, for many taxpayers who do not have 25 percent or 28 percent capital gains/losses, the process is relatively simple. For these taxpayers, the netting process involves first combining short-term gains and losses and separately combining 0/15/20 percent gains and losses (including any losses carried over from prior years). If, after this step, both short-term and long-term categories yield gains—*or* if they both yield losses—the netting process is complete. Otherwise, the taxpayer will combine the short- and long-term outcomes against each other to yield a final net gain or net loss (which may be classified as either short-term or long-term depending on which outcome is greater). Net short-term capital gains are taxed at the same rate as ordinary income. Net long-term gains are taxed at 20 percent to the extent the taxpayer's taxable income exceeds the maximum 15 percent rate breakpoint based on filing status; at 0 percent to the extent taxable income is below the maximum zero rate breakpoint based on filing status; and at 15 percent otherwise.

Taxpayers can deduct up to $3,000 ($1,500 if married filing separately) of net capital losses against ordinary income. Net capital losses in excess of $3,000 ($1,500 if married filing separately) retain their short- or long-term character and are carried forward and treated as though they were incurred in the next year. Short-term losses are applied first to reduce ordinary income when the taxpayer recognizes both short- and long-term net capital losses. Capital loss carryovers for individuals never expire.

Example 7-7 shows the netting process when taxpayers have long-term capital gains and losses only in the 0/15/20 percent group.

Example 7-7

Jeb Landers has recently retired and now wants to pursue his lifelong dream of owning a sailboat. To come up with the necessary cash, he sells the following investments:

Stock	Market Value	Basis	Capital Gain/Loss	Scenario 1 Type	Scenario 2 Type
A	$40,000	$ 5,000	$ 35,000	Long	Short
B	20,000	30,000	(10,000)	Long	Short
C	20,000	12,000	8,000	Short	Long
D	17,000	28,000	(11,000)	Short	Long

Based on the information in Scenario 1, what are the amount and nature of Jeb's capital gains and losses?

Answer: $22,000 net capital gain (treated as long-term capital gain), computed as follows:

The $8,000 short-term gain on Stock C is netted against the $11,000 short-term loss on Stock D, yielding a net short-term capital loss of $3,000. Next, the $35,000 long-term gain on Stock A is netted against the $10,000 long-term loss on Stock B, producing a net long-term capital gain of $25,000. Because the outcome of combining the short-term gains and losses and combining the long-term gains and losses results in differing outcomes, the net short-term loss of $3,000 is combined with the net long-term gain of $25,000, resulting in a net capital gain of $22,000.

What if: Consider the original facts, except that Scenario 2 dictates the long- and short-term capital gains. What are the amount and character of Jeb's net gain (or loss) on the sale of the shares in this situation?

Answer: $22,000 net short-term capital gain, computed as follows:

The short-term gain from Stock A is netted with the loss from Stock B to produce a $25,000 net short-term capital gain [$35,000 + ($10,000)]. Next, the loss from Stock D and the gain from Stock C are combined to produce a net long-term capital loss of $3,000 [($11,000) + $8,000]. The results from the short-term netting and long-term netting are combined to reach a $22,000 net short-term capital gain [$25,000 + ($3,000)].

When taxpayers have long-term capital gains/losses that include 25 percent and 28 percent gains, the netting process becomes more complex. To briefly summarize, the netting process separates capital gains and losses into short-term and three different long-term categories (based on the maximum rate applicable to the long-term gains). Although the process is complex, the underlying intuition is to have taxpayers net all long-term capital gains and losses together, allowing long-term losses to offset the highest rate long-term gains first. Then, taxpayers use **net long-term capital losses** to offset net short-term gains or **net short-term capital losses** to offset net long-term gains.

After completing the netting process, taxpayers must calculate the tax consequences of the resulting outcomes. As before, **net short-term capital gains** are taxed at the same rate as ordinary income. **Net long-term capital gains** are taxed at a maximum of 28 percent if from the collectible and §1202 category, a maximum of 25 percent if from the unrecaptured §1250 gain category, or 0/15/20 percent for all other long-term capital gains. In the 0/15/20 percent category, net long-term gains are taxed at 20 percent to the extent the taxpayer's taxable income exceeds the maximum 15 percent rate breakpoint based on filing status; at 0 percent to the extent taxable income is below the maximum zero rate breakpoint based on filing status; and at 15 percent otherwise.[29] We discuss the taxation of capital gains in more detail later in the chapter.

The following provides a simplified version of the capital gains and losses netting process when taxpayers sell capital assets with 28 percent gains and 25 percent types of gains and losses. The chapter appendix provides a more detailed step-by-step guide of the capital gains netting process.

To begin, sort all capital gains and losses into two primary categories: short-term and long-term. The long-term capital gains and losses then must be sorted further into three additional categories: 28 percent, 25 percent, and 0/15/20 percent. Combine gains and losses within each of the four categories to result in a net gain or net loss in each (the 25 percent category will never have a loss).

If after netting each category, a net loss remains in the 28 percent or 0/15/20 percent category, these losses will be used to offset the highest taxed gains in the long-term category first (e.g., 28 percent, then 25 percent, then 0/15/20 percent), moving to the next highest taxed category as the gains in each category are completely offset with losses.

Once all the long-term losses have been used to offset long-term gains, any remaining long-term losses may be used to offset net short-term gains (if any). If, instead, long-term gains remain after using all long-term losses, net short-term losses may be used to offset the remaining long-term gains, beginning with the highest taxed gains, until the losses are exhausted or no gains remain. The gain remaining is called a **net capital gain** (net long-term capital gains in excess of net short-term capital losses).

At this point in the process, two possible scenarios emerge: Only gains remain or only losses remain in the groups. The remaining capital losses are treated as discussed above. The tax on the remaining gains is determined as described in the next section.

Example 7-8 shows the netting process using the simplified process when taxpayers also sell long-term capital assets and recognize gains subject to the 25 percent and/or 28 percent capital gains rates.

Example 7-8

What if: Assume that in addition to selling stocks, Jeb sold gold coins and a rental home as follows:

Capital Asset	Market Value	Tax Basis	Capital Gain/Loss	Scenario 1 Type
A stock	$ 40,000	$ 5,000	$ 35,000	Long 0/15/20%
B stock	20,000	30,000	(10,000)	Long 0/15/20%
C stock	20,000	12,000	8,000	Short
D stock	17,000	28,000	(11,000)	Short
Gold coins	4,000	3,000	1,000	Long 28%
Rental home	200,000	80,000	120,000	Long 25% and 0/15/20%*
Overall gain			$143,000	

*$50,000 of the gain is 25 percent gain and the remaining $70,000 is 0/15/20 percent gain.

(continued on page 7-16)

[29]Note that the maximum zero rate breakpoint does not coincide directly with the end of a tax bracket amount for any filing status. Similarly, the maximum 15 percent rate breakpoint does not match up with the end of a tax bracket.

Assuming Jeb did not sell any other capital assets during the year, he recognizes an overall capital gain of $143,000. What is (are) the maximum tax rate(s) applicable to this gain?

Answer: $95,000 of gain is subject to a 0/15/20 percent maximum rate and $48,000 of gain is subject to a 25 percent maximum rate, computed as follows:

Jeb first sorts the gains and losses into short-term and long-term categories, resulting in a ($3,000) net short-term capital loss and long-term amounts totaling $146,000. Jeb will next sort the long-term amounts into gains and losses. The gain from Stock A and the loss from Stock B are placed in the 0/15/20 percent category, the gain from the gold coins is placed in the 28 percent category, $50,000 of the gain from the sale of the rental home is placed in the 25 percent category, and the remaining $70,000 gain from the rental home is placed in the 0/15/20 percent category. The sum of the gains and losses in each category results in a 28 percent net gain of $1,000, a 25 percent gain of $50,000, and a net $95,000 gain in the 0/15/20 percent category.

Jeb then uses the $3,000 net short-term capital loss to offset the $1,000 gain in the 28 percent category (the highest taxed gain). The remaining $2,000 loss [$1,000 gain on gold + ($3,000) net short-term loss] next offsets gains in the 25 percent category (the next highest taxed gain), resulting in $48,000 gain [$50,000 gain from the rental home + ($2,000) remaining net short-term loss] taxed at 25 percent.

The netting process is complete at this point because the net short-term capital loss does not offset all of the gains in the long-term rate categories and only gains remain in the long-term rate categories.

Jeb's netting process is reflected in the following table:

Description	Short-Term	Long-Term 28%	Long-Term 25%	Long-Term 0/15/20%
Stock C	$8,000			
Stock D	(11,000)			
Step 1:	(3,000)			
Coins		$ 1,000		
Unrecaptured §1250 Gain			$50,000	
Remaining Gain from Rental Property				$70,000
Stock A				35,000
Stock B				(10,000)
Step 2:		$ 1,000	$50,000	$95,000
Step 6:	(3,000) →	→ (3,000)		
		$(2,000) →	→ (2,000)	
			$48,000	
Summary			$48,000	$95,000
Maximum Rate			25%	0/15/20%

THE KEY FACTS

25 Percent and 28 Percent Rate Capital Gains

- Certain gains from the sale of depreciable real property held long term are taxed at a maximum rate of 25 percent (unrecaptured §1250 gain).
- Gains from collectibles and from qualified small business stock not held for five years are taxed at a maximum rate of 28 percent.
- When taxpayers have 25 percent or 28 percent rate capital gains, the netting process requires that losses be applied to higher-rate groups before lower-rate groups.
- When taxable income without long-term capital gains exceeds the maximum 15 percent rate amount, 25 and 28 percent capital gains are taxed at their maximum rate. Otherwise, applicable capital gains rates must be adjusted to reflect their inclusion in lower ordinary income rate brackets.

Reporting capital gains and losses. When taxpayers sell capital assets, they report the details of their sales on Form 8949 (dates of sale and purchase are additional items provided on Form 8949).[30] Brokerage firms will provide taxpayers with details of securities transactions on Form 1099-B (Exhibit 7-6). Taxpayers will be required to maintain their own documentation for other capital asset sales. After listing their sales on Form 8949, taxpayers then use Schedule D to summarize the sales and apply the basic capital gains netting process. Exhibits 7-7 and 7-8 illustrate how Jeb would report his stock sales in Example 7-7, Scenario 1.

[30]If the taxpayer receives Form 1099-B from their broker and no adjustments are required, the taxpayer may aggregate their short-term (long-term) transactions reported on their Form 1099-Bs as a one-line entry directly on Schedule D, line 1a (8a). In this case, Form 8949 is not required for these transactions.

EXHIBIT 7-6 Jeb's Form 1099-B

☐ VOID ☐ CORRECTED

PAYER'S name, street address, city or town, state or province, country, ZIP or foreign postal code, and telephone no. CONTINENTAL FINANCIAL SERVICES LLC 844 WASHINGTON BLVD JERSEY CITY, NJ 07310	Applicable checkbox on Form 8949 Box D	OMB No. 1545-0715 2021 Form 1099-B	**Proceeds From Broker and Barter Exchange Transactions**
	1a Description of property (Example: 100 sh. XYZ Co.) 100 SH STOCK A		
	1b Date acquired 11/07/18	1c Date sold or disposed 3/08/21	
PAYER'S TIN 19-****245 / RECIPIENT'S TIN ***-**-3344	1d Proceeds $ 40,000	1e Cost or other basis $ 5,000	**Copy 1 For State Tax Department**
	1f Accrued market discount $	1g Wash sale loss disallowed $	
RECIPIENT'S name JEB LANDERS	2 Short-term gain or loss ☐ Long-term gain or loss ☑ Ordinary ☐	3 If checked, proceeds from: Collectibles ☐ QOF ☐	
Street address (including apt. no.) 1234 MAIN ST	4 Federal income tax withheld $	5 If checked, noncovered security ☐	
City or town, state or province, country, and ZIP or foreign postal code KANSAS CITY, KS 77379-4939	6 Reported to IRS: Gross proceeds ☑ Net proceeds ☐	7 If checked, loss is not allowed based on amount in 1d ☐	
Account number (see instructions)	8 Profit or (loss) realized in 2021 on closed contracts $	9 Unrealized profit or (loss) on open contracts—12/31/2020 $	
CUSIP number / FATCA filing requirement ☐	10 Unrealized profit or (loss) on open contracts—12/31/2021 $	11 Aggregate profit or (loss) on contracts $	
14 State name / 15 State identification no. / 16 State tax withheld $ $	12 If checked, basis reported to IRS ☐	13 Bartering $	

Form 1099-B www.irs.gov/Form1099B Department of the Treasury - Internal Revenue Service

Source: irs.gov.

Calculating Tax Liability on Net Capital Gains So, we've learned how to determine the *maximum* tax rates applicable to different types of capital gains. How do we go about actually calculating how these gains affect the taxpayer's tax liability? Follow these basic guidelines:

- If the taxpayer's ordinary income (total taxable income excluding long-term capital gains and qualified dividends) is above the maximum 15 percent rate breakpoint, the capital gains for each of the 0/15/20 percent, 25 percent, and 28 percent groups are taxed at their maximum rates.
- If the taxpayer's taxable income (including capital gains and qualified dividends) is below the maximum zero rate breakpoint, the capital gains for the 0/15/20 percent group are taxed at 0 percent, and the 25 percent and 28 percent gains are taxed at the taxpayer's ordinary rate. Thus, the taxpayer's tax is calculated using the ordinary tax rates on the taxpayer's taxable income including the 25 percent and 28 percent gains and excluding the 0/15/20 percent gains, which are taxed at 0 percent.
- For other situations, use the following steps to determine the tax on the gains:[31]

Step 1: Fill up the 10, 12, 22, 24, 32, 35, and 37 percent tax rate brackets with taxable income, exclusive of long-term capital gains (and qualified dividends) subject to preferential rates.

Step 2: Next, if there is any remaining space below the beginning of the 32 percent bracket after Step 1, add any 25 percent rate capital gains to the amount from Step 1 until reaching the end of the 24 percent bracket. This 25 percent rate capital gain is taxed at the ordinary rates provided in the tax rate schedule.

Step 3: Next, if, after including all of the 25 percent gain (Step 2), there is still space remaining below the beginning of the 32 percent bracket, add any 28 percent rate

[31]§1(h).

EXHIBIT 7-7 Jeb's Form 8949

Form **8949**

Department of the Treasury
Internal Revenue Service

Sales and Other Dispositions of Capital Assets

▶ Go to *www.irs.gov/Form8949* for instructions and the latest information.

▶ File with your Schedule D to list your transactions for lines 1b, 2, 3, 8b, 9, and 10 of Schedule D.

OMB No. 1545-0074

2021

Attachment Sequence No. **12A**

Name(s) shown on return: **Jeb Landers**

Social security number or taxpayer identification number

Before you check Box A, B, or C below, see whether you received any Form(s) 1099-B or substitute statement(s) from your broker. A substitute statement will have the same information as Form 1099-B. Either will show whether your basis (usually your cost) was reported to the IRS by your broker and may even tell you which box to check.

Part I **Short-Term.** Transactions involving capital assets you held 1 year or less are generally short-term (see instructions). For long-term transactions, see page 2.

Note: You may aggregate all short-term transactions reported on Form(s) 1099-B showing basis was reported to the IRS and for which no adjustments or codes are required. Enter the totals directly on Schedule D, line 1a; you aren't required to report these transactions on Form 8949 (see instructions).

You *must* check Box A, B, *or* C below. Check only one box. If more than one box applies for your short-term transactions, complete a separate Form 8949, page 1, for each applicable box. If you have more short-term transactions than will fit on this page for one or more of the boxes, complete as many forms with the same box checked as you need.

☑ **(A)** Short-term transactions reported on Form(s) 1099-B showing basis was reported to the IRS (see **Note** above)

☐ **(B)** Short-term transactions reported on Form(s) 1099-B showing basis **wasn't** reported to the IRS

☐ **(C)** Short-term transactions not reported to you on Form 1099-B

1 (a) Description of property (Example: 100 sh. XYZ Co.)	(b) Date acquired (Mo., day, yr.)	(c) Date sold or disposed of (Mo., day, yr.)	(d) Proceeds (sales price) (see instructions)	(e) Cost or other basis. See the **Note** below and see *Column (e)* in the separate instructions	Adjustment, if any, to gain or loss. If you enter an amount in column (g), enter a code in column (f). See the separate instructions. (f) Code(s) from instructions	(g) Amount of adjustment	(h) Gain or (loss). Subtract column (e) from column (d) and combine the result with column (g)
Stock C	**3/1/22**	**11/15/22**	**20,000**	**12,000**			**8,000**
Stock D	**2/2/22**	**6/9/21**	**17,000**	**28,000**			**(11,000)**
2 Totals. Add the amounts in columns (d), (e), (g), and (h) (subtract negative amounts). Enter each total here and include on your Schedule D, **line 1b** (if **Box A** above is checked), **line 2** (if **Box B** above is checked), or **line 3** (if **Box C** above is checked) ▶			**37,000**	**40,000**			**(3,000)**

Note: If you checked Box A above but the basis reported to the IRS was incorrect, enter in column (e) the basis as reported to the IRS, and enter an adjustment in column (g) to correct the basis. See *Column (g)* in the separate instructions for how to figure the amount of the adjustment.

For Paperwork Reduction Act Notice, see your tax return instructions. Cat. No. 37768Z Form **8949** (2021)

EXHIBIT 7-7 Jeb's Form 8949 (*continued*)

Form 8949 (2021) Attachment Sequence No. **12A** Page **2**

Name(s) shown on return. Name and SSN or taxpayer identification no. not required if shown on other side	**Social security number or taxpayer identification number**
Jeb Landers	

Before you check Box D, E, or F below, see whether you received any Form(s) 1099-B or substitute statement(s) from your broker. A substitute statement will have the same information as Form 1099-B. Either will show whether your basis (usually your cost) was reported to the IRS by your broker and may even tell you which box to check.

Part II **Long-Term.** Transactions involving capital assets you held more than 1 year are generally long-term (see instructions). For short-term transactions, see page 1.

Note: You may aggregate all long-term transactions reported on Form(s) 1099-B showing basis was reported to the IRS and for which no adjustments or codes are required. Enter the totals directly on Schedule D, line 8a; you aren't required to report these transactions on Form 8949 (see instructions).

You *must* check Box D, E, *or* F below. Check only one box. If more than one box applies for your long-term transactions, complete a separate Form 8949, page 2, for each applicable box. If you have more long-term transactions than will fit on this page for one or more of the boxes, complete as many forms with the same box checked as you need.

☑ **(D)** Long-term transactions reported on Form(s) 1099-B showing basis was reported to the IRS (see **Note** above)
☐ **(E)** Long-term transactions reported on Form(s) 1099-B showing basis **wasn't** reported to the IRS
☐ **(F)** Long-term transactions not reported to you on Form 1099-B

1 (a) Description of property (Example: 100 sh. XYZ Co.)	(b) Date acquired (Mo., day, yr.)	(c) Date sold or disposed of (Mo., day, yr.)	(d) Proceeds (sales price) (see instructions)	(e) Cost or other basis. See the **Note** below and see *Column (e)* in the separate instructions	**Adjustment, if any, to gain or loss.** If you enter an amount in column (g), enter a code in column (f). **See the separate instructions.** (f) Code(s) from instructions	(g) Amount of adjustment	(h) **Gain or (loss).** Subtract column (e) from column (d) and combine the result with column (g)
Stock A	**11/7/19**	**3/6/22**	**40,000**	**5,000**			**35,000**
Stock B	**7/6/18**	**9/1/22**	**20,000**	**30,000**			**(10,000)**
2 Totals. Add the amounts in columns (d), (e), (g), and (h) (subtract negative amounts). Enter each total here and include on your Schedule D, **line 8b** (if **Box D** above is checked), **line 9** (if **Box E** above is checked), or **line 10** (if **Box F** above is checked) ▶			**60,000**	**35,000**			**25,000**

Note: If you checked Box D above but the basis reported to the IRS was incorrect, enter in column (e) the basis as reported to the IRS, and enter an adjustment in column (g) to correct the basis. See *Column (g)* in the separate instructions for how to figure the amount of the adjustment.

Form **8949** (2021)

Source: irs.gov.

EXHIBIT 7-8 Jeb's Schedule D

SCHEDULE D (Form 1040)

Department of the Treasury Internal Revenue Service (99)

Capital Gains and Losses

▶ Attach to Form 1040, 1040-SR, or 1040-NR.
▶ Go to *www.irs.gov/ScheduleD* for instructions and the latest information.
▶ Use Form 8949 to list your transactions for lines 1b, 2, 3, 8b, 9, and 10.

OMB No. 1545-0074
2021
Attachment Sequence No. 12

Name(s) shown on return: Jeb Landers | Your social security number

Did you dispose of any investment(s) in a qualified opportunity fund during the tax year? ☐ Yes ☐ No
If "Yes," attach Form 8949 and see its instructions for additional requirements for reporting your gain or loss.

Part I **Short-Term Capital Gains and Losses—Generally Assets Held One Year or Less** (see instructions)

See instructions for how to figure the amounts to enter on the lines below. This form may be easier to complete if you round off cents to whole dollars.	(d) Proceeds (sales price)	(e) Cost (or other basis)	(g) Adjustments to gain or loss from Form(s) 8949, Part I, line 2, column (g)	(h) Gain or (loss) Subtract column (e) from column (d) and combine the result with column (g)
1a Totals for all short-term transactions reported on Form 1099-B for which basis was reported to the IRS and for which you have no adjustments (see instructions). However, if you choose to report all these transactions on Form 8949, leave this line blank and go to line 1b				
1b Totals for all transactions reported on Form(s) 8949 with **Box A** checked	37,000	40,000		(3,000)
2 Totals for all transactions reported on Form(s) 8949 with **Box B** checked				
3 Totals for all transactions reported on Form(s) 8949 with **Box C** checked				

4 Short-term gain from Form 6252 and short-term gain or (loss) from Forms 4684, 6781, and 8824	4	
5 Net short-term gain or (loss) from partnerships, S corporations, estates, and trusts from Schedule(s) K-1	5	
6 Short-term capital loss carryover. Enter the amount, if any, from line 8 of your **Capital Loss Carryover Worksheet** in the instructions	6	( )
7 **Net short-term capital gain or (loss).** Combine lines 1a through 6 in column (h). If you have any long-term capital gains or losses, go to Part II below. Otherwise, go to Part III on the back	7	(3,000)

Part II **Long-Term Capital Gains and Losses—Generally Assets Held More Than One Year** (see instructions)

See instructions for how to figure the amounts to enter on the lines below. This form may be easier to complete if you round off cents to whole dollars.	(d) Proceeds (sales price)	(e) Cost (or other basis)	(g) Adjustments to gain or loss from Form(s) 8949, Part II, line 2, column (g)	(h) Gain or (loss) Subtract column (e) from column (d) and combine the result with column (g)
8a Totals for all long-term transactions reported on Form 1099-B for which basis was reported to the IRS and for which you have no adjustments (see instructions). However, if you choose to report all these transactions on Form 8949, leave this line blank and go to line 8b				
8b Totals for all transactions reported on Form(s) 8949 with **Box D** checked	60,000	35,000		25,000
9 Totals for all transactions reported on Form(s) 8949 with **Box E** checked				
10 Totals for all transactions reported on Form(s) 8949 with **Box F** checked				

11 Gain from Form 4797, Part I; long-term gain from Forms 2439 and 6252; and long-term gain or (loss) from Forms 4684, 6781, and 8824	11	
12 Net long-term gain or (loss) from partnerships, S corporations, estates, and trusts from Schedule(s) K-1	12	
13 Capital gain distributions. See the instructions	13	
14 Long-term capital loss carryover. Enter the amount, if any, from line 13 of your **Capital Loss Carryover Worksheet** in the instructions	14	( )
15 **Net long-term capital gain or (loss).** Combine lines 8a through 14 in column (h). Then, go to Part III on the back	15	25,000

For Paperwork Reduction Act Notice, see your tax return instructions. Cat. No. 11338H **Schedule D (Form 1040) 2021**

Data provided on Form 1040 Schedule D.
Source: irs.gov.

capital gain until reaching the end of the 24 percent bracket. This 28 percent rate capital gain is taxed at the ordinary rates provided in the tax rate schedule.

Step 4: Next, if there is room below the maximum zero rate breakpoint after applying Step 3, add any 0/15/20 percent rate capital gain until reaching the maximum zero rate breakpoint. This 0/15/20 percent rate capital gain is taxed at 0 percent. If there is additional 0/15/20 percent capital gain that increases taxable income above the maximum zero rate breakpoint, add the 0/15/20 percent capital gain until reaching the maximum 15 percent rate breakpoint. This 0/15/20 percent capital gain is taxed at 15 percent. If there is additional 0/15/20 percent capital gain that increases taxable income above the maximum 15 percent rate breakpoint, this 0/15/20 percent capital gain is taxed at 20 percent.

Step 5: Finally, any remaining 25 percent rate capital gain (not taxed in Step 2) is taxed at 25 percent. Any remaining 28 percent rate capital gain (not taxed in Step 3) is taxed at 28 percent. If, however, a taxpayer's tax liability would be lower using the ordinary tax rates for all ordinary income and capital gains (which is possible but not typical), the taxpayer would simply determine their tax liability based on ordinary tax rates.

Example 7-9

What if: Let's return to the facts of Example 7-8, in which Jeb recognized a $48,000 25 percent net capital gain and a $95,000 0/15/20 percent net capital gain. Also, assume that Jeb's taxable income before considering the net capital gains is $10,000. His filing status is single. What is Jeb's gross tax liability for the year?

Answer: $22,627, computed as follows:

Amount and Type of Income	Applicable Rate	Tax	Explanation
$10,000; ordinary	10%	$ 1,000.00	$10,000 × 10%. All of Jeb's $10,000 of ordinary income is taxed at 10 percent (see single tax rate schedule for this and other computations).
$275; 25 percent rate capital gains	10%	27.50	$275 × 10%. The end of Jeb's 10 percent bracket is $10,275 minus $10,000 already taxed. Jeb's ordinary tax rate of 10 percent is lower than the maximum 25 percent rate for these gains, so it is taxed at the lower ordinary rate.
$31,500; 25 percent rate capital gains	12%	3,780.00	$31,500 × 12%. The end of Jeb's 12 percent bracket is $41,775 minus $10,275 ($10,000 + $275) already taxed. Jeb's ordinary tax rate of 12 percent is lower than the maximum 25 percent rate for these gains, so it is taxed at the lower ordinary rate.
$16,225; 25 percent rate capital gains	22%	3,569.50	$16,225 × 22%. $48,000 total 25 percent gain minus $31,500 gain already taxed at 12 percent and $275 taxed at 10 percent. Jeb's ordinary tax rate of 22 percent is lower than the maximum 25 percent rate for these gains, so it is taxed at the lower ordinary rate.
$95,000; 15 percent rate capital gains	15%	14,250.00	$95,000 × 15%. All of the 15 percent gain is between Jeb's maximum zero rate breakpoint ($41,675) and the maximum 15 percent rate breakpoint ($459,750), so it is all taxed at 15 percent.
Gross tax liability		**$22,627.00**	

(continued on page 7-22)

What if: Suppose Jeb's 0/15/20 percent capital gains were $450,000 rather than $95,000. What is Jeb's gross tax liability for the year?

Answer: $78,289.50, computed as follows:

Amount and Type of Income	Applicable Rate	Tax	Explanation
$10,000; ordinary	10%	$ 1,000.00	$10,000 × 10%. All of Jeb's $10,000 of ordinary income is taxed at 10 percent (see single tax rate schedule for this and other computations).
$275; ordinary	10%	27.50	$275 × 10%. The end of Jeb's 10 percent bracket is $10,275 minus $10,000 already taxed. Jeb's ordinary tax rate of 10 percent is lower than the maximum 25 percent rate for these gains, so it is taxed at the lower ordinary rate.
$31,500; 25 percent rate capital gains	12%	3,780.00	$31,500 × 12%. The end of Jeb's 12 percent bracket is $41,775 minus $10,275 ($10,000 + $275) already taxed. Jeb's ordinary tax rate of 12 percent is lower than the maximum 25 percent rate for these gains, so it is taxed at the lower ordinary rate.
$16,225; 25 percent rate capital gains	22%	3,569.50	$16,225 × 22%. $48,000 total 25 percent gain minus $31,500 gain already taxed at 12 percent and $275 taxed at 10 percent. Jeb's ordinary tax rate of 22 percent is lower than the maximum 25 percent rate for these gains, so it is taxed at the lower ordinary rate.
$401,750; 0/15/20 percent rate capital gains	15%	60,262.50	$401,750 × 15%. $401,750 represents the 0/15/20 percent gain that is below the maximum 15 percent rate breakpoint ($459,750) after including the other taxable amounts ($459,750 – $16,225 – $31,500 – $275 – $10,000). This gain is taxed at 15 percent.
$48,250; 0/15/20 percent rate capital gains	20%	9,650.00	$48,250 × 20%. The remaining 0/15/20 percent gain ($450,000 – $401,750) that is above the maximum 15 percent rate breakpoint ($459,750). This gain is taxed at the maximum 20 percent.
Gross tax liability		**$78,289.50**	

TAXES IN THE REAL WORLD Ooops! Even the IRS Doesn't Get It Right All the Time!

The Tax Cuts and Jobs Act (TCJA) of 2017 was a pervasive change to the tax system, and one of the key political issues was that the system needed to be simplified. President Trump directed Treasury to simplify the tax forms such that individual taxpayers could file their returns on forms the size of a postcard. The jury is still out as to whether the new forms simplified taxpayers' filing, but one thing is for sure . . . it is not easier if the form is incorrect!

That's right! The IRS made an error in the Tax Worksheet included in the Instructions for Schedule D (Form 1040). This form and worksheet report taxpayers' capital gains and losses and guide them through the netting process discussed in this chapter. For taxpayers that reported 28 percent (collectible) gains/losses or 25 percent (unrecaptured §1250) gains, the new schedule did not correctly calculate the tax with the new TCJA regular tax rates and brackets. The IRS corrected the calculation on May 16, 2019, so any tax returns filed with forms downloaded after that date will be unaffected.

The IRS says that taxpayers that filed before the correction was made do not need to file an amended return. "The IRS is reviewing all potentially impacted filed returns, including those filed before May 16, 2019, and will send correction notices to any affected taxpayers. Taxpayers who overpaid their tax due to the error will receive refunds. If you filed an amended return because you opted to recalculate your regular tax using the new worksheet to see if it changed, the IRS is currently processing those amended returns."

Source: IRS, "Error in Tax Calculation in Schedule D Tax Worksheet (Form 1040)," www.irs.gov/forms-pubs/update-to-error-in-tax-calculation-in-2018-schedule-d-tax-worksheet-form-1041.

Limits for Capital Loss Deductions

We've discussed the general rule that taxpayers may deduct capital losses against capital gains in the netting process, and that individual taxpayers may deduct up to \$3,000 (\$1,500 if married filing separately) of net capital losses against ordinary income in a given year. This general rule is subject to certain exceptions, however, as described below.

Losses on the Sale of Personal-Use Assets We've seen that personal-use assets fall within the category of capital assets. When taxpayers sell personal-use assets, what are the tax consequences? Consider an engaged taxpayer who calls off the wedding plans. After getting the ring back from his former partner, the taxpayer sells the engagement ring for more than its purchase price. Does he recognize a taxable gain? Absolutely—the gain from the sale of a personal-use asset is taxable even though it was not purchased for its appreciation potential. The tax rate on the gain depends on the amount of time between the purchase and selling date, and on the netting process involving the seller's other capital gains and losses during the year. What if a taxpayer sold their car for less than the purchase price? Can the seller deduct the capital loss? Unfortunately, no—losses on the sale of personal-use assets are *not* deductible and therefore never become part of the netting process.

Capital Losses on Sales to Related Persons When taxpayers sell capital assets at a loss to related persons, they are not able to deduct the loss.[32] As we describe in detail in the Property Dispositions chapter, the related person acquiring the asset may eventually be allowed to deduct all, a portion, or none of the disallowed loss on a subsequent sale.

Wash Sales Consider the case of a taxpayer attempting to do some tax planning near the end of the year: She has invested in the stock of several corporations; some of these investments have appreciated, while others have declined in value. The taxpayer wants to capture the tax benefit of the stock losses in the current year to offset ordinary income (up to \$3,000) or to offset other capital gains she has already recognized during the year. However, she can't deduct the losses until she sells the stock. Why might this be a problem? If the taxpayer believes that the stocks with unrealized losses are likely to appreciate in the near future, she may prefer *not* to sell those stocks but rather to keep them in her investment portfolio. What might this taxpayer do to deduct the losses while continuing to hold the investment in the stocks? For one, she might be tempted to sell the stocks and then immediately buy them back. Or she might buy more of the same stock and then sell the stock she originally held to recognize the losses. With this strategy, she hopes to realize (and then recognize or deduct) the losses and, at the end of the day, still hold the stocks in her investment portfolio.

Although that might sound like a great plan, certain **wash sale** tax rules prevent this strategy from accomplishing the taxpayer's objective.[33] A wash sale occurs when an investor sells or trades stock or securities at a loss *and* within 30 days *either before or after* the day of sale buys substantially identical stocks or securities.[34] Because the day of sale is included but not the day of acquisition, the 30 days before and after period creates a 61-day window during which the wash sale provisions may apply. When the wash sale provisions apply to a sale of stock, realized losses are not recognized; instead, the amount of *the unrecognized loss is added to the basis of the newly*

[32]§267(a).

[33]§1091.

[34]Substantially identical stocks or securities include contracts or options to buy substantially identical securities. However, corporate bonds and preferred stock are not generally considered substantially identical to common stock of the same corporation.

acquired stock. Congress created this rule to prevent taxpayers from accelerating losses on securities that have declined in value without actually altering their investment in the securities. The 61-day period ensures that taxpayers cannot deduct losses from stock sales without exposing themselves to the risk that the stock they sold will subsequently increase in value. Interestingly, because Bitcoin is considered property rather than a security, absent new legislation, the wash sale provisions don't apply to Bitcoin (or other crypto assets). Given the volatile nature of Bitcoin, many Bitcoin investors sell and immediately buy the Bitcoin back in order to recognize the losses while still owning the Bitcoin. Some suggest that the fact that the wash sale rules don't apply to Bitcoin contributes to its volatility.

Example 7-10

What if: Suppose Courtney owns 100 shares of Cisco stock that she purchased in June 2019 for $50 a share. On December 21, 2022, Courtney sells the shares for $40 a share to generate cash for the holidays. This sale generates a capital loss of $1,000 [$4,000 sale proceeds (100 × $40) – $5,000 tax basis ($50 × 100)]. Later, however, Courtney decides that Cisco might be a good long-term investment. On January 3, 2023 (13 days later), Courtney purchases 100 shares of Cisco stock for $41 a share ($4,100).

How much of the realized $1,000 long-term capital loss can Courtney recognize or deduct on her 2022 tax return?

Answer: Zero. Because Courtney sold the stock at a loss and purchased the same stock within the 61-day period centered on the date of sale (30 days before December 21 and 30 days after December 21), the wash sale rules disallow the loss in 2022. Had Courtney waited another 18 days to repurchase the Cisco shares, she could have avoided the wash sale rules. In that case, under the general rules for capital loss deductibility, Courtney *would* be able to deduct a $1,000 long-term capital loss from the sale against her ordinary income on her 2022 income tax return.

What tax basis will Courtney have in the Cisco stock she purchased (or repurchased) on January 3, 2023?

Answer: $5,100. Under the wash sale rules, Courtney adds the $1,000 disallowed loss to the basis of the stock she purchased on January 3. Thus, she now owns 100 shares of Cisco stock with a $5,100 basis in the shares, which is $1,000 more than she paid for it.

What if: How much of the loss would Courtney have recognized if she had only purchased 40 shares of Cisco stock instead of 100 shares on January 3, 2023?

Answer: $600. The wash sale rules disallow the loss to the extent taxpayers acquire other shares in the 61-day window. In this situation, Courtney only acquired 40 percent (40 of 100) of the shares she sold at a loss within the window. Consequently, she must disallow 40 percent, or $400, of the loss, and she is allowed to deduct the remaining $600 loss.

THE KEY FACTS

Capital Gains and Losses

- Tax on the appreciation of capital assets is deferred until the asset is sold.
  - The longer the holding period, the greater the after-tax rate of return for a given before-tax rate of return.
- Tracking the basis of stock sold
  - FIFO method is the default.
  - Specific identification is allowed.
- Capital gains and losses
  - Long-term capital gain if the asset is held more than a year before sold; short-term otherwise.
  - Net long-term capital gains are taxed at the maximum 0/15/20 percent rate.
  - ($3,000) net capital loss is deductible annually against ordinary income.
  - Losses on personal-use assets are not deductible.
  - Losses on wash sales are not deductible but are added to the basis of new shares acquired.
- Basic tax planning strategies
  - Hold capital assets for more than a year before selling.
  - Sell loss capital assets to offset gains.

ETHICS

In December, T. D. Weber evaluates his stock portfolio and finds that his DLW Inc. common stock has declined in value since he purchased it. He decides to sell the DLW stock on December 15. However, he would like to retain an interest in the company. So, knowing that he needs to avoid the wash sale rules, when he sells the common stock on December 15 and deducts the loss on his return for the year, T. D. simultaneously purchases an equivalent amount of preferred stock in DLW Inc. On January 17 of the next year, he sells the preferred stock and repurchases DLW common stock. What do you think of his strategy from an ethical perspective?

Balancing Tax Planning Strategies for Capital Assets with Other Goals

When taxpayers invest in capital assets and hold the assets for more than a year, they receive at least two benefits. First, they are able to defer recognizing gains on the assets until they sell them—the longer the deferral period, the lower the present value of the capital gains tax when taxpayers ultimately sell the assets. Second, they pay taxes on the gains at preferential rates. These tax advantages provide taxpayers with greater after-tax rates of return on these investments than they would obtain from less tax-favored assets that earn equivalent before-tax rates of return. Investors who quickly sell investments pay taxes on gains at higher, ordinary rates and incur significantly greater transaction costs than those who hold them for a longer period. Nevertheless, taxpayers should balance the tax benefits available for holding assets with the risk that the asset values will have declined by the time they want to sell the assets.

Example 7-11

What if: Assume Courtney decides to purchase Intel stock for $100,000. She plans to hold half the shares for five years to purchase the Park City home and hold the other half for eight years to pay for Deron's education. If the Intel stock grows at a constant 8 percent before-tax rate and does not pay any dividends, how much cash will Courtney accumulate after taxes for the Park City home?

Answer: $69,946, computed as follows:

Description	Amount	Explanation
(1) Proceeds from sale	$ 73,466	[$50,000 × (1 + .08)^5]
(2) Basis in fund shares	50,000	
(3) Gain realized on sale	$ 23,466	(1) − (2)
(4) Tax rate on gain	× 15%	Preferential rate for long-term capital gain.*
(5) Tax on gain	$ 3,520	(3) × (4)
After-tax cash for Park City home	**$69,946**	(1) − (5)

*Assumes Courtney doesn't have any capital losses.

How much cash will Courtney accumulate after taxes for Deron's education?

Answer: $86,165, computed as follows:

Description	Amount	Explanation
(1) Proceeds from sale	$92,547	[$50,000 × (1 + .08)^8]
(2) Basis in fund shares	50,000	
(3) Gain realized on sale	$42,547	(1) − (2)
(4) Tax rate on gain	× 15%	Preferential rate for long-term capital gain.*
(5) Tax on gain	$ 6,382	(3) × (4)
After-tax cash for education goal	**$86,165**	(1) − (5)

*Assumes Courtney doesn't have capital losses.

When investing in capital assets, taxpayers run the risk that some of their investments may decline in value. Thus, a productive strategy for managing investments in capital assets is to sell investments with built-in losses. This strategy is commonly referred to as "loss harvesting." By selectively selling loss assets, taxpayers can reduce their taxes by deducting up to $3,000 against their ordinary income and by reducing the amount of capital gains that would otherwise be subject to tax during the year. This is particularly beneficial for taxpayers who have short-term capital gains that will be taxed at higher ordinary rates absent offsetting capital losses. Note, however, that taxpayers should not sell investments to gain tax benefits if they believe the potential economic benefit of holding the investment outweighs the tax benefits of selling the stock. Also, keep in mind that capital losses on stock sales may not be deductible due to the wash sale rules discussed above.

PORTFOLIO INCOME SUMMARY

As we've discussed the tax consequences of various investments up to this point in the chapter, we have proceeded from the least tax-advantaged (taxed annually at ordinary rates) to the most tax-advantaged (tax deferred at capital gains rates). By moving along this continuum from investments taxed annually at ordinary rates (corporate bonds[35]) to investments taxed annually at capital gains rates (dividend-paying stock), investors are in essence employing the conversion planning strategy referred to repeatedly throughout this text. As they move from dividend-paying stock to growth stock, which provides tax deferral in addition to preferential tax rates, taxpayers combine the conversion strategy with the basic strategy of shifting income from one time period to another.

In this chapter and elsewhere in this text, we emphasize that tax planning must not be done in a vacuum or without considering all relevant parties and taxpayers' economic and personal objectives. Because investments typically are not designed to accommodate the specific needs of each individual investor, considering the other party in the deal is not as relevant when investing as it is in other transactions. However, it is vital that investors carefully balance the tax characteristics of their investment options with the other attributes of their investment options, such as risk and liquidity.

LO 7-3

INVESTMENT INTEREST EXPENSE AND NET INVESTMENT INCOME TAX

Now that we've discussed how *income* from various forms of investments is taxed, let's explore the deductibility of expenses taxpayers incur to acquire or maintain their investments. Beginning in 2018, the only expense associated with investments that remains deductible is **investment interest expense.**[36]

When taxpayers borrow money to acquire investments, the interest expense they pay on the loan is investment interest expense. For example, if you borrow funds to buy stock, any interest you pay on the loan would be considered investment interest expense. Investment interest expense may be deductible as an itemized deduction.[37] It is, however, subject to a limitation. Technically, a taxpayer's investment interest expense deduction for the year is limited to the taxpayer's **net investment income** for the year.[38] In addition, to the extent taxpayers borrow to purchase investments that produce tax-exempt income, such as municipal bonds, they are not allowed to deduct the related interest expense.[39]

[35]We refer here to corporate bonds issued or acquired at face value.

[36]Prior to 2018, investment expenses (including expenses for investment management fees, fees to collect interest and dividends, safe deposit box rental fees, attorney and accounting fees that are necessary to produce investment income, and investment adviser fees) were deductible as an itemized deduction but subject to limitations. These expenses are no longer deductible. However, rental expenses are deductible under §212, as we discuss in the Individual Deductions chapter. Investment expenses from rental and royalty-related activities are deductible as for AGI and not as itemized deductions and thus remain deductible.

[37]§265.

[38]The investment interest expense limitation is calculated on Form 4952.

[39]§163.

To avoid confusion with the *net investment income tax,* we use the term *investment income* rather than the term *net investment income* to discuss the investment interest expense limitation. Because investment expenses are not deductible, net investment income is simply gross investment income. Gross investment income includes interest, annuity, and royalty income not derived in the ordinary course of a trade or business. It also includes net *short-term* capital gains and nonqualified dividends. However, investment income generally does not include capital gains and qualified dividends taxed at a preferential rate.

Example 7-12

What if: Suppose that during the year, Courtney recognized the following income from investments: $1,500 of qualified dividends and $500 of taxable interest. What is Courtney's investment income for purposes of determining her investment interest expense deduction limitation?

Answer: $500. The taxable interest is included, and the qualified dividends are excluded because they are taxed at a preferential rate.

Taxpayers may deduct their investment interest expense up to the amount of their investment income. Any investment interest expense in excess of investment income is carried over and treated as though it was incurred in the next year, when it is subject to the same limitations. The carryover amount never expires. That is, taxpayers can carry over the excess investment interest expense until they generate sufficient investment income to deduct it.

Example 7-13

What if: Continuing with Example 7-12, suppose that in July of this year, Courtney purchased a parcel of undeveloped land as an investment for $120,000. She made a $20,000 down payment and financed the remaining $100,000 with a loan from her local credit union. The interest rate on the loan was 5 percent, payable annually. During the year, Courtney paid $2,500 in interest expense on the loan. Because the loan was used to purchase an investment, the interest expense is investment interest expense. Courtney has investment income of $500 from interest. What amount of this investment interest expense is Courtney allowed to deduct this year?

Answer: $500. Although she incurred $2,500 of investment interest expense, her deduction for the current year is limited to her $500 investment income (see Example 7-12). The $2,000 of investment interest expense that is not deductible this year is carried forward until Courtney generates enough investment income to deduct it.

Congress allows taxpayers to *elect to include* preferentially taxed income in investment income if they are willing to subject this income to tax at the ordinary (not preferential) tax rates. Taxpayers who make this election benefit from increasing their investment income and thus increasing their current year investment interest expense deduction. However, this additional deduction comes at a price because they must subject their capital gains and qualified dividends included in investment income (that would have been taxed at preferential rates if not for the election) to ordinary tax rates.[40]

[40]Note that the election is not an all-or-nothing proposition. Taxpayers can elect to include all or only a portion of their preferentially taxed capital gains and qualified dividends in investment income. However, the amount they include in investment income is subject to tax at ordinary tax rates.

Example 7-14

What if: In Examples 7-12 and 7-13, we discovered that Courtney paid $2,500 of investment interest expense during the year but was only able to deduct $500 of the interest expense because her net investment income was only $500. However, as indicated in Example 7-12, Courtney also received $1,500 of qualified dividends that were *excluded* from the investment income computation. Courtney may elect to increase her investment income by the amount of the qualified dividends (and increase her investment interest expense deduction), but by doing so, she must subject the qualified dividends to her ordinary tax rate (assume a 32 percent ordinary tax rate) instead of the preferential rate (15 percent). Thus, Courtney is faced with a choice of whether to include the $1,500 dividend in investment income and tax it at ordinary rates (Alternative 1) or exclude it from investment income and tax it at preferential rates (Alternative 2). How much more investment interest expense is she allowed to deduct under Alternative 1 than Alternative 2?

Answer: $1,500 more under Alternative 1, saving $225 in taxes, computed as follows:

Alternative 1: *Include the $1,500 dividends in investment income.*

Description	Amount	Explanation
(1) Increase in investment income	$1,500	Elect to include dividends in investment income.
(2) Increase in investment interest expense deduction	**1,500**	Investment interest expense deduction increased from $500 to $2,000.
(3) Tax benefit from additional deduction	480	(2) × 32%
(4) Tax cost of taxing dividends at ordinary rate	255	(1) × (32% − 15%)
(5) Current savings from election to include dividends in net investment income	225	(3) − (4)
(6) Investment interest expense carryover	$ 500	$2,500 total − $2,000 deducted

Alternative 2: *Exclude the $1,500 dividends from investment income.*

Description	Amount	Explanation
Forgone tax benefit available *this year* under Alternative 1	$ 225	Under Alternative 2, Courtney doesn't receive the tax savings available under Alternative 1.
(1) Increase in investment interest expense carryover	1,500	Investment interest expense not deducted under Alternative 2.
Total investment interest expense carryover	$2,000	(1) + $500 investment interest expense carryover under Alternative 1.

THE KEY FACTS

Investment Interest Expense

- Interest expense on loans used to purchase taxable investments.
- Itemized deduction.
- Deductible to the extent of investment income.
- Investment income includes interest, annuity, and other investment-type income not taxed at the preferential rate (net capital gains and qualified dividends).
- Taxpayers can elect to include net capital gains and qualified dividends in investment income but must tax them at the ordinary (not the preferential) rate.
- Investment interest expense not deducted carries forward indefinitely.

Whether it makes sense to elect to include net capital gains and qualified dividends in investment income depends on the taxpayer's circumstances and personal preferences. As we see in Example 7-14, Courtney could save $225 this year by electing to include this income in investment income. However, by doing so, she is forgoing $1,500 of investment interest expense carryover ($2,000 − $500) that would be available to offset ordinary income in future years.

Net Investment Income Tax

A net investment income tax is imposed on net investment income.[41] The tax imposed is 3.8 percent of the lesser of (a) net investment income or (b) the excess of modified

[41]§1411. For purposes of the net investment income tax (NIIT), the definition of net investment income differs from that of investment income in the previous section. Net investment income for purposes of the NIIT includes interest, dividends, annuities, royalties, rents, income from passive activities, and gains from the disposition of assets generating these types of income. Allowable related deductions (including rental property taxes and related state income taxes) reduce income to obtain net investment income.

adjusted gross income over $250,000 for married-joint filers and surviving spouses, $125,000 for married-separate filers, and $200,000 for other taxpayers. Modified adjusted gross income equals adjusted gross income increased by income excluded under the foreign-earned income exclusion less any disallowed deductions associated with the foreign-earned income exclusion. The tax is calculated and reported on Form 8960. Additional details and examples of the tax are provided in the Individual Income Tax Computation and Tax Credits chapter.

PASSIVE ACTIVITY INCOME AND LOSSES

LO 7-4

Thus far we have discussed how taxpayers may invest in business- and income-producing activities and earn various forms of income that are taxed as *portfolio income.* For example, taxpayers acquiring stock in a **C corporation** that files tax returns and pays taxes or taxpayers purchasing bonds issued by a corporation are taxed on the portfolio income these investments generate in the form of dividends and interest. On the other hand, a taxpayer may passively invest directly in an income-producing enterprise by purchasing rental property. Similarly, a taxpayer could passively invest in a partial interest in a trade or business or rental activity by acquiring an ownership interest in a **flow-through entity** that doesn't pay taxes, such as a partnership, limited liability company (taxed as a partnership), or an S corporation (taxed similar to a partnership by shareholders' election). This section addresses the taxation of these passive activities.

Whether an investor makes a direct investment in rental property or makes an indirect investment in a business or rental activity through a partnership, limited liability company, or S corporation, the *actual operating income or loss* from these investments flows through to the taxpayer as it is earned and is treated as ordinary income or ordinary loss. If trade or business or rental activities (held either directly or indirectly through flow-through entities) generate ordinary operating income, taxpayers report it on their tax returns and it is taxed at ordinary rates. However, if these activities generate operating losses, the operating losses must clear three hurdles to be deductible currently. The three loss limits are the tax-basis, **at-risk amount,** and **passive activity loss rules.**

The tax-basis hurdle limits a taxpayer's deductible operating losses to the taxpayer's tax basis in the business or rental activity. This limitation is very similar to loss limitations that apply when a taxpayer sells an investment asset such as corporate stock or another similar capital asset. Recall that the formula for determining gain or loss on an exchange is the amount realized less the taxpayer's adjusted basis in the property. If a taxpayer were to sell an asset for nothing, the loss would be the amount of the tax basis in the property, but no more.

Obviously, in order to apply the tax-basis loss limitation, we must first determine the taxpayer's tax basis in the activity. Very generally speaking, the tax basis is the taxpayer's investment in the activity adjusted for certain items (namely, income, debt, and investments). The adjustments are beyond the scope of this chapter.

When a loss from a business or business-related activity clears the tax-basis hurdle, it next must clear an at-risk amount hurdle on its journey toward deductibility.[42] The at-risk rules are meant to limit the ability of investors to deduct "artificial" ordinary losses produced with certain types of debt. These rules serve to limit ordinary losses to a taxpayer's economic risk in an activity. Generally, a taxpayer is considered to be "at risk" in an activity to the extent of any cash personally contributed to the activity and certain other adjustments similar (but not identical) to those for tax basis.[43] Because the computation of the tax basis and the at-risk amount are so similar, a taxpayer's tax basis and at-risk amount in the activity are frequently the same, so that when they clear the tax-basis hurdle for deducting a loss, they also clear the at-risk amount hurdle. If the at-risk amount

[42]§465.

[43]A detailed discussion of these adjustments is beyond the scope of this chapter.

does differ from the tax basis, the at-risk amount will be less than the tax basis. Losses that do not clear the at-risk amount hurdle are suspended until the taxpayer generates more at-risk amounts to absorb the loss or until the activity is sold, when they may offset the seller's gain from the disposition of the activity.

Example 7-15

What if: Assume that instead of investing solely in assets that generate portfolio income, Courtney used $10,000 of the inheritance from Gramps to acquire a 5 percent interest in a limited partnership (a flow-through entity) called Color Comfort Sheets (CCS). Courtney's share of CCS's loss for the year is $15,000. What amount of this loss is Courtney allowed to deduct after applying the tax basis and at-risk amount limitations?

Answer: $10,000. Because Courtney's tax basis and at-risk amount in her CCS interest are both $10,000 (the amount of cash invested), the tax-basis and at-risk amount limitations result in the same limitation. Thus, Courtney may deduct $10,000 of the $15,000 loss before considering the passive activity loss limits discussed below.

Even when a taxpayer has sufficient tax basis and sufficient amounts at risk to absorb a loss from a business-related activity, the loss may still be limited by the passive activity loss rules. To combat the thriving **tax shelter** industry that existed by marketing investments to wealthy investors designed primarily to generate ordinary losses that could be used to shield other income from tax, Congress introduced the passive activity loss rules.[44] Specifically, these rules limit the ability of investors in certain passive activities involving interests in trades or businesses and in rental property, including real estate, to use their ordinary losses from these activities currently to reduce taxable income from other sources.[45] The passive activity loss rules are applied to any losses remaining *after* applying the tax-basis and at-risk loss limits.

Passive Activity Definition

The passive activity loss (PAL) rules define a passive activity as "any activity which involves the conduct of a trade or business, and in which the taxpayer does not materially participate."[46] According to the tax code, participants in rental activities, including rental real estate, and limited partners in partnerships are generally deemed to be passive participants, and participants in all other trade or business activities are passive unless their involvement in an activity is "regular, continuous, and substantial." Clearly, these terms are quite subjective and difficult to apply. Fortunately, regulations provide more certainty in this area by listing seven separate tests for material participation.[47] An individual, other than a limited partner, can be classified as a material participant in an activity by meeting any one of the seven tests in Exhibit 7-9. Therefore, investors who purchase rental property or an interest in a trade or business without intending to be involved in the management of the trade or business are classified as passive participants, and these activities are classified as passive activities with respect to them.

[44]§469, enacted in 1986.

[45]Before passage of the passive activity loss rules, the at-risk amount rules in §465 were adopted in an attempt to limit the ability of investors to deduct "artificial" ordinary losses. Given the similarity of the at-risk amount and tax-basis computations, especially for real estate investments, the at-risk amount rules were not entirely successful at accomplishing this objective. The passive activity loss rules were adopted as a backstop to the at-risk amount rules, and both sets of rules may potentially apply to a given activity.

[46]§469(c).

[47]Reg. §1.469-5T.

EXHIBIT 7-9 Tests for Material Participation

Individuals are generally considered material participants for the activity if they meet any *one* of these tests:

1. The individual participates in the activity more than 500 hours during the year.
2. The individual's activity constitutes substantially all of the participation in such activity by all individuals, including nonowners.
3. The individual participates more than 100 hours during the year, and the individual's participation is not less than any other individual's participation in the activity.
4. The activity qualifies as a "significant participation activity" (more than 100 hours spent during the year) and the aggregate of all "significant participation activities" is greater than 500 hours for the year.
5. The individual materially participated in the activity for any 5 of the preceding 10 taxable years.
6. The individual materially participated for any three preceding years in any personal service activity (personal services in health, law, engineering, architecture, accounting, actuarial science, performing arts, or consulting).
7. Taking into account all the facts and circumstances, the individual participates on a regular, continuous, and substantial basis during the year.

Income and Loss Categories

Under the passive activity loss rules, each item of a taxpayer's income or loss for the year is placed in one of three categories. Losses from the *passive* category cannot offset income from other categories. The three different categories are as follows (see Exhibit 7-10):

1. *Passive activity income or loss*—income or loss from an activity in which the taxpayer is not a material participant.
2. *Portfolio income*—income from investments including capital gains and losses, dividends, interest, annuities, and royalties.
3. *Active business income*—income from sources in which the taxpayer is a material participant. For individuals, this includes salary and self-employment income. Thus, an individual with income in this category is no longer an investor with respect to this source of income given that we define investors in this chapter as individuals with portfolio and/or passive income and losses.

The impact of segregating taxpayers' income into these categories is to limit their ability to apply passive activity losses against income in the other two categories. In effect, passive activity losses are suspended and remain in the passive income or loss category until the taxpayer generates passive income, either from the passive activity

EXHIBIT 7-10 Income and Loss Categories

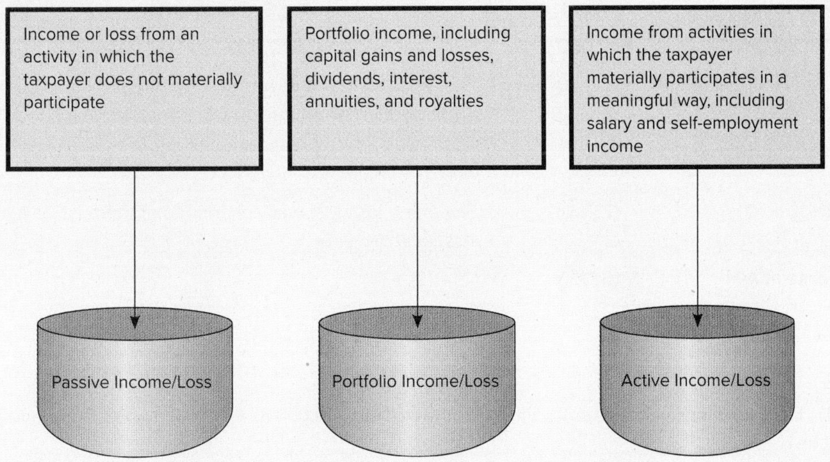

producing the loss or from some other passive activity, or until the taxpayer sells the entire activity that generated the passive loss in a taxable transaction. On the sale, current and suspended passive losses from the activity are first applied to reduce gain from the sale of the activity, then to reduce net passive income from other passive activities, and then to reduce nonpassive income.[48] However, these passive losses that are allowed when the activity is sold may be limited by the excess business loss rules discussed in the Individual Deductions chapter.[49]

Example 7-16

THE KEY FACTS

Passive Activities

- Ordinary losses from flow-though entities and other enterprises will be classified as passive if the taxpayer is not a material participant.
- Losses from limited partnerships and from rental activities, including rental real estate, are generally deemed to be passive losses.
- Passive activity loss rules limit losses from passive activities to passive income from other sources.
  - Active business income such as salary and self-employment income is not passive income.
  - Investment-type income such as interest and dividends is portfolio income, not passive income.
  - Passive losses in excess of passive income are suspended and deductible against passive income in the future or when the taxpayer sells the passive activity generating the loss.
  - Income from passive activities is subject to the net investment income tax.

What if: Let's return to the facts in Example 7-15, in which Courtney's share of CCS loss is $15,000, her tax basis in her CCS interest is $10,000, and her at-risk amount in the activity is also $10,000. Further assume that Courtney received $170,000 in salary, $4,000 of taxable interest income from corporate bonds, $3,000 of dividends, and $5,000 of long-term capital gains. Finally, assume that Courtney also owns a rental condominium that generated $8,000 of net income. How would each of these income or loss items be allocated among the passive, portfolio, and active income and loss categories?

Answer: Courtney's $10,000 loss from CCS remaining after applying the tax-basis and at-risk loss limits is placed in the passive category because, as a limited partner, Courtney did not materially participate in the activity. Further, her $8,000 of net income from her rental property is included in the passive category because rental activities are generally considered to be passive. The $4,000 of taxable interest income, $3,000 of dividends, and $5,000 of long-term capital gains are all included in the portfolio income category. Finally, the $170,000 of salary is included in the active income category.

What if: What is Courtney's AGI for the year assuming, other than the items described above, no other items affect her AGI?

Answer: $182,000, computed as follows:

Description	Amount	Explanation
(1) Active income	$170,000	Salary
(2) Portfolio income	12,000	Interest of $4,000; dividends of $3,000; $5,000 of long-term capital gains.
(3) Passive income	0	$10,000 passive loss that clears tax-basis and at-risk hurdles and $8,000 of passive income. However, the passive loss clearing the basis and at-risk amount hurdles is deductible only to the extent of passive income. The suspended passive activity loss is ($2,000).
AGI	**$182,000**	(1) + (2) + (3)

What if: In addition to the facts above, assume that at the beginning of next year Courtney sells her limited partnership interest for $12,000. If Courtney's tax basis on the date of sale is $0, what effect does the sale have on her AGI?

Answer: $10,000 increase in AGI, computed as follows:

Description	Amount	Explanation
(1) Capital gain	$12,000	Gain recognized = $12,000 – $0 tax basis
(2) Ordinary loss	0	The ($5,000) loss that was suspended at the basis level is not deductible on the sale. This loss expires unused. There was no loss suspended at the at-risk level or it would have been deductible on the sale.
(3) Ordinary loss	(2,000)	This is the loss that was suspended at the passive activity loss level last year.
Increase in AGI	**$10,000**	(1) + (2) + (3)

[48]§469(g).

[49]§461(l). The excess business loss rules limit these losses to $270,000 or $540,000 for 2022, depending on filing status.

Rental Real Estate Exception to the Passive Activity Loss Rules

Tax laws are renowned for exceptions to rules and, not surprisingly, the general rule that passive activity losses cannot be used to offset nonpassive types of income is subject to a few important exceptions. The one we choose to discuss here applies to lower- to middle-income individuals with rental real estate.[50] A taxpayer who is an **active participant in a rental activity** may be allowed to deduct up to $25,000 of the rental loss against other types of income. To be considered an active participant, the taxpayer must (1) own at least 10 percent of the rental property and (2) participate in the process of making management decisions such as approving new tenants, deciding on rental terms, and approving repairs and capital expenditures.

Consistent with a number of tax benefits, the exception amount for active owners is phased out as adjusted gross income increases. The $25,000 maximum exception amount is phased out by 50 cents for every dollar the taxpayer's adjusted gross income (before considering the rental loss) exceeds $100,000. Consequently, the entire $25,000 deduction is phased out when the taxpayer's adjusted gross income reaches $150,000.

THE KEY FACTS

Rental Real Estate Losses

- Rental real estate exception to passive loss rules
  - Applies to active participants in rental property.
  - Deduct up to $25,000 of rental real estate loss against ordinary income.
  - $25,000 maximum deduction phased out by 50 cents for every dollar of AGI over $100,000 (excluding the rental loss deduction).
  - Fully phased out at $150,000 of AGI.

Example 7-17

What if: Assume that Jeb Landers, Courtney's uncle, owns and rents a condominium. Jeb is involved in approving new tenants for the rental home and in managing its maintenance. During the year, he reported a net loss of $5,000 from the rental activity, and he had sufficient tax-basis and at-risk amounts to absorb the loss. Further, his only sources of income during the year were $126,000 of salary and $22,000 of long-term capital gains. Given Jeb's $5,000 loss from his rental home, how much of the loss can he deduct currently, and what is his passive activity loss carryover?

Answer: Jeb's rental loss deductible in the current year is $1,000, and his passive loss carryover is $4,000. Because Jeb meets the definition of an "active participant" and has adjusted gross income of less than $150,000 before considering his rental loss, he may deduct a portion of the loss against his other income. His $1,000 deduction is computed as follows:

Description	Amount	Explanation
(1) Maximum deduction available before phase-out	$25,000	
(2) Phase-out of maximum deduction	24,000	[($148,000 – 100,000) × .5]
(3) Maximum deduction in current year	$ 1,000	(1) – (2)
(4) Rental loss in current year	5,000	
(5) Rental loss deductible in current year	**1,000**	Lesser of (3) or (4)
Passive activity loss carryover	**$ 4,000**	(4) – (3)

What if: Assume that Jeb's salary for the year had been $50,000 and he reported $22,000 from the sale of his stock. How much of his rental loss could he deduct currently?

Answer: Because Jeb's adjusted gross income would be only $72,000 under this scenario, he could deduct his entire $5,000 rental loss during the year.

Net Investment Income Tax on Net Passive Income

Earlier in this chapter we noted that taxpayers with modified AGI over certain thresholds are required to pay a 3.8 percent tax on their net investment income (in addition to the income tax). In calculating net investment income for this tax, taxpayers must include their net passive income.

[50]Section 469(c)(7) provides another important exception to the general rule that all real estate activities are passive. To overcome this presumption, taxpayers must spend more than half their time working in real estate trades or businesses and for more than 750 hours during the year. This exception benefits individuals who spend a substantial amount of time in activities like real estate development and construction.

Example 7-18

What if: Suppose Courtney has income from her salary of $170,000. Assume that in addition to this income, Courtney also owns 50 percent of an S corporation in which she does not materially participate. The S corporation is profitable and generates $105,000 of flow-through income to her this year. Courtney paid $5,000 of state income taxes related to the S corporation income. Thus, her net investment income from the activity is $100,000. How much net investment income tax will Courtney owe?

Answer: $2,660, calculated as follows:

Description	Amount	Explanation
(1) Net investment income	$100,000	Income from passive investment
(2) Modified AGI	270,000	$170,000 salary + $100,000 S corporation income
(3) Modified AGI threshold	200,000	
(4) Excess modified AGI above threshold	70,000	(2) − (3)
(5) Net investment income tax base	70,000	Lesser of (1) or (4)
Net investment income tax	**$ 2,660**	(5) × 3.8%

What if: Assume that Courtney spends 525 hours participating in the activity of the S corporation during the year. How much net investment income tax will she owe?

Answer: $0. Because Courtney materially participates in the S corporation, the flow-through income is no longer passive income, and she will not be subject to the net investment income tax.

CONCLUSION

Investors and their advisers face numerous tax rules that apply to investment income. Understanding these rules is important, not only to comply with the tax law, but also to make wise investment choices. Investments differ in terms of their potential for implementing the conversion and shifting tax planning strategies. Failing to consider these strategies when investing will lead to less-than-optimal results. By carefully weighing nontax investment objectives along with the tax characteristics of different investment options, informed investors will be better equipped to select investments appropriate for them.

Appendix A: Detailed Step-By-Step Guide to the Capital Gains Netting Process

In this appendix, we provide a more detailed step-by-step guide to the capital gains and losses netting process including 25 percent and 28 percent gains.

Step 1: Net all short-term capital gains and short-term capital losses, including any short-term capital loss carried forward from the prior year. A net positive amount is a **net short-term capital gain.** A net negative amount is a net short-term capital loss. If there are no long-term capital gains or losses, the netting process is complete. Otherwise, continue to Step 2.

Step 2: Separate long-term capital gains and losses into three rate groups (28 percent, 25 percent, and 0/15/20 percent). Place any net long-term capital loss carried over from the prior year into the 28 percent rate group. Sum the gains and losses within each group. The outcome will be a net 28 percent gain or loss, a 25 percent gain (there are no 25 percent losses), and/or a net 0/15/20 percent gain or loss. Proceed to Step 3.

Step 3: (a) If neither the 0/15/20 percent nor the 28 percent rate group from Step 2 nets to a gain, transfer the net loss (if any) in the 0/15/20 percent rate group to the 28 percent rate group, combine it with the loss in that group (if any), and proceed to Step 4.

(b) If none of the long-term rate groups from Step 2 nets to a loss, proceed to Step 6.

(c) Combining net gains and losses in long-term rate groups:

i. If Step 2 results in net losses in both the 28 percent and 0/15/20 percent rate groups, combine the net losses and then apply them to offset gains in the 25 percent rate group. If the losses exceed the gain, the result is a net long-term capital loss. Proceed to Step 4. If the gain exceeds the losses, the result is a net long-term capital gain. Proceed to Step 6.

ii. If the Step 2 outcomes include a net loss in the 28 percent rate group and net gains in the other rate groups, apply the net loss from the 28 percent rate group to the gain in the 25 percent rate group until the 25 percent rate group gain is reduced to zero. Then offset any remaining 28 percent rate group loss against the net gain in the 0/15/20 percent rate group. If the net loss from the 28 percent rate group exceeds the net gains from the other rate groups, the net loss is a net long-term capital loss. Proceed to Step 4. If gain remains in the 25 percent and/or 0/15/20 percent rate groups after applying the loss, the result is a net long-term capital gain. Proceed to Step 6.

iii. If the amounts from Step 2 include a net loss in the 0/15/20 percent rate group and net gains in the 28 percent and/or the 25 percent rate groups, apply the net loss from the 0/15/20 percent rate group to the net gain in the 28 percent rate group until the net gain is reduced to zero. Then offset any remaining loss against the gain in the 25 percent rate group. If the net loss from the 0/15/20 percent rate group exceeds the net gains from the other rate groups, the net loss is a net long-term capital loss. Proceed to Step 4. If gain remains in the 28 percent and/or 25 percent rate groups after applying the loss, the result is a net long-term capital gain. Proceed to Step 6.

Step 4: If there is no net short-term capital gain or loss from Step 1, the netting process is complete; apply the net capital loss deduction limitation ($3,000, or $1,500 if married filing separately) and ignore the remaining steps. If the result from Step 1 is a net short-term capital loss *and* the result from Step 3 is a net long-term capital loss, the netting process is complete: Apply the net capital loss deduction limitation and ignore the remaining steps. Otherwise, continue on to Step 5.

Step 5: If Step 1 produces a net short-term capital gain *and* Step 3 produces a net long-term capital loss, combine the net short-term capital gain and the net long-term capital loss.

(a) If the outcome is a net loss, the netting process is complete. Apply the net capital loss deduction limitation described previously.

(b) If the outcome is a net gain, the net gain is treated the same as a net short-term capital gain and is taxed at ordinary rates. The netting process is complete.

Step 6: If there is no net short-term capital gain or loss from Step 1, the netting process is complete. The tax on the net long-term capital gain (also called a net capital gain) remaining in each long-term group is determined as described in the next section. If the Step 1 outcome is a net short-term capital gain, skip to Step 7. If the Step 1 outcome is a net short-term capital loss *and* Step 3 results in a net gain in any (or all) of the long-term rate groups, first use the short-term capital loss to offset the gain in the 28 percent rate group (if any), then the gain in the 25 percent rate group (if any), and finally the gain in the 0/15/20 percent rate group (if any).

(a) If the net short-term capital loss exceeds all gains in the long-term rate groups, the netting process is complete. Apply the net capital loss deduction limitation described previously.

(b) If the net short-term capital loss does not offset all of the gain in any (or all) of the long-term rate groups, the netting process is complete. The result is a **net capital gain** (net long-term capital gains in excess of net short-term capital losses). The tax on the gain remaining in each long-term group is determined as described in the next section.

Step 7: If Step 1 produces a net short-term capital gain *and* Step 3 produces a net long-term capital gain(s), the netting process is complete. The tax on the remaining gains is determined as described in the section Calculating Tax Liability on Net Capital Gains.

Summary

LO 7-1 Explain how interest income and dividend income are taxed.

- Investors seeking current income invest in interest-bearing securities or dividend-paying stocks.
- Interest income received from certificates of deposit, U.S. Treasury securities, corporate bonds, and other similar investments is typically taxed annually at ordinary rates.
- Accrued market discount on bonds and interest earned on U.S. savings bonds is taxed at sale or maturity, while original issue discount on bonds is taxed annually.
- Bond premiums increase the tax basis of bonds and affect the amount of capital gains or losses investors report.
- Taxpayers may elect to amortize bond premiums to reduce the amount of annual interest reported on bonds purchased at a premium.
- Dividend income, like interest income, is taxed when it is received. However, most dividend income currently is taxed at preferential capital gains rates.

LO 7-2 Compute the tax consequences associated with the disposition of capital assets, including the netting process for calculating gains and losses.

- When taxpayers sell stock, they may determine the basis of the stock using the FIFO method (default) or the specific identification method (by election).
- Capital assets held for more than one year generate long-term capital gains or losses on sale or disposition. Other capital assets generate short-term capital gains or losses on sale or disposition.
- Generally, net long-term capital gains in excess of net short-term losses are taxed at either a 0, 15, or 20 percent tax rate, depending on the taxpayer's income.
- Unrecaptured §1250 gain is taxed at a maximum 25 percent rate, and gains from collectibles and §1202 stock are taxed at a maximum 28 percent rate.
- Up to $3,000 of net capital losses are deductible against ordinary income for the year.
- A taxpayer's capital gains and losses for the year are reported on Form 8949 and Schedule D of Form 1040.
- Wash sale provisions prevent taxpayers from selling stock or securities at a loss, deducting the loss, and replacing the stock sold with the same stock or substantially identical securities within 30 days either before or after the day of sale.
- Losses on the disposition of property held for personal use are not deductible.
- Because of the deferral of the capital gains tax, after-tax rates of return from capital assets will increase as an investor's investment horizon increases.

Calculate the deduction for investment interest expense. LO 7-3

- Investment expenses are not deductible.
- Investment interest expense is deductible to the extent of net investment income.
- Because investment expenses are not deductible, net investment income is equivalent to gross investment income.
- Preferentially taxed capital gains and qualified dividends are not included in investment income unless the taxpayer elects to tax them as ordinary income.

Apply tax-basis, at-risk amount, and passive activity loss limits to losses from passive investments. LO 7-4

- A taxpayer's share of operating losses from passive flow-through entities and other trade or business activities are deductible to the extent they clear the tax-basis, at-risk, and passive activity loss hurdles.
- A taxpayer's ordinary losses from flow-through entities and other trade or business activities may be classified as passive if the taxpayer's involvement is not regular, continuous, and substantial.
- A taxpayer's operating losses from rental activities are, with limited exceptions, deemed to be passive regardless of the taxpayer's activity level.
- A taxpayer's losses from passive activity are limited to passive income from all other sources until disposition of the activity. On disposition, current and prior losses from passive activities can be used but may be subject to the excess business loss limitations.
- A rental real estate exception allows taxpayers to deduct up to $25,000 of operating losses from rental real estate annually provided they are actively involved in managing the rental real estate and have adjusted gross income of less than $150,000.

KEY TERMS

accrued market discount (7-4)
active participant in a rental activity (7-33)
amortization (7-3)
amount realized (7-8)
at-risk amount (7-29)
basis (7-4)
bond discount (7-3)
bond premium (7-3)
bonds (7-2)
C corporation (7-29)
capital assets (7-7)
certificate of deposit (CD) (7-2)
collectibles (7-11)
dividends (7-2)
exchange traded funds (ETF) (7-2)
ex-dividend date (7-6)
face value (7-2)
first-in, first-out (FIFO) method (7-9)
flow-through entity (7-29)
investment income (7-2)
investment interest expense (7-26)
long-term capital gains or losses (7-10)
market discount (7-4)
market premium (7-4)
maturity (7-4)
maturity value (7-2)
maximum 15 percent rate amount (7-11)
maximum zero percent rate amount (7-10)
mutual funds (7-2)
net capital gain (7-15)
net investment income (7-26)
net long-term capital gains (7-15)
net long-term capital losses (7-14)
net short-term capital gains (7-15)
net short-term capital losses (7-14)
operating income (7-2)
operating losses (7-2)
original issue discount (OID) (7-3)
passive activity loss rules (7-29)
passive investments (7-2)
portfolio investments (7-2)
qualified dividends (7-6)
qualified small business stock (7-11)
short-term capital gains or losses (7-10)
specific identification method (7-9)
tax basis (7-8)
tax shelter (7-30)
Treasury bonds (7-3)
Treasury notes (7-3)
unrecaptured §1250 gain (7-11)
U.S. savings bonds (7-3)
wash sale (7-23)
zero-coupon bonds (7-3)

DISCUSSION QUESTIONS

Discussion Questions are available in Connect®.

1. Describe how interest income and dividend income are taxed. What are the similarities and differences in their tax treatment? LO 7-1
2. What is the underlying policy rationale for the current tax rules applicable to interest income and dividend income? LO 7-1

LO 7-1 3. Compare and contrast the tax treatment of interest from a Treasury bond and qualified dividends from corporate stock.

LO 7-1 4. How are Treasury notes and Treasury bonds treated for federal and state income tax purposes?

LO 7-1 5. Why would taxpayers generally prefer the tax treatment of market discount to the treatment of original issue discount on corporate bonds?

LO 7-1 6. In what ways are U.S. savings bonds treated more favorably for tax purposes than corporate bonds?

planning LO 7-1 7. When should investors consider making an election to amortize the market discount on a bond into income annually? [*Hint:* See §1278(b).]

LO 7-1 8. Why might investors purchase interest-paying securities rather than dividend-paying stocks?

LO 7-1 9. Compare and contrast the tax treatment of dividend-paying stocks and growth stocks.

LO 7-2 10. What is the definition of a capital asset? Give three examples of capital assets.

LO 7-2 11. Why does the tax law allow a taxpayer to defer gains accrued on a capital asset until the taxpayer actually sells the asset?

LO 7-2 12. Why does the tax law provide preferential rates on certain capital gains?

LO 7-2 13. What is the deciding factor in determining whether a capital gain is a short-term or long-term capital gain?

LO 7-2 14. What methods may taxpayers use to determine the adjusted basis of stock they have sold?

LO 7-2 15. What tax rate applies to net short-term capital gains?

LO 7-2 16. What limitations are placed on the deductibility of capital losses for individual taxpayers?

LO 7-2 17. What happens to capital losses that are not deductible in the current year?

LO 7-2 18. Are all long-term capital gains taxable at the same maximum rate? If not, what rates may apply to long-term capital gains?

planning LO 7-2 19. This year, David, a taxpayer in the highest tax rate bracket, has the option to purchase either stock in a Fortune 500 company or qualified small business stock in his friend's corporation. All else being equal, which of the two will he prefer from a tax perspective if he intends to hold the stock for six years? Which would he prefer if he only plans to hold the stock for two years?

LO 7-2 20. What is a "wash sale"? What is the purpose of the wash sale tax rules?

LO 7-2 21. Nick does not use his car for business purposes. If he sells his car for less than he paid for it, does he get to deduct the loss for tax purposes? Why or why not?

planning LO 7-2 22. Describe three basic tax planning strategies available to taxpayers investing in capital assets.

planning LO 7-2 23. Clark owns stock in BCS Corporation that he purchased in January of the current year. The stock has appreciated significantly during the year. It is now December of the current year, and Clark is deciding whether or not he should sell the stock. What tax and nontax factors should Clark consider before making the decision on whether to sell the stock now?

LO 7-3 24. Are dividends and capital gains considered to be investment income for purposes of determining the amount of a taxpayer's deductible investment interest expense for the year?

LO 7-3 25. How is the amount of net investment income determined for a taxpayer?

LO 7-3 26. What limitations are placed on the deductibility of investment interest expense? What happens to investment interest expense that is not deductible because of the limitations?

LO 7-3 27. When taxpayers borrow money to buy municipal bonds, are they allowed to deduct interest expense on the loan? Why or why not?

28. What types of losses may potentially be characterized as passive losses? LO 7-3
29. What are the implications of treating losses as passive? LO 7-4
30. Discuss the treatment of suspended passive losses upon the sale of a passive activity. LO 7-4
31. What tests are applied to determine if losses should be characterized as passive? LO 7-4
32. All else being equal, would a taxpayer with passive losses prefer to have wage income or passive income? LO 7-4 planning

PROBLEMS

Select problems are available in Connect®.

33. Hassnein recently deposited $20,000 in a savings account paying a guaranteed interest rate of 4 percent for the next 10 years. If Hassnein expects his marginal tax rate to be 22 percent for the next 10 years, how much interest will he earn after-tax for the first year of his investment? How much interest will he earn after-tax for the second year of his investment if he withdraws enough cash every year to pay the tax on the interest he earns? How much will he have in the account after 4 years? How much will he have in the account after 7 years? LO 7-1
34. Dana intends to invest $30,000 in either a Treasury bond or a corporate bond. The Treasury bond yields 5 percent before tax, and the corporate bond yields 6 percent before tax. Assuming Dana's federal marginal rate is 24 percent and her marginal state rate is 5 percent, which of the two options should she choose? If she were to move to another state where her marginal state rate would be 10 percent, would her choice be any different? Assume that Dana itemizes deductions. LO 7-1
35. At the beginning of his current tax year, David invests $12,000 in original issue U.S. Treasury bonds with a $10,000 face value that mature in exactly 10 years. David receives $700 in interest ($350 every six months) from the Treasury bonds during the current year, and the yield to maturity on the bonds is 5 percent. LO 7-1
    a) How much interest income will he report this year if he elects to amortize the bond premium?
    b) How much interest will he report this year if he does not elect to amortize the bond premium?
36. Seth invested $20,000 in Series EE savings bonds on April 1. By December 31, the published redemption value of the bonds had increased to $20,700. How much interest income will Seth report from the savings bonds in the current year absent any special election? LO 7-1
37. At the beginning of her current tax year, Angela purchased a zero-coupon corporate bond at original issue for $30,000 with a yield to maturity of 6 percent. Given that she will not actually receive any interest payments until the bond matures in 10 years, how much interest income will she report this year assuming semiannual compounding of interest? LO 7-1
38. At the beginning of his current tax year, Eric bought a corporate bond with a maturity value of $50,000 from the secondary market for $45,000. The bond has a stated annual interest rate of 5 percent payable on June 30 and December 31, and it matures in five years on December 31. Absent any special tax elections, how much interest income will Eric report from the bond this year and in the year the bond matures? LO 7-1
39. Hayley recently invested $50,000 in a public utility stock paying a 3 percent annual dividend. If Hayley reinvests the annual dividend she receives net of any taxes owed on the dividend, how much will her investment be worth in four years if the dividends paid are qualified dividends? (Hayley's marginal income tax rate is 32 percent.) What will her investment be worth in four years if the dividends are nonqualified? LO 7-1

LO 7-1 planning

40. Five years ago, Kate purchased a dividend-paying stock for $10,000. For all five years, the stock paid an annual dividend of 4 percent before tax and Kate's marginal tax rate was 24 percent. Every year Kate reinvested her after-tax dividends in the same stock. For the first two years of her investment, the dividends qualified for the 15 percent capital gains rate; however, for the last three years the 15 percent dividend rate was repealed and dividends were taxed at ordinary rates.
   a) What is the current value (at the beginning of year 6) of Kate's investment assuming the stock has not appreciated in value?
   b) What will Kate's investment be worth three years from now (at the beginning of year 9) assuming her marginal tax rate increases to 35 percent for the next three years?

LO 7-2

41. John bought 1,000 shares of Intel stock on October 18, 2018, for $30 per share plus a $750 commission he paid to his broker. On December 12, 2022, he sells the shares for $42.50 per share. He also incurs a $1,000 fee for this transaction.
   a) What is John's adjusted basis in the 1,000 shares of Intel stock?
   b) What amount does John realize when he sells the 1,000 shares?
   c) What is the gain/loss for John on the sale of his Intel stock? What is the character of the gain/loss?

LO 7-2

42. Dahlia is in the 32 percent tax rate bracket and has purchased the following shares of Microsoft common stock over the years:

Date Purchased	Shares	Basis
7/10/2012	400	$12,000
4/20/2013	300	10,750
1/29/2014	500	12,230
11/02/2016	250	7,300

If Dahlia sells 800 shares of Microsoft for $40,000 on December 20, 2022, what is her capital gain or loss in each of the following assumptions?
   a) She uses the FIFO method.
   b) She uses the specific identification method and she wants to minimize her current-year capital gain.

LO 7-2 research

43. Karyn loaned $20,000 to her co-worker to begin a new business several years ago. If her co-worker declares bankruptcy on June 22 of the current year, is Karyn allowed to deduct the bad debt loss this year? If she can deduct the loss, what is the character of the loss?

LO 7-2

44. Sue has 5,000 shares of Sony stock that have an adjusted basis of $27,500. She sold the 5,000 shares of stock for cash of $10,000, and she also received a piece of land as part of the proceeds. The land was valued at $20,000 and had an adjusted basis to the buyer of $12,000. What is Sue's gain or loss on the sale of 5,000 shares of Sony stock?

LO 7-2

45. Matt and Meg Comer are married and file a joint tax return. They do not have any children. Matt works as a history professor at a local university and earns a salary of $70,000. Meg works part time at the same university. She earns $33,000 a year. The couple does not itemize deductions. Other than salary, the Comers' only other source of income is from the disposition of various capital assets (mostly stocks).
   a) What is the Comers' tax liability for 2022 if they report the following capital gains and losses for the year?

Short-term capital gains	$ 9,000
Short-term capital losses	(2,000)
Long-term capital gains	15,000
Long-term capital losses	(6,000)

b) What is the Comers' tax liability for 2022 if they report the following capital gains and losses for the year?

Short-term capital gains	$ 1,500
Short-term capital losses	0
Long-term capital gains	13,000
Long-term capital losses	(10,000)

46. Grayson (single) is in the 24 percent tax rate bracket and has sold the following stocks in 2022: LO 7-2

Stock	Date Purchased	Basis	Date Sold	Amount Realized
Stock A	1/23/1998	$ 7,250	7/22/2022	$ 4,500
Stock B	4/10/2022	14,000	9/13/2022	17,500
Stock C	8/23/2020	10,750	10/12/2022	15,300
Stock D	5/19/2012	5,230	10/12/2022	12,400
Stock E	8/20/2022	7,300	11/14/2022	3,500

a) What is Grayson's net short-term capital gain or loss from these transactions?
b) What is Grayson's net long-term gain or loss from these transactions?
c) What is Grayson's overall net gain or loss from these transactions?
d) What amount of the gain, if any, is subject to the preferential rate for certain capital gains?

47. George bought the following amounts of Stock A over the years: LO 7-2

	Date Purchased	Number of Shares	Adjusted Basis
Stock A	11/21/1996	1,000	$24,000
Stock A	3/18/2002	500	9,000
Stock A	5/22/2011	750	27,000

On October 12, 2022, he sold 1,200 of his shares of Stock A for $38 per share.

a) How much gain/loss will George have to recognize if he uses the FIFO method of accounting for the shares sold?
b) How much gain/loss will George have to recognize if he specifically identifies the shares to be sold by telling his broker to sell all 750 shares from the 5/22/2011 purchase and 450 shares from the 11/21/1996 purchase?

48. During the current year, Ron and Anne sold the following assets: LO 7-2

Capital Asset	Market Value	Tax Basis	Holding Period
L stock	$ 50,000	$41,000	> 1 year
M stock	28,000	39,000	> 1 year
N stock	30,000	22,000	< 1 year
O stock	26,000	33,000	< 1 year
Antiques	7,000	4,000	> 1 year
Rental home	300,000*	90,000	> 1 year

*$30,000 of the gain is 25 percent gain (from accumulated depreciation on the property).

a) Given that Ron and Anne have taxable income of only $20,000 (all ordinary) before considering the tax effect of their asset sales, what is their gross tax liability for 2022 assuming they file a joint return?
b) Given that Ron and Anne have taxable income of $400,000 (all ordinary) before considering the tax effect of their asset sales, what is their gross tax liability for 2022 assuming they file a joint return?

49. In 2022, Tom and Alejandro Jackson (married filing jointly) have $200,000 of taxable income before considering the following events: LO 7-2

a) On May 12, 2022, they sold a painting (art) for $110,000 that was inherited from Grandma on July 23, 2020. The fair market value on the date of Grandma's death was $90,000, and Grandma's adjusted basis of the painting was $25,000.

b) They applied a long-term capital loss carryover from 2021 of $10,000.

c) They recognized a $12,000 loss on the 11/1/2022 sale of bonds (acquired on 5/12/2012).

d) They recognized a $4,000 gain on the 12/12/2022 sale of IBM stock (acquired on 2/5/2022).

e) They recognized a $17,000 gain on the 10/17/2022 sale of rental property (the only §1231 transaction), of which $8,000 is reportable as gain subject to the 25 percent maximum rate and the remaining $9,000 is subject to the 0/15/20 percent maximum rates (the property was acquired on 8/2/2016).

f) They recognized a $12,000 loss on the 12/20/2022 sale of bonds (acquired on 1/18/2022).

g) They recognized a $7,000 gain on the 6/27/2022 sale of BH stock (acquired on 7/30/2013).

h) They recognized an $11,000 loss on the 6/13/2022 sale of QuikCo stock (acquired on 3/20/2015).

i) They received $500 of qualified dividends on 7/15/2022.

Complete the required capital gains netting procedures and calculate the Jacksons' 2022 tax liability.

LO 7-2

50. For 2022, Sherri has a short-term loss of $2,500 and a long-term loss of $4,750.

a) How much loss can Sherri deduct in 2022?

b) How much loss will Sherri carry over to 2023, and what is the character of the loss carryover?

LO 7-2

51. Three years ago, Adrian purchased 100 shares of stock in X Corp. for $10,000. On December 30 of year 4, Adrian sells the 100 shares for $6,000.

a) Assuming Adrian has no other capital gains or losses, how much of the loss is Adrian able to deduct on their year 4 tax return?

b) Assume the same facts as in part (a), except that on January 20 of year 5, Adrian purchases 100 shares of X Corp. stock for $6,000. How much loss from the sale on December 30 of year 4 is deductible on Adrian's year 4 tax return? What basis does Adrian take in the stock purchased on January 20 of year 5?

LO 7-2

52. Christopher sold 100 shares of Cisco stock for $5,500 in the current year. He purchased the shares several years ago for $2,200. Assuming his ordinary income tax rate is 24 percent and he has no other capital gains or losses, how much tax will he pay on this gain?

LO 7-2

53. Christina, who is single, purchased 100 shares of Apple Inc. stock several years ago for $3,500. During her year-end tax planning, she decided to sell 50 shares of Apple for $1,500 on December 30. However, two weeks later, Apple introduced its latest iPhone, and she decided that she should buy the 50 shares (cost of $1,600) of Apple back before prices skyrocket.

a) What is Christina's deductible loss on the sale of 50 shares? What is her basis in the 50 new shares?

b) Assume the same facts, except that Christina repurchased only 25 shares for $800. What is Christina's deductible loss on the sale of 50 shares? What is her basis in the 25 new shares?

LO 7-2
research

54. Arden purchased 300 shares of AMC common stock several years ago for $1,500. On April 30, Arden sold the shares of AMC common for $500 and then purchased 250 shares of AMC preferred stock two days later for $700. The AMC preferred stock is not convertible into AMC common stock. What is Arden's deductible loss from the sale of the 300 shares of AMC common stock?

LO 7-2
planning

55. Shaun bought 300 shares of Dental Equipment Inc. several years ago for $10,000. Currently the stock is worth $8,000. Shaun's marginal tax rate this year is 24 percent, and he has no other capital gains or losses. Shaun expects to have a marginal rate of 32 percent next year, but he also expects to have a long-term capital gain of $10,000. To minimize taxes, should Shaun sell the stock on December 31 of this year or January 1 of next year (ignore the time value of money)?

56. Mickey and Jenny Porter file a joint tax return, and they itemize deductions. The Porters incur $2,000 in investment expenses. They also incur $3,000 of investment interest expense during the year. The Porters' income for the year consists of $150,000 in salary and $2,500 of interest income. LO 7-3

a) What is the amount of the Porters' investment interest expense deduction for the year?

b) What would their investment interest expense deduction be if they also had a ($2,000) long-term capital loss?

57. On January 1 of year 1, Nick and Rachel Sutton purchased a parcel of undeveloped land as an investment. The purchase price of the land was $150,000. They paid for the property by making a down payment of $50,000 and borrowing $100,000 from the bank at an interest rate of 6 percent per year. At the end of the first year, the Suttons paid $6,000 of interest to the bank. During year 1, the Suttons' only source of income was salary. On December 31 of year 2, the Suttons paid $6,000 of interest to the bank and sold the land for $210,000. They used $100,000 of the sale proceeds to pay off the $100,000 loan. The Suttons itemize deductions and are subject to a marginal ordinary income tax rate of 32 percent. LO 7-3 planning

a) Should the Suttons treat the capital gain from the land sale as investment income in year 2 in order to minimize their year 2 tax bill? If so, how much could the Suttons save?

b) How much does this cost or save them in year 2?

58. George recently received a great stock tip from his friend, Mason. George didn't have any cash on hand to invest, so he decided to take out a $20,000 loan to facilitate the stock acquisition. The loan terms are 8 percent interest with interest-only payments due each year for five years. At the end of the five-year period, the entire loan principal is due. When George closed on the loan on April 1, 2022, he decided to invest $16,000 in stock and to use the remaining $4,000 to purchase a four-wheel recreation vehicle. George is unsure how he will treat the interest paid on the $20,000 loan. In 2022, George paid $1,200 interest expense on the loan. For tax purposes, how should he treat the 2022 interest expense? (*Hint:* Visit www.irs.gov and consider IRS Publication 550.) LO 7-3 research

59. Larry recently invested $20,000 (tax basis) in purchasing a limited partnership interest in which he will have no management rights in the company. His at-risk amount is also $20,000. In addition, Larry's share of the limited partnership loss for the year is $2,000, his share of income from a different limited partnership is $1,000, and he has $3,000 of dividend income from the stock he owns. How much of Larry's $2,000 loss from the limited partnership can he deduct in the current year? LO 7-4

60. Rubio recently invested $20,000 (tax basis) in purchasing a limited partnership interest in which he will have no management rights in the company. His at-risk amount is $15,000. In addition, Rubio's share of the limited partnership loss for the year is $22,000, his share of income from a different limited partnership is $5,000, and he has $40,000 in wage income and $10,000 in long-term capital gains. LO 7-4

a) How much of Rubio's $22,000 loss is allowed considering only the tax-basis loss limitations?

b) How much of the loss from part (a) is allowed under the at-risk limitations?

c) How much of Rubio's $22,000 loss from the limited partnership can he deduct in the current year considering all limitations?

61. Molly Grey (single) acquired a 30 percent limited partnership interest in Beau Geste LLP several years ago for $48,000. At the beginning of year 1, Molly has tax basis and an at-risk amount of $20,000. In year 1, Beau Geste incurs a loss of $180,000 and does not make any distributions to the partners. LO 7-4

- In year 1, Molly's AGI (excluding any income or loss from Beau Geste) is $60,000. This includes $10,000 of passive income from other passive activities.
- In year 2, Beau Geste earns income of $30,000. In addition, Molly contributes an additional $30,000 to Beau Geste during year 2. Molly's AGI in year 2 is $63,000 (excluding any income or loss from Beau Geste). This amount includes $8,000 in income from her other passive investments.

a) Based on the above information, determine the following amounts:
- At-risk amount at the end of year 1.
- At-risk amount at the end of year 2.
- Losses allowed under the at-risk rules in year 2.
- Total suspended passive losses at the end of year 1.
- Total suspended at-risk losses at the end of year 2.
- Deductible losses in year 1.
- Year 2 AGI after considering Beau Geste events.

b) Briefly describe actions Molly Grey could undertake in year 2 to utilize any suspended passive losses from year 1.

LO 7-4

62. Anwer owns a rental home and is involved in maintaining it and approving renters. During the year, he has a net loss of $8,000 from renting the home. His other sources of income during the year are a salary of $111,000 and $34,000 of long-term capital gains. How much of Anwer's $8,000 rental loss can he deduct currently if he has no sources of passive income?

COMPREHENSIVE PROBLEM

Select problems are available in Connect®.

tax forms

63. During 2022, your clients, Mr. and Mrs. Howell, owned the following investment assets:

Investment Assets	Date Acquired	Purchase Price	Broker's Commission Paid at Time of Purchase
300 shares of IBM common	11/22/2019	$ 10,350	$ 100
200 shares of IBM common	4/3/2020	43,250	300
3,000 shares of Apple preferred	12/12/2020	147,000	1,300
2,100 shares of Cisco common	8/14/2021	52,500	550
420 shares of Vanguard mutual fund	3/2/2022	14,700	No-load fund*

*No commissions are charged when no-load mutual funds are bought and sold.

Because of the downturn in the stock market, Mr. and Mrs. Howell decided to sell most of their stocks and the mutual fund in 2022 and to reinvest in municipal bonds. The following investment assets were sold in 2022:

Investment Assets	Date Sold	Sale Price	Broker's Commission Paid at Time of Sale
300 shares of IBM common	5/6	$ 13,700	$ 100
3,000 shares of Apple preferred	10/5	221,400	2,000
2,100 shares of Cisco common	8/15	63,250	650
451 shares of Vanguard mutual fund	12/21	15,700	No-load fund*

*No commissions are charged when no-load mutual funds are bought and sold.

The Howells' broker issued them Form 1099-B showing the sales proceeds net of the commissions paid. For example, the IBM sales proceeds were reported as $13,600 on the Form 1099-B they received.

In addition to the sales reflected in the table above, the Howells provided you with the following additional information concerning 2022:

- The Howells received Form 1099-B from the Vanguard mutual fund reporting a $900 long-term capital gain distribution. This distribution was reinvested in 31 additional Vanguard mutual fund shares on 6/30/2022.

- In 2016, Mrs. Howell loaned $6,000 to a friend who was starting a new multilevel marketing company called LD3. The friend declared bankruptcy in 2022, and Mrs. Howell has been notified she will not be receiving any repayment of the loan.
- The Howells have a $2,300 short-term capital loss carryover and a $4,800 long-term capital loss carryover from prior years.
- The Howells did not instruct their broker to sell any particular lot of IBM stock.
- The Howells earned $3,000 in municipal bond interest, $3,000 in interest from corporate bonds, and $4,000 in qualified dividends.
- Assume the Howells have $130,000 of wage income during the year.

Required:

a) Go to the IRS website (www.irs.gov) and download the most current version of Form 8949 and Form 1040 Schedule D. Use Form 8949 and page 1 of Schedule D to compute net long-term and short-term capital gains. Complete Form 8949 even though the brokerage firm may have reported everything correctly and no adjustments are necessary. Then, compute the Howells' tax liability for the year (ignoring the alternative minimum tax and any phase-out provisions) assuming they file a joint return, they have no dependents, they don't make any special tax elections, and their itemized deductions total $30,000. Assume that asset bases are reported to the IRS.

b) Are there any tax planning recommendations related to the stock sales that you should have shared with the Howells before their decision to sell?

c) Assume the Howells' short-term capital loss carryover from prior years is $82,300 rather than $2,300 as indicated above. If this is the case, how much short-term and long-term capital loss carryovers remain to be carried beyond 2022 to future tax years?

UWorld | ROGER CPA Review

UWorld Roger CPA Review

Sample CPA Exam questions from Roger CPA Review are available in Connect as support for the topics in this text. These Multiple Choice Questions and Task-Based Simulations include expert-written explanations and solutions and provide a starting point for students to become familiar with the content and functionality of the actual CPA Exam.

chapter

8 Individual Income Tax Computation and Tax Credits

Learning Objectives

Upon completing this chapter, you should be able to:

LO 8-1 Determine a taxpayer's regular tax liability.

LO 8-2 Compute a taxpayer's alternative minimum tax liability.

LO 8-3 Calculate a taxpayer's net investment income tax, and employment and self-employment tax liability.

LO 8-4 Compute a taxpayer's allowable child tax credit, child and dependent care credit, American opportunity tax credit, lifetime learning credit, and earned income credit.

LO 8-5 Explain how to compute a taxpayer's underpayment, late filing, and late payment penalties.

Drazen/E+/Getty Images

Storyline Summary

Taxpayers:	Courtney Wilson (she/her/hers), age 40, and Courtney's mother, Dorothy "Gram" Weiss (she/her/hers), age 70
Family description:	Courtney is divorced with a son, Deron (he/him/his), age 10, and a daughter, Ellen (she/her/hers), age 20. Gram is currently residing with Courtney.
Location:	Kansas City, Missouri
Employment status:	Courtney works as an architect for EWD. Gram is retired.
Filing status:	Courtney is head of household. Gram is single.
Current situation:	Courtney and Gram have computed their taxable income. Now they are trying to determine their tax liability, tax refund, or additional taxes due and whether they owe any payment-related penalties.

Courtney has already determined her taxable income. Now she's working on computing her tax liability. She knows she owes a significant amount of regular income tax on her employment and business activities. However, she's not sure how to compute the tax on the dividends she received from Home Depot and is worried that she may be subject to the alternative minimum tax this year. Finally, Courtney knows she owes some self-employment taxes on her business income. Courtney would like to determine whether she is eligible to claim any tax credits, such as the child tax credit for her two children and education credits because she paid for a portion of her daughter Ellen's tuition at the University of Missouri–Kansas City this year. Courtney is hoping that she has paid enough in taxes during the year to avoid underpayment penalties. She's planning on filing her tax return and paying her taxes on time.

Gram's tax situation is much more straightforward. She needs to determine the regular income tax on her taxable income. Her income is so low she knows she need not worry about the alternative minimum tax, and she believes she doesn't owe any self-employment tax. Gram didn't prepay any taxes this year, so she is concerned that she might be required to pay an underpayment penalty. She plans to file her tax return and pay her taxes by the looming due date.

(to be continued . . .)

In earlier chapters we've learned how to compute taxable income for taxpayers such as Courtney and Gram. This chapter describes how to determine a taxpayer's tax liability for the year. The process is not as easy as simply applying taxable income to the applicable tax rate schedule or tax table. Taxpayers may generate taxable income that is taxed at rates not provided in the tax rate schedules or tax tables. Taxpayers also may be required to pay taxes in addition to the regular income tax. This chapter also describes tax credits taxpayers may use to reduce their gross taxes payable. We conclude the chapter by describing taxpayer filing requirements and identifying certain penalties taxpayers may be required to pay when they underpay or are late paying their taxes. We start our coverage by explaining how to compute one's regular tax liability.

LO 8-1

REGULAR FEDERAL INCOME TAX COMPUTATION

Once taxpayers have determined their taxable income, they are ready to compute their gross tax from a series of progressive tax rates called a **tax rate schedule.**

Tax Rate Schedules

Congress has constructed four different tax rate schedules for individuals. The applicable tax rate schedule is determined by the taxpayer's filing status, which we discussed in depth in the Individual Income Tax Overview, Dependents, and Filing Status chapter. Recall that a taxpayer's filing status is one of the following:

1. Married filing jointly.
2. Qualifying widow or widower, also referred to as surviving spouse.
3. Married filing separately.
4. Head of household.
5. Single.

As we described in the chapter An Introduction to Tax, a tax rate schedule is composed of several ranges of income taxed at different (increasing) rates. Each separate range of income subject to a different tax rate is referred to as a **tax bracket.** While each filing status has its own tax rate schedule (married filing jointly and qualifying widow or widower use the same rate schedule), all tax rate schedules consist of tax brackets taxed at 10 percent, 12 percent, 22 percent, 24 percent, 32 percent, 35 percent, and 37 percent. However, the width or range of income within each bracket varies by filing status. In general, the tax brackets are widest and higher levels of income are taxed at the lowest rates for the married filing jointly filing status, followed by the head of household filing status, single filing status, and, finally, the married filing separately filing status.

The tax rate schedule for each filing status is provided in Appendix C. Notice that the married filing separately schedule is the same as the married filing jointly schedule except that the taxable income levels listed in the schedule are exactly one-half the taxable income levels for married filing jointly.

Example 8-1

As we determined in the Individual Deductions chapter, Courtney files under the head of household filing status and her 2022 taxable income is $145,070 (see Exhibit 6-12).

What if: For now, let's *assume* that all of Courtney's income is taxed as ordinary income. That is, assume that none of her income is taxed at a preferential rate (some is, but we'll address this in a bit). What is the tax on her taxable income?

Answer: $27,153. Using the head of household tax rate schedule, her taxable income falls in the 24 percent marginal tax rate bracket, in between $89,050 and $170,050, so her tax is computed as follows:

Description	Amount	Explanation
(1) Base tax	$ 13,708	From head of household tax rate schedule for taxpayer with taxable income in 24% bracket.
(2) Income taxed at marginal tax rate	56,020	$145,070 – $89,050 from head of household tax rate schedule.
(3) Marginal tax rate	24%	From head of household tax rate schedule.
(4) Tax on income at marginal tax rate	13,444.80	(2) × (3)
Tax on taxable income	**$ 27,153**	(1) + (4), rounded

Example 8-2

As we determined in the Individual Deductions chapter, Gram files under the single filing status. In the Individual Deductions chapter we calculated her 2022 taxable income to be $890 (see Exhibit 6-14). None of her income is taxed at a preferential rate. What is the tax on her taxable income using the tax rate schedules?

Answer: $89 ($890 × 10%).

For administrative convenience and to prevent low- and middle-income taxpayers from making mathematical errors using a tax rate schedule, the IRS provides **tax tables** that present the gross tax for various amounts of taxable income under $100,000 and filing status (it's impractical to provide a table for essentially unlimited amounts of income). Taxpayers with taxable income less than $100,000 generally must use the tax tables to determine their tax liability.[1]

Because the tax tables generate nearly the same tax as calculated from the tax rate schedule, we use the tax rate schedules throughout this chapter.

Marriage Penalty or Benefit

An interesting artifact of the tax rate schedules is that they can impose what some refer to as a **marriage penalty,** but they may actually produce a **marriage benefit.** A marriage penalty (benefit) occurs when, for a given level of income, a married couple incurs a greater (lesser) tax liability by using the married filing jointly tax rate schedule to determine the tax on their joint income than they would have owed (in total) if each spouse had used the single tax rate schedule to compute the tax on their individual incomes. Exhibit 8-1 explores the marriage penalty in a scenario in which both spouses earn income and another in which only one spouse earns income. As the exhibit illustrates, the marriage penalty applies to couples with two wage earners with high incomes, but a marriage benefit applies to couples with single breadwinners. For couples with two wage earners with moderate to low incomes, there is typically not a marriage penalty or benefit.

Exceptions to the Basic Tax Computation

In certain circumstances, taxpayers cannot completely determine their final tax liability from their tax rate schedule or tax table. Taxpayers must perform additional computations to determine their tax liability (1) when they recognize long-term capital gains or receive dividends that are taxed at preferential (lower) rates or (2) when the taxpayer is a child and the child's unearned income is taxed using the parents' tax rates. We describe these additional computations in detail below.

[1]Exceptions to this requirement include taxpayers subject to the kiddie tax, with qualified dividends or long-term capital gains, or claiming the foreign-earned income exclusion. You may view the tax tables in the instructions for Form 1040 located at www.irs.gov.

EXHIBIT 8-1 2022 Marriage Penalty (Benefit): Two-Income vs. Single-Income Married Couple*

Married Couple	Taxable Income	Tax if Filing Jointly (1)	Tax if Filing Single† (2)	Marriage Penalty (Benefit) (1) – (2)
Scenario 1: *Two wage earners*				
Spouse 1	$350,000		$ 96,253	
Spouse 2	350,000		96,253	
Combined	$700,000	$193,549	$192,506	$ 1,043
Scenario 2: *One wage earner*				
Spouse 1	$700,000		$221,955	
Spouse 2	0		0	
Combined	$700,000	$193,549	$221,955	$(28,406)

*This analysis assumes the taxpayers do not owe any alternative minimum tax (discussed below).
†Married couples do not actually have the option of filing as single. If they choose not to file jointly, they must file as married filing separately.

Preferential Tax Rates for Capital Gains and Dividends As we described in detail earlier in the text, certain capital gains and qualified dividends are taxed at a lower or **preferential tax rate** relative to other types of income. In general, the preferential tax rate is 0 percent, 15 percent, or 20 percent.[2] The preferential tax rates vary with the taxpayer's taxable income. See Appendix C for the tax brackets by filing status that apply to preferentially taxed capital gains and dividends. Taxpayers with income subject to the preferential rate (long-term capital gains and qualified dividends) can use the following three-step process to determine their tax liability.

Step 1: Split taxable income into the portion that is subject to the preferential rate and the portion taxed at the ordinary rates.

Step 2: Compute the tax separately on each type of income. Note that the income that is not taxed at the preferential rate is taxed at the ordinary tax rates using the tax rate schedule for the taxpayer's filing status.

Step 3: Add the tax on the income subject to the preferential tax rates and the tax on the income subject to the ordinary rates. This is the taxpayer's regular tax liability.

Example 8-3

Courtney's taxable income of $145,070 includes $700 of qualified dividends from Home Depot (Example 5-8). What is her tax liability on her taxable income?

Answer: $27,090, computed at head of household rates as follows:

Description	Amount	Explanation
(1) Taxable income	$145,070	Exhibit 6-12
(2) Preferentially taxed income	700	Example 5-8
(3) Income taxed at ordinary rates	$144,370	(1) – (2)

[2]As we discovered earlier in the text, some types of income may be taxed at a preferential rate of 28 percent or 25 percent. In addition, as we discuss later in this chapter, dividends and capital gains for higher-income taxpayers are subject to the 3.8 percent net investment income tax.

Description	Amount	Explanation
(4) Tax on income taxed at ordinary rates	$ 26,985	[$13,708 + ($144,370 – $89,050) × 24%], rounded
(5) Tax on preferentially taxed income	105	(2) × 15% (Preferential tax rate for taxpayer filing head of household with income between $55,800 and $488,500)
Tax on taxable income	**$27,090**	(4) + (5)

In this example, what is Courtney's tax savings from having the dividends taxed at the preferential rate rather than the ordinary rate?

Answer: $63. $700 × (24% – 15%). This is the amount of the dividend times the difference in the ordinary and preferential tax rates.

What if: Assume that Courtney's taxable income is $498,500, including $15,000 of qualified dividends taxed at the preferential rate. What would be Courtney's tax liability under these circumstances?

Answer: $144,229, computed using the head of household tax rate schedule as follows:

Description	Amount	Explanation
(1) Taxable income	$ 498,500	
(2) Preferentially taxed income	15,000	
(3) Income taxed at ordinary rates	483,500	(1) – (2)
(4) Tax on income at ordinary tax rates	$ 141,479	$47,836 + [($483,500 – $215,950) × 35%] (See tax rate schedule for head of household.)
(5) Tax on preferentially taxed income	2,750	[($5,000 × 15%) + ($10,000 × 20%)]*
Tax	**$144,229**	(4) + (5), rounded

*Courtney had $15,000 of preferentially taxed income. $10,000 of her dividends fall in the 20 percent preferential tax bracket ($498,500 taxable income – $488,500 end of 20 percent preferential tax bracket; see preferential tax rate schedule for head of household). The remaining $5,000 is taxed at 15 percent (15 percent bracket for preferentially taxed income extends from $55,801 to $488,500 for head of household).

Kiddie Tax Parents can reduce their family's income tax bill by shifting income that would otherwise be taxed at their higher tax rates to their children whose income is taxed at lower rates. However, as we described in the Gross Income and Exclusions chapter, under the assignment of income doctrine, taxpayers cannot simply assign or transfer income to other parties. Earned income, or income from services or labor, is taxed to the person who earns it. Thus, it's difficult for a parent to shift *earned* income to a child. However, unearned income or income from property such as dividends from stocks or interest from bonds is taxed to the *owner* of the property. Thus, a parent can shift unearned income to a child by transferring actual ownership of the income-producing property to the child. By transferring ownership, the parent runs the risk that the child will sell the asset or use it in a way unintended by the parent. However, this risk is relatively small for parents transferring property ownership to younger children.

The tax laws reduce parents' ability to shift unearned income to children through the so-called **kiddie tax.** The kiddie tax provisions apply (or potentially apply) to a child if (1) the child is under 18 years old at year-end, (2) the child is 18 at year-end but their earned income does *not* exceed half of their support, or (3) the child is over age 18 but under age 24 at year-end and is a full-time student during the year, and their earned income does not exceed half of their support (excluding scholarships).[3] The kiddie tax does not apply to a married child filing a joint tax return or to a child without living parents. In general terms, if the kiddie tax applies, children must pay tax on a certain amount of their **net unearned income** (discussed below) at their parents' marginal tax rate rather than at their own marginal tax rate, unless the parents' marginal tax rate on the income (the preferential tax rate if the income is long-term capital gain or qualified dividends) would be lower than the child's marginal tax rate.[4]

The kiddie tax base is the child's net unearned income. Net unearned income is the *lesser* of (1) the child's gross *unearned income* minus $2,300[5] or (2) the child's taxable income (the child is not taxed on more than their taxable income).[6] Consequently, the kiddie tax does not apply unless the child has *unearned* income in *excess* of $2,300. Thus, the kiddie tax limits, but does not eliminate, the tax benefit gained by a family unit when parents transfer income-producing assets to children.

Example 8-4

What if: Suppose that during 2022, Deron received $5,300 in interest from an IBM bond, and he received another $2,100 in interest income from a money market account that his parents have been contributing to over the years. Is Deron potentially subject to the kiddie tax?

Answer: Yes. Deron is younger than 18 years old at the end of the year and his net unearned income exceeds $2,300.

What are Deron's taxable income and corresponding tax liability?

Answer: $6,250 taxable income and $1,339 tax liability, calculated as follows:

Description	Amount	Explanation
(1) Gross income/AGI	$ 7,400	$5,300 interest from IBM bond + $2,100 interest. All unearned income.
(2) Standard deduction	1,150	Minimum for taxpayer claimed as a dependent on another return (no earned income, so must use minimum).
(3) Taxable income	**$6,250**	(1) – (2)
(4) Gross unearned income minus $2,300	5,100	(1) – $2,300
(5) Net unearned income	$ 5,100	Lesser of (3) or (4)
(6) Kiddie tax	$ 1,224	(5) × 24%; see Example 8-3 (use Courtney's marginal tax rate of 24% because she is the custodial parent).
(7) Taxable income taxed at Deron's rate	1,150	(3) – (5)
(8) Tax on taxable income using Deron's tax rates	$ 115	(7) × 10%; see single filing status, $1,150 taxable income.
Deron's total tax liability	**$1,339**	(6) + (8)

THE KEY FACTS

Tax Rates

- Regular tax rates
  - Schedule depends on filing status.
  - Progressive tax rate schedules with tax rates ranging from 10 percent to 37 percent.
  - Marriage penalty (benefit) occurs because dual-earning spouses pay more (less) combined tax than if they each filed single.
- Preferential tax rates
  - Net long-term capital gains and qualified dividends generally taxed at 0 percent, 15 percent, or 20 percent.
- Kiddie tax
  - Unearned income in excess of $2,300 is taxed at parent's marginal tax rate if child is (1) under age 18, (2) 18 but earned income does not exceed one-half of support, or (3) over 18 and under 24, full-time student, and earned income does not exceed one-half of support.

[3]§1(g)(2)(A).

[4]§1(g).

[5]The $2,300 consists of the child's minimum standard deduction of $1,150 (even if the child is entitled to a larger standard deduction) plus an extra $1,150. If the child itemizes deductions, then the calculation becomes more complex and is beyond the scope of this text.

[6]§1(g)(4).

What if: Assume Deron's only source of income is qualified dividends of $5,300 (unearned income). What are his taxable income and tax liability?

Answer: Taxable income is $4,150; tax liability is $450, computed as follows:

Description	Amount	Explanation
(1) Gross income/(AGI)	$ 5,300	Qualified dividends, all unearned income.
(2) Standard deduction	1,150	Minimum for taxpayer claimed as a dependent on another return (all unearned income, so must use minimum).
(3) Taxable income	**$4,150**	(1) − (2)
(4) Gross unearned income minus $2,300	3,000	(1) − $2,300
(5) Net unearned income	$ 3,000	Lesser of (3) or (4)
(6) Kiddie tax	$ 450	(5) × 15%; see Example 8-3 (use Courtney's marginal tax rate of 15% on net capital gains and qualified dividends because she is the custodial parent).
(7) Taxable income taxed at Deron's rate	1,150	(3) − (5)
(8) Tax on taxable income using Deron's tax rates	$ 0	(7) × 0%; see single tax rate schedule for preferentially taxed dividends.
Deron's total tax liability	**$ 450**	(6) + (8)

As we've just described, all individual taxpayers must pay federal income taxes on their federal taxable income. However, taxpayers may be liable for other federal taxes in addition to the regular tax liability. Many taxpayers are also required to pay the alternative minimum tax, and some working taxpayers are required to pay employment or self-employment taxes. We delve into these additional taxes below.

ALTERNATIVE MINIMUM TAX

LO 8-2

Each year, a number of taxpayers are required to pay the **alternative minimum tax (AMT)** in addition to their regular tax liability. The **alternative minimum tax system** was implemented in 1986 (earlier variations date back to the late 1960s) to ensure that taxpayers generating income pay some *minimum* amount of income tax each year. The tax is targeted at higher-income taxpayers who are benefiting from or are perceived by the public to be benefiting from the excessive use (more than Congress intended) of tax preference items such as exclusions, deferrals, and deductions to reduce or even eliminate their tax liabilities.

In general terms, the alternative minimum tax is a tax on an *alternative* tax base meant to more closely reflect economic income than the regular income tax base. Thus, the **alternative minimum tax (AMT) base** is more inclusive (or more broadly defined) than is the regular income tax base. To compute their AMT, taxpayers first compute their regular income tax liability. Then they compute the AMT base and multiply the base by the applicable alternative tax rate.[7] They must pay the AMT only when the tax on the AMT base exceeds their regular tax liability.

Alternative Minimum Tax Formula

Regular taxable income is the starting point for determining the alternative minimum tax. As the AMT formula in Exhibit 8-2 illustrates, taxpayers make several "plus" and "minus" adjustments to regular taxable income to compute alternative minimum

[7]The rate of the alternative minimum tax (AMT) is set below that of the income tax with the objective of avoiding the perception that the AMT is an additional assessment.

EXHIBIT 8-2 Formula for Computing the Alternative Minimum Tax

	Regular Taxable Income
Plus:	Standard deduction if taxpayer deducted the standard deduction in computing regular taxable income
Plus or *Minus:*	Other adjustments*
Equals:	Alternative minimum taxable income
Minus:	AMT exemption amount (if any)
Equals:	Tax base for AMT
Times:	AMT rate
Equals:	Tentative minimum tax
Minus:	Regular tax
Equals:	Alternative minimum tax

*Technically, some of these adjustments are referred to as preference items and some are referred to as adjustments. We refer to all of these items as *adjustments* for simplicity's sake.

taxable income (AMTI). They then arrive at the AMT base by subtracting an AMT exemption from AMTI. Taxpayers multiply the AMT base by the AMT rate to determine their **tentative minimum tax (TMT).** Finally, to determine their alternative minimum tax, taxpayers subtract their regular tax liability from the tentative minimum tax. The alternative minimum tax is the *excess* of the tentative minimum tax over the regular tax. If the regular tax liability equals or exceeds the tentative minimum tax, taxpayers need not pay any AMT. Individual taxpayers compute their AMT on Form 6251 (see Exhibit 8-4).

Alternative Minimum Taxable Income In order to compute alternative minimum taxable income (AMTI), taxpayers make several **alternative minimum tax adjustments** to regular taxable income. Many of these are plus adjustments that are added to regular taxable income to reach AMTI, and some are minus adjustments that are subtracted from regular taxable income to determine AMTI. Consequently, these adjustments tend to expand the regular income tax base to more closely reflect economic income.

Adjustments. Taxpayers first add back to regular taxable income the standard deduction amount, but only if they deducted it in determining taxable income. Taxpayers add back the standard deduction because it is a deduction that does not reflect an actual economic outflow from the taxpayer. Taxpayers are then required to make several adjustments to compute AMTI. Exhibit 8-3 describes the most common of these adjustments, and Exhibit 8-4 presents Form 6251, which taxpayers use to calculate the AMT. Because 2022 forms were not available at press time, we present the 2021 form as an example of the form.

The major itemized deductions that are deductible for both regular tax and AMT purposes using the *same limitations* are:

- Charitable contributions.
- Home mortgage interest expenses.
- Gambling losses.

Some deductions are deductible for regular tax and AMT purposes but have different limitations. For example, interest income that is tax exempt for regular tax purposes but included in the AMT base is included in investment income for determining the AMT investment interest expense deduction. Also, medical expenses are subject to a 10% of AGI floor for AMT purposes, instead of the 7.5% of AGI floor for regular tax purposes.

EXHIBIT 8-3 Common AMT Adjustments

Adjustment	Description
Plus adjustments:	
Tax-exempt interest from private activity bonds	Taxpayers must add back interest income that was excluded for regular tax purposes if the bonds were used to fund private activities (privately owned baseball stadium or private business subsidies) and not for the public good (build or repair public roads). However, taxpayers do not add back interest income from private activity bonds if the bonds were issued in either 2009 or 2010. Taxpayers do not personally make the determination of whether a bond is a private activity bond. Instead, interest from private activity bonds is denoted as such on Form 1099 that taxpayers receive.
Real property and personal property taxes deducted as itemized deductions	Deductible for regular tax purposes (subject to $10,000 limitation for state and local tax deductions), but not for AMT purposes.
State income or sales taxes	Deductible for regular tax purposes (subject to $10,000 limitation for state and local tax deductions), but not for AMT purposes.
Plus or Minus adjustment:	
Depreciation	Taxpayers must compute their depreciation expense for AMT purposes. For certain types of assets, the regular tax method is more accelerated than the AMT method. In any event, if the regular tax depreciation exceeds the AMT depreciation, this is a plus adjustment. If the AMT depreciation exceeds the regular tax depreciation, this is a minus adjustment.
Minus adjustments:	
State income tax refunds included in regular taxable income	Because state income taxes paid are not deductible for AMT purposes, refunds are not taxable (they do not increase the AMT base).
Gain or loss on sale of depreciable assets	Due to differences in regular tax and AMT depreciation methods, taxpayers may have a different adjusted basis (cost minus accumulated depreciation) for regular tax and for AMT purposes. Thus, they may have a different gain or loss for regular tax purposes than they do for AMT purposes. If regular tax gain exceeds AMT gain, this is a minus adjustment. Because AMT accumulated depreciation will never exceed regular tax accumulated depreciation, this would never be a plus adjustment.

Example 8-5

Courtney continued to work on her AMT computation by determining the other adjustments she needs to make to determine her alternative minimum taxable income (AMTI). What is Courtney's AMTI?

Answer: $155,150, computed as follows:

Description	Amount	Explanation
(1) Taxable income	$145,070	Exhibit 6-12
Plus adjustments:		
(2) Tax-exempt interest on Cincinnati bond used to pay for renovations to major league baseball stadium (Private activity bond: assume issued in 2016)	500	Example 5-22
(3) Itemized deduction for taxes	10,000	Example 6-14
Minus adjustments:		
(4) State income tax refund included in regular taxable income	(420)	Example 5-3
Alternative minimum taxable income	**$155,150**	Sum of (1) through (4)

EXHIBIT 8-4 2021 Form 6251 (Page 1 of 2)

Form **6251**

Department of the Treasury
Internal Revenue Service (99)

Alternative Minimum Tax—Individuals

▶ Go to *www.irs.gov/Form6251* for instructions and the latest information.
▶ Attach to Form 1040, 1040-SR, or 1040-NR.

OMB No. 1545-0074
2021
Attachment Sequence No. 32

Name(s) shown on Form 1040, 1040-SR, or 1040-NR | Your social security number

Part I Alternative Minimum Taxable Income (See instructions for how to complete each line.)

1	Enter the amount from Form 1040 or 1040-SR, line 15, if more than zero. If Form 1040 or 1040-SR, line 15, is zero, subtract line 14 of Form 1040 or 1040-SR from line 11 of Form 1040 or 1040-SR and enter the result here. (If less than zero, enter as a negative amount.)	1	
2a	If filing Schedule A (Form 1040), enter the taxes from Schedule A, line 7; otherwise, enter the amount from Form 1040 or 1040-SR, line 12a	2a	
b	Tax refund from Schedule 1 (Form 1040), line 1 or line 8z	2b	( )
c	Investment interest expense (difference between regular tax and AMT)	2c	
d	Depletion (difference between regular tax and AMT)	2d	
e	Net operating loss deduction from Schedule 1 (Form 1040), line 8a. Enter as a positive amount	2e	
f	Alternative tax net operating loss deduction	2f	( )
g	Interest from specified private activity bonds exempt from the regular tax	2g	
h	Qualified small business stock, see instructions	2h	
i	Exercise of incentive stock options (excess of AMT income over regular tax income)	2i	
j	Estates and trusts (amount from Schedule K-1 (Form 1041), box 12, code A)	2j	
k	Disposition of property (difference between AMT and regular tax gain or loss)	2k	
l	Depreciation on assets placed in service after 1986 (difference between regular tax and AMT)	2l	
m	Passive activities (difference between AMT and regular tax income or loss)	2m	
n	Loss limitations (difference between AMT and regular tax income or loss)	2n	
o	Circulation costs (difference between regular tax and AMT)	2o	
p	Long-term contracts (difference between AMT and regular tax income)	2p	
q	Mining costs (difference between regular tax and AMT)	2q	
r	Research and experimental costs (difference between regular tax and AMT)	2r	
s	Income from certain installment sales before January 1, 1987	2s	( )
t	Intangible drilling costs preference	2t	
3	Other adjustments, including income-based related adjustments	3	
4	**Alternative minimum taxable income.** Combine lines 1 through 3. (If married filing separately and line 4 is more than $752,800, see instructions.)	4	

Part II Alternative Minimum Tax (AMT)

5 Exemption.

IF your filing status is . . .	AND line 4 is not over . . .	THEN enter on line 5 . . .
Single or head of household	$ 523,600	$ 73,600
Married filing jointly or qualifying widow(er)	1,047,200	114,600
Married filing separately	523,600	57,300

If line 4 is **over** the amount shown above for your filing status, see instructions. **5**

6	Subtract line 5 from line 4. If more than zero, go to line 7. If zero or less, enter -0- here and on lines 7, 9, and 11, and go to line 10	6	
7	• If you are filing Form 2555, see instructions for the amount to enter. • If you reported capital gain distributions directly on Form 1040 or 1040-SR, line 7; you reported qualified dividends on Form 1040 or 1040-SR, line 3a; **or** you had a gain on both lines 15 and 16 of Schedule D (Form 1040) (as refigured for the AMT, if necessary), complete Part III on the back and enter the amount from line 40 here. • **All others:** If line 6 is $199,900 or less ($99,950 or less if married filing separately), multiply line 6 by 26% (0.26). Otherwise, multiply line 6 by 28% (0.28) and subtract $3,998 ($1,999 if married filing separately) from the result.	7	
8	Alternative minimum tax foreign tax credit (see instructions)	8	
9	Tentative minimum tax. Subtract line 8 from line 7	9	
10	Add Form 1040 or 1040-SR, line 16 (minus any tax from Form 4972), and Schedule 2 (Form 1040), line 2. Subtract from the result Schedule 3 (Form 1040), line 1 and any negative amount reported on Form 8978, line 14 (treated as a positive number). If zero or less, enter -0-. If you used Schedule J to figure your tax on Form 1040 or 1040-SR, line 16, refigure that tax without using Schedule J before completing this line. See instructions	10	
11	**AMT.** Subtract line 10 from line 9. If zero or less, enter -0-. Enter here and on Schedule 2 (Form 1040), line 1	11	

For Paperwork Reduction Act Notice, see your tax return instructions. Cat. No. 13600G Form **6251** (2021)

Source: irs.gov.

AMT Exemption To help ensure that most taxpayers aren't required to pay the alternative minimum tax, Congress allows taxpayers to deduct an **alternative minimum tax (AMT) exemption** amount to determine their alternative minimum tax base.[8] The amount of the exemption depends on the taxpayer's filing status. The exemption is phased out (reduced) by 25 cents for every dollar the AMTI exceeds the threshold amount. Exhibit 8-5 identifies, by filing status, the base exemption amount, the phase-out threshold, and the range of AMTI over which the exemption is phased out for 2022.[9]

EXHIBIT 8-5 **2022 AMT Exemptions**

Filing Status	Exemption	Phase-Out Begins at This Level of AMTI	Phase-Out Complete for This Level of AMTI
Married filing jointly	$118,100	$1,079,800	$1,552,200
Married filing separately	59,050	539,900	776,100
Head of household and single	75,900	539,900	843,500

Example 8-6

What is Courtney's AMT base?

Answer: $79,250, computed by subtracting her allowable exemption amount from her AMTI as follows:

Description	Amount	Explanation
(1) AMTI	$155,150	Example 8-5
(2) Full AMT exemption (head of household)	75,900	Exhibit 8-5
(3) Exemption phase-out threshold	539,900	Exhibit 8-5
(4) AMTI in excess of exemption phase-out threshold	0	(1) – (3)
(5) Exemption phase-out percentage	25%	
(6) Exemption phase-out amount	0	(4) × (5), rounded
(7) Deductible exemption amount	75,900	(2) – (6)
AMT base	**$ 79,250**	(1) – (7)

What if: Suppose Courtney's AMTI is $700,000. What is Courtney's AMT base?

Answer: $664,125, computed as follows:

Description	Amount	Explanation
(1) AMTI	$ 700,000	
(2) Full AMT exemption (head of household)	75,900	Exhibit 8-5
(3) Exemption phase-out threshold	539,900	Exhibit 8-5
(4) AMTI in excess of exemption phase-out	160,100	(1) – (3)
(5) Exemption phase-out percentage	25%	
(6) Exemption phase-out amount	40,025	(4) × (5)
(7) Deductible exemption amount	35,875	(2) – (6)
AMT base	**$664,125**	(1) – (7)

THE KEY FACTS

Alternative Minimum Tax (AMT)

- Implemented to ensure taxpayers pay some minimum level of income tax.
- AMT base
  - More broad than regular income tax base.
  - No deductions for standard deduction, state income taxes, and property taxes, in addition to other adjustments.
- AMT exemption amounts for 2022
  - $118,100 married filing jointly.
  - $59,050 married filing separately.
  - $75,900 single or head of household.
  - Phased out by 25 cents for each dollar of AMTI over threshold.
- AMT rates
  - 26 percent on first $206,100 of AMT base ($103,050 for married taxpayers filing separately).
  - 28 percent on AMT base in excess of $206,100 ($103,050 for married taxpayers filing separately) .

(continued)

[8]Similar to standard deduction amounts, the AMT exemption is indexed for inflation. The phase-out threshold amounts are also indexed annually for inflation.

[9]The AMT exemption for a child subject to the kiddie tax is limited in 2022 to the lesser of (a) the AMT exemption amount in Exhibit 8-5 for the child's filing status (reduced by any exemption phase-out amount) or (b) the child's earned income plus $8,200.

- Net long-term capital gains and qualified dividends taxed at same preferential rates used for regular tax purposes.
- AMT is the excess of tentative minimum tax (tax on AMT base) over regular tax liability.

Tentative Minimum Tax and AMT Computation Taxpayers compute the tentative minimum tax by multiplying the AMT base by the applicable AMT rates. The 2022 AMT tax rate schedule consists of the following two brackets:

- 26 percent on the first $206,100 (indexed for inflation annually) of AMT base for all taxpayers other than married taxpayers filing separately ($103,050, indexed for inflation annually, for married taxpayers filing separately).
- 28 percent on AMT base in excess of $206,100 (indexed for inflation annually) for all taxpayers other than married taxpayers filing separately ($103,050, indexed for inflation annually, for married taxpayers filing separately).

However, for AMT purposes, long-term capital gains and qualified dividends are taxed at the same preferential rate as they were taxed for regular tax purposes (generally 0 percent, 15 percent, or 20 percent).

Example 8-7

Courtney's AMT base is $79,250. However, Courtney also received $700 in dividends that are included in the base but are subject to a tax rate of 15 percent even under the AMT system. The remaining $78,550 ($79,250 – $700) is taxed at the normal AMT rates. What is Courtney's tentative minimum tax?

Answer: $20,528, computed as follows:

Description	Amount	Explanation
(1) AMT base	$ 79,250	Example 8-6
(2) Dividends taxed at preferential rate	700	Example 8-3
(3) Tax on qualified dividends	105	Example 8-3
(4) AMT base taxed at regular AMT rates	78,550	(1) – (2)
(5) Regular AMT tax rate	26%	For AMT base below $206,100.
(6) Tax on AMT base taxed at regular AMT rates	20,423	(4) × (5)
Tentative minimum tax	**$20,528**	(3) + (6)

Taxpayers subtract their regular tax liability from their tentative minimum tax to determine their AMT.[10] If the taxpayer's regular tax liability is equal to or exceeds the tentative minimum tax liability, the taxpayer does not owe any AMT.

Example 8-8

What is Courtney's alternative minimum tax liability?

Answer: $0, computed as follows:

Description	Amount	Explanation
(1) Tentative minimum tax	$20,528	Example 8-7
(2) Regular tax liability	27,090	Example 8-3
Alternative minimum tax	**$ 0**	(1) – (2) ($0 if negative)

Courtney owes $0 alternative minimum tax in addition to her regular tax liability.

In some situations, taxpayers who pay the AMT are entitled to a **minimum tax credit** to use when the regular tax exceeds the tentative minimum tax. They can use the credit to offset regular tax but not below the tentative minimum tax for that year.[11]

[10]As might be expected, self-employment taxes and the net investment income tax are not considered as part of a taxpayer's regular tax liability in determining whether a taxpayer owes AMT.

[11]The credit applies only when the taxpayer has positive adjustments that will reverse and become negative adjustments in the future. For example, depreciation, gain or loss on asset sales, and incentive stock option bargain element adjustments fall into this category. Due to the nature of her adjustments, Courtney does not qualify for the minimum tax credit.

ADDITIONAL TAXES

LO 8-3

In addition to regular income taxes, taxpayers are often subject to additional taxes. In the following paragraphs, we discuss three of the most common additional taxes: the net investment income tax, and employment and self-employment taxes.

Net Investment Income Tax Higher-income taxpayers are required to pay a 3.8 percent tax on net investment income. For purposes of the **net investment income tax,** net investment income equals the sum of:

1. Gross income from interest, dividends, annuities, royalties, and rents (unless these items are derived in a trade or business to which the net investment income tax does not apply).
2. Income from a trade or business that is a passive activity or a trade or business of trading financial instruments or commodities.
3. Net gain from disposing of property (other than property held in a trade or business in which the net investment income tax does not apply).[12]
4. Less the allowable deductions that are allocable to items 1, 2, and 3.

Tax-exempt interest, veterans' benefits, excluded gain from the sale of a principal residence, distributions from qualified retirement plans, and any amounts subject to self-employment tax are not subject to the net investment income tax.

The tax imposed is 3.8 percent of the lesser of (1) net investment income or (2) the excess of modified adjusted gross income over $250,000 for married-joint filers and surviving spouses, $125,000 for married-separate filers, and $200,000 for other taxpayers. Modified adjusted gross income equals adjusted gross income increased by income excluded under the foreign-earned income exclusion less any disallowed deductions associated with the foreign-earned income exclusion.[13]

THE KEY FACTS

Net Investment Income Tax

3.8 percent tax on lesser of (a) net investment income or (b) excess of modified AGI over applicable threshold based on filing status.

Example 8-9

Courtney's AGI (and modified AGI) is $187,000, and her investment income consists of $321 of taxable interest, $700 of dividends, and $5,000 of rental income (see Exhibit 6-7 and Exhibit 6-8).[14] How much net investment income tax will Courtney owe?

Answer: $0. Because Courtney's modified AGI ($187,000) is less than the $200,000 threshold for the net investment income tax for a taxpayer filing as head of household, she will not be subject to the tax.

What if: Assume that Courtney's AGI (and modified AGI) is $225,000. How much net investment income tax will Courtney owe?

Answer: $229, calculated as follows:

Description	Amount	Explanation
(1) Net investment income	$ 6,021	$321 interest + $700 dividends + $5,000 rental income
(2) Modified AGI	225,000	
(3) Modified AGI threshold	200,000	
(4) Excess modified AGI above threshold	25,000	(2) − (3)
(5) Net investment income tax base	6,021	Lesser of (1) or (4)
Net investment income tax	**$ 229**	(5) × 3.8%

[12]However, the income, gain, or loss attributable to invested working capital of a trade or business is subject to the net investment income tax. §1411(c)(3).

[13]Taxpayers compute the net investment income tax using Form 8960.

[14]Courtney's rental income would be considered investment income for purposes of the net investment income tax because it would be considered income from a trade or business that is a passive activity.

Employment and Self-Employment Taxes

As we discussed in the chapter An Introduction to Tax, employees and self-employed taxpayers must pay employment (or self-employment) taxes known as FICA taxes.[15] The FICA tax consists of a Social Security and a Medicare component that are payable by both employees and employers. The **Social Security tax** is intended to provide basic pension coverage for the retired and disabled. The **Medicare tax** helps pay medical costs for qualified individuals. Because Social Security and Medicare taxes are paid by working taxpayers but received by retired taxpayers, Social Security and Medicare taxes represent intergenerational transfers. The Social Security tax rate is 12.4 percent on the tax base (limited to $147,000 in 2022), and the Medicare tax rate is 2.9 percent on the tax base. An **additional Medicare tax** of .9 percent applies on the tax base in excess of $200,000 ($125,000 for married filing separately; $250,000 for married filing jointly). Below we discuss how these taxes apply for employees, employers, and self-employed taxpayers.

THE KEY FACTS

Employee FICA Tax

- Tax base is employee salary or wages.
- Social Security tax
  - 6.2 percent rate on tax base.
  - 2022 tax base limit is $147,000.
- Medicare tax
  - 1.45 percent rate on tax base.
  - Tax base unlimited.
- Additional Medicare tax
  - .9 percent rate on tax base in excess of $200,000 ($125,000 for married filing separately; $250,000 for married filing jointly).

Employee FICA Taxes Payable Both employees and employers have to pay **FICA taxes** on employee salary, wages, and other compensation paid by employers. The Social Security tax rate for employees is 6.2 percent of their salary or wages (tax base limited to $147,000 in 2022), the Medicare tax rate for employees is 1.45 percent of their salary or wages, and the additional Medicare tax rate is .9 percent on salary or wages in excess of $200,000 ($125,000 for married filing separately; $250,000 of combined salary or wages for married filing jointly).

Employers withhold the employees' FICA tax liabilities from the employees' paychecks for both the Social Security tax and the Medicare tax. For the additional Medicare tax, employers are required to withhold the tax at a rate of .9 percent for any salary or wages above $200,000, irrespective of the taxpayer's filing status (e.g., single, married filing separately, married filing jointly, or head of household).[16] Taxpayers use Form 8959, Additional Medicare Tax, to determine their liability for the additional Medicare tax and report all of the additional Medicare tax withheld as a tax payment on Form 1040, Schedule 2, line 11.

Employers also must pay their portion of the Social Security tax (6.2 percent of employee salary or wages) and Medicare tax (1.45 percent of employee salary or wages, regardless of the amount of salary or wages). In contrast to employees, employers are not subject to the additional Medicare tax on employee salary or wages.

Example 8-10

While she was attending school full time, Ellen received $15,000 in wages working part time for an off-campus employer during the year. How much in FICA taxes should Ellen's employer have withheld from her paychecks during the year?

Answer: $1,148, computed as follows:

Description	Amount	Explanation
(1) Wages	$15,000	
(2) Social Security tax rate	6.2%	
(3) Social Security tax	930	(1) × (2)
(4) Medicare tax rate	1.45%	
(5) Medicare tax	218	(1) × (4)
FICA taxes withheld	**$ 1,148**	(3) + (5)

[15]FICA stands for Federal Insurance Contributions Act.

[16]To avoid a potential underpayment penalty, taxpayers can request additional income tax withholding or make estimated tax payments to pay any Medicare tax that otherwise would have been owed upon filing their tax return.

Example 8-11

During 2022, Courtney received a total of $162,800 in employee compensation from EWD. Recall that the compensation consisted of $138,000 in wages, $4,800 performance bonus, $6,000 discount for architectural design services, $4,000 compensation for a below-market loan, and $10,000 forgiveness of debt (see Exhibit 5-4). What is her FICA tax liability on this income?

Answer: $11,475, computed as follows:

Description	Amount	Explanation
(1) Compensation subject to FICA tax	$162,800	
(2) Social Security tax base limit for 2022	147,000	
(3) Compensation subject to Social Security tax	147,000	Lesser of (1) or (2)
(4) Social Security tax rate	6.2%	
(5) Social Security tax	9,114	(3) × (4)
(6) Medicare tax rate	1.45%	
(7) Medicare tax	2,361	(1) × (6), rounded
FICA taxes	**$ 11,475**	(5) + (7)

What amount of FICA taxes for the year must EWD pay on Courtney's behalf?

Answer: $11,475, which includes $9,114 of Social Security tax ($147,000 × 6.2%) and $2,361 of Medicare tax ($162,800 × 1.45%).

What if: Suppose Courtney received a total of $220,000 in employee compensation. What would be her FICA tax liability on this income?

Answer: $12,484, computed as follows:

Description	Amount	Explanation
(1) Compensation subject to FICA tax	$220,000	
(2) Social Security tax base limit for 2022	147,000	
(3) Compensation subject to Social Security tax	147,000	Lesser of (1) or (2)
(4) Social Security tax rate	6.2%	
(5) Social Security tax	9,114	(3) × (4)
(6) Medicare tax rate	1.45%	
(7) Compensation subject to Medicare tax	220,000	(1)
(8) Medicare tax	3,190	(6) × (7)
(9) Additional Medicare tax rate	.9%	
(10) Compensation subject to additional Medicare tax	20,000	Greater of [(1) – $200,000] or $0
(11) Additional Medicare tax	180	(9) × (10)
FICA taxes	**$ 12,484**	(5) + (8) + (11)

What amount of FICA taxes for the year must EWD pay on Courtney's behalf?

Answer: $12,304, which includes $9,114 of Social Security tax ($147,000 × 6.2%) and $3,190 of Medicare tax ($220,000 × 1.45%). Employers do not pay the additional Medicare tax.

Employees who work for multiple employers within a calendar year may receive aggregate compensation that exceeds the Social Security tax base but does not exceed it with any employer. Because each employer is required to withhold Social Security taxes on the employee's wages until the employee has reached the tax base limit *with that employer,* the employee may end up paying Social Security tax in excess of the required maximum. As it does in situations in which excess Medicare tax has been withheld, the IRS treats the excess Social Security tax paid through withholding as an additional federal income tax payment (or credit) on Schedule 3, line 11 and page 2, line 31 of Form 1040. The government refunds the excess withholding to the employee through either lower taxes payable with the tax return or a larger tax refund. Employers, on the other hand, are not able to recover excess Social Security taxes paid on behalf of their employees.

Example 8-12

What if: Suppose Courtney worked for her former employer, Landmark Architects Inc. (LA), in Cincinnati, for two weeks in January 2022 before moving to Kansas City. During those two weeks, Courtney would have earned $4,000 in salary. LA would have withheld $306 in FICA taxes from her final paycheck consisting of $248 of Social Security taxes ($4,000 × 6.2%) and $58 of Medicare taxes ($4,000 × 1.45%). How much excess Social Security tax would have been withheld from Courtney's combined salaries from LA and EWD during 2022?

Answer: $248 ($4,000 wages earned with LA × 6.2% Social Security rate). Due to the $147,000 Social Security tax base limit for the year, Courtney's Social Security tax liability is limited to $9,114 ($147,000 × 6.2%). However, through employer withholding, she would have paid a total of $9,362 in Social Security taxes, consisting of $248 withheld by LA ($4,000 × 6.2%) and $9,114 withheld by EWD ($147,000 × 6.2%). Thus, given these facts, Courtney's *excess* Social Security tax withheld was $248 ($9,362 − $9,114). Courtney would get this amount back from the government through either lower taxes payable with her tax return or a larger tax refund.

Self-Employment Taxes While employees share their FICA (Social Security and Medicare) tax burden with employers, self-employed taxpayers must pay the *entire* FICA tax burden on their self-employment earnings.[17] Like FICA taxes for employees, self-employment taxes consist of both Social Security and Medicare taxes. Because their FICA taxes are based on their self-employment earnings, FICA taxes for self-employed taxpayers are referred to as **self-employment taxes.** The base for the Social Security component of the self-employment tax is limited to $147,000. The base for the Medicare portion of the self-employment tax is unlimited. Taxpayers use Schedule SE to determine their Social Security tax and 2.9 percent Medicare tax on self-employment earnings, and they use Form 8959 to determine the additional Medicare tax on self-employment earnings. Although applied to self-employment earnings, the additional Medicare tax is not considered technically a part of the self-employment tax. The process for determining the taxpayer's self-employment taxes (and additional Medicare tax) payable requires the following steps:

Step 1: Compute the amount of the taxpayer's net income from self-employment activities that is subject to self-employment taxes. This is generally the taxpayer's net income from **Schedule C** of Form 1040. Schedule C reports the taxpayer's self-employment-related income and expenses.

Step 2: Multiply the amount from Step 1 by 92.35 percent. The product is called **net earnings from self-employment.** Because self-employed taxpayers are responsible for paying the entire amount of their FICA taxes, they are allowed an implicit deduction for the 7.65 percent "employer's portion" of the taxes,

[17]As we discussed in the Gross Income and Exclusions and Individual Deductions chapters, self-employed taxpayers report their self-employment earnings on Schedule C of Form 1040. Individuals who are partners in partnerships and who are actively involved in the partnerships' business activities may be required to pay self-employment taxes on the income they are allocated from the partnerships. They would report these earnings on Schedule E of Form 1040.

leaving 92.35 percent (100% – 7.65%) of the full amount subject to self-employment taxes. Note that the 7.65 percent consists of the 6.2 percent Social Security tax and 1.45 percent Medicare tax. Net earnings from self-employment is the base for the self-employment tax. If net earnings from self-employment is less than $400, the taxpayer is not subject to self-employment tax (but is still subject to income tax on the earnings).

Step 3: Compute the Social Security tax. The Social Security tax component of the self-employment tax equals 12.4 percent [the combined Social Security tax rate for employer and employee (6.2% + 6.2% = 12.4%)] multiplied by the lesser of (a) the taxpayer's net earnings from self-employment (from Step 2) or (b) $147,000 (the maximum tax base for the Social Security tax).

Step 4: Compute the Medicare tax. The Medicare tax component of the self-employment tax equals 2.9 percent [the combined Medicare tax rate for employer and employee (1.45% + 1.45% = 2.9%)] multiplied by the net earnings from self-employment (from Step 2).

Step 5: Compute the additional Medicare tax. The additional Medicare tax due on net self-employment earnings equals .9 percent multiplied by the greater of (1) zero or (2) net earnings from self-employment (from Step 2) less $200,000 ($125,000 for married filing separately; $250,000 for married filing jointly). The additional Medicare tax is considered an "employee" tax (and not a "self-employment" tax).

Note that, as we discussed in the Individual Deductions chapter, taxpayers are allowed to deduct the employer portion of their self-employment taxes as a for AGI deduction.

Example 8-13

What if: Assume that Courtney's only income for the year is her $18,000 in net self-employment income from her weekend consulting business. What amount of self-employment taxes and additional Medicare tax would Courtney be required to pay on this income?

Answer: $2,543 self-employment taxes and $0 of additional Medicare tax, computed as follows:

Step 1: $18,000 of net self-employment income subject to self-employment taxes.

Step 2: $18,000 × .9235 = $16,623. This is net earnings from self-employment.

Step 3: $16,623 × 12.4% = $2,061. This is Courtney's Social Security tax payable for her self-employment income.

Step 4: $16,623 × 2.9% = $482. This is Courtney's Medicare tax payable for her self-employment income.

Step 5: $0. Because Courtney's net earnings from self-employment do not exceed $200,000, she does not have an additional Medicare tax liability.

Total $2,543 self-employment taxes [sum of Steps (3) and (4)] and **$0** of additional Medicare tax [Step (5)].

Under these circumstances, Courtney would be able to deduct $1,272 as a for AGI deduction (Schedule 1, Form 1040) for the employer portion of self-employment taxes she paid [i.e., $16,623 × (6.2% + 1.45%)].

When a taxpayer receives both employee compensation and self-employment earnings in the same year, the calculation of Social Security and additional Medicare taxes is a bit more complicated. For the Social Security tax component, the taxpayer's total earnings subject to the Social Security tax are capped at $147,000. In these situations, the taxpayer's Social Security tax liability on the employee compensation is determined as if the employee had no self-employment income. The taxpayer then computes their Social Security tax on their net earnings from self-employment. This ordering is favorable for taxpayers because it allows them to use up all or a portion of the Social Security tax base limit with their employee income (taxed at 6.2 percent) before they determine the Social Security tax on their net earnings from self-employment (taxed at 12.4 percent). Consequently, if an employee's wages exceed the Social Security tax base limitation, they are not required to pay any Social Security tax on their self-employment earnings.

Likewise, the additional Medicare tax calculation is more complicated when (1) the taxpayer receives both employee compensation and self-employment earnings or (2) the taxpayer files married jointly with a spouse receiving employee compensation or net self-employment earnings. For taxpayers not filing married jointly, the additional Medicare tax equals .9 percent of the taxpayer's salary or wages and net self-employment earnings in excess of $200,000 ($125,000 for married filing separately). For married filing jointly taxpayers, the additional Medicare tax equals .9 percent of the taxpayer's and their spouse's salary or wages and net self-employment earnings in excess of $250,000.

The calculation of the taxpayer's Social Security and Medicare taxes on self-employment earnings in these settings can be determined as follows:[18]

Social Security Tax:

Step 1: Determine the limit on the Social Security portion of the self-employment tax base by subtracting the employee compensation from the Social Security tax base limit ($147,000 in 2022) (not below $0).

Step 2: Determine the net earnings from self-employment (self-employment earnings times 92.35 percent).

Step 3: Multiply the lesser of Steps 1 and 2 by 12.4 percent. This is the amount of Social Security taxes due on the self-employment income.

Medicare Tax:

Step 4: Multiply the amount from Step 2 by 2.9 percent, the combined Medicare tax rate for employer and employee.

Additional Medicare Tax:

Step 5: Add the amount from Step 2 and the taxpayer's compensation. If married filing jointly, also add the spouse's compensation and net earnings from self-employment (spouse's self-employment earnings times 92.35 percent).

Step 6: Multiply the greater of [(a) zero or (b) the amount from Step 5 minus $200,000 ($125,000 for married filing separately; $250,000 for married filing jointly)] by .9 percent.

Step 7: Take the amount from Step 6 and subtract the amount of the .9 percent additional Medicare tax withheld by the taxpayer's employer (and their spouse's employer if married filing jointly). This is the .9 percent additional Medicare tax due on the self-employment income.

[18]If net earnings from self-employment is less than $400 ($433 in self-employment earnings times 92.35%), the taxpayer is not subject to self-employment tax (but the taxpayer is still subject to income tax on the earnings).

Example 8-14

In 2022, Courtney received $162,800 in taxable compensation from EWD (see Example 8-11) and $18,000 in self-employment income from her weekend consulting activities (see Example 6-2). What are Courtney's *self-employment taxes* and additional Medicare tax payable on her $18,000 of income from self-employment? Assume that Courtney's employer correctly withheld $9,114 of Social Security tax and $2,361 of Medicare tax.

Answer: $482 of self-employment taxes and $0 of additional Medicare tax, computed as follows:

Description	Amount	Explanation
(1) Social Security tax base limit less employee compensation subject to Social Security tax	$ 0	$147,000 − $147,000, limited to $0
(2) Net earnings from self-employment	16,623	$18,000 × 92.35%
(3) Social Security portion of self-employment tax	0	[Lesser of Step (1) or (2)] × 12.4%
(4) Medicare tax	482	Step (2) × 2.9%
(5) Sum of taxpayer's compensation and net earnings from self-employment	179,423	$162,800 + Step (2)
(6) [Greater of (a) zero or (b) the amount from Step (5) minus $200,000] × 0.9%	0	0 × 0.9%
(7) Step (6) less any additional Medicare tax withheld by Courtney's employer	0	0 − 0
Total	$ 482	(3) + (4) + (7). [**$482** of self-employment taxes {(3) + (4)} and **$0** of additional Medicare tax]

As we reported in Example 6-6, Courtney is entitled to a $241 for AGI deduction (Schedule 1, Form 1040) for the employer portion of the $482 self-employment taxes she incurred during the year ($16,623 × 1.45% employer portion of the Medicare tax rate = $241).

Example 8-15

What if: Let's change the facts and assume that Courtney received $100,000 of taxable compensation from EWD in 2022, and she received $180,000 in self-employment income from her consulting activities. What amount of self-employment taxes and additional Medicare tax is Courtney required to pay on her $180,000 of business income? Assume that Courtney's employer correctly withheld $6,200 of Social Security tax, $1,450 of Medicare tax, and $0 of additional Medicare tax.

Answer: $11,245, consisting of $10,649 of self-employment taxes and $596 of additional Medicare tax, computed as follows:

Description	Amount	Explanation
(1) Social Security tax base limit less employee compensation subject to Social Security tax	$ 47,000	$147,000 − $100,000, limited to $0
(2) Net earnings from self-employment	166,230	$180,000 × 92.35%
(3) Social Security portion of self-employment tax	5,828	[Lesser of Step (1) or (2)] × 12.4%
(4) Medicare tax	4,821	Step (2) × 2.9%, rounded

(continued on page 8-20)

Description	Amount	Explanation
(5) Sum of taxpayer's compensation and net earnings from self-employment	266,230	$100,000 + Step (2)
(6) [Greater of (a) zero or (b) the amount from Step (5) minus $200,000] × 0.9%	596	$66,230 × 0.9%, rounded
(7) Step (6) less any additional Medicare tax withheld by Courtney's employer	596	$596 – $0
Total	$ 11,245	(3) + (4) + (7) [**$10,649** of self-employment taxes {(3) + (4)} and **$596** of additional Medicare tax]

What if: Now let's assume that Courtney is married and files jointly. Assume that Courtney received $100,000 of taxable compensation from EWD in 2022 and $180,000 in self-employment income from her weekend consulting activities. In addition, her spouse received $75,000 of taxable compensation from his employer. What amount of self-employment taxes and additional Medicare tax is Courtney required to pay on her $180,000 of business income? Assume that Courtney's employer correctly withheld $6,200 of Social Security tax, $1,450 of Medicare tax, and $0 of additional Medicare tax, and that her spouse's employer correctly withheld $4,650 of Social Security tax, $1,088 of Medicare tax, and $0 of additional Medicare tax.

Answer: $11,470, consisting of $10,649 of self-employment taxes and $821 of additional Medicare tax, computed as follows:

Description	Amount	Explanation
(1) Social Security tax base limit less employee compensation subject to Social Security tax	$ 47,000	$147,000 – $100,000, limited to $0
(2) Net earnings from self-employment	166,230	$180,000 × 92.35%
(3) Social Security portion of self-employment tax	5,828	[Lesser of Step (1) or (2)] × 12.4%
(4) Medicare portion of self-employment tax	4,821	Step (2) × 2.9%, rounded
(5) Sum of taxpayer's and spouse's compensation and net earnings from self-employment	341,230	$100,000 + $75,000 + Step (2)
(6) [Greater of (a) zero or (b) the amount from Step (5) minus $250,000] × 0.9%	821	$91,230 × 0.9%, rounded
(7) Step (6) less any additional Medicare tax withheld by Courtney's employer and her husband's employer	821	$821 – $0
Total	$ 11,470	(3) + (4) + (7) [**$10,649** of self-employment taxes {(3) + (4)} and **$821** of additional Medicare tax]

Unlike employees, whose employers withhold tax throughout the year on their behalf, self-employed taxpayers must satisfy their self-employment tax obligations through periodic, usually quarterly, estimated tax payments. Taxpayers who are employed and self-employed (an employee with a business on the side, like Courtney) may have their employers withhold enough taxes to cover their income, self-employment, and additional Medicare tax obligations. Any self-employment or additional Medicare taxes not paid through these mechanisms must be paid with the self-employed taxpayer's individual tax return.

(continued from page 8-1 . . .)

Courtney was enjoying her work with EWD, but she also really liked her weekend consulting work. A couple of months ago, after she had played an integral part in completing a successful project, her boss jokingly mentioned that, if Courtney ever decided to leave EWD to work for herself as a full-time consultant, EWD would love to hire her back for contract work. This caused Courtney to start thinking about the possibilities of starting her own consulting business. She always had some interest in working for herself, but she is not at a point in her life where she can take significant financial risks even if it might mean a more satisfying career. Courtney knows that before making such a move she would need to seriously consider the nontax issues associated with self-employment and learn more about the tax consequences of working as an independent contractor. She is particularly interested in the tax consequences of working for EWD as an independent contractor (contract worker) relative to working for EWD as an employee. ■

Employee vs. Self-Employed (Independent Contractor) Determining whether an individual should be taxed as an **employee** or as an **independent contractor** can be straightforward or quite complex, depending on the specific arrangement between the parties. In its published guidance, the IRS stipulates that an employer/employee relationship exists when the party for whom services are performed has the right to direct or control the individual performing services.[19] To assist taxpayers in deciding whether the party receiving services has the requisite amount of control over the individual providing services, the IRS has published a list of 20 factors to consider.[20] A few of the factors suggesting independent contractor rather than employee status include the contractor's ability to:

1. Set their own working hours.
2. Work part time.
3. Work for more than one firm.
4. Realize either a profit or a loss from the activities.
5. Perform work somewhere other than on an employer's premises.
6. Work without frequent oversight.

When these factors are absent, individuals are more likely to be classified as employees. Rather than simply summing the number of factors in favor of independent contractor status and those in favor of employee status, however, taxpayers and their advisers should use the factors as guides in determining the overall substance of the contractual relationship.

Whether a taxpayer is classified as an employee or as an independent contractor (self-employed) has both tax and nontax consequences to the employer and the taxpayer. The best classification for the taxpayer is situation-specific.

Employee vs. independent contractor comparison. The two primary *tax* differences between independent contractors and employees relate to (1) the amount of FICA taxes payable and (2) the deductibility of business expenses (and possibly the qualified business income deduction).[21] However, there are several nontax factors to consider as well.

THE KEY FACTS

Employee vs. Independent Contractor

- Employees
  - Less control over how, when, and where to perform duties.
  - Pay 6.2 percent Social Security tax subject to limit.
  - Pay 1.45 percent Medicare tax.
  - Pay additional Medicare tax of .9 percent on salary or wages above $200,000 ($125,000 for married filing separately; $250,000 of combined salary or wages for married filing jointly).
- Independent contractors
  - More control over how, when, and where to perform duties.
  - Report income and expenses on Form 1040, Schedule C.
  - Pay 12.4 percent Social Security tax subject to limit of $147,000 in 2022.
  - Pay Medicare tax of 2.9 percent.

(continued)

[19]IRS Publication 1779, "Independent Contractor or Employee."

[20]Rev. Rul. 87-41.

[21]Also, independent contractors generally receive a Form 1099-NEC from each client reporting the gross income they received from the client during the year. Employees receive Form W-2 reporting the compensation the employee received from the employer during the year.

- Pay additional Medicare tax of .9 percent on net self-employment earnings above $200,000 ($125,000 for married filing separately; $250,000 of combined salary or wages for married filing jointly).
- Self-employment tax base is 92.35 percent of net self-employment income.
- Deduct the employer portion of self-employment taxes paid for AGI.

In the previous section, we detailed how to determine the FICA taxes payable for employees and independent contractors (self-employed taxpayers). In terms of the deductibility of business expenses, as we discussed earlier in the text, *employees* who incur unreimbursed business expenses relating to their employment cannot deduct these expenses. In contrast, self-employed independent contractors are able to deduct expenses relating to their business activities as for AGI deductions, which they can deduct without restriction. Subject to the limitations discussed earlier in the text, self-employed independent contractors may also claim the deduction for qualified business income. While these factors appear to favor independent contractor status over employee status, independent contractors typically incur more costs in doing business than employees.

When taxpayers are classified as independent contractors rather than employees, they are not eligible for nontaxable fringe benefits available to employees, such as health care insurance, retirement plan benefits, and others. Further, independent contractors are responsible for paying their estimated tax liability throughout the year because the employer does not withhold taxes from an independent contractor's pay. However, as we mentioned above, taxpayers are allowed to deduct the employer portion of the self-employment taxes they pay.

From the employer's perspective, it is generally less costly to hire an independent contractor than an employee because the employer need not provide these benefits or withhold or pay any FICA taxes on behalf of an independent contractor. As a result, an employer may be willing to offer an apparently higher level of taxable compensation to an independent contractor than to a similarly situated employee. However, after considering all relevant factors, the taxpayer may do better receiving less compensation as an employee than slightly higher compensation as an independent contractor.

ETHICS

Sudipta is an accounting major who works during the day and takes classes in the evening. They were excited to finally land their first accounting job doing the books for a local dry cleaners. In their new job, Sudipta works 30 hours a week at the dry cleaners' main office. Their excitement quickly dampened when they realized that their new employer was not withholding any income taxes or FICA taxes from their paycheck. Apparently, Sudipta's employer is treating them as an independent contractor. Sudipta likes the job, appreciates the money earned, but recognizes that they should be treated as an employee instead of an independent contractor. What would you do if you were Sudipta?

Example 8-16

What if: Let's compare Courtney's compensation as an employee with EWD to her compensation if she were to work for EWD as an independent contractor. Assume Courtney works an average of 40 hours per week for 50 weeks per year to earn a salary of $100,000; in addition, she receives fringe benefits including a 5 percent contribution to her retirement plan, life insurance coverage, and health insurance coverage. Would Courtney be "made whole" in terms of her hourly rate if EWD agreed to pay her $52.50 an hour for her contract work (5 percent more than her hourly rate as an employee)?

Answer: Not very likely. As an independent contractor, Courtney must pay more costly self-employment taxes (at nearly twice the rate of employment taxes) under the new arrangement. In addition, she will be ineligible for the nontaxable fringe benefits (retirement plan contributions, life insurance, and health coverage) she was receiving as an employee and will not receive as a contractor. Although she would benefit from the qualified business income deduction, the related tax benefits and higher pay as an independent contractor are not likely to offset the value of the nontaxable fringe benefits she would receive as an employee and the additional cost of the self-employment tax.

We've described how to calculate a taxpayer's regular tax liability, alternative minimum tax liability, net investment income tax liability, Social Security and Medicare tax liability, additional Medicare tax liability, and self-employment tax liability. These tax liabilities sum to a taxpayer's gross tax liability. While Gram's gross tax is simply her regular income tax liability of $89 (see Example 8-2), Courtney's gross tax liability includes other taxes. Courtney's gross tax liability is calculated in Exhibit 8-6.

EXHIBIT 8-6 Courtney's Gross Tax

Description	Amount	Explanation
(1) Regular federal income tax	$27,090	Example 8-3
(2) Alternative minimum tax	0	Example 8-8
(3) Self-employment tax	482	Example 8-14
Gross tax liability	$27,572	(1) + (2) + (3)

Taxpayers reduce their gross tax by tax credits and tax prepayments (withholding and estimated tax payments) for the year. As indicated in Exhibit 8-7, if the gross tax exceeds the tax credits and prepayments, the taxpayer owes additional taxes when they file their tax return. In contrast, if the prepayments exceed the gross tax after applying tax credits, the taxpayer is entitled to a tax refund. We next explore available tax credits and conclude the chapter by dealing with taxpayer prepayments.

EXHIBIT 8-7 Formula for Computing Net Tax Due or Refund

Gross tax
Minus: Tax credits
Minus: Prepayments
Net tax due (refund)

TAX CREDITS

LO 8-4

Congress provides a considerable number of credits for taxpayers. **Tax credits** reduce a taxpayer's *tax liability* dollar-for-dollar. In contrast, deductions reduce *taxable income* dollar-for-dollar, but the tax savings deductions generated depend on the taxpayer's marginal tax rate. Because tax credits generate tax savings independent of a taxpayer's marginal tax rate, they are a popular tax policy tool for avoiding the perception that tax benefits for certain tax policies are distributed disproportionately to taxpayers with higher incomes and corresponding higher marginal tax rates. Further, tax credits are powerful tax policy tools because they directly affect taxes due. By using tax credits, policy makers can adjust the magnitude of the tax effects of tax policy without changing tax rates.

Tax credits can be either nonrefundable or refundable. A **nonrefundable credit** may reduce a taxpayer's gross tax liability to zero, but if the amount of the credit exceeds the amount of the taxpayer's gross tax liability, the credit in excess of the gross tax liability is not refunded to the taxpayer. It expires without ever providing tax benefits, unless it can be carried over to a different year. Refundable credits in excess of a taxpayer's gross tax liability are refunded to the taxpayer.

Tax credits are generally classified into one of three categories: nonrefundable personal, refundable personal, or business credits, depending on the nature of the credit. The primary exception to this general rule is the foreign tax credit. The foreign tax credit is a hybrid between personal and business credits because, like nonrefundable personal credits, it reduces the taxpayer's liability before business credits, but, like business credits, unused foreign tax credits can be carried over to use in other years.

THE KEY FACTS

Child Tax Credit

- Taxpayers may claim a $2,000 credit for each qualifying child under age 17 (under age 18 for 2021 only) or $500 credit for other qualifying dependents.
- For 2021 only, taxpayers could claim an additional $1,000 child tax credit per qualifying child (additional $1,600 child tax credit per qualifying child under age six at year-end).
- The child tax credit (and, separately, the 2021 additional child tax credit) is phased out for taxpayers with AGI above applicable thresholds.
  - Taxpayer loses $50 for every $1,000 or portion thereof that AGI exceeds applicable threshold.

Nonrefundable Personal Credits

Congress provides many nonrefundable personal tax credits to generate tax relief for certain groups of individuals. For example, the child tax credit (partially refundable in most tax years) provides tax relief for taxpayers who provide a home for dependent children, and the child and dependent care credit provides tax relief for taxpayers who incur expenses to care for their children and other dependents in order to work. The American opportunity tax credit (partially refundable) and the lifetime learning credit help taxpayers pay for the cost of higher education. Because the child tax credit, the child and dependent care credit, and the American opportunity tax credit and lifetime learning credit are some of the most common personal credits that are typically nonrefundable, we discuss them in detail.

Child Tax Credit Taxpayers may claim a $2,000 **child tax credit** for *each qualifying child* [same definition for dependency purposes—see §152(c) and the Individual Income Tax Overview, Dependents, and Filing Status chapter] who is under age 17 (under age 18 for 2021 only) at the end of the year and who is claimed as their dependent.[22] To claim the credit for a qualifying child, the taxpayers must provide the qualifying child's Social Security number on the tax return.

Taxpayers may also claim a $500 credit for qualifying dependents other than qualifying children for whom the $2,000 credit is claimed. Social Security numbers are not required to be reported to claim the $500 child tax credit for these dependents. The credit is subject to phase-out based on the taxpayer's AGI. The phase-out threshold depends on the taxpayer's filing status and is provided in Exhibit 8-8.

EXHIBIT 8-8 Child Tax Credit Phase-Out Threshold

Filing Status	Phase-Out Threshold
Married filing jointly	$400,000
Married filing separately	200,000
Head of household and single	200,000

Source: §24(a).

The total amount of the base credit is phased out, but not below zero, by $50 for each $1,000 *or portion thereof* by which the taxpayer's AGI exceeds the applicable threshold. Taxpayers can determine their allowable child tax credit after the phase-out by using the following four steps:

Step 1: Determine the excess AGI by subtracting the threshold amount (see Exhibit 8-8) from the taxpayer's AGI.

Step 2: Divide the excess AGI from Step 1 by 1,000 and round up to the next whole number.

Step 3: Multiply the amount from Step 2 by $50. This is the amount of the total credit that is phased out or disallowed.

Step 4: Subtract the amount from Step 3 from the total base credit before phase-out (limited to $0) to determine the allowable base child tax credit.

[22]§24(a).

Because the phase-out is based upon a fixed amount ($50) rather than a percentage, the phase-out range varies according to the amount of credit claimed.[23]

Example 8-17

Both Ellen and Deron are Courtney's qualifying children. Courtney may claim the $2,000 child tax credit for Deron because he is under age 17 at the end of the year. Courtney cannot claim the $2,000 child tax credit for Ellen because she is not under age 17 at the end of the year, but Courtney may claim the $500 credit for Ellen because she is a qualified dependent. What amount of the tax credit is Courtney allowed to claim for Deron and Ellen after accounting for the credit phase-out?

Answer: $2,500. Because Courtney's AGI of $187,000 (Exhibit 6-5) does not exceed the $200,000 phase-out threshold (Exhibit 8-8), she may claim the full credit of $2,000 for Deron and $500 for Ellen.

What if: Suppose Courtney's AGI is $230,000. How much of the tax credit may she claim for Deron and Ellen?

Answer: $1,000, computed as follows:

Description	Amount	Explanation
(1) AGI	$230,000	
(2) Phase-out threshold	200,000	Exhibit 8-8
(3) AGI in excess of threshold	30,000	(1) – (2)
(4) Credit phase-out increment	30	(3)/1,000
(5) Credit phase-out	1,500	(4) × 50
(6) Credit before phase-out	2,500	$2,000 for Deron; $500 for Ellen
Credit after phase-out	**$ 1,000**	(6) – (5)

Additional Child Tax Credit for 2021 Only For 2021 only, the $2,000 child tax credit was increased to $3,000 per qualifying child ($3,600 for children under age six at the end of the year).[24] There was no corresponding increase for the $500 child tax credit for other qualifying dependents. The 2021 additional $1,000 child tax credit per qualifying child (additional $1,600 child tax credit per qualifying child under age six) was subject to a separate phase-out from the base $2,000 child tax credit per qualifying child. The $1,000 ($1,600) additional child tax credit was phased out by $50 for each $1,000 or portion thereof by which the taxpayer's AGI exceeds the applicable threshold shown in Exhibit 8-9.

EXHIBIT 8-9 Additional Child Tax Credit for 2021 Phase-Out Threshold

Filing Status	Phase-Out Threshold
Married filing jointly	$150,000
Married filing separately	75,000
Head of household and single	112,500

[23]In 2022 and most other years, the child tax credit is partially refundable. The $500 child tax credit for qualifying dependents other than qualifying children is not refundable. The refundable portion of the child tax credit is the lesser of (1) $1,500 per each qualifying child for which the $2,000 credit is claimed, (2) the taxpayer's earned income in excess of $2,500 times 15 percent, or (3) the amount of the unclaimed portion of the otherwise nonrefundable credit. Thus, if a taxpayer has enough tax liability to absorb the nonrefundable portion of the credit, the refundable portion is reduced to zero. The computation is modified for taxpayers with three or more qualifying children. For 2021, the child tax credit (and the 2021 additional child tax credit) is fully refundable for taxpayers with their principal place of abode in the United States for more than half the year or for residents of Puerto Rico. For all other taxpayers in 2021, the child tax credit is partially refundable. See IRS Publication 972 for more information relating to the child tax credit.

[24]The additional child tax credit had not been extended to 2022 as of press time. In 2021 only, the IRS was directed through enacted tax law to make advance payments to taxpayers of 50 percent of their eligible child tax credits. Taxpayers who received advance payments in excess of their allowable child tax credit generally were required to repay the excess amount as additional tax liability on their 2021 returns (subject to exception for taxpayers with AGI below specified thresholds).

Example 8-18

Assume the tax year is 2021, Courtney has an AGI of $187,000, and we have determined that she may claim the $2,000 child tax credit for Deron, age 9 in 2021. What additional child tax credit could Courtney claim for Deron in 2021 after accounting for the phase-out?

Answer: $0, computed as follows:

Description	Amount	Explanation
(1) AGI	$187,000	
(2) Phase-out threshold	112,500	Exhibit 8-9
(3) AGI in excess of threshold	74,500	(1) – (2)
(4) Credit phase-out increment	75	(3)/1,000, rounded up
(5) Credit phase-out	3,750	(4) × 50
(6) Additional child tax credit before phase-out	1,000	$1,000 for Deron
Additional child tax credit after phase-out	$ 0	(6) – (5), limited to zero

What if: Suppose that it is 2021 and Courtney's AGI was $120,000. How much additional child tax credit could Courtney claim for Deron in 2021 after accounting for the phase-out?

Answer: $600, computed as follows:

Description	Amount	Explanation
(1) AGI	$120,000	
(2) Phase-out threshold	112,500	Exhibit 8-9
(3) AGI in excess of threshold	7,500	(1) – (2)
(4) Credit phase-out increment	8	(3)/1,000, rounded up
(5) Credit phase-out	400	(4) × 50
(6) Additional child tax credit before phase-out	1,000	$1,000 for Deron
Additional child tax credit after phase-out	$ 600	(6) – (5), limited to zero

THE KEY FACTS

Child and Dependent Care Credit

- Designed to help taxpayers who work or seek work when they must provide care for dependents.
- Nonrefundable except in 2021.
- Based on maximum qualifying expenditures multiplied by the rate based on AGI.

Child and Dependent Care Credit The child and dependent care credit is a tax subsidy to help taxpayers pay the cost of providing care for their dependents to allow taxpayers to work or look for work. The amount of the credit is based on the amount of the taxpayer's expenditures to provide care for one or more qualifying persons. A qualifying person includes (1) a dependent under the age of 13 and (2) a dependent or spouse who is physically or mentally incapable of caring for herself or himself and who lives in the taxpayer's home for more than half the year.

The amount of expenditures eligible for the credit is the *least* of the following three amounts:

1. The total amount of dependent care expenditures for the year.
2. $3,000 for one qualifying person ($8,000 in 2021 only) or $6,000 for two or more qualifying persons ($16,000 in 2021 only).
3. The taxpayer's earned income including wages, salary, or other taxable employee compensation, or net earnings from self-employment. Married taxpayers must file a joint tax return and the amount of earned income for purposes of the dependent care credit limitation is the earned income of the lesser-earning spouse.[25]

Expenditures for care qualify whether the care is provided outside or within the home. But they do *not* qualify if the caregiver is a dependent relative or child of

[25]If the lesser-earning spouse cannot work due to a disability or is a full-time student, the lesser-earning spouse is *deemed* to have earned $250 a month if the couple is computing the credit for one qualifying person or $500 a month if the couple is computing the credit for more than one qualifying person.

the taxpayer.[26] The amount of the credit is calculated by multiplying qualifying expenditures by the appropriate credit percentage. The credit percentage is based upon the taxpayer's AGI level and begins at 35 percent for taxpayers with AGI of $15,000 or less. The maximum dependent care credit is 20 percent for taxpayers with AGI over $43,000.[27] The child and dependent care credit was fully refundable in 2021 for taxpayers with their principal abode in the U.S. for more than half the year. For all other taxpayers and all other years, the credit is nonrefundable. Exhibit 8-10 provides the dependent care percentage for different levels of AGI.

EXHIBIT 8-10 Child and Dependent Care Credit Percentage

If AGI is over	But not over	Then the percentage is
$ 0	$15,000	35%
15,000	17,000	34
17,000	19,000	33
19,000	21,000	32
21,000	23,000	31
23,000	25,000	30
25,000	27,000	29
27,000	29,000	28
29,000	31,000	27
31,000	33,000	26
33,000	35,000	25
35,000	37,000	24
37,000	39,000	23
39,000	41,000	22
41,000	43,000	21
43,000	No limit	20

Source: §21.

Example 8-19

What if: Suppose that this year, Courtney paid a neighbor $3,200 to care for her 10-year-old son, Deron, so Courtney could work. Would Courtney be allowed to claim the child and dependent care credit for the expenditures she made for Deron's care?

Answer: Yes. (1) Courtney paid for Deron's care to allow her to work and (2) Deron is a qualifying person for purposes of the credit because (a) he is Courtney's dependent and (b) he is under 13 years of age at the end of the year.

What amount of child and dependent care credit, if any, would Courtney be allowed to claim for the $3,200 she spent to provide Deron's care given her AGI is $187,000?

(continued on page 8-28)

[26]§21(e)(6).

[27]In 2021 only, the credit percentage begins at 50 percent for taxpayers with AGI of $125,000 or less and is reduced to zero for taxpayers with AGI of $440,000 or more. The credit percentage is decreased by 1 percent for every $2,000 (or increment thereof) of AGI above $125,000 until the credit percentage is reduced to 20 percent (for taxpayers with AGI over $183,000). The credit percentage is 20 percent for taxpayers with AGI over $183,000 but not over $400,000. For taxpayers with AGI over $400,000, the credit percentage is decreased by 1 percent for every $2,000 (or increment thereof) of AGI above $400,000 until the credit percentage is reduced to 0 percent (for taxpayers with AGI over $438,000).

Answer: $600, computed as follows:

Description	Amount	Explanation
(1) Dependent care expenditures	$ 3,200	
(2) Limit on qualifying expenditures for one dependent	3,000	
(3) Courtney's earned income	180,800	$162,800 compensation from EWD + $18,000 business income (see Example 8-14)
(4) Expenditures eligible for credit	3,000	Least of (1), (2), and (3)
(5) Credit percentage rate	20%	AGI over $43,000 (see Exhibit 8-10)
Dependent care credit	**$ 600**	(4) × (5)

What if: If Courtney's AGI (and her earned income) were only $31,500, what would be her child and dependent care credit?

Answer: $780, computed as follows:

Description	Amount	Explanation
(1) Dependent care expenditures	$ 3,200	
(2) Limit on qualifying expenditures for one dependent	3,000	
(3) Courtney's earned income	31,500	
(4) Expenditures eligible for credit	3,000	Least of (1), (2), and (3)
(5) Credit percentage rate	26%	AGI between $31,000 and $33,0000 (see Exhibit 8-10)
Dependent care credit	**$ 780**	(4) × (5)

Education Credits Congress provides the American opportunity tax credit (AOTC) and the lifetime learning credit to encourage taxpayers and their dependents to obtain higher education by reducing the costs of the education. In contrast to the payment rules discussed for the deduction for qualified education expenses, taxpayers may claim credits for eligible expenditures made for themselves, their dependents, and third parties on behalf of the taxpayers' dependents.[28] If a student is claimed as a dependent of another taxpayer, only that taxpayer may claim the education credits (even if the dependent or another third party actually pays the education expenses).[29] Married taxpayers filing separate returns are not eligible for the AOTC or the lifetime learning credit.

The AOTC is available for students in their first four years of postsecondary (post high school) education. To qualify, students must be enrolled in a qualified postsecondary educational institution at least half time.[30] The amount of the credit is 100 percent of the first $2,000 of eligible expenses paid by the taxpayer (or another person) plus 25 percent of the next $2,000 of eligible expenses paid by the taxpayer (or another person). Thus, the maximum AOTC for eligible expenses paid for any one person is $2,500 [$2,000 + (25% × $2,000)]. To be eligible for the 2022 credit, taxpayers must pay the eligible expenses in 2022 for any academic period beginning in 2022 or in the first three months of 2023.[31]

Eligible expenses for the AOTC include tuition, fees, and course materials (cost of books and other materials) needed for courses of instruction at an eligible educational

[28]§25A(g)(3).

[29]If a third party pays the education expenses of a student claimed as a dependent by another taxpayer, the dependent is deemed to have paid the education expenses and the taxpayer claiming the student as a dependent is allowed to claim the credit for the expenses.

[30]§25A(b). Generally, eligible institutions are those eligible to participate in the federal student loan program [§25A(f)(2)].

[31]Reg. §1.25A-3(e).

institution.[32] The AOTC is applied on a *per student* basis. Consequently, a taxpayer with three eligible dependents can claim a maximum AOTC of $2,500 for *each* dependent. The AOTC is subject to phase-out based on the taxpayer's AGI. The credit is phased out pro rata for taxpayers with AGI between $80,000 and $90,000 ($160,000 and $180,000 for married taxpayers filing jointly).[33] Forty percent of a taxpayer's allowable AOTC is refundable.[34]

Example 8-20

Courtney paid $2,000 of tuition and $300 for books for Ellen to attend the University of Missouri–Kansas City during the summer following the end of her first year. What is the maximum American opportunity tax credit (AOTC) (before phase-out) Courtney may claim for these expenses?

Answer: $2,075. Because the cost of tuition and books is an eligible expense, Courtney may claim a maximum AOTC before phase-out of $2,075 [($2,000 × 100%) + ($2,300 − $2,000) × 25%].

How much AOTC is Courtney allowed to claim on her 2022 tax return (how much can she claim after applying the phase-out)?

Answer: $0. Because Courtney's AGI exceeds the head of household limit of $90,000, she is not allowed to claim any AOTC.

What if: How much AOTC would Courtney have been allowed to claim on her 2022 tax return if she were married and filed a joint return with her husband (assuming the couple's AGI is $162,000)?

Answer: $1,867, computed as follows:

Description	Amount	Explanation
(1) AOTC before phase-out	$ 2,075	
(2) AGI	162,000	
(3) Phase-out threshold	160,000	
(4) Excess AGI	2,000	(2) − (3)
(5) Phase-out range for married taxpayer filing jointly	20,000	$180,000 − $160,000
(6) Phase-out percentage	10%	(4)/(5)
(7) Phase-out amount	208	(1) × (6)
AOTC after phase-out	**$ 1,867**	(1) − (7)

What if: Suppose Courtney could claim a $1,867 AOTC in 2022 (after phase-out). How much of this credit would be refundable?

Answer: $747 ($1,867 × 40%).

THE KEY FACTS

Education Credits

- American opportunity tax credit
  - Qualifying expenses include tuition for a qualifying student incurred during the first four years at a qualifying institution of higher education.
  - Maximum credit of $2,500 per student calculated as percentage of maximum of $4,000 qualifying expenses.
  - Subject to phase-out for taxpayers with AGI in excess of $80,000 ($160,000 married filing jointly).
- Lifetime learning credit
  - Qualifying expenses include costs at a qualifying institution associated with acquiring or improving job skills.
  - Maximum credit of $2,000 per taxpayer calculated as percentage of maximum of $10,000 in annual expenses.
  - Subject to phase-out for taxpayers with AGI in excess of $80,000 ($160,000 married filing jointly).

The lifetime learning credit is a nonrefundable credit that applies to the cost of tuition and fees (but generally not books) for any course of instruction to acquire or improve a taxpayer's job skills.[35] This includes the cost of professional or graduate school tuition

[32]§25A(i)(3). Eligible expenses for both the AOTC and the lifetime learning credit must be reduced by scholarships received to pay for these expenses or other amounts received as reimbursements for the expenses (Pell grants, employer-sponsored reimbursement plans, educational IRAs, 529 plans, and the like). Students can elect to include a portion or all of scholarships in taxable income to take the tax credit for expenditures that would have been offset by the scholarships. The cost of room and board or other personal expenses do not qualify as eligible expenses for either the AOTC or the lifetime learning credit.

[33]§25A(i)(4).

[34]§25A(i)(5). The refundability of the tax credit is not applicable to a taxpayer who is a child subject to the "kiddie tax" rules—i.e., a child (a) who does not file a joint return, (b) who has at least one living parent, and (c) who is either (1) under 18 years old at year-end, (2) 18 at year-end with earned income that does not exceed half of their support, or (3) over age 18 but under age 24 at year-end, is a full-time student during the year, and has earned income that does not exceed half of their support.

[35]§25A(f)(1).

(expenses are not limited to those incurred in the first four years of postsecondary education). The credit is equal to 20 percent of eligible expenses up to an annual maximum of $10,000 of eligible expenses (maximum of $2,000). The credit for a year is based on the amount paid during that year for an academic period beginning in that year or the first three months of the following year.

In contrast to the American opportunity tax credit, the lifetime learning credit limit applies to the taxpayer. Thus, a married couple filing a joint tax return or taxpayer with multiple eligible dependents can claim a maximum lifetime learning credit of only $2,000 for the year. Like the AOTC, the credit is phased out pro rata for taxpayers with AGI between $80,000 and $90,000 ($160,000 and $180,000 for married taxpayers filing jointly).[36]

Example 8-21

Courtney paid $1,550 to attend a class at the local university to help her improve her job skills. How much lifetime learning credit can Courtney claim before applying the phase-out?

Answer: $310 ($1,550 × 20%)

How much lifetime learning credit is Courtney allowed to claim on her 2022 tax return (how much can she claim after applying the phase-out)?

Answer: $0. Because Courtney's AGI exceeds the head of household limit of $90,000, she is not allowed to claim any lifetime learning credit.

For expenses that qualify for both the AOTC and lifetime learning credit (tuition and fees during the first four years of postsecondary education), taxpayers may choose which credit to use, but they may not claim both credits for the same student in the same year.

Example 8-22

What if: Suppose Courtney paid $5,000 of tuition for Ellen to attend the University of Missouri–Kansas City during the summer following the end of her first year. Further assume that Courtney's AGI is $45,000, so her education credits are not subject to phase-out. Courtney would be allowed to claim the maximum AOTC of $2,500 on the first $4,000 of the qualifying educational expenditures. Assuming Courtney used $4,000 of the educational expenses to claim the maximum AOTC, would she be allowed to deduct (or claim the lifetime credit on) the remaining $1,000 of tuition costs ($5,000 total expenses − $4,000 maximum AOTC expenses)?

Answer: No. If Courtney claims any AOTC for Ellen's expenditures, she is not allowed to deduct or claim a lifetime learning credit for Ellen's expenditures (even for the expenses not used in computing the AOTC).

Refundable Personal Credits

Several personal credits are refundable, the most common of which is the earned income credit, which we discuss below.

Earned Income Credit The **earned income credit** is a refundable credit that is designed to help offset the effect of employment taxes on compensation paid to low-income taxpayers and to encourage lower-income taxpayers to seek employment. Because it is refundable (if the credit exceeds the tax after considering nonrefundable credits, the taxpayer receives a refund for the excess), it is sometimes referred to as a *negative income tax*. The credit is available for qualified individuals who have earned income for the year.[37] Qualified individuals generally include (1) those who have at least one qualifying child (same definition of qualifying child for dependent purposes—see the Individual Income Tax Overview, Dependents, and Filing Status chapter) and (2) those who do not have a qualifying child for the taxable year but who live in the United States for more

[36]§25A(d).
[37]§32.

than half the year, are at least 25 years old but younger than 65 at the end of the year, and are not a dependent of another taxpayer.[38] Earned income includes wages, salaries, tips, and other employee compensation included in gross income and net earnings from self-employment. Taxpayers with investment income such as interest, dividends, and capital gains in excess of $10,300 are ineligible for the credit.[39]

The amount of the credit depends on the taxpayer's filing status, the number of the taxpayer's qualifying children who live in the home for more than half of the year, and the amount of the taxpayer's earned income. To be eligible for the credit, married taxpayers generally must file a joint tax return. The credit is computed by multiplying the appropriate credit percentage times the taxpayer's earned income up to a maximum amount. The credit percentage depends upon the number of qualifying children in the home and is subject to a phase-out based upon AGI (or earned income if greater). As summarized in Exhibit 8-11, the earned income credit increases as taxpayers receive earned income up to the maximum amount of earned income eligible for the credit. However, as taxpayers earn more income, the credit begins to phase out and is completely eliminated once taxpayers' earned income reaches established levels.

EXHIBIT 8-11 2022 Earned Income Credit Table

Qualifying Children	(1) Maximum Earned Income Eligible for Credit	(2) Credit %	(3) Maximum Credit (1) × (2)	(4) Credit Phase-Out for AGI (or earned income if greater) over This Amount	(5) Phase-Out Percentage	No Credit When AGI (or earned income if greater) Equals or Exceeds This Amount (4) + [(3)/(5)]
Married taxpayers filing joint returns						
0	$ 7,320	7.65%	$ 560	$15,290	7.65%	$22,610
1	10,980	34	3,733	26,260	15.98	49,622
2	15,410	40	6,164	26,260	21.06	55,529
3+	15,410	45	6,935	26,260	21.06	59,187
All taxpayers *except* married taxpayers filing joint returns						
0	$ 7,320	7.65%	$ 560	$ 9,160	15.30%	$16,480
1	10,980	34	3,733	20,130	15.98	43,492
2	15,410	40	6,164	20,130	21.06	49,399
3+	15,410	45	6,935	20,130	21.06	$53,057

Source: Rev. Proc. 2021-45 and §32.

Example 8-23

Courtney's earned income for the year is $180,800 (Example 8-19) and her AGI is $187,000 (Exhibit 6-5). Deron and Ellen both qualify as Courtney's qualifying children. What amount of earned income credit is Courtney entitled to claim on her 2022 tax return?

Answer: $0. Courtney's AGI (which is greater than her earned income) exceeds the $49,399 limit for unmarried taxpayers with two qualifying children. Consequently, Courtney is not allowed to claim any earned income credit.

What if: Assume Courtney's only source of income for the year was $30,000 in salary. Also assume Courtney's AGI for the year was $30,000. What would be Courtney's earned income credit in these circumstances?

(continued on page 8-28)

[38]For 2021, the age requirements were that the taxpayer must be at least 19 at year-end (at least age 24 at year-end if the taxpayer is a student during at least five months in the year; at least age 18 at year-end if the taxpayer is a qualified former foster youth or a qualified homeless youth).

[39]§32(i).

Answer: $4,085, computed as follows:

Description	Amount	Explanation
(1) Earned income	$30,000	
(2) Maximum earned income eligible for earned income credit for taxpayers filing as head of household with two qualifying children	15,410	Exhibit 8-11
(3) Earned income eligible for credit	15,410	Lesser of (1) and (2)
(4) Earned income credit percentage for taxpayer with two qualifying children	40%	
(5) Earned income credit before phase-out	6,164	(3) × (4)
(6) Phase-out threshold begins at this level of AGI (or earned income if greater)	20,130	See Exhibit 8-11 for head of household filing status and two qualifying children.
(7) Greater of (a) AGI or (b) earned income, less the phase-out threshold	9,870	(1) – (6). In this example, AGI equals earned income.
(8) Phase-out percentage	21.06%	See Exhibit 8-11.
(9) Credit phase-out amount	2,079	(7) × (8), rounded
Earned income credit after phase-out	**$ 4,085**	(5) – (9)

TAXES IN THE REAL WORLD Taking a Bite Out of Earned Income Tax Credit Abuse

The IRS has special reporting requirements (Form 8867) for tax professionals filing tax returns that include an earned income tax credit. Form 8867, the Paid Preparer's Earned Income Credit Checklist, is intended to ensure that tax professionals use appropriate due diligence in determining the amount of, and a taxpayer's eligibility for, the earned income tax credit.

Why the extra concern with the earned Income tax credit? Because the earned income tax credit is a refundable tax credit, the potential for abuse (fraudulent claim) is quite high. Only paid tax preparers are required to complete the form, and failure to do so can result in a $500 penalty for each failure.

Sources: See Form 8867 and §6695(g).

Special Tax Credit For 2021 To provide additional taxpayer relief in 2021 during the pandemic, Congress enacted the individual recovery credit. This credit only applied in 2021 and provided that eligible taxpayers [individuals other than (a) nonresident aliens or (b) individuals who are dependents of other taxpayers] were allowed an income tax credit of $1,400 ($2,800 for married taxpayers filing joint) plus $1,400 for each dependent. The credit was reduced ratably for taxpayers with AGI over $75,000 ($112,500 for a head of household; $150,000 for married taxpayers filing joint) and completely phased out at $80,000 ($120,000 for head of household; $160,000 for married taxpayers filing joint). To accelerate relief during 2021, the IRS issued advanced payment of the credits (i.e., stimulus payments) to taxpayers based upon their 2019 tax return information (or 2020 if their 2020 tax return was already filed). Taxpayers who received advance payments in excess of the credits actually allowed based upon their 2021 tax information were not required to repay the excess amount. If a taxpayer received a lower advance payment than allowed based upon their 2021 tax information, the taxpayer could claim the additional amount allowed as a credit on their 2021 tax return. Because of the advance payment of the credit and no need to repay any excess credit, only those taxpayers not receiving advance payment for their full credit allowed claimed the tax credit on their 2021 tax return.

Example 8-24

Assuming Courtney and Gram had their same respective AGI in 2020 and 2021 as in 2022 ($187,000 and $15,590, respectively), what amount of individual recovery credit would each have received?

Answer: $0 for Courtney and $1,400 for Gram. Courtney would not have been eligible for the advanced payment/credit because both her 2020 and 2021 AGI of $187,000 exceeds $120,000, the AGI level in which the advance payment/credit is completely phased out. Gram was eligible for a $1,400 advance payment/credit as an eligible individual with no dependents. She would have received the full $1,400 advance payment/credit because her AGI of $15,590 was below $75,000, the AGI level in which the advance payment/credit begins phase-out.

Other Refundable Personal Credits Other refundable personal tax credits include a portion of the child tax credit (discussed above), a portion of the AOTC (discussed above), excess FICA withholdings (see discussion above under FICA taxes), and taxes withheld on wages and estimated tax payments. We address withholdings and estimated taxes in the next section, when we discuss tax prepayments.

Business Tax Credits

Business tax credits are designed to provide incentives for taxpayers to hire certain types of individuals or to participate in certain business activities. For example, Congress provides the employment tax credit to encourage businesses to hire certain unemployed individuals, and it provides the research and development credit to encourage businesses to expend funds to develop new technology. Business tax credits are *nonrefundable* credits. However, when business credits other than the foreign tax credit (discussed below) exceed the taxpayer's gross tax for the year, the credits are carried back 1 year and forward 20 years to use in years when the taxpayer has sufficient gross tax liability to use them.

Why discuss business credits in an individual tax chapter? We discuss business credits here because self-employed individuals may qualify for them. Also, individuals may be allocated business credits from flow-through entities (partnerships, LLCs, and S corporations). Finally, individuals working as employees overseas or receiving dividends from investments in foreign securities may qualify for the foreign tax credit.

Foreign Tax Credit U.S. citizens must pay U.S. tax on their worldwide income. However, when they generate some or all of their income in other countries, they generally are required to pay income taxes to the foreign country where they earned their income. Without some form of tax relief, taxpayers earning income overseas would be double-taxed on this income. When taxpayers pay income taxes to foreign countries, for U.S. tax purposes they may treat the payment in one of three ways: (1) as we discussed in the Gross Income and Exclusions chapter when we introduced the foreign-earned income exclusion, taxpayers may exclude the foreign-earned income from U.S. taxation (in which case they would not deduct or receive a credit for any foreign taxes paid); (2) they may include the foreign income in their gross income and deduct the foreign taxes paid as itemized deductions; or (3) they may include foreign income in gross income and claim a foreign tax credit for the foreign taxes paid. Here, we discuss the foreign tax credit.

The foreign tax credit helps reduce the double tax taxpayers may face when they pay income taxes on foreign-earned income to the United States and to foreign countries. Taxpayers are allowed to claim a foreign tax credit, against their U.S. tax liability, for the income taxes they pay to foreign countries.[40] In certain situations, taxpayers may not be able to claim the full amount of foreign tax paid as a credit. This restriction may apply when the taxpayer's foreign tax rate is higher than the U.S. tax rate on the foreign earnings. Taxpayers generally benefit from claiming credits rather than deductions for foreign taxes paid because credits reduce their liabilities dollar-for-dollar. However, when the

[40]§904.

foreign tax credit is restricted (see above), taxpayers may benefit by claiming deductions for the taxes paid instead of credits because itemized foreign tax deductions are not subject to the $10,000 limit that applies to itemized state and local taxes.

As we discussed above, the foreign tax credit may be limited in circumstances in which a taxpayer's effective foreign tax rate exceeds their U.S. tax rate. In addition, as a nonrefundable credit, it can reduce the taxpayer's tax liability only to zero (but not create a refund). When the use of a foreign tax credit is limited, taxpayers may carry back unused credits 1 year and carry forward the credits up to 10 years.[41]

Tax Credit Summary

Exhibit 8-12 identifies several tax credits and for each credit identifies the credit type, notes the IRC section allowing the credit, and describes the credit.

EXHIBIT 8-12 Summary of Selected Tax Credits

Credit	Type of Credit	IRC	Description
Child and dependent care credit	Nonrefundable personal	§21	Credit for taxpayers who pay dependent care expenses due to their employment activities.
Credit for elderly and disabled	Nonrefundable personal	§22	Credit for elderly low-income taxpayers who retire because of a disability.
Adoption expense credit	Nonrefundable personal	§23	Credit for qualified adoption-related expenses.
Child tax credit	Nonrefundable and refundable personal	§24	Credit for providing home for dependent children under the age of 17.
American opportunity tax credit	Nonrefundable and refundable personal	§25A	Credit for higher education expenses for the first four years of postsecondary education.
Lifetime learning credit	Nonrefundable personal	§25A	Credit for higher education expenses.
Saver's credit	Nonrefundable personal	§25B	Credit for contributing to qualified retirement plans.
Residential energy	Nonrefundable personal	§25D	Credit for qualified expenditures for solar electric property, solar water heating property, fuel cell property, wind energy property, and qualified geothermal heat pump property.
Earned income credit	Refundable personal	§32	Credit to encourage low-income taxpayers to work.
Premium tax credit	Refundable personal	§36B	Credit for health insurance purchased through an exchange for individuals and families with household incomes between 100% and 400% of the poverty line.
Credit for increasing research activities	Business	§41	Credit to encourage research and development.
Employer-provided child care credit	Business	§45F	Credit for providing child care for employees.
Small employer health insurance credit	Business	§45R	Credit to encourage employer-provided health insurance.
Rehabilitation credit	Business	§47	Credit for expenditures to renovate or restore older business buildings.
Energy credit	Business	§48	Credit for businesses that invest in energy conservation measures.
Work opportunity credit	Business	§51	Credit for hiring certain qualified veterans.
Foreign tax credit	Hybrid business and personal	§904	Credit to reduce effects of double taxation of foreign income.

[41]See IRS Publication 514, "Foreign Tax Credit for Individuals," for more information about the foreign tax credit.

Credit Application Sequence

As we've discussed, credits are applied against a taxpayer's gross tax. However, we still must describe what happens when the taxpayer's allowable credits exceed the taxpayer's gross tax. Keep in mind that nonrefundable personal credits and business credits may be used to reduce a taxpayer's gross tax to zero, but not below zero.[42] In contrast, by definition, a refundable credit may reduce a taxpayer's gross tax below zero. This excess refundable credit generates a tax refund for the taxpayer.

When a nonrefundable personal credit exceeds the taxpayer's gross tax, it reduces the gross tax to zero, but the excess credit (credit in excess of the taxpayer's gross tax) disappears. That is, the taxpayer may not carry over any excess nonrefundable personal credits to use in other years. However, when a business credit or foreign tax credit exceeds the gross tax, it reduces the taxpayer's gross tax to zero, but the excess credit may be carried forward or back to be used in other years when the taxpayer has sufficient gross tax to use the credit (subject to certain time restrictions discussed above).

Because the tax treatment of excess credits depends on the type of credit, it is important to identify the sequence in which taxpayers apply the credits when they have more than one type of credit for the year. In this case, they apply the credits against their gross tax in the following order: (1) nonrefundable personal credits, (2) business credits, and (3) refundable credits. This sequence maximizes the chances that taxpayers will receive full benefit for their tax credits.

Because, as we discuss above, the foreign tax credit is a hybrid credit subject to a unique set of application rules, we exclude it from our general discussion on applying credits. Exhibit 8-13 summarizes the order in which the credits are applied against gross tax and indicates the tax treatment of any excess credits.

EXHIBIT 8-13 Credit Application

Credit Type	Order Applied	Excess Credit
Nonrefundable personal	First	Lost
Business	Second	Carryback and carryover
Refundable personal	Last	Refunded

Example 8-25

What if: As we describe in Example 8-2, Gram's gross tax liability is $89. For illustrative purposes, let's assume Gram is entitled to an $800 nonrefundable personal tax credit, a $700 business tax credit, and a $600 refundable personal tax credit. What is the amount of Gram's refund or taxes due?

Answer: $600 refund. Gram would apply these credits as follows:

Description	Amount	Treatment of Excess Credit
Gross tax liability	$ 89	Example 8-2
Nonrefundable personal credits	(89)	$711 ($800 – $89) excess credit expires unused
Business credits	0	$700 carried back one year or forward 20 years (10 years for foreign tax credit)
Refundable personal credits	**$(600)**	Generates $600 tax refund to Gram

[42]In general, nonrefundable personal credits can offset a taxpayer's regular tax and AMT (§26) but not self-employment tax. The limitation on business credits is more complex. We limit our discussion here to basic concepts. See §38(c) for the detailed limitations.

LO 8-5

TAXPAYER PREPAYMENTS AND FILING REQUIREMENTS

After determining their tax liabilities, taxpayers must file a tax return and pay any additional tax due or receive a refund. When they don't pay enough taxes during the year or are late filing their tax return or paying their taxes due, they may be subject to certain penalties.

Prepayments

The income tax must be paid on a *pay-as-you-go* basis. This means it must be prepaid via **withholding** from salary or through periodic **estimated tax payments** during the tax year. Employees pay tax through withholding, and self-employed taxpayers generally pay taxes through estimated tax payments. Employers are required to withhold taxes from an employee's wages based upon the employee's marital status, exemptions, and estimated annual pay. Wages include both cash and noncash remuneration for services, and employers remit withholdings to the government on behalf of employees. At the end of the year, employers report the amounts withheld to each employee via Form W-2. Estimated tax payments are required of employees only if withholdings are insufficient to meet the taxpayer's tax liability. For calendar-year taxpayers, estimated tax payments are due on April 15, June 15, and September 15 of the current year and January 15 of the following year. If the due date falls on a Saturday, Sunday, or holiday, it is automatically extended to the next day that is not a Saturday, Sunday, or holiday.

Example 8-26

Courtney's gross tax liability for the year, including federal income tax, alternative minimum tax, and self-employment taxes, is $27,572 (see Exhibit 8-6), and her net tax liability is $25,072 after the $2,500 child tax credit (see Example 8-17). However, because she had only $21,072 withheld from her paycheck by EWD (per her Form W-2 received from her employer), she underpaid $4,000 for the year ($25,072 − $21,072). Because Courtney did not pay her full tax liability, she may be subject to underpayment penalties discussed below. If she had been aware that her withholding would be insufficient, she could have increased her withholding at any time during the year (even in her December paycheck) or made estimated tax payments of $1,000 on April 15, June 15, and September 15 in 2022 and January 17, 2023 ($4,000/4). Because January 15 is a Sunday and January 16 is a holiday, the last quarterly estimated payment is due on January 17.

What if: If Courtney were self-employed (instead of employed by EWD) and thus had no tax withholdings by an employer, she would be required to pay quarterly estimated tax payments. In this scenario, she would need to pay $6,268 ($25,072/4 = $6,268) by April 15, June 15, and September 15 of 2022 and $6,268 by January 17, 2023, to cover her gross tax liability of $25,072.

Underpayment Penalties When taxpayers like Courtney fall behind on their tax prepayments, they may be subject to an **underpayment penalty.**[43] Taxpayers with unpredictable income streams may be particularly susceptible to this penalty because it is difficult for them to accurately estimate their tax liability for the year. To help taxpayers who may not be able to predict their earnings for the year and to provide some margin of error for those who can, the tax laws provide some **safe-harbor provisions.** Under these provisions, taxpayers can avoid underpayment penalties if their withholdings and estimated tax payments equal or exceed one of the following two safe harbors: (1) 90 percent of their *current tax liability* or (2) 100 percent of their *previous-year tax liability* (110 percent for individuals with AGI greater than $150,000).

[43]§6654.

These two safe harbors determine on a quarterly basis the minimum tax prepayments that a taxpayer must have made to avoid the underpayment penalty. The first safe harbor requires that a taxpayer must have paid at least 22.5 percent (90 percent/4 = 22.5 percent) of the *current*-year liability via withholdings or estimated tax payments by April 15 to avoid the underpayment penalty for the first quarter. Similarly by June 15, September 15, and January 15, the taxpayer must have paid 45 percent (22.5 percent × 2), 67.5 percent (22.5 percent × 3), and 90 percent (22.5 percent × 4), respectively, of the current-year liability via withholding or estimated tax payments to avoid the underpayment penalty in the second, third, and fourth quarters.[44] In determining taxpayers' prepayments for a quarter, tax withholdings are generally treated as though they are withheld evenly throughout the year. In contrast, estimated tax payments are credited to the taxpayer's account when they are remitted.

Example 8-27

Because all Courtney's prepayments were made through withholding by EWD, the payments are treated as though they were made evenly throughout the year. What are Courtney's actual and required withholdings under the 90 percent safe-harbor provision throughout the year? See Example 8-26 for Courtney's actual withholding and required withholding amounts.

Answer: See the following table:

Dates	(1) Actual Withholding (rounded)	(2) Required Withholding (rounded)	(1) – (2) Over- (Under-) Withheld
April 15, 2022	$5,268 ($21,072 × .25)	$5,641 ($25,072 × .9 × .25)	$ (373)
June 15, 2022	$10,536 ($21,072 × .50)	$11,282 ($25,072 × .9 × .50)	(746)
September 15, 2022	$15,804 ($21,072 × .75)	$16,924 ($25,072 × .9 × .75)	(1,120)
January 17, 2023	$21,072	$22,565 ($25,072 × .9 × 1)	(1,493)

It looks like Courtney is underwithheld in each quarter.

THE KEY FACTS

Taxpayer Prepayments and Underpayment Penalties

- Taxpayers prepay their tax via withholding from salary or through periodic estimated tax payments during the tax year.
- Estimated tax payments are required only if withholdings are insufficient to meet the taxpayer's tax liability.
- For calendar-year taxpayers, estimated tax payments are due on April 15, June 15, and September 15 of the current year and January 15 of the following year.
- Taxpayers can avoid an underpayment penalty if their withholdings and estimated tax payments equal or exceed one of two safe harbors.
- The underpayment penalty is determined by multiplying the federal short-term interest rate plus 3 percentage points by the amount of tax underpayment per quarter.

The second safe harbor requires that by April 15, June 15, September 15, and January 15, the taxpayer must have paid 25 percent, 50 percent (25 percent × 2), 75 percent (25 percent × 3), and 100 percent (25 percent × 4), respectively, of the *previous*-year tax liability (110 percent of the previous-year tax liability for individuals with AGI greater than $150,000), via withholding or estimated tax payments, to avoid the underpayment penalty in the first, second, third, and fourth quarters.

A taxpayer who does not satisfy either of the safe-harbor provisions can compute the underpayment penalty owed using Form 2210, Underpayment of Estimated Tax by Individuals, Estates, and Trusts. The underpayment penalty is determined by multiplying the **federal short-term interest rate** plus 3 percentage points by the amount of tax

[44]As an alternative method of estimating safe harbor, taxpayers can compute 90 percent of the current liability using the seasonal method. This method allows taxpayers to estimate 90 percent of their current tax liability by annualizing their taxable income earned through the month prior to the payment date (e.g., through March for April 15, May for June 15, and August for September 15). Taxpayers with uneven taxable income throughout the year with smaller taxable income earlier in the year benefit from this method.

underpayment per quarter. For purposes of this computation, the quarterly tax underpayment is the difference between the taxpayer's quarterly withholding and estimated tax payments and the required minimum tax payment under the first or second safe harbor (whichever is less). If the taxpayer does not complete Form 2210 and remit the underpayment penalty with the taxpayer's tax return, the IRS will compute and assess the penalty for the taxpayer.

Example 8-28

In the previous example, we discovered that Courtney was underwithheld in each quarter based on the first (90 percent of current year) safe-harbor provision. Assuming Courtney was underwithheld by even more under the second (100 percent of prior year) safe-harbor provision, she is required to pay an underpayment penalty based on the underpayments determined using the first safe-harbor provision. Assuming the federal short-term rate is 1 percent, what is Courtney's underpayment penalty for 2022?

Answer: $37, computed as follows:

Description	First Quarter	Second Quarter	Third Quarter	Fourth Quarter
Underpayment	$373	$746	$1,120	$1,493
Times: Federal rate + 3% (1% + 3%)	× 4%	× 4%	× 4%	× 4%
	$ 15	$ 30	$ 45	$ 60
Times one-quarter of a year[45]	× 25%	× 25%	× 25%	× 25%
Underpayment penalty per quarter	$ 4	$ 7	$ 11	$ 15

That's a lot of work to figure out a $37 penalty: ($4 + $7 + $11 + $15).

As a matter of administrative convenience, taxpayers are not subject to underpayment penalties if they had no tax liability in the previous year, or if their tax payable is less than $1,000 after subtracting their withholding amounts (but not estimated payments).

Example 8-29

Gram's tax liability for the year is $89 (Example 8-2), but she did not have any taxes withheld during the year, and she did not make any estimated tax payments. What is Gram's underpayment penalty?

Answer: $0. Because Gram's $89 tax payable after subtracting her withholding amounts ($89 tax – $0 withholding) is less than $1,000, she is not subject to an underpayment penalty.

Filing Requirements

Individual taxpayers are required to file a tax return only if their gross income exceeds certain thresholds, which vary based on the taxpayer's filing status and age. However, a taxpayer may prefer to file a tax return even when not required to do so. For example, a taxpayer with gross income less than the threshold may want to file a tax return to receive a refund of income taxes withheld. In general, the thresholds are simply the applicable standard deduction amount for the different filing statuses.[46]

[45]Form 2210 actually computes the penalty per quarter based on the number of days in the quarter divided by the number of days in the year. For simplicity, we assume this ratio is per quarter.

[46]§6012. Filing requirements for individuals who are dependents of other taxpayers are subject to special rules that consider the individual's unearned income, earned income, and gross income. See IRS Publication 17, "Your Federal Income Tax."

Individual tax returns are due on April 15 for calendar-year individuals (the fifteenth day of the fourth month following year-end). If the due date falls on a Saturday, Sunday, or holiday, it is automatically extended to the next day that is not a Saturday, Sunday, or holiday. Taxpayers unable to file a tax return by the original due date can request (by that same deadline) a six-month extension to file, which is granted automatically by the IRS. The extension gives the taxpayer additional time to file the tax return, but it does *not* extend the due date for paying the tax.

THE KEY FACTS

Filing Requirements and Filing-Related Penalties

- Filing requirements vary based on the taxpayer's filing status, age, and gross income.
- Individual tax returns are due on April 15 for calendar-year individuals. If the due date falls on a Saturday, Sunday, or holiday, it is automatically extended to the next day that is not a Saturday, Sunday, or holiday.
- Taxpayers unable to file a tax return by the original due date can request a six-month extension to file.
- The tax law imposes penalties on taxpayers who do not file a tax return (by the original due date plus extension) or pay the tax owed (by the original due date).

Late Filing Penalty The tax law imposes a **late filing penalty** on taxpayers who do not file a tax return by the required date (the original due date plus extension).[47] The penalty equals 5 percent of the amount of tax owed for each month (or fraction of a month) that the tax return is late, with a maximum penalty of 25 percent (reached over five months). For fraudulent failure to file, the penalty is 15 percent of the amount of tax owed per month, with a maximum penalty of 75 percent. If the taxpayer owes no tax as of the due date of the tax return (plus extension), the tax law does not impose a late filing penalty.

Late Payment Penalty An extension allows the taxpayer to delay filing a tax return but does not extend the due date for tax payments. If a taxpayer fails to pay the entire balance of tax owed by the original due date of the tax return, the tax law imposes a **late payment penalty** from the due date of the return until the taxpayer pays the tax.[48] The late payment penalty equals .5 percent of the amount of tax owed for each month (or fraction of a month) that the tax is not paid, with a maximum penalty of 25 percent (reached over 50 months).

If the late filing penalty and late payment penalty both apply in the same month, the late filing penalty of 5 percent for the month (and its corresponding maximum penalty of 25 percent) is reduced by the .5 percent late payment penalty for the month. If the fraudulent late filing penalty applies, a similar reduction applies to the 15 percent monthly penalty and maximum 75 percent penalty. In contrast, the late payment penalty of .5 percent and its corresponding maximum penalty of 25 percent are not reduced by the late filing penalty when they both apply. Thus, when both the late filing penalty and late payment penalty apply, the combined total penalty can be as high as 47.5 percent (22.5 percent for late filing and 25 percent for late payment) when both penalties apply for their maximum periods. Similarly, when both the fraudulent late filing penalty and late payment apply, the combined total penalty can be as high as 97.5 percent (72.5 percent for fraudulent late filing and 25 percent for late payment).

Example 8-30

Courtney filed her tax return on April 10 and included a check with the return for $4,037 made payable to the United States Treasury. The $4,037 consisted of her underpaid tax liability of $4,000 (Example 8-26) and her $37 underpayment penalty (Example 8-28).

What if: If Courtney had waited until May 1 to file her return and pay her taxes, what late filing and late payment penalties would she owe?

Answer: Her combined late filing penalty and late payment penalty would be $200 ($4,000 late payment × 5 percent × 1 month or portion thereof—the combined penalty is limited to 5 percent per month).

TAX SUMMARY

Courtney's and Gram's net taxes due, including an underpayment penalty for Courtney, are provided in Exhibits 8-14 and 8-16, respectively. Exhibit 8-15 illustrates how this information would be presented on Courtney's tax return by providing Courtney's Form 1040, page 2. We use 2021 forms, as 2022 forms were not available at press time.

[47] §6651.

[48] §6651. As we discussed in the Tax Compliance, the IRS, and Tax Authorities chapter, the tax law also assesses interest on any tax underpayments until the tax is paid (§6601).

EXHIBIT 8-14 Courtney's Net Tax Payable

Description	Amount	Explanation
(1) Regular federal income tax	$ 27,090	Example 8-3
(2) Alternative minimum tax	0	Example 8-8
(3) Self-employment tax	482	Example 8-14
(4) Gross tax	$ 27,572	(1) + (2) + (3)
(5) Tax credits	$ (2,500)	Example 8-17
(6) Prepayments	$(21,072)	Example 8-26
(7) Underpayment penalties	37	Example 8-28
Tax and penalties due with tax return	$ 4,037	(4) − (5) − (6) + (7)

EXHIBIT 8-15 Courtney's Net Tax Payable (as presented on her Form 1040, page 2)

Form 1040 (2021) Page **2**

Line	Description	Box	Amount	Line	Amount
16	**Tax** (see instructions). Check if any from Form(s): 1 ☐ 8814 2 ☐ 4972 3 ☐			16	27,090
17	Amount from Schedule 2, line 3			17	
18	Add lines 16 and 17			18	27,090
19	Nonrefundable child tax credit or credit for other dependents from Schedule 8812			19	2,500
20	Amount from Schedule 3, line 8			20	
21	Add lines 19 and 20			21	2,500
22	Subtract line 21 from line 18. If zero or less, enter -0-			22	24,590
23	Other taxes, including self-employment tax, from Schedule 2, line 21			23	482
24	Add lines 22 and 23. This is your **total tax** ►			24	25,072
25	Federal income tax withheld from:				
a	Form(s) W-2	25a	21,072		
b	Form(s) 1099	25b			
c	Other forms (see instructions)	25c			
d	Add lines 25a through 25c			25d	21,072
26	2021 estimated tax payments and amount applied from 2020 return			26	
27a	Earned income credit (EIC)	27a			
	Check here if you were born after January 1, 1998, and before January 2, 2004, and you satisfy all the other requirements for taxpayers who are at least age 18, to claim the EIC. See instructions ► ☐				
b	Nontaxable combat pay election	27b			
c	Prior year (2019) earned income	27c			
28	Refundable child tax credit or additional child tax credit from Schedule 8812	28			
29	American opportunity credit from Form 8863, line 8	29			
30	Recovery rebate credit. See instructions	30			
31	Amount from Schedule 3, line 15	31			
32	Add lines 27a and 28 through 31. These are your **total other payments and refundable credits** ►			32	
33	Add lines 25d, 26, and 32. These are your **total payments** ►			33	21,072
Refund 34	If line 33 is more than line 24, subtract line 24 from line 33. This is the amount you **overpaid**			34	
35a	Amount of line 34 you want **refunded to you.** If Form 8888 is attached, check here ► ☐			35a	
Direct deposit? See instructions. ►b	Routing number ► c Type: ☐ Checking ☐ Savings				
►d	Account number				
36	Amount of line 34 you want **applied to your 2022 estimated tax** ►	36			
Amount You Owe 37	**Amount you owe.** Subtract line 33 from line 24. For details on how to pay, see instructions ►			37	4,037
38	Estimated tax penalty (see instructions) ►	38	37		

If you have a qualifying child, attach Sch. EIC.

Source: irs.gov.

EXHIBIT 8-16 Gram's Tax Payable

Description	Amount	Explanation
(1) Gross tax	$89	Example 8-2
(2) Alternative minimum tax	0	
(3) Self-employment tax	0	
(4) Gross tax	$89	(1) + (2) + (3)
(5) Tax credits	0	
(6) Prepayments	0	
(7) Penalties	0	
Tax due with return	$89	(4) − (5) − (6) + (7)

CONCLUSION

This chapter reviewed the process for determining an individual's gross and net tax liability. We discovered that taxpayers may be required to pay regular federal income tax, alternative minimum tax, and employment-related tax. Taxpayers are able to offset their gross tax liability dollar-for-dollar with various types of tax credits and by the amount of tax they prepay during the year. Taxpayers must pay additional taxes with their tax return or they may receive a refund when they file their tax return, depending on their gross tax liability and their available tax credits and tax prepayments. The previous chapters have covered the basic individual tax formula. The next three chapters address issues relevant for taxpayers involved in business activities.

Summary

Determine a taxpayer's regular tax liability. **LO 8-1**

- Individual income is taxed using progressive tax rate schedules with rates ranging from 10 percent to 37 percent.
- Marginal tax rates depend on filing status and amount of taxable income.
- Progressive tax rate schedules may lead to either a marriage penalty or a marriage benefit for married taxpayers.
- Long-term capital gains and qualified dividends are taxed at either 0 percent, 15 percent, or 20 percent, depending on the amount of taxable income.
- Strategies to shift investment income from parents to children are limited by the "kiddie tax," whereby children's investment income is taxed using the parents' marginal tax rate.

Compute a taxpayer's alternative minimum tax liability. **LO 8-2**

- The AMT was designed to ensure that higher-income taxpayers pay some minimum level of income tax.
- The AMT base is broader than the regular income tax base. The AMT base is designed to more closely reflect economic income, as opposed to regular taxable income.
- The starting point for calculating AMT is regular taxable income. To compute AMTI, taxpayers add back items that are not deductible for AMT purposes (but were deducted for regular tax purposes) and items taxable for AMT purposes (but tax exempt or deferred for regular tax purposes). Taxpayers then subtract the allowable AMT exemption to generate the AMT base. They then apply the AMT rates and compare the product (the tentative minimum tax) to their regular tax liability. They owe AMT if the tentative minimum tax exceeds the regular tax liability.
- The AMT exemption depends on the taxpayer's filing status and is subject to a phase-out of 25 cents for each dollar of AMTI over the specific thresholds based on filing status.
- The 2022 AMT tax rates are 26 percent up to $206,100 of AMT base ($103,050 of AMT base for married taxpayers filing separately) and 28 percent thereafter. However, long-term capital gains and qualified dividends are subject to the same preferential rate at which they are taxed for regular tax purposes.
- The amount of the AMT is the excess of the tentative minimum tax over the taxpayer's regular tax liability.

Calculate a taxpayer's net investment income tax, and employment and self-employment tax liability. **LO 8-3**

- A 3.8 percent tax is levied on net investment income for higher-income taxpayers.
- Employees' wages are subject to FICA tax. For employees, the Social Security component is 6.2 percent, the Medicare component is 1.45 percent, and the additional Medicare tax is .9 percent. For employers, the Social Security component is 6.2 percent and the Medicare component is 1.45 percent. The Social Security tax applies to the first $147,000 of salary or wages in 2022. The tax base on the Medicare tax is unlimited. The additional Medicare tax applies to employees (not employers) on salary or wages above $200,000 ($125,000 for married filing separately; $250,000 of combined salary or wages for married filing jointly).
- Self-employed taxpayers pay self-employment tax on their net self-employment income (92.35 percent of their net Schedule C income). They pay Social Security tax of 12.4 percent and Medicare tax of 2.9 percent on their net self-employment income. The Social Security

tax applies to the first $147,000 of net Schedule C income in 2022. The base for the Medicare tax is unlimited. Self-employed taxpayers are also subject to the additional Medicare tax of .9 percent on net self-employment earnings in excess of $200,000 ($125,000 for married filing separately; $250,000 of combined salary or wages for married filing jointly).

- The determination as to whether to treat a worker as an independent contractor or as an employee for tax purposes is a subjective test based in large part on the extent of control the worker has over things such as the nature, timing, and location of work performed.
- Independent contractors are able to deduct ordinary and necessary business expenses as for AGI deductions. Employees cannot deduct unreimbursed employee business expenses.
- Independent contractors may deduct the employer portion of their self-employment taxes paid during the year. Employees may not deduct their FICA taxes.
- Independent contractors are required to pay self-employment tax, which represents the employer and employee portions of FICA taxes. Further, independent contractors must pay estimated taxes on their income because the employer does not withhold taxes from the independent contractor's paychecks.
- Hiring independent contractors is generally less costly for employers than is hiring employees. Employers do not pay FICA taxes, withhold taxes, or provide fringe benefits for independent contractors.

LO 8-4 Compute a taxpayer's allowable child tax credit, child and dependent care credit, American opportunity tax credit, lifetime learning credit, and earned income credit.

- Tax credits are generally classified into one of three categories: business, nonrefundable personal, or refundable personal credits.
- Nonrefundable personal tax credits provide tax relief to specified groups of individuals.
- The child tax credit is $2,000 for a qualifying child under the age of 17 and $500 for other qualified dependents.
- For 2021 only, taxpayers could claim an additional $1,000 child tax credit per qualifying child (additional $1,600 child tax credit per qualifying child under age six).
- The child and dependent care credit is provided to help taxpayers pay the cost of providing care for their dependents and allow taxpayers to work or to look for work.
- The American opportunity tax credit provides a credit for a percentage of the costs of the first four years of a student's college education. Forty percent of the credit is refundable.
- The lifetime learning credit provides a credit for a percentage of the costs for instruction in a postsecondary degree program or the costs to acquire or improve a taxpayer's job skills.
- Nonrefundable credits are first used to reduce a taxpayer's gross tax but cannot reduce the gross tax below zero. Any excess credit is lost unless it is allowed to be carried to a different tax year.
- The earned income credit is refundable but subject to a very complex calculation.
- To provide additional taxpayer relief in 2021, the individual recovery credit provided eligible taxpayers an income tax credit of $1,400 ($2,800 for married taxpayers filing joint) plus $1,400 for each dependent.
- Business credits reduce the tax after applying nonrefundable credits. Any credit in excess of the remaining tax is generally allowed to be carried over or back to be used in other years.
- Refundable credits are the last credit applied to the tax after applying nonrefundable and business credits. Any refundable credit in excess of the remaining tax is treated as an overpayment and refunded to the taxpayer.

LO 8-5 Explain how to compute a taxpayer's underpayment, late filing, and late payment penalties.

- The income tax must be prepaid via withholding from salary or through periodic estimated tax payments during the tax year. Estimated tax payments are required only if withholdings are insufficient to meet the taxpayer's tax liability. For calendar-year taxpayers, estimated tax payments are due on April 15, June 15, and September 15 of the current year and January 15 of the following year.
- Taxpayers can avoid an underpayment penalty if their withholdings and estimated tax payments equal or exceed one of two safe harbors: (1) 90 percent of current-year tax or (2) 100 percent of previous-year tax (110 percent if AGI exceeds $150,000). If the taxpayer does not satisfy either of the safe-harbor provisions, the underpayment penalty is determined

by multiplying the federal short-term interest rate plus 3 percentage points by the amount of tax underpayment per quarter.

- Individual taxpayers are required to file a tax return only if their *gross income* exceeds certain thresholds, which vary based on the taxpayer's filing status, age, and gross income.
- Individual tax returns are due on April 15 for calendar-year individuals. Taxpayers unable to file a tax return by the original due date can request a six-month extension to file.
- The tax law imposes penalties on taxpayers who do not file a tax return (by the original due date plus extension) or pay the tax owed (by the original due date). The failure-to-file penalty equals 5 percent of the amount of tax owed for each month (or fraction thereof) that the tax return is late, with a maximum penalty of 25 percent. The late payment penalty equals .5 percent of the amount of tax owed for each month (or fraction thereof) that the tax is not paid. The combined maximum penalty that may be imposed for late filing and late payment is 5 percent per month (25 percent in total). The late filing and late payment penalties are higher if fraud is involved.

KEY TERMS

additional Medicare tax (8-14)
alternative minimum tax (AMT) (8-7)
alternative minimum tax adjustments (8-8)
alternative minimum tax (AMT) base (8-7)
alternative minimum tax (AMT) exemption (8-11)
alternative minimum tax system (8-7)
business tax credits (8-33)
child tax credit (8-24)
earned income credit (8-30)
employee (8-21)
estimated tax payments (8-36)
federal short-term interest rate (8-37)
FICA taxes (8-14)
independent contractor (8-21)
kiddie tax (8-5)
late filing penalty (8-39)
late payment penalty (8-39)
marriage benefit (8-3)
marriage penalty (8-3)
Medicare tax (8-14)
minimum tax credit (8-12)
net earnings from self-employment (8-16)
net investment income tax (8-13)
net unearned income (8-6)
nonrefundable credit (8-23)
preferential tax rate (8-4)
safe-harbor provisions (8-36)
Schedule C (8-16)
self-employment taxes (8-16)
Social Security tax (8-14)
tax bracket (8-2)
tax credits (8-23)
tax rate schedule (8-2)
tax tables (8-3)
tentative minimum tax (TMT) (8-8)
underpayment penalty (8-36)
withholding (8-36)

DISCUSSION QUESTIONS

Discussion Questions are available in Connect®.

1. What is a tax bracket? What is the relationship between filing status and the width of the tax brackets in the tax rate schedule? LO 8-1
2. In 2022, for a taxpayer with $50,000 of taxable income, without doing any actual computations, which filing status do you expect to provide the lowest tax liability? Which filing status provides the highest tax liability? LO 8-1
3. What is the tax marriage penalty and when does it apply? Under what circumstances would a couple experience a tax marriage benefit? LO 8-1
4. Once they've computed their taxable income, how do taxpayers determine their regular tax liability? What additional steps must taxpayers take to compute their tax liability when they have preferentially taxed income? LO 8-1
5. Are there circumstances in which preferentially taxed income (long-term capital gains and qualified dividends) is taxed at the same rate as ordinary income? Explain. LO 8-1 research
6. Augustana received $100,000 of qualified dividends this year. Under what circumstances might the entire $100,000 of income not be taxed at the same rate? LO 8-1

LO 8-1 7. What is the difference between earned and unearned income?

LO 8-1 8. What is the kiddie tax? Explain.

LO 8-1 9. Does the kiddie tax eliminate the tax benefits gained by a family when parents transfer income-producing assets to children? Explain.

LO 8-1 10. Does the kiddie tax apply to all children no matter their age? Explain.

LO 8-1 11. Lauren is 17 years old. She reports earned income of $3,000 and unearned income of $6,200. Is it likely that she is subject to the kiddie tax? Explain.

LO 8-2 12. In very general terms, how is the alternative minimum tax system different from the regular income tax system? How is it similar?

LO 8-2 13. Describe, in general terms, why Congress implemented the AMT.

LO 8-2 14. Do taxpayers always add back the standard deduction when computing alternative minimum taxable income? Explain.

LO 8-2 15. The starting point for computing alternative minimum taxable income is regular taxable income. What are some of the plus adjustments, plus or minus adjustments, and minus adjustments to regular taxable income to compute alternative minimum taxable income?

LO 8-2 16. Describe what the AMT exemption is and who is and isn't allowed to deduct the exemption. How is it similar to the standard deduction, and how is it dissimilar?

LO 8-1 LO 8-2 17. How do the AMT tax rates compare to the regular income tax rates?

LO 8-2 18. Is it possible for a taxpayer who pays AMT to have a marginal tax rate higher than the stated AMT rate? Explain.

LO 8-2 19. What is the difference between the tentative minimum tax (TMT) and the AMT?

LO 8-3 20. Are an employee's entire wages subject to the FICA tax? Explain.

LO 8-3 21. Bobbie works as an employee for Altron Corp. for the first half of the year and for Betel Inc. for the rest of the year. She is relatively well paid. What FICA tax issues is she likely to encounter? What FICA tax issues do Altron Corp. and Betel Inc. need to consider?

LO 8-3 22. Compare and contrast an employee's FICA tax payment responsibilities with those of a self-employed taxpayer.

LO 8-3 23. When a taxpayer works as an employee and as a self-employed independent contractor during the year, how does the taxpayer determine their employment and self-employment taxes payable?

LO 8-3 24. What are the primary factors to consider when deciding whether a worker should be considered an employee or a self-employed taxpayer for tax purposes?

LO 8-3 25. How do the tax consequences of being an employee differ from those of being self-employed?

LO 8-3 planning 26. Mike wanted to work for a CPA firm, but he also wanted to work on his parents' farm in Montana. Because the CPA firm wanted Mike to be happy, it offered to let him work for the firm as an independent contractor during the fall and winter and return to Montana to work for his parents during the spring and summer. He was very excited to hear that the firm was also going to give him a 5 percent higher "salary" for the six months he would be working for the firm over what he would have made over the same six-month period if he worked full time as an employee (i.e., an increase from $30,000 to $31,500). Should Mike be excited about his 5 percent raise? Why or why not? What counteroffer could Mike reasonably suggest?

LO 8-4 27. How are tax credits and tax deductions similar? How are they dissimilar?

LO 8-4 28. What are the three types of tax credits? Explain why it is important to distinguish between the different types of tax credits.

LO 8-4 29. Explain why there are such a large number and variety of tax credits.

LO 8-4 30. What is the difference between a refundable and nonrefundable tax credit?

LO 8-4 31. Is the child tax credit a refundable or nonrefundable credit? Explain.

32. Diane has a job working three-quarter time. She hired a relative to take care of her two small children so Diane could work. Do Diane's child care payments to her relative qualify for the child and dependent care credit in 2022? Explain. LO 8-4
33. The amount of the child and dependent care credit is based on the amount of the taxpayer's expenditures to provide care for one or more qualifying persons. Who is considered to be a qualifying person for this purpose? LO 8-4
34. Compare and contrast the lifetime learning credit with the American opportunity tax credit. LO 8-4
35. Jennie's grandmother paid her tuition this fall to State University (an eligible educational institution). Jennie is claimed as a dependent by her parents, but she also files her own tax return. Can Jennie claim an education credit for the tuition paid by her grandmother? What difference would it make, if any, if Jennie did not qualify as a dependent of her parents (or anyone else)? LO 8-4 research
36. Why is the earned income credit referred to as a negative income tax? LO 8-4
37. Under what circumstances can a college student qualify for the earned income credit? LO 8-4
38. How are business credits similar to personal credits? How are they dissimilar? LO 8-4
39. When a U.S. taxpayer pays income taxes to a foreign government, what options does the taxpayer have when determining how to treat the expenditure on their U.S. individual income tax return? LO 8-4
40. Describe the order in which different types of tax credits are applied to reduce a taxpayer's tax liability. LO 8-4
41. Describe the two methods that taxpayers use to prepay their taxes. LO 8-5
42. What are the consequences of a taxpayer underpaying their tax liability throughout the year? Explain the safe-harbor provisions that may apply in this situation. LO 8-5
43. Describe how the underpayment penalty is calculated. LO 8-5
44. What determines if a taxpayer is required to file a tax return? If a taxpayer is not required to file a tax return, does this mean that the taxpayer should not file a tax return? LO 8-5
45. What is the due date for individual tax returns? What extensions are available? LO 8-5
46. Describe the consequences for failure to file a tax return and late payment of taxes owed. LO 8-5

PROBLEMS

Select problems are available in Connect®.

47. Whitney received $75,000 of taxable income in 2022. All of the income was salary from her employer. What is her income tax liability in each of the following alternative situations? LO 8-1
    a) She files under the single filing status.
    b) She files a joint tax return with her spouse. Together their taxable income is $75,000.
    c) She is married but files a separate tax return. Her taxable income is $75,000.
    d) She files as a head of household.
48. In 2022, Lisa and Fred, a married couple, had taxable income of $300,000. If they were to file separate tax returns, Lisa would have reported taxable income of $125,000 and Fred would have reported taxable income of $175,000. What is the couple's marriage penalty or benefit? LO 8-1

LO 8-1

49. In 2022, Jasmine and Thomas, a married couple, had taxable income of $150,000. If they were to file separate tax returns, Jasmine would have reported taxable income of $140,000 and Thomas would have reported taxable income of $10,000. What is the couple's marriage penalty or benefit?

LO 8-1

50. Lacy is a single taxpayer. In 2022, her taxable income is $44,000. What is her tax liability in each of the following alternative situations?
   a) All of her income is salary from her employer.
   b) Her $44,000 of taxable income includes $1,000 of qualified dividends.
   c) Her $44,000 of taxable income includes $5,000 of qualified dividends.

LO 8-1

51. In 2022, Sheryl is claimed as a dependent on her parents' tax return. Her parents report taxable income of $550,000 (married filing jointly). Sheryl did not provide more than half her own support. What is Sheryl's tax liability for the year in each of the following alternative circumstances?
   a) She received $7,000 from a part-time job. This was her only source of income. She is 16 years old at year-end.
   b) She received $7,000 of interest income from corporate bonds she received several years ago. This is her only source of income. She is 16 years old at year-end.
   c) She received $7,000 of interest income from corporate bonds she received several years ago. This is her only source of income. She is 20 years old at year-end and is a full-time student.
   d) She received $7,000 of qualified dividend income. This is her only source of income. She is 16 years old at year-end.

LO 8-1

52. In 2022, Carson is claimed as a dependent on his parents' tax return. His parents report taxable income of $200,000 (married filing jointly). Carson's parents provided most of his support. What is Carson's tax liability for the year in each of the following alternative circumstances?
   a) Carson is 17 years old at year-end and earned $14,000 from his summer job and part-time job after school. This was his only source of income.
   b) Carson is 23 years old at year-end. He is a full-time student and earned $14,000 from his summer internship and part-time job. He also received $5,000 of qualified dividend income.

LO 8-2

53. Brooklyn files as a head of household for 2022. They claimed the standard deduction of $19,400 for regular tax purposes. Their regular taxable income was $80,000. What is Brooklyn's AMTI?

LO 8-2

54. Sylvester files as a single taxpayer during 2022. He itemizes deductions for regular tax purposes. He paid charitable contributions of $7,000, real estate taxes of $1,000, state income taxes of $4,000, and mortgage interest of $2,000 on $30,000 of acquisition indebtedness on his home. Sylvester's regular taxable income is $100,000. What is Sylvester's AMTI?

LO 8-2

tax forms

55. In 2022, Nadia has $100,000 of regular taxable income. She itemizes her deductions as follows: real property taxes of $1,500, state income taxes of $2,000, and mortgage interest expense of $10,000 (acquisition indebtedness of $200,000). In addition, she receives tax-exempt interest of $1,000 from a municipal bond (issued in 2006) that was used to fund a new business building for a (formerly) out-of-state employer. Finally, she received a state tax refund of $300 from the prior year.
   a) What is Nadia's AMTI this year if she deducted $15,000 of itemized deductions last year (including a total of $4,000 of real property taxes and state income taxes) and did not owe any AMT last year? Complete Form 6251 (through line 4) for Nadia.
   b) What is Nadia's AMTI this year if she deducted the standard deduction last year and did not owe any AMT last year? Complete Form 6251 (through line 4) for Nadia.

56. In 2022, Sven is single and has $120,000 of regular taxable income. He itemizes his deductions as follows: real property tax of $2,000, state income tax of $4,000, and mortgage interest expense of $15,000 (acquisition debt of $300,000). He also has a positive AMT depreciation adjustment of $500. What is Sven's alternative minimum taxable income (AMTI)? Complete Form 6251 (through line 4) for Sven. LO 8-2 tax forms

57. Olga is married and files a joint tax return with her husband. What amount of AMT exemption may she deduct under each of the following alternative circumstances? LO 8-2
   a) Her AMTI is $390,000.
   b) Her AMTI is $1,180,000.
   c) Her AMTI is $1,600,000.

58. Corbett's AMTI is $600,000. What is his AMT exemption under the following alternative circumstances? LO 8-2
   a) He is married and files a joint return.
   b) He is married and files a separate return.
   c) His filing status is single.
   d) His filing status is head of household.

59. In 2022, Juanita is married and files a joint tax return with her husband. What is her tentative minimum tax in each of the following alternative circumstances? LO 8-2
   a) Her AMT base is $100,000, all ordinary income.
   b) Her AMT base is $250,000, all ordinary income.
   c) Her AMT base is $100,000, which includes $10,000 of qualified dividends.
   d) Her AMT base is $250,000, which includes $10,000 of qualified dividends.

60. Steve's tentative minimum tax for 2022 is $245,000. What is his AMT if LO 8-2
   a) His regular tax is $230,000?
   b) His regular tax is $250,000?

61. In 2022, Janet and Ray are married filing jointly. They have five dependent children under 18 years of age. Janet and Ray's taxable income is $2,400,000, and they itemize their deductions as follows: state income taxes of $10,000 and mortgage interest expense of $25,000 (acquisition debt of $300,000). What is Janet and Ray's AMT? Complete Form 6251 for Janet and Ray. LO 8-2 tax forms

62. In 2022, Deon and NeNe are married filing jointly. Deon and NeNe's taxable income is $1,090,000, and they itemize their deductions as follows: real property taxes of $10,000, charitable contributions of $30,000, and mortgage interest expense of $40,000 ($700,000 acquisition debt for home). What is Deon and NeNe's AMT? Complete Form 6251 for Deon and NeNe. LO 8-2 tax forms

63. Henrich is a single taxpayer. In 2022, his taxable income is $480,000. What are his income tax and net investment income tax liability in each of the following alternative scenarios? LO 8-1 LO 8-3
   a) All of his income is salary from his employer. Assume his modified AGI is $520,000.
   b) His $480,000 of taxable income includes $2,000 of long-term capital gain that is taxed at preferential rates. Assume his modified AGI is $520,000.
   c) His $480,000 of taxable income includes $55,000 of long-term capital gain that is taxed at preferential rates. Assume his modified AGI is $520,000.
   d) Now assume that Henrich has $195,000 of taxable income, which includes $50,000 of long-term capital gain that is taxed at preferential rates. Assume his modified AGI is $210,000.

LO 8-3

64. Brooke, a single taxpayer, works for Company A for all of 2022, earning a salary of $50,000.
    a) What is her FICA tax obligation for the year?
    b) Assume Brooke works for Company A for half of 2022, earning $50,000 in salary, and she works for Company B for the second half of 2022, earning $100,000 in salary. What is Brooke's FICA tax obligation for the year?

LO 8-3

65. Rasheed works for Company A, earning $350,000 in salary during 2022. Assuming he is single and has no other sources of income, what amount of FICA tax will Rasheed pay for the year?

LO 8-3

66. Alice is single and self-employed in 2022. Her net business profit on her Schedule C for the year is $160,000. What are her self-employment tax liability and additional Medicare tax liability for 2022?

LO 8-3

67. Kyle, a single taxpayer, worked as a freelance software engineer for the first three months of 2022. During that time, he earned $44,000 of self-employment income. On April 1, 2022, Kyle took a job as a full-time software engineer with one of his former clients, Hoogle Inc. From April through the end of the year, Kyle earned $178,000 in salary. What amount of FICA taxes (self-employment and employment related) does Kyle owe for the year?

LO 8-3

68. Eva received $60,000 in compensation payments from JAZZ Corp. during 2022. Eva incurred $5,000 in business expenses relating to her work for JAZZ Corp. JAZZ did not reimburse Eva for any of these expenses. Eva is single and deducts a standard deduction of $12,950. Based on these facts, answer the following questions:
    a) Assume that Eva is considered to be an *employee.* What amount of FICA taxes is she required to pay for the year?
    b) Assume that Eva is considered to be an *employee.* What is her regular income tax liability for the year?
    c) Assume that Eva is considered to be a *self-employed contractor.* What are her self-employment tax liability and additional Medicare tax liability for the year?
    d) Assume that Eva is considered to be a *self-employed contractor.* What is her regular tax liability for the year?

LO 8-3
research

69. Terry Hutchison worked as a self-employed lawyer until two years ago, when he retired. He used the cash method of accounting in his business for tax purposes. Five years ago, Terry represented his client ABC Corporation in an antitrust lawsuit against XYZ Corporation. During that year, Terry paid self-employment taxes on all of his income. ABC won the lawsuit, but Terry and ABC could not agree on the amount of his earnings. Finally, this year, the issue got resolved and ABC paid Terry $90,000 for the services he provided five years ago. Terry plans to include the payment in his gross income, but because he spends most of his time playing golf and absolutely no time working on legal matters, he does not intend to pay self-employment taxes on the income. Is Terry subject to self-employment taxes on this income?

LO 8-4

70. Trey has two dependents, his daughters, ages 14 and 18, at year-end. Trey files a joint return with his spouse. What amount of child tax credit (either as a child or a qualifying dependent) will Trey be able to claim in 2022 for his daughters under each of the following alternative situations?
    a) His AGI is $100,000.
    b) His AGI is $420,000.
    c) His AGI is $420,100, and his daughters are ages 10 and 12.

71. Julie paid a day care center to watch her two-year-old son while she worked as a computer programmer for a local start-up company. What amount of child and dependent care credit can Julie claim in 2022 in each of the following alternative scenarios? LO 8-4
   a) Julie paid $2,000 to the day care center, and her AGI is $50,000 (all salary).
   b) Julie paid $10,000 to the day care center, and her AGI is $50,000 (all salary).
   c) Julie paid $4,000 to the day care center, and her AGI is $25,000 (all salary).
   d) Julie paid $2,000 to the day care center, and her AGI is $14,000 (all salary).
   e) Julie paid $4,000 to the day care center, and her AGI is $14,000 ($2,000 salary and $12,000 unearned income).

72. In 2022, Elaine paid $2,800 of tuition and $600 for books for her dependent son to attend State University this past fall as a freshman. Elaine files a joint return with her husband. What is the maximum American opportunity tax credit that Elaine can claim for the tuition payment and books in each of the following alternative situations? LO 8-4
   a) Elaine's AGI is $80,000.
   b) Elaine's AGI is $168,000.
   c) Elaine's AGI is $184,000.

73. In 2022, Laureen is currently single. She paid $2,800 of qualified tuition and related expenses for each of her twin daughters Sheri and Meri to attend State University as freshmen ($2,800 each, for a total of $5,600). Sheri and Meri qualify as Laureen's dependents. Laureen also paid $1,900 for her son Ryan's (also Laureen's dependent) tuition and related expenses to attend his junior year at State University. Finally, Laureen paid $1,200 for herself to attend seminars at a community college to help her improve her job skills. What is the maximum amount of education credits Laureen can claim for these expenditures in each of the following alternative scenarios? LO 8-4 planning
   a) Laureen's AGI is $45,000.
   b) Laureen's AGI is $95,000.
   c) Laureen's AGI is $45,000, and Laureen paid $12,000 (not $1,900) for Ryan to attend graduate school (i.e., his fifth year, not his junior year).

74. In 2022, Amanda and Jaxon Stuart have a daughter who is 1 year old. The Stuarts are full-time students and are both 23 years old. Their only sources of income are gains from stock they held for three years before selling and wages from part-time jobs. What is their earned income credit in the following alternative scenarios if they file jointly? LO 8-4
   a) Their AGI is $15,000, consisting of $12,000 of capital gains and $3,000 of wages.
   b) Their AGI is $15,000, consisting of $10,000 of lottery winnings (unearned income) and $5,000 of wages.
   c) Their AGI is $28,000, consisting of $23,000 of wages and $5,000 of lottery winnings (unearned income).
   d) Their AGI is $28,000, consisting of $5,000 of wages and $23,000 of lottery winnings (unearned income).
   e) Their AGI is $10,000, consisting of $10,000 of lottery winnings (unearned income).

LO 8-4

75. In 2022, Zach is single with no dependents. He is not claimed as a dependent on another's return. All of his income is from salary, and he does not have any for AGI deductions. What is his earned income credit in 2022 in the following alternative scenarios?
   a) Zach is 29 years old, and his AGI is $5,000.
   b) Zach is 29 years old, and his AGI is $10,000.
   c) Zach is 29 years old, and his AGI is $19,000.
   d) Zach is 17 years old, and his AGI is $5,000.

LO 8-4

76. This year Luke has calculated his gross tax liability at $1,800. Luke is entitled to a $2,400 nonrefundable personal tax credit, a $1,500 business tax credit, and a $600 refundable personal tax credit. In addition, Luke has had $2,300 of income taxes withheld from his salary. What is Luke's net tax due or refund?

LO 8-5 planning

77. This year Lloyd, a single taxpayer, estimates that his tax liability will be $10,000. Last year, his total tax liability was $15,000. He estimates that his tax withholding from his employer will be $7,800.
   a) Is Lloyd required to increase his withholding or make estimated tax payments this year to avoid the underpayment penalty? If so, how much?
   b) Assuming Lloyd does not make any additional payments, what is the amount of his underpayment penalty? Assume the federal short-term rate is 5 percent.

LO 8-5 planning

78. This year, Paula and Simon (married filing jointly) estimate that their tax liability will be $200,000. Last year, their total tax liability was $170,000. They estimate that their tax withholding from their employers will be $175,000. Are Paula and Simon required to increase their withholdings or make estimated tax payments this year to avoid the underpayment penalty? If so, how much?

LO 8-5 planning

79. This year, Santhosh, a single taxpayer, estimates that his tax liability will be $100,000. Last year, his total tax liability was $15,000. He estimates that his tax withholding from his employer will be $35,000. Is Santhosh required to increase his withholding or make estimated tax payments this year to avoid the underpayment penalty? If so, how much?

LO 8-5

80. For the following taxpayers, determine if they are required to file a tax return in 2022.
   a) Ricko, single taxpayer, with gross income of $15,000.
   b) Fantasia, head of household, with gross income of $17,500.
   c) Ken and Barbie, married taxpayers with no dependents, with gross income of $20,000.
   d) Dorothy and Rudolf, married taxpayers, both age 68, with gross income of $25,500.
   e) Janyce, single taxpayer, age 73, with gross income of $13,500.

LO 8-5

81. For the following taxpayers, determine the due date of their tax returns.
   a) Jerome, a single taxpayer, is not requesting an extension this year. Assume the due date falls on a Tuesday.
   b) Lashaunda, a single taxpayer, requests an extension this year. Assume the extended due date falls on a Wednesday.
   c) Barney and Betty, married taxpayers, do not request an extension this year. Assume the due date falls on a Sunday and the next day is a holiday.
   d) Fred and Wilma, married taxpayers, request an extension this year. Assume the extended date falls on a Saturday.

LO 8-5 planning

82. Determine the amount of the late filing and late payment penalties that apply for the following taxpayers.
   a) Jolene filed her tax return by its original due date but did not pay the $2,000 in taxes she owed with the return until one and a half months later.
   b) Oscar filed his tax return and paid his $3,000 tax liability five months late.

COMPREHENSIVE PROBLEMS

Select problems are available in Connect®.

83. In 2022, Jack is single and has two children, ages 10 and 12. Jack works full time and earns an annual salary of $195,000 as a consultant. Jack files as a head of household and does not itemize his deductions. In the fall of this year, he was recently offered a position with another firm that would pay him an additional $45,000.

    a) Calculate the marginal tax rate on the additional income, excluding employment taxes, to help Jack evaluate the offer.

    b) Calculate the marginal tax rate on the additional income, including employment taxes, to help Jack evaluate the offer.

84. Reba Dixon is a fifth-grade schoolteacher who earned a salary of $38,000 in 2022. She is 45 years old and has been divorced for four years. She receives $1,200 of alimony payments each month from her former husband (divorced in 2016). Reba also rents out a small apartment building. This year Reba received $50,000 of rental payments from tenants, and she incurred $19,500 of expenses associated with the rental.

tax forms

Reba and her daughter Heather (20 years old at the end of the year) moved to Georgia in January of this year. Reba provides more than one-half of Heather's support. They had been living in Colorado for the past 15 years, but ever since her divorce, Reba has been wanting to move back to Georgia to be closer to her family. Luckily, last December, a teaching position opened up and Reba and Heather decided to make the move. Reba paid a moving company $2,010 to move their personal belongings, and she and Heather spent two days driving the 1,426 miles to Georgia.

Reba rented a home in Georgia. Heather decided to continue living at home with her mom, but she started attending school full time in January and throughout the rest of the year at a nearby university. She was awarded a $3,000 partial tuition scholarship this year, and Reba helped out by paying the remaining $500 tuition cost. If possible, Reba thought it would be best to claim the education credit for these expenses.

Reba wasn't sure if she would have enough items to help her benefit from itemizing on her tax return. However, she kept track of several expenses this year that she thought might qualify if she was able to itemize. Reba paid $5,800 in state income taxes and $12,500 in charitable contributions during the year. She also paid the following medical-related expenses for herself and Heather:

Insurance premiums	$7,952
Medical care expenses	1,100
Prescription medicine	350
Nonprescription medicine	100
New contact lenses for Heather	200

Shortly after the move, Reba got distracted while driving and ran into a street sign. The accident caused $900 in damage to the car and gave her whiplash. Because the repairs were less than her insurance deductible, she paid the entire cost of the repairs. Reba wasn't able to work for two months after the accident. Fortunately, she received $2,000 from her disability insurance. Her employer, the Central Georgia School District, paid 60 percent of the premiums on the policy as a nontaxable fringe benefit, and Reba paid the remaining 40 percent portion.

A few years ago, Reba acquired several investments with her portion of the divorce settlement. This year she reported the following income from her investments: $2,200 of interest income from corporate bonds and $1,500 interest income from City of Denver municipal bonds. Overall, Reba's stock portfolio appreciated by $12,000, but she did not sell any of her stocks.

Heather reported $6,200 of interest income from corporate bonds she received as gifts from her father over the last several years. This was Heather's only source of income for the year.

Reba had $10,000 of federal income taxes withheld by her employer. Heather made $1,000 of estimated tax payments during the year. Reba did not make any estimated payments.

Required:

a) Determine Reba's federal income taxes due or taxes payable for the current year. Complete pages 1 and 2, Schedule 1, and Schedule 3 of Form 1040 for Reba.
b) Is Reba allowed to file as a head of household or single?
c) Determine the amount of FICA taxes Reba was required to pay on her salary.
d) Determine Heather's federal income taxes due or payable.

tax forms

85. Sandy and John Ferguson got married eight years ago and have a seven-year-old daughter, Samantha. In 2022, Sandy worked as a computer technician at a local university, earning a salary of $152,000, and John worked part time as a receptionist for a law firm, earning a salary of $29,000. Sandy also does some Web design work on the side and reported revenues of $4,000 and associated expenses of $750. The Fergusons received $800 in qualified dividends and a $200 refund of their state income taxes. The Fergusons always itemize their deductions, and their itemized deductions were well over the standard deduction amount last year.

The Fergusons reported making the following payments during the year:

- State income taxes of $4,400. Federal tax withholding of $21,000.
- Alimony payments to Sandy's former spouse of $10,000 (divorced in 2014).
- Child support payments for Sandy's child with her former spouse of $4,100.
- $12,200 of real property taxes.
- John was reimbursed $600 for employee business expenses he incurred. He was required to provide documentation for the expenses to his employer.
- $3,600 to Kid Care day care center for Samantha's care while Sandy and John worked.
- $14,000 interest on their home mortgage ($400,000 acquisition debt).
- $3,000 interest on a $40,000 home-equity loan. They used the loan to pay for a family vacation and new car.
- $15,000 cash charitable contributions to qualified charities.
- Donation of used furniture to Goodwill. The furniture had a fair market value of $400 and cost $2,000.

Required:

What is the Fergusons' 2022 federal income taxes payable or refund, including any self-employment tax and AMT, if applicable? Complete Form 1040, pages 1 and 2; Schedule 1, Schedule 2, and Schedule 3 of Form 1040; and Form 6251 for Sandy and John.

UWorld | ROGER CPA Review

UWorld Roger CPA Review

Sample CPA Exam questions from Roger CPA Review are available in Connect as support for the topics in this text. These Multiple Choice Questions and Task-Based Simulations include expert-written explanations and solutions and provide a starting point for students to become familiar with the content and functionality of the actual CPA Exam.

chapter **9**

Business Income, Deductions, and Accounting Methods

Learning Objectives

Upon completing this chapter, you should be able to:

- **LO 9-1** Identify common business deductions.
- **LO 9-2** Determine the limits on deducting business expenses.
- **LO 9-3** Describe accounting periods available to businesses.
- **LO 9-4** Apply cash and accrual methods to determine business income and expense deductions.

Tony Anderson/DigitalVision/Getty Images

Storyline Summary

Taxpayer:	Rick Grime (he/him/his)
Location:	San Antonio, Texas
Family description:	Unmarried
Employment status:	Rick quit his landscaping job in Dallas and moved to San Antonio to start a business as a self-employed landscaper.

Rick Grime graduated from Texas A&M University with a degree in agronomy, and for the past few years has been employed by a landscape architect in Dallas. Nearly every day Rick shared ideas with his employer about improving the business. Rick finally decided to take his ideas and start his own landscaping business in his hometown of San Antonio, Texas. In mid-April, Rick left his job and moved to San Antonio. Once in town, Rick discovered a lot of things are necessary to start a business. First, Rick registered his new business name (Green Acres Landscaping, LLC) and established a bank account for the business. Next, Rick rented a used sport utility vehicle (SUV) and a shop for the place of business. Rick didn't know much about accounting for business activities, so a CPA, Jane Bronson, was hired to advise Rick. Jane and Rick decided that Green Acres would operate as a sole proprietorship, but Jane suggested that as the business grew, Rick might want to consider organizing it as a different type of legal entity. Operating as a corporation, for instance, would allow Rick to invite new investors or business partners to help fund future expansion. Rick formally started his business on May 1. Initially, Rick spent a lot of time attracting new customers, and figured he would hire employees as needs warranted.

(to be continued . . .)

Previous chapters have emphasized the process of determining gross income and deductions for *individuals*. This chapter describes the process for determining income for *businesses*. Keep in mind that the concepts in this chapter generally apply to all types of tax entities, including sole proprietorships (such as Green Acres), partnerships, entities taxed as partnerships (such as LLCs), S corporations, and C corporations.[1] Because Rick is a sole proprietor, our examples emphasize business income and deductions from his personal perspective. Proprietors report business income on Schedule C of their individual income tax returns.

Schedule C income is subject to both individual income and self-employment taxes. Entities, other than sole proprietorships, report income on tax forms separate from the owners' tax returns. For example, partnerships report taxable income on Form 1065, S corporations report taxable income on Form 1120-S, and C corporations report taxable income on Form 1120. Of all these entity types, generally only C corporations pay taxes on their income.

BUSINESS GROSS INCOME

In most respects, the rules for determining business gross income are the same as for determining gross income for individuals. Gross income includes "all income from whatever source derived."[2] Generally speaking, income from a business includes gross profit from inventory sales (i.e., sales minus cost of goods sold), income from services provided to customers, and income from renting property to customers. Just like individuals, a business is allowed to exclude certain types of realized income from gross income, such as municipal bond interest. Unlike wage earners, businesses can be subject to complex rules and limitations discussed later in this chapter. However, most *small* businesses are exempt from these rules as determined under a gross receipts test.

Gross Receipts Test for Determining Small Businesses

A business that qualifies as a *small* business under a **gross receipts test** is exempt from certain complex accounting provisions (discussed later in the chapter) for each year in which it meets the test. A business meets the gross receipts test for 2022 if its average annual gross receipts for the three prior taxable years does not exceed $27 million.[3] For example, if a corporation reported gross receipts of $26 million, $25 million, and $29 million in 2019, 2020, and 2021, respectively, it would meet the gross receipts test for 2022 ($26.7 million in average gross receipts over the prior three years). However, if it reported $32 million of gross receipts in 2021, rather than $29 million, it would fail the gross receipts test for 2022 ($27.7 million in average gross receipts over the prior three years) and would not qualify as a small business for 2022. For purposes of the test, gross receipts includes total sales (net of returns and allowances but not cost of goods sold), amounts received for services, and income from investments (including tax-exempt interest).[4] When the business has not been in existence for three prior tax years, the test is conducted for the years that it was in existence. Also, in the case of a taxable year of less than 12 months (a *short* year), the amount of gross receipts must be annualized by multiplying the gross receipts for the short period by 12 and dividing the result by the number of months in the short period.

[1] S corporations are treated as flow-through entities (S corporation income is taxed to its owners), while C corporations are taxed as separate taxable entities. The choice of the organizational form for a business is a complex decision that is beyond the scope of this chapter.

[2] §61(a).

[3] §448(c). The gross receipts threshold amount is indexed for inflation. The gross receipts threshold was $25 million for 2018 and $26 million for 2019 through 2021.

[4] Temp. Reg. §1.448-1T(f)(2)(iv)(A). Gross receipts from the sale of a capital asset is reduced by the adjusted basis in the asset.

The gross receipts test is an annual test. It is possible a business might qualify under the the gross receipts test in year 1 but experience a surge in gross receipts and not qualify in year 2. Hence, businesses that experience volatile gross receipts may find that they qualify in one year but not the next if gross receipts vary substantially around the $27 million cutoff.

Example 9-1

What if: Suppose that Green Acres is a C corporation and a calendar-year taxpayer. Suppose further that Green Acres reported gross receipts of $20 million in 2019, $25 million in 2020, and $30 million in 2021. In 2022, is Green Acres a small business under the gross receipts test?

Answer: Yes. The average of gross receipts for the previous three-tax-year period is $25 million ($75 million divided by 3). Because average gross receipts doesn't exceed $27 million, Green Acres qualifies as a small business under the gross receipts test in 2022.

What if: Suppose that Green Acres began business operations on January 1, 2020, and reported $22 million in gross receipts for that year. In 2021, Green Acres reported $30 million in gross receipts. Is Green Acres a small business in 2022 under the gross receipts test?

Answer: Yes. The average of gross receipts for the two-tax-year period in which Green Acres conducted business is $26 million ($52 million divided by 2). Because average gross receipts doesn't exceed $27 million, Green Acres qualifies as a small business in 2022.

What if: Suppose that Green Acres began business operations on July 1, 2021, and reported $15 million in gross receipts for the six months of 2021, a short year. Does Green Acres qualify as a small business in 2022 under the gross receipts test?

Answer: No. For purposes of the gross receipts test, the gross receipts for the six-month 2021 tax year is annualized by multiplying $15 million by 12 and dividing the result by 6 (the number of months in the short period 2021). Thus, gross receipts for Green Acres in 2021 is $30 million ($180 million divided by 6). Because average gross receipts is more than $27 million, Green Acres is not considered to be a small business in 2022.

TAXES IN THE REAL WORLD Is a *Hard Fork* a taxable event?

A hard fork refers to a radical change to the protocols of a blockchain network. In simple terms, a hard fork splits a single cryptocurrency into two. On August 1, 2017, Bitcoin experienced a hard fork, and a second cryptocurrency, called Bitcoin Cash, was created. Every holder of a unit of Bitcoin received the same number of Bitcoin Cash units.

In 2021, the IRS concluded that the Bitcoin hard fork is a taxable event if the taxpayer had control over the resulting second cryptocurrency. Hence, a taxpayer who held 1 Bitcoin unit with a private key was subject to tax in 2017 on the value of the Bitcoin Cash unit received in the hard fork.

In contrast, another taxpayer owned Bitcoin through an account at CEX, a cryptocurrency exchange. Rather than the taxpayer, CEX had sole control over the private key to 100 units of Bitcoin. The taxpayer owned one unit of the 100 total Bitcoin units held by CEX. Because CEX was uncertain of Bitcoin Cash's security and viability, it chose not to support Bitcoin Cash at the time of the hard fork. As a result, the taxpayer was unable to access any Bitcoin Cash through the account with CEX. The taxpayer was only subject to tax in 2018 on the value of the Bitcoin Cash unit after CEX initiated support for Bitcoin Cash in 2018, allowing the taxpayer to buy, sell, send, receive, transfer, or exchange the 1 unit in their account. The IRS noted that the character of the gain depended on whether the virtual currency is a capital asset in the hands of the taxpayer.

Source: Chief Counsel Advice CCA 202114020.

BUSINESS DEDUCTIONS

LO 9-1

Because Congress intended for taxable income to reflect the *net* increase in wealth from a business, it is only fair that a business is allowed to deduct expenses incurred to generate business income. Typically, Congress provides *specific* statutory rules authorizing

THE KEY FACTS

Business Expenses

- Business expenses must be incurred in pursuit of profits, not personal goals.
- A deduction must be ordinary and necessary (appropriate and helpful).
- Only reasonable amounts are allowed as deductions.

deductions. However, as you can see from the following excerpt from §162, the provision authorizing business deductions is relatively broad and ambiguous:

> There shall be allowed as a deduction all the ordinary and necessary expenses paid or incurred during the taxable year in carrying on any trade or business. . . .[5]

Taxpayers can deduct expenses for "trade or business" activities, but the law does not define the phrase "trade or business."[6] However, it is implicit that the primary objective of a "business" activity is to make a profit. Thus, the law requires that a business expense be made in the pursuit of profit rather than the pursuit of other, presumably personal, motives.

Ordinary and Necessary

Business expenditures must be both **ordinary and necessary** to be deductible. An *ordinary* expense is an expense that is normal or appropriate for the business under the circumstances.[7] To be considered ordinary, an expense need not be typical or repetitive in nature. For example, a business could deduct the legal fees it expends to defend itself in an antitrust suit. Although an antitrust suit would be atypical and unusual for most businesses, defending the suit would probably be deemed ordinary because it would be expected under the circumstances. A *necessary* expense is an expense that is helpful or conducive to the business activity, but the expenditure need not be essential or indispensable. For example, a deduction for metric tools would qualify as ordinary and necessary even if there was only a small chance that a repair would require these tools. The "ordinary and necessary" requirements are applied on a case-by-case basis, and while the deduction depends on individual circumstances, the IRS is often reluctant to second-guess business decisions. Exhibit 9-1 presents examples of expenditures that are ordinary and necessary for typical businesses.

EXHIBIT 9-1 Examples of Typical Ordinary and Necessary Business Expenses

• Advertising	• Office expenses
• Car and truck expenses	• Rent
• Depreciation	• Repairs
• Employee compensation and benefits	• Supplies
• Insurance	• Travel
• Interest	• Utilities
• Legal fees	• Wages

Example 9-2

Rick provides a small waiting room for clients. Rick paid $50 for several books to occupy clients while waiting for appointments. These are hardcover books with photographs and illustrations of landscape designs. Rick believes that the books will inspire new designs and alleviate boredom for potential clients. Can Rick deduct the $50 cost as a business expense?

Answer: Yes, the $50 is ordinary and necessary. The phrase *ordinary and necessary* is interpreted as *helpful or conducive to business activity*. In Rick's situation, it seems highly unlikely that the IRS or a court would conclude that the cost of these books is not ordinary and necessary.

What if: Suppose that Rick's hobby was pre-Columbian art. Would Rick be able to deduct the cost of a new treatise on determining provenance of this art if he placed this book in his waiting room?

[5]§162(a). It is important to note that the cost of goods sold is not a deduction. Instead, it automatically reduces gross income from sales and requires no statutory authority. See *Doyle v. Mitchell Brothers Co.,* 247 U.S. 179 (1918), *aff'g* 235 Fed. 686 (6th Cir. 1916).

[6]§212 contains a sister provision to §162 allowing deductions for ordinary and necessary expenses incurred for the production of income ("investment expenses") and for the management and maintenance of property (including expenses incurred in renting property in situations when the rental activity is not considered to be a trade or business). A business activity, sometimes referred to as a trade or business, requires a relatively high level of involvement or effort from the taxpayer. Unlike business activities, investments are profit-motivated activities that don't require a high degree of taxpayer involvement or effort.

[7]*Welch v. Helvering,* 290 U.S. 111 (1933).

Answer: No. It seems unlikely that Rick's prospective clients would share Rick's interest in pre-Columbian art, much less how to determine provenance. Hence, it seems highly likely that the IRS or a court would conclude that Rick purchased the treatise for personal rather than business reasons and that the cost of this book is not ordinary and necessary.

ETHICS

Sheri is an attorney who operates as a sole practitioner. Despite a busy schedule, in the past Sheri found time for family. This year Sheri took on two new important clients and hired a personal assistant to help manage Sheri's schedule and make timely court filings. Occasionally, Sheri asked the assistant to assist with personal tasks such as buying groceries. Do you think that Sheri should treat the assistant's entire salary as a business expense? Would your answer be any different if personal assistants were to commonly perform these tasks for other busy professionals, such as corporate executives and accountants? How would the cost of a personal assistant differ from the cost of having groceries delivered?

Reasonable in Amount

Ordinary and necessary business expenses are deductible only *to the extent* they are **reasonable in amount.** The courts have interpreted this requirement to mean that an expenditure is not reasonable when it is extravagant or exorbitant.[8] If the expenditure is extravagant in amount, the courts presume the excess amount is spent for personal rather than business reasons and is not deductible.

Determining whether an expenditure is reasonable is not an exact science, and, not surprisingly, taxpayers and the IRS may have different opinions. Generally, the courts and the IRS test for extravagance by comparing the amount of the expense to a market price or an **arm's-length amount.** An amount is reasonable if it is within the range of amounts typically charged in the market by unrelated persons. When an amount exceeds this range, the underlying issue becomes *why* a profit-motivated taxpayer would make an excessive payment. Hence, reasonableness is most likely to be an issue when a payment is made to an individual related to the taxpayer or when the taxpayer enjoys some incidental benefit from the expenditure.

Example 9-3

During the busy part of the year, Rick could not keep up with all the work. Therefore, he hired four part-time employees and paid them the market rate of $20 an hour to mow and trim lawns. When things finally slowed down in late fall, Rick released his four part-time employees. Rick paid a total of $21,000 in compensation to the four employees.

Rick still needed some extra help now and then, so he hired his brother, Tom, on a part-time basis. Tom performed the same duties as the prior part-time employees. However, Rick paid Tom $35 per hour because Tom is a college student and Rick wanted to provide some additional support for Tom's education. At year-end, Tom had worked a total of 100 hours and received $3,500 from Rick. What amount can Rick deduct for the compensation he paid to his employees?

Answer: $23,000. Rick can deduct the entire $21,000 paid to the four part-time employees. However, he can only deduct $20 an hour for Tom's compensation because the extra $15 per hour Rick paid Tom is unreasonable in amount.[9] The remaining $15 per hour is considered a personal (nondeductible) gift from Rick to Tom. Hence, Rick can deduct a total of $23,000 for compensation expense this year [$21,000 + ($20 × 100)].

(continued on page 9-6)

[8]§162(a); *Comm'r v. Lincoln Elec. Co.*, 176 F.2d 815 (6th Cir. 1949).

[9]In practice, this distinction is rarely cut and dried. Rick may be able to argue for various reasons that Tom's work is worth more than $20 an hour, but perhaps not as much as $35 per hour. We use this example to illustrate the issue of reasonable expenses and not to discuss the merits of what actually is reasonable compensation to Tom.

What if: Suppose that Tom was able to mow twice as many lawns as other employees in the same amount of time and also provide the same quality of work. What is the deductible amount of the $3,500 under these circumstances?

Answer: $3,500. Rick can now deduct an additional $1,500 because Tom's quality of work justifies twice the salary paid to other employees.

LO 9-2

LIMITATIONS ON BUSINESS DEDUCTIONS

THE KEY FACTS

Limitations on Business Deductions

- No business deductions are allowable for expenditures that are against public policy (bribes) or are political contributions.
- Expenditures that benefit a period longer than 12 months generally must be capitalized.
- No deductions are allowable for expenditures associated with the production of tax-exempt income.
- Personal expenditures are not deductible.

For a variety of reasons, Congress specifically prohibits or limits a business's ability to deduct certain expenditures that appear to otherwise meet the general business expense deductibility requirements.

Expenditures against Public Policy

Businesses occasionally incur fines and penalties and may even pay illegal bribes and kickbacks. However, these payments are not deductible for tax purposes.[10] Congress disallows these expenditures under the rationale that allowing them would subsidize illegal activities and frustrate public policy. Interestingly enough, businesses conducting an illegal activity (i.e., selling stolen goods or conducting illegal gambling) are allowed to offset gross income with the cost of the illegal goods (the cost of goods sold) and deduct other ordinary and necessary business expenses incurred in conducting the illegal business activity. However, they are not allowed to deduct fines, penalties, bribes, or illegal kickbacks.[11] Of course, the IRS is probably more concerned that many illegal businesses fail to report *any* income than that illegal businesses overstate deductions.[12]

Example 9-4

In July, the city fined Rick $200 for violating the city's watering ban when he watered a newly installed landscape. Later, Rick donated $250 to the mayor's campaign for reelection. Can Rick deduct these expenditures?

Answer: No. Rick cannot deduct either the fine or the political contribution as a business expense because the tax laws specifically prohibit deductions for these expenditures.

Political Contributions and Lobbying Costs

Perhaps to avoid the perception that the federal government subsidizes taxpayer efforts to influence politics, the tax laws prohibit deductions for political contributions and most lobbying expenses.[13]

[10] §162(c); Reg. §1.162-21. This prohibition applies to fines and penalties imposed by a government or governmental unit unless the taxpayer establishes that the payment is either restitution, remediation, or required to come into compliance with the law. Fines and penalties imposed by other organizations, such as a fine levied by NASCAR or the NFL, would be fully deductible if the payment otherwise qualified as an ordinary and necessary business expense.

[11] *Comm'r v. Sullivan,* 356 U.S. 27 (1958). In addition, no deduction is allowed for any settlement, payout, or attorney fees related to sexual harassment or abuse if the payments are subject to a nondisclosure agreement.

[12] §280E explicitly prohibits dealers in illegal drugs from deducting any business expenses associated with this "business" activity. This prohibition remains on marijuana producers despite the legalization of marijuana under some state laws. However, drug dealers and marijuana producers are still able to deduct cost of goods sold because cost of goods sold is technically a reduction in gross income (return of capital) and not a business expense. See Reg. §1.61-3(a).

[13] §162(e).

Capital Expenditures

Whether a business uses the cash or the accrual method of accounting, it must capitalize expenditures for *tangible* assets such as buildings, machinery and equipment, furniture and fixtures, and similar property that have useful lives of more than one year (12 months).[14] For tax purposes, businesses recover the cost of capitalized tangible assets (other than land) either by immediate expensing (when allowed by law) or through depreciation.

Businesses also capitalize the cost to create or acquire *intangible* assets such as patents, purchased goodwill, start-up costs, and organizational expenditures.[15] They recover the costs of capitalized intangible assets either through amortization (when the tax laws allow them to do so) or upon disposition of the assets.[16] Prepaid expenses are also subject to capitalization, but there is a special exception that we discuss under accounting methods later in this chapter.

Expenses Associated with the Production of Tax-Exempt Income

Expenses that generate *tax-exempt* income are not allowed to offset taxable income. For example, this restriction disallows interest expense deductions for businesses that borrow money and invest the loan proceeds in municipal (tax-exempt) bonds. It also disallows deductions for life insurance premiums businesses pay on policies that cover the lives of officers or other key employees and compensate the business for the disruption and lost income related to a key employee's death. Because the death benefit from the life insurance policy is not taxable, a business is not allowed to deduct the insurance premium expense associated with this nontaxable income.

Example 9-5

Rick employs Joan, an arborist who specializes in trimming trees and treating local tree ailments. Joan generates a great deal of revenue for Rick's business, but Joan is over 60 and suffers from MS. In November, Rick purchased a "key employee" term life insurance policy on Joan's life. Rick paid $720 in premiums for a policy that pays Rick (Green Acres) a $20,000 death benefit if Joan passes away during the next 12 months. Can Rick deduct the life insurance premium?

Answer: No. Rick cannot deduct the $720 premium on the life insurance policy because the life insurance proceeds from the policy are tax-exempt.

What if: Suppose Rick purchased the life insurance policy on Joan's life and allowed Joan to name the beneficiary. Again, Rick paid a $720 premium for a policy that pays the beneficiary a $20,000 death benefit if Joan dies in the next 12 months. What amount of life insurance policy premium can Rick deduct?

Answer: $720. In this scenario, Rick can deduct the entire premium of $720 as a *compensation* expense because the benefit of the policy inures to Joan (she names the beneficiary), and not to Rick's business.

Personal Expenditures

Taxpayers are not allowed to deduct **personal expenses** unless the expenses are "expressly" authorized by a provision in the law.[17] While the tax laws do not expressly define what constitutes a *personal* expense, the statute identifies "personal, living, or family expenses" as nondeductible examples. Hence, at a minimum, the costs of food, clothing, and shelter are assumed to be personal and nondeductible. Of course, there are the inevitable exceptions when otherwise personal items are specially adapted to business use. For example, taxpayers may deduct the cost of uniforms or special clothing they purchase for use in their business if the clothing is not appropriate to wear as ordinary clothing outside the place of business. However, when the clothing is adaptable as ordinary clothing, the cost of the clothing is a nondeductible personal expenditure.

[14]Reg. §1.263(a)-2(d)(4). The act of recording the asset is sometimes referred to as *capitalizing* the expenditure.

[15]Reg. §1.263(a)-4(b). The extent to which expenditures for intangible assets must be capitalized is explored in *Indopco v. Comm'r*, 503 U.S. 79 (1992).

[16]See §§195, 197, and 248 for provisions that allow taxpayers to amortize the cost of certain intangible assets such as start-up costs and purchased goodwill.

[17]§262(a).

Example 9-6

Rick spent $500 to purchase special coveralls that identify his landscaping service and provide a professional appearance. How much of the cost for the clothing can Rick deduct as a business expense?

Answer: $500. While the cost of clothing is inherently personal, Rick can deduct the $500 cost of the coveralls because, due to the design and labeling on the coveralls, they are not suitable for ordinary use.

Many business owners, particularly small business owners such as sole proprietors, may be tempted to use business funds to pay for items that are entirely personal in nature. For example, a sole proprietor could use the business checking account to pay for family groceries. These expenditures, even though funded by the business, are not deductible.

Educational expenses constitute another exception. Expenditures made by a taxpayer for business education, including tuition and books, may be motivated by business aspirations. However, educational expenditures are not deductible as business expenses unless the taxpayer is self-employed and the education *maintains or improves skills* required by the individual in an *existing* trade or business. Education expenses necessary to meet minimum requirements for an occupation are not deductible. For example, tuition payments for courses to satisfy the education requirement to sit for the CPA exam are not deductible. These courses would qualify the taxpayer for a *new* trade or business rather than improving his skills in an existing trade or business.

Mixed-Motive Expenditures

THE KEY FACTS

Mixed-Motive Expenditures

- Special limits are imposed on expenditures that have both personal and business benefits.
- Entertainment expenses are generally not deductible.
- For 2022, the cost of business meals provided by restaurants is 100 percent deductible. Other business meals are typically 50 percent deductible.
- Contemporaneous written records of business purpose are required.

Business owners in general, and owners of small or closely held businesses in particular, often make expenditures that are motivated by *both* business and personal concerns. These **mixed-motive expenditures** are of particular concern to lawmakers and the IRS because of the tax incentive to disguise nondeductible personal expenses as deductible business expenses. Thus, deductions for business expenditures accompanied by personal benefits are closely monitored and restricted. The rules for determining the amount of *deductible* mixed-motive expenditures depend on the type of expenditure. The most common restrictions determine the deductible portion of mixed-motive expenditures for meals, travel and transportation, and the use of property for both business and personal purposes.

Like personal expenses, entertainment expenditures are generally not deductible as business expenses. Entertainment is defined in the regulations as any activity that is of a type generally considered to constitute entertainment, amusement, or recreation. Activities at night clubs, theaters, country clubs, and sporting events are all considered entertainment.[18] Two notable exceptions to the ban on deducting entertainment expenses include expenditures primarily for the benefit of the taxpayer's employees and entertainment expenses designed and treated as compensation. For example, an employer could deduct as compensation an all-expense paid holiday provided to an outstanding employee.

Some business expenditures are deductible despite being related to personal, living, or family needs of an individual; for example, the cost of a hotel room maintained by an employer for lodging of his employees while in business travel status. Another example is the cost for using an automobile in the active conduct of trade or business even though the auto might also be used for routine personal purposes such as commuting to and from work.

Because everyone needs to eat, meals also contain a significant personal element. In addition, meals are also often associated with entertainment activities. However, the cost or a portion of the cost of a meal can sometimes qualify as a business expense. To qualify as a business expense, the cost of food and beverages must meet several requirements. First, as with all business expenses, a meal must be ordinary and necessary under the circumstances and the amount must be reasonable (not extravagant). Second, the taxpayer or an employee must be present when the meal is furnished, and the meal must be provided to a current or potential client or business contact. Finally, if the meal is provided during or at an entertainment activity, the meal must be purchased separately from the entertainment or the cost stated separately on invoices or receipts.[19]

[18]Reg. §§1.274-2(b) and 1.274-11.

[19]§274(k), (n); Notices 2018-76 and 2021-25; Prop. Reg. §1.274-11(b)(ii).

Business deductions for food and beverages are generally limited to 50 percent of the cost. However, for 2022 (and 2021) the cost of food and beverages for business meals is 100 percent deductible as long as the expense is for food or beverages provided by a *restaurant* (presumably including take-out and delivery).[20] Also fully deductible are the costs of food and beverages when the amounts paid are treated as employee compensation.[21] For example, when a business rewards a high-performing salesperson with an all-inclusive vacation, the cost of the vacation including food and beverages is fully deductible. Likewise, the cost of food and beverages provided during employee recreational activities is fully deductible when the activity is not limited to highly compensated individuals. For example, the cost of meals and beverages would be fully deductible for a buffet and open bar at a holiday party for employees.

Example 9-7

Rick invited two prospective clients to a professional basketball game. Rick purchased tickets to attend the game in a suite where food and beverages would be provided by a wine and cheese specialty store that does not qualify as a restaurant. Rick paid $850 for the tickets and $540 for the food and beverages. Assuming that these amounts were not extravagant, what amount can Rick deduct as a business expense?

Answer: Rick can deduct $270 [$540 × 50%] as a business expense because the cost of the food was stated separately from the cost of the tickets. The cost of the tickets to the game is a nondeductible entertainment expense. If the food and beverages were provided by a restaurant, then Rick could deduct their full cost ($540).

What if: Suppose that Rick purchased the tickets for $1,500 and that the cost of the tickets included food and beverages. What amount of the expenditures can Rick deduct as a business expense?

Answer: Zero. The cost of meals must be stated separately from the cost of the entertainment.

What if: Suppose that Rick invited all of his employees to a company picnic where he paid $1,250 for food and beverages. What amount of the expenditures can Rick deduct as a business expense?

Answer: $1,250. The cost of food and beverages is fully deductible for employee recreational events that are not limited to highly compensated employees.

What if: Suppose Rick took a prospective client to his favorite restaurant and paid $200 for a meal. What amount could Rick deduct as a business expense?

Answer: $200 if the meal was not extravagant. For 2022, the entire cost of a business meal is deductible when provided by a restaurant.

Travel and Transportation Under certain conditions, sole proprietors and self-employed taxpayers may deduct the cost of travel and transportation for business purposes. *Transportation* expenses relate to the direct cost of transporting the taxpayer to and from remote business sites. In contrast, the cost of commuting between the taxpayer's home and regular place of business is personal and, therefore, not deductible. If the taxpayer uses a vehicle for business, the taxpayer can deduct the costs of operating the vehicle plus depreciation on the vehicle's tax basis. Alternatively, in lieu of deducting these costs, the taxpayer may simply deduct a standard amount for each business mile driven. The standard mileage rate represents the per-mile cost of operating an automobile (including depreciation or lease payments).[22] For 2022, the standard mileage rate is 58.5 cents per mile. To be deductible, the transportation must be for business reasons. If the transportation is primarily for personal purposes, the cost is not deductible.

[20]Section 210 of the Taxpayer Certainty and Disaster Tax Relief Act of 2020 amends Code Sec. 274(n)(2) to allow for 100 percent deduction of expenses for food and beverages paid to or incurred at a restaurant after December 31, 2020, and prior to January 1, 2023. Notice 2021-15 defines restaurant to mean a business that sells food or beverages to retail customers for immediate consumption regardless of whether the food or beverages are consumed on the business's premises.

[21]§274(e)(20) and Reg. §1.274-12(c). Importantly, the cost of food and beverages is only 50 percent deductible for breakroom snacks because this benefit does not qualify as compensation or recreational activities.

[22]This mileage rate is updated periodically (sometimes more than once a year) to reflect changes in the cost of operating a vehicle. Once a taxpayer uses the actual cost method including depreciation for determining automobile deductions, the taxpayer is not allowed to switch to the standard mileage rate method. If the taxpayer uses the mileage method, they can switch to the cost method in a subsequent year but must compute depreciation using the straight-line method.

Example 9-8

Rick decided to lease an SUV to drive between his shop and various work sites. Rick carefully documents the business use of the SUV (8,100 miles this year) and his operating expenses ($5,335 this year, including $3,935 for gas, oil, and repairs and $1,400 for lease payments). At no time does Rick use the SUV for personal purposes. What amount of these expenses may Rick deduct as business expenses?

Answer: $5,335. Because Rick uses the SUV in his business activities, he can deduct (1) the $5,335 cost of operating and leasing the SUV or (2) $4,739 for the 8,100 business miles driven this year (58.5 cents per mile × 8,100 miles). Assuming Rick chooses to deduct operating expenses and lease payments in lieu of using the mileage rate, he can deduct $5,335. However, by choosing to deduct the actual operating expense, Rick will forgo the option of using the mileage rate in the future.

In contrast to transportation expenses, *travel* expenses are only deductible if the taxpayer is *away from home* overnight while traveling. This distinction is important because, besides the cost of transportation, the deduction for **travel expenses** includes the cost of meals (limited to 50 percent unless provided by a restaurant), lodging, and incidental expenses. A taxpayer is considered to be away from home overnight if the travel is away from the primary place of business and of sufficient duration to require sleep or rest (typically this will be overnight).

When a taxpayer travels solely for business purposes, *all* of the costs of travel are deductible (but only 50 percent of meals unless provided by a restaurant). When the travel has both business and personal aspects, the deductibility of the transportation costs depends upon whether business is the *primary* purpose for the trip. If the primary purpose of a trip is business, the transportation costs are fully deductible, but meals (50 percent unless provided by a restaurant), lodging, and incidental expenditures are limited to those incurred during the business portion of the travel.[23] If the taxpayer's primary purpose for the trip is personal, the taxpayer may not deduct *any* transportation costs to arrive at the location but may deduct meals (limited to 50 percent unless provided by a restaurant), lodging, transportation, and incidental expenditures for the *business* portion of the trip. The primary purpose of a trip depends upon facts and circumstances and is often the subject of dispute.

The rule for business travel is modified somewhat if a trip abroad includes both business and personal activities. Like the rule for domestic travel, if foreign travel is primarily for personal purposes, then only those expenses directly associated with business activities are deductible. However, unlike the rule for domestic travel, when foreign travel is primarily for business purposes, a portion of the round-trip transportation costs is not deductible. The nondeductible portion is typically computed based on a ratio of the proportion of personal days to total days (travel days count as business days).[24]

Example 9-9

Rick paid a $300 registration fee for a three-day course in landscape design. The course was held in upstate New York (Rick paid $625 for airfare to attend) and he spent four days away from home. He spent the last day sightseeing. During the trip, Rick paid $150 a night for three nights' lodging, $50 a day for meals at restaurants, and $70 a day for a rental car. What amount of these travel-related expenditures may Rick deduct as business expenses?

[23]Note that travel days are considered business days. Also, special limitations apply to a number of travel expenses that are potentially abusive, such as luxury water travel, foreign conventions, conventions on cruise ships, and travel expenses associated with taking a companion.

[24]Foreign transportation expense is deductible without prorating under special circumstances detailed in §274(c). For example, the cost of getting abroad is fully deductible if the travel is for one week or less or if the personal activity constitutes less than one-fourth of the travel time.

Answer: $1,435 for business travel and $300 for business education. The primary purpose for the trip appears to be business because Rick spent three days on business activities versus one day on personal activities. He can deduct travel costs, computed as follows:

Deductible Travel Costs

Description	Amount	Explanation
Airfare	$ 625	Primary purpose is business
Lodging	450	3 business days × $150 a day
Meals	150	3 business days × $50 a day
Rental car	210	3 business days × $70 a day
Total business travel expenses	**$1,435**	

What if: Assume Rick stayed in New York for 10 days, spending 3 days at the seminar and 7 days sightseeing. What amount could he deduct?

Answer: In this scenario Rick can deduct $810 for the lodging, meals, and rental car and $300 for business education. Rick would not be able to deduct the $625 cost of airfare because the trip is primarily personal, as evidenced by the seven days of personal activities compared to only three days of business activities.

Deductible Travel Costs

Description	Amount	Explanation
Airfare	$ 0	Primary purpose is personal
Lodging	450	3 business days × $150 a day
Meals	150	3 business days × $50 a day
Rental car	210	3 business days × $70 a day
Total business travel expenses	**$810**	

What if: Assume the original facts in the example except Rick traveled to London (rather than upstate New York) for 10 days, spending 6 days at the seminar and 4 days sightseeing. What amount could he deduct?

Answer: In this scenario, Rick can deduct $1,995 for travel (computed below) and $300 for business education.

Deductible Travel Costs

Description	Amount	Explanation
Airfare to London	$ 375	6 business days/10 total days × $625
Lodging in London	900	6 business days × $150 a day
Meals	300	6 business days × $50 a day
Rental car	420	6 business days × $70 a day
Total business travel expenses	**$1,995**	

Rick is allowed to deduct $375 of the $625 airfare (60 percent) because he spent 6 of the 10 days on the trip conducting business activities.

Property Use Several types of property may be used for both business and personal purposes. For example, business owners often use automobiles, computers, or cell phones for both business and personal purposes.[25] However, because expenses relating to these assets are deductible only to the extent the assets are used for business purposes, taxpayers must allocate the expenses between the business and personal use portions. For example, if a full year's expense for a business asset is $1,000, but the asset is only used for business purposes 90 percent of the time, then only $900 of expense can be deducted ($1,000 × 90%).

[25]These types of assets are referred to as "listed property." However, cell phones and computers are specifically exempted from the definition of listed property under §280F(d)(4)(A).

Example 9-10

Rick occasionally uses his personal auto (a BMW) to drive to interviews with prospective clients and to drive back and forth between his shop and various work sites. This year Rick carefully recorded that the BMW was driven 500 miles for business activities and 10,000 miles in total. What expenses associated with the BMW may Rick deduct if Rick incurred $6,120 in operating costs for his BMW?

Answer: $306. Rick can deduct the business portion (of his total operating costs based upon the percentage of business miles driven to total miles driven [500 business miles/10,000 total miles]). Hence, Rick will deduct 5 percent of $6,120, or $306, as business travel. Alternatively, Rick could use the business mileage rate of 58.5 cents a mile to determine his business travel expense.

Record Keeping and Other Requirements Because distinguishing business purposes from personal purposes is a difficult and subjective task, the tax laws include provisions designed to help the courts and the IRS determine the business element of mixed-motive transactions. Under these provisions, taxpayers must maintain specific, written, contemporaneous records (of time, amount, and business purpose) for mixed-motive expenses. For example, the cost of business meals is deductible (limited to 50% unless provided by a restaurant), but only if the taxpayer can properly document the five requirements described above.[26]

Limitation on Business Interest Deductions

THE KEY FACTS

Business Interest Limitation

- The deduction of business interest expense is limited to business interest income plus 30 percent of the business's adjusted taxable income.
- The business interest limitation does not apply to businesses qualifying as small businesses under the $27 million gross receipts test.
- Adjusted taxable income is taxable income allocable to the business computed without interest income and before depreciation and interest expense deductions.
- Disallowed business interest expense can be carried forward indefinitely.

The deduction of interest paid or accrued on indebtedness allocable to a trade or business is subject to limitation. The purpose of this limitation is to limit the extent to which a business utilizes debt to avoid income taxes. Specifically, business interest is broadly defined as an amount that is paid, received, or accrued as compensation for the use or forbearance of money under the terms of an instrument or contractual arrangement. The amount of the deduction is, in general, limited to the sum of (1) *business interest income* and (2) 30 percent of the *adjusted taxable income* of the taxpayer for the taxable year. As a matter of equity, Congress allows business interest deductions to offset business interest income. The latter is defined as the amount of interest income includable in gross income that is properly allocable to a trade or business. The limitation does not apply to a business that qualifies as a small business under the $27 million gross receipts test discussed in the gross income section of the chapter.

Calculating the Interest Limitation Adjusted taxable income represents the taxable income allocable to the business activity. This income is defined as taxable income of the taxpayer computed without regard to (1) any item of income, gain, deduction, or loss that is not properly allocable to a trade or business; (2) any business interest expense or business interest income; (3) the amount of any net operating loss deduction; (4) deductions allowable for depreciation, amortization, or depletion; and (5) any deduction for qualified business income under §199A.[27]

When computing the limit, business interest expense does not include investment interest expense, and business interest income does not include investment income. For example, business interest expense would include interest paid on a loan used to purchase business equipment, but it would not include interest paid on a loan to purchase stock or bonds for investment purposes. The amount of any business interest expense not allowed as a deduction for any taxable year is carried forward indefinitely. If the average gross receipts of the business in any given year falls below a three-year average of $27 million indexed for inflation, then the interest (including any carryforwards) becomes fully deductible (i.e., it is no longer subject to the business interest limitation).

[26]§274 requires substantiation of all elements of travel, including sufficient corroborating evidence. Although there are a few exceptions to this rule, approximations and estimates are generally not sufficient. Also, taxpayers must maintain records to deduct the business portion of mixed-use assets such as cars used for both business and personal purposes. Note that when the taxpayer is unable to substantiate other deductions, the court may estimate the deductible amount under the *Cohan* rule [*George Cohan v. Comm'r,* 39 F.2d 540 (2d Cir. 1930)].

[27]Adjusted taxable income of the taxpayer cannot be less than zero. Under §163(j), the interest expense disallowance is determined at the filer level, but special rules apply to pass-through entities. For years before 2022, adjusted taxable income was also reduced for depreciation, amortization, and depletion.

Example 9-11

What if: Suppose that at the beginning of the year Rick borrowed $300,000 to provide liquidity for starting up Green Acres. Suppose further that at year-end Rick had reported $9,000 in interest expense on the business loan. In addition, Green Acres reported $70,000 of revenue from services and incurred $47,000 of other deductible expenses (excluding interest expense and $5,000 of depreciation). What amount of interest can Rick deduct as a business expense for Green Acres?

Answer: $9,000. Green Acres is not subject to the business interest expense limitation because Rick's gross receipts do not exceed the $27 million average gross receipts test.

What if: Suppose the interest expense limitation applies to Green Acres. What amount of business interest expense could Rick deduct for Green Acres?

Answer: $6,900. Green Acres generated $23,000 of adjusted taxable income. Adjusted taxable income is the amount of revenue less expense before interest expense and after adding back depreciation ($70,000 – ($47,000)). The 2022 business interest limitation is 30 percent of the $23,000 of adjusted taxable income, or $6,900. The $2,100 of disallowed interest expense from 2022 would be carried over to 2023.

Losses on Dispositions of Business Property

Businesses are generally allowed to deduct losses incurred when selling or disposing of business assets. The calculation of losses from business property dispositions can be complex, but the main idea is that businesses realize and recognize a loss when the asset's tax basis exceeds the sale proceeds. To prevent businesses and related persons from working together to defer taxes, the tax laws generally limit the deduction of business losses when property is sold to a related person. For this purpose, related persons generally include family members, partnerships, and controlled corporations. Related persons are discussed in more detail in the next section of this chapter, and the calculation of the loss limitation is discussed in the Property Dispositions chapter.

Example 9-12

What if: Assume that in late October, Rick purchased a used trailer to transport equipment to work sites. Rick bought the trailer for what he thought was a bargain price of $1,000. However, shortly after Rick acquired it, the axle snapped and was not repairable. Rick was forced to sell the trailer to a parts shop for $325. What amount can Rick deduct as a loss from the trailer sale?

Answer: $675 is deductible as a business loss because the trailer was a business asset. The loss is calculated as the amount realized of $325 minus adjusted basis of $1,000. (Note that Rick is not allowed to deduct depreciation on the trailer because he disposed of it in the same year he acquired it.)

What if: Suppose that Rick sold the trailer to a parts shop owned by his father. What amount can Rick deduct as a loss from the trailer sale?

Answer: Zero. However, Rick's father may be able to utilize Rick's loss if the trailer is later sold by the father.

Business Casualty Losses

Businesses can also incur deductible losses when their assets are stolen, damaged, or completely destroyed by a force outside the control of the business. These events are called casualties.[28] Businesses deduct casualty losses in the year the casualty occurs or, in the case of theft, the year the theft is discovered. The amount of the loss deduction depends on whether the asset is completely destroyed or only partially destroyed. When its asset is *completely* destroyed (or stolen), the business calculates the loss by substituting the insurance proceeds, if any, for the amount realized. That is, the loss is the amount of insurance proceeds minus the adjusted tax basis of the asset. If the asset is damaged but not completely destroyed, the amount of the loss is the amount of the insurance proceeds

[28]Casualties are unexpected events driven by forces outside the control of the taxpayer that damage or destroy a taxpayer's property. §165 lists "fire, storm, and shipwreck" as examples of casualties.

minus the *lesser* of (1) the asset's adjusted tax basis or (2) the decline in the value of the asset due to the casualty. For individuals, business casualty losses and casualty losses associated with rentals and royalties are deducted for AGI.

Example 9-13

What if: Suppose Rick acquires business equipment this year for $5,000, but a fire damages the equipment shortly after it is acquired and before it can be placed in service. After the fire the equipment was worth $3,500 and insurance reimbursed Rick for $1,000. What would be the amount of his business casualty loss?

Answer: $500. The loss is the insurance proceeds ($1,000) reduced by the lesser of the decline in value, $1,500 (computed as $5,000 – $3,500), or the adjusted tax basis, $5,000. The calculation follows:

Insurance proceeds	$ 1,000
Minus decline in value	−1,500
Casualty loss deduction	**$ (500)**

What if: Suppose that the fire completely destroyed the equipment. What would be the amount of Rick's business casualty loss?

Answer: $4,000. The loss is the insurance proceeds ($1,000) reduced by the adjusted tax basis, $5,000.

LO 9-3

ACCOUNTING PERIODS

After identifying a business's taxable income and deductible business expenses, it is necessary to identify the period in which income and deductions are to be measured. Businesses must report their income and deductions over a fixed **accounting period** or **tax year.** A full tax year consists of 12 full months. A tax year can consist of a period less than 12 months (a short tax year) in certain circumstances. For instance, a business may report income for such a short year in its first year of existence (for example, it reports income on a calendar year-end and starts business after January 1) or in its final year of existence (for example, a calendar-year business ends its business before December 31). Short tax years in a business's initial or final year are treated the same as full years. A business also may have a short year when it changes its tax year, and this can occur when the business is acquired by new owners. In these situations, special rules may apply for computing taxable income and the tax liability of the business.[29]

There are three types of tax years, each with different year-ends:

1. A calendar year ends on December 31.
2. A **fiscal year** ends on the last day of a month other than December.
3. A 52/53-week year. This is a fiscal year that ends on the same day of the week that is the last such day in the month or on the same day of the week nearest the end of the month. For example, a business could adopt a 52/53-week fiscal year that (1) ends on the last Saturday in July each year or (2) ends on the Saturday closest to the end of July (although this Saturday might be in August rather than July).[30]

THE KEY FACTS

Accounting Periods

- Individuals and proprietorships generally account for income using a calendar year-end.
- Corporations are allowed to choose a fiscal year.
- Partnerships and other flow-through entities generally use a tax year consistent with their owners' tax years.

Not all types of tax years are available to all types of businesses. The rules for determining the tax years available to the business depend on whether the business is a sole proprietorship, a **flow-through entity,** or a C corporation. These rules are summarized as follows:

- *Sole proprietorships:* Because individual proprietors must report their business income on their individual returns, proprietorships use a calendar-year-end to report their business income on their tax returns.[31]

[29]§443. Discussion of tax consequences associated with these short years is beyond the scope of this text.

[30]Businesses with inventories, such as retailers, can benefit from 52/53-week year-ends. These year-ends can facilitate inventory counts (e.g., the store is closed, such as over a weekend) and financial reporting.

[31]Virtually all individual taxpayers use a calendar-year tax year.

- *Flow-through entities:* Partnerships and S corporations are flow-through entities (partners and S corporation owners report the entity's income directly on their own tax returns), and these entities generally must adopt tax years consistent with the owners' tax years.[32] Because owners are allocated income from flow-through entities on the last day of the entity's taxable year, the tax laws impose the tax year consistency requirement to minimize income tax deferral opportunities for the owners.
- *C corporations:* C corporations are generally allowed to select a calendar, fiscal, or 52/53-week year-end.

A business adopts a calendar year-end or fiscal year-end by filing its initial tax return. In contrast, a business adopts a 52/53-week year-end by filing a special election with the IRS. Once a business establishes its tax year, it generally must receive permission from the IRS to change.

Example 9-14

Rick is a calendar-year taxpayer. What tax year must Rick use to report income from Green Acres?

Answer: Calendar year. This is true even though Rick began his business in May of this year. He will calculate income and expense for his landscaping business over the calendar year and include business income and deductions from May through December of this year on Schedule C of his individual tax return.

What if: Suppose that Rick formed Green Acres as a C corporation for tax purposes at the time he began his business. What tax year could Green Acres adopt?

Answer: If Green Acres were operated as a C corporation, it could elect a calendar year-end, a fiscal year-end, or a 52/53-week year-end. If it were an S corporation, it likely would use a calendar year-end. If Rick opted to have Green Acres adopt a calendar year-end, the first tax return for Green Acres would only cover the eight months from May through December (a short year).

ACCOUNTING METHODS

LO 9-4

Once a business adopts a tax year, it must determine which items of income and deduction to recognize during a particular year. Generally speaking, the taxpayer's **accounting methods** determine the tax year in which a business recognizes a particular item of income or deduction. Because accounting methods affect the *timing* of when a taxpayer reports income and deductions, these methods are especially important for taxpayers considering a timing strategy to defer taxable income or accelerate deductions.[33]

Financial and Tax Accounting Methods

Many businesses are required to generate financial statements for nontax business reasons. For example, publicly traded corporations must file financial statements with the Securities and Exchange Commission (SEC) based on generally accepted accounting principles (GAAP). Also, privately owned businesses borrowing money from banks are often required to generate financial statements under GAAP so that the lender can evaluate the business's creditworthiness. In reporting financial statement income, businesses have incentives to select accounting methods permissible under GAAP that *accelerate income* and *defer deductions.*

In contrast, for tax planning purposes, businesses have incentives to choose accounting methods that defer income and accelerate deductions. This natural tension between financial reporting incentives and tax reporting incentives may be the reason the tax laws generally require businesses to use the same accounting methods for tax purposes that they use for

[32]See §706 for the specific restrictions on year-ends for partnerships and §1378 for restrictions on S corporations. If they can show a business purpose (a difficult task), both partnerships and S corporations can adopt year-ends other than those used by their owners.

[33]Accounting methods determine *when* income or a deduction is recognized but do not determine *whether* an item of income is taxable or an expense is deductible.

financial accounting purposes, a *consistency* requirement. In other words, in many circumstances, if businesses want to defer taxable income, they must also defer book income.[34]

Sometimes the tax laws require businesses to use specific accounting methods for tax purposes regardless of what accounting method is used for financial reporting purposes. With certain restrictions, businesses first select their *overall* accounting method and then choose accounting methods for *specific* items or transactions.

Overall Accounting Method

Businesses must choose an overall method of accounting to track and report their business activities for tax purposes. The overriding requirement for all tax accounting methods is that the method must "clearly reflect income" and be applied consistently.[35] The two overall methods of accounting are the cash method and the accrual method. Although businesses are generally free to choose either the cash or accrual method, C corporations and partnerships with C corporation partners are generally required to use the accrual method if they do not qualify as a small business under the gross receipts test discussed previously.[36] Businesses that qualify under the gross receipts test do not need to request the consent of the IRS to elect the cash method. Businesses also may choose to keep some accounts on the cash method and others on the accrual method. This method is sometimes called a hybrid or mixed accounting method, but technically the method is still classified as a form of cash method.

Cash Method A business using the cash method of accounting recognizes revenue when property or services are actually or constructively received. This is generally true no matter when the business sells the goods or performs the service that generates the revenue. Keep in mind that a cash-method business receiving payments in *noncash* form (as property or services) must recognize the noncash payments as gross income when the goods or services are received.

Likewise, a business adopting the cash method generally recognizes deductions when the expense is paid. Thus, the timing of the liability giving rise to the expense is usually irrelevant. For example, a cash-method business would deduct office supply expense when payment is made rather than when the supplies are ordered or received. Also, in certain circumstances, a business expending cash on ordinary and necessary business expenses may not be allowed to *currently* deduct the expense at the time of the payment. For example, cash-method taxpayers (and accrual-method taxpayers) are not allowed to deduct expenditures that create future benefits. Hence, a business using either the cash or accrual method must generally capitalize prepaid interest and other prepayments that create tangible or intangible assets.

However, it can be difficult and time-consuming for small businesses to capitalize the multitude of prepaid expenditures that create benefits for a relatively brief period of time. For this reason, regulations provide a **12-month rule** that simplifies the process of determining whether to capitalize or immediately expense payments that create benefits for a relatively brief period of time, such as insurance, security, rent, and warranty service contracts. When a business prepays business expenses, it may *immediately* deduct the prepayment if (1) the contract period does not last more than a year *and* (2) the contract period does not extend beyond the end of the taxable year following the tax year in which the taxpayer makes the payment.[37] If the prepaid expense does not meet both these

[34]§446(a). Businesses that use different accounting methods for book and tax income must typically file a Schedule M-1 or Schedule M-3 that reconciles the results from the two accounting methods.

[35]§446(b).

[36]Businesses that are defined as tax shelters cannot qualify for the cash method under §448(a). A business on the cash basis that fails the gross receipts test must change to the accrual method of accounting. However, if the same business qualifies under the gross receipts test in a subsequent year, the business may elect to use the cash basis again.

[37]§263(a).

criteria, the business must capitalize the prepaid amount and amortize it over the length of the contract whether the business uses the cash or accrual method of accounting.[38]

Example 9-15

On July 1 of this year, Rick paid $1,200 for a 12-month insurance policy that covers his business property from accidents and casualties from July 1 of this year through June 30 of next year. How much of the $1,200 expenditure may Rick deduct this year if he uses the cash method of accounting for his business activities?

Answer: $1,200. Because the insurance coverage does not exceed 12 months and does not extend beyond the end of next year, Rick is allowed to deduct the entire premium payment under the 12-month rule.

What if: Suppose the insurance policy was for 12 months, but the policy ran from February 1 of next year through January 31 of the following year. How much of the expenditure may Rick deduct this year if he uses the cash method of accounting for his business activities?

Answer: $0. Even though the contract period is 12 months or less, Rick is required to capitalize the cost of the prepayment for the insurance policy because the contract period extends beyond the end of next year. Hence, he will amortize the cost beginning next year.

What if: Suppose Rick had paid $1,200 for an *18-month* policy beginning July 1 of this year and ending December 31 of next year. How much may he deduct this year if he uses the cash method of accounting for his business activities?

Answer: $400. In this scenario, because the policy exceeds 12 months, Rick is allowed to deduct the portion of the premium pertaining to this year. Hence, this year, he would deduct $400 [(6 months/18 months) x $1,200]. He would deduct the remaining $800 in the next year.

(continued from page 9-1 . . .)
Rick's CPA, Jane, informed him that he needs to select an overall method of accounting for Green Acres to compute its taxable income. Jane advised Rick to use the cash method. However, Rick wanted to prepare GAAP financial statements and use the accrual method of accounting. Rick believed that if Green Acres was going to become a big business, it needed to act like a big business. Finally, after much discussion, Rick and Jane reached a compromise. For the first year, they decided they would track Green Acres's business activities using both the cash *and* the accrual methods. In addition, they would also keep GAAP-based books for financial purposes. When filing time comes, Rick must choose which method to use in reporting taxable income. Jane told Rick that he could wait until he filed his tax return to select the overall accounting method for tax purposes. ■

Accrual Method Businesses using the accrual method to determine taxable income follow rules similar to GAAP with two basic differences. First, the requirements for recognizing taxable income tend to be structured to recognize income earlier than the recognition rules for financial accounting. Second, the requirements for accruing tax deductions tend to be structured to recognize less accrued expenses than the recognition rules for financial reporting purposes. These differences reflect the underlying objectives of financial accounting income and taxable income. The objective of financial accounting is to provide useful information to stakeholders such as creditors, prospective investors, and shareholders. Because financial accounting methods are designed to guard against businesses overstating their profitability to these users, financial accounting tends to bias against *overstating* income. In contrast, the government's main objective for writing tax laws is to collect revenues. Thus, tax accounting rules for accrual-method businesses tend to bias against *understating* income.

[38] Reg §1.263(a)-4(f). This 12-month rule applies to both cash-method and accrual-method taxpayers. However, for accrual-method taxpayers to deduct prepaid expenses, they must meet both the 12-month rule requirements and the economic performance requirements discussed in the Accrual Deductions section.

Accrual Income

Businesses using the accrual method of accounting generally recognize income when they meet the *all-events test.* This test is sometimes referred to as the fixed and determinable test.

All-Events Test for Income The all-events test requires that businesses recognize income when (1) all events have occurred that determine or fix their right to receive the income and (2) the amount of the income can be determined with reasonable accuracy.[39] Assuming the amount of income can be determined with reasonable accuracy, businesses meet the all-events requirement on the *earliest* of the following three dates:

1. When they complete the task required to earn the income. Businesses earn income for services as they provide the services, and they generally earn income from selling property when the title of the property passes to the buyer.
2. When the payment for the task is due from the customer.
3. When the business receives payment for the task.

Alternatively, the all-events test is deemed to be satisfied when an income item is recognized on an applicable financial statement (AFS), even if it has yet to satisfy any of the above three criteria.[40]

Example 9-16

In early fall, Rick contracted with a dozen homeowners to landscape their yards. Rick agreed to do the work for an aggregate of $11,000. Rick and his crew started in the fall and completed the jobs in December of this year. However, he didn't mail the bills until after the holidays and didn't receive any payments until the following January. When must Rick recognize the income from this work?

Answer: Under the accrual method, Rick would recognize the entire $11,000 as income this year because his right to the income is fixed at year-end, when Rick and his crew complete the work. Under the cash method, however, Rick would not recognize the $11,000 as income until next year, when he receives it.

THE KEY FACTS

Revenue Recognition under the Accrual Method

- Income is recognized when earned (all-events) or received (if earlier).
- Under the all-events test, income is earned when the business has the right to receive payment or when recognized in the applicable financial statement, if earlier.
- Taxpayers can generally elect to defer recognition of prepaid (unearned) income if the income is also deferred for financial accounting purposes.
- However, the deferral of income is an accounting method election and deferred income must be recognized in the year after deferral (e.g., the tax deferral only lasts for one year).

Taxation of Advance Payments of Income (Unearned Income)

In some cases, taxpayers receive income payments before they actually earn the income.[41] Taxpayers using the cash method include these payments in gross income in the year the payment is received. When an accrual-method taxpayer must include unearned income in gross income depends, in part, on the type of income. For example, all taxpayers must recognize interest and rental income immediately upon receipt (i.e., the income is taxable when received even if is not yet earned).

For other types of income, accrual-method businesses can elect to defer recognition of unearned income for one year. Specifically, businesses using the accrual method may elect to defer recognizing advance payments for goods or services until the next tax year.[42] This one-year deferral method does not apply if the income is actually earned by the end of the year of receipt or if the unearned income is recognized for financial reporting purposes. In addition, this is an accounting method election that once elected can only be revoked with the permission of the Commissioner.

[39]Reg. §1.451-1(a).

[40]§451(b). Applicable financial statements are described in §451(b)(3).

[41]Unlike advance payments, businesses are not required to recognize security deposits as income because there is an obligation to return the deposit [*Comm'r v. Indianapolis Power & Light Co.*, 493 U.S. 203 (1990)].

[42]§451(c).

Example 9-17

In late November 2022, Rick received a $7,200 payment in advance from a client for monthly landscaping services from December 1, 2022, through November 30, 2024 ($300 a month for 24 months). When must Rick recognize the income from the advance payment for services?

Answer: Under the accrual method, if Rick elects the deferral method to account for advance payments, he would initially recognize the $300 income he earned in December 2022. In 2023, he would recognize the remaining $6,900 (rather than only the $3,600 related to 2022) because he is not allowed to defer the prepayments for more than a year. If Rick does not elect the deferral method, he would recognize the entire prepayment of $7,200 as income upon receipt in 2022. Under the cash method, Rick would recognize the entire prepayment, $7,200, as income upon receipt in 2022.

What if: Suppose that rather than receiving payment in advance for services, Rick's client paid $7,200 in 2022 for landscape supplies that Rick purchased in 2022 and provided in 2023. When must Rick recognize the income from the advance payment for goods?

Answer: Using the accrual method, if Rick elects the deferral method to account for advance payments, he would not recognize any income in 2022 because none of the income had been earned in 2022. Rick would then recognize the entire $7,200 (less the cost of goods sold) in 2023. If Rick did not elect the deferral method, he would recognize the entire $7,200 (less the cost of the goods) in 2022. Under the cash method, Rick would recognize the entire $7,200 (less the cost of goods sold) in 2022.

Inventories

When producing, buying, or selling goods is an income-producing activity, taxpayers are required to keep inventories of goods, including raw materials and work in process, to determine the cost of goods sold. In addition, taxpayers who are required to keep inventory records also must use the accrual method of accounting for purchases and sales.[43] This requirement applies regardless of whether the taxpayer uses the cash or the accrual method as the overall method of accounting. Hence, the cost of inventory must include the purchase price of raw materials (minus any discounts), direct costs (manufacturing), shipping costs, and any indirect costs allocated to the inventory under the **uniform cost capitalization (UNICAP) rules** (discussed next).[44]

However, under §471(c), small businesses qualifying under the gross receipts test discussed previously can opt to account for goods as nonincidental materials or use the accounting method that conforms to the taxpayer's financial accounting treatment of inventory. Generally, nonincidental materials are tracked on the taxpayer's books and records, either through records of consumption or by periodic physical inventory. Amounts paid to acquire or produce nonincidental materials are generally deductible in the tax year in which the materials are used in the taxpayer's operations or are consumed in the taxpayer's operations. The IRS interprets "used or consumed" to mean that nonincidental materials are deductible when taxpayers sell the inventory.

For example, suppose a company stores machine repair parts for which it keeps records of purchases and consumption. The company can choose to treat the parts either under the method conforming to its financial accounting or as nonincidental materials. If the parts are treated as nonincidental materials and the parts are used in the business, the company can deduct the costs of parts in the tax year the part is removed from storage. If, however, the parts are a component of a finished good, then the cost of the part can only be deducted at the time the taxpayer incurs the cost or delivers the finished goods, whichever is later.[45]

THE KEY FACTS

Inventories

- C corporations and partnerships with C corporation partners must use the accrual method to account for inventories unless they qualify as a small business under the gross receipts test. Small businesses can account for inventories either as nonincidental materials or use the inventory method used for financial reporting.
- The UNICAP rules require capitalization of most indirect costs of production, but businesses that qualify as a small business under the gross receipts test are exempt from UNICAP.
- The LIFO method is allowed if it is also used for financial reporting purposes (a conformity rule).

[43]Reg. §1.446-1(c)(2).

[44]Inventory valuation allowances are generally not allowed, but taxpayers can adopt the lower of cost or market method of inventory valuation. In addition, under certain conditions specific goods not salable at normal prices can be valued at bona fide selling prices less direct cost of disposition.

[45]Reg. §1.162-3(a)(1); Prop. Reg. §1.471-1(b)(4). Note that nonincidental materials can only be accounted for using the first-in, first-out (FIFO); specific identification; or average cost methods. The last-in, first-out (LIFO) method and the lower of cost or market method may not be used.

The ability to account for goods as nonincidental materials was intended to simplify accounting for small businesses by exempting them from having to allocate indirect costs to inventory. However, small businesses are still required to record beginning and ending inventories even when the business chooses to treat goods as nonincidental materials or use the inventory method on the taxpayer's books. In addition, small business accounting for inventories is subject to the overriding requirement that all accounting methods must ultimately clearly reflect income.

Example 9-18

What if: Suppose that Green Acres (Rick) commences to manufacture an organic lawn supplement. Green Acres would purchase compost from local farms and blend the compost with minerals. Green Acres would then package the mix and sell the packages to local retailers. Under these circumstances, would Green Acres be required to keep inventories of raw materials, work in process, and goods for sale?

Answer: Yes. Green Acres must keep inventories because producing and selling goods is an income-producing activity. However, because it is a small business under the gross receipts test, Green Acres need not use the accrual method of accounting for its purchases and sales. Green Acres either can elect to treat the raw materials, work-in-process, and finished products as nonincidental materials or can use the accounting method that conforms to the method Green Acres uses for financial reporting. In either case, Green Acres must keep records of its beginning and ending inventories.

What if: Suppose that Green Acres purchased and paid for compost in 2022 and elected to account for the purchase as nonincidental materials. However, the compost was used in producing lawn supplements sold in 2023. Can Green Acres deduct the cost of the compost in 2022?

Answer: No, the cost of the compost used is deducted in 2023. While Green Acres incurred the cost in 2022, the deduction is allowed in the year the goods were delivered because it is the later date.

Uniform Capitalization The tax laws require large businesses that account for inventories to capitalize certain direct and indirect costs associated with inventories (called the UNICAP rules for uniform capitalization). However, businesses that qualify as a small business under the gross receipts test need not apply UNICAP rules.[46] Congress enacted UNICAP primarily for two reasons. First, the rules accelerate tax revenues for the government by deferring deductions for the capitalized costs until the business sells the associated inventory. Thus, there is generally a one-year lag between when businesses initially capitalize the costs and when they deduct them. Second, Congress designed the "uniform" rules to reduce variation in the costs businesses include in inventory, and Congress intended these provisions to apply to large manufacturers and resellers.

Under these uniform cost capitalization rules, large businesses are generally required to capitalize more costs to inventory for tax purposes than they capitalize under financial accounting rules. Under GAAP, businesses generally include in inventory only those costs incurred within their production facility. In contrast, the UNICAP rules require businesses to allocate to inventory the costs they incur inside the production facility and the costs they incur outside the facility to support production (or inventory acquisition) activities. For example, under the UNICAP provisions, a business must capitalize at least a portion of the compensation paid to employees in its purchasing department, general and administrative department, and even its information technology department, to the extent these groups provide support for the production process. In contrast, businesses immediately expense these items as period costs for financial accounting purposes. The regulations provide guidance on the costs that must be allocated to inventory. Selling, advertising, and research are specifically identified as costs that do not have to be allocated to inventory under the UNICAP provisions.[47]

[46]§263A(i).

[47]Reg. §1.263A–1(e)(3)(iii).

Example 9-19

What if: Green Acres sells trees, but Rick anticipates that the business will sell flowers, shrubs, and other plants in future years. Ken is Rick's employee in charge of purchasing inventory. Ken's compensation this year is $30,000, and Rick estimates that Ken spends about 5 percent of his time acquiring inventory and the remaining time working on landscaping projects. Assuming Green Acres is required to apply the UNICAP rules, how would Ken's compensation be allocated?

Answer: If the UNICAP rules applied to Green Acres (Rick), $1,500 ($30,000 × 5%) of Ken's compensation would be allocated to the cost of the inventory Green Acres acquired this year. In contrast, Ken's entire salary would be expensed as a period cost for financial accounting purposes.

What if: Suppose that Green Acres began operations on September 1, 2021, and reported $5 million in gross receipts from services and sales of trees, flowers, shrubs, and other plants for the four months in the 2021 short year. Is Green Acres required to apply the UNICAP rules in 2022?

Answer: No, because average annual gross receipts in the period prior to 2022 is less than $27 million. For purposes of the gross receipts test, the gross receipts for the four-month 2021 tax year is annualized by multiplying $5 million by 12 and dividing the result by 4 (the number of months in the short period 2021). Thus, gross receipts for Green Acres in 2021 is $15 million ($60 million divided by 4).

Inventory Cost-Flow Methods Once a business determines the cost of its inventory, it must use an inventory cost-flow method to determine its cost of goods sold. Three primary cost-flow methods are (1) the **first-in, first-out (FIFO) method;** (2) the **last-in, first-out (LIFO) method;** and (3) the **specific identification method,** although the LIFO method cannot be used to account for inventories of nonincidental materials. Businesses might be inclined to use FIFO or LIFO methods when they sell similar, relatively low-cost, high-volume products such as cans of soup or barrels of oil. These methods simplify inventory accounting because the business need not track the individual cost of each item it sells. In contrast, businesses that sell distinct, relatively high-cost, low-volume products might be more likely to adopt the specific identification method. For example, jewelry and used-car businesses would likely use the specific identification method to account for their cost of sales. In general terms, when costs are increasing, a business using the FIFO method will report a higher gross margin than if it used the LIFO method. The opposite is true if costs are decreasing.

Example 9-20

In late August, Green Acres (Rick) purchased 10 oak saplings (immature trees) for a total purchase price of $3,000. In September, 12 more were purchased for a total price of $3,900, and in late October, 15 more were purchased for $5,000. The total cost of each lot of trees was determined as follows:

Purchase Date	Trees	Direct Cost	Other Costs	Total Cost
August 20	10	$ 3,000	$ 350	$ 3,350
September 15	12	3,900	300	4,200
October 22	15	5,000	400	5,400
Totals	37	$11,900	$1,050	$12,950

Before the end of the year, Green Acres sold 20 of the oak saplings (5 from the August lot, 5 from the September lot, and 10 from the October lot) for cash. To illustrate the effects of inventory accounting, assume that Green Acres is considering keeping inventory records for financial reporting purposes under various methods. What is Green Acres's gross profit from sales of oak saplings if the sales revenue totaled $14,000 (all collected by year-end), and what is its ending oak sapling inventory under the FIFO, LIFO, and specific identification cost-flow methods?

(continued on page 9-22)

Answer: Under the accrual method, Rick's (Green Acres) gross profit from sapling sales and its ending inventory balance for the remaining oak saplings under the FIFO, LIFO, and specific identification cost-flow methods are as follows:

Description	FIFO	LIFO	Specific ID
Sales	$14,000	$14,000	$14,000
Cost of goods sold	−6,850	−7,150	−7,025
Gross profit	$ 7,150	$ 6,850	$ 6,975
Ending inventory:			
August 20 trees	$ 0	$ 3,350	$ 1,675
September 15 trees	700	2,450	2,450
October 22 trees	5,400	0	1,800
Total ending inventory	**$ 6,100**	**$ 5,800**	**$ 5,925**

If the gross receipts test is satisfied, Rick could record the trees as nonincidental materials. However, Rick would still need to count the trees and adopt a flow assumption. For example, Rick could adopt the average cost method and calculate the average cost of trees by summing the cost of trees in inventory at the beginning of the year with the cost of purchased trees and dividing by the total trees (beginning inventory plus purchases). In this example, the cost of purchasing 37 trees was $12,950 (average of $350 per tree), so the cost of selling 20 trees would be $7,000 (20 times $350).

When costs are subject to inflation over time, a business would get the best of both worlds if it adopted the FIFO method for financial reporting purposes and the LIFO method for tax purposes. Not surprisingly, the tax laws require that a business can use LIFO for tax purposes only if it also uses LIFO for financial reporting purposes.[48] While this "conformity" requirement may not matter to entities not required to generate financial reports, it can be very restrictive to publicly traded corporations.

Accrual Deductions

Generally, when accrual-method businesses incur an expense, they account for it by crediting a liability account or by crediting cash if the expense is paid. Sometimes the amount of the expense must be estimated. For example, a business might have to estimate the expenses associated with future warranty claims to match with current sales. Typically, estimated expenses result in a reserve account, which can be described as a contingent liability.

To claim a tax deduction for an accrued expense, the expense must meet two tests: (1) an **all-events test** *and* (2) an **economic performance test.**[49] The all-events test for recognizing deductions is similar to the all-events test for recognizing income. That is, the events that establish the liability giving rise to the deduction must have occurred and the amount of the liability must be determinable with reasonable accuracy. However, the additional economic performance requirement makes the deduction recognition rules more stringent than the income recognition rules. As a result, businesses are generally prohibited from deducting estimated expenses or reserves. In other words, economic performance must have occurred for a business to claim a deduction.[50]

[48]§472(c).
[49]§461(h).
[50]§461.

TAXES IN THE REAL WORLD Economic Performance and Cost of Goods Sold

During 2008 and 2009, a limited liability company called Bluescape paid around $180 million to acquire hundreds of thousands of acres of mineral and lease interests in four states. Bluescape planned to explore for natural gas on these leases and produce the gas for sale. Bluescape claimed on its tax return for those years about $160 million in cost of goods sold for natural gas exploration and mining. However, during those years, Bluescape did not actually drill for gas and did not report any gross receipts or sales attributable to the sale of natural gas.

Upon audit, the IRS disallowed the cost of goods sold arguing that Bluescape did not satisfy the all-events test and the economic performance requirement in §461(h)(1). Bluescape responded by arguing that the economic performance requirement does not apply to amounts included in cost of goods sold. They claimed, instead, that the cost of goods sold is an offset against gross receipts used to compute gross income. Hence, cost of goods sold is governed by §451 and not subject to economic performance.

Bluescape petitioned the Tax Court, which then posed a question to both parties: Can a taxpayer recognize cost of goods sold before it has any gross receipts from the sale of goods? In his opinion, Judge Pugh noted that under Reg §1.61-3(a), gross income is calculated by subtracting the cost of goods sold from gross receipts. Bluescape argued, however, that "matching" of cost of goods sold and gross receipts is not required under the regulations and that cost of goods sold should be recognized in the year the taxpayer assumes the obligations to drill the wells.

In finding for the IRS, the judge noted the gap in the taxpayer's logic that cost of goods sold serves as an offset against gross receipts but that cost of goods sold need not "match" gross receipts. The court held that taxpayers can only offset cost of goods sold against gross receipts from sales of goods. Unfortunately, the court did not answer the dispute over whether the economic performance requirement applies to the cost of goods sold.

Source: BRC Operating Co. LLC v. Comm'r, TC Memo 2021-59.

Example 9-21

On November 1 of this year, Rick agreed to a one-year $6,000 contract with Ace Advertising to produce a radio ad campaign. Ace agreed that Rick would owe nothing under the contract unless the sales for Green Acres increase a minimum of 25 percent over the next six months. What amount, if any, may Rick deduct this year for this contract under the accrual and cash methods?

Answer: Under the accrual method, Rick is not allowed to recognize *any* deduction this year for the liability. Even though Ace will have completed two months of advertising for Green Acres by the end of the year, the guarantee means that the liability is not fixed until and unless the sales increase by 25 percent. Under the cash method, Rick would not deduct any of the cost of the campaign this year because he has not paid anything to Ace.

THE KEY FACTS

Accrual of Business-Expense Deductions

- Both all-events and economic performance tests are required for deducting accrued business expenses.
- The all-events test requires the events that establish the liability giving rise to the expense must have occurred and the amount of the liability must be determinable with reasonable accuracy.
- Economic performance generally requires that the underlying activity generating the liability has occurred in order for the associated expense to be deductible.

Economic Performance Even when businesses meet the all-events test, they still must clear the economic performance hurdle to recognize the tax deduction. Congress added the economic performance requirement because in some situations, taxpayers claimed current deductions under the all events test, but delayed the event triggering payment of the associated cash expenditures for years. Thus, the delayed payment reduced the real (present value) cost of the deduction. This requirement specifies that businesses cannot deduct an expense until the underlying activity generating the associated liability has occurred. Thus, an accrual-method business is not allowed to deduct a prepaid business expense even if it qualifies to do so under the 12-month rule (discussed above) unless it also has met the economic performance test with respect to the liability associated with the expense.

The specific requirements for the economic performance test differ based on whether the liability has arisen from:

- Receiving goods or services *from* another person.
- Use of property (renting or leasing property *from* another person).
- Providing goods or services *to* another person.
- Certain activities creating **payment liabilities.**

Receiving goods or services from another person. When a business receives goods or services from another person, the business deducts the expense associated with the liability when the other person provides the goods or services (assuming the all-events test is met for the liability). However, there is an exception when a business actually pays the liability before the other person provides the goods or services. In this circumstance, the business can elect to treat the actual payment as economic performance as long as it reasonably expects the other person to provide the goods or the services within 3½ months after the payment.[51]

Example 9-22

On December 22, 2022, Rick signed a contract with PickUp LLC to clean and sweep Rick's shop during 2023. Rick agreed to pay PickUp $300 per month for the service, a total of $3,600. Rick paid $1,000 of the cost as a down payment and agreed to pay the remaining $2,600 in 2023. What amount associated with this service is Rick allowed to deduct in 2022 and 2023 under the accrual method and, alternatively, under the cash method?

Answer: Under the accrual method, Rick is not entitled to a deduction in 2022. Rick will deduct his full $3,600 service costs in 2023. Even though Rick paid for part of the services in 2022, economic performance only occurs as the services are provided to the taxpayer. Under the cash method, Rick would deduct $1,000 (his down payment) in 2022 and the remainder in 2023 when he pays the remainder on the contract.

What if: Suppose that Rick only contracted with PickUp to provide cleaning services for the first three months of 2023 and paid $900 on December 22, 2022. What amount associated with this service is Rick allowed to deduct in 2022 and 2023?

Answer: Under the accrual method, Rick is allowed to deduct $900 in 2022 because Rick actually paid this amount in 2022 and he reasonably expected YNF to complete the services within 3½ months after he made the payment. Under the cash method, Rick also deducts the $900 payment in 2022.

Renting or leasing property from another person. When a business enters into an agreement to use property (rent or lease property) from another person, economic performance occurs over the term of the lease. Thus, the business is allowed to deduct the rental expense over the term of the lease.

Example 9-23

On May 1, 2022, Rick paid $7,200 in advance to rent his shop for 12 months ($600 per month). What amount may Rick deduct for rent in 2022 if he accounts for his business activities using the accrual method?

Answer: $4,800 ($600 × 8 months' use). Even though the rent is a prepaid business expense under the 12-month rule (the contract period is for 12 months and the contract period does not extend beyond 2023), he can only deduct the rent expense over the term of the lease because that is when economic performance occurs.

[51]Reg. §1.461-4(d)(6).

What if: Assuming the original facts, what amount of the $7,200 rental payment may Rick deduct in 2022 if he is using the cash method of accounting for his business?

Answer: $7,200. In this case, Rick may deduct the expense under the 12-month rule. Rick is not required to meet the economic performance requirement to deduct the expense because the economic performance requirements apply to accrual-method taxpayers, but not cash-method taxpayers.

Example 9-24

On November 1, 2022, Rick paid $2,400 to rent a trailer for 24 months. What amount of this payment may Rick deduct and when may he deduct it?

Answer: Under the accrual method, even though Rick paid the entire rental fee in advance, economic performance occurs over the 24-month rental period. Thus, Rick deducts $200 for the trailer rental in 2022, $1,200 in 2023, and $1,000 in 2024. Because the rental period exceeds 12 months, the amount and timing of the deductions are the same under the cash method.

Providing goods or services to another person. Businesses liable for providing goods or services to other persons meet the economic performance test as they provide the goods or services that satisfy the liability.

Example 9-25

In the summer, Rick landscaped a city park. As part of this contract, Rick agreed to remove a fountain from the park if requested by the city parks committee. In December 2022, the committee decided to have Rick remove the fountain. Rick began the removal in December, and he accrued $850 of expenses associated with this work on December 31. Rick completed the removal work in the spring of 2023 and paid accrued expenses of $1,500 on March 31. What amounts will Rick deduct for the removal project and when may he deduct them?

Answer: Under the accrual method, Rick is allowed to deduct his accrued expenses as he provides the services. Consequently, in 2022 Rick can deduct $850 for the cost of the services provided in 2022 and the additional $650 in 2023. In 2023, Rick can deduct the remaining $685 cost of the services. Under the cash method, Rick can only deduct the $1,500 of expenses when paid in 2023.

Payment liabilities. Economic performance occurs for certain liabilities only when the business actually pays the liability. Thus, accrual-method businesses incurring payment liabilities are essentially on the cash method for deducting the associated expenses. Exhibit 9-2 describes different categories of these payment liabilities.

EXHIBIT 9-2 Categories of Payment Liabilities

Economic performance occurs when the taxpayer pays liabilities associated with:

- Workers' compensation, tort, breach of contract, or violation of law.
- Rebates and refunds.
- Awards, prizes, and jackpots.
- Insurance, warranties, and service contracts provided *to* the business. (*Note:* This relates to insurance, warranties, and product service contracts that cover the taxpayer and *not* a warranty that the taxpayer provides to others.)
- Taxes.[52]
- Other liabilities not provided for elsewhere.

[52]While taxes are generally not deducted until they are paid, §461(c) allows businesses to elect to accrue the deduction for real property taxes ratably over the tax period instead of deducting them when they actually pay them.

Exhibit 9-3 describes the requirements for economic performance for the different types of liabilities.

EXHIBIT 9-3 Economic Performance

Taxpayer incurs liability from	Economic performance occurs
Receiving goods and services *from* another person.	When the goods or services are provided to the taxpayer or with payment if the taxpayer reasonably expects actual performance within 3½ months.
Renting or leasing property *from* another person.	Ratably over the time period during which the taxpayer is entitled to use the property or money.
Providing goods and services *to* another person.	When the taxpayer incurs costs to satisfy the liability or provide the goods and services.
Activities creating "payment" liabilities.	When the business actually makes payment.
Interest expense.	As accrued. This technically does not fall within the economic performance rules, but it is a similar concept.

Recurring item exception. One of the most common exceptions to economic performance is the **recurring item** exception. This exception is designed to reduce the administrative cost of applying economic performance to expenses that occur on a regular basis. Under this exception, accrual-method taxpayers can deduct certain accrued expenses even if economic performance has not occurred by year-end.[53] A recurring item is a liability that is expected to recur in future years and either the liability is not material in amount or deducting the expense in the current year more properly matches with revenue. Payment liabilities, such as insurance, rebates, and refunds, are deemed to meet the matching requirement.[54] In addition, the all-events test must be satisfied at year-end and actual economic performance of the item must occur within a reasonable time after year-end (but prior to the filing of the tax return, which could be up to 8½ months after year-end with an extension). As a final note, the recurring item exception does not apply to workers' compensation or tort liabilities.

Example 9-26

If clients are not completely satisfied with his landscaping work, Rick offers a $200 refund with no questions asked. Near the end of 2022, Rick had four clients request refunds, so Rick incurred the liability for the refunds this year. However, Rick was busy during the holiday season, so he didn't pay the refunds until January 2023. Ignoring the recurring item exception, when can Rick deduct the customer refunds under the cash and accrual methods?

Answer: Because refunds are payment liabilities, under the accrual method economic performance does not occur until Rick actually pays the refunds. Consequently, Rick deducts the $800 of refunds in 2023 even though the liability for the refunds met the all-events test in 2022. Under the cash method, Rick would not deduct the refunds until he paid them in 2023.

What if: Suppose that Rick received $800 of refund requests at year-end. Under what conditions could Rick deduct the refunds in 2022 if he elects to use accrual accounting and the recurring item exception?

Answer: Typically, to claim accrual method deductions under the recurring item exception, either the accrued expense must not be material in amount or a 2022 deduction must better match 2022 revenue than 2023 revenue. Rick doesn't need to worry about the matching requirement because under the regulations, refunds are deemed to meet the matching requirement for purposes of the recurring item exception. Also, actual economic performance (payment) must occur within a reasonable time after year-end (but not longer than 8½ months or the filing of the tax return). Note once Rick elects to use the recurring item exception for refunds, he must follow this method for refunds in future periods.

[53] §461(h)(3).
[54] Reg. §1.461-5(b)(5)(ii).

Bad Debt Expense When accrual method businesses sell a product or a service on credit, they debit accounts receivable and credit sales revenue for both financial and tax purposes. However, when a business is unable to collect the full amount of their accounts receivable, they incur bad debt expense (a customer owes them a debt that the customer will not or can not pay). For financial reporting purposes, the business estimates the amount of the bad debt at year end and creates a reserve account, the allowance for doubtful accounts. However, for tax purposes, businesses are only allowed to deduct bad debt expense when the debt actually becomes worthless within the taxable year.[55] Consequently, for tax purposes, when businesses determine which specific debts are uncollectible, they are entitled to a deduction. This method of determining bad debt expense for tax purposes is called the **direct write-off method.** In contrast, the method used for financial reporting purposes is called the **allowance method.** As an aside, businesses using the cash method of accounting are *not* allowed to deduct bad debt expenses because they do not include receivables in taxable income.

Example 9-27

At year-end, Rick estimates that about $900 of the receivables for his services will be uncollectible, but he has identified only one client, Jared, who will definitely not pay his bill. Jared, who has skipped town, owes Rick $280 for landscaping this fall. What amount of bad debt expense may Rick deduct for the year under the accrual method?

Answer: For financial reporting purposes, Rick recognizes a $900 bad debt expense. However, for tax purposes, under the direct write-off method, Rick can deduct only $280—the amount associated with specifically writing off Jared's receivable. Under the cash method, Rick would not be able to claim any deduction because he did not receive a payment from Jared and thus did not recognize income on the amount Jared owed him.

Limitations on Accruals To prevent businesses and related persons from working together to defer taxes, the tax laws prevent an accrual-method business from accruing (and deducting) an expense for a liability owed to a related person using the cash method until the related person recognizes the income associated with the payment.[56] For this purpose, related persons include:

- Family members, including parents, siblings, and spouses.
- Shareholders and C corporations when the shareholder owns more than 50 percent of the corporation's stock.[57]
- Owners of partnerships and S corporations no matter the ownership percentage.[58]

This issue frequently arises in situations in which a business using the accrual method employs the owner or a relative of an owner. The business is not allowed to deduct compensation expense owed to the related person until the year in which the related person includes the compensation in income. However, this related-person limit extends beyond compensation to any accrued expense the business owes to a related cash-method taxpayer.

For compensation paid to unrelated persons, an accrual method business generally deducts compensation expense as employees perform services. However, a business is not allowed to deduct compensation accrued at year-end unless it actually pays the compensation (including bonuses, vacation pay, and other forms of compensation) within 2½ months of year-end.

Example 9-28

In December, Rick asked his retired father, Lee, to help him finish a landscaping job. By the end of 2022, Rick owed Lee $2,000 of (reasonable) compensation for his efforts, which he paid in January 2023. What amount of this compensation may Rick deduct and when may he deduct it?

(continued on page 9-28)

[55] §166(a).

[56] §267(a).

[57] Certain constructive ownership rules apply in determining ownership percentages for this purpose. See §267(c).

[58] See §267(b) for related-person definitions.

Answer: If Rick uses the accrual method and Lee the cash method, Rick will not be able to deduct the $2,000 compensation expense until 2023. Rick is Lee's son, so Rick and Lee are "related" persons for tax purposes. Consequently, Rick can deduct the compensation only when Lee includes the payment in his taxable income in 2023. If Rick uses the cash method, he will deduct the expense when he pays it in January 2023.

What if: Suppose that Rick owed the $2,000 in compensation to Megan, an unrelated employee, instead of Lee. Can Rick deduct the compensation in 2022 even though he did not pay the compensation until January 2023?

Answer: Yes, Rick can deduct compensation in the year accrued (2022) if the compensation is paid within the *first* 2½ months following the end of Rick's taxable year. If Rick waits to pay the compensation until after March 15, 2023, he would deduct the compensation in the year he pays it.

Comparison of Accrual and Cash Methods

From a business perspective, the two primary advantages of adopting the cash method over the accrual method are that (1) the cash method provides the business with more flexibility to time income and deductions by accelerating or deferring payments (timing tax planning strategy) and (2) bookkeeping for the cash method is easier. For example, a cash-method taxpayer could defer revenue by waiting to bill clients for goods or services until after year-end, thereby increasing the likelihood that customers would send payment after year-end. There are some concerns with this tax strategy. For example, delaying the bills might increase the likelihood that the customers will not pay their bills at all.

The primary advantage of the accrual method over the cash method is that it better matches revenues and expenses. For that reason, external financial statement users who want to evaluate a business's financial performance prefer the accrual method. Consistent with this idea, the cash method is not allowed for financial reporting under GAAP.

Although the cash method is by far the predominate accounting method among sole proprietors, it is less common in other types of businesses. As we noted previously, tax laws generally prohibit large C corporations and large partnerships with corporate partners from using the cash method of accounting.[59] Exhibit 9-4 details the basic differences in accounting for income and deductions under the accrual and cash methods of accounting.

Example 9-29

At year-end, Rick determined that Green Acres had collected a total of $78,000 of service revenue and $12,575 in other expenses (not described elsewhere in examples but listed in Exhibit 9-5). Rick is debating whether to adopt the cash or accrual method. To help him resolve his dilemma, Jane calculates Green Acres's taxable income under the cash and accrual methods assuming that Rick elects to account for the cost of goods as nonincidental materials (summarized in Exhibit 9-5). What are the differences between the two calculations?

Answer: Jane provided the following summary of the differences between taxable income under the cash method and taxable income under the accrual method:

Description	(1) Accrual	(2) Cash	(1) − (2) Difference	Example
Revenue:				
Credit sales	11,000	0	+11,000	9-16
Prepaid revenue	300	7,200	−6,900	9-17
Expenses:				
Prepaid services	0	−1,000	+1,000	9-22
Prepaid rent expense	−4,800	−7,200	+2,400	9-23
Bad debts	−280	0	−280	9-27
Total difference (accrual income > cash income)			**+7,220**	

After comparing the revenue and expenses recognized under the two accounting methods, Jane explains that the selection of the accrual method for Green Acres means that Rick will be taxed on an additional $7,220 of income this year.

[59]Recall businesses are able to adopt the cash method when they qualify as a small business under the gross receipts test.

EXHIBIT 9-4 Comparison of Cash and Accrual Methods

Income or Expense Item	Cash Method	Accrual Method
Income recognition.	Actually or constructively received.	Taxable once the all-events test is satisfied or the income is recognized in the financial statements.
Unearned rent and interest income.	Taxable on receipt.	Taxable on receipt.
Advance payment for goods and services.	Taxable on receipt.	Taxed when received, or taxpayers can elect to be taxed in the year following receipt if not earned by end of year of receipt.
General deduction recognition.	Deduct when paid; economic performance does not apply.	Deduct once all-events test and economic performance test are both satisfied.
Expenditures for tangible assets with a useful life of more than one year.	Capitalize and apply cost recovery.	Same as the cash method.
Expenditures for intangible assets other than prepaid business expenses.	Capitalize and amortize if provision in code allows it.	Same as the cash method.
Prepaid business expenses.	Immediately deductible. However, amortize if contract period exceeds 12 months or extends beyond the end of the next taxable year.	Same as cash method for payment liabilities; otherwise, apply all-events and economic performance tests to ascertain when to capitalize and amortize.
Prepaid interest expense.	Not deductible until interest accrues.	Same as the cash method.
Bad debt expense.	Not deductible because sales on account not included in income.	Deduct under direct write-off method.

The business income for Green Acres under the accrual and cash methods is summarized in Exhibit 9-5. After reflecting on these numbers and realizing that he would recognize $7,220 more taxable income (and self-employment income subject to self-employment tax) this year under the accrual method, Rick determined that it made sense to instead adopt the cash method of accounting for Green Acres. Rick would make this election when he includes Green Acres's business income calculated using the cash method on Schedule C of his individual tax return. Exhibit 9-6 presents Rick's Schedule C for Green Acres using the cash method of accounting.

Adopting an Accounting Method

We've seen that businesses use overall accounting methods (cash, accrual, or hybrid) and many specific accounting methods (inventory cost-flow assumption, methods of accounting for prepaid income for goods and services, and methods for accounting for prepaid expenses, among other methods) to account for their business activities. For tax purposes, it's important to understand how and when a business technically adopts an accounting method because once it does so, it must get the IRS's permission to change the method.

Businesses generally elect their accounting methods by using them on their tax returns. However, when the business technically adopts a method depends on whether it is a **permissible accounting method** or an **impermissible accounting method.** So far, our discussion has emphasized accounting methods permissible under the tax laws. A business adopts a permissible accounting method by using and reporting the tax results of the method for at least one year. However, businesses may unwittingly (or intentionally) use impermissible accounting methods. For example, a business using the allowance method for determining bad debt expense for tax purposes is using an impermissible accounting method because the tax laws prescribe the use of the direct write-off method for determining bad debt expense. A business adopts an impermissible method by using and reporting the results of the method for two consecutive years.

EXHIBIT 9-5 Green Acres's Net Business Income

Description	Cash	Accrual	Example
Income			
Service revenue:			
Landscaping revenue	$78,000	$ 78,000	9-29
December landscape service	0	11,000	9-16
Prepaid landscape services	7,200	300	9-17
Sales of inventory:			
Tree sales	14,000	14,000	9-20
Total receipts and sales	**$99,200**	**$103,300**	
Cost of Goods Sold (non-incidental materials)	−7,000	−7,000	9-20
Gross Profit	**$92,200**	**$ 96,300**	
Car and truck expense:			
SUV operating expense	5,335	5,335	9-8
BMW operating expense	306	306	9-10
Insurance	1,200	1,200	9-15
Rent:			
Shop	7,200	4,800	9-23
Trailer	200	200	9-24
Travel and business meals:			
Travel to NY seminar	1,435	1,435	9-9
Business dinner with clients	270	270	9-7
Wages and subcontractor fees:			
Part-time employees	23,000	23,000	9-3
Full-time employee (Ken)	30,000	30,000	9-19
Fountain removal (part-time employee)	850	850	9-25
Fence installation (prepaid subcontractor)	1,000	0	9-22
Other expenses:			
Books for waiting room	50	50	9-2
Education—seminar	300	300	9-9
Uniforms	500	500	9-6
Bad debts	0	280	9-27
Other expenses (not in examples):			
Advertising	1,160	1,160	
Depreciation	4,000	4,000	
Interest	300	300	
Legal and professional services	1,040	1,040	
Office expense	1,500	1,500	
Repairs and maintenance	1,975	1,975	
Taxes and licenses	400	400	
Utilities	2,200	2,200	
Total deductions	**$91,221**	**$ 88,101**	
Net Business Income	**$ 7,979**	**$ 15,199**	

Changing Accounting Methods

Once a business has adopted an accounting method, it must generally receive permission to change the method, regardless of whether it is a permissible or an impermissible method. There are three important exceptions to this general rule that apply to small businesses that qualify under the gross receipts test. Small businesses are allowed to switch to use the cash method, treat inventories as nonincidental materials, and ignore the UNICAP rules when the gross receipts test is satisfied.[60]

[60]§§448(d)(7), 471(c)(4), 263A(i)(3), respectively. These changes in accounting method are treated as initiated by the taxpayer and no longer need the consent of the Secretary.

EXHIBIT 9-6 Green Acres Schedule C

SCHEDULE C (Form 1040)
Department of the Treasury Internal Revenue Service (99)

Profit or Loss From Business
(Sole Proprietorship)

▶ Go to *www.irs.gov/ScheduleC* for instructions and the latest information.
▶ Attach to Form 1040, 1040-SR, 1040-NR, or 1041; partnerships must generally file Form 1065.

OMB No. 1545-0074
2021
Attachment Sequence No. 09

Name of proprietor: RICK GRIME — Social security number (SSN): 000-00-0000

A Principal business or profession, including product or service (see instructions): LANDSCAPING — B Enter code from instructions ▶ 5 7 1 6 3 0

C Business name. If no separate business name, leave blank. GREEN ACRES LANDSCAPING — D Employer ID number (EIN) (see instr.) 0 0 0 0 0 0 0 0 0

E Business address (including suite or room no.) ▶ BUCKSNORT STREET
City, town or post office, state, and ZIP code SAN ANTONIO TX 78208

F Accounting method: (1) ☑ Cash (2) ☐ Accrual (3) ☐ Other (specify) ▶

G Did you "materially participate" in the operation of this business during 2021? If "No," see instructions for limit on losses . ☑ Yes ☐ No

H If you started or acquired this business during 2021, check here ▶ ☑

I Did you make any payments in 2021 that would require you to file Form(s) 1099? See instructions ☐ Yes ☑ No

J If "Yes," did you or will you file required Form(s) 1099? ☐ Yes ☐ No

Part I Income

1	Gross receipts or sales. See instructions for line 1 and check the box if this income was reported to you on Form W-2 and the "Statutory employee" box on that form was checked ▶ ☐	1	99,200
2	Returns and allowances	2	
3	Subtract line 2 from line 1	3	99,200
4	Cost of goods sold (from line 42)	4	7,000
5	**Gross profit.** Subtract line 4 from line 3	5	92,200
6	Other income, including federal and state gasoline or fuel tax credit or refund (see instructions)	6	
7	**Gross income.** Add lines 5 and 6 ▶	7	92,200

Part II Expenses. Enter expenses for business use of your home **only** on line 30.

8	Advertising	8	1,160	18	Office expense (see instructions)	18	1,500
9	Car and truck expenses (see instructions)	9	5,641	19	Pension and profit-sharing plans	19	
10	Commissions and fees	10		20	Rent or lease (see instructions):		
11	Contract labor (see instructions)	11	1,000	a	Vehicles, machinery, and equipment	20a	7,400
12	Depletion	12		b	Other business property	20b	
13	Depreciation and section 179 expense deduction (not included in Part III) (see instructions)	13	4,000	21	Repairs and maintenance	21	1,975
				22	Supplies (not included in Part III)	22	
				23	Taxes and licenses	23	400
				24	Travel and meals:		
14	Employee benefit programs (other than on line 19)	14		a	Travel	24a	1,435
15	Insurance (other than health)	15	1,200	b	Deductible meals (see instructions)	24b	270
16	Interest (see instructions):			25	Utilities	25	2,200
a	Mortgage (paid to banks, etc.)	16a	300	26	Wages (less employment credits)	26	53,850
b	Other	16b		27a	Other expenses (from line 48)	27a	850
17	Legal and professional services	17	1,040	b	**Reserved for future use**	27b	

28	**Total expenses** before expenses for business use of home. Add lines 8 through 27a ▶	28	84.221
29	Tentative profit or (loss). Subtract line 28 from line 7	29	7,979
30	Expenses for business use of your home. Do not report these expenses elsewhere. Attach Form 8829 unless using the simplified method. See instructions. **Simplified method filers only:** Enter the total square footage of (a) your home: ______ and (b) the part of your home used for business: ______. Use the Simplified Method Worksheet in the instructions to figure the amount to enter on line 30	30	0
31	**Net profit or (loss).** Subtract line 30 from line 29. • If a profit, enter on both **Schedule 1 (Form 1040), line 3,** and on **Schedule SE, line 2.** (If you checked the box on line 1, see instructions). Estates and trusts, enter on **Form 1041, line 3.** • If a loss, you **must** go to line 32.	31	7,979

32 If you have a loss, check the box that describes your investment in this activity. See instructions.
• If you checked 32a, enter the loss on both **Schedule 1 (Form 1040), line 3,** and on **Schedule SE, line 2.** (If you checked the box on line 1, see the line 31 instructions.) Estates and trusts, enter on **Form 1041, line 3.**
• If you checked 32b, you **must** attach **Form 6198.** Your loss may be limited.

32a ☑ All investment is at risk.
32b ☐ Some investment is not at risk.

For Paperwork Reduction Act Notice, see the separate instructions. Cat. No. 11334P **Schedule C (Form 1040) 2021**

Source: irs.gov.

For accounting method changes unrelated to qualifying as a small business under the gross receipts test, a taxpayer must request permission to change accounting methods by filing Form 3115 with the IRS. The IRS automatically approves certain types of accounting method changes (such as described above), but for others the business must provide a good business purpose for the change and pay a fee. The IRS also requires permission when a business must change from using an impermissible method; this requirement helps the IRS to certify that the business properly makes the transition to a permissible method. In essence, the IRS requires the business to report its own noncompliance. Why would a business do so? Besides complying with the tax laws, a business might report its own noncompliance to receive leniency from the IRS. Without getting into the details, the IRS is likely to assess fewer penalties and less interest expense for noncompliance when the business reports the noncompliance before the IRS discovers it on its own.

Tax Consequences of Changing Accounting Methods When a business changes from one accounting method to another, the business determines its taxable income for the year of change using the new method. Furthermore, the business must make an adjustment to taxable income that effectively represents the cumulative difference, as of the beginning of the tax year, between the amount of income (or deductions) recognized under the old accounting method and the amount that would have been recognized for all prior years if the new method had been applied. This adjustment is called a **§481 adjustment.** The §481 adjustment prevents the duplication or omission of items of income or deduction due to a change in accounting method. If the §481 adjustment increases taxable income, the taxpayer generally recognizes the total adjustment spread evenly over four years beginning with the year of the change (25 percent of the full adjustment each year).[61] If the adjustment decreases taxable income, the taxpayer typically recognizes it entirely in the year of change.

Example 9-30

What if: Suppose that at the end of 2022, Green Acres has $24,000 of accounts receivable. Assuming Green Acres uses the cash method of accounting in 2022, it would not include the $24,000 of receivables in income in determining its 2022 taxable income. Suppose further that Rick decides to switch Green Acres to the accrual method of accounting in 2023 by filing a Form 3115 and receiving permission from the IRS. What is Rick's §481 adjustment for his change in accounting method from the cash to the accrual method, and when will he include the full adjustment in his taxable income?

Answer: Rick's positive §481 full adjustment is $24,000, which will be added to his taxable income over four years in equal increments. Hence, Rick will have a $6,000 annual increase to income beginning in 2023 and ending in 2026. Because Rick is using the accrual method in 2023, he would *not* include payments he receives for the $24,000 in receivables from sales made in 2022. Instead, Rick would be required to make a §481 adjustment to ensure that he does not *omit* these items from taxable income.

What if: Suppose that at the end of 2022, Green Acres has $4,000 of accounts payable instead of $24,000 of accounts receivable. What is the full §481 adjustment and when will he include the adjustment in his taxable income?

Answer: In this instance, Green Acres would have a negative (income-decreasing) §481 adjustment of $4,000 because the $4,000 of expenses would have accrued in 2022 but would not have been deducted in 2022. Hence, Green Acres would be entitled to deduct the full $4,000 as a negative §481 adjustment amount in 2023 (income-decreasing adjustments are made in the year of change rather than spread over four years).

[61]Rev. Proc. 2015-13. There are multiple exceptions to the general rule. For example, taxpayers with positive §481 adjustments less than $25,000 can elect to recognize the entire amount in the year of change. Rev. Proc. 2002-19.

CONCLUSION

This chapter discusses issues relating to business income and deductions. We learned that the income rules for businesses are very similar to those for individuals and that businesses may deduct only ordinary and necessary business expenses and other business expenses specifically authorized by law. We also described several business expense limitations and discussed the accounting periods and methods businesses may use in reporting taxable income to the IRS. The issues described in this chapter are widely applicable to all types of business entities, including sole proprietorships, partnerships, S corporations, and C corporations.

Summary

Identify common business deductions. **LO 9-1**

- Ordinary and necessary business expenses are allowed as deductions to calculate net income from activities entered into with a profit motive.
- Only reasonable amounts are allowed as business expense deductions. Extravagant or excessive amounts are likely to be characterized by personal motives and are disallowed.

Determine the limits on deducting business expenses. **LO 9-2**

- To pass the gross receipts test for 2022, a business cannot have average annual gross receipts in excess of $27 million for the three prior years. This limit is indexed for inflation.
- The law specifically prohibits deducting expenses that are against public policy (such as fines or bribes) and expenses that produce tax-exempt income.
- Entertainment is not a deductible business expense, but the cost of business meals is 50 percent deductible (100 percent if purchased from a restaurant) under specific circumstances.
- Expenses benefiting more than 12 months must be capitalized, and special limits and recordkeeping requirements are applied to business expenses that may have personal benefits, such as meals and travel.
- Except for businesses qualifying under the gross receipts test, business interest can only be deducted to the extent of business interest income plus 30 percent of the business's adjusted taxable income. Adjusted taxable income is taxable income before depreciation and interest deductions allocable to the business activity. Disallowed business interest expense can be carried forward indefinitely.
- Losses on the sale of business assets are typically deductible. However, losses on sales to related persons, such as family members, cannot be deducted in the year of sale.
- Special calculations are necessary for deductions such as the deduction for casualty losses. The deduction when an asset is damaged (not destroyed) is limited to the lesser of the reduction in value or the adjusted tax basis of the asset.

Describe accounting periods available to businesses. **LO 9-3**

- Accounting periods and methods are chosen at the time of filing the first tax return.
- There are three types of tax years—calendar year, fiscal year, and 52/53-week year—and each tax year is distinguished by year-end.

Apply cash and accrual methods to determine business income and expense deductions. **LO 9-4**

- Under the cash method, taxpayers recognize revenue when they actually or constructively receive property or services and they recognize deductions when they actually pay the expense. C corporations and partnerships with C corporation partners, but not tax shelters, can elect to use the cash method if the business passes the gross receipts test.
- Under the accrual method, the all-events test requires that income be recognized when all the events have occurred that are necessary to fix the right to receive payments and the amount of the payments can be determined with reasonable accuracy, but no later than the income is recognized in the financial statements.
- Businesses where sales are an income-producing factor must elect an inventory method and account for sales and purchases under the accrual method.

- Taxpayers who meet the gross receipts test, however, can account for sales either under the method used for financial reporting or as nonincidental materials.
- Under the accrual method, accrued expenses can be deducted only when the all-events test and the economic performance test both have been met. The application of the economic performance test depends, in part, on the type of business expense.
- Changes in accounting method or accounting period typically require the consent of the IRS and a §481 adjustment to taxable income. A negative adjustment is included in income for the year of change, whereas a positive adjustment is spread over four years.

KEY TERMS

§481 adjustment (9-32)
12-month rule (9-16)
accounting methods (9-15)
accounting period (9-14)
all-events test (9-22)
allowance method (9-27)
arm's-length amount (9-5)
direct write-off method (9-27)
economic performance test (9-22)
first-in, first-out (FIFO) method (9-21)
fiscal year (9-14)
flow-through entity (9-14)
gross receipts test (9-2)
impermissible accounting method (9-29)
last-in, first-out (LIFO) method (9-21)
mixed-motive expenditures (9-8)
ordinary and necessary (9-4)
payment liabilities (9-24)
permissible accounting method (9-29)
personal expenses (9-7)
reasonable in amount (9-5)
recurring item (9-26)
specific identification method (9-21)
tax year (9-14)
travel expenses (9-10)
uniform cost capitalization (UNICAP) rules (9-19)

DISCUSSION QUESTIONS

Discussion Questions are available in Connect®.

LO 9-1
1. What is an "ordinary and necessary" business expenditure?

LO 9-1
2. Explain how cost of goods is treated when a business sells inventory.

LO 9-1
3. Whether a business expense is "reasonable in amount" is often a difficult question. Explain why determining reasonableness is difficult, and describe a circumstance where reasonableness is likely to be questioned by the IRS.

LO 9-1
4. Jake is a professional dog trainer who purchases and trains dogs for use by law enforcement agencies. Last year Jake purchased 500 bags of dog food from a large pet food company at an average cost of $30 per bag. This year, however, Jake purchased 500 bags of dog food from a local pet food company at an average cost of $45 per bag. Under what circumstances would the IRS likely challenge the cost of Jake's dog food as unreasonable?

LO 9-2
5. What kinds of deductions are prohibited as a matter of public policy? Why might Congress deem it important to disallow deductions for expenditures that are against public policy?

LO 9-2
6. Provide an example of an expense associated with the production of tax-exempt income, and explain what might happen if Congress repealed the prohibition against deducting expenses incurred to produce tax-exempt income.

LO 9-2 research
7. Peggy is a rodeo clown, and this year she expended $1,000 on special "funny" clothes and outfits. Peggy would like to deduct the cost of these clothes as work-related because she refuses to wear the clothes unless she is working. Under what circumstances can Peggy deduct the cost of her clown clothes?

LO 9-2
8. Jimmy is a sole proprietor of a small dry-cleaning business. This month Jimmy paid for his groceries by writing checks from the checking account dedicated to the dry-cleaning business. Why do you suppose Jimmy is using his business checking account rather than his personal checking account to pay for personal expenditures?

LO 9-2
9. Troy operates an editorial service that often entertains prospective authors to encourage them to use Troy's service. This year Troy paid $3,000 for the cost of meals and

$6,200 for the cost of entertaining authors. Describe the conditions under which Troy can deduct a portion of the cost of the meals as a business expense.

10. Susmita purchased a car this year and uses it for both business and personal purposes. Susmita drove the car 11,000 miles on business trips and 9,000 miles for personal transportation. Describe how Susmita will determine the amount of deductible expenses associated with the auto. LO 9-2
11. What expenses are deductible when a taxpayer combines both business and personal activities on a trip? How do the rules for international travel differ from the rules for domestic travel? LO 9-1 LO 9-2
12. Clyde lives and operates a sole proprietorship in Dallas, Texas. This year Clyde found it necessary to travel to Fort Worth (about 25 miles away) for legitimate business reasons. Is Clyde's trip likely to qualify as "away from home"? Why would this designation matter? LO 9-2
13. Describe the record-keeping requirements for deducting business expenses, including mixed-motive expenditures. LO 9-2
14. Describe the computation of the limit placed on the business interest deduction. Is the disallowed business interest ever deductible? LO 9-2
15. Describe the gross receipts test and identify how this test relates to the business interest deduction. LO 9-2
16. Explain the difference between calculating a loss deduction for a business asset that was partially damaged in an accident and calculating a loss deduction for a business asset that was stolen or completely destroyed in an accident. LO 9-2
17. How does a casualty loss on a business asset differ when the asset is stolen as opposed to destroyed in a fire? LO 9-2
18. What is the difference between a full tax year and a short tax year? Describe circumstances in which a business may have a short tax year. LO 9-3
19. Explain why a taxpayer might choose one tax year-end over another if given a choice. LO 9-3
20. Compare and contrast the different year-ends available to sole proprietorships, flow-through entities, and C corporations. LO 9-3
21. Why does the law generally require partnerships to adopt a tax year consistent with the year used by the partners? LO 9-3
22. How does an entity choose its tax year? Is it the same process no matter the type of tax year-end the taxpayer adopts? LO 9-3
23. Explain when an expenditure should be "capitalized" based upon accounting principles. From time to time, it is suggested that all business expenditures should be deducted when incurred for tax purposes. Do you agree with this proposition, and if so, why? LO 9-4
24. Describe the 12-month rule for determining whether and to what extent businesses should capitalize or immediately deduct prepaid expenses such as insurance or security contracts. Explain the apparent rationale for this rule. LO 9-4
25. Explain why Congress sometimes mandates that businesses use particular accounting methods while other times Congress is content to require businesses to use the same accounting methods for tax purposes that they use for financial accounting purposes. LO 9-4
26. Why is it not surprising that specific rules differ between tax accounting and financial accounting? LO 9-4
27. The cash method of accounting is generally preferred by taxpayers. Describe two types of businesses that are not allowed to use the cash method. LO 9-4
28. Fred is considering using the accrual method for his next business venture. Explain to Fred the conditions for recognizing income for tax purposes under the accrual method. LO 9-4
29. Describe the all-events test for determining income, and describe how to determine the date on which the all-events test has been met. LO 9-4

LO 9-4 30. Compare and contrast the tax treatment for rental income received in advance with advance payments for goods and services.

LO 9-4 research 31. Jack operates a large home repair business as a sole proprietorship. Besides providing services, Jack also sells home repair supplies to homeowners. However, these sales constitute a relatively small portion of Jack's income. Describe the conditions under which Jack would need to account for sales and purchases of plumbing supplies using the accrual method. (*Hint:* Read §471(c) and Reg. §1.471-1.)

LO 9-4 32. Describe why Congress enacted the UNICAP rules, and describe an exception to these rules.

LO 9-4 33. Compare and contrast financial accounting rules with the tax rules under UNICAP (§263A). Explain whether the UNICAP rules tend to accelerate or defer income relative to the financial accounting rules.

LO 9-4 34. Compare and contrast the tests for accruing income and those for accruing deductions for tax purposes.

LO 9-4 35. Compare and contrast when taxpayers are allowed to deduct the cost of warranties provided by others to the taxpayer (i.e., purchased by the taxpayer) and when taxpayers are allowed to deduct the costs associated with warranties they provide (sell) to others.

LO 9-4 36. Describe when economic performance occurs for the following expenses:

a) Workers' compensation

b) Rebates and refunds

c) Insurance, warranties, and service contracts provided *to* the business

d) Taxes

LO 9-4 37. On December 31 of the current year, a taxpayer prepays an advertising company to provide advertising services for the next 10 months. Using the 12-month rule and the economic performance rules, contrast when the taxpayer would be able to deduct the expenditure if the taxpayer uses the cash method of accounting versus if the taxpayer uses the accrual method of accounting.

LO 9-4 38. Compare and contrast how bad debt expense is determined for financial accounting purposes and how the deduction for bad debts is determined for accrual-method taxpayers. How do cash-method taxpayers determine their bad debt expense for accounts receivable?

LO 9-4 39. Describe the related-person limitation on accrued deductions. What tax savings strategy is this limitation designed to thwart?

LO 9-4 40. What are the relative advantages of the cash and accrual methods of accounting?

LO 9-4 41. Describe how a business adopts a permissible accounting method. Explain whether a taxpayer can adopt an impermissible accounting method.

LO 9-4 42. Describe why the IRS might be skeptical of permitting requests for changes in accounting method without a good business purpose.

LO 9-4 43. Describe two specific accounting methods that are treated as initiated by the taxpayer without any need for consent of the IRS when the business qualifies under the gross receipts test.

LO 9-4 44. What is a §481 adjustment, and what is the purpose of this adjustment?

PROBLEMS

Select problems are available in Connect®.

LO 9-1 45. Manny hired his brother's firm to provide accounting services to his business. During the current year, Manny paid his brother's firm $82,000 for services even though other firms were willing to provide the same services for $40,000. How much of this expenditure, if any, is deductible as an ordinary and necessary business expenditure?

46. Michelle operates several food trucks. Indicate the amount (if any) that she can deduct as an ordinary and necessary business deduction in each of the following situations, and explain your solution. LO 9-1 LO 9-2
   a) Michelle moves her food truck between various locations on a daily rotation. Last week, Michelle was stopped for speeding. She paid a fine of $125 for speeding, including $80 for legal advice in connection with the ticket.
   b) Michelle paid $750 to reserve a parking place for her food truck for the fall football season outside the local football stadium. Michelle also paid $95 for tickets to a game for her children.
   c) Michelle provided a candidate with free advertising painted on her truck during the candidate's campaign for city council. Michelle paid $500 to have the ad prepared and an additional $200 to have the ad removed from the truck after the candidate lost the election.
   d) Michelle realized a $1,200 loss when she sold one of her food trucks to her father, a related party.

47. Indicate the amount (if any) that Josh can deduct as an ordinary and necessary business deduction in each of the following situations, and explain your solution. LO 9-1 LO 9-2
   a) Josh borrowed $50,000 from First State Bank using his business assets as collateral. He used the money to buy City of Blanksville bonds. Over the course of a year, Josh paid interest of $4,200 on the borrowed funds, but he received $3,500 of interest on the bonds.
   b) Josh purchased a piece of land for $45,000 in order to get a location to expand his business. He also paid $3,200 to construct a new driveway for access to the property.
   c) This year Josh paid $15,000 to employ the mayor's son in the business. Josh would typically pay an employee with these responsibilities about $10,000, but the mayor assured Josh that after his son was hired, some city business would be coming his way.
   d) Josh paid his brother, a mechanic, $3,000 to install a robotic machine for Josh's business. The amount he paid to his brother is comparable to what he would have paid to an unrelated person to do the same work. Once the installation was completed by his brother, Josh began calibrating the machine for operation. However, by the end of the year, he had not started using the machine in his business.

48. Armelio operates a business that acts as a sales representative for firms that produce and sell precious metals to electronics manufacturers. Armelio contacts manufacturers and convinces them to sign contracts for the delivery of metals. Armelio's company earns a commission on the sales. This year, Armelio contacted a jeweler to engrave small lapel buttons for each client. Armelio paid $20 each for the lapel buttons, and the jeweler charged Armelio an additional $7 for engraving. The electronics manufacturers, however, prohibit their employees from accepting gifts related to sales contracts. Can Armelio deduct the cost of the lapel buttons as business gifts? LO 9-2 research

49. Melissa recently paid $400 for round-trip airfare to San Francisco to attend a business conference for three days. Melissa also paid the following expenses: $250 fee to register for the conference, $300 per night for three nights' lodging, $200 for meals in restaurants, and $150 for cab fare. LO 9-2
   a) What amount of these costs can Melissa deduct as business expenses?
   b) Suppose that while Melissa was on the coast, she also spent two days sightseeing the national parks in the area. To do the sightseeing, she paid $1,000 for transportation, $800 for lodging, and $450 for meals during this part of her trip, which she considers personal in nature. What amount of these costs can Melissa deduct as business expenses?

c) Suppose that Melissa made the trip to San Francisco primarily to visit the national parks and only attended the business conference as an incidental benefit of being present on the coast at that time. What amount of the airfare can Melissa deduct as a business expense?

d) Suppose that Melissa's permanent residence and business were located in San Francisco. She attended the conference in San Francisco and paid $250 for the registration fee. She drove 100 miles over the course of three days and paid $90 for parking at the conference hotel. In addition, she spent $150 for breakfast and dinner over the three days of the conference. She bought breakfast on the way to the conference hotel, and she bought dinner on her way home each night from the conference. What amount of these costs can Melissa deduct as business expenses?

LO 9-2

50. Sasha is a self-employed taxpayer. They recently spent $1,000 for airfare to travel to Italy. What amount of the airfare is deductible in each of the following alternative scenarios?

a) Sasha's trip was entirely for personal purposes.

b) On the trip, Sasha spent eight days on personal activities and two days on business activities.

c) On the trip, Sasha spent seven days on business activities and three days on personal activities.

d) Sasha's trip was entirely for business purposes.

LO 9-2

51. Ryan is self-employed. This year Ryan used his personal auto for several long business trips. Ryan paid $1,500 for gasoline on these trips. His depreciation on the car if he was using it fully for business purposes would be $3,000. During the year, he drove his car a total of 12,000 miles (a combination of business and personal travel).

a) Ryan can provide written documentation of the business purpose for trips totaling 3,000 miles. What business expense amount can Ryan deduct (if any) for these trips?

b) Ryan estimates that he drove approximately 1,300 miles on business trips, but he can only provide written documentation of the business purpose for trips totaling 820 miles. What business expense amount can Ryan deduct (if any) for these trips?

LO 9-1 LO 9-2

52. Haru is a self-employed cash-method, calendar-year taxpayer who made the following cash payments related to his business this year. Calculate the after-tax cost of each payment assuming Haru has a 37 percent marginal tax rate.

a) $500 fine for speeding while traveling to a client meeting.

b) $800 of interest on a short-term loan incurred in September and repaid in November. Half of the loan proceeds was used immediately to pay salaries and the other half was invested in municipal bonds until November.

c) $600 for office supplies in May of this year. Haru used half of the supplies this year, and he will use the remaining half by February of next year.

d) $450 for several pairs of work boots. Haru expects to use the boots about 80 percent of the time in his business and the remainder of the time for hiking. Consider the boots to be a form of clothing.

LO 9-2

53. Heather is an attorney who paid $15,000 to join a country club in order to meet potential clients. This year she also paid $4,300 in greens fees when golfing with clients and paid an additional $1,700 for meals with clients in the clubhouse. Under what circumstances, if any, can Heather deduct all or part of the $21,000 paid to the country club this year?

54. Sarah is a cash-method, calendar-year taxpayer, and she is considering making the following cash payments related to her business. Calculate the after-tax cost of each payment assuming she is subject to a 37 percent marginal tax rate. LO 9-1 LO 9-2
    a) $2,000 payment for next year's property taxes on her place of business.
    b) $800 to reimburse the cost of meals at restaurants incurred by employees while traveling for the business.
    c) $1,200 for football tickets to entertain out-of-town clients during contract negotiations.
    d) $500 contribution to the mayor's reelection campaign.
55. Red Inc. is a C corporation and a calendar-year taxpayer. Red reports sales of $24 million in 2019, $28.3 million in 2020, and $32 million in 2021. LO 9-2
    a) Is Red subject to the business interest limitation in 2022?
    b) Suppose that besides sales, Red also reports sales returns of $3.1 million in each year 2019–2021. Is Red subject to the business interest limitation in 2022?
    c) Suppose that Red began business on January 1, 2020, and reported gross receipts of $25.3 million in 2020 and $28.9 million in 2021. Is Red subject to the business interest limitation in 2022?
    d) Suppose that Red began business operations on October 1, 2021, and reported $6.2 million in gross receipts for the three-month 2021 short year. Is Red subject to the business interest limitation in 2022?
56. Renee operates a proprietorship selling collectibles over the Web. This year, Renee's business reported revenue of $95.5 million and deducted $88.6 million in expenses and loss carryovers. Her business deductions included cost of goods sold of $48.5 million, sales commissions paid of $16.9 million, $10.5 million of interest paid on a mortgage, $10.7 million of depreciation, and $2 million deduction for a net operating loss carryover. LO 9-2
    a) What is Renee's adjusted taxable income for purposes of calculating the limitation on business interest expense?
    b) What is the maximum amount of business interest expense that Renee can deduct this year, and how is the disallowed interest expense (if any) treated?
    c) Suppose that Renee's revenue includes $5 million of business interest income. What is the maximum amount of business interest expense that could be deducted this year under the business interest limitation?
57. This year, Amy purchased $2,000 of equipment for use in her business. However, the machine was damaged in a traffic accident while Amy was transporting the equipment to her business. Note that because Amy did not place the equipment into service during the year, she does not claim any depreciation or cost recovery expense for the equipment. LO 9-2
    a) After the accident, Amy had the choice of repairing the equipment for $1,800 or selling the equipment to a junk shop for $300. Amy sold the equipment. What amount can Amy deduct for the loss of the equipment?
    b) Suppose that after the accident, Amy repaired the equipment for $800. What amount can Amy deduct for the loss of the equipment?
    c) Suppose that after the accident, Amy could not replace the equipment so she had the equipment repaired for $2,300. What amount can Amy deduct for the loss of the equipment?
58. In July of this year, Stephen started a proprietorship called ECR (which stands for electric car repair). ECR uses the cash method of accounting, and Stephen has produced the following financial information for this year: LO 9-3 tax forms
    - ECR collected $81,000 in cash for repairs completed during the year and an additional $3,200 in cash for repairs that will commence after year-end.

- Customers owe ECR $14,300 for repairs completed this year, and while Stephen isn't sure which bills will eventually be paid, he expects to collect all but about $1,900 of these revenues next year.

ECR has made the following expenditures:

Interest expense	$ 1,250
Shop rent ($1,500 per month)	27,000
Utilities	1,075
Contract labor	8,250
Compensation	21,100
Liability insurance premiums ($350 per month)	4,200
Term life insurance premiums ($150 per month)	1,800

The interest paid relates to interest accrued on a $54,000 loan made to Stephen in July of this year. Stephen used half of the loan to pay for 18 months of shop rent, and the remainder he used to upgrade his personal wardrobe. In July, Stephen purchased 12 months of liability insurance to protect against liability should anyone be injured in the shop. ECR has only one employee (the remaining workers are contract labor), and this employee thoroughly understands how to repair an electric propulsion system. On November 1 of this year, Stephen purchased a 12-month term life policy that insures the life of this "key" employee. Stephen paid Gecko Insurance Company $1,800; in return, Gecko promises to pay Stephen a $40,000 death benefit if this employee dies any time during the next 12 months.

Complete a draft of the front page of Stephen's Schedule C.

LO 9-4 planning

59. Nicole is a calendar-year taxpayer who accounts for her business using the cash method. On average, Nicole sends out bills for about $12,000 of her services on the first of each month. The bills are due by the end of the month, and typically 70 percent of the bills are paid on time and 98 percent are paid within 60 days.
   a) Suppose that Nicole is expecting a 2 percent reduction in her marginal tax rate next year. Ignoring the time value of money, estimate the tax savings for Nicole if she postpones mailing the December bills until January 1 of next year.
   b) Describe how the time value of money affects your calculations.
   c) Would this tax savings strategy create any additional business risks? Explain.

LO 9-4

60. Jeremy is a calendar-year taxpayer who sometimes leases his business equipment to local organizations. He recorded the following receipts this year. Indicate the extent to which these payments are taxable income to Jeremy this year if Jeremy is (1) a cash-method taxpayer and (2) an accrual-method taxpayer.
   a) $1,000 deposit from the Ladies' Club, which wants to lease a trailer. The club will receive the entire deposit back when the trailer is returned undamaged.
   b) $800 from the Ladies' Club for leasing the trailer from December of this year through March of next year ($200 per month).
   c) $300 lease payment received from the Men's Club this year for renting Jeremy's trailer last year. Jeremy billed the club last year, but recently he determined that the Men's Club would never pay him, so he was surprised when he received the check.

LO 9-4

61. Brown Thumb Landscaping is a calendar-year, accrual-method taxpayer. In September, Brown Thumb negotiated a $14,000 contract for services it would provide to the city in November of the current year. The contract specifies that Brown Thumb will receive $4,000 in October as a down payment for these services, and it will receive the remaining $10,000 in January of next year.
   a) How much income from this $14,000 contract will Brown Thumb recognize in the current year? Explain.
   b) How much income from this $14,000 contract will Brown Thumb recognize in the current year if it uses the cash method of accounting?

c) Suppose that the total amount to be paid under the contract with the city is estimated at $14,000 but may be adjusted to $12,000 next year during the review of the city budget. What amount from the contract, if any, should Brown Thumb recognize as income this year? Explain.

d) Suppose that in addition to the basic contract, Brown Thumb will be paid an additional $3,000 if its city landscape design wins the annual design competition next year. Should Brown Thumb accrue $3,000 revenue this year? Why or why not?

62. In January of year 0, Justin paid $4,800 for an insurance policy that covers his business property for accidents and casualties. Justin is a calendar-year taxpayer who uses the cash method of accounting. What amount of the insurance premium may Justin deduct in year 0 in each of the following alternative scenarios? LO 9-4

a) The policy covers the business property from April 1 of year 0 through March 31 of year 1.

b) The policy begins on February 1 of year 1 and extends through January 31 of year 2.

c) Justin pays $6,000 for a 24-month policy that covers the business from April 1, year 0, through March 31, year 2.

d) Instead of paying an insurance premium, Justin pays $4,800 to rent his business property from April 1 of year 0 through March 31 of year 1.

63. Binu teaches golf lessons at a country club under a business called Binu's Pure Swings (BPS). Binu operates this business as a sole proprietorship on the accrual basis of accounting. Use the following accounting information for BPS to complete the firm's Schedule C: LO 9-4 tax forms

This year BPS billed clients for $86,700 and collected $61,000 in cash for golf lessons completed during the year. In addition, BPS collected an additional $14,500 in cash for lessons that will commence after year-end. Binu hopes to collect about half of the outstanding billings next year, but the rest will likely be written off.

Besides providing private golf lessons, BPS also contracted with the country club to staff the driving range. This year, BPS billed the country club $27,200 for the service. The club paid $17,000 of the amount but disputed the remainder. By year-end, the dispute had not been resolved, and while Binu believes BPS is entitled to the money, the remaining $10,200 has not been paid.

BPS has accrued the following expenses (explained below):

Advertising (in the clubhouse)	$13,150
Pro golf teachers' membership fees	860
Supplies (golf tees, balls, etc.)	4,720
Club rental	6,800
Malpractice insurance	2,400
Accounting fees	8,820

The expenditures were all paid for this calendar year, with several exceptions. First, Binu initiated his golfer's malpractice insurance on June 1 of this year. The $2,400 insurance bill covers the last six months of this calendar year and the first six months of next year. At year-end, Binu had only paid $600 but has assured the insurance agent the remaining $1,800 will be paid early next year. Second, the amount paid for club rental ($100 per week) represents rental charges for the last 6 weeks of the previous year, the 52 weeks in this calendar year, and the first 10 weeks of next year. Binu has also mentioned that BPS only pays for supplies that are used at the club. Although BPS could buy the supplies for half the cost elsewhere, Binu likes to "throw some business" to the golf pro shop because it is operated by his brother.

Complete a draft of Parts I and II on the front page of a Schedule C for BPS.

LO 9-4

64. Stephanie began her consulting business this year, and on April 1 Stephanie received a $9,000 payment for full payment on a three-year service contract (under the contract, Stephanie is obligated to provide advisory services for the next three years). Stephanie has elected to use the accrual method of accounting for her business.
   a) What is the minimum amount of income Stephanie should recognize for tax purposes this year if she recognizes $2,250 of income for financial accounting purposes?
   b) What is the minimum amount of income Stephanie will recognize next year for tax purposes?

LO 9-4

65. This year, Amber purchased a business that processes and packages landscape mulch. Approximately 20 percent of management time, space, and expenses are spent on this manufacturing process.

		Costs	Tax Inventory
Material:	Mulch and packaging	$ 500,000	?
	Administrative supplies	25,000	?
Salaries:	Factory labor	1,200,000	?
	Sales & advertising	350,000	?
	Administration	520,000	?
Property taxes:	Factory	460,000	?
	Offices	270,000	?
Depreciation:	Factory	800,000	?
	Offices	150,000	?

   a) At the end of the year, Amber's accountant indicated that the business had processed 10 million bags of mulch, but only 1 million bags remained in the ending inventory. What is Amber's tax basis in her ending inventory if the UNICAP rules are used to allocate indirect costs to inventory? (Assume direct costs are allocated to inventory according to the level of ending inventory. In contrast, indirect costs are first allocated by time spent and then according to level of ending inventory.)
   b) Under what conditions could Amber's business avoid having to apply UNICAP rules to allocate indirect costs to inventory for tax purposes?

LO 9-4

66. Suppose that David has elected to account for inventories and has adopted the last-in, first-out (LIFO) inventory-flow method for his business inventory of widgets (purchase prices below).

Widget	Purchase Date	Direct Cost	Other Costs	Total Cost
#1	August 15	$2,100	$100	$2,200
#2	October 30	2,200	150	2,350
#3	November 10	2,300	100	2,400

In late December, David sold one widget, and next year David expects to purchase three more widgets at the following estimated prices:

Widget	Purchase Date	Estimated Cost
#4	Early spring	$2,600
#5	Summer	2,260
#6	Fall	2,400

   a) What cost of goods sold and ending inventory would David record if he elects to use the LIFO method this year?
   b) If David sells two more widgets next year, what will be his cost of goods sold and ending inventory next year under the LIFO method?

c) How would you answer (a) and (b) if David had initially selected the first-in, first-out (FIFO) method instead of LIFO?

d) Suppose that David initially adopted the LIFO method but wants to apply for a change to FIFO next year. What would be his §481 adjustment for this change, and in what year(s) would he make the adjustment?

67. On November 1 of this year, Jaxon borrowed $50,000 from Bucksnort Savings and Loan for use in his business. In December, Jaxon paid interest of $4,500 relating to the 12-month period from November of this year through October of next year. LO 9-4

a) How much interest, if any, can Jaxon deduct this year if his business uses the cash method of accounting for tax purposes?

b) How much interest, if any, can Jaxon deduct this year if his business uses the accrual method of accounting for tax purposes?

68. Matt hired Apex Services to repair his business equipment. On November 1 of this year, Matt paid $2,000 for the repairs that he expects to begin in early March of next year. LO 9-4

a) What amount of the cost of the repairs can Matt deduct this year if he uses the cash method of accounting for his business?

b) What amount of the cost of the repairs can Matt deduct this year if he uses the accrual method of accounting for his business?

c) What amount of the cost of the repairs can Matt deduct this year if he uses the accrual method, and he expects the repairs to be done by early February?

d) What amount of the cost of the repairs can Matt deduct this year if he uses the cash method of accounting, and he expects the repairs to be done by early February?

69. Circuit Corporation (CC) is a calendar-year, accrual-method taxpayer. CC manufactures and sells electronic circuitry. On November 15 of this year, CC enters into a contract with Equip Corp (EC) that provides CC with exclusive use of EC's specialized manufacturing equipment for the five-year period beginning on January 1 of next year. Pursuant to the contract, CC pays EC $100,000 on December 30 of this year. How much of this expenditure is CC allowed to deduct this year and next year? LO 9-4

70. This year Elizabeth agreed to a three-year service contract with an engineering consulting firm to improve efficiency in her factory. The contract requires Elizabeth to pay the consulting firm $1,500 for each instance that Elizabeth requests its assistance. The contract also provides that Elizabeth only pays the consultants if their advice increases efficiency as measured 12 months from the date of service. This year Elizabeth requested advice on three occasions, and she has not yet made any payments to the consultants. LO 9-4

a) How much should Elizabeth deduct this year under this service contract if she uses the accrual method of accounting?

b) How much should Elizabeth deduct this year under this service contract if she uses the cash method of accounting?

71. Travis is a professional landscaper. He provides his clients with a one-year (12-month) warranty for retaining walls he installs. In June of this year, Travis installed a wall for an important client, Sheila. In early November, Sheila informed Travis that the retaining wall had failed. To repair the wall, Travis paid $700 cash for additional stone that he delivered to Sheila's location on November 20 of this year. Travis also offered to pay a mason $800 to repair the wall. Due to some bad weather and the mason's work backlog, the mason agreed to begin the work by the end of January of the next year. Even though Travis expected the mason to finish LO 9-4

the project by the end of February, Travis informed the mason that he would only pay the mason the $800 when he completed the job.

a) Assuming Travis is an accrual-method taxpayer, how much can he deduct this year from these activities?

b) Assuming Travis is a cash-method taxpayer, how much can he deduct this year from these activities?

LO 9-4
research

72. Adam elects the accrual method of accounting for his business. What amount of deductions does Adam recognize this year for the following transactions?

a) Adam guarantees that he will refund the cost of any goods sold to a client if the goods fail within a year of delivery. In December of this year, Adam agreed to refund $2,400 to clients, and he expects to make payment in January of next year.

b) On December 1 of this year, Adam paid $480 for a one-year contract with CleanUP Services to clean his store. The agreement calls for services to be provided on a weekly basis.

c) Adam was billed $240 for annual personal property taxes on his delivery van. Because this was the first time Adam was billed for these taxes, he did not make payment until January of next year. However, he considers the amounts immaterial.

LO 9-4

73. Rebecca is a calendar-year taxpayer who operates a business. She made the following business-related expenditures in December of this year. Indicate the amount of these payments that she may deduct this year under both the cash method of accounting and the accrual method of accounting.

a) $2,000 for an accountant to evaluate the accounting system of Rebecca's business. The accountant spent three weeks in January of next year working on the evaluation.

b) $2,500 for new office furniture. The furniture was delivered on January 15 of next year.

c) $3,000 for property taxes payable on her factory.

d) $1,500 for interest on a short-term bank loan relating to the period from November 1 of this year through March 31 of next year.

LO 9-4

74. BCS Corporation is a calendar-year, accrual-method taxpayer. BCS was formed and started its business activities on January 1 of this year. It reported the following information for the year. Indicate BCS's deductible amount for this year in each of the following alternative scenarios.

a) BCS provides two-year warranties on products it sells to customers. For its current-year sales, BCS estimated and accrued $200,000 in warranty expense for financial accounting purposes. During this year, BCS actually spent $30,000 repairing its product under the warranty.

b) BCS accrued an expense of $50,000 for amounts it anticipated it would be required to pay under the workers' compensation act. During the year, BCS actually paid $10,000 for workers' compensation–related liabilities.

c) In June of this year, a display of BCS's product located in its showroom fell and injured a customer. The customer sued BCS for $500,000. The case is scheduled to go to trial next year. BCS anticipates that it will lose the case and this year accrued a $500,000 expense on its financial statements.

d) Assume the same facts as in (c) except that BCS was required to pay $500,000 to a court-appointed escrow fund this year. If BCS loses the case next year, the money from the escrow fund will be transferred to the customer suing BCS.

e) On December 1 of this year, BCS acquired equipment from Equip Company. As part of the purchase, BCS signed a separate contract that provided that Equip would warranty the equipment for two years (starting on December 1 of this year). The extra cost of the warranty was $12,000, which BCS finally paid to Equip in January of next year.

75. This year William provided $4,200 of services to a large client on credit. Unfortunately, this client has recently encountered financial difficulties and has been unable to pay William for the services. Moreover, William does not expect to collect for his services. William has "written off" the account and would like to claim a deduction for tax purposes. LO 9-4
   a) What amount of deduction for bad debt expense can William claim this year if he uses the accrual method?
   b) What amount of deduction for bad debt expense can William claim this year if he uses the cash method?

76. Dustin has a contract to provide services to Dado Enterprises. In November of this year, Dustin billed Dado $10,000 for the services he rendered during the year. Dado is an accrual-method proprietorship that is owned and operated by Dustin's father. LO 9-4
   a) What amount of revenue must Dustin recognize this year if Dustin uses the cash method and Dado remits payment and Dustin receives payment for the services in December of this year? What amount can Dado deduct this year?
   b) What amount of revenue must Dustin recognize this year if Dustin uses the accrual method and Dado remits payment for the services in December of this year? What amount can Dado deduct this year?
   c) What amount of revenue must Dustin recognize this year if Dustin uses the cash method and Dado remits payment for the services in January of this year? What amount can Dado deduct this year?
   d) What amount of revenue must Dustin recognize this year if Dustin uses the accrual method and Dado remits payment for the services in January of next year? What amount can Dado deduct this year?

77. Nancy operates a business that uses the accrual method of accounting. In December, Nancy asked her brother, Hank, to provide her business with consulting advice. Hank billed Nancy for $5,000 of consulting services in year 0 (a reasonable amount), but Nancy was only able to pay $3,000 of the bill by the end of this year. However, Nancy paid the remainder of the bill in the following year. LO 9-4
   a) How much of the $5,000 consulting services will Hank include in his income this year if he uses the cash method of accounting? What amount can Nancy deduct this year for the consulting services?
   b) How much of the $5,000 consulting services will Hank include in his income this year if he uses the accrual method of accounting? What amount can Nancy deduct this year for the consulting services?

78. Erin is considering switching her business from the cash method to the accrual method at the beginning of next year. Determine the amount and timing of her §481 adjustment assuming the IRS grants Erin's request in the following alternative scenarios. LO 9-4
   a) At the end of this year, Erin's business has $15,000 of accounts receivable and $18,000 of accounts payable that have not been recorded for tax purposes.
   b) At the end of this year, Erin's business reports $25,000 of accounts receivable and $9,000 of accounts payable that have not been recorded for tax purposes.

COMPREHENSIVE PROBLEMS

Select problems are available in Connect®.

79. Joe operates a business that locates and purchases specialized assets for clients, among other activities. Joe uses the accrual method of accounting, but he doesn't keep any significant inventories of the specialized assets that he sells. Joe reported

the following financial information for his business activities during this year. Determine the effect of each of the following transactions on the taxable business income.

a) Joe has signed a contract to sell gadgets to the city. The contract provides that sales of gadgets are dependent upon a test sample of gadgets operating successfully. In December of this year, Joe delivers $12,000 worth of gadgets to the city that will be tested in March of next year. Joe purchased the gadgets especially for this contract and paid $8,500.

b) Joe paid $180 in July of this year to entertain a visiting out-of-town client. The client didn't discuss business with Joe during this visit, but Joe wants to maintain good relations to encourage additional business next year.

c) On November 1 of this year, Joe paid $600 for premiums providing for $40,000 of "key man" insurance on the life of Joe's accountant over the next 12 months.

d) At the end of this year, Joe's business reports $9,000 of accounts receivable. Based upon past experience, Joe believes that at least $2,000 of his new receivables will be uncollectible.

e) In December of this year, Joe rented equipment to complete a large job. Joe paid $3,000 in December because the rental agency required a minimum rental of three months ($1,000 per month). Joe completed the job before year-end, but he returned the equipment at the end of the lease.

f) Joe hired a new sales representative as an employee and sent them to Dallas for a week to contact prospective out-of-state clients. Joe ended up reimbursing his employee $300 for airfare, $350 for lodging, and $250 for meals at restaurants (the sales representative provided adequate documentation to substantiate the business purpose for the meals). Joe requires the employee to account for all expenditures to be reimbursed.

g) Joe uses his BMW (a personal auto) to travel to and from his residence to his factory. However, he switches to a business vehicle if he needs to travel after he reaches the factory. In September of this year, the business vehicle broke down and he was forced to use the BMW both to travel to and from the factory and to visit work sites. He drove 120 miles visiting work sites and 46 miles driving back and forth between the factory and his home. Joe uses the standard mileage rate to determine his auto-related business expenses.

h) Joe paid a visit to his parents in Dallas over the Christmas holidays this year. While he was in the city, Joe spent $50 to attend a half-day business symposium. Joe paid $200 for airfare, $50 for meals provided during the symposium, and $20 on cab fare to the symposium.

80. Jack, a geologist, had been debating for years whether or not to venture out on his own and operate his own business. He had developed a lot of solid relationships with clients, and he believed that many of them would follow him if he were to leave his current employer. As part of a New Year's resolution, Jack decided he would finally do it. Jack put his business plan together, and on January 1 of this year, Jack opened his doors for business as a C corporation called Geo-Jack (GJ). Jack is the sole shareholder. Jack reported the following financial information for the year (assume GJ reports on a calendar year, uses the accrual method of accounting, and elects to account for inventory).

a) In January, GJ rented a small business office about 12 miles from Jack's home. GJ paid $10,000, which represented a damage deposit of $4,000 and rent for two years ($3,000 annually).

b) GJ earned and collected $290,000 performing geological-related services and selling its specialized digging tool [see part (i)].

c) GJ received $50 interest from municipal bonds and $2,100 interest from other investments.

d) GJ purchased some new equipment in February for $42,500. It claimed depreciation on these assets during the year in the amount of $6,540.

e) GJ paid $7,000 to buy luxury season tickets for Jack's parents for State U football games.

f) GJ paid Jack's father $10,000 for services that would have cost no more than $6,000 if Jack had hired any other local business to perform the services. While Jack's dad was competent, he does not command such a premium from his other clients.

g) In an attempt to get his name and new business recognized, GJ paid $7,000 for a one-page ad in the *Geologic Survey*. It also paid $15,000 in radio ads to be run through the end of December.

h) GJ leased additional office space in a building downtown. GJ paid rent of $27,000 for the year.

i) In November, Jack's office was broken into, and equipment valued at $5,000 was stolen. The tax basis of the equipment was $5,500. Jack received $2,000 of insurance proceeds from the theft.

j) GJ incurred a $4,000 fine from the state government for digging in an unauthorized digging zone.

k) GJ contributed $3,000 to lobbyists for their help in persuading the state government to authorize certain unauthorized digging zones.

l) On July 1, GJ paid $1,800 for an 18-month insurance policy for its business equipment. The policy covers the period July 1 of this year through December 31 of next year.

m) GJ borrowed $20,000 to help with the company's initial funding needs. GJ used $2,000 of funds to invest in municipal bonds. At the end of the year, GJ paid the $1,200 of interest expense that accrued on the loan during the year.

n) Jack lives 12 miles from the office. He carefully tracked his mileage and drove his truck 6,280 miles between the office and his home. He also drove an additional 7,200 miles traveling between the office and client sites. Jack did not use the truck for any other purposes. He did not keep track of the specific expenses associated with the truck. However, while traveling to a client site, Jack received a $150 speeding ticket. GJ reimbursed Jack for business mileage and for the speeding ticket.

o) GJ purchased two season tickets (20 games) to attend State U baseball games for a total of $1,100. Jack took existing and prospective clients to the games to maintain contact and find further work. This was very successful for Jack as GJ gained many new projects through substantial discussions with the clients following the games.

p) GJ paid $3,500 for meals at restaurants when sales employees met with prospective clients.

q) GJ had a client who needed Jack to perform work in Florida. Because Jack had never been to Florida before, he booked an extra day and night for sightseeing. Jack spent $400 for airfare and booked a hotel for three nights ($120/night). (Jack stayed two days for business purposes and one day for personal purposes.) He also rented a car for $45 per day. The client provided Jack's meals while Jack was doing business, but GJ paid all expenses.

r) GJ paid a total of $10,000 of wages to employees during the year, and cost of goods sold was $15,000.

Required:

a) What is GJ's net business income for tax purposes for the year?

b) As a C corporation, does GJ have a required tax year? If so, what would it be?

c) If GJ were a sole proprietorship, would it have a required tax year-end? If so, what would it be?

d) If GJ were an S corporation, would it have a required tax year-end? If so, what would it be?

81. Rex loves to work with his hands and is very good at making small figurines. Three years ago, Rex opened Bronze Age Miniatures (BAM) for business as a sole proprietorship. BAM produces miniature characters ranging from sci-fi characters (his favorite) to historical characters like George Washington (the most popular). Business has been going very well for him, and he has provided the following information relating to his business. Calculate the business taxable income for BAM assuming that BAM elects to account for its inventory of miniatures.

a) Rex received approval from the IRS to switch from the cash method of accounting to the accrual method of accounting effective January 1 of this year. At the end of last year, BAM reported accounts receivable that had not been included in income under the accrual method of $14,000 and accounts payable that had not been deducted under the accrual method of $5,000.

b) In March, BAM sold 5,000 miniature historical figures to History R Us Inc. (HRU), a retailer of historical artifacts and figurines, for $75,000.

c) HRU was so impressed with the figurines that it purchased in March that it wanted to contract with BAM to continue to produce the figurines for it for the next three years. HRU paid BAM $216,000 ($12 per figurine) on October 30 of this year to produce 500 figurines per month for 36 months beginning on November 1 of this year. BAM delivered 500 figurines on November 30 and again on December 30. Rex elects to use the deferral method to account for the transaction.

d) Though the sci-fi figurines were not quite as popular, BAM sold 400 figurines at a sci-fi convention in April. Rex accepted cash only and received $11,000 for these sales.

e) In January, BAM determined that it would not be able to collect on $2,000 of its beginning-of-the-year receivables, so it wrote off $2,000 of specific receivables. BAM sold 100,000 other figurines on credit for $120,000. BAM estimates that it will be unable to collect 5 percent of the sales revenue from these sales, but it has not been able to specifically identify any accounts to write off.

f) Assume that BAM correctly determined that its cost of goods sold using an appropriate inventory method is $54,000 this year.

g) The sci-fi convention in April was held in Chicago, Illinois. Rex attended the convention because he felt it was a good opportunity to gain new customers and to get new ideas for figurines. He paid $350 round-trip airfare, $100 for entrance to the convention, $210 for lodging, $65 for cab fare, and $110 for meals at restaurants during the trip. He was busy with business activities the entire trip.

h) On August 1, BAM purchased a 12-month insurance policy that covers its business property for accidents and casualties through July 31 of next year. The policy cost BAM $3,600.

i) BAM reported depreciation expense of $8,200 for this year.

j) Rex had previously operated his business out of his garage, but in January he decided to rent a larger space. He entered into a lease agreement on February 1 and paid $14,400 ($1,200 per month) to possess the space for the next 12 months (February of this year through January of next year).

k) Before he opened his doors for business, Rex spent $30,000 investigating and otherwise getting ready to do business. He expensed $5,000 immediately and is amortizing the remainder using the straight-line method over 180 months.

l) In December, BAM agreed to a 12-month, $8,000 contract with Advertise-With-Us (AWU) to produce a radio ad campaign. BAM paid $3,000 up front (in December of this year), and AWU agreed that BAM would owe the remaining $5,000 only if BAM's sales increased by 15 percent over the 9-month period after the contract was signed.

m) In November of this year, BAM paid $2,500 in business property taxes (based on asset values) covering the period December 1 of this year through November 30 of next year. In November of last year, BAM paid $1,500 for business property taxes (based on asset values) covering the period December 1 of last year through November 30 of this year.

82. Bryan followed in his father's footsteps and entered into the carpet business. He owns and operates I Do Carpet (IDC). Bryan prefers to install carpet only, but in order to earn additional revenue, he also cleans carpets and sells carpet-cleaning supplies. Compute his taxable income for the current year considering the following items:

a) IDC contracted with a homebuilder in December of last year to install carpet in 10 new homes being built. The contract price of $80,000 includes $50,000 for materials (carpet). The remaining $30,000 is for IDC's service of installing the carpet. The contract also stated that all money was to be paid up front. The homebuilder paid IDC in full on December 28 of last year. The contract required IDC to complete the work by January 31 of this year. Bryan purchased the necessary carpet on January 2 and began working on the first home January 4. He completed the last home on January 27 of this year.

b) IDC entered into several other contracts this year and completed the work before year-end. The work cost $130,000 in materials, and IDC elects to immediately deduct supplies. Bryan billed out $240,000 but only collected $220,000 by year-end. Of the $20,000 still owed to him, Bryan wrote off $3,000 he didn't expect to collect as a bad debt from a customer experiencing extreme financial difficulties.

c) IDC entered into a three-year contract to clean the carpets of an office building. The contract specified that IDC would clean the carpets monthly from July 1 of this year through June 30 three years hence. IDC received payment in full of $8,640 ($240 a month for 36 months) on June 30 of this year.

d) IDC sold 100 bottles of carpet stain remover this year for $5 per bottle (it collected $500). Rex sold 40 bottles on June 1 and 60 bottles on November 2. IDC had the following carpet-cleaning supplies on hand for this year, and IDC has elected to use the LIFO method of accounting for inventory under a perpetual inventory system:

Purchase Date	Bottles	Total Cost
November last year	40	$120
February this year	35	112
July this year	25	85
August this year	40	140
Totals	140	$457

e) On August 1 of this year, IDC needed more room for storage and paid $900 to rent a garage for 12 months.

f) On November 30 of this year, Bryan decided it was time to get his logo on the sides of his work van. IDC hired We Paint Anything Inc. (WPA) to do the job. It paid $500 down and agreed to pay the remaining $1,500 upon completion of the job. WPA indicated it wouldn't be able to begin the job until January 15 of next year, but the job would only take one week to complete. Due to circumstances beyond its control, WPA wasn't able to complete the job until April 1 of next year, at which time IDC paid the remaining $1,500.

g) In December, Bryan's son, Aiden, helped him finish some carpeting jobs. IDC owed Aiden $600 (reasonable) compensation for his work. However, Aiden did not receive the payment until January of next year.

h) IDC also paid $1,000 for interest on a short-term bank loan relating to the period from November 1 of this year through March 31 of next year.

83. Hank started a new business, Hank's Donut World (HW for short), in June of last year. He has requested your advice on the following specific tax matters associated with HW's first year of operations. Hank has estimated HW's income for the first year as follows:

Revenue:		
Donut sales	$252,000	
Catering revenues	71,550	$ 323,550
Expenditures:		
Donut supplies	$124,240	
Catering expense	27,910	
Salaries to shop employees	52,500	
Rent expense	40,050	
Accident insurance premiums	8,400	
Other business expenditures	6,850	−259,950
Net income		$ 63,600

HW operates as a sole proprietorship, and Hank reports on a calendar year. Hank uses the cash method of accounting and plans to do the same with HW (HW has no inventory of donuts because unsold donuts are not salable). HW does not purchase donut supplies on credit, nor does it generally make sales on credit. Hank has provided the following details for specific first-year transactions:

- A small minority of HW clients complained about the catering service. To mitigate these complaints, Hank's policy is to refund dissatisfied clients 50 percent of the catering fee. By the end of the first year, only two HW clients had complained but had not yet been paid refunds. The expected refunds amount to $1,700, and Hank reduced the reported catering fees for the first year to reflect the expected refund.
- In the first year, HW received a $6,750 payment from a client for catering a monthly breakfast for 30 consecutive months beginning in December. Because the payment didn't relate to last year, Hank excluded the entire amount when he calculated catering revenues.
- In July, HW paid $1,500 to ADMAN Co. for an advertising campaign to distribute fliers advertising HW's catering service. Unfortunately, this campaign violated a city code restricting advertising by fliers, and the city fined HW $250 for the violation. HW paid the fine, and Hank included the fine and the cost of the campaign in "other business" expenditures.
- In July, HW also paid $8,400 for a 24-month insurance policy that covers HW for accidents and casualties beginning on August 1 of the first year. Hank deducted the entire $8,400 as accident insurance premiums.
- In May of the first year, Hank signed a contract to lease the HW donut shop for 10 months. In conjunction with the contract, Hank paid $2,000 as a damage deposit and $8,050 for rent ($805 per month). Hank explained that the damage deposit was refundable at the end of the lease. At this time, Hank also paid $30,000 to lease kitchen equipment for 24 months ($1,250 per month). Both leases began on June 1 of the first year. In his estimate, Hank deducted these amounts ($40,050 in total) as rent expense.
- Hank signed a contract hiring WEGO Catering to help cater breakfasts. At year-end, WEGO asked Hank to hold the last catering payment for the year, $9,250, until after January 1 (apparently because WEGO didn't want to report the income on its tax return). The last check was delivered to WEGO in January after the end of the first year. However, because the payment related to the first year of operations, Hank included the $9,250 in last year's catering expense.

- Hank believes that the key to the success of HW has been hiring Jimbo Jones to supervise the donut production and manage the shop. Because Jimbo is such an important employee, HW purchased a "key-employee" term life insurance policy on his life. HW paid a $5,100 premium for this policy, and it will pay HW a $40,000 death benefit if Jimbo passes away any time during the next 12 months. The term of the policy began on September 1 of last year, and this payment was included in "other business" expenditures.
- In the first year, HW catered a large breakfast event to celebrate the city's anniversary. The city agreed to pay $7,100 for the event, but Hank forgot to notify the city of the outstanding bill until January of this year. When he mailed the bill in January, Hank decided to discount the charge to $5,500. On the bill, Hank thanked the mayor and the city council for their patronage and asked them to "send a little more business our way." This bill is not reflected in Hank's estimate of HW's income for the first year of operations.

Required:

a) Hank files his personal tax return on a calendar year, but he has not yet filed last year's personal tax return, nor has he filed a tax return reporting HW's results for the first year of operations. Explain when Hank should file the tax return for HW, and calculate the amount of taxable income generated by HW last year.

b) Determine the taxable income that HW will generate if Hank chooses to account for the business under the accrual method.

c) Describe how your solution might change if Hank incorporated HW before he commenced business last year.

84. R.E.M., a calendar-year corporation and Athens, Georgia, band, recently sold tickets ($20,000,000) for concerts scheduled in the United States for next year and the following two years. For financial statement purposes, R.E.M. will recognize the income from the ticket sales when it performs the concerts, and R.E.M is obligated to return the ticket payments should a concert be cancelled. For tax purposes, R.E.M. uses the accrual method and would prefer to defer the income from the ticket sales until after the concerts are performed. This is the first time that it has sold tickets one or two years in advance. Michael Stipe has asked for your advice. Write a memo to Michael explaining your findings.

UWorld | ROGER CPA Review

UWorld Roger CPA Review

Sample CPA Exam questions from Roger CPA Review are available in Connect as support for the topics in this text. These Multiple Choice Questions and Task-Based Simulations include expert-written explanations and solutions and provide a starting point for students to become familiar with the content and functionality of the actual CPA Exam.

chapter

10 Property Acquisition and Cost Recovery

Learning Objectives

Upon completing this chapter, you should be able to:

LO 10-1 Describe the cost recovery methods for recovering the cost of personal property, real property, intangible assets, and natural resources.

LO 10-2 Determine the applicable cost recovery (depreciation) life, method, and convention for tangible personal and real property and the deduction allowable under basic MACRS.

LO 10-3 Calculate the deduction allowable under the additional special cost recovery rules (§179, bonus, and listed property).

LO 10-4 Calculate the deduction for amortization.

LO 10-5 Explain cost recovery of natural resources and the allowable depletion methods.

Adam Sternin/Cavan Images/Image Source

Storyline Summary

Taxpayer:	Teton Mountaineering Technology, LLC (Teton)—a calendar-year, single-member LLC (treated as a sole proprietorship for tax purposes)
Location:	Cody, Wyoming
President/ Founder:	Steve Dallimore (he/him/his)
Current situation:	Teton has acquired property for its manufacturing operations and wants to understand the tax consequences of property acquisitions.

Several years ago while climbing the Black Ice Couloir (pronounced "cool-wahr") in Grand Teton National Park, Steve Dallimore and his buddy got into a desperate situation. The climbers planned to move fast and light and be home before an approaching storm reached the Tetons. But just shy of the summit, climbing conditions forced them to turn back. Huddled in a wet sleeping bag in a dark snow cave waiting for the tempest to pass, Steve had an epiphany—he conceived of a design for a better ice-climbing tool. Since that moment, Steve has been working toward making his dream—designing and selling his own line of climbing equipment—a reality. Steve spent the next few years planning his business while continuing his current sales career. In December 2020, Steve decided to exercise his stock options, leave his sales position, and start Teton Mountaineering Technology (Teton). At the beginning of 2021, Steve identified a location for his business in Cody, Wyoming, and purchased a building and some equipment to begin his business. He soon discovered that he needed help dealing with the tax issues related to his business assets.

(to be continued . . .)

Steve obviously has many issues to address and decisions to make. In this chapter, we focus on the tax issues relating to the assets Steve acquires for use in his new business. In particular, we explain how Teton determines its cost recovery (depreciation, amortization, and depletion) deductions for the assets in the year the business begins and in subsequent years.[1] These deductions can generate significant tax savings for companies in capital-intensive industries.

This chapter explores the tax consequences of acquiring new or used property, depreciation methods businesses may use to recover the cost of their assets, and other special cost recovery incentives. The Tax Cuts and Jobs Act of 2017 (TCJA) made many changes to the way taxpayers determine their depreciation deductions. Although these changes dramatically accelerate the depreciation deductions for many assets, they do not apply to all assets. Therefore, it is important to understand the basic depreciation rules as we discuss in more detail later in the chapter. To begin, we discuss the amount that is subject to cost recovery. We then discuss the basic depreciation rules using the assets Steve acquires for his business in 2021. We follow basic depreciation rules by discussing the special incentives using Steve's 2022 asset acquisitions.[2] We also address the tax consequences of using intangible assets and natural resources in business activities.

COST RECOVERY AND TAX BASIS FOR COST RECOVERY

LO 10-1

Most businesses make a significant investment in property, plant, and equipment that is expected to provide benefits over a number of years. Both for financial accounting and generally for tax accounting purposes, businesses must capitalize the cost of assets with a useful life of more than one year (on the balance sheet) rather than expense the cost immediately. Businesses are allowed to use various methods to allocate the cost of these assets over time because the assets are subject to wear, tear, and obsolescence.

The method of **cost recovery** depends on the nature of the underlying asset. **Depreciation** is the method of deducting the cost of *tangible* personal and real property (other than land) over time. **Amortization** is the method of deducting the cost of **intangible assets** over time. Finally, **depletion** is the method of deducting the cost of natural resources over time. Exhibit 10-1 summarizes these concepts.

EXHIBIT 10-1 Assets and Cost Recovery

Asset Type	Cost Recovery Method
Personal property comprises tangible assets such as automobiles, equipment, and machinery.	Depreciation
Real property comprises buildings and land (although land is nondepreciable).	Depreciation
Intangible assets are nonphysical assets such as goodwill and patents.	Amortization
Natural resources are commodities that are considered valuable in their natural form such as oil, coal, timber, and gold.	Depletion

Generally, a significant portion of a firm's assets consists of property, plant, equipment, intangibles, or even natural resources. In most cases, this holds true for small businesses like Teton and also for large publicly traded companies. For example, Exhibit 10-2 describes the assets held by Weyerhaeuser, a publicly traded timber company. As indicated in Exhibit 10-2, Weyerhaeuser has over $2 billion in property and equipment (net of depreciation) and $11.8 billion in timber (net of depletion), together comprising over 80 percent of its assets.

[1]Cost recovery is the common term used to describe the process by which businesses allocate the cost of their fixed assets over the time period in which the assets are used.

[2]The rules for basic depreciation that we discuss for the 2021 assets are the same as for assets acquired in 2022.

EXHIBIT 10-2 Weyerhaeuser Assets

Assets (in millions) per 2020 10-K Statement	2020	2019
Total current assets	$ 1,609	$ 1,611
Property and equipment, net (Note 7)	2,013	1,969
Construction in progress	73	130
Timber and timberlands at cost, less depletion charged to disposal	11,827	11,929
Minerals and mineral rights, less depletion	268	281
Deferred tax assets (Note 20)	120	72
Other assets	401	414
Total assets	$16,311	$16,406

Attention to detail is important because the **tax basis** of an asset must be reduced by the cost recovery deductions allowed or *allowable.* If a business fails to deduct (by mistake or error) the allowable amount of depreciation for the year, the business still must reduce the asset's tax basis by the depreciation the taxpayer could have deducted under the method the business is using to depreciate the asset. This means that the business will never receive a tax benefit for the amount of depreciation it failed to deduct.[3]

THE KEY FACTS

Initial Basis

- An asset's initial basis includes all costs needed to purchase the asset, prepare it for use, and begin using it.
- Initial basis is usually the same for book and tax purposes.
- Special basis rules apply when personal-use assets are converted to business use and when assets are acquired through tax-deferred transactions, gifts, or inheritances.

Basis for Cost Recovery

Businesses may begin recouping the cost of purchased business assets once they begin using the asset in their business (i.e., they place it in service).[4] Once the business establishes its cost in an asset, the business recovers the cost of the asset through cost recovery deductions such as depreciation, amortization, or depletion. The amount of an asset's cost that has yet to be recovered through cost recovery deductions is called the asset's **adjusted basis** or tax basis.[5] An asset's adjusted basis can be computed by subtracting the accumulated depreciation (or amortization or depletion) from the asset's initial or historical basis.[6]

For most assets, the initial basis is the cost plus all the expenses to purchase, prepare for use, and begin using the asset. These expenses include sales tax, shipping costs, and installation costs. The financial accounting and tax rules for computing an asset's basis are very similar. Thus, a purchased asset's initial basis is generally the same for both tax

[3]If a business discovers that it failed to claim allowable depreciation in a previous year, it can deduct the depreciation it failed to claim in prior years in the current year by filing an automatic consent to a change in accounting method using Form 3115 (Rev. Procs. 2002-9, 2004-11, and 2015-14).

[4]Basis is defined under §1012. The mere purchase of an asset does not trigger cost recovery deductions. A business must begin using the asset for business purposes (place it in service) in order to depreciate the asset. However, because businesses generally acquire and place assets in service at the same time, we refer to these terms interchangeably throughout the chapter.

[5]Throughout the chapter, we use several different terms to refer to an asset's tax basis. The differences in these terms are somewhat subtle but can often be important. For example, an asset's initial basis refers to the tax basis of an asset at the time the taxpayer initially acquires the asset. If a taxpayer purchases the asset, the initial basis is the same as its cost. However, if a taxpayer acquires the asset through means other than purchase (e.g., gift, inheritance, tax-deferred transaction, or conversion from personal use), the initial basis will typically differ from the asset's cost. We discuss some of these differences in the Property Dispositions chapter. The broad term *tax basis* refers to an asset's carrying value for tax purposes at a given point in time. When an asset's initial basis is recovered through depreciation, amortization, or depletion, the asset's tax basis is often referred to as the adjusted tax basis, or sometimes simply the adjusted basis. It is not common to use the term adjusted tax basis for assets that are not subject to cost recovery. For example, the tax basis for a common stock investment would typically be referred to simply as its tax basis rather than its adjusted tax basis. Finally, the depreciable basis of an asset refers to the amount of the initial basis that can be depreciated over time using the regular depreciation rules. In many cases, the depreciable basis and the initial basis are the same—for example, in the case of real property (i.e., buildings). However, the depreciable basis may differ from the initial basis when taxpayers take advantage of special incentives (such as §179 expensing or bonus depreciation, discussed later in the chapter) that accelerate an asset's cost recovery in the year it is placed in service.

[6]§1011.

and book purposes.[7] So how do taxpayers know whether they should immediately deduct the cost of an asset or capitalize and depreciate it? Taxpayers generally capitalize assets with useful lives over one year, but there are exceptions to this rule. The Treasury has issued regulations that are quite lengthy (over 200 pages) and complex to guide taxpayers in answering this question.[8] The regulations provide a *de minimis* safe harbor that allows taxpayers to immediately deduct low-cost personal property items used in their business. The definition of "low-cost" depends on whether the taxpayer has an applicable financial statement, which generally means a certified, audited financial statement. If taxpayers have an applicable financial statement, they may use the *de minimis* safe harbor to immediately deduct amounts paid for tangible property up to $5,000 per invoice or item.[9] If taxpayers don't have an applicable financial statement, they may use the safe harbor to deduct amounts up to $2,500 per invoice or item. Taxpayers generally use the invoice amount to determine whether they meet the safe harbor; however, if the total invoice amount exceeds the $5,000/$2,500 threshold and the invoice provides detailed cost information about each item, taxpayers may immediately deduct individual items that are less than the threshold amount. Taxpayers must capitalize the cost of personal property that does not fall under the *de minimis* safe harbor provision.[10]

When a business acquires multiple assets for one purchase price, the tax laws require the business to determine a cost basis for each separate asset. For example, for Teton's building purchase, Teton must treat the building and land as separate assets. In these types of acquisitions, businesses determine the initial basis of each asset by allocating a portion of the purchase price to each asset based on that asset's value relative to the total value of all the assets the business acquired in the same purchase. The asset values are generally determined by an appraisal.[11]

Example 10-1

Steve determined that he needed machinery and office furniture for a manufacturing facility and a design studio (located in Cody, Wyoming). During 2021, Steve purchased the following assets and incurred the following costs to prepare the assets for business use. His cost basis in each asset is determined as follows:

Asset	Date Acquired	(1) Purchase Price	(2) Business Preparation Costs	(1) + (2) Cost Basis
Office furniture	2/3/21	$ 20,000		$ 20,000
Warehouse	5/1/21	270,000*	$5,000 (minor modifications)	275,000
Land (10 acres)	5/1/21	75,000*		75,000
Machinery	7/22/21	600,000	$10,000 (delivery and setup)	610,000
Delivery truck (used)	8/17/21	25,000		25,000

*Note that the warehouse and the land were purchased together for $345,000. Steve and the seller determined that the value (and cost) of the warehouse was $270,000 and the value (and cost) of the land was $75,000.

What if: Assume Steve acquired a printer for $800 on July 9. Would he immediately deduct the cost of the printer or capitalize it?

Answer: Assuming that Steve has a policy to expense items costing $2,500 or less for nontax purposes, he would be able to immediately deduct the cost of the printer under the *de minimis* safe harbor.[12]

[7]However, special basis rules apply when an asset is acquired through a tax-deferred transaction. See discussion in the Property Dispositions chapter.

[8]Reg. §§1.263(a)-1, -2, -3.

[9]Taxpayers must have accounting procedures in place at the beginning of the year treating items costing less than a specified dollar figure as an expense for nontax purposes.

[10]Separate rules apply when taxpayers purchase materials and supplies to be used in their business (Reg. §1.162-3).

[11]Reg. §1.167(a)-5.

[12]Later in this chapter, we discuss alternative ways to immediately deduct the cost of certain assets (§179 expensing and bonus depreciation). The first step, however, is to determine if it must be capitalized or immediately deducted under the Treasury regulations for §263.

When a business incurs additional costs associated with an asset after the asset has been placed in service, are these costs immediately deducted or are they capitalized? In general, the answer depends on whether the expenditure constitutes routine maintenance on the asset or whether it results in a "betterment, restoration, or new or different use for the property."[13] Taxpayers can immediately deduct the costs if they meet the routine maintenance safe harbor rules provided in the Treasury regulations.[14] Routine maintenance is defined as preventative or cyclical maintenance that is an essential part of the ongoing care and upkeep of a building or building system. Building systems include the critical systems of a building such as electrical, HVAC, security, and lighting. Costs related to the replacement of damaged or worn parts with comparable and commercially available replacement parts arising from inspecting, cleaning, and testing of the property are immediately deductible when the taxpayer fully expects to perform the activity more than once during a 10-year period (for buildings and structures related to buildings), or more than once during the property's class life (for property other than buildings).

Example 10-2

What if: Suppose that Steve's business requires an annual safety certification on all its equipment and machinery. As a result of a required inspection of the machinery, Steve finds a defect in the engine blade (not a major component) of one of his machines and must replace the engine blade at a cost of $3,000. Can Steve immediately deduct the cost of the new engine blade?

Answer: Steve's business requires an annual safety certification inspection; thus, Steve meets the requirement of reasonably expecting to perform the activity more than once during the machinery's class life. Assuming that Steve replaces the engine blade with a comparable, commercially available part, he may immediately deduct the $3,000 cost of the new engine blade.

If the routine maintenance safe harbor rules do not apply, then taxpayers must determine whether the costs result in a betterment, restoration, or adaptation for a new or different use for the property.[15] If so, they must capitalize the costs; if not, they may immediately deduct the costs.[16] For example, if the roof of Teton's warehouse was completely replaced because it was leaking, Steve would be required to capitalize the costs to replace the roof as a restoration because a significant portion (100 percent) of a major component was replaced. If Teton needed to replace only 10 percent of the roof, Steve would most likely be able to immediately deduct the costs.[17]

Special rules apply when determining the tax basis of assets converted from personal to business use or assets acquired through a tax-deferred exchange, gift, or inheritance. If an asset is used for personal purposes and is later converted to business (or rental) use, the basis for cost recovery purposes is the *lesser* of (1) the cost basis of the asset or (2) the fair market value of the asset on the date of conversion to business use.[18] This rule prevents taxpayers from converting a nondeductible personal loss into a deductible business loss. For example, if Steve had purchased a truck for $20,000 several

[13]Reg. §1.263(a)-3.

[14]The routine maintenance safe harbor is discussed in Reg. §1.263(a)-3(i). In addition to the routine maintenance safe harbor, the regulations provide an additional safe harbor for small taxpayers. This safe harbor allows taxpayers with average annual gross receipts over the last three years of $10 million or less to immediately deduct amounts paid for maintenance and improvement on buildings with an unadjusted basis of $1 million or less if the amounts expended are less than the lesser of 2 percent of the building's unadjusted basis or $10,000 [Reg. §1.263(a)-3(h)].

[15]Reg. §1.263(a)-3.

[16]The regulations provide detailed guidelines for taxpayers to use to establish when they have expenditures related to these three distinct concepts. Coverage of these concepts is beyond the scope of this chapter. See Reg. §1.263(a)-3 for details.

[17]Steve may have an opportunity to expense the cost of the roof under §179 (discussed later in the chapter) if the property meets the definition of real property for purposes of the expensing provision.

[18]Reg. §§1.167(g)-1, 1.168(i)-4(b). However, this rule creates an interesting situation when selling converted assets. The taxpayer uses the lower of the adjusted basis or the fair market value at the time of the conversion for computing loss but uses the adjusted basis to compute a gain.

years ago for personal use but decided to use it as a delivery truck when its value had declined to $15,000, his basis in the truck for cost recovery purposes would be $15,000. The $5,000 decline in the truck's value from $20,000 to $15,000 would be a nondeductible personal loss to Steve, and the reduction in basis ensures that he will not be allowed to deduct the loss as a business loss.

Assets acquired through a tax-deferred transaction, such as a like-kind exchange (like-kind exchanges are discussed later in the Property Dispositions chapter), generally take the same basis the taxpayer had in the property that the taxpayer transferred in the transaction. Assets acquired by gift have a carryover basis. This means that the taxpayer's basis in property received through a gift is generally the same basis the transferor had in the property.[19] For example, if Steve's parents gave him equipment worth $45,000 to help him start his business and his parents had purchased the equipment 10 years earlier for $25,000, Steve's basis in the equipment would be $25,000 (the same basis his parents had in the equipment). Assets acquired through inheritance generally receive a basis equal to the fair market value on the transferor's date of death.[20] For example, if Steve inherited a building worth $90,000 from his grandfather, who originally paid $35,000 for it, Steve's basis would be $90,000 (its fair market value at date of death) because Steve acquired it through an inheritance.

ETHICS

Catherine Travis is starting a new business. She has several assets that she wants to use in her business that she has been using personally. Because she plans to convert several assets from personal to business use, she will need to find out how much each asset is worth so she can determine her basis for depreciating the assets. Catherine has decided that getting an appraisal would be too costly, so she simply uses her cost basis for the assets. What do you think of Catherine's strategy for determining her business asset bases?

DEPRECIATION

LO 10-2

THE KEY FACTS

Tax Depreciation

To depreciate an asset, a business must determine:

- Original basis
- Depreciation method
- Recovery period
- Depreciation convention

As a preface to this section, the TCJA made many changes to how taxpayers will recover the cost of their assets for the next several years. In this chapter, we discuss the depreciation provisions both before and after the TCJA effective dates for several reasons. First, existing assets continue to follow the rules in place before the tax law change; therefore, for assets placed in service before the effective dates of the TCJA, taxpayers will need to understand the rules in effect at the time the assets were placed in service. Second, the new provisions provide very generous deductions for personal property; however, taxpayers may opt out of these provisions and instead follow the pre-TCJA rules. Taxpayers with losses may opt to forgo the large depreciation deductions provided under the TCJA to reduce their losses, which may be subject to limitations (e.g., NOL limitations and excess business loss limitations). These taxpayers would then use the standard depreciation methods used prior to the TCJA. Third, for assets that do not qualify for the special provisions in the TCJA, taxpayers must fall back to the standard depreciation methods used under prior law. For example, some states do not allow the additional depreciation provided by the TCJA. Taxpayers doing business in these states will need to follow the basic depreciation rules in place prior to TCJA. Finally, the TCJA expanded §179 expensing (effective for assets placed in service after December 31, 2017) and extended bonus depreciation (effective for assets placed in service after September 27, 2017); however, bonus depreciation is temporary and is scheduled to begin phasing out for assets placed in service after December 31, 2022. Therefore, it is important to understand the rules in effect both before and after the effective date of the TCJA.

With that in mind, we proceed by discussing the basic rules for determining depreciation. In this section, we consider how Steve can depreciate the assets he acquired in 2021

[19]§1015. The basis may be increased if the transferor is required to pay gift tax on the transfer [see §1015(d)]. In addition, special dual basis rules apply if the basis in the gifted property at the gift date is greater than its fair market value.

[20]§1014. In certain circumstances, the estate can elect an alternative valuation date six months after death.

assuming he does not want to use any of the special depreciation provisions. We then discuss the special rules (§179, bonus depreciation, and listed property), which were modified and expanded by the TCJA.

Since 1986, businesses have calculated their tax depreciation using the **Modified Accelerated Cost Recovery System (MACRS)**—which is pronounced "makers" by tax accountants.[21] Compared to financial (book) depreciation, MACRS tax depreciation is quite simple. To compute MACRS depreciation for an asset, the business need only know the asset's *depreciable basis,* the date it was placed in service, the applicable *depreciation method,* the asset's **recovery period** (or depreciable "life"), and the applicable depreciation *convention* (used to compute the amount of depreciation deductible in the year of acquisition and the year of disposition). The method, recovery period, and convention vary based on whether the asset is **personal property** or **real property.** Before we turn our attention to the determination of the depreciation deduction for personal property, it is important to emphasize that there may be a difference in when an asset is acquired and when it is placed in service. Being placed in service requires that the property is in a condition or state of readiness and availability for a specifically assigned function. This requirement is often met when an asset is acquired but may not be when additional installation is required or modifications must be made to ready the asset for its intended use.[22]

Personal Property Depreciation

Personal property includes all tangible property, such as computers, automobiles, furniture, machinery, and equipment, other than real property. Note that *personal* property and *personal-use* property are not the same thing. Personal property denotes any property that is not real property (e.g., building and land), while personal-use property is any property used for personal purposes (e.g., a personal residence is personal-use property even though it is real property). Personal property is relatively short-lived and subject to obsolescence, as compared to real property.

Depreciation Method MACRS provides three acceptable methods for depreciating personal property: 200 percent (double) declining balance (DB), 150 percent declining balance, and straight-line.[23] The 200 percent declining balance method is the default method. This method takes twice the straight-line percentage of depreciation in the first year and continues to take twice the straight-line percentage on the asset's declining basis until switching to the straight-line method in the year that the straight-line method over the remaining life provides a greater depreciation expense. Fortunately, as we describe below, the IRS provides depreciation tables to simplify the calculations.

Profitable businesses with relatively high marginal tax rates generally choose to use the 200 percent declining balance method because it generates the largest depreciation deduction in the early years of the asset's life and, thus, the highest current-year, after-tax cash flows. For tax planning purposes, taxpayers that currently have lower marginal tax rates but expect their marginal tax rates to increase in the near future may elect to use the straight-line method because that method generates less depreciation in the early years of the asset's life, relatively, and more depreciation in the later years when their marginal tax rates may increase.

Example 10-3

If Teton wants to accelerate its current MACRS depreciation deductions to the extent possible, what method should it use to depreciate its office furniture, machinery, and delivery truck?

Answer: The 200 percent declining balance method (default). Teton could elect to use either the 150 percent declining balance or the straight-line method if it wants a less-accelerated method for determining its depreciation deductions.

[21] IRS Publication 946 provides a useful summary of MACRS depreciation.

[22] Reg. §1.167(a)-11(e)(1)(1); *Brown v. Comm'r,* TC Memo 2013-275.

[23] MACRS includes two depreciation systems: the general depreciation system (GDS) and the alternative depreciation system (ADS). MACRS provides three methods under GDS (200 percent DB, 150 percent DB, and straight-line) and one method under ADS (straight-line).

Each year, businesses elect the depreciation method for the assets placed in service during *that year.* Specifically, businesses elect one depreciation method for all similar assets they acquire that year.[24] Thus, if a business acquires several different machines during the year, it must use the same method to depreciate all of the machines. However, the methods may differ for machines acquired in different tax years.

Depreciation Recovery Period For financial accounting purposes, an asset's recovery period (depreciable life) is based on its taxpayer-determined estimated useful life. In contrast, for tax purposes, an asset's recovery period is predetermined by the IRS in Rev. Proc. 87-56. This revenue procedure helps taxpayers categorize each of their assets based upon the property's description. Once the business has determined the appropriate categories for its assets, it can use the revenue procedure to identify the recovery period for all assets in a particular category. For example, Teton placed office furniture in service during the year. By examining the excerpt from Rev. Proc. 87-56 provided in Exhibit 10-3, you can see that Category or Asset Class 00.11 includes office furniture and that assets in this category, including Teton's office furniture, have a recovery period of seven years (emphasis in excerpt added through bold text).[25]

EXHIBIT 10-3 Excerpt from Revenue Procedure 87-56

Description of Assets Included	Years		
Specific depreciable assets used in all business activities, except as noted:	**Class Life**	**General Recovery Period**	**Alternative Recovery Period**
00.11 Office Furniture, Fixtures, and Equipment: Includes furniture and fixtures that are not a structural component of a building. Includes such assets as desks, files, safes, and communications equipment. Does not include communications equipment that is included in other classes.	10	7	10
00.12 Information Systems: Includes computers and their peripheral equipment used in administering normal business transactions and the maintenance of business records.	6	5	5
00.241 Light General Purpose Trucks: Includes trucks for use over the road (actual unloaded weight less than 13,000 pounds) . . .	4	5	5
34.0 Manufacture of Fabricated Metal Products Special Tools: Includes assets used in the production of metal cans, tinware . . .	12	7	12

While even this small excerpt from Rev. Proc. 87-56 may seem a bit intimidating, you can classify the vast majority of business assets acquired by knowing a few common recovery periods. Exhibit 10-4 lists the most commonly purchased assets and their recovery periods.

To this point, our discussion has emphasized computing regular MACRS depreciation for new assets. Does the process change when businesses acquire used assets? No, it is exactly the same. For example, Teton purchased a *used* delivery truck. The fact that the truck is used does not change its MACRS recovery period. No matter how long the

[24]Technically, similar assets are assets in the same property class (with the same recovery period).

[25]The "alternative" recovery period in Rev. Proc. 87-56 refers to an asset's life under the alternative depreciation system referred to as ADS (which we discuss later in this chapter). The class life referred to in Rev. Proc. 87-56 refers to the midpoint of the asset depreciation range (ADR) applicable under pre-ACRS and has little or no meaning under MACRS.

previous owner used the truck, Teton will restart the five-year recovery period for light general-purpose trucks to depreciate the delivery truck (see Exhibit 10-4).

Under MACRS, the tax recovery period for machinery and equipment is seven years. Using Rev. Proc. 87-56, Teton has determined the cost recovery periods for the personal property it purchased and placed in service during 2021. Exhibit 10-5 summarizes this information.

EXHIBIT 10-4 **Recovery Period for Most Common Business Assets**

Asset Description (Summary of Rev. Proc. 87-56)	Recovery Period
Cars, light general-purpose trucks, and computers and peripheral equipment	5 years
Office furniture, fixtures, and equipment	7 years
Qualified improvement property (straight-line method)	15 years

EXHIBIT 10-5 **Teton Personal Property Summary (Base Scenario)**

Asset	Date Acquired	Quarter Acquired	Cost Basis	Recovery Period	Reference
Office furniture	2/3/21	1st	$ 20,000	7	Example 10-1; Exhibit 10-3
Machinery	7/22/21	3rd	610,000	7	Example 10-1; Exhibit 10-3
Delivery truck	8/17/21	3rd	25,000	5	Example 10-1; Exhibit 10-3
Total personal property			**$655,000**		

Depreciation Conventions Once a business has determined the depreciation methods and recovery periods for the assets it placed in service during the year, it then must determine the applicable depreciation conventions. The depreciation convention specifies the portion of a full-year's depreciation the business can deduct for an asset in the year the asset is first placed in service *and* in the year the asset is sold. For *personal property,* taxpayers must use either the **half-year convention** or the **mid-quarter convention.** But taxpayers are *not* free to choose between the two conventions. The half-year convention applies most of the time; however, under certain conditions, taxpayers are required to use the mid-quarter convention (discussed below). The depreciation convention is determined annually for the assets placed in service in that year. Once the convention is determined for the assets acquired during the year, the convention remains the same for the entire recovery period for those assets. For example, if a taxpayer placed assets in service in year 1 and was required to use the mid-quarter convention for year 1, depreciation calculated in year 2 for these assets would continue using the mid-quarter convention even though the taxpayer may not be required to use the mid-quarter convention for assets placed in service in year 2.

Before MACRS, taxpayers were required to use the half-year convention for all personal property placed in service during the year. However, Congress believed that many businesses took unfair advantage of the half-year convention by purposely acquiring assets at the end of the year that they otherwise would have acquired at the beginning of the next taxable year. Thus, businesses received one-half of a year's depreciation for assets that they used for only a small portion of the year. Even though the half-year convention is the default convention, policy makers introduced the *mid-quarter convention* under MACRS to limit or prevent this type of opportunistic behavior. Nevertheless, as we discuss below, the new tax laws allow taxpayers to accelerate their cost recovery deductions no matter when during the year the assets are placed in service. Consequently, the mid-quarter convention may have limited application to assets placed in service under current law.

Half-year convention. The half-year convention allows one-half of a full-year's depreciation in the year the asset is placed in service (and in the year in which it is disposed), regardless of when it was actually placed in service. For example, when the half-year convention applies to a calendar-year business, an asset placed in service on either February 3 or August 17 is treated as though it was placed in service on July 1, which is the middle of the calendar year. Thus, under this convention, Teton would deduct one-half of a year's depreciation for the machinery, office furniture, and delivery truck even though it acquired the machinery, delivery truck, and office furniture at various times during the year (see Exhibit 10-5). The half-year convention is built into the depreciation tables provided by the IRS, which simplifies the depreciation calculation for the year the asset is placed into service.

THE KEY FACTS

Half-Year Convention

- One-half of a year's depreciation is allowed in the first and the last years of an asset's life.
- The IRS depreciation tables automatically account for the half-year convention in the acquisition year.
- If an asset is disposed of before it is fully depreciated, only one-half of the table's applicable depreciation percentage is allowed in the year of disposition.

Mid-quarter convention. Businesses must use the mid-quarter convention when *more* than 40 percent of their total *tangible personal property* that they place in service during the year is placed in service during the *fourth* quarter. Under the mid-quarter convention, businesses treat assets *as though* they were placed in service during the middle of the *quarter* in which the business actually placed the assets into service. For example, when the mid-quarter convention applies, if a business places an asset in service on December 1 (in the fourth quarter), it must treat the asset as though it was placed in service on November 15, which is the middle of the fourth quarter. Consequently, the business deducts only one-half of a quarter's depreciation in the year the asset is placed in service (depreciation for the second half of November and the entire month of December). In addition, if the mid-quarter convention applies, businesses must use the convention for *all* tangible personal property placed in service during the year—even assets placed in service in quarters other than the fourth quarter. The mid-quarter test is applied after the §179 expense but before bonus depreciation (discussed later in the chapter), meaning that to the extent property is expensed under §179, it is not included in the mid-quarter test. The IRS depreciation tables have built in the mid-quarter convention to simplify the calculations.

For assets placed in service under the TCJA regime (effective for assets acquired after September 27, 2017), the mid-quarter convention will be largely irrelevant as businesses can use either §179 or 100 percent bonus depreciation to recover the cost in full in the year of acquisition. However, for assets placed in service before TCJA and for assets that fail to qualify for §179 and bonus depreciation, the mid-quarter convention continues to apply.

Calculating Depreciation for Personal Property Once a business has identified the applicable method, recovery period, and convention for personal property, tax depreciation is relatively easy to calculate because the Internal Revenue Service provides depreciation percentage tables in Rev. Proc. 87-57. The percentages in the depreciation tables for tangible personal property incorporate the method and convention. Accordingly, there are separate tables for each combination of depreciation method (200 percent declining balance, 150 percent declining balance, and straight-line) and convention (half-year and mid-quarter; each quarter has its own table). To determine the depreciation for an asset for the year, use the following steps:

Step 1: Determine the appropriate convention (half-year or mid-quarter) by determining whether more than 40 percent of qualified property was placed in service in the last quarter of the tax year.

Step 2: Locate the applicable table provided in Rev. Proc. 87-57 (reproduced in Appendix A of this chapter).

Step 3: Select the column that corresponds with the asset's recovery period.

Step 4: Find the row identifying the year of the asset's recovery period.

The tables are constructed so that the intersection of the row and column provides the percentage of the asset's *depreciable basis* that is deductible as depreciation expense for the particular year. As we discuss later, the depreciable basis used for basic depreciation is the initial basis less the amount of §179 expense and bonus depreciation taken on the asset. Thus, depreciation expense for a particular asset is the product of the percentage from the table and the asset's *depreciable basis.*

Applying the Half-Year Convention Consider Table 1 in Appendix A at the end of the chapter that shows the depreciation percentages for MACRS 200 percent declining balance using the half-year convention. If a seven-year asset is placed into service during the current year, the depreciation percentage is 14.29 percent [the intersection of row 1 (year 1) and the seven-year property column].

Notice from Table 1 that the depreciation percentages for five-year property extend for six years and the percentages for seven-year property extend for eight years. Why does it take six years to fully depreciate an asset with a five-year recovery period and eight years for a seven-year asset? Because the business does not deduct a full-year's depreciation in the first year, an entire year of depreciation is effectively split between the first and last years. For example, when the half-year convention applies to a five-year asset, the taxpayer deducts one-half of a year's depreciation in year 1 and one-half of a year's depreciation in year 6.

Example 10-4

Teton is using the 200 percent declining balance method and half-year convention to compute depreciation on its 2021 personal property additions. What is Teton's 2021 depreciation deduction for these assets?

Answer: $95,027, computed as follows:

Asset	Date Placed in Service	(1) Original Basis	(2) Rate	(1) × (2) Depreciation
Office furniture	February 3	$ 20,000	14.29%	$ 2,858
Machinery	July 22	610,000	14.29%	87,169
Used delivery truck	August 17	25,000	20.00%	5,000
Total				**$95,027**

Because the office furniture and machinery have a seven-year recovery period and it is the first year for depreciation, the depreciation rate is 14.29 percent (see Table 1). The depreciation rate for the used delivery truck (five-year property) is 20 percent (see Table 1) and is determined in a similar manner.

Calculating depreciation for assets in years after the year of acquisition is also relatively simple. Again, using Table 1 to compute depreciation for the second year, the taxpayer would multiply the asset's initial basis by the percentage in the *year 2* row; in the following year, the taxpayer would use the percentage in the *year 3* row; and so on.

Example 10-5

What if: Assume that Teton holds the tangible personal property it acquired and placed in service in 2021 until the assets are fully depreciated. Using the IRS-provided tables (see Table 1), how would Teton determine its depreciation expense for 2021 through 2028?

Answer: See the following table:

(*continued on page 10-12*)

Depreciation over Asset Recovery Period					
Recovery Period	Year	7-Year Office Furniture	7-Year Machinery	5-Year Delivery Truck	Yearly Total
1	2021	$ 2,858	$ 87,169	$ 5,000	$ 95,027
2	2022	4,898	149,389	8,000	162,287
3	2023	3,498	106,689	4,800	114,987
4	2024	2,498	76,189	2,880	81,567
5	2025	1,786	54,473	2,880	59,139
6	2026	1,784	54,412	1,440	57,636
7	2027	1,786	54,473	N/A	56,259
8	2028	892	27,206	N/A	28,098
Accumulated Depreciation		$20,000	$610,000	$25,000	$655,000

Half-year convention for year of disposition. Businesses often sell or dispose of assets before they fully depreciate them. Recall that the half-year convention applies in both the year of acquisition and the year of disposition. Note, however, that the tables can't anticipate when a business may dispose of an asset. Accordingly, the tables only provide depreciation percentages for assets assuming the asset won't be disposed of before it is fully depreciated. That is, for each year in the asset's recovery period, the tables provide a percentage for an entire year's depreciation. So, to calculate the depreciation for the year of disposition, the business first calculates depreciation for the *entire year* as if the property had not been disposed of. Then the business applies the half-year convention by multiplying the full-year's depreciation by 50 percent (one-half of a year's depreciation).[26] Note, however, that if a business acquires and disposes of an asset in the same tax year, it is not allowed to claim any depreciation on the asset.

Example 10-6

What if: Assume that Teton sells all of its office furniture in 2022 (the year after it buys it). What is Teton's depreciation for the office furniture in the year of disposition (2022)?

Answer: $2,449, calculated using the MACRS Half-Year Convention table (Table 1) as follows:

Asset	Amount	Explanation
(1) Office furniture	$20,000	Original basis
(2) Depreciation percentage	24.49%	Seven-year property, year 2
(3) Full year of depreciation	$ 4,898	(1) × (2)
(4) Half-year convention percentage	50%	Depreciation limit in year of disposal
Depreciation in year of disposal	**$ 2,449**	(3) × (4)

What if: Assume that Teton sold all of its office furniture in year 1 (the year it bought it and placed it in service). How much depreciation expense can Teton deduct for the office furniture in year 1?

Answer: $0. A business is not allowed to claim any depreciation expense for assets it acquires and disposes of in the same tax year.

[26]Suppose Teton sells the five-year delivery truck in year 6 on January 5. What depreciation percentage should Teton use for purposes of determining year 6 depreciation? Teton should take one-half year's depreciation on the truck. The percentage shown in Table 1 for the year of an asset's recovery period (in this case, year 6) already reflects the half-year convention, so Teton would take $1,440 of depreciation regardless of when during year 6 the truck was sold.

Applying the Mid-Quarter Convention When the mid-quarter convention applies, the process for computing depreciation is the same as it is when the half-year convention applies, except that businesses use a separate table for each quarter. After categorizing the assets by recovery period and grouping them into quarters, businesses consult the Mid-Quarter Convention tables (Tables 2a–2d in Appendix A to this chapter) to determine the depreciation percentage for each asset group.

The depreciation deduction for an asset is the product of the asset's original basis and the percentage from the table.

Example 10-7

What if: For this example, assume the machinery Teton placed in service in Exhibit 10-5 was placed in service on November 1, 2021, rather than July 22. What is Teton's 2021 depreciation for its personal property additions?

Answer: $30,527, computed as follows:

Asset	Purchase Date	Quarter	Original Basis	Rate	Depreciation
Office furniture (7-year)	February 3	1st	$ 20,000	25.00%	$ 5,000
Delivery truck (5-year)	August 17	3rd	25,000	15.00%	3,750
Machinery (7-year)	November 1	4th	610,000	3.57%	21,777
					$30,527

The mid-quarter convention applies because more than 40 percent of the assets were placed in service during the last quarter of the year ($610,000/$655,000 = 93% placed in service in the last quarter). The office furniture percentage of 25 percent is located in Table 2a. See the columns for property placed into service during the first quarter (first two columns); select the seven-year recovery period column (last column), and the year 1 row. The process for determining the percentage for the delivery truck and machinery follows the same method, using Table 2c and Table 2d, respectively.

THE KEY FACTS

Mid-Quarter Convention

- The mid-quarter convention is required when more than 40 percent of personal property is placed in service during the fourth quarter of the tax year.
- Each quarter has its own depreciation table. Once the mid-quarter convention applies, the taxpayer must continue to use it over the assets' entire recovery period.
- If an asset is disposed of before it is fully depreciated, use the formula given to determine the allowable depreciation in the year of disposition.

The process for calculating depreciation for assets in years after acquisition is the same as the process we described for the half-year convention except the taxpayer uses the MACRS Mid-Quarter Convention tables for the appropriate quarter rather than the MACRS Half-Year Convention table (Table 1).

Mid-quarter convention for year of disposition. Calculating depreciation expense in the year of sale or disposition is a bit more involved when the mid-quarter convention applies than when it does not. When the mid-quarter convention applies, the asset is treated as though it is sold in the middle of the quarter of which it was actually sold. The process for calculating mid-quarter convention depreciation for the year of sale is exactly the same as the process for using the half-year convention, except that instead of multiplying the full-year's depreciation by 50 percent, the business multiplies the amount of depreciation it would have been able to claim on the asset if it had not sold the asset (a full-year's depreciation) by the applicable percentage in Exhibit 10-6.

EXHIBIT 10-6 Mid-Quarter Convention Percentage of Full-Year's Depreciation in Year of Disposition

Quarter of Disposition	Percentage	Calculation*
1st	12.5%	1.5/12
2nd	37.5	4.5/12
3rd	62.5	7.5/12
4th	87.5	10.5/12

*The calculation is the number of months the taxpayer is deemed to have held the asset in the year of disposition divided by 12 months in the year.

Example 10-8

What if: Assume that Teton depreciates its personal property under the mid-quarter convention (Example 10-7) and that it sells its office furniture in the third quarter of 2022. The office furniture ($20,000 original basis) was placed into service during the first quarter of 2021 and has a seven-year recovery period. What is Teton's 2022 depreciation deduction for the office furniture?

Answer: $2,679, computed as follows:

Description	Amount	Explanation
(1) Original basis	$20,000	Example 10-7
(2) 2022 depreciation percentage	21.43%	Table 2a, mid-quarter, first quarter table, 7-year property, year 2
(3) Full-year's depreciation	$ 4,286	(1) × (2)
(4) Percentage of full-year's depreciation in year of disposition if mid-quarter convention applies	62.5%	From Exhibit 10-6; asset disposed of in third quarter
Depreciation in year of disposition	**$ 2,679**	(3) × (4)

THE KEY FACTS

Real Property Depreciation

- Real property is depreciated using the straight-line method.
- Real property uses the mid-month convention.
- Residential property has a recovery period of 27.5 years.
- Nonresidential property placed in service on or after May 13, 1993, has a life of 39 years.
- Nonresidential property placed in service after December 31, 1986, but before May 13, 1993, has a recovery period of 31.5 years.

Real Property

For depreciation purposes, real property is classified as land, *residential rental property,* or *nonresidential property.* Land is nondepreciable. Residential rental property consists of dwelling units such as houses, condominiums, and apartment complexes. Residential rental property has a 27.5-year recovery period. Nonresidential property consists of all other buildings (office buildings, manufacturing facilities, shopping malls, and the like). Nonresidential property placed in service on or after May 13, 1993, has a 39-year recovery period, and nonresidential property placed in service after December 31, 1986, but before May 13, 1993, has a 31.5-year recovery period. Exhibit 10-7 summarizes the recovery periods for real property.[27]

EXHIBIT 10-7 Recovery Period for Real Property

Asset Description (Summary from Rev. Proc. 87-57)	Recovery Period
Residential	27.5 years
Nonresidential property placed in service on or after May 13, 1993	39 years
Nonresidential property placed in service after December 31, 1986, but before May 13, 1993	31.5 years

If a building is substantially improved (e.g., expanded) at some point after the initial purchase, the building addition is treated as a new asset with the same recovery period of the original building. For example, if Teton expanded its warehouse 10 years after the building was placed in service, the expansion or building addition would be depreciated as a *new, separate* asset over 39 years because it is nonresidential property.

An important area of tax practice related to real property is cost segregation (see Taxes in the Real World on this later in the chapter). This practice attempts to partition or divide the costs of a building into two or more categories. The first category is the building itself, which has a recovery period as noted in Exhibit 10-7. The second category is building components (tangible personal property associated with the building such as electrical and plumbing fixtures that have a shorter recovery period and accelerated depreciation

[27]§179(f)(2) classifies the following improvements to nonresidential real property as eligible for immediate expensing: roofs; heating, ventilation, and air-conditioning systems; fire protection and alarm systems; and security systems. In addition, §179(f)(1) allows qualified improvements (any improvement to an interior portion of a nonresidential building placed in service after the date the building was placed in service) to be eligible for §179. Qualified improvements do not include expansions, additions of elevators/escalators, or improvements to the internal structural framework of the building; therefore, these items are not eligible to be immediately deducted under §179 [§168(e)(6)(B)].

method). Cost segregation utilizes engineers and construction experts who divide the costs between real and tangible personal property. This can generate significant tax savings due to the difference in the present value of the tax savings from the accelerated depreciation deductions associated with personal property relative to real property.

TAXES IN THE REAL WORLD Cost Segregation

Consider a taxpayer who purchases a strip mall for $1 million, excluding land, in July. Typically, the taxpayer records the purchase as a 39-year asset and depreciates it using a straight-line method according to the MACRS rules for depreciating real property. After five years, the taxpayer would have claimed $114,330 of depreciation deductions on the property. Is it possible for the taxpayer to accelerate the depreciation deductions on the property to take advantage of the timing tax planning strategy? Yes, with the help of a cost segregation study!

Cost segregation is the process of identifying personal property assets that are included in the purchase price of real property such as a strip mall. Cost segregation separates out the personal property from the real property for tax reporting purposes. Personal property includes a building's nonstructural elements, exterior land improvements, and indirect construction costs. Now suppose a cost segregation study on the strip mall identifies 5-year property of $200,000, 15-year property of $250,000, and 39-year property of $550,000. The taxpayer would claim $345,562 of depreciation expense over the 5-year period, even without considering bonus depreciation on the identified personal property. Taking bonus depreciation into consideration, the total depreciation over the five years would be $512,882, an increase of almost $398,552 in deductions over the 5-year period!

Applicable Method All depreciable real property is depreciated for tax purposes using the straight-line method. This is generally consistent with depreciation methods used for financial accounting purposes.

Applicable Convention All real property is depreciated using the mid-month convention. The **mid-month convention** allows the owner of real property to expense one-half of a month's depreciation for the month in which the property was placed in service (and in the month of the year it is sold as well). This is true regardless of whether the asset was placed in service at the beginning or at the end of the month. For example, if Teton placed its warehouse into service on May 1 (or on *any* other day in May), it would deduct *one-half* of a month's depreciation for May and then full depreciation for the months June through December.

Depreciation Tables Just as it does for personal property, the IRS provides depreciation tables for real property. The depreciation tables for 27.5-year, 31.5-year, and 39-year real property are reproduced as Tables 3, 4, and 5, respectively, in Appendix A. The percentage of the asset's basis that is depreciated in a particular year is located at the intersection of the month the asset was placed in service (column) and the year of depreciation (row).

Example 10-9

As indicated in Example 10-1, Teton's cost basis in the warehouse it purchased on May 1, 2021, is $275,000. What is Teton's 2021 and 2022 depreciation on its warehouse?

Answer: $4,414 in 2021 and $7,051 in 2022, calculated as follows:

Warehouse	Method	Recovery Period	Date Placed in Service	(1) Basis	(2) Rate*	(1) × (2) Depreciation
2020	SL	39	5/1/2021	$275,000	1.605%	**$4,414**
2021	SL	39	5/1/2021	275,000	2.564%	**7,051**

(continued on page 10-16)

What if: What would be Teton's 2021 and 2022 depreciation if, instead of a warehouse, the building was an apartment building that it rented to Teton's employees?

Answer: $6,251 in 2021 and $9,999 in 2022, calculated as follows:

Apartment Bldg.	Method	Recovery Period	Date Placed in Service	(1) Basis	(2) Rate†	(1) × (2) Depreciation
2020	SL	27.5	5/1/2021	$275,000	2.273%	**$6,251**
2021	SL	27.5	5/1/2022	275,000	3.636%	**9,999**

*The 1.605 percent for the year is found in the 39-year table (Table 5, in Appendix A) in the fifth column (fifth month) and first row (first year).

†The 2.273 percent for the year is found in the 27.5-year table (Table 3, in Appendix A) in the fifth column (fifth month) and first row (first year).

When using depreciation tables for real property, it is important to stay in the month column corresponding with the month the property was originally placed in service.[28] Thus, to calculate depreciation for real property placed in service in May (the fifth month), businesses will *always* (for each year of depreciation) find the current-year rate factor in the fifth column for that asset. This is true even if the asset is sold in a subsequent year in July (it's easy to make the mistake of using the seventh column to calculate the depreciation for the year of disposition in this situation).

Mid-month convention for year of disposition. Businesses deduct one-half of a month's depreciation in the month they sell or otherwise dispose of real property. For example, if Teton sold its warehouse on March 5 of year 2, it would deduct two and one-half months of depreciation in that year for the warehouse (depreciation for January, February, and one-half of March). Calculating depreciation deduction in the year of sale or disposition for mid-month convention assets is similar to the calculation under the mid-quarter convention. When the mid-month convention applies, the asset is treated as though it is sold in the *middle of the month* in which it was actually sold. The simplest process for calculating mid-month convention depreciation for the year of sale consists of the following four steps:

Step 1: Determine the amount of depreciation deduction for the asset as if the asset was held for the entire year.

Step 2: Subtract one-half of a month from the month in which the asset was sold (if sold in the third month, subtract .5 from 3 to get 2.5). (Subtract half of a month because the business is treated as though the asset was disposed of in the middle of the third month—not the end.)

Step 3: Divide the amount determined in Step 2 by 12 months (2.5/12). This is the fraction of the full-year's depreciation the business is eligible to deduct.

Step 4: Multiply the Step 3 outcome by the full depreciation determined in Step 1.

These steps are summarized in the following formula:

Mid-month depreciation for year of disposition

$$= \text{Full-year's depreciation} \times \frac{(\text{Month in which asset was disposed of} - .5)}{12}$$

[28]Failure to do so will result in the wrong depreciation expense and is technically a change in accounting method (which requires filing of Form 3115 with the IRS).

(continued from page 10-1 . . .)

During 2021, Teton had huge success, generating a large profit. To continue to grow the business and increase Teton's production capacity, Steve acquired more assets in 2022. He has heard about ways to "write off" the costs of business assets and wants to learn more.

(to be continued . . .)

Example 10-10

What if: Assume that Teton sells its warehouse on March 5, 2022 (the year after Teton buys it). What is Teton's depreciation for the warehouse in the year of disposition?

Answer: $1,469, computed using the four-step procedure outlined above as follows.

Step 1: Determine full-year's depreciation: $275,000 × 2.564%* = $7,051

Step 2: 3 (month sold) – .5 = 2.5

Step 3: 2.5/12

Step 4: $7,051 × 2.5/12 = **$1,469** (see formula above)

*The 2.564 percent (full-year percentage) in Step 1 is obtained from the MACRS Mid-Month table for 39-year property (Table 5) placed in service during the fifth month (year 2 row).

SPECIAL RULES RELATING TO COST RECOVERY

LO 10-3

In addition to the basic MACRS rules, several additional provisions affect the depreciation of personal property. Congress often uses these special rules for economic stimulus or to curb perceived taxpayer abuses. For many businesses, the calculation of MACRS depreciation for personal property will become a thing of the past due to the recent expansion of these special rules. It is worth noting, however, that Congress did not make all of the provisions permanent. For example, bonus depreciation is effective for property placed in service before January 1, 2023, with a subsequent four-year phase-out. We discuss these special rules below.

Immediate Expensing (§179) Policy makers created §179 as an incentive to help small businesses purchasing qualified property. This incentive is commonly referred to as the **§179 expense** or *immediate expensing* election.[29] This provision will have limited application because bonus depreciation (discussed below) allows taxpayers to immediately deduct assets' initial bases. As discussed earlier in the chapter, businesses must generally depreciate an asset's initial basis over the asset's recovery period. However, under §179, businesses may elect to immediately expense up to $1,080,000 (up from $1,050,000 in 2021) of qualified property placed in service during 2022.[30,31] Businesses can also use immediate expensing for off-the-shelf computer software and qualified real property.[32] Qualified property does not include property with prior use by the taxpayer reacquiring the property. Businesses may also elect to deduct less than the maximum. When businesses elect to deduct a certain amount of §179 expense, they immediately expense all or a portion of an asset's basis or several assets' bases. To reflect this immediate depreciation, they must reduce the basis of the asset or assets (to which they applied the §179 amount) *before* they compute MACRS depreciation (from the tables).

Exhibit 10-8 shows the assets Teton acquires in 2022.

EXHIBIT 10-8 Teton's 2022 Asset Acquisitions

Asset	Cost	Date Placed in Service
Computers & information systems	$ 920,000	March 3
Delivery truck	80,000	May 26
Machinery	1,200,000	August 15
Total	$2,200,000	

[29]Intangibles and tangible personal property that are used less than 50 percent for business and most real property are not eligible for immediate expensing.

[30]The maximum allowable expense under §179 is indexed for inflation beginning with years after 2018.

[31]These maximum amounts are per tax return. Thus, if an individual has multiple businesses with asset acquisitions, the taxpayer may only deduct up to these maximum amounts for the combined businesses.

[32]Qualified real property means improvements to nonresidential real property placed in service after the date the building was placed in service, including roofs; heating, ventilation, and air-conditioning; fire protection and alarm systems; and security systems.

Example 10-11

What if: Assume Teton is eligible for and elects to immediately deduct $800,000 of §179 expense against the basis of the machinery acquired in 2022 (see Exhibit 10-8). (Note that Teton could have elected to deduct up to $1,080,000.) What is the amount of Teton's current-year depreciation deduction, including regular MACRS depreciation and the §179 expense on its machinery (assuming the half-year convention applies and that Teton elects out of bonus depreciation)?

Answer: $857,160, computed as follows:

Description	Amount	Explanation
(1) Machinery	$1,200,000	Exhibit 10-8
(2) §179 expense	800,000	
(3) Remaining basis in machinery	$ 400,000	(1) – (2)
(4) MACRS depreciation rate for 7-year machinery	14.29%	Rate from Table 1
(5) MACRS depreciation expense on machinery	$ 57,160	(3) × (4)
Total depreciation on machinery	**$ 857,160**	(2) + (5)

What if: Assume that Teton was eligible for and elected to claim the maximum amount of §179 expense. What would be its total current-year depreciation deduction, including MACRS depreciation and §179 expense (assuming the half-year convention applies and that Teton elects out of bonus depreciation)?

Answer: $1,097,148, computed as follows:

Description	Amount	Explanation
(1) Machinery	$ 1,200,000	Exhibit 10-8
(2) §179 expense	1,080,000	Maximum expense in 2022
(3) Remaining basis in machinery	$ 120,000	(1) – (2)
(4) MACRS depreciation rate for 7-year machinery	14.29%	Rate from Table 1
(5) MACRS depreciation expense on machinery	$ 17,148	(3) × (4)
Total depreciation on machinery	**$ 1,097,148**	(2) + (5)

Limits on immediate expensing. The maximum amount of §179 expense a business may elect to claim for the year is subject to a phase-out limitation. Under the phase-out limitation, businesses must reduce the $1,080,000 maximum available expense dollar-for-dollar for the amount of *qualified property* placed in service during 2022 over a $2,700,000 threshold (up from $2,620,000 in 2021).[33] Thus, if a business places $3,780,000 ($2,700,000 threshold plus $1,080,000) or more of tangible personal property into service during 2022, its maximum available §179 expense for the year is $0. The phased-out portion of the maximum expense disappears and does *not* carry over to a subsequent year.

Businesses may elect to claim the §179 expense for the year up to the maximum amount available (after computing the phase-out—see the previous example). When a business elects to claim a certain amount of §179 expense, it must reduce the basis of the asset(s) to which the expense is applied. It then computes regular depreciation on the remaining basis after reducing the basis of the asset(s) for the §179 expense.

[33]The threshold under §179 is indexed for inflation beginning with years after 2018.

Example 10-12

What if: Let's assume that during 2022, Teton placed into service $2,400,000 of machinery (up from the $1,200,000 amount in Exhibit 10-8), $920,000 of computers, and an $80,000 delivery truck, for a total of $3,400,000 tangible *personal* property placed in service for the year. What is Teton's maximum §179 expense after applying the phase-out limitation?

Answer: $380,000, computed as follows:

Description	Amount	Explanation
(1) Property placed in service in 2022	$3,400,000	
(2) Threshold for §179 phase-out	2,700,000	2022 amount [§179(b)(2)]
(3) Phase-out of maximum §179 expense	700,000	(1) – (2)
(4) Maximum §179 expense before phase-out	1,080,000	§179(b)(1)
Maximum §179 expense after phase-out*	**$ 380,000**	(4) – (3)

*Note that this is the maximum expense after phase-out but *before* the taxable income limitation we discuss next.

What if: Assume further that on November 13, Teton acquired and placed in service a storage building costing $400,000. Taking the building into account, what is Teton's maximum §179 amount after the phase-out?

Answer: $380,000, the same answer as above. The phase-out is based on the amount of qualified property placed in service during the year. Because the warehouse is *real property* (not qualified), its acquisition has no effect on Teton's maximum §179 expense.

A business's *deductible* §179 expense is limited to the taxpayer's business income after deducting all expenses (including regular and bonus depreciation) except the §179 expense. Consequently, the §179 expense cannot create or extend a business's net operating loss. Taxpayers' business income includes income from all businesses. For example, a sole proprietor's business income for purposes of §179 would include the income not only from all Schedules C but also from regular wages. If a business claims more §179 expense than it is allowed to deduct due to the taxable income limitation, it carries the excess forward (indefinitely) and deducts it in a subsequent year, subject to the taxable income limitation (but not the phase-out limitation) in the subsequent year.[34]

Example 10-13

What if: Let's assume the facts in Example 10-12, where Teton's maximum §179 expense after applying the phase-out limitation is $380,000. Also assume that Teton elects to claim the entire $380,000 expense and it chooses to apply it against the machinery. Further assume that Teton elects out of bonus depreciation and reports $400,000 of taxable income before deducting any §179 expense and depreciation. What amount of total depreciation (including §179 expense) is Teton able to deduct on the machinery for the year?

Answer: $400,000, computed as follows:

Description	Amount	Explanation
(1) Machinery	$2,400,000	Example 10-12
(2) Elected §179 expense	380,000	
(3) Remaining basis	$2,020,000	(1) – (2)
(4) MACRS depreciation rate for 7-year machinery, year 1	14.29%	See Table 1
(5) MACRS depreciation expense on machinery	$ 288,658	(3) × (4)
(6) Deductible §179 expense	111,342	Taxable income limitation ($400,000 – $288,658)
(7) Total depreciation expense on machinery for the year	**$ 400,000**	(5) + (6)
(8) Excess §179 expense	$ 268,658	(2) – (6)

(continued on page 10-20)

THE KEY FACTS

§179 Expenses

- $1,080,000 of tangible personal property can be immediately expensed in 2022.
- Businesses are eligible for the full amount of this expense when tangible personal property placed in service is less than $2,700,000. Beginning at $2,700,000, the §179 expense is phased out, dollar-for-dollar. When assets placed in service reach $3,780,000, no §179 expense can be taken.
- §179 expenses are also limited to a business's taxable income before the §179 expense. §179 expenses cannot create losses.

[34]Businesses typically elect to expense only the currently deductible amount because the taxable income limitation may also limit their §179 expense in future years just as it does for the current year. Electing the amount deductible after the taxable income limitation also maximizes the current-year depreciation deduction.

What is the amount of Teton's excess §179 expense (elected expense in excess of the deductible amount due to the taxable income limitation), and what does Teton do with it for tax purposes?

Answer: $268,658. See the above table for the computation (line 8). Teton carries this $268,658 excess §179 expense forward to future years and may deduct it subject to the taxable income limitation. Note that the depreciable basis of the machinery remaining after the §179 expense is $2,020,000 because the depreciable basis is reduced by the full $380,000 of §179 expense elected even though the deductible §179 expense was limited to $111,342 in the current year.

Choosing the assets to immediately expense. Businesses qualifying for immediate expensing are allowed to choose the asset or assets (from tangible personal property placed in service during the year) they immediately expense under §179. If a business's objective is to maximize its current depreciation deduction, it should immediately expense the asset with the lowest first-year cost recovery percentage including bonus depreciation (discussed in the next section).[35,36]

Example 10-14

What if: Let's assume that on June 1, Teton placed into service five-year property costing $1,400,000 and seven-year property costing $1,400,000 and had no other fixed asset additions during the year. Further assume that Teton is not subject to the taxable income limitation for the §179 expense. What is Teton's depreciation deduction (including §179 expense) if it elects to apply the full §179 expense against the five-year property (Scenario A)? What is its depreciation deduction if it applies the full §179 expense against its seven-year property (Scenario B)? Assume Teton elects out of bonus depreciation.

Answer: $1,344,060 if it applies the full §179 expense to the five-year property (Scenario A) and $1,405,728 if it applies it to the seven-year property (Scenario B). See the computations below:

Description	(Scenario A) §179 Expense on 5-Year Property	(Scenario B) §179 Expense on 7-Year Property	Explanation
(1) Original basis	$1,400,000	$1,400,000	
(2) Elected §179 expense	1,080,000	1,080,000	Maximum expense
(3) Remaining basis	320,000	320,000	(1) − (2)
(4) MACRS depreciation rate	20%	14.29%	See Table 1
(5) MACRS depreciation expense	$ 64,000	$ 45,728	(3) × (4)
(6) Deductible §179 expense	1,080,000	1,080,000	Maximum §179 expense allowed this year.
(7) MACRS depreciation on other property	200,060	280,000	This is the depreciation on the $1,400,000 7-year property in the 5-year column ($1,400,000 × 14.29% = $200,060) and on the $1,400,000 5-year property in the 7-year column ($1,400,000 × 20% = $280,000).
Total depreciation expense	**$1,344,060**	**$1,405,728**	(5) + (6) + (7)

Note that Teton deducts $61,668 more in depreciation expense if it applies the §179 expense to the seven-year property.

[35]Reg. §1.168(d)-1(b)(4)(i).

[36]Looking at Tables 2a and 2c in Appendix A, if a business has to choose between immediately expensing seven-year property placed in service in the first quarter or five-year property placed in service in the third quarter, which asset should it elect to expense under §179 if it wants to maximize its current-year depreciation expense? The answer is the five-year asset because its first-year depreciation percentage is 15 percent, while the seven-year asset's first-year depreciation percentage is 25 percent. Finally, note that businesses reduce the basis of the assets for the §179 expense before computing whether the mid-quarter convention applies.

Bonus Depreciation Since 2001, businesses have had the ability to immediately deduct a percentage of the acquisition cost of qualifying assets under rules known as **bonus depreciation.**[37] The percentage allowable for each tax year during this period has changed many times, ranging from 30 percent to 100 percent. Just prior to the TCJA, the bonus percentage was 50 percent. However, the TCJA increased the percentage to 100 percent for qualified property acquired after September 27, 2017. This provision (and the enhancement of §179) simplifies the depreciation calculation for many businesses because they can deduct the full amount of certain assets placed in service during the year.[38] There are several nuances of this provision that businesses need to consider. We discuss them in this section.

Bonus depreciation is mandatory for all taxpayers that qualify. However, taxpayers may elect out of bonus depreciation (on a property class basis) by attaching a statement to their tax return indicating they are electing not to claim bonus depreciation.[39] That is, taxpayers can elect out of bonus depreciation for all of their five-year class property but still claim bonus depreciation for all of their seven-year property acquisitions. The election to opt out of bonus depreciation is made annually. Businesses in a loss position may want to elect out of bonus depreciation to reduce these losses because their ability to deduct the losses in the future may be limited by other provisions of the tax code. In addition, businesses may want to elect out of bonus depreciation and use §179 instead because §179 allows taxpayers to pick and choose carefully which assets to expense, whereas bonus depreciation is all-or-nothing based on property class. For taxpayers claiming the deduction, bonus depreciation is calculated after the §179 expense but before regular MACRS depreciation.[40] Bonus depreciation is a temporary provision, and the percentage phases out as shown in Exhibit 10-9.[41]

Qualified property. Taxpayers must first determine whether the assets acquired during the year are eligible for bonus depreciation. To qualify, property must be new or used property (as long as the property has not previously been used by the taxpayer within the past five years)[42] and must generally have a regular depreciation life of 20 years or less.

EXHIBIT 10-9 Bonus Depreciation Percentages

Placed in Service	Bonus Depreciation Percentage
September 28, 2017–December 31, 2022	100 percent
2023	80 percent
2024	60 percent
2025	40 percent
2026	20 percent
2027 and after	None

[37]§168(k)(1).

[38]Many states do not allow bonus depreciation, so businesses will be required to calculate their depreciation using basic MACRS for those state tax returns.

[39]§168(k)(7). Property classes are broader categories of the asset classes discussed in Rev. Proc. 87-56. There are eight property classes of assets: 3-year, 5-year, 7-year, 10-year, 15-year, 20-year, residential rental property, and nonresidential real property.

[40]Reg. §1.168(k)-1(a)(2)(iii), (d)(3) Example (2).

[41]§168(k)(6).

[42]§168(k)(2)(E)(ii). Taxpayers may not use bonus depreciation for assets received as a gift or inheritance, for like-kind property (unless the taxpayer pays money in addition to the exchanged property), for property received in tax-deferred exchanges (reorganizations), or for property acquired from a related entity.

Example 10-15

What if: Assume that Teton claims bonus depreciation for the eligible personal property acquired in Exhibit 10-8.

Asset	Date Acquired	Cost Basis	Recovery Period
Computers & information systems	3/3/2022	$ 920,000	5
Delivery truck	5/26/2022	80,000	5
Machinery	8/15/2022	1,200,000	7
Total		$2,200,000	

Assuming Teton elects no §179 expense, what is Teton's bonus depreciation?

Answer: $2,200,000, computed as follows:

Description	Amount	Explanation
(1) Qualified property	$ 2,200,000	
(2) Bonus depreciation rate	100%	§168(k)(1)(A), (6)(A)(i)
Bonus depreciation	**$2,200,000**	(1) × (2)

What if: Assume that the delivery truck does not qualify for bonus depreciation and that Teton elects the maximum §179 expense. What is Teton's bonus depreciation?

Answer: $1,150,000, computed as follows:

Description	Amount	Explanation
(1) §179 qualified property	$ 2,200,000	
(2) §179 expense	1,080,000	Maximum expense
(3) Remaining basis	$ 1,120,000	(1) − (2)
(4) Remaining amount eligible for bonus depreciation	1,120,000	Remaining amount relates to the computers and the machinery. Because the truck is not eligible for bonus depreciation, we apply $80,000 of §179 expense first to the truck to maximize the current-year depreciation deduction. We next apply the remaining $1,000,000 of §179 expense ($1,080,000 − $80,000) to the machinery (7-year), which reduces its basis to $200,000 ($1,200,000 − $1,000,000).
(5) Bonus depreciation rate	100%	§168(k)(1)(A), (6)(A)(i)
Bonus depreciation	**$1,120,000**	(4) × (5)

What if: Assuming Teton elects the maximum §179 and bonus depreciation, what is Teton's total depreciation on its personal property?

Answer: $2,200,000. Teton is able to fully depreciate its tangible personal property placed in service in 2022 due to a combination of §179 ($1,080,000) and bonus depreciation ($1,120,000). Teton does not need to calculate regular MACRS depreciation on any of its tangible personal property. Alternatively, Teton could elect to take §179 on the delivery truck only and use bonus depreciation on the remaining assets. This option would produce $80,000 of §179 expense and $2,120,000 of bonus depreciation, for a total of $2,200,000.

THE KEY FACTS

Listed Property

- When an asset is used for both personal and business use, calculate the business-use percentage.
- If the business-use percentage is above 50 percent, the allowable depreciation is limited to the business-use percentage.
- If a listed property's business-use percentage ever falls to or below 50 percent, depreciation for all previous years is retroactively restated using the MACRS straight-line method.

Listed Property Most business-owned assets are used for business rather than personal purposes. For example, Weyerhaeuser employees probably have little or no personal interest in using Weyerhaeuser's timber-harvesting equipment during their free time. In contrast, business owners and employees may find some business assets, such as company automobiles or laptop computers, conducive to personal use.

Business assets that tend to be used for both business and personal purposes are referred to as **listed property.** For example, automobiles, other means of transportation (planes, boats, and recreation vehicles), and even digital cameras are considered to be listed property. The tax law limits the allowable depreciation on listed property to the portion of the asset used for business purposes.

How do taxpayers compute depreciation for listed property? First, they must determine the percentage of business versus personal use of the asset for the year. If the business-use percentage for the year exceeds 50 percent, the deductible depreciation is limited to the full annual depreciation multiplied by the business-use percentage for the year. Listed property used in trade or business more than 50 percent of the time is eligible for the §179 expensing election and bonus depreciation (limited to the business-use percentage).

Example 10-16

What if: Assume that, in addition to the assets Teton purchased in 2022 presented in Exhibit 10-8, it also purchased a new digital camera for $4,000 that its employees use for business on weekdays. On weekends, Steve uses the camera for his photography hobby. Because the camera is listed property, Teton must assess the business-use percentage to properly calculate its deductible depreciation for the camera. Assuming that Teton determines the business-use percentage to be 75 percent, what is Teton's depreciation deduction on the camera for the year (ignoring bonus depreciation and §179 expensing)?

Answer: $600, computed as follows:

Description	Amount	Explanation
(1) Initial basis of camera	$4,000	
(2) MACRS depreciation rate	20%	5-year property, year 1, half-year convention
(3) Full MACRS depreciation expense	$ 800	(1) × (2)
(4) Business-use percentage	75%	
Depreciation deduction for year	**$ 600**	(3) × (4)

When the business-use percentage of an asset is 50 percent or less, the business must compute depreciation for the asset using the MACRS *straight-line* method over the MACRS ADS (alternative depreciation system) recovery period.[43] For five-year assets such as automobiles, the assets on which the personal-use limitation is most common, the MACRS ADS recovery period is also 5 years. However, for seven-year assets, the ADS recovery period is generally 10 years.[44]

If a business initially uses an asset more than 50 percent of the time for business (and appropriately adopts the 200 percent declining balance method, §179, or bonus depreciation) but subsequently its business use drops to 50 percent or below, the depreciation expense for all prior years must be recomputed as if the business had been using the straight-line depreciation over the ADS recovery period the entire time. The business must then recapture any excess accelerated depreciation (including §179 and bonus depreciation) it deducted over the straight-line depreciation that it should have deducted by adjusting the current-year depreciation. In practical terms, taxpayers can use the following five steps to determine their current depreciation expense for the asset:

Step 1: Compute depreciation for the year it drops to 50 percent or below using the straight-line method (this method also applies to all subsequent years).

Step 2: Compute the amount of depreciation the taxpayer would have deducted if the taxpayer had used the straight-line method over the ADS recovery period for

[43]This is the alternative recovery period listed in Rev. Proc. 87-56. See §168(g)(3)(C); Reg. §1.280F-3T(d)(1).

[44]However, there are exceptions to this general rule. For example, the ADS recovery period for certain machinery for food and beverages is 12 years and the ADS recovery period for machinery for tobacco products is 15 years. Thus, it is important to check Rev. Proc. 87-56 to verify the ADS recovery period in these situations.

all prior years (recall that depreciation is limited to the business-use percentage in those years).

Step 3: Compute the amount of depreciation (including §179 and bonus depreciation) the taxpayer actually deducted on the asset for all prior years.

Step 4: Subtract the amount from Step 2 from the amount in Step 3. The difference is the prior-year accelerated depreciation in excess of straight-line depreciation.

Step 5: Subtract the excess accelerated depreciation determined in Step 4 from the current-year, straight-line depreciation in Step 1. This is the taxpayer's allowable depreciation expense on the asset for the year. If the prior-year excess depreciation from Step 4 exceeds the current-year, straight-line depreciation in Step 1, the taxpayer is not allowed to deduct any depreciation on the asset for the year and must recognize additional ordinary income for the amount of the excess.

This five-step process is designed to place the taxpayer in the same position it would have been in had it used straight-line depreciation during all years of the asset's life.

Example 10-17

What if: Assume that, consistent with Example 10-16, in 2022 Teton used the camera 75 percent of the time for business purposes and deducted $600 depreciation expense on the camera. However, in year 2, Teton's business-use percentage falls to 40 percent. What is Teton's depreciation deduction for the camera in year 2?

Answer: $20, computed using the five-step process described above as follows:

Description	Amount	Explanation*
(1) Straight-line depreciation in current year	$320	$4,000/5 years × 40 percent business-use percentage (Step 1)
(2) Prior-year, straight-line depreciation	300	$4,000/5 × 50 percent (half-year convention) × 75 percent business-use percentage (Step 2)
(3) Prior-year accelerated depreciation	600	Example 10-16 (prior example)
(4) Excess accelerated depreciation	300	(3) – (2) (Step 4)
Allowable current-year depreciation	**$ 20**	(1) – (4) (Step 5)

*Note that the MACRS ADS recovery period (five years) for digital cameras (qualified technological equipment) is the same as the standard MACRS recovery period (five years).

What if: Now assume that, in 2022, Teton took bonus depreciation and deducted $3,000 depreciation expense ($4,000 × 100% × 75%) on the camera. However, in year 2, Teton's business-use percentage falls to 40 percent. What is Teton's depreciation deduction for the camera in year 2?

Answer: $0 depreciation deduction and $2,380 of ordinary income because excess accelerated depreciation exceeds current-year straight-line depreciation, computed as follows:

Description	Amount	Explanation
(1) Straight-line depreciation in current year	$ 320	$4,000/5 years × 40 percent business use (Step 1)
(2) Prior-year, straight-line depreciation	300	$4,000/5 × 50 percent (half-year convention) × 75 percent business-use percentage from year 1 (Step 2)
(3) Prior-year accelerated depreciation	3,000	Bonus depreciation
(4) Excess accelerated depreciation	2,700	(3) – (2) (Step 4)
Income required to be recognized	**$(2,380)**	(1) – (4) (Step 5)

Luxury Automobiles As we discussed in the Business Income, Deductions, and Accounting Methods chapter, §162 limits business deductions to those considered to be "ordinary, necessary, and reasonable" to prevent subsidizing (i.e., giving a tax deduction for) unwarranted business expenses. Although these terms are subject to interpretation, most taxpayers agree that for purposes of simply transporting passengers for business-related purposes, the cost of acquiring and using a Ford Focus is more likely to be ordinary, necessary, and reasonable than the cost of acquiring and using a Ferrari California—although perhaps not as exhilarating. Because either vehicle should be able to transport an employee or business owner from the office to a business meeting, the Ford Focus should be just as effective at accomplishing the business purpose as the Ferrari.

If this is true, why should the government help taxpayers pay for expensive cars with tax savings from large depreciation deductions associated with automobiles? Congress decided it shouldn't. Therefore, with certain exceptions we discuss below, the tax laws generally limit the annual depreciation deduction for automobiles. Each year, the IRS provides a maximum depreciation schedule for automobiles placed in service during that particular year.[45] In 2022, taxpayers are allowed to expense $8,000 of bonus depreciation above the otherwise allowable maximum depreciation (maximum depreciation of $18,200).[46] Exhibit 10-10 summarizes these schedules for automobiles placed in service for each year from 2022 back to 2019.

THE KEY FACTS

Luxury Vehicles

- Depreciation on automobiles weighing less than 6,000 pounds is subject to luxury auto provisions.
- Luxury automobiles have a maximum depreciation limit for each year.
- Listed property rules are also applicable to luxury automobiles.

EXHIBIT 10-10 Automobile Depreciation Limits

Recovery Year	Year Placed in Service			
	2022*	2021	2020	2019
1	10,200**	10,200**	10,100**	10,100**
2	16,400	16,400	16,100	16,100
3	9,800	9,800	9,700	9,700
4 and after	5,860	5,860	5,760	5,760

*As of press date, the IRS had not released the 2022 limitations for automobiles, so throughout the chapter we use the same limitations as in 2021 for 2022.

**$8,000 additional depreciation is allowed when bonus depreciation is claimed [§168(k)(2)(F)].

Ignoring bonus depreciation for a moment, taxpayers placing automobiles into service during the year determine depreciation for the automobiles by first computing regular MACRS depreciation (using the appropriate convention). They then compare it to the maximum depreciation amount for the first year of the recovery period based on the IRS-provided tables. Taxpayers are allowed to deduct the lesser of the two. Each subsequent year, taxpayers should compare the regular MACRS amount with the limitation amount and deduct the lesser of the basic MACRS depreciation or the limitation. In 2022, if the half-year convention applies, the table limits the depreciation on automobiles placed in service during the year costing more than $51,000.[47] Automobiles to which the depreciation

[45]These limitations are indexed for inflation and change annually. Section 280F(a)(1)(A) provides the 2018 limitations for automobiles.

[46]§168(k)(2)(F)(i).

[47]Using the 2021 limitation amounts for 2022, the full first-year depreciation on an automobile costing $51,000 is $10,200 ($50,500 × 20 percent). This is the amount of the first-year limit for automobiles placed in service in 2021.

limits apply are commonly referred to as **luxury automobiles.**[48] Comparing the lifetime depreciation for two cars—say, a 2023 Honda Civic and a 2023 Porsche 911—we can see that the annual depreciation deduction is lower and the recovery period much shorter for the Civic than for the Porsche. As the next example illustrates, the Porsche will take 16 years to fully depreciate!

Example 10-18

What is the maximum annual depreciation deduction available for 2022 (year 1) on a 2023 Honda Civic costing $19,150 and a 2023 Porsche 911 costing $112,000 (ignoring bonus depreciation)?

Answer: $3,830 for the Honda and $10,200 for the Porsche. See the following depreciation schedules for each automobile.

Luxury Auto Depreciation*

Year/Make	**2023 Honda Civic**	**2023 Porsche 911**
Model	DX 2dr Coupe	Carrera 4S
Price	$19,150	$112,000
Depreciation		
Year 1	**$ 3,830**	**$ 10,200**
Year 2	6,128	16,400
Year 3	3,677	9,800
Year 4	2,206	5,860
Year 5	2,206	5,860
Year 6	1,103	5,860
Years 7–15		5,860
Year 16		5,280

The depreciation schedule for the Honda Civic follows the standard depreciation amounts calculated under MACRS because these annual amounts are lower than the limitations. The Honda is fully depreciated in year 6. The MACRS depreciation amounts for the Porsche, however, exceed the limitations, so the schedule shows the limited amount of depreciation each year. The limitations extend the recovery period for the Porsche to 16 years—however, it is unlikely the business will actually hold the Porsche for that long.

*Note that we use the 2021 limitations for the 2022 amounts in this example.

The luxury automobile limitations don't apply to vehicles weighing more than 6,000 pounds (for example, large SUVs) and those that charge for transportation, such as taxi cabs, limousines, and hearses. It also excludes delivery trucks and vans. Thus, taxpayers owning these vehicles are allowed to claim §179, bonus, and regular MACRS depreciation expense for these vehicles.[49]

Just like taxpayers using other types of listed property, taxpayers using automobiles exceeding the automobile limitation for business and personal purposes may deduct depreciation on the asset only to the extent of business use. Business use is determined by miles driven for business purposes relative to total miles driven for the year.[50] Consequently,

[48]Correspondingly, the depreciation limits on automobiles are commonly referred to as the *luxury auto depreciation limits.*

[49]§280F(d)(5)(A).

[50]As an alternative to deducting depreciation expense and other costs of operating an automobile, taxpayers using automobiles for both personal and business purposes may deduct a standard mileage rate for each mile of business use. In 2022 the business mileage rate is 58.5 cents per mile. Once a taxpayer uses the standard mileage rate, they may not switch back to actual costs.

if a taxpayer places a luxury automobile into service in 2022 and uses the automobile 90 percent of the time for business purposes during the year (9,000 miles for business and 1,000 miles of personal use), the owner's depreciation (ignoring bonus depreciation) on the auto for the year is limited to $9,180 (year 1 full depreciation of $10,200 × 90 percent business use—see Exhibit 10-10).[51] Further, if the business use falls to 50 percent or less in any subsequent year, just as with other listed property, the taxpayer must use the straight-line method of depreciation and reduce depreciation expense by the amount of excess accelerated depreciation (see Example 10-17). However, because straight-line depreciation is also limited by the luxury auto depreciation limits, it may turn out that the taxpayer doesn't have any excess accelerated depreciation.

Automobiles and §179. Are taxpayers allowed to deduct §179 expensing on luxury automobiles? The answer is yes, but . . . the luxury car limitation in 2022 is $10,200, and this limit applies regardless of whether the taxpayer claims regular MACRS depreciation or §179 expensing on the car. So, for cars that cost more than $51,000, the taxpayer doesn't benefit by electing §179 because the regular MACRS depreciation deduction would be greater than $10,200 and would be limited to $10,200. For cars that cost less than $51,000, taxpayers could benefit by electing to take $10,200 of §179 expense on the car to boost the depreciation deduction in the first year. For instance, in Example 10-18, the regular MACRS depreciation amount for the Honda Civic in the first year was $3,830. By electing §179, a taxpayer could increase the first-year depreciation deduction to $10,200.

Recall that large SUVs (those weighing more than 6,000 pounds) are not subject to the luxury car limitations. Therefore, a taxpayer will calculate its regular MACRS depreciation each year without the limitations for passenger cars. For these vehicles, taxpayers may take a §179 expense amount of $27,000 in 2022 (up from $26,200 in 2021) in the acquisition year in addition to their MACRS depreciation (calculated after the §179 expense).[52]

Automobiles and bonus depreciation. But wait! Why don't taxpayers simply use bonus depreciation to fully recover the cost of their automobiles in the year they buy the vehicle? For passenger cars (automobiles weighing 6,000 pounds or less), the luxury automobile limitations still apply. With bonus depreciation, taxpayers are allowed to increase the limitation in the first year by $8,000, making the first-year limit $18,200 in 2022.

Example 10-19

What if: Suppose Teton purchases a $60,000 car, which is used 100 percent of the time for business purposes. Teton would like to claim bonus depreciation. What is Teton's depreciation deduction for the car in 2022?

Answer: $18,200, calculated as follows:

Description	Amount	Explanation
(1) Automobile	$ 60,000	
(2) Bonus percentage	100%	§168(k)(1), (6)(A)(i)
(3) Bonus depreciation	$60,000	(1) × (2)
(4) Luxury automobile limitation	18,200	Luxury automobile limitation [$10,200 [§280F(a)(1)] + $8,000 [§168(k)(2)(F)]]
Year 1 depreciation	**$18,200**	Lesser of (3) or (4)

[51]Even if the business-use percentage multiplied by the MACRS depreciation is greater than the $10,200 maximum, the depreciation amount is limited to the maximum depreciation amount times the business-use percentage.

[52]This amount is indexed for inflation for years after 2018 [§179(b)(6)].

However, in years 2–6 (recovery period for passenger cars), taxpayers must again compare the regular MACRS amount in each year to the automobile limitation in Exhibit 10-10 for the year. If the taxpayer claims bonus depreciation, then, technically, all of the allowable depreciation was taken in year 1 (100 percent bonus depreciation) even though the taxpayer was limited by the automobile limitations. This means that there is no regular depreciation remaining for years 2–6. So, absent a special rule, taxpayers would not be allowed to claim *any* depreciation for those years. The remaining cost to be recovered would occur beginning in year 7 using the limitation for year 4 and after ($5,860 per Exhibit 10-10). Fortunately, the IRS provides a way (safe harbor) for taxpayers to continue to take depreciation in years 2–6 when they claim bonus depreciation.[53] This method applies to automobiles that have an initial basis greater than $18,200 (the first-year depreciation limitation for luxury automobiles) when taxpayers have not elected out of 100 percent bonus depreciation.

Under the IRS method, taxpayers first subtract the annual first-year limitation ($18,200) from the initial basis to determine the asset's adjusted depreciable basis. The taxpayer then multiplies the asset's adjusted depreciable basis by the applicable percentage in the MACRS table for each year (years 2–6) and then compares that to the annual depreciation limitation for each year (see Exhibit 10-10). The depreciation deduction for years 2–6 is the lesser of these two numbers. Starting in year 7, the taxpayer may deduct up to the year 4 and after automobile limitation until the auto is fully depreciated. This method is illustrated in the following example:

Example 10-20

What if: Assume the same facts as in Example 10-19. What is Teton's annual depreciation deduction on the car after the first year?

Answer: Determined as follows:

Taxable Year	Depreciation Limitations	Annual Depreciation	Deductible Depreciation under the Safe Harbor
2022	$18,200	$18,200 ($10,200 limitation + $8,000 additional bonus depreciation)	$18,200
2023	16,400	$13,376 [adjusted depreciable basis of $41,800 ($60,000 less $18,200 depreciation taken in the first year) × 32% depreciation rate from Appendix Table 1]	13,376
2024	9,800	$8,026 ($41,800 × 19.2%)	8,026
2025	5,860	$4,815 ($41,800 × 11.52%)	4,815
2026	5,860	$4,815 ($41,800 × 11.52%)	4,815
2027	5,860	$2,408 ($41,800 × 5.76%)	2,408
2028	5,860	N/A	$5,860 (lesser of limitation or remaining basis of $8,360)
2029	5,860	N/A	$2,500 (lesser of limitation of $5,860 or remaining basis of $2,500)

Can taxpayers avoid this calculation? Yes! There are at least two ways to avoid having to calculate depreciation on cars in this way. First, taxpayers can elect out of bonus depreciation. By electing out of bonus, taxpayers would calculate the depreciation on automobiles as the lesser of the regular MACRS depreciation or the limitation amount from Exhibit 10-10 for each year. The downside of electing out of bonus depreciation for automobiles is that the election must be done on a property class basis. Automobiles are in the five-year property class, but so are computers and office machinery (calculators and

[53]Rev. Proc. 2019-13.

copiers). So, if taxpayers elect out of bonus for automobiles, they also elect out for other assets included in the five-year property class. The second way to avoid this calculation is to purchase SUVs that weigh more than 6,000 pounds instead of passenger cars. These large SUVs are not subject to the listed property automobile limitations. Taxpayers can deduct the full cost of these vehicles in the first year under the bonus depreciation rules.

Depreciation for the Alternative Minimum Tax Individuals are subject to tax under the alternative minimum tax (AMT) system.[54] In determining their alternative minimum taxable income, individuals may be required to recalculate their depreciation expense. For AMT purposes, the allowable recovery period and conventions are the same for all depreciable assets as they are for regular tax purposes.[55] However, for AMT purposes, businesses are not allowed to use the 200 percent declining balance method to depreciate tangible personal property. Rather, they must choose from the 150 percent declining balance method or the straight-line method to depreciate the property for AMT purposes. The difference between regular tax depreciation and AMT depreciation is an adjustment that is either added to or subtracted from regular taxable income in computing the alternative minimum tax base.[56] In contrast, the §179 expense and bonus depreciation are equally deductible for both regular tax and AMT purposes. If a taxpayer claims bonus depreciation, there is no adjustment for AMT. Depreciation of real property is the same for both regular tax and AMT purposes.

Depreciation Summary Teton's depreciation for 2022 on all its assets is summarized in Exhibit 10-11, and Exhibit 10-12 presents Teton's depreciation as it would be reported on its tax return on Form 4562 (assuming Teton does not elect §179 and elects out of bonus depreciation for assets acquired in 2021). We use the 2021 forms for Teton's depreciation because the 2022 forms are not yet available.

EXHIBIT 10-11 Teton's 2022 Depreciation Expense

	Date Acquired	Original Basis	§179 Expense	Remaining Basis	Bonus Depreciation	Remaining Basis	Depreciation Expense	Reference
2021 Assets								
Machinery	7/22/2021	$ 610,000	–	$610,000	–	$610,000	$ 149,389	Example 10-5
Office furniture	2/3/2021	20,000	–	20,000	–	20,000	4,898	Example 10-5
Delivery truck	8/17/2021	25,000	–	25,000	–	25,000	8,000	Example 10-5
Warehouse	5/1/2021	275,000	–	275,000	–	275,000	7,051	Example 10-9
Land	5/1/2021	75,000	–	75,000	–	75,000	–	N/A
2022 Assets								
Computers & info systems	3/3/2022	920,000	–	920,000	920,000	–	–	Example 10-15 *What if* scenario
Delivery truck	5/26/2022	80,000	80,000	–	–	–	–	Example 10-15 *What if* scenario
Machinery	8/15/2022	1,200,000	1,000,000	200,000	200,000	–	–	Example 10-15 *What if* scenario
§179 Expense							1,080,000	Example 10-15 *What if* scenario
Bonus depreciation							1,120,000	Example 10-15 *What if* scenario
Total 2022 Depreciation Expense							**$2,369,338**	

[54]Corporations are not subject to the alternative minimum tax.

[55]This is true for assets placed in service after 1998.

[56]If the taxpayer elected either the 150 percent declining balance or the straight-line method for regular tax depreciation of tangible personal property, then there is no AMT adjustment with respect to that property.

EXHIBIT 10-12 **Teton's Form 4562 Parts I–IV for Depreciation (Assumes $1,500,000 of taxable income before the §179 expense)**

Form **4562**

Department of the Treasury
Internal Revenue Service (99)

Depreciation and Amortization
(Including Information on Listed Property)
▶ Attach to your tax return.
▶ Go to *www.irs.gov/Form4562* for instructions and the latest information.

OMB No. 1545-0172
2021
Attachment Sequence No. **179**

Name(s) shown on return	Business or activity to which this form relates	Identifying number
Steve Dallimore	**Teton Mountaineering Technologies LLC**	

Part I **Election To Expense Certain Property Under Section 179**
Note: If you have any listed property, complete Part V before you complete Part I.

1	Maximum amount (see instructions)	1	**1,080,000**
2	Total cost of section 179 property placed in service (see instructions)	2	**2,200,000**
3	Threshold cost of section 179 property before reduction in limitation (see instructions)	3	**2,700,000**
4	Reduction in limitation. Subtract line 3 from line 2. If zero or less, enter -0-	4	**-0-**
5	Dollar limitation for tax year. Subtract line 4 from line 1. If zero or less, enter -0-. If married filing separately, see instructions	5	**1,080,000**

6 (a) Description of property	(b) Cost (business use only)	(c) Elected cost
Machinery	**1,200,000**	**1,000,000**
Delivery Truck	**80,000**	**80,000**

7	Listed property. Enter the amount from line 29 ... 7		
8	Total elected cost of section 179 property. Add amounts in column (c), lines 6 and 7	8	**1,080,000**
9	Tentative deduction. Enter the **smaller** of line 5 or line 8	9	**1,080,000**
10	Carryover of disallowed deduction from line 13 of your 2020 Form 4562	10	
11	Business income limitation. Enter the smaller of business income (not less than zero) or line 5. See instructions	11	**1,080,000**
12	Section 179 expense deduction. Add lines 9 and 10, but don't enter more than line 11	12	**1,080,000**
13	Carryover of disallowed deduction to 2022. Add lines 9 and 10, less line 12 ▶ 13		

Note: Don't use Part II or Part III below for listed property. Instead, use Part V.

Part II **Special Depreciation Allowance and Other Depreciation (Don't** include listed property. See instructions.)

14	Special depreciation allowance for qualified property (other than listed property) placed in service during the tax year. See instructions	14	**1,120,000**
15	Property subject to section 168(f)(1) election	15	
16	Other depreciation (including ACRS)	16	

Part III **MACRS Depreciation (Don't** include listed property. See instructions.)

Section A

17	MACRS deductions for assets placed in service in tax years beginning before 2021	17	**169,338**
18	If you are electing to group any assets placed in service during the tax year into one or more general asset accounts, check here ▶ ☐		

Section B—Assets Placed in Service During 2021 Tax Year Using the General Depreciation System

(a) Classification of property	(b) Month and year placed in service	(c) Basis for depreciation (business/investment use only—see instructions)	(d) Recovery period	(e) Convention	(f) Method	(g) Depreciation deduction
19a 3-year property						
b 5-year property						
c 7-year property						
d 10-year property						
e 15-year property						
f 20-year property						
g 25-year property			25 yrs.		S/L	
h Residential rental property			27.5 yrs.	MM	S/L	
			27.5 yrs.	MM	S/L	
i Nonresidential real property			39 yrs.	MM	S/L	
				MM	S/L	

Section C—Assets Placed in Service During 2021 Tax Year Using the Alternative Depreciation System

20a Class life					S/L	
b 12-year			12 yrs.		S/L	
c 30-year			30 yrs.	MM	S/L	
d 40-year			40 yrs.	MM	S/L	

Part IV **Summary** (See instructions.)

21	Listed property. Enter amount from line 28	21	
22	**Total.** Add amounts from line 12, lines 14 through 17, lines 19 and 20 in column (g), and line 21. Enter here and on the appropriate lines of your return. Partnerships and S corporations—see instructions	22	**2,369,388**
23	For assets shown above and placed in service during the current year, enter the portion of the basis attributable to section 263A costs ... 23		

For Paperwork Reduction Act Notice, see separate instructions. Cat. No. 12906N Form **4562** (2021)

Source: irs.gov.

AMORTIZATION

LO 10-4

Businesses recover the cost of intangible assets through amortization rather than depreciation. Intangible assets in the form of capitalized expenditures, such as capitalized **research and experimentation (R&E) costs** or **covenants not to compete,** do not have physical characteristics. Nonetheless, they may have determinable lives. While research and experimentation costs may have an indeterminate life, a covenant not to compete, for example, would have a life equal to the stated term of the contractual agreement. When the life of intangible assets cannot be determined, taxpayers recover the cost of the assets when they dispose of them—unless they are assigned a specific tax recovery period.

For tax purposes, an intangible asset can be placed into one of the following four general categories:

1. §197 purchased intangibles.
2. Organizational expenditures and start-up costs.
3. Research and experimentation costs.
4. Patents and copyrights.

Businesses amortize all intangible assets in these categories using the straight-line method for both financial accounting and tax purposes.

Section 197 Intangibles

When a business purchases the *assets* of another business for a single purchase price, the business must determine the initial basis of each of the assets it acquired in the transaction. To determine basis, the business must allocate a portion of the purchase price to each of the individual assets acquired in the transaction. Generally, under this approach, each asset acquired (cash, machinery, and real property, for example) takes an initial basis equal to its fair market value. However, some of the assets acquired in the transaction may not appear on the seller's balance sheet. In fact, a substantial portion of a business's value may exist in the form of intangible assets such as customer lists, patents, trademarks, trade names, goodwill, going-concern value, covenants not to compete, and so forth. Nearly all these assets are amortized according to §197 of the Internal Revenue Code—hence, they are often referred to **§197 intangibles.**

According to §197, these assets have a recovery period of 180 months (15 years), *regardless of their useful life*.[57] For example, when a business buys an existing business, the owner selling the business often signs a covenant not to compete for a specified period such as 5 years.[58] Even though a five-year covenant not to compete clearly has a fixed and determinable life, it must be amortized over 180 months (15 years). The **full-month convention** applies to the amortization of purchased intangibles. This convention allows taxpayers to deduct an entire month's amortization for the month of purchase and all subsequent months in the year. The full-month convention also applies in the month of sale or disposition.[59]

THE KEY FACTS

§197 Intangible Assets

- Purchased intangibles are amortized over a period of 180 months, regardless of their explicitly stated lives.
- The full-month convention applies to amortizable assets.

[57] Section 197 was Congress's response to taxpayers manipulating the valuation and recovery periods assigned to these purchased intangibles.

[58] A covenant not to compete is a contract between the seller of a business and its buyer that the seller will not operate a similar business that would compete with the previous business for a specified period of time.

[59] Reg. §1.197-2(g)(1)(i) illustrates the special rules that apply when a taxpayer sells a §197 intangible or the intangible becomes worthless and the taxpayer's basis in the asset exceeds the sale proceeds (if any). A business may recognize a loss on the sale or disposition only when the business does not hold any other §197 assets that the business acquired in the *same initial transaction*. Otherwise, the taxpayer may not deduct the loss on the sale or disposition until the business sells or disposes of *all* of the other §197 intangibles that it purchased in the same initial transaction. The same loss disallowance rule applies if a §197 intangible expires before it is fully amortized.

Example 10-21

What if: Assume that on January 30, 2022, Teton acquires a competitor's assets for $350,000.[60] Of the $350,000 purchase price, $125,000 is allocated to tangible assets and $225,000 is allocated to §197 intangible assets (patent, $25,000; customer list with a three-year life, $50,000; and goodwill, $150,000).[61] For each of the first three years, Teton would deduct one-fifteenth of the basis of each asset as amortization expense. What is Teton's accumulated amortization and remaining basis in each of these §197 intangibles after three years?

Answer: See the table below:

Description	Patent	Customer List	Goodwill
Initial basis	$25,000	$50,000	$150,000
Accumulated amortization (3/15 of original basis)	(5,000)	(10,000)	(30,000)
Remaining basis	$20,000	$40,000	$120,000

When a taxpayer sells a §197 intangible for more than its basis, the taxpayer recognizes gain. We describe how to characterize this type of gain in the next chapter.

TAXES IN THE REAL WORLD The Case of How Sports Owners Pay Lower Tax Rates Than the Stadium Beer Server

ProPublica, an investigative journalism nonprofit, obtained proprietary IRS data on thousands of America's wealthiest individuals. Among other things, these data revealed the tax rates of some of the sports team owners and compared them to the tax rates of players and even stadium employees. Their analysis showed that the owners often paid the lowest tax rate! As an example, Steve Ballmer, owner of the Los Angeles Clippers, had a federal income tax rate of 12 percent on $656 million in 2019. That same year, LeBron James (LA Lakers) paid a federal income tax rate of 35.9 percent on $124 million, and Adelaide Avila (Staples Center employee) had a federal income tax rate of 14.1 percent on $44,810. So, how does this happen? The answer relates to how the price of a sports franchise is treated under the U.S. tax code. A sports team's most valuable assets are generally its TV and player contracts. These assets can represent upward of 90 percent of the team's value. When the franchise is acquired, the purchase price is allocated to the team's assets, which are then subject to depreciation or, more importantly in this instance, amortization rules. Under §197, the intangible assets acquired with a business purchase are amortized and deducted over a 15-year period. These amortization deductions can turn profits into what looks like a huge tax loss. As the owner of the franchise, Ballmer and others can use these losses to offset other income. LeBron James's and Adelaide Avila's incomes are typically subject to ordinary income tax rates with no benefit from amortization.

Source: Based on Robert Faturechi, Justin Elliott, and Ellis Simani, "The Billionaire Playbook: How Sports Owners Use Their Teams to Avoid Millions in Taxes," *ProPublica* (July 8, 2021), www.propublica.org/article/the-billionaire-playbook-how-sports-owners-use-their-teams-to-avoid-millions-in-taxes.

Organizational Expenditures and Start-Up Costs

Organizational expenditures include expenditures to form and organize a business in the form of a corporation or an entity taxed as a partnership.[62] Organizational expenditures typically include costs of organizational meetings, state fees, accounting service costs incident to organization, and legal service expenditures such as document drafting,

[60] If a business acquires a corporation's stock (rather than assets), there is no goodwill assigned for tax purposes, and the purchase price simply becomes the basis of the stock purchased.

[61] A customer list is the value assigned to current customers (i.e., the lists that will allow the new owner to capture future benefits from the current customers).

[62] §248 for corporations and §709 for partnerships. Sole proprietorships cannot deduct organizational expenditures.

taking minutes of organizational meetings, and creating terms of the original stock certificates. These costs are generally incurred prior to the starting of business (or shortly thereafter) but relate to creating the business entity. The costs of selling or marketing stock do *not* qualify as organizational expenditures and cannot be amortized.[63]

Example 10-22

What if: Suppose Teton was organized as a corporation rather than a sole proprietorship (sole proprietorships cannot deduct organizational expenditures). Steve paid $35,000 of legal costs to Scott, Tang, and Malan to draft the corporate charter and articles of incorporation; $10,000 to Harvey and Stratford for accounting fees related to the organization; and $7,000 for organizational meetings, $5,000 for stock issuance costs, and $1,000 for state fees related to the incorporation. What amounts of these expenditures qualify as organizational expenditures?

Answer: $53,000, computed as follows (with the exception of the stock issuance costs, each of Teton's expenses qualifies as an amortizable organizational expenditure):

Description	Qualifying Organizational Expenditures
Legal drafting of corporate charter and articles of incorporation	$ 35,000
Accounting fees related to organization	10,000
Organizational meetings	7,000
Stock issuance costs	0
State incorporation fees	1,000
Total	**$53,000**

THE KEY FACTS

Organizational Expenditures and Start-Up Costs

- Taxpayers may immediately expense up to $5,000 of organizational expenditures and $5,000 of start-up costs.
- The immediate expense rule has a dollar-for-dollar phase-out that begins at $50,000 for organizational expenditures and for start-up costs. Thus, when organizational expenditures or start-up costs exceed $55,000, there is no immediate expensing.

Businesses may *immediately expense* up to $5,000 of organizational expenditures.[64] However, corporations and partnerships incurring more than $50,000 in organizational expenditures must phase out (reduce) the $5,000 immediate expense amount dollar-for-dollar for expenditures exceeding $50,000. Thus, businesses incurring at least $55,000 of organizational expenditures are not allowed to immediately expense any of the expenditures.

Example 10-23

What if: Suppose Teton is a corporation and it wants to maximize its first-year organizational expenditure deduction. As described in Example 10-22, Teton incurred $53,000 of organizational expenditures in year 1. How much of the organizational expenditures can Teton immediately deduct in year 1?

Answer: $2,000, computed as follows:

Description	Amount	Explanation
(1) Maximum immediate expense	$ 5,000	§248(a)(1)
(2) Total organizational expenditures	53,000	Example 10-22
(3) Phase-out threshold	50,000	§248(a)(1)(B)
(4) Immediate expense phase-out	$ 3,000	(2) – (3)
(5) Allowable immediate expense	**$ 2,000**	(1) – (4), but not below zero
Remaining organizational expenditures	$51,000*	(2) – (5)

*As we discuss below, Teton amortizes the remaining organizational expenditures over 180 months beginning in the month it starts business.

(continued on page 10-34)

[63]These costs are called syndication costs and are capitalized and deducted on the final tax return.

[64]§248(a)(1) for corporations or §709 for partnerships.

What if: Assuming that Teton is a corporation and that it incurred $41,000 of organizational expenditures in year 1, how much of the organizational expenditures could Teton immediately expense in year 1?

Answer: $5,000, computed as follows:

Description	Amount	Explanation
(1) Maximum immediate expense	$ 5,000	§248(a)(1)
(2) Total organizational expenditures	41,000	
(3) Phase-out threshold	50,000	§248(a)(1)(B)
(4) Immediate expense phase-out	$ 0	(2) – (3), limit to zero
(5) Allowable immediate expense	**$ 5,000**	(1) – (4)
Remaining organizational expenditures	$36,000*	(2) – (5)

*As we discuss below, Teton amortizes the remaining organizational expenditures over 180 months beginning in the month it starts business.

What if: Assuming that Teton is a corporation and it incurred $60,000 of organizational expenditures in year 1, how much of the organizational expenditures could Teton immediately expense in year 1?

Answer: $0, computed as follows:

Description	Amount	Explanation
(1) Maximum immediate expense	$ 5,000	§248(a)(1)
(2) Total organizational expenditures	60,000	
(3) Phase-out threshold	50,000	§248(a)(1)(B)
(4) Immediate expense phase-out	$10,000	(2) – (3)
(5) Allowable immediate expense	**$ 0**	(1) – (4), limited to zero
Remaining organizational expenditures	$60,000*	(2) – (5)

*As we discuss below, Teton amortizes the remaining organizational expenditures over 180 months beginning in the month it starts business.

Businesses amortize organizational expenditures that they do not immediately expense using the straight-line method over a recovery period of 15 years (180 months beginning in the month it starts business).

Example 10-24

What if: Assume Teton is a corporation and it amortizes the $51,000 of organizational expenditures remaining after it immediately expenses $2,000 of the costs (see the first *what if* scenario in Example 10-23). If Teton began business on February 1 of year 1, how much total cost recovery expense for the organizational expenditures is Teton able to deduct in year 1? How much cost recovery expense will Teton be able to deduct in year 2?

Answer: $5,117 in year 1 and $3,400 in year 2, computed as follows:

Description	Amount	Explanation
(1) Total organizational expenditures	$53,000	Example 10-22
(2) Amount immediately expensed	2,000	Example 10-23
(3) Expenditures subject to straight-line amortization	$51,000	(1) – (2)
(4) Recovery period in months	180	15 years; §248(a)(2)
(5) Monthly straight-line amortization	283.33	(3)/(4)
(6) Teton business months during year 1	× 11	February through December
(7) Year 1 straight-line amortization	$ 3,117	(5) × (6) (using full-month convention)
Total year 1 cost recovery expense for organizational expenditures	**$ 5,117**	(2) + (7)
Total year 2 cost recovery expense	**$ 3,400**	(3)/15 years

Start-up costs are costs businesses incur to, not surprisingly, start up a business.[65] Start-up costs apply to sole proprietorships, entities taxed as partnerships, and corporations.[66] These costs include costs associated with investigating the possibilities of and actually creating or acquiring a trade or business. For example, costs Teton incurs in deciding whether to locate the business in Cody, Wyoming, or Bozeman, Montana, are start-up costs. Start-up costs also include costs that would normally be deductible as ordinary business expenses except that they don't qualify as business expenses because they are incurred before the trade or business activity actually begins. For example, costs Teton incurs to train its employees before the business begins are start-up costs.

The rules for immediately expensing and amortizing start-up costs are the same as those for immediately expensing and amortizing organizational expenditures. Consequently, businesses incurring at least $55,000 of start-up costs are not allowed to immediately expense any of the costs. The limitations are computed separately for organizational expenditures and for start-up costs. Thus, a business could immediately expense $5,000 of organizational expenditures and $5,000 of start-up costs in its first year of business in addition to the 15-year amortization amount.

Example 10-25

What if: Assume that in January of year 1 (before it began business on February 1), Teton spent $4,500 investigating the climbing hardware market, creating company logos, and determining the locations for both the office and manufacturing facility. The $4,500 of expenditures qualify as start-up costs. How much of the $4,500 of start-up costs is Teton allowed to immediately expense?

Answer: All $4,500. Teton is allowed to immediately expense the entire $4,500 because its total start-up costs do not exceed $50,000.

Exhibit 10-13 illustrates the timing of organizational expenditures, start-up costs, and normal trade or business expenses.

EXHIBIT 10-13 Summary of Timing for Organizational Expenditures, Start-Up Costs, and Normal Trade or Business Expenses

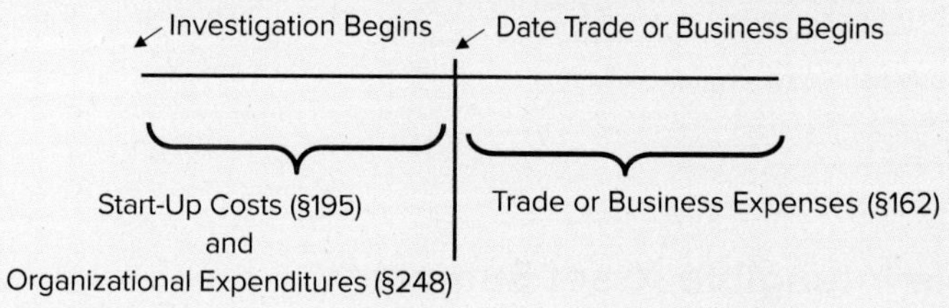

Research and Experimentation Expenditures

To stay competitive, businesses often invest in activities they believe will generate innovative products or significantly improve their current products or processes. These research and experimentation costs include expenditures for research laboratories, including salaries, materials, and other related expenses. In tax years beginning after December 31, 2021, these costs are capitalized and amortized ratably over 5 years beginning with the midpoint of the year in which the costs were incurred. Research and experimentation expenditures attributable to research conducted outside the United States are capitalized and amortized ratably over a period of 15 years for tax years beginning after December 31, 2021.[67] However, when

[65]§195.

[66]Recall that rules for amortizing organizational expenditures apply only to corporations and partnerships.

[67]See §174. For tax years beginning before January 1, 2022, businesses could immediately expense research and experimentation costs or elect to capitalize the costs and amortize them. The research and experimentation credit is also available to some businesses.

a business receives a patent relating to the expenditures, it must stop amortizing the costs. When the business obtains a patent, it adds any remaining basis in the costs to the basis of the patent and it amortizes the basis of the patent over the patent's life (see discussion below).

Patents and Copyrights

The manner in which a business amortizes a patent or copyright depends on whether the business directly purchases the patent or copyright or whether it creates it. Businesses directly purchasing patents or copyrights (not in an asset acquisition to which §197 applies) amortize the cost over the remaining life of the patents or copyrights.[68] Businesses that create patents or copyrights amortize the cost or basis of the self-created intangible assets over their legal lives. The costs included in the basis of a self-created patent or copyright include legal costs, fees, and, as we discussed above, unamortized research and experimentation expenditures associated with the creation of the patent or copyright. However, because the patent approval process is slow, the unamortized research and experimentation costs included in the patent's basis are likely to be relatively small because, with a five-year recovery period, the research and experimentation costs would likely be mostly or even fully amortized by the time the patent is approved.

Example 10-26

In September of year 1, Teton purchased a patent with a remaining life of 10 years from Chouinard Equipment for $60,000. What amount of amortization expense is Teton allowed to deduct for the patent in year 1? In year 2?

Answer: $2,000 in year 1 and $6,000 in year 2, computed as follows:

Description	Amount	Explanation
(1) Cost of patent	$60,000	
(2) Remaining life of patent in months	120	10 years
(3) Monthly amortization	$ 500	(1)/(2)
(4) Months in year 1 Teton held patent	× 4	September through December
(5) Monthly straight-line amortization (year 1)	**$ 2,000**	(3) × (4)
(6) Unamortized cost of patent at end of year 1	$58,000	(1) – (5)
(7) Monthly straight-line amortization (year 2)	$ 6,000	(3) × 12 months

Amortizable Intangible Asset Summary

Exhibit 10-14 summarizes the different types of amortizable intangible assets, identifies the recovery period of these assets, and describes the applicable amortization method for each asset. Exhibit 10-14 also identifies the applicable convention for each type of amortizable intangible asset and identifies the financial accounting treatment for recovering the cost of the intangible assets under GAAP.

Exhibit 10-15 presents Teton's amortization expense as it would be reported on its tax return on Form 4562 (the exhibit assumes that Teton is a corporation so it can amortize organizational expenditures). We use the 2021 form because the 2022 form is not yet available. The amortization is reported on line 43 because it is Teton's second year in business. The amortization amount of $9,400 is from organizational expenditures of $3,400 (Example 10-24) and a patent, $6,000 (Example 10-26). The amortization would be reported on line 42 (with more detail) had this been Teton's first year in business.

[68]§167(f).

EXHIBIT 10-14 Summary of Amortizable Assets

Asset Description	Recovery Period	Applicable Method	Applicable Convention	Financial Accounting Treatment
§197 purchased intangibles, including goodwill, trademarks, patents, and covenants not to compete[69]	180 months	Straight-line	Full-month, beginning with month of purchase	ASC 350 tests for annual impairment
Organizational expenditures and start-up costs that are required to be capitalized	180 months	Straight-line	Full-month, in month business begins	AICPA SOP 98-5
Research and experimentation costs	Ratably over 5 years	Straight-line	Midpoint of the tax year in which the costs are paid or incurred	Expensed
Self-created patents and copyrights	Actual life	Straight-line	Full-month, in month intangible is obtained	Expensed
Purchased patents and copyrights	Remaining life	Straight-line	Full-month, in month intangible is obtained	Expensed

EXHIBIT 10-15 Teton Form 4562 Part VI for Amortization of Organizational Expenditures and Patent

Part VI Amortization

(a) Description of costs	(b) Date amortization begins	(c) Amortizable amount	(d) Code section	(e) Amortization period or percentage	(f) Amortization for this year
42 Amortization of costs that begins during your 2021 tax year (see instructions):					
43 Amortization of costs that began before your 2021 tax year				43	9,400
44 **Total.** Add amounts in column (f). See the instructions for where to report				44	9,400

Form **4562** (2021)

Source: irs.gov.

(continued from page 10-16 . . .)

Teton was developing some additional employee parking on a lot adjacent to the warehouse when the excavation crew discovered a small gold deposit. Steve called his friend Ken, who had some experience in mining precious metals, to see what Ken thought of the find. Ken was impressed and offered Steve $1,500,000 for the rights to the gold. Steve accepted the offer on Teton's behalf. ■

DEPLETION

LO 10-5

Depletion is the method taxpayers use to recover their capital investment in natural resources. Depletion is a particularly significant deduction for businesses in the mining, oil and gas, and forestry industries. These businesses generally incur depletion expense as they use the natural resource. Specifically, businesses compute annual depletion expense under both the cost and percentage depletion methods and deduct the larger of the two.[70]

[69]A patent or copyright that is part of a basket purchase (several assets together) is treated as a §197 intangible. A patent or copyright that is purchased separately is simply amortized over its remaining life [§167(f)].

[70]Depletion of timber and major integrated oil companies must be calculated using only the cost depletion method (i.e., no percentage depletion is available).

Under **cost depletion,** taxpayers must estimate or determine the number of recoverable units or reserves (tons of coal, barrels of oil, or board feet of timber, for example) that remain at the beginning of the year and allocate a pro rata share of the property's adjusted basis to each unit. To determine the cost depletion amount, taxpayers then multiply the per-unit basis amount by the number of units sold during the year.[71]

Example 10-27

THE KEY FACTS

Depletion

- Cost depletion involves estimating resource reserves and allocating a pro rata share of basis based on the number of units extracted.
- Percentage depletion is determined by a statutory percentage of gross income that is permitted to be expensed each year. Different resources have different statutory percentages (e.g., gold, tin, coal).
- Taxpayers may expense the larger of cost or percentage depletion.

Ken's cost basis in the gold is the $1,500,000 he paid for it. Based on a mining engineer's estimate that the gold deposit probably holds 1,000 ounces of gold, Ken can determine his cost depletion. What is Ken's cost depletion for year 1 and year 2, assuming he extracts and sells 300 and 700 ounces of gold in year 1 and year 2, respectively?

Answer: $450,000 in year 1 and $1,050,000 in year 2, computed as follows:

Description	Amount	Explanation
(1) Cost basis in gold	$ 1,500,000	
(2) Estimated ounces of gold	1,000	
(3) Per-ounce cost depletion rate	1,500	(1)/(2)
(4) Year 1 ounces sold	300	
(5) Year 1 cost depletion	**$ 450,000**	(3) × (4)
(6) Basis remaining after year 1 depletion	1,050,000	(1) − (5)
(7) Year 2 ounces sold	700	
(8) Year 2 cost depletion	**$1,050,000**	(7) × (3)
Basis remaining after year 2 depletion	$ 0	(6) − (8)

Ken is not eligible for cost depletion after year 2 because as of the end of year 2, his cost basis has been reduced to $0.

Because the cost depletion method requires businesses to estimate the number of units of the resource they will actually extract, it is possible that their estimate will prove to be inaccurate. If they underestimate the number of units, they will fully deplete the cost basis of the resource before they have fully extracted the resource. Once they have recovered the entire cost basis of the resource, businesses are not allowed to use cost depletion to determine depletion expense. They may, however, continue to use percentage depletion (see discussion below). If a business overestimates the number of units to be extracted, it will still have basis remaining after the resource has been fully extracted. In these situations, the business deducts the unrecovered basis once it has sold all the remaining units.

The amount of **percentage depletion** for a natural resource business activity is determined by multiplying the *gross income* from the resource extraction activity by a fixed percentage based on the type of natural resource, as indicated in Exhibit 10-16.[72]

EXHIBIT 10-16 Applicable Percentage Depletion Rates

Statutory Percentage	Natural Resources (partial list)
5 percent [§613(b)(6)]	Gravel, pumice, and stone
14 percent [§613(b)(3)]	Asphalt rock, clay, and other metals
15 percent [§613(b)(2)]	Gold, copper, oil shale, and silver
15 percent [§613A(c)(1)]	Domestic oil and gas
22 percent [§613(b)(1)]	Platinum, sulfur, uranium, and titanium

[71]§612.

[72]§613.

In many cases, percentage depletion may generate *larger* depletion deductions than cost depletion. Recall that taxpayers are allowed to deduct the greater of cost or percentage depletion. Businesses reduce their initial basis in the resource when they deduct percentage depletion. However, once the initial basis is exhausted, they are allowed to continue to deduct percentage (but not cost) depletion. This provides a potentially significant governmental subsidy to extraction businesses that have completely recovered their costs in a natural resource.[73]

Note that businesses deduct percentage depletion when they *sell* the natural resource, and they deduct cost depletion in the year they *produce* or *extract* the natural resource. Also, percentage depletion cannot exceed 50 percent (100 percent in the case of oil and gas properties) of the taxable income from the natural resource business activity before considering the depletion expense, while cost depletion has no such limitation.

Example 10-28

In Example 10-27, Ken determined his cost depletion expense for the gold. However, because he is allowed to deduct the greater of cost or percentage depletion each year, he set out to determine his percentage depletion for year 2. Assuming that Ken has gross (taxable) income from the gold mining activity before depletion expense of $2,000,000 ($500,000), $6,000,000 ($4,500,000), and $6,000,000 ($5,000,000) in year 1, year 2, and year 3, respectively, what is his percentage depletion expense for each of these three years?

Answer: $250,000, $900,000, and $900,000 for years 1, 2, and 3, respectively, computed as follows:

Description	Year 1	Year 2	Year 3	Explanation
(1) Taxable income from activity (before depletion expense)	$ 500,000	$4,500,000	$5,000,000	
(2) Gross income	$2,000,000	$6,000,000	$6,000,000	
(3) Percentage	× 15%	× 15%	× 15%	Exhibit 10-16
(4) Percentage depletion expense before limit	$ 300,000	$ 900,000	$ 900,000	(2) × (3)
(5) 50 percent of taxable income limitation	$ 250,000	$2,250,000	$2,500,000	(1) × 50%
Allowable percentage depletion	**$ 250,000**	**$ 900,000**	**$ 900,000**	Lesser of (4) or (5)

Finally, as we discussed above, a business's depletion deduction is the greater of either the annual cost or percentage depletion.

Example 10-29

Based on his computations of cost depletion and percentage depletion, Ken was able to determine his deductible depletion expense. Using the cost and percentage depletion computations from Examples 10-27 and 10-28, what is Ken's deductible depletion expense for years 1, 2, and 3?

Answer: $450,000 for year 1, $1,050,000 for year 2, and $900,000 for year 3, computed as follows:

Tax Depletion Expense	Year 1	Year 2	Year 3	Explanation
(1) Cost depletion	$ 450,000	$ 1,050,000	$ 0	Example 10-27
(2) Percentage depletion	$ 250,000	$ 900,000	$ 900,000	Example 10-28
Allowable expense	**$450,000**	**$1,050,000**	**$900,000**	Greater of (1) or (2)

[73]Percentage depletion in excess of basis is an AMT preference item.

CONCLUSION

This chapter describes and discusses how businesses recover the costs of their tangible and intangible assets. Cost recovery is important because it represents a significant tax deduction for many businesses. Businesses must routinely make choices that affect the amount and timing of these deductions. Further understanding cost recovery basics helps businesses determine how to compute and characterize the gain and loss they recognize when they sell or otherwise dispose of business assets. We address the interaction between cost recovery deductions and gain and loss on property dispositions in the next chapter.

Appendix A MACRS Tables

TABLE 1 MACRS Half-Year Convention

	Depreciation Rate for Recovery Period					
Year	**3-Year**	**5-Year**	**7-Year**	**10-Year**	**15-Year**	**20-Year**
1	33.33%	20.00%	14.29%	10.00%	5.00%	3.750%
2	44.45	32.00	24.49	18.00	9.50	7.219
3	14.81	19.20	17.49	14.40	8.55	6.677
4	7.41	11.52	12.49	11.52	7.70	6.177
5		11.52	8.93	9.22	6.93	5.713
6		5.76	8.92	7.37	6.23	5.285
7			8.93	6.55	5.90	4.888
8			4.46	6.55	5.90	4.522
9				6.56	5.91	4.462
10				6.55	5.90	4.461
11				3.28	5.91	4.462
12					5.90	4.461
13					5.91	4.462
14					5.90	4.461
15					5.91	4.462
16					2.95	4.461
17						4.462
18						4.461
19						4.462
20						4.461
21						2.231

TABLE 2a MACRS Mid-Quarter Convention: *For property placed in service during the first quarter*

	Depreciation Rate for Recovery Period	
Year	**5-Year**	**7-Year**
1	35.00%	25.00%
2	26.00	21.43
3	15.60	15.31
4	11.01	10.93
5	11.01	8.75
6	1.38	8.74
7		8.75
8		1.09

TABLE 2b **MACRS Mid-Quarter Convention:** *For property placed in service during the second quarter*

Depreciation Rate for Recovery Period		
Year	5-Year	7-Year
1	25.00%	17.85%
2	30.00	23.47
3	18.00	16.76
4	11.37	11.97
5	11.37	8.87
6	4.26	8.87
7		8.87
8		3.34

TABLE 2c **MACRS Mid-Quarter Convention:** *For property placed in service during the third quarter*

Depreciation Rate for Recovery Period		
Year	5-Year	7-Year
1	15.00%	10.71%
2	34.00	25.51
3	20.40	18.22
4	12.24	13.02
5	11.30	9.30
6	7.06	8.85
7		8.86
8		5.53

TABLE 2d **MACRS Mid-Quarter Convention:** *For property placed in service during the fourth quarter*

Depreciation Rate for Recovery Period		
Year	5-Year	7-Year
1	5.00%	3.57%
2	38.00	27.55
3	22.80	19.68
4	13.68	14.06
5	10.94	10.04
6	9.58	8.73
7		8.73
8		7.64

TABLE 3 Residential Rental Property Mid-Month Convention Straight-Line—27.5 Years

	Month Property Placed in Service											
Year	1	2	3	4	5	6	7	8	9	10	11	12
1	3.485%	3.182%	2.879%	2.576%	2.273%	1.970%	1.667%	1.364%	1.061%	0.758%	0.455%	0.152%
2–9	3.636	3.636	3.636	3.636	3.636	3.636	3.636	3.636	3.636	3.636	3.636	3.636
10	3.637	3.637	3.637	3.637	3.637	3.637	3.636	3.636	3.636	3.636	3.636	3.636
11	3.636	3.636	3.636	3.636	3.636	3.636	3.637	3.637	3.637	3.637	3.637	3.637
12	3.637	3.637	3.637	3.637	3.637	3.637	3.636	3.636	3.636	3.636	3.636	3.636
13	3.636	3.636	3.636	3.636	3.636	3.636	3.637	3.637	3.637	3.637	3.637	3.637
14	3.637	3.637	3.637	3.637	3.637	3.637	3.636	3.636	3.636	3.636	3.636	3.636
15	3.636	3.636	3.636	3.636	3.636	3.636	3.637	3.637	3.637	3.637	3.637	3.637
16	3.637	3.637	3.637	3.637	3.637	3.637	3.636	3.636	3.636	3.636	3.636	3.636
17	3.636	3.636	3.636	3.636	3.636	3.636	3.637	3.637	3.637	3.637	3.637	3.637
18	3.637	3.637	3.637	3.637	3.637	3.637	3.636	3.636	3.636	3.636	3.636	3.636
19	3.636	3.636	3.636	3.636	3.636	3.636	3.637	3.637	3.637	3.637	3.637	3.637
20	3.637	3.637	3.637	3.637	3.637	3.637	3.636	3.636	3.636	3.636	3.636	3.636
21	3.636	3.636	3.636	3.636	3.636	3.636	3.637	3.637	3.637	3.637	3.637	3.637
22	3.637	3.637	3.637	3.637	3.637	3.637	3.636	3.636	3.636	3.636	3.636	3.636
23	3.636	3.636	3.636	3.636	3.636	3.636	3.637	3.637	3.637	3.637	3.637	3.637
24	3.637	3.637	3.637	3.637	3.637	3.637	3.636	3.636	3.636	3.636	3.636	3.636
25	3.636	3.636	3.636	3.636	3.636	3.636	3.637	3.637	3.637	3.637	3.637	3.637
26	3.637	3.637	3.637	3.637	3.637	3.637	3.636	3.636	3.636	3.636	3.636	3.636
27	3.636	3.636	3.636	3.636	3.636	3.636	3.637	3.637	3.637	3.637	3.637	3.637
28	1.97	2.273	2.576	2.879	3.182	3.485	3.636	3.636	3.636	3.636	3.636	3.636
29							0.152	0.455	0.758	1.061	1.364	1.667

TABLE 4 Nonresidential Real Property Mid-Month Convention Straight-Line—31.5 Years (for assets placed in service before May 13, 1993)

	Month Property Placed in Service											
Year	1	2	3	4	5	6	7	8	9	10	11	12
1	3.042%	2.778%	2.513%	2.249%	1.984%	1.720%	1.455%	1.190%	0.926%	0.661%	0.397%	0.132%
2–7	3.175	3.175	3.175	3.175	3.175	3.175	3.175	3.175	3.175	3.175	3.175	3.175
8	3.175	3.174	3.175	3.174	3.175	3.174	3.175	3.175	3.175	3.175	3.175	3.175
9	3.174	3.175	3.174	3.175	3.174	3.175	3.174	3.175	3.174	3.175	3.174	3.175
10	3.175	3.174	3.175	3.174	3.175	3.174	3.175	3.174	3.175	3.174	3.175	3.174
11	3.174	3.175	3.174	3.175	3.174	3.175	3.174	3.175	3.174	3.175	3.174	3.175
12	3.175	3.174	3.175	3.174	3.175	3.174	3.175	3.174	3.175	3.174	3.175	3.174
13	3.174	3.175	3.174	3.175	3.174	3.175	3.174	3.175	3.174	3.175	3.174	3.175
14	3.175	3.174	3.175	3.174	3.175	3.174	3.175	3.174	3.175	3.174	3.175	3.174
15	3.174	3.175	3.174	3.175	3.174	3.175	3.174	3.175	3.174	3.175	3.174	3.175
16	3.175	3.174	3.175	3.174	3.175	3.174	3.175	3.174	3.175	3.174	3.175	3.174
17	3.174	3.175	3.174	3.175	3.174	3.175	3.174	3.175	3.174	3.175	3.174	3.175
18	3.175	3.174	3.175	3.174	3.175	3.174	3.175	3.174	3.175	3.174	3.175	3.174
19	3.174	3.175	3.174	3.175	3.174	3.175	3.174	3.175	3.174	3.175	3.174	3.175
20	3.175	3.174	3.175	3.174	3.175	3.174	3.175	3.174	3.175	3.174	3.175	3.174
21	3.174	3.175	3.174	3.175	3.174	3.175	3.174	3.175	3.174	3.175	3.174	3.175
22	3.175	3.174	3.175	3.174	3.175	3.174	3.175	3.174	3.175	3.174	3.175	3.174
23	3.174	3.175	3.174	3.175	3.174	3.175	3.174	3.115	3.174	3.175	3.174	3.175
24	3.175	3.174	3.175	3.174	3.175	3.174	3.175	3.174	3.175	3.174	3.175	3.174
25	3.174	3.175	3.174	3.175	3.174	3.175	3.174	3.175	3.174	3.175	3.174	3.175
26	3.175	3.174	3.175	3.174	3.175	3.174	3.175	3.174	3.175	3.174	3.175	3.174
27	3.174	3.175	3.174	3.175	3.174	3.175	3.174	3.175	3.174	3.175	3.174	3.175
28	3.175	3.174	3.175	3.174	3.175	3.174	3.175	3.174	3.175	3.174	3.175	3.174
29	3.174	3.175	3.174	3.175	3.174	3.175	3.174	3.175	3.174	3.175	3.174	3.175
30	3.175	3.174	3.175	3.174	3.175	3.174	3.175	3.174	3.175	3.174	3.175	3.174
31	3.174	3.175	3.174	3.175	3.174	3.175	3.174	3.175	3.174	3.175	3.174	3.175
32	1.720	1.984	2.249	2.513	2.778	3.042	3.175	3.174	3.175	3.174	3.175	3.174
33							0.132	0.397	0.661	0.926	1.190	1.455

TABLE 5 Nonresidential Real Property Mid-Month Convention Straight-Line—39 Years (for assets placed in service on or after May 13, 1993)

	Month Property Placed in Service											
Year	1	2	3	4	5	6	7	8	9	10	11	12
1	2.461%	2.247%	2.033%	1.819%	1.605%	1.391%	1.177%	0.963%	0.749%	0.535%	0.321%	0.107%
2–39	2.564	2.564	2.564	2.564	2.564	2.564	2.564	2.564	2.564	2.564	2.564	2.564
40	0.107	0.321	0.535	0.749	0.963	1.177	1.391	1.605	1.819	2.033	2.247	2.461

Summary

LO 10-1 Describe the cost recovery methods for recovering the cost of personal property, real property, intangible assets, and natural resources.

- Tangible personal and real property (depreciation), intangibles (amortization), and natural resources (depletion) are all subject to cost recovery.
- An asset's initial basis is the amount that is subject to cost recovery. Generally, an asset's initial basis is its purchase price, plus the cost of any other expenses incurred to get the asset in working condition.
- The taxpayer's basis of assets acquired in a tax-deferred exchange is the same basis the taxpayer transferred to acquire the property received.
- Expenditures on an asset are either expensed currently or capitalized as a new asset. Expenditures for routine or general maintenance of the asset are expensed currently. Expenditures that better, restore, or adapt an asset to a new use are capitalized.
- When acquiring a business and purchasing a bundle of property, the basis of each asset is determined as the fair market value of the asset.

LO 10-2 Determine the applicable cost recovery (depreciation) life, method, and convention for tangible personal and real property and the deduction allowable under basic MACRS.

- Tax depreciation is calculated under the Modified Accelerated Cost Recovery System (MACRS).
- MACRS for tangible personal property is based upon the recovery period (Rev. Proc. 87-56), method (200 percent declining balance, 150 percent declining balance, and straight-line), and convention (half-year or mid-quarter).
- Real property is divided into two groups for tax purposes: residential rental and nonresidential. The recovery period is 27.5 years for residential property and 31.5 years or 39 years for nonresidential property, depending on when the property was placed in service. The depreciation method is straight-line and the convention is mid-month.

LO 10-3 Calculate the deduction allowable under the additional special cost recovery rules (§179, bonus, and listed property).

- §179 allows taxpayers to expense qualified property. The deduction is limited by the amount of property placed in service and taxable income.
- Bonus depreciation allows taxpayers to immediately deduct 100 percent of qualified property in the year of acquisition.
- Listed property includes automobiles, other means of transportation, and assets that tend to be used for both business and personal purposes. Depreciation is limited to the expense multiplied by business-use percentage. Special rules apply if business use is less than or equal to 50 percent.
- Additional limitations apply to luxury automobiles.

LO 10-4 Calculate the deduction for amortization.

- Intangible assets (such as patents, goodwill, and trademarks) have their costs recovered through amortization.
- Intangible assets are amortized (straight-line method) using the full-month convention except research and experimentation costs, which use a mid-year convention.
- Intangibles are divided into four types (§197 purchased intangibles, start-up costs and organizational expenditures, research and experimentation, and self-created intangibles).

LO 10-5 Explain cost recovery of natural resources and the allowable depletion methods.

- Depletion allows a taxpayer to recover their capital investment in natural resources.
- Two methods of depletion are available, and the taxpayer must calculate both and take the one that results in the larger depletion deduction each year.
- Cost depletion allows taxpayers to estimate the number of units and then allocate a pro rata share of the basis to each unit extracted during the year.
- Percentage depletion allows the taxpayer to take a statutory determined percentage of gross income as an expense. Deductions are not limited to basis.

KEY TERMS

§179 expense (10-17)
§197 intangibles (10-31)
adjusted basis (10-3)
amortization (10-2)
bonus depreciation (10-21)
cost depletion (10-38)
cost recovery (10-2)
covenants not to compete (10-31)
depletion (10-2)
depreciation (10-2)
full-month convention (10-31)
half-year convention (10-9)
intangible assets (10-2)
listed property (10-23)
luxury automobiles (10-26)
mid-month convention (10-15)
mid-quarter convention (10-9)
Modified Accelerated Cost Recovery System (MACRS) (10-7)
organizational expenditures (10-32)
percentage depletion (10-38)
personal property (10-7)
real property (10-7)
recovery period (10-7)
research and experimentation (R&E) costs (10-31)
start-up costs (10-35)
tax basis (10-3)

DISCUSSION QUESTIONS

Discussion Questions are available in Connect®.

1. Explain why certain long-lived assets are capitalized and recovered over time rather than immediately expensed. LO 10-1
2. Explain the differences and similarities between personal property, real property, intangible property, and natural resources. Also, provide an example of each type of asset. LO 10-1
3. Explain the similarities and dissimilarities between depreciation, amortization, and depletion. Describe the cost recovery method used for each of the four asset types (personal property, real property, intangible property, and natural resources). LO 10-1
4. Is an asset's initial or cost basis simply its purchase price? Explain. LO 10-1
5. Compare and contrast the basis of property acquired via purchase, conversion from personal use to business or rental use, tax-deferred exchange, gift, and inheritance. LO 10-1
6. Explain why the expenses incurred to get an asset in place and operable should be included in the asset's basis. LO 10-1
7. Graber Corporation runs a long-haul trucking business. Graber incurs the following expenses: replacement tires, oil changes, and a transmission overhaul. Which of these expenditures may be deducted currently and which must be capitalized? Explain. LO 10-1
8. MACRS depreciation requires the use of a recovery period, method, and convention to depreciate tangible personal property assets. Briefly explain why each is important to the calculation. LO 10-2
9. Can a taxpayer with very little current-year income choose to not claim any depreciation deduction for the current year and thus save depreciation deductions for the future when the taxpayer expects to be more profitable? LO 10-2
10. What depreciation methods are available for tangible personal property? Explain the characteristics of a business likely to adopt each method. LO 10-2 planning
11. If a business places several different assets in service during the year, must it use the same depreciation method for all assets? If not, what restrictions apply to the business's choices of depreciation methods? LO 10-2
12. Describe how you would determine the MACRS recovery period for an asset if you did not already know it. LO 10-2

research LO 10-2 13. Compare and contrast the recovery periods used by MACRS and those used under generally accepted accounting principles (GAAP).

LO 10-2 14. What are the two depreciation conventions that apply to tangible personal property under MACRS? Explain why Congress provides two methods.

LO 10-2 15. A business buys two identical tangible personal property assets for the same price. It buys one at the beginning of the year and one at the end of the year. Under what conditions would the taxpayer's depreciation on each asset be exactly the same? Under what conditions would it be different?

LO 10-2 16. AAA Inc. acquired a machine in year 1. In May of year 3, it sold the asset. Can AAA find its year 3 depreciation percentage for the machine on the MACRS table? If not, what adjustment must AAA make to its full-year depreciation percentage to determine its year 3 depreciation?

LO 10-2 17. There are two recovery period classifications for real property. What reasons might Congress have to allow residential real estate a shorter recovery period than nonresidential real property?

LO 10-2 18. Discuss why Congress has instructed taxpayers to depreciate real property using the mid-month convention as opposed to the half-year convention used for tangible personal property.

research LO 10-2 19. If a taxpayer has owned a building for 10 years and decides that it should make significant improvements to the building, what is the recovery period for the improvements?

LO 10-2 20. Compare and contrast computing the depreciation deduction for tangible personal property versus computing the depreciation deduction for real property under both the regular tax and alternative tax systems.

LO 10-3 21. Discuss how the property limitation restricts large businesses from taking the §179 expense.

LO 10-3 22. Explain the two limitations placed on the §179 deduction. How are they similar? How are they different?

LO 10-3 23. Compare and contrast the types of businesses that would and would not benefit from the §179 expense.

LO 10-3 24. What strategies will help a business maximize its current depreciation deductions (including §179)? Why might a taxpayer choose *not* to maximize its current depreciation deductions?

LO 10-3 25. Why might a business claim a reduced §179 expense amount in the current year rather than claiming the maximum amount available?

LO 10-3 26. Describe assets that are listed property. Why do you think Congress requires them to be "listed"?

LO 10-3 27. Are taxpayers allowed to claim depreciation on assets they use for both business and personal purposes? What are the tax consequences if the business use drops from above 50 percent in one year to below 50 percent in the next?

LO 10-3 28. Discuss why Congress limits the amount of depreciation deduction businesses may claim on certain automobiles.

LO 10-3 29. Compare and contrast how a Land Rover SUV and a Mercedes-Benz sedan are treated under the luxury auto rules. Also include a discussion of the similarities and differences in available §179 expense.

LO 10-4 30. What is a §197 intangible? How do taxpayers recover the costs of these intangibles? How do taxpayers recover the cost of a §197 intangible that expires (such as a covenant not to compete)?

31. Compare and contrast the tax and financial accounting treatment of goodwill. Are taxpayers allowed to deduct amounts associated with self-created goodwill? LO 10-4
32. Compare and contrast the similarities and differences between organizational expenditures and start-up costs for tax purposes. LO 10-4
33. Discuss the method used to determine the amount of organizational expenditures or start-up costs that may be immediately expensed in the year a taxpayer begins business. LO 10-4
34. Explain the amortization convention applicable to intangible assets. LO 10-4
35. Compare and contrast the recovery periods of §197 intangibles, organizational expenditures, start-up costs, and research and experimentation expenses. LO 10-4
36. Compare and contrast the cost and percentage depletion methods for recovering the costs of natural resources. What are the similarities and differences between the two methods? LO 10-5
37. Explain why percentage depletion has been referred to as a government subsidy. LO 10-5

PROBLEMS

Select problems are available in Connect®. McGraw Hill connect

38. Jose purchased a delivery van for his business through an online auction. His winning bid for the van was $24,500. In addition, Jose incurred the following expenses before using the van: shipping costs of $650; paint to match the other fleet vehicles at a cost of $1,000; registration costs of $3,200, which included $3,000 of sales tax and an annual registration fee of $200; wash and detailing for $50; and an engine tune-up for $250. What is Jose's cost basis for the delivery van? LO 10-1
39. Emily purchased a building to store inventory for her business. The purchase price was $760,000. Emily also paid legal fees of $300 to acquire the building. In March, Emily incurred $2,000 to repair minor leaks in the roof (from storm damage earlier in the month) and $5,000 to make the interior suitable for her finished goods. What is Emily's cost basis in the new building? LO 10-1 research
40. In January, Prahbu purchased for $90,000 a new machine for use in an existing production line of his manufacturing business. Assume that the machine is a unit of property and is not a material or supply. Prahbu pays $2,500 to install the machine, and after the machine is installed, he pays $1,300 to perform a critical test on the machine to ensure that it will operate in accordance with quality standards. On November 1, the critical test is complete, and Prahbu places the machine in service on the production line. On December 3, Prahbu pays another $3,300 to perform periodic quality control testing after the machine is placed in service. How much will Prahbu be required to capitalize as the cost of the machine? LO 10-1 research
41. Dennis contributed business assets to a new business in exchange for stock in the company. The exchange did not qualify as a tax-deferred exchange. The fair market value of these assets was $287,000 on the contribution date. Dennis's original basis in the assets he contributed was $143,000, and the accumulated depreciation on the assets was $78,000. LO 10-1
    a) What is the business's basis in the assets it received from Dennis?
    b) What would be the business's basis if the transaction qualified as a tax-deferred exchange?
42. Brittany started a law practice as a sole proprietor. She owned a computer, printer, desk, and file cabinet she purchased during law school (several years ago) that she is planning to use in her business. What is the depreciable basis LO 10-1

that Brittany should use in her business for each asset, given the following information?

Asset	Purchase Price	FMV at Time Converted to Business Use
Computer	$5,500	$3,800
Printer	3,300	3,150
Desk	4,200	4,000
File cabinet	3,200	3,225

LO 10-1 43. Meg O'Brien received a gift of some small-scale jewelry manufacturing equipment that her father had used for personal purposes for many years. Her father originally purchased the equipment for $1,500. Because the equipment is out of production and no longer available, the property is currently worth $4,000. Meg has decided to begin a new jewelry manufacturing trade or business. What is her depreciable basis for depreciating the equipment?

LO 10-1 44. Gary inherited a Maine summer cabin on 10 acres from his grandmother. His grandparents originally purchased the property for $500 in 1950 and built the cabin at a cost of $10,000 in 1965. His grandfather died in 1980, and when his grandmother recently passed away, the property was appraised at $500,000 for the land and $700,000 for the cabin. Because Gary doesn't currently live in New England, he decided that it would be best to put the property to use as a rental. What is Gary's basis in the land and in the cabin?

LO 10-1 45. Wanting to finalize a sale before year-end, on December 29, WR Outfitters sold to Bob a warehouse and the land for $125,000. The appraised fair market value of the warehouse was $75,000, and the appraised value of the land was $100,000.

a) What is Bob's basis in the warehouse and in the land?

b) What would be Bob's basis in the warehouse and in the land if the appraised value of the warehouse was $50,000 and the appraised value of the land was $125,000?

c) Which appraisal would Bob likely prefer?

LO 10-2 46. At the beginning of the year, Poplock began a calendar-year, dog-boarding business called Griff's Palace. Poplock bought and placed in service the following assets during the year:

Asset	Date Acquired	Cost Basis
Computer equipment	3/23	$ 5,000
Dog-grooming furniture	5/12	7,000
Pickup truck	9/17	10,000
Commercial building	10/11	270,000
Land (one acre)	10/11	80,000

Assuming Poplock does not elect §179 expensing and elects not to use bonus depreciation, answer the following questions:

a) What is Poplock's year 1 depreciation deduction for each asset?

b) What is Poplock's year 2 depreciation deduction for each asset?

LO 10-2 47. DLW Corporation acquired and placed in service the following assets during the year:

Asset	Date Acquired	Cost Basis
Computer equipment	2/17	$ 10,000
Furniture	5/12	17,000
Commercial building	11/1	270,000

Assuming DLW does not elect §179 expensing and elects not to use bonus depreciation, answer the following questions:

a) What is DLW's year 1 cost recovery for each asset?

b) What is DLW's year 3 cost recovery for each asset if DLW sells these assets on 1/23 of year 3?

48. At the beginning of the year, Anna began a calendar-year business and placed in service the following assets during the year: LO 10-2

Asset	Date Acquired	Cost Basis
Computers	1/30	$ 28,000
Office desks	2/15	32,000
Machinery	7/25	75,000
Office building	8/13	400,000

Assuming Anna does not elect §179 expensing and elects not to use bonus depreciation, answer the following questions:

a) What is Anna's year 1 cost recovery for each asset?

b) What is Anna's year 2 cost recovery for each asset?

49. Parley needs a new truck to help him expand Parley's Plumbing Palace. Business has been booming, and Parley would like to accelerate his tax deductions as much as possible (ignore §179 expense and bonus depreciation for this problem). On April 1, Parley purchased a new delivery van for $25,000. It is now September 26 and Parley, already in need of another vehicle, has found a deal on buying a truck for $22,000 (all fees included). The dealer tells him if he doesn't buy the truck (Option 1), it will be gone tomorrow. There is an auction (Option 2) scheduled for October 5 where Parley believes he can get a similar truck for $21,500, but there is also a $500 auction fee. Parley makes no other asset acquisitions during the year. LO 10-2 planning

a) Which option allows Parley to generate more depreciation deductions this year (the vehicles are not considered to be luxury autos)?

b) Assume the original facts, except that the delivery van was placed in service one day earlier on March 31 rather than April 1. Which option generates more depreciation deduction?

50. Way Corporation disposed of the following tangible personal property assets in the current year. Assume that the delivery truck is not a luxury auto. Calculate Way Corporation's 2022 depreciation deduction (ignore §179 expense and bonus depreciation for this problem). LO 10-2

Asset	Date Acquired	Date Sold	Convention	Original Basis
Furniture (7-year)	5/12/18	7/15/22	HY	$ 55,000
Machinery (7-year)	3/23/19	3/15/22	MQ	72,000
Delivery truck* (5-year)	9/17/20	3/13/22	HY	20,000
Machinery (7-year)	10/11/21	8/11/22	MQ	270,000
Computer (5-year)	10/11/22	12/15/22	HY	80,000

*Used 100 percent for business.

51. On November 10 of year 1, Javier purchased a building, including the land it was on, to assemble his new equipment. The total cost of the purchase was $1,200,000; $300,000 was allocated to the basis of the land, and the remaining $900,000 was allocated to the basis of the building. LO 10-2

a) Using MACRS, what is Javier's depreciation deduction on the building for years 1 through 3?

b) What would be the year 3 depreciation deduction if the building was sold on August 1 of year 3?

c) Answer the question in part (a), except assume the building was purchased and placed in service on March 3 instead of November 10.

d) Answer the question in part (a), except assume that the building is residential property.

e) What would be the depreciation for 2022, 2023, and 2024 if the property were nonresidential property purchased and placed in service November 10, 2005 (assume the same original basis)?

LO 10-2

52. Carl purchased an apartment complex for $1.1 million on March 17 of year 1. Of the purchase price, $300,000 was attributable to the land the complex sits on. He also installed new furniture into half of the units at a cost of $60,000.

a) What is Carl's allowable depreciation deduction for his real property for years 1 and 2?

b) What is Carl's allowable depreciation deduction for year 3 if the real property is sold on January 2 of year 3?

LO 10-2 LO 10-3

53. Evergreen Corporation (calendar-year-end) acquired the following assets during the current year:

Asset	Date Placed in Service	Original Basis
Machinery	October 25	$ 70,000
Computer equipment	February 3	10,000
Used delivery truck*	August 17	23,000
Furniture	April 22	150,000

*The delivery truck is not a luxury automobile.

a) What is the allowable depreciation on Evergreen's property in the current year, assuming Evergreen does not elect §179 expense and elects out of bonus depreciation?

b) What is the allowable depreciation on Evergreen's property in the current year if Evergreen does not elect out of bonus depreciation?

LO 10-2 LO 10-3

54. Convers Corporation (calendar-year-end) acquired the following assets during the current tax year:

Asset	Date Placed in Service	Original Basis
Machinery	October 25	$ 70,000
Computer equipment	February 3	10,000
Delivery truck*	March 17	23,000
Furniture	April 22	150,000
Total		$253,000

*The delivery truck is not a luxury automobile.

In addition to these assets, Convers installed qualified real property (MACRS, 15 year, 150% DB) on May 12 at a cost of $300,000.

a) What is the allowable MACRS depreciation on Convers's property in the current year assuming Convers does not elect §179 expense and elects out of bonus depreciation?

b) What is the allowable MACRS depreciation on Convers's property in the current year assuming Convers does not elect out of bonus depreciation (but does not take §179 expense)?

55. Harris Corp. is a technology start-up in its second year of operations. The company didn't purchase any assets this year but purchased the following assets in the prior year: LO 10-2 LO 10-3

Asset	Placed in Service	Basis
Office equipment	August 14	$10,000
Manufacturing equipment	April 15	68,000
Computer system	June 1	16,000
Total		$94,000

Harris did not know depreciation was tax deductible until it hired an accountant this year and didn't claim any depreciation deduction in its first year of operation.

a) What is the maximum amount of depreciation deduction Harris Corp. can deduct in its second year of operation?

b) What is the basis of the office equipment at the end of the second year?

56. AMP Corporation (calendar-year-end) has 2022 taxable income of $1,900,000 for purposes of computing the §179 expense. During 2022, AMP acquired the following assets: LO 10-2 LO 10-3

Asset	Placed in Service	Basis
Machinery	September 12	$1,550,000
Computer equipment	February 10	365,000
Office building	April 2	480,000
Total		$2,395,000

a) What is the maximum amount of §179 expense AMP may deduct for 2022?

b) What is the maximum total depreciation, including §179 expense, that AMP may deduct in 2022 on the assets it placed in service in 2022, assuming no bonus depreciation?

57. Assume that TDW Corporation (calendar-year-end) has 2022 taxable income of $650,000 for purposes of computing the §179 expense. The company acquired the following assets during 2022: LO 10-2 LO 10-3

Asset	Placed in Service	Basis
Machinery	September 12	$2,270,000
Computer equipment	February 10	263,000
Furniture	April 2	880,000
Total		$3,413,000

a) What is the maximum amount of §179 expense TDW may deduct for 2022?

b) What is the maximum total depreciation, including §179 expense, that TDW may deduct in 2022 on the assets it placed in service in 2022, assuming no bonus depreciation?

58. Assume that Timberline Corporation has 2022 taxable income of $240,000 for purposes of computing the §179 expense. It acquired the following assets in 2022: LO 10-2 LO 10-3

Asset	Purchase Date	Basis
Furniture (7-year)	December 1	$ 450,000
Computer equipment (5-year)	February 28	90,000
Copier (5-year)	July 15	30,000
Machinery (7-year)	May 22	480,000
Total		$1,050,000

a) What is the maximum amount of §179 expense Timberline may deduct for 2022? What is Timberline's §179 carryforward to 2023, if any?

b) What would Timberline's maximum depreciation deduction be for 2022 assuming no bonus depreciation?

c) What would Timberline's maximum depreciation deduction be for 2022 if the machinery cost $3,500,000 instead of $480,000 and assuming no bonus depreciation?

LO 10-2 LO 10-3 planning

59. Dain's Diamond Bit Drilling purchased the following assets this year. Assume its taxable income for the year was $53,000 for purposes of computing the §179 expense (assume no bonus depreciation).

Asset	Purchase Date	Original Basis
Drill bits (5-year)	January 25	$ 90,000
Drill bits (5-year)	July 25	95,000
Commercial building	April 22	220,000

a) What is the maximum amount of §179 expense Dain's may deduct for the year?

b) What is Dain's maximum depreciation deduction for the year (including §179 expense)?

c) If the January drill bits' original basis was $2,875,000, what is the maximum amount of §179 expense Dain's may deduct for the year?

d) If the January drill bits' original basis was $3,875,000, what is the maximum amount of §179 expense Dain's may deduct for the year?

LO 10-2 LO 10-3 research

60. Assume that ACW Corporation has 2022 taxable income of $1,500,000 for purposes of computing the §179 expense. The company acquired the following assets during 2022 (assume no bonus depreciation):

Asset	Placed in Service	Basis
Machinery	September 12	$ 470,000
Computer equipment	February 10	70,000
Delivery truck	August 21	93,000
Qualified real property (MACRS, 15 year, 150% DB)	April 2	1,380,000
Total		$2,013,000

a) What is the maximum amount of §179 expense ACW may deduct for 2022?

b) What is the maximum *total* depreciation that ACW may deduct in 2022 on the assets it placed in service in 2022?

LO 10-2 LO 10-3

61. Chaz Corporation has taxable income in 2022 of $312,000 for purposes of computing the §179 expense and acquired the following assets during the year:

Asset	Placed in Service	Basis
Office furniture	September 12	$ 780,000
Computer equipment	February 10	930,000
Delivery truck	August 21	68,000
Qualified real property (MACRS, 15 year, 150% DB)	September 30	1,500,000
Total		$3,278,000

What is the maximum *total* depreciation deduction that Chaz may deduct in 2022?

LO 10-2 LO 10-3 planning research

62. Woolard Supplies (a sole proprietorship) has taxable income in 2022 of $240,000 before any depreciation deductions (§179, bonus, or MACRS) and placed some office furniture into service during the year. The furniture does not qualify for bonus depreciation.

Asset	Placed in Service	Basis
Office furniture (used)	March 20	$1,200,000

a) If Woolard elects $50,000 of §179, what is Woolard's total depreciation deduction for the year?

b) If Woolard elects the maximum amount of §179 for the year, what is the amount of deductible §179 expense for the year? What is the *total* depreciation that Woolard may deduct in 2022? What is Woolard's §179 carryforward amount to next year, if any?

c) Woolard is concerned about future limitations on its §179 expense. How much §179 expense should Woolard expense this year if it wants to maximize its depreciation this year and avoid any carryover to future years?

63. Assume that Sivart Corporation has 2022 taxable income of $1,750,000 for purposes of computing the §179 expense and acquired several assets during the year. Assume the delivery truck does not qualify for bonus depreciation. LO 10-2 LO 10-3 planning

Asset	Placed in Service	Basis
Machinery	June 12	$1,440,000
Computer equipment	February 10	70,000
Delivery truck—used	August 21	93,000
Furniture	April 2	310,000
Total		$1,913,000

a) What is the maximum amount of §179 expense Sivart may deduct for 2022?

b) What is the maximum *total* depreciation (§179, bonus, MACRS) that Sivart may deduct in 2022 on the assets it placed in service in 2022?

64. Acorn Construction (calendar-year-end C corporation) has had rapid expansion during the last half of the current year due to the housing market's recovery. The company has record income and would like to maximize its cost recovery deduction for the current year. Acorn provided you with the following information: LO 10-2 LO 10-3 planning

Asset	Placed in Service	Basis
New equipment and tools	August 20	$3,800,000
Used light-duty trucks	October 17	2,000,000
Used machinery	November 6	525,000
Total		$6,325,000

The used assets had been contributed to the business by its owner in a tax-deferred transaction.

a) What is Acorn's maximum cost recovery deduction in the current year?

b) What planning strategies would you advise Acorn to consider?

65. Phil owns a ranch business and uses four-wheelers to do much of his work. Occasionally, though, he and his boys will go for a ride together as a family activity. During year 1, Phil put 765 miles on the four-wheeler that he bought on January 15 for $6,500. Of the miles driven, only 175 miles were for personal use. Assume four-wheelers qualify to be depreciated according to the five-year MACRS schedule and the four-wheeler was the only asset Phil purchased this year. LO 10-3

a) Calculate the allowable depreciation for year 1 (ignore the §179 expense and bonus depreciation).

b) Calculate the allowable depreciation for year 2 if total miles were 930 and personal-use miles were 400 (ignore the §179 expense and bonus depreciation).

LO 10-3

66. Assume that Ernesto purchased a digital camera on July 10 of year 1 for $3,000. In year 1, 80 percent of his camera usage was for his business and 20 percent was for personal photography activities. This was the only asset he placed in service during year 1. Ignoring any potential §179 expense and bonus depreciation, answer the questions for each of the following alternative scenarios:
   a) What is Ernesto's depreciation deduction for the camera in year 1?
   b) What would be Ernesto's depreciation deduction for the camera in year 2 if his year 2 usage was 75 percent business and 25 percent for personal use?
   c) What would be Ernesto's depreciation deduction for the camera in year 2 if his year 2 usage was 45 percent business and 55 percent for personal use?

LO 10-3

67. Lina purchased a new car for use in her business during 2022. The auto was the only business asset she purchased during the year, and her business was extremely profitable. Calculate her maximum depreciation deductions (including §179 expense unless stated otherwise) for the automobile in 2022 and 2023 (Lina doesn't want to take bonus depreciation for 2022 or 2023) in the following alternative scenarios (assuming half-year convention for all):
   a) The vehicle cost $35,000, and business use is 100 percent (ignore §179 expense).
   b) The vehicle cost $80,000, and business use is 100 percent.
   c) The vehicle cost $80,000, and she used it 80 percent for business.
   d) The vehicle cost $80,000, and she used it 80 percent for business. She sold it on March 1 of year 2.
   e) The vehicle cost $80,000, and she used it 20 percent for business.
   f) The vehicle cost $80,000 and is an SUV that weighs 6,500 pounds. Business use was 100 percent.

LO 10-2 LO 10-3
planning

68. Tamika Meer purchased a new car for use in her business during 2022 for $75,000. The auto was the only business asset she purchased during the year, and her business was very profitable. Calculate Tamika's maximum depreciation deductions for the automobile in 2022 and 2023 under the following scenarios:
   a) Tamika does not want to take §179 expense and she elects out of bonus depreciation.
   b) Tamika wants to maximize her 2022 depreciation using bonus depreciation.

LO 10-2 LO 10-3

69. Burbank Corporation (calendar-year-end) acquired the following property this year:

Asset	Placed in Service	Basis
Used copier	November 12	$ 7,800
New computer equipment	June 6	14,000
Furniture	July 15	32,000
New delivery truck	October 28	19,000
Luxury auto	January 31	70,000
Total		$142,800

Burbank acquired the copier in a tax-deferred transaction when the shareholder contributed the copier to the business in exchange for stock.
   a) Assuming no bonus or §179 expense, what is Burbank's maximum cost recovery deduction for this year?
   b) Assuming Burbank would like to maximize its cost recovery deductions by claiming bonus and §179 expense, which assets should Burbank immediately expense?
   c) What is Burbank's maximum cost recovery deduction this year assuming it elects §179 expense and claims bonus depreciation?

70. Paul Vote purchased the following assets this year (ignore §179 expensing and bonus depreciation when answering the questions below): LO 10-3 research

Asset	Purchase Date	Basis
Machinery	May 12	$ 23,500
Computers	August 13	20,000
Warehouse	December 13	180,000

a) What is Paul's allowable MACRS depreciation for the property?
b) What is Paul's allowable alternative minimum tax (AMT) depreciation for the property? You will need to find the AMT depreciation tables to compute the depreciation.

71. After several profitable years running her business, Ingrid decided to acquire the assets of a small competing business. On May 1 of year 1, Ingrid acquired the competing business for $300,000. Ingrid allocated $50,000 of the purchase price to goodwill. Ingrid's business reports its taxable income on a calendar-year basis. LO 10-4 research
a) How much amortization expense on the goodwill can Ingrid deduct in year 1, year 2, and year 3?
b) In lieu of the original facts, assume that Ingrid purchased only a phone list with a useful life of five years for $10,000. How much amortization expense on the phone list can Ingrid deduct in year 1, year 2, and year 3?

72. Juliette formed a new business to sell sporting goods this year. The business opened its doors to customers on June 1. Determine the amount of start-up costs Juliette can immediately expense (not including the portion of the expenditures that are amortized over 180 months) this year in the following alternative scenarios: LO 10-4
a) She incurred start-up costs of $2,000.
b) She incurred start-up costs of $45,000.
c) She incurred start-up costs of $53,500.
d) She incurred start-up costs of $63,000.
e) How would you answer parts (a) through (d) if she formed a partnership or a corporation and she incurred the same amount of organizational expenditures rather than start-up costs (how much of the organizational expenditures would be immediately deductible)?

73. Nicole organized a new corporation. The corporation began business on April 1 of year 1. She made the following expenditures associated with getting the corporation started: LO 10-4

Expense	Date	Amount
Attorney fees for articles of incorporation	February 10	$32,000
March 1–March 30 wages	March 30	4,500
March 1–March 30 rent	March 30	2,000
Stock issuance costs	April 1	20,000
April 1–May 30 wages	May 30	12,000

a) What is the total amount of the start-up costs and organizational expenditures for Nicole's corporation?
b) What amount of the start-up costs and organizational expenditures may the corporation immediately expense in year 1 (excluding the portion of the expenditures that are amortized over 180 months)?
c) What amount can the corporation deduct as amortization expense for the organizational expenditures and for the start-up costs for year 1 [not including the amount determined in part (b)]?
d) What would be the total allowable organizational expenditures if Nicole started a sole proprietorship instead of a corporation?

LO 10-4

74. Bethany incurred $20,000 in research and experimental costs for developing a specialized product during July 2022. Bethany went through a lot of trouble and spent $10,000 in legal fees to receive a patent for the product in August 2024. Bethany expects the patent to have a remaining useful life of 10 years.
   a) What amount of research and experimental expenses for 2022, 2023, and 2024 may Bethany deduct?
   b) How much *patent* amortization expense would Bethany deduct in 2024?
   c) If Bethany chose to capitalize but *not* amortize the research and experimental expenses she incurred in 2022, how much patent amortization expense would Bethany deduct in2024?

LO 10-5

75. Last Chance Mine (LCM) purchased a coal deposit for $750,000. It estimated it would extract 12,000 tons of coal from the deposit. LCM mined the coal and sold it, reporting gross receipts of $1 million, $3 million, and $2 million for years 1 through 3, respectively. During years 1–3, LCM reported net income (loss) from the coal deposit activity in the amount of ($20,000), $500,000, and $450,000, respectively. In years 1–3, LCM extracted 13,000 tons of coal as follows:

(1)	(2)	(2)/(1)	Tons Extracted per Year		
Tons of Coal	Basis	Depletion Rate	Year 1	Year 2	Year 3
12,000	$750,000	$62.50	2,000	7,200	3,800

   a) What is LCM's cost depletion for years 1, 2, and 3?
   b) What is LCM's percentage depletion for each year (the applicable percentage for coal is 10 percent)?
   c) Using the cost and percentage depletion computations from parts (a) and (b), what is LCM's actual depletion expense for each year?

COMPREHENSIVE PROBLEMS

Select problems are available with Connect®.

tax forms

76. Karane Enterprises, a calendar-year manufacturer based in College Station, Texas, began business in 2021. In the process of setting up the business, Karane has acquired various types of assets. Below is a list of assets acquired during 2021:

Asset	Cost	Date Placed in Service
Office furniture	$ 150,000	02/03/2021
Machinery	1,560,000	07/22/2021
Used delivery truck*	40,000	08/17/2021

*Not considered a luxury automobile.

During 2021, Karane was very successful (and had no §179 limitations) and decided to acquire more assets in 2022 to increase its production capacity. These are the assets acquired during 2022:

Asset	Cost	Date Placed in Service
Computers & info. system	$ 400,000	03/31/2022
Luxury auto*	80,000	05/26/2022
Assembly equipment	1,200,000	08/15/2022
Storage building	700,000	11/13/2022

*Used 100% for business purposes.

Karane generated taxable income in 2022 of $1,732,500 for purposes of computing the §179 expense limitation.

a) Compute the maximum 2021 depreciation deductions, including §179 expense (ignoring bonus depreciation).
b) Compute the maximum 2022 depreciation deductions, including §179 expense (ignoring bonus depreciation).
c) Compute the maximum 2022 depreciation deductions, including §179 expense, but now assume that Karane would like to take bonus depreciation.
d) Now assume that during 2022, Karane decides to buy a competitor's assets for a purchase price of $1,350,000. Compute the maximum 2022 cost recovery, including §179 expense and bonus depreciation. Karane purchased the following assets for the lump-sum purchase price:

Asset	Cost	Date Placed in Service
Inventory	$220,000	09/15/2022
Office furniture	230,000	09/15/2022
Machinery	250,000	09/15/2022
Patent	198,000	09/15/2022
Goodwill	2,000	09/15/2022
Building	430,000	09/15/2022
Land	20,000	09/15/2022

e) Complete Part I of Form 4562 for part (b) (use the most current form available).

77. While completing undergraduate school work in information systems, Dallin Bourne and Michael Banks decided to start a technology support company called eSys Answers. During year 1, they bought the following assets and incurred the following start-up fees: **tax forms**

Year 1 Assets	Purchase Date	Basis
Computers (5-year)	October 30, Y1	$15,000
Office equipment (7-year)	October 30, Y1	10,000
Furniture (7-year)	October 30, Y1	3,000
Start-up costs	October 30, Y1	17,000

In April of year 2, they decided to purchase a customer list from a company providing virtually the same services, started by fellow information systems students preparing to graduate. The customer list cost $10,000, and the sale was completed on April 30. During their summer break, Dallin and Michael passed on internship opportunities in an attempt to really grow their business into something they could do full time after graduation. In the summer, they purchased a small van (for transportation, not considered a luxury auto) and a pinball machine (to help attract new employees). They bought the van on June 15, Y2, for $15,000 and spent $3,000 getting it ready to put into service. The pinball machine cost $4,000 and was placed in service on July 1, Y2.

Year 2 Assets	Purchase Date	Basis
Van	June 15, Y2	$18,000
Pinball machine (7-year)	July 1, Y2	4,000
Customer list	April 30, Y2	10,000

Assume that eSys Answers does not claim any §179 expense or bonus depreciation.

a) What are the maximum cost recovery deductions for eSys Answers for Y1 and Y2?
b) Complete eSys Answers's Form 4562 for Y1 (use the most current form available).
c) What is eSys Answers's basis in each of its assets at the end of Y2?

78. Diamond Mountain was originally thought to be one of the few places in North America to contain diamonds, so Diamond Mountain Inc. (DM) purchased the land for $1,000,000. Later, DM discovered that the only diamonds on the mountain had been planted there and the land was worthless for mining. DM engineers discovered a new survey technology and discovered a silver deposit estimated at 5,000 pounds on Diamond Mountain. DM immediately bought new drilling equipment and began mining the silver.

In years 1–3 following the opening of the mine, DM had net (gross) income of $200,000 ($700,000), $400,000 ($1,100,000), and $600,000 ($1,450,000), respectively. Mining amounts for each year were as follows: 750 pounds (year 1), 1,450 pounds (year 2), and 1,800 pounds (year 3). At the end of year 2, engineers used the new technology (which had been improving over time) and estimated there was still an estimated 6,000 pounds of silver deposits.

DM also began a research and experimentation project with the hopes of gaining a patent for its new survey technology. Diamond Mountain Inc. chose to capitalize research and experimentation expenditures and to amortize the costs over 60 months or until it obtained a patent on its technology. In March of year 1, DM spent $95,000 on research and experimentation. DM spent another $75,000 in February of year 2 for research and experimentation. DM realizes benefits from the research and experimentation expenditures when the costs are incurred. In September of year 2, DM paid $20,000 of legal fees and was granted the patent in October of year 2 (the entire process of obtaining a patent was unusually fast). The patent's life is 20 years.

Answer the following questions regarding DM's activities (assume that DM tries to maximize its deductions if given a choice).

a) What is DM's depletion expense for years 1–3?

b) What is DM's research and experimentation amortization for years 1 and 2?

c) What is DM's basis in its patent, and what is its amortization for the patent in year 2?

UWorld | ROGER CPA Review
YOUR WORLD OF LEARNING

UWorld Roger CPA Review

Sample CPA Exam questions from Roger CPA Review are available in Connect as support for the topics in this text. These Multiple Choice Questions and Task-Based Simulations include expert-written explanations and solutions and provide a starting point for students to become familiar with the content and functionality of the actual CPA Exam.

chapter

11 Property Dispositions

Learning Objectives

Upon completing this chapter, you should be able to:

LO 11-1 Calculate the amount of gain or loss recognized on the disposition of assets used in a trade or business.

LO 11-2 Describe the general character types of gain or loss recognized on property dispositions.

LO 11-3 Calculate depreciation recapture.

LO 11-4 Describe the tax treatment of unrecaptured §1250 gains.

LO 11-5 Describe the tax treatment of §1231 gains or losses, including the §1231 netting process.

LO 11-6 Explain common deferral exceptions to the general rule that realized gains and losses are recognized currently.

Mike Kemp/Blend Images

Storyline Summary

Taxpayer:	Teton Mountaineering Technology, LLC (Teton)—a calendar-year, single-member LLC (treated as a sole proprietorship for tax purposes)
President:	Steve Dallimore (he/him/his)
Location:	Cody, Wyoming

By most measures, Teton Mountaineering Technology, LLC (Teton), has become a success, with sponsored climbers summiting the world's highest peaks, satisfied customers creating brand loyalty, and profitability improving steadily. However, after several years of operation, some of Teton's machinery is wearing out and must be replaced. Further, because Teton has outgrown its manufacturing capacity, Steve is considering whether to expand the company's current facility or sell it and build a new one in a different location. Steve would like to know how any asset dispositions will affect his tax bill.

Steve has found a willing buyer for some of Teton's land, and he has options for trading the land. For tax purposes, does it matter whether he sells or trades the land? Steve also has questions about how to best manage Teton's acquisitions and dispositions of real property. It all seems a bit overwhelming. . . . He picks up the phone and dials his tax accountant's number. ■

You can imagine why Steve might be eager to reach out to his accountant. Tax accounting widely impacts business decisions: What are the tax consequences of selling, trading, or even abandoning business assets? Are the tax consequences the same whether taxpayers sell machinery, inventory, or investment assets? Does it matter for tax purposes whether Teton is structured as a sole proprietorship or a corporation when it sells its warehouse? If Steve sells his personal sailboat, car, or furniture, what are the tax consequences?

In the previous chapter, we explained the tax consequences associated with purchasing assets and recovering the cost of the assets through depreciation, amortization, or depletion. This chapter explores fundamental tax issues associated with property dispositions (sales, trades, or other dispositions). We focus on the disposition of tangible assets, but the same principles apply to the sale of intangible assets and natural resources.

LO 11-1

DISPOSITIONS

Taxpayers can dispose of assets in many ways. For example, a taxpayer could sell an asset, donate it to charity, trade it for a similar asset, take it to the landfill, or have it destroyed in a natural disaster. No matter how it is accomplished, every asset disposition triggers a realization event for tax purposes. To calculate the amount of gain or loss taxpayers realize when they sell assets, they must determine the amount realized on the sale and the *adjusted basis* of each asset they are selling.

Amount Realized

Simply put, the **amount realized** by a taxpayer from the sale or other disposition of an asset is everything of *value* received from the buyer *less* any selling costs.[1] Although taxpayers typically receive cash when they sell property, they may also accept marketable securities, notes receivable, cryptocurrency, similar assets, or any combination of these items as payment. Additionally, taxpayers selling assets such as real property subject to loans or mortgages may receive some debt relief. In this case, they would increase their amount realized by the amount of debt relief (the buyer's assumption of the seller's liability increases the seller's amount realized). The amount realized computation is captured in the following formula:

Amount realized = Cash received + Fair market value of other property
+ Buyer's assumption of liabilities − Seller's expenses

Example 11-1

Teton wants to upgrade its old manufacturing machinery that is wearing out. On November 1 of the current year, Teton sells the machinery for $230,000 cash and marketable securities valued at $70,500. Teton paid a broker $500 to find a buyer. What is Teton's amount realized on the sale of the machinery?

Answer: $300,000, computed as follows:

Description	Amount	Explanation
(1) Cash received	$ 230,000	
(2) Marketable securities received	70,500	
(3) Broker commission paid	(500)	
Amount realized	**$300,000**	(1) + (2) + (3)

[1] *Chapin v. Comm'r*, 50-1 USTC ¶ 9171 (8th Cir. 1950).

Determination of Adjusted Basis

In the previous chapter, we discussed the basis for cost recovery and focused on purchased assets in which the initial basis is the asset's cost. However, taxpayers may acquire assets without purchasing them. For example, a taxpayer may acquire an asset as a gift or as an inheritance. In either case, the taxpayer does not purchase the asset, so the taxpayer's initial basis in the asset must be computed as something other than purchase price. Although there are many situations when an asset's initial basis is not the asset's cost, we focus on three cases: gifts, inherited assets, and property converted from personal use to business use.

Gifts A gift is defined as a transfer of property proceeding from a detached and disinterested generosity or out of affection, respect, admiration, charity, or like impulses.[2] The initial basis of gift property to a recipient (donee) depends on whether the value of the asset exceeds the donor's basis on the date of the gift. If the fair market value of the asset on the date of the gift is greater than the donor's basis, then the asset's initial basis to the recipient of the gift will be the same as the donor's basis.[3] That is, the donor's basis carries over to the donee.

If the donor's basis is greater than the fair market value of the asset at the date of the gift, then special dual basis rules apply. A dual basis means that the gift property has one basis to the donee if the donee sells the property at a price above the donor's basis and a different basis if the donee sells the property at a price below the fair market value at the date of the gift. Interestingly, the donee will not know the basis for calculating gain or loss until the donee sells the property. Thus, the basis of gifted property that has declined in value depends on the sales price of the asset subsequent to the gift. The donee uses the carryover basis if the asset is sold for a gain (sales price > donor's basis), whereas the donee uses the fair market value at the date of the gift if the asset is sold for a loss (sales price < FMV at date of gift). If the asset sells at a price between the donor's basis and the fair market value at the date of the gift, then the donee's basis at the time of the sale is set equal to the selling price and the donee does not recognize gain or loss on the sale. The dual basis rule prevents the transfer of unrealized losses from one taxpayer to another by gift.

When the dual basis rules apply, the donee's holding period of the asset depends on whether the gift property subsequently sells for a gain or loss. If the donor's basis is used to determine the gain, the holding period includes that of the donor. If the fair market value at the date of the gift is used to figure the loss, the holding period starts on the date of the gift. If the asset subsequently sells at a price between the donor's basis and the fair market value at the date of the gift, the holding period is irrelevant because there is no recognized gain or loss.

Inherited Property For inherited property, the general rule is that the heir's basis in property passing from a decedent to the heir is the fair market value on the date of the decedent's death.[4] The holding period of inherited property is deemed to be long term regardless of how long the heir owns the property.[5]

Property Converted from Personal Use to Business Use The basis for determining the gain or loss on the sale of converted property depends on whether the property appreciated or declined in value during the time the property was used personally. For appreciated property (i.e., the fair market value at the date of the conversion is greater than the taxpayer's basis in the property), the taxpayer will use their basis to calculate depreciation and gain or loss at disposition.

[2] *Comm'r v. Duberstein,* 363 U.S. 278 (1960), *rev'g* 265 F.2d 28 (6th Cir. 1959), *rev'g* TC Memo 1958-4.

[3] §1015(a). The basis to the donee may be increased if the donor is required to pay gift tax on the gift.

[4] §1014(a)(1). An alternate valuation date may be used to determine the basis to the heirs if elected by the estate.

[5] §1223(9).

For property with a basis greater than value, taxpayers may try to convert nondeductible personal losses to business losses by converting the property into business property and then selling it. In order to prevent this from occurring, the dual basis rules apply. If the fair market value at the date of conversion is below the taxpayer's basis, the taxpayer will use the fair market value at the date of conversion as the basis for calculating loss and will use the basis at date of conversion to calculate gain. The fair market value at the date of conversion is also the basis used to calculate depreciation on property that has declined in value prior to the conversion regardless of whether the taxpayer subsequently sells the property for a gain or a loss. After conversion, the taxpayer adjusts the basis (whether gain or loss) for depreciation deductions from the date of conversion to the date of disposition. If the property later sells for an amount that falls between the adjusted basis for gain and the adjusted basis for loss, the basis for the sale is treated as the sales price so that the taxpayer does not recognize gain or loss on the sale.[6]

Example 11-2

Assume that Steve received 100 shares of FZL stock from his grandfather on January 8. On the date of the gift, the stock was worth $15,000. Steve's grandfather originally purchased the stock 10 years earlier for $10,000. What is Steve's initial basis in the stock?

Answer: Because the stock had appreciated in value while Steve's grandfather owned it, Steve's initial basis is a carryover basis of $10,000.

What if: Assume that on the date of the gift, the fair market value of the stock was $8,000. What is Steve's initial basis in the stock?

Answer: Steve's initial basis depends on the price for which he later sells the stock. If Steve sells the stock six months later at a price greater than $10,000, his basis is the $10,000 carryover basis. He will recognize a long-term capital gain because his holding period is 10½ years (i.e., it includes the time his grandfather owned the stock). If he sells the stock six months later at a price less than $8,000, his basis is $8,000, the fair market value at the date of the gift. He will recognize a short-term capital loss because his holding period is only six months (i.e., it begins on the date of the gift). If he sells the stock for a price that is between $10,000 and $8,000, his basis is the sales price and he recognizes no gain or loss (his holding period does not matter).

What if: Assume that Steve inherited the stock from his grandfather on January 8. What is Steve's initial basis if the fair market value is (a) $15,000 and (b) $8,000 at the time of his grandfather's death?

Answer: Steve's initial basis is the fair market value at the date of his grandfather's death regardless of whether the value is greater or less than his grandfather's original cost. If the fair market value is $15,000, Steve's initial basis is $15,000. If the fair market value is $8,000, Steve's initial basis is $8,000. Steve's holding period is long-term regardless of how long he actually holds the stock because it is inherited property.

What if: Assume Steve owns some mountaineering equipment that he uses personally and purchased two years ago for $4,000. On March 20, he converts the equipment into business-use property when the fair market value of the equipment is $5,000. What is Steve's initial basis in the equipment for business purposes?

Answer: Because the equipment appreciated in value before Steve converted it to business use, his basis is his original cost of $4,000. Steve will use the $4,000 as his initial basis for calculating cost recovery and determining his adjusted basis when he sells or otherwise disposes of the equipment.

What if: Assume that the equipment that Steve converts from personal to business use has a fair market value of $3,000 at the date of conversion. What is Steve's initial basis in the equipment for business purposes?

Answer: The equipment declined in value before Steve converted it to business use. In order to prevent Steve from converting his $1,000 personal loss into a business loss, his initial basis for business purposes will depend on whether he subsequently sells the equipment at a gain or loss. His initial basis for loss (and cost recovery) is the $3,000 fair market value at the conversion date. His initial basis for gain is his $4,000 original cost.

[6]Reg. §§1.165-9(b)(2), 1.167(g)-1.

What if: Assume that the equipment that Steve converts from personal to business use has a fair market value of $3,000 at the date of conversion. Two years later, after taking $500 of depreciation deductions, he sells the equipment for $3,300. What is Steve's adjusted basis in the equipment for purposes of determining the gain or loss on the disposition?

Answer: Steve's initial basis for loss was the $3,000 fair market value at the conversion date, and his initial basis for gain was the $4,000 original cost. At the time of the sale, the adjusted basis for loss is $2,500, and the adjusted basis for gain is $3,500. Because the sales price falls between the adjusted basis for gain and the adjusted basis for loss, the adjusted basis is assumed to be equal to the sales price of $3,300, resulting in no gain or loss.

The **adjusted basis** for determining the gain or loss on the sale of an asset is the initial basis (however determined) reduced by depreciation or other types of cost recovery deductions allowed (or allowable) on the property. The adjusted basis of an asset can be determined using the following formula:

Adjusted basis = Initial basis − Cost recovery allowed (or allowable)

Example 11-3

To determine its realized gain or loss on the sale, Teton must calculate the adjusted basis of the machinery it sold in Example 11-1 for $300,000. Teton originally purchased the machinery for $610,000 three years ago. For tax purposes, Teton depreciated the machinery using MACRS (seven-year recovery period, 200 percent declining-balance method, and half-year convention).

The machinery's adjusted basis at the time of the sale is $228,658, computed as follows:

Description	Basis	Explanation
(1) Initial basis	$ 610,000	Example 10-1
(2) Year 1	(87,169)	Example 10-5
(3) Year 2	(149,389)	Example 10-5
(4) Year 3	(106,689)	Example 10-5
(5) Year 4	(38,095)	$76,189 (Example 10-5) × 50% (half-year convention)
(6) Accumulated depreciation	(381,342)	(2) + (3) + (4) + (5)
Adjusted basis	**$228,658**	(1) + (6)

Because businesses generally use more highly accelerated depreciation methods for tax purposes than they do for book purposes, the adjusted tax basis of a particular asset is likely to be lower than the adjusted book basis.

Realized Gain or Loss on Disposition

The amount of gain or loss taxpayers realize on a sale or other disposition of assets is simply the amount they realize minus their adjusted basis in the disposed assets.[7] The formula for computing **realized gain or loss** is as follows:

Gain or (loss) realized = Amount realized − Adjusted basis

Example 11-4

In Example 11-1 we learned that Teton sold machinery for a total amount realized of $300,000, and in Example 11-3 we learned that its basis in the machinery was $228,658. What is Teton's realized gain or loss on the sale of the machinery?

(continued on page 11-6)

[7]§1001(a).

Answer: $71,342, computed as follows:

Description	Amount	Explanation
(1) Amount realized	$300,000	Example 11-1
(2) Adjusted basis	(228,658)	Example 11-3
Gain realized	**$ 71,342**	(1) + (2)

Exhibit 11-1 details the important formulas necessary to determine realized tax gains and losses.

EXHIBIT 11-1 Summary of Formulas for Computing Gain or Loss Realized on an Asset Disposition

Gain (loss) realized = Amount realized − Adjusted basis; where

- Amount realized = Cash received + Fair market value of other property + Buyer's assumption of seller's liabilities − Seller's expenses
- Adjusted basis = Initial basis − Cost recovery deductions

So far, our examples have used one of Teton's asset sales to demonstrate how to compute gain or loss realized when property is sold. However, as we describe in Exhibit 11-2, Teton disposed of several assets during the year. We refer to this exhibit throughout the chapter as a reference point for discussing the tax issues associated with property dispositions.

EXHIBIT 11-2 Teton's Asset Dispositions:* Realized Gain (Loss) for Tax Purposes

Assets	(1) Amount Realized	(2) Initial Basis	(3) Accumulated Depreciation	(4) [(2) − (3)] Adjusted Basis	(5) [(1) − (4)] Gain (Loss) Realized
Machinery	$300,000	$610,000	$381,342	$228,658	$ 71,342
Office furniture	23,000	20,000	14,000	6,000	17,000
Delivery truck	2,000	25,000	17,500	7,500	(5,500)
Warehouse	350,000	275,000	15,000	260,000	90,000
Land	175,000	75,000	0	75,000	100,000
Total gain realized					$272,842

*These are the assets initially purchased by Teton in Example 10-1. In this chapter, we assume that Teton has been in business for four years. For simplicity, we assume Teton did not previously elect any §179 immediate expensing and opted out of bonus depreciation.

Recognized Gain or Loss on Disposition

THE KEY FACTS

- Realized gain or loss:
  - Amount realized less adjusted basis.
- Recognized gain or loss:
  - A realized gain or loss reported on the taxpayer's current-year return.

As a general rule, taxpayers realizing gains and losses during a year must recognize the gains or losses. **Recognized gains or losses** are gains (losses) that increase (decrease) taxpayers' gross income.[8] Thus, taxpayers must report recognized gains and losses on their tax returns. Although taxpayers must immediately recognize the vast majority of realized gains and losses, in certain circumstances they may be allowed to defer recognizing gains to subsequent periods, or they may be allowed to permanently exclude the gains from taxable income. However, taxpayers may also be required to defer losses to later periods and, in more extreme cases, they may have their realized losses permanently disallowed. We address certain tax-deferred provisions later in the chapter.

[8]Recall under the return of capital principle we discussed in the Gross Income and Exclusions chapter, when a taxpayer sells an asset, the taxpayer's adjusted basis is a return of capital and not a deductible expense.

CHARACTER OF GAIN OR LOSS

LO 11-2

In order to determine how a recognized gain or loss affects a taxpayer's income tax liability, the taxpayer must determine the *character* or type of gain or loss recognized. Ultimately, every gain or loss is characterized as either ordinary or capital (long-term or short-term gains or losses). As described below, businesses may recognize §1231 gains or losses on property dispositions that require some intermediary steps, but even these gains or losses are eventually characterized as ordinary or capital (long-term).

The character of a gain or loss is important because gains and losses of different characters are treated differently for tax purposes. For example, ordinary income (loss) is generally taxed at ordinary rates (fully deductible against ordinary income). However, capital gains may be taxed at preferential (lower) rates, while deductions for capital losses are subject to certain restrictions. The character of the gains or losses taxpayers recognize when they sell assets depends on the character of the assets they are selling. The character of an asset depends on how the taxpayer used the asset and how long the taxpayer owned the asset (i.e., the holding period) before selling it.

In general terms, property can be used in a trade or business, treated as inventory or accounts receivable of a business, held for investment, or used for personal purposes. The holding period may be short term (one year or less) or long term (more than a year). Exhibit 11-3 provides a table showing the character of assets (ordinary, capital, or §1231) depending on how taxpayers used the assets and the length of time they held the property before selling it.

THE KEY FACTS

Character of Assets

- Ordinary assets
  - Assets created or used in a taxpayer's trade or business.
  - Business assets held for one year or less.
- Capital assets
  - Assets held for investment purposes.
  - Assets held for personal-use purposes.
- §1231 assets
  - Depreciable assets and land used in a trade or business held for *more* than one year.

EXHIBIT 11-3 Character of Assets Depending on Property Use and Holding Period

	Property Use		
Holding Period	Trade or Business	Investment or Personal-Use Assets*	Inventory and Accounts Receivable
Short term (one year or less)	Ordinary	Short-term capital	Ordinary
Long term (more than one year)	§1231†	Long-term capital	Ordinary

*Gains on the sale of personal-use assets are taxable, but losses on the sale of personal-use assets are not deductible.
†As we describe later in the chapter, gain or loss is eventually characterized as ordinary or capital (long-term).

TAXES IN THE REAL WORLD Buyer Beware!

In February 2021, Elon Musk, Tesla's CEO, announced that Tesla would accept Bitcoin as payment in exchange for its products. But buyer beware! If buyers choose to pay with Bitcoin, they may face a higher tax bill. The IRS treats Bitcoin as property and not currency. What that means is that when taxpayers use Bitcoin to pay for products or services, the IRS treats it as a sale of an asset. Because Bitcoin's price has increased from about $11,000 in September 2020 to $58,000 in February 2021, most uses of Bitcoin will require taxpayers to report a gain on their tax return. For example, if a taxpayer acquired a Tesla Model S in February 2021 for $58,000 in Bitcoin purchased three months earlier for $18,000, they would have a gain of $40,000. The tax on the gain at a rate of 37 percent (short-term capital gains rate) would be $14,800, increasing the price of the car by 25.5 percent!

Source: Based on Spencer Jakab, "Tesla Versus the Taxman," *The Wall Street Journal* (March 26, 2021), www.wsj.com/articles/tesla-versus-the-taxman-11616767630.

Ordinary Assets

Ordinary assets are generally assets created or used in a taxpayer's trade or business. For example, inventory is an **ordinary asset** because it is held for sale to customers in the ordinary course of business. Accounts receivable are ordinary assets because receivables are generated from the sale of inventory or business services. Other assets used in a trade or business such as machinery and equipment are also considered to be ordinary assets if they have been used in a business for *one year or less*. For example, if Teton purchased a forklift for the warehouse but sold it six months later, the gain or loss would be ordinary. When taxpayers sell ordinary assets at a gain, they recognize an ordinary gain that is taxed at ordinary rates. When taxpayers sell ordinary assets at a loss, they deduct the loss against other ordinary income.

Capital Assets

A **capital asset** is generally something held for investment (e.g., stocks and bonds) for the **production of income** (i.e., a for-profit activity that doesn't rise to the level of a trade or business) or for personal use (e.g., your car, house, or personal computer).[9] Whether an asset qualifies as a capital asset depends on the purpose for which the taxpayer uses the asset. Thus, the same asset may be considered a capital asset to one taxpayer and an ordinary asset to another taxpayer. For example, a piece of land held as an investment because it is expected to appreciate in value over time is a capital asset to that taxpayer. However, the same piece of land held as inventory by a real estate developer would be an ordinary asset. Finally, the same piece of land would be a §1231 asset if the taxpayer held it for more than one year and used it in a trade or business (e.g., as a parking lot).

Individual taxpayers generally prefer capital gains to ordinary income because certain capital gains are taxed at lower rates and capital gains may offset capital losses that cannot be deducted against ordinary income. Individuals also prefer ordinary losses to capital losses because ordinary losses are deductible without limit, while individuals may deduct only $3,000 of net capital losses against ordinary income each year. Corporate taxpayers may prefer capital gains to ordinary income because capital gains may offset capital losses that they would not be allowed to offset otherwise. C corporations are not allowed to deduct net capital losses, but they are allowed to carry net capital losses back three years and forward five years to offset net gains from capital assets in those years. Exhibit 11-4 reviews the treatment of capital gains and losses for individuals and corporations.

Section 1231 Assets

Section 1231 assets are depreciable assets and land used in a trade or business (including rental property) held by taxpayers for *more* than one year.[10] At a general level, when a taxpayer sells a §1231 asset, the taxpayer recognizes a §1231 gain or loss. As discussed above, however, ultimately §1231 gains or losses are characterized as ordinary or capital on a taxpayer's return. When taxpayers sell multiple §1231 assets during the year, they combine or "net" their §1231 gains and §1231 losses together. If the netting results in a net §1231 gain, the net gain is treated as a long-term capital gain. If the netting results in a net §1231 loss, the net loss is treated as an ordinary loss. Because net §1231 gains are treated as capital gains and §1231 losses are treated as ordinary losses, §1231 assets are tax-favored relative to other types of assets.

As we discuss below, §1231 gains on individual depreciable assets may be recharacterized as ordinary income under the depreciation recapture rules. However, because land is not depreciable, when taxpayers sell or otherwise dispose of land that qualifies as §1231 property, the gain or loss from the sale is always characterized as a §1231 gain or loss. Thus, we refer to land as a pure §1231 asset.

[9]§1221 defines what is not a capital asset. Broadly speaking, a *capital asset* is any property *other than* property used in a trade or business (e.g., inventory, manufacturing equipment) or accounts (or notes) receivable acquired in a business from the sale of services or property.

[10]As noted above, property used in a trade or business and held for one year or less is ordinary income property.

EXHIBIT 11-4 Review of Capital Gains and Losses

Taxpayer Type	Preferential Rates	Loss Limitations
Individuals	• Net capital gains on assets held more than one year are taxed at 15% (0% to the extent taxable income including the gain is below the maximum 0% breakpoint and 20% to the extent taxable income including capital gains is above the maximum 15% breakpoint). When determining which capital gains tax rate applies, capital gains that fall within the range of taxable income specified in the tax rate schedules are included in taxable income last.) • Unrecaptured §1250 gains on real property held more than one year remaining after the netting process are taxed at a maximum rate of 25%. • Net gains on collectibles held for more than a year and qualified small business stock (§1202) are taxed at a maximum rate of 28%. • Net gains from capital assets held one year or less are taxed at ordinary rates.	• Individuals may annually deduct up to $3,000 of net capital losses against ordinary income. • Losses can be carried forward indefinitely but not carried back.
C Corporations	• No preferential rates; taxed at ordinary rates.	• No offset against ordinary income. • Net capital losses can generally be carried back three years and forward five years to offset net gains from capital assets in those years.

Example 11-5

In order to acquire another parcel of land to expand its manufacturing capabilities, Teton sold five acres of land that it had been using in its trade or business for $175,000. Teton purchased the land several years ago for $75,000. What are the amount and character of Teton's gain recognized on the land?

Answer: $100,000 §1231 gain, calculated as follows:

Description	Amount	Explanation
(1) Amount realized	$ 175,000	
(2) Original basis and current adjusted basis	75,000	
Gain (loss) realized and recognized	**$100,000**	(1) − (2) §1231 gain

What if: Assume that Teton sold the land for $50,000. What would be the character of the $25,000 loss it would recognize?

Answer: §1231 loss.

What if: Assume that the land was the only asset Teton sold during the year. How would the §1231 gain or §1231 loss on the sale ultimately be characterized on its tax return?

Answer: If Teton recognized a §1231 gain on the sale, it would be characterized as a long-term capital gain on its return. If Teton recognized a §1231 loss on the sale, it would be characterized as an ordinary loss.

LO 11-3

DEPRECIATION RECAPTURE

Although Congress intended for businesses to receive favorable treatment on economic gains from the economic *appreciation* of §1231 assets, it did not intend for this favorable treatment to apply to gains that were created artificially through depreciation deductions that offset ordinary income. For example, if a taxpayer purchases an asset for $100 and sells it three years later for the same amount, we would generally agree that there is no economic gain on the disposition of the asset. However, if the taxpayer claimed depreciation deductions of $70 during the three years of ownership, the taxpayer would recognize a $70 gain on the disposition simply because the depreciation deductions reduced the asset's adjusted basis. Depreciation is an ordinary deduction that offsets income that would otherwise be taxed at ordinary rates.

Absent tax rules to the contrary, the gain recognized by the taxpayer upon the sale of the asset would be treated as long-term capital gain and would be taxed at a preferential rate (for individuals). Thus, depreciation deductions save taxes at the ordinary rate, but the gains created by depreciation generate income taxed at a preferential rate. This potential asymmetrical treatment led Congress to implement the concept of **depreciation recapture.** Depreciation recapture potentially applies to gains (but not losses) on the sale of depreciable or amortizable business property. When depreciation recapture applies, it changes the character of the gain on the sale of a §1231 asset (all or a portion of the gain) from §1231 gain into ordinary income. Note, however, that depreciation recapture does not affect losses recognized on the disposition of §1231 assets.

The method for computing the amount of depreciation recapture depends on the type of §1231 asset the taxpayer is selling (personal property or real property). As presented in Exhibit 11-5, §1231 assets can be categorized as pure §1231 assets (land), §1245 assets (personal property), or §1250 assets (real property). Whether personal or real property is sold, it is important to understand that depreciation recapture changes only the *character* but not the *amount* of gain recognized.

EXHIBIT 11-5 §1231 Asset Types

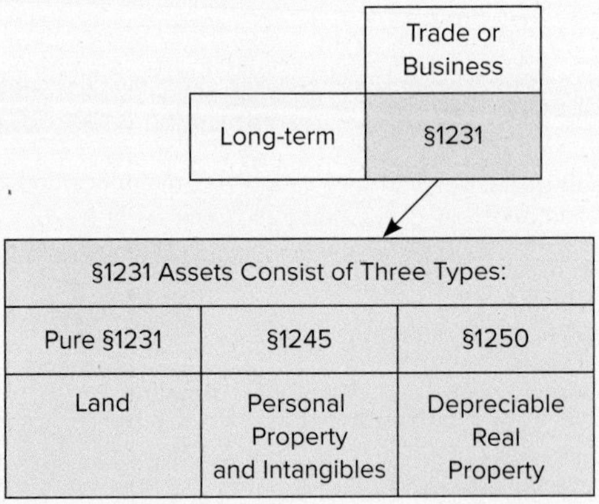

Section 1245 Property

Tangible personal property (e.g., machinery, equipment, and automobiles) and amortizable intangible property (e.g., patents, copyrights, and purchased goodwill) are a subset of §1231 property known as **§1245 property.**[11] The gain from the sale of §1245 property is characterized as ordinary income to the extent the gain was created by depreciation or amortization deductions. The amount of *ordinary income* (§1245 depreciation recapture) taxpayers

[11]An exception in the law is that §1245 property also includes nonresidential real property placed in service between 1981 and 1986 (ACRS) for which the taxpayer elected accelerated depreciation.

recognize when they sell §1245 property is the lesser of (1) recognized gain on the sale *or* (2) total accumulated depreciation (or amortization) on the asset.[12] The remainder of any recognized gain is characterized as §1231 gain.[13] The sum of the ordinary income (due to depreciation recapture) and the §1231 gain on the sale equals the *total* gain recognized because depreciation recapture changes only the character of the gain, not the amount.

When taxpayers sell or dispose of §1245 property, they encounter one of the following three scenarios involving gain or loss:

Scenario 1: They recognize a gain created solely through depreciation deductions.

Scenario 2: They recognize a gain created through both depreciation deductions and actual asset appreciation.

Scenario 3: They recognize a loss.

The following discussion considers each of these scenarios.

THE KEY FACTS

§1245 Assets

- Personal property and amortizable intangible assets are §1245 assets.
- The lesser of (1) gain recognized or (2) accumulated depreciation is recaptured (characterized) as ordinary income under §1245.
- Any remaining gain is §1231 gain.
- There is no depreciation recapture on assets sold at a loss.

Scenario 1: Gain Created Solely through Cost Recovery Deductions Most §1231 assets that experience wear and tear or obsolescence generally do not appreciate in value. Thus, when a taxpayer sells these types of assets at a gain, the gain is usually created because the taxpayer's depreciation deductions associated with the asset reduced the asset's adjusted basis faster than the real decline in the asset's economic value. That is, the entire gain is artificially generated through depreciation, and absent these deductions, the taxpayer would recognize a loss on the sale of the asset. Therefore, the entire gain on the disposition is recaptured (or recharacterized) as ordinary income under §1245 (recall that without depreciation recapture, the gain would be §1231 gain, which can generate long-term capital gain and could create a double benefit for the taxpayer: ordinary depreciation deductions and preferentially taxed capital gain upon disposition).

Example 11-6

As indicated in Exhibit 11-2, Teton sold machinery for $300,000. What are the amount and character of the gain Teton recognizes on the sale?

Answer: $71,342 of ordinary income under the §1245 depreciation recapture rules and $0 of §1231 gain, computed as follows:

Machinery Sale: Scenario 1
(Original scenario sales price = $300,000)

Description	Amount	Explanation
(1) Amount realized	$300,000	Exhibit 11-2
(2) Original basis	610,000	Exhibit 11-2
(3) Accumulated depreciation	381,342	Exhibit 11-2
(4) Adjusted basis	$228,658	(2) − (3)
(5) Gain (loss) recognized	71,342	(1) − (4)
(6) Ordinary income (§1245 depreciation recapture)	**$ 71,342**	Lesser of (3) or (5)
§1231 gain	**0**	(5) − (6)

Note that in this situation, because Teton's entire gain is created through depreciation deductions reducing the basis, the entire gain is treated as ordinary income under §1245.

(continued on page 11-12)

[12]Section 1245 recapture is commonly referred to as "full" depreciation recapture because it may cause a taxpayer to recapture the entire accumulated depreciation amount as ordinary income. Section 1245 recapture applies notwithstanding any other provision of the Internal Revenue Code (i.e., depreciation recapture takes precedence over all other tax rules, such as installment sales).

[13]As a practical matter, taxpayers are unlikely to recognize any §1231 gain on the disposition of personal property because the real economic value of most tangible personal property does not increase over time as the property is used.

What if: What would be the amount and character of Teton's gain without the depreciation recapture rules?

Answer: $71,342 of §1231 gain. Note that the recapture rules change the character of the gain but not the amount of the gain.

Both §179 expensing and bonus depreciation allow taxpayers to accelerate the depreciation taken on assets in the year of acquisition. Under current law, many taxpayers will fully deduct the cost of acquired assets. These provisions, however, require that taxpayers reduce the basis of the assets by the amount of accumulated depreciation. When taxpayers deduct the full cost of an asset under these rules, the asset's basis is reduced to zero. As a result, taxpayers will have larger gains than under prior law, and the gains will typically be ordinary in character.

Scenario 2: Gain Due to Both Cost Recovery Deductions and Asset Appreciation Assets subject to cost recovery deductions may actually *appreciate* in value over time. When these assets are sold, the recognized gain must be divided into ordinary gain from depreciation recapture and §1231 gain. The portion of the gain created through cost recovery deductions is recaptured as ordinary income. The remaining gain (i.e., the gain due to economic appreciation) is §1231 gain.

Example 11-7

What if: Let's assume the same facts as in Example 11-6 and Exhibit 11-2, except that Teton sells the machinery for $620,000. What are the amount and character of the gain Teton would recognize on this sale?

Answer: $381,342 of ordinary income under the §1245 depreciation recapture rules and $10,000 of §1231 gain due to the asset's economic appreciation, computed as follows:

Machinery Sale: Scenario 2
(Assumed sales price = $620,000)

Description	Amount	Explanation
(1) Amount realized	$ 620,000	
(2) Original basis	610,000	Exhibit 11-2
(3) Accumulated depreciation	381,342	Exhibit 11-2
(4) Adjusted basis	$ 228,658	(2) – (3)
(5) Gain (loss) recognized	391,342	(1) – (4)
(6) Ordinary income (§1245 depreciation recapture)	**$381,342**	Lesser of (3) or (5)
§1231 gain	**$ 10,000**	(5) – (6)

Note that taxpayers can quickly determine their §1231 gain (if any) when they sell §1245 property by subtracting the asset's *initial* basis from the amount realized. For example, in Example 11-7, the §1231 gain is $10,000 ($620,000 amount realized less the $610,000 original basis).

Scenario 3: Asset Sold at a Loss Many §1231 assets, such as computer equipment or automobiles, tend to decline in value faster than the corresponding depreciation deductions reduce the asset's adjusted basis. When taxpayers sell or dispose of these assets before the assets are fully depreciated, they recognize a loss on the disposition. Because the depreciation recapture rules don't apply to losses, taxpayers selling §1245 property at a loss recognize a §1231 loss.

Example 11-8

What if: Let's assume the same facts as in Example 11-6 and Exhibit 11-2, except that Teton sells the machinery for $180,000. What are the amount and character of the gain or loss Teton would recognize on this sale?

Answer: A $48,658 §1231 loss, computed as follows:

Machinery Sale: Scenario 3
(Assumed sales price = $180,000)

Description	Amount	Explanation
(1) Amount realized	$180,000	
(2) Initial basis	610,000	Exhibit 11-2
(3) Accumulated depreciation	381,342	Exhibit 11-2
(4) Adjusted basis	$228,658	(2) − (3)
(5) Gain (loss) recognized	(48,658)	(1) − (4)
(6) Ordinary income (§1245 depreciation recapture)	$ 0	Lesser of (3) or (5) (limited to $0)
§1231 (loss)	**$(48,658)**	(5) − (6)

Exhibit 11-6 graphically illustrates the §1245 depreciation recapture computations for the machinery sold in Scenarios 1, 2, and 3, presented in Examples 11-6, 11-7, and 11-8, respectively.[14]

EXHIBIT 11-6 Machinery §1245 Depreciation Recapture Scenarios 1, 2, and 3

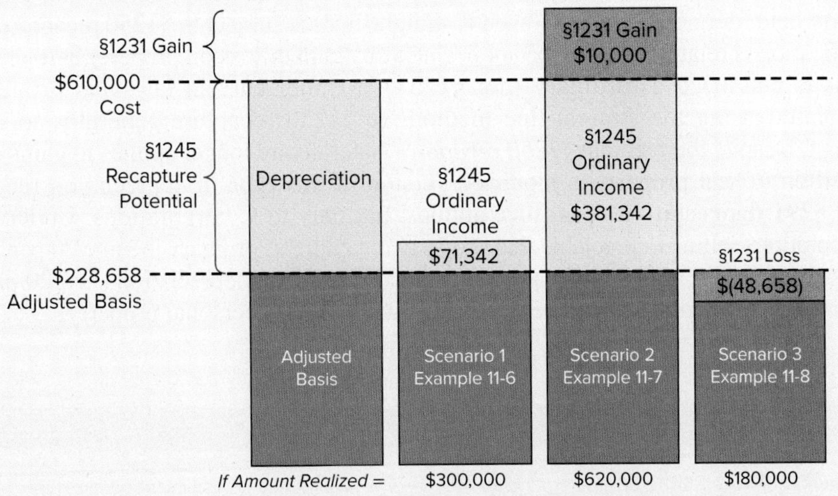

Example 11-9

In Example 11-6 (Scenario 1), we characterized the gain Teton recognized when it sold its machinery. For completeness, let's characterize the gain or loss Teton recognized on the other two §1245 assets it sold during the year (see Exhibit 11-2). Teton sold its office furniture for $23,000 and its delivery truck for $2,000. What are the amount and character of gain or loss Teton recognizes on the sale of the office furniture and the delivery truck?

(continued on page 11-14)

[14]The authors thank PwC for allowing us to use this exhibit.

Answer: Office furniture: $14,000 ordinary income and $3,000 §1231 gain. Delivery truck: $5,500 §1231 loss. The computations supporting the answers are as follows:

Description	Office Furniture	Delivery Truck	Explanation
(1) Amount realized	$ 23,000	$ 2,000	Exhibit 11-2
(2) Initial basis	20,000	25,000	Exhibit 11-2
(3) Accumulated depreciation	14,000	17,500	Exhibit 11-2
(4) Adjusted basis	$ 6,000	$ 7,500	(2) – (3)
(5) Gain (loss) recognized	17,000	(5,500)	(1) – (4)
(6) Ordinary income (§1245 depreciation recapture)	**$14,000**	**$ 0**	Lesser of (3) or (5), limited to $0
§1231 gain (loss)	**$ 3,000**	**$(5,500)**	(5) – (6)

Section 1250 Depreciation Recapture for Real Property

Depreciable real property, such as an office building or a warehouse, sold at a gain is *not* subject to §1245 depreciation recapture. Rather, it is potentially subject to a different type of recapture called §1250 depreciation recapture. Thus, depreciable real property is frequently referred to as **§1250 property.** Under §1250, when depreciable real property is sold at a gain, the amount of gain recaptured as ordinary income is limited to *additional* depreciation, defined as the excess of *accelerated* depreciation deductions on the property over the amount that would have been deducted if the taxpayer had used the straight-line method of depreciation to depreciate the asset. In addition, depreciation taken on property held for one year or less (even if straight-line) is subject to §1250 recapture. This classification is relatively unimportant because any gain or loss on property held one year or less is classified as ordinary (not §1231).[15] Under current law, real property is depreciated using the straight-line method, so §1250 recapture generally no longer applies.[16] Despite the fact that *§1250 recapture* generally no longer applies to gains on the disposition of real property, a modified version of this type of depreciation recapture called **§291 depreciation recapture** applies, but only to C corporations. Under §291, C corporations selling depreciable real property recapture as ordinary income 20 percent of the lesser of (1) the recognized gain or (2) the accumulated depreciation (i.e., 20 percent of what §1245 recapture would be if the asset was tangible personal property).

Example 11-10

What if: Suppose that Teton was organized as a C corporation and that, as described in Exhibit 11-2, it sold its existing warehouse. Let's assume the same facts: Teton sold the warehouse for $350,000, it initially purchased the warehouse for $275,000, and it has deducted $15,000 of straight-line depreciation deductions as of the date of the sale. What is Teton's recognized gain on the sale and what is the character of its gain on the sale?

[15]Section 1250 recapture is commonly referred to as *partial depreciation recapture.*

[16]Accelerated depreciation was allowed for real property placed in service before 1987. Such property had a maximum recovery period of 19 years, which means that as of 2005 all of this property is now fully depreciated under both the accelerated and straight-line depreciation methods. One instance where §1250 recapture might apply is for qualified leasehold improvements placed in service before 2018 and depreciated over 15 years.

Answer: $90,000 gain recognized; $3,000 ordinary income and $87,000 §1231 gain, computed as follows:

Description	Amount	Explanation
(1) Amount realized	$350,000	Exhibit 11-2
(2) Initial basis	275,000	Exhibit 11-2
(3) Accumulated depreciation	15,000	Exhibit 11-2
(4) Adjusted basis	$260,000	(2) − (3)
(5) Gain (loss) recognized	**$ 90,000**	(1) − (4)
(6) Lesser of accumulated depreciation or recognized gain	15,000	Lesser of (3) or (5)
(7) §291 recapture (ordinary income)	**$ 3,000**	20% × (6)
§1231 gain	**$ 87,000**	(5) − (7)

OTHER PROVISIONS AFFECTING THE RATE AT WHICH GAINS ARE TAXED

LO 11-4

Other provisions, other than depreciation recapture, may affect the rate at which gains are taxed. The first potentially applies when individuals sell §1250 property at a gain, and the second potentially applies when taxpayers sell property to related persons at a gain.

Unrecaptured §1250 Gain for Individuals

Except for assets held one year or less and select instances for qualified leasehold property, neither C corporations nor individuals recognize §1250 recapture on the sale of §1250 property when it is sold at a gain. Instead, C corporations recognize §291 recapture as ordinary income on the sale of these assets. Individuals, however, do not recognize ordinary income from the sale of §1250 property when it is held long term. Rather, individual taxpayers treat a gain resulting from the disposition of §1250 property as a §1231 gain and combine it with other §1231 gains and losses to determine whether a net §1231 gain or a net §1231 loss results for the year.

After the §1231 netting process (described below), if the gain on the sale of the §1250 property is ultimately determined to be a long-term capital gain, the taxpayer must determine the rate at which the gain will be taxed. Tax policy makers have determined that the portion of the gain caused by depreciation deductions reducing the basis, called **unrecaptured §1250 gain,** should be taxed at a maximum rate of 25 percent (taxed at the ordinary rate if the ordinary rate is lower than 25 percent) and not the 0/15/20 percent rate generally applicable to other types of long-term capital gains. Consequently, when an individual sells §1250 property at a gain, the amount of the gain taxed at a maximum rate of 25 percent is the *lesser* of (1) the recognized gain or (2) the accumulated depreciation on the asset.[17] Thus, the amount of unrecaptured §1250 gain is the same as the depreciation recapture would be if it were §1245 property. The remainder of the gain is taxed at a maximum rate of 0/15/20 percent.[18]

THE KEY FACTS

Unrecaptured §1250 Gains

- Depreciable real property sold at a gain is §1250 property but is no longer subject to §1250 recapture unless it is held 12 months or less and bought and sold in different years.
- The lesser of the (1) recognized gain or (2) accumulated depreciation on the assets is called *unrecaptured* §1250 gain.
- Unrecaptured §1250 gain is §1231 gain that, if ultimately characterized as a long-term capital gain, is taxed at a maximum rate of 25 percent.

Example 11-11

Teton bought its warehouse for $275,000, depreciated it $15,000, and sold it for $350,000. What are the amount and character of the gain Teton (and thus Steve) reports on the sale? (Recall that income of sole proprietorships is taxed directly to the owner of the business.)

(continued on page 11-16)

[17]The amount taxed at a maximum rate of 25 percent cannot exceed the amount of the taxpayer's net §1231 gain.

[18]These rates (25 or 0/15/20 percent) apply to net §1231 gains after a netting process for capital gains, which we discuss in a different chapter.

Answer: $90,000 of §1231 gain, which includes $15,000 of unrecaptured §1250 gain, computed as follows:

Description	Amount	Explanation
(1) Amount realized	$350,000	Exhibit 11-2
(2) Original basis	275,000	Exhibit 11-2
(3) Accumulated depreciation	15,000	Exhibit 11-2
(4) Adjusted basis	$260,000	(2) – (3)
(5) Gain (loss) recognized	90,000	(1) – (4)
(6) Unrecaptured §1250 gain	$ 15,000	Lesser of (3) or (5)
(7) Remaining §1231 gain	$ 75,000	(5) – (6)
Total §1231 gain	**$ 90,000**	(6) + (7)

What if: Suppose Steve's marginal ordinary tax rate is 32 percent. What amount of tax will he pay on the gain (assuming no other asset dispositions)?

Answer: $15,000, computed as follows:

Description	(1) Gain	(2) Rate	(1) × (2) Tax	Explanation
Long-term capital gain (unrecaptured §1250 gain portion)	$15,000	25%	$ 3,750	This is the gain due to depreciation deductions.
Long-term capital gain (15% portion)	75,000	15%	11,250	Taxed at 15% because Steve's taxable income including the capital gain is below the maximum 15%/20% breakpoint.
Totals	$90,000		**$15,000**	

Because Steve did not sell any other §1231 assets during the year, the entire §1231 gain is treated as a long-term capital gain that is split into a portion taxed at 25 percent and a portion taxed at 15 percent.

THE KEY FACTS

§1239 Related-Person Transactions

- All gain recognized from selling property that is a depreciable asset to a related buyer is ordinary income (regardless of the character of the asset to the seller).
- Related persons are defined in §1239 and include:
  - An individual and the individual's controlled corporation or partnership.
  - A taxpayer and any trust in which the taxpayer (or spouse) is a beneficiary.

Characterizing Gains on the Sale of Depreciable Property to Related Persons

Under §1239, when a taxpayer sells property to a *related person* and the property is depreciable property to the *buyer,* the entire gain on the sale is characterized as ordinary income to the *seller.*[19] Without this provision, related taxpayers could create tax savings by currently generating capital or §1231 gains through selling appreciated assets to related persons who would receive future ordinary deductions through depreciation expense on the basis of the property (stepped up to fair market value through the sale) acquired in the transaction.

The §1239 provision is different from depreciation recapture in the sense that the seller is required to recognize ordinary income for depreciation deductions the buyer will receive *in the future,* while depreciation recapture requires taxpayers to recognize ordinary income for depreciation deductions they have received *in the past.* In both cases, however, the tax laws are designed to provide symmetry between the character of deductions an asset generates and the character of income the asset generates when it is sold.

[19]§1239. §707(b)(2) contains a similar provision for partnerships.

For purposes of §1239, a related person includes an individual and their controlled (more than 50 percent owned) corporation or partnership or a taxpayer and any trust in which the taxpayer (or spouse) is a beneficiary.[20]

Example 11-12

What if: Suppose that Teton is organized as a C corporation and Steve is the sole shareholder. Steve sells equipment that he was using for personal purposes to Teton for $90,000 (he originally purchased the equipment for $80,000). The equipment was a capital asset to Steve because he had been using it for personal purposes (he did not depreciate it). What are the amount and character of the gain Steve would recognize on the sale?

Answer: $10,000 of ordinary income (amount realized $90,000 − $80,000 adjusted basis). Even though Steve is selling what is a capital asset to him, because it is a depreciable asset to Teton and because Steve and Teton are considered to be related persons, Steve is required to characterize the entire amount of gain as ordinary under §1239. Without the §1239 provision, Steve would have recognized a capital gain.

Exhibit 11-7 provides a flowchart for determining the character of gains and losses on the taxable sale of assets used in a trade or business.

CALCULATING NET §1231 GAINS OR LOSSES

LO 11-5

Once taxpayers determine the amount and character of gain or loss they recognize on *each* §1231 asset they sell during the year, they still have work to do to determine whether the gains or losses will be treated as ordinary or capital. After recharacterizing §1231 gain as ordinary income under the §1245 and §291 (if applicable) depreciation recapture rules and the §1239 recharacterization rules, the remaining §1231 gains and losses are netted together.[21] Recall that a portion of the §1231 gains may include unrecaptured §1250 gains that are taxed at a maximum of 25 percent. When netting the §1231 losses against §1231 gains, the losses first offset regular §1231 gains before offsetting unrecaptured §1250 gains. If the gains exceed the losses, the net gain becomes a long-term capital gain (a portion of which may be taxed at the maximum rate of 25 percent). If the losses exceed the gains, the net loss is treated as an ordinary loss.

A taxpayer could obtain significant tax benefits by discovering a way to have all §1231 gains treated as long-term capital gains and all §1231 losses treated as ordinary losses. The *annual* netting process makes this task impossible for a *particular* year. However, a taxpayer who owns multiple §1231 assets could sell the §1231 loss assets at the end of year 1 and the §1231 gain assets at the beginning of year 2. The taxpayer could benefit from this strategy in three ways: (1) accelerating losses into year 1, (2) deferring gains until year 2, and (3) favorably characterizing the gains and losses due to the §1231 netting process. The **§1231 look-back rule** limits the benefits from implementing this strategy.

THE KEY FACTS

Netting and Look-Back Rule

- §1231 gains and losses from individual asset dispositions are annually netted together.
- Net §1231 gains may be recharacterized as ordinary income under the §1231 look-back rule.

Section 1231 Look-Back Rule

The §1231 look-back rule is a *nondepreciation* recapture rule that applies in situations like the one we just described to turn what would otherwise be §1231 gain into ordinary income. That is, the rule affects the character but not the amount of gains on which a

[20]Additional related persons for purposes of §1239 include two corporations that are members of the same controlled group, a corporation and a partnership if the same person owns more than 50 percent of both entities, two S corporations controlled by the same person, and an S corporation and a C corporation controlled by the same person.

[21]If any of the §1231 gains and losses result from casualty or theft, these gains and losses are netted together first. If a net loss results, the net loss from §1231 casualty and theft events is treated as ordinary loss. Net gains from casualty and theft are treated as other §1231 gains and continue through the normal §1231 netting process.

EXHIBIT 11-7 Sale of Assets Used in a Business

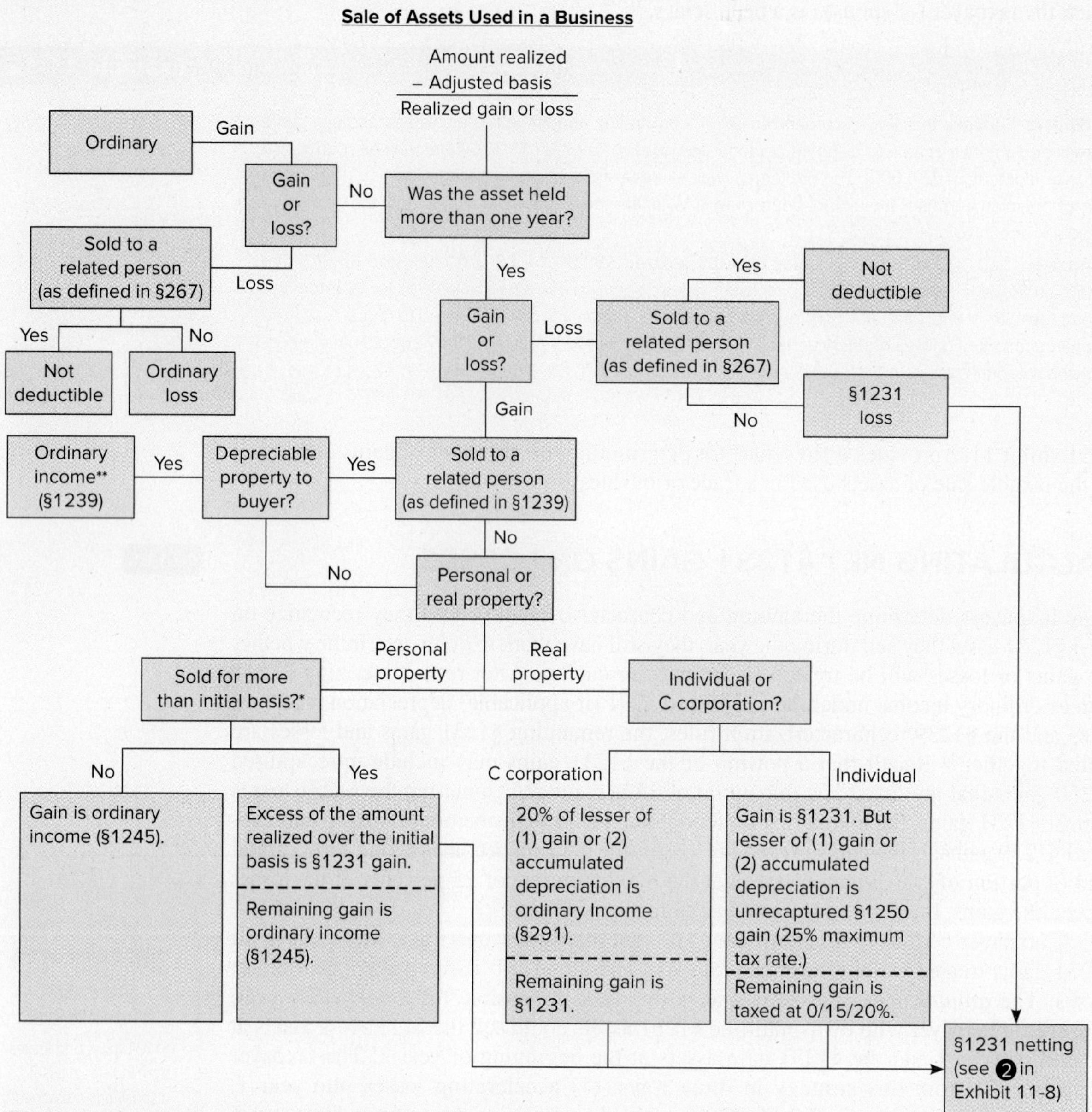

*This treatment assumes the asset was initially purchased by the taxpayer.

**Technically, §1245 recapture precedes the §1239 reclassification; however, from a practical perspective, the income will all be ordinary under either §1239 or §1245.

taxpayer is taxed. In general terms, the §1231 look-back rule is designed to require taxpayers who recognize net §1231 gains in the current year to recapture (recharacterize) current-year gains as ordinary to the extent the taxpayer deducted ordinary net §1231 losses in prior years. Without the look-back rule, taxpayers could carefully time the year in which the §1231 assets were sold to maximize the tax benefits.

In specific terms, the §1231 look-back rule indicates that when a taxpayer recognizes a net §1231 gain for a year, the taxpayer must "look back" to the *five-year* period preceding the current tax year to determine whether, during that period, the taxpayer recognized any **nonrecaptured net §1231 losses,** which are losses that were deducted as ordinary losses that have not caused subsequent §1231 gains to be recharacterized as ordinary income. The taxpayer starts the process by looking back to the year five years prior to the beginning of the current year. If the taxpayer has recognized a net §1231 loss in that period and has not previously recaptured the loss (by causing a subsequent §1231 gain to be recharacterized as ordinary) in a subsequent year (but prior to the current year), the taxpayer must recharacterize the *current-year* net §1231 gain as ordinary income to the extent of that prior-year nonrecaptured net §1231 loss. If the current-year net §1231 gain includes unrecaptured §1250 gains, the look-back rule requires the unrecaptured §1250 gains to be recharacterized as ordinary before other §1231 gains. The prior-year loss is then considered "recaptured," to the extent it caused the current-year gain to be treated as ordinary income.

If the current-year net §1231 gain exceeds the nonrecaptured net §1231 loss from the year five years prior, the taxpayer repeats the process for the year four years prior, and then three years prior, and so on. A prior year's nonrecaptured net losses are not netted against the current year's gains (they don't offset the current-year gains); rather, they cause the taxpayer to recharacterize a net §1231 gain or a portion of that gain (that would otherwise be characterized as a long-term capital gain) as ordinary income in the current year.

Example 11-13

What if: Suppose that Teton began business in year 1 and that it recognized a $7,000 net §1231 loss in year 1. Assume that the current year is year 6 and that Teton reports a ***net*** §1231 gain of $25,000 for the year. Teton did not recognize any §1231 gains or losses in years 2–5. For year 6, what would be the ultimate character of the $25,000 net §1231 gain?

Answer: $7,000 ordinary income and $18,000 long-term capital gain. Because it recognized a net §1231 loss in year 1, it must recharacterize $7,000 of its net §1231 gain in year 6 as ordinary income. The remaining $18,000 §1231 gain is taxed as long-term capital gain.

What if: Assume the same facts as above, except that Teton also recognized a $2,000 net §1231 loss in year 5. For year 6, what would be the ultimate character of the $25,000 net §1231 gain?

Answer: $9,000 ordinary income and $16,000 long-term capital gain. Note that the overall gain is still $25,000, but to the extent of the $7,000 loss in year 1 and the $2,000 loss in year 5, the §1231 gain is recharacterized as ordinary income under the §1231 look-back rule.

ETHICS

Emma Bean operates a real estate development company and wants to sell some of her business equipment and a piece of land that is used as a parking lot for her business. She expects to realize a $10,000 loss on the equipment and a $15,000 gain on the land. Emma has talked to her accountant and has learned about the look-back rule for §1231 property. To avoid any negative effects, she has decided to game the system and sell the land this year and then sell the equipment early next year. What do you think about her strategy to avoid the look-back rule?

As we've mentioned before, ultimately, all of a taxpayer's §1231 gains and losses must be characterized as ordinary or capital for purposes of determining the taxpayer's tax liability. Exhibit 11-8 summarizes the process of characterizing §1231 gains and losses as ordinary or capital.

The following provides details on Steps 1–3 from Exhibit 11-8:

Step 1: Apply the *depreciation* recapture rules (and the §1239 rule) to §1231 assets sold at a gain (any recaptured amounts become ordinary).

Step 2: Net the remaining §1231 gains with the §1231 losses. The §1231 losses offset regular §1231 gains before the unrecaptured §1250 gains. If the netting process yields a §1231 loss, the net §1231 loss becomes an ordinary loss.

Step 3: If the netting process produces a net §1231 gain, the taxpayer applies the §1231 look-back rule to determine if any of the remaining §1231 gain should be recharacterized as ordinary gain. Under the look-back rule, the unrecaptured §1250 gains will be recharacterized before the regular §1231 gains. Any gain remaining after applying the look-back rule is treated as long-term capital gain (including unrecaptured §1250 gain). This gain is included in the capital gains netting process.

EXHIBIT 11-8 §1231 Netting Process

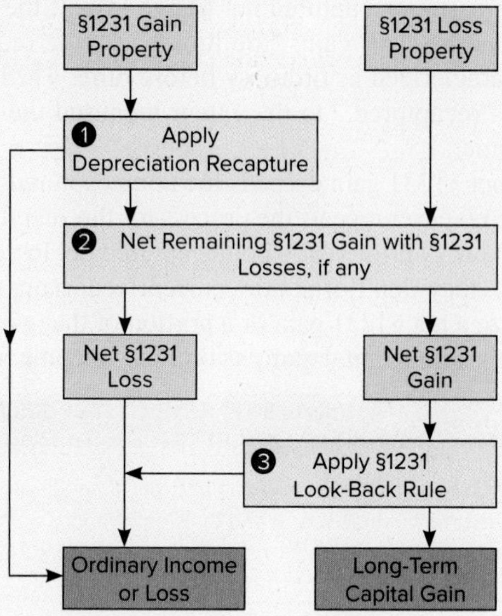

GAIN OR LOSS SUMMARY

As indicated in Exhibit 11-2, Teton sold several assets during the year. Exhibit 11-9 summarizes the character of the gain or loss Teton (and thus Steve) recognized on each asset sale.

So, how would this information be reported on Steve's tax return? Exhibit 11-10 provides Steve's Form 4797, which summarizes Teton's property transactions and divides the gains and losses between the ordinary gain of $95,342 and the §1231 gain of $177,500. Because the net §1231 gain is treated as a long-term capital gain, it flows to Steve's Schedule D (the form for reporting capital gains and losses). Steve's Schedule D is presented in Exhibit 11-11.

EXHIBIT 11-9 Summary of Teton Gains and Losses on Property Dispositions

Asset	(1) §1245 Ordinary Gain	(2) Total Ordinary Gain	(3) §1231 Gain (Loss)	(2) + (3) Total Gain
Machinery	$71,342	$71,342	$ 0	$ 71,342
Office furniture	14,000	14,000	3,000	17,000
Delivery truck	0	0	(5,500)	(5,500)
Warehouse	0	0	90,000*	90,000
Land	0	0	100,000	100,000
§1231 look-back	0	10,000	(10,000)†	0
Totals	$85,342	$95,342	$177,500*	$272,842

*Because the warehouse is §1231 property, the $90,000 gain is included in the §1231 gain (loss) column. Further, $15,000 of the $90,000 gain is considered unrecaptured §1250 gain (see Example 11-11).

†This exhibit assumes that Teton had $10,000 of net §1231 losses in the prior five years. Following the application of the look-back rule, $172,500 of the §1231 gains will be treated as long-term capital gains taxed at 0/15/20 percent and $5,000 of the §1231 gains will be treated as long-term capital gains taxed at a maximum rate of 25 percent.

EXHIBIT 11-10 Teton's (on Steve's return) Form 4797

Form **4797**

Department of the Treasury
Internal Revenue Service

Sales of Business Property

(Also Involuntary Conversions and Recapture Amounts Under Sections 179 and 280F(b)(2))

▶ Attach to your tax return.
▶ Go to *www.irs.gov/Form4797* for instructions and the latest information.

OMB No. 1545-0184
2021
Attachment Sequence No. 27

Name(s) shown on return	Identifying number
Steve Dallimore (Teton Mountaineering Technology, LLC)	

1a	Enter the gross proceeds from sales or exchanges reported to you for 2021 on Form(s) 1099-B or 1099-S (or substitute statement) that you are including on line 2, 10, or 20. See instructions	1a	
b	Enter the total amount of gain that you are including on lines 2, 10, and 24 due to the partial dispositions of MACRS assets	1b	
c	Enter the total amount of loss that you are including on lines 2 and 10 due to the partial dispositions of MACRS assets	1c	

Part I **Sales or Exchanges of Property Used in a Trade or Business and Involuntary Conversions From Other Than Casualty or Theft—Most Property Held More Than 1 Year** (see instructions)

2 (a) Description of property	(b) Date acquired (mo., day, yr.)	(c) Date sold (mo., day, yr.)	(d) Gross sales price	(e) Depreciation allowed or allowable since acquisition	(f) Cost or other basis, plus improvements and expense of sale	(g) Gain or (loss) Subtract (f) from the sum of (d) and (e)
Delivery truck	Yr 0	Yr 4	2,000	17,500	25,000	(5,500)
Land	Yr 0	Yr 4	175,000	0	75,000	100,000

3	Gain, if any, from Form 4684, line 39	3	
4	Section 1231 gain from installment sales from Form 6252, line 26 or 37	4	
5	Section 1231 gain or (loss) from like-kind exchanges from Form 8824	5	
6	Gain, if any, from line 32, from other than casualty or theft	6	93,000
7	Combine lines 2 through 6. Enter the gain or (loss) here and on the appropriate line as follows	7	187,500
	Partnerships and S corporations. Report the gain or (loss) following the instructions for Form 1065, Schedule K, line 10, or Form 1120-S, Schedule K, line 9. Skip lines 8, 9, 11, and 12 below.		
	Individuals, partners, S corporation shareholders, and all others. If line 7 is zero or a loss, enter the amount from line 7 on line 11 below and skip lines 8 and 9. If line 7 is a gain and you didn't have any prior year section 1231 losses, or they were recaptured in an earlier year, enter the gain from line 7 as a long-term capital gain on the Schedule D filed with your return and skip lines 8, 9, 11, and 12 below.		
8	Nonrecaptured net section 1231 losses from prior years. See instructions	8	10,000
9	Subtract line 8 from line 7. If zero or less, enter -0-. If line 9 is zero, enter the gain from line 7 on line 12 below. If line 9 is more than zero, enter the amount from line 8 on line 12 below and enter the gain from line 9 as a long-term capital gain on the Schedule D filed with your return. See instructions	9	177,500

Part II **Ordinary Gains and Losses** (see instructions)

10 Ordinary gains and losses not included on lines 11 through 16 (include property held 1 year or less):

11	Loss, if any, from line 7	11	( )
12	Gain, if any, from line 7 or amount from line 8, if applicable	12	10,000
13	Gain, if any, from line 31	13	85,342
14	Net gain or (loss) from Form 4684, lines 31 and 38a	14	
15	Ordinary gain from installment sales from Form 6252, line 25 or 36	15	
16	Ordinary gain or (loss) from like-kind exchanges from Form 8824	16	
17	Combine lines 10 through 16	17	95,342
18	For all except individual returns, enter the amount from line 17 on the appropriate line of your return and skip lines a and b below. For individual returns, complete lines a and b below.		
a	If the loss on line 11 includes a loss from Form 4684, line 35, column (b)(ii), enter that part of the loss here. Enter the loss from income-producing property on Schedule A (Form 1040), line 16. (Do not include any loss on property used as an employee.) Identify as from "Form 4797, line 18a." See instructions	18a	
b	Redetermine the gain or (loss) on line 17 excluding the loss, if any, on line 18a. Enter here and on Schedule 1 (Form 1040), Part I, line 4	18b	95,342

For Paperwork Reduction Act Notice, see separate instructions. Cat. No. 13086I Form **4797** (2021)

EXHIBIT 11-10 **Teton's (on Steve's return) Form 4797 (*continued*)**

Form 4797 (2021) Page **2**

Part III **Gain From Disposition of Property Under Sections 1245, 1250, 1252, 1254, and 1255** (see instructions)

19 (a) Description of section 1245, 1250, 1252, 1254, or 1255 property:	(b) Date acquired (mo., day, yr.)	(c) Date sold (mo., day, yr.)
A **Machinery**	**Yr 0**	**Yr 4**
B **Office furniture**	**Yr 0**	**Yr 4**
C **Warehouse**	**Yr 0**	**Yr 4**
D		

These columns relate to the properties on lines 19A through 19D. ▶		Property A	Property B	Property C	Property D
20 Gross sales price (**Note:** *See line 1a before completing.*)	20	300,000	23,000	350,000	
21 Cost or other basis plus expense of sale	21	610,000	20,000	275,000	
22 Depreciation (or depletion) allowed or allowable	22	381,342	14,000	15,000	
23 Adjusted basis. Subtract line 22 from line 21	23	228,658	6,000	260,000	
24 Total gain. Subtract line 23 from line 20	24	71,342	17,000	90,000	
25 **If section 1245 property:**					
a Depreciation allowed or allowable from line 22	25a	381,342	14,000		
b Enter the **smaller** of line 24 or 25a	25b	71,342	14,000		
26 **If section 1250 property:** If straight line depreciation was used, enter -0- on line 26g, except for a corporation subject to section 291.					
a Additional depreciation after 1975. See instructions	26a				
b Applicable percentage multiplied by the **smaller** of line 24 or line 26a. See instructions	26b				
c Subtract line 26a from line 24. If residential rental property **or** line 24 isn't more than line 26a, skip lines 26d and 26e	26c				
d Additional depreciation after 1969 and before 1976	26d				
e Enter the **smaller** of line 26c or 26d	26e				
f Section 291 amount (corporations only)	26f				
g Add lines 26b, 26e, and 26f	26g			0	
27 **If section 1252 property:** Skip this section if you didn't dispose of farmland or if this form is being completed for a partnership.					
a Soil, water, and land clearing expenses	27a				
b Line 27a multiplied by applicable percentage. See instructions	27b				
c Enter the **smaller** of line 24 or 27b	27c				
28 **If section 1254 property:**					
a Intangible drilling and development costs, expenditures for development of mines and other natural deposits, mining exploration costs, and depletion. See instructions	28a				
b Enter the **smaller** of line 24 or 28a	28b				
29 **If section 1255 property:**					
a Applicable percentage of payments excluded from income under section 126. See instructions	29a				
b Enter the **smaller** of line 24 or 29a. See instructions	29b				

Summary of Part III Gains. Complete property columns A through D through line 29b before going to line 30.

30 Total gains for all properties. Add property columns A through D, line 24	30	178,342
31 Add property columns A through D, lines 25b, 26g, 27c, 28b, and 29b. Enter here and on line 13	31	85,342
32 Subtract line 31 from line 30. Enter the portion from casualty or theft on Form 4684, line 33. Enter the portion from other than casualty or theft on Form 4797, line 6	32	93,000

Part IV **Recapture Amounts Under Sections 179 and 280F(b)(2) When Business Use Drops to 50% or Less** (see instructions)

		(a) Section 179	(b) Section 280F(b)(2)
33 Section 179 expense deduction or depreciation allowable in prior years	33		
34 Recomputed depreciation. See instructions	34		
35 Recapture amount. Subtract line 34 from line 33. See the instructions for where to report	35		

Form **4797** (2021)

Source: irs.gov.

EXHIBIT 11-11 Steve's Schedule D (Assumes Steve had no other capital gains and losses other than those incurred by Teton)

SCHEDULE D
(Form 1040)

Department of the Treasury
Internal Revenue Service (99)

Capital Gains and Losses

▶ Attach to Form 1040, 1040-SR, or 1040-NR.
▶ Go to *www.irs.gov/ScheduleD* for instructions and the latest information.
▶ Use Form 8949 to list your transactions for lines 1b, 2, 3, 8b, 9, and 10.

OMB No. 1545-0074
2021
Attachment Sequence No. **12**

Name(s) shown on return: **Steve Dallimore** | **Your social security number**

Did you dispose of any investment(s) in a qualified opportunity fund during the tax year? ☐ **Yes** ☐ **No**
If "Yes," attach Form 8949 and see its instructions for additional requirements for reporting your gain or loss.

Part I Short-Term Capital Gains and Losses—Generally Assets Held One Year or Less (see instructions)

See instructions for how to figure the amounts to enter on the lines below. This form may be easier to complete if you round off cents to whole dollars.	(d) Proceeds (sales price)	(e) Cost (or other basis)	(g) Adjustments to gain or loss from Form(s) 8949, Part I, line 2, column (g)	(h) Gain or (loss) Subtract column (e) from column (d) and combine the result with column (g)
1a Totals for all short-term transactions reported on Form 1099-B for which basis was reported to the IRS and for which you have no adjustments (see instructions). However, if you choose to report all these transactions on Form 8949, leave this line blank and go to line 1b .				
1b Totals for all transactions reported on Form(s) 8949 with **Box A** checked				
2 Totals for all transactions reported on Form(s) 8949 with **Box B** checked				
3 Totals for all transactions reported on Form(s) 8949 with **Box C** checked				

4 Short-term gain from Form 6252 and short-term gain or (loss) from Forms 4684, 6781, and 8824 . .	**4**	
5 Net short-term gain or (loss) from partnerships, S corporations, estates, and trusts from Schedule(s) K-1	**5**	
6 Short-term capital loss carryover. Enter the amount, if any, from line 8 of your **Capital Loss Carryover Worksheet** in the instructions	**6**	( )
7 **Net short-term capital gain or (loss).** Combine lines 1a through 6 in column (h). If you have any long-term capital gains or losses, go to Part II below. Otherwise, go to Part III on the back	**7**	

Part II Long-Term Capital Gains and Losses—Generally Assets Held More Than One Year (see instructions)

See instructions for how to figure the amounts to enter on the lines below. This form may be easier to complete if you round off cents to whole dollars.	(d) Proceeds (sales price)	(e) Cost (or other basis)	(g) Adjustments to gain or loss from Form(s) 8949, Part II, line 2, column (g)	(h) Gain or (loss) Subtract column (e) from column (d) and combine the result with column (g)
8a Totals for all long-term transactions reported on Form 1099-B for which basis was reported to the IRS and for which you have no adjustments (see instructions). However, if you choose to report all these transactions on Form 8949, leave this line blank and go to line 8b .				
8b Totals for all transactions reported on Form(s) 8949 with **Box D** checked				
9 Totals for all transactions reported on Form(s) 8949 with **Box E** checked				
10 Totals for all transactions reported on Form(s) 8949 with **Box F** checked.				

11 Gain from Form 4797, Part I; long-term gain from Forms 2439 and 6252; and long-term gain or (loss) from Forms 4684, 6781, and 8824	**11**	177,500
12 Net long-term gain or (loss) from partnerships, S corporations, estates, and trusts from Schedule(s) K-1	**12**	
13 Capital gain distributions. See the instructions	**13**	
14 Long-term capital loss carryover. Enter the amount, if any, from line 13 of your **Capital Loss Carryover Worksheet** in the instructions	**14**	( )
15 **Net long-term capital gain or (loss).** Combine lines 8a through 14 in column (h). Then, go to Part III on the back	**15**	177,500

For Paperwork Reduction Act Notice, see your tax return instructions. Cat. No. 11338H **Schedule D (Form 1040) 2021**

Source: irs.gov.

LO 11-6

TAX-DEFERRED TRANSACTIONS

Taxpayers realizing gains and losses when they sell or exchange property must immediately recognize the gain for tax purposes unless a specific provision in the tax code says otherwise. Under certain tax provisions, taxpayers defer or delay recognizing a gain or loss until a subsequent period. We first explore tax provisions that allow taxpayers to defer recognizing realized gains. Congress allows taxpayers to defer recognizing gains in certain types of exchanges because the exchange itself does not provide the taxpayers with the wherewithal (cash) to pay taxes on the realized gain if the taxpayers were required to immediately recognize the gain. Also, taxpayers are in the same economic position before and after the exchange (e.g., owning similar property). In particular, we discuss common **tax-deferred transactions** such as like-kind exchanges, involuntary conversions, installment sales, and other business-related transactions such as business formations and reorganizations.

Like-Kind Exchanges

Taxpayers involved in a business may have valid reasons to trade business assets to others for similar business assets. For example, a taxpayer may want to trade land used in its business for a different parcel of land in a better location. As we discussed earlier in this chapter, taxpayers exchanging property *realize* gains (or losses) on exchanges just as taxpayers do by selling property for cash. However, taxpayers exchanging property for property are in a different situation than taxpayers selling the same property for cash. Taxpayers exchanging one piece of business property for another haven't changed their relative economic position because both before and after the exchange they hold similar assets for use in their business. Further, exchanges of property do not generate the wherewithal (cash) for the taxpayers to pay taxes on the gain they realize and recognize on the exchanges. While taxpayers selling property for cash must immediately recognize gain on the sale, taxpayers exchanging property for assets other than cash must defer recognizing gain (or loss) realized on the exchange if they meet certain requirements. This type of deferred gain (or loss) transaction is commonly referred to as a **like-kind exchange** or §1031 exchange.[22]

Like-kind exchange treatment can provide taxpayers with significant tax advantages by allowing them to defer gain (and current taxes payable) that would otherwise be recognized immediately.[23] For an exchange to qualify as a like-kind exchange for tax purposes, the transaction must meet the following three criteria:

1. Real property is exchanged "solely for like-kind" property.
2. Both the real property given up and the real property received in the exchange by the taxpayer are and will be either "used in a trade or business" or "held for investment" by the taxpayer.
3. The exchange must meet certain time restrictions.[24]

Below, we discuss each of these requirements in detail.

Definition of Like-Kind Property Real property is eligible for like-kind treatment while personal property is not.[25] Real property is considered to be like-kind with any other type of real property as long as the real property is used in a trade or business or held for

[22]Like-kind exchanges are defined in §1031 of the Internal Revenue Code.

[23]Financial accounting rules require businesses to recognize (for financial accounting purposes) any gain they realize in a like-kind exchange transaction.

[24]Prior to 2018, personal property could be exchanged under the like-kind exchange rules.

[25]Regulations under §1031 issued in December 2020 provide clarification and guidance as to what constitutes real property. Property that is considered inherently permanent (e.g., in-ground swimming pools, parking facilities, fences, silos) is listed in Reg. §1.1031(a)-3(a)(2).

investment. For example, from Teton's perspective, its warehouse on 10 acres is considered to be like-kind with a nearby condominium, a 20-acre parcel of raw land across town, or even a Manhattan skyscraper. Real property held for sale in the course of ordinary business is not eligible for like-kind treatment, so taxpayers whose business is to buy and sell real property cannot do so using the like-kind exchange rules.[26] In addition, real property located in the United States and real property located outside the United States are not like-kind.

THE KEY FACTS

Like-Kind Property

- Real property
  - All real property used in a trade or business or held for investment is considered "like-kind" with other real property used in a trade or business or held for investment.
- Ineligible property
  - Personal property.
  - Domestic property exchanged for property used in a foreign country and all property used in a foreign country.
  - Real property held for sale.

Property Use Even when property meets the definition of like-kind property, taxpayers can exchange the property in a qualifying like-kind exchange only if they used the transferred property in a trade or business or for investment *and* they will use the property received in the exchange in a trade or business or for investment. For example, Teton could exchange its warehouse on 10 acres for a 200-acre parcel of land it intends to hold as an investment in a qualifying like-kind exchange because Teton was using the warehouse in its business and it will hold the land as an investment. However, if Steve exchanged his cabin in Maine for a personal residence in Wyoming, the exchange would not qualify because Steve used the Maine residence for personal purposes, and he would be using the Wyoming property for personal rather than business or investment purposes. In fact, even if Steve were renting out his Maine cabin (meaning it qualifies as investment property) when he exchanged it for his principal residence in Wyoming, the exchange would not qualify for like-kind exchange treatment because *both* properties must meet the use test for Steve (the personal residence does not qualify as business or investment property).

Timing Requirements for a Like-Kind Exchange The like-kind rules require an exchange of real property for real property; however, a simultaneous exchange may not be practical or possible. For example, taxpayers may not always be able to immediately (or even eventually) find another party who is willing to exchange properties with them. In these situations, taxpayers often use **third-party intermediaries** to facilitate like-kind exchanges.

THE KEY FACTS

Timing Requirements

- Like-kind property exchanges may involve intermediaries.
- Taxpayers must identify replacement like-kind property within 45 days of giving up their real property.
- Like-kind property must be received within 180 days of when the taxpayer transfers real property in a like-kind exchange.

When a third party is involved, the taxpayer transfers the like-kind property to the intermediary, who then sells the property and uses the proceeds to acquire the new property for the taxpayer.[27] Because the third party must sell the taxpayer's old property and locate and purchase suitable replacement property, this process is subject to delay. Does a delay in the completion of the exchange disqualify an otherwise allowable like-kind exchange? Not necessarily. The tax laws do not require a simultaneous exchange of assets, but they do impose some timing requirements to ensure that a transaction is completed within a reasonable time in order to qualify as a **deferred like-kind exchange** (not simultaneous)—often referred to as a "*Starker* exchange."[28]

The two timing rules applicable to like-kind exchanges are that (1) the taxpayer must *identify* the like-kind replacement property within 45 days after transferring the property given up in the exchange and (2) the taxpayer must receive the replacement like-kind property within 180 days (or the due date of the tax return including extensions) after the taxpayer initially transfers property in the exchange.[29,30] The time limits force the

[26]§1031(a)(2).

[27]Exchanges involving third-party intermediaries are very common with real estate exchanges. For real estate, taxpayers must use a "qualified exchange intermediary," such as a title company, and cannot use a personal attorney (because attorneys are considered to be the taxpayer's agent).

[28]The term "*Starker* exchange" refers to a landmark court case that first allowed deferred exchanges [*Starker v. United States,* 79-2 USTC ¶ 9541 (9th Cir. 1979)]. The rules for deferred exchanges are found in §1031(a)(3). The tax laws also allow for reverse like-kind exchanges, where replacement property is acquired before the taxpayer transfers the like-kind property.

[29]The taxpayer must identify at least one like-kind asset; however, because failure to obtain the asset disqualifies the transaction from having deferred like-kind exchange status, the taxpayer may identify up to three alternatives to hedge against the inability to obtain the first identified asset. Generally, a taxpayer must obtain only one to facilitate the exchange [see Reg. §1.1031(k)-1(c)(4)].

[30]The identification period begins on the date the taxpayer transfers the property and ends at midnight on the 45th day after the transfer. Similarly, the exchange period begins on the date of the transfer and ends at midnight on the earlier of the 180th day after the transfer or the due date (including extensions) for the taxpayer's tax return. Reg. §1.1031(k)-1(b)(2).

taxpayer to close the transaction within a specified time period in order to be able to report the tax consequences of the transaction. Exhibit 11-12 provides a diagram of a like-kind exchange involving a third-party intermediary.

EXHIBIT 11-12 Diagram of Deferred or *Starker* Exchange

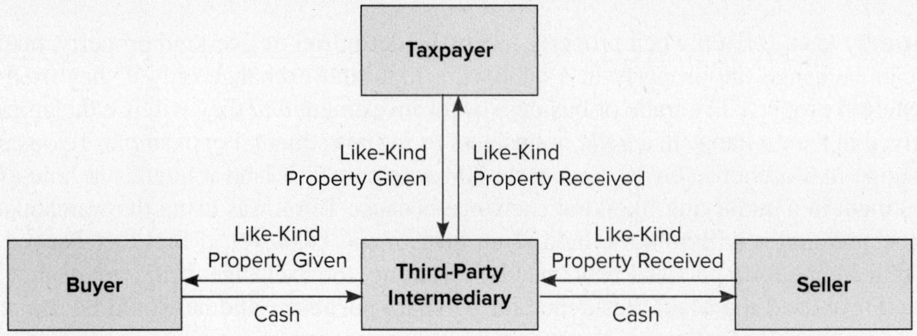

When a taxpayer fails to meet the timing requirements, the exchange fails to qualify for like-kind treatment and is fully taxable.

Example 11-14

What if: Suppose that on August 4 of year 1 Steve transferred a parcel of real property that he was holding as an investment to a third-party intermediary with the intention of exchanging the property for another suitable investment property. By what date does Steve need to identify the replacement property?

Answer: September 18 of year 1, which is 45 days after Steve transferred the property to the intermediary.

Assuming Steve identifies the replacement property within the 45-day time period, by what date does he need to receive the replacement property in order to qualify for like-kind exchange treatment?

Answer: January 31 of year 2, which is 180 days from August 4, the date he transferred the property to the intermediary.

Tax Consequences When Like-Kind Property Is Exchanged Solely for Like-Kind Property As we've discussed, when taxpayers exchanging property meet the like-kind exchange requirements, they do not recognize gain or loss on the exchange. They also establish or receive a **substituted basis** in the like-kind property they receive. That is, they exchange the basis they have in the property they are giving up and transfer it to the basis of the property they are receiving.[31]

Example 11-15

Teton trades land worth $29,500 (tax basis of $18,000) for land in a different location that is also worth $29,500. How much gain does Teton recognize on this exchange?

Answer: $0. Teton's exchange qualifies as a like-kind exchange, and the $11,500 realized gain ($29,500 amount realized – $18,000 tax basis) is deferred.

What is Teton's tax basis in the new land?

Answer: $18,000, the basis it had in the old land it exchanged.

[31]If the real property received is depreciable, the taxpayer continues to depreciate the new property as if it were the old property.

Tax Consequences of Transfers Involving Like-Kind and Non-Like-Kind Property (Boot) A practical problem with like-kind exchanges is that the value of the like-kind property the taxpayer transfers may differ from the value of the like-kind property the taxpayer receives in the exchange. In these situations, the party transferring the lesser-valued asset must also transfer additional property to the other party to equate the values. When this additional property or **boot** (non-like-kind property) is transferred, the party giving the boot recognizes gain or loss on the transfer of the boot portion of the exchange. If the boot transferred is cash, there is no gain or loss for the transferor. However, the like-kind property exchanged will still qualify for gain deferral.

When a taxpayer receives boot, it appears as though the transaction fails the first like-kind exchange requirement that like-kind property be exchanged solely for like-kind property. Nevertheless, if a taxpayer receives boot in addition to like-kind property, the transaction can still qualify for like-kind exchange treatment, but the taxpayer is required to recognize realized gain *to the extent of the boot received*.[32] As a practical matter, this means the taxpayer's recognized gain is the *lesser of* (1) gain realized or (2) boot received.

The reason a taxpayer must recognize gain is that the taxpayer is essentially selling a portion of the like-kind property for the boot in a taxable exchange. The receipt of boot triggers taxable gain (but not taxable loss) in an otherwise qualifying like-kind exchange. If the taxpayer transfers loss property (adjusted basis is greater than fair market value) in a qualifying like-kind exchange, the taxpayer defers recognition of the loss until the taxpayer sells or disposes of the loss property in a taxable transaction—so it may be important for tax planning purposes to avoid the like-kind exchange rules if the taxpayer wishes to currently recognize the loss.[33] When a taxpayer recognizes gain in a like-kind exchange, the character of the gain depends on the character of the asset transferred by the taxpayer (the depreciation recapture rules apply when characterizing gains).

THE KEY FACTS

Like-Kind Exchanges Involving Boot

- Non-like-kind property is known as *boot*.
- When boot is given as part of a like-kind transaction:
  - The asset received is recorded in two parts: (1) property received in exchange for like-kind property and (2) property received in a sale (bought by the boot).
- When boot is received:
  - Boot received usually creates recognized gain.
  - Gain recognized is lesser of gain realized or boot received.

Example 11-16

What if: Suppose that Teton trades land with a value of $29,500 and a tax basis of $18,000 for land in a different location valued at $27,500. To equate the value of the property exchanged, the other party also pays Teton $2,000. What gain or loss does Teton realize on the exchange and what gain or loss does Teton recognize on the exchange?

Answer: $11,500 realized gain and $2,000 recognized gain, calculated as follows:

Description	Amount	Explanation
(1) Amount realized from land	$ 27,500	Fair market value of new land
(2) Amount realized from boot (cash)	2,000	
(3) Total amount realized	29,500	(1) + (2)
(4) Adjusted basis	18,000	
(5) Gain realized	**$11,500**	(3) – (4)
Gain recognized	**$ 2,000**	Lesser of (2) or (5)

What is the character of Teton's $2,000 gain?

Answer: §1231 gain. Teton includes the gain in its §1231 netting process.

What if: Suppose the same facts as above, except that Teton's tax basis in the land was $29,000. What amount of gain would Teton recognize on the exchange?

Answer: $500. Teton recognizes the lesser of (1) $500 gain realized ($29,500 – $29,000) or (2) $2,000 boot received.

[32]§1031(b).

[33]§1031(a) states that no gain or loss is recognized in a qualifying like-kind exchange.

When taxpayers receive like-kind property and boot in a like-kind exchange, their basis in the like-kind property can be computed in two ways, as shown in Exhibit 11-13.

EXHIBIT 11-13 Like-Kind Basis Calculation

Simplified Method	Method under §1031(d)
Fair market value of like-kind property received	Adjusted basis of like-kind property surrendered
− Deferred gain, or	+ Adjusted basis of boot given
+ Deferred loss	+ Gain recognized
= Basis of like-kind property received	− Fair market value of boot received
	− Loss recognized
	= Basis of like-kind property received

The basis of boot received in the exchange is the boot's fair market value. The formula for computing basis ensures that the taxpayer's deferred gain or loss on the exchange (i.e., the gain or loss realized that is not recognized) is captured in the difference between the value and the basis of the new property received. Consequently, taxpayers defer realized gains or losses on qualifying like-kind exchanges; they do not exclude them. Taxpayers will ultimately recognize the entire gain or loss when they dispose of the new asset in a fully taxable transaction.[34]

Example 11-17

What if: Assume the facts in Example 11-16, where Teton exchanged land with a value of $29,500 and tax basis of $18,000 for land valued at $27,500 and $2,000 cash. Teton recognized $2,000 of gain on the exchange. What is Teton's basis in the new land it received from the dealer?

Answer: $18,000, computed using the simplified method, as follows:

Description	Amount	Explanation
(1) Amount realized from land	$ 27,500	Fair market value of new land
(2) Amount realized from boot (cash)	2,000	
(3) Total amount realized	$ 29,500	(1) + (2)
(4) Tax basis of land	18,000	
(5) Gain realized	$ 11,500	(3) − (4)
(6) Gain recognized	$ 2,000	Lesser of (2) or (5)
(7) Deferred gain	9,500	(5) − (6)
Basis in new land	**$18,000**	(1) − (7)

Anything a taxpayer receives in an exchange other than like-kind property is considered boot. This includes cash, other property, or even the amount of a taxpayer's liability transferred to (assumed by) the other party in the exchange. Let's return to the previous example. If, instead of paying Teton $2,000 in cash, the buyer had assumed Teton's $2,000 liability secured by Teton's old land, the tax consequences would have been identical. The buyer relieved Teton of $2,000 of debt, and the debt relief would be treated the same as if the buyer had paid Teton cash and Teton had paid off its $2,000 liability. Generally, when a taxpayer both transfers and receives boot in an otherwise qualifying like-kind exchange, the taxpayer must recognize any realized gain to the extent of the boot received. That is, the taxpayer is not allowed to offset boot received with boot paid.[35]

[34]Additionally, the deferred gain is subject to depreciation recapture when the asset is eventually disposed of in a taxable disposition.

[35]However, Reg. §1.1031(j)-1 provides an exception where multiple like-kind exchanges are made in a single exchange.

EXHIBIT 11-14 **Form 8824, Part III (From exchange in Example 11-15)**

Form 8824 (2021) Page **2**

Name(s) shown on tax return. Do not enter name and social security number if shown on other side. | **Your social security number**

Steve Dallimore (Teton Mountaineering Technologies, LLC)

Part III **Realized Gain or (Loss), Recognized Gain, and Basis of Like-Kind Property Received**

Caution: If you transferred **and** received **(a)** more than one group of like-kind properties, or **(b)** cash or other (not like-kind) property, see ***Reporting of multi-asset exchanges*** in the instructions.

Note: Complete lines 12 through 14 **only** if you gave up property that was not like-kind. Otherwise, go to line 15.

12	Fair market value (FMV) of other property given up. See instructions	12			
13	Adjusted basis of other property given up	13			
14	Gain or (loss) recognized on other property given up. Subtract line 13 from line 12. Report the gain or (loss) in the same manner as if the exchange had been a sale			14	
	Caution: If the property given up was used previously or partly as a home, see ***Property used as home*** in the instructions.				
15	Cash received, FMV of other property received, plus net liabilities assumed by other party, reduced (but not below zero) by any exchange expenses you incurred. See instructions			15	0
16	FMV of like-kind property you received			16	29,500
17	Add lines 15 and 16			17	29,500
18	Adjusted basis of like-kind property you gave up, net amounts paid to other party, plus any exchange expenses **not** used on line 15. See instructions			18	18,000
19	**Realized gain or (loss).** Subtract line 18 from line 17			19	11,500
20	Enter the smaller of line 15 or line 19, but not less than zero			20	0
21	Ordinary income under recapture rules. Enter here and on Form 4797, line 16. See instructions			21	0
22	Subtract line 21 from line 20. If zero or less, enter -0-. If more than zero, enter here and on Schedule D or Form 4797, unless the installment method applies. See instructions			22	0
23	**Recognized gain.** Add lines 21 and 22			23	0
24	Deferred gain or (loss). Subtract line 23 from line 19. If a related party exchange, see instructions			24	11,500
25	**Basis of like-kind property received.** Subtract line 15 from the sum of lines 18 and 23. See instructions			25	18,000

Source: irs.gov.

However, when the taxpayer receives boot in the form of liability relief, the taxpayer is allowed to net any boot paid against the (liability) boot received when determining gain recognized.[36]

THE KEY FACTS

Exchanged Basis

- The basis of like-kind property received is the fair market value of the new asset minus deferred gain or plus deferred loss on the exchange (unless boot is given).
  - When no gain is recognized on the exchange, the basis of the new property is the same as the taxpayer's basis in the old like-kind property.
- The basis of boot received is the fair market value of the boot.

Reporting Like-Kind Exchanges Like-kind exchange transactions are reported on Form 8824. Exhibit 11-14 presents the computations from Form 8824 reflecting the like-kind exchange of the land in Example 11-15.

Involuntary Conversions

Usually, when taxpayers sell, exchange, or abandon property, they intend to do so. However, sometimes taxpayers may involuntarily dispose of property due to circumstances beyond their control. The tax law refers to these types of property dispositions as **involuntary conversions.**[37] Involuntary conversions occur when property is partially or wholly destroyed by a natural disaster or accident, stolen, condemned, or seized via eminent domain by a governmental agency. Tragic examples of this include the results of Hurricanes Harvey, Irma, and Maria in 2017 and the wildfires in California in 2020. Even in situations when taxpayers experience a loss of property due to theft, disaster, or other circumstances, they might realize a gain for tax purposes if they receive replacement property or insurance proceeds in excess of their basis in the property that was stolen or destroyed.

Taxpayers may experience a tremendous financial hardship if they are required to recognize the realized gain in these circumstances. For example, let's consider a business

[36]Further details of this important exception are beyond the scope of our discussion. See the examples provided in Reg. §1.1031(d)-2 for further guidance.

[37]§1033.

THE KEY FACTS

Involuntary Conversions

- Gain is deferred when appreciated property is involuntarily converted in an accident or natural disaster.
- Basis of property directly converted is carried over from the old property to the new property.
- In an indirect conversion, gain recognized is the lesser of:
  - Gain realized or
  - Amount of reimbursement the taxpayer does not reinvest in qualified property.
- Qualified replacement property must be of a similar or related use to the original property.

that acquired a building for $100,000. The building appreciates in value, and when it is worth $150,000, it is destroyed by fire. The building is fully insured at its replacement cost, so the business receives a check from the insurance company for $150,000. The problem for the business is that it realizes a $50,000 gain on this involuntary conversion ($150,000 insurance proceeds minus $100,000 basis in property without considering depreciation). Assuming the business's income is taxed at a 32 percent marginal rate, it must pay $16,000 of tax on the insurance money it receives. That leaves it with only $134,000 to replace property worth $150,000. This hardly seems equitable. Congress provides special tax laws to allow taxpayers to defer the gains on such *involuntary* conversions.

Taxpayers may defer realized gains on both direct and indirect involuntary conversions. **Direct conversions** occur when taxpayers receive a direct property replacement for the involuntarily converted property. For example, a municipality that is widening its streets may seize land from a taxpayer through its eminent domain and compensate the taxpayer with another parcel of similar value. In this case, the taxpayer would not recognize gain on the exchange of property and would take a basis in the new parcel of land equal to the taxpayer's basis in the land that was claimed by the municipality. Just as with like-kind exchanges, an exchanged basis (basis of old property exchanged for basis of new property) ensures that the gain built into the new property (i.e., fair market value minus adjusted basis) includes the same gain that was built into the old property.

Indirect conversions occur when taxpayers receive money for the involuntarily converted property through insurance reimbursement or some other type of settlement. Taxpayers meeting the involuntary conversion requirements may *elect* to either recognize or defer realized gain on the conversions. Indirect conversions are more common than direct conversions. Taxpayers can defer realized gains on indirect conversions *if* they acquire **qualified replacement property** within a prescribed time limit, which is generally two years (three years in the case of condemnation) after the close of the tax year in which they receive the proceeds.[38,39]

In contrast to the like-kind exchange rules, both personal and real property can qualify for the tax treatment under the involuntary conversion rules. Qualified replacement property is defined somewhat narrowly; to qualify, it must be similar *and* related in service or use.[40] For example, a bowling alley is not qualified replacement property for a pool hall, even though both are real properties used for entertainment purposes. This definition is stricter than the like-kind exchange rules that would allow the bowling alley to be exchanged for any other real property, including a pool hall. In addition, the involuntary conversion rules allow a taxpayer's personal residence (personal-use property) to qualify for gain deferral; however, qualified replacement property of a personal residence is restricted to another residence. Taxpayers recognize realized gain to the extent that they do not reinvest the reimbursement proceeds in qualified property. However, just as in like-kind exchanges, taxpayers do not recognize more gain than they realize on involuntary conversions. That is, a taxpayer's recognized gain on an involuntary conversion can be determined by the following formula: Recognized gain on an involuntary conversion is equal to the *lesser of* (1) the gain realized on the conversion or (2) the amount of reimbursement the taxpayer does *not reinvest* in qualified property.

The character of any gain recognized in an involuntary conversion depends on the nature of the asset that was converted—including depreciation recapture, if applicable. The basis of the replacement property in an involuntary conversion is calculated using the

[38]Condemnation occurs when a local, state, or federal government seizes private property and compensates the owner but does not require the owner's approval. Governments accomplish a condemnation through the power of eminent domain, which essentially means the government takes private property for public use.

[39]§1033(a)(2)(B). The time period varies depending on the type of property converted. Additionally, the IRS may consent to an extension of the time period for replacement.

[40]The similar and related-use test has been developed through a variety of administrative pronouncements and judicial law.

simplified method described for like-kind exchange property (see Exhibit 11-13, Simplified Method). That is, the basis of the replacement property is the fair market value of the new property minus the deferred gain on the conversion.

Example 11-18

What if: Assume that one of Teton's employees was in a traffic accident while driving a delivery van. The employee escaped without serious injury, but the van was totally destroyed. Before the accident, Teton's delivery van had a fair market value of $15,000 and an adjusted basis of $11,000 (the cost basis was $15,000 and accumulated depreciation on the van was $4,000). Teton received $15,000 of insurance proceeds to cover the loss. Teton was considering two alternatives for replacing the van: Alternative 1 was to purchase a new delivery van for $20,000 and Alternative 2 was to purchase a used delivery van for $14,000. What gain or loss does Teton recognize under Alternative 1 and Alternative 2?

Answer: $0 gain recognized under Alternative 1 and $1,000 gain recognized under Alternative 2 (see computations below). Teton qualifies for a deferral because the new property (delivery van) has a similar and related use to the old property (delivery van). But it must recognize gain under Alternative 2 because it did not reinvest all of the insurance proceeds in a replacement van.

What is Teton's basis in the replacement property it acquired under Alternative 1 and Alternative 2?

Answer: $16,000 in Alternative 1 and $11,000 in Alternative 2, computed as follows:

Description	Alternative 1 Amount	Alternative 2 Amount	Explanation
(1) Amount realized	$15,000	$15,000	
(2) Adjusted basis	11,000	11,000	
(3) Gain realized	4,000	4,000	(1) – (2)
(4) Insurance proceeds	15,000	15,000	
(5) Proceeds reinvested	15,000	14,000	
(6) Amount not reinvested	0	1,000	(4) – (5)
(7) Gain recognized	**0**	**1,000**	Lesser of (3) or (6)*
(8) Deferred gain	4,000	3,000	(3) – (7)
(9) Value of replacement property	20,000	14,000	
Basis of replacement property	**16,000**	**11,000**	(9) – (8)

*The character of the $1,000 recognized gain is ordinary income under §1245 (lesser of gain recognized or accumulated depreciation).

Involuntary conversions share several characteristics with like-kind exchanges, such as the concept of qualified property, time period restrictions, the method of computing gain recognized (lesser of realized gain or cash received in addition to qualifying property), and basis calculation (gain or loss from old property remains built into new property). However, there are two important differences between like-kind exchanges and involuntary conversions. First, involuntary conversion rules allow taxpayers to defer gains on both personal and real property (business, investment, or personal-use property), whereas the like-kind exchange rules limit the deferral treatment to only real property (business or investment use). Second, taxpayers experiencing a loss from involuntary conversion may immediately deduct the loss as a casualty loss, either as a business loss or as a personal loss, if incurred in a federally declared disaster area, depending on the nature of the loss.

Installment Sales

In general, when taxpayers sell property for cash and collect the entire sale proceeds in one lump-sum payment, they immediately recognize gain or loss for tax purposes. However, taxpayers selling property don't always collect the sale proceeds in one lump sum from the buyer. For example, the buyer may make a down payment in the year of sale and

THE KEY FACTS

Installment Sales

- Sale of property where the seller receives at least one payment in a taxable year subsequent to the year of disposition of the property.
- Must recognize a portion of gain on each installment payment received.
- Gains from installment sales are calculated as follows:
  - Gross profit percentage = Gross profit/Contract price
  - Gain recognized = Gross profit percentage × Principal payment received in the year
- Inventory, marketable securities, and depreciation recapture cannot be accounted for under installment sale rules.
- Installment sale rules do not apply to losses.

then agree to pay the remainder of the sale proceeds over a period of time. This type of arrangement is termed an **installment sale.** For tax purposes, an installment sale is any sale of property where the seller receives at least one payment in a taxable year subsequent to the year of disposition of the property.[41]

Taxpayers selling property via an installment sale realize gains to the extent the selling price (the amount realized) exceeds their adjusted basis in the property sold. The installment sale rules stay true to the wherewithal-to-pay concept and allow taxpayers selling property in this manner to use the installment method of recognizing *gain* on the sale over time.[42] The installment method does not apply to property sold at a loss. Under the installment method, taxpayers determine the amount of realized gain on the transaction, and they recognize the gain pro rata as they receive the installment payments. So, by the time they have received all the installment payments, they will have recognized all the initial realized gain.[43] For financial accounting purposes, businesses selling property on an installment basis generally immediately recognize the realized gain on their financial statements.[44]

To calculate the amount of gain the taxpayer (seller) must recognize on each installment payment received, the seller must compute the gross profit percentage on the transaction. The gross profit percentage is calculated as follows:

$$\text{Gross profit percentage} = \frac{\text{Gross profit}}{\text{Contract price}}$$

Gross profit is calculated as the sales price minus the adjusted basis of the property being sold. The contract price is the sales price less the seller's liabilities that are assumed by the buyer. The gross profit percentage indicates the percentage of the contract price that will ultimately be recognized as gain. To calculate the portion of a particular payment that is currently recognized as gain, the seller multiplies the amount of the payments received during the year (including the year of sale) by the gross profit percentage (note that once established, the gross profit percentage does not change). As in fully taxable transactions, the character of gain recognized by taxpayers using the installment method is determined by the character of the asset sold.

The formula for determining the basis of an installment note receivable is:

$$(1 - \text{Gross profit percentage}) \times \text{Remaining principal payments on note}$$

Because the gross profit percentage reflects the percentage of the installment payments that will be recognized as gain, (1 – Gross profit percentage) is the percentage that is not recognized as gain because it reflects a return of capital (basis).

Example 11-19

What if: Suppose Teton decides to sell five acres of land adjacent to the warehouse for $100,000. The basis for the land is $37,500. Teton agrees to sell the property for four equal payments of $25,000—one now (in year 1) and the other three on January 1 of the next three years—plus interest. What amount of gain does Teton realize on the sale and what amount of gain does it recognize in year 1?

[41] §453(b)(1).

[42] For tax purposes, a taxpayer selling qualifying property on an installment basis at a gain is required to use the installment method of reporting the recognized gain from the transaction. However, taxpayers are allowed to elect out of using the installment method [§453(d)].

[43] Because the seller in an installment sale is essentially lending money to the buyer, the buyer makes the required installment payments to the seller and the buyer pays interest to the seller for the money the buyer is borrowing. Any interest income received by the seller is immediately taxable as ordinary income. Special rules apply regarding interest for installment sales of more than $150,000 (see §453A).

[44] One exception is that the installment sale method, similar to the tax installment method, is used for financial accounting purposes when there is doubt that the business will collect the receivable.

Answer: The realized gain on the transaction is $62,500 ($100,000 amount realized less $37,500 adjusted basis), and the year 1 recognized gain is $15,625, computed as follows:

Description	Amount	Explanation
(1) Sales price	$100,000	
(2) Adjusted basis	37,500	
(3) Gross profit	**$ 62,500**	(1) – (2)
(4) Contract price	$100,000	(1) – assumed liabilities (-0-)
(5) Gross profit percentage	62.5%	(3)/(4)
(6) Payment received in year 1	$ 25,000	
Gain recognized in year 1	**$ 15,625**	(5) × (6)

Because Teton used the land in its trade or business and it held the land for more than a year, the character of the gain is §1231 gain.

Gains Ineligible for Installment Reporting

Not all gains are eligible for installment sale reporting. Taxpayers selling marketable securities or inventory on an installment basis may not use the installment method to report gain on the sales. Similarly, any depreciation recapture (including §1245, §1250, and §291 depreciation recapture) is not eligible for installment reporting and must be recognized in the year of sale.[45] However, the §1231 gain remaining after the depreciation recapture can be recognized using the installment method. To ensure that any depreciation recapture is not taxed twice (once immediately and then a second time as payments are received), taxable recapture-related gains that are taxable in the year of sale are *added to* the adjusted basis of the property sold to determine the gross profit percentage. The increase in basis reduces the gain realized, which also reduces the gross profit percentage and the amount of future gain that will ultimately be recognized as the taxpayer receives the installment payments. Installment sales are reported on Form 6252.

Example 11-20

What if: Assume that Teton agrees to sell some of its machinery for $90,000 for two equal payments of $45,000 plus interest. Teton's original basis was $80,000 and accumulated depreciation on the machinery was $30,000. Teton will receive one payment in year 1 (the current year) and the other payment in year 2. What are the amount and character of the gain Teton recognizes on the sale in year 1?

Answer: $30,000 ordinary income and $5,000 of §1231 gain, computed as follows:

Description	Amount	Explanation
(1) Sales price	$ 90,000	
(2) Initial basis	80,000	
(3) Accumulated depreciation	(30,000)	
(4) Adjusted basis	$ 50,000	(2) + (3)
(5) Realized gain (loss)	$ 40,000	(1) – (4)
(6) Ordinary income from depreciation recapture (not eligible for installment reporting)	**$30,000**	Ordinary income; lesser of (3) or (5)
(7) Gain eligible for installment reporting	$ 10,000	(5) – (6)
(8) Contract price	$ 90,000	(1) – assumed liabilities (-0-)
(9) Gross profit percentage	11.11%	(7)/(8)
(10) Payment received in year 1	$ 45,000	
Installment (§1231) gain recognized in year 1	**$ 5,000**	(10) × (9)

What are the amount and character of the gain Teton recognized upon receipt of the payment in year 2?

Answer: $5,000 of §1231 gain ($45,000 payment received × 11.11% gross profit percentage).

[45]§453(i). Unrecaptured §1250 gain is eligible for deferral but is recognized first upon gain recognition when cash payments are received [Reg. §1.453-12(a)].

Other Tax-Deferred Provisions

Several tax law provisions allow businesses to change the form or organization of their business while deferring the realized gains for tax purposes. For example, a sole proprietor can form the business as a corporation or contribute assets to an existing corporation and defer the gain realized on the exchange of assets for an ownership interest in the business entity.[46] Without the tax-deferred provision, the tax cost of forming a corporation may be large enough to deter taxpayers from doing so. Tax-deferral rules also apply to taxpayers forming partnerships or contributing assets to partnerships.[47] In still other corporate transactions, such as mergers or reorganizations, corporations can often do so in tax-deferred transactions.[48] While these transactions generally result in deferred gain or loss for the involved parties, the specific details of these topics can easily fill entire chapters. Further coverage is beyond the scope of this chapter (see later chapters for coverage of §351 and §721 tax-deferred transactions).

THE KEY FACTS

Related-Person Losses

- Related persons are defined in §267 and include certain family members, related corporations, and other entities.
- Losses on sales to related persons are not deductible by the seller.
- The related-person buyer may subsequently deduct the previously disallowed loss *to the extent of the gain* on the sale to an unrelated third party.

Related-Person Loss Disallowance Rules

Taxpayers selling business or investment property at a loss to unrelated persons are generally able to deduct the loss.[49] This makes sense in most situations because taxpayers are selling the property for less than their remaining investment (adjusted basis) in the property, and after the sale, the taxpayer's investment in the property is completely terminated. In contrast, when a taxpayer sells property at a loss to a related person, they effectively retain some element of control over the property through the related person. Consistent with this idea, §267(a) disallows recognition of losses on sales to related persons. Under §267, related persons include individuals with family relationships, including siblings, spouses, ancestors, and lineal descendants. Related persons also include an individual and a corporation if the individual owns more than 50 percent of the value of the stock of the corporation.[50]

Example 11-21

What if: Suppose Teton is formed as a C corporation and Steve is its sole shareholder. Teton is looking to make some long-term investments to fund its anticipated purchase of a new manufacturing facility. Steve currently owns 1,000 shares of stock in his previous company, Northeastern Corp., which he intends to sell in the near future. Steve initially paid $40 a share for the stock, but the stock is currently valued at $30 a share. While Steve believes the stock has good long-term potential, he needs cash now to purchase a personal residence in Cody, Wyoming. Steve believes selling the shares to Teton makes good sense because he can deduct the loss and save taxes now, and Teton can benefit from the expected long-term appreciation of the stock. If Steve sells 1,000 shares of Northeastern Corp. stock to Teton for $30 per share, what amount of loss will he realize and what amount of loss will he recognize for tax purposes?

Answer: $10,000 loss realized and $0 loss recognized, determined as follows:

Description	Amount	Explanation
(1) Amount realized on sale	$30,000	(1,000 × $30)
(2) Adjusted basis in stock	40,000	(1,000 × $40)
(3) Loss realized on sale	**(10,000)**	(1) − (2)
Loss recognized on sale	**$ 0**	Losses on sales to related persons are disallowed.

Because Steve owns more than 50 percent of Teton (he owns 100 percent), Steve and Teton are considered to be related persons. Consequently, Steve is not allowed to recognize any loss on the sale.

[46]§351.

[47]§721.

[48]Section 368(a) contains the numerous variations and requirements of these tax-deferred reorganizations.

[49]Capital losses are subject to certain limitations for individuals and corporate taxpayers (§1211).

[50]§267(a). The related-person rules include both direct ownership as well as indirect ownership (ownership attributed to the taxpayer from related persons). See §267(c) for a description of the indirect ownership rules.

Although taxpayers are not allowed to immediately deduct losses when they sell property to the related person, the related-person buyer may be able to subsequently deduct the disallowed loss by selling the property to an *unrelated* third party at a gain. The rules follow:

- If the related-person buyer sells the property at a gain (the related-person buyer sells it for more than their purchase price) greater than the disallowed loss, the entire loss that was disallowed for the related-person seller is deductible by the buyer.
- If the related-person buyer subsequently sells the property and the related-person seller's disallowed loss exceeds the related-person buyer's gain on the subsequent sale, the related-person buyer may only deduct or offset the previously disallowed loss *to the extent of the gain* on the sale to the unrelated third party—the remaining disallowed loss expires unused.
- If the related-person buyer sells the property for less than their purchase price from the related-person seller, the disallowed loss expires unused.
- The holding period for the related-person buyer begins on the date of the sale between the related persons.[51]

Example 11-22

What if: Let's return to Example 11-21, where Steve sold 1,000 shares of Northeastern Corp. stock to Teton for $30,000. As we discovered in that example, Steve realized a $10,000 loss on the sale, but he was not allowed to deduct it because Steve and Teton are related persons. Let's assume that a few years after Teton purchased the stock from Steve, Teton sells the Northeastern Corp. stock to an unrelated third party. What gain or loss does *Teton* recognize when it sells the stock in each of three scenarios, assuming it sells the stock for $37,000 in Scenario 1, $55,000 in Scenario 2, and $25,000 in Scenario 3?

Answer: $0 gain or loss in Scenario 1, $15,000 gain in Scenario 2, and $5,000 loss in Scenario 3, computed as follows:

Description	Scenario 1	Scenario 2	Scenario 3	Explanation
(1) Amount realized	$37,000	$ 55,000	$25,000	
(2) Adjusted basis	30,000	30,000	30,000	Example 11-21 (Teton's purchase price)
(3) Realized gain (loss)	$ 7,000	$ 25,000	$ (5,000)	(1) – (2)
(4) Benefit of Steve's ($10,000) disallowed loss	(7,000)	(10,000)	0	Loss benefit limited to realized gain.
Recognized gain (loss)	**$ 0**	**$15,000**	**$(5,000)**	(3) + (4)

In Scenario 1, $3,000 of Steve's $10,000 remaining disallowed loss expires unused. In Scenario 3, Steve's entire $10,000 disallowed loss expires unused.

CONCLUSION

This chapter describes and discusses the tax consequences associated with sales and other types of property dispositions. We've learned how to determine the amount of gain or loss taxpayers recognize when they sell or otherwise dispose of property, and we've learned how to determine the character of these gains and losses. Tax accountants who understand the rules and concepts of property dispositions are able to comply with the tax law and advise clients of potential tax planning opportunities and avoid pitfalls associated with various tax-deferred provisions.

[51]Reg. §1.267(d)-1(c)(3).

Summary

LO 11-1 Calculate the amount of gain or loss recognized on the disposition of assets used in a trade or business.

- Dispositions occur in the form of sales, trades, or other realization events.
- Gain realized is the amount realized less the adjusted basis of an asset.
- Amount realized is everything of value received in the transaction less any selling costs.
- Adjusted basis is the historical cost or initial basis of an asset less any cost recovery deductions applied against the asset.
- Gain realized on asset dispositions is not always recognized.

LO 11-2 Describe the general character types of gain or loss recognized on property dispositions.

- Recognized gains must be characterized as ordinary, capital, or §1231. An asset's character is a function of the asset's use and holding period.
- Ordinary assets are derived from normal transactions of the business (revenues and accounts receivable), the sale of short-term trade or business assets, and depreciation recapture.
- Capital assets are assets that are held either for investment or for personal use (a taxpayer's principal residence).
- Section 1231 assets consist of property used in a taxpayer's trade or business that has been held for more than one year.
- Net §1231 gains are treated as long-term capital gains, and net §1231 losses are treated as ordinary losses.

LO 11-3 Calculate depreciation recapture.

- Section 1231 assets, other than land, are subject to cost recovery deductions (depreciation), which generate ordinary deductions.
- Gains that are created through depreciation deductions are subject to depreciation recapture. Any remaining gain is §1231 gain.
- Depreciation recapture does not change the amount of the gain but simply converts or recharacterizes the gain from §1231 to ordinary.
- Different recapture rules apply to tangible personal property (§1245) and real property (§291 for C corporations only and §1250).

LO 11-4 Describe the tax treatment of unrecaptured §1250 gains.

- When individuals sell §1250 property at a gain, the portion of the gain generated by depreciation deductions is called unrecaptured §1250 gain.
- This gain is a §1231 gain that, when treated as a capital gain after the §1231 netting process, flows into the capital gain/loss process (see the Investments chapter) and is taxed at a maximum rate of 25 percent.
- If a taxpayer sells an asset at a gain to a related person and the asset is a depreciable asset to the related person, the seller must characterize the entire gain as ordinary income.

LO 11-5 Describe the tax treatment of §1231 gains or losses, including the §1231 netting process.

- After applying the depreciation recapture rules, taxpayers calculate the net §1231 gain or loss.
- If a net §1231 loss results, the loss will become ordinary and offset ordinary income.
- If a net §1231 gain results, the §1231 look-back rule must be applied.
- After applying the look-back rule, any remaining net §1231 gain is a long-term capital gain.

LO 11-6 Explain common deferral exceptions to the general rule that realized gains and losses are recognized currently.

- Like-kind exchanges involve trading or exchanging real property used in a business or held for investment for similar real property. The gain is deferred unless boot or non-like-kind property is received.

- Involuntary conversions are the losses on property through circumstances beyond taxpayers' control. Reasons include natural disasters, accidents, theft, or condemnation.
- Installment sales occur when any portion of the amount realized is received in a year subsequent to the disposition. A portion of the gain is initially deferred but then recognized over time as payments are received.
- §267 related-person losses are disallowed, but the related-person buyer may be able to deduct the disallowed loss if they subsequently sell the property at a gain.

KEY TERMS

§291 depreciation recapture (11-14)
§1231 assets (11-8)
§1231 look-back rule (11-17)
§1245 property (11-10)
§1250 property (11-14)
adjusted basis (11-5)
amount realized (11-2)
boot (11-27)
capital asset (11-8)
deferred like-kind exchange (11-25)
depreciation recapture (11-10)
direct conversions (11-30)
indirect conversions (11-30)
installment sale (11-32)
involuntary conversions (11-29)
like-kind exchange (11-24)
nonrecaptured net §1231 losses (11-18)
ordinary asset (11-7)
production of income (11-8)
qualified replacement property (11-30)
realized gain or loss (11-5)
recognized gains or losses (11-6)
substituted basis (11-26)
tax-deferred transactions (11-24)
third-party intermediaries (11-25)
unrecaptured §1250 gain (11-15)

DISCUSSION QUESTIONS

Discussion Questions are available in Connect®.

1. Compare and contrast different ways in which a taxpayer triggers a realization event by disposing of an asset. LO 11-1
2. Potomac Corporation wants to sell a warehouse that it has used in its business for 10 years. Potomac is asking $450,000 for the property. The warehouse is subject to a mortgage of $125,000. If Potomac accepts Wyden Inc.'s offer to give Potomac $325,000 in cash and assume full responsibility for the mortgage on the property, what amount does Potomac realize on the sale? LO 11-1
3. Montana Max sells a 2,500-acre ranch for $1,000,000 in cash, a note receivable of $1,000,000, and debt relief of $2,400,000. He also pays selling commissions of $60,000. In addition, Max agrees to build a new barn on the property (cost $250,000) and spend $100,000 upgrading the fence on the property before the sale. What is Max's amount realized on the sale? LO 11-1
4. Hawkeye sold farming equipment for $55,000. It bought the equipment four years ago for $75,000, and it has since claimed a total of $42,000 in depreciation deductions against the asset. Explain how to calculate Hawkeye's adjusted basis in the farming equipment. LO 11-1
5. When a taxpayer sells an asset, what is the difference between realized and recognized gain or loss on the sale? LO 11-1
6. What does it mean to characterize a gain or loss? Why is characterizing a gain or loss important? LO 11-2
7. Explain the difference between ordinary, capital, and §1231 assets. LO 11-2
8. Discuss the reasons why individuals generally prefer capital gains over ordinary gains. Explain why corporate taxpayers might prefer capital gains over ordinary gains. LO 11-2
9. Dakota Conrad owns a parcel of land he would like to sell. Describe the circumstances in which the sale of the land would generate §1231 gain or loss, ordinary gain or loss, or capital gain or loss. Also, describe the circumstances under which Dakota would not be allowed to deduct a loss on the sale. LO 11-2

LO 11-2 10. Lincoln Brown has used a piece of land in their business for the past five years. The land qualifies as §1231 property. It is unclear whether Lincoln will have to recognize a gain or loss when they eventually sell the asset. Lincoln asks their accountant how the gain or loss would be characterized if they decide to sell. The accountant says that selling §1231 assets gives sellers "the best of both worlds." Explain what the accountant means by this statement.

LO 11-3 11. Explain Congress's rationale for depreciation recapture.

LO 11-3 12. Compare and contrast §1245 recapture and §1250 recapture.

LO 11-3 13. Why is depreciation recapture not required when assets are sold at a loss?

LO 11-3 14. What are the similarities and differences between the tax benefit rule and depreciation recapture?

LO 11-3 LO 11-4 15. Are both corporations and individuals subject to depreciation recapture when they sell depreciable real property at a gain? Explain.

LO 11-4 16. How is unrecaptured §1250 gain for individuals similar to depreciation recapture? How is it different?

LO 11-4 17. Explain why gains from depreciable property sold to a related taxpayer are treated as ordinary income under §1239.

LO 11-5 18. Bingaman Resources sold two depreciable §1231 assets during the year. One asset resulted in a large gain (the asset was sold for more than it was purchased) and the other resulted in a small loss. Describe the §1231 netting process for Bingaman.

LO 11-5 19. Jeraldine believes that when the §1231 look-back rule applies, the taxpayer deducts a §1231 loss in a previous year against §1231 gains in the current year. Explain whether Jeraldine's description is correct.

LO 11-5 20. Explain the purpose behind the §1231 look-back rule.

LO 11-5 21. Does a taxpayer apply the §1231 look-back rule in a year when the taxpayer recognizes a net §1231 loss? Explain.

LO 11-4 LO 11-5 22. Describe the circumstances in which an individual taxpayer with a net §1231 gain will have different portions of the gain taxed at different rates.

LO 11-6 23. Rocky and Bullwinkle Partnership sold a parcel of land during the current year and realized a gain of $250,000. Rocky and Bullwinkle did not recognize gain related to the sale of the land on its tax return. Is this possible? Explain how a taxpayer could realize a gain but not recognize it.

LO 11-6 24. Why does the tax code allow taxpayers to defer gains on like-kind exchanges? How do the tax laws ensure that the gains (or losses) are deferred and not permanently excluded from a taxpayer's income?

LO 11-6 25. Describe the like-kind property requirements for real property for purposes of qualifying for a like-kind exchange. Explain whether land held for investment by a corporation will qualify as like-kind property with land held by an individual for personal use.

LO 11-6 26. Salazar Inc., a Colorado company, is relocating to a nearby town. It would like to trade its real property for some real property in the new location. While Salazar has found several prospective buyers for its real property and has also located several properties that are acceptable in the new location, it cannot find anyone willing to trade Salazar Inc. for its property in a like-kind exchange. Explain how a third-party intermediary could facilitate Salazar's like-kind exchange.

LO 11-6 27. Minuteman wants to enter into a like-kind exchange by exchanging its old New England manufacturing facility for a ranch in Wyoming. Minuteman is using a third-party intermediary to facilitate the exchange. The purchaser of the manufacturing facility wants to complete the transaction immediately, but, for various reasons, the ranch transaction will not be completed for three to four months. Will this delay cause a problem for Minuteman's desire to accomplish this through a like-kind exchange? Explain.

28. Olympia Corporation, of Kittery, Maine, wants to exchange its manufacturing facility for Bangor Company's warehouse. Both parties agree that Olympia's building is worth $100,000 and that Bangor's building is worth $95,000. Olympia would like the transaction to qualify as a like-kind exchange. What could the parties do to equalize the value exchanged but still allow the exchange to qualify as a like-kind exchange? How would the necessary change affect the tax consequences of the transaction? LO 11-6

29. Compare and contrast the similarities and differences between like-kind exchanges and involuntary conversions for tax purposes. LO 11-6

30. What is an installment sale? How do the tax laws ensure that taxpayers recognize all the gain they realize on an installment sale? How is depreciation recapture treated in an installment sale? Explain the gross profit ratio and how it relates to gains recognized under installment method sales. LO 11-6

31. Mr. Kyle owns stock in a local publicly traded company. Although the stock price has declined since he purchased it two years ago, he likes the long-term prospects for the company. If Kyle sells the stock to his sister because he needs some cash for a down payment on a new home, is the loss deductible? If Kyle is right and the stock price increases in the future, how is his sister's gain computed if she sells the stock? LO 11-6

PROBLEMS

Select problems are available in Connect®.

32. Rafael sold an asset to Jamal. What is Rafael's amount realized on the sale in each of the following alternative scenarios? LO 11-1
    a) Rafael received $80,000 cash and a vehicle worth $10,000. Rafael also paid $5,000 in selling expenses.
    b) Rafael received $80,000 cash and was relieved of a $30,000 mortgage on the asset he sold to Jamal. Rafael also paid a commission of $5,000 on the transaction.
    c) Rafael received $20,000 cash, a parcel of land worth $50,000, and marketable securities of $10,000. Rafael also paid a commission of $8,000 on the transaction.

33. Alan Meer inherits a hotel from his grandmother, Mary, on February 11 of the current year. Mary bought the hotel for $730,000 three years ago. Mary deducted $27,000 of cost recovery on the hotel before her death. The fair market value of the hotel in February is $725,000. (Assume that the alternative valuation date is not used.) LO 11-1
    a) What is Alan's adjusted basis in the hotel?
    b) If the fair market value of the hotel at the time of Mary's death was $500,000, what is Alan's basis?

34. Shasta Corporation sold a piece of land to Bill for $45,000. Shasta bought the land two years ago for $30,600. What gain or loss does Shasta realize on the transaction? LO 11-1

35. Lassen Corporation sold a machine to a machine dealer for $25,000. Lassen bought the machine for $55,000 and has claimed $15,000 of depreciation expense on the machine. What gain or loss does Lassen realize on the transaction? LO 11-1

36. Hannah Tywin owns 100 shares of MM Inc. stock. She sells the stock on December 11 for $25 per share. She received the stock as a gift from her Aunt Pam on March 20 of this year when the fair market value of the stock was $18 per share. Aunt Pam originally purchased the stock seven years ago at a price of $12 per share. What are the amount and character of Hannah's recognized gain on the stock? LO 11-1 LO 11-2

LO 11-1 LO 11-2

37. On September 30 of last year, Rex received some investment land from Holly as a gift. Holly's basis was $50,000 and the land was valued at $40,000 at the time of the gift. Holly acquired the land five years ago. What are the amount and character of Rex's recognized gain (loss) if he sells the land on May 12 this year at the following prices?
    a) $32,000
    b) $70,000
    c) $45,000

LO 11-1 LO 11-2

38. Franco converted a building from personal to business use in May 2019 when the fair market value was $55,000. He purchased the building in July 2016 for $80,000. On December 15 of this year, Franco sells the building for $40,000. On the date of sale, the accumulated depreciation on the building is $5,565. What is Franco's recognized gain or loss on the sale?

LO 11-2

39. Identify each of Avery Corporation's following assets as an ordinary, capital, or §1231 asset.
    a) Two years ago, Avery used its excess cash to purchase a piece of land as an investment.
    b) Two years ago, Avery purchased land and a warehouse. It uses these assets in its business.
    c) Manufacturing machinery Avery purchased earlier this year.
    d) Inventory Avery purchased 13 months ago that is ready to be shipped to a customer.
    e) Office equipment Avery has used in its business for the past three years.
    f) 1,000 shares of stock in Plaid Corporation that Avery purchased two years ago because it was a good investment.
    g) Account receivable from a customer with terms 2/10, net 30.
    h) Machinery Avery held for three years and then sold at a loss of $10,000.

LO 11-3 LO 11-4

40. In year 0, Canon purchased a machine to use in its business for $56,000. In year 3, Canon sold the machine for $42,000. Between the date of the purchase and the date of the sale, Canon depreciated the machine by $32,000.
    a) What are the amount and character of the gain or loss Canon will recognize on the sale, assuming that it is a partnership?
    b) What are the amount and character of the gain or loss Canon will recognize on the sale, assuming that it is a corporation?
    c) What are the amount and character of the gain or loss Canon will recognize on the sale, assuming that it is a corporation and the sale proceeds were increased to $60,000?
    d) What are the amount and character of the gain or loss Canon will recognize on the sale, assuming that it is a corporation and the sale proceeds were decreased to $20,000?

LO 11-3 LO 11-4

41. In year 0, Longworth Partnership purchased a machine for $40,000 to use in its business. In year 3, Longworth sold the machine for $35,000. Between the date of the purchase and the date of the sale, Longworth depreciated the machine by $22,000.
    a) What are the amount and character of the gain or loss Longworth will recognize on the sale?
    b) What are the amount and character of the gain or loss Longworth will recognize on the sale if the sale proceeds are increased to $45,000?
    c) What are the amount and character of the gain or loss Longworth will recognize on the sale if the sale proceeds are decreased to $15,000?

42. On August 1 of year 0, Dirksen purchased a machine for $20,000 to use in its business. On December 4 of year 0, Dirksen sold the machine for $18,000. LO 11-3 LO 11-4

a) What are the amount and character of the gain or loss Dirksen will recognize on the sale?

b) Dirksen depreciated the machinery using MACRS (seven-year recovery period). What are the amount and character of the gain or loss Dirksen will recognize on the sale if the machine is sold on January 15 of year 1 instead?

43. Rayburn Corporation has a building that it bought during year 0 for $850,000. It sold the building in year 5. During the time it held the building, Rayburn depreciated it by $100,000. What are the amount and character of the gain or loss Rayburn will recognize on the sale in each of the following alternative situations? LO 11-3 LO 11-4

a) Rayburn receives $840,000.

b) Rayburn receives $900,000.

c) Rayburn receives $700,000.

44. Moran owns a building he bought during year 0 for $150,000. He sold the building in year 6. During the time he held the building, he depreciated it by $32,000. What are the amount and character of the gain or loss Moran will recognize on the sale in each of the following alternative situations? LO 11-3 LO 11-4

a) Moran received $145,000.

b) Moran received $170,000.

c) Moran received $110,000.

45. Hart, an individual, bought an asset for $500,000 and has claimed $100,000 of depreciation deductions against the asset. Hart has a marginal tax rate of 32 percent. Answer the questions presented in the following alternative scenarios (assume Hart had no property transactions other than those described in the problem): LO 11-3 LO 11-4 LO 11-5 planning

a) What are the amount and character of Hart's recognized gain or loss if the asset is tangible personal property sold for $450,000? What effect does the sale have on Hart's tax liability for the year?

b) What are the amount and character of Hart's recognized gain or loss if the asset is tangible personal property sold for $550,000? What effect does the sale have on Hart's tax liability for the year?

c) What are the amount and character of Hart's recognized gain or loss if the asset is tangible personal property sold for $350,000? What effect does the sale have on Hart's tax liability for the year?

d) What are the amount and character of Hart's recognized gain or loss if the asset is a nonresidential building sold for $450,000? What effect does the sale have on Hart's tax liability for the year?

e) Now assume that Hart is a C corporation. What are the amount and character of its recognized gain or loss if the asset is a nonresidential building sold for $450,000? What effect does the sale have on Hart's tax liability for the year (assume a 21 percent tax rate)?

f) Assuming that the asset is real property, which entity type should be used to minimize the taxes paid on real estate gains?

46. Luke sold a building and the land on which the building sits to his wholly owned corporation, Studemont Corp., at fair market value. The fair market value of the building was determined to be $325,000; Luke built the building several years ago at a cost of $200,000. Luke had claimed $45,000 of depreciation on the building. The fair market value of the land was determined to be $210,000 at the time of the sale; Luke purchased the land many years ago for $130,000. LO 11-4

a) What are the amount and character of Luke's recognized gain or loss on the building?

b) What are the amount and character of Luke's recognized gain or loss on the land?

LO 11-5

47. Buckley, an individual, began business two years ago and has never sold a §1231 asset. Buckley has owned each of the assets since he began the business. In the current year, Buckley sold the following business assets:

Asset	Accumulated Original Cost	Depreciation	Gain/Loss
Computers	$ 6,000	$ 2,000	$(3,000)
Machinery	10,000	4,000	(2,000)
Furniture	20,000	12,000	7,000
Building	100,000	10,000	(1,000)

Assuming Buckley's marginal ordinary income tax rate is 32 percent, answer the questions for the following alternative scenarios:

a) What is the character of Buckley's gains or losses for the current year? What effect do the gains and losses have on Buckley's tax liability?

b) Assume that the amount realized increased so that the building was sold at a $6,000 gain instead. What is the character of Buckley's gains or losses for the current year? What effect do the gains and losses have on Buckley's tax liability?

c) Assume that the amount realized increased so that the building was sold at a $15,000 gain instead. What is the character of Buckley's gains or losses for the current year? What effect do the gains and losses have on Buckley's tax liability?

LO 11-3 LO 11-4 LO 11-5

48. Lily Tucker (single) owns and operates a bike shop as a sole proprietorship. In 2022, she sells the following long-term assets used in her business:

Asset	Sales Price	Cost	Accumulated Depreciation
Building	$230,000	$200,000	$52,000
Equipment	80,000	148,000	23,000

Lily's taxable income before these transactions is $190,500. What are Lily's taxable income and tax liability for the year?

LO 11-3 LO 11-4 LO 11-5

49. Shimmer Inc. is a calendar-year-end, accrual-method corporation. This year, it sells the following long-term assets:

Asset	Sales Price	Cost	Accumulated Depreciation
Building	$650,000	$642,000	$37,000
Sparkle Corporation stock	130,000	175,000	n/a

Shimmer does not sell any other assets during the year, and its taxable income before these transactions is $800,000. What are Shimmer's taxable income and tax liability for the year?

LO 11-5 planning

50. Aruna, a sole proprietor, wants to sell two assets that she no longer needs for her business. Both assets qualify as §1231 assets. The first is machinery and will generate a $10,000 §1231 loss on the sale. The second is land that will generate a $7,000 §1231 gain on the sale. Aruna's ordinary marginal tax rate is 32 percent.

a) Assuming she sells both assets in December of year 1 (the current year), what effect will the sales have on Aruna's tax liability?

b) Assuming that Aruna sells the land in December of year 1 and the machinery in January of year 2, what effect will the sales have on Aruna's tax liability for each year?

c) Explain why selling the assets in separate years will result in greater tax savings for Aruna.

51. Bourne Guitars, a corporation, reported a $157,000 net §1231 gain for year 6. LO 11-5

a) Assuming Bourne reported $50,000 of nonrecaptured net §1231 losses during years 1–5, what amount of Bourne's net §1231 gain for year 6, if any, is treated as ordinary income?

b) Assuming Bourne's nonrecaptured net §1231 losses from years 1–5 were $200,000, what amount of Bourne's net §1231 gain for year 6, if any, is treated as ordinary income?

52. Tonya Jefferson (single), a sole proprietor, runs a successful lobbying business in Washington, D.C. She doesn't sell many business assets, but she is planning on retiring and selling her historic townhouse, from which she runs her business, to buy a place somewhere sunny and warm. Tonya's townhouse is worth $1,000,000 and the land is worth another $1,000,000. The original basis in the townhouse was $600,000, and she has claimed $250,000 of depreciation deductions against the asset over the years. The original basis in the land was $500,000. Tonya has located a buyer that would like to finalize the transaction in December of the current year. Tonya's marginal ordinary income tax rate is 35 percent, and her capital gains tax rate is 20 percent. LO 11-5 planning

a) What amount of gain or loss does Tonya recognize on the sale? What is the character of the gain or loss? What effect does the gain or loss have on her tax liability?

b) In addition to the original facts, assume that Tonya reports the following nonrecaptured net §1231 loss:

Year	Net §1231 Gains/(Losses)
Year 1	$(200,000)
Year 2	0
Year 3	0
Year 4	0
Year 5	0
Year 6 (current year)	?

What amount of gain or loss does Tonya recognize on the sale? What is the character of the gain or loss? What effect does the gain or loss have on her year 6 (the current year) tax liability?

c) As Tonya's tax adviser, you suggest that Tonya sell the townhouse in year 7 in order to reduce her taxes. What amount of gain or loss does Tonya recognize on the sale in year 7?

53. Morgan's Water World (MWW), an LLC, opened several years ago. MWW has reported the following net §1231 gains and losses since it began business. Net §1231 gains shown are before the look-back rule. LO 11-5

Year	Net §1231 Gains/(Losses)
Year 1	$ (11,000)
Year 2	5,000
Year 3	(21,000)
Year 4	(4,000)
Year 5	17,000
Year 6	(43,000)
Year 7 (current year)	113,000

What amount, if any, of the current year (year 7) $113,000 net §1231 gain is treated as ordinary income?

LO 11-5

54. Hans runs a sole proprietorship. Hans has reported the following net §1231 gains and losses since he began business. Net §1231 gains shown are before the look-back rule.

Year	Net §1231 Gains/(Losses)
Year 1	$(65,000)
Year 2	15,000
Year 3	0
Year 4	0
Year 5	10,000
Year 6	0
Year 7 (current year)	50,000

a) What amount, if any, of the year 7 (current year) $50,000 net §1231 gain is treated as ordinary income?

b) Assume that the $50,000 net §1231 gain occurs in year 6 instead of year 7. What amount of the gain would be treated as ordinary income in year 6?

LO 11-6

55. Independence Corporation needs to replace some of the assets used in its trade or business and is contemplating the following exchanges:

Exchange	Asset Given Up by Independence	Asset Received by Independence
A	Office building in Chicago, IL	Piece of land in Toronto, Canada
B	Large warehouse on 2 acres	Small warehouse on 22 acres
C	Office building in Green Bay, WI, used in the business	Apartment complex in Newport Beach, CA, that will be held as an investment

Determine whether each exchange qualifies as a like-kind exchange. Also, explain the rationale for why each qualifies or does not qualify as a like-kind exchange.

LO 11-6

56. Kase, an individual, purchased some property in Potomac, Maryland, for $150,000 approximately 10 years ago. Kase is approached by a real estate agent representing a client who would like to exchange a parcel of land in North Carolina for Kase's Maryland property. Kase agrees to the exchange. What is Kase's realized gain or loss, recognized gain or loss, and basis in the North Carolina property in each of the following alternative scenarios?

a) The transaction qualifies as a like-kind exchange, and the fair market value of each property is $675,000.

b) The transaction qualifies as a like-kind exchange, and the fair market value of each property is $100,000.

LO 11-6
research

57. Longhaul Real Estate exchanged a parcel of land it held for sale in Bryan, Texas, for a warehouse in College Station, Texas. Will the exchange qualify for like-kind treatment?

LO 11-6
research
planning

58. Twinbrook Corporation needed to upgrade to a larger manufacturing facility. Twinbrook first acquired a new manufacturing facility for $2,100,000 cash and then transferred the facility it was using (building and land) to White Flint Corporation for $2,000,000 three months later. Does the exchange qualify for like-kind exchange treatment? (*Hint:* Examine Revenue Procedures 2000-37 and 2004-51.) If not, can you propose a change in the transaction that will allow it to qualify?

LO 11-6
research

59. Woodley Park Corporation currently owns two parcels of land (parcel 1 and parcel 2). It owns a warehouse facility on parcel 1. Woodley needs to acquire a new and larger manufacturing facility. Woodley was approached by Blazing Fast Construction (which specializes in prefabricated warehouses) about acquiring Woodley's existing warehouse on parcel 1. Woodley indicated that it would prefer to exchange its

existing facility for a new and larger facility in a qualifying like-kind exchange. Blazing Fast indicated that it could construct a new manufacturing facility on parcel 2 to Woodley's specification within four months. Woodley and Blazing Fast agreed to the following arrangement. First, Blazing Fast would construct the new warehouse on parcel 2 and then relinquish the property to Woodley within four months. Woodley would then transfer the warehouse facility and land parcel 1 to Blazing Fast. All of the property exchanged in the deal was identified immediately and the construction was completed within 180 days. Does the exchange of the new building for the old building and parcel 1 qualify as a like-kind exchange? [*Hint*: See *DeCleene v. Comm'r*, 115 TC 457 (2000).]

60. Metro Corp. traded building A for building B. Metro originally purchased building A for $50,000, and building A's adjusted basis was $25,000 at the time of the exchange. What is Metro's realized gain or loss, recognized gain or loss, and adjusted basis in building B in each of the following alternative scenarios? **LO 11-6**
    a) The fair market value of building A and of building B is $40,000 at the time of the exchange. The exchange does not qualify as a like-kind exchange.
    b) The fair market value of building A and of building B is $40,000. The exchange qualifies as a like-kind exchange.
    c) The fair market value of building A is $35,000, and building B is valued at $40,000. Metro exchanges building A and $5,000 cash for building B. Building A and building B are like-kind property.
    d) The fair market value of building A is $45,000, and Metro trades building A for building B valued at $40,000 and $5,000 cash. Building A and building B are like-kind property.
61. Prater Inc. enters into an exchange in which it gives up its warehouse on 10 acres of land and receives a tract of land. A summary of the exchange is as follows: **LO 11-6**

Transferred	FMV	Original Basis	Accumulated Depreciation
Warehouse	$300,000	$225,000	$45,000
Land	50,000	50,000	
Mortgage on warehouse	30,000		
Cash	20,000	20,000	

Assets received	FMV
Land	$340,000

What are Prater's realized and recognized gain on the exchange and its basis in the assets it received in the exchange?

62. Baker Corporation owned a building located in Kansas. Baker used the building for its business operations. Last year, a tornado hit the property and completely destroyed it. This year, Baker received an insurance settlement. Baker had originally purchased the building for $350,000 and had claimed a total of $100,000 of depreciation deductions against the property. What are Baker's realized and recognized gain or (loss) on this transaction and what is its basis in the new building in the following alternative scenarios? **LO 11-6**
    a) Baker received $450,000 in insurance proceeds and spent $450,000 rebuilding the building during the current year.
    b) Baker received $450,000 in insurance proceeds and spent $500,000 rebuilding the building during the current year.
    c) Baker received $450,000 in insurance proceeds and spent $400,000 rebuilding the building during the current year.
    d) Baker received $450,000 in insurance proceeds and spent $450,000 rebuilding the building during the next three years.

LO 11-6

63. Russell Corporation sold a parcel of land valued at $400,000. Its basis in the land was $275,000. For the land, Russell received $50,000 in cash in year 0 and a note providing that Russell will receive $175,000 in year 1 and $175,000 in year 2 from the buyer.
   a) What is Russell's realized gain on the transaction?
   b) What is Russell's recognized gain in year 0, year 1, and year 2?

LO 11-6

64. In year 0, Javens Inc. sold machinery with a fair market value of $400,000 to Chris. The machinery's original basis was $317,000, and Javens's accumulated depreciation on the machinery was $50,000, so its adjusted basis to Javens was $267,000. Chris paid Javens $40,000 immediately (in year 0) and provided a note to Javens indicating that Chris would pay Javens $60,000 a year for six years beginning in year 1. What are the amount and character of the gain that Javens will recognize in year 0? What amount and character of the gain will Javens recognize in years 1 through 6?

LO 11-6
research

65. Ken sold a rental property for $500,000. He received $100,000 in the current year and $100,000 each year for the next four years. Of the sales price, $400,000 was allocated to the building, and the remaining $100,000 was allocated to the land. Ken purchased the property several years ago for $300,000. When he initially purchased the property, he allocated $225,000 of the purchase price to the building and $75,000 to the land. Ken has claimed $25,000 of depreciation deductions over the years against the building. Ken had no other sales of §1231 or capital assets in the current year. For the year of the sale, determine Ken's recognized gain or loss and the character of Ken's gain, and calculate Ken's tax due because of the sale (assuming his marginal ordinary tax rate is 32 percent). (*Hint:* See the examples in Reg. §1.453-12.)

LO 11-6
planning

66. Hill Corporation is in the leasing business and faces a marginal tax rate of 21 percent. It has leased a building to Whitewater Corporation for several years. Hill bought the building for $150,000 and claimed $20,000 of depreciation deductions against the asset. The lease term is about to expire and Whitewater would like to acquire the building. Hill has been offered two options:

Option	Details
Like-kind exchange	Whitewater would provide Hill with a like-kind building. The like-kind building has a fair market value of $135,000.
Installment sale	Whitewater would provide Hill with two payments of $69,000. It would use the proceeds to purchase another building that it could also lease.

Ignoring time value of money, which option provides the greater after-tax value for Hill, assuming it is indifferent between the proposals based on nontax factors?

LO 11-6

67. Deirdre sold 100 shares of stock to her brother, James, for $2,400. Deirdre purchased the stock several years ago for $3,000.
   a) What gain or loss does Deirdre recognize on the sale?
   b) What amount of gain or loss does James recognize if he sells the stock for $3,200?
   c) What amount of gain or loss does James recognize if he sells the stock for $2,600?
   d) What amount of gain or loss does James recognize if he sells the stock for $2,000?

COMPREHENSIVE PROBLEMS

Select problems are available in Connect®.

68. Two years ago, Bethesda Corporation bought a delivery truck for $30,000 (not subject to the luxury auto depreciation limits). Bethesda used MACRS 200 percent declining balance and the half-year convention to recover the cost of the truck, but it did not elect §179 expensing and opted out of bonus depreciation. Answer the questions for the following alternative scenarios.
    a) Assuming Bethesda used the truck until it sold it in March of year 3, what depreciation expense can it claim on the truck for years 1 through 3?
    b) Assume that Bethesda claimed $18,500 of depreciation expense on the truck before it sold it in year 3. What are the amount and character of the gain or loss if Bethesda sold the truck in year 3 for $17,000 and incurred $2,000 of selling expenses on the sale?
    c) Assume that Bethesda claimed $18,500 of depreciation expense on the truck before it sold it in year 3. What are the amount and character of the gain or loss if Bethesda sold the truck in year 3 for $35,000 and incurred $3,000 of selling expenses on the sale?
69. Hauswirth Corporation sold (or exchanged) a warehouse in year 0. Hauswirth bought the warehouse several years ago for $65,000, and it has claimed $23,000 of depreciation expense against the building.
    a) Assuming that Hauswirth receives $50,000 in cash for the warehouse, compute the amount and character of Hauswirth's recognized gain or loss on the sale.
    b) Assuming that Hauswirth exchanges the warehouse in a like-kind exchange for some land with a fair market value of $50,000, compute Hauswirth's realized gain or loss, recognized gain or loss, deferred gain or loss, and basis in the new land.
    c) Assuming that Hauswirth receives $20,000 in cash in year 0 and a $50,000 note receivable that is payable in year 1, compute the amount and character of Hauswirth's gain or loss in year 0 and in year 1.
70. Fontenot Corporation sold some machinery to its majority owner Gray (an individual who owns 60 percent of Fontenot). Fontenot purchased the machinery for $100,000 and has claimed a total of $40,000 of depreciation expense deductions against the property. Gray will provide Fontenot with $10,000 cash today and provide a $100,000 note that will pay Fontenot $50,000 one year from now and $50,000 two years from now. **research**
    a) What gain or loss does Fontenot realize on the sale?
    b) What are the amount and character of the gain or loss that Fontenot must recognize in the year of sale (if any) and each of the two subsequent years? (*Hint:* Use the Internal Revenue Code and start with §453; please give appropriate citations.)
71. Moab Inc. manufactures and distributes high-tech biking gadgets. It has decided to streamline some of its operations so that it will be able to be more productive and efficient. Because of this decision, it has entered into several transactions during the year. **tax forms**

    Part (1): Determine the gain/loss realized and recognized in the current year for each of these events. Also determine whether the gain/loss recognized will be §1231, capital, or ordinary.
    a) Moab Inc. sold a machine that it used to make computerized gadgets for $27,300 cash. It originally bought the machine for $19,200 three years ago and has taken $8,000 in depreciation.
    b) Moab Inc. held stock in ABC Corp., which had a value of $12,000 at the beginning of the year. That same stock had a value of $15,230 at the end of the year.
    c) Moab Inc. sold some of its inventory for $7,000 cash. This inventory had a basis of $5,000.

d) Moab Inc. disposed of an office building with a fair market value of $75,000 for another office building with a fair market value of $55,000 and $20,000 in cash. It originally bought the office building seven years ago for $62,000 and has taken $15,000 in depreciation.

e) Moab Inc. sold some land held for investment for $28,000. It originally bought the land for $32,000 two years ago.

f) Moab Inc. sold another machine for a note payable in four annual installments of $12,000. The first payment was received in the current year. It originally bought the machine two years ago for $32,000 and has claimed $9,000 in depreciation expense against the machine.

g) Moab Inc. sold stock it held for eight years for $2,750. It originally purchased the stock for $2,100.

h) Moab Inc. sold another machine for $7,300. It originally purchased this machine six months ago for $9,000 and has claimed $830 in depreciation expense against the asset.

Part (2): From the recognized gains/losses determined in part (1), determine the net §1231 gain/loss, the net ordinary gain/loss, and the net capital gain/loss Moab will recognize on its tax return. Moab Inc. also has $2,000 of nonrecaptured net §1231 losses from previous years.

Part (3): Complete Moab Inc.'s Form 4797 for the year. Use the most current form available.

research

72. Vertovec Inc., a large local consulting firm in Utah, hired several new consultants from out of state last year to help service its expanding list of clients. To aid in relocating the consultants, Vertovec Inc. purchased the consultants' homes in their prior location if the consultants were unable to sell their homes within 30 days of listing them for sale. Vertovec Inc. bought the homes from the consultants for 5 percent less than the list price and then continued to list the homes for sale. Each home Vertovec Inc. purchased was sold at a loss. By the end of last year, Vertovec had suffered a loss totaling $250,000 from the homes. How should Vertovec treat the loss for tax purposes? Write a memo to Vertovec Inc. explaining your findings and any planning suggestions that you may have if Vertovec Inc. continues to offer this type of relocation benefit to newly hired consultants.

tax forms

73. WAR (We Are Rich) has been in business since 1989. WAR is an accrual-method sole proprietorship that deals in the manufacturing and wholesaling of various types of golf equipment. Hack & Hack CPAs has filed accurate tax returns for WAR's owner since WAR opened its doors. The managing partner of Hack & Hack (Jack) has gotten along very well with the owner of WAR—Mr. Someday Woods (single). However, in early 2022, Jack Hack and Someday Woods played a round of golf, and Jack, for the first time ever, beat Mr. Woods. Mr. Woods was so upset that he fired Hack & Hack and has hired you to compute his 2022 taxable income. Mr. Woods was able to provide you with the following information from prior tax returns. The taxable income numbers reflect the results from all of Mr. Woods's activities *except for the items separately stated.* You will need to consider how to handle the separately stated items for tax purposes. Also, note that the 2017–2021 numbers do not reflect capital loss carryovers.

Description	2017	2018	2019	2020	2021
Ordinary taxable income	$ 4,000	$ 2,000	$94,000	$170,000	$250,000
Other items not included in ordinary taxable income					
Net gain (loss) on disposition of §1231 assets	3,000	10,000		(6,000)	
Net long-term capital gain (loss) on disposition of capital assets	(15,000)	1,000	(7,000)		(7,000)

In 2022, Mr. Woods had taxable income in the amount of $480,000 *before* considering the following events and transactions that transpired in 2022:

a) On January 1, 2022, WAR purchased a plot of land for $100,000 with the intention of creating a driving range where patrons could test their new golf equipment. WAR never got around to building the driving range; instead, WAR sold the land on October 1, 2022, for $40,000.

b) On August 17, 2022, WAR sold its golf testing machine, "Iron Byron," and replaced it with a new machine, "Iron Tiger." "Iron Byron" was purchased and installed for a total cost of $22,000 on February 5, 2018. At the time of sale, "Iron Byron" had an adjusted tax basis of $4,000. WAR sold "Iron Byron" for $25,000.

c) In the months October through December 2022, WAR sold various assets to come up with the funds necessary to invest in WAR's latest and greatest invention—the three-dimple golf ball. Data on these assets are provided below:

Asset	Placed in Service (or Purchased)	Sold	Initial Basis	Accumulated Depreciation	Selling Price
Someday's black leather sofa (used in office)	4/4/21	10/16/22	$ 3,000	$ 540	$ 2,900
Someday's office chair	3/1/20	11/8/22	8,000	3,000	4,000
Marketable securities	2/1/19	12/1/22	12,000	0	20,000
Land held for investment	7/1/21	11/29/22	45,000	0	48,000
Other investment property	11/30/20	10/15/22	10,000	0	8,000

d) Finally, on May 7, 2022, WAR decided to sell the building where it tested its plutonium shaft and lignite head drivers. WAR purchased the building on January 5, 2010, for $190,000 ($170,000 for the building, $20,000 for the land). At the time of the sale, the accumulated depreciation on the building was $50,000. WAR sold the building (with the land) for $300,000. The fair market value of the land at the time of sale was $45,000.

Part (1): Compute Mr. Woods's taxable income *after* taking into account the transactions described above.

Part (2): Compute Mr. Woods's tax liability for the year. (Ignore any net investment income tax for the year and assume the 20 percent qualified business income deduction is included in taxable income before these transactions.)

Part (3): Complete Mr. Woods's Form 8949, Schedule D, and Form 4797 (use the most current version of these schedules) to be attached to his Form 1040. Assume that asset bases are not reported to the IRS.

74. Fizbo Corporation is in the business of breeding and racing horses. Fizbo has taxable income of $5,000,000 other than from these transactions. It has nonrecaptured §1231 losses of $10,000 from 2018 and $13,000 from 2016.

Consider the following transactions that occur during 2022:

a) A building with an adjusted basis of $300,000 is totally destroyed by fire. Fizbo receives insurance proceeds of $400,000 but does not plan to replace the building. The building was built 12 years ago at a cost of $420,000 and was used to provide lodging for employees.

b) Fizbo sells four acres of undeveloped farmland (used for grazing) for $50,000. Fizbo purchased the land 15 years ago for $15,000.

c) Fizbo sells a racehorse for $250,000. The racehorse was purchased four years ago for $200,000. Total depreciation taken on the racehorse was $160,000.

d) Fizbo exchanges equipment that was purchased three years ago for $300,000 for $100,000 of IBM common stock. The adjusted basis of the equipment is $220,000. If straight-line depreciation had been used, the adjusted basis would be $252,000.

e) On November 1, Fizbo sold XCON stock for $50,000. Fizbo had purchased the stock on December 12, 2021, for $112,000.

Part (1): After *all* netting is complete, what is Fizbo's total amount of income from these transactions to be treated as ordinary income or loss? What is its capital gain or loss?

Part (2): What is Fizbo's taxable income for the year after including the effects of these transactions?

UWorld Roger CPA Review

Sample CPA Exam questions from Roger CPA Review are available in Connect as support for the topics in this text. These Multiple Choice Questions and Task-Based Simulations include expert-written explanations and solutions and provide a starting point for students to become familiar with the content and functionality of the actual CPA Exam.

chapter

12 Compensation

Learning Objectives

Upon completing this chapter, you should be able to:

LO 12-1 Determine the tax implications of compensation in the form of salary and wages from the perspectives of the employee and the employer.

LO 12-2 Describe the tax implications of various forms of equity-based compensation from the perspectives of the employee and the employer.

LO 12-3 Compare and contrast taxable and nontaxable fringe benefits and explain their tax consequences for the employee and the employer.

Ronnarong Thanuthattaphong/123RF

Storyline Summary

Taxpayers:	Julie (she/her/hers) and Ethan (he/him/his) Clark
Location:	San Diego, California
Employment status:	Julie—mid-level executive at Premier Computer Corporation (PCC); current salary $240,000 Ethan—mechanical engineer; current salary $70,000
Filing status:	Married filing jointly
Dependents:	Two children
Marginal ordinary tax rate:	24 percent
Long-term capital gain rate:	15 percent
Current situation:	Julie is considering an offer for the VP of marketing position with Technology Products Inc. (TPI).
Taxpayer:	TPI (a C corporation)
Location:	San Diego, California
Ownership:	Publicly traded corporation
Industry:	Manufacturer of high-technology products
CEO:	Daniella Hewitt
Current situation:	Recruiting Julie Clark for VP of marketing position

Julie and Ethan Clark and their two children have lived in San Diego, California, for some time. Julie has decided her career is at a crossroads. Her employment as a mid-level executive for Premier Computer Corporation (PCC) is going well, but the work is not as challenging as it used to be. She suspects that, given her skills and abilities, she could put her career on the fast track with the right opportunity, engaging in more fulfilling work and gaining a significant increase in compensation.

Julie was sitting at her desk contemplating her career when she received yet another call from a corporate headhunter. While she usually quickly dismissed such calls, this time her interest and curiosity were piqued and she gave her full attention. He asked if she had any interest in a vice president (VP) of marketing position with a publicly traded company located nearby. After the headhunter answered a few of her questions, Julie gave him the go-ahead to set up an interview.

A couple of weeks later, Julie had been through two rounds of interviews for the VP of marketing position when she received a call informing her that she was the one Technology Products Inc. (TPI) wanted for the job, and that an offer letter with the details was on its way. The letter indicated TPI was offering a $280,000 salary (a significant increase from her current salary). TPI was also offering her several types of equity-based compensation and some attractive fringe benefits. While excited by the letter, Julie knew she needed to learn more about the equity-based compensation alternatives and the other forms of compensation TPI was offering before she could adequately evaluate the offer and reach a decision.

(to be continued . . .)

As TPI's letter to Julie illustrates, employers are able to offer many different forms of compensation to employees. They can pay some compensation now and also defer some to the future. Each type of compensation has unique tax and nontax consequences.

This chapter addresses the tax and nontax consequences of *current* compensation packages from both the employee's and the employer's perspectives. For discussion about deferred compensation, see the Retirement Savings and Deferred Compensation chapter.

LO 12-1

SALARY AND WAGES

Current compensation paid to **employees** in the form of **salary** and **wages** has tax consequences for both employees and employers. Below, we address the tax (and nontax) considerations of salary and wages from the employee's perspective, followed by the employer's perspective.

THE KEY FACTS

Employment-Related Forms

- **Form W-2**
  - Summarizes an employee's taxable salary and wages.
  - Provides annual federal and state withholding information.
  - Generated by employer on an annual basis.
- **Form W-4**
  - Supplies an employee's withholding information to an employer.
  - Generated by employee.
- **Form 1099-NEC**
  - Summarizes an independent contractor's or nonemployee's taxable compensation.
  - Generated by the person or entity paying the compensation.

Employee Considerations for Salary and Wages

Employees receiving salary generally earn a fixed amount of compensation for the year no matter how many hours they work. In addition, salaried employees may be eligible for bonuses if they satisfy certain criteria. In contrast, employees receiving wages generally get paid on an hourly, daily, or piecework basis. Salary, bonus(es), and wages are all taxed to employees as ordinary income. Employees generally recognize income from salary and wages as they receive it.[1] As we discussed in detail in the Individual Income Tax Computation and Tax Credits chapter, employees must pay **FICA taxes** on their wages.[2] FICA taxes consist of both a Social Security and a Medicare component.

At the end of each year, employees receive a **Form W-2** (see Exhibit 12-1) from their employers, summarizing their compensation and the various amounts withheld from their paychecks during the year.[3] Employees simply report their compensation on page 1, line 1, of the federal Form 1040 and report their federal income taxes withheld on line 25 of page 2.[4] Self-employed taxpayers receive a Form 1099-NEC indicating the nonemployee compensation they received, and they report the amount on Schedule C.

Tax Withholding When employees begin employment with a company, they complete a **Form W-4** to supply the information the company needs in order to determine how much tax to withhold from each paycheck. Specifically, employees use Form W-4 to indicate (1) their anticipated filing status (e.g., single or married filing jointly), (2) whether the taxpayer has multiple jobs or a working spouse, (3) the number of children qualifying for the child tax credit and other dependents, and (4) whether the employee has other adjustments (additional income or deductions) or wants extra withholding for each pay period.

Employer Considerations for Salary and Wages

Deductibility of Salary and Wage Payments Employers receive a deduction for reasonable salaries, wages, and other compensation paid to employees.[5] Determining whether compensation is reasonable in amount is a **facts and circumstances test** that requires considering the duties of the employee, the complexities of the business, and the

[1]Reg. §1.451-1(a).

[2]FICA stands for Federal Insurance Contributions Act.

[3]Compensation received by taxpayers who are self-employed is not considered to be salary and wages.

[4]The 2021 forms were used because the 2022 forms were unavailable at press time.

[5]§162(a)(1). As we discuss in the Business Income, Deductions, and Accounting Methods chapter, all business expenses (not just compensation) must be reasonable in amount to be fully deductible.

EXHIBIT 12-1 Form W-2

22222	a Employee's social security number	OMB No. 1545-0008

b Employer identification number (EIN)	1 Wages, tips, other compensation	2 Federal income tax withheld
c Employer's name, address, and ZIP code	3 Social security wages	4 Social security tax withheld
	5 Medicare wages and tips	6 Medicare tax withheld
	7 Social security tips	8 Allocated tips
d Control number	9	10 Dependent care benefits
e Employee's first name and initial Last name Suff.	11 Nonqualified plans	12a Code
	13 Statutory employee ☐ Retirement plan ☐ Third-party sick pay ☐	12b Code
	14 Other	12c Code
		12d Code
f Employee's address and ZIP code		

15 State Employer's state ID number	16 State wages, tips, etc.	17 State income tax	18 Local wages, tips, etc.	19 Local income tax	20 Locality name

Form **W-2 Wage and Tax Statement** **2021** Department of the Treasury—Internal Revenue Service

Copy 1—For State, City, or Local Tax Department

Source: irs.gov.

amount of salary compared with the income of the business, prevailing rates of compensation, and external comparison to other businesses, among other things. The amount of compensation paid in excess of the amount considered reasonable is not deductible. The reasonable compensation limit typically applies to closely held businesses where either the employee is an owner of the business or the employee is a relative of the business owner. If the IRS determines that the shareholder/employee compensation is unreasonable, the nondeductible portion of the compensation may be recharacterized as a dividend to the shareholder/employee.[6]

The timing of the compensation deduction depends on the employer's method of accounting. Cash-method employers generally deduct compensation when they pay employees.[7] Accrual-method employers generally deduct compensation as the employees perform services.[8] This general rule for accrual-method employers holds even in situations when the employer accrues and fixes compensation expense in one year but actually pays the employee in the subsequent year, as long as the employer makes the payment within 2½ months after the employer's year-end. If the employer pays the employee more than 2½ months after the employer's year-end, the compensation is considered deferred compensation and is not deductible by the employer until the employee receives the payment

[6]Reg. §1.162-8.

[7]Reg. §1.461-1(a)(1).

[8]Reg. §1.461-1(a)(2). See the Business Income, Deductions, and Accounting Methods chapter for a detailed discussion of the cash and accrual accounting methods.

and recognizes the compensation as income.[9] Because most employers pay compensation to employees each month (or more frequently), the 2½-month rule is likely to be more of an issue for other types of accrued compensation such as one-time, year-end bonuses or vacation pay than it is for compensation paid each pay period.

Example 12-1

When does PCC deduct the $240,000 salary it paid to Julie in the current year?

Answer: All $240,000 would be deducted in the current year.

What if: Suppose that PCC paid Julie $240,000 of salary and a bonus of $20,000 for the current year. The bonus was fixed before year-end and paid on February 1 of the subsequent year. When would PCC deduct the compensation paid to Julie?

Answer: All $260,000 would be deducted in the current year because the salary and bonus were fixed in the current year and the bonus was paid within 2½ months after PCC's year-end.

What if: Using the same facts as in the previous what-if scenario, now assume that the bonus was paid on April 1 of the subsequent year. When would PCC deduct the compensation paid to Julie?

Answer: $240,000 in the current year and $20,000 in the subsequent year. The bonus would be deductible in the subsequent year because it was not paid within 2½ months after PCC's year-end.

The after-tax cost of providing salary is generally much less than the before-tax cost.[10] While profitable corporations now have a 21 percent tax rate, the marginal tax rate for other businesses (sole proprietorships and flow-through entities) could be as high as 37 percent. The formula for computing the after-tax cost of salary (the cost after subtracting the tax savings from the deduction), or any deductible expense, for that matter, is as follows:

$$\text{After-tax cost of salary} = \text{Deductible expenditure (salary)} \times (1 - \text{Marginal tax rate})$$

Example 12-2

For PCC, what are the before-tax and after-tax costs of paying Julie a $240,000 salary (ignoring FICA taxes)?

Answer: $240,000 before-tax cost and $189,600 after-tax cost, computed as follows:

Description	Amount	Explanation
Before-tax cost of salary:		
(1) **Salary**	**$240,000**	
(2) 1 – Marginal tax rate	× 79%	(1 – 21%). Corporate tax rate is 21%.
After-tax cost of salary	**$189,600**	(1) × (2)

THE KEY FACTS

Compensation Deductibility for Accrual-Method Taxpayers

- Compensation expense accrued at end of year *is generally* deductible if fixed and paid within 2½ months of year-end.
- Compensation expense accrued at end of year *is not* deductible until fixed and paid if the employer and employee are related persons.

Compensation deduction restrictions. Special compensation deduction rules may apply when the employer and employee are considered to be related persons and when an employee is considered to be a "covered employee." We discuss each of these situations in the next few paragraphs.

When an accrual-method employer and a cash-method employee are considered to be "related persons," the employer is not allowed to deduct compensation accrued at year-end until it actually pays the employee, even if the payment is within 2½ months of

[9]Reg. §1.404(b)-1T(A-2).

[10]As discussed in the Individual Income Tax Computation and Tax Credits chapter, employers are required to pay FICA taxes on employees' compensation. Employers may also be required to pay other expenses based on employee wages such as workers' compensation insurance.

year-end.[11] This rule prevents employers and employees with close relationships from accelerating the deduction for the employer while deferring the income to the employee. For this purpose, a corporate employer and an employee are considered to be related persons if the employee owns directly or indirectly more than 50 percent of the value of the corporate employer's stock.[12] Employees are treated as indirectly owning any stock owned by employees' spouses, siblings, ancestors (parents, grandparents, etc.), and lineal descendants (children, grandchildren, etc.).

Example 12-3

What if: Suppose that PCC paid Julie $240,000 of salary during the current year and a bonus of $20,000 that was fixed before year-end and paid on February 1 of the subsequent year. Further, assume that Julie and her father own 10 percent and 45 percent of the PCC stock, respectively. When would PCC deduct the compensation paid to Julie?

Answer: $240,000 of salary would be deductible in the current year and the $20,000 bonus would be deductible in the subsequent year. The bonus is not deductible to PCC (an accrual-method employer) until the year that Julie (the cash-method, related person) receives and recognizes the bonus as income. Julie is a related person to PCC because her direct ownership (10 percent of PCC stock) plus her indirect ownership (45 percent of PCC stock attributed to her from her father) is greater than 50 percent.

THE KEY FACTS

Limits on Salary Deductibility of Publicly Traded Corporations

- $1 million maximum annual compensation deduction per covered employee.
  - Covered employees are the CEO, CFO, and the three other highest-compensated officers.
  - A covered employee for any year beginning after 2016 will be considered a covered employee by the employer for all future years.
  - Limit does not apply to performance-based compensation contracts in existence on November 2, 2017, that have not been materially modified.

For taxable years beginning on or after January 1, 2018, the deduction for compensation with respect to a covered employee of a publicly held corporation is limited to $1 million per year for each covered employee. Amounts in excess of $1 million are never deductible.[13] For this purpose, compensation includes all taxable amounts paid to the employee. Covered employees include the principal executive officer (CEO), principal financial officer (CFO), and the three highest-paid officers other than the CEO and CFO in the current year. Additionally, if an employee was a covered employee for any year beginning after December 31, 2016, that employee will be considered a covered employee in all subsequent years. That is, once an employee is a covered employee, that person will always be a covered employee to the employer, even when the employment relationship ends for any reason.[14] The covered employee deduction limitation applies to all publicly traded corporations and certain other corporations.[15]

Example 12-4

Julie's potential employer had been actively searching for a new CEO. The board of directors eventually chose Daniella Hewitt. During negotiations, Daniella indicated she wanted a $1.5 million salary and a performance-based bonus of $1 million upon reaching certain performance objectives. If the board of directors agreed to her request, and the performance objectives were met, what are TPI's before-tax and after-tax costs of paying Daniella (a covered employee) a $1.5 million salary and a $750,000 bonus during the current year?

(continued on page 12-6)

[11]§267(a)(2).

[12]See §267(b) for the complete definition of related persons.

[13]§162(m).

[14]For example, compensation paid to a beneficiary after the employee's death or to a former spouse under a domestic relations order would be nondeductible to the extent the compensation exceeds the $1 million limit.

[15]The limit applies to private debt issuers and foreign private issuers that meet the definition of a publicly held corporation (even if not subject to the Securities Exchange Act). T.D. 9932 provides some additional guidance.

Answer: $2,500,000 before-tax cost and $2,040,000 after-tax cost, computed as follows:

Description	Amount	Explanation
Before-tax cost of compensation		
(1) **Salary**	**$1,500,000**	
(2) **Bonus**	**$ 750,000**	
(3) Total compensation	$ 2,250,000	(1) + (2)
(4) Deductible compensation	$ 1,000,000	Limited to $1,000,000 because Daniella is a covered employee.
(5) Marginal tax rate	× 21%	Corporate tax rate.
(6) Tax savings from compensation deduction	$ 210,000	(4) × (5)
After-tax cost of compensation	**$2,040,000**	(3) − (6)

For taxable years beginning prior to January 1, 2018, and for compensation paid under a binding contract in existence on November 2, 2017 (that has not been materially modified after that date), the $1 million per year deduction limitation does not apply to performance-based compensation (e.g., stock option compensation, performance-based bonuses, and commissions).

Example 12-5

Julie's potential employer was still paying compensation to its former CEO during 2022. Under the compensation contract, which was in existence before November 2, 2017, TPI paid the former CEO a salary of $1.5 million and a $1 million performance-based bonus. What are TPI's before-tax and after-tax costs of paying the former CEO (a covered employee) a $1.5 million salary and a $1.1 million performance-based bonus during 2022?

Answer: $2,500,000 before-tax cost and $2,159,000 after-tax cost, computed as follows:

Description	Amount	Explanation
Before-tax cost of compensation		
(1) **Salary**	**$1,500,000**	
(2) **Bonus**	**$1,100,000**	Performance based
(3) Total compensation	$ 2,600,000	(1) + (2)
(4) Deductible compensation	$ 2,100,000	$1,000,000 limitation on (1) + performance-based bonus (2)
(5) Marginal tax rate	× 21%	Corporate tax rate
(6) Tax savings from compensation deduction	$ 441,000	(4) × (5)
After-tax cost of compensation	**$2,159,000**	(3) − (6)

Note that the after-tax cost of the compensation is lower than the after-tax cost of the compensation in Example 12-4 because performance-based compensation is deductible for contracts in existence before November 2, 2017. This provides an incentive to keep preexisting contracts in place for covered employees.

What if: What are TPI's before-tax and after-tax costs of paying a noncovered employee a $1.5 million salary and a $1.1 million performance-based bonus during 2022?

Answer: $2,500,000 before-tax cost and $2,054,000 after-tax cost, computed as follows:

Description	Amount	Explanation
Before-tax cost of compensation:		
(1) **Compensation**	**$1,500,000**	
(2) **Commissions**	**$1,100,000**	
(3) Total compensation	$ 2,600,000	(1) + (2)
(4) Deductible compensation	$ 2,600,000	No limitation to compensation for a noncovered employee.
(5) Marginal tax rate	× 21%	Corporate tax rate is 21%.
(6) Tax savings from compensation deduction	$ 546,000	(4) × (5)
After-tax cost of compensation	**$2,054,000**	(3) − (6)

Due to the $1 million limitation, the after-tax cost of compensation for a covered employee is higher than for a noncovered employee.

TAXES IN THE REAL WORLD Are CEOs Cutting Jobs but Keeping Their Massive Bonuses?

In 2020, Hertz, Office Depot, NBC, and United Airlines all announced big layoffs when the COVID-19 pandemic has hit our economy. The big question is whether executives are cutting their own compensation, including massive bonuses.

While some executives at Disney, Dick's Sporting Goods, General Electric, Lyft, and Marriott have announced pay cuts—often to zero—other executives are not so generous. Other SEC filings in 2020 show that average CEO compensation rose 14% to $21.3 million. Time will tell whether CEOs and other executives share the pain that many of their employees are experiencing. Changes in compensation have tax consequences as well. For companies laying off noncovered employees, the cash savings will be the after-tax cost of the compensation rather than the actual compensation due to the loss of tax deductions. For the reduction in CEO salaries, the cash savings depend on whether the compensation contracts met the binding contract in existence on November 2, 2017, or not. However, the relative cash savings for reductions in covered employee compensation will be larger than the savings for noncovered employees because of the limitations in place with respect to tax deductions for covered employees.

EQUITY-BASED COMPENSATION

LO 12-2

(continued from page 12-1 . . .)

As she read TPI's offer letter more carefully, Julie discovered that on the first day of January following her acceptance of the offer, she would be granted 200 nonqualified stock options (NQOs), 50 incentive stock options (ISOs), and 10,000 shares of restricted stock. Each stock option would allow her to purchase up to 100 shares of stock (200 NQOs allow her to acquire/purchase up to 20,000 shares and 50 ISOs allow her to acquire/purchase up to 5,000 shares) at a fixed price equal to the market value of TPI stock on the date of grant. As she read on, Julie noticed that she would not be able to exercise either type of stock option (purchase the TPI stock at the exercise price) until the options vest (i.e., the options become legally hers) two years after the grant date. Further, Julie understood that, after the restricted stock vests (one year from the grant date on January 1), she would be free to do what she wanted with the shares. The last detail Julie noticed when reading this part of the offer letter was that both types of options expire 10 years from the grant date. She understood this to mean that if she did not exercise her options sometime before their expiration date, she would forfeit them. Julie also remembered that the HR director mentioned that TPI was considering granting restricted stock units (RSUs) in the future. Julie wondered if restricted stock and RSUs were the same thing.

Although it was obvious to Julie that the value of the options and restricted stock would increase as the share price of TPI increased from the current share price of $5 per share, she remained unsure about the terminology used in this section of the letter. She realized that she needs to learn more about the economic and tax implications of stock options, restricted stock, and possibly RSUs before making her decision.

(to be continued . . .)

THE KEY FACTS

Equity-Based Compensation

- Stock options
  - Allow employees to purchase stock at a definitive price.
- Restricted stock
  - Form of compensation that provides actual stock ownership to employees after restrictions lapse.
- Restricted stock units
  - Grant valued in terms of company stock, but company stock is not issued at the time of the grant. After vesting, the company distributes shares or the cash equivalent of the number of shares used to value the unit.

Equity-based compensation such as stock options and restricted stock provides risks and potential rewards not available with other forms of compensation.[16] If the employer's stock price increases after it grants options and restricted stock, employees can be rewarded handsomely. On the other hand, if the employer's stock price doesn't increase, the stock options will expire worthless, and the value of the restricted stock will be limited.

By using equity-based compensation, employers are able to provide their employees actual ownership in the entity. When employees hold stock and/or stock options, their compensation is more directly tied to the fortunes of their employer and its shareholders—that is, employees' compensation increases in tandem with the stock price. This philosophy is reflected in an excerpt from Adobe's 2021 proxy statement, presented in Exhibit 12-2.

EXHIBIT 12-2 Excerpt from Adobe's 2021 Proxy Statement

Goals of Equity Compensation

We use equity compensation to motivate and reward strong corporate performance and to retain valued executive officers. We also use equity incentive awards as a means to attract and recruit qualified executives. We believe that equity awards serve to align the interests of our Named Executive Officers (NEOs) with those of our stockholders by rewarding them for growing the value of the company. By having a significant percentage of our NEOs' target tax deductible compensation (TDC) payable in the form of multi-year equity and, thus, subject to higher risk and longer vesting than cash compensation, our NEOs are motivated to take actions that will benefit Adobe and its stockholders in the long term.

See page 40 of proxy statement: www.adobe.com/content/dam/cc/en/investor-relations/pdfs/ADBE-Proxy2021.pdf.

THE KEY FACTS

Stock Option Terminology

- *Nonqualified stock options* (NQOs) are any options that don't meet the requirements for being classified as ISOs.
- *Incentive stock options* (ISOs) satisfy certain tax code requirements to provide favorable tax treatment to employees.
- The *grant date* is the date employees are initially allocated stock options.

(continued)

In addition to its motivational effects, equity-based compensation also provides cash-flow benefits to employers. How? Unless employers purchase their own stock in a market transaction to satisfy option exercises and stock grants, there are no cash outflows associated with this form of compensation. In fact, employers actually *receive* cash from their employees in the amount of the exercise price on the options exercised. There are a couple of downsides to this benefit.

First, employers experience the opportunity cost of selling shares at a discounted price to employees rather than selling them at fair market value on the open market. Second, when employers issue new shares to satisfy option exercises and stock grants, the total number of shares outstanding increases, and, therefore, earnings per share are diluted. Employers can avoid diluting earnings per share if they use their cash reserves to buy back shares before issuing shares as equity-based compensation. However, from a cash-flow perspective, this is no different from paying cash compensation.

[16]As with other forms of compensation, equity-based compensation is subject to FICA.

Stock Options

Stock options are a form of equity-based compensation that gives the employee the legal right to buy employer stock at a set price between the date the stock options **vest** and the expiration date of the options.[17] The stipulated price at which employees can purchase the employer stock is referred to as the **exercise price** or the **strike price.** At any point between the vesting and expiration dates, the employee may exercise the option by paying the employer the exercise price. Stock options have several important characteristics: (1) employees have no incentive to exercise options when the employer's share price is below the exercise price; (2) once the option vests, the employee must use cash to purchase the employer's stock; and (3) once purchased, the employer stock is subject to investment risk. As suggested in Exhibit 12-3, the value of stock option awards depends on the exercise price, the company's future share price, the exercise date of the options, and the timing for selling the shares received from the **option exercise.**

- The *exercise date* is the date that employees purchase stock using their options.
- The *vesting date* is the time when stock options granted can be exercised.
- The *exercise price* (or *strike price*) is the amount paid to the employer to acquire shares with stock options.
- The *bargain element* is the difference between the fair market value of stock and the exercise price on the exercise date.

Example 12-6

What if: Given the assumptions in the stock option timeline shown in Exhibit 12-3, what is Julie's economic loss from her stock options if TPI's stock price falls to $3 per share before the vesting date and remains there until after the options' expiration date?

Answer: Zero. If TPI's stock price never exceeds the $5 per share exercise price before the expiration date of the options, Julie will not exercise her options to purchase TPI shares, and those options will expire worthless.

If the employer's stock appreciates so that the stock price exceeds the exercise price, the options are valuable, and the employee will almost certainly exercise the options. The exercise of the option to purchase the employer's stock requires the payment of cash equal to the exercise price. Employees who exercise options to purchase employer stock experience an increase in before-tax net worth equal to the difference between the market value of the acquired shares and the exercise price on the date of exercise. This difference is called the **bargain element.**

Example 12-7

Given the assumptions in the stock option timeline shown in Exhibit 12-3, how much would it cost Julie to exercise all her options at the end of year 3 (before taxes), and what would Julie's economic gain before taxes be if she were to immediately exercise the options and sell the shares?[18]

Answer: $125,000 cost to exercise; $375,000 economic gain before taxes, calculated as follows:

Description	Amount	Explanation
(1) Shares acquired	25,000	(20,000 NQOs and 5,000 ISOs)
(2) Exercise price	$ 5	Exhibit 12-3
(3) **Cash needed to exercise**	**$125,000**	(1) × (2)
(4) Market price	$ 20	Exhibit 12-3
(5) Market value of shares	$ 500,000	(1) × (4)
Economic gain before taxes (bargain element)	**$375,000**	(5) – (3)

[17]Vesting dates are frequently specified as future calendar dates, or they may be triggered when certain events occur (i.e., predefined performance objectives are met or the company has been sold).

[18]According to the facts presented in Exhibit 12-3, Julie could have exercised her options as early as the vesting date for her options at the beginning of year 3. We assume she waits one year to exercise her options to better illustrate the implications of deferring the option exercise beyond the vesting date. In reality, it is quite common for employees to exercise at least a portion of their stock options on the vesting date.

EXHIBIT 12-3 Sample Timeline for Nonqualified and Incentive Stock Options

The economic and tax consequences of Julie's initial stock option award depend on the future share price of TPI, at the time Julie decides to exercise her options, and at the time Julie sells the shares received from the option exercise. The stock option examples in this chapter initially draw from the timeline below for the necessary assumptions regarding these key variables.

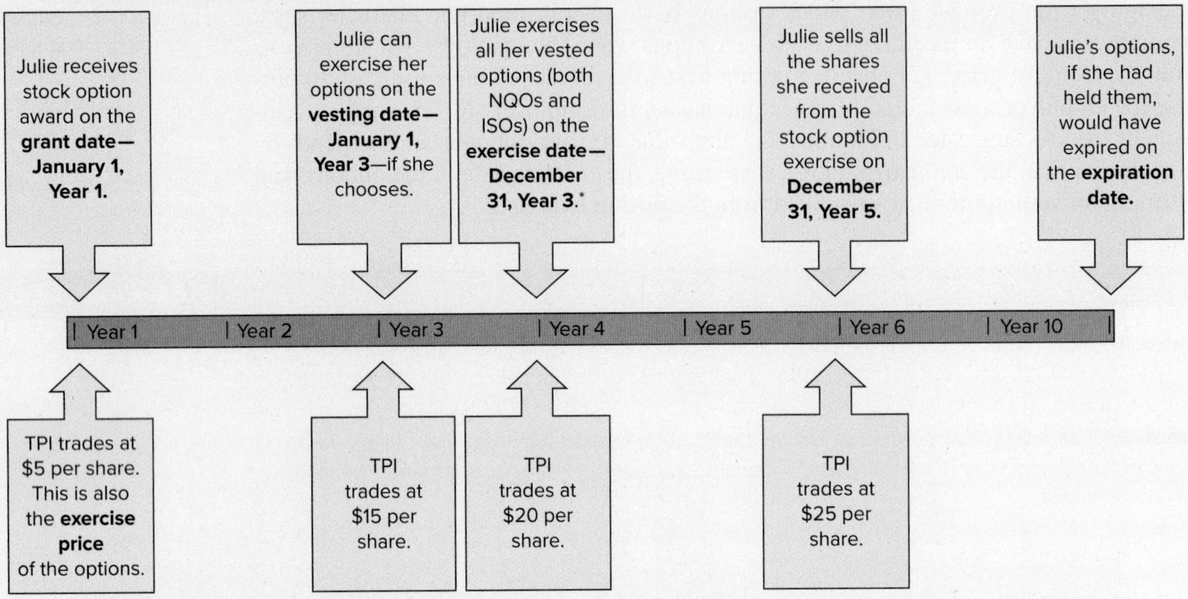

*Julie will acquire 20,000 shares of TPI (200 NQOs × 100 shares per NQO) with NQOs and 5,000 shares of TPI (50 ISOs × 100 shares per ISO) with ISOs. In total, Julie will acquire 25,000 shares of TPI.

TPI will receive $125,000 from Julie when she exercises her options. If new shares are issued, however, TPI's earnings per share will drop relative to what it would have been had the new shares not been issued. If, to avoid dilution of its earnings per share, TPI purchases its own shares from the market instead of issuing new shares, it would pay $500,000 (25,000 shares purchased × $20 per share), resulting in total cash outflows of $375,000 net of the $125,000 Julie paid in to exercise her options.

In certain circumstances, an employee may engage in a cashless exercise or same-day sale. A **cashless exercise** is a technique that uses a brokerage firm to borrow funds in the amount of the exercise price (plus any associated brokerage fees) and then a portion of the sales proceeds is used to pay back the borrowed funds. A **same-day sale** typically does not require the employee to pay for the stock, but rather allows them to receive cash in the amount of the difference between the fair market value of the stock and the exercise price. Three primary reasons exist for a cashless exercise or same-day sale. First, the employee may not have enough cash on hand to cover the cost of exercising the options. Second, the employee may not have enough cash on hand to cover the future tax liability from exercising the options. Third, because the employee bears investment risk with respect to the employer stock, the employee might want to diversify her investment portfolio by selling the employer's stock and investing in other stocks.

Employee Tax Considerations for Stock Options Stock options are classified for tax purposes as either **nonqualified stock options (NQOs)** or **incentive stock options (ISOs).** There are three important dates for employee stock options: the grant date, vesting date, and exercise date. While all three of these dates have economic consequences, only the exercise date has tax consequences to the employee. The employee's tax consequences on the exercise date depend on whether the employee is exercising NQOs or ISOs.

Nonqualified options. Most employer stock options are NQOs. When NQOs are exercised, an employee reports ordinary income equal to the bargain element on the shares of the employer stock acquired (as if they had sold the stock)—whether they hold the share's sell the shares immediately.[19] The employee's basis in the newly acquired shares is equal to the fair market value of the shares on the exercise date. Thus, the basis includes the exercise price plus the ordinary income the taxpayer recognizes on the exercise (i.e., the bargain element) and the holding period for the shares begins on the exercise date. When the employee eventually sells these shares, the employee will recognize a long- or short-term capital gain, depending on the holding period, on the difference between the sales price and the employee's basis in the shares.

Example 12-8

Assume that Julie exercises her NQOs when the employer stock price is $20 per share (see Exhibit 12-3). On the exercise date, Julie acquires 20,000 shares of TPI stock and pays TPI the exercise price of $5 per share. What are the tax consequences to Julie on the exercise of her NQOs?

Answer: $300,000 of ordinary income, equal to the bargain element, on the exercise of the NQOs, calculated as follows:

Description	Amount	Explanation
(1) Shares acquires with NQOs	20,000	
(2) Market price per share	$ 20	Exhibit 12-3
(3) Exercise Price	5	Exhibit 12-3
(4) Bargain element per share	$ 15	(2) – (3)
Bargain element (ordinary income)	**$300,000**	(1) × (4)

What is Julie's basis in the 20,000 shares she acquired through NQOs?

Answer: $400,000 [$100,000 (20,000 shares × $5 per share exercise price) + $300,000 (bargain element taxed as ordinary income)].

What if: Suppose that five years after Julie exercised her NQOs and acquired 20,000 TPI shares with a basis of $20 per share, she sold all of her shares for $25 per share. What is the amount and character of the gain she will recognize on the sale?

Answer: $100,000 long-term capital gain, calculated as follows:

Description	Amount	Explanation
(1) Amount realized (sales proceeds)	$ 500,000	20,000 shares × $25
(2) Tax basis	400,000	See basis calculation above
Long-term capital gain recognized	**$100,000**	(1) – (2)

What if: Suppose Julie sold the shares for $25 per share six months after she exercised them. What is the character of the $100,000 gain she recognized on the sale?

Answer: Short-term capital gain because she held the shares for one year or less before selling.

Incentive stock options. Relative to NQOs the granting of ISOs is less common. ISOs are sometimes referred to as statutory or qualified stock options. If the employee *holds ISOs for at least two years after the grant date and the employee holds the stock received from exercising ISOs for at least one year after the exercise date,* the

[19]Income from the bargain element is reported on an employee's Form W-2, and the applicable income and payroll taxes are withheld.

employee gains two important tax benefits.[20] First, the realized gain on the bargain element is deferred for regular tax purposes until the stock is subsequently sold.[21] Second, the character of the gain on the subsequent stock sale is recognized as long-term capital gain rather than as ordinary income. Holding the number of options granted constant, employees generally prefer ISOs to NQOs due to the potential tax benefits for ISOs. The employee's basis in shares acquired through exercising ISOs is equal to the exercise price paid and the holding period for the shares begins on the exercise date. If the employee meets the required holding period requirements (described above) with respect to the ISOs the employee will recognize a long-term capital gain on the difference between the sales price and the employee's basis in the shares upon subsequent disposition.

Example 12-9

Assume that Julie exercises her ISOs when the employer stock price is $20 per share (see Exhibit 12-3). On the exercise date, Julie acquires 5,000 shares of TPI stock and pays TPI the exercise price of $5 per share. What are the tax consequences to Julie on the exercise of her ISOs?

Answer: $0, there are no regular tax consequences on the ISO exercise, because Julie held the shares at least two years after the grant date and one year after the exercise date. Julie's realized gain is the bargain element of $75,000 [5,000 shares × $15 ($20 market price less $5 exercise price)], which is deferred until Julie sells the stock.

What is Julie's basis in the 5,000 shares she acquired through ISOs?

Answer: $25,000 is the regular tax basis (5,000 shares acquired × $5 per share exercise price).

What if: Suppose that five years after Julie exercised her ISOs and acquired 5,000 TPI shares with a basis of $5 per share, she sold all of her shares for $25 per share. What is the amount and character of the gain she will recognize on the sale?

Answer: $100,000 long-term capital gain, calculated as follows:

Description	Amount	Explanation
(1) Amount realized (sales proceeds)	$ 125,000	5,000 shares × $25
(2) Tax basis	25,000	See basis calculation above
Long-term capital gain recognized	**$100,000**	(1) − (2)

When an employee holding an ISO fails to meet either of the holding periods—*holding the options for at least two years after the grant date and holding the stock for at least one year after the exercise date*—the sale of stock is classified as a **disqualifying disposition,** and the bargain element (i.e., sales price minus exercise price) is taxed at the time of the stock sale as ordinary income—essentially the same treatment as a NQO but recognized on the date of the stock sale rather than the exercise date. Thus, when holders of ISOs execute same-day sales, or hold the shares for less than one year after exercise, they forgo the potential tax benefits of deferring the gain and having the bargain element taxed at lower capital gains rates—but they also eliminate the investment risk they would otherwise have to bear by holding the stock long enough to meet two-year-from-grant-date and one-year-from-exercise holding period requirements.

[20]§422(a)(1).

[21]When taxpayers exercise ISOs, the bargain element is added to their alternative minimum taxable income, which increases the likelihood that the employee will have an alternative minimum tax (AMT) liability. We discuss the alternative minimum tax in the Individual Income Tax Computation and Tax Credits chapter.

Example 12-10

What If: Assume that Julie exercised her ISOs and executed a same-day sale of the 5,000 shares on the vesting date (January 1, year 3) when the share price was $15. What are the amount and character of income she will recognize on these transactions?

Answer: $50,000 of ordinary income, as calculated below. Because Julie's sale is a disqualifying disposition, the transactions are recast as though she exercised NQOs.

Description	Amount	Explanation
(1) Shares acquired with ISOs that were disqualified (became NQOs)	5,000	
(2) Market price per share	$ 15	
(3) Exercise price	5	Exhibit 12-3
(4) Bargain element per share	$ 10	(2) − (3)
Bargain element (ordinary income)	**$50,000**	(1) × (4)

What If: Assume that Julie exercised her ISOs and sold the 5,000 shares nine months after exercise (September 1, year 4) when the share price was $13. What are the amount and character of income she will recognize on these transactions?

Answer: $40,000 of ordinary income, as calculated below. Because Julie's sale is a disqualifying disposition and the market price of the employer's stock has declined since the exercise date, the bargain element is the difference between the fair market value on the date of the disqualifying disposition and the exercise price.

Description	Amount	Explanation
(1) Shares acquired with ISOs that were disqualified 9 months later	5,000	
(2) Per share market price on date of disqualifying disposition	$ 13	
(3) Exercise price	5	Exhibit 12-3
(4) Bargain element per share	$ 8	(2) − (3)
Ordinary income	**$40,000**	(1) × (4)

THE KEY FACTS

Incentive Stock Options (ISOs)

- No tax consequences on grant date.
- No tax consequences on vesting date.
- No regular tax consequences on exercise date if employee holds stock for two years from grant date and one year from exercise date.
  - If holding requirements are not met (if there is a disqualifying disposition), the options become an NQO.
- For AMT, the bargain element is included in AMT income on the exercise date.
- When employee sells stock, employee recognizes long-term capital gain or loss on difference between selling price and exercise price.
- Employers receive no deduction unless employee doesn't meet holding period requirements.

TAXES IN THE REAL WORLD Stock Options

Elon Musk co-founded Tesla in 2003. In 2010, Tesla went public. Fast forward to 2012, Tesla was building cars by hand and producing only about five cars a week. Needless to say, Tesla was struggling and its stock price was $6.06 per share when the market closed on August 12, 2012. To create incentives for Elon to grow the company, Tesla's Board of Directors created a nonqualified stock option (NQOs) plan on August 13, 2012, with 10 milestones. The NQO plan granted Elon the right to exercise or acquire 26,374,505 Tesla shares at an exercise price of $6.24 per share (both the number of shares and exercise price have been adjusted for a 5-1 stock split occurring on August 31, 2020). The plan indicated that the options vest in ten equal installments based on Tesla's attainment of operational and market capitalization milestones, and that these NQOs expire on August 13, 2022.

Elon did what many founders do, he held onto most of the options even as the stock price rose. Tesla's 2021 proxy statement disclosed that in October of 2021 Elon still held NQOs to exercise 22,862,050 more Tesla shares at the $6.24 exercise price and that he must exercise (use) them or lose them by August 13, 2022. The problem is that each time Elon exercises a

(continued on page 12-14)

NQO to acquire a share, he must pay Tesla the $6.24 exercise price and pay the IRS $375 in income taxes (see how the $375 tax liability is calculated below). When a NQO is exercised, the taxpayer must include the value of the bargain element (the difference between the current market price of the stock and the exercise price) into taxable income. For each share acquired through the NQO exercise, Elon will include the $1,013.02 ($1,019.26 market price – $6.24 exercise price) bargain element into taxable income and pay taxes of $375 ($1,013.02 bargain element × 37% the highest marginal tax rate). Assuming he exercises all the NQOs, Elon will pay Tesla $143 million ($6.24 × 22,862,050 shares) for the exercised shares. He will also recognize $23.3 billion (22,862,050 shares × $1,013.02 bargain element) in taxable income and pay $8.6 billion ($23.2 billion × 37%) more in federal income tax.

Even though Elon currently owns a staggering 177,032,165 Tesla shares (based on his December 28, 2021 SEC filing) and has a net worth of $227 billion—making him the world's richest man—all that wealth isn't liquid. Elon has said that he would prefer to keep all of his Tesla shares—stating that he was the first to put money into Tesla, and he wants to be the last one to take money out. But without selling shares, it would be difficult and very likely he would not have enough cash to pay Tesla the $143 million for NQO exercises to acquire the shares and still be able to pay the IRS $8.6 billion in taxes on the income from the NQO exercise.

Elon's strategy became clear during November and December of 2021, when he filed 11 reports with the SEC disclosing that all of the remaining 2012 NQOs were exercised to acquire 22,862,050 Tesla shares. Additionally, the SEC disclosures reveal that Elon sold 9,880,662 Tesla share using same-day sales for $10.1 billion, which provides him with enough cash to pay for both the NQO exercises and taxes. The NQOs exercised, the Tesla market price, NQO exercise price, and same-day sale prices were all obtained from Elon's SEC filings which also noted that "the shares of common stock were sold solely to satisfy the reporting person's tax withholding obligations related to the exercise of stock options."

In 2018, Tesla's Board of Directors granted Elon another set of stock options with rights to purchase 33,773,400 more Tesla shares, which vest to Elon as Tesla reaches 12 additional operational and market capitalization milestones. So sometime between now and 2028 (when the new set of stock options expire) things might get interesting again.

Employer Tax Considerations for Stock Options As is true for employees, an employer's tax treatment of stock options depends on whether the options are NQOs or ISOs.

Nonqualified options. With NQOs, employers deduct the bargain element that employees recognize as compensation or ordinary income when the employees exercise NQOs.[22] From the employer's perspective, no other date is relevant for tax purposes.

Example 12-11

What if: Suppose that in year 3, Julie exercises NQOs to acquire 20,000 shares of TPI and reports $300,000 of ordinary income for the bargain element of the exercise (see Example 12-8). How much compensation expense for Julie's stock option exercise can TPI deduct in year 3?

Answer: $300,000. TPI can deduct the bargain element of Julie's exercise.

Note that this tax deduction is not tied to a cash payment. Thus, unless employers purchase their own shares to satisfy their employees' stock option exercises, they'll be entitled to a tax deduction without incurring any cash outflows.

[22]The employer's deduction is limited for covered employees with compensation over the $1 million limit.

Incentive stock options. Employers typically don't view ISOs as favorably as NQOs because (1) ISOs don't provide them with the same tax benefits (no tax deduction) and (2) the administrative requirements can be burdensome. That is, as long as the employee doesn't sell the stock in a disqualifying disposition, the employer will not get a tax deduction for ISOs. For this reason, employers lose potential tax benefits by issuing ISOs rather than NQOs. On the other hand, start-up companies or employers with net operating losses may actually benefit by issuing ISOs instead of NQOs. Due to their zero percent tax rate, companies in this position don't lose tax benefits by granting ISOs; however, because of the potential tax benefits ISOs provide to their employees relative to NQOs, they may be able to persuade their employees to accept relatively fewer ISOs than NQOs.

ETHICS

Many companies use stock options as a form of equity compensation—to motivate executives and key employees. Some stock option issuers have either backdated and/or repriced stock options. Backdating is an illegal practice by which a company chooses a date in the past when the stock price was at its lowest point in order to maximize executive compensation. Stock option repricing is used when stock options are underwater (i.e., the market price is below the strike price). Repricing simply resets the strike price to a price below the current market price. While backdating options is illegal and obviously unethical, what do you think about the practice of repricing stock options?

Accounting issues. The Financial Accounting Standards Board (FASB) has mandated the expensing of stock options (both NQOs and ISOs) for financial accounting purposes for years beginning on or after January 1, 2006.[23] Companies must estimate the economic value of options on the grant date and then amortize these costs on a straight-line basis over the vesting period of the options.[24]

Example 12-12

What if: Assume that an accounting employee benefits specialist calculated the economic value of Julie's stock option grant (NQOs and ISOs) to be $32,000. Also assume that Julie's options vest 50 percent in year 1 (the year of the grant) and 50 percent in year 2. What compensation expense for financial accounting would TPI report for Julie's stock options in year 1 and year 2?

Answer: $16,000 ($32,000 × 50%) in year 1 and $16,000 in year 2.

THE KEY FACTS

Stock Option Expense: GAAP vs. Tax

- For tax purposes, employers deduct the bargain element of NQOs on the exercise date but receive no tax deduction for ISOs unless they become disqualified.
- For GAAP purposes, employers expense the estimated value of the option pro rata over the vesting period.

As you probably realize by now, the tax rules governing the treatment of stock options differ markedly from generally accepted accounting principles in terms of both the amount and the timing of the stock option expense. To compare the tax and book treatment, we present TPI's book expense and tax deduction resulting from its stock option grant to Julie (given prior assumptions) in Exhibit 12-4.

The tremendous difference between the book and tax numbers presented in Exhibit 12-4 is driven by the increase in TPI's share price, from $5 on the grant date to $20 on the exercise date. The economic valuation of the stock options used to determine the book expense did not factor in the stock appreciation before exercise.

[23]Accounting Standards Codification (ASC) Topic 718, Stock Compensation.

[24]Although the exercise price of compensatory stock options typically equals the stock price on the grant date, compensatory options are, nevertheless, economically valuable on the grant date. They have economic value because the stock price may eventually exceed the exercise price before the options expire. To determine economic value, companies typically use either the Black-Scholes option pricing model or the binomial option pricing model.

EXHIBIT 12-4 **TPI's Tax Deductions and Book Expense from Stock Option Grant to Julie**

	Tax Deduction if Stock Price Increases	Tax Deduction if Stock Price Decreases	Book Expense
Year 1	$ 0	$0	$16,000
Year 2	0	0	16,000
Year 3	300,000	0*	0

*There would be no exercise because the exercise price exceeds the stock price.

Restricted Stock

When an employee receives a **restricted stock** award, the employee receives actual stock with voting rights and the right to receive dividends if any are declared. However, until the restrictions lapse on the vesting date, the employee cannot sell the stock. If the employee does not meet the vesting requirements (e.g., the employee quits before the stock vests), the employee forfeits the shares. Exhibit 12-5 provides a timeline of an employee's restricted stock award.

EXHIBIT 12-5 **Sample Timeline for Restricted Stock**

If Julie doesn't make any special tax elections, the economic and tax consequences of Julie's initial restricted stock award depend on the future share price of TPI, on the vesting date of the restricted stock. The restricted stock examples in this chapter initially draw from the timeline below for the necessary assumptions regarding these key variables.

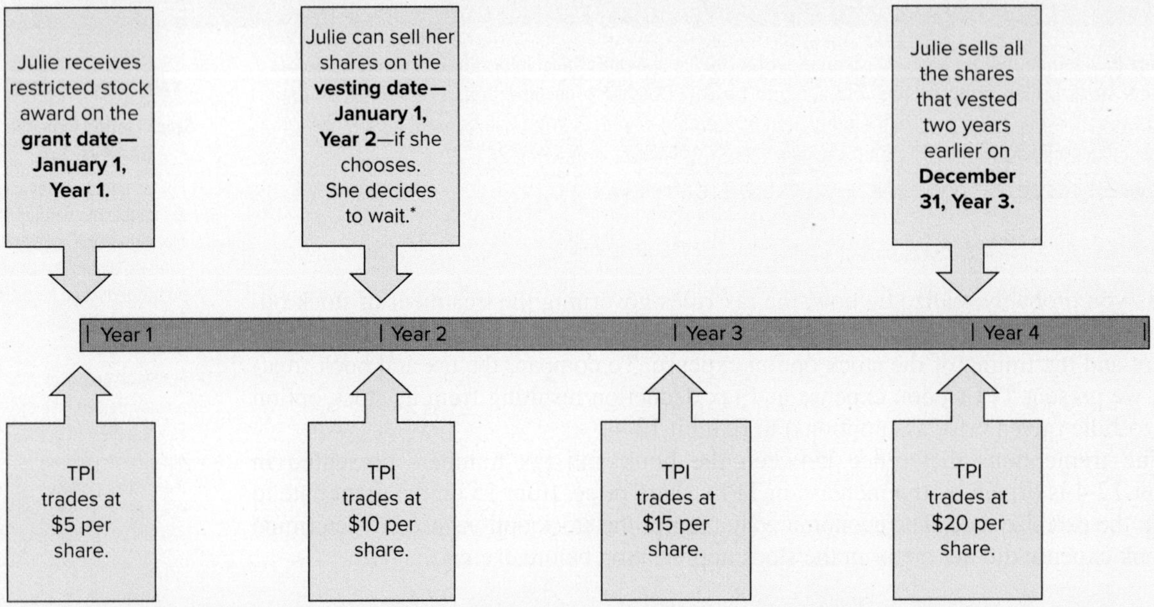

*As stipulated in her offer letter, Julie is able to sell the 10,000 shares of TPI stock when the restrictions lapse on the vesting date (January 1 of year 2).

Example 12-13

Given the assumptions regarding the 10,000 shares of restricted stock that will vest on January 1, year 2 (see Exhibit 12-5), how much would Julie's wealth increase (before taxes) on the vesting date if TPI's stock is trading at $10 on January 1, year 2?

Answer: Julie's wealth would increase by $100,000 (10,000 shares × $10 per share) before taxes.

What if: Assuming that the stock decreased to $3 per share on the vesting date, and no dividends were declared, by how much would Julie's wealth increase or decrease on the vesting date?

Answer: $30,000 increase (10,000 shares × $3 per share). Until the vesting date, Julie was not entitled to any economic benefit from the restricted stock. On the vesting date, however, she is entitled to stock valued at $30,000. Thus, the vesting of Julie's restricted stock increases her wealth even though the stock price has decreased between the grant date and vesting date (unlike stock options, which would be worthless).

THE KEY FACTS

Restricted Stock

- On vesting date, employee recognizes market value of stock as ordinary income.
- Employee takes fair market value basis in stock.
- Holding period for stock begins on vesting date.
- If employee never vests, employer receives no deduction for basis in stock.
- Employer deducts value of stock on vesting date.

Employee Tax Considerations for Restricted Stock Restricted stock is taxed like NQOs with two important distinctions: While employees receiving NQOs are taxed on the bargain element of the shares when they exercise their options, employees receiving restricted stock are taxed on the *full fair market value* of the shares *on the date the restrictions lapse*. They are taxed on the fair market value of the stock because they received the stock without any payment requirements (contrast this with the exercise price paid for stock options).[25] The taxpayer's basis in the stock when the restrictions lapse is the fair market value of the stock on the day the restrictions lapse (vesting date). The employee's holding period for the stock begins on the vesting date. Any subsequent change in stock price will result in capital gain or loss to the employee upon sale of the stock.

Example 12-14

Assume that the restricted stock vests in year 2 when the market price is $10 per share (see Exhibit 12-5). What are the amount and character of the income Julie recognizes in year 2?

Answer: $100,000 of ordinary income (10,000 shares × $10 per share).

Assume the same facts as above and that Julie sells the shares in year 4 when the market price is $20 per share. What are the amount and character of the income she will recognize on the sale?

Answer: $100,000 long-term capital gain, calculated as follows:

Description	Amount	Explanation
(1) Amount realized	$ 200,000	10,000 shares × $20 per share
(2) Tax basis	100,000	FMV on vesting date
Long-term capital gain	**$100,000**	(1) – (2)

What if: Assume the original facts except that Julie sells the shares in year 4 and the market price is now $4 per share. What are the amount and character of the gain or loss she recognizes on the sale?

Answer: $60,000 long-term capital loss, calculated as follows:

Description	Amount	Explanation
(1) Amount realized	$ 40,000	10,000 shares × $4 per share
(2) Adjusted basis	100,000	FMV on vesting date
Long-term capital loss	**$(60,000)**	(1) – (2)

THE KEY FACTS

Restricted Stock *with* Section 83(b) Election

- On grant date, employee recognizes market value of stock as ordinary income.
- Employee takes fair market value basis in stock.
- Holding period for stock begins on grant date.
- If employee never vests, employer receives no deduction for basis in stock.
- Employer deducts value of stock on grant date.

83(b) election. An **83(b) election** accelerates the ordinary income recognition on the fair market value of a restricted stock award from the vesting date (when the restrictions lapse) to the grant date. Simply put, the 83(b) election allows the taxpayer to treat the

[25]The income recognized when the restrictions lapse is compensation income that is subject to FICA and other payroll taxes.

restricted stock award as if there were no restrictions for tax purposes (the legal restrictions still exist, however). Employees may make the election no later than 30 days after the grant date. The election is irrevocable. While accelerating income is generally undesirable from a tax planning perspective (see the Tax Planning Strategies and Related Limitations chapter), if an employee receives restricted stock worth a relatively low value, it almost always makes sense to make the election because the taxes paid currently are relatively small compared to the potential future tax savings. If the employee believes the employer's stock value will increase between the grant date and the date the restrictions lapse, the election converts appreciation that would have been taxed as compensation at ordinary income rates into a capital gain that is taxed at more favorable long-term capital gain rates (assuming the shares are held for more than one year after the grant date).

Example 12-15

What if: How much tax on the restricted stock will Julie pay in year 1 if she does not make an 83(b) election?

Answer: $0. The stock has not vested yet, so she has no income.

What if: How much tax on the restricted stock will Julie pay in year 1 if she makes an 83(b) election?

Answer: $12,000 [$50,000 ordinary income (10,000 shares × $5 per share) × 24 percent marginal ordinary tax rate].

What if: How much tax will Julie pay in year 2 on the restricted stock (the year the restricted stock vests) if she does not make an 83(b) election in year 1 (the stock is trading at $10 per share on the vesting date)?

Answer: $24,000 [$100,000 ordinary income (10,000 shares × $10 per share) × 24 percent marginal ordinary tax rate].

What if: How much tax will Julie pay in year 2 on the restricted stock if she makes an 83(b) election in year 1?

Answer: $0. With the 83(b) election, Julie treats the stock as though it vested in year 1, not year 2, so she does not have a taxable event in year 2 when the stock actually vests.

What if: How much tax will Julie pay in year 3 on the restricted stock when she sells the stock for $20 per share (on December 31) if she *does not* make an 83(b) election in year 1?

Answer: $15,000 {[$200,000 (10,000 × $20) − $100,000 tax basis (fair market value on vesting date in year 2)] × 15 percent long-term capital gains rate}.

What if: How much tax will Julie pay in year 3 on the restricted stock when she sells the stock for $20 per share (on December 31) if she makes the 83(b) election in year 1?

Answer: $22,500 {[$200,000 (10,000 × $20) − $50,000 tax basis (fair market value in year 1 when she makes the 83(b) election)] × 15 percent long-term capital gains rate}.

What if: Given the analyses above, what amount of taxes would Julie save by making an 83(b) election (ignoring the time value of money)?

Answer: $4,500 ($39,000 in taxes without election − $34,500 in taxes with election), computed as follows:

Taxes Payable

Description	Without Election	With Election
Year 1 taxes on ordinary income	$ 0	$ 12,000
Year 2 taxes on ordinary income	24,000	0
Year 4 taxes on long-term capital gains	15,000	22,500
Total taxes	**$39,000**	**$34,500**

Note that Julie reduces her total taxes payable because the election allows her to convert $50,000 of income from ordinary income taxed at 24 percent into a long-term capital gain taxed at 15 percent. However, in order to have a greater portion of her gains taxed at the preferential capital gains rate, Julie gave up some tax deferral when she had to pay part of her tax liability sooner when she accelerated $50,000 of income from year 3 into year 1.

Also note that this computation overstates to some degree the benefits of making the 83(b) election because it ignores the time value of money.

Employees making the 83(b) election essentially trade off some additional current tax now in order to convert ordinary income into a long-term capital gain later. Accordingly, the 83(b) election is advisable when the potential for growth in the stock value is high and the employee has the ability to pay the additional taxes due. If an employee makes an 83(b) election and then forfeits the stock for any reason, the employee cannot deduct the loss on the forfeiture.[26] Thus, the risk of making the election is that if the employee forfeits the stock, the employee will have paid tax on value never received.

Employer Tax Considerations for Restricted Stock Like the tax treatment of NQOs, the employer's deduction for restricted stock equals the amount of ordinary income reported by its employees on receipt of the restricted stock. The timing of the deduction is determined by the employee's decision regarding the 83(b) election. If the employee makes an 83(b) election, the employer claims the deduction in the year the restricted stock is granted. Otherwise, the employer claims a deduction when the restrictions lapse.

The accounting treatment for restricted stock is similar to the accounting treatment for stock options.[27] If grants of restricted stock vest over time, the market value of restricted stock on the *date of grant* is expensed pro rata over the vesting period.

Example 12-16

What if: Given the assumptions in Exhibit 12-5, what amounts can TPI deduct for tax purposes in year 1 and in year 2 assuming Julie *does not* make an 83(b) election?

Answer: $0 in year 1 and $100,000 in year 2 (10,000 shares of restricted stock vested × $10 per share market price at vesting date).

What if: What amounts can TPI deduct in year 1 and in year 2 if Julie *does* make an 83(b) election?

Answer: $50,000 in year 1 (10,000 shares of restricted stock awarded × $5 per share market price on the grant date) and $0 in year 2.

What is TPI's compensation expense for financial accounting purposes for Julie's restricted stock in year 1 and in year 2?

Answer: $50,000 book expense in year 1. Because the value of Julie's restricted stock award on the date of grant is $50,000, TPI expenses the award on its books over the vesting period, which, in this case, is just one year (it has a one-year vesting period).

Restricted stock units (RSUs). Restricted stock units (RSUs) are units that are valued in employer stock at the time of grant. However, unlike restricted stock, upon settlement RSUs can be exchanged for employer stock, cash, or some combination of cash and stock depending upon the terms of the RSU agreement. RSUs do not provide dividend income or voting rights because actual shares are not owned by the employee; however, some employers contractually pay a dividend equivalent to the employee. RSUs are growing in popularity and are used by companies like Apple (see Exhibit 12-6) and Amazon. The value of the RSUs is

THE KEY FACTS

Restricted Stock Expense: GAAP vs. Tax

- For tax purposes, employers deduct the market value of stock when the employee recognizes income.
- For GAAP purposes, employers deduct the market value at grant date over the vesting period.

EXHIBIT 12-6 Excerpt from Apple Inc.'s 2020 Proxy Statement

Long-Term Equity Awards
The equity component of our named executive officers' compensation emphasizes long-term shareholder value creation through performance-based and time-based RSU awards.

Performance-Based RSUs. RSU awards with performance-based vesting are a substantial, at-risk component of our named executive officers' compensation tied to Apple's long-term performance. The number of performance-based RSUs that vest depends on Apple's total shareholder return relative to the other companies in the S&P 500 ("Relative TSR") for the performance period. The Compensation Committee chose Relative TSR as a straightforward and objective metric to evaluate our performance against the performance of other companies and to align the interests of our named executive officers with the interests of our shareholders in creating long-term value.

[26]Reg. §1.83-2(a).
[27]ASC Topic 718.

> We measure Relative TSR for the applicable performance period based on the change in each company's stock price during that period, taking into account any dividends paid during that period, which are assumed to be reinvested in the stock. A 20-trading-day averaging period is used to determine the beginning and ending stock price values used to calculate the total shareholder return of Apple and the other companies in the S&P 500. This averaging period mitigates the impact on the long-term Relative TSR results of one-day or short-term stock price fluctuations at the beginning or end of the performance period. The change in stock price value from the beginning to the end of the period is divided by the beginning stock price value to determine total shareholder return.
>
> **Time-Based RSUs.** RSU awards with time-based vesting align the interests of our named executive officers with the interests of our shareholders by promoting the stability and retention of a high-performing executive team over the longer term. Vesting schedules for time-based awards are generally longer than typical peer company practices and require continuous service over multiple years, as described below.

See page 40 of proxy statement: https://d18rn0p25nwr6d.cloudfront.net/CIK-0000320193/492dd75b-15df-4826-ba30-8828289290cf.pdf.

taxed to the employee as ordinary income when the restrictions lapse. Unlike restricted stock, employees with RSUs cannot make an 83(b) election. Employers receive a deduction equal to the fair market value of the RSUs when the RSUs vest (restrictions lapse).

Qualified Equity Grants Employees of publicly traded companies have access to an efficient market to liquidate equity-based compensation when liquidity needs arise. In contrast, employees of private corporations do not have an efficient market to help them alleviate liquidity constraints created through purchasing and/or paying tax liabilities on equity-based compensation. To alleviate this liquidity inequity, the tax laws allow employees of private corporations to elect to defer for up to five years the income tax liability for equity-based compensation in the form of a **qualified equity grant**.[28]

A qualified equity grant is a grant of qualified stock of an eligible corporation that is received by a qualified employee. Qualified stock is either an NQO or RSU issued as compensation to a qualified employee.[29] A qualified employee is an employee of an eligible corporation who is not an excluded employee. An excluded employee is an employee who owns at least 1 percent of the stock of the corporation at any time in the prior 10 years or a covered employee of the employer at any time.[30] An eligible corporation is a nonpublicly traded corporation that grants NQOs or RSUs to at least 80 percent of its domestic employees.[31] Qualified equity grants are designed specifically to help the rank-and-file employees of these private companies. Qualified employees must make an 83(i) election [similar to an 83(b) election] no later than 30 days after (1) the first date the employee's right to the RSU is substantially vested or is transferable, whichever occurs earlier, or (2) the date the employee exercises an NQO.[32] Instead of including income at the exercise of an NQO or the vesting of an RSU, the employee's qualified equity grant is taxable at the earliest of the following dates: (1) the date the qualified stock is transferrable, (2) the date the employee becomes an "excluded employee," (3) the date on which any stock of the employer becomes publicly traded, (4) the date that is five years after the rights of the employee in such qualified stock are transferable or are not subject to a substantial risk of forfeiture, or (5) the date the employee revokes the 83(i) election.[33]

Equity-Based Compensation Summary

To summarize our discussion of the tax treatment of equity-based compensation, Exhibit 12-7 highlights the general tax treatment of NQOs, ISOs, and restricted stock on

[28]Section 83(i) applies to options exercised or RSUs settled after December 31, 2017. Notice 2018-97 gives additional guidance, including an option for employers to opt out of allowing employees to make the deferral election.

[29]§83(i)(2).

[30]§83(i)(3).

[31]§83(i)(2).

[32]§83(i)(4).

[33]§83(i)(2). Additional details of qualified equity grants are beyond the scope of this text.

a per-share basis from both employee and employer perspectives given an arbitrary time series of share prices. In addition to showing future share prices, the exhibit assumes options are exercisable for the share price on the grant date.

EXHIBIT 12-7 Reportable Income and Deductions from Equity-Based Compensation (for given time frame and stock prices)

	Party Affected	NQOs	ISOs	Restricted Stock
Grant date				
Year 1	Employee	No effect	No effect	No effect
Stock Price = $1 Exercise Price = $1	Employer	No effect	No effect	No effect
Vesting date				
Year 4	Employee	No effect	No effect	$6/share ordinary income
Stock price = $6/share	Employer	No effect	No effect	$6/share ordinary deduction
Exercise date				
Year 6	Employee	$10/share ordinary income	No effect*	N/A
Stock price = $11	Employer	$10/share ordinary deduction	No effect	N/A
Sale date				
Year 8	Employee	$5/share LT capital gain	$15/share LT capital gain	$10/share LT capital gain
Stock price = $16/share	Employer	No effect	No effect	No effect

*$10 per share is included in alternative minimum taxable income.

FRINGE BENEFITS

LO 12-3

(continued from page 12-8 . . .)

The final section of TPI's offer letter indicated Julie would receive fringe benefits in the form of health and dental insurance (value of $18,000), $750,000 of group-term life insurance, a biennial $30,000 automobile allowance, employer educational assistance, and a flexible spending account for medical expenses. ■

Employees generally receive most of their compensation in the form of cash salary or wages. However, employers often provide noncash benefits to employees in addition to their cash compensation. These **fringe benefits** range from the common (e.g., health insurance) to the exotic (e.g., use of a corporate aircraft). As a general rule, because fringe benefits are employee compensation, they are taxable to the employee upon receipt. In fact, fringe benefits are specifically mentioned in the definition of gross income. As we indicated in the Gross Income and Exclusions chapter, §61(a) indicates that "gross income means all income from whatever source derived, including . . . (1) Compensation for services, including fees, commissions, *fringe benefits,* and similar items" (emphasis added). This definition of income notwithstanding, the tax law specifically *excludes* certain fringe benefits from an employee's gross income. Thus, some fringe benefits are taxable, while others are not.

THE KEY FACTS

Taxable Fringe Benefits

- Employees recognize compensation or ordinary income on all benefits received unless specifically excluded by the tax law.
- Employees treat benefits received like taxable cash compensation, both of which are subject to FICA.
- Employers deduct cost and pay employer's share of FICA taxes on benefit.

Taxable Fringe Benefits

Taxable fringe benefits are fringe benefits not specifically excluded from gross income. Congress views many of the taxable fringe benefits as luxuries and chooses not to subsidize them. Taxable fringe benefits include such things as below-market interest rate loans (see discussion in the Gross Income and Exclusions chapter), gym memberships, season tickets to the local NBA team, an automobile allowance for a personal automobile, moving expense reimbursements, and anything else not specifically excluded by the tax law. Employers generally provide taxable fringe benefits to executives and higher-salaried employees rather than to their rank-and-file employees.

Employee Considerations for Taxable Fringe Benefits From an employee's perspective, taxable fringe benefits are taxed just like cash. Taxable fringe benefits cost employees the amount of tax they must pay on the benefits.

Example 12-17

Julie's offer includes a biennial auto allowance of up to $30,000. That is, every other year, TPI will reimburse Julie for an automobile purchase up to $30,000. TPI provides this benefit to executives who interact with the public on a regular basis. Julie purchases a Toyota 4Runner with a retail price of $45,000. What income tax is Julie required to pay if she applies the auto allowance toward the purchase? What is Julie's after-tax cost of the automobile if her marginal tax rate is 24 percent (ignoring FICA and sales taxes)?

Answer: $7,200 in income taxes and $12,200 of after-tax cost, computed as follows:

Description	Amount	Explanation
(1) Fair market value of Toyota	$ 45,000	
(2) Automobile allowance	30,000	Taxable fringe benefit
(3) Julie's additional cost	$ 15,000	(1) − (2)
(4) **Income tax on allowance**	**7,200**	(2) × 24%
Total after-tax cost	**$22,200**	(3) + (4)

From Julie's perspective, this is a pretty good deal—particularly if she was willing to pay the market price for the car without the allowance.

Employees may prefer a taxable benefit to an equivalent amount of cash when they benefit from employer-provided quantity or group discounts associated with the benefit. For example, many companies pay employees' premiums for **group-term life insurance** as a fringe benefit, in part because they can purchase the insurance at a lower rate than employees could individually. However, employees must recognize a certain amount of gross income when employers pay life insurance premiums for employee policies with a death benefit in excess of $50,000.[34] Consequently, a portion of the group-term life insurance benefit is taxable and a portion is nontaxable. In these circumstances, the employer determines the employee's taxable amount using a table provided in the Treasury Regulations. An excerpt of this table is provided in Exhibit 12-8.[35] To compute the annual taxable benefit, taxpayers use the following steps:

Step 1: Subtract $50,000 from the death benefit of their employer-provided group-term life insurance policy.

Step 2: Divide the Step 1 result by $1,000.

Step 3: Multiply the result from Step 2 by the cost per $1,000 of protection for one month from the table (Exhibit 12-8) based on the taxpayer's age.

Step 4: Multiply the outcome of Step 3 by the number of months the benefit was received during the taxable year.

[34]§79.

[35]Reg. §1.79-3(d)(2) provides an age-based table and instructions for how to calculate the employee's includable amount.

EXHIBIT 12-8 Uniform Premiums for $1,000 of Group-Term Life Insurance Protection

5-Year Age Bracket	Cost per $1,000 of Protection for One Month
Under 25	$0.05
25 to 29	.06
30 to 34	.08
35 to 39	.09
40 to 44	.10
45 to 49	.15
50 to 54	.23
55 to 59	.43
60 to 64	.66
65 to 69	1.27
70 and above	2.06

Reg. §1.79-3(d)(2) and also published in IRS Publication 15-B.

Example 12-18

Julie's offer from TPI includes $750,000 of group-term life insurance. TPI's cost to provide Julie the insurance is $500 per year. If Julie were to purchase the insurance herself, she would pay $2,000 per year. Assume that Julie is 37 years old. Based on the Treasury's table (see Exhibit 12-8), the monthly premium per $1,000 of insurance is $.09. What is Julie's taxable compensation included in gross income from receiving the group-term life insurance benefit? What does this benefit cost Julie (ignoring FICA taxes)?

Answer: $756 included in Julie's gross income and $181 in income taxes paid, calculated as follows. Julie's cost is the income and Medicare taxes she must pay on the compensation.

Group-Term Life Insurance Description	Amount	Explanation
(1) Insurance coverage	$750,000	Provided by employer
(2) Excluded coverage	(50,000)	Nontaxable portion
(3) Taxable benefit	$700,000	(1) + (2) (Step 1)
(4) Divide by 1,000	1,000	Divide by 1,000 (Step 2)
(5) Result of Step 2	700	(3)/(4)
(6) Monthly cost per $1,000	× 0.09	Taxable portion per $1,000 (from Exhibit 12-8)
(7) Monthly benefit	$ 63	(5) × (6) (Step 3)
(8) Months	× 12	Annualize monthly taxable amount
(9) Annual taxable benefit	**$ 756**	(7) × (8) (Step 4)
Income taxes paid	**$ 181**	(9) × 24%

Note that Julie's income tax cost is not based on TPI's actual cost ($500) of providing the policy.

Taxpayers receiving taxable fringe benefits may experience some financial strain because they must pay tax on the benefits. Frequently, when employers provide taxable fringe benefits to senior executives, they also provide the executives enough cash to cover the taxes so the benefit(s) costs the executive essentially nothing.[36] This is commonly referred to as a *gross-up*. For example, ConocoPhillips's 2021 proxy statement reveals that it made payments of $20.1 million to R. M. Lance, its chairman, including $3,202 for

[36]Companies generally choose a formula to determine how much cash (gross-up) they need to pay the employee in addition to the taxable benefit to ensure the benefit costs the employee nothing.

a tax reimbursement gross-up.[37] Employees can choose to forgo a benefit if they prefer not to pay taxes on it.

Employer Considerations for Taxable Fringe Benefits Like employees, employers treat taxable fringe benefits just like cash compensation. That is, the employer has an outlay for the cost of the benefit and deducts its *cost* of the benefit for tax purposes, not the *value* of the benefit to the employee.[38] As we mention above, employers are often able to purchase fringe benefits at a lower cost than individual employees can. For example, employers may receive a group discount for purchasing life insurance, automobiles, financial or tax planning services, or accident insurance.

Example 12-19

In Example 12-19, TPI provided Julie with $750,000 of group-term life insurance. Its cost of providing the entire $750,000 of coverage is $500 per year. If Julie were to purchase the policy herself, it would cost her $2,000 per year. What is TPI's after-tax cost of the partially taxable group-term life insurance benefit it provided to Julie?

Answer: TPI's after-tax cost of the benefit provided is $395, calculated as follows:

Description	Amount	Explanation
(1) Cost of policy	$500	
(2) Income tax benefit	105	(1) × 21%
Total after-tax cost	**$395**	(1) – (2)

Finally, employers may discriminate between employees when providing benefits. That is, they can select which employees receive benefits and which do not. Not surprisingly, the more highly compensated employees tend to receive these benefits. For example, as described in an excerpt from Walmart's 2021 proxy statement in Exhibit 12-9, Walmart's perquisite and supplemental benefits provide certain officers with use of the company aircraft. Walmart is unlikely to offer these same benefits to its hourly sales associates.

EXHIBIT 12-9 Excerpt from Walmart's 2021 Proxy Statement

What perquisites and other benefits do our NEOs receive?

Our NEOs receive a limited number of perquisites and supplemental benefits. We cover the cost of annual physical examinations for our NEOs and provide each NEO with personal use of our aircraft for a limited number of hours each year. Our NEOs also receive company-paid life and accidental death and dismemberment insurance. Additionally, our NEOs are entitled to benefits available to our officers, such as participation in the Deferred Compensation Matching Plan, and benefits available to associates generally, including a Walmart discount card, a limited 15% match on purchases of Shares through our Associate Stock Purchase Plan, participation in our 401(k) Plan, medical benefits, and foreign business travel insurance. We provide these perquisites and supplemental benefits to attract talented executives to our company and to retain our current executives, and we believe their limited cost is outweighed by the benefits to our company.

See page 65 of proxy statement: https://corporate.walmart.com/media-library/document/2021-proxy-statement/_proxyDocument?id=00000178-f54e-db6f-adfe-fdcf45560000.

[37]A tax gross-up is an additional payment made to an employee to offset or partially offset the cost of taxes on a benefit received.

[38]The employer also has an outlay for the cost of the employer's share of FICA taxes on the taxable portion of benefits it provides to employees and receives a deduction for the FICA taxes paid.

TAXES IN THE REAL WORLD Fringe Benefits

Comcast Takes Off

At Comcast, the company's executive usage of aircraft paid for by the company has taken off. According to two excerpts from Comcast's 2021 Proxy Statement, this amount exceeds $3.6 million:

> For security and business reasons, Company practices and policy strongly encourage, and in some cases may require, Mr. Roberts to use Company-provided aircraft for business and personal travel. Our other NEOs also have access to Company-provided aircraft for personal travel, as it affords all of our NEOs greater security, allows travel time to be used productively and enables them to be immediately available to respond to business priorities from any location.
>
> Our policy allows an NEO to bring guests, such as family members, on flights on Company-provided aircraft. The NEOs are required to pay us for personal use of Company-provided aircraft in amounts determined by Company policy. The NEOs are imputed income for costs related to use of Company-provided aircraft when required under Internal Revenue Code guidelines. We do not reimburse the NEOs for any taxes incurred as a result of imputed income. In addition, the Internal Revenue Code limits the amount that we can deduct for the personal use of Company-provided aircraft to the amount recognized as income by our executives who use the aircraft; the amounts in the table above do not include our 2020 disallowed tax deduction of $3.6 million resulting from the personal use of Company-provided aircraft by our NEOs and any guests.
>
> The amounts reflected for each NEO on account of personal use of Company-provided aircraft indicate the extent to which the incremental cost of such use exceeds the amount paid to us by the NEO. The aggregate incremental cost for a personal flight on a charter plane is the cost of the flight as charged to us by the charter company. The aggregate incremental cost for a personal flight taken on a third party-owned plane that is serviced by us includes all variable costs attributable to that flight (including for repositioning flights), such as fuel, trip and allocable maintenance expenses and third-party lease payments. The aggregate incremental cost for a personal flight on a Company plane includes all variable costs for the year, such as fuel, maintenance and other trip expenses, to arrive at a variable cost per hour that we then multiply by the number of hours the NEO used the aircraft for personal travel (including the hours for repositioning flights). These methodologies exclude fixed costs, as these costs do not change based on usage. For all other benefits that would otherwise be considered perquisites, our NEOs are required to pay us in full (and have paid us in full) for such benefits.

Corporate Use of Personal Aircraft

> In connection with Mr. Roberts' use of an aircraft he leases from a third party, we have agreed to provide various operational services for the aircraft for Mr. Roberts and his immediate family members, including by providing pilots and performing general operational and maintenance services. Pursuant to this agreement, Mr. Roberts is responsible for reimbursing us for the costs we incur in operating and maintaining the aircraft. For 2020, Mr. Roberts paid us an aggregate of approximately $418,000 related to this agreement.

Source: See pages 47–48 and 66 of Comcast's 2021 proxy statement: "Notice of 2021 Annual Meeting of Stockholders and Proxy Statement," https://www.cmcsa.com/static-files/5e1868f1-1e29-44db-a35a-9a2253f928d5.

Nontaxable Fringe Benefits

For policy reasons, Congress specifically excludes certain fringe benefits, such as health insurance, from employees' gross income to encourage employers to provide these benefits.[39] We refer to excluded benefits as **nontaxable fringe benefits.** Other nontaxable fringe benefits enable taxpayers to become or stay employed, including meals or lodging for the convenience of the employer, educational assistance, dependent-care benefits, and transportation-related benefits. Finally, some benefits are excluded for simplicity's sake, such as no-additional-cost services, qualified employee discounts, and *de minimis* (small) fringe benefits. Exhibit 12-10 provides a partial list of nontaxable fringe benefits, and in the text that follows, we discuss these benefits in more detail.

[39]The nontaxable fringe benefits are listed with "items specifically excluded from gross income" in §§101–140 of the Internal Revenue Code. Employers are generally prohibited from discriminating among employees with respect to nontaxable fringe benefits (i.e., they cannot offer them only to executives). This chapter indicates whether or not discrimination for a particular benefit is allowed. However, further discussion of the discrimination rules is beyond the scope of this text.

EXHIBIT 12-10 Common Forms of Nontaxable Fringe Benefits

Benefit	Description
Group-term life insurance [§79]	Employer-paid premiums on up to $50,000 group-term life insurance policies are excluded from employees' income.
Health benefits [§§105–106]	Employer-paid premiums covering health, medical, and dental insurance and the benefits provided through the insurance.
Meals or lodging for the convenience of the employer [§119]*	Meals provided on employer's premises and lodging provided by the employer as a condition of employment are excluded from an employee's income. For 2021 and 2022, meals are 50% deductible by the employer, 100% deductible if purchased at a restaurant.
Employee educational assistance [§127]	Up to $5,250 exclusion for tuition, books, and fees. See IRS Publication 970, *Tax Benefits for Education*. The $5,250 exclusion also applies to eligible student loan repayments made by an employer on qualified education loans for the education of the employee (but not of the spouse or dependent).
Dependent-care benefits [§129]	Up to $5,000 exclusion for cost of providing care for a dependent who is under 13 years old or a dependent who is disabled.
No-additional-cost services [§132(a)(1)]	Benefits that don't cost the employer a material amount.
Qualified employee discounts [§132(a)(2)]	Reduced prices on employer's product within certain limits.
Working condition fringe benefits [§132(a)(3)]*	A benefit provided by an employer that would be deductible as an ordinary and necessary business expense by the employee if the employee rather than the employer paid the expense.
De minimis fringe benefits [§132(a)(4)]*	Relatively small and infrequently provided benefits.
Qualified transportation fringe benefits [§132(a)(5)]*	Mass transit passes up to monthly limit of $280, qualified parking up to monthly limit of $280, or use of company-owned carpool vehicles (vans).
Cafeteria plans [§125]	A plan where employees can choose from among various nontaxable fringe benefits or cash. Taxable to the extent employees receive cash.
Flexible spending [§125]	Flexible spending accounts (FSAs) allow employees to set aside a portion of their before-tax salary for payment of health and/or dependent-care benefits. These amounts generally must be used by the end of the year or within the first two and a half months of the next plan year, or employees forfeit the unused balance.[40] For 2022, the amount of before-tax salary an employee may set aside for medical expenses is limited to $2,850, the carryover limit to 2023 is $570, and the before-tax amount that may be set aside for dependent-care expenses is limited to $5,000.

*Employer may discriminate in providing this benefit.

Group-Term Life Insurance As we mentioned in the taxable benefits section, employees may exclude from income the employer-provided benefit for the first $50,000 of group-term life insurance.[41] Any remaining group-term life insurance benefit is taxable

[40]For 2020 through 2022, employers can elect to extend the grace period to 12 months after the plan year (to 2021 and 2022) to use any unused health and dependent care benefits. As of the printing date, the 12 month grace period is not available for carryovers from 2022 to 2023.

[41]§79.

(see Example 12-19). An employer may not discriminate between employees in providing nontaxable group-term life insurance benefits.

Health and Accident Insurance and Benefits When employers pay for **health and accident insurance** for an employee, and the employee's spouse and dependents, the benefit is excluded from the employee's gross income.[42] For example, if TPI pays health premiums of $18,000 for Julie and her family, Julie is not required to include this $18,000 fringe benefit in her gross income.[43] Further, when employees receive cash reimbursements for medical care, they can exclude the reimbursement from gross income.[44] For example, if TPI reimburses Julie for $450 of medical co-payments she makes during the year, Julie excludes the $450 from gross income. Generally, employers may not discriminate between employees when providing health and accident insurance benefits.[45]

Meals and Lodging for the Convenience of the Employer The value of certain meals and lodging the employer provides to an employee may be excluded from an employee's gross income if the benefit meets two criteria: (1) the meals and lodging are provided on the employer's business premises to the employee (and the employee's spouse and dependents, if any) and (2) the meals and lodging are provided for the convenience of the employer.[46] For example, employers may provide meals at their place of business so employees can continue working efficiently without taking time off to go out to eat. Accounting firms frequently provide meals to tax professionals working late during tax season. Employees submitting receipts for meals may exclude the reimbursement from income. For 2021 and 2022, employers are allowed to deduct 100 percent of the cost of meals purchased from a restaurant and 50 percent of other meals, as discussed in the Business Income, Deductions, and Accounting Methods chapter.[47] Employers may generally discriminate between employees in providing **for the convenience of the employer benefits.**

TAXES IN THE REAL WORLD Free Lunch

Apple, Google, and Facebook are famous for their cafeterias, which have been chronicled in *Bon Appetit* and other foodie magazines. These cafeterias are light years ahead of the dorm cafeteria you ate in as a college freshman. And better yet, meals are either free or almost free for employees. However, the secret is out—and now the IRS is questioning whether these benefits are taxable or nontaxable. To be considered nontaxable, the benefit has to be provided "for the convenience of the employer" rather than as a way to attract and compensate employees. These companies are arguing that without these cafeterias, employees will be away from the company premises more and lose the opportunity to talk together, both of which are detrimental to the employer. Under recently passed legislation, the meals would be 100 percent deductible if these types of cafeterias qualify as restaurants. The IRS defines a "restaurant" as "a business that prepares and sells food or beverages to retail customers for immediate consumption, regardless of whether the food or beverages are consumed on the business's premises." If these cafeterias don't qualify as a restaurant, the meals would be 50 percent deductible.

[42]§106.

[43]If Julie were to purchase the health insurance with after-tax dollars, the equivalent would be $23,684 [$18,000/(1 – .24 marginal tax rate)].

[44]§105(b). However, reimbursement in excess of costs is included in income.

[45]However, employers may exclude part-time employees from participation.

[46]§119(a)(1).

[47]§274(n).

Example 12-20

What if: Assume that last year Julie purchased 25 meals, at a cost of $500, on evenings when she worked late. Julie turned in expense reports and receipts for the meals totaling $500, which PCC reimbursed. What is the amount Julie must include in income?

Answer: Julie will not include the value of any of the overtime meals in income because they were provided for PCC's convenience.

In some situations, employers may provide lodging for employees and require employees to live on the business premises as a condition of their employment. In these cases, employees may exclude the value of the lodging from gross income.[48] For example, an employer may require an apartment complex manager to live in an apartment in the complex (free of charge) so the employee can respond to tenant needs, provide security, and handle emergencies. The apartment manager can exclude the value of the lodging from gross income.

Employee Educational Assistance Employees can exclude from income up to $5,250 of employee **educational assistance benefits** covering tuition, books, and fees.[49] The $5,250 exclusion also applies to eligible student loan repayments made by an employer on qualified education loans for the education of the employee (but not of the spouse or dependent). Amounts received in excess of this limit are taxed as compensation to the employee. (See IRS Publication 970 for details related to education benefits.) This includes amounts employers provide for employee undergraduate- or graduate-level courses or for courses that lead to a professional degree. Amounts excluded from income cannot qualify for educational credits (such as the American opportunity tax credit and the lifetime learning credit).

Dependent-Care Benefits Employees can exclude up to $5,000 for benefits paid or reimbursed by employers for caring for children under age 13 or dependents or spouses who are physically or mentally unable to care for themselves.[50] Excluded amounts do not qualify for the child and dependent care credit (see the Individual Income Tax Computation and Tax Credits chapter).

No-Additional-Cost Services Employees can exclude the value of **no-additional-cost services.** These are any services employers provide to employees in the ordinary course of business that generate no substantial costs to the employer (including opportunity costs).[51] For example, airline companies can provide employees with free flight benefits on a space-available basis, hoteliers can allow employees to use vacant hotel rooms, and telephone companies can provide free basic phone service to their employees—all without the employees recognizing gross income. Exhibit 12-11 describes no-cost benefits that airline companies like United Airlines provide to their employees.

EXHIBIT 12-11 Flight Benefits

United Airlines, like most other airlines, offers the following flight benefits to employees:
Love traveling around the world? So do we. Enjoy unlimited standby travel and discounted rates on airline tickets to anywhere United flies. Whether it's backpacking through Europe or a long weekend in Guam, you can see and do it all.

United Airlines. "Benefits and Travel Privileges," www.united.com/ual/en/us/fly/company/career/benefits.html.

[48]§119(a)(2).

[49]§127(a)(2). The discrimination and eligibility rules are provided in §127(b)(2).

[50]§129.

[51]§132(a)(1).

Example 12-21

What if: Assume that Julie's current employer, PCC, has a division that provides wireless Internet service and virus protection software. Because PCC has such a large contract with a national provider, its contract has sufficient bandwidth to allow employees to use the service without incurring additional cost. The market value of the services is $1,080 per year. What amount of this benefit must Julie include in her gross income?

Answer: $0. Julie may exclude the value of the wireless Internet service from her income because it qualifies as a no-additional-cost service under §132.

Qualified Employee Discounts Employers frequently allow employees to purchase the employer's goods and services at a discount. Employees may exclude **qualified employee discounts** from income as long as they don't acquire *goods* at a discount greater than the average gross profit percentage for the employer's goods.[52] This can be a fairly significant nontaxable benefit to employees, particularly for higher-priced products. For example, Ford Motor Company allows employees a substantial discount on its Ford and Lincoln brand cars. United Airlines advertises their benefits as follows: "Love traveling around the world? So do we. Enjoy unlimited standby travel and discounted rates on airline tickets to anywhere United flies. Whether it's backpacking through Europe or a long weekend in Guam, you can see and do it all." Employees may also exclude qualified employee discounts on *services* as long as the discount is not more than 20 percent off the retail price offered to customers. From a nontax perspective, employers can use this qualified fringe benefit to entice and retain employees.

Example 12-22

What if: Assume that Julie's current employer, PCC, allows all employees to purchase computers (both laptops and desktops) from its retail stores at a discount. Julie purchased two computers during the current year: a laptop for $1,600 (retails for $2,100, with a cost to PCC of $1,500) and a desktop for $1,300 (retails for $1,800, with a cost of $1,250). Julie saved $500 ($2,100 – $1,600) on the laptop and $500 ($1,800 – $1,300) on the desktop. Assume that PCC's average gross profit percentage is 25 percent. What amount of the discount must Julie include in her gross income?

Answer: Julie must include $50 in her gross income. The $50 of income is from the desktop because the employee discount of $500 ($1,800 retail price less the $1,300 purchase price) exceeds the $450 discount allowed ($1,800 retail price × 25% average gross profit percentage). The $500 savings on the laptop may be excluded from her income because the savings are less than the $525 ($2,100 × 25%) allowable qualified employee discount.

What if: Suppose that the laptop Julie purchased for $1,600 has a cost of $1,700 (instead of $1,500, as stated above). What amount of the tax savings on the laptop must Julie include in her gross income?

Answer: Zero for the laptop because Julie's employee discount of $500 is still less than the allowable qualified employee discount of $525 ($2,100 × 25%). The qualified discount is tied to PCC's gross profit percentage, not the purchase price of a specific item.

What if: Assume that Julie's current employer, PCC, allows all employees to receive one free computer each year. Julie selected the laptop (retails for $2,100, with a cost to PCC of $1,500) as her free computer. What amount must Julie include in gross income?

(continued on page 12-30)

[52]§132(a)(2).

Answer: $1,575. PCC is allowed to offer employees a qualified discount of $525 ($2,100 × 25%). Because Julie's discount of $2,100 ($0 paid less $2,100) exceeds the allowable discount of $525, she must include $1,575 in gross income (actual discount of $2,100 less the allowable discount of $525). Employee discounts only qualify as an allowable qualified employee discount to the extent they don't exceed the employer's gross profit percentage.

Working Condition Fringe Benefits Employees may exclude from income any benefit or reimbursement of a benefit provided by an employer. For example, if a company or firm reimburses its employees for professional licensing costs or dues (e.g., CPA or bar fees or AICPA dues), the reimbursement may be excluded from an employee's income.[53] Additionally, telephones or computers provided to employees for business use may be excluded. Employers may discriminate between employees with respect to **working condition fringe benefits.**

Example 12-23

What if: Assume that Julie's employer reimburses executives for business-related continuing education courses as well as travel costs related to such education. Julie attended a certificate (nondegree program) course at the University of Chicago this year. Her costs were as follows: $2,500 for the course, $600 for airfare, $800 for hotels, $400 for meals, and $200 for books and course materials. PCC reimbursed Julie for the entire $4,500 ($2,500 + $600 + $800 + $400 + $200). What amount of the reimbursement must Julie include in her gross income?

Answer: $0. The reimbursement qualifies as a working condition fringe benefit.

What if: Assume that Ethan's employer allows all of its engineers to take home products for consumer testing and evaluation. For example, Ethan is currently designing a new disc brake system for mountain bikes. So Ethan is allowed to check out up to three mountain bikes at a time to see how various brake systems work. The annual rental value of products Ethan uses is $2,500. What amount of the annual rental value must Ethan include in his gross income?

Answer: $0. The value of the consumer testing products is an excludable working condition fringe benefit.

***De Minimis* Fringe Benefits** Employees can also exclude from income occasional or incidental ***de minimis* fringe benefits.**[54] These typically include occasional personal use of a copy machine, company-sponsored picnics, noncash traditional holiday gifts (Thanksgiving turkey or Christmas ham), and occasional tickets to sporting or theatrical events. Employers are allowed to discriminate between employees when providing *de minimis* fringe benefits. Who do you think gets to use a company's NBA tickets—the new employee or the boss?

Qualified Transportation Fringe Benefits Employees may exclude from income the value of certain transportation benefits they receive from employers, whether employers pay for these benefits directly or reimburse employees for the transportation costs.[55] **Qualified transportation fringe benefits** eligible for exclusion include the value of company-owned carpool vehicles for commuting to and from work, the cost of mass transit passes, and the cost of qualified parking near the workplace. In 2022, the maximum exclusion for the carpool vehicle and mass transit pass is $280 per month, and the maximum exclusion for the qualified parking benefit is also up to $280 per month. Employers may discriminate with respect to these benefits.

[53] Employees can exclude reimbursements from their income if they properly document their expenses through expense reports, mileage logs, and receipts.

[54] §132(a)(4).

[55] §132(a)(5). Qualified transportation fringe benefits are defined in §132(f).

Cafeteria Plans and Flexible Spending Accounts Employers generally choose the benefits they make available to employees. Some employers offer a standard package of benefits that employees can either take or leave. Standard benefits typically include health and dental insurance for the employee and family, dependent care benefits, and group-term life insurance for the employee. However, a standard benefit plan is not optimal for all employees because each employee has individual needs. So how can employers tailor their benefits to the needs of employees? The answer is through a cafeteria plan and flexible spending accounts.

Under a **cafeteria plan,** employers determine the total cost of benefits they are willing to provide for each employee. Each employee then either chooses (or buys) benefits up to the determined amount from a menu of nontaxable fringe benefits or may receive a cash equivalent in lieu of forgone benefits.[56] However, cash received from a cafeteria plan is taxable compensation to employees. Cafeteria plans are popular because each employee may desire different types of nontaxable fringe benefits. For example, if an employer provides $3,000 of dependent-care benefits to every employee, the benefits would be worthless to employees without dependents. Through a cafeteria plan, employees can select the benefits best suited to their needs. For example, instead of selecting dependent-care benefits, an employee with no dependents could choose any combination of nontaxable benefits such as dental insurance, educational benefits, or cash if no other benefits are desirable.

Employers can also offer **flexible spending accounts (FSAs),** which allow employees to set aside a portion of their before-tax salary for payment of either health and/or dependent-care benefits. These plans allow employees to set aside either employee contributions (on a before-tax basis) or employer contributions (a leftover cafeteria plan amount) to pay for medical-related expenses (such as co-payments and prescriptions) or dependent care. The 2022 limit for medical-related expenses is $2,850. Generally, amounts placed in flexible spending accounts must be used for qualifying benefits during the FSA plan year (which is often the calendar year). Employees must use the amount elected during the FSA plan year. However, employers may offer one of two options: (1) allow up to $570 to be carried to the next FSA plan year or (2) provide a grace period of 2½ extra months to use the remaining balance, but excess amounts are forfeited by the employee.

Employee and Employer Considerations for Nontaxable Fringe Benefits Nontaxable fringe benefits are very attractive to employees because their after-tax cost of these benefits is zero.[57] Employees do not pay for the after-tax cost of the benefits, and they are not taxed on the value of the benefits they receive. In contrast to taxable fringe benefits, nontaxable fringe benefits cannot, with a few exceptions noted above, be provided on a discriminatory basis (that is, they cannot be given to some employees and not others). Employers deduct the cost of providing the benefits, which, thanks to group or quantity discounts, can be considerably lower than the cost to the employee of purchasing the benefit(s) separately. Employers may deduct the cost of providing nontaxable fringe benefits except for qualified parking, qualified transportation fringe benefits, and 100 percent of meals purchased from a restaurant (2021 and 2022 only) and provided for the convenience of the employer on the employer's premises, and 50 percent of other meals. IRS Publication 15-B, *Employer's Tax Guide to Fringe Benefits* (available at www.irs.gov), provides tax guidance for employers providing fringe benefits.

> **THE KEY FACTS**
>
> **Nontaxable Fringe Benefits**
>
> - Specifically identified in the Code.
> - Employee excludes benefit from taxable income.
> - Employer deducts the cost when goods or services are provided to the taxpayer.

Tax Planning with Fringe Benefits

The fact that employees can exclude nontaxable fringe benefits from gross income, while employers can deduct the cost of providing them (just as they deduct the cost of taxable fringe benefits), gives rise to compensation-related tax planning opportunities that may benefit both the employee and the employer.

[56]§125.

[57]Furthermore, there are nontax reasons for employees to value nontaxable benefits, such as the fact that many employer-provided group health insurance plans allow for preexisting health conditions, whereas employees may not be able to obtain health insurance plans that cover preexisting health conditions on their own.

Example 12-24

In its offer letter, TPI indicates Julie will receive employer educational assistance. Let's assume TPI has proposed to reimburse Julie $5,000 a year for her educational expenses. What amount of this employee educational assistance reimbursement would be a nontaxable fringe benefit to Julie?

Answer: All $5,000. Julie can exclude up to $5,250 per year (see Exhibit 12-10) as an employee educational assistance fringe benefit.

What if: Assume that TPI will not reimburse Julie's educational expenses unless Julie is willing to accept a reduction in salary. Assuming Julie is subject to a 24 percent marginal tax rate, how much salary should Julie be willing to forgo to receive the $5,000 of nontaxable employee educational assistance fringe benefit (ignoring FICA taxes)?

Answer: $6,579, computed as follows:

Description	Amount	Explanation
(1) Annual fringe benefit	$5,000	
(2) Marginal ordinary tax rate	24%	
Before-tax compensation required to pay for annual fringe benefit	**$6,579**	(1)/[1 − (2)]

Example 12-25

What if: Assume that instead of an educational benefit, TPI will pay Julie $6,579 of salary that she can then use to pay for her educational expenses. What is TPI's after-tax cost of paying $6,579 of salary to Julie?

Answer: $5,197, calculated as follows:

Description	Amount	Explanation
(1) Taxable salary paid	$ 6,579	
(2) Income tax benefit	(1,382)	(1) × 21%
Total after-tax cost of salary	**$5,197**	(1) + (2)

What if: Assume that TPI will provide Julie $5,000 of employee educational assistance qualified fringe benefits. What will be its after-tax cost of paying the $5,000 nontaxable fringe benefit to Julie?

Answer: $3,950, calculated as follows:

Description	Amount	Explanation
(1) Nontaxable fringe benefit paid	$ 5,000	
(2) Income tax benefit	(1,050)	(1) × 21%
Total after-tax cost of nontaxable benefit	**$3,950**	(1) + (2)

Can an employer and an employee work together to implement the conversion tax planning strategy to make both the employee and the employer better off by substituting desired nontaxable fringe benefits for taxable salary in the compensation package? The answer is yes!

Example 12-26

What if: As shown in Example 12-25, Julie is indifferent between receiving (1) $6,579 in salary or (2) $5,000 in nontaxable employee educational assistance benefits. Consequently, if TPI paid Julie $5,000 in nontaxable benefits and any amount of additional salary, she would be better off than she would be by receiving no educational assistance and $6,579 in salary. As shown in Example 12-26, TPI would be better off after taxes by providing Julie with (1) $5,000 in nontaxable benefits (cost of

$3,950) rather than (2) salary of $6,579 (after-tax cost of $5,197). What amount of salary could TPI provide in addition to the $5,000 of nontaxable benefits to make it indifferent between providing the educational assistance and the additional salary or providing salary of $6,579?

Answer: $1,578 additional salary, calculated as follows:

Description	Amount	Explanation
(1) After-tax cost of salary	$ 5,197	Example 12-26
(2) After-tax cost of fringe benefit	3,950	Example 12-26
(3) After-tax cost of additional salary	$ 1,247	(1) − (2)
(4) After-tax cost percentage	79%	(1 − .21)
Additional before-tax salary	**$1,578**	(3)/(4)

To summarize, if TPI reimburses Julie's educational expenses and provides her with additional salary of any amount below $1,578, it will be better off than it would be by not providing the educational expenses and paying her $6,579 in salary. Julie is better off if TPI reimburses her educational expenses and gives her any additional salary than she is if it doesn't reimburse her educational expenses but pays her $6,579 of salary.

Fringe Benefits Summary

Fringe benefits, both taxable and nontaxable, can make up a significant portion of an employee's compensation. Fringe benefits are taxable unless the tax laws specifically exclude them from gross income. Taxable fringe benefits usually represent a luxury perk, while nontaxable fringe benefits are generally excluded for public policy reasons. At this point, you should be able to distinguish between taxable and nontaxable fringe benefits. Exhibit 12-12 presents an excerpt from Disney Company's 2021 proxy statement. Read through the excerpt and see whether you can identify which of the benefits received by CEO Robert Iger are taxable and which are nontaxable.

Iger's taxable benefits include the personal air travel, security, wellness-related purposes, reimbursement for financial consulting, and perhaps part of the group-term life insurance. His nontaxable benefits include theme park access (a no-additional-cost service), merchandise discounts (qualified employee discount), occasional sporting events (*de minimis* fringe benefit), educational expense reimbursements, health insurance, and group-term life insurance (some of this coverage may be taxable).

Recall the fringe benefits included in Julie's offer letter: health and dental insurance (valued at $18,000), $750,000 of group-term life insurance, a biennial $30,000 automobile allowance, and a flexible spending account for medical expenses (no amounts

EXHIBIT 12-12 Excerpt from Disney Company's 2021 Proxy Statement Dealing with Fringe Benefits

The following table identifies the incremental cost of each perquisite or personal benefit that exceeded the greater of $25,000 or 10% of the total amount of perquisites and personal benefits for a named executive officer in fiscal 2020.

Fiscal 2020 Perquisites and Personal Benefits					
Executive	Year	Personal Air Travel	Security	Other	Total
Robert A. Iger	2020	$157,639	$767,127	$157,990	$1,082,756

The incremental cost to the Company of the items specified above was determined as follows:

- Personal air travel: the actual catering costs, landing and ramp fees, fuel costs and lodging costs incurred by flight crew plus a per hour charge based on the average hourly maintenance costs for the aircraft during the year for flights that were purely personal in nature, and a pro rata portion of catering costs where personal

(continued)

EXHIBIT 12-12 *(continued)*

guests accompanied a named executive officer on flights that were business in nature. Where a personal flight coincided with the repositioning of an aircraft following a business flight, only the incremental costs of the flight compared to an immediate repositioning of the aircraft are included. As noted on page 28 above, Mr. Iger and Mr. Chapek are required for security reasons to use corporate aircraft for all of their personal travel.

- Security: the actual costs incurred by the Company for providing security equipment and services.

The "Other" column in the table above includes, to the extent a NEO elected to receive any of these benefits, the incremental cost to the Company of the vehicle benefit, personal air travel (except for the NEOs whose personal air travel is separately identified in the "personal air travel" column in the table above), reimbursement of up to $1,000 per calendar year for wellness-related purposes such as fitness and nutrition management, and reimbursement of expenses for financial consulting. With respect to Mr. Iger, the "Other" column also includes $130,840 for the filing fee and related legal fees incurred in connection with a filing by Mr. Iger under the Hart-Scott-Rodino Antitrust Improvements Act that was required as a result of Mr. Iger's participation in the Company's equity compensation program.

The NEOs also were eligible to receive the other benefits described in the Compensation Discussion and Analysis under the discussion of "Benefits and Perquisites" in the "Compensation Program Elements" section, which involved no incremental cost to the Company or are offered through group life, health or medical reimbursement plans that are available generally to all of the Company's salaried employees.

See page 45 of proxy statement: https://thewaltdisneycompany.com/app/uploads/2021/01/2021-Proxy-Statement.pdf.

given—assume she elects $1,500). She also received a reimbursement of $5,000 of educational expenses (see Example 12-24). Which of these benefits are taxable and which are nontaxable? Exhibit 12-13 summarizes how each of these benefits is classified for tax purposes, Julie's after-tax benefit, and TPI's after-tax cost.

EXHIBIT 12-13 Summary of Julie's Nonsalary Benefits from TPI

Benefit	Nontaxable Fringe	Taxable Fringe	Employee After-Tax Benefit	Employer After-Tax Cost
Auto allowance		×	**$22,800** ($30,000 − $7,200) (Example 12-18)	**$23,700** [$30,000 × (1 − .21)]
Health and dental insurance	×		**$18,000** [$18,000 × (1 − .0)]	**$14,220** [$18,000 × (1 − .21)]
Flexible spending account	×		**$1,500** [$1,500 × (1 − .0)]	**$1,185** [$1,500 × (1 − .21)]
Parking reimbursement	×		**$2,400** [$2,400 × (1 − .0)]	**$2,400** [$2,400 × (1 − .0)]
Group-term life insurance	×	×	**$1,605** ($2,000 − $395) (Examples 12-19, 20)	**$395** [$500 × (1 − .21)] (Example 12-20)
Education assistance benefits	×		**$5,000** [($5,000 × (1 − .0)] (Example 12-25)	**$3,950** [$5,000 × (1 − .21)] (Example 12-26)
Total			**$51,305**	**$45,850**

CONCLUSION

Individuals and employers routinely make choices involving compensation issues. As they do so, they must understand how alternative forms of compensation are taxed. In this chapter, we have discussed the tax compliance and planning implications associated with common types of payment including salary and wages, equity-based compensation (such as stock options and restricted stock), and taxable and nontaxable fringe benefits from both employee and employer perspectives. Throughout, we have emphasized that both tax and nontax issues must be considered in the broader context of compensation planning. Armed with the information provided in this chapter, future employees and employers can approach the compensation decisions they will undoubtedly face with more confidence and insight.

Summary

Determine the tax implications of compensation in the form of salary and wages from the perspectives of the employee and the employer. LO 12-1

- Employees are taxed on salary and wages at ordinary income rates.
- Employees use Form W-4 to supply their employer with withholding information. Employees can use the W-4 to manage withholding throughout the year because withholding is treated as though it is withheld evenly throughout the year for estimated tax purposes.
- Cash-method employers deduct wages when paid. Accrual-method employers deduct wages when accrued as long as the wages are paid within 2½ months of year-end. If paid after 2½ months of year-end, wages are deductible when the employee recognizes the income (when paid). When an employer accrues wages to a related-person employee (more than 50 percent ownership), the wages are not deductible until the employee recognizes the income (when received).
- Employers' after-tax cost of wages is the cost of the wages minus the tax benefit of the deduction for the wages.
- For publicly traded corporations, the tax deduction for compensation paid to covered employees (the CEO, CFO, and the three other most highly compensated officers) is limited to $1,000,000 per year per individual.

Describe the tax implications of various forms of equity-based compensation from the perspectives of the employee and the employer. LO 12-2

- Stock options and restricted stock are common forms of equity-based compensation. Although both reward employees for increases in the stock price of their employers, there are fundamental economic differences between them.
- Stock options are either nonqualified stock options (NQOs) or incentive stock options (ISOs) for tax purposes.
- Employees recognize ordinary income equal to the bargain element on NQOs when they are exercised. Employers are able to deduct the bargain element when NQOs are exercised. Any appreciation in the value of shares subsequent to the exercise of NQOs is treated as a capital gain by employees when the shares are sold.
- If certain holding period requirements are met, employees exercising ISOs don't recognize any income until the shares received from the exercised options are sold. When the shares are sold, the difference between the exercise price and the share price is a long-term capital gain (assuming appreciation). Employers are not permitted a deduction for ISOs.
- Generally, employees prefer ISOs and employers prefer NQOs because of differences in the way the two types of options are taxed.
- Employers treat stock options differently for book and tax purposes.
- Employees recognize ordinary income from restricted stock equal to the fair market value of the stock on the vesting date. Employers receive a corresponding tax deduction.
- Employees may elect to recognize taxable income from restricted stock on the date it is received rather than on the vesting date if they make an 83(b) election. Although this election accelerates the recognition of income, it gives the employee the ability to convert ordinary income from further appreciation into a capital gain.
- Restricted stock units (RSUs) are units valued in employer stock at the time of grant, but unlike restricted stock, upon settlement RSUs can be exchanged for employer stock, cash, or some combination of cash and stock depending upon the terms of the RSU agreement.

- Qualified employees may elect to defer recognition of taxable income from a qualified equity grant if they make an 83(i) election. A qualified equity grant is a grant of qualified stock of an eligible corporation that is received by a qualified employee.

LO 12-3 Compare and contrast taxable and nontaxable fringe benefits and explain their tax consequences for the employee and the employer.

- Fringe benefits are taxable to the employee unless the Code specifically excludes the benefit from gross income. Taxable fringe benefits are generally luxury perks, such as corporate air travel and security.
- Nontaxable fringe benefits include up to $50,000 of group-term life insurance, health benefits, meals and lodging for the convenience of the employer, educational assistance, dependent-care benefits, qualified employee discounts, and qualified transportation benefits (among others).

KEY TERMS

83(b) election (12-17)
bargain element (12-9)
cafeteria plan (12-31)
cashless exercise (12-10)
***de minimis* fringe benefits (12-30)**
disqualifying disposition (12-12)
educational assistance benefits (12-28)
employee (12-2)
exercise date (12-10)
exercise price (12-9)
facts and circumstances test (12-2)
FICA taxes (12-2)
flexible spending accounts (FSA) (12-31)
for the convenience of the employer benefits (12-27)
Form W-2 (12-2)
Form W-4 (12-2)
fringe benefits (12-21)
grant date (12-10)
group-term life insurance (12-22)
health and accident insurance (12-27)
incentive stock options (ISOs) (12-10)
no-additional-cost services (12-28)
nonqualified stock options (NQOs) (12-10)
nontaxable fringe benefits (12-25)
option exercise (12-9)
qualified employee discounts (12-29)
qualified equity grant (12-20)
qualified transportation fringe benefits (12-30)
restricted stock (12-16)
salary (12-2)
same-day sale (12-10)
strike price (12-9)
taxable fringe benefits (12-21)
vest (12-9)
vesting date (12-10)
wages (12-2)
working condition fringe benefits (12-30)

DISCUSSION QUESTIONS

Discussion Questions are available in Connect®.

LO 12-1 1. Nicole and Braxton are each 50 percent shareholders of NB Corporation. Nicole is also an employee of the corporation. NB is a calendar-year taxpayer and uses the accrual method of accounting. The corporation pays its employees monthly on the first day of the month after the salary is earned by the employees. What issues must NB consider with respect to the deductibility of the wages it pays to Nicole if Nicole is Braxton's sister? What issues arise if Nicole and Braxton are unrelated?

LO 12-1 2. Holding all else equal, does an employer with a higher marginal tax rate or lower marginal tax rate have a lower after-tax cost of paying a particular employee's salary? Explain.

LO 12-1 3. What *nontax* reasons explain why a corporation may choose to cap its executives' salaries at $1 million?

LO 12-1 4. What *tax* reasons explain why a corporation may choose to cap its executives' salaries at $1 million?

LO 12-2 5. From an *employee* perspective, how are ISOs treated differently from NQOs for tax purposes? In general, for a given number of options, which type of stock options should employees prefer?

6. From an *employer* perspective, how are ISOs treated differently from NQOs for tax purposes? In general, for a given number of options, which type of stock options should employers prefer? LO 12-2
7. Why do employers use stock options in addition to salary to compensate their employees? For employers, are stock options treated more favorably than salary for tax purposes? Explain. LO 12-2
8. What is a "disqualifying disposition" of ISOs, and how does it affect employees who have exercised ISOs? LO 12-2
9. Compare and contrast how employers record book and tax expense for stock options. LO 12-2
10. How is the tax treatment of restricted stock different from that of NQOs? How is it similar? LO 12-2
11. Matt just started work with Boom Zoom Inc., a manufacturer of credit-card-sized devices for storing and playing back music. Due to the popularity of its devices, analysts expect Boom Zoom's stock price to increase dramatically. In addition to his salary, Matt received Boom Zoom restricted stock. How will Matt's restricted stock be treated for tax purposes? Should Matt consider making the 83(b) election? What are the factors he should consider in making this decision? From a tax perspective, would this election help or hurt Boom Zoom? LO 12-2
12. What risks are assumed by employees making an 83(b) election on a restricted stock grant? LO 12-2
13. Explain the differences and similarities between fringe benefits and salary as forms of compensation. LO 12-3
14. When an employer provides group-term life insurance to an employee, what are the tax consequences to the employee? What are the tax consequences to the employer? LO 12-3
15. Compare and contrast the employer's tax consequences of providing taxable versus nontaxable fringe benefits. LO 12-3
16. Mike is working his way through college and trying to make ends meet. Tara, a friend, is graduating soon and tells Mike about a really great job opportunity. She is the onsite manager for an apartment complex catering to students. The job entails working in the office for about 10 hours a week, collecting rent each month, and answering after-hours emergency calls. The owner of the apartment complex requires the manager to live onsite as a condition of employment. The pay is $20 per hour, plus a rent-free apartment (worth about $800 per month). Tara then tells him the best part: The rent-free apartment is tax-free. Knowing that you are a tax student, Mike asks you if the rent-free apartment is really tax-free or if Tara is mistaken. Explain to Mike whether the compensation for the apartment is really a nontaxable fringe benefit. LO 12-3
17. Assume that your friend has accepted a position working as an accountant for a large automaker. As a signing bonus, the employer provides the traditional cash incentive but also provides the employee with a vehicle not to exceed a retail price of $25,000. Explain to your friend whether the value of the vehicle is included, excluded, or partially included in the employee's gross income. LO 12-3
18. Explain why an employee might accept a lower salary to receive a nontaxable fringe benefit. Why might an employee *not* accept a lower salary to receive a nontaxable fringe benefit? LO 12-3
19. Describe a cafeteria plan and discuss why an employer would provide a cafeteria plan for its employees. LO 12-3
20. Explain why Congress allows employees to receive certain fringe benefits tax-free but others are taxable. LO 12-3
21. Explain the policy reason for including the value of a country club membership provided to an executive as a taxable fringe benefit. LO 12-3
22. Describe the circumstances in which an employee may not value a nontaxable fringe benefit. LO 12-3

PROBLEMS

Select problems are available in Connect®.

LO 12-1

23. North Inc. is a calendar-year C corporation, accrual-basis taxpayer. At the end of year 1, North accrued and deducted the following bonuses for certain employees for financial accounting purposes:
    - $7,500 for Lisa Tanaka, a 30 percent shareholder.
    - $10,000 for Jared Zabaski, a 35 percent shareholder.
    - $12,500 for Helen Talanian, a 20 percent shareholder.
    - $5,000 for Steve Nielson, a 0 percent shareholder.

    Unless stated otherwise, assume these shareholders are unrelated.

    How much of the accrued bonuses can North Inc. deduct in year 1 under the following alternative scenarios?

    a) North paid the bonuses to the employees on March 1 of year 2.
    b) North paid the bonuses to the employees on April 1 of year 2.
    c) North paid the bonuses to employees on March 1 of year 2 and Lisa and Jared are related to each other, so they are treated as owning each other's stock in North.
    d) North paid the bonuses to employees on March 1 of year 2 and Lisa and Helen are related to each other, so they are treated as owning each other's stock in North.

LO 12-1

24. Jorgensen High Tech Inc. is a calendar-year, accrual-method taxpayer. At the end of year 1, Jorgensen accrued and deducted the following bonuses for certain employees for financial accounting purposes:
    - $40,000 for Ken.
    - $30,000 for Jayne.
    - $20,000 for Jill.
    - $10,000 for Justin.

    How much of the accrued bonuses can Jorgensen deduct in year 1 under the following alternative scenarios?

    a) Jorgensen paid the bonuses to the employees on March 1 of year 2.
    b) Jorgensen paid the bonuses to the employees on April 1 of year 2.
    c) Jorgensen paid the bonuses to the employees on March 1 of year 2, and there is a requirement that the employee must remain employed with Jorgensen on the payment date to receive the bonus.
    d) Jorgensen paid the bonuses to the employees on March 1 of year 2, and there is a requirement that the employee must remain employed with Jorgensen on the payment date to receive the bonus; if not, the forfeited bonus is reallocated to the other employees.

LO 12-1

25. Lynette is the CEO of publicly traded TTT Corporation and earns a salary of $200,000 in the current year. What is TTT Corporation's after-tax cost of paying Lynette's salary excluding FICA taxes?

LO 12-1

26. Marcus is the CEO of publicly traded ABC Corporation and earns a salary of $1,500,000. What is ABC's after-tax cost of paying Marcus's salary?

LO 12-2

tax forms

27. Cammie received 100 NQOs (each option provides a right to purchase 10 shares of MNL stock for $10 per share). She started working for MNL Corporation four years ago (5/1/Y1) when MNL's stock price was $8 per share. Now (8/15/Y5) that MNL's stock price is $40 per share, she intends to exercise all of her options. After acquiring the 1,000 MNL shares with her stock options, she held the shares for over one year and sold (on 10/1/Y6) them at $60 per share.
    a) What are Cammie's taxes due on the grant date (5/1/Y1), exercise date (8/15/Y5), and sale date (10/1/Y6), assuming her ordinary marginal rate is 32 percent and her long-term capital gains rate is 15 percent?

b) What are MNL Corporation's tax savings on the grant date (5/1/Y1), exercise date (8/15/Y5), and sale date (10/1/Y6)?

c) Complete Cammie's Form 8949 and Schedule D for the year of sale. Also assume that the sale transaction of the MNL Corporation stock was not reported to Cammie on a Form 1099-B.

28. Yost received 300 NQOs (each option gives Yost the right to purchase 10 shares of Cutter Corporation stock for $15 per share). At the time he started working for Cutter Corporation three years ago, Cutter's stock price was $15 per share. Yost exercised all of his options when the share price was $26 per share. Two years after acquiring the shares, he sold them at $47 per share. LO 12-2 planning

a) What are Yost's taxes due on the grant date, exercise date, and sale date, assuming his ordinary marginal rate is 35 percent and his long-term capital gains rate is 15 percent?

b) What are Cutter Corporation's tax consequences (amount of deduction and tax savings from deduction) on the grant date, the exercise date, and the date Yost sold the shares?

c) Assume that Yost is "cash poor" and needs to engage in a same-day sale in order to buy his shares. Due to his belief that the stock price is going to increase significantly, he wants to maintain as many shares as possible. How many shares must he sell in order to cover his purchase price and taxes payable on the exercise?

d) Assume that Yost's options were exercisable at $20 and expired after five years. If the stock only reached $18 during its high point during the five-year period, what are Yost's tax consequences on the grant date, the exercise date, and the date the shares are sold, assuming his ordinary marginal rate is 35 percent and his long-term capital gains rate is 15 percent?

29. Haven received 200 NQOs (each option gives him the right to purchase 20 shares of Barlow Corporation stock for $7 per share) at the time he started working for Barlow Corporation three years ago when its stock price was $7 per share. Now that Barlow's share price is $50 per share, he intends to exercise all of his options. After acquiring the 4,000 Barlow shares with his stock options, he intends to hold the shares for more than one year and then sell the shares when the price reaches $75 per share. LO 12-2

a) What are Haven's taxes due on the grant date, exercise date, and sale date, assuming his ordinary marginal rate is 32 percent and his long-term capital gains rate is 15 percent?

b) What are the cash flow effects for Barlow Corporation resulting from Haven's option exercise? How would it change if Barlow's marginal rate were 0 percent?

30. Mark received 10 ISOs (each option gives him the right to purchase 10 shares of Hendricks Corporation stock for $5 per share) at the time he started working for Hendricks Corporation five years ago, when Hendricks's stock price was $5 per share. Now that Hendricks's share price is $35 per share, Mark intends to exercise all of his options and hold all of his shares for more than one year. Assume that more than a year after exercise, Mark sells the stock for $35 a share. LO 12-2

a) What are Mark's taxes due on the grant date, the exercise date, and the date he sells the shares, assuming his ordinary marginal rate is 32 percent and his long-term capital gains rate is 15 percent?

b) What are Hendricks's tax consequences on the grant date, the exercise date, and the date Mark sells the shares?

31. Antonio received 40 ISOs (each option gives him the right to purchase 20 shares of Zorro stock for $3 per share) at the time he started working for Zorro Corporation six years ago. Zorro's stock price was $3 per share at the time. Now that Zorro's stock price is $50 per share, Antonio intends to exercise all of his options and immediately sell all the shares he receives from the options exercise. LO 12-2

a) What are Antonio's taxes due on the grant date, the exercise date, and the date the shares are sold, assuming his ordinary marginal rate is 32 percent and his long-term capital gains rate is 15 percent?

b) What are Zorro's tax consequences on the grant date, the exercise date, and the date Antonio sells the shares?

c) What are the cash flow effects of these transactions to Antonio, assuming his ordinary marginal rate is 24 percent and his long-term capital gains rate is 15 percent?

d) What are the cash flow effects to Zorro resulting from Antonio's option exercise?

LO 12-2 planning

32. Harmer Inc. is now a successful company. In the early days (before it became profitable), it issued ISOs to its employees. Now Harmer is trying to decide whether to issue NQOs or ISOs to its employees. Initially, Harmer would like to give each employee 20 options (each option allows the employee to acquire one share of Harmer stock). For purposes of this problem, assume that the options are exercised in three years (*three years from now*) and that the underlying stock is sold in five years (*five years from now*). Assume that taxes are paid at the same time the income generating the tax is recognized. Also assume the following facts:

- The after-tax discount rate for both Harmer Inc. and its employees is 10 percent.
- The corporate tax rate is 21 percent.
- The personal (employee) ordinary income tax rate is 37 percent.
- The personal (employee) long-term capital gains rate is 20 percent.
- The exercise price of the options is $7.
- The market price of Harmer at date of grant is $5.
- The market price of Harmer at date of exercise is $25.
- The market price of Harmer at date of sale is $35.

Answer the following questions:

a) Considering these facts, which type of option plan, NQO or ISO, should Harmer prefer? Explain.

b) Assuming Harmer issues NQOs, what is Harmer's tax benefit from the options for each employee in the year each employee exercises the NQOs?

c) Assuming Harmer issues ISOs, what is the tax benefit to Harmer in the year the ISOs are exercised?

d) Which type of option plan should Harmer's employees prefer?

e) What is the present value of each employee's after-tax cash flows from year 1 through year 5 if the employees receive ISOs?

f) What is the present value of each employee's after-tax cash flows from year 1 through year 5 if the employees receive NQOs?

g) How many NQOs would Harmer have to grant to keep its employees indifferent between NQOs and 20 ISOs?

LO 12-2

33. On January 1, year 1, Dave received 1,000 shares of restricted stock from his employer, RRK Corporation. On that date, the stock price was $7 per share. Dave's restricted shares will vest at the end of year 2. He intends to hold the shares until the end of year 4, when he intends to sell them to help fund the purchase of a new home. Dave predicts the share price of RRK will be $30 per share when his shares vest and will be $40 per share when he sells them.

a) If Dave's stock price predictions are correct, what are the taxes due on these transactions to Dave if his ordinary marginal rate is 32 percent and his long-term capital gains rate is 15 percent?

b) If Dave's stock price predictions are correct, what are the tax consequences of these transactions to RRK?

LO 12-2

34. On January 1, year 1, Dave received 1,000 shares of restricted stock from his employer, RRK Corporation. On that date, the stock price was $7 per share. On receiving the restricted stock, Dave made the 83(b) election. Dave's restricted shares will vest at the end of year 2. He intends to hold the shares until the end of year 4,

when he intends to sell them to help fund the purchase of a new home. Dave predicts the share price of RRK will be $30 per share when his shares vest and $40 per share when he sells them. Assume that Dave's price predictions are correct, and answer the following questions:

a) What are Dave's taxes due if his ordinary marginal rate is 32 percent and his long-term capital gains rate is 15 percent?

b) What are the tax consequences of these transactions to RRK?

35. On January 1, year 1, Jessica received 10,000 shares of restricted stock from her employer, Rocket Corporation. On that date, the stock price was $10 per share. On receiving the restricted stock, Jessica made an 83(b) election. Jessica's restricted shares will all vest at the end of year 4. After the shares vest, she intends to sell them immediately to fund an around-the-world cruise. Unfortunately, Jessica decided that she couldn't wait four years and she quit her job to start her cruise on January 1, year 3. LO 12-2

a) What are Jessica's taxes due in year 1 assuming her marginal tax rate is 35 percent and her long-term capital gains rate is 15 percent?

b) What are Jessica's taxes due in year 3 assuming her marginal tax rate is 35 percent and her long-term capital gains rate is 15 percent?

36. On May 1, year 1, Anna received 5,000 shares of restricted stock from her employer, Jarbal Corporation. On that date, the stock price was $5 per share. On receiving the restricted stock, Anna made an 83(b) election. Anna's restricted shares will all vest on May 1, year 3. After the shares vest, she intends to sell them immediately to purchase a condo. True to her plan, Anna sold the shares immediately after they vested. LO 12-2

a) What is Anna's ordinary income in year 1?

b) What is Anna's gain or loss in year 3 if the stock is valued at $1 per share on the day the shares vest?

c) What is Anna's gain or loss in year 3 if the stock is valued at $9 per share on the day the shares vest?

d) What is Anna's gain or loss in year 3 if the stock is valued at $5 per share on the day the shares vest?

37. On January 1, year 1, Tyra started working for Hatch Corporation. New employees must choose immediately between receiving 7 NQOs (each NQO provides the right to purchase for $5 per share 10 shares of Hatch stock) or 50 restricted shares. Hatch's stock price is $5 on Tyra's start date. Either form of equity-based compensation will vest in two years. Tyra believes that the stock will be worth $15 per share in two years and $25 in four years, when she will sell the stock. Tyra's marginal tax rate is 32 percent and her long-term capital gains rate is 15 percent. Assuming that Tyra's price predictions are correct, answer the following questions (ignore present value, and use nominal dollars): LO 12-2 planning

a) What are the cash-flow effects to Tyra in the year she receives the options, in the year the options vest and she exercises the options, and in the year she sells the stock if she chooses the NQOs?

b) What are the cash-flow effects to Tyra in the year she receives the restricted stock, in the year the stock vests, and in the year she sells the stock if Tyra chooses the restricted stock?

c) What are the cash-flow effects to Tyra in the year she receives the restricted stock, in the year the stock vests, and in the year she sells the stock if she makes an 83(b) election?

d) What recommendation would you give Tyra? Explain.

38. Nicole's employer, Poe Corporation, provides her with an automobile allowance of $20,000 every other year. Her marginal tax rate is 32 percent. Answer the following questions relating to this fringe benefit. LO 12-3

a) What is Nicole's after-tax benefit if she receives the allowance this year?

b) What is Poe's after-tax cost of providing the auto allowance?

LO 12-3
research

39. Bills Corporation runs a defense contracting business that requires security clearance. To prevent unauthorized access to its materials, Bills requires its security personnel to be on duty except for a 15-minute break every two hours. Because the nearest restaurants are a 25-minute round trip, Bills provides free lunches to its security personnel. Bills has never included the value of these meals in its employees' compensation. Bills is currently under audit, and the IRS agent wants to deny Bills a deduction for past meals. The agent also wants Bills to begin including the value of the meals in employee compensation starting with the current year. As Bills's tax adviser, provide a recommendation on whether to appeal the agent's decision. [*Hint:* See *Boyd Gaming Corp. v. Comm'r,* 177 F.3d 1096, 99-1 USTC ¶ 50,530 (9th Cir. 1999) (Acq.).)

LO 12-3
planning

40. Lars Osberg, a single taxpayer with a 35 percent marginal tax rate, desires health insurance. Volvo, his employer, has a 21 percent marginal tax rate. The health insurance will cost Lars $8,500 to purchase if he pays for it himself through the health exchange (Lars's AGI is too high to receive any tax deduction for the insurance as a medical expense). Answer the following questions about this benefit.
    a) What is the maximum amount of before-tax salary Lars would give up to receive health insurance from Volvo?
    b) What would be the after-tax cost to Volvo to provide Lars with health insurance if it could purchase the insurance through its group plan for $5,000?
    c) Assume that Volvo could purchase the insurance for $5,000. Lars is interested in getting health insurance, and he is willing to receive a lower salary in exchange for the health insurance. What is the least amount by which Volvo would be willing to reduce Lars's salary while agreeing to pay his health insurance?
    d) Will Volvo and Lars be able to reach an agreement by which Volvo will provide Lars with health insurance?

LO 12-3
planning

41. Seiko's current salary is $85,000. Her marginal tax rate is 32 percent, and she fancies European sports cars. She purchases a new auto each year. Seiko is currently a manager for Idaho Office Supply. Her friend, knowing of her interest in sports cars, tells her about a manager position at the local BMW and Porsche dealer. The new position pays $75,000 per year, but it allows employees to purchase one new car per year at a discount of $15,000. This discount qualifies as a nontaxable fringe benefit. In an effort to keep Seiko as an employee, Idaho Office Supply offers her a $10,000 raise. Answer the following questions about this analysis.
    a) What is the annual after-tax cost to Idaho Office Supply if it provides Seiko with the $10,000 increase in salary?
    b) Financially, which offer is better for Seiko on an after-tax basis, and by how much? (Assume that Seiko is going to purchase the new car whether she switches jobs or not.)
    c) What salary would Seiko need to receive from Idaho Office Supply to make her financially indifferent (after taxes) between receiving additional salary from Idaho Office Supply and accepting a position at the auto dealership?

LO 12-1 LO 12-3

42. JDD Corporation provides the following benefits to its employee Ahmed (age 47):

Salary	$300,000
Health insurance	10,000
Dental insurance	2,000
Life insurance	3,000
Dependent care	5,000
Professional dues	500
Personal use of company jet	200,000

The life insurance is a group-term life insurance policy that provides $200,000 of coverage for Ahmed. Assuming Ahmed is subject to a marginal tax rate of 32 percent, what is his after-tax benefit of receiving each of these benefits?

43. Gray's employer is now offering group-term life insurance. The company will provide each employee with $100,000 of group-term life insurance. It costs Gray's employer $300 to provide this amount of insurance to Gray each year. Assuming that Gray is 52 years old, determine the monthly premium that Gray must include in gross income as a result of receiving the group-term life insurance benefit. LO 12-3

44. Brady recently graduated from SUNY–New Paltz with his bachelor's degree. He works for Makarov & Company CPAs. The firm pays his tuition ($10,000 per year) for him so that he can receive his Master of Science in Taxation, which will qualify him to sit for the CPA exam. How much of the $10,000 tuition benefit does Brady need to include in gross income? LO 12-3

45. Meg works for Freedom Airlines in the accounts payable department. Meg and all other employees receive free flight benefits (for the employee, family, and 10 free buddy passes for friends per year) as part of its employee benefits package. If Meg uses 30 flights with a value of $12,350 this year, how much must she include in her compensation this year? LO 12-3

46. Sharmilla works for Shasta Lumber, a local lumber supplier. The company annually provides each employee with a Shasta Lumber shirt so that employees look branded and advertise for the business while wearing the shirts. Are Shasta's employees required to include the value of the shirts in income? LO 12-3 research

47. LaMont works for a company in downtown Chicago. The company encourages employees to use public transportation (to save the environment) by providing them with transit passes at a cost of $285 per month. LO 12-3 research
    a) If LaMont receives one pass (worth $285) each month, how much of this benefit must he include in his gross income each year?
    b) If the company provides each employee with $285 per month in parking benefits, how much of the parking benefit must LaMont include in his gross income each year?

48. Jarvie loves to bike. In fact, he has always turned down better-paying jobs to work in bicycle shops where he gets an employee discount. At Jarvie's current shop, Bad Dog Cycles, each employee is allowed to purchase four bicycles a year at a discount. Bad Dog has an average gross profit percentage on bicycles of 25 percent. During the current year, Jarvie bought the following bikes: LO 12-3

Description	Retail Price	Cost	Employee Price
Specialized road bike	$3,200	$2,000	$2,240
Rocky Mountain mountain bike	3,800	3,200	3,040
Trek road bike	2,700	2,000	1,890
Yeti mountain bike	3,500	2,500	2,800

    a) What amount is Jarvie required to include in taxable income from these purchases?
    b) What amount of deductions is Bad Dog allowed to claim from these transactions?

49. Matt works for Fresh Corporation. Fresh offers a cafeteria plan that allows each employee to receive $15,000 worth of benefits each year. The menu of benefits is as follows: LO 12-1 LO 12-3

Benefit	Cost
Health insurance—single	$ 5,000
Health insurance—with spouse	$ 8,000
Health insurance—with spouse and dependents	$11,000
Dental and vision	$ 1,500
Dependent care—any specified amount up to $5,000	Variable
Adoption benefits—any specified amount up to $5,000	Variable
Cash—any specified amount up to $15,000 plan benefit	Variable
401(k)—any specified amount up to $10,000	Variable

For each of the following independent circumstances, determine the amount of income Matt must recognize and the amount of deduction Fresh may claim:

a) Matt selects the single health insurance benefit and places $10,000 in his 401(k).

b) Matt selects the single health insurance benefit, is reimbursed $5,000 for dependent care, and takes the remainder in cash.

c) Matt selects the single health insurance benefit and is reimbursed for $10,000 of dependent care.

d) Matt gets married and selects the health insurance with spouse benefit and takes the rest in cash to help pay for the wedding.

e) Matt elects to take all cash.

COMPREHENSIVE PROBLEMS

Select problems are available in Connect®.

tax forms

50. Pratt is ready to graduate and leave College Park. His future employer (Ferndale Corp.) offers the following four compensation packages from which Pratt may choose. Pratt will start working for Ferndale on January 1, year 1.

Benefit Description	Option 1	Option 2	Option 3	Option 4
Salary	$60,000	$50,000	$45,000	$45,000
Health insurance	No coverage	5,000	5,000	5,000
Restricted stock	0	0	1,000 shares	0
NQOs	0	0	0	100 options

Assume that the restricted stock is 1,000 shares that trade at $5 per share on the grant date (January 1, year 1); shares are expected to be worth $10 per share on the vesting date at the end of year 1; and no 83(b) election is made. Assume that the NQOs (100 options) each allows the employee to purchase 10 shares at $5 exercise price. The stock trades at $5 per share on the grant date (January 1, year 1) and is expected to be worth $10 per share on the vesting date at the end of year 1, and the options are exercised and sold at the end of the year. Also assume that Pratt spends on average $3,000 on health-related costs that will be covered by insurance if he had coverage or is an after-tax expense if he isn't covered by insurance (treat this as a cash outflow). Assume that Pratt's marginal tax rate is 35 percent. (Ignore FICA taxes and time value of money considerations).

a) What is the after-tax value of each compensation package for year 1?

b) If Pratt's sole consideration is maximizing after-tax value for year 1, which scheme should he select?

c) Assuming Pratt chooses Option 3 and sells the stock on the vesting date (on the last day of year 1), complete Pratt's Schedule D and Form 8949 for the sale of the restricted stock.

51. Santini's new contract for 2022 indicates the following compensation and benefits:

Benefit Description	Amount
Salary	$130,000
Health insurance	9,000
Restricted stock grant	2,500
Bonus	5,000
Hawaii trip	4,000
Group-term life insurance	1,600
Parking ($ per month)	3,720

Santini is 54 years old at the end of 2022. He is single and has no dependents. Assume that the employer matches dollar-for-dollar for the first $6,000 that the employee contributes to his 401(k) during the year. The restricted stock grant is 500 shares granted when the market price was $5 per share. Assume that the stock vests on December 31, 2022, and that the market price on that date is $7.50 per share. Also assume that Santini is willing to make any elections to reduce equity-based compensation taxes. The Hawaii trip was given to him as the outstanding salesperson for 2021. The group-term life policy gives him $150,000 of coverage. Assume that Santini does not itemize deductions for the year. Determine Santini's taxable income and income tax liability for 2022.

52. Sylvana is given a job offer with two alternative compensation packages to choose from. The first package offers her $250,000 annual salary with no qualified fringe benefits. The second package offers $235,000 annual salary plus health and life insurance benefits. If Sylvana were required to purchase the health and life insurance benefits herself, she would need to pay $10,000 annually after taxes. Assume her marginal tax rate is 35 percent. planning
   a) Which compensation package should she choose, and by how much would she benefit in after-tax dollars by choosing this package?
   b) Assume the second package offers $230,000 plus benefits instead of $235,000 plus benefits. Which compensation package should she choose, and by how much would she benefit in after-tax dollars by choosing this package?

53. In the current year, Jill, age 35, received a job offer with two alternative compensation packages to choose from. The first package offers her a $90,000 annual salary with no qualified fringe benefits and requires her to pay $3,500 a year for parking and to purchase life insurance at a cost of $1,000. The second package offers an $80,000 annual salary, employer-provided health insurance, annual free parking (worth $330 per month), $200,000 of life insurance (purchasing on her own would have been $1,000 annually), and free flight benefits (she estimates that it will save her $5,000 per year). If Jill chooses the first package, she will purchase the health and life insurance benefits herself at a cost of $1,000 annually after taxes and spend another $5,000 in flights while traveling. Assume her marginal tax rate is 32 percent. planning
   a) Which compensation package should she choose, and by how much would she benefit in after-tax dollars by choosing this compensation package instead of the alternative package?
   b) Assume the first package offers a $100,000 salary instead of a $90,000 salary, and the other benefits and costs are the same. Which compensation package should she choose, and by how much would she benefit in after-tax dollars by choosing this package?

UWorld | ROGER CPA Review

UWorld Roger CPA Review

Sample CPA Exam questions from Roger CPA Review are available in Connect as support for the topics in this text. These Multiple Choice Questions and Task-Based Simulations include expert-written explanations and solutions and provide a starting point for students to become familiar with the content and functionality of the actual CPA Exam.

chapter

13 Retirement Savings and Deferred Compensation

Learning Objectives

Upon completing this chapter, you should be able to:

LO 13-1 Describe the tax and nontax aspects of employer-provided defined benefit plans from both the employer's and the employee's perspectives.

LO 13-2 Explain and determine the tax consequences associated with employer-provided defined contribution plans, including traditional 401(k) and Roth 401(k) plans.

LO 13-3 Describe the tax implications of deferred compensation from both the employer's and the employee's perspectives.

LO 13-4 Compare and determine the tax consequences of traditional and Roth IRAs (individual retirement accounts).

LO 13-5 Describe retirement savings account options for self-employed taxpayers and compute the limitations for deductible contributions to these accounts.

LO 13-6 Compute the saver's credit.

Michaeljung/iStock/Getty Images

Tina Hillman has just completed her last exam, finally fulfilling the requirements for a bachelor's degree in accounting. It is the end of June, and she will finally have some time to vacation and see her family before September, when she will start her professional career working in the tax department of Corporate Business Associates (CBA). While Tina is looking forward to the time off, she is also eager to start making money instead of just spending it. She had a great experience during her internship at CBA last year. She had some challenging but enjoyable work assignments, and she got along very well with her co-workers.

Storyline Summary

Taxpayer:	Tina Hillman (she/her/hers)
Location:	Chicago, Illinois
Employment status:	Graduating student about to begin career in the tax department of Corporate Business Associates
Starting salary:	$60,000 per year
Filing status:	Single
Dependents:	None
Marginal tax rate:	Current year 12 percent, next year 22 percent
Taxpayer:	Lisa Whitlark (she/her/hers)
Location:	Chicago, Illinois
Employment status:	Recently promoted to chief financial officer (CFO) for Corporate Business Associates
Salary:	$400,000
Filing status:	Married, filing jointly
Marginal tax rate:	32 percent
Dependents:	Spouse and three children
Taxpayer:	Dave Allan (he/him/his)
Location:	Chicago, Illinois
Employment status:	Recently retired as CFO for Corporate Business Associates after 20 years of employment with the company
Salary at retirement:	$500,000
Retirement benefits:	Participant in Corporate Business Associates's defined benefit plan, 401(k) plan, and nonqualified deferred compensation plan
Filing status:	Married filing jointly
Dependents:	Spouse
Marginal tax rate:	35 percent for current year
Taxpayer:	Corporate Business Associates (CBA)
Location:	Chicago, Illinois
Marginal tax rate:	21 percent
Status:	Publicly traded corporation

Overall, she is excited about the work opportunities she will have at CBA.

Tina recently received an information packet about the benefits available to her as a CBA employee. The information indicated that Tina would be eligible to participate in CBA's 401(k) retirement plan on January 1 of next year. Tina plans on contributing to the plan as soon as she is eligible because CBA matches every dollar contributed by the employee with $2 contributed by the company. In the meantime, Tina wonders whether she has any retirement savings options during the current year while she waits to become eligible to participate in CBA's retirement plan.

Lisa Whitlark

Lisa Whitlark is finally getting used to her new responsibilities. She was recently promoted to the position of chief financial officer (CFO) for CBA. Lisa applied for the position a few months ago when CBA announced that Dave Allan, the former CFO, would be retiring. Lisa had been working as CBA's tax director for the last 10 years. As a top executive of the company, Lisa is now eligible to participate in CBA's nonqualified deferred compensation plan. She didn't have this option as a tax director. Lisa knows she should consider both tax and nontax factors when deciding whether and to what extent she will participate in the nonqualified deferred compensation plan.

Dave Allan

Dave Allan couldn't believe that he was actually going to retire at the end of the year. Looking back, his successful career had passed so quickly. At age 72, he is now ready to move on and spend time seeing the world with his wife. Dave's retirement plans are going to be quite expensive. Fortunately, he has accumulated substantial retirement benefits during his CBA career. Dave will be receiving retirement benefits from CBA's defined benefit plan, 401(k) plan, and nonqualified deferred compensation plan. He knows he has some choices about the timing and amounts of his distributions from these plans. Dave wants to be sure to evaluate both the tax and the nontax consequences before making these decisions. ■

At different stages in their careers, taxpayers are likely to face issues similar to those confronting Tina, Lisa, and Dave. Saving for retirement is not always easy because it requires forgoing cash now in order to receive benefits at some point in the future. However, not saving for retirement can be a costly mistake because it's not likely that government-promised Social Security benefits alone will satisfy most taxpayers' retirement needs.[1]

Many employers help employees save for retirement by sponsoring retirement plans on employees' behalf. These plans may be "qualified" retirement plans or "nonqualified" deferred compensation plans. Qualified plans are subject to certain restrictions not applicable to nonqualified plans. Both qualified and nonqualified plans are useful tools through which employers can accomplish various compensation-related goals while helping employees save for retirement. In this chapter, we discuss the tax and nontax consequences for both employers and employees of qualified retirement plans [e.g., 401(k)] and nonqualified plans, including issues relating to contributions to and distributions from these plans. We also discuss individually managed retirement savings plans available to individual taxpayers [e.g., individual retirement accounts (IRAs)] and qualified retirement plans available to self-employed taxpayers (SEP IRAs). For all of these plans,

[1]The 2021 Social Security Trustees report indicates that the Social Security Trust Fund reserves are projected to become depleted in 2033 (last year, it was projected to be depleted in 2034), at which time the income would be sufficient to pay 76 percent of scheduled benefits. See https://www.ssa.gov/OACT/TR/2021/tr2021.pdf (p. 5).

either employees are allowed to defer taxes on the savings until they receive the payments in retirement or, for certain types of plans, employees are able to exclude the retirement payments from income entirely.

EMPLOYER-PROVIDED QUALIFIED PLANS

Traditional **qualified retirement plans** grew from a congressional concern that, if left unregulated, employers might not adequately fund and protect employee pension benefits and might be tempted to provide lavish retirement plans to highly compensated employees such as executives and business owners to the detriment of rank-and-file employees. To address these concerns, Congress mandated that employer-provided plans receive tax-favored qualified plan status only if they meet certain requirements, thus ensuring that the plan does not discriminate against rank-and-file employees and promised benefits are secure. Over the years, the rules addressing these issues have evolved, but the concept of a qualified plan eligible for favorable tax treatment remains the same.

Employer-provided qualified plans can be generally classified as **defined benefit plans** or **defined contribution plans.** As the name suggests, defined benefit plans spell out the specific benefit the employee will receive upon retirement. Because the defined benefit plan specifies the amount of payments (i.e., the plan defines the benefit to be received by the employee) the employer will pay to the employee in retirement (usually a percentage of their salary based on the number of years the employee worked for the employer), a defined benefit plan is commonly referred to as a pension plan. In contrast, defined contribution plans specify the maximum annual contributions that employers will contribute to the plan and the amount that employees may contribute to the plan. A common defined contribution plan is a 401(k) plan. While we explore both basic plan types below, we emphasize defined contribution plans because they are much more common than defined benefit plans. Later in the chapter, we describe and discuss non-employer-provided plans such as IRAs and retirement accounts for self-employed taxpayers such as SEP IRAs.

DEFINED BENEFIT PLANS

LO 13-1

Defined benefit plans are traditional pension plans used by many older and more established companies and tax-exempt organizations. These plans provide standard retirement benefits to employees based on a fixed formula. The formula to determine an employee's standard retirement benefit is usually a function of years of service working for the employer sponsoring the plan and the level of the employee's compensation as they near retirement. For example, an employer may offer a defined benefit plan that pays retiring employees 2 percent for each full year of service, up to a maximum of 60 percent (i.e., 30 years of service), of the average of the employee's three highest consecutive calendar years of compensation. However, the amount of compensation used in calculating the maximum retirement benefit allowed under the tax law for a particular year is restricted to the annual compensation limit for that year. Consequently, if a retiring employee's compensation for a year is above the limit for that particular year, the annual limit amount is used in the retirement benefit calculation. The annual compensation limit is $280,000 for 2019, $285,000 for 2020, $290,000 for 2021, and $305,000 for 2022.[2] For employees who begin receiving retirement benefits in 2022, the maximum annual benefit they can receive is the *lesser* of (1) 100 percent of the average of the employee's *three* highest consecutive calendar years of compensation, limited to the annual compensation limitation for each of the three years, or (2) $245,000.[3]

[2]§401(a)(17). This limitation is indexed for inflation.

[3]§415(b)(1). The maximum benefit is indexed for inflation.

Example 13-1

Corporate Business Associates (CBA) provides a defined benefit plan for its employees. The plan uses a fixed formula to determine employee benefits. The formula specifies a benefit of 3 percent for each year of service, up to a maximum of 90 percent (30 years of service), of the average of the employee's three highest consecutive calendar years of compensation up to the annual compensation limitation for each year. In January of 2022, Dave retired from CBA. On the date of retirement, Dave had been a CBA employee for 20 years. His highest three consecutive calendar years of annual compensation were $420,000 in 2019, $450,000 in 2020, and $480,000 in 2021. What is Dave's annual benefit from the defined benefit plan that he will begin receiving in 2022?

Answer: $171,000 a year. The benefit is calculated by multiplying 60 percent (3 percent for each of his 20 years of service) by $285,000 (the average of his highest three years of salary, limited to the annual compensation limit of $280,000 for 2019, $285,000 for 2020, and $290,000 for 2021 because his actual compensation is higher than the limit for each of these three years).

What if: Assume the same facts except that Dave had worked for 30 years. What is the annual benefit he will receive from the plan in 2022?

Answer: $245,000. His annual benefit is the lesser of (1) $256,500, his accrued benefit calculated by multiplying 90 percent (3 percent for each of his 30 years of service) by $285,000 (the average of his highest three consecutive calendar years of salary, limited to the annual compensation limit of $280,000 for 2019, $285,000 for 2020, and $290,000 for 2021) or (2) $245,000, the annual defined benefit limit in 2022.

THE KEY FACTS

Defined Benefit Plans

- Employer specifies benefit employee receives on retirement based on years of service and salary. The maximum compensation that can be taken into account for purposes of determining an employee's benefit is limited to the annual compensation limitation for that particular year.
- The annual compensation limitation is $280,000 for 2019, $285,000 for 2020, $290,000 for 2021, and $305,000 for 2022.
- The maximum annual benefit for employees who begin receiving benefits in 2022 is the lesser of (1) 100 percent of the average of the employee's three highest consecutive calendar years of compensation, limited to the annual compensation limitation, or (2) $245,000.
- Employee must vest to receive benefits using at a minimum
  - 5-year cliff vesting schedule.
  - 7-year graded vesting schedule.

Vesting

As we've discussed, an employee's retirement benefit from a defined benefit plan is based on the number of years the employee works for the employer sponsoring the plan. When an employee works for an employer for only a short time before leaving, the employee's benefit depends on their salary, the number of full years worked for the employer, and the employer's vesting schedule. **Vesting** is the process of becoming legally entitled to a certain right or property. Thus, an employee vests in retirement benefits (i.e., becomes legally entitled to the retirement benefits) once they have met certain requirements set forth by the employer. The most restrictive vesting requirements an employer can impose on a qualified defined benefit plan are a five-year "cliff" or a seven-year graded vesting schedule.[4] Under the **cliff vesting** option, after a certain period of time, benefits vest all at once. With a **graded vesting** schedule, the employee's vested benefit increases each full year the employee works for the employer. Exhibit 13-1 features the five-year cliff and seven-year graded minimum vesting schedules for defined benefit plans.

EXHIBIT 13-1 Defined Benefit Plans Minimum Vesting Schedules*

Full Years of Service	5-Year Cliff	7-Year Graded
1	0%	0%
2	0	0
3	0	20
4	0	40
5	100	60
6	N/A	80
7	N/A	100

*Percent of employee benefit no longer subject to forfeiture.

Source: §411(a).

[4]§411(a) specifies maximum vesting periods for employer contributions to qualified plans. Employers are allowed to adopt more generous vesting requirements such as immediate vesting if they choose.

Example 13-2

What if: CBA provides a defined benefit plan to its employees. Under the plan, employees earn a benefit equal to 2 percent, for every full year of service, of the average of their three highest years of compensation. CBA implements a seven-year graded vesting schedule as part of the plan. If Tina works for CBA for four years, earning annual salaries of $60,000, $65,000, $70,000, and $75,000, and then leaves to work for another employer, what annual benefit will she be entitled to receive when she is eligible to begin receiving payments (i.e., what is her vested benefit)?

Answer: $2,240, computed as follows:

Description	Amount	Explanation
(1) Average of three highest years of salary	$70,000	($65,000 + 70,000 + 75,000)/3
(2) Benefit percentage	× 8%	Four years of service × 2 percent per year
(3) Full annual benefit	$ 5,600	(1) × (2)
(4) Vesting percentage	× 40%	Four years of service on 7-year graded vesting schedule (see Exhibit 13-1)
Vested benefit	**$ 2,240**	(3) × (4) = Amount that she is allowed to keep

Tina would forfeit her unvested benefit of $3,360 ($5,600 − $2,240 vested benefit). Note that the $2,240 vested benefit would not grow anymore because this is a defined benefit plan and the $2,240 is the defined benefit the taxpayer will receive upon eligibility (as we discuss later, this is usually after the taxpayer reaches a certain age).

What if: Assume the same facts except that CBA uses a five-year cliff vesting schedule. What would be Tina's vested benefit?

Answer: $0. She did not work for CBA for five years, so her benefits in CBA's defined benefit plan do not vest.

Distributions

When their benefits have vested, employees are entitled to receive future distributions according to the provisions of the plan. These distributions are taxable as ordinary income in the year received.[5] Distributions from defined benefit plans (and defined contribution plans) are subject to early distribution requirements and to minimum distribution requirements. Distributions violating these requirements are penalized. However, because defined benefit plans typically don't permit payout arrangements that would trigger the early distribution or minimum distribution penalties, these penalties are of greater concern to participants in defined contribution plans. Consequently, we address these penalties in more detail when we discuss distributions from defined contribution plans.

Nontax Considerations

From a nontax perspective, a defined benefit plan imposes administrative burdens and risks on the employer sponsoring the plan. A significant amount of work is required to track employee benefits and to compute the employer's required contributions to the plan. Because defined benefit plans require employers to provide particular benefits to employees on retirement, the employer bears the investment risk associated with investments within the plan. Beyond the additional administrative costs and risks, defined benefit plans impose significant funding costs on employers relative to alternative retirement plans. Consequently, in recent years, many employers have begun replacing defined benefit plans with defined contribution plans.

THE KEY FACTS

Defined Benefit Plans

- Employer, not employee, bears investment risk of plan.
- Early and minimum distribution rules apply but are usually not restrictive.

[5]Distributions of both defined benefit plans and defined contribution plans are reported to taxpayers on Form 1099-R.

TAXES IN THE REAL WORLD Define Your Benefit and Let the Deductions Flow

Because defined benefit plans create significantly more administrative burdens and economic risks for employers than defined contribution plans, they are less popular with employers. However, self-employed taxpayers and taxpayers running family businesses may be able to use defined benefit plans to contribute significantly more to qualified retirement plans on behalf of themselves and working family members than they would otherwise be able to contribute. Former Florida governor Jeb Bush provides Exhibit A for this strategy.

Bush released his tax returns in July 2015. His tax returns reported that he claimed deductions for payments to "pension and profit-sharing plans" that averaged $350,000 a year for the previous five years. Bush's (completely legal) defined benefit plan was set up for two people working for his consulting firm, Jeb Bush & Associates LLC. Those in the know believe the plan likely covered him and his son, Jeb Bush Jr. The $350,000 annual contribution average is more than three times the contribution limit otherwise allowable for a defined contribution plan. Why was Bush able to contribute so much more to a defined benefit plan than he could have contributed to a defined contribution plan?

Under a defined benefit plan, the business is allowed to contribute as much as required to fund the expected benefit it must pay to the recipient. Because Bush started the plan when he was nearing retirement age, the business was allowed to contribute (and deduct) significantly more to fund his retirement than if he had started the plan when he had a longer time to work before retirement. In contrast, contributions to defined contribution plans are limited to $67,500 per year (in 2022) for taxpayers who are at least 50 years of age (and $61,000 per year for those who are not), no matter when they are planning to retire.

This strategy has become increasingly important for professionals such as doctors, dentists, and lawyers because it may allow them to reduce their taxable income below certain income limits, which allows them to claim the qualified business income deduction (a current tax break for owners of flow-through entities). Even before the qualified business income deduction was enacted (effective in 2018), defined benefit plans had become increasingly popular with small business owners. Between 2010 and 2016, the number of small businesses adopting such plans increased by about 300 percent.

Sources: Based on Mark Maremont, "Pension Plan Cut Jeb Bush's Taxes," *The Wall Street Journal*, updated July 2, 2015, www.wsj.com/articles/jeb-bushs-pension-cut-his-taxes-1435858574; Ben Steverman, "Rich Professionals Barred from Tax Break Find Pension Painkiller," *Accounting Today* (August 15, 2018), www.accountingtoday.com/articles/rich-professionals-barred-from-tax-break-by-tcja-find-pension-plan-painkiller?utm_campaign=daily-aug%2016%20 2018&utm_medium=email&utm_source=newsletter&eid=40744e9c9e4c98282e2f0457b669c70d.

LO 13-2

DEFINED CONTRIBUTION PLANS

THE KEY FACTS

Traditional Defined Contribution Plans: Overview

- Employer specifies amount it will contribute to employee's retirement account each year, *not* the amount the employee will receive at retirement.
  - Employers typically match employee contributions.
- Employee chooses how funds are invested and bears investment risk.

Defined contribution plans provide an alternate way for employers to help employees save for retirement. While defined contribution plans and defined benefit plans have similar overall objectives, they are different in important ways. First, in a defined contribution plan, employers maintain a separate account for *each* participating employee. Second, defined contribution plans specify the annual contributions the employer will make to the employee's separate account, rather than specifying the ultimate benefit the employee will receive from the plan. Third, employees are often allowed to contribute to their own defined contribution plans, and in many instances they contribute to their own accounts more than their employers do. Finally, employees are generally free to choose how amounts in their retirement accounts are invested (subject to the options available in the plan). If investments in the plan perform well, employees benefit; if they perform poorly, employees suffer the financial consequences. Thus, defined contribution plans shift funding responsibility and investment risk from the employer to the employee.

Employers may provide different types of defined contribution plans, such as 401(k) plans (used by for-profit companies), 403(b) plans (used by nonprofit organizations, including educational institutions), 457 plans (used by government agencies), profit-sharing plans, and money-purchase pension plans.[6] They may even offer multiple defined contribution plans. Due to their popularity, we use 401(k) plans here to represent the general category of defined contribution plans. However, no matter which type of defined contribution plan(s) employers provide, employers must ensure that their plans meet certain requirements relating to annual contribution limits and vesting requirements. Also, to a greater extent than with defined benefit plans, participants in defined contribution plans should be careful to avoid the penalties associated with either early distributions or insufficient minimum distributions from these plans (discussed later in the chapter).

Employer Matching

Employers, but not employees, typically contribute to certain defined contribution plan types such as profit-sharing plans (contributions may be made based on a fixed formula based on profits or may be at the employer's discretion) and money-purchase plans (contributions are a fixed percentage of the employee's compensation). In contrast, employees themselves contribute to 401(k)-type plans. Many employers also "match" employee contributions to these plans.

When deciding whether to contribute to a 401(k) plan, employees should take into account the matching policies of their employers. The match can range from a small percentage (e.g., 25 cents on the dollar) to a multiple of the employee's contribution (e.g., for every dollar contributed by employee, employer contributes $3). A dollar-for-dollar match gives employees a 100 percent immediate, no-risk return on their contributions. Thus, whenever possible, employees should contribute enough to receive the full match from the employer.

Example 13-3

Tina's offer from CBA includes participation in its 401(k) plan effective the beginning of next year. The plan's formula provides that CBA will match employee contributions on a two-for-one basis up to employee contributions of 4 percent of the employee's annual salary. Next year when she's eligible, Tina will contribute 4 percent of her salary to the plan. Assuming a $60,000 salary for next year, how much will Tina contribute and how much will CBA contribute to Tina's 401(k) account?

Answer: Tina will contribute $2,400 ($60,000 × 4%) to her 401(k) account and CBA will contribute $4,800 ($2,400 × 2) to Tina's 401(k) account.

TAXES IN THE REAL WORLD Take the Money and Run!

In its report "How America Saves 2021," Vanguard reports that the most common employer match for employer-sponsored defined contribution plans is $.50 for every dollar contributed by the employee on the first 6 percent of the employee's income. When your employer is willing to give you money, you should find a way to take it if you can. Nevertheless, Vanguard's report indicates that for the 2020 calendar year, 34 percent of employees participating in defined contribution plans did not contribute enough to receive the full employer match. The report also indicates that 18 percent of participating employees contributed exactly enough to receive the full match but did not contribute beyond that and 48 percent of participating employees contributed more than enough to receive the full match.

Source: https://institutional.vanguard.com/content/dam/inst/vanguard-has/insights-pdfs/21_CIR_HAS21_HAS_FSreport.pdf.

THE KEY FACTS

Traditional Defined Contribution Plans: Contribution Limits

- 2022 overall contribution limits for sum of employer and employee contributions:
  - Lesser of $61,000 ($67,500 for employees 50 years old by year-end) or 100 percent of employee's annual compensation.
- 2022 employee contribution limit to 401(k) plan:
  - $20,500 or
  - $27,000 for employees 50 years old by year-end.

Contribution Limits

For 2022, the sum of employer *and* employee contributions to an employee's defined contribution account(s) is limited to the *lesser* of (1) $61,000 ($67,500 for employees

[6]401(k), 403(b), and 457 plans are named for the Internal Revenue Code sections describing the plans.

who are at least 50 years of age by the end of the year) or (2) 100 percent of the employee's compensation for the year.[7] *Employee* contributions to an employee's 401(k) account are limited to $20,500 (or $27,000 for employees who reach age 50 by the end of the year).[8] While this limit applies only to employee contributions, the $61,000 (or $67,500) limit still applies to the sum of employer and employee contributions. For example, if an employee under age 50 contributes the maximum $20,500 to their employer-sponsored 401(k) plan in 2022, the employer's contribution would be limited to $40,500 ($61,000 – $20,500).[9] Because of this limit on employer contributions, highly compensated employees may not be able to maximize the employee contribution and also receive the full employer match available to other employees.

Example 13-4

Before Dave retires at the end of 2022, he continues to contribute to his CBA-sponsored 401(k) account. CBA matches employee contributions on a two-for-one basis up to 4 percent of the employee's salary. Dave is 72 years old at the end of the year; he earned a salary of $600,000 during the year and contributed $27,000 to his 401(k) account. How much will CBA contribute to Dave's 401(k) account?

Answer: $40,500 [$67,500 (Dave is 50+ years old) – $27,000 (Dave's contribution)]. Without the limitation, CBA would have contributed $48,000 ($600,000 × 4% × 2) to Dave's account.

What if: Assume Dave contributed $22,500 to his 401(k) account. What would CBA contribute to Dave's 401(k)?

Answer: $45,000. Note that this is a better deal for Dave because $67,500 ends up in his 401(k) account just as it would if he were to contribute $27,000. In this what-if scenario, however, Dave contributed only $22,500 instead of $27,000.

Vesting

When employees contribute to a defined contribution plan, they are fully vested in the accrued benefit from those contributions (employee contributions plus earnings on employee contributions). However, employees vest in the accrued benefit from employer contributions (employer contributions plus earnings on employer contributions) based on the plan's vesting schedule. When they do not maintain separate accounts for the employee contributions and the employer contributions (one account has both employee and employer contributions plus earnings), the accrued benefit from employee contributions is calculated by multiplying the total accrued benefit in the account by the ratio of employee contributions to total contributions (employee plus employer) to the account.[10] The accrued benefit from employer contributions is the difference between the total accrued benefit and the accrued benefit from employee contributions.

The minimum vesting requirements for defined contribution plans are a bit more accelerated than the five-year cliff and seven-year graded vesting schedules applicable to defined benefit plans. For defined contribution plans, employers have the option of providing three-year cliff or six-year graded vesting. These minimum vesting schedules are presented in Exhibit 13-2.

[7]§415(c)(1). The amount is indexed for inflation under §415(d)(1)(C). Note that the increase in the limit for taxpayers age 50 and older increases the amount the employee can contribute but does not affect the limit the employer can contribute.

[8]§402(g)(1). The amount is indexed for inflation under §402(g)(4).

[9]If an employee participates in more than one defined contribution plan, these limits apply to the total employee and employer contributions to all defined contribution plans. Thus, in a situation where the employee participates in more than one defined contribution plan, the contribution limits for any one defined contribution plan may be less than the overall contribution limits described here.

[10]§411(c).

EXHIBIT 13-2 Defined Contribution Plans Minimum Vesting Schedules*

Full Years of Service with Employer	3-Year Cliff	6-Year Graded
1	0%	0%
2	0	20
3	100	40
4	N/A	60
5	N/A	80
6	N/A	100

*Percent of employer contributions no longer subject to forfeiture.

Source: §411(a).

Example 13-5

What if: Suppose that in three and one-half years the balance in Tina's 401(k) account is $33,000. In total, Tina has contributed $9,000 to the account and CBA has contributed $18,000. Also assume that Tina is 40 percent vested in her accrued benefit from CBA contributions. What is Tina's vested benefit in her 401(k) account?

Answer: $19,800 [$11,000 accrued benefit from her contributions + $8,800, which is 40 percent of the $22,000 accrued benefit from CBA contributions], as described below. Tina is fully vested in the $11,000 accrued benefit from her contributions ($33,000 total accrued benefit in account × $9,000 employee contributions/$27,000 total contributions to her account) and 40 percent vested in the $22,000 accrued benefit from CBA contributions ($33,000 total accrued benefit in account minus $11,000 accrued benefit from her contributions).

THE KEY FACTS

Traditional Defined Contribution Plans: Vesting and After-Tax Cost

- Employee must vest to be entitled to employer contributions (and earnings on those contributions) using:
  - 3-year cliff vesting schedule.
  - 6-year graded vesting schedule.
- Employee contributes before-tax amounts (contributions are deductible).
- After-tax cost is before-tax contribution minus tax savings from contribution.

After-Tax Cost of Contributions to Traditional (non-Roth) Defined Contribution Plans

Employer-sponsored traditional defined contribution plans include all plans except Roth 401(k) plans (discussed below). Employees effectively deduct their contributions to traditional defined contribution plans because contributions are removed from their taxable salary (they are, however, still subject to FICA taxes on funds contributed to defined contribution plans).[11] Consequently, the after-tax cost of a contribution to a traditional defined contribution plan is the contribution amount minus the tax savings generated by the deduction from the contribution.

Example 13-6

Tina contributed $2,400 to her CBA-sponsored traditional 401(k) account in her first full calendar year with CBA. Given Tina's marginal tax rate of 22 percent, what is the after-tax cost of her $2,400 contribution?

Answer: $1,872, computed as follows:

Description	Amount	Explanation
(1) Contribution amount	$ 2,400	Cost of contribution before tax savings
(2) Tax savings from contribution	(528)	$2,400 deduction × 22 percent marginal tax rate
After-tax cost of contribution	**$1,872**	(1) + (2)

[11]Employees pay the same FICA taxes no matter how much they contribute to defined contribution plans.

Distributions from Traditional Defined Contribution Plans

When employees receive distributions (i.e., withdraw funds) from traditional defined contribution plans, the distributions are taxed as ordinary income. However, when employees receive distributions from these plans either too early or too late, they must pay a penalty in addition to the income taxes they owe on the distributions. Generally, employees who receive distributions before they reach

- 59½ years of age or
- 55 years of age *and* have separated from service (retired or let go by employer)

are subject to a 10 percent nondeductible penalty on the amount of the early distributions.[12]

Example 13-7

What if: Assume that when she reaches 60 years of age, Lisa Whitlark retires from CBA and receives a $60,000 distribution from her traditional 401(k) account in the year she retires. Assuming her marginal ordinary tax rate is 32 percent, what amount of tax and penalty will Lisa pay on the distribution?

Answer: $19,200 taxes ($60,000 × 32%) + $0 penalty (she is over 59½ years of age on date of distribution).

What if: Assume that when Lisa is 57 years of age and still employed by CBA, she requests and receives a $60,000 distribution from her traditional 401(k) account. What amount of tax and penalty is Lisa required to pay on the distribution?

Answer: $19,200 taxes ($60,000 × 32%) + $6,000 penalty ($60,000 × 10%).

What if: Assume that Lisa's employment is terminated by CBA when she is 57 years old. In that same year, Lisa requests and receives a $60,000 distribution from her traditional 401(k) account. What amount of tax and penalty is Lisa required to pay on the distribution?

Answer: $19,200 taxes ($60,000 × 32%) + $0 penalty (she is over 55 years of age and she no longer works for CBA).

THE KEY FACTS

Traditional Defined Contribution Plans: Distributions

- Taxed at ordinary rates.
- 10 percent penalty on early distributions:
  - Before 59½ years of age if not retired or
  - Before 55 years of age if retired or let go.
- Required minimum distributions:
  - Must begin receiving by April 1 of the later of (1) the year after the year in which taxpayer reaches 72 years of age or (2) the year after the year in which the employee retires.
  - Must receive required minimum distributions each year after retirement year.
  - 50 percent penalty to the extent required minimum distributions are not made.

Taxpayers who fail to receive a required minimum distribution for (pertaining to) a particular year are also penalized. The year for which taxpayers must receive their *first* required minimum distribution is the *later* of:

- The year in which the employee reaches 72 years of age.
- The year in which the employee retires.

Taxpayers must receive their first required minimum distribution no later than April 1 of the year after the year to which the distribution pertains.[13] Taxpayers generally must receive required minimum distributions for subsequent years by the end of the year to which they pertain. Thus, a retired taxpayer who turns 72 years of age in 2022 must receive a required minimum distribution for 2022 by April 1, 2023. The same taxpayer must also receive a required minimum distribution for 2023 by December 31, 2023.

The amount of the required minimum distribution for a particular year is the taxpayer's account balance at the end of the year *prior to* the year to which the distribution pertains, multiplied by a percentage from a life expectancy table called the "Uniform Lifetime Table." The percentage is based on the distribution period (in years), which depends on the taxpayer's age at the end of the year to which the distribution pertains. An abbreviated version of the table applicable for distributions in 2022 and subsequent years is presented in Exhibit 13-3.

[12]See §72(t)(2) for other exceptions to the 10 percent penalty.

[13]The amount of the required minimum distribution *for the year* in which a retired employee turns 72 is the same whether the employee receives the distribution in the year they turn 72 or whether they defer receiving the distribution until the next year (no later than April 1).

EXHIBIT 13-3 Abbreviated Uniform Lifetime Table for Distributions in 2022

Age of Participant	Distribution Period	Applicable Percentage*
72	27.4	3.65
73	26.5	3.77
74	25.5	3.92
75	24.6	4.07
76	23.7	4.22
77	22.9	4.37
78	22.0	4.55

*The applicable percentage is calculated by dividing 1 by the relevant distribution period.

Source: Treasury Decision 9930 (November 8, 2020), https://public-inspection.federalregister.gov/2020-24723.pdf.

Example 13-8

What if: Suppose that Dave retires from CBA in 2022 at age 74 (and he is still 74 at year-end). When must he receive his required minimum distribution for 2022 from his traditional 401(k) account?

Answer: By April 1, 2023.

What if: Assuming Dave retires in 2022 and that his traditional 401(k) account balance on December 31, 2021, was $3,500,000, what is the amount of the required minimum distribution Dave must receive by April 1, 2023?

Answer: $137,200 ($3,500,000 × 3.92%). The percentage from the Uniform Life Table for determining the required minimum distribution is based on Dave's age at the end of 2022, which is 74 years old.

What if: Assuming Dave's traditional 401(k) account balance on December 31, 2022, is $3,700,000, what is the amount of the required minimum distribution for 2023 that Dave must receive sometime during 2023 (in addition to the $137,200 distribution by April 1)? The applicable percentage for a 75-year-old in 2023 is 4.07 percent.

Answer: $150,590 ($3,700,000 × 4.07%) must be received by Dave during 2023.

The consequences for failing to receive timely required minimum distributions from defined contribution plans are even more severe than for receiving distributions too early. Taxpayers incur a 50 percent nondeductible penalty on the amount of a required minimum distribution (RMD) they should have received but did not (the penalty is payable as an additional tax for the calendar year containing the last day on which the amount is required to be distributed). The taxpayer reports this additional tax on Form 5329, "Additional Taxes on Qualified Plans (Including IRAs) and Other Tax-Favored Accounts," part IX. It is vital that payouts from defined contribution plans be monitored to avoid not only the 10 percent premature distribution penalty but also the 50 percent penalty for failing to receive timely required minimum distributions.

Example 13-9

What if: In the previous example, we determined that Dave must receive a required minimum distribution of $137,200 from his traditional 401(k) account by April 1, 2023. If Dave does not receive any distribution before April 1, 2023, what penalty will he be required to pay?

Answer: $68,600 ($137,200 × 50%). Dave will pay this penalty as an other tax on his 2023 tax return on Form 5329, part IX. This nondeductible penalty is a strong incentive to take the required minimum distributions, or at least to take the penalty into consideration when developing a distribution plan.

What if: Assume that Dave received his first distribution from his traditional 401(k) account on March 1, 2023, in the amount of $100,000, but he did not receive any other distributions before April 1, 2023. What required minimum distribution penalty is Dave required to pay relating to his first required minimum distribution?

Answer: $18,600 [($137,200 RMD − $100,000 actual distribution) × 50%].

In contrast to defined benefit plans, defined contribution plans often provide distribution options that could trigger the penalty for early distributions for the unwary. For example, an employee who retires (or is fired) and takes a lump-sum distribution from their defined contribution account in a year before the year in which they turn 55 will be subject to a 10 percent early-distribution penalty on the entire amount of the distribution. Employees who receive such lump-sum distributions may avoid the 10 percent penalty by electing to "roll over" (deposit) the distributions into one of the individually managed retirement plans we discuss later in this chapter.

After-Tax Rates of Return for Traditional Defined Contribution Plans

For a given before-tax rate of return and a constant tax rate, the longer the taxpayer defers distributions from a traditional defined contribution plan, the greater the taxpayer's after-tax rate of return on the retirement account because deferring the distribution reduces the present value of the taxes paid on the distribution. A taxpayer's after-tax rate of return also depends on the taxpayer's marginal tax rate at the time they contribute to the plan and at the time they receive distributions from the plan. All else equal, the higher the marginal tax rate at the time of contribution to the plan, the higher the after-tax rate of return (the higher tax rate increases the tax savings from the deduction); likewise, the lower the marginal tax rate at the time of the distribution from the plan, the higher the after-tax rate of return (the lower rate reduces the taxes from the distribution).

Of course, any employer contributions to an employee's account, such as CBA's two-for-one matching contributions to Tina's account, significantly increase the after-tax rate of return (and after-tax accumulation) because the contributions increase the employee's after-tax proceeds, but the employee's cost of these contributions is zero.

Exhibit 13-4 summarizes the tax aspects of defined benefit and defined contribution plans.

Roth 401(k) Plans

THE KEY FACTS

Roth 401(k) Defined Contribution Plans

- Employees but not employers may contribute.
  - Employers contribute only to traditional 401(k) plans.
- Contributions are not deductible.
- Same contribution limits as for traditional 401(k) plans.

Employers that provide **traditional 401(k)** plans to employees may also provide **Roth 401(k)** plans. As we discuss below, employee tax consequences for Roth 401(k) plans differ from tax consequences of other traditional defined contribution plans.

When employers provide a Roth 401(k) plan, employees may elect to contribute to the plan instead of or in addition to contributing to a traditional 401(k) plan. However, *employer* contributions to an employee's 401(k) account must go to the employee's traditional 401(k) account rather than to the employee's Roth 401(k) account. Consequently, the balance in an employee's Roth 401(k) account must consist only of the employee's contributions and earnings on those contributions. Because employers providing Roth 401(k) plans to employees are not allowed to contribute to the Roth plans, employers are required to maintain traditional 401(k) accounts for each employee participating in the Roth 401(k) plan.

In contrast to contributions to traditional 401(k) plans, employee contributions to Roth 401(k) accounts are *not* deductible and, therefore, do not produce any immediate tax savings for employees. Therefore, employees wanting to contribute a certain amount to a Roth 401(k) plan must earn more than the contribution amount in order to have the desired contribution amount remaining *after* paying taxes on the amount they earn. For example, assume an employee with a 22 percent marginal tax rate wants to contribute $2,000 to a Roth 401(k) account. To earn the funds to make this contribution, the employee must earn $2,564 [2.000/(1 – .22)] before taxes. The tax on the $2,564 of income is $564 ($2,564 × 22%). This leaves the taxpayer with $2,000 after taxes ($2,564 before taxes minus $564 in taxes) to contribute to the Roth 401(k) account.

EXHIBIT 13-4 Defined Benefit Plan versus Defined Contribution Plan Summary

	Defined Benefit Plan	Defined Contribution Plan
Benefits	• Specifies benefit employee receives on retirement. • Maximum benefit in 2022 is the lesser of (1) 100 percent of average of three highest consecutive calendar years of compensation, limited to the annual compensation limitation for each of the three years, or (2) $245,000. The annual compensation limits are as follows: $280,000 for 2019, $285,000 for 2020, $290,000 for 2021, and $305,000 for 2022.	• Specifies the amounts employer and employee contribute to the account. • Ultimate benefit depends on earnings on contributions.
Payout type	• Life annuity. • Lump-sum distribution of the present value of standard benefit.	• Life annuity. • Lump sum. • Fixed number of years.
Funding requirements	• Employers fund increase in expected future liability each year.	• No funding requirement other than to make required contributions to employee accounts.
Employer's contributions tax deductible?	• Yes.	• Yes, but limited to 25 percent of aggregate employee annual compensation.
Employee's contributions tax deductible?	• No employee contributions.	• Yes, subject to limitations on the amount that can be contributed [$20,500 ($27,000 if 50 years of age or older at end of year) maximum contribution to 401(k) plan in 2022.
Contribution limits	• Not applicable.	• In 2022, lesser of (1) $61,000 ($67,500 for taxpayers at least 50 years of age at end of year) or (2) 100 percent of the employee's compensation for year.
Other factors	• All employees paid from same account. • Heavy administrative burden. • Employers make investment choices and assume investment risk.	• Separate accounts for each employee. • Employees assume investment risk.
Vesting requirements	• 5-year cliff or 7-year graded	• 3-year cliff or 6-year graded • Employee contributions vest immediately.
Distributions	• Taxed as ordinary income. • No 10 percent penalty if either 59½ years of age or 55 years of age and retired. • Minimum distributions required by April 1 of year after the later of (1) year employee reaches 72 or (2) year employee retires.	• Taxed as ordinary income (except Roth-type accounts). • No 10 percent penalty if either 59½ years of age or 55 years of age and retired. • Minimum distribution requirements same as for defined benefit plan.

Example 13-10

THE KEY FACTS

Roth 401(k) Defined Contribution Plans

- Qualified distributions are not taxable.
  - Account must be open for five years before distribution.
  - Employee must be at least 59½ at time of distribution.
- Nonqualified distributions.
  - Distributions of account earnings are taxable and subject to 10 percent penalty if taxpayer is not either 59½ years of age or 55 and retired.
  - Distributions of contributions are not taxed or penalized.
  - Distribution × ratio of contributions to account balance is nontaxable. The remainder of distribution is from account earnings.
- After-tax rate of return equals before-tax rate of return.

What if: Let's assume that CBA offers a Roth 401(k) plan in addition to its traditional 401(k) plan. In her first full calendar year of employment with CBA, Tina elects to contribute 4 percent of her $60,000 salary to CBA's Roth 401(k) plan instead of CBA's traditional 401(k) plan. What is Tina's after-tax cost of this $2,400 contribution (her marginal tax rate is 22 percent)?

Answer: $2,400. Her after-tax cost is her $2,400 contribution because the contribution does not generate any tax savings.

What is Tina's before-tax cost of the contribution? That is, how much did Tina need to earn before taxes to fund the $2,400 after-tax contribution?

Answer: $3,077. Because her marginal tax rate is 22 percent, she needs to earn $3,077 before taxes [$2,400/(1 − .22)] to have $2,400 to contribute to the Roth 401(k) after taxes [$3,077 × (1 − .22)]. When she contributes $2,400 *after taxes* to the Roth 401(k), she is contributing $3,077 *before taxes.*

While contributions to Roth 401(k) accounts are not deductible and, as a result, do not generate any current tax savings, *qualified* distributions from Roth 401(k) accounts are excluded from gross income. Because contributions to Roth 401(k) accounts are not deductible and qualified distributions from Roth 401(k) accounts are not taxable, the before-tax rate of return equals the after-tax rate of return on Roth 401(k) accounts. Note also that because qualified Roth 401(k) distributions are excluded from income, in contrast to traditional 401(k) distributions, they do not increase AGI and thus do not cause AGI-based tax benefit phase-outs (e.g., itemized deduction for medical expenses and certain tax credits), and they do not cause an increase in the taxation of the recipient's Social Security benefits (see the Gross Income and Exclusions chapter for a discussion of the taxation of Social Security benefits).

Example 13-11

What if: In the previous example, Tina contributed $2,400 to her Roth 401(k) account in her first calendar year on the job with CBA. Let's assume that Tina leaves this contribution in the account until she retires in 40 years at the age of 63, that her contribution earns an annual 8 percent before-tax rate of return, and that her marginal tax rate will be 30 percent when she receives the distribution. How much will Tina have accumulated after taxes if she withdraws the initial contribution and all the earnings on the contribution when she retires?

Answer: $52,139 ($2,400 × 1.08^{40}). Tina's contribution does not generate any tax savings and she does not pay any taxes on the accumulated earnings distributed to her at the end of the 40-year period. Note that Tina's after-tax rate of return on her $2,400 after-tax contribution is exactly 8 percent, the same as the before-tax rate of return. With a Roth 401(k), the after-tax rate of return should always equal the before-tax rate of return because the contributions are not deductible and distributions are not taxable.

Qualified distributions from Roth 401(k) accounts are those made after the employee's account has been open for five taxable years (beginning January 1 of the year of the first contribution) *and* the employee is at least 59½ years of age. All other distributions are nonqualified distributions. When a taxpayer receives a *nonqualified* distribution from a Roth 401(k) account, the tax consequences of the distribution depend on the extent to which the distribution is from the account earnings and the extent to which it is from the employee's contributions to the account. Nonqualified distributions of account *earnings* are fully taxable. Nonqualified distributions of account earnings are also generally subject to a 10 percent early distribution penalty unless the taxpayer is either 59½ years of age at the time of the distribution or at least 55 years of age and retired at the time of the distribution.

Nonqualified distributions of the taxpayer's account *contributions* are not subject to tax because the taxpayer did not deduct these amounts when they were contributed. If less than the entire balance in the account is distributed, the nontaxable portion of the distribution is calculated by multiplying the amount of the distribution by the ratio of account contributions to the total account balance. This formula is very similar to the formula described in the Gross Income and Exclusions chapter for determining the nontaxable portion of an annuity payment.

Example 13-12

What If: In the previous example, Tina contributed $2,400 to CBA's Roth 401(k) plan, her account generated an 8 percent before-tax rate of return, and she withdrew the entire balance 40 years after the contribution. Let's assume that at the end of year 6 Tina needs cash, so she withdraws $1,000 from the account when the account balance is $3,808 and her marginal tax rate is 24 percent. How much tax and penalty, if any, is Tina required to pay on this nonqualified distribution?

Answer: $89 tax and $37 penalty, computed as follows:

Description	Amount	Explanation
(1) Contribution to Roth 401(k) (nondeductible)	$2,400	Beginning of year 1
(2) Account balance end of year 6	3,808	$2,400 × 1.08^6$
(3) Nonqualified distribution end of year 6	1,000	
(4) Percentage of distribution that is not taxable	63.03%	(1)/(2)
(5) Nontaxable portion of distribution	630	(3) × (4)
(6) Taxable portion of distribution	370	(3) − (5)
(7) Marginal tax rate in year 6	24%	
(8) Regular income tax on distribution	**89**	**(6) × (7)**
(9) Penalty tax percentage for early distributions	10%	
(10) Penalty tax on early distribution	**37**	**(6) × (9)**
Total tax and penalty on early distribution	$ 126	(8) + (10)

Finally, note that the minimum distribution requirements applicable to traditional 401(k) accounts also apply to Roth 401(k) accounts.

Comparing Traditional Defined Contribution Plans and Roth 401(k) Plans

We've described and discussed the tax consequences associated with participating in traditional and Roth 401(k) plans. So which is better for employees? If given a choice, to which type of 401(k) plan should you direct your contributions? While many factors should be considered in making this decision, perhaps the most important is the taxpayer's current marginal tax rate (the rate in the year of contributions) compared to the taxpayer's expected future marginal tax rate (the expected rate in the year of distributions). Taxpayers generally should prefer traditional 401(k) plans when their current marginal rate is higher (i.e., greater tax savings derived from deductions) than their expected future marginal rate (i.e., lower tax cost on income from distributions), and they should prefer Roth 401(k) plans when their current marginal rate is lower than their expected future tax rate.

When future rates are higher than current rates, taxpayers should generally prefer Roth 401(k) plans because the forgone tax savings from a nondeductible contribution are smaller when the marginal tax rate is lower and the tax savings from excluding the distribution from income are greater when the marginal tax rate is higher. While current and expected future marginal tax rates are important to consider, other factors relevant to this decision include the uncertainty of future tax rates and the taxpayer's risk tolerance for this uncertainty, and the way a taxpayer reinvests the tax savings from contributions to traditional 401(k) plans. A detailed discussion of all factors relevant to this decision is beyond the scope of this text. Exhibit 13-5 summarizes and compares the tax consequences of traditional 401(k) plans and Roth 401(k) plans.

EXHIBIT 13-5 Traditional 401(k) Plan versus Roth 401(k) Plan Summary

	Traditional 401(k) Plans	Roth 401(k) Plans
Employer contributions allowed	• Yes.	• No.
Tax consequences to employer	• Contributions deductible when paid.	• Not applicable.
Tax consequences to employee	• Contributions are deductible.	• Contributions are not deductible.
Distributions	• Taxed as ordinary income. • No 10 percent penalty if the taxpayer is at least 59½ years of age or at least 55 years of age and retired at time of distribution. • If life annuity or joint and survivor annuity, no penalty even if not 55 years of age. • Minimum distributions required by April 1 of the later of (1) the year after the year in which the employee reaches age 72 or (2) the year after the year in which the employee retires. • Failure to meet minimum distribution timing and amount requirements triggers 50 percent penalty.	• Qualified distributions not taxed. • Qualified distributions when account is open for at least five taxable years and employee has reached age 59½. • No 10 percent penalty on taxable part of nonqualified distribution if the taxpayer is at least 59½ years of age or at least 55 years of age and retired at time of distribution. • If life annuity or joint and survivor annuity, no penalty even if not 55 years of age. • Minimum distribution requirements and penalties are the same as for traditional 401(k) plans. • If nonqualified distribution, nontaxable percentage of distribution is the ratio of contributions to total account value.

LO 13-3

NONQUALIFIED DEFERRED COMPENSATION PLANS

So far, our discussion has emphasized the tax and nontax aspects of employer-provided *qualified* defined benefit and defined contribution plans. In addition to or perhaps in lieu of these types of qualified plans, employers may offer **nonqualified deferred compensation** plans to certain employees.

Nonqualified Plans versus Qualified Defined Contribution Plans

Deferred compensation plans permit employees to defer current salary (similar to contributing current salary) in exchange for a future payment from the employer. From an employee's perspective, the tax consequences of contributions to and distributions from nonqualified plans are similar to those for qualified defined contribution plans. For example, just as with defined contribution plans, employee contributions to nonqualified deferred compensation (NQDC) plans reduce the employee's taxable income in the year of contribution.[14] Also, just as with qualified plans, employees are not taxed on the balance in their accounts until they receive distributions. Finally, like distributions from qualified plans, distributions from NQDC plans are taxed as ordinary income.

[14]Technically, employees participating in NQDC plans defer the receipt of current salary and employers credit the employee's account for the amount of the deferral. This has the same effect as if the employee had actually made a deductible contribution (for AGI) to their account, as an employee participating in a defined contribution plan would do.

Example 13-13

CBA provides a nonqualified deferred compensation plan under which executives (not rank-and-file employees) may elect to defer up to 10 percent of their salary. Dave Allan has been participating in the plan by deferring a portion of his salary each year for the last 15 years. The balance in his deferred compensation account is currently $2,000,000. In keeping with a fixed-payment schedule Dave elected under the plan, he receives a $50,000 distribution this year. What amount of tax must Dave pay on the distribution? (Recall that Dave's marginal tax rate is 35 percent.)

Answer: $17,500 ($50,000 × .35).

For employers, NQDC plans are treated differently from qualified plans. For example, because nonqualified plans are not subject to the same restrictions that govern qualified plans, employers may discriminate in terms of who they allow to participate in the plan. In practice, employers generally restrict participation in nonqualified plans to more highly compensated employees. Employers are also not required to fund nonqualified plans. That is, they are not required to formally set aside and accumulate funds specifically to pay the deferred compensation obligation when it comes due. Rather, they typically retain funds deferred by employees under the plan, use the funds for business operations, and pay the deferred compensation out of their general funds when the deferred compensation becomes payable.

Because employers retain, control, and generate income on funds deferred by employees under nonqualified plans, employers are allowed to deduct only *actual payments* of deferred compensation to employees.[15] That is, employers cannot deduct the amount of deferred compensation they accrue each year. Thus, for tax purposes, an employer may not deduct the deferred compensation when an employee initially earns it, even though the company becomes liable for the deferred compensation payment. In contrast, for financial accounting purposes, companies generally expense deferred compensation in the year employees earn it and record a corresponding deferred compensation liability.[16]

Employee Considerations

Should employees participate in nonqualified plans when given the chance? The decision obviously involves several considerations. First, employees must decide whether the benefits they expect to receive from qualified retirement plans (or other sources) will be adequate to provide for their expected costs during retirement. Next, they should consider whether they can afford to defer current salary. This may not be a significant concern for most eligible participants, however, because nonqualified plans are generally available only to highly compensated employees who may not have the liquidity concerns that lower-compensated employees may face. Also, employees should consider the expected after-tax rate of return on the deferred salary relative to what they could earn by receiving that salary currently and personally investing it.

Generally, larger employers allow employees participating in nonqualified plans to choose how their deferred compensation will be invested from among alternative investments provided under the plan (e.g., money market, various bond funds, and stock funds, among others). However, because employers do not actually invest compensation deferred under the plan on the employee's behalf, the employer credits the employee's account *as if* the employee's contributions had been invested in the employee's deemed investment choices. For example, the Coca-Cola company provides a nonqualified deferred compensation plan under which "Eligible participants may defer up to 80 percent

THE KEY FACTS

Nonqualified Deferred Compensation Plans

- Employee defers current income in exchange for future payment.
  - Employee is taxed when payment is received.
  - Employee generally selects investment choices up front to determine return on deferral.
  - Just as for traditional deferred compensation plans, after-tax rate of return depends on before-tax rate of return, marginal tax rate at time of deferral, and marginal tax rate at time of distribution.
  - Payment is not guaranteed. If employer doesn't pay, employee becomes unsecured creditor.

[15]Technically, for tax purposes, accrued compensation that is not paid within 2.5 months of year-end is considered to be deferred compensation.

[16]Employers record additional expense and liability for financial accounting purposes as earnings on the deferred compensation accumulate.

of base salary and up to 95 percent of their annual incentive." Further, under the plan, "Participants' accounts may or may not appreciate and may depreciate depending on the performance of their deemed investment choices."[17]

Just as with qualified defined contribution plans, other than Roth 401(k) plans, an employee's after-tax rate of return on deferred compensation depends on the employee's investment choices *and* on the employee's marginal tax rates at the time of the contribution and at the time of the distribution.

Example 13-14

As a new executive with CBA, Lisa Whitlark is eligible to participate in the company's nonqualified deferred compensation (NQDC) plan. Recall that CBA provides a plan under which executives may elect to defer up to 10 percent of their salary. In her first year with CBA, Lisa elects to defer $40,000 of salary ($400,000 × 10%) under the plan. Because her current marginal income tax rate is 32 percent, she saves $12,800 in taxes by deferring the salary ($40,000 × 32%). Consequently, her after-tax cost of deferring the compensation is $27,200 ($40,000 − $12,800). Lisa plans to receive a distribution from the nonqualified plan in 20 years when she expects her marginal tax rate to be 32 percent. She selects a stock index fund as her deemed investment choice. She expects the fund to provide an 8 percent before-tax rate of return on her $40,000 deferral. What will Lisa receive after taxes in 20 years from her current-year $40,000 deferral?

Answer: $126,778 after-tax accumulation, computed as follows:

Description	Amount	Explanation
Contribution to plan	$ 40,000	Deferral of 10 percent of her current salary
Times future value factor	$\times 1.08^{20}$	8 percent annual rate of return for 20 years
Future value of deferred compensation	$ 186,438	Value of deferral/distribution 20 years after deferral
Minus: taxes payable on distribution	(59,660)	$186,438 value of account × 32 percent marginal tax rate
After-tax proceeds from distribution	**$126,778**	Value of account minus taxes payable on distribution

Deferring salary to a future period can be an effective tax planning technique, particularly when the employee anticipates their marginal tax rate will be lower in the year they will receive the deferred compensation than it is in the year the employee defers the salary. In fact, if employees had complete flexibility as to when they could receive distributions from deferred compensation plans, they would likely accelerate distributions from deferred compensation plans into years they knew with certainty would have relatively low marginal tax rates. This strategy is limited, however, by rules requiring employees to specify the timing of the future payments when they decide to participate in deferred compensation plans.[18]

Employees considering participating in nonqualified deferred compensation plans should also consider the potential financial risks of doing so. Recall that employers are not required to fund nonqualified plans. So there's always the possibility that the employer may become bankrupt and not have the funds to pay the employee on the scheduled distribution dates. If the employer is not able to make the payments, the employee becomes an unsecured creditor of the company and may never receive

[17]The Coca Cola Company 2020 Proxy Statement, p. 100, https://investors.coca-colacompany.com/filings-reports/proxy-statements/content/0001206774-21-000597/0001206774-21-000597.pdf.

[18]§409A. These rules do provide, however, that specified payments from deferred compensation plans may commence while employees are still employed.

the full compensation owed to them. Consequently, the employee should evaluate the financial stability of the company when deciding whether to defer compensation under the employer's plan.

Employer Considerations

It's pretty clear that nonqualified plans can provide significant benefits to employees. How might employers benefit from providing nonqualified plans? First, employers may benefit if they are able to earn a better rate of return on the deferred compensation than the rate of return they are required to pay employees participating in the plan. In addition, employers can use nonqualified plans to achieve certain hiring objectives. For example, nonqualified plans could be a component of a compensation package a company may use to attract prospective executives. Deferred compensation can also be used to compensate an employee when the employer's percentage contribution to the employee's qualified retirement account is limited by the annual contribution limit. Deferred compensation is not subject to the qualified retirement account contribution limits.

Likewise, deferring compensation may be an important tax planning tool for employers when their current marginal tax rates are low (they are experiencing net operating losses so their current marginal tax rate is 0 percent) and they expect their future marginal tax rates when deferred compensation is paid to be significantly higher because they expect to return to profitability (unless tax rates change, the marginal rate would be 21 percent). In effect, deferring compensation into a year with a higher marginal tax rate increases the after-tax benefit of the compensation deduction, which reduces the after-tax cost of the compensation to the employer.

Exhibit 13-6 summarizes and compares qualified retirement plans and nonqualified deferred compensation plans.

THE KEY FACTS

Nonqualified Deferred Compensation Plans

- Employer promises to pay deferred compensation at some point in future.
  - Deduct when paid to employee.
  - Not required to fund obligation.
  - Use to accomplish compensation objectives such as providing more deferred compensation to employees who are over contribution limits on qualified plans.
  - Employer's marginal tax rates at time of deferral relative to those at time of payment affect after-tax cost of providing deferred compensation relative to current compensation.

EXHIBIT 13-6 **Qualified Plans versus Nonqualified Plans Summary**

	Qualified Plans	Nonqualified Plans
Types	• Defined benefit (pension). • Defined contribution [401(k)].	• Deferred compensation.
Requirements	• May not discriminate against "rank-and-file" employees of the company. • Funding or contribution requirements. • Vesting requirements.	• May discriminate. • Generally provided to executives and highly compensated employees. • No formal funding requirements (employee is essentially an unsecured creditor). • No formal vesting requirements.
Tax consequences to employers	• Immediately deduct contributions to plan (amount funded).	• No deduction until paid to employee.
Tax consequences to employees	• Employee contributions deductible unless to Roth-type account. • Earnings deferred until distributed to employee. • Employer contributions not immediately taxed. • Distributions from non-Roth accounts treated as ordinary income.	• Employee contributions (or deferrals) are deductible. • Taxed as ordinary income when received. • Earnings deferred until distributed to employee.

INDIVIDUALLY MANAGED QUALIFIED RETIREMENT PLANS

We've covered tax and nontax issues relating to both qualified and nonqualified employer-sponsored retirement savings plans. However, not all employers provide retirement savings plans, and when they do, some employees may not be eligible to participate, while others who are eligible may elect not to participate in these plans. The tax laws provide opportunities for these taxpayers to provide for their own retirement security through individually managed retirement plans. The **individual retirement account (IRA)** is the most common of the individually managed retirement plans. Other types of individually managed plans are available to self-employed taxpayers.

LO 13-4

INDIVIDUAL RETIREMENT ACCOUNTS

Taxpayers who meet certain eligibility requirements can contribute to **traditional IRAs,** to **Roth IRAs,** or to both. Just like traditional and Roth 401(k) plans, traditional IRAs and Roth IRAs have different tax characteristics. In fact, in most respects, the tax characteristics of traditional 401(k) plans mirror those of traditional IRAs, and the tax characteristics of Roth 401(k) plans mirror those of Roth IRA accounts. To minimize redundancy, we focus on the tax characteristics that differ between employer-sponsored 401(k) plans and individually managed IRAs.

Traditional IRAs

THE KEY FACTS

Traditional IRAs

- 2022 deductible contribution limit:
  - Lesser of $6,000 or earned income.
  - For taxpayers over 50, lesser of $7,000 or earned income.
- If taxpayers participate in employer-provided plan:
  - For 2022, deduction limit phased out for single taxpayers with MAGI between $68,000 and $78,000, and for married filing jointly taxpayers with MAGI between $109,000 and $129,000.
  - Special rules if one spouse is covered by plan and the other is not.

Deductible Contributions Deductible contributions to IRAs are for AGI deductions. The maximum deductible contribution for a taxpayer in 2022 depends on the taxpayer's age, as follows:

- $6,000 deduction limit if the taxpayer is less than 50 years of age at year-end.[19,20]
- $7,000 deduction limit if the taxpayer is at least 50 years of age at year-end.[21]

The deductible contribution limit may be further restricted depending on the following factors:

- The taxpayer's participation in an employer-sponsored retirement plan.
- The taxpayer's filing status.
- The amount of the taxpayer's earned income.
- The taxpayer's modified AGI (MAGI). For purposes of determining the deductible amount of traditional IRA contributions, MAGI is the taxpayer's AGI disregarding the IRA deduction itself and certain other items.[22]

Unmarried taxpayers not participating in an employer-sponsored retirement plan may deduct IRA contributions up to the *lesser* of:

- $6,000 ($7,000 for taxpayers at least 50 years of age at year-end).
- Earned income.

[19]Lump-sum distributions from qualified plans other than Roth 401(k)s received prior to retirement are frequently rolled over into traditional IRA accounts to avoid the 10 percent premature distribution penalty and current taxation. Rollover contributions are not subject to normal contribution limits for traditional IRAs.

[20]The IRA contribution limit is indexed for inflation.

[21]The $1,000 increase in the deduction limit for older taxpayers is granted to allow taxpayers nearing retirement age to "catch up" on contributions they may have not made in previous years.

[22]§219(g)(3).

Earned income generally includes income actually earned through the taxpayer's efforts, such as wages, salaries, tips, and other employee compensation, plus the amount of the taxpayer's net earnings from self-employment. Alimony income is also considered earned income for this purpose.

Example 13-15

In the year she graduated from college, Tina earned $25,000. She earned $5,000 in salary working part time while she was in school, and she earned $20,000 in salary working for CBA from September through December. To get an early start saving for retirement, she contributed $5,000 to a *traditional* IRA [recall that Tina is not eligible to participate in CBA's 401(k) retirement plan until January of next year]. How much of this contribution may Tina deduct?

Answer: $5,000. Because Tina is not participating in an employer-sponsored retirement plan during the current year, she may deduct the full $5,000 contribution as a for AGI deduction, reducing her AGI from $25,000 to $20,000.

For *unmarried taxpayers* who actively participate in an employer-sponsored retirement plan, the deduction limits are the same as for those who do not participate, except that the maximum deduction is phased out based on the taxpayer's MAGI, as follows:

- No phase-out if MAGI is equal to or less than $68,000.
- Proportional phase-out of full limit for MAGI between $68,000 and $78,000. [The phase-out percentage is computed as follows: (MAGI – $68,000) divided by ($78,000 – $68,000). For example, if MAGI is $69,000, the taxpayer loses 10 percent of deduction limit.]
- Full phase-out (no deduction) if MAGI is equal to or greater than $78,000.

Married taxpayers can make deductible contributions to separate IRAs (i.e., an IRA for each spouse) subject to limitations. If the married couple files jointly, before any AGI-based phase-out amounts (discussed below), the maximum deduction for the spouse with the *higher* amount of earned income is the same as it is for unmarried taxpayers [$6,000 ($7,000 if at least 50 years of age at year-end) or earned income if it is less]. However, the maximum deduction for the spouse with the *lower* amount of earned income is limited to the lesser of:

- $6,000 ($7,000 if this spouse is at least 50 years of age at year-end) or
- Total earned income of both spouses reduced by deductible and nondeductible contributions to the higher-earning spouse's traditional IRA and by contributions to the higher-earning spouse's Roth IRA.[23]

The contribution to the lesser-earning spouse's IRA is called a **spousal IRA.** The money in the account belongs to the lower-earning spouse no matter who earned the funds for the contribution.

If a spouse is an active participant in an employer's retirement plan and the couple files jointly, the maximum deduction for that spouse's contribution is phased out based on the *couple's* MAGI as follows:

- No phase-out if the couple's MAGI is equal to or less than $109,000.
- Proportional phase-out of full limit for MAGI between $109,000 and $129,000 (for example, if the couple's MAGI is $115,000, the couple loses 30 percent of deductible contribution limit).
- Full phase-out (no deduction) if MAGI is equal to or greater than $129,000.

[23]§219(c).

If one spouse is an active participant in an employer's retirement plan and the other is not and the couple files jointly, the deduction for the spouse who is not an active participant is phased out based on the couple's MAGI as follows (the phase-out applies whether the spouse is the higher- or lower-earning spouse):

- No phase-out if the couple's MAGI is equal to or less than $204,000.
- Proportional phase-out of full limit for MAGI between $204,000 and $214,000.
- Full phase-out (no deduction) if MAGI is equal to or greater than $214,000.

Married taxpayers who file separately may also make deductible contributions to an IRA. The maximum deduction is the lesser of:

- $6,000 ($7,000 if taxpayer is at least 50 years of age at year-end).
- The taxpayer's earned income.

However, if either spouse is an active participant in an employer's retirement plan and they file separately, then each spouse's deductible contribution (including the nonactive participant spouse's contribution) is phased out over that spouse's MAGI as follows:

- No phase-out if the taxpayer's MAGI is $0 (also no tax benefit of deducting).
- Proportional phase-out of full limit for MAGI between $0 and $10,000.
- Full phase-out (no deduction) if MAGI is equal to or greater than $10,000.

If the couple files separate tax returns and did not live with each other at any time during the year, they will be treated as unmarried taxpayers for purposes of the IRA deduction limitations. Appendix A at the end of this chapter provides a flowchart for identifying traditional IRA deduction limitations.

THE KEY FACTS

Traditional IRAs

- If taxpayer does not participate in employer-provided plan but spouse does
  - Deduction limit phased out for MAGI between $204,000 and $214,000.
- Distribution taxed as ordinary income
  - If distribution before taxpayer is 59½, 10 percent penalty generally applies.

Example 13-16

In her first full calendar year working for CBA, Tina earns $60,000. Because she contributes $2,400 of her salary to CBA's 401(k) plan, her MAGI is $57,600 ($60,000 – $2,400). Tina would like to make the maximum deductible contribution to her IRA. Assuming the 2022 limitations apply, how much is she allowed to deduct?

Answer: $6,000. Because Tina is a participant in CBA's retirement plan, the $6,000 deduction limit is subject to phase-out. However, because Tina's MAGI is less than the beginning of the phase-out threshold ($66,000), she is allowed to deduct the maximum contribution.

What if: Assume that in her first full calendar year working for CBA, Tina earns $71,000. Because she contributes $2,400 of her salary to CBA's 401(k) plan, her MAGI is $68,600 ($71,000 – $2,400). Tina would like to make the maximum deductible contribution to her IRA. How much is she allowed to deduct (using 2022 limits)?

Answer: $5,640. The deductible amount before considering MAGI limitations is $6,000. However, because Tina is a participant in CBA's retirement plan, the $6,000 deduction limit is subject to phase-out. Because Tina's MAGI is 6 percent of the way through the $68,000–$78,000 phase-out range for a single taxpayer [($68,600 – $68,000)/($78,000 – $68,000)], the $6,000 deductible contribution limit is reduced by 6 percent, to $5,640 [$6,000 × (1 – .06)]. So, $5,640 is the maximum deductible contribution she can make to her traditional IRA.

What if: Assume that Tina is married and files a joint return with her spouse Steve. Tina participates in CBA's 401(k) plan and she receives $60,000 in salary from CBA for the year. Steve is a full-time student and is unemployed. Assuming the couple's MAGI is $60,000, what is Tina's maximum deductible IRA contribution for the year? What is Steve's maximum deductible IRA contribution for the year?

Answer: Tina's maximum deductible contribution for the year is $6,000. Because Tina is married, files a joint return, and reports MAGI under $109,000 with her husband, her contribution is not phased out at all even though she is an active participant in CBA's retirement plan.

Steve's maximum deductible contribution for the year is also $6,000. Because Steve reports less earned income than Tina (in fact, he doesn't report any earned income for the year), his deductible IRA contribution is limited to the lesser of (1) $6,000 or (2) $54,000 ($60,000 – $6,000), which is the couple's earned income minus Tina's deductible IRA contribution.

What if: Assume the same facts as the preceding what-if example except that Tina and Steve file separately. What is each spouse's maximum deductible IRA contribution for the year?

Answer: $0 for Tina and $0 for Steve. Tina is ineligible to make a deductible IRA contribution because her MAGI of $60,000 exceeds the $10,000 phase-out limit, and Steve may not make a deductible contribution to the IRA because he does not report any earned income.

Nondeductible Contributions Taxpayers whose maximum deductible contribution is phased out based on MAGI can still make *nondeductible* contributions up to the overall contribution limit. Further, taxpayers who are able to deduct IRA contributions can designate otherwise deductible contributions as nondeductible. When a taxpayer makes a nondeductible contribution to a traditional IRA during the year, the taxpayer must file Form 8606, "Nondeductible IRAs," to inform the IRS of the amount of the taxpayer's nondeductible contributions for the year. Nondeductible contributions create basis in the taxpayer's IRA that is not taxed on distribution.

The overall limit of the sum of deductible and nondeductible contributions (including Roth IRAs—see below) is $6,000 per year ($7,000 for taxpayers who are at least 50 years of age at year-end). Earned income limitations (including the spousal IRA limits) that apply to deductible IRA contributions also apply to nondeductible contributions. That is, a taxpayer must have earned income in order to make nondeductible contributions to a traditional IRA, with the exception of a spouse who is contributing to a spousal IRA. The earnings on nondeductible contributions grow tax-deferred until the taxpayer receives distributions from the IRA (see discussion below). Thus, most taxpayers making nondeductible contributions to traditional IRAs would likely do better by contributing directly to a Roth IRA, if eligible, instead of making nondeductible contributions to traditional IRAs. Another alternative would be transferring the nondeductible contributions into a Roth IRA (termed a "backdoor" Roth IRA contribution). We discuss Roth IRAs after discussing traditional IRAs.

Taxpayers may contribute to an IRA up until the unextended tax return due date (generally, April 15 of the subsequent year). That is, as long as the taxpayer makes a contribution to the IRA by April 15 of year 2, the contribution counts as though it were made during year 1 (the prior calendar year). However, when a taxpayer makes a year 1 contribution in year 2, the taxpayer needs to specify to the IRA custodian that the contribution is intended to be a year 1 rather than a year 2 contribution.

Distributions Just like distributions from traditional 401(k) plans, distributions from traditional IRAs are generally taxed as ordinary income to the taxpayer. Taxpayers withdrawing funds from traditional IRAs before reaching the age of 59½ are also generally subject to a 10 percent early-distribution penalty on the amount of the withdrawal. Distributions exempt from the early distribution penalties include account proceeds distributed in the form of a life annuity (i.e., a fixed payment each month or year over the taxpayer's life) and account proceeds used for qualifying medical expenses (but only to the extent the expenses exceed the 7.5 percent of AGI floor even if the taxpayer does not itemize deductions), health insurance premiums for the owner, qualified higher education expenses, qualified child births or adoptions (limited to $5,000), or first-time home purchases (proceeds for a first-time home purchase are limited to $10,000).[24] Taxpayers must receive their first required minimum distribution by April 1 of the year following the year in which they reach 72 years of age. Whether the taxpayer is retired or not is irrelevant for determining IRA required minimum distributions.

Taxpayers are eligible to complete a qualified charitable distribution (QCD) if they have reached age 70½ years by the time of the distribution. A QCD is a distribution from a traditional IRA (not a Roth or a SEP IRA) made directly by the IRA trustee to a qualified charitable organization.[25] The benefit of a QCD is that it counts as a distribution for required minimum distribution (RMD) purposes, but the distribution is excluded from the

[24]§72(t). A first-time homebuyer is someone who did not own a principal residence in the two years before acquiring the new home [see §72(t)(8)(D)].

[25]§408(d)(8).

taxpayer's gross income (because it is excluded from income, the charitable donation is not deductible as a charitable contribution).[26] A distribution can qualify as a QCD only to the extent the distribution would have been included in gross income before considering the QCD exclusion (i.e., distributions of nondeductible contributions do not count as QCDs). The QCD annual limit is $100,000 per IRA owner. Therefore, each spouse could complete a $100,000 QCD for married couples filing jointly. The QCD provides an alternative to a taxpayer receiving a taxable distribution from the IRA and then donating the funds to a charitable organization. Therefore, a QCD would benefit older taxpayers who regularly make charitable donations but do not have enough other itemized deductions in total to gain full tax savings from the charitable donations itemized deductions. A taxpayer completing a QCD would also report a lower AGI than they would without the QCD. Consequently, the taxpayer would receive tax benefits from the QCD for tax items that are phased out or reduced based on AGI (e.g., floor for medical expense deductions, taxability of social security income, threshold for net investment income tax, etc.). By making a QCD, the taxpayer effectively converts a potential itemized deduction for the charitable donation (from AGI deduction) into a for AGI deduction because the QCD reduces gross income (and therefore AGI) from what it would have been if the taxpayer had received the distribution without the QCD.

When a taxpayer receives a distribution from a traditional IRA to which nondeductible contributions have been made, the taxpayer is taxed on the earnings generated by the nondeductible contributions but not on the actual nondeductible contributions. When taxpayers receive partial distributions from an IRA to which they have made nondeductible contributions (i.e., they have basis in the IRA), each distribution consists of a taxable and a nontaxable component (the nontaxable component is the portion that comes out of the taxpayer's IRA basis). The portion of the distribution that is nontaxable is the ratio of the nondeductible contribution to the total account balance at the time of the distribution.[27] This is exactly the same formula used in Example 13-12 to determine the nontaxable portion of nonqualified distributions from Roth 401(k) accounts and is similar to the formula described in the Gross Income and Exclusions chapter for determining the nontaxable portion of an annuity payment. Taxpayers report distributions from traditional IRAs with nondeductible contributions on Form 8606, "Nondeductible IRAs," part I.

THE KEY FACTS

Roth IRAs

- Contributions are not deductible.
- Same contribution limits as traditional IRAs but
  - For 2022, contribution phases out for MAGI between $129,000 and $144,000 for unmarried taxpayers and between $204,000 and $214,000 for married taxpayers filing jointly.
- Qualified distributions are not taxable.
  - To qualify, account must be open for at least five years before distribution and distribution must be made after taxpayer reaches 59½ years of age (among others).
- Nonqualified distributions of account earnings
  - Taxed at ordinary rates and subject to 10 percent penalty if the taxpayer is not at least 59½ years of age at the time of the distribution.
- Distributions come first from contributions and then from account earnings.

Roth IRAs

As an alternative to a traditional IRA, taxpayers meeting certain requirements can contribute to a Roth IRA. Contributions to a Roth IRA are *not* deductible, and *qualifying* distributions from a Roth IRA are *not* taxable.

Contributions Roth IRAs are subject to the same annual contribution limits as traditional IRAs [the lesser of $6,000 ($7,000 if at least age 50 at year-end) or earned income]. Further, the same spousal IRA rules that apply to traditional IRAs apply to Roth IRA contributions. These limits apply to the sum of a taxpayer's contributions to deductible IRAs, nondeductible IRAs, and Roth IRAs.

Whether taxpayers participate in an employer-sponsored retirement plan or not, the Roth IRA contribution limitation phases out based on modified AGI (MAGI) as follows:[28]

Unmarried taxpayers

- No phase-out if the taxpayer's MAGI is $129,000 or below.
- Proportional phase-out of full limit for MAGI between $129,000 and $144,000.
- Full phase-out (no contribution) if MAGI is $144,000 or higher.

[26]Note that taxpayers can make qualified charitable contributions if they are 70½ years of age at the time of the distribution, but taxpayers are not required to make RMDs unless they are 72 years of age at year-end.

[27]If the taxpayer has multiple IRAs at the time of the distribution, all IRAs except for Roth IRAs are combined and treated as one IRA.

[28]§408A(c)(3)(B)(i).

Married taxpayers filing jointly

- No phase-out if the taxpayer's MAGI is $204,000 or below.
- Proportional phase-out of full limit for MAGI between $204,000 and $214,000.
- Full phase-out (no contribution) if MAGI is $214,000 or higher.

Married taxpayers filing separately

- No phase-out if the taxpayer's MAGI is $0.
- Proportional phase-out of full limit if taxpayer's MAGI is between $0 and $10,000.
- Full phase-out (no contribution) if taxpayer's MAGI is equal to or greater than $10,000.

MAGI for purposes of the Roth IRA contribution limits is the same as MAGI for traditional IRA except it does not include income from rolling (or converting) a traditional retirement account into a Roth IRA. Appendix B at the end of this chapter provides a flowchart for determining Roth IRA contribution limits.

Taxpayers who exceed the MAGI thresholds for contributing to a Roth IRA are not eligible to contribute directly to a Roth IRA. However, these taxpayers may still make a "backdoor" Roth IRA contribution. To make a backdoor Roth IRA contribution, the taxpayer would contribute to a traditional IRA and then convert or roll over the funds in the traditional IRA into a Roth IRA. If the contribution going into the traditional IRA was not deductible, transferring the contribution to a Roth IRA is not taxable.[29]

Distributions *Qualified* distributions from Roth IRAs are not taxable. A qualified distribution is a distribution from funds or earnings from funds in a Roth IRA if the distribution occurs at least five years after the taxpayer opened the Roth IRA[30] and meets one of the following requirements:

- Distribution is made on or after the date the taxpayer reaches 59½ years of age.
- Distribution is made to a beneficiary (or to the estate of the taxpayer) on or after the death of the taxpayer.
- Distribution is attributable to the taxpayer being disabled.
- Distribution is used to pay qualified acquisition costs for first-time homebuyers (limited to $10,000).[31]

All other distributions are considered to be *nonqualified* distributions.

Nonqualified distributions are not necessarily taxable, however. Because taxpayers do not deduct Roth IRA contributions, they are able to withdraw the contributions tax-free at any time. However, nonqualified distributions of the *earnings* of a Roth IRA are taxable as ordinary income. The distributed earnings are also subject to a 10 percent penalty unless the taxpayer is 59½ years of age at the time of the distribution.[32] Nonqualified distributions are deemed to come:

- First from the taxpayer's contributions (nontaxable),
- Then from account earnings after the total contributions have been distributed [note that this is different from the comparable rule for Roth 401(k)s and traditional IRAs with nondeductible contributions].

Roth IRA distributions are reported on Form 8606, "Nondeductible IRAs," part III.

[29] If the taxpayer has before-tax amounts in the IRA or in the taxpayer's other IRAs, a portion of the amount transferred into the Roth IRA would be taxable, thus negating some of the benefit of the backdoor Roth.

[30] The five-year period starts on January 1 of the year in which the contribution was made and ends on the last day of the fifth taxable year. See Reg. §1.408A-6, Q&A-2 and Q&A-5(b).

[31] §408A(d)(2).

[32] See §72(t)(2) for other exceptions to the penalty.

Because distributions from Roth IRAs come first from contributions, taxpayers can treat the Roth IRA as an emergency savings account to the extent of their contributions without incurring penalties if they need to withdraw the contributions.

ETHICS

Ryan had just finished a finance class and had learned about the importance of the time value of money. With this knowledge, he wanted to start saving for retirement. Last year Ryan had a job and earned $2,000. After paying his expenses, he placed the remaining $500 in a savings account in the bank. This year, however, Ryan decided to focus on his studies, so he did not earn any income. He paid his living expenses through student loans. At the end of the current year, Ryan contributed $400 to a Roth IRA. On his tax return for the year, Ryan reported $400 of self-employment income (even though he didn't earn any). Why did Ryan report this "phantom" income? What do you think of his strategy?

Example 13-17

What if: Assume that when Tina started working for CBA, she made a one-time contribution of $4,000 to a Roth IRA. Years later, she retired at the age of 65 when the value of her Roth IRA was $60,000. If Tina receives a $10,000 distribution from her Roth IRA, what amount of taxes (and penalty, if applicable) must she pay on the distribution (assume her ordinary marginal rate is 30 percent)?

Answer: $0 taxes and $0 penalty. Qualified Roth IRA distributions are not taxable.

What if: Assume the same facts as above, except that Tina received a $10,000 distribution when she was 57 years of age. What amount of taxes and penalty, if applicable, is she required to pay on the distribution (assume a 30 percent ordinary marginal rate)?

Answer: $2,400 in total, consisting of $1,800 in taxes ($6,000 earnings distributed × 30 percent marginal tax rate) and $600 penalty ($6,000 earnings × 10 percent penalty rate). Because Tina has not reached age 59½ at the time of the distribution, this is a nonqualified distribution. Consequently, she is taxed on the $6,000 distribution of earnings ($10,000 distribution – $4,000 contribution). She is penalized on the distribution of earnings because she is not 59½ years of age at the time of the distribution.

What if: Assume that when Tina was 62 years old, she opened a Roth IRA, contributing $4,000. Three years later, Tina withdrew the entire account balance of $5,000. What amount of taxes (and penalty, if applicable) must Tina pay on the distribution (assume her marginal tax rate is 30 percent)?

Answer: $300 of taxes ($1,000 earnings × 30 percent marginal tax rate) but $0 penalty. The distribution is a nonqualified distribution because Tina did not have the Roth IRA open for five years before receiving the distribution. Consequently, she must pay tax on the $1,000 earnings portion of the distribution ($5,000 – $4,000), but she is not penalized on the distribution because she was over 59½ years of age at the time of the distribution.

In contrast to taxpayers with traditional IRAs, taxpayers are *not* required to take minimum distributions from Roth IRAs.

Converting a Traditional IRA to a Roth IRA

Many taxpayers made contributions to traditional IRAs before Roth IRAs were available. Some taxpayers may have contributed to traditional IRAs and then later decided they would prefer to have funds in a Roth IRA than a traditional IRA due to their beliefs about current and future tax rates. The tax laws accommodate these taxpayers by allowing them to convert an IRA (and other qualified defined contribution plans including SEP IRAs, discussed later in the chapter) to a Roth IRA.[33] Taxpayers can do this via direct transfer

[33]See Notice 2009-75.

from the IRA to the Roth IRA, or the taxpayer can receive a distribution from a traditional IRA and then contribute the funds to a Roth IRA. The act of receiving a distribution and contributing funds to another qualified retirement account is called a **rollover.** The process of moving funds from a traditional IRA to a Roth IRA is called a conversion. When taxpayers convert a traditional IRA into a Roth IRA via direct transfer or rollover, the entire amount coming out of the traditional IRA is taxed at ordinary rates (except for the portion deemed to come from nondeductible contributions, if any). In the case of a direct transfer, the amount transferred is not subject to the 10 percent early distribution penalty tax. However, in the case of a rollover, the amount distributed to the taxpayer is potentially subject to the 10 percent penalty to the extent the taxpayer fails to contribute the amount of the distribution that was taxable to the Roth IRA within 60 days of the withdrawal from the traditional IRA.[34] Taxpayers report conversions from traditional IRAs and SEP IRAs (discussed in self-employment retirement account sections) on Form 8606, "Nondeductible IRAs," part II.

Example 13-18

What if: Let's assume that in the year she graduated from college and began working for CBA, Tina made a fully deductible $4,000 contribution to a *traditional* IRA. Three years later, when her marginal tax rate is 22 percent, she converted the traditional IRA into a Roth IRA by directly transferring the entire $5,000 account balance into a Roth IRA. What amount of taxes is she required to pay on the conversion?

Answer: $1,100 ($5,000 × 22%). The entire $5,000 directly transferred from the traditional to the Roth IRA is taxed at 22 percent but is not subject to the 10 percent early withdrawal penalty.

What if: What amount of tax and penalty would Tina be required to pay if she converted the traditional IRA into a Roth IRA through a rollover by taking a $5,000 distribution from the traditional IRA and contributing the funds to a Roth IRA?

Answer: Tina would owe $1,100 in tax ($5,000 × 22%). The entire distribution is taxable to Tina. She would not owe any penalty tax as long as she contributed the $5,000 to the Roth IRA within 60 days of receiving the distribution.

What if: What amount of penalty would Tina be required to pay if she converted the traditional IRA into a Roth IRA through a rollover by taking a $5,000 distribution from the traditional IRA, paying the $1,100 tax liability with funds from the distribution, and contributing $3,900 to the Roth IRA within 60 days of the distribution?

Answer: She must pay a $110 penalty. The penalty is 10 percent of the $1,100 that she withdrew from the IRA and did not contribute to the Roth IRA ($5,000 − $3,900).

Why would anyone want to convert from a traditional IRA to a Roth IRA and pay taxes currently in order to avoid paying taxes later? Typically, a conversion from a traditional IRA to a Roth IRA makes sense when a taxpayer's marginal tax rate is currently low (i.e., when the tax cost of the conversion is low) and expected to be significantly higher in the future (i.e., when the expected benefit of the conversion is high). (See other reasons for converting in the next section comparing traditional and Roth IRAs.) Note that high-income taxpayers may not be allowed to contribute to Roth IRAs due to the AGI restrictions on contribution limits. However, because currently there is no AGI restriction on who may convert from a traditional IRA (or other qualified defined contribution plan) to a Roth IRA, high-income taxpayers who would like to fund a Roth IRA may do so through a conversion.[35]

THE KEY FACTS

Roth IRAs

Conversions of traditional IRA to Roth IRA through direct transfers or rollovers:

- Amount transferred or withdrawn from traditional IRA is fully taxable (amount from nondeductible contributions is not taxable) but not penalized.
- Taxpayer must contribute full amount withdrawn to Roth IRA account within 60 days of withdrawal.
- Amounts withdrawn but not contributed are subject to tax and 10 percent penalty (nondeductible contributions withdrawn are not subject to tax or penalty).

[34]§408(d)(3). Most taxpayers have the IRA custodian directly transfer the funds from the traditional IRA to the Roth IRA. With direct transfers, the 60-day rule does not apply because the taxpayer never touches the cash. Taxpayers who roll over funds from a traditional IRA (or other traditional retirement account) to a Roth IRA must wait at least five years from the date of the rollover to withdraw the funds from the rollover in order to avoid a 10 percent penalty on the distribution [§408A(d)(3)(F)].

[35]§408A(c)(3). This includes backdoor Roth IRA contributions discussed earlier in the chapter.

Comparing Traditional and Roth IRAs

So, which type of IRA is better for taxpayers? The tax considerations are very similar to those we already discussed when we compared traditional and Roth 401(k) plans. In general, after-tax rates of return from traditional IRAs will exceed those from Roth IRAs when marginal tax rates decline. However, after-tax rates of return from Roth IRAs will exceed those from traditional IRAs when tax rates increase.

Unrelated to marginal tax rates, Roth IRAs have other advantages relative to traditional IRAs, as follows:

- The minimum distribution requirements for traditional IRAs do not apply to Roth IRAs. This provision permits owners of Roth IRAs to use their accounts to generate tax-free income long after retirement.
- Taxpayers can withdraw their Roth contributions tax-free at any time without paying tax or paying a penalty. Taxpayers who withdraw their traditional IRA contributions are taxed on the distribution and potentially penalized.

Exhibit 13-7 summarizes tax-related requirements for traditional and Roth IRAs.

EXHIBIT 13-7 Traditional IRA versus Roth IRA Summary

	Traditional IRA	Roth IRA
Contributions requirements	• Taxpayer must not be a participant in an employer-sponsored plan or, if participating in an employer-provided plan, must meet certain income thresholds. Those above the threshold will have deductible portion of contribution phased out. • Contributions allowed no matter the taxpayer's age.	• No deduction allowed for contributions. Must meet certain income requirements to be able to contribute to a Roth IRA. • Contributions allowed no matter the taxpayer's age.
Contributions	• Deductible unless taxpayer is a participant in an employer plan and has high AGI. • Nondeductible contributions allowed.	• Not deductible. • May not contribute if high AGI.
Maximum contribution	• Lesser of $6,000 per taxpayer ($7,000 for taxpayers at least 50 years of age at year-end) or earned income. • The contribution limits apply to the sum of contributions to traditional deductible IRAs, nondeductible IRAs, and Roth IRAs for the year. • For married couples filing jointly, contributions for the lesser-earning spouse may not exceed the total earned income of both spouses reduced by deductible and nondeductible contributions to the other spouse's traditional IRA and by contributions to the other spouse's Roth IRA.	• Same as traditional IRA.
Contribution dates	• Can contribute up to unextended tax return due date, generally April 15.	• Same as traditional IRA.
Distributions	• Generally taxed as ordinary income. • If made before age 59½, generally subject to 10 percent penalty. • If nondeductible contribution made, allocate distribution between taxable and nontaxable amounts similar to annuity rules. • Minimum distributions required by April 1 of the year after the year in which the taxpayer reaches age 72. • Failure to meet minimum distribution timing and amount requirements triggers 50 percent penalty.	• Qualified distributions are not taxed. • Generally, distributions are qualified after account has been open for five years and employee has reached the age of 59½. • Nonqualified distributions are not taxed to the extent of prior contributions. • Nonqualified distributions of earnings are subject to tax at ordinary rates and are also subject to a 10 percent penalty if the taxpayer is not at least 59½ years of age at the time of the distribution. • No minimum distribution requirements.

TAXES IN THE REAL WORLD How to Turn a Retirement Nest Egg into a Golden Egg

Peter Thiel, founder of PayPal, used a Roth IRA as a vehicle to create an enormous amount of wealth that will never be taxed. An estimate from an article published online in June 2021 puts the balance in his Roth IRA at around $5 billion. So, how did he do it? Let's go back to 1999 when it got started. In 1999, single taxpayers with income under $110,000 could contribute up to $2,000 annually to a Roth IRA. Thiel's income for the year was just over $73,000, so he was able to contribute to a Roth. Thiel used the funds contributed to the Roth IRA to purchase founders' shares in PayPal. More specifically, he acquired 1.7 million shares in PayPal for $1,700. That's only $.001 per share. After 1999, Thiel did not contribute any more funds to his Roth IRA. In 2002, the year eBay purchased PayPal, Thiel sold the PayPal shares in his Roth account and, by the end of the year, his Roth IRA was worth about $28.5 million. From there, Thiel used the cash in the account to make other investments, including shares in other companies such as Palantir and Facebook, before they went public. By the end of 2008, Thiel's Roth IRA was worth about $870 million and, as noted above, has grown to about $5 billion. Assuming he leaves funds in his Roth IRA until April 11, 2027, when he turns 59½ years of age, he will be able to withdraw the funds tax free.

Thiel's big advantage is that, as an "insider," he was able to buy shares in a private company at what appears to be something significantly below market value. And he's not the only one benefiting from these types of valuations. While undervaluing assets acquired in a retirement account is typically not allowed, valuation can be a subjective determination. In any event, Congress has considered and is currently considering legislation to restrict the taxpayers' ability to accumulate large amounts of wealth in retirement accounts. Some prior proposals include provisions that are designed to prevent taxpayers from stuffing undervalued assets into Roth IRAs, requiring taxpayers with Roth IRA balances over $5 million to take distributions from the Roth IRA over time, and limiting taxpayers' ability to convert from traditional retirement accounts to Roth IRAs. A wealth tax proposal has also been proposed. Under this proposal, a wealth tax would be imposed on households with a net worth of over $50 million. We will have to wait and see when and if these types of tax provisions will become law. In the meantime, for some taxpayers, their Roth IRA is like a golden goose.

Sources: Justin Elliott, Patricia Callahan, and James Bandler, "The Ultrawealthy Have Hijacked Roth IRAs. The Senate Finance Chair Is Eyeing a Crackdown.," *ProPublica* (June 25, 2021), www.propublica.org/article/the-ultrawealthy-have-hijacked-roth-iras-the-senate-finance-chair-is-eyeing-a-crackdown; and Justin Elliott, Patricia Callahan, and James Bandler, "Lord of the Roths: How Tech Mogul Peter Thiel Turned a Retirement Account for the Middle Class into a $5 Billion Tax-Free Piggy Bank," *ProPublica* (June 25, 2021), www.propublica.org/article/lord-of-the-roths-how-tech-mogul-peter-thiel-turned-a-retirement-account-for-the-middle-class-into-a-5-billion-dollar-tax-free-piggy-bank.

SELF-EMPLOYED RETIREMENT ACCOUNTS

LO 13-5

We've discussed retirement savings opportunities available to employees. However, many taxpayers are self-employed small business owners who do not have access to employer-sponsored plans.[36] Moreover, individually managed retirement plans such as traditional and Roth IRAs are not particularly attractive to self-employed taxpayers due to the relatively low contribution limits on these plans. What retirement savings options, then, are available to the self-employed?

Congress has created a number of retirement savings plans for self-employed taxpayers. Two of the more popular are simplified employee pension (SEP) IRAs and individual (or "self-employed" or "solo") 401(k) plans. These are defined contribution plans that generally work the same way as employer-provided plans. That is, amounts set aside in these plans are deducted from income, earnings are free of tax until distributed, and distributions from the plans are fully taxable.[37] As we discuss below, these plans differ in

THE KEY FACTS

Self-Employed Retirement Accounts

- Popular plans include SEP IRAs and individual 401(k)s.
- Similar to (non-Roth) qualified defined contribution plans.
  - Contributions are deductible and distributions are taxable.

[36]Because sole proprietorships with self-employment income are very common, we assume in our examples and explanations here that any self-employment income originates from a sole proprietorship. In some cases, however, partners and LLC members may also have self-employment income from a partnership or LLC.

[37]"Keogh" self-employed defined benefit plans are also an option. Generally, defined benefit plans are attractive to older, self-employed individuals with profitable businesses because they allow for greater deductible contributions. However, they are usually more costly to maintain than the defined contribution plans we mention here.

terms of their annual contribution limits. They also have different nontax characteristics, including their suitability for businesses with employees other than the owner and their administration costs. As you might expect, these factors should be considered when self-employed small business owners choose a retirement plan.[38] We describe SEP IRAs and individual 401(k) plans below.[39]

Simplified Employee Pension (SEP) IRA

A simplified employee pension (SEP) can be administered through an individual retirement account (IRA) called a **SEP IRA.**[40] The owner of a sole proprietorship can make annual contributions directly to a SEP IRA. For 2022, the annual contribution is limited to the *lesser* of:

- $61,000 or
- 20 percent of Schedule C net income, after reducing Schedule C net income by the deduction for the employer's portion of self-employment taxes paid (50 percent of the self-employment taxes paid).[41]

In general, the self-employment tax base is 92.65 percent of Schedule C net income (termed "net earnings from self-employment"). The self-employment tax rate is 15.3 percent of the first $147,000 of self employment tax base plus 2.9 percent on the amount above $147,000 (2022 limits). See the Individual Income Tax Computation and Tax Credits chapter for details on computing self-employment tax.

Contributions can be made up to the extended due date of the tax return.[42] While taxpayers are not allowed to make nondeductible contributions to SEP IRAs (no Roth option), they can convert funds in a SEP IRA to a Roth IRA. This would have the same effect as backdoor Roth IRA contributions through nondeductible traditional IRA contributions except the limit would be much higher (i.e., potentially $61,000 vs. $6,000, depending on income) because the SEP IRA contribution would be deductible and the Roth conversion would be taxable. The deduction and the income would offset, so there would be no immediate tax cost or tax savings associated with the conversion.

Example 13-19

What if: Dave (assume age 64) reports Schedule C net income of $40,000 during the current year. If he sets up a SEP IRA for himself, what is the maximum contribution he may make to the plan (assuming he has no other self-employment income and he has no income as an employee)?

Answer: $7,435, computed as follows:

Description	Amount	Explanation
(1) First limit on contribution	$61,000	
(2) Schedule C net income minus the self-employment tax deduction	37,174	$40,000 − ($40,000 × .9235 × 15.3% × 50%)
(3) Percentage for limitation based on (2)	20%	
(4) Second limit on contribution	7,435	(2) × (3)
Maximum contribution	**$7,435**	Lesser of (1) or (4)

[38]Many investment firms provide comparisons to help taxpayers select self-employed retirement plans. For example, see www.fidelity.com/retirement/small-business/compare-plans-chart.

[39]A Savings Incentive Match Plans for Employees (SIMPLE) IRA is another popular form of retirement plan for the self-employed. For those earning lower amounts of self-employment income, the contribution limits for a SIMPLE IRA are generally higher than contribution limits for SEP IRAs.

[40]§408(k).

[41]Note that for SEP IRAs, no catch-up contributions are allowed for taxpayers 50 years of age and older.

[42]§404(h). This is October 15 for a calendar-year taxpayer.

What if: Assume Dave is 48 years old at the end of the year. What is his maximum deductible contribution?

Answer: $7,435. Dave's maximum deductible contribution for a SEP IRA does not depend on his age.

What if: Suppose Dave reports $310,000 of Schedule C net income rather than $40,000. What is his maximum deductible contribution to his SEP IRA account?

Answer: $59,347, the lesser of (1) $61,000 or (2) $59,347 {20% × [$310,000 − ({(310,000 × .9235 − $147,000) × 2.9% × 50%} + {$147,000 × 15.3% × 50%})]}.

THE KEY FACTS

Self-Employed Retirement Accounts

SEP IRA 2022 contribution limit.

- Lesser of (1) $61,000 or (2) 20 percent of Schedule C net income (after reducing Schedule C net income by the deduction for the employer's portion of self-employment taxes paid).

Nontax Considerations If a sole proprietor has hired employees, the sole proprietor *must* contribute to the employees' respective SEP IRAs based on their compensation. Because owners may view this requirement as being too costly, the SEP IRA is best suited for sole proprietors who do not have employees or who are willing to provide generous benefits to their employees. From an administrative perspective, SEP IRAs are easy to set up and have relatively low administrative costs from year to year.

Individual 401(k) Plans

Individual 401(k) plans are strictly for sole proprietors (and their spouses who work for the business) who do not have employees. Under this type of plan, for 2022, the sole proprietor can contribute the lesser of:

- $61,000 ($67,500 if at least 50 years old at year-end) or
- 20 percent of Schedule C net income, after reducing Schedule C net income by the deduction for the employer's portion of self-employment taxes paid (50 percent of self-employment taxes paid) plus an additional $20,500 (employee's contribution).

Further, if the sole proprietor is at least 50 years of age by the end of the tax year, the proprietor may contribute an *additional* $6,500 as a catch-up contribution. Thus, a self-employed taxpayer with sufficient self-employment earnings who is at least 50 years of age at year-end could contribute up to $67,500 to an individual 401(k) for 2022 ($61,000 + $6,500). The overall limit consists of $20,500 ($27,000 if 50 years of age at year-end) of "employee" contributions (note that SEP IRAs don't have employee contributions) and employer contributions of $61,000 (or $67,500 if age 50 or over) minus the employee contributions. Taxpayers can set up an individual Roth IRA to receive employee contributions but not employer contributions.

Finally, even though individual 401(k) contribution limits provide for taxpayers to contribute an additional $20,500 or $27,000 (this includes the additional $6,500 for taxpayers at least 50 years of age at year-end) relative to a SEP IRA, a taxpayer's individual 401(k) contributions for the year are not allowed to exceed the taxpayer's Schedule C net income minus the self-employment tax deduction. Consequently, a taxpayer with limited self-employment income may not be able to take full advantage of the additional $20,500 ($27,000) employee contribution limit available to individual 401(k)s relative to SEP IRAs.

THE KEY FACTS

Self-Employed Retirement Accounts

Individual 401(k) 2022 contribution limit.

- Lesser of (1) $61,000 or (2) 20 percent of Schedule C net income (after reducing Schedule C net income by the deduction for the employer's portion of self-employment taxes paid) plus $20,500. The additional $20,500 is allowed as an "employee" contribution.
- Taxpayers who are at least 50 years old at the end of the year may contribute an additional $6,500 per year (maximum of $67,500, if self-employment earnings are sufficient). The additional contribution limit is considered to be an "employee contribution."
- Contribution cannot exceed Schedule C net income minus self-employment tax deduction.

Nontax Considerations As we mentioned above, the individual 401(k) plan is not available for sole proprietors with employees, so providing benefits to employees under the plan is not a concern. However, the administrative burden of establishing, operating, and maintaining a 401(k) plan is potentially higher than it is for the other self-employed plans.

Example 13-20

What if: Suppose that Dave is 64 years old at the end of the year, reports $40,000 of Schedule C net income, and has no other sources of income. What is the maximum amount he can contribute to an individual 401(k) account?

Answer: $34,435, computed as follows:

Description	Amount	Explanation
(1) Annual limit on contribution	$ 61,000	
(2) Schedule C net income minus the self-employment tax deduction	37,174	$40,000 – ($40,000 × .9235 × 15.3% × 50%)
(3) Percentage for limitation based on (2)	20%	
(4) Limit on employer's contribution	7,435	(2) × (3)
(5) Limit on employee's contribution	20,500	
(6) Second limitation	27,935	(4) + (5)
(7) Maximum contribution before catch-up contribution	27,935	Lesser of (1) or (6)
(8) Catch-up contribution	6,500	Dave is 64 years old at year-end
Maximum contribution	**$34,435**	(7) + (8), not to exceed (2)

Example 13-21

What if: Assume Dave is 48 years old at the end of the year, reports $40,000 of Schedule C net income, and has no other sources of income. What is his maximum deductible contribution to his individual 401(k) account?

Answer: $27,935. This is the same as the amount he could contribute as a 64-year-old (see prior example), minus the $6,500 catch-up adjustment ($34,435 – $6,500).

What if: Assume the same facts as above except that Dave (age 64) earned $10,000 of Schedule C net income rather than $40,000. What is his maximum deductible contribution to his individual 401(k)?

Answer: $9,294, computed as follows (Dave's contribution is limited to his Schedule C net income minus self-employment tax deduction):

Description	Amount	Explanation
(1) First limit on contribution	$61,000	
(2) Schedule C net income minus self-employment tax deduction	9,294	$10,000 – ($10,000 × .9235 × 15.3% × 50%)
(3) Percentage for limitation based on (2)	20%	
(4) Limit on employer's contribution	1,859	(2) × (3)
(5) Limit on employee's contribution	20,500	
(6) Second limitation	22,359	(4) + (5)
(7) Maximum contribution before income limitation	22,359	Lesser of (1) or (6)
Maximum contribution	**$ 9,294**	Lesser of (7) and (2)

Example 13-22

What if: Assume Dave (age 64) earned $400,000 of Schedule C net income. What is his maximum deductible contribution to his individual 401(k)?

Answer: $67,500, computed as follows:

Description	Amount	Explanation
(1) First limit on contribution	$ 61,000	
(2) Schedule C net income minus self-employment tax deduction	385,530	$400,000 − {[(400,000 × .9235 − 147,000) × 2.9% × 50%] + [147,000 × 15.3% × 50%]}
(3) Percentage for limitation based on (2)	20%	
(4) Limit on employer's contribution	77,106	(2) × (3)
(5) Limit on employee's contribution	20,500	
(6) Second limitation	97,606	(4) + (5)
(7) Maximum contribution before catch-up contribution	61,000	Lesser of (1) or (6)
(8) Catch-up contribution	6,500	Dave is 64 years old at year-end.
Maximum contribution	**$ 67,500**	(7) + (8), not to exceed (2)

SAVER'S CREDIT

LO 13-6

To encourage middle- and low-income taxpayers to take advantage of the retirement savings opportunities discussed in this chapter, Congress provides an additional saver's credit for an individual's elective contribution of up to $2,000 to any of the qualified retirement plans discussed in this chapter, including employer-sponsored qualified plans, traditional and Roth IRA plans, and self-employed qualified plans. The credit is provided *in addition to* any deduction the taxpayer is allowed for contributing to a retirement account. It is calculated by multiplying the taxpayer's contribution, up to a maximum of $2,000, by the applicable percentage depending on the taxpayer's filing status and AGI. The credit is nonrefundable. Exhibit 13-8 provides the applicable percentages for 2022 according to a taxpayer's filing status and AGI.[43]

THE KEY FACTS

Saver's Credit

- Credit for taxpayers contributing to qualified plan.
- Credit is based on contributions up to $2,000, taxpayer's filing status, and AGI.
  - Phased out as AGI increases.
  - Maximum credit is $1,000.
  - Unavailable for married filing jointly taxpayers with AGI over $68,000, head of household taxpayers with AGI above $51,000, and all other taxpayers with AGI above $34,000.

EXHIBIT 13-8 2022 Applicable Percentages for Saver's Credit by Filing Status and AGI

Applicable Percentage	Joint Filers AGI	Heads of Household AGI	All Other Filers AGI
50%	$0 to $41,000	$0 to $30,750	$0 to $20,500
20	$41,001 to $44,000	$30,751 to $33,000	$20,501 to $22,000
10	$44,001 to $68,000	$33,001 to $51,000	$22,001 to $34,000
No credit available	Above $68,000	Above $51,000	Above $34,000

[43]For this purpose, AGI is determined without considering the foreign-earned income exclusion provided for U.S. residents living abroad under §911.

In addition to restricting the credit to taxpayers with AGI below a certain threshold, the credit is also restricted to individuals who are 18 years of age or older, are not claimed as dependents by another taxpayer, and are not full-time students at a qualified educational organization during each of five calendar months of the taxpayer's tax year.[44] Although limited in scope, the saver's credit provides some tax benefits for those taxpayers who qualify.

Example 13-23

What if: Tina earned $25,000 during the year she began working for CBA. She earned $5,000 in salary working part time while she was in school and $20,000 in salary working for CBA from September through December. To get an early start saving for retirement, assume she contributed $4,000 to a traditional IRA. Because Tina did not participate in an employer-sponsored retirement plan during the current year, she may deduct the full $4,000 contribution as a for AGI deduction, reducing her AGI from $25,000 to $21,000. What amount of saver's credit, if any, is Tina allowed to claim, assuming she was a full-time student during four months of the year?

Answer: $400 ($2,000 × 20 percent applicable credit).

What if: What saver's credit may Tina claim if her AGI were $15,000?

Answer: $1,000 ($2,000 × 50 percent applicable credit).

CONCLUSION

The decisions that employees like Tina, Lisa, and Dave must deal with highlight the role that tax issues play in this important area. Employers, like their employees, must also pay careful attention to tax considerations when deciding on retirement savings vehicles to offer their employees. Further, as has been a recurring theme throughout this book, nontax issues play an equal, if not more important, role in the retirement savings decisions of both employees and employers.

[44]§152(f)(2).

Appendix A (Page 1) Traditional IRA Deduction Limitations

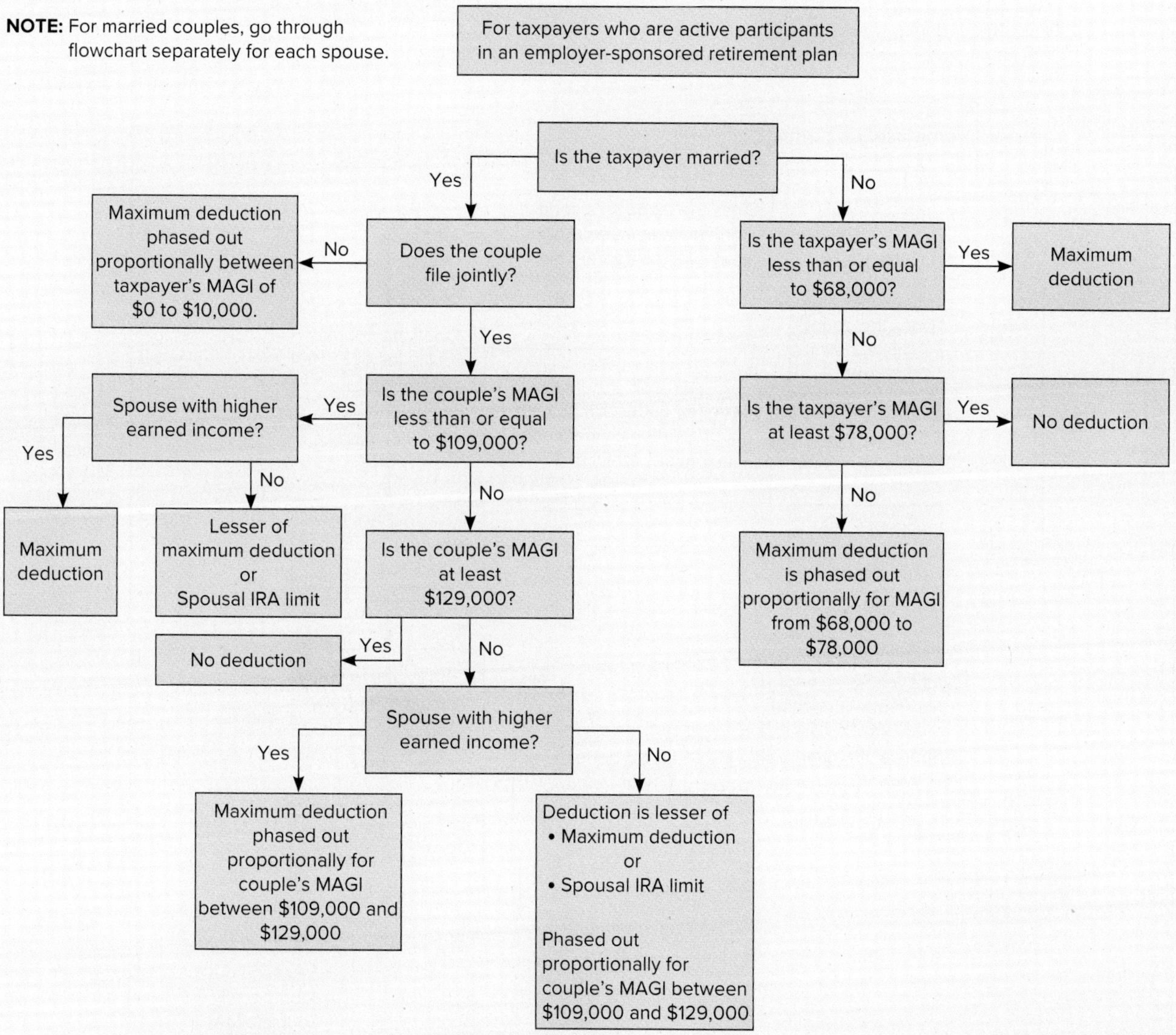

Spousal IRA Limit.
Total earned income of both spouses reduced by contributions to deductible IRAs, nondeductible IRAs, and Roth IRAs made by higher-earning spouse.

Maximum Deduction
Least of:
- $6,000 ($7,000 if at least age 50 at year-end)
- Taxpayer's earned income for year

NOTES: The sum of the taxpayer's deductible IRA contributions, nondeductible IRA contributions, and Roth IRA contributions cannot exceed $6,000 (or $7,000 if the taxpayer is at least 50 years old at year-end). MAGI generally is AGI disregarding the deduction for the IRA contribution itself.

(Page 2) Traditional IRA Deduction Limitations

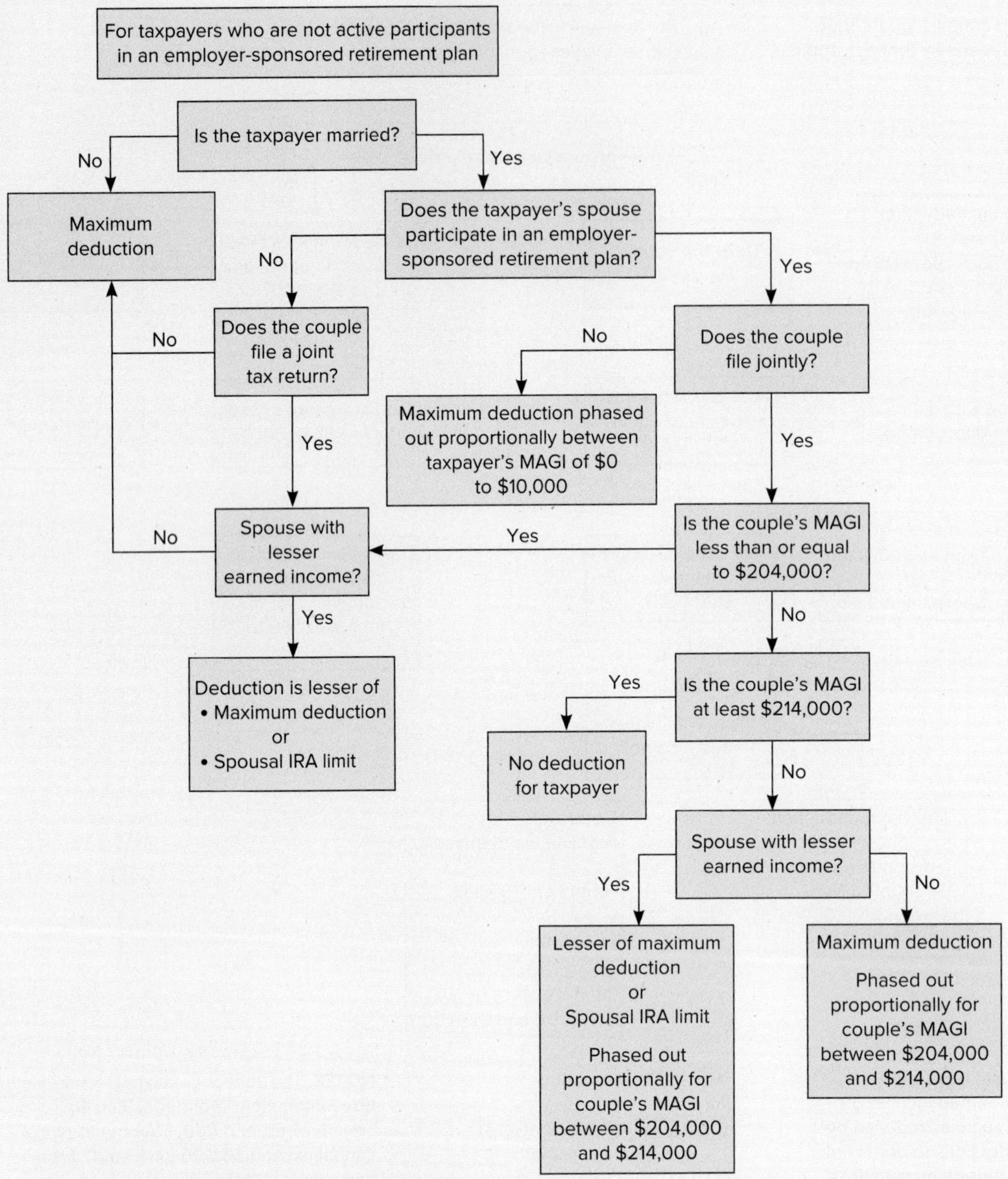

Spousal IRA Limit.
Total earned income of both spouses reduced by contributions to deductible IRAs, nondeductible IRAs, and Roth IRAs made by higher-earning spouse.

Maximum Deduction
Least of:
- $6,000 ($7,000 if at least age 50 at year-end)
- Taxpayer's earned income for year

NOTES: The sum of the taxpayer's deductible IRA contributions, nondeductible IRA contributions, and Roth IRA contributions cannot exceed $6,000 (or $7,000 if the taxpayer is at least 50 years old at year-end). MAGI generally is AGI disregarding the deduction for the IRA contribution itself.

Appendix B Roth IRA Contribution Limits

NOTE: For married couples, go through flowchart for each spouse separately.

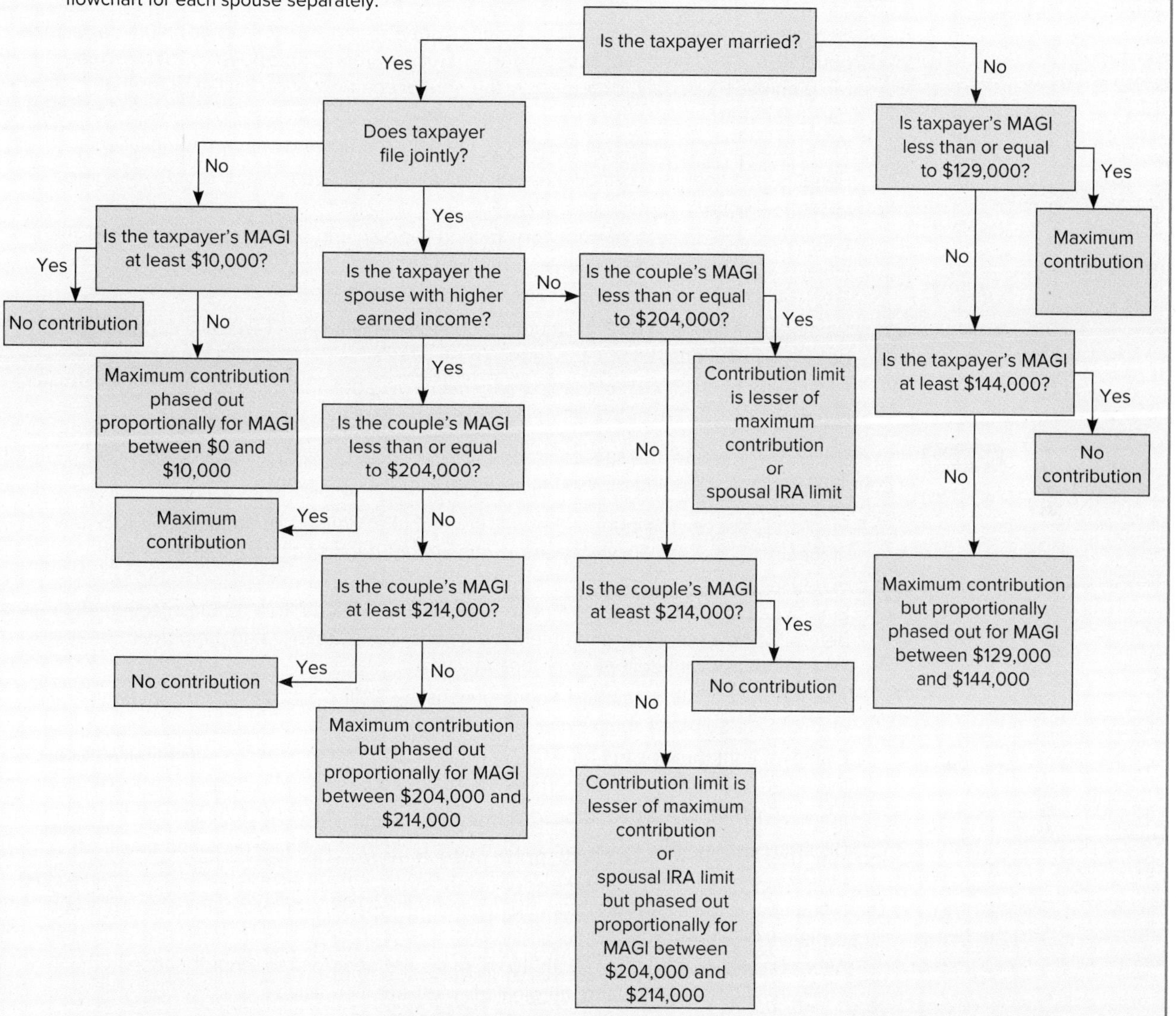

Spousal IRA Limit.
Total earned income of both spouses reduced by contributions to deductible IRAs, nondeductible IRAs, and Roth IRAs.

Maximum Contribution Lesser or
- $6,000 ($7,000 if the taxpayer is at least age 50 at year-end) and
- Taxpayer's earned income

NOTES: The sum of the taxpayer's deductible IRA contributions, nondeductible IRA contributions, and Roth IRA contributions cannot exceed $6,000 (or $7,000 if the taxpayer is at least 50 years old at year-end). MAGI is AGI disregarding any IRA deduction and income generated by rolling over a traditional IRA into a Roth IRA.

Summary

LO 13-1 Describe the tax and nontax aspects of employer-provided defined benefit plans from both the employer's and the employee's perspectives.

- Benefits are determined based on years of service and salary. The maximum compensation that can be taken into account for a particular year for purposes of determining the employee's benefit is capped by the annual compensation limitation for that particular year.
- The maximum annual benefit is capped and adjusted upward annually for inflation.
- Benefits vest over time using (at a minimum) either a five-year cliff or seven-year graded vesting schedule.
- Employers deduct cash contributions to fund the plan and employees treat cash distributions as ordinary income in the year received.
- Employers bear investment risk with defined benefit plans.
- Premature distribution and minimum distribution penalties don't typically apply to defined benefit distributions.
- Because of the high cost of funding and maintaining defined benefit plans, they are waning in popularity.

LO 13-2 Explain and determine the tax consequences associated with employer-provided defined contribution plans, including traditional 401(k) and Roth 401(k) plans.

- Employers specify the amount they will contribute to defined contribution plans instead of the annual benefit. However, employers are not permitted to contribute to Roth 401(k) plans.
- Employees may contribute to either a traditional 401(k) or a Roth 401(k) account, and they determine how employer and employee contributions are invested. Employees bear investment risk with defined contribution plans.
- Annual employer and employee contributions are limited and maximum contribution amounts are adjusted annually for inflation.
- Employer contributions to traditional plans vest over time using (at a minimum) either a three-year cliff or six-year graded vesting schedule.
- Employers deduct their contributions to traditional defined contribution plans.
- Distributions from traditional 401(k) plans are taxable at ordinary rates and qualified distributions from Roth 401(k) plans are not taxable.
- Distributions from both traditional 401(k) and Roth 401(k) plans are subject to early and minimum distribution penalties.
- After-tax rates of return from Roth 401(k) plans are generally superior to those from traditional 401(k) plans when marginal tax rates are increasing.

LO 13-3 Describe the tax implications of deferred compensation from both the employer's and the employee's perspectives.

- Employees elect to defer current salary in exchange for promised future payments from the employer.
- Because the employer's promise of future payment is unsecured, employees recognize ordinary income when future payments are received. Employers wait to deduct payments until cash is actually paid.
- The after-tax rate of return and costs from deferred compensation arrangements to employees and employers depend on the current and future marginal tax rates of both the employee and the employer.
- Deferred compensation can be used to overcome constraints imposed on employer contributions to an employee's qualified retirement account.
- Employees bear more risk with deferred compensation relative to other forms of retirement savings because employees are unsecured creditors of their employers and because the investments upon which their compensation is based have risk.

Compare and determine the tax consequences of traditional and Roth IRAs (individual retirement accounts). LO 13-4

- The same inflation-adjusted annual contribution limits apply to both traditional IRAs and Roth IRAs.
- The deduction for traditional IRA contributions is phased out for taxpayers covered by a retirement plan at work and with modified AGI above certain inflation-adjusted amounts. Special rules pertain for spouses not covered by an employer plan.
- The ability to contribute to a Roth IRA is phased out for individuals with modified AGI above certain inflation-adjusted amounts.
- Distributions from traditional IRAs are taxed at ordinary rates. A 10 percent early distribution penalty generally applies to distributions from traditional IRAs received before age 59½.
- Taxpayers can make qualified charitable distributions (QCDs) from traditional IRAs if they are at least 70½ years of age at the time of the distribution. The distribution counts toward any RMD requirements and is excluded from gross income. It does not also count as a charitable donation itemized deduction.
- Distributions from Roth IRAs received after a Roth IRA account has been open for at least five years and after the recipient reaches age 59½ are not taxable. The earnings component of any distributions not meeting these requirements is generally taxable and subject to the 10 percent early distribution penalty.
- Taxpayers generally prefer Roth IRAs to traditional IRAs when they expect their marginal tax rates to increase.

Describe retirement savings account options for self-employed taxpayers and compute the limitations for deductible contributions to these accounts. LO 13-5

- Self-employed individuals may set up their own qualified pension plans such as SEP IRAs and individual 401(k) plans.
- Contribution limits generally parallel those for employer-sponsored plans, allowing self-employed individuals to have the same access to qualified plans that employees have.
- Self-employed individuals with employees may have to incur the cost of covering their employees when they establish a qualified retirement plan.

Compute the saver's credit. LO 13-6

- Individuals may receive up to a $1,000 tax credit for contributions they make to IRAs and employer-sponsored qualified plans.
- The amount of the credit is a function of the taxpayer's filing status and AGI.

KEY TERMS

cliff vesting (13-4)
defined benefit plans (13-3)
defined contribution plans (13-3)
graded vesting (13-4)
individual retirement account (IRA) (13-20)
nonqualified deferred compensation (13-16)
qualified retirement plans (13-3)
rollover (13-27)
Roth 401(k) (13-12)
Roth IRA (13-20)
SEP IRA (13-30)
spousal IRA (13-21)
traditional 401(k) (13-12)
traditional IRA (13-20)
vesting (13-4)

DISCUSSION QUESTIONS

Discussion Questions are available in Connect®.

1. How are defined benefit plans different from defined contribution plans? How are they similar? LO 13-1 LO 13-2
2. Describe how an employee's benefit under a defined benefit plan is computed. LO 13-1
3. True or False. Both Sato and Kiran have worked for JBP Corp. and have participated in JBP's defined benefit plan for the past 20 years. Sato's annual salary over the prior three years was $800,000 and Kiran's annual salary over the prior three LO 13-1

years was $500,000. Assuming both retire effective January 1 of the current year, Sato's annual retirement payment from the defined benefit plan will be higher than Kiran's annual retirement payment. Explain.

LO 13-1 LO 13-2
4. What does it mean to vest in a defined benefit or defined contribution plan?

LO 13-1 LO 13-2
5. Compare and contrast the minimum vesting requirements for defined benefit plans and defined contribution plans.

LO 13-1 LO 13-2
6. What are the nontax advantages and disadvantages of defined benefit plans relative to defined contribution plans?

LO 13-1
7. Describe the maximum annual benefit that taxpayers may receive under defined benefit plans.

LO 13-1
8. Describe the distribution or payout options available to taxpayers participating in qualified defined benefit plans. How are defined benefit plan distributions to recipients taxed?

LO 13-1 LO 13-2
9. Describe the minimum distribution requirements for defined benefit plans. Are these requirements typically an item of concern for taxpayers? Explain.

LO 13-1 LO 13-2
10. Compare and contrast the employer's responsibilities for providing a defined benefit plan to employees relative to providing a defined contribution plan.

LO 13-2
11. Describe how an employee's benefit under a defined contribution plan is determined.

LO 13-2
12. Is there a limit to how much an employer and/or employee may contribute to an employee's defined contribution account(s) for the year? If so, describe the limit.

LO 13-2 planning
13. Cami (age 52 and married) was recently laid off as part of her employer's reduction in workforce program. Cami's annual AGI was usually around $50,000. Shortly after Cami's employment was terminated, her employer distributed the balance of her employer-sponsored 401(k) account to her. What could Cami do to avoid being assessed the 10 percent early distribution penalty?

LO 13-2
14. When may employees begin to receive defined contribution plan distributions without penalty?

LO 13-2
15. Describe the circumstances under which distributions from defined contribution plans are penalized. What are the penalties?

LO 13-2 research
16. Brady Corporation has a profit-sharing plan that allocates 10 percent of all after-tax income to employees. The profit sharing is allocated to individual employees based on relative employee compensation. The profit-sharing contributions vest to employees under a six-year graded plan. If an employee terminates their employment before fully vesting, the plan allocates the forfeited amounts among the remaining participants according to their account balances. Is this forfeiture allocation policy discriminatory, and will it cause the plan to lose its qualified status? (*Hint:* Use Rev. Rul. 81-10 to help formulate your answer.)

LO 13-2
17. What does it mean if an employer "matches" employee contributions to 401(k) plans?

planning LO 13-2
18. What nontax factor(s) should an employee consider when deciding whether and to what extent to participate in an employer's 401(k) plan?

LO 13-2
19. What are the differences between a traditional 401(k) and a Roth 401(k) plan?

LO 13-2
20. Can employers match employee contributions to Roth 401(k) plans? Explain.

LO 13-2
21. Describe the annual limitation on employer and employee contributions to traditional 401(k) and Roth 401(k) plans.

LO 13-2 LO 13-3
22. When a company is limited by the tax laws in the amount it can contribute to an employee's 401(k) plan, what will it generally do to make the employee whole? Is this likely an issue for rank-and-file employees? Why or why not?

planning LO 13-2
23. From a tax perspective, how would taxpayers determine whether they should contribute to a traditional 401(k) or a Roth 401(k)?

24. Could a taxpayer contributing to a traditional 401(k) plan earn an after-tax return *greater* than the before-tax return? Explain. LO 13-2
25. Explain the *tax* similarities and differences between qualified defined contribution plans and nonqualified deferred compensation plans from an *employer's* perspective. LO 13-2 LO 13-3
26. Explain the *tax* similarities and differences between qualified defined contribution plans and nonqualified deferred compensation plans from an *employee's* perspective. LO 13-2 LO 13-3
27. Explain the *nontax* similarities and differences between qualified defined contribution plans and nonqualified deferred compensation plans from an *employer's* perspective. LO 13-2 LO 13-3
28. Explain the *nontax* similarities and differences between qualified defined contribution plans and nonqualified deferred compensation plans from an *employee's* perspective. LO 13-2 LO 13-3
29. From a *tax* perspective, what issues does an employee need to consider in deciding whether to defer compensation under a nonqualified deferred compensation plan or to receive it immediately? LO 13-3 planning
30. From a *nontax* perspective, what issues does an employee need to consider in deciding whether to defer compensation under a nonqualified deferred compensation plan or to receive it immediately? LO 13-3 planning
31. What are reasons why companies provide nonqualified deferred compensation plans for certain employees? LO 13-3
32. Are companies allowed to decide who can and cannot participate in nonqualified deferred compensation plans? Briefly explain. LO 13-3
33. How might the ultimate benefits to an employee who participates in a qualified retirement plan of a company differ from the ultimate benefits to an employee who participates in a nonqualified deferred compensation plan of the company if the company experiences bankruptcy before the employee is scheduled to receive the benefits? LO 13-1 LO 13-2 LO 13-3
34. Deductions for traditional IRAs and contributions to Roth IRAs are phased out based on modified AGI (MAGI). In general terms, how does MAGI for purposes of determining the traditional IRA deduction differ from AGI, and how does it differ from MAGI for purposes of determining whether a taxpayer can contribute to a Roth IRA? LO 13-4
35. What are the primary tax differences between traditional IRAs and Roth IRAs? LO 13-4
36. Describe the circumstances in which it would be more favorable for a taxpayer to contribute to a traditional IRA rather than a Roth IRA, and vice versa. LO 13-4 planning
37. What are the requirements for a taxpayer to make a deductible contribution to a traditional IRA? Why do the tax laws impose these restrictions? LO 13-4
38. What is the limitation on a deductible IRA contribution for 2022? LO 13-4
39. Compare the minimum distribution requirements for traditional IRAs to those of Roth IRAs. LO 13-4
40. What is a qualified charitable donation (QCD), who is eligible to complete a QCD, and how would a taxpayer benefit from a QCD? LO 13-4 planning
41. How are qualified distributions from Roth IRAs taxed? How are nonqualified distributions taxed? LO 13-4
42. Explain when a taxpayer will be subject to the 10 percent penalty when receiving distributions from a Roth IRA. LO 13-4
43. Is a taxpayer who contributed to a traditional IRA able to convert the funds to a Roth IRA? If yes, explain the tax consequences of the conversion. LO 13-4
44. What is a "backdoor" Roth IRA contribution, and when is it useful? LO 13-4 LO 13-5 planning

LO 13-4 45. Assume a taxpayer makes a nondeductible contribution to a traditional IRA. How does the taxpayer determine the taxability of distributions from the IRA on reaching retirement?

LO 13-4 46. When a taxpayer receives a nonqualified distribution from a Roth IRA, is the entire amount of the distribution treated as taxable income? Explain.

LO 13-5 47. What types of retirement plans are available to self-employed taxpayers?

LO 13-5 48. Compare and contrast the annual limitations on deductible contributions to SEP IRAs and individual 401(k) accounts for self-employed taxpayers.

planning LO 13-5 49. What are the nontax considerations for self-employed taxpayers deciding whether to set up a SEP IRA or an individual 401(k)?

LO 13-6 50. What is the saver's credit, and who is eligible to receive it?

LO 13-6 51. What is the maximum saver's credit available to taxpayers? What taxpayer characteristics are relevant to the determination?

LO 13-6 52. How is the saver's credit computed?

PROBLEMS

Select problems are available in Connect®.

LO 13-1 53. Haley has an annual salary of $1,000,000 in 2019, 2020, and 2021. She is thinking about retiring at the beginning of 2022 after working for XYZ Corp. and participating in XYZ Corp.'s defined benefit plan. If XYZ Corp.'s defined benefit plan pays employees 3 percent for every year of service for the average of their three highest years of compensation, what is the minimum number of years of service that would maximize Haley's benefit if she were to retire at the beginning of 2022? Assuming she worked the minimum number of years to receive the maximum benefit, what would her annual defined benefit plan payment be in retirement?

LO 13-1 54. Javier recently graduated and started his career with DNL Inc. DNL provides a defined benefit plan to all employees. According to the terms of the plan, for each full year of service working for the employer, employees receive a benefit of 1.5 percent of their average salary over their highest three years of compensation from the company. Employees may accrue only 30 years of benefit under the plan (45 percent). Determine Javier's annual benefit on retirement, before taxes, under each of the following scenarios:

a) Javier works for DNL for three years and three months before he leaves for another job. Javier's annual salary was $55,000, $65,000, $70,000, and $72,000 for years 1, 2, 3, and 4, respectively. DNL uses a five-year cliff vesting schedule.

b) Javier works for DNL for three years and three months before he leaves for another job. Javier's annual salary was $55,000, $65,000, $70,000, and $72,000 for years 1, 2, 3, and 4, respectively. DNL uses a seven-year graded vesting schedule.

c) Javier works for DNL for six years and three months before he leaves for another job. Javier's annual salary was $75,000, $85,000, $90,000, and $95,000 for years 4, 5, 6, and 7, respectively. DNL uses a five-year cliff vesting schedule.

d) Javier works for DNL for six years and three months before he leaves for another job. Javier's annual salary was $75,000, $85,000, $90,000, and $95,000 for years 4, 5, 6, and 7, respectively. DNL uses a seven-year graded vesting schedule.

e) Javier works for DNL for 32 years and three months before retiring. Javier's annual salary was $175,000, $185,000, $190,000, and $195,000 for his final 4 years of employment. Note that in the year he retired, he didn't work for the entire year, so he received only a portion of the annual salary for that year.

55. Alicia has been working for JMM Corp. for 32 years. Alicia participates in JMM's defined benefit plan. Under the plan, for every year of service for JMM, she is to receive 2 percent of the average salary of her three highest consecutive calendar years of compensation from JMM. She retired on January 1, 2022. Before retirement, her annual salary was $570,000, $600,000, and $630,000 for 2019, 2020, and 2021. What is the maximum benefit Alicia can receive in 2022? LO 13-1

56. Allie received a $50,000 distribution from her 401(k) account this year that she established while working for Big Stories Inc. Assuming her marginal ordinary tax rate is 24 percent, how much tax and penalty will Allie pay on the distribution under the following circumstances? LO 13-2
   a) Allie is 45 and still employed with Big Stories Inc.
   b) Allie is 56 and was terminated from Big Stories Inc. this year.
   c) Allie is 67 and retired.

57. Tim has worked for one employer his entire career. While he was working, he participated in the employer's defined contribution plan [traditional 401(k)]. At the end of 2022, Tim retires. The balance in his defined contribution plan at the end of 2021 was $2,000,000. LO 13-2 tax forms
   a) What is Tim's required minimum distribution for 2022 that must be distributed in 2023 if he is 68 years old at the end of 2022?
   b) What is Tim's required minimum distribution for 2022 if he turns 72 during 2022? When must he receive this distribution?
   c) What is Tim's required minimum distribution for 2022 that must be distributed in 2023 if he turns 75 years old in 2022?
   d) Assuming that Tim is 76 years old at the end of 2022 and his marginal tax rate is 32 percent, what amount of his distribution will he have remaining after taxes if he receives only a distribution of $50,000 for 2022?
   e) Complete Form 5329, page 2, to report the minimum distribution penalty in question d). Use the most recent form available.

58. Matthew (48 at year-end) develops cutting-edge technology for SV Inc., located in Silicon Valley. In 2022, Matthew participates in SV's money purchase pension plan (a defined contribution plan) and in his company's 401(k) plan. Under the money purchase pension plan, SV contributes 15 percent of an employee's salary to a retirement account for the employee up to the amount limited by the tax law. Because it provides the money purchase pension plan, SV does not contribute to the employee's 401(k) plan. Matthew would like to maximize his contribution to his 401(k) account after SV's contribution to the money purchase plan. LO 13-2
   a) Assuming Matthew's annual salary is $400,000, what amount will SV contribute to Matthew's money purchase plan? What can Matthew contribute to his 401(k) account in 2022?
   b) Assuming Matthew's annual salary is $240,000, what amount will SV contribute to Matthew's money purchase plan? What can Matthew contribute to his 401(k) account in 2022?
   c) Assuming Matthew's annual salary is $60,000, what amount will SV contribute to Matthew's money purchase plan? What amount can Matthew contribute to his 401(k) account in 2022?
   d) Assume the same facts as in part (c), except that Matthew is 54 years old at the end of 2022. What amount can Matthew contribute to his 401(k) account in 2022?

59. In 2022, Maggy (34 years old) is an employee of YBU Corp. YBU provides a 401(k) plan for all its employees. According to the terms of the plan, YBU contributes 50 cents for every dollar the employee contributes. The maximum employer LO 13-2 planning

contribution under the plan is 15 percent of the employee's salary (if allowed, YBU contributes until the employee has contributed 30 percent of her salary).

a) Maggy worked for YBU Corporation for 3½ years before deciding to leave effective July 1, 2022. Maggy's annual salary during this time was $45,000, $52,000, $55,000, and $60,000 (she only received half of her $60,000 2022 salary). Assuming Maggy contributed 8 percent of her salary (including her 2022 salary) to her 401(k) account, what is Maggy's vested account balance when she leaves YBU (exclusive of account earnings)? Assume YBU uses three-year cliff vesting.

b) Using the same facts as in part (a), assume YBU uses six-year graded vesting. What is Maggy's vested account balance when she leaves YBU (exclusive of account earnings)?

c) Maggy wants to maximize YBU's contribution to her 401(k) account in 2022. How much should Maggy contribute to her 401(k) account assuming her annual salary is $100,000 (and assuming she works for YBU for the entire year)?

d) Using the same facts as in part (c), assume Maggy is 55 years old rather than 34 years old at the end of the year. How much should Maggy contribute to her 401(k) account?

LO 13-2 60. In 2022, Nina contributes 10 percent of her $100,000 annual salary to her 401(k) account. She expects to earn a 7 percent before-tax rate of return. Assuming she leaves this (and any employer contributions) in the account until she retires in 25 years, what is Nina's after-tax accumulation from her 2022 contributions to her 401(k) account?

a) Assume Nina's marginal tax rate at retirement is 30 percent.

b) Assume Nina's marginal tax rate at retirement is 20 percent.

c) Assume Nina's marginal tax rate at retirement is 40 percent.

LO 13-2 61. Kathleen, age 56, works for MH Inc. in Dallas, Texas. Kathleen contributes to a Roth 401(k), and MH contributes to a traditional 401(k) on her behalf. Kathleen has contributed $30,000 to her Roth 401(k) over the past six years. The current balance in her Roth 401(k) account is $50,000, and the balance in her traditional 401(k) is $40,000. Kathleen needs cash because she is taking a month of vacation to travel the world. Answer the following questions relating to distributions from Kathleen's retirement accounts assuming her marginal tax rate for ordinary income is 24 percent.

a) If Kathleen receives a $10,000 distribution from her traditional 401(k) account, how much will she be able to keep after paying taxes and penalties, if any, on the distribution?

b) If Kathleen receives a $10,000 distribution from her Roth 401(k) account, how much will she be able to keep after paying taxes and penalties, if any, on the distribution?

c) If Kathleen retires from MH and then receives a $10,000 distribution from her traditional 401(k), how much will she be able to keep after paying taxes and penalties, if any, on the distribution?

d) If Kathleen retires from MH and then receives a $10,000 distribution from her Roth 401(k), how much will she be able to keep after paying taxes and penalties, if any, on the distribution?

e) Assume the original facts except that Kathleen is 60 years of age, not 56. If Kathleen receives a $10,000 distribution from her Roth 401(k) (without retiring), how much will she be able to keep after paying taxes and penalties, if any, on the distribution?

LO 13-2 62. In 2022, Nitai (age 40) contributes 10 percent of his $100,000 annual salary to a Roth 401(k) account sponsored by his employer, AY Inc. AY Inc. matches employee contributions to the employee's traditional 401(k) account dollar-for-dollar up to 10 percent of the employee's salary. Nitai expects to earn a 7 percent before-tax rate of return. Assume he leaves the contributions in the Roth 401(k) and traditional 401(k) accounts until he retires in 25 years and that he makes no additional contributions to either account. What are Nitai's after-tax proceeds from the Roth 401(k) and traditional 401(k) accounts after he receives the distributions, assuming his marginal tax rate at retirement is 30 percent?

63. Marissa participates in her employer's nonqualified deferred compensation plan. For 2022, she is deferring 10 percent of her $320,000 annual salary. Assuming this is her only source of income and her marginal income tax rate is 32 percent, how much *tax* does Marissa save in 2022 by deferring this income (ignore payroll taxes)? LO 13-3 planning

64. Clayton participates in his employer's nonqualified deferred compensation plan. For 2022, he is deferring 10 percent of his $320,000 annual salary. Assuming this is his only source of income and his marginal income tax rate is 32 percent, how much does deferring Clayton's income save his employer (after taxes) in 2022? The employer's marginal tax rate is 21 percent (ignore payroll taxes). LO 13-3

65. Leslie participates in IBO's nonqualified deferred compensation plan. For 2022, she is deferring 10 percent of her $300,000 annual salary. Based on her deemed investment choice, Leslie expects to earn a 7 percent before-tax rate of return on her deferred compensation, which she plans to receive in 10 years. Leslie's marginal tax rate in 2022 is 32 percent. IBO's marginal tax rate is 21 percent (ignore payroll taxes in your analysis). LO 13-3 planning
    a) Assuming Leslie's marginal tax rate in 10 years (when she receives the distribution) is 33 percent, what is Leslie's after-tax accumulation on the deferred compensation?
    b) Assuming Leslie's marginal tax rate in 10 years (when she receives the distribution) is 20 percent, what is Leslie's after-tax accumulation on the deferred compensation?
    c) Assuming IBO's cost of capital is 8 percent after taxes, how much deferred compensation should IBO be willing to pay Leslie that would make it indifferent between paying 10 percent of Leslie's current salary or deferring it for 10 years?

66. XYZ Corporation has a deferred compensation plan under which it allows certain employees to defer up to 40 percent of their salary for five years. For purposes of this problem, ignore payroll taxes in your computations. LO 13-3 planning
    a) Assume XYZ has a marginal tax rate of 21 percent for the foreseeable future and earns an after-tax rate of return of 8 percent on its assets. Joel Johnson, XYZ's VP of finance, is attempting to determine what amount of deferred compensation XYZ should be willing to pay in five years that would make XYZ indifferent between paying the current salary of $10,000 and paying the deferred compensation. What amount of deferred compensation would accomplish this objective?
    b) Assume Julie, an XYZ employee, has the option of participating in XYZ's deferred compensation plan. Julie's marginal tax rate is 37 percent, and she expects the rate to remain constant over the next five years. Julie is trying to decide how much deferred compensation she will need to receive from XYZ in five years to make her indifferent between receiving the current salary of $10,000 and receiving the deferred compensation payment. If Julie takes the salary, she will invest it in a taxable corporate bond paying interest at 5 percent annually (after taxes). What amount of deferred compensation would accomplish this objective?

67. In 2022, LeSean (age 51 and single) has earned income of $3,000. He also has $30,000 of unearned (capital gain) income. LO 13-4
    a) If he does not participate in an employer-sponsored plan, what is the maximum deductible IRA contribution LeSean can make in 2022?
    b) If he does participate in an employer-sponsored plan, what is the maximum deductible IRA contribution LeSean can make in 2022?
    c) If he does not participate in an employer-sponsored plan, what is the maximum deductible IRA contribution LeSean can make in 2022 if he has earned income of $10,000?

LO 13-4

68. William is a single writer (age 35) who recently decided that he needs to save more for retirement. His 2022 AGI before the IRA contribution deduction is $69,000 (all earned income).
   a) If he does not participate in an employer-sponsored plan, what is the maximum deductible IRA contribution William can make in 2022?
   b) If he does participate in an employer-sponsored plan, what is the maximum deductible IRA contribution William can make in 2022?
   c) Assume the same facts as in part (b), except William's AGI before the IRA contribution deduction is $79,000. What is the maximum deductible IRA contribution William can make in 2022?

LO 13-4

69. In 2022, Susan (44 years old) is a highly successful architect and is covered by an employee-sponsored plan. Her husband Dan (47 years old), however, is a Ph.D. student and unemployed. Compute the maximum deductible IRA contribution for each spouse in the following alternative situations.
   a) Susan's salary and the couple's AGI before any IRA contribution deductions is $207,000. The couple files a joint tax return.
   b) Susan's salary and the couple's AGI before any IRA contribution deductions is $133,000. The couple files a joint tax return.
   c) Susan's salary and the couple's AGI before any IRA contribution deductions is $83,000. The couple files a joint tax return.
   d) Susan's salary and her AGI before the IRA contribution deduction is $83,000. Dan reports $5,000 of AGI before the IRA contribution deduction (earned income). The couple files separate tax returns.

LO 13-4
tax forms

70. In 2022, Rashaun (62 years old) retired and planned on immediately receiving distributions (making withdrawals) from his traditional IRA account. The balance of his IRA account is $160,000 (before reducing it for withdrawals/distributions described below). Over the years, Rashaun has contributed $40,000 to the IRA. Of his $40,000 contributions, $30,000 was *nondeductible* and $10,000 was *deductible*. Assume Rashaun did not make any contributions to the account during 2022.
   a) If Rashaun currently withdraws $20,000 from the IRA, how much tax will he be required to pay on the withdrawal if his marginal tax rate is 24 percent?
   b) If Rashaun currently withdraws $70,000 from the IRA, how much tax will he be required to pay on the withdrawal if his marginal tax rate is 28 percent?
   c) Using the information provided in part (b), complete Form 8606, part I, to report the taxable portion of the $70,000 distribution (withdrawal). Use the most current form available.

LO 13-4
planning

71. Jaden (single) has a traditional IRA to which he has made only deductible contributions. At the end of 2022, Jaden is 74 years old. Jaden's required minimum distribution (RMD) from his IRA for 2022 is $5,000. Before considering the RMD, Jaden's AGI is $100,000. Jaden does not itemize deductions. What is Jaden's AGI after considering the RMD under each of the following alternative scenarios?
   a) Jaden receives the RMD and donates the $5,000 distribution proceeds to a qualifying charity.
   b) Jaden directs the IRA trustee to transfer the $5,000 distribution directly to a qualifying charity as a qualified charitable donation (QCD).
   c) True or False. Based on the information provided, Jaden's taxable income is the same whether he makes a QCD or not. Explain.

LO 13-4

72. Brooklyn has been contributing to a traditional IRA for seven years (all deductible contributions) and has a total of $30,000 in the account. In 2022, she is 39 years old and has decided that she wants to get a new car. She withdraws $20,000 from the IRA to help pay for the car. She is currently in the 24 percent marginal tax bracket.

What amount of the withdrawal, after tax considerations, will Brooklyn have available to purchase the car?

73. Jackson and Ashley Turner (both 45 years old) are married and want to contribute to a Roth IRA for Ashley. In 2022, their AGI is $209,000. Jackson and Ashley each earned half of the income. LO 13-4
    a) How much can Ashley contribute to her Roth IRA if they file a joint return?
    b) How much can Ashley contribute if she files a separate return?
    c) Assume that Ashley earned all of the couple's income and that she contributed the maximum amount she is allowed to contribute to a Roth IRA. What amount can be contributed to Jackson's Roth IRA?

74. Harriet and Harry Combs (both 37 years old) are married, and both want to contribute to a Roth IRA. In 2022, their AGI before any IRA contribution deductions is $50,000. Harriet earned $46,000 and Harry earned $4,000. LO 13-4
    a) How much can Harriet contribute to her Roth IRA if they file a joint return?
    b) How much can Harriet contribute if she files a separate return?
    c) How much can Harry contribute to his Roth IRA if they file separately?

75. Michael is single and 35 years old. He is a participant in his employer's sponsored retirement plan. How much can Michael contribute to a Roth IRA in 2022 in each of the following alternative situations? LO 13-4
    a) Michael's AGI before the IRA contribution deduction is $50,000. Michael contributed $3,000 to a traditional IRA.
    b) Michael's AGI is $80,000 before any IRA contributions.
    c) Michael's AGI is $155,000 before any IRA contributions.

76. George (age 42 at year-end) has been contributing to a traditional IRA for years (all deductible contributions), and his IRA is now worth $25,000. He is planning on converting the entire balance to a Roth IRA account. George's marginal tax rate is 24 percent. LO 13-4
    a) What are the tax consequences to George if he takes $25,000 out of the traditional IRA and contributes the entire amount into a Roth IRA one week after receiving the distribution?
    b) What are the tax consequences to George if he takes $25,000 out of the traditional IRA, pays the taxes due from the traditional IRA distribution, and contributes what's left from the distribution to the Roth IRA one week after receiving the distribution?
    c) What are the tax consequences to George if he takes $25,000 out of the traditional IRA, keeps $10,000 to pay taxes and to make a down payment on a new car, and contributes what's left from the distribution to the Roth IRA one week after receiving the distribution?

77. Jimmer has contributed $15,000 to his Roth IRA, and the balance in the account is $18,000. In the current year, Jimmer withdrew $17,000 from the Roth IRA to pay for a new car. If Jimmer's marginal ordinary income tax rate is 24 percent, what amount of tax and penalty, if any, is Jimmer required to pay on the withdrawal in each of the following alternative situations? LO 13-4
    a) Jimmer opened the Roth account 44 months before he withdrew the $17,000, and Jimmer is 62 years of age.
    b) Jimmer opened the Roth account 44 months before he withdrew the $17,000, and Jimmer is age 53.
    c) Jimmer opened the Roth account 76 months before he withdrew the $17,000, and Jimmer is age 62.
    d) Jimmer opened the Roth account 76 months before he withdrew the $17,000, and Jimmer is age 53.

LO 13-4 planning

78. John is trying to decide whether to contribute to a Roth IRA or a traditional IRA. He plans on making a $5,000 contribution to whichever plan he decides to fund. He currently pays tax at a 32 percent marginal income tax rate, but he believes that his marginal tax rate in the future will be 28 percent. He intends to leave the money in the Roth IRA or traditional IRA for 30 years, and he expects to earn a 6 percent before-tax rate of return on the account.
    a) How much will John accumulate after taxes if he contributes to a Roth IRA (consider only the funds contributed to the Roth IRA)?
    b) How much will John accumulate after taxes if he contributes to a traditional IRA (consider only the funds contributed to the traditional IRA)?
    c) Without doing any computations, explain whether the traditional IRA or the Roth IRA will generate a greater after-tax rate of return.

LO 13-4

79. Sherry, who is 52 years of age, opened a Roth IRA three years ago. She has contributed a total of $12,000 to the Roth IRA ($4,000 a year). The current value of the Roth IRA is $16,300. In the current year, Sherry withdraws $14,000 of the account balance to purchase a car. Assuming Sherry's marginal tax rate is 24 percent, how much of the $14,000 withdrawal will she retain after taxes to fund her car purchase?

LO 13-4

80. Seven years ago, Halle (currently age 41) contributed $4,000 to a Roth IRA account. The current value of the Roth IRA is $9,000. In the current year, Halle withdraws $8,000 of the account balance to use as a down payment on her first home. Assuming Halle's marginal tax rate is 24 percent, how much of the $8,000 withdrawal will she retain after taxes to fund the down payment on her house?

LO 13-4 research planning

81. Yuki (age 45 at year-end) has been contributing to a traditional IRA for years (all deductible contributions), and her IRA is now worth $50,000. She is trying to decide whether she should convert her traditional IRA into a Roth IRA. Her current marginal tax rate is 24 percent. She plans to withdraw the entire balance of the account in 20 years, and she expects to earn a before-tax rate of return of 5 percent on her retirement accounts and a 4 percent after-tax rate of return on all investments outside of her retirement accounts. For each of the following alternative scenarios, indicate how much more or less Yuki will accumulate after taxes in 20 years if she converts her traditional IRA into a Roth IRA. Be sure to include the opportunity cost of having to pay taxes on the conversion.
    a) When she withdraws the retirement funds in 20 years, she expects her marginal tax rate to be 35 percent.
    b) When she withdraws the retirement funds in 20 years, she expects her marginal tax rate to be 18 percent.
    c) Assume the same facts as in part (b), except that she earns a 3 percent after-tax rate of return on investments outside of the retirement accounts.
    d) In general terms, reconcile your answer from part (b) with your answer to part (c) (no numbers required).

LO 13-4 research

82. Sarah was contemplating making a contribution to her traditional individual retirement account for 2022. She determined that she would contribute $6,000 to her IRA, and she deducted $6,000 for the contribution when she completed and filed her 2022 tax return on February 15, 2023. Two months later, on April 15, Sarah realized that she had not yet actually contributed the funds to her IRA. On April 15, she went to the post office and mailed a $6,000 check to the bank holding her IRA. The bank received the payment on April 19. In which year is Sarah's $6,000 contribution deductible?

83. Elvira is a self-employed taxpayer who turns 42 years old at the end of the year (2022). In 2022, her net Schedule C income was $130,000. This was her only source of income. This year, Elvira is considering setting up a retirement plan. What is the maximum amount Elvira may contribute to the self-employed plan in each of the following situations? LO 13-5 planning

a) She sets up a SEP IRA.

b) She sets up an individual 401(k).

84. Hope is a self-employed taxpayer who turns 54 years old at the end of the year (2022). In 2022, her net Schedule C income was $130,000. This was her only source of income. This year, Hope is considering setting up a retirement plan. What is the maximum amount Hope may contribute to the self-employed plan in each of the following situations? LO 13-5 planning

a) She sets up a SEP IRA.

b) She sets up an individual 401(k).

85. Rita is a self-employed taxpayer who turns 39 years old at the end of the year (2022). In 2022, her net Schedule C income was $300,000. This was her only source of income. This year, Rita is considering setting up a retirement plan. What is the maximum amount Rita may contribute to the self-employed plan in each of the following situations? LO 13-5

a) She sets up a SEP IRA.

b) She sets up an individual 401(k).

86. Reggie is a self-employed taxpayer who turns 59 years old at the end of the year (2022). In 2022, his net Schedule C income was $300,000. This was his only source of income. This year, Reggie is considering setting up a retirement plan. What is the maximum amount he may contribute to the self-employed plan in each of the following situations? LO 13-5

a) He sets up a SEP IRA.

b) He sets up an individual 401(k).

87. Desmond is 25 years old, and he participates in his employer's 401(k) plan. During the year, he contributed $3,000 to his 401(k) account. What is Desmond's saver's credit in each of the following alternative scenarios? LO 13-6

a) Desmond is not married and has no dependents. His AGI after deducting his 401(k) contribution is $35,000.

b) Desmond is not married and has no dependents. His AGI after deducting his 401(k) contribution is $17,500.

c) Desmond files as a head of household and has an AGI of $44,000.

d) Desmond and his spouse file jointly and report an AGI of $30,000 for the year.

88. Penny is 57 years old, and she participates in her employer's 401(k) plan. During the year, she contributed $2,000 to her 401(k) account. Penny's AGI is $36,000 after deducting her 401(k) contribution. What is Penny's saver's credit in each of the following alternative scenarios? LO 13-6

a) Penny is not married and has no dependents.

b) Penny files as a head of household and has three dependents.

c) Penny files as a head of household and has one dependent.

d) Penny is married and files a joint return with her spouse. They have three dependents.

e) Penny files a separate tax return from her husband. She claims two dependent children on her return.

COMPREHENSIVE PROBLEMS

Select problems are available in Connect®.

89. Jacquiline is unmarried and age 32. Even though she participates in an employer-sponsored retirement plan, Jacquiline contributed $3,000 to a traditional IRA during the year. Jacquiline files as a head of household, her AGI before the contribution is $43,000, and her marginal tax rate is 12 percent. What is the after-tax cost of her $3,000 traditional IRA contribution?

90. Ian retired in December of 2021 at the age of 71 (his birthday is January 6). Ian's retirement account was valued at $490,000 at the end of 2020 and $500,000 at the end of 2021. He has had all of his retirement accounts open for 15 years. What is Ian's required minimum distribution for 2022 under each of the following alternative scenarios?
    a) Ian's retirement account is a traditional 401(k) account.
    b) Ian's retirement account is a Roth 401(k) account.
    c) Ian's retirement account is a traditional IRA.
    d) Ian's retirement account is a Roth IRA.

91. Alex is 31 years old and has lived in Los Alamos, New Mexico, for the last four years, where he works at the Los Alamos National Laboratory (LANL). LANL provides employees with a 401(k) plan, and for every $1 an employee contributes (up to 9 percent of the employee's salary), LANL contributes $3 (a 3-to-1 match). The plan provides a six-year graded vesting schedule. Alex is now in his fifth year working for LANL, and his current-year salary is $170,000. Alex's marginal tax rate is 24 percent in 2022. Answer the following questions relating to Alex's retirement savings in 2022.
    a) Assume that over the past four years, Alex has contributed $45,000 to his 401(k) and his employer has contributed $115,000 to the plan. The plan has an account balance of $175,000. What is Alex's vested account balance in his 401(k)?
    b) Because Alex considers his employer's matching contributions "free money," he wants to maximize the amount of LANL's contributions. What is the least amount Alex can contribute and still maximize LANL's contribution?
    c) In need of cash to build a home theater, Alex withdrew $30,000 from his traditional 401(k) account. What amount of the withdrawal, after taxes and penalties, will Alex have available to complete his project?
    d) Assume that Alex contributes $10,000 to his traditional 401(k) account this year. Also assume that in 30 years, Alex retires (at age 61) and withdraws the $10,000 contribution made this year *and* all the earnings generated by the contribution. Also assume that his marginal tax rate at the time he retires is 24 percent. Ignore any prior or subsequent contributions to his plan. If Alex earns a 6 percent annual before-tax rate of return, what are his after-tax proceeds from the distribution?
    e) Assume that Alex is 74 years old at the end of the year, and retired, and that his marginal tax rate is 24 percent. His account balance in his traditional 401(k) was $1,250,000 at the end of last year. What is the minimum distribution Alex must receive from his 401(k) account for this year? If Alex receives a $43,000 distribution from his 401(k) account (his only distribution during the year), what amount will he be able to keep after taxes and penalties (if any)?

92. Tommy (age 47) and his wife Michelle (age 49) live in Columbus, Ohio, where Tommy works for Callahan Auto Parts (CAP) as the vice president of the brakes division. Tommy's 2022 salary is $360,000. CAP allows Tommy to participate in its nonqualified deferred compensation plan, in which participants can defer 15 percent of their salary for five years. Tommy also participates in CAP's qualified 401(k) plan. Tommy's current marginal tax rate is 24 percent, and CAP's current marginal tax rate is 21 percent.

a) Assuming Tommy earns a 6 percent *after-tax* rate of return and he expects his marginal tax rate to be 30 percent in five years, what before-tax deferred compensation payment in five years would make him indifferent between receiving the deferred compensation payment or 15 percent of his salary now (ignore payroll taxes)?

b) Assuming CAP has an 8 percent *after-tax* rate of return and expects its marginal tax rate to be 35 percent in five years, how much would it be willing to pay in five years to be indifferent between paying the deferred compensation or paying 15 percent of Tommy's salary now (ignore payroll taxes)?

c) Will Tommy and CAP be able to come to an agreement on deferring Tommy's salary?

d) Assume that Tommy and Michelle have an AGI of $111,000 before IRA deductions by either spouse. The AGI includes $10,000 that Michelle earned working part time (but she does not participate in an employer-sponsored retirement plan). Tommy and Michelle file a joint return. What is the maximum deductible contribution Tommy and Michelle may make to a traditional IRA?

e) Tommy has a balance of $55,000 in his traditional IRA. Because Tommy believes his marginal tax rate will increase from his current rate of 22 percent, he would like to convert his traditional IRA into a Roth IRA. What are the tax consequences to Tommy if he takes $55,000 out of the IRA, pays the taxes due from the traditional IRA distribution, and contributes what is left from the distribution to the Roth IRA?

93. Gerry (age 56) and Elaine (age 54) have been married for 12 years and file a joint tax return. The couple lives in an apartment in downtown Manhattan. Gerry's father, Mortey, recently retired from Del Boca Vista Corporation (DBVC), where he worked for many years. Mortey participated in DBVC's defined benefit plan. Elaine is an editor and works for Pendent Publishing earning an annual $150,000 salary in 2022. Gerry is a self-employed, stand-up comedian and had net business income of $46,000 in 2022. At the advice of their neighbor, Gerry, Elaine, and Mortey have come to you for help in answering several retirement savings–related questions.

a) The DBVC defined benefit plan specifies a benefit of 1.5 percent for each year of service, up to a maximum of 30 percent (20 years of service), of the average of the employee's three highest consecutive calendar years of salary. Mortey worked for the company for 25 years and earned $75,000, $78,000, and $84,000 over his final three years of service. What is Mortey's annual benefit from DBVC's defined benefit plan?

b) Elaine has worked at Pendent Publishing since January 1, 2018. The company offers a defined contribution plan. It matches 100 percent of employee contributions to the plan up to 6 percent of her salary. Prior to 2022 Elaine had contributed $40,000 to the plan, and her employer had contributed $28,000 to the plan. In 2022, Elaine contributed $17,000 to her traditional 401(k). What is the amount of her employer's matching contribution for 2022? Assuming the company uses a six-year graded vesting schedule, what is Elaine's vested balance in the plan at the end of 2022? (For simplicity, disregard the plan's earnings.)

c) Elaine tells you that her employer has offered her $30,000 in 10 years to defer 10 percent of her current salary (defer $15,000). Assuming that the couple's marginal tax rate is currently 32 percent, they earn an after-tax rate of return of 8 percent, and they expect their marginal tax rate to be 28 percent in 10 years, should Elaine accept her company's offer? What is the minimum amount she should be willing to accept (ignoring nontax factors and payroll taxes)?

d) Gerry has a SEP IRA and would like to contribute as much as possible to this account. What is the maximum contribution Gerry can make to his SEP IRA in 2022?

e) Assuming Gerry had an individual 401(k), what is the maximum amount he could contribute to the plan in 2022?

f) Gerry also has a traditional IRA with an account balance of $12,000. He would like to convert the traditional IRA to a Roth IRA. Gerry would like to pay the least amount of tax possible from the conversion. Assume the couple's marginal tax rate is 32 percent. What is the least amount of tax Gerry will be required to pay on the conversion?

g) Assume that Gerry converted his traditional IRA into a Roth IRA six years ago (rather than in 2022) when the balance was $8,000 and that the account balance is now $20,000. Gerry has not made any contributions to his Roth IRA (other than the original conversion from his traditional IRA). The couple is considering buying their first home and would like to pay as much down as possible. They have heard from their friends that they can take the funds from their Roth IRA and use it to buy their first home. Are their friends correct? What would you advise them to do?

h) Assume that Gerry and Elaine made total contributions of $20,000 to their qualified retirement accounts in 2022. Also assume that their AGI is $40,500. What is the amount of their saver's credit for 2022?

UWorld | ROGER CPA Review

UWorld Roger CPA Review

Sample CPA Exam questions from Roger CPA Review are available in Connect as support for the topics in this text. These Multiple Choice Questions and Task-Based Simulations include expert-written explanations and solutions and provide a starting point for students to become familiar with the content and functionality of the actual CPA Exam.

chapter

14 Tax Consequences of Home Ownership

Learning Objectives

Upon completing this chapter, you should be able to:

LO 14-1 Determine whether a home is considered a principal residence, a residence (not principal), or a nonresidence for tax purposes.

LO 14-2 Compute the taxable gain on the sale of a residence.

LO 14-3 Determine the amount of the home mortgage interest deduction.

LO 14-4 Discuss the deductibility of real property taxes.

LO 14-5 Explain the tax issues and consequences associated with rental use of the home.

LO 14-6 Compute the limitations on home office deductions.

FatCamera/iStock/Getty Images

Storyline Summary

Taxpayers:	Tyler (he/him/his) and Jasmine Jefferson (she/her/hers)
Location:	Chicago, Illinois
Employment status:	Tyler—Newly hired VP of Sales for GLO Corporation, earning an annual salary of $320,000. Jasmine—graphic designer, earning an annual salary of $37,000.
Filing status:	Married filing jointly
Dependents:	Two children
Marginal tax rate:	32 percent

With the extra income Tyler Jefferson is earning in his new position as VP of Sales for GLO Corporation, his family now has greater financial flexibility, but with the money come new possibilities. For one, Tyler and Jasmine Jefferson would like to sell their current home and purchase a larger one closer to Tyler's work. Fortunately, the value of their home has increased considerably since they purchased it, which should allow them to make a substantial down payment on a new home. Still, they would need to acquire financing to make the purchase. Jasmine likes the idea of buying a vacation home in Scottsdale, Arizona. Besides the great weather (she and Tyler both love golf), Scottsdale has the added benefit of being near Jasmine's family. Jasmine is trying to pitch the second-home idea to Tyler by suggesting that, to help defray the costs, they could rent out the house when they're not there. Finally, Jasmine is seriously considering a transition to self-employment as a graphic designer, which she believes would allow her to make substantially more money and have higher job satisfaction. She believes that, with her experience and contacts, she can find enough clients to keep busy most of the time—and she very much likes the idea of setting aside a room in their primary home as her workplace. ■

When making these decisions, the Jeffersons should consider the tax consequences of their actions. For example, will the gain on the sale of their current home be taxable? Will the interest expense on the new home be fully deductible? Should they pay points to obtain a lower interest rate on the home loan? If they rent out the vacation home for part of the year, how do they account for the related income and expenses for tax purposes? If Jasmine sets up a home office, will the Jeffersons be allowed any tax deductions for expenses relating to their home? This chapter answers these and other relevant questions for the Jeffersons and for others interested in the tax consequences of home ownership.

LO 14-1

IS A DWELLING UNIT A PRINCIPAL RESIDENCE, RESIDENCE, OR NONRESIDENCE?

The starting point for identifying the tax consequences of home ownership is first determining whether the taxpayer owns a **dwelling unit.** If a property is not a dwelling unit, then the tax rules of home ownership discussed in this chapter do not apply. A dwelling unit is property that provides a place suitable for people to occupy (live and sleep). A taxpayer may use a dwelling unit solely for personal use, for some mixture of personal and rental use, or solely for rental use. For tax purposes, a dwelling unit includes the following:

- House
- Condominium
- Mobile home
- Boat
- Other similar property[1]

A single structure may contain more than one dwelling unit. For example, if a basement in a house contains basic living accommodations (i.e., sleeping space, toilet and cooking facilities) and is separately occupied, the basement would be considered a separate dwelling unit apart from the main floor. However, a single room in a home that is separately occupied would not be considered to be a separate dwelling unit unless the room itself contains basic living accommodations.

Each year, the dwelling unit is classified as either a residence or a nonresidence (i.e., rental property) based on how the taxpayer used the unit for that year. The dwelling unit (we refer to a dwelling unit and a "home" interchangeably) is considered to be a residence if the taxpayer's number of personal-use days of the home is more than the greater of:

1. 14 days or
2. 10 percent of the number of rental days during the year.[2]

Thus, to determine whether a dwelling unit is a residence or not, the taxpayer must calculate the number of days the home (dwelling unit) was used for personal use during the year and the number of days the home was rented out during the year. So what counts as a day of personal use and what counts as a day of rental use? A day of personal use includes any day for which:

- The taxpayer (owner) or any other owner of the home stays in the home.
- A relative of an owner stays in the home, even if the relative pays full fair market value rent, unless the home is the relative's principal residence (discussed below).
- A nonowner stays in the home under a vacation home exchange or swap arrangement with the owner.
- The taxpayer rents out the property for less than fair market value.[3]

[1]§280A(f)(1)(B). A dwelling unit does not include a hotel, motel, inn, or similar establishment.
[2]§280A(d)(1).
[3]§280A(d)(2).

A day of rental use includes any day for which:

- The taxpayer rents out the property at fair market value.
- The home is being repaired or maintained for rental use.

Days when the home is available for rent, but not actually rented out, *do not count* as either personal or rental days.

When a dwelling unit is determined to be a residence, the taxpayer must determine whether the residence is the taxpayer's **principal residence** in order to determine certain tax consequences associated with the property (for certain purposes, the taxpayer need only determine whether the property is a residence). What makes a residence a "principal" residence? When a taxpayer lives in more than one residence during the year, the determination of which residence is the principal residence depends on the facts and circumstances, such as:

- The amount of time the taxpayer spends at each residence during the year.
- The proximity of each residence to the taxpayer's place of employment.
- The principal place of abode of the taxpayer's immediate family (i.e., where they live and sleep).
- The taxpayer's mailing address for bills and correspondence.

To summarize, with respect to a particular taxpayer for a particular year, a dwelling unit or home can be classified as either a:

- Principal residence,
- Residence (not principal), or
- Nonresidence (rental property).

We refer to these property classifications throughout the chapter as we describe the tax consequences of home ownership. Exhibit 14-1 lists deductions and other tax provisions available for each property type. We discuss each of these tax provisions, including limitations, throughout the chapter. Also, Appendix A at the end of this chapter provides a flowchart for determining the tax status of a home used for rental purposes.

EXHIBIT 14-1 Tax Provisions by Property Type

	Property Type		
Tax Provision	**Principal Residence**	**Residence (not principal)**	**Nonresidence**
Home mortgage interest deductions (from AGI deduction)	X	X	
Home mortgage insurance (from AGI deduction)	X	X	
Real property taxes (from AGI deduction)	X	X	X
Deductions associated with rental use, if any (for AGI deduction)	X	X	X
Exclusion of gain on sale of home	X	X*	X*
Forgiveness of debt on home foreclosure (income exclusion)	X		

*Must have previously been a principal residence to qualify.

We begin our discussion by considering the tax consequences associated with personal use of the home. We then discuss the tax consequences of rental use of the home, and we conclude the chapter by discussing the tax consequences of business use of the home.

THE KEY FACTS

Tax and Nontax Consequences of Home Ownership

- Nontax consequences
  - Large financial investment.
  - Potential for big return (or loss) on investment with use of leverage.
  - Risk of default on home loan.
  - Time and costs of maintenance.
  - Limited mobility.
- Tax consequences
  - Deductible interest expense.
  - Excludable gain on sale.
  - Deductible real property taxes on home.
  - Rental and business-use possibilities.

PERSONAL USE OF THE HOME

To buy or to rent? This is a difficult question with no absolute answer. The decision to purchase a home is a significant one that includes both nontax and tax considerations. Primary nontax factors favoring home ownership include the home's potential to appreciate as an investment. As the value of the home increases, so does the homeowner's net worth.

A home is frequently an individual's most significant financial investment in terms of overall wealth. Therefore, home ownership also carries significant potential risk. When real estate values decline, the owner's net worth also declines. Homeowners borrowing funds to purchase their home have the potential to achieve high returns on their cash investment due to the power of leverage (i.e., the homeowner provides the down payment and the bank lends the rest of the cash necessary to purchase the home), but a home is by no means a liquid asset. Furthermore, homeowners must assume the risk associated with the possible default on the loan. If the owner does not make the mortgage payments required by the terms of the loan, the lender may repossess the home. Homeowners also are responsible for the cost or effort required to repair, maintain, and landscape the home. Finally, because building, buying, selling, and moving in or out of a home are expensive and time-consuming tasks, home ownership reduces the ability to relocate to take advantage of new opportunities.

On the tax side, the government seems to favors taxpayer home ownership, given the deductions made available to homeowners that are unavailable to renters. Besides the deduction for interest payments made on home mortgages, other tax benefits of home ownership include the potential deduction of real estate taxes paid on the home, the exclusion of gain on the sale of the home, and the deduction of expenses relating to business offices in the home. Homeowners also may gain tax benefits associated with owning and renting a vacation home. We address the tax consequences of home ownership throughout this chapter.

LO 14-2 Exclusion of Gain on Sale of Personal Residence

When a taxpayer sells a personal residence, they *realize* a gain or a loss calculated by subtracting the tax basis of the home from the amount they receive from the buyer (minus selling costs). The basis of the residence depends on how the taxpayer acquired the home. The general rules for determining the basis of the home are as follows:

- Purchase: the cost of the home.
- Inheritance: the fair market value of the home on the date of the decedent's death (the person who has died and bequested the property).
- Gift: the donor's basis.
- Conversion of rental home to residence: the taxpayer's basis in the rental home at the time of the conversion.

Because a personal residence is a capital asset, the gain a taxpayer recognizes by selling the residence is a capital gain. However, because a personal residence is also a personal-use asset, the loss on the sale of a personal residence is a nondeductible personal loss.[4] This is an important limitation for many taxpayers when the housing market is depressed. When a taxpayer sells a personal residence at a gain, the tax consequences are generally more favorable. In fact, taxpayers meeting certain requirements are allowed to exclude a certain amount of realized gain on the sale.[5] The maximum exclusion depends on filing status as follows:

- $500,000 for married filing jointly taxpayers.
- $250,000 for all other taxpayers.

Gain in excess of the excludable amount generally qualifies as long-term capital gain subject to tax at preferential rates. Further, gain in excess of the exclusion amount is considered to be investment income for purposes of determining the 3.8 percent net investment income tax discussed in the Individual Income Tax Computation and Tax Credits chapter.

[4]§165(c).
[5]§121.

Requirements To qualify for the exclusion, the taxpayer must meet both an ownership and a use test for the residence:

> *Ownership test:* The taxpayer must have owned the property for a total of two or more years during the five-year period ending on the date of the sale. The ownership test prevents a taxpayer from purchasing a home, fixing it up, and soon thereafter selling it and excluding the gain—a real estate investment practice termed **flipping.** In these circumstances, the gain is primarily due to the taxpayer's efforts in remodeling the home, not to general appreciation in the value of the property.
>
> *Use test:* The taxpayer must have *used* the property as their principal residence (see earlier discussion) for a total of two or more years during the five-year period ending on the date of the sale. The exclusion provision was designed to provide tax benefits to homeowners rather than investors or landlords. The use test helps ensure that taxpayers using the exclusion have realized gains from selling the home they actually lived in as opposed to selling an investment or rental property.

Note that the periods of ownership and use need not be continuous, nor do they need to cover the same two-year period. In fact, a taxpayer could rent a home and live in it as their principal residence during 2017 and then again during 2019, purchase the home and rent it to someone else during 2020 and 2021, and then sell the home at the beginning of 2022—and *still* meet the ownership and use tests!

THE KEY FACTS

Exclusion of Gain on Sale of Personal Residence

- Must meet ownership and use tests.
  - Must own home for at least two of five years before sale.
  - Must use home as principal residence for at least two of five years before sale.
  - For married couples to qualify for maximum exclusion on a joint return, one spouse must meet the ownership test and both spouses must meet the use test.

Example 14-1

The Jeffersons sold their home in Denver, Colorado, before moving to Chicago. They sold the Denver home for $450,000. The Jeffersons initially purchased the home for $350,000. They owned and lived in the home (as their principal residence) for four years before selling. How much of the $100,000 gain realized on the sale ($450,000 – $350,000) do they recognize?

Answer: $0. The Jeffersons qualified for the full exclusion available to married couples filing jointly because they met the ownership and use tests. Consequently, they are allowed to exclude the entire $100,000 of gain and could have excluded up to $500,000 of gain on the sale.

How do the ownership and use tests apply to married couples filing joint returns? Married couples filing joint returns are eligible for the full $500,000 exclusion if at least one spouse meets the ownership test and *both* spouses meet the use test. However, if at least one spouse meets the ownership test, but only one spouse meets the use test, the couple's exclusion is limited to $250,000 on the couple's joint tax return.

Example 14-2

What if: Suppose that after Tyler and Jasmine were married, Jasmine moved into Tyler's home located in Denver, Colorado. Tyler had purchased the home two years before the marriage. After the marriage, the couple lived in the home together as their principal residence for four years before selling the home and moving to Chicago. Tyler was the sole owner of the home for the entire six years he resided in the home. Would gain on the sale of the home qualify for the $500,000 exclusion available to married couples filing jointly even though Jasmine was never an owner of the home?

Answer: Yes. Gain on the sale qualifies for the full $500,000 exclusion available to married couples filing jointly because Tyler has met the ownership test, and both Tyler and Jasmine have met the use test.

What if: Suppose that Tyler and Jasmine lived in the home together for only one year before selling it. Would the couple be allowed to exclude any gain on the sale?

Answer: Yes; however, because Jasmine does not meet the use test, they would qualify only for the $250,000 exclusion even if they were to file a joint return.

If a widow or widower sells a home that they owned and occupied with the decedent spouse (the spouse who died), the surviving spouse is entitled to the full $500,000 exclusion provided they sell the home within two years after the date of death of the spouse. Finally, once a taxpayer claims a home sale exclusion, they are not eligible to claim another exclusion until at least two years pass from the time of the first sale (however, see the unforeseen circumstances discussion for an exception to this general rule).

General rule exceptions for nonqualified use, unforeseen circumstances, and depreciation. In certain circumstances, taxpayers who otherwise meet the ownership and use requirements may have their exclusion limited under a "nonqualified use" provision. In other circumstances, taxpayers who fail the ownership and/or use tests are allowed to exclude gain on the sale of their residence under an employment, health, or an "unforeseen" circumstances provision. Finally, taxpayers who have claimed depreciation deductions on their home for rental or business use (see discussion later in the chapter) may be required to recognize gain on the sale of their residence that otherwise would have been excluded. Let's first discuss the nonqualified use provision.

Under the general rules for the home sale exclusion, taxpayers could exclude gain on the sale of a vacation home or rental property (including gain accrued while it was not a principal residence) simply by moving into the property and using it as their principal residence for two years before selling it. To limit a taxpayer's ability to benefit from this strategy, the nonqualified use provision reduces the taxpayer's otherwise excludable gain on the home sale if, on or after January 1, 2009, the taxpayer used or uses the home for something other than a principal residence (termed *nonqualified use*).[6] The period of nonqualified use does not include any portion of the five-year period ending on the date of the sale that is after the last date that such property is used as the principal residence of the taxpayer or the taxpayer's spouse. This exception allows the taxpayer time to sell the principal residence after moving out of it without having to count the time the house is available for sale as nonqualified use (if it were considered to be nonqualified use, the amount of gain the taxpayer would be eligible to exclude would be reduced).

If the nonqualified use limitation applies, the percentage of the realized gain that must be recognized is the ratio of the period of nonqualified use divided by the period of time the taxpayer owned the home (both the nonqualified use and the home ownership periods do not include the date of sale). Note that this provision does not reduce the maximum exclusion; it reduces the amount of realized gain eligible for exclusion.

Example 14-3

What if: Suppose the Jeffersons purchased home 1 on January 1, 2019, for $350,000. They lived in home 1 as their principal residence until January 1, 2022, when they moved into a new principal residence (home 2). They finally sold home 1 on January 1, 2024, for $450,000. What amount of the $100,000 gain on the sale of home 1 ($450,000 amount realized – $350,000 basis) do the Jeffersons recognize?

Answer: $0. The Jeffersons meet the ownership and use tests (they owned and used home 1 as their principal residence for at least two of the five years prior to January 1, 2024), so they qualify for a maximum exclusion of $500,000. Further, the gain eligible for the exclusion is *not* reduced because the Jeffersons stopped using home 1 as a principal residence after December 31, 2021, and they sold the home within five years of this date.

What if: Assume the same facts as above, except that on January 1, 2023, the Jeffersons moved back into home 1 and used it as their principal residence until they sold it for $450,000 on January 1, 2024. What amount of the $100,000 gain on the sale of home 1 do the Jeffersons recognize?

Answer: $20,000. The Jeffersons meet the ownership and use tests for home 1 and therefore qualify for the maximum potential $500,000 exclusion. However, because they stopped using the home as their principal residence for a period on or after January 1, 2009 (nonqualified use from January 1, 2022–December 31, 2022), and they used the home as their principal residence immediately before selling (January 1, 2023–December 31, 2023), the gain eligible for exclusion must be reduced. The percentage of the gain that is not eligible for exclusion is 20 percent, which is the period of nonqualified use (one year: January 1, 2022–December 31, 2022) divided by the total period of time the Jeffersons owned the home (five years: January 1, 2019–December 31, 2023). Therefore, the Jeffersons must reduce their realized gain eligible for exclusion by $20,000 ($100,000 gain × 20% reduction percentage), allowing them to exclude $80,000 of the $100,000 gain from gross income.

[6] §121(b)(5).

Sometimes taxpayers are unable to meet the two-year requirements for the ownership and use tests due to changes in employment, health, or unforeseen circumstances.[7] For example, a taxpayer may be forced to sell their home before meeting the ownership and use requirements due to a job transfer to another city. In such cases, the *maximum* exclusion amount ($500,000 for married filing jointly, $250,000 otherwise) is reduced based on the amount of time the taxpayer owned and used the home as a principal residence before selling. For example, if a single taxpayer owned and used a home as a principal residence for six months before selling due to unforeseen circumstances, the maximum exclusion would be $62,500, which is one-fourth of what it would be otherwise (6 months of ownership and use divided by 24 months required under the general rule, multiplied by the full $250,000 exclusion for single taxpayers). The maximum exclusion available to a taxpayer selling under these circumstances is expressed in the formula presented in Exhibit 14-2.

THE KEY FACTS

Exclusion of Gain on Sale of Personal Residence

- Exclusion amount
  - $500,000 for married couples filing joint returns.
  - $250,000 for other taxpayers.
  - Gain eligible for exclusion may be reduced for a period of nonqualified use.
  - Unforeseen circumstances provision: *Maximum exclusion* = Full exclusion × Months of qualifying ownership and use/24 months.

EXHIBIT 14-2 Formula for Determining Maximum Home Sale Exclusion in Unforeseen Circumstances

Maximum exclusion in unforeseen circumstances = Full exclusion × Qualifying months/24 months

where

Full exclusion = $250,000 for single taxpayers or $500,000 for taxpayers filing a joint return.

Qualifying months = the number of months the taxpayer met the ownership and use requirements for the home before selling it.

24 months = the number of months the taxpayer must own and use the home as a principal residence to qualify for the full exclusion.[8]

Source: Reg. §1.121-3(g).

Example 14-4

What if: Let's assume that when the Jeffersons moved from Denver, they purchased a home in Chicago for $375,000 and moved into the home on July 1, 2021. In January of 2022, Tyler accepted a work opportunity with a different employer located in Miami, Florida. On February 1, 2022, the Jeffersons sold their home for $395,000 and permanently relocated to Miami. How much of the $20,000 realized gain ($395,000 – $375,000) on their Chicago home sale must the Jeffersons recognize in taxable income?

Answer: $0. The Jeffersons lived in the home for only seven months (July 1, 2021, to January 31, 2022), so they do not meet either the ownership or the use test to qualify for the maximum exclusion. However, under the unforeseen circumstances provision, they are eligible for a reduced maximum exclusion computed as follows: 500,000 (maximum exclusion) × 7 (qualifying months)/24 = $145,833. Because the amount they are able to exclude ($145,833) exceeds the $20,000 gain they realized on the sale, they are able to exclude all $20,000 and recognize $0 gain.

What if: Assume the same facts, except that the Jeffersons realized a $150,000 gain on the sale of their home. How much of the realized gain would they recognize and at what rate would this gain be taxed?

Answer: $150,000 gain realized minus $145,833 exclusion = $4,167 short-term capital gain (the home is a capital asset that the Jeffersons did not own for more than one year). Assuming the Jeffersons did not recognize any other capital gains during the year, the $4,167 would be taxed at the Jeffersons' 32 percent marginal tax rate (see storyline summary at beginning of chapter).

Note, as the previous example illustrates, that under the so-called unforeseen circumstances provision, it is the *full exclusion amount* that is reduced, not necessarily the excludable gain. Consequently, if a taxpayer's gain on the sale of a residence is less than the maximum exclusion (after the unforeseen circumstances adjustment), the taxpayer may still be able to exclude the entire amount of the gain.

[7]See Reg. §1.121-3 for qualifications and examples of acceptable circumstances. For instance, the IRS has ruled that a couple's need to move because of a birth of a second child was an unforeseen circumstance (LTR 201628002).

[8]Taxpayers may choose to use the number of days the taxpayer fully qualified for the exclusion divided by 730 days.

Finally, taxpayers who used their home for business purposes (i.e., they deducted home office expenses) or rental purposes are not allowed to exclude gain attributable to depreciation deductions on the home incurred after May 6, 1997. Rather, this gain is treated as unrecaptured §1250 gain and is subject to a maximum 25 percent tax rate (see the Property Dispositions chapter for a detailed discussion of unrecaptured §1250 gain).

Exclusion of gain from debt forgiveness on foreclosure of home mortgage. Prior to 2007, if a lender foreclosed (took possession of) a taxpayer's principal residence, sold the home for less than the taxpayer's outstanding mortgage, and forgave the taxpayer for the remainder of the debt, the taxpayer was required to include the debt forgiveness in their gross income. From January 1, 2007, through December 31, 2020, taxpayers who realized income from this situation were allowed to exclude up to $2 million of debt forgiveness if the debt was secured by the taxpayer's principal residence (i.e., the principal residence was collateral for the loan) and the debt was incurred to acquire, construct, or substantially improve the home.[9] For debt forgiven after December 31, 2020, and prior to January 1, 2026, the maximum amount of debt forgiveness that may be excluded from gross income is reduced from $2 million to $750,000. The taxpayer must apply the excluded amount of debt forgiveness income to reduce the basis of the principal residence, but not below zero.

LO 14-3

Home Mortgage Interest Deduction

A primary tax benefit of owning a home is that taxpayers are generally allowed to deduct the interest they pay on their home mortgage loans as an itemized deduction. Taxpayers generate tax savings and reduce the after-tax cost of their mortgage payments to the extent of their deductible interest payments. Note that taxpayers benefit from mortgage interest deductions only to the extent that mortgage interest (when added to other itemized deductions) exceeds the standard deduction.

Example 14-5

During the current year, Tyler and Jasmine own a home with an average mortgage balance of $400,000. They pay interest at 3 percent annually on the loan, and they qualify to deduct the interest expense as an itemized deduction. The Jeffersons' marginal income tax rate is 32 percent, and before counting mortgage interest, their itemized deductions exceed the standard deduction for married filing jointly taxpayers. What are the before- and after-tax costs of their mortgage interest expense for the year?

Answer: $12,000 before-tax cost and $8,160 after-tax cost, computed as follows:

Description	Amount	Explanation
(1) Before-tax interest expense	**$12,000**	$400,000 × 3% (all tax deductible)
(2) Marginal tax rate	× 32%	
(3) Tax savings from interest expense	3,840	(1) × (2)
After-tax cost of interest expense	**$ 8,160**	(1) − (3)

Note that the $3,840 tax savings generated by the mortgage interest expense deduction reduces the after-tax cost of their monthly mortgage payment by an average of $320 ($3,840/12).

What if: Assume the original facts except that before counting the mortgage interest expense, the Jeffersons' itemized deductions were $6,000 below the standard deduction. How much tax savings would the $12,000 mortgage interest expense generate for the Jeffersons?

Answer: $1,920 ($6,000 × 32%). The first $6,000 of mortgage interest expense increases the Jeffersons' itemized deductions to equal the standard deduction but does not affect their taxable

[9]§108(a)(1)(E) and (h). This larger $2 million exclusion amount also applied to qualifying debt forgiven in 2021 if the debt is forgiven pursuant to a written agreement that was entered into in 2020.

income. The remaining $6,000 increases itemized deductions above the standard deduction and thus reduces taxable income, producing tax savings.

What if: Assume that instead of buying a home, the Jeffersons rented a home and paid $1,667 a month for rent expense. What would be the before- and after-tax costs of the $20,000 annual rental payments?

Answer: $20,000 before-tax cost and $20,000 after-tax cost. Because rental payments are not deductible, they do not generate tax savings, so the before- and after-tax costs of the rental payments are the same.

However, despite the tax savings from buying versus renting a home, it is important to consider that nontax factors could favor renting over purchasing a home.

Acquisition Indebtedness Taxpayers are allowed to deduct interest paid on the principal amount of **acquisition indebtedness** (subject to the limitation discussed below) owed by them as an itemized deduction. For tax purposes, acquisition indebtedness is any debt secured by a **qualified residence** that is incurred in acquiring, constructing, or substantially improving the residence but only to the extent that the amount borrowed does not exceed the limits described below. Thus, a loan secured by the home after the taxpayer has acquired or constructed the home may be called a "home equity loan" by the bank, but it would be treated as acquisition indebtedness for tax purposes only to the extent the loan proceeds were used to substantially improve the home and, when combined with the existing acquisition indebtedness, do not exceed the acquisition indebtedness limit described below. To be able to determine whether a loan qualifies as acquisition indebtedness for tax purposes, it's important to define a couple of terms.

Debt secured by residence: A debt is secured by a residence when the residence is used as collateral for the loan. If the owner does not make the payments on the loan, the lender may take possession of or force a sale of the home to satisfy the owner's responsibility for the debt.

Qualified residence: A qualified residence is the taxpayer's principal residence *and* one other residence (see previous discussion for definition of the terms *principal residence* and *residence*). For a taxpayer with *more* than two residences, the property to be treated as the second qualified residence is an annual election—that is, the taxpayer can choose to deduct interest related to a particular second home one year and a different second home the next. The second residence is often a vacation home where the taxpayer resides part time.

TAXES IN THE REAL WORLD A Nonowner Can Be an Owner

Deducting home mortgage interest paid as acquisition indebtedness generally requires that the home be legally owned by the taxpayer claiming the deduction. However, the term *owner* not only is defined to be the person listed on the property deed but, in certain circumstances, also can be a taxpayer found to be an "equitable owner" under state law.

John Wainwright was friends with a homeowner in Bethesda, Maryland, for over 35 years. In 2006, Wainwright and his friend refinanced the friend's mortgage in order to make certain renovations to the home. Wainwright became a co-borrower along with his friend on the mortgage. However, the ownership deed to the home was not altered and only his friend remained listed as the legal owner of the home. Wainwright and his friend lived in the friend's home during 2010 and 2011. Although Wainwright did not own the home, he was legally obligated as a co-borrower to repay the loan. Wainwright paid all of the mortgage payments and maintained the property during the tax years in question.

The IRS denied the home mortgage deduction claimed by Wainwright because Wainwright did not legally own the home. However, despite the lack of actual ownership, the Tax Court considered various state law factors to determine if Wainwright was still an "equitable owner" such that he had the benefits

(*continued*)

and burden of owning the property. Key factors used included the duty to maintain the property, risk of loss, obligation to pay taxes, and other charges as well as the right to use the property.

Based upon the various state law factors analyzed, the Tax Court ruled that Wainwright was an equitable owner, and because he paid the mortgage, he was entitled to deduct the home mortgage interest deduction during the tax years in question.

Source: John Wainwright v. Comm'r, T.C. Memo 2017-70.

THE KEY FACTS

Home Mortgage Interest Deduction

- Deduction allowed for home mortgage interest on acquisition indebtedness.
  - Principal residence and one other residence.
- Acquisition indebtedness
  - Proceeds used to acquire or substantially improve a qualified residence.
  - Limited to $1,000,000 if incurred prior to 12/16/2017.
  - Limited to $750,000 if incurred after 12/15/2017.

Limitation on Acquisition Indebtedness For purposes of determining the deductible amount of mortgage interest expense, the amount of acquisition indebtedness is limited to a fixed amount based on when the indebtedness originated. For acquisition indebtedness incurred after December 15, 2017, the amount of acquisition indebtedness is limited to $750,000 ($375,000 for married taxpayers filing separately). For acquisition indebtedness incurred before December 16, 2017, the amount of acquisition indebtedness is limited to $1,000,000 ($500,000 for married taxpayers filing separately), even if the debt is **refinanced** after December 15, 2017.[10] When a taxpayer has both acquisition indebtedness incurred before December 16, 2017, and acquisition indebtedness incurred after December 15, 2017, the $750,000 ($375,000) limit is reduced (not below zero) by the acquisition indebtedness incurred before December 16, 2017. The higher $1,000,000 limit continues to apply to any debt incurred after December 15, 2017, to refinance debt incurred prior to December 16, 2017, to the extent the amount of the refinancing does not exceed the amount of the pre–December 16, 2017, existing debt. This exception for the refinancing of debt will not apply after (1) the expiration of the term of the original debt or (2) the earlier of the expiration of the first refinancing of the debt or 30 years after the date of the first refinancing.

Example 14-6

What if: Assume that in January of 2022, the Jeffersons purchased a home in Chicago costing $900,000 by making a down payment of $100,000 and taking out an $800,000 loan secured by the home. During the year, the Jeffersons paid $24,000 of interest on the mortgage. How much of the interest are the Jeffersons allowed to deduct?

Answer: $22,500 ($24,000 × $750,000/$800,000). Interest on $750,000 of $800,000 is deductible because the acquisition indebtedness was incurred after December 15, 2017, so the acquisition indebtedness is limited to $750,000 for purposes of determining their deductible mortgage interest.

What if: Assume that in December of 2021, the Jeffersons purchased a home in Chicago costing $800,000 by making a down payment of $100,000 and taking out a $700,000 loan secured by the home. During 2022, the Jeffersons paid $21,000 of interest on the mortgage (and no principal). In addition, on July 1, 2022, the Jeffersons borrowed $20,000 through a loan called a "home equity loan" by the bank (the loan was secured by the home) and they paid $600 of interest on this loan in 2022. The Jeffersons used $15,000 of the proceeds from this loan to finish the basement in their home, and they used $5,000 of the proceeds as a down payment on a new car. How much home mortgage interest can the Jeffersons deduct in 2022?

Answer: $21,450 [$21,000 + $450 ($15,000/$20,000 × $600]. The Jeffersons can deduct all $21,000 of interest on the $700,000 loan because the entire loan is acquisition indebtedness. However, because only $15,000 of the $20,000 "home equity loan" is acquisition debt for tax purposes ($15,000 of the $20,000 was used to substantially improve the home), the Jeffersons can deduct interest on only $15,000 of the loan. Thus, the Jeffersons can deduct $450 of interest on the additional $20,000 loan ($15,000/$20,000 × $600), and the remaining $150 of interest is nondeductible personal interest.

What if: Assume that on December 1, 2017, the Jeffersons purchased a home in Chicago costing $900,000 by making a down payment of $100,000 and taking out an $800,000 loan secured by the

[10]§163(h)(3)(F). For tax years prior to 2018, taxpayers could deduct interest paid on up to $100,000 of home-equity indebtedness ($50,000 if married filing separately) as an itemized deduction (in addition to the acquisition indebtedness limit) no matter how they used the loan proceeds. However, for tax years after 2017, as discussed above, interest on home equity indebtedness is no longer deductible unless the loan qualifies as acquisition indebtedness.

home. During 2022, the Jeffersons paid $39,000 of interest on the mortgage. How much of the interest are the Jeffersons allowed to deduct?

Answer: $39,000. All of the interest is deductible because the acquisition indebtedness was incurred before December 16, 2017, and it is under the $1,000,000 limit.

What if: Assume that on December 1, 2017, the Jeffersons purchased a home in Chicago costing $900,000 by making a down payment of $100,000 and taking out an $800,000 loan secured by the home. In June of 2023, the Jeffersons refinanced the remaining $770,000 balance of the loan to get a lower interest rate. Are the Jeffersons allowed to deduct all the interest on the refinanced loan?

Answer: Yes. The Jeffersons can deduct all of the interest on the refinanced loan even though the balance exceeds $750,000 because the original acquisition indebtedness occurred before December 16, 2017, when the acquisition debt limit was $1,000,000.

Once acquisition indebtedness is established for a qualifying residence (or for the sum of two qualifying residences), principal payments reduce it and only additional indebtedness secured by the residence(s) *and* incurred to substantially improve the residence(s) increases acquisition indebtedness. Does refinancing affect the amount of indebtedness? Unless the taxpayer uses proceeds from the refinance to substantially improve the residence, the refinanced loan is treated as acquisition debt only to the extent that the principal amount of the refinancing does not exceed the amount of the acquisition debt immediately before the refinancing. Consequently, the amount borrowed in excess of the remaining principal on the original loan that is not used to substantially improve the residence does not qualify as acquisition indebtedness. Interest on the "excess" part of this loan is not deductible as acquisition indebtedness.[11] However, such interest may be deductible as investment interest or business interest depending on how the loan proceeds were used.

At the end of each year, taxpayers receive a **Form 1098** (see Exhibit 14-3) that reports the amount of mortgage interest paid by the borrower to a reporting lender (box 1). In addition, this form also provides the taxpayer with relevant information necessary to determine the deductibility of mortgage interest paid, including the outstanding mortgage principal balance (box 2), mortgage origination date (box 3), and whether or not the loan is secured by the taxpayer's principal residence (boxes 7 and 8). While Form 1098 provides key information, the form itself is not sufficient to determine the deductibility of the mortgage interest paid. For instance, a taxpayer would also need to determine if the borrowed funds constituted acquisition indebtedness.

Example 14-7

What if: Assume the Jeffersons purchased a home in Chicago costing $430,000 by making a down payment of $30,000 and taking out a $400,000 loan secured by the home. What is the Jeffersons' acquisition indebtedness?

Answer: $400,000. This is debt secured by a qualified residence that is incurred in acquiring, constructing, or substantially improving the residence.

What if: Now assume that when they moved to Chicago, the Jeffersons purchased a home costing $430,000 by making a down payment of $400,000, and taking out a $30,000 loan secured by the home. During the next few years, the Jeffersons paid $10,000 of principal on the loan, thereby reducing the loan balance to $20,000. Subsequently, needing cash, the Jeffersons refinanced their mortgage by taking out a loan, secured by their residence, for $150,000. With the $150,000 they paid off the $20,000 balance on the original loan and used the $130,000 of extra cash for purposes unrelated to the home. After the refinance, what is the Jeffersons' acquisition indebtedness?

Answer: $20,000, the same amount as before the refinance. The only way to increase acquisition indebtedness once it is established is to borrow money to substantially improve the home. Thus, the

(continued on page 14-12)

[11]When taxpayers have multiple acquisition debt loans that, when combined, exceed the acquisition debt limit, they can determine the deductible interest expense using either the simplified or the exact method described in Reg. §1.163-10T(d) and (e), respectively.

Jeffersons' interest deductions on the home will be limited to the interest expense on the $20,000 acquisition indebtedness.

What if: Assume the same facts as the previous what-if scenario except now suppose the Jeffersons used $40,000 of the cash from the loan to build a new garage on their property. After the refinance, what is the Jeffersons' acquisition indebtedness?

Answer: $60,000 ($20,000 original loan principal + $40,000 used to substantially improve the home).

TAXES IN THE REAL WORLD Double-Take on Home-Related Interest Deductions

Taxpayers (other than married taxpayers filing separately) are allowed to deduct interest paid on up to either $1,000,000 or $750,000 of acquisition indebtedness (depending on when the debt occurred) on their principal residence (and one other residence). In 2012, the Tax Court concluded that the indebtedness limit for interest deductions is a per-residence(s) limit and not a per-taxpayer limit. For example, if two unmarried taxpayers jointly acquire (in 2022) and reside in a home, the qualifying debt limit for both taxpayers combined would be $750,000. However, in 2015, the 9th Circuit Court of Appeals overruled the 2012 Tax Court decision and concluded that the qualifying debt limit applies on a per-taxpayer basis and not a per-residence(s) basis. In 2016, the IRS acquiesced to this decision (2016-31 IRB 193). Consequently, two unmarried taxpayers who jointly acquire a home in 2022 can each deduct interest on up to $750,000 of acquisition debt ($1,500,000 of acquisition debt in total). If the two taxpayers were married, together they would be able to deduct interest on up to only $750,000 of acquisition debt. Now, that's a marriage penalty!

Source: *Voss v. Comm'r*, 2015-2 USTC ¶ 50,427 (9th Cir. 2015), *rev'g Sophy v. Comm'r*, 138 TC 204 (2012).

EXHIBIT 14-3 Form 1098

☐ CORRECTED (if checked)

RECIPIENT'S/LENDER'S name, street address, city or town, state or province, country, ZIP or foreign postal code, and telephone no.

*Caution: The amount shown may not be fully deductible by you. Limits based on the loan amount and the cost and value of the secured property may apply. Also, you may only deduct interest to the extent it was incurred by you, actually paid by you, and not reimbursed by another person.

OMB No. 1545-1380

2021

Form **1098**

Mortgage Interest Statement

1 Mortgage interest received from payer(s)/borrower(s)*
$

RECIPIENT'S/LENDER'S TIN

PAYER'S/BORROWER'S TIN

2 Outstanding mortgage principal
$

3 Mortgage origination date

4 Refund of overpaid interest
$

5 Mortgage insurance premiums
$

PAYER'S/BORROWER'S name

6 Points paid on purchase of principal residence
$

Street address (including apt. no.)

7 ☐ If address of property securing mortgage is the same as PAYER'S/BORROWER'S address, the box is checked, or the address or description is entered in box 8.

City or town, state or province, country, and ZIP or foreign postal code

8 Address or description of property securing mortgage

9 Number of properties securing the mortgage

10 Other

Account number (see instructions)

Copy B
For Payer/ Borrower

The information in boxes 1 through 9 and 11 is important tax information and is being furnished to the IRS. If you are required to file a return, a negligence penalty or other sanction may be imposed on you if the IRS determines that an underpayment of tax results because you overstated a deduction for this mortgage interest or for these points, reported in boxes 1 and 6; or because you didn't report the refund of interest (box 4); or because you claimed a nondeductible item.

11 Mortgage acquisition date

Form **1098** (Keep for your records) www.irs.gov/Form1098 Department of the Treasury - Internal Revenue Service

Source: irs.gov.

Mortgage Insurance Taxpayers are allowed to deduct as qualified residence interest expense premiums paid or accrued on mortgage insurance (insurance premiums paid by the borrower to protect the lender against the borrower defaulting on the loan). To qualify, the premiums for the mortgage insurance must be paid or accrued in connection with acquisition indebtedness on a qualified residence and must be paid by December 31, 2021. The deduction does not apply to mortgage insurance contracts issued before January 1, 2007. The (itemized) deduction is phased out by 10 percent for every $1,000 ($500 for married taxpayers filing separately), or fraction thereof, that the taxpayer's AGI exceeds $100,000 ($50,000 for married taxpayers filing separately).[12]

Points A home buyer arranging financing for a home typically incurs several loan-related fees or expenses, including "points." A **point** is 1 percent of the principal amount of the loan. In general, borrowers pay points to lenders in exchange for reduced interest rates on loans. However, borrowers may also pay lenders for other purposes (e.g., to compensate lenders for the service of providing the loan). In order for taxpayers to deduct points, the points must be paid for a reduced interest rate (rather than for the service of providing the loan).[13] However, to minimize possible disputes regarding the deductibility of points and as a matter of administrative convenience, the IRS will treat points as deductible qualified residence interest if the following requirements are met:[14]

1. The **settlement statement**—a document that details the monies paid out and received by the buyer and seller as part of the loan transaction—must clearly designate the amounts as points payable in connection with the loan, for example, as "loan origination charge," "loan discount," or "discount points." These amounts are typically provided on lines 801 and 802 of the settlement statement. (See Appendix B at the end of this chapter for a sample settlement statement for the Jeffersons.)
2. The amounts must be computed as a percentage of the stated principal amount of the loan.
3. The amounts paid must conform to an established business general practice of charging points for loans in the area in which the residence is located, and the amount of the points paid must not exceed the amount generally charged in that area.
4. The amounts must be paid in connection with the acquisition of the taxpayer's *principal residence* and the loan *must be secured by that residence* (i.e., the deduction for points is not available for points paid in connection with a loan for a second home). Points paid on a home acquisition loan in excess of the acquisition debt limit are not deductible.
5. The buyer must provide enough funds in the down payment on the home to at least equal the cost of the points (i.e., the buyer is not allowed to borrow from the lender to pay the points). However, points paid by the *seller* to the lender in connection with the taxpayer's loan are treated as paid directly by the taxpayer. Consequently, such points are generally deductible by the buyer.

Note that points paid in *refinancing* a home loan (i.e., financing the home again with a new loan, typically at a lower interest rate) are not immediately deductible by the homeowner. These points must be amortized and deducted on a straight-line basis over the life of the loan.[15]

Now that we understand how points are treated for tax purposes, let's consider the home buyer's decision whether to pay points to obtain a lower interest rate on a home loan. From an economic standpoint, the buyer must choose between (1) paying extra money up front and having lower monthly mortgage payments or (2) paying less initially and having larger monthly payments.

[12]§163(h)(3)(E).

[13]§461(g)(2).

[14]Rev. Proc. 94-27.

[15]See the Tax Compliance, the IRS, and Tax Authorities chapter research memo and *J.R. Huntsman v. Comm'r,* 90-2 USTC ¶ 50,340 (8th Cir. 1990), *rev'g* 91 TC 917 (1988), for a limited exception to this rule.

When the taxpayer can afford to pay points, deciding whether to do so generally requires a "break-even" analysis. Essentially, the taxpayer determines how long it will take to recoup the after-tax cost of the point(s) through the after-tax interest savings on the loan. Generally speaking, the longer the taxpayer plans on staying in the home and maintaining the loan (not refinancing it), the more likely it is financially beneficial to pay points to obtain a lower interest rate. However, paying points can be costly if, after too short a time, the taxpayer sells the home or refinances the home loan. In these situations, the taxpayer may not reach the break-even point. Further, because the deduction for points is an itemized deduction, paying points only generates tax savings to the extent the points paid (when combined with other itemized deductions) exceed the standard deduction.

Example 14-8

Tyler and Jasmine are seeking financing for their new $800,000 home. They are paying $500,000 down and borrowing the remaining $300,000, to be paid back over 30 years. They have the choice of paying 2 discount points ($6,000) and getting a fixed interest rate of 3 percent or paying no discount points and getting a fixed interest rate of 4 percent. Assume the points meet the immediate deductibility requirements, the Jeffersons' marginal tax rate is 32 percent, they pay interest only (no principal) for the first three years of the loan, and their other itemized deductions exceed the standard deduction. What is the Jeffersons' break-even point for paying the points?

Answer: Two years, calculated as follows:

Loan summary: $300,000; 4 percent rate with no points or 3 percent rate with 2 points ($6,000). Assume the Jeffersons pay interest only (no principal) for the first three years.

Description	Amount	Calculation
(1) Initial cash outflow from paying points	$(6,000)	$300,000 × 2%
(2) Tax benefit from deducting points	1,920	(1) × 32%
(3) After-tax cost of points	(4,080)	(1) + (2)
(4) Before-tax *savings per year* from 3% vs. 4% interest rate	3,000	$300,000 × (4% − 3%)
(5) *Forgone tax benefit per year* of higher interest rate	(960)	(4) × 32%
(6) After-tax savings per year of 3% vs. 4% interest rate	$ 2,040	(4) + (5)
Break-even point in years	**2 years**	(3)/(6)

The break-even analysis in Example 14-8, while a useful exercise, oversimplifies the calculations a bit. Why? Because it doesn't take into account the present value of the tax savings or the increasing principal that would be paid on a traditional principal-and-interest-type loan. In reality, the cost of the points is immediate, while the savings come later—so the break-even point on a present value basis is likely a little longer than two years. Also, the more principal paid on the loan, the lower the amount of interest paid each month—so savings from the lower interest rate decline over time, which would also extend the break-even point.

Because points paid on a refinancing are deducted over the life of the loan, the break-even point for paying points on a refinanced mortgage is longer than the break-even point for an original mortgage of the same amount.

Example 14-9

What if: Assume that the Jeffersons have a $300,000 mortgage on their home. They have decided to refinance with a new 30-year mortgage in order to get a lower interest rate. The Jeffersons have the option of paying 2 discount points ($6,000) and obtaining a 3 percent interest rate or obtaining a 4 percent rate with no discount points. Assume the Jeffersons' marginal tax rate is 32 percent, they pay interest only on the loan for the first three years (no principal), and the Jeffersons' other itemized deductions exceed the standard deduction amount. What is the Jeffersons' approximate break-even point in years for paying the points on the refinance?

Answer: 2.85 years, calculated as follows:

Loan summary: $300,000; 4 percent rate with no points or 3 percent rate with 2 points ($6,000). Assume the Jeffersons pay interest only (no principal) for the first three years.

Description	Points	Notes
(1) Initial cash outflow from paying points	$(6,000)	$300,000 × 2%
(2) Tax benefit from deducting points	0	
(3) After-tax cost of points	(6,000)	(1) + (2)
(4) Before-tax savings per year from 3% vs. 4% interest rate	3,000	$300,000 × (4% − 3%)
(5) Forgone tax benefit per year of higher interest payments	(960)	(4) × 32%
(6) After-tax savings per year of 3% vs. 4% interest rate	2,040	(4) + (5)
(7) Annual tax savings from amortizing points	64	(1)/30 years × 32%
(8) Annual after-tax cash flow benefit of paying points	$ 2,104	(6) + (7)
Break-even point in years	**2.85 years**	(3)/(8)

The reason for the longer break-even point is that the points effectively cost more because they are not immediately deductible on a refinance.

Real Property Taxes

LO 14-4

Owners of personal residences and other types of real estate such as land, rental properties, business buildings, and other types of real property are generally required to pay **real property taxes.** These taxes are assessed by local governments and are based on the fair market value of the property.[16] Real property taxes support general public welfare by providing funding for local public needs such as schools and roads.

Local governments set the tax rates applied to the value of the property annually based on their financial needs for the year. The applicable rates may depend on the type of real estate. For example, the tax rate for real estate used in a business may be higher than the rates for residential real property. Taxpayers conducting self-employment activities can deduct real property tax payments from business income as for AGI deductions. For individual owners, such payments are for AGI deductions from rental income. For other individuals, real property taxes are deductible as itemized deductions. However, the itemized deduction for all taxes combined [state and local income (or sales), U.S. real property, and personal property tax] is limited to $10,000 ($5,000 for married taxpayers filing separately). Foreign property taxes paid by taxpayers are not deductible as itemized deductions.

Taxpayers are not allowed to deduct fees paid for setting up water and sewer services or for assessments for local benefits such as streets and sidewalks.[17] They generally add these expenditures to the basis of their property.

Frequently, homeowners pay their real estate taxes through an **escrow (holding) account** with their mortgage lender. Each monthly payment to the lender includes an amount that represents roughly one-twelfth of the anticipated real property taxes for the year. The actual tax payment (or payments if the taxes are due more than once a year) is made by the mortgage company with funds accumulated in the escrow account. The homeowner gets to deduct the property taxes when they are paid to the taxing jurisdiction, not when the homeowner makes payments for these taxes to the escrow account.

Who is responsible for paying the taxes when an owner sells a personal residence or other type of real estate during the year? Is it the owner at the time the taxes are due?

THE KEY FACTS

Real Estate Taxes

- Apply to homes, land, business buildings, and other types of real estate.
- Deduction for all taxes combined (including state income taxes and U.S. real property taxes) limited to $10,000.
- Homeowners frequently pay real property tax bill through an escrow account.
  - Deduction timing is based on date of payment of taxes to governmental body, not date of deposits to the escrow account.
- When homeowners sell home during year:
  - Deduction is based on the proportion of the year the taxpayer lived in the home, no matter who actually pays the tax.

[16]Local governments tend to understate the fair market value of property when appraising it to minimize the chances that the taxpayer will contest the appraisal.

[17]Reg. §1.164-4(a).

Who receives the corresponding tax deduction? In most situations, the buyer and seller divide the responsibility for the tax payments based on the portion of the property tax year that each party held the property. This allocation of taxes between buyer and seller is generally spelled out in the settlement statement when the sale becomes final (see Appendix B to this chapter for a sample settlement statement for the Jeffersons). For tax purposes, it doesn't matter who actually pays the tax, although generally the current owner has the responsibility to do so. As long as the taxes are paid, the tax deduction is based on the relative amount of time each party owned the property during the year (or the period over which the property taxes are payable).[18]

Example 14-10

On February 1, Tyler and Jasmine purchased a new home for $800,000. At the time of the purchase, it was estimated that the property tax bill on the home for the year would be $8,000 ($800,000 × 1%). Assume that the tax bill is paid and that the property tax bill is based on a calendar year. During the year, the Jeffersons paid $15,000 in state income taxes, and they did not pay any taxes other than state income taxes and real property taxes during the year. What is their itemized deduction for taxes for the year?

Answer: $10,000. Before even considering real property taxes, the Jeffersons reached the $10,000 itemized deduction limit with the state income taxes they paid. Consequently, the real property taxes do not increase their itemized deductions.

What if: Assume the same facts except that the Jeffersons did not pay any taxes other than real property taxes during the year. What would be their itemized deduction for taxes for the year?

Answer: $7,333. Because the seller lived in the home for one-twelfth of the year (January) and the Jeffersons lived in the home for eleven-twelfths of the year (February through December), the seller will deduct $667 of the property taxes (one-twelfth) and the Jeffersons will deduct $7,333. Consequently, the Jeffersons could have deducted up to $2,667 ($10,000 − $7,333) of other taxes for the year.

LO 14-5

RENTAL USE OF THE HOME

THE KEY FACTS

Rental Use of the Home

- Tax treatment depends on amount of personal and rental use. The three categories are:
  (1) Residence with minimal rental use (personal residence).
  (2) Residence with significant rental use (vacation home).
  (3) Nonresidence (rental property).

A taxpayer with the financial means to do so may purchase a second home as a vacation home, a rental property, or a combination of the two. A taxpayer may own a second home outright or may share ownership with others through a timeshare or fractional ownership arrangement. Or a taxpayer may rent out their home or part of their home using an online service such as Airbnb or VRBO. The nontax benefits of owning a second home include a fixed vacation destination, the ability to trade the use of the home with an owner of a home in a different location, the opportunity to generate income through rentals, and the potential appreciation of the second home as an investment. The nontax costs of owning a second home include the initial purchase cost, maintenance costs, the inconvenience of dealing with renters or property managers, and the downside risk associated with holding the second home as an investment.

The tax consequences of owning a second home depend on whether the home qualifies as a residence (see discussion at the beginning of the chapter) and on the number of days the taxpayer rents out the home. The home is categorized in one of three ways:

1. Residence with minimal rental use (rented for 14 or fewer days).
2. Residence with significant rental use (rented for 15 or more days).
3. Nonresidence.

[18]The seller gets a deduction (subject to the $10,000 limit) for the taxes allocable for the period of time up to and including the day before the date of the sale. The taxes allocable to the day of the sale through the end of the property tax year are deductible by the buyer. See §164(d).

Recall that, as we discussed earlier in the chapter, a dwelling unit is considered a "residence" for tax purposes if the taxpayer uses the home for personal purposes for *more than* the greater of 14 days or 10 percent of the number of rental days during the year. For example, if a taxpayer rents their home for 200 days and uses it for personal purposes for 21 days or more, the home is considered to be a residence for tax purposes. If the same taxpayer used the home for personal purposes for 20 days, the home would be considered a nonresidence for tax purposes.

THE KEY FACTS

Rental Use of the Home

- Residence with minimal rental use.
  - Taxpayer lives in the home at least 15 days and rents it 14 or fewer days.
  - Exclude all rental income.
  - Don't deduct rental expenses (other than mortgage interest and real property taxes).

Residence with Minimal Rental Use

The law is simple for taxpayers who rent out a residence for a minimal amount of time during the year (i.e., they live in it for at least 15 days and they rent it for 14 or fewer days). These taxpayers are not required to include the gross receipts in rental income, and they are not allowed to deduct any expenses related to the rental.[19] They are, however, allowed to claim as itemized deductions any home mortgage interest and real property taxes on the home (subject to limits discussed above).

Example 14-11

The Jeffersons purchased a vacation home in a golf community in Scottsdale, Arizona, in January. They spent 10 days vacationing in the home in early March and another 15 days vacationing in the home in mid-December. In early February, they rented the home for 14 days to a group of golfers who were in town to attend a PGA Tour golf tournament and play golf. The Jeffersons received $6,000 in rent from the group, and the Jeffersons incurred $1,000 of expenses relating to the rental home (other than mortgage interest and real property taxes). The Jeffersons did not rent out the property again for the rest of the year. How much will the $5,000 net income ($6,000 – $1,000) from the rental increase their taxable income?

Answer: Zero! Because the Jeffersons lived in the home for at least 15 days and rented out the home for 14 or fewer days during the year, they do not report the rental income to the IRS, and they do not deduct expenses associated with the rental. The Jeffersons saved $1,600 in taxes by excluding the $5,000 of net rental income ($5,000 net income × 32% marginal tax rate). Note that they can also claim the mortgage interest and real property taxes (subject to the $10,000 itemized deduction limit for taxes) on the property for the *full year* as itemized deductions.

ETHICS

Carey and Pat were good friends and neighbors in an upscale neighborhood near several highly rated golf courses in Arizona. During the winter, both Carey and Pat decided to rent their homes (at a premium) to groups of golfers from the New York area who wanted to get out of the snow and enjoy sunshine and golf for a couple of weeks during the winter. While their homes were rented, Carey and Pat vacationed together in Cancun. In January 2022, Carey rented his home for 14 days and received $14,000 in rent. Pat also rented his home for the same 14 days and received $16,000 in rent. Near the end of the 14-day rental period, Pat got a call from the renters, who wanted to extend their stay for one day. Pat agreed to the extension and charged the group $2,000 for the extra day. When preparing his 2022 tax return, Pat discovered that taxpayers who rent their home for more than 14 days are required to report all their rental income on their tax returns. Pat didn't think it was fair that he had to pay taxes on the rental income while Carey did not just because Pat rented his home for one more day than Carey in 2022. Consequently, Pat decided that he had rented his property for 14 days and given the renters the last day for free. What do you think about Pat's approach to solving his tax problem?

[19]§280A(g).

THE KEY FACTS

Rental Use of the Home

- Residence with significant rental use.
  - Rental use is 15 days or more and personal use exceeds the greater of (1) 14 days or (2) 10 percent of rental days.
  - Deduct direct rental expenses such as advertising and commissions for real estate agents.
  - Allocate home-related expenses between rental use and personal use.
  - Interest and taxes allocated to personal use are deducted as itemized deductions (subject to relevant limitations); all other expenses allocated to personal use are not deductible.
  - IRS method allocates interest and taxes to rental use based on rental use to total use for the year.
  - Tax Court method allocates interest and taxes to rental use based on rental use to total days in entire year.
  - Rental deductions other than tier 1 expenses are limited to gross rental revenue. When limited, deduct tier 1 expenses first, then tier 2, and finally tier 3 expenses.

A taxpayer with a strategically located second (or even first) home can take advantage of this favorable tax rule by renting the property to those in town to attend high-profile events such as the Olympics, the Masters golf tournament, the Super Bowl, and Mardi Gras—and excluding potentially large rental payments from taxable income.

Residence with Significant Rental Use (Vacation Home)

When a home qualifies as a residence and the taxpayer rents out the home for 15 days or more, rental revenue is included in gross income, expenses to obtain tenants (i.e., advertising and commissions for real estate agents) are fully deductible as direct rental expenses, and expenses relating to the home are allocated between personal and rental use. The expenses allocated to personal use are not deductible except as permitted as itemized deductions under nonrental tax provisions. (These deductions are reported on Schedule A of Form 1040 and include mortgage interest, real property taxes, and certain casualty losses on the home.) All other expenses allocated to personal use are not deductible. Expenses are *generally* allocated to rental use based on the ratio of the number of days of rental use to the total number of days the property was used for rental and personal purposes. All expenses not allocated to rental use are allocated to personal use. The only potential exception to the general allocation rule is the allocation of mortgage interest expense and real property taxes. The IRS and the Tax Court disagree on how to allocate these particular expenses. Under the IRS method, these expenses are allocated the same way as all other expenses. However, under the Tax Court method, interest and taxes are allocated to rental use based on the ratio of days the property was rented over the number of days in the year, rather than the number of days the property was used for any purpose during the year.[20] The **IRS** and **Tax Court allocation methods** are described in Exhibit 14-4.

EXHIBIT 14-4 Tax Court versus IRS Method of Allocating Expenses

Rental Allocation	IRS Method	Tax Court Method
Mortgage interest and property taxes	$\text{Expense} \times \frac{\text{Total rental days}}{\text{Total days used}}$	$\text{Expense} \times \frac{\text{Total rental days}}{\text{Days in year}}$
All other expenses	$\text{Expense} \times \frac{\text{Total rental days}}{\text{Total days used}}$	$\text{Expense} \times \frac{\text{Total rental days}}{\text{Total days used}}$

The Tax Court justifies its allocation method by emphasizing that interest expense and property taxes accrue over the entire year regardless of the level of personal or rental use. Taxpayers generally choose the approach most beneficial to them. Determining which method is more favorable for a particular taxpayer depends on the taxpayer's facts and circumstances, as discussed below.

What is deductible if you rent part of your dwelling unit but not the whole thing, such as a single bedroom or perhaps a basement of a two-level single-family residence? The taxpayer is required to divide the total expenses between those that are attributable

[20]The Tax Court method of allocating these expenses is also referred to as the *Bolton* method after the taxpayer in the court case in which the Tax Court approved this method of allocating deductions. While the court case initially was tried in the Tax Court, the decision in favor of the taxpayer was appealed to the Ninth Circuit Court, which also ruled in favor of the taxpayer and sanctioned the use of the Tax Court or *Bolton* method of allocating interest expense. *Bolton v. Comm'r,* 82-2 USTC ¶ 9699 (9th Cir. 1982), *aff'g* 77 TC 104 (1981).

to the rental portion versus the personal-use portion. Expenses that relate only to the rented portion of the dwelling unit (e.g., carpet or painting expenses for that room only) do not have to be prorated between rental and non-rental use. The two most common methods of prorating shared expenses between rental and non-rental use are the method based upon the number of rented rooms divided by the number of rooms in the dwelling unit or using the square footage of the rental room divided by the total square footage of the dwelling unit. Under either method, the taxpayer multiplies each category of shared expenses by the allocation percentage determined under the selected allocation method to arrive at the expenses allocated to determine the rental expenses of the dwelling unit.

Example 14-12

What if: Suppose the Jeffersons rented a spare bedroom in their principal residence for the entire 2022 tax year. The spare room measures 300 square feet, and the total square footage of their residence is 3,000 square feet. Assume that the Jeffersons incur the following expenses during the 2022 tax year:

Description	Amount
Repairing the drywall and repainting the spare room	$ 1,000
Replacing a broken window in the spare room	450
Property taxes (entire residence)	2,500
Mortgage interest (entire residence)	12,000
Utilities (entire residence)	2,000

What is the amount of rental expenses allocated to the spare room assuming the Jeffersons are using the square footage method to allocate expenses?

Answer: $3,100 ($1,450 + $1,650). The $1,450 of expenses for the wall/repainting repair and the broken window are exclusive to the spare room and thus are allocated to the spare bedroom. The property taxes, mortgage interest, and utilities are expenses of the entire home and thus must be prorated between the spare bedroom and the remainder of the home. The allocation percentage for the spare bedroom is 10% (calculated as 300 square feet for the spare room/3,000 square feet for the entire dwelling unit). As a result, $1,650 of the total $16,500 of the entire home ($2,500 + $12,000 + $2,000) would also be thus are allocated to the spare room.

Deducting Rental Expenses of Vacation Home When the gross rental revenue for the year exceeds the sum of direct rental expenses and expenses allocated to the rental use of the home, the taxpayer is allowed to deduct all rental expenses in full. However, when the sum of direct rental expenses and expenses allocated to the rental use of the home exceeds the rental revenue, the deductibility of the expenses depends on the type of expenses. In these situations, taxpayers assign each of the rental expenses into one of three categories or "tiers." Tier 1 expenses include expenses to obtain tenants and potentially mortgage interest expense and real property taxes allocated to the rental use of the home.[21] Tier 2 expenses include all expenses allocated to rental use of the home that are not tier 1 expenses or tier 3 expenses. Tier 3 expense is depreciation expense allocated to the rental use of the home.[22]

[21]Technically, expenses to obtain tenants (advertising and commissions for real estate agents) are a reduction in gross rental income for tax purposes. However, we classify them as tier 1 expenses to simplify the discussion. Tier 1 expenses also include certain casualty losses allocated to the rental use of the home. In this chapter, we focus on mortgage interest and real property taxes because they are much more common.

[22]Tier 3 expenses also include casualty losses allocated to the home that are not tier 1 expenses.

If the taxpayer claims the standard deduction, all mortgage interest expense and real property taxes allocated to rental use of the home are tier 2 expenses. If the taxpayer itemizes deductions, whether mortgage interest expense and real property taxes allocated to rental use of the home are treated as tier 1 expenses or as tier 2 expenses is determined as follows:[23]

1. All mortgage interest expense on acquisition indebtedness is a tier 1 expense. Any remaining mortgage interest expense is a tier 2 expense.[24]
2. If the sum of the taxpayer's state and local income (or sales) tax and nonrental property taxes equals or exceeds the $10,000 tax deduction limit ($5,000 if married filing separately), all rental real property taxes are tier 2 expenses.
3. If the sum of the taxpayer's state and local income (or sales) tax and nonrental property taxes is less than the $10,000 tax deduction limit ($5,000 if married filing separately), all rental real property taxes are tier 1 expenses up to the difference between the tax deduction limit and the taxpayer's nonrental state and local taxes. The remaining rental real property taxes are tier 2 expenses. For example, if the taxpayer's itemized deduction for (nonrental) state and local taxes is $8,000 and the rental real property taxes are $3,000, then $2,000 ($10,000 – $8,000) of the rental real property taxes is tier 1 and $1,000 ($3,000 – $2,000) of the rental real property taxes is tier 2.

After categorizing rental expenses into the three tiers, the taxpayer first deducts tier 1 expenses in full. This is true even when tier 1 expenses exceed the gross rental revenue.[25] Second, the taxpayer deducts tier 2 expenses.[26] However, tier 2 expense deductions are limited to the gross rental revenue in excess of tier 1 expenses. Any tier 2 expenses not deducted in the current year due to the income limitation are suspended and carried forward to the next year as tier 2 expenses. Finally, the taxpayer deducts tier 3 expense (depreciation calculated using the straight-line method over 27.5 years). The tier 3 expense deduction is limited to the gross rental revenue in excess of the sum of tier 1 and tier 2 expenses. Any tier 3 expenses not deductible due to the gross income limitation are suspended and carried forward to the subsequent year. Nondeductible tier 3 expenses do not reduce the taxpayer's tax basis in the home. The three-tier deduction sequence is designed to maximize taxpayer rental deductions for expenses that would be deductible even without any rental use of the home (most commonly, mortgage interest and real property taxes) and to minimize allowable depreciation deductions for the home. The tier 1, 2, and 3 expenses for rental property are summarized in Exhibit 14-5.

Because the IRS method allocates more mortgage interest expense and property taxes to rental use than the Tax Court method, the IRS method is generally more beneficial when either the taxpayer claims the standard deduction or the gross income limitation does not apply (all rental expenses are immediately deductible as for AGI deductions). Conversely, because the Tax Court method allocates more mortgage interest expense and property taxes to personal use of the property, the Tax Court method is generally more beneficial when the taxpayer itemizes deductions and the gross income limitation applies. However, because these are only general rules, taxpayers should analyze their specific facts and circumstances to determine whether the IRS method or the Tax Court method is more advantageous. In any event, use of the Tax Court method likely involves more risk of IRS scrutiny than the IRS method.

[23]Program Manager Technical Advice 2019-001.

[24]Mortgage interest expense on nonacquisition indebtedness allocated to personal use of the home is nondeductible.

[25]The rental activity associated with a home that falls into the residence-with-significant-rental-use category is not considered to be a passive activity, so income or loss generated from the activity is not considered to be passive income or passive loss [§469(j)]. See discussion of passive loss rules below.

[26]§280A(c)(5). Also, see Worksheet 1 in IRS Publication 527, *Residential Rental Property (Including Rental of Vacation Homes),* for information on deducting rental expenses on vacation homes.

EXHIBIT 14-5 Rental Expenses by Tier and Deduction Sequence

Tier 1
Expenses for obtaining tenants (such as advertising expense and commissions for real estate agents) and rental mortgage interest expense and real property taxes the taxpayer would be able to deduct as itemized deductions if the taxpayer did not rent the property at all.

↓

Tier 2
All other expenses allocated to the rental activity except depreciation expense, including payments for utilities, maintenance, and other expenses

↓

Tier 3
Depreciation expense

Example 14-13

At the beginning of the year, the Jeffersons purchased a vacation home in Scottsdale, Arizona, for $500,000 ($400,000 for the building and $100,000 for the land). They paid $200,000 down and financed the remaining $300,000 with a 6 percent mortgage secured by the home. During the year, the Jeffersons used the home for personal purposes for 30 days and rented it out for 200 days. Thus, the home falls in the residence-with-significant-rental-use category. They received $37,500 of rental revenue and incurred $500 of rental advertising expenses. How are their expenses allocated to the rental use under the IRS and Tax Court methods? The Jeffersons are deducting $10,000 of state and local income and nonrental real property taxes as itemized deductions on their 2022 tax return.

Answer: See the following summary of allocation of expenses associated with the home:

Allocation Method to Rental Use

Expense	Amount	Tier	IRS Method (200/230)	Tax Court Method (200/365 Tier 1, 200/230 other)
Advertising*	$ 500	1	$ 500	$ 500
Interest	18,000	1	15,652	9,863
Total tier 1 expenses	**$18,500**	**1**	**$16,152**	**$10,363**
Real estate taxes**	5,000	2	4,348	2,740
Utilities	4,500	2	3,913	3,913
Repairs	1,800	2	1,565	1,565
Insurance	3,500	2	3,043	3,043
Maintenance	3,200	2	2,783	2,783
Total tier 2 expenses	**$18,000**	**2**	**$15,652**	**$14,044**
Tier 3: Depreciation	**$13,939**	**3**	**$12,121**	**$12,121**
Total expenses	$ 50,439			

*Advertising is a direct expense of the rental, so it is fully deductible against rental revenue.
**Rental real property taxes are tier 2 expenses because the Jeffersons incurred at least $10,000 of state and local income and nonrental real property taxes.

(continued on page 14-22)

Net Income from Rental	IRS Method	Tax Court Method
Rental receipts	$37,500	$ 37,500
Less tier 1 expenses	(16,152)	(10,363)
Income after tier 1 expenses	21,348	27,137
Less tier 2 expenses	(15,652)	(14,044)
Income after tier 2 expenses	5,696	13,093
Less tier 3 expenses (limited to income after tier 2 expenses)	(5,696)	(12,121)
Taxable rental income	**$ 0**	**$ 972**
Interest itemized deduction	$ 2,348	$ 8,137
Real property tax itemized deduction	0	0
Deductible rental expenses (sum of tier 1, 2, and 3 expenses)	37,500	36,528
Total itemized and rental expenses	**$39,848**	**$44,665**

At first glance, it appears that the Tax Court method is more favorable for the Jeffersons. After all, the Jeffersons are able to claim $4,817 more total deductions under the Tax Court method compared to the IRS method ($44,665 – $39,848). While the IRS method allows the Jeffersons to deduct $972 more for AGI (rental) deductions than the Tax Court method ($37,500 – $36,528), the Tax Court method allows the Jeffersons to potentially deduct $5,789 more in mortgage interest expense ($8,137 – $2,348) as an itemized deduction. However, on closer inspection, it is not clear whether the Tax Court or the IRS method is more favorable for two reasons. First, the Jeffersons are allowed to carry over to next year the $6,425 ($12,121 – $5,696) of depreciation expense that they did not deduct this year under the IRS method. That is, they were not able to deduct the $6,425 this year, but they will be able to deduct it in a subsequent year if they generate enough rental income. Second, the Jeffersons report $1,608 ($4,348 – $2,740) more in deductible real property taxes attributable to the rental activity under the IRS method than under the Tax Court method. Because the Jeffersons exceed the $10,000 limit on the itemized deduction for taxes, the additional $1,608 allocated to personal use provides them with no tax benefit. The Tax Court gives the Jeffersons more deductions in the current year, but the IRS method gives them more deductions in the current plus future years (assuming they generate enough income from the rental).

Taxpayers report their rental activities on Schedule E of Form 1040. Deductible rental expenses are for AGI deductions. Exhibit 14-6 displays the completed Schedule E for the Jeffersons' Scottsdale vacation home using the Tax Court method. Note that net rental income is considered to be investment income for purposes of determining the 3.8 percent net investment income tax (discussed in the Individual Income Tax Computation and Tax Credits chapter).

TAXES IN THE REAL WORLD Airbnb Anyone?

Online home rental communities such as Airbnb, HomeAway, and VRBO provide a marketplace that connects travelers looking for lodging with taxpayers seeking rental income from renting all (or part) of their homes. Online rental communities continue to grow as travelers increasingly seek lodging bargains. For example, reportedly, Airbnb's revenue for 2020 was $3.4 billion (see https://news.airbnb.com/airbnb-fourth-quarter-and-full-year-2020-financial-results/). Total 2020 revenue was down only 22% year-over-year despite the travel impact of COVID-19. Taxpayers renting entire homes or even just a bedroom on Airbnb must deal with the tax consequences discussed in the Rental Use of the Home section of this chapter. See https://assets.airbnb.com/eyguidance/us.pdf for a discussion of the tax consequences of those renting their homes (consistent with the discussion in this chapter).

EXHIBIT 14-6 (PART I) Jeffersons' Schedule E for Vacation Home Rental

SCHEDULE E (Form 1040)
Department of the Treasury Internal Revenue Service (99)

Supplemental Income and Loss
(From rental real estate, royalties, partnerships, S corporations, estates, trusts, REMICs, etc.)
▶ Attach to Form 1040, 1040-SR, 1040-NR, or 1041.
▶ Go to *www.irs.gov/ScheduleE* for instructions and the latest information.

OMB No. 1545-0074
2021
Attachment Sequence No. 13

Name(s) shown on return: TYLER AND JASMINE JEFFERSON
Your social security number: 321-54-9876

Part I **Income or Loss From Rental Real Estate and Royalties** **Note:** If you are in the business of renting personal property, use **Schedule C.** See instructions. If you are an individual, report farm rental income or loss from **Form 4835** on page 2, line 40.

A Did you make any payments in 2021 that would require you to file Form(s) 1099? See instructions . . . . . . ☐ Yes ☑ No
B If "Yes," did you or will you file required Form(s) 1099? . . . . . . ☐ Yes ☐ No

1a	Physical address of each property (street, city, state, ZIP code)
A	2020 CACTUS WAY, SCOTTSDALE, ARIZONA 85054
B	
C	

1b	Type of Property (from list below)	2 For each rental real estate property listed above, report the number of fair rental and personal use days. Check the **QJV** box only if you meet the requirements to file as a qualified joint venture. See instructions.		Fair Rental Days	Personal Use Days	QJV
A	1		A	200	30	☐
B			B			☐
C			C			☐

Type of Property:
1 Single Family Residence
2 Multi-Family Residence
3 Vacation/Short-Term Rental
4 Commercial
5 Land
6 Royalties
7 Self-Rental
8 Other (describe)

Income:	**Properties:**		A	B	C
3	Rents received	3	37,500		
4	Royalties received	4			
Expenses:					
5	Advertising	5	500		
6	Auto and travel (see instructions)	6			
7	Cleaning and maintenance	7	2,783		
8	Commissions	8			
9	Insurance	9	3,043		
10	Legal and other professional fees	10			
11	Management fees	11			
12	Mortgage interest paid to banks, etc. (see instructions)	12	9,863		
13	Other interest	13			
14	Repairs	14	1,565		
15	Supplies	15			
16	Taxes	16	2,740		
17	Utilities	17	3,913		
18	Depreciation expense or depletion	18	12,121		
19	Other (list) ▶	19			
20	Total expenses. Add lines 5 through 19	20	36,528		
21	Subtract line 20 from line 3 (rents) and/or 4 (royalties). If result is a (loss), see instructions to find out if you must file **Form 6198**	21	972		
22	Deductible rental real estate loss after limitation, if any, on **Form 8582** (see instructions)	22	( )	( )	( )

23a	Total of all amounts reported on line 3 for all rental properties	23a	37,500
b	Total of all amounts reported on line 4 for all royalty properties	23b	
c	Total of all amounts reported on line 12 for all properties	23c	9,863
d	Total of all amounts reported on line 18 for all properties	23d	12,121
e	Total of all amounts reported on line 20 for all properties	23e	36,528
24	**Income.** Add positive amounts shown on line 21. **Do not** include any losses	24	972
25	**Losses.** Add royalty losses from line 21 and rental real estate losses from line 22. Enter total losses here	25	( )
26	**Total rental real estate and royalty income or (loss).** Combine lines 24 and 25. Enter the result here. If Parts II, III, IV, and line 40 on page 2 do not apply to you, also enter this amount on Schedule 1 (Form 1040), line 5. Otherwise, include this amount in the total on line 41 on page 2	26	972

For Paperwork Reduction Act Notice, see the separate instructions. Cat. No. 11344L **Schedule E (Form 1040) 2021**

Source: irs.gov.

Nonresidence (Rental Property)

For property (i.e., dwelling units) in this category, the taxpayer includes the rental revenue in gross income and deducts all rental expenses *allocated to the rental use* of the property as for AGI deductions (all on Form 1040, Schedule E). When the property is used for even a day for personal purposes, the expenses must be allocated between the rental usage and the personal usage.[27] This same allocation rule applies to all shared expenses between the nonresidence dwelling unit and other dwelling units located within the same structure (e.g., a rented basement in a single-family home). Allocating expenses between rental and personal is important because the law does not allow the taxpayer to deduct mortgage interest that is not allocated to rental use since the taxpayer does not meet the minimum personal use required for the deduction (the home is not a residence—see earlier discussion). However, the taxpayer is still allowed to deduct, as an itemized deduction, real property taxes that are not allocated to the rental property (subject to the $10,000 deduction limitation for taxes). In contrast to the case for a residence with significant rental use, the rental expenses deduction for a nonresidence is not limited to gross income. However, a rental loss from a nonresidence is considered a passive loss and thus is subject to the passive activity loss limitations discussed below.[28]

Example 14-14

What if: Suppose that at the beginning of the year, the Jeffersons purchased a vacation home in Scottsdale, Arizona, for $400,000. They paid $100,000 down and financed the remaining $300,000 with a 6 percent mortgage secured by the home. During the year, the Jeffersons *did not use the home for personal purposes* and they rented the home for 200 days. They received $37,500 in gross rental revenue for the year and incurred $50,439 of expenses relating to the rental property. How much can the Jeffersons deduct in this situation?

Answer: The good news is that the deductions are not limited to gross income from the rental so they can tentatively deduct all $50,439, generating a $12,939 loss on the property ($37,500 – $50,439). The bad news is that, as we discuss below, the loss may not be immediately deductible due to the passive activity loss limitations.

THE KEY FACTS

Rental Use of the Home

- Nonresidence
  - Rental use is at least 1 day and personal use is no more than the *greater* of (1) 14 days or (2) 10 percent of rental days.
  - Allocate expenses to rental use and personal use.
  - Rental deductions in excess of rental income are deductible subject to passive loss limitation rules.
  - Interest expense allocated to personal use is not deductible.

Exhibit 14-7 summarizes the tax rules relating to a home used for rental purposes depending on the extent of rental (and personal) use. Appendix A to this chapter provides a flowchart summarizing the implementation of these rules.

Losses on Rental Property A rental property can be a great investment that gets the best of all worlds. It could (1) appreciate in value, (2) produce annual positive cash flow (rental receipts exceed expenses other than depreciation), and (3) generate tax losses that reduce the taxes the owner is required to pay on other sources of income. Consider the Jeffersons' second-home property, purchased for $400,000 and used primarily as a rental home (see Example 14-14), which we'll assume has appreciated to $440,000 by the end of 2022. The property has appreciated by $40,000, produced a positive cash flow of $1,000 [$37,500 rental income minus expenses other than depreciation of $36,500 ($50,439 total expenses minus depreciation expense of $13,939)], and generated a net tax loss of $12,939. This loss apparently saves the Jeffersons $4,140 in taxes ($12,939 × 32% marginal tax rate).

Thus, the increase in the Jeffersons' wealth from their second-home investment for the year appears to be $45,140 ($40,000 appreciation + $1,000 rental cash flow + $4,140 tax savings). But as noted elsewhere in this text, when a tax outcome seems too good to be true, it usually is. Read on.

Passive activity loss rules. In the Investments chapter, we introduced the passive activity loss rules that indicate taxpayers may only deduct passive losses for a year to the

[27]§280A(e).

[28]If the home rental is deemed to be a not-for-profit activity, deductions allocated to the rental are nondeductible.

EXHIBIT 14-7 Summary of Tax Rules Relating to Home Used for Rental Purposes

	Residence with Minimal Rental Use	Residence with Significant Rental Use	Nonresidence
Classification test	Reside in home for at least 15 days and rent home for 14 or fewer days during the year.	Rent home for 15 days or more and use home for personal purposes for more than the greater of (1) 14 days or (2) 10 percent of the total rental days.	Rent home for at least 1 day, and personal use does not exceed the greater of (1) 14 days or (2) 10 percent of the rental days.
Rental revenue	Exclude from gross income.	Include in gross income.	Include in gross income.
Direct rental expenses unrelated to home use	Not deductible.	Fully deductible for AGI (loss not subject to passive activity loss rules).	Deductible for AGI but subject to passive activity loss rules.
Treatment of mortgage interest and real property taxes	Deductible as itemized deductions.	Allocated to rental days and are deductible as either tier 1 or 2 rental expenses. To the extent interest and taxes are tier 1 expenses, they are deductible immediately. Otherwise, they are grouped with other rental expenses. Interest and taxes allocated to personal-use days are potentially deductible as itemized deductions subject to the limitations on home mortgage interest and taxes.	Allocated between personal-use days and rental days; interest and taxes allocated to rental days are deductible as rental expenses; taxes allocated to personal-use days are deductible as itemized deductions (subject to the $10,000 deduction limit for taxes); interest allocated to personal-use days is not deductible.
Treatment of all other expenses	Not deductible.	Allocated between personal-use days and rental days; expenses allocated to personal-use days are not deductible; expenses allocated to rental days are deductible as rental expenses to the extent of rental revenue minus the sum of direct rental expenses and tier 1 rental mortgage interest and real property taxes.	Rental expenses in excess of rental income minus the sum of direct rental expenses and tier 1 rental mortgage interest, and real property taxes are carried forward to the next year.
Excess expenses	Not applicable.	Rental expenses in excess of rental income minus the sum of direct rental expenses and tier 1 rental mortgage interest, and real property taxes are carried forward to the next year.	Not applicable; rental expenses are deductible, even if they create a rental loss.

THE KEY FACTS

Rental Losses

- Losses on home rentals in the nonresidence-use category are passive losses.
- Passive loss rules generally limit deductions for losses from passive activities such as rental to passive income from other sources.
  - Passive losses in excess of passive income are suspended and deductible against passive income in the future or when the taxpayer sells the passive activity generating the loss.
- Rental real estate exception to passive loss rules:
  - Applies to active participants in rental property.
  - Deduct up to $25,000 of rental real estate loss against ordinary income.
  - $25,000 maximum deduction phased out by 50 cents for every dollar of AGI over $100,000 (excluding the rental loss deduction); fully phased out at $150,000 of AGI.

extent of their passive income. We also learned that, by definition, a rental real estate activity (including a dwelling unit that falls in the nonresidence category) is considered to be a passive activity.[29] Because they are passive losses, losses from rental properties are generally not allowed to offset other ordinary or investment type income. However,

[29]Recall that homes falling into the significant-personal-and-rental-use category are not passive activities. See §469(j).

as we also discussed in the Investments chapter, a taxpayer who is an **active participant in a rental activity** may be allowed to deduct up to $25,000 of the rental loss against nonpassive income.[30] Consistent with a number of tax benefits, the exception amount for active owners is phased out as adjusted gross income increases: The $25,000 maximum exception amount is phased out by 50 cents for every dollar the taxpayer's adjusted gross income (before considering the rental loss) exceeds $100,000. Consequently, the entire $25,000 is phased out when the taxpayer's adjusted gross income reaches $150,000.

Example 14-15

Suppose the Jeffersons incurred a $12,939 passive loss from their Scottsdale rental home (as described in Example 14-14), and they did not receive any passive income during the year. Assuming that their current-year AGI before considering the rental loss is $250,000 and they are considered to be active participants in the rental activity, how much of the rental loss are the Jeffersons allowed to deduct this year under the rental real estate exception to the passive activity loss rules?

Answer: $0. Because their adjusted gross income exceeds $150,000, the $25,000 deduction exception to the passive activity loss rules is completely phased out. Consequently, the Jeffersons are not allowed to deduct any of the $12,939 rental loss for the year.

What if: How much of the $12,939 loss could the Jeffersons deduct for the year if their adjusted gross income (before considering the rental loss) were $120,000?

Answer: In this case, they could deduct the entire $12,939 loss. The $25,000 exception amount would be reduced by a $10,000 phase-out [50 cents × ($120,000 − $100,000)]. The maximum amount of the rental loss that can offset ordinary income would therefore be reduced from $25,000 to $15,000 ($25,000 − $10,000 phased out). However, because their loss is less than $15,000, they may deduct the entire $12,939 rental loss against their other sources of income for the year.

Are passive losses from rental real estate activities that taxpayers are not allowed to deduct in the current year permanently disallowed? No, these losses are suspended until the taxpayer generates passive income or sells the property that generated the passive loss. On the sale, in addition to reporting gain or loss from the sale of the property, the taxpayer is allowed to deduct suspended passive losses against ordinary income.

LO 14-6

BUSINESS USE OF THE HOME

THE KEY FACTS

Home Office Deduction

- Deductibility limits on expenses allocated to home office.
  - The expenses are deducted for AGI, but deductions may be subject to income limitation.
  - If deduction is limited by income limitation, apply the same tiered system used for rental property when tier 2 and tier 3 deductions are limited to gross rental income minus tier 1 expenses.

(continued)

Because a personal residence is a personal-use asset, utility payments and depreciation due to wear and tear are not deductible expenses. However, self-employed taxpayers (not employees) who use their home—or at least part of their home—for business purposes may be able to deduct expenses associated with their home use if they meet certain stringent requirements.[31]

To qualify for **home office deductions,** a taxpayer must use their home—or part of their home—*exclusively and regularly* as either:

1. The principal place of business for any of the taxpayer's trade or businesses or
2. A place to meet with patients, clients, or customers in the normal course of business.

[30]§469(i).

[31]§280A. If taxpayers rent the home they occupy and they meet the requirements for business use of the home, they can deduct part of the rent they pay. To determine the amount of the deduction, multiply the rental payment by the percentage of the home used for business purposes.

Taxpayers fail the exclusive use test if they use the area of the home in question for any personal purpose.

Example 14-16

What if: Jasmine recently quit her job as an employee for an advertising firm because, with the move to the new home, the commute was too long. She has decided to start working as a self-employed graphic designer. She uses a large room in the basement of the Jeffersons' new home as her office. The room has been wired for all her office needs. Once or twice a week, Tyler sits at the desk in the room and surfs the Web to read up on his favorite sports teams. Is the office space eligible for a home office deduction?

Answer: No. The office is not used exclusively for Jasmine's business. Tyler's personal use of the office disqualifies the office for the home office deduction.

- Taxpayers can elect the simplified method to report home office expenses.
  - Deduct allowable business use square footage (limited to 300 sq. feet) × $5 per square foot.
  - Deduction limited to gross business revenue (minus business expenses unrelated to home).
  - No carryover of excess deduction to subsequent year.
  - Deduct all property taxes and mortgage interest as itemized deductions.
  - Do not deduct depreciation expense so basis in home is unaffected by home office expense deduction (under the simplified method).
- Depreciation expense.
  - Reduces basis in home.
  - Gain on sale due to depreciation deductions after May 6, 1997, is ineligible for exclusion.
  - This gain is taxed at a maximum 25 percent rate as unrecaptured §1250 gain.

The taxpayer is not required to meet the exclusive use test in order to claim the home office deduction to the extent the taxpayer either:

- Uses part of the home for the storage of inventory or product samples.
- Uses part of the home as a day care facility.

When a taxpayer has more than one business location, including the home, which is the taxpayer's principal place of business? This is a facts-and-circumstances determination based upon:

- The relative importance of the activities performed at each place where the taxpayer conducts business (more income from an activity generally means it is a more important activity) and
- The total time spent doing work at each location.

However, by definition, a taxpayer's principal place of business also includes the place of business used by the taxpayer for the administrative or management activities of the taxpayer's trade or business, if there is no other fixed location of the trade or business where the taxpayer conducts substantial administrative or management activities of the trade or business.[32]

If a taxpayer meets with clients or patients in her home during the normal course of business, they qualify for the home office deduction even if the home is not their principal place of business. However, the clients or patients must visit the taxpayer's home *in person.* Communication through telephone calls or other types of communication technology does not qualify.

Example 14-17

What if: Jasmine recently quit her job as an employee for an advertising firm because, with the move to the new home, the commute was too long. She has decided to start working as a self-employed graphic designer. She uses a large room in the basement of the Jeffersons' new home as her office. The room has been wired for all her office needs. The Jeffersons use the room exclusively for Jasmine's graphic design business use. Does this space qualify for the home office deduction?

Answer: Yes. While Jasmine will spend a good deal of time meeting with clients outside her home office, she has no other fixed location for her trade or business. Further, the office is used exclusively for business purposes. Consequently, the office qualifies for the home office deduction subject to certain limitations described below.

[32]§280A(c)(1).

TAXES IN THE REAL WORLD If You Want the Bathroom to Qualify as a Part of a Home Office, You Better Lock It and Keep the Key

The IRS and a taxpayer with seven years of IRS work experience have battled over home office expenses in the Tax Court. The taxpayer operated an accounting business, and he used a bedroom in his residence exclusively for his accounting business. The taxpayer included the bathroom adjacent to the bedroom in his home office square footage. However, because the taxpayer testified that his children and personal guests occasionally used the bathroom, the Tax Court determined that the bathroom was not used exclusively for business purposes (the children and personal guests may beg to differ), and it disallowed the expenses associated with the bathroom square footage.

Source: Luis Bulas v. Comm'r, TC Memo 2011-201.

Direct versus Indirect Expenses

When taxpayers qualify for home office deductions, they are allowed to deduct only actual home expenses that are related—either directly or indirectly—to their business. Direct expenses are expenses incurred in maintaining the room or part of the home that is set aside for business use. They include painting or costs of other repairs to the area. These expenses are deductible in full as home office expenses. Indirect expenses are expenses incurred in maintaining and using the entire home. Indirect expenses include insurance, utilities, interest, real property taxes, general repairs, and depreciation on the home as if it were used entirely for business purposes. Depreciation on the home is calculated using nonresidential real property depreciation tables (straight-line depreciation over 39 years). In contrast to direct expenses that are fully deductible, only indirect expenses *allocated* to the home office space are deductible.

How do taxpayers allocate indirect expenses to the home office space? If the rooms in the home are roughly of equal size, the taxpayer may allocate the indirect expenses to the business portion of the home based on the number of rooms. In a 10-room home, a taxpayer using one room for qualifying business use is allowed to deduct 10 percent of the indirect expenses. Or the taxpayer may allocate indirect expenses based on the square footage of the business-use room relative to the total square footage in the home. If the home is 5,000 square feet and the home office is 250 square feet, the taxpayer may deduct 5 percent of the indirect expenses. Unrelated expenses such as painting a room not used for business purposes or repairing the garage door are not deductible.

In lieu of allocating actual expenses to home office use, the IRS allows taxpayers to use an optional simplified method for computing home office expenses.[33] Under the simplified method, taxpayers are not allowed to deduct any *actual* expenses relating to qualified business use of the home (including depreciation). Instead, taxpayers electing the simplified method deduct, subject to limitations described below, the allowable business use square footage of the office (not to exceed 300 square feet) multiplied by $5 per square foot. Thus, this method generates a maximum deduction of $1,500 (300 square feet × $5 per square foot). In addition, taxpayers using this method are allowed to deduct all of their home mortgage interest and real property taxes as itemized deductions. Taxpayers may choose from year to year whether to use the simplified method or the actual expense method.

[33]Rev. Proc. 2013-13.

Example 14-18

The Jeffersons moved into their new $800,000, 6,000-square-foot home on February 1 (the home building was valued at $600,000, and the land was valued at $200,000). Jasmine quit her job and set up a 420-square-foot home office in the basement on that same date. Through the end of the calendar year, the Jeffersons incurred several expenses relating to their home (see table below). Assuming they qualify for the home office deduction, they would sum the direct expenses and the indirect expenses allocated to the office. They would allocate the indirect expenses based on the square footage of the office compared to the rest of the home. Using the actual expense method, what amount of home-related expenses would qualify as home office expenses?

Answer: $4,575. See allocation below. All direct expenses and 7 percent of the indirect expenses would be allocated to the home office (420 office square footage/6,000 home square footage). The Jeffersons would allocate the expenses as follows:

Expenses	Type	(A) Amount	(B) Office %	(A) × (B) Home Office Expense
Painting office	Direct	$ 200	100%	$ 200
Real property taxes	Indirect	11,000	7	770
Home interest expense	Indirect	27,917	7	1,954
Electricity	Indirect	2,600	7	182
Gas and other utilities	Indirect	2,500	7	175
Homeowner's insurance	Indirect	5,000	7	350
Depreciation	Indirect	13,482	7	944
Total expenses		$62,699		**$4,575**

The expenses attributable to the home office are deductible subject to the limitations discussed below. Also, as discussed below, the Jeffersons are able to deduct the home interest expense not allocated to the home office as an itemized deduction.

What if: Suppose Jasmine elects to use the simplified method for determining home office expenses. What would be the amount of their home office expenses?

Answer: $1,500 (300 square feet × $5 per square foot). Even though the Jeffersons' home office is 420 square feet, for purposes of the home office expense under the simplified method, the square footage is limited to 300 square feet.

What if: Suppose the Jeffersons elect to use the simplified method for home office expenses. What amount of home mortgage interest expenses and real property taxes would they be able to deduct as itemized deductions?

Answer: Home mortgage interest expense of $27,917 and $10,000 of real property tax as an itemized deduction. The Jeffersons paid $15,000 in state income taxes, and consequently the $26,000 of taxes they paid in total ($11,000 + $15,000) are limited because of the $10,000 itemized deduction limit on taxes.

Limitations on Deductibility of Expenses

The process for determining the home office expense deduction using the actual expense method is similar to the process used to determine deductions for vacation homes. When net business income (net Schedule C income) before the home office deduction exceeds total home office expenses (before applying any limitations), all home office expenses are deductible. However, when home office expenses exceed net Schedule C income before the home office deduction, the deduction is potentially limited.

In these situations, taxpayers first assign each home office expense to one of three categories or tiers. Tier 1 expenses include certain mortgage interest expense and real property taxes allocated to the business use of the home. Tier 2 expenses include all expenses allocated to business use of the home that are not tier 1 expenses or tier 3 expenses. Tier 3 expense is depreciation expense.

If the taxpayer claims the standard deduction, the mortgage interest and property taxes allocated to the home office are tier 2 expenses. If the taxpayer itemizes deductions, whether mortgage interest expense and real property taxes allocated to business use of the home are treated as tier 1 expenses or as tier 2 expenses is determined as follows:

1. All mortgage interest expense on acquisition indebtedness is a tier 1 expense. Any remaining mortgage interest expense is a tier 2 expense.[34]
2. If the sum of the taxpayer's state and local income (or sales) tax and non–home business property taxes equals or exceeds the $10,000 tax deduction limit ($5,000 if married filing separately), all business real property taxes are tier 2 expenses.
3. If the sum of the taxpayer's state and local income (or sales) tax and non–home business property taxes is less than the $10,000 tax deduction limit ($5,000 if married filing separately), all business real property taxes are tier 1 expenses up to the difference between the tax deduction limit and the taxpayer's non–home business state and local taxes. The remaining home business real property taxes are tier 2 expenses. For example, if the taxpayer's itemized deduction for (non–home business) state and local taxes is $8,000 and the home business real property taxes are $3,000, then $2,000 ($10,000 – $8,000) of the home business real property taxes are tier 1 and $1,000 ($3,000 – $2,000) of the home business real property taxes are tier 2.

Taxpayers first deduct tier 1 expenses in full, even when they exceed net Schedule C income before the home office deduction.[35] Second, taxpayers deduct tier 2 expenses. However, deductible tier 2 expenses are limited to net Schedule C income before home office deductions minus tier 1 expenses (that is, deducting tier 2 expenses cannot create a net Schedule C loss). Any tier 2 expenses not deductible due to the income limitation are suspended and carried forward to the next year, subject to the same limitations. Finally, taxpayers deduct tier 3 expense. The deductible tier 3 expense is limited to net Schedule C income before the home office deduction minus the sum of tier 1 and deductible tier 2 expenses (tier 3 expenses cannot create a net Schedule C loss). The nondeductible portion of tier 3 expenses is carried forward to the next year, subject to the same limitations.

Under the simplified method, the expense, as calculated by multiplying the square footage by the $5 application rate, is limited to net Schedule C income before home office deductions. Further, taxpayers using the simplified method in a particular year may not carry over expenses disallowed by the income limitation, and they may not deduct expenses carried over to that year under the actual expense method. However, disallowed expenses under the actual expense method can be carried over to a subsequent year in which the taxpayer uses the actual expense method for determining the home office expense deduction.

Example 14-19

For the year, Jasmine generated $4,000 of net business income before the home office deduction from her graphic design business. Her home office expenses before limitation total $4,575 (see Example 14-18). The expenses consist of painting the office, $200; real property taxes, $770; home interest expense, $1,954; electricity, $182; gas and other utilities, $175; homeowner's insurance, $350; and depreciation, $944. What is the total amount of tier 1, tier 2, and tier 3 expenses? The Jeffersons are deducting $10,000 of state and local income and non–home business real property taxes as itemized deductions on their 2022 tax return.

[34]Mortgage interest expense on nonacquisition indebtedness allocated to personal use of the home is nondeductible.

[35]§280A(c)(5).

Answer: Tier 1 expenses are $1,954 (home interest expense); tier 2 expenses are $1,677 (real property taxes, $770; painting office, $200; electricity, $182; gas and other utilities, $175; and homeowner's insurance, $350); and tier 3 expense is $944 (depreciation).

What is Jasmine's net income from the business after claiming the home office deduction, and what expenses, if any, will she carry over to next year?

Answer: $0 net income, as shown in the table below. She will carry over $575 ($944 minus $369) of depreciation expense.

Expenses	Net Income from Business
Gross business receipts	$4,000
Less tier 1 expenses	(1,954)
Income after tier 1 expenses	$2,046
Less tier 2 expenses	(1,677)
Income after tier 2 expenses	$ 369
Less tier 3 expenses	(369)
Taxable business income	**$ 0**

Due to the income limitation, Jasmine is allowed to deduct only $369 of the $944 depreciation expense. She will carry over the remaining $575 to next year to deduct as a home office expense (tier 3) subject to the same limitations.

What if: Suppose Jasmine uses the simplified method of determining home office expenses. What amount of the $1,500 expense (300 square feet × $5 application rate) will she be allowed to deduct?

Answer: She can deduct all $1,500 because the home office expense is less than the $4,000 net business income before the home office deduction.

What if: Assume the same facts as in the previous what-if scenario except that net business income before the home office deduction is now $1,200. What amount of the $1,500 home office expense will Jasmine be allowed to deduct?

Answer: $1,200. The home office expense deduction under the simplified method is limited to net business income before the home office deduction. Jasmine is not allowed to carry over the $300 nondeductible portion of the expense to a subsequent year ($1,500 total expense − $1,200 deductible expense).

When a taxpayer deducts depreciation as a home office expense, the depreciation expense reduces the basis of the taxpayer's home. Consequently, when the taxpayer sells the home, the gain on the sale will be greater than it would have been had the taxpayer not deducted depreciation expense. Further, the gain on the sale of the home attributable to depreciation deductions (incurred after May 6, 1997) is not eligible to be excluded under the home sale exclusion provision. Rather, the gain is treated as unrecaptured §1250 gain and is subject to a maximum 25 percent tax rate (see the Property Dispositions chapter for a detailed discussion of unrecaptured §1250 gain).

Example 14-20

At the beginning of the year, the Jeffersons' basis in their home was $800,000. Jasmine's first-year home office deductions included $369 in depreciation expense. What is the Jeffersons' adjusted basis in the home at the end of the year?

Answer: $799,631 ($800,000 − $369 deductible depreciation expense).

What if: Now suppose that the Jeffersons meet the ownership and use tests for the home sale exclusion and they sell the home for $900,000. Assume the only depreciation expense the Jeffersons have deducted is the $369 they deducted in the year they bought the home. Consequently, their adjusted

(continued on page 14-32)

basis in the home on the date of sale is $799,631 and they realize a gain of $100,369 on the sale. How much of the gain, if any, must they recognize on the sale?

Answer: $369. They can exclude $100,000 of gain. However, they are not allowed to exclude the remaining $369 gain caused by the depreciation expense for the home office. The Jeffersons must pay $92 of tax on the gain ($369 × 25% unrecaptured §1250 gain).

Taxpayers using the simplified method for deducting home office expenses are not allowed to deduct depreciation expense. Consequently, the simplified method does not affect the taxpayer's adjusted basis in the home. However, if a taxpayer switches from the simplified method in one year to the actual expense method in a subsequent year, the taxpayer is required to use modified depreciation tables to compute depreciation expense under the actual expense method.

Allowing taxpayers to deduct part of their home-related expenses as business expenses creates temptations for taxpayers to deduct home-related expenses that don't meet the deduction requirements. Not surprisingly, the IRS is very concerned about taxpayers inappropriately deducting expenses relating to their home. Consequently, expenses for business use of the home are some of the most highly scrutinized deductions available to taxpayers. Self-employed taxpayers claiming home office deductions must file a Form 8829, "Expenses for Business Use of Your Home," when deducting home office expenses on a tax return. With the high level of scrutiny applied to home office expenses, taxpayers should be sure to have documentation available to support their deductions. Exhibit 14-8 includes Form 8829 for Jasmine based on the information in Examples 14-17 and 14-18.

CONCLUSION

When deciding whether to invest in a home as a principal residence, a vacation home, or even a rental home, prospective owners should consider both nontax and tax factors relating to the ownership of the property. The tax code includes several provisions favorable to homeowners. This chapter is intended to provide current and prospective homeowners with enough insight on tax and nontax consequences of home ownership to allow them to make informed investment and compliance decisions when applicable.

EXHIBIT 14-8

Form **8829**

Department of the Treasury
Internal Revenue Service (99)

Expenses for Business Use of Your Home

► File only with Schedule C (Form 1040). Use a separate Form 8829 for each home you used for business during the year.
► Go to *www.irs.gov/Form8829* for instructions and the latest information.

OMB No. 1545-0074
2021
Attachment Sequence No. **176**

Name(s) of proprietor(s): JASMINE JEFFERSON
Your social security number: 674-65-6564

Part I Part of Your Home Used for Business

1	Area used regularly and exclusively for business, regularly for daycare, or for storage of inventory or product samples (see instructions)			1	420
2	Total area of home			2	6,000
3	Divide line 1 by line 2. Enter the result as a percentage			3	7 %
	For daycare facilities not used exclusively for business, go to line 4. All others, go to line 7.				
4	Multiply days used for daycare during year by hours used per day	4	hr.		
5	If you started or stopped using your home for daycare during the year, see instructions; otherwise, enter 8,760	5	hr.		
6	Divide line 4 by line 5. Enter the result as a decimal amount	6	.		
7	Business percentage. For daycare facilities not used exclusively for business, multiply line 6 by line 3 (enter the result as a percentage). All others, enter the amount from line 3 ▶			7	7 %

Part II Figure Your Allowable Deduction

			(a) Direct expenses	(b) Indirect expenses		
8	Enter the amount from Schedule C, line 29, **plus** any gain derived from the business use of your home, **minus** any loss from the trade or business not derived from the business use of your home. See instructions.				8	4,000
	See instructions for columns (a) and (b) before completing lines 9–22.					
9	Casualty losses (see instructions)	9		27,917		
10	Deductible mortgage interest (see instructions)	10		11,000		
11	Real estate taxes (see instructions)	11		38,917		
12	Add lines 9, 10, and 11	12				
13	Multiply line 12, column (b), by line 7	13		2,724		
14	Add line 12, column (a), and line 13				14	2,724
15	Subtract line 14 from line 8. If zero or less, enter -0-				15	1,276
16	Excess mortgage interest (see instructions)	16				
17	Excess real estate taxes (see instructions)	17				
18	Insurance	18		5,000		
19	Rent	19				
20	Repairs and maintenance	20	200			
21	Utilities	21		5,100		
22	Other expenses (see instructions)	22				
23	Add lines 16 through 22	23		10,100		
24	Multiply line 23, column (b), by line 7	24		707		
25	Carryover of prior year operating expenses (see instructions)	25				
26	Add line 23, column (a), line 24, and line 25				26	907
27	Allowable operating expenses. Enter the **smaller** of line 15 or line 26				27	907
28	Limit on excess casualty losses and depreciation. Subtract line 27 from line 15				28	369
29	Excess casualty losses (see instructions)	29				
30	Depreciation of your home from line 42 below	30		944		
31	Carryover of prior year excess casualty losses and depreciation (see instructions)	31				
32	Add lines 29 through 31				32	944
33	Allowable excess casualty losses and depreciation. Enter the **smaller** of line 28 or line 32				33	369
34	Add lines 14, 27, and 33				34	4,000
35	Casualty loss portion, if any, from lines 14 and 33. Carry amount to **Form 4684**. See instructions				35	
36	**Allowable expenses for business use of your home.** Subtract line 35 from line 34. Enter here and on Schedule C, line 30. If your home was used for more than one business, see instructions. ▶				36	4,000

Part III Depreciation of Your Home

37	Enter the **smaller** of your home's adjusted basis or its fair market value. See instructions	37	800,000
38	Value of land included on line 37	38	200,000
39	Basis of building. Subtract line 38 from line 37	39	600,000
40	Business basis of building. Multiply line 39 by line 7	40	42,000
41	Depreciation percentage (see instructions)	41	2.247 %
42	Depreciation allowable (see instructions). Multiply line 40 by line 41. Enter here and on line 30 above	42	944

Part IV Carryover of Unallowed Expenses to 2022

43	Operating expenses. Subtract line 27 from line 26. If less than zero, enter -0-	43	
44	Excess casualty losses and depreciation. Subtract line 33 from line 32. If less than zero, enter -0-	44	575

For Paperwork Reduction Act Notice, see your tax return instructions. Cat. No. 13232M Form **8829** (2021)

Department of the Treasury—Internal Revenue Service. "Form 1040." Accessed October 14, 2019. https://www.irs.gov/pub/irs-pdf/f8829.pdf.

Appendix A Flowchart of Tax Rules Relating to Home Used for Rental Purposes (page 1)

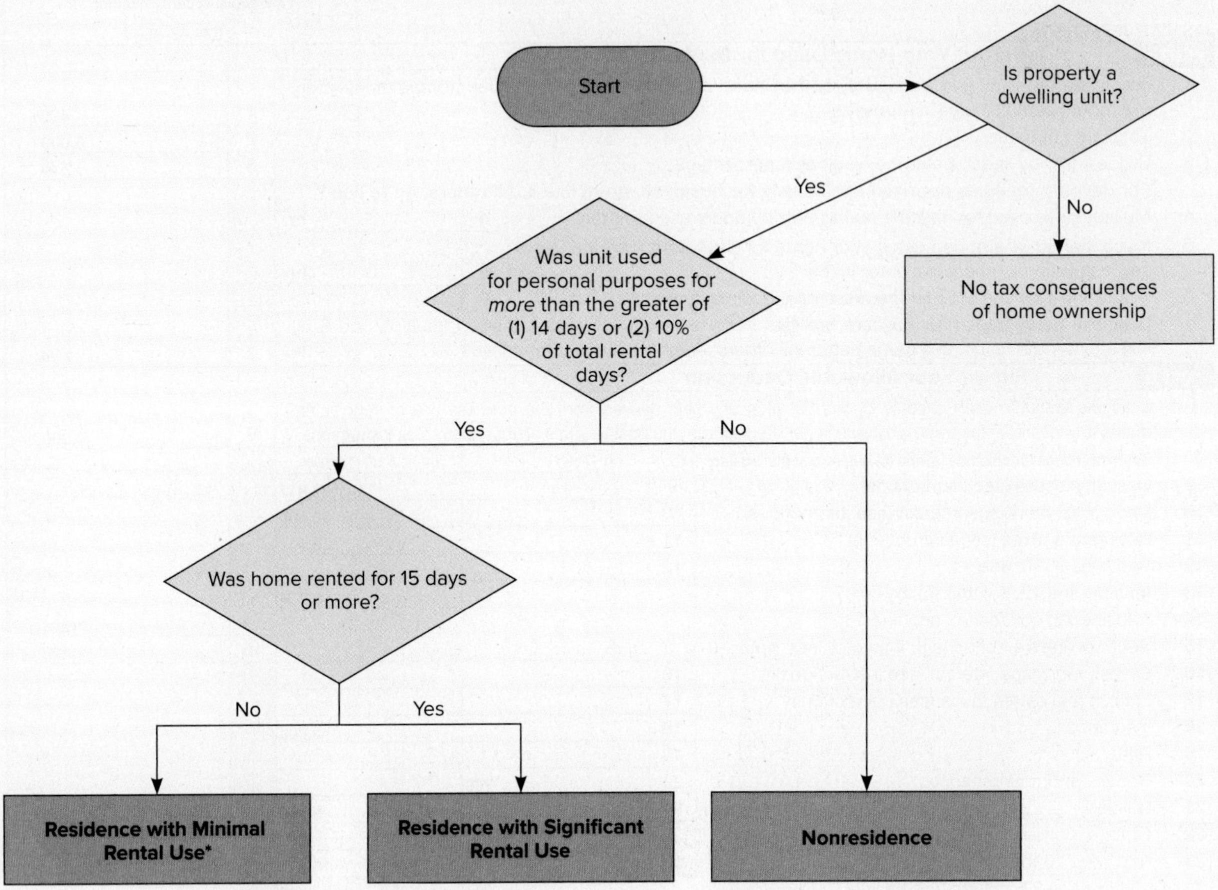

*Depending on facts and circumstances, residence may or may not be taxpayer's principal residence for year.

(page 2)

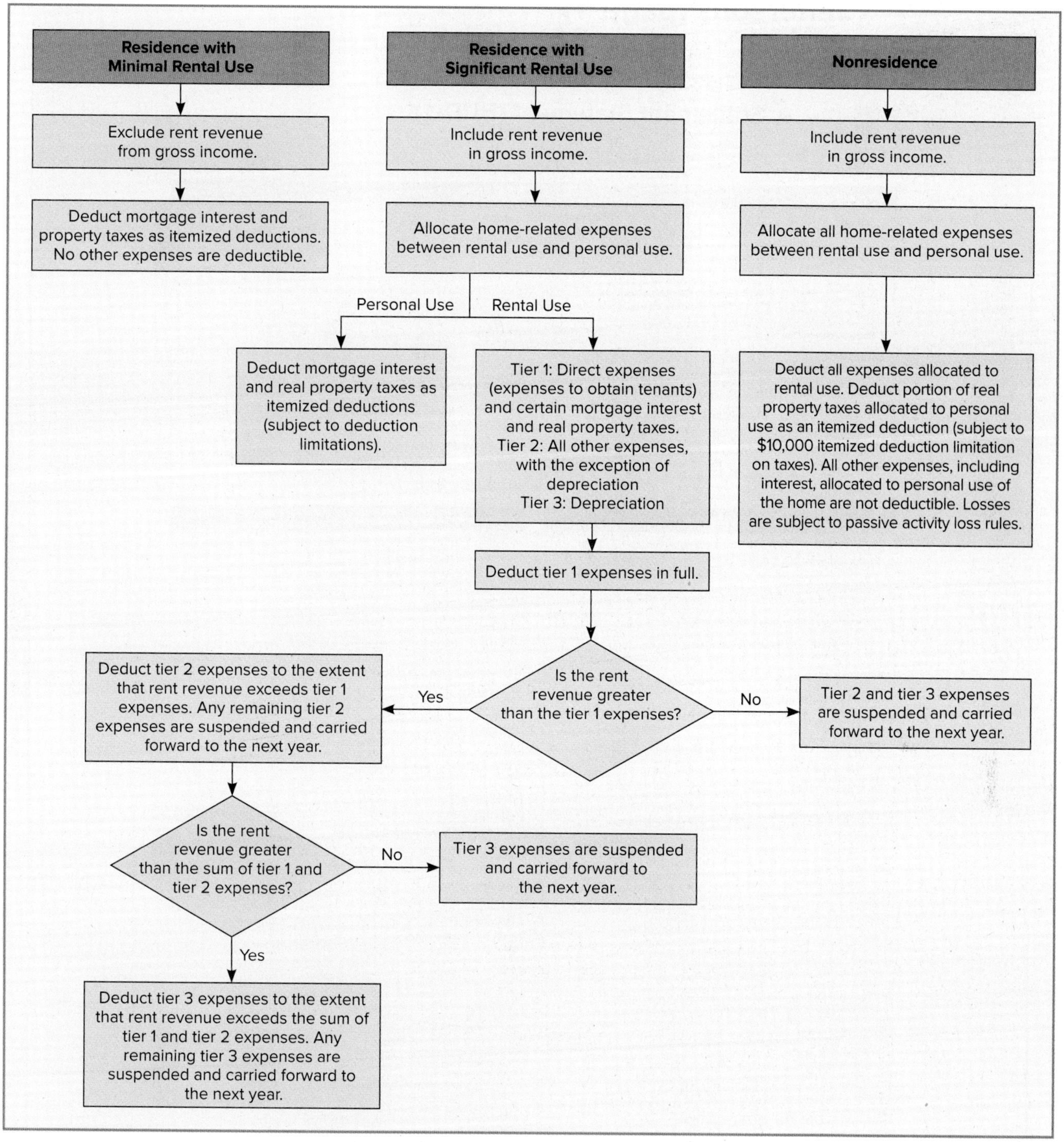
Residence with Minimal Rental Use
Exclude rent revenue from gross income.
Deduct mortgage interest and property taxes as itemized deductions. No other expenses are deductible.
Residence with Significant Rental Use
Include rent revenue in gross income.
Allocate home-related expenses between rental use and personal use.
Personal Use
Rental Use
Deduct mortgage interest and real property taxes as itemized deductions (subject to deduction limitations).
Tier 1: Direct expenses (expenses to obtain tenants) and certain mortgage interest and real property taxes.
Tier 2: All other expenses, with the exception of depreciation
Tier 3: Depreciation
Deduct tier 1 expenses in full.
Is the rent revenue greater than the tier 1 expenses?
Yes
No
Deduct tier 2 expenses to the extent that rent revenue exceeds tier 1 expenses. Any remaining tier 2 expenses are suspended and carried forward to the next year.
Tier 2 and tier 3 expenses are suspended and carried forward to the next year.
Is the rent revenue greater than the sum of tier 1 and tier 2 expenses?
No
Tier 3 expenses are suspended and carried forward to the next year.
Yes
Deduct tier 3 expenses to the extent that rent revenue exceeds the sum of tier 1 and tier 2 expenses. Any remaining tier 3 expenses are suspended and carried forward to the next year.
Nonresidence
Include rent revenue in gross income.
Allocate all home-related expenses between rental use and personal use.
Deduct all expenses allocated to rental use. Deduct portion of real property taxes allocated to personal use as an itemized deduction (subject to $10,000 itemized deduction limitation on taxes). All other expenses, including interest, allocated to personal use of the home are not deductible. Losses are subject to passive activity loss rules.

Appendix B Sample Settlement Statement for the Jeffersons (page 1)

OMB Approval No. 2502-0265

A. Settlement Statement (HUD-1)

B. Type of Loan

1. ☐ FHA 2. ☐ RHS 3. ☒ Conv. Unins. 4. ☐ VA 5. ☐ Conv. Ins.	6. File Number: 1355	7. Loan Number: 6788	8. Mortgage Insurance Case Number:	

C. Note: This form is furnished to give you a statement of actual settlement costs. Amounts paid to and by the settlement agent are shown. Items marked "(p.o.c.)" were paid outside the closing; they are shown here for informational purposes and are not included in the totals.

D. Name & Address of Borrower: Tyler Jefferson Jasmine Jefferson 225 El Tejon Dr. Chicago, IL 60612	E. Name & Address of Seller: Ian Sabin 525 Roberts Ln. Glencoe, IL 60022	F. Name & Address of Lender: First Bank of Chicago 125 Decatur St. Chicago, IL 60612
G. Property Location: 225 El Tejon Dr. Chicago, IL 60612 Lot 1, Block 2, Dozier Estates Cook County, Illinois	H. Settlement Agent: Beardsley Settlement Group Place of Settlement: 425 McCray St., Chicago, IL 60612	I. Settlement Date: 1/31/2022

J. Summary of Borrower's Transaction		K. Summary of Seller's Transaction	
100. Gross Amount Due from Borrower		**400. Gross Amount Due to Seller**	
101. Contract sales price	$800,000.00	401. Contract sales price	$800,000.00
102. Personal property		402. Personal property	
103. Settlement charges to borrower (line 1400)	$13,476.00	403.	
104.		404.	
105.		405.	
Adjustment for items paid by seller in advance		**Adjustment for items paid by seller in advance**	
106. City/town taxes to		406. City/town taxes to	
107. County taxes to		407. County taxes to	
108. Assessments to		408. Assessments to	
109.		409.	
110.		410.	
111.		411.	
112.		412.	
120. Gross Amount Due from Borrower	$813,476.00	**420. Gross Amount Due to Seller**	$800,000.00
200. Amount Paid by or in Behalf of Borrower		**500. Reductions In Amount Due to seller**	
201. Deposit or earnest money	$20,000.00	501. Excess deposit (see instructions)	
202. Principal amount of new loan(s)	$300,000.00	502. Settlement charges to seller (line 1400)	$51,700.00
203. Existing loan(s) taken subject to		503. Existing loan(s) taken subject to	
204.		504. Payoff of first mortgage loan	
205.		505. Payoff of second mortgage loan	
206.		506.	
207.		507.	
208.		508.	
209.		509.	
Adjustments for items unpaid by seller		**Adjustments for items unpaid by seller**	
210. City/town taxes to		510. City/town taxes to	
211. County taxes 1/1/2022 to 1/31/2022	$1,000.00	511. County taxes 1/1/2022 to 1/31/2022	$1,000.00
212. Assessments to		512. Assessments to	
213.		513.	
214.		514.	
215.		515.	
216.		516.	
217.		517.	
218.		518.	
219.		519.	
220. Total Paid by/for Borrower	$321,000.00	**520. Total Reduction Amount Due Seller**	$52,700.00
300. Cash at Settlement from/to Borrower		**600. Cash at Settlement to/from Seller**	
301. Gross amount due from borrower (line 120)	$813,476.00	601. Gross amount due to seller (line 420)	$800,000.00
302. Less amounts paid by/for borrower (line 220)	($321,000.00)	602. Less reductions in amounts due seller (line 520)	($52,700.00)
303. Cash ☒ **From** ☐ **To Borrower**	$492,476.00	**603. Cash** ☒ **To** ☐ **From Seller**	$747,300.00

The Public Reporting Burden for this collection of information is estimated at 35 minutes per response for collecting, reviewing, and reporting the data. This agency may not collect this information, and you are not required to complete this form, unless it displays a currently valid OMB control number. No confidentiality is assured; this disclosure is mandatory. This is designed to provide the parties to a RESPA covered transaction with information during the settlement process.

Source: www.HUD.gov.

(page 2)

L. Settlement Charges			
700. Total Real Estate Broker Fees based on price $800,000 @ 6.0% = $48,000		Paid From Borrower's Funds at Settlement	Paid From Seller's Funds at Settlement
Division of commission (line 700) as follows :			
701. $ 24,000.00 to Selling Agent Co.			
702. $ 24,000.00 to Listing Agent Co.			
703. Commission paid at settlement			$48,000.00
704.			
800. Items Payable in Connection with Loan			
801. Our origination charge 1.0% $ 3,000.00	(from GFE #1)		
802. Your credit or charge (points) for the specific interest rate chosen 2.0% $ 6,000.00	(from GFE #2)		
803. Your adjusted origination charges	(from GFE #A)	$9,000.00	
804. Appraisal fee to Drumgoole Appraisal Co.	(from GFE #3)	$400.00	
805. Credit report to O'Brien Credit Check Inc.	(from GFE #3)	$40.00	
806. Tax service to	(from GFE #3)		
807. Flood certification to	(from GFE #3)		
808.			
809.			
810.			
811.			
900. Items Required by Lender to be Paid in Advance			
901. Daily interest charges from 1/31/2022 to 2/10/2022 @ $ 41.10 /day	(from GFE #10)	$411.00	
902. Mortgage insurance premium for months to	(from GFE #3)		
903. Homeowner's insurance for years to	(from GFE #11)		
904.			
1000. Reserves Deposited with Lender			
1001. Initial deposit for your escrow account	(from GFE #9)		
1002. Homeowner's insurance 2 months @ $ 100.00 per month $ 200.00			
1003. Mortgage insurance months @ $ per month $			
1004. Property Taxes 11 months @ $ 1,000.00 per month $ 11,000.00			
1005. months @ $ per month $			
1006. months @ $ per month $			
1007. Aggregate Adjustment -$			
1100. Title Charges			
1101. Title services and lender's title insurance	(from GFE #4)	$250.00	
1102. Settlement or closing fee Beardsley Settlement Group $			$300.00
1103. Owner's title insurance Title Insurance Co.	(from GFE #5)	$3,250.00	
1104. Lender's title insurance $			
1105. Lender's title policy limit $			
1106. Owner's title policy limit $			
1107. Agent's portion of the total title insurance premium to $			
1108. Underwriter's portion of the total title insurance premium to $			
1109. Document Preparation to Buckles & Pitts, L.L.P			$200.00
1110.			
1111.			
1200. Government Recording and Transfer Charges			
1201. Government recording charges	(from GFE #7)		
1202. Deed $ 40.00 Mortgage $ 50.00 Release $			$90.00
1203. Transfer taxes	(from GFE #8)		
1204. City/County tax/stamps Deed $ 450.00 Mortgage $ 350.00			$800.00
1205. State tax/stamps Deed $ 1,250.00 Mortgage $ 1,000.00			$2,250.00
1206.			
1300. Additional Settlement Charges			
1301. Required services that you can shop for	(from GFE #6)		
1302. Survey to Beardsley Settlement Group $		$125.00	
1303. Pest Inspection to Clark's Pest Control $			$60.00
1304.			
1305.			
1400. Total Settlement Charges (enter on lines 103, Section J and 502, Section K)		$13,476.00	$51,700.00

Source: www.HUD.gov.

Summary

LO 14-1 Determine whether a home is considered a principal residence, a residence (not principal), or a nonresidence for tax purposes.

- A dwelling unit includes a house, condominium, mobile home, boat, or similar property.
- A dwelling unit is considered to be a residence if the taxpayer's personal use of the unit (home) exceeds the greater of (1) 14 days or (2) 10 percent of the rental days during the year.
- Personal use includes days when the taxpayer or other owners stay in the home; a relative of the owner stays in the home (even if the relative pays full fair market value, unless the relative is using the home as a principal residence); a nonowner stays in the home under a vacation home exchange or swap arrangement; or the taxpayer rents out the property for less than fair market value.
- Rental use includes days the taxpayer rents out the property at fair market value and days spent repairing or maintaining the home for rental use.
- Days when the home is available for rent but not rented out do not count as personal or rental days.
- When a taxpayer owns more than one residence, the principal residence is determined based on the facts and circumstances, such as total time spent living in each residence.
- For a particular taxpayer for a particular year, a dwelling unit or home can be classified as a principal residence, residence (not principal), or nonresidence (rental property).

LO 14-2 Compute the taxable gain on the sale of a residence.

- If they meet ownership and use requirements, married taxpayers filing jointly may exclude up to $500,000 of gain on the sale of their principal residence. Other taxpayers may exclude up to $250,000 of gain on the sale of their principal residence.
- To qualify for the exclusion on the sale of real estate, taxpayers must own and use the home as their principal residence for two of the five years preceding the sale.
- The amount of gain eligible for exclusion may be reduced if on or after January 1, 2009, the taxpayer uses the home for a purpose other than as a principal residence.

LO 14-3 Determine the amount of the home mortgage interest deduction.

- Depending on when the debt was incurred, taxpayers may deduct interest on up to either $1,000,000 or $750,000 of acquisition indebtedness for their principal residence and one other residence.
- A loan secured by the home (called a "home equity loan" by the bank) is treated as acquisition indebtedness only to the extent the taxpayer uses the loan proceeds to substantially improve the home.
- Taxpayers may immediately deduct points paid (discount points and loan origination fees) on qualifying home mortgages used to acquire the taxpayer's principal residence if they meet certain requirements. Qualifying points paid on a loan refinancing are deductible over the life of the loan.

LO 14-4 Discuss the deductibility of real property taxes.

- Taxpayers deduct real property taxes when the taxes are paid to the taxing jurisdiction and not when the taxes are paid to an escrow account.
- When real property is sold during the year, the property tax deduction for the property is allocated to the buyer and seller based on the portion of the year that each holds the property, no matter which party pays the taxes.
- The itemized deduction for all taxes combined (state income, real property, and personal property tax) is limited to $10,000 ($5,000 for married taxpayers filing separately).

LO 14-5 Explain the tax issues and consequences associated with rental use of the home.

- Taxpayers who live in a home for 15 days or more and rent the home out for 14 days or less (a residence with minimal rental use) do not include gross rental receipts in taxable income and do not deduct rental expenses.

- Taxpayers who both reside in and rent out a home for a significant portion of the year (a residence with significant rental use) include rental revenue in gross income, deduct direct rental expenses not relating to the home (expenses to obtain tenants), and allocate home-related expenses between personal use and rental use of the home. They deduct mortgage interest expense and real property taxes allocated to the rental use of the home as for AGI deductions (to the extent they would have been deductible as itemized deductions had the taxpayer not rented the property) and the mortgage interest expense and real property taxes allocated to the personal use of the home as itemized deductions (subject to limitations). The remaining deductions allocated to the rental use of the home are deductible in a particular sequence, and the amount of these deductions cannot exceed rental revenue in excess of direct rental expenses and rental mortgage interest and real property taxes.
- Net rental income reported on Schedule E is potentially subject to the net investment income tax discussed in the Individual Income Tax Computation and Tax Credits chapter. This tax applies to net investment income for high-income taxpayers.
- Taxpayers who rent out a home with minimal or no personal use (nonresidence) include rental receipts in income and deduct all rental expenses. In this situation, expenses exceeding income are subject to the passive activity loss rules.
- Taxpayers may be able to deduct up to $25,000 of passive loss on their rental home if they are active participants with respect to the property. This deduction is phased out for taxpayers with adjusted gross income between $100,000 and $150,000.

Compute the limitations on home office deductions. LO 14-6

- To deduct expenses relating to a home office, the taxpayer must be self-employed and use the home office exclusively and regularly for business purposes.
- Home-related expenses are allocated between business expenses and personal expenses based on the size of the office relative to the size of the home.
- Mortgage interest and real property taxes allocated to business use of the home are deductible in full without regard to the income of the business to the extent they would have been deductible as itemized deductions if the taxpayer did not have any business use of the home.
- Other expenses allocated to the business use of the home are deducted in a particular sequence. The deduction for these expenses cannot exceed the taxpayer's net Schedule C income (before home office expenses) minus the mortgage interest and real property taxes allocated to business use of the home.
- Taxpayers electing the simplified method for claiming home office expenses may deduct $5 per square foot up to 300 square feet.

KEY TERMS

acquisition indebtedness (14-9)
active participant in a rental activity (14-26)
dwelling unit (14-2)
escrow (holding) account (14-15)
flipping (14-5)
Form 1098 (14-11)
home office deductions (14-26)
IRS allocation method (14-18)
point (14-13)
principal residence (14-3)
qualified residence (14-9)
real property taxes (14-15)
refinanced (14-10)
settlement statement (14-13)
Tax Court allocation method (14-18)

DISCUSSION QUESTIONS

Discussion Questions are available in Connect®. Mc Graw Hill connect

1. How does a taxpayer determine whether a dwelling unit is treated as a residence or nonresidence for tax purposes? LO 14-1
2. For tax purposes, does a residence need to be situated at a fixed location? Explain. LO 14-1
3. When determining whether a dwelling unit is treated as a residence or a nonresidence for tax purposes, what constitutes a day of personal use and what constitutes a day of rental use? LO 14-1

LO 14-1 4. A taxpayer owns a home in Salt Lake City, Utah, and a second home in St. George, Utah. How does the taxpayer determine which home is their principal residence for tax purposes?

LO 14-2 5. What are the ownership and use requirements a taxpayer must meet to qualify for the exclusion of gain on the sale of a residence?

LO 14-2 6. Under what circumstances, if any, can a taxpayer fail to meet the ownership and use requirements but still be able to exclude all of the gain on the sale of a principal residence?

LO 14-2 7. Under what circumstances can a taxpayer meet the ownership and use requirements for a residence but still *not* be allowed to exclude all realized gain on the sale of the residence?

LO 14-2 8. A taxpayer purchases and lives in a home for a year. The home appreciates in value by $50,000. The taxpayer sells the home and purchases a new home. What information do you need to obtain to determine whether the taxpayer is allowed to exclude the gain on the sale of the first home?

LO 14-3 9. Juanita owns a principal residence in New Jersey, a cabin in Montana, and a houseboat in Washington. All of these properties have mortgages incurred before 2017 on which Juanita pays interest. What limits, if any, apply to Juanita's home mortgage interest deductions? Explain whether deductible interest is deductible for AGI or from AGI.

LO 14-3 10. For purposes of determining a taxpayer's deductible home mortgage interest, does it matter when the taxpayer incurred the debt to acquire the home? Explain.

LO 14-3 11. Lars and Leigha saved up for years before they purchased their dream home. They were considering (1) using all of their savings to make a large down payment on the home (90 percent of the value of the home) and barely scraping by without backup savings or (2) making a more modest down payment (50 percent of the value of the loan) and holding some of the savings in reserve as needed if funds got tight. They decided to make a large down payment because they figured they could always refinance the home to pull some equity out of it if they needed cash. What advice would you give them about the tax consequences of their decision?

LO 14-3 12. Is it possible for a taxpayer to have more than one loan that is treated as acquisition indebtedness for tax purposes, even if one of the loans is considered to be a "home equity loan" by the bank lending the money?

LO 14-3 13. Why might it be good advice from a tax perspective to think hard before deciding to quickly pay down mortgage debt?

LO 14-3 14. Does the deductible amount of a taxpayer's home mortgage interest potentially depend on when the taxpayer executed the mortgage? Explain.

LO 14-3 15. Compare and contrast the characteristics of a deductible point from a nondeductible point on a first home mortgage.

LO 14-3 16. Is the break-even period generally longer for points paid to reduce the interest rate on initial home loans or points paid for the same purpose on a refinance? Explain.

planning LO 14-3 17. Under what circumstances is it likely to be economically beneficial to pay points to reduce the interest rate on a home loan?

LO 14-3 18. Harry decides to finance his new home with a 30-year fixed mortgage. Because he figures he will be in this home for a long time, he decides to pay a fully deductible discount point on his mortgage to reduce the interest rate. Assume that Harry itemizes deductions and has a constant marginal tax rate over time. Will the time required to recover the cost of the discount point be shorter or longer if Harry makes extra principal payments starting in the first year (as opposed to not making any extra principal payments)? Explain.

LO 14-3 LO 14-4 19. Consider the settlement statement in Appendix B to this chapter. What amounts on the statement are the Jeffersons allowed to deduct on their 2022 tax return? Indicate the settlement statement line number for each deductible amount (discuss any issues that must be addressed to determine deductibility) and label each deduction as a for AGI deduction or a from AGI deduction.

20. A taxpayer sells a piece of real property in year 1. The amount of year 1 real property taxes is estimated at the closing of the sale and the amounts are allocated between the buyer and the taxpayer. At the end of year 1, the buyer receives a property tax bill that is higher than the estimate. After paying the tax bill, the buyer contacts the taxpayer at the beginning of year 2 and asks the taxpayer to pay the taxpayer's share of the shortfall. The taxpayer sends a check to the buyer. Should the taxpayer be concerned that they won't get to deduct the extra tax payment because it was paid to the buyer and not to the taxing jurisdiction? Explain. LO 14-4
21. Are real property taxes subject to any deduction limitations? Explain. LO 14-4
22. Is a homeowner allowed a property tax deduction for amounts included in the monthly mortgage payment that are earmarked for property taxes? Explain. LO 14-4
23. Is it possible for a taxpayer to receive rental income that is not subject to taxation? Explain. LO 14-5 planning
24. Halle just acquired a vacation home. She plans on spending several months each year vacationing in the home and renting out the property for the rest of the year. She is projecting tax losses on the rental portion of the property for the year. She is not too concerned about the losses because she is confident she will be able to use the losses to offset her income from other sources. Is her confidence misplaced? Explain. LO 14-5
25. A taxpayer is planning to stay in their second home for the entire month of September but not any other days during the year. They would like the home to fall into the residence-with-significant-rental-use category for tax purposes. What is the maximum number of days they can rent out the home and have it qualify? LO 14-5 planning
26. Compare and contrast the IRS method and the Tax Court method for allocating expenses between personal use and rental use for vacation homes. Include the Tax Court's justification for departing from the IRS method in your answer. LO 14-5
27. In what circumstances is the IRS method for allocating expenses between personal use and rental use for vacation homes more beneficial to a taxpayer than the Tax Court method, and when is the Tax Court method generally more beneficial? LO 14-5
28. Under what circumstances would a taxpayer who generates a loss from renting a home that is not a residence be able to fully deduct the loss? What potential limitations apply? LO 14-5
29. Describe the circumstances in which a taxpayer acquires a home and rents it out and is not allowed to deduct a portion of the interest expense on the loan the taxpayer used to acquire the home. LO 14-5
30. Is it possible for a rental property to generate a positive annual cash flow and at the same time produce a loss for tax purposes? Explain. LO 14-5
31. How are the tax issues associated with home offices and vacation homes used as rentals similar? How are the tax issues or requirements dissimilar? LO 14-5 LO 14-6
32. Can both employees and self-employed taxpayers claim the home office deduction? Explain. LO 14-6
33. How do self-employed taxpayers report home office deductions on their tax returns? LO 14-6
34. For taxpayers qualifying for home office deductions, what are considered to be indirect expenses of maintaining the home? How are these expenses allocated to personal and home office use? Can taxpayers choose to calculate home office expenses without regard to actual expenses allocated to the home office? Explain. LO 14-6
35. What limitations exist for self-employed taxpayers in deducting home office expenses, and how does the taxpayer determine which expenses are deductible and which are not in situations when the overall amount of the home office deduction is limited? LO 14-6

LO 14-2 LO 14-6

36. A self-employed taxpayer deducts home office expenses including depreciation expense. The taxpayer then sells the home at a $100,000 gain. Assuming the taxpayer meets the ownership and use tests, does the full gain qualify for exclusion? Explain.

PROBLEMS

Select problems are available in Connect®.

LO 14-1

37. Several years ago, Junior acquired a home that he vacationed in part of the time and rented out part of the time. During the current year, Junior:

- Personally stayed in the home for 22 days.
- Rented it to his favorite brother at a discount for 10 days.
- Rented it to his least-favorite brother for 8 days at the full market rate.
- Rented it to his friend at a discounted rate for 4 days.
- Rented the home to third parties for 58 days at the market rate.
- Did repair and maintenance work on the home for 2 days.
- Marketed the property and made it available for rent for 150 days during the year (but did not rent it out).

How many days of personal use and how many days of rental use did Junior experience on the property during the year?

LO 14-1

38. Seo-yeon owns a condominium. In each of the following alternative situations, determine whether the condominium should be treated as a residence or a nonresidence for tax purposes.

a) Seo-yeon lives in the condo for 19 days and rents it out for 22 days.
b) Seo-yeon lives in the condo for 8 days and rents it out for 9 days.
c) Seo-yeon lives in the condo for 80 days and rents it out for 120 days.
d) Seo-yeon lives in the condo for 30 days and rents it out for 320 days.

LO 14-2

39. Leticia and Stephanie Sims purchased a home in Spokane, Washington, for $400,000. They moved into the home on February 1 of year 1. They lived in the home as their primary residence until June 30 of year 5, when they sold the home for $700,000.

a) What amount of gain on the sale of the home are the Sims required to include in taxable income?
b) Assume the original facts, except that Leticia and Stephanie live in the home until January 1 of year 3, when they purchase a new home and rent out the original home. They finally sell the original home on June 30 of year 5 for $700,000. Ignoring any issues relating to depreciation taken on the home while it is being rented, what amount of realized gain on the sale of the home are the Simses required to include in taxable income?
c) Assume the same facts as in part (b), except that the Sims live in the home until January of year 4, when they purchase a new home and rent out the first home. What amount of realized gain on the sale of the home will the Sims include in taxable income if they sell the first home on June 30 of year 5 for $700,000?
d) Assume the original facts, except that Stephanie moves in with Leticia on March 1 of year 3 and the couple is married on March 1 of year 4. Under state law, the couple jointly owns Leticia's home beginning on the date they are married. On December 1 of year 3, Stephanie sells her home that she lived in before she moved in with Leticia. She excludes the entire $50,000 gain on the sale on her individual year 3 tax return. What amount of gain must the couple recognize on the sale in June of year 5?

40. Salvador and Jenna Porter purchased a home in Kenosha, Wisconsin, for $400,000. They moved into the home on February 1 of year 1. They lived in the home as their primary residence until November 1 of year 1, when they sold the home for $500,000. The Porters' marginal ordinary tax rate is 35 percent. LO 14-2
   a) Assume that the Porters sold their home and moved because they didn't like their neighbors. How much gain will the Porters recognize on their home sale? At what rate, if any, will the gain be taxed?
   b) Assume the Porters sell the home because Jenna's employer transfers her to an office in Texas. How much gain will the Porters recognize on their home sale?
   c) Assume the same facts as in part (b), except that the Porters sell their home for $700,000. How much gain will the Porters recognize on the home sale?
   d) Assume the same facts as part (b), except that on December 1 of year 0 the Porters sold their home in Kenosha and excluded the $300,000 gain from income on their year 0 tax return. How much gain will the Porters recognize on the sale of their Kenosha home?
41. Steve Pratt, who is single, purchased a home in Riverside, California, for $400,000. He moved into the home on February 1 of year 1. He lived in the home as his primary residence until June 30 of year 5, when he sold the home for $700,000. LO 14-2
   a) What amount of gain will Steve be required to recognize on the sale of the home?
   b) Assume the original facts, except that the home is Steve's vacation home and he vacations there four months each year. Steve does not ever rent the home to others. What gain must Steve recognize on the home sale?
   c) Assume the original facts, except that Steve married Giuseppina on February 1 of year 3 and the couple lived in the home until they sold it in June of year 5. Under state law, Steve owned the home by himself. How much gain must Steve and Giuseppina recognize on the sale (assume they file a joint return in year 5)?
42. Celia has been married to Daryl for 52 years. The couple has lived in their current home for the last 20 years. In October of year 0, Daryl passed away. Celia sold their home and moved into a condominium. What is the maximum exclusion Celia is entitled to if she sells the home on December 15 of year 1? LO 14-2
43. Sarah (single) purchased a home on January 1, 2008, for $600,000. She eventually sold the home for $800,000. What amount of the $200,000 gain on the sale does Sarah recognize in each of the following alternative situations? (Assume accumulated depreciation on the home is $0 at the time of the sale.) (Round all intermediary percentages to two decimal places.) LO 14-2
   a) Sarah used the home as her principal residence through December 31, 2019. She used the home as a vacation home from January 1, 2020, until she sold it on January 1, 2023.
   b) Sarah used the property as a vacation home through December 31, 2019. She then used the home as her principal residence from January 1, 2020, until she sold it on January 1, 2023.
   c) Sarah used the home as a vacation home from January 1, 2008, until January 1, 2022. She used the home as her principal residence from January 1, 2022, until she sold it on January 1, 2023.
   d) Sarah used the home as a vacation home from January 1, 2008, through December 31, 2016. She used the home as her principal residence from January 1, 2017, until she sold it on January 1, 2023.
44. Troy (single) purchased a home in Hopkinton, Massachusetts, on January 1, 2007, for $300,000. He sold the home on January 1, 2022, for $320,000. How much gain must Troy recognize on his home sale in each of the following alternative situations? LO 14-2
   a) Troy rented out the home from January 1, 2007, through November 30, 2008. He lived in the home as his principal residence from December 1, 2008, through the date of sale. Assume accumulated depreciation on the home at the time of sale was $7,000.

b) Troy lived in the home as his principal residence from January 1, 2007, through December 31, 2017. He rented out the home from January 1, 2018, through the date of the sale. Assume accumulated depreciation on the home at the time of sale was $2,000.

c) Troy lived in the home as his principal residence from January 1, 2007, through December 31, 2019. He rented out the home from January 1, 2020, through the date of the sale. Assume accumulated depreciation on the home at the time of sale was $0.

d) Troy rented out the home from January 1, 2007, through December 31, 2017. He lived in the home as his principal residence from January 1, 2018, through December 31, 2018. He rented out the home from January 1, 2019, through December 31, 2019, and lived in the home as his principal residence from January 1, 2020, through the date of the sale. Assume accumulated depreciation on the home at the time of sale was $0.

LO 14-3

45. Javier and Anita Sanchez purchased a home on January 1, 2022, for $600,000 by paying $200,000 down and borrowing the remaining $400,000 with a 7 percent loan secured by the home. The loan requires interest-only payments for the first five years. The Sanchezes would itemize deductions even if they did not have any deductible interest. The Sanchezes' marginal tax rate is 32 percent.

a) What is the after-tax cost of the interest expense to the Sanchezes in 2022?

b) Assume the original facts, except that the Sanchezes rent a home and pay $21,000 in rent during the year. What is the after-tax cost of their rental payments in 2022?

c) Assuming the interest expense is their only itemized deduction for the year and that Javier and Anita file a joint return, have great eyesight, and are under 60 years of age, what is the after-tax cost of their 2022 interest expense?

LO 14-3

46. Javier and Anita Sanchez purchased a home on January 1 of year 1 for $1,000,000 by paying $200,000 down and borrowing the remaining $800,000 with a 6 percent loan secured by the home. The Sanchezes made interest-only payments on the loan in years 1 and 2.

a) Assuming year 1 is 2017, how much interest would the Sanchezes deduct in year 2?

b) Assuming year 1 is 2022, how much interest would the Sanchezes deduct in year 2?

c) Assume year 1 is 2022 and by the beginning of year 4, the Sanchezes have paid down the principal amount of the loan to $500,000. In year 4, they borrow an additional $100,000 through a loan secured by the home in order to finish their basement. The new loan carries a 7 percent interest rate and is termed a "home equity loan" by the lender. What amount of interest can the Sanchezes deduct on the $100,000 loan?

d) Assume year 1 is 2022, and by the beginning of year 4, the Sanchezes have paid down the principal amount of the loan to $500,000. In year 4, they borrow an additional $100,000 through a loan secured by the home in order to purchase a new car. The new loan carries a 7 percent interest rate and is termed a "home equity loan" by the lender. What amount of interest can the Sanchezes deduct on the $100,000 loan?

LO 14-3

47. Lewis and Laurie are married and jointly own a home valued at $240,000. They recently paid off the mortgage on their home. The couple borrowed money from the local credit union in January of 2022. How much interest may the couple deduct in each of the following alternative situations? (Assume they itemize deductions no matter the amount of interest.)

a) The couple borrows $40,000, and the loan is secured by their home. The credit union calls the loan a "home equity loan." Lewis and Laurie use the loan proceeds for purposes unrelated to the home. The couple pays $1,600 interest on the loan during the year, and the couple files a joint return.

b) The couple borrows $110,000, and the loan is secured by their home. The credit union calls the loan a "home equity loan." Lewis and Laurie use the loan proceeds to add a room to their home. The couple pays $5,200 interest on the loan during the year, and the couple files a joint return.

48. On January 1 of year 1, Arthur and Aretha Franklin purchased a home for $1.5 million by paying $200,000 down and borrowing the remaining $1.3 million with a 7 percent loan secured by the home. The Franklins paid interest only on the loan for year 1, year 2, and year 3 (unless stated otherwise). LO 14-3

a) What is the amount of interest expense the Franklins may deduct in year 3 assuming year 1 is 2017?

b) What is the amount of interest expense the Franklins may deduct in year 2 assuming year 1 is 2021?

c) Assume that year 1 is 2022 and that in year 2, the Franklins pay off the entire loan, but at the beginning of year 3, they borrow $300,000 secured by the home at a 3 percent rate. They make interest-only payments on the loan during the year, and they use the loan proceeds for purposes unrelated to the home. What amount of interest expense may the Franklins deduct in year 3 on this loan?

49. On January 1 of 2022, Jason and Jill Marsh acquired a home for $500,000 by paying $400,000 down and borrowing $100,000 with a 3 percent loan secured by the home. On January 1 of 2023, the Marshes needed cash, so they refinanced the original loan by taking out a new $250,000, 3 percent loan. With the $250,000 proceeds from the new loan, the Marshes paid off the original $100,000 loan and used the remaining $150,000 to fund their son's college education. LO 14-3

a) What amount of interest expense on the refinanced loan may the Marshes deduct in 2023?

b) Assume the original facts, except that the Marshes use the $150,000 cash from the refinancing to add two rooms and a garage to their home. What amount of interest expense on the refinanced loan may the Marshes deduct in 2023?

50. Jennifer has been living in her current principal residence for three years. Six months ago, Jennifer decided that she would like to purchase a second home near a beach so she can vacation there for part of the year. Despite her best efforts, Jennifer has been unable to find what she is looking for. Consequently, Jennifer recently decided to change plans. She purchased a parcel of land for $200,000 with the intention of building her second home on the property. To acquire the land, she borrowed $200,000 secured by the land. Jennifer would like to know whether the interest she pays on the loan (before construction on the house is completed) is deductible as mortgage interest. LO 14-3 research

a) How should Jennifer treat the interest if she has begun construction on the home and plans to live in the home in 12 months from the time construction began?

b) How should Jennifer treat the interest if she hasn't begun construction on the home but plans to live in the home in 15 months?

c) How should Jennifer treat the interest if she has begun construction on the home but doesn't plan to live in the home for 37 months from the time construction began?

51. Rajiv and Laurie Amin are recent college graduates looking to purchase a new home. They are purchasing a $200,000 home by paying $20,000 down and borrowing the other $180,000 with a 30-year loan secured by the home. The Amins have the option of (1) paying no discount points on the loan and paying interest at 3 percent or (2) paying 1 discount point on the loan and paying interest of 2.5 percent. Both loans require the Amins to make interest-only payments for the first five years. Unless otherwise stated, the Amins itemize deductions irrespective of the amount of interest expense. The Amins are in the 24 percent marginal ordinary income tax bracket. LO 14-3 planning

a) Assuming the Amins *do not itemize deductions,* what is the break-even point for paying the point to get a lower interest rate?

b) Assuming the Amins do itemize deductions, what is the break-even point for paying the point to get a lower interest rate?

c) Assume the original facts, except that the amount of the loan is $300,000. What is the break-even point for the Amins for paying the point to get a lower interest rate?

d) Assume the original facts, except that the $180,000 loan is a refinance instead of an original loan. What is the break-even point for paying the point to get a lower interest rate?

e) Assume the original facts, except that the amount of the loan is $300,000 and the loan is a refinance and not an original loan. What is the break-even point for paying the point to get a lower interest rate?

LO 14-4

52. Peter and Shaline Johnsen moved into a home in a new subdivision. Theirs was one of the first homes in the subdivision. During the year, they paid $1,500 in real property taxes to the state government, $500 to the developer of the subdivision for an assessment to pay for the sidewalks, and $900 for real property taxes on land they hold as an investment. What amount of property taxes are the Johnsens allowed to deduct assuming their itemized deductions exceed the standard deduction amount before considering any property tax deductions and they pay $5,000 of state income taxes for the year and no other deductible taxes?

LO 14-4

53. Jesse Brimhall is single. In 2022, his itemized deductions were $9,000 before considering any real property taxes he paid during the year. Jesse's adjusted gross income was $70,000 (also before considering any property tax deductions). In 2022, he paid real property taxes of $3,000 on property 1 and $1,200 of real property taxes on property 2. He did not pay any other deductible taxes during the year.

a) If property 1 is Jesse's primary residence and property 2 is his vacation home (he does not rent it out at all), what is his taxable income after taking property taxes into account?

b) If property 1 is Jesse's business building (he owns the property) and property 2 is his primary residence, what is his taxable income after taking property taxes into account (ignore the deduction for qualified business income)?

c) If property 1 is Jesse's primary residence and property 2 is a parcel of land he holds for investment, what is his taxable income after taking property taxes into account?

LO 14-4

54. Craig and Karen Conder purchased a new home on May 1 of year 1 for $200,000. At the time of the purchase, it was estimated that the real property tax rate for the year would be 1 percent of the property's value. How much in property taxes on the new home are the Conders allowed to deduct under each of the following circumstances? Assume the Conders' itemized deductions exceed the standard deduction before considering property taxes and the property tax is the only deductible tax they pay during the year.

a) The property tax estimate proves to be accurate. The seller and the Conders paid their share of the tax. The full property tax bill is paid to the taxing jurisdiction by the end of the year.

b) The actual property tax bill was 1.05 percent of the property's value. The Conders paid their share of the estimated tax bill and the entire difference between the 1 percent estimate and the 1.05 percent actual tax bill, and the seller paid the rest. The full property tax bill is paid to the taxing jurisdiction by the end of the year.

c) The actual property tax bill was .95 percent of the property's value. The seller paid their share of taxes based on the 1 percent estimate, and the Conders paid the difference between what the seller paid and the amount of the final tax bill. The full property tax bill is paid to the taxing jurisdiction by the end of the year.

55. Kirk and Lorna Newbold purchased a new home on August 1 of year 1 for $300,000. At the time of the purchase, it was estimated that the real property tax rate for the year would be .5 percent of the property's value. Because the taxing jurisdiction collects taxes on a July 1 year-end, it was estimated that the Newbolds would be required to pay $1,375 in property taxes for the property tax year relating to August through June of year 2 ($300,000 × .005 × 11/12). The seller would be required to pay the $125 for July of year 1. Along with their monthly payment of principal and interest, the Newbolds paid $125 to the mortgage company to cover the property taxes. The mortgage company placed the money in escrow and used the funds in the escrow account to pay the property tax bill in July of year 2. The Newbolds' itemized deductions exceed the standard deduction before considering real property taxes, and they don't pay any other deductible taxes during the year. LO 14-4

a) How much in real property taxes can the Newbolds deduct for year 1?

b) How much in real property taxes can the Newbolds deduct for year 2?

c) Assume the original facts, except that the Newbolds were not able to collect $125 from the seller for the property taxes for July of year 1. How much in real property taxes can the Newbolds deduct for year 1 and year 2?

d) Assume the original facts, except that the tax bill for July 1 of year 1 through June 30 of year 2 turned out to be $1,200 instead of $1,500. How much in real property taxes can the Newbolds deduct in year 1 and year 2?

56. Jenae and Terry Hutchings own a parcel of land as tenants by entirety. That is, they both own the property, but when one of them dies, the other becomes the sole owner of the property. For nontax reasons, Jenae and Terry decide to file separate tax returns for the current year. Jenae paid the entire $3,000 property tax bill for the land. How much of the $3,000 property tax payment is each spouse entitled to deduct in the current year assuming they pay no other deductible taxes during the year? LO 14-4 research

57. Dillon rented his personal residence at Lake Tahoe for 14 days while he was vacationing in Ireland. He resided in the home for the remainder of the year. Rental income from the property was $6,500. Expenses associated with use of the home for the entire year were as follows: LO 14-5

Real property taxes	$ 3,100
Mortgage interest	12,000
Repairs	1,500
Insurance	1,500
Utilities	3,900
Depreciation	13,000

a) What effect does the rental have on Dillon's AGI?

b) What effect does the rental have on Dillon's itemized deductions (assuming he itemizes deductions before considering deductions associated with the home)?

Use the following facts to answer problems 58 and 59.

Tamar owns a condominium near Cocoa Beach in Florida. In 2022, she incurs the following expenses in connection with her condo:

Insurance	$1,000
Advertising expense	500
Mortgage interest	3,500
Property taxes	900
Repairs & maintenance	650
Utilities	950
Depreciation	8,500

During the year, Tamar rented out the condo for 75 days, receiving $10,000 of gross income. She personally used the condo for 35 days during her vacation. Tamar's itemized deduction for nonrental taxes is less than $10,000 by more than the property taxes allocated to the rental use of the property.

LO 14-5

tax forms

58. Assume Tamar uses the IRS method of allocating expenses to rental use of the property.
   a) What is the total amount of for AGI (rental) deductions Tamar may deduct in the current year related to the condo?
   b) What is the total amount of itemized deductions Tamar may deduct in the current year related to the condo?
   c) If Tamar's basis in the condo at the beginning of the year was $150,000, what is her basis in the condo at the end of the year?
   d) Assume that gross rental revenue was $2,000 (rather than $10,000). What amount of for AGI deductions may Tamar deduct in the current year related to the condo (assuming she itemizes deductions before considering deductions associated with the condo)?
   e) Assuming that gross rental revenue was $2,000 (rather than $10,000) and that Tamar's itemized deduction for taxes is $10,000 before considering property taxes allocated to rental use of the property, what amount of for AGI deductions may Tamar deduct in the current year related to the condo?
   f) Using the original facts, complete Tamar's Form 1040, Schedule E, for this property. Also, partially complete Tamar's Form 1040, Schedule A, to include her from AGI deductions related to the condo.

LO 14-5

59. Assume Tamar uses the Tax Court method of allocating expenses to rental use of the property.
   a) What is the total amount of for AGI (rental) deductions Tamar may deduct in the current year related to the condo (assuming she itemizes deductions before considering deductions associated with the condo)?
   b) What is the total amount of itemized deductions Tamar may deduct in the current year related to the condo?
   c) If Tamar's basis in the condo at the beginning of the year was $150,000, what is her basis in the condo at the end of the year?
   d) Assume that gross rental revenue was $2,000 (rather than $10,000). What amount of for AGI deductions may Tamar deduct in the current year related to the condo?

Use the following facts to answer problems 60, 61, and 62.
Alexa owns a condominium near Cocoa Beach in Florida. In 2022, she incurs the following expenses in connection with her condo:

Insurance	$ 2,000
Mortgage interest	6,500
Property taxes	2,000
Repairs & maintenance	1,400
Utilities	2,500
Depreciation	14,500

During the year, Alexa rented out the condo for 100 days. She did not use the condo at all for personal purposes during the year. Alexa's AGI from all sources other than the rental property is $200,000. Unless otherwise specified, Alexa has no sources of passive income.

LO 14-5

60. Assume Alexa receives $30,000 in gross rental receipts.
   a) What effect do the expenses associated with the property have on her AGI?
   b) What effect do the expenses associated with the property have on her itemized deductions?

LO 14-5

61. Assuming Alexa receives $20,000 in gross rental receipts, answer the following questions:
   a) What effect does the rental activity have on her AGI for the year?

b) Assuming that Alexa's AGI from other sources is $90,000, what effect does the rental activity have on Alexa's AGI? Alexa makes all decisions with respect to the property.

c) Assuming that Alexa's AGI from other sources is $120,000, what effect does the rental activity have on Alexa's AGI? Alexa makes all decisions with respect to the property.

d) Assume that Alexa's AGI from other sources is $200,000. This consists of $150,000 salary, $10,000 of dividends, $25,000 of long-term capital gain, and net rental income from another rental property in the amount of $15,000. What effect does the Cocoa Beach condo rental activity have on Alexa's AGI?

62. Assume that in addition to renting the condo for 100 days, Alexa uses the condo for 8 days of personal use. Also assume that Alexa receives $30,000 of gross rental receipts, her itemized deductions exceed the standard deduction before considering expenses associated with the condo, and her itemized deduction for non–home business taxes is less than $10,000 by more than the real property taxes allocated to rental use of the home. Answer the following questions: LO 14-5 planning

a) What is the total amount of for AGI deductions relating to the condo that Alexa may deduct in the current year? Assume she uses the IRS method of allocating expenses between rental and personal days.

b) What is the total amount of from AGI deductions relating to the condo that Alexa may deduct in the current year? Assume she uses the IRS method of allocating expenses between rental and personal days.

c) Would Alexa be better or worse off after taxes in the current year if she uses the Tax Court method of allocating expenses?

63. Brooke owns a sole proprietorship in which she works as a management consultant. She maintains an office in her home where she meets with clients, prepares bills, and performs other work-related tasks. The home office is 300 square feet, and the entire house is 4,500 square feet. Brooke incurred the following home-related expenses during the year. Brooke itemizes her deductions, and her itemized deduction for non–home business taxes is less than $10,000 by more than the real property taxes allocated to business use of the home. Unless indicated otherwise, assume Brooke uses the actual expense method to compute home office expenses. LO 14-6 tax forms

Real property taxes	$ 3,600
Interest on home mortgage	14,000
Operating expenses of home	5,000
Depreciation	12,000
Repairs to home theater room	1,000

a) What amount of each of these expenses is allocated to the home office?

b) What are the total amounts of tier 1, tier 2, and tier 3 expenses, respectively, allocated to the home office?

c) If Brooke reported $2,000 of Schedule C net income before the home office expense deduction, what is the amount of her home office expense deduction, and what home office expenses, if any, would she carry over to next year?

d) Assuming Brooke reported $2,000 of Schedule C income before the home office expense deduction, complete Form 8829 for Brooke's home office expense deduction. Also assume the value of the home is $500,000 and the adjusted basis of the home (exclusive of land) is $468,019.

e) Assume that Brooke uses the simplified method for computing home office expenses. If Brooke reported $2,000 of Schedule C net income before the home office expense deduction, what is the amount of her home office expense deduction, and what home office expenses, if any, would she carry over to next year?

Use the following facts to answer problems 64 and 65.
Rita owns a sole proprietorship in which she works as a management consultant. She maintains an office in her home (500 square feet) where she meets with clients, prepares bills, and performs other work-related tasks. Her business expenses, other than home office expenses, total $5,600. The following home-related expenses have been allocated to her home office under the actual expense method for calculating home office expenses.

Real property taxes	$1,600
Interest on home mortgage	5,100
Operating expenses of home	800
Depreciation	1,600

Also, assume that, not counting the sole proprietorship, Rita's AGI is $60,000. Rita itemizes deductions, and her itemized deduction for non–home business taxes is less than $10,000 by more than the real property taxes allocated to business use of the home.

LO 14-6 planning

64. Assume Rita's consulting business generated $15,000 in gross income.
   a) What is Rita's home office deduction for the current year?
   b) What would Rita's home office deduction be if her business generated $10,000 of gross income instead of $15,000? (Answer for both the actual expense method and the simplified method.)
   c) Given the original facts, what is Rita's AGI for the year?
   d) Given the original facts, what types and amounts of expenses will she carry over to next year?

LO 14-6

65. Assume Rita's consulting business generated $13,000 in gross income for the current year. Further, assume Rita uses the actual expense method for computing her home office expense deduction.
   a) What is Rita's home office deduction for the current year?
   b) What is Rita's AGI for the year?
   c) Assuming the original facts, what types and amounts of expenses will she carry over to next year?

LO 14-6 research

66. Boodeesh is contemplating running a consulting business out of her home. She has a large garage apartment in her backyard that would be perfect for her business. Given that the garage apartment is separate from her house (about 30 feet behind her house), would the office be considered part of her home for purposes of the home office rules?

LO 14-2 LO 14-6

67. Alisha, who is single, owns a sole proprietorship in which she works as a management consultant. She maintains an office in her home where she meets with clients, prepares bills, and performs other work-related tasks. She purchased the home at the beginning of year 1 for $400,000. Since she purchased the home and moved into it, she has been able to deduct $10,000 of depreciation expenses to offset her consulting income. At the end of year 3, Alisha sold the home for $500,000. What is the amount of taxes Alisha will be required to pay on the gain from the sale of the home? Alisha's ordinary marginal tax rate is 32 percent. (Ignore the net investment income tax.)

COMPREHENSIVE PROBLEMS

Select problems are available in Connect®.

McGraw Hill connect

planning

68. Derek and Meagan Jacoby recently graduated from State University, and Derek accepted a job in business consulting while Meagan accepted a job in computer programming. Meagan inherited $75,000 from her grandfather, who recently passed away. The couple is debating whether they should buy or rent a home. They located a rental home that meets their needs. The monthly rent is $2,250. They also found a

three-bedroom home that would cost $475,000 to purchase. The Jacobys could use Meagan's inheritance for a down payment on the home. Thus, they would need to borrow $400,000 to acquire the home. They have the option of paying 2 discount points to receive a fixed interest rate of 2.5 percent on the loan or paying no points and receiving a fixed interest rate of 3.75 percent for a 30-year fixed loan.

Though anything could happen, the couple expects to live in the home for no more than five years before relocating to a different region of the country. Derek and Meagan don't have any school-related debt, so they will save the $75,000 if they don't purchase a home. Also, consider the following information:

- The couple's marginal tax rate is 24 percent.
- Regardless of whether they buy or rent, the couple will itemize their deductions and have the ability to deduct all of the property taxes from the purchase of a residence.
- If they buy, the Jacobys would purchase and move into the home on January 1, 2022.
- If they buy the home, the property taxes for the year are $3,600.
- Disregard loan-related fees not mentioned above.
- If the couple does not buy a home, they will put their money into their taxable annuity account, where they earn 5 percent annual interest.
- Assume that all unstated costs are equal between the buy and rent options.

Required:

Help the Jacobys with their decisions by answering the following questions:

a) If the Jacobys decide to rent the home, what is their after-tax cost of the rental for the first year? (Include income from the annuity account in your analysis.)

b) What is the approximate break-even point in years (or months) for paying the points to receive a reduced interest rate? (To simplify this computation, assume the Jacobys will make interest-only payments, and ignore the time value of money.)

c) What is the after-tax cost (in interest and property taxes) of living in the home for 2022? Assume that the Jacobys' interest rate is 3.75 percent, they do not pay discount points, they make interest-only payments for the first year, and the value of the home does not change during the year.

d) Assume that on March 1, 2022, the Jacobys sold their home for $525,000 so that Derek and Meagan could accept job opportunities in a different state. The Jacobys used the sale proceeds to (1) pay off the $400,000 principal of the mortgage, (2) pay a $10,000 commission to their real estate broker, and (3) make a down payment on a new home in the different state. However, the new home cost only $300,000. What gain or loss do the Jacobys realize and recognize on the sale of their home, and what amount of taxes must they pay on the gain, if any? (Assume they make interest-only payments on the loan.)

e) Assume the same facts as in part (d), except that the Jacobys sell their home for $450,000 and they pay a $7,500 commission. What effect does the sale have on their 2022 income tax liability? Recall that the Jacobys are subject to an ordinary marginal tax rate of 24 percent, and assume that they do not have any other transactions involving capital assets in 2022.

69. James and Kate Sawyer were married on New Year's Eve of 2021. Before their marriage, Kate lived in New York and worked as a hair stylist for one of the city's top salons. James lives in Atlanta, where he works for a public accounting firm earning an annual salary of $100,000. After their marriage, Kate left her job in New York and moved into the couple's newly purchased, 3,200-square-foot home in Atlanta. Kate incurred $2,200 of moving expenses. The couple purchased the home on January 3, 2022, by paying $100,000 down and obtaining a $400,000 mortgage for the remainder. The interest rate on this loan was 3 percent, and the Sawyers made interest-only payments on the loan through June 30, 2022 (assume they paid exactly one-half of a year's worth of interest on this loan by June 30). On July 1, 2022, the

Sawyers borrowed an additional $50,000, secured by the home, in order to make home improvements (the loan was called a "home equity loan" by the lender). The interest rate on the loan was 3 percent (assume they paid exactly one-half of a year's worth of interest on this loan by year-end).

Shortly after moving into the new home, Kate started a new business called Kate's Beauty Cuts LLC. She set up shop in a 384-square-foot corner room of the couple's home and began to get it ready for business. The room conveniently had a door to the outside, providing customers direct access to the shop. Kate paid $2,100 to have the carpet replaced with a tile floor. She also paid $1,200 to have the room painted with vibrant colors and $650 to have the room rewired for appropriate lighting. Kate ran an ad in the local newspaper and officially opened her shop on January 24, 2022. By the end of the year, Kate's Beauty Cuts LLC generated $40,000 of *net* income before considering the home office deduction. The Sawyers incurred the following home-related expenditures during 2022:

- $4,200 of real property taxes.
- $2,000 for homeowner's insurance.
- $2,400 for electricity.
- $1,500 for gas and other utilities.

They determined depreciation expense for their entire house was $17,424.

Also, on March 2, Kate was able to finally sell her one-bedroom Manhattan condominium for $478,000. She purchased the condo, which she had lived in for six years prior to her marriage, for $205,000.

Kate owns a vacation home in Myrtle Beach, South Carolina. She purchased the home several years ago, largely as an investment. To help cover the expenses of maintaining the home, James and Kate decided to rent the home out. They rented the home for a total of 106 days at fair market value (this included 8 days that they rented the home to James's brother Jack). In addition to the 106 days, Kate allowed a good friend and customer, Clair, to stay in the home for half-price for 2 days. James and Kate stayed in the home for 6 days for a romantic getaway and another 3 days in order to do some repair and maintenance work on the home. The rental revenues from the home in 2022 were $18,400. The Sawyers incurred the following expenses associated with the home:

- $9,100 of interest (assume not limited by acquisition debt limit).
- $3,400 of real property taxes.
- $1,900 for homeowner's insurance.
- $1,200 for electricity.
- $1,600 for gas, other utilities, and landscaping.
- $5,200 for depreciation.

Required:

Determine the Sawyers' taxable income for 2022. Disregard self-employment taxes and the qualified business income deduction. Assume the couple paid $4,400 in state income taxes and files a joint return. For determining deductible home office expenses and allocating expenses to the rental, the Sawyers would like to use the methods that minimize their overall taxable income for the year.

UWorld | ROGER CPA Review

UWorld Roger CPA Review

Sample CPA Exam questions from Roger CPA Review are available in Connect as support for the topics in this text. These Multiple Choice Questions and Task-Based Simulations include expert-written explanations and solutions and provide a starting point for students to become familiar with the content and functionality of the actual CPA Exam.

chapter

15 Business Entities Overview

Learning Objectives

Upon completing this chapter, you should be able to:

LO 15-1 Discuss the legal and other nontax characteristics of different types of legal business entities.

LO 15-2 Describe the different types of business entities for tax purposes.

LO 15-3 Identify fundamental differences in tax characteristics across business entity types.

Gyorgy Barna/Shutterstock

Storyline Summary

Taxpayer:	Nicole Johnson (she/her/hers)
Location:	Salt Lake City, Utah
Employment status:	State government employee with entrepreneurial ambitions

Nicole Johnson is currently employed by the Utah Chamber of Commerce in Salt Lake City, Utah. While she enjoys the relatively short workweeks, she eventually would like to work for herself. In her current position, she deals with a lot of successful entrepreneurs who have become role models for her. Nicole has also developed an extensive list of contacts that should prove valuable when she starts her own business. It has taken a while, but Nicole believes she has finally developed a viable new business idea. Her idea is to design and manufacture bed sheets that have various colored patterns and are made of unique fabric blends. The sheets look great and are extremely comfortable whether the bedroom is warm or cool. She has had several friends try out her prototype sheets, and they have consistently given the sheets rave reviews. With this encouragement, Nicole started giving serious thought to making "Color Comfort Sheets" a moneymaking enterprise.

Nicole has enough business background to realize that she is embarking on a risky path, but one, she hopes, with significant potential rewards. After creating some initial income projections, Nicole realized that it will take a few years for the business to become profitable.

While Nicole's original plan was to start the business by herself, she is considering seeking out another equity owner so that she can add financial resources and business experience to the venture. Nicole feels like she has a grasp on her business plan, but she still needs to determine how to organize the business for tax purposes. After doing some research, Nicole learned that she should consider many factors in order to determine the "best" entity type for her business. Each type of entity has advantages and disadvantages from both tax and nontax perspectives, and the best entity for a business depends on the goals, outlook, and strategy for that particular business and its owners. She understands that she has more work to do to make an informed decision.

(to be continued . . .)

This chapter explores various types of legal business entities and then discusses business entities available for tax purposes. We outline some of the pros and cons of each business entity type from both nontax and tax perspectives, as we help Nicole determine how she will organize her business to best accomplish her goals. Subsequent chapters provide additional detail concerning the tax characteristics of each business entity type.

LO 15-1

BUSINESS ENTITY LEGAL CLASSIFICATION AND NONTAX CHARACTERISTICS

When forming new business ventures, entrepreneurs can choose to house their operations under one of several basic business entity types. These business entities differ in terms of their legal and tax considerations. In fact, as we discuss in more depth below, the legal classification of a business may be different from its tax classification. These business entities differ in terms of the formalities that entrepreneurs must follow to create them, the legal rights and responsibilities conferred on the entities and their owners, and the tax rules that determine how the business entities and owners will be taxed on income generated by the entities. CPAs are frequently asked to help clients choose the best entity choice for their businesses.

Legal Classification

Generally, a business entity legally may be classified as a **corporation,** a **limited liability company (LLC),** a **general partnership (GP),** a **limited partnership (LP),** or a **sole proprietorship** (not formed as an LLC).[1] Under state law, corporations are recognized as legal entities separate from their owners (i.e., shareholders). Business owners legally form corporations by filing **articles of incorporation** with the state in which they organize the business. State laws also recognize limited liability companies (LLCs) as legal entities separate from their owners (i.e., members). Business owners create limited liability companies by filing either, depending on the state, a **certificate of organization** or **articles of organization** with the state in which they are organizing the business.

Partnerships are formed under state partnership statutes, and the degree of formality required depends on the type of partnership being formed. General partnerships may be formed by written agreement among the partners, called a **partnership agreement,** or they may be formed informally without a written agreement when two or more owners join together in an activity to generate profits. Although general partners are not required to file partnership agreements with the state, general partnerships are still considered to be legal entities separate from their owners under state laws. Unlike general partnerships, limited partnerships are usually organized by written agreement and typically must file a **certificate of limited partnership** to be recognized by the state.[2]

Finally, for state law purposes, sole proprietorships are *not* treated as legal entities separate from their individual owners, unless they are formed as a single-member LLC. As a result, sole proprietors are not required to formally organize their businesses with the state, and they hold title to business assets in their own names rather than in the name of their businesses.

Nontax Characteristics

Rather than identify and discuss all possible nontax entity characteristics, we compare and contrast several prominent nontax characteristics across the different legal entity types.

[1]Variations of these entities include limited liability partnerships (LLPs), limited liability limited partnerships (LLLPs), professional limited liability companies (PLLCs), and professional corporations (PCs).

[2]Similar to limited partnerships, LLPs, LLLPs, PLLCs, and PCs must register with the state to receive formal recognition.

Responsibility for Liabilities Whether the business entity or the owner(s) is ultimately responsible for paying the liabilities of the business depends on the type of entity. Under state law, the corporation itself, not its shareholders, is responsible for payment of its liabilities.[3] Similarly, LLCs and not their members are responsible for the liabilities of the business.[4] For entities formed as partnerships, all general partners are ultimately responsible for the liabilities of the partnership. In contrast, limited partners are not responsible for the partnership's liabilities.[5] However, limited partners are not allowed to actively participate in the activities of the business.

Finally, if a business is conducted as a sole proprietorship, the individual owner is responsible for the liabilities of the business. However, individual business owners may organize their businesses as single-member LLCs. In exchange for observing the formalities of organizing as an LLC, they receive the liability protection available to LLC members.[6]

Rights, Responsibilities, and Legal Arrangements among Owners State corporation laws specify the rights and responsibilities of corporations and their shareholders. For example, to retain limited liability protection for shareholders, corporations must create, regularly update, and comply with a set of bylaws (i.e., internal rules governing how the corporation is run). They must have a board of directors. They must have regular board meetings and regular (at least annual) shareholder meetings, and they must keep minutes of these meetings. They must also issue shares of stock to owners (i.e., shareholders) and maintain a stock ledger reflecting stock ownership. They must comply with annual filing requirements specified by the state of incorporation, pay required filing fees, and pay required corporate taxes, if any. Consequently, shareholders have no flexibility to alter their legal treatment with respect to one another (rights are determined solely by stock ownership, not by agreements), with respect to the corporation, or with respect to outsiders. In contrast, while state laws provide default provisions specifying rights and responsibilities of LLCs and their members, members have the flexibility to alter their arrangement by spelling out, through an operating agreement, the management practices of the entity and the rights and responsibilities of the members consistent with their wishes. Thus, LLCs allow more flexible business arrangements than do corporations.

Like LLC statutes, state partnership laws provide default provisions specifying the partners' legal rights and responsibilities for dealing with each other absent an agreement to the contrary. Because partners have the flexibility to depart from the default provisions, they frequently craft partnership agreements that are consistent with their preferences.

Although in many instances having the flexibility to customize business arrangements is desirable, sometimes inflexible governance rules mandated by state statute are needed to limit the participation of owners in management when their participation becomes impractical. For example, when businesses decide to "go public" with an **initial public offering (IPO)** on one of the public securities exchanges, they usually solicit a

THE KEY FACTS

Legal Classification and Nontax Characteristics of Business Entities

- State law generally classifies business entities as either corporations, limited liability companies, general partnerships, limited partnerships, or sole proprietorships.
- Corporations and limited liability companies shield all their owners against the entity's liabilities.
- Corporations are less flexible than other business entities but are generally better suited to going public.

[3]Payroll tax liabilities are an important exception to this general rule. Shareholders of closely held corporations may be held responsible for these liabilities.

[4]When closely held corporations and LLCs borrow from banks or other lenders, shareholders or members are commonly asked to personally guarantee the debt. To the extent they do this, they become personally liable to repay the loan in the event the corporation or LLC is unable to repay it.

[5]Limited liability limited partnerships (LLLPs) are limited partnerships in which general and limited partners are protected from the liabilities of the entity. Also, professional service businesses such as accounting firms and law firms are generally not allowed to operate as corporations, LLCs, or limited partnerships. These businesses are frequently organized as limited liability partnerships (LLPs), professional limited liability companies (PLLCs), or professional corporations (PCs). Owners of a PLLC or a PC are protected from liabilities of the entity other than liabilities stemming from their own negligence. LLPs do not provide protection against liabilities stemming from a partner's own negligence or from the LLP's contractual liabilities.

[6]Shareholders of corporations and LLC members are responsible for liabilities stemming from their own negligence.

vast pool of potential investors to become corporate shareholders.[7] State corporation laws prohibit shareholders from directly amending corporate governance rules and from directly participating in management—they have only the right to vote for corporate directors or officers. In comparison, LLC members generally have the right to amend the LLC operating agreement, provide input, and manage LLCs. Obviously, managing a publicly traded business would be next to impossible if thousands of owners had the legal right to change operating rules and directly participate in managing the enterprise.

Exhibit 15-1 summarizes several nontax characteristics of different types of legal business entities.

EXHIBIT 15-1 Business Types: Legal Entities and Nontax Characteristics

Nontax Characteristics	Corporation	LLC	General Partnership	Limited Partnership	Sole Proprietorship
Must formally organize with state	Yes	Yes	No	Yes	No*
Responsibility for liabilities of business	Entity	Entity	General partner(s)	General partner(s)	Owner†
Legal arrangement among owners	Not flexible	Flexible	Flexible	Flexible	Not applicable
Suitable for initial public offering	Yes	No	No	No‡	No

*A sole proprietor must organize with the state if forming a single-member LLC.
†The owner is not responsible for the liabilities of the business if the sole proprietorship is organized as an LLC. However, the owner is responsible for liabilities stemming from personal negligence and for any liabilities the owner personally guarantees.
‡While it is uncommon, certain limited partnerships are eligible for IPOs.

As summarized in Exhibit 15-1, corporations and LLCs have the advantage in liability protection, LLCs and partnerships have an advantage over other entities in terms of legal flexibility, and corporations have the advantage when owners want to take a business public.

(continued from page 15-1 . . .)

As an initial step in the process of selecting the type of legal entity to house Color Comfort Sheets (CCS), Nicole began to research other nontax issues that might be relevant to her decision. Early in her research she realized that the other nontax benefits unique to traditional corporations were relevant primarily to large, publicly traded corporations. Although Nicole was very optimistic about CCS's prospects, she knew it would likely be a long time, if ever, before CCS would go public. However, she remained interested in limiting her own and other potential investors' liability in the new venture, so she began to dig a little deeper. As she perused the State of Utah website, she learned that corporations and LLCs are the only legal business entities that can completely shield investors from liabilities. Although Nicole doesn't anticipate any trouble from her future creditors, she decides to limit her choice of legal entity to either a corporation or LLC.

At this point in her information-gathering process, Nicole is leaning toward the LLC option because she is not sure she wants to deal with board meetings and all the other formalities of operating a corporation; however, she decides to assemble a five-year forecast of CCS's expected operating results and to learn a little more about the way corporations and LLCs are taxed before making a final decision.

(to be continued . . .)

[7]The vast majority of IPOs involve corporate shares; however, limited partnership interests are occasionally sold in IPOs. Like shareholders, limited partners are typically not allowed to participate in management. Limited partnerships are used for public offerings in lieu of corporations when they qualify for favorable partnership tax treatment available to some publicly traded partnerships.

BUSINESS ENTITY TAX CLASSIFICATION

LO 15-2

A business's legal form may be different from its tax form. We discussed the legal form of business entities in the previous section. We now discuss the tax form of business entities. In general terms, for tax purposes, business entities can be classified as either separate taxpaying entities or **flow-through entities.** Separate taxpaying entities pay tax on their own income. In contrast, flow-through entities generally don't pay taxes because income from these entities flows through to their business owners, who are responsible for paying tax on the income.

How do we determine whether a particular business entity is treated as a separate taxpaying entity or as a flow-through entity for tax purposes? According to Treasury Regulations, commonly referred to as the "check-the-box" regulations, entities that are legal corporations under state law are treated as **C corporations** for tax purposes by default. These corporations and their shareholders are subject to tax provisions in Subchapter C (and not Subchapter S) of the Internal Revenue Code.[8] C corporations report their taxable income to the IRS on Form 1120, "U.S. Corporation Income Tax Return." However, shareholders of *legal* corporations may qualify to make a special tax election known as an "S" election, thus permitting the corporation to be taxed as a flow-through entity called an **S corporation.**[9] S corporations and their shareholders are subject to tax provisions in Subchapter S of the Internal Revenue Code. S corporations report the results of their operations to the IRS on Form 1120-S, "U.S. Income Tax Return for an S Corporation."

> **THE KEY FACTS**
>
> **Tax Classification of Legal Entities**
>
> - Incorporated entities (i.e., legal corporations) are C corporations for tax purposes unless they make a valid S election.
> - Unincorporated entities are taxed as partnerships if they have more than one owner.
> - Unincorporated entities are taxed as sole proprietorships if held by a single individual or as disregarded entities if held by a single entity.
> - Unincorporated entities may elect to be treated as C corporations, or they may elect to be taxed as S corporations, if eligible.

Also under the check-the-box regulations, unincorporated entities are, by default, treated as flow-through entities.[10] However, owners of an unincorporated entity can still elect to have their business taxed as a C corporation instead of as the default flow-through entity.[11] In fact, the owner(s) of an unincorporated entity could elect to have the business taxed as a C corporation and then make a second election to have the "C corporation" taxed as an S corporation (provided that it meets the S corporation eligibility requirements).[12] Before making such elections, however, the business owner(s) would need to be convinced that the move makes sense from a tax perspective.[13] Tax entity elections do not change nontax entity choice considerations because tax elections do not affect the legal classification of the entity.

Finally, entities that are not taxed as C or S corporations are treated for tax purposes as either partnerships, sole proprietorships, or **disregarded entities** (considered to be the same entity as the owner).[14] Entities with more than one owner are taxed as partnerships.[15] Partnerships report their operating results to the IRS on Form 1065, "U.S. Return of Partnership Income." Entities with only one *individual* owner such as sole proprietorships and **single-member LLCs** are taxed as sole proprietorships.[16] Income from businesses taxed as sole proprietorships is reported on Schedule C, "Profit or Loss from Business," of Form 1040, "U.S. Individual Income Tax Return." Similarly, unincorporated entities with only one *corporate* owner, typically a single-member LLC, are disregarded for tax purposes. Thus, income and losses from this single, corporate-member LLC are reported as if they had originated from a division of the corporation and are reported directly on the single-member corporation's tax return. Exhibit 15-2 provides a flowchart for determining the tax form of a business entity under the check-the-box regulations. Taxpayers check the box by filing Form 8832, "Entity Classification Election."

[8]Reg. §301.7701-3(a).

[9]§1362(a). Because §1361 limits the number and type of shareholders of corporations qualifying to make an S election, some corporations are ineligible to become S corporations.

[10]Reg. §301.7701-3(b). However, §7704 mandates that unincorporated publicly traded entities be taxed as corporations unless their income predominately consists of certain types of passive income.

[11]Reg. §301.7701-3(a).

[12]In general, a noncorporate entity that is eligible to elect to be treated as a corporation can elect to be treated as a corporation for tax purposes and as an S corporation in one step by filing a timely S corporation election.

[13]As presented in Exhibit 15-3, compared to corporations, unincorporated entities taxed as partnerships have more favorable ownership requirements and more favorable tax treatment on nonliquidating and liquidating distributions of noncash property.

[14]Reg. §301.7701-3(a).

[15]Reg. §301.7701-3(b)(i).

[16]Reg. §301.7701-3(b)(ii).

EXHIBIT 15-2 Determining the Tax Form of a Business Entity Under Check-the-Box Regulations

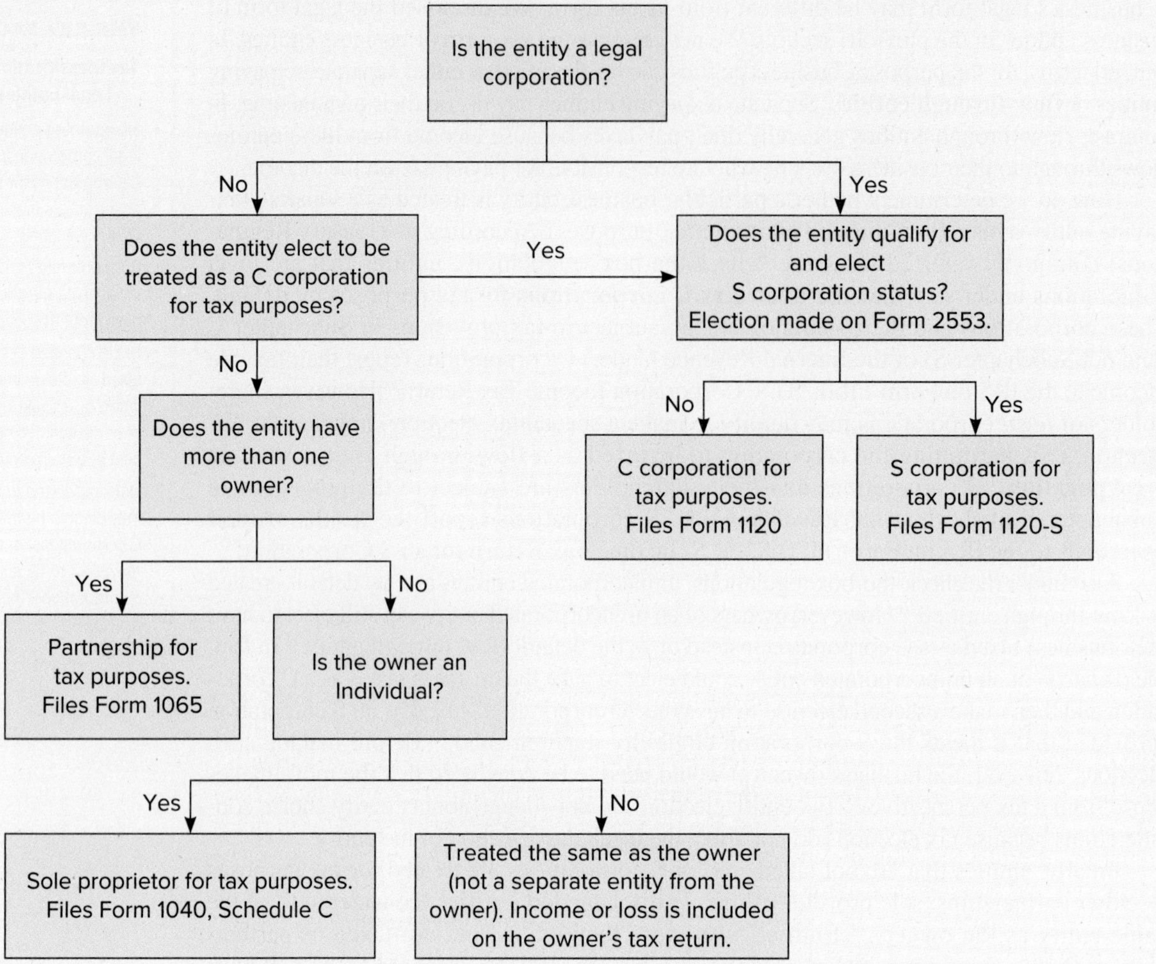

To summarize, although there are other types of legal entities, there are really only four categories of business entities recognized by the U.S. tax system, as follows:

1. C corporation (separate taxpaying entity; income reported on Form 1120).
2. S corporation (flow-through entity; income reported on Form 1120-S).
3. Partnership (flow-through entity; income reported on Form 1065).
4. Sole proprietorship (flow-through entity; income reported on Form 1040, Schedule C).

Example 15-1

What if: Assume Nicole legally forms CCS as a corporation (with only common stock) by filing articles of incorporation with the state. What are her options for classifying CCS for tax purposes if she is the only shareholder of CCS?

Answer: Nicole may treat CCS as either a C corporation or an S corporation. The default classification is a C corporation for tax purposes. However, given the facts provided, CCS is eligible to make an election to be taxed as an S corporation.[17]

[17] §1361(b).

What if: Assume Nicole legally forms CCS as an LLC (with only one class of ownership rights) by filing articles of organization with the state. What are her options for classifying CCS for tax purposes if she is the only member of CCS?

Answer: The default classification for CCS is a sole proprietorship because CCS is unincorporated with one individual member. However, Nicole may elect to have CCS taxed as a C corporation or as an S corporation. CCS can be taxed as a C corporation because unincorporated entities may elect to be taxed as corporations. Further, eligible entities taxed as corporations can elect to be taxed as S corporations. Later in the chapter, we discuss reasons why LLC owners may prefer to be taxed as S corporations.

What if: Assume Nicole legally forms CCS as an LLC and allows other individuals or business entities to become members in return for contributing their cash, property, or services to CCS. What is the default tax classification of CCS under these assumptions?

Answer: Partnership. The default tax classification for unincorporated entities with more than one owner is a partnership.

It might seem at this point that owners of business entities classified as flow-through entities would be treated the same for tax purposes; however, that is true only in a general sense. We see in this and other chapters that there are subtle and not-so-subtle differences in ways the owners of ventures classified as S corporations, partnerships, and sole proprietorships are taxed.[18]

BUSINESS ENTITY TAX CHARACTERISTICS

LO 15-3

In choosing from the available options for the tax form of business entities, owners and their advisers must carefully consider whether tax rules that apply to a particular tax classification would be either more or less favorable than tax rules under alternative tax classifications. The specific tax rules they must compare and contrast are unique to their situations; however, certain key differences in the tax rules tend to be relevant in many scenarios. We turn our attention to the taxation of business entity income, owner compensation, and the tax treatment of entity losses because these are a few of the most important tax characteristics to consider when selecting the tax form of the entity. Later in the chapter we preview other tax factors that differ between entities, and we identify the chapter where each factor is discussed in more detail.

Taxation of Business Entity Income

The taxation of a business entity's income depends on whether the entity is a flow-through entity or a C corporation. The income of a flow-through entity is taxed once to the owner when the income "flows through" or is allocated (on paper) to entity owners at the end of the year, whether or not the income is distributed to them. The income is included on the owners' tax returns as if they had earned the income themselves. The income also increases the owners' basis in their ownership interest in the entity to ensure that the income is not taxed a second time if an owner sells their partnership interest or if the owner receives a distribution from the entity. A distribution from a flow-through entity reduces the owner's basis in their ownership interest and is therefore treated as a nontaxable return of capital rather than a taxable distribution of income. C corporation income, however, is taxed twice. The income is first taxed to the corporation at the corporate tax rate. A C corporation's income is taxed a second time (taxed to the shareholders) when the shareholders sell their stock or the corporation distributes the income as a dividend.[19]

[18]The Business Income, Deductions, and Accounting Methods chapter explains how sole proprietors are taxed, and the Forming and Operating Partnerships and Dispositions of Partnership Interests and Partnership Distributions chapters describe how partners are taxed. Finally, the S Corporations chapter explains how S corporation shareholders are taxed.

[19]Distributions to C corporation shareholders are taxed as dividends to the extent they come from the "earnings and profits" (similar to economic income) of corporations.

Example 15-2

What if: Suppose Nicole formed CCS by contributing $100,000 in cash in exchange for CCS stock. In the first year of operations, CCS reported $10,000 of business income. On the last day of the year, CCS distributed $6,000 to Nicole. How much taxable income will Nicole recognize for the year on these transactions, and what is her stock basis in CCS at year-end assuming she operated CCS as a C corporation compared to operating it as an S corporation (flow-through entity)?

Answer: If CCS is organized as a C corporation, Nicole will recognize $6,000 of dividend income on the distribution and her basis in her CCS stock at year-end will be $100,000 (the amount of her original contribution). If CCS is organized as an S corporation, Nicole will be personally taxed on the $10,000 of business income allocated to her, but she will not be taxed on the $6,000 distribution because the distribution will be treated as a return of capital. Nicole's basis in her S corporation stock at the end of the year will be $104,000 ($100,000 original basis for contribution + $10,000 income allocation – $6,000 distribution). See the following for computations:

Description	C Corporation	S Corporation (flow-through)	Explanation
(1) Original basis in CCS ownership interest (stock)	$ 100,000	$ 100,000	Basis is equal to the cost (cash contributed)
(2) Business income	10,000	10,000	
(3) Income taxed at entity level	10,000	0	C corporation income taxed at corporate level
(4) Flow-through income taxed to Nicole	0	10,000	Nicole is a 100% owner and thus is taxed on 100% of the S corporation income.
(5) Nicole's stock basis at end of year before distribution	100,000	110,000	(1) + (4)
(6) Distribution	6,000	6,000	
(7) **Taxable portion of distribution**	**6,000**	**0**	Distribution from C corporation is a taxable dividend to Nicole. Distribution from S corporation is not taxable because distribution does not exceed basis [i.e., (6) is not greater than (5)].
(8) Nontaxable portion of distribution	0	6,000	(6) – (7)
Nicole's basis in CCS stock at year-end after distribution	**$100,000**	**$104,000**	(5) – (8)

In this example, all $10,000 of business income is taxed at the entity level for the C corporation and $6,000 of the $10,000 is also taxed to Nicole when she receives the dividend distribution. In the C corporation form, the $4,000 that was not taxed twice this year will eventually be taxed to Nicole as a dividend when it is distributed to her or as a capital gain when she sells her stock [the corporation stock has appreciated in value by $4,000 during the year ($104,000 FMV end of year – $100,000 FMV beginning of year)]. If CCS is organized as an S corporation, the $10,000 business income earned by CCS is taxed only once. That is, the income is taxed to Nicole, not CCS, when it is allocated to Nicole. The distribution to Nicole is not taxed because it represents a return of her capital (investment).

The Taxation of Flow-Through Entity Business Income The tax that flow-through entity owners pay on the entity's business income depends in large part on the owner's marginal income tax rate. The top marginal individual tax rate is currently 37 percent. Nevertheless, flow-through entity owners' tax burden on the flow-through income also depends on whether the income is eligible for the deduction for qualified business income, whether it is subject to the net investment income tax, whether it is subject to self-employment tax, and/or whether it is subject to the additional Medicare tax. Below, we discuss the deduction for qualified business income, the net investment income tax, the self-employment tax, the additional Medicare tax, and the overall tax rate on flow-through entity income (assuming the owners are individuals).

Deduction for qualified business income. The deduction for **qualified business income (QBI)** is deductible by individuals but not by business entities.[20] However, the amount of the deduction is based on the amount of QBI allocated to individuals from flow-through entities (i.e., S corporations, partnerships, and sole proprietorships). The QBI deduction is a from AGI deduction (i.e., it does not impact AGI) and is deductible by taxpayers even if they claim the standard deduction instead of itemizing deductions. Qualified business income is generally the net business income from a qualified trade or business conducted in the United States. Subject to a taxable income limit and to a wage-based limitation (the wage-based limitation is discussed after the next example), taxpayers can deduct 20 percent of the amount of QBI allocated to them from the business entity reduced by other deductions attributable to the QBI such as the taxpayer's self-employment tax deduction, self-employed health insurance deduction, and self-employed retirement plan contribution deductions [i.e., the QBI deduction before the wage-based limitation is {(QBI − self-employment tax deduction − self-employed health insurance deduction − self-employment retirement plan contributions) × 20 percent}]. Note that, as discussed below, guaranteed payments are not included in the calculation of the QBI deduction. Thus, the deduction for the self-employment tax on the guaranteed payment does not reduce QBI.[21]

The taxable income limit for the QBI deduction is 20 percent of the taxpayer's taxable income before the QBI deduction that is taxed at ordinary rates (net capital gains and qualified dividends are not included in the QBI tax base because they are taxed at a preferential tax rate). The taxable income limit represents the maximum deduction the taxpayer can claim after applying the specified service requirement and the wage-based limitation (both discussed below) to the QBI deduction.

To qualify as QBI, the business income must be from a business *other than* a **specified service trade or business.** In general, a specified service trade or business includes certain service businesses such as services in the fields of health, law, accounting, actuarial science, performing arts, consulting, athletics, financial services, brokerage services, or any trade or business where the principal asset of such trade or business is the reputation or skill of one or more of its employees or that involves the performance of services that consist of investing and investment management trading or dealing in securities, partnership interests, or commodities.[22] Qualified business income does not include income earned as an employee, guaranteed payments received by a partner (see owner compensation discussion below), or investment-type income such as capital gains, dividends, and investment interest income. In 2022, if the taxpayer's taxable income before the QBI deduction is less than $170,050 ($340,100 if married filing jointly), the specified service requirement does not apply. That is, the taxpayer is allowed to claim the QBI deduction even if the business income is from a specified service trade or business, but employee income, guaranteed payments, and investment income are not eligible for the QBI no matter the taxpayer's income level. However, for taxpayers with taxable income above $170,050 ($340,100 if married filing jointly), the specified service trade or business requirement phases in pro rata (i.e., the deduction phases out) over a $50,000 range ($100,000 if married filing jointly). Thus, the specified service requirement is completely phased in (i.e., the

[20]§199A.

[21]Reg. §1.199A-3(b)(1)(vi). The self-employment tax deduction is allocated between the guaranteed payment (not QBI) and the business income allocation (QBI) based on the relative amounts of these income items included in the taxpayer's gross income.

[22]§199A(d)(2). See Reg. §1.199A-5 for discussion of what constitutes a specified trade or business in each of the fields referenced in §199A(d)(2).

deduction is fully phased out if the business income is from a specified service trade or business) for taxpayers with taxable income before the QBI deduction of at least \$220,050 (\$440,100 if married filing jointly).[23]

Example 15-3

What if: Assume that CCS allocates \$50,000 of business income to Nicole and the business income is from a specified service trade or business. Also, assume that Nicole's deduction for self-employment taxes paid on the business income allocation included in QBI is \$3,532, Nicole is married and files a joint return with her spouse, and the taxable income on their joint tax return is \$600,000 before the QBI deduction (all of the income is taxed at ordinary rates). What is Nicole's QBI deduction before considering the wage-based limitation?

Answer: \$0 QBI deduction. Because the income is from a specified service trade or business and the taxable income on Nicole's joint tax return of \$600,000 is greater than \$440,100, the specified service trade or business requirement is fully phased in. Consequently, the QBI deduction is fully phased out.

What if: Assume that CCS allocates \$50,000 of business income to Nicole and that the business income is from a specified service trade or business. Also, assume that Nicole's deduction for self-employment taxes paid on the business allocation included in QBI is \$3,532, Nicole is married and files a joint tax return with her spouse, and the taxable income on their joint tax return is \$300,000 before the QBI deduction (all of the taxable income is taxed at ordinary rates). What is Nicole's QBI deduction before considering the wage-based limitation but after considering the taxable income limitation?

Answer: \$9,294 QBI deduction, computed as follows:

Description	Amount	Explanation
(1) Qualified business income	\$ 50,000	Not from a specified service
(2) Self-employment tax deduction	3,532	Based on self-employment taxes paid on self-employment income included in QBI
(3) Base for QBI deduction	\$ 46,468	(1) − (2)
(4) QBI deduction rate	20%	
(5) QBI deduction before specified service requirement	9,294	(3) × (4)
(6) Deduction phase-out due to specified service requirement	0	Taxable income before QBI deduction is less than \$340,100
(7) QBI deduction before the taxable income limitation	\$ 9,294	(5) − (6)
(8) Taxable income limitation	\$300,000	Taxable income (before QBI deduction) taxed at ordinary rates
QBI deduction	**\$ 9,294**	Lesser of (7) or (8)

What if: Assume that CCS allocates \$50,000 of business income to Nicole and that the business income is from a specified service trade or business. Also, assume that Nicole's deduction for self-employment taxes paid on the business allocation included in QBI is \$3,532, Nicole is married and files a joint return with her spouse, and the taxable income on their joint tax return is \$400,000 before the QBI deduction. All of the taxable income is taxed at ordinary rates except for \$15,000 of qualified dividends. What is Nicole's QBI deduction before considering the wage-based limitation but after considering the taxable income limitation?

[23]The phase-out thresholds for both the specified service trade or business requirement and the wage-based limitation are indexed for inflation.

Answer: $3,727 QBI deduction, computed as follows:

Description	Amount	Explanation
(1) Qualified business income	$ 50,000	Not from a specified service
(2) Self-employment tax deduction	3,532	Based on self-employment taxes paid on self-employment income included in QBI
(3) Base for QBI deduction	$ 46,468	(1) − (2)
(4) QBI deduction rate	20%	
(5) QBI deduction before specified service requirement	$ 9,294	(3) × (4)
(6) Taxable income before QBI deduction	400,000	
(7) Taxable income threshold for specified service T or B requirement phase-in	340,100	
(8) Taxable income over threshold	$ 59,900	(6) − (7)
(9) Percentage through specified service T or B requirement phase-in (deduction phase-out) range for MFJ tax return	59.9%	(8)/100,000
(10) Deduction phase-out due to specified service requirement	5,567	(5) × (9)
(11) QBI deduction before the taxable income limit	$ 3,727	(5) − (10)
(12) Taxable income limitation	$385,000	Taxable income (before QBI deduction) taxed at ordinary rates ($400,000 − $15,000)
QBI deduction	**$ 3,727**	Lesser of (11) or (12)

Under the wage-based limitation, the QBI deduction cannot exceed the greater of (1) 50 percent of the wages paid with respect to the qualified trade or business or (2) the sum of 25 percent of the wages with respect to the qualified trade or business plus 2.5 percent of the unadjusted basis of all qualified property used in the qualified trade or business immediately after the acquisition.[24] For purposes of the wage-based limitation, each partner or S corporation shareholder is treated as having paid wages for the year equal to their allocable share from the partnership or S corporation. The wage-based limitation only applies to taxpayers with taxable income in 2022 in excess of $170,050 ($340,100 if married filing jointly). The wage-based limitation phases in pro rata (i.e., the amount that would be deductible without the limit phases out) over a $50,000 range ($100,000 if married filing jointly). Thus, the wage-based limitation is completely phased in for taxpayers with taxable income before the QBI deduction of at least $220,050 ($440,100 if married filing jointly).

Example 15-4

What if: Assume that CCS allocates $50,000 of business income to Nicole, the business income is *not* from a specified service trade or business, and CCS allocated $15,000 of wages to Nicole for purposes of determining the wage-based limitation (assume there is no qualified property). Also, assume that Nicole's deduction for self-employment taxes paid on the business allocation included in

(continued on page 15-12)

[24]Qualified property is generally tangible, depreciable property used in a qualified trade or business during the year.

QBI is $3,532, Nicole is married and files a joint return with her spouse, and the taxable income on their joint tax return is $600,000 before the QBI deduction (all taxable income is taxed at ordinary rates). What is Nicole's QBI deduction?

Answer: $7,500 QBI deduction, computed as follows:

Description	Amount	Explanation
(1) Qualified business income	$ 50,000	Not from a specified service
(2) Self-employment tax deduction	3,532	Based on self-employment taxes paid on self-employment income included in QBI
(3) Base for QBI deduction	$ 46,468	(1) − (2)
(4) QBI deduction rate	20%	
(5) QBI deduction before wage limit	$ 9,294	(3) × (4)
(6) 50% of wages paid allocated to Nicole	7,500	$15,000 wages allocated to Nicole × 50%
(7) QBI deduction before taxable income limit	7,500	Lesser of (5) or (6)
(8) Taxable income limit	$600,000	
QBI deduction	**$ 7,500**	Lesser of (7) or (8)

Because Nicole's taxable income before the QBI deduction of $600,000 exceeds $440,100, the wage-based limitation is fully phased in (the limit applies in full), so Nicole's QBI deduction is limited to $7,500, which is 50% of the wages she is allocated from CCS.

What if: Assume the original facts except that the business income allocated to Nicole was from a specified service trade or business. What would be Nicole's QBI deduction?

Answer: $0 QBI deduction. The income is from a specified service trade or business and Nicole's taxable income on her joint tax return before the QBI deduction is greater than $440,100. Consequently, the specified service requirement is fully phased in and the deduction is fully phased out before considering the wage-based limitation.

What if: Assume the original facts (business income is not from a specified service trade or business) except Nicole's taxable income on her joint tax return is $300,000 before the QBI deduction and all the income is taxed at ordinary rates.

Answer: $9,294 QBI deduction. Because Nicole's joint taxable income before the QBI deduction is below $340,100, the wage-based limitation does not apply and Nicole would be able to claim a $9,294 QBI deduction.

What if: Assume the same facts as the prior what-if scenario except that $292,000 of the $300,000 of taxable income is qualified dividends and long-term capital gains taxed at the preferential 15% tax rate. That is, only $8,000 of the $300,000 is taxed at ordinary rates. What would be Nicole's QBI deduction?.

Answer: $8,000 QBI deduction. Without imposing the taxable income limitation, the QBI deduction would be $9,294. However, the taxable income limitation is $8,000 because that was the amount of taxable income before the QBI deduction taxed at ordinary rates. Consequently, the taxable income limitation restricts the QBI deduction to $8,000 in this scenario.

What if: Assume the original facts (business income is not from a specified service trade or business) except that Nicole's taxable income is $410,000 before the QBI deduction (all income taxed at ordinary rates). What would be Nicole's QBI deduction?

Answer: $8,040 QBI deduction, computed as follows:

Description	Amount	Explanation
(1) Qualified business income	$ 50,000	Not from a specified service
(2) Self-employment tax deduction	3,532	Based on self-employment taxes paid on self-employment income included in QBI
(3) Base for QBI deduction	$ 46,468	(1) – (2)
(4) QBI deduction rate	20%	
(5) QBI deduction before wage-based limit	$ 9,294	(3) × (4)
(6) Full wage-based limitation	7,500	
(7) Deduction disallowed if wage-based limit applies in full	$ 1,794	(5) – (6) (limited to $0)
(8) Taxable income before QBI deduction	410,000	
(9) Taxable income threshold for phase-in of wage-based limitation (phase-out of deduction)	340,100	
(10) Taxable income over threshold	$ 69,900	(8) – (9)
(11) Percentage through wage-based limitation phase-in (deduction phase-out)	69.9%	(10)/$100,000
(12) Deduction disallowed after partial phase-in of wage-based limitation	1,254	(7) × (11)
(13) QBI deduction before taxable income limit	$ 8,040	(5) – (12)
(14) Taxable income limit	$410,000	
QBI deduction	**$ 8,040**	Lesser of (13) or (14)

When the business income is from a specified service trade or business, both the specified service trade or business limitation and the wage-based limitation are phased in based on taxable income before the QBI. The QBI deduction computation can become complex when both limits are partially phased in. Describing the process of partial phase-in of both limitations simultaneously is beyond the scope of this text.

Net investment income tax. When an owner of a business entity taxed as a partnership or a shareholder of an S corporation does not work for the entity (that is, the owner is a passive owner or investor in the entity), the business income allocated to the taxpayer is considered to be "passive" income.[25] Because passive income is considered to be investment income for purposes of the net investment income tax, passive owners of flow-through entities may be required to pay net investment income tax on income allocated to them from the business (minus related investment expenses). Note that traditional types of investment income such as dividends, capital gains and interest income are also included in the net investment income tax base. The net investment income tax rate is 3.8 percent of the lesser of (1) net investment income (gross investment income minus investment expenses) or (2) AGI in excess of a threshold amount. The threshold amount is $250,000 for married taxpayers filing jointly and surviving spouses, $125,000 for married taxpayers filing separately, and $200,000 for all other taxpayers.[26]

[25]§469. We discuss specific tests for determining when an owner is a passive investor in the Forming and Operating Partnerships chapter.

[26]§1411. The thresholds are not indexed for inflation.

Self-employment tax. Business owners who receive and/or are allocated self-employment income from their businesses are subject to self-employment tax on the income. Whether a flow-through entity's business income allocated to an owner is considered to be self-employment income to the owner depends on the type of entity and the owner's involvement in the entity's business activities. An S corporation's business income allocated to a shareholder is not self-employment income to the shareholder. In contrast, a sole proprietorship's income is self-employment income to the sole proprietor. For owners of entities taxed as partnerships, the determination of whether business income allocations are subject to self-employment tax isn't as clear as it is for S corporations and sole proprietorships. For entities taxed as partnerships, whether business income is self-employment income to an owner depends on the owner's involvement in the entity's business activities.[27]

The tax base for the self-employment tax is **net earnings from self-employment.** Net earnings from self-employment is 92.35 percent of the taxpayer's self-employment income (from all sources).[28] For example, if a taxpayer reported net income of $100,000 as a sole proprietor on Schedule C, was allocated $50,000 of business income from a partnership in which the taxpayer was actively involved in the business (assume no guaranteed payment—we discuss guaranteed payments later in the chapter), and was allocated $10,000 of business income from an S corporation in which the taxpayer was actively involved in the business, the taxpayer's self-employment income would be $150,000 [$100,000 sole proprietor income + $50,000 business income from partnership (business income from S corporation is not self-employment income)]. The taxpayer's tax base for the self-employment tax would be $138,525 ($150,000 × .9235). For 2022, the first $147,000 of net earnings from self-employment is taxed at 15.3 percent, and net earnings from self-employment above $147,000 is taxed at 2.9 percent.[29] The $147,000 is called the **social security wage base limitation** (adjusted annually based on the national average wage index). The $147,000 limitation is reduced by the amount of employee compensation received during the year (i.e., wages or salary) when computing the self-employment tax. Taxpayers can deduct 50 percent of the self-employment tax paid as a for AGI deduction (i.e., deducted when computing AGI). Consequently, a taxpayer who paid $20,000 of self-employment tax would deduct $10,000 of the tax for AGI ($20,000 × .50). Finally, it is important to note that the self-employment tax is computed separately for each spouse even if a married couple files a joint return (i.e., the self-employment tax is an individual computation rather than a joint computation).

Example 15-5

What if: Assume that Nicole chooses to form CCS as an S corporation. In 2022, assume that Nicole is allocated $30,000 of business income from CCS and $20,000 of business income from a partnership in which Nicole is actively involved in the business. What are Nicole's self-employment tax liability and self-employment tax deduction for the year?

[27]We discuss more details of determining whether business income allocated to partners is self-employment income in the Forming and Operating Partnerships chapter.

[28]§1402. Taxing 92.35 percent of self-employment income for self-employment tax and additional Medicare tax purposes provides the taxpayer with a built-in 7.65 percent deduction for the employer's portion of the 15.3 percent self-employment tax.

[29]The 15.3 percent rate consists of a 12.4 percent Social Security portion (6.2 percent of the 12.4 percent is the employer portion of the self-employment tax and the other 6.2 percent is the employee portion) and a 2.9 percent Medicare portion (1.45 percent of the 2.9 percent is the employer portion and the other 1.45 percent is the employee portion). There is no limit on the 2.9 percent Medicare portion of the self-employment tax.

Answer: $2,826 self-employment tax liability and $1,413 self-employment tax deduction, computed as follows:

Description	Amount	Explanation
(1) Self-employment income	$20,000	$20,000 allocation from partnership is self-employment income, but $30,000 allocation from the S corporation is not.
(2) Net earnings from self-employment (SE tax base)	18,470	(1) × 92.35%
(3) Self-employment tax rate	15.3%	Rate is 15.3% on first $147,000 of net earnings from self-employment and 2.9% on the amount over $147,000.
(4) Self-employment tax liability	**$ 2,826**	**(2) × (3)**
Self-employment tax deduction	**$ 1,413**	(4) × 50 percent

What if: Assume the original facts except that the income allocation from the partnership is $200,000. What would be Nicole's self-employment tax liability and self-employment tax deduction?

Answer: $23,584 self-employment tax liability and $11,792 self-employment tax deduction, computed as follows:

Description	Amount	Explanation
(1) Self-employment income	$200,000	$200,000 allocation from partnership is self-employment income, but $30,000 allocation from S corporation is not.
(2) Net earnings from self-employment (SE tax base)	184,700	(1) × 92.35 percent
(3) Self-employment tax rate up to $147,000	15.3%	Rate on first $147,000 of net earnings from self-employment
(4) Self-employment tax rate on net earnings from self-employment above $147,000	2.9%	Rate on net earnings from self-employment above $147,000
(5) Self-employment tax liability	**$ 23,584**	(3) × $147,000 + (4) × [(2) – $147,000] (i.e., $22,491 + $1,093)
Self-employment tax deduction	**$ 11,792**	(5) × 50 percent

What if: Assume the same facts as in the previous what-if except that Nicole also received $170,000 in salary compensation from an employer (not CCS). What would be Nicole's self-employment tax liability and self-employment tax deduction?

Answer: $5,356 self-employment tax liability ($184,700 × 2.9%) and $2,678 self-employment tax deduction ($5,356 × 50%). Because Nicole's salary exceeds the $147,000 social security wage base limitation for 2022, the remaining wage base limit is reduced to zero for purposes of determining her self-employment tax, and the entire amount of earnings from self-employment is taxed at 2.9%.

Additional Medicare tax. In addition to the self-employment tax, business owners who receive or are allocated self-employment income from their businesses potentially must pay additional Medicare tax on the income. The tax rate for the additional Medicare tax is .9 percent and the tax base is the sum of the taxpayer's (and spouse's, if married filing jointly) net earnings from self-employment (from all sources) and compensation earned as an employee minus a threshold amount. The threshold amount is $250,000 for married taxpayers filing jointly and surviving spouses, $125,000 for married taxpayers filing separately, and $200,000 for all other taxpayers. Thus, for example, a single taxpayer who was allocated $240,000 of self-employment income (assuming no other self-employment income and no employee compensation) would have $221,640 of net earnings from self-employment ($240,000 × .9235) and would owe $195 of additional Medicare tax [($221,640 – $200,000) × .009].[30]

The additional Medicare tax is computed jointly for married couples filing a joint return. Thus, net earnings from self-employment from both spouses (and compensation earned as employees, if any) is combined to determine the excess of net earnings from self-employment over the $250,000 threshold amount for married taxpayers filing a joint tax return. Taxpayers are not allowed to deduct any of the additional Medicare tax they pay.

Example 15-6

What if: Assume that Nicole chooses to form CCS as an S corporation. She makes the following assumptions:

- CCS's taxable income is $500,000, and all of the income is business income.
- Nicole's marginal ordinary tax rate is 37 percent (this assumes she has other sources of income).
- Nicole is eligible for the full deduction for qualified business income on the flow-through income from CCS (i.e., no limitations apply).
- The income is not passive income and is therefore not subject to the net investment income tax.
- Because CCS is an S corporation, the flow-through business income from CCS is not self-employment income to Nicole.

What is the overall tax rate on CCS's business income?

Answer: 29.6 percent, computed as follows:

Description	Amount	Explanation
(1) Business income allocated to Nicole	$500,000	
(2) Deduction for qualified business income	(100,000)	(1) × 20 percent
(3) Net taxable income to Nicole from CCS	$400,000	(1) + (2)
(4) Owner's marginal income tax rate	37%	
(5) Owner-level income tax	$148,000	(3) × (4)
Overall tax rate on business income allocation	**29.6%**	(5)/(1)

What if: Assume the original facts except that the income from CCS is not eligible for the deduction for qualified business income. What is the overall tax rate on CCS's business income?

Answer: 37 percent. The entire $500,000 business income is taxed to Nicole at her marginal ordinary tax rate of 37 percent.

What if: Assume the original facts except the income from CCS is not eligible for the deduction for qualified business income and Nicole is a passive investor in CCS and must pay the 3.8 percent net investment income tax on the income. What is the overall tax rate on the income of CCS?

Answer: 40.8 percent. The full $500,000 of business income is taxed to Nicole at her marginal ordinary tax rate of 37 percent plus the net investment income tax rate of 3.8 percent.

[30]The threshold amounts are not indexed for inflation.

Example 15-7

What if: Assume that Nicole forms CCS as an LLC with another investor (as equal owners) so that CCS is taxed as a partnership. Nicole makes the following assumptions:

- CCS earns business income of $1,000,000, and Nicole's share of the business income is $500,000 (i.e., Nicole is allocated 50 percent of the CCS business income).
- Nicole's marginal ordinary tax rate is 37 percent.
- Nicole is entitled to the deduction for qualified business income on the flow-through income from CCS (minus her self-employment tax deduction) without limitation.
- Because Nicole works full time for the entity, the business income allocated to her is self-employment income.
- The CCS business income is Nicole's only source of self-employment income.
- Nicole's spouse received $300,000 of salary for the year.
- Nicole's entire net earnings from self-employment from the income allocation is subject to the .9 percent additional Medicare tax (i.e., Nicole's spouse's salary is over the $250,000 threshold amount, so the entire amount of Nicole's net earnings from self-employment is subject to the additional Medicare tax).

What is the overall tax rate on the CCS business income allocated to Nicole?

Answer: 35.82 percent, computed as follows:

Description	Amount	Explanation
(1) Business income allocated to Nicole	$500,000	$1,000,000 × .5
(2) Net earnings from self-employment	461,750	(1) × .9235
(3) Deduction for 50 percent of self-employment tax (for AGI deduction)	(15,809)	(7) × .5
(4) Deduction for qualified business income (from AGI deduction)	(96,838)	[(1) + (3)] × 20%
(5) Income net of Nicole's deductions	$387,353	(1) + (3) + (4)
(6) Owner-level income tax	143,321	(5) × 37%
(7) Self-employment tax	31,619	$147,000 × .153 + [(2) – $147,000] × .029
(8) Additional Medicare tax	4,156	(2) × .009 [Nicole's spouse's employee compensation income exceeds $250,000 threshold amount before considering (2)]
(9) Total tax paid on CCS business income allocations	$179,096	(6) + (7) + (8)
Overall tax rate on business income allocation	**35.82%**	(9)/(1)

What if: Assume the original facts except that the business income allocation is not qualified business income (QBI). That is, assume Nicole does not claim the QBI deduction. What is the overall tax rate on the CCS business income allocated to Nicole?

Answer: 42.99 percent. The only difference between the original and new facts in this what-if example is that Nicole would pay an additional $35,830 in income tax ($96,838 QBI deduction × 37 percent tax rate). Consequently, the overall taxes due on the business income allocation would be $214,926 ($179,096 + $35,830), and the overall tax rate would be 42.99 percent ($214,926/$500,000).

What if: Assume the original facts except Nicole's marginal self-employment tax rate is 2.9 percent because she has other sources of self-employment income that put her net earnings from self-employment over the $147,000 cutoff for the 15.3 percent rate.

What is the overall tax rate on the CCS business income allocated to Nicole?

(continued on page 15-18)

Answer: 32.71 percent, computed as follows:

Description	Amount	Explanation
(1) Business income allocated to Nicole	$500,000	$1,000,000 × .5
(2) Net earnings from self-employment	461,750	(1) × .9235
(3) Deduction for 50 percent of self-employment tax (for AGI deduction)	(6,695)	(7) × .5
(4) Deduction for qualified business income (from AGI deduction)	(98,661)	[(1) + (3)] × 20 percent
(5) Income net of Nicole's deductions	$394,644	(1) + (3) + (4)
(6) Owner-level income tax	146,018	(5) × 37%
(7) Self-employment tax	13,391	(2) × .029
(8) Additional Medicare tax	4,156	(2) × .009
(9) Total tax paid on CCS business income allocations	$163,565	(6) + (7) + (8)
Overall tax rate on business income allocation	**32.71%**	(9)/(1)

What if: Assume the original facts except the income from CCS is not eligible for the QBI deduction and Nicole is a passive investor in CCS. Consequently, she must pay the net investment income tax on the entire income allocation, but she is not required to pay the self-employment tax or the additional Medicare tax on the income allocation. What is the overall tax rate on the CCS business income allocated to Nicole?

Answer: 40.8 percent. The entire $500,000 business income allocation is taxed to Nicole at her marginal ordinary tax rate of 37 percent plus the net investment income tax rate of 3.8 percent.

In summary, while income from a flow-through entity is taxed only once, the overall tax rate on the entity's business income depends on whether the income (and thus the owner) qualifies for the QBI deduction and whether the income is subject to the net investment tax or is considered to be self-employment income.

Overall Tax Rate of C Corporation Income C corporations are taxed on their taxable income at a flat 21 percent rate. The tax rate on the second level of tax on a C corporation's income depends on whether the shareholder is an individual (or S corporation because S corporation income flows through to shareholders who are individuals), a C corporation, an **institutional shareholder,** a tax-exempt entity, or a foreign entity. Determining the overall tax rate on a tax entity's income is an important factor when making the tax entity choice for a business.

Individual shareholders. The tax rate on dividends to individual taxpayers depends on the individual's taxable income. High-income taxpayers are taxed on dividends at a 20 percent rate, low-income taxpayers are taxed at a 0 percent rate, and others are taxed on dividends at a 15 percent rate.[31] Also, as discussed above, taxpayers with (modified) AGI in excess of a threshold amount pay an additional 3.8 percent net investment income tax on dividends.

[31]To the extent the dividend income increases a taxpayer's taxable income beyond specific "breakpoints," the dividend is taxed at a higher rate. For 2022, the breakpoint between the 0 and 15 percent rates is $83,350 for married taxpayers filing jointly, $55,800 for head of household filers, and $41,675 for all other taxpayers. The breakpoint between the 15 percent and 20 percent rates is $517,200 for married taxpayers filing jointly, $258,600 for married taxpayers filing separately, $459,750 for single taxpayers, and $488,500 for head of household filers.

Example 15-8

What if: Assume that Nicole operates CCS as a C corporation and she makes the following assumptions:

- CCS earns taxable income of $500,000.
- CSS will distribute all of its after-tax earnings annually as a dividend.
- Nicole's marginal ordinary tax rate is 37 percent and her dividend tax rate is 23.8 percent (20% income tax on the dividend plus an additional 3.8% of net investment tax on the dividend).

What is the overall tax rate on CCS's taxable income?

Answer: 39.8 percent, computed as follows:

Description	Amount	Explanation
(1) Taxable income	$500,000	
(2) Corporate tax rate	21%	Flat corporate tax rate
(3) Corporate-level tax	$105,000	(1) × (2) [first level of tax]
(4) Income remaining after taxes and amount distributed as a dividend	$395,000	(1) − (3)
(5) Dividend tax rate	23.8%	20% dividend rate + 3.8% net investment income tax rate
(6) Shareholder-level tax on dividend	$ 94,010	(4) × (5) [second level of tax]
(7) Total tax paid on corporate taxable income	$199,010	(3) + (6)
Overall tax rate on corporate taxable income	**39.8%**	(7)/(1)

Note that the overall rate is not 44.8 percent (21 percent corporate rate + 23.8 percent shareholder rate) because the amount of corporate-level tax (i.e., $105,000) is income that is not taxed twice (it is paid to the government, not to the shareholders).

What if: Assume that Nicole operates CCS as a C corporation and she makes the following assumptions:

- CCS earns taxable income of $500,000.
- CCS distributes 25 percent of its after-tax earnings as a dividend and retains the rest to grow the business.
- Nicole's marginal ordinary tax rate is 37 percent and her dividend tax rate is 23.8 percent (including both income and net investment income tax.

What is the overall tax rate on CCS's taxable income?

Answer: 25.7 percent, computed as follows:

Description	Amount	Explanation
(1) Taxable income	$500,000	
(2) Corporate tax rate	21%	Flat corporate tax rate
(3) Corporate-level tax	$105,000	(1) × (2) [first level of tax]
(4) Income remaining after taxes	$395,000	(1) − (3)
(5) Dividend	$ 98,750	(4) × 25% distributed
(6) Tax rate on dividend	23.8%	20% dividend rate + 3.8% net investment income tax rate
(7) Shareholder-level tax on dividend	$ 23,503	(5) × (6) [second level of tax]
(8) Total tax paid on corporate taxable income	$128,503	(3) + (7)
Overall tax rate on corporate taxable income	**25.7%**	(8)/(1)

The overall tax rate is lower in this situation because CCS retains most of its after-tax income and thus protects that portion of its income from immediate double taxation. If CCS retained all of its after-tax earnings, the current overall tax rate on its income would have been 21 percent (the corporate tax rate). Also, note that while the overall tax rate is lower when CCS distributes less of its income, Nicole also receives less cash from the business.

Shareholders that are C corporations. Shareholders that are C corporations are taxed on dividends at 21 percent, the same rate as they are taxed on other income. In addition, dividends received by a corporation are potentially subject to another (third) level of tax when the corporation receiving the dividend distributes its earnings as dividends to its shareholders. This potential for more than two levels of tax on the same before-tax earnings prompted Congress to allow corporations to claim the **dividends-received deduction (DRD).** In the next chapter, we discuss the DRD in detail, but the underlying concept is that a corporation *receiving* a dividend is allowed to deduct a certain percentage of the dividend from its taxable income to offset the potential for additional layers of taxation on the dividend when it distributes the dividend to its shareholders. The dividends-received deduction percentage is 50, 65, or 100 percent of the dividend received, depending on the level of the recipient corporation's ownership in the dividend-paying corporation's stock. The DRD is 50 percent if the shareholder corporation owns less than 20 percent of the distributing corporation; 65 percent if it owns at least 20 percent but less than 80 percent of the distributing corporation; and 100 percent if the shareholder corporation owns at least 80 percent of the distributing corporation. Thus, a corporation's net tax rate on a dividend received is 10.5 percent if it claims a 50 percent DRD [.21 tax rate × (1 − .5 DRD)], 7.35 percent if it claims a 65 percent DRD [.21 tax rate × (1 − .65 DRD)], and 0 percent if it claims a 100 percent DRD [.21 × (1 − 1.0 DRD)].

Example 15-9

What if: Assume that Nicole invites a C corporation to invest in CCS in exchange for a 10 percent share in the company. Nicole makes the following assumptions as part of her calculations:

- CCS is a C corporation.
- CCS earns taxable income of $500,000.
- CCS will pay out all of its after-tax earnings annually as a dividend.

Given these assumptions, what would be the overall tax rate on a C corporate investor's share of CCS's income given that the shareholder corporation would be eligible for the 50 percent dividends-received deduction?

Answer: 29.3 percent, computed as follows:

Description	Amount	Explanation
(1) Taxable income	$500,000	
(2) Corporate tax rate	21%	Flat corporate tax rate
(3) Entity-level tax	$105,000	(1) × (2) [first level of tax]
(4) After-tax income	$395,000	(1) − (3)
(5) Corporate investor's dividend	$ 39,500	(4) × 10%
(6) Dividend income net of DRD	$ 19,750	(5) × (1 − 50% DRD)
(7) Corporate investor's share of entity-level tax	$ 10,500	(3) × 10% investor's share
(8) Corporate investor's tax on dividend net of DRD	$ 4,148	(6) × 21% corporate tax rate
(9) Total tax paid on corporate taxable income	$ 14,648	(7) + (8)
Overall tax rate on corporate taxable income	**29.3%**	(9)/[(1) × 10% investor's share]

Note: The income of the corporate shareholder will be taxed again when the corporate shareholder distributes it to its own shareholders.

Institutional shareholders. Pension and retirement funds are some of the largest institutional shareholders of corporations. However, these entities do not pay shareholder-level tax on the dividends they receive. Ultimately, retirees pay the second tax on this income when they receive retirement distributions from these funds. While retirees pay the second tax at ordinary rates, not reduced dividend rates, they are able to defer the tax until they receive distributions.

Tax-exempt organizations. Tax-exempt organizations such as charitable organizations, churches, universities, and political organizations are exempt from tax on their investment income, including dividend income from investments in corporate stock. In general, tax-exempt organizations are required to annually file Form 990, "Return of Organization Exempt from Income Tax."[32] While tax-exempt organizations don't pay tax on their investment income, they may be required to pay tax on unrelated business income (UBI) they generate. The tax is called the unrelated business income tax (UBIT). **Unrelated business income** is income from a trade or business, regularly carried on, that is not substantially related to the charitable, educational, or other purpose that is the basis of the organization's exemption. The tax rate is equal to the C corporation tax rate (21 percent). The UBIT is imposed so that tax-exempt organizations don't have an unfair tax advantage compared to taxable businesses when the taxable and tax-exempt entities are both involved in business activities. If an organization has $1,000 or more of gross income for the year from unrelated business activities, the organization must file Form 990-T, "Exempt Organization Business Income Tax Return" (generally due the 15th day of the 5th month after the end of its tax year). Further, tax-exempt organizations must pay estimated tax if they expect their tax for the year to be $500 or more.[33]

Foreign shareholders. Foreign investors may be eligible for reduced rates on dividend income depending on the tax treaty, if any, their country of residence has signed with the United States.

Double tax on C corporation income. As we discuss and illustrate above, C corporation income is subject to **double taxation.** The first tax is paid by the corporation when it earns the income, and the second tax is paid by the shareholders when the earnings are distributed to shareholders as dividends. Can C corporations avoid the second level of tax entirely by not paying dividends? The answer is generally no. Even when corporations retain after-tax income, their shareholders pay the second level of tax at capital gains rates on the undistributed income when they sell their stock because the undistributed income indirectly increases the value of their stock and thus increases shareholders' gains when they sell the stock. Assuming the shareholder is an individual and the shareholder owns stock in a corporation for more than a year, the gain is taxed at the same rates as the tax rates on qualified dividends discussed above (0, 15, or 20 percent plus 3.8 percent net investment income tax for higher-income taxpayers). Because this second level of tax is deferred until taxpayers sell their stock, the longer they hold the stock, the less the tax cost is on a present value basis. In the extreme, taxpayers can avoid the second level of income tax completely on their stock appreciation by holding the stock until death. At death, gain built into the stock is eliminated because the stock takes basis equal to the value of the stock on the date of death.[34]

[32]See www.irs.gov/charities-non-profits/annual-exempt-organization-return-who-must-file for exceptions as to which tax-exempt entities are required to file Form 990.

[33]A detailed discussion of tax-exempt organizations is beyond the scope of this text. See www.irs.gov/charities-non-profits/exempt-organization-types and related links for more details.

[34]§1014. High net worth taxpayers may be required to pay estate tax on the value of the stock at death.

Shareholders other than individuals face different tax consequences when they sell their shares. When shareholders that are C corporations eventually sell the stock, they are taxed on capital gains at the corporate rate of 21 percent. Consequently, income from stock appreciation may expose income to *more* than two levels of taxation because capital gains from selling stock do not qualify for the dividends-received deduction. Also, institutional shareholders don't pay tax when they sell their stock and recognize capital gains. However, retirees generally pay tax on the gains at ordinary rates when they receive distributions from their retirement accounts. Also, tax-exempt shareholders do not pay tax on capital gains from selling stock, and foreign investors are generally not subject to U.S. tax on their capital gains from selling corporate stock.

Finally, the tax law provides incentives for C corporations to distribute income rather than to retain it for the purpose of avoiding the second level of tax. First, **personal holding companies** (closely held corporations generating primarily investment income) are subject to a 20 percent **personal holding company tax** on their undistributed income.[35] Second, corporations that retain earnings for the purpose of avoiding the second level of tax are subject to a 20 percent **accumulated earnings tax** on the retained earnings.[36] Corporations are not considered to be retaining earnings for tax avoidance purposes and are not subject to the accumulated earnings tax to the extent they (1) reinvest the earnings in assets necessary for their business or (2) retain liquid assets for reasonable planned needs of the business.

Under the tax rate system prior to 2018, flow-through entities were generally considered to be superior to corporations for tax purposes because they generated income that was taxed only once, while corporations produced income that was taxed twice, with the first level of tax imposed at a rate comparable to the individual tax rate. However, for years after 2017, the corporate tax rate is significantly lower than the maximum individual tax rate. Further, as described above, tax law effective beginning in 2018 provides a deduction for qualified business income (QBI) for individuals who are owners of flow-through entities. This tax legislation makes the optimal choice of entity based on overall tax rates of the entity's business income less clear than it was under prior law. It is important to note, however, that the corporate tax rate reduction is a permanent change, while the QBI deduction is scheduled to expire in 2026.[37] The overall tax rate on a flow-through entity's business income depends on whether the flow-through entity's business income is eligible for the QBI deduction and whether the income is subject to the net investment income tax or the self-employment tax and the additional Medicare tax. For C corporations, the overall tax rate depends in large part on the extent to which the corporation distributes its after-tax earnings as a dividend to its shareholders. As we saw in Example 15-6, the overall tax rate on CCS's taxable income as a flow-through entity (S corporation) ranged from 29.6 percent to 40.8 percent, depending on whether the QBI deduction and the net investment income tax applied. In Example 15-8, the overall tax rate on CCS's taxable income as a C corporation ranged from 21 percent, when CCS retained all of its after-tax income, to 39.8 percent, when it distributed all of its after-tax income.

Owner Compensation Entity owners who work for the entity are compensated in different ways, depending on the entity type. Owners of S corporations and C corporations receive compensation as employees. Owners of entities taxed as partnerships receive compensation in the form of guaranteed payments. Sole proprietors don't receive separate compensation payments because a sole proprietorship is the same taxable entity as the individual sole proprietor (this is true even when the proprietorship is organized as a single-member LLC).

S corporations and C corporations deduct the wages paid to employees (including shareholders who are employees) to calculate the entity's business income. They also pay

[35]§541.

[36]§§531–533.

[37]While the corporate tax rate has no scheduled expiration date, future legislation could change the rate.

(and deduct) the employer's portion of the FICA tax (Social Security tax plus Medicare tax) on the employee's behalf. In 2022, the employer's portion of the tax is 7.65 percent of the employee's first $147,000 of employee compensation plus 1.45 percent of employee compensation above $147,000. The shareholder-employee is taxed on the wages received at ordinary rates and is required to pay the employee's portion of the FICA tax, which is generally the same as the employer's portion. When considering both the employer's and the employee's portions of the FICA tax, the overall FICA tax rate is 15.3 percent of the first $147,000 of wages and 2.9 percent of the rest. This is the same rate as the self-employment tax rate. Also, similar to self-employment income, employee compensation is subject to the additional Medicare tax when the taxpayer's AGI is over the threshold amount (discussed previously).

Entities taxed as partnerships deduct guaranteed payments made to owners working for the entity. However, the entity is not required to pay FICA tax on the owner-worker's behalf because guaranteed payments are self-employment income to the recipient, and self-employment taxes are the sole responsibility of the owner-worker.[38] The owner-workers are taxed on the amount of the guaranteed payment at ordinary rates and are required to pay self-employment tax and potentially additional Medicare tax on the income, depending on their income level (see prior discussion on computing the self-employment tax and additional Medicare tax). A sole proprietorship does not pay deductible compensation to the sole proprietor. In general, all of the income of a sole proprietorship is self-employment income and, consequently, is subject to self-employment tax and additional Medicare tax.

Owner compensation from certain entity types provides potential tax planning opportunities. For S corporations, business income allocations to owners are not subject to FICA or self-employment tax. However, salary and wages paid to owner-employees are subject to FICA tax. (Recall that the combined employer/employee FICA rate is the same as the self-employment tax rate.) Consequently, as we discuss in the S Corporations chapter, S corporations have a tax incentive to pay lower salary/wages to shareholder-employees who are subject to FICA tax so there is more business income to allocate to shareholder-employees who are not subject to FICA tax (lower deductible wages mean higher business income allocations). Further, S corporations have an incentive to reduce wages to shareholder-employees in order to increase business income because employee compensation is not eligible for the deduction for qualified business income, but business income allocations to shareholders are eligible. In the extreme, S corporations may prefer to pay zero wages to shareholder-employees in order to maximize business income allocations to them. However, to the extent an S corporation pays an S corporation shareholder an unreasonably low salary for services provided, the IRS may reclassify some of the shareholder's business income allocation as salary.[39]

In contrast to S corporations, entities taxed as partnerships don't have an incentive to decrease guaranteed payments in order to increase business income allocations in an attempt to save self-employment taxes to owners. This is because both guaranteed payments and business income allocations are self-employment income to the owner-worker. However, similar to S corporations, entities taxed as partnerships have an incentive to reduce guaranteed payments to owner-workers in order to increase business income allocations to them because guaranteed payments are not eligible for the qualified business income deduction, but allocations of business income are eligible. Finally, relative to both S corporations and entities taxed as partnerships, sole proprietorships may be the most advantageous for purposes of maximizing the qualified business income deduction in certain situations. This is because the sole proprietorship's qualified business income is not reduced by a deduction for compensation paid to the owner/sole proprietor (but it is reduced by the sole proprietor's deduction for self-employment taxes paid).

[38] Taxpayers pay self-employment tax on self-employment income and FICA taxes on employee compensation.

[39] See www.forbes.com/sites/anthonynitti/2014/02/04/tax-geek-tuesday-reasonable-compensation-in-the-s-corporation-arena/#2f467d5f4790 for a more detailed discussion of this potential tax planning strategy.

Example 15-10

What if: Assume that Nicole and a second investor are equal (50%) owners in CCS. Both Nicole and the other investor provide similar services to CCS, and both receive the same amount of annual compensation. For the year, CCS's business income before the compensation deduction is $200,000 (Nicole's share is $100,000). What are the total FICA/self-employment tax and income taxes payable by Nicole and CCS as they relate to Nicole's services, assuming CCS is either an S corporation (S Corp 1) that pays $10,000 of compensation for Nicole's services, an S corporation (S Corp 2) that pays $6,000 for Nicole's services, or a partnership (Partnership) that pays $10,000 for Nicole's services? Further assume that Nicole's marginal ordinary income tax rate is 35% and that her marginal self-employment tax rate is 2.9% (she has self-employment income from other sources that exceed the $147,000 Social Security wage base limit).

Note: The numbers in computations below provide entity-related information as it pertains to Nicole only. The results for the second investor would be exactly the same as the results for Nicole, but results for the second investor are not included here for simplicity. The overall tax numbers for the entity (for both owners combined) can be calculated simply by doubling the number in each cell in the example results.

Answer: Total FICA/self-employment tax and income taxes payable by Nicole are $36,262 for S Corp 1, $35,757 for S Corp 2, and $37,209 for Partnership.

Description	S Corp 1	S Corp 2	Partnership	Explanation
(1) Business income before compensation deduction (Nicole's portion only)	$100,000	$100,000	$100,000	Nicole's share of entity income before compensation deduction ($200,000 × 50%) for Nicole's share
(2) Compensation deduction for services provided by Nicole only	10,000	6,000	10,000	Treated as salary to Nicole in S corporation scenarios and as a guaranteed payment in the partnership scenario
(3) FICA tax rate for employer on employee's salary	7.65%	7.65%	N/A	FICA rate on employer's portion of FICA liability based on salary. No employer FICA liability on guaranteed payments.
(4) FICA paid and deducted by employer	765	459	N/A	(2) × (3)
(5) Business income (Nicole's portion)	$ 89,235	$ 93,541	$ 90,000	(1) – (2) – (4)
(6) Nicole's FICA tax on salary	765	459	N/A	(2) × (3). Employee's portion is same as employer's portion (7.65%).
(7) Self-employment tax	0	0	2,678	[(2) + (5)] × .9235 × .029. Business income and compensation are self-employment income for partner but not for S corporation shareholder.
(8) Self-employment tax deduction	0	0	1,339	(7) × 50%
(9) Combined entity and owner FICA (or self-employment) tax	$ 1,530	$ 918	$ 2,678	(4) + (6) + (7)
(10) Income taxed at ordinary tax rates	$ 99,235	$ 99,541	$ 98,661	(2) + (5) – (8)
(11) Income taxes	$ 34,732	$ 34,839	$ 34,531	(10) × 35%
Total FICA/self-employment tax and income taxes	**$ 36,262**	**$ 35,757**	**$ 37,209**	(9) + (11)

S Corp 2 has a lower tax burden than S Corp 1 ($35,757 vs. $36,262, respectively). S Corp 2's tax burden is lower than S Corp 1's tax burden solely due to S Corp 2 paying less compensation (salary) to Nicole than does S Corp 1. Also, both S Corp 1 and S Corp 2 have a lower tax burden compared to Partnership ($36,262 and $35,757 vs. $37,209, respectively). The primary reason for this is that all of the partnership income is subject to self-employment tax at 2.9%, and for the S corporations, only the salary is subject to FICA tax (combined employer and employee rate is 15.3%). The difference would be much larger if CCS were Nicole's only source of self-employment income because the self-employment tax rate on the partnership income would be 15.3% rather than 2.9%.

What if: What is Nicole's QBI deduction based on the income from each of the three entities assuming that the business income is QBI and that the QBI wage-based limitations do not apply?

Answer: For the S corporation entities, the QBI deduction is the business income [line (5)] × 20%. The QBI deduction based on S Corp 1's income is $17,847, and the QBI deduction based on S Corp 2's income is $18,708. However, in the case of the partnership, the business income must be reduced by the deduction for self-employment taxes paid to arrive at QBI. Nicole's QBI deduction under the partnership entity form is $17,732 {[(5) – (8)] × 20%}.

In this example, the S corporation tax form provides more tax benefits than the partnership tax form. This example illustrates a reason why taxpayers who form an LLC may elect to have the entity taxed as an S corporation rather than as a partnership. The LLC legal form of entity can protect owners from liability while the S corporation tax form can reduce taxes. However, the tax entity form decision should be made based on the facts specific to the situation rather than a general rule of thumb.

TAXES IN THE REAL WORLD Reasonable Compensation Must Be, Well, Reasonable

As we've discussed in this chapter, an S corporation shareholder who also works as an employee for the business must pay FICA tax on the salary received. Further, the S corporation must also pay payroll taxes on the salary. In contrast, neither the shareholder nor the business pays payroll tax on business income allocated to S corporation shareholders. Thus, shareholders and the S corporation have incentives to keep salaries low so that less income is subject to payroll taxes. The IRS insists that shareholders providing services be paid a reasonable salary for their services, and the IRS is likely to challenge the amount of the salary when it identifies a salary that may be unreasonably low. The IRS and taxpayers have had many court battles over whether salary paid to the shareholders is unreasonably low based on the extent and nature of the services the shareholder provides to the S corporation. In *David E. Watson, P.C. v. United States,* Mr. Watson, an employee/shareholder in an S corporation, received only $24,000 in annual salary from the S corporation but received distributions of almost $200,000 per year (in 2002 and 2003 when the Social Security wage base limitation was $84,900 and $87,000, respectively). At trial, an expert witness for the IRS testified that the value of the taxpayer's services to the business was about $91,000 per year. The court concluded that any reasonable person in Mr. Watson's position would expect to earn significantly more than what he was being paid in salary and that his $24,000 salary wasn't enough to support Mr. Watson's lifestyle. The court ruled for the IRS, resulting in a portion of the distributions being recast as taxable salary. Further, Mr. Watson (and the S corporation) was required to pay employment taxes, penalties, and interest.

In *J.D. & Associates v. United States,* Mr. Dahl, the sole shareholder of an S corporation, J.D. & Associates, was paid a salary between $19,000 and $30,000 each year but received annual distributions in the $50,000 range. It turns out that the salary paid to Mr. Dahl, a CPA, was lower than the salary paid to other employees who were providing only administrative services to the business. Needless to say, the taxpayer lost that case too and ended up paying payroll taxes on distributions that were recast as salary.

In these types of cases, the S corporation bears the burden of proving that the compensation paid to the shareholder is reasonable. Obviously, the burden is much easier to manage when the salaries are actually reasonable.

Sources: David E. Watson, P.C. v. United States, 109 AFTR2d 2012-1059 (8th Cir. 2012); and *J.D. & Associates v. United States,* No. 3:04-cv-59, 2006 U.S. Dist. LEXIS 117266 (D.N.D. June 5, 2006).

For C corporations, tax planning opportunities have potentially shifted with the steep reduction in the corporate tax rate relative to individual rates, effective beginning in 2018. Prior to the rate reduction, corporations could avoid the heavy cost of double taxation of their income by paying deductible salaries to shareholder-employees. This income would be taxed once to the employee at ordinary rates that were similar to the corporate rate. The IRS could evaluate compensation to an employee-shareholder to determine if the compensation was unreasonably high for the work the employee-shareholder was doing and, to the extent it was, reclassify the excess compensation as nondeductible dividends. Currently, however, with the corporate tax rate significantly lower than the maximum individual rate, corporations have an incentive to pay lower salaries to shareholder-employees in order to have more of their income taxed at the lower corporate rate. By reducing deductible salaries, more of the corporate income is subject to tax at the lower 21 percent tax rate. If the income is paid in the form of salaries, it is subject to the individual rate (the top rate is 37 percent) and subject to both the employer's and the employee's portions of the FICA tax. This type of strategy is more likely to be useful for closely held corporations where all of the owners work for the corporation. It remains to be seen how the IRS will respond to such strategies.

While the overall tax rate of an entity's income and the tax treatment of owner compensation are important entity choice factors, it is also important to consider the tax treatment of the entity's losses and other tax characteristics when choosing a tax entity for a new business.

ETHICS

Meghna is the sole shareholder and CEO of BQT. BQT is a very profitable S corporation. Until recently, Meghna's salary was in line with the salaries of comparable CEOs. However, Meghna recently learned that she could reduce her tax burden if she were to reduce her salary. In particular, by lowering her salary, Meghna would receive less employee compensation that is subject to FICA tax and is not eligible for the qualified business income deduction, and she would be allocated more business income that is not subject to FICA tax and qualifies for the qualified business income deduction. After considering the potential benefits, Meghna decided to cut her salary in half. Do you think Meghna's decision is ethical? Why or why not?

Deductibility of Entity Losses When a C corporation's tax deductions exceed its income for the year, the excess is called a **net operating loss (NOL).** While NOLs provide no tax benefit to C corporations for the year they incur them, corporations may use NOLs to offset corporate taxable income and reduce corporate taxes in other years. The specific tax treatment for an NOL depends on when the NOL was generated. For NOLs generated in tax years beginning before 2018, the carry forward period is 20 years and the carry back period is two years. These carryovers can offset up to 100 percent of taxable income before the NOL deduction in carryover years. For NOLs generated in tax years beginning after 2017 and before 2021, the carryforward period is indefinite and the carryback period is five years. The NOL carryovers can offset up to 100 percent of taxable income before the NOL deduction in tax years beginning before 2021. However, in tax years beginning after 2020, the NOL carryovers from 2018–2020 tax years can offset up to only 80 percent of taxable income remaining after deducting NOL carryovers from NOLs incurred in tax years beginning before 2018. Finally, for NOLs generated in tax years beginning after 2020, the NOLs may be carried forward indefinitely but may not be carried back. In carryover years, the NOL can offset up to only 80 percent of taxable income remaining after deducting NOL carryovers from NOLs incurred in tax years beginning before 2018.[40] NOL carryovers are deducted on a FIFO basis (oldest first, to the extent deductible). In any event, losses from C corporations are *not* available to offset shareholders' personal income.

[40]We discuss the net operating loss deduction in more detail in the Corporate Operations chapter.

In contrast to losses generated by C corporations, losses generated by sole proprietorships and other flow-through entities are generally available to offset owners' personal income, subject to certain restrictions. For example, the owner of an entity taxed as a partnership or an S corporation shareholder may deduct losses from the entity only to the extent of the owner's basis in their ownership interest in the flow-through entity. In addition, deductibility of losses from flow-through entities may be further limited by the at-risk limitation and/or the passive activity loss limitation. The at-risk limitation is similar to the basis limitation but is slightly more restrictive (i.e., the amount at risk is generally the same as the owner's basis in their ownership interest). Consequently, if the taxpayer clears the basis limitation, they typically clear the at-risk limitation for deduction. The passive activity loss limitation typically applies to individual investors who are passive investors in the flow-through entities. For passive investors, the business activities of the entity are called passive activities. In these circumstances, taxpayers can deduct losses from passive activities only to the extent they have income from other passive activities (or when they sell their interest in the activity). Due to the complex nature of these limitations, we defer a detailed discussion of these limitations until the Forming and Operating Partnerships chapter.

Individual taxpayers are also not allowed to deduct an "excess business loss" for the year. An **excess business loss** is the excess of aggregate business deductions for the year over the sum of aggregate business gross income or gain of the taxpayer plus a threshold amount. The threshold amount for 2022 is $540,000 for married taxpayers filing jointly and $270,000 for other taxpayers. The amounts are adjusted annually for inflation. Excess business losses include business losses from sole proprietorships, entities taxed as partnerships, and S corporations. In the case of an S corporation or an entity taxed as a partnership, the limit applies at the owner level. Excess business losses are carried forward and used in subsequent years. The excess business loss limitation applies to losses that are otherwise deductible after applying the basis, at-risk, and passive loss rules. See the Forming and Operating Partnerships chapter for more details.

The ability to deduct flow-through losses against other sources of income can be a significant issue for owners of new businesses because new businesses tend to report losses early on as the businesses get established. If owners form a new business as a C corporation, the corporate-level losses provide no current tax benefit to the shareholders. The fact that C corporation losses are trapped at the corporate level can impose a higher tax cost for shareholders initially doing business as a C corporation relative to a flow-through entity such as an S corporation or an entity taxed as a partnership.

TAXES IN THE REAL WORLD Will Entity Selection Be Affected by the Tax Law Changes Effective in 2018?

In its Statistics of Income Tax Report (see below), the Internal Revenue Service reported the following information relating to tax entity selection by business owners as of 2015 (the most recent year reported). Sole proprietorships were the most common, followed by S corporations, entities taxed as partnerships, and then C corporations. Nevertheless, C corporations by far generated the most business entity receipts and net income. Under tax legislation effective in 2018, the C corporation tax rate has been reduced from 35 percent to 21 percent and owners of flow-through entities are allowed a new deduction for qualified business income generated by the entity. Going forward, how do you expect the percentage of each entity type to change, if at all, under the new tax system? Is it likely we will see a shift toward C corporations as the entity of choice?

The Blackstone Group Inc., the largest alternative investment firm in the world, converted from a publicly traded partnership to a corporation (C corporation for tax purposes), effective July 1, 2019. By converting, Blackstone expects to provide value to its shareholders. Stephen Schwarzman, Blackstone chairperson, CEO, and co-founder, said, "We are converting our firm from a publicly traded partnership to a

(continued)

THE KEY FACTS
Taxation of Entity Income

- Flow-through entity income is taxed at the owner's tax rate. Individuals are taxed at a top marginal income rate of 37 percent on business income allocated to them from a flow-through entity.
- Flow-through entity owners who receive qualified business income from a flow-through entity are allowed to claim a qualified business income deduction equal to 20 percent of the qualified business income allocated to them (reduced by certain deductions and subject to certain limitations).
- Business income allocations to passive owners of flow-through entities may be subject to the 3.8 percent net investment income tax.
- Business income allocated to S corporation shareholders is not subject to self-employment tax.
- Owners of entities taxed as a partnership may be subject to self-employment tax on business income allocations, depending on the owner's involvement in the business activities.
- Sole proprietors are subject to self-employment tax on the sole proprietorship's income.
- C corporation taxable income is subject to a flat 21 percent tax rate.
- The maximum tax rate on dividends for Individuals who are C corporation shareholders is generally 20 percent. Further, certain taxpayers may be charged a 3.8 percent net investment income tax on dividends and capital gains.
- C corporation shareholders that are themselves C corporations are generally eligible to receive a 50 percent or greater dividends-received deduction (DRD).

(continued)

- C corporation shareholders who are individuals generally pay capital gains taxes when shares are sold at a gain.
- S corporation and C corporation shareholders receive employee compensation for work they do for the entity.
- Owner-workers for entities taxed as a partnership receive compensation in the form of guaranteed payments. Guaranteed payments are self-employment income.

corporation. This change will make it vastly easier to buy and own Blackstone stock. It eliminates the burdensome K-1 tax forms. Blackstone will also become eligible for several market indicies. And these benefits come at what we expect to be a modest tax cost."* Mr. Schwarzman's comments suggest that while Blackstone had important nontax reasons to convert to a corporation, the recent reduction in the corporate tax rate from 35 percent to 21 percent significantly reduced the tax cost of converting to the point that the conversion made sense from an economical perspective. Would Blackstone have converted if the rate hadn't dropped? Probably not, but who knows for sure?

	Number of Entities	Business Receipts	Net Income (including deficits)
Totals for all entities	35,060,997	$33,812,762,216	$3,145,991,627
Entity Type	**Percentage**	**Percentage**	**Percentage**
C corporations	4.60	59.58	36.71
S corporations	12.80	21.73	17.79
General partnerships	1.66	1.08	2.89
Limited partnerships	1.16	2.92	7.76
LLCs (taxed as partnerships)	7.17	9.28	7.87
Sole proprietorships (nonfarm)	71.95	4.27	10.55
Other	.66	1.14	16.43

*Blackstone.com, April 18, 2019,http://site-174789.bcvp0rtal.com/.
Source: www.irs.gov/statistics/soi-tax-stats-integrated-business-data,Table 3: Selected financial data on businesses, 2015.

Example 15-11

What if: Assume that Nicole organizes CCS as a C corporation and that, in spite of her best efforts as CEO of the company, CCS reports a tax loss of $50,000 in its first year of operation (2022). Also assume that Nicole's marginal tax rate is 37 percent and the taxable income on her joint tax return is $500,000 (all ordinary income) before considering the CCS tax loss. How much tax will CCS pay for 2022, and how much tax will Nicole (and her spouse) pay on the $500,000 of other taxable income on their joint return if CCS is organized as a C corporation?

Answer: CCS will pay $0 in taxes because it reports a loss for tax purposes. However, CCS can carry the loss over to future years and can use the loss to offset up to 80 percent of its taxable income in a given year (before the NOL deduction itself). Because Nicole may not use the CCS loss to offset any of the ordinary income on her joint return, Nicole (and her spouse) must pay $185,000 in taxes. See the computations in the table below.

What if: Suppose CCS is organized as an S corporation and Nicole's stock basis in CCS before the 2022 loss is $100,000. How much tax will CCS pay for 2022, and how much tax will Nicole (and her spouse) pay on the $500,000 of ordinary income on the joint tax return?

Answer: CCS will pay $0 taxes (S corporations are not tax-paying entities) and Nicole (and spouse) will pay $166,500 in taxes. See the computations in the table below.

Description	C Corporation	S Corporation (flow-through)	Explanation
(1) Taxable income (loss)	$ (50,000)	$ (50,000)	
(2) CCS corporate-level tax	**$ 0**	**$ 0**	No taxable income
(3) Nicole's other income	$ 500,000	$ 500,000	
(4) CCS loss available to offset Nicole's other income	$ 0	$ (50,000)	$0 if C corporation; (1) if S corporation (flow-through entity)
(5) Nicole's other income reduced by entity loss	$ 500,000	$ 450,000	(3) + (4)
(6) Nicole's marginal ordinary tax rate	37%	37%	
Nicole's tax on other income	**$185,000**	**$166,500**	(5) × (6)

What if: Suppose CCS is organized as an S corporation and Nicole's stock basis before the $50,000 loss in 2022 is $100,000. Further, assume that Nicole does not participate in CCS's business activities; that is, assume she is a passive investor in the business entity. How much tax will Nicole (and her spouse) pay on the $500,000 of other ordinary income?

Answer: $185,000. Because Nicole is a passive investor, she is not allowed to deduct the loss allocated to her this year. She must carry it over and use it in future years (this assumes neither Nicole nor her spouse has income from other investments in which they are passive investors).

As the example above illustrates, owners' ability to immediately use start-up losses from flow-through entities to offset income from other sources is a tax advantage of flow-through entities over C corporations.

Exhibit 15-3 summarizes general rules for different tax characteristics by tax entity type.

EXHIBIT 15-3 General Rules for Tax Characteristics by Tax Entity Type*

Tax Characteristic	C Corporation	S Corporation	Partnership	Sole Proprietorship
Tax Form (or schedule) filed	Form 1120	Form 1120-S	Form 1065	Schedule C (Form 1040)
Taxation of entity income	Entity pays tax on its income and shareholders pay tax on dividends or when they sell their stock (i.e., double taxation).	Flows through to owners and is taxed once to owners as if owners had earned income (no double taxation). Income allocation increases each owner's stock basis and loss allocation decreases stock basis.	Flows through to owners and is taxed once to owners as if owners had earned income (no double taxation). Income allocation increases each owner's basis in ownership interest and loss allocation decreases basis in ownership interest.	Taxed once on the owner's tax return.** Owner does not have separate ownership basis in sole proprietorship even if the entity is formed as an LLC.
Are owners (who are individuals) potentially eligible for QBI deduction based on entity's income?	N/A	Yes, potentially eligible for QBI deduction based on business income allocation to owner.	Yes, potentially eligible for QBI deduction based on business income allocation to owner.	Yes
Compensation paid to owners for services	Treated as salary to owner/employee. Deductible by entity in computing entity's taxable income.	Treated as salary to owner/employee. Deductible by entity in computing entity's business income.	Guaranteed payment to partner providing service. Deductible by entity in computing entity's business income.	No compensation paid to owner.
Are owners subject to self-employment tax on compensation received for services provided to entity?	No***	No***	Yes	N/A
Is business income allocation to or earned by owners subject to self-employment tax?	N/A	No.	Yes, for general partners. No for limited partners. Yes, for LLC members who provide significant services for entity.	Yes.

(continued)

Tax Characteristic	C Corporation	S Corporation	Partnership	Sole Proprietorship
Are owners potentially subject to the additional Medicare tax on compensation received from the entity and on the entity's business income allocated to or earned by owner?	Yes, for compensation. N/A for business income.	Yes, for compensation. No, for business income allocation.	Yes, for compensation (guaranteed payment). Yes, for business income allocation that is subject to self-employment tax.	N/A for compensation. Yes, for business income.
Are distributions taxable to owners?	Yes, distributions are taxable as dividends.	No, to the extent of shareholder's basis in stock. Amount in excess of stock basis is capital gain.	No, to the extent of owner's basis in ownership interest. Amount above basis in ownership interest is capital gain.	N/A
Are owners potentially subject to net investment income tax on entity's income?	Yes, for dividends received and capital gain on sale of stock.	Yes, for capital gain on sale of stock, traditional investment income that flows through to shareholder, and business income allocated to shareholder to the extent the shareholder is a passive investor in the entity.	Yes, for capital gain on sale of ownership interest, traditional investment income that flows through to partner, and business income allocated to partner to the extent the shareholder is a passive investor in the entity.	N/A
Entity losses	Net losses (NOLs) stay at the entity level carry over to offset income in other years.	Deductible at the owner level to extent losses clear basis, at-risk, and passive loss hurdles. Amount of deductible loss for a year is restricted to annual excess loss limitation (based on filing status). Loss over limit carries over to next year. Limit applies to individual taxpayers.	Deductible at the owner level to extent losses clear basis, at-risk, and passive loss hurdles. Deduction for losses are subject to the excess loss deduction limitation as described in the S Corp. column.	Net loss can potentially offset individual's income from other sources. Net loss can carry over to other years under individual NOL provisions. Deduction for losses are subject to the at-risk, passive loss, and excess loss deduction limitations.
Is contribution of appreciated property to entity taxable (includes entity formation)?****	No to shareholder and no to corporation if shareholder(s) has control of corporation after property contribution.	No to shareholder and no to corporation if shareholder(s) has control of corporation after property contribution.	No to partner (member) and no to partnership. Control not required.	N/A
Are liquidations taxable?****	Generally, entity gain to extent FMV of property distributed exceeds property's basis. Shareholder recognizes capital gain (loss) to extent value of property received exceeds (is less than) stock basis in entity. Liquidations of 80%+ owned subsidiary into parent are not taxable.	Yes, entity gain that flows through to shareholders to extent FMV of property distributed exceeds property's basis. Shareholder recognizes capital gain (loss) to extent value of property received exceeds (is less than) stock basis.	No to entity or to owners.	N/A
Other	See Exhibit 15-4.	See Exhibit 15-4.	See Exhibit 15-4.	See Exhibit 15-4.

*This table provides the general rules. There are exceptions to most of the general rules. Exceptions are covered elsewhere in text.
**Entity and owner are same. Income flows from Schedule C to front page of Form 1040.
***Salary is not subject to self-employment tax, but it is subject to FICA tax. The employee pays half the FICA tax, and the entity pays the other half.
****This topic is not covered in detail in this chapter but is included here for completeness. See Exhibit 15-4 for text chapters that cover these topics in more detail.

OTHER TAX CHARACTERISTICS

There are many tax factors that differ across entities and can influence the entity selection decision. Exhibit 15-4 provides an overview of these tax characteristics. The exhibit describes the general rules for each tax characteristic as it relates to C corporations, S corporations, entities taxed as partnerships, and sole proprietorships, and it ranks the entities on each characteristic (1 is most tax favorable). Finally, it identifies the chapters where detail on these tax characteristics can be found.

Converting to Other Business Entity Types

With the significant reduction in corporate tax rates from tax legislation effective beginning in 2018, owners of existing flow-through entities may reevaluate their entity status and determine whether they prefer to have their entity taxed as a C corporation rather than as a flow-through entity (see the Taxes in the Real World box in this chapter discussing The Blackstone Group's conversion from a partnership to a C corporation). Fortunately for flow-through entity owners wanting to change entity type, it is easy and inexpensive to convert flow-through entities, including sole proprietorships, into C corporations. Owners of S corporations can revoke their election to be taxed as an S corporation and be taxed as a C corporation (see the S Corporations chapter for details on this process). As we discussed in the Business Entity Tax Classification section of this chapter, owners of entities taxed as partnerships and sole proprietors doing business as an LLC can retain the same legal entity type but make a check-the-box election to be taxed as a C corporation. Alternatively, owners of entities taxed as a partnership and sole proprietors can contribute the assets of the business entity to a newly formed corporation in a tax-deferred transaction without any special tax elections.[41] However, because this alternative involves creating a new legal entity, nontax factors (e.g., the cost of creating a new entity, changing the asset title to a new entity, etc.) may make this option less desirable than the check-the-box election to be taxed as a C corporation.

Conversely, because tax laws currently allow a deduction for qualified business income and slightly lower individual tax rates, C corporation shareholders may prefer to have their business taxed as a flow-through entity rather than as a C corporation. Shareholders of existing corporations really have only two options for converting into flow-through entities. First, shareholders of C corporations could make an election to treat the corporation as an S corporation (flow-through entity), if they are eligible to do so. This option is not available for many corporations due to the tax rule restrictions prohibiting certain corporations from operating as S corporations.[42] The only other option is for the shareholders to liquidate the corporation and form the business as an entity taxed as a partnership or sole proprietorship for tax purposes. This may not be a viable option, however, because the taxes imposed on liquidating corporations with appreciated assets can be punitive, even with the low current corporate tax rate. As described in Exhibit 15-4, liquidating corporations are taxed on the appreciation in the assets they distribute to their shareholders in liquidation. Further, shareholders of liquidating corporations are also taxed on the difference between the fair market value of the assets they receive from the liquidating corporation and the tax basis in their stock. Effectively, the total double-tax cost of liquidating a corporation can swamp expected tax savings from operating as a flow-through entity. The tax cost of liquidating an entity is a factor to consider when making the tax entity choice for a business.

[41] §351; Rev. Rul. 84-111.

[42] See the S Corporations chapter for details on making the S corporation election.

EXHIBIT 15-4 **Comparison of Tax Characteristics across Entities**

Tax Characteristic	C Corporation	Entity Taxed as Partnership	S Corporation	Sole Proprietorship	Summary
Owner limits	At least one shareholder.	At least two owners.	Not more than 100 shareholders; no corporations, partnerships, nonresident aliens, or certain trusts.	Not applicable.	Limitations are least strict for C corporations and most strict for S corporations. S corporations are the only entity with significant owner limitations. More detail for this factor is discussed in the S Corporations chapter.
Rank[1]	1	2	3	N/A	
Owner contributions of appreciated property to entity	Tax deferred to shareholder if certain requirements are met.	Tax deferred to owner.	Tax deferred to shareholder if certain requirements are met.	Not applicable.	This factor favors entities taxed as partnerships because partners are not required to meet special requirements in order to avoid recognizing gain on the contribution of appreciated property to the partnership, but shareholders of both C and S corporations are required to meet certain requirements to avoid recognizing gain on such contributions to the corporation. More detail for this factor is provided in the Corporate Formation, Reorganization, and Liquidation, the Forming and Operating Partnerships, and the S Corporations chapters.
Rank	2	1	2	N/A	
Accounting periods	Generally, any tax year that ends on the last day of any month.[2]	Generally, must use tax year that matches tax year of owners (special rules when not all owners have same tax year-end).	Calendar year.	Generally a calendar year.	C corporations generally have the most flexibility to select their year-end. But because C corporations are not flow-through entities, this is not a real advantage or disadvantage from a tax perspective. Partnerships generally are not free to choose their year-end, but they can have a year-end that is a different year-end from some of the owners. Because this allows some partners to defer reporting income, this factor favors partnerships over S corporations. S corporations generally have the same calendar year-end as their shareholders. More detail for this factor is provided in the Business Income, Deductions, and Accounting Methods, the Forming and Operating Partnerships, and the S Corporations chapters.
Rank	2	1	2	2	
Overall accounting method	Must use accrual method unless average annual gross receipts are $27 million or less.[3,4]	Generally, allowed to use cash or accrual method.	Generally, allowed to use cash or accrual method.	Cash or accrual method.	Entities taxed as partnerships, S corporations, and sole proprietorships generally have more flexibility to choose their overall accounting method than do C corporations with average annual gross receipts over $27 million. The cash method makes it easier for these entities to plan the timing of income and expenses than does the accrual method. More detail for this factor is provided in the Business Income, Deductions, and Accounting Methods, the Corporate Operations, the Forming and Operating Partnerships, and the S Corporations chapters.
Rank	4	1	1	1	
Allocation of income or loss items to owners	Not applicable	Allocations based on partnership agreement (can differ from ownership percentages).	Allocations based on stock ownership percentages.	Not applicable	This factor applies to partnerships and S corporations only. Partnerships have more flexibility than S corporations to determine how to allocate income and loss items to entity owners. More detail for this factor is provided in the Forming and Operating Partnerships and the S Corporations chapters.
Rank	N/A	1	2	N/A	

Tax Characteristic	C Corporation	Entity Taxed as Partnership	S Corporation	Sole Proprietorship	Summary
Share of flow-through entity debt included in basis of owner's equity interest	Not applicable	Increase basis in ownership interest by owner's share of entity's debt.	No increase in stock basis for debt of entity (special rules if shareholder lends money to S corporation).	Not applicable	Partners are allowed to increase the basis in their ownership interest by their share of the partnership's debt; S corporation shareholders generally are not. This factor favors partnerships over S corporations. More detail for this factor is provided in the the Forming and Operating Partnerships and the S Corporations chapters.
Rank	N/A	1	2	N/A	
Nonliquidating distributions of noncash property	Gains recognized on distributions of appreciated property and losses disallowed on distributions of depreciated property.	Generally no gain or loss recognized on noncash property distributions.	Same as C corporation.	Not applicable	This factor favors partnerships for distributions of appreciated and depreciated property. More detail for this factor is provided in the Corporate Taxation: Nonliquidating Distributions, the Dispositions of Partnership Interests and Partnership Distributions, and the S Corporations chapters.
Rank	2	1	1	N/A	
Liquidating distributions	Gain and loss generally recognized (certain losses disallowed). Liquidations of 80+ owned subsidiary into parent are tax deferred.	Generally no gain or loss recognized.	Gain and loss recognized (certain losses disallowed).	Not applicable	This factor tends to favor partnerships if the liquidating entities have gain assets, and it tends to favor corporations if the entities have loss assets. More detail for this factor is provided in the Corporate Formation, Reorganization, and Liquidation, the Dispositions of Partnership Interests and Partnership Distributions, and the S Corporations chapters.
Rank	1	1	1	N/A	

[1]"Rank" orders the entities based on the particular characteristic (1 is most favorable).

[2]C corporations that qualify as personal service corporations (PSCs) are generally required to use a calendar year. In general, a personal service corporation is a corporation whose shareholders perform professional services such as law, engineering, and accounting. See §448(d)(2) for more detail.

[3]The $27 million limit applies for tax years beginning in 2022, and the limit is indexed for inflation. The entity meets the gross receipts test for a taxable year if its annual gross receipts for the three-taxable-year period ending with the taxable year that precedes such taxable year does not exceed $27 million.

[4]C corporations that are qualified personal service corporations are required to use the cash method.

Example 15-12

What if: Assume we are years down the road and that Nicole is the sole shareholder of CCS (a C corporation). CCS's assets have a fair market value of $10 million and adjusted tax basis of $6 million ($4 million built-in gain). Further assume that the corporate tax rate is 21 percent, Nicole's stock basis in CCS is $2 million, and her marginal tax rate on long-term capital gains is 23.8 percent (20 percent capital gains rate + 3.8 percent net investment income tax). How much tax would CCS and Nicole be required to pay if CCS were to liquidate in order to form an LLC?

Answer: $2,544,080. This would be a steep tax price to pay for changing from a C corporation to an LLC.

Description	Amount	Explanation
(1) FMV of CCS assets	$10,000,000	
(2) Adjusted basis of CCS assets	6,000,000	
(3) CCS taxable income on liquidation	$ 4,000,000	(1) − (2)
(4) Corporate tax rate	21%	
(5) Entity-level tax	$ 840,000	(3) × (4)
(6) After-tax assets distributed to Nicole	9,160,000	(1) − (5)
(7) Nicole's stock basis	2,000,000	
(8) Nicole's long-term capital gain on distribution	$ 7,160,000	(6) − (7)
(9) Nicole's marginal tax rate on gain	23.8%	
(10) Shareholder-level tax	$ 1,704,080	(8) × (9)
Total entity- and shareholder-level tax on liquidation	**$ 2,544,080**	(5) + (10)

(continued from page 15-4 . . .)
Nicole quickly determined she would legally form CCS as an LLC in Utah. This would provide her with limited liability and allow her complete flexibility for determining the tax entity type of CCS. If at some point she wanted to convert CCS into a corporation in Utah, she was advised that she could make the conversion simply by filing some paperwork.

Nicole's five-year forecast of CCS's expected operating results showed that CCS would generate losses for the first three years and then become very profitable thereafter. With these projections in hand, Nicole first considered forming CCS as a partnership for tax purposes (she was planning on bringing in another investor) or electing to become an S corporation. Nicole determined that income allocated to her from CCS would be eligible for the deduction for qualified business income whether she operated CCS as a partnership or an S corporation. She then compared the specific tax rules applicable to partnerships and S corporations before deciding her preference between the two tax entity types. She identified some differences that could sway her decision one way or the other. Supporting a decision to select a partnership, Nicole learned she would likely be able to deduct the projected losses in the early years from CCS more quickly with a partnership compared with an S corporation because she could include a share of the partnership's debt in her tax basis in her ownership interest (whereas she would not be able to include a share of the S corporation's debt in the tax basis of her ownership interest). Nicole also hoped to attract corporate investors, and she discovered that a partnership can have corporate partners but that S corporations are not permitted to have corporate shareholders. Supporting a decision to select an S corporation, Nicole learned that S corporations appear to have a compelling advantage over partnerships in reducing the self-employment tax of owners active in managing their businesses. Nicole decided that she preferred a partnership over an S corporation because she would be willing to potentially incur additional self-employment taxes with a partnership in exchange for the ability to deduct her losses sooner and for the freedom to solicit corporate investors.

Nicole then turned her attention to whether she preferred to operate CCS as a C corporation or a partnership for tax purposes. Favoring the partnership tax entity choice was the fact that Nicole would be able to immediately deduct initial losses of the business against her personal taxable income. Favoring the C corporation choice was the overall tax rate on the CCS income when it becomes profitable. She reasoned that the corporate tax rate is significantly lower than her marginal individual tax rate and she planned to grow CCS by having CCS retain rather than distribute its income and subject it to a second level of tax. Consequently, Nicole determined that the overall tax rate to CCS income would be significantly lower if she operated CCS as a C corporation. Further, as a C corporation she would be able to solicit corporate owners and eventually take CCS public if the opportunity were to present itself (to do this she would have to convert to a legal corporation). After much thought and analysis, Nicole chose to make the election necessary to have CCS taxed as a C corporation. With this big decision out of the way, Nicole could focus on applying for a small business loan from her local bank and on having her attorney take the necessary steps to formally organize CCS as a limited liability company. ■

CONCLUSION

Any time a new business is formed, and periodically thereafter as circumstances change (such as relevant tax law), business owners must carefully evaluate what type of business entity will maximize the after-tax profits from their business ventures. Many of the key factors to consider in the entity selection decision-making process are outlined in this chapter. When making the entity selection decision, owners must carefully balance the tax and nontax characteristics unique to the entities available to them. This chapter explains how various legal entities are treated for tax purposes and how certain tax characteristics differ between entity types. Moreover, it also identifies some of the more important nontax issues that come to bear on the choice of entity decision. With this understanding, taxpayers and their advisers will be better prepared to face this frequently encountered business decision. In the Forming and Operating Partnerships chapter, we return to Nicole and Color Comfort Sheets LLC to examine the tax rules that apply to Nicole and other members in CCS as they form the entity for tax purposes and begin business operations.

Summary

Discuss the legal and other nontax characteristics of different types of legal business entities. **LO 15-1**

- Business entities that differ in terms of their legal characteristics include corporations, limited liability companies, general partnerships, limited partnerships, and sole proprietorships.
- Corporations are formally organized by filing articles of incorporation with the state. They are legally separate entities and protect their shareholders from the liabilities of the corporation. State corporation laws dictate interactions between corporations and shareholders.

As a result, shareholders have limited flexibility to customize their business arrangements with the corporation and other shareholders. State corporate governance rules do, however, facilitate initial public offerings.

- Limited liability companies are formally organized by filing articles of organization with the state. Like corporations, they are separate legal entities that shield their members from liabilities. In contrast to corporations, state LLC statutes give members a great deal of latitude in customizing their business arrangements with the LLC and other members.
- General partnerships may be organized informally without state approval, but limited partnerships must file a certificate of limited partnership with the state to organize. Although they are considered to be legally separate entities, they provide either limited or no liability protection for partners. While limited partners in limited partnerships have liability protection, general partners are fully exposed to the liabilities of the partnership. General and limited partnerships are given a great deal of latitude in customizing their partnership agreements.
- Sole proprietorships are businesses legally indistinguishable from their sole individual owners. As such, they are very flexible but provide no liability protection. Sole proprietors can obtain liability protection by converting to a single-member LLC.

LO 15-2 Describe the different types of business entities for tax purposes.

- The four categories of business entities recognized by our tax system include C corporations, S corporations, partnerships, and sole proprietorships.
- Legal corporations that don't make the S election are treated as C corporations and therefore pay taxes. All other entities recognized for tax purposes are flow-through entities.
- Legal corporations that qualify for and make the S election are treated as S corporations.
- Unincorporated entities with more than one owner are treated as partnerships unless they elect to be taxed as a corporation. If the entity elects to be taxed as a corporation, it can further elect to be taxed as an S corporation if it meets the S corporation requirements.
- Unincorporated entities with one owner are treated as sole proprietorships, where the sole owner is an individual, or as disregarded entities otherwise. If a sole proprietor converts to a single-member LLC, the LLC can elect to be taxed as a corporation. It can further elect to be taxed as an S corporation.

LO 15-3 Identify fundamental differences in tax characteristics across business entity types.

- Flow-through entity income is taxed once at the owner level. For individual owners, the top rate is 37 percent. Flow-through income may also be subject to the net investment income tax for passive investors or the self-employment tax for those involved in the business activities of a partnership or sole proprietorship.
- Flow-through business owners are eligible to deduct 20 percent of their qualified business income (minus the self-employed health insurance deduction, the self-employment tax deduction, and the deduction for contributions to self-employed retirement plans) as a from AGI deduction that is not an itemized deduction. The deduction is subject to certain limitations determined at the individual level.
- Qualified business income is generally nonservice business income generated in the United States. The deduction is subject to a wage-based limitation and a taxable income limitation.
- Flow-through entity business income allocated to passive owners is subject to the 3.8 percent net investment income tax for taxpayers with AGI over a threshold dependent on filing status.
- Self-employment income is subject to self-employment tax and additional Medicare tax.
- S corporation business income allocated to shareholders is not self-employment income.
- Sole proprietorship income is self-employment income to the sole proprietor.
- Whether business income of entities taxed as a partnership is self-employment income to an owner depends on the owner's involvement in the entity's business activities.
- Corporate taxable income is taxed at the corporate level and again at the shareholder level. The corporate tax rate is a flat 21 percent. The second level of tax is paid at the shareholder level when the corporation distributes after-tax earnings as a dividend or when the shareholder sells the stock. The tax rate for the second level of tax depends on the type of shareholder.

- Dividends and long-term capital gains are taxed at a top rate of 23.8 percent (20 percent dividend plus 3.8 percent net investment income tax). Corporate shareholders are taxed on dividends and capital gains at the corporate tax rate. However, corporations are entitled to deduct 50, 65, or 100 percent of dividends received based on the extent of their ownership in the distributing corporation.
- Corporations can defer the second level of tax by not distributing their after-tax income. However, corporations that retain earnings for tax avoidance rather than business purposes may be subject to the accumulated earnings tax or the personal holding company tax. These taxes reduce the incentive for corporations to retain earnings in order to avoid the second level of tax. Corporations are allowed to retain earnings to invest in their business.
- Business entity owners who work for the entity are compensated in different ways, depending on the type of entity.
- S corporation and C corporation shareholders who work for the entity receive employee compensation.
- Owners who work for entities taxed as partnerships receive guaranteed payments that are self-employment income to the owner-worker.
- Sole proprietors don't receive compensation from the business because the sole proprietorship and the sole proprietor are the same entity for tax purposes.
- Operating losses from S corporations and entities taxed as partnerships flow through to the owners. Owners may deduct these losses only to the extent of the basis in their ownership interest. The losses must also clear "at-risk" limitations and passive activity loss limitations in order for the owners to deduct the loss.
- The at-risk limitation is similar to the basis limitation. The passive activity loss limitations typically apply to individual investors who do little, if any, work relating to the business activities of the flow-through entity (referred to as *passive* activities to the individual investors). In these circumstances, taxpayers can deduct such losses only to the extent they have income from other passive activities.
- Flow-through entity individual owners are not allowed to deduct an excess business loss for the year ($540,000 for married couples filing jointly; $270,000 for other taxpayers). This provision potentially limits losses that would otherwise be deductible after applying the at-risk and passive activity loss limitations.
- Shareholders can mitigate the double tax by increasing the time they hold shares before selling.
- C corporation losses are referred to as net operating losses (NOLs).
- The specific tax rules for a corporation's ability to deduct net operating losses depends on the year in which the NOL is incurred. Different rules apply for NOLs originating in tax years beginning before 2018, beginning after 2017 and before 2021, and beginning after 2020.
- C corporations may have one or many shareholders. S corporations may have one shareholder and as many as 100 unrelated shareholders; but corporations, nonresident aliens, partnerships, and certain trusts may not be S corporation shareholders. Partnerships must have at least two partners but are not restricted to a maximum number of partners. Sole proprietorships may have only one owner.
- Gains and income from contributing appreciated property to business entities are more easily deferred with partnerships compared to C and S corporations.
- S corporations, partnerships, and sole proprietorships are generally required to use tax year-ends conforming to the tax year-ends of their owners. C corporations may use any tax year-end.
- C corporations generally must use the accrual method unless they are a smaller corporation (average gross receipts of $27 million or less in the prior three years). S corporations may use either the cash or accrual method of accounting. Partnerships generally may use either the cash or accrual method. Sole proprietorships may use either the cash or accrual method.
- Income and losses may be specially allocated to partners based on the partnership agreement. This gives partnerships a great deal of flexibility in determining how the risks and rewards of the enterprise are shared among partners. In contrast, income and losses must be allocated pro rata to S corporation shareholders consistent with their ownership percentages.

- Partners, but not S corporation shareholders, may add their share of entity debt to the basis in their ownership interest.
- Generally, distributions of appreciated property trigger gain at both the corporate and shareholder levels when made to shareholders of C corporations, trigger gain at the corporate level when made to S corporation shareholders, and don't trigger any gain at all when made to partners.
- On liquidation, C and S corporations will generally recognize gains and losses on distributed assets. In contrast, partnerships and their partners generally do not recognize gains or losses on liquidating distributions.
- Converting a flow-through entity into a C corporation for tax purposes is generally fairly easy and inexpensive to do. S corporation shareholders can revoke the S corporation election; partnerships (and sole proprietorships formed as LLCs) can check the box to be taxed as a corporation; and partnerships and sole proprietors can contribute assets to a corporate entity in tax-deferred transactions.
- C corporations wanting to convert to a flow-through entity have two options. They may elect to become an S corporation if eligible, or they may liquidate the corporation and organize as a new entity. Taxes from liquidating C corporations can be significant when C corporations have appreciated assets.

KEY TERMS

accumulated earnings tax (15-22)
articles of incorporation (15-2)
articles of organization (15-2)
C corporations (15-5)
certificate of limited partnership (15-2)
certificate of organization (15-2)
corporation (15-2)
disregarded entities (15-5)
dividends-received deduction (DRD) (15-20)
double taxation (15-21)
excess business loss (15-27)
flow-through entities (15-5)
general partnership (GP) (15-2)
initial public offering (IPO) (15-3)
institutional shareholder (15-18)
limited liability company (LLC) (15-2)
limited partnership (LP) (15-2)
net earnings from self-employment (15-14)
net operating loss (NOL) (15-26)
partnership agreement (15-2)
personal holding companies (15-22)
personal holding company tax (15-22)
qualified business income (QBI) (15-9)
S corporation (15-5)
single-member LLCs (15-5)
social security wage base limitation (15-14)
sole proprietorship (15-2)
specified service trade or business (15-9)
unrelated business income (15-21)

DISCUSSION QUESTIONS

Discussion Questions are available in Connect®.

LO 15-1 1. What are the most common legal entities used for operating a business? How are these entities treated similarly and differently for state law purposes?

LO 15-1 2. How do business owners create legal entities? Is the process the same for all entities? If not, what are the differences?

LO 15-1 3. What is an operating agreement for an LLC? Are operating agreements required for limited liability companies? If not, why might it be important to have one?

LO 15-1 4. Explain how legal business entities differ in terms of the liability protection they provide their owners.

LO 15-1 5. Why is it a nontax advantage for corporations to be able to trade their stock on the stock market?

LO 15-1 6. How do legal corporations protect shareholders from liability? If you formed a small corporation, would you be able to avoid repaying a bank loan from your community bank if the corporation went bankrupt? Explain.

LO 15-1 LO 15-2 7. Other than corporations, are there other legal business entities that offer liability protection? Are any of them taxed as flow-through entities? Explain.

8. In general, how are unincorporated business entities classified for tax purposes? LO 15-2
9. Can unincorporated legal business entities ever be treated as corporations for tax purposes? Can legal corporations ever be treated as flow-through entities for tax purposes? Explain. LO 15-2
10. What are the differences, if any, between the legal and tax classifications of business entities? LO 15-2
11. What types of business entities does the U.S. tax system recognize? LO 15-2
12. For flow-through business entities with individual owners, how many times is flow-through entity income taxed, who pays the tax, and what is the tax rate? LO 15-3
13. What is the qualified business income deduction, and how does it affect the tax rate on flow-through business entity income? LO 15-3
14. Daria is considering investing in one of two partnerships that will build, own, and operate a hotel. One is located in Canada and one is located in Arizona. Assuming both investments will generate the same before-tax rate of return, which entity should Daria invest in when considering the after-tax consequences of the investment? Assume Daria's marginal tax rate is 37 percent, she will be a passive investor in the business, and she will report the flow-through income from either entity on her tax return. Explain (ignore any foreign tax credit issues). LO 15-3 planning
15. Is business income allocated from a flow-through business entity to its owner's self-employment income? Explain. LO 15-3
16. Did tax lax law changes effective in 2018 increase or decrease the amount of the double tax on C corporation income? Explain. LO 15-3
17. Who pays the first level of tax on a C corporation's income? What is the tax rate applicable to the first level of tax? LO 15-3
18. Who pays the second level of tax on a C corporation's income? What is the tax rate applicable to the second level of tax, and when is it levied? LO 15-3
19. Is it possible for shareholders to defer or avoid the second level of tax on corporate income altogether? Briefly explain. LO 15-3
20. How does a corporation's decision to pay dividends affect its overall tax rate? LO 15-3
21. Is it possible for the overall tax rate on corporate taxable income to be lower than the tax rate on flow-through entity taxable income? If so, under what conditions would you expect the overall corporate tax rate to be lower? LO 15-3
22. Assume Congress increases individual tax rates on ordinary income while leaving all other tax rates unchanged. How would this change affect the overall tax rate on corporate taxable income? How would this change affect overall tax rates for owners of flow-through business entities? LO 15-3
23. Assume Congress increases the dividend tax rate to the ordinary tax rate while leaving all other tax rates unchanged. How would this change affect the overall tax rate on corporate taxable income? LO 15-3
24. Evaluate the following statement: "When dividends and long-term capital gains are taxed at the same rate, the overall tax rate on corporate income is the same whether the corporation distributes its after-tax earnings as a dividend or whether it reinvests the after-tax earnings to increase the value of the corporation." LO 15-3
25. If XYZ Corporation is a shareholder of BCD Corporation, how many times will BCD's before-tax income potentially be taxed? Has Congress provided any tax relief for this result? Explain. LO 15-3
26. How many times is income from a C corporation taxed if a retirement fund is the owner of the corporation's stock? Explain. LO 15-3
27. Do tax-exempt organizations pay tax on dividends received from C corporations? Do tax-exempt organizations pay tax on business income earned? Explain. LO 15-3

LO 15-3 28. For tax purposes, how is the compensation paid to an S corporation shareholder similar to compensation paid to an owner of an entity taxed as a partnership? How is it different?

LO 15-3 29. Why might it be a good tax planning strategy for an S corporation with one shareholder to pay a salary to the shareholder on the low end of what the services are potentially worth?

LO 15-3 30. When a C corporation reports a loss for the year, can shareholders use the loss to offset their personal income? Why or why not?

LO 15-3 31. Is a current-year net operating loss of a C corporation available to offset income from the corporation in other years? Explain.

LO 15-3 32. Would a corporation with a small amount of current-year taxable income (before the net operating loss deduction) and a large net operating loss carryover have a tax liability for the current year? Explain.

LO 15-3 33. In its first year of existence, SMS, an S corporation, reported a business loss of $10,000. Sewon, SMS's sole shareholder, reports $50,000 of taxable income from sources other than SMS. What must you know to determine whether she can deduct the $10,000 loss against her other income? Explain.

LO 15-3 34. ELS, an S corporation, reported a business loss of $1,000,000. Ethan, ELS's sole shareholder, is involved in ELS's daily business activities, and he reports $1,200,000 of taxable income from sources other than ELS. What must you know in order to determine how much, if any, of the $1,000,000 loss Ethan may deduct in the current year? Explain.

LO 15-3 35. Why are S corporations less favorable than C corporations and entities taxed as partnerships in terms of owner-related limitations?

LO 15-3 36. Are C corporations or flow-through entities (S corporations and entities taxed as partnerships) more flexible in terms of selecting a tax year-end? Why are the tax rules in this area different for C corporations and flow-through business entities?

LO 15-3 37. Which tax entity types are generally allowed to use the cash method of accounting?

LO 15-3 38. According to the tax rules, how are profits and losses allocated to owners of entities taxed as partnerships (partners or LLC members)? How are they allocated to S corporation shareholders? Which entity permits greater flexibility in allocating profits and losses?

LO 15-3 39. Compare and contrast the FICA tax burden of S corporation shareholder-employees and LLC members (assume the LLC is taxed as a partnership) receiving compensation for working for the entity (guaranteed payments) and business income allocations to S corporation shareholders and LLC members assuming the owners are actively involved in the entity's business activities. How does your analysis change if the owners are not actively involved in the entity's business activities?

LO 15-3 40. Explain how liabilities of an LLC (taxed as a partnership) or an S corporation affect the amount of tax losses from the entity that limited liability company members and S corporation shareholders may deduct. Do the tax rules favor LLCs or S corporations?

LO 15-3 41. Compare the entity-level tax consequences for C corporations, S corporations, and business entities taxed as partnerships for both nonliquidating and liquidating distributions of noncash property. Do the tax rules tend to favor one entity type more than the others? Explain.

LO 15-3 42. If business entities taxed as partnerships and S corporations are both flow-through entities for tax purposes, why might an owner prefer one form over the other for tax purposes? List separately the tax factors supporting the decision to operate a business entity as an entity taxed either as a partnership or as an S corporation.

LO 15-3 43. What are the tax advantages and disadvantages of converting a C corporation into an LLC taxed as a partnership?

PROBLEMS

Select problems are available in Connect®.

44. Visit your state's official website and review the information there related to forming and operating business entities in your state. Write a short report explaining the steps for organizing a business in your state and summarizing any tax-related information you found. LO 15-1 research

45. Kiyara (single) is a 50 percent shareholder of Guardian Corporation (an S corporation). Kiyara does not do any work for Guardian Corp. Guardian Corp. reported $300,000 of business income for the year (2022). Before considering her business income allocation from Guardian Corp. and the self-employment tax deduction (if any), Kiyara's adjusted gross income was $250,000 (all employee salary). Kivara has $40,000 in itemized deductions. Answer the following questions for Kiyara. LO 15-3
    a) What is Kiyara's self-employment tax liability?
    b) Assuming the income allocated to Kiyara is qualified business income, what is Kiyara's deduction for qualified business income? Assume Kiyara's share of wages paid by Guardian Corp. is $50,000 and her share in the unadjusted basis of qualified property used by Guardian was $200,000.
    c) What is Kiyara's net investment income tax liability (assume no investment expenses)?
    d) What is Kiyara's additional Medicare tax liability (include all earned income in computing the tax)?

46. Mason (single) is a 50 percent shareholder in Angels Corp. (an S Corporation). Mason receives a $180,000 salary working full time for Angels Corp. Angels Corp. reported $400,000 of taxable business income for the year (2022). Before considering his business income allocation from Angels and the self-employment tax deduction (if any), Mason's adjusted gross income is $180,000 (all salary from Angels Corp.). Mason claims $50,000 in itemized deductions. Answer the following questions for Mason. LO 15-3
    a) What is Mason's self-employment tax liability?
    b) Assuming the business income allocated to Mason is income from a specified service trade or business, what is Mason's deduction for qualified business income? Ignore the wage-based limitation when computing the deduction.
    c) Assume the same facts as question (b), except that Angels Corp. reported $150,000 of taxable business income for the year. What is Mason's deduction for qualified business income? Ignore the wage-based limitation when computing the deduction.
    d) Assuming the original facts, what is Mason's net investment income tax liability (assume no investment expenses)?
    e) Assuming the original facts, what is Mason's additional Medicare tax liability?

47. Sofia (single) is a 50 percent owner in Beehive LLC (taxed as a partnership). Sofia does not do any work for Beehive. Beehive LLC reported $600,000 of taxable business income for the year (2022). Before considering her 50 percent business income allocation from Beehive and the self-employment tax deduction (if any), Sofia's adjusted gross income is $150,000 (all employee salary). Sofia has $35,000 in itemized deductions. Answer the following questions for Sofia. LO 15-3
    a) What is Sofia's self-employment tax liability?
    b) Assuming the income allocated to Sofia is not from a specified service trade or business, what is Sofia's deduction for qualified business income? Assume Sofia's share of wages paid by Beehive LLC is $130,000 and her share in the unadjusted basis of qualified property used by Beehive was $300,000.

c) What is Sofia's net investment income tax liability (assume no investment expenses)?

d) What is Sofia's additional Medicare tax liability?

LO 15-3

48. Omar (single) is a 50 percent owner in Cougar LLC (taxed as a partnership). Omar works half time for Cougar and receives guaranteed payment of $50,000. Cougar LLC reported $450,000 of business income for the year (2022). Before considering his 50 percent business income allocation from Cougar and the self-employment tax deduction (if any), Omar's adjusted gross income is $210,000 (includes $50,000 guaranteed payment from Cougar and $160,000 salary from a different employer). Omar reports itemized deductions of $40,000. Answer the following questions for Omar.

a) What is Omar's self-employment tax liability?

b) What would be Omar's self-employment tax liability if he didn't receive any salary.

c) Assume the original facts and that the business income allocated to Omar is not from a specified service. What is Omar's deduction for qualified business income? Assume that 81.82 percent of the self-employment tax is from self-employment income included in QBI [i.e., $225,000 business income allocation/$275,000 (business income allocation plus guaranteed payment)]. That is, the $50,000 guaranteed payment is not qualified business income. Ignore the wage-based limitation.

d) What is Omar's net investment income tax liability (assume no investment expenses)?

e) What is Omar's additional Medicare tax liability?

LO 15-3

49. Jacob is a member of WCC (an LLC taxed as a partnership). Jacob was allocated $100,000 of business income from WCC for the year. Jacob's marginal income tax rate is 37 percent. The business allocation is subject to 2.9 percent of self-employment tax and .9 percent additional Medicare tax.

a) What is the amount of tax Jacob will owe on the income allocation if the income is not qualified business income?

b) What is the amount of tax Jacob will owe on the income allocation if the income is qualified business income (QBI) and Jacob qualifies for the full QBI deduction?

LO 15-3

50. Amanda would like to organize BAL as either an LLC (taxed as a sole proprietorship) or a C corporation. In either form, the entity is expected to generate an 8 percent annual before-tax return on a $500,000 investment. Amanda's marginal income tax rate is 37 percent, and her tax rate on qualified dividends and net capital gains is 20%. Assume that BAL will distribute half of its after-tax earnings every year as a dividend if it is formed as a C corporation. Assume the income is not eligible for the QBI deduction. Further, when computing your answers, include the self-employment tax (use a 2.9% marginal rate for self-employment income because Amanda has salary over $147,000 from her employer) but not the additional Medicare tax or the net investment income tax.

a) How much cash after taxes would Amanda receive from her investment in the first year if BAL is organized as an LLC? What if BAL is organized as a C corporation?

b) What is the overall tax rate on BAL's income in the first year if BAL is organized as an LLC or as a C corporation?

c) At a high level, explain the primary factors contributing to differences between entities in cash flow and overall tax rate on business income.

51. Sandra would like to organize LAB (a legal corporation) as either an S corporation or a C corporation for tax purposes. In either form, the entity is expected to generate an 8 percent annual before-tax return on a $500,000 investment. Sandra's marginal income tax rate is 37 percent and her tax rate on qualified dividends and net capital gains is 20 percent. LAB's income is not qualified business income (QBI), so Sandra is not allowed to claim the QBI deduction. Assume that LAB will distribute all of its earnings after entity-level taxes every year. Ignore the additional Medicare tax and the net investment income tax when computing your answers. LO 15-3
   a) How much cash after taxes would Sandra receive from her investment in the first year if LAB is organized as either an S corporation or a C corporation?
   b) What is the overall tax rate on LAB's income in the first year if LAB is organized as an S corporation or as a C corporation?
   c) At a high level, explain the differences between entity types in after-tax cash flow and overall tax rate on business income.

52. Tremaine would like to organize UTA as either an S Corporation or a C corporation. In either form, the entity will generate a 9 percent annual before-tax return on a $1,000,000 investment. Tremaine's marginal income tax rate is 37 percent, and his tax rate on dividends and capital gains is 23.8 percent (including the net investment income tax). If Tremaine organizes UTA as an S corporation, he will be allowed to claim the deduction for qualified business income. Also, because Tremaine will participate in UTA's business activities, the income from UTA will not be subject to the net investment income tax. Assume that UTA will pay out 25 percent of its after-tax earnings every year as a dividend if it is formed as a C corporation. LO 15-3 research
   a) How much cash after taxes would Tremaine receive from his investment in the first year if UTA is organized either as an S corporation or as a C corporation?
   b) What is the overall tax rate on UTA's income in the first year if UTA is organized as an S corporation or as a C corporation?
   c) What is the overall tax rate on UTA's income in the first year if it is organized as an S corporation, but UTA's income is not qualified business income?
   d) What is the overall tax rate on UTA's income if it is organized as an S corporation, UTA's income is not qualified business income, and Tremaine is a passive investor in UTA?

53. Marathon Inc. (a C corporation) reported $1,000,000 of taxable income in the current year. During the year, it distributed $100,000 as dividends to its shareholders as follows: LO 15-3 tax forms
   - $5,000 to Guy, a 5 percent individual shareholder.
   - $15,000 to Little Rock Corp., a 15 percent shareholder (C corporation).
   - $80,000 to other shareholders.

   a) How much of the dividend payment did Marathon deduct in determining its taxable income?
   b) Assuming Guy's marginal ordinary tax rate is 37 percent, how much tax will he pay on the $5,000 dividend he received from Marathon Inc. (including the net investment income tax)?
   c) What amount of tax will Little Rock Corp. pay on the $15,000 dividend it received from Marathon Inc. (50 percent dividends-received deduction)?
   d) Complete Form 1120 Schedule C for Little Rock Corp. to reflect its dividends-received deduction (use the most recent Form 1120 Schedule C available).
   e) On what line on page 1 of Little Rock Corp.'s Form 1120 is the dividend from Marathon Inc. reported, and on what line of Little Rock Corp.'s Form 1120 is its dividends-received deduction reported?

LO 15-3
research

54. After several years of profitable operations, Javell, the sole shareholder of JBD Inc., a C corporation, sold 22 percent of her JBD stock to ZNO Inc., a C corporation in a similar industry. During the current year, JBD reports $1,000,000 of after-tax income. JBD distributes all of its after-tax earnings to its two shareholders in proportion to their shareholdings. How much tax will ZNO pay on the dividend it receives from JBD? What is ZNO's tax rate on the dividend income (after considering the DRD)? [*Hint:* See §243.]

LO 15-3

55. Mackenzie is considering conducting her business, Mac561, as either a single-member LLC or an S corporation. Assume her marginal ordinary income tax rate is 37 percent, her marginal FICA rate on employee compensation is 1.45 percent, her marginal self-employment tax rate is 2.9 percent (her other self-employment income and/or salary exceeds the $147,000 wage base limit for the 12.4 percent Social Security tax portion of the self-employment tax), and any employee compensation or self-employment income she receives is subject to the .9 percent additional Medicare tax. Also, assume Mac561 generated $200,000 of business income before considering the deduction for compensation Mac561 pays to Mackenzie and Mackenzie can claim the full qualified business income deduction on Mac561's business income allocated to her. Determine Mackenzie's after-tax cash flow from the entity's business income and any compensation she receives from the business under the following assumptions:
    a) Mackenzie conducted Mac561 as a single-member LLC.
    b) Mackenzie conducted Mac561 as an S corporation and she received a salary of $100,000. All business income allocated to her is also distributed to her.
    c) Mackenzie conducted Mac561 as an S corporation and she received a salary of $20,000. All business income allocated to her is also distributed to her.
    d) Which entity/compensation combination generated the most after-tax cash flow for Mackenzie? What are the primary contributing factors favoring this combination?

LO 15-3

56. SCC corporation (a calendar-year C corporation) has a net operating loss (NOL) carryover to 2022 in the amount of $30,000. How much tax will SCC pay for 2022 if it reports taxable income from operations of $20,000 before considering loss carryovers under the following assumptions?
    a) The NOL originated in 2017.
    b) The NOL originated in 2018.

LO 15-3

57. Willow Corp. (a calendar-year C corporation) reported taxable income before the net operating loss deduction (NOL) in the amount of $100,000 in 2022. Willow had an NOL carryover of $90,000 to 2022. How much tax will Willow Corp. pay in 2022, what is its NOL carryover to 2023, and when will the NOL expire under the following assumptions?
    a) $50,000 of the NOL carryover was generated in 2016 and $40,000 of the NOL carryover was generated in 2017.
    b) $40,000 of the NOL was generated in 2016 and $50,000 was generated in 2021.

LO 15-3

58. Damarcus is a 50 percent owner of Rockit (a business entity). In the current year, Rockit reported a $100,000 business loss. Answer the following questions associated with each of the following alternative scenarios.
    a) Rockit is organized as a C corporation and Damarcus works full time as an employee for Rockit. Damarcus has a $20,000 basis in his Rockit stock. How much of Rockit's loss is Damarcus allowed to deduct against his other income?
    b) Rockit is organized as an LLC taxed as a partnership. Fifty percent of Rockit's loss is allocated to Damarcus. Damarcus works full time for Rockit (he is not considered to be a passive investor in Rockit). Damarcus has a $20,000 basis and at-risk amount in his ownership interest in Rockit. Damarcus does not report

income or loss from any other business activity investments. How much of the $50,000 loss allocated to him by Rockit is Damarcus allowed to deduct this year?

c) Rockit is organized as an LLC taxed as a partnership. Fifty percent of Rockit's loss is allocated to Damarcus. Damarcus does not work for Rockit at all (he is a passive investor in Rockit). Damarcus has a $20,000 basis and at-risk amount in his ownership interest in Rockit. Damarcus does not report income or loss from any other business activity investments. How much of the $50,000 loss allocated to him by Rockit is Damarcus allowed to deduct this year?

d) Rockit is organized as an LLC taxed as a partnership. Fifty percent of Rockit's loss is allocated to Damarcus. Damarcus works full time for Rockit (he is not considered to be a passive investor in Rockit). Damarcus has a $70,000 basis and at-risk amount in his ownership interest in Rockit. Damarcus does not report income or loss from any other business activity investments. How much of the $50,000 loss allocated to him by Rockit is Damarcus allowed to deduct this year?

e) Rockit is organized as an LLC taxed as a partnership. Fifty percent of Rockit's loss is allocated to Damarcus. Damarcus does not work for Rockit at all (he is a passive investor in Rockit). Damarcus has a $20,000 basis and at-risk amount in his ownership interest in Rockit. Damarcus reports $10,000 of income from another business activity in which he is a passive investor. How much of the $50,000 loss allocated to him by Rockit is Damarcus allowed to deduct this year?

59. Danni is a single 30 percent owner of Kolt (a business entity). In the current year, Kolt reported a $1,000,000 business loss. Answer the following questions associated with each of the following alternative scenarios: LO 15-3

a) Kolt is organized as a C corporation and Danni works 20 hours a week as an employee for Kolt. Danni has a $200,000 basis in her Kolt stock. How much of Kolt's loss is Danni allowed to deduct this year against her other income?

b) Kolt is organized as an LLC taxed as a partnership. Thirty percent of Kolt's loss is allocated to Danni. Danni works 20 hours a week on Kolt business activities (she is not considered to be a passive investor in Kolt). Danni has a $400,000 basis in her Kolt ownership interest, and she also has a $400,000 at-risk amount in her investment in Kolt. Danni does not report income or loss from any other business activity investments. How much of the $300,000 loss allocated to her from Kolt is Danni allowed to deduct this year?

c) Kolt is organized as an LLC taxed as a partnership. Thirty percent of Kolt's loss is allocated to Danni. Danni is not involved in Kolt business activities. Consequently, she is considered to be a passive investor in Kolt. Danni has a $400,000 basis and at-risk amount in her ownership interest in Kolt. Danni does not report income or loss from any other business activity investments. How much of the $300,000 loss allocated to her from Kolt is Danni allowed to deduct this year?

60. Mustafa, Mickayla, and Taylor are starting a new business (MMT). To get the business started, Mustafa is contributing $200,000 for a 40 percent ownership interest, Mickayla is contributing a building with a value of $200,000 and a tax basis of $150,000 for a 40 percent ownership interest, and Taylor is contributing legal services for a 20 percent ownership interest. What amount of gain or income is each owner required to recognize under each of the following alternative situations? [*Hint:* Look at §§351 and 721.] LO 15-3 research

a) MMT is formed as a C corporation.

b) MMT is formed as an S corporation.

c) MMT is formed as an LLC (taxed as a partnership).

61. Dave and his friend Stewart each owns 50 percent of KBS. During the year, Dave received $75,000 compensation for services he performed for KBS during the year. He performed a significant amount of work for the entity, and he was heavily LO 15-3 research

involved in management decisions for the entity (he was not a passive investor in KBS). After deducting Dave's compensation, KBS reported taxable income of $30,000. How much FICA and/or self-employment tax is Dave required to pay on his compensation and his share of the KBS income if KBS is formed as a C corporation, an S corporation, or a limited liability company (taxed as a partnership) (ignore the .9 percent additional Medicare tax)? How much FICA tax would the entity be required to pay on the compensation paid to Dave?

LO 15-3
research

62. Rondo and his business associate, Larry, are considering forming a business entity called R&L, but they are unsure about whether to form it as a C corporation, an S corporation, or an LLC taxed as a partnership for tax purposes. Rondo and Larry would each invest $50,000 in the business. Thus, each owner would take an initial basis in his ownership interest of $50,000 no matter which entity type is formed. Shortly after the formation of the entity, the business borrowed $30,000 from the bank. If applicable, this debt will be shared equally between the two owners.
    a) After taking the loan into account, what is Rondo's tax basis in his R&L stock if R&L is formed as a C corporation?
    b) After taking the loan into account, what is Rondo's tax basis in his R&L stock if R&L is formed as an S corporation?
    c) After taking the loan into account, what is Rondo's tax basis in his R&L ownership interest if R&L is formed as an LLC and taxed as a partnership?

LO 15-3
research

63. Haruki and Bob have owned and operated SOA as a C corporation for a number of years. When they formed the entity, Haruki and Bob each contributed $100,000 to SOA. Each has a current basis of $100,000 in his SOA ownership interest. Information on SOA's assets at the end of year 5 is as follows (SOA does not have any liabilities):

Assets	FMV	Adjusted Basis	Built-in Gain
Cash	$200,000	$200,000	$ 0
Inventory	80,000	40,000	40,000
Land and building	220,000	170,000	50,000
Total	$500,000		

At the end of year 5, SOA liquidated and distributed half of the land and building, half of the inventory, and half of the cash remaining after paying taxes (if any) to each owner. Assume that, excluding the effects of the liquidating distribution, SOA's taxable income for year 5 is $0.
    a) What are the amount and character of gain or loss SOA will recognize on the liquidating distribution?
    b) What are the amount and character of gain or loss Haruki will recognize when he receives the liquidating distribution of cash and property? Recall that his stock basis is $100,000 and he is treated as having sold his stock for the liquidation proceeds.

COMPREHENSIVE PROBLEMS

Select problems are available with Connect®.

Mc Graw Hill connect

planning
research

64. Daisy Taylor has developed a viable new business idea. Her idea is to design and manufacture cookware that remains cool to the touch when in use. She has had several family members and friends try out her prototype cookware, and they have consistently given the cookware rave reviews. With this encouragement, Daisy started giving serious thought to starting up a business called "Cool Touch Cookware" (CTC).

Daisy understands that it will take a few years for the business to become profitable. She would like to grow her business and perhaps at some point "go public" or sell the business to a large retailer.

Daisy, who is single, decided to quit her full-time job so that she could focus all of her efforts on the new business. Daisy had some savings to support her for a while, but she did not have any other source of income. She was able to recruit Kesha and Aryan to join her as initial equity investors in CTC. Kesha has an MBA and a law degree. She was employed as a business consultant when she decided to leave that job to work with Daisy and Aryan. Aryan owns a *very* profitable used car business. Because buying and selling used cars takes all his time, he is interested in becoming only a passive investor in CTC. He wanted to get in on the ground floor because he really likes the product and believes CTC will be wildly successful. While CTC originally has three investors, Daisy and Kesha have plans to grow the business and seek more owners and capital in the future.

The three owners agreed that Daisy would contribute land and cash for a 30 percent interest in CTC, Kesha would contribute services (legal and business advisory) for the first two years for a 30 percent interest, and Aryan would contribute cash for a 40 percent interest. The plan called for Daisy and Kesha to be actively involved in managing the business, while Aryan would not be. The three equity owners' contributions are summarized as follows:

Daisy Contributed	FMV	Adjusted Basis	Ownership Interest
Land (held as investment)	$120,000	$70,000	30%
Cash	30,000		
Kesha Contributed			
Services	$150,000		30
Aryan Contributed			
Cash	$200,000		40

Working together, Daisy and Kesha made the following five-year income and loss projections for CTC. They anticipate the business will be profitable and that it will continue to grow after the first five years.

Cool Touch Cookware
5-Year Income and Loss Projections

Year	Income (Loss)
1	$(200,000)
2	(80,000)
3	(20,000)
4	60,000
5	180,000

With plans for Daisy and Kesha to spend a considerable amount of their time working for and managing CTC, the owners would like to develop a compensation plan that works for all parties. Down the road, they plan to have two business locations (in different cities). Daisy would take responsibility for the activities of one location and Kesha would take responsibility for the other. Finally, they would like to arrange for some performance-based financial incentives for each location.

To get the business activities started, Daisy and Kesha determined CTC would need to borrow $800,000 to purchase a building to house its manufacturing facilities and its administrative offices (at least for now). Also, in need of additional cash, Daisy and Kesha arranged to have CTC borrow $300,000 from a local bank and borrow $200,000 cash from Aryan. CTC would pay Aryan a market rate of interest on the loan, but there was no fixed date for principal repayment.

Required:

Identify significant tax and nontax issues or concerns that may differ across entity types and discuss how they are relevant to the choice of entity decision for CTC.

research

65. Cool Touch Cookware (CTC) has been in business for about 10 years now. Daisy and Kesha are each 50 percent owners of the business. They initially established the business with cash contributions. CTC manufactures unique cookware that remains cool to the touch when in use. CTC has been fairly profitable over the years. Daisy and Kesha have both been actively involved in managing the business. They have developed very good personal relationships with many customers (both wholesale and retail) that, Daisy and Kesha believe, keep the customers coming back.

    On September 30 of the current year, CTC had all of its assets appraised. Below is CTC's balance sheet, as of September 30, with the corresponding appraisals of the fair market value of all of its assets. Note that CTC has several depreciated assets. CTC uses the hybrid method of accounting. It accounts for its gross margin–related items under the accrual method, and it accounts for everything else using the cash method of accounting.

Assets	Adjusted Tax Basis	FMV
Cash	$150,000	$150,000
Accounts receivable	20,000	15,000
Inventory*	90,000	300,000
Equipment	120,000	100,000
Investment in XYZ stock	40,000	120,000
Land (used in the business)	80,000	70,000
Building	200,000	180,000
Total assets	$700,000	$935,000†
Liabilities		
Accounts payable	$ 40,000	
Bank loan	60,000	
Mortgage on building	100,000	
Equity	500,000	
Total liabilities and equity	$700,000	

*CTC uses the LIFO method for determining the adjusted basis of its inventory. Its basis in the inventory under the FIFO method would have been $110,000.

†In addition, Daisy and Kesha had the entire business appraised at $1,135,000, which is $200,000 more than the value of the identifiable assets.

From January 1 of the current year through September 30, CTC reported the following income:

Ordinary business income	$530,000
Dividends from XYZ stock	12,000
Long-term capital losses	15,000
Interest income	3,000

Daisy and Kesha are considering changing the business form of CTC.

Required:

a) Assume CTC is organized as a C corporation. Identify significant tax and nontax issues associated with converting CTC from a C corporation to an S corporation. [*Hint:* See §§1374 and 1363(d).]

b) Assume CTC is organized as a C corporation. Identify significant tax and nontax issues associated with converting CTC from a C corporation to an LLC. Assume CTC converts to an LLC (taxed as a partnership) by distributing its assets to its shareholders, who then contribute the assets to a new LLC. [*Hint:* See §§331, 336, and 721(a).]

c) Assume that CTC is a C corporation with a net operating loss carryforward as of the beginning of the year in the amount of $500,000 and that the NOL originated in 2019. Identify significant tax and nontax issues associated with converting CTC from a C corporation to an LLC (taxed as a partnership). Assume CTC converts to an LLC by distributing its assets to its shareholders, who then contribute the assets to a new LLC. [*Hint:* See §§172(a), 331, 336, and 721(a).]

66. Amy is evaluating the cash flow consequences of organizing her business entity SHO as an LLC (taxed as a sole proprietorship), an S corporation, or a C corporation. She used the following assumptions to make her calculations:

a) For all entity types, the business reports $22,000 of business income before deducting compensation paid to Amy and payroll taxes SHO pays on Amy's behalf.

b) All entities use the cash method of accounting.

c) If Amy organizes SHO as an S corporation or a C corporation, SHO will pay Amy a $5,000 annual salary (assume the salary is reasonable for purposes of this problem). For both the S and C corporations, Amy will pay 7.65 percent FICA tax on her salary and SHO will also pay 7.65 percent FICA tax on Amy's salary (the FICA tax paid by the entity is deductible by the entity).

d) Amy's marginal ordinary income tax rate is 35 percent, and her income tax rate on qualified dividends and net capital gains is 15 percent.

e) Amy's marginal self-employment tax rate is 15.3 percent.

f) Amy pays a .9 percent additional Medicare tax on salary and net earnings from self-employment (i.e., her salary and net earnings from self-employment are over the threshold for the tax).

g) Amy pays a 3.8 percent net investment income tax on dividends and net capital gains (i.e., AGI on joint tax return is over threshold by more than any net investment income she receives).

h) Assume that for purposes of the qualified business income deduction, the business income is not from a specified service and neither the wage-based limitation nor the taxable income limitation applies to limit the deduction.

i) If SHO is formed as an S corporation or a C corporation, SHO will distribute all of its earnings after paying entity level taxes and after deducting salary and related FICA taxes paid to Amy.

Required:

a) Fill in the cells in the table below to identify cash flows associated with the income from the business if the business is formed as an LLC (sole proprietorship), S corporation, or C corporation for tax purposes. Enter cash outflows as negative numbers.

Cash flow	LLC (Sole prop)	S Corporation	C Corporation
Business income	$22,000	$22,000	$22,000
FICA taxes paid by Amy			
FICA taxes paid by SHO			
Self-employment tax paid by Amy			
Federal income tax paid by SHO			
Additional Medicare tax paid by Amy			
Net investment income tax paid by Amy			
Federal income tax paid by Amy*			
Cash remaining after taxes			

*Remember to consider account flow-through income, qualified dividends, the self-employment tax deduction, and the qualified business income deduction in calculation.

b) At a high level, describe the factors causing differences in the after-tax cash flows from each entity, given that the before-tax cash flows are the same (don't use dollar amounts in the explanation).

UWorld | ROGER CPA Review

UWorld Roger CPA Review

Sample CPA Exam questions from Roger CPA Review are available in Connect as support for the topics in this text. These Multiple Choice Questions and Task-Based Simulations include expert-written explanations and solutions and provide a starting point for students to become familiar with the content and functionality of the actual CPA Exam.

chapter

16 Corporate Operations

Learning Objectives

Upon completing this chapter, you should be able to:

LO 16-1 Describe the corporate income tax formula and discuss tax considerations relating to corporations' accounting periods and accounting methods.

LO 16-2 Identify common permanent and temporary book–tax differences and compute a corporation's taxable income and associated income tax liability.

LO 16-3 Describe a corporation's tax return reporting and estimated tax payment obligations.

mentatdgt/Shutterstock

Storyline Summary

Premiere Computer Corporation (PCC)

Medium-sized publicly traded company

Manufactures and sells computers and computer-related equipment

Calendar-year taxpayer

Elise Brandon (she/her/hers)

Newly hired tax associate for a large public accounting firm

Currently assigned to review the federal income tax return for PCC

Today was Elise's first day on the job as a tax associate for a large public accounting firm. Shortly after she arrived, Aminah, a tax manager, introduced herself and took Elise around the office to meet some of the people with whom Elise would be working. After the introductions, Aminah told Elise she would like her to review the federal tax return for Premiere Computer Corporation (PCC).

PCC is a medium-sized publicly traded C corporation that manufactures computers and computer-related equipment. PCC has been a client of the firm for several years. Overall, PCC has been a fairly profitable company, but last year the company experienced a bit of a setback, incurring its first tax loss in many years.

Elise was excited about her opportunity. She was confident her accounting education had adequately prepared her to successfully complete the assignment. When Aminah spoke with Elise about the assignment, Aminah advised Elise to first review PCC's tax return and tax return workpapers from last year to get an idea about how to review the current-year tax return. Next, she should start with the audited numbers on the income statement and examine the book-to-tax adjustments that caused taxable income to differ from PCC's book net income before income taxes. Aminah counseled Elise to identify those book and tax differences as being "temporary" or "permanent" because Elise was eventually going to compute the company's accounting "income tax provision" from this information. Aminah encouraged Elise to keep her posted on her progress and ask questions when necessary to keep the project on budget. ■

In this chapter we explore the process of computing and reporting taxable income for C corporations. As we discussed in the Business Entities Overview chapter, C corporations are taxpaying entities separate from their shareholders. Each year, C corporations are required to compute their taxable income and pay tax on the income. In contrast to individuals, C corporations often compute taxable income by starting with their book (financial accounting) income and making adjustments for book–tax differences.

LO 16-1

CORPORATE TAXABLE INCOME FORMULA

The formulas for computing corporate taxable income and individual taxable income are similar in some respects and different in others. Exhibit 16-1 compares the corporate income tax formula with the individual tax formula.

EXHIBIT 16-1 Corporate and Individual Tax Formulas

	Corporate Tax Formula	Individual Tax Formula
	Gross income	Gross income
Minus	Deductions	For AGI deductions
Equals		Adjusted gross income
Minus		From AGI deductions: (1) Greater of: (a) Standard deduction or (b) Itemized deductions (2) Charitable contribution deduction for taxpayers who do not itemize deductions* (3) Deduction for qualified business income
Equals	Taxable income	Taxable income
Times	Tax rates	Tax rates
Equals	Regular income tax liability	Regular income tax liability
Add	Other taxes	Other taxes
Equals	Total tax	Total tax
Minus	Credits	Credits
Minus	Prepayments	Prepayments
Equals	Taxes due (or refund)	Taxes due (or refund)

*The charitable contribution for nonitemizers applies for 2021 but, as of press time, the deduction had not been extended to 2022.

THE KEY FACTS

Corporate Taxable Income Formula and Accounting Periods and Methods

- The corporate tax formula is similar to the individual tax formula, but corporations don't claim the deduction for qualified business income and they don't itemize deductions or deduct the standard deduction.
- In 2022, corporations with annual average gross receipts of $27 million or less over the three prior tax years (or a shorter period for new corporations) may use the cash method.

Corporations compute gross income in the same way as other types of business entities and individual taxpayers. Similar to other businesses, corporations are permitted to deduct ordinary and necessary business expenditures (see discussion in the Business Income, Deductions, and Accounting Methods chapter). However, in contrast to individuals, corporations cannot claim the deduction for qualified business income and corporations do not itemize deductions or deduct a standard deduction. Consequently, the formula for computing a corporation's taxable income is relatively straightforward.

Accounting Periods and Methods

In the Business Income, Deductions, and Accounting Methods chapter, we discussed accounting periods and methods for all types of business entities. We learned that corporations measure their taxable income over a tax year and that their tax year must be the same as their financial accounting year. A C corporation generally elects its tax year when it files its first income tax return. A C corporation is able to adopt a calendar or any fiscal year-end that matches its financial accounting year-end.

A corporation's choice of accounting methods determines when income and deductions are recognized. As we discuss in the Business Income, Deductions, and Accounting Methods chapter, accounting methods include overall methods of accounting (accrual method, cash method, or hybrid method) and accounting methods for individual items such as inventory (for example, LIFO or FIFO) or depreciation (accelerated or straight-line). For tax purposes, corporations have some flexibility in choosing methods of accounting for individual items or transactions. However, corporations generally are required to use the accrual method of accounting.[1] For tax purposes, corporations with annual average gross receipts of $27 million or less for the three years prior to the current tax year (2022) can elect to use the cash method of accounting.[2] Corporations that have not been in existence for at least three years compute their annual average gross receipts over the prior periods they have been in existence to determine if they are permitted to use the cash method of accounting.

COMPUTING CORPORATE TAXABLE INCOME

LO 16-2

To compute taxable income, most corporations begin with **book (financial reporting) income** after income tax expense and then make adjustments for **book–tax differences** to reconcile to the tax numbers.[3]

Book–Tax Differences

Many items of income and expense are accounted for differently for book and tax purposes. The following discussion describes common book–tax differences applicable to corporations. Each book–tax difference can be classified as "unfavorable" or "favorable" depending on its effect on taxable income relative to book income. A book–tax difference that requires an add-back to book income to compute taxable income is an **unfavorable book–tax difference** because it increases taxable income (and, therefore, taxes payable) relative to book income. A book–tax difference that requires corporations to subtract the difference from book income in computing taxable income is a **favorable book–tax difference** because it decreases taxable income (and, therefore, taxes payable) relative to book income.

In addition to the favorable or unfavorable distinction, book–tax differences can be categorized as permanent or temporary. **Permanent book–tax differences** arise from items that are income or deductions during the year for either book or tax purposes but not both. Permanent differences *do not reverse* over time, so over the long term, the *total* amount of income or deductions for the items differs for book and tax purposes. In contrast, **temporary book–tax differences** reverse over time such that, over the long term, corporations recognize the same amount of income or deductions for the items on their income statements as they recognize on their tax returns. Temporary book–tax differences arise because the income or deduction items are included in financial accounting income in one year and in taxable income in a different year. Temporary book–tax differences that are *initially* favorable (unfavorable) become unfavorable (favorable) in future years when they reverse.

[1]See the Business Income, Deductions, and Accounting Methods chapter for a detailed discussion of determining the timing of taxable income and tax deductions under the accrual method.

[2]§448. Other special types of corporations such as qualified family farming corporations and qualified personal service corporations may use the cash method of accounting. A C corporation that fails the $27 million gross receipts test is precluded from using the cash method for the year in which the test is not satisfied but can resume using the cash method in future years in which the test is satisfied. The $27 million annual average gross receipts test threshold is indexed for inflation.

[3]This chapter generally assumes that generally accepted accounting principles (GAAP) are used to determine book income numbers.

> **THE KEY FACTS**
>
> **Computing Corporate Regular Taxable Income**
>
> - Corporations reconcile from book income to taxable income.
>   - Favorable (unfavorable) book–tax differences decrease (increase) taxable income relative to book income.
>   - Permanent book–tax differences arise in one year and never reverse.
>   - Temporary book–tax differences arise in one year and reverse in subsequent years.

Distinguishing between permanent and temporary book–tax differences is important for several reasons. First, as we discuss later in the chapter, large corporations are *required to disclose* their permanent and temporary book–tax differences on a schedule attached to their tax returns. Second, the distinction is useful for those responsible for tracking book–tax differences for purposes of computing the corporation's income tax expense on its income statement. For temporary book–tax differences, it is important to understand how the items were accounted for in previous years to appropriately account for current-year reversals. In contrast, for permanent book–tax differences, corporations need only consider current-year amounts to determine book–tax differences. Finally, as we discuss in more detail in the Accounting for Income Taxes chapter, permanent differences impact a company's effective tax rate whereas temporary differences generally do not. Below we describe common book–tax differences.

Common Permanent Book–Tax Differences As we describe in the Business Income, Deductions, and Accounting Methods chapter, businesses, including corporations, exclude certain income items from gross income, and they are not allowed to deduct certain expenditures for tax purposes. Because these income items are included in book income, and the expenditures are deductible for financial reporting purposes, they generate permanent book–tax differences. Exhibit 16-2 identifies several permanent book–tax differences associated with items we discuss in the Business Income, Deductions, and Accounting Methods chapter; explains their tax treatment; and identifies whether the items create favorable or unfavorable book–tax differences.

EXHIBIT 16-2 Common Permanent Book–Tax Differences Associated with Items Discussed in the Business Income, Deductions, and Accounting Methods Chapter

Description	Explanation	Difference
Interest income from municipal bonds	Income included in book income but excluded from taxable income	Favorable
Death benefit from life insurance on key employees	Income included in book income but excluded from taxable income	Favorable
Interest expense on loans to acquire investments generating tax-exempt income	Deductible for book purposes, but expenses incurred to generate tax-exempt income are not deductible for tax purposes	Unfavorable
Life insurance premiums for which corporation is beneficiary	Deductible for book purposes, but expenses incurred to generate tax-exempt income (life insurance death benefit) are not deductible for tax purposes	Unfavorable
Meals expense	Fully deductible for book purposes but generally only 50 percent deductible for tax purposes. However, for 2022 (and 2021), the cost of meals purchased from restaurants (including take-out and delivery) is fully deductible for tax purposes.[4]	Unfavorable
Fines and penalties and political contributions	Deductible for book purposes but not for tax purposes	Unfavorable
Entertainment expense	Deductible for book purposes but not deductible for tax purposes	Unfavorable
Federal income tax expense	Deductible for book purposes but not deductible for tax purposes	Unfavorable

[4]IRS Notice 2021-25 provides guidance on what is and is not considered to be a restaurant.

Example 16-1

Elise reviewed PCC's prior-year tax return and its current-year trial balance. She discovered that PCC earned $12,000 of interest income from City of San Diego municipal bonds, expensed $34,000 for premiums on key employee life insurance policies, and expensed $28,000 for business-related meals purchased from restaurants. What amount of permanent book–tax differences does PCC report from these transactions? Are the differences favorable or unfavorable?

Answer: See Elise's summary of these items below:

Item	Adjustment (Favorable) Unfavorable	Notes
Interest income from City of San Diego municipal bonds	$(12,000)	Income excluded from gross income.
Premiums paid for key employee life insurance policies	34,000	Premiums paid to insure lives of key company executives are not deductible for tax purposes.
Meals expense	0	No book–tax difference because meals were purchased from restaurants.

Federal income tax expense. Corporations deduct federal income tax expense (called a "provision for income taxes") in determining their book income [determined under FASB ASC (Accounting Standards Codification) Topic 740]. However, they are not allowed to deduct federal income tax expense for tax purposes.[5] Federal income tax expense is an unfavorable, permanent difference when the corporation is reconciling after-tax book income with taxable income.

Example 16-2

What if: Assume that PCC's audited financial reporting income statement indicates that its federal income tax provision (expense) is $2,000,000.[6] What is PCC's book–tax difference for the year associated with this expense? Is the difference favorable or unfavorable? Is it permanent or temporary?

Answer: $2,000,000 unfavorable, permanent book–tax difference because PCC is not allowed to deduct federal income tax expense for tax purposes.

Common Temporary Book–Tax Differences Corporations experience temporary book–tax differences because the accounting methods they apply to determine certain items of income and expense for financial reporting purposes differ from those they use for tax purposes. Unlike permanent book–tax differences, temporary book–tax differences balance out over time, so corporations eventually recognize the same amount of income or deduction for the particular item. Exhibit 16-3 identifies common temporary book–tax differences associated with items we discuss in other chapters. Exhibit 16-4 summarizes PCC's temporary book–tax differences described in Exhibit 16-3.

[5]§275(a)(1).

[6]Note that this example is presented in what-if form because this is not the income tax expense PCC will report in its financial statements. We compute PCC's actual income tax expense in the Accounting for Income Taxes chapter.

EXHIBIT 16-3 Common Temporary Book–Tax Differences Associated with Items Discussed in Other Chapters

Description	Explanation	Initial Difference*
Depreciation expense (Property Acquisition and Cost Recovery chapter)	Difference between depreciation expense for tax purposes and depreciation expense for book purposes.	Favorable
Gain or loss on disposition of depreciable assets (Property Dispositions chapter)	Difference between gain or loss for tax and book purposes when a corporation sells or disposes of depreciable property. Difference generally arises because depreciation expense, and thus the adjusted basis of the asset, is different for tax and book purposes. This difference is essentially the reversal of the book–tax difference for the depreciation expense on the asset sold or disposed of.	Unfavorable
Bad debt expense (Business Income, Deductions, and Accounting Methods chapter)	Direct write-off method for tax purposes; allowance method for book purposes.	Unfavorable
Unearned rent revenue (Business Income, Deductions, and Accounting Methods chapter)	Taxable on receipt but recognized when earned for book purposes.	Unfavorable
Deferred compensation (Business Income, Deductions, and Accounting Methods chapter)	Deductible when accrued for book purposes but deductible when paid for tax purposes if accrued but not paid within 2.5 months after year-end. Also, accrued compensation to shareholders owning more than 50 percent of the corporation is not deductible until paid.	Unfavorable
Organizational expenditures and start-up costs (Property Acquisition and Cost Recovery chapter)	Immediately deducted for book purposes but capitalized and amortized for tax purposes (limited immediate expensing allowed for tax).	Unfavorable
Warranty expense and other estimated expenses (Business Income, Deductions, and Accounting Methods chapter)	Estimated expenses deducted for book purposes, but actual expenses deducted for tax purposes.	Unfavorable
UNICAP (§263A) (Business Income, Deductions, and Accounting Methods chapter)	Certain expenditures deducted for book purposes but capitalized to inventory for tax purposes. Difference reverses when inventory is sold. There is an exception for taxpayers with an annual average of $27 million or less in gross receipts over the three prior years.	Unfavorable
Interest expense [§163(j)] (Business Income, Deductions, and Accounting Methods chapter)	The deduction for interest expense is disallowed to the extent it exceeds the sum of business interest income and 30 percent of adjusted taxable income (ATI). There is an exception for taxpayers with an annual average of $27 million or less in gross receipts over the three prior years. Unused amounts can be carried forward indefinitely. ATI is defined as taxable income computed without regard to any business interest expense or business interest income. It also excludes depreciation and amortization.	Unfavorable
Installment sales (§453) (Property Dispositions chapter)	When qualifying property is sold and the selling taxpayer receives payment in a taxable year subsequent to the year of disposition, under the installment method, the taxpayer recognizes realized gain (but not loss) pro rata over time as the payments are collected. Gain from property dispositions are generally recognized for book purposes in the year of disposition.	Favorable
Like-kind exchange (§1031) (Property Dispositions chapter)	Realized gain (or loss) is deferred for tax purposes when a taxpayer exchanges property for other qualifying real property in an exchange that meets certain timing requirements. Gain or loss is generally recognized immediately for book purposes.	Favorable

*Note that each of the initial book–tax differences will reverse over time [the initially favorable (unfavorable) book–tax differences will reverse to become unfavorable (favorable) book–tax differences in the future].

EXHIBIT 16-4 PCC's Temporary Book–Tax Differences Associated with Items Discussed in Other Chapters

Item	(1) Books (Dr) Cr	(2) Tax (Dr) Cr	(2) − (1) Difference (Favorable) Unfavorable
Depreciation expense	$(2,400,000)	$(3,100,000)	$(700,000)
Gain on fixed-asset disposition	54,000	70,000	16,000
Bad debt expense	(165,000)	(95,000)	70,000
Warranty expense	(580,000)	(410,000)	170,000
Deferred compensation	(300,000)	(450,000)	(150,000)

Example 16-3

What if: Assume that PCC started business on July 1, 2021. PCC incurred $100,000 of organizational expenditures that it expensed immediately for books and capitalized to amortize over 180 months for tax purposes. What was PCC's book–tax difference associated with organizational expenditures in 2021? What is the book–tax difference associated with organizational expenditures for 2022? Are these book–tax differences favorable or unfavorable? Are they permanent or temporary?

Answer: For 2021, the book–tax difference is $96,667 unfavorable ($100,000 book expense and $3,333 amortization tax deduction) temporary difference. For books the entire $100,000 was expensed in 2021, but for tax only $3,333 was amortized ($100,000 × 6/180 months). After 2021, the remaining basis in the organizational expenditures was $0 for books and $96,667 for tax. For 2022, the book–tax difference is $6,667 favorable ($0 book expense and $6,667 amortization tax deduction) temporary difference. Because the entire amount of organizational expenditures was expensed on the books in 2021, there are no organizational expenditures remaining to expense for book purposes. However, for tax purposes, PCC can deduct $6,667 of amortization for tax purposes ($100,000 × 12/180 months). PCC will continue amortizing the organizational expenditures for 162 more months (13.5 years). All of the tax amortization will result in a favorable, temporary book–tax difference after 2021.

TAXES IN THE REAL WORLD Are Large Corporations Paying Enough in Taxes?

In a report dated April 2021, the Institute of Taxation and Economic Policy (ITEP) indicated that, based on an analysis of financial statements and notes to the financial statements, 55 corporations paid $0 taxes in 2020 despite reporting significant pre-tax profit for book purposes. Corporations on the list included Archer Daniels Midland, FedEx, Nike, Dish Network, and Salesforce. The report indicates that "tax breaks" such as deducting the bargain element of nonqualified stock options or accelerated depreciation on business asset purchases (e.g., 100% bonus depreciation) or the Research and Experimentation Credit (for research and development) are the reason(s) some corporations are not paying taxes, even though they are reporting profits on their financial statements. Some may perceive this as an injustice and determine that the system is flawed because large, profitable corporations aren't paying their fair share of taxes. In an article published by the Tax Foundation, the author points out that there may be legitimate reasons why a corporation may pay $0 taxes despite reporting profits for book purposes. The article points out that, first and foremost, the accounting rules (GAAP) that determine book income are different from tax laws that determine taxable income. Book and taxable income serve different purposes. For example, tax laws allow accelerated depreciation deductions or tax credits for research to companies that invest in capital or perform research and development because Congress wants to encourage companies to invest in business and research and development. The article also points out that the IRS is closely watching large corporations. The IRS audit rate for large corporations is

(continued on page 16-8)

near 50 percent, while the overall audit rate for other corporations is 0.7 percent. Further, the Joint Committee on Taxation reviews C corporation refunds in excess of $5 million. Finally, large companies pay taxes in foreign countries that add to their overall tax bill without increasing their U.S. tax bill. The article concludes that it is a mistake to determine that something is amiss when a corporation has a $0 tax bill because Congress makes the tax laws that corporations are following and Congress could change the tax rules to conform more closely to book rules, if it wished to do so. In the end, different people have different opinions about whether large corporations are paying enough taxes. What's your opinion?

Sources: Matthew Gardner and Steve Wamhoff, "55 Corporations Paid $0 Federal Taxes on 2020 Profits," ITEP, April 2, 2021, https://itep.org/55-profitable-corporations-zero-corporate-tax/; and Erica York, "Explaining the GAAP between Book and Taxable Income," Tax Foundation, June 3, 2021, https://taxfoundation.org/corporations-zero-corporate-tax/.

Dividends and stock ownership related. Corporations receiving dividends from other corporations may account for the dividends in different ways for book and tax purposes. For tax purposes, corporations receiving dividends include the dividends in gross income.[7] For financial reporting purposes, accounting for the dividend depends on the receiving corporation's level of stock ownership in the distributing corporation. The *general* rules for such investments are summarized as follows:

- If the receiving (shareholder) corporation owns less than 20 percent of the stock of the distributing corporation, the receiving corporation includes the dividend in both book and taxable income (i.e., no book–tax difference on the dividend). In addition, if the corporate shareholder is holding the stock investment for trading (i.e., purchased the stock with the intent to sell it within a short period, usually less than a year), the shareholder corporation includes the unrealized gain or loss for the year on that stock in book income but not taxable income. The unrealized gain or loss for the year results in a temporary book–tax difference that will completely reverse when the shareholder corporation sells the stock.
- If the receiving corporation owns at least 20 percent but not more than 50 percent of the distributing corporation's stock, the receiving corporation usually includes a pro rata portion of the distributing corporation's earnings in its book income under the "equity method of accounting" (ASC Topic 323) and does not include the dividend in its income, resulting in a temporary favorable or unfavorable book–tax difference for the difference between the pro rata share of equity income reported on the books and the dividend amount reported on the tax return.
- If the receiving corporation owns more than 50 percent of the distributing corporation's stock, the receiving corporation and the distributing corporation usually consolidate their financial reporting books (ASC Topic 810) and the intercompany dividend is eliminated (book–tax difference beyond the scope of this text).[8]

Example 16-4

What if: Assume that PCC owns 30 percent of the stock of BCS, a U.S. corporation, and applies the equity method of accounting for book purposes. During 2022, BCS distributed a $40,000 dividend to PCC. Also, BCS reported $100,000 of net income for 2022 on its financial statements. Based on this information, what is PCC's 2022 book–tax difference relating to the dividend and its investment in BCS (ignore the dividends-received deduction)? Is the difference favorable or unfavorable?

[7]As we discuss later in the chapter, corporations are generally entitled to deduct a certain percentage of the dividends received based on the level of the receiving corporation's ownership in the distributing corporation.

[8]Note that at least 80 percent ownership is required to file a consolidated tax return.

Answer: $10,000 unfavorable book–tax difference, computed as follows:

Description	Amount	Explanation
(1) Dividend received in 2022 (included in 2022 taxable income but not in book income)	$ 40,000	
(2) BCS 2022 net income on financial statements	$ 100,000	
(3) PCC's ownership in BCS stock	30%	
(4) PCC's book income from BCS investment	$ 30,000	(2) × (3)
Unfavorable book–tax difference associated with dividend	**$ 10,000**	(1) − (4)

What if: Assume the same facts as above, except that PCC owns 10 percent of BCS rather than 30 percent. What would be PCC's 2022 book–tax difference relating to the $40,000 dividend and its investment in BCS (ignore the dividends-received deduction)? Assume that PCC's basis (and value) in its BCS stock on January 1 is $1,000,000 and its value in its BCS stock on December 31 is $1,050,000.

Answer: $0 book–tax difference on the dividend because PCC includes the $40,000 dividend in income for both book and tax purposes. $50,000 favorable book–tax difference for the unrealized gain in PCC's BCS stock that is recognized for book purposes but not for tax purposes.

Goodwill acquired in an acquisition. When a corporation acquires the stock of another corporation in a cash (taxable) transaction, the tax basis of each asset of the target corporation remains unchanged. Self-created intangibles such as a patent retain a tax basis of zero or close to zero and do not get written up to fair value as they do for book purposes. The accounting rules (ASC Topic 805) require the target corporation's identifiable assets to be reported at fair value, with any residual amount allocated to book goodwill. This book goodwill will not have a corresponding tax basis. Such book goodwill generally is subject to impairment testing (private companies can elect to amortize the book goodwill over 10 years, however). A book–tax difference does not arise until the goodwill is written off as impaired, at which time the book expense creates a (permanent) unfavorable difference.

In less-frequent acquisitions, the acquiring corporation may acquire the assets of another business directly in a taxable transaction. When this occurs, the assets acquired are assigned a tax basis equal to their fair market value. Any excess of the consideration paid over the net fair value of the tangible and intangible assets acquired is allocated to tax goodwill, which is amortizable over 15 years (180 months).[9] In this case, the goodwill has both a tax and a book basis, which may be the same or different because of differences in the purchase price computation. As the corporation amortizes the goodwill for tax purposes, the resulting book–tax difference is treated as a favorable temporary difference (if book and tax goodwill are different, the accounting becomes more complex and is beyond the scope of this book). If the corporation writes the goodwill off as impaired in a future period, the excess of book goodwill impaired over the remaining goodwill tax basis is treated as an unfavorable temporary book–tax difference (assuming the original tax and book goodwill were equal).

Example 16-5

What if: Suppose that on July 1, 2022, PCC acquired the assets of another business in a taxable acquisition. As part of the transaction, PCC recognized $180,000 of goodwill for both financial accounting and tax purposes. During 2022, PCC amortized $6,000 of the goodwill for tax purposes ($180,000/180 months × 6 months during the year) and did not impair any of the goodwill for financial accounting purposes. What was PCC's book–tax difference associated with this goodwill in 2022? Is it a favorable or unfavorable difference? Is the difference permanent or temporary?

(continued on page 16-10)

[9]§197. Self-created goodwill is not amortizable for tax purposes.

Answer: $6,000 favorable, temporary book–tax difference. The amount of capitalized goodwill is the same for book and tax purposes, and PCC deducted $6,000 of the goodwill for tax purposes and none for book purposes.

What if: Assume that at the end of 2023, PCC recorded a $30,000 goodwill impairment expense on its income statement. What is PCC's book–tax difference associated with its goodwill during 2023? Is the difference favorable or unfavorable? Is the difference permanent or temporary?

Answer: $18,000 unfavorable, temporary book–tax difference, computed as follows:

Description	Amount	Explanation
(1) Goodwill initially recorded on 7/1/22 acquisition	$180,000	
(2) Goodwill impairment recorded in 2023	$ 30,000	This write-down is expensed for book purposes.
(3) Months over which goodwill is amortized for tax purposes.	180	15 years × 12 months = 180 months
(4) Tax goodwill amortization expense for 2023	$ 12,000	[(1)/(3)] × 12 months
Unfavorable book–tax temporary difference associated with goodwill in 2023	**$ 18,000**	(2) − (4)

Corporate-Specific Deductions and Associated Book–Tax Differences

Certain deductions and corresponding limitations apply specifically to corporations. In this section, we introduce these deductions and identify book–tax differences associated with the deductions.

Stock Options Corporations often compensate executives and other employees with stock options. Stock options allow recipients to acquire stock in the corporation issuing the options at a predetermined price over a specified period of time. To acquire the stock, employees exercise the options and pay the **exercise price.** The exercise price is usually at or above the stock price on the day the options are issued to the employee. For example, when a corporation's stock is trading for $10 per share, a corporation might issue (or grant) 100 stock options to an employee that allow the employee to purchase up to 100 shares of the corporation's stock for $10 a share. In most cases, after receiving the options, employees must wait a certain amount of time (called the **requisite service period)** before they are able to exercise them (they must wait until the options **vest** before they can exercise them). If employees stop working for the corporation before the options vest, they forfeit the options.

Stock options are valuable to employees when the stock price appreciates above the exercise price because, when the options vest, employees can purchase the stock at a below-market price. Stock options are a popular form of compensation because they provide incentives for employees receiving the options to work to increase the value of the corporation's stock and thereby benefit themselves and other stockholders.

For tax purposes, the tax treatment to the corporation (and the employee) depends on whether the options are **incentive stock options (ISOs)** (less common, more administrative requirements for the corporation to qualify) or **nonqualified stock options (NQOs)** (more common, options that don't qualify as ISOs).[10] Corporations issuing ISOs

[10]Employees do not recognize any compensation income when they exercise incentive stock options. However, for nonqualified options, they recognize compensation (ordinary) income for the difference between the value of the stock and the exercise price on the date of exercise. This chapter emphasizes the tax treatment of the options from the corporation's perspective. Requirements for options to qualify as incentive stock options are more restrictive than the requirements for nonqualified stock options. The formal requirements for incentive stock options are beyond the scope of this text.

generally do not deduct compensation expense associated with the options for tax purposes. In contrast, for NQOs, corporations deduct for tax purposes the difference between the fair market value of the stock and the exercise price of the option (called the **bargain element**) as compensation expense in the year in which employees exercise the stock options.

For book purposes (ASC Topic 718), corporations are required to recognize *book expense* for stock options they grant. Corporations are required to estimate the fair value of the options at the time they issue them (i.e., on the **grant date**). They then deduct (or expense) the value of the options for book purposes as employee compensation over the employee's requisite service period (i.e., over the **vesting period**). For ISOs, the book compensation expense is an unfavorable permanent difference (book deduction but no tax deduction).

Example 16-6

What if: Assume that on January 1, 2022, PCC issued 10,000 incentive stock options (ISOs) with an estimated fair value of $6 per option. The options vest at the end of four years. For 2022, PCC records a $15,000 compensation expense related to the ISOs (10,000 options × $6/4 years). What is PCC's 2022 book–tax difference associated with the incentive stock options? Would the difference be favorable or unfavorable? Would the difference be permanent or temporary?

Answer: $15,000 unfavorable, permanent difference. PCC does not deduct compensation expense related to the ISOs for tax purposes.

Nonqualified options (NQOs) can generate both temporary and permanent book–tax differences. Corporations recognize unfavorable book–tax difference each year equal to the value of the options that vest during the year but are not exercised (book deduction but no tax deduction). The unfavorable book–tax differences completely reverse (corporations recognize a favorable temporary book–tax difference equal to the previous unfavorable book–tax differences) in the year the employee exercises the stock options.

When an employee exercises an NQO, the tax deduction, which is the difference between the fair market value of the stock purchased and the exercise price on the exercise date, likely will differ from the compensation expense recorded on the income statement over the requisite service period (i.e., the estimated value of the options for book purposes). The corporation recognizes a favorable permanent book–tax difference in the amount by which the tax deduction exceeds the total book expense for the options, and the corporation recognizes an unfavorable permanent book–tax difference in the amount by which the total book expenses for the options exceed the tax deduction.

Example 16-7

On January 1, 2022, PCC granted 20,000 NQOs with an estimated $10 fair value per option ($200,000 total fair value). Each option entitled the recipient to purchase one share of PCC stock for $10 a share (the per share price of PCC stock on January 1, 2022, when the options were granted). The options vested at the end of the day on December 31, 2023. No options were exercised in 2022 or 2023. For 2022 and 2023, PCC deducts compensation expense of $100,000 for book purposes. What is PCC's book–tax difference associated with the nonqualified options in 2022? in 2023? Is the difference favorable or unfavorable? Is it permanent or temporary?

Answer: $100,000 unfavorable, temporary book–tax difference in both 2022 and 2023. PCC reports $100,000 of compensation expense for book purposes in 2022 and 2023 and $0 for tax purposes (no options were exercised in 2022 or 2023).

(continued on page 16-12)

What if: Assume the same facts as above and that on March 1, 2024, employees exercised all 20,000 options at a time when the PCC stock was trading at $25 per share. What is PCC's book–tax difference associated with the stock options in 2024? Is it a permanent difference or a temporary difference? Is it favorable or unfavorable?

Answer: $200,000 favorable, temporary book–tax difference in 2024 and a $100,000 favorable permanent book–tax difference. PCC claims a $300,000 tax deduction in 2024, equal to the number of shares purchased (20,000) times the bargain element of $15 per option exercised ($25 – $10). PCC does not deduct any additional compensation expense for book purposes in 2024 because the vesting period ended in 2023. $200,000 of the tax deduction is a reversal of the total 2022–2023 unfavorable, temporary book–tax difference. The excess $100,000 tax deduction is a favorable permanent difference.

Exhibit 16-5 summarizes the book and tax treatments of stock options.

EXHIBIT 16-5 Book and Tax Treatment of Stock Options

Description	Book Deduction	Tax Deduction	Book–Tax Difference
Incentive stock option	Initial estimated fair value of stock options/ requisite service period	No deduction	Unfavorable, permanent
Nonqualified stock option (in years before exercise)	Initial estimated fair value of stock options/ requisite service period	No deduction until exercise	Unfavorable, temporary
Nonqualified stock option (in year of exercise)	Initial estimated fair value of stock options/ requisite service period	Bargain element*	Favorable, temporary (reversing unfavorable, temporary difference in prior years)
			Favorable, permanent difference if the bargain element exceeds the initial estimated value of stock options; unfavorable permanent difference otherwise

*The bargain element is the difference between the fair market value of the stock and the exercise price on the date the employee exercises the stock options.

TAXES IN THE REAL WORLD Facebook's NQO Tax Benefits

When Facebook filed its registration statement for its initial public offering (IPO) in February 2012, it was revealed that CEO Mark Zuckerberg had been granted nonqualifying stock options (NQOs) to purchase 120 million additional shares of the company for 6 cents per share. The company also informed potential investors that Mr. Zuckerberg intended to exercise these options when the company became a publicly traded company. Mr. Zuckerberg subsequently exercised his option to purchase 60 million additional Facebook shares prior to the IPO at a time when the value of the shares was $2,276,677,500. This transaction (fair value of the Facebook stock on the exercise date less the exercise price) simultaneously created a tax deduction for Facebook and compensation income to Mr. Zuckerberg of approximately $2.3 billion! The company's tax benefit of $800 million also created an $800 million tax bill for Mr. Zuckerberg. In total, employees of Facebook exercised 135.5 million NQOs in 2012, resulting in a tax benefit to the company of more than $1 billion, of which $451 million was recovered as a refund for taxes paid in 2010–2011. The cash proceeds received by the company from the employees' exercise of the NQOs was only $17 million.

In 2018, 2019, and 2020, Facebook employees exercised stock options and provided the company with excess tax benefits of approximately $659 million, $174 million, and $531 million, respectively. Since going public, Facebook has reported more than $50 billion of U.S. net income, yet the company reports a federal net operating loss carryover as of December 31, 2020, of $10.62 billion! Most of this difference results from the book–tax differences in stock option compensation reported on the income statements and the tax returns over this period.

Source: All of the information is publicly available on Facebook's Form 10-K and Proxy Statement for 2012, 2018, 2019, and 2020.

Net Capital Losses For corporations, all net capital gains (long- and short-term) are included in taxable income and taxed at the 21 percent corporate tax rate. Nevertheless, corporations generally prefer capital gains to ordinary income capital gains because corporations can deduct capital losses only to the extent of capital gains.[11] That is, corporations cannot deduct a net capital loss for the year (excess of capital losses over capital gains for the year). In contrast, individual taxpayers may deduct up to $3,000 ($1,500 if married filing separately) of net capital losses in computing taxable income.[12]

When corporations recognize net capital losses for a year, they are permitted to carry the capital losses back three years, called a **net capital loss carryback,** and forward five years, called a **net capital loss carryover,** to offset net capital gains in the three years before the current tax year and then to offset net capital gains in the five years after the current tax year.[13] The net capital loss carrybacks and carryovers must be applied in a particular order. If a corporation reports a net capital loss in year 4, it must first carry back the loss to year 1, then year 2, and then year 3. If the net capital loss remains after the carryback period, the corporation carries the loss forward to year 5 first, then year 6, then year 7, then year 8, and finally year 9. If the net capital loss carryover has not been fully absorbed by the end of the fifth year after it was incurred (i.e., year 9), the carryover expires unused.

Although corporations may carry back net capital losses, they may not carry back a net capital loss if doing so creates or increases a net operating loss of the corporation (excess of deductions over income) in the year to which it is carried back (see discussion of net operating losses in the next section).[14]

For financial reporting purposes, corporations deduct net capital losses in the year they are incurred. Thus, corporations recognizing net capital losses report unfavorable book–tax differences in the year they incur the losses and favorable book–tax differences in the year they use net capital loss carrybacks or carryovers to offset net capital gains.

Example 16-8

During 2022, PCC sold Intel stock at a $12,000 gain and also reported a $40,000 capital loss on the disposition of land held for investment. PCC has not recognized a net capital gain or loss since 2018. PCC has a net operating loss carryover from 2021 in the amount of $24,000. What is PCC's net capital loss for the year?

Answer: $28,000 loss [$12,000 + ($40,000)]. Because PCC did not recognize any net capital gains in 2019, 2020, or 2021, it may not carry back the loss (note that PCC could not carry back the loss to 2021 in any event because it recognized a net operating loss in that year as evidenced by its net operating loss carryover from 2021).

(continued on page 16-14)

[11]§1211(a).

[12]§1211(b). Individuals are also allowed to carry net capital losses forward indefinitely.

[13]§1212(a).

[14]§1212(a)(1)(A)(ii). To allow a corporation to carry back a net capital loss to absorb capital gains in a net operating loss year would increase the NOL carryover amount of the net capital loss used to offset the capital gain. This freed-up NOL would have a 20-year or indefinite carryover (depending on the year incurred) rather than the 5-year carryover of the net capital loss.

What amount of book–tax difference does this loss generate? Is the difference favorable or unfavorable? Is it temporary or permanent?

Answer: $28,000 unfavorable, temporary book–tax difference.

What if: Assume that in 2022, PCC reported a net capital loss of $28,000 and that it reported a $7,000 net capital gain in 2019, no net capital gain or loss in 2020, and a $4,000 net capital gain in 2021. What is the amount of its net capital loss carryover to 2023? PCC reported a net operating loss in 2021 but did not report a net operating loss in either 2019 or 2020.

Answer: $21,000. PCC first carries back the $28,000 loss to 2019, offsetting the $7,000 net capital gain in that year. PCC then carries the remaining $21,000 loss [($28,000) + $7,000] back to 2021. However, because PCC reported a net operating loss in 2021, it is not allowed to offset the $4,000 net capital gain with the net capital loss carryback. Consequently, the $21,000 unused net capital loss carryover is carried forward to 2023.

What if: Suppose PCC did not recognize any net capital gains in prior years but that next year (2023) it recognizes a net capital gain of $5,000 (before considering any capital loss carryovers). What will be its book–tax difference associated with capital gains and losses next year? Is it favorable or unfavorable? Is it temporary or permanent?

Answer: Next year, PCC would report a $5,000 favorable, temporary book–tax difference because it would be allowed to deduct $5,000 of its $28,000 net capital loss carryover for tax purposes. This is a reversal of $5,000 of the $28,000 unfavorable, temporary book–tax difference from the prior year. PCC would carry over the remaining $23,000 loss for up to four more years.

Net Operating Losses Compare the tax burdens of A Corporation and B Corporation. A Corporation reports $1,000,000 of taxable income and pays $210,000 of tax in year 1 and again in year 2. In contrast, B Corporation reports a $2,000,000 loss in year 1 and $4,000,000 of taxable income in year 2. Absent any special tax provisions, B Corporation would pay no tax in year 1 but $840,000 of tax in year 2. Over the same two-year period, both A Corporation and B Corporation reported $2,000,000 of (net) taxable income, yet B Corporation paid twice the tax A Corporation paid ($840,000 vs. $420,000).

The inequity for B Corporation in this situation is that, because it is required to report taxable income on an annual basis, it receives no tax benefit for its $2,000,000 loss (deductions in excess of gross income) in year 1. To ease the tax burden on corporations that aren't consistently profitable (for tax purposes), the tax laws allow those that report deductions in excess of gross income in a particular year to carry over the excess deductions to reduce taxable income and taxes payable in years when gross income exceeds deductions. This excess of deductions over gross income is referred to as a **net operating loss (NOL).** NOLs may be carried forward to deduct against positive taxable income in future years, and certain NOLs may be carried back to deduct against positive taxable income in prior years. When a NOL is carried forward to a future year, it is referred to as a **net operating loss carryover,** and when it is carried back to a prior year, it is called a **net operating loss carryback.**

When computing a corporation's net operating loss for the current year, a corporation may not deduct a NOL generated in a different year. Further, a corporation may deduct a net capital loss carryover against a net capital gain arising in the current year in calculating its current-year NOL, but, as described previously, it may not deduct a net capital loss carryback against a net capital gain in calculating its current-year NOL.

The specific rules for deducting NOL carryovers and carrybacks depend on the year in which the NOL was created.[15] When a corporation has multiple NOL carryovers, it uses the oldest first (i.e., FIFO order). The NOL deduction rules are summarized in Exhibit 16-6.

[15]In certain situations, corporations that experience a "change in ownership" may have NOL deductions limited under §382. Details relating to the §382 limitations are beyond the scope of this text.

EXHIBIT 16-6 Net Operating Loss Carryback and Carryover Summary*

Tax Year NOL Originated	Carrybacks	Carryovers
Beginning before 2018	Back two years.** Can offset 100% of taxable income before the NOL deduction in carryback years.	Forward 20 years. Can offset 100% of taxable income before the NOL deduction.
Beginning after 2017 and before 2021	Back five years.** Can offset up to 100% of taxable income before the NOL deduction in carryback years.	Carried forward indefinitely. Can offset up to 100% of taxable income before the NOL deduction in tax years beginning before 2021. In tax years beginning after 2020, can offset up to 80 percent of taxable income after deducting NOL carryovers from NOLs originating in tax years beginning before 2018.
Beginning after 2020	Not allowed.	Carried forward indefinitely. Can offset up to 80 percent of taxable income remaining after deducting NOL carryovers from NOLs originating in tax years beginning before 2018.

*In certain situations, when a corporation with a NOL experiences an "ownership change," the NOL deduction may be limited beyond the restrictions described in this exhibit (see §382). A discussion of these rules are beyond the scope of this text.

**A corporation can elect to forgo the NOL carryback and simply carry the NOL forward to future years. Also, if a corporation carries back a NOL, it must carry it back to the earliest year first (i.e., two years prior or five years prior, depending on the year the NOL originated).

Example 16-9

What if: In 2022, PCC reported taxable income of $250,000 before the NOL deduction. Assume that PCC has a NOL carryover from 2021 in the amount of $300,000 (this assumes PCC elected to forgo the carryback). What is PCC's 2022 taxable income and its NOL carryover to 2023?

Answer: $50,000 taxable income ($250,000 – $200,000), with a $100,000 NOL carryover to 2023 ($300,000 – $200,000). The NOL can be carried forward indefinitely. PCC can deduct the 2021 NOL carryover against 80 percent of 2022 taxable income before the NOL deduction ($250,000 × 80% = $200,000 limitation on the NOL carryover).

What if: Assume the $300,000 NOL originated in 2017 (the $300,000 is what remained after the two-year carryback) and PCC broke even each year from 2018 through 2021. What are PCC's 2022 taxable income and NOL carryover to 2023?

Answer: $0 taxable income ($250,000 – $250,000), with a $50,000 NOL carryover to 2023 ($300,000 – $250,000). PCC can deduct 100 percent of the pre-2018 NOL against taxable income in carryover years (2023 would be the sixth year of the 20-year carryover period).

What if: Assume that in 2022, PCC reported taxable income of $250,000 before the NOL deduction. Also assume that PCC has a NOL carryover from 2016 in the amount of $210,000 and a NOL carryover from 2019 in the amount of $200,000. What are PCC's 2022 taxable income and its NOL carryover to 2023?

Answer: $8,000 taxable income, with a $168,000 NOL carryover from 2019 to 2023. For 2022, PCC can deduct the full $210,000 NOL carryover from 2016. This leaves $40,000 of taxable income before the deduction for the 2019 NOL ($250,000 – $210,000). PCC can then deduct $32,000 of the 2019 NOL ($40,000 × 80%). Thus, taxable income is $8,000 ($250,000 – $210,000 – $32,000). PCC can carry over indefinitely the remaining $168,000 NOL from 2019 ($200,000 – $32,000), subject to the 80 percent limitation.

What if: Assume that in 2022 PCC reported $120,000 of deductions and $90,000 of gross income (including $6,000 of net capital gain). Also assume PCC has a $15,000 NOL carryover from 2021 and an $8,000 net capital loss carryover from 2021. What are PCC's net operating loss and capital loss carryovers to 2023, and when do they expire?

Answer: $15,000 net operating loss carryover from 2021 that can be carried forward indefinitely, a $36,000 net operating loss carryover from 2022 that can be carried forward indefinitely, and a $2,000 net capital loss carryover from 2021 that expires at the end of 2026 if unused. PCC's 2021 NOL is unused in 2022 because PCC reports a NOL in 2022 and is not allowed to deduct its NOL carryover in determining its 2022 NOL. In 2022, PCC is able to offset the $6,000 net capital gain included in gross income with $6,000 of the $8,000 net capital loss carryover from 2022. This reduces PCC's gross income to $84,000 ($90,000 – $6,000) and increases its deductions in excess of gross income (its current-year NOL) to $36,000 ($120,000 – $84,000). Finally, PCC's 2022 capital loss carryover is reduced by the $6,000 absorbed portion to $2,000 ($8,000 – $6,000 used in 2022).

For financial reporting purposes, corporations report losses in the year they incur them. Consequently, corporations report unfavorable temporary book–tax differences in the year they generate NOLs. Because corporations do not deduct NOL carryovers in determining book income, they report favorable *temporary* book–tax differences in the year they deduct the NOL carryovers for tax purposes. A corporation reports its NOL carryovers on Schedule K (line 12 on 2021 form) of Form 1120.

Example 16-10

What if: Assume that PCC incurred a $24,000 net operating loss in 2021 that it carried over to reduce 2022 taxable income from $100,000 (before the NOL deduction) to $76,000 (after the NOL deduction). What is PCC's current-year book–tax difference associated with its NOL carryover? Is the difference favorable or unfavorable? Is it permanent or temporary?

Answer: $24,000 favorable, temporary book–tax difference. The net operating loss carryover from the prior year is deductible for tax purposes but not for book purposes. The NOL carryover from 2021 is fully deductible because it did not reduce 2022 taxable income by more than 80 percent (it reduced it by 24 percent).

Charitable Contributions Similar to individuals, corporations are allowed to deduct charitable contributions to qualified charitable organizations.[16] However, the income-based deduction limitations and the timing rules are a little different for corporations than they are for individual taxpayers. In general, corporations are allowed to deduct the amount of money they contribute, the fair market value of **capital gain property** they donate (i.e., property that would generate long-term capital gain if sold), and the adjusted basis of **ordinary income property** they donate (i.e., all other property). This chapter emphasizes the tax consequences of cash donations by corporations to qualified charities.

Generally, corporations are allowed to deduct charitable contributions at the time they make payment to charitable organizations (subject to an overall taxable income limitation we discuss below). However, corporations using the accrual method of accounting can deduct contributions in the year *before* they actually pay the contribution when (1) their board of directors approves the payment and (2) they actually pay the contributions within three and one-half months of their tax year (two and one-half months for corporations with a June 30 year-end).[17]

Example 16-11

On December 1, 2022, the PCC board of directors approved a $110,000 cash contribution to the American Red Cross (ARC). For financial reporting purposes, PCC accrued and expensed the donation in 2022 for book purposes. PCC transferred the cash to the ARC on March 1, 2023. Does PCC report a book–tax difference associated with the charitable contribution (assume the taxable income limitation does not apply)?

Answer: No book–tax difference. For tax purposes, as an accrual-method taxpayer, PCC may deduct the $110,000 contribution in 2022 because it paid the donation to the ARC within three and one-half months after year-end.

What if: Assume the same facts as above, except that PCC transferred the cash to the ARC on April 30, 2023. Does PCC report a book–tax difference associated with the charitable contribution (assume the taxable income limitation does not apply)?

Answer: Yes, PCC reports a $110,000 unfavorable, temporary book–tax difference in 2022. A calendar-year-end corporation such as PCC must pay the charitable contribution by the 15th day of the fourth month after its year-end (April 15). This book–tax difference will reverse and become a $110,000 favorable, temporary book–tax difference in 2023 when PCC makes the payment to the ARC and deducts the contribution.

[16]§170(a). The IRS Tax Exempt Organization Search (https://apps.irs.gov/app/eos/) allows you to search an organization to determine if it is a qualified charity eligible to receive tax-deductible charitable contributions.

[17]§170(a)(2).

A corporation's deduction for qualified charitable contributions is limited to a percentage of a corporation's **charitable contribution limit modified taxable income.** For 2022, the percentage is 10 percent. For 2021 (and 2020), the percentage was 25 percent for qualified contributions and 10 percent for nonqualified contributions. For this purpose, qualified charitable contributions are cash contributions made to public charities and private operating foundations (except contributions to donor advised funds or supporting organizations) by a corporation that *elects* to apply the 25 percent limit. A corporation's charitable contribution limit modified taxable income is its taxable income *before* deducting the following:

1. *Any* charitable contributions.
2. The dividends-received deduction (DRD) (discussed below).
3. Net capital loss *carrybacks*.

Net capital loss and NOL *carryovers are deductible* in determining a corporation's charitable contribution limit modified taxable income. Net capital loss *carrybacks* are *not deductible* for charitable contribution limitation purposes because they are unknown when corporations must determine the limitation (they arise in a future year).

Due to the income percentage limitation, a corporation's charitable contribution deduction for the year is the *lower* of (1) the amount of charitable contributions to qualifying charities (including charitable contribution carryovers—discussed below) or (2) the applicable percentage of the corporation's charitable contribution limit modified taxable income.

THE KEY FACTS

Charitable Contributions

- Charitable contribution deductions
  - Deductible when they accrue if approved by board of directors and paid within 3.5 months of year-end (2.5 months for corporations with a June 30 year-end).
  - Deductions limited to 10 percent of charitable contribution deduction modified taxable income in 2022. In 2021, deductions limited to 25 percent for qualified contributions from electing corporations and 10 percent otherwise.
  - Contributions in excess of the charitable contribution limit are carried forward up to five years.

Example 16-12

What if: Assume that PCC's 2022 taxable income *before* considering the charitable contribution limitation was $100,000. Further, assume the taxable income computation includes an $18,000 charitable contribution deduction, a $10,000 DRD, a $24,000 NOL carryover deduction from 2020, a $4,000 net capital loss carryover deduction (offsets $4,000 of capital gain), and a $25,000 depreciation deduction. Under these circumstances, what would be PCC's 2022 deductible charitable contribution after applying the income percentage limitation?

Answer: $12,800 deductible charitable contribution, computed as follows:

Description	Amount	Explanation
(1) Taxable income before charitable contribution limitation	$100,000	
(2) Charitable contribution deduction before limitation	18,000	Not deductible in computing limitation
(3) Dividends-received deduction	10,000	Not deductible in computing limitation
(4) Charitable contribution limit modified taxable income*	$128,000	Sum of (1) through (3)
(5) Tax deduction limitation percentage	10%	10% limit for 2022
(6) Charitable contribution deduction limitation	$ 12,800	(4) × (5)
(7) Charitable contribution deduction for year	**$ 12,800**	Lesser of (2) or (6)
Charitable contribution carryover (expires if unused by the end of 2027)	$ 5,200	(2) – (7)

*Note that the NOL and net capital loss carryovers are not added back to compute line (4) because they are deductible in determining the charitable contribution limit modified taxable income.

What if: Assume this was a qualified contribution in 2021. What would be PCC's charitable contribution deduction for 2021?

Answer: $18,000. Because this is 2021 and it is a qualified contribution (taxpayer is eligible and elects to use the 25% modified charitable contribution limitation, the deduction is the lesser of (1) $32,000 ($128,000 × 25% charitable deduction limit percentage) or (2) $18,000, the amount of the actual contribution.

Corporations making current-year charitable contributions in excess of the income limitation may carry forward the excess for up to five years after the year in which the carryover arises. Carryovers are absorbed on a first-in, first-out (FIFO) basis and are applied after the current-year contribution deduction. Corporations can deduct the carryover in future years to the extent the income limitation does not restrict deductions for charitable contributions corporations actually make in those years. Unused carryovers expire after five years.

Example 16-13

What if: Assume the same facts as in the previous example, where PCC reported a $12,800 charitable contribution deduction and a $5,200 charitable contribution carryover. What would be PCC's book–tax difference associated with the charitable contribution? Would it be favorable or unfavorable? Would it be permanent or temporary?

Answer: $5,200 unfavorable, temporary book–tax difference. The amount of the carryover was not deductible for tax in the current year, but it was expensed for books. When PCC deducts the charitable contribution carryover, it will report a $5,200 favorable, temporary book–tax difference.

Corporations report *unfavorable, temporary* book–tax differences to the extent the modified taxable income limitation restricts the amount of their charitable contribution tax deduction. That is, they recognize unfavorable, temporary book–tax differences in the amount of the charitable contribution carryover they generate for the year. Conversely, corporations report *favorable, temporary* book–tax differences when they deduct charitable contribution carryovers because they deduct the carryovers for tax purposes but not book purposes.

Example 16-14

In 2022, PCC donated a total of $700,000 of cash to the American Red Cross. Elise knew she had to apply the 10 percent taxable income limitation to verify the amount PCC deducted for tax purposes. For 2022, PCC's taxable income before any charitable contribution, NOL carryovers from prior years, and dividends-received deduction was $6,287,000 (see Exhibit 16-8 later in the text for the computation). What is PCC's charitable contribution deduction for the year, assuming the donation is a qualified charitable contribution? What is its charitable contribution carryover to next year, if any?

Answer: $626,300 charitable contribution deduction and $73,700 charitable contribution carry-over, computed as follows:

Description	Amount	Explanation
(1) Taxable income before *any* charitable contribution, NOL carryover from previous year, and DRD	$6,287,000	Exhibit 16-8
(2) NOL *carryover* from previous year (from Example 16-10)	(24,000)	Deductible in determining taxable income limit
(3) Charitable contribution limit modified taxable income	$6,263,000	(1) + (2)
(4) Total charitable contributions for year	$ 700,000	
(5) Tax deduction limitation percentage	10%	Percentage limitation for qualified contributions
(6) Charitable contribution deduction limitation	$ 626,300	(3) × (5)
(7) Charitable contribution deduction for year	**$ 626,300**	Lesser of (4) or (6)
Charitable contribution carryover (expires if unused by the end of 2027)	**$ 73,700**	(4) − (7)

What is PCC's book–tax difference associated with its charitable contribution? Is the difference favorable or unfavorable? Is it permanent or temporary?

Answer: $73,700 unfavorable, temporary book–tax difference.

Dividends-Received Deduction When corporations receive dividends from other corporations, the dividends are included in taxable income and taxed at the 21 percent corporate tax rate. However, corporations are allowed to claim a dividends-received deduction (DRD) that reduces the actual tax they pay on the dividends.[18] The DRD is designed to mitigate the extent to which corporate earnings are subject to three (or perhaps even more) levels of taxation. Corporate taxable income is subject to triple taxation when a corporation pays tax on its income and then distributes its after-tax income to shareholders that are corporations. Corporate shareholders are taxed on the dividends, creating the second tax. When corporate shareholders distribute their after-tax earnings as dividends to their shareholders, the income is taxed for a third time. The dividends-received deduction reduces the amount of the second-level tax and thus mitigates the impact of triple taxation (or more) of earnings that corporations distribute as dividends.

Corporations generally compute their dividends-received deduction by multiplying the dividend amount by 50 percent, 65 percent, or 100 percent, depending on the receiving corporation's level of ownership in the distributing corporation's stock. Exhibit 16-7 summarizes the stock ownership thresholds and the corresponding dividends-received deduction percentage. Only dividends received from domestic corporations are eligible for this DRD. Certain dividends from 10-percent-or-more-owned foreign corporations are eligible for a 100 percent DRD, which is discussed in the chapter The U.S. Taxation of Multinational Transactions.

THE KEY FACTS

Dividends-Received Deduction

- Dividends-received deduction
  - Generally lesser of deduction percentage (50 percent, 65 percent, or 100 percent) based on ownership × DRD modified taxable income.
  - Limitation doesn't apply if full DRD creates or increases a corporation's NOL.
  - Generates favorable, permanent book–tax difference.

EXHIBIT 16-7 Stock Ownership and Dividends-Received Deduction Percentage

Receiving Corporation's Stock Ownership in Distributing Corporation's Stock	Dividends-Received Deduction Percentage
Less than 20 percent	50%
At least 20 percent but less than 80 percent	65
80 percent or more[19]	100

Example 16-15

During 2022, PCC received a $30,000 dividend from Apple Inc. PCC owns less than 1 percent of the Apple Inc. stock. What is PCC's DRD associated with the dividend?

Answer: $15,000 ($30,000 × 50%).

What if: PCC's marginal tax rate on the dividend *before* considering the effect of the dividends-received deduction is 21 percent. What is PCC's marginal tax rate on the Apple Inc. dividend income *after* considering the dividends-received deduction?

Answer: 10.5 percent marginal tax rate on dividend income, computed as follows:

Description	Amount	Explanation
(1) Dividend from Apple	$ 30,000	
(2) The percentage DRD	50%	Less than 20 percent ownership in Apple
(3) Dividends-received deduction	**$15,000**	(1) × (2)
(4) Dividend subject to taxation after DRD	$ 15,000	(1) − (3)
(5) Marginal ordinary tax rate	21%	
(6) Taxes payable on dividend *after* DRD	$ 3,150	(4) × (5)
Marginal tax rate on dividend *after* DRD	**10.5%**	(6)/(1)

[18]§243. Also, §246(c) describes certain dividends that are ineligible for the dividends-received deduction.

[19]To qualify for the 100 percent dividends-received deduction, the receiving and distributing corporations must be in the same affiliated group, as described in §1504. The 80 percent ownership requirement is the minimum ownership level required for inclusion in the same affiliated group.

Deduction limitation. The dividends-received deduction is limited to the product of the applicable dividends-received deduction percentage (see Exhibit 16-7) and **DRD modified taxable income.**[20] DRD modified taxable income is the dividend-receiving corporation's taxable income *before* deducting the following:

- DRD.
- NOL deduction.
- Net capital loss carrybacks (but after deducting net capital loss carryovers).[21]

Example 16-16

What if: Suppose that during 2022, PCC received a $30,000 dividend from Apple Inc. and that PCC owns less than 1 percent of the Apple Inc. stock. Further assume that PCC's taxable income before the dividends-received deduction was $50,000 in Scenario A and $25,000 in Scenario B. To arrive at the taxable income under both scenarios (before the DRD), PCC deducted a $3,000 NOL carryover and a $4,000 net capital loss carryover. What is PCC's dividends-received deduction associated with the dividend in Scenario A and in Scenario B?

Answer: $15,000 in Scenario A and $14,000 in Scenario B, computed as follows:

Description	Scenario A	Scenario B	Explanation
(1) Taxable income before the dividends-received deduction (includes dividend income)	$ 50,000	$ 25,000	
(2) NOL carryover	3,000	3,000	
(3) DRD modified taxable income	$ 53,000	$ 28,000	(1) + (2)
(4) Dividend income	$ 30,000	$ 30,000	
(5) Dividends-received deduction percentage based on ownership	50%	50%	§243(a)
(6) Dividends-received deduction before limitation	$ 15,000	$ 15,000	(4) × (5)
(7) Dividends-received deduction limitation	$ 26,500	$ 14,000	(3) × (5)
DRD deductible	**$15,000**	**$14,000**	Lesser of (6) or (7)

Note that the net capital loss carryover is deductible in determining the DRD modified taxable income, so it is not added back to taxable income to arrive at DRD modified taxable income.

The modified taxable income limitation *does not apply* if, after deducting the *full* dividends-received deduction (dividend × DRD percentage), a corporation reports a current-year net operating loss. That is, if, after deducting the full dividends-received deduction, the corporation has a net operating loss, the corporation is allowed to deduct the *full* dividends-received deduction no matter the amount of the modified taxable income limitation.[22] As the following example illustrates, this rule can cause some unusual results.

Example 16-17

What if: Let's assume that PCC reports gross income of $80,000, *including* $40,000 of dividend income from TOU Corp. PCC owns 25 percent of TOU Corp. stock, so its applicable DRD percentage is 65 percent (see Exhibit 16-7). Finally, let's consider two alternative scenarios. In Scenario A, PCC reports $54,000 of business expenses deductible in determining its DRD modified taxable income. In Scenario B, PCC reports $55,000 of business expenses deductible in determining its DRD modified taxable income. For each scenario, what is PCC's DRD modified taxable income? For each scenario, what is PCC's dividends-received deduction?

[20]When corporations receive dividends from multiple corporations with different deduction percentages, according to §246(b)(3), the limitations first apply to the 65 percent dividends-received deduction and then the 50 percent dividends-received deduction.

[21]§246(b)(1).

[22]§246(b)(2).

Scenario A Answer: $26,000 DRD modified taxable income; $16,900 dividends-received deduction (see computation below).

Scenario B Answer: $25,000 DRD modified taxable income; $26,000 dividends-received deduction, computed as follows:

Description	Scenario A	Scenario B	Explanation
(1) Gross income other than dividends	$ 40,000	$ 40,000	
(2) Dividend income	40,000	40,000	
(3) Gross income	$ 80,000	$ 80,000	(1) + (2)
(4) Business expenses deductible in determining the DRD modified taxable income	54,000	55,000	
(5) DRD modified taxable income (note this is taxable income before the DRD)	**$26,000**	**$25,000**	(3) – (4)
(6) Full dividends-received deduction	$ 26,000	$ 26,000	(2) × 65%
(7) DRD modified taxable income limitation	16,900	16,250	(5) × 65%
(8) Taxable income (loss) after deducting full DRD	0	(1,000)	(5) – (6)
DRD deductible	**$16,900**	**$26,000**	Lesser of (6) or (7) unless (8) is negative, then (6)

Compare the results in Scenario A and Scenario B in the previous example. In Scenario B, PCC's DRD is $9,100 larger than it is in Scenario A ($26,000 – $16,900), despite the fact that the only difference in the two scenarios is that PCC reports $54,000 of business expenses in Scenario A and $55,000 of business expenses in Scenario B. Interestingly, in this example, PCC is able to increase its DRD by $9,100 for a $40,000 dividend simply by incurring $1,000 more in expenses (or potentially even $1 more).

Because the dividends-received deduction is strictly a tax deduction and not a book deduction, *any* dividends-received deduction creates a *favorable, permanent* book–tax difference.

Example 16-18

From her review of PCC's dividend income computations, Elise determined that the only dividend PCC received during the year was a $30,000 dividend from Apple Inc., a U.S. corporation. Because PCC owns a very small percentage of Apple Inc. stock (less than 1 percent), Elise determined that PCC was entitled to a 50 percent dividends-received deduction. PCC's modified taxable income before any NOL and DRD is $4,721,250. What is PCC's book–tax difference associated with its dividends-received deduction? Is the difference favorable or unfavorable? Is it permanent or temporary?

Answer: $15,000 favorable, permanent book–tax difference, computed as follows:

Description	Amount	Explanation
(1) Taxable income before NOL and DRD (DRD modified taxable income)	$4,721,250	Exhibit 16-8 ($4,697,250 + 24,000 NOL)
(2) Dividend income	$ 30,000	Exhibit 16-8
(3) Applicable DRD percentage	50%	Owns less than 20 percent of Apple Inc.
(4) Full dividends-received deduction	$ 15,000	(2) × (3)
(5) Dividends-received deduction taxable income limitation	$2,360,625	(1) × (3)
(6) Book deductible dividends-received deduction	0	No book DRD
(7) Tax-deductible dividends-received deduction	$ 15,000	Lesser of (4) or (5)
(Favorable) permanent book–tax difference	**$ (15,000)**	(6) – (7)

Taxable Income Summary

Exhibit 16-8 presents Elise's template for reconciling PCC's book and taxable income. Note that the template does not follow the typical financial accounting

EXHIBIT 16-8 **PCC Book–Tax Reconciliation Template**

Description	Book Income (Dr) Cr	Book–Tax Adjustments (Dr)[†]		Taxable Income (Dr) Cr
Revenue from sales	$60,000,000			$60,000,000
Cost of goods sold	(38,000,000)			(38,000,000)
Gross profit	$22,000,000			$22,000,000
Other income:				
Dividend income	30,000			30,000
Interest income	120,000	(12,000)[Ex. 1]		108,000
Capital gains (losses)	(28,000)		28,000[Ex. 8]	0
Gain on fixed asset dispositions	54,000		16,000[Exh. 4]	70,000
Gross income	$22,176,000			$22,208,000
Expenses:				
Compensation	(9,868,000)			(9,868,000)
Deferred compensation	(300,000)	(150,000)[Exh. 4]		(450,000)
Stock option compensation	(100,000)		100,000[Ex. 7]	0
Bad debt expense	(165,000)		70,000[Exh. 4]	(95,000)
Charitable contributions	Moved below			
Depreciation	(2,400,000)	(700,000)[Exh. 4]		(3,100,000)
Advertising	(1,920,000)			(1,920,000)
Warranty expenses	(580,000)		170,000[Exh. 4]	(410,000)
Meals	(14,000)			(14,000)
Life insurance premiums	(34,000)		34,000[Ex. 1]	0
Other expenses	(64,000)			(64,000)
Federal income tax expense	(2,000,000)*		2,000,000[Ex. 2]	0
Total expenses *before* charitable contribution, NOL, and DRD	(17,445,000)			(15,921,000)
Income *before* charitable contribution, NOL, and DRD	4,731,000			$ 6,287,000
NOL carryover from prior year		(24,000)[Ex. 10]		(24,000)
Taxable income for charitable contribution limitation purposes				6,263,000
Charitable contributions	(700,000)		73,700[Ex. 14]	(626,300)
Taxable income before DRD				5,636,700
Dividends-received deduction (DRD)		(15,000)[Ex. 18]		(15,000)
Book/taxable income	**$ 4,031,000**	**$(901,000)**	**$2,491,700**	**$5,621,700**

*This number is used only for illustrative purposes. In the Accounting for Income Taxes chapter, we compute the correct federal income tax expense (also referred to as the federal income tax provision).

[†]Note that the superscript by each book–tax difference identifies the example (Ex.) or exhibit (Exh.) where the adjustment is calculated. Also note that the debit numbers are favorable book–tax adjustments while credit numbers are unfavorable book–tax adjustments.

format because it organizes the information to facilitate the taxable income computation. In particular, it puts the deductions in the sequence in which they are deducted for tax purposes.

Corporate Income Tax Liability

Corporations compute their pre-credit federal income tax liability by applying a 21 percent rate to taxable income.

Example 16-19

Elise determined that PCC's taxable income is $5,621,700. What is its income tax liability?

Answer: $1,180,557, computed as $5,621,700 × 21%.

COMPLIANCE

LO 16-3

Corporations report their taxable income on Form 1120. Exhibit 16-9 presents the front page of PCC's current-year Form 1120 through the tax liability.

Form 1120 includes a schedule for corporations to report their book–tax differences and reconcile their book and taxable income. Corporations with total assets of less than $10,000,000 report their book–tax differences on Schedule M-1. Corporations with total assets of $10,000,000 or more are required to report their book–tax differences on Schedule M-3.[23] Because corporations report book–tax differences as adjustments to book income to compute taxable income on either Schedule M-1 or M-3, these book-to-tax adjustments are often referred to as **Schedule M adjustments, M adjustments,** and even "Ms" (plural version of M).

Because PCC's total assets are $9,500,000 (see Exhibit 16-9, line D), it may complete a Schedule M-1 rather than a Schedule M-3. Exhibit 16-10 presents PCC's completed Schedule M-1 based on the information provided in Exhibit 16-8. Schedule M-1 is a relatively short schedule, and it does not require corporations to provide much detail about the nature of their book–tax differences.

The schedule begins on line 1 with book income after taxes. The left-hand column includes all unfavorable book–tax differences (add-backs to book income to arrive at taxable income). In general, the top part of the left column is for income items and the bottom part is for expense items. The right-hand column consists of all favorable book–tax differences. The top part of the right column is for income items and the bottom part includes expense items.

Finally, note that Schedule M-1 (and Schedule M-3) reconciles to taxable income *before* the net operating loss deduction and the dividends-received deduction.[24] Consequently, to fully reconcile book and taxable income, corporations must deduct net operating loss carryovers and dividends-received deductions from line 10 on Schedule M-1 (or the amount on line 30d on Schedule M-3).

[23]Corporations with at least $10 million but less than $50 million in total assets at tax year-end are permitted to file Schedule M-1 in place of Schedule M-3, Parts II and III. Schedule M-3, Part I, lines 1–12 continue to be required for these taxpayers. Corporations with $10 million to $50 million in total assets may voluntarily file Schedule M-3 Parts II and III rather than Schedule M-1.

[24]Schedule M-1 (and Schedule M-3) reconciles to line 28 on Form 1120. Line 28 is taxable income before the net operating loss and special deductions (the dividends-received deduction).

EXHIBIT 16-9 PCC Form 1120 page 1, through tax refund

Form **1120** Department of the Treasury Internal Revenue Service

U.S. Corporation Income Tax Return

For calendar year 2021 or tax year beginning ________, 2021, ending ________, 20 ___

▶ Go to *www.irs.gov/Form1120* for instructions and the latest information.

OMB No. 1545-0123 **2021**

A Check if:
- 1a Consolidated return (attach Form 851) ☐
- b Life/nonlife consolidated return ☐
- 2 Personal holding co. (attach Sch. PH) ☐
- 3 Personal service corp. (see instructions) ☐
- 4 Schedule M-3 attached ☐

TYPE OR PRINT
- Name: **Premier Computer Corporation**
- Number, street, and room or suite no. If a P.O. box, see instructions.: **4810 East Crown Drive**
- City or town, state or province, country, and ZIP or foreign postal code: **Denver, CO 80239**

B Employer identification number: **12-3456789**

C Date incorporated: **01/01/2001**

D Total assets (see instructions): $ **9,500,000**

E Check if: (1) ☐ Initial return (2) ☐ Final return (3) ☐ Name change (4) ☐ Address change

Section	Line	Description			Line	Amount
Income	1a	Gross receipts or sales	1a	60,000,000		
	b	Returns and allowances	1b			
	c	Balance. Subtract line 1b from line 1a			1c	60,000,000
	2	Cost of goods sold (attach Form 1125-A)			2	38,000,000
	3	Gross profit. Subtract line 2 from line 1c			3	22,000,000
	4	Dividends and inclusions (Schedule C, line 23)			4	30,000
	5	Interest			5	108,000
	6	Gross rents			6	
	7	Gross royalties			7	
	8	Capital gain net income (attach Schedule D (Form 1120))			8	
	9	Net gain or (loss) from Form 4797, Part II, line 17 (attach Form 4797)			9	70,000
	10	Other income (see instructions—attach statement)			10	
	11	**Total income.** Add lines 3 through 10 ▶			11	22,208,000
Deductions (See instructions for limitations on deductions.)	12	Compensation of officers (see instructions—attach Form 1125-E) ▶			12	1,500,000
	13	Salaries and wages (less employment credits)			13	8,818,000
	14	Repairs and maintenance			14	
	15	Bad debts			15	95,000
	16	Rents			16	
	17	Taxes and licenses			17	
	18	Interest (see instructions)			18	
	19	Charitable contributions			19	626,300
	20	Depreciation from Form 4562 not claimed on Form 1125-A or elsewhere on return (attach Form 4562)			20	3,100,000
	21	Depletion			21	
	22	Advertising			22	1,920,000
	23	Pension, profit-sharing, etc., plans			23	
	24	Employee benefit programs			24	
	25	Reserved for future use			25	
	26	Other deductions (attach statement) Warranties 410,000 + Meals 14,000 + Other expenses 64,000			26	488,000
	27	**Total deductions.** Add lines 12 through 26 ▶			27	16,547,300
	28	Taxable income before net operating loss deduction and special deductions. Subtract line 27 from line 11.			28	5,660,700
	29a	Net operating loss deduction (see instructions)	29a	24,000		
	b	Special deductions (Schedule C, line 24)	29b	15,000		
	c	Add lines 29a and 29b			29c	39,000
Tax, Refundable Credits, and Payments	30	**Taxable income.** Subtract line 29c from line 28. See instructions			30	5,621,700
	31	Total tax (Schedule J, Part I, line 11)			31	1,180,557
	32	Reserved for future use			32	
	33	Total payments and credits (Schedule J, Part III, line 23)			33	1,328,000
	34	Estimated tax penalty. See instructions. Check if Form 2220 is attached ▶ ☐			34	
	35	**Amount owed.** If line 33 is smaller than the total of lines 31 and 34, enter amount owed			35	
	36	**Overpayment.** If line 33 is larger than the total of lines 31 and 34, enter amount overpaid			36	147,443
	37	Enter amount from line 36 you want: **Credited to 2022 estimated tax ▶**	**Refunded ▶**		37	147,443

Sign Here

Under penalties of perjury, I declare that I have examined this return, including accompanying schedules and statements, and to the best of my knowledge and belief, it is true, correct, and complete. Declaration of preparer (other than taxpayer) is based on all information of which preparer has any knowledge.

▶ Signature of officer — Date ▶ Title

May the IRS discuss this return with the preparer shown below? See instructions. ☐ Yes ☐ No

Paid Preparer Use Only

Print/Type preparer's name	Preparer's signature	Date	Check ☐ if self-employed	PTIN
Firm's name ▶			Firm's EIN ▶	
Firm's address ▶			Phone no.	

For Paperwork Reduction Act Notice, see separate instructions. Cat. No. 11450Q Form **1120** (2021)

Source: irs.gov.

EXHIBIT 16-10 Form 1120, Schedule M-1

Schedule M-1 **Reconciliation of Income (Loss) per Books With Income per Return**

Note: The corporation may be required to file Schedule M-3. See instructions.

1	Net income (loss) per books	4,031,000	7	Income recorded on books this year not included on this return (itemize):	
2	Federal income tax per books	2,000,000		Tax-exempt interest $ 12,000	
3	Excess of capital losses over capital gains .	28,000			
4	Income subject to tax not recorded on books this year (itemize): **gain on disposition of fixed assets**	16,000			12,000
5	Expenses recorded on books this year not deducted on this return (itemize):		8	Deductions on this return not charged against book income this year (itemize):	
a	Depreciation . . . . $		a	Depreciation . . $ 700,000	
b	Charitable contributions . $ 73,700		b	Charitable contributions $	
c	Travel and entertainment . $			**deferred compensation 150,000**	850,000
	Other 374,000 see statement 1	447,700	9	Add lines 7 and 8	862,000
6	Add lines 1 through 5	6,522,700	10	Income (page 1, line 28)—line 6 less line 9	5,660,700

Schedule M-1
Statement 1
Other expenses recorded on books this year not deducted on this return

Compensation expense (stock options)	$100,000
Bad debt expense	70,000
Warranty expense	170,000
Life insurance premiums	34,000
Total other expenses	$374,000

Source: irs.gov.

Example 16-20

In reviewing her work on PCC's tax return, Elise wanted to check to make sure that she could reconcile from the bottom line of Schedule M-1 to PCC's taxable income. She noted that line 10 of PCC's Schedule M-1 was $5,660,700. How should Elise reconcile from this number to PCC's taxable income?

Answer: Start with the amount on line 10 and subtract PCC's NOL carryover and its DRD, as illustrated below:

Description	Amount	Explanation
(1) Schedule M-1 taxable income reconciliation total	$ 5,660,700	Form 1120, Schedule M-1, line 10
(2) Net operating loss deduction	(24,000)	Exhibit 16-8
(3) Dividends-received deduction	(15,000)	Exhibit 16-8
Taxable income	**$5,621,700**	(1) + (2) + (3)

Schedule M-3 requires corporations to report significantly more information than Schedule M-1 does. For example, Schedule M-3 includes more than 60 specific types of book–tax differences, while Schedule M-1 includes only 10 summary lines. Furthermore,

Schedule M-3 requires corporations to identify each book–tax difference as either temporary or permanent. The IRS created Schedule M-3 in hopes of providing a better and more efficient starting point for agents to identify and scrutinize large dollar compliance issues.

Form 1120 also requires corporations to complete Schedule M-2, which provides a reconciliation of the corporation's beginning and ending balance in its unappropriated retained earnings from its financial accounting balance sheet (reported on Schedule L). Corporations with total receipts and total assets of less than $250,000 are not required to complete Schedules L, M-1, and M-2.

ETHICS

Your client traditionally provides free doughnuts and coffee from a local convenience store (not considered to be a restaurant) to its employees every Friday morning to help boost morale. Corporations can generally deduct 50 percent of the cost of food provided to employees. However, food costs at "mentoring events" is 100 percent deductible. Following the tax director's proposal, the Friday events have been recharacterized as "mentoring events" by having someone from management make a few remarks about professional development. What do you think of the corporation's approach to maximizing its deduction for meals on its tax return? Would it matter that the client could easily purchase the coffee and doughnuts from a doughnut shop?

Consolidated Tax Returns An affiliated group of corporations may elect to file a **consolidated tax return**—that is, the group files a tax return as if it were one entity for tax purposes. An **affiliated group** exists when one corporation owns at least 80 percent of (1) the total voting power and (2) the total stock value of another corporation.[25] Filing a consolidated tax return allows the losses of one group member to offset the income of other members. Further, income from certain intercompany transactions is deferred until realized through a transaction outside of the affiliated group. However, losses from certain intercompany transactions are also deferred until realized through a transaction outside of the affiliated group.

Affiliated groups cannot file a consolidated tax return unless they elect to do so. Because the election is binding on subsequent years, it should be made with care. Consolidated tax returns may impose additional administrative and compliance costs on the taxpayers. The consolidated tax return laws are very complex and beyond the scope of this text.[26] Further, the rules for consolidated reporting for financial statement purposes are different from the tax rules.

Corporate Tax Return Due Dates and Estimated Taxes

The tax return due date for most C corporations (those with a tax year-end other than June 30) is three and one-half months after the corporation's year-end. Thus, a calendar-year corporation's unextended tax return due date is April 15. Corporations requesting an

[25]§1504(a).

[26]The tax rules for consolidated tax returns are provided primarily in the regulations under §1502.

extension can extend the due date for filing their tax returns (not for paying the taxes) for six months (October 15 for calendar-year corporations). Corporations with a June 30 year-end have a September 15 due date (the 15th day of the third month following the end of the fiscal year), and the extended due date is seven months after the regular due date (April 15).

Corporations with a federal income tax liability of $500 or more are required to pay their tax liability for the year in quarterly estimated installments.[27] The installments are due on the 15th day of the 4th, 6th, 9th, and 12th months of their tax year.[28] When corporations file their tax returns, they determine whether they must pay estimated tax underpayment penalties. Generally, corporations are subject to underpayment penalties if they did not pay 25 percent, 50 percent, 75 percent, and 100 percent of their required annual payment with their first, second, third, and fourth installment payments, respectively.[29] The required annual payment is the *least* of:

1. 100 percent of the tax liability on the prior year's return, but only if there was a positive tax liability on the return and the prior-year return covered a 12-month period (however, see discussion of the exception that applies to corporations with taxable income above $1 million).
2. 100 percent of the current-year tax liability (corporations usually don't rely on this method to compute the required payment because they won't know what their current-year liability is until they complete their tax returns—after the estimated tax due dates).
3. 100 percent of the estimated current-year tax liability using the annualized income method (discussed below).[30]

From a cash management perspective (considering the time value of money), it generally makes sense for corporations to make the *minimum* required estimated payment installments for each quarter. Thus, as each estimated tax due date approaches, corporations will generally compute the required estimated payment under the prior-year tax method (if available) and under the annualized method and pay the lesser of the two.

The **annualized income method** is perhaps the most popular method of determining estimated tax payments (particularly for corporations that can't use the prior-year tax liability to compute their current-year estimated tax payment obligations) because corporations can use this method as a safe harbor to avoid estimated payment penalties. Under this method, corporations measure their taxable income as of the end of each quarter and then annualize (project) the amount to calculate their estimated taxable income and tax liability for the year. They use the estimated annual tax liability at the end of each quarter to calculate the minimum required estimated payment for that quarter. Corporations use the first-quarter taxable income to project their annual tax liability for the *first- and second-quarter* estimated tax payments. They use taxable income at the end of the second quarter to calculate the third-quarter estimated tax payment requirement, and taxable income at the end of the third quarter to calculate their fourth-quarter payment requirement. Exhibit 16-11 shows the formula for computing estimated taxable income under the annualized income method.

THE KEY FACTS

Tax Compliance

- Corporations report taxable income on Form 1120.
- Corporations with total assets of less than $10M report book–tax differences on Schedule M-1 of Form 1120. Otherwise, they are required to report book–tax differences on Schedule M-3.
- The tax return due date is 3.5 months after year-end (2.5 months for corporations with a June 30 year-end).
  - Extensions extend the due date for filing Form 1120 (not for paying taxes) for six additional months after year-end (seven months for corporations with a June 30 year-end).
- An affiliated group may file a consolidated tax return.
- Corporations pay expected annual tax liability through estimated tax payments.
  - Installments due in the 4th, 6th, 9th, and 12th months of their taxable year.
- Underpayment penalties apply if estimated tax payments are inadequate.

[27]§6655.

[28]§6655(c).

[29]§6665(d).

[30]§6655(e).

EXHIBIT 16-11 Estimated Taxable Income Computation under Annualized Income Method

Installment	(1) Taxable Income (first __ months of year)	(2) Annualization Factor	(1) × (2) Annual Estimated Taxable Income
First quarter	3	12/3 = 4	
Second quarter	3	12/3 = 4	
Third quarter	6	12/6 = 2	
Fourth quarter	9	12/9 = 1.3333	

Example 16-21

PCC determined its taxable income at the close of the first, second, and third quarters as follows:

Quarter-End	Cumulative Taxable Income
First	$1,000,000
Second	3,200,000
Third	4,000,000

What is its annual estimated taxable income for estimated tax payment purposes as of the end of the first, second, third, and fourth quarters, respectively?

Answer: $4,000,000 for the first and second quarters, $6,400,000 for the third quarter, and $6,666,667 for the fourth quarter, computed as follows:

Installment	(1) Taxable Income	(2) Annualization Factor	(1) × (2) Annual Estimated Taxable Income
First quarter	$1,000,000	12/3 = 4	**$4,000,000**
Second quarter	1,000,000	12/3 = 4	**4,000,000**
Third quarter	3,200,000	12/6 = 2	**6,400,000**
Fourth quarter	5,000,000	12/9 = 1.333	**6,666,667**

Once corporations have determined their annual estimated taxable income for each quarter, they can use the formulas in Exhibit 16-12 to compute the required estimated tax installments for each quarter under the annualized income method.

EXHIBIT 16-12 Estimated Taxable Income Computation under Annualized Income Method

Installment	(1) Annual Estimated Taxable Income	(2) Tax on Estimated Taxable Income	(3) Percentage of Tax Required to Be Paid	(4) [(2) × (3)] Required Cumulative Payment	(5) Prior Cumulative Payment	(4) – (5) Required Estimated Tax Payment
First quarter			25%			
Second quarter			50			
Third quarter			75			
Fourth quarter			100			

Example 16-22

Based on the estimated taxable income in the previous example, what are PCC's required estimated tax payments for the year under the annualized income method?

Answer: $210,000 for the first and second quarters, $588,000 for the third quarter, and $392,000 for the fourth quarter, computed as follows:

Installment	(1) Annual Estimated Taxable Income	(2) Tax on Estimated Taxable Income	(3) Percentage of Tax Required to Be Paid	(4) [(2) × (3)] Required Cumulative Payment	(5) Prior Cumulative Payments	(4) – (5) Required Estimated Tax Payment
First quarter	$4,000,000	$ 840,000	25%	$ 210,000	$ 0	**$210,000**
Second quarter	4,000,000	840,000	50	420,000	210,000	**210,000**
Third quarter	6,400,000	1,344,000	75	1,008,000	420,000	**588,000**
Fourth quarter	6,666,667	1,400,000	100	1,400,000	$1,008,000	**392,000**

Can PCC use its prior-year tax liability to determine its current-year estimated tax payments?

Answer: No. PCC reported a net operating loss last year and did not pay taxes, so it may not use its prior-year tax liability to determine its current-year estimated tax payments.

Can PCC use its current-year tax liability to determine its current-year estimated tax payments?

Answer: Yes. As we determined in Example 16-19, PCC's actual tax liability for the year is $1,180,557. So, PCC could have avoided estimated tax penalties by paying in $295,139 each quarter ($1,180,557 × 25%). However, it did not know this amount when it was required to make its estimated tax payments, so it would likely have used the annualized income method of determining its estimated tax payments to protect itself from penalties.

"Large" corporations, defined as corporations with over $1,000,000 of taxable income in *any* of the three years prior to the current year,[31] may use the prior-year tax liability to determine their first-quarter estimated tax payments only. If they use the prior-year tax liability to determine their first-quarter payment, their second-quarter payment must catch up their estimated payments. That is, the second-quarter payment must be large enough for the sum of the first- and second-quarter payments to equal or exceed 50 percent of the corporation's projected current-year tax liability.[32]

Example 16-23

What if: Assume that in 2021 PCC reported taxable income of $2,000,000 and a tax liability of $420,000. Further, PCC determined its required estimated tax payments under the annualized method as described in the previous example. What would be PCC's required minimum estimated tax payments for each quarter for 2022? (Ignore the current-year tax requirement because PCC is unsure what its current-year tax will be.)

(continued on page 16-30)

[31]§6655(g)(2).
[32]§6655(d).

Answer: $105,000 for the first quarter, $315,000 for the second quarter, $588,000 for the third quarter, and $392,000 for the fourth quarter, computed as follows:

Installment	(1) Estimated Tax Payment under Prior-Year Tax Exception	(2) Estimated Tax Payment under Annualized Method	(3) Required Cumulative Payment for Quarter × [sum of the lesser of (1) or (2) through quarter x]	(4) Prior Cumulative Payments	(5) [(3) − (4)] Required Estimated Tax Payment
First quarter	$105,000*	$210,000	$ 105,000	$ 0	**$105,000**
Second quarter	Not applicable*	210,000	420,000	105,000	**315,000**
Third quarter	Not applicable*	588,000	1,008,000	420,000	**588,000**
Fourth quarter	Not applicable*	320,000	1,400,000	1,008,000	**392,000**

*Because PCC is a large corporation, it may determine its first-quarter estimated tax payment using its prior-year liability ($420,000 × 25% = $105,000). However, it must use the annualized method to determine its second-, third-, and fourth-quarter required payments.

With its second installment, PCC must have paid in $420,000. Because it only paid in $105,000 with the first-quarter installment, it must pay $315,000 with its second-quarter payment.

What if: Assume the same facts as above, except that last year PCC paid $200,000 in tax and PCC is not a large corporation. What would be PCC's required minimum estimated tax payments for each quarter (ignore the current-year tax requirement)?

Answer: $50,000 for the first quarter, $50,000 for the second quarter, $50,000 for the third quarter, and $50,000 for the fourth quarter, computed as follows:

Installment	(1) Estimated Tax Payment under Prior Year Tax Exception ($200,000/4)	(2) Estimated Tax Payment under Annualized Method	(3) Required Cumulative Payment for Quarter × [sum of the lesser of (1) or (2) through quarter x]	(4) Prior Cumulative Payments	(5) [(3) − (4)] Required Estimated Tax Payment
First quarter	$50,000	$210,000	$ 50,000	$ 0	**$50,000**
Second quarter	50,000	210,000	100,000	50,000	**50,000**
Third quarter	50,000	588,000	150,000	100,000	**50,000**
Fourth quarter	50,000	320,000	200,000	150,000	**50,000**

PCC can use the prior-year tax to determine its minimum required estimated tax payments.

Corporations that have underpaid their estimated taxes for any quarter must pay an underpayment penalty calculated on Form 2220. The amount of the penalty is based on the underpayment rate (or interest rate), the amount of the underpayment, and the period of the underpayment. The interest rate is generally the federal short-term interest rate plus 3 percent. The period of the underpayment is the due date for the installment through the earlier of (1) the date the payment is made or (2) the due date of the tax return without extensions. The penalties are not deductible.[33]

CONCLUSION

A C corporation is a separate taxpaying entity from its stockholders. Consequently, it must compute and report its own taxable income to the IRS. This chapter described the process of computing a corporation's taxable income and the associated tax liability

[33] §6655(b)(2).

for C corporations. We learned that book income (after taxes) is the starting point for calculating taxable income. Corporations adjust their book income for book–tax differences that arise because they account for many items of income and deduction differently for book purposes than they do for tax purposes. Some of these book–tax differences are temporary (the differences balance out over time), and some are permanent in nature (they don't balance out over the long term). As we discover in the next chapter, the distinction between temporary and permanent book–tax differences is critical for corporations computing their income tax expense or benefit for financial accounting purposes.

Summary

Describe the corporate income tax formula and discuss tax considerations relating to corporations' accounting periods and accounting methods. **LO 16-1**

- A corporation's taxable income is gross income minus deductions.
- The corporate tax formula is similar to the individual formula except that corporations don't claim the qualified business income deduction and they don't itemize deductions or deduct a standard deduction.
- Corporations may generally elect any tax year for reporting their taxable income, but the year must coincide with their financial accounting year.
- The timing of a corporation's income and deductions depends on the corporation's overall accounting method and its methods for specific transactions.
- Corporations are generally required to use the accrual overall method of accounting. However, smaller corporations may be allowed to use the cash method.

Identify common permanent and temporary book–tax differences and compute a corporation's taxable income and associated income tax liability. **LO 16-2**

- Corporations typically compute taxable income by starting with book income and adjusting for book–tax differences.
- Book–tax differences are favorable when they reduce taxable income relative to book income and unfavorable when they increase it.
- Book–tax differences are permanent when the amount of an income or deduction item is different for book and tax purposes and the amount will not reverse in the future.
- Book–tax differences are temporary when the amount of an income or deduction item is different for book and tax purposes in the current year but the same for book and tax purposes over the long term. That is, temporary book–tax differences reverse over time.
- Common permanent book–tax differences include interest from municipal bonds (favorable), life insurance premiums on policies covering key employees (unfavorable), one-half of nonrestaurant-provided meals expense, entertainment expense, and federal income tax expense, among others.
- Common temporary book–tax differences include depreciation expense, gain or loss on sale of depreciable assets, bad-debt expense, purchased goodwill amortization, and warranty expense, among others.
- Stock options granted when FASB ASC Topic 718 applies can generate temporary and permanent book–tax differences.
- Corporations may not deduct net capital losses for tax purposes. However, they may carry them back three years and forward five years to offset net capital gains in those other years.
- Net operating losses incurred in tax years beginning before 2018 can be carried forward up to 20 years (and back 2 years) and can offset up to 100 percent of taxable income (before the NOL deduction) in a given year.
- Net operating losses incurred in tax years beginning after 2017 and before 2021 can be carried back five years and forward indefinitely. These NOLs can offset 100 percent of taxable income before the NOL deduction for tax years beginning before 2021. For tax years beginning after 2020, they can offset up to 80 percent of taxable income after deducting NOL carryovers from tax years beginning before 2018.

- Net operating losses incurred in tax years beginning after 2020 can be carried forward indefinitely but may not be carried back. They can offset up to 80 percent of taxable income after deducting NOL carryovers from tax years beginning before 2018.
- When corporations have NOL carryovers from multiple years, they apply the oldest first to offset taxable income in a given year.
- When computing their net operating losses for the year, corporations may not deduct net operating losses from other years or net capital loss carrybacks.
- Subject to limitation, corporations can deduct the amount of money, the fair market value of capital gain property, and the adjusted basis of ordinary income property they donate to charity.
- The charitable contribution deduction limit is 10 percent of taxable income before deducting the charitable contribution, the dividends-received deduction, and net capital loss carrybacks. Amounts in excess of the limitation can be carried forward for up to five years.
- Corporations are allowed a deduction for dividends received to help mitigate potential triple taxation of the income distributed as a dividend. The amount of the deduction depends on the corporation's ownership in the distributing corporation. The deduction is 50 percent if the ownership is less than 20 percent; the deduction is 65 percent if the ownership is at least 20 percent but less than 80 percent; and the deduction is 100 percent if the ownership is 80 percent or more.
- The dividends-received deduction (DRD) is subject to a taxable income limitation. This limitation does not apply if the full DRD extends or creates a net operating loss for the corporation in the current year.
- A corporation's tax rate is 21 percent.

LO 16-3 Describe a corporation's tax return reporting and estimated tax payment obligations.

- Corporations file their tax returns on Form 1120, which is due three and one-half months after the corporation's year-end. Corporations with a June 30 year-end must file within two and one-half months after year-end (through 2026). Corporations can apply for a six-month extension of the due date for filing (seven months for corporations with a June 30 year-end).
- Small corporations report their book–tax differences on Schedule M-1 of Form 1120. Large corporations (assets of $10 million or more) report them on Schedule M-3. Schedule M-3 requires much more detail than Schedule M-1.
- Corporations pay income taxes through estimated tax payments. Each payment should be 25 percent of their required annual payment. The installments are due on the 15th day of the 4th, 6th, 9th, and 12th months of the corporation's taxable year.
- Corporations' required annual payment is the least of (1) 100 percent of their current-year tax liability, (2) 100 percent of their prior-year tax liability (but only if they had a positive tax liability in the prior year), or (3) 100 percent of the estimated current-year tax liability using the annualized income method. Large corporations may rely on (2) only to compute their first-quarter estimated payment requirement.

KEY TERMS

affiliated group (16-26)
annualized income method (16-27)
bargain element (16-11)
book (financial reporting) income (16-3)
book–tax differences (16-3)
capital gain property (16-16)
charitable contribution limit modified taxable income (16-17)
consolidated tax return (16-26)
DRD modified taxable income (16-20)
exercise price (16-10)
favorable book–tax difference (16-3)
grant date (16-11)
incentive stock option (ISO) (16-10)
M adjustments (16-23)
net capital loss carryback (16-13)
net capital loss carryover (16-13)
net operating loss (NOL) (16-14)
net operating loss carryback (16-14)
net operating loss carryover (16-14)
nonqualified stock option (NQO) (16-10)
ordinary income property (16-16)
permanent book–tax differences (16-3)
requisite service period (16-10)
Schedule M adjustments (16-23)
temporary book–tax differences (16-3)
unfavorable book–tax difference (16-3)
vest (16-10)
vesting period (16-11)

DISCUSSION QUESTIONS

Discussion Questions are available in Connect®.

1. In general terms, identify the similarities and differences between the corporate taxable income formula and the individual taxable income formula. LO 16-1
2. Is a corporation's choice of its tax year independent from its year-end for financial accounting purposes? LO 16-1
3. Can C corporations use the cash method of accounting? Explain. LO 16-1
4. Briefly describe the process of computing a corporation's taxable income assuming the corporation must use GAAP to determine its book income. LO 16-2
5. What role do a corporation's audited financial statements play in determining its taxable income? LO 16-2
6. What is the difference between favorable and unfavorable book–tax differences? LO 16-2
7. What is the difference between permanent and temporary book–tax differences? LO 16-2
8. Why is it important to be able to determine whether a particular book–tax difference is permanent or temporary? LO 16-2
9. Describe the relation between the book–tax differences associated with depreciation expense and the book–tax differences associated with gain or loss on disposition of depreciable assets. LO 16-2
10. A Corporation owns stock in B Corporation, and A Corporation receives a dividend from B Corporation. Ignoring the dividends-received deduction, what book–tax differences will A report for the year relating to its investment in B? Explain. LO 16-2
11. Describe how goodwill with a zero basis for tax purposes but not for book purposes leads to a permanent book–tax difference when the book goodwill is written off as impaired. LO 16-2
12. Describe how purchased goodwill leads to temporary book–tax differences. LO 16-2
13. Describe the book–tax differences that arise from incentive stock options. LO 16-2
14. Describe the book–tax differences that arise from nonqualified stock options. LO 16-2
15. How do corporations account for capital gains and losses for tax purposes? How is this different from the way individuals account for capital gains and losses? LO 16-2
16. What are the common book–tax differences relating to accounting for capital gains and losses? Do these differences create favorable or unfavorable book-to-tax adjustments? LO 16-2
17. What are the carryover and carryback periods for a net operating loss? Does a corporation have the option to choose the years to which it carries back a NOL? Explain. LO 16-2
18. Distinguish the tax treatment of a NOL incurred in 2017, a NOL incurred in 2020, and a NOL incurred in 2022. LO 16-2
19. When a corporation has NOL carryovers arising in different years, can it choose which NOL carryover to deduct first in a given year? Explain. LO 16-2
20. A corporation commissioned an accounting firm to recalculate the way it accounted for leasing transactions. With the new calculations, the corporation was able to file amended tax returns for the past few years that increased the corporation's net operating loss carryover from $3,000,000 to $5,000,000. Was the corporation wise to pay the accountants for their work that led to the increase in the NOL carryover? What factors should be considered in making this determination? LO 16-2
21. Compare and contrast the general rule for determining the amount of the charitable contribution if the corporation contributes capital gain property versus ordinary income property. LO 16-2
22. Which limitations might restrict a corporation's deduction for a cash charitable contribution in 2022? Explain how to determine the amount of the limitation. LO 16-2
23. For tax purposes, what happens to a corporation's charitable contributions that are not deducted in the current year because of the taxable income limitation? LO 16-2

LO 16-2 24. What are common book–tax differences relating to corporate charitable contributions? Are these differences favorable or unfavorable?

LO 16-2 25. Why does Congress provide the dividends-received deduction for corporations receiving dividends?

LO 16-2 26. How does a corporation determine the percentage for its dividends-received deduction? Explain.

LO 16-2 27. What limitations apply to the amount of the allowable dividends-received deduction?

LO 16-2 28. How many tax brackets are there in the corporate tax rate schedule?

LO 16-3 29. How is Schedule M-1 similar to and different from Schedule M-3? How does a corporation determine whether it must complete Schedule M-1 or Schedule M-3 when it completes its tax return?

LO 16-3 30. What is the due date for a calendar-year corporation tax return Form 1120 for 2022? Is it possible to extend the due date? Explain.

LO 16-3 31. How does a corporation determine the minimum amount of estimated tax payments it must make to avoid underpayment penalties? How do these rules differ for large corporations?

LO 16-3 32. Describe the annualized income method for determining a corporation's required estimated tax payments. What advantages does this method have over other methods?

PROBLEMS

Select problems are available in Connect®.

LO 16-1 33. LNS Corporation reports book revenue of $2,000,000. Included in the $2,000,000 is $15,000 of tax-exempt interest income. LNS reports $1,345,000 in ordinary and necessary business expenses. What is LNS Corporation's taxable income for the year?

LO 16-1 34. ATW Corporation currently uses the FIFO method of accounting for its inventory for book and tax purposes. Its beginning inventory for the current year was $8,000,000. Its ending inventory for the current year was $7,000,000. If ATW had been using the LIFO method of accounting for its inventory, its beginning inventory would have been $7,000,000 and its ending inventory would have been $5,500,000.

a) How much more in taxes did ATW Corporation pay for the current year because it used the FIFO method of accounting for inventory rather than the LIFO method?

b) Why would ATW use the FIFO method of accounting if doing so causes it to pay more taxes on a present value basis? (Note that the tax laws don't allow corporations to use the LIFO method of accounting for inventory unless they also use the LIFO method of accounting for inventory for book purposes.)

LO 16-1 35. ELS Corporation reported gross receipts for 2019–2021 for Scenarios A, B, and C as follows:

Year	Scenario A	Scenario B	Scenario C
2019	$26,000,000	$25,000,000	$27,500,000
2020	$27,000,000	$27,000,000	$27,000,000
2021	$27,900,000	$29,500,000	$26,500,000

a) Is ELS allowed to use the cash method of accounting in 2022 under Scenario A?

b) Is ELS allowed to use the cash method of accounting in 2022 under Scenario B?

c) Is ELS allowed to use the cash method of accounting in 2022 under Scenario C?

LO 16-2 36. On its year 1 financial statements, Seatax Corporation, an accrual-method taxpayer, reported federal income tax expense of $570,000. On its year 1 tax return, it reported a tax liability of $650,000. During year 1, Seatax made estimated tax payments of $700,000. What book–tax difference, if any, associated with its federal income tax expense should Seatax have reported when computing its year 1 taxable income? Is the difference favorable or unfavorable? Is it temporary or permanent?

37. Assume Maple Corp. has just completed the third year of its existence (year 3). The table below indicates Maple's ending book inventory for each year and the additional §263A costs it was required to include in its ending inventory. Maple immediately expensed these costs for book purposes. In year 2, Maple sold all of its year 1 ending inventory, and in year 3 it sold all of its year 2 ending inventory. LO 16-2

	Year 1	Year 2	Year 3
Ending book inventory	$2,400,000	$2,700,000	$2,040,000
Additional §263A costs	60,000	70,000	40,000
Ending tax inventory	$2,460,000	$2,770,000	$2,080,000

a) What book–tax difference associated with its inventory did Maple report in year 1? Was the difference favorable or unfavorable? Was it permanent or temporary?
b) What book–tax difference associated with its inventory did Maple report in year 2? Was the difference favorable or unfavorable? Was it permanent or temporary?
c) What book–tax difference associated with its inventory did Maple report in year 3? Was the difference favorable or unfavorable? Was it permanent or temporary?

38. JDog Corporation owns stock in Oscar Inc. valued at $2,000,000 at the beginning of the year and $2,200,000 at year-end. JDog received a $10,000 dividend from Oscar Inc. What temporary book–tax differences associated with its ownership in Oscar stock will JDog report for the year in the following alternative scenarios (income difference only—ignore the dividends-received deduction)? LO 16-2
a) JDog owns 5 percent of the Oscar Inc. stock. Oscar's income for the year was $500,000.
b) JDog owns 40 percent of the Oscar Inc. stock. Oscar's income for the year was $500,000.

39. On July 1 of year 1, Riverside Corp. (RC), a calendar-year taxpayer, acquired the assets of another business in a taxable acquisition. When the purchase price was allocated to the assets purchased, RC determined it had purchased $1,200,000 of goodwill for both book and tax purposes. At the end of year 1, RC determined that the goodwill had not been impaired during the year. In year 2, however, RC concluded that $200,000 of the goodwill had been impaired and wrote down the goodwill by $200,000 for book purposes. LO 16-2
a) What book–tax difference associated with its goodwill should RC report in year 1? Is it favorable or unfavorable? Is it permanent or temporary?
b) What book–tax difference associated with its goodwill should RC report in year 2? Is it favorable or unfavorable? Is it permanent or temporary?

40. Assume that on January 1, year 1, ABC Inc. issued 5,000 stock options with an estimated value of $10 per option. Each option entitles the owner to purchase one share of ABC stock for $25 a share (the per share price of ABC stock on January 1, year 1, when the options were granted). The options vest at the end of the day on December 31, year 2. All 5,000 stock options were exercised in year 3 when the ABC stock was valued at $31 per share. Identify ABC's year 1, 2, and 3 tax deductions and book–tax differences (indicate whether permanent and/or temporary) associated with the stock options under the following alternative scenarios: LO 16-2
a) The stock options are incentive stock options.
b) The stock options are nonqualified stock options.

41. Assume that on January 1, year 1, XYZ Corp. issued 1,000 nonqualified stock options with an estimated value of $4 per option. Each option entitles the owner to purchase one share of XYZ stock for $14 a share (the per share price of XYZ stock on January 1, year 1, when the options were granted). The options vest 25 percent a year (on December 31) for four years (beginning with year 1). All 500 stock options that had vested to that point were exercised in year 3 when the XYZ stock was valued at $20 per share. No other options were exercised in year 3 or year 4. Identify XYZ's LO 16-2

year 1, 2, 3, and 4 tax deductions and book–tax difference (identify as permanent and/or temporary) associated with the stock options.

LO 16-2 42. What book–tax differences in year 1 and year 2 associated with its capital gains and losses would ABD Inc. report in the following alternative scenarios? Identify each book–tax difference as favorable or unfavorable and as permanent or temporary.

a)

	Year 1	Year 2
Capital gains	$20,000	$5,000
Capital losses	8,000	0

b)

	Year 1	Year 2
Capital gains	$ 8,000	$5,000
Capital losses	20,000	0

c)

	Year 1	Year 2
Capital gains	$ 0	$50,000
Capital losses	25,000	30,000

d)

	Year 1	Year 2
Capital gains	$ 0	$40,000
Capital losses	25,000	0

e) Answer for year 6 only.

	Year 1	Years 2–5	Year 6
Capital gains	$ 0	$ 0	$15,000
Capital losses	10,000	0	0

f) Answer for year 7 only.

	Year 1	Years 2–6	Year 7
Capital gains	$ 0	$ 0	$15,000
Capital losses	10,000	0	0

LO 16-2 43. What book–tax differences in year 1 and year 2 associated with its capital gains and losses would DEF Inc. report in the following alternative scenarios? Identify each book–tax difference as favorable or unfavorable and as permanent or temporary.

a) In year 1, DEF recognized a loss of $15,000 on land that it had held for investment. In year 1, it also recognized a $30,000 gain on equipment it had purchased a few years ago. The equipment sold for $50,000 and had an adjusted basis of $20,000. DEF had deducted $40,000 of depreciation on the equipment. In year 2, DEF recognized a capital loss of $2,000.

b) In year 1, DEF recognized a loss of $15,000 on land that it had held for investment. It also recognized a $20,000 gain on equipment it had purchased a few years ago. The equipment sold for $50,000 and had an adjusted basis of $30,000. DEF had deducted $15,000 of tax depreciation on the equipment. There were no capital asset transactions in year 2.

LO 16-2 44. B12 Corp. is currently in the sixth year of its existence (2022). In 2017–2021, it reported the following income and (losses) (before net operating loss carryovers or carrybacks).

2017	$ (70,000)
2018	(30,000)
2019	60,000
2020	140,000
2021	(225,000)
2022	300,000

What is B12's 2022 taxable income after the NOL deduction (assume it does not elect to forgo any carrybacks, if applicable)? What is its 2022 book–tax difference associated with its NOL? Is it favorable or unfavorable? Is it permanent or temporary?

45. In 2022 Hill Corporation reported a net operating loss of $10,000 that it carried forward to 2023. In 2022 Hill also reported a net capital loss of $3,000 that it carried forward to 2023. In 2023, ignoring any carryovers from other years, Hill reported a loss for tax purposes of $50,000. The current-year loss includes a $12,000 net capital gain. What is Hill's 2023 net operating loss? LO 16-2

46. WCC Corp. has a $100,000 net operating loss carryover to 2022 from a previous year. Assume that it reported $75,000 of taxable income in 2022 (before the net operating loss deduction) and $30,000 of taxable income in 2023 (before the net operating loss deduction). LO 16-2
   a) What is WCC's taxable income in 2022 and 2023 (after the net operating loss deduction), assuming the $100,000 NOL carryover originated in 2017?
   b) What is WCC's taxable income in 2022 and 2023 (after the net operating loss deduction), assuming the $100,000 NOL carryover originated in 2020 and WCC elected to forgo the NOL carry back option?
   c) Assuming the same facts as in part (b), what is WCC's book–tax difference associated with the NOL in 2022 and in 2023? Identify the book–tax difference for each year as permanent or temporary.

47. In 2022, SML Corp. reported taxable income of $100,000 before any NOL deduc tions. SML has a $170,000 NOL carryover that originated in 2017 and a $90,000 NOL carryover that originated in 2020. What is SML's 2022 taxable income after the NOL deduction (assuming it elects to forgo any NOL carryback)? What NOLs can SML carry over to 2023? LO 16-2

48. Cedar Corporation reported a $25,000,000 net operating loss in 2022. It also has a $100,000 NOL carryover from 2017. In 2023, Cedar reported taxable income before any NOL carryovers of $20,000,000. What is Cedar's taxable income in 2023 after the NOL deduction, and what is its NOL carryover, if any, to 2024? LO 16-2

49. Golf Corp. (GC), a calendar-year, accrual-method corporation, held its directors' meeting on December 15 of year 1. During the meeting, the board of directors authorized GC to pay a $75,000 charitable contribution to the World Golf Foundation, a qualifying charity. LO 16-2
   a) If GC actually pays $50,000 of this contribution on January 15 of year 2 and the remaining $25,000 on or before April 15 of year 2, what book–tax difference will it report associated with the contribution in year 1 (assume the income limit does not apply)? Is it favorable or unfavorable? Is it permanent or temporary?
   b) Assuming the same facts as in part (a), what book–tax difference will GC report in year 2 (assume the income limit does not apply)? Is it favorable or unfavorable?
   c) If GC actually pays $50,000 of this contribution on January 15 of year 2 and the remaining $25,000 on May 15 of year 2, what book–tax difference will it report associated with the contribution in year 1 (assume the income limit does not apply)? Is it favorable or unfavorable? Is it permanent or temporary?
   d) Assuming the same facts as in part (c), what book–tax difference will GC report in year 2 (assume the income limit does not apply)? Is it favorable or unfavorable?

50. In 2022, OCC Corp. made a charitable donation of $400,000 to the International Rescue Committee (a qualifying charity). For the year, OCC reported taxable income of $1,500,000 before deducting any charitable contributions, before deducting its $20,000 dividends-received deduction, and before deducting its $40,000 NOL carryover from last year. LO 16-2
   a) What amount of the $400,000 donation is OCC allowed to deduct for tax purposes in 2022, what is the carryover to 2023, and when does the carryover expire?

b) Assume that in 2023, OCC did not make any charitable donations and that it is allowed to deduct its full charitable contribution carryover, if any, from 2022. What book–tax difference associated with the charitable contributions will OCC report in 2023? Is the difference favorable or unfavorable? Is it permanent or temporary?

LO 16-2

51. In 2022, LAA Inc. made a charitable donation of $100,000 to the Trevor Project (a qualifying charity). For the year, LAA reported taxable income of $550,000, which included a $100,000 charitable contribution deduction (before limitation), a $50,000 dividends-received deduction, and a $10,000 net operating loss carryover from 2021. What is LAA Inc.'s charitable contribution deduction for 2022?

LO 16-2
research

52. Coattail Corporation (CC) manufactures and sells women's and children's coats. This year, CC donated 1,000 coats to a qualified public charity. The charity distributed the coats to needy women and children throughout the region. At the time of the contribution, the fair market value of each coat was $80. Determine the amount of CC's charitable contribution (the taxable income limitation does not apply) for the coats, assuming the following:

a) CC's adjusted basis in each coat was $30.

b) CC's adjusted basis in each coat was $10.

LO 16-2
research

53. Maple Corp. owns several pieces of highly valued paintings that are on display in the corporation's headquarters. This year, it donated one of the paintings valued at $100,000 (adjusted basis of $25,000) to a local museum for the museum to display. What is the amount of Maple Corp.'s charitable contribution deduction for the painting (assuming income limitations do not apply)? What would be Maple's deduction if the museum sold the painting one month after it received it from Maple? (Assume Maple Corp. had prior knowledge of the museum's intention to sell the painting after receiving it.)

LO 16-2

54. Riverbend Inc. received a $200,000 dividend from stock it held in Hobble Corporation. Riverbend's taxable income is $2,100,000 before deducting the dividends-received deduction (DRD), a $40,000 NOL carryover, and a $100,000 charitable contribution.

a) What is Riverbend's deductible DRD assuming it owns 10 percent of Hobble Corporation?

b) Assuming the facts in part (a), what is Riverbend's marginal tax rate on the dividend after taking the DRD into account?

c) What is Riverbend's DRD assuming it owns 60 percent of Hobble Corporation?

d) Assuming the facts in part (c), what is Riverbend's marginal tax rate on the dividend?

e) What is Riverbend's DRD assuming it owns 85 percent of Hobble Corporation (and is part of the same affiliated group)?

f) Assuming the facts in part (e), what is Riverbend's marginal tax rate on the dividend?

LO 16-2

55. Wasatch Corp. (WC) received a $200,000 dividend from Tager Corporation (TC). WC owns 15 percent of the TC stock. Compute WC's deductible DRD in each of the following situations:

a) WC's taxable income (loss) without the dividend income or the DRD is $10,000.

b) WC's taxable income (loss) without the dividend income or the DRD is $(10,000).

c) WC's taxable income (loss) without the dividend income or the DRD is $(99,000).

d) WC's taxable income (loss) without the dividend income or the DRD is $(101,000).

e) WC's taxable income (loss) without the dividend income or the DRD is $(500,000).

f) What is WC's book–tax difference associated with its DRD in part (a)? Is the difference favorable or unfavorable? Is it permanent or temporary?

56. Compute SWK Inc.'s tax liability for each of the following scenarios: LO 16-3
a) SWK's taxable income is $60,000.
b) SWK's taxable income is $275,000.
c) SWK's taxable income is $50,000,000.

57. Last year, TBA Corporation, a calendar-year taxpayer, reported a tax liability of $100,000. TBA confidently anticipates a current-year tax liability of $240,000. What minimum estimated tax payments should TBA make for the first, second, third, and fourth quarters, respectively (ignore the annualized income method), assuming the following: LO 16-3
a) TBA is not considered to be a large corporation for estimated tax purposes.
b) TBA is considered to be a large corporation for estimated tax purposes.

58. Last year, BTA Corporation, a calendar-year taxpayer, reported a net operating loss of $10,000 and a $0 tax liability. BTA confidently anticipates a current-year tax liability of $240,000. What minimum estimated tax payments should BTA make for the first, second, third, and fourth quarters, respectively (ignore the annualized income method), assuming the following: LO 16-3
a) BTA is not considered to be a large corporation for estimated tax purposes.
b) BTA is considered to be a large corporation for estimated tax purposes.

59. For the current year, LNS Corporation reported the following taxable income at the end of its first, second, and third quarters. What are LNS's minimum first-, second-, third-, and fourth-quarter estimated tax payments, using the annualized income method? LO 16-3

Quarter-End	Cumulative Taxable Income
First	$1,000,000
Second	1,600,000
Third	2,400,000

60. Last year, JL Corporation's tax liability was $900,000. For the current year, JL Corporation reported the following taxable income at the end of its first, second, and third quarters (see table below). What are JL's minimum required first-, second-, third-, and fourth-quarter estimated tax payments (ignore the actual current-year tax safe harbor)? LO 16-3 planning

Quarter-End	Cumulative Taxable Income
First	$ 500,000
Second	1,250,000
Third	2,250,000

61. Last year, Cougar Corp. (CC) reported a net operating loss of $25,000. In the current year, CC expected its current-year tax liability to be $260,000, so it made four equal estimated tax payments of $65,000 each. Cougar closed its books at the end of each quarter. The following schedule reports CC's taxable income at the end of each quarter: LO 16-3

Quarter-End	Cumulative Taxable Income
First	$ 300,000
Second	700,000
Third	1,000,000
Fourth	1,500,000

CC's current-year tax liability on $1,500,000 of taxable income is $315,000. Does CC owe underpayment penalties on its estimated tax payments? If so, for which quarters does it owe the penalty?

COMPREHENSIVE PROBLEMS

Select problems are available in Connect®.

62. Compute MV Corp.'s 2022 taxable income given the following information relating to its year 1 activities. Also, compute MV's Schedule M-1 assuming that MV's federal income tax expense for book purposes is $100,000.
    - Gross profit from inventory sales of $500,000 (no book–tax differences).
    - Dividends MV received from 25 percent–owned corporation of $100,000 (assume this is also MV's pro rata share of the distributing corporation's earnings).
    - Expenses *other than* DRD, charitable contribution (CC), and net operating loss (NOL) are $350,000 (no book–tax differences).
    - NOL carryover from 2021 of $10,000.
    - Cash charitable contribution of $120,000.
63. Compute HC Inc.'s current-year taxable income given the following information relating to its current-year (2022) activities. Also, compute HC's Schedule M-1 assuming that HC's federal income tax expense for book purposes is $30,000.
    - Gross profit from inventory sales of $310,000 (no book–tax differences).
    - Dividends HC received from 28 percent–owned corporation of $120,000 (this is also HC's pro rata share of the corporation's earnings).
    - Expenses *other than* DRD, charitable contribution (CC), and net operating loss (NOL) are $300,000 (no book–tax differences).
    - NOL carryover from prior year of $12,000.
    - Cash charitable contribution of $50,000.

tax forms

64. Timpanogos Inc. is an accrual-method, calendar-year corporation. For 2022, it reported financial statement income after taxes of $1,342,000. Timpanogos provided the following information relating to its 2022 activities:

Life insurance proceeds as a result of CEO's death	$ 200,000
Revenue from sales (for both book and tax purposes)	2,000,000
Premiums paid on the key-person life insurance policies; the policies have no cash surrender value	21,000
Charitable contributions	180,000
Cost of goods sold for book and tax purposes	300,000
Interest income on tax-exempt bonds	40,000
Interest paid on loan obtained to purchase tax-exempt bonds	45,000
Rental income payments received and earned in 2022	15,000
Rental income payments received in 2021 but earned in 2022	10,000
Rental income payments received in 2022 but not earned by year-end	30,000
Tax depreciation	55,000
Book depreciation	25,000
Net capital loss	42,000
Federal income tax expense for books in 2022	310,000

Required:

a) Reconcile book income to taxable income for Timpanogos Inc. Be sure to start with book income and identify all of the adjustments necessary to arrive at taxable income.
b) Identify each book–tax difference as either permanent or temporary.

c) Complete Schedule M-1 for Timpanogos.
d) Compute Timpanogos Inc.'s tax liability.

65. XYZ is a calendar-year corporation that began business on January 1, 2022. For the year, it reported the following information in its current-year audited income statement. Notes with important tax information are provided below.

tax forms

Required:
Identify the book-to-tax adjustments for XYZ.

a) Reconcile book income to taxable income and identify each book–tax difference as temporary or permanent.
b) Compute XYZ's income tax liability.
c) Complete XYZ's Schedule M-1.
d) Complete XYZ's Form 1120, page 1 (use the most current form available). Ignore estimated tax penalties when completing this form.
e) Determine the quarters for which XYZ is subject to penalties for the underpayment of estimated taxes (see assumptions and estimated tax information below).

XYZ Corp. Income Statement for Current Year	**Book Income**	**Book to Tax Adjustments (Dr.)**	**Cr.**	**Taxable Income**
Revenue from sales	$ 40,000,000			
Cost of goods sold	(27,000,000)			
Gross profit	$ 13,000,000			
Other income:				
Income from investment in corporate stock	300,000[1]			
Interest income	20,000[2]			
Capital gains (losses)	(4,000)			
Gain or loss from disposition of fixed assets	3,000[3]			
Miscellaneous income	50,000			
Gross income	$ 13,369,000			
Expenses:				
Compensation	(7,500,000)[4]			
Stock option compensation	(200,000)[5]			
Advertising	(1,350,000)			
Repairs and maintenance	(75,000)			
Rent	(22,000)			
Bad debt expense	(41,000)[6]			
Depreciation	(1,400,000)[7]			
Warranty expenses	(70,000)[8]			
Charitable donations	(500,000)[9]			
Meals (all from restaurants)	(18,000)			
Goodwill impairment	(30,000)[10]			
Organizational expenditures	(44,000)[11]			
Other expenses	(140,000)[12]			
Total expenses	$(11,390,000)			
Income before taxes	$ 1,979,000			
Provision for income taxes	(400,000)[13]			
Net income after taxes	$ 1,579,000			

Notes

1. XYZ owns 30 percent of the outstanding Hobble Corp. (HC) stock. HC reported $1,000,000 of income for the year. XYZ accounted for its investment in HC under the equity method, and it recorded its pro rata share of HC's earnings for the year. HC also distributed a $200,000 dividend to XYZ. For tax purposes, HC reports the actual dividend received as income, not the pro rata share of HC's earnings.
2. Of the $20,000 interest income, $5,000 was from a City of Seattle bond, $7,000 was from a Tacoma City bond, $6,000 was from a fully taxable corporate bond, and the remaining $2,000 was from a money market account.
3. This gain is from equipment that XYZ purchased in February and sold in December (i.e., it does not qualify as §1231 gain).
4. This includes total officer compensation of $2,500,000 (no one officer received more than $1,000,000 compensation).
5. This amount is the portion of incentive stock option compensation that was expensed during the year (recipients are officers).
6. XYZ actually wrote off $27,000 of its accounts receivable as uncollectible.
7. Tax depreciation was $1,900,000.
8. In the current year, XYZ did not make any actual payments on warranties it provided to customers.
9. XYZ made $500,000 of cash contributions to charities during the year.
10. On July 1 of this year, XYZ acquired the assets of another business. In the process, it acquired $300,000 of goodwill. At the end of the year, XYZ wrote off $30,000 of the goodwill as impaired.
11. XYZ expensed all of its organizational expenditures for book purposes. XYZ expensed the maximum amount of organizational expenditures allowed for tax purposes.
12. The other expenses do not contain any items with book–tax differences.
13. This is an estimated tax provision (federal tax expense) for the year. Assume that XYZ is not subject to state income taxes.

Estimated Tax Information

XYZ made four equal estimated tax payments totaling $360,000 ($90,000 per quarter). For purposes of estimated tax liabilities, assume XYZ was in existence in 2021 and that in 2021 it reported a tax liability of $500,000. During 2022, XYZ determined its taxable income at the end of each of the four quarters as follows:

Quarter-End	Cumulative Taxable Income (Loss)
First	$ 400,000
Second	1,100,000
Third	1,400,000

Finally, assume that XYZ is not a large corporation for purposes of estimated tax calculations.

UWorld Roger CPA Review

Sample CPA Exam questions from Roger CPA Review are available in Connect as support for the topics in this text. These Multiple Choice Questions and Task-Based Simulations include expert-written explanations and solutions and provide a starting point for students to become familiar with the content and functionality of the actual CPA Exam.

chapter

17 Accounting for Income Taxes

Learning Objectives

Upon completing this chapter, you should be able to:

LO 17-1 Describe the objectives of FASB ASC Topic 740, *Income Taxes,* and the income tax provision process.

LO 17-2 Calculate the current and deferred income tax expense or benefit components of a company's income tax provision.

LO 17-3 Determine how to calculate a valuation allowance.

LO 17-4 Explain how a company accounts for its uncertain income tax positions under FASB ASC Topic 740.

LO 17-5 Describe how a company computes and discloses the components of its effective tax rate.

mentatdgt/Shutterstock

Storyline Summary

Elise Brandon (she/her/hers)

Employment status:	Tax associate for a large public accounting firm.

Assigned to prepare the federal income tax provision and income-tax-related balance sheet accounts and footnote disclosures for Premiere Computer Corporation, a nonaudit client.

Premiere Computer Corporation
Medium-sized publicly traded company.
Manufactures and sells computers and computer-related equipment. Calendar-year taxpayer.

Tax rate:	21 percent.

Elise felt a great sense of accomplishment when she completed her review of the federal income tax return for Premiere Computer Corporation (PCC). She was glad the return was filed on time and did not need to be extended. With the tax return filed, Elise was assigned to help the PCC tax department compute the federal **income tax provision** (financial income tax expense) for the company's soon-to-be-published income statement and to determine the correct amounts in the company's income-tax-related balance sheet accounts.[1] She also was given responsibility for helping prepare the income tax note to the financial statements.[2]

Elise was aware that, as a result of the stringent independence requirements imposed by the Sarbanes-Oxley Act, her colleagues in the tax group were getting a lot of engagements to help prepare the income tax provision for nonaudit clients. In fact, her firm considered accounting for income taxes to be a "core competency" for all tax staff and prepared a training course for everyone. Having recently attended the firm's training on the subject, Elise was eager to apply her new knowledge to an actual client situation. She knew that developing her skill set in this complex topic would make her more valuable to her firm and her clients.

(to be continued . . .)

[1]The tax provision is typically completed in the month or two following year-end, whereas the filing date of the tax return is several months later. Due to the chapter sequence, Elise will complete the provision after the tax return from the Corporate Operations chapter. We discuss the timing of the provision and return later in the chapter.

[2]In today's post-Sarbanes-Oxley environment, staff from public accounting firms that are not a company's auditors often are hired to help prepare the company's income tax provision under FASB ASC Topic 740 because many companies do not have staff with the expertise to make this calculation.

Most of the items of income (revenue) and deductions (expenses) that are included in a company's taxable income also are included in the company's net (book) income before taxes. Not all of these items are included in the computations in the same accounting period, however, which creates a "temporary" mismatch of the amounts of these items included in taxable income and pretax book income in a given year. Other items are included in only one of the computations, which creates a "permanent" mismatch of the amount of these items included in taxable income and pretax book income. A company must take these temporary and permanent differences into account in computing its income tax expense or (benefit) on the income statement and its deferred income taxes payable (liabilities) or refundable (assets) on the balance sheet.

FASB Accounting Standards Codification Topic 740, *Income Taxes* (hereafter, ASC 740), governs the computation and disclosure of a company's income tax provision (expense or benefit) and its expected future income tax liabilities or benefits related to "events" that have been recorded on either the financial statement or the tax return. ASC 740 deals with the majority of accounting and reporting guidance related to income taxes. Accounting for income taxes guidance related to accounting for investments under the equity method, stock compensation, business combinations, foreign currency translation, and industry subtopics such as real estate, entertainment, and oil and gas is embedded within the ASC topic that deals with each of these issues. The Emerging Issues Task Force (EITF)[3] and the Securities and Exchange Commission continue to provide guidance on issues related to accounting for income taxes.

A company's failure to accurately compute the income tax provision and related balance sheet accounts can lead to the issuance of a material weakness statement by the auditor and, in some cases, a restatement of the financial statements. Not surprisingly, individuals who understand these complex and sometimes counterintuitive rules are in great demand by public accounting firms and industry.

This chapter discusses the basic rules for how a company computes and discloses its current-year income tax provision and its future income tax consequences, using the facts related to Premiere Computer Corporation in the Corporate Operations chapter. We focus on the portion of the provision that relates to federal income taxes.

LO 17-1

ACCOUNTING FOR INCOME TAXES AND THE INCOME TAX PROVISION PROCESS

In addition to filing its federal, state and local, and non-U.S. income tax returns, Premiere Computer Corporation, along with all other U.S. publicly traded corporations and many privately held corporations, must prepare financial statements in accordance with generally accepted accounting principles (GAAP) issued by the FASB (Financial Accounting Standards Board). Under GAAP, a company includes as part of its income statement a "provision" for the income tax expense or benefit that is associated with the pretax net income or loss reported on the income statement. The income tax provision includes not only current-year taxes payable or refundable, but also future income tax consequences, that result from differences in the timing of when an item is reported on the tax return compared to the financial statement. The company records the amount of future income tax benefits as a **deferred tax asset** and the amount of future income tax obligations as a **deferred tax liability** on its balance sheet. Practitioners use the term "provision" to refer to either all of the income tax expense reported in the financial statements or the specific components of income tax expense such as "the current tax provision" or the "deferred tax provision." It is often a matter of context to determine how the term is being used. In this chapter, we use the term *provision* in both contexts. The income tax provision process refers to the entire income tax process, whereas the current or deferred tax provisions refer to individual components of the process.

[3]The Emerging Issues Task Force is a committee of accounting practitioners who assist the Financial Accounting Standards Board in providing timely guidance on emerging issues and the implementation of existing standards.

TAXES IN THE REAL WORLD Material Weaknesses in Tax Reporting

Taxes remain a primary area for internal control issues due to their size and complexity of the issues. The consequences of errors can be severe. As an example, on October 29, 2019, Mattel Inc. announced the completion of a whistleblower investigation into accounting errors that occurred in 2017. The investigation found that in the third quarter of 2017, Mattel Inc. understated its income tax expense by reducing its deferred tax valuation allowance by $109 million, understating its loss. Rather than disclose the error to the CEO and the board, the company changed its accounting for an intangible asset in the fourth quarter of 2017, which resulted in correcting the third quarter error. As a result of the investigation, Mattel determined there were material weaknesses in its internal control over financial reporting. To remediate the identified issues, Mattel restated its 2016–2018 annual financial statements and replaced several financial employees, including the CFO, controller, and Senior Vice President of Tax. In addition, Mattel's outside auditor replaced its lead audit partner and other key members of the audit team.

Source: Based on Mattel Inc.'s 8-K filing dated October 29, 2019. Available at https://investors.mattel.com/node/31261/html.

Why Is Accounting for Income Taxes So Complex?

The basic principles that underlie ASC 740 are fairly straightforward, but the application of ASC 740 can be very complex. Much of the complexity is due to the fact that the U.S. tax laws are complex and often ambiguous. In addition, companies frequently prepare their financial statements (Form 10-K) much earlier than their corresponding tax returns. For example, a calendar-year corporation generally files its Form 10-K with the SEC in February or early March, but it might not file its federal income tax return (Form 1120) with the Internal Revenue Service (IRS) until October.[4] As a result, management often must exercise a high degree of judgment in estimating the income tax return positions currently and in future years when a tax return position might be challenged by the tax authorities. After the tax return has been filed, it may take a number of years before it is audited by the IRS and the final tax liability is determined.[5] For example, Microsoft Corporation disclosed in its Form 10-K for the year ended June 30, 2021, that the IRS is auditing Microsoft's tax returns for 2004–2017.

Objectives of ASC 740

ASC 740 applies only to *income* taxes levied by the U.S. federal government, U.S. state and local governments, and non-U.S. (foreign) governments. The FASB defines an *income tax* as a tax *based on income*. This definition excludes property taxes, excise taxes, sales taxes, and value-added taxes. Companies report nonincome taxes as expenses in the computation of their net income before taxes.

ASC 740 has two primary objectives. One is to "recognize the amount of taxes payable or refundable in the current year," referred to as the **current tax liability (asset).**[6] A second objective is to "recognize deferred tax liabilities and assets for the future tax consequences of events that have been recognized in an entity's financial statements or tax returns."[7] Both objectives relate to reporting a company's income tax amounts on the balance sheet, not on the income statement. The FASB refers to this method as the "asset

[4]The due date for a federal income tax return filed by a calendar-year corporation is April 15, but corporations can request a six-month extension to October 15 by filing Form 7004 and paying any remaining tax liability.

[5]Although the statute of limitations for a filed income tax return is three years, large corporations often agree to extend the statute for a longer period of time to allow the IRS to audit the return. As a result, a corporation's tax return may not be audited for five or more years from the date it is filed.

[6]ASC 740-10-10-1(a).

[7]Accounting Standards Update No. 2018-05. Income Taxes (Topic 740). March 2018.

and liability approach" to accounting for income taxes.[8] The FASB chose this approach because it is the most consistent with the definitions in FASB Concepts Statement No. 6, *Elements of Financial Statements,* and produces the most useful and understandable information.[9] So, some of the complexity of the income tax provision comes from meeting these two objectives.

To compute the deferred tax liability or asset, a company calculates the future tax effects attributable to temporary book and tax differences and **tax carryovers.**[10] As you learned in the Corporate Operations chapter, temporary differences generally can be thought of as revenue (income) or expenses (deductions) that will appear on both the income statement and the tax return but in different periods. Temporary differences that cause cumulative taxable income to be less than cumulative pretax book income create deferred tax liabilities. Thus, deferred tax liabilities represent future tax obligations resulting from the reversal of favorable originating book–tax differences. In contrast, temporary differences that cause cumulative taxable income to exceed cumulative pretax book income create deferred tax assets, which represent future tax benefits resulting from the reversal of unfavorable originating book–tax differences.

Examples 17-1 and 17-2 illustrate the two objectives of ASC 740.

Example 17-1

What if: Suppose PPC begins business in year 1. PPC uses the accrual method of accounting for book purposes and the cash method for tax purposes and has a 25 percent tax rate. The company has two sources of revenue in year 1: $100 of interest income and $100 from the sale of services on account. In year 2, PPC again earns $100 of interest income but does not sell any additional services. It receives $100 from its customer in payment for the year 1 sale. The company does not have any expenses other than income taxes in years 1 and 2. How would these transactions be reflected in PPC's income statement if PPC reported its income taxes as calculated on its tax return (i.e., no deferred taxes)?

Answer:

	Book (Accrual Method)			Tax (Cash Method)	
	Year 1	**Year 2**		**Year 1**	**Year 2**
Revenue	$200	$100	Income	$100	$200
Expenses	0	0	Deductions	0	0
Pretax income	$200	$100	Taxable income	$100	$200
			Tax bill	$ 25	$ 50
Tax expense					
Current tax expense (using tax bill amount)	25	50			
Deferred tax expense	N/A	N/A			
Net income	$175	$ 50			
Effective tax rate (tax expense/pretax income)	12.5%	50%			

In year 1, PPC has $200 of income for book purposes; however, because PPC did not receive payment for the sale of its services in year 1, it will only report the interest income on its year 1 tax return, resulting in a $25 tax bill ($100 × 25 percent). If PPC reports the $25 tax bill as its financial tax expense, year 1 net income is $175 and its effective tax rate is 12.5 percent ($25/$200). In year 2, PPC reports the $100 of interest income for book purposes and $200 of taxable income because it includes the $100 payment on the sale of services from year 1. At a 25 percent tax rate, PPC's tax bill is $50 ($200 × 25 percent). Consequently, in year 2 PPC reports $50 of net income and an effective tax rate of 50 percent!

[8]FAS 109, ¶63. (This paragraph was not codified in ASC 740.)
[9]FAS 109, ¶63.
[10]ASC 740-10-25-2(b).

As shown in Example 17-1, this reporting causes large swings in net income and the effective tax rate that have little to do with the company's operations, making it difficult for shareholders and other interested parties of the financial statements to interpret the company's performance. To prevent these situations, GAAP requires the use of the accrual method of accounting, which is designed to better align expenses (like taxes) with revenues. So, under accrual accounting, the effects of transactions in specific years should be accounted for in the year of the transaction regardless of the cash flow. ASC 740 provides the guidance for companies to report their income tax expense in accordance with these accrual accounting principles. For PPC's situation, ASC 740 requires PPC to report the tax expense associated with both the interest income and the sale of services in year 1 regardless of when the tax is paid to the taxing authority—that is, it is required to report both the current and deferred income tax expenses.

Example 17-2

What if: How would PPC's income statement be reported using ASC 740 principles?

Answer:

	Book (Accrual Method)			**Tax (Cash Method)**	
	Year 1	**Year 2**		**Year 1**	**Year 2**
Revenue	$200	$100	Revenue	$100	$200
Expenses	0	0	Expenses	0	0
Pretax income	$200	$100	Taxable income	$100	$200
			Tax bill	$ 25	$ 50
Tax expense					
Current tax expense	25	50			
Deferred tax expense*	25	(25)			
Net income	$150	$ 75			
Effective tax rate (tax expense/ pretax income)	25%	25%			

*We will discuss the calculation of the deferred tax expense later in the chapter.

Example 17-2 shows that PPC's net income and effective tax rate now reflect the effects of PPC's operations for each of those years. Notice that the fluctuation in the effective tax rate has disappeared.

The Income Tax Provision Process

The tax provision process refers to the process of determining the current and deferred income tax expense or (benefit) for the income statement and the tax payable or receivable and deferred tax assets and liabilities for the balance sheet. In addition, the process includes preparing the related footnote disclosures for a company's financial reporting. A company typically begins this process by computing the two components of its income tax provision (current and deferred) separately (independently) for each category of income tax (U.S. federal, U.S. state and local, and international) and then combining the components to produce the total income tax expense or (benefit). We can summarize the formula to compute a company's total income tax expense or (benefit) as:

Total income tax expense (benefit) = Current income tax expense (benefit)
+ Deferred income tax expense (benefit)

A company computes its federal income tax provision using a five-step process. These steps are:

1. Identify all permanent and temporary differences and tax carryover amounts and calculate the current income tax provision (ASC 740 Objective 1).
2. Determine the ending balances in the balance sheet deferred tax asset and liability accounts (ASC 740 Objective 2).
3. Calculate the deferred income tax provision and the total income tax provision.
4. Evaluate the need for a valuation allowance for gross deferred tax assets.
5. Evaluate the need for an uncertain tax benefit reserve.

Example 17-3

Before she began the income tax provision process for 2022, Elise knew she needed to get the ending balances in PCC's deferred tax accounts from the prior year. Accordingly, she retrieved PCC's balance sheet for the current and prior years (Exhibit 17-1) and the deferred tax component of the company's income tax note (Exhibit 17-2).

EXHIBIT 17-1 PCC Balance Sheet at 12/31/2022 and 12/31/2021

	12/31/2022	12/31/2021
Assets		
Current Assets		
Cash	$ 6,933,480	$ 10,776,380
Municipal bonds	300,000	300,000
Accounts receivable	20,750,000	17,250,000
Less: Allowance for bad debts	(415,000)	(345,000)
Accounts receivable (net)	20,335,000	16,905,000
Inventory	5,175,000	4,312,500
Total current assets	$ 32,743,480	$ 32,293,880
Noncurrent Assets		
Fixed assets	$ 70,000,000	$ 60,000,000
Less: Accumulated depreciation	(14,400,000)	(12,054,000)
Fixed assets (net)	55,600,000	47,946,000
Investments	1,647,960	1,597,960
Goodwill	180,000	180,000
Total noncurrent assets	$ 57,427,960	$ 49,723,960
Total assets	$ 90,171,440	$ 82,017,840
Liabilities and Shareholders' Equity		
Current Liabilities		
Accounts payable	$ 24,015,600	$ 20,013,000
Reserve for warranties	600,000	430,000
Total current liabilities	$ 24,615,600	$ 20,443,000
Noncurrent Liabilities		
Long-term debt	$ 40,000,000	$ 40,000,000
Deferred compensation	1,050,000	1,200,000
Deferred tax liabilities*	2,187,570	2,187,570
Total noncurrent liabilities	$ 43,237,570	$ 43,387,570
Total liabilities	$ 67,853,170	$ 63,830,570
Shareholders' Equity		
Common stock (par value = $1)	$ 500,000	$ 500,000
Additional paid-in capital	5,100,000	5,000,000
Retained earnings	16,718,270	12,687,270
Total shareholders' equity	$ 22,318,270	$ 18,187,270
Total liabilities and shareholders' equity	$ 90,171,440	$ 82,017,840

*Deferred tax liabilities have not yet been updated for current year.

Looking at Exhibit 17-2, what income tax accounts appear on PCC's balance sheet from the prior year?

Answer: PCC has a net deferred tax liability of $2,187,570, which is the sum of the deferred tax assets and liabilities. A net deferred tax liability results when deferred tax liabilities exceed deferred tax assets. A net deferred tax asset results when deferred tax assets exceed deferred tax liabilities.

Since its inception, has PCC had net favorable or unfavorable temporary differences?

Answer: Because PCC has a net deferred tax liability at the end of 2021, PCC has a future tax obligation related to the reversal of book–tax differences that were favorable when they originated. The future tax obligation indicates that the company has had cumulative pretax net income that has exceeded its cumulative taxable income.

EXHIBIT 17-2 PCC Deferred Tax Accounts at 12/31/2021

Deferred Tax Assets	
Allowance for bad debts	$ 72,450
Reserve for warranties	90,300
Net operating loss carryover	5,040
Deferred compensation	252,000
Net capital loss carryover	—
Contribution carryover	—
Total deferred tax assets	$ 419,790
Valuation allowance for deferred tax assets	—
Deferred tax assets, net of valuation allowance	$ 419,790
Deferred Tax Liabilities	
Depreciation	(2,607,360)
Total deferred tax liabilities	$(2,607,360)
Net deferred tax liabilities	$(2,187,570)

CALCULATING A COMPANY'S INCOME TAX PROVISION

LO 17-2

(continued from page 17-1 . . .)

Elise gathered the financial statement and tax return data she needed to get started, beginning with the workpaper template she reviewed to verify PCC's taxable income. (Exhibit 17-3 reproduces the book–tax reconciliation template from Exhibit 16-8, excluding the estimated book federal income tax expense of $2,000,000.) Elise identified each of the book–tax adjustments as being either permanent (P) or temporary (T). She was ready to begin the process of computing PCC's federal income tax provision using the five-step method she had learned at firm training.

(to be continued . . .)

Step 1: Identify All Permanent and Temporary Differences and Tax Carryover Amounts and Calculate the Current Income Tax Provision (ASC 740 Objective 1)

Permanent Differences As you learned in the Corporate Operations chapter, book–tax differences can be classified into different categories (permanent or temporary). Some differences will appear on either the income statement or the tax return but not on both. ASC 740 does not provide a label for these types of differences; however, in practice they are referred to as **permanent book–tax differences.** Examples of items that affect only the income statement are tax-exempt interest income and nondeductible fines. Items that appear only on the tax return include the dividends-received deduction and the excess tax over book benefit from the exercise of nonqualified stock options.

EXHIBIT 17-3 PCC Book–Tax Reconciliation Template for 2022

Premiere Computer Corporation				
Income Statement for Current Year	Book Income	Book–Tax Adjustments (Dr)	Book–Tax Adjustments Cr	Taxable Income
Revenue from sales	$ 60,000,000			$ 60,000,000
Cost of goods sold	(38,000,000)			(38,000,000)
Gross profit	$ 22,000,000			$ 22,000,000
Other income:				
Dividend income	30,000			30,000
Interest income (P)	120,000	(12,000)		108,000
Capital gains (losses) (T)	(28,000)		28,000	0
Gain on fixed asset dispositions (T)	54,000		16,000	70,000
Gross income	$ 22,176,000			$ 22,208,000
Expenses:				
Compensation	(9,868,000)			(9,868,000)
Deferred compensation (T)	(300,000)	(150,000)		(450,000)
Stock option compensation (T)	(100,000)		100,000	0
Bad debt expense (T)	(165,000)		70,000	(95,000)
Charitable contributions (T)	(700,000)		73,700	(626,300)
Depreciation (T)	(2,400,000)	(700,000)		(3,100,000)
Advertising	(1,920,000)			(1,920,000)
Warranty expenses (T)	(580,000)		170,000	(410,000)
Meals	(14,000)			(14,000)
Life insurance premiums (P)	(34,000)		34,000	0
Other expenses	(64,000)			(64,000)
Total expenses *before* NOL, DRD	$(16,145,000)			$(16,547,300)
Income *before* NOL, DRD	$ 6,031,000			$ 5,660,700
NOL carryover from prior year (T)	0	(24,000)		(24,000)
Dividends-received deduction (P)	0	(15,000)		(15,000)
Book/taxable income	**$ 6,031,000**	**$(901,000)**	**$491,700**	**$ 5,621,700**

A company does not take permanent differences into account in computing its deferred tax assets and liabilities. Permanent differences enter into the company's computation of taxable income and thus affect the current tax expense or benefit, either increasing or decreasing it. As a result, permanent differences usually affect a company's **effective tax rate**—or its total income tax expense/pretax net income—and appear as part of the company's reconciliation of its effective tax rate with its statutory U.S. tax rate (21 percent). We discuss this and other ASC 740 disclosure requirements in a later section of this chapter.

Exhibit 17-4 provides a list of common permanent differences you will encounter in practice.

EXHIBIT 17-4 Common Permanent Differences

Life insurance proceeds	Disallowed premiums on officers' life insurance
Tax-exempt interest income	Dividends-received deduction
Nondeductible tax penalties and fines	The windfall tax benefit from exercise of nonqualified stock options
Political contributions	Entertainment expenses
Disallowed business-related meals*	Tax credits**

*For 2021 and 2022, meals purchased from restaurants are fully deductible and will not result in a permanent difference.

**Tax credits are permanent differences for ASC 740; however, they are not a book-tax reconciling item. Rather, tax credits reduce tax expense directly.

Example 17-4

Elise went back to the template she used to review PCC's taxable income and identified the book–tax adjustments that were considered permanent in nature. What are PCC's permanent differences, and are they favorable or unfavorable?

Answer: A net unfavorable permanent difference of $7,000, computed as follows:

Permanent Differences	(Favorable) Unfavorable
Tax-exempt interest income	$(12,000)
Life insurance premiums	34,000
Dividends-received deduction	(15,000)
Net unfavorable permanent difference	**$ 7,000**

Example 17-5

Elise used the net unfavorable permanent difference of $7,000 to adjust PCC's pretax income. What is PCC's pretax income adjusted for permanent differences?

Answer: $6,038,000, computed as follows:

PCC pretax income	$ 6,031,000
Net unfavorable permanent difference	$ 7,000
PCC pretax income adjusted for permanent differences	**$ 6,038,000**

Elise remembered that her instructor at ASC 740 training referred to this intermediate computation as a company's **book equivalent of taxable income.** That is, this amount represents the book income that ultimately will be taxable, either currently or in the future.

Temporary Differences and Tax Carryover Amounts In contrast to permanent differences, **temporary book–tax differences** reverse over time such that, over the long term, corporations recognize the same amount of income or deductions for the items on their income statements as they recognize on their tax returns. Temporary book–tax differences arise because the income or deduction items are included in financial accounting income in one year and in taxable income in a different year. Temporary book–tax differences that are *initially* favorable (unfavorable) become unfavorable (favorable) in future years when they reverse. The distinction between permanent and temporary book–tax differences is not all that important in calculating the current tax provision, but it is useful to identify them at this stage because only temporary differences and tax carryovers create deferred tax assets and liabilities and the deferred tax provision.

Exhibit 17-5 lists common temporary differences.[11] Refer to the Corporate Operations chapter for more details on the book and tax treatment of these temporary differences.

EXHIBIT 17-5 Common Temporary Differences

Depreciation	Reserves for bad debts (uncollectible accounts)
Accrued vacation pay	Inventory costs capitalized under §263A
Prepayments of income	Warranty reserves
Installment sale income	Stock option expense
Pension plan deductions	Accrued bonuses and other compensation
Accrued contingency losses	Net operating loss and net capital loss carryovers
Business interest expense	

[11]The standard practice to determine temporary differences is to compare book and tax balance sheet basis differences. Companies that do not keep formal tax balance sheets may "roll forward" cumulative book and tax differences from prior years and must periodically prove out the balances to book and tax bases.

Example 17-6

Elise uses the book–tax reconciliation (see Exhibit 17-3) to identify PCC's temporary differences. What are PCC's temporary differences?

Answer: PCC has several temporary difference in the current year, which Elise summarizes as follows:

Temporary Differences	Amount
Net capital loss carryover	$ 28,000
Gain on fixed asset dispositions	16,000
Deferred compensation	(150,000)
Stock option compensation	100,000
Bad debt expense	70,000
Charitable contribution carryover	73,700
Depreciation	(700,000)
Warranty expense	170,000
NOL carryover from 2021	(24,000)
Total temporary differences	**$(416,300)**

Temporary differences that reduce taxable income are shown in parentheses and represent favorable book–tax differences. For the year, PCC has a net (favorable) temporary difference of $(416,300).

Temporary differences arise in one reporting period and reverse in later periods. Which of PCC's temporary differences are reversals of differences that arose in a prior period?

Answer: The gain on fixed asset dispositions, deferred compensation, and NOL carryover from 2021 are reversals. For example, the NOL carryover originated in a prior year but can be used in the current period to reduce taxable income. The use of the NOL deduction will reverse the deferred tax effects from the prior period. So, it is important to identify these reversals for the calculation of the deferred tax assets and liabilities, which we discuss in Step 2 of the income tax provision process.

Calculate the Current Income Tax Expense or (Benefit) (ASC 740 Objective 1)

In many respects, the computation of the current portion of a company's tax provision appears to be straightforward. **Current income tax expense (benefit)** is generally defined as

> [t]he amount of income taxes paid or payable (or refundable) for a year as determined by applying the provisions of the enacted tax law to the taxable income or excess of deductions over revenues for that year.[12]

In most cases, the major component of a company's current income tax expense or benefit is the income tax liability or refund from its current-year operations. Exhibit 17-6 shows a common formula used to calculate this component of the current income tax expense or benefit.

Although Exhibit 17-6 shows the calculation of the main component of the current income tax expense, there are other items that enter into the computation that do not appear on the company's income tax return (Form 1120), which add to the complexity of the computation. In practice, the tax provision is usually completed several months before the tax

EXHIBIT 17-6 Current Tax Expense Formula

	Pretax book income or loss
+/−	Book–tax permanent differences
+/−	Book–tax temporary differences
=	Taxable income
×	Applicable tax rate
=	Current income tax expense

[12]Statement of Financial Accounting Standards No. 109, Accounting for Income Taxes, February 1992. This definition was not codified in ASC 740.

return is filed and must rely on some estimates of the book–tax differences. These estimates often result in differences between the provision calculations of current tax expense and the tax return amounts, and the differences are corrected in the next year with return to provision adjustments that affect the current tax expense in the year the difference is discovered (usually the subsequent tax year). Other items that produce differences include prior-year income tax refunds from current-year carrybacks of a net capital loss,[13] IRS audit adjustments from prior-year tax returns,[14] and changes in the company's **uncertain tax positions**—a company's reserve for taxes it has not paid but could pay in the future for positions taken on the current- and prior-year income tax returns.[15]

Example 17-7

Elise uses her summary of permanent and temporary differences to verify her earlier computation of PCC's taxable income. Does using her summary of PCC's permanent and temporary differences verify her earlier computation?

Answer: Yes!

	PCC pretax net income	$ 6,031,000
+	Net permanent difference (from Example 17-4)	7,000
−	Net temporary differences (from Example 17-6)	(416,300)
=	**PCC taxable income**	**$5,621,700**

What is PCC's current income tax expense?

Answer: $1,180,557, computed as follows:

PCC taxable income	$ 5,621,700
Applicable tax rate	× 21%
PCC current income tax expense (income tax payable)	**$1,180,557**

Because Elise has completed the tax return (in the Corporate Operations chapter) before our discussion of the income tax provision process, we will not see any differences between the tax return and the provision for book–tax differences, which eliminates the need for any return to provision adjustments.

(continued from page 17-7 . . .)

Having calculated the current portion of PCC's income tax provision, Elise turned her attention to computing the deferred component of PCC's income tax provision. Although not required by ASC 740, firms commonly keep a separate tax basis balance sheet to compute the deferred tax accounts. Fortunately for Elise, PCC had created a formal **tax accounting balance sheet**[16] for computing its deferred tax provision (see Exhibit 17-8). Elise would need to compare the changes in the book–tax basis differences from the beginning of the year to the end of the year for each account she identified as being a temporary difference. ■

[13]Requested on Form 1139, Corporation Application for Tentative Refund, or Form 1120X, Amended U.S. Corporation Income Tax Return.

[14]Agreed to on Form 5701, Notice of Proposed Adjustment.

[15]Calculated in the uncertain tax position workpapers.

[16]Schedule L of Form 1120 requests that the taxpayer report its financial statement balance sheet.

Step 2: Determine the Ending Balances in the Balance Sheet Deferred Tax Asset and Liability Accounts (ASC 740 Objective 2)

Think back to Example 17-1 in which PPC's net income and effective tax rate fluctuated simply because of the tax effects of PPC's temporary difference and Example 17-2, where including the future tax effects of the temporary differences smoothed out the fluctuation. In this section, we determine how to measure the deferred tax assets and liabilities, which is the start to calculating the deferred income tax provision.

THE KEY FACTS

Identifying Taxable and Deductible Temporary Differences

- ASC 740 defines a temporary difference as a difference between the financial reporting and tax basis of an asset or liability that will create a future tax liability or benefit when the difference reverses.
- A taxable temporary difference results from an excess of book carrying value over tax basis for assets and from an excess of tax basis over book carrying value for liabilities.
- The future tax cost associated with a taxable temporary difference is recorded on the balance sheet as a deferred tax liability.
- A deductible temporary difference results from an excess of tax basis over book carrying value for assets and from an excess of book carrying value over tax basis for liabilities.
- The future tax benefit associated with a deductible temporary difference is recorded on the balance sheet as a deferred tax asset.

Identifying Taxable and Deductible Temporary Differences Deferred tax assets and liabilities are a result of temporary differences in which the book and tax treatments of certain items occur in different periods. In the Corporate Operations chapter and in calculating the current tax expense in Step 1 of the income tax provision process, these temporary differences were classified as favorable and unfavorable depending on whether they decreased or increased taxable income relative to book income. Because the standard focuses on the balance sheet, ASC 740 uses different terminology for temporary differences.

ASC 740 formally defines a *temporary difference* as:

> [a] difference between the tax basis of an asset or liability . . . and its reported amount in the financial statements that will result in taxable or deductible amounts in future years when the reported amount of the asset or liability is recovered or settled, respectively.[17]

Note that the standard evaluates temporary differences based on their impact in *future* periods rather than their impact on the current period and thus labels the differences as either taxable or deductible temporary differences based on what effect the temporary difference will have when it reverses. These temporary differences result from differences in the book and tax bases of a company's assets and liabilities and reflect the cumulative amount of temporary differences over the life of the company. Taxable temporary differences (associated with deferred tax liabilities) will increase taxable income in the future when they reverse, whereas deductible temporary differences (associated with deferred tax assets) will reduce taxable income in the future when they reverse.

Taxable Temporary Difference From a balance sheet perspective, a **taxable temporary difference**[18] (TTD) generally arises when the financial reporting (book) basis of an asset exceeds its corresponding tax basis or when the financial reporting (book) basis of a liability is less than its corresponding tax basis. Subsequent recovery of the financial statement balance sheet basis of the asset or payment of the balance sheet liability will cause taxable income to exceed book income, by either creating a tax gain or reducing a tax deduction. The future tax cost associated with a taxable temporary difference is recorded on the balance sheet as a deferred tax liability. The bases differences that produce taxable temporary differences generally arise when (1) revenues or gains are taxable *after* they are recognized in net income (e.g., gross profit from an installment sale) (category 1) and (2) expenses or losses are deductible on the tax return *before* they reduce net income (e.g., excess tax depreciation over financial accounting depreciation) (category 2) (See Exhibit 17-7).[19]

[17]Accounting Standards Update No. 2016-16. Income Taxes (Topic 740). October 2016.

[18]ASC 740-10-25-23.

[19]Consistent with the terminology introduced in the Corporate Operations chapter, a "favorable" book–tax adjustment is one that reduces current-year taxable income compared to current-year net income.

EXHIBIT 17-7 Sources of Taxable and Deductible Temporary Differences

Taxable Temporary Differences	Deductible Temporary Differences
1. Revenues or gains that are taxable after they are recognized in financial income	3. Revenues or gains that are taxable before they are recognized in financial income
2. Expenses or losses that are deductible before they are recognized in financial income	4. Expenses or losses that are deductible after they are recognized in financial income

Deductible Temporary Difference From a balance sheet perspective, a **deductible temporary difference**[20] (DTD) occurs when the financial reporting (book) basis of an asset is less than its corresponding tax basis or the financial reporting (book) basis of a liability exceeds its corresponding tax basis. Subsequent recovery of the financial reporting balance sheet basis of the asset or payment of the balance sheet liability will cause taxable income to be less than book income, by either creating a tax loss or increasing a tax deduction. The future tax benefit associated with a deductible temporary difference is recorded on the balance sheet as a deferred tax asset.

Book and tax basis differences that produce deductible generally arise when (1) revenues or gains are taxable *before* they are recognized in net income (e.g., prepayments of subscriptions) (category 3) and (2) expenses or losses are deductible on the tax return *after* they reduce net income (e.g., reserves for product warranty or uncollectible accounts) (category 4). Deductible temporary differences also can arise from items that cannot be associated with a particular asset or liability for financial accounting purposes but produce revenue (income) or expense (deduction) that has been recognized in the financial statement and will result in taxable or deductible amounts in future years. For example, a net operating loss carryover and a net capital loss carryover create temporary differences in the year they arise without being associated with a specific asset or liability. Temporary differences that do not have balance sheet accounts, such as net operating loss carryovers, net capital loss carryovers, and charitable contribution carryovers, must be tracked to ensure that the appropriate adjustment is made to a company's deferred tax asset accounts when the carryover is used on a future tax return.

In order to determine the taxable and deductible temporary differences, companies must create a tax basis balance sheet. For many of the assets and liabilities listed on the book balance sheet, the tax and book bases will be the same. However, when accounting methods differ between book and tax that result in temporary differences, the tax basis will be different from the book basis. For example, the net carrying value of fixed assets will differ between book and tax due to differences in the way depreciation is calculated: usually straight-line for book and MACRS for tax. Similarly, the book and tax bases of accounts receivable differ because the accounting methods for determining bad debts differs: the allowance method for book and the direct charge off method for tax. Determining the tax basis for liabilities is slightly less straightforward. The regulations provide some guidelines to help determine the tax basis of an obligation.[21] An obligation is a tax liability if and to the extent the obligation:

1. creates or increases basis or results in cash (e.g., bank loan);
2. provides an immediate tax deduction (e.g., accounts payable);[22] or
3. is a nondeductible expense for computing taxable income (e.g., accrued fines expense).

If an obligation meets one of these criteria, it will have a tax basis. Exhibit 17-8 shows PCC's tax basis balance sheet comparing the prior year with current year amounts.

[20]ASC 740-10-25-23.

[21]Reg. §1.752-1(a)(4)

[22]To be immediately deductible, an expense must meet the all events test (fixed and determinable) and the requirements of economic performance. See the Business Income, Deductions, and Accounting Methods chapter for more details.

EXHIBIT 17-8 **PCC's Tax Basis Balance Sheet for 12/31/2021 and 12/31/2022**

	12/31/2022	12/31/2021
Assets		
Cash	$ 6,933,480	$10,776,380
Municipal bonds	300,000	300,000
Accounts receivable	20,750,000	17,250,000
Less: Allowance for bad debts	–	–
Accounts receivable (net)	20,750,000	17,250,000
Inventory	5,175,000	4,312,500
Fixed assets	70,000,000	60,000,000
Less: Accumulated depreciation	(27,500,000)	(24,470,000)
Fixed assets (net)	42,500,000	35,530,000
Investments	1,647,960	1,597,960
Goodwill	180,000	180,000
Total assets	$77,486,440	$69,946,840
Liabilities		
Accounts payable	$24,015,600	$20,013,000
Reserve for warranties	–	–
Long term debt	40,000,000	40,000,000
Deferred compensation	–	–
Deferred tax liabilities*	N/A	N/A
Total liabilities	$64,015,600	$60,013,000
Shareholders' Equity		
Common stock	$ 500,000	$ 500,000
Additional paid-in capital	5,000,000	5,000,000
Retained earnings*	N/A	N/A
Total liabilities and shareholders' equity	$69,515,600	$65,513,000

*Tax basis balance sheets do not include these accounts

Example 17-8

PCC has provided its book (Exhibit 17-1) and tax (Exhibit 17-8) basis balance sheets. Elise identifies differences in the balances in several accounts. She isolates the accounts with differences as an initial step in determining the taxable and deductible temporary differences and the deferred tax liabilities (DTLs) and deferred tax assets (DTAs). Elise summarizes the differences and produces the following table:

PCC Balance Sheet (select items)	**Book Basis DR/(CR)**		**Tax Basis**	
	12/31/2022	**12/31/2021**	**12/31/2022**	**12/31/2021**
Accounts receivable (net)	$20,335,000	$16,905,000	$20,750,000	$17,250,000
Fixed assets (net)	55,600,000	47,946,000	42,500,000	35,530,000
Reserve for warranties	(600,000)	(430,000)	–	–
Deferred compensation	(1,050,000)	(1,200,000)	–	–
Additional paid-in capital (stock option expense)	(5,100,000)	(5,000,000)	(5,000,000)	(5,000,000)

Why is the tax basis for the reserve for warranties and deferred compensation zero?

Answer: Neither of these book liabilities meets the definition for a tax liability. The warranty reserve and the deferred compensation do not provide an immediate tax deduction because the related expenses do not meet the all events test (not fixed) and therefore do not create tax basis. These items also do not meet the other two criteria because they do not create cash and they will eventually be deductible.

By comparing the book and tax bases of the assets and liabilities, we can determine the taxable and deductible temporary differences. TTDs occur for assets (liabilities) when the book basis is greater (less) than the tax basis. Conversely, DTDs arise for assets (liabilities) when the book basis is less (greater) than the tax basis. For example, using the end of year book and tax bases in the accounts receivable from Example 17-8, the end of year difference is $415,000 ($20,750,000 tax basis less $20,335,000 book basis). Because this difference relates to an asset and the book basis is less than the tax basis, the difference results in a deductible temporary difference.

Example 17-9

What are PCC's taxable and deductible temporary differences at the beginning and end of the year? What is the change in the cumulative temporary differences?

Answer:

	Cumulative Temporary Differences DTD/(TTD)		Change in Cumulative Temporary Differences
	End of Year (Tax – Book)	Beginning of Year (Tax – Book)	(Ending – Beginning)
(1) Accounts receivable (net)	$ 415,000	$ 345,000	$ 70,000
(2) Fixed assets (net)	(13,100,000)	(12,416,000)	(684,000)
(3) Reserve for warranties	600,000	430,000	170,000
(4) Deferred compensation	1,050,000	1,200,000	(150,000)
(5) Additional paid-in capital (stock option expense)	100,000	–	100,000

Elise has set up her workpaper so that positive amounts are deductible temporary differences (DTDs) and negative amounts are taxable temporary differences (TTDs). Because DTDs generate DTAs and TTDs generate DTLs, this formatting convention will help her as she determines how these amounts need to be recorded on the balance sheet.

Some temporary differences are not directly related to an asset or liability on the balance sheet. For example, tax attributes such as NOL carryovers, capital loss carryovers, credit carryovers, and other carryovers are not tied to any specific asset or liability and as a result will not appear on either a book or tax balance sheet. These items produce deductible temporary differences and must be tracked separately in the tax workpapers.

Example 17-10

Elise reviewed her schedules of favorable and unfavorable temporary differences (from Example 17-6) and notices that for the most part, the change in temporary differences for these items matches the temporary differences she identified when calculating the current tax provision. However, Elise notices that the change in the temporary difference for fixed assets is $684,000 and does not match the depreciation book–tax difference she used for the tax provision. Why doesn't the depreciation difference match the cumulative temporary difference change for fixed assets?

Answer: The depreciation temporary difference that Elise used for the current provision of $700,000 only represents part of the cumulative temporary difference related to fixed assets. A missing item is the temporary difference related to the gain on the sale of fixed assets of $16,000. This difference represents the reversal of the difference in depreciation that was taken on the asset while PCC used it. So, this difference is included in the overall fixed asset difference from the book and tax basis balance sheets. Elise reconciles the difference by combining the $(700,000) favorable depreciation difference with the $16,000 unfavorable difference from the sale to obtain a total $684,000 favorable temporary difference for fixed assets, which matches the taxable temporary difference she calculated using the balance sheet approach.

(continued on page 17-16)

Elise also notices that some items are missing from the temporary items she identified in the book–tax reconciliation. Which temporary differences are missing?

Answer: The missing items include the NOL, net capital loss, and charitable contribution carryovers. These items are tax items for which there is no book basis and must be tracked separately in the tax workpapers. Elise adds them to her cumulative temporary differences.

	Cumulative Temporary Differences DTD/(TTD)		Change in Temporary Differences
	Ending (Tax – Book)	**Beginning (Tax – Book)**	**(Ending – Beginning)**
(1) NOL carryover	–	$24,000	$(24,000)
(2) Net capital loss carryover	$28,000	–	28,000
(3) Charitable contribution carryover	73,700	–	73,700

Once the TTDs and DTDs are identified, they are used to determine the deferred tax assets and liabilities reported on the book balance sheet. The future tax obligation of a taxable temporary difference is recorded on the balance sheet as a deferred tax liability. Conversely the future tax benefit of a deductible temporary difference is recorded as a deferred tax asset. The company computes its deferred tax assets and liabilities using the **enacted tax rate** that is expected to apply to taxable income in the period(s) in which the deferred tax assets and liabilities are expected to be settled.[23] For example, in Example 17-9, we determined that the end of year DTD related to the accounts receivable balance is $415,000. To calculate the deferred tax asset related to this DTD, we multiply the DTD by the enacted tax rate of 21 percent resulting in a DTA of $87,150 ($415,000 × 21%) at the end of the year.

Example 17-11

Elise's next step is to determine the deferred tax assets and liabilities to be included on the financial balance sheet. Using the temporary differences from Example 17-9 and the enacted tax rate of 21 percent, she determines the beginning and ending DTAs and DTLs.

	DTA/(DTL) @ 21%		
PCC Balance Sheet (select items)	**Ending**	**Beginning**	**Explanation**
Accounts receivable (net) (allowance for bad debts)	$ 87,150	$ 72,450	Example 17-9, line (1) × 21%
Fixed assets (net) (depreciation)	(2,751,000)	(2,607,360)	Example 17-9, line (2) × 21%
Reserve for warranties	126,000	90,300	Example 17-9, line (3) × 21%
Deferred compensation	220,500	252,000	Example 17-9, line (4) × 21%
Additional paid-in capital (stock option expense)	21,000	–	Example 17-9, line (5) × 21%
Other temporary differences			
NOL carryover	–	5,040	Example 17-10, line (1) × 21%
Net capital loss carryover	5,880	–	Example 17-10, line (2) × 21%
Charitable contribution carryover	15,477	–	Example 17-10, line (3) × 21%
Totals	$(2,274,993)	$(2,187,570)	

[23]ASC 740-10-30-2.

Which of the amounts in the table above represent DTAs and which represent DTLs?

Answer: Elise has set up her workpaper such that DTAs are positive amounts and DTLs are negative (i.e., in parentheses). This convention is typical in financial accounting formatting for debits and credits. PCC's DTAs include the accounts receivable (net), reserve for warranties, deferred compensation, additional paid-in capital (representing the stock option expense temporary difference), NOL carryover, net capital loss carryover, and charitable contribution carryover. Fixed assets (depreciation) is the only DTL for PCC.

Summary of PCC's DTAs and DTLs

	Ending	Beginning
DTA	$ 476,007	$ 419,790
DTL	(2,751,000)	(2,607,360)
Totals	(2,274,993)	(2,187,570)

Using a template that tracks the cumulative changes in the book–tax differences related to book and tax balance sheet accounts becomes especially important when a company's enacted tax rate changes. For example, the Tax Cuts and Jobs Act reduced the corporate tax rate to 21 percent for tax years beginning after December 31, 2017. The bill was signed by the president on December 22, 2017. As a result, corporations were required to revalue their U.S. deferred tax assets and liabilities existing on December 22, 2017, to reflect the lower tax rate. This discussion points to the fact that the focus of ASC 740 is to have the balance sheet deferred tax accounts reflect the tax benefit or obligation when the underlying temporary differences reverse in a future period.

THE KEY FACTS

Computing the Deferred Income Tax Expense (Benefit)

- Identify current-year changes in taxable and deductible temporary differences.
- Determine ending balances in each deferred tax asset and liability balance sheet account.
- Identify carryovers (net operating loss, net capital loss, charitable contributions) not on the balance sheet.
- The current-year deferred income tax expense or benefit is the difference between the deferred tax asset and liability balances at the beginning of the year and the end of the year, as well as changes in tax carryovers.

Step 3: Calculate the Deferred Income Tax Provision and the Total Income Tax Provision

Deferred Income Tax Provision The deferred income tax expense or benefit portion of a company's tax provision reflects the change during the year in a company's balance sheet deferred tax liabilities or assets.[24] This information provides investors and other interested parties with a measure of a company's expected future income-tax-related cash inflows or outflows resulting from book-tax differences that are temporary in nature or from tax carryovers. Once the beginning and ending DTAs and DTLs have been determined, calculating the deferred income tax expense or benefit is relatively straightforward. The deferred tax expense or benefit is calculated as the change in the *net* deferred tax asset or liability for the period (EOY net DTL or DTA minus BOY net DTL or DTA). An increase (decrease) in a net DTA produces a deferred tax benefit (expense). Conversely, an increase (decrease) in a net DTL produces a deferred income tax expense (benefit).

Example 17-12

Elise now has the pieces to determine PCC's deferred income tax expense or benefit for 2022. Using the solution from Example 17-11, what is PCC's deferred income tax provision for 2022?

Answer: $87,423 deferred tax expense, computed as follows:

Summary

	Ending	Beginning	Change
DTA	$ 476,007	$ 419,790	$ 56,217
DTL	(2,751,000)	(2,607,360)	(143,640)
Net DTL	$(2,274,993)	$(2,187,570)	**$ (87,423)**

PCC's net deferred tax liability increased during the year, indicating a larger net future tax obligation; thus, the $87,423 increase represents PCC's deferred income tax expense for the year.

[24]ASC 740-10-20 Glossary.

Total Income Tax Provision Recall that ASC 740 has two objectives. The first is to "recognize the amount of tax payable or refundable in the current year,"[25] and the second is to "recognize deferred tax liabilities and assets for the future tax consequences of events that have been recognized in an entity's financial statements or tax returns."[26] The first relates to the current income tax provision and the second to the deferred income tax provision. Although the current income tax expense or benefit and the deferred income tax expense or benefit may be affected by other complexities not yet discussed, once these amounts are determined, the total tax expense is the sum of the two.

Example 17-13

What is PCC's total income tax provision for 2022?

Answer: $1,267,980 total income tax expense, computed as:

Current income tax expense	$ 1,180,557	Example 17-7
Deferred income tax expense	87,423	Example 17-12
Total income tax expense	**$1,267,980**	

There is a straightforward back-of-the-envelope method of verifying the ASC 740 approach to calculating PCC's total tax provision. Under the assumption that all temporary differences will appear on a tax return in a current or future period, the total tax provision should reflect the tax that ultimately will be paid on pretax net income adjusted for permanent differences. Remember from Example 17-5 that this amount is sometimes referred to as a company's *book equivalent of taxable income*. The total income tax provision should equal the company's tax rate times its book equivalent of taxable income. We emphasize that this approach to computing a company's income tax provision is not in accordance with GAAP and will not provide the correct answer when there are changes in a company's income tax rate or other items that affect the current tax expense (e.g., UTPs, carrybacks, return to provision adjustments, and audit adjustments).

Example 17-14

Elise retrieved her computation of PCC's book equivalent of taxable income (from Example 17-5), as follows:

PCC pretax net income	$6,031,000
Net unfavorable permanent difference	7,000
PCC book equivalent of taxable income	$6,038,000

What is PCC's total tax provision using book equivalent of taxable income as a base?

Answer: $1,267,980, computed as follows:

PCC's book equivalent of taxable income	$ 6,038,000
	× 21%
PCC's total tax provision	**$1,267,980**

This computation confirms the computation made under ASC 740 from Example 17-13.

[25]ASC 740-10-10-1(a)

[26]Accounting Standards Update No. 2018-05, Income Taxes (Topic 740), March 2018.

Journal Entries Once the calculations have been completed to determine the current and deferred income tax expense, the journal entries must be made to record the income tax effects on the financial statements. To record a current income tax expense, the journal entry follows this format:

Current income tax expense	XXX	
Income taxes payable		XXX

If the company instead has a current income tax benefit, the journal entry format would be:

Income taxes receivable	XXX	
Current income taxes expense		XXX

For the deferred provision, the journal entry records the changes in the deferred tax assets and liabilities as well as the deferred tax expense or benefit. The general format of the journal entry for a company where the change in the deferred tax liabilities is greater than the change in the deferred tax assets is:

Deferred income tax expense	XXX	
Deferred tax asset	XXX	
Deferred tax liability		XXX

The journal entry will change depending on whether the deferred tax assets and liabilities increase or decrease and their relative amounts. The deferred tax expense or benefit is the balancing amount of the entry. For example, if the change in the deferred tax assets is greater than the change in the deferred tax liabilities, the journal entry would appear in the following format:

Deferred tax asset	XXX	
Deferred income tax benefit		XXX
Deferred tax liability		XXX

Example 17-15

What tax accounting journal entry does Elise make to record PCC's current income taxes?

Answer:

Current income tax expense	$1,180,557		Example 17-7
Income taxes payable		$1,180,557	

What tax accounting journal entry does Elise make to record PCC's deferred income taxes?

Answer:

Deferred income tax expense	$87,423		Example 17-12
Deferred income tax asset	$56,217		
Deferred income tax liability		$143,640	

LO 17-3

DETERMINING WHETHER A VALUATION ALLOWANCE IS NEEDED

Step 4: Evaluate the Need for a Valuation Allowance for Gross Deferred Tax Assets

ASC 740 specifically precludes PCC, or any company, from discounting (i.e., recording the present value of) the deferred income tax liability or asset related to a temporary difference based on when the asset is expected to be recovered or the liability settled. The FASB debated whether discounting deferred income tax assets and liabilities would provide more relevant information to investors, but ultimately it decided that the complexity and cost of making the computation outweighed any benefits investors and creditors might receive.[27]

Rather than discounting, ASC 740 requires that a company evaluate each of its gross deferred income tax assets on the balance sheet and assess the likelihood the expected tax benefit will be *realized* in a future period. The income tax benefits reflected in the deferred tax assets can be realized (i.e., converted into cash) only if the company expects to have sufficient taxable income or tax liability in the future or carryback period to absorb the unused tax deductions or credits before they expire.

> **THE KEY FACTS**
>
> **Determining Whether a Valuation Allowance Is Needed**
>
> - A valuation allowance is required if it is more likely than not that some or all of the deferred tax asset will not be realized in the future.
> - To make this determination, a company must determine its sources of future (or past) taxable income.
>   - Taxable income in carryback years.
>   - Reversing taxable temporary differences in future years.
>   - Expected taxable income in future years from other than reversing taxable temporary differences.
>   - Expected taxable income in future taxable years from implementing tax planning strategies.
> - A company must evaluate positive and negative evidence in deciding whether a valuation allowance is needed.
> - A company must monitor whether increases or decreases should be made to the valuation allowance account every quarter.

Determining the Need for a Valuation Allowance

Under ASC 740, if a company determines that it is more likely than not (i.e., a likelihood greater than 50 percent) that some portion or all of the deferred tax assets will not be realized in a future period, it must offset the deferred tax assets with a **valuation allowance** to reflect the amount the company does not expect to realize in the future.[28] Valuation allowances operate as *contra accounts* to the deferred income tax assets on the balance sheet, much like the allowance for bad debts a company must estimate for its accounts receivable. Companies usually disclose the amount of the valuation allowance in the income tax footnote to the financial statements.

Management must assess whether it is more likely than not that a deferred income tax asset will *not* be realized in the future based on all available evidence, both positive and negative. ASC 740 identifies four sources of potential future taxable income, two of which are objective and two of which are subjective and determined by management judgment.[29] The objective sources are (1) future reversals of existing taxable temporary differences and (2) taxable income in prior carryback year(s). The subjective sources are (1) expected future taxable income exclusive of reversing temporary differences and carryovers and (2) tax planning strategies.

Future Reversals of Existing Taxable Temporary Differences Existing taxable temporary differences provide taxable income when they are recovered in a future period. For example, the recovery of the excess of an asset's financial accounting (book) basis over its tax basis, whether through sale or depreciation, will cause taxable income to be higher than pretax net income in the periods in which the excess financial accounting basis is recovered. If the reversing taxable temporary differences provide sufficient future taxable income to absorb the reversing deductible temporary differences, the company does not record a valuation allowance against the deferred tax asset. In the case of NOL carryovers from years beginning after December 31, 2017, only 80 percent of the reversing taxable temporary differences can be used as a source of future taxable income because these NOL carryovers can only offset up to 80 percent of taxable income. Refer to the Corporate Operations chapter for more details related to NOL carryover usage.

[27]FAS 109, ¶¶198–199. (These paragraphs were not codified in ASC 740.)

[28]ASC 740-10-30-5(e).

[29]ASC 740-10-30-18.

Taxable Income in Prior Carryback Year(s) The company does not record a valuation allowance if the tax benefit from the realization of a deferred income tax asset can be carried back to a prior year that has sufficient taxable income (or capital gain net income in the case of a net capital loss carryback) or tax liability (in the case of a credit) to absorb the realized tax benefit.

Expected Future Taxable Income Exclusive of Reversing Temporary Differences and Carryovers ASC 740 allows a company to consider taxable income it expects to earn in future periods in determining whether a valuation allowance is necessary. The company might support its predictions of future taxable income with evidence of existing contracts or a sales backlog that will produce enough taxable income to realize the deferred tax asset when it reverses. In addition, the company could demonstrate that it has a strong earnings history if a deferred tax asset arises from a loss that could be considered out of the ordinary and not from a continuing condition. Firms in cyclical industries, such as automobile manufacturers, builders, and airlines, traditionally have cited a history of past income as evidence of expected future income.

Tax Planning Strategies The most subjective source of future taxable income to support the realization of a deferred income tax asset is the company's ability and willingness to employ tax strategies in those future periods to create the taxable income needed to absorb the deferred tax asset. ASC 740 allows a company to consider actions it might take to create sufficient taxable income to absorb a deferred income tax asset, provided such actions (1) are prudent and feasible, (2) are actions an enterprise would take only to prevent an operating loss or tax credit carryovers from expiring unused, and (3) would result in realization of the deferred tax assets.

The company does not have to implement the strategy to avoid recording a valuation allowance, but management must be willing and able to execute the strategy if the need arises. Tax planning strategies could include (1) selling and leasing back operating assets, (2) changing inventory accounting methods (e.g., from LIFO to FIFO), (3) refraining from making voluntary contributions to the company pension plan, (4) electing to capitalize certain expenditures (e.g., research and development costs) rather than deduct them currently, (5) selling noncore assets, (6) converting tax-exempt investments into taxable investments, and (7) electing the alternative depreciation system (i.e., straight line instead of declining balance).

Negative Evidence That a Valuation Allowance Is Needed ASC 740 requires that a company consider negative evidence as well as positive evidence in determining whether it is more likely than not that a deferred income tax asset will not be realized in the future. Negative evidence includes (1) cumulative (book) losses in recent years; (2) a history of net operating losses, net capital losses, and credits expiring unused; (3) an expectation of losses in the near future; and (4) unsettled circumstances that, if resolved unfavorably, will result in losses from continuing operations in future years (e.g., the loss of a patent on a highly profitable drug).[30] As a general rule, public accounting firms interpret "recent years" with regard to cumulative book losses as a rolling 12 quarters (i.e., 36 months). As with all general rules, there are exceptions depending on the industry.

Valuation Allowance Journal Entries If the company determines that it is more likely than not that its deferred tax assets will not be fully realized, it will need to record the valuation allowance as a contra-asset account to its deferred tax assets as follows:

Deferred tax expense	*XXX*	
Valuation allowance		*XXX*

[30]ASC 740-10-30-21.

When setting up the valuation allowance, the offsetting part of the journal entry is to the deferred income tax expense. It will not affect the current tax provision. Note that this journal entry is similar to the journal entry required to set up an allowance for doubtful accounts (debit: bad debt expense, credit: allowance for doubtful accounts).

Each reporting period, the valuation allowance must be evaluated to determine if it is still needed. If management determines that a deferred tax asset will never be realized (e.g., DTA from a NOL that expires), the DTA will need to be written off. The format for the journal entry would be as follows:

Valuation allowance	*XXX*	
Deferred tax asset		*XXX*

Note that this entry affects only the balance sheet because the income tax expense effect occurred when the valuation allowance was initially set up. There may also be situations when management evaluates new facts and circumstances and determines that the realizability of the deferred tax asset has increased such that the valuation allowance is no longer needed. The valuation allowance would need to be reduced or eliminated using a journal entry of the following form:

Valuation allowance	*XXX*	
Deferred tax benefit		*XXX*

In these situations, the reduction or elimination of the valuation allowance decreases the deferred tax expense and provides a benefit, increasing book income. Because the valuation allowance requires substantial judgment, auditors pay close attention to changes in the account.

TAXES IN THE REAL WORLD Berkshire Hathaway's $29 Billion Gift from Congress

When Berkshire Hathaway released its highly anticipated Form 10-K for 2017, the company announced that its gain in net worth for the year was $65.3 billion, but as CEO Warren Buffett noted, "A large portion of our gain did not come from anything we accomplished at Berkshire. The $65 billion gain is nonetheless real—rest assured of that. But only $36 billion came from Berkshire's operations. The remaining $29 billion was delivered to us in December when Congress rewrote the U.S. Tax Code."[31] What was the source of this $29 billion? Deferred tax accounting! At September 30, 2017, Berkshire Hathaway had a net deferred tax liability on its balance sheet of $85 billion, most of which was tax-effected at 35 percent (the statutory tax rate). When Congress reduced the corporate tax rate to 21 percent, Berkshire Hathaway was required to revalue this liability at 21 percent to the extent the associated taxable temporary differences were associated with U.S. book–tax differences. Using a back-of-the-envelope calculation, the $85 billion deferred tax liability translates to approximately $240 billion of book–tax differences ($85/.35). Valued at 21 percent, this net book–tax difference would translate to a deferred tax liability of $51 billion. Berkshire Hathaway would reduce its net deferred tax liability from $85 billion to $51 billion. The $34 billion reduction in the balance sheet basis would be accompanied by a decrease in deferred tax expense of $34 billion, thus increasing net income after tax and, ultimately, retained earnings (net worth) by $34 billion. The company stated in its Form 10-K that the benefit from revaluing its deferred tax accounts was approximately $30 billion.

[31]Warren Buffett, "Warren Buffett's Letter to the Shareholders of Berkshire Hathaway, Inc.," February 24, 2018. www.berkshirehathaway.com/letters/2017ltr.pdf.

Example 17-16

Elise created a workpaper that listed PCC's ending balances in its deferred tax assets and liabilities at December 31, 2022 (from Example 17-11), as follows:

PCC Deferred Tax Accounts at 12/31/2022

Deferred tax assets	
Allowance for bad debts	$ 87,150
Reserve for warranties	126,000
Net operating loss carryover	0
Deferred compensation	220,500
Stock option compensation	21,000
Net capital loss carryover	5,880
Charitable contribution carryover	15,477
Total deferred tax assets	**$ 476,007**
Deferred tax liabilities	
Depreciation	(2,751,000)
Total deferred tax liabilities	$ (2,751,000)
Net deferred tax liabilities	**$(2,274,993)**

What *positive* evidence should Elise consider in her evaluation as to whether PCC should record a valuation allowance against some or all of the deferred tax assets?

Answer: PCC has an excess of deferred tax liabilities over deferred tax assets of $2,274,993. When the book–tax depreciation difference reverses in the future, this will provide PCC with enough taxable income to absorb the reversing deferred tax assets.

What *negative* evidence should Elise consider in her evaluation as to whether PCC should record a valuation allowance against some or all of the deferred tax assets?

Answer: The deferred tax asset related to the charitable contribution carryover has a short carryover expiration date (five years). Elise may need to schedule out when the depreciation differences will reverse to determine if the reversals alone will provide PCC with enough taxable income to absorb the contribution carryover within the next five years.

More problematic, the net capital loss carryover has both a short carryover expiration date (five years) and requires PCC to recognize net capital gains in future periods to absorb the net capital loss. A reversal of the book–tax depreciation temporary difference will not provide PCC with net capital gain to absorb the net capital loss carryover.

What other sources of *positive* evidence should Elise consider in her evaluation as to whether PCC should record a valuation allowance against the deferred tax asset related to the net capital loss carryover?

Answer: Two additional sources of positive evidence are management's projections of future taxable income from sources other than reversing taxable temporary differences and future taxable income from tax planning strategies. Because PCC is in the business of manufacturing and selling computer-related equipment, any additional taxable income it generates from selling additional equipment will produce ordinary income. The company likely will have to rely on an assertion that management has a "prudent" *tax planning strategy* it would be willing to use to generate net capital gain in the future. An example of such a strategy might be management's willingness to sell a parcel of land held for investment to generate a capital gain sufficient to absorb the net capital loss.

After discussing with management its assessment of the company's sources of future taxable income, Elise concurred with management that the company did not need to record a valuation allowance for 2022.

What if: Assume PCC determined that a valuation allowance is required for the capital loss carryover. What journal entry would be required to reflect the valuation allowance?

Answer: The journal entry PCC would need to make to set up the valuation allowance would be as follows:

Deferred tax expense	$5,880	
Valuation allowance		$5,880

The impact of this journal entry would be to increase PCC's deferred tax expense for the year.

Example 17-17

What if: Assume PCC has had pretax book losses of $5,000,000 and $2,500,000 in 2020 and 2021, respectively. How might this additional fact influence Elise's assessment about the need for a valuation allowance?

Answer: PCC would have a cumulative pretax book loss of $1,469,000 over the past 36 months at December 31, 2022 (combined book losses of $7,500,000 in excess of 2022 pretax book income of $6,031,000 from Exhibit 17-3). ASC 740 states that a cumulative loss "in recent years" is considered objective negative evidence that may be hard to overcome. Elise would have to consider other sources of positive evidence that will outweigh the "significant" negative evidence in this situation. Often, the national office of the public accounting firm will make the determination as to whether a valuation allowance is required when a client experiences a 36-month cumulative loss.

Example 17-18

What if: Assume PCC just lost a big account to its competitor, but the company reported cumulative net income in the current and prior two years. How might this additional fact influence Elise's assessment about the need for a valuation allowance?

Answer: Expectations of future events can outweigh historic results. In this case, Elise would have to seriously consider whether a valuation allowance would be required to the extent that reversing taxable temporary differences would not absorb expected future losses.

LO 17-4

THE KEY FACTS

Accounting for Uncertain Tax Positions

- ASC 740 requires a two-step process for determining whether a tax benefit can be recognized in the financial statements.
  - A company first determines whether it is more likely than not that its tax position on a particular account will be sustained on IRS examination based on its technical merits.
  - A company then computes the amount it expects to be able to recognize.
- The measurement process requires the company to make a cumulative probability assessment of all likely outcomes of the audit and litigation process.
  - The company recognizes the amount that has a greater than 50 percent probability of being sustained on examination and subsequent litigation.
  - The amount not recognized is recorded as a liability on the balance sheet.

ACCOUNTING FOR UNCERTAINTY IN INCOME TAX POSITIONS

Step 5: Evaluate the Need for an Uncertain Tax Benefit Reserve

As you have learned in your study of the U.S. income tax laws, the answer to every tax question is not always certain. Taxpayers and the IRS can differ in their opinions as to whether an expenditure is deductible or must be capitalized, or whether income is taxable or is deferred or exempt from taxation. When irresolvable disputes arise, the taxpayer can petition the courts to resolve the tax treatment of a transaction. Taxpayers and the IRS can appeal decisions of the lower courts to the appellate courts and ultimately to the U.S. Supreme Court.

Taxpayers also take tax positions that can be disputed by state and local taxing authorities and international tax authorities. For example, the taxpayer and a state (international) tax authority may differ on whether the taxpayer has earned income in that jurisdiction and should pay tax on such income. The courts may not resolve this issue for many years after the original transaction takes place. If the courts do not resolve the issue in the taxpayer's favor, the taxpayer will be subject to interest and possible penalties on the tax owed.

For financial accounting purposes, a company must determine whether it can record the current or future tax benefits from an uncertain tax position in its financial statement for the period in which the transaction takes place, knowing that the ultimate resolution of the tax position may not be known until some time in the future.

Statement of Financial Accounting Standards No. 109 as originally written provided no specific guidance on how to deal with uncertain tax positions. As a result, companies generally applied the principles of FAS 5, *Accounting for Contingencies* (codified as ASC Topic 450), to uncertain tax positions. The FASB became concerned that companies were not applying FAS 5 uniformly, leading to diversity in practice and financial statements that were not comparable. After much debate, the FASB issued FASB Interpretation (FIN) No. 48, *Accounting for Uncertainty in Income Taxes—An Interpretation of FASB Statement No. 109,* in July 2006, effective for years beginning after December 15, 2006.

FIN 48 has been codified in ASC 740-10 but continues to be commonly referred to as FIN 48. We use both references (ASC 740-10 (FIN 48)) throughout the chapter to minimize confusion when referring to the topic. The objective of ASC 740-10 (FIN 48) is to provide a uniform approach to recording and disclosing tax benefits resulting from tax positions that are considered to be uncertain.

ASC 740-10 (FIN 48) applies a two-step process to evaluating tax positions. ASC 740-10 refers to the first step as *recognition*.[32] The second step is referred to as *measurement*.[33] Under ASC 740-10, the company records the largest amount of the benefit, as calculated on a cumulative probability basis, which is more likely than not to be realized on the ultimate settlement of the tax position.

Application of ASC Topic 740 to Uncertain Tax Positions

ASC 740 applies to all *tax positions* dealing with income taxes. As a result, it pertains to a tax position taken on a current or previously filed tax return and a tax position that will be taken on a future tax return that is reflected in the financial statements as a deferred tax asset or liability. ASC 740-10 (FIN 48) also applies to tax positions that result in permanent differences (e.g., the dividends-received deduction and credits) and to decisions not to file a tax return in a particular jurisdiction. For example, assume a company deducts an expenditure on its current tax return, which the IRS may challenge on audit in a future period. The deduction produces a net operating loss that will be carried forward and offset against future taxable income. ASC 740-10 (FIN 48) addresses whether the company can *recognize* the deferred tax asset related to the NOL carryover on its balance sheet. Once the recognition hurdle has been overcome, the company must then evaluate whether it is more likely than not that the deferred tax asset will be *realized* in the future period (i.e., whether a valuation allowance should be recorded).

Step 1: Recognition A company first must determine whether it is more likely than not that its tax position on a particular account will be sustained on IRS examination based on its technical merits. If the company believes this threshold has been met, it can record (recognize) the tax benefit of the tax position on its financial statements as a reduction in its current tax expense or an increase in its deferred tax benefit. The company must presume the IRS will examine this tax position with full knowledge of all relevant information. However, in deciding whether the more-likely-than-not threshold has been met, the company can take into account how the tax position might be resolved if litigated. This requires the company to evaluate the sources of authority that address this issue (i.e., the tax law, regulations, legislative history, IRS rulings, and court opinions).

Step 2: Measurement After the company determines that the more-likely-than-not recognition threshold has been met, it must compute the amount of the tax benefit to recognize in its financial statements. ASC 740-10 (FIN 48) states that the tax position is to be measured as:

> the largest amount of tax benefit that is greater than 50 percent likely of being realized upon ultimate settlement with a taxing authority that has full knowledge of all relevant information.[34]

This measurement process requires the company to make a cumulative probability assessment of all likely outcomes of the audit and litigation process. The company then recognizes the amount that has a greater than 50 percent probability of being sustained on examination and subsequent litigation.

[32]ASC 740-10-25-5 through 25-7.
[33]ASC 740-10-30-7.
[34]ASC 740-10-30-7.

Example 17-19

Assume PCC had taken a research credit of $500,000 on its 2022 tax return. There was some discussion about whether all of the company's activities qualified for the credit.

What threshold must be met before PCC can *recognize* any of the tax benefit from the "uncertain" portion of the research credit on its financial statements?

Answer: PCC must determine that it is more likely than not that its tax position on the research credit will be sustained by the IRS on examination based on its technical merits.

Example 17-20

PCC determined that it was more likely than not that the tax position in Example 17-19 would be sustained on audit and litigation. The tax department calculated the probability of receiving a full or partial benefit after resolution of the issue as follows:

Potential Estimated Tax Benefit	Individual Probability of Being Realized (%)	Cumulative Probability of Being Realized (%)
$500,000	60	60
300,000	25	85
200,000	10	95
0	5	100

Based on these probabilities, how much of the uncertain tax benefit of $500,000 can PCC recognize?

Answer: $500,000. PCC can recognize all $500,000 of the research credit tax benefit because this amount is the largest amount that has a greater than 50 percent cumulative probability of being realized on the ultimate settlement of the tax position.

Uncertain Tax Benefit Reserve Journal Entries The amount of the tax benefit that is not recognized ("unrecognized tax benefit") is recorded as a liability on the balance sheet (usually labeled as "Income Taxes Payable"). The corresponding "debit" to record the balance sheet liability is to *current* income tax expense (or a decrease in income tax benefit).

Current income tax expense	*XXX*	
Income taxes payable		*XXX*

If the company expects the uncertain tax position to be resolved in the next 12 months, the balance sheet payable is characterized as current. Otherwise, the payable is characterized as being noncurrent. The increase in tax expense is added to the current portion of the provision under the theory that this is an on-demand liability.

Example 17-21

What if: Assume PCC's tax department had assessed the cumulative probabilities of sustaining the $500,000 research credit tax benefit as follows:

Potential Estimated Tax Benefit	Individual Probability of Being Realized (%)	Cumulative Probability of Being Realized (%)
$500,000	40	40
300,000	30	70
200,000	20	90
0	10	100

Based on these probabilities, how much of the uncertain tax benefit of $500,000 can PCC recognize?

Answer: $300,000. PCC can recognize $300,000 of the research credit tax benefit because this amount is the largest amount that has a greater than 50 percent cumulative probability of being realized on the ultimate settlement of the tax position. This translates into management believing that $300,000 of the uncertain research credit will be sustained on audit.

What would be PCC's journal entry to record the portion of the tax benefit that cannot be recognized?

Answer: PCC would establish a liability for the $200,000 difference between the amount of the benefit received on the current-year tax return ($500,000) and the amount the company ultimately expects to receive ($300,000). PCC would record the following journal entry:

Current income tax expense	$200,000	
Income taxes payable		$200,000

The Income Taxes Payable account is characterized as noncurrent on the balance sheet if PCC does not expect the "uncertain tax position" (UTP) to be resolved within the next 12 months. The uncertain tax benefit is recorded as a current tax expense because this is the additional amount of taxes PCC would pay if it prepared its tax return by deducting only $300,000 of the uncertain research credit instead of $500,000.

Subsequent Events

ASC 740-10 (FIN 48) requires a company to monitor subsequent events (e.g., the issuance of new regulations, rulings, court opinions) that might change the company's assessment that a tax position will be sustained on audit and litigation. As facts and circumstances change, a company must reevaluate the tax benefit amount it expects to realize in the future. For example, the Treasury might issue a regulation or ruling that clarifies its tax position on a particular item. This regulation could change a company's assessment that its tax position meets the more-likely-than-not threshold required for recognition.

In July 2015, the U.S. Tax Court held in favor of Altera, Inc., that the IRS's challenge to its transfer pricing methodology (intercompany cost sharing for the development of intangibles) was invalid. After the decision, the IRS filed an appeal with the U.S. Court of Appeals for the Ninth Circuit. The Ninth Circuit court held 2-1 in favor of the IRS, but one of the judges favoring the IRS died and the case was remanded back to the Ninth Circuit for a new hearing. At that time, Microsoft Corp., which had a similar tax-related uncertain tax position, concluded that no adjustment should be made to the company's uncertain tax benefit balance because there was still uncertainty as to the ultimate outcome of the case. On the other hand, Juniper Networks viewed the *Altera* decision as new information that allowed the company to reduce its uncertain tax benefit related to its cost-sharing arrangements. The different reactions of these two companies to the same court case decision illustrates that the application of this accounting pronouncement is subject to management judgment. On June 7, 2019, a three-judge panel of the Ninth Circuit Court of Appeals reversed the Tax Court decision.[35] The IRS issued a new directive (www.irs.gov/businesses/corporations/withdrawal-of-directive-lbi-04-0118-005) instructing examiners to open new examinations on the issue. On June 22, 2020, the U.S. Supreme Court denied to hear Altera's appeal; thus, the 9th Circuit decision stands (926 F.3d 1061 (2019)). Microsoft Corp.'s 2020 annual report shows continued uncertainty in its uncertain tax positions related to its transfer pricing. Juniper Networks's 2020 annual report (latest available) includes an additional charge of $20.1 million to its uncertain tax benefit reserve in response to the Supreme Court denial to hear the case.

[35] *Altera v. Comm'r,* 926 F.3d 1061 (9th Cir. 2019).

Interest and Penalties

ASC 740-10 (FIN 48) requires a company to accrue interest and any applicable penalties on liabilities it establishes for potential future tax obligations. The interest (net of the tax benefit from deducting it on a future tax return when paid) and penalties (which are not tax deductible) can be treated as part of the company's UTP-related income tax expense and income tax payable or can be recognized as interest or penalties separate from the UTP-related income tax expense. ASC 740-10 (FIN 48) only requires that the company apply its election consistently from period to period. This election creates the potential for diversity in practice. For example, General Motors Corporation treats accrued interest and penalties on its uncertain tax positions as part of its selling, general, and administrative expenses, while Ford Motor Company treats accrued interest and penalties on its uncertain tax positions as part of its income tax provision.

Disclosures of Uncertain Tax Positions

One of the most controversial aspects of ASC 740-10 (FIN 48) is its expansion of the disclosure requirements related to liabilities recorded due to uncertain tax positions (UTPs). ASC 740-10 (FIN 48) requires the company to roll forward all unrecognized tax benefits (UTBs) on a worldwide aggregated basis. Specific line items must disclose (1) the gross amounts of increases and decreases in liabilities related to uncertain tax positions as a result of tax positions taken during a prior period, (2) the gross amounts of increases and decreases in liabilities related to uncertain tax positions as a result of tax positions taken during the current period, (3) the amounts of decreases in liabilities related to uncertain tax positions relating to settlements with taxing authorities, and (4) reductions in liabilities related to uncertain tax positions as a result of a lapse of the applicable statute of limitations (the taxing authority can no longer audit the tax return on which the tax position was taken). The UTP disclosure by Microsoft Corporation is illustrated in Exhibit 17-9.

EXHIBIT 17-9 The UTP Disclosure of Microsoft Corporation

The aggregate changes in the balance of unrecognized tax benefits were as follows:

	(In millions)		
Year Ended June 30,	**2021**	**2020**	**2019**
Balance, beginning of year	**$13,792**	$13,146	$11,961
Decreases related to settlements	**(195)**	(31)	(316)
Increases for tax positions related to the current year	**790**	647	2,106
Increases for tax positions related to prior years	**461**	366	508
Decreases for tax positions related to prior years	**(297)**	(331)	(1,113)
Decreases due to lapsed statutes of limitations	**(1)**	(5)	0
Balance, end of year	**$14,550**	$13,792	$13,146

Source: Microsoft Corporation, "Annual Report 2021," July 31, 2021, Note 12—Income Taxes.

Opponents of ASC 740-10 (FIN 48) worried that the UTB disclosures would provide the IRS with a "roadmap" to a company's uncertain tax positions.[36] The ASC 740-10 (FIN 48) disclosures have not provided the IRS with the hoped-for details because the UTP disclosure does not identify the tax jurisdictions to which the uncertain tax positions relate.

[36]Jesse Drucker, "Lifting the Veil on Tax Risk—New Accounting Rule Lays Bare a Firm's Liability If Transaction Is Later Disallowed by the IRS," *The Wall Street Journal,* May 25, 2007.

Schedule UTP (Uncertain Tax Position) Statement

Since 2010, large corporations have been required to file Schedule UTP, Uncertain Tax Position Statement, with their Form 1120. Schedule UTP was designed to increase transparency and efficiency in identifying audit issues and help the IRS prioritize the selection of issues and taxpayers for audit. Schedule UTP requires corporations to report any federal income tax position for which an unrecognized tax benefit has been recorded in an audited financial statement. A corporation must identify the IRC section or sections relating to the position, indicate whether the position involves a temporary or permanent difference, identify whether the tax position is a major tax position (i.e., 10 percent or more of the total), rank the tax position by size, and provide a "concise" description of the UTP. Corporations with assets of $10 million or more that issue audited financial statements and have one or more reported uncertain tax positions must file Schedule UTP.

ETHICS

Miguel Castillo, senior manager in the tax group in the Boston office of Bean Counters LLP, an international professional services firm, was reviewing the workpapers related to the uncertain tax positions prepared by his biggest client, Pro Vision Inc. Miguel noticed that the client took the position that it did not need to record an uncertain tax benefit for a significant transaction because it had a "should level" opinion from its law firm. (A "should level" tax opinion means that the law firm believes there is a 70 to 90 percent probability that the tax benefit from the transaction will be allowed if litigated.) When Miguel asked to see the tax opinion, he was told by the firm's tax director that the company did not want to disclose the item for fear the IRS also would ask to see the opinion. Miguel has always had a good working relationship with the tax staff at Pro Vision and trusts their integrity.

Should Miguel take the tax director's word when auditing the company's reserve for uncertain tax positions? What would you do if you were in Miguel's position?

FINANCIAL STATEMENT DISCLOSURE AND COMPUTING A CORPORATION'S EFFECTIVE TAX RATE

LO 17-5

Balance Sheet Classification

ASC 740 requires publicly traded and privately held companies to classify all deferred tax assets and liabilities on their balance sheets as noncurrent.

Income Tax Footnote Disclosure

In addition to the above balance sheet disclosure requirements, ASC 740 mandates that a company disclose the components of the net deferred tax assets and liabilities reported on its balance sheet and the total valuation allowance recognized for deferred tax assets.[37] Most companies provide this information in a footnote to the financial statements (often referred to as the *income tax footnote*). Publicly traded companies must disclose the approximate "tax effect" of each type of temporary difference and carryover that gives rise to a *significant* portion of the net deferred tax liabilities and deferred tax assets.[38] Privately held (nonpublic) companies need to disclose only the types of significant temporary differences, without disclosing the tax effects of each type. ASC 740 does not

[37]ASC 740-10-50-2.

[38]ASC 740-10-50-6.

define the term *significant,* although the SEC requires a publicly traded company to disclose separately the components of its total deferred tax assets and liabilities that are 5 percent or more of the total balance.[39] Exhibit 17-10 provides the disclosure of PCC's deferred tax accounts in its income tax footnote.

ASC 740 also requires publicly traded companies to disclose the significant components of their income tax provision (expense or benefit) attributable to continuing operations in

EXHIBIT 17-10 PCC's Income Tax Note to Its Financial Statements

NOTE 5 INCOME TAXES

The Company's income (loss) from continuing operations before the income tax provision by taxing jurisdiction is as follows:

	2022
United States	$6,031,000

The provision (benefit) for income taxes is as follows:

Current tax provision (benefit)	
Federal (U.S.)	$1,180,557
Deferred tax expense (benefit)	
Federal (U.S.)	87,423
Income tax provision	$1,267,980

The significant components of the Company's deferred tax assets and liabilities as of December 31, 2022, are as follows:

	2022
Deferred tax *assets*	
Allowance for bad debts	$ 87,150
Reserve for warranties	126,000
Deferred compensation	220,500
Stock option compensation	21,000
Net capital loss carryover	5,880
Contribution carryover	15,477
Total deferred tax assets	$ 476,007
Valuation allowance	0
Deferred tax assets net of valuation allowance	$ 476,007
Deferred tax *liabilities*	
Depreciation	$(2,751,000)
Total deferred tax liabilities	$(2,751,000)
Net deferred tax liabilities	$(2,274,993)

The net capital loss carryover and the contribution carryover expire after 2027 if unused.

A reconciliation of income taxes computed by applying the statutory U.S. income tax rate to the Company's income before income taxes to the income tax provision is as follows:

	2022
Amount computed at the statutory U.S. tax rate (21%)	$1,266,510
Tax-exempt income	(2,520)
Nondeductible life insurance premiums	7,140
Dividends-received deduction	(3,150)
Income tax provision	$1,267,980

The cash amount paid during 2022 for income taxes, net of refunds, was $1,180,557.

[39]ASC 740-10-50-8; SEC Regulation S-X, §210.4-08(h).

either the financial statements or a note thereto.[40] These components include the (1) current tax expense or benefit, (2) deferred tax expense or benefit, (3) benefits of operating loss carryovers, (4) adjustments of a deferred tax liability or asset for enacted changes in tax laws or rates, and (5) adjustments of the beginning-of-the-year balance of a valuation allowance because of a change in circumstances that causes a change in management's judgment about the realizability of the recognized deferred tax assets.

Computation and Reconciliation of the Income Tax Provision with a Company's *Hypothetical* Tax Provision (Effective Tax Rate Reconciliation) ASC 740 requires a company to reconcile its (a) reported income tax provision attributable to continuing operations with (b) the amount of income tax expense that would result from applying its U.S. statutory tax rate to its pretax net income or loss from continuing operations.[41] Alternately, a company can present the reconciliation in terms of tax rates, comparing its statutory tax rate with its effective tax rate (income tax provision/pretax income from continuing operations).

Differences between a company's income tax provision and its hypothetical tax provision can arise from several sources. Income taxes paid to a state or municipality increase a company's total income tax provision over its hypothetical income tax expense. Income taxes paid to a jurisdiction outside the United States can increase or decrease a company's total income tax provision over its hypothetical income tax expense, depending on whether the jurisdiction taxes the company's income at more or less than the U.S. statutory rate. Permanent differences also affect the computation of a company's income tax provision. Favorable permanent differences (e.g., tax-exempt income) decrease the income tax provision relative to the hypothetical income tax provision. Unfavorable permanent differences (e.g., nondeductible fines and penalties) increase the income tax provision relative to the hypothetical income tax provision.

ASC 740 requires a publicly traded company to disclose the estimated amount and nature of each significant reconciling item, which the SEC defines as an amount equal to or greater than 5 percent of the hypothetical provision. The SEC requires nonpublicly traded companies to disclose the nature of significant reconciling items but not the reconciling amount.

Example 17-22

Elise used her schedule of permanent differences (from Example 17-4) to reconcile PCC's income tax provision ($1,267,980, from Example 17-13) with the company's hypothetical income tax provision. The permanent differences from Example 17-4 are reproduced below:

Permanent Differences	(Favorable) Unfavorable
Tax-exempt interest income	$(12,000)
Life insurance premiums	34,000
Dividends-received deduction	(15,000)

PCC's pretax net income from continuing operations in 2022 is $6,031,000 (from Exhibit 17-10).

What is PCC's *hypothetical* income tax provision for 2022?

Answer: $1,266,510, computed as $6,031,000 × 21 percent.

(continued on page 17-32)

[40]ASC 740-10-50-9.

[41]ASC 740-10-50-12. The income tax provision computed using the statutory tax rate is often referred to as the *hypothetical income tax expense*.

What is PCC's *effective tax rate* for 2022?

Answer: 21.02 percent, computed as $1,267,980/$6,031,000.

PCC's reconciliation of its hypothetical income tax provision with its actual income tax provision in 2022 was presented in Exhibit 17-10. The tax cost or benefit from each permanent difference is computed by multiplying the permanent difference (from above) times 21 percent.

Answer:

	2022
Amount computed at statutory U.S. tax rate (21%)	$1,266,510
Tax-exempt income	(2,520)
Nondeductible life insurance premiums	7,140
Dividends-received deduction	(3,150)
Income tax provision	$1,267,980

The SEC requires its registrants to separately disclose only those components of their effective tax rate reconciliations that equal or exceed 5 percent of the "hypothetical" tax expense. In the above reconciliation, PCC would only be required to separately disclose the items that equal or exceed $63,326 ($1,266,510 × 5%). None of the reconciling items exceed this amount. All of the reconciling items could be netted in the reconciliation.

Provide a reconciliation of PCC's statutory income tax rate (21 percent) with its actual effective tax rate (21.02 percent) in 2022. The percentage effect of each permanent difference is computed by dividing the tax cost or benefit from the item (from above) by PCC's pretax net income ($6,031,000).

Answer:

	2022
Statutory U.S. tax rate	21.00%
Tax-exempt income	(0.042)
Nondeductible life insurance premiums	0.118
Dividends-received deduction	(0.052)
Effective tax rate	21.02%

PCC's income tax note to its financial statements (Exhibit 17-10) provides the disclosure of PCC's reconciliation of its effective tax rate.

Importance of a Corporation's Effective Tax Rate The effective tax rate often serves as a benchmark for companies in the same industry. However, nonrecurring events can sometimes have a significant impact on the effective tax rate. To mitigate the impact of such aberrational events, companies and their investors may use (at least for internal purposes) a different measure of effective tax rate that backs out one-time and nonrecurring events and assumes profitable operations in each jurisdiction in which it operates. This effective tax rate is referred to as the company's **structural tax rate.** The structural effective tax rate often is viewed as more representative of the company's effective tax rate from its normal (recurring) operations. In our example, PCC does not appear to have any nonrecurring reconciling items, which would make its effective tax rate and its structural tax rate the same.

Analysts often compute a company's **cash tax rate,** the cash taxes paid divided by pretax book income, in their evaluation of the company's tax efficiency.[42] As the name implies, the cash tax rate excludes deferred taxes. PCC's cash tax rate in 2022 is 19.57 percent ($1,180,557/$6,031,000). Companies that have significant favorable temporary differences can have a cash tax rate that is much lower than their accounting effective tax rate.

Interim Period Effective Tax Rates

In addition to annual reports (Form 10-K), PCC also must report earnings on a quarterly basis (Form 10-Q). ASC 740-270, *Interim Reporting,* governs the preparation of these quarterly statements. ASC 740-270-30-6 states that "[a]t the end of each interim period the entity should make its best estimate of the effective tax rate expected to be applicable for the full fiscal year"[43] and apply this rate to the income reported in the quarterly statement. A company must reconsider its estimate of the annual rate each quarter. When the estimate changes, the company must adjust the cumulative tax provision for the year-to-date earnings to reflect the new expected annual rate. The adjusting amount becomes the company's income tax provision for the quarter.

FASB PROJECTS RELATED TO ACCOUNTING FOR INCOME TAXES

As part of its Disclosure Framework project, the FASB has proposed expanding the information to be provided in the income tax footnote. In particular, the FASB is considering whether to require companies to report pretax income from continuing operations, the associated income tax provision, and cash taxes paid as either U.S. or non-U.S. The FASB also wants increased disclosure regarding the nature and amounts of the valuation allowance recorded and released during the reporting period. The FASB issued an Accounting Statement Update in December 2019 (ASU No. 2019-12) to simplify certain reporting requirements of ASC 740 relating to loss entities and interim reporting.

CONCLUSION

In this chapter we discussed the basic rules that govern the computation of a company's U.S. income tax provision. As a result of increased SEC and Public Company Accounting Oversight Board (PCAOB) scrutiny, the need for individuals who understand these rules has increased dramatically. The FASB requires a company to take a balance sheet approach to computing its current and future (deferred) tax liabilities or benefits (assets). The income tax provision that appears on a company's income statement becomes the amount necessary to adjust the beginning balances of these accounts to their appropriate ending balances. The FASB and SEC also impose disclosure requirements for how a company reports its tax accounts in the financial statement amounts and notes to the financial statements.

[42]ASC Topic 230, *Statement of Cash Flows,* requires an enterprise to separately disclose income taxes paid as part of the statement itself or in a note to the financial statements (usually the income taxes note or a supplemental cash flow note).

[43]Financial Accounting Foundation, "FASB Exposure Draft: Proposed Accounting Standards Update. Income Taxes (Topic 740)," May 14, 2019. https://asc.fasb.org/imageRoot/07/120320407.pdf.

Summary

LO 17-1 Describe the objectives of FASB ASC Topic 740, *Income Taxes,* and the income tax provision process.

- Objectives of ASC 740:
  - To recognize a current income tax liability or asset for the company's taxes payable or refundable in the current year.
  - To recognize a deferred income tax liability or asset for the income tax effects of the company's temporary differences and carryovers.
- The income tax provision process consists of five steps:
  1. Identify all permanent and temporary differences and tax carryover amounts and calculate the current income tax provision (ASC 740 Objective 1).
  2. Determine the ending balances in the balance sheet deferred tax asset and liability accounts (ASC 740 Objective 2).
  3. Calculate the deferred income tax provision and the total income tax provision.
  4. Evaluate the need for a valuation allowance for gross deferred tax assets.
  5. Evaluate the need for an uncertain tax benefit reserve.

LO 17-2 Calculate the current and deferred income tax expense or benefit components of a company's income tax provision.

- The company first adjusts its pretax net income or loss for permanent and temporary book–tax differences to compute taxable income or loss. The company then applies the appropriate tax rate to taxable income (loss) to compute the tax return current tax expense or benefit.
- The company adjusts its tax return income tax liability or benefit for audit refunds or deficiencies from prior-year tax returns and for income tax benefits from stock option exercises treated as permanent differences.
- A company computes its deferred income tax expense or benefit by applying the applicable tax rate to the change in the cumulative balance sheet temporary differences between the financial accounting basis of an asset or liability and its corresponding tax basis from the beginning of the year to the end of the year.
- The future tax benefits from deductible temporary differences are recorded as deferred tax assets.
- The future tax costs of favorable taxable temporary differences are recorded as deferred tax liabilities.

LO 17-3 Determine how to calculate a valuation allowance.

- If a company determines that it is more likely than not (a greater than 50 percent probability) that some portion or all of the deferred tax assets will not be realized in a future period, it must offset the deferred tax assets with a valuation allowance to reflect the amount the company does not expect to realize in the future.
- The determination as to whether it is more likely than not that a deferred tax asset will not be realized in the future must be based on all available evidence, both positive and negative.
- ASC 740 identifies four sources of prior and future taxable income to consider: (1) future reversals of existing taxable temporary differences, (2) taxable income in prior carryback year(s), (3) expected future taxable income exclusive of reversing temporary differences and carryovers, and (4) expected income from tax planning strategies.

LO 17-4 Explain how a company accounts for its uncertain income tax positions under FASB ASC Topic 740.

- A company must determine whether it can record the tax benefits from an "uncertain" tax position in its financial statement for the period in which the transaction takes place, knowing that the ultimate resolution of the tax position may not be known until some future period.

- ASC 740 applies a two-step process to evaluating uncertain tax positions:
  - Recognition: A company must determine whether it is more likely than not (a greater than 50 percent probability) that a tax position will be sustained upon examination by the IRS or other taxing authority, including resolution of any appeals within the court system, based on the technical merits of the position.
  - Measurement: If the tax position meets the more-likely-than-not threshold (a subjective determination), the company must determine the amount of the benefit to record in the financial statements.
- Under ASC 740, the amount to be recorded is the largest amount of the benefit, as calculated on a cumulative probability basis, that is more likely than not to be realized on the ultimate settlement of the tax position.

Describe how a company computes and discloses the components of its effective tax rate. LO 17-5

- For annual periods beginning after December 15, 2016, ASC 740 requires a business entity to disclose all of its deferred tax liabilities and assets as noncurrent on its balance sheet.
- A company also is required to present the "significant" components of the income tax provision (expense or benefit) attributable to continuing operations.
- ASC 740 requires publicly traded companies to reconcile their reported income tax expense (benefit) from continuing operations with the *hypothetical* tax expense that would have resulted from applying the domestic federal statutory rate to pretax income from continuing operations. Alternatively, the company can compute an *effective tax rate* from its continuing operations and reconcile it with the domestic federal statutory rate (21 percent).
- A company computes its effective tax rate by dividing its income tax provision (benefit) from continuing operations by its pretax net income from continuing operations.
- Items that cause the effective tax rate to differ from the statutory tax rate include permanent differences, audit adjustments, state and local taxes, and international taxes.

KEY TERMS

book equivalent of taxable income (17-9)
cash tax rate (17-33)
current income tax expense (benefit) (17-10)
current tax liability (asset) (17-3)
deductible temporary differences (17-13)
deferred tax asset (17-2)
deferred tax liability (17-2)
effective tax rate (17-8)
enacted tax rate (17-16)
income tax provision (17-1)
permanent book–tax differences (17-7)
structural tax rate (17-32)
tax accounting balance sheet (17-11)
tax carryovers (17-4)
taxable temporary difference (17-12)
temporary book–tax differences (17-9)
uncertain tax positions (17-11)
valuation allowance (17-20)

DISCUSSION QUESTIONS

Discussion Questions are available in Connect®.

1. Identify some of the reasons why accounting for income taxes is complex. LO 17-1
2. True or False: ASC 740 applies to all taxes paid by a corporation. Explain. LO 17-1
3. True or False: ASC 740 is the sole source for the rules that apply to accounting for income taxes. Explain. LO 17-1
4. How does the fact that most corporations file their financial statements several months before they file their income tax returns complicate the income tax provision process? LO 17-1
5. What distinguishes an *income tax* from other taxes? LO 17-1
6. Briefly describe the five-step process by which a company computes its income tax provision. LO 17-1

LO 17-2 7. What are the two components of a company's income tax provision? What does each component represent about a company's income tax provision?

LO 17-2 8. True or False: All differences between book and taxable income, both permanent and temporary, affect a company's effective tax rate. Explain.

LO 17-2 9. When does a temporary difference resulting from an expense (deduction) create a taxable temporary difference? A deductible temporary difference?

LO 17-2 10. When does a temporary difference resulting from income create a taxable temporary difference? A deductible temporary difference?

LO 17-2 11. Briefly describe what is meant by the *asset and liability* or *balance sheet* approach taken by ASC 740 with respect to computing a corporation's deferred tax provision.

LO 17-2 12. Why are cumulatively favorable temporary differences referred to as taxable temporary differences?

LO 17-2 13. Why are cumulatively unfavorable temporary differences referred to as deductible temporary differences?

LO 17-2 14. In addition to the current-year tax return taxes payable or refundable, what other transactions can affect a company's current income tax provision?

LO 17-2 LO 17-4 15. What is an unrecognized tax benefit, and how does it affect a company's current income tax expense?

LO 17-2 16. True or False: When Congress changes the corporate tax rates, only the current-year book–tax temporary differences are measured using the new rates. Explain.

LO 17-2 17. True or False: All temporary differences have a financial accounting basis. Explain.

LO 17-3 18. What is the purpose behind a valuation allowance as it applies to deferred tax assets?

LO 17-3 19. What is the difference between *recognition* and *realization* in the recording of a deferred tax asset on a balance sheet?

LO 17-3 20. Briefly describe the four sources of taxable income a company evaluates in determining if a valuation allowance is necessary.

LO 17-3 21. Which of the four sources of taxable income are considered objective and which are considered subjective? Which of these sources generally receives the most weight in analyzing whether a valuation allowance is necessary?

LO 17-3 22. What are the elements that define a tax planning strategy as it applies to determining if a valuation allowance is necessary? Provide an example where a tax planning strategy may be necessary to avoid recording a valuation allowance.

LO 17-3 23. When does a company remove a valuation allowance from its balance sheet?

LO 17-3 24. What is a company's *book equivalent of taxable income*?

LO 17-4 25. What motivated the FASB to issue ASC 740-10 (FIN 48)?

LO 17-4 26. Briefly describe the two-step process a company must undertake when it evaluates whether it can record the tax benefit from an uncertain tax position under ASC 740-10 (FIN 48).

LO 17-4 27. Distinguish between *recognition* and *measurement* as they relate to the computation of unrecognized tax benefits under ASC 740-10 (FIN 48).

LO 17-4 28. What is a *tax position* as it relates to the application of ASC 740-10 (FIN 48) to uncertain tax positions?

LO 17-4 29. True or False: A company determines its unrecognized tax benefits with respect to a transaction only at the time the transaction takes place; subsequent events are ignored. Explain.

LO 17-4 30. True or False: ASC 740-10 (FIN 48) requires that a company treat potential interest and penalties related to an unrecognized tax benefit as part of its income tax provision. Explain.

LO 17-4 31. Where on the balance sheet does a company report its unrecognized tax benefits?

32. Why did many companies oppose ASC 740-10 (FIN 48) when it was first proposed? LO 17-4
33. How does a company disclose deferred tax assets and liabilities on its balance sheet? LO 17-5
34. Under what conditions can a company net its deferred tax assets with its deferred tax liabilities on the balance sheet? LO 17-5
35. True or False: A publicly traded company must disclose all of the components of its deferred tax assets and liabilities in a footnote to the financial statements. Explain. LO 17-5
36. What is a company's *hypothetical* income tax provision, and what is its importance in a company's disclosure of its income tax provision in the tax footnote? LO 17-5
37. Briefly describe the difference between a company's effective tax rate, cash tax rate, and structural tax rate. LO 17-5

PROBLEMS

Select problems are available in Connect®.

38. Which of the following taxes is *not* accounted for under ASC 740? LO 17-1
    a) Income taxes paid to the U.S. government.
    b) Income taxes paid to the French government.
    c) Income taxes paid to the city of Detroit.
    d) Property taxes paid to the city of Detroit.
    e) All of the above taxes are accounted for under ASC 740.
39. Which of the following organizations can issue rules that govern accounting for income taxes? LO 17-1
    a) FASB.
    b) SEC.
    c) IRS.
    d) Both (a) and (b) above.
    e) All of the above organizations.
40. Find the paragraph(s) in ASC 740 that deals with the following items (access ASC 740 on the FASB website, www.fasb.org, and then click on "Standards"). You will need a username and password from your instructor. LO 17-1 research
    a) The objectives and basic principles that underlie ASC 740.
    b) Examples of book–tax differences that create temporary differences.
    c) The definition of a *tax planning strategy*.
    d) Examples of positive evidence in the valuation allowance process.
    e) Rules relating to financial statement disclosure.
41. Bautista Corporation reported pretax book income of $1,000,000. Included in the computation were favorable temporary differences of $200,000, unfavorable temporary differences of $50,000, and favorable permanent differences of $100,000. Compute the company's current income tax expense or benefit. LO 17-2
42. Cass Corporation reported pretax book income of $10,000,000. During the current year, the reserve for bad debts increased by $100,000. In addition, tax depreciation exceeded book depreciation by $200,000. Cass Corporation sold a fixed asset and reported book gain of $50,000 and tax gain of $75,000. Finally, the company received $250,000 of tax-exempt life insurance proceeds from the death of one of its officers. Compute the company's current income tax expense or benefit. LO 17-2

LO 17-2 43. Grand Corporation reported pretax book income of $600,000. Tax depreciation exceeded book depreciation by $400,000. In addition, the company received $300,000 of tax-exempt municipal bond interest. The company's prior-year tax return showed taxable income of $50,000. Compute the company's current income tax expense or benefit.

LO 17-2 44. Akoto Corporation reported pretax book income of $2,000,000. Tax depreciation exceeded book depreciation by $500,000. During the year, the company capitalized $250,000 into ending inventory under §263A. Capitalized inventory costs of $150,000 in beginning inventory were deducted as part of cost of goods sold on the tax return. Compute the company's taxes payable or refundable.

LO 17-2 45. Choi Company determined that the book basis of its office building exceeded the tax basis by $800,000. This basis difference is properly characterized as:

a) A permanent difference.
b) A taxable temporary difference.
c) A deductible temporary difference.
d) A favorable book–tax difference.
e) Both (b) and (d) above are correct.

LO 17-2 46. Abbot Company determined that the book basis of its allowance for bad debts is $100,000. There is no corresponding tax basis in this account. The basis difference is properly characterized as:

a) A permanent difference.
b) A taxable temporary difference.
c) A deductible temporary difference.
d) A favorable book–tax difference.
e) Both (b) and (d) above are correct.

LO 17-2 47. Which of the following items is *not* a temporary book–tax basis difference?

a) Warranty reserve accruals.
b) Accelerated depreciation.
c) Capitalized inventory costs under §263A.
d) Nondeductible stock option compensation from exercising an ISO.
e) All of the above are temporary differences.

LO 17-2 48. Which of the following book–tax differences does *not* create a favorable temporary book–tax basis difference?

a) Tax depreciation for the period exceeds book depreciation.
b) Bad debts charged off in the current period exceed the bad debts accrued in the current period.
c) Inventory costs capitalized under §263A deducted as part of current-year tax cost of goods sold are less than the inventory costs capitalized in ending inventory.
d) Vacation pay accrued for tax purposes in a prior period is deducted in the current period.
e) All of the above create a favorable temporary book–tax difference.

LO 17-2 49. Lodge Inc. reported pretax book income of $5,000,000. During the year, the company increased its reserve for warranties by $200,000. The company deducted $50,000 on its tax return related to warranty payments made during the year. What is the impact on taxable income compared to pretax book income of the book–tax difference that results from these two events?

a) Favorable (decreases taxable income).
b) Unfavorable (increases taxable income).
c) Neutral (no impact on taxable income).

50. Which of the following book–tax basis differences results in a deductible temporary difference? LO 17-2
  a) Book basis of a fixed asset exceeds its tax basis.
  b) Book basis of a pension-related liability exceeds its tax basis.
  c) Prepayment of income included on the tax return but not on the income statement (the transaction is recorded as a liability on the balance sheet).
  d) All of the above result in a deductible temporary difference.
  e) Both (b) and (c) result in a deductible temporary difference.

51. Kumara Corporation reported pretax book income of $1,000,000. Kumara also reports an increase in the taxable temporary differences of $200,000, an increase in the deductible temporary differences of $50,000, and favorable permanent differences of $100,000. Assuming a tax rate of 21 percent, compute the company's deferred income tax expense or benefit. LO 17-2

52. Song Inc. reported pretax book income of $10,000,000. During the current year, the reserve for bad debts increased by $100,000. In addition, tax depreciation exceeded book depreciation by $200,000. Song Inc. sold a fixed asset and reported book gain of $50,000 and tax gain of $75,000. Finally, the company received $250,000 of tax-exempt life insurance proceeds from the death of one of its officers. Assuming a tax rate of 21 percent, compute the company's deferred income tax expense or benefit. LO 17-2

53. Li Corporation reported pretax book income of $600,000. Tax depreciation exceeded book depreciation by $400,000. In addition, the company received $300,000 of tax-exempt municipal bond interest. The company's prior-year tax return showed taxable income of $50,000. Assuming a tax rate of 21 percent, compute the company's deferred income tax expense or benefit. LO 17-2

54. Identify the following items as creating a temporary book–tax difference, a permanent book–tax difference, or no book–tax difference. LO 17-2

Item	Temporary Difference	Permanent Difference	No Difference
Reserve for warranties			
Accrued pension liability			
Goodwill not amortized for tax purposes but subject to impairment under ASC Topic 350			
Nondeductible meal expenses			
Life insurance proceeds			
Net capital loss carryover			
Nondeductible fines and penalties			
Accrued vacation pay liability paid within the first two and one-half months of the next tax year			

55. Which of the following items is *not* a permanent book–tax difference? LO 17-2
  a) Tax-exempt interest income.
  b) Tax-exempt insurance proceeds.
  c) Windfall tax benefits from the exercise of a nonqualified stock option (NQO).
  d) Nondeductible meal expenses.
  e) First-year expensing under §179.

56. Rimas Corporation reported pretax book income of $1,000,000. Included in the computation were favorable temporary differences of $200,000, unfavorable temporary differences of $50,000, and favorable permanent differences of $100,000. Compute the company's book equivalent of taxable income. Use this number to compute the company's total income tax provision or benefit. LO 17-2

LO 17-2 57. Burcham Corporation reported pretax book income of $600,000. Tax depreciation exceeded book depreciation by $400,000. In addition, the company received $300,000 of tax-exempt municipal bond interest. The company's prior-year tax return showed taxable income of $50,000. Compute the company's book equivalent of taxable income. Use this number to compute the company's total income tax provision or benefit.

LO 17-3 58. Arain Corporation has total deferred tax assets of $3,000,000 at year-end. Management is assessing whether a valuation allowance must be recorded against some or all of the deferred tax assets. What level of assurance must management have, based on the weight of available evidence, that some or all of the deferred tax assets will not be realized before a valuation allowance is required?

a) Probable.
b) More likely than not.
c) Realistic possibility.
d) Reasonable.
e) More than remote.

LO 17-3 59. Which of the following would *not* be considered positive evidence in determining whether Arain Corporation needs to record a valuation allowance for some or all of its deferred tax assets?

a) The company forecasts future taxable income because of its backlog of orders.
b) The company has unfavorable temporary differences that will create future taxable income when they reverse.
c) The company has tax-planning strategies that it can implement to create future taxable income.
d) The company has cumulative net income over the current and prior two years.
e) The company had a net operating loss carryover expire in the current year.

LO 17-3 60. As of the beginning of the year, Gratiot Company recorded a valuation allowance of $200,000 against its deferred tax assets of $1,000,000. The valuation allowance relates to a net operating loss carryover from the prior year. During the year, management concludes that the valuation allowance is no longer necessary because it forecasts sufficient taxable income to absorb the NOL carryover. What is the impact of management's reversal of the valuation allowance on the company's effective tax rate?

a) Increases the effective tax rate.
b) Decreases the effective tax rate.
c) No impact on the effective tax rate.

LO 17-3 61. Which of the following would be considered negative evidence in determining whether Gratiot Corporation needs to record a valuation allowance for some or all of its deferred tax assets?

a) The company forecasts future taxable income because of its backlog of orders.
b) The company has a cumulative net loss over the current and prior two years.
c) The company has unfavorable temporary differences that will create future taxable income when they reverse.
d) The company had a net operating loss carryover expire in the current year.
e) Both (b) and (d) constitute negative evidence in assessing the need for a valuation allowance.

LO 17-3 62. Saginaw Inc. completed its first year of operations with a pretax loss of $500,000. The tax return showed a net operating loss of $600,000, which the company will carry forward. The $100,000 book–tax difference results from excess tax depreciation over book depreciation. Management has determined that it should record a valuation allowance equal to the net deferred tax asset. Assuming the current tax expense is zero, prepare the journal entries to record the deferred tax provision and the valuation allowance.

63. Access the 2017 Form 10-Ks for General Motors, Inc. and Berkshire Hathaway. What was the impact of the Tax Cuts and Jobs Act on their income tax provision for 2017? Why was the impact in opposite directions (i.e., in one case the provision increased and in the other it decreased)? LO 17-3 research

64. Montcalm Corporation has total deferred tax assets of $3,000,000 at year-end. Of that amount, $1,000,000 results from the current expensing of an expenditure that the IRS might assert must be capitalized on audit. Management is trying to determine if it should not recognize the deferred tax asset related to this item under ASC 740-10 (FIN 48). What confidence level must management have that the item will be sustained on audit before it can recognize any portion of the deferred tax asset under ASC 740-10 (FIN 48)? LO 17-4
   a) Probable.
   b) More likely than not.
   c) Realistic possibility.
   d) Reasonable.
   e) More than remote.

65. Which of the following statements about uncertain tax positions (UTP) is correct? LO 17-4
   a) UTP applies only to tax positions accounted for under ASC 740 taken on a filed tax return.
   b) UTP applies to all tax positions accounted for under ASC 740, regardless of whether the item is taken on a filed tax return.
   c) UTP deals with both the recognition and realization of deferred tax assets.
   d) If a tax position meets the more-likely-than-not standard, the entire amount of the deferred tax asset or current tax benefit related to the tax position can be recognized under ASC 740.
   e) Statements (b), (c), and (d) are correct.

66. Cadillac Square Corporation determined that $1,000,000 of its research and development tax credit on its current-year tax return was uncertain but that it was more likely than not to be sustained on audit. Management made the following assessment of the company's potential tax benefit from the deduction and its probability of occurring. LO 17-4

Potential Estimated Benefit (000s)	Individual Probability of Occurring (%)	Cumulative Probability of Occurring (%)
$1,000,000	40	40
750,000	25	65
500,000	20	85
0	15	100

What amount of the tax benefit related to the uncertain tax position from the research and development tax credit can Cadillac Square Corporation recognize in calculating its income tax provision in the current year?

67. How would your answer to the previous problem change if management determined that there was only a 50/50 chance any portion of the $1,000,000 research and development tax credit would be sustained on audit? LO 17-4

LO 17-4

68. As part of its UTP assessment, Penobscot Company records interest and penalties related to its unrecognized tax benefit of $500,000. Which of the following statements about recording this amount is most correct?
   a) Penobscot must include the amount in its income tax provision.
   b) Penobscot must record the amount separate from its income tax provision.
   c) Penobscot can elect to allocate a portion of the amount to both its income tax provision and its general and administrative expenses provided the company discloses which option it has chosen.
   d) Penobscot can elect to record the entire amount as part of its income tax provision or separate from its income tax provision, provided the company discloses which option it has chosen.
   e) Statements (c) and (d) are both correct.

LO 17-5 research

69. What was Facebook's accounting effective tax rate for 2020? What items caused the company's accounting effective tax rate to differ from the "hypothetical" tax rate of 21 percent? What was the company's cash effective tax rate for 2020? What factors cause a company's cash tax rate to differ from its accounting effective tax rate? You can access Facebook's Form 10-K for 2020 at the company's website or the SEC EDGAR website.

LO 17-5

70. Beacon Corporation recorded the following deferred tax assets and liabilities:

Current deferred tax assets	$ 650,000
Current deferred tax liabilities	(400,000)
Noncurrent deferred tax assets	1,000,000
Noncurrent deferred tax liabilities	(2,500,000)
Net deferred tax liabilities	$ 1,250,000)

All of the deferred tax accounts relate to temporary differences that arose as a result of the company's U.S. operations. Which of the following statements describes how Beacon should disclose these accounts on its balance sheet?
   a) Beacon reports a net deferred tax liability of $1,250,000 on its balance sheet as noncurrent.
   b) Beacon nets the deferred tax assets and the deferred tax liabilities and reports a net deferred tax asset of $1,650,000 and a net deferred tax liability of $2,900,000 on its balance sheet.
   c) Beacon can elect to net the current deferred tax accounts and the noncurrent tax accounts and report a net current deferred tax asset of $250,000 and a net deferred tax liability of $1,500,000 on its balance sheet.
   d) Beacon is required to net the current deferred tax accounts and the noncurrent deferred tax accounts and report a net current deferred tax asset of $250,000 and a net deferred tax liability of $1,500,000 on its balance sheet.

LO 17-5

71. ASC 740 requires a company to disclose those components of its deferred tax assets and liabilities that are considered
   a) Relevant.
   b) Significant.
   c) Important.
   d) Major.

LO 17-5

72. Which of the following temporary differences creates a deferred tax asset?
   a) Allowance for bad debts.
   b) Goodwill amortization for tax, but not book, purposes.
   c) Cumulative excess of tax over book depreciation.
   d) Inventory capitalization under §263A.
   e) Both (a) and (d) create a deferred tax asset.

73. Which formula represents the calculation of a company's effective tax rate? LO 17-5
   a) Income taxes paid/Taxable income.
   b) Income taxes paid/Pretax income from continuing operations.
   c) Income tax provision/Taxable income.
   d) Income tax provision/Pretax income from continuing operations.
74. Which of the following items is *not* a reconciling item in the effective tax rate reconciliation in the income tax footnote? LO 17-5
   a) State income taxes.
   b) Foreign income taxes.
   c) Accrued pension liabilities.
   d) Dividends-received deduction.
   e) Tax-exempt municipal bond interest.
75. Hafnaoui Company reported pretax net income from continuing operations of $800,000 and taxable income of $500,000. The book–tax difference of $300,000 was due to a $200,000 favorable temporary difference relating to depreciation, an unfavorable temporary difference of $80,000 due to an increase in the reserve for bad debts, and a $180,000 favorable permanent difference from the receipt of life insurance proceeds. LO 17-5
   a) Compute Hafnaoui Company's current income tax expense.
   b) Compute Hafnaoui Company's deferred income tax expense or benefit.
   c) Compute Hafnaoui Company's effective tax rate.
   d) Provide a reconciliation of Hafnaoui Company's effective tax rate with its hypothetical tax rate of 21 percent.
76. Which of the following pronouncements should a company consult in computing its quarterly income tax provision? LO 17-5
   a) ASC Topic 740.
   b) ASC Topic 230.
   c) ASC Topic 718.
   d) ASC Topic 810.
   e) SarbOX §404.

COMPREHENSIVE PROBLEMS

Select problems are available with Connect®.

77. You have been assigned to compute the income tax provision for Motown Memories Inc. (MM) as of December 31, 2022. The company's income statement for 2022 is provided below:

Motown Memories Inc. Statement of Operations at December 31, 2022	
Net sales	$50,000,000
Cost of sales	28,000,000
Gross profit	$22,000,000
Compensation	$ 2,000,000
Selling expenses	1,500,000
Depreciation and amortization	4,000,000
Other expenses	500,000
Total operating expenses	$ 8,000,000
Income from operations	$14,000,000
Interest and other income	1,000,000
Income before income taxes	$15,000,000

You identified the following permanent differences:

Interest income from municipal bonds	$50,000
Nondeductible entertainment expenses	20,000
Nondeductible fines	5,000

MM prepared the following schedule of temporary differences from the beginning of the year to the end of the year:

Motown Memories Inc.
Temporary Differences Scheduling Template

Taxable Temporary Differences	BOY Deferred Taxes	Current-Year Change	EOY Cumulative T/D	EOY Deferred Taxes
Accumulated depreciation	$(1,680,000)	$(1,000,000)	$(9,000,000)	**$(1,890,000)**

Deductible Temporary Differences	BOY Deferred Taxes	Current-Year Change	EOY Cumulative T/D	EOY Deferred Taxes
Allowance for bad debts	$ 42,000	$ 50,000	$ 250,000	$ 52,500
Reserve for warranties	21,000	20,000	120,000	25,200
Inventory §263A adjustment	50,400	60,000	300,000	63,000
Deferred compensation	10,500	10,000	60,000	12,600
Accrued pension liabilities	630,000	250,000	3,250,000	682,500
Total	**$753,900**	**$390,000**	**$3,980,000**	**$835,800**

Required:

a) Compute MM's current income tax expense or benefit for 2022.
b) Compute MM's deferred income tax expense or benefit for 2022.
c) Prepare a reconciliation of MM's total income tax provision with its hypothetical income tax expense of 21 percent in both dollars and rates.

78. You have been assigned to compute the income tax provision for Tulip City Flowers Inc. (TCF) as of December 31, 2022. The company's income statement for 2022 is provided below:

Tulip City Flowers Inc.
Statement of Operations at December 31, 2022

Net sales	$20,000,000
Cost of sales	12,000,000
Gross profit	$ 8,000,000
Compensation	$ 500,000
Selling expenses	750,000
Depreciation and amortization	1,250,000
Other expenses	1,000,000
Total operating expenses	$ 3,500,000
Income from operations	$ 4,500,000
Interest and other income	25,000
Income before income taxes	$ 4,525,000

You identified the following permanent differences:

Interest income from municipal bonds	$10,000
Nondeductible stock compensation	5,000
Nondeductible fines	1,000

TCF prepared the following schedule of temporary differences from the beginning of the year to the end of the year:

Tulip City Flowers Inc.
Temporary Differences Scheduling Template

Taxable Temporary Differences	BOY Deferred Taxes	Current-Year Change	EOY Cumulative T/D	EOY Deferred Taxes
Accumulated depreciation	$(1,050,000)	$(500,000)	$(5,500,000)	$(1,155,000)

Deductible Temporary Differences	BOY Deferred Taxes	Current-Year Change	EOY Cumulative T/D	EOY Deferred Taxes
Allowance for bad debts	$ 21,000	$ 10,000	$ 110,000	$ 23,100
Prepaid income	0	20,000	20,000	4,200
Deferred compensation	10,500	10,000	60,000	12,600
Accrued pension liabilities	105,000	100,000	600,000	126,000
Total	**$136,500**	**$140,000**	**$790,000**	**$165,900**

Required:

a) Compute TCF's current income tax expense or benefit for 2022.
b) Compute TCF's deferred income tax expense or benefit for 2022.
c) Prepare a reconciliation of TCF's total income tax provision with its hypothetical income tax expense of 21 percent in both dollars and rates.

79. Access the 2020 Form 10-K for Facebook, Inc., and answer the following questions. **research**

Required:

a) Using information from the company's Income Statement and Income Taxes footnote, what was the company's effective tax rate for 2020? Show how the rate is calculated.
b) Using information from the Statement of Cash Flows, calculate the company's cash tax rate.
c) What does the company's Income Taxes note tell you about where the company earns its international income? Why does earning income in these countries cause the effective tax rate to decrease?
d) What item creates the company's largest deferred tax asset? Explain why this item creates a deductible temporary difference.
e) What item creates the company's largest deferred tax liability? Explain why this item creates a taxable temporary difference.
f) How does the company classify its income taxes payable related to its unrecognized tax benefits on the balance sheet?
g) How does the company treat interest and penalties related to its unrecognized tax benefits?

80. Spartan Builders Corporation is a builder of high-end housing with locations in major metropolitan areas throughout the Midwest. At June 30, 2022, the company has deferred tax assets totaling $10 million and deferred tax liabilities of $5 million, all of which relate to U.S. temporary differences. Reversing taxable temporary differences and taxable income in the carryback period can be used to support approximately $2 million of the $10 million gross deferred tax asset. The remaining $8 million of gross deferred tax assets will have to come from future taxable income.

The company has historically been profitable. However, significant losses were incurred in fiscal years 2020 and 2021. These two years reflect a cumulative loss of $10 million ($7 million of which was due to a write-down of inventory), with losses of $3 million expected in 2022. Beginning in fiscal 2023, management decided to get out of the metropolitan Chicago market, which had become oversaturated with new houses.

Evaluate the company's need to record a valuation allowance for the $10 million of gross deferred tax assets. What positive and negative evidence would you weigh?

UWorld | ROGER CPA Review

UWorld Roger CPA Review

Sample CPA Exam questions from Roger CPA Review are available in Connect as support for the topics in this text. These Multiple Choice Questions and Task-Based Simulations include expert-written explanations and solutions and provide a starting point for students to become familiar with the content and functionality of the actual CPA Exam.

chapter

18 Corporate Taxation: Nonliquidating Distributions

Learning Objectives

Upon completing this chapter, you should be able to:

LO 18-1 Recognize the tax framework applying to property distributions from a corporation to a shareholder.

LO 18-2 Compute a corporation's earnings and profits and a shareholder's dividend income.

LO 18-3 Explain the taxation of stock distributions.

LO 18-4 Discern the tax consequences of stock redemptions.

LO 18-5 Describe the tax consequences of a partial liquidation to the corporation and its shareholders.

Sam Edwards/OJO Images/age fotostock

Storyline Summary

Taxpayer:	Jim Wheels (he/him/his)
Location:	East Lansing, Michigan
Status:	Co-owner of Spartan Cycle and Repair (75 percent)
Taxpayer:	Ginny Gears (she/her/hers)
Location:	East Lansing, Michigan
Status:	Co-owner of Spartan Cycle and Repair (25 percent)

Jim Wheels and Ginny Gears are old friends who met years ago at the Mid-Michigan Cycling Club. Members of the club, including Ginny, often found it difficult to get parts and have their bicycles repaired locally. Because of his experience from working at a bicycle shop during his undergraduate days, Jim was the club's local bike repair expert. Ginny majored in marketing at Michigan State University (MSU) and was eager to put marketing and management to work in a real business. Consequently, Jim and Ginny often discussed the feasibility of operating a high-end bicycle shop in East Lansing, Michigan.

A few years ago, Jim and Ginny decided to start Spartan Cycle and Repair (SCR). Their business had humble beginnings, as most start-up companies do. By borrowing from Jim's father, Walt, they raised $50,000 of capital needed to purchase inventory and the necessary repair tools. They also leased a vacant building on Grand River Avenue. On the advice of their accountant, Jim and Ginny organized their company as a C corporation, with Jim owning 75 percent of the corporation's stock and Ginny owning the remaining 25 percent. Jim's responsibilities include repairing bikes and deciding which bicycle brands to carry, while Ginny is responsible for managing and marketing the business. Jim works approximately 10 hours per week at the store and receives a modest salary of $15,000 per year. Ginny works half time at the store and currently receives a salary of $25,000 per year.

Since the company's inception, Jim and Ginny have used most of the company's profits to pay back the loan to Jim's father and expand the store's inventory and marketing activities. By the end of this year, SCR had become very successful, as evidenced by the significant amount of cash ($300,000) in the company's bank accounts. Over a latte at the local gourmet coffee shop, Jim and Ginny decided it was time to think about distributing some of the company's profits to reward their hard work. Jim admitted he liked the look of a dark green BMW that retailed for approximately $48,000. Ginny was a bit more restrained and wanted to put a down payment on a condominium in the newly developed Evergreen Commons being constructed near their store. The down payment would require $16,000. The latest proposal is for SCR to distribute $64,000 at year-end ($48,000 to Jim and $16,000 to Ginny).

(to be continued . . .)

At some point during the life of a company, especially in the case of a closely held business, the shareholders will likely want to distribute some of the company's accumulated profits. If the business is operated as a C corporation, the company can distribute its *after-tax* profits to its shareholders in the form of a **dividend, stock redemption,** or, in rare cases, a **partial liquidation.** This chapter addresses the tax consequences to the corporation and its shareholders when a C corporation makes distributions to its shareholders.[1]

LO 18-1

TAXATION OF PROPERTY DISTRIBUTIONS

The characterization of a distribution from a C corporation to a shareholder has important tax consequences to both the shareholders and the corporation. If the tax law characterizes the distribution as a dividend rather than compensation, the corporation may not deduct the amount paid in computing its taxable income. In addition, the shareholder must include the dividend received in gross income. The nondeductibility of the distribution by the corporation, coupled with the taxation of the distribution to the shareholder, creates *double taxation* of the corporation's income, first at the corporate level and then at the shareholder level. The double taxation of distributed corporate income has been a fundamental principle of the U.S. income tax since 1913.

Historically, tax planning focused on eliminating or mitigating one level of taxation on C corporation earnings. For example, if the distribution can instead be characterized as salary, bonus, interest, or rent, the corporation can deduct the amount paid in computing its taxable income, thereby avoiding the corporate income tax on this incremental payment. It is also important to recall that the corporate tax rate (21 percent) is significantly lower than the maximum individual tax rate (37 percent). However, the individual marginal tax rate on dividends is generally below the top individual tax rate. Hence, it is conceivable that some taxpayers may save taxes by choosing to have a business entity taxed as a C corporation. In other words, depending on the timing and form of distributions of profits, subjecting a business to double taxation may be preferable to operating the business as a flow-through entity and subjecting the income to a single tax at a higher individual rate.

LO 18-2

DETERMINING THE DIVIDEND AMOUNT FROM EARNINGS AND PROFITS

Overview

When a corporation distributes property to shareholders in their capacity as shareholders, the distributions are characterized as dividend income, return of capital, and/or capital gain. The portion characterized as dividend income is included in gross income. In contrast, a return of capital is not considered income, but rather a reduction in the shareholder's tax basis in the stock. If the nondividend portion of the distribution exceeds the tax basis of the stock, then the excess distribution (above basis) is taxed as a capital gain from the sale of the shares.[2]

Corporate distributions of "property" usually take the form of cash, but distributions can also consist of other tangible or intangible property. Special rules apply when a corporation distributes its own stock to its shareholders.[3]

Dividends Defined

A dividend is any distribution of property made by a corporation to its shareholders from earnings and profits (E&P). Congress created E&P to be a measure of the corporation's

[1]Corporations subject to the corporate tax are referred to as *C corporations* because Subchapter C (§§301–385) governs the tax consequences of distributions between a corporation and its shareholders. If Jim and Ginny had elected to operate their business through an S corporation or partnership, the entity-level taxation of the company's earnings would be eliminated.

[2]§301(c).

[3]§305.

economic earnings available for distribution to its shareholders. Hence, earnings and profits is similar in concept to financial accounting retained earnings. Corporations keep two separate E&P accounts. One is called **current earnings and profits** that is comparable to the economic income earned in the current period. The other account represents the undistributed earnings and profits accumulated in all prior years and is called **accumulated earnings and profits.**

Each year corporations compute their *current* E&P by making specific adjustments to taxable income (discussed below). When both current and accumulated E&P are positive, distributions can be treated as dividends up to the available amount of E&P (current plus accumulated). Any E&P that is not distributed to shareholders becomes the amount of *accumulated* E&P at the beginning of the next taxable year. Distributions reduce E&P but cannot produce (or increase) a deficit (a negative balance) in E&P. In other words, a corporation cannot distribute E&P if there is a deficit in E&P, and only losses can create a deficit in E&P. A corporation that makes a distribution in excess of its available E&P (i.e., a return of capital and/or capital gain to shareholders) must report the distribution on Form 5452 and include a calculation of its E&P balance to support the tax treatment.

Example 18-1

Jim owns 75 percent of the Spartan Cycle and Repair (SCR) stock, while Ginny owns the remaining 25 percent. Jim has a tax basis in his SCR stock of $24,000. Ginny's tax basis in her SCR stock is $10,000.

What if: Assume SCR has current earnings and profits (E&P) of $30,000 and no accumulated earnings and profits. At year-end, SCR makes a $64,000 distribution—a $48,000 distribution to Jim and a $16,000 distribution to Ginny.

What is the tax treatment of the distribution to Jim and Ginny?

Answer: Only $30,000 of the $64,000 distribution is treated as a dividend. The distribution is first deemed to be paid from current E&P to each shareholder in proportion to their ownership interest on the date of the distribution: $22,500 to Jim ($30,000 × 75%) and $7,500 to Ginny ($30,000 × 25%). The $34,000 distribution in excess of current E&P ($64,000 – $30,000) is then deemed to be paid from accumulated E&P in proportion to ownership interests. However, because there is no accumulated E&P, the distribution in excess of E&P is first treated as a return of capital and then capital gain once basis is exhausted.

Jim treats the $48,000 distribution for tax purposes as follows:

- $22,500 is treated as a dividend.
- $24,000 is a nontaxable reduction in his stock tax basis (return of capital).
- $1,500 is treated as gain from the deemed sale of his stock (capital gain).

Note that a return of capital cannot reduce a shareholder's stock basis below zero. Amounts paid in excess of stock basis result in gain recognition.

Ginny treats the $16,000 distribution for tax purposes as follows:

- $7,500 is treated as a dividend.
- $8,500 from E&P is a nontaxable reduction in her stock tax basis (return of capital).
- Ginny has no capital gain because the distribution did not exceed the tax basis of her SCR stock.

What is Jim's tax basis in his SCR stock after the distribution? What is Ginny's tax basis in her SCR stock after the distribution?

Answer: Jim has a zero basis in the SCR stock, while Ginny has a remaining tax basis of $1,500 ($10,000 – $8,500) in the SCR stock.

TAXES IN THE REAL WORLD Keeping Track of Tax Basis Is Important

When a corporation makes a distribution that is treated as a return of capital (i.e., a distribution in excess of E&P), it is incumbent on each shareholder to establish their basis for the stock in determining the extent to which the distribution is a nontaxable return of capital or a capital gain. The burden of proving the basis of the stock is on the shareholder, as a taxpayer, Mr. Visconti, ultimately discovered.

(continued)

To avoid income taxes on a corporate distribution, a shareholder must establish that the distribution is in respect to the corporation's stock, there is an absence of earnings and profits, and the stock basis is in excess of the distribution. The government charged Mr. Visconti with tax evasion for failing to pay capital gains taxes on a corporate distribution in excess of earnings and profits. At trial, focus was on whether the taxpayer could prove that the distributions did not exceed the stock basis.

Visconti argued the stock had a basis of $13.13 million. Checks were presented showing that Visconti paid $4.9 million to purchase the stock. Visconti also argued that the value of property contributed to the corporation increased the tax basis to $8.25 million. However, Visconti provided no evidence of the property's value or basis aside from his own estimate. In contrast, the government's evidence consisted of testimony of a CPA who testified that the property Visconti transferred to the corporation was only valued at $6.25 million. The government also presented bank records and a statement that Visconti submitted in divorce proceedings. These documents showed that the corporation had previously distributed $12.25 million to Visconti. Hence, the government argued that Visconti had a zero basis in his stock.

At trial, the district court ruled that Visconti's statements were insufficient to support the $8.25 million valuation or rebut the government's evidence. Hence, the court precluded Visconti's return-of-capital defense. On appeal, the Ninth Circuit Court held that the trial court did not abuse its discretion in finding that Visconti failed to establish a factual basis for a return-of-capital defense.

When a shareholder is unable to establish his basis for the stock, the IRS will treat the shareholder as having a zero basis in the stock. Hence, it pays for shareholders to be prepared and keep records of corporate contributions and distributions.

Source: United States v. Visconti, 122 AFTR2d 2018-5976 (9th Cir. 2018).

THE KEY FACTS

Adjustments to Taxable Income (Loss) to Compute Current E&P

- A corporation makes the following adjustments to taxable income to compute current E&P:
  - Include certain income that is excluded from taxable income.
  - Disallow certain expenses that are deducted in computing taxable income.
  - Deduct certain expenses that are not deductible in computing taxable income.
  - Defer deductions or accelerate income due to separate accounting methods required for E&P purposes.

Computing Earnings and Profits

The concept of earnings and profits has been part of the tax laws since 1916. Although Congress has never provided a precise definition, E&P is supposed to represent the economic income eligible for distribution to shareholders. Consistent with this rationale, E&P includes both taxable and nontaxable income, indicating that Congress intended E&P to represent a corporation's economic income. As a result, shareholders may be taxed on distributions of income even if the income was not taxable to the corporation.

A corporation begins the computation of current E&P with taxable income or loss. It then makes adjustments required by the Internal Revenue Code or the accompanying regulations and IRS rulings. These adjustments fall into four broad categories:

1. Certain nontaxable income is included in E&P.
2. Certain deductions do not reduce E&P.
3. Certain nondeductible expenses reduce E&P.
4. The timing of certain items of income and deduction is modified for E&P calculations because separate accounting methods are required for E&P purposes.[4]

Nontaxable Income Included in Current E&P Tax-exempt income represents economic income that can be distributed to shareholders. Thus, tax-exempt income is included in current E&P. Common examples of tax-exempt income included in current E&P are tax-exempt municipal interest and tax-exempt life insurance proceeds.

Example 18-2

SCR reported $5,000 of tax-exempt interest from its investment in City of East Lansing municipal bonds. What effect does the tax-exempt interest income have on current earnings and profits, if any?

Answer: The tax-exempt interest income is included in current earnings and profits thereby increasing current E&P by $5,000 because it reflects economic income.

[4]§312.

Deductible Expenses That Do Not Reduce Current E&P Deductions that require no cash outlay by the corporation or are carryovers from another tax year do not represent current economic outflows and cannot be used to reduce current E&P. Examples include the dividends-received deduction, net capital loss carryovers from a different tax year, net operating loss carryovers from a different tax year, and charitable contribution carryovers from a prior tax year.[5]

Nondeductible Expenses That Reduce Current E&P A corporation reduces its current E&P for certain expenditures that are not deductible in computing its taxable income but require a cash outflow. Examples of such expenses include:

- Federal income taxes paid or accrued (depending on the corporation's method of accounting).
- Expenses incurred in earning tax-exempt income (such income is included in E&P).
- Current-year charitable contributions in excess of the taxable income percentage limitation (there is no percentage limitation for E&P purposes).
- Premiums on life insurance contracts in excess of the increase in the policy's cash surrender value.
- Current-year net capital loss (there is no limit on capital losses for E&P purposes).
- Nondeductible meal expenses.
- Nondeductible entertainment expenses.
- Nondeductible lobbying expenses and political contributions.
- Nondeductible penalties and fines.
- Disallowed business interest expense.

Items Requiring Separate Accounting Methods for E&P Purposes A corporation must generally use the same accounting methods for computing both E&P and taxable income. For example, a gain or loss deferred for income tax purposes under the like-kind exchange rules (§1031) or the involuntary conversion rules is also deferred for calculating E&P. A corporation using the accrual method for income tax purposes generally must use the accrual method for E&P purposes. However, there are important differences between the accounting methods used to compute taxable income and current E&P. Hence, the adjustments to taxable income reflect differences in both the recognition and the timing of certain items of income and expense. The list of adjustments in deriving current E&P from taxable income is somewhat lengthy; some adjustments are positive and others are negative.

Some types of income deferred from current-year taxable income must be included in the computation of current E&P in the year in which the transaction occurs. For example, a corporation that defers gains under the installment method for income tax purposes must still include the deferred gain in current E&P. This difference reverses in future years when the installment payments are received, thereby triggering recognition of the deferred gain. In these years, the gain increases taxable income but is not included in current E&P.

Certain expenses currently deducted in the computation of taxable income are deferred in computing E&P.[6] For example, organizational expenditures, which can be

[5]The deduction allowed for employee exercises of nonqualified stock options reduces current E&P because the bargain element of the option reflects an economic cost to the corporation (even though it does not require a cash outflow from the corporation).

[6]§312(n) was added in 1984 to "ensure that a corporation's earnings and profits more closely conform to its economic income."

deducted currently or amortized for income tax purposes, must be capitalized for E&P purposes. Depreciation must be computed using the prescribed E&P method. For property acquired after 1986, the alternative depreciation system (ADS) must be used. This system requires that assets be depreciated using the asset depreciation range.[7] Also, bonus depreciation is not allowed for E&P purposes. This generally results in more accelerated depreciation for taxable income purposes than for E&P purposes. Further, amounts expensed under §179 (first-year expensing) must be amortized over five years for E&P purposes.

For any given year, adjustments in this category may increase or decrease current E&P because these adjustments are timing differences that reverse over time.

Example 18-3

This year, SCR reported taxable income of $10,000 and paid federal income tax of $2,100. SCR reported the following items of income and expense:

- $50,000 of depreciation, including bonus depreciation.
- $700 dividends-received deduction.
- $3,000 net operating loss carryover.
- $5,000 of tax-exempt interest.
- $6,000 of entertainment expense.
- $4,000 net capital loss from the current year.

For E&P purposes, depreciation computed under the alternative depreciation system is $30,000.

What is SCR's current E&P?

Answer: $26,600, computed as follows:

Taxable income	$ 10,000
Add:	
Tax-exempt interest income	5,000
Dividends-received deduction	700
NOL carryover	3,000
Excess of income tax depreciation over E&P depreciation	20,000
Subtract:	
Federal income taxes	(2,100)
Entertainment expense	(6,000)
Net capital loss for the current year	(4,000)
Current E&P	**$26,600**

What if: Assume that for taxable income purposes, SCR also reported a tax-deferred gain of $100,000 as the result of a §1031 (like-kind) exchange and deferred $75,000 of gain from an installment sale during the year. What is SCR's current E&P under these circumstances?

Answer: Current E&P would equal $101,600 ($26,600 + $75,000). Deferred gains from §1031 exchanges are not included in the computation of current E&P, but realized gain from current-year installment sales is included in current E&P. In future years, SCR would compute current E&P by reducing taxable income by any gain included in taxable income from the prior-year installment sale.

What if: Assume the original facts except that SCR also reported a $50,000 net capital loss for the current year (rather than a $4,000 loss). What is SCR's current E&P under these circumstances?

Answer: Current E&P would be a negative $19,400 ($26,600 + $4,000 − $50,000). E&P can be negative, but E&P cannot be driven below zero by distributions.

[7] §168(g)(2).

Exhibit 18-1 provides a summary of common adjustments to taxable income to compute current E&P. The IRC does not impose a statute of limitations on the computation of E&P. Hence, many corporations (public and private) may mistakenly fail to compute E&P until after years of operations. This delay makes the computation difficult because the annual adjustments necessary to derive the current E&P from taxable income may not have been well documented and because it is necessary to derive the current E&P for each year to calculate accumulated E&P.

EXHIBIT 18-1 Template for Computing Current Earnings and Profits

Taxable Income (Net Operating Loss)

Add: **Exclusions from Taxable Income**

- Tax-exempt bond interest income.
- Life insurance proceeds.
- Federal tax refunds (if a cash-method taxpayer).
- Increase in cash surrender value of corporate-owned life insurance policy.

Add: **Deductions Allowed for Tax Purposes but Not for E&P**

- Dividends-received deduction.
- NOL deduction.
- Net capital loss carryforwards.
- Contribution carryforwards.
- Organizational expenditures.

Subtract: **Deductions Allowed for E&P Purposes but Not for Tax Purposes**

- Federal income taxes paid or accrued.
- Expenses of earning tax-exempt income.
- Current-year charitable contributions in excess of the taxable income limitation.
- Nondeductible premiums on life insurance policies.
- Current-year net capital loss.
- Penalties and fines.
- Nondeductible portion of meal expense.
- Entertainment expenses.
- Disallowed lobbying expenses, dues, and political contributions.
- Decrease in cash surrender value of corporate-owned life insurance policy.
- Disallowed business interest expense.

Add or Subtract: **Timing Differences Due to Separate Accounting Methods for Taxable Income and E&P**

- Installment method. Add deferred gain under installment method in year of sale and subtract recognized gain in subsequent years.
- Depreciation. Compare taxable income depreciation to E&P depreciation (other than §179 expense) under regular tax rules to E&P depreciation (bonus depreciation is not allowed). Add back difference if taxable income depreciation exceeds E&P depreciation. Subtract difference if E&P depreciation exceeds taxable income depreciation for the year.
- §179 expense. Immediately deductible for taxable income purposes. Deductible over five years for E&P purposes. Add back in year of §179 expense but subtract in subsequent years.
- Inventory. If LIFO is used for tax purposes, FIFO must be used for E&P calculations.
- Gain or loss on sale of depreciable assets. Subtract greater taxable gain (lesser taxable loss) due to lower asset basis for taxable income purposes than for E&P purposes. This is a reversal of the depreciation deduction adjustment.
- Long-term contracts. Percentage completion method is required for E&P. Compare the income recognized under both methods. Add back if more income is recognized under the completed contract method; subtract if more income is recognized under the percentage completion method.
- Depletion. Must use the cost depletion method for E&P purposes. If using percentage depletion for taxable income, add back the difference if percentage depletion exceeds cost depletion for the year. Otherwise, subtract the excess of cost depletion over percentage depletion for the year.

Equals: **Current Earnings and Profits**

Ordering of E&P Distributions

Corporations must refer to both current and accumulated E&P accounts in determining the amount of distributions that are deemed to be dividends. Distributions are designated as dividends in the following order:

1. Distributions are dividends up to the balance of current E&P.
2. Distributions in excess of current E&P are dividends up to the balance in accumulated E&P.

Under these ordering rules, whether a distribution is characterized as a dividend depends on whether the balances in these two accounts are positive or negative. As a result, there are only four possible scenarios:

1. Positive current E&P, positive accumulated E&P.
2. Positive current E&P, negative accumulated E&P.
3. Negative current E&P, positive accumulated E&P.
4. Negative current E&P, negative accumulated E&P.

Positive Current E&P and Positive Accumulated E&P Corporate distributions are deemed to be paid out of current E&P first. If distributions exceed current E&P, the amount distributed from current E&P is allocated pro rata to all the distributions made during the year. The amount of distributions in excess of current E&P come from accumulated E&P and distributions are allocated to the accumulated E&P in the chronological order in which the distributions were made.[8] This ordering of distributions is particularly important when distributions exceed current E&P and either the identity of the shareholders receiving the distributions changes or a shareholder's percentage ownership changes during the year. Because current E&P is calculated at year-end, it can be difficult to determine the dividend status of a distribution at the time of the distribution.

Example 18-4

What if: Assume SCR reported current E&P of $40,000 and the balance in accumulated E&P was $16,000. On December 31, SCR distributed $48,000 to Jim and $16,000 to Ginny. What amount of dividend income do Jim and Ginny report, and what is accumulated E&P for SCR at the beginning of next year?

Answer: Jim and Ginny report $42,000 and $14,000 of dividend income, respectively. The distribution is first deemed to be paid from current E&P to each shareholder in proportion to their ownership interest on the date of the distribution: $30,000 to Jim ($40,000 × 75%) and $10,000 to Ginny ($40,000 × 25%). The $24,000 distribution in excess of current E&P ($64,000 – $40,000) is then deemed to be paid from accumulated E&P ($16,000) in proportion to ownership interests ($12,000 to Jim and $4,000 to Ginny). The remaining distribution of $8,000 ($64,000 total minus $40,000 current E&P and $16,000 accumulated E&P) is a return of capital. Hence, Jim will reduce his stock basis by $6,000 and Ginny will reduce her stock basis by $2,000.

SCR has a zero balance in accumulated E&P at the beginning of the next year because all current and accumulated E&P was distributed during the current year.

What if: Assume that SCR's current E&P is $40,000 and its accumulated E&P is $15,000. Also, assume that Jim is the sole shareholder of SCR and that he received a $45,000 distribution on June 1. Assume that after the June distribution Jim sold all his SCR shares to Ginny for $12,000. Ginny received a $15,000 distribution on December 31. What are the amount and the character of each distribution?

Answer: Jim has a $45,000 dividend, and Ginny has a $10,000 dividend with a $5,000 return of capital. The $40,000 of current E&P is allocated between the two distributions in proportion to total distributions. Hence, $30,000 ($40,000 × $45,000/$60,000) is allocated to the first distribution and $10,000 ($40,000 × $15,000/$60,000) is allocated to the second distribution. After current E&P is exhausted, accumulated E&P is then allocated in chronological order. Thus, because Jim's distribution took place before Ginny's distribution, Jim's distribution ($15,000) is allocated to accumulated E&P, leaving $0 in remaining accumulated E&P to be allocated to Ginny's distribution. Because Ginny is allocated only $10,000 of E&P, the excess distribution of $5,000 ($15,000 – $10,000) is treated as a nontaxable reduction of her basis in the SCR stock. Ginny's basis is reduced to $2,000 ($12,000 – $10,000). Refer to Exhibit 18-2 to see how this fact pattern would be presented on a Form 5452.

[8] Reg. §1.316-2(b); Rev. Rul. 74-164.

EXHIBIT 18-2 Corporate Report of Nondividend Distributions

Form **5452**
(Rev. October 2018)
Department of the Treasury
Internal Revenue Service

Corporate Report of Nondividend Distributions

▶ For calendar year ending December 31, ______
▶ Attach to the corporation's income tax return.
▶ Go to *www.irs.gov/Form5452* for instructions and the latest information.

OMB No. 1545-0123

Name: **SCR CORPORATION**
Employer identification number: **00-0000000**

A Has the corporation filed a Form 5452 for a prior calendar year? ▶ ☐ Yes ☑ No
If "Yes," enter the applicable year(s) ______

B Are any of the distributions part of a partial or complete liquidation? ▶ ☐ Yes ☑ No
If "Yes," attach explanation.

C Are any of the distributions from an S corporation's accumulated adjustments account? ▶ ☐ Yes ☑ No
If "Yes," enter the balance at the beginning of the tax year ______

D Earnings and Profits (See **Supporting Information** in instructions.)

- Accumulated earnings and profits (since February 28, 1913) at the beginning of the tax year ▶ $ **15,000**
- Actual earnings and profits for the current tax year ▶ $ **40,000**

E Shareholders at Date of Last Dividend Payment

- Number of individuals **1**
- Number of partnerships ______
- Number of corporations and other shareholders **1**

F Corporate Distributions (see instructions)

Date Paid	Total Amount Paid (Common (C), Preferred (P), Other (O))	Amount Per Share	Amount Paid During Calendar Year From Earnings & Profits Since February 28, 1913 — From the Current Year	Accumulated	Total	Percentage Taxable	Amount Paid During Calendar Year From Other Than Earnings & Profits Since February 28, 1913	Percentage Nontaxable
JUNE 1	$ 45,000 (C)	$ 1	$ 30,000	$ 15,000	$ 45,000	100 %	$	%
DEC 31	15,000 (C)	1	10,000		10,000	67	5,000	33
Totals	$ 60,000 (C)		$ 40,000	$ 15,000	$ 55,000		$ 5,000	

For Paperwork Reduction Act Notice, see the instructions. Cat. No. 11881T Form **5452** (Rev. 10-2018)

Source: irs.gov.

Positive Current E&P and Negative Accumulated E&P In this scenario, distributions deemed paid out of current E&P are taxable as dividends. Because accumulated E&P has a negative balance, distributions in excess of current E&P will be treated as a return of capital. If the nondividend distribution exceeds the stock basis, the excess is then treated as a capital gain.

Example 18-5

What if: Assume SCR reported current E&P of $60,000, but the balance in accumulated E&P is negative $20,000. On December 31, SCR distributed $48,000 to Jim and $16,000 to Ginny. Jim has a tax basis in his SCR stock of $24,000. Ginny's tax basis in her SCR stock is $10,000. What amount of income will Jim and Ginny report?

Answer: Jim and Ginny will report $45,000 and $15,000 of dividend income, respectively. The distribution is first deemed to be paid from current E&P ($45,000 to Jim and $15,000 to Ginny). No additional amount is treated as a dividend because current E&P has been exhausted and SCR has negative accumulated E&P.

What tax basis will Jim and Ginny have in their SCR stock after the distribution?

Answer: The distribution in excess of current E&P ($3,000 to Jim, $1,000 to Ginny) would be treated as a return of capital. Neither will recognize any gain because they both have sufficient tax basis in their SCR stock. Jim's tax basis in his SCR stock after the distribution would be $21,000 ($24,000 – $3,000), and Ginny's tax basis in her SCR stock after the distribution would be $9,000 ($10,000 – $1,000).

What is SCR's balance in accumulated E&P at the end of the year/beginning of next year.?

Answer: SCR has a $20,000 deficit (negative) balance in accumulated E&P at the end of the current year/beginning of the next year.

Negative Current E&P and Positive Accumulated E&P When current E&P is negative, the tax status of a distribution is determined by the available accumulated E&P on the *date* of the distribution. The available accumulated E&P is computed by allocating the negative current E&P up to the distribution date (but not including the distribution date) and then subtracting the allocated amount from accumulated E&P. The deficit in current earnings and profits can be prorated throughout the year using months or days, or the allocation can be made by closing the books and specifically identifying when the current earnings and profits was incurred. Distributions in excess of available E&P in this scenario are treated as return of capital, and any nondividend distribution in excess of stock basis is treated as a capital gain.

Example 18-6

What if: Assume SCR reported current E&P deficit (negative) of $20,000. However, the balance in accumulated E&P at the beginning of the year was $60,000. On July 1, SCR distributed $48,000 to Jim and $16,000 to Ginny. Jim has a tax basis in his SCR stock of $24,000. Ginny's tax basis in her SCR stock is $10,000. What amount of dividend income do Jim and Ginny report?

Answer: Jim and Ginny report $37,500 and $12,500 of dividend income, respectively. Because current E&P is negative, SCR must determine its available E&P on the distribution date. SCR prorates the full-year negative current E&P to June 30 [6 months/12 months × ($20,000) = ($10,000)]. The negative current E&P of $10,000 is subtracted from the balance in accumulated E&P on the date prior to the distribution ($60,000) to compute the available accumulated E&P as of the end of the day June 30 ($50,000). Because their distributions were made at the same time, Jim is allocated 75 percent of the total E&P (75% × $50,000 = $37,500) and Ginny is allocated the remaining 25 percent (25% × $50,000 = $12,500).

What tax basis do Jim and Ginny have in their SCR stock after the distribution?

Answer: $13,500 for Jim and $6,500 for Ginny. The amount in excess of available E&P ($10,500 to Jim, $3,500 to Ginny) is treated as a return of capital. Jim reduces the basis in his SCR stock to $13,500 ($24,000 – $10,500). Ginny reduces the basis in her SCR stock to $6,500 ($10,000 – $3,500).

What is SCR's balance in accumulated E&P at the end of the year?

Answer: Negative $10,000. Note that the distribution in excess of available E&P does not reduce E&P because it would generate a deficit in E&P. Only a loss can produce a deficit in E&P, as follows:

Accumulated E&P beginning balance	$ 60,000
Prorated negative current E&P, 1/1–6/30	(10,000)
Dividend distribution (July 1)	(50,000)
Prorated negative current E&P, 7/1–12/31	(10,000)
Accumulated E&P ending balance (deficit)	**$(10,000)**

Negative Current E&P and Negative Accumulated E&P When current E&P and accumulated E&P are both negative, none of the distribution is treated as a dividend. Distributions will be return of capital to extent of stock basis. Any distribution in excess of stock basis is treated as a capital gain.

Example 18-7

What if: Assume SCR reported current E&P of negative $50,000. The balance in accumulated E&P at the beginning of the year was negative $60,000. Jim has a tax basis in his SCR stock of $24,000. Ginny's tax basis in her SCR stock is $10,000. On December 31 of this year, SCR distributed $48,000 to Jim and $16,000 to Ginny. What amount of dividend income do Jim and Ginny report this year?

Answer: Neither Jim nor Ginny recognizes any dividend income from this distribution. Because current E&P and accumulated E&P are negative, the entire distribution would be treated as a return of capital/capital gain.

Will Jim or Ginny recognize any capital gain as a result of the distribution, and what is the tax basis in the SCR stock for Jim and Ginny at year-end?

Answer: Jim has a capital gain of $24,000, the amount by which the distribution exceeds the tax basis in his SCR stock ($48,000 – $24,000). Ginny has a capital gain of $6,000, the amount by which the distribution exceeds the tax basis in her SCR stock ($16,000 – $10,000). Both Jim and Ginny have a zero basis in their SCR stock at year-end.

What is SCR's balance in accumulated E&P at the end of the year?

Answer: A deficit (negative) balance of $110,000, the sum of the accumulated E&P deficit of $60,000 plus the negative current E&P of $50,000.

Exhibit 18-3 summarizes the rules for determining whether a distribution represents dividend income. When both balances are positive, the distribution is treated as a dividend to the extent of current E&P at year-end and then to the extent of the balance of accumulated E&P. A distribution in excess of current and accumulated E&P is treated as a return of capital/capital gain. When current E&P is negative and accumulated E&P is positive, distributions are dividend income to the extent of accumulated E&P after netting against the deficit in current E&P (up to the date of the distribution). The distribution reduces accumulated E&P but not below zero. When accumulated E&P is negative and current E&P is positive, distributions are dividend income to the extent of current E&P. Finally, when both balances are negative, the distribution is treated as a return of capital/capital gain and the deficits in E&P are unaffected.

EXHIBIT 18-3 Summary of E&P Status and Taxability of Cash Distributions

	Balance in Accumulated E&P at the Time of the Distribution	
Balance in Current E&P at the Time of the Distribution	**Negative**	**Positive**
Negative	Distributions are a return of capital/ capital gain.	Distributions are dividend income to the extent of current E&P and the balance of accumulated E&P.[9]
Positive	Distributions are dividend income to the extent of current E&P.	Distributions are dividend income to the extent of accumulated E&P after netting against deficit in current E&P incurred up to the date of the distribution.

[9]When there are multiple distributions, current E&P is allocated to each distribution based on relative FMVs and AE&P is allocated chronologically.

THE KEY FACTS

Dividend Distributions

The amount of a distribution equals:

- Cash distributed.
- Increased by fair market value of noncash property distributed.
- Reduced by any liabilities assumed by the shareholder on property received.
- The amount distributed is a dividend to the extent of available E&P (see Exhibit 18-3).

Distributions of Noncash Property to Shareholders

On occasion, a shareholder will receive a distribution of property other than cash. The dividend sourcing rules, described in Exhibit 18-3, apply to both cash and noncash distributions. However, noncash distributions can be more complex for two reasons. First, any liability attached to the property affects the amount distributed, and second, any difference between the value and the tax basis of the property affects the calculation of E&P. In addition, noncash distributions can have income tax consequences to the distributing corporation. To begin, when noncash property is received, the shareholder determines the amount distributed as follows:

	Money received
+	Fair market value of other property received
−	Liabilities assumed by the shareholder on property received
	Amount distributed[10]

Example 18-8

What if: Assume that rather than distributing $16,000 of cash to Ginny, SCR distributes $15,000 in cash and a Fuji custom touring bike that has a fair market value of $1,000. Suppose that SCR has current E&P of $100,000 (including the impact of the distribution on current E&P) and no accumulated E&P. What amount of dividend income will Ginny report this year?

Answer: $16,000. Ginny would include the $15,000 plus the $1,000 fair market value of the bicycle in her gross income as a dividend.

As a general rule, a shareholder's tax basis in noncash property received as a dividend equals the property's fair market value.[11] Although liabilities affect the amount of the distribution, liabilities do not affect the new basis of the distributed property. In other words, the basis of the property received consists of the taxable distribution plus the liabilities assumed by the shareholder. The fair market value is determined as of the date of the distribution.

Example 18-9

What is Ginny's tax basis in the bicycle she received as a dividend in the previous example?

Answer: $1,000. Ginny has a tax basis in the bicycle of $1,000, the bicycle's fair market value.

Example 18-10

What if: Assume that, instead of distributing $48,000 in cash to Jim, SCR distributes a parcel of land that SCR previously purchased for $60,000. The land has a fair market value of $60,000 and a mortgage of $12,000 attached to it. Jim assumes the mortgage on the land. Suppose that SCR has current E&P of $100,000 and no accumulated E&P. How much dividend income does Jim recognize on the distribution?

Answer: $48,000. Jim recognizes dividend income in an amount equal to the land's fair market value of $60,000, less the mortgage he assumes on the land in the amount of $12,000.

What is Jim's tax basis in the land he receives?

Answer: $60,000. Jim receives a tax basis equal to the land's fair market value. Jim has a $60,000 basis in the land because he recognized $48,000 of income and assumed $12,000 of debt.

[10] §301(b).

[11] §301(d).

Effect of Noncash Property Distributions on Taxable Income When a corporation distributes noncash property to shareholders, the corporation recognizes a taxable gain on the distribution to the extent that the fair market value of the property distributed exceeds the corporation's adjusted tax basis in the property.[12] In contrast, if the fair market value of the property distributed is less than the corporation's adjusted tax basis in the property, the corporation does not recognize a deductible loss for computing taxable income.

Example 18-11

What if: Assume SCR has an adjusted tax basis of $650 in the Fuji custom touring bike (for both income tax and E&P purposes) that it distributes to Ginny (see the facts in Example 18-8). How much taxable gain, if any, does SCR recognize when it distributes the bicycle to Ginny? Recall the FMV of the bicycle is $1,000.

Answer: $350. SCR recognizes a taxable gain of $350 on the distribution of the bicycle to Ginny ($1,000 – $650). Because the bike is considered inventory, SCR would characterize the gain as ordinary income.

What if: Assume SCR has an adjusted tax basis of $1,200 in the Fuji custom touring bike that it distributes to Ginny. The bicycle's fair market value has declined to $1,000 because it is an outdated model. How much loss, if any, does SCR recognize when it distributes the bicycle to Ginny?

Answer: $0. SCR is not permitted to recognize a loss on the distribution of the bicycle to Ginny.

What if: Suppose SCR *sells* the bicycle to Ginny for $1,000. How much loss, if any, can SCR recognize if it sells the bicycle to Ginny?

Answer: $200. SCR is permitted to recognize a loss on the sale of property to a shareholder provided it does not run afoul of the related-person loss rules found in §267. To be a related person, Ginny must own *more than* 50 percent of SCR, which she does not in this scenario.

Liabilities The amount of any liability assumed by the shareholder can also affect the recognized gain. When a liability assumed by the shareholder is greater than the distributed property's fair market value, the property's fair market value is deemed to be the amount of the liability assumed by the shareholder.[13] If the liability assumed is less than the property's fair market value, the gain recognized on the distribution is still the excess of the property's fair market value over its tax basis (i.e., the liability is ignored by the distributing corporation).

Example 18-12

What if: Assume SCR distributes a parcel of land to Jim that SCR had purchased previously purchased for possible expansion. The land has a fair market value of $60,000 and a remaining mortgage of $12,000 attached to it. SCR has a tax basis in the land of $20,000, and Jim assumes the mortgage on the land. How much gain, if any, does SCR recognize when it distributes the land to Jim?

Answer: $40,000 ($60,000 – $20,000). Because the mortgage assumed by Jim is less than the land's fair market value, SCR recognizes gain in an amount equal to the excess of the land's fair market value over its tax basis.

What if: Assume the mortgage assumed by Jim is $75,000 instead of $12,000. The land has a fair market value of $60,000, and SCR has a tax basis in the land of $20,000. Jim will assume the mortgage on the land. How much gain, if any, does SCR recognize when it distributes the land to Jim?

Answer: $55,000 ($75,000 – $20,000). Because the mortgage assumed by Jim exceeds the land's fair market value, SCR treats the land's fair market value as $75,000 and recognizes gain in an amount equal to the excess of the mortgage assumed over its tax basis. Because the mortgage exceeds the value of the property, Jim is treated as receiving a distribution of $0 and will take a basis in the land of $75,000.

[12]§311.

[13]§311(b)(2) refers to §336(b).

THE KEY FACTS

Effect of Distributions on E&P

E&P is reduced by distributions as follows:

- Cash distributed.
- E&P adjusted tax basis of noncash *depreciated* property (fair market value less than or equal to its E&P adjusted tax basis).
- Fair market value of noncash *appreciated* property.
- Noncash property distributions are reduced by any liabilities assumed by the shareholder on property received.
- E&P reductions for distributions cannot cause E&P to drop below zero.

Effect of Noncash Property Distributions on E&P As we discuss below, noncash property distributions to shareholders can affect a corporation's current E&P and accumulated E&P.

Current E&P. Noncash property distributions can affect current E&P in two ways. First, current E&P is reduced by the income taxes paid (or payable) on the taxable gain (fair market value of property distributed in excess of the property's adjusted tax basis). Second, current E&P is increased to the extent the fair market value of the property distributed exceeds the E&P basis of the property. For most types of property, the corporation's E&P basis is the same as the corporation's taxable income basis, so the taxable gain on the distribution is equal to the current E&P gain on the distribution. However for certain types of property (e.g., inventory and depreciable assets), a corporation's income tax basis for the property is different from the E&P basis of the property (e.g., inventory may have a LIFO basis for taxable income purposes but must have a FIFO basis for E&P purposes and the adjusted basis of certain depreciable assets may differ for taxable income and E&P purposes because the accumulated depreciation for income tax is different from accumulated depreciation for E&P purposes). In these situations, the taxable gain will be different from the current E&P gain. When a corporation distributes property with a fair market value that is lower than the E&P basis of the property, the corporation does not deduct the loss in determining current E&P.

Accumulated E&P. To reflect the fact that a distribution reduces a corporation's economic resources to pay dividends in future years, a corporation reduces its accumulated E&P at the end of the current year. The amount of the reduction depends on whether the distributed property was appreciated or depreciated for E&P purposes. When a corporation distributes *appreciated* property (fair market value in excess of E&P adjusted tax basis), the distribution reduces accumulated E&P at year-end by the fair market value of the property distributed. However, when a corporation distributes *depreciated* property (E&P adjusted tax basis in excess of fair market value of the property), the distribution reduces accumulated E&P at the end of the year by the E&P adjusted tax basis of the property. When the distributed property is subject to a liability, the amount of the liability assumed by the shareholder(s) increases accumulated E&P essentially netting the liability against the distribution of the property. Recall, however, distributions cannot cause accumulated E&P to drop below zero and cannot increase a negative balance in E&P.

Example 18-13

What if: Assume the same facts as in Example 18-12. SCR distributed land to Jim that has a fair market value of $60,000 and a remaining mortgage of $12,000 attached to it. SCR has an income tax and E&P adjusted tax basis in the land of $20,000. Jim has assumed the mortgage on the land. SCR has current E&P of $100,000, which includes the net gain of $31,600 from distribution of the land ($40,000 gain less a related tax liability of $8,400) and accumulated E&P at the beginning of the year of $500,000. What is SCR's balance in accumulated E&P at the end of this year (i.e., the beginning of next year) as a result of the distribution of the land to Jim?

Answer: $552,000, computed as follows:

Accumulated E&P, beginning of this year	$ 500,000
Current E&P	100,000
Fair market value of land distributed	(60,000)
Liability assumed by Jim	12,000
Balance of accumulated E&P, at year-end (beginning of next year)	**$552,000**

[14]§312(a), (b).

What if: Assume SCR has current E&P of $40,000, which includes the net gain of $31,600 from the land distribution ($40,000 gain less a related tax liability of $8,400) and accumulated E&P of $500,000. What is SCR's beginning balance in accumulated E&P at the end of this year (i.e., the beginning of next year) as a result of the distribution of the land to Jim?

Answer: $492,000, computed as follows:

Accumulated E&P, beginning of this year	$ 500,000
Current E&P	40,000
Fair market value of land distributed	(60,000)
Liability assumed by Jim	12,000
Beginning balance, accumulated E&P, next year	**$492,000**

What if: Assume the land distributed to Jim has a tax and E&P basis to SCR of $75,000 instead of $20,000. SCR has current E&P of $100,000 ($15,000 loss on the distribution is not allowed in computing current E&P). SCR has accumulated E&P at the beginning of the year of $500,000. What is SCR's beginning balance in accumulated E&P at the beginning of next year after taking the distribution of the land into account?

Answer: $537,000, computed as follows:

Accumulated E&P, beginning of this year	$ 500,000
Current E&P	100,000
E&P basis of land distributed	(75,000)
Liability assumed by Jim	12,000
Balance of accumulated E&P at year-end (beginning of next year)	**$537,000**

TAXES IN THE REAL WORLD Tax Planning for Distributions

Visteon Corporation is a global technology company that designs, engineers, and manufactures innovative cockpit electronics and connected car solutions for the world's major vehicle manufacturers. During 2008 and 2009, weakened economic conditions triggered a global economic recession that severely impacted the automotive sector. Visteon filed voluntary petitions for reorganization relief in 2009, but the company has been profitable since it emerged from bankruptcy in 2010.

Visteon had two technology-focused core businesses: vehicle cockpit electronics and thermal energy management. The company's vehicle cockpit electronics product line includes audio systems, infotainment systems, driver information systems, and electronic control modules. In order to focus its operations on automotive cockpit electronics, Visteon sold a subsidiary at a pretax gain of approximately $2.3 billion. The sale was completed on June 9, 2015, and Visteon's net cash proceeds from the sale were approximately $2.7 billion. Visteon then announced a plan to return $2.5 billion–$2.75 billion of cash to its shareholders through a series of actions including a special distribution. Ultimately, Visteon actually distributed approximately $1.75 billion on January 22, 2016.

Is there a tax reason why Visteon might have delayed the distribution from 2015 until 2016?

One possibility is that Visteon had a large deficit in its accumulated E&P at the beginning of 2015 from prior losses. However, the gain on the sale of the subsidiary created significant 2015 current E&P. Recall that distributions are dividends to the extent of current E&P even when there is a deficit in accumulated E&P. If true, then Visteon's special distribution in 2015 would have been characterized entirely as a dividend to its shareholders. However, by waiting until 2016 to make the distribution, it is possible that a significant portion of the distribution was treated as a nontaxable return of capital to shareholders instead of a taxable dividend. This is because Visteon's available E&P (beginning-of-year accumulated E&P plus current E&P) was significantly less than the distribution amount.

Sources: Visteon Corporation 2014 and 2015 Forms 10-K and annual reports.

LO 18-3

STOCK DISTRIBUTIONS

Rather than distribute cash to its shareholders, a corporation may instead distribute additional shares of its own stock (or rights to acquire additional shares) to shareholders. A publicly held corporation is likely to distribute additional shares of stock to promote shareholder goodwill (it allows the corporation to retain cash and still provide shareholders with tangible evidence of their interest in corporate earnings) or to reduce the market price of its outstanding shares (the stock distribution reduces the price of shares by increasing their number, making the stock more accessible to a wider range of shareholders). For example, a 5 percent stock distribution will increase the number of shares outstanding by 5 percent. Hence, a shareholder holding 100 shares will own 105 shares after a 5 percent stock distribution. Corporations may also declare a **stock split,** in which the number of shares outstanding is increased by the ratio of the split. For example, a 2-for-1 stock split would double the number of shares outstanding. Hence, a shareholder holding 100 shares will own 200 shares after a 2-for-1 stock split. Stock splits are sometimes used by public corporations to keep stock prices accessible to a diverse group of investors.

Tax Consequences to Shareholders Receiving a Stock Distribution

Nontaxable Stock Distributions In theory, stock splits and pro rata stock distributions do not provide shareholders with any increase in value. This is because these distributions do not change a shareholder's interest in the corporation except that the shareholder now owns more pieces of paper (shares of stock). As a result, these distributions are generally not included in the shareholders' gross income.[15]

In a nontaxable stock distribution, each shareholder allocates a portion of their tax basis from the stock on which the distribution was issued to the newly issued stock based on the relative fair market value (FMV) of the stock.[16] In the case of a simple distribution of common stock or a stock split where the stock distributed is identical to the stock from which the distribution is made (same class and same fair market value), the new per-share tax basis is the original tax basis divided by the total number of shares held (including the new shares).

For example, assume a shareholder owns 100 shares of Acme Corporation stock, for which they paid $3,000. Acme declares a 100 percent stock distribution and sends the shareholder an additional 100 shares of stock. The shareholder will now own 200 shares of stock with the same tax basis of $3,000. The basis of each share of stock decreases from its original $30 per share ($3,000/100) to $15 per share ($3,000/200). The holding period of the new stock includes the holding period for which the shareholder held the old stock.[17]

Example 18-14

Jim has a tax basis in his SCR stock of $24,000. Ginny's tax basis in her SCR stock is $10,000. Jim owns 75 of the 100 shares of outstanding SCR stock, while Ginny owns the remaining 25 shares.

What if: Assume that SCR declares a 100 percent stock distribution. As a result, Jim will own 150 shares of SCR stock and Ginny will own the remaining 50 shares.

Is the stock distribution taxable to Jim and Ginny?

Answer: No. The stock distribution to Jim and Ginny is nontaxable because it is made pro rata to the shareholders (that is, the distribution did not change their proportional ownership of SCR).

[15] §305(a). To be nontaxable, a stock distribution must meet two conditions: (1) It must be made with respect to the corporation's common stock and (2) it must be pro rata with respect to all shareholders (i.e., the shareholders' relative equity positions do not change as a result of the distribution).

[16] §307.

[17] §1223(4).

What is the tax basis of each share of SCR stock now held by Jim and Ginny?

Answer: Jim's original tax basis of $24,000 is divided among 150 shares. Hence, each one of Jim's shares has a basis of $160. Ginny's original tax basis of $10,000 is divided among 50 shares. Hence, each one of Ginny's shares has a basis of $200.

THE KEY FACTS

Tax Consequences of Stock Distributions

- Pro rata stock distributions generally are nontaxable.
- Shareholders allocate basis from the pre-distribution shares of stock to the recently acquired shares of stock based on relative fair market value.
- Non–pro rata (disproportionate) stock distributions are treated as a property distribution that is taxed as a dividend up to the corporation's E&P.

Taxable Stock Distributions Non–pro rata (i.e., disproportionate) stock distributions generally are treated as a property distribution and characterized as dividends to the extent of the distributing corporation's E&P.[18] This makes sense because the recipient has now received something of value: an increase in the shareholder's claim on the corporation's income and assets. For example, a corporation may give its shareholders the choice between a cash or a stock distribution. In this case, shareholders who elect to receive stock in lieu of money will be treated as having received a property distribution equal to the fair market value of the stock received, and the shareholder will have a tax basis in the new stock equal to its fair market value.

Example 18-15

What if: Assume that SCR declares a 10 percent stock distribution but offers Jim and Ginny the choice between more stock or $100 per share in cash. Is the distribution taxable to Jim if he elects to receive 15 shares of stock worth $1,600? If Jim has received a taxable distribution, what is the character of the income?

Answer: Yes, Jim is taxed on $1,600, the fair value of the stock, because the distribution has the potential to change the proportionate ownership interests in SCR. If Jim elected the cash, he would be taxed on the cash distribution of $1,500. If Jim elected the stock, the distribution would be a property distribution treated as a dividend to the extent of SCR's earnings and profits.

STOCK REDEMPTIONS

LO 18-4

(continued from page 18-1. . .)

In the original storyline, Jim and Ginny raised some of the initial capital they needed to start SCR by borrowing $50,000 from Jim's father, Walt. An alternate strategy would have been to issue 25 additional shares of SCR stock to Walt in return for $50,000. This change in facts would reduce Jim's ownership percentage in SCR to 60 percent (75 shares/125 shares). Ginny's ownership percentage would decrease to 20 percent (25 shares/125 shares). Walt would own the remaining 20 percent. We will assume this change in facts to continue the storyline.

Walt does not participate in the management of the company. In fact, he was hoping to cash out of SCR when it became profitable and use the money to put a down payment on a condominium in a retirement community near Orlando, Florida. With the SCR stock valued at $5,000 per share ($125,000 in total), Walt saw an opportunity to realize his retirement dream. Jim and Ginny saw it as a chance to own all SCR's stock, eliminating a potential source of discord should Jim's father disapprove of the way they are managing the company.

By the end of this year, SCR will have sufficient cash to buy back some or all of Walt's shares of SCR stock. Jim and Ginny were wondering about the potential tax consequences to SCR and Walt under various redemption plans. In particular, Jim and Ginny wanted to know whether there was a tax difference between (1) buying back 5 of Walt's shares this year and the remaining 20 shares equally over the next four years (at 5 shares per year) and (2) buying back all 25 shares this year using an installment note that would pay Walt 20 percent of the purchase price in each of the next five years plus interest. ■

[18]§305(b). A technical discussion of all the rules that apply to determining whether a stock distribution is taxable is beyond the scope of this text.

Publicly held corporations buy back (redeem) their stock from existing shareholders for many and varied reasons. For example, a corporation may have excess cash and limited investment opportunities, or management may feel the stock is undervalued. Management may see a large redemption as a way to get shareholders or stock analysts to reconsider their valuation of the company or as a way to selectively buy out dissenting shareholders who have become disruptive. Reducing the number of outstanding shares also increases earnings per share (by reducing the number of shares in the denominator of the calculation) and potentially increases the stock's market price.[19]

Privately held corporations often use stock redemptions for other reasons, such as to shift ownership control from older to younger family members who do not have the resources to purchase shares directly or to buy out dissatisfied, disinterested, or deceased shareholders. In addition, redemptions of an ex-spouse's stock can provide liquidity in a divorce agreement and eliminate the individual from management or ownership in the company. Finally, redemptions can provide cash to satisfy estate taxes imposed on the estate of a deceased shareholder of the company.

The Form of a Stock Redemption

A stock redemption is an acquisition by a corporation of its stock from a shareholder in exchange for property. It is irrelevant whether the stock acquired by the corporation is cancelled, retired, or held as treasury stock.[20] The term *property* in this context has the same meaning as it does for distributions (i.e., cash and noncash property).

Stock redemptions take the form of an exchange in which the shareholders give up stock in the corporation for property, usually cash. If the form of the transaction is respected, shareholders compute gain or loss (capital gain or loss if the stock is held as an investment) by comparing the amount realized (money and the fair market value of other property received) with their tax basis in the stock exchanged.

Without any tax law restrictions, a sole shareholder of a corporation could circumvent the dividend rules by structuring distributions to have the form of an exchange (i.e., a stock redemption). For example, rather than have the corporation make a $100,000 dividend distribution, the shareholder could have the corporation buy back $100,000 of stock from the shareholder. If the shareholder had a tax basis of $60,000 in the stock redeemed, the amount of income reported on the shareholder's tax return would decrease from $100,000 (dividend) to $40,000 (capital gain). At present, both amounts would be taxed at the same preferential tax rate (20 percent is the highest capital gains tax rate), assuming the shareholder held the stock for more than a year. In contrast to a dividend, a capital gain can be offset with capital losses. Similar to a dividend, however, the sole shareholder would continue to own 100 percent of the corporation before and after the stock redemption.

Form is not always respected in a redemption, however. The tax law may determine (or the IRS may argue) that the transaction is, in substance, a distribution of earnings, the tax consequences of which should be determined under the dividend rules we discussed above.

The IRC provides both objective/mechanical tests (so-called **bright-line tests**) and subjective/judgmental tests to distinguish when a redemption should be treated as an exchange or a potential dividend.[21] The result is an intricate set of rules that the corporation and its shareholders must navigate carefully to ensure that the shareholders receive the tax treatment they desire. This is especially true in closely held family corporations, where the majority of stock is held by people related to each other through birth or marriage.

[19]It is also important to note that corporations are not taxed on gains or losses resulting from transactions in their own stock. §1032.

[20]§317(b).

[21]§302. The IRC also defines when sale treatment is appropriate in some special circumstances. For example, §303 defines when sale treatment is allowed for redemptions of stock to pay death taxes.

While individual shareholders prefer sale treatment, corporate shareholders generally have more incentive for dividend treatment. Dividends from domestic corporations are eligible for the dividends-received deduction (DRD) (usually 50 or 65 percent), whereas a capital gain is not eligible for the DRD. A corporation might prefer exchange treatment if the redemption results in a loss, if the corporation has capital loss carryovers, or if its stock tax basis as a percentage of the redemption price exceeds the DRD ratio.

Redemptions That Reduce a Shareholder's Ownership Interest

The IRC allows a shareholder to treat a redemption as an exchange if the transaction meets one of three change-in-ownership tests: the substantially disproportionate test, the complete termination test, or the not essentially equivalent to a dividend test.[22] These ownership tests consider the effect of each redemption from the shareholder's perspective.

Redemptions That Are Substantially Disproportionate The IRC states in §302(b)(2) that a redemption will be treated as an exchange if the redemption is "substantially disproportionate with respect to the shareholder." A shareholder meets this requirement by satisfying the three objective ("bright-line") *stock ownership tests:*

1. Immediately after the exchange, the shareholder owns less than 50 percent of the total combined voting power of all classes of stock entitled to vote.
2. The shareholder's percentage ownership of voting stock after the redemption is less than 80 percent of their percentage ownership before the redemption.
3. The shareholder's percentage ownership of the aggregate fair market value of the corporation's common stock (voting and nonvoting) after the redemption is less than 80 percent of their percentage ownership before the redemption.[23]

For example, suppose a shareholder owns 60 percent of a corporation's stock prior to a redemption. To satisfy the 80 percent test, this shareholder must own less than 48 percent of the outstanding stock after a redemption (60% × 80% = 48%). Note that in this instance the redemption would also satisfy the 50 percent test (48 percent is less than 50 percent). Note also, that a redemption reduces that number of shares outstanding, and this must be taken into account in calculating the ownership tests. In contrast, suppose the same shareholder owns 70 percent before a redemption. In this case, a redemption that satisfies the 80 percent reduction test (70% × 80% = 56%) will not satisfy the 50 percent test.

The determination as to whether a shareholder meets both the 50 percent and 80 percent tests is made on a shareholder-by-shareholder basis. If multiple shareholders have shares redeemed, some shareholders can satisfy the test while others do not. If a shareholder owns multiple classes of common stock (voting and nonvoting), the less-than-80-percent of fair market value test is applied to the shareholder's aggregate ownership of the common stock rather than on a class-by-class basis.

Example 18-16

What if: Assume Walt is not related to either Jim or Ginny. This year, SCR redeemed five shares of Walt's stock in exchange for $25,000. Walt has a tax basis in the five shares of SCR stock of $10,000 ($2,000 per share). What is the tax treatment of the stock redemption to Walt under §302(b)(2)?

Answer: $25,000 dividend to the extent of SCR's E&P. Prior to the redemption, Walt owned 20 percent of SCR (25/125 shares). After the redemption, his ownership percentage in SCR dropped to 16.67 percent (20/120 shares). This redemption does not satisfy the substantially disproportionate

(continued on page 18-20)

[22]§302(b)(1), (2), (3), respectively.

[23]§302(b)(2).

test. After the redemption, Walt owns less than 50 percent of SCR stock, but his ownership percentage after the redemption (16.67 percent) does not fall below 80 percent of his ownership percentage prior to the redemption (80% × 20% = 16%). Walt will not be able to treat the redemption as an exchange under this change-in-ownership test. Unless he can satisfy one of the other change-in-ownership tests, Walt will have a $25,000 dividend, assuming SCR has sufficient E&P, rather than a $15,000 capital gain ($25,000 – $10,000).

How many shares of stock would SCR have to redeem from Walt to guarantee exchange treatment under the substantially disproportionate test?

Answer: For Walt to meet the 80 percent test, SCR must redeem six shares of stock. The computation is made as follows:

$$\frac{25 - x}{125 - x} < 16\%, \text{ where } x \text{ is the number of shares to be redeemed}$$

Using some algebra, we can compute x to be 5.95, rounded up to six shares.[24] If SCR redeems six shares from Walt, his ownership percentage after the redemption will be 15.97 percent (19/119 shares), which now meets the 80 percent test. The redemption of this one additional share transforms the transaction from a $30,000 dividend (6 shares × $5,000) to an $18,000 capital gain ($30,000 – $12,000).

In determining whether the 50 percent and 80 percent tests are met, an individual shareholder must take into account the **constructive ownership** or stock attribution rules found in §318. Under certain circumstances, the stock attribution rules require that stock owned by other persons (individuals and entities) that are related to the redeeming shareholder are considered to be constructively owned (we also refer to this as indirect ownership) by the redeeming shareholder for purposes of determining whether the shareholder has met the change-in-stock-ownership tests. The purpose of the attribution rules is to prevent shareholders from dispersing stock ownership to either family members who have similar economic interests or entities controlled by the shareholder to avoid having a stock redemption characterized as a dividend.

Family attribution. Individuals are treated as owning the shares of stock owned by their spouse, children, grandchildren, and parents. Stock owned constructively through the family attribution rule cannot be reattributed to another family member through the family attribution rule.

Example 18-17

Return to the amended storyline in which Walt is Jim's father and, in exchange for contributing $50,000, he received 25 shares of SCR stock and 20 percent ownership of the company. This year, SCR redeems 6 shares of stock from Walt in exchange for $30,000. Walt has a tax basis in the 6 shares of stock redeemed of $12,000 ($2,000 per share). What is the tax treatment of the stock redemption to Walt under §302(b)(2)?

Answer: $30,000 dividend to the extent of SCR's E&P.

Prior to the redemption, Walt owned 20 percent of SCR (25/125 shares) directly. Under the family attribution rules, Walt is treated as constructively owning the shares of SCR stock owned by Jim (75 shares). In applying the substantially disproportionate change-in-stock-ownership tests, Walt is treated as owning 100 shares of SCR stock (25 + 75), or 80 percent of the SCR stock (100/125 shares). After the redemption, Walt's ownership percentage in SCR drops to 79 percent (94/119 shares). This redemption does not satisfy the substantially disproportionate test because Walt is deemed to own more than 50 percent of the SCR stock after the redemption. As a result, Walt will have a $30,000 dividend, assuming SCR has sufficient E&P, rather than an $18,000 capital gain ($30,000 – $12,000).

[24]Multiplying both sides by $(125 - x)$, we get $25 - x = 20 - .16x$. Moving x to the right side of the equation and the integers to the left side of the equation, we get $5 = .84x$. Solving for x, we get $x = 5.95$.

An interesting question relates to what happens to the tax basis of stock redeemed that is not used in determining the shareholder's tax consequences. This occurs in a redemption treated as a dividend, where the tax basis of the stock redeemed is not subtracted from the amount received from the corporation. Under the current rules, the tax basis of the stock redeemed is added to the tax basis of any shares still held by the shareholder.

Example 18-18

In the preceding example, SCR redeemed six shares of stock from Walt for $30,000, and the transaction was treated as a dividend because of the application of the family attribution rules. Walt had a tax basis in the 6 shares of stock redeemed of $12,000 ($2,000 per share), but this tax basis was not used in determining their taxable income from the transaction.

What is Walt's tax basis in the remaining 19 shares of SCR stock?

Answer: $50,000. Walt adds the unused $12,000 tax basis in the 6 shares redeemed to the tax basis of the remaining 19 shares. The tax basis in these remaining shares increases to $50,000, the original tax basis of the 25 shares.

If the shareholder no longer holds any shares, the tax basis transfers to the stock held by those persons who caused the shareholder to have dividend treatment under the attribution rules.[25]

Attribution from entities to owners or beneficiaries. Owners or beneficiaries of entities can be deemed to own shares of stock owned by the entity itself. Under these rules, partners are deemed to own a pro rata share of their partnership's stock holdings (i.e., a partner who has a 10 percent interest in a partnership is deemed to own 10 percent of any stock owned by the partnership). Beneficiaries are deemed to own a pro rata share of the stock owned by the trust or estate of which they are a beneficiary. Shareholders are deemed to own a pro rata share of their corporation's stock holdings, but only if they own at least 50 percent of the value of the corporation's stock. Other attribution rules, such as family attribution, apply in determining if this 50 percent test is met.

Example 18-19

What if: Assume that Walt is not Jim's father, and besides the 25 shares of SCR that he owns directly, he is a 40 percent partner in a partnership that also owns 25 shares in SCR. The other 60 percent of the partnership is owned by his neighbors, Fred and Ethel, who are unrelated to Walt. How many shares of SCR is Walt treated as owning directly and indirectly through the partnership?

Answer: 35 shares. Walt owns 25 shares directly and another 10 shares indirectly. Walt is treated as indirectly owning a pro rata share of SCR stock owned by the partnership; in this example, 40 percent times 25 shares is 10 shares.

What if: Assume now that Walt is a 40 percent shareholder in Acme Corporation, which owns 25 shares in SCR. The other 60 percent of Acme shares is owned by his neighbors, Fred and Ethel, who are unrelated to Walt. How many shares of SCR is Walt treated as owning indirectly through Acme Corporation?

Answer: 0 shares. None of the shares owned by Acme Corporation are attributed to Walt under the constructive ownership rules because Walt does not own at least 50 percent of the stock of Acme Corporation. Stock owned by a corporation (Acme in this example) is attributed to a shareholder only if the shareholder owns at least 50 percent of the corporation's stock. In this case, Walt owns only 40 percent of Acme, and, therefore, SCR shares owned by Acme are not attributed to Walt.

What if: Assume now that Walt is a 60 percent shareholder in Acme Corporation, which owns 25 shares in SCR. The other 40 percent of Acme shares is owned by his neighbors, Fred and Ethel, who are unrelated to Walt. How many shares of SCR is Walt treated as owning indirectly through Acme Corporation?

Answer: 15 shares. Walt is treated as indirectly owning a pro rata share of SCR stock owned by Acme; in this example, 60 percent times 25 shares. A portion of Acme's stock in SCR is attributed to Walt because Walt owns at least 50 percent of the stock of Acme Corporation.

[25]Reg. §1.302-2.

Attribution from owners or beneficiaries to entities. Entities can be deemed to own other stock owned by their owners or beneficiaries. Under these rules, a partnership is deemed to own 100 percent of the shares owned by its partners. A trust or estate is deemed to own 100 percent of the shares owned by its beneficiaries. A corporation is deemed to own 100 percent of the shares owned by a shareholder who owns at least 50 percent of the value of the corporation's stock (direct plus indirect (constructive) ownership). Stock that is deemed owned by an entity cannot be reattributed to the other owners in the entity under the entity-to-owner rules previously discussed (this is known as *sideways attribution*).

Example 18-20

What if: Assume that Walt owns 25 shares of SCR and he is a 40 percent partner in a partnership. The other 60 percent of the partnership is owned by Walt's neighbors, Fred and Ethel, who are unrelated to Walt. How many shares of SCR is the partnership treated as owning indirectly through Walt?

Answer: 25 shares. Stock in a corporation (SCR) is attributed from an owner in an entity (Walt) to the entity (the partnership) in full. Under the owner-to-entity attribution rule, all of Walt's 25 shares would be attributed to the partnership as long as Walt had any ownership interest in the partnership.

What if: Assume the same facts as in the previous what-if example except that the partnership is now Acme Corporation. How many shares of SCR is Acme treated as owning indirectly through Walt?

Answer: 0 shares. Because the entity (Acme) is a corporation, the owner in the entity (Walt) must own at least 50 percent of the stock of the entity (Acme) in order for there to be any attribution from the owner (Walt) to the entity (Acme).

What if: Assume the same facts as in the previous what-if example except that Walt owns 60 percent of Acme Corporation. How many shares of SCR is Acme Corporation treated as owning indirectly through Walt?

Answer: 25 shares. Because the entity (Acme) is a corporation and the owner (Walt) owns at least 50 percent of the entity (Acme), all of Walt's 25 shares in SCR are attributed to Acme Corporation.

Option attribution. A person having an option to purchase stock is deemed to indirectly own the stock that the option entitles the person to purchase.

Complete Redemption of the Stock Owned by a Shareholder A redemption will be treated as an exchange if it is in "complete redemption of all of the stock of the corporation owned by the shareholder."[26] This test seems redundant with the substantially disproportionate test discussed above; after all, a complete redemption seemingly satisfies the 50 percent and 80 percent tests. The difference is in the application of the family attribution rules discussed above.

The stock attribution rules also apply to a complete redemption. This presents a potential problem in family-owned corporations in which the only (or majority) shareholders are parents, children, and grandchildren. Parents who have all their stock redeemed will be will not be able to qualify for sale or exchange treatment if their children or grandchildren continue to own the remaining stock in the corporation because of the operation of the family attribution rules. To provide family members with relief in these situations, shareholders can waive (ignore) the family attribution rules in a complete redemption of their stock.[27] As usual, there are some strings attached.

The first requirement is that the shareholder has no interest in the corporation immediately after the exchange as a "shareholder, employee, director, officer or consultant."[28] These relations to the corporation are referred to as prohibited interests. The second

[26]§302(b)(3).
[27]§302(c)(2).
[28]§302(c).

requirement is that the shareholder does not acquire a prohibited interest within 10 years after the redemption, unless by inheritance (this is known as the *10-year look-forward rule*). Finally, the shareholder must agree to notify the IRS district director within 30 days if a prohibited interest is acquired within 10 years after the redemption. The shareholder can still be a creditor of the corporation (e.g., the parents can receive a corporate note in return for their stock if the corporation does not have the cash on hand to finance the redemption).

Example 18-21

Return to the amended storyline in which Walt is Jim's father and he owns 25 shares of SCR stock. Assume SCR redeemed all 25 of his shares this year for $125,000, and for the year SCR has current E&P of $500,000. Walt's tax basis in the SCR shares is $50,000 (25 × $2,000). Under the family attribution rules, Walt would still be treated as indirectly owning 75 percent of the SCR stock (Jim would own 75 of the remaining 100 shares in SCR). The $125,000 payment would be treated as a taxable dividend to the extent of SCR's E&P.

What happens to the unused $50,000 tax basis in the SCR stock redeemed?

Answer: The tax basis transfers to Jim's stock, giving Jim a tax basis in his SCR stock of $74,000 ($24,000 + $50,000).

How can Walt change the tax treatment of the complete redemption?

Answer: Because Walt has redeemed all his shares, he can waive the family attribution rules, provided he files an agreement with the IRS and does not retain a prohibited interest in SCR (e.g., as an employee or consultant). By waiving the family attribution rules, Walt will be treated as not owning any SCR stock and, thus, will be able to treat the redemption as an exchange and report a capital gain of $75,000 ($125,000 − $50,000).

Redemptions That Are Not Essentially Equivalent to a Dividend A redemption will also be treated as an exchange if it is "not essentially equivalent to a dividend."[29] This is a subjective determination that turns on the facts and circumstances of each case. To satisfy this requirement, there must be a "meaningful" reduction in the shareholder's ownership interest in the corporation as a result of the redemption.[30] Neither the IRS nor the courts provide any mechanical tests to make this determination. The courts generally look at the substance of the transaction to determine if the redemption is a sale or a disguised dividend. As a result of the potential for litigation, shareholder reliance on this test is typically a last resort.

Although the courts have held that a shareholder's interest can include the right to vote and exercise control, participate in current and accumulated earnings, or share in net assets on liquidation, the IRS generally looks at the change in voting power as the key factor. The shareholder's voting power must decrease and be below 50 percent as a result of the exchange before this test can be considered.[31] As before, the stock attribution rules apply to these types of redemptions. Shareholders generally turn to this test to provide exchange treatment for redemptions when they cannot meet any of the other tests discussed previously.

[29]§302(b)(1).

[30]*United States v. Davis,* 397 U.S. 301, 313 (1970).

[31]In Rev. Rul. 76-385, the IRS held that in the case of a "small, minority shareholder, whose relative stock interest is minimal and who exercises no control over the affairs of the corporation," any reduction in proportionate interest is "meaningful." In this ruling, the shareholder's ownership percentage decreased from .0001118% to .0001081%, which would not be considered a "meaningful" reduction by most standards. Because the reduction in stock ownership did not meet the substantially disproportionate tests of §302(b)(2), the shareholder's only hope for exchange treatment was to qualify under §302(b)(1).

TAXES IN THE REAL WORLD Form Sometimes Prevails over Substance

Jon Dickinson was a shareholder and CFO for Geosyntec Consultants, Inc. (GCI), a privately held corporation. With authorization from the GCI board of directors, Dickinson donated appreciated long-term GCI shares to a qualified charity, Fidelity Investments Charitable Gift fund (Gift Fund). GCI immediately redeemed the donated shares for cash (i.e., the Gift Fund sold stock back to the corporation for cash). Because the Gift Fund is a tax-exempt charity, it recognized no gain on the redemption. Dickinson, in turn, claimed a charitable contribution deduction for the fair market value of the donated stock. The IRS argued that the transaction should be recast as though GCI redeemed Dickinson's stock for cash and then Dickinson donated the cash to the charity. In this scenario, Dickinson would be taxed on the appreciation in the donated stock.

At trial, Dickinson presented contemporaneous evidence that he relinquished all ownership rights in the shares at the time of the donation. GCI's letters to the Gift Fund confirmed the ownership transfer, and the Gift Fund's letters to Dickinson explained that the charity had "exclusive legal control" over the donated shares. The Tax Court held that where control is relinquished, the form of the transaction (donation then redemption) takes precedence over the substance of the transaction (redemption then donation). In this case, the tax consequences follow from the form of the transaction regardless of whether the donation was closely followed by a redemption or whether there was a preexisting "understanding" that the stock would be redeemed. Thus, Dickinson was able to claim a donation for the appreciated stock and was not taxed on the redemption.

Source: Jon Dickinson, et ux. v. Comm'r, TC Memo 2020-128.

Example 18-22

What if: Assume Walt is not related to Jim or Ginny. This year, SCR redeemed five shares of his stock in exchange for $25,000. Walt has a tax basis in the five shares of SCR stock of $10,000 ($2,000 per share). Assume that SCR has sufficient E&P to cover any distribution. What is the tax treatment of the stock redemption to Walt under the *not essentially equivalent to a dividend* test?

Answer: $15,000 capital gain.

Prior to the redemption, Walt owned 20 percent of SCR (25/125 shares). After the redemption, his ownership percentage in SCR drops to 16.67 percent (20/120 shares). This redemption does not satisfy the substantially disproportionate test, which would treat the redemption as an exchange. Walt can argue that the redemption should be treated as an exchange because it was *not essentially equivalent to a dividend.* Walt's ownership percentage decreased (20 percent to 16.67 percent) and is below 50 percent after the redemption. However, the result Walt seeks (exchange treatment) is not guaranteed. For peace of mind, he might prefer having SCR redeem one additional share and have the certainty that the redemption will be treated as an exchange under §302(b)(2).

Example 18-23

What if: Assume Walt is Jim's father, and SCR redeemed five shares of his stock in exchange for $25,000. Walt has a tax basis in the five shares of SCR stock of $10,000 ($2,000 per share), and SCR has sufficient E&P to cover any distribution. What is the tax treatment of the stock redemption to Walt under the *not essentially equivalent to a dividend* test?

Answer: $25,000 dividend to the extent of SCR's E&P.

Prior to the redemption, Walt is treated as owning 80 percent of SCR (25 shares directly and 75 shares through Jim). After the redemption, his ownership percentage in SCR drops to 79 percent (95/120 shares). This redemption does not satisfy the *not essentially equivalent to a dividend* test because Walt is treated as owning more than 50 percent of the SCR stock.

Tax Consequences to the Distributing Corporation

The corporation distributing property to shareholders in a redemption generally recognizes gain on the distribution of appreciated property but is not permitted to recognize loss on the distribution of property with a fair market value less than its tax basis.[32]

If the redemption is treated as a distribution, the corporation reduces its accumulated E&P at the end of the year by the cash distributed and the greater of the fair market value or the adjusted tax basis of other property distributed.[33] If the redemption is treated as an *exchange,* the corporation reduces E&P at the date of distribution by the percentage of stock redeemed (i.e., if 60 percent of the stock is redeemed, E&P available at the time of the distribution is reduced by 60 percent), not to exceed the fair market value of the property distributed.[34] When dividend distributions and redemption distributions are made in the same taxable year, the dividend distributions are allocated to E&P first and then the redemptions reduce the remaining E&P on a per share basis.[35]

The distributing corporation cannot deduct expenses incurred in a stock redemption.[36] The corporation can, however, deduct interest on debt incurred to finance a redemption.

THE KEY FACTS

Stock Redemptions Treated as Exchanges

- A stock redemption is treated as an exchange if it meets one of the following three tests:
  - Substantially disproportionate with respect to the shareholders.
  - In complete termination of the shareholder's interest.
  - Not essentially equivalent to a dividend.
- The following attribution rules are used to determine if one of the three tests is met:
  - Family attribution.
  - Entity-to-owner attribution (pro rata).
  - Owner-to-entity attribution (100 percent).
  - Options.
- A corporation reduces its E&P as a result of a stock redemption as follows:
  - If the distribution is treated as an exchange, E&P is reduced by the lesser of (1) the amount distributed or (2) the percentage of stock redeemed times accumulated E&P at the redemption date.
  - If the distribution is treated as a distribution, E&P is reduced using the dividend rules.

Example 18-24

What if: Assume SCR redeemed all of the 25 shares owned by Walt in exchange for $125,000. The stock redeemed represents 20 percent of the total stock outstanding. Walt has a tax basis in his SCR shares of $50,000. Further assume that Walt treated the redemption as an exchange because he waived the family attribution rules and filed an agreement with the IRS.[37] As a result, Walt recognized a capital gain of $75,000 ($125,000 − $50,000). The redemption took place on December 31, on which date SCR had accumulated E&P at the end of the year (including current E&P for year) of $500,000. SCR did not make any distributions during the year.

By what amount does SCR reduce its E&P as a result of this redemption?

Answer: $100,000. SCR reduces E&P by the lesser of (1) $100,000 (20% × $500,000) or (2) $125,000, the amount paid to Walt in the redemption.

What if: Assume E&P was $1,000,000 at the end of the year. By what amount does SCR reduce its available E&P as a result of this redemption?

Answer: $125,000. SCR reduces E&P by the lesser of (1) $200,000 (20% × $1,000,000) or (2) $125,000, the amount paid to Walt in the redemption.

PARTIAL LIQUIDATIONS

LO 18-5

Corporations sometimes contract their operations either by distributing the stock of a subsidiary to their shareholders or by selling the business. In the case of a sale, the corporation may distribute the proceeds from the sale to its shareholders in partial liquidation of the corporation. The distribution may require the shareholders to tender shares of stock back to the corporation or may be pro rata to all the shareholders without an actual exchange of stock.

The tax treatment of a distribution received in a partial liquidation depends on the type of entity receiving the distribution.[38] All *noncorporate* shareholders (partnerships,

[32]§311(a), (b).

[33]§312(a), (b).

[34]§312(n)(7).

[35]See Rev. Rul. 74-338 and Rev. Rul. 74-339 for discussion of how to determine E&P when a corporation redeems stock and makes a distribution to shareholders during the year.

[36]§162(k).

[37]The requirements for this agreement are found in Reg. §1.302-4T.

[38]§302(b)(4).

THE KEY FACTS

Tax Consequences to Shareholders in a Partial Liquidation of a Corporation

- Noncorporate shareholders receive exchange treatment.
- Corporate shareholders determine their tax consequences using the change-in-stock-ownership rules that apply to stock redemptions.

LLCs, individuals, etc.) receive exchange treatment. This entitles the individual to sale or exchange treatment with respect to the gain or loss recognized on the actual or deemed exchange. If the shareholder is not required to tender stock to the corporation in return for the property received, the shareholder computes gain or loss recognized on the exchange by calculating the tax basis of the shares that would have been transferred to the corporation had the transaction been a stock redemption.

All *corporate* shareholders are subject to the change-in-stock-ownership rules that apply to stock redemptions. This usually results in dividend treatment because partial liquidations almost always involve pro rata distributions. Corporate shareholders generally prefer dividend treatment because of the availability of the dividends-received deduction, although the benefit of the dividends-received deduction is mitigated because a partial liquidating distribution to a corporate shareholder is treated as an extraordinary dividend under §1059 which requires corporations to reduce their stock basis by the amount of the dividends received deduction.

For a distribution to be in partial liquidation of the corporation, it must be either "not essentially equivalent to a dividend" (as determined at the corporate level) or the result of the termination of a "qualified trade or business."[39] The technical requirements to meet these requirements are beyond the scope of this text.

TAXES IN THE REAL WORLD A Partial Liquidation in Dutch Auction Tender Offer

XBiotech is a Canadian biotech company that trades on NASDAQ (XBIT). In December 2019, the company sold a subsidiary, True Human antibody Bermekimab, to Janssen Biotech, Inc. (Janssen), a subsidiary of Johnson & Johnson. Upon closing, XBiotech received $750 million, with the possibility that the company could also receive up to $600 million subject to other conditions. The company announced plans to use the sale proceeds for a new research program and to return remaining funds to shareholders.

In January 2020, the company announced that it planned to use $420 million to repurchase shares in a Dutch auction tender offer. In a Dutch auction tender offer, the company sets a price range for the offering, in this case $30–$33. Shareholders interested in tendering their shares offer a price where they are willing to sell. At expiration, the company adds up the shares tendered, starting at the minimum price, until they reach the number of shares they are seeking, in this case 33%. The highest price of that group is the price the company will pay for all shares tendered at or below that price.

According to the company, Canadian shareholders will treat the offer as a taxable dividend. However, U.S. shareholders who participate in the tender will be entitled to treat the offer as a redemption under §302. Specifically, the company indicated in the tender offer that it intends for the sale to be treated as a partial liquidation under §302(e). As a partial liquidation, noncorporate shareholders would be entitled to treat the redemption as a sale regardless of whether it qualifies as substantially disproportionate. Of course, the company suggests that shareholders should consult with tax advisers because treatment as a partial liquidation depends on the facts and circumstances, and the IRS may disagree with this position.

Source: Schedule TO (pages 39–40), filed with the SEC by XBiotech Inc. on January 14, 2020.

CONCLUSION

This chapter explains that a corporation can distribute cash and other property to its shareholders in alternative ways. The most common forms are dividend distributions and stock buybacks (redemptions). The form chosen to make such a distribution affects the tax consequences to the recipients (shareholders) as well as the corporation itself. In some cases, the tax laws or the tax administrators can ignore the form of the transaction and assess tax based on the substance of the transaction. This is common in the case of stock redemptions that can be taxed as dividend payments. The tax rules that apply to distinguishing between substance and form often are complex, and taxpayers and their tax advisers must evaluate them carefully before making a decision.

[39]§302(e).

Summary

Recognize the tax framework applying to property distributions from a corporation to a shareholder. **LO 18-1**

- Subchapter C of the Internal Revenue Code (IRC) provides guidelines and rules for determining the tax status of distributions from a C corporation to its shareholders.
- When a corporation distributes property to persons in their capacity as shareholders, all or a portion of the distribution could be characterized as a dividend.
- If the distribution is of property other than cash, the distributing corporation recognizes gain but not loss on the distribution.

Compute a corporation's earnings and profits and a shareholder's dividend income. **LO 18-2**

- The IRC defines a dividend as any distribution of property made by a corporation to its shareholders out of its current or accumulated earnings and profits (E&P).
- Similar in concept to financial accounting retained earnings, E&P is meant to represent accumulated economic income.
- A corporation must keep two E&P accounts: current E&P and accumulated E&P. Current E&P is computed on the last day of each tax year.
- The IRC and the related regulations list four basic types of adjustments that a corporation must make to its taxable income to compute current E&P.
    - Inclusion of income that is excluded from taxable income.
    - Disallowance of certain expenses that are deducted in computing taxable income.
    - Deduction of certain expenses that are excluded from the computation of taxable income.
    - Separate accounting methods required for E&P purposes that result in both positive and negative adjustments to taxable income.
- The shareholder recognizes a corporate distribution as dividend income up to the amount of E&P. The distribution is the sum of cash received plus the fair market value of property received less any liabilities assumed.
- Distributions reduce accumulated E&P but cannot produce a deficit in E&P.
- The distributing corporation recognizes gain, but not loss, on the distribution of noncash property.
- A corporation reduces accumulated E&P by the amount of cash distributed, the E&P basis of depreciated (loss) property distributed, and the fair market value of appreciated property distributed, net of any liability assumed by the shareholders.

Explain the taxation of stock distributions. **LO 18-3**

- The general rule is that a stock distribution (stock dividend or split) is not taxable.
- The basis of the "new" stock received is computed by allocating basis from the existing stock based on relative fair market value.
- The holding period of the new stock includes the holding period of the existing stock on which the new stock was distributed.
- Non–pro rata stock distributions usually are treated as taxable dividends to the recipients.

Discern the tax consequences of stock redemptions. **LO 18-4**

- If a redemption is treated as an exchange, the shareholder computes gain or loss by comparing the amount realized (money and property received) with the adjusted tax basis of the stock surrendered.
    - The character of the gain or loss is capital.
    - The basis of noncash property received is its fair market value.
    - The holding period of the property received begins at the date of receipt.
- If the redemption is treated as a dividend, the shareholder will recognize dividend income (to the extent of corporate E&P) equal to the cash and fair market value of other property received.
    - The basis of the property received is its fair market value.
- Redemptions can be treated as exchanges in transactions in which the shareholder's ownership interest in the corporation has been "meaningfully" reduced relative to other shareholders as a result of the redemption.

- There are three change-in-stock-ownership tests that entitle the shareholder to exchange treatment in a redemption.
- A redemption will be treated as an exchange if the redemption is "not essentially equivalent to a dividend."
  - This is a facts and circumstances determination (subjective).
  - To satisfy this requirement, the courts or IRS must conclude that there has been a "meaningful" reduction in the shareholder's ownership interest in the corporation as a result of the redemption.
- A redemption will be treated as an exchange if the redemption is "substantially disproportionate with respect to the shareholder," defined as follows:
  - Immediately after the exchange, the shareholder owns less than 50 percent of the total combined voting power of all classes of stock entitled to vote.
  - The shareholder's percentage ownership of voting stock after the redemption is less than 80 percent of the percentage ownership before the redemption.
  - The shareholder's percentage ownership of the aggregate fair market value of the corporation's common stock (voting and nonvoting) after the redemption is less than 80 percent of the percentage ownership before the redemption.
- A redemption will be treated as an exchange if the redemption is in "complete redemption of all of the stock of the corporation owned by the shareholder."
- In determining whether the change-in-stock-ownership tests are met, each shareholder's percentage change in ownership in the corporation before and after a redemption must take into account constructive ownership (attribution) rules.
- The attribution rules cause stock owned by other persons to be treated as owned by (attributed to) the shareholder for purposes of determining whether the shareholder has met any of the change-in-stock-ownership tests to receive exchange treatment.
  - Family attribution. Individuals are treated as owning the shares of stock owned by their spouse, children, grandchildren, and parents.
  - Attribution from entities to owners or beneficiaries.
    - Partners are deemed to own a pro rata share of their partnership's stock holdings (i.e., a partner who has a 10 percent interest in a partnership is deemed to own 10 percent of any stock owned by the partnership).
    - Shareholders are deemed to own a pro rata share of their corporation's stock holdings, but only if they own at least 50 percent of the value of the corporation's stock.
  - Attribution from owners or beneficiaries to entities.
    - Partnerships are deemed to own 100 percent of the stock owned by partners (i.e., a partnership is deemed to own 100 percent of the stock owned by a 10 percent partner).
    - Attribution to a corporation only applies to shareholders owning 50 percent or more of the value of the corporation's stock.
  - Option attribution. A person having an option to purchase stock is deemed to own the stock that the option entitles the person to purchase.
- Shareholders can waive the family attribution rules in a complete redemption of their stock if certain conditions are met.
  - The shareholder has not retained a prohibited interest in the corporation immediately after the exchange (e.g., as a shareholder, employee, director, officer, or consultant).
  - The shareholder does not acquire a prohibited interest within 10 years after the redemption, unless by inheritance (the 10-year look-forward rule).
  - The shareholder agrees to notify the IRS district director within 30 days if a prohibited interest is acquired within 10 years (by filing an agreement with the IRS).
- If the redemption is treated as a dividend by the shareholder, the corporation generally reduces its E&P by the cash distributed and the fair market value of other property distributed.
- If the redemption is treated as an exchange by the shareholder, the corporation reduces E&P at the date of distribution by the percentage of stock redeemed (i.e., if 50 percent of the stock is redeemed, E&P is reduced by 50 percent), not to exceed the fair market value of the property distributed.

Describe the tax consequences of a partial liquidation to the corporation and its shareholders. LO 18-5

- For a distribution to be a partial liquidation, it must be "not essentially equivalent to a dividend" (as determined at the corporate level, not the shareholder level). The distribution automatically meets this test if the distribution is the result of the termination of a "qualified trade or business."
- The tax treatment of a distribution received in partial liquidation of a corporation depends on the identity of the shareholder receiving it.
  - All noncorporate shareholders get exchange treatment.
  - All corporate shareholders are subject to the stock redemption change-in-ownership rules, which usually result in dividend treatment because partial liquidations are almost always pro rata distributions.

KEY TERMS

accumulated earnings and profits (18-3)
bright-line tests (18-18)
constructive ownership (18-20)
current earnings and profits (18-3)
dividend (18-2)
partial liquidation (18-2)
stock redemption (18-2)
stock split (18-16)

DISCUSSION QUESTIONS

Discussion Questions are available in Connect®.

1. What is meant by the phrase "double taxation of corporate income"? LO 18-1
2. How does the double taxation of corporate distributions affect whether an individual chooses to operate a business as a C corporation or a flow-through entity? LO 18-1
3. Historically, taxpayers have implemented strategies to mitigate or eliminate the effects of double taxation. Why might taxpayers think twice before implementing such strategies today? Explain. LO 18-1
4. Why might a shareholder who is also an employee prefer receiving a dividend instead of compensation from a corporation? LO 18-1
5. What are the three potential tax treatments of a cash distribution to a shareholder? Are these potential tax treatments elective by the shareholder? LO 18-2
6. In general, what is the concept of earnings and profits (E&P) designed to represent? LO 18-2
7. How does the *current earnings and profits* account differ from the *accumulated earnings and profits* account? LO 18-2
8. Assume a calendar-year corporation has positive current E&P of $120 and a deficit in accumulated E&P of ($200). Under this circumstance, a cash distribution of $100 to the corporation's sole shareholder at year-end will not be treated as a dividend because total E&P is negative. True or false? Explain. LO 18-2
9. Assume a calendar-year corporation has a deficit in current E&P of ($120) and positive beginning accumulated E&P of $120. Under this circumstance, a cash distribution of $120 to the corporation's sole shareholder on June 30 will not be treated as a dividend because total E&P on December 31 is $0. True or false? Explain. LO 18-2
10. List the four general categories of adjustments that a corporation makes to taxable income or net loss to compute current E&P. What is the rationale for making these adjustments? LO 18-2
11. Assuming adequate amounts of corporate E&P, what is the formula for determining the amount of a noncash distribution a shareholder must include in gross income? LO 18-2
12. What income tax issues must a corporation consider before it makes a noncash distribution to a shareholder? LO 18-2
13. Assuming adequate E&P, will the shareholder's tax basis in noncash property received equal the amount included in gross income as a dividend (assuming adequate E&P)? Under what circumstances will the amounts be different, if any? LO 18-2

LO 18-2 14. A shareholder receives appreciated noncash property in a corporate distribution and assumes a liability attached to the property. How does the assumption of a liability affect the amount of dividend reported in gross income, assuming adequate E&P?

LO 18-2 15. A shareholder receives appreciated noncash property in a corporate distribution and assumes a liability attached to the property. How does this assumption affect the amount of gain the corporation recognizes? From the corporation's perspective, does it matter if the liability assumed by the shareholder exceeds the property's gross fair market value?

LO 18-2 16. When a shareholder receives a noncash distribution of property that is encumbered by a liability (the shareholder assumes the liability on the distribution), how does the shareholder determine the amount of the distribution?

LO 18-2 17. A corporation distributes *depreciated* noncash property to a shareholder. What impact does the distribution have on the corporation's earnings and profits

LO 18-2 18. A corporation distributes *appreciated* noncash property to a shareholder. What impact does the distribution have on the corporation's earnings and profits?

LO 18-3 19. Why might a corporation issue a stock distribution to its shareholders?

LO 18-3 20. What tax issue arises when a shareholder receives a nontaxable stock distribution?

LO 18-3 21. In general, what causes a stock distribution to be taxable to the recipient?

LO 18-4 22. What are the potential tax consequences to a shareholder who participates in a stock redemption?

LO 18-4 23. What stock ownership tests must be met before a shareholder receives exchange treatment under the substantially disproportionate change-in-stock-ownership test in a stock redemption? Why is a change-in-stock-ownership test used to determine the tax status of a stock redemption?

LO 18-4 24. What are the criteria necessary to meet the "not essentially equivalent to a dividend" change-in-stock-ownership test in a stock redemption?

LO 18-4 25. When might a shareholder have to rely on the "not essentially equivalent to a dividend" test in arguing that a stock redemption should be treated as an exchange for tax purposes?

LO 18-4 26. Explain why the tax law imposes constructive stock ownership rules on stock redemptions.

LO 18-4 27. Which members of a family are included in the family attribution rules? Is there any rationale for the family members included in the test?

LO 18-4 28. Ilya and Olga are brother and sister. Ilya owns 200 shares of stock in Parker Corporation. Is Olga deemed to own Ilya's 200 shares under the family attribution rules that apply to stock redemptions?

LO 18-4 29. Maria has all her stock in May Corporation redeemed. Under what conditions will Maria treat the redemption as an exchange and recognize capital gain or loss?

LO 18-4 30. What must a shareholder do to waive the family attribution rules in a complete redemption of stock?

LO 18-4 31. How does a corporation's adjustment to earnings and profits differ based on the tax treatment of a stock redemption to the shareholder (i.e., as either a dividend or exchange)?

LO 18-5 32. How does the tax treatment of a partial liquidation differ from a stock redemption?

LO 18-5 33. Reveille Corporation experienced a complete loss of its lumber mill as the result of a fire. The company received $2 million from the insurance company. Rather than rebuild, Reveille decided to distribute the $2 million to its two shareholders. No stock was exchanged in return. Under what conditions will the distribution meet the requirements necessary to be treated as a partial liquidation and not a dividend? Why does it matter to the shareholders?

PROBLEMS

Select problems are available in Connect®.

34. Gopher Corporation reported taxable income of $500,000 this year. Gopher paid a dividend of $100,000 to its sole shareholder, Sven Anderson. The dividend meets the requirements to be a qualified dividend, and Sven is subject to a tax rate of 15 percent on the dividend. What is the income tax imposed on the corporate income earned by Gopher and the income tax on the dividend distributed to Sven? LO 18-1

35. Bulldog Corporation reported taxable income of $500,000 this year, before any deduction for any payment to its sole shareholder and employee, Rojas. Bulldog chose to pay a bonus of $100,000 to Rojas at year-end. The bonus meets the requirements to be "reasonable" and is therefore deductible by Bulldog. Rojas is subject to a marginal tax rate of 35 percent on the bonus. What is the income tax imposed on the corporate income earned by Bulldog and the income tax on the bonus paid to Rojas? LO 18-1

36. Hawkeye Company reports current E&P of $300,000 this year and accumulated E&P at the beginning of the year of $200,000. Hawkeye distributed $400,000 to its sole shareholder, Ray, on December 31 of this year. Ray's tax basis in his Hawkeye stock before the distribution is $75,000. LO 18-2
    a) How much of the $400,000 distribution is treated as a dividend to Ray?
    b) What is Ray's tax basis in the Hawkeye stock after the distribution?
    c) What is Hawkeye's balance in accumulated E&P as of January 1 of next year?

37. Jayhawk Company reports current E&P of $300,000 and a deficit in accumulated E&P of ($200,000). Jayhawk distributed $400,000 to its sole shareholder, Rock, on the last day of the year. Rock's tax basis in the Jayhawk stock before the distribution is $75,000. LO 18-2
    a) How much of the $400,000 distribution is treated as a dividend to Rock?
    b) What is Rock's tax basis in the Jayhawk stock after the distribution?
    c) What is Jayhawk's balance in accumulated E&P on the first day of next year?

38. This year, Sooner Company reports a deficit in current E&P of ($300,000). Its accumulated E&P at the beginning of the year was $200,000. Sooner distributed $400,000 to its sole shareholder, Boomer, on June 30 of this year. Boomer's tax basis in the Sooner stock before the distribution is $75,000. LO 18-2
    a) How much of the $400,000 distribution is treated as a dividend to Boomer?
    b) What is Boomer's tax basis in the Sooner stock after the distribution?
    c) What is Sooner's balance in accumulated E&P on the first day of next year?

39. This year, Bobcat Company reports a deficit in current E&P of ($300,000) that accrued evenly throughout the year. At the beginning of the year, Bobcat's accumulated E&P was $200,000. Bobcat distributed $200,000 to its sole shareholder, Melanie, on June 30 of this year. Melanie's tax basis in the Bobcat stock before the distribution was $75,000. LO 18-2 tax forms
    a) How much of the $200,000 distribution is treated as a dividend to Melanie?
    b) What is Melanie's tax basis in the Bobcat stock after the distribution?
    c) What is Bobcat's balance in accumulated E&P on the first day of next year?
    d) Prepare a draft of Bobcat's Form 5452 for this year. You may assume that the June 30 distribution was Bobcat's first and only distribution.

40. Lone Star Company is a calendar-year corporation, and this year Lone Star reported $100,000 in current E&P that accrued evenly throughout the year. At the beginning of the year, Lone Star's accumulated E&P was $12,000. At the beginning of the LO 18-2 tax forms

year, Lone Star's sole shareholder was Matt. Lone Star declared $30,000 in cash distributions on each of the following dates: March 31, June 30, September 30, and December 31.

a) How much of the $120,000 in total distributions will be treated as dividends?

b) Suppose that Matt sold half of the shares to Chris on June 1 for $40,000. How much dividend income will Matt recognize this year?

c) If Matt's basis in the Lone Star shares was $7,000 at the beginning of the year, how much capital gain will he recognize on the sale and distributions from Lone Star?

d) Prepare a draft of Lone Star's Form 5452 for this year.

LO 18-2 41. This year, Jolt Inc. reported $40,000 of taxable income before any charitable contribution deduction. Assume the 10% of taxable income limitation applies to the contribution because Jolt did not make the necessary election to use the 25% of taxable income limitation. Jolt contributed $10,000 this year to Goodwill Industries, a public charity. Compute the company's current E&P.

LO 18-2 42. Boilermaker Inc. reported taxable income of $500,000 this year and paid federal income taxes of $105,000. Not included in the company's computation of taxable income is tax-exempt income of $20,000, disallowed meals and entertainment expenses of $30,000, and disallowed expenses related to the tax-exempt income of $1,000. Boilermaker deducted depreciation of $100,000 on its tax return. Under the alternative (E&P) depreciation method, the deduction would have been $60,000. Compute the company's current E&P.

LO 18-2 43. Gator Inc. reported taxable income of $1,000,000 this year and paid federal income taxes of $210,000. Included in the company's computation of taxable income is gain from the sale of a depreciable asset of $50,000. The income tax basis of the asset was $100,000. The E&P basis of the asset using the alternative depreciation system was $175,000. Compute the company's current E&P.

LO 18-2 44. Paladin Inc. reported taxable income of $1,000,000 this year and paid federal income taxes of $210,000. The company reported a capital gain from sale of investments of $150,000, which was partially offset by a $100,000 net capital loss carryover from last year, resulting in a net capital gain of $50,000 included in taxable income. Compute the company's current E&P.

LO 18-2 45. Volunteer Corporation reported taxable income of $500,000 *from operations* this year. During the year, the company made a distribution of land to its sole shareholder, Rocky. The land's fair market value was $75,000 and its tax and E&P basis to Volunteer was $25,000. Rocky assumed a mortgage attached to the land of $15,000. The company had accumulated E&P of $750,000 at the beginning of the year.

a) Compute Volunteer's taxable income and federal income tax.

b) Compute Volunteer's current E&P.

c) Compute Volunteer's accumulated E&P at the beginning of next year.

d) What amount of dividend income does Rocky report because of the distribution?

e) What is Rocky's income tax basis in the land received from Volunteer?

LO 18-2 46. Tiger Corporation reported taxable income of $500,000 *from operations* this year. During the year, the company made a distribution of land to its sole shareholder, Mike. The land's fair market value was $75,000, and its tax and E&P basis to Tiger was $125,000. Mike assumed a mortgage attached to the land of $15,000. The company had accumulated E&P of $750,000 at the beginning of the year.

a) Compute Tiger's taxable income and federal income tax.

b) Compute Tiger's current E&P.

c) Compute Tiger's accumulated E&P at the beginning of next year.

d) What amount of dividend income does Mike report because of the distribution?

e) What is Mike's tax basis in the land he received from Tiger?

47. Illini Corporation reported taxable income of $500,000 *from operations* for this year. During the year, the company made a distribution of an automobile to its sole shareholder, Carly. The auto's fair market value was $30,000, and its adjusted tax basis to Illini was $0. The auto's E&P adjusted tax basis was $15,000. Illini had accumulated E&P of $1,500,000. LO 18-2

a) Compute Illini's taxable income and federal income tax.

b) Compute Illini's current E&P.

c) Compute Illini's accumulated E&P at the beginning of next year.

d) What amount of dividend income does Carly report because of the distribution?

e) What is Carly's tax basis in the auto received from Illini?

48. Beaver Corporation reported taxable income of $500,000 *from operations* this year. During the year, the company made a distribution of land to its sole shareholder, Eugenia. The land's fair market value was $20,000, and its income tax and E&P adjusted tax basis to Beaver was $50,000. Eugenia assumed a mortgage on the land of $25,000. Beaver Corporation had accumulated E&P of $1,500,000. LO 18-2

a) Compute Beaver's taxable income and federal income tax.

b) Compute Beaver's current E&P.

c) Compute Beaver's accumulated E&P at the beginning of next year.

d) What amount of dividend income does Eugenia report because of the distribution?

49. Tiny and Tim each owns half of the 100 outstanding shares of Flower Corporation. This year, Flower reported taxable income of $6,000. In addition, Flower received $20,000 of life insurance proceeds due to the death of an employee (Flower paid $500 in life insurance premiums this year). Flower had $5,000 of accumulated E&P at the beginning of the year. LO 18-2 tax forms research

a) What is Flower's current E&P?

b) Flower distributed $6,000 on February 15 and $30,000 on August 1. What total amount of dividends will Tiny and Tim report?

c) What amount of capital gain (if any) would Tiny and Tim report on the distributions in part (b) if their stock bases are $2,000 and $10,000, respectively?

d) What form would Flower use to report nondividend distributions?

e) On what form (line) would Tiny and Tim report nondividend distributions?

50. Hoosier Corporation declared a 2-for-1 stock split (shareholders received one share of stock for each share they already owned) to all shareholders of record on March 25 of this year. Hoosier reported current E&P of $600,000 and accumulated E&P of $3,000,000. The total fair market value of the stock distributed was $1,500,000. Barbara owned 1,000 shares of Hoosier stock with a tax basis of $100 per share. LO 18-3

a) What amount of taxable dividend income, if any, does Barbara recognize this year? Assume the fair market value of the stock was $150 per share on March 25 of this year.

b) What is the income tax basis in the new and existing stock Barbara owns in Hoosier Corporation, assuming the distribution is tax-free?

c) How does the stock distribution affect Hoosier's accumulated E&P at the beginning of next year?

LO 18-3 51. Badger Corporation declared a stock distribution to all shareholders of record on March 25 of this year. Shareholders will receive 1 share of Badger stock for each 10 shares of stock they already own. Madison owns 1,000 shares of Badger stock with a tax basis of $100 per share. The fair market value of the Badger stock was $110 per share on March 25 of this year.

a) What amount of taxable dividend income, if any, does Madison recognize this year?

b) What is the tax basis in Madison's new and existing stock in Badger Corporation, assuming the distribution is nontaxable?

c) How would you answer parts (a) and (b) if Badger offered shareholders a choice between receiving 1 additional share of Badger stock for each 10 Badger shares held or receiving $120 cash in lieu of an additional share of stock?

LO 18-4 52. Wildcat Company is owned equally by Evan and his sister Sara, each of whom holds 1,000 shares in the company. Sara wants to reduce her ownership in the company, and it was decided that the company will redeem 500 of her shares for $25,000 per share on December 31 of this year. Sara's tax basis in each share is $5,000. Wildcat has current E&P of $10,000,000 and at the beginning of the year accumulated E&P is $50,000,000.

a) What are the amount and character (capital gain or dividend) recognized by Sara because of the stock redemption?

b) What is the tax basis in the remaining 500 shares Sara owns in the company?

c) By what amount does Wildcat reduce its E&P because of the redemption?

LO 18-4 53. Flintstone Company is owned equally by Fred and his sister Wilma, each of whom holds 1,000 shares in the company. Wilma wants to reduce her ownership in the company, and it was decided that the company will redeem 250 of her shares for $25,000 per share on December 31 of this year. Wilma's tax basis in each share is $5,000. Flintstone has current E&P of $10,000,000 and accumulated E&P at the beginning of the year is $50,000,000.

a) What are the amount and character (capital gain or dividend) recognized by Wilma because of the stock redemption, assuming only the "substantially disproportionate with respect to the shareholder" test is applied?

b) Given your answer to part (a), what is the tax basis in the remaining 750 shares Wilma owns in the company?

c) By what amount does Flintstone reduce its E&P because of the redemption?

d) What other argument might Wilma make to treat the redemption as an exchange?

LO 18-4 54. Acme Corporation has 1,000 shares outstanding. Joan and Tin are married, and each of them owns 20 shares of Acme. Joan and Tin's daughter, Kara, also owns 20 shares of Acme. Joan is an equal partner with Jeri in the J&J partnership, and this partnership owns 60 shares of Acme. Jeri is not related to Joan or Tin. How many shares of Acme is Kara deemed to own under the stock attribution rules?

LO 18-4 55. Bedrock Inc. is owned equally by Barney and his wife Betty, each of whom holds 1,000 shares in the company. Betty wants to reduce her ownership in the company, and it was decided that the company will redeem 500 of her shares for $25,000 per share on December 31 of this year. Betty's tax basis in each share is $5,000. Bedrock has current E&P of $10,000,000 and accumulated E&P of $50,000,000.

a) What are the amount and character (capital gain or dividend) recognized by Betty because of the stock redemption, assuming only the "substantially disproportionate with respect to the shareholder" test is applied?

b) Given your answer to part (a), what is the tax basis in the remaining 500 shares Betty owns in the company?

c) By what amount does Bedrock reduce its E&P because of the redemption?

d) Can Betty argue that the redemption is "not essentially equivalent to a dividend" and should be treated as an exchange?

56. In the previous problem, assume that Betty and Barney are not getting along and have separated due to marital discord (although they are not legally separated). In fact, they cannot even stand to talk to each other anymore and communicate only through their accountant. Betty wants to argue that she should not be treated as owning any of Barney's stock in Bedrock because of their hostility toward each other. Can family hostility be used as an argument to void the family attribution rules? Consult Rev. Rul. 80-26; *Robin Haft Trust v. Comm'r,* 510 F.2d 43 (1st Cir. 1975); *Metzger Trust v. Comm'r,* 693 F.2d 459 (5th Cir. 1982); and *Cerone v. Comm'r,* 87 TC 1 (1986). LO 18-4 research

57. Boots Inc. is owned equally by Muhammad and his daughter Isabel, each of whom holds 1,000 shares in the company. Muhammad wants to retire from the company, and it was decided that the company will redeem all 1,000 of Muhammad's shares for $25,000 per share on December 31 of this year. Muhammad's tax basis in each share is $500. Boots Inc. has current E&P of $1,000,000 and at the beginning of the year accumulated E&P is $5,000,000. LO 18-4

a) What must Muhammad do to ensure that the redemption will be treated as an exchange?

b) If Muhammad remained as the chair of the board after the redemption, what are the amount and character of income (capital gain or dividend) that Muhammad will recognize this year?

c) If Muhammad treats the redemption as a dividend, what happens to the stock basis in the 1,000 shares redeemed?

58. In the previous problem, Isabel would like to have Muhammad stay on as a consultant after all his shares are redeemed. Boots would pay Muhammad a modest salary of $500 per month. Isabel wants to know if there is any *de minimis* rule such that Muhammad would not be treated as having retained a prohibited interest in the company because the salary is so small. Consult *Lynch v. Comm'r,* 801 F.2d 1176 (9th Cir. 1986), *reversing* 83 TC 597 (1984); *Seda v. Comm'r,* 82 TC 484 (1984); and *Cerone v. Comm'r,* 87 TC 1 (1986). LO 18-4 research

59. Limited Brands recently repurchased 68,965,000 of its shares, paying $29 per share. The total number of shares outstanding before the redemption was 473,223,066. The total number of shares outstanding after the redemption was 404,258,066. Assume your client owned 20,000 shares of stock in The Limited. What is the minimum number of shares she must tender to receive exchange treatment under the "substantially disproportionate with respect to the shareholder" change-in-ownership rules? LO 18-4 planning

60. Cougar Company is owned equally by Cat and a partnership that is owned equally by his father and two unrelated individuals. Cat and the partnership each owns 3,000 shares in the company. Cat wants to reduce his ownership in the company and decided that the company will redeem 1,500 of his shares for $25,000 per share. Cat's tax basis in each share is $5,000. What are the income tax consequences to Cat because of the stock redemption, assuming the company has earnings and profits of $10 million? LO 18-4

LO 18-4
planning

61. Oriole Corporation, a privately held company, has one class of voting common stock, of which 1,000 shares are issued and outstanding. The shares are owned as follows:

Larry	400
Ivan (Larry's son)	200
Gabi (Larry's daughter)	200
Cali (unrelated)	200
Total	1,000

Larry is considering retirement and would like to have the corporation redeem all his shares for $400,000.

a) What action is necessary if Larry wants to guarantee that the redemption will be treated as an exchange?

b) Could Larry act as a consultant to the company and still have the redemption treated as an exchange?

LO 18-4
research

62. Using the facts in the previous problem, Oriole Corporation proposes to pay Larry $100,000 and an installment note that pays $30,000 per year for the next 10 years plus a market rate of interest. Will this arrangement allow Larry to treat the redemption as an exchange? Consult §453(k)(2)(A).

LO 18-4

63. EG Corporation redeemed 200 shares of stock from one of its shareholders in exchange for $200,000. The redemption represented 20 percent of the corporation's outstanding stock. The redemption was treated as an exchange by the shareholder. By what amount does EG reduce its total E&P because of the redemption under the following E&P assumptions?

a) EG's total E&P at the time of the distribution was $2,000,000.

b) EG's total E&P at the time of the distribution was $500,000.

LO 18-4
research

64. Spartan Corporation redeemed 25 percent of its shares for $2,000 on July 1 of this year, in a transaction that qualified as an exchange under §302(a). Spartan's accumulated E&P at the beginning of the year was $2,000. Its current E&P is $12,000. Spartan made dividend distributions of $1,000 on June 1 and $4,000 on August 31. Determine the beginning balance in Spartan's accumulated E&P at the beginning of the next year. See Rev. Rul. 74-338 and Rev. Rul. 74-339 for help in making this calculation.

LO 18-4

65. Bonnie and Clyde are the only two shareholders in Getaway Corporation. Bonnie owns 60 shares with a basis of $3,000, and Clyde owns the remaining 40 shares with a basis of $12,000. At year-end, Getaway is considering different alternatives for redeeming some shares of stock. Evaluate whether each of the following stock redemption transactions will qualify for sale and exchange treatment.

a) Getaway redeems 10 of Bonnie's shares for $2,000. Getaway has $20,000 of E&P at year-end and Bonnie is unrelated to Clyde.

b) Getaway redeems 25 of Bonnie's shares for $4,000. Getaway has $20,000 of E&P at year-end and Bonnie is unrelated to Clyde.

c) Getaway redeems 10 of Clyde's shares for $2,500. Getaway has $20,000 of E&P at year-end and Clyde is unrelated to Bonnie.

LO 18-4
research

66. Brent, Matt, Chris, Brad, and Anwer are five unrelated shareholders who each owns 20 of the 100 outstanding shares of Aggie Corporation. On June 30 of this year, Aggie distributed $100,000 in cash to the shareholders. On September 30 of this

year, Aggie redeemed all Anwer's shares for $80,000. Aggie had $45,000 of accumulated E&P at the beginning of the year and reported $120,000 of current E&P at year-end. What is Aggie's accumulated E&P at the beginning of next year? Consult Rev. Rul. 74-338. (*Hint:* Determine the tax status of the redemption and then calculate the effect of the June distribution on current E&P.)

67. Nail Corporation made a distribution of $500,000 to Rusty in partial liquidation of the company on December 31 of this year. Rusty, an individual, owns 100 percent of Nail Corporation. The distribution was in exchange for 50 percent of Rusty's stock in the company. At the time of the distribution, the shares had a fair market value of $200 per share. Rusty's tax basis in the shares was $50 per share. Nail had total E&P of $8,000,000 at the time of the distribution. LO 18-5
    a) What are the amount and character (capital gain or dividend) of any income or gain recognized by Rusty because of the partial liquidation?
    b) Assuming Nail made no other distributions to Rusty during the year, by what amount does Nail reduce its total E&P because of the partial liquidation?

68. Wolverine Corporation made a distribution of $500,000 to Deer Inc. in partial liquidation of the company on December 31 of this year. Deer owns 100 percent of Wolverine Corporation. The distribution was in exchange for 50 percent of Deer's stock in the company. At the time of the distribution, the shares had a fair market value of $200 per share. Deer's tax basis in the shares was $50 per share. Wolverine had total E&P of $8,000,000 at the time of the distribution. LO 18-5
    a) What are the amount and character (capital gain or dividend) of any income or gain recognized by Deer because of the partial liquidation?
    b) Assuming Wolverine made no other distributions to Deer during the year, by what amount does Wolverine reduce its total E&P because of the partial liquidation?

COMPREHENSIVE PROBLEMS

Select problems are available in Connect®.

69. Lanco Corporation, an accrual-method corporation, reported taxable income of $1,460,000 this year. Included in the computation of taxable income were the following items:

    - MACRS depreciation of $200,000. Depreciation for earnings and profits purposes is $120,000.
    - A net capital loss carryover of $10,000 from last year.
    - A net operating loss carryover of $25,000 from last year.
    - $65,000 capital gain from the distribution of land to the company's sole shareholder (see below).

    Not included in the computation of taxable income were the following items:

    - Tax-exempt income of $5,000.
    - Life insurance proceeds of $250,000.
    - Excess current-year charitable contribution of $2,500 (to be carried over to next year).
    - Tax-deferred gain of $20,000 on a like-kind exchange.
    - Nondeductible life insurance premium of $3,500.
    - Nondeductible interest expense of $1,000 on a loan used to buy tax-exempt bonds.

Lanco's accumulated E&P at the beginning of the year was $2,400,000. During the year, Lanco made the following distributions to its sole shareholder, Luigi:

- June 30: $50,000.
- September 30: Parcel of land with a fair market value of $75,000. Lanco's adjusted tax basis in the land was $10,000. Luigi assumed an existing mortgage on the property of $15,000.

Required:

a) Compute Lanco's current E&P.

b) Compute the amount of dividend income reported by Luigi this year because of the distributions.

c) Compute Lanco's accumulated E&P at the beginning of next year.

70. Petoskey Stone Quarry Inc. (PSQ), a calendar-year, accrual-method C corporation, provides landscaping supplies to local builders in northern Michigan. PSQ has always been a family-owned business and has a single class of voting common stock outstanding. The 500 outstanding shares are owned as follows:

Nick	150
Abigail (Nick's daughter)	50
Charlie (Nick's son)	50
Sandler (Nick's father)	100
Amy (Sandler's sister)	150
Total shares	500

Nick serves as president of PSQ, and his father, Sandler, serves as chair of the board. Amy is the company's CFO, and Abigail and Charlie work as employees of the company. Sandler would like to retire and sell his shares back to the company. The fair market value of the shares is $500,000. Sandler's tax basis is $10,000. The redemption is tentatively scheduled to take place on December 31 of this year. At the beginning of the year, PSQ had accumulated earnings and profits of $2,500,000. The company projects current E&P of $200,000. The company intends to pay pro rata cash dividends of $300 per share to its shareholders on December 1 of this year.

Required:

a) Assume the redemption takes place as planned on December 31 and no elections are made by the shareholders.

  1) What amount of dividend or capital gain will Sandler recognize because of the stock redemption?

  2) How will the tax basis of Sandler's stock be allocated to the remaining shareholders?

b) What must Sandler and the other shareholders do to change the tax results you calculated in part (a)?

research

71. Thriller Corporation has one class of voting common stock, of which 1,000 shares are issued and outstanding. The shares are owned as follows:

Joe	400
Miguel (Joe's son)	200
Lili (Joe's daughter)	200
Vinnie (unrelated)	200
Total shares	1,000

Thriller Corporation has current E&P of $400,000 for this year and accumulated E&P on January 1 of this year of $60,000. During this year, the corporation made the following distributions to its shareholders:

03/31: Distributed $100 per share to each shareholder ($100,000 in total).

06/30: Distributed $100 per share to each shareholder ($100,000 in total).

09/30: Distributed $100 per share to each shareholder ($100,000 in total).

12/31: Redeemed all of Vinnie's shares for $250,000 in cash.

Required:

a) Determine the tax status of each distribution made this year.

b) Compute the corporation's accumulated E&P on January 1 of next year.

c) Joe is considering retirement and would like to have the corporation redeem all his shares for $100,000 plus a 10-year note with a fair market value of $300,000. What action must Joe consider to ensure that the redemption will be treated as an exchange? Could Joe still act as a consultant to the company?

d) Thriller Corporation must pay attorney fees of $5,000 to facilitate the stock redemptions. Is this fee deductible?

UWorld Roger CPA Review

Sample CPA Exam questions from Roger CPA Review are available in Connect as support for the topics in this text. These Multiple Choice Questions and Task-Based Simulations include expert-written explanations and solutions and provide a starting point for students to become familiar with the content and functionality of the actual CPA Exam.

chapter

19 Corporate Formation, Reorganization, and Liquidation

Learning Objectives

Upon completing this chapter, you should be able to:

LO 19-1 Review the taxation of property dispositions.

LO 19-2 Recognize the tax consequences to the parties to a tax-deferred corporate formation.

LO 19-3 Identify the different forms of taxable and tax-deferred acquisitions.

LO 19-4 Determine the tax consequences to the parties to a corporate acquisition.

LO 19-5 Calculate the tax consequences that apply to the parties to a complete liquidation of a corporation.

Sergey Ryzhov/123RF

Storyline Summary

Spartan Cycle and Repair

Privately held company located in East Lansing, Michigan, that sells and repairs high-end bicycles

Jim Wheels (he/him/his)

Co-owner of Spartan Cycle and Repair (75 percent)

Ginny Gears (she/her/hers)

Co-owner of Spartan Cycle and Repair (25 percent)

360 Air

Privately held company in East Lansing, Michigan, that sells snowboarding equipment

Al Pine (he/him/his)

Owner of 360 Air

Wolverine Cycles and Repair

Privately held company in Ann Arbor, Michigan
Sells and repairs high-end bicycles

Pam Peloton (she/her/hers)

Owner of Wolverine Cycles and Repair

Jim Wheels and Ginny Gears are excited about the growth of their business, Spartan Cycle and Repair (SCR). The business has a solid base of loyal customers and is showing a healthy profit, and now Jim and Ginny are ready for some new challenges. They have considered both expanding the bicycle business to a new geographic region and branching out into a new line of business. Given the seasonal nature of the demand for bicycle products and repair in Michigan, Jim and Ginny favor a complementary line of business that would provide them with a source of income during the winter months. Ginny is impressed with the growing popularity of snowboarding. Factors that have contributed to this growth include low equipment costs, easily attained skills, a "coolness" attractive to young people, and the sport's inclusion in the Olympic Games.

Jim and Ginny are aware of a small snowboarding store in East Lansing called 360 Air, which is also the name of a daring snowboarding maneuver. The business is owned and operated as a sole proprietorship by Al Pine, a rather free-spirited individual whose enthusiasm for the sport is not matched by business acumen.

Jim and Ginny feel that with some additional capital investment and marketing effort, they could turn Al's snowboarding business into a profitable operation. They set up a meeting with Al to discuss how they could become partners in his business enterprise.

After some negotiation, Jim, Ginny, and Al agree to jointly operate the snowboarding business as a corporation taxed as a C corporation. As part of incorporating the business, each individual will make a contribution of property or services to the corporation in return for stock. Al will contribute existing snowboard inventory, a building (with associated land), and a separate parcel of land in return for 50 percent of the stock in 360 Air. The corporation will assume the existing mortgage on the property. Jim will contribute cash in exchange for 40 percent of the stock, and Ginny will contribute marketing services in return for 10 percent of the stock.

Each of the parties wants to know the income tax implications of incorporating Al's ongoing business. In addition, Jim is wondering whether the manner in which they are intending to create the corporation is tax efficient and whether there are other issues they should consider that would lessen the current and future tax burdens of both the corporation and its new shareholders.

(to be continued . . .)

When creating a business, the owners must choose an organizational form for operations. The choice of tax entity affects whether and how the income or loss generated by the business is taxed at the entity level and the owner level. At some point during the life of a business, the owners may decide to change its tax status. In the case of an ongoing business, such as 360 Air, changing from proprietorship to corporate status will require the transfer of assets and liabilities by the owners in return for stock in the corporation. These property transfers have important tax implications. A transfer of assets or liabilities to a corporation in exchange for stock triggers realization of gains and losses and may cause shareholders to recognize gains in the year of the transfer. In addition, shareholders will need to calculate the tax basis of their stock, and the corporation will need to calculate the basis of the assets and liabilities received in the transfer.

LO 19-1

REVIEW OF THE TAXATION OF PROPERTY DISPOSITIONS

This section provides a brief review of tax rules that apply to transfers of property to a corporation in exchange for stock and other property. Before gain or loss is recognized (included in taxable income), it must first be realized. **Realization** generally occurs when a transaction takes place (that is, when there is an exchange of property rights between two persons).

Exhibit 19-1 provides a template for computing gain or loss realized by a party to a property transaction.

EXHIBIT 19-1 Computing Gain or Loss Realized in a Property Transaction

	Amount realized (received)
−	Adjusted tax basis of the property transferred
	Gain (+) or loss (−) realized

Source: §1001(a).

The **amount realized** is computed using the template in Exhibit 19-2.

EXHIBIT 19-2 Computing the Amount Realized in a Property Transaction

	Cash received
+	Fair market value of other property received
+	Liabilities assumed by the transferee on the transferred property
–	Selling expenses incurred in the transaction
–	Liabilities assumed by the transferor on any property received in the exchange
	Amount realized

Source: §1001(b).

A property's **adjusted tax basis** is calculated using the template in Exhibit 19-3.

EXHIBIT 19-3 Computing a Property's Adjusted Tax Basis in a Property Transaction

	Acquisition basis
+	Capital improvements
–	Accumulated depreciation/Cost recovery
	Adjusted tax basis

Source: §1011.

THE KEY FACTS

Overview of the Taxation of Property Transactions

- Gain or loss is realized when a person engages in a transaction (an exchange of property rights with another person).
- Gain or loss realized is computed by subtracting the transferor's adjusted tax basis in the property exchanged from the amount realized in the exchange.
- Gain or loss realized is recognized (included in the computation of taxable income) unless exempted or deferred by a provision of the tax laws.

The entire amount of gain or deductible loss realized is recognized unless otherwise excluded or deferred by other provisions of the law.[1] Gain or loss that is excluded from gross income will never be recognized. Gain or deductible loss that is deferred is merely postponed to a future period.

TAX-DEFERRED TRANSFERS OF PROPERTY TO A CORPORATION

LO 19-2

A realization event occurs when shareholders transfer cash and noncash property to a corporation in return for stock in the corporation. Transfers of assets to corporations occurs in the formation of a corporation, but it can also happen in subsequent transactions with an existing corporation. Unless the transfer meets certain requirements, the transaction is treated as a taxable sale or exchange of the shareholder's property to the corporation. That is, the taxpayer is treated as selling the property to the corporation for the corporation's stock (and any other property transferred from the corporation to the shareholder). The stock can be common or preferred, voting, or nonvoting.[2] We discussed the tax consequences of a sale or exchange of property in depth in the Property Dispositions chapter. To summarize, shareholders would recognize gain or loss by the difference between the value of the corporate stock and other assets received in the exchange and the adjusted tax basis of the assets contributed to the corporation.

[1] §1001(c). Realized losses must first be deductible to be recognized. Nondeductible losses are never recognized.

[2] A category of stock with different rights (e.g., voting rights, dividend rights, liquidation rights) is referred to as a class of stock.

In §351, Congress provides for the deferral of gain or loss on qualifying transfers of property to a corporation in exchange for stock in order to remove tax consequences as an impediment to conducting business in the corporate form. Congress justifies tax deferral because shareholders maintain an interest in the property transferred through a different form of ownership (i.e., from direct ownership to indirect ownership through stock). In other words, the shareholders making the transfer have not substantively disposed of their ownership of the property.

Gain or loss deferred in the transfer of property to a corporation in return for stock is reflected in the shareholder's adjusted tax basis in the stock received in exchange for the transferred property.[3] Consequently, when the shareholder defers a gain on the transfer, the stock basis will be lower than the fair market value of the stock by the amount of the gain. When the shareholder defers a loss on the transfer, the stock basis will be higher than the fair market value of the stock by the amount of the loss.

Transactions Subject to Tax Deferral

For shareholders to receive tax deferral in a transfer of property to a corporation, the transferors must meet all three requirements in §351 as follows:

1. One or more shareholders must transfer *property* to a corporation.
2. Shareholders who transfer property to the corporation (i.e., the transferors) must receive *stock* of the transferee corporation in exchange for the property they transfer.
3. Immediately after the transfer, the transferors, together, must *control* the corporation to which they transferred the property.

Each of these requirements is discussed below. When the requirements are met, deferral of gain or loss in a §351 transaction is mandatory. Section 351 applies to transfers of property to both C corporations and S corporations.

Section 351 applies only to those **persons** who transfer property to the corporation in exchange for stock (i.e., shareholders). A *person* is defined for tax purposes to include individuals, corporations, partnerships, and fiduciaries (estates and trusts).[4] Thus, §351 allows individuals like Al to form a corporation and also allows existing corporations, such as General Electric, to employ §351 when creating a subsidiary. Also, the corporation receiving the property in exchange for its own stock does not recognize gain or loss on the transaction.[5]

Meeting the Section 351 Tax Deferral Requirements

The shareholders transferring property (the *transferors*) to a corporation (the *transferee*) must meet several requirements for the transfer to be tax-deferred. Some of these requirements are not precisely defined in either the IRC or the regulations. As a result, much of what we understand about the parameters of §351 has developed over time as the IRS and the courts have interpreted the law. This incremental approach to understanding the meaning of the law is common throughout Subchapter C of the Internal Revenue Code.[6]

Section 351 Applies Only to the Transfer of Property to the Corporation

Property includes money, tangible assets, and intangible assets (e.g., company name, patents, customer lists, trademarks, and logos). Services are, however, excluded from the

[3]§358.

[4]§7701(a)(1).

[5]§1032. Note, however, that under GAAP a corporation will record contributed property at fair value for book purposes. Hence, a contribution of property under §351 will give rise to book–tax differences because different amounts of depreciation will be recorded for book and tax purposes.

[6]Subchapter C encompasses §§301–385 and provides the tax rules for the corporate transactions discussed in this chapter.

definition of property. Thus, a person who receives stock in return for services generally has compensation equal to the fair market value of the stock received.[7]

Example 19-1

As part of the formation of the corporation, Ginny received 10 percent of the stock in 360 Air, valued at $60,000, in exchange for services in setting up the corporation. Will Ginny recognize the $60,000 of value realized on the transaction?

Answer: Yes. Ginny must recognize compensation income of $60,000 as a result of this exchange because services are not considered property under §351.

What if: Suppose Ginny created a distinctive logo for the company and in exchange received 10 percent of the stock in 360 Air, valued at $60,000. Assume the adjusted tax basis of the slogan is zero because Ginny created it. Will Ginny recognize the $60,000 gain realized on the transfer of the slogan?

Answer: No. Ginny will not recognize the $60,000 gain realized because intangibles are considered property under §351.

The Property Transferred to the Corporation Must Be Exchanged for Stock of the Corporation When property is transferred to a corporation in exchange for stock and other property, only the portion of the property exchanged for stock will qualify for tax deferral. Property (other than stock in the transferee corporation) received by shareholders is referred to as **boot.** The receipt of boot will cause the shareholder (transferor) to recognize gain, but not loss, realized on the exchange. We will discuss the details of this computation later in the chapter.

The type of stock a shareholder can receive in a §351 exchange is quite flexible and includes voting or nonvoting and common or preferred stock. Stock for purposes of §351 does not include stock warrants, rights, or options.[8] Property transferred in exchange for debt of the corporation is not eligible for deferral under §351.

Example 19-2

What if: Suppose Ginny received a five-year note (debt) in 360 Air valued at $60,000 in exchange for contributing machinery. The original cost of the machinery was $70,000, and Ginny has depreciated it to a basis of zero. Will Ginny defer recognition of the $60,000 gain realized on the transfer of the machinery?

Answer: No. Section 351 provides for deferral only when the transferor of property receives stock in return. Ginny must recognize the entire $60,000 gain.

The Transferor(s) of Property to the Corporation Must Be in Control of the Corporation, in the Aggregate, Immediately after the Transfer Control for purposes of §351 is defined as the ownership of 80 percent or more of the total combined voting power of all voting stock that is issued and outstanding, and 80 percent or more of the total number of shares of each class of nonvoting stock.[9]

[7]An individual who receives stock subject to "restrictions" (e.g., they must remain with the company for a certain number of years) does not report compensation income until the restrictions attached to the stock are lifted (§83). Under §83(b), as an alternative the individual can elect to value the stock on the date received and report that amount as income.

[8]§351(g) identifies nonqualified preferred stock as boot but nonqualified preferred stock will count as equity for purposes of determining control of the corporation. Nonqualified preferred stock generally has characteristics that cause it to more resemble debt than equity.

[9]§368(c). Voting power is generally defined as the ability of the shareholders to elect members of the corporation's board of directors.

Whether the control test is met is based on the collective ownership of the shareholders transferring property to the corporation immediately after the transfer. Keep in mind that this group of shareholders (i.e., the transferors) is composed only of those who have transferred property, which does not include services, in exchange for stock. In addition, the aggregate ownership (not the change in ownership) of these shareholders immediately after the transfer must meet the 80 percent threshold.

ETHICS

Malik owns appreciated property and wants to use this property to start a business with Lance. Malik is considering making a contribution of the property to a newly organized corporation in exchange for 100 percent of the corporate stock. Malik then plans to give half of the stock to Lance in exchange for managing the business. Do you think this transaction will qualify for §351 treatment? Does it make any difference if Lance is Malik's son? Suppose Malik promises that the stock transfer won't occur for a month after making the contribution of property. Does this make any difference? Compare Rev. Rul. 54-96, with *Intermountain Lumber Co.*, 65 TC 1025 (1976).

Example 19-3

What if: Assume Ginny was hesitant to join with Jim and Al in the incorporation of 360 Air. Instead, after six months, Ginny changed her mind and received a 10 percent interest in 360 Air stock in exchange for intangibles that qualified as property under §351. The stock was valued at $60,000, and Ginny's adjusted tax basis in the intangibles was zero. Will Ginny defer recognition of the $60,000 gain realized on the exchange under §351?

Answer: No. Ginny is the only transferor and does not control (80 percent or more of) 360 Air immediately after the transfer. As a result, Ginny must recognize the $60,000 gain.

What if: Suppose Ginny joined with Jim and Al in forming 360 Air and received 25 percent of the corporation's stock in exchange for services. The stock was valued at $150,000. Al and Jim received the remaining 75 percent of the stock in the company in exchange for appreciated property. Will Al and Jim defer recognition of gain they realize on the exchange of the appreciated property under §351?

Answer: No. Taking into account only the stock received in exchange for property, Al and Jim do not collectively control 360 Air immediately after the transaction. Al and Jim own only 75 percent, not 80 percent. Consequently, the transaction is not eligible for deferral under §351, and all gain realized is recognized.

Generally, when a shareholder transfers both services and property to the corporation in exchange for stock, that shareholder is generally considered to be a transferor of property for purposes of the control test. However, if the primary purpose for the shareholder's transfer of property to the corporation is to qualify the exchange of another person under §351, that shareholder would be considered to be a transferor of property only if the value of the stock received for property is not of "relatively small value" compared to the value of the stock received for services.[10] The IRS has stated that, for ruling purposes, property will not be of "relatively small value" if it equals at least 10 percent of the value of the stock received for the services provided.[11]

Example 19-4

What if: Let's say Ginny joined with Jim and Al in the incorporation of 360 Air primarily to qualify Jim and Al for §351 treatment. Ginny received 25 percent of the corporation's stock in exchange for services and intangibles treated as property. The stock was valued at $150,000. The services were valued at $125,000 and the intangibles were valued at $25,000. Al and Jim received the remaining 75 percent of the stock in the company in exchange for appreciated property. Using the IRS standards

[10] Reg. §1.351-1(a)(1)(ii). Note that the determination of relative value is a factual issue.

[11] Rev. Proc. 77-37.

for rulings, will Al and Jim defer recognition of gain they realize on the exchange of the appreciated property under §351?

Answer: Yes. The stock Ginny received in exchange for the intangibles exceeds 10 percent of the value of the stock received for the services ($25,000/$125,000 = 20%). For purposes of determining control, Ginny will qualify as a transferor, and all of the stock received in 360 Air will qualify as having been received for property. Al, Jim, and Ginny will be treated as collectively receiving 100 percent of the 360 Air stock in exchange for property. Hence, Al and Jim will defer gain realized on their exchanges of property for stock. Ginny will recognize compensation of $125,000 on the exchange, but Ginny will defer recognizing any gain realized on the transfer of the intangibles.

What if: Assume Ginny's services were valued at $140,000 and the intangibles were valued at $10,000. Using the IRS standards for rulings, will Al and Jim defer recognition of gain they realize on the exchange of the appreciated property under §351?

Answer: No, because Ginny's primary purpose in transferring the intangible property was to qualify the transfer for deferral. The fair market value of the stock received for the intangibles is less than 10 percent of the stock received for services ($10,000/$140,000 = 7.14%). As a result, the IRS will not consider Ginny to be a transferor of property for ruling purposes, and none of Ginny's stock will count in the control test. Al, Jim, and Ginny are treated as having received collectively only 75 percent of 360 Air stock in exchange for property. Consequently, §351 does not apply to any of the transferors of the property to 360 Air.

This same rule applies to subsequent transfers of property by an existing shareholder to accommodate a new shareholder's transfer of property to an established corporation. The regulations state that stock received for property that is of "relatively small value" in comparison to the value of the stock already owned will not be considered issued in return for property (i.e., the shareholder making the contribution will not be included in the control test) if the "primary purpose" of the transfer is to qualify the exchange of another person under §351. The IRS has stated that, for ruling purposes, an existing shareholder must contribute property that has a fair market value of at least 10 percent of the value of the stock already owned to be included in the control test.[12]

Example 19-5

What if: Assume Jim and Ginny were 100 percent shareholders of SCR and wanted to bring Al on board as a 20 percent shareholder. Al will transfer appreciated property to SCR in return for stock in SCR valued at $100,000. Will Al defer recognizing any gain realized on the transfer under §351?

Answer: No. Al does not control SCR "immediately after" the exchange, taking into account only the stock Al owns in SCR.

What if: Suppose Jim agreed to make an additional property contribution to SCR at the same time as Al's transfer in order to help Al qualify his transfer under §351. Jim's 75 percent ownership interest in SCR was valued at $300,000 at the time of Al's transfer. Using the IRS standards for rulings, how much property (fair market value) must Jim contribute to SCR to have his ownership of stock in SCR counted in determining if Al qualifies for deferral under §351?

Answer: $30,000. For the "accommodation transfer" to be respected by the IRS, Jim must contribute property with a fair market value of 10 percent or more of the fair market value of his existing stock in SCR (10% × $300,000).

THE KEY FACTS

Requirements for Tax Deferral in a Corporate Formation

- Tax deferral applies to transfers of *property* to a corporation.
- The persons transferring property to a corporation must receive only stock in the corporation in return.
- The persons transferring property to a corporation must collectively control the corporation after the transaction.
- Control is defined as ownership of 80 percent or more of the corporation's voting stock and 80 percent or more of each class of nonvoting stock.

(continued)

Tax Consequences When a Shareholder Receives No Boot

As discussed above, when an exchange qualifies under §351, the shareholder's gain or loss realized on the exchange is deferred. This deferral is generally reflected in the shareholder's basis in stock received in the exchange (the deferred gain or loss is built into the stock's tax basis). When no boot is involved, the adjusted tax basis of stock received in a tax-deferred §351 exchange equals the adjusted tax basis of the property transferred less any liabilities assumed by the corporation.[13] The stock is said to have a **substituted basis.** That is, the

[12]Rev. Proc. 77-37.

[13]§358(a).

- Generally, all stock received by the transferor counts for the control test, unless the stock is received solely in exchange for services.

adjusted tax basis of the property transferred is substituted for the adjusted tax basis of the property received.[14] Exhibit 19-4 provides a template for computing the adjusted tax basis of stock received in a tax-deferred §351 transaction.

EXHIBIT 19-4 Computing the Adjusted Tax Basis of Stock Received in a Tax-Deferred Section 351 Transaction with No Boot

	Cash contributed
+	Adjusted tax basis of other property contributed
−	Liabilities assumed by the corporation on property contributed
	Adjusted tax basis of stock received

Source: §358(a).

Example 19-6

As part of the formation of 360 Air, Al transferred inventory, a building, and land to the corporation in return for 50 percent of the corporation's stock (50 shares). The property transferred to the corporation had the following fair market values and adjusted tax bases:

	FMV	Adjusted Tax Basis
Inventory	$ 25,000	$ 15,000
Building	150,000	60,000
Land	200,000	100,000
Total	$375,000	$175,000

In addition, the corporation assumed a mortgage of $75,000 attached to the building and land. The fair market value of the 360 Air stock Al received in the exchange was $300,000. Al realizes a gain of $200,000 on the transfer, computed as follows:

	Fair market value of 360 Air stock received	$ 300,000
+	Mortgage assumed by 360 Air	75,000
	Amount realized	$ 375,000
−	Adjusted tax basis of the property transferred	175,000
	Gain realized	$ 200,000

Assuming Al meets the requirements under §351 to defer recognizing the $200,000 gain realized, what is his tax basis in the 50 shares of 360 Air stock he receives in the exchange?

Answer: $100,000. Al's tax basis in the stock must reflect the gain he defers in the exchange. Al computes tax basis in the 360 Air stock as follows:

	Adjusted tax basis of property contributed	$ 175,000
−	Mortgage assumed by 360 Air	75,000
	Tax basis of 360 Air stock received	**$100,000**

If Al subsequently were to sell his 360 Air stock for its fair market value of $300,000, he would recognize a capital gain of $200,000 ($300,000 − $100,000), an amount equal to the gain he deferred previously.

What if: Assume Al did not meet the requirements under §351 and was required to recognize the $200,000 gain realized. What is Al's tax basis in the 50 shares of 360 Air stock received in the exchange?

Answer: $300,000. Al's tax basis in his stock equals its fair market value. If Al subsequently sells his 360 Air stock for $300,000, he will not recognize any further gain.

[14]§7701(a)(44) uses the term *exchanged basis property* for this type of property.

Tax Consequences When a Shareholder Receives Boot

A shareholder who receives property other than stock (boot) recognizes gains (but not losses) in an amount not to exceed the lesser of (1) the gain realized or (2) the fair market value of the boot received. We calculate the amount of gain recognized when boot is received in a §351 transaction by allocating the boot received to each contributed property using the relative fair market values of the properties.[15] The amount of gain recognized with respect to each asset is the lesser of the gain realized or the boot allocated to such asset. The character of the recognized gain (i.e., capital gain, §1231 gain, ordinary income) is determined by the character of the asset.

Example 19-7

What if: Suppose Al received 40 shares of 360 Air stock with a fair market value of $315,000 plus $60,000 in return for inventory, a building, and land used in his business and transferred to the corporation. The property transferred to the corporation had the following fair market values and adjusted bases:

	FMV	Adjusted Tax Basis	Gain Realized
Inventory	$ 25,000	$ 15,000	$ 10,000
Building	150,000	60,000	90,000
Land	200,000	100,000	100,000
Total	$375,000	$175,000	$200,000

What amount of gain does Al recognize on receipt of the $60,000 boot, and what is its character (ordinary income or §1231 gain)?

Answer: The $60,000 constitutes boot received and causes Al to recognize some or all of the gain realized on each asset in the transfer. Al apportions the $60,000 of boot to each of the properties transferred to the corporation based on their relative fair market values. Al recognizes gain on each property transferred in an amount equal to the lesser of the gain realized or the fair market value of the boot apportioned to the property. The computation is made for each property separately, as follows:

Inventory	
Fair market value of 360 Air stock and cash received	$ 25,000
Less adjusted tax basis of the inventory transferred	−15,000
(1) Gain realized	$ 10,000
(2) Boot apportioned (25/375 × $60,000)	4,000
Gain recognized: lesser of (1) or (2)	**$ 4,000**
Character of gain recognized: ordinary income	
Building	
Fair market value of 360 Air stock and cash received	$ 150,000
Less adjusted tax basis of the building transferred	−60,000
(1) Gain realized	$ 90,000
(2) Boot apportioned (150/375 × $60,000)	24,000
Gain recognized: lesser of (1) or (2)	**$ 24,000**
Character of gain recognized: §1231[16]	

(continued on page 19-10)

[15]In Rev. Rul. 68-55 and Rev. Rul. 85-164, the IRS adopted the proportionate method of allocating gain. However, neither the Code nor the regulations proscribe an allocation mechanism.

[16]If Al owned more than 50 percent of 360 Air after the transfer, the gain would be treated as ordinary income under §1239(a). Section 1239 converts §1231 gain to ordinary income if the transferor of the property owns more than 50 percent of the corporation and the property is depreciable in the hands of the transferee. The gain also could be unrecaptured §1250 gain subject to a maximum tax rate of 25 percent.

	Land	
	Fair market value of 360 Air stock and cash received	$ 200,000
−	Less tax basis of the land transferred	−100,000
	(1) Gain realized	$ 100,000
	(2) Boot apportioned (200/375 × $60,000)	32,000
	Gain recognized: lesser of (1) or (2)	**$ 32,000**
	Character of gain recognized: §1231	

Al recognizes total gain of $60,000 on this transfer ($4,000 + $24,000 + $32,000) and defers recognition of $140,000 of the $200,000 gain realized ($200,000 – $60,000).

What if: Suppose the land has a tax basis of $250,000. What amount of gain or loss would Al recognize?

Answer: The $60,000 of boot must still be apportioned among the assets based on relative fair market values. However, Al cannot recognize any of the realized loss on the land because boot only causes gain realized to be recognized. The recomputation for the land is as follows:

	Land	
	Fair market value of 360 Air stock and cash received	$200,000
−	Less adjusted tax basis of the building transferred	−250,000
	(1) Loss realized	($ 50,000)
	(2) Boot apportioned (200/375 × $60,000)	32,000
	No loss is recognized	

Al recognizes total gain of $28,000 from receipt of the building and inventory ($24,000 + $4,000). Al defers recognition of $72,000 of gain realized ($6,000 + $66,000) from receipt of the building and inventory and all of the $50,000 loss realized from receipt of the land.

Boot received in a §351 transaction receives a tax basis equal to its fair market value.[17] Al must adjust the tax basis in his 360 Air stock to take into account the boot received and the gain recognized. Exhibit 19-5 provides a template for computing stock basis when boot is received in a §351 transaction.

EXHIBIT 19-5 Computing the Tax Basis of Stock in a Section 351 Transaction When Boot Is Received

	Cash contributed
+	Adjusted tax basis of other property contributed
+	Gain recognized on the transfer
−	Fair market value of boot received
−	Liabilities assumed by the corporation on property contributed
	Tax basis of stock received

Source: §358(a)(1).

Example 19-8

Return to the original facts in Example 19-7, in which Al received $60,000 and recognized $60,000 gain in the exchange. What is Al's tax basis in the 360 Air stock?

Answer: $175,000. Al computes the tax basis in the 360 Air stock as follows:

	Adjusted tax basis of property contributed	$ 175,000
+	Gain recognized on the exchange	60,000
−	Fair market value of boot (cash) received	60,000
	Tax basis of stock received	**$175,000**

[17] §358(a)(2).

If Al subsequently sells the 360 Air stock for its current fair market value of $315,000, he would recognize a gain of $140,000 ($315,000 − $175,000), an amount equal to the gain he deferred in the exchange.

Assumption of Shareholder Liabilities by the Corporation

When a business is formed as a corporation in a §351 exchange, the newly formed corporation frequently assumes the outstanding liabilities of the business, such as accounts payable or mortgages. An important tax issue is whether the assumption of liabilities by the new corporation constitutes boot received by the shareholder transferring the liabilities to the corporation. After all, the shareholder does receive something other than stock in the transaction—that is, relief from debt.

Under the general rule, the corporation's assumption of a shareholder's liability attached to property transferred (e.g., the mortgage attached to the building and land transferred by Al to 360 Air) is *not* treated as boot received by the shareholder.[18] However, an exception to this general rule is described below.

Tax-Avoidance Transactions If *any* of the liabilities assumed by the corporation are contributed with the purpose of avoiding the federal income tax or if there is no corporate business purpose for the assumption, *all* liabilities assumed are treated as boot to the shareholder.[19] The "avoidance" motive may be present where the corporation assumes debt created by the shareholders immediately prior to the contribution of the encumbered assets. Completing this transaction is essentially equivalent to having the corporation pay the shareholder cash in exchange for the property. The "no business purpose" motive can also be present when shareholders have the corporation assume their personal liabilities (i.e., a home mortgage or car payments).

Example 19-9

What if: Suppose that when incorporating 360 Air, Jim transferred a parcel of land in exchange for 40 percent of the corporation's stock (40 shares valued at $80,000). The land's fair market value was $100,000, and its tax basis to Jim was $35,000. The land was subject to a $20,000 mortgage that 360 Air assumed on the transfer. Jim borrowed the $20,000 from a bank (using the land as collateral) shortly before transferring the land to 360 Air. Jim used the mortgage proceeds to pay for a new car. Assuming the transfer qualifies under §351 and that the mortgage has a tax-avoidance purpose, what gain or loss does Jim recognize on the transfer?

Answer: $20,000 gain recognized. Jim realized a $65,000 gain on the land transfer ($100,000 fair market value minus $35,000 basis). Because the mortgage has a tax-avoidance purpose, the $20,000 relief of debt is treated as boot received by Jim on the exchange. Consequently, he must recognize gain in the amount of the lesser of (1) the $65,000 realized gain or (2) the $20,000 boot received.

What if: Supposing the liability did not have a tax-avoidance purpose, what gain would Jim recognize on the exchange?

Answer: $0. Because the liability is not considered to be boot, Jim is allowed to defer the entire gain realized on the exchange.

Liabilities in Excess of Basis Even when liabilities are not treated as boot, under §357(c) the taxpayer is required to recognize gain to the extent the liabilities assumed by the corporation exceed the aggregate adjusted tax basis of the properties transferred by the shareholder. The character of §357(c) gain recognized should be based on the character of the transferred assets, but this rule is inadequate if the transfer includes two or more

[18]§357(a).
[19]§357(b).

assets of differing character. The regulations indicate that the character of the gain in this situation should be determined by allocating the gain according to the relative fair market value of the transferred assets. Some tax commentators argue that allocating the gain to assets based on their relative built-in gains is a more appropriate alternative method of allocating gain across the transferred assets because it does not allocate gain to loss assets.

ETHICS

Lisa is the sole proprietor of a business that manufactures solar panels. This week Lisa was approached to exchange her business assets for shares in Burns Power. As part of the exchange, Lisa is requiring Burns Power to assume the home equity loan on her home. Do you think that Lisa should argue that there is no tax-avoidance motive in this arrangement? Suppose that Lisa established her business five years ago by investing funds from a home equity loan. Does this make any difference?

Example 19-10

What if: Assume Al transferred inventory, a building, and land to 360 Air in return for 50 percent of the corporation's stock (50 shares) with a fair market value of $175,000. The corporation will assume a mortgage of $200,000 attached to the land and building. The properties transferred have fair market values and tax bases as follows:

	FMV	Adjusted Tax Basis
Inventory	$ 25,000	$ 15,000
Building	150,000	60,000
Land	200,000	100,000
Total	$375,000	$175,000

Al realizes a gain of $200,000 on the transfer, computed as follows:

	Fair market value of 360 Air stock received	$ 175,000
+	Mortgage assumed by 360 Air	200,000
	Amount realized	$ 375,000
−	Adjusted tax basis of the property transferred	175,000
	Gain realized	**$200,000**

What amount of gain, if any, does Al recognize on the transfer, assuming all of the other requirements of §351 are met?

Answer: $25,000, the excess of the mortgage assumed by 360 Air ($200,000) over the aggregate adjusted tax basis of the property Al transferred to the corporation ($175,000). Al defers gain of $175,000. The character of the $25,000 gain is determined by allocating the gain to the contributed assets and treating the gain in accordance with the character of each asset. For example, in this case 6.67 percent of the $25,000 gain ($25/$375) would be allocated to the inventory and taxed as ordinary income.

What is Al's tax basis in the 360 Air stock?

Answer: $0, computed as follows:

	Adjusted tax basis of property contributed	$175,000
+	Gain recognized on the exchange	25,000
−	Mortgage assumed by 360 Air	200,000
	Tax basis of stock received	**$ 0**

If Al sold his 360 Air stock for $175,000 (its current fair market value), he would recognize a gain of $175,000 ($175,000 – $0), an amount equal to the gain he deferred in the exchange.

There is a special exception for the assumption of liabilities the payment of which would give rise to a deduction. The assumption of such liabilities is disregarded in determining whether the liabilities assumed exceed basis.[20] Examples are a corporation assuming the accounts payable of a cash-method sole proprietorship and a subsidiary assuming "payment liabilities" (e.g., accrued vacation pay) of an accrual-method corporation.

Example 19-11

What if: Suppose Al transferred inventory, a building, and land to 360 Air in return for 50 percent of the corporation's stock (50 shares) with a fair market value of $175,000. The corporation will assume cash-method accounts payable of $200,000. The properties transferred have fair market values and tax bases as follows:

	FMV	Adjusted Tax Basis
Inventory	$ 25,000	$ 15,000
Building	150,000	60,000
Land	200,000	100,000
Total	$375,000	$175,000

Al realizes a gain of $200,000 on the transfer, computed as follows:

	Fair market value of 360 Air stock received	$ 175,000
+	Payables assumed by 360 Air	200,000
	Amount realized	$ 375,000
−	Adjusted tax basis of the property transferred	175,000
	Gain realized	**$200,000**

What amount of gain, if any, does Al recognize in the transfer, assuming all of the other requirements of §351 are met?

Answer: $0. Al defers recognition of the entire gain of $200,000. The assumption of the cash-method payables is disregarded in computing whether the liabilities assumed exceed the aggregate tax basis of the property transferred. The reason for disregarding the payables is that Al has no basis in this asset (the payables are not recognized by a cash-basis taxpayer). The corporation will recognize a deduction or an asset once payment is made on the payables.

What is Al's tax basis in the 360 Air stock?

Answer: $175,000, computed as follows:

	Adjusted basis of property contributed	$ 175,000
+	Gain recognized on the exchange	0
−	Payables assumed by 360 Air	0
	Tax basis of stock received	**$175,000**

If Al subsequently sells his 360 Air stock for $175,000 (its current fair market value), he will recognize a gain of $0 ($175,000 − $175,000). This result seems odd at first glance because the gain deferred before was $200,000. However, by transferring the payables to 360 Air, Al is forgoing a $200,000 deduction that he would have received if he paid off the liabilities while operating as a sole proprietorship. This $200,000 "loss" exactly offsets the $200,000 gain he realized when 360 Air assumed the payables, resulting in a net gain of $0.

Tax Consequences to the Transferee Corporation

The corporation receiving property in exchange for its stock does not recognize gain or loss realized on the transfer.[21] In transactions that do not qualify for §351, the corporation will have a fair market value tax basis in the property. In a §351 transaction, the corporation will

[20]§357(c)(3). Note that this exception is not available when the liabilities are used to create basis in assets, such as payables related to the purchase of tools.

[21]§1032.

have an adjusted tax basis in the property that equals the property's adjusted tax basis in the transferor's hands.[22] The transferred property is said to have a **carryover basis** (i.e., the corporation "carries over" the shareholder's basis and holding period in the transferred property).[23] To the extent the shareholder's adjusted tax basis carries over to the corporation and the property is §1231 property or a capital asset, the shareholder's holding period also carries over (it *tacks* to the property).[24] This could be important in determining if subsequent gain or loss recognized on the disposition of the property qualifies as a §1231 gain or loss or a long-term capital gain or loss.

If the shareholder recognizes gain as a result of the property transfer, either because the shareholder received boot or the liabilities assumed by the corporation in the exchange exceeded the adjusted tax basis of the property contributed by the shareholder, the corporation increases its tax basis in each asset by the gain recognized on that asset. Exhibit 19-6 provides a template for computing the tax basis of each asset received by the corporation in a §351 transaction.

EXHIBIT 19-6 Computing the Tax Basis of Each Asset Received by the Corporation in a Section 351 Transaction

	Adjusted tax basis of the asset contributed by the shareholder
+	Gain recognized by the shareholder on the transfer of the asset to the corporation
	Adjusted tax basis of the asset received

Source: §362(a).

Example 19-12

Let's return to the facts in Example 19-7 in which Al received 40 shares of 360 Air stock with a fair market value of $315,000 and $60,000 in return for his transfer of inventory, a building, and land to the corporation. The $60,000 received by Al constituted boot received and caused him to recognize gain on the transfer. The $60,000 was allocated to each of the properties transferred to the corporation based on their relative fair market values. Al recognized gain on each property transferred in an amount equal to the lesser of the gain realized or the fair market value of the boot allocated to the property. Al's tax results from this transaction can be summarized as follows:

	Adjusted Tax Basis	Gain Recognized
Inventory	$ 15,000	$ 4,000
Building	60,000	24,000
Land	100,000	32,000
Total	$175,000	$60,000

What tax basis does 360 Air take in each of the properties it receives from Al in the exchange?

Answer: 360 Air will carry over Al's adjusted tax basis in the property transferred and will increase the adjusted tax basis by gain recognized by Al on the transfer. The corporation's adjusted tax basis in each of the three properties is as follows:

	Adjusted Tax Basis	Gain Recognized	360 Air Adjusted Tax Basis
Inventory	$ 15,000	$ 4,000	$ 19,000
Building	60,000	24,000	84,000
Land	100,000	32,000	132,000
Total	$175,000	$60,000	$235,000

360 Air also will carry over Al's holding period in the building and land transferred because they are §1231 assets.

[22]§362(a).

[23]See §1223(2) and note that §7701(a)(43) refers to this type of property as *transferred basis property*.

[24]§1223(1).

Tax law limits the ability of a shareholder to transfer a built-in loss to a corporation in a §351 transaction. Without this limitation, a shareholder could create a duplicate loss, one loss for the shareholder and a second loss for the corporation. In particular, if the aggregate adjusted tax basis of property transferred to a corporation by a shareholder in a §351 transfer exceeds the aggregate fair market value of the assets, the aggregate adjusted tax basis of the assets in the hands of the transferee corporation cannot exceed their aggregate fair market value.[25] When determining whether the aggregate adjusted basis of the property transferred to a corporation exceeds the aggregate fair market value of the assets in a §351 transfer, gains recognized by the shareholders are included in the aggregate adjusted tax basis of the assets. The aggregate reduction in tax basis is allocated among the assets transferred in proportion to their respective built-in losses immediately before the transfer. As an alternative, the transferor and transferee can elect to have the transferor reduce her stock basis to fair market value (the duplicate loss is eliminated at either the corporate or shareholder level).

Example 19-13

What if: Assume Al transferred a building and land to the corporation in return for 50 percent of the corporation's stock (50 shares). The property transferred to the corporation had the following fair market values and adjusted tax bases:

	FMV	Adjusted Tax Basis
Building	$ 75,000	$100,000
Land	200,000	100,000
Total	$275,000	$200,000

The fair market value of the 360 Air stock Al received in the exchange was $275,000.

Assuming the transfer meets the requirements under §351 to defer recognizing the $75,000 net gain realized, what is Al's tax basis in the 50 shares of 360 Air stock received in the exchange?

Answer: $200,000. In this case, the aggregate fair market value of the property transferred to the corporation exceeds the aggregate adjusted tax basis of the property. As a result, Al's tax basis in the stock equals the aggregate adjusted tax basis of the property transferred.

What are the adjusted tax bases of the building and land held by 360 Air?

Answer: The building has a carryover basis of $100,000, and the land has a carryover basis of $100,000. Because the aggregate fair market value of the assets transferred to the corporation exceeds the aggregate adjusted tax basis of the property, 360 Air applies the general basis carryover rules. The building retains its built-in loss of $25,000 at the corporate level.

What if: Suppose Al transferred a building and land to the corporation in return for 50 percent of the corporation's stock (50 shares). The property transferred to the corporation had the following fair market values and adjusted bases:

	FMV	Adjusted Tax Basis
Building	$ 75,000	$200,000
Land	200,000	100,000
Total	$275,000	$300,000

The fair market value of the 360 Air stock Al received in the exchange was $275,000.

Assuming the transfer meets the requirements under §351 to defer recognizing the $25,000 net loss realized, what is Al's tax basis in the 50 shares of 360 Air stock he receives in the exchange?

Answer: $300,000. In this case, the aggregate adjusted tax basis of the property transferred to the corporation exceeds the aggregate fair market value of the property. Assuming he doesn't elect to reduce his stock basis to fair market value, Al's tax basis in the stock received will equal the adjusted basis of the assets transferred.

(continued on page 19-16)

[25]§362(e)(2).

What is the adjusted tax basis of the building and land held by 360 Air?

Answer: An aggregate adjusted tax basis of $275,000. Because the aggregate fair market value of the property transferred to the corporation is less than the aggregate adjusted tax basis of the property, 360 Air must reduce the aggregate adjusted tax basis of the property to their aggregate fair market value. The allocation is made to those assets that have a built-in loss; in this example, this includes only the building. The adjusted tax basis of the building will be reduced to $175,000 ($200,000 – $25,000 net built-in loss). The adjusted tax basis of the land will retain its carryover basis of $100,000. This adjustment eliminates the net $25,000 built-in loss at the corporate level.

What alternative election can Al and 360 Air make with respect to these basis reduction rules?

Answer: Al and the corporation can jointly elect to have Al reduce his stock basis to its fair market value of $275,000. The corporation would take a carryover basis of $200,000 in the building and a carryover basis of $100,000 in the land.

What if: Suppose Al transferred a building and land to the corporation in return for 40 percent of the corporation's stock (40 shares). The property transferred to the corporation had the following fair market values and adjusted bases:

	FMV	Adjusted Tax Basis
Building	$ 75,000	$200,000
Land	200,000	100,000
Total	$275,000	$300,000

In the exchange, Al received 360 Air stock worth $220,000 plus $55,000 in cash. Assuming the transfer qualifies under §351, how much gain or loss, if any, will Al recognize on the exchange?

Answer: $40,000 gain recognized. The cash (i.e., boot) is allocated between the building and land in proportion to the relative values, and gain is recognized to the lesser of boot received or realized gain. In this case, $40,000 of boot allocated to the land triggers $40,000 of recognized gain, calculated as follows:

		Building	Land
	Fair market value of stock received	$ 60,000	$160,000
+	Cash received (allocated by relative FMV)	+15,000	+40,000
	Amount realized	$ 75,000	$200,000
–	Adjusted tax basis of assets transferred	−200,000	−100,000
	Gain or (loss) realized	$(125,000)	$100,000
	Gain or (loss) recognized	**$ 0***	**$ 40,000**

*Realized loss is not recognized in a §351 exchange, even when boot is received.

What is Al's tax basis in the 40 shares of 360 Air stock received in the exchange?

Answer: $285,000. Assuming he does not elect to reduce his stock basis to fair market value, Al's tax basis in the stock received will equal the $300,000 adjusted basis of the assets less the $55,000 in cash received plus the $40,000 recognized gain.

What is the adjusted tax basis of the building and land held by 360 Air?

Answer: The aggregate basis is $275,000. Specifically, the basis in the building is $135,000 and the basis in the Land is $140,000. The aggregate tax basis of the assets in the hands of the transferee corporation must first be adjusted upward for any gain recognized by the transferor. Hence, 360 Air must first increase the aggregate basis by the $40,000 recognized gain from $300,000 to $340,000. After increasing the basis of the land for the gain recognized, the aggregate built-in loss is measured as the difference between the $340,000 aggregate basis ($200,000 + $100,000 + $40,000) and the $275,000 aggregate FMV of the transfer ($60,000 + $160,000 + $55,000). The $65,000 reduction in basis ($340,000 – 275,000) is allocated to the loss assets, but in this case the building is the only asset with a built-in loss and receives the reduction in basis.

		Building	Land
	Carryover basis	$200,000	$100,000
+	Gain recognized by Al		+40,000
–	Aggregate built-in loss ($340,000 – $275,000)	−65,000	
	Air 360 adjusted tax basis	$135,000	$140,000

Other Issues Related to Incorporating an Ongoing Business

Depreciable Assets Transferred to a Corporation To the extent a property's adjusted tax basis carries over from the shareholder, the corporation in effect steps into the shoes of the shareholder and continues to depreciate the carryover basis portion of the property's adjusted tax basis using the shareholder's depreciation schedule.[26] Any additional tax basis (from recognition of gain due to boot received) is treated as a separate asset and is subject to a separate depreciation election (i.e., this one physical asset is treated as two separate tax assets for depreciation purposes).

Example 19-14

Let's return to the facts in Examples 19-7 and 19-12. Recall that Al received 40 shares of 360 Air stock with a fair market value of $315,000 and $60,000 in return for his transfer of inventory, a building, and land to the corporation. The cash received by Al constituted boot received and caused him to recognize $60,000 of gain on the transfer. 360 Air takes Al's tax basis in the property and increases it by the gain recognized by Al on the transfer. The corporation's adjusted tax basis in each of the three properties is as follows:

	Adjusted Tax Basis	Gain Recognized	360 Air Adjusted Tax Basis
Inventory	$ 15,000	$ 4,000	$ 19,000
Building	60,000	24,000	84,000
Land	100,000	32,000	132,000
Total	$175,000	$60,000	$235,000

360 Air also will carry over Al's holding period in the building and land transferred because they are §1231 assets. How will 360 Air compute the depreciation deduction on the building for the year of the transfer? For this problem, let's assume that the transfer occurs on January 1. Furthermore, let's assume that Al originally purchased the building for $67,400 in September five years ago and has claimed $7,400 of straight-line depreciation over a 39-year recovery period using a mid-month convention.

Answer: 360 Air carries over Al's depreciation schedule for the building with respect to the $60,000 original basis, but 360 Air depreciates the additional $24,000 as a new asset. With respect to the carryover basis portion of the building, 360 Air uses Al's original cost of $67,400 in the building to calculate the depreciation computation. Al is entitled to ½ month of depreciation on the building in the year of transfer ($67,400 × .02564 × .5/12 = $72), and the corporation is entitled to the remaining 11.5 months of depreciation of $1,656 ($67,400 × .02564 × 11.5/12 = $1,656). The corporation treats the additional $24,000 of basis as a new asset and applies the proper depreciation rate to calculate the additional depreciation. Because the transfer took place in January, 360 Air would be entitled to 11.5 months of depreciation (recall the mid-month convention). Hence, 360 Air would claim additional depreciation of $591 ($24,000 × .02461 = $591) for a total depreciation deduction of $2,247 (i.e., $1,656 + $591).

Practitioners often advise against transferring appreciated property (especially real estate) into a closely held corporation. By doing so the shareholder creates two assets with the same built-in gain as the original property (the stock received in the hands of the shareholder and the building owned by the corporation). The federal government can now collect taxes twice on the same gain, once when the corporation sells the property received and a second time when the shareholder sells the stock. You will notice that Congress is not concerned by a duplication of gain result, only a duplication of loss result. By retaining the property outside the corporation, the shareholder can lease the property to the corporation, thereby reducing the corporation's taxable income through

[26]§168(i)(7)(B)(ii).

rent deductions. Note, however, that there may be valid state tax reasons to own the property inside a corporation, such as lower property taxes.

Contributions to Capital

A **contribution to capital** is a transfer of property to a corporation by a shareholder or nonshareholder for which no stock or other property is received in return. The corporation receiving the property is not taxed on the receipt of the property if the property is contributed by a shareholder.[27] If the property is contributed by a shareholder, the corporation takes a carryover tax basis in the property.[28] If the property is contributed by a nonshareholder (e.g., a city contributes land to induce a corporation to locate its operations there), the corporation recognizes the value of the contributed property as income and takes a fair market value basis in the property.

A capital contribution generally is not a taxable event to the shareholder because the shareholder does not receive any additional consideration in return for the transfer. A shareholder making a capital contribution gets to increase the tax basis in her existing stock in an amount equal to the tax basis of the property contributed.

TAXES IN THE REAL WORLD A Meaningless Gesture?

When a shareholder contributes assets or cash to a solely owned corporation, it would seem that §351 couldn't apply unless the transfer is made "solely in exchange for stock." Unfortunately, there is no other authority that directly addresses the tax consequences should a shareholder make a contribution to capital where the shareholder receives nothing in exchange for the property. Recently, the IRS "has become aware of transactions that purport to result in holding periods for corporate stock that are longer than the period of economic investment." Apparently, some enterprising consultants have attempted to utilize this absence of authority to argue that the contribution would not affect the holding period of the stock. Here's a version of the deal that worries the IRS:

> Shareholder creates corporation with negligible contribution on January 1, Year 1. On March 1, Year 1, Shareholder invests a substantial amount of money in property that appreciates in value. On August 1, Year 1, Shareholder transfers the appreciated property to Corporation for no consideration. On February 1, Year 2, Shareholder sells all of the stock in Corporation for a price that reflects the unrealized appreciation in the property, so that gain is recognized to Shareholder. Shareholder claims that all the stock has a holding period exceeding one year (from January 1, Year 1).

In a memorandum, the Office of Chief Counsel argues that despite the absence of any consideration, §351 applies to this transaction and the shareholder takes a bifurcated (split) basis in his shares with a short-term holding period for the amount representing the August contribution of property. The Chief Counsel argues that issuing stock to the sole shareholder represents a "meaningless gesture" that should not be used to alter the economic substance of the transaction.

The memorandum also provides a second illustration where the sole shareholder contributes cash instead of property. After the contribution, the corporation invests the cash in property that then appreciates and the shareholder again sells his shares. The Chief Counsel rejects the shareholder's argument that the gain on the sale of the shares is entirely long term, again arguing that issuing stock in exchange for the cash would be a meaningless gesture.

Suppose that in this latter illustration, the shareholder didn't make any additional contribution but instead had let the corporation borrow the funds to invest in the property. Do you think the subsequent sale of the shares be treated as long term or short term?

Source: AM 2020-005, available at www.irs.gov/pub/lanoa/am-2020-005.pdf.

[27]§118.

[28]§362(a)(2).

Section 1244 Stock

Stock is generally a capital asset in the hands of the shareholders, and gains or losses from sale or exchange are capital in nature. For individuals, long-term capital gains are taxed at a maximum tax rate of 20 percent. Losses can only offset capital gains plus $3,000 of ordinary income per year. Section 1244 allows a shareholder to treat a loss on the sale or exchange of stock that qualifies as §1244 stock as an ordinary loss.

Section 1244 applies only to individual shareholders who are the original recipients of the stock. The maximum amount of loss that can be treated as an ordinary loss under §1244 is $50,000 per year ($100,000 in the case of married, filing jointly shareholders). For shareholders to qualify for this tax benefit, the corporation from which they received stock must have been a small business corporation when the stock was issued. The Code defines a small business corporation as one in which the aggregate amount of money and other property received in return for the stock or as a contribution to capital did not exceed $1 million. In our story line, 360 Air qualifies as a small business corporation.

There is an additional requirement that for the five taxable years preceding the year in which the stock is sold, the corporation must have derived more than 50 percent of its aggregate gross receipts from an *active* trade or business. 360 Air meets this test as well. Section 1244 provides a tax benefit to entrepreneurs who create a risky start-up company that ultimately fails.

Example 19-15

What if: Assume Al received 50 shares of 360 Air stock (50 percent of the outstanding stock) with a fair market value of $300,000 in return for transferring a building and land to the corporation in a transaction that qualified under §351. As a result of the transfer, Al received a tax basis in the 50 shares of $200,000 ($4,000 per share). Suppose that over time the snowboarding business declined due to a change in weather patterns in Michigan. As a result, Al's 50 shares were worth $50,000 ($1,000 per share). Needing some cash, Al sold all 50 shares to Jim for $50,000 and recognized a $150,000 loss [$50,000 – ($4,000 × 50 shares)]. 360 Air qualifies as a small business corporation under §1244. Al has no capital gains in the year of the sale. How much of the loss can Al deduct if he held his stock at least five years, assuming current tax rules, and he is married, filing a joint tax return and does not have other capital gains or losses? What is the character of the loss (capital or ordinary)?

Answer: $103,000, $100,000 of which is ordinary loss and $3,000 of which is capital loss that can reduce up to $3,000 of ordinary income. The remaining $47,000 loss is carried forward as a capital loss.

What tax planning advice would you give Al to maximize the tax treatment of the loss from sale of the stock?

Answer: Section 1244 imposes an annual limit on the amount of the loss that can be treated as ordinary. To maximize the tax value of his loss, Al should sell enough shares of 360 Air stock to generate a $100,000 loss this year and sell the remaining amount to generate a $50,000 loss next year. In that way, the entire $150,000 loss will be treated as ordinary loss. Of course, delaying the sale of shares is risky because the stock could continue to lose value. Al would need to weigh the tax benefits of the delay against the risk of additional loss.

TAXABLE AND TAX-DEFERRED CORPORATE ACQUISITIONS

LO 19-3

(continued from page 19-2 . . .)

Jim Wheels and Ginny Gears are excited about their new business venture with Al Pine. It seems to solve their need to find a source of revenues during the winter months, when the demand for bicycles declines significantly. With that challenge met, Jim and Ginny have turned their attention to expanding their bicycle business to a new geographic region. At the recent Tour de Gaslight race sponsored by the Michigan Bicycle Racing

Association, Jim struck up a conversation with Pam Peloton, owner of Wolverine Cycles and Repair (WCR) in Ann Arbor, Michigan. Pam mentioned she is planning to move to Colorado and is looking to sell her business. Jim can see lots of synergies in buying WCR. He and Ginny are familiar with the biking community in Ann Arbor, and they understand the economics of operating a business in a college town. Ginny is also excited about the possibility of expanding their company to Ann Arbor.

A meeting has been set up with Pam to explore the possible acquisition of her business. Pam operates Wolverine Cycles and Repair as a C corporation, which gives Jim and Ginny the opportunity to consider buying the assets of the business directly or buying Pam's stock in the corporation. If they take the stock acquisition route, Jim and Ginny need to consider whether they want to operate their new company as a subsidiary of Spartan Cycle and Repair or in a lateral ownership arrangement (in which their two companies would be "brother-sister" corporations). Operating WCR as a subsidiary of SCR would allow Jim and Ginny to file a consolidated tax return with SCR. Pam is concerned about the tax consequences of each of these options, as are Jim and Ginny.

(to be continued . . .)

At some point in the life of a successful business, its owners likely will consider expanding its scope or geographic location. Businesses can grow internally through expansion or externally by acquiring an existing business. Jim and Ginny prefer to buy Pam's existing business to expand to a new geographic location. Because Pam operates the business as a C corporation, Jim and Ginny have multiple options. Jim and Ginny first need to consider whether they will personally acquire the business or have SCR acquire the business. Second, they must determine whether they will purchase the assets or the stock of the corporation. Finally, they need to determine the type of consideration to use in the acquisition (SCR stock or cash). Each of these options can result in different tax consequences for the buyer and the seller. Thus, besides negotiating a purchase price, Jim and Ginny will also need to negotiate the form of the transaction with Pam.

This section of the chapter considers the basic ways in which a corporation or its shareholders can acquire the stock or assets of another corporation and the tax consequences that follow the form of the acquisition. This is an extremely complicated and technical area of the tax law. A thorough discussion of all the ways in which an acquisition can take place likely would take up most or all of a semester. As a result, our discussion is limited to the basic types of corporate acquisitions.

THE KEY FACTS

Tax Model for Corporate Acquisitions

- The acquiring corporation can acquire the target corporation through either a stock or asset acquisition.
- The acquisition can be structured as either taxable or tax-deferred.
- Taxable asset acquisitions allow the acquiring corporation to step up the tax basis of the assets acquired to fair value.
- In stock acquisitions and tax-deferred asset acquisitions, the adjusted tax basis of the target corporation's assets remains at the assets' carryover basis (generally, cost less accumulated depreciation).

The Acquisition Tax Model

When negotiating an acquisition, management of the acquiring corporation must decide whether to acquire the target corporation's assets or stock and what consideration to use (equity, debt, and/or cash). The form of the transaction and the consideration paid will jointly determine the tax status of the transaction.[29] Nontax considerations, such as the ease of transferring stock or the existence of contingent liabilities, often dictate the form of an acquisition by a publicly traded corporation. In contrast, privately held corporations are more likely to make tax considerations a priority.

The shareholders of the target corporation must decide what consideration to demand in return for their stock or assets in the corporation. Cash provides liquidity and does not decline in value after the acquisition is announced, but it also causes the transaction to be fully or partially taxable to the seller. Receiving equity in the acquiring corporation may

[29]The form of the transaction and the consideration paid to shareholders does not affect the financial accounting treatment of the acquisition. ASC 805-10-25-1 requires that all business combinations be accounted for using the purchase method.

allow shareholders to defer paying tax on gain realized on the exchange, but the sellers must accept the risk that the acquiring corporation's stock will decline in value after the deal is announced or consummated.

The technical tax (and accounting) rules that apply to corporate acquisitions are extremely complex. Because the statutory language governing reorganizations is sparse, the IRS and courts often must decide whether the form of a tax-deferred reorganization transaction meets both the literal language of the statute and the substance of the judicial doctrines that underlie the reorganization provisions. As a result, the reorganization area is heavily laden with administrative and judicial pronouncements. Our goal is to provide you with a basic overview of the most common types of corporate acquisitions that you will see discussed in the business press.

Exhibit 19-7 summarizes the four basic types of transactions that can effect an acquisition of another company. The buyer can purchase either stock or assets in a transaction that is either taxable or tax-deferred (in whole or in part) to the seller. The buyer and seller must jointly and simultaneously decide on the form and consideration of the transaction.

EXHIBIT 19-7 Types of Corporate Acquisitions

	Asset Purchase	Stock Purchase
Taxable	Cash or debt generally (Cell 1)	Cash or debt generally (Cell 2)
Tax-Deferred Reorganization	Type A or Type C reorganization using equity (Cell 3)	Type B reorganization using voting equity only (Cell 4)

Often, the buyer and seller have different tax incentives (they want to be in different cells), and this requires both sides to negotiate a compromise arrangement that satisfies both parties. For example, the buyer likely prefers to acquire the target corporation's assets in a taxable asset transaction (cell 1). By purchasing the target corporation's assets in a taxable asset acquisition, the acquiring corporation gets a stepped-up tax basis in the assets equal to fair market value. To the extent the acquiring corporation can allocate the purchase price to depreciable or amortizable assets, this increases future depreciation or amortization deductions on the acquiring corporation's tax return. It is not uncommon in an acquisition involving publicly traded corporations for goodwill to comprise over 70 percent of the purchase price. If the acquiring corporation can achieve a tax basis in the goodwill, the basis can be amortized over 15 years.[30] If the acquiring corporation makes the acquisition using a tax-deferred technique (cell 3 or cell 4) or purchases stock (cell 2), then the tax basis of the acquired assets will not generally be stepped up to fair value and goodwill will have a zero tax basis. Hence, the acquiring company will be ineligible for increased depreciation and amortization deductions.

In contrast to the buyer, the seller likely prefers a tax-deferred transaction (cell 3 or cell 4) because any tax on the appreciation will be postponed. If deferral of the gain isn't possible, then the seller would prefer to sell the stock in a taxable transaction (cell 2) because any gain on the stock will be taxed as capital gains. However, neither of these options provides the acquiring corporation with a stepped-up tax basis in the assets, greatly reducing the future value of the acquisition to the buyer. The seller would likely be reluctant to sell the assets of the corporation in a taxable asset transaction (cell 1) because the seller would be required to pay both the corporate tax on appreciation of the assets and the individual capital gains tax on the appreciation of the stock. Of course, the buyer might be able to overcome the seller's reluctance by offering a sufficiently high purchase price.

[30]§197.

LO 19-4

TAX CONSEQUENCES TO A CORPORATE ACQUISITION

(continued from page 19-20 . . .)

As part of the negotiations with Pam, Jim and Ginny have examined WCR's balance sheet that compares adjusted tax basis with a recent valuation of the assets' fair market values. Pam has held the WCR stock for 10 years, and her tax basis in the stock is $50,000. WCR is an accrual-method taxpayer, and as a result, the payables have a tax basis. That is, the corporation deducted the expenses related to the payables when the expenses were accrued. These facts are summarized as follows:

	FMV	Adjusted Tax Basis	Appreciation
Cash	$ 10,000	$ 10,000	
Receivables	5,000	5,000	
Inventory	20,000	10,000	$ 10,000
Building	80,000	50,000	30,000
Land	120,000	60,000	60,000
Total	$235,000	$135,000	$100,000
Payables	$ 4,000	$ 4,000	
Mortgage*	31,000	31,000	
Total	$ 35,000	$ 35,000	

*The mortgage was attached to the building and land.

Jim and Ginny agree to pay Pam $300,000 for the business, an amount that is $100,000 more than the net fair market value of the assets less the liabilities listed on the balance sheet ($235,000 – $35,000). The additional $100,000 reflects an amount to be paid for the company's customer list, valued at $25,000, with the remaining $75,000 allocated to goodwill.

With the price apparently settled, Jim, Ginny, and Pam now must agree on the form the transaction will take.

(to be continued . . .)

Taxable Acquisitions

A corporation can acquire an ongoing business through the purchase of its stock or assets in return for cash, debt, equity, or a combination thereof. Cash purchases of stock are the most common form of corporate acquisition. Using cash to acquire another company has several nontax advantages; most notably, the acquiring corporation does not "acquire" the target corporation's shareholders in the transaction. There are disadvantages to using cash, particularly if the acquiring corporation must incur additional expensive debt to fund the purchase.

If SCR purchases the assets directly from WCR in return for cash (cell 1 in Exhibit 19-7), WCR will recognize gain or loss on the sale of each individual asset, including goodwill. If the sale results in WCR recognizing gain on self-created goodwill or other intangibles such as customer lists, these are capital assets that result in capital gains. In contrast, SCR will treat amounts allocated to purchased goodwill and other intangibles as assets eligible for amortization. WCR may cease to exist as a separate corporation and could liquidate by transferring the net after-tax proceeds received from SCR to its shareholder. If WCR liquidates, Pam recognizes gain or loss on the exchange of her WCR stock for the cash received.

Example 19-16

What if: Assume SCR will purchase WCR's assets for $300,000 and assume the company's liabilities of $35,000. WCR will realize $335,000 ($300,000 + $35,000), which it will allocate to each of the assets sold, as follows:

	Allocation	Adjusted Tax Basis	Gain Realized
Cash	$ 10,000	$ 10,000	$ 0
Receivables	5,000	5,000	0
Inventory	20,000	10,000	10,000
Building	80,000	50,000	30,000
Land	120,000	60,000	60,000
Customer list	25,000	0	25,000
Goodwill	75,000	0	75,000
Total	$335,000	$135,000	$200,000

What amount of gain or loss does WCR recognize on the sale of its assets, and what is the character of the gain or loss (ordinary income, §1231, or capital)?

Answer: WCR recognizes total gain of $200,000, and WCR pays a corporate-level tax of $42,000 ($200,000 × 21 percent). The character of the gain will be as follows:

	Gain Recognized	Character
Inventory	$ 10,000	Ordinary income
Building	30,000	Ordinary (§291) and §1231
Land	60,000	§1231
Customer list	25,000	Capital gain
Goodwill	75,000	Capital gain
Total	**$200,000**	

What if: Suppose that WCR opts to go out of existence (liquidate) by exchanging the $258,000 net amount realized after taxes ($300,000 − $42,000) for Pam's WCR stock. What amount of gain or loss will Pam recognize on the exchange of her WCR stock for the after-tax proceeds from the sale ($258,000)?

Answer: Pam recognizes a long-term capital gain of $208,000 ($258,000 − $50,000 stock basis) and pays a shareholder-level tax of $31,200 ($208,000 × 15%, assuming it is not subject to the net investment income tax and that Pam's total taxable income is not above the breakpoint for the 15%/20% capital gains tax rate). The total tax paid using this form of acquisition is $73,200 ($42,000 + $31,200). Pam is left with $226,800 after taxes ($300,000 − $42,000 − $31,200).

Although unattractive to Pam, this deal provides SCR (Jim and Ginny) with the maximum tax benefits. The building will have an increased tax basis of $30,000. The customer list and goodwill will have a tax basis of $25,000 and $75,000, respectively, and SCR can amortize these assets over 15 years on a straight-line basis.[31]

If SCR acquires WCR by acquiring Pam's stock for cash (cell 2 in Exhibit 19-7), WCR retains its tax and legal identity. The adjusted tax basis of WCR's assets, which will remain unchanged, will not reflect SCR's tax basis (purchase price) in WCR's stock.

[31]§197. Note that goodwill is not currently amortized for financial accounting purposes, and the determination of goodwill for accounting purposes under ASC 805-30-30-1 differs from the determination of goodwill for tax purposes under §1060. Hence, even a taxable acquisition can give rise to a book–tax difference because different amounts of goodwill exist for tax and book purposes.

Example 19-17

What if: Suppose instead that SCR purchases the WCR stock from Pam for $300,000. What amount of gain or loss does WCR recognize in this transaction?

Answer: WCR will not recognize gain on this form of acquisition because it has not sold any assets directly to SCR.

What amount and character of gain or loss does Pam recognize in this transaction?

Answer: Pam recognizes long-term capital gain of $250,000 ($300,000 – $50,000 stock basis) and pays a shareholder-level tax of $37,500 ($250,000 × 15%). Pam will be left with $262,500 after taxes ($300,000 – $37,500), which is $35,700 more than a direct asset sale ($262,500 – $226,800).

Although attractive to Pam, this deal will not be as attractive (from a tax perspective) as a direct asset sale to SCR (Jim and Ginny). Rather than $80,000, the building will retain its adjusted tax basis of $50,000. In addition, the customer list and goodwill will have a zero tax basis to WCR because they are self-created assets. The adjusted tax basis of WCR's other assets will remain at $135,000. SCR has a tax basis in the WCR stock equal to the purchase price of $300,000.

A tax-efficient outcome would be achieved if the acquisition could be structured so that (1) Pam can treat the transaction as a stock sale and pay a single level of capital gains tax on the gain recognized from the sale and (2) SCR can treat the transaction as an asset purchase and receive a step-up in basis of the assets to fair market value. This alternative is sometimes available in transactions where a corporate taxpayer purchases 80 percent or more of another corporation's stock within a 12-month period. In such cases, SCR can make a **§338(g) election** to treat the stock purchase as a deemed asset purchase.

Like most things that appear too good to be true, this election does not come without some cost. The calculation of these tax costs is extremely technical and beyond the scope of this text. In big-picture terms, WCR is treated as if it is selling its assets prior to the transaction and then repurchasing them at fair market value. This deemed sale of assets causes WCR to recognize gain on assets that have appreciated in value. SCR, as the buyer, bears this tax cost because the fair market value of WCR will be reduced by the tax paid. In almost all cases, this tax cost negates the tax benefits of getting a step-up in basis in WCR's assets and is rarely elected. For example, it rarely makes economic sense to pay income taxes on a $100 gain just to increase the basis of an asset by $100. The additional tax on the $100 gain would very likely outweigh the present value of the savings from an additional $100 of current and future depreciation deductions. However, this election might be tax-efficient if WCR has net operating losses or net capital losses that can be used to offset gain from the deemed sale of its assets.

If the target corporation is a subsidiary of the seller, the acquiring corporation and seller can make a joint **§338(h)(10) election** and have the seller report the gain from the deemed sale of the target corporation's assets on its tax return in lieu of reporting the actual gain from the sale of the target corporation stock. The technical rules that apply to §338(h)(10) elections are also beyond the scope of this text, but these elections often make sense when the seller has loss carryovers to offset any recognized gains. These elections, which are more common than the regular §338(g) election, often achieve tax savings to both parties to the transaction. For example, Dow Chemical sold its AgroFresh subsidiary to a group of investors in 2015. The buyer and seller made a joint §338(h)(10) election, which allowed AgroFresh to record a stepped-up tax basis for its asset. In this instance, the §338(h)(10) election provided almost $400 million in cash tax benefits from amortizing or depreciating the step-up in basis.

Tax-Deferred Acquisitions

As previously discussed, the tax law allows taxpayers to organize a corporation in a tax-deferred manner under §351. The tax law also allows taxpayers to *reorganize* their corporate structure in a tax-deferred manner. For tax purposes, the term **reorganization** encompasses acquisitions and dispositions of corporate assets (including the stock of subsidiaries) and a corporation's restructuring of its capital structure, place of incorporation, or company name. The Code provides tax deferral to the corporation(s) involved in the reorganization (the parties to the reorganization) and the shareholders if the transaction meets one of seven statutory definitions[32] and satisfies the judicial doctrines that underlie the reorganization statutes. As before, tax deferral in corporate reorganizations is predicated on the seller's receiving a continuing ownership interest in the assets transferred, in the form of equity in the acquiring corporation.

The statutory language governing corporate reorganizations is rather sparse. It should not be surprising, then, that the IRS and the courts frequently must interpret how changes in the facts related to a transaction's form affect its tax status. Our goal is to acquaint you with the basic principles that underlie all corporate reorganizations and provide you with an understanding of the most common forms of corporate acquisitions that are tax-deferred.

Judicial Doctrines That Underlie All Tax-Deferred Reorganizations

Continuity of Interest Tax deferral in a reorganization is based on the presumption that the shareholders of the acquired (target) corporation retain a continuing ownership (equity) interest in the target corporation's assets or historic business through their ownership of stock in the acquiring corporation. There is no **bright-line test** to establish whether **continuity of interest (COI)** has been met, although the regulations provide an example that says COI has been satisfied when the shareholders of the target corporation, in the aggregate, receive equity equal to 40 percent or more of the total value of the consideration received.[33]

Continuity of Business Enterprise For a transaction to qualify as a tax-deferred reorganization, the acquiring corporation must continue the target corporation's historic business or continue to use a *significant* portion of the target corporation's historic business assets in a business. This principle is called **Continuity of business enterprise (COBE).** For example, the regulations suggest that in an acquisition of a corporation with three equal business lines, an acquirer will meet COBE if one line of business is continued without interruption. Whether the historic business assets retained are "significant" is a facts-and-circumstances test, which adds to the administrative and judicial rulings that are part and parcel of the reorganization landscape. COBE does not apply to the historic business or assets of the acquiring corporation; the acquiring corporation can sell off its assets after the reorganization without violating the COBE requirement.

Business Purpose Test As early as 1935, the Supreme Court stated that transactions with "no business or corporate purpose" should not receive tax deferral even if they comply with the statutory requirements.[34] To meet the business purpose test, the acquiring corporation must be able to show a significant business purpose for engaging in the transaction (other than tax avoidance).

[32]The types of corporate reorganizations are defined in §368(a)(1).

[33]Reg. §1.368-1T(e)(2)(v), Example 10.

[34]*Gregory v. Helvering,* 293 U.S. 465 (1935).

Type A Asset Acquisitions

Type A reorganizations (cell 3 in Exhibit 19-7) are statutory **mergers** or **consolidations.**[35] In a merger, either the acquired (target) corporation or the acquiring corporation will cease to exist. For example, SCR could acquire the assets and liabilities of WCR by transferring SCR shares to Pam in exchange for her WCR stock, and WCR would no longer exist. This type of merger is an *upstream* or *forward* acquisition because the target is merged into the acquiring corporation. Alternatively, the target corporation could be the surviving entity, and this type of acquisition is a *downstream* or *reverse* acquisition. In a consolidation, two corporations (e.g., SCR and WCR) transfer their assets and liabilities to a newly formed corporation in return for stock in the new corporation, after which the original corporations (SCR and WCR) both cease to exist.

In a Type A reorganization, the target corporation shareholders defer recognition of gain or loss realized on the receipt of stock of the acquiring corporation. Similar to a §351 transaction, if a target corporation shareholder receives money or other property (boot) from the acquiring corporation or its acquisition subsidiary, the shareholder recognizes *gain* to the extent of the money and fair market value of other property received (not to exceed the gain realized). The shareholder's tax basis in the stock received is a *substituted basis* of the stock transferred plus any gain recognized less any money and the fair market value of other property received. The target corporation's assets remain the same at their (historic) adjusted tax basis in a Type A merger.

Exhibit 19-8 provides an illustration of a Type A merger. The consideration that can be paid to Pam is relatively flexible in a Type A merger; the only limitation on the consideration is that the transaction must satisfy the COI requirement (at least 40 percent of the consideration must be SCR stock). The stock used to satisfy the COI test can be voting or nonvoting, common or preferred.

EXHIBIT 19-8 Form of a Type A Merger

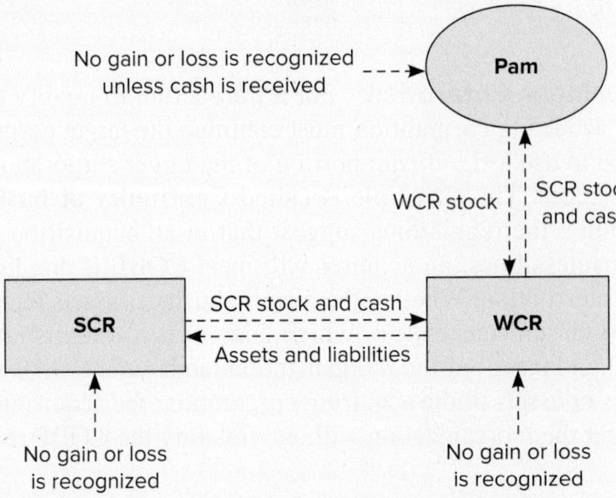

Example 19-18

What if: Assume WCR will merge into SCR in a Type A reorganization. Under the terms of the deal, SCR will pay Pam $300,000 in SCR stock, after which WCR will merge into SCR. Pam's tax basis in the WCR stock is $50,000. What amount of gain will Pam *realize* on the exchange of WCR stock for SCR stock?

Answer: $250,000 ($300,000 – $50,000)

[35]"Type A reorganizations" are so named because they are described in §368(a)(1)(A). Likewise, Type B and Type C reorganizations are described in subparagraphs (B) and (C) of §368, respectively.

What amount of gain will Pam *recognize* on the exchange of her WCR stock for SCR stock?

Answer: $0. Pam defers the entire $250,000 gain realized because only stock was transferred (no boot).

What is Pam's tax basis in the SCR stock?

Answer: $50,000. Because the entire gain is deferred, Pam's tax basis in the SCR stock is a substituted basis from the WCR stock. This preserves the gain deferred for future recognition if Pam should choose to sell the SCR stock in the future for $300,000.

What is the tax basis of each of the assets SCR receives from WCR in the merger?

Answer: SCR receives a carryover tax basis in each of the assets received (e.g., the tax basis of the goodwill and customer list will be zero).

What if: Suppose instead Pam wants some cash as well as SCR stock in the transaction. What is the maximum amount of cash Pam can receive from SCR and not violate the COI rule as illustrated in the regulations?

Answer: $180,000 ($300,000 × 60%). Pam can receive a maximum of 60 percent of the consideration in cash and not violate the COI rule under the regulations.

What if: Assume Pam receives $100,000 in cash plus $200,000 in SCR stock in exchange for all of her WCR stock in a Type A merger. What amount of gain will Pam *realize* on the exchange?

Answer: $250,000 ($300,000 – $50,000)

What amount of gain will Pam *recognize* on the exchange?

Answer: $100,000. Pam must recognize gain in an amount that is the lesser of the gain realized or the boot received. Pam defers the $150,000 gain.

What is Pam's tax basis in her SCR stock?

Answer: $50,000, computed as follows:

	Adjusted basis of WCR stock exchanged	$ 50,000
+	Gain recognized on the exchange	100,000
–	Fair market value of boot (cash) received	100,000
	Tax basis of stock received	**$ 50,000**

This calculation preserves the gain deferred for future recognition if Pam sells her SCR stock in the future for at least $200,000 ($200,000 – $50,000 = $150,000).

TAXES IN THE REAL WORLD What the Heck Is a SPAC?

When a private company wants its shares to be publicly traded, then historically it would hire an investment bank to provide advice, underwrite, and assist in issuing shares in the new public company. This process is called an initial public offering (IPO), and it involves regulatory review that can take months to finalize. Ultimately, there is no guarantee with an IPO that the company will ultimately go public if stock market conditions become unfavorable before the IPO is approved.

A reverse merger is a popular alternative to an IPO because the process is simpler, shorter, and less expensive. In a reverse merger, a private company becomes a public company by purchasing control of another public company. The shareholders of the private company receive sufficient stock in the public company to control its board of directors. Once the merger is complete, the firm has greater access to capital markets and can issue additional shares of stock to pursue corporate acquisitions, and investors gain the ability to liquidate their holdings.

The way a *special purpose acquisition company* (SPAC) works is that a *sponsor* creates a publicly listed *shell* corporation by selling shares to investors. This shell company does not operate a business, but instead only holds cash contributed by investors. The sponsor then looks for a private company to merge with the shell company in a reverse merger. When the sponsor identifies a target company and completes the merger, the target company gets the money in the shell company and the investors in the shell company get shares of the target company, which are publicly traded.

(*continued on page 19-28*)

Besides its speed and simplicity, a SPAC allows more speculative companies to get funding at an earlier stage than under an IPO. Rather than relying on reviews by the SEC and investment banks as in an IPO, investors in a SPAC rely on the sponsor who formed the SPAC to investigate the target company. This can allow the target company to become publicly traded using optimistic projections rather than the audited financial records that would be required to be reviewed in an IPO.

Reverse mergers are typically treated as Type A tax-deferred acquisitions. Hence, the target company retains all of its tax characteristics and tax attributes, as does the acquiring (SPAC) corporation. All that changes is the identity of the publicly traded corporation.

Sources: SEC Investor Alert, "What You Need to Know About SPACs—Updated Investor Bulletin," on the web at www.sec.gov/oiea/investor-alerts-and-bulletins/what-you-need-know-about-spacs-investor-bulletin.

There are several potential disadvantages to structuring the transaction as a statutory merger. Pam will become a shareholder of SCR, and the historic adjusted tax basis of WCR's assets and liabilities will carry over to SCR. Going back to the facts in Example 19-18, Pam will not owe any tax on the transaction, but she will not receive any cash. Finally, WCR will cease to exist as a separate corporation. Jim and Ginny expressed a desire to operate WCR as an independent corporation. To accomplish this, SCR will need to transfer the WCR assets and liabilities to a newly created subsidiary under §351. SCR will incur the additional cost to re-title the assets a second time and pay any state transfer tax on the transfer of the assets. Jim and Ginny can avoid this latter cost by employing a variation of a Type A reorganization called a *forward (upstream) triangular merger.*

Forward Triangular Merger In a forward triangular merger, the acquiring corporation creates a subsidiary corporation (called, perhaps, SCR Acquisition Subsidiary in our example) that holds stock of the acquiring corporation. The target corporation then merges into this subsidiary with its shareholders (Pam in this case) receiving stock of the acquiring corporation (SCR) in exchange for the stock of the target corporation (WCR). In our example, when the dust clears, WCR assets and liabilities are isolated in a wholly owned subsidiary of SCR. Exhibit 19-9 provides an illustration of a forward triangular merger for determining the tax consequences to the parties in our fictional transaction.

EXHIBIT 19-9 Form of a Forward Triangular Merger

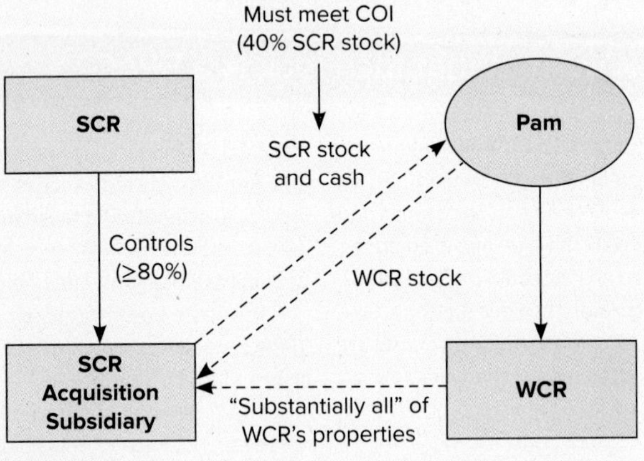

This type of merger is a common vehicle for effecting mergers when the parent corporation stock is publicly traded or the parent corporation is a holding company. For a forward triangular merger to be effective, the transaction must satisfy the requirements to be a straight Type A merger and one additional requirement: The acquisition subsidiary must acquire "substantially all" of the target corporation's properties in the exchange. In Rev. Proc. 77-37, the IRS announced in making rulings on triangular forward acquisitions, it would interpret "substantially all" to mean 90 percent of the fair market value of the target corporation's *net* properties and 70 percent of the fair market value of the target corporation's *gross* properties. For example, to qualify for an IRS ruling as a tax-deferred forward triangular merger, SCR would need to acquire 90 percent of WCR's net properties, or \$270,000 (90% × \$300,000). In addition, SCR would need to acquire 70 percent of WCR's gross value, or \$234,500 (\$335,000 × 70%).

Reverse Triangular Merger Another variation of a Type A reorganization is the *reverse (downstream) triangular merger*. Suppose that WCR holds valuable assets that cannot be easily transferred to another corporation (perhaps employment contracts or licenses). In this scenario, it would not be prudent to merge WCR into SCR or merge it into a subsidiary because these valuable assets would be lost when WCR ceased to exist. In a reverse triangular merger, the acquiring corporation still creates a subsidiary corporation that holds stock of the acquiring corporation. However, it is the acquisition subsidiary that merges into the target corporation. Again, the shareholders of the target corporation (Pam) receive stock of the acquiring corporation (SCR) in exchange for the stock of the target corporation (WCR). When the dust clears, however, the target corporation (WCR) is still intact, albeit as a wholly owned subsidiary of the acquiring corporation. Reverse triangular mergers are desirable because the transaction preserves the target corporation's existence. Exhibit 19-10 provides an illustration of a reverse triangular merger for determining the tax consequences to the parties in our fictional transaction.

EXHIBIT 19-10 Form of a Reverse Triangular Merger

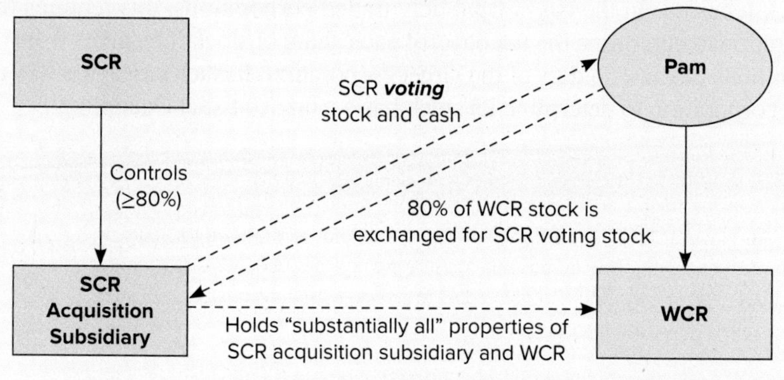

Three additional requirements must be met to satisfy the requirements for tax deferral in a reverse triangular merger. First, after the transaction the acquiring corporations must hold "substantially all" of the properties of both the target corporation and the acquisition subsidiary, excluding the property transferred to the shareholders. Second, in the exchange, the target corporation's shareholders must transfer an amount of stock in the target corporation that constitutes control of the target corporation (80 percent or more of the target stock). Finally, the target corporation's shareholders must receive *voting stock* of the acquiring corporation in return for target stock that constitutes control of the target corporation. For example, if the SCR Acquisition Subsidiary acquires 100 percent of WCR's stock in the exchange, at least 80 percent of the consideration the SCR Acquisition Subsidiary pays Pam must be in the form of SCR voting stock.

This last requirement often presents too high a hurdle in acquisitions in which the acquiring corporation wants to use a combination of cash and stock to acquire the target corporation. Publicly traded corporations are very sensitive to the amount of stock they use in an acquisition because of the negative effect it can have on the company's earnings per share (issuing additional stock increases the denominator in the earnings per share computation).

Type B Stock-for-Stock Reorganizations

Type B reorganizations (cell 4 in Exhibit 19-7) are often referred to as **stock-for-stock acquisitions.** The requirements for a tax-deferred Type B reorganization are very restrictive. In particular, the acquiring corporation (SCR) must acquire control (80 percent or more ownership) of the target corporation (WCR) using solely the voting stock of the acquiring corporation. Additional consideration of as little as \$1 can taint the transaction and

THE KEY FACTS

Forms of a Tax-Deferred Asset Acquisition

- Statutory Type A merger
  - Must meet state law requirements to be a merger or consolidation.
  - Judicial requirements of COI, COBE, and business purpose must be met.
- Forward triangular merger
  - Must meet requirements to be a straight Type A merger.
  - The target corporation merges into an acquisition subsidiary (80 percent or more shares owned by the acquiring corporation).
  - The acquisition subsidiary must acquire "substantially all" of the target corporation's properties in the exchange.
- Reverse triangular merger
  - Must meet requirements to be a straight Type A merger.
  - The acquisition subsidiary merges into the target corporation.
  - The target corporation must hold "substantially all" of the acquisition subsidiary's properties and its own properties after the exchange.
  - The acquisition subsidiary must receive in the exchange 80 percent or more of the target corporation's stock in exchange for voting stock of the acquiring corporation.

THE KEY FACTS

Forms of a Tax-Deferred Stock Acquisition

- Stock-for-stock B reorganization
  - The acquiring corporation must exchange solely voting stock for stock of the target corporation.
  - The acquiring corporation must control (own 80 percent or more of) the target corporation after the transaction.
  - The target corporation shareholders take a substituted tax basis in the acquiring corporation stock received in the exchange.
  - The acquiring corporation takes a carryover tax basis in the target corporation stock received in the exchange.

EXHIBIT 19-11 Form of a Type B Reorganization

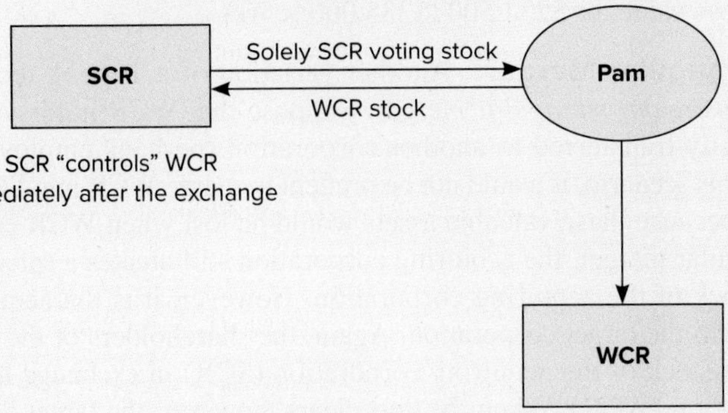

cause it to be fully taxable to the shareholders of the target corporation (Pam). Not surprisingly, Type B reorganizations are rare among publicly traded corporations. Exhibit 19-11 provides an illustration of the form of a Type B merger using our fictional example.

In a Type B reorganization, Pam will defer recognition of any gain or loss realized and take a substituted basis in the SCR stock. SCR takes a carryover basis (from Pam) in the WCR stock received. In the case of publicly traded corporations, this requires the acquiring corporation to determine the tax basis of each share of stock it receives from thousands or even millions of shareholders of the target corporation. In such cases, the IRS allows the acquiring corporation to determine its stock basis using statistical sampling.

Example 19-19

What if: Suppose SCR will exchange SCR voting stock for all of Pam's WCR stock in a Type B stock-for-stock reorganization. Pam's tax basis in WCR stock is $50,000. The fair market value of the SCR stock is $300,000. What amount of gain will Pam *realize* on the exchange of WCR stock for SCR stock?

Answer: $250,000 ($300,000 – $50,000)

What amount of gain will Pam *recognize* on the exchange of WCR stock for SCR stock?

Answer: $0. Pam defers the entire $250,000 gain realized because only SCR stock is received (no boot).

What is Pam's tax basis in the SCR stock?

Answer: $50,000. Because the entire gain is deferred, Pam's tax basis in the SCR stock is a substituted basis from the WCR stock. This preserves the gain deferred for future recognition if Pam should choose to sell the SCR stock in the future for its fair market value of $300,000.

What is SCR's tax basis in the WCR stock received in the exchange?

Answer: $50,000. SCR receives a substituted tax basis equal to Pam's basis in her WCR stock.

What is WCR's adjusted tax basis in the assets after the exchange?

Answer: The adjusted tax basis of WCR's assets remains the same (e.g., the tax basis of the goodwill and customer list will be zero).

What if: Suppose Pam received $10,000 plus $290,000 of SCR stock in the transaction. How does this change in facts affect Pam's tax consequences?

Answer: This transaction will not qualify as a Type B reorganization and the entire realized gain of $250,000 is recognized. For a Type B reorganization to be tax-deferred, Pam cannot receive any cash. Given her desire to move to Colorado, this limitation likely will be a deal breaker.

There are many variations of corporate acquisitions and reorganizations that we do not discuss in this chapter because of complexity. Suffice it to say that tax experts in mergers and acquisitions have a toolbox of ideas and alternatives that allow for countless ways to structure a transaction and achieve tax deferral for the parties to the reorganization. For the novice entering this field of taxation, such variety can be both exhilarating and exasperating. Our goal in this section is to provide you with a glimpse of this intricate area of taxation. A summary of the tax-deferred reorganizations discussed in this section, along with the other forms of tax-deferred reorganizations, is provided in Exhibit 19-12.

EXHIBIT 19-12 Summary of Tax-Deferred Corporate Reorganizations

Form of Reorganization	Description
Statutory Merger Type A	One corporation acquires the assets and liabilities of another corporation in return for stock or a combination of stock and cash. The acquisition is tax-deferred if the transaction satisfies the continuity of interest, continuity of business enterprise, and business purpose test requirements.
Forward Triangular	The acquiring corporation uses stock of its *parent* corporation to acquire the target corporation's stock, after which the target corporation merges into the acquiring corporation. To be tax-deferred, the transaction must meet the requirements to be a Type A merger. In addition, the acquiring corporation must use *solely* the stock of its parent corporation and acquire "substantially all" of the target corporation's property in the transaction.
Reverse Triangular	The acquiring corporation uses stock of its parent corporation to acquire the target corporation's stock, after which the acquiring corporation merges into the target corporation (which becomes a subsidiary of the parent corporation). To be tax-deferred, the transaction must satisfy three requirements: (1) the surviving corporation must hold "substantially all" of the properties of both the surviving and the merged corporations, (2) the target shareholders must transfer in the exchange an amount of stock in the target that constitutes control of the target (80 percent or more of the target's stock), and (3) the target shareholders must receive parent corporation voting stock in return.
Type B	The acquiring corporation uses its voting stock (or the voting stock of its parent corporation) to acquire control (80 percent voting power and 80 percent of nonvoting stock) of the target corporation. To be tax-deferred, the target shareholders must receive *solely* voting stock of the acquiring corporation.
Type C	The acquiring corporation uses its voting stock (or the voting stock of its parent corporation) to acquire "substantially all" of the target corporation's assets. The end result of a Type C reorganization resembles a Type A reorganization. The major difference between a Type C reorganization and a Type A reorganization is that state law governs the form of the Type A merger, while the Internal Revenue Code governs the form of the Type C reorganization.
Type D	Nondivisive Type D: A corporation transfers all or part of its assets to another corporation, and immediately after the transfer the shareholders of the transferor corporation own at least 50 percent of the voting power or value of the transferee corporation. Divisive Type D: A corporation transfers all or part of its assets to another corporation, and immediately after the transfer the shareholders of the transferor corporation own at least 80 percent of the transferee corporation.
Type E	Type E reorganizations are often referred to as recapitalizations. Stock in the corporation (e.g., common) is exchanged for a different class of stock (e.g., preferred) or securities (debt). Recapitalizations can range from an amendment in the corporate charter to a change in the redemption price or liquidating value of stock to an actual exchange of stock between the corporation and its shareholder(s).
Type F	Type F reorganizations are described as a "mere change in identity, form, or place of organization" of a single corporation. A corporation uses a Type F reorganization to change its corporate name or its state (country) of incorporation.
Type G	Type G reorganizations are often referred to as bankruptcy reorganizations. In a Type G reorganization, the corporation transfers all or a part of its assets to another corporation in a Title 11 case, and the stock of the corporation receiving the assets is distributed in a transaction that is tax-deferred.

Tax law also allows corporations to divide by transferring stock of a subsidiary to shareholders in a pro rata distribution (spin-off) or a non–pro rata distribution (split-off).[36] The technical details of these transactions are beyond the scope of this text.

[36]§355.

TAXES IN THE REAL WORLD Consolidations and Acquisitions in Oil

Innovations and unexpected events, such as recessions, can roil whole industries, resulting in waves of corporate acquisitions as firms try to retrench and reorganize. In 2017, the oil and gas industry was trying to recover from a recession and the fracking boom was about to upend the industry further.

One result was that Noble Energy (NYSE: NBL) agreed to exchange stock and cash to acquire Clayton Williams Energy Inc. (NYSE: CWEI). Under the agreement, CWEI shareholders would receive cash of $34.75 and approximately 3.722 NBL shares for each CWEI share. The ratio of cash and stock was to be adjusted so that the total value of the NBL stock issued would not be less than 75 percent of the total merger consideration. According to SEC filings, the qualification of the transaction as a "reorganization" within the meaning of §368(a) of the Internal Revenue Code of 1986 is a condition to the deal.

While fracking led to an earlier boom, the pandemic at the beginning of 2020 caused another severe recession for oil and gas. This time, however, Noble was the target and not the acquirer. On August 24, 2020, Noble Energy entered into a definitive agreement with Chevron (NYSE: CVX) under which Chevron would acquire all the outstanding shares of Noble in exchange for Chevron shares. Again, the deal depended on the transaction qualifying as a "reorganization" organized as a downstream triangular merger (Noble survives as a subsidiary of Chevron).

Sources: Clayton Williams Energy Inc. proxy dated March 23, 2017; and Nobel Energy proxy dated August 26, 2020.

LO 19-5

COMPLETE LIQUIDATION OF A CORPORATION

(continued from page 19-22 . . .)

After several years of trying to get 360 Air off the ground, Jim, Ginny, and even Al realize that there is not enough demand for snowboarding products in East Lansing to make their business venture profitable. Reluctantly, the three owners have decided to liquidate the corporation and have constructed the company's tax accounting balance sheet, which is reproduced below.

	FMV	Adjusted Tax Basis	Difference
Cash	$138,000	$138,000	
Receivables	2,000	2,000	
Inventory	10,000	12,000	$ (2,000)
Building	150,000	48,000	102,000
Land	200,000	100,000	100,000
Total	$500,000	$300,000	$200,000

The parties agree that 360 Air will sell off the inventory, building, and land and collect the remaining receivables. After the sale, 360 Air will pay taxes of $42,000 (21% × $200,000) on the gains and divide the remaining $458,000 in cash ($500,000 − $42,000) pro rata between the three shareholders (50 percent to Al, 40 percent to Jim, and 10 percent to Ginny). ■

The owners of a corporation may decide at some point to discontinue the corporation's business activities. They may make this decision because the corporation is not profitable, the officers and shareholders wish to change the organizational form of the business (e.g., to a flow-through entity), or the owners want to consolidate operations (e.g., a subsidiary is liquidated into the parent corporation).

A complete liquidation occurs when a corporation acquires all its stock from all its shareholders in exchange for all its net assets, after which the corporation ceases to do business. For tax purposes, a corporation files Form 966 ("Corporate Dissolution or Liquidation") to inform the IRS of its intention to liquidate its tax existence. The form should be filed within 30 days after the board of directors resolve to liquidate the corporation.

Tax Consequences to the Shareholders in a Complete Liquidation

The tax consequences to a shareholder in a complete liquidation depend on (1) whether the shareholder is incorporated and (2) what percentage of the corporation the shareholder owns. In general, all *noncorporate* shareholders receiving liquidating distributions have a fully taxable transaction.[37] The shareholders treat the property received as full payment in exchange for the stock transferred. They compute capital gain or loss by subtracting the stock's tax basis from the money and fair market value of property received in return. If a shareholder assumes the corporation's liabilities on property received as a liquidating distribution, this reduces the amount realized by the amount of the liabilities assumed when computing the realized gain or loss. The shareholder's tax basis in the property received equals the property's fair market value.

Example 19-20

As a result of the liquidation of 360 Air, Ginny received cash of $45,800 (representing her 10 percent ownership in the company's assets of $458,000 after all debts were paid). Ginny's tax basis in the 360 Air stock is $60,000.

What amount of gain or loss will Ginny *realize* and *recognize* on the exchange of 360 Air stock for 360 Air assets?

Answer: Ginny will realize a loss of $14,200, computed as the amount realized of $45,800 less the tax basis of $60,000. Ginny will recognize a $14,200 long-term capital loss. The entire amount could be deductible to the extent of Ginny's capital gains. Otherwise, Ginny can offset this loss against capital gains and deduct an additional $3,000 of net capital loss. Any unused capital loss would carry forward.

As a result of the complete liquidation of 360 Air, Jim received $183,200 cash (representing his 40 percent ownership in the company's assets of $458,000). Jim's tax basis in 360 Air is $240,000, an amount equal to the cash contributed when the corporation was formed.

What amount of gain or loss will Jim *realize* on the exchange of his 360 Air stock for 360 Air assets?

Answer: $56,800 loss, the amount realized ($183,200) less Jim's tax basis in the stock ($240,000).

What amount of loss will Jim *recognize* on the exchange, and what is the character of the loss?

Answer: $56,800 long-term capital loss. The entire amount could be deductible to the extent of Jim's capital gains. Otherwise, Jim can offset this loss against capital gains and deduct an additional $3,000 of net capital loss. Any unused capital loss would carry forward.

What if: Suppose that the land owned by 360 Air consists of two parcels, the building is located on parcel #1 which has a value of $50,000 and an adjusted basis of $40,000. Parcel #2 is an undeveloped tract of land with a value of $150,000 and an adjusted basis of $60,000. Suppose further that rather than sell parcel #2, 360 Air distributed parcel #2 and $79,000 cash to Al. This consideration represents Al's 50 percent interest in the net fair market value of the company (50% × $458,000). Al's tax basis in the 360 Air stock is $100,000. What amount of gain or loss will Al *realize* and *recognize* on the exchange of the 360 Air stock for 360 Air assets?

Answer: $129,000 realized and recognized gain. The gain is computed as the amount realized ($150,000 + $79,000 = $229,000) less Al's adjusted tax basis in the stock ($100,000). The gain is taxable as a long-term capital gain.

What is Al's tax basis in the land he receives in the liquidation?

Answer: $150,000. Al takes a tax basis in the land equal to its fair market value.

[37] §331.

Liquidating distributions to corporate shareholders are also taxable unless the corporation owns 80 percent or more of the stock (voting power and value). Corporate shareholders owning 80 percent or more of the stock of the liquidating corporation do not recognize gain or loss on the receipt of liquidating distributions.[38] This nonrecognition treatment is mandatory. The adjusted tax basis in the property transferred carries over to the corporate shareholder receiving the liquidating distribution.[39] This deferral provision allows a group of corporations under common control to reorganize their organizational structure without recognizing gain.

Example 19-21

What if: Suppose 360 Air was a 100-percent-owned subsidiary of SCR, and 360 Air is liquidated into SCR. SCR has a tax basis in its 360 Air stock of $300,000. What amount of gain or loss will SCR *realize* on the complete liquidation of 360 Air stock for 360 Air assets?

Answer: $200,000 ($500,000 – $300,000).

What amount of gain will SCR *recognize* on the exchange?

Answer: $0. The gain is not recognized because SCR owns 80 percent or more of 360 Air.

What is SCR's adjusted tax basis in the assets and liabilities it receives in the liquidation?

Answer: SCR will inherit a carryover tax basis in 360 Air's assets and liabilities.

Tax Consequences to the Liquidating Corporation in a Complete Liquidation

The tax consequences to the liquidating corporation depend on the tax treatment applied to the shareholder to whom the property was distributed.

Taxable Liquidating Distributions Typically, a liquidating corporation recognizes all gains and certain losses on taxable liquidating distributions of property to shareholders.[40] The liquidating corporation does not recognize loss if the loss property is distributed to a related person and either (1) the distribution is non pro rata (to the related person) or (2) the distributed asset is disqualified property.[41] A distribution of loss property is non pro rata unless the related person only receives in the distribution an interest in the loss property equal to the related party's ownership interest. A *related person* is defined as a shareholder who owns more than 50 percent of the value of the stock in the liquidating corporation.[42] *Disqualified property* is property acquired within five years of the date of distribution in a tax-deferred §351 transaction or as a nontaxable contribution to capital.

[38]§332(a). Corporate shareholders must meet the 80 percent ownership test from the time the plan is adopted until the plan is complete. Under §1504(a)(2), the corporation must own 80 percent or more of both voting power and value of the shares of the liquidating corporation. Besides corporate ownership, deferral also includes additional requirements for asset distributions.

[39]§334(b)(1).

[40]§336(a).

[41]§336(d)(1).

[42]§267(b) defines related persons and includes constructive ownership rules under §267(c).

Example 19-22

360 Air made taxable liquidating distributions to Jim, Ginny, and Al during the current year. Al owns 50 percent of the stock, Ginny owns 10 percent, and Jim owns 40 percent. Assume for purposes of this example that 360 Air made a pro rata distribution of each asset to its three shareholders. The company's tax accounting balance sheet at the time of the distribution is shown below:

	FMV	Adjusted Tax Basis	Difference
Cash	$138,000	$138,000	
Receivables	2,000	2,000	
Inventory	10,000	12,000	$ (2,000)
Building	150,000	48,000	102,000
Land	200,000	100,000	100,000
Total	$500,000	$300,000	$200,000

What amount of gain or loss does 360 Air recognize as a result of the distribution?

Answer: $200,000. 360 Air recognizes all gains and losses on the distribution of its assets in the following amounts and character:

	Gain (Loss) Recognized	Character
Inventory	$ (2,000)	Ordinary income
Building	102,000	Ordinary (§291) and §1231
Land	100,000	§1231
Net gain	**$200,000**	

Note that the gain or loss on the complete liquidation is identical to gains and losses that would result if 360 Air had sold all of its assets at fair market value.

What if: Assume Jim owned 60 percent of the stock and 360 Air proposed distributing the assets other than the land to Jim. The company's tax accounting balance sheet at the time of the distribution is shown below:

	FMV	Adjusted Tax Basis	Difference
Cash	$138,000	$138,000	
Receivables	2,000	2,000	
Inventory	10,000	12,000	$ (2,000)
Building	150,000	48,000	102,000
Land	200,000	100,000	100,000
Total	$500,000	$300,000	$200,000

What amount of gain or loss would 360 Air recognize as a result of the distribution?

Answer: $202,000 gain, as calculated below. 360 Air would recognize gains but could not recognize the $2,000 inventory loss because the distribution is non pro rata (Jim's interest in the inventory was only 60% but he received 100%) and the loss property is distributed to a related person (Jim owns more than 50 percent of the stock).

	Gain (Loss) Recognized	Character
Inventory	$ 0	
Building	102,000	Ordinary (§291) and §1231
Land	100,000	§1231
Net gain	**$202,000**	

(continued on page 19-36)

What if: Assume that Ginny owned 40 percent of the stock and that 360 Air proposed distributing the inventory, the building, and cash to Ginny. What amount of gain or loss would 360 Air recognize as a result of this distribution?

Answer: $200,000. 360 Air would now recognize the $2,000 loss on the distribution of the inventory because the inventory (loss property) was not distributed to a related person. To the extent loss property is distributed to an unrelated person, such as Ginny (she owns less than 50%), the loss is deductible even if the distribution of the loss property is non pro rata.

A second loss disallowance rule potentially applies to property acquired by the corporation in a §351 transaction or as a contribution to capital. The loss built in at the time of acquisition is not recognized if the property is distributed or sold after the corporation adopts a plan of liquidation and if a principal purpose of the §351 transaction or the contribution was to allow the liquidating corporation to recognize the loss.[43] This rule prevents a built-in loss (adjusted tax basis in excess of fair market value) from being recognized by treating the basis of the property distributed or sold as its fair market value at the time it was contributed to the corporation. This prohibited tax-avoidance purpose is presumed if the property is acquired within two years before the corporation adopts a plan of liquidation. The presumption can be overcome if the corporation can show that there was a corporate business purpose for contributing the property to the corporation.

Example 19-23

What if: Suppose Al transferred a building and land to 360 Air in return for 50 percent of the corporation's stock (50 shares) in a transaction that qualified under §351. The property transferred to the corporation had the following fair market values and adjusted tax bases:

	FMV	Adjusted Tax Basis
Building	$ 75,000	$100,000
Land	200,000	100,000
Total	$275,000	$200,000

In this case, the aggregate fair market value of the property transferred to the corporation exceeds the aggregate adjusted basis of the property. As a result, the building will retain its carryover basis of $100,000 and subsequent built-in loss of $25,000.

What if: If the building and land are either sold or distributed to Al in complete liquidation of his ownership of 360 Air stock within two years of the §351 transaction, will 360 Air be able to deduct the $25,000 loss on the distribution of the building?

Answer: It depends. Because the sale or liquidating distribution is made pursuant to a plan of complete liquidation adopted within two years of the §351 transaction, the presumption is that Al contributed the property to 360 Air for tax avoidance purposes (i.e., to allow the corporation to deduct the built-in loss). The corporation can rebut this presumption by demonstrating that the contribution of the property by Al had a corporate business purpose at the time of the §351 transaction. In addition, the corporation could argue that he did not have a tax avoidance motive because at the time of his original transfer, Al transferred assets with a net built-in gain.

[43] §336(d)(2).

Tax Deferred Liquidating Distributions The liquidating corporation does not recognize gain or loss on distributions of property to an 80 percent corporate shareholder.[44] If a shareholder receives tax deferral in the liquidation, the liquidating corporation cannot recognize any loss, even on distributions to shareholders who receive taxable distributions.[45]

Example 19-24

What if: Assume 360 Air was a 100-percent-owned subsidiary of SCR, and SCR liquidated 360 Air. SCR has a tax basis in its 360 Air stock of $300,000. The company's tax accounting balance sheet at the time of the distribution is shown below:

	FMV	Adjusted Tax Basis	Difference
Cash	$138,000	$138,000	
Receivables	2,000	2,000	
Inventory	10,000	12,000	$ (2,000)
Building	150,000	48,000	102,000
Land	200,000	100,000	100,000
Total	$500,000	$300,000	$200,000

What amount of gain or loss does 360 Air *recognize* as a result of the liquidation?

Answer: $0. 360 Air does not recognize any gain or loss on the liquidation.

What if: Suppose 360 Air was 80 percent owned by SCR and 20 percent owned by Jim. 360 Air distributed the inventory plus $90,000 to Jim in complete liquidation of his stock. Can 360 Air recognize the $2,000 inventory loss?

Answer: No. 360 Air cannot recognize the loss even though Jim is not a related person and has a taxable distribution. When one shareholder is not taxable on a liquidating distribution (SCR), the liquidating corporation cannot recognize any losses on the distribution of property to any shareholder.

THE KEY FACTS

Tax Consequences of a Complete Liquidation

- Shareholders other than corporations that own 80 percent or more of the liquidating corporation's stock recognize gain and usually loss in a complete liquidation of the corporation.
- Corporations that own 80 percent or more of the liquidating corporation's stock (vote and value) do not recognize gain or loss in a complete liquidation of the corporation.
- Shareholders recognizing gain or loss take a tax basis in property received in the complete liquidation equal to its fair market value.
- Corporate shareholders that defer recognizing gain or loss take an adjusted tax basis in property received in the complete liquidation equal to its carryover basis.

Liquidation-related expenses, including the cost of preparing and effectuating a plan of complete liquidation, are deductible by the liquidating corporation on its final Form 1120. Deferred or capitalized expenditures such as organizational expenditures also are deductible on the final tax return.

CONCLUSION

This chapter discussed some of the important tax rules that apply during the life cycle of a C corporation. As the storyline indicates, forming a corporation generally does not create any tax to any of the parties to the transaction. Gain or loss realized by the shareholders on the transfer of property to the corporation is deferred until a later date, when either the shareholder sells his ownership interest or the corporation liquidates. Subsequent acquisitions of new businesses or dispositions of existing businesses also can be achieved in a tax-deferred manner. However, failure to meet all the requirements can convert a tax-deferred transaction into a taxable transaction. A complete liquidation of a corporation generally is a fully taxable transaction to the shareholders and the liquidating corporation, except in the case where a subsidiary is liquidated into its parent corporation.

[44] §337(a).

[45] §336(d)(3).

Summary

LO 19-1 Review the taxation of property dispositions.

- A person realizes gain or loss as a result of engaging in a transaction, which is defined as an exchange of property rights with another person.
- Gain or loss realized is computed by subtracting the adjusted tax basis of property transferred in the exchange from the amount realized in the exchange.
- The amount realized is computed as cash received plus the fair market value of other property received plus any liabilities assumed by the transferee on the property transferred, reduced by selling expenses and any liabilities assumed by the transferor on property received in the exchange.
- The general tax rule is that gain or loss realized is recognized (included in the computation of taxable income) unless a specific tax rule exempts the gain or loss from being recognized (permanently) or defers such recognition until a future date.

LO 19-2 Recognize the tax consequences to the parties to a tax-deferred corporate formation.

- Section 351 applies to transactions in which one or more persons transfer property to a corporation in return for stock, and immediately after the transfer, these same persons control the corporation to which they transferred the property.
- If a transaction meets these requirements, the transferors of property (shareholders) do not recognize (defer) gain or loss realized on the transfer of the property to the corporation.
  - Shareholders contributing property to a corporation in a §351 transaction compute gain or loss realized by subtracting the adjusted tax basis of the contributed property from the fair market value of the consideration they receive in return (amount realized).
  - Gain, but not loss, is recognized when property other than the corporation's stock (boot) is received in the exchange.
  - Gain is recognized in an amount equal to the *lesser of* the gain realized or the fair market value of boot received.
  - The tax basis of stock received in the exchange equals the adjusted tax basis of the property transferred, less any liabilities assumed by the corporation on the property contributed (substituted basis).
  - The shareholder's stock basis is increased by any gain recognized and reduced by the fair market value of any boot received.
- The corporation receiving property for its stock in a §351 exchange does not recognize (excludes) gain or loss realized on the transfer.
  - The adjusted tax basis of the property received by the corporation equals the property's adjusted tax basis in the transferor's hands (carryover basis).
  - The asset's tax basis is increased by any gain recognized by the shareholder on the transfer of the property to the corporation.

LO 19-3 Identify the different forms of taxable and tax-deferred acquisitions.

- Corporations can be acquired in taxable asset or stock purchases.
- Corporations can be acquired in tax-deferred asset or stock purchases.
- To be tax-deferred, an acquisition must meet certain IRC and judicial doctrines to qualify as reorganization.
  - The judicial requirements, now summarized in the regulations, require continuity of interest, continuity of business enterprise, and business purpose.
- In a Type A tax-deferred acquisition, the target corporation's assets and liabilities are merged into the acquiring corporation (stock-for-assets exchange).
  - Type A acquisitions involving publicly traded corporations often use an acquisition subsidiary (triangular merger) to acquire the target corporation's assets and liabilities.
- In a Type B tax-deferred acquisition, the shareholders of the target corporation exchange their stock for stock of the acquiring corporation (stock-for-stock exchange).
  - Type B acquisitions prohibit the use of cash in the exchange.

Determine the tax consequences to the parties to a corporate acquisition. **LO 19-4**

- Shareholders participating in a taxable asset or stock transaction compute gain or loss realized by subtracting the adjusted basis of the stock they surrender to the acquiring corporation from the fair market value of the consideration they receive in the exchange.
- Shareholders participating in a tax-deferred reorganization defer gain and loss realized in the exchange unless cash (boot) is received.
  - Shareholders receiving boot recognize gain, but not loss, in an amount equal to the lesser of the gain realized or the fair market value of the boot received.
- The corporation does not recognize gain on the distribution of its own stock in exchange for property in a reorganization.
- The stock received in return for stock in a tax-deferred reorganization has a tax basis equal to the tax basis of the stock surrendered in the exchange (substituted basis).
- The shareholder's stock basis is increased by any gain recognized and reduced by cash or other boot received.
- The assets transferred to the corporation in a tax-deferred reorganization carry over the tax basis of the shareholders contributing the property (carryover basis).

Calculate the tax consequences that apply to the parties to a complete liquidation of a corporation. **LO 19-5**

- Noncorporate shareholders receiving a distribution in complete liquidation of their corporation recognize gain and (usually) loss in the exchange.
- Tax deferral is extended to corporate shareholders that own 80 percent or more of the liquidating corporation.
- The liquidating corporation recognizes gain and (usually) loss on the distribution of property to those shareholders who are taxable on the distribution.
- The liquidating corporation cannot deduct losses on property distributed to a related person if the distribution of loss property is non–pro rata or the loss property is disqualified property.
- A loss cannot be deducted on the distribution or sale of property after the corporation adopts the plan of liquidation, but only if the property was previously contributed to the corporation in a §351 transaction whose principal purpose was to avoid tax.
- The liquidating corporation cannot deduct losses on property distributed if one of the persons receiving the liquidation is not taxable on the distribution (a corporate shareholder owning 80 percent or more of the stock).
- The liquidating corporation does not recognize gain or loss on the distribution of property to a corporate shareholder owning 80 percent or more of the stock.
- The tax basis of each asset received by the shareholder in a taxable complete liquidation equals the asset's fair market value on the date of the distribution.
- The adjusted tax basis of each asset received by a corporate shareholder (owning 80 percent or more of the stock) in a tax-deferred complete liquidation carries over from the liquidating corporation.

KEY TERMS

§338(g) election (19-24)
§338(h)(10) election (19-24)
adjusted tax basis (19-3)
amount realized (19-3)
boot (19-5)
bright-line test (19-25)
carryover basis (19-14)
consolidations (19-26)
continuity of business enterprise (COBE) (19-25)
continuity of interest (COI) (19-25)
contribution to capital (19-18)
mergers (19-26)
persons (19-4)
realization (19-2)
reorganization (19-25)
stock-for-stock acquisitions (19-29)
substituted basis (19-7)

DISCUSSION QUESTIONS

Discussion Questions are available in Connect®.

LO 19-1 1. Discuss the difference between realization and recognition in a property transaction.

LO 19-1 2. What information must a taxpayer gather to determine the *amount realized* in a property transaction?

LO 19-1 3. Distinguish between exclusion and deferral in a property transaction.

LO 19-1 4. Contrast how a taxpayer's tax basis in property received in a property transaction will be affected if the transaction results in gain exclusion versus gain deferral.

LO 19-1 5. What information must a taxpayer gather to determine the *adjusted tax basis* of property exchanged in a property transaction?

LO 19-2 6. Why does Congress provide tax deferral on the formation of a corporation?

LO 19-2 7. List the key statutory requirements that must be met before a corporate formation is tax deferred under §351.

LO 19-2 8. What is the definition of *control* for purposes of §351? Why does Congress require the shareholders to control a corporation to receive tax deferral?

LO 19-2 9. What is a *substituted basis* as it relates to stock received in exchange for property in a §351 transaction? What is the purpose of attaching a substituted basis to stock received in a §351 transaction?

LO 19-2 10. Explain whether the receipt of boot by a shareholder in a §351 transaction causes the transaction to be fully taxable.

LO 19-2 11. Explain whether a corporation's assumption of shareholder liabilities will always constitute boot in a §351 transaction.

LO 19-2 12. How does the tax treatment differ in cases where liabilities are assumed with a tax avoidance purpose versus where liabilities assumed exceed basis?

LO 19-2 13. What is a *carryover basis* as it relates to property received by a corporation in a §351 transaction? What is the purpose of attaching a carryover basis to property received in a §351 transaction?

LO 19-2 14. Under what circumstances does property received by a corporation in a §351 transaction not receive a carryover basis? What is the reason for this rule?

LO 19-2 15. How does a corporation depreciate an asset received in a §351 transaction in which no gain or loss is recognized by the transferor of the property?

LO 19-2 16. Are the tax consequences the same whether a shareholder contributes property to a corporation in a §351 transaction or as a capital contribution? Explain.

LO 19-2 17. Why might a corporation prefer to characterize an instrument as debt rather than equity for tax purposes? Are the holders of the instrument indifferent as to its characterization for tax purposes?

LO 19-2 18. Under what conditions is it advantageous for a shareholder to hold §1244 stock? Why did Congress bestow these tax benefits on holders of such stock?

LO 19-3 19. Explain when an acquiring corporation would prefer to buy the target corporation's assets directly in an acquisition.

LO 19-3 20. Do the shareholders of the target corporation usually prefer to sell the stock or the assets of the target corporation? Explain.

LO 19-3 21. What is the congressional purpose for allowing tax deferral on transactions that meet the definition of a corporate reorganization?

LO 19-3 22. Describe the advantages (if any) of using a reverse triangular form of reorganization in acquiring other corporations.

LO 19-3 23. What are the key differences in the tax law requirements that apply to forward versus reverse triangular mergers?

LO 19-3 24. What are the key differences in the tax law requirements that apply to a Type A stock-for-assets acquisition versus a Type B stock-for-stock acquisition?

25. How does the form of a regular §338(g) election compare and contrast to a §338(h)(10) election? LO 19-4
26. What tax benefits does the buyer hope to obtain by making a §338(g) or §338(h)(10) election? Describe how this election might affect the value offered for the target corporation. LO 19-4
27. In a stock acquisition, describe the difference (if any) between the *adjusted tax basis of assets* held by an acquired corporation and the *tax basis of the shares* held by a corporate acquirer. LO 19-4
28. What is the presumption behind the continuity of ownership interest (COI) requirement in a tax-deferred acquisition? How do the target shareholders determine if COI is met in a Type A reorganization? LO 19-4
29. W Corporation will acquire all of the assets and liabilities of Z Corporation in a Type A merger, after which W Corporation will sell off all of its assets and liabilities and focus solely on Z Corporation's business. Explain whether the transaction will be taxable because W Corporation fails the continuity of business enterprise (COBE) test. LO 19-4
30. Compare how a shareholder computes tax basis in stock received from the acquiring corporation in a forward triangular merger versus a Type B merger. LO 19-4
31. Do all shareholders receive the same tax treatment in a complete liquidation of a corporation? Explain. LO 19-5
32. Describe when a corporate shareholder must defer gains and losses on the receipt of distributions of property from the complete liquidation of a subsidiary corporation. LO 19-5
33. Is it true that a corporation recognizes all gains and losses on liquidating distributions of property to noncorporate shareholders? Explain. LO 19-5
34. Under what circumstances must a corporate shareholder recognize gains in a complete liquidation? LO 19-5
35. Under what circumstances will a liquidating corporation be allowed to recognize loss in a non–pro rata distribution? LO 19-5
36. Compare and contrast the built-in loss duplication rule as it relates to §351 with the built-in loss disallowance rule as it applies to a complete liquidation. LO 19-5

PROBLEMS

Select problems are available in Connect®.

37. Ramon incorporated his sole proprietorship by transferring inventory, a building, and land to the corporation in return for 100 percent of the corporation's stock. The property transferred to the corporation had the following fair market values and adjusted tax bases: LO 19-2

	FMV	Adjusted Tax Basis
Inventory	$ 10,000	$ 4,000
Building	50,000	30,000
Land	100,000	50,000
Total	$160,000	$84,000

The fair market value of the corporation's stock received in the exchange equaled the fair market value of the assets transferred to the corporation by Ramon.

a) What amount of gain or loss does Ramon *realize* on the transfer of the property to his corporation?
b) What amount of gain or loss does Ramon *recognize* on the transfer of the property to his corporation?
c) What is Ramon's basis in the stock received in the new corporation?

LO 19-2
planning

38. Carla incorporated her sole proprietorship by transferring inventory, a building, and land to the corporation in return for 100 percent of the corporation's stock. The property transferred to the corporation had the following fair market values and adjusted tax bases:

	FMV	Adjusted Tax Basis
Inventory	$ 20,000	$ 10,000
Building	150,000	100,000
Land	250,000	300,000
Total	$420,000	$410,000

The corporation also assumed a mortgage of $120,000 attached to the building and land. The fair market value of the corporation's stock received in the exchange was $300,000.

a) What amount of gain or loss does Carla *realize* on the transfer of the property to the corporation?

b) What amount of gain or loss does Carla *recognize* on the transfer of the property to her corporation?

c) What is Carla's basis in the stock received in the new corporation?

d) Would you advise Carla to transfer the building and land to the corporation? What tax benefits might be generated if Carla kept the building and land and leased it to the corporation?

LO 19-2

39. Ivan incorporated his sole proprietorship by transferring inventory, a building, and land to the corporation in return for 100 percent of the corporation's stock. The property transferred to the corporation had the following fair market values and adjusted tax bases:

	FMV	Adjusted Tax Basis
Inventory	$ 10,000	$15,000
Building	50,000	40,000
Land	60,000	30,000
Total	$120,000	$85,000

The fair market value of the corporation's stock received in the exchange equaled the fair market value of the assets transferred to the corporation by Ivan. The transaction met the requirements to be tax-deferred under §351.

a) What amount of gain or loss does Ivan *realize* on the transfer of the property to the corporation?

b) What amount of gain or loss does Ivan *recognize* on the transfer of the property to the corporation?

c) What is Ivan's basis in the stock received in the new corporation?

d) What is the corporation's adjusted tax basis in each of the assets received in the exchange?

e) Would the stock held by Ivan qualify as §1244 stock? Why is this determination important for Ivan?

LO 19-2

40. Zhang incorporated her sole proprietorship by transferring inventory, a building, and land to the corporation in return for 100 percent of the corporation's stock. The property transferred to the corporation had the following fair market values and adjusted tax bases:

	FMV	Adjusted Tax Basis
Inventory	$ 20,000	$ 10,000
Building	150,000	100,000
Land	230,000	300,000
Total	$400,000	$410,000

The corporation also assumed a mortgage of $100,000 attached to the building and land. The fair market value of the corporation's stock received in the exchange was $300,000. The transaction met the requirements to be tax-deferred under §351.

a) What amount of gain or loss does Zhang *realize* on the transfer of the property to the corporation?
b) What amount of gain or loss does Zhang *recognize* on the transfer of the property to the corporation?
c) What is Zhang's tax basis in the stock received in the exchange?
d) What is the corporation's adjusted tax basis in each of the assets received in the exchange?

Assume the corporation assumed a mortgage of $500,000 attached to the building and land. Assume the fair market value of the building is now $250,000 and the fair market value of the land is $530,000. The fair market value of the stock remains $300,000.

e) How much, if any, gain or loss does Zhang *recognize* on the exchange assuming the revised facts?
f) What is Zhang's tax basis in the stock received in the exchange?
g) What is the corporation's adjusted tax basis in each of the assets received in the exchange?

41. Sam and Devon agree to go into business together selling college-licensed clothing. According to the agreement, Sam will contribute inventory valued at $100,000 in return for 80 percent of the stock in the corporation. Sam's tax basis in the inventory is $60,000. Devon will receive 20 percent of the stock in return for providing accounting services to the corporation (these qualify as organizational expenditures). The accounting services are valued at $25,000. LO 19-2 planning

a) What amount of income gain or loss does Sam *realize* on the formation of the corporation? What amount, if any, does Sam *recognize*?
b) What is Sam's tax basis in the stock received in return for his contribution of property to the corporation?
c) What amount of income, gain, or loss does Devon *realize* on the formation of the corporation? What amount, if any, does Devon *recognize*?
d) What is Devon's tax basis in the stock received in return for the contribution of services to the corporation?

Assume Devon received 25 percent of the stock in the corporation in return for his services.

e) What amount of gain or loss does Sam *recognize* on the formation of the corporation?
f) What is Sam's tax basis in the stock received in return for the contribution of property to the corporation?
g) What amount of income, gain, or loss does Devon *recognize* on the formation of the corporation?
h) What is Devon's tax basis in the stock received in return for the contribution of services to the corporation?
i) What tax advice could you give Sam and Devon to change the tax consequences?

42. Jekyll and Hyde formed a corporation (Halloween Inc.) on October 31 to develop a drug to address split personalities. Jekyll will contribute a patented formula valued at $200,000 in return for 50 percent of the stock in the corporation. Hyde will contribute an experimental formula worth $120,000 and medical services in exchange for the remaining stock. Jekyll's tax basis in the patented formula is $125,000, whereas Hyde has a basis of $15,000 in his experimental formula. LO 19-2 tax forms research

a) Describe the tax consequences of the transaction.
b) Prepare the §351 statement that must be included with the return.

LO 19-2

43. Ramona and Hermione formed Wiley Corporation on January 2. Ramona contributed cash of $200,000 in return for 50 percent of the corporation's stock. Hermione contributed a building and land with the following fair market values and adjusted tax bases in return for 50 percent of the corporation's stock:

	FMV	Adjusted Tax Basis
Building	$ 75,000	$ 20,000
Land	175,000	80,000
Total	$250,000	$100,000

To equalize the exchange, Wiley Corporation paid Hermione $50,000 in addition to her stock.

a) What amount of gain or loss does Ramona *realize* on the formation of the corporation? What amount, if any, does Ramona *recognize*?

b) What is Ramona's tax basis in the stock received in return for the contribution of property to the corporation?

c) What amount of gain or loss does Hermione *realize* on the formation of the corporation? What amount, if any, does she *recognize*?

d) What is Hermione's tax basis in the stock received in return for the contribution of property to the corporation?

e) What adjusted tax basis does Wiley Corporation take in the land and building received from Hermione?

Assume Hermione's adjusted tax basis in the land was $200,000.

f) What amount of gain or loss does Hermione *realize* on the formation of the corporation? What amount, if any, does she *recognize*?

g) What adjusted tax basis does Wiley Corporation take in the land and building received from Hermione?

Assume Hermione's adjusted tax basis in the land was $250,000.

h) What amount of gain or loss does Hermione *realize* on the formation of the corporation? What amount, if any, does she *recognize*?

i) What adjusted tax basis does Wiley Corporation take in the land and building received from Hermione?

j) What election can Hermione and Wiley Corporation make to allow Wiley Corporation to take a carryover basis in the land?

LO 19-2
planning

44. This year, Jack O. Lantern incurred a $60,000 loss on the worthlessness of his stock in the Creepy Corporation (CC). The stock, which Jack purchased in 2005, met all of the §1244 stock requirements at the time of issue. In December of this year, Jack's wife, Jill, also incurred a $75,000 loss on the sale of Eerie Corporation (EC) stock that she purchased in July 2005 and that also satisfied all of the §1244 stock requirements at the time of issue. Both corporations are operating companies.

a) How much of the losses incurred on the two stock sales can Jack and Jill deduct this year, assuming they do not have capital gains in the current or prior years?

b) Assuming they did not engage in any other property transactions this year, how much of a net capital loss will carry over to next year for Jack and Jill?

c) What would be the tax treatment for the losses if Jack and Jill reported only $60,000 of taxable income this year, excluding the securities transactions?

d) What tax planning suggestions can you offer the Lanterns to increase the tax benefits of these losses?

LO 19-2

45. Breslin Inc. made a capital contribution of investment property to its 100-percent-owned subsidiary, Crisler Company. The investment property had a fair market value of $3,000,000 and a tax basis to Breslin of $2,225,000.

a) What are the tax consequences to Breslin Inc. on the contribution of the investment property to Crisler Company?

b) What is the tax basis of the investment property to Crisler Company after the contribution to capital?

46. Nareh joined Jim in forming DBJ Corp. Nareh contributed appreciated land for 90 percent of the stock in DBJ. Jim received 10 percent of the DBJ stock valued at $15,000. Determine Jim's tax consequences in each of the following alternative scenarios. LO 19-2
   a) Jim received the stock in exchange for providing computer-related services for the corporation. What amount of income or gain does Jim recognize on the exchange? What is Jim's basis in the stock received in the exchange?
   b) Jim contributed the rights to a patent he owned to DBJ in exchange for the DBJ stock. The patent was worth $15,000 and Jim's basis in the patent was $8,000. How much gain does Jim recognize on the exchange? What is Jim's basis in the DBJ stock?

47. Carole, Karmen, and Charles formed ABC Corporation. Carole received 60 percent of the stock in ABC Corporation in exchange for appreciated property, Karmen received 30 percent of the stock in ABC Corporation in exchange for legal services, and Charles received 10 percent of the stock in ABC Corporation in exchange for cash. LO 19-2
   a) Must Carole recognize the gain she realized on the transfer of the appreciated property?
   b) Suppose that, instead of receiving the entire 30 percent of the ABC Corporation stock in exchange for legal services, Karmen received 10 percent of the ABC Corporation stock in exchange for her legal services and she received 20 percent of the ABC Corporation stock in exchange for cash (i.e., she transferred both services and property to ABC Corporation). Must Carole recognize gain on the transfer of appreciated property?

48. Camila and Kelly invited Ben to join them in forming Aero, a plane-chartering company, as a corporation. Ben did not want to join at the time and declined their invitation. More than a year later, Ben changed his mind and transferred appreciated property to Aero in exchange for 45 percent of Aero stock. Is Ben required to recognize the realized gain on the transaction? LO 19-2

49. Kristine transferred investment property she has owned for six years to XYZ Corporation in exchange for 40 percent of the corporation's stock (40 shares valued at $160,000) at the time XYZ was incorporated. The property's adjusted tax basis was $90,000 and its fair market value was $160,000. Assume the transfer qualifies under §351. LO 19-2
   a) What gain or loss does Kristine recognize on the transfer?
   b) What is her basis in the stock received in the exchange?
   c) What is Kristine's holding period in the stock?

50. Jasmine transferred land she held as an investment (fair market value $140,000; basis $110,000) in exchange for 50 percent of Kandy Corporation stock (40 shares valued at $100,000) and $40,000 cash in a qualifying §351 exchange. What is the amount of gain Jasmine recognizes on the transfer and its character? LO 19-2

51. Jorge contributed land he held as an investment (fair market value $120,000; adjusted tax basis $55,000) and inventory (fair market value $80,000; adjusted tax basis $75,000) to ABC Corporation in exchange for 50 percent of the ABC stock (50 shares valued at $160,000) and $40,000 cash in a qualifying §351 exchange. LO 19-2
   a) What amount of gain does Jorge recognize on the exchange? What is the character of the gain? What would be Jorge's tax basis in his ABC stock after the exchange?
   b) Assume the same facts except that Jorge received $40,000 of business property from ABC instead of $40,000 cash. What is the amount of gain Jorge would recognize on the exchange and its character?
   c) Assume the original facts in this example except that the inventory had an adjusted tax basis of $90,000 so that Jorge realized a $10,000 loss on the inventory (he still realized a $65,000 gain on the land). How much gain or loss would Jorge recognize on the exchange?

LO 19-2

52. In forming Parts Inc. as a corporation, Candice transferred inventory to Parts Inc. in exchange for 30 percent of the corporation's stock (60 shares valued at $130,000). The inventory's fair market value was $147,000 and its adjusted tax basis to Candice was $75,000. The inventory was subject to a $17,000 liability that Parts Inc. assumed on the transfer. Candice borrowed the $17,000 from the bank (using the inventory as collateral) shortly before transferring the inventory to Parts Inc. and used the loan proceeds to pay for a family vacation to Europe.
    a) Assuming the transfer qualifies under §351 and that the liability has a tax-avoidance purpose, what gain or loss will Candice recognize on the transfer?
    b) Assuming the original facts, what is Candice's basis in the stock received in the exchange?
    c) Suppose the liability does not have a tax-avoidance purpose. What gain will Candice recognize on the transfer?
    d) Assuming the facts in part (c), what is Candice's basis in the stock received in the exchange?

LO 19-2

53. Johanne transferred investment property to S&J Corporation in exchange for 60 percent of the S&J Corporation stock (60 shares valued at $115,000). The property's fair market value was $190,000 and its adjusted tax basis to Johanne was $60,000. The investment property was subject to a $75,000 mortgage that S&J Corporation assumed on the transfer (not treated as boot).
    a) Assuming the transfer qualifies under §351, what is the amount of the gain Johanne must recognize on the exchange and its character?
    b) What is Johanne's tax basis in the S&J stock received in the exchange?
    c) Assume that in addition to the investment property, Johanne transferred inventory with a fair market value of $30,000 and an adjusted tax basis of $20,000 for additional S&J Corporation stock. What is the amount of gain Johanne must recognize on the exchange of the investment property and inventory for stock and its character?
    d) Assuming the facts in (c), what is Johanne's basis in the S&J stock received in the exchange?
    e) Assume the original facts except that the liability assumed by S&J Corporation would give rise to a deduction when paid. What is the amount of gain Johanne must recognize on the exchange and its character?
    f) Assuming the facts in (e), what is Johanne's basis in the S&J stock received in the exchange?

LO 19-2

54. When incorporating Spotfree, a cleaning company, Jayne transferred accounts receivable (fair market value $20,000 and $0 tax basis) and $12,000 of accounts payable from her cash-method sole proprietorship to Spotfree in exchange for Spotfree stock valued at $8,000. Assume the transfer qualifies under §351.
    a) What is the amount of the gain Jayne must recognize on the exchange and its character?
    b) What is Jayne's basis in the Spotfree stock received in the exchange?

LO 19-3
research

55. On January 21, 2020, FB Financial Corporation agreed to acquire Franklin Financial Network, Inc., a Tennessee bank corporation, in a tax-deferred acquisition. The Form 8-K for FB (NYSE ticker FBK, cik 00011649749) describes the transaction and was filed with the SEC on August 18, 2020. You can access the Form 8-K at the SEC's Investor website (www.sec.gov/ix?doc=/Archives/edgar/data/1649749/000119312520222966/d38613d8k.htm). Read "Item 2.01, Completion of Acquisition or Disposition of Assets" and determine which form of merger(s) was used to accomplish the acquisition.

56. On August 1, 2019, Salesforce completed its business combination with Tableau Software, Inc. The Form 8-K for Salesforce (NYSE ticker CRM) describes the transaction and was filed with the SEC on August 1, 2019. You can access the Form 8-K at the SEC's Investor website (www.sec.gov/Archives/edgar/data/1108524/000119312519169276/d764344d8k.htm). Read "Item 1.01, Entry into a Material Definitive Agreement" and determine which form of reorganization was used to complete the acquisition. LO 19-3 research

57. Amy and Brian were investigating the acquisition of a tax accounting business, Bottom Line Inc. (BLI). As part of their discussions with the sole shareholder of the corporation, Ernesto Young, they examined the company's tax accounting balance sheet. The relevant information is summarized as follows: LO 19-4

	FMV	Adjusted Tax Basis	Appreciation
Cash	$ 10,000	$ 10,000	
Receivables	15,000	15,000	
Building	100,000	50,000	$ 50,000
Land	225,000	75,000	150,000
Total	$350,000	$150,000	$200,000
Payables	$ 18,000	$ 18,000	
Mortgage*	112,000	112,000	
Total	$130,000	$130,000	

*The mortgage is attached to the building and land.

Ernesto was asking for $400,000 for the company. His tax basis in the BLI stock was $100,000. Included in the sales price was an unrecognized customer list valued at $100,000. The unallocated portion of the purchase price ($80,000) will be recorded as goodwill.

a) What amount of gain or loss does BLI recognize if the transaction is structured as a direct asset sale to Amy and Brian? What amount of corporate-level tax does BLI pay as a result of the transaction?

b) What amount of gain or loss does Ernesto recognize if the transaction is structured as a direct asset sale to Amy and Brian, and BLI distributes the after-tax proceeds [computed in question (a)] to Ernesto in liquidation of his stock?

c) What are the tax benefits, if any, to Amy and Brian as a result of structuring the acquisition as a direct asset purchase?

58. Using the same facts in problem 57, assume Ernesto agrees to sell his stock in BLI to Amy and Brian for $400,000. LO 19-4

a) What amount of gain or loss does BLI recognize if the transaction is structured as a stock sale to Amy and Brian? What amount of corporate-level tax does BLI pay as a result of the transaction?

b) What amount of gain or loss does Ernesto recognize if the transaction is structured as a stock sale to Amy and Brian?

c) What are the tax benefits, if any, to Amy and Brian as a result of structuring the acquisition as a stock sale?

59. Rather than purchase BLI directly (as in problems 57 and 58), Amy and Brian will have their corporation, Spartan Tax Services (STS), acquire the business from Ernesto in a tax-deferred Type A merger. Amy and Brian would like Ernesto to continue to run BLI, which he agreed to do if he could obtain an equity interest in STS. As part of the agreement, Amy and Brian propose to pay Ernesto $200,000 plus voting stock in STS worth $200,000. Ernesto will become a 10 percent shareholder in STS after the transaction. LO 19-4

a) Will the continuity of ownership interest (COI) requirements for a straight Type A merger be met? Explain.

b) What amount of gain or loss does BLI recognize if the transaction is structured as a Type A merger? What amount of corporate-level tax does BLI pay as a result of the transaction, assuming a tax rate of 21 percent?

c) What amount of gain or loss does Ernesto recognize if the transaction is structured as a Type A merger?

d) What is Ernesto's tax basis in the STS stock he receives in the exchange?

e) What is the adjusted tax basis of each of the BLI assets held by STS after the merger?

LO 19-4 60. Jakub and Sylvia propose to have their corporation, Wolverine Universal (WU), acquire another corporation, EMU Inc., in a tax-deferred triangular merger using an acquisition subsidiary of WU. The sole shareholder of EMU, Edie Eagle, will receive $250,000 plus $150,000 of WU voting stock in the transaction.

a) Can the transaction be structured as a forward triangular merger? Explain why or why not.

b) Can the transaction be structured as a reverse triangular merger? Explain why or why not.

LO 19-4 61. Jakub and Sylvia propose to have their corporation, Wolverine Universal (WU), acquire another corporation, EMU Inc., in a stock-for-stock Type B acquisition. The sole shareholder of EMU, Edie Eagle, will receive $400,000 of WU voting stock in the transaction. Edie's tax basis in the EMU stock is $100,000.

a) What amount of gain or loss does Edie recognize if the transaction is structured as a stock-for-stock Type B acquisition?

b) What is Edie's tax basis in the WU stock received in the exchange?

c) What is the tax basis of the EMU stock held by WU after the exchange?

LO 19-5 62. Shauna and Danielle decided to liquidate their jointly owned corporation, Woodward Fashions Inc. (WFI). After liquidating its remaining inventory and paying off its remaining liabilities, WFI had the following tax accounting balance sheet:

	FMV	Adjusted Tax Basis	Appreciation
Cash	$200,000	$200,000	
Building	50,000	10,000	$ 40,000
Land	150,000	90,000	60,000
Total	$400,000	$300,000	$100,000

Under the terms of the agreement, Shauna will receive the $200,000 cash in exchange for her 50 percent interest in WFI. Shauna's tax basis in her WFI stock is $50,000. Danielle will receive the building and land in exchange for her 50 percent interest in WFI. Danielle's tax basis in her WFI stock is $100,000. Assume for purposes of this problem that the cash available to distribute to the shareholders has been reduced by any tax paid by the corporation on gain recognized as a result of the liquidation.

a) What amount of gain or loss does WFI recognize in the complete liquidation?

b) What amount of gain or loss does Shauna recognize in the complete liquidation?

c) What amount of gain or loss does Danielle recognize in the complete liquidation?

d) What is Danielle's tax basis in the building and land after the complete liquidation?

LO 19-5 63. Tiffany and Carlos decided to liquidate their jointly owned corporation, Royal Oak Furniture (ROF). After liquidating its remaining inventory and paying off its remaining liabilities, ROF had the following tax accounting balance sheet:

	FMV	Adjusted Tax Basis	Appreciation (Depreciation)
Cash	$200,000	$200,000	
Building	50,000	10,000	$ 40,000
Land	150,000	200,000	(50,000)
Total	$400,000	$410,000	$(10,000)

Under the terms of the agreement, Tiffany will receive the $200,000 cash in exchange for her 50 percent interest in ROF. Tiffany's tax basis in her ROF stock is $50,000. Carlos will receive the building and land in exchange for his 50 percent interest in ROF. His tax basis in the ROF stock is $100,000. Assume for purposes of this problem that the cash available to distribute to the shareholders has been reduced by any tax paid by the corporation on gain recognized as a result of the liquidation.

a) What amount of gain or loss does ROF recognize in the complete liquidation?
b) What amount of gain or loss does Tiffany recognize in the complete liquidation?
c) What amount of gain or loss does Carlos recognize in the complete liquidation?
d) What is Carlos's adjusted tax basis in the building and land after the complete liquidation?

Assume Tiffany owns 40 percent of the ROF stock and Carlos owns 60 percent. Tiffany will receive $160,000 in the liquidation and Carlos will receive the land and building plus $40,000.

e) What amount of gain or loss does ROF recognize in the complete liquidation?
f) What amount of gain or loss does Tiffany recognize in the complete liquidation?
g) What amount of gain or loss does Carlos recognize in the complete liquidation?
h) What is Carlos's adjusted tax basis in the building and land after the complete liquidation?

64. Jefferson Millinery Inc. (JMI) decided to liquidate its wholly owned subsidiary, 8 Miles High Inc. (8MH). 8MH had the following tax accounting balance sheet: LO 19-5

	FMV	Adjusted Tax Basis	Appreciation
Cash	$200,000	$200,000	
Building	50,000	10,000	$ 40,000
Land	150,000	90,000	60,000
Total	$400,000	$300,000	$100,000

a) What amount of gain or loss does 8MH recognize in the complete liquidation?
b) What amount of gain or loss does JMI recognize in the complete liquidation?
c) What is JMI's adjusted tax basis in the building and land after the complete liquidation?

65. Jones Mills Inc. (JMI) decided to liquidate its wholly owned subsidiary, Most Help, Inc. (MH). MH had the following tax accounting balance sheet. LO 19-5

	FMV	Adjusted Tax Basis	Appreciation
Cash	$200,000	$200,000	
Building	50,000	10,000	$40,000
Land	150,000	200,000	(50,000)
Total	$400,000	$410,000	$(10,000)

a) What amount of gain or loss does MH recognize in the complete liquidation?
b) What amount of gain or loss does JMI recognize in the complete liquidation?
c) What is JMI's adjusted tax basis in the building and land after the complete liquidation?

COMPREHENSIVE PROBLEMS

Select problems are available in Connect®.

66. Several years ago, your client, Brooks Robertson, started an office cleaning service. His business was very successful, owing much to his legacy as the greatest defensive third baseman in major league history and his nickname, "The Human Vacuum Cleaner." Brooks operated his business as a sole proprietorship and used the cash method of accounting. Brooks was advised by his attorney that it is too risky to operate his business as a sole proprietorship and that he should incorporate to limit his liability. Brooks has come to you for advice on the tax implications of incorporation. His balance sheet is presented below. Under the terms of the incorporation, Brooks would transfer the assets to the corporation in return for 100 percent of the company's common stock. The corporation would also assume the company's liabilities (payables and mortgage).

Balance Sheet

	Adjusted Tax Basis	FMV
Assets		
Accounts receivable	$ 0	$ 5,000
Cleaning equipment (net)	25,000	20,000
Building	50,000	75,000
Land	25,000	50,000
Total assets	$100,000	$150,000
Liabilities		
Accounts payable	$ 0	$ 10,000
Salaries payable	0	5,000
Mortgage on land and building	35,000	35,000
Total liabilities	$ 35,000	$ 50,000

Required:

Answer the following questions:

a) How much gain or loss (on a per-asset basis) does Brooks *realize* on the transfer of each asset to the corporation?

b) How much, if any, gain or loss (on a per-asset basis) does Brooks *recognize*?

c) How much gain or loss, if any, must the corporation recognize on the receipt of the assets of the sole proprietorship in exchange for the corporation's stock?

d) What tax basis does Brooks have in the corporation's stock?

e) What is the corporation's adjusted tax basis in each asset it receives from Brooks?

f) How would you answer the question in part (b) if Brooks had taken back a 10-year note worth $25,000 plus stock worth $75,000 plus the liability assumption?

g) Will Brooks be able to transfer the accounts receivable to the corporation and have the corporation recognize the income when the receivable is collected?

h) Brooks was depreciating the equipment (200 percent declining balance) and building (straight-line) using MACRS when it was held inside the proprietorship. How will the corporation depreciate the equipment and building? Assume Brooks owned the equipment for four years (seven-year property) and the building for six years.

i) Will the corporation be able to deduct the liabilities when paid? Will it matter which accounting method (cash or accrual) the corporation uses?

j) Would you advise Brooks to transfer the land and building to the corporation? What other tax strategy might you suggest to Brooks with respect to the realty?

67. Your client, Midwest Products Inc. (MPI), is a closely held, calendar-year, accrual-method corporation located in Fowlerville, Michigan. MPI has two operating divisions. One division manufactures lawn and garden furniture and decorative objects (furniture division), while the other division manufactures garden tools and hardware (tool division). MPI's single class of voting common stock is owned as follows:

	Shares	Adjusted Tax Basis	FMV
Iris Green	300	$2,000,000	$3,000,000
Rose Ruby	100	1,200,000	1,000,000
Lily White	100	800,000	1,000,000
Totals	500	$4,000,000	$5,000,000

The three shareholders are unrelated.

Outdoor Living Company (OLC), a publicly held, calendar-year corporation doing business in several midwestern states, has approached MPI about acquiring its furniture division. OLC has no interest in acquiring the tool division, however. OLC's management has several strong business reasons for the acquisition, the most important of which is to expand the company's market into Michigan. Iris, Rose, and Lily are amenable to the acquisition, provided it can be accomplished in a tax-deferred manner.

OLC has proposed the following transaction for acquiring MPI's furniture division. On April 30 of this year, OLC will create a whollly owned subsidiary, OLC Acquisition Inc. (OLC-A). OLC will transfer to the subsidiary 60,000 shares of OLC voting common stock and $2,000,000. The current fair market value of the OLC voting stock is $50 per share ($3,000,000 in total). Each of the three MPI shareholders will receive a pro rata amount of OLC stock and cash.

As part of the agreement, MPI will sell the tool division before the acquisition, after which MPI will merge into OLC-A under Michigan and Ohio state laws (a forward triangular merger). Pursuant to the merger agreement, OLC-A will acquire all of MPI's assets, including 100 percent of the cash received from the sale of the tool division ($2,000,000), and will assume all of MPI's liabilities. The cash from the sale of the tool division will be used to modernize and upgrade much of the furniture division's production facilities. OLC's management is convinced that the cash infusion, coupled with new management, will make MPI's furniture business profitable. OLC management has no plans to liquidate OLC-A into OLC at any time subsequent to the merger. After the merger, OLC-A will be renamed Michigan Garden Furniture Inc.

a) Determine whether the proposed transaction meets the requirements to qualify as a tax-deferred forward triangular merger. Consult Rev. Rul. 88-48 and Rev. Rul. 2001-25 in thinking about the premerger sale of the tool division assets.

b) Could the proposed transaction qualify as a reverse triangular merger if OLC-A merged into MPI? If not, how would the transaction have to be restructured to meet the requirements to be a reverse triangular merger?

68. Rex and Felix are the sole shareholders of Dogs and Cats Corporation (DCC). After several years of operation using the accrual method, they decided to liquidate the corporation and operate the business as a partnership. Rex and Felix hired a lawyer to draw up the legal papers to dissolve the corporation, but they need some tax advice from you, their trusted accountant. They are hoping you will find a way for them to liquidate the corporation while minimizing their total income tax liability.

Rex has a tax basis in his shares of $60,000 and Felix has a tax basis in his shares of $30,000. DCC's tax accounting balance sheet at the date of liquidation is as follows:

	Adjusted Tax Basis	FMV
Assets		
Cash	$ 30,000	$ 30,000
Accounts receivable	10,000	10,000
Inventory	10,000	20,000
Equipment	30,000	20,000
Building	15,000	30,000
Land	5,000	40,000
Total assets	$100,000	$ 150,000
Liabilities		
Accounts payable		$ 5,000
Mortgage payable—Building		10,000
Mortgage payable—Land		10,000
Total liabilities		$ 25,000
Shareholders' Equity		
Common stock—Rex (80%)		$ 100,000
Common stock—Felix (20%)		25,000
Total shareholders' equity		$ 125,000

a) Compute the gain or loss recognized by Rex, Felix, and DCC on a complete liquidation of the corporation assuming each shareholder receives a pro rata distribution of the corporation's assets and assumes a pro rata amount of the liabilities.

b) Compute the gain or loss recognized by Rex, Felix, and DCC on a complete liquidation of the corporation assuming that Felix received cash in lieu of his pro rata share of assets and liabilities.

Assume Felix received the accounts receivable and equipment and assumed the accounts payable for the following two questions.

c) Will Felix recognize any income when he collects the accounts receivable?

d) Will Felix be able to take a deduction when he pays the accounts payable?

Assume Rex is a corporate shareholder of DCC for the following two questions.

e) Compute the gain or loss recognized by Rex, Felix, and DCC on a complete liquidation of the corporation assuming each shareholder receives a pro rata distribution of the corporation's assets and assumes a pro rata amount of the liabilities.

f) Compute the gain or loss recognized by Rex, Felix, and DCC on a complete liquidation of the corporation assuming Felix receives $25,000 in cash and Rex receives the remainder of the assets and assumes all of the liabilities.

Assume the equipment was contributed by Rex to DCC in a §351 transaction two months prior to the liquidation. At the time of the contribution, the property's fair market value was $25,000.

g) Would the tax result change if the property was contributed one year ago? Two years ago? Three years ago?

69. Newman Corporation owns 90 shares of SP Corporation. The remaining 10 shares are owned by Kenny (an individual). After several years of operations, Newman decided to liquidate SP Corporation by distributing the assets to Newman and Kenny. The tax basis of Newman's shares is $10,000, and the tax basis of Kenny's shares is $7,000. SP reported the following balance sheet at the date of liquidation:

tax forms

research

	Adjusted Tax Basis	FMV
Cash	$12,000	$ 12,000
Accounts receivable	8,000	8,000
Stock investment	2,000	10,000
Land	40,000	70,000
Total assets	$62,000	$100,000
Common stock—Newman (90%)		$ 90,000
Common stock—Kenny (10%)		10,000
Total shareholder equity		$100,000

a) Compute the gain or loss recognized by SP, Newman, and Kenny on a complete liquidation of the corporation, where SP distributes $10,000 of cash to Kenny and the remaining assets to Newman.

b) Compute the gain or loss recognized by SP, Newman, and Kenny on a complete liquidation of the corporation, where SP distributes the stock investment to Kenny and the remaining assets to Newman. Assume that SP's tax rate is zero.

c) What form needs to be filed with the liquidation of SP?

UWorld ROGER CPA Review

UWorld Roger CPA Review

Sample CPA Exam questions from Roger CPA Review are available in Connect as support for the topics in this text. These Multiple Choice Questions and Task-Based Simulations include expert-written explanations and solutions and provide a starting point for students to become familiar with the content and functionality of the actual CPA Exam.

chapter

20 Forming and Operating Partnerships

Learning Objectives

Upon completing this chapter, you should be able to:

LO 20-1 Describe tax flow-through entities and determine whether they are taxed as partnerships or S corporations.

LO 20-2 Resolve tax issues applicable to partnership formations and other acquisitions of partnership interests, including gain recognition to partners and tax basis for partners and partnerships.

LO 20-3 Determine the appropriate accounting periods and methods for partnerships.

LO 20-4 Calculate and characterize a partnership's ordinary business income or loss and its separately stated items, and demonstrate how to report these items to partners.

LO 20-5 Explain the importance of a partner's tax basis in her partnership interest and the adjustments that affect it.

LO 20-6 Apply the tax-basis, at-risk, passive activity loss, and excess business loss limits to losses from partnerships.

Gyorgy Barna/Shutterstock

Storyline Summary

Nicole Johnson (she/her/hers)

Location:	Salt Lake City, Utah
Status:	Managing member of Color Comfort Sheets LLC
Filing status:	Married to Tom Johnson
Marginal tax rate:	35 percent unless otherwise stated

Sarah Walker (she/her/hers)

Location:	Salt Lake City, Utah
Status:	Managing member of Color Comfort Sheets LLC
Filing status:	Married to Blaine Walker
Marginal tax rate:	24 percent unless otherwise stated

Chanzz Inc.

Location:	Salt Lake City, Utah
Business:	Managing sports franchises
Status:	Nonmanaging member of Color Comfort Sheets LLC
Filing status:	C corporation with a June 30 year-end
Marginal tax rate:	21 percent

In the Business Entities Overview chapter, we introduced you to Nicole Johnson, who decided to turn her sheet-making hobby into a full-time business called Color Comfort Sheets (CCS). In the Business Entities Overview chapter, she organized the business a a C corporation. However, for purposes of this chapter, we assume that in early 2021, Nicole decided to organize her new enterprise as a limited liability company. Once the business was organized, she turned her attention to raising capital for the business from other investors and a bank loan. Although her limited savings would clearly not be enough to get CCS started, she was willing to contribute a parcel of land in the industrial section of town that she had inherited five years ago from her grandfather. Her friend and mentor Sarah Walker offered to contribute time and money to help CCS get off the ground.

With Sarah on board, things seemed to be coming together nicely for Nicole. However, the amount her bank was willing to loan to CCS was not enough to fully capitalize it, and Nicole and Sarah were unable to invest any more cash into the business to make up the shortfall. Hoping to obtain the additional funding they needed, Nicole and Sarah visited Chance Armstrong, a successful local sports-team owner who had a reputation for being willing to take a chance on new ventures. After listening to Nicole and Sarah's proposal, Chance agreed to invest the additional cash needed to fully fund CCS. Rather than use his personal funds, however, Chance planned to have his closely held corporation, Chanzz Inc., invest in CCS. Unlike Nicole and Sarah, who would take an active role in managing CCS, Chanzz Inc., with everyone's agreement, would not play a part in running the company. By the end of March, CCS had cash, land on which to build its manufacturing facility and offices, and owners who were excited and willing to work hard to make it a successful company.

(to be continued . . .)

In this chapter, we review the options for operating a business with multiple owners as a **flow-through entity.** In addition, we explain the basic tax consequences of forming and operating business entities taxed as partnerships by examining the specific tax consequences of forming and operating Color Comfort Sheets as a limited liability company (LLC) taxed as a partnership.

LO 20-1 FLOW-THROUGH ENTITIES OVERVIEW

Income earned by flow-through entities is usually not taxed at the entity level. Instead, the *owners* of flow-through entities are taxed on the share of entity-level income allocated to them. Thus, unlike income earned by **C corporations,** income from flow-through entities is taxed only once—when it "flows through" to owners of these entities.[1]

Flow-through entities with multiple owners are governed by two somewhat different sets of rules in our tax system.[2] Unincorporated business entities such as **general partnerships, limited partnerships,** and **limited liability companies (LLCs)** are treated as partnerships under the rules provided in **Subchapter K** of the Internal Revenue Code unless they elect to be taxed as corporations.[3] In contrast, owners of entities that are taxed as corporations may elect to treat them as flow-through entities under the rules in **Subchapter S.** These corporations are called **S corporations.** See the Business Entities Overview chapter for further detail regarding the tax treatment of different entity types.

There are many similarities and a few important differences between the tax rules for partnerships and S corporations. Our focus in this chapter and the next is on the tax rules for partnerships. Then, in the S Corporations chapter, we turn our attention to the tax treatment of S corporations and their shareholders.

TAXES IN THE REAL WORLD Hedge Funds

We can scarcely read the financial press these days without encountering some reference to hedge funds. Hedge funds are private investment funds that have grown in popularity in recent years; they were estimated to have over $8.24 trillion in assets under management at the end of 2020.[4] According to a report by the Congressional Research Service, most hedge funds are organized as partnerships and their investors are taxed as limited partners.[5]

[1]The "check the box" rules determine how various legal entities should be classified for tax purposes. See the discussion in the Business Entities Overview chapter for a more detailed explanation of these rules.

[2]Unincorporated entities with one individual owner are taxed as *sole proprietorships*. The tax rules relevant to *sole proprietorships* are discussed in the Business Income, Deductions, and Accounting Methods chapter. In addition to sole proprietorships, other specialized forms of flow-through entities such as real estate investment trusts and regulated investment companies are authorized by the Internal Revenue Code. A discussion of these entities is beyond the scope of this chapter.

[3]Publicly traded partnerships may be taxed as corporations. The tax treatment of publicly traded partnerships is more fully developed in the Business Entities Overview chapter.

[4]"Private Fund Statistics, Fourth Calendar Quarter 2020," SEC Division of Investment Management (www.sec.gov), August 4, 2021.

[5]Congressional Research Service, "Taxation of Carried Interest," R46477, July 9, 2020.

Aggregate and Entity Concepts

When Congress adopted Subchapter K in 1954, it had to debate whether to follow an **entity approach** and treat tax partnerships as entities separate from their partners or to apply an **aggregate approach** and treat partnerships simply as an aggregation of the partners' separate interests in the assets and liabilities of the partnership. In the end, Congress decided to apply both concepts in formulating partnership tax law. For instance, one of the most basic tenets of partnership tax law—that partnerships don't pay taxes—reflects the aggregate approach. However, Congress also adopted other partnership tax rules that fall more squarely on the side of the entity approach. For example, the requirement that partnerships, rather than partners, make most tax elections represents the entity concept. Throughout this and the following chapter, we highlight examples where one or the other basic approach underlies a specific partnership tax rule.

PARTNERSHIP FORMATIONS AND ACQUISITIONS OF PARTNERSHIP INTERESTS

LO 20-2

Acquiring Partnership Interests When Partnerships Are Formed

When a partnership is formed, and afterwards, partners may transfer cash, other tangible or intangible property, and services to the partnership in exchange for an equity interest called a **partnership interest.** Partnership interests represent the bundle of economic rights granted to partners under the partnership agreement (or operating agreement for an LLC).[6] These rights include the right to receive a share of the partnership net assets if the partnership is liquidated, called a **capital interest,** and the right or obligation to receive a share of *future* profits or *future* losses, called a **profits interest.**[7] It is quite common for partners contributing property to receive both capital and profits interests in the exchange. Partners who contribute services instead of property frequently receive only profits interests. The distinction between capital and profits interests is important because the tax rules for partnerships are sometimes applied to them differently.

Contributions of Property Partnership formations are similar to other tax-deferred transactions, such as like-kind exchanges and corporate formations, because realized gains and losses from the exchange of contributed property for partnership interests are either fully or partially deferred for tax purposes, depending on the specifics of the transaction. The rationale for permitting taxpayers to defer realized gains or losses on property contributed to partnerships is identical to the rationale for permitting tax deferral when corporations are formed.[8] From a practical perspective, the tax rules in this area allow entrepreneurs to organize their businesses without having to pay taxes. In addition, these rules follow the aggregate theory of partnership taxation because they recognize that partners contributing property to a partnership still own the contributed property, albeit a smaller percentage, because other partners will also indirectly own the contributed property through their partnership interests.

Gain and loss recognition. As a general rule, neither partnerships nor partners recognize gain or loss when they contribute property to partnerships.[9] This applies to property contributions when a partnership is initially formed and to subsequent property contributions. In this context, the term *property* is defined broadly to include a wide variety of both tangible and intangible assets but not services. The general rule facilitates contributions of property with **built-in gains,** meaning the fair market value is greater than the tax basis, but it

THE KEY FACTS

Property Contributions

- Partners don't generally recognize gain or loss when they contribute property to partnerships.
- Initial tax basis for partners contributing property = Basis of contributed property − Liability securing contributed property + Partnership liabilities allocated to contributing partner + Gain recognized by the contributing partner.
- Contributing partner's holding period in a partnership interest depends on the type of property contributed.

[6]The partnership books reflect partners' shares of the partnership's net assets in their individual capital accounts.

[7]An interest in the future profits or losses of a partnership is customarily referred to as a profits interest rather than a profits/loss interest.

[8]The Corporate Formation, Reorganization, and Liquidation chapter discusses the tax rules related to corporate formations.

[9]§721.

discourages contributions of property with **built-in losses,** meaning the fair market value is less than the tax basis. In fact, partners holding property with built-in losses are usually better off from a tax perspective selling the property, recognizing the associated tax loss, and contributing the cash from the sale to the partnership so it can acquire property elsewhere.

Example 20-1

What if: Assume Nicole contributes land to CCS with a fair market value of $120,000 and a basis of $20,000. What amount of gain or loss would she recognize on the contribution?

Answer: None. Under the general rule for contributions of appreciated property, Nicole will not recognize any of the $100,000 built-in gain from her land.

What if: Suppose Chanzz Inc. contributed equipment with a fair market value of $120,000 and a tax basis of $220,000 to CCS. What amount of the gain or loss would Chanzz Inc. recognize on the contribution?

Answer: None. Chanzz Inc. would not recognize any of the $100,000 built-in loss on the equipment. However, if Chanzz Inc. sold the property to an unrelated person and contributed $120,000 in cash instead of the equipment, it could recognize the $100,000 built-in tax loss. If, for some reason, the equipment Chanzz planned to contribute was uniquely suited to CCS's operations, Chanzz could obtain the same result by selling the equipment to Sarah and contributing the cash received from the sale to CCS. Sarah would then contribute the equipment to CCS.

Partner's initial tax basis in partnership interest. Among other things, partners need to determine the tax basis in their partnership interest to properly compute their taxable gains and losses when they sell their partnership interest. A partner's tax basis in a partnership interest is referred to as that partner's **outside basis.** In contrast, the partnership's basis in its assets is its **inside basis.** As we progress through this and the next chapter, you'll see other important reasons for calculating a partner's outside tax basis.

Calculating a partner's initial tax basis in a partnership interest acquired by contributing property and/or cash is relatively straightforward if the partnership doesn't have any liabilities. The partner will simply have a basis in the partnership interest equivalent to the tax basis of the property and cash contributed.[10] This rule ensures that realized gains and losses on contributed property are merely deferred until either the contributing partner sells the partnership interest or the partnership sells the contributed property.

Example 20-2

What if: Assume that Sarah contributed $120,000 in cash to CCS in exchange for her partnership interest and that CCS had no liabilities. What is Sarah's outside basis in her partnership interest after the contribution?

Answer: Sarah's basis is $120,000, the amount of cash she contributed to CCS.

What if: Assume Nicole contributed land with a fair market value of $120,000 and a basis of $20,000 and CCS had no liabilities. What is Nicole's outside tax basis in CCS?

Answer: Nicole's outside basis in CCS is $20,000, the basis of the property she contributed to CCS. If Nicole immediately sold her interest in CCS for $120,000 (the value of the land she contributed), she would recognize a gain of $100,000—exactly the amount she would have recognized if she had sold the land instead of contributing it to CCS.

When partnerships have liabilities, a few additional steps are required to determine each partners' tax basis in their respective partnership interests. First, all partners must include their shares of the partnership's liabilities in calculating their own outside bases because partnership tax law treats them as each borrowing their own proportionate shares of the partnership's liabilities and then contributing the borrowed cash to acquire their respective partnership interests.[11] You can understand the necessity for this basis increase by recalling that the basis of any purchased asset increases by the amount of any borrowed funds used to purchase it.

Partnerships may have either **recourse liabilities** or **nonrecourse liabilities** or both, and the specific approach to allocating partnership liabilities to individual partners differs

[10]§722.

[11]§752(a).

for each. These two types of liabilities are also frequently referred to in practice as recourse and nonrecourse debt. The fundamental difference between the two types of liabilities lies in the legal responsibility partners assume for ultimately paying the liability. Recourse liabilities are those for which at least one partner has economic risk of loss—that is, they may have to legally satisfy the liability with their own funds. For example, the unsecured liabilities of general partnerships, such as payables, are recourse liabilities because general partners are legally responsible for the liabilities of the partnership. Recourse liabilities are usually allocated to the partners who will ultimately be responsible for paying them.[12] The partners must consider their partner guarantees, other agreements, and state partnership or LLC statutes in making this determination.

Nonrecourse liabilities, in contrast, don't provide creditors the same level of legal recourse against partners. Nonrecourse liabilities such as mortgages are typically secured by real property and only give lenders the right to obtain the secured property in the event the partnership defaults on the liability. Because partners are responsible for paying nonrecourse liabilities only to the extent the partnership generates sufficient profits, such liabilities are generally allocated according to partners' profit-sharing ratios. We discuss an exception to this general rule later in the chapter.[13] The basic rules for allocating recourse and nonrecourse liabilities are summarized in Exhibit 20-1.

EXHIBIT 20-1 **Basic Rules for Allocating Partnership Liabilities to Partners**

Type of liability	Allocation Method
Recourse	Allocated to partners with ultimate responsibility for paying liability
Nonrecourse	Allocated according to partners' profit-sharing ratios

The legal structure of entities taxed as partnerships also influences the way partners characterize and allocate partnership liabilities. Recourse liabilities in limited partnerships are typically allocated only to general partners because, as we discuss in the Business Entities Overview chapter, limited partners are legally protected from a limited partnership's recourse creditors.[14] Limited partners, however, may be allocated recourse liabilities if they forgo their legal protection by guaranteeing some or all of the recourse liabilities. Similarly, LLC members generally treat LLC liabilities as nonrecourse liabilities because they, like corporate shareholders, are shielded from the LLC's creditors. However, like limited partners, LLC members may treat liabilities as recourse liabilities to the extent they contractually assume risk of loss by agreeing to be legally responsible for paying the liabilities.[15]

Example 20-3

Sarah and Chanzz Inc. initially each contributed $120,000, and CCS borrowed $60,000 from a bank when CCS was formed. The bank required Nicole, Sarah, and Chanzz Inc. to personally guarantee the bank loan. The terms were structured so each of the members would (1) be responsible for a portion of the liability equal to the percentage of CCS losses allocated to each member (one-third each) and (2) have no right of reimbursement from either CCS or the other members of CCS. How much of the $60,000 bank liability was allocated to each member?

(continued on page 20-6)

[12]Reg. §1.752-2. Under the regulations, partners' obligations for paying recourse liabilities are determined by assuming a hypothetical, worst-case scenario where partnership assets (including cash) become worthless, and the resulting losses are then allocated to partners. The partners who legally would be responsible for partnership recourse liabilities under this scenario must be allocated the recourse liabilities. A detailed description of this approach for allocating recourse liabilities is beyond the scope of this book.

[13]Reg. §1.752-3 provides the rules for allocating nonrecourse liabilities, some of which are beyond the scope of this text.

[14]Recall from the Business Entities Overview chapter that, in limited partnerships, general partners' liability is unlimited, whereas limited partners' liability is usually limited to the amount they have invested.

[15]It's actually quite common for banks and other lenders to require LLC members to personally guarantee loans made to LLCs.

Answer: Each member is allocated $20,000. The liability is treated as recourse liability because the members are personally guaranteeing it. Because each guarantees one-third of the liability, the $60,000 liability is allocated equally among them.

What if: Assuming the $60,000 bank loan is CCS's only liability, what is Sarah's outside basis in her CCS interest after taking her share of CCS's bank liability into account?

Answer: Sarah's basis is $140,000 ($120,000 + $20,000) and consists of her cash contribution plus her share of CCS's $60,000 bank loan.

Another step is needed to determine a partner's outside basis when the partnership assumes the *liability of the partner* secured by property the partner contributes to the partnership. Essentially, contributing partners must treat their own liability relief as deemed cash distributions from the partnership that reduce their individual outside bases.[16] If the liability securing the contributed property is a *nonrecourse liability,* the amount of the liability in excess of the basis of the contributed property is allocated solely to the contributing partner, and the remaining liability is allocated to all partners according to their profit-sharing ratios.[17]

Example 20-4

What if: Nicole contributed $10,000 of cash and land with a fair market value of $150,000 and basis of $20,000 to CCS when it was formed. The land was encumbered by a $40,000 nonrecourse mortgage executed three years before. Recalling that CCS already had a $60,000 bank loan before Nicole's contribution, what outside tax bases do Nicole, Sarah, and Chanzz Inc. have in their CCS interests?

Answer: Their outside bases are $36,666, $146,666, and $146,666, respectively. Nicole, Sarah, and Chanzz Inc. would determine their initial tax bases as illustrated in the table below:

Description	Nicole	Sarah	Chanzz Inc.	Explanation
(1) Basis in contributed land	$ 20,000			
(2) Cash contributed	10,000	$ 120,000	$ 120,000	Example 20-3
(3) Members' share of $60,000 recourse bank loan	20,000	20,000	20,000	Example 20-3
(4) Nonrecourse mortgage in excess of basis in contributed land	20,000			Nonrecourse liability > basis is allocated only to Nicole
(5) Remaining nonrecourse mortgage	6,666	6,666	6,666	33.33% × [$40,000 – (4)]
(6) Relief from mortgage liability	(40,000)			
Members' initial outside basis in CCS	**$36,666**	**$146,666**	**$146,666**	Sum of (1) through (6)

Although in many instances partners don't recognize gains on property contributions, there is an important exception to the general rule that may apply when property secured by a liability is contributed to a partnership. In these situations, the contributing partner recognizes gain *only if* the cash deemed to have been received from a partnership

[16]§752(b).

[17]Reg. §1.752-3(a)(2).

distribution exceeds the contributing partner's tax basis in the partnership interest prior to the deemed distribution.[18] Any gain recognized is generally treated as capital gain.[19]

Example 20-5

What if: Assume Sarah and Chanzz Inc., but *not* Nicole, personally guarantee all $100,000 of CCS's liabilities ($60,000 bank loan + $40,000 mortgage on land). How much gain, if any, would Nicole recognize on her contribution to CCS, and what would be the outside basis in her CCS interest?

Answer: Nicole would recognize $10,000 gain and have a $0 outside basis, computed as follows:

Description	Amount	Explanation
(1) Basis in contributed land	$ 20,000	Example 20-4
(2) Cash contributed	10,000	Example 20-4
(3) Nicole's share of liabilities	0	Sarah and Chanzz guaranteed all of CCS's liabilities, including the mortgage on land, thereby turning them into recourse liabilities that should be allocated only to Sarah and Chanzz.
(4) Liability relief	(40,000)	Nicole was relieved of mortgage on land.
(5) Liability relief in excess of basis in contributed land and cash	$(10,000)	Sum of (1) through (4)
(6) Capital gain recognized	10,000	(5) with opposite sign
Nicole's outside tax basis in CCS	**$ 0**	(5) + (6)

Partner's holding period in partnership interest. Because a partnership interest is a capital asset, the partner's holding period in the interest determines whether gains or losses from the disposition of the partnership interest are short-term or long-term capital gains or losses. The length of a partner's holding period for a partnership interest acquired by contributing property depends on the nature of the assets the partner contributed. When partners contribute capital assets or §1231 assets (§1231 assets are assets used in a trade or business and held for more than one year), the holding period of the contributed property "tacks on" to the holding period of the partnership interest.[20] Otherwise, it begins on the day the partnership interest is acquired.

Example 20-6

What if: Assume Nicole contributed only land held for investment that she had held for five years in exchange for her partnership interest. One month after contributing the property, she sold her partnership interest and recognized a capital gain. Is the gain long-term or short-term?

Answer: The gain is long-term because the five-year holding period of the land is tacked on to Nicole's holding period for her partnership interest. She is treated as though she held the partnership interest for five years and one month at the time she sells it.

Partnership's tax basis and holding period in contributed property. Just as partners must determine their outside basis in their partnership interests after contributing property, partnerships must establish their inside basis in the contributed property. Measuring both

[18]§731(a). However, §707(a)(2)(B) provides that deemed cash received from the relief of liability should be considered as sale proceeds rather than a distribution when circumstances indicate the relief of liability constitutes a disguised sale. Further discussion of disguised sale transactions is beyond the scope of this book.

[19]§731(a). This is equivalent to increasing what would have been a negative basis by the recognized gain to arrive at a zero basis. This mechanism ensures that partners will be left with an initial tax basis of zero any time they recognize gain from a property contribution.

[20]Reg. §1.1223-1(a).

the partner's outside basis and the partnership's inside basis is consistent with the entity theory of partnership taxation. To ensure built-in gains and losses on contributed property are ultimately recognized if partnerships sell contributed property, partnerships generally take a tax basis in the property equal to the contributing partner's tax basis in the property at the time of the contribution.[21] Like the tax basis of contributed property, a partnership retains the holding period of contributed assets.[22] In fact, the only tax attribute of contributed property that *doesn't* carry over to the partnership is the character of contributed property. Whether gains or losses on dispositions of contributed property are capital or ordinary usually depends on the manner in which the partnership uses contributed property.[23]

Example 20-7

What if: Assume CCS used the land Nicole contributed in its business for one month and then sold it for its fair market value of $150,000. What are the amount and character of the gain CCS would recognize on the sale? (See Example 20-4.)

Answer: CCS recognizes $130,000 of §1231 gain. Nicole held the land as a capital asset, and her basis in the land prior to the formation of CCS was $20,000. Because CCS receives a carryover basis in the land of $20,000, it recognizes $130,000 of gain when it sells the land for $150,000 ($110,000 in cash and $40,000 of liability relief minus $20,000 basis in land). Also, because CCS used the land in its business and because Nicole's five-year holding period carries over to CCS, the land qualifies as a §1231 asset to CCS, and CCS recognizes §1231 gain when the land is sold. Note that $130,000 of gain is recognized regardless of whether (1) Nicole sells the land, recognizes the gain, and contributes cash to CCS or (2) CCS sells the land shortly after it is contributed and recognizes the gain.

Unlike entities taxed as corporations, entities taxed as partnerships track the equity of their owners using a **capital account** for each owner. The methodology for maintaining owners' capital accounts depends on the approach these entities use to prepare their financial statements. For example, an entity preparing GAAP financial statements would track each owner's share of the equity using **GAAP capital accounts** maintained using generally accepted accounting principles.

In addition to tracking the inside basis of its assets for tax purposes, partnerships not required to produce GAAP financial statements may decide to use tax basis, as well as tax income and expense recognition rules, to maintain their books. Under this approach, a new partnership would prepare its initial balance sheet using the tax basis for its assets. In addition, it would create a **tax capital account** for each new partner, reflecting the tax basis of any property the partner contributed (net of any liability securing the property) and the partner's cash contributions. Because each new partner's tax capital account measures that partner's equity in the partnership using tax accounting rules, it will later be adjusted to include the partner's share of earnings and losses, contributions, and distributions.

Besides satisfying bookkeeping requirements, a partnership's tax basis balance sheet can provide useful tax-related information. For example, we can calculate each partner's share of the inside basis of partnership assets by adding each one's share of liabilities to their respective tax capital accounts. Interestingly, partners who acquire their interests by contributing property (without having to recognize any gain) will have an *outside basis* equal to their share of the partnership's total inside basis. However, as we discuss more fully in the Dispositions of Partnership Interests and Partnership Distributions chapter, partners' inside and outside bases will likely be different when they purchase existing partnership interests.

As another alternative to maintaining GAAP capital accounts, partnerships may also maintain their partners' capital accounts using accounting rules prescribed in the §704(b) tax regulations.[24] In fact, many partnership agreements require the partnership to

[21]§723.

[22]§1223(2).

[23]§702(b). However, §724 provides some important exceptions to this general rule for contributions of certain receivables, inventory, and capital loss property.

[24]Reg. §1.704-1(b)(2)(iv).

maintain **§704(b) capital accounts** for the partners in addition to tax basis capital accounts. Partnerships set up §704(b) capital accounts in much the same way as tax capital accounts, except that §704(b) capital accounts reflect the fair market value rather than the tax basis of contributed assets. Once a partnership begins operations, it can adjust §704(b) capital accounts so they continue to reflect the fair market value of partners' capital interests as accurately as possible. Partnerships may prefer this approach over simply maintaining tax capital accounts because §704(b) capital accounts may be a better measure of the true value of partners' capital interests.

(continued from page 20-2 . . .)
Before forming CCS, its members agreed to keep its books using the tax basis of contributed assets and tax income and expense recognition rules. After receiving the cash and property contributions from its members and borrowing $60,000 from Nicole's bank, CCS prepared the tax basis balance sheet in Exhibit 20-2.

Once CCS was organized in March 2021, it built a small production facility on the commercial land Nicole had contributed, purchased and installed the equipment needed to produce sheets, and hired and trained workers—all before the actual production and marketing of the sheets. After production began on July 1, 2021, CCS started selling its sheets to local specialty bedding stores, but this local market was limited. To create additional demand for their product, the members of CCS decided to draw on Sarah's marketing expertise to develop an advertising campaign targeted at home and garden magazines. All members of CCS agreed Sarah would receive, on December 31, 2021, an additional *capital interest* in CCS with a liquidation value of $20,000 *and* an increase in her profit-and-loss-sharing ratio from 1/3 to 40 percent (leaving the other members each with a 30 percent share of profits and losses), to compensate her for the time she would spend on this additional project. At this point, CCS's liability remained at $100,000.

(to be continued . . .)

EXHIBIT 20-2 Color Comfort Sheets LLC

Balance Sheet March 31, 2021	Tax Basis	§704(b)/FMV*
Assets:		
Cash	$310,000	$310,000
Land	20,000	150,000
Totals	$330,000	$460,000
Liabilities and Capital:		
Long-term liabilities	$100,000	$100,000
Capital—Nicole	(10,000)	120,000
Capital—Sarah	120,000	120,000
Capital—Chanzz Inc.	120,000	120,000
Totals	$330,000	$460,000

*The §704(b)/FMV balance sheet is also provided to illustrate the difference in the two approaches to maintaining partners' capital accounts.

Contribution of Services So far we've assumed partners receive their partnership interests in exchange for contributed property. They may also receive partnership interests in exchange for services they provide to the partnership. For example, an attorney or other service provider might accept a partnership interest in lieu of cash payment for services provided as part of a partnership formation. Similarly, ongoing partnerships may compensate their employees with partnership interests to reduce compensation-related cash payments and motivate employees to behave more like owners. Unlike property contributions, services contributed in exchange for partnership interests may create immediate tax consequences to both the contributing partner *and* the partnership, depending on the nature of the partnership interest received.[25]

Capital interests. Partners who receive unrestricted capital interests in exchange for services have the right to receive a share of the partnership's capital if it liquidates.[26] Because capital interests represent a current economic entitlement amenable to measurement, partners receiving capital interests for services must treat the amount they would receive if the partnership were to liquidate, or the **liquidation value**[27] of the capital interest, as ordinary income at the time they receive their interest.[28] In addition, the tax basis in the capital interest received by the **service partner** will equal the amount of ordinary income recognized, and the holding period will begin on the date the service partner receives the capital interest. The partnership either deducts or capitalizes the value of the capital interest, depending on the nature of the services the partner provides. For example, a real estate partnership would capitalize the value of a capital interest compensating a partner for architectural drawings used for a real estate development project.[29] Conversely, the same partnership would deduct the value of a capital interest compensating a partner for providing property management services. When the partnership deducts the value of capital interests used to compensate partners for services provided, it allocates the deduction only to the partners *not* providing services, or **nonservice partners,** because they are the partners transferring capital to the new service partner.[30]

Example 20-8

What if: What are the income and deductions allocated to Sarah and CCS if Sarah receives a capital interest with a $20,000 liquidation value for her marketing services?

Answer: As summarized below, Sarah has $20,000 of ordinary income, and CCS receives a $20,000 ordinary deduction. However, this deduction must be split equally between Nicole and Chanzz Inc. because, in effect, they transferred a portion of their capital to Sarah.

Description	Sarah	Nicole	Chanzz Inc.	Explanation
(1) Ordinary income	$20,000			Liquidation value of capital interest
Ordinary deduction		$(10,000)	$(10,000)	Capital shift from nonservice partners (1) × .5

[25]Rev. Procs. 93-27 and 2001-43. In 2005, the Treasury issued Prop. Reg. §1.704-1, which will change certain elements of current tax law when it is adopted as a final regulation. The concepts and examples discussed here are consistent with both current law and the proposed regulation.

[26]Certain restrictions, such as vesting requirements, may be placed on partnership interests received for services. We limit our discussion here to unrestricted partnership interests.

[27]Proposed regulations in this area also allow the parties in this transaction to use the fair market value of partnership interests as a measure of value rather than liquidation value.

[28]The ordinary income recognized by the service partner is treated as a "guaranteed payment" by the service partner. Guaranteed payments are discussed more fully later in this chapter.

[29]§263(a).

[30]The preamble to Prop. Reg. §1.721-1(b) also applies the varying interest rule of §706(d)(1) to the admission of a service partner.

Profits interests. It's fairly common for partnerships to compensate service partners with profits rather than capital interests. Profits interests are fundamentally different from capital interests because the only economic benefit they provide is the right to share in the future profits of the partnership. Unlike capital interests, profits interests have no liquidation value at the time they are received. Nonservice partners generally prefer to compensate service partners with profits interests because they don't have to forgo their current share of capital in the partnership and may not ever have to give up anything if the partnership is ultimately unprofitable. Thus, a profits interest is more risky than a capital interest from the perspective of the service partner.

The tax rules applicable to profits interests differ from those pertaining to capital interests due to the fundamental economic differences between them. Because there is no immediate liquidation value associated with a profits interest, the service partner typically will not recognize income and the nonservice partners will not be allocated deductions.[31] However, future profits and losses attributable to the profits interest are allocated to the service partner (and away from the nonservice partners) as they are generated. At this point, the service partner will have a capital interest equal to the share of the undistributed profits of the partnership possessed by that service partner. In addition, the partnership must adjust liability allocations based on profit-and-loss-sharing ratios to reflect the service partner's new or increased share of profits and losses.

Example 20-9

What if: Assuming Sarah received only a profits interest for her marketing services instead of the capital interest she received in Example 20-8, what are the tax consequences to Sarah, Nicole, Chanzz Inc., and CCS?[32]

Answer: Sarah would not be required to recognize any income, and CCS would not deduct or capitalize any costs. As CCS generates future profits, Sarah will receive a greater share of the profits than she would have otherwise received, and the other two members will receive a correspondingly smaller share. In addition, Sarah will have a capital interest equal to her share of any undistributed future profits. Finally, with the increase in Sarah's profit-and-loss-sharing ratio from 1/3 to 40 percent, liability allocations among the partners will change to reflect Sarah's additional entitlement. Note that the liability allocations affect each partner's outside basis. The change in liability allocations is reflected in the table below:

Description	Sarah	Nicole	Chanzz Inc.	Explanation
(1) Increase in liability allocation	$5,334			Loss-sharing ratio increases from 1/3 to 40 percent, or 6.67 percent ($60,000 recourse bank loan × 6.67% increase in loss-sharing ratio) + ($20,000 nonrecourse mortgage not allocated solely to Nicole × 6.67% increase in profit-sharing ratio).
Decrease in liability allocation		$(2,667)	$(2,667)	(1) × .5

[31]Rev. Proc. 93-27 indicates that income is recognized by the service partner "if the profits interest relates to a substantially certain and predictable stream of income," if the partner disposes of the profits interest within two years, or "if the profits interest is a limited partnership interest in a 'publicly traded partnership'."

[32]It is common for partnerships to grant a profits interest without an accompanying capital interest.

Example 20-10

When compared with Example 20-9, what are the tax consequences to Sarah, Nicole, and Chanzz Inc. associated with the capital interest (liquidation value of $20,000) and profits interest Sarah receives for her marketing services?

Answer: The tax consequences associated with giving Sarah *both* a capital interest and a profits interest are summarized in the table below:

Description	Sarah	Nicole	Chanzz Inc.	Explanation
(1) Ordinary income	$20,000			Liquidation value of capital interest
Ordinary deduction		$(10,000)	$(10,000)	Capital shift from nonservice partners, (1) × .5
(2) Increase in liability allocation	5,334			Loss-sharing ratio increases from 1/3 to 40 percent, or 6.67 percent [($60,000 recourse bank loan × 6.67% increase in loss-sharing ratio) + ($20,000 nonrecourse mortgage not allocated solely to Nicole × 6.67% increase in profit-sharing ratio)].
Decrease in liability allocation		$(2,667)	$(2,667)	(2) × .5

TAXES IN THE REAL WORLD Carried Interests

In debates over tax policy, politicians in the news have frequently discussed *carried interests* as if everyone within earshot understands the term. However, judging from the public's confusion over the issue, not everyone does.

Carried interests are nothing more than profits interests granted to managing partners and key employees of private equity and other similar investment partnerships. Industry norms suggest that typical carried interests provide managing partners with a 20 percent (and sometimes greater) share of profits when partnership investments are eventually sold. When these investments have been held for the long term, gains from their sale allocated to carried interest holders are often taxed at favorable, long-term capital gains rates. However, under current law portfolio assets in investment funds must be held for more than three years before gains allocated to carried interest holders are eligible for long-term capital gains treatment.[33]

The benefits of these types of carried-interest arrangements are twofold: Any income managing partners receive is deferred until partnership investments are sold, and when the income is finally recognized, it is frequently taxed at favorable, long-term capital gains rates. To some politicians and their supporters, this result seems unfair given that carried interests are economically equivalent to deferred salary and thus should be taxed at higher ordinary rates.

Source: For a more detailed description of carried interests, see "Business Taxation: What Is Carried Interest and How Should It Be Taxed?" in *The Tax Policy Briefing Book* at www.taxpolicycenter.org.

Organizational Expenditures, Start-Up Costs, and Syndication Costs When partnerships are formed, they typically incur some costs that must be capitalized rather than expensed for tax purposes because they will benefit the partnership over its entire lifespan. This category of expenses includes **organizational expenditures** associated with legally forming a partnership (such as attorney and accountant fees), **syndication costs** to promote and sell partnership interests, and **start-up costs** that would normally be deducted as business expenses except that they are incurred before the start of active trade or business. However, with the exception of syndication costs,[34] which are not deductible, the partnership may elect to amortize these costs. The Property Acquisition and Cost

[33]§1061(a).

[34]Syndication costs are typically incurred by partnerships whose interests are marketed to the public. Thus, syndication expenses are unusual in closely held partnerships.

Recovery chapter provides additional detail about immediately expensing or amortizing business organizational expenditures and start-up costs.

Acquisitions of Partnership Interests after Formation

After a partnership has been formed and begins operating, new or existing partners can acquire partnership interests in exchange for contributing property and/or services, in which case the tax rules discussed above in the context of forming a partnership still apply. Or new partners may purchase partnership interests from existing partners. Partners who purchase their partnership interests don't have to be concerned with recognizing taxable income when they receive their interests. However, in each of these scenarios, they must still determine the initial tax basis and holding period in their partnership interests. Exhibit 20-3 summarizes the rules for determining the outside basis of partnership interests when they are received in exchange for contributed property or services or when they are purchased.

THE KEY FACTS

Acquisitions of Partnership Interests

- Contributing partner's tax basis and holding period in contributed property carry over to the partnership.
- If service partners report ordinary income, the partnership either expenses or capitalizes the amount depending on the nature of the services provided.
- The tax basis of a purchased partnership interest = Purchase price + Partnership liability allocated to partner, and the holding period begins on the purchase date.

EXHIBIT 20-3 Summary of Partner's Outside Basis and Holding Period by Acquisition Method

Acquisition Method	Outside Basis	Holding Period
Contribute Property	= Basis of contributed property − Liability relief + Liability allocation + Gain recognized.	If property contributed is a capital or §1231 asset, holding period includes holding period of contributed property; otherwise begins on date interest received.
Contribute Services	= Liquidation value of capital interest + Liability allocation. Equals liability allocation if only profits interest received.	Begins on date interest received.
Purchase	= Cost basis[35] + Liability allocation.	Begins on date interest purchased.

Example 20-11

CCS had overall operating losses from July 1, 2021 (when it began operating), through June 30, 2022. Because of the losses, Chanzz Inc. decided to sell its 30 percent interest in CCS (Chanzz Inc.'s original 1/3 interest in CCS was reduced to 30 percent at the end of 2021 when Sarah's interest was increased to compensate her for services provided) on June 30, 2022, to Greg Randall. Like Chanzz Inc., Greg will be a nonmanaging member and will guarantee a portion of CCS liabilities. Greg paid Chanzz Inc. $100,000 for his interest in CCS and was allocated a 30 percent share of CCS liabilities (CCS's liabilities remained at $100,000 on June 30, 2022). What are Greg's outside basis and holding period in CCS?

Answer: Greg's outside basis of $124,000 in CCS includes the $100,000 amount he paid to purchase the interest plus his $24,000 share of CCS's total $80,000 liabilities available to be allocated to all members ($60,000 recourse bank loan and $20,000 of nonrecourse mortgage remaining after allocating the first $20,000 to Nicole). Greg's holding period in his CCS interest begins on June 30, 2022.

PARTNERSHIP ACCOUNTING: TAX ELECTIONS, ACCOUNTING PERIODS, AND ACCOUNTING METHODS

LO 20-3

A newly formed partnership must adopt its required tax year-end and decide whether it intends to use either the cash or accrual method as its overall method of accounting. As discussed in the Business Income, Deductions, and Accounting Methods chapter, an entity's tax year-end determines the cutoff date for including income and deductions in a particular tax return, and its overall accounting method determines when income and

[35]§742.

deductions are recognized for tax purposes. Partnerships must frequently make other tax-related elections as well.

Tax Elections

New partnerships determine their accounting periods and make tax elections, including the election of overall accounting method, the election to expense a portion of organizational expenditures and start-up costs, and the election to expense tangible personal property. Who formally makes all these elections? In theory, either the partnership or the partners themselves could do so. However, with just a few exceptions, the partnership tax rules rely on the entity theory of partnership taxation and make the partnership responsible for tax elections.[36] In many instances, the partnership makes elections in conjunction with filing its annual tax return. For example, it selects an accounting method and determines whether to elect to amortize organizational expenditures or start-up costs by simply applying its elections in calculating ordinary business income on its first return. The partnership makes other tax elections by filing a separate document with the IRS, such as Form 3115, when it elects to change an accounting method.

Example 20-12

How will CCS elect its overall accounting method after it begins operations?

Answer: Nicole, Sarah, and Chanzz Inc. may jointly decide on an overall accounting method or, in their LLC operating agreement, they may appoint one of the members to be responsible for making this and other tax elections. Once they have made this decision, CCS makes the election by simply using the chosen accounting method when preparing its first return.

THE KEY FACTS

Partnership Accounting: Tax Elections, Accounting Periods, and Methods

- Partnerships are responsible for making most tax elections.
- A partnership's taxable year is the majority interest taxable year, the common taxable year of the principal partners, or the taxable year providing the least aggregate deferral to the partners.
- Partnerships are generally eligible to use the cash method for 2022 unless they have corporate partners and average gross receipts over the three prior years of greater than $27 million (this number is indexed for inflation).

Accounting Periods

Required Year-Ends Because partners include their share of partnership income or loss in their taxable year ending with the partnership taxable year, or within which the partnership taxable year falls, any partnership tax year other than that of the partners will result in some degree of tax deferral for some or all of the partners.[37] Exhibit 20-4 reflects the tax deferral a partner with a calendar year-end would receive if the corresponding partnership had a January 31 year-end.

EXHIBIT 20-4 Partner Defers 11 Months of Income for One Year

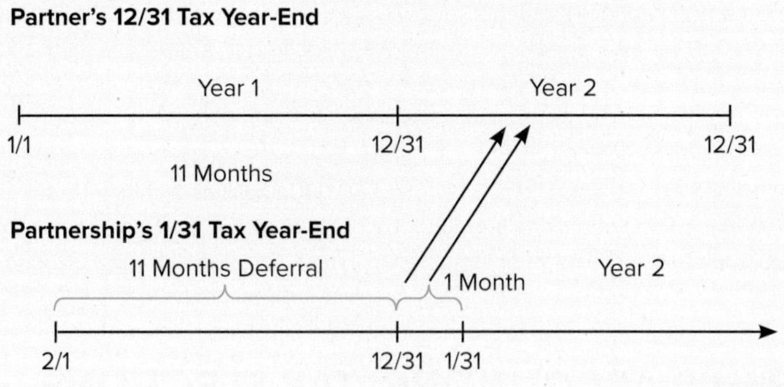

The partner reports the partnership's year 1 income earned from February 1 until January 31 in the partner's second calendar year (i.e., the year within which the partnership's January 31 year-end falls). As a result, the partner defers reporting for one year the

[36]§703(b). Certain elections are made at the partner level.

[37]§706(a).

11 months of income allocated from February 1 through December 31 of that partner's first calendar year.

The government's desire to reduce the aggregate tax deferral of partners (i.e., the sum of the deferrals for each individual partner) provides the underlying rationale behind the rules requiring certain partnership taxable year-ends. Partnerships are generally required to use one of three possible tax year-ends and, under certain circumstances, are allowed other alternative year-ends.[38] As illustrated in Exhibit 20-5, they must follow a series of steps to determine the appropriate year-end.

EXHIBIT 20-5 Steps to Determine a Partnership's Year-End

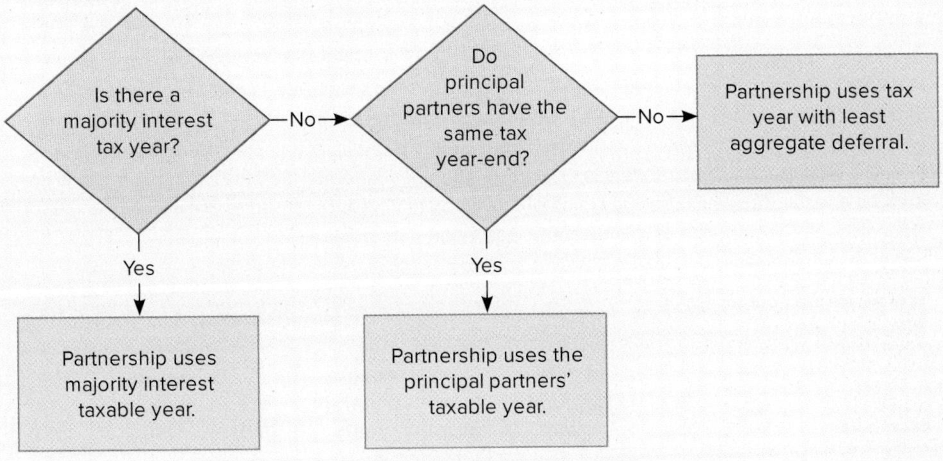

The first potential required tax year is the **majority interest taxable year,** the taxable year of one or more partners who together own more than 50 percent of the capital and profits interests in the partnership.[39] However, there may not be a majority interest taxable year when several partners have different year-ends. For example, if a partnership has two partners with 50 percent capital and profits interests and each has a different tax year, there will be no majority interest taxable year. In that case, the partnership next applies the principal partners test to determine its year-end.

Under the **principal partners** test, the required tax year is the taxable year the principal partners *all* have in common. For this purpose, principal partners are those who have a 5 percent or more interest in the partnership profits and capital.[40] Consider a partnership with two calendar-year partners, each with a 20 percent capital and profits interest, and 30 additional fiscal year-end partners, each with less than a 5 percent capital and profits interest. In this scenario, the required taxable year of the partnership is a calendar year, corresponding with the taxable year of the partnership's only two principal partners. If, as in the earlier example, the partnership had two 50 percent capital and profits partners with different tax years, it would then use the tax year providing the "least aggregate deferral" to the partners, unless it is eligible to elect an alternative year-end.[41]

The tax year with the **least aggregate deferral** is the one among the tax years of the partners that provides the partner group as a whole with the smallest amount of aggregate tax deferral. Under this approach, the total tax deferral is measured under each potential tax year mathematically by weighting each partner's months of deferral under the potential tax year by each partner's *profits* percentage and then summing the weighted months of deferral for all the partners.

[38]See Rev. Proc. 2002-38 and §444 for additional information concerning these options.

[39]§706(b)(1)(B)(i).

[40]§706(b)(3).

[41]Reg. §1.706-1(b)(3).

Example 20-13

When CCS began operating in 2021, it had two calendar-year-end members, Nicole and Sarah, and one member with a June 30 year-end, Chanzz Inc. What tax year-end must CCS use for 2021?

Answer: CCS must use the calendar year as its taxable year unless it was eligible for an alternative year-end. Although Chanzz Inc. had a June 30 taxable year, Nicole and Sarah both had calendar year-ends. Because Nicole and Sarah each initially owns 1/3 of the capital and profits of CCS, and together they own greater than 50 percent of the profits and capital of CCS, the calendar year is the required taxable year for CCS because it is the majority interest taxable year.

What if: Assume CCS initially began operating with three members: Nicole, a calendar-year-end member with a 20 percent profits and capital interest; Chanzz Inc., a June 30 year-end member with a 40 percent profits and capital interest; and Telle Inc., a September 30 year-end member with a 40 percent profits and capital interest. What tax year-end must CCS use for 2021?

Answer: CCS would be required to use a June 30 year-end unless it was eligible for an alternative year-end. CCS does not have a majority interest taxable year because no partner or group of partners with the same year-end owns more than 50 percent of the profits and capital interests in CCS. Also, because all three principal partners in CCS have different year-ends, the principal partner test is not met. As a result, CCS must decide which of three potential year-ends—June 30, September 30, or December 31—will provide its members the least aggregate deferral. The table below illustrates the required computations:

Possible Year-Ends			12/31 Year-End		6/30 Year-End		9/30 Year-End	
Members	**%**	**Tax Year**	**Months Deferral* (MD)**	**% × (MD)**	**Months Deferral* (MD)**	**% × (MD)**	**Months Deferral* (MD)**	**% × (MD)**
Nicole	20	12/31	0	0	6	1.2	3	.6
Chanzz Inc.	40	6/30	6	2.4	0	0	9	3.6
Telle Inc.	40	9/30	9	3.6	3	1.2	0	0
Total aggregate deferral				6		**2.4**		4.2

*Months deferral equals number of months between the proposed year-end and partner's year-end.

June 30 is the required taxable year-end because it provides members with the least aggregate tax deferral (2.4 is less than 6 and 4.2).

Accounting Methods

Although partnerships may use the accrual method freely, they may not use the cash method under certain conditions because it facilitates the deferral of income and acceleration of deductions. For example, partnerships with C corporation partners are generally not eligible to use the cash method[42] for 2022 unless their average annual gross receipts for the three prior taxable years do not exceed $27 million (this number is indexed for inflation) and they otherwise qualify.[43] Entities generally eligible to use the overall cash method of accounting must nevertheless use the accrual method to account for the purchase and sale of inventory in 2022 unless they have average annual gross receipts over the prior three years of $27 million (this number is indexed for inflation) or less.

[42]§448(a)(2). In addition, §448(a)(3) prohibits partnerships classified as "tax shelters" from electing the cash method.

[43]§448(b)(3). If a partnership has not been in existence for at least three years, this test is applied based on the number of years it has been in existence. See the Business Income, Deductions, and Accounting Methods chapter for more details on the gross receipts test.

Example 20-14

When CCS began operations, its members decided it should elect the cash method of accounting if eligible to do so. Would having a corporate member—Chanzz Inc.—prevent it from electing the cash method?

Answer: Not necessarily. Although Chanzz Inc. was a founding member of CCS, its ownership share would not affect the partnership's eligibility to use the cash method unless CCS's average annual gross receipts were to exceed the threshold that would require it to use the accrual method.

REPORTING THE RESULTS OF PARTNERSHIP OPERATIONS

LO 20-4

The first section in the Internal Revenue Code dealing with partnerships states emphatically that partnerships are flow-through entities: "A partnership as such shall not be subject to the income tax imposed by this chapter. Persons carrying on business as partners shall be liable for income tax only in their separate or individual capacities."[44] This feature of partnership taxation explains why entities taxed as partnerships are sometimes favored over entities taxed as corporations, whose shareholders are subject to a double tax—once when the income is earned and again when it is distributed to shareholders as a dividend or when the shares are sold.

TAXES IN THE REAL WORLD Publicly Traded Partnerships

Would it surprise you to know that many private equity firms are organized as partnerships for tax purposes? Even more surprising may be the fact that some well-known private equity funds—including Oaktree Capital Group and Oz Management—are publicly traded. Publicly traded firms are typically taxed as corporations even if they are legally structured as partnerships or, in the case of these private equity firms, as limited partnerships. However, relying on a provision in the tax code, these private equity funds are able to maintain their tax status as partnerships after their public offerings.[45] Thus, investors purchasing shares in these funds are buying investments that are subject to only one level of taxation but, like shares in a corporation, can be readily traded in a public securities market.

Ordinary Business Income (Loss) and Separately Stated Items

Although partnerships are not taxpaying entities, they are required to file information returns annually. They also distribute information to each partner detailing the amount *and* character of items of income and loss flowing through the partnership.[46] Partners must report these income and loss items on their tax returns even if they don't receive cash distributions from the partnership during the year.

When gathering this information for their partners, partnerships must determine each partner's share of **ordinary business income (loss)** and **separately stated items.** Partnership ordinary business income (loss) is all partnership income (loss) exclusive of any separately stated items of income (loss). Separately stated items share one common characteristic—they are treated differently from a partner's share of ordinary business income (loss) for tax purposes. To better understand why certain items must be separately disclosed to partners, consider how two particular separately stated items, dividend income and net capital losses, might affect an individual partner's tax liability. Qualified dividend income allocated to individual partners is taxed at either a 0 percent, 15 percent,

THE KEY FACTS

Reporting the Results of Partnership Operations

- Partnerships file annual information returns reporting their ordinary business income (loss) and separately stated items.
- Ordinary business income (loss) = Partnership overall income or loss exclusive of separately stated items.
- Separately stated items change partners' tax liabilities according to each partner's unique situation (e.g., tax bracket, capital gains/losses, etc.).

[44] §701.

[45] §7704.

[46] Other items, such as tax credits, may also flow through the partnership to partners.

or 20 percent rate, depending on individual partners' level of taxable income.[47] In a similar vein, individual partners without capital gains during the year may deduct up to $3,000 in net capital loss (i.e., capital losses in excess of capital gains) against their ordinary income, while other individual partners with capital gains may deduct more.[48] If a partnership's dividends and capital losses were simply buried in the computation of its overall income or loss for the year, the partner would be unable to apply these specific tax rules to their unique situation and determine their correct tax liability.

The tax code specifically enumerates several common separately stated items, including short-term capital gains and losses, long-term capital gains and losses, §1231 gains and losses, charitable contributions, and dividends.[49] Many more items are considered under regulations issued by the Treasury Department.[50] Exhibit 20-6 lists several other common separately stated items.

EXHIBIT 20-6 Common Separately Stated Items

- Interest income
- Guaranteed payments
- Net earnings (loss) from self-employment
- Tax-exempt income
- Net rental real estate income
- Investment interest expense
- Royalties
- §179 deduction

Example 20-15

After constructing a building and purchasing equipment in its first year of operations ending on December 31, 2021, CCS invested $15,000 of its remaining idle cash in stocks and bonds. CCS's books reflected an overall loss (computed on a tax basis) for the year of $80,000. Included in the $80,000 loss were $2,100 of dividend income, $1,200 of short-term capital gains, and a $20,000 deduction for the capital interest transferred to Sarah at the end of 2021 (see Example 20-10). How much ordinary business loss and what separately stated items are allocated to the CCS members for the taxable year ended December 31, 2021?

Answer: As reflected in the table below, CCS has $63,300 of ordinary business loss. In addition, it has $2,100 of dividend income, $1,200 in short-term capital gains, and $20,000 of ordinary deduction (related to the capital interest Sarah received) that are separately stated items. To Nicole, Sarah, and Chanzz Inc., CCS would report $21,100 of ordinary business loss, $700 of dividend income, and $400 of short-term capital gain. In addition, CCS would report $20,000 of ordinary income to Sarah for the capital interest she received, and a $10,000 deduction to Nicole and Chanzz Inc. reflecting the amount of partnership capital they relinquished.

Description	CCS	Nicole $\left(\frac{1}{3}\right)$	Sarah $\left(\frac{1}{3}\right)$	Chanzz Inc. $\left(\frac{1}{3}\right)$
2021 overall net tax loss	$(80,000)			
Less:				
Dividends	2,100			
Short-term capital gains	1,200			
Ordinary deduction for Sarah's capital interest	(20,000)			
Ordinary business loss	$(63,300)	$(21,100)	$(21,100)	$(21,100)
Separately stated Items:				
Dividends	2,100	700	700	700
Short-term capital gains	1,200	400	400	400
Ordinary income for capital interest to Sarah	20,000		20,000	
Ordinary deduction for capital interest to Sarah	(20,000)	(10,000)		(10,000)

[47]§1(h).
[48]§1211.
[49]§702.
[50]Reg. §1.702-1(a).

Nicole and Sarah will treat their shares of CCS's ordinary business loss as an *ordinary* loss and include it along with their shares of dividend income and short-term capital gain in their individual tax returns for the year.[51] Chanzz Inc. will also include its share of these items in its annual tax return. But because Chanzz is a C corporation, different tax rules apply to its share of dividend income and short-term capital gains. For example, Chanzz will be entitled to the 50 percent dividends-received deduction, while Nicole and Sarah will pay tax on their share of dividend income at individual capital gains rates.

Notice that the character of separately stated items is determined at the partnership level rather than at the partner level.[52] This treatment reflects the entity theory.

Example 20-16

What if: Assume Chanzz Inc. is an investments dealer rather than a sports franchise operator. How would Chanzz Inc. classify its share of the $1,200 gain from the securities sold by CCS during 2021?

Answer: Chanzz Inc. would classify its share of the $1,200 as short-term capital gains. Because the securities CCS sold were capital assets to CCS, the gain on the sale is a capital gain even though the securities would be inventory (an ordinary asset) if sold by Chanzz Inc. That is, we determine the character of the income at the partnership level, not the partner level.

Guaranteed Payments In addition to dividends, capital gains and losses, and other routine separately stated items, **guaranteed payments** are also a very common separately stated item for partners who receive them. As their name suggests, guaranteed payments are fixed amounts paid to partners regardless of whether the partnership shows a profit or loss for the year.[53] We can think of them—and some partnerships treat them—as economically equivalent to cash salary payments made to partners for services provided.[54] Specifically, they are typically deducted in computing a partnership's ordinary income or loss for the year. Though included in a partnership's ordinary business income (loss) computation, guaranteed payments must, nevertheless, be separately stated to the partners who receive them. This separate reporting serves the same purpose as providing W-2 forms to employees. Because guaranteed payments are similar to salary payments, partners treat them as ordinary income.

(continued from page 20-9. . .)
Because Sarah received an additional capital interest for marketing services she provided at the end of 2021, she held a 40 percent capital and profits interest, and Nicole and Chanzz Inc. each held a 30 percent capital and profits interest at the beginning of 2022. After Sarah's initial work in formulating a marketing strategy in 2021, Nicole suggested they hire a permanent employee to oversee product marketing. However, because they were unable to find a suitable candidate, Sarah continued to shoulder the product marketing responsibilities in addition to her normal role as a managing member of CCS. To compensate Sarah for her additional workload, all members of CCS agreed that CCS would provide Sarah a $10,000 guaranteed payment for her marketing efforts in 2022. Exhibit 20-7 provides CCS's income statement for 2022. ■

[51]Nicole and Sarah would report their share of ordinary business loss on Schedule E, their share of dividend income on Schedule B, and their share of short-term capital gain on Schedule D of Form 1040.

[52]§702(b).

[53]§707(c).

[54]Fringe benefits that partners receive for services provided such as medical insurance and group-term life insurance are also treated as guaranteed payments. In addition to compensating partners for services provided, guaranteed payments are also made to partners for the use of capital.

EXHIBIT 20-7 Color Comfort Sheets LLC

Income Statement December 31, 2022	
Sales revenue	$ 40,000
Cost of goods sold	(20,000)
Employee wages	(50,000)
Depreciation expense	(18,000)
Guaranteed payments	(10,000)
Miscellaneous expenses	(2,800)
Dividend income	500
Long-term capital gains	300
Overall net loss	$(60,000)

Example 20-17

Given CCS's operating results for 2022 presented in Exhibit 20-7, how much ordinary business loss and what separately stated items will it report on its return for the year? How will it allocate these amounts to its members?

Answer: The table below displays CCS's ordinary business loss and separately stated items and the allocation of these amounts to CCS's members:

Description	CCS	Nicole 30%	Sarah 40%	Chanzz Inc. 30% × 6/12*	Greg 30% × 6/12*
Sales revenue	$ 40,000				
Cost of goods sold	(20,000)				
Employee wages	(50,000)				
Depreciation expense	(18,000)				
Guaranteed payment to Sarah	(10,000)				
Miscellaneous expenses	(2,800)				
Ordinary business loss	$(60,800)	$(18,240)	$(24,320)	$(9,120)	$(9,120)
Separately stated to partners					
Dividends	500	150	200	75	75
Long-term capital gains	300	90	120	45	45
Guaranteed payment			10,000		

*As we noted in Example 20-11, Chanzz Inc. sold its 30 percent interest in CCS to Greg Randall on June 30, 2021. Therefore, the items related to Chanzz Inc.'s original 30 percent interest must be allocated between Chanzz Inc. and Greg Randall.[55]

THE KEY FACTS

Guaranteed Payments and Self-Employment Income

- Guaranteed payments are separately stated items, are treated as ordinary income by partners receiving them, and are either capitalized or expensed by partnerships.
- Guaranteed payments for services are always treated as self-employment income.
- Shares of ordinary business income (loss) are always treated as self-employment income (loss) by general partners and never treated as self-employment income (loss) by limited partners.
- Shares of ordinary business income (loss) may or may not be treated by LLC members as self-employment income (loss), depending on the extent of their involvement with the LLC.

Self-Employment Tax Individual partners, like sole proprietors, may be responsible for paying **self-employment taxes** in addition to income taxes on their share of business income from partnerships.[56] The degree to which partners are responsible for self-employment taxes depends on their legal status as general partners, limited partners, or LLC members and their business activities. General partners report guaranteed payments for services they provide and their share of ordinary business income (loss) as self-employment income (loss) because they are actively involved in managing the partnership. Limited partners, on the other hand, are generally not allowed under state law to participate in the management of limited partnerships. Therefore, their share of ordinary business income (loss) is conceptually more like investment income than trade or business income. As a result, ordinary business income (loss) allocated to limited partners is not subject to

[55]We assume here that the items are allocated based on the number of months the interest was held. See the Dispositions of Partnership Interests and Partnership Distributions chapter for additional detail regarding methods to account for partners' varying interests in a partnership when a partnership interest is sold.

[56]The Business Entities Overview chapter more fully discusses earned income and related self-employment taxes.

self-employment tax. However, if limited partners receive guaranteed payments for services provided to the partnership, they treat those payments as self-employment income.

Because LLC members may be either managing or nonmanaging members, the approach to taxing their share of ordinary business income (loss) for self-employment tax purposes does depend to some degree on their level of involvement in the LLC.[57] Tax rules in this area were developed before LLCs became popular, however, so the IRS has not issued any authoritative guidance to help LLCs decide whether to characterize their members' shares of ordinary business income (loss) as self-employment income (loss). However, a proposed regulation issued by the Treasury and later withdrawn can assist partnerships in drawing the line between aggressive and conservative positions in this area.[58] The proposed regulation provides that LLC members who have personal liability for the liabilities of the LLC by reason of being an LLC member, who have authority to contract on behalf of the LLC, *or* who participate more than 500 hours in the LLC's trade or business during the taxable year should be classified as general partners when applying the self-employment tax rules.

Historically, the lack of authoritative guidance in this area has resulted in a predictable diversity of practice. Indeed, some aggressive taxpayers and their advisers have ignored the proposed regulation entirely and claimed that managing members of LLCs or members providing significant services to their LLCs are similar to limited partners and shouldn't have to pay self-employment taxes at all. This approach has been invalidated by a string of court decisions.[59] These decisions follow the spirit of the proposed regulation in that they provide that LLC members either with management control or that actively participate in the trade or business of an LLC should be treated as general partners for self-employment tax purposes and be subject to self-employment tax on their share of ordinary business income.[60] The same criteria are used to determine if a loss is a self employment loss. If it is, it offsets other sources of self employment income in determining self employment tax.

Example 20-18

For *2022*, should CCS classify Sarah's $10,000 guaranteed payment as self-employment income?

Answer: Yes. The law is clear with respect to guaranteed payments to LLC members—they are always treated as self-employment income.

Using the proposed regulation, will CCS classify Sarah's $24,320 (see Example 20-17) share of ordinary business loss for *2022* as a self-employment loss?

Answer: Yes. Under the proposed regulations, an LLC member who has personal liability for LLC liabilities or the ability to contract on behalf of the LLC, or who spends more than 500 hours participating in the business of the LLC, is classified as a general partner when applying the self-employment tax rules. Given Sarah's status as a managing member of CCS, at least one but probably all three criteria for classifying her share of CCS's ordinary business loss as self-employment loss will apply. Although these rules have not been finalized and are therefore not authoritative, the IRS would likely follow them because they represent its current thinking on the matter. Applying the law this way, CCS will report a $14,320 self-employment loss ($24,320 share of ordinary business loss + $10,000 guaranteed payment) as a separately stated item to Sarah so she can properly compute her self-employment tax liability on her individual return. If Sarah has no other sources of self-employment income, Sarah would not be liable for self-employment tax. Otherwise, she would be able to use her self-employment loss from CCS to reduce or eliminate her self-employment income from other sources.

Example 20-19

Using the proposed regulation, will CCS classify Nicole's $18,240 (see Example 20-17) share of ordinary business loss for *2022* as a self employment loss?

Answer: Yes. Because Nicole, like Sarah, is involved in the day-to-day management of CCS, it will classify her entire share of ordinary business loss as a self employment loss, consistent with its

(continued on page 20-22)

[57]Guaranteed payments to LLC members are clearly subject to self-employment tax because they are similar to salary payments.

[58]Prop. Reg. §1.1402(a)-2.

[59]See *Renkemeyer, Campbell & Weaver, LLP v. Comm'r,* 136 TC 137 (2011); *Riether v. United States,* 919 F. Supp. 2d 1140 (D.N.M. 2012); *Castigliola,* TC Memo 2017-62.

[60]Of course, these cases also suggest that the opposite should also be true: LLC members without management control or that don't provide significant services should be treated as limited partners for self-employment tax purposes.

classification of Sarah's share of ordinary business loss, and report the amount as a separately stated item to Nicole.

Under the proposed regulation, will CCS treat Greg's $9,120 share of ordinary business loss for *2022* as a self employment loss?

Answer: Yes. CCS will treat Greg's share of ordinary business loss as a self employment loss because he has guaranteed a portion of CCS's liabilities. CCS's total self-employment loss is $41,680, consisting of Sarah's $14,320 self-employment loss (an amount that includes Sarah's share of ordinary business loss offset by her guaranteed payment), Nicole's $18,240 self-employment loss, and Greg's $9,120 self-employment loss.

Limitation on Business Interest Expense As explained in the Business Income, Deductions, and Accounting Methods chapter, the deduction for business interest expense is limited to the sum of (1) business interest income and (2) 30 percent of the adjusted taxable income of the taxpayer for the taxable year.[61] For entities taxed as partnerships, this limitation is applied at the partnership level first. Under this approach, any business interest expense of a partnership that is not disallowed due to the limitation is taken into account in determining the partnership's ordinary business income or loss for the year.

In contrast, disallowed business interest expense is allocated and separately stated to partners, reducing the basis in their partnership interests.[62] Subsequently, the disallowed business interest expense is carried forward indefinitely at the partner level until the partnership has excess business interest expense limitation to allocate to the partners. This will occur whenever the partnership's business interest expense limitation exceeds the partnership's business interest expense in a given year. Generally, partners may deduct their carried-forward disallowed interest expense from a given partnership in any future year to the extent they have excess business interest expense limitation (the adjusted taxable income equivalent is separately stated to partners[63]) from the same partnership.

The limitation on business interest expense does not apply to partnerships in 2022 with average annual gross receipts for the prior three years that do not exceed $27 million (indexed for inflation). As a result, the limitation on business interest expense will apply to only a relatively small number of large partnerships.

Deduction for Qualified Business Income As we more fully discuss in the Business Entities Overview chapter, noncorporate owners of flow-through entities, including partnerships, may deduct 20 percent of the qualified business income allocated to them from the entity subject to certain limitations. Qualified business income is the net business income from a qualified trade or business conducted in the United States. In a partnership setting, qualified business income would typically not include a partnership's ordinary business income from most service-related businesses and would also not include a partnership's investment income such as capital gains, dividends, and investment interest income.[64] Further, guaranteed payments received by partners for services provided to the partnership are, by definition, not considered to be qualified business income.

[61]§163(j).

[62]§163(j)(4).

[63]Under §163(j)(4)(A)(ii), a partner's share of adjusted taxable income is increased by the partner's distributive share of the partnership's "excess taxable income." Per §163(j)(4)(C), excess taxable income is mathematically equivalent to the amount of a partnership's excess business interest expense limitation divided by 30 percent.

[64]Section 199A(d)(2) excludes income from certain specified service trades or businesses from the definition of qualified business income. A specified service trade or business is defined as any trade or business involving the performance of services in the fields of health, law, accounting, actuarial science, performing arts, consulting, athletics, financial services, brokerage services, or any trade or business where the principal asset of such trade or business is the reputation or skill of one or more of its employees or which involves the performance of services that consist of investing and investment management trading, or dealing in securities, partnership interests, or commodities. The definition specifically excludes architecture and engineering from the definition. Reg. §1.199A-5 provides additional details regarding the definition of specified service trades or businesses. The specified service trade or business requirement does not apply to taxpayers with taxable income (before the deduction) below a certain threshold and the requirement phases in over a range of taxable income above the threshold [see §199A(d)(3)].

To facilitate a partner's calculation of the 20 percent deduction, partnerships must disclose certain items to the partners. First, the partnership must disclose each partner's share of qualified business income for the separate qualified trade or businesses within the partnership. Further, the partnership must also disclose for each qualified trade or business within the partnership any additional information required for the partners to calculate the limitations on the deduction applied at the partner level.[65]

Net Investment Income Tax

An individual partner's share of gross income from interest, dividends, annuities, royalties, or rents is included in the partner's net investment income when calculating the net investment income tax.[66] In addition, the partner's share of income from a trade or business that is a passive activity, income from a trade or business of trading financial instruments or commodities, and any net gain from disposing of property (other than property used in a trade or business that is not a passive activity) is also included in the partner's net investment income.[67]

Allocating Partners' Shares of Income and Loss

Partnership tax rules provide partners with tremendous flexibility in allocating overall profit and loss as well as specific items of profit and loss to partners, as long as partners agree to the allocations and they have "substantial economic effect." Partnership allocations designed to accomplish business objectives other than reducing taxes will generally have substantial economic effect.[68] If they are not defined in the partnership agreement or do not have substantial economic effect, allocations to partners must be made in accordance with the "partners' interests in the partnership."[69] According to tax regulations, the partners' interests in the partnership are a measure of the partners' economic arrangement and should be determined by considering factors such as their capital contributions, distribution rights, and interests in economic profits and losses (if different from their interests in taxable income and loss). Partnership allocations inconsistent with partners' capital interests or overall profit-and-loss-sharing ratios are called **special allocations.**

Although special allocations are made largely at the discretion of the partnership, certain special allocations of gains and losses from the sale of partnership property are mandatory. Specifically, when property contributed to a partnership with built-in gains (fair market value greater than tax basis) or built-in losses (tax basis greater than fair market value) is subsequently sold, the partnership must allocate, to the extent possible, the built-in gain or built-in loss (at the time of the contribution) solely to the contributing partner and then allocate any remaining gain or loss to all the partners in accordance with their profit-and-loss-sharing ratios.[70] This rule prevents contributing partners from shifting their built-in gains and built-in losses to other partners.

[65]Under §199A(b)(2)(B), the deduction cannot exceed the greater of 50 percent of the wages paid with respect to the qualified trade or business or the sum of 25 percent of the wages with respect to the qualified trade or business plus 2.5 percent of the unadjusted basis, immediately after acquisition, of all qualified property in the qualified trade or business. Partners are allocated their share of qualified wages and the unadjusted basis of qualified property so that they may properly calculate the limitations at their level. These limitations do not apply to taxpayers with taxable income (before the deduction) below a certain threshold, and the limitations phase in over a range of taxable income above the threshold [see §199A(b)(3)].

[66]§1411. The tax imposed is 3.8 percent of the lesser of (a) net investment income or (b) the excess of modified adjusted gross income over $250,000 for married-joint filers and surviving spouses, $125,000 for married-separate filers, and $200,000 for other taxpayers. Modified adjusted gross income equals adjusted gross income increased by income excluded under the foreign-earned income exclusion less any disallowed deductions associated with the foreign-earned income exclusion.

[67]§1411(c)(2)(A). For purposes of computing the net investment income tax, a partner's status as either active or passive with respect to an activity is determined according to the §469 passive activity loss rules explained later in this chapter.

[68]Reg. §1.704-1 defines the requirements allocations must satisfy to have substantial economic effect.

[69]§704(b).

[70]§704(c). In addition to requiring built-in gains and losses to be specially allocated to contributing partners, §704(c) also requires depreciation to be specially allocated to noncontributing partners. Tax regulations permit partners to choose among several methods for making these required special allocations. Further discussion of these methods is beyond the scope of this book.

Example 20-20

What if: Assume that at the beginning of 2022, Nicole and Sarah decide to organize CCS's marketing efforts by region. Nicole will take responsibility for marketing in the western United States, and Sarah will take responsibility for marketing in the eastern United States. All members agree that CCS's provision for allocating profits and losses in the operating agreement should be amended to provide Nicole and Sarah with better incentives. Specifically, CCS would like to allocate the first 20 percent of profits or losses from each region to Nicole and Sarah. Then, it will allocate any remaining profits or losses from each region among the members in proportion to their profits interests at the end of 2022—40 percent to Sarah and 30 percent each to Nicole and Greg. Will CCS's proposed special allocation of profits and losses be accepted by the IRS?

Answer: Yes. Because CCS is a partnership for federal income tax purposes, it can make special allocations to members, and because the allocations are designed to accomplish a business objective other than tax reduction, the IRS will accept them.[71]

What if: Assume that the land Nicole contributed to CCS had a fair market value of $150,000 and a tax basis of $20,000 (see original facts in Example 20-1) and was sold by CCS for $150,000 of consideration almost immediately after it was contributed. How would the resulting $130,000 gain be allocated among the members of CCS?

Answer: Nicole's built-in gain of $130,000 at the time of contribution must be allocated exclusively to her to prevent it from being shifted to other CCS members. Shifting the gain to other members could lower the overall tax liability of the CCS members if Sarah's and Greg's marginal tax rates are lower than Nicole's marginal tax rate, or it could increase it if their marginal rates are higher.

What if: Suppose CCS held the land Nicole contributed for one year and then sold it on March 31, 2022, for $180,000 instead of $150,000. How should the resulting $160,000 gain be allocated to Nicole, Sarah, and Chanzz Inc.?

Answer: The allocations are $139,000 to Nicole, $12,000 to Sarah, and $9,000 to Chanzz Inc., as reflected in the table below:

Description	CCS	Nicole 30%	Sarah 40%	Chanzz Inc. 30%
Total gain from sale of land	$160,000			
Less:				
Special allocation to Nicole of built-in gain	(130,000)	$ 130,000		
Post-contribution appreciation in land	30,000	9,000	$ 12,000	$ 9,000
Total gain allocations		**$139,000**	**$12,000**	**$9,000**

Partnership Compliance Issues

Although partnerships don't pay taxes, they are required to file **Form 1065,** U.S. Return of Partnership Income (shown in Exhibit 20-8), with the IRS by the 15th day of the third month after their year-end (March 15th for a calendar-year-end partnership). Partnerships may receive an automatic six-month extension to file by filing **Form 7004** with the IRS before the original due date of the return.[72] Page 1 of Form 1065 details the calculation of the partnership's ordinary business income (loss) for the year, and page 4, **Schedule K,** lists the partnership's ordinary business income (loss) and separately stated items. In addition to preparing Form 1065, the partnership is also responsible for preparing a Schedule K-1 for each partner detailing the partner's individual share of the partnership's ordinary business income (loss) and separately stated items for the year. Once prepared, Schedule K-1s are included with Form 1065 when it is filed, and they are also separately

[71]Reg. §1.704-1(b)(5), Example 10, suggests that this type of special allocation would not violate the substantial economic effect rules.

[72]Under §6698, late filing penalties apply if the partnership fails to file by the normal or extended due date for the return. For 2022 returns, the penalty is $220 ($210 for 2021 returns) times the number of partners in the partnership times the number of months (or fraction thereof) the return is late, up to a maximum of 12 months.

EXHIBIT 20-8 (PART I) **Page 1 Form 1065 CCS's 2022 Ordinary Business Loss (on 2021 forms)**

Form **1065**

Department of the Treasury
Internal Revenue Service

U.S. Return of Partnership Income

For calendar year 2021, or tax year beginning ________, 2021, ending ________, 20____.

▶ Go to *www.irs.gov/Form1065* for instructions and the latest information.

OMB No. 1545-0123

2021

A Principal business activity **Manufacturing**	Type or Print	Name of partnership **Color Comfort Sheets**	D Employer identification number **000072359**
B Principal product or service **Textile Products**		Number, street, and room or suite no. If a P.O. box, see instructions. **375 East 450 South**	E Date business started **April 1, 2021**
C Business code number **31400**		City or town, state or province, country, and ZIP or foreign postal code **Salt Lake City, UT 84608**	F Total assets (see instructions) $ **370,000**

G Check applicable boxes: (1) ☐ Initial return (2) ☐ Final return (3) ☐ Name change (4) ☐ Address change (5) ☐ Amended return

H Check accounting method: (1) ☑ Cash (2) ☐ Accrual (3) ☐ Other (specify) ▶

I Number of Schedules K-1. Attach one for each person who was a partner at any time during the tax year ▶ 3

J Check if Schedules C and M-3 are attached . . . ▶ ☐

K Check if partnership: (1) ☐ Aggregated activities for section 465 at-risk purposes (2) ☐ Grouped activities for section 469 passive activity purposes

Caution: Include **only** trade or business income and expenses on lines 1a through 22 below. See instructions for more information.

Section	Line	Description			Line	Amount
Income	1a	Gross receipts or sales	1a	40,000		
	b	Returns and allowances	1b			
	c	Balance. Subtract line 1b from line 1a			1c	40,000
	2	Cost of goods sold (attach Form 1125-A)			2	20,000
	3	Gross profit. Subtract line 2 from line 1c			3	20,000
	4	Ordinary income (loss) from other partnerships, estates, and trusts (attach statement)			4	
	5	Net farm profit (loss) (attach Schedule F (Form 1040))			5	
	6	Net gain (loss) from Form 4797, Part II, line 17 (attach Form 4797)			6	
	7	Other income (loss) (attach statement)			7	
	8	**Total income (loss).** Combine lines 3 through 7			8	20,000
Deductions (see instructions for limitations)	9	Salaries and wages (other than to partners) (less employment credits)			9	50,000
	10	Guaranteed payments to partners			10	10,000
	11	Repairs and maintenance			11	
	12	Bad debts			12	
	13	Rent			13	
	14	Taxes and licenses			14	
	15	Interest (see instructions)			15	
	16a	Depreciation (if required, attach Form 4562)	16a	18,000		
	b	Less depreciation reported on Form 1125-A and elsewhere on return	16b		16c	18,000
	17	Depletion **(Do not deduct oil and gas depletion.)**			17	
	18	Retirement plans, etc.			18	
	19	Employee benefit programs			19	
	20	Other deductions (attach statement)			20	2,800
	21	**Total deductions.** Add the amounts shown in the far right column for lines 9 through 20			21	80,800
	22	**Ordinary business income (loss).** Subtract line 21 from line 8			22	60,800
Tax and Payment	23	Interest due under the look-back method—completed long-term contracts (attach Form 8697)			23	
	24	Interest due under the look-back method—income forecast method (attach Form 8866)			24	
	25	BBA AAR imputed underpayment (see instructions)			25	
	26	Other taxes (see instructions)			26	
	27	**Total balance due.** Add lines 23 through 26			27	
	28	Payment (see instructions)			28	
	29	**Amount owed.** If line 28 is smaller than line 27, enter amount owed			29	
	30	**Overpayment.** If line 28 is larger than line 27, enter overpayment			30	

Sign Here

Under penalties of perjury, I declare that I have examined this return, including accompanying schedules and statements, and to the best of my knowledge and belief, it is true, correct, and complete. Declaration of preparer (other than partner or limited liability company member) is based on all information of which preparer has any knowledge.

▶ Signature of partner or limited liability company member ▶ Date

May the IRS discuss this return with the preparer shown below? See instructions. ☐ Yes ☐ No

Paid Preparer Use Only

Print/Type preparer's name	Preparer's signature	Date	Check ☐ if self-employed	PTIN
Firm's name ▶			Firm's EIN ▶	
Firm's address ▶			Phone no.	

For Paperwork Reduction Act Notice, see separate instructions. Cat. No. 11390Z Form **1065** (2021)

Source: irs.gov.

EXHIBIT 20-8 (PART II) Page 4 Form 1065 CCS's 2022 Schedule K (on 2021 forms)

Form 1065 (2021) Page 4

Section	Line	Schedule K Partners' Distributive Share Items		Line	Total amount
Income (Loss)	1	Ordinary business income (loss) (page 1, line 22)		1	(60,800)
	2	Net rental real estate income (loss) (attach Form 8825)		2	
	3a	Other gross rental income (loss)	3a		
	b	Expenses from other rental activities (attach statement)	3b		
	c	Other net rental income (loss). Subtract line 3b from line 3a		3c	
	4	Guaranteed payments: a Services 4a 10,000 b Capital 4b			
		c Total. Add lines 4a and 4b		4c	10,000
	5	Interest income		5	0
	6	Dividends and dividend equivalents: a Ordinary dividends		6a	500
		b Qualified dividends 6b 500 c Dividend equivalents 6c			
	7	Royalties		7	
	8	Net short-term capital gain (loss) (attach Schedule D (Form 1065))		8	
	9a	Net long-term capital gain (loss) (attach Schedule D (Form 1065))		9a	300
	b	Collectibles (28%) gain (loss)	9b		
	c	Unrecaptured section 1250 gain (attach statement)	9c		
	10	Net section 1231 gain (loss) (attach Form 4797)		10	
	11	Other income (loss) (see instructions) Type ▶		11	
Deductions	12	Section 179 deduction (attach Form 4562)		12	
	13a	Contributions		13a	
	b	Investment interest expense		13b	
	c	Section 59(e)(2) expenditures: (1) Type ▶ (2) Amount ▶		13c(2)	
	d	Other deductions (see instructions) Type ▶		13d	
Self-Employment	14a	Net earnings (loss) from self-employment		14a	(41,680)
	b	Gross farming or fishing income		14b	
	c	Gross nonfarm income		14c	20,000
Credits	15a	Low-income housing credit (section 42(j)(5))		15a	
	b	Low-income housing credit (other)		15b	
	c	Qualified rehabilitation expenditures (rental real estate) (attach Form 3468, if applicable)		15c	
	d	Other rental real estate credits (see instructions) Type ▶		15d	
	e	Other rental credits (see instructions) Type ▶		15e	
	f	Other credits (see instructions) Type ▶		15f	
International Transactions	16	Attach Schedule K-2 (Form 1065), Partners' Distributive Share Items-International, and check this box to indicate that you are reporting items of international tax relevance ☐			
Alternative Minimum Tax (AMT) Items	17a	Post-1986 depreciation adjustment		17a	
	b	Adjusted gain or loss		17b	
	c	Depletion (other than oil and gas)		17c	
	d	Oil, gas, and geothermal properties—gross income		17d	
	e	Oil, gas, and geothermal properties—deductions		17e	
	f	Other AMT items (attach statement)		17f	
Other Information	18a	Tax-exempt interest income		18a	
	b	Other tax-exempt income		18b	
	c	Nondeductible expenses		18c	
	19a	Distributions of cash and marketable securities		19a	
	b	Distributions of other property		19b	
	20a	Investment income		20a	500
	b	Investment expenses		20b	
	c	Other items and amounts (attach statement)			
	21	Total foreign taxes paid or accrued		21	

Form 1065 (2021)

Source: irs.gov.

EXHIBIT 20-8 (PART III) **2022 Schedule K-1 for Sarah Walker (on 2021 forms); CCS Operates as an LLC**

651121

☐ Final K-1 ☐ Amended K-1 OMB No. 1545-0123

Schedule K-1 (Form 1065) **2021**

Department of the Treasury
Internal Revenue Service

For calendar year 2021, or tax year

beginning / / 2021 ending / /

Partner's Share of Income, Deductions, Credits, etc. ▶ **See back of form and separate instructions.**

Part I Information About the Partnership

A Partnership's employer identification number
00072359

B Partnership's name, address, city, state, and ZIP code
Color Comfort Sheets

C IRS center where partnership filed return ▶ Ogden, UT

D ☐ Check if this is a publicly traded partnership (PTP)

Part II Information About the Partner

E Partner's SSN or TIN (Do not use TIN of a disregarded entity. See instructions.)
498-88-3426

F Name, address, city, state, and ZIP code for partner entered in E. See instructions.
Sarah Walker
540 Laurel Lane
Holladay, UT 84609

G ☒ General partner or LLC member-manager ☐ Limited partner or other LLC member

H1 ☒ Domestic partner ☐ Foreign partner

H2 ☐ If the partner is a disregarded entity (DE), enter the partner's:
TIN ______ Name ______

I1 What type of entity is this partner? Individual

I2 If this partner is a retirement plan (IRA/SEP/Keogh/etc.), check here ▶ ☐

J Partner's share of profit, loss, and capital (see instructions):

	Beginning	Ending
Profit	40 %	40 %
Loss	40 %	40 %
Capital	40 %	40 %

Check if decrease is due to sale or exchange of partnership interest . ▶ ☐

K Partner's share of liabilities:

	Beginning	Ending
Nonrecourse . . .	$	$ 12,000
Qualified nonrecourse financing . . .	$ 8,000	$ 8,000
Recourse . . .	$ 24,000	$ 24,000

Check this box if Item K includes liability amounts from lower tier partnerships ▶ ☐

L **Partner's Capital Account Analysis**

Beginning capital account . . .	$ 100,000
Capital contributed during the year . . .	$ 20,000
Current year net income (loss) . . .	$ (24,000)
Other increase (decrease) (attach explanation)	$
Withdrawals and distributions . . .	$ ( )
Ending capital account	$ 96,000

M Did the partner contribute property with a built-in gain (loss)?
☐ **Yes** ☒ **No** If "Yes," attach statement. See instructions.

N **Partner's Share of Net Unrecognized Section 704(c) Gain or (Loss)**
Beginning . . . . $
Ending . . . . $

Part III Partner's Share of Current Year Income, Deductions, Credits, and Other Items

1 Ordinary business income (loss)	(24,320)	**14** Self-employment earnings (loss)	A (14,320)
2 Net rental real estate income (loss)			C 8,000
3 Other net rental income (loss)		**15** Credits	
4a Guaranteed payments for services	10,000		
4b Guaranteed payments for capital		**16** Schedule K-3 is attached if checked . . . . ▶ ☐	
4c Total guaranteed payments	10,000	**17** Alternative minimum tax (AMT) items	
5 Interest income			
6a Ordinary dividends	200		
6b Qualified dividends	200	**18** Tax-exempt income and nondeductible expenses	
6c Dividend equivalents			
7 Royalties			
8 Net short-term capital gain (loss)		**19** Distributions	
9a Net long-term capital gain (loss)	120		
9b Collectibles (28%) gain (loss)		**20** Other information	
9c Unrecaptured section 1250 gain			A 200
10 Net section 1231 gain (loss)			Z See attached schedule
11 Other income (loss)			
12 Section 179 deduction		**21** Foreign taxes paid or accrued	
13 Other deductions			

22 ☐ More than one activity for at-risk purposes*
23 ☐ More than one activity for passive activity purposes*

*See attached statement for additional information.

For IRS Use Only

For Paperwork Reduction Act Notice, see the Instructions for Form 1065. www.irs.gov/Form1065 Cat. No. 11394R **Schedule K-1 (Form 1065) 2021**

Source: irs.gov.

provided to all partners (each partner receives a Schedule K-1 with that partner's income and loss allocations). Beginning with returns filed for 2021, partnerships with income earned outside the United States will also be required to include Schedules K-2 and K-3 with their returns. These new schedules will provide partners with the uniform and detailed information they need to calculate their U.S. income tax liability stemming from the partnership's international operations and investments. Exhibit 20-8, parts I through III, displays CCS's return, showing the operating results we summarized in Example 20-17, and Sarah's actual Schedule K-1, reflecting the facts and conclusions in Examples 20-17 and 20-18.[73]

LO 20-5

ADJUSTING A PARTNER'S TAX BASIS IN PARTNERSHIP INTEREST

Earlier in this chapter, we discussed how partners measure their outside tax basis in their partnership interests when they contribute property or services to partnerships in exchange for their partnership interests, or when they purchase partnership interests from an existing partner. Unlike the basis in a stock or other similar investment, which is usually stable, the basis in a partnership interest is dynamic and must be *adjusted* as the partnership generates income and losses, changes its liability levels, and makes distributions to partners. These annual adjustments to a partner's tax basis are required to ensure partners don't double-count taxable income/gains and deductible expenses/losses, either when they sell their partnership interests or when they receive partnership distributions. They also ensure tax-exempt income and nondeductible expenses are not ultimately taxed or deducted.

Partners make the following adjustments to the basis in their partnership interests annually:

- Increase for actual and deemed cash contributions to the partnership during the year.[74]
- Increase for partner's share of ordinary business income and separately stated income/gain items.
- Increase for partner's share of tax-exempt income.
- Decrease for actual and deemed cash distributions during the year.[75,76]
- Decrease for partner's share of nondeductible expenses (fines, penalties, etc.).
- Decrease for partner's share of ordinary business loss and separately stated expense/loss items.[77]
- Decrease for partner's share of disallowed business interest expense.[78]

Partners first adjust their outside bases for items that increase basis, then for distributions, then by nondeductible expenses, and then by deductible expenses and losses to the extent any basis remains after prior adjustments.[79] Basis adjustments that decrease basis may never reduce a partner's tax basis below zero.[80]

Example 20-21

Given the events that affected CCS and its members during *2021*, what tax basis did Nicole, Sarah, and Chanzz Inc. have in their ownership interests at the end of 2021?

[73]We use 2021 forms because 2022 forms were unavailable at press time.

[74]Recall that partners are deemed to have made a cash contribution to the partnership when they are allocated an additional share of partnership liabilities.

[75]Recall that partners are deemed to have received a cash distribution from the partnership when they are relieved of partnership liabilities.

[76]Property distributions to partners are also treated as basis reductions. We discuss property distributions at length in the Dispositions of Partnership Interests and Partnership Distributions chapter.

[77]Per §704(d)(3)(B), a partner does not reduce the basis in her interest by her share of any appreciation in property contributed by the partnership to a charitable organization.

[78]§163(j)(4)(B)(iii).

[79]Reg. §1.704-1(d)(2).

[80]§705(a)(2).

Answer: Their tax bases in their CCS interests were $4,000, $152,000, and $114,000, respectively. Their individual tax basis calculations at the end of 2021 are illustrated in the table below:

Description	Nicole	Sarah	Chanzz Inc.	Explanation
(1) Initial tax basis (including liability)	$36,666	$ 146,666	$ 146,666	Example 20-4
(2) Dividends	700	700	700	Example 20-15
(3) Short-term capital gains	400	400	400	Example 20-15
(4) Liability reallocation (deemed cash contribution/distribution)	(2,667)	5,334	(2,667)	Example 20-10
(5) Sarah's capital interest	(10,000)	20,000	(10,000)	Examples 20-10, 20-15
(6) CCS's ordinary business loss	(21,100)	(21,100)	(21,100)	Example 20-15
Tax basis on 12/31/21	**$ 4,000**	**$152,000**	**$114,000**	Sum of (1) through (6)

What if: Suppose Sarah sold her LLC interest but forgot to include her share of short-term capital gains when computing her basis to determine her gain on the sale. What are the tax implications of Sarah's mistake?

Answer: Sarah would be double-taxed on the amount of the short-term capital gain. She was initially taxed on her share of the short-term capital gain allocation, and she will be taxed a second time when she recognizes $400 more long-term capital gain on the sale than she would have had she included her share of the gain in her basis.

What if: Assume Sarah was allocated $700 of tax-exempt municipal bond income instead of dividend income. What will happen if she neglects to increase her basis in CCS by the $700 tax-exempt income?

Answer: If Sarah were to sell her interest in CCS for a price reflecting the tax-exempt income received, she would, in effect, be converting tax-exempt income into taxable capital gain.

Example 20-22

In addition to the other events of *2022*, CCS increased its liabilities from $100,000 to $130,000 in the second half of the year. The $30,000 increase was attributable to accounts payable owed to suppliers. Unlike the case of the $60,000 bank loan, the members did not guarantee any of the accounts payable. Therefore, the accounts payable are considered a nonrecourse liability because CCS is an LLC. Given this information, what are Nicole's, Sarah's, and Greg's tax bases in their CCS interests at the end of *2022*?

Answer: The bases in their CCS interests are $0, $140,000, and $124,000, respectively. Nicole, Sarah, and Greg would determine their tax basis in CCS at the end of *2022* as illustrated in the table below:

Description	Nicole 30%	Sarah[81] 40%	Greg 30%	Explanation
(1) Tax basis on 1/1/22	$ 4,000	$ 152,000		Example 20-21
(2) Greg's purchase of Chanzz Inc.'s interest			$ 124,000	Example 20-11
(3) Dividends	150	200	75	Example 20-17
(4) Long-term capital gains	90	120	45	Example 20-17
(5) Increase in nonrecourse liability from accounts payable (deemed cash contribution)	9,000	12,000	9,000	$30,000 × member's profit-sharing ratio
(6) CCS's ordinary business loss	(18,240)	(24,320)	(9,120)	Example 20-17
Preliminary tax basis	(5,000)	140,000	124,000	Sum of (1) through (6)
Tax basis on 12/31/22	**$ 0***	**$140,000**	**$124,000**	*Nicole's basis can't go below zero.

[81]Recall that Sarah received a $10,000 cash guaranteed payment for services she performed in 2022. Cash guaranteed payments generally don't have a direct impact on the recipient partner's tax basis because they are similar to salary payments.

THE KEY FACTS

Partner's Basis Adjustments

- A partner will increase the tax basis in her partnership interest for:
  - Contributions.
  - Share of ordinary business income.
  - Separately stated income/gain items.
  - Tax-exempt income.
- A partner will decrease the tax basis in her partnership interest for:
  - Cash distributions.
  - Share of nondeductible expenses.
  - Share of ordinary business loss.
  - Separately stated expense/loss items.
  - Share of disallowed business interest expense
- A partner's tax basis may not be negative.

Cash Distributions in Operating Partnerships

Even after a partnership has been formed, partners are likely to continue to receive actual and deemed cash distributions. For example, excess cash may be distributed to partners to provide them with cash flow to pay their taxes or simply for consumption, and deemed cash distributions occur as partnerships pay down their liabilities. The principles underlying the calculation of a partner's tax basis highlight the fact that partners are taxed on income as the partnership earns it instead of when it distributes it. If cash is distributed when partners have a positive tax basis in their partnership interests, the distribution effectively represents a distribution of profits that have been previously taxed, a return of capital previously contributed by the partner to the partnership, a distribution of cash the partnership has borrowed, or some combination of the three. Thus, as long as a cash distribution does not exceed a partner's outside basis before the distribution, it reduces the partner's tax basis but is not taxable. However, as we highlighted in our discussion of property contributions earlier in this chapter, cash distributions (deemed or actual) in excess of a partner's basis are taxable gains and are generally treated as capital gains.[82]

Example 20-23

What if: In Example 20-22, we determined that Sarah's basis in her partnership interest was $140,000. Assume that in addition to the facts provided in that example, Sarah received a $10,000 distribution in *2022*. What will her basis in CCS (i.e., her outside basis) be at the end of the year?

Answer: Sarah's outside basis will be $130,000. After making only her positive adjustments for the year (positive adjustments come before negative adjustments such as distributions), she has an outside basis of $164,320, which is greater than the $10,000 distribution. Thus, the distribution is not taxable because it does not exceed her outside basis before adjusting for the distribution. Sarah will also reduce her outside basis by the $10,000 distribution in addition to the $24,320 reduction for her share of the ordinary business loss, leaving her with an ending outside basis of $130,000 ($164,320 – $10,000 – $24,320).

What problem will be created if Sarah does not reduce her basis by the $10,000 distribution?

Answer: After she receives the $10,000 distribution, the value of Sarah's interest will decrease by $10,000. If she doesn't reduce her tax basis by the distribution, selling her interest will produce a $10,000 artificial tax loss.

LO 20-6

LOSS LIMITATIONS

While partners generally prefer not to invest in partnerships with operating losses, these losses generate current tax benefits when partners can deduct them against other sources of taxable income. Unlike capital losses, which are of limited usefulness if taxpayers don't also have capital gains, ordinary losses from partnerships are deductible against any type of taxable income. However, they are deductible on the partner's tax return only when they clear four separate hurdles: (1) tax-basis, (2) at-risk amount, and (3) passive activity. In addition, for losses that clear each of the three hurdles, (4) partners are not allowed to deduct excess business losses, as described below.

Tax-Basis Limitation

A partner's outside or tax basis in the partnership interest limits the amount of partnership losses the partner can use to offset other sources of income. In theory, a partner's outside basis represents the amount a partner has invested in a partnership (or may have to invest to satisfy the partner's liability obligations). As a result, partners may not utilize partnership losses in excess of their investment or outside basis in their partnership interests. Any losses allocated in excess of their basis must be suspended and carried forward indefinitely until they have sufficient basis to utilize the losses.[83] Any suspended losses

[82]§731.

[83]§704(d).

remaining when partners sell or otherwise dispose of their interests are lost forever. Among other things, partners may create additional tax basis by making capital contributions, by guaranteeing more partnership liability, and by helping their partnership to become profitable.

Example 20-24

In Example 20-22 we discovered Nicole was allocated $5,000 of ordinary loss in excess of her tax basis for 2022, leaving her with a tax basis of $0 at the end of 2022. What does Nicole do with this loss?

Answer: Nicole will carry forward all $5,000 of ordinary loss in excess of her tax basis indefinitely until her tax basis in her CCS interest becomes positive. To the extent her tax basis increases in the future, the tax-basis limitation will no longer apply to her ordinary loss. Even then, however, the at-risk, passive activity loss, and/or excess business loss limitations may ultimately apply to constrain her ability to deduct the loss on her future tax returns.

What if: Assuming Nicole is allocated $4,000 of income from CCS in *2023*, how much of her $5,000 suspended loss will clear the tax basis hurdle in *2023*?

Answer: Nicole's basis will initially increase by $4,000. Then she can apply $4,000 of her suspended loss against this basis increase, leaving her tax basis at $0 and holding a remaining suspended loss of $1,000. The $4,000 loss clearing the tax-basis hurdle must still clear the at-risk, passive activity loss, and excess business loss hurdles before Nicole can deduct it on her return.

At-Risk Amount Limitation

The at-risk amount hurdle or limitation is more restrictive than the tax-basis limitation because it excludes a type of liability normally included in a partner's tax basis. We have already highlighted the distinction between recourse and nonrecourse liabilities and noted that partners allocated recourse liabilities have economic risk of loss, while partners allocated nonrecourse liabilities have no risk of loss. Instead, the risk of loss on nonrecourse liabilities is borne by lenders. The **at-risk rules** in §465 were adopted to limit the ability of partners to use nonrecourse liabilities as a means of creating tax basis to use losses from tax shelter partnerships expressly designed to generate losses for the partners. The at-risk rules limit partners' losses to their amount "at risk" in the partnership—their **at-risk amount.** Generally, a partner's at-risk amount is the same as the partner's tax basis except that, with one exception, the partner's share of certain nonrecourse liabilities is not included in the at-risk amount. Specifically, the only nonrecourse liabilities considered to be at risk are nonrecourse real estate mortgages from commercial lenders that are unrelated to borrowers. This type of liability is called **qualified nonrecourse financing.**[84] In addition to qualified nonrecourse financing, partners are considered to be at risk to the extent of cash and the tax basis of property contributed to the partnership. Further, partners are at risk for any partnership recourse liabilities allocated to them.

Partners apply the at-risk limitation after the tax-basis limitation. Any partnership losses that would otherwise have been allowed under the tax-basis limitation are further limited to the extent they exceed a partner's at-risk amount. Losses limited under the at-risk rules are carried forward indefinitely until the partner generates additional at-risk amounts to utilize the losses, or until they are applied to reduce any gain from selling the partnership interest.

THE KEY FACTS

Loss Limitations

- Partnership losses in excess of a partner's tax basis are suspended and carried forward until additional basis is created.
- Remaining partnership losses are further suspended by the at-risk rules to the extent a partner is allocated nonrecourse liabilities not secured by real property.
- If a partner is not a material participant or the partnership is involved in rental activities, losses remaining after application of the tax-basis and at-risk limitations may be used only against other passive income or when the partnership interest is sold.
- Losses remaining after applying the tax basis, at-risk, and passive activity loss limitations are only deductible to the extent they do not add to or create an excess business loss at the partner level.

Example 20-25

In Example 20-22, we discovered Nicole was allocated an ordinary business loss of $18,240. There we also learned that of this loss, $13,240 cleared the tax-basis hurdle and $5,000 did not. How much of the $13,240 ordinary business loss that clears the tax-basis hurdle will clear the at-risk amount hurdle?

(continued on page 20-32)

[84]§465(b)(6).

Answer: $4,240. The table below summarizes and compares Nicole's calculations to determine her tax-basis and at-risk limitations for 2021:

Example	Description	Tax Basis	At-Risk Amount	Explanation
20-22	(1) Nicole's tax basis on 1/1/22	$ 4,000	$ 4,000	Nicole's tax basis and at-risk amount are the same because she was allocated only recourse liability and qualified nonrecourse financing.
20-22	(2) Dividends	150	150	
20-22	(3) Long-term capital gains	90	90	
20-22	(4) Nonrecourse accounts payable	9,000	0	
	(5) Tax basis and at-risk amount before ordinary business loss	13,240	4,240	Sum of (1) through (4)
20-22	(6) Ordinary business loss	(18,240)		
	(7) Loss clearing the tax-basis hurdle	(13,240)		Loss limited to (5)
	Loss suspended by tax-basis hurdle	$ (5,000)		(6) – (7)
	(8) Loss clearing tax-basis hurdle		(13,240)	(7)
	(9) Loss clearing at-risk hurdle		**(4,240)**	Loss limited to (5)
	Loss suspended by at-risk hurdle		$ (9,000)	(8) – (9)

Although Nicole's $9,000 share of the nonrecourse accounts payable added in 2022 and her investment income of $240 allow her to create enough tax basis in her interest in 2022 to get $13,240 of her $18,240 ordinary business loss past the tax-basis limitation, she is not at risk with respect to her $9,000 share of accounts payable because an LLC's accounts payable are general nonrecourse liability. Therefore, $9,000 of the $13,240 ordinary business loss clearing the tax-basis hurdle is suspended under the at-risk limitation. As a result, Nicole has two separate losses to carry forward: a $5,000 ordinary loss limited by her tax basis in her CCS interest and a $9,000 ordinary loss limited by the at-risk rules, leaving $4,240 of ordinary loss that she may deduct on her 2022 return.

Passive Activity Loss Limitation

Prior to 1986, partners with sufficient tax basis and at-risk amounts were able to utilize ordinary losses from their partnerships to offset portfolio income (i.e., interest, dividends, and capital gains), salary income, and self-employment income from partnerships and other trades or businesses. During this time, a partnership tax shelter industry thrived by marketing to wealthy investors partnership interests designed primarily to generate ordinary losses they could use to shield other income from tax. To combat this practice, Congress introduced the **passive activity loss (PAL) rules.**[85] These rules were enacted as a backstop to the at-risk rules and are applied after the tax-basis and at-risk limitations. Thus, depending on their situation, partners may have to overcome *three separate hurdles* before finally reporting partnership ordinary losses on their returns. In a nutshell, the PAL rules limit the ability of partners in rental real estate partnerships and other partnerships they don't actively manage (passive activities) from using their ordinary losses from these activities (remaining after the application of the tax-basis and at-risk limitations) to reduce other sources of taxable income.

Passive Activity Defined The passive activity rules define a passive activity as "any activity which involves the conduct of a trade or business,[86] and in which the taxpayer does not materially participate."[87] According to the IRC and Treasury regulations, participants in

[85]§469. The passive activity loss rules apply primarily to individuals but also to estates, trusts, closely held C corporations, and personal service corporations.

[86]The term *trade or business* is also deemed to include property held for the production of income, such as rental property.

[87]irs.gov.

rental activities, including rental real estate,[88] and limited partners without management rights are automatically deemed to be passive participants. In addition, participants in all other activities are passive unless their involvement in an activity is "regular, continuous, and substantial." Clearly, these terms are quite subjective and difficult to apply. Fortunately, regulations provide more certainty in this area by enumerating seven separate tests for material participation.[89] An individual, other than a limited partner, can be classified as a material participant in activities, other than rental activities, by meeting any *one* of the seven tests in Exhibit 20-9.

EXHIBIT 20-9 Tests for Material Participation

1. The individual participates in the activity more than 500 hours during the year.
2. The individual's activity constitutes substantially all the participation in such activity by individuals.
3. The individual participates more than 100 hours during the year and the individual's participation is not less than any other individual's participation in the activity.
4. The activity qualifies as a "significant participation activity" (individual participates for more than 100 hours during the year) and the aggregate of all other "significant participation activities" is greater than 500 hours for the year.
5. The individual materially participated in the activity for any 5 of the preceding 10 taxable years.
6. The activity involves personal services in health, law, accounting, architecture, and so on, and the individual materially participated for any three preceding years.
7. Taking into account all the facts and circumstances, the individual participates on a regular, continuous, and substantial basis during the year.

TAXES IN THE REAL WORLD Donald Trump's Tax Losses

During his run for the presidency in the fall of 2016, the first page of Donald Trump's New York State resident tax return for 1995 was mailed anonymously to the *New York Times*. When the *Times* subsequently published the first page of President Trump's New York State return, it showed that he reported a loss for the year of nearly $16 million from "rental real estate, royalties, partnerships, S corporations, trusts, etc." Given President Trump's status as a real estate developer and owner, it is likely that a significant portion of this loss originated from rental real estate activities held in partnership form. These partnerships frequently generate losses because they are able to deduct depreciation, interest, and other operating costs in determining their taxable income.

President Trump's return also showed that he used the $16 million loss to offset business income of $3.4 million, $6,000 in wages, and $7.4 million in interest he reported earning the same year. For many taxpayers, losses from rental real estate are presumed to be passive losses and therefore may not be used to offset active and portfolio income. So, how was Donald Trump able to use the portion of his $16 million loss attributable to rental real estate to legally shelter his other sources of income? President Trump was likely able to take advantage of the "real estate professional" exception found in §469(c)(6) of the Code. This exception permits individuals that are heavily involved in real property trades or businesses to overcome the presumption that their losses from rental real estate are passive and then go on to establish that their losses are active under one of the material participation tests found in the tax regulations.

Income and Loss Baskets Under the passive activity loss rules, each item of a partner's income or loss from all sources for the year is placed in one of three categories, or "baskets." Losses from the *passive basket* are not allowed to offset income from other baskets. The three baskets are (see Exhibit 20-10):

1. *Passive activity income or loss*—income or loss from an activity, including partnerships, in which the taxpayer is not a material participant.

[88]Section 469(b)(7) provides an important exception to the general rule that all real estate activities are passive. To overcome this presumption, taxpayers must spend more than half their time working in trades or businesses materially participating in real estate activities and more than 750 hours materially participating in real estate activities during the year. This exception benefits partners that spend a substantial amount of time in partnership activities like real estate development and construction. Moreover, §469(i) permits individual taxpayers to treat up to $25,000 of losses from rental real estate as active losses each year.

[89]Reg. §1.469-5T.

2. *Portfolio income*—income from investments, including capital gains and losses, dividends, interest, annuities, and royalties.
3. *Active business income*—income from sources, including partnerships, in which the taxpayer is a material participant. For individuals, this includes salary and self-employment income.

EXHIBIT 20-10 Income and Loss Baskets

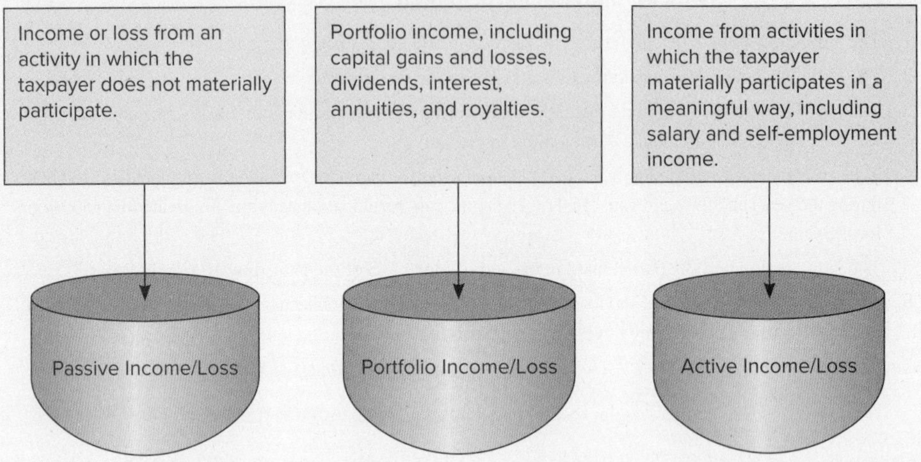

The impact of segregating a partner's income in these baskets is to limit their ability to apply passive activity losses against income in the other two baskets. In effect, passive activity losses are suspended and remain in the passive income or loss basket until the taxpayer generates current-year passive income, either from the passive activity producing the loss or from some other passive activity, or until the taxpayer sells the activity that generated the passive loss.[90] On the sale of the activity, the taxpayer would classify gain or loss from the sale as current-year passive income or loss, and they would treat a net passive loss from the activity (i.e., suspended prior-year passive losses, plus current-year passive losses, plus or minus any passive loss or income from the sale) as passive to the extent the taxpayer has passive income in the year from other activities. Finally, the taxpayer would treat any remaining net losses from the activity that had been sold as nonpassive losses.[91]

ETHICS

Several years ago, Lou, together with his friend Carlo, opened an Italian restaurant in their neighborhood. The venture was formed as an LLC, with Lou receiving a 75 percent ownership interest and Carlo receiving the remaining 25 percent ownership interest. While Lou was primarily responsible for operating the restaurant, Carlo came in only on weekends because he held a full-time job elsewhere. To document the time he spent in the restaurant, Carlo recorded the number of hours he had worked in a logbook at the end of every shift. This year, because of a downturn in the local economy, the restaurant showed a loss for the first time. To be able to deduct his share of this loss when he files his tax return, Carlo would like to establish that he worked more than 500 hours during the year and is therefore a material participant in the restaurant. His logbook shows that he worked for 502 hours during the year; however, he rounded up to the nearest hour at the end of every shift to simplify his record keeping. For example, if he worked 4 hours and 25 minutes during a shift, he wrote 5 hours in the logbook. Should Carlo claim that he is a material participant on the basis of the hours recorded in his logbook and deduct his share of the loss? What would you do?

[90]Under §469(k), this rule is even more restrictive for publicly traded partnerships. Passive activity losses from these partnerships may only be utilized to offset future passive income from the same partnership generating the passive activity loss.

[91]§469(g)(1)(A).

Example 20-26

As indicated in Example 20-22, Greg was allocated a $9,120 ordinary loss for 2022 and had a $124,000 tax basis at year-end *after* adjusting his tax basis in his CCS interest for the loss. Given that Greg was allocated $9,000 of nonrecourse liability from accounts payable during 2022, what is Greg's at-risk amount at the end of the year?

Answer: $115,000. Greg's at-risk amount is calculated by subtracting his $9,000 share of nonrecourse liability from his $124,000 tax basis.

Given Greg's status as a silent or nonmanaging member of CCS, how much of his $9,120 ordinary loss can he deduct in 2022 if he has no other sources of passive income?

Answer: None. Because Greg's tax basis and at-risk amount are large relative to his $9,120 ordinary loss, the tax-basis and at-risk hurdles don't limit his loss. However, Greg's $9,120 loss would be classified as a passive loss and suspended until Greg receives passive income from another source—hopefully CCS—or until he disposes of his interest in CCS.

What could Greg do to deduct any losses from CCS in the future?

Answer: He could satisfy one of the seven tests in Exhibit 20-9 to be classified as a material participant in CCS, thereby converting his future CCS losses from passive to active losses. Or he could become a passive participant in some other activity, producing trade or business income that could be offset by any future passive losses from CCS. Or he could sell his interest in CCS.

Excess Business Loss Limitation

Noncorporate taxpayers are not allowed to deduct an **excess business loss** for the year, including business losses from entities taxed as partnerships.[92] Rather, excess business losses are carried forward and used in subsequent years. The excess business loss limitation applies to losses that are otherwise deductible under the tax-basis, at-risk, and passive loss rules. An excess business loss for the year is the excess of the sum of business deductions for the year over the sum of aggregate business gross income or gain of the taxpayer plus a threshold amount. The threshold amount for losses reported in 2022 is $540,000 for married taxpayers filing jointly and $270,000 for other taxpayers. The amounts are indexed for inflation. In the case of partnership business losses, the provision applies at the partner level.

Example 20-27

From Example 20-25 we learned that Nicole would report $150 of dividend income and $90 of long-term capital gains from CCS on her 2022 tax return. Further, we learned that $4,240 of her $18,240 ordinary loss allocation from CCS for 2022 cleared both the tax-basis and at-risk hurdles, leaving a total of $14,000 ($9,000 + $5,000) ordinary loss suspended and carried forward. How much of the $4,240 of ordinary loss can Nicole actually deduct on her tax return, given her status as a managing member of CCS?

Answer: Because Nicole is a managing member of CCS, it is likely she will satisfy at least one of the seven tests for material participation in Exhibit 20-9. As a result, she will treat the $4,240 ordinary loss clearing the tax-basis and at-risk hurdles as an active loss. Because Nicole's $4,240 active business loss is less than the $540,000 threshold amount for married taxpayers filing jointly, she does not have an excess business loss and may fully deduct this loss on her tax return.

What if: Suppose that Nicole's share of the 2022 ordinary loss from CCS remaining after applying the tax basis and at-risk limitation was $544,000 rather than $4,240. How much of the loss would be deductible on her return?

Answer: $540,000. Deductible net business losses are limited to $540,000 for taxpayers married filing jointly. The $4,000 excess business loss would be carried forward and used in subsequent years.

What if: Assume Nicole was not a managing member of CCS during 2022 and could not satisfy one of the seven material participation tests in Exhibit 20-9. How much of the $4,240 ordinary loss could she deduct on her tax return, assuming she has no other sources of passive income?

Answer: None. Under this assumption, the $4,240 is a passive activity loss and suspended until Nicole either receives some passive income from CCS (or from some other source) or sells her interest in CCS. In the end, her entire $18,240 loss from 2022 would be suspended: $5,000 due to the tax-basis limitation, $9,000 due to the at-risk limitation, and $4,240 due to the passive activity loss limitation.

[92] §461(1).

CONCLUSION

This chapter explained the relevant tax rules pertaining to forming and operating partnerships. Specifically, we introduced important tax issues arising from partnership formations, including partner gain or loss recognition and the calculation of inside and outside basis. In addition, we explained accounting periods and methods, allocations of partners' ordinary income (loss) and separately stated items, basis adjustments, and loss limitation rules in the context of an operating partnership. Although it would seem that partnership tax law should be relatively straightforward given that partnerships don't pay taxes, by now you may have come to realize quite the opposite is true. The Dispositions of Partnership Interests and Partnership Distributions chapter continues our discussion of partnership tax law with a focus on dispositions of partnership interests and partnership distributions.

Summary

LO 20-1 Describe tax flow-through entities and determine whether they are taxed as partnerships or S corporations.

- Unincorporated business entities with more than one owner are taxed as partnerships unless they elect to be taxed as corporations.
- Owners of entities taxed as corporations may elect to have them treated as flow-through entities by filing an S election with the IRS.
- Though partnerships and S corporations are both flow-through entities, the tax rules that apply to them differ.
- Partnership tax rules reflect both the aggregate and entity concepts.

LO 20-2 Resolve tax issues applicable to partnership formations and other acquisitions of partnership interests, including gain recognition to partners and tax basis for partners and partnerships.

- As a general rule, partners don't recognize gain or loss when they contribute property to partnerships in exchange for a partnership interest.
- Partnership recourse liabilities are allocated to partners with ultimate responsibility for paying the liabilities, and nonrecourse liabilities are allocated to partners using profit-sharing ratios.
- Partners contributing property encumbered by a liability may have to recognize gain, depending on the basis of the property and the amount of the liability.
- Partners contributing property to a partnership will have an initial tax basis in their partnership interest equal to the basis of contributed property less any liability relief plus their share of any partnership liabilities and any gain they recognize.
- Partners receiving partnership interests by contributing capital assets or §1231 assets have a holding period in their partnership interest that includes the holding period of the contributed property. If they contribute any other type of property instead, their holding period begins on the date the partnership interest is received.
- Partnerships with contributed property have a tax basis and holding period in the property equal to the contributing partner's tax basis and holding period.
- Partners who receive capital interests in exchange for services must report the liquidation value of the capital interest as ordinary income, and the partnership either deducts or capitalizes an equivalent amount depending on the nature of the services provided.
- Partners who receive profits interest in exchange for services don't report any income. However, they share in any subsequent partnership profits and losses.
- Partners who purchase partnership interests have a tax basis in their interests equal to the purchase price plus their shares of partnership liabilities, and their holding periods begin on the date of purchase.

LO 20-3 Determine the appropriate accounting periods and methods for partnerships.

- Partnerships, rather than individual partners, are responsible for making most tax elections.
- The Code mandates that partners include their share of income (loss) or other partnership items for "any taxable year of the partnership ending within or with the taxable year of the partner."

- Partnerships must use a tax year-end consistent with the majority interest taxable year, the taxable year of the principal partners, or the year-end providing the least aggregate deferral for the partners.
- For 2022, partnerships with C corporation partners and average annual gross receipts over $27 million (indexed for inflation) may not use the cash method of accounting. Partnerships eligible to use the overall cash method of accounting must still use the accrual method to account for the purchase and sale of inventory in 2022 unless they have average annual gross receipts over the prior three years of $27 million (indexed for inflation) or less. Otherwise, partnerships may use either the cash or accrual method of accounting.

Calculate and characterize a partnership's ordinary business income or loss and its separately stated items, and demonstrate how to report these items to partners. **LO 20-4**

- Partnerships must file Form 1065, U.S. Return of Partnership Income, with the IRS annually and must provide each partner with a Schedule K-1 detailing the partner's share of ordinary business income (loss) and separately stated items.
- Separately stated items include short-term and long-term capital gains and losses, dividends, §1231 gains and losses, and other partnership items that may be treated differently at the partner level.
- The character of separately stated items is determined at the partnership rather than at the partner level.
- Guaranteed payments are typically fixed payments made to partners for services provided to the partnership. They are treated as ordinary income by partners who receive them and are either deducted or capitalized by the partnership depending on the nature of services provided.
- Guaranteed payments to any type of partner (or LLC member) and general partners' shares of ordinary business income (loss) are treated as self-employment income (loss).
- Limited partners' shares of ordinary business income (loss) are not treated as self-employment income (loss).
- Though the tax law is uncertain in this area, all or a portion of LLC members' shares of ordinary business income (loss) should be classified as self-employment income (loss) if members are significantly involved in managing the LLC.
- Partnerships provide a great deal of flexibility because they may specially allocate their income, gains, expenses, losses, and other partnership items, as long as the allocations have "substantial economic effect" or are consistent with partners' interests in the partnership. Special allocations of built-in gain or loss on contributed property to contributing partners are mandatory.

Explain the importance of a partner's tax basis in her partnership interest and the adjustments that affect it. **LO 20-5**

- Partners must make specified annual adjustments to the tax basis in their partnership interests to ensure that partnership taxable income/gain or deductible expense/loss items are not double-taxed or deducted twice and to ensure that partnership tax-exempt income or nondeductible expense is not taxed or deducted.
- Partners increase the tax basis in their interests by their actual or deemed cash contributions, shares of ordinary business income, separately stated income/gain items, and shares of tax-exempt income.
- Partners decrease the tax basis in their interests by their actual or deemed cash distributions, shares of ordinary business loss, separately stated expense/loss items, and shares of nondeductible expenses.
- A partner's tax basis in the partnership interest may never be reduced below zero.
- Cash distributions that are less than a partner's tax basis in her partnership interest immediately before the distribution are not taxable. However, cash distributions in excess of a partner's tax basis in her partnership interest immediately before the distribution are generally taxable as capital gain.

Apply the tax-basis, at-risk amount, passive activity loss, and excess business loss limits to losses from partnerships. **LO 20-6**

- In order for losses to provide tax benefits to partners, partnership losses must clear the tax-basis, at-risk, and passive activity loss hurdles (in that order).
- Partnership losses in excess of a partner's tax basis are suspended and may be utilized only when additional tax basis is created.

- Losses clearing the tax-basis hurdle may be utilized only to the extent of the partner's at-risk amount. A partner's at-risk amount generally equals that partner's tax basis (before any reduction for current-year losses) less the share of nonrecourse liability that is not secured by real estate.
- If a partner is not a material participant in the partnership or if the partnership is involved in rental activities, losses clearing the tax-basis and at-risk hurdles may be reported on the partner's tax return only when that partnership or other sources generate passive income or when the partnership interest is sold.
- If an individual partner is a material participant in the partnership, losses clearing the tax-basis and at-risk hurdles may only be reported on the partner's tax return for 2022 to the extent that the partner has business income from other sources plus a threshold amount of $540,000 for married taxpayers filing jointly and $270,000 for other taxpayers.

KEY TERMS

§704(b) capital accounts (20-9)
aggregate approach (20-3)
at-risk amount (20-31)
at-risk rules (20-31)
built-in gain (20-3)
built-in losses (20-4)
C corporations (20-2)
capital account (20-8)
capital interest (20-3)
entity approach (20-3)
excess business loss (20-35)
flow-through entity (20-2)
Form 1065 (20-24)
Form 7004 (20-24)
GAAP capital accounts (20-8)
general partnerships (20-2)
guaranteed payments (20-19)
inside basis (20-4)
least aggregate deferral (20-15)
limited liability companies (LLC) (20-2)
limited partnerships (20-2)
liquidation value (20-10)
majority interest taxable year (20-15)
nonrecourse liabilities (20-4)
nonservice partners (20-10)
ordinary business income (loss) (20-17)
organizational expenditures (20-12)
outside basis (20-4)
partnership interest (20-3)
passive activity loss (PAL) rules (20-32)
principal partners (20-15)
profits interest (20-3)
qualified nonrecourse financing (20-31)
recourse liabilities (20-4)
S corporation (20-2)
Schedule K (20-24)
self-employment taxes (20-20)
separately stated items (20-17)
service partner (20-10)
special allocations (20-23)
start-up costs (20-12)
Subchapter K (20-2)
Subchapter S (20-2)
syndication costs (20-12)
tax capital account (20-8)

DISCUSSION QUESTIONS

Discussion Questions are available in Connect®.

LO 20-1 1. What is a *flow-through entity,* and what effect does this designation have on how business entities and their owners are taxed?

LO 20-1 2. What types of business entities are taxed as flow-through entities?

LO 20-1 3. Compare and contrast the aggregate and entity concepts for taxing partnerships and their partners.

LO 20-2 4. What is a partnership interest, and what specific economic rights or entitlements are included with it?

LO 20-2 5. What is the rationale for requiring partners to defer most gains and all losses when they contribute property to a partnership?

LO 20-2 6. Under what circumstances is it possible for partners to recognize gain when contributing property to partnerships?

LO 20-2 7. What are *inside basis* and *outside basis,* and why are they relevant for taxing partnerships and partners?

LO 20-2 8. What are *recourse* and *nonrecourse liability,* and how is each generally allocated to partners?

9. How does the amount of liability allocated to a partner affect the amount of gain a partner recognizes when contributing property secured by a liability? LO 20-2
10. What is a tax-basis capital account, and what type of tax-related information does it provide? LO 20-2
11. Distinguish between a capital interest and a profits interest, and explain how partners and partnerships treat each when exchanging them for services provided. LO 20-2
12. How do partners who purchase a partnership interest determine the tax basis and holding period of their partnership interests? LO 20-2
13. Why do you think partnerships, rather than the individual partners, are responsible for making most of the tax elections related to the operation of the partnership? LO 20-3
14. If a partner with a taxable year-end of December 31 is in a partnership with a March 31 taxable year-end, how many months of deferral will the partner receive? Why? LO 20-3
15. In what situation will there be a common year-end for the principal partners when there is no majority interest taxable year? LO 20-3
16. Explain the least aggregate deferral test for determining a partnership's year-end and discuss when it applies. LO 20-3
17. When are partnerships eligible to use the cash method of accounting? LO 20-3
18. What is a partnership's ordinary business income (loss), and how is it calculated? LO 20-4
19. What are some common separately stated items, and why must they be separately stated to the partners? LO 20-4
20. Is the character of partnership income/gains and expenses/losses determined at the partnership or partner level? Why? LO 20-4
21. What are guaranteed payments, and how do partnerships and partners treat them for income and self-employment tax purposes? LO 20-4
22. How do general and limited partners treat their share of ordinary business income for self-employment tax purposes? LO 20-4
23. What challenges do LLCs face when deciding whether to treat their members' shares of ordinary business income as self-employment income? LO 20-4
24. How much flexibility do partnerships have in allocating partnership items to partners? LO 20-4
25. What are the basic tax-filing requirements imposed on partnerships? LO 20-4
26. In what situations do partners need to know the tax basis in their partnership interests? LO 20-5
27. Why does a partner's tax basis in a partnership interest need to be adjusted annually? LO 20-5
28. What items will increase a partner's basis in the partnership interest? LO 20-5
29. What items will decrease a partner's basis in the partnership interest? LO 20-5
30. What hurdles (or limitations) must partners overcome before they can ultimately deduct partnership losses on their tax returns? LO 20-6
31. What happens to partnership losses allocated to partners in excess of the tax basis in their partnership interests? LO 20-6
32. In what sense is the at-risk loss limitation rule more restrictive than the tax-basis loss limitation rule? LO 20-6
33. How do partners measure the amount they have at risk in the partnership? LO 20-6
34. In what order are the loss limitation rules applied to limit partners' losses from partnerships? LO 20-6
35. How do partners determine whether they are passive participants in partnerships when applying the passive activity loss limitation rules? LO 20-6
36. Under what circumstances can partners with passive losses from partnerships deduct their passive losses? LO 20-6

PROBLEMS

Select problems are available in Connect®.

LO 20-2

37. Joseph contributed $22,000 in cash and equipment with a tax basis of $5,000 and a fair market value of $11,000 to Berry Hill Partnership in exchange for a partnership interest.
    a) What is Joseph's tax basis in his partnership interest?
    b) What is Berry Hill's basis in the equipment?

LO 20-2

38. Lance contributed investment property worth $500,000, purchased three years ago for $200,000 cash, to Cloud Peak LLC in exchange for an 85 percent profits and capital interest in the LLC. Cloud Peak owes $300,000 to its suppliers but has no other liabilities.
    a) What is Lance's tax basis in his LLC interest?
    b) What is Lance's holding period in his interest?
    c) What is Cloud Peak's basis in the contributed property?
    d) What is Cloud Peak's holding period in the contributed property?

LO 20-2

39. Rania contributed equipment worth $200,000, purchased 10 months ago for $250,000 cash and used in her sole proprietorship, to Sand Creek LLC in exchange for a 15 percent profits and capital interest in the LLC. Rania agreed to guarantee all $15,000 of Sand Creek's accounts payable, but she did not guarantee any portion of the $100,000 nonrecourse mortgage securing Sand Creek's office building. Other than the accounts payable and mortgage, Sand Creek does not have any liabilities to other creditors.
    a) What is Rania's initial tax basis in her LLC interest?
    b) What is Rania's holding period in her interest?
    c) What is Sand Creek's initial basis in the contributed property?
    d) What is Sand Creek's holding period in the contributed property?

LO 20-2
planning

40. Harry and Sally formed the Evergreen Partnership by contributing the following assets in exchange for a 50 percent capital and profits interest in the partnership:

	Basis	Fair Market Value
Harry:		
Cash	$ 30,000	$ 30,000
Land	100,000	120,000
Totals	$130,000	$150,000
Sally:		
Equipment used in a business	200,000	150,000
Totals	$200,000	$150,000

    a) How much gain or loss will Harry recognize on the contribution?
    b) How much gain or loss will Sally recognize on the contribution?
    c) How could the transaction be structured in a different way to get a better result for Sally?
    d) What is Harry's tax basis in his partnership interest?
    e) What is Sally's tax basis in her partnership interest?
    f) What is Evergreen's tax basis in its assets?
    g) Following the format in Exhibit 20-2, prepare a tax basis balance sheet for the Evergreen partnership showing the tax capital accounts for the partners.

LO 20-2

41. Cosmo contributed land with a fair market value of $400,000 and a tax basis of $90,000 to the Y Mountain Partnership in exchange for a 25 percent profits and capital interest in the partnership. The land is secured by a $120,000 nonrecourse liability. Other than this nonrecourse liability, Y Mountain Partnership does not have any liability.
    a) How much gain will Cosmo recognize from the contribution?
    b) What is Cosmo's tax basis in his partnership interest?

42. When High Horizon LLC was formed, Maude contributed the following assets in exchange for a 25 percent capital and profits interest in the LLC: LO 20-2

	Basis	Fair Market Value
Maude:		
Cash	$ 20,000	$ 20,000
Land*	100,000	360,000
Totals	$120,000	$380,000

*Nonrecourse liability secured by the land equals $160,000.

Hiro, Harold, and Sofiya each contributed $220,000 in cash for a 25 percent profits and capital interest. LO 20-2

a) How much gain or loss will Maude and the other members recognize?
b) What is Maude's tax basis in her LLC interest?
c) What tax basis do Hiro, Harold, and Sofiya have in their LLC interests?
d) What is High Horizon's tax basis in its assets?
e) Following the format in Exhibit 20-2, prepare a tax basis balance sheet for High Horizon LLC showing the tax capital accounts for the members.

43. Kevan, Jerry, and Dave formed Albee LLC. Jerry and Dave each contributed $245,000 in cash. Kevan contributed the following assets: LO 20-2

	Basis	Fair Market Value
Kevan:		
Cash	$ 15,000	$ 15,000
Land*	120,000	440,000
Totals	$135,000	$455,000

*Nonrecourse liability secured by the land equals $210,000.

Each member received a one-third capital and profits interest in the LLC.

a) How much gain or loss will Jerry, Dave, and Kevan recognize on the contributions?
b) What is Kevan's tax basis in his LLC interest?
c) What tax basis do Jerry and Dave have in their LLC interests?
d) What is Albee LLC's tax basis in its assets?
e) Following the format in Exhibit 20-2, prepare a tax basis balance sheet for Albee LLC showing the tax capital accounts for the members. What is Kevan's share of the LLC's inside basis?
f) If the lender holding the nonrecourse liability secured by Kevan's land required Kevan to guarantee 1/3 of the liability and Jerry to guarantee the remaining 2/3 of the liability when Albee LLC was formed, how much gain or loss will Kevan recognize?
g) If the lender holding the nonrecourse liability secured by Kevan's land required Kevan to guarantee 1/3 of the liability and Jerry to guarantee the remaining 2/3 of the liability when Albee LLC was formed, what are the members' tax bases in their LLC interests?

44. Malak has decided to contribute some equipment she previously used in her sole proprietorship in exchange for a 10 percent profits and capital interest in Fast Choppers LLC. Malak originally paid $200,000 cash for the equipment. Since then, the tax basis in the equipment has been reduced to $100,000 because of tax depreciation, and the fair market value of the equipment is now $150,000. LO 20-2 research

a) Must Malak recognize any of the potential §1245 recapture when she contributes the machinery to Fast Choppers? [*Hint:* See §1245(b)(3).]

b) What cost recovery method will Fast Choppers use to depreciate the machinery? [*Hint:* See §168(i)(7).]

c) If Fast Choppers were to immediately sell the equipment Malak contributed for $150,000, how much gain would Malak recognize, and what is its character? [*Hint:* See §§1245 and 704(c).]

LO 20-2 research

45. Ansel purchased raw land three years ago for $200,000 to hold as an investment. After watching the value of the land drop to $150,000, he decided to contribute it to Mountainside Developers LLC in exchange for a 5 percent capital and profits interest. Mountainside plans to develop the property and will treat it as inventory, like all the other real estate it holds.

a) If Mountainside sells the property for $150,000 after holding it for one year, how much gain or loss does it recognize, and what is the character of the gain or loss? [*Hint:* See §724.]

b) If Mountainside sells the property for $125,000 after holding it for two years, how much gain or loss does it recognize, and what is the character of the gain or loss?

c) If Mountainside sells the property for $150,000 after holding it for six years, how much gain or loss does it recognize, and what is the character of the gain or loss?

LO 20-2 research

46. Claude purchased raw land three years ago for $1,500,000 to develop into lots and sell to individuals planning to build their dream homes. Claude intended to treat this property as inventory, like his other development properties. Before completing the development of the property, however, he decided to contribute it to South Peak Investors LLC when it was worth $2,500,000, in exchange for a 10 percent capital and profits interest. South Peak's strategy is to hold land for investment purposes only and then sell it later at a gain.

a) If South Peak sells the property for $3,000,000 four years after Claude's contribution, how much gain or loss is recognized, and what is its character? [*Hint:* See §724.]

b) If South Peak sells the property for $3,000,000 five and one-half years after Claude's contribution, how much gain or loss is recognized, and what is its character?

LO 20-2 research

47. Kamal contributed $10,000 in cash and a capital asset he had held for three years with a fair market value of $20,000 and tax basis of $10,000 for a 5 percent capital and profits interest in Green Valley LLC.

a) If Kamal sells his LLC interest 13 months later for $30,000 when the tax basis in his partnership interest is still $20,000, how much gain does he report, and what is its character?

b) If Kamal sells his LLC interest two months later for $30,000 when the tax basis in his partnership interest is still $20,000, how much gain does he report, and what is its character? [*Hint*: See Reg. §1.1223-3.]

LO 20-2

48. Connie recently provided legal services to the Winterhaven LLC and received a 5 percent interest in the LLC as compensation. Winterhaven currently has $50,000 of accounts payable and no other liabilities. The current fair market value of Winterhaven's capital is $200,000.

a) If Connie receives a 5 percent capital interest only, how much income must she report, and what is her tax basis in the LLC interest?

b) If Connie receives a 5 percent profits interest only, how much income must she report, and what is her tax basis in the LLC interest?

c) If Connie receives a 5 percent capital and profits interest, how much income must she report, and what is her tax basis in the LLC interest?

49. Mary and Scott formed a partnership that maintains its records on a calendar-year basis. The balance sheet of the MS Partnership at year-end is as follows: LO 20-2

	Basis	Fair Market Value
Cash	$ 60	$ 60
Land	60	180
Inventory	72	60
	$192	$300
Mary	$ 96	$150
Scott	96	150
	$192	$300

At the end of the current year, Kari will receive a one-third capital interest only in exchange for services rendered. Kari's interest will not be subject to a substantial risk of forfeiture, and the costs for the type of services she provided are typically not capitalized by the partnership. For the current year, the income and expenses from operations are equal. Consequently, the only tax consequences for the year are those relating to the admission of Kari to the partnership.

a) Compute and characterize any gain or loss Kari may have to recognize as a result of her admission to the partnership.
b) Compute Kari's basis in her partnership interest.
c) Prepare a balance sheet of the partnership immediately after Kari's admission showing the partners' tax capital accounts and capital accounts stated at fair market value.
d) Calculate how much gain or loss Kari would have to recognize if, instead of a capital interest, she received a profits interest.

50. Dave LaCroix recently received a 10 percent capital and profits interest in Cirque Capital LLC in exchange for consulting services he provided. If Cirque Capital had paid an outsider to provide the advice, it would have deducted the payment as compensation expense. Cirque Capital's balance sheet on the day Dave received his capital interest appears below: LO 20-2

	Basis	Fair Market Value
Assets:		
Cash	$150,000	$ 150,000
Investments	200,000	700,000
Land	150,000	250,000
Totals	$500,000	$1,100,000
Liabilities and capital:		
Nonrecourse liabilities	$100,000	$ 100,000
Tatsuki*	200,000	500,000
Robert*	200,000	500,000
Totals	$500,000	$1,100,000

*Assume that Tatsuki's basis and Robert's basis in their LLC interests equal their tax basis capital accounts plus their respective shares of nonrecourse liabilities.

a) Compute and characterize any gain or loss Dave may have to recognize as a result of his admission to Cirque Capital.
b) Compute each member's tax basis in his LLC interest immediately after Dave's receipt of his interest.
c) Prepare a balance sheet for Cirque Capital immediately after Dave's admission showing the members' tax capital accounts and their capital accounts stated at fair market value.

d) Compute and characterize any gain or loss Dave may have to recognize as a result of his admission to Cirque Capital if he receives only a profits interest.

e) Compute each member's tax basis in his LLC interest immediately after Dave's receipt of his interest if Dave receives only a profits interest.

LO 20-2

51. Last December 31, Ramon sold the 10 percent interest in the Del Sol Partnership that he had held for two years to Garrett for $400,000. Prior to selling his interest, Ramon's basis in Del Sol was $200,000, which included a $100,000 share of nonrecourse liabilities allocated to him.

a) What is Garrett's tax basis in his partnership interest?

b) If Garrett sells his partnership interest three months after receiving it and recognizes a gain, what is the character of his gain?

LO 20-3

52. Broken Rock LLC was recently formed with the following members:

Name	Tax Year-End	Capital/Profits %
George Allen	December 31	33.33%
Elanax Corp.	June 30	33.33
Elizabeth Cheam	December 31	33.34

What is the required taxable year-end for Broken Rock LLC?

LO 20-3

53. Granite Slab LLC was recently formed with the following members:

Name	Tax Year-End	Capital/Profits %
Nelson Black	December 31	22.0%
Brittany Jones	December 31	24.0
Lone Pine LLC	June 30	4.5
Red Spot Inc.	October 31	4.5
Pale Rock Inc.	September 30	4.5
Thunder Ridge LLC	July 31	4.5
Alpensee LLC	March 31	4.5
Lakewood Inc.	June 30	4.5
Streamside LLC	October 31	4.5
Burnt Fork Inc.	October 31	4.5
Snowy Ridge LP	June 30	4.5
Whitewater LP	October 31	4.5
Straw Hat LLC	January 31	4.5
Wildfire Inc.	September 30	4.5

What is the required taxable year-end for Granite Slab LLC?

LO 20-3

54. Tall Tree LLC was recently formed with the following members:

Name	Tax Year-End	Capital/Profits %
Eddie Robinson	December 31	40%
Pitcher Lenders LLC	June 30	25
Perry Homes Inc.	October 31	35

What is the required taxable year-end for Tall Tree LLC?

LO 20-3

55. Rock Creek LLC was recently formed with the following members:

Name	Tax Year-End	Capital/Profits %
Mark Banks	December 31	35%
Highball Properties LLC	March 31	25
Chavez Builders Inc.	November 30	40

What is the required taxable year-end for Rock Creek LLC?

56. Ryan, Dahir, and Bill have operated Broken Feather LLC for the last four years using a calendar year-end. Each has a one-third interest. Since they began operating, their busy season has run from June through August, with 35 percent of their gross receipts coming in July and August. The members would like to change their tax year-end and have asked you to address the following questions: LO 20-3 research

a) Can they change to an August 31 year-end and, if so, how do they make the change? [*Hint:* See Rev. Proc. 2002-38.]

b) Can they change to a September 30 year-end, and, if so, how do they make the change? [*Hint:* See §444.]

57. Ashlee, Hiroki, Kate, and Albee LLC each owns a 25 percent interest in Tally Industries LLC, which generates annual gross receipts of over $10 million. Ashlee, Hiroki, and Kate manage the business, but Albee LLC is a nonmanaging member. Although Tally Industries has historically been profitable, for the last three years losses have been allocated to the members. Given these facts, the members want to know whether Tally Industries can use the cash method of accounting. Why or why not? [*Hint:* See §448(b)(3).] LO 20-3 research

58. Turtle Creek Partnership had the following revenues, expenses, gains, losses, and distributions: LO 20-4

Sales revenue	$ 40,000
Long-term capital gains	2,000
Cost of goods sold	(13,000)
Depreciation—MACRS	(3,000)
Amortization of organization costs	(1,000)
Guaranteed payments to partners for general management	(10,000)
Cash distributions to partners	(2,000)

a) Given these items, what is Turtle Creek's ordinary business income (loss) for the year?

b) What are Turtle Creek's separately stated items for the year?

59. Georgio owns a 20 percent profits and capital interest in Rain Tree LLC. For the current year, Rain Tree had the following revenues, expenses, gains, and losses: LO 20-4

Sales revenue	$ 70,000
Gain on sale of land (§1231)	11,000
Cost of goods sold	(26,000)
Depreciation—MACRS	(3,000)
§179 deduction*	(10,000)
Employee wages	(11,000)
Nondeductible fines and penalties	(3,000)
Municipal bond interest	6,000
Short-term capital gains	4,000
Guaranteed payment to Sandra	(3,000)

*Assume the §179 property placed in service limitation does not apply.

a) How much ordinary business income (loss) is allocated to Georgio for the year?

b) What are Georgio's separately stated items for the year?

60. Richard Mendez and two friends from law school recently formed Mendez and Associates as a limited liability partnership (LLP). Income from the partnership will be split equally among the partners. The partnership will generate fee income primarily from representing clients in bankruptcy and foreclosure matters. While some attorney friends have suggested that partners' earnings will be self-employment income, other attorneys they know from their local bar association meetings claim just the opposite. After examining relevant authority, explain how you would advise Mendez and Associates on this matter. [*Hint:* See §1402(a)(13) and *Renkemeyer, Campbell & Weaver LLP v. Comm'r,* 136 TC 137 (2011).] LO 20-4 research

LO 20-4

61. The partnership agreement of the G&P general partnership states that Gary will receive a guaranteed payment of $13,000, and that Gary and Prudence will share the remaining profits or losses in a 45/55 ratio. For year 1, the G&P partnership reports the following results:

Sales revenue	$70,000
Gain on sale of land (§1231)	8,000
Cost of goods sold	(38,000)
Depreciation—MACRS	(9,000)
Employee wages	(14,000)
Cash charitable contributions	(3,000)
Municipal bond interest	2,000
Other expenses	(2,000)

a) Compute Gary's share of ordinary income (loss) and separately stated items to be reported on his year 1 Schedule K-1, including his self-employment income (loss).
b) Compute Gary's share of self-employment income (loss) to be reported on his year 1 Schedule K-1, assuming G&P is a limited partnership and Gary is a limited partner.
c) What do you believe Gary's share of self-employment income (loss) to be reported on his year 1 Schedule K-1 should be, assuming G&P is an LLC and Gary spends 2,000 hours per year working there full time?

LO 20-4
research

62. Hoki Poki, a cash-method general partnership, recorded the following items for its current tax year:

Rental real estate income	$ 2,000
Sales revenue	70,000
§1245 recapture income	8,000
Interest income	2,000
Cost of goods sold	(38,000)
Depreciation—MACRS	(9,000)
Supplies expense	(1,000)
Employee wages	(14,000)
Investment interest expense	(1,000)
Partner's medical insurance premiums paid by Hoki Poki	(3,000)

As part of preparing Hoki Poki's current-year return, identify the items that should be included in computing its ordinary business income (loss) and those that should be separately stated. [*Hint:* See Schedule K-1 and related preparer's instructions at www.irs.gov.]

LO 20-4
research

63. On the last day of its current tax year, Buy Rite LLC received $300,000 when it sold a machine it had purchased for $200,000 three years ago to use in its business. At the time of the sale, the basis in the equipment had been reduced to $100,000 due to tax depreciation taken. How much did the members' self-employment earnings from Buy Rite increase when the equipment was sold? [*Hint:* See §1402(a)(3).]

LO 20-4

64. Jhumpa, Stewart, and Kelly are all one-third partners in the capital and profits of Firewalker General Partnership. In addition to their normal share of the partnership's annual income, Jhumpa and Stewart receive an annual guaranteed payment of $10,000 each to compensate them for additional services they provide. Firewalker's income statement for the current year reflects the following revenues and expenses:

Sales revenue	$340,000
Interest income	3,300
Long-term capital gains	1,200
Cost of goods sold	(120,000)
Employee wages	(75,000)
Depreciation expense	(28,000)
Guaranteed payments	(20,000)
Miscellaneous expenses	(4,500)
Overall net income	$ 97,000

a) Given Firewalker's operating results, how much ordinary business income (loss) and what separately stated items [including the partners' self-employment earnings (loss)] will it report on its return for the year?
b) How will it allocate these amounts to its partners?
c) How much self-employment tax will each partner pay assuming none has any other source of income or loss?

65. This year, Darrel's distributive share from Alcove Partnership includes $6,000 of interest income, $3,000 of dividend income, and $70,000 ordinary business income. LO 20-4
a) Assume that Darrel materially participates in the partnership. How much of his distributive share from Alcove Partnership is potentially subject to the net investment income tax?
b) Assume that Darrel does not materially participate in the partnership. How much of his distributive share from Alcove Partnership is potentially subject to the net investment income tax?

66. This year, Agustin's distributive share from Eden Lakes Partnership includes $8,000 of interest income, $4,000 of net long-term capital gains, $2,000 net §1231 gain from the sale of property used in the partnership's trade or business, and $83,000 of ordinary business income. LO 20-4
a) Assume that Agustin materially participates in the partnership. How much of his distributive share from Eden Lakes Partnership is potentially subject to the net investment income tax?
b) Assume that Agustin does not materially participate in the partnership. How much of his distributive share from Eden Lakes Partnership is potentially subject to the net investment income tax?

67. Lane and Cal each owns 50 percent of the profits and capital of HighYield LLC. HighYield owns a portfolio of taxable bonds and municipal bonds, and each year the portfolio generates approximately $10,000 of taxable interest and $10,000 of tax-exempt interest. Lane's marginal tax rate is 35 percent, while Cal's marginal tax rate is 12 percent. To take advantage of the difference in their marginal tax rates, Lane and Cal want to modify their operating agreement to specially allocate all of the taxable interest to Cal and all of the tax-exempt interest to Lane. Until now, Lane and Cal had been allocated 50 percent of each type of interest income. LO 20-4 research
a) Is HighYield's proposed special allocation acceptable under current tax rules? Why or why not? [*Hint:* See Reg. §1.704-1(b)(2)(iii)(b) and (5) Example (5).]
b) If the IRS ultimately disagrees with HighYield's special allocation, how will it likely reallocate the taxable and tax-exempt interest among the members? [*Hint:* See Reg. §1.704-1(b)(5) Example (5)(ii).]

68. Mustafa's tax basis in his partnership interest at the beginning of the year was $10,000. If his share of the partnership liabilities increased by $10,000 during the year and his share of partnership income for the year is $3,000, what is his tax basis in his partnership interest at the end of the year? LO 20-5

69. Carmine was allocated the following items from Piccolo LLC for last year: LO 20-5

Ordinary business loss
Nondeductible penalties
Tax-exempt interest income
Short-term capital gain
Cash distributions

Rank these items in terms of the order in which they should be applied to adjust Carmine's tax basis in Piccolo for the year (some items may be of equal rank).

LO 20-5

70. Oscar, Felix, and Marv are all one-third partners in the capital and profits of Eastside General Partnership. In addition to their normal share of the partnership's annual income, Oscar and Felix receive annual guaranteed payments of $7,000 to compensate them for additional services they provide. Eastside's income statement for the current year reflects the following revenues and expenses:

Sales revenue	$420,000
Dividend income	5,700
Short-term capital gains	2,800
Cost of goods sold	(210,000)
Employee wages	(115,000)
Depreciation expense	(28,000)
Guaranteed payments	(14,000)
Miscellaneous expenses	(9,500)
Overall net income	$ 52,000

In addition, Eastside owed creditors $120,000 at the beginning of the year but managed to pay down its liabilities to $90,000 by the end of the year. All partnership liabilities are allocated equally among the partners. Finally, Oscar, Felix, and Marv had a tax basis of $80,000 in their interests at the beginning of the year.

a) What tax basis do the partners have in their partnership interests at the end of the year?

b) Assume the partners began the year with a tax basis of $10,000 and all the liabilities were paid off on the last day of the year. How much gain will the partners recognize when the liabilities are paid off? What tax basis do the partners have in their partnership interests at the end of the year?

LO 20-5

71. Pam, Sergei, and Mercedes are all one-third partners in the capital and profits of Oak Grove General Partnership. Partnership liabilities are allocated among the partners in accordance with their capital and profits interests. In addition to their normal share of the partnership's annual income, Pam and Sergei receive annual guaranteed payments of $20,000 each to compensate them for additional services they provide. Oak Grove's income statement for the current year reflects the following revenues and expenses:

Sales revenue	$476,700
Dividend income	6,600
§1231 losses	(3,800)
Cost of goods sold	(245,000)
Employee wages	(92,000)
Depreciation expense	(31,000)
Guaranteed payments	(40,000)
Miscellaneous expenses	(11,500)
Overall net income	$ 60,000

In addition, Oak Grove owed creditors $90,000 at the beginning of the year and $150,000 at the end, and Pam, Sergei, and Mercedes had a tax basis of $50,000 in their interests at the beginning of the year. Also, on December 31 of the current year, Sergei and Mercedes agreed to increase Pam's capital and profits interests from 1/3 to 40 percent in exchange for additional services she provided to the partnership. The current liquidation value of the additional capital interest Pam received is $40,000.

a) What tax basis do the partners have in their partnership interests at the end of the year?

b) If, in addition to the expenses listed above, the partnership donated $12,000 to a political campaign, what tax basis do the partners have in their partnership interests at the end of the year assuming the liquidation value of the additional capital interest Pam received at the end of the year remains at $40,000?

72. Laura Davis is a member in a limited liability company that has historically been profitable but is expecting to generate losses in the near future because of a weak local economy. In addition to the hours she works as an employee of a local business, she currently spends approximately 150 hours per year helping to manage the LLC. Other LLC members work approximately 175 hours per year each in the LLC, and the time Laura and other members spend managing the LLC has remained constant since she joined the company three years ago. Laura's tax basis and amount at risk are large compared to her share of projected losses; however, she is concerned that her ability to deduct her share of the projected losses will be limited by the passive activity loss rules. LO 20-6 research

 a) As an LLC member, will Laura's share of losses be presumed to be passive as they are for limited partners? Why or why not? [*Hint:* See §469(h)(2); *Garnett v. Comm'r,* 132 TC 368 (2009); and Prop. Reg. §1.469-5(e)(3)(i).]
 b) Assuming Laura's losses are not presumed to be passive, is she devoting sufficient time to the LLC to be considered a material participant? Why or why not?
 c) What would you recommend to Laura to help her achieve a more favorable tax outcome?

73. Alfonso began the year with a tax basis in his partnership interest of $30,000. His share of partnership liabilities at the beginning and end of the year consists of $4,000 of recourse liabilities and $6,000 of nonrecourse liabilities. During the year, he was allocated $40,000 of partnership ordinary business loss. Alfonso does not materially participate in this partnership, and he has $1,000 of passive income from other sources. LO 20-6

 a) How much of Alfonso's loss is limited by his tax basis?
 b) How much of Alfonso's loss is limited by his at-risk amount?
 c) How much of Alfonso's loss is limited by the passive activity loss rules?

74. Nareh began the year with a tax basis of $45,000 in her partnership interest. Her share of partnership liabilities consists of $6,000 of recourse liabilities and $10,000 of nonrecourse liabilities at the beginning of the year and $6,000 of recourse liabilities and $13,000 of nonrecourse liabilities at the end of the year. During the year, she was allocated $65,000 of partnership ordinary business loss. Nareh does not materially participate in this partnership, and she has $4,000 of passive income from other sources. LO 20-6

 a) How much of Nareh's loss is limited by her tax basis?
 b) How much of Nareh's loss is limited by her at-risk amount?
 c) How much of Nareh's loss is limited by the passive activity loss rules?

75. Juan Diego began the year with a tax basis in his partnership interest of $50,000. During the year, he was allocated $20,000 of partnership ordinary business income, $70,000 of §1231 losses, and $30,000 of short-term capital losses and received a cash distribution of $50,000. LO 20-5 LO 20-6 research

 a) What items related to these allocations does Juan Diego actually report on his tax return for the year? [*Hint:* See Reg. §1.704-1(d)(2) and Rev. Rul. 66-94.]
 b) If any deductions or losses are limited, what are the carryover amounts, and what is their character? [*Hint:* See Reg. §1.704-1(d).]

76. Farell is a member of Sierra Vista LLC. Although Sierra Vista is involved in a number of different business ventures, it is not currently involved in real estate either as an investor or as a developer. On January 1, year 1, Farell has a $100,000 tax basis in his LLC interest that includes his $90,000 share of Sierra Vista's general liabilities. By the end of the year, Farell's share of Sierra Vista's general liabilities have increased to $100,000. Because of the time he spends in other endeavors, Farell does not materially participate in Sierra Vista. His share of the Sierra Vista losses for year 1 LO 20-6

is $120,000. As a partner in the Riverwoods Partnership, he also has year 1, Schedule K-1 passive income of $5,000. Farell is single and has no other sources of business income or loss.

a) Determine how much of the Sierra Vista loss Farell will currently be able to deduct on his tax return for year 1, and list the losses suspended due to tax-basis, at-risk, and passive activity loss limitations.

b) Assuming Farell's Riverwoods K-1 indicates passive income of $30,000, determine how much of the Sierra Vista loss he will ultimately be able to deduct on his tax return for year 1, and list the losses suspended due to tax-basis, at-risk, and passive activity loss limitations.

c) Assuming Farell is deemed to be an active participant in Sierra Vista, determine how much of the Sierra Vista loss he will ultimately be able to deduct on his tax return for year 1, and list the losses suspended due to tax-basis, at-risk, and passive activity loss limitations.

d) Assuming Farell is deemed to be an active participant in Sierra Vista, and he also has a $280,000 loss from a sole proprietorship, determine how much total trade or business loss Farell will deduct on his return in year 1.

LO 20-6
research

77. Jenkins has a one-third capital and profits interest in the Maverick General Partnership. On January 1, year 1, Maverick has $120,000 of general liabilities and Jenkins has a $50,000 tax basis (including his share of Maverick's liabilities) in his partnership interest. During the year, Maverick incurred a $30,000 nonrecourse liability that is not secured by real estate. Because Maverick is a rental real estate partnership, Jenkins is deemed to be a passive participant in Maverick. His share of the Maverick losses for year 1 is $75,000. Jenkins is not involved in any other passive activities, and this is the first year he has been allocated losses from Maverick.

a) Determine how much of the Maverick loss Jenkins will currently be able to deduct on his tax return for year 1, and list the losses suspended due to tax-basis, at-risk, and passive activity loss limitations.

b) If Jenkins sells his interest on January 1, year 2, what happens to his suspended losses from year 1? [*Hint:* See §706(c)(2)(A); Reg. §1.704-1(d)(1); Prop. Reg. §1.465-66(a); and *Sennett v. Comm'r,* 80 TC 825 (1983).]

LO 20-6
research

78. Suki and Steve own 50 percent capital and profits interests in Lorinda LLC. Lorinda operates the local minor league baseball team and owns the stadium where the team plays. Although the liability incurred to build the stadium was paid off several years ago, Lorinda owes its general creditors $300,000 (at the beginning of the year) that is not secured by firm property or guaranteed by any of the members. At the beginning of 2022, Suki and Steve had a tax basis of $170,000 in their LLC interests, including their share of liabilities owed to the general creditors. Shortly before the end of the year, they each received a $10,000 cash distribution, even though Lorinda's ordinary business loss for the year was $400,000. Because of the time commitment to operate a baseball team, both Suki and Steve spent more than 1,500 hours during the year operating Lorinda. Both Suki and Steve are single, and neither of them has any business income or losses from other sources.

a) Determine how much of the Lorinda loss Suki and Steve will each be able to deduct on their current tax returns, and list their losses suspended by the tax-basis, at-risk, and passive activity loss limitations.

b) Assume that some time before receiving the $10,000 cash distribution, Steve is advised by his tax adviser that his marginal tax rate will be abnormally high during the current year because of an unexpected windfall. To help Steve utilize more of the losses allocated from Lorinda in the current year, his adviser recommends refusing the cash distribution and personally guaranteeing $100,000 of Lorinda's liabilities, without the right to be reimbursed by Suki. If Steve follows his adviser's recommendations, how much additional Lorinda loss can he deduct on his current tax return? How does Steve's decision affect the amount of loss Suki can deduct on her current return and the amount and type of her suspended losses?

79. Ray and Matias own 50 percent capital and profits interests in Alpine Properties LLC. Alpine builds and manages rental real estate, and Ray and Matias each works full time (over 1,000 hours per year) managing Alpine. Alpine's liabilities (at both the beginning and end of the year) consist of $1,500,000 in nonrecourse mortgages obtained from an unrelated bank and secured by various rental properties. At the beginning of the current year, Ray and Matias each had a tax basis of $250,000 in his respective LLC interest, including his share of the nonrecourse mortgage liability. Alpine's ordinary business losses for the current year totaled $600,000, and neither member is involved in other activities that generate passive income. LO 20-6 research

a) How much of each member's loss is suspended because of the tax-basis limitation?

b) How much of each member's loss is suspended because of the at-risk limitation?

c) How much of each member's loss is suspended because of the passive activity loss limitation? [*Hint:* See §469(c)(7).]

d) If both Ray and Matias are single and Ray has a current-year loss of $50,000 from a sole proprietorship, how much trade or business loss can each deduct on his tax return in the current year?

COMPREHENSIVE PROBLEMS

Select problems are available in Connect®.

80. Aaron, Deanne, and Keon formed the Blue Bell General Partnership at the beginning of the current year. Aaron and Deanne each contributed $110,000, and Keon transferred an acre of undeveloped land to the partnership. The land had a tax basis of $70,000 and was appraised at $180,000. The land was also encumbered with a $70,000 nonrecourse mortgage for which no one was personally liable. All three partners agreed to split profits and losses equally. At the end of the first year, Blue Bell made a $7,000 principal payment on the mortgage. For the first year of operations, the partnership records disclosed the following information: tax forms

Sales revenue	$470,000
Cost of goods sold	410,000
Operating expenses	70,000
Long-term capital gains	2,400
§1231 gains	900
Charitable contributions	300
Municipal bond interest	300
Salary paid as a guaranteed payment to Deanne (not included in expenses)	3,000

a) Compute the adjusted basis of each partner's interest in the partnership immediately after the formation of the partnership.

b) List the separate items of partnership income, gains, losses, and deductions that the partners must show on their individual income tax returns that include the results of the partnership's first year of operations.

c) Using the information generated in answering parts (a) and (b), prepare Blue Bell's page 1 and Schedule K to be included with its Form 1065 for its first year of operations, along with Schedule K-1 for Deanne.

d) What are the partners' adjusted bases in their partnership interests at the end of the first year of operations?

tax forms

81. The TimpRiders LP has operated a motorcycle dealership for a number of years. Amir is the limited partner, Francesca is the general partner, and they share capital and profits equally. Francesca works full time managing the partnership. Both the partnership and the partners report on a calendar-year basis. At the start of the current year, Amir and Francesca had bases of $10,000 and $3,000, respectively, and the partnership did not have any liabilities. During the current year, the partnership reported the following results from operations:

Net sales	$650,000
Cost of goods sold	500,000
Operating expenses	160,000
Short-term capital loss	2,000
Tax-exempt interest	2,000
§1231 gain	6,000

On the last day of the year, the partnership distributed $3,000 each to Amir and Francesca.

a) What outside basis do Amir and Francesca have in their partnership interests at the end of the year?

b) How much of their losses are currently not deductible by Amir and Francesca because of the tax-basis limitation?

c) To what extent does the passive activity loss limitation apply in restricting their deductible losses for the year?

d) Using the information provided, prepare TimpRiders's page 1 and Schedule K to be included with its Form 1065 for the current year. Also, prepare a Schedule K-1 for Amir and Francesca.

82. LeBron, Dennis, and Susan formed the Bar T LLC at the beginning of the current year. LeBron and Dennis each contributed $200,000 and Susan transferred several acres of agricultural land she had purchased two years earlier to the LLC. The land had a tax basis of $50,000 and was appraised at $300,000. The land was also encumbered with a $100,000 nonrecourse mortgage (i.e., qualified nonrecourse financing) for which no one was personally liable. The members plan to use the land and cash to begin a cattle-feeding operation. Susan will work full time operating the business, but LeBron and Dennis will devote less than two days per year to the operation.

All three members agree to split profits and losses equally. At the end of the first year, Bar T had accumulated $40,000 of accounts payable jointly guaranteed by LeBron and Dennis and had made a $9,000 principal payment on the mortgage. None of the members have passive income from other sources or business income from other sources. LeBron and Dennis are married, while Susan is single.

For the first year of operations, the partnership records disclosed the following information:

Sales revenue	$620,000
Cost of goods sold	380,000
Operating expenses	670,000
Dividends	1,200
Municipal bond interest	300
Salary paid as a guaranteed payment to Susan (not included in expenses)	10,000
Cash distributions split equally among the members at year-end	3,000

a) Compute the tax basis of each member's interest immediately after the formation of the LLC.
b) When does each member's holding period for his or her LLC interest begin?
c) What are Bar T's tax basis and holding period in its land?
d) What is Bar T's required tax year-end?
e) What overall methods of accounting were initially available to Bar T?
f) List the separate items of partnership income, gains, losses, deductions, and other items that will be included in each member's Schedule K-1 for the first year of operations. Use the proposed self-employment tax regulations to determine each member's self-employment income or loss.
g) What are the members' tax bases in their LLC interests at the end of the first year of operations?
h) What are the members' at-risk amounts in their LLC interests at the end of the first year of operations?
i) How much loss from Bar T, if any, will the members be able to deduct on their individual returns from the first year of operations?

UWorld YOUR WORLD OF LEARNING | ROGER CPA Review

UWorld Roger CPA Review

Sample CPA Exam questions from Roger CPA Review are available in Connect as support for the topics in this text. These Multiple Choice Questions and Task-Based Simulations include expert-written explanations and solutions and provide a starting point for students to become familiar with the content and functionality of the actual CPA Exam.

chapter

21 Dispositions of Partnership Interests and Partnership Distributions

Learning Objectives

Upon completing this chapter, you should be able to:

- **LO 21-1** Determine the tax consequences to the buyer and seller of the disposition of a partnership interest, including the amount and character of gain or loss recognized.
- **LO 21-2** List the reasons for distributions, and compare operating and liquidating distributions.
- **LO 21-3** Determine the tax consequences of proportionate operating distributions.
- **LO 21-4** Determine the tax consequences of proportionate liquidating distributions.
- **LO 21-5** Explain the significance of disproportionate distributions.
- **LO 21-6** Explain the rationale for special basis adjustments, determine when they are necessary, and calculate the special basis adjustment for dispositions and distributions.

Andresr/E+/Getty Images

Storyline Summary

Taxpayer:	Color Comfort Sheets LLC
Location:	Salt Lake City, Utah
Owners and interests:	Nicole Johnson (she/her/hers), managing member—30 percent interest
	Sarah Walker (she/her/hers), managing member—40 percent interest
	Greg Randall (he/him/his), nonmanaging member—30 percent interest

In January 2023,* Nicole and Sarah sit in the Color Comfort Sheets (CCS) LLC office discussing the current state of business affairs over a cup of coffee. They both agree they are not doing as well as they had hoped after two years of running the business. Their main topic of discussion this morning is how to turn the business around. Both women know the viability of the business is at stake if they can't figure out how to make it profitable . . . and soon.

As Nicole and Sarah brainstorm various ideas, Nicole's administrative assistant interrupts to announce a phone call from Olivia Winsted, the media mogul. Nicole takes the call. On her top-rated television talk show, Olivia occasionally promotes a product to her viewers based on her own successful experience using it. Apparently, one of Olivia's viewers sent her a set of Color Comfort sheets, and Olivia is so happy with the product that she wants to promote it on her show in about two weeks. Nicole and Sarah are, of course, thrilled with this news. Products Olivia has endorsed in the past have become wildly successful. The focus of Nicole and Sarah's meeting changes dramatically. Now they have to figure out how they can gear up for an immediate increase in production. Nicole and Sarah's analysis of the accounting records reveals that CCS is in a precarious cash position—the business is down to its last $10,000.

Nicole and Sarah immediately call Greg to fill him in on the news. Greg is as thrilled as they are to hear that Olivia will promote their sheets and agrees to kick in an additional $30,000. Nicole says she will contribute $30,000 and Sarah antes up another $40,000.

The following couple of weeks fly by in a whirlwind of work—phone calls, meetings with bankers, and production scheduling. Olivia's special guest for the show is the popular film star Tom Hughes, promoting his soon-to-be-released movie *Global Warfare*. Tom is good-natured and expresses interest in the sheets. During the show, he announces he will order a set as soon as the broadcast is over. Nicole and Sarah anticipate orders will roll in. Sure enough, before Olivia has even said goodbye to her studio audience, CCS's website traffic has picked up and the phone lines are hopping with new orders.

By the end of 2023, CCS's financial situation has completely turned around; business is booming, the accounting records show a healthy profit, and the members feel comfortable the trend will continue. Greg decides it is time to talk to Nicole and Sarah about cashing out his investment.

(to be continued. . .)

*To allow the storyline to continue from the previous chapter, this chapter begins in 2023 with CCS treated as a partnership for tax purposes. We assume the 2022 tax laws apply for 2023 and subsequent years.

This chapter explores the tax consequences associated with selling partnership interests and distributing partnership assets to partners. In the Business Entities Overview chapter, we learned that Color Comfort Sheets LLC actually elected to be taxed as a C corporation. In this chapter, we assume it did not make this election, leaving it to be taxed as a partnership.

LO 21-1

BASICS OF SALES OF PARTNERSHIP INTERESTS

As we've seen in preceding chapters, owners of various business entities receive returns on their investments, either when the business makes distributions or upon the sale of their business interest. Corporate shareholders may sell their stock to other investors or back to the corporation. Likewise, partners may dispose of their interest in several ways—by selling to a third party, selling to another partner, or transferring the interest back to the partnership. The payments in a disposition (sale) can come from either another owner of the partnership or a new partner; in either case, the sale proceeds come from outside the partnership.

Selling a **partnership interest** raises unique issues because of the flow-through nature of the entity. For example, is the interest a separate asset, or does the disposition represent the sale of the partner's share of each of the partnership's assets? To the extent the tax rules follow an entity approach, the interest is considered a separate asset and a sale of the partnership interest is very similar to the sale of corporate stock. That is, the partner simply recognizes capital gain or loss on the sale, based on the difference between the sales price and the partner's tax basis in the partnership interest. Alternately, to the extent the tax rules use the aggregate approach, the disposition represents a sale of the partner's share of each of the partnership's assets. This approach adds some complexity because of the differing character and holding periods of the partnership assets—ordinary, capital, and §1231. The selling partner also has the additional task of allocating the sales proceeds among the underlying assets in order to determine the gain or loss on each.

Rather than strictly following one approach, the tax rules end up being a mixture of the two approaches (see the Forming and Operating Partnerships chapter for a more detailed discussion of the entity and aggregate approaches). When feasible, the entity approach controls; however, if the result distorts the amount or character of income, then the aggregate approach dominates. We discuss the tax consequences of sales of partnership interests by first taking the perspective of the seller (partner), followed by a discussion from the perspective of the buyer (new investor).

Seller Issues

The seller's primary tax concern in a partnership interest sale is calculating the amount and character of gain or loss on the sale. The selling partner calculates the gain or loss as the difference between the amount realized and the **outside basis** in the partnership interest determined on the date of the sale.[1] Because selling partners are no longer responsible for their share of the partnership liabilities, any debt relief increases the amount that partners *realize* from the sale under general tax principles.

[1]Partners determine their outside basis as discussed in the Forming and Operating Partnerships chapter. Importantly, the outside basis includes the selling partner's share of distributive income for the year to the date of the sale.

Example 21-1

Last year, Chanzz Inc. sold its 30 percent interest in CCS on June 30 to Greg Randall, a wealthy local entrepreneur, to limit its exposure to any further losses. Greg anticipated that CCS would become profitable in the near future and paid Chanzz Inc. $100,000 for its interest in CCS. Chanzz's share of CCS liabilities as of June 30 was $24,000. Chanzz Inc.'s outside basis in its CCS interest at the sale date was $105,000 (including its share of CCS's liabilities). What amount of gain or loss did Chanzz recognize on the sale?

Answer: $19,000 gain, computed as follows:

Description	Amount	Explanation
(1) Cash and fair market value of property received	$100,000	
(2) Debt relief	24,000	
(3) Amount realized	$124,000	(1) + (2)
(4) Outside basis in CCS interest	105,000	
Recognized gain	**$ 19,000**	(3) – (4)

THE KEY FACTS

Sale of Partnership Interest

- Seller issues:
  - Gain or loss calculation.
    Amount realized:
    Cash and fair market value of property received
    Plus: Debt relief
    Less: Outside basis in partnership interest
    Equals: Realized gain or loss
  - Some of seller's gain or loss may be ordinary if hot assets are present inside the partnership.
  - Tax year closes with respect to selling partner when the entire interest is sold.
- Buyer issues:
  - Outside basis—cost of the partnership interest plus share of partnership's liabilities.
  - Inside basis—generally equals selling partner's inside basis at sale date.

The character of the gain or loss from a sale of a partnership interest is generally short-term or long-term capital gain or loss depending on the selling partner's holding period.[2] However, a portion of the gain or loss will be ordinary if a seller realizes any gain or loss attributable to **unrealized receivables** or **inventory items.**[3] Practitioners often refer to these assets that give rise to ordinary gains and losses as **hot assets.**[4] Let's discuss that term further because these assets are central to determining the tax treatment of many transactions in this chapter.

Hot Assets As you might expect, unrealized receivables include the right to receive payment for (1) "goods delivered, or to be delivered,"[5] or (2) "services rendered, or to be rendered."[6] For cash-method taxpayers, unrealized receivables include amounts earned but not yet received (accounts receivable). Accrual-method taxpayers, however, do not consider accounts receivable as unrealized receivables because they have already realized and recognized these items as ordinary income. Unrealized receivables also include items the partnership would treat as ordinary income if it sold the assets for its fair market value, such as depreciation recapture under §1245.[7]

[2]§§731, 741.

[3]§751(a). Partnerships are required to provide Form 8308, Report of a Sale or Exchange of Certain Partnership Interests, to all the parties to the sale as well as to the IRS. Selling partners include this form with their tax returns as well as a statement detailing the calculation of any ordinary gain from the sale of their interest. Practically speaking, these calculations are made with information provided by the partnership.

[4]There are actually two definitions of *inventory items* in §751. Section 751(a) *inventory items* are defined in §751(d) to include *all* inventory items. However, under §751(b), the definition includes only *substantially appreciated* inventory. For purposes of determining the character of gain or loss from the sale of partnership interests, the term *inventory items* includes all inventory as in §751(a). However, these two definitions have created some confusion when using the term *hot assets*. In this chapter, we use the term *hot assets* to refer to unrealized receivables and all inventory items as in §751(a). The definition under §751(b) becomes more relevant when determining the tax treatment in a disproportionate distribution (discussed only briefly later in the chapter).

[5]§751(c)(1).

[6]§751(c)(2).

[7]§751(c).

Inventory items include classic inventory, defined as property held for sale to customers in the ordinary course of business, but also, more broadly, any assets that are *not* capital assets or §1231 assets.[8] Under this definition, assets such as equipment or real estate used in the business but not held for more than a year and all accounts receivable are considered inventory. This broad definition means cash, capital assets, and §1231 assets are the only properties not considered inventory.[9]

Example 21-2

CCS's balance sheet last year as of the date of Chanzz's sale of its CCS interest to Greg follows:

Color Comfort Sheets LLC
June 30, 2022

	Tax Basis	FMV
Assets		
Cash	$ 27,000	$ 27,000
Accounts receivable	0	13,000
Investments	15,000	12,000
Inventory	1,000	1,000
Equipment (acc. depr. = $20,000)	80,000	86,000
Building	97,000	97,000
Land	20,000	150,000
Totals	$240,000	$386,000
Liabilities and capital		
Long-term debt	$100,000*	
Capital—Nicole	(49,000)	
—Sarah	108,000	
—Chanzz	81,000	
Totals	$240,000	

*Of the $100,000 of long-term debt, $20,000 is allocated solely to Nicole. The remaining $80,000 is allocated to all three owners according to their profit-sharing ratios (30 percent to Nicole, 40 percent to Sarah, and 30 percent to Greg).

Which of CCS's assets are considered hot assets under §751(a)?

Answer: The hot assets are accounts receivable of $13,000 and $6,000 depreciation recapture (§1245) potential ($86,000 – $80,000) in the equipment. The accounts receivable are unrealized receivables because CCS has not included them in income for tax purposes under CCS's cash accounting method. The depreciation recapture is also considered an unrealized receivable under §751(a). Inventory would be considered a hot asset; however, because the tax basis and fair market value are equal, it will not affect the character of any gain recognized on the sale.

[8]§751(d)(1).

[9]This broad definition of inventory includes all unrealized receivables except for recapture. Recapture items are excluded from the definition of inventory items simply because recapture is not technically an asset; rather, it is merely a portion of gain that results from the sale of property. Recapture is, however, considered an unrealized receivable (i.e., hot asset) under §751(a). This idea is important in determining whether inventory is substantially appreciated for purposes of determining the §751 assets for distributions, as we discuss later in the chapter.

Example 21-3

Review CCS's balance sheet as of the end of 2023.

Color Comfort Sheets LLC
December 31, 2023

	Tax Basis	FMV
Assets		
Cash	$390,000	$ 390,000
Accounts receivable	0	40,000
Inventory	90,000	200,000
Investments	60,000	105,000
Equipment (acc. depr. = $50,000)	150,000	200,000
Building (acc. depr. = $10,000)	90,000	100,000
Land—original	20,000	160,000
Land—investment	140,000	270,000
Totals	$940,000	$1,465,000
Liabilities and capital		
Accounts payable	$ 80,000	
Long-term debt	0	
Mortgage on original land	40,000	
Mortgage on investment land	120,000	
Capital—Nicole	119,000	
—Sarah	332,000	
—Greg	249,000	
Totals	$940,000	

What amount of CCS's assets are considered to be hot assets as of December 31, 2023?

Answer: The hot assets include inventory with a fair market value of $200,000 and unrealized receivables consisting of $50,000 of depreciation recapture potential on the equipment and $40,000 of accounts receivable.

When selling an interest in a partnership that holds hot assets, a partner modifies the calculation of the gain or loss to ensure the portion that relates to hot assets is properly characterized as ordinary income. The process for determining the gain or loss follows:

Step 1: Calculate the total gain or loss recognized by subtracting outside basis from the amount realized.

Step 2: Calculate the partner's share of gain or loss from hot assets as if the partnership sold these assets at their fair market value. This represents the ordinary portion of the gain or loss.

Step 3: Finally, subtract the ordinary portion of the gain or loss obtained in Step 2 from the total gain or loss from Step 1. This remaining amount is the capital gain or loss from the sale.[10,11]

[10]The partner must also determine if any portion of the capital gain or loss relates to collectibles (28 percent capital gain property) or to unrecaptured §1250 gains (25 percent capital gain property). This is typically referred to as the *look-through rule*.

[11]Any capital gain from the sale of a partnership interest is potentially subject to the 3.8 percent net investment income tax unless the gain is allocable to trade or business assets held by the partnership that generate trade or business income not subject to the tax. See Prop. Reg. §1.1411-7 for a detailed discussion of this concept.

Example 21-4

In Example 21-1, we are reminded that Chanzz Inc. sold its interest in CCS to Greg Randall for $100,000 cash on June 30, 2022. As a result, Chanzz recognized a gain of $19,000 on the sale. What was the character of Chanzz's gain?

Answer: $5,700 of ordinary income and $13,300 of capital gain, determined as follows:

Step 1: Determine the total gain or loss: $19,000 gain (from Example 21-1).

Step 2: Determine the ordinary gain or loss recognized from hot assets:

Asset	(1) Basis	(2) FMV	(3) Gain/Loss (2) – (1)	Chanzz's Share 30% × (3)
Accounts receivable	$ 0	$13,000	$13,000	$3,900
Equipment	80,000	86,000	6,000	1,800
Total ordinary income				**$5,700**

Step 3: Determine the capital gain or loss:

Description	Amount	Explanation
(1) Total gain	$ 19,000	From Step 1
(2) Ordinary income from §751(a)	5,700	From Step 2
Capital gain*	**$13,300**	(1) – (2)

*Because Chanzz sold its interest in CCS more than one year after it acquired its interest in CCS, this gain is long-term capital gain.

Example 21-5

What if: Assume the same facts as in Example 21-1, except Greg paid Chanzz only $82,800 cash for its interest in CCS. What would be the amount and character of Chanzz's gain or loss?

Answer: $5,700 of ordinary income and capital loss of $3,900, determined as follows:

Step 1: Determine the total gain or loss recognized:

Description	Amount	Explanation
(1) Cash and fair market value of property received	$ 82,800	
(2) Debt relief	24,000	Chanzz's share of CCS's allocable debt (30% × $80,000)
(3) Amount realized	$106,800	(1) + (2)
(4) Outside basis in CCS interest	105,000	
Gain recognized	$ 1,800	(3) – (4)

Step 2: Determine the ordinary gain or loss from hot assets:

Asset	(1) Basis	(2) FMV	(3) Gain/Loss (2) – (1)	Chanzz's Share 30% × (3)
Accounts receivable	$ 0	$13,000	$13,000	$ 3,900
Equipment	80,000	86,000	6,000	1,800
Total ordinary income				**$5,700**

Step 3: Determine the capital gain or loss:

Description	Amount	Explanation
(1) Total gain	$ 1,800	From Step 1
(2) Ordinary income from §751(a)	5,700	From Step 2
Capital loss*	**$(3,900)**	(1) – (2)

*Because Chanzz sold its interest in CCS more than one year after it acquired its interest in CCS, this loss is long-term capital loss.

ETHICS

Sarah recently sold her partnership interest for significantly more than her outside basis in the interest. Two separate appraisals were commissioned at the time of the sale to estimate the value of the partnership's hot assets and other assets. The first appraisal estimates the value of the hot assets at approximately $750,000, while the second appraisal estimates the value of these assets at approximately $500,000. Given that the partnership's inside basis for its hot assets is $455,000, Sarah intends to use the second appraisal to determine the character of the gain from the sale of her partnership interest. Is it appropriate for Sarah to ignore the first appraisal when determining her tax liability from the sale of her partnership interest?

Buyer and Partnership Issues

A new investor in a partnership is, of course, concerned with determining how much to pay for the partnership interest. However, a new partner's primary tax concerns are about the outside basis in the partnership interest and that partner's share of the inside basis of the partnership's assets. In general, for a sale transaction, the new investor's outside basis in this interest will be equal to the cost that investor paid for the partnership interest.[12] To the extent that the new investor shares in the partnership liabilities, his share of partnership liabilities increases his outside basis in his interest.

Example 21-6

When Greg Randall acquired Chanzz's 30 percent interest in CCS for $100,000 on June 30, 2022 (see Example 21-1), he guaranteed his share of CCS's liabilities just as Chanzz had done. As a result, Greg will be allocated his share of CCS's allocable liabilities in accordance with his 30 percent profit-sharing ratio. What is the outside basis of Greg's acquired interest?

Answer: $124,000, determined as follows:

Description	Amount	Explanation
(1) Initial tax basis in CSS	$100,000	Cash paid to Chanzz Inc.
(2) Share of CCS's liabilities	24,000	30% × CCS's allocable liabilities of $80,000
Outside basis in CSS	**$124,000**	(1) + (2)

The partnership experiences very few tax consequences when a partner sells their interest.[13] The sale does not generally affect a partnership's **inside basis** in its assets.[14]

[12] §1012. The outside basis in a partnership interest will depend, in part, on how the new investor obtains the interest. For example, a gift generally results in a carryover basis, whereas an inherited interest typically results in a basis equal to the fair market value as of the date of the decedent's death.

[13] Later in the chapter, we discuss situations in which the new investor's share of the partnership's asset bases is adjusted after a sale of a partnership interest under §754. Throughout this section, we assume that the partnership does not have a §754 election in effect.

[14] §743.

The new investor typically "steps into the shoes" of the selling partner to determine their share of the partnership's inside basis of the partnership assets. Consequently, the new investor's share of inside basis is equal to the selling partner's share of inside basis at the sale date. Recall from the preceding chapter that each partner has a tax capital account that reflects the tax basis of property and cash contributed by the partner, the partner's share of profits and losses, and distributions to the partner. In a sale of a partnership interest, the selling partner's tax capital account carries over to the new investor.[15]

Example 21-7

Refer to Example 21-2 for CCS's balance sheet as of June 30, 2022. What is Greg's share of CCS's inside basis in its assets immediately after purchasing Chanzz's 30 percent interest in CCS?

Answer: Greg's share is $105,000: the sum of Chanzz's tax capital account of $81,000 and its share of CCS's liabilities of $24,000. Greg simply steps into Chanzz's place after the acquisition. In Example 21-6, we determined Greg's outside basis in his interest to be $124,000. A sale of a partnership interest often results in a difference between the new investor's inside and outside bases because the outside basis in his interest is the price paid based on fair market value and the inside basis is generally the seller's share of tax basis in the partnership assets.

Varying Interest Rule If a partner's interest in a partnership increases or decreases during the partnership's tax year, the partnership income or loss allocated to the partner for the year must be adjusted to reflect their *varying interest* in the partnership.[16] Partners' interests increase when they contribute property or cash to a partnership[17] or purchase a partnership interest. Conversely, partners' interests decrease when they receive partnership distributions[18] or sell all or a portion of their partnership interests. Upon the sale of a partner's entire interest, the partnership tax year closes for the *selling* partner only. Regulations allow partners to choose between two possible methods for allocating income or loss to partners when their interests change during the year.[19] The first method allows the partnership to prorate income or loss to partners with varying interests, while the second method sanctions an interim closing of the partnership's books.

Example 21-8

CCS had a $60,000 overall business loss for the 2022 calendar year. The issue of how to allocate the 2022 loss between Chanzz Inc. and Greg was easily resolved because CCS's operating agreement specifies the proration method to allocate income or loss when members' interests in CCS change during the year. How much of CCS's 2022 loss will Chanzz be allocated under the proration method?

Answer: Chanzz is allocated a loss of $9,000, which includes its share of CCS's loss but for only one-half the year ($60,000 × 30% share × 6/12 months).[20] On the sale date, Chanzz decreases its outside basis in CCS by the $9,000 loss to determine its adjusted tax basis to use in calculating its gain or loss on the sale of its interest.

[15]An exception occurs when the selling partner contributes to the partnership property with a built-in loss. Only the contributing partner is entitled to that loss [see the Forming and Operating Partnerships chapter and §704(c)(1)(C)]. Therefore, when a new investor buys a partnership interest from a partner that contributed built-in loss property, the new investor reduces the inside basis and tax capital account by the amount of the built-in loss in the contributed property at the contribution date.

[16]§706(d)(1).

[17]If all partners simultaneously contribute property or cash with a value proportionate to their interests, their relative interests will not change.

[18]If all partners receive distributions with a value proportionate to their interests, their relative interests will not change.

[19]Reg. §1.706-1(c).

[20]Reg. §1.706-4(c)(3) requires the calendar-day convention when using the proration method. For the sake of mathematical simplicity, we use number of months here and elsewhere in the chapter when applying the proration method.

Example 21-9

What if: If CCS's overall loss through June 30 was $20,000, how much of the $60,000 overall loss for 2022 will Chanzz and Greg Randall be allocated under an interim closing of the books?

Answer: CCS will allocate $6,000 of loss (30% × $20,000) to Chanzz and $12,000 of loss (30% × $40,000) to Greg.

TAXES IN THE REAL WORLD Changing the Way Companies Dispose of a Business

Corporate takeovers seemed to be the transaction du jour during the 1990s, but many practitioners are predicting joint ventures will be the defining deal currently and in coming years. We regularly see articles in *The Wall Street Journal* describing how firms are starting up joint ventures or strategic alliances—or exiting them. For example, Volvo and Waymo announced in 2020 a $300 million joint venture to develop self-driving cars.

The increase in the number of joint ventures and their possible dissolution or disposition brings an increasing need to understand the partnership tax rules and regulations. More than ever before, corporate tax executives find they must advise senior management on the opportunities and pitfalls of structuring joint ventures and investments as partnerships or LLCs under Subchapter K of the Internal Revenue Code.

BASICS OF PARTNERSHIP DISTRIBUTIONS

LO 21-2

Like shareholders receiving corporate dividend distributions, partners often receive distributions of the partnership profits, known as **operating distributions.** Recall that owners of flow-through entities are taxed currently on their business income regardless of whether the business distributes it. As a result, partners may require cash distributions in order to make quarterly estimated tax payments on their shares of business income. Usually, the general partners (or managing members of LLCs) determine the amount and timing of distributions; however, the partnership (operating) agreement may stipulate some distributions.

Partners may also receive **liquidating distributions.** Because the market for partnership interests is much smaller than for publicly traded stock, partners may have a difficult time finding buyers for their interests. Partnership agreements also often limit purchasers of an interest to the current partner group, to avoid adding an unwanted partner. If the current partner group either cannot or does not want to purchase the interest, the partnership can instead distribute assets to terminate a partner's interest. These liquidating distributions are similar in form to corporate redemptions of a shareholder's stock. They can also terminate the partnership. We first explore the tax consequences of operating distributions and then examine the tax treatment for liquidating distributions.

LO 21-3

Operating Distributions

A distribution from a partnership is an operating distribution when the partners continue their interests afterwards. Operating distributions are usually made to distribute the business profits to the partners but can also reduce a partner's capital interest. The partnership may distribute cash or other assets. Let's look at the tax consequences of distributions of money, and then at the tax consequences of distributing property other than money.

THE KEY FACTS

Operating Distributions

- **Gain or loss recognition:** Partners generally do not recognize gain or loss. One exception occurs when the partnership distributes money only and the amount is greater than the partner's outside basis in their interest.

(continued)

Operating Distributions of Money Only The general rule for operating distributions states that a partnership does not recognize gain or loss on the distribution of property or money.[21,22] Nor do the general tax rules require a partner to recognize gain or loss when receiving distributed property or money.[23] The partner simply reduces the outside basis in the partnership interest by the amount of cash distributed and the inside basis of any property distributed. In general, the partnership's basis in its remaining assets remains unchanged.[24]

Example 21-10

- **Basis of distributed assets:** Partners generally take a carryover basis in distributed assets. If the partnership distribution includes property and the combined inside basis of the distributed property is greater than the partner's outside basis in their interest, the bases of the distributed property will be reduced.
- **Remaining outside basis:** In general, partners reduce outside basis by the amount of money distributed and the inside basis of distributed property.

What if: Suppose CCS makes its first distribution to the owners on December 31, 2023: $250,000 each to Nicole and Greg and $333,333 to Sarah. After taking into account their distributive shares of CCS's income for the year, the owners have the following predistribution bases in their CCS interests:

Owner	Outside Basis
Nicole	$205,000
Sarah	420,000
Greg	334,000

What are the tax consequences (gain or loss and basis in CCS interest) of the distribution to Sarah?

Answer: Sarah does not recognize any gain or loss on the distribution. She reduces her outside basis in her interest from $420,000 to $86,667 ($420,000 – $333,333) after the distribution.

The general rule of no gain is impractical when the partner receives a greater amount of money than their outside basis in their partnership interest. They cannot defer gain to the extent of the excess amount because the outside basis is insufficient for a full reduction. Therefore, the partner reduces their outside basis in their interest to zero[25] and recognizes gain (generally capital) to the extent the amount of money distributed is greater than their outside basis.[26] A partner *never* recognizes a loss from an *operating* distribution.

Example 21-11

What if: Suppose that in the December 31, 2023, distribution Nicole's distribution consists of $250,000 cash. Her outside basis in her CCS interest is $205,000 before the distribution. What are Nicole's gain or loss and basis in her CCS interest after the distribution?

Answer: Nicole has $45,000 capital gain and $0 basis in CCS. Because she receives only money in the distribution, she decreases her outside basis to $0 and must recognize a $45,000 capital gain ($250,000 distribution – $205,000 basis). She recognizes gain because she receives a cash distribution in excess of her outside basis in her CCS interest.

Operating Distributions That Include Property Other Than Money If a partnership makes a distribution that includes property *other than money,* the partners face the problem of determining how much outside basis in their interests to allocate to the

[21]For distribution purposes, money includes cash, deemed cash from reductions in a partner's share of liabilities, and the fair market value of certain marketable securities.

[22]§731(b).

[23]§731.

[24]However, if the partnership has a §754 election in effect or if there is a substantial basis reduction, the partnership basis of its remaining assets must be adjusted following a distribution according to §§734(b) and 755.

[25]§733.

[26]§731(a)(1).

distributed property.[27] Under the general rule, the partner takes a basis in the distributed property equal to the partnership's basis in the property. This is called a **carryover basis.**[28] The tax rules define the order in which to allocate outside basis in a partnership interest to the bases of distributed assets. First, the partner allocates the outside basis in their interest to any money received and then to other property as a carryover basis. The remainder is the partner's outside basis in the partnership interest after the distribution.

Example 21-12

What if: Suppose CCS's December 31, 2023 distribution to Sarah consists of $133,333 cash and investments (other than marketable securities) with a fair market value of $200,000 and an adjusted basis of $115,000. Sarah has a predistribution outside basis in her CCS interest of $420,000. What are the tax consequences (Sarah's gain or loss, basis of distributed assets, outside basis of CCS interest, and CCS's gain or loss) of the distribution?

Answer: Sarah recognizes no gain or loss on the distribution. To determine her bases in the distributed assets, she first allocates $133,333 to the cash and then takes a carryover basis in the investments so her basis in the investments is $115,000. Sarah reduces her outside basis in CCS by $248,333 ($133,333 cash + $115,000 basis of investments). Her outside basis in CCS after the distribution is $171,667 ($420,000 – $248,333). CCS does not recognize any gain or loss on the distribution.

When the partnership distributes property (other than money) with a basis that exceeds the remaining outside basis in the interest (after the allocation to any money also distributed), the partner assigns the remaining outside basis in the interest to the distributed assets,[29] and the partner's outside basis in the interest is reduced to zero.[30] The first allocation of outside basis in the interest goes to money, then to hot assets, and finally to other property.[31] In this case, the partner's basis in the property received in the distribution will be less than the property's basis in the hands of the partnership.

Example 21-13

What if: Suppose Nicole's December 31, 2023, distribution consists of $150,000 cash and investments (other than marketable securities) with a fair market value of $100,000 and an adjusted basis of $90,000 to CCS. Nicole's outside basis in her CCS interest is $205,000 before the distribution. What are Nicole's tax consequences (gain or loss, basis of distributed assets, and outside basis in CCS interest) of the distribution?

Answer: Nicole recognizes no gain or loss and takes a basis of $55,000 in the investments. Her outside basis in CCS is $0, computed as follows:

Description	Amount	Explanation
(1) Nicole's outside basis in CCS	$205,000	
(2) Cash distribution	150,000	
(3) Remaining basis	$ 55,000	(1) – (2); remaining outside basis to be allocated to the distributed investments
(4) Inside basis of investments	90,000	
(5) Basis in investments	55,000	Lesser of (3) or (4)
Nicole's outside basis in CCS	**$ 0**	(3) – (5)

[27]In this context, money includes certain marketable securities [§731(c)(1)(A)]. The special rules in §731(c) for the treatment of distributed marketable securities are beyond the scope of this book.

[28]§732(a).

[29]§732(a)(2).

[30]§733.

[31]If multiple assets are distributed, then the outside basis in a partnership interest will be allocated in accordance with §732(c). We discuss these rules later in conjunction with liquidating distributions.

Because a partner's outside basis in a partnership interest includes their share of the partnership liabilities, the outside basis in a partnership interest must reflect any changes in a partner's share of partnership liabilities resulting from a distribution. In essence, a partner treats a reduction of their share of liabilities as a distribution of cash.[32] If the partner increases their share of liabilities, the increase is treated as a cash contribution to the partnership.

Example 21-14

What if: Suppose Greg receives land held for investment with a fair market value of $250,000 (inside basis is $140,000) as his distribution from CCS on December 31, 2023. He agrees to assume the $120,000 mortgage on the land after the distribution. His outside basis in his CCS interest is $334,000 before considering the distribution. What are the tax consequences (gain or loss, basis of distributed assets, and outside basis in his CCS interest) of the distribution to Greg?

Answer: Greg does not recognize any gain or loss on the distribution. His basis in the land is $140,000 and his post-distribution outside basis in CCS is $278,000, determined as follows:

Description	Amount	Explanation
(1) Greg's predistribution outside basis	$ 334,000	
(2) Mortgage assumed by Greg	120,000	
(3) Greg's predistribution share of mortgage	36,000	(2) × 30% ownership
(4) Deemed cash contribution from debt assumption	$ 84,000	(2) – (3)
(5) Greg's outside basis in CCS after debt changes	418,000	(1) + (4)
(6) Greg's basis in distributed land	140,000	Carryover basis from CCS
Greg's post-distribution outside basis in CCS	**$278,000**	(5) – (6)

Greg must first consider the effects of changes in debt before determining the effects of the distribution. The tax rules treat him as making a net contribution of $84,000 cash to the partnership, the difference between the full mortgage he assumes and his predistribution share of the debt. Greg then allocates $140,000 of his outside basis in his CCS interest to the land and reduces his outside basis in CCS accordingly.

LO 21-4

Liquidating Distributions

In contrast to an operating distribution in which the partners retain a continuing interest in the partnership after the distribution, a liquidating distribution terminates a partner's interest in the partnership. Like operating distributions, a liquidating distribution can be made to just one partner or to multiple partners simultaneously. For example, if outside investors or current partners do not have sufficient cash or inclination to purchase a partner's interest, the partnership agreement often allows a partner wishing to cash out to receive a liquidating distribution from the partnership in lieu of selling the interest. On the other end of the spectrum, all the partners may agree at some point to end the partnership, because they have lost interest in continuing it or because it has not been profitable. In such cases, the partnership may distribute all its assets to the partners in a complete liquidation of the partnership. Once a partnership has been terminated in this manner, it must file a final return covering the period from the beginning of its tax year through the date of termination. Subsequently, it no longer has any tax filing obligations. A partnership termination is analogous to a complete corporate liquidation (discussed in the Corporate Formation, Reorganization, and Liquidation chapter).

The tax issues related to partnership liquidating distributions are basically twofold: (1) to determine whether the partner receiving the distribution recognizes gain or loss and (2) to allocate the partner's outside basis in their interest to the assets received in the liquidating distribution. The rationale behind the rules for liquidating distributions is simply to have the partner's outside basis in their interest carry over to the assets received by the partner. In some instances, the partner receiving the distribution will not recognize gain or loss on the distribution, and the tax basis in the distributed assets will be the same in

[32]§752(b).

the partner's hands as they were inside the partnership. Unfortunately, this simple outcome rarely occurs. Thus, the rules in this area stipulate when gain or loss must be recognized by partners receiving such distributions and describe how they must allocate their outside basis in their interests to the distributed assets received.

Gain or Loss Recognition in Liquidating Distributions In general, neither partnerships nor partners recognize gain or loss from liquidating distributions. However, there are exceptions. For example, when a terminated partner receives more money in the distribution than their outside basis in the interest, they will recognize gain.[33] See Example 21-11 for an illustration in the context of operating distributions.

In contrast to operating distributions, a partner may recognize a *loss* from a liquidating distribution, but only when two conditions are met: (1) The distribution includes only cash, unrealized receivables, and/or inventory *and* (2) the partner's outside basis in their partnership interest is greater than the sum of the *inside bases* of the distributed assets.[34] The loss on the distribution is a capital loss to the partner.

Commonly, the terminated partner's share of partnership debt decreases after a liquidating distribution. Any reduction in the partner's share of liabilities is considered a distribution of money to the partner and reduces the partner's outside basis in their interest available for allocation of basis to other assets, including inventory and unrealized receivables.

Example 21-15

What if: Suppose on December 31, 2023, CCS liquidates Greg's interest in the LLC by distributing to him cash of $206,000 and inventory with a fair market value of $103,000 (adjusted basis is $43,000). Greg's share of CCS's liabilities as of the liquidation is $66,000. On December 31, 2023, Greg's outside basis in CCS is $334,000, including his share of CCS's liabilities. What is Greg's gain or loss on the liquidation of his CCS interest?

Answer: Greg recognizes a capital loss of $19,000 from the liquidating distribution, computed as follows:

Description	Amount	Explanation
(1) Outside basis in CCS before distribution	$334,000	
(2) Debt relief	66,000	Deemed cash distribution
(3) Outside basis in CCS after considering debt relief	$268,000	(1) – (2)
(4) Basis of property distributed (cash + inventory)	249,000	($206,000 + $43,000)
Gain (loss) on distribution	**$(19,000)**	(4) – (3)

Greg recognizes a loss because he meets the two necessary conditions: (1) He receives only cash and inventory in the distribution *and* (2) the sum of the adjusted inside bases of the distributed assets is less than his outside basis in his CCS interest ($249,000 inside basis in assets versus $268,000 CCS outside basis after deemed cash distribution).

THE KEY FACTS

Gain or Loss Recognition in Liquidating Distributions

- **Generally:** Partners and partnerships do not recognize gain or loss.
- **Exceptions:**
  - **Gain:** Partner recognizes gain when partnership distributes money and the amount exceeds the partner's outside basis in the partnership interest.
  - **Loss:** Partner recognizes loss when two conditions are met: (1) Distribution consists of only cash and hot assets and (2) the partner's outside basis in the partnership interest exceeds the sum of the bases of the distributed assets.

Basis in Distributed Property A key theme of the partnership tax rules is the idea that the partnership acts merely as a conduit for the partners' business activities. Thus, the rules attempt to keep the basis of the assets the same regardless of whether the partner or the partnership has possession of them. Moving assets in and out of the partnership should therefore have few meaningful tax consequences. The primary objective of the basis rules in liquidating distributions is to allocate the partner's entire outside basis in the partnership interest to the assets the partner receives in the liquidating distribution. The allocation essentially depends on two things: (1) the partnership's bases in distributed assets relative to the partner's outside basis in the interest and (2) the type of property distributed—whether it is money, hot assets, or other property. For purposes of distributions, hot assets include unrealized receivables (including potential depreciation recapture) and inventory, as we've defined above. We discuss each of the possible scenarios in Exhibit 21-1 in turn.

[33]These rules are very similar to those for operating distributions. When a partner receives money only in complete termination of the partnership interest, any gain on distribution cannot be deferred through a basis adjustment. Therefore, the partner recognizes the gain.

[34]§731(a)(2).

EXHIBIT 21-1 Alternative Scenarios for Determining Basis in Distributed Property

Type of Property Distributed	Partner's Outside Basis Is *Greater* Than Inside Bases of Distributed Assets	Partner's Outside Basis Is *Less* Than Inside Bases of Distributed Assets
Money only	Scenario 1	Scenario 3
Money and hot assets	Scenario 1	Scenario 4
Other property included in distribution[35]	Scenario 2	Scenario 5

Partner's Outside Basis in an Interest Is Greater Than Inside Bases of Distributed Assets

Scenario 1: Distributions of money, inventory, and/or unrealized receivables. If the partnership distributes only money, inventory, and/or unrealized receivables (ordinary income property) and the partner's outside basis in the interest is greater than the sum of the inside bases of the distributed assets, the partner recognizes a capital loss.[36] The partner assigns a basis to the distributed assets equal to the partnership's inside basis in the assets, and the remaining outside basis in the interest is equal to the recognized loss.[37]

Example 21-16

What if: Suppose Greg has an outside basis in CCS of $334,000, including his share of liabilities of $66,000. In a liquidating distribution, he receives $159,000 cash and inventory with a fair market value and basis of $49,000. Will Greg recognize a gain or loss? Explain.

Answer: Greg will recognize a capital loss of $60,000 on the liquidation, computed as follows:

Description	Amount	Explanation
(1) Outside basis in CCS before distribution	$ 334,000	
(2) Debt relief	66,000	Deemed cash distribution
(3) Outside basis after considering debt relief	$ 268,000	(1) – (2)
(4) Basis of property distributed (cash + inventory)	208,000	($159,000 + $49,000)
Gain (loss) on distribution	**$ (60,000)**	(4) – (3)

In this case, Greg is unable to defer his loss without changing its character. Greg clearly cannot adjust the basis in the cash to defer the loss. *If* he were able to increase his basis in the distributed inventory, he could defer the loss. However, this would produce an ordinary loss of $60,000 when Greg sells the inventory.[38] Greg must recognize a $60,000 capital loss when he receives the liquidating distribution. This requirement ensures Greg does not convert a capital loss into an ordinary loss.

Scenario 2: Other property included in distributions. This scenario is similar to the first scenario except that property other than money, inventory, and unrealized receivables is also distributed. Recall that when other property is also distributed, the liquidating partner must allocate all the outside basis in that partner's interest to the distributed assets. We determined in Scenario 1 that when the partnership distributes only money and/or hot

[35]This category includes distributions that include other property in addition to or instead of either money or unrealized receivables or inventory. For example, the distributions in this category can include any combination of money, unrealized receivables, and inventory as long as other property is also distributed.

[36]§731(a)(2).

[37]§§732(c)(1), 731(a)(2). To prevent a partner from converting a capital loss from their investment into an ordinary loss, the tax law prohibits increasing their basis in unrealized receivables and inventory and requires the partner to recognize a capital loss.

[38]If the inventory distributed to Greg is also considered inventory in his hands, the eventual sale of the inventory will generate ordinary income. If the inventory is a capital asset to Greg, a sale of the asset within five years of the distribution will generate ordinary income. After five years, the gain or loss will be capital.

assets and the total inside basis of the distributed assets is less than the partner's outside basis in their interest, it is impossible to allocate the entire outside basis to the distributed assets without changing the character of a resulting loss. Thus, a partner never increases the bases of distributed hot assets. However, when the partnership distributes other property, in addition to money and/or hot assets, the partner can adjust the basis of the *other* property without converting ordinary gains to capital, and the liquidating partner will not currently recognize any gain or loss from the distribution.

Example 21-17

What if: Suppose CCS has no liabilities or hot assets and distributes $50,000 in cash and land with a fair market value of $160,000 and a basis of $20,000 to Greg in complete liquidation of his CCS interest. Greg has an outside basis in CCS of $268,000 prior to the distribution. What is Greg's recognized gain or loss on the distribution?

Answer: Greg does not recognize any gain or loss. He receives money and other property with a total basis of $70,000, which is less than his outside basis of $268,000. Greg first reduces his outside basis by the amount of money he receives, and he assigns his remaining outside basis to the land as follows:

Description	Amount	Explanation
(1) Outside basis in CCS before distribution	$268,000	
(2) Basis allocated to money distributed	50,000	
Remaining outside basis assigned to land	$218,000	(1) – (2)

Note that Greg increases the basis of the other property received in liquidation (land) from $20,000 to $218,000 in order to allocate his entire outside basis to the distributed assets. If Greg holds the distributed land as a personal use asset, he may never be able to receive a tax benefit for the basis increase.

Example 21-17 illustrates the required basis increase in a very simple situation. In reality, liquidating distributions may include several types of assets. In these situations, to allocate the outside basis in a partnership interest to the distributed assets, the partner implements the following, more detailed process:[39]

Step 1: The partner first determines their outside basis net of any debt relief, and then allocates that amount to any money, inventory, and unrealized receivables equal to the partnership's basis in these assets. The partner also assigns a basis to the other distributed property in an amount equal to the partnership's basis in those assets.

Step 2: The partner then allocates the remaining outside basis (full outside basis less the amounts assigned in Step 1) to the other distributed property that has unrealized appreciation to the extent of that appreciation. Thus, if an asset has an adjusted basis to the partnership of $500 and a fair market value of $700, the partner will allocate the first $200 of remaining basis to that asset.[40]

Step 3: The partner allocates any remaining basis to all other property in proportion to the relative *fair market values* of the other property.

$$\text{Basis allocation} = \text{Remaining basis} \times \frac{\text{FMV}_{\text{asset}}}{\text{Sum of FMV}_{\text{distributed other property}}}$$

[39]§732(c)(2).

[40]If the remaining outside basis in a partnership interest is insufficient to allocate the full amount of appreciation to the distributed assets in this step, then the partner will allocate the remaining basis in this step to the appreciated assets based on their relative appreciation.

Example 21-18

What if: Suppose CCS makes the following distribution to Greg in liquidation of his CCS interest:

Asset	CCS Tax Basis	Fair Market Value
Cash	$181,000	$181,000
Inventory	43,000	103,000
Investment A	5,000	12,000
Investment B	10,000	13,000

Greg's basis in his CCS interest as of the liquidation is $334,000, including his $66,000 share of CCS's liabilities. What is Greg's recognized gain or loss on the distribution? What are Greg's bases in the distributed assets following the liquidation?

Answer: Greg recognizes no gain or loss on the distribution. Greg's bases in the distributed assets are:

Cash	$181,000
Inventory	43,000
Investment A	21,120
Investment B	22,880
Total	$268,000

Because Greg receives other property in the distribution and the distributed asset bases are less than Greg's outside basis in CCS (Scenario 2), he will allocate his outside basis in CCS as follows:

First, Greg determines his allocable basis:

Description	Amount	Explanation
(1) Basis in CCS before distribution	$334,000	
(2) Debt relief	66,000	Greg's 30% share of CCS's liabilities
Allocable basis	$268,000	(1) – (2)

Next, Greg allocates his remaining outside basis in CCS of $268,000 to the distributed assets by following the allocation process.

Description	Amount	Explanation
Step 1:		
(1) Allocable basis	$268,000	See above
(2) Basis assigned to cash	181,000	
(3) Basis assigned to inventory	43,000	
(4) Initial basis assigned to Investment A	5,000	
(5) Initial basis assigned to Investment B	10,000	
(6) Required basis increase	$ 29,000	(1) – (2) – (3) – (4) – (5) Initial assignment of basis is less than Greg's allocable CCS basis
Step 2:		
(7) Additional basis assigned to Investment A	$ 7,000	Unrealized appreciation on Investment A (FMV of $12,000 less basis of $5,000)
(8) Additional basis assigned to Investment B	3,000	Unrealized appreciation on Investment B (FMV of $13,000 less basis of $10,000)
(9) Remaining required basis increase after Step 2	$ 19,000	(6) – (7) – (8)

Step 3:

In Step 3, Greg allocates the required remaining basis increase to the distributed investments based on their relative fair market values using:

$$\textbf{Basis allocation} = \textbf{Remaining basis} \times \frac{\textbf{FMV}_{\textbf{asset}}}{\textbf{Sum of FMV}_{\textbf{distributed other property}}}$$

(10) Additional basis allocated to other property: Investment A	\$9,120	Basis allocation = \$19,000 × (\$12,000/\$25,000) = \$9,120
(11) Additional basis allocated to other property: Investment B	\$9,880	Basis allocation = \$19,000 × (\$13,000/\$25,000) = \$9,880

Thus, Greg's bases in the investments are \$21,120 (Investment A) and \$22,880 (Investment B):

Description	Inv. A	Explanation	Inv. B	Explanation
(12) Initial basis assignment	\$ 5,000	From (4) above	\$ 10,000	From (5) above
(13) Basis assigned in Step 2	7,000	From (7) above	3,000	From (8) above
(14) Basis assigned in Step 3	9,120	From (10) above	9,880	From (11) above
Greg's bases in investments	**\$21,120**	(12) + (13) + (14)	**\$22,880**	(12) + (13) + (14)

Partner's Outside Basis in an Interest Is Less Than Inside Bases of Distributed Assets

Scenario 3: Distributions of money only. A partner recognizes a gain (generally capital) if the partnership distributes money (only) that exceeds the partner's outside basis in their interest. Example 21-11 illustrates the tax consequences for this scenario in the context of an operating distribution.

Scenario 4: Distributions of money, inventory, and/or unrealized receivables. In liquidating distributions when the partner's outside basis in their interest is less than the inside bases of the distributed assets and the partnership distributes money and property other than money, the partner reduces the basis in the noncash property distributed but does not recognize gain or loss. This basis reduction may apply to hot assets as well as other property because the tax law does not restrict *reducing* the basis of ordinary income assets. However, the tax law does prescribe a particular sequence for the required reductions.

If the partnership distributes only money, inventory, and unrealized receivables, the partner reduces the basis of the hot assets distributed, assuming money doesn't exceed basis. The required decrease in the basis of the distributed assets is equal to the difference between the partner's outside basis in their interest and the partnership's inside basis in the distributed assets. The partner first assigns basis to money and then to other assets received in an amount equal to the assets' inside bases. Then the partner allocates the required *decrease* to the assets with unrealized depreciation, to reduce or eliminate any existing losses built into the distributed assets.[41] Finally, the partner allocates any remaining required decrease to the distributed assets in proportion to their *adjusted bases* (AB), after considering the preceding steps and using the following equation:

$$\text{Basis allocation} = \text{Required decrease} \times \frac{\text{AB}_{\text{asset}}}{\text{Sum of AB}_{\text{distributed assets}}}$$

[41]If the required decrease is insufficient to allocate the full amount of depreciation to the distributed assets in this step, then the partner will allocate the remaining required decrease in this step to the depreciated assets based on their relative unrealized depreciation.

Example 21-19

What if: Suppose CCS makes the following distribution to Greg in liquidation of his CCS interest:

Asset	CCS Tax Basis	Fair Market Value
Cash	$256,000	$256,000
Inventory A	50,000	129,000
Inventory B	25,000	6,000
Total	$331,000	

Greg's basis in his CCS interest as of the liquidation is $334,000, including his $66,000 share of CCS's liabilities. What is Greg's recognized gain or loss on the distribution? What is Greg's basis in the distributed assets following the liquidation?

Answer: Greg does not recognize any gain or loss. His basis in the cash is $256,000; his basis in Inventory A is $10,714; and his basis in Inventory B is $1,286, computed as follows:

First, Greg reduces his outside basis in CCS by his $66,000 debt relief, such that his outside basis allocable to distributed assets is $268,000 ($334,000 − $66,000). He must allocate this remaining basis to the distributed assets using the following steps:

Description	Amount	Explanation
Step 1:		
(1) Allocable basis	$268,000	Basis in CCS of $334,000 − debt relief of $66,000
(2) Basis assigned to cash	256,000	
(3) Initial basis assigned to Inventory A	50,000	
(4) Initial basis assigned to Inventory B	25,000	
(5) Required basis decrease	$ (63,000)	(1) − (2) − (3) − (4): Initial assignment of basis exceeds Greg's allocable CCS basis
Step 2:		
(6) Required decrease to Inventory B	(19,000)	Unrealized depreciation on Inventory B (FMV of $6,000 less basis of $25,000)
(7) Remaining required basis decrease	$ (44,000)	(5) − (6)
(8) Interim adjusted basis of Inventory B	6,000	(4) + (6)

Step 3:

In Step 3, Greg decreases the basis of the inventory in proportion to their relative adjusted bases determined in Step 2 using the following allocation:

$$\textbf{Basis allocation} = \textbf{Required decrease} \times \frac{\textbf{AB}_{\textbf{asset}}}{\textbf{Sum of AB}_{\textbf{distributed assets}}}$$

(9) Required decrease to Inventory A	$(39,286)	Basis reduction = $(44,000) × ($50,000/$56,000)
(10) Required decrease to Inventory B	(4,714)	Basis reduction = $(44,000) × ($6,000/$56,000)
Final basis of Inventory A	**$10,714**	(3) + (9)
Final basis of Inventory B	**$ 1,286**	(8) + (10)

Example 21-20

What if: Suppose CCS makes the following distribution to Greg in liquidation of his CCS interest:

Asset	CCS Tax Basis	Fair Market Value
Cash	$242,000	$242,000
Accounts receivable	0	12,000
Inventory	72,000	120,000
Total	$314,000	

Greg's basis in his CCS interest as of the liquidation is $334,000, including his $66,000 share of CCS's liabilities. What is Greg's recognized gain or loss on the distribution? What is Greg's basis in the assets he receives in the liquidating distribution?

Answer: Greg does not recognize any gain or loss on the liquidation. His asset bases are:

Cash	$242,000
Accounts receivable	0
Inventory	26,000
Total	$268,000

Greg computes the basis as follows:

As a preliminary step to the allocation, he reduces his outside basis in CCS by his $66,000 debt relief, leaving an allocable outside basis of $268,000 ($334,000 − $66,000). He allocates this basis to the distributed assets using the following steps:

Description	Amount	Explanation
Step 1:		
(1) Allocable basis	$268,000	Basis in CCS of $334,000 − debt relief of $66,000
(2) Basis assigned to cash	242,000	
(3) Initial basis assigned to accounts receivable	0	
(4) Initial basis assigned to inventory	72,000	
(5) Required basis decrease	$ (46,000)	(1) − (2) − (3) − (4): Initial assignment of basis exceeds Greg's allocable CCS basis

Step 2: N/A because no assets have unrealized depreciation.

Step 3: In Step 3, Greg decreases the basis of the accounts receivable and inventory in proportion to their relative adjusted bases using the following reduction:

$$\textbf{Basis allocation} = \textbf{Required decrease} \times \frac{\mathbf{AB}_{\text{asset}}}{\textbf{Sum of } \mathbf{AB}_{\text{distributed assets}}}$$

Description	Amount	Explanation
(6) Required basis decrease to accounts receivable	$ 0	Basis reduction = $(46,000) × ($0/$72,000)
(7) Required basis decrease to inventory	(46,000)	Basis reduction = $(46,000) × ($72,000/$72,000)
Final basis of accounts receivable	0	(3) + (6)
Final basis of inventory	**$26,000**	(4) + (7)

Note that in this scenario, the tax rules recharacterize a portion ($46,000) of Greg's ultimate gain from capital gain to ordinary income. The sum of the bases of the distributed assets ($314,000) exceeds Greg's allocable outside basis in CCS ($268,000) by $46,000. Absent the allocation rules illustrated in Example 21-20, this would have been a capital gain to Greg. Instead, as we discuss below, the basis decrease to the hot assets will cause Greg to recognize any gain as ordinary upon sale of these assets.

Scenario 5: Other property included in distributions. Our final scenario is similar to Scenario 4 except the partnership distributes other property in addition to or instead of money and/or inventory and unrealized receivables. The terminating partner does not recognize gain or loss; rather, the partner first decreases the basis in the other property distributed before decreasing the basis in any distributed hot assets. The process for assigning basis to the distributed assets is similar to the method we described above, although the required basis decrease is applied first to other property before reducing the basis of any hot assets.[42] The procedure for determining the basis adjustment to other property is as follows:

Step 1: The partner first determines the outside basis in their interest net of any debt relief and then allocates that amount to any money, inventory, and unrealized receivables equal to the partnership's basis in these assets. The partner also assigns a basis to any other property equal to the partnership's basis in the other property distributed.

Step 2: The partner then allocates the required decrease (outside basis less partnership adjusted basis in distributed assets) to the other property that has unrealized depreciation to the extent of that depreciation to eliminate inherent losses. Thus, if an asset has an adjusted basis to the partnership of $700 and a fair market value of $600, the asset's basis is first reduced by $100 (unrealized depreciation).

Step 3: If any required decrease remains after accounting for the inherent losses in the distributed assets, the partner then allocates it to all other property in proportion to their *adjusted bases*. The adjusted bases used in this step are the bases from Step 2. We can determine the allocation as follows:

$$\text{Basis reduction} = \text{Required decrease} \times \frac{AB_{\text{asset}}}{\text{Sum of } AB_{\text{all distributed other property}}}$$

Example 21-21

What if: Suppose CCS makes the following distribution to Greg in liquidation of his CCS interest:

Asset	CCS Tax Basis	Fair Market Value
Cash	$187,000	$187,000
Inventory	70,000	162,000
Investment A	10,000	7,000
Investment B	10,000	18,000
Total	$277,000	

Greg's basis in his CCS interest as of the liquidation is $334,000, including his $66,000 share of CCS's liabilities. What is Greg's recognized gain or loss on the distribution? What is Greg's basis in the distributed assets following the liquidation?

[42] §732(c)(3).

Answer: Greg does not recognize any gain or loss. His asset bases are as follows:

Cash	$187,000
Inventory	70,000
Investment A	4,530
Investment B	6,470
Total	$268,000

Greg's basis in these assets is determined as follows:

Greg first determines his allocable basis of $268,000 by reducing his CCS basis ($334,000) for the deemed cash distribution relating to his $66,000 share of the reduction in CCS's debt.

Description	Amount	Explanation
Step 1:		
(1) Allocable basis	$268,000	Basis in CCS of $334,000 – debt relief of $66,000
(2) Basis assigned to cash	187,000	
(3) Initial basis assigned to Inventory	70,000	
(4) Initial basis assigned to Investment A	10,000	
(5) Initial basis assigned to Investment B	10,000	
(6) Required basis decrease	$ (9,000)	(1) – (2) – (3) – (4) – (5): Initial assignment of basis exceeds Greg's allocable CCS basis
Step 2:		
(7) Required basis decrease to Investment A	$ (3,000)	Unrealized depreciation on Investment A (FMV of $7,000 less basis of $10,000)
(8) Remaining required basis decrease	(6,000)	(6) – (7)
(9) Interim basis of Investment A	7,000	(4) + (7)

Step 3: In Step 3, Greg decreases the basis of the other property (Investments A and B) in proportion to their relative adjusted bases (after Step 2) using the following allocation:

$$\textbf{Basis reduction} = \textbf{Required decrease} \times \frac{\textbf{AB}_{\textbf{asset}}}{\textbf{Sum of AB}_{\textbf{all distributed other property}}}$$

(10) Required basis decrease to Investment A	$ (2,470)	Basis reduction = $(6,000) × ($7,000/$17,000)
(11) Required basis decrease to Investment B	(3,530)	Basis reduction = $(6,000) × ($10,000/$17,000)
Final basis of Investment A	**$ 4,530**	(9) + (10)
Final basis of Investment B	**$ 6,470**	(5) + (11)

Character and Holding Period of Distributed Assets For both operating and liquidating distributions, the character of distributed assets in the hands of the partner may stay the same as it was in the partnership in order to reduce the opportunity for converting ordinary income into capital gain with such distributions. Thus, if a partner sells certain assets with ordinary character after the distribution, the partner will recognize ordinary income from the sale.[43] These assets include §751(d) inventory and §751(c) unrealized receivables. For inventory items, the ordinary income "taint" will remain for five years after the distribution. For unrealized receivables, a subsequent sale at any time after the distribution will result in ordinary income. The reverse is not true, however. If a partnership distributes a capital asset that would be characterized as inventory in the hands of the terminating partner, the partner will have ordinary income from an eventual sale, not capital gain or loss. To ensure the character of any distributed long-term capital gain property retains its character to the partner, the partner's holding period generally includes the partnership's holding period.[44]

Example 21-22

Greg has decided to cash out his investment in CCS in order to invest in another project in which he can more actively participate. After speaking with Nicole and Sarah about different options, the three owners decide Greg can cash out using one of two options.

Option 1: CCS will liquidate Greg's interest by distributing cash of $242,000, accounts receivable worth $12,000 (adjusted basis is $0), and inventory worth $120,000 (adjusted basis is $72,000).

Option 2: Nicole and Sarah will purchase Greg's interest in CCS. Nicole agrees to purchase two-thirds of Greg's interest for $249,333 cash and Sarah agrees to purchase the remaining one-third for $124,667 cash.

Greg's basis in his 30 percent CCS interest is $334,000, including his share of CCS's liabilities of $66,000. Either event would occur on December 31, 2023, when CCS's balance sheet is as follows:

Color Comfort Sheets LLC
December 31, 2023

	Tax Basis	FMV
Assets		
Cash	$390,000	$ 390,000
Accounts receivable	0	40,000
Inventory	90,000	200,000
Investments	60,000	105,000
Equipment (cost = $200,000)	150,000	200,000
Building (cost = $100,000)	90,000	100,000
Land—original	20,000	160,000
Land—investment	140,000	270,000
Totals	$940,000	$1,465,000
Liabilities and capital		
Accounts payable	$ 80,000	
Long-term debt	0	
Mortgage on original land	40,000	
Mortgage on investment land	120,000	
Capital—Nicole	119,000	
—Sarah	332,000	
—Greg	249,000	
Totals	$940,000	

[43]§735(a).

[44]§735(b).

What are the tax consequences (amount and character of recognized gain or loss, basis in assets) for Greg under each option?

Answer: *Option 1:* Greg recognizes no gain or loss on the liquidating distribution. His bases in the distributed assets are:

Cash	$242,000
Accounts receivable	0
Inventory	26,000
Total	$268,000

Option 2: Greg recognizes ordinary income of $60,000 and a long-term capital gain of $46,000.

The tax consequences of both options are determined as follows:

Option 1: The distribution allows Greg to defer recognizing any gain or loss on the liquidation. Example 21-20 provides the details of the analysis. Greg has debt relief in an amount equal to his $66,000 share of CCS's liabilities. The debt relief is treated as a distribution of cash, so Greg reduces his outside basis in CCS by this amount from $334,000 to $268,000. The difference between the $314,000 sum of the inside bases of the distributed cash and inventory ($242,000 + $72,000) and his outside basis is $46,000 ($314,000 – $268,000) and represents a required *decrease* to the bases of assets distributed in liquidation. Greg follows the prescribed method illustrated in Example 21-20 to compute his asset bases (i.e., the accounts receivable will have a basis equal to zero and the inventory basis will be reduced by $46,000 from $72,000 to $26,000).

The basis reduction for these assets allows Greg to defer recognizing a $46,000 gain on the liquidation. The cost to accomplish the deferral is that if Greg sells the inventory and the accounts receivable immediately after the distribution, he will recognize ordinary income of $106,000, as follows:

Amount realized:		
Cash (equal to FMV of accounts receivable and inventory)	$ 12,000	
	120,000	$132,000
Less: Adjusted basis		
Accounts receivable	0	
Inventory	26,000	26,000
Ordinary income		$106,000

The $106,000 ordinary income is $46,000 greater than the inherent gain on these assets of $60,000 ($132,000 – $72,000) had the partnership sold the assets. If Greg selects Option 1, he will not recognize income on the liquidation until he sells the inventory and collects (or sells) the accounts receivable, thereby leaving himself flexibility on the timing of gain recognition.

Option 2: In this option, Greg sells his CCS interest to Nicole and Sarah and receives cash of $374,000 ($249,333 from Nicole and $124,667 from Sarah). Greg computes his total gain or loss as follows:

Amount realized:		
Cash	$374,000	
Debt relief	66,000	$440,000
Less: Basis in CCS interest		334,000
Realized and recognized gain		$106,000

Next, Greg determines the character of the gain from the sale by first identifying the gain related to hot assets.

Hot Asset—CCS	(1) Basis	(2) FMV	(3) Gain/Loss (2) – (1)	Greg's Share 30% × (3)
Accounts receivable	$ 0	$ 40,000	$ 40,000	$12,000
Inventory	90,000	200,000	110,000	33,000
Equipment	150,000	200,000	50,000	15,000
Total ordinary income				$60,000

(continued on page 21-24)

The final step for Greg is to determine the capital gain or loss by subtracting the ordinary portion from the total gain.

Total gain	$106,000
Less: ordinary income from §751(a)	(60,000)
Capital gain	$ 46,000

If he chooses Option 2, Greg will recognize $60,000 of ordinary income and $46,000 of capital gain in 2024.

Example 21-23

Given the tax consequences to Greg in the previous example, should he have CCS liquidate his interest (Option 1) or should he sell his interest (Option 2)?

Answer: Under Option 1 (the liquidation), Greg is able to defer all recognition of gain until he later sells the distributed assets. This provides him flexibility as to when he pays tax on the liquidating distribution. However, when he recognizes any income upon subsequent sales, the character of the income will be ordinary and taxed at ordinary rates. Under Option 2, Greg must recognize income immediately upon the sale: $60,000 of ordinary income and $46,000 of long-term capital gain. He has no future tax liability related to the liquidating distribution. The capital gain could be taxed at a rate as high as 23.8 percent (including the 3.8% net investment income tax). An additional consideration is that under Option 2 Greg receives cash, rather than a mix of cash and other assets. If he wants to immediately invest the proceeds in another venture, he may prefer a pure cash payment.

(continued from page 21-1 . . .)
Greg takes the liquidating distribution option (Option 1) offered by CCS to avoid recognizing a gain currently. Although this option doesn't give him as much cash as a sale would have, Greg figures it is enough for another investment and he can avoid paying tax on the distribution this year.

For the first time, CCS has only two owners—Nicole and Sarah. After liquidating Greg's interest, Nicole's interest has increased to 43 percent and Sarah's to 57 percent. Both women are happy with that outcome, although they are sorry to lose Greg's investment in the business. ■

LO 21-5

DISPROPORTIONATE DISTRIBUTIONS

Up to this point in the chapter, our distribution examples have either assumed or represented that each partner received a pro rata share of the partnership's unrealized appreciation in its ordinary assets, as specified in the partnership agreement based on the partner's capital interests. In practice, distributions may not always reflect each partner's proportionate share of the appreciation in hot assets.[45] Both operating and liquidating distributions can be **disproportionate distributions.** Without going into all the details of these complex rules, let's briefly discuss the implications of distributions in which partners receive either more or less than their share of the unrealized appreciation or losses in so-called hot assets [assets defined in §751(b) as **substantially appreciated inventory** and

[45]A thorough discussion of these issues is beyond the scope of this chapter. Therefore, we will abbreviate our discussion just to give a flavor for the issues and consequences of these disproportionate distributions.

unrealized receivables].[46] Note that the definition of hot assets for purposes of disproportionate distributions includes only *substantially appreciated* inventory, not *all* inventory [as is the case under §751(a), the definition we used to characterize the gain in dispositions of partnership interests]. Inventory is considered substantially appreciated if its fair market value is greater than 120 percent of its basis.

Suppose a partner receives less than their share of the appreciation in hot assets in a liquidating distribution. This may occur, for example, if a partner receives only cash in a liquidating distribution from a partnership with hot assets. Rather than only applying the rules we discussed above, the partner must treat part of the distribution as a sale or exchange.[47] Basically, the disproportionate distribution rules treat the partner as having sold their share of hot assets to the partnership in exchange for "cold" [non-§751(b)] assets. This deemed sale generates an ordinary gain or loss to the partner on the deemed sale, essentially equal to their share of the appreciation or depreciation in the portion of hot assets not distributed to them. From the partnership's perspective, the partnership is deemed to have purchased the hot assets from the partner in exchange for the distributed cold assets. Therefore, the *partnership* recognizes a capital or §1231 gain or loss equal to the remaining partners' inherent gain or loss in the distributed cold assets. The effects are reversed if a partner receives more than their share of the appreciation in a partnership's hot assets when the partner receives all or predominately hot assets in a distribution.[48] The rules are meant to ensure that partners cannot convert ordinary income into capital gain through distributions. Thus, they require that partners will ultimately recognize their share of the partnership ordinary income regardless of the form of their distributions.

THE KEY FACTS

Disproportionate Distributions

- **When?**
  When a distribution changes a partner's relative share of unrealized appreciation or losses in a partnership's hot assets.
- **Why?**
  To prevent partners from converting ordinary income into capital gains through distributions.
- **How?**
  Partner and partnership must treat part of the distribution as a sale or exchange, which may change the character and timing of income or losses that are recognized.

Example 21-24

What if: Suppose CCS distributes $328,000 in cash to Greg Randall on December 31, 2023, in complete liquidation of Greg's 30 percent interest in CCS. Greg's basis in his CCS interest before the distribution is $334,000. Assume CCS's balance sheet is as follows:

Color Comfort Sheets LLC
December 31, 2023

	Tax Basis	FMV
Assets		
Cash	$700,000	$ 700,000
Inventory	240,000	440,000
Totals	$940,000	$1,140,000
Liabilities and capital		
Liabilities	$240,000	
Capital—Nicole	119,000	
—Sarah	332,000	
—Greg	249,000	
Totals	$940,000	

(continued on page 21-26)

[46]Unrealized receivables include the accounts receivable of a cash-method taxpayer, the excess of the fair market value over basis of accounts receivable for accrual-method taxpayers, and depreciation recapture. The definition of substantially appreciated inventory is broader than simply goods primarily held for sale to customers. It also includes property that would not be classified as capital assets or §1231 assets if sold by the partnership. As a result, receivables are included as "inventory."

[47]§751(b).

[48]The partner would generally recognize capital gain on the deemed sale and the partnership would recognize ordinary income.

Is this distribution disproportionate? What are the implications of the distribution?

Answer: The CCS balance sheet as of December 31, 2023, indicates that CCS's inventory is a hot asset given that its fair market value is more than 120 percent of its basis ($440,000/$240,000 = 183.33%). Further, the CCS balance sheet indicates that the fair market value of Greg's share of the unrealized appreciation in CCS's hot assets for purposes of disproportionate distributions [§751(b)] is $60,000, or 30 percent of the $200,000 unrealized appreciation in inventory ($440,000 FMV – $240,000 adjusted basis). Because Greg receives only cash in the distribution, he has not received a proportionate share of the unrealized appreciation in CCS's hot assets. He could only have received a share of the appreciation in the hot assets if he had actually received hot assets in the distribution. Thus, the distribution will be disproportionate.

The tax law treats Greg as having sold his share of the hot assets for cold assets, and he will recognize ordinary income equal to his share of the appreciation on the hot assets not distributed, or $60,000. Absent this provision in the tax law, all of Greg's gains from the distribution would have been treated as capital gains. CCS does not recognize any gain or loss because it has no appreciation in the assets (cash) used to "purchase" the hot assets.

LO 21-6

SPECIAL BASIS ADJUSTMENTS

Recall that when an existing partner sells their partnership interest, the partnership's inside basis is generally unaffected by the sale. This creates a discrepancy between the new partner's outside basis in their interest (cost) and that partner's share of the partnership's inside basis, which artificially changes the potential income or loss at the partnership level. For example, earlier in the chapter we considered a scenario in which Greg Randall purchased Chanzz's 30 percent interest in CCS for $82,800 (see the *what-if* scenario in Example 21-5). Greg's outside basis in CCS after the acquisition is $106,800, reflecting the cash payment of $82,800 and his share of CCS's debt at the time of the acquisition, $24,000. However, Greg's share of CCS's inside basis in its assets is $105,000 (see Example 21-7). This is the outcome because the sale does not affect CCS's inside basis and Greg simply steps into Chanzz's shoes for determining his share of the inside basis. The discrepancy reflects Chanzz's unrecognized share in the net appreciation of CCS's assets (which Greg paid full value for) as of the sale date and causes Greg to be temporarily overtaxed when CCS sells these appreciated assets.

Example 21-25

What if: Assume that Greg acquires his 30 percent interest in CCS from Chanzz for $82,800 (see Example 21-5). Under this assumption, if CCS sells its accounts receivable for their fair market value of $13,000 (adjusted basis is $0) (see Example 21-2 for CCS's balance sheet as of June 30, 2022, the acquisition date), what are the amount and character of gain that Greg recognizes on the sale?

Answer: When CCS sells the accounts receivable, it recognizes $13,000 of ordinary income, of which $3,900 (30 percent) is allocated to Greg. However, when Chanzz sold its interest to Greg, Chanzz was already taxed on the $3,900 allocated portion of that ordinary income under §751(a), and Greg paid full value for his interest in the receivables when he acquired his 30 percent interest in CCS. This means Greg will be taxed on the $3,900 again in 2022, and his outside basis in CCS will increase by $3,900. Because Greg paid fair market value for his share of the receivables, he should not have any income when they are sold at fair market value. Eventually, when Greg disposes of his CCS interest, his ultimate gain (or loss) on the disposition will be $3,900 less because of the increase to his outside basis from this additional income; meanwhile, he is overtaxed on the receivables. Greg must report ordinary income today for an offsetting capital loss (or reduced capital gain) in the future when he disposes of his interest.

The tax rules allow the partnership to make an election for a **special basis adjustment** to eliminate discrepancies between partners' inside and outside bases and to correct the artificial income or loss at the partnership level.[49] For the most part, basis discrepancies arise in three situations: following *sales* of partnership interests, following *distributions* when a partner receives an asset that takes more or less basis outside the partnership than it had on the inside, and following *distributions* when a partner recognizes a gain or loss on the distribution. Once a partnership makes a §754 election, the partnership is required to

[49]§754. The election is made by including a written statement declaring that the partnership is making the §754 election with the partnership return when filed for the year the election is to take effect.

make special basis adjustments for all subsequent sales of partnership interests and partnership distributions. The election can be revoked only with permission from the IRS.

Even without a §754 election in effect, the partnership must adjust its bases if the partnership has a **substantial built-in loss** at the time a partner sells their partnership interest. A substantial built-in loss exists if the partnership's aggregate inside basis in its property exceeds the property's fair market value by more than $250,000 when a transfer of an interest occurs or when the purchasing partner would be allocated a loss of more than $250,000 if the partnership assets were sold for fair market value immediately after the sale.[50]

Similarly, a mandatory basis adjustment in partnership assets is required when a **substantial basis reduction** occurs in connection with a partnership distribution. A substantial basis reduction is triggered either when a partner recognizes a loss of more than $250,000 from a partnership distribution or when a partner takes a basis in distributed property exceeding the basis in that property prior to the distribution[51] by more than $250,000.

Although the election is made under §754, the actual authorization of the special basis adjustment is governed by two separate code sections, depending on which situation gives rise to the adjustment: (1) sale of partnership interest, §743(b), or (2) distributions, §734(b). These two sections determine the amount of the adjustment, and §755 then stipulates how the adjustment is allocated among partnership assets. The relationships among these code sections are depicted in Exhibit 21-2.

THE KEY FACTS

Special Basis Adjustments

- **How to elect?**
  Partnership makes a §754 election and then makes a special basis adjustment whenever (1) a new partner purchases a partnership interest or (2) a partner recognizes a gain or loss in a distribution or (3) a partner takes a basis in distributed property that differs from the partnership's basis in the property prior to the distribution.
- **When mandatory?**
  (1) When a partner sells a partnership interest and the partnership has a substantial built-in loss at the time of sale or (2) when a partnership has a substantial basis reduction from a distribution.
- **Why?**
  To prevent partners from being temporarily overtaxed or undertaxed after a partnership interest is transferred or after a distribution occurs.

EXHIBIT 21-2 Special Basis Adjustments

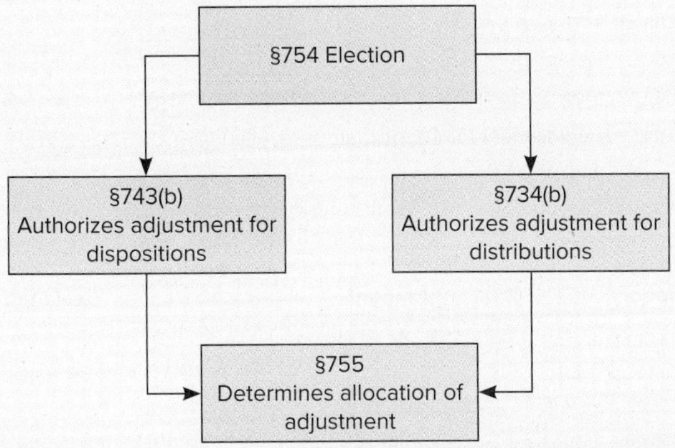

Special Basis Adjustments for Dispositions

The special basis adjustment the partnership makes when an existing partner sells their partnership interest is designed to give the new partner an inside basis in the partnership assets equal to their outside basis in the partnership interest. The basis adjustment in these cases applies *only* to the new partner. The inside bases of the continuing partners remain unchanged, so their income and losses will continue to be accurately allocated. The adjustment is equal to the difference between the new partner's outside basis in their interest and their share of the inside basis of the partnership's assets.[52] The new partner's outside basis is generally equal to the cost of their partnership interest plus their share of partnership liabilities.[53] The special basis adjustment must then be allocated to the assets under allocation rules in §755, which are beyond the scope of this text.

[50] §743(d). In this context, a transfer generally refers to sales, exchanges, or transfers at death, not gift transfers.

[51] §734(d).

[52] §743(b).

[53] A partner's share of inside basis is also labeled *previously taxed capital* [Reg. §1.743-1(d)]. The technical calculation is determined as follows (but generally equals the partner's tax capital account): (1) the amount of cash the partner would receive on liquidation after a hypothetical sale of all the partnership assets for their fair market value after the sale of the partnership interest, plus (2) the amount of taxable loss allocated to the partner from the hypothetical sale, less (3) the amount of taxable gain allocated to the partner from the hypothetical sale.

Example 21-26

What if: Suppose Greg acquired Chanzz's 30 percent interest in CCS on June 30, 2022, for $82,800. CCS's balance sheet as of the sale date is assumed to be as follows:

Color Comfort Sheets LLC
June 30, 2022

	Tax Basis	FMV
Assets		
Cash	$ 27,000	$ 27,000
Accounts receivable	0	13,000
Investments	15,000	12,000
Inventory	1,000	1,000
Equipment (cost = $100,000)	80,000	86,000
Building	97,000	97,000
Land	20,000	150,000
Totals	$240,000	$386,000
Liabilities and capital		
Long-term debt	$100,000	
Capital—Nicole	(49,000)	
—Sarah	108,000	
—Chanzz	81,000	
Totals	$240,000	

What is the special basis adjustment for Greg's purchase, assuming CCS has a §754 election in effect at the sale date?

Answer: $1,800, the difference between Greg's outside basis in his CCS interest and inside basis of CCS's assets, calculated as follows:

Description	Amount	Explanation
(1) Cash purchase price	$ 82,800	
(2) Greg's share of CCS debt	24,000	$80,000 × 30% (see Example 21-2)
(3) Initial basis in CCS	$106,800	(1) + (2)
(4) Greg's inside basis	105,000	Chanzz's tax capital ($81,000) plus share of CCS debt ($24,000) (see Example 21-7)
Special basis adjustment	**$ 1,800**	(3) − (4)

When a new partner's positive special basis adjustment is allocated to depreciable or amortizable assets, the new partner will benefit from additional depreciation or amortization. In some cases, the amounts can be quite substantial, and a new partner may be willing to pay more for a partnership interest with a §754 election in place than for a partnership interest without it.

TAXES IN THE REAL WORLD Sports Team Owners Garner Tax Deductions from Amortization

Professional sports team franchises are typically organized as partnerships for tax purposes. When a new owner purchases an interest in a professional sports team from an existing owner, the new owner is purchasing an interest in a business with assets that mainly consist of intangible assets such as goodwill, trademarks, licenses, broadcasting rights, and player contracts. As a result, the new owner usually receives a positive special basis adjustment that is allocated almost entirely to their share of these intangible assets. To be more specific, news sources report that 90 percent or more of the purchase price the new owner pays is typically allocated as a positive special basis adjustment to intangible assets. Because this special positive basis adjustment is amortizable over 15 years, the new owner will effectively be able to deduct nearly their entire investment in the team against their other sources of income over the remaining 15 years. Though this same tax advantage is available in other types of businesses taxed as partnerships, it has become somewhat controversial given the public visibility of professional sports teams and their owners.

Source: www.propublica.org/article/the-billionaire-playbook-how-sports-owners-use-their-teams-to-avoid-millions-in-taxes.

Special Basis Adjustments for Distributions

As with dispositions of partnership interests, partnership distributions may cause the partners' outside basis in their partnership interests to differ from their inside basis in partnership assets. This usually occurs when a partner recognizes a gain or loss on a distribution or when a partner's basis in the distributed property is different from the partnership's basis in the property prior to the distribution. In contrast to the special basis adjustment for sales of partnership interests, the special basis adjustment for distributions affects the common basis of *partnership* property and not merely one partner's basis adjustment.

The special basis adjustment can either increase or decrease the basis in the partnership assets. A **positive basis adjustment** will *increase* the basis in the partnership assets (1) when a partner receiving distributed property recognizes a gain on the distribution (for instance, in operating distributions where the partner receives money in excess of that partner's outside basis in their partnership interest) and (2) when a partner receiving distributed property takes a basis in the property less than the partnership's basis in the property. The positive adjustment will equal the sum of the gain recognized by the partners receiving a cash distribution in excess of their basis or the amount of the basis reduction in distributed property.

In Example 21-11, CCS distributed $250,000 cash to Nicole on December 31, 2023, as part of an operating distribution. Because Nicole's outside basis in her CCS interest before the distribution was $205,000 and she received only money in the distribution, Nicole was required to recognize a $45,000 gain on the distribution. If CCS had a §754 election in effect, it would have a positive special basis adjustment from the distribution of $45,000.

A **negative basis adjustment** will *decrease* the basis in partnership assets (1) when a partner receiving distributed property in a liquidating distribution recognizes a loss on the distribution and (2) when a partner receiving distributed property takes a basis in the property greater than the partnership's basis in the property.

The negative adjustment will equal the sum of the recognized loss or the amount of the basis increase in property distributed to partners. Recall from our previous discussion of distributions that negative adjustments can occur only in liquidating distributions. Only then does a partner recognize a loss or increase the distributed property's basis over its basis prior to the distribution.

In Example 21-15, CCS liquidated Greg's 30 percent interest by distributing cash of $206,000 and inventory with a fair market value of $103,000 (adjusted basis is $43,000). Because Greg's outside basis in his CCS interest after considering his debt relief ($268,000) was greater than the sum of the bases of the property distributed ($249,000), Greg recognized a loss of $19,000 on the liquidation. If CCS had a §754 election in effect at the time of this liquidation, CCS would have a negative basis adjustment of $19,000.

The allocation of the special basis adjustment among the partnership's remaining assets after a distribution is intended to offset any gain or loss any partners remaining in the partnership after the distribution would have recognized twice absent the adjustment. The process of allocating the adjustment for distributions is prescribed in §755, and these procedures are beyond the scope of this text.

CONCLUSION

The tax rules for partnership dispositions and distributions are among the most complex in the Internal Revenue Code. This chapter provided an overview of these rules and in some cases plunged into the complexity. We discussed the calculation of gains and losses from the sale of a partnership interest, as well as the basis implications of the purchase to a new investor. In doing so, we discussed how *hot assets* might affect the gain or loss. The chapter also explained the basic rules for determining the tax treatment of partnership distributions.

We illustrated how partnership elections might affect the partnership's basis in assets following partnership interest dispositions or distributions. In general, the tax rules are designed to avoid having business owners make decisions based on tax rules rather than on business principles; however, making this goal a reality provides for some challenging applications.

Summary

LO 21-1 Determine the tax consequences to the buyer and seller of the disposition of a partnership interest, including the amount and character of gain or loss recognized.

- Sellers are primarily concerned about their realized and recognized gain or loss on the sale of their partnership interest.
- Sellers' debt relief is included in the amount realized from the sale.
- Buyers' main tax concerns are determining their basis in the partnership interest they acquire and their inside bases of the partnership assets.
- The outside basis in a buyer's interest after an acquisition is generally equal to the cost that buyer paid plus the share of partnership liabilities allocated to that partner. A buyer's inside basis is generally the same as the seller's inside basis at the sale date.
- The sale of a partnership interest does not generally affect a partnership's inside basis in its assets.
- A partnership's tax year closes for the selling partner upon the sale of a partnership interest.
- Hot assets include unrealized receivables and inventory items.
- Unrealized receivables include the rights to receive payment for goods delivered or to be delivered, or services rendered or to be rendered, as well as items that would generate ordinary income if the partnership sold the asset for its fair market value, such as depreciation recapture.
- There are actually two definitions of inventory items. The first, under §751(a), applies to sales of partnership interests and includes all classic inventory items and assets that are *not* capital or §1231 assets. The second definition of inventory [§751(b)] applies primarily to distributions and includes only substantially appreciated inventory.
- Sellers classify gains and losses from the sale of partnership interests as ordinary to the extent the gain relates to hot assets.
- Hot assets are also important in determining whether a distribution is proportionate or disproportionate.

LO 21-2 List the reasons for distributions, and compare operating and liquidating distributions.

- Distributions from a flow-through entity are one mechanism to return business profits or capital to the owners of the entity.
- Distributions may also be used to liquidate an owner's interest in the business or to completely terminate the business.
- Operating distributions include distributions in which the owner retains an interest in the business.

LO 21-3 Determine the tax consequences of proportionate operating distributions.

- Partnerships do not generally recognize gain or loss on the distribution of property.
- Most operating distributions do not result in gain or loss to the partner receiving the distribution. Gains and losses are deferred through basis adjustments to the distributed assets and basis of the partnership interest.

- A partner recognizes a gain from an operating distribution if they receive a distribution of money that exceeds the basis in their partnership interest.
- Partners never recognize losses from operating distributions.

Determine the tax consequences of proportionate liquidating distributions. **LO 21-4**

- The tax issues in liquidating distributions are primarily twofold: (1) determining whether the liquidating partner recognizes a gain or loss and (2) allocating the liquidating partner's basis in the partnership interest to the distributed assets.
- A partner recognizes a gain only when receiving more money than that partner's basis in the partnership interest.
- A partner recognizes a loss only when the partnership distributes cash and hot assets and the partner's basis in the partnership interest is greater than the sum of the bases of the assets the partner receives in the distribution.
- In all other cases, a partner does not recognize gains or losses from a liquidating distribution; rather, the partner will simply allocate the basis in the partnership interest to the distributed assets.
- The key to the allocation process is to focus on two factors: (1) the type of property distributed and (2) whether the total basis in distributed assets is larger or smaller than the partner's basis in the partnership interest.
- The character of the distributed assets usually stays the same to the partner as in the partnership.

Explain the significance of disproportionate distributions. **LO 21-5**

- Disproportionate distributions occur when the assets distributed in either operating or liquidating distributions do not represent the partner's proportionate share of the partnership's unrealized appreciation in its hot and cold assets.
- A disproportionate distribution causes a shift in the proportion of ordinary income and capital gain income from the partnership. Therefore, the rules require the partner to treat the disproportionate portion of a distribution as a sale or exchange.
- If a partner receives more cold assets than the proportionate share owned by that partner in a distribution, the partner will generally recognize ordinary income in an amount equal to that partner's share of the appreciation in the hot assets not distributed to the partner. If a partner receives more hot assets than the proportionate share owned, the partner will recognize capital gain equal to that partner's share of the appreciation in cold assets not distributed to the partner.
- The disproportionate distribution rules ensure that partners cannot convert ordinary income into capital gain through distributions.

Explain the rationale for special basis adjustments, determine when they are necessary, and calculate the special basis adjustment for dispositions and distributions. **LO 21-6**

- Discrepancies between a partner's inside and outside bases may cause a partner to be overtaxed or undertaxed, at least temporarily. Special basis adjustment rules allow the partnership to eliminate discrepancies between inside and outside bases to correct any artificial income or loss at the partnership level.
- Basis discrepancies may occur following the acquisition of a partnership interest and following distributions where a partner receives more or less than their share of the inside basis in the partnership property.
- When purchasing a partnership interest, a new partner may receive a special basis adjustment equal to the difference between the new partner's outside basis in the partnership interest and their share of inside basis in the partnership's assets if the partnership has a §754 election in effect.
- A special basis adjustment is mandatory even without a §754 election in effect when a partnership has a substantial built-in loss at the time a partnership interest is transferred.
- When a partner recognizes a gain from a distribution or takes a basis in distributed property less than the partnership's basis in the property, the partnership will have a positive special basis adjustment to increase the basis in the partnership's assets.
- When a partner recognizes a loss from a liquidating distribution or takes a basis in distributed property greater than the partnership's basis in the property, the partnership will have a negative special basis adjustment to decrease the basis in partnership assets.

KEY TERMS

carryover basis (21-11)
disproportionate distributions (21-24)
hot assets (21-3)
inside basis (21-7)
inventory items (21-3)
liquidating distributions (21-9)
negative basis adjustment (21-29)
operating distributions (21-9)
outside basis (21-2)
partnership interest (21-2)
positive basis adjustment (21-29)
special basis adjustment (21-26)
substantial basis reduction (21-27)
substantial built-in loss (21-27)
substantially appreciated inventory (21-24)
unrealized receivables (21-3)

DISCUSSION QUESTIONS

Discussion Questions are available in Connect®.

LO 21-1 1. Joey is a 25 percent owner of Loopy LLC. He no longer wants to be involved in the business. What options does Joey have to exit the business?

LO 21-1 2. Compare and contrast the aggregate and entity approaches for a sale of a partnership interest.

LO 21-1 3. What restrictions might prevent a partner from selling their partnership interest to a third party?

LO 21-1 4. Explain how a partner's debt relief affects their amount realized in a sale of a partnership interest.

LO 21-1 5. Under what circumstances will the gain or loss on the sale of a partnership interest be characterized as ordinary rather than capital?

LO 21-1 6. What are *hot assets,* and why are they important in the sale of a partnership interest?

LO 21-1 7. For an accrual-method partnership, are accounts receivable considered unrealized receivables? Explain.

LO 21-1 8. Can a partnership have unrealized receivables if it has no accounts receivable?

LO 21-1 9. How do hot assets affect the character of gain or loss on the sale of a partnership interest?

LO 21-1 10. Under what circumstances can a partner recognize both gain and loss on the sale of a partnership interest?

LO 21-1 11. Absent any special elections, what effect does a sale of a partnership interest have on the partnership?

research LO 21-1 12. Generally, a selling partner's capital account carries over to the purchaser of the partnership interest. Under what circumstances will this not be the case?

LO 21-2 13. What distinguishes operating from liquidating distributions?

LO 21-3 14. Under what circumstances will a partner recognize a gain from an operating distribution?

LO 21-3 15. Under what circumstances will a partner recognize a loss from an operating distribution?

LO 21-3 16. In general, what effect does an operating distribution have on the partnership?

LO 21-3 17. If a partner's outside basis is less than the partnership's inside basis in distributed assets, how does the partner determine their basis of the distributed assets in an operating distribution?

LO 21-4 18. Under what conditions will a partner recognize gain in a liquidating distribution?

LO 21-4 19. Under what conditions will a partner recognize loss in a liquidating distribution?

LO 21-4 20. Describe how to determine the basis a partner has in distributed assets in cases in which a partnership distributes only money, inventory, and/or unrealized receivables in a liquidating distribution.

LO 21-4 21. How does a partner determine their basis in distributed assets when the partnership distributes other property in addition to money and hot assets?

22. SBT partnership distributes $5,000 cash and a parcel of land with a fair market value of $40,000 and a $25,000 basis to the partnership to Sam (30 percent partner). What factors must Sam and SBT consider in determining the tax treatment of this distribution? LO 21-5 planning
23. Discuss the underlying concern to tax policy makers in distributions in which a partner receives more or less than his share of the partnership's hot assets. LO 21-5
24. In general, how do the disproportionate distribution rules ensure that partners recognize their share of partnership ordinary income? LO 21-5
25. Why would a new partner who pays more for a partnership interest than the selling partner's outside basis want the partnership to elect a special basis adjustment? LO 21-6 planning
26. List two common situations that will cause a partner's inside and outside bases to differ. LO 21-6
27. Explain why a partnership might not want to make a §754 election to allow special basis adjustments. LO 21-6
28. When might a new partner have an upward basis adjustment following the acquisition of a partnership interest? LO 21-6
29. When are partnerships mandated to adjust the basis of their assets (inside basis) when a partner sells a partnership interest or receives a partnership distribution? LO 21-6

PROBLEMS

Select problems are available in Connect®. Mc Graw Hill connect

30. Jerry is a 30 percent partner in the JJM Partnership when he sells his entire interest to Lucia for $56,000 cash. At the time of the sale, Jerry's basis in JJM is $32,000. JJM does not have any debt or hot assets. What is Jerry's gain or loss on the sale of his interest? LO 21-1
31. Amina is a 30 percent partner in the AOM Partnership when she sells her entire interest to Hope for $72,000 cash. At the time of the sale, Amina's basis in AOM is $44,000 (which includes her $6,000 share of AOM liabilities). AOM does not have any hot assets. What is Amina's gain or loss on the sale of her interest? LO 21-1
32. Allison, Keesha, and Steven each owns an equal interest in KAS Partnership, a calendar-year-end, cash-method entity. On January 1 of the current year, Steven's basis in his partnership interest is $27,000. During January and February, the partnership generates $30,000 of ordinary income and $4,500 of tax-exempt income. On March 1, Steven sells his partnership interest to Juan for a cash payment of $45,000. The partnership has the following assets and no liabilities at the sale date: LO 21-1

	Tax Basis	FMV
Cash	$30,000	$30,000
Land held for investment	30,000	60,000
Totals	$60,000	$90,000

a) Assuming KAS's operating agreement provides for an interim closing of the books when partners' interests change during the year, what is Steven's basis in his partnership interest on March 1 just prior to the sale?
b) What are the amount and character of Steven's recognized gain or loss on the sale?
c) What is Juan's initial basis in the partnership interest?
d) What is the partnership's basis in the assets following the sale?

33. Gamila, James, Helen, and Carlos each owns an equal interest in GJHC Partnership, a calendar-year-end, cash-method entity. On January 1 of the current year, James's basis in his partnership interest is $62,000. For the taxable year, the partnership LO 21-1

generates $80,000 of ordinary income and $30,000 of dividend income. For the first five months of the year, GJHC generates $25,000 of ordinary income and no dividend income. On June 1, James sells his partnership interest to Robert for a cash payment of $70,000. The partnership has the following assets and no liabilities at the sale date:

	Tax Basis	FMV
Cash	$ 27,000	$ 27,000
Land held for investment	80,000	100,000
Totals	$107,000	$127,000

a) Assuming GJHC's operating agreement provides that the proration method will be used to allocate income or loss when partners' interests change during the year, what is James's basis in his partnership interest on June 1 just prior to the sale?

b) What are the amount and character of James's recognized gain or loss on the sale?

c) If GJHC uses an interim closing of the books, what are the amount and character of James's recognized gain or loss on the sale?

LO 21-1

34. At the end of last year, Milena, a 35 percent partner in the five-person LAMEC Partnership, has an outside basis of $60,000, including her $30,000 share of LAMEC debt. On January 1 of the current year, Milena sells her partnership interest to MaryLynn for a cash payment of $45,000 and the assumption of her share of LAMEC's debt.

a) What are the amount and character of Milena's recognized gain or loss on the sale?

b) If LAMEC has $100,000 of unrealized receivables as of the sale date, what are the amount and character of Milena's recognized gain or loss?

c) What is MaryLynn's initial basis in the partnership interest?

LO 21-1

35. Marco, Jaclyn, and Carrie formed Daxing Partnership (a calendar-year-end entity) by contributing cash 10 years ago. Each partner owns an equal interest in the partnership and has an outside basis in their partnership interest of $104,000. On January 1 of the current year, Marco sells his partnership interest to Ryan for a cash payment of $137,000. The partnership has the following assets and no liabilities as of the sale date:

	Tax Basis	FMV
Cash	$ 18,000	$ 18,000
Accounts receivable	0	12,000
Inventory	69,000	81,000
Equipment	180,000	225,000
Stock investment	45,000	75,000
Totals	$312,000	$411,000

The equipment was purchased for $240,000, and the partnership has taken $60,000 of depreciation. The stock was purchased seven years ago.

a) What are the *hot assets* [§751(a)] for this sale?

b) What is Marco's gain or loss on the sale of his partnership interest?

c) What is the character of Marco's gain or loss?

d) What are Ryan's inside and outside bases in the partnership on the date of the sale?

LO 21-1

36. Franklin, Jefferson, and Washington formed the Independence Partnership (a calendar-year-end entity) by contributing cash 10 years ago. Each partner owns an equal interest in the partnership and has an outside basis in his partnership interest of $104,000. On January 1 of the current year, Franklin sells his partnership interest to

Adams for a cash payment of $122,000. The partnership has the following assets and no liabilities as of the sale date:

	Tax Basis	FMV
Cash	$ 18,000	$ 18,000
Accounts receivable	0	12,000
Inventory	69,000	81,000
Equipment	180,000	225,000
Stock investment	45,000	30,000
Totals	$312,000	$366,000

The equipment was purchased for $240,000, and the partnership has taken $60,000 of depreciation. The stock was purchased seven years ago.

a) What is Franklin's overall gain or loss on the sale of his partnership interest?

b) What is the character of Franklin's gain or loss?

37. Travis and Alix Weber are equal partners in the Tralix Partnership, which does not have a §754 election in place. Alix sells one-half of her interest (25 percent) to Michael Tomei for $30,000 cash. Just before the sale, Alix's basis in her entire partnership interest is $75,000, including her $30,000 share of the partnership liabilities. Tralix's assets on the sale date are as follows: LO 21-1

	Tax Basis	FMV
Cash	$ 40,000	$ 40,000
Inventory	30,000	90,000
Land held for investment	80,000	50,000
Totals	$150,000	$180,000

a) What are the amount and character of Alix's recognized gain or loss on the sale?

b) What is Alix's basis in her remaining partnership interest?

c) What is Michael's basis in his partnership interest?

d) What is the effect of the sale on the partnership's basis in the assets?

38. Newton is a one-third owner of ProRite Partnership. Newton has decided to sell his interest in the business to Dunja for $50,000 cash plus the assumption of his share of ProRite's liabilities. Assume Newton's inside and outside bases in ProRite are equal. ProRite shows the following balance sheet as of the sale date: LO 21-1

	Tax Basis	FMV
Assets		
Cash	$ 80,000	$ 80,000
Receivables	25,000	25,000
Inventory	40,000	85,000
Land	30,000	20,000
Totals	$175,000	$210,000
Liabilities and capital		
Liabilities	$ 60,000	
Capital—Newton	38,333	
—Barbara	38,334	
—Liz	38,333	
Totals	$175,000	

What are the amount and character of Newton's recognized gain or loss?

LO 21-3

39. Coy and Matt are equal partners in the Matcoy Partnership. Each partner has a basis in his partnership interest of $28,000 at the end of the current year, prior to any distribution. On December 31, each receives an operating distribution. Coy receives $10,000 cash. Matt receives $3,000 cash and a parcel of land with a $7,000 fair market value and a $4,000 basis to the partnership. Matcoy has no debt or hot assets.
    a) What is Coy's recognized gain or loss? What is the character of any gain or loss?
    b) What is Coy's ending basis in his partnership interest?
    c) What is Matt's recognized gain or loss? What is the character of any gain or loss?
    d) What is Matt's basis in the distributed property?
    e) What is Matt's ending basis in his partnership interest?

LO 21-3

40. Santiago and Lauren are equal partners in the PJenn Partnership. The partners formed the partnership seven years ago by contributing cash. Prior to any distributions, the partners have the following bases in their partnership interests:

Partner	Outside Basis
Santiago	$22,000
Lauren	22,000

On December 31 of the current year, the partnership makes a pro rata operating distribution of:

Partner	Distribution
Santiago	Cash $25,000
Lauren	Cash $18,000
	Property $7,000 (FMV)
	($2,000 basis to partnership)

    a) What are the amount and character of Santiago's recognized gain or loss?
    b) What is Santiago's remaining basis in his partnership interest?
    c) What are the amount and character of Lauren's recognized gain or loss?
    d) What is Lauren's basis in the distributed assets?
    e) What is Lauren's remaining basis in her partnership interest?

LO 21-3

41. Adam and Alyssa are equal partners in the PartiPilo Partnership. The partners formed the partnership three years ago by contributing cash. Prior to any distributions, the partners have the following bases in their partnership interests:

Partner	Outside Basis
Adam	$12,000
Alyssa	12,000

On December 31 of the current year, the partnership makes a pro rata operating distribution of:

Partner	Distribution
Adam	Cash $16,000
Alyssa	Cash $8,000
	Property $8,000 (FMV)
	($6,000 basis to partnership)

    a) What are the amount and character of Adam's recognized gain or loss?
    b) What is Adam's remaining basis in his partnership interest?
    c) What are the amount and character of Alyssa's recognized gain or loss?
    d) What is Alyssa's basis in the distributed assets?
    e) What is Alyssa's remaining basis in her partnership interest?

42. Rania has a $68,000 basis in her 50 percent partnership interest in the KD Partnership before receiving a current distribution of $6,000 cash and land with a fair market value of $35,000 and a basis to the partnership of $18,000. LO 21-3
   a) What are the amount and character of Rania's recognized gain or loss?
   b) What is Rania's basis in the land?
   c) What is Rania's remaining basis in her partnership interest?

43. Pam has a $27,000 basis (including her share of debt) in her 50 percent partnership interest in the Meddoc Partnership before receiving any distributions. This year Meddoc makes a current distribution to Pam of a parcel of land with a $40,000 fair market value and a $32,000 basis to the partnership. The land is encumbered with a $15,000 mortgage (the partnership's only liability). LO 21-3
   a) What are the amount and character of Pam's recognized gain or loss?
   b) What is Pam's basis in the land?
   c) What is Pam's remaining basis in her partnership interest?

44. Two years ago, Kimberly became a 30 percent partner in the KST Partnership with a contribution of investment land with a $10,000 basis and a $16,000 fair market value. On January 2 of this year, Kimberly has a $15,000 basis in her partnership interest, and none of her pre-contribution gain has been recognized. On January 2 Kimberly receives an operating distribution of a tract of land (not the contributed land) with a $12,000 basis and an $18,000 fair market value. LO 21-3 research
   a) What are the amount and character of Kimberly's recognized gain or loss on the distribution?
   b) What is Kimberly's remaining basis in KST after the distribution?
   c) What is KST's basis in the land Kimberly contributed after Kimberly receives this distribution?

45. Rufus is a one-quarter partner in the Adventure Partnership. On January 1 of the current year, Adventure distributes $13,000 cash to Rufus in complete liquidation of his interest. Adventure has only capital assets and no liabilities at the date of the distribution. Rufus's basis in his partnership interest is $18,500. LO 21-4
   a) What are the amount and character of Rufus's recognized gain or loss?
   b) What are the amount and character of Adventure's recognized gain or loss?
   c) If Rufus's basis is $10,000 at the distribution date rather than $18,500, what are the amount and character of Rufus's recognized gain or loss?

46. The Taurin Partnership (a calendar-year-end entity) has the following assets as of December 31 of the current year: LO 21-4

	Tax Basis	FMV
Cash	$ 45,000	$ 45,000
Accounts receivable	15,000	30,000
Inventory	81,000	120,000
Totals	$141,000	$195,000

On December 31, Taurin distributes $15,000 of cash, $10,000 (FMV) of accounts receivable, and $40,000 (FMV) of inventory to Emma (a one-third partner) in termination of her partnership interest. Emma's basis in her partnership interest immediately prior to the distribution is $40,000.
   a) What are the amount and character of Emma's recognized gain or loss on the distribution?
   b) What is Emma's basis in the distributed assets?
   c) If Emma's basis before the distribution was $55,000 rather than $40,000, what is Emma's recognized gain or loss and what is her basis in the distributed assets?

LO 21-4

47. Melissa, Nicole, and Miguel are equal partners in the Opto Partnership (a calendar-year-end entity). Melissa decides she wants to exit the partnership and receives a proportionate distribution to liquidate her partnership interest on January 1. The partnership has no liabilities and holds the following assets as of January 1:

	Tax Basis	FMV
Cash	$18,000	$18,000
Accounts receivable	0	24,000
Stock investment	7,500	12,000
Land	30,000	36,000
Totals	$55,500	$90,000

Melissa receives one-third of each of the partnership assets. She has a basis in her partnership interest of $25,000.

a) What are the amount and character of any recognized gain or loss to Melissa?

b) What is Melissa's basis in the distributed assets?

c) What are the tax implications (amount and character of gain or loss and basis of assets) to Melissa if her outside basis is $11,000 rather than $25,000?

d) What are the amount and character of any recognized gain or loss from the distribution to Opto?

LO 21-4
planning

48. Lonnie Davis has been a general partner in the Highland Partnership for many years and is also a sole proprietor in a separate business. To spend more time focusing on his sole proprietorship, he plans to leave Highland and will receive a liquidating distribution of $50,000 in cash and land with a fair market value of $100,000 (tax basis of $120,000). Immediately before the distribution, Lonnie's basis in his partnership interest is $350,000, which includes his $50,000 share of partnership debt. Highland Partnership does not hold any hot assets.

a) What are the amount and character of any gain or loss to Lonnie?

b) What is Lonnie's basis in the land?

c) What are the amount and character of Lonnie's gain or loss if he holds the land for 13 months as investment property and then sells it for $100,000?

d) What are the amount and character of Lonnie's gain or loss if he places the land into service in his sole proprietorship and then sells it 13 months later for $100,000?

e) Do your answers to parts (c) and (d) suggest a course of action that would help Lonnie to achieve a more favorable tax outcome?

LO 21-4

49. AJ is a 30 percent partner in the Trane Partnership, a calendar-year-end entity. On January 1, AJ has an outside basis in his interest in Trane of $73,000, which includes his share of the $50,000 of partnership liabilities. Trane generates $42,000 of income during the year and does not make any changes to its liabilities. On December 31, Trane makes a proportionate distribution of the following assets to AJ to terminate his partnership interest:

	Tax Basis	FMV
Inventory	$55,000	$65,000
Land	30,000	25,000
Totals	$85,000	$90,000

a) What are the tax consequences (gain or loss, basis adjustments) of the distribution to Trane?

b) What are the amount and character of any recognized gain or loss to AJ?

c) What is AJ's basis in the distributed assets?

d) If AJ sells the inventory four years after the distribution for $70,000, what are the amount and character of his recognized gain or loss?

50. Mikaere's basis in the Jimsoo Partnership is $53,000. In a proportionate liquidating distribution, Mikaere receives cash of $7,000 and two capital assets: (1) Land A with a fair market value of $20,000 and a basis to Jimsoo of $16,000 and (2) Land B with a fair market value of $10,000 and a basis to Jimsoo of $16,000. Jimsoo has no liabilities. LO 21-4

a) How much gain or loss will Mikaere recognize on the distribution? What is the character of any recognized gain or loss?

b) What is Mikaere's basis in the distributed assets?

c) If the two parcels of land had been inventory to Jimsoo, what are the tax consequences to Mikaere (amount and character of gain or loss and basis in distributed assets)?

51. Megan and Matthew are equal partners in the J & J Partnership (a calendar-year-end entity). On January 1 of the current year, they decide to liquidate the partnership. Megan's basis in her partnership interest is $100,000, and Matthew's is $35,000. The two partners receive identical distributions, with each receiving the following assets: LO 21-4

	Tax Basis	FMV
Cash	$30,000	$30,000
Inventory	5,000	6,000
Land	500	1,000
Totals	$35,500	$37,000

a) What are the amount and character of Megan's recognized gain or loss?

b) What is Megan's basis in the distributed assets?

c) What are the amount and character of Matthew's recognized gain or loss?

d) What is Matthew's basis in the distributed assets?

52. Markell's basis in the Markit Partnership is $58,000. In a proportionate liquidating distribution, Markell receives the following assets: LO 21-4

	Tax Basis	FMV
Cash	$ 8,000	$ 8,000
Land A	20,000	45,000
Land B	20,000	25,000

a) How much gain or loss will Markell recognize on the distribution? What is the character of any recognized gain or loss?

b) What is Markell's basis in the distributed assets?

53. Danner Inc. has a $395,000 capital loss carryover that will expire at the end of the current tax year if it is not used. Also, Danner Inc. has been a general partner in the Talisman Partnership for three years and plans to end its involvement with the partnership by receiving a liquidating distribution. Initially, all parties agreed that Danner Inc.'s liquidating distribution would include $50,000 in cash and land with a fair market value of $400,000 (tax basis of $120,000). Immediately before the distribution, Danner's basis in its partnership interest is $150,000, which includes its $100,000 share of partnership debt. Talisman Partnership does not hold any hot assets. LO 21-4 planning

a) What are the amount and character of any gain or loss to Danner Inc.?

b) What is Danner Inc.'s basis in the land?

c) Can you suggest a course of action that would help Danner Inc. avoid the expiration of its capital loss carryover?

LO 21-1 LO 21-5 planning

54. Bella Partnership is an equal partnership in which each of the partners has a basis in their partnership interest of $10,000. Bella reports the following balance sheet:

	Tax Basis	FMV
Assets		
Inventory	$20,000	$30,000
Land	10,000	15,000
Totals	$30,000	$45,000
Liabilities and capital		
Capital—Toby	$10,000	
—Kaelin	10,000	
—Andrew	10,000	
Totals	$30,000	

a) Identify the *hot assets* if Toby decides to sell his partnership interest. Are these assets "hot" for purposes of distributions?
b) If Bella distributes the land to Toby in complete liquidation of his partnership interest, what tax issues should be considered?

LO 21-1 LO 21-6

55. Fatima pays $120,000 cash for Brittany's one-third interest in the Westlake Partnership. Just prior to the sale, Brittany's basis in Westlake is $96,000. Westlake reports the following balance sheet:

	Tax Basis	FMV
Assets		
Cash	$ 96,000	$ 96,000
Land	192,000	264,000
Totals	$288,000	$360,000
Liabilities and capital		
Capital—Amy	$ 96,000	
—Brittany	96,000	
—Ben	96,000	
Totals	$288,000	

a) What are the amount and character of Brittany's recognized gain or loss on the sale?
b) What is Fatima's basis in her partnership interest? What is Fatima's inside basis?
c) If Westlake were to sell the land for $264,000 shortly after the sale of Brittany's partnership interest, how much gain or loss would the partnership recognize?
d) How much gain or loss would Fatima recognize if the land were sold for $264,000?
e) Suppose Westlake has a §754 election in place. What is Fatima's special basis adjustment? How much gain or loss would Fatima recognize on a subsequent sale of the land in this situation?

LO 21-1 LO 21-6

56. Elaine pays $40,000 cash for Martha's one-third interest in Lakewood Partnership. Just prior to the sale, Martha's basis in Lakewood is $140,000. Lakewood reports the following balance sheet:

	Tax Basis	FMV
Assets		
Cash	$ 50,000	$ 50,000
Land	370,000	70,000
Totals	$420,000	$120,000
Liabilities and capital		
Capital—Mary	140,000	
—Martha	140,000	
—Margaret	140,000	
Totals	$420,000	

Assume the land had been purchased several years ago and the partnership does not have a §754 election in place.

a) What are the amount and character of Martha's recognized gain or loss on the sale?
b) What is Elaine's basis in her partnership interest?
c) If Lakewood were to sell the land for $70,000 shortly after the sale of Martha's partnership interest, how much gain or loss would Elaine recognize?

57. Cliff's basis in his Aero Partnership interest is $11,000. Cliff receives a distribution of $22,000 cash from Aero in complete liquidation of his interest. Aero is an equal partnership with the following balance sheet: LO 21-4 LO 21-6

	Tax Basis	FMV
Assets		
Cash	$22,000	$22,000
Investment	8,800	8,800
Land	2,200	35,200
Totals	$33,000	$66,000
Liabilities and capital		
Capital—Chris	$11,000	
—Cliff	11,000	
—Cooper	11,000	
Totals	$33,000	

a) What are the amount and character of Cliff's recognized gain or loss? What is the effect on the partnership assets?
b) If Aero has a §754 election in place, what is the amount of the special basis adjustment?

58. Erin's basis in her Kiybron Partnership interest is $3,300. Erin receives a distribution of $2,200 cash from Kiybron in complete liquidation of her interest. Kiybron is an equal partnership with the following balance sheet: LO 21-4 LO 21-6

	Tax Basis	FMV
Assets		
Cash	$2,200	$2,200
Stock (investment)	1,100	2,200
Land	6,600	2,200
Totals	$9,900	$6,600
Liabilities and capital		
Capital—Erin	$3,300	
—Carl	3,300	
—Grace	3,300	
Totals	$9,900	

a) What are the amount and character of Erin's recognized gain or loss? What is the effect on the partnership assets?
b) If Kiybron has a §754 election in place, what is the amount of the special basis adjustment?

59. Helen's basis in Haywood Partnership is $270,000. Haywood distributes all the land to Helen in complete liquidation of her partnership interest. The partnership reports the following balance sheet just before the distribution: LO 21-4 LO 21-6

	Tax Basis	FMV
Assets		
Cash	$220,000	$220,000
Stock (investment)	480,000	220,000
Land	110,000	220,000
Totals	$810,000	$660,000
Liabilities and capital		
Capital—Charles	$270,000	
—Esther	270,000	
—Helen	270,000	
Totals	$810,000	

a) What are the amount and character of Helen's recognized gain or loss? What is the effect on the partnership assets?

b) If Haywood has a §754 election in place, what is the amount of the special basis adjustment?

LO 21-4 LO 21-6

60. Lauren's basis in Driftwood Partnership is $510,000. Driftwood distributes all the land to Lauren in complete liquidation of her partnership interest. The partnership reports the following balance sheet just before the distribution:

	Tax Basis	FMV
Assets		
Cash	$ 370,000	$ 370,000
Stock (investment)	910,000	370,000
Land	250,000	370,000
Totals	$1,530,000	$1,110,000
Liabilities and capital		
Capital—Esteban	$ 510,000	
—Kylie	510,000	
—Lauren	510,000	
Totals	$1,530,000	

a) What are the amount and character of Lauren's recognized gain or loss?

b) If Driftwood does not have a §754 election in place, what is the amount of the special basis adjustment, if any?

COMPREHENSIVE PROBLEMS

Select problems are available in Connect®. connect

61. Joaquin is a 30 percent partner in the SBD Partnership, a calendar-year-end entity. As of the end of this year, Joaquin has an outside basis in his interest in SBD of $188,000, which includes his share of the $60,000 of partnership liabilities. On December 31, SBD makes a proportionate distribution of the following assets to Joaquin:

	Tax Basis	FMV
Cash	$ 40,000	$ 40,000
Inventory	55,000	65,000
Land	30,000	45,000
Totals	$125,000	$150,000

a) What are the tax consequences (amount and character of recognized gain or loss, basis in distributed assets) of the distribution to Joaquin if the distribution is an operating distribution?

b) What are the tax consequences (amount and character of recognized gain or loss, basis in distributed assets) of the distribution to Joaquin if the distribution is a liquidating distribution?

c) Compare and contrast the results from parts (a) and (b).

planning

62. Paolo is a 50 percent partner in the Capri Partnership and has decided to terminate his partnership interest. Paolo is considering two options as potential exit strategies. The first is to sell his partnership interest to the two remaining 25 percent partners, Giuseppe and Isabella, for $105,000 cash and the assumption of Paolo's share of Capri's liabilities. Under this option, Giuseppe and Isabella would each pay $52,500

for half of Paolo's interest. The second option is to have Capri liquidate Paolo's partnership interest with a proportionate distribution of the partnership assets. Paolo's basis in his partnership interest is $110,000, including Paolo's share of Capri's liabilities. Capri reports the following balance sheet as of the termination date:

	Tax Basis	FMV
Assets		
Cash	$ 80,000	$ 80,000
Receivables	40,000	40,000
Inventory	50,000	80,000
Land	50,000	60,000
Totals	$220,000	$260,000
Liabilities and capital		
Liabilities	$ 50,000	
Capital—Paolo	85,000	
—Giuseppe	42,500	
—Isabella	42,500	
Totals	$220,000	

a) If Paolo sells his partnership interest to Giuseppe and Isabella for $105,000, what are the amount and character of Paolo's recognized gain or loss?

b) Giuseppe and Isabella each has a basis in Capri of $55,000 before any purchase of Paolo's interest. What are Giuseppe's and Isabella's bases in their partnership interests following the purchase of Paolo's interest?

c) If Capri liquidates Paolo's partnership interest with a proportionate distribution of the partnership assets ($25,000 deemed cash from debt relief, $15,000 of actual cash, and half of the remaining assets), what are the amount and character of Paolo's recognized gain or loss?

d) If Capri liquidates Paolo's interest, what is Paolo's basis in the distributed assets?

e) Compare and contrast Paolo's options for terminating his partnership interest. Assume Paolo's marginal tax rate is 35 percent and his capital gains rate is 15 percent.

63. Carrie D'Lake, Reed A. Green, and Doug A. Divot share a passion for golf and decide to go into the golf club manufacturing business together. On January 2, 2022, D'Lake, Green, and Divot form the Slicenhook Partnership, a general partnership. Slicenhook's main product will be a perimeter-weighted titanium driver with a patented graphite shaft. All three partners plan to actively participate in the business. The partners contribute the following property to form Slicenhook: tax forms

Partner	Contribution
Carrie D'Lake	Land, FMV $460,000 Basis $460,000, Mortgage $60,000
Reed A. Green	$400,000
Doug A. Divot	$400,000

Carrie had recently acquired the land with the idea that she would contribute it to the newly formed partnership. The partners agree to share in profits and losses equally. Slicenhook elects a calendar year-end and the accrual method of accounting.

In addition, Slicenhook received a $1,500,000 recourse loan from Big Bank at the time the contributions were made. Slicenhook uses the proceeds from the loan and the cash contributions to build a state-of-the-art manufacturing facility ($1,200,000), purchase equipment ($600,000), and produce inventory ($400,000). With the remaining cash, Slicenhook invests $45,000 in the stock of a privately owned graphite research company and retains $55,000 as working cash.

Slicenhook operates on a just-in-time inventory system so it sells all inventory and collects all sales immediately. That means that at the end of the year, Slicenhook does not carry any inventory or accounts receivable balances. During 2022, Slicenhook has the following operating results:

Sales		$1,126,000
Cost of goods sold		400,000
Interest income from tax-exempt bonds		900
Qualified dividend income from stock		1,500
Operating expenses		126,000
Depreciation (tax)		
§179 on equipment	$39,000	
Equipment	81,000	
Building	24,000	144,000
Interest expense on debt		120,000

The partnership is very successful in its first year. The success allows Slicenhook to use excess cash from operations to purchase $15,000 of tax-exempt bonds (you can see the interest income already reflected in the operating results). The partnership also makes a principal payment on its loan from Big Bank in the amount of $300,000 and a distribution of $100,000 to each of the partners on December 31, 2022.

The partnership continues its success in 2023 with the following operating results:

Sales		$1,200,000
Cost of goods sold		420,000
Interest income from tax-exempt bonds		900
Qualified dividend income from stock		1,500
Operating expenses		132,000
Depreciation (tax)		
Equipment	$147,000	
Building	30,000	177,000
Interest expense on debt		96,000

The operating expenses include a $1,800 trucking fine that one of its drivers incurred for reckless driving and speeding and meals expense of $6,000 (the meals were not provided by a restaurant).

By the end of 2023, Reed has had a falling out with Carrie and Doug and has decided to leave the partnership. He has located a potential buyer for his partnership interest, Indie Ruff. Indie has agreed to purchase Reed's interest in Slicenhook for $730,000 in cash and the assumption of Reed's share of Slicenhook's debt. Carrie and Doug, however, are not certain that admitting Indie to the partnership is such a good idea. They want to consider having Slicenhook liquidate Reed's interest on January 1, 2024. As of January 1, 2024, Slicenhook has the following assets:

	Tax Basis	FMV
Cash	$ 876,800	$ 876,800
Investment—tax exempts	15,000	18,000
Investment stock	45,000	45,000
Equipment—net of dep.	333,000	600,000
Building—net of dep.	1,146,000	1,440,000
Land	460,000	510,000
Total	$2,875,800	$3,489,800

Carrie and Doug propose that Slicenhook distribute the following to Reed in complete liquidation of his partnership interest:

	Tax Basis	FMV
Cash	$485,000	$485,000
Investment stock	45,000	45,000
Equipment—$200,000 cost, net of dep.	111,000	200,000
Total	$641,000	$730,000

Slicenhook has not purchased or sold any equipment since its original purchase just after formation.

a) Determine each partner's recognized gain or loss upon formation of Slicenhook.

b) What is each partner's initial tax basis in Slicenhook on January 2, 2022?

c) Prepare Slicenhook's opening tax basis balance sheet as of January 2, 2022.

d) Using the operating results, what are Slicenhook's ordinary income and separately stated items for 2022 and 2023? What amount of Slicenhook's income for each period would each of the partners receive?

e) Using the information provided, prepare Slicenhook's page 1 and Schedule K to be included with its Form 1065 for 2022. Also, prepare a Schedule K-1 for Carrie.

f) What are Carrie's, Reed's, and Doug's bases in their partnership interest at the end of 2022 and 2023?

g) If Reed sells his interest in Slicenhook to Indie Ruff, what are the amount and character of his recognized gain or loss? What is Indie's basis in the partnership interest?

h) What is Indie's inside basis in Slicenhook? What effect would a §754 election have on Indie's inside basis?

i) If Slicenhook distributes the assets proposed by Carrie and Doug in complete liquidation of Reed's partnership interest, what are the amount and character of Reed's recognized gain or loss? What is Reed's basis in the distributed assets?

j) Compare and contrast Reed's options for terminating his partnership interest. Assume Reed's marginal ordinary rate is 35 percent and his capital gains rate is 15 percent.

UWorld | ROGER CPA Review

UWorld Roger CPA Review

Sample CPA Exam questions from Roger CPA Review are available in Connect as support for the topics in this text. These Multiple Choice Questions and Task-Based Simulations include expert-written explanations and solutions and provide a starting point for students to become familiar with the content and functionality of the actual CPA Exam.

chapter

22 S Corporations

Learning Objectives

Upon completing this chapter, you should be able to:

LO 22-1 Describe the requirements and process to elect S corporation status.

LO 22-2 Explain the events that terminate the S corporation election.

LO 22-3 Describe operating issues relating to S corporation accounting periods and methods, and explain income and loss allocations and separately stated items.

LO 22-4 Explain stock-basis calculations, loss limitations, determination of self-employment income, and fringe benefit rules that apply to S corporation shareholders.

LO 22-5 Apply the tax rules for S corporation operating distributions and liquidating distributions.

LO 22-6 Describe the taxes that apply to S corporations, estimated tax requirements, and tax return filing requirements.

Gyorgy Barna/Shutterstock

Storyline Summary

Taxpayers:	Nicole Johnson (she/her/hers), Sarah Walker (she/her/hers), and Chance Armstrong (he/him/his)
Location:	Salt Lake City, Utah
Status:	Shareholders of newly formed Color Comfort Sheets Inc. (CCS)
Situation:	Formed CCS as a corporation and have elected to have the entity taxed as an S corporation

In the Business Entities Overview chapter, we met Nicole Johnson, who turned her sheet-making hobby into a full-time business called Color Comfort Sheets (CCS). In this chapter, we assume Nicole formed CCS as a corporation, intending to elect S corporation tax status.

When starting the business, Nicole had cash to contribute to CCS but not enough to meet initial needs. She convinced her friend Sarah Walker to invest in CCS and fortunately, after listening to Nicole and Sarah's proposal, local sports team owner Chance Armstrong also agreed to invest. Nicole and Sarah would take an active role in managing CCS; Chance would not. Nicole contributed a parcel of land and cash in exchange for one-third of CCS's stock. Sarah and Chance each contributed cash for one-third of the stock. With funding in place, CCS began operating on January 1, 2021. However, with the excitement (and turmoil) of starting the new business, it took Nicole, Sarah, and Chance a while to talk with their accountant about electing S corporation status. After several discussions, they filed their S election on May 1, 2021. ■

In this chapter, we discuss the tax characteristics of an **S corporation,** a hybrid entity that shares some characteristics with C corporations and some with partnerships.[1] S corporations either are incorporated under state law, have the same legal protections as C corporations, and have elected S corporation status or, as we discuss in the Business Entities Overview chapter, they are noncorporate business entities (e.g., an LLC) that have elected to be treated as a corporation, and then elected S corporation status. S corporations are governed by the same corporate tax rules that apply in the organization, liquidation, and reorganization of C corporations. However, unlike a C corporation, an S corporation is a flow-through entity and shares many tax similarities with partnerships. For example, basis calculations for S corporation shareholders and partners are similar, the income or loss of an S corporation flows through to its owners, and distributions are generally not taxed to the extent of the owner's basis.

Throughout this chapter, we highlight the tax similarities between S corporations and C corporations and between S corporations and partnerships, while focusing on the unique rules that apply to S corporations. These rules are more complex for S corporations that were once C corporations with previously undistributed **earnings and profits (E&P).**

LO 22-1

S CORPORATION ELECTIONS

Formations

The same rules for forming and contributing property govern S and C corporations. As discussed earlier in the text, §351 and related provisions apply when one or more persons transfer property to a corporation (C or S) in return for stock, and immediately after the transfer, these persons control the corporation. These rules allow shareholders meeting the requirements to defer gains they realize when they transfer appreciated property to the corporation in exchange for stock. Note that similar rules apply to formations and property contributions to partnerships under §721. One important difference, however, is that partnership tax rules do not impose a control requirement to defer gains (see the Forming and Operating Partnerships chapter for partnership contributions).

THE KEY FACTS

S Corporation Qualification Requirements

- Only U.S. citizens or residents, estates, certain trusts, and certain tax-exempt organizations may be S corporation shareholders.
- S corporations may have no more than 100 shareholders.
- For purposes of the 100-shareholder limit, family members and their estates count as only one shareholder.

S Corporation Qualification Requirements

Unlike C corporations and partnerships, S corporations are limited as to type and number of owners (shareholders).[2] Only U.S. citizens or residents, estates, certain trusts, and certain tax-exempt organizations may be shareholders. No S or C corporations (legal corporations or treated as a corporation for tax purposes) or partnerships can be shareholders.[3] S corporations may have no more than 100 shareholders; family members and their estates count as one shareholder. Family members include a common ancestor (not more than six generations removed) and their lineal descendants and their lineal descendants' spouses (or former spouses).[4] Under this broad definition, great-grandparents, grandparents, parents, children, siblings, grandchildren, great-grandchildren, aunts, uncles, cousins, and the respective spouses are family members for this purpose. A practical implication of these limits is that large, publicly traded corporations cannot elect to be treated as S corporations.

[1]S corporations get their name from Subchapter S of the Internal Revenue Code, which includes code sections 1361–1379.

[2]§1361.

[3]Grantor trusts, qualified Subchapter S trusts, electing small business trusts, certain testamentary trusts, and voting trusts can own S corporation stock. A discussion of these trusts is beyond the scope of this chapter. Eligible tax-exempt shareholders include qualified retirement plan trusts or charitable, religious, educational, etc., organizations that are tax-exempt under §501. A single-owned LLC (not electing to be taxed as a corporation) owned by a permissible shareholder (e.g., an individual) may also be an S corporation shareholder. In this case, the LLC would be a disregarded entity and the LLC owner would be considered the shareholder.

[4]The common ancestor (living or not, owning shares or not) must not be more than six generations removed from the youngest generation of shareholder family members determined at the later of the S corporation election date or the date the first member of the respective family holds the S corporation's stock.

Example 22-1

What if: Suppose CCS was formed with Nicole Johnson, Sarah Walker, and Chanzz Inc., a legal corporation owned by Chance Armstrong, as shareholders. Would CCS be eligible to elect S corporation status?

Answer: No. Because one of its shareholders is a corporation (Chanzz Inc.), CCS would not be eligible to elect S corporation status.

What if: Suppose Nicole, Sarah, and Chance recruited 97 U.S. residents to become shareholders of CCS. Meanwhile, Nicole gave several of her CCS shares to her grandfather and his spouse as a wedding gift and to her first cousin as an MBA graduation gift. After the transfer, CCS had 103 shareholders. Can CCS elect S corporation status?

Answer: Yes. Nicole (descendant of common ancestor), her first cousin (descendant of common ancestor), her grandfather (common ancestor), and her grandfather's spouse (spouse of common ancestor) are treated as *one* shareholder for purposes of the 100-shareholder limit.

TAXES IN THE REAL WORLD Planning to Launch the Next Uber? May Want to Rethink That S Election

If you are planning to launch the next great start-up company with aspirations to create the next Uber, you may want to rethink an S corporation election. Many start-up companies with plans for uber growth (pun intended) seek outside investors through venture capital firms. Venture capital firms are generally organized as limited partnerships with an LLC or corporation serving as general partner. Either way, a limited partnership cannot be a shareholder in an S corporation. Thus, if you are planning to launch the next Uber, operating as an S corporation may not be a viable option. Note, however, an S corporation can receive funding from angel investors directly (high-net-worth individuals) and still maintain S corporation status as long as the 100-shareholder limit is not exceeded.

THE KEY FACTS

S Corporation Election

- An eligible corporation must make an affirmative election to be treated as an S corporation.
- Eligible corporations meet the type and number of shareholder requirements, are domestic corporations for tax purposes, are not specifically identified as ineligible corporations, and have only one class of stock.
- To elect S corporation status, the corporation makes a formal election using Form 2553.

S Corporation Election

An eligible corporation must make an affirmative election to be treated as an S corporation.[5] In addition to meeting the shareholder requirements above, it must:

- Be a domestic corporation for tax purposes (created or organized in the United States or under U.S. law or the law of any state in the United States).
- Not be a specifically identified ineligible corporation.[6]
- Have only one class of stock.

A corporation is considered to have only one class of stock if all its outstanding shares provide identical distribution and liquidation rights. Differences in voting powers are permissible. In general, debt instruments do not violate the single-class-of-stock requirement unless they are treated as equity elsewhere under the tax law.[7] In addition, §1361 provides safe-harbor rules to ensure that debt obligations are not recharacterized as a second class of stock.[8]

[5]§1362(a).

[6]Ineligible corporations include financial institutions using the reserve method of accounting under §585, insurance companies, corporations allowed a tax credit for income from Puerto Rico and from U.S. possessions under §936, corporations previously electing Domestic International Sales Corporation status, and corporations treated as a taxable mortgage pool.

[7]See §385 for factors considered in determining whether debt should be considered as equity for tax purposes.

[8]§1361(c)(5)(A) provides that straight debt issued during an S corporation year (i.e., not during a C corporation year) will not be treated as a second class of stock. Section 1361(c)(5)(A) defines straight debt as debt characterized by a written unconditional promise to pay on demand or on a specified date a certain sum in money if (1) the interest rate and interest payment dates are not contingent on profits, the borrower's discretion, or similar factors; (2) the debt is not convertible into stock; and (3) the creditor is an individual (other than a nonresident alien), an estate, a qualified trust, or a person who is actively and regularly engaged in the business of lending money.

Example 22-2

What if: Suppose Nicole were a resident of Toronto, Canada, and while she formed CCS in Canada under Canadian law, she still planned to do business in the United States. Is CCS eligible to elect S corporation status in the United States?

Answer: No. CCS would not be eligible for S corporation treatment because it was neither organized in the United States nor formed under U.S. laws.

What if: Suppose Nicole resided in Seattle and formed CCS under the state laws of Washington but planned to do a significant amount of business in Canada. Would CCS be eligible to elect S corporation status?

Answer: Yes, because CCS was formed under the laws of a U.S. state.

To formally elect S corporation status effective as of the beginning of the current tax year, the corporation uses **Form 2553,** Election by a Small Business Corporation, either in the prior tax year or on or before the 15th day of the third month of the current tax year.[9] Elections made after the 15th day of the third month of a year are effective at the beginning of the following year. All shareholders on the date of the election must consent to the election.

Example 22-3

What if: Suppose Nicole formed CCS as a C corporation in 2021 with a calendar tax year and finally got around to electing S corporation status on February 20, 2022. What is the earliest effective date of the S election?

Answer: January 1, 2022.

What if: Suppose Nicole formed CCS as a C corporation in 2021 with a calendar tax year and made the S election on March 20, 2022. When is the S election effective?

Answer: It is effective January 1, 2023, because Nicole made the election after March 15, 2022.

Even when the corporation makes the election on or before the 15th day of the third month of its tax year, the election will not be effective until the subsequent year if (1) the corporation did not meet the S corporation requirements for each day of the current tax year before it made the S election or (2) one or more shareholders who held the stock in the corporation during the current year and before the S corporation election was made did not consent to the election (e.g., a shareholder disposes of their stock in the corporation in the election year before the election is made and fails to consent to the S election).[10]

Example 22-4

What if: Suppose in 2021 Nicole formed CCS as a C corporation (calendar tax year) with Nicole, Sarah, and Chanzz Inc. (a C corporation) as shareholders. On January 2, 2022, Chanzz Inc. sold all its shares to Chance Armstrong. On January 31, 2022, CCS filed an S corporation election, with Nicole, Sarah, and Chance all consenting to the election. What is the earliest effective date of the S election?

[9]§1362(b). When the IRS determines that taxpayers have reasonable cause for making late elections, it has the authority to treat late elections as timely [§1362(b)(5)]. Rev. Proc. 2013-30 provides a simplified method to provide relief for late elections by submitting Form 2553 to the IRS with a statement that explains that (a) there was either reasonable cause for the late election or the late election was inadvertent and (b) the taxpayer acted diligently to correct the mistake upon discovery.

[10]§1362(b)(2). Requiring all shareholders who own stock in an S corporation during the year to consent to the election ensures that shareholders who dispose of their stock before the election do not suffer adverse tax consequences from an election to which they did not consent.

Answer: January 1, 2023. Because CCS had an ineligible shareholder (Chanzz Inc.) during 2022, the election is not effective until the beginning of 2023.

What if: Suppose in 2021 Nicole formed CCS as a C corporation (calendar tax year) with Nicole, Sarah, and Chance as shareholders. On January 30, 2022, Chance sold his shares to Nicole. On February 15, 2022, CCS filed an S election, with Nicole and Sarah consenting to the election. Chance, however, did not consent to the election. What is the earliest effective date of the S election?

Answer: January 1, 2023. Because Chance was a shareholder until January 30, 2022, and he did not consent to the S election in 2022, the S election is not effective until the beginning of 2023, the year after the election.

The timing of the election may be especially important for C corporations with net operating losses. The reason: Net operating losses attributable to C corporation years generally cannot be carried over to the S corporation. Thus, it may be beneficial to delay the S election until the corporation has utilized its net operating losses.[11]

S CORPORATION TERMINATIONS

LO 22-2

Once the S election becomes effective, the corporation remains an S corporation until the election is terminated. The termination may be voluntary or involuntary.

Voluntary Terminations

The corporation can make a *voluntary revocation* of the S election if shareholders holding more than 50 percent of the S corporation stock (including nonvoting shares) agree.[12] The corporation files a statement with the IRS revoking the election made under §1362(a) and stating the effective date of the revocation and the number of shares issued and outstanding. In general, voluntary revocations made on or before the 15th day of the third month of the year are effective as of the beginning of the year. A revocation after this period is effective the first day of the following tax year. Alternatively, an S corporation may specify the termination date as long as the date specified is on or after the date the revocation is made.[13]

Example 22-5

What if: Suppose CCS had been initially formed as an S corporation with a calendar year-end. After a couple of years, things were going so well that Nicole and Sarah (each one-third shareholders) wanted to terminate the S election and take CCS public. However, Chance (also a one-third shareholder) was opposed to the S election termination. Can Nicole and Sarah terminate the S election without Chance's consent?

Answer: Yes. To revoke the election, Nicole and Sarah need to own more than 50 percent of the shares, and together they own 66.7 percent.

What if: If Nicole and Sarah file the revocation on February 15, 2023, what is the effective date of the S corporation termination (assuming they do not specify one)?

Answer: January 1, 2023. If they file the S corporation revocation after March 15, 2023, it becomes effective January 1, 2024. Alternatively, CCS could have specified an effective date of the S corporation's termination (in 2023 or after) as long as it was on or after the date the revocation was made.

[11]Later in this chapter we discuss one exception to the rule that disallows net operating loss carryovers from C corporation to S corporation years. See the discussion of the S corporation built-in gains tax.

[12]§1362(d)(1)(B).

[13]§1362(d)(1)(D).

ETHICS

Suppose Chance Armstrong is a U.S. resident but a French citizen. His mother has recently been diagnosed with a terminal illness, and Chance has decided to move back to France to take care of his mother and her affairs. He anticipates that he will live in France for several years and that he will no longer be considered a U.S. resident. If you were Sarah or Nicole, how would you react to Chance's decision to move? Would you ignore the impact it may have on CCS's S corporation status? Would you pressure Chance to sell his CCS stock to you?

Involuntary Terminations

Involuntary terminations can result from failure to meet requirements (by far the most common reason) or from an excess of passive investment income.

Failure to Meet Requirements A corporation's S election is automatically terminated if the corporation fails to meet the requirements. The termination is effective on the date it fails the S corporation requirements. If the IRS deems the termination inadvertent, it may allow the corporation to continue to be treated as an S corporation if, within a reasonable period after the inadvertent termination, the corporation takes the necessary steps to meet the S corporation requirements.[14]

Example 22-6

What if: Suppose CCS was formed as a calendar-year S corporation with Nicole Johnson, Sarah Walker, and Chance Armstrong as equal shareholders. On June 15, 2022, Chance sold his CCS shares to his solely owned C corporation, Chanzz Inc. Is CCS's S election still in effect at the beginning of 2023? If not, when was it terminated?

Answer: No, the election was automatically terminated on June 15, 2022, when Chanzz Inc. became a shareholder because S corporations may not have corporate shareholders.

Excess of Passive Investment Income If an S corporation has *earnings and profits* from a previous C corporation year (or through a tax-deferred reorganization with a corporation that has earnings and profits), its election is terminated if the S corporation has passive investment income in excess of 25 percent of gross receipts for three consecutive years. If the S corporation has never operated as a C corporation or does not have C corporation earnings and profits (either by prior distribution of C corporation earnings and profits, or simply by not having earnings and profits at the effective date of the S election), this provision does not apply.

For purposes of the passive investment income test, **gross receipts** are the total amount of revenues received—including net capital gains from the sale of capital assets and gain (not offset by losses) from the sale of stock and securities—or accrued under the corporation's accounting method, *not* reduced by returns, allowances, cost of goods sold, or deductions. **Passive investment income (PII)** includes gross receipts from royalties, rents, dividends, interest (including tax-exempt interest), and annuities.[15] While net capital gain income is included in gross receipts, it is *not* considered passive investment income. S corporation election terminations due to excess passive investment income are effective on the first day of the year following the third consecutive tax year with excess passive investment income.

[14]§1362(f). Because the restrictions on S corporation ownership are so specific and exact, many S corporations require their shareholders, as a condition of stock ownership, to enter into a shareholder agreement. These agreements generally restrict the ability of shareholders to transfer their stock ownership to any disqualified shareholder.

[15]PII excludes certain rents (e.g., rents derived from the active trade or business of renting property, produced film rents, income from leasing self-produced tangible property, temporary parking fees, etc.).

Example 22-7

What if: Suppose CCS was initially formed as an S corporation with a calendar year-end. During its first three years, it reported passive investment income in excess of 25 percent of its gross receipts. Is CCS's S election terminated under the excess passive investment income test? If so, what is the effective date of the termination?

Answer: No, the excess passive investment income test does not apply to CCS in this situation because CCS has never operated as a C corporation; consequently, it does not have C corporation earnings and profits.

What if: Suppose CCS was initially formed as a C corporation with a calendar year-end. After a very profitable first year of operations, CCS elected S corporation status, effective January 1, 2022. During 2023, 2024, and 2025, it reported passive investment income in excess of 25 percent of its gross receipts and had undistributed earnings and profits from its C corporation year. Is CCS's S election terminated under the excess passive investment income test? If so, what is the effective date of the termination?

Answer: Yes, it is terminated. Because CCS has C corporation earnings and profits from 2021 and excess passive investment income for three consecutive years as an S corporation, its S election is terminated, effective January 1, 2026.

Short Tax Years

S corporation election terminations frequently create an S corporation *short tax year* (i.e., a reporting year less than 12 months) and a C corporation short tax year. The corporation must then allocate its income for the full year between the S and the C corporation years, using the number of days in each short year (the daily method). Or it may use the corporation's normal accounting rules to allocate income to the actual period in which it was earned (the specific identification method).[16] Both short tax year returns are due on the corporation's customary tax return due date (with normal extensions available).

Example 22-8

What if: Suppose CCS was formed as a calendar-year S corporation with Nicole Johnson, Sarah Walker, and Chance Armstrong as equal shareholders. On June 15, 2022, Chance sold his CCS shares (one-third of all shares) to his solely owned C corporation, Chanzz Inc., terminating CCS's S election on June 15, 2022. Assume CCS reported the following business income for 2022:

Period	Income
January 1 through June 14 (165 days)	$100,000
June 15 through December 31 (200 days)	265,000
January 1 through December 31, 2022 (365 days)	$365,000

If CCS uses the daily method of allocating income between the S corporation short tax year (January 1–June 14) and the C corporation short tax year (June 15–December 31), how much income will it report on its S corporation short tax year return and its C corporation short tax year return for 2022?

Answer: S corporation short tax year = $165,000 ($365,000/365 days × 165 days); C corporation short tax year = $200,000 ($365,000/365 days × 200 days).

(continued on page 22-8)

THE KEY FACTS

S Corporation Terminations and Reelections

- The S election may be revoked by shareholders holding more than 50 percent of the S corporation's stock (including nonvoting shares).

(continued)

[16]Use of the specific identification method requires that all shareholders at any time during the S corporation short year and the shareholders on the first day of the C corporation short year consent to the election using the specific identification method [§1362(e)(3)(A)]. However, an S corporation must use the specific identification method to allocate income between the short years (the per day allocation method is not allowed) if there is a sale or exchange of 50 percent or more of the corporation's stock during the year [§1362(e)(6)(D)].

- A corporation's S election is automatically terminated if (1) the S corporation fails to meet the S corporation requirements or (2) the S corporation has earnings and profits from a previous C corporation year and has passive investment income in excess of 25 percent of gross receipts for three consecutive years.
- A corporation losing its S corporation status must wait until the beginning of the fifth year after the election is terminated to elect S corporation status again.

What if: If CCS uses the specific identification method to allocate income, how much will it allocate to the S corporation short tax year and how much will it allocate to the C corporation short tax year?

Answer: S corporation short tax year, $100,000; C corporation short tax year, $265,000.

Note that if the entity wanted to minimize the income subject to taxation as a C corporation, it would use the daily method of allocating income.

S Corporation Reelections

After terminating or voluntarily revoking S corporation status, the corporation may elect it again, but it generally must wait until the beginning of the fifth tax year *after* the tax year in which it terminated the election.[17] Thus, if the election was terminated effective the first day of the tax year, the corporation must wait five full years to again become an S corporation.

Example 22-9

What if: Let's return to the facts of Example 22-8. CCS was formed as a calendar-year S corporation with Nicole Johnson, Sarah Walker, and Chance Armstrong as equal shareholders. On June 15, 2022, Chance sold his CCS shares (one-third of all shares) to his solely owned C corporation, Chanzz Inc., terminating CCS's S election on June 15, 2022. Absent permission from the IRS (see text below), what is the earliest date CCS may again elect to be taxed as an S corporation?

Answer: January 1, 2027. This is the fifth tax year after the year in which the termination became effective.

What if: Assume on February 1, 2022, CCS voluntarily elected to revoke its S corporation status effective January 1, 2023. Absent IRS permission, what is the earliest CCS may again elect to be taxed as an S corporation?

Answer: January 1, 2028. This is the fifth year after the year in which the termination became effective.

The IRS may consent to an earlier election under a couple of conditions: (1) if the corporation is now more than 50 percent owned by shareholders who were not owners at the time of termination or (2) if the termination was not reasonably within the control of the corporation or shareholders with a substantial interest in the corporation and was not part of a planned termination by the corporation or shareholders. Given the potential adverse consequences of an S election termination, the corporation should carefully monitor compliance with the S corporation requirements.

LO 22-3

OPERATING ISSUES

Accounting Methods and Periods

Like partnerships, S corporations determine their accounting periods and make accounting method elections at the entity level. An S corporation makes most of its elections (e.g., electing out of bonus depreciation) in conjunction with the filing of its annual tax return and some by filing a separate request with the IRS. (For example, an application to change accounting methods is filed on Form 3115, separate from the S corporation's tax return.) For an S corporation previously operating as a C corporation, all prior accounting methods carry over to the S corporation.

[17]§1362(g).

Recall that both C corporations and partnerships with C corporation partners face restrictions on using the cash method. S corporations do not. They may choose the cash, accrual, or a hybrid method unless selling inventory is a material income-producing factor for them. In that case, they generally must account for gross profit (sales minus cost of goods sold) using the accrual method, even if they are otherwise cash-method taxpayers.[18] Hence, they would use the hybrid method.

Tax laws also specify permissible tax years for S corporations, but they are a little less cumbersome than for partnerships. S corporations must use a calendar year-end unless they can establish a business purpose for an alternative year-end or a natural business year-end. For example, a business that receives 25 percent or more of gross receipts for the previous three years in the last two months of the year-end requested would qualify for a noncalendar year-end.[19]

THE KEY FACTS

Operating Issues

- S corporations are generally required to adopt a calendar tax year.
- S corporations allocate profits and losses to shareholders pro rata, based on the number of outstanding shares each shareholder owns on each day of the tax year.
- S corporations determine each shareholder's share of ordinary business income (loss) and separately stated items.
- Ordinary business income (loss) is all income (loss) exclusive of any separately stated items of income (loss). Separately stated items are tax items that are treated differently from a shareholder's share of ordinary business income (loss) for tax purposes.

Income and Loss Allocations

S corporations, like partnerships, are flow-through entities, and thus their profits and losses flow through to their shareholders annually for tax purposes. As we discussed in the Forming and Operating Partnerships chapter, partnerships have considerable flexibility in making special profit and loss allocations to their partners. In contrast, S corporations must allocate profits and losses pro rata, based on the number of outstanding shares each shareholder owns on each day of the tax year.[20]

An S corporation generally allocates income or loss items to shareholders on the last day of its tax year.[21] If a shareholder sells their shares during the year, they will report their share of S corporation income and loss allocated to the days they owned the stock (including the day of sale) using a pro rata allocation. If *all shareholders with changing ownership percentages* during the year agree, the S corporation can instead use its normal accounting rules to allocate income and loss (and other separately stated items, discussed below) to the specific periods in which it realized income and losses.

Example 22-10

What if: Assume CCS was formed as a calendar-year S corporation with Nicole Johnson, Sarah Walker, and Chance Armstrong as equal (one-third) shareholders. On June 14, 2022, Chance sold his CCS shares to Nicole. CCS reported the following business income for 2022:

Period	Income
January 1 through June 14 (165 days)	$100,000
June 15 through December 31 (200 days)	265,000
January 1 through December 31, 2022 (365 days)	$365,000

How much 2022 income is allocated to each shareholder if CCS uses the daily method of allocating income?

(continued on page 22-10)

[18]Section 471(c)(1) provides an exception to this general rule. Specifically, S corporations are not required to use the accrual method if (a) for 2022, they have average gross receipts of $27 million or less for the three prior tax years; (b) they choose not to keep an inventory; and (c) their method of accounting (i) treats inventory as nonincidental material or supplies deducted when first used or consumed or (ii) conforms to their financial accounting treatment for inventories. For these S corporations, the accrual method is not required for inventories.

[19]§1378(b). In addition, S corporations, like partnerships, have the option of electing an alternative taxable year under §444.

[20]§§1366(a), 1377(a).

[21]§1366(a).

Answer: Nicole's allocation is $188,333; Sarah's is $121,667; and Chance's is $55,000, calculated as follows.

Individual	(1) January 1–June 14	(2) June 15–December 31	(1) + (2) Total 2022 Allocation
Nicole	$55,000 ($365,000/365 × 165 × 1/3)	$133,333 ($365,000/365 × 200 × 2/3)	**$188,333**
Sarah	$55,000 ($365,000/365 × 165 × 1/3)	$66,667 ($365,000/365 × 200 × 1/3)	**121,667**
Chance	$55,000 ($365,000/365 × 165 × 1/3)	$0	**55,000**
Totals	$165,000	$200,000	$ 365,000

How much 2022 income is allocated to each shareholder if CCS uses its normal accounting rules to allocate income to the specific periods in which it was actually earned?

Answer: Nicole's allocation is $210,000 ($100,000 × 1/3 + $265,000 × 2/3); Sarah's is $121,667 ($365,000 × 1/3); and Chance's is $33,333 ($100,000 × 1/3).

Separately Stated Items

Like partnerships, S corporations are required to file tax returns (Form 1120-S, U.S. Income Tax Return for an S Corporation) annually. In addition, on Form 1120-S, Schedule K-1, they supply information to each shareholder detailing the amount *and* character of items of income and loss flowing through the S corporation.[22] Shareholders must report these income and loss items on their respective tax returns even if they do not receive cash distributions during the year.

S corporations determine each shareholder's share of ordinary business income (loss) and separately stated items. Like partnerships, **ordinary business income (loss)** (also referred to as *nonseparately stated income or loss*) is all income (loss) exclusive of any separately stated items of income (loss). **Separately stated items** are tax items that are treated differently from a shareholder's share of ordinary business income (loss) for tax purposes. The character of each separately stated item is determined at the S corporation level rather than at the shareholder level. The list of common separately stated items for S corporations is similar to that for partnerships, with a couple of exceptions. (For example, S corporations do not report self-employment income and do not have guaranteed payments.) Exhibit 22-1 lists several common separately stated items. See Form 1120-S,

EXHIBIT 22-1 Common Separately Stated Items

- Short-term capital gains and losses
- Long-term capital gains and losses
- §1231 gains and losses
- Dividends
- Interest income
- Charitable contributions
- Tax-exempt income
- Net rental real estate income
- Investment interest expense
- §179 deduction
- Foreign taxes
- §199A qualified business income, allocated wages, and unadjusted basis of qualified property (included in a statement attached to Schedule K-1)

[22]Other items, such as tax credits and informational items such as AMT adjustments, also flow through from the S corporation to its shareholders and are reported to shareholders on Form 1120-S, Schedule K-1.

Schedule K-1 (and related instructions) for a comprehensive list of separately stated items.[23] Similar to partners in a partnership, S corporation shareholders are allowed a 20 percent deduction for §199A qualified business income, calculated and subject to limitations at the shareholder level. See the Business Entities Overview chapter for a discussion of the deduction. Informational items related to the deduction calculation (e.g., §199A qualified business income; W-2 wages paid by the S corporation, including owner's compensation; and unadjusted basis of qualified property) are reported to shareholders in a statement included with Form 1120-S, Schedule K-1.

S corporations may hold stock in C corporations, and any dividends S corporations receive will flow through to their shareholders. However, S corporations are not entitled to claim the dividends-received deduction that is available to C corporations.

Assuming CCS operated as a C corporation in 2021 and an S corporation in 2022, Exhibit 22-2 presents the results of operations. CCS's S election was not effective until January 1, 2022, because the shareholders filed the S election after the required date for it to be effective in 2021.

EXHIBIT 22-2

Color Comfort Sheets
Income Statement
December 31, 2021 and 2022

	2021 C Corporation	2022 S Corporation
Sales revenue	$220,000	$ 520,000
Cost of goods sold	(50,000)	(115,000)
Salary to owners Nicole and Sarah	(70,000)	(90,000)
Employee wages	(45,000)	(50,000)
Depreciation expense	(15,000)	(20,000)
Miscellaneous expenses	(4,000)	(5,000)
Interest income (from investments)	3,000	6,000
Dividend income	1,000	3,000
Overall net income	$ 40,000	$ 249,000

Example 22-11

Given that CCS was a C corporation for tax purposes in 2021 and an S corporation in 2022, and its operating results in Exhibit 22-2, what amounts of ordinary business income and separately stated items are allocated to CCS's shareholders for 2021?

Answer: $0 ordinary business income and $0 separately stated items. Because CCS is a C corporation in 2021, its income does *not* flow through to its shareholders.

Based on the information in Exhibit 22-2, what amounts of ordinary business income and separately stated items are allocated to CCS's shareholders for 2022? Assume CCS has qualified property with an unadjusted basis of $300,000 for purposes of the deduction for qualified business income.

(continued on page 22-12)

[23]S corporations with average annual gross receipts for the prior three years that exceed $27 million in 2022 are subject to the 30 percent of taxable income limitation on the deduction for business interest expense. See the Business Income, Deductions, and Accounting Methods chapter. The limitation applies at the S corporation level, not at the shareholder level. In years where the adjusted taxable income limitation is binding, the disallowed business interest does not reduce S corporation income or reduce shareholder basis. Instead, the S corporation carries the disallowed business interest forward to the next year and applies the limitation calculation in that year. Any business interest deduction allowed reduces S corporation income (and shareholder basis). When the adjusted taxable income limitation applies but is not binding, the S corporation reports any excess taxable income to its shareholders as an information item so that shareholders can use the excess taxable income in calculating their deductible business interest expense from non–S corporation sources (e.g., from a sole proprietorship) if they are subject to the taxable income limitation.

Answer: See the following table for the allocations:

Description	CCS	Allocations Nicole 1/3	Sarah 1/3	Chance 1/3
2022 overall net income less:	$249,000			
Dividends	3,000			
Interest income	6,000			
Ordinary Business Income	$240,000	**$80,000**	**$80,000**	**$80,000**
Separately Stated Items:				
Interest income	6,000	**2,000**	**2,000**	**2,000**
Dividends	3,000	**1,000**	**1,000**	**1,000**
Qualified Business Income				
Informational Items:				
§199A qualified business income	240,000	80,000	80,000	80,000
§199A allocated wages	140,000	46,667	46,667	46,666
§199A unadjusted basis of qualified property	300,000	100,000	100,000	100,000

Nicole, Sarah, and Chance will treat their shares of CCS's ordinary business income as *ordinary* income and include it, along with their shares of interest and dividend income, in their individual tax returns for the year.[24] Qualified business income does not include interest income because it was not allocable to the trade or business. Allocated wages include the $50,000 wages paid to employees and $90,000 wages paid to owners.

LO 22-4

SHAREHOLDER'S BASIS

Just as partners must determine their bases in their partnership interests, S corporation shareholders must determine their bases in S corporation stock to determine the gain or loss they recognize when they sell the stock, the taxability of distributions, and the deductibility of losses.

Initial Basis An S corporation shareholder calculates their *initial basis* upon formation of the corporation, like a C corporation shareholder. (See earlier discussion in text on corporate formation.) Specifically, the shareholder's basis in stock received in the exchange equals the tax basis of the property transferred, less any liabilities assumed by the corporation on the property contributed (*substituted basis*). The shareholder's stock basis is increased by any gain recognized; it is reduced by the fair market value of any property received other than stock.[25] If, on the other hand, the shareholder purchased the S corporation stock from another shareholder or the corporation, the new shareholder's basis is simply the purchase price of the stock.[26]

[24]Nicole, Sarah, and Chance would report their share of ordinary business income on Schedule E and their share of interest and dividend income on Schedule B of Form 1040.

[25]§358. This assumes the shareholder meets the §351 requirements. If the shareholder's exchange with the corporation does not meet these requirements, the shareholder's basis in the stock is its fair market value.

[26]If the shareholder acquires the stock by gift, their basis in the stock is the lesser of the donor's basis (increased for any gift taxes paid on the stock's appreciation) or the fair market value of the stock. In contrast, if the shareholder acquires the stock by bequest, their basis in the stock is the stock's fair market value on the date of the decedent's death adjusted to reflect any income in respect of the decedent.

Example 22-12

At the beginning of 2021, Nicole contributed $30,000 of cash and land with a fair market value of $130,000 and an adjusted basis of $125,000 to CCS. The land was encumbered by a $40,000 mortgage executed three years before. Sarah and Chance each contributed $120,000 of cash to CCS. What tax bases do Nicole, Sarah, and Chance have in their CCS stock at the beginning of 2021?

Answer: Nicole's basis is $115,000 ($30,000 cash + $125,000 adjusted basis of land − $40,000 mortgage assumed), Sarah's basis is $120,000, and Chance's basis is $120,000.

Annual Basis Adjustments While C corporation rules govern the initial stock basis of an S corporation shareholder, subsequent calculations more closely resemble the partnership rules. Specifically, an S corporation shareholder's stock basis is dynamic and must be *adjusted annually* to ensure that (1) taxable income/gains and deductible expenses/losses are *not* double-counted by shareholders either when they sell their shares or when they receive S corporation distributions (for example, because shareholders are taxed on the S corporation's income annually, they should not be taxed again when they receive distributions of the income) and (2) tax-exempt income and nondeductible expenses are not ultimately taxed or deducted.

S corporation shareholders make the following adjustments to their stock basis annually, in the order listed:

- Increase for any capital contributions to the S corporation during the year.
- Increase for shareholder's share of ordinary business income and separately stated income/gain items (including tax-exempt income).
- Decrease for distributions during the year.
- Decrease for shareholder's share of nondeductible expenses (e.g., fines and penalties).
- Decrease for shareholder's share of ordinary business loss and separately stated expense/loss items.[27]

As with a partnership, adjustments that decrease basis may never reduce an S corporation shareholder's tax basis below zero.[28]

S corporation shareholders are not allowed to include any S corporation debt in their stock basis. Recall that partners *are* allowed to include their share of partnership debt in the basis of their partnership interests. One implication of this difference is that, everything else equal, an S corporation shareholder's basis will be lower than a partner's basis, due to the exclusion of debt (however, see the discussion of *debt basis* for S corporation shareholders below).

THE KEY FACTS

S Corporation Shareholder's Basis Adjustments

- A shareholder will *increase* the tax basis in their stock for:
  - Capital contributions.
  - Share of ordinary business income.
  - Separately stated income/gain items.
  - Tax-exempt income.
- A shareholder will *decrease* the tax basis in their stock for:
  - Cash distributions.
  - Share of nondeductible expenses.
  - Share of ordinary business loss.
  - Separately stated expense/loss items.
- A shareholder's tax basis may not be negative.

Example 22-13

Given the shareholders' 2021 bases in their CCS stock in Example 22-12 (Nicole, $115,000; Sarah, $120,000; and Chance, $120,000), what basis does each have at the end of 2022, after taking into account the information in Exhibit 22-2 (but before taking into account any distributions, which are discussed below)?

(continued on page 22-14)

[27]Reg. §1.1367-1(g).
[28]§1367(a)(2).

Answer: Nicole, $198,000; Sarah, $203,000; and Chance, $203,000, computed as follows:

Description	Nicole	Sarah	Chance	Explanation
(1) Initial tax basis	$ 115,000	$ 120,000	$ 120,000	Example 22-12
(2) Ordinary business income	80,000	80,000	80,000	Example 22-11
(3) Interest income	2,000	2,000	2,000	Example 22-11
(4) Dividends	1,000	1,000	1,000	Example 22-11
Tax basis in stock at end of 2022	**$198,000**	**$203,000**	**$203,000**	(1) + (2) + (3) + (4)

Note that the shareholders do not include any portion of CCS's debt in their stock basis.

What if: Suppose that, in addition to the amounts in Exhibit 22-2, CCS also recognized $1,200 of tax-exempt interest income in 2022. Nicole's share of this separately stated item is $400. Taking this allocation into account, what is Nicole's stock basis at the end of 2022?

Answer: It is $198,400 ($198,000 + $400). The tax-exempt income allocated to Nicole as a separately stated item increases her tax basis to ensure that she is never taxed on her share of the tax-exempt income.

Loss Limitations

S corporations have loss-limitation rules similar to those for partnerships. For an S corporation shareholder to deduct a loss, the loss must clear three separate hurdles: (1) tax-basis, (2) at-risk amount, and (3) passive activity.[29] In addition, for losses that clear each of the three hurdles, S corporation shareholders are not allowed to deduct excess business losses as described below.

Tax-Basis Limitation S corporation shareholders may not deduct losses in excess of their stock basis. Recall they are not allowed to include debt in their basis; partners are. This restriction makes it more likely that the tax-basis limitation will apply to S corporation shareholders than to similarly situated partners. Losses not deductible due to the tax-basis limitation are not necessarily lost. Rather, they are suspended until the shareholder generates additional basis. The carryover period for the suspended loss is indefinite. However, if the shareholder sells the stock before creating additional basis, the suspended loss disappears unused.

Example 22-14

What if: Suppose at the beginning of 2023, Nicole's basis in her CCS stock was $14,000. During 2023, CCS reported a $60,000 ordinary business loss and no separately stated items. How much of the ordinary loss is allocated to Nicole?

Answer: The loss allocation is $20,000 ($60,000 × 1/3).

How much of the $20,000 loss clears the tax-basis hurdle for deductibility in 2023?

Answer: The amount of Nicole's basis in her CCS stock, or $14,000. The remaining $6,000 of loss does not clear the tax-basis hurdle; it is suspended until Nicole generates additional basis.

A shareholder can mitigate the disadvantage of not including S corporation debt in stock basis by loaning money directly to the S corporation. These loans create **debt basis,** separate from stock basis. Losses are limited first to the shareholder's tax basis in S corporation stock and *then* to the shareholder's basis in any direct loans made to the S corporation.[30]

[29]S corporations are also subject to the hobby loss rules in §183 that limit loss deductions for activities not engaged in for profit.

[30]§1366(d)(1)(B). These must be direct loans to the corporation. Thus, shareholders do not get debt basis when they guarantee a loan of the S corporation, although they would to the extent they had to "make good" on their guarantee obligation.

Specifically, if the total amount of items (besides distributions) that decrease the shareholder's basis for the year exceeds the shareholder's stock basis, the excess amount decreases the shareholder's debt basis. Like stock basis, debt basis cannot be decreased below zero. In subsequent years, any net increase in basis for the year restores first the shareholder's debt basis (up to the outstanding debt amount) and then the shareholder's stock basis. If the S corporation repays the debt owed to the shareholder before the shareholder's debt basis is restored, any loan repayment in excess of the shareholder's debt basis will trigger a taxable gain to the shareholder.

Example 22-15

What if: Suppose at the beginning of 2023, Nicole's basis in her CCS stock was $14,000. During 2023, Nicole loaned $8,000 to CCS, and CCS reported a $60,000 ordinary business loss and no separately stated items. How much of the $20,000 ordinary loss allocated to Nicole clears the tax-basis hurdle for deductibility in 2023?

Answer: All $20,000. The first $14,000 of the loss reduces her stock basis to $0, and the remaining $6,000 reduces her debt basis to $2,000 ($8,000 – $6,000).

What if: Suppose in 2024, CCS allocated $9,000 of ordinary business income to Nicole and no separately stated items. What are Nicole's CCS stock basis and debt basis at the end of 2024, assuming CCS did not pay back any debt?

Answer: Her stock basis is $3,000; her debt basis is $8,000. The income first restores debt basis to the outstanding debt amount and then increases her stock basis.

At-Risk Amount Limitation Like partners in partnerships, S corporation shareholders are subject to the *at-risk* rules. They may deduct S corporation losses only to the extent of their **at-risk amount** in the S corporation, as defined in §465. With one notable exception, an S corporation shareholder's at-risk amount is the sum of the shareholder's stock and debt bases. The primary exception relates to nonrecourse loans (i.e., loans that do not allow lenders to pursue anything other than the collateral securing the loans) and is designed to ensure that shareholders are deemed at risk only when they have an actual risk of loss. Specifically, an S corporation shareholder taking out a nonrecourse loan to make a capital contribution (either cash or other property) to the S corporation generally creates stock basis (equal to the basis of property contributed) in the S corporation but increases the amount at risk by only the net fair market value of the shareholder's property, if any, used as collateral to secure the nonrecourse loan.[31] The collateral's net fair market value is determined at the loan date.

Likewise, if the shareholder takes out a nonrecourse loan to make a direct loan to the S corporation, the loan creates debt basis but increases the amount at risk only by the net fair market value of the shareholder's property, if any, used as collateral to secure the nonrecourse loan. When the stock basis plus debt basis is different from the at-risk amount, S corporation shareholders apply the tax-basis loss limitation first, and then the at-risk limitation. Losses limited under the at-risk rules are carried forward indefinitely until the shareholder generates additional at-risk amounts to utilize them or sells the S corporation stock.

THE KEY FACTS

Loss Limitations

- S corporation losses in excess of a shareholder's tax basis and at-risk amount are suspended and carried forward until additional basis and amounts at risk are created.
- Upon S election termination, shareholders may create additional stock basis during the post-termination transition period to utilize losses limited by the basis or at-risk rules.
- The passive activity loss rules limit the ability of S corporation shareholders to deduct losses of the S corporation unless the shareholders are actively managing the business.

Post-Termination Transition Period Loss Limitation The voluntary or involuntary termination of a corporation's S election creates a problem for shareholders with suspended losses due to the basis and at-risk rules. The reason: These losses are generally not deductible after the S termination date. Shareholders can obtain some relief provided by §1366(d)(3), which allows them to treat any suspended losses existing at the S termination date as occurring on the last day of the **post-termination transition period (PTTP).** In general, the PTTP begins on the day after the last day of the corporation's last

[31]§465(b)(2)(B). In some circumstances (beyond the scope of this text), shareholders do not create stock basis (or debt basis) for capital contributions (or shareholder loans to the S corporation) that are funded by nonrecourse loans.

taxable year as an S corporation and ends on the later of (a) one year after the last S corporation day or (b) the due date for filing the return for the last year as an S corporation (including extensions).[32]

This rule allows the shareholder to create additional stock basis by making additional capital contributions during the PTTP and to utilize suspended losses based on their *stock* basis (but not debt basis) at the end of the period. Any suspended losses utilized at the end of the PTTP reduce the shareholder's basis in the stock. Any losses not utilized at the end of the period are lost forever.

Example 22-16

What if: Suppose CCS terminated its S election on July 17, 2023. At the end of the S corporation's short tax year ending on July 17, Nicole's stock basis and at-risk amounts were both zero (she has never had debt basis), and she had a suspended loss of $15,000. Nicole made additional capital contributions of $10,000 on February 20, 2024, and $7,000 on September 6, 2024. When does the PTTP end for CCS? How much loss may Nicole deduct, and what is her basis in the CCS stock at the end of the PTTP?

Answer: For loss deduction purposes, CCS's PTTP ends on September 15, 2024. That date represents (b) in the "later of (a) or (b)" alternative—(a) one year after the last S corporation day, which would be July 17, 2024, or (b) the due date for filing the return for the last year as an S corporation, including extensions, which would be September 15, 2024, assuming CCS extends its tax return. (Note that the short tax year S corporation return is due the same time as the short tax year C corporation return.) Nicole may deduct the entire $15,000 suspended loss because her basis at the end of the PTTP and before the loss deduction is $17,000. (That amount is calculated as a carryover basis of $0 on the last S corporation day plus $17,000 capital contributions during the PTTP.) Nicole's basis in CCS stock after the loss deduction is $2,000 ($17,000 basis at the end of the PTTP less the $15,000 loss deduction).

What if: Suppose Nicole made her second capital contribution on October 22, 2024, instead of September 6, 2024. How much loss can Nicole deduct, and what is her basis in CCS stock at the end of the PTTP?

Answer: The loss deduction is $10,000: Nicole's stock basis at the end of the PTTP and before her loss deduction is only $10,000 because the $7,000 capital contribution occurred after the end of the PTTP. Nicole's basis in the CCS stock at the end of the PTTP and after the loss deduction is zero ($10,000 basis less $10,000 loss deduction). Her basis then increases to $7,000 on October 22, 2024, but the $5,000 suspended loss is lost forever.

Passive Activity Loss Limitation S corporation shareholders, just like partners, are subject to the **passive activity loss (PAL) rules.** There are no differences in the application of these rules for S corporations; the definition of a passive activity, the tests for material participation, the income and loss baskets, and the passive activity loss carryover rules described in the Forming and Operating Partnerships chapter are exactly the same. Thus, as in partnerships, the passive activity loss rules limit the ability of S corporation shareholders to deduct losses unless they are involved in actively managing the business.[33]

Example 22-17

What if: Suppose in 2024, CCS incurred an ordinary business loss and allocated the loss equally to its shareholders. Assuming Nicole, Sarah, and Chance all had adequate stock basis and at-risk amounts to absorb the losses, which of the three shareholders would be least likely to deduct the loss due to the passive activity limitation rules?

Answer: Chance. Because he is not actively involved in managing CCS's business activities, any loss allocated to him is a passive activity loss.

[32]§1377(b)(1)(A). Section 1377(b) indicates that the PTTP also includes the 120-day period beginning on the date of a determination (not the date of the actual termination) that the corporation's S election had terminated for a previous taxable year.

[33]§469.

Excess Business Loss Limitation Taxpayers are not allowed to deduct an **excess business loss** for the year. Rather, an excess business loss is carried forward to subsequent years. The excess business loss limitation applies to losses that are otherwise deductible under the tax-basis, at-risk, and passive loss rules. An excess business loss for the year is the excess of aggregate business deductions for the year over the sum of aggregate business gross income or gain of the taxpayer plus a threshold amount indexed for inflation. The threshold amount for 2022 is $540,000 for married taxpayers filing jointly and $270,000 for other taxpayers.[34] In the case of partnership or S corporation business losses, the provision applies at the partner/shareholder level.

Self-Employment Income

You might wonder whether an S corporation shareholder's allocable share of ordinary business income (loss) is classified as self-employment income for tax purposes. The answer is no, even when the shareholder actively works for the S corporation.[35]

When a shareholder does work as an employee of and receives a salary from an S corporation, the S corporation treats this salary payment like that made to any other employee: For Social Security taxes, it withholds 6.2 percent of the shareholder's salary or wages subject to the wage limitation ($147,000 in 2022); for Medicare taxes, it withholds 1.45 percent of the shareholder's salary or wages (no limit); and for the additional Medicare tax, it withholds .9 percent of the shareholder's salary or wages above $200,000 (no limit).[36] In addition, the S corporation must pay its portion of the Social Security tax (6.2 percent of the shareholder's salary or wages subject to the $147,000 wage limitation in 2022) and Medicare tax (1.45 percent of the shareholder's salary or wages, regardless of the amount of salary or wages). In contrast to shareholder-employees, S corporations are not subject to the additional Medicare tax on employee salary or wages.

Because of this stark contrast between the treatment of ordinary business income and that of shareholder salaries, S corporation shareholders may desire to avoid payroll taxes by limiting or even eliminating their salary payments. However, if they work as employees, they are required to pay themselves a reasonable salary for the services they perform. If they pay themselves an unreasonably low salary, the IRS may attempt to reclassify some or all of the S corporation's ordinary business income as shareholder salary!

TAXES IN THE REAL WORLD The Benefits of an S Corporation

U.S. President Joe Biden appears to be a fan of S corporations. His 2017 and 2018 tax returns reveal that a large portion of his income came from an S corporation, CelticCapri Corp., that was established for his speaking and writing engagements after his book release of *Promise Me, Dad*. President Biden earned almost $3 million from CelticCapri but only reported $300,000 of compensation as CelticCapri's employee. By doing so, Biden avoided employment or self-employment taxes on the bulk of CelticCapri's earnings.

Source: Eric Yauch, "Biden Took 'Astounding' Tax Positions in Business Planning," *Taxnotes.com*, July 11, 2019.

[34]In 2020, the CARES Act suspended the excess business loss limitation for 2018, 2019, and 2020. Thus, taxpayers were able to deduct excess business losses arising from these years.

[35]Rev. Rul. 59-221.

[36]Although employee liability for the additional Medicare tax varies based on filing status ($250,000 combined salary or wages for married filing jointly; $125,000 salary or wages for married filing separate; $200,000 salary or wages for all other taxpayers), employers are required to withhold the additional Medicare tax on salary or wages above $200,000 irrespective of the taxpayer's filing status.

Net Investment Income Tax

Just like partners in a partnership, S corporation shareholders are subject to a 3.8 percent net investment income tax on their share of an S corporation's gross income from interest, dividends, annuities, royalties, rents, a trade or business that is a passive activity or a trade or business of trading financial instruments or commodities, and any net gain from disposing of property (other than property held in a trade or business in which the net investment income tax does not apply), less any allowable deductions from these items.[37,38] Likewise, any gain from the sale of S corporation stock (or distribution in excess of basis) is subject to the net investment income tax to the extent it is allocable to assets held by the S corporation that would have generated a net gain subject to the net investment income tax if all S corporation assets were sold at fair market value.[39]

Fringe Benefits

True to their hybrid status, S corporations are treated in part like C corporations and in part like partnerships with respect to tax deductions for qualifying employee fringe benefits.[40] For shareholder-employees who own 2 percent or less of the entity, the S corporation receives C corporation tax treatment. That is, it gets a tax deduction for qualifying fringe benefits, and the benefits are nontaxable to *all* employees. For shareholder-employees who own more than 2 percent of the S corporation, it receives partnership treatment.[41] That is, it gets a tax deduction, but the otherwise-qualifying fringe benefits are taxable to the shareholder-employees who own more than 2 percent.[42]

Fringe benefits taxable to this group include employer-provided health insurance[43] (§106), group-term life insurance (§79), meals and lodging provided for the convenience of the employer (§119), and benefits provided under a cafeteria plan (§125). Examples of benefits that are nontaxable to more-than-2-percent shareholder-employees (and partners in a partnership) include employee achievement awards (§74), qualified group legal services plans (§120), educational assistance programs (§127), dependent care assistance programs (§129), no-additional-cost services (§132), qualified employee discounts (§132), working-condition fringe benefits (§132), *de minimis* fringe benefits (§132), on-premises athletic facilities (§132), and medical savings accounts (§220).

[37]Interest, dividend, annuity, royalty, and rent income derived in the *ordinary* course of a trade or business that is not passive and does not involve financial instrument or commodity trading is exempt from the net investment income tax.

[38]The tax imposed is 3.8 percent of the lesser of (a) net investment income or (b) the excess of modified adjusted gross income over $250,000 for married-joint filers and surviving spouses, $125,000 for married-separate filers, and $200,000 for other taxpayers. Modified adjusted gross income equals adjusted gross income increased by income excluded under the foreign earned income exclusion less any disallowed deductions associated with the foreign earned income exclusion.

[39]See Prop. Reg. §1.1411-7.

[40]Qualifying fringe benefits are nontaxable to the employee. Other fringe benefits (nonqualifying) are taxed as compensation to employees.

[41]§1372(a).

[42]The §318 indirect stock ownership rules apply (see the Corporate Taxation: Nonliquidating Distributions chapter) for purposes of determining which shareholders own more than 2 percent.

[43]Note, however, that shareholders who own more than 2 percent are allowed to deduct their insurance costs as for AGI deductions [§162(l)].

DISTRIBUTIONS

LO 22-5

S corporations face special rules when accounting for operating distributions of cash or other property and liquidating distributions.[44]

Operating Distributions

The rules for determining the shareholder-level tax consequences of operating distributions depend on the S corporation's history; specifically whether, at the time of the distribution, it has accumulated *earnings and profits* from a previous year as a C corporation. (See the discussion earlier in text of C corporation earnings and profits.) We consider both situations—with and without accumulated earnings and profits.

S Corporation with No C Corporation Accumulated Earnings and Profits

Two sets of historical circumstances could apply here: (1) An entity may have been an S corporation since inception or (2) it may have been converted from a C corporation but not have C corporation accumulated earnings and profits at the time of the distribution. In both cases, as long as there are no C corporation accumulated earnings and profits, the rules for accounting for the distribution are very similar to those applicable to distributions to partners. That is, shareholder distributions are nontaxable to the extent of the shareholder's stock basis determined after increasing the stock basis for income allocations for the year.[45] If a distribution exceeds the shareholder's stock basis, the shareholder has a capital gain equal to the excess distribution amount.

Example 22-18

What if: Suppose CCS has been an S corporation since its inception. On June 1, 2024, CCS distributed $30,000 to Nicole. Her basis in her CCS stock on January 1, 2024, was $20,000. For 2024, Nicole was allocated $15,000 of ordinary income from CCS and no separately stated items. What are the amount and character of income Nicole recognizes on the distribution, and what is her basis in her CCS stock after the distribution?

Answer: Nicole has $0 income from the distribution and $5,000 basis in stock after the distribution ($35,000 − $30,000). Her stock basis for determining the taxability of the distribution is $35,000, or her beginning basis of $20,000 plus the $15,000 income allocation for the year (which is taxable to Nicole).

What if: Assume the same facts except that CCS distributed $40,000 to Nicole rather than $30,000. What are the amount and character of income Nicole recognizes on the distribution, and what is her basis in her CCS stock after the distribution?

Answer: Nicole has a $5,000 long-term capital gain (she has held her CCS stock more than one year) and $0 basis in her stock (the distribution reduced her stock basis to $0).

What if: Suppose CCS began in 2021 as a C corporation and elected to be taxed as an S corporation in its second year of operations. In 2021, it distributed all its earnings and profits as a dividend, so it did not have any earnings and profits at the end of 2021. In 2022, it distributed $30,000 to Nicole when her basis in her stock was $35,000. What are the amount and character of income she recognizes on the distribution, and what is her basis in her CCS stock after the distribution?

Answer: Nicole has $0 income on the distribution and $5,000 basis in stock after the distribution ($35,000 − $30,000). Because CCS did not have C corporation earnings and profits at the time of the distribution, her outcome is the same as if CCS had been taxed as an S corporation since inception.

[44]The §302 stock redemption rules that determine whether a distribution in redemption of a shareholder's stock should be treated as a distribution or a sale or exchange apply to both C corporations and S corporations. See discussion on redemptions in the Corporate Taxation: Nonliquidating Distributions chapter.

[45]§1368(d).

THE KEY FACTS

Cash Operating Distributions for S Corporations

- For S corporations without E&P: Distributions are nontaxable to the extent of the shareholder's stock basis. If a distribution exceeds the shareholder's stock basis, the shareholder has a capital gain equal to the excess distribution amount.
- For S corporations with E&P: Distributions are deemed to be paid from (1) the AAA (nontaxable to the extent of basis and taxed as capital gain thereafter), (2) existing accumulated E&P (taxable as dividends), and (3) the shareholder's remaining basis in the S corporation stock, if any (nontaxable to the extent of basis and taxed as capital gain thereafter).

S Corporation with C Corporation Accumulated Earnings and Profits When an S corporation has accumulated earnings and profits (E&P) from prior C corporation years, the distribution rules are a bit more complex. These rules are designed to ensure that shareholders cannot avoid tax on dividend distributions out of C corporation accumulated E&P by simply electing S corporation status and then distributing the accumulated E&P. For S corporations in this situation, the tax laws require the corporation to maintain an **accumulated adjustments account (AAA)** to determine the taxability of S corporate distributions. The AAA represents the cumulative income or losses for the period the corporation has been an S corporation. It is calculated as:

The beginning-of-year AAA balance
\+ Separately stated income/gain items (excluding tax-exempt income)
\+ Ordinary income
− Separately stated losses and deductions
− Ordinary losses
− Nondeductible expenses that are not capital expenditures (except deductions related to generating tax-exempt income)
− Distributions out of AAA[46]
= End-of-year AAA balance

Unlike a shareholder's stock basis, the AAA may have a negative balance. However, the reduction for distributions may not cause the AAA to go negative or to become more negative. Also, unlike stock basis, the AAA is a corporate-level account rather than a shareholder-specific account.

Example 22-19

CCS was originally formed as a C corporation and reported 2021 taxable income (and earnings and profits) of $40,000 (see Exhibit 22-2). Effective the beginning of 2022, it elected to be taxed as an S corporation. In 2022, CCS reported $249,000 of overall income (including separately stated items—see Exhibit 22-2). What is the amount of CCS's AAA for 2022 before considering the effects of distributions?

Answer: $249,000, computed as follows:

Description	Amount	Explanation
(1) Separately stated income	$ 9,000	$6,000 interest income + $3,000 dividend income (see Exhibit 22-2)
(2) Ordinary business income	240,000	Example 22-11
AAA before distributions	**$249,000**	(1) + (2)

What if: Assume that during 2022, CCS distributed $300,000 to its shareholders. What is CCS's AAA at the end of 2022?

Answer: AAA is $0 because the distribution cannot cause AAA to be negative.

What if: Instead of reporting $249,000 of income during 2022, assume that during 2022 CCS reported an ordinary business loss of $45,000, a separately stated charitable contribution of $5,000, and a $6,000 distribution to its shareholders. What is CCS's AAA at the end of 2022?

Answer: AAA is ($50,000). CCS decreases its AAA by the $45,000 business loss and the $5,000 charitable contribution. AAA before distributions is ($50,000). CCS does not decrease AAA by the $6,000 distribution to its shareholders because the distribution cannot cause AAA to be negative or make it more negative.

[46]§1368(e)(1)(C). If the current-year income and loss items net to make a negative adjustment to the AAA, the net negative adjustment from these items is made to the AAA *after* any AAA reductions for distributions (i.e., the reduction in AAA for distributions is made before the net negative adjustment for current-year income and loss items).

S corporation distributions are deemed to be paid from the following sources in the order listed:[47]

1. The AAA (to the extent it has a positive balance).[48]
2. Existing accumulated earnings and profits from years when the corporation operated as a C corporation.
3. The shareholder's stock basis.[49]

S corporation distributions from the AAA (the most common distributions) are treated the same as distributions when the S corporation does not have E&P. They are nontaxable to the extent of the shareholder's basis, and they create capital gains if they exceed the shareholder's stock basis. If an S corporation makes a distribution from accumulated E&P, the distribution is taxable to shareholders as a dividend. (See the discussion earlier in the text for the calculation of corporate E&P.) Once an S corporation's accumulated E&P is fully distributed, the remaining distributions reduce the shareholder's remaining basis in the S corporation stock (if any) and are nontaxable. Any excess distributions are treated as capital gain.

Example 22-20

What if: Assume at the end of 2022, before considering distributions, CCS's AAA was $24,000 and its accumulated E&P from 2021 was $40,000. Also assume Nicole's basis in her CCS stock is $80,000. If CCS distributes $60,000 on July 1 ($20,000 to each shareholder), what are the amount and character of income Nicole must recognize on her $20,000 distribution, and what is her stock basis in CCS after the distribution?

Answer: $12,000 dividend income and $72,000 stock basis after the distribution, computed as follows:

Description	Amount	Explanation
(1) Total distribution	$ 60,000	
(2) CCS's AAA beginning balance	24,000	
(3) Distribution from AAA	24,000	Lesser of (1) or (2)
(4) Distribution in excess of AAA	36,000	(1) – (3)
(5) Nicole's share of AAA distribution	8,000	(3) × 1/3 (nontaxable reduction of stock basis)
(6) Nicole's beginning stock basis	80,000	
(7) Nicole's ending stock basis	**72,000**	(6) – (5)
(8) CCS's E&P balance	40,000	
(9) Dividend distribution (from E&P)	36,000	Lesser of (4) or (8)
Nicole's share of dividend	**$12,000**	(9) × 1/3

[47]S corporations may elect to have distributions treated as being first paid out of existing accumulated earnings and profits from C corporation years to avoid the excess net passive income tax. We discuss the excess net passive income tax later in the chapter.

[48]Prior to 1983, S corporations' shareholders were taxed on undistributed taxable income as a deemed distribution. This undistributed income is referred to as *previously taxable income (PTI)*. For S corporations with PTI, distributions are considered to be paid out of PTI (if there is any remaining that has not been distributed) after any distributions out of their AAA. These distributions are also nontaxable to the extent of basis and reduce both the shareholder's basis and PTI.

[49]Technically, the distributions come from the Other Adjustments Account (OAA) and then any remaining shareholder equity accounts (e.g., common stock, paid-in capital). The OAA starts at zero at the S corporation's inception; is increased for tax-exempt income; and is decreased by expenses related to tax-exempt income, any federal taxes paid that are attributable to a C corporation tax year, and any S corporation distributions after the AAA and accumulated E&P have been reduced to zero. As with the AAA, the reduction for distributions may not cause the OAA to go negative or to increase a negative balance. Because from the shareholder's perspective distributions out of the OAA and equity accounts both reduce the shareholder's stock basis, we do not discuss the OAA or other equity accounts in detail.

Property Distributions At times, S corporations distribute appreciated property to their shareholders. When they do so, S corporations recognize gain as though they had sold the appreciated property for its fair market value just prior to the distribution.[50] (This rule contrasts with the partnership provisions for property distributions but is consistent with the C corporation rules.) Shareholders who receive the distributed property recognize their distributive share of the deemed gain and increase their stock basis accordingly. On the other hand, S corporations do not recognize losses on distributions of property whose value has declined.

For the shareholder, the amount of a property distribution is the fair market value of the property received (minus any liabilities the shareholder assumes on the distribution). The rules we described above apply in determining the extent to which the amount of the distribution is a nontaxable reduction of basis, a capital gain for a distribution in excess of basis, or a taxable dividend to the shareholder.[51] (See the rules for the taxability of distributions for S corporations with and without C corporation accumulated earnings and profits.) Shareholders take a fair market value basis in the property received in the distribution.

Example 22-21

What if: Assume that at the end of 2023, CCS distributes long-term capital gain property (fair market value of $24,000, basis of $15,000) to each shareholder (aggregate property distribution of $72,000 with an aggregate basis of $45,000). At the time of the distribution, CCS has no corporate E&P and Nicole has a basis of $10,000 in her CCS stock. How much gain, if any, does CCS recognize on the distribution? How much income does Nicole recognize as a result of the distribution?

Answer: CCS recognizes $27,000 of long-term capital gain, and Nicole recognizes $14,000 of long-term capital gain, computed as follows:

Description	Amount	Explanation
(1) FMV of distributed property	$ 72,000	
(2) CCS's basis in distributed property	45,000	
(3) CCS's LTCG on distribution	**$27,000**	(1) − (2)
(4) Nicole's share of LTCG from CCS	9,000	(3) × 1/3
(5) Nicole's stock basis after gain allocation	19,000	$10,000 beginning basis + (4)
(6) Distribution to Nicole	24,000	(1) × 1/3
(7) Nicole's stock basis after distribution	$ 0	(5) − (6), limited to $0
(8) LTCG to Nicole on distribution in excess of stock basis	5,000	(6) in excess of (5)
Nicole's total LTCG on distribution	**$14,000**	(4) + (8)

THE KEY FACTS

Property Distributions

- S corporations recognize gains but not losses when they distribute property to their shareholders.
- For shareholders, the amount of the distribution is the fair market value of the property received (minus any liabilities the shareholder assumes on the distribution).
- The rules for determining the taxability of property distributions at the shareholder level are the same as those for cash distributions.
- Shareholders take a fair market value basis in the property received in the distribution.

Post-Termination Transition Period Distributions Recall the special tax rules relating to suspended losses at the S corporation termination date. Similarly, §1371(e) provides for special treatment of any S corporation distribution *in cash* after an S election termination and during the post-termination transition period (PTTP). Such cash distributions are nontaxable to the extent they do not exceed the corporation's AAA balance and the individual shareholder's basis in the stock.

[50]§311(b). In addition, the S corporation may incur entity-level tax if the distributed property had built-in gains related to when the corporation converted to an S corporation. We discuss the built-in gains tax later in the chapter.

[51]Note that while S corporation shareholders reduce their stock basis by the fair market value of the property received, partners receiving property distributions from partnerships generally reduce the basis in their partnership interests by the adjusted basis of the distributed property.

The PTTP for post-termination distributions is generally the same as the PTTP for deducting suspended losses, discussed above. For determining the taxability of distributions, the PTTP generally begins on the day after the last day of the corporation's last taxable year as an S corporation; it ends on the later of (a) one year after the last S corporation day or (b) the due date for filing the return for the last year as an S corporation (including extensions).[52,53]

Liquidating Distributions

Liquidating distributions of a shareholder interest in an S corporation follow corporate tax rules rather than partnership rules. For a complete liquidation of the S corporation, the rules under §§331 and 336 (see discussion of C corporation liquidating distributions earlier in the text) govern the tax consequences. S corporations generally recognize gain *or* loss on each asset they distribute in liquidation (recall that S corporations recognize gain but not loss on operating distributions of noncash property). These gains and losses are allocated to the S corporation shareholders, increasing or decreasing their stock basis. In general, shareholders recognize gain on the distribution if the value of the property exceeds their stock basis; they recognize loss if their stock basis exceeds the value of the property.

Example 22-22

What if: Assume that at the end of 2024, CCS liquidates by distributing long-term capital gain property (fair market value of $20,000, basis of $12,000) to each shareholder (aggregate property distribution of $60,000 with an aggregate basis of $36,000). At the time of the distribution, CCS has no corporate E&P and Nicole has a basis of $25,000 in her CCS stock. How much gain or loss, if any, does CCS recognize on the distribution? How much gain or loss does Nicole recognize as a result of the distribution?

Answer: CCS recognizes $24,000 of long-term capital gain and Nicole recognizes $5,000 of net long-term capital loss, computed as follows:

Description	Amount	Explanation
(1) FMV of distributed property	$ 60,000	
(2) CCS's basis in distributed property	36,000	
(3) **CCS's LTCG on distribution**	**$24,000**	(1) – (2)
(4) Nicole's share of LTCG from CCS	8,000	(3) × 1/3
(5) Nicole's stock basis after gain allocation	33,000	$25,000 beginning basis + (4)
(6) Distribution to Nicole	20,000	(1) × 1/3
(7) Nicole's LTCL on liquidating distribution	(13,000)	(6) – (5)
Nicole's net LTCL on distribution	**(5,000)**	(4) + (7)

[52]§1377(b)(1)(A). For purposes of the taxability of distributions, the PTTP also includes (1) the 120-day period that begins on the date of any determination (court decision, closing agreement, and so on) from an IRS audit that occurs after the S election has been terminated and adjusts the corporation's income, loss, or deduction during the S period and (2) the 120-day period beginning on the date of a determination (not the date of the actual termination) that the corporation's S election had terminated for a previous taxable year [§1377(b)(1)(B), (C)].

[53]In addition to the general rules that apply to PTTP distributions, there is a special rule that applies to distributions from an "eligible terminated S corporation" that occur *after* the PTTP. Specifically, distributions from an eligible terminated S corporation that occur after the PTTP are treated as paid *pro rata* from its accumulated adjustments account and from its earnings and profits. An eligible terminated S corporation is any C corporation that (i) was an S corporation on December 21, 2017; (ii) revoked its S corporation election during the two-year period beginning on December 22, 2017; and (iii) had the same owners on December 22, 2017, and on the revocation date (in identical proportions).

LO 22-6

S CORPORATION TAXES AND FILING REQUIREMENTS

THE KEY FACTS

Built-in Gains Tax

- The built-in gains tax applies only to S corporations that have a net unrealized built-in gain at the time they convert from C corporations and that recognize net built-in gains during the built-in gains tax recognition period.
- The net unrealized built-in gain represents the net gain (if any) that the corporation would recognize if it sold each asset at its fair market value.
- Recognized built-in gains (losses) include the gain (loss) for any asset sold during the year [limited to the unrealized gain (loss) for the specific asset at the S conversion date].

Although S corporations are flow-through entities generally not subject to tax, three potential taxes apply to S corporations that previously operated as C corporations: the built-in gains tax, excess net passive income tax, and LIFO recapture tax. The built-in gains tax is the most common of the three and will be our starting point.

Built-in Gains Tax

Congress enacted the built-in gains tax to prevent C corporations from avoiding corporate taxes on sales of appreciated property by electing S corporation status. The **built-in gains tax** applies only to an S corporation that has a *net unrealized built-in gain* at the time it converts from a C corporation. Further, for the built-in gains tax to apply, the S corporation must subsequently recognize net built-in gains during the **built-in gains tax recognition period.**[54] The built-in gains tax recognition period is the five-year period beginning with the first day of the first taxable year the corporation operates as an S corporation.

What exactly is a **net unrealized built-in gain?** Measured on the first day of the corporation's first year as an S corporation, it represents the net gain (if any) the corporation would recognize if it sold each asset at its fair market value. For this purpose, we net gains and losses to determine whether indeed there is a net unrealized gain at the conversion date. The corporation's accounts receivable and accounts payable are also part of the computation: Under the cash method, accounts receivable are gain items and accounts payable are loss items. If the S corporation has a net unrealized gain at conversion, it must compute its net recognized built-in gains for each tax year during the applicable built-in gain recognition period to determine whether it is liable for the built-in gains tax.

Example 22-23

- The net recognized built-in gain is limited to the lowest of (a) the net recognized built-in gain less any net operating loss (NOL) and net capital loss carryovers, (b) the net unrealized built-in gain not yet recognized, and (c) the corporation's taxable income for the year using the C corporation tax rules.

CCS uses the accrual method of accounting. At the beginning of 2022, it owned the following assets (but leased its manufacturing facility and its equipment):

Asset	Fair Market Value (FMV)	Adjusted Basis (AB)	Built-in Gain (Loss)
Cash	$ 80,000	$ 80,000	$ 0
Accounts receivable	20,000	20,000	0
Inventory (FIFO)	130,000	110,000	20,000
Land	100,000	125,000	(25,000)
Totals	$330,000	$335,000	$ (5,000)

What is CCS's net unrealized built-in gain when it converts to an S corporation on January 1, 2022?

Answer: CCS has $0 net unrealized built-in gain. It has a net unrealized built-in loss, so it is not subject to the built-in gains tax.

What if: Suppose CCS's inventory is valued at $155,000 instead of $130,000. What is its net unrealized built-in gain?

Answer: $20,000. The $45,000 built-in gain on the inventory is netted against the $25,000 built-in loss on the land.

Recognized built-in gains for an S corporation year include (1) the gain for any asset sold during the year (limited to the unrealized gain for the specific asset at the S conversion date) and (2) any income received during the current year attributable to pre–S corporation years (such as collection on accounts receivable for cash-method S corporations). Likewise, recognized built-in losses for a year include (1) the loss for any asset sold during the year (limited to the unrealized loss for the specific asset at the S conversion date) and (2) any deduction during the current year attributable to pre–S corporation years (such as

[54]§1374.

deductions for accounts payable for cash-method S corporations). The net recognized built-in gain for any year is limited to *the least of:*

1. The net of the recognized built-in gains and losses for the year.
2. The net unrealized built-in gains as of the S election date less the net recognized built-in gains in previous years. (This restriction ensures the net recognized built-in gains during the recognition period do not exceed the net unrealized gain at the S conversion date.)
3. The corporation's taxable income for the year, using the C corporation tax rules exclusive of the dividends-received deduction and net operating loss deduction.

If taxable income limits the net recognized built-in gain for any year [item (3) above], the excess gain is treated as a recognized built-in gain in the next tax year, *but only if* the next tax year is in the built-in gains tax recognition period. After the net recognized built-in gain to be taxed has been determined using the limitations above, it should be reduced by any net operating loss (NOL) or net capital loss carryovers from prior C corporation years.[55] This base is then multiplied by the corporate tax rate (21 percent) to determine the built-in gains tax. The built-in gains tax paid by the S corporation is allocated to the shareholders as a loss. The character of the allocated loss (ordinary, capital, §1231) depends on the nature of assets that give rise to the built-in gains tax. Specifically, the loss is allocated proportionately among the character of the recognized built-in gains resulting in the tax.[56] For planning purposes, the S corporation should consider when to recognize built-in losses to reduce its exposure to the built-in gains tax. That is, the company could seek to recognize built-in losses in years with recognized built-in gains in order to avoid the built-in gains tax.

Example 22-24

What if: Suppose CCS had a net unrealized built-in gain of $20,000. In addition to other transactions in 2022, CCS sold inventory it owned at the beginning of the year; that inventory had built-in gain at the beginning of the year of $40,000 (FMV $150,000; cost basis $110,000). If CCS had been a C corporation in 2022, its taxable income would have been $200,000. How much built-in gains tax must CCS pay in 2022?

Answer: It must pay $4,200 ($20,000 × 21%) in built-in gains tax. CCS must pay a 21 percent tax on the least of (a) $40,000 (recognized built-in gain on inventory), (b) $20,000 (initial net unrealized gain), and (c) $200,000 (taxable income computed as if CCS were a C corporation for 2022). It will reduce the amount of ordinary business income it would otherwise allocate to its shareholders by $4,200—the amount of the built-in gains tax—because the entire amount of the tax is due to inventory sales.

What if: Assume the same facts as above (an initial net unrealized gain of $20,000) except CCS sold two assets that had built-in gains at the time CCS became an S corporation. CCS sold a capital asset with a built-in gain of $10,000 and inventory with a built-in gain of $40,000. CCS will still pay a $4,200 built in gains tax. This tax will be allocated as a loss to its shareholders. What is the character of the $4,200 loss?

Answer: It is an $840 capital loss [$4,200 × ($10,000 capital gain/$50,000 total recognized built-in gain)] and a $3,360 ordinary loss [$4,200 × ($40,000 ordinary income from inventory sale/$50,000 total recognized built-in gain)].

What if: Assume that in addition to the initial facts in the example, CCS also had a net operating loss from 2021 (the year it operated as a C corporation) of $15,000. CCS has no NOLs from tax years beginning before 2018. How much built-in gains tax will CCS have to pay in 2022?

Answer: It will pay $1,050 ($5,000 × 21%). CCS is allowed to offset $15,000 of the $20,000 recognized portion of the initial net unrealized gain by its $15,000 net operating loss carryover from 2021. Note that because CCS's net operating loss originated after 2017, the net operating loss deduction could not exceed 80 percent of CCS's taxable income, determined before the post-2017 net operating loss deduction ($20,000 × 80% = $16,000). Thus, the full $15,000 net operating loss can be used to offset the $20,000 built-in gain.

(continued on page 22-26)

[55] Net capital loss carryovers only reduce built-in gains that are capital gains. For net operating losses originating in tax years beginning after 2017, the net operating loss deduction is limited to 80 percent of taxable income, determined after deducting pre-2018 NOLs but before deducting the post-2017 NOLs. The 80 percent of taxable income limitation only applies for tax years beginning after 2020.

[56] §1366(f)(2).

What if: Suppose CCS had a net unrealized built-in gain of $20,000. In addition to other transactions in 2022, CCS sold inventory it owned at the beginning of the year; that inventory had built-in gain at the beginning of the year of $40,000 (FMV $150,000; AB $110,000). If CCS had been a C corporation in 2022, its taxable income would have been $4,000. How much built-in gains tax would CCS have to pay in 2022?

Answer: $840 ($4,000 × 21%). CCS must pay a 21 percent tax on the least of (a) $40,000 (recognized built-in gain on inventory), (b) $20,000 (initial net unrealized gain), and (c) $4,000 (taxable income computed as if CCS were a C corporation for 2022). Because the tax was limited due to the taxable income limitation, the excess gain of $16,000 ($20,000 recognized built-in gain minus $4,000 gain on which CCS paid tax) is treated as a recognized built-in gain in 2023.

Excess Net Passive Income Tax

THE KEY FACTS

Excess Net Passive Income Tax

- The excess net passive income tax applies only to S corporations that previously operated as C corporations *and* at the end of the year have accumulated earnings and profits from a prior C corporation year.
- This tax applies when passive investment income exceeds 25 percent of gross receipts.
- Passive investment income includes gross receipts from royalties, rents, dividends, interest (including tax-exempt interest), and annuities.

If an S corporation previously operated as a C corporation *and* has accumulated earnings and profits at the end of the year from a prior C corporation year, it may be subject to the **excess net passive income tax.**[57] Congress created this tax to encourage S corporations to distribute their accumulated earnings and profits from prior C corporation years. It does not apply to S corporations that never operated as a C corporation, or to S corporations without earnings and profits from prior C corporation years.

The tax is levied on the S corporation's **excess net passive income,** computed as follows:

$$\text{Excess net passive income} = \text{Net passive investment income} \times \frac{\text{Passive investment income} - (25\% \times \text{Gross receipts})}{\text{Passive investment income}}$$

Note that an S corporation has excess net passive income only when (1) it has net passive investment income and (2) its passive investment income exceeds 25 percent of its gross receipts. For purposes of determining excess net passive income, *gross receipts* is the total amount of revenues (including passive investment income) received or accrued under the corporation's accounting method, and not reduced by returns, allowances, cost of goods sold, or deductions. Gross receipts include net capital gains from the sales or exchanges of capital assets and gains from the sales or exchanges of stock or securities (losses do not offset gains). As defined previously in the chapter, passive investment income includes gross receipts from royalties, rents, dividends, interest (including tax-exempt interest), and annuities. **Net passive investment income** is passive investment income decreased by any expenses connected with producing that income.

The excess net passive income tax is imposed on excess net passive income at the corporate tax rate (21 percent). For purposes of computing the tax, excess net passive income is limited to taxable income computed as if the corporation were a C corporation (excluding net operating losses). The formula for determining the tax is:

$$\text{Excess net passive income tax} = 21\% \times \text{Excess net passive income}$$

Each item of passive investment income that flows through to shareholders is reduced by an allocable share of the excess net passive income tax. The portion of the tax allocated to each item of passive investment income is the amount of the item divided by the total amount of passive investment income.

The IRS may waive the excess net passive income tax in some circumstances—for example, if the S corporation determined in good faith it did not have accumulated earnings and profits at the end of the tax year and within a reasonable period distributed earnings and profits it identified later.[58]

[57]§1375.

[58]§1375(d).

Example 22-25

During 2022, CCS reported the following income (see Exhibit 22-2):

Description	2022 (S Corporation)
Sales revenue	$ 520,000
Cost of goods sold	(115,000)
Salary to owners Nicole and Sarah	(90,000)
Employee wages	(50,000)
Depreciation expense	(20,000)
Miscellaneous expenses	(5,000)
Interest income	6,000
Dividend income	3,000
Overall net income	$ 249,000

What are CCS's passive investment income, net passive investment income, and gross receipts for 2022?

Answer: The amounts are $9,000 passive income ($6,000 interest income + $3,000 dividends); $9,000 net passive investment income (because CCS has $0 expenses in producing passive investment income); and $529,000 gross receipts ($520,000 sales revenue + $3,000 dividends + $6,000 interest income).

What is CCS's excess net passive income tax in 2022, if any?

Answer: Zero. CCS has accumulated earnings and profits from 2021 (see Exhibit 22-2), but it owes zero excess net passive income tax because its passive investment income is less than 25 percent of its gross receipts [$9,000 < $132,250 ($529,000 × 25%)].

What if: Suppose CCS has passive investment income of $180,000 ($120,000 interest + $60,000 dividends), expenses associated with the passive investment income of $20,000, and gross receipts of $700,000 ($520,000 + $180,000). Also, if CCS were a C corporation, its taxable income would have been $249,000; assume it had accumulated earnings and profits of $40,000. What is CCS's excess net passive income tax, if any? What effect, if any, would the excess net passive income tax have on interest and dividends allocated to the shareholders?

Answer: The base for the tax is limited to the lesser of (a) excess net passive income of $4,444 [($180,000 passive investment income – $20,000 expenses associated with passive investment income) × ($180,000 – 25% × $700,000)/$180,000] or (b) $249,000 (CCS's taxable income if it had been a C corporation). Thus, the base for the tax is limited to $4,444, and the tax is $933 (21% × $4,444).

Interest and dividends allocated to the shareholders will be reduced by the excess net passive income tax. The interest income allocated to shareholders will be reduced by $622 [$933 tax × ($120,000 interest/$180,000 total passive investment income)], and dividend income will be reduced by $311 [$933 × ($60,000 dividend/$180,000)].

What if: Suppose CCS has passive investment income of $180,000, expenses associated with the passive investment income of $20,000, and gross receipts of $700,000 ($520,000 + $180,000). Also, if CCS were a C corporation, its taxable income would have been $2,000; assume it had accumulated earnings and profits of $40,000. What is CCS's excess net passive income tax, if any?

Answer: The base for the tax is limited to the lesser of (a) excess net passive investment income of $4,444 [$160,000 × ($180,000 – 25% × $700,000)/$180,000] or (b) $2,000 (taxable income if CCS had been a C corporation). So the tax is $420 (21% × $2,000).

Remember, if an S corporation pays the net excess passive income tax for three years in a row, its S election will be terminated by the excess passive income test.

LIFO Recapture Tax

C corporations that elect S corporation status and use the LIFO inventory method are subject to the **LIFO recapture tax.** The purpose of this tax is to prevent former C corporations from avoiding built-in gains tax by using the LIFO method of accounting for their inventories.

Specifically, a LIFO method S corporation would not recognize built-in gains unless the corporation invaded its LIFO layers during the built-in gains tax recognition period.

The LIFO recapture tax requires the C corporation to include the **LIFO recapture amount** in its gross income in the last year it operates as a C corporation.[59] That amount equals the excess of the inventory basis computed using the FIFO method over the inventory basis computed using the LIFO method at the end of the corporation's last tax year as a C corporation. In addition to being included in gross income (and taxed at the C corporation's tax rate), the LIFO recapture amount also increases the corporation's adjusted basis in its inventory at the time it converts to an S corporation. The basis increase reduces the amount of net unrealized gain subject to the built-in gains tax.

The corporation pays the LIFO recapture tax (technically a C corporation tax) in four annual installments. The first installment is due on or before the due date (not including extensions) of the corporation's last *C corporation* tax return. The final three annual installments are due each year on or before the due date (not including extensions) of the *S corporation*'s tax return.

The LIFO recapture tax does not preclude the S corporation from using the LIFO method, but it obviously does accelerate the gain attributable to differences between LIFO and FIFO for inventory existing at the time of the S corporation election.

Example 22-26

What if: Suppose CCS uses the LIFO method of accounting for its inventory and elected S corporation status effective January 1, 2023. Assume that at the end of 2022, the basis of the inventory under the LIFO method was $90,000. Under the FIFO method, the basis of the inventory would have been $100,000. Finally, CCS's taxable income in 2022 was $40,000. What amount of LIFO recapture tax must CCS pay?

Answer: CCS must pay $2,100 [($100,000 FIFO inventory basis − $90,000 LIFO inventory basis) × 21%, the corporate tax rate]. CCS would increase its basis in its inventory by $10,000, to $100,000, as of the end of 2022, its last year as a C corporation. This would reduce the unrealized net built-in gain on the inventory.

When is CCS required to pay the tax?

Answer: CCS must pay $525 by April 15, 2023 (the unextended due date of the C corporation tax return); March 15, 2024; March 15, 2025; and March 15, 2026. March 15 is the annual tax return due date for calendar-year-end S corporation returns without extensions (see discussion below).

Estimated Taxes

THE KEY FACTS

S Corporation Estimated Tax and Filing Requirements

- S corporations owing the built-in gains tax or excess net passive investment income tax (but not the LIFO recapture tax) must pay the tax based on estimated tax rules similar to C corporations.
- S corporations file Form 1120-S to report the results of their operations for the year. They request a filing extension on Form 7004.

The estimated tax rules for S corporations generally follow the rules for C corporations: S corporations with a federal income tax liability of $500 or more due to the built-in gains tax or excess net passive income tax must estimate their tax liability for the year and pay it in four quarterly estimated installments. However, an S corporation is not required to make estimated tax payments for the LIFO recapture tax.[60]

Filing Requirements

S corporations are required to file **Form 1120-S** with the IRS by the 15th day of the third month after the S corporation's year-end (e.g., March 15 for a calendar-year-end S corporation). S corporations may receive an automatic six-month extension by filing **Form 7004** with the IRS prior to the original due date of the return.[61] Thus, the extended due date of an S corporation tax return is generally September 15.

Exhibit 22-3 presents page 1 of CCS's Form 1120-S (for its 2022 activities), CCS's partial Schedule K, and Nicole's Schedule K-1 (we use 2021 forms because 2022 forms were unavailable at the time this book went to press). Note the K-1 of the 1120-S is

[59]§1363(d).

[60]Rev. Proc. 94-61.

[61]Under §6698, late-filing penalties apply if the S corporation fails to file by the normal or extended due date for the return.

EXHIBIT 22-3, PART I CCS's 2022 Form 1120-S (on 2021 form)

Form **1120-S** | Department of the Treasury Internal Revenue Service

U.S. Income Tax Return for an S Corporation

▶ Do not file this form unless the corporation has filed or is attaching Form 2553 to elect to be an S corporation.
▶ Go to *www.irs.gov/Form1120S* for instructions and the latest information.

OMB No. 1545-0123 | 2021

For calendar year 2021 or tax year beginning , 2021, ending , 20

A S election effective date: January 1, 2022	Name: Color Comfort Sheets	D Employer identification number: 24-4681012
B Business activity code number (see instructions): 314000	TYPE OR PRINT — Number, street, and room or suite no. If a P.O. box, see instructions.: 375 East 450 South	E Date incorporated: January 1, 2021
C Check if Sch. M-3 attached ☐	City or town, state or province, country, and ZIP or foreign postal code: Salt Lake City, UT 84103	F Total assets (see instructions): $ 370,000

G Is the corporation electing to be an S corporation beginning with this tax year? See instructions. ☑ Yes ☐ No
H Check if: (1) ☐ Final return (2) ☐ Name change (3) ☐ Address change (4) ☐ Amended return (5) ☐ S election termination
I Enter the number of shareholders who were shareholders during any part of the tax year . . . ▶ 3
J Check if corporation: (1) ☐ Aggregated activities for section 465 at-risk purposes (2) ☐ Grouped activities for section 469 passive activity purposes

Caution: Include **only** trade or business income and expenses on lines 1a through 21. See the instructions for more information.

Section	Line	Description	Box	Amount	Line	Amount
Income	1a	Gross receipts or sales	1a	520,000		
	b	Returns and allowances	1b			
	c	Balance. Subtract line 1b from line 1a			1c	520,000
	2	Cost of goods sold (attach Form 1125-A)			2	115,000
	3	Gross profit. Subtract line 2 from line 1c			3	405,000
	4	Net gain (loss) from Form 4797, line 17 (attach Form 4797)			4	
	5	Other income (loss) (see instructions—attach statement)			5	
	6	**Total income (loss).** Add lines 3 through 5 ▶			6	405,000
Deductions (see instructions for limitations)	7	Compensation of officers (see instructions—attach Form 1125-E)			7	90,000
	8	Salaries and wages (less employment credits)			8	50,000
	9	Repairs and maintenance			9	
	10	Bad debts			10	
	11	Rents			11	
	12	Taxes and licenses			12	
	13	Interest (see instructions)			13	
	14	Depreciation not claimed on Form 1125-A or elsewhere on return (attach Form 4562)			14	20,000
	15	Depletion **(Do not deduct oil and gas depletion.)**			15	
	16	Advertising			16	
	17	Pension, profit-sharing, etc., plans			17	
	18	Employee benefit programs			18	
	19	Other deductions (attach statement)			19	5,000
	20	**Total deductions.** Add lines 7 through 19 ▶			20	165,000
	21	**Ordinary business income (loss).** Subtract line 20 from line 6			21	240,000
Tax and Payments	22a	Excess net passive income or LIFO recapture tax (see instructions)	22a			
	b	Tax from Schedule D (Form 1120-S)	22b			
	c	Add lines 22a and 22b (see instructions for additional taxes)			22c	
	23a	2021 estimated tax payments and 2020 overpayment credited to 2021	23a			
	b	Tax deposited with Form 7004	23b			
	c	Credit for federal tax paid on fuels (attach Form 4136)	23c			
	d	Add lines 23a through 23c			23d	
	24	Estimated tax penalty (see instructions). Check if Form 2220 is attached ▶ ☐			24	
	25	**Amount owed.** If line 23d is smaller than the total of lines 22c and 24, enter amount owed			25	
	26	**Overpayment.** If line 23d is larger than the total of lines 22c and 24, enter amount overpaid			26	
	27	Enter amount from line 26: **Credited to 2022 estimated tax ▶** **Refunded ▶**			27	

Sign Here — Under penalties of perjury, I declare that I have examined this return, including accompanying schedules and statements, and to the best of my knowledge and belief, it is true, correct, and complete. Declaration of preparer (other than taxpayer) is based on all information of which preparer has any knowledge.

▶ Signature of officer | Date | ▶ Title | May the IRS discuss this return with the preparer shown below? See instructions. ☐ Yes ☐ No

Paid Preparer Use Only				
Print/Type preparer's name	Preparer's signature	Date	Check ☐ if self-employed	PTIN
Firm's name ▶			Firm's EIN ▶	
Firm's address ▶			Phone no.	

For Paperwork Reduction Act Notice, see separate instructions. Cat. No. 11510H Form **1120-S** (2021)

Source: irs.gov.

EXHIBIT 22-3, PART II CCS's 2022 Partial Schedule K (on 2021 form)

Schedule K **Shareholders' Pro Rata Share Items**

Section	Line	Description	Box	Amount	Line	Total amount
Income (Loss)	1	Ordinary business income (loss) (page 1, line 21)			1	240,000
	2	Net rental real estate income (loss) (attach Form 8825)			2	
	3a	Other gross rental income (loss)	3a			
	b	Expenses from other rental activities (attach statement)	3b			
	c	Other net rental income (loss). Subtract line 3b from line 3a			3c	
	4	Interest income			4	6,000
	5	Dividends: **a** Ordinary dividends			5a	3,000
		b Qualified dividends	5b	3,000		
	6	Royalties			6	
	7	Net short-term capital gain (loss) (attach Schedule D (Form 1120-S))			7	
	8a	Net long-term capital gain (loss) (attach Schedule D (Form 1120-S))			8a	
	b	Collectibles (28%) gain (loss)	8b			
	c	Unrecaptured section 1250 gain (attach statement)	8c			
	9	Net section 1231 gain (loss) (attach Form 4797)			9	
	10	Other income (loss) (see instructions) . . . Type ▶			10	

Source: irs.gov.

EXHIBIT 22-3, PART III Nicole's 2022 Schedule K-1 (on 2021 form)

671121

☐ Final K-1 ☐ Amended K-1 OMB No. 1545-0123

Schedule K-1 (Form 1120-S) **2021**

Department of the Treasury
Internal Revenue Service

For calendar year 2021, or tax year

beginning / / 2021 ending / /

Shareholder's Share of Income, Deductions, Credits, etc. ▶ See separate instructions.

Part I Information About the Corporation

A Corporation's employer identification number
24-4681012

B Corporation's name, address, city, state, and ZIP code
Color Comfort Sheets
375 East 450 South
Salt Lake City, UT 84103

C IRS Center where corporation filed return
Ogden, UT

D Corporation's total number of shares
Beginning of tax year 3,000
End of tax year 3,000

Part II Information About the Shareholder

E Shareholder's identifying number
123-45-6789

F Shareholder's name, address, city, state, and ZIP code
Nicole Johnson
811 East 8320 South
Sandy, UT 84094

G Current year allocation percentage . . . 33.333333 %

H Shareholder's number of shares
Beginning of tax year 1000
End of tax year 1000

I Loans from shareholder
Beginning of tax year . . . . . $
End of tax year . . . . $

For IRS Use Only

Statement on Qualified Business Income Items:

Line 17, Code V:
QBI income: $80,000
QBI wages: $46,667
QBI unadjusted basis: $100,000

* Not a specified service trade or business

Part III Shareholder's Share of Current Year Income, Deductions, Credits, and Other Items

Line	Item	Amount	Line	Item	Amount
1	Ordinary business income (loss)	80,000	13	Credits	
2	Net rental real estate income (loss)				
3	Other net rental income (loss)				
4	Interest income	2,000			
5a	Ordinary dividends	1,000			
5b	Qualified dividends	1,000	14	Schedule K-3 is attached if checked . . . . ▶ ☐	
6	Royalties		15	Alternative minimum tax (AMT) items	
7	Net short-term capital gain (loss)				
8a	Net long-term capital gain (loss)				
8b	Collectibles (28%) gain (loss)				
8c	Unrecaptured section 1250 gain				
9	Net section 1231 gain (loss)		16	Items affecting shareholder basis	
10	Other income (loss)				
			17	Other information	
			A		3,000
11	Section 179 deduction		V		STMT
12	Other deductions				

18 ☐ More than one activity for at-risk purposes*
19 ☐ More than one activity for passive activity purposes*

* See attached statement for additional information.

For Paperwork Reduction Act Notice, see the Instructions for Form 1120-S. www.irs.gov/Form1120S Cat. No. 11520D Schedule K-1 (Form 1120-S) 2021

Source: irs.gov.

different from the K-1 of the partnership Form 1065. In contrast to the 1065 Schedule K-1, the 1120-S Schedule K-1 does not report self-employment income, does not allocate entity-level debt to shareholders, and does not allow for shareholders to have profit-and-loss-sharing ratios that are different from shareholders' percentage of stock ownership.

COMPARING C AND S CORPORATIONS AND PARTNERSHIPS

Exhibit 22-4 compares tax consequences for C corporations, S corporations, and partnerships discussed in this chapter.

EXHIBIT 22-4 Comparison of Tax Consequences for C and S Corporations and Partnerships

Tax Characteristic	C Corporation	S Corporation	Partnership/LLC
Forming or contributing property to an entity	No gain or loss on contribution of appreciated or depreciated property if transferors of property have control (as defined in §351) after transfer.	Same as C corporation.	Same as C and S corporations except no control requirement (§721 applies to partnerships).
Type of owner restrictions	No restrictions.	Only individuals who are U.S. citizens or residents, certain trusts, and tax-exempt organizations.	No restrictions.
Number of owner restrictions	No restrictions.	Limited to 100 shareholders. (Family members and their estates count as one shareholder.)	Must have more than one owner.
Election	Default status if corporation under state law.	Must formally elect to have corporation taxed as S corporation.	Default status if unincorporated; must have more than one owner.
Income and loss allocations	Not allocated to shareholders.	Income and loss flow through to owners based on ownership percentages.	Income and loss flow through to owners but may be allocated based on something other than ownership percentages (special allocations).
Entity debt included in stock (or partnership interest) basis	No	Generally no. However, loans made from shareholder to corporation create debt basis. Losses may be deducted to extent of stock basis and then debt basis.	Yes. All entity liabilities are allocated to basis of partners.
Loss limitations	Losses remain at corporate level.	Losses flow through but subject to tax-basis limitation, at-risk limitation, passive activity limitations, and excess business loss limitation.	Same as S corporations.
Self-employment income status of ordinary income allocations	Not applicable.	Not self-employment income.	May be self-employment income depending on partner's status.
Salary to owners permitted	Yes	Yes	Generally no. Salary-type payments are guaranteed payments subject to self-employment tax.
Fringe benefits	Can pay nontaxable fringe benefits to owners.	Can pay nontaxable fringe benefits to owners who own 2 percent or less of stock.	May not pay nontaxable fringe benefits to owners.
Operating distributions: Owner tax consequences	Taxable as dividends to extent of earnings and profits.	Generally not taxable to extent of owner's basis.	Same as S corporations.
Operating distributions: Entity tax consequences	Gain on distribution of appreciated property; no loss on distribution of depreciated property.	Same as C corporations.	Generally no gain or loss on distribution of property.
Liquidating distributions	Corporation and shareholders generally recognize gain or loss on distributions.	Same as C corporations.	Partnership and partners generally do not recognize gain or loss on liquidating distributions.

(*continued*)

EXHIBIT 22-4 *(concluded)*

Tax Characteristic	C Corporation	S Corporation	Partnership/LLC
Entity-level taxes	Yes, based on corporate tax rate schedule.	Generally no, but may be required to pay built-in gains tax, excess passive investment income tax, or LIFO recapture tax if converting from C to S corporation.	No
Tax year	Last day of any month or 52/53-week year.	Generally calendar year.	Based on tax year of owners.

CONCLUSION

This chapter highlights the rules specific to S corporations and compared S corporations to C corporations and partnerships. S corporations are true hybrid entities: They share characteristics with C corporations (the tax rules that apply in organizing and liquidating a corporation). They also share characteristics with partnerships (the flow-through of the entity's income and loss to its owners, ability to make nontaxable distributions to the extent of the owner's basis, and basis calculations for owners).

Although many S corporation attributes follow from the C corporation or partnership rules, several specific attributes unique to S corporations may be particularly important in choosing an entity form or operating an S corporation in a tax-efficient manner. These attributes include unique S corporation taxes, the rules for how debt enters into the basis calculations and loss limitation rules for S corporations, and the rules for how distributions are taxed for S corporations previously operating as C corporations.

Summary

LO 22-1 Describe the requirements and process to elect S corporation status.

- Shareholders of S corporations are able to defer realized gains when they contribute property to the corporation if they have control of the corporation after the contribution.
- S corporations are limited in the type of owners they may have. Only individuals who are U.S. citizens or residents, certain trusts, and certain tax-exempt organizations may be shareholders of S corporations.
- S corporations may have no more than 100 shareholders. For this purpose, family members and their estates count as one shareholder. Family members include a common ancestor and their lineal descendants and their lineal descendants' spouses (or former spouses).
- S corporations may have only one class of stock. The stock may have differences in voting rights between shares, but all stock must have identical rights with respect to corporate distribution and liquidation proceeds.
- The S corporation election is made on Form 2553. All shareholders on the date of the election must consent to the election.
- To be effective for the current year, the election must be filed in the prior tax year or on or before the 15th day of the third month of the year. Even then, the election may not be effective in certain circumstances.

LO 22-2 Explain the events that terminate the S corporation election.

- The S corporation election may be voluntarily revoked by shareholders owning more than 50 percent of the S corporation stock. In general, revocations made on or before the 15th day of the third month of the year are effective as of the beginning of the year, and revocations after that date are effective on the first day of the next year. Alternatively, the shareholders may choose an alternate date that is not before the revocation election is filed.

- An S corporation's election is automatically terminated on the date it fails to meet the S corporation requirements.
- If an S corporation has earnings and profits from a previous C corporation year, its S election is terminated if it has passive investment income in excess of 25 percent of gross receipts for three consecutive years.
- When an S corporation election is terminated midyear, the corporation files a short tax year return for the period it was an S corporation and a short tax year return for the portion of the year it was a C corporation. It can allocate the income on a per-day basis, or it may specifically identify the income to each period.
- When an S corporation's S election is terminated, it may not reelect S status until the beginning of the fifth tax year after the tax year in which the election was terminated.

Describe operating issues relating to S corporation accounting periods and methods, and explain income and loss allocations and separately stated items. LO 22-3

- When C corporations elect to become S corporations, all prior accounting methods carry over to the S corporation.
- S corporations are generally required to use a calendar tax year.
- Income and losses are allocated to S corporation shareholders pro rata based on the number of outstanding shares each shareholder owns on each day of the tax year, or, with shareholder consent, it may use its normal accounting rules to allocate income and loss to the shareholders.
- S corporations determine their ordinary business income and separately stated items for the year and allocate these to the shareholders during the year.
- Separately stated items are tax items treated differently at the shareholder level than a shareholder's share of ordinary business income.

Explain stock-basis calculations, loss limitations, determination of self-employment income, and fringe benefit rules that apply to S corporation shareholders. LO 22-4

- An S corporation shareholder's initial basis in their stock is generally the basis of the property contributed to the corporation minus liabilities assumed by the corporation on the contribution.
- S corporation shareholders adjust their stock basis annually. They increase it for (in this order) capital contributions to the S corporation during the year, the shareholder's share of ordinary business income, and separately stated income/gain items. They decrease it for distributions during the year, the shareholder's share of nondeductible expenses, and the shareholder's share of ordinary business loss and separately stated expense/loss items. The basis may not be reduced below zero.
- S corporation shareholders are not allowed to include the S corporation's debt in their stock basis. However, they are allowed to create *debt basis* for the amount of loans they make directly to the S corporation. Debt basis can absorb S corporation losses (see below).
- For an S corporation shareholder to deduct them, S corporation losses must clear three separate hurdles: (1) tax-basis limitation in stock (and debt), (2) at-risk amount limitation, and (3) passive activity loss limitation. In addition, for losses that clear each of the three separate hurdles, S corporation shareholders are not allowed to deduct excess business losses.
- Losses suspended at a particular level remain suspended until the shareholder creates additional tax-basis or at-risk amounts, clears the passive loss hurdle, or sells their stock in the S corporation.
- If a shareholder's stock and debt bases are reduced by loss allocations and then increased by subsequent income allocations, the income allocation first increases the debt basis to the debt's outstanding amount before increasing the stock basis.
- When an S corporation's S election is terminated, S corporation shareholders can deduct their share of S corporation losses on the last day of the post-termination transition period as long as the losses are able to clear the three loss limitation hurdles.
- Allocation of ordinary business income is not self-employment income to S corporation shareholders.
- If S corporation shareholders are employees of the corporation, their wages are subject to employment taxes.

- S corporation shareholders are subject to the net investment income tax on their share of an S corporation's gross income from interest, dividends, annuities, royalties, rents, a trade or business that is a passive activity or a trade or business of trading financial instruments or commodities, and generally any net gain from disposing of property, less any allowable deductions from these items.
- Many fringe benefits that are nontaxable to other S corporation employees are taxable to employees who own more than 2 percent of the S corporation.

LO 22-5 Apply the tax rules for S corporation operating distributions and liquidating distributions.

- Operating distributions from S corporations without accumulated earnings and profits from C corporation years are nontaxable to the extent of the shareholder's basis and then taxable as capital gain to the extent they exceed the shareholder's stock basis.
- Operating distributions from S corporations with accumulated earnings and profits from C corporation years are a nontaxable reduction in stock basis to the extent of the S corporation's accumulated adjustments account, a dividend to the extent of the corporation's earnings and profits, and then a nontaxable return of capital to the extent of the stock basis. Amounts in excess of the stock basis are capital gain.
- The accumulated adjustments account represents the cumulative income or losses for the period the corporation has been an S corporation.
- When S corporations distribute appreciated property to shareholders, they must recognize gain on the distribution (the gain is allocated to the shareholders). When they distribute loss property, they are not allowed to deduct the losses. In either case, the fair market value of the property (reduced by liabilities) is the amount of the distribution to the shareholders.
- When an S election is terminated, cash distributions during the post-termination transition period are nontaxable to the shareholder to the extent of the S corporation's accumulated adjustments account and the shareholder's stock basis.
- S corporations making liquidating distributions recognize gain or loss on the distributions. The gains or losses are allocated to the shareholders. The shareholders compare the amount received in the liquidating distribution to their stock basis to determine if they recognize gain or loss on the distributions.

LO 22-6 Describe the taxes that apply to S corporations, estimated tax requirements, and tax return filing requirements.

- S corporations that were formerly C corporations may be required to pay the built-in gains tax. The tax applies if the S corporation had a net unrealized built-in gain at the time it converted to an S corporation. It must pay the tax when it recognizes these net built-in gains during its first five years operating as an S corporation.
- The base for the tax is limited to the least of (1) the net of the recognized built-in gains and losses for the year, (2) the net unrealized built-in gains as of the date of the S election date less the net recognized built-in gains in previous years, and (3) the corporation's taxable income for the year using the C corporation tax rules [excluding the dividends-received deduction and net operating loss (NOL) deduction]. The base is then reduced by any NOL or net capital loss carryovers from prior C corporation years.
- S corporations that were formerly C corporations and have C corporation earnings and profits must pay the excess net passive income tax when their passive investment income exceeds 25 percent of their gross receipts.
- The formula for the excess net passive income tax is 21 percent (the corporate tax rate) × {Net passive investment income × [Passive investment income − (25% × Gross receipts)]/Passive investment income}.
- C corporations that elect to be taxed as S corporations and that use the LIFO method of accounting for inventories must pay the LIFO recapture tax. The tax is the C corporation's tax rate times the excess of the inventory valued under the LIFO method over the inventory valued under the FIFO method at the time the S election became effective. The corporation pays one-quarter of the tax on its final C corporation tax return and the final three installments on its S corporation tax return for the first three years it is an S corporation.
- S corporations that must pay the built-in gains tax or the excess passive income tax generally must pay estimated taxes in four quarterly installments. They are not required to make estimated tax payments for the LIFO recapture tax.

- S corporations file Form 1120-S by the 15th day of the third month after the tax year-end (generally March 15).
- S corporations may receive a six-month extension by filing Form 7004.
- On Form 1120-S, S corporations report ordinary business income and separately stated items on Schedule K. Each shareholder's portion of items on Schedule K is reported to the shareholder on their Schedule K-1.

KEY TERMS

accumulated adjustments account (AAA) (22-20)
at-risk amount (22-15)
built-in gains tax (22-24)
built-in gains tax recognition period (22-24)
debt basis (22-14)
earnings and profits (E&P) (22-2)
excess business loss (22-17)
excess net passive income (22-26)
excess net passive income tax (22-26)
Form 1120-S (22-28)
Form 2553 (22-4)
Form 7004 (22-28)
gross receipts (22-6)
LIFO recapture amount (22-28)
LIFO recapture tax (22-27)
net passive investment income (22-26)
net unrealized built-in gain (22-24)
ordinary business income (loss) (22-10)
passive activity loss (PAL) rules (22-16)
passive investment income (PII) (22-6)
post-termination transition period (PTTP) (22-15)
S corporation (22-2)
separately stated items (22-10)

DISCUSSION QUESTIONS

Discussion Questions are available in Connect®.

1. In general terms, how are C corporations different from and similar to S corporations? LO 22-1
2. What are the limitations on the number and type of shareholders an S corporation may have? How are these limitations different from restrictions on the number and type of shareholders C corporations or partnerships may have? LO 22-1
3. Why can't large, publicly traded corporations be treated as S corporations? LO 22-1
4. How do the tax laws treat family members for purposes of limiting the number of owners an S corporation may have? LO 22-1
5. Super Corp. was organized under the laws of the state of Montana. It issued common voting stock and common nonvoting stock to its two shareholders. Is Super Corp. eligible to elect S corporation status? Why or why not? LO 22-1
6. Karen is the sole shareholder of a calendar-year-end C corporation she formed last year. If she elects S corporation status this year on February 20, when will the election become effective and why? What if she had made the election on March 20? LO 22-1
7. JB Corporation is a C corporation owned 80 percent by Jacob and 20 percent by Bauer. Jacob would like JB to make an S election, but Bauer is opposed to the idea. Can JB elect to be taxed as an S corporation without Bauer's consent? Explain. LO 22-1
8. In what circumstances could a calendar-year C corporation make an election on February 1, year 1, to be taxed as an S corporation in year 1 but not have the election effective until year 2? LO 22-1
9. Theodore, Alvin, and Simon are equal shareholders of Timeless Corp. (an S corporation). Simon wants to terminate the S election, but Theodore and Alvin disagree. Can Simon unilaterally elect to have the S election terminated? If not, what would Simon need to do to have the S election terminated? LO 22-2
10. Juanita is the sole shareholder of Belize Corporation (a calendar-year S corporation). She is considering revoking the S election. It is February 1, year 1. What options does Juanita have for timing the effective date of the S election revocation? LO 22-2
11. Describe the circumstances in which an S election may be involuntarily terminated. LO 22-2

LO 22-2 12. Describe a situation in which a former C corporation that elected to be taxed as an S corporation may have its S election automatically terminated, but a similarly situated corporation that has always been taxed as an S corporation would not.

LO 22-2 13. When a corporation's S election is terminated midyear, what options does the corporation have for allocating the annual income between the S corporation short year and the C corporation short year?

LO 22-2 14. On June 1, year 1, Jasper Corporation's S election was involuntarily terminated. What is the earliest Jasper may be taxed as an S corporation again? Are there any exceptions to the general rule? Explain.

LO 22-3 15. Apple Union (AU), a C corporation with a March 31 year-end, uses the accrual method of accounting. If AU elects to be taxed as an S corporation, what will its year-end and method of accounting be (assuming no special elections)?

LO 22-3 16. Compare and contrast the method of allocating income or loss to owners for partnerships and for S corporations.

LO 22-3 17. Why must an S corporation report separately stated items to its shareholders? How is the character of a separately stated item determined? How does the S corporation report this information to each shareholder?

LO 22-3 18. How do S corporations report dividends they receive? Are they entitled to a dividends-received deduction? Why or why not?

LO 22-4 19. Shawn receives stock in an S corporation when it is formed in a tax-deferred transaction by contributing land with a tax basis of $50,000 and encumbered by a $20,000 mortgage. What is Shawn's initial basis in his S corporation stock?

LO 22-4 20. Why is a shareholder's basis in an S corporation stock adjusted annually?

LO 22-4 21. What adjustments are made annually to a shareholder's basis in S corporation stock, and in what order? What impact do these adjustments have on a subsequent sale of stock?

LO 22-4 22. Can a shareholder's basis in S corporation stock ever be adjusted to a negative number? Why or why not?

LO 22-4 23. Describe the three hurdles a taxpayer must pass if they want to deduct a loss from their share in an S corporation. What other loss limitation rule may impact the deductibility of losses from an S corporation?

LO 22-4 24. Is a shareholder allowed to increase their basis in S corporation stock by their share of the corporation's liabilities, as partners are able to increase the basis of their ownership interest by their share of partnership liabilities? Explain.

LO 22-4 25. How does a shareholder create *debt basis* in an S corporation? How is debt basis similar and dissimilar to stock basis?

LO 22-4 26. When an S corporation shareholder has suspended losses due to the tax-basis or at-risk amount limitation, are they allowed to deduct the losses if the S corporation status is terminated? Why or why not?

LO 22-4 27. When considering C corporations, the IRS checks to see whether salaries paid are too large. In S corporations, however, it usually must verify that salaries are large enough. Account for this difference.

LO 22-4 28. How does the tax treatment of employee fringe benefits reflect the hybrid nature of the S corporation?

LO 22-4 29. If a corporation has been an S corporation since inception, describe how its operating distributions to its shareholders are taxed to the shareholders.

LO 22-4 30. How are the tax consequences of a cash distribution different from those of a noncash property distribution to both the S corporation and the shareholders?

LO 22-5 31. What role does debt basis play in determining the taxability of operating distributions to S corporation shareholders?

LO 22-5 32. What does the accumulated adjustments account represent? How is it adjusted year by year? Can it have a negative balance?

33. If an S corporation with accumulated E&P makes a distribution, from what accounts (and in what order) is the distribution deemed to be paid? LO 22-5
34. Under what circumstances could a corporation with earnings and profits make a nontaxable distribution to its shareholders after the S election termination? LO 22-5
35. How do the tax consequences of S corporation liquidating distributions differ from the tax consequences of S corporation operating distributions at both the corporate and shareholder levels? LO 22-5
36. When is an S corporation required to pay a built-in gains tax? LO 22-6
37. When is an S corporation required to pay the excess net passive income tax? LO 22-6
38. Is the LIFO recapture tax a C corporation tax or an S corporation tax? Explain. LO 22-6
39. When must an S corporation make estimated tax payments? LO 22-6
40. On what form does an S corporation report its income to the IRS? When is the tax return due? What information does the S corporation provide to shareholders to allow them to complete their tax returns? LO 22-6
41. Compare and contrast S corporations, C corporations, and partnerships in terms of tax consequences at formation, shareholder restrictions, income allocation, basis calculations, compensation to owners, taxation of distributions, and accounting periods. LO 22-6

PROBLEMS

Select problems are available in Connect®.

42. Janelle wants to create an S corporation called J's Dance Shoes (JDS). Describe how the items below affect her eligibility for an S election. LO 22-1
    a) Because Janelle wants all her shareholders to have an equal say in the future of JDS, she gives them equal voting rights and decides shareholders who take a more active role in the firm will have priority in terms of distribution and liquidation rights.
    b) Janelle decides to incorporate under the state laws of Utah because that is where she lives. Once she gets her business up and running, however, she plans on doing extensive business in Mexico.
43. Lucy and Ricky Ricardo live in Los Angeles, California. After they were married, they started a business named ILL Corporation (a C corporation). For state law purposes, the shares of stock in ILL Corp. are listed under Ricky's name only. Ricky signed Form 2553 electing to have ILL taxed as an S corporation for federal income tax purposes, but Lucy did not sign. Given that California is a community property state, is the S election for ILL Corp. valid? LO 22-1 research
44. Maria has been operating Mansfield Park as a C corporation and decides she would like to make an S election. What is the earliest the election will become effective under each of these alternative scenarios? LO 22-1
    a) Maria is on top of things and makes the election on January 1, 2022.
    b) Maria is mostly on top of things and makes the election on January 15, 2022.
    c) Maria makes the election on February 10, 2022. She needed a little time to convince a C corporation shareholder to sell its stock to a qualifying shareholder. That process took all of January, and she was glad to have it over with.
    d) Maria makes the election on March 14, 2022.
    e) Maria makes the election on February 5, 2022. One of the shareholders refused to consent to the S election. They sold their shares (on January 15, 2022) to another shareholder who consented to the election.
45. Missy is 1 of 100 unrelated shareholders of Dalmatian, an S corporation. She is considering selling her shares. Under the following alternative scenarios, would the S election be terminated? Why or why not? LO 22-2

a) Missy wants to sell half her shares to a friend, a U.S. citizen, so they can rename their corporation 101 Dalmatians.

b) Missy's mother's family wants to be involved with the corporation. Missy splits half her shares evenly among her aunt, uncle, grandfather, and two cousins.

c) Missy sells half her Dalmatian stock to her husband's corporation.

LO 22-2

46. Cathy, Heathcliff, and Isabelle are equal shareholders in Wuthering Heights (WH), an S corporation. Heathcliff has decided he would like to terminate the S election. In the following alternative scenarios, indicate whether the termination will occur, and indicate the date if applicable (assume no alternative termination dates are selected).

a) Cathy and Isabelle both decline to agree to the termination. Heathcliff files the termination election anyway on March 14, 2022.

b) Isabelle agrees with the termination, but Cathy strongly disagrees. The termination is filed on February 16, 2022.

c) The termination seems to be the first thing all three could agree on. They file the election to terminate on March 28, 2022.

d) The termination seems to be the first thing all three could agree on. They file the election to terminate on February 28, 2022.

e) Knowing the other two disagree with the termination, on March 16, 2022, Heathcliff sells 1 of his 50 shares to his maid, who recently moved back to Bulgaria, her home country.

LO 22-2

47. Assume the following S corporations, gross receipts, passive investment income, and corporate E&P. Will any of these corporations have its S election terminated due to excessive passive income? If so, in what year? All became S corporations at the beginning of year 1.

a) Clarion Corp.

Year	Gross Receipts	Passive Investment Income	Corporate Earnings and Profits
1	$1,353,458	$250,000	$321,300
2	1,230,389	100,000	321,300
3	1,139,394	300,000	230,000
4	1,347,039	350,000	100,000
5	1,500,340	400,000	0

b) Hanson Corp.

Year	Gross Receipts	Passive Investment Income	Corporate Earnings and Profits
1	$1,430,000	$247,000	$138,039
2	700,380	200,000	100,000
3	849,000	190,000	100,000
4	830,000	210,000	80,000
5	1,000,385	257,390	80,000

c) Jelena Corp.

Year	Gross Receipts	Passive Investment Income	Corporate Earnings and Profits
1	$1,000,458	$250,000	$0
2	703,000	300,480	0
3	800,375	400,370	0
4	900,370	350,470	0
5	670,000	290,377	0

d) Nazmul Corp.

Year	Gross Receipts	Passive Investment Income	Corporate Earnings and Profits
1	$1,100,370	$250,000	$500
2	998,000	240,000	400
3	800,350	230,000	300
4	803,000	214,570	200
5	750,000	200,000	100

48. Hughie, Dewey, and Louie are equal shareholders in HDL, an S corporation. HDL's S election terminates under each of the following alternative scenarios. When is the earliest it can again operate as an S corporation? LO 22-2

a) The S election terminates on August 1, year 2, because Louie sells half his shares to his uncle Walt, a citizen and resident of Scotland.

b) The S election terminates effective January 1, year 3, because on August 1, year 2, Hughie and Dewey vote (2 to 1) to terminate the election.

49. Winkin, Blinkin, and Nod are equal shareholders in SleepEZ, an S corporation. In the conditions listed below, how much income should each report from SleepEZ for 2022 under both the daily allocation and the specific identification allocation methods? Refer to the following table for the timing of SleepEZ's income. LO 22-3

Period	Income
January 1 through March 15 (74 days)	$125,000
March 16 through December 31 (291 days)	345,500
January 1 through December 31, 2022 (365 days)	$470,500

a) There are no sales of SleepEZ stock during the year.

b) On March 15, 2022, Blinkin sells his shares to Nod.

c) On March 15, 2022, Winkin and Nod each sells his shares to Blinkin.

Use the following information to complete problems 50 and 51:

UpAHill Corporation (an S Corporation)
Income Statement
December 31, Year 1 and Year 2

	Year 1	Year 2
Sales revenue	$175,000	$310,000
Cost of goods sold	(60,000)	(85,000)
Salary to owners Jack and Jill	(40,000)	(50,000)
Employee wages	(15,000)	(20,000)
Depreciation expense	(10,000)	(15,000)
Miscellaneous expenses	(7,500)	(9,000)
Interest income (unrelated to business)	2,000	2,500
Qualified dividend income	500	1,000
Overall net income	$ 45,000	$134,500

50. Jack and Jill are owners of UpAHill, an S corporation. They own 25 and 75 percent, respectively. LO 22-3 tax forms

a) What amount of ordinary income and separately stated items are allocated to them for years 1 and 2 based on the information above? Assume that UpAHill Corporation has $100,000 of qualified property (unadjusted basis) in both years.

b) Complete UpAHill's Form 1120-S, Schedule K, for year 1.

c) Complete Jill's Form 1120-S, Schedule K-1, for year 1.

LO 22-3 LO 22-4

51. Assume Jack and Jill, 25 and 75 percent shareholders, respectively, in UpAHill Corporation, have tax bases in their shares at the beginning of year 1 of $24,000 and $56,000, respectively. Also assume no distributions were made. Given the income statement above, what are their tax bases in their shares at the end of year 1?

Use the following information to complete problems 52 and 53:

Falcons Corporation (an S Corporation)
Income Statement
December 31, Year 1 and Year 2

	Year 1	Year 2
Sales revenue	$300,000	$430,000
Cost of goods sold	(40,000)	(60,000)
Salary to owners Julio and Milania	(40,000)	(80,000)
Employee wages	(25,000)	(50,000)
Depreciation expense	(20,000)	(40,000)
Section 179 expense	(30,000)	(50,000)
Interest income (related to business)	12,000	22,500
Municipal bond income	1,500	4,000
Government fines	0	(2,000)
Overall net income	$158,500	$174,500
Distributions	$ 30,000	$ 50,000

LO 22-3

tax forms

52. Julio and Milania are owners of Falcons Corporation, an S corporation. Each owns 50 percent of Falcons Corporation. In year 1, Julio and Milania each received distributions of $15,000 from Falcons Corporation.
    a) What amount of ordinary income and separately stated items are allocated to them for year 1 based on the information above? Assume that Falcons Corporation has $200,000 of qualified property (unadjusted basis).
    b) Complete Falcons's Form 1120-S, Schedule K, for year 1.
    c) Complete Julio's Form 1120-S, Schedule K-1, for year 1.

LO 22-3

tax forms

53. In year 2, Julio and Milania each received distributions of $25,000 from Falcons Corporation.
    a) What amount of ordinary income and separately stated items are allocated to them for year 2 based on the information above? Assume that Falcons Corporation has $200,000 of qualified property (unadjusted basis).
    b) Complete Falcons's Form 1120-S, Schedule K, for year 2.
    c) Complete Milania's Form 1120-S, Schedule K-1, for year 2.

LO 22-4

54. Harriet, Herm, and Ronde formed an S corporation called Innovet. Harriet and Herm both contributed cash of $25,000 to get things started. Ronde was a bit short on cash but had a parcel of land valued at $60,000 (basis of $50,000) that he decided to contribute. The land was encumbered by a $35,000 mortgage. What tax bases will each of the three have in their stock of Innovet?

LO 22-4

55. Sunita is a one-third owner in Bikes-R-Us, an S corporation that experienced a $45,000 loss this year (year 1). If her stock basis is $10,000 at the beginning of the year, how much of this loss clears the hurdle for deductibility (assume the at-risk limitation equals the tax-basis limitation)? If she cannot deduct the whole loss, what happens to the remainder? Is she able to deduct her entire loss if she sells her stock at year-end?

LO 22-4

56. Assume the same facts as in the previous problem, except that at the beginning of year 1 Sunita loaned Bikes-R-Us $3,000. In year 2, Bikes-R-Us reported ordinary income of $12,000. What amount is Sunita allowed to deduct in year 1? What are her stock and debt bases in the corporation at the end of year 1? What are her stock and debt bases in the corporation at the end of year 2?

57. Birch Corp., a calendar-year corporation, was formed three years ago by its sole shareholder, James, who has operated it as an S corporation since its inception. Last year, James made a direct loan to Birch Corp. in the amount of $5,000. Birch Corp. has paid the interest on the loan but has not yet paid any principal. (Assume the loan qualifies as debt for tax purposes.) For the year, Birch experienced a $25,000 business loss. What amount of the loss clears the tax-basis limitation, and what is James's basis in his Birch Corp. stock and Birch Corp. debt in each of the following alternative scenarios? LO 22-4
    a) At the beginning of the year, James's basis in his Birch Corp. stock was $45,000 and his basis in his Birch Corp. debt was $5,000.
    b) At the beginning of the year, James's basis in his Birch Corp. stock was $8,000 and his basis in his Birch Corp. debt was $5,000.
    c) At the beginning of the year, James's basis in his Birch Corp. stock was $0 and his basis in his Birch Corp. debt was $5,000.

58. Timo is the sole owner of Jazz Inc., an S corporation. On October 31, 2022, Timo executed an unsecured demand promissory note of $15,000 and transferred the note to Jazz (Jazz could require Timo to pay it $15,000 on demand). When Timo transferred the note to Jazz, his tax basis in his Jazz stock was $0. On January 31, 2023, Timo paid the $15,000 to Jazz as required by the promissory note. For the taxable year ending December 31, 2022, Jazz incurred a business loss of $12,000. How much of the loss clears the stock and debt basis hurdles for deductibility? LO 22-4 research

59. Chandra was the sole shareholder of Pet Emporium, which was originally formed as an S corporation. When Pet Emporium terminated its S election on August 31, 2021, Chandra had a stock basis and an at-risk amount of $0. Chandra also had a suspended loss from Pet Emporium of $9,000. What amount of the suspended loss is Chandra allowed to deduct, and what is her basis in her Pet Emporium stock, at the end of the post-termination transition period under the following alternative scenarios (assume Pet Emporium files for an extension to file its tax returns)? LO 22-4
    a) Chandra makes capital contributions of $7,000 on August 30, 2022, and $4,000 on September 14, 2022.
    b) Chandra makes capital contributions of $5,000 on September 1, 2022, and $5,000 on September 30, 2022.
    c) Chandra makes a capital contribution of $10,000 on August 31, 2022.
    d) Chandra makes a capital contribution of $10,000 on October 1, 2022.

60. Dejan owns stock in two S corporations, Blue and Green. He actively participates in the management of Blue but maintains ownership in Green only as a passive investor. Dejan has no other business investments. Both Blue and Green anticipate a loss this year, and Dejan's basis in his stock of both corporations is $0. All else equal, if Dejan plans on making a capital contribution to at least one of the corporations this year, to which firm should he contribute in order to increase his chances of deducting the loss allocated to him from the entity? Why? LO 22-4 planning

61. In the past several years, Shakira had loaned money to Shakira Inc. (an S corporation) to help the corporation keep afloat in a downturn. Her stock basis in the S corporation is now $0, and she has deducted $40,000 in losses, reducing her debt basis from $100,000 to $60,000. Things appear to be turning around this year, and Shakira Inc. repaid Shakira $20,000 of the $100,000 outstanding loan. What is Shakira's income, if any, on the partial loan repayment? LO 22-4 planning

62. Adam Fleeman, a skilled carpenter, started a home improvement business with Tom Collins, a master plumber. Adam and Tom are concerned about the payroll taxes they will have to pay. Assume they form an S corporation and each earns a salary of $80,000 from the corporation; in addition, they expect their share of business profits to be $60,000 each. How much Social Security tax and Medicare tax (or self-employment tax) will Adam, Tom, and their corporation have to pay on their salary and profits? LO 22-4

LO 22-4 planning

63. Using the facts in problem 62, could Adam and Tom lower their payroll tax exposure if they operated their business as a partnership? Why or why not?

LO 22-4

64. This year, Justin B.'s share of S corporation income includes $4,000 of interest income, $5,000 of dividend income, and $40,000 of net income from the corporation's professional service business activity.

a) Assume that Justin B. materially participates in the S corporation. How much of his S corporation income is potentially subject to the net investment income tax?

b) Assume that Justin B. does not materially participate in the S corporation. How much of his S corporation income is potentially subject to the net investment income tax?

LO 22-4

65. Friends Jackie (0.5 percent owner), Jermaine (1 percent owner), Marlon (2 percent owner), Janet (86 percent owner), and Tito (10.5 percent owner) are shareholders in Jackson 5 Inc. (an S corporation). As employees of the company, each receives health insurance ($10,000 per year benefit), dental insurance ($2,000 per year benefit), and free access to a workout facility located at company headquarters ($500 per year benefit). What are the tax consequences of these benefits for each shareholder and for Jackson 5 Inc.?

LO 22-5

66. Maple Corp., a calendar-year corporation, was formed three years ago by its sole shareholder, Jian, who immediately elected S corporation status. On December 31 of the current year, Maple distributed $30,000 cash to Jian. What are the amount and character of gain Jian must recognize on the distribution in each of the following alternative scenarios?

a) At the time of the distribution, Jian's basis in his Maple Corp. stock was $35,000.

b) At the time of the distribution, Jian's basis in his Maple Corp. stock was $8,000.

c) At the time of the distribution, Jian's basis in his Maple Corp. stock was $0.

LO 22-5

67. Oak Corp., a calendar-year corporation, was formed three years ago by its sole shareholder, Glover, and has always operated as a C corporation. However, at the beginning of this year, Glover made a qualifying S election for Oak Corp., effective January 1. Oak Corp. did not have any C corporation earnings and profits on that date. On June 1, Oak Corp. distributed $15,000 to Glover. What are the amount and character of gain Glover must recognize on the distribution, and what is his basis in his Oak Corp. stock in each of the following alternative scenarios?

a) At the time of the distribution, Glover's basis in his Oak Corp. stock was $35,000.

b) At the time of the distribution, Glover's basis in his Oak Corp. stock was $8,000.

c) At the time of the distribution, Glover's basis in his Oak Corp. stock was $0.

LO 22-5

68. On January 1, 2022, Janna has a tax basis of $15,000 in her Mimikaki stock (Mimikaki has been an S corporation since inception). In 2022, Janna was allocated $20,000 of ordinary income from Mimikaki. What are the amount and character of gain she recognizes from end-of-the-year distributions in each of the following alternative scenarios, and what is her stock basis following each distribution?

a) Mimikaki distributes $10,000 to Janna.

b) Mimikaki distributes $20,000 to Janna.

c) Mimikaki distributes $30,000 to Janna.

d) Mimikaki distributes $40,000 to Janna.

LO 22-5

69. Assume the following year 2 income statement for Johnstone Corporation, which was a C corporation in year 1 and elected to be taxed as an S corporation beginning in year 2. Johnstone's earnings and profits at the end of year 1 were $10,000. Marcus is Johnstone's sole shareholder, and he has a stock basis of $40,000 at the end of year 1. What is Johnstone's accumulated adjustments account at the end of

year 2, and what amount of dividend income does Marcus recognize on the year 2 distribution in each of the following alternative scenarios?

Johnstone Corporation Income Statement December 31, Year 2	Year 2 (S Corporation)
Sales revenue	$150,000
Cost of goods sold	(35,000)
Salary to owners	(60,000)
Employee wages	(50,000)
Depreciation expense	(4,000)
Miscellaneous expenses	(4,000)
Interest income	10,000
Overall net income	$ 7,000

a) Johnstone distributed $6,000 to Marcus in year 2.
b) Johnstone distributed $10,000 to Marcus in year 2.
c) Johnstone distributed $16,000 to Marcus in year 2.
d) Johnstone distributed $26,000 to Marcus in year 2.

70. At the end of the year, before distributions, Bombay (an S corporation) has an accumulated adjustments account balance of $15,000 and accumulated E&P of $20,000 from a previous year as a C corporation. During the year, Nicolette (a 40 percent shareholder) received a $20,000 distribution (the remaining shareholders received $30,000 in distributions). What are the amount and character of gain Nicolette must recognize from the distribution? What is her basis in her Bombay stock at the end of the year? (Assume her stock basis is $40,000 after considering her share of Bombay's income for the year but before considering the effects of the distribution.) LO 22-5

71. Pine Corp., a calendar-year corporation, was formed three years ago by its sole shareholder, Alejandro, who has always operated it as a C corporation. However, at the beginning of this year, Alejandro made a qualifying S election for Pine Corp., effective January 1. Pine Corp. reported $70,000 of C corporation earnings and profits on the effective date of the S election. This year (its first S corporation year), Pine Corp. reported business income of $50,000. Alejandro's basis in his Pine Corp. stock at the beginning of the year was $15,000. What are the amount and character of income or gain Alejandro must recognize on the following alternative distributions, and what is his basis in his Pine Corp. stock at the end of the year? LO 22-5

a) Alejandro received a $40,000 distribution from Pine Corp. at the end of the year.
b) Alejandro received a $60,000 distribution from Pine Corp. at the end of the year.
c) Alejandro received a $130,000 distribution from Pine Corp. at the end of the year.
d) Alejandro received a $150,000 distribution from Pine Corp. at the end of the year.

72. Carolina Corporation, an S corporation, has no corporate E&P from its years as a C corporation. At the end of the year, it distributes a small parcel of land to its sole shareholder, Shadiya. The fair market value of the parcel is $70,000, and its tax basis is $40,000. Shadiya's basis in her stock is $14,000. Assume Carolina Corporation reported $0 taxable income before considering the tax consequences of the distribution. LO 22-5

a) What amount of gain or loss, if any, does Carolina Corporation recognize on the distribution?
b) How much gain must Shadiya recognize (if any) as a result of the distribution, what is her basis in her Carolina Corporation stock after the distribution, and what is her basis in the land?

c) What is your answer to part (a) if the fair market value of the land is $25,000 rather than $70,000?

d) What is your answer to part (b) if the fair market value of the land is $25,000 rather than $70,000?

LO 22-5 73. Miley decided to terminate the S corporation election of her solely owned corporation on October 17, 2021 (effective immediately), in preparation for taking it public. Miley had previously elected S corporation status on January 1, 2020. At the time of the election, the corporation had an accumulated adjustments account balance of $150,000 and $450,000 of accumulated E&P from prior C corporation years, and Miley had a basis in her S corporation stock of $135,000. During 2022, Miley's corporation reported $0 taxable income or loss. Also, during 2022 the corporation made distributions to Miley of $80,000 and $60,000. How are these distributions taxed to Miley assuming the following?

a) Both distributions are in cash. The first was paid on June 15, 2022, and the second was paid on November 15, 2022.

b) Both distributions are in cash. The first was paid on June 15, 2022, and the second was paid on September 30, 2022.

c) Assume the same facts as in part (b), except the June 15 distribution was a property (noncash) distribution (fair market value of distributed property equal to basis).

LO 22-6 74. Alabama Corporation, an S corporation, liquidates this year by distributing a parcel of land to its sole shareholder, Mark Ingram. The fair market value of the parcel is $50,000, and its tax basis is $30,000. Mark's basis in his stock is $25,000.

a) What amount of gain or loss, if any, does Alabama Corporation recognize on the distribution?

b) How much gain must Mark recognize (if any) as a result of the distribution, and what is his basis in the land?

c) What is your answer to part (a) if the fair market value of the land is $20,000 rather than $50,000?

d) What is your answer to part (b) if the fair market value of the land is $20,000 rather than $50,000?

LO 22-6 75. Rivendell Corporation uses the accrual method of accounting and has the following assets as of the end of 2021. Rivendell converted to an S corporation on January 1, 2022.

Asset	Adjusted Basis	FMV
Cash	$ 40,000	$ 40,000
Accounts receivable	30,000	30,000
Inventory	130,000	60,000
Land	100,000	125,000
Totals	$300,000	$255,000

a) What is Rivendell's net unrealized built-in gain at the time it converted to an S corporation?

b) Assuming the land was valued at $200,000, what would be Rivendell's net unrealized gain at the time it converted to an S corporation?

c) Assuming the land was valued at $125,000 but that the inventory was valued at $85,000, what would be Rivendell's net unrealized gain at the time it converted to an S corporation?

LO 22-6 76. Virginia Corporation is a calendar-year corporation. At the beginning of 2022, its election to be taxed as an S corporation became effective. Virginia Corp.'s balance sheet at the end of 2021 reflected the following assets (it did not have any earnings and profits from its prior years as a C corporation).

Asset	Adjusted Basis	FMV
Cash	$ 20,000	$ 20,000
Accounts receivable	40,000	40,000
Inventory	90,000	200,000
Land	150,000	175,000
Totals	$300,000	$435,000

In 2022, Virginia Corp. reported business income of $50,000 (this would have been its taxable income if it were still a C corporation). What is Virginia's built-in gains tax in each of the following alternative scenarios?

a) During 2022, Virginia Corp. sold inventory it owned at the beginning of the year for $100,000. The basis of the inventory sold was $55,000.

b) Assume the same facts as in part (a), except Virginia Corp. had a net operating loss carryover of $24,000 from its time as a C corporation.

c) Assume the same facts as in part (a), except that if Virginia Corp. were a C corporation, its taxable income would have been $1,500.

77. Tempe Corporation is a calendar-year corporation. At the beginning of 2022, its election to be taxed as an S corporation became effective. Tempe Corp.'s balance sheet at the end of 2021 reflected the following assets (it did not have any earnings and profits from its prior years as a C corporation): LO 22-6

Asset	Adjusted Basis	FMV
Cash	$ 20,000	$ 20,000
Accounts receivable	40,000	40,000
Inventory	160,000	200,000
Land	150,000	120,000
Totals	$370,000	$380,000

Tempe Corp.'s business income for the year was $40,000 (this would have been its taxable income if it were a C corporation). During 2022, Tempe Corp. sold all of the inventory it owned at the beginning of the year for $210,000.

a) What is its built-in gains tax in 2022?

b) Assume the original facts, except that if Tempe Corp. were a C corporation, its taxable income would have been $7,000. What is its built-in gains tax in 2022?

c) Assume the original facts, except the land was valued at $140,000 instead of $120,000. What is Tempe Corp.'s built-in gains tax in 2022?

78. Wood Corporation was a C corporation in 2021 but elected to be taxed as an S corporation in 2022. At the end of 2021, its earnings and profits were $15,500. The following table reports Wood Corp.'s (taxable) income for 2022 (its first year as an S corporation). LO 22-6

Wood Corporation Income Statement December 31, 2022	
Sales revenue	$150,000
Cost of goods sold	(35,000)
Salary to owners	(60,000)
Employee wages	(50,000)
Depreciation expense	(4,000)
Miscellaneous expenses	(4,000)
Interest income	8,000
Qualified dividend income	2,000
Overall net income	$ 7,000

What is Wood Corporation's excess net passive income tax for 2022?

LO 22-6

79. Calculate Anaheim Corporation's excess net passive income tax in each of the following alternative scenarios:

a) Passive investment income, $100,000; expenses associated with passive investment income, $40,000; gross receipts, $120,000; taxable income if a C corporation, $40,000; corporate E&P, $30,000.

b) Passive investment income, $100,000; expenses associated with passive investment income, $70,000; gross receipts, $120,000; taxable income if a C corporation, $1,200; corporate E&P, $30,000.

c) Passive investment income, $100,000; expenses associated with passive investment income, $40,000; gross receipts, $120,000; taxable income if a C corporation, $40,000; corporate E&P, $0.

LO 22-5 LO 22-6 planning

80. Inuk is the sole shareholder of Tex Corporation. Inuk first formed Tex as a C corporation. However, in an attempt to avoid having Tex's income double-taxed, Inuk elected S corporation status for Tex several years ago. On December 31, 2022, Tex reports $5,000 of earnings and profits from its years as a C corporation and $50,000 in its accumulated adjustments account from its activities as an S corporation (including its 2022 activities). Inuk discovered that for the first time Tex was going to have to pay the excess net passive income tax. Inuk wanted to avoid having to pay the tax, but he determined the only way to avoid the tax was to eliminate Tex's E&P by the end of 2022. He determined that, because of the distribution ordering rules (AAA first), he would need to have Tex immediately (in 2022) distribute $55,000 to him. This would clear out Tex's accumulated adjustments account first and then eliminate Tex's C corporation earnings and profits in time to avoid the excess net passive income tax. Inuk was not sure Tex could come up with $55,000 of cash or property in time to accomplish his objective. Does Inuk have any other options to eliminate Tex's earnings and profits without first distributing the balance in Tex's accumulated adjustments account?

LO 22-6 planning

81. Farve Inc. recently elected S corporation status. At the time of the election, the company had $10,000 of accumulated earnings and profits and a net unrealized gain of $1,000,000 associated with land it had invested in (although some parcels had an unrealized loss). In the next couple of years, most of the income the company expects to generate will be in the form of interest and dividends (approximately $200,000 per year). However, in the future, the company will want to liquidate some of its current holdings in land and possibly reinvest in other parcels. What strategies can you recommend for Farve Inc. to help reduce its potential tax liability as an S corporation?

LO 22-6

82. Until the end of year 0, Magic Carpets (MC) was a C corporation with a calendar year-end. At the beginning of year 1, it elected to be taxed as an S corporation. MC uses the LIFO method to value its inventory. At the end of year 0, under the LIFO method, its inventory of rugs was valued at $150,000. Under the FIFO method, the rugs would have been valued at $170,000. How much LIFO recapture tax must MC pay, and what is the due date of the first payment under the following alternative scenarios?

a) MC's regular taxable income in year 0 was $65,000.

b) MC's regular taxable income in year 0 was $200,000.

COMPREHENSIVE PROBLEMS

Select problems are available in Connect®.

planning

83. Knowshon, sole owner of Moreno Inc., is contemplating electing S status for the corporation (Moreno Inc. is currently taxed as a C corporation). Provide recommendations related to Knowshon's election under the following alternative scenarios:

a) At the end of the current year, Moreno Inc. has a net operating loss of $800,000 carryover from 2021. Beginning next year, the company expects to return to profitability. Knowshon projects that Moreno will report profits of $400,000, $500,000, and $600,000 over the next three years. What suggestions do you have regarding the timing of the S election? Explain.

b) How would you answer part (a) if Moreno Inc. had been operating profitably for several years and thus had no net operating loss?

c) While several of Moreno Inc.'s assets have appreciated in value (to the tune of $2,000,000), the corporation has one property—some land in a newly identified flood zone—that has declined in value by $1,500,000. Knowshon plans on selling the loss property in the next year or two. Assume that Moreno does not have a net operating loss. What suggestions do you have for timing the sale of the flood zone property, and why?

84. Barry Porter and Winnie Weeks are considering making an S election on March 1, 2023, for their C corporation, Omniocular. However, first they want to consider the implications of the following information: planning

- Winnie is a U.S. citizen and resident.
- Barry is a citizen of the United Kingdom but a resident of the United States.
- Barry and Winnie each owns 50 percent of the voting power in Omniocular. However, Barry's stock provides him with a claim on 60 percent of the Omniocular assets in liquidation.
- Omniocular was formed under Arizona state law, but it plans on eventually conducting some business in Mexico.

a) Is Omniocular eligible to elect S corporation status? If so, when is the election effective?

For the remainder of the problem, assume Omniocular made a valid S election effective January 1, 2023. Barry and Winnie each owns 50 percent of the voting power and has an equal claim on Omniocular's assets in liquidation. In addition, consider the following information:

- Omniocular reports on a calendar tax year.
- Omniocular's earnings and profits as of December 31, 2022, were $55,000.
- Omniocular's 2022 taxable income was $15,000.
- Omniocular's assets at the end of 2022 are as follows:

Omniocular Assets
December 31, 2022

Asset	Adjusted Basis	FMV
Cash	$ 50,000	$ 50,000
Accounts receivable	20,000	20,000
Investments in stocks and bonds	700,000	700,000
Investment in land	90,000	100,000
Inventory (LIFO)	80,000*	125,000
Equipment	40,000	35,000
Totals	$980,000	$1,030,000

*$110,000 under FIFO accounting.

- On March 31, 2023, Omniocular sold the land for $42,000.
- In 2023, Omniocular sold all the inventory it had on hand at the beginning of the year. This was the only inventory it sold during the year.

Other Income/Expense Items for 2023	
Sales revenue	$155,000
Salary to owners	(50,000)
Employee wages	(10,000)
Depreciation expense	(5,000)
Miscellaneous expenses	(1,000)
Interest income	40,000
Qualified dividend income	65,000

- Assume that if Omniocular were a C corporation for 2023, its taxable income would have been $88,500.

b) How much LIFO recapture tax is Omniocular required to pay, and when is it due?
c) How much built-in gains tax, if any, is Omniocular required to pay?
d) How much excess net passive income tax, if any, is Omniocular required to pay?
e) Assume Barry's basis in his Omniocular stock was $40,000 on January 1, 2023. What is his stock basis on December 31, 2023?

For the following questions, assume that after electing S corporation status, Barry and Winnie had a change of heart and filed an election to terminate Omniocular's S election, effective August 1, 2024.

- In 2024, Omniocular reported the following income/expense items:

Description	January 1—July 31, 2024 (213 days)	August 1—December 31, 2024 (153 days)	January 1—December 31, 2024
Sales revenue	$ 80,000	$185,000	$265,000
Cost of goods sold	(40,000)	(20,000)	(60,000)
Salaries to Barry and Winnie	(60,000)	(40,000)	(100,000)
Depreciation expense	(7,000)	(2,000)	(9,000)
Miscellaneous expenses	(4,000)	(3,000)	(7,000)
Interest income	6,000	5,250	11,250
Overall net income (loss)	$(25,000)	$125,250	$100,250

f) For tax purposes, how would you recommend Barry and Winnie allocate income between the short S corporation year and the short C corporation year if they would like to minimize double taxation of Omniocular's income?
g) Assume in part (f) that Omniocular allocates income between the short S and C corporation years in a way that minimizes the double taxation of its income. If Barry's stock basis in his Omniocular stock on January 1, 2024, is $50,000, what is his stock basis on December 31, 2024?
h) When is the earliest tax year in which Omniocular can be taxed as an S corporation again?

85. Agustina, Bobby, and Claudia are equal owners in Lafter, an S corporation that was a C corporation several years ago. While Agustina and Bobby actively participate in running the company, Claudia has a separate day job and is a passive owner. Consider the following information for 2022:

- As of January 1, 2022, Agustina, Bobby, and Claudia each has a basis in Lafter stock of $15,000 and a debt basis of $0. On January 1, the stock basis is also the at-risk amount for each shareholder.
- Bobby and Claudia also are passive owners in Aggressive LLC, which allocated business income of $14,000 to each of them in 2022. Neither has any other source of passive income (besides Lafter, for Claudia).

- On March 31, 2022, Agustina lends $5,000 of her own money to Lafter.
- Anticipating the need for basis to deduct a loss, on April 4, 2022, Bobby takes out a $10,000 loan to make a $10,000 capital contribution to Lafter. Bobby uses his automobile ($12,000 fair market value) as the sole collateral for his loan (nonrecourse).
- Lafter has an accumulated adjustments account balance of $45,000 as of January 1, 2022.
- Lafter has C corporation earnings and profits of $15,000 as of January 1, 2022.
- During 2022, Lafter reports a business loss of $75,000, computed as follows:

Sales revenue	$ 90,000
Cost of goods sold	(85,000)
Salary to Agustina	(40,000)
Salary to Bobby	(40,000)
Business (loss)	$(75,000)

- Lafter also reported $12,000 of tax-exempt interest income.

a) What amount of Lafter's 2022 business loss of $75,000 are Agustina, Bobby, and Claudia allowed to deduct on their individual tax returns? What are each owner's stock basis and debt basis (if applicable) and each owner's at-risk amount with respect to the investment in Lafter at the end of 2022?

- During 2023, Lafter made several changes to its business approach and reported $18,000 of business income, computed as follows:

Sales revenue	$208,000
Cost of goods sold	(90,000)
Salary to Agustina	(45,000)
Salary to Bobby	(45,000)
Marketing expense	(10,000)
Business income	$ 18,000

- Lafter also reported a long-term capital gain of $24,000 in 2023.
- Lafter made a cash distribution on July 1, 2023, of $20,000 to each shareholder.

b) What amount of gain/income does each shareholder recognize from the cash distribution on July 1, 2023?

86. While James Craig and his former classmate Paul Dolittle both studied accounting at school, they ended up pursuing careers in professional cake decorating. Their company, Good to Eat (GTE), specializes in custom-sculpted cakes for weddings, birthdays, and other celebrations. James and Paul formed the business at the beginning of 2022, and each contributed $50,000 in exchange for a 50 percent ownership interest. GTE also borrowed $200,000 from a local bank. Both James and Paul had to personally guarantee the loan. Both owners provide significant services for the business. The following information pertains to GTE's 2022 activities: **tax forms**

- GTE uses the cash method of accounting (for both book and tax purposes) and reports income on a calendar-year basis.
- GTE received $450,000 of sales revenue and reported $210,000 of cost of goods sold (it did not have any ending inventory).
- GTE paid $30,000 compensation to James, $30,000 compensation to Paul, and $40,000 of compensation to other employees (assume these amounts include applicable payroll taxes, if any).
- GTE paid $15,000 of rent for a building and equipment, $20,000 for advertising, $14,000 in interest expense, $4,000 for utilities, and $2,000 for supplies.

- GTE contributed $5,000 to charity.
- GTE received a $1,000 qualified dividend from a great stock investment (it owned 2 percent of the corporation distributing the dividend), and it recognized $1,500 in short-term capital gain when it sold some of the stock.
- On December 1, 2022, GTE distributed $20,000 to James and $20,000 to Paul.
- GTE has qualified property of $300,000 (unadjusted basis).

Required:

a) Assume James and Paul formed GTE as an S corporation.

- Complete GTE's Form 1120-S, page 1; Form 1120-S, Schedule K; and Paul's Form 1120-S, Schedule K-1 (note that you should use 2021 tax forms).
- Compute the tax basis of Paul's stock in GTE at the end of 2022.
- What amount of Paul's income from GTE is subject to FICA or self-employment taxes?
- What amount of income, including its character, will Paul recognize on the $20,000 distribution he receives on December 1?
- What amount of tax does GTE pay on the $1,000 qualified dividend it received?

b) Assume James and Paul formed GTE as an LLC.

- Complete GTE's Form 1065, page 1; Form 1065, Schedule K; and Paul's Form 1065, Schedule K-1 (note that you should use 2021 tax forms).
- Compute the tax basis of Paul's ownership interest in GTE at the end of 2022.
- What amount of Paul's income from GTE is subject to FICA or self-employment taxes?
- What amount of income, including its character, will Paul recognize on the $20,000 distribution he receives on December 1?
- What amount of tax does GTE pay on the $1,000 qualified dividend it received?

c) Assume James and Paul formed GTE as a C corporation.

- Complete GTE's Form 1120, page 1 (note that you should use the 2021 tax form).
- Compute the tax basis of Paul's stock in GTE at the end of 2022.
- What amount of Paul's income from GTE is subject to FICA or self-employment taxes?
- What amount of income, including its character, will Paul recognize on the $20,000 distribution he receives on December 1?
- What amount of tax does GTE pay on the $1,000 qualified dividend it received?

UWorld | ROGER CPA Review

UWorld Roger CPA Review

Sample CPA Exam questions from Roger CPA Review are available in Connect as support for the topics in this text. These Multiple Choice Questions and Task-Based Simulations include expert-written explanations and solutions and provide a starting point for students to become familiar with the content and functionality of the actual CPA Exam.

chapter

23 State and Local Taxes

Learning Objectives

Upon completing this chapter, you should be able to:

LO 23-1 Describe the primary types of state and local taxes.

LO 23-2 Determine whether a business has sales tax nexus and calculate its sales tax withholding responsibilities.

LO 23-3 Identify whether a business has income tax nexus and determine its state income tax liabilities.

Robert Dziewulski/dziewul/123RF

Storyline Summary

Taxpayer:	Ken Brody (he/him/his)
Location:	Idaho
Status:	Sole owner of Wild West River Runners Inc., a C corporation
Situation:	Ken owns retail stores in Idaho and Wyoming that sell merchandise locally; operates a Wyoming-based Internet store; and provides services in Idaho, Tennessee, Washington, and Wyoming. He must determine the company's state and local tax liabilities.

Ken Brody owns Wild West River Runners Incorporated (Wild West), an Idaho C corporation. Wild West offers guided white-water rafting adventures in Idaho, Tennessee, Washington, and Wyoming. It also operates retail stores in Idaho and Wyoming and an Internet-based retail store based in Wyoming. Wild West's retail stores sell only locally (they never ship merchandise), but the salesclerks often refer customers to the Internet store (www.wildwestriverrunners.com). Most employees are seasonal (teachers or college students). During the off-season, a few guides make sales visits with Ken and operate the retail stores. Also during the off-season, Ken attends the annual 10-day Raft and River Show in Phoenix, Arizona, and travels the country promoting Wild West's guided river adventures.

Wild West's Form 1120, U.S. Corporation Income Tax Return, shows federal taxable income for the current year of $53,289, and it must calculate its state and local tax liabilities. Because Wild West operates a multistate business, it must identify the states in which it must collect sales tax, collect the sales tax and remit it to the respective states, determine the states in which it must file income tax returns, and file income tax returns reflecting its taxable income for each state in which it must file. ■

Like a lot of other businesses, Wild West is a multistate operation. From a business perspective, multistate businesses generally have access to a larger economic base than those operating in a single state. However, with this economic opportunity come complexity and additional tax burdens.

LO 23-1 STATE AND LOCAL TAXES

The primary purpose of state and local taxes is to raise revenue to finance state and local governments. All 50 states and the District of Columbia have some combination of three primary revenue sources: sales and use tax, income or franchise tax, and property tax.[1] This chapter focuses on sales and use taxes (i.e., excise taxes levied on the sale or use of tangible personal property within a state) and taxes based on *net* income (i.e., income taxes).[2]

Like federal tax law, state tax law includes the following:

- Legislative law (state constitution and tax code).
- Administrative law (regulations and rulings).
- Judicial law (tax court cases).

While businesses deal with a single federal tax code, there are different tax codes or laws for each state. This makes state tax research particularly challenging. State tax agencies, such as the California Franchise Tax Board and the New York Department of Finance and Taxation, administer the law and promulgate regulations for their particular states.[3] Federal and state courts interpret the law when a state's tax authority and businesses cannot agree on its interpretation or constitutionality. Because of constitutionality questions, judicial law plays a significantly more important role in state tax law than in federal tax law. It is impractical, if not impossible, to study each individual state statute in one text. Instead, this chapter addresses the most important state and local tax principles at a conceptual level.

The most important question Wild West, or any other business, must answer is whether it is subject to a state's taxing regime. The answer depends on the business's state of **commercial domicile** and whether the business has **nexus** (either sales tax nexus or income tax nexus) in that state. We will discuss both sales tax nexus and income tax nexus in this chapter. Commercial domicile is the state where a business is headquartered and directs its operations; this location may be different from the place of incorporation.[4] A business must always collect and remit sales tax from its customers and pay income tax in the state where it is domiciled. **Nondomiciliary businesses**—businesses not domiciled or headquartered in a state—are subject to taxing authorities only where they have nexus. Nexus is the sufficient (or minimum) connection between a business and a state that subjects the business to the state's tax system.

Wild West's commercial domicile is Idaho because it is headquartered there. Consequently, it must collect and remit Idaho sales tax and pay Idaho income tax. Yet, as detailed in Exhibit 23-1, it has activities and sales in other states, and therefore it must collect sales tax and pay income tax in the states in which it has nexus.

[1]State and local jurisdictions may also tax or levy the following: personal property, capital stock, business licensing, transfer, incorporation, excise, severance, payroll, disability, unemployment, fuel, and telecommunication.

[2]This chapter discusses corporate income and franchise taxes interchangeably. Franchise taxes are imposed for the right to conduct business within a state. Most franchise taxes (such as the California Franchise Tax) are calculated based on net income.

[3]A great resource for guidance and forms from specific states can be found on the Federation of Tax Administrators website, www.taxadmin.org/state-tax-forms.

[4]Some companies (e.g., Adobe Inc.) are incorporated in one state (e.g., Delaware) but domiciled or headquartered in another (e.g., California). These companies pay taxes in both states (although sometimes just a capital stock tax applies in the state of incorporation if there are no activities other than incorporation within a state).

EXHIBIT 23-1 Wild West's Activities and Sales by State

Wild West In-State Activities

State	Sale of Goods	Sale of Services	Employees	Property	Commercial Domicile
Arizona	✓				
California	✓				
Colorado	✓				
Idaho	✓	✓	✓	✓	✓
Tennessee	✓	✓	✓	✓	
Washington	✓	✓	✓	✓	
Wyoming	✓	✓	✓	✓	

Wild West Sales

State	Goods	Services	Total	Transactions
Arizona	$ 89,242	$ 0	$ 89,242	215
California	132,045	0	132,045	489
Colorado	75,002	0	75,002	163
Idaho	167,921	625,003	792,924	1,043
Tennessee	45,331	357,061	402,392	753
Washington	41,982	377,441	419,423	812
Wyoming	185,249	437,755	623,004	941
Totals	$736,772	$1,797,260	$2,534,032	4,416

When a business sells tangible personal property that is included in a state's sales tax base, it must collect and remit the **sales tax** on a periodic basis if it has sales tax nexus in that state.[5] Exhibit 23-2 provides an overview of who bears the burden of sales taxes (i.e., who must pay and who must collect and remit sales tax to the state). Sales tax liability accrues on certain sales of tangible personal property within the state. For example, Wild West's Idaho retail store collects sales tax on goods sold in Idaho stores and remits the tax

EXHIBIT 23-2 State Sales and Use Tax Process

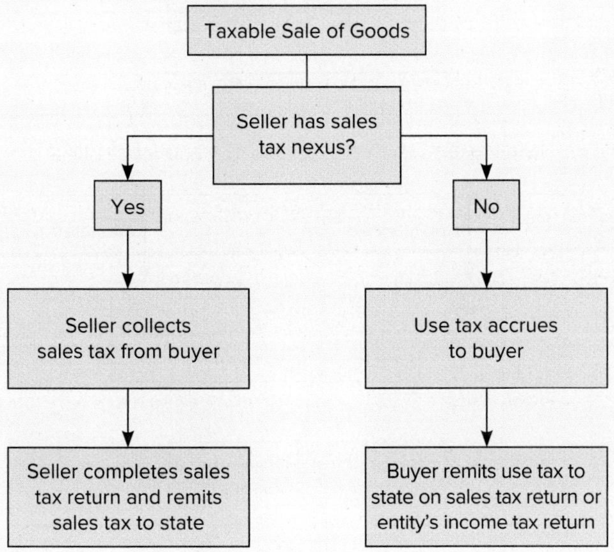

[5]Businesses remit the sales taxes collected from customers to the state on a sales tax return, which is filed on a monthly, quarterly, or annual basis depending on the size of the liability and the state law thresholds.

to the Idaho Department of Revenue. **Use tax** liability accrues in the state where purchased property will be used when no sales tax was paid at the time of purchase. The use tax applies only when a seller in one state ships goods to a customer in a different state and the seller is not required to collect the sales tax (i.e., the seller does not have sales tax nexus in the state to which the goods are shipped). For example, Colorado customers ordering through Wild West's Wyoming-based Internet store (which has no Colorado sales tax nexus) are required to accrue and remit the Colorado use tax (i.e., usually through their personal income tax returns).[6] Businesses with sales tax nexus in a state are legally responsible for remitting the sales tax even when they fail to collect it, and they generally record the sales tax liability on their financial statements.

Businesses engaged in **interstate commerce** must also deal with income tax–related issues. If a business meets certain requirements creating income tax nexus, it may be required to remit income tax to that state. The general process of determining a business's state income tax liability is highlighted in Exhibit 23-3. The **state tax base** is computed by making adjustments to federal taxable income. The adjustments are necessary to account for differences between federal income tax laws and state income tax laws. Then we divide the state tax base into **business income** and **nonbusiness income.** Business income (i.e., income from business activities) is subject to **apportionment** among states where income tax nexus and a filing requirement exist, based on the extent of the business's activities and property in various states. Nonbusiness income (i.e., all income except business income—generally investment income) is subject to **allocation,** or assignment directly to the business's state of commercial domicile. For states in which the business has income tax nexus and a filing requirement, state taxable income is the sum of the business income apportioned to that state plus the nonbusiness income allocated to that state. The business computes its state tax liability for that particular state by multiplying state taxable income by the state's tax rate.

Let's now look in more depth at sales tax and net income–based taxes, the nexus requirements, and the calculation of each tax.

EXHIBIT 23-3 State Income Tax Process

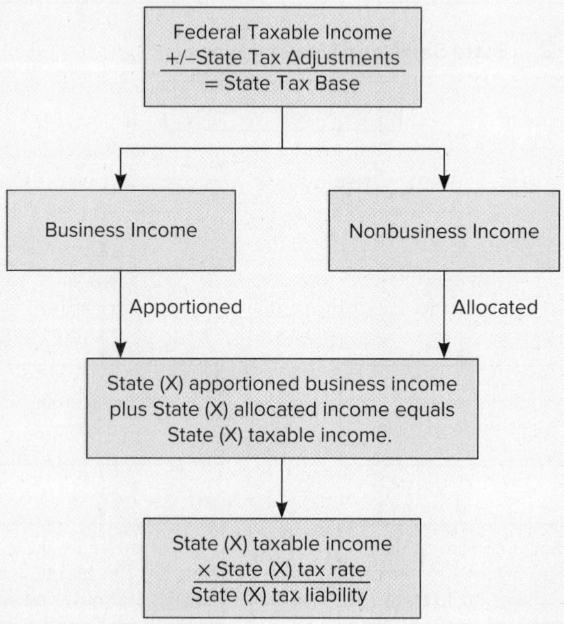

[6]Individuals remit their use tax by adding their use tax liability to a line on their individual income tax return. Businesses remit their use tax by adding it to any sales tax collected from customers on their sales and use tax return.

SALES AND USE TAXES

LO 23-2

Forty-five states and the District of Columbia impose sales taxes; Alaska, Delaware, Montana, New Hampshire, and Oregon do not. Sales tax must be collected on the state's sales tax base. Generally, sales of tangible personal property are subject to the tax. Most states also tax restaurant meals, rental car usage, hotel room rentals (often at higher tax rates than general sales), and some services (which vary widely by state). Purchases of inventory for resale are generally exempt from the sales tax.[7] For example, Wild West's rafting equipment purchases for resale are exempt from sales tax because inventory is taxed when sold, but the office furniture purchased for use in the business is taxable because it represents a final sale. Items that are included in the sales tax base vary from state to state. Many states exempt food (except prepared restaurant food) because taxing food is considered to be regressive; that is, it imposes a proportionally higher tax burden on lower-income taxpayers, who spend a greater proportion of their income on food and other necessities. Most states also exempt sales of real property, intangible property, and services. However, many states are expanding the types of services subject to sales tax in order to increase their sales tax revenue.[8]

TAXES IN THE REAL WORLD Is It Candy or Is It Food?

Items subject to the sales tax vary from state to state. Historically, New York taxed the sale of large marshmallows but exempted the sale of small marshmallows. Large and small marshmallows were treated differently because large marshmallows were considered to be candy, which was included in the sales tax base, while small marshmallows were considered to be a food ingredient and therefore excluded from the sales tax base. Currently, all marshmallows are taxed as a food ingredient.

The Washington state legislature passed a law subjecting candy to sales tax a few years ago. Any item containing flour was considered a food item, not candy. As a result, Twix bars were exempt because the cookie has flour as an ingredient, while Starburst candy was subject to sales tax. Within a year, Washington voters repealed the tax on candy through a ballot initiative.

Sales Tax Nexus

Have you ever wondered why sometimes you pay sales tax on goods purchased over the Internet and sometimes you don't? The answer is it depends on whether the seller has **sales tax nexus** in the state where the goods are being shipped to. A business is required to collect sales tax from customers in a state only if it has sales tax nexus in the destination state. For example, if you purchase a book from a local bookstore, you will pay sales tax, but if you purchase the book from some online sellers, you won't pay sales tax unless the book is being shipped to a state where the seller has sales tax nexus. As a result, understanding when a business has sales tax nexus can be extremely important for profitability, business modeling, and compliance. Exhibit 23-4 provides an excerpt from the 2020 annual report for Wayfair, a prominent online seller, in which it describes how the Court's Wayfair decision is not expected to have a significant impact on its business.

The Commerce Clause of the U.S. Constitution gives Congress the authority "[t]o regulate Commerce with foreign Nations, and among the several States, and with the Indian Tribes." The purpose of the Commerce Clause is to place limits on taxation to enhance or increase interstate commerce. Because Congress has never exercised its Commerce Clause right with respect to sales tax, the courts have historically determined sales tax nexus thresholds. Businesses that establish sales tax nexus with a state but fail to properly collect sales tax and remit it to the state can create significant liabilities that may need to be disclosed for financial reporting purposes.[9]

THE KEY FACTS

Sales Tax Nexus

- Nexus is the sufficient connection between a business and a state that allows a state to levy a tax on the business.
- Historically, sales tax nexus was established through the physical presence of salespeople or property within a state.
- On June 21, 2018, the Supreme Court ruled that economic nexus is also established for an online seller when either $100,000 of sales or 200 sales transactions are made to customers within a state during a year.

[7]Most states grant a reseller's certificate, which exempts purchases of inventory for resale from sales tax.
[8]For example, Connecticut taxes services such as tax preparation.
[9]Sales tax liabilities are ASC Topic 450 contingencies.

EXHIBIT 23-4 Excerpt from Wayfair's 2020 Annual Report

From the Form 10-K

Collection of Sales or Other Similar Taxes

Wayfair has historically collected and remitted sales tax based on the locations of its physical operations. On June 21, 2018, the U.S. Supreme Court rendered a 5-4 majority decision in South Dakota v. Wayfair Inc., 17-494. Among other things, the Court held that a state may require an out-of-state seller with no physical presence in the state to collect and remit sales taxes on goods the seller ships to consumers in the state, overturning existing court precedent. Several states and other taxing jurisdictions have presented, or indicated that they may present, Wayfair with sales tax assessments. The aggregate assessments received as of December 31, 2020 are not material to Wayfair's business and Wayfair does not expect the Court's decision to have a significant impact on its business.

Source: Wayfair 2020 Annual Report.

Prior to June 21, 2018, sales tax nexus was established through a business having *physical presence* within a state. Physical presence was established through either (1) salespeople (or independent contractors representing a business) entering a state to obtain sales or (2) tangible property (such as a company-owned truck that made deliveries) being located within a state.[10] In *National Bellas Hess* (1967), the U.S. Supreme Court held that an out-of-state mail-order company (nondomiciliary) did not have a sales tax collection responsibility because it lacked physical presence (even though it mailed catalogs and advertised in the state).[11] Subsequently, in *Quill Corp.* (1992), the U.S. Supreme Court reaffirmed that out-of-state (nondomiciliary) businesses must have a physical presence in the state before the state may require a business to collect sales tax from in-state customers.[12]

On June 21, 2018, the U.S. Supreme Court reversed its physical presence standard for online sellers in favor of an economic nexus standard in its *Wayfair* decision.[13] The new economic nexus standard allows a state to impose a sales tax collection responsibility on businesses (including non-U.S. businesses) when the following six criteria are met: (1) businesses selling less than $100,000 in sales or having less than 200 sales transactions are excluded; (2) no retroactive tax is collected; (3) there is a single, state-level administration of sales taxes; (4) there is a simplified tax rate structure; (5) there are uniform definitions and other rules; and (6) the state provides software for sales tax collection and provides immunity to businesses that rely on the software. Currently, all states imposing a sales tax have now adopted the new economic nexus standard for sales tax. Missouri's law will not be effective until January 1, 2023.

Even after the *Wayfair* decision, it remains unclear whether the physical presence and economic sales tax nexus standards now apply simultaneously or whether the economic nexus standard has completely replaced the physical presence standard for all businesses. For example, does a business that has a physical presence in a state but has less than $100,000 in sales or 200 sales transactions have sales tax nexus in that state? A strict reading of most of these newly implemented economic nexus laws indicates that online sellers meeting the economic standard are treated as if they have a physical presence within the state. For this reason, many professionals believe that the nexus standards apply simultaneously—but only time will help businesses resolve this question.

[10]*Scripto, Inc. v. Carson,* 362 U.S. 207 (1960). Scripto hired independent salespeople to represent the company in Florida. The Supreme Court held that these salespeople were agents of Scripto, who established the physical presence necessary to create sales tax nexus.

[11]*Nat'l Bellas Hess, Inc. v. Dep't of Rev. of the State of Ill.,* 386 U.S. 753 (1967).

[12]*Quill Corp. v. North Dakota,* 504 U.S. 298 (1992).

[13]*South Dakota v. Wayfair, Inc.,* 138 S. Ct. 2080 (2018).

Example 23-1

Wild West sends promotional brochures from Idaho to its Arizona and Colorado clients. Wild West generated current-year sales of $89,242 on 215 sales transactions and $75,002 on 163 sales transactions within Arizona and Colorado, respectively. Prior to the *Wayfair* decision, Wild West didn't collect Arizona or Colorado sales tax or file sales tax returns. Wild West has neither employees nor property in Arizona or Colorado. Assume that Arizona and Colorado both adopted the new economic nexus standard under *Wayfair.* Does Wild West have sales tax nexus in Arizona and/or Colorado?

Answer: Yes in Arizona and no in Colorado. Wild West has met the new economic nexus standard of $100,000 in sales or 200 sales transactions within Arizona because of its 215 sales transactions, but not in Colorado, where it had only 163 sales transactions and its sales revenue from those transactions was less than $100,000. Wild West has economic sales tax nexus in Arizona, but not in Colorado, Therefore, Wild West has an Arizona sales tax collection responsibility.

What if: Assume that in addition to mailing promotional brochures, Ken visits Colorado on promotional trips. Does Wild West have sales tax nexus in Colorado under these circumstances?

Answer: Probably yes. Prior to Colorado adopting the new economic nexus standard, the presence of Wild West's representatives would have created physical presence nexus. Colorado law now treats online sellers that meet the economic nexus standard as if they had physical presence in that state. So Wild West should probably assume that the physical presence of the promotional trips creates sales tax nexus in Colorado.

What if: Assume the original facts except that Wild West had $110,000 in sales and 250 sales transactions with Colorado customers during the year. Does Wild West have sales tax nexus in Colorado under these circumstances?

Answer: Yes. The new economic nexus standard has been met because Wild West exceeds both $100,000 in sales and 200 sales transactions in Colorado during the year.

Sales Tax Liability

Typically, sellers with sales tax nexus collect sales tax from their customers at the time of sale. For example, Wild West collects sales tax on river rafting equipment it sells from its retail store but not on river guiding *services* it provides. If the seller doesn't have sales tax nexus and chooses not to collect the sales tax, then the customer is responsible for remitting a use tax (at the same tax rate as sales tax) to the state in which the property is located and used. If the buyer is charged a sales tax in another state, the buyer will have a use tax liability for the incremental amount if the state where the property is located and used has a higher sales tax rate than the state where the item was purchased.

Example 23-2

Wild West generated current-year sales of $75,002 within Colorado on its 163 sales transactions to Colorado customers. Wild West received $3,500 from a customer named Casey Jarvie residing in Boulder, Colorado. Of this amount, $500 was for personal rafting equipment shipped to Boulder, where the sales tax rate is 8.845 percent. The remaining $3,000 was payment for a four-day river raft adventure on the Salmon River in Idaho. Colorado adopted the new economic nexus standard. Does Wild West have a responsibility to collect sales tax from Casey?

Answer: No. Wild West is below the economic nexus standard, has no physical presence, and does not have sales tax nexus in Colorado; therefore, it has no Colorado sales tax collection requirement.

Because Wild West has no sales tax collection responsibility, does Casey have a use tax liability to the state of Colorado? If so, in what amount?

(continued on page 23-8)

Answer: Yes. Casey is responsible for remitting $44.23 of use tax ($500 × 8.845%) on his personal Colorado state income tax return for the purchase of the personal rafting equipment in Colorado. He is not required to pay Colorado use tax on the river raft adventure purchase because Wild West provided an out-of-state service (no sales tax is due on the services in Idaho either).

What if: If Casey had Wild West hold the goods until he arrived in Burley, Idaho, to pick them up at the time of the trip (assume the sales tax rate in Burley, Idaho, is 6 percent), would Wild West have sales tax collection responsibility? If so, what is the sales tax amount? Would Casey have a Colorado use tax liability?

Answer: Yes. Because Wild West has physical presence in Idaho, it is required to collect $30 ($500 × 6%) of sales tax and remit it to Idaho. Casey would also have a $14.23 Colorado use tax liability ($44.23 reduced by the $30 remitted to Idaho) in this scenario.

ETHICS

Jill is a Virginia resident who purchased $1,500 of personal use items from various small Internet retailers during the year. None of these retailers meets the new economic nexus standard and they do not collect sales taxes from Jill. While completing her personal tax return using a popular software package, Jill was asked to report her online purchases. After entering these purchases, she noticed that $75 of "use tax" was added to her state tax liability. Jill has never paid this tax in the past. She decided to delete the online purchase information she had previously entered. What do you think of Jill's failure to report her Virginia use tax?

Many states have now implemented marketplace seller rules for companies like Amazon, eBay, and Etsy. Rather than applying the economic nexus standard to the small reseller, these states apply the economic nexus standard at the marketplace level. This forces the marketplace to collect and remit sales tax.

Large companies often must file sales tax returns in all 45 states, and the District of Columbia, that have sales taxes.[14] This administrative burden is further increased by the fact that more than 7,500 tax jurisdictions (including counties, cities, school districts, and other divisions) impose sales taxes, and several hundred jurisdictions have rates change annually at various times throughout the year.[15] The sales tax administrative burden can also be large for small businesses. For example, a local pizzeria that delivers can sometimes be subject to a half-dozen sales tax rates if its delivery services cross city, county, or even school district boundaries.

ETHICS

Oklahoma has notice and reporting requirements that require nondomiciliary businesses without sales tax nexus to report all the necessary information to help the Department of Revenue collect its use tax from resident individuals and domiciliary businesses. Assume you are responsible for resolving sales tax issues for an online retailer from another state. You believe that Oklahoma's notice and reporting requirements are unconstitutional based on a seminar you attended and the advice of your accounting firm. Would you recommend that your company comply with these notice and reporting laws? Would your opinion change if the court issued an injunction prohibiting the state from enforcing the new law?

[14]Some counties or political subdivisions of states without state sales taxes (such as Kenai Peninsula Borough in Alaska) impose a county or local sales tax.

[15]Software companies provide sales tax solutions that help companies with the administrative burden. However, they generally fail to indemnify or compensate businesses against errors in their software that result in uncollected sales taxes, which creates a liability for the business.

Example 23-3

Recall from Exhibit 23-1 that Wild West has sales in Arizona, California, Colorado, Idaho, Tennessee, Washington, and Wyoming. Also recall that it has property and employees in Idaho, Tennessee, Washington, and Wyoming. In which states does Wild West have sales tax nexus and, therefore, sales tax collection responsibility?

Answer: Wild West's physical presence of employees and real and personal property create sales tax nexus in Idaho, Tennessee, Washington, and Wyoming. Additionally, under the new economic nexus standard for sales taxes, Wild West will have sales tax nexus in Arizona and California. Wild West will have under $100,000 in sales and less than 200 sales transactions with Colorado customers and will not have sales tax nexus in Colorado.

Using the sales data provided in Exhibit 23-1, how much sales tax must Wild West remit? Assume the following (hypothetical) sales tax rates: Arizona, 8.6 percent; California, 9.5 percent; Idaho, 6 percent; Tennessee, 9.25 percent; Washington, 7.7 percent; and Wyoming, 6 percent.

Answer: It must remit $48,835, computed as follows:

State	(1) Taxable Sales	(2) Rate	(1) × (2) Sales Tax Due
Arizona	$ 89,242	8.60%	$ 7,675
California	132,045	9.50%	12,544
Idaho	167,921	6.00%	10,075
Tennessee	45,331	9.25%	4,193
Washington	41,982	7.70%	3,233
Wyoming	185,249	6.00%	11,115
Totals	**$661,770**		**$48,835**

Remember, services are not generally subject to sales tax.

TAXES IN THE REAL WORLD Groupon

Have you ever bought a restaurant meal from Groupon? Did you know there is a tax issue complicating these types of purchases? Suppose you pay $25 for a $50 voucher good at your favorite restaurant. You just scored a great deal. Groupon collects the $25 and pays the restaurant $12.50. You show up and order $50 worth of food, and the server brings you the bill. How much sales tax should the restaurant collect from you on the prepared food (which is a taxable item)? You received $50 worth of prepared food (one possible tax base), but you paid only $25 (another possible tax base), and the restaurant received only $12.50 (a third possible tax base). What is the nature of the $12.50 retained by Groupon? Did it provide a good (taxable) or a service (not taxable)? Most restaurants currently collect tax on the entire $50 benefit you received. However, some states have started providing guidance.

INCOME TAXES

LO 23-3

Forty-four states impose an income tax on corporations; South Dakota and Wyoming impose no corporate income tax and Nevada, Ohio, Texas, and Washington impose a gross-receipts tax.[16] Forty-three states tax individuals on income earned through partnerships and S corporations.[17] This chapter focuses on C corporations, but the same

[16]Several states (such as California and New York) impose a franchise tax rather than an income tax. Because franchise taxes are generally based upon net income, they are essentially the same as income taxes.

[17]These states tax individuals, including the income that flows through from partnerships and S corporations (although New Hampshire and Tennessee tax only dividends and interest). The following states do not tax individuals: Alaska, Florida, Nevada, South Dakota, Texas, Washington, and Wyoming.

principles generally apply to flow-through entities. Most states imposing income-based taxes conform to an entity's federal tax status. For example, most states treat an S corporation as a flow-through entity and tax only the owner of the entity. However, a few states impose minimum taxes on flow-through entities. For example, California imposes a minimum tax of $800 or a 1.5 percent tax on the income of all flow-through entities, including partnerships (and LLCs taxed as partnerships) and S corporations.

Businesses must pay income tax in their state of commercial domicile (i.e., where they are headquartered). For example, Wild West is both incorporated and domiciled in Idaho and is therefore subject to Idaho's income tax regime. Until a few decades ago, many businesses believed they were virtually exempt from state income taxes in states other than their state of commercial domicile. However, in *Complete Auto Transit,* the U.S. Supreme Court spelled out four criteria for determining whether states can tax nondomiciliary businesses and whether the tax imposed is discriminatory against nondomiciliary businesses (i.e., businesses domiciled in another state).[18] First, a sufficient connection, or **income tax nexus,** must exist between the state and the business. Second, a state may tax only a fair portion of a business's income. Businesses must be able to divide or apportion income among the states where an income tax filing requirement exists. Third, the tax cannot be constructed to discriminate against nonresident businesses. For example, states cannot impose a higher tax rate on nondomiciliary businesses than domiciliary businesses. Fourth, the taxes paid must be fairly related to the services the state provides the business. For example, states provide businesses access to their courts, economic base, infrastructure, and so forth.

Businesses must answer the following questions to determine their state income tax liabilities:

- In which state(s) does it have income tax nexus?
- If income tax nexus exists, is the company protected from paying income taxes by Public Law 86-272?
- If the business is related to other entities, should it file separate state income tax returns, or should it include the activities of the related entities on a single state income tax return?
- What adjustments to federal taxable income must the business make to calculate state taxable income for each state in which it is required to file?
- If it has income tax nexus in more than one state, how is income divided among the various states in which the business is required to file tax returns?

THE KEY FACTS

Income Tax Nexus

- Income tax nexus is created through physical presence of salespeople or property.
- Sellers of tangible personal property, even when income tax nexus exists, can be protected from an income tax liability under Public Law 86-272.
  - As long as in-state activities are limited to solicitation.
- Several states are now asserting economic income tax nexus.

Income Tax Nexus

Income tax nexus can be created through either physical presence or economic factors.[19] Historically, income tax nexus has been created through the physical presence of salespeople or property in that state. Physical presence in a state always creates income tax nexus in that state. More recently, states are pursuing nexus through economic presence to capture additional tax revenue. However, even when physical presence or economic presence creates income tax nexus for sellers of tangible personal property, these sellers may be protected from paying income taxes if their activities within a state are limited to certain "protected" activities as described by **Public Law 86-272.**

[18]*Complete Auto Transit, Inc. v. Brady,* 430 U.S. 274 (1977).

[19]Until 1959, there was a common and persistent belief among businesses that state tax accrued only in the business's state of commercial domicile. In 1959, the U.S. Supreme Court allowed Minnesota to tax an Iowa-based business [*Nw. States Portland Cement Co. v. Minnesota,* 358 U.S. 450 (1959)]. As discussed in the next section, Congress passed Public Law 86-272 seven months later.

Economic Presence Many states assert that because they provide the infrastructure for nonresident companies to do business in the state (e.g., Internet, phone connections, and roads), nonresident companies doing business in the state have an economic presence in the state and thus have **economic income tax nexus** in the state, even when they don't have a physical presence in the state.[20] For example, West Virginia asserted income tax nexus and an income tax liability on a business (MBNA Bank) that merely solicited credit card customers through advertising and phone calls without having physical presence (employees or property) in the state. The West Virginia Supreme Court upheld the assertion, and the U.S. Supreme Court denied MBNA's *writ of certiorari*. However, some experts believe West Virginia's law to be unconstitutional and that the U.S. Supreme Court's refusal to hear the case was designed to urge Congress to resolve the uncertainty surrounding income tax nexus issues. Economic presence is most often measured through the factor presence test (see the Taxes in the Real World box Factor Presence Nexus).

TAXES IN THE REAL WORLD Economic Income Tax Nexus

While several states have asserted economic income tax nexus through state courts, the Multistate Tax Commission (MTC) adopted the Factor Presence Nexus Standard in 2002 (MTC Policy Statement 02-02). The MTC is an intergovernmental state tax agency created by the Multistate Tax Compact. Factor Presence asserts that if any business exceeds any of the following criteria for a given state, it is deemed to have economic income tax nexus:

- $50,000 of property,
- $50,000 of payroll,
- $500,000 of sales, or
- 25 percent of total property, payroll, or sales.

In 2021, the MTC updated its Statement on P.L. 86-272 for the first time in 20 years. The MTC now claims that many Internet-based transactions are unprotected activities creating income tax nexus. These standards are attempts change the game by making Public Law 86-272 irrelevant, and it should make all companies not filing income tax returns in a state concerned because of potential income tax liabilities.

Example 23-4

What if: Assume Wild West's Internet store receives and fills an order from a West Virginia customer. Wild West has no physical presence in West Virginia. Does Wild West have economic income tax nexus in West Virginia?

Answer: Unlikely, but perhaps. West Virginia's assertion that economic presence creates income tax nexus could happen. If a court were to uphold the MTC's Statement on P.L. 86-272 or the West Virginia sales exceed $500,000 or 25 percent of sales from all sources, it could create economic nexus.

Protection under Public Law 86-272 Public Law 86-272 protects or places limits on states' power to impose income taxes on certain nondomiciliary businesses. Businesses that sell only tangible personal property within a state are protected from paying income taxes, even in a state where income tax nexus exists, if they meet all of the criteria

[20]The Supreme Court's *Quill* decision, which has now been vacated, gave credibility to the concept of economic presence creating income tax nexus. In *Quill,* the court said that while physical presence was required for sales tax nexus, "nexus for other taxes may be different." States have interpreted that nexus for other taxes, including an income tax, could be created through economic presence. Several more recent cases have given de facto income tax nexus to businesses without the requisite physical presence [*Geoffrey, Inc. v. S.C. Tax Comm'n,* 313 S.C. 15 (1993); *Lanco, Inc. v. Dir., Div. of Taxation,* 188 N.J. 380, 908 A.2d 176 (2006); *Tax Comm'r of W. Va. v. MBNA Am. Bank, N.A.,* 640 S.E.2d 226 (W. Va. 2006)].

listed below. One common strategy businesses protected by Public Law 86-272 use is to file a "zero" income tax return in the protected state to start the statute of limitations running—businesses list their name and address and write "protected by Public Law 86-272" on the top of page 1 of the income tax return. Businesses that provide services along with selling tangible personal property, or that sell real property or intangibles, are not protected by Public Law 86-272 and therefore are subject to a state's income tax. Businesses are protected from paying income taxes, even when income tax nexus exists, if (and only if) *all* the following apply:

- The tax is based on net income.[21]
- The taxpayer sells only tangible personal property in that state.
- The taxpayer's in-state activities are limited to solicitation of sales (see the discussion below for the definition of *solicitation*).
- The taxpayer participates in interstate commerce.
- The taxpayer is nondomiciliary.
- The taxpayer approves orders outside the state.
- The taxpayer delivers goods from outside the state through a common carrier.[22]

Example 23-5

What if: Assume that Wild West sends employees into Oregon to visit retail stores and solicit orders of rafting equipment only. Does the presence of Wild West's employees in Oregon create income tax nexus in Oregon? If income tax nexus exists, would Wild West have an income tax filing requirement in Oregon?

Answer: Yes. The physical presence of representatives creates income tax nexus. However, because Wild West is a seller of tangible personal property in Oregon, its Oregon activities are protected under Public Law 86-272. Thus, while income tax nexus is created for Wild West in Oregon, Wild West has no obligation to file an Oregon income tax return.

What if: Assume that Ken or other Wild West sales representatives enter Oregon to solicit customers for both rafting equipment and white-water adventures. Does the presence of Wild West's employees create income tax nexus in Oregon? If income tax nexus exists, would Wild West have an income tax filing requirement in Oregon?

Answer: Yes. The physical presence of representatives creates income tax nexus. Additionally, because solicitation of services is not a protected activity under Public Law 86-272, Wild West will have to file an income tax return in Oregon.

Solicitation. Public Law 86-272 protects **solicitation** of tangible personal property but doesn't clearly define the term *solicitation.* In *Wisconsin v. Wrigley,* however, the U.S. Supreme Court addressed the definition.[23] Wrigley, a chewing gum manufacturer, based in Chicago, Illinois, had sales representatives and a regional manager in Wisconsin. Sales meetings in Wisconsin were held both in the manager's basement and in a rented hotel space. The sales representatives had company cars, a stock of gum, display racks, and promotional literature. The sales activities included handing out promotional materials, free samples, and free display racks; replacing stale gum; handling billing disputes; and occasionally filling orders from their stock of gum and issuing an agency stock check (a bill) to customers. All other orders were sent to Illinois for acceptance and were filled by a common carrier from outside of Wisconsin. In *Wrigley,* the U.S.

[21]Taxes calculated based on gross receipts or other bases are not protected by Public Law 86-272.

[22]"Common carrier" is a general term referring to delivery businesses (such as FedEx, UPS, DHL, or USPS).

[23]*Wis. Dep't of Rev. v. William Wrigley, Jr. Co.,* 505 U.S. 214 (1992).

Supreme Court determined the following activities performed within Wisconsin met the definition of solicitation:

- Soliciting by any form of advertising.
- Carrying samples and promotional materials for display or distribution without charge.
- Passing inquiries or complaints to the home office.
- Checking a customer's inventory for reorder.
- Maintaining a sample room for two weeks or less; this is known as the **trade show rule.**
- Recruiting, training, and evaluating sales reps using homes or hotels.
- Owning or furnishing personal property and autos used in sales activities.

The U.S. Supreme Court held the following activities do *not* meet the definition of solicitation and, therefore, create an income tax filing requirement with the state in which they take place:

- Making repairs.
- Collecting delinquent accounts.
- Investigating creditworthiness.
- Installing or supervising the installation of property.
- Providing training for employees other than sales representatives.
- Approving or accepting orders.
- Repossessing property.
- Securing deposits.
- Maintaining an office (other than an in-home office).

If sales representatives know and understand these solicitation rules, they can help businesses avoid income tax liability in states where a business wants to avoid paying income taxes.

TAXES IN THE REAL WORLD Independent Contractors Create Nexus

One of the biggest current issues for out-of-state retailers is the manner in which warranty work is performed. For example, assume you buy a new laptop for school from an online retailer because the price is unbeatable. Two months later you are told by customer support that the hard drive needs to be replaced and you need to ship the computer from Lawrence, Kansas, to Austin, Texas, for repair. You respond that you cannot go a week without your computer, so the retailer agrees to have a local repair shop in Kansas do the repair for you. Many companies wrongly assume that hiring an independent representative to do in-state warranty work does not create income tax nexus. The hiring of the independent contractor is an agency relationship that creates income tax nexus for the out-of-state Texas retailer in Kansas. The MTC issued guidance (MTC Nexus Bulletin 95-1) on this issue more than two decades ago—and taxpayers challenging the ruling have lost time and time again. Retailers with these issues quickly find themselves liable for both current and past income taxes as well as for sales taxes.

Example 23-6

Assume Wild West's Oregon sales representatives give store employees free white-water gloves and pass on customer complaints to the home office. Do these activities create an income tax filing requirement for Wild West in Oregon?

(continued on page 23-14)

Answer: No. Even though the presence of sales representatives creates income tax nexus, giving samples (without charge) and passing on customer complaints, suggestions, and customer inquiries are protected sales activities under Public Law 86-272. Therefore, Wild West is protected from an Oregon income tax filing requirement.

What if: While in Oregon, several sales representatives accept checks for down payments on merchandise, repair faulty merchandise, and perform credit checks. Do these activities create an income tax filing requirement for Wild West in Oregon?

Answer: Yes. Each of these activities is an unprotected sales activity, and any or all of these activities will create an Oregon income tax filing requirement for Wild West.

Example 23-7

What if: Assume that Ken and other Wild West employees visit Colorado retail stores and hold slideshows about summer rafting trips. After the slideshows, Ken and the other guides interact with and gather information from potential white-water rafting customers. Do these solicitation activities create an income tax filing requirement?

Answer: Yes. The presence of sales representatives creates income tax nexus. Additionally, because Wild West is soliciting for services, rather than tangible personal property, Public Law 86-272 does not protect them from Colorado's income tax.

Does a one-time sales activity violation create a potential income tax filing requirement? Technically, yes. However, the *Wrigley* decision indicates that *de minimis* (i.e., immaterial) activities may be excluded. The decision whether an activity is *de minimis* is a subjective one, however, based on relevant facts and circumstances.

Example 23-8

Assume that Wild West's sales representatives occasionally investigate creditworthiness and occasionally repossess property in Oregon. Can Wild West avoid income tax liability?

Answer: Possibly. Even though the physical presence of sales representatives in Oregon creates income tax nexus and the sales representatives performed unprotected activities, Wild West could argue that these unprotected activities are *de minimis* because they are not material to its overall operations within Oregon. However, these activities put Wild West at risk and could lead to an income tax liability.

Now that we've explored income tax nexus, let's determine Wild West's income tax nexus and filing requirements.

Example 23-9

Wild West is domiciled in Idaho and has physical presence through property and employees whose activities exceed protected solicitation in Idaho, Tennessee, Washington, and Wyoming. Recall from Exhibit 23-1 that Wild West has sales in the following states: Arizona, California, Colorado, Idaho, Tennessee, Washington, and Wyoming. Where does Wild West have income tax nexus?

Answer: Wild West has income tax nexus in Idaho, Tennessee, Washington, and Wyoming. It has income tax nexus in Idaho because of commercial domicile, physical presence of retail stores (where orders are accepted), and the provision of services. Wild West has income tax nexus in Tennessee and Washington because of the provision of services. Wild West has income tax nexus in Wyoming because of the physical presence of retail stores, Internet-based store, and the provision of services.

Where does Wild West have an income tax filing requirement?

Answer: Wild West has an income tax filing requirement in Idaho, Tennessee, Washington, and Wyoming. Wild West will file income tax returns in Idaho and Tennessee. Wild West will not file in Wyoming because Wyoming does not impose a corporate income tax. Washington imposes a gross receipts tax (business and occupation tax) rather than an income tax. Wild West will file a Washington gross receipts tax return, as we discuss in Example 23-21.

Entities Included on Income Tax Return

When a business operates as more than one legal entity, the way it files its tax return(s) becomes an issue. Some states require a **separate tax return** for each entity with an income tax filing requirement in the state, and others require a **unitary tax return** (i.e., one tax return) for a group of related entities.[24]

Separate Tax Returns A separate-return state requires only those businesses with an income tax filing requirement in the state to file an income tax return. This is generally true even when a group of companies file together on a federal consolidated tax return.[25] Historically, many states east of the Mississippi River (except Illinois) were separate-return states; however, many states have begun shifting away from separate-return requirements over the last decade. Today, 28 states impose taxes on unitary groups.

Example 23-10

Wild West has income tax nexus in Tennessee because its employees provide services within the state and it owns property there. Must Wild West file a Tennessee income tax return?

Answer: Yes. Wild West must file a Tennessee income tax return because it has income tax nexus in Tennessee and it exceeds the protections offered by Public Law 86-272.

What if: Assume that Tennessee is a separate return state and Wild West splits into two separate corporations: one that runs retail stores (Wild West Retail) and one that provides the guided rafting services (Wild West Services). How would the split affect Wild West's Tennessee income tax filing requirements (even though Tennessee recently became a unitary state, answer the question as though Tennessee is still a separate-return state)?

Answer: Wild West would file two separate income tax returns: one for Wild West Retail and one for Wild West Services. Both companies would have income tax nexus in Tennessee because Wild West Retail's stores do more than solicit sales of tangible personal property and Wild West Service's activities are not protected activities under Public Law 86-272.

THE KEY FACTS

Entities Included on a Tax Return

- Separate-return states require a separate return for each entity that has an income tax filing requirement in the state.
- Unitary states require members of a unitary group to file a single tax return reflecting the combined income of the unitary group if any member of the unitary group has an income tax filing requirement.
  - Any of three factors characterizes a unitary group: functional integration, centralization of management, and economies of scale.

While separate tax returns are simple, the income reported on separate tax returns can easily be manipulated through related-entity transactions (i.e., through transfer pricing, for example). A historical tax planning technique was to use passive investment companies (PICs), in which a company simply created a subsidiary and transferred ownership of its trademarks and patents to an entity within a state that did not tax royalties, interest, and other similar types of intangible income (e.g., within a state such as Delaware or Nevada that does not tax these items). The PIC then charged a royalty for use of the intangible, which generated a deductible business expense in the state used and created income in a little- or no-tax state. States have implemented laws to fight this type of planning, and many other states have responded by adopting unitary filing requirements. Such "tax planning" opportunities are not available if the related entities are required to file a unitary tax return.

Unitary Tax Returns Historically, only states west of the Mississippi River, and Illinois, were unitary-return states. However, since 2004, the following states have adopted unitary return filing requirements: Colorado, Connecticut, Georgia, Kentucky, Maine, Massachusetts, Michigan, Minnesota, New Hampshire, New Jersey, New Mexico, New York, Ohio, Rhode Island, Tennessee, Vermont, and Wisconsin. Whether a business must file one tax return with other businesses or entities depends on whether these businesses are considered to be a "unitary" group of entities.

[24]The separate versus unitary discussion is a complex and complicated discussion even at the graduate tax level. However, a basic understanding of the terminology and concepts can be useful for all accounting professionals.

[25]Some states also allow combined reporting, a setting where more than one corporation file together on the same income tax return. However, the tax is calculated as if each corporation filed a separate return and was taxed separately.

In *Mobil,* the U.S. Supreme Court identified the following three factors that can be used to establish whether a group of businesses is unitary:

- Functional integration (vertical or horizontal integration or knowledge transfer).
- Centralization of management (interlocking directors, common officers, or rotation of management between companies).
- Economies of scale (group discounts or other efficiencies due to size).[26]

The unitary concept considers the integration and flow of value, rather than the business's legal form and ownership structure, in establishing which companies file a tax return together. Taxpayers must consider each of the three factors to determine whether multiple businesses will be treated as one for state tax purposes.

The important concept here is that companies filing a federal consolidated tax return may have to file separately for state purposes, and companies not filing a federal consolidated tax return may be required to file as a unitary group in some states.[27] A unitary tax return group includes all members meeting the unitary criteria—whether they have an income tax filing requirement in that state or not.[28] Unitary businesses usually have a flow of value between the various businesses. For example, raw materials or components can flow between businesses or one entity may borrow funds from another. The unitary concept pervades activities in the entire state income tax computation, including computing taxable income, computing apportionment percentages (discussed later in the chapter), and identifying income tax return filing requirements. The primary difference between separate and unitary states is that separate-return states tax the entire apportioned income of each separate business by requiring each business entity to file a separate tax return while unitary-return states tax the entire unitary group using a smaller apportioned percentage.

Example 23-11

What if: As in the previous example, assume Wild West is divided into two separate corporations: Wild West Retail (WWR) and Wild West Services (WWS). Ken owns and manages both companies. The rafting services company purchases all its rafting equipment from the retail stores company. Guides for the rafting company stop at the retail store before trips so customers can purchase any necessary gear, and the store refers customers looking for guided rafting to the rafting services company. Assume the two companies use the same marketing and accounting firms and receive discounts for having multiple bank accounts and insurance policies. Using the *Mobil* factors (i.e., functional integration, centralization of management, and economies of scale), are WWR and WWS part of a unitary group in a unitary state like Idaho?

Answer: Yes. WWR and WWS would likely be considered a unitary group and thus would combine income and file a single unitary tax return in each unitary state. The two companies likely share some integration in that their customer bases have significant overlap, and WWS purchases its equipment from WWR. They share centralization of management in that both are owned and operated by the same individual (Ken). The two companies have some economies of scale because they receive discounts for using the same accounting, banking, insurance, and marketing vendors. Businesses do not have to meet all three factors to be considered a unitary group, but WWR and WWS probably do. As a result, WWR and WWS would likely file a unitary (single) Idaho income tax return.

State Taxable Income

Companies doing business in multiple states must identify the tax return due dates, procedures for filing tax return extensions, and other administrative requirements specific to each state. Businesses must also calculate state taxable income for each state in which

[26] *Mobil Oil Corp. v. Comm'r of Taxes,* 445 U.S. 425 (1980).

[27] In some cases, different divisions of a single corporation can be separated, and in others a partnership and corporation can be joined.

[28] Entities without an income tax filing requirement will usually have apportionment factors that are zero. While their incomes increase the unitary group's income, their zero apportionment factors decrease the apportionment factors to the state. Therefore, the inclusion of entities without an income tax filing requirement is usually considered to be nondiscriminatory.

they must file tax returns. Federal taxable income before special deductions (Form 1120, Page 1, Line 28) is generally the starting point for computing state taxable income. Just as corporations reconcile from book income to taxable income to compute federal income tax (see the Corporate Operations chapter), businesses must reconcile from federal taxable income to state taxable income to compute state taxable income. This requires them to identify **federal/state adjustments** or differences for *each specific state* before apportioning the income to a particular state in which they have an income tax filing requirement.

Rather than starting from scratch, most states conform to the federal tax law in some way. Most "piggyback" their state tax laws on the federal tax laws (state tax codes generally follow the Internal Revenue Code).[29] Idaho generally conforms to the current Code. Consequently, Wild West will not report many federal/state adjustments. Other states adopt a specific version of the Code (i.e., the Code as of a specific date). For example, California adopts the Code as of January 1, 2015. This method requires more federal/state adjustments because every subsequent change to the Internal Revenue Code results in less conformity between the state law and the federal tax law. Corporations should carefully examine federal/state adjustments because states may not fully conform with recent federal tax law changes including bonus depreciation, deemed repatriation, interest deductions, and international provisions, including the participation exemption, global intangible low-taxed income (GILTI), and foreign-derived intangible income (FDII). Income tax software helps practitioners correctly calculate the federal/state adjustments necessary to compute state taxable income.

Because states cannot tax federal interest income (interest from Treasury notes, for example), all states require a negative adjustment (reduction in federal taxable income in adjusting to state taxable income) for federal interest income. Most states require a positive adjustment for state income tax deductions because they *do not* allow businesses to deduct state income taxes, and they require a positive adjustment for state and local bond interest income if the bond is from another state (i.e., they tax out-of-state bond interest income).[30]

States' tax instruction booklets generally describe common federal/state tax adjustments applicable for that state, but these descriptions are often incomplete and particularly problematic for states with low federal tax conformity. While it is impractical to identify all potential federal/state adjustments, Exhibit 23-5 provides a list of common federal/state adjustments and identifies each as a positive adjustment (state income increasing) or a negative adjustment (state income decreasing).

EXHIBIT 23-5 Common Federal/State Adjustments

Positive Adjustments (Increasing Taxable Income)

State and local income taxes
State and local bond interest income from bonds in other states
Federal dividends-received deduction
Federal income tax refunds (only in states where federal tax is allowed as a deduction)
Intercompany expenses associated with related persons (for separate-return states)*
MACRS depreciation over state depreciation
Federal bonus depreciation

Negative Adjustments (Decreasing Taxable Income)

U.S. obligation interest income (T-bills, notes, and bonds)
State dividends-received deduction
Foreign dividend gross-up
State income tax refunds included on federal return
State depreciation over federal depreciation

*Approximately 20 separate-return states require a positive adjustment of intercompany royalties, interest, and other expenses between related persons. The disallowance prevents companies from extracting profits from high-tax states and placing them in low- or no-tax states.

[29]Also, states may conform or not conform to administrative authority such as Treasury Regulations, Revenue Procedures, and Revenue Rulings.

[30]Thirty-three of the 46 states with an income tax require a positive adjustment for state and local income tax expenses deducted on the federal return.

Example 23-12

Wild West properly included, deducted, or excluded the following items on its federal tax return in the current year:

Item	Amount	Federal Treatment
Idaho income tax	$27,744	Deducted on federal return
Tennessee income tax	18,152	Deducted on federal return
Washington gross receipts tax	6,201	Deducted on federal return
Idaho bond interest income	5,000	Excluded from federal return
Federal T-note interest income	1,500	Included on federal return

Given federal taxable income of $53,289, what is Wild West's state tax base for Idaho and for Tennessee?

Answer: The Idaho state tax base is $97,685; for Tennessee it is $102,685. Bases are calculated as follows:

Federal Taxable Income	Idaho	Tennessee	Source
Wild West	$ 53,289	$ 53,289	Storyline
Positive Adjustments			
Idaho income tax	$ 27,744	$ 27,744	Idaho tax is not deducted.
Tennessee income tax	18,152	18,152	Tennessee tax is not deducted.
Washington gross receipts tax	0	0	Washington tax is not a positive adjustment because it is not an income-based tax.
State bond interest	0	5,000	States exempt their own interest only.
Total positive adjustments	$ 45,896	$ 50,896	
Negative Adjustments			
Federal interest	($ 1,500)	($ 1,500)	Federal interest is not taxable for state purposes.
Total negative adjustments	($ 1,500)	($ 1,500)	
State tax base	**$97,685**	**$102,685**	Federal + Positive − Negative

THE KEY FACTS

Dividing Income among States with Income Tax Nexus

- Business income is apportioned based on some combination of the following factors:
  - Sales
  - Payroll
  - Property
- Nonbusiness income is allocated.
- Investment income is allocated to the state of commercial domicile.
- Rents and royalties are generally allocated to the state where the property is used.

Dividing State Tax Base among States

All state taxable income is taxed in the state of commercial domicile unless the business is taxable in more than one state. An interstate business must separate its business income (earned from business operations) from nonbusiness income (primarily from investments, including rents and royalties). The business must fairly *apportion* its business income among the states in which it conducts business in a manner that creates income tax filing requirements, whereas it *allocates* or assigns nonbusiness income to a specific state (usually the state of commercial domicile).[31]

Business Income Business income includes all revenues earned in the ordinary course of business—sales less cost of goods sold and other expenses. Business income is fairly apportioned or divided across the states with an income tax filing requirement.[32] If

[31]The Multistate Tax Commission (MTC) has provided guidance on the division of income between states in Article IV of its Compact. The Compact can be found at www.mtc.gov. Also, see the Uniform Division of Income Tax Purposes Act that many states have adopted. Some states are treating all income as business income, and therefore have no separation of business and nonbusiness income.

[32]*Complete Auto Transit, Inc. v. Brady,* 430 U.S. 274 (1977).

a business has income tax nexus or a filing requirement with more than one state, it has the right to apportion income to that state—even if the state does not actually impose a tax (e.g., Wyoming).[33]

Example 23-13

Recall from Example 23-12 that Wild West's Idaho and Tennessee state tax bases were $97,685 and $102,685, respectively. Wild West's federal tax return shows the following items of investment income: dividends of $6,000, interest income of $16,005 (which includes $14,505 of bank interest and $1,500 of federal government interest but excludes $5,000 from Idaho bond interest), and rental income of $18,000. What is Wild West's business income for Idaho and Tennessee?

Answer: Idaho and Tennessee business income amounts are $59,180 and $59,180, respectively, calculated as follows:

Description	Idaho	Tennessee	Explanation
(1) State tax base	$ 97,685	$102,685	Example 23-12
(2) Dividends	6,000	6,000	Federal tax return
(3) Interest income	14,505	19,505	$14,505 (bank interest) + $5,000 of Idaho bond interest (for Tennessee only)
(4) Rental income	18,000	18,000	Federal tax return
(5) Nonbusiness income	$ 38,505	$ 43,505	(2) + (3) + (4)
Business income	**$59,180**	**$ 59,180**	(1) − (5)

Apportionment formula. States set the apportionment formula for income based on some combination of the following factors: sales, payroll, and property. For each state in which it establishes income tax nexus, the business calculates the factors as the ratio of (1) total sales, payroll, or property in a specific state to (2) total sales, payroll, or property everywhere. The sales factor is calculated as follows:

$$\text{Sales factor in state } X = \frac{\text{Total sales in state } X}{\text{Total sales in all states}}$$

The sales factor includes all gross business receipts net of returns, allowances, and discounts.[34] The general rules for determining the amount of sales to include in the sales factor calculation are:

- Sales of tangible personal property are sourced to the destination state (i.e., the state where the personal property is delivered and used).
- If the business does not have income tax nexus in the destination state, sales are generally "thrown back" to the state from which the property is shipped; this is called the **throwback rule.**[35] For example, if Wild West ships goods from Idaho to Montana, where it does not have income tax nexus, the sales are treated as if they are Idaho sales.

[33]Creating income tax nexus in states without an income tax creates "nowhere income"—income that is not taxed anywhere.

[34]There is substantial variation in the apportionment factor across states.

[35]Some states don't have a throwback rule and some states such as California have a double-throwback rule. This rule applies to drop shipments from a state without income tax nexus. For example, if a California company ships goods from Arizona into Colorado and the company has income tax nexus in neither Arizona nor Colorado, the sales are thrown back from Colorado into Arizona and then thrown back again from Arizona to California.

- Dock sales should be sourced to the good's ultimate destination (e.g., sales picked up by an out-of-state buyer at the seller's in-state dock rather than being shipped to the buyer's out-of-state location).
- Sales of services are generally apportioned to the state in which the services are performed (California and Illinois are exceptions to this general rule, but the list of states that apportion services to the state in which the services are consumed is growing).
- Government sales are sourced in the state from which they were shipped.

TAXES IN THE REAL WORLD Sourcing Receipts from Sales of Services and Intangible Property

The last 20 years have seen a shift from the use of the equally weighted three-factor formula to the adoption of a single sales-factor formula for apportionment purposes. This shift has made the method of calculating the sales factor more important for both taxpayers and tax administrators. Additionally, over the same period, there has been a significant shift from a goods-based economy to an intangibles- and service-based economy. Consequently, many states have changed their apportionment method for services. While sales of services were traditionally sourced to the state from which the services were provided, many states have now shifted the sourcing to the market (state) where the services are consumed—a destination approach. This means that, in many cases, two states are trying to tax the same services. For example, if an Idaho-based marketing firm creates a campaign for a California-based retailer, both states may assert the right to tax the transaction. Idaho will source the sale to the state in which the marketing campaign was created (Idaho) and California will source the sale to the state where the services will be used (California). Alternatively, if the facts were reversed, neither state would assert the right to tax the sale.

Example 23-14

Recall from Exhibit 23-1 that Wild West reported sales of $2,534,032. The sales are split between goods and services and sourced by state as follows:

Wild West Sales

State	Goods	Services	Total
AZ	$ 89,242	$ 0	$ 89,242
CA	132,045	0	132,045
CO	75,002	0	75,002
ID	**167,921**	**625,003**	**792,924**
TN	**45,331**	**357,061**	**402,392**
WA	41,982	377,441	419,423
WY	185,249	437,755	623,004
Totals	**$736,772**	**$1,797,260**	**$2,534,032**

Recall from Example 23-9 that Wild West has income tax nexus in Idaho, Tennessee, Washington, and Wyoming. Washington has a gross receipts tax and Wyoming does not tax corporations. What are the sales apportionment factors for Idaho and Tennessee?

Answer: The apportionment factors for Idaho and Tennessee are 31.29 percent and 15.88 percent, respectively, calculated from figures in the Total column in the sales table above:

$$\text{Idaho} \quad \frac{\$792{,}924}{\$2{,}534{,}032} = 31.29\%$$

$$\text{Tennessee} \quad \frac{\$402{,}392}{\$2{,}534{,}032} = 15.88\%$$

Note the Arizona, California, and Colorado sales are thrown back to Wyoming because the sales were made through the Internet store based in Wyoming and Wild West does not have an income tax filing requirement in Arizona, California, or Colorado.

Payroll is generally defined as total compensation paid to employees.[36] The payroll factor is calculated as follows:

- Payroll includes salaries, commissions, bonuses, and other forms of compensation.
- Payroll does not include amounts paid to independent contractors.
- Payroll for each employee is apportioned to a single state (payroll for employees who work in more than one state is sourced to the state where they perform the majority of services).

Example 23-15

Wild West's payments for wages are $737,021, sourced to the states as follows:

Payroll State	Wild West Wages
Idaho	**$201,032**
Tennessee	**148,202**
Washington	115,021
Wyoming	272,766
Total	**$737,021**

What are the payroll apportionment factors for Idaho and Tennessee?

Answer: The payroll apportionment factors for Idaho and Tennessee are 27.28 percent and 20.11 percent, respectively, calculated from the payroll table above:

$$\text{Idaho} \quad \frac{\$201{,}032}{\$737{,}021} = 27.28\%$$

$$\text{Tennessee} \quad \frac{\$148{,}202}{\$737{,}021} = 20.11\%$$

Property generally includes both real and tangible personal property, but not intangible property.[37] The general rules for determining the property factors are:

- Use the average property values for the year [(beginning + ending)/2].
- Value property at historical cost rather than adjusted basis (do not subtract accumulated depreciation in determining value).
- Include property in transit (such as inventory) in the destination state.

36The payroll definition varies by state.

37Property definitions may vary slightly by state.

- Include only business property (values of rented investment properties are excluded).
- Include rented or leased business property by multiplying the annual rent by 8 and adding this value to the average owned-property factor.[38]

Example 23-16

The historical cost of Wild West's property (before subtracting accumulated depreciation) owned at the beginning and end of the year and rented during the year, by state, is as follows:

Property			
State	**Beginning**	**Ending**	**Rented**
Idaho	$1,042,023	$1,203,814	$36,000
Tennessee	502,424	531,984	0
Washington	52,327	65,829	60,000
Wyoming	1,420,387	1,692,373	0
Total	$3,017,161	$3,494,000	$96,000

What are the property apportionment factors for Idaho and Tennessee?

Answer: The property apportionment factors for Idaho and Tennessee are 35.07 percent and 12.85 percent, respectively, computed as follows:

Property and Rents Total					
	Owned Property			Rented Property	
State	**Beginning**	**Ending**	**Average**	**Rents × 8**	**Total**
Idaho	**$1,042,023**	**$1,203,814**	**$1,122,919**	**$288,000**	**$1,410,919**
Tennessee	**502,424**	**531,984**	**517,204**		**517,204**
Washington	52,327	65,829	59,078	$480,000	539,078
Wyoming	1,420,387	1,692,373	1,556,380		1,556,380
Total	**$3,017,161**	**$3,494,000**	**$3,255,581**		**$4,023,581**

Idaho $\frac{\$1,410,919}{\$4,023,581} = 35.07\%$

Tennessee $\frac{\$517,204}{\$4,023,581} = 12.85\%$

The average amount for each state from the subtotal property table is added to the inclusion amount from the subtotal rent table to reach the total property numerator for each state.

Historically, most states used an equally weighted three-factor apportionment formula, which was required by the Model Tax Compact (MTC). This method adds together the sales, payroll, and property factors and divides the total by 3 to arrive at the apportionment factor (percentages) for each state. Over time most states shifted to a double-weighted sales factor (doubling the sales factor and then adding the payroll and property factors, and dividing the total by 4). Currently, 28 states have moved to a single-weighted sales factor formula that eliminates the payroll and property factors altogether. California is an example of a state that requires corporations to use a single-weighted sales factor. All else equal, increasing the weight of the sales factor in the apportionment formula tends to decrease the tax liabilities of in-state businesses and increases the tax liabilities of out-of-state businesses. This result occurs because in-state businesses tend to

[38]The annual rent is multiplied by 8 to approximate the value of the rental property.

have higher payroll and property factors relative to their sales factors where headquartered, and out-of-state businesses tend to have higher sales factors than payroll and property factors in nondomiciliary states.

TAXES IN THE REAL WORLD Apportionment: The *Gillette* Decision

On December 31, 2015, the California Supreme Court reversed the California Court of Appeals decision in *Gillette Co. v. Franchise Tax Board* [196 Cal. Rptr. 3d 486, 363 P.3d 94 (2015)]. The California Court of Appeals had held that a taxpayer could apportion its income to California using the Model Tax Compact's evenly weighted three-factor formula, despite statutory language mandating the use of a three-factor, double-weighted sales formula for most corporations for the years at issue.

The California Supreme Court reversed this decision and concluded that the California Legislature may properly preclude a taxpayer from relying on the Model Tax Compact's election provision. On October 12, 2016, the U.S. Supreme Court denied the *Gillette* appeal. The Minnesota, Oregon, and Texas Supreme Courts recently reached the same decision as California. Similarly, the Michigan Appellate Court reversed a 2015 decision favoring IBM, and the Michigan Supreme Court denied the consolidated appeal of IBM and 50 other companies.[39]

The U.S. Supreme Court has denied *writ of certiorari* in these cases, and it is unclear whether taxpayers can ultimately win this argument. As a result, the single-weighted sales factor formula or methodology appears to be constitutional and will likely see continued growth and adoption by the remaining states.

Example 23-17

Wild West must apportion its business income to Idaho and Tennessee. Its Idaho sales, payroll, and property factors are 31.29 percent, 27.28 percent, and 35.07 percent, respectively. Its Tennessee sales, payroll, and property factors are 15.88 percent, 20.11 percent, and 12.85 percent, respectively. These factors are aggregated from Examples 23-14, 23-15, and 23-16. What are Wild West's apportionment factors in both states if they use a double-weighted sales factor?

Answer: The apportionment factors for Idaho and Tennessee are 31.23 percent and 16.18 percent, respectively.

Factor	Idaho	Tennessee	Explanation
(1) Sales	31.29%	15.88%	Example 23-14
(2) Sales	31.29	15.88	Example 23-14
(3) Payroll	27.28	20.11	Example 23-15
(4) Property	35.07	12.85	Example 23-16
Apportionment factor	**31.23%**	**16.18%**	[(1) + (2) + (3) + (4)]/4

What if: Assume Tennessee uses an equally weighted three-factor apportionment formula. What is Wild West's Tennessee apportionment factors?

Answer: The apportionment factor for Tennessee is 16.28 percent. Tennessee's apportionment factor would now be calculated as follows:

Factor	Tennessee	Explanation
(1) Sales	15.88%	
(2) Payroll	20.11	
(3) Property	12.85	
Apportionment factor	**16.28%**	[(1) + (2) + (3)]/3

What if: Assume Idaho uses a single-weighted sales factor apportionment formula. What would Wild West's apportionment factor be?

Answer: The apportionment factor for Idaho would be 31.29 percent. Idaho's apportionment factor would now simply be Wild West's Idaho sales factor. No payroll or property factor would be needed for Idaho.

[39] *Int'l Bus. Machines Corp. v. Dep't of Treasury,* Docket No. 327359, 316 Mich. App. 346 (July 21, 2016).

Nonbusiness Income We've said nonbusiness income includes all income except business income. Common types of nonbusiness income and the rules for allocating each type to specific states include:[40]

- Allocate interest and dividends to the state of commercial domicile (except interest on working capital, which is business income).
- Allocate rental income to the state where the property generating the rental income is located.
- Allocate royalties to the state where the property is used (if the business has income tax nexus in that state; if not, allocate royalties to the state of commercial domicile).
- Allocate capital gains from investment property to the state of commercial domicile.
- Allocate capital gains from selling rental property to the state where the rental property is located.

Example 23-18

Wild West reports nonbusiness income as follows:

Wild West			
Description	**Idaho**	**Tennessee**	**Explanation**
Dividends	$ 6,000	$ 6,000	From Example 23-13
Interest	14,505	19,505	From Example 23-13
Rental income	18,000	18,000	From Example 23-13
Allocable total	$38,505	$43,505	

Wild West's commercial domicile is in Idaho. Its rental income is for real property located in Wyoming. To which state(s) should the firm allocate its nonbusiness income?

Answer: $20,505 to Idaho and $18,000 to Wyoming, calculated as follows:

Wild West		
State	**Amount**	**Explanation**
Idaho	**$20,505**	$6,000 dividends + $14,505 interest income
Tennessee	0	
Washington	0	
Wyoming	**18,000**	Rental income
Total	$ 38,505	

State Income Tax Liability

It is relatively easy to calculate a business's state taxable income and state tax after separating business and nonbusiness income, apportioning business income, and allocating nonbusiness income. Specifically, state taxable income is calculated by multiplying business income by the apportionment factor and then adding any nonbusiness income allocated to the state.

[40]Multistate Tax Compact, Article IV, Division of Income, para. 4. Note that a few states treat all income as business income.

Example 23-19

What if: Assume Idaho and Tennessee have a flat income tax rate of 7.6 percent and 6.5 percent, respectively. What is Wild West's income tax liability for Idaho and Tennessee?

Answer: Its income tax liabilities in Idaho and Tennessee are $2,963 and $622, respectively, computed as follows:

Description	Idaho	Tennessee	Explanation
(1) State tax base	$97,685	$102,685	Example 23-12
(2) Allocable income	(38,505)	(43,505)	Example 23-18
(3) Business income	$59,180	$ 59,180	(1) – (2)
(4) Apportionment factor	31.23%	16.18%	Example 23-17
(5) Apportioned income	$18,482	$ 9,575	(3) × (4)
(6) Allocable income	20,505	0	Example 23-18
(7) State taxable income	$38,987	$ 9,575	(5) + (6)
(8) Tax rate	7.6%	6.5%	
Tax liability	**$ 2,963**	**$ 622**	(7) × (8)

Nonincome-Based Taxes

Several states have nonincome-based taxes (other than sales tax). Washington has the business and occupation (B&O) tax, which is a gross receipts tax. Texas has the margin tax, the lesser of a gross margin tax or gross receipts tax (e.g., many states are treating the Texas margin tax as a tax based on net income). Many states are imposing nonincome-based taxes to increase revenues from nondomiciliary businesses because the nexus for nonincome-based taxes is different.

Remember that Public Law 86-272 only protects businesses from the imposition of income-based taxes. Therefore, physical or economic presence is all that is necessary for the imposition of a nonincome-based tax. While nonincome-based taxes are largely beyond the scope of this text, recognizing that a different nexus standard exists for nonincome-based taxes is vitally important.

Example 23-20

What if: The Texas margin tax is calculated on the least of (1) revenue less cost of goods sold, (2) 70 percent of sales revenue, (3) revenue minus compensation, or (4) revenue minus $1 million. Assume that Wild West sends employees into Texas to visit retail stores and solicit orders of rafting equipment. Would the presence of Wild West employees create nonincome-based tax nexus for the Texas margin tax?

Answer: Yes. Because the tax is nonincome-based (it is not based on *net* income), Wild West is not protected by Public Law 86-272. Therefore, the physical presence of salespeople soliciting sales of tangible personal property creates a nonincome-based tax nexus (but it would *not* have created an income tax filing requirement if the tax were based on net income).

Some states impose nonincome-based taxes on all businesses, not just the businesses taxable at the federal level. For example, Texas imposes the margin tax on C corporations, S corporations, partnerships, and sole proprietorships that have limited liability. The calculation of a nonincome-based tax is detailed in Example 23-21.

Example 23-21

Wild West has nexus in Washington and is subject to that state's business and occupation (B&O) tax. The tax is .471 percent of gross receipts for retailers and 1.5 percent of gross receipts on services. Wild West's gross receipts from retail sales and services in Washington are $41,982 and $377,441, respectively (from Exhibit 23-1). Calculate Wild West's B&O tax.

(continued on page 23-26)

Answer: Wild West's B&O tax is $5,860, calculated as follows:

Activity	(1) Receipts	(2) Rate	(1) × (2) Tax
Retailing	$ 41,982	0.471%	$ 198
Services	377,441	1.500%	5,662
B&O tax			**$5,860**

CONCLUSION

In this chapter, we discussed the fundamentals of state and local taxation with an emphasis on sales tax nexus, income tax nexus, sales tax, and net income-based corporate taxes. State and local taxes currently make up a significant portion of many businesses' total tax burden and also consume a significant portion of the tax department's time.

Sales tax nexus was traditionally established through physical presence but has shifted to economic sales tax nexus under the *Wayfair* decision. Companies selling tangible personal property must collect sales tax from their customers (where sales tax nexus exists) and remit it to the various states. Income tax nexus can be created through either physical or economic presence. However, even when income tax nexus exists, sellers of tangible personal property are protected from income tax filing requirements by Public Law 86-272 if certain criteria are met.

Businesses subject to multijurisdictional taxation—taxation by more than one government—have many issues in common. A business located in San Diego, California, but also doing business in Tucson, Arizona, will be subject to California and Arizona tax. If it also does business in Rosarito, Mexico, it will be subject to both U.S. and Mexico federal taxes. State and local taxation and international taxation bring up many of the same issues. For both, businesses must determine which jurisdiction has the right to tax a transaction (nexus) and how to divide income among different jurisdictions. The next chapter examines the taxation of multinational transactions.

Summary

LO 23-1 Describe the primary types of state and local taxes.

- The primary purpose of state and local taxes is to raise revenue.
- Like federal tax law, state tax law is composed of legislative, administrative, and judicial law.
- Judicial law plays a more important role in state tax law than federal tax law because constitutionality is a primary concern for state tax laws.
- The most important question any taxpayer must answer is whether it is subject to a state's taxing regime.
- Nexus is the connection between a business and a state sufficient to subject the business to the state's tax system. We cover two types of nexus: sales tax nexus and income tax nexus.
- When a business sells tangible personal property, sales and/or use tax is due. If the seller has sales tax nexus, the seller must collect and remit the tax to the state. Otherwise, the buyer is responsible for paying the use tax.
- Businesses engaged in interstate commerce that have income tax nexus and an income tax filing requirement must pay income tax.

LO 23-2 Determine whether a business has sales tax nexus and calculate its sales tax withholding responsibilities.

- Forty-five states and the District of Columbia impose sales taxes. The items subject to sales tax vary from state to state.

- Businesses are required to collect sales tax on sales only if they have sales tax nexus in that state.
- For nondomiciliary businesses, sales tax nexus may be created through either economic activity or physical presence.

Identify whether a business has income tax nexus and determine its state income tax liabilities. LO 23-3

- Forty-four states impose an income tax on corporations, and 43 states impose an income tax on income from partnerships and S corporations.
- Businesses must pay income tax in their state of commercial domicile, and nondomiciliary firms may be subject to tax if they have income tax nexus in the state.
- Income tax nexus can be created through either physical or economic presence. Income tax nexus creates an income tax filing requirement unless a business is protected by Public Law 86-272. Public Law 86-272 protects sellers of tangible personal property from the income tax filing requirement—even when income tax nexus exists—if the business activities within the state are limited to solicitation. However, recent changes to the MTC's Statement on P.L. 86-272 suggest indicate that a push towards economic nexus may have arrived.
- Businesses divide or apportion their income among the states where they have established income tax nexus.
- Some states require a separate income tax return for each entity with income tax nexus, and others require a unitary (single) tax return for a group of related entities as long as one of the entities has established income tax nexus in the state.
- Businesses must calculate state taxable income for each state in which they must file a tax return—this requires businesses to identify federal/state adjustments.
- Firms adjust federal taxable income to arrive at their state taxable base.
- The state taxable base of an interstate business is generally separated into business and nonbusiness income: Business income is apportioned across states using a general formula, and nonbusiness income is allocated to specific states using specific rules.
- Business income is apportioned using some combination of sales, payroll, and property factors.

KEY TERMS

allocation (23-4)
apportionment (23-4)
business income (23-4)
commercial domicile (23-2)
economic income tax nexus (23-11)
federal/state adjustments (23-17)
income tax nexus (23-10)
interstate commerce (23-4)
nexus (23-2)
nonbusiness income (23-4)
nondomiciliary businesses (23-2)
Public Law 86-272 (23-10)
sales tax (23-3)
sales tax nexus (23-5)
separate tax return (23-15)
solicitation (23-12)
state tax base (23-4)
throwback rule (23-19)
trade show rule (23-13)
unitary tax return (23-15)
use tax (23-4)

DISCUSSION QUESTIONS

Discussion Questions are available in Connect®. Mc Graw Hill connect

1. Why do states and local jurisdictions assess taxes? LO 23-1
2. Compare and contrast the relative importance of judicial law to state and local and federal tax law. LO 23-1
3. Describe briefly the nexus concept and explain its importance to state and local taxation. LO 23-1
4. What is the difference, if any, between the state of a business's commercial domicile and its state of incorporation? LO 23-1
5. What types of property sales are subject to sales tax, and why might a state choose to exclude the sales of certain types of property from the sales tax base? LO 23-1
6. In what circumstances would a business be subject to income taxes in more than one state? LO 23-1

LO 23-1 7. Describe how the failure to collect sales tax can result in a larger tax liability for a business than failing to pay income taxes.

LO 23-2 8. Discuss why restaurant meals, rental cars, and hotel receipts are often taxed at a higher-than-average sales tax rate.

LO 23-2 9. Compare and contrast general sales tax nexus rules under the *Quill* and *Wayfair* decisions.

LO 23-2 10. What is the difference between a sales tax and a use tax?

LO 23-2 11. Renée operates Scandinavian Imports, a furniture shop in Olney, Maryland, that ships goods to customers in all 50 states. Scandinavian Imports also appraises antique furniture and has recently conducted in-home appraisals in the District of Columbia, Maryland, Pennsylvania, and Virginia. Online appraisals have been done for customers in California, Minnesota, New Mexico, and Texas. Determine where Scandinavian Imports has sales tax nexus.

LO 23-2 12. Web Music, located in Gardnerville, Nevada, is a new online music service that allows inexpensive legal music downloads. Web Music prides itself on having the fastest download times in the industry. It achieved this speed by leasing server space from 10 regional servers dispersed across the country. Discuss where Web Music has sales tax nexus.

LO 23-2 13. Discuss possible reasons why the Commerce Clause was included in the U.S. Constitution.

LO 23-2 14. Describe the administrative burden businesses face in collecting sales taxes.

LO 23-3 15. Compare and contrast the rules determining where domiciliary and nondomiciliary businesses must file state income tax returns.

LO 23-3 16. Lars operates Keep Flying Incorporated, a used airplane parts business, in Laramie, Wyoming. Lars employs sales agents who visit mechanics in all 50 states to solicit orders. All orders are sent to Wyoming for approval, and all parts are shipped via common carrier. The sales agents are always on the lookout for wrecked, abandoned, or salvaged aircraft with rare parts because they receive substantial bonuses for purchasing and salvaging these parts and shipping them to Wyoming. Discuss the states where Keep Flying has income tax nexus.

LO 23-3 17. Explain changes in the U.S. economy that have made Public Law 86-272 partially obsolete. Provide an example of a company for which Public Law 86-272 works well and one for which it does not.

LO 23-3 18. Climb Higher is a distributor of high-end climbing gear located in Paradise, Washington. Its sales personnel regularly perform the following activities in an effort to maximize sales:

- Carry swag (free samples) for distribution to climbing shop employees.
- Perform credit checks of new customers to reduce delivery time of the first order of merchandise.
- Check customer inventory for proper display and proper quantities.
- Accept returns of defective goods.

Identify which of Climb Higher's sales activities are protected and unprotected activities under the *Wrigley* Supreme Court decision.

LO 23-3 19. Describe a situation in which it would be advantageous for a business to establish income tax nexus in a state.

LO 23-3 20. States are arguing for economic income tax nexus; provide at least one reason for and one reason against the validity of economic income tax nexus.

LO 23-3 21. Explain the difference between separate-return states and unitary-return states.

LO 23-3 22. Explain the rationale for the factors (functional integration, centralization of management, and economies of scale) that determine whether two or more businesses form a unitary group under the *Mobil* decision.

LO 23-3 23. Compare and contrast the reasons why book/tax and federal/state adjustments are necessary for interest income.

24. Compare and contrast the ways a multistate business divides business and nonbusiness income among states. LO 23-3
25. Contrast the treatment of government sales and dock sales for the sales apportionment factor. LO 23-3
26. Most states have increased the weight of the sales factor for the apportionment of business income. What are some of the possible reasons for this change? LO 23-3
27. Compare and contrast federal/state tax differences and book/federal tax differences. LO 23-3

PROBLEMS

Select problems are available in Connect®.

28. Crazy Eddie Incorporated manufactures baseball caps and distributes them across the northeastern United States. The firm is incorporated and headquartered in New York and sells to customers in Connecticut, Delaware, Massachusetts, New Jersey, New York, Ohio, and Pennsylvania. It has sales reps only where discussed in the scenarios below. Determine whether Crazy Eddie has sales tax nexus in each of the following states, assuming these states have adopted *Wayfair:* LO 23-2
    a) Crazy Eddie is incorporated and headquartered in New York. It also has property, employees, salespeople, and intangibles in New York.
    b) Crazy Eddie has a warehouse, personal property, and employees in Connecticut.
    c) Crazy Eddie has two customers in Delaware. Crazy Eddie receives orders over the phone and ships goods to its Delaware customers using FedEx.
    d) Crazy Eddie has independent sales representatives in Massachusetts who distribute baseball-related items for over a dozen companies.
    e) Crazy Eddie has salespeople who visit New Jersey. They follow procedures that comply with Public Law 86-272 by sending orders to New York for acceptance. The goods are shipped to New Jersey by FedEx.
    f) Crazy Eddie provides graphic design services to another manufacturer located in Ohio. While the services are performed in New York, Crazy Eddie's designers visit Ohio at least quarterly to deliver the new designs and receive feedback.
    g) Crazy Eddie receives online orders from its Pennsylvania clients. Because the orders are so large, the goods are delivered weekly on Crazy Eddie's trucks.
29. Brad Carlton operates Carlton Collectibles, a rare-coin shop in Washington, D.C., that ships coins to collectors in all 50 states. Carlton also provides appraisal services upon request. During the last several years, the appraisal work has been done either in the D.C. shop or at the homes of private collectors in Maryland and Virginia. Determine the jurisdictions in which Carlton Collectibles has sales tax nexus, assuming these states have enacted *Wayfair* legislation. LO 23-2
30. Melanie operates Mel's Bakery in Foxboro, Massachusetts, and has retail stores in Connecticut, Maine, Massachusetts, New Hampshire, and Rhode Island. Mel's Bakery also ships specialty breads nationwide upon request. Determine Mel's Bakery's sales tax collection responsibility and calculate the sales tax liability for Massachusetts, Connecticut, Maine, New Hampshire, Rhode Island, and Texas, based on the following information: LO 23-2
    a) The Massachusetts stores have $500,000 in sales. Massachusetts's sales tax rate is 5 percent; assume it exempts food items.
    b) The Connecticut retail stores have $400,000 in sales ($300,000 from in-store sales and $100,000 from catering) and $10,000 in delivery charges for catering activities. Connecticut sales tax is 6 percent and excludes food products but taxes prepared meals (catering). Connecticut also imposes sales tax on delivery charges on taxable sales.

c) Mel's Bakery's Maine retail store has $250,000 of sales ($200,000 for take-out and $50,000 of in-store sales). Maine has a 5 percent sales tax rate and a 7 percent sales tax rate on prepared food; it exempts other food purchases.

d) The New Hampshire retail stores have $250,000 of dine-in sales. New Hampshire is one of five states with no sales tax. However, it has a room and meals tax rate of 8 percent. New Hampshire considers any food or beverage served by a restaurant for consumption on or off the premises to be a meal.

e) Mel's Bakery's Rhode Island stores earn $300,000 in sales. The Rhode Island sales tax rate is 7 percent and its restaurant surtax is 1 percent. Rhode Island considers Mel's Bakery to be a restaurant because its retail store has seating.

f) One of Mel's Bakery's best customers relocated to Texas, which imposes an 8.25 percent state and local sales tax rate but exempts bakery products. This customer entertains guests regularly and made 10 orders totaling $15,000 of food items this year. Assume Texas only has a sales threshold of $500,000 to establish an economic nexus.

LO 23-2
research

31. Cuyahoga County, Ohio, has a sales tax rate of 8 percent. Determine the state, local, and transit (a local transportation district) portions of the rate. You can find resources on the State of Ohio website, including the following link: www.tax.ohio.gov/Portals/0/tax_analysis/tax_data_series/sales_and_use/salestaxmap.pdf.

LO 23-2

32. Kai operates the Surf Shop in Laie, Hawaii, which designs, manufactures, and customizes surfboards. Hawaii has a hypothetical 4 percent excise tax rate, technically paid by the seller. However, the state also allows "tax on tax" to be charged, which effectively means a customer is billed 4.166 percent of the sales price. Determine the sales tax the Surf Shop must collect and remit—or the use tax liability the customer must pay—for each of the following orders:

a) Kalani, a Utah customer, places an Internet order for a $1,000 board that will be shipped to Provo, Utah, where the local sales tax rate is 6.85 percent.

b) Nick, an Alabama resident, comes to the retail shop on vacation and has a $2,000 custom board made. Nick uses the board on vacation and then has the Surf Shop ship it to Tuscaloosa, Alabama, where the sales tax rate is 9 percent.

c) Jim, a Michigan resident, places an order for a $2,000 custom board at the end of his vacation. Upon completion, the board will be shipped to Ann Arbor, Michigan, where the sales tax rate is 6 percent.

d) Scott, a Nebraska resident, sends his current surfboard to the Surf Shop for a custom paint job. The customization services come to $800. The board is shipped to Lincoln, Nebraska, where the sales tax rate is 7.25 percent.

LO 23-2
planning

33. Last year, Reggie, a Los Angeles, California, resident, began selling autographed footballs through Trojan Victory (TV) Incorporated, a California corporation. TV has never collected sales tax. Last year it had sales as follows: California ($100,000), Arizona ($10,000), Oregon ($15,000), New York ($50,000), and Wyoming ($1,000). Most sales are made over the Internet and shipped by common carrier. Determine how much sales tax TV should have collected in each of the following situations:

a) California treats the autographed footballs as tangible personal property subject to an 8.25 percent sales tax rate. Answer for California.

b) California treats the autographed footballs as part tangible personal property ($50,000) and part services ($50,000), and tangible personal property is subject to an 8.25 percent sales tax rate. Answer for California.

c) TV has no property or other physical presence in New York (10.25 percent) or Wyoming (5 percent). Answer for New York and Wyoming.

d) TV has Reggie deliver a few footballs to fans in Arizona (5.6 percent sales tax rate) and Oregon (no sales tax) while attending football games there. Answer for Arizona and Oregon.

e) Related to part (d), can you make any suggestions that would decrease TV's Arizona sales tax liability?

34. LeMond Incorporated, a Wisconsin corporation, runs bicycle tours in several states. LeMond also has a Wisconsin retail store and an Internet store that ships to out-of-state customers. The bicycle tours operate in Colorado, North Carolina, and Wisconsin, where LeMond has employees and owns and uses tangible personal property. LeMond has real property only in Wisconsin and logs the following sales: LO 23-2

LeMond Sales

State	Goods	Services	Total
Arizona	$ 34,194	$ 0	$ 34,194
California	110,612	0	110,612
Colorado	25,913	356,084	381,997
North Carolina	16,721	225,327	242,048
Oregon	15,431	0	15,431
Wisconsin	241,982	877,441	1,119,423
Totals	$444,853	$1,458,852	$1,903,705

Assume the following hypothetical tax rates: Arizona (5.6 percent), California (7.75 percent), Colorado (8 percent), North Carolina (6.75 percent), Oregon (no sales tax), and Wisconsin (5 percent). How much sales tax must LeMond collect and remit, assuming these states, except California, have adopted *Wayfair* legislation?

35. Kashi Corporation is the U.S. distributor of fencing (sword fighting) equipment imported from Europe. It is incorporated in Virginia and headquartered in Arlington, Virginia; it ships goods to all 50 states. Kashi's employees attend regional and national fencing competitions, where they maintain temporary booths to market their goods. Determine whether Kashi has income tax nexus and a filing requirement in the following situations: LO 23-3 planning

a) Kashi is incorporated and headquartered in Virginia. It also has property, employees, salespeople, and intangibles in Virginia. Determine whether Kashi has income tax nexus in Virginia.

b) Kashi has employees who live in Washington, D.C., and Maryland, but they perform all their employment-related activities in Virginia. Does Kashi have income tax nexus in Washington, D.C., and Maryland?

c) Kashi has two customers in North Dakota. It receives their orders over the phone and ships goods to them using FedEx. Determine whether Kashi has income tax nexus in North Dakota.

d) Kashi has independent sales representatives in Illinois who distribute fencing and other sports-related items for many companies. Does Kashi have income tax nexus in Illinois?

e) Kashi has salespeople who visit South Carolina for a regional fencing competition for a total of three days during the year. They send all orders to Virginia for credit approval and acceptance, and Kashi ships the goods into South Carolina by FedEx. Determine whether Kashi has income tax nexus in South Carolina.

f) Kashi has sales reps who visit California for a national fencing competition and several regional competitions for a total of 17 days during the year. They send all orders to Virginia for credit approval and acceptance. The goods are shipped by FedEx into California. Does Kashi have income tax nexus in California?

g) Kashi receives online orders from its Pennsylvania client. Because the orders are so large, the goods are delivered weekly on Kashi's trucks. Does Kashi have income tax nexus in Pennsylvania?

h) In addition to shipping goods, Kashi provides fencing lessons in Virginia and Maryland locations. Determine whether Kashi has income tax nexus in Virginia and Maryland.

i) Given that Kashi ships to all 50 states, are there locations that would decrease Kashi's overall state income tax burden if income tax nexus were created there?

LO 23-3

36. Gary Holt LLP provides tax and legal services regarding the tax-exempt bond issues of state and local jurisdictions. Gary typically provides the services from his New York offices. However, for large issuances he and his staff occasionally travel to another state to complete the work. Determine whether the firm has income tax nexus in the following situations:
   a) Gary Holt LLP is a New York partnership and headquartered in New York. It also has property and employees in New York. Does it have income tax nexus in New York?
   b) Gary Holt LLP has employees who live in New Jersey and Connecticut and perform all their employment-related activities in New York. Does it have income tax nexus in New Jersey and/or Connecticut?
   c) Gary Holt LLP has two customers in California. Gary personally travels there to finalize the Alameda County bond issuance. Does it have income tax nexus in California?

LO 23-3

37. Root Beer Inc. (RBI) is incorporated and headquartered in Seattle, Washington. RBI runs an Internet business, www.makerootbeer.com, and sells bottling equipment and other supplies for making homemade root beer. It also has an Oregon warehouse from which it ships goods. Determine whether RBI has income tax nexus in the following situations:
   a) RBI is incorporated and headquartered in Washington and has property and employees in Oregon and Washington. Determine whether RBI has income tax nexus in Oregon and Washington.
   b) RBI has hundreds of customers in California but no physical presence (no employees or property). Does it have income tax nexus in California?
   c) RBI has 500 New York customers but no physical presence (no employees or property). Determine whether RBI has income tax nexus in New York.

LO 23-3

38. Rockville Enterprises manufactures woodworking equipment and is incorporated and based in Evansville, Indiana. All of its real property is in Indiana. Rockville Enterprises employs a large sales force that travels throughout the United States. Determine whether each of the following is a protected activity in nondomiciliary states under Public Law 86-272:
   a) Rockville Enterprises advertises in Wisconsin using television, radio, and newspapers.
   b) Rockville Enterprises's employees in Illinois check the credit of potential customers.
   c) Rockville Enterprises maintains a booth at an industry trade show in Arizona for 10 days.
   d) Sales representatives check the inventory of a Tennessee customer to make sure it has enough stock and that the stock is properly displayed.
   e) Rockville Enterprises holds a management seminar executive retreat for corporate executives over four days in Florida.
   f) Sales representatives supervise the repossession of inventory from a customer in Maine that is not making payments on time.
   g) Rockville Enterprises provides automobiles to Idaho and Montana sales representatives.
   h) An Alabama sales representative accepts a customer deposit on a large order.
   i) Colorado sales reps carry display racks and promotional materials that they place in customers' retail stores without charge.

LO 23-3
research

39. Software Incorporated is a sales and use tax software vendor that provides customers with a license to download and use its software on their machines. Software retains ownership of the software. It has customers in New Jersey and West Virginia. Determine whether Software has economic income tax nexus in these states based on the following decisions: *Lanco, Inc. v. Director, Division of Taxation,* 188 N.J. 380, 908 A.2d 176 (2006), and *Tax Commissioner of West Virginia v. MBNA America Bank, N.A.,* 640 S.E.2d 226 (W. Va. 2006).

LO 23-3
research

40. Peter Inc., a Kentucky corporation, owns 100 percent of Suvi Inc., a Mississippi corporation. Peter and Suvi file a consolidated federal tax return. Peter has income

tax nexus in Kentucky and South Carolina; Suvi has income tax nexus in Mississippi and South Carolina. Kentucky, Mississippi, and South Carolina are separate-return states. In which states must Peter and Suvi file tax returns? Can they file a consolidated return in any states? Explain. (*Hint:* Use South Carolina Form SC 1120 and the related instructions.)

41. Use California Publication 1061 (2020) to identify the various tests California uses to determine whether two or more entities are part of a unitary group. The publication can be found here: www.ftb.ca.gov/forms/2020/2020-1061-publication.pdf. LO 23-3 research

42. Bulldog Incorporated is a Georgia corporation. It properly included, deducted, or excluded the following items on its federal tax return in the current year: LO 23-3 tax forms research

Item	Amount	Federal Treatment
Georgia income taxes	$25,496	Deducted on federal return
Tennessee income taxes	13,653	Deducted on federal return
Washington gross receipts tax	3,105	Deducted on federal return
Georgia bond interest income	10,000	Excluded from federal return
Federal T-note interest income	4,500	Included on federal return
Bonus depreciation	15,096	Deducted on federal return

Use Georgia's Corporate Income Tax Form 600 and Instructions to determine what federal/state adjustments Bulldog needs to make for Georgia. Bulldog's federal taxable income was $194,302. Calculate its Georgia state tax base and complete Schedule 1, page 1, of Form 600 for Bulldog.

43. Herger Corporation does business in California, Nevada, and Oregon and has income tax nexus in these states as well. Herger's California state tax base was $921,023 after making the required federal/state adjustments. Herger's federal tax return contains the following items: LO 23-3

Item	Amount
Federal T-note interest income	$ 5,000
Nevada municipal bond interest income	3,400
California municipal bond interest income	6,000
Interest expense related to T-note interest income	1,400
Royalty income	100,000
Travel expenses	9,025

Determine Herger's business income.

44. Bad Brad sells used semitrucks and tractor trailers in the Texas panhandle. Bad Brad has sales as follows: LO 23-3

Bad Brad	
State	**Sales**
Colorado	$ 234,992
New Mexico	675,204
Oklahoma	402,450
Texas	1,085,249
Total	$2,397,895

Bad Brad is a Texas corporation. Answer the questions in each of the following alternative scenarios.

a) Bad Brad has income tax nexus in Colorado, New Mexico, Oklahoma, and Texas. What are the Colorado, New Mexico, Oklahoma, and Texas sales apportionment factors?

b) Bad Brad has income tax nexus in Colorado and Texas. Oklahoma and New Mexico sales are shipped from Texas (a throwback state). What are the Colorado and Texas sales apportionment factors?

c) Bad Brad has income tax nexus in Colorado and Texas. Oklahoma and New Mexico sales are shipped from Texas (a throwback state); $200,000 of Oklahoma sales were to the federal government. What are the Colorado and Texas sales apportionment factors?

d) Bad Brad has income tax nexus in Colorado and Texas. Oklahoma and New Mexico sales are shipped from Texas (assume Texas is a nonthrowback state). What are the Colorado and Texas sales apportionment factors?

LO 23-3 45. Nicole's Salon, a Louisiana corporation, operates beauty salons in Arkansas, Louisiana, and Tennessee. The salons' payrolls by state are as follows:

Nicole's Salon

State	Payroll
Arkansas	$ 130,239
Louisiana	309,192
Tennessee	723,010
Total	$1,162,441

What are the payroll apportionment factors for Arkansas, Louisiana, and Tennessee in each of the following alternative scenarios?

a) Nicole's Salon has income tax nexus in Arkansas, Louisiana, and Tennessee.

b) Nicole's Salon has income tax nexus in Arkansas, Louisiana, and Tennessee, but $50,000 of the Arkansas amount is paid to independent contractors.

LO 23-3 46. Delicious Dave's Maple Syrup, a Vermont corporation, has property in the following states:

	Property	
State	Beginning	Ending
Maine	$ 923,032	$ 994,221
Massachusetts	103,311	203,109
New Hampshire	381,983	283,021
Vermont	873,132	891,976
Total	$2,281,458	$2,372,327

What are the property apportionment factors for Maine, Massachusetts, New Hampshire, and Vermont in each of the following alternative scenarios?

a) Delicious Dave's has income tax nexus in each of the states.

b) Delicious Dave's has income tax nexus in each of the states, but the Maine total includes $400,000 of investment property that Delicious rents out (unrelated to its business).

c) Delicious Dave's has income tax nexus in each of the states, but it also pays $50,000 to rent property in Massachusetts.

LO 23-3 47. Susie's Sweet Shop has the following sales, payroll, and property factors:

Item	Iowa	Missouri
Sales	69.20%	32.01%
Payroll	88.00%	3.50%
Property	72.42%	24.04%

What are Susie's Sweet Shop's Iowa and Missouri apportionment factors under each of the following alternative scenarios?

a) Iowa and Missouri both use a three-factor apportionment formula.

b) Iowa and Missouri both use a four-factor apportionment formula that double-weights sales.

c) Iowa uses a three-factor formula and Missouri uses a single-factor apportionment formula (based solely on sales).

48. Brady Corporation is a Nebraska corporation, but it owns business and investment property in surrounding states as well. Determine the state where each item of income is allocated. LO 23-3
   a) $15,000 of dividend income.
   b) $10,000 of interest income.
   c) $15,000 of rental income for South Dakota property.
   d) $20,000 of royalty income for intangibles used in South Dakota (where income tax nexus exists).
   e) $24,000 of royalty income from Kansas (where income tax nexus does not exist).
   f) $15,000 of capital gain from securities held for investment.
   g) $30,000 of capital gain on real property located in South Dakota.
49. Ashton Corporation is headquartered in Pennsylvania and has a state income tax base there of $500,000. Of this amount, $50,000 was nonbusiness income. Ashton's Pennsylvania apportionment factor is 42.35 percent. The nonbusiness income allocated to Pennsylvania was $32,000. Assuming a Pennsylvania corporate tax rate of 8.25 percent, what is Ashton's Pennsylvania state tax liability? LO 23-3

COMPREHENSIVE PROBLEMS

Select problems are available in Connect®.

50. Cloud computing is the use of hosted computer facilities through the Internet. Gmail, RIA Checkpoint, and even your iPhone are some applications of cloud computing. Please research the following questions. research
   a) If HP provides a customized bundle of servers, storage, network and security software, and business application software to a customer in Washington State, how is it taxed?
   b) Is HP leasing tangible personal property, which is taxable, or providing a nontaxable service?
   c) Is the buyer of HP's product subject to Washington sales tax?
   d) Is HP subject to Washington's B&O tax?
51. Sharon Inc. is headquartered in State X and owns 100 percent of Carol Corp., Josey Corp., and Janice Corp., which form a single unitary group. Assume sales operations are within the solicitation bounds of Public Law 86-272. Each of the corporations has operations in the following states:

Domicile State	Sharon Inc. State X (throwback)	Carol Corp. State Y (throwback)	Josey Corp. State Z (nonthrowback)	Janice Corp. State Z (nonthrowback)
Dividend income	$ 1,000	$ 200	$ 300	$ 500
Business income	50,000	30,000	10,000	10,000
Sales: State X	70,000	10,000	10,000	10,000
State Y		40,000	5,000	
State Z		20,000	20,000	10,000
State A	20,000			
State B	10,000			10,000
Property: State X	50,000	20,000		10,000
State Y		80,000		
State Z			25,000	20,000
State A	50,000			
Payroll: State X	10,000	10,000		
State Y		40,000		
State Z			3,000	10,000
State A				10,000

Compute the following for State X assuming a tax rate of 15 percent.

a) Calculate the State X apportionment factor for Sharon Inc., Carol Corp., Josey Corp., and Janice Corp.

b) Calculate the business income apportioned to State X.

c) Calculate the taxable income for State X for each company.

d) Determine the tax liability for State X for the entire group.

52. Happy Hippos (HH) is a manufacturer and retailer of New England crafts headquartered in Camden, Maine. HH provides services and has sales, employees, property, and commercial domicile as follows:

Happy Hippos In-State Activities

State	Sales	Employees	Property	Services	Commercial Domicile
Connecticut	✓	✓		✓	
Maine	✓	✓	✓	✓	✓
Massachusetts	✓	✓			
New York	✓				
Rhode Island	✓	✓			
Vermont	✓	✓	✓	✓	

HH's sales of goods and services by state are as follows:

Happy Hippos Sales

State	Goods	Services	Total
Connecticut	$ 78,231	$ 52,321	$130,552
Maine	292,813	81,313	374,126
Massachusetts	90,238		90,238
New York	129,322		129,322
Rhode Island	98,313		98,313
Vermont	123,914	23,942	147,856
Totals	$812,831	$157,576	$970,407

HH has federal taxable income of $282,487 for the current year. Included in federal taxable income are the following income and deductions:

- $12,000 of Vermont rental income.
- City of Orono, Maine, bond interest of $10,000.
- $10,000 of dividends.
- $2,498 of state tax refund included in income.
- $32,084 of state net income tax expense.
- $59,234 of federal depreciation.

Other relevant facts include:

- Assume that the New York sales are to a single customer who is a retailer and can provide a valid New York reseller's certificate.
- Maine state depreciation for the year was $47,923, and Maine doesn't allow deductions for state income taxes.
- The employees present in Connecticut, Massachusetts, and Rhode Island are salespeople who perform only activities protected by Public Law 86-272.
- Assume that each of the states is a separate-return state.

HH's payroll is as follows:

Payroll	
State	**Wages**
Connecticut	$ 94,231
Maine	392,195
Massachusetts	167,265
Rhode Island	92,391
Vermont	193,923
Total	$940,005

HH's property is as follows:

Property			
State	**Beginning**	**Ending**	**Rented**
Maine	$ 938,234	$ 937,652	
Vermont	329,134	428,142	$12,000
Total	$1,267,368	$1,365,794	$12,000

Required:

a) Determine the states in which HH has sales tax nexus, assuming these states have passed *Wayfair* legislation.

b) Calculate the sales tax HH must remit assuming the following (hypothetical) sales tax rates:

- Connecticut (6 percent)
- Maine (8 percent)
- Massachusetts (7 percent)
- New York (8.875 percent)
- Rhode Island (5 percent)
- Vermont (9 percent)

c) Determine the states in which HH has income tax nexus and an income tax filing requirement.

d) Determine HH's state tax base for Maine, assuming federal taxable income of $282,487.

e) Calculate business and nonbusiness income.

f) Determine HH's Maine apportionment factors using the three-factor method (assume that Maine is a throwback state).

g) Calculate HH's business income apportioned to Maine.

h) Determine HH's allocation of nonbusiness income to Maine.

i) Determine HH's Maine taxable income.

j) Calculate HH's Maine income tax liability, assuming a Maine income tax rate of 5 percent.

UWorld Roger CPA Review

Sample CPA Exam questions from Roger CPA Review are available in Connect as support for the topics in this text. These Multiple Choice Questions and Task-Based Simulations include expert-written explanations and solutions and provide a starting point for students to become familiar with the content and functionality of the actual CPA Exam.

chapter

24 The U.S. Taxation of Multinational Transactions

Learning Objectives

Upon completing this chapter, you should be able to:

LO 24-1 Describe the basic U.S. framework for taxing multinational transactions and the role of the foreign tax credit limitation.

LO 24-2 Apply the U.S. source rules for common items of gross income and deductions.

LO 24-3 Explain the role of income tax treaties in international tax planning.

LO 24-4 Identify creditable foreign taxes and compute the foreign tax credit limitation.

LO 24-5 Compare the advantages and disadvantages of the different forms of doing business outside the United States.

LO 24-6 Explain the basic U.S. anti-deferral tax regime and identify common sources of subpart F income.

Karin Dreyer/Tetra images/Getty Images

Storyline Summary

Detroit Doughnut Depot (3D)

Privately held company located in Detroit, Michigan. Operated as a C corporation for U.S. tax purposes. Makes and sells fresh baked goods, homemade sandwiches, and premium coffee and tea drinks.

Owner:	Lily Green (she/her/hers)
Filing status:	Married filing jointly
Marginal tax rate:	24 percent

Lily Green was excited about the growth of her coffee and baked goods business since she opened her store in downtown Detroit in 2015. From its humble beginnings, the Detroit Doughnut Depot (3D) had attracted a solid base of loyal customers who appreciated the freshness and organic ingredients that set the company's products apart from its competitors. Many of Lily's customers were commuters from nearby Windsor, Canada. They often asked Lily whether she ever considered opening a store in Windsor, where they thought she would find a receptive customer base. Lily was intrigued by the idea of "going global" with her business, but she knew she needed to find someone to help her understand the U.S. and Canadian income tax implications of expanding her business to Windsor. Her first questions dealt with how and when she would be subject to Canadian tax and whether her Canadian activities also would be subject to U.S. tax. ■

Lily Green is about to take part in a growing trend of expansion by U.S. businesses into international markets. In 1983, gross receipts of non-U.S. subsidiaries of U.S. multinational corporations totaled approximately $720 billion; by 2019, that number exceeded $7.7 trillion, over a tenfold increase.[1] Net income increased from $57 billion in 1983 to $1.5 trillion in 2019. Companies such as Google Inc. and Apple Inc. report a significant amount of revenue from international operations. For example, Alphabet Inc. (Google) reported revenue from its international operations of $97 billion in the calendar year ended 2020, approximately 53 percent of its total revenue.[2] Apple Inc. reported net sales of $365.8 billion in fiscal 2021, approximately 63 percent of which came from outside the United States.

As dramatic as the outflow of investment from the United States has been, the inflow of investment by non-U.S. businesses and individuals into the United States has been just as impressive. According to the U.S. Bureau of Economic Analysis, the total amount of foreign-owned assets in the United States increased by more than 1,000 percent between 1989 and 2020, to $32.3 trillion.[3] U.S. subsidiaries of non-U.S. companies currently employ 7.9 million Americans.[4] Familiar non–U.S. headquartered companies with large U.S. operations include BP Global (United Kingdom), Toyota Motor Corporation (Japan), Honda Motor Corporation (Japan), Nissan Group (Japan), Nestlé S.A. (Switzerland), Sony Corporation (Japan), GlaxoSmithKline PLC (United Kingdom), Volkswagen AG (Germany), Samsung Group (South Korea), BMW AG (Germany), Bridgestone Corporation (Japan), Bayer AG (Germany), and Philips Electronics N.V. (Netherlands).

This chapter provides a basic overview of the income tax consequences related to transactions that span more than one national tax jurisdiction (in our storyline, the United States and Canada). We focus primarily on the U.S. tax rules that apply to **outbound transactions,** involving the establishment of a **foreign branch** or formation of a foreign corporation, where a U.S. person engages in a transaction that occurs outside the United States or involves a non-U.S. person.[5] We also discuss briefly the U.S. tax rules that apply to **inbound transactions,** where a non-U.S. person engages in a transaction that occurs within the United States or involves a U.S. person. Most of the U.S. income tax rules that apply to multinational transactions are found in subchapter N of the Internal Revenue Code (IRC) (§§861–999).

LO 24-1 THE U.S. FRAMEWORK FOR TAXING MULTINATIONAL TRANSACTIONS

When a U.S. person engages in a transaction that involves a country outside the United States, there arises the issue as to which tax authority or authorities have jurisdiction (i.e., the legal right) to tax that transaction. All governments (national, state, and local) must adopt a basis on which to claim the right to tax income. The criteria they choose to assert their right to tax a person or transaction is called **nexus.** At the national level, governments most often determine nexus by either the taxpayer's citizenship or residence, called **residence-based jurisdiction,** or the geographic source of income, called **source-based jurisdiction.**

THE KEY FACTS

Basic Framework for U.S. Taxation of Multinational Transactions

- The United States taxes citizens and residents on their worldwide income and nonresidents on their U.S. source income.
- U.S. corporations owning 10 percent or more of a foreign corporation receive a 100 percent dividends-received deduction for dividends received from these corporations.

(continued)

[1]Bureau of Economic Analysis, *U.S. Direct Investment Abroad: Financial and Operating Data for U.S. Multinational Companies,* available at www.bea.gov.

[2]As a reference point, Google Inc. reported a *loss* of $42.3 million in 2005 from international operations.

[3]Bureau of Economic Analysis, *U.S. Net International Investment Position Year 2020* (updated September 30, 2021), available at www.bea.gov.

[4]Global Business Alliance, data available at www.globalbusiness.org.

[5]As used in this chapter, a "person" includes an individual, corporation, partnership, trust, estate, or association. §7701(a)(1). The "United States," as used in this context, includes only the 50 states and the District of Columbia. §7701(a)(9).

Once nexus has been established, a government must decide how to allocate and apportion a person's income and expenses to its tax jurisdiction. Under a residence-based approach, a country taxes the worldwide income of the person earning the income. Under a source-based approach, a country taxes only the income earned within its boundaries. When applying a source-based approach, a government must develop source rules to allocate and apportion income and expenses to its jurisdiction. Within the United States, states use apportionment formulas that take into account sales, property, and payroll, or some combination of these factors, to apportion income and expenses to their tax jurisdiction.[6]

Income earned by a citizen or resident of one country that has its source in another country can be taxed by both countries. The country where the taxpayer resides can assert residence-based jurisdiction, whereas the country where the income is earned can apply geographic source–based jurisdiction. To mitigate such double taxation and to promote international commerce, governments often allow their residents a tax credit for foreign income taxes paid on *foreign source* income. National governments also enter into income tax treaties with other national governments to mitigate the double taxation of income earned by residents of one country in the other country. Under a treaty, both countries may agree not to tax income earned within their boundaries by a resident of the other country.

The United States applies both residence-based jurisdiction and source-based jurisdiction in asserting its right to tax income. The U.S. government taxes *citizens* and *residents* on their worldwide income, regardless of source (i.e., residence-based jurisdiction).[7] In the Tax Cuts and Jobs Act (TCJA), enacted on December 22, 2017, Congress replaced the worldwide approach with a more territorial approach for U.S. corporations owning 10 percent or more of a foreign corporation. The TCJA allows these 10 percent U.S. corporate shareholders a 100 percent dividends-received deduction to the extent the earnings distributed do not exceed a "normal rate of return" (defined as 10 percent) on the foreign corporation's tangible assets. In contrast, the U.S. government only taxes *nonresidents* on income that is "U.S. source" or is connected with the operation of a U.S. trade or business (i.e., source-based jurisdiction).

- A noncitizen is treated as a U.S. resident for income tax purposes if the individual is a permanent resident (has a green card) or meets a substantial presence test.
- Nonresident income is characterized as either ECI or FDAP income.
  - ECI income is taxed on a net basis using the U.S. graduated tax rates.
  - FDAP income is taxed on a gross basis through a flat withholding tax.
- The U.S. allows citizens and residents a tax credit for foreign income taxes paid on foreign source income.
- U.S. corporations do not receive a foreign tax credit on dividend income from foreign corporations eligible for the 100 percent dividends-received deduction.
- The foreign tax credit is limited to the percentage of foreign source taxable income to total taxable income times the pre-credit income tax on total taxable income.

U.S. Taxation of a Nonresident

U.S. source income earned by a nonresident is classified into two categories for U.S. tax purposes: (1) **effectively connected income (ECI)** and (2) **fixed and determinable, annual or periodic (FDAP) income.** Income that is effectively connected with a U.S. trade or business is subject to *net taxation* (i.e., gross income minus deductions) at the U.S. tax rate. A nonresident reports such income and related deductions on a U.S. tax return, either a Form 1120F for a nonresident corporation or a Form 1040NR for a nonresident individual. FDAP income, which generally is passive income such as dividends, interest, rents, or royalties, is subject to a *withholding tax* regime applied to gross income. The payor of the FDAP income withholds the tax at the statutory rate (30 percent under U.S. tax law), unless reduced under a treaty arrangement, and remits it to the government. The recipient of the FDAP income usually does not have to file a tax return and does not reduce the FDAP income by any deductions. Most countries, including Canada, apply a similar tax regime to U.S. persons earning income within their jurisdiction.[8]

[6]See the State and Local Taxes chapter for a more thorough discussion of how states apportion income.

[7]The United States is one of two countries, the other being Eritrea, that applies full worldwide taxation based on citizenship as well as residency.

[8]Canada applies a 25 percent withholding tax rate on dividends, rents, and royalties unless reduced under a treaty. Under the U.S.–Canada income tax treaty, the withholding tax on shareholders owning less than 10 percent of a corporation's stock is 15 percent, and 5 percent otherwise.

Example 24-1

Lily decided to open a store in Windsor, Canada, from which she will sell baked goods and sandwiches prepared in her U.S. store and transported daily across the border. She elected to operate the store as an unincorporated division, or branch, of Detroit Doughnut Depot (3D) for Canadian tax purposes. Will 3D be subject to tax in Canada on any taxable income it earns through its Windsor store?

Answer: Yes. 3D will have nexus in Canada because it operates a business there (residence-based jurisdiction). As a result, Canada and the province of Ontario will tax the branch's Canadian-source taxable income.

How will Canada tax 3D's Canadian-source taxable income?

Answer: Canada will apply the appropriate corporate tax rate(s) to the branch's taxable income (gross income less deductions). For 2022, the general Canadian corporate net tax rate is a flat 15 percent after abatements. The province of Ontario also will impose an income tax between 3.2 and 11.5 percent on the branch's taxable income.

What if: Assume 3D does not operate a business in Canada but owns 5 percent of the stock in a Canadian corporation that pays 3D a C$100 dividend each year.[9] How will Canada tax 3D on the dividend income it receives from its investment in the stock of the Canadian company?

Answer: Canada will apply a flat withholding tax of 15 percent on the gross amount of the dividend. This is the rate imposed under the U.S.–Canada income tax treaty.[10]

Definition of a Resident for U.S. Tax Purposes

An individual who is not a U.S. citizen is characterized for U.S. tax purposes as either a **resident alien** or a **nonresident alien.** An individual becomes a U.S. resident by satisfying one of two tests found in the Code.[11] Under the first test, sometimes referred to as the *green card test,* if an individual possesses a permanent resident visa ("green card") at any time during the calendar year, that individual is treated as a resident. Under the second test, sometimes referred to as the *substantial presence test,* an individual who is *physically present* in the United States for 31 days or more during the current calendar year *and* the number of days of physical presence during the current calendar year, plus one-third times the number of days of physical presence during the first preceding year, plus one-sixth times the number of days of physical presence during the second preceding year, equals or exceeds 183 days, becomes a U.S. resident.[12] As we will discuss later in the chapter, these rules often are modified by treaties between the United States and other countries to limit instances in which an individual might be taxed as a resident by more than one country.

As always, there are a number of exceptions. For example, international students and teachers generally are exempt from the physical presence test for five and two years, respectively. Individuals who are present in the United States during the current year for less than 183 days and who establish that they have a "closer connection" to another country can elect to be exempt from the physical presence test.[13] Other exemptions apply to individuals who experience unexpected medical conditions while in the United States and to commuters from Canada and Mexico who have a U.S. employer.

The residence of a corporation for U.S. tax purposes generally is determined by the entity's country of incorporation. Other countries may determine the residency of

[9]The national currency of Canada is the Canadian dollar, abbreviated C$.

[10]Article X of the U.S.–Canada income tax treaty.

[11]§7701(b).

[12]For purposes of this test, a full day is considered any part of a day.

[13]An individual usually satisfies the closer connection test by demonstrating that they have a "tax home" in another country. A tax home is defined as the taxpayer's regular place of business or *regular place of abode.*

corporations for tax purposes using different standards. For example, the United Kingdom (UK) also typically treats businesses incorporated in the UK as residents for UK tax purposes. However, the UK also considers companies incorporated outside of the UK to be UK tax residents if their central management and control are located in the UK.

Example 24-2

What if: Assume that for quality-control purposes, Lily has decided to do all the baking for her Windsor store in Detroit. Every morning a Windsor employee drives a van to Detroit and picks up the baked goods for sale in Windsor. One of her Windsor employees, Stan Lee Cupp, made the two-hour trip on 132 different days during 2022. He was not physically present in the United States prior to 2022. Will Stan be considered a U.S. resident in 2022 applying only the substantial presence test? Stan is a Canadian citizen and resident.

Answer: No. Although he is physically present in the United States for more than 30 days in 2022, Stan does not satisfy the 183-day test when applying the formula [132 + (1/3 × 0) + (1/6 × 0) = 132].

What if: Assume Stan continues to be physically present in the United States for 132 days in 2023 and again in 2024. Will Stan be considered a U.S. resident in 2023 or 2024 applying only the substantial presence test?

Answer: 2023: No. He does not satisfy the 183-day test when applying the formula [132 + (1/3 × 132) + (1/6 × 0) = 176].

2024: Yes. He now satisfies the 183-day test when applying the formula [132 + (1/3 × 132) + (1/6 × 132) = 198].

Does Stan qualify for any exceptions that allow him to avoid being treated as a U.S. resident in 2024?

Answer: Yes. Stan can avoid being treated as a U.S. resident under the closer connection test because he was physically present in the United States for less than 183 days in 2024 and his tax home is in Canada. If Stan is in the United States for 183 days or more, he will have to rely on the U.S.–Canada income tax treaty to avoid being considered a U.S. resident for income tax purposes (to be discussed in more detail later in the chapter).

Overview of the U.S. Foreign Tax Credit System

For U.S. taxpayers subject to worldwide taxation of their income, the United States mitigates the double taxation of foreign source income by allowing U.S. taxpayers to claim a **foreign tax credit (FTC)** for foreign income taxes paid on *foreign source* income not eligible for exemption from U.S. tax. Generally, the United States taxes foreign source income to the extent the foreign taxing jurisdiction did not tax the income at a rate equal to or greater than the U.S. tax rate of 21 percent. The United States does not allow a current-year credit for taxes paid in excess of the U.S. tax rate, however. The United States attempts to achieve this residual tax approach through the **foreign tax credit limitation,** which is computed as follows:

$$\frac{\text{Foreign source taxable income}}{\text{Total taxable income}} \times \text{Precredit U.S. tax on total taxable income}$$

For tax years beginning after December 31, 2017, the foreign tax credit limitation is computed separately for foreign branch income along with three additional categories of foreign source income. We first address the foreign branch income category because it is the most straightforward. We discuss the other categories of foreign source income later in this chapter. Generally, taxpayers can carry any unused (excess) FTC for the current year back to the previous tax year and then forward to the next 10 tax years.

Example 24-3

Lily's store in Windsor is an immediate success and reports taxable income on its Canadian operations of C$50,000 for 2022. 3D paid a combined national and provincial income tax of C$9,100 on its taxable income. Because 3D operates the Windsor store as a branch, it also must report the income on its U.S. corporate income tax return along with taxable income from its Detroit operations.[14]

Assuming a translation rate of C$1:US$0.80, 3D reports the Canadian taxable income on its U.S. tax return as $40,000 and reports the Canadian income taxes as $7,280. 3D also reports taxable income from its U.S. operations of $160,000. The company's U.S. income tax on $200,000 of taxable income from all sources is $42,000 before any credit for the income taxes paid to Canada. 3D's income from its Windsor operations is classified as "foreign branch income" for foreign tax credit purposes (we discuss the significance of foreign branch income later in the chapter).

Using the above facts, what is the foreign tax credit limitation that applies to 3D's Canadian income taxes for 2022?

Answer: $8,400, computed as $40,000/$200,000 × $42,000,

where:

$40,000 = Foreign source taxable income
$200,000 = Taxable income from all sources
$42,000 = Pre-credit U.S. tax on total taxable income

What is 3D's net U.S. tax after subtracting the available foreign tax credit?

Answer: $34,720, computed as $42,000 – $7,280. 3D has an "excess foreign tax credit limitation" of $1,120 (i.e., $8,400 FTC limitation – $7,280 Canadian income taxes). That is, 3D could have incurred an additional $1,120 of foreign taxes and received a foreign tax credit for them as well.

What is 3D's average tax rate on its taxable income from all sources for 2022?

Answer: 21 percent, computed as ($7,280 + $34,720)/$200,000.

What if: Assume 3D pays Canadian income taxes of C$12,800 ($10,240) for 2022 (a Canadian tax rate of 26.5 percent). What is its net U.S. tax after subtracting the available foreign tax credit?

Answer: $33,600, computed as $42,000 – $8,400.

The foreign tax credit limitation limits the foreign tax credit to $8,400. 3D now has an "excess foreign tax credit" of $1,840 ($10,240 – $8,400), which 3D can carry forward 10 years.

Given the above scenario, what is 3D's average tax rate on its taxable income from all sources for 2022?

Answer: 21.92 percent, computed as ($10,240 + $33,600)/$200,000. The FTC limitation prevents 3D from getting a current-year tax credit on income taxes paid in excess of the U.S. rate of 21 percent.

LO 24-2

U.S. SOURCE RULES FOR GROSS INCOME AND DEDUCTIONS

Many of the U.S. tax rules that apply to multinational transactions require taxpayers to determine the jurisdictional (i.e., geographic) source (U.S. or foreign) of their gross income.[15] The source rules determine whether income and related deductions are from sources within or without the United States. All developed countries have source-of-income rules, although most practitioners consider the U.S. rules to be the most complex in the world.

[14]Because 3D is a "small corporation," the Ontario tax rate is 3.2 percent, which, added to the federal tax rate of 15 percent, creates a combined tax rate of 18.2 percent. Large corporations are subject to a combined tax rate of 26.5 percent if operating in Ontario.

[15]The U.S. federal income tax source rules are found in §§861–865 and the accompanying regulations.

The U.S. source-of-income rules are important to *non-U.S. persons* because they limit the scope of U.S. taxation to only their U.S. source income. For *U.S. persons,* the primary purpose of the U.S. source-of-income rules is to calculate *foreign source taxable income* in the numerator of the foreign tax credit limitation. Except in the case of dividends from foreign corporations eligible for the 100 percent dividends-received deduction, the United States imposes a tax on the worldwide income of U.S. persons, regardless of its source or the U.S. person's residence. The United States cedes *primary jurisdiction* to foreign governments to tax U.S. persons on income earned outside the United States while retaining the *residual* right to tax foreign source income to the extent it has not been "fully taxed" by the foreign government. The net result is that the United States taxes foreign source income earned by U.S. persons at a rate that theoretically reflects the difference between the U.S. tax rate and the foreign tax rate imposed on the income.

U.S. persons must understand the source-of-income rules in other situations. For example, U.S. citizens and residents employed outside the United States may be eligible to exclude a portion of their *foreign source earned income* from U.S. taxation under §911.[16] In addition, U.S. persons who pay U.S. source FDAP income to foreign payees (e.g., interest or dividends) usually are required to withhold U.S. taxes on such payments.[17] U.S. corporations receive a 100 percent dividends-received deduction (DRD) on the "foreign-source portion" of dividends received from 10 percent-or-more-owned foreign corporations.

The source-of-income rules are definitional in nature; they do not impose a tax liability, create income, or allow a deduction. Although the primary focus of the source rules is on where the economic activity that generates income takes place, the U.S. government also uses the source rules to advance a variety of international tax policy objectives.

THE KEY FACTS

Source Rules

- The source rules determine whether income and deductions are treated as U.S. source or foreign source.
- For a U.S. taxpayer, the source rules primarily determine foreign taxable income in the calculation of the foreign tax credit limitation.
- For a non-U.S. taxpayer, the source rules determine what income is subject to U.S. taxation.

Source-of-Income Rules

The Internal Revenue Code defines nine classes of gross income from sources within the United States[18] and nine classes of gross income from sources outside the United States.[19] A summary of the general rules that apply to common sources of income follows. A detailed discussion of all the exceptions to these rules is beyond the scope of this text.

Interest As a general rule, the taxpayer looks to the residence of the party *paying* the interest (i.e., the borrower) to determine the geographic source of interest received. A borrower's residence is established at the time the interest is paid. Factors that determine an individual's residence include the location of the individual's family; whether the person buys a home, pays foreign taxes, and engages in social and community affairs; and the length of time spent in a country. Under these general rules, interest income is U.S. source income if it is paid by the United States or the District of Columbia, a noncorporate U.S. resident, or a U.S. corporation. Although interest income paid by a U.S. bank to a nonresident (e.g., an international student attending a U.S. university) is U.S. source income, such interest is exempt from U.S. withholding or other income taxation.[20] This exception is designed to attract foreign capital to U.S. banks.

[16]If certain conditions are met, a U.S. individual can exclude up to $112,000 of foreign earned income from U.S. taxation in 2022 plus additional earnings equal to excess "foreign housing expenses" under §911.

[17]§1441.

[18]§861(a).

[19]§862(a).

[20]§§871(i)(2)(A), 881(d).

Example 24-4

3D was dissatisfied with the 1 percent interest rate it received on its checking account at Bank of America in Detroit. Lily's investment adviser suggested the company invest $50,000 in five-year bonds issued by the Canadian government with an annual interest rate of 3 percent. During 2022, 3D received C$1,500 in interest from the bonds. Per the U.S.–Canada treaty, the Canadian government did not withhold taxes on the payment.

What is the source, U.S. or foreign, of the interest Lily receives on the bonds?

Answer: Foreign source. The source of interest income depends on the residence of the borrower at the time the interest is paid. The Canadian government is considered a resident of Canada for U.S. source rule purposes.

Dividends In general, the source of dividend income is determined by the residence of the corporation paying the dividend. Residence usually is determined by the corporation's country of incorporation or organization (in some countries, such as the United Kingdom, a corporation's residence may also be determined by where its central management is located).

Example 24-5

As part of diversifying its investment portfolio, 3D purchased 200 shares of Scotiabank (Bank of Nova Scotia, Canada). In 2022, Scotiabank paid 3D dividends of C$400. Scotiabank withheld C$60 in taxes (15 percent) on the payment.

What is the source, U.S. or foreign, of the dividend 3D receives on the stock?

Answer: Foreign source. The source of dividend income depends on the residence of the payor of the dividend. Scotiabank is headquartered in Toronto, Canada, and is a resident of Canada for U.S. source rule purposes.

Compensation for Services The source of compensation received for "labor or personal services" is determined by the location where the service is performed. The IRS and the courts have held that the term includes activities of employees, independent contractors, artists, entertainers, athletes, and even corporations offering "personal services" (e.g., accounting). The IRC provides a limited **commercial traveler exception,** in which personal service compensation earned by nonresidents within the United States is *not* treated as U.S. source if the individual meets the following criteria:

- The individual was present in the United States for not more than 90 days during the current taxable year;[21]
- Compensation for the services does not exceed $3,000; and
- The services are performed for a nonresident alien, foreign corporation, or foreign partnership or for the foreign office of a domestic corporation.[22]

The United States frequently modifies the limitations on length of stay and compensation through treaty agreements. In most cases, the 90-day limit is extended to 183 days, and no dollar limit is put on the amount of compensation received.

Compensation for services performed within and outside of the United States must be allocated between U.S. and foreign sources. An individual who receives compensation,

[21]For purposes of this test, a full day is considered to be any part of a day.

[22]§861(a)(3)(A)–(C).

other than compensation in the form of fringe benefits, as an employee for labor or personal services performed partly within and partly outside the United States is required to source such compensation on a *time basis.* An individual who receives compensation as an employee for labor or personal services performed partly within and partly outside the United States in the form of fringe benefits (e.g., additional amounts paid for housing or education) is required to source such compensation on a *geographic basis;* that is, determined by the employee's principal place of work.

Example 24-6

What if: Assume that for quality-control purposes Lily decided to do all the baking for her Windsor store in Detroit. Every morning a Windsor employee drives a truck to Detroit and picks up the baked goods for sale in Windsor. One of her Windsor employees, Stan Lee Cupp, made the 2-hour trip on 120 different days during 2022 (240 hours spent in the United States). 3D paid Stan a salary of C$50,000 during 2022. He worked a total of 1,920 hours during 2022. Assume the translation rate is C$1:US$0.80. How much U.S. source compensation does Stan have in 2022? Base your computation on hours worked.

Answer: $5,000 (C$50,000 × 240/1,920 × $0.80). Stan sources his salary for U.S. tax purposes based on where he performed the services. Using hours worked, Stan spent 12.5 percent of his time performing services in the United States (240/1,920).

Using only the exception found in the IRC, will Stan be subject to U.S. tax on his U.S. source wages in 2022?

Answer: Yes. Stan fails the commercial traveler exception. He is in the United States for more than 90 days during 2022.

What if: Assume Stan limits his trips to 90 days during 2022 (180 hours spent in the United States). Using only the IRC exception, will Stan be subject to U.S. tax on his U.S. source salary in 2022?

Answer: Yes. Stan still fails the commercial traveler exception. Although he is in the United States for not more than 90 days, his U.S. source salary is $3,750 (C$50,000 × 180/1,920 × $0.80), which exceeds $3,000.

As we discuss later in the chapter, the U.S.–Canada income tax treaty significantly liberalizes the commercial traveler exception, thus allowing Stan to spend more time in the United States without being taxed by the U.S. government on his U.S. source wages.

Rents and Royalties Rent has its source where the property generating the rent is located. Royalty income has its source where the intangible property or rights generating the royalty are used. Royalties include payments related to intangibles such as patents, copyrights, secret processes and formulas, goodwill, trademarks, trade brands, and franchises. An intangible is "used" in the country that protects the owner against its unauthorized use.

Example 24-7

In 2022, 3D rented its Windsor store from a Canadian owner for C$2,500 per month, for a total of C$30,000. Under the U.S.–Canada income tax treaty, 3D must withhold U.S. taxes at a 30 percent rate on rent payments that flow from the United States to Canada if the rent is U.S. source income. Will 3D have to withhold taxes on the rent payments it makes in 2022?

Answer: No. The rent is considered foreign source income because the store that is rented is located in Canada.

TAXES IN THE REAL WORLD Taxing Professional Golfers

One of the issues that the IRS has struggled with is whether to characterize fees paid to foreign professional golf and tennis players pursuant to on-course/on-court endorsement contracts (e.g., contracts that require wearing a company's logo or using its equipment) as income from royalties or income from personal services, or both. A Tax Court case dealing with a well-known professional golfer illustrates the complexities of this issue.

The first case involved Retief Goosen, a PGA tour member and winner of the 2001 U.S. Open Championship.* Mr. Goosen was a citizen of South Africa and a resident of the United Kingdom, but he spent most of his time competing in the United States and Europe.

Mr. Goosen entered into several endorsement and appearance agreements with sponsors that allowed the sponsor to use his name and likeness to advertise and promote the sponsor's products or in connection with advertising and promoting a specific tournament or event. The "on-course" endorsement agreements required him to wear or use the sponsor's products during golf tournaments, whereas the "off-course" endorsement agreements did not have this requirement.

Mr. Goosen reported all his prize money from golf tournaments and appearance fees in the United States as "effectively connected" income taxable in the United States. He characterized his endorsement fees from on-course endorsements as 50 percent royalty income and 50 percent personal services income. He sourced the personal services income from the on-course endorsement fees to the United States based on the number of days he played within the United States over the total number of days he played golf for the year. Mr. Goosen characterized his endorsement fees from the off-course endorsement agreements as 100 percent royalty income. The IRS argued that the sponsors primarily paid Mr. Goosen to perform personal services, which included playing golf and carrying or wearing the sponsors' products.

The Tax Court awarded a partial victory to both parties. The court found that Mr. Goosen's name had a value beyond his golf skills and abilities for which his sponsors paid a substantial amount of money for the right to use his name and likeness. The sponsors also valued Mr. Goosen's play at tournaments, as evidenced by the fact that the sponsors conditioned the full endorsement fee on his playing in 36 tournaments a year. The court thus held that his performance of services and the use of his name and likeness were equally important and characterized 50 percent of the endorsement fees from the on-course endorsement agreements as royalty income and 50 percent of the fees as personal services income.

The court held that Mr. Goosen's earnings from playing golf in the United States were effectively connected U.S. source income. The on-course endorsement and appearance fees and his on-course royalty income also were held to be U.S. source effectively connected income because payment depended on whether he played a specified number of tournaments. Both categories of income were taxed at U.S. tax rates.

The court held that income Mr. Goosen received from off-course endorsement agreements did not depend on whether he played in golf tournaments. Thus, the income was not effectively connected with a U.S. trade or business and was thus subject to a 30 percent withholding tax to the extent it was treated as U.S. source income.

**Retief Goosen v. Comm'r,* 136 TC No. 27 (June 9, 2011).

Gain or Loss from Sale of Real Property In general, gain or loss from the sale of real property (i.e., realty) has its source where the property is located.

Gain or Loss from Sale of Purchased Personal Property Under the general rule, gain or loss from the sale of purchased personal (nonrealty) property, including intangible assets and stock, has its source based on the seller's residence. There are many exceptions to this general rule. In particular, gross income (i.e., sales minus cost of goods sold) from the sale of purchased inventory is sourced where title passes. Title is deemed to pass at the time when, and the place where, the seller's rights, title, and interest in the property are transferred to the buyer.

Gain or Loss from Sale of Manufactured Inventory Gain or loss from the sale of manufactured inventory has its source based on the physical location of the assets used to produce the inventory.

Source-of-Deduction Rules

After determining the source of gross income as being from U.S. or foreign sources, a taxpayer may be required to **allocate** and **apportion** allowable deductions to gross income from each geographical source to compute taxable income from U.S. and foreign sources. For a U.S. taxpayer, this allocation and apportionment process identifies the foreign source deductions that are subtracted from foreign source gross income in computing foreign source taxable income in the numerator of the foreign tax credit (FTC) limitation computation. A non-U.S. taxpayer with gross income that is effectively connected with a U.S. trade or business must identify the U.S. source deductions that are subtracted from U.S. gross income to compute U.S. taxable income.

U.S. and non-U.S. taxpayers can have different motivations in seeking to deduct (or not deduct) expenses from either foreign source or U.S. source gross income. A U.S. taxpayer seeking to maximize the foreign tax credit limitation will want to allocate as few deductions to foreign source gross income as possible, the goal being to make the ratio of foreign source taxable income to taxable income from all sources as close to 100 percent as possible (or whatever ratio is needed to absorb any excess credits). Non-U.S. taxpayers operating in a low-tax-rate country (i.e., a tax rate less than the U.S. rate) have a tax incentive to allocate as many deductions to U.S. source income as possible to minimize their U.S. tax liability. Non-U.S. taxpayers operating in a high-tax-rate country (i.e., a tax rate greater than the U.S. rate) have a worldwide tax incentive to allocate as many deductions to foreign source income as possible to minimize their worldwide tax liability.

ETHICS

International Contractors, Inc., has been hired by the U.S. government to build roads and bridges in Spartania, a country with which the United States recently signed a treaty. To facilitate the issuance of visas and licenses to begin construction, an official from the Spartanian government asked for 100 "facilitating payments" (also known as "grease payments") of $5,000 each from the company. These payments were customary in Spartania and did not violate Spartanian law. The company intended to expense the $500,000 payment in its financial statements. It was not clear if these payments violated the Foreign Corrupt Practices Act. To avoid IRS and possible Department of Justice scrutiny, the company's tax director suggested that the payment be described as "taxes and licenses" on the tax return (line 17 of Form 1120) without further details. What do you think of the tax director's advice? What tax and other consequences might result from taking this advice?

General Principles of Allocation and Apportionment The IRC provides very broad language in describing how to allocate deductions to U.S. and foreign source gross income. The regulations attempt to match deductions with the gross income such deductions were incurred to produce.[23] Matching usually is done based on the "factual relationship" of the deduction to gross income. Deductions that can be directly associated with a particular item of income (e.g., machine depreciation with manufacturing gross profit) are referred to as **definitely related deductions.** Deductions not directly associated with a particular item of gross income (e.g., medical expenses, property taxes, standard deduction) are referred to as **not definitely related deductions** and are allocated to all gross income.

[23]Reg. §1.861-8 provides the general rules for allocating and apportioning deductions to U.S. and foreign source gross income.

The regulations require the taxpayer to first allocate (i.e., associate) deductions to the class or classes of gross income such deductions were incurred to produce. The taxpayer then apportions the deductions between, in most cases, foreign source and U.S. source gross income. The regulations allow the taxpayer to apportion deductions using a method that reflects the factual relationship between the deduction and the grouping of gross income. Examples include units sold, gross sales or receipts, and gross income.

Example 24-8

Return to the facts in Example 24-3. Lily's store in Windsor reported taxable income on its Canadian operations of C$50,000 for 2022. For U.S. tax purposes, foreign source taxable income was $40,000 (C$50,000 × 0.80). 3D paid a combined national and provincial income tax of C$9,100 ($7,280) on its taxable income (at a tax rate of 18.2 percent). The company reported the $40,000 taxable income on its U.S. corporate income tax return along with $160,000 of taxable income from its Detroit operations. 3D's U.S. income tax on $200,000 of taxable income is $42,000 before any credit for the income taxes paid to Canada.

Included in the computation of taxable income was a deduction of $50,000 for advertising that 3D incurred to promote its stores in Detroit and Windsor. 3D elected to apportion the advertising deduction based on sales. For 2022, Detroit sales were $400,000 and Windsor sales were C$125,000 ($100,000). How much of the $50,000 advertising deduction does 3D apportion to its foreign source taxable income for FTC purposes?

Answer: $10,000, computed as $100,000/$500,000 × $50,000,

where:

$100,000 = Canadian sales

$500,000 = Total sales

$50,000 = Advertising deduction

Using the above facts, what is the foreign tax credit limitation that applies to 3D's Canadian income taxes for 2022?

Answer: $6,300, computed as ($40,000 – $10,000)/$200,000 × $42,000,

where:

$40,000 = Foreign source taxable income ***before*** apportionment of any advertising deduction

$10,000 = Apportioned advertising deduction

$200,000 = Taxable income from all sources

$42,000 = Pre-credit U.S. tax on taxable income from all sources

Apportioning some of the advertising deduction to the numerator of 3D's FTC limitation ratio reduces the amount of foreign income taxes that are creditable in 2022. 3D gets a foreign tax credit of $6,300 because the FTC limitation is less than the foreign taxes paid. 3D now has a foreign tax credit carryforward of $980 ($7,280 – $6,300).

Special Apportionment Rules Special apportionment rules apply to nine categories of deductions, most notably interest expense, research and experimentation, state and local income taxes, losses on property disposition, and charitable contributions.[24] These special apportionment rules are very complicated, and the details are beyond the scope of this text. However, the basic rules for apportioning interest expense and research and experimentation costs are discussed below.

[24]The other deductions are stewardship expenses attributable to dividends received, supportive expenses, net operating losses, and legal and accounting fees.

Interest expense is allocated to all gross income based on the assets that generated such income. Interest expense is apportioned based on average tax book value for the year. Assets are attributed to income based on the source and type of income they generate, have generated, or may reasonably be expected to generate. A taxpayer using the tax book value method can elect to use the alternative depreciation system (ADS)[25] on U.S. assets solely for purposes of apportioning interest expense.

Example 24-9

Expanding on the facts in Example 24-8, 3D borrowed $100,000 from Bank of America in Detroit and paid interest expense of $6,000 in 2022. 3D apportions this interest expense between U.S. and foreign source income using average tax book value. 3D's U.S. assets had an average tax book value of $250,000, and its foreign assets had an average tax book value of $50,000 in 2022. How much of the $6,000 interest deduction does 3D apportion to its foreign source taxable income for FTC purposes? Assume the limitation on business interest does not apply.

Answer: $1,000, computed as $50,000/$300,000 × $6,000,
where:

$50,000 = Average tax book value of Canadian assets
$300,000 = Total average tax book value of all of 3D's assets
$6,000 = Interest expense

Taking into account the apportioned advertising deduction and interest deduction determined in the previous example, what is the foreign tax credit limitation that applies to 3D's Canadian income taxes for 2022?

Answer: $6,090, computed as ($40,000 – $10,000 – $1,000)/$200,000 × $42,000,
where:

$40,000 = Foreign source taxable income before apportioned advertising and interest expense
$10,000 = Apportioned advertising expense
$1,000 = Apportioned interest expense
$200,000 = Taxable income from all sources
$42,000 = Pre-credit U.S. tax on taxable income from all sources

Allocation of a portion of the interest expense to the numerator of 3D's FTC limitation ratio further reduces the amount of foreign taxes that are creditable in 2022. 3D now has an excess foreign tax credit of $1,190 ($7,280 – $6,090).

Research and experimentation (R&E) expenditures must be apportioned between U.S. and foreign source income using the sales method. Under this method, taxpayers apportion 50 percent of R&E expenditures based on where the research is conducted, and they apportion the remaining 50 percent based on the proportion of U.S. and foreign sales to worldwide sales. State and local income taxes are allocated to the gross income with respect to which such state income taxes are imposed. Charitable contributions and the dividends-received deductions generally are allocated to U.S. source income. The allocation and apportionment rules of these deductions are complex and beyond the scope of this text.

The foreign tax credit limitation is computed on Form 1118 (corporations) or Form 1116 (individuals). Exhibit 24-1 presents a completed Form 1118 for the cumulative facts in Examples 24-3, 24-8, and 24-9. This is a 2021 form because the 2022 form was not available when we went to press.

[25]This alternative approach to calculating tax depreciation is more fully described in the Property Acquisition and Cost Recovery chapter.

EXHIBIT 24-1 Form 1118: Foreign Tax Credit—Corporations, Schedules A, B, and H for 3D Corporation (cumulative facts from Examples 24-3, 24-8, and 24-9)

Form **1118** (Rev. December 2021) Department of the Treasury Internal Revenue Service

Foreign Tax Credit—Corporations

▶ Attach to the corporation's tax return.

▶ Go to *www.irs.gov/Form1118* for instructions and the latest information.

OMB No. 1545-0123

Attachment Sequence No. **118**

For calendar year 20 , or other tax year beginning , 20 , and ending , 20

Name of corporation: 3D Corporation

Employer identification number

Use a separate Form 1118 for each applicable category of income (see instructions).

a Separate Category (Enter code—see instructions.) . . . ▶ FB

b If code 901j is entered on line a, enter the country code for the sanctioned country (see instructions) . . . ▶

c If one of the RBT codes is entered on line a, enter the country code for the treaty country (see instructions) . . . ▶

Schedule A **Income or (Loss) Before Adjustments** *(Report all amounts in U.S. dollars. See* **Specific Instructions.***)*

	1. EIN or Reference ID Number (see instructions)*	2. Foreign Country or U.S. Possession (enter two-letter code—use a separate line for each) (see instructions)	Gross Income or (Loss) From Sources Outside the United States: 3. Inclusions Under Sections 951(a)(1) and 951A (see instructions) (a) Exclude Gross-Up	3. (b) Gross-Up (section 78)	4. Dividends (see instructions)	5. Interest
A		CN				
B						
C						
Totals (add lines A through C) ▶						

	6. Gross Rents, Royalties, and License Fees	7. Sales	8. Gross Income From Performance of Services	9. Currency Gain	10. Currency Gain Code (see instructions)	11. Other (attach schedule)	12. Total (add columns 3(a) through 9 and 11)
A		40,000					40,000
B							
C							
Totals		40,000					40,000

	13. Allocable Deductions: (a) Dividends Received Deduction (see instructions)	(b) Deduction Allowed Under Section 250(a)(1)(A)—Foreign Derived Intangible Income	(c) Deduction Allowed Under Section 250(a)(1)(B)—Global Intangible Low-Taxed Income	Rental, Royalty, and Licensing Expenses: (d) Depreciation, Depletion, and Amortization	(e) Other Allocable Expenses	(f) Expenses Allocable to Sales Income	(g) Expenses Allocable to Gross Income From Performance of Services
A						10,000	
B							
C							
Totals						10,000	

	13. Allocable Deductions (continued): (h) Currency Loss	(i) Currency Loss Code (see instructions)	(j) Other Allocable Deductions (attach schedule) (see instructions)	(k) Total Allocable Deductions (add columns 13(a) through 13(h) and 13(j))	14. Apportioned Share of Deductions (enter amount from applicable line of Schedule H, Part I, column (b), and Schedule H, Part II, column (d))	15. Net Operating Loss Deduction	16. Total Deductions (add columns 13(k) through 15)	17. Total Income or (Loss) Before Adjustments (subtract column 16 from column 12)
A				10,000	1,000		11,000	29,000
B								
C								
Totals				10,000	1,000		11,000	29,000

*For section 863(b) income, NOLs, income from RICs, high-taxed income, section 951A, and reattribution of income by reason of disregarded payments, use a single line (see instructions). Also, for reporting branches that are QBUs, use a separate line for each such branch.

For Paperwork Reduction Act Notice, see separate instructions. Cat. No. 10900F Form **1118** (Rev. 12-2021)

Source: irs.gov.

EXHIBIT 24-1 Form 1118: Foreign Tax Credit—Corporations, Schedules A, B, and H for 3D Corporation (cumulative facts from Examples 24-3, 24-8, and 24-9) *(continued)*

Form 1118 (Rev. 12-2021) Page 2

Schedule B **Foreign Tax Credit** *(Report all foreign tax amounts in U.S. dollars.)*

Part I—Foreign Taxes Paid, Accrued, and Deemed Paid *(see instructions)*

	1. Credit Is Claimed for Taxes (check one): ☑ Paid ☐ Accrued		2. Foreign Taxes Paid or Accrued (attach schedule showing amounts in foreign currency and conversion rate(s) used) — Tax Withheld at Source on:					
	Date Paid	Date Accrued	(a) Dividends	(b) Distributions of Previously Taxed Earnings and Profits	(c) Branch Remittances	(d) Interest	(e) Rents, Royalties, and License Fees	(f) Other
A	various							
B								
C								
Totals (add lines A through C) ▶								

	2. Foreign Taxes Paid or Accrued (attach schedule showing amounts in foreign currency and conversion rate(s) used) *(continued)* — Other Foreign Taxes Paid or Accrued on:				
	(g) Sales	(h) Services Income	(i) Other	(j) Total Foreign Taxes Paid or Accrued (add columns 2(a) through 2(i))	3. Tax Deemed Paid (see instructions)
A	7,280			7,280	
B					
C					
Totals	7,280			7,280	

Part II—Separate Foreign Tax Credit *(Complete a* ***separate*** *Part II for* ***each*** *applicable category of income.)*

Line	Description				
1a	Total foreign taxes paid or accrued (total from Part I, column 2(j))	1a	7,280		
b	Foreign taxes paid or accrued by the corporation during prior tax years that were suspended due to the rules of section 909 and for which the related income is taken into account by the corporation during the current tax year (see instructions)	1b			
2	Total taxes deemed paid (total from Part I, column 3)	2			
3	Reductions of taxes paid, accrued, or deemed paid (enter total from Schedule G, Part I)	3	( )		
4	Taxes reclassified under high-tax kickout	4			
5	Enter the sum of any carryover of foreign taxes (from Schedule K, line 3, column (xiv), and from Schedule I, Part III, line 3) plus any carrybacks to the current tax year	5			
6	Total foreign taxes (combine lines 1a through 5)			6	7,280
7	Enter the amount from the applicable column of Schedule J, Part I, line 11 (see instructions). If Schedule J is **not** required to be completed, enter the result from the "Totals" line of column 17 of the applicable Schedule A			7	29,000
8a	Total taxable income from all sources (enter taxable income from the corporation's tax return)	8a	200,000		
b	Adjustments to line 8a (see instructions)	8b			
c	Subtract line 8b from line 8a			8c	200,000
9	Divide line 7 by line 8c. Enter the resulting fraction as a decimal (see instructions). If line 7 is greater than line 8c, enter 1			9	.145
10	Total U.S. income tax against which credit is allowed (regular tax liability (see section 26(b)) minus any American Samoa economic development credit)			10	42,000
11	Multiply line 9 by line 10			11	6,090
12	Increase in limitation (section 960(c))			12	
13	Credit limitation (add lines 11 and 12) (see instructions)			13	6,090
14	**Separate foreign tax credit** (enter the smaller of line 6 or line 13). Enter here and on the appropriate line of Part III ▶			14	6,090

Form **1118** (Rev. 12-2021)

Form 1118 (Rev. 12-2021) Page 3

Schedule B **Foreign Tax Credit** *(Report all foreign tax amounts in U.S. dollars.) (continued)*

Part III—Summary of Separate Credits *(Enter amounts from Part II, line 14, for* ***each*** *applicable category of income.* ***Do not*** *include taxes paid to sanctioned countries.)*

Line	Description				
1	Credit for taxes on section 951A category income	1			
2	Credit for taxes on foreign branch category income	2	6,090		
3	Credit for taxes on passive category income	3			
4	Credit for taxes on general category income	4			
5	Credit for taxes on section 901(j) category income (combine all such credits on this line)	5			
6	Credit for taxes on income re-sourced by treaty (combine all such credits on this line)	6			
7	Total (add lines 1 through 6)			7	
8	Reduction in credit for international boycott operations (see instructions)			8	
9	**Total foreign tax credit** (subtract line 8 from line 7). Enter here and on the appropriate line of the corporation's tax return ▶			9	6,090

Source: irs.gov.

EXHIBIT 24-1 **Form 1118: Foreign Tax Credit—Corporations, Schedules A, B, and H for 3D Corporation (cumulative facts from Examples 24-3, 24-8, and 24-9) *(continued)***

Form 1118 (Rev. 12-2021) Page **11**

Schedule H **Apportionment of Certain Deductions** *(Complete only once for all categories of income.) (continued)*

Part II—Interest Deductions, All Other Deductions, and Total Deductions

	(a) Average Value of Assets—Check Method Used: ☑ Tax book value ☐ Alternative tax book value		**(b)** Interest Deductions		**(c)** All Other Deductions (attach schedule) (see instructions)	**(d)** Totals (add the amounts from columns (b)(iii), (b)(iv), and (c)) **Additional note:** With respect to each applicable statutory grouping, enter the amount in column (d) of line 3a(2), 3b(2), 3c(2), 3d(2), 3e(2), or 3f(2) below in column 14 of the corresponding Schedule A.
	(i) Nonfinancial Corporations	**(ii)** Financial Corporations	**(iii)** Nonfinancial Corporations	**(iv)** Financial Corporations		
1a Totals (see instructions)	300,000		6,000			
b Amounts specifically allocable under Temporary Regulations section 1.861-10T(e)						
c Other specific allocations under Temporary Regulations section 1.861-10T						
d Assets excluded from apportionment formula						
2 Total to be apportioned (subtract the sum of lines 1b, 1c, and 1d from line 1a)	300,000		6,000			
3 Apportionment among statutory groupings (see instructions):						
a Enter code FB						
(1) Section 245A dividend	0		0			
(2) Other	50,000		1,000			
(3) Total line a	50,000		1,000			
b Enter code						
(1) Section 245A dividend						
(2) Other						
(3) Total line b						
c Enter code						
(1) Section 245A dividend						
(2) Other						
(3) Total line c						
d Enter code						
(1) Section 245A dividend						
(2) Other						
(3) Total line d						
e Enter code						
(1) Section 245A dividend						
(2) Other						
(3) Total line e						
f Enter code						
(1) Section 245A dividend						
(2) Other						
(3) Total line f						
4 **Total foreign** (add lines 3a(3), 3b(3), 3c(3), 3d(3), 3e(3), and 3f(3)) ▶	50,000		1,000			

Section 904(b)(4) Adjustments

5 Expenses Allocated and Apportioned to Foreign Source Section 245A Dividend. Enter the sum of amounts in column (d) of lines 3a(1), 3b(1), 3c(1), 3d(1), 3e(1), and 3f(1). Include this line 5 result as a negative amount on Schedule B, Part II, line 8b	5	
6 Enter expenses allocated and apportioned to U.S. source section 245A dividend. Include this line 6 amount as a negative amount on Schedule B, Part II, line 8b	6	

Form **1118** (Rev. 12-2021)

Source: irs.gov.

OPERATING ABROAD THROUGH A FOREIGN CORPORATION

The Tax Cuts and Jobs Act (TCJA of 2017) made significant changes to the taxation of foreign source income earned through a foreign corporation owned by *domestic corporations* that meet certain ownership requirements. In particular, U.S. corporations that meet the definition of a *U.S. shareholder* of such foreign corporation (i.e., owns 10 percent or more of the voting power or value of the foreign corporation) are eligible for a 100 percent dividends-received deduction (also known as a *participation exemption*) on earnings remitted by the foreign corporation that have not previously been subject to the deemed dividend rules of subpart F or GILTI (to be discussed later in the chapter).[26] Any foreign income taxes paid on income eligible for the exemption are not creditable or deductible on the U.S. shareholder's U.S. tax return.

The enactment of this deduction moves the United States toward a territorial tax system for corporations and puts the United States in line with most other countries in the taxation of foreign source active trade or business income.

[26]§§245A, 951(a), 951A(a).

Example 24-10

Assume the same facts as Example 24-3 except that Detroit Donut Depot (3D) decides to operate its Windsor operations through a wholly owned Canadian corporation rather than as a foreign branch. In 2022, the Canadian corporation reported taxable income of C$50,000 and paid a combined national and provincial income tax of C$9,100 on its taxable income. The C$50,000 is not subject to U.S. taxation because it is active trade or business income earned through a foreign corporation. In 2023, the Canadian subsidiary pays a dividend of C$10,000 to the U.S. corporation. The dividend is subject to a 5 percent withholding tax (C$500) under the U.S.–Canada treaty. How much of the dividend is subject to U.S. taxation, and are any of the foreign taxes imposed on the income distributed creditable?

Answer: $0 income is subject to U.S. taxation and $0 foreign taxes are creditable. The dividend is eligible for a 100 percent dividends-received deduction, and any Canadian taxes paid on such income are not creditable or deductible on 3D's U.S. tax return.

Foreign-Derived Intangible Income Current tax rules give U.S. C corporations that sell goods and services an incentive to export such products and services from the United States, and to hold intellectual property in the United States. For tax years beginning after December 31, 2017, gross profit derived from certain export sales or services provided to persons outside the United States, referred to as **foreign-derived intangible income (FDII),** is eligible for a tax deduction equal to 37.5 percent of FDII, which reduces the effective tax rate imposed on such income to 13.125 percent (21 percent × 62.5 percent).[27] The FDII deduction is computed on Form 8993, Section 250 Deduction for Foreign-Derived Intangible Income and Global Intangible Low-Taxed Income.

The computation of FDII is extremely complex, as are many of the international tax provisions. In general terms, the deduction applies to income from sales of property intended for foreign use or services provided to any person not located in the United States in excess of a "normal return" on U.S. assets used in the production of the product or services. A normal return is defined as 10 percent of **qualified business asset investment (QBAI).** QBAI is defined as the tax basis of depreciable property used in the production of the products sold (to both U.S. and foreign customers), assuming straight-line depreciation.

Example 24-11

Assume 3D, a Detroit-based C corporation, had $175,000 of net income (gross income less allocated deductions) from sales of baked goods to U.S. customers and $25,000 of net income from sales of baked goods to the Canadian store for sale to Canadian customers in 2022. Also assume 3D had QBAI of $300,000. What is 3D's deduction for FDII in 2022?

Answer: $7,969. 3D has net income of $170,000 in excess of 10 percent of QBAI [$200,000 – (.10 × $300,000)]. Of that amount, $21,250 ($25,000/$200,000 × $170,000) is considered FDII and eligible for the 37.5 percent deduction. The FDII deduction allowed in computing 3D's taxable income is $7,969 ($21,250 × 37.5 percent). The actual calculation is much more complex than this and is beyond the scope of this text.

TREATIES

LO 24-3

A tax treaty is a bilateral agreement between two contracting countries in which each agrees to modify its own tax laws to achieve reciprocal benefits. The general purpose of an income tax treaty is to eliminate or reduce the impact of double taxation so that residents paying taxes to one country will not have the full burden of taxes in the other country. The United States signed its first income tax treaty with France in 1939. The United States now has income tax treaties with 67 countries as of the date we went to press. Exhibit 24-2 provides a list of the countries with which the United States has

[27]§250.

EXHIBIT 24-2 Countries with Which the United States Has Income Tax Treaties

Australia	India	Philippines
Austria	Indonesia	Poland
Bangladesh	Ireland	Portugal
Barbados	Israel	Romania
Belgium	Italy	Russian Federation
Bulgaria	Jamaica	Slovak Republic
Canada	Japan	Slovenia
China, People's Republic of	Kazakhstan	South Africa
Commonwealth of Independent States[a]	Korea, Republic of	Spain
Cyprus	Latvia	Sri Lanka
Czech Republic	Lithuania	Sweden
Denmark	Luxembourg	Switzerland
Egypt	Malta	Thailand
Estonia	Mexico	Trinidad and Tobago
Finland	Morocco	Tunisia
France	Netherlands	Turkey
Germany	New Zealand	Ukraine
Greece	Norway	United Kingdom
Hungary	Pakistan	Venezuela
Iceland		

[a]Armenia, Azerbaijan, Belarus, Georgia, Kyrgyzstan, Moldova, Tajikistan, Turkmenistan, and Uzbekistan.
Source: Internal Revenue Service, "Publication 901: U.S. Tax Treaties," www.irs.gov/pub/irs-pdf/p901.pdf.

THE KEY FACTS

Treaties

- Treaties are designed to encourage cross-border trade by reducing or eliminating the double taxation of such income by the countries that are party to the treaty.
- Treaties define whether and when a resident of one country has nexus in the other country.
- Treaties reduce or eliminate the withholding tax imposed on cross-border payments such as interest, dividends, and royalties.

income tax treaties. U.S. treaties generally do not affect the U.S. taxation of U.S. citizens, residents, and domestic corporations because such taxpayers are taxed on a worldwide basis.

Treaties reduce or eliminate the tax on income earned in one contracting country by a resident of the other contracting country. For example, most U.S. treaties provide a low withholding tax rate or an exemption from tax on various types of investment income (i.e., interest, dividends, gains from sale of stock, and royalties) that otherwise would be subject to a high withholding tax.[28] For individuals, U.S. treaties often provide exemption from taxation by the host country on wages or self-employment income earned in the treaty country, provided the individual does not spend more than 183 days in that other country. U.S. businesses generally are not taxed on business profits earned in the host treaty country unless they conduct that business through a **permanent establishment.** A permanent establishment generally is a fixed place of business such as an office or factory, although employees acting as agents can create a permanent establishment. Treaties also provide "tiebreaker" rules for determining the country in which an individual will be considered a resident for treaty purposes.

Example 24-12

What if: Lily is trying to determine whether 3D would be subject to Canadian taxation under two different scenarios: (1) she opens a store in Windsor and operates it as a branch of 3D or (2) she prepares the baked goods in Detroit and ships them to Windsor-area grocery stores using the company's van. Article VII of the U.S.–Canada income tax treaty states that the business profits of a U.S. resident are taxed in Canada only if the business operates in Canada through a permanent establishment.

[28]Absent a treaty, the United States imposes a withholding tax rate of 30 percent on payments of FDAP income to nonresidents.

Article V defines a permanent establishment as including a place of management, a branch, an office, a factory, and a workshop. Under the U.S.–Canada treaty, will 3D be subject to Canadian tax on taxable income earned through its Windsor store?

Answer: Yes. A branch is defined as a permanent establishment. Canada can tax 3D's Canadian source taxable income under Article VII of the U.S.–Canada treaty.

Under the U.S.–Canada treaty, will 3D be subject to Canadian tax on taxable income earned by selling goods to grocery stores in Windsor directly?

Answer: No. 3D does not have a permanent establishment in Canada on these sales. Canada will not tax income from these sales under Article VII of the U.S.–Canada treaty.

Example 24-13

What if: Assume that for quality-control purposes Lily decided to do all the baking for her Windsor store in Detroit. Every morning a Windsor employee drives a van to Detroit and picks up the baked goods for sale in Windsor. One of her Windsor employees, Stan Lee Cupp, made the two-hour trip on 200 different days during 2022. Article IV of the U.S.–Canada income tax treaty states that, in cases where an individual is considered a resident of both countries under their respective tax laws, the individual will be considered a resident of the country in which they have a permanent home. Stan has a home only in Canada, and Canada still considers him to be a Canadian resident. Will Stan be considered a U.S. resident in 2022 applying only the substantial presence test?

Answer: Yes. Stan is physically present in the United States for more than 30 days in 2022 and satisfies the 183-day test when applying the formula [200 + (1/3 × 0) + (1/6 × 0) = 200].

Will Stan be considered a U.S. resident in 2022 under the U.S.–Canada treaty?

Answer: No. Under the tiebreaker rules in the U.S.–Canada treaty, Stan is considered to be a resident only of Canada for income tax purposes because that is where he has his permanent home. The United States can tax Stan only on income that is considered to be from U.S. sources.

Example 24-14

What if: Return to the facts in Example 24-6. Stan made the 2-hour trip from Windsor to Detroit and back on 120 different days during 2022 (240 hours). 3D paid Stan a salary of C$50,000 ($40,000) during 2022. He worked a total of 240 days (1,920 hours) during 2022. Article XV of the U.S.–Canada income tax treaty states that a Canadian resident individual earning wages in the United States will be exempt from U.S. tax on his or her U.S. source wages if the wages do not exceed $10,000 or the individual is present in the United States for no more than 183 days. Under the U.S.–Canada treaty, will Stan be subject to U.S. tax on his U.S. source compensation in 2022?

Answer: No. Stan is exempt from U.S. tax on his wages because under the apportionment rules for compensation (discussed in Example 24-6), he has only $5,000 of U.S. source compensation, computed as (240/1,920) × $40,000,

where:

240 = Number of hours worked in the United States

1,920 = Total number of hours worked

$40,000 = Total compensation in U.S. dollars

What if: Assume Stan received wages from 3D of $100,000 in 2022. Under the U.S.–Canada treaty, will Stan be subject to U.S. tax on his U.S. source compensation in 2022?

Answer: No. Even though Stan has U.S. source wages of $12,500 (240/1,920 × $100,000), Stan was in the United States for less than 184 days, and therefore he is exempt from U.S. tax on his U.S. source compensation.

LO 24-4

FOREIGN TAX CREDITS

THE KEY FACTS

Foreign Tax Credits

- Only income taxes can be claimed as a credit on a U.S. tax return.
- The current-year foreign tax credit cannot exceed the FTC limitation.
- The FTC limitation is applied to four separate categories (baskets) of foreign source income: passive, general, foreign branch, and GILTI.

The United States taxes the worldwide income of U.S. partnerships, trusts and estates, U.S. citizens, and resident aliens. U.S. corporations continue to be taxed on all income other than dividends received from foreign corporations eligible for the 100 percent dividends-received deduction (DRD). As we have discussed, U.S. persons earning foreign source income may be subject to multiple taxation on such income by the United States and the country in which the individual resides or where the income is earned. For example, a U.S. citizen who earns income in France may be subject to taxation by both governments. Without any relief from such multiple taxation, U.S. taxpayers would have little incentive to do business outside the United States.

FTC Limitation Categories of Taxable Income

Earlier in the chapter, when we discussed the foreign tax credit, we assumed that all foreign source income was from one category (foreign branch income). However, as a policy matter, the U.S. government must decide whether, and to what extent, U.S. taxpayers should segregate foreign source income subject to different tax rates and compute a separate FTC limitation for different categories of foreign source income. Since 1976, the United States has required persons claiming the foreign tax credit to segregate foreign source income by category of income. Practitioners often refer to each income category as an **FTC basket.** Historically, there were two primary categories of FTC income: **passive category income** and **general category income.**[29] Beginning in 2018, two more categories of FTC income were added: foreign branch income and **global intangible low-taxed income (GILTI).** The "basket" approach is intended to limit blending opportunities (i.e., high-tax foreign source income and low-tax foreign source income) to income that is in the same category.

Passive Category Income Passive category income generally is investment-type income that traditionally is subject to low foreign taxes, usually in the form of withholding taxes. Passive category income includes interest, dividends not eligible for the 100 percent DRD, rents, royalties, and annuities.

General Category Income Income not treated as passive category income, foreign branch income, or GILTI is defined as general category income.

Foreign Branch Income Foreign branch income generally is defined to be business profits earned through one or more unincorporated qualified business units (branches). Earlier in the chapter, we discussed and illustrated how the foreign tax credit limitation applies to foreign branch income.

GILTI Income A new category of foreign source income to be discussed later in this chapter.

Example 24-15

What if: Suppose 3D's branch operations in Windsor generated C$50,000 ($40,000) of taxable income and paid Canadian tax of C$9,250 ($7,400). The branch income meets the definition of qualified branch income for FTC purposes. In addition, 3D received a dividend of C$1,000 ($800) from its stock investment in Scotiabank. Under the U.S.–Canada treaty, Scotiabank withheld C$150 ($120) in taxes (15 percent) on the payment. The withholding tax is eligible for the foreign tax credit, and the dividend meets the definition of passive category income for FTC purposes. 3D has taxable income from all

[29]§904(d).

sources of $200,000 (including the dividend) in 2022 and a pre-credit U.S. income tax of $42,000. In computing its FTC for 2022, can 3D combine the branch income with the dividend in calculating its FTC limitation? Assume the exchange rate is C$1:$0.80.

Answer: No. The branch income and the dividend cannot be blended because they are in different income categories for FTC limitation purposes.

How much of the $7,520 ($7,400 + $120) in Canadian taxes can 3D claim as an FTC in 2022?

Answer: $7,520.

3D must compute separate FTC limitations for the branch income and the dividend, as follows:

Branch income: $40,000/$200,000 × $42,000 = $8,400

Dividend income: $800/$200,000 × $42,000 = $168

3D can take a credit for the full amount of the withholding tax on the dividend and a full credit for taxes paid on the branch income because the foreign taxes associated with each FTC basket are less than the FTC limitation for each basket.

What if: Assume the branch income is subject to Canadian income tax of C$13,240 ($10,600). How much of the $10,720 in Canadian taxes can 3D take as a credit in 2022?

Answer: $8,520, computed as $8,400 + $120.

The FTC for the branch income is now limited to $8,400, as computed previously. 3D can carry forward the excess FTC of $2,200 ($10,600 – $8,400) for 10 years.

Creditable Foreign Taxes

The foreign tax credit is available only for foreign taxes the United States considers to be *income* taxes in the U.S. sense. In general, a tax resembles the U.S. concept of an income tax when it is applied to net income.[30] Taxes that do not qualify as income taxes include property taxes, customs taxes, sales taxes, and value-added taxes. U.S. taxpayers can deduct noncreditable foreign taxes. On an annual basis, U.S. taxpayers also can elect to deduct foreign income taxes in lieu of claiming the credit. This election might make sense if the taxpayer does not expect to be able to use the credit during the 10-year carryforward period. Foreign taxes generally are translated into U.S. dollars using the average exchange rate for the year, regardless of when the tax is actually paid.[31] U.S. taxpayers can elect to translate withholding taxes using the exchange rate on the day the tax is withheld. This election makes translation of the withholding tax consistent with the translation of the payment (e.g., dividend, interest, royalty) into U.S. dollars, which is done using the exchange rate on the date of payment, which is referred to as the **spot rate.**

Direct Taxes Direct foreign income taxes are income taxes paid directly by the U.S. taxpayer.[32] For example, the income taxes 3D pays to the Canadian government on its branch operations in Windsor are direct foreign income taxes and are eligible for a credit on the company's U.S. tax return.

In Lieu of Taxes Taxes that do not qualify as income taxes can still be creditable if they are imposed in lieu of an income tax.[33] The most common example is a withholding tax imposed on gross income such as dividends, interest, and royalties. These taxes technically do not meet the definition of an income tax because they are imposed on gross, rather than net, income. Governments impose these taxes for administrative purposes in lieu of requiring the recipient of the income to file an income tax return.

[30]There has been much litigation and many IRS rulings over whether a tax paid to another country qualifies as an income tax in the U.S. sense. See Reg. §1.901-2(a)(1) for the definition of a tax "in the U.S. sense."

[31]§986(a)(1)(A).

[32]Direct foreign income taxes are creditable under §901.

[33]In lieu of income taxes are creditable under §903.

LO 24-5

PLANNING FOR INTERNATIONAL OPERATIONS

The organizational form through which a U.S. person does business or invests outside the United States affects the timing and scope of U.S. taxation of foreign source income or loss reported by the business or investment. U.S. corporations conducting international operations directly (e.g., through a branch) or through a flow-through entity (such as a partnership) are subject to U.S. tax or receive a U.S. tax benefit currently on income or loss from those operations. Foreign source income earned by a foreign corporation owned by U.S. persons (e.g., a Canadian subsidiary of a U.S. corporation) generally is not subject to U.S. taxation until such income is repatriated to the U.S. shareholder as interest, rent, royalty, or a management fee (i.e., U.S. taxation of such income is deferred to a future period). Dividends paid to domestic corporations from 10-percent-or-more-owned foreign corporations are exempt from U.S. taxation because they are eligible for a 100 percent DRD.

The organizational form chosen can help a U.S. person reduce worldwide taxation by:

- Exempting from U.S. taxation income not subject to the subpart F or GILTI deemed dividend rules.
- Reducing foreign taxes in high-tax jurisdictions through tax-deductible payments (e.g., rent, interest, royalties, and management fees) to lower-tax jurisdictions.
- Taking advantage of tax incentives provided by host jurisdictions (e.g., a tax holiday on profits for a specified time period).
- Using transfer pricing to shift profits from a high-tax jurisdiction to a low-tax jurisdiction.
- Taking advantage of tax treaties to reduce withholding taxes on cross-border payments.

Hybrid entities such as limited liability companies can provide the U.S. investor with the legal advantages of the corporate form (i.e., limited liability, continuity of life, transferability of interests) and the tax advantages of the partnership or branch form (e.g., flow-through of losses and flow-through of foreign taxes to individual investors).

Each organizational form offers a U.S. person investing abroad with advantages and disadvantages. Most U.S. businesses operate abroad through either a subsidiary or hybrid entity. Corporation status provides the U.S. investor with protection against liabilities of the subsidiary, entitles the subsidiary to treaty benefits in its dealings outside the country of incorporation, and generally insulates the subsidiary's business income from U.S. taxation until such income is repatriated back to the United States. Conversely, losses incurred in the subsidiary are not currently deductible on the investor's U.S. tax return.

THE KEY FACTS

Organizational Forms for Conducting International Operations

- A U.S. taxpayer doing business outside the United States can choose between a branch, partnership, corporation, or hybrid entity.
- A hybrid entity is an entity that is treated as a flow-through entity for U.S. tax purposes and a corporation for foreign tax purposes (or vice versa).
- A U.S. taxpayer elects the U.S. tax status of a hybrid entity by checking the box on Form 8832.
- "Per se" entities are not eligible for the check-the-box election.

Check-the-Box Hybrid Entities

Through regulations, the U.S. Treasury allows U.S. taxpayers to elect the *U.S. tax status* of eligible entities by checking the box on Form 8832, Entity Classification Election. Where the U.S. person owns 100 percent of the entity, that person can choose corporation status or branch status; the latter often is referred to as a **disregarded entity** because it is disregarded for U.S. tax purposes. Where more than one U.S. person owns the entity, the taxpayers can choose corporation status or partnership status. Such an entity is referred to as a hybrid entity. A multiple-person-owned hybrid entity for which corporation status is elected is referred to as a **reverse hybrid entity.** Certain designated "per se" foreign entities are not eligible for this elective treatment. These ineligible entities tend to be entities that can be publicly traded in their host countries (e.g., a German A.G., Dutch N.V., U.K. PLC, Spanish S.A., or Canadian corporation). The entire list is printed in the Instructions to Form 8832. In Canada, a

U.S. corporation or individual must operate through an unlimited liability company (ULC) organized under the laws of Nova Scotia, Alberta, or British Columbia to achieve the benefits of operating through a hybrid entity.

Hybrid entities offer U.S. investors much flexibility in avoiding the U.S. anti-deferral rules found in subpart F, which we discuss in the next section. However, there are drawbacks to operating through a hybrid entity. In particular, a hybrid entity organized outside the United States may not be eligible for treaty benefits because it is not recognized as a resident of the United States by the host country. For example, the U.S.–Canada treaty does not extend treaty benefits to distributions from a ULC to its U.S. investors. Distributions from a Nova Scotia ULC to its U.S. parent company in the form of dividends or royalties will be subject to a 25 percent withholding tax instead of a 5 percent or 10 percent withholding tax, respectively, under the U.S.–Canada treaty. Exhibit 24-3 lists the advantages and disadvantages of operating outside the United States through different organizational forms.

EXHIBIT 24-3 Advantages and Disadvantages of Operating Outside the United States in Different Organizational Forms

Branch

Advantages

- Foreign losses are currently deductible on the U.S. tax return.
- Foreign taxes imposed on income earned through the branch are eligible for the direct foreign tax credit.
- A branch qualifies as a permanent establishment and is eligible for treaty benefits.

Disadvantages

- Profits are subject to immediate U.S. taxation.
- The U.S. corporation must have 100 percent control over its international operations (joint ventures are not available).

Subsidiary

Advantages

- Separate entity status insulates the U.S. parent corporation against certain types of liabilities.
- Distributions from 10-percent-or-more owned foreign corporations are eligible for a 100 percent DRD when distributed as a dividend.
- Certain payments (e.g., management fees, royalties) made to the U.S. parent corporation may be deductible in the host country only if the payor is a corporation.

Disadvantages

- Losses are not deductible on the U.S. tax return for tax purposes.
- Certain foreign source income may be subject to the subpart F and GILTI rules, which increase the administrative costs of operating as a subsidiary.

Hybrid Entity Treated as a Flow-Through Entity

Advantages

- Foreign losses are currently deductible on the U.S. tax return.
- Foreign taxes imposed on income earned through the hybrid entity are eligible for the direct foreign tax credit.
- The U.S. corporation can operate as a joint venture.
- Certain payments (e.g., management fees, royalties, interest) made to the U.S. parent corporation are deductible in the foreign jurisdiction.

Disadvantages

- Profits are subject to immediate U.S. taxation.
- Dividend, interest, and royalty payments to the United States are not eligible for reduced treaty withholding taxes.

Example 24-16

Lily expects her Canadian operations to be profitable for the foreseeable future. She has plans to expand her operations throughout the province of Ontario and hopefully throughout all of Canada. Lily is trying to decide whether she should change the organizational form of her Canadian operations from a branch to a corporation or perhaps a hybrid entity. Can Lily organize her Canadian operations as a hybrid entity in Ontario for U.S. tax purposes?

Answer: No. Hybrid entities (unlimited liability companies) in Canada can be organized only in the provinces of Nova Scotia, Alberta, and British Columbia.

What are the primary income tax reasons for organizing the Canadian operations as a corporation for U.S. tax purposes?

Answer: There are several. Operating as a corporation allows for exemption from U.S. taxation on income earned by the Canadian operations when it is distributed to 3D as a dividend. In addition, 3D can loan money or lease its trademarks to the Canadian corporation and transfer income from Canada to the United States in the form of tax-deductible interest expense or royalty payments.

Are there any compelling nontax reasons for organizing the Canadian operations as a corporation for U.S. tax purposes?

Answer: Yes. Corporate form limits 3D's liability in Canada to its Canadian assets. In addition, operating as a corporation allows the company to hold itself out as a Canadian business to its customers and borrow money directly from Canadian banks.

When drawing an organizational chart of a multinational company, we often designate the different organizational forms with symbols. Exhibit 24-4 shows the symbols for each of the common organizational forms U.S. taxpayers use to do business outside the United States and their tax status for U.S. tax purposes (we will refer back to this exhibit in Exhibit 24-5).

EXHIBIT 24-4 Symbols for Different Organizational Forms and Their U.S. Tax Status

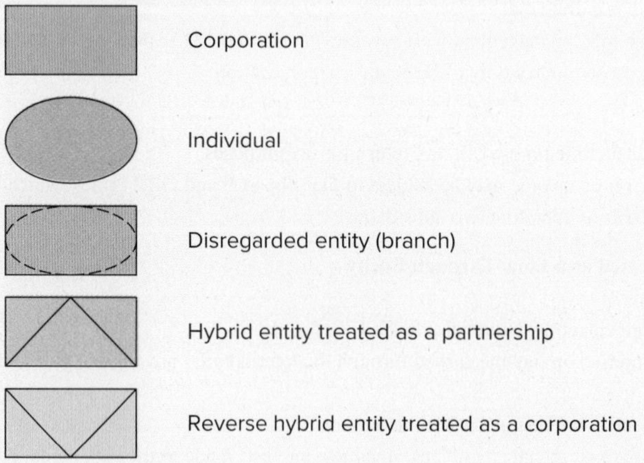

LO 24-6

U.S. ANTI-DEFERRAL RULES

Deferral of U.S. taxation on all foreign source income earned through a foreign subsidiary would invite tax planning strategies that shift income to low-tax countries to minimize worldwide taxation. U.S. individuals and corporations could transfer investment assets to subsidiaries located in low- or no-tax countries, called **tax havens,** and earn low-tax or tax-exempt income until such time as the money was repatriated to the United States.

The United States has debated whether to allow full deferral on all foreign earnings since 1937, when the U.S. government enacted its first "anti-deferral" rules applying to foreign personal holding companies. Congress, with urging from President Kennedy, enacted more expansive anti-deferral rules in subpart F of subchapter N of the IRC in 1962.[34]

In a nutshell, subpart F requires certain *U.S. shareholders* in a **controlled foreign corporation (CFC)** to include in their gross income their pro rata share of specified categories of "tainted" income earned by the CFC during the current year—**subpart F income** and global intangible low-taxed income (GILTI)—regardless of whether such income is repatriated as a dividend (i.e., the income is treated as if it were paid out to the shareholders as a deemed dividend at the end of the CFC's taxable year). The deemed dividend is translated into U.S. dollars using the average exchange rate for the year. The technical rules that determine the amount of the deemed dividend to be included in income are among the most complex provisions in the IRC.

THE KEY FACTS

U.S. Anti-Deferral Rules

- Income described in subpart F of subchapter N of the IRC defines income that is not eligible for deferral from U.S. taxation when earned by a foreign corporation.
- Subpart F income generally includes foreign personal holding company income and foreign base company sales income.
- Subpart F applies only to U.S. shareholders of a CFC.
- *De minimis* and full inclusion rules apply to exclude or increase the amount of a CFC's income subject to the deemed dividend regime of subpart F.
- In addition to subpart F income, U.S. shareholders of a CFC must also include their share of GILTI in their gross income.

Definition of a Controlled Foreign Corporation

A controlled foreign corporation (CFC) is defined as any foreign corporation in which U.S. shareholders collectively own more than 50 percent of the total combined voting power of all classes of stock entitled to vote or the total value of the corporation's stock on any day during the CFC's tax year.[35] For purposes of subpart F, a U.S. shareholder is any U.S. person who owns or is deemed to own 10 percent or more of the voting power or value of the corporation's stock.[36] The term **United States person** means a citizen or resident of the United States, a domestic partnership, a domestic corporation, or any U.S. estate or trust, but it excludes certain residents of U.S. possessions.

Indirect (constructive) ownership rules are used in the calculation of both the 50 percent test for determining CFC status and the 10 percent test for determining who is a U.S. shareholder.[37] These rules are similar to the indirect ownership rules found in §318 (see the Corporate Taxation: Nonliquidating Distributions chapter) and include family attribution (spouse, children, grandchildren, and parents), entity-to-owner attribution, and owner-to-entity attribution. A detailed discussion of the other attribution rules is beyond the scope of this chapter.

Example 24-17

What if: Assume Lily decided to partner with a Canadian investor, Maurice Richard, to expand her operations into Quebec through a Canadian corporation to be called Quebec Doughnut Depot (QDD). As part of the creation of QDD, Maurice contributed enough cash to the corporation to become a 50 percent shareholder in the corporation, with Lily owning the remaining 50 percent. Will QDD be a controlled foreign corporation (CFC) for U.S. tax purposes?

Answer: No. Lily is the only U.S. person who qualifies as a U.S. shareholder for purposes of determining whether QDD is a CFC for U.S. tax purposes. Because Lily owns only 50 percent of QDD (not *more than* 50 percent), the corporation is not considered a CFC.

What if: Suppose Lily organized QDD with her spouse, Red, and Maurice, with each owning one-third of the company's stock. Will QDD be a CFC for U.S. tax purposes?

(continued on page 24-26)

[34]§§951–965.

[35]§957(a).

[36]§951(b).

[37]§958(b).

Answer: Yes. Lily and Red are both U.S. persons who qualify as U.S. shareholders for purposes of determining whether QDD is a CFC for U.S. tax purposes (each owns at least 10 percent of the QDD stock). Because they collectively own more than 50 percent of QDD, the corporation is a CFC.

What if: Suppose Lily organized QDD with her spouse, Red, and Maurice, with Lily owning 49 percent, Red owning 2 percent, and Maurice owning 49 percent of the company's stock. Will QDD be a CFC for U.S. tax purposes?

Answer: Yes. Lily is deemed to own Red's 2 percent stock interest in QDD under the family attribution rules, making her a U.S. shareholder owning 51 percent of QDD's stock.

Definition of Subpart F Income

Subpart F income generally can be characterized as low-taxed passive income or as portable income earned by a CFC. Passive income, otherwise referred to as **foreign personal holding company income,** includes interest, dividends, rents, royalties, annuities, gains from the sale of certain foreign property, foreign currency exchange rate gains, net income from certain commodities transactions, and income equivalent to interest. There are complex exceptions involving payments between CFCs in the same country, export financing interest, and rents and royalties derived in the active conduct of a trade or business. Subpart F income does not include dividends, interest, rents, and royalties received by one CFC from a related CFC to the extent the payment is attributable to non–subpart F income of the payor. That is, the taxpayer "looks through" the payment to the income from which it was paid.

Example 24-18

What if: Assume that 3D organized its Windsor operations as a wholly owned Canadian subsidiary, Canadian Doughnut Depot Company (CDD). Now suppose CDD reported taxable income from its bakery operations of C$75,000 in 2022. CDD also purchased 1,000 shares of stock (less than 1 percent) in Thorntons PLC, a United Kingdom corporation that makes fine chocolate. During 2022, CDD received dividends of £1,000, which translated into C$1,500.[38] Thorntons withheld £100 (C$150) of U.K. taxes on the payment (a 10 percent withholding tax under the U.K.–Canada treaty). Does the dividend from Thorntons to CDD constitute subpart F income to 3D in 2022?

Answer: Yes. Dividends from investments by a CFC in a non-CFC are considered foreign personal holding company income under subpart F.

Also included in subpart F income is **foreign base company sales income,** which is defined as income derived by a CFC from the sale or purchase of personal property (e.g., inventory) to or from a related person (a U.S. shareholder owning more than 50 percent of the CFC or a corporation that is 50-percent-or-more owned by the CFC) when the property is manufactured and sold outside the CFC's country of incorporation.[39] Similar rules apply to foreign base company services income.

Together, a CFC's foreign personal holding company income, foreign base company sales income, and foreign base company services income are defined as a CFC's **foreign base company income.** For most CFCs, foreign base company income represents the largest single category of subpart F income.

This category of subpart F income was included because many countries offer incentives to multinational corporations to locate holding companies or sales companies within their borders by imposing no or a low tax on investment income or export sales. These companies are referred to as base companies because they operate primarily as profit centers and are located in a different country than where the economic activity (i.e., manufacture, sales, or service) takes place.

[38]The currency of the United Kingdom is the pound sterling, abbreviated £.

[39]§954(d).

Without any anti-deferral rules, a U.S. multinational corporation could shift profits to a foreign base company by selling goods to the base company at an artificially low transfer price. The base company could then resell the goods at a higher price to the ultimate customer in a different country. The profit earned by the base company would be subject to the lower (or no) tax imposed by the tax haven country. The base company thus would become a depository for the multinational company's excess funds, which could be invested in an active business or in passive investment assets outside the United States.

Example 24-19

What if: Assume in 2022 that 3D set up a corporation in the Cayman Islands through which it intended to transfer its products from the United States to its operations in Canada. Under this plan, 3D would "sell" its products, made in the United States, to the subsidiary in the Cayman Islands at a low transfer price, after which the Cayman Islands subsidiary would resell the products to CDD at a high transfer price. The goal would be to locate as much profit as possible in a low-tax country (the Cayman Islands has no corporate income tax). Will profit from the sale of goods from the Cayman Islands subsidiary to CDD constitute subpart F income to 3D in 2022?

Answer: Yes. The Cayman Islands profit is considered foreign base company sales income under subpart F because the goods are manufactured outside the Cayman Islands by a related person (3D) and sold outside the Cayman Islands. 3D will be treated as having received a deemed dividend equal to the profit from the Cayman Islands subsidiary.

Several exceptions serve to exclude all or a portion of a CFC's subpart F income from current taxation to the U.S. shareholders. A *de minimis rule* excludes all gross income from being treated as foreign base company income if the sum of the CFC's gross foreign base company income is less than the lesser of 5 percent of gross income or $1 million. A *full inclusion rule* treats all the CFC's gross profit as foreign base company income if more than 70 percent of the CFC's gross income is foreign base company income. In addition, a taxpayer can *elect* to exclude "high-tax" subpart F income from the deemed dividend rules. High-tax subpart F income is taxed at an effective tax rate that is 90 percent or more of the highest U.S. statutory rate. For a U.S. corporation, the current rate is 18.9 percent (90% × 21%). The calculation of the effective tax rate is complex and beyond the scope of this text.

Example 24-20

Return to the facts in Example 24-18, in which CDD reported taxable income from its bakery operations of C$75,000 in 2022 and received dividends of £1,000 from Thorntons PLC, which translated into C$1,500. Assume CDD has gross income of C$125,000 in 2022. In Example 24-18, we determined that the dividend constitutes subpart F income for U.S. tax purposes. Will 3D have a deemed dividend of this subpart F income in 2022?

Answer: No. The dividend is less than the lesser of 5 percent of CDD's gross income ($6,250) or $1 million and is not subject to the deemed dividend rules under the *de minimis rule*.

Only those U.S. shareholders who own stock in the CFC on the last day in the CFC's taxable year are treated as having received their pro rata share of any subpart F deemed dividend.

The computation of the deemed dividend related to subpart F income is exceptionally complicated and requires the CFC to allocate both deductions and taxes paid to subpart F gross income. The formula for this computation can be found in worksheets in the instructions to Form 5471, Information Return of U.S. Persons with Respect to Certain Foreign Corporations. In addition, the U.S. shareholder receives a foreign tax credit for income taxes paid on the subpart F income.[40]

[40]§960.

Subpart F income of the CFC treated as a deemed dividend under subpart F becomes *previously taxed earnings and profits* and subsequently can be distributed to the shareholders without being included in the shareholder's income a second time. A foreign currency gain or loss on repatriation of such income is included in (deducted from) the shareholders' income.

Planning to Avoid Subpart F Income

U.S. multinational corporations expanding outside the United States often use hybrid entities as a tax-efficient means to avoid the subpart F rules. Tax aligning a U.S. corporation's international supply chain has become a frequent objective in international tax planning. Accomplishing this goal requires the formation of a foreign holding company (Foreign HoldCo) treated as a corporation for U.S. tax purposes (and thus eligible for deferral from U.S. taxation). The holding company owns the stock of hybrid entities set up to conduct each of the components of the company's foreign operations: financing (FinanceCo), manufacturing (OpCo), distribution (DistribCo), and intellectual property (IPCo). The holding company is strategically located in a country that lightly taxes dividend income paid by the hybrid entities. The hybrid entities also are strategically located in countries that tax the income from such operations (e.g., interest or royalties paid by the operating company to the finance company or intellectual property company) at a low tax rate.

For instance, Ireland taxes manufacturing and intellectual property income at 12.5 percent. Because these operations are conducted through hybrid entities, transactions between the entities (e.g., payments of interest, rents, or royalties from one entity to another), which otherwise would create subpart F income, are ignored for U.S. tax purposes but respected for foreign tax purposes because the hybrid entity is treated as a corporation in the country in which it is organized. This allows for the free flow of cash between foreign operations without the intrusion of the U.S. tax laws and the reduction of taxes in high-tax countries through cross-border payments that are deductible in the country in which the hybrid entity is located. Exhibit 24-5 illustrates a template for such an international operation.[41]

EXHIBIT 24-5 A Tax-Aligned International Organizational Chart (see Exhibit 24-4 for explanation of symbols)

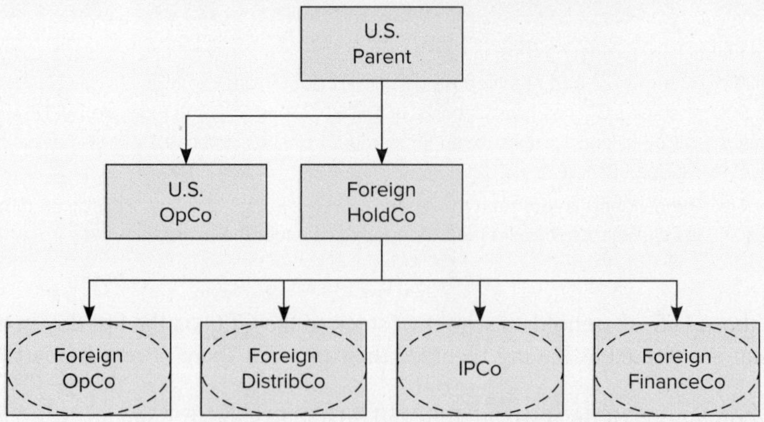

Source: U.S. Senate Committee on Homeland Security & Governmental Affairs, "Exhibits from Hearing on Offshore Profit Shifting and the U.S. Tax Code—Part 2 (Apple Inc.)," www.hsgac.senate.gov.

[41]In hearings held on May 21, 2013, Senator Carl Levin accused Apple Inc. of avoiding billions of U.S. taxes by structuring its overseas operations to route royalty income to low-tax jurisdictions. See www.hsgac.senate.gov/subcommittees/investigations/hearings/offshore-profit-shifting-and-the-us-tax-code_-part-2 for more details.

TAXES IN THE REAL WORLD Apple Inc.'s $37 Billion Repatriation Tax

As part of the transition toward a territorial tax system in the Tax Cuts and Jobs Act of 2017, Congress enacted a one-time deemed repatriation tax on unrepatriated earnings and profits of U.S. multinational companies that were previously deferred from U.S. taxation. Congress enacted this deemed repatriation tax to prevent earnings that had been deferred from U.S. taxation under the previous tax rules to avoid permanent exemption from U.S. taxation under the new 100 percent DRD rules. The repatriation tax is calculated as 15.5 percent times the component of earnings that is considered cash and cash equivalents and 8 percent times the component of earnings that is considered "illiquid" (for example, a building). The U.S. corporation determines its earnings as the greater of the earnings on November 2, 2017, or year-end (December 31, 2017, for a calendar-year corporation).

Apple Inc. had, by most estimates, unrepatriated earnings subject to the repatriation tax of more than $250 billion, almost all of which was in cash. The company announced in its Form 10-K for September 28, 2018, that its repatriation tax was $37.3 billion! The good news for Apple Inc. is that the tax law gives companies subject to the repatriation tax eight years in which to pay the tax, interest-free! Had Apple Inc. distributed its foreign earnings under the pre-TCJA rules, it would have incurred a U.S. tax of more than $75 billion, so the deemed repatriation tax saved the company a significant amount of potential future taxes—which, of course, would only have been paid if Apple Inc. actually repatriated the earnings.

Global Intangible Low-Taxed Income

The tax rules that apply to a category of foreign earnings known as Global Intangible Low-Taxed Income (GILTI) add an additonal anti-deferral regime on top of the existing subpart F income regime for U.S. shareholders in CFCs. These rules apply to a CFC's "nonroutine" GILTI. Most of the details of this tax are beyond the scope of this text. You should understand, however, that the goal of the GILTI tax is to subject CFC income (other than subpart F income) that exceeds a "normal rate of return" (10 percent of its invested foreign assets or QBAI) to treatment similar to subpart F income (deemed dividend).

All U.S. shareholders include their share of pretax GILTI in their gross income. U.S. *corporate* shareholders are then allowed a deduction equal to 50 percent of GILTI

TAXES IN THE REAL WORLD Corporate Inversions

In the years leading up to the passage of the Tax Cuts and Jobs Act in 2017, a number of large corporations headquartered in the United States such as Allergan, Mylan, and Johnson Controls changed their tax residence from the United States to tax haven countries like Ireland and the Netherlands through cross-border mergers with foreign corporations. These transactions were commonly referred to as "corporate inversions." To a great extent, the international provisions adopted as part of the TCJA were designed to deter new inversions and incentivize inverted companies to return to the United States. These international rule changes included a reduction in U.S. corporate tax rates from 35 percent to 21 percent, the creation of a new 37.5 percent deduction for foreign-derived intangible income reported in the United States, and the introduction of a new tax levied on the U.S. shareholders of controlled foreign corporations with GILTI (foreign earnings of controlled foreign corporations that exceed a 10 percent return on certain foreign assets).

Though it will take some time before the full impact of the TCJA is fully understood, it appears that it may indeed be having the intended impact on corporate location decisions. For example, Mylan and Allergan PLC, both inverted pharmaceutical companies, returned to the United States in 2020. Mylan returned by way of a merger with a subsidiary of Pfizer, Inc., and Allergan PLC through a sale to AbbVie Inc.

for 2018 through 2025, which decreases to 37.5 percent beginning in 2026. As a result, the effective tax rate on GILTI when U.S. *corporate* shareholders are allowed the 50 percent deduction is 10.5 percent for tax years prior to 2026. U.S. *corporate* shareholders are also eligible for an FTC of up to 80 percent of foreign taxes paid on their share of GILTI; however, as noted earlier in the chapter, the foreign tax credit limitation is applied separately to income in the GILTI basket and any excess foreign tax credits are not eligible to be carried back or forward. For U.S. corporate shareholders, the U.S. tax on GILTI generally will be zero if the foreign tax rate paid on the GILTI is at least 13.125 percent. In contrast, U.S. *individual* shareholders will typically be taxed on GILTI at rates as high as 40.8 percent (the 37 percent rate on ordinary income plus the 3.8 percent rate on net investment income) because they are not eligible for any deduction or FTC on their share of GILTI.[42] Many U.S. multinational companies with significant offshore intangibles (e.g., Apple, Microsoft, Alphabet, and Coca-Cola) will be subject to the new tax. Taxpayers compute their GILTI on Form 8992, U.S. Calculation of Global Intangible Low-Taxed Income, and the related deduction is computed on Form 8993, Section 250 Deduction for Foreign-Derived Intangible Income and Global Intangible Low-Taxed Income.

BASE EROSION AND PROFIT-SHIFTING INITIATIVES AROUND THE WORLD

The Organization for Economic Cooperation and Development (OECD) has embarked on a "base erosion and profit shifting" (BEPS) initiative. Its goal is to provide "governments with solutions for closing the gaps in existing international rules that allow corporate profits to 'disappear' or be artificially shifted to low/no tax environments, where little or no economic activity takes place."[43] The BEPS initiative, which began in 2013, was prompted by estimates that governments around the world were losing between $100 and $240 billion per year in tax revenues due to aggressive tax planning by multinational corporations. The OECD issued 15 "actions" in October 2015 that focused on transfer pricing, harmful tax practices, and treaty shopping and urged more transparent reporting ("country-by-country reporting" of income and taxes paid). Adoption of these actions by governments around the world will dramatically change the way multinational corporations plan their international operations and develop their information systems, as well as the way taxing agencies audit the tax returns filed by these corporations.

More recently, the OECD, issued its "Statement on a Two Pillar Solution to the Address the Tax Challenges Arising from the Digitalization of the Economy" in October 2021.[44] This action is a continuation of the BEPS initiative it had begun earlier and focuses on two specific areas that it refers to as "pillars". The first, "Pillar One" would shift tax revenues to the countries where companies sell to customers as opposed to where the companies are located, and the second, "Pillar Two", establishes a global 15 percent

[42]U.S. individual shareholders may elect under §962 to have their GILTI inclusions taxed as if they had been received by domestic corporations. This election, however, also requires that a portion of subsequent distributions of GILTI to an electing shareholder be taxed as dividend income.

[43]Organization for Economic Cooperation and Development (OECD), "Reforms to the International Tax System for Curbing Avoidance by Multinational Enterprises," May 10, 2015, www.oecd.org/ctp/oecd-presents-outputs-of-oecd-g20-beps-project-for-discussion-at-g20-finance-ministers-meeting.htm.

[44]Organization for Economic Cooperation and Development (OECD), "Statement on a Two-Pillar Solution to Address the Tax Challenges Arising from the Digitalisation of the Economy," October 8, 2021, www.oecd.org/tax/beps/statement-on-a-two-pillar-solution-to-address-the-tax-challenges-arising-from-the-digitalisation-of-the-economy-october-2021.pdf.

minimum tax rate on large corporations with profits reported in OECD countries that agree to participate.

As of the date we go to press, 137 OECD countries have signed on to this new approach to international taxation. The impact of this transformational agreement will not be immediate, however. To conform, each of these countries will be required to enact substantial changes to their current tax laws.

Consistent with the BEPS objectives, the IRC includes a **base erosion and anti-abuse tax (BEAT)** minimum tax. Under this provision, U.S. corporations with annual average gross receipts of at least $500 million for the three tax-year periods ending with the preceding tax year are required to pay a minimum tax amount of 10 percent (12.5 percent for tax years beginning after December 31, 2025) of a corporation's modified taxable income determined by adding back to regular taxable income cross-border outbound payments such as interest, royalties, and rents.[45] Because it is a minimum tax, the BEAT will only apply when the minimum tax amount exceeds a corporation's regular income tax liability. In effect, the BEAT serves as a minimum tax on outbound payments made by U.S. corporations to related foreign persons that reduce the U.S. tax base. The BEAT only applies when the "base erosion" deductions exceed 3 percent of total deductions. The details of this tax are beyond the scope of this text.

In addition, the European Union (EU) has aggressively gone after U.S. multinational companies for special arrangements with low-tax countries such as Ireland and Luxembourg that lowered the tax paid in these countries through transfer pricing. The European Commission ruled in September 2016 that Apple Inc. had received more than $14.5 billion of "illegal" tax benefits from Ireland and demanded that the Irish government recoup these lost taxes. However, the European Union's General Court announced in July 2020 that it was overturning this decision because there was not sufficient evidence to show that Apple had broken EU rules. This did not end the battle, however, because the European Commission subsequently announced it would appeal the decision to a higher court. At the date of publication, the issue remains unresolved.

CONCLUSION

In this chapter we discussed some of the important U.S. tax rules that apply to U.S. persons who expand their business operations outside the United States. As the storyline indicates, a U.S. business that wants to expand its markets outside the United States must decide on an organizational form through which to conduct its business. Establishing a physical presence in another country generally subjects the profits of the business to taxation in the host country and potentially in the United States as well.

Treaties between the United States and other countries can provide beneficial tax treatment to a U.S. company's operations, employees, and cross-border payments. Where a cross-border transaction is subject to both foreign and U.S. taxation, the United States provides relief in the form of a foreign tax credit for foreign income taxes paid on foreign income that is reported on a U.S. tax return. These credits can be reduced by the foreign tax credit limitation. By operating through a foreign corporation, a U.S. corporation can repatriate foreign source income to the United States as a dividend and avoid residual U.S. taxation by receiving a 100 percent dividends-received deduction. Certain types of income are not subject to exemption if earned through a controlled foreign corporation (CFC). The use of hybrid entities outside the United States provides U.S. companies with the ability to shift income and move cash across jurisdictions without being subject to deemed dividends under subpart F.

[45] §59A.

Summary

LO 24-1 Describe the basic U.S. framework for taxing multinational transactions and the role of the foreign tax credit limitation.

- Countries most often determine nexus by either the geographic source of the income (source-based jurisdiction) or the taxpayer's citizenship or residence (residence-based jurisdiction).
  - Under a residence-based approach, a country taxes the worldwide income of the person earning the income.
  - Under a source-based approach, a country taxes only the income earned within its boundaries.
- The U.S. government taxes citizens and residents on their worldwide income, regardless of source (residence-based jurisdiction).
  - An individual who is not a citizen will be treated as a U.S. resident for income tax purposes if they are considered a permanent resident (have a green card) or satisfy a substantial presence test.
- The U.S. government only taxes nonresidents on income that is "U.S. source" or is connected with the operation of a U.S. trade or business (source-based jurisdiction).
- To alleviate (mitigate) potential double taxation and to promote international commerce, governments often allow their residents a tax credit for foreign income taxes paid on foreign source income or exempt dividends from foreign corporations from U.S. taxation.
- Dividends remitted to U.S. corporate shareholders from 10-percent-or-more-owned foreign corporations qualify for a 100 percent dividends-received deduction and are exempt from residual U.S. taxation.

LO 24-2 Apply the U.S. source rules for common items of gross income and deductions.

- The U.S. source rules determine whether income and related deductions are from sources within or outside of the United States.
  - The U.S. source-of-income rules are important to non-U.S. persons because they limit the scope of U.S. taxation of their worldwide income.
  - For U.S. persons, the primary purpose of the U.S. source-of-income rules is to calculate foreign source taxable income in the numerator of the foreign tax credit limitation.
- The Internal Revenue Code defines eight classes of gross income from sources within the United States and eight classes of gross income from sources outside of the United States.
  - As a general rule, the taxpayer looks to the borrower's residence to determine the geographic source of interest received.
  - In general, the source of dividend income is determined by the residence of the corporation paying the dividend.
  - The source of compensation received for labor or personal services is determined by the location where the service is performed.
  - Rent has its source where the property generating the rent is located.
  - Royalty income has its source where the intangible property or the rights generating the royalty are used.
- After determining the source of gross income as being from U.S. or foreign sources, a taxpayer may be required to allocate and apportion allowable deductions to gross income from each geographical source to compute taxable income from U.S. and foreign sources.
  - The IRC provides very broad language in describing how to allocate deductions to U.S. and foreign source gross income.
  - The regulations attempt to match deductions with the gross income such deductions were incurred to produce, usually based on the "factual relationship" of the deduction to gross income.
  - Special apportionment rules apply to nine categories of deductions, most notably interest, research and experimentation, state and local income taxes, losses on property disposition, and charitable contributions.

Explain the role of income tax treaties in international tax planning. **LO 24-3**

- A tax treaty is a bilateral agreement between two contracting countries in which each agrees to modify its own tax laws to achieve reciprocal benefits.
- The general purpose of an income tax treaty is to eliminate or reduce (mitigate) the impact of double taxation so that residents paying taxes to one country will not have the full burden of taxes in the other country.
- The United States currently has income tax treaties with over sixty countries.
- Most U.S. treaties provide a low withholding tax rate or an exemption from tax on various types of investment income (interest, dividends, gains from the sale of stock, and royalties) that would otherwise be subject to a high withholding tax.

Identify creditable foreign taxes and compute the foreign tax credit limitation. **LO 24-4**

- The foreign tax credit is available only for foreign taxes the United States considers to be income taxes.
- Creditable foreign income taxes can be direct or "in lieu of" income taxes.
- Taxpayers must compute a separate FTC limitation for each category ("basket") of foreign source taxable income.
  - Passive category income generally is investment-type income that traditionally is subject to low foreign taxes (usually in the form of withholding taxes).
  - Foreign branch income is business profit earned through unincorporated operations located outside the United States.
  - GILTI is a new category of income based on returns in excess of a fixed rate of return on certain assets held by foreign corporations.
  - Income not treated as passive category income, foreign branch income, or GILTI is defined as general category income. General category income includes gross income from an active trade or business, financial services income, and shipping income.
  - A taxpayer computes the FTC limitation by multiplying the ratio of foreign source taxable income to taxable income from all sources by its pre-credit U.S. tax, as follows:

$$\frac{\text{Foreign source taxable income}}{\text{Taxable income from all sources}} \times \text{Pre-credit U.S. tax}$$

Compare the advantages and disadvantages of the different forms of doing business outside the United States. **LO 24-5**

- A U.S. person can do business outside the United States through a branch, partnership, corporation, or hybrid entity.
- A hybrid entity is an entity that is treated as a flow-through entity for U.S. tax purposes and a corporation for foreign tax purposes (or vice versa).
- A U.S. taxpayer elects the U.S. tax status of a hybrid entity by "checking the box" on Form 8832.
  - Certain designated per se foreign entities are not eligible for this elective treatment.

Explain the basic U.S. anti-deferral tax regime and identify common sources of subpart F income. **LO 24-6**

- Subpart F requires certain U.S. shareholders in a controlled foreign corporation (CFC) to include in their current gross income their pro rata share of specified categories of "tainted" income earned by the CFC during the current year (*subpart F income*).
- A controlled foreign corporation is defined as any foreign corporation in which U.S. shareholders collectively own more than 50 percent of the total combined voting power of all classes of stock entitled to vote or the total value of the corporation's stock on any day during the CFC's tax year.
  - Constructive ownership rules are used in the calculation of both the 50 percent test for determining CFC status and the 10 percent test for determining who is a U.S. shareholder.
- Subpart F income generally can be characterized as low-taxed passive income or "portable" income earned by a CFC.
  - Foreign personal holding company income includes interest, dividends, rents, royalties, and gains from the sale of certain foreign property.

- Foreign base company sales income is income derived by a CFC from the sale or purchase of personal property to (or from) a related person when the property is manufactured and sold outside the CFC's country of incorporation.
- There are several exceptions that serve to exclude all or a portion of a CFC's subpart F income from current taxation to the U.S. shareholders.
  - A *de minimis rule* excludes all gross income from being treated as foreign base company income if the sum of the CFC's gross foreign base company income is less than the lesser of 5 percent of gross income or $1 million.
  - A *full inclusion rule* treats all of the CFC's gross income as foreign base company income if more than 70 percent of the CFC's gross income is foreign base company income.
  - GILTI is high-return income earned through a foreign corporation.

KEY TERMS

allocate (24-11)
apportion (24-11)
base erosion and anti-abuse tax (BEAT) (24-31)
commercial traveler exception (24-8)
controlled foreign corporation (CFC) (24-25)
definitely related deductions (24-11)
disregarded entity (24-22)
effectively connected income (ECI) (24-3)
fixed and determinable, annual or periodic (FDAP) income (24-3)
foreign base company income (24-26)
foreign base company sales income (24-26)
foreign branch (24-2)
foreign personal holding company income (24-26)
foreign tax credit (FTC) (24-5)
foreign tax credit limitation (24-5)
foreign-derived intangible income (FDII) (24-17)
FTC basket (24-20)
general category income (24-20)
global intangible low-taxed income (GILTI) (24-20)
hybrid entity (24-22)
inbound transaction (24-2)
nexus (24-2)
nonresident alien (24-4)
not definitely related deductions (24-11)
outbound transaction (24-2)
passive category income (24-20)
permanent establishment (24-18)
qualified business asset investment (QBAI) (24-17)
residence-based jurisdiction (24-2)
resident alien (24-4)
reverse hybrid entity (24-22)
source-based jurisdiction (24-2)
spot rate (24-21)
subpart F income (24-25)
tax haven (24-25)
United States person (24-25)

DISCUSSION QUESTIONS

Discussion Questions are available in Connect®.

LO 24-1 1. Distinguish between an outbound transaction and an inbound transaction from a U.S. tax perspective.

LO 24-1 2. What are the major U.S. tax issues that apply to an inbound transaction?

LO 24-1 3. What are the major U.S. tax issues that apply to an outbound transaction?

LO 24-1 4. How does a residence-based approach to taxing worldwide income differ from a source-based approach to taxing the same income?

LO 24-1 5. Henri is a resident of the United States for U.S. tax purposes and earns $10,000 from an investment in a French company. Will Henri be subject to U.S. tax under a residence-based approach to taxation? A source-based approach?

LO 24-1 6. What are the two categories of income that can be taxed by the United States when earned by a nonresident? How does the United States tax each category of income?

LO 24-1 7. Maria is not a citizen of the United States, but she spends 180 days per year in the United States on business-related activities. Under what conditions will Maria be considered a resident of the United States for U.S. tax purposes?

8. Natasha is not a citizen of the United States, but she spends 200 days per year in the United States on business. She does not have a green card. True or False: Natasha will always be considered a resident of the United States for U.S. tax purposes because of her physical presence in the United States. Explain. LO 24-1
9. Why does the United States allow U.S. taxpayers to claim a credit against their pre-credit U.S. tax for foreign income taxes paid? LO 24-1
10. What role does the foreign tax credit limitation play in U.S. tax policy? LO 24-1
11. Why are the income source rules important to a U.S. citizen or resident? LO 24-2
12. Why are the income source rules important to a U.S. nonresident? LO 24-2
13. Carol receives $500 of dividend income from Microsoft Inc., a U.S. company. True or False: Absent any treaty provisions, Carol will be subject to U.S. tax on the dividend regardless of whether she is a resident or nonresident. Explain. LO 24-2
14. Pavel, a citizen and resident of Russia, spent 100 days in the United States working for his employer, Yukos Oil, a Russian corporation. Under what conditions will Pavel be subject to U.S. tax on the portion of his compensation earned while working in the United States? LO 24-2
15. What are the potential U.S. tax benefits from engaging in an export sale? LO 24-2
16. True or False: A taxpayer will always prefer deducting an expense against U.S. source income and not foreign source income when filing a tax return in the United States. Explain. LO 24-2
17. Distinguish between *allocation* and *apportionment* in sourcing deductions in computing the foreign tax credit limitation. LO 24-2
18. Distinguish between a *definitely related deduction* and a *not definitely related deduction* in the allocation and apportionment of deductions to foreign source taxable income. LO 24-2
19. Briefly describe the method for apportioning interest expense to foreign source taxable income in the computation of the foreign tax credit limitation. LO 24-2
20. What is the primary goal of the United States in negotiating income tax treaties with other countries? LO 24-3
21. What is a *permanent establishment,* and why is it an important part of most income tax treaties? LO 24-3
22. Why is a treaty important to a nonresident investor in U.S. stocks and bonds? LO 24-3
23. Why is a treaty important to a nonresident worker in the United States? LO 24-3
24. Why does the United States use a "basket" approach in the foreign tax credit limitation computation? LO 24-4
25. True or False: All dividend income received by a U.S. taxpayer is classified as passive category income for foreign tax credit limitation purposes. Explain. LO 24-4
26. True or False: All foreign taxes are creditable for U.S. tax purposes. Explain. LO 24-4
27. What is a hybrid entity for U.S. tax purposes? Why is a hybrid entity a popular organizational form for a U.S. company expanding its international operations? What are the potential drawbacks to using a hybrid entity? LO 24-5
28. What is a "per se" entity under the check-the-box rules? LO 24-5
29. What are the requirements for a foreign corporation to be a *controlled foreign corporation* for U.S. tax purposes? LO 24-6
30. Why does the United States not allow exclusion of all foreign source income earned by a controlled foreign corporation? LO 24-6
31. True or False: A foreign corporation owned equally by 11 U.S. individuals can never be a controlled foreign corporation. Explain. LO 24-6
32. What is foreign base company sales income? Why does the United States include this income in its definition of subpart F income? LO 24-6

LO 24-6 33. True or False: Subpart F income is always treated as a deemed dividend to the U.S. shareholders of a controlled foreign corporation. Explain.

LO 24-6 34. What is global intangible low-tax income (GILTI)? How and when is the GILTI of controlled foreign corporations taxed?

LO 24-6 35. True or False: All outbound payments from a U.S. corporation to a related foreign subsidiary are subject to the BEAT minimum tax. Explain.

PROBLEMS

Select problems are available in Connect®.

LO 24-1 36. Diya, a citizen and resident of Country A, received a $1,000 dividend from a corporation organized in Country B. Which statement best describes the taxation of this income under the two different approaches to taxing foreign income?

a) Country B will not tax this income under a residence-based jurisdiction approach but will tax this income under a source-based jurisdiction approach.

b) Country B will tax this income under a residence-based jurisdiction approach but will not tax this income under a source-based jurisdiction approach.

c) Country B will tax this income under both a residence-based jurisdiction approach and a source-based jurisdiction approach.

d) Country B will not tax this income under either a residence-based jurisdiction approach or a source-based jurisdiction approach.

LO 24-1 37. Spartan Corporation, a U.S. corporation, reported $2 million of pretax income from its business operations in Spartania, which were conducted through a foreign branch. Spartania taxes branch income at 15 percent, and the United States taxes corporate income at 21 percent.

a) If the United States provided no mechanism for mitigating double taxation, what would be the total tax (U.S. and foreign) on the $2 million of branch profits?

b) Assume the United States allows U.S. corporations to exclude foreign source income from U.S. taxation. What would be the total tax on the $2 million of branch profits?

c) Assume the United States allows U.S. corporations to claim a deduction for foreign income taxes. What would be the total tax on the $2 million of branch profits?

d) Assume the United States allows U.S. corporations to claim a credit for foreign income taxes paid on foreign source income. What would be the total tax on the $2 million of branch profits? What would be your answer if Spartania taxed branch profits at 30 percent?

LO 24-1 38. Lars is a citizen and resident of Belgium. He has a full-time job in Belgium and has lived there with his family for the past 10 years. In 2020, Lars came to the United States for the first time. The sole purpose of his trip was business. He intended to stay in the United States for only 180 days, but he ended up staying for 210 days because of unforeseen problems with his business. Lars came to the United States again on business in 2021 and stayed for 180 days. In 2022 he came back to the United States on business and stayed for 70 days. Determine if Lars meets the U.S. statutory definition of a resident alien in 2020, 2021, and 2022 under the substantial presence test.

LO 24-1 research 39. Use the facts in problem 38. If Lars meets the statutory requirements to be considered a resident of both the United States and Belgium, what criteria does the U.S.–Belgium treaty use to "break the tie" and determine Lars's country of residence? Look at Article 4 of the 2007 U.S.–Belgium income tax treaty, which you can find on the IRS website, www.irs.gov.

40. How does the U.S.–Belgium treaty define a *permanent establishment* for determining nexus? Look at Article 5 of the 2007 U.S.–Belgium income tax treaty, which you can find on the IRS website, www.irs.gov. LO 24-1 research

41. Mackinac Corporation, a U.S. corporation, reported total taxable income of $5 million. Taxable income included $1.5 million of foreign source taxable income from the company's branch operations in Canada. All of the branch income is foreign branch income. Mackinac paid Canadian income taxes of $375,000 (as translated) on its branch income. Compute Mackinac's allowable foreign tax credit. LO 24-1

42. Waco Leather Inc., a U.S. corporation, reported total taxable income of $5 million. Taxable income included $1.5 million of foreign source taxable income from the company's branch operations in Mexico. All of the branch income is foreign branch income. Waco paid Mexican income taxes of $300,000 on its branch income. Compute Waco's allowable foreign tax credit. LO 24-1

43. Valley View Inc., a U.S. corporation, formed a wholly owned Mexican corporation to conduct manufacturing and selling operations in Mexico. In its first year of operations, the Mexican corporation reported taxable income of Mex$5,000,000 and paid Mexican income tax of Mex$1,500,000 on its taxable income. In the second year of its operations, the Mexican subsidiary pays a dividend of Mex$2,000,000 to Valley View Inc. The dividend is subject to a 10 percent withholding tax (Mex$200,000) under the U.S.–Mexico treaty. Assume the currency translation rate for both years is Mex$1:US$.05. LO 24-2
    a) Assuming that Valley View Inc.'s Mexican subsidiary does not have any subpart F income or global intangible low-tax income (GILTI), how much taxable income would Valley View Inc. report in U.S. dollars from its Mexican subsidiary's first year of operations?
    b) How much of the dividend from the Mexican subsidiary is subject to U.S. taxation, and are any of the Mexican taxes imposed on the income distributed creditable in the U.S.?
    c) If Valley View Inc. only held 5 percent of the Mexican corporation stock, how much of the dividend from the Mexican corporation would be subject to U.S. taxation, and would any of the Mexican taxes imposed on the income distributed be creditable in the U.S.?

44. Petoskey Stone Inc., a U.S. corporation, received the following sources of income during the current year. Identify the source of each item as either U.S. or foreign. LO 24-2
    a) Interest income from a loan to its German subsidiary.
    b) Dividend income from Granite Corporation, a U.S. corporation.
    c) Royalty income from its Irish subsidiary for use of a trademark.
    d) Rent income from its Canadian subsidiary for its use of a warehouse located in Wisconsin.

45. Carmen SanDiego, a U.S. citizen, is employed by General Motors Corporation, a U.S. corporation. On April 1, 2022, GM relocated Carmen to its Brazilian operations for the remainder of 2022. Carmen was paid a salary of $120,000 and was employed on a 5-day-week basis. As part of her compensation package for moving to Brazil, Carmen also received a housing allowance of $25,000. Carmen's salary was earned ratably over the 12-month period. During 2022 Carmen worked 260 days, 195 of which were in Brazil and 65 of which were in Michigan. How much of Carmen's total compensation is treated as foreign source income for 2022? Why might Carmen want to maximize her foreign source income in 2022? LO 24-2

46. Sam Smith is a citizen and bona fide resident of Great Britain (United Kingdom). During the current year, Sam received the following income: LO 24-2
    - Compensation of $30 million from performing concerts in the United States.
    - Cash dividends of $10,000 from a French corporation's stock.

- Interest of $6,000 on a U.S. corporation bond.
- Interest of $2,000 on a loan made to a U.S. citizen residing in Australia.
- Gain of $80,000 on the sale of stock in a U.S. corporation.

Determine the source (U.S. or foreign) of each item of income Sam received.

Income	Source
Income from concerts	
Dividend from French corporation	
Interest on a U.S. corporation bond	
Interest of $2,000 on a loan made to a U.S. citizen residing in Australia	
Gain of $80,000 on the sale of stock in a U.S. corporation	

LO 24-2

47. Spartan Corporation, a U.S. company, manufactures green eyeshades for sale in the United States and Europe. All manufacturing activities take place in Michigan. During the current year, Spartan sold 10,000 green eyeshades to European customers at a price of $10 each. Each eyeshade costs $4 to produce. For each independent scenario, determine the source of the gross income from sale of the green eyeshades.
   a) All of Spartan's production assets are located in the United States.
   b) Half of Spartan's production assets are located outside the United States.

LO 24-2
planning

48. Falmouth Kettle Company, a U.S. corporation, sells its products in the United States and Europe. During the current year, selling, general, and administrative (SG&A) expenses included:

Personnel department	$ 500
Training department	350
President's salary	400
Sales manager's salary	200
Other general and administrative	550
Total SG&A expenses	$2,000

Falmouth had $12,000 of gross sales to U.S. customers and $3,000 of gross sales to European customers. Gross income (sales minus cost of goods sold) from domestic sales was $3,000, and gross profit from foreign sales was $1,000. Apportion Falmouth's SG&A expenses to foreign source income using the following methods:
   a) Gross sales.
   b) Gross income.
   c) If Falmouth wants to maximize its foreign tax credit limitation, which method produces the better outcome? Assume the FDII deduction does not apply.

LO 24-2
planning

49. Owl Vision Corporation (OVC) is a North Carolina corporation engaged in the manufacture and sale of contact lenses and other optical equipment. The company handles its export sales through sales branches in Belgium and Singapore. The average tax book value of OVC's assets for the year was $200 million, of which $160 million generated U.S. source income and $40 million generated foreign source income. OVC's total interest expense was $20 million. What amount of the interest expense will be apportioned to foreign source income under the tax book value method?

LO 24-2
planning

50. Riverbend Semiconductor Corporation (RSC) is an Arizona corporation engaged in the manufacture and sale of semiconductors and other computer equipment. RSC spent $3 million on research and experimentation costs, and all its research and experimentation activity was conducted in the United States. The company handles its export sales through sales branches in Ireland and Taiwan. Total foreign sales from the foreign branches were $8 million and worldwide sales were $20 million.

What amount of the total research and experimentation expense will be apportioned to foreign source income?

51. Coleen is a citizen and bona fide resident of Ireland. During the current year, she received the following income: LO 24-3 research

- Cash dividends of $2,000 from a U.S. corporation's stock.
- Interest of $1,000 on a U.S. corporation bond.
- Royalty of $100,000 from a U.S. corporation for use of a patent she developed.
- Rent of $3,000 from U.S. individuals renting her cottage in Maine.

Identify the U.S. withholding tax rate on the payment of each item of income under the U.S.–Ireland income tax treaty and cite the appropriate treaty article. You can access the 1997 U.S.–Ireland income tax treaty on the IRS website, www.irs.gov.

Income	Withholding Tax Rate	Treaty Article
Cash dividends of $2,000		
Interest of $1,000		
Royalty of $100,000		
Rent of $3,000		

52. Gameco, a U.S. corporation, operates gambling machines in the United States and abroad. Gameco conducts its operations in Europe through a Dutch B.V., which is treated as a branch for U.S. tax purposes. Gameco also licenses game machines to an unrelated company in Japan. During the current year, Gameco paid the following foreign taxes, translated into U.S. dollars at the appropriate exchange rate: LO 24-4

Foreign Taxes	Amount (in $)
National income taxes	1,000,000
City (Amsterdam) income taxes	100,000
Value-added tax	150,000
Payroll tax (employer's share of social insurance contributions)	400,000
Withholding tax on royalties received from Japan	50,000

Identify Gameco's creditable foreign taxes.

53. Sombrero Corporation, a U.S. corporation, operates through a branch in Espania. Management projects that the company's pretax income in the next taxable year will be $100,000: $80,000 from U.S. operations and $20,000 from the Espania branch. Espania taxes corporate income at a rate of 30 percent. LO 24-4 planning

a) If management's projections are accurate, what will be Sombrero's excess foreign tax credit in the next taxable year? Assume all of the income is foreign branch income.

b) Management plans to establish a second branch in Italia. Italia taxes corporate income at a rate of 10 percent. What amount of income will the branch in Italia have to generate to eliminate the excess credit generated by the branch in Espania?

54. Chapeau Company, a U.S. corporation, operates through a branch in Champagnia. The source rules used by Champagnia are identical to those used by the United States. For 2022, Chapeau has $2,000 of gross income: $1,200 from U.S. sources and $800 from sources within Champagnia. The $1,200 of U.S. source income and $700 of the foreign source income are attributable to manufacturing activities in Champagnia (foreign branch income). The remaining $100 of foreign source income is passive category interest income. Chapeau had $500 of expenses other than taxes, all of which are allocated directly to manufacturing income ($200 of which is apportioned to foreign sources). Chapeau paid $150 of income taxes to Champagnia on its manufacturing income. The interest income was subject to a 10 percent withholding tax of $10. Compute Chapeau's allowable foreign tax credit in 2022. LO 24-4

LO 24-5 research

55. Identify the "per se" companies for which a check-the-box election cannot be made for U.S. tax purposes in the countries listed below. Consult the Instructions to Form 8832, which can be found on the "Forms & Instructions" site on the IRS website, www.irs.gov.
   a) Japan
   b) Germany
   c) Netherlands
   d) United Kingdom
   e) People's Republic of China

LO 24-5 research

56. Eagle Inc., a U.S. corporation, intends to create a *Limitada* (limited liability company) in Brazil in 2022 to manufacture pitching machines. The company expects the operation to generate losses of US$2,500,000 during its first three years of operations. Eagle would like the losses to flow through to its U.S. tax return and offset its U.S. profits.
   a) Can Eagle "check the box" and treat the *Limitada* as a disregarded entity (branch) for U.S. tax purposes? Consult the Instructions to Form 8832, which can be found on the "Forms & Instructions" site on the IRS website, www.irs.gov.
   b) Assume management's projections were accurate and Eagle deducted $75,000 of branch losses on its U.S. tax return from 2022–2024. On January 1, 2025, the fair market value of the *Limitada*'s net assets exceeded Eagle's tax basis in the assets by US$5 million. What are the U.S. tax consequences of checking the box on Form 8832 and converting the *Limitada* to a corporation for U.S. tax purposes?

LO 24-6

57. Identify whether the corporations described below are controlled foreign corporations.
   a) Shetland PLC, a U.K. corporation, has two classes of stock outstanding, 75 shares of class AA stock and 25 shares of class A stock. Each class of stock has equal voting power and value. Angus owns 35 shares of class AA stock and 20 shares of class A stock. Angus is a U.S. citizen who resides in England.
   b) Mihai and Gina, both U.S. citizens, own 5 percent and 10 percent, respectively, of the voting stock and value of DaVinci S.A., an Italian corporation. Mihai and Gina are also equal partners in Roma Corporation, an Italian corporation that owns 50 percent of the DaVinci stock.
   c) Pierre, a U.S. citizen, owns 45 of the 100 shares outstanding in Vino S.A., a French corporation. Pierre's father, Pepe, owns 8 shares in Vino. Pepe also is a U.S. citizen. The remaining 47 shares are owned by non-U.S. individuals.

LO 24-6

58. USCo owns 100 percent of the following corporations: Dutch N.V., Germany A.G., Australia PLC, Japan Corporation, and Brazil S.A. During the year, the following transactions took place. Determine whether these transactions result in Subpart F income.
   a) Germany A.G. owns an office building that it leases to unrelated persons. Germany A.G. engaged an independent managing agent to manage and maintain the office building and performs no activities with respect to the property.
   b) Dutch N.V. leased office machines to unrelated persons. Dutch N.V. performed only incidental activities and incurred nominal expenses in leasing and servicing the machines. Dutch N.V. is not engaged in the manufacture or production of the machines and does not add substantial value to the machines.
   c) Dutch N.V. purchased goods manufactured in France from an unrelated contract manufacturer and sold them to Germany A.G. for consumption in Germany.
   d) Australia PLC purchased goods manufactured in Australia from an unrelated person and sold them to Japan Corporation for use in Japan.

59. USCo manufactures and markets electrical components. USCo operates outside the United States through a number of CFCs, each of which is organized in a different country. These CFCs derived the following income for the current year. Determine the amount of income that USCo must report as a deemed dividend under Subpart F in each scenario. LO 24-6

a) F1 has gross income of $5 million, including $200,000 of foreign personal holding company interest and $4.8 million of gross income from the sale of inventory that F1 manufactured at a factory located within its home country.

b) F2 has gross income of $5 million, including $4 million of foreign personal holding company interest and $1 million of gross income from the sale of inventory that F2 manufactured at a factory located within its home country.

COMPREHENSIVE PROBLEMS

Select problems are available in Connect®.

60. Spartan Corporation manufactures quidgets at its plant in Sparta, Michigan. Spartan sells its quidgets to customers in the United States, Canada, England, and Australia.

Spartan markets its products in Canada and England through branches in Toronto and London, respectively. Spartan reported total gross income on U.S. sales of $15,000,000 and total gross income on Canadian and U.K. sales of $5,000,000, split equally between the two countries. Spartan paid Canadian income taxes of $600,000 on its branch profits in Canada and U.K. income taxes of $700,000 on its branch profits in the United Kingdom. Spartan financed its Canadian operations through a $10 million capital contribution, which Spartan financed through a loan from Bank of America. During the current year, Spartan paid $600,000 in interest on the loan.

Spartan sells its quidgets to Australian customers through its wholly owned Australian subsidiary. Spartan reported gross income of $3,000,000 on sales to its subsidiary during the year. The subsidiary paid Spartan a dividend of $670,000 on December 31 (the withholding tax is 0 percent under the U.S.–Australia treaty). Spartan paid Australian income taxes of $330,000 on the income repatriated as a dividend.

a) Compute Spartan's foreign source gross income and foreign tax (direct and withholding) for the current year.

b) Assume 20 percent of the interest paid to Bank of America is allocated to the numerator of Spartan's FTC limitation calculation. Compute Spartan Corporation's FTC limitation using your calculation from part (a) and any excess FTC or excess FTC limitation (all of the foreign source income is put in the foreign branch FTC basket).

61. Windmill Corporation manufactures products in its plants in Iowa, Canada, Ireland, and Australia. Windmill conducts its operations in Canada through a 50-percent-owned joint venture, CanCo. CanCo is treated as a corporation for U.S. and Canadian tax purposes. An unrelated Canadian investor owns the remaining 50 percent. Windmill conducts its operations in Ireland through a wholly owned subsidiary, IrishCo. IrishCo is a controlled foreign corporation for U.S. tax purposes. Windmill conducts its operations in Australia through a wholly owned hybrid entity, KiwiCo. KiwiCo is treated as a branch for U.S. tax purposes and a corporation for Australian tax purposes. Windmill also owns a 5 percent interest in a Dutch corporation, TulipCo.

During 2022, Windmill reported the following foreign source income from its international operations and investments.

	CanCo	IrishCo	KiwiCo	TulipCo
Dividend income				
Amount	$45,000	$28,000		$20,000
Withholding tax	2,250	1,400		3,000
Interest income				
Amount	30,000			
Withholding tax	0	0		
Branch income				
Taxable income			$93,000	
AUS income taxes			31,000	

Note: CanCo and KiwiCo derive all of their earnings from active business operations.

a) Classify the income received by Windmill into the appropriate FTC baskets.

b) Windmill has $1,250,000 of U.S. source gross income. Windmill also incurred SG&A of $300,000 that is apportioned between U.S. and foreign source income based on the gross income in each basket. Assume KiwiCo's gross income is $200,000. Compute the FTC limitation for each basket of foreign source income.

tax forms

62. Euro Corporation, a U.S. corporation, operates through a branch in Germany. During 2022, the branch reported taxable income of $1,000,000 and paid German income taxes of $300,000. In addition, Euro received $50,000 of dividends from its 5 percent investment in the stock of Maple Leaf Company, a Canadian corporation. The dividend was subject to a withholding tax of $5,000. Euro reported U.S. taxable income from its manufacturing operations of $950,000. Total taxable income was $2,000,000. Pre-credit U.S. taxes on the taxable income were $420,000. Included in the computation of Euro's taxable income were "definitely allocable" expenses of $500,000, 50 percent of which were related to the German branch taxable income.

Complete pages 1 and 2 of Form 1118 for just the foreign branch income reported by Euro. You can use the fill-in form available on the IRS website, www.irs.gov.

research

63. USCo, a U.S. corporation, has decided to set up a headquarters subsidiary in Europe. Management has narrowed its location choice to either Spain, Ireland, or Switzerland. The company has asked you to research some of the income tax implications of setting up a corporation in these three countries. In particular, management wants to know what tax rate will be imposed on corporate income earned in the country and the withholding rates applied to interest, dividends, and royalty payments from the subsidiary to USCo.

To answer the tax rate question, consult KPMG's *Corporate Tax Rates Table 2011–2021,* which you can access at https://home.kpmg.com/xx/en/home/services/tax/tax-tools-and-resources/tax-rates-online/corporate-tax-rates-table.html. To answer the withholding tax questions, consult the treaties between the United States and Spain, Ireland, and Switzerland, which you can access at www.irs.gov (type in "treaties" as your search word).

UWorld | ROGER CPA Review

UWorld Roger CPA Review

Sample CPA Exam questions from Roger CPA Review are available in Connect as support for the topics in this text. These Multiple Choice Questions and Task-Based Simulations include expert-written explanations and solutions and provide a starting point for students to become familiar with the content and functionality of the actual CPA Exam.

chapter

25 Transfer Taxes and Wealth Planning

Learning Objectives

Upon completing this chapter, you should be able to:

LO 25-1 Describe federal transfer taxes.

LO 25-2 Calculate the federal gift tax.

LO 25-3 Compute the federal estate tax.

LO 25-4 Understand how income and transfer taxation interact to affect wealth planning.

Ekaterina Kholyavskaya/THIETVU/mangostar/123RF

Storyline Summary

Taxpayers:	Harry (he/him/his) and Bob (he/him/his) Smith, brothers, ages 63 and 69, respectively. Frank's Frozen Pizzas Inc. (FFP) is a family business organized as a C corporation.
Description:	Harry is married to his second spouse, Wilma (she/her/hers), age 38, and has a daughter, Dina (age 35, she/her/hers); a son-in-law, Steve (he/him/his); and a grandson, George (age 6, he/him/his). Bob, a widower, is recently deceased and has a son, Nate (age 28, he/him/his).
Location:	Ann Arbor, Michigan
Status:	Harry and Bob were both previously employed by FFP and they inherited the FFP shares from their father in 1990. Bob retired from FFP and subsequently died this year.
Current situation:	Harry is planning to retire as CEO of FFP. Nate is Bob's executor.

Harry and Bob Smith were brothers and owners of a small privately held corporation, Frank's Frozen Pizzas Inc. (FFP). Their father, Frank, established the business 40 years ago, and Harry and Bob each inherited half of FFP's outstanding shares upon Frank's death. At the time of Frank's death in 1990, FFP was worth about $1 million, but the business is now debt-free and has a value of $9 million. FFP's success didn't come easily. Over the years, Harry and Bob were employed as executive officers and worked long, hard hours. After the death of his spouse in 2005, Bob retired on his FFP pension. Since that time, Harry has served as CEO of FFP. Both Harry and Bob have transferred some of their FFP shares to other family members. Bob has given 20 percent of the shares in FFP to his son, Nate, and Harry has transferred a like amount to a trust established for Dina (his daughter) and George (his grandson).

Harry recently decided that he wants to retire from FFP and spend more time traveling and enjoying his family. Harry believes that Nate would like to assume responsibilities as CEO, and Dina has agreed to support Nate's decisions. Harry plans to begin an orderly transfer of his FFP stock to Dina to provide a future source of support for her and George. Besides his FFP stock, Harry has accumulated considerable personal assets to help maintain his lifestyle during retirement. Although Wilma, Harry's spouse, owns significant assets, Harry also wants to provide for Wilma's eventual support. Finally, while Harry believes taxes and lawyers are necessary evils, he wants to avoid any unnecessary fees or taxes associated with the transfer of his assets. Hence, Harry would like advice on how to make his gifts in the most tax-efficient manner possible.

(to be continued . . .)

LO 25-1

INTRODUCTION TO FEDERAL TRANSFER TAXES

In this chapter, we explain the structure of the federal transfer taxes and begins with background on transfer taxes. We then describe details of the federal gift and estate taxes and conclude with a description of wealth planning.

Beginnings

In 1916 Congress imposed an estate tax on transfers of property at death. Transfers at death are dictated by the **last will and testament** of the deceased, and such transfers are called **testamentary transfers.** The transfer tax system was expanded in 1924 to include a gift tax on lifetime transfers called **inter vivos transfers** (*inter vivos* is from the Latin meaning "during the life of"). Eventually, a generation-skipping tax was also added to prevent people from avoiding taxes by transferring assets to younger generations (making transfers to grandchildren rather than to children). Together, this trio of taxes represents one way of reducing the potential wealth society's richest families might accumulate over several generations. (Recall that neither gifts nor inheritances are included in recipients' gross income.)

Common Features of Integrated Transfer Taxes

The two primary federal transfer taxes, the gift tax and the estate tax, were originally enacted separately and operated independently. In 1976 they were combined into a *unified* transfer tax scheme that applies a progressive tax rate schedule to cumulative transfers. In other words, the gift and estate taxes now are integrated to operate in unison.

This integrated formula takes into account the cumulative effect of transfers in previous periods when calculating the tax on a transfer in a current period. Likewise, it takes lifetime transfers into account to compute the tax on assets transferred at death. As you'll see in the tax formulas, taxable transfers in prior years are added to the current-year transfers, and the tax is computed on total (cumulative) transfers. The tax on the prior-year transfers is subtracted from the total tax to avoid taxing prior-year transfers twice. This calculation ensures that the current transfers will be taxed at a marginal tax rate as high as or higher than the rate applicable to the prior-year transfers. Exhibit 25-1 presents the unified transfer tax rate schedule for estate and gift taxes that has been in effect since 2013. As presented in Exhibit 25-1, the transfer tax rate is progressive on taxable transfers up to $1 million at which point the tentative tax is $345,800. Over $1 million, the rate is a flat 40 percent.

EXHIBIT 25-1 **Unified Transfer Tax Rates***

Tax Base Equal to or Over	Not Over	Tentative Tax	Plus	of Amount Over
$ 0	$ 10,000	$ 0	18%	$ 0
10,000	20,000	1,800	20	10,000
20,000	40,000	3,800	22	20,000
40,000	60,000	8,200	24	40,000
60,000	80,000	13,000	26	60,000
80,000	100,000	18,200	28	80,000
100,000	150,000	23,800	30	100,000
150,000	250,000	38,800	32	150,000
250,000	500,000	70,800	34	250,000
500,000	750,000	155,800	37	500,000
750,000	1,000,000	248,300	39	750,000
1,000,000		345,800	40	1,000,000

THE KEY FACTS

Common Features of the Unified Transfer Taxes

- Property transfers, whether made by gift or at death, are subject to transfer tax using a progressive tax rate schedule.
- The applicable credit exempts cumulative transfers of up to $12.06 million.
- Each transfer tax allows a deduction for transfers to charities and surviving spouses (the charitable and marital deductions, respectively).

Another common feature of the integrated transfer taxes is the **applicable credit.** This credit, previously known as the *unified credit,* was enacted in 1977, and it applies to both the gift tax and the estate tax. The credit is designed to prevent the application of transfer tax to taxpayers who either would not accumulate a relatively large amount of property transfers during their lifetime and/or would not have a relatively large transfer passing to heirs upon their death. The value of cumulative taxable transfers a person can make without exceeding the applicable credit is called the **exemption equivalent** or, alternately, the *applicable exclusion amount.*

Exhibit 25-2 presents the applicable exclusion amounts for both the estate and gift taxes since 1986. Except for the period between 2004 and 2010 (inclusive), the base exclusion amount has been the same for both the estate and gift taxes. Beginning in 2011, the base amount was set at $5 million and is indexed for inflation. In 2018, Congress increased the base exclusion amount from $5 million to $10 million for the years 2018 through 2025. The base exclusion amount is scheduled to revert to $5 million in 2026.[1]

EXHIBIT 25-2 The Exemption Equivalent/Applicable Exclusion Amount

Year of Transfer	Gift Tax	Estate Tax
1986	$ 500,000	$ 500,000
1987–1997	600,000	600,000
1998	625,000	625,000
1999	650,000	650,000
2000–2001	675,000	675,000
2002–2003	1,000,000	1,000,000
2004–2005	1,000,000	1,500,000
2006–2008	1,000,000	2,000,000
2009–2010*	1,000,000	3,500,000
2011	5,000,000	5,000,000
2012	5,120,000	5,120,000
2013	5,250,000	5,250,000
2014	5,340,000	5,340,000
2015	5,430,000	5,430,000
2016	5,450,000	5,450,000
2017	5,490,000	5,490,000
2018	11,180,000	11,180,000
2019	11,400,000	11,400,000
2020	11,580,000	11,580,000
2021	11,700,000	11,700,000
2022	12,060,000	12,060,000

*The estate tax was optional for decedents dying in 2010. In lieu of the estate tax, executors could opt to have the adjusted tax basis of the assets in the gross estate carry over to the heirs of the decedent. The applicable credit and exemption are zero for taxpayers who opt out of the estate tax in 2010.

The value of the applicable credit depends on both the transfer tax rates and the exemption equivalent that apply in the year of the transfer. Because the tax rates can change over time and because the exemption equivalent changes with inflation adjustments, we can best calculate the applicable credit by tracking the exemption equivalent and converting it into the applicable credit using the *current* tax rate schedule. Consequently, in 2022, the amount of the applicable credit for a transfer made in 2011 will be $1,945,800 ($345,800 on the first million and 40 percent on the remaining four million) regardless of the amount of the actual applicable credit in 2011. In other words, the applicable credit for the current year is always calculated using the tax rate schedule for the current year.

The exemption equivalent is $12.06 million for transfers made in 2022. Under the tax rate schedule for 2022, the applicable credit would be $4,769,800. The amount is calculated

[1]If the exclusion amount at the time of a taxpayer's death is less than the cumulative exclusion amount used to reduce gift taxes in earlier periods, Reg. §20.2010-2(c) provides that the exclusion amount at the time of death governs for purposes of computing the estate tax. For example, suppose a taxpayer made taxable gifts of $9 million that were fully sheltered from gift tax by an exclusion, but the basic exclusion amount on the taxpayer's death was only $6.8 million. In this case, the taxpayer's estate tax would be computed using the $9 million exclusion amount allowed in computing the gift tax payable on the prior gift.

in three steps, as follows: (1) the tax on the first million is $345,800; (2) the tax on the next $11.06 million is calculated at 40 percent or $4.424 million; (3) the total tax is the sum of the two parts $4,424,000 + $345,800 = $4,769,800.

A third common feature of the unified tax system is the application of two deductions. Each transfer tax provides an unlimited deduction for charitable contributions and a generous **marital deduction** for transfers to a spouse. The marital deduction allows almost unfettered transfers between spouses. In contrast to the income tax where a married couple can elect to file a single joint return, both individuals are required to file separate transfer tax returns.

A final important feature of the transfer taxes is the valuation of transferred property. Property transferred via gift or at death is valued at fair market value. While fair market value is simple in concept, it is very complicated to apply. For purposes of the transfer taxes, fair market value is defined by the *willing-buyer, willing-seller rule* as follows:

> The price at which such property would change hands between a willing buyer and a willing seller, neither being under any compulsion to buy or to sell, and both having reasonable knowledge of the relevant facts.[2]

Fair market value is determined based on the facts and circumstances for each individual property. Determining value is relatively simple for properties that have an active market. For example, stocks and bonds traded on exchanges or over the counter are valued at the mean of the highest and lowest selling prices. Unfortunately, the valuation of many other properties, especially realty, is very difficult. The large number of court cases resolving contentious values testifies to the difficulties in applying the willing-buyer, willing-seller rule.

LO 25-2

THE FEDERAL GIFT TAX

The gift tax is levied on individual taxpayers for all *taxable* gifts made during a calendar year. As noted above, each *individual* who makes a gift in excess of the annual exclusion amount must file a gift tax return (Form 709) by April 15 of the following year.[3] Exhibit 25-3 presents the complete formula for the federal gift tax in two parts. In the first part, taxable gifts are calculated for each donee, and in the second, the gift tax is calculated using aggregate taxable gifts to all donees. We begin the first part by identifying transfers that constitute gifts.

EXHIBIT 25-3 The Federal Gift Tax Formula

	***Part 1:* Calculate taxable gifts for each individual donee:**
	Total Current Gifts
Minus	½ of split gifts (other half included in spouse's current gifts)
Plus	½ of split gifts by spouse
Minus	Annual exclusion ($16,000 per donee)
Minus	Marital and charitable deductions
Equals	Current Taxable Gifts
	***Part 2:* Sum taxable gifts for all donees and calculate tax:**
	Total Current Taxable Gifts
Plus	Prior taxable gifts
Equals	Cumulative taxable gifts
Times	Current tax rates
Equals	Cumulative tax
Minus	Tax at current rates on prior taxable gifts
Minus	Unused applicable credit at current rates
Equals	Gift tax payable

[2]Reg. §25.2512-1.

[3]A gift tax return reporting taxable gifts must be filed by April 15 following year-end if a taxpayer has made *any* taxable gifts during the current calendar year *or wishes to elect* gift-splitting. When taxpayers request extensions for their individual income tax returns, they also receive a six-month extension for filing their gift tax returns.

Transfers Subject to Gift Tax

The gift tax is imposed on lifetime transfers of property for less than **adequate consideration.** Typically, a gift is made in a personal context such as between family members, but the satisfaction of an obligation to support is not considered a gift. For example, tuition payments for a dependent child's education satisfy a support obligation. On the other hand, transfers motivated by affection or other personal motives, including transfers associated with marriage, are gratuitous and potentially subject to the tax. The gift tax is imposed once a gift has been completed, and this occurs when the **donor** relinquishes control of the property and the **donee** accepts the gift.[4] For example, deposits made to a joint bank account are not complete gifts because the donor (depositor) can withdraw the deposit at any time. The gift will be complete at the time the donee withdraws cash from the account.

THE KEY FACTS

Gifts Excluded from the Gift Tax

- Incomplete and revocable gifts.
- Payments for support obligations or debts.
- Contributions to political parties or candidates.
- Medical and educational expenses paid on behalf of an unrelated individual.

TAXES IN THE REAL WORLD Gifts or Compensation?

In the 1990s, Burt Kroner was in the business of credit counseling. During this period, Kroner was introduced to Haring, a "high-net-worth British citizen with residences and business interests in various non-U.S. jurisdictions." Haring invested in Kroner's credit counseling business and hired him to assist with investing in discounted privately held mortgages. Unfortunately, Kroner was prohibited from participating in these investments due to a noncompete agreement.

In 2005, Mr. Haring experienced a "liquidity event" with respect to these mortgage investments, and Kroner received a two-to-three-minute phone call from Haring to inform him of a "surprise" bank transfer. Haring's tax attorneys drafted a note stating that the transfers were gifts. The note was signed by Haring and dated January 18, 2005.

Despite not having personal contact with Haring since 2002, over the period 2005–2007 Kroner received $24.875 million in wire transfers from Haring that were coordinated by Haring's attorney. Based on the note and a call with Haring, Kroner's tax attorney advised him that the transfers were excludable from income as gifts. The IRS audited Kroner's returns and disagreed with his characterization. The dispute landed in the Tax Court.

The court stated that to qualify as a gift requires "detached and disinterested" generosity. When a donee has rendered services to a donor, a payment for the services is not a gift even if the transferor had no legal compulsion to pay the remuneration. Despite warning Kroner that Haring's intention in making the transfers was critical evidence, Haring refused to testify. Instead, Kroner relied on his testimony and Haring's note to establish the intent of the transfers.

After observing the candor, sincerity, and demeanor of the witnesses, the court found Kroner's story unconvincing. The court described the testimony as self-serving and evasive. The court noted that Haring did not draft the note and that there was no credible evidence to suggest that it came from detached and disinterested generosity.

Source: Burt Kroner v. Comm'r, TC Memo 2020-73.

In some instances, a donor may relinquish some control over transferred property but retain other powers that can influence the enjoyment or disposition of the property. If the retained powers are important, the transfer will not be a complete gift.[5] For example, a transfer of property to a trust will not be a complete gift if the grantor retains the ability to revoke the transfer. If the grantor releases the powers, then the gift will generally be complete at that time because the property is no longer subject to the donor's control. For example, a distribution of property from a revocable trust is a complete gift because the grantor no longer has the ability to revoke the distribution.

[4]Under Reg. §25.2511-2, a gift is complete only when the donor has departed with control of property so that he has no power to change the disposition of the property. If property is subject to a reserved power, the gift may be wholly or partially incomplete depending on the scope of the power. Also, if a donee refuses or disclaims a gift under §2518, the gift is incomplete.

[5]Section 2514 addresses the treatment of general powers of appointment.

Example 25-1

On July 12 of this year, Harry transferred $250,000 of FFP stock to a new trust. He gave the trustee directions to pay income to Dina for the next 20 years and then remit the remainder to Dina's son George. Harry named a bank as trustee but retained the power to revoke the trust in case he should need additional assets after retirement. Is the transfer of the stock a complete gift?

Answer: No. Harry retains sufficient control that the transfer of the stock to the trust is an incomplete gift.

What if: Suppose $11,000 of trust income was distributed to Dina at year-end. Is the transfer of the cash to Dina a complete gift?

Answer: Yes. With the payment, Harry has relinquished control over the $11,000, and, thus, it is a complete gift.

What if: Suppose Harry releases his power to revoke the trust at a time when the shares of FFP in the trust are valued at $225,000. Would this release cause the transfer of the stock to be a complete gift, and, if so, what is the amount of the gift?

Answer: Yes. By releasing his powers, Harry has relinquished control over the entire trust, and the value of the trust at that time, $225,000, would be a complete gift.

There are several important exceptions to the taxation of gifts. For example, political contributions are not gifts. Also, the payment of medical or educational expenses on behalf of another individual is not considered a gift if the payments are made directly to the health care provider or to the educational institution. To avoid confusing a division of property with a gift, a transfer of property in conjunction with a divorce is not considered to be a gift if the property is transferred within three years of the divorce under a written property settlement. Also, special rules apply to transfers of certain types of property, such as life insurance and jointly held property. To make a complete gift of a life insurance policy, the donor must give the donee all the incidents of ownership, including the power to designate beneficiaries.

Special rules apply to the purchase or transfer of property with joint (i.e., multiple) owners. The two most common forms of joint ownership are **joint tenancy** (also called **joint tenancy with right of survivorship**) and **tenancy in common.** In joint tenancy, each owner owns an equal share of the property, whereas ownership proportions can vary for property held as tenants-in-common. When property is purchased or ownership is transferred, each of the joint owners is responsible for providing or receiving their proportionate share of funds. When one of the joint owners provides a disproportionate share of funds, that owner is treated as having made a gift to the other owners. The gift is the amount necessary to pay for the other party's interest in the property. For example, suppose the donor pays $80,000 toward the purchase of $100,000 in realty held in equal proportions with the donee (i.e., the donee provides only $20,000 of the purchase price). The donor is deemed to make a gift of $30,000 to the donee, the difference between the value of the joint interest ($100,000 ÷ 2 = $50,000) and the consideration provided by the donee ($20,000).

ETHICS

Carol is a retired engineer who has three adult children and several grandchildren. This year Rudy, Carol's youngest son, approached Carol for a $40,000 business loan. Although Rudy had no collateral for the loan and did not sign any written promise to repay the money, Carol still transferred the funds to Rudy's account. Do you think Carol should file a gift tax return for the transfer? Suppose Carol has no intention of demanding repayment but has not told anyone so. Does this make any difference?

Example 25-2

This year Harry helped purchase a residence for use by Dina and her spouse Steve. The price of the residence was $250,000, and the title named Harry and Steve joint tenants with the right of survivorship. Harry provided $210,000 of the purchase price and Steve the remaining $40,000. Has Harry made a complete gift, and if so, in what amount?

Answer: Yes, Harry made a complete gift to Steve of $85,000, calculated by subtracting the amount paid by Steve from the price of his ownership interest ($125,000 − $40,000).

What if: Suppose Steve didn't provide any part of the purchase price for his half interest in the property. What is the amount of the gift?

Answer: In this case, Harry made a complete gift to Steve of half the purchase price, $125,000.

Valuation Gifts are taxed at the fair market value of the donated property on the date the gift becomes complete. Remember that despite the valuation of a gift at fair market value, the donee generally takes a carryover basis for income tax purposes.[6]

Valuation of remainders and other temporal interests. Assigning value to unique property is difficult enough, but sometimes we must also assign a value to a stream of payments over time or a payment to be made in the future. The right to currently enjoy property or receive income payments from property is called a **present interest.** In contrast, the right to receive income or property in the future is called a **future interest.** A present right to possess and/or collect income from property may not be permanent; if the right is granted for a specific period of time or until the occurrence of a specific event, it is a **terminable interest.** For example, the right to receive income payments from property for 10 years is a terminable interest. Another terminable interest is the right to possess property and/or receive income for the duration of someone's life, and this right is called a **life estate.** The person whose life determines the duration of the life estate is called the *life tenant.*

At the end of a terminable interest, the property will pass to another owner, the person holding the future interest. In a **reversion,** it returns to the original owner. If it goes to a new owner, the right to the property is called a **remainder** and the owner is called a **remainderman.** For example, the right to own property after a 10-year income interest has ended is a future interest held by the remainderman. The right to property after the termination of a life estate is also called a remainder.

Future interests are common when property is placed in a trust. **Trusts** are legal entities established by a person called the **grantor.** Trusts are administered by a **trustee** and generally contain property called the **corpus** (principal) of the trust. The trustee has a **fiduciary duty** to manage the property in the trust for the benefit of a **beneficiary** or beneficiaries. This duty requires the trustee to administer the trust in an objective and impartial manner and not favor one beneficiary over another.

Because a future interest is essentially a promise of a future payment, we estimate the value of the remainder by discounting the future payment to a present value using a market rate of interest. For example, suppose property worth $100 is placed in a trust with the income to be paid to an income beneficiary each year for 10 years, after which time the property accumulated in the trust will be distributed. The remainder is a future interest with a value we estimate by calculating the present value of a payment of $100 in 10 years as follows:

$$\text{Value of remainder} = \frac{\text{Future payment}}{(1 + r)^n}$$

where r is the market rate of interest and n is the number of years. The interest rate used for this calculation is published monthly by the Treasury as the §7520 rate.[7] If the §7520 rate is 6 percent, we calculate the value of a remainder of $100 placed in trust for 10 years as follows:

$$\text{Value of remainder} = \frac{\$100}{(1 + .06)^{10}} = \frac{\$100}{1.791} = \$55.83$$

THE KEY FACTS

Valuation of Remainders and Income Interests

- Future interests are valued at present value, calculated by estimating the time until the present interest expires.
- The present value calculation uses the §7520 interest rate published by the Treasury.
- If the present interest is measured by a person's life (a life estate), then we estimate the delay by reference to the person's life expectancy as published in IRS tables.
- The value of a present interest, such as an income interest or life estate, is determined by subtracting the value of the remainder interest from the total value of the property.

[6]The carryover basis may be increased for any gift tax paid (after 1976) on the appreciation of the property.

[7]The §7520 rate is 120 percent of the applicable federal mid-term rate in effect during the month of the transaction. The IRS publishes this rate each month in a Revenue Ruling. For example, in Revenue Ruling 2022-1, the IRS announced that this rate was 0.53% for January, 2022.

The value of property consists of the present interest (the right to income) and the future interest (the remainder). Hence, once we have estimated the value of the remainder, we compute the value of the income interest as the difference between the value of the remainder and the total value of the property.

Value of income interest = Total value − Value of remainder
= \$100 − \$55.83
= \$44.17

If the terminable interest is a life estate, the valuation of the remainder is a bit more complicated because payment of the remainder is delayed by the duration of the life estate. To estimate this delay, the calculation is based on the number of years the life tenant is expected to live. To facilitate the calculation, the regulations provide a table (Table S) that calculates the discount factor by including the life tenant's age at the time of transfer. Exhibit 25-4 includes a portion of Table S from the regulation with interest rates by column and the age of the life tenant by row.

EXHIBIT 25-4 Discount Factors for Estimating the Value of Remainders

Regulation §20.2031-7(d)(7)
Table S.—Based on Life Table 2000CM Single Life Remainder Factors
Applicable on or after May 1, 2009

	Interest rate									
Age	**4.2%**	**4.4%**	**4.6%**	**4.8%**	**5.0%**	**5.2%**	**5.4%**	**5.6%**	**5.8%**	**6.0%**
0	.06083	.05483	.04959	.04501	.04101	.03749	.03441	.03170	.02931	.02721
1	.05668	.05049	.04507	.04034	.03618	.03254	.02934	.02652	.02403	.02183
2	.05858	.05222	.04665	.04178	.03750	.03373	.03042	.02750	.02492	.02264
3	.06072	.05420	.04848	.04346	.03904	.03516	.03173	.02871	.02603	.02366
4	.06303	.05634	.05046	.04530	.04075	.03674	.03319	.03006	.02729	.02483
5	.06547	.05861	.05258	.04726	.04258	.03844	.03478	.03153	.02866	.02610
6	.06805	.06102	.05482	.04935	.04453	.04026	.03647	.03312	.03014	.02749
⋮										
35	.19692	.18423	.17253	.16174	.15178	.14258	.13408	.12621	.11892	.11217
36	.20407	.19119	.17931	.16833	.15818	.14879	.14009	.13204	.12457	.11764
37	.21144	.19838	.18631	.17515	.16481	.15523	.14635	.13811	.13046	.12335
38	.21904	.20582	.19357	.18222	.17170	.16193	.15287	.14444	.13661	.12932
⋮										
86	.79825	.79044	.78278	.77524	.76783	.76055	.75340	.74636	.73944	.73264
87	.80921	.80176	.79443	.78722	.78014	.77316	.76630	.75956	.75292	.74638
88	.81978	.81268	.80569	.79880	.79203	.78536	.77880	.77234	.76598	.75971
89	.82994	.82317	.81651	.80995	.80349	.79712	.79085	.78467	.77859	.77259

Source: Reg. §20.2031-7(d)(7) Table S.

Example 25-3

Harry transferred \$500,000 of FFP stock to the DG Trust, whose trustee is directed to pay income to Dina for her life and, upon Dina's death, pay the remainder to George (or his estate). At the time of the gift, Dina was 35 years old and the §7520 interest rate was 5.8 percent. What are the values of the gift of the life estate and of the remainder interest?

Answer: Harry made a \$59,460 gift of the remainder to George and a \$440,540 gift of the life estate to Dina. Under Table S (see Exhibit 25-4), the percentage of the property that represents the value of George's remainder is .11892. Thus, George's remainder is valued at \$59,460 (\$500,000 × .11892). Dina's life estate (the income interest) is the remaining value of \$440,540 (\$500,000 − \$59,460).

The Annual Exclusion One of the most important aspects of the gift tax is the **annual exclusion,** which operates to eliminate "small" gifts from the gift tax base. The amount of the exclusion has been revised upward periodically over the years and is now indexed for inflation.[8] In 2022, the annual exclusion amount is $16,000.

The annual exclusion is available to offset gifts made to *each* donee regardless of the number of donees in any particular year. For example, in 2022 a donor could give $16,000 in cash to each of 10 donees without exceeding the annual exclusion. One important limitation to the annual exclusion is that it applies only to gifts of *present* interests; that is, with limited exceptions, a gift of a future interest is not eligible for an annual exclusion.

Example 25-4

When Harry transferred $500,000 of FFP stock to the DG Trust (Example 25-3), he simultaneously made two taxable gifts: a life estate to Dina and a remainder to George. What is the amount of the taxable gift of the life estate to Dina and the remainder interest to George, after taking the annual exclusion into account?

Answer: Dina's life estate is a present interest and would qualify for the annual exclusion. However, George's remainder is a future interest and will not qualify for the annual exclusion. Harry would file a Form 709 to report total taxable gifts of $484,000, consisting of a $424,540 taxable gift to Dina ($440,540 less the annual exclusion of $16,000) and a taxable gift of $59,460 to George (no annual exclusion is available for a future interest).

Description	Dina	George	Harry's Gift Tax Return
Current gifts	$440,540	$59,460	$500,000
Annual exclusion	−16,000	−0	−16,000
Taxable gifts	$424,540	$59,460	$484,000

THE KEY FACTS

Annual Exclusion

- In 2022, gifts of present interests qualify for an annual exclusion of $16,000 per donee.
- A present interest is the ability to use property or receive income presently.
- Gifts of future interests placed in trust for a minor can also qualify for the exclusion.

The prohibition on annual exclusions for gifts of future interests means that most gifts will qualify for an annual exclusion only if the donee has a present interest (the ability to immediately use the property or the income from it). However, a special exception applies to future interests given to "minors" (defined as individuals under the age of 21). Gifts in trust for a minor are future interests if the minor does not have the ability to access the income or property until reaching the age of majority. These gifts will still qualify for the annual exclusion as long as the property can be used to support the minor and any remaining property is distributed to the child once they reach age 21.[9]

Example 25-5

Harry transferred $48,500 of cash to the George Trust. The trustee of the George Trust has the discretion to distribute income or corpus (principal) for George's benefit and is required to distribute all assets to George (or his estate) not later than George's 21st birthday. Is this gift eligible for the annual exclusion? If so, what is the amount of the taxable gift?

Answer: Yes, Harry will be entitled to an annual exclusion for the transfer despite the fact that George's interest is a future one because the gift is in trust for the support of a minor and the property must distribute the assets to George once he reaches age 21. The amount of the gift is $48,500, reduced to a taxable gift of $32,500 after applying the $16,000 annual exclusion.

[8]The exclusion is indexed for inflation in such a way that the amount of the exclusion only increases in increments of $1,000. The annual exclusion was $10,000 from 1981 through 2001, but was $11,000 for 2002 through 2005, $12,000 for 2006 through 2008, $13,000 for 2009 through 2012, $14,000 from 2012 through 2017, $15,000 from 2018 through 2021, and $16,000 in 2022.

[9]§2503(c). The courts have created another exception to the present interest rule called *Crummey power.* [See *Clifford Crummey v. Comm'r,* 397 F.2d 82 (9th Cir. 1968).] A discussion of this exception is beyond the scope of this text.

Taxable Gifts

In Part 1 of the formula in Exhibit 25-3, **current gifts** are accumulated for each donee, and this amount includes all gifts completed during the calendar year for each individual. Current gifts do not include transfers exempted from the tax, such as political contributions. Several adjustments are made to calculate current **taxable gifts** for each donee. As we've seen, each taxpayer is allowed an annual exclusion applied to the cumulative gifts of present interests made during the year to *each* donee. Next, if a married couple elects to split gifts (discussed below), half of each gift is included in the current gifts of each spouse. The marital deduction for gifts to spouses and the charitable deduction for gifts to charity are the last adjustments to calculate taxable gifts for each donee. We discuss each in turn.

Gift-Splitting Election Married couples have the option to *split gifts,* allowing them to treat *all* gifts made in a year as if each spouse had made one-half of each gift. In a **community-property state,** both spouses automatically own equal shares in most property acquired during the marriage.[10] Hence, a gift of community property is divided between the spouses equally. In **common-law states,** one spouse can own a disproportionate amount of property because the spouse earns most of the income. The gift-splitting election provides a mechanism for married couples in common-law states to achieve the same result as couples receive automatically in community-property states.[11]

Example 25-6

Wilma and Harry live in Michigan, a common-law state. For the holidays, Wilma gave cash gifts of $35,000 to Steve and $41,000 to Dina. Wilma and Harry did not elect to split gifts. What is the amount of Wilma's taxable gifts?

Answer: $44,000. After using her annual exclusion (both gifts are present interests), Wilma has made taxable gifts of $19,000 to Steve ($35,000 – $16,000) and $25,000 to Dina ($41,000 – $16,000).

What if: Suppose Wilma and Harry elect gift-splitting this year. How would your answer change?

Answer: Wilma and Harry each made taxable gifts of $6,000. Under gift-splitting, Wilma and Harry are each treated as making a current gift of $17,500 to Steve and $20,500 to Dina. After the annual exclusion, both Wilma and Harry made a $1,500 taxable gift to Steve [($35,000 ÷ 2) – $16,000 = $1,500]. In addition, both Wilma and Harry made a $4,500 taxable gift to Dina [($41,000 ÷ 2) – $16,000 = $4,500].

What if: Suppose Wilma and Harry lived in Texas (a community-property state), and Wilma made the same gifts from community property.

Answer: Even without electing gift-splitting, Wilma and Harry will each be treated as making a taxable gift of $6,000. Under state law, each spouse is automatically treated as gifting half the value of any gifts made from community property. After the annual exclusion, both Wilma and Harry made a $1,500 taxable gift to Steve [($35,000 ÷ 2) – $16,000], and each made a $4,500 taxable gift to Dina [($41,000 ÷ 2) – $16,000].

THE KEY FACTS

Marital Deduction

- Gifts of property to a spouse may be deducted in computing taxable gifts.
- Transfers of terminable interests in property, such as a life estate, will not generally qualify for the deduction.
- The deduction is limited to the value of property included in taxable gifts.

Besides increasing the application of the annual exclusion, a gift-splitting election also increases the likelihood that taxable gifts will be taxed at lower tax rates or any gift tax will be offset by applicable credits. To utilize gift-splitting, each spouse must be a citizen or resident of the United States, be married at the time of the gift, and not remarry during the remainder of the calendar year. The election is made by both spouses by consenting on each other's gift tax return. Split gifts are computed separately in each return, and the tax is calculated for each spouse separately on their respective returns. Taxpayers make this election annually, and it applies to all gifts completed by either spouse during the calendar year. As a result of the election, both spouses share joint and several liability for any gift tax due.

Marital Deduction The marital deduction was originally enacted to equalize the treatment of spouses residing in common-law states with those residing in community-property

[10]Depending upon state law, the ownership of property acquired by either spouse prior to a marriage is not automatically divided equally between the spouses. In other words, property owned prior to the marriage is not necessarily community property and continues to belong to the original owner.

[11]There are nine community-property states: Arizona, California, Idaho, Louisiana, Nevada, New Mexico, Texas, Washington, and Wisconsin.

states. In community-property states, the ownership of most property *acquired* during a marriage is automatically divided between the spouses. In common-law states, one spouse can own a disproportionate amount of property if that spouse earns most of the income. Absent the marital deduction, in a common-law state, a transfer between spouses to equalize the ownership of property would be treated as a taxable gift. However, because transfers to spouses are eligible for a marital deduction, no taxable gift results from such a transfer.

The marital deduction is subject to two limits. First, the amount is limited to the value of the gift after the annual exclusion. Second, transfers of **nondeductible terminable interests** do not qualify for a marital deduction. A nondeductible terminable interest is a property interest transferred to the spouse that terminates when some event occurs or after a specified amount of time, when the property is transferred to another.

Example 25-7

After his decision to retire, Harry gave Wilma a piece of jewelry that is a family heirloom valued at $50,000. What is the amount of the taxable gift from this transfer?

Answer: Zero. This gift will qualify for an annual exclusion, and the amount remaining after subtracting the annual exclusion qualifies for the marital deduction. The taxable gift is calculated below:

Description	Amount
Current gift	$ 50,000
Less: Annual exclusion	−16,000
Less: Marital deduction	−34,000
Taxable gift	$ 0

What if: Suppose Harry transferred $200,000 to a trust with directions to pay income to Wilma for her life (a life estate). After Wilma's death, the corpus of the trust would then pass to Dina (the remainder). What is the amount of this taxable gift if Wilma is age 38 at the time and the §7520 interest rate is 5 percent?

Answer: The total taxable gift is $184,000. This transfer is actually two gifts, a gift of a present interest to Wilma (a life estate) and a future interest to Dina (the remainder). The gift of the remainder is valued at $34,340 using Wilma's age and the §7520 interest rate from Table S in Exhibit 25-4 ($200,000 × .17170). The remainder does not qualify for an annual exclusion because it is a future interest. The gift of the life estate is a present interest valued at $165,660 ($200,000 – $34,340), and it qualifies for the annual exclusion. The taxable gifts are calculated below:

Description	Dina (remainder)	Wilma (life estate)
Current gifts	$34,340	$165,660
Less: Annual exclusion (life estate)	−0	−16,000
Less: Marital deduction	−0	−0
Taxable gift	$34,340	$149,660

When the life estate is given to a spouse, it does not qualify for the marital deduction because it will terminate upon a future event (Wilma's death) and then pass to another person (Dina).

The limitation on the deductible terminable interests ensures that property owned by a married couple is subject to a transfer tax when the property is eventually transferred from the couple (as opposed to between the spouses).[12] If a life estate were eligible for a marital deduction, it would not be taxed at the time of the gift, nor would any value be taxed upon the spouse's death (the life estate disappears with his or her death). Hence, a marital deduction is available only for spousal transfers that will eventually be included in the recipient spouse's estate.[13]

[12]Qualified terminable interest properties (QTIPs for short) are an exception to the nondeductibility of terminable interest property. To qualify, the taxpayer must agree to have qualifying terminable interests included in the estate of the spouse. A detailed discussion of this election is beyond the scope of this text.

[13]To be eligible for the marital deduction, the spouse must be entitled to all of the income from the property payable at least annually, and no person has the power to appoint any part of the property to anyone other than the spouse until the death of the spouse.

Charitable Deduction The amount of the charitable deduction is also limited to the value of the gift after subtracting the annual exclusion. Requirements for an organization to qualify as a charity for purposes of the gift tax charitable deduction are quite similar to those for the income tax deduction (i.e., the entity must be organized for religious, charitable, scientific, educational, or other public purposes, including governmental entities). Unlike the income tax deduction, however, the charitable deduction has no income tax percentage limitation. In addition, as long as the qualifying charity receives the donor's entire interest in the property, no gift tax return need be filed (assuming the donor has no other taxable gifts). Finally, a transfer to a charity also qualifies for an income tax deduction (subject to the AGI percentage limits on the income tax charitable deduction).

Example 25-8

Harry donated $155,000 in cash to State University. What is the amount of the taxable gift?

Answer: Zero. The gift qualifies for the charitable gift tax deduction, as calculated below.

Description	Amount
Current gift	$ 155,000
Less: Annual exclusion	−16,000
Less: Charitable deduction	−139,000
Taxable gift	$ 0

Note that Harry can also claim an income tax deduction for the transfer.

Computation of the Gift Tax

Part 2 of the formula in Exhibit 25-3 provides the method for calculating the gift tax. It begins by summing the taxable gifts made for all donees during a calendar year.

Example 25-9

Harry and Wilma did not make any gifts from community property and did not elect to gift-split this year (see Example 25-6). What is the value of Harry's current taxable gifts this year?

Answer: Harry made $585,500 of taxable gifts, calculated using Part 1 of the formula in Exhibit 25-3 as follows:

Gifted Property	Donee	Value	Explanation
1. Residence	Steve	$ 85,000	Example 25-2
Less: Annual exclusion		−16,000	
2. DG Trust—life estate	Dina	440,540	Example 25-3
Less: Annual exclusion		−16,000	
3. DG Trust—remainder	Dina	59,460	Example 25-3
4. George Trust	George	48,500	Example 25-5
Less: Annual exclusion		−16,000	
5. Jewelry	Wilma	50,000	Example 25-7
Less: Annual exclusion		−16,000	
Less: Marital deduction	Wilma	−34,000	
6. Donation	State University	155,000	Example 25-8
Less: Annual exclusion		−16,000	
Less: Charitable deduction	State University	−139,000	
Harry's current taxable gifts		**$ 585,500**	

The amounts of the marital and charitable deductions are limited to the value of the property included in taxable gifts.

Will Wilma be required to file a gift tax return this year? If so, what is the amount of her taxable gifts?

Answer: Wilma must also file a gift tax return this year because her current gifts exceed the available annual exclusion amounts. Wilma's taxable gifts sum to $44,000, calculated as follows:

Gifted Property	Donee	Value	Explanation
1. Cash gift	Steve	$ 35,000	Example 25-6
Less: Annual exclusion		−16,000	
2. Cash gift	Dina	41,000	Example 25-6
Less: Annual exclusion		−16,000	
Wilma's current taxable gifts		**$ 44,000**	

What if: What is the amount of Harry and Wilma's taxable gifts if they elect to gift-split?

Answer: Harry and Wilma each made $306,750 of taxable gifts, calculated as follows:

				Gift-Splitting	
Gifted Property	**Harry**	**Wilma**	**Donee**	**Harry**	**Wilma**
1. Gift of a residence	$ 85,000		Steve	$ 42,500	$ 42,500
Less: Annual exclusion	−16,000			−16,000	
2. Cash gift		$ 35,000	Steve	17,500	17,500
Less: Annual exclusion		−16,000			−16,000
3. Transfer to DG trust	440,540		Dina	220,270	220,270
Less: Annual exclusion	−16,000			−16,000	
4. Cash gift		41,000	Dina	20,500	20,500
Less: Annual exclusion		−16,000			−16,000
5. DG Trust—remainder	59,460		George	29,730	29,730
6. George Trust	48,500		George	24,250	24,250
Less: Annual exclusion	−16,000			−16,000	−16,000
7. Gift of jewelry	50,000		Wilma	50,000	
Less: Annual exclusion	−16,000			−16,000	
Less: Marital deduction	−34,000			−34,000	
8. Donation to State U	155,000		State U	77,500	77,500
Less: Annual exclusion	−16,000			−16,000	−16,000
Less: Charitable deduction	−139,000			−61,500	−61,500
Total	**$ 585,500**	**$ 44,000**		**$306,750**	**$306,750**

Note that absent gift-splitting, Harry and Wilma made taxable gifts totaling $629,500 ($585,500 + $44,000), but under gift-splitting that reduced to $613,500 ($306,750 + $306,750) because Wilma was able to use an additional $16,000 annual exclusion for her portion of the gift to the George Trust. Neither Harry nor Wilma was able to use any additional annual exclusions for the gifts to Steve and Dina because they had already used annual exclusions to these two donees. If they were to elect to gift-split, Harry and Wilma would be jointly and severally liable for the gift taxes.

Tax on Current Taxable Gifts The first step to computing the gift tax on current taxable gifts is to add prior taxable gifts to current taxable gifts. The purpose of adding gifts from previous periods is to increase the tax base and thereby increase the marginal tax rate applied to current gifts. To prevent double taxation of prior taxable gifts, the gift tax on prior taxable gifts is subtracted from the tax on total transfers. Two elements of the tax on prior taxable gifts are important to understand. First, the tax is calculated on prior taxable gifts ignoring whether any applicable credit was claimed on the gifts in the prior year. Second, the tax on prior taxable gifts is computed using the *current* tax rate schedule (the tax rates for the year of the prior transfer are not relevant). The difference between the tax on cumulative taxable gifts and prior taxable gifts is the tax on the current taxable gifts.

Applicable Credit The last adjustment in the formula is for the *unused* portion of the applicable credit. Recall that the applicable credit is calculated using the current tax rate schedule applied to the exemption equivalent ($12.06 million for 2022). The exemption equivalent can change over time because it is indexed for inflation. Thus, as the exemption equivalent changes, the applicable credit on the exemption equivalent also changes.

Example 25-10

Assume that Harry made a taxable gift of $1,500,000 in 2007. At that time, the exemption equivalent for the gift tax was $1 million, so Harry paid gift taxes on $500,000. Harry has not made any taxable gifts since 2007. This year, however, Harry made taxable gifts of $585,500. What is Harry's gift tax on the transfer?

Answer: Harry will report cumulative taxable gifts of $2,085,500, but he will not owe any gift tax this year. The calculation is as follows:

Current taxable gifts	$ 585,500	
Prior taxable gifts	1,500,000	
Cumulative taxable gifts	$2,085,500	
Tax on cumulative taxable gifts (at current rates)		$ 780,000
Less: Current tax on prior taxable gifts ($1.5 million)		−545,800
Tax on current taxable gifts		$ 234,200
Applicable credit on current taxable gifts		−234,200
Gift tax due		$ 0

What is Harry's unused exemption equivalent?

At the end of 2022, Harry has $10,474,500 of unused exemption equivalent remaining ($12,060,000 − $1,000,000 − $585,500). Harry used $1 million of his exemption equivalent in 2007, and this year he used another $585,500 (the amount of exemption equivalent necessary to offset the current taxable gift).

What if: Suppose Harry made a taxable gift of $3,500,000 in 2007, and at that time, the exemption equivalent was $1 million. What should Harry report this year as his cumulative taxable gifts, gift tax on cumulative taxable gifts, gift tax on current taxable gifts, applicable credit for current tax on prior taxable gifts, and gift tax due? What is Harry's unused exemption equivalent?

Answer: Harry should report cumulative taxable gifts of $4,085,500 and gift tax on cumulative gifts of $1,580,000. Harry, however, owes no gift tax because of the applicable credit. The calculation is as follows:

Current taxable gifts	$ 585,500	
Prior taxable gifts	3,500,000	
Cumulative taxable gifts	$4,085,500	
Tax on cumulative taxable gifts (at current rates)		$ 1,580,000
Less: Current tax on prior taxable gifts ($3.5 million)		−1,345,800
Tax on current taxable gifts		234,200
Applicable credit on current taxable gifts		−234,200
Gift tax due		$ 0

At the end of 2022, Harry would have $10,474,500 of exemption equivalent remaining ($12,060,000 − $1,000,000 − $585,500). Note that Harry paid gift tax in 2007 because his taxable gifts far exceeded the exemption equivalent of $1 million in 2007. However, the amount of gift tax that was paid in 2007 is not relevant for calculating Harry's current tax. All calculations in the current year are made using the current tax rate schedule (not the one that applied in prior years).

What are Wilma's gift tax due and unused exemption equivalent?

Answer: Zero gift tax due. Wilma has used $44,000 of her exemption equivalent. Hence, at the end of 2022, Wilma has $12,016,000 ($12,060,000 – $44,000) of exemption equivalent remaining.

Wilma's current taxable gifts	$44,000	
Prior taxable gifts	+0	
Cumulative taxable gifts	$44,000	
Tax on cumulative taxable gifts (at current rates)		$ 9,160
Less: Current tax on prior taxable gifts		–0
Tax on current taxable gifts		$ 9,160
Applicable credit on current taxable gifts		–9,160
Gift tax due		$ 0

Example 25-11

What if: Suppose that Harry made a taxable gift of $8 million in 2011 (when the exemption equivalent was $5 million) and made current taxable gifts of $20 million. In this example, Harry has cumulative transfers of $28 million, and because he used $5 million of exemption equivalent in 2011, he has an unused exemption equivalent of $7.06 million ($12.06 million minus $5 million). The unused applicable credit is $2.824 million, calculated by subtracting the tax on the $5 million previously used exemption ($1,945,800) from the tax on the $12.06 million current exemption ($4,769,800). The gift tax due is calculated below using the tax formula in Exhibit 25-3:

Gift Tax Calculation Tracking the Applicable Credit on the Unused Exemption Equivalent

Description	Tax Amounts
Gift tax on cumulative transfers of $28 million	$11,145,800
Less gift tax on $8 million of prior taxable gifts	–3,145,800
Less gift tax on unused exemption equivalent of $7.06 million	–2,824,000
Gift tax due	$ 5,176,000

The gift tax formula requires donors to keep track of the unused applicable credit to calculate the tax due. Fortunately, there is a shortcut method for calculating the gift tax when cumulative taxable transfers exceed $1 million. Rather than track the tax on the exemption equivalent, instead subtract gifts from prior periods and the unused exemption equivalent from the cumulative taxable transfers to calculate the taxable transfers in the current period. If the cumulative transfers exceed $1 million, the tax is computed using a flat 40% tax rate. Here's how the shortcut works in this example:

Gift Tax Calculation Using the Shortcut

Description	Exemption Equivalent
Cumulative taxable transfers ($8 million plus $20 million)	$28,000,000
Less total taxable gifts in prior periods	–8,000,000
Less ***unused*** exemption equivalent ($12.06 – $5 million)	–7,060,000
Taxable transfers in this period	$12,940,000
Times marginal tax rate (40%)	× 40%
Gift tax on current gifts at the current tax rate	$ 5,176,000

To recap, rather than track the tax on the exemption equivalent, subtract taxable gifts from prior periods and the unused exemption equivalent from total taxable transfers. As long as taxable transfers exceed $1 million, the tax is calculated by multiplying the difference by the marginal tax rate, 40 percent.

Exhibit 25-5 presents the first page of the 2021 gift tax return Form 709 (using the 2022 exemption equivalent) for Harry Smith (Form 709 for 2022 was not available as of press date).

EXHIBIT 25-5 **Page 1 of Form 709 Gift Tax Return for Harry Smith**

Form **709**

Department of the Treasury
Internal Revenue Service

United States Gift (and Generation-Skipping Transfer) Tax Return

▶ Go to *www.irs.gov/Form709* for instructions and the latest information.
(For gifts made during calendar year 2021)
▶ See instructions.

OMB No. 1545-0020

2021

1 Donor's first name and middle initial HARRY	2 Donor's last name SMITH	3 Donor's social security number 000-00-0000
4 Address (number, street, and apartment number) 2813 ELMWOOD		5 Legal residence (domicile) WASHTENAW, MICHIGAN
6 City or town, state or province, country, and ZIP or foreign postal code ANN ARBOR, MI 48109		7 Citizenship (see instructions) USA

Part 1—General Information

Line		Yes	No
8	If the donor died during the year, check here ▶ ☐ and enter date of death ______ , ______ .		
9	If you extended the time to file this Form 709, check here ▶ ☐		
10	Enter the total number of donees listed on Schedule A. Count each person only once ▶		
11a	Have you (the donor) previously filed a Form 709 (or 709-A) for any other year? If "No," skip line 11b	✓	
b	Has your address changed since you last filed Form 709 (or 709-A)?		✓
12	**Gifts by husband or wife to third parties.** Do you consent to have the gifts (including generation-skipping transfers) made by you and by your spouse to third parties during the calendar year considered as made one-half by each of you? (See instructions.) (If the answer is "Yes," the following information must be furnished and your spouse must sign the consent shown below. **If the answer is "No," skip lines 13–18.**)		✓
13	Name of consenting spouse — 14 SSN		
15	Were you married to one another during the entire calendar year? See instructions		
16	If line 15 is "No," check whether ☐ married ☐ divorced or ☐ widowed/deceased, and give date. See instructions ▶		
17	Will a gift tax return for this year be filed by your spouse? If "Yes," mail both returns in the same envelope		
18	**Consent of Spouse.** I consent to have the gifts (and generation-skipping transfers) made by me and by my spouse to third parties during the calendar year considered as made one-half by each of us. We are both aware of the joint and several liability for tax created by the execution of this consent.		

Consenting spouse's signature ▶ **Date ▶**

Line		Yes	No
19	Have you applied a DSUE amount received from a predeceased spouse to a gift or gifts reported on this or a previous Form 709? If "Yes," complete Schedule C		✓

Part 2—Tax Computation

Line		Line	Amount
1	Enter the amount from Schedule A, Part 4, line 11	1	585,500
2	Enter the amount from Schedule B, line 3	2	1,500,000
3	Total taxable gifts. Add lines 1 and 2	3	2,085,500
4	Tax computed on amount on line 3 (see *Table for Computing Gift Tax* in instructions)	4	780,000
5	Tax computed on amount on line 2 (see *Table for Computing Gift Tax* in instructions)	5	545,800
6	Balance. Subtract line 5 from line 4	6	234,200
7	Applicable credit amount. If donor has DSUE amount from predeceased spouse(s) or Restored Exclusion Amount, enter amount from Schedule C, line 5; otherwise, see instructions	7	4,769,800
8	Enter the applicable credit against tax allowable for all prior periods (from Sch. B, line 1, col. C)	8	345,800
9	Balance. Subtract line 8 from line 7. Do not enter less than zero	9	4,424,000
10	Enter 20% (0.20) of the amount allowed as a specific exemption for gifts made after September 8, 1976, and before January 1, 1977. See instructions	10	0
11	Balance. Subtract line 10 from line 9. Do not enter less than zero	11	4,424,000
12	Applicable credit. Enter the smaller of line 6 or line 11	12	234,200
13	Credit for foreign gift taxes (see instructions)	13	
14	Total credits. Add lines 12 and 13	14	234,200
15	Balance. Subtract line 14 from line 6. Do not enter less than zero	15	0
16	Generation-skipping transfer taxes (from Schedule D, Part 3, col. G, total)	16	
17	Total tax. Add lines 15 and 16	17	0
18	Gift and generation-skipping transfer taxes prepaid with extension of time to file	18	
19	If line 18 is less than line 17, enter **balance due.** See instructions	19	
20	If line 18 is greater than line 17, enter **amount to be refunded**	20	

Attach check or money order here.

Sign Here

Under penalties of perjury, I declare that I have examined this return, including any accompanying schedules and statements, and to the best of my knowledge and belief, it is true, correct, and complete. Declaration of preparer (other than donor) is based on all information of which preparer has any knowledge.

May the IRS discuss this return with the preparer shown below? See instructions. ☐ Yes ☐ No

▶ Signature of donor — Date

Paid Preparer Use Only

Print/Type preparer's name	Preparer's signature	Date	Check ☐ if self-employed	PTIN
Firm's name ▶			Firm's EIN ▶	
Firm's address ▶			Phone no.	

For Disclosure, Privacy Act, and Paperwork Reduction Act Notice, see the instructions for this form. Cat. No. 16783M Form **709** (2021)

Source: irs.gov.

(continued from page 25-1. . .)

Early this year Bob was injured in an auto accident. Unable to recover from his injuries, he died after two days in the hospital. Bob is survived by his son Nate, who is also the executor of Bob's estate. Nate is now collecting his father's assets, and he would like help in preparing Bob's federal estate tax return. ■

THE FEDERAL ESTATE TAX

LO 25-3

The estate tax is designed to tax the value of property owned or controlled by an individual at death, the decedent. Because federal gift and estate taxes are integrated, taxable gifts affect the tax base for the estate tax. Exhibit 25-6 presents the estate tax formula.

EXHIBIT 25-6 The Federal Estate Tax Formula

	Gross estate
Minus	Expenses, debts, and losses
Equals	Adjusted gross estate
Minus	Marital and charitable deductions
Equals	Taxable estate
Plus	Adjusted taxable gifts
Equals	Cumulative taxable transfers (the tax base)
Times	Current tax rates
Equals	Tax on cumulative transfers
Minus	Gift taxes payable on adjusted taxable gifts at current rates
Equals	Tentative tax
Minus	Full applicable credit calculated using current tax rates
Equals	Gross estate tax

The Gross Estate

Property possessed by or owned (titled) by a decedent at the time of death is generally referred to as the **probate estate** because the transfer of this property is carried out by a probate court. **Probate** is the process of gathering property possessed by or titled in the name of a decedent at the time of death, paying the debts of the decedent, and transferring the ownership of any remaining property to the decedent's **heirs.** Property in the probate estate can include cash, stocks, jewelry, clothing, and realty owned by or titled in the name of the deceased at the time of death. The person appointed by the court to carry out the will is called the **executor.** If the decedent does not have a valid will at the time of death, the person is said to die *intestate*.

The **gross estate** is broader than the probate estate. The gross estate consists of (1) the fair market value of property possessed or owned by a decedent at death *plus* (2) the value of certain automatic property transfers that take effect at death.[14] Property transfers that take effect only at death are not in the probate estate because the transfer takes place just as death occurs. Hence, the probate court does not need to effect a transfer. Establishing a trust to hold the title to property is another method of avoiding probate. The ownership of property transferred to these living trusts automatically vests in a designated beneficiary upon the occurrence of an event, such as death of the donor.

[14]§2033. The principle of increasing the gross estate for transfers taking effect at death began with gifts in contemplation of death. So-called deathbed gifts were a device used to avoid the estate tax in the years before enactment of the gift tax.

Example 25-12

What if: Nate took an inventory of his father's property in preparation for distributing assets according to Bob's will. Nate must report this preliminary inventory of personal and investment property to the probate court. Bob's property includes the following:

Property	Fair Market Value
Auto	$ 33,000
Clothes, furniture, and personal effects	48,000
Smith painting (original cost/initial estimated value)	25,000
Checking and savings accounts	75,250
FFP stock	19,500,000
Residence	400,000
Other investments	8,200
Total	$20,089,450

What amount of this property is included in Bob's gross estate?

Answer: Bob's gross estate includes the value of *all* the above property, or $20,089,450, because he owned these assets at his death (i.e., these assets are included in Bob's probate estate). In this example, Bob's gross estate and his probate estate are identical, but this would not be the case if Bob owned property that transferred automatically on his death.

What if: Suppose Bob was also entitled to a pension distribution of $15,000 but had not yet received the check at the time of his death. Would this value also be included in Bob's probate estate and therefore gross estate?

Answer: Yes. Although Bob had not received the check, he was legally entitled to the property at the time of his death, and therefore it will be included in both his probate estate and his gross estate.

TAXES IN THE REAL WORLD Income in Respect of a Decedent

Individual retirement accounts are one of the most common properties inherited from a decedent, and retirement accounts owned by the decedent are included in the gross estate. When the retirement account consists of income accrued by the decedent but untaxed at the time of death, the untaxed income is called income in respect of a decedent (IRD). Because this income was never included in the decedent's gross income (i.e., not subject to income tax during the decedent's life), distributions from the inherited retirement account are included in the gross income of the beneficiary who inherits the account.

For example, suppose that at Bob's death he owned a traditional IRA (all pretax) worth $1 million, and Nate was the beneficiary of Bob's IRA. The $1 million would be included in Bob's gross estate, and when Nate takes a distribution from the IRA, the distribution would be included in Nate's gross income. However, when Nate takes a distribution from the IRA, he would be eligible to claim a deduction for the estate tax imposed on the IRA. The deduction is allowed as an itemized deduction under §691(c) but is not subject to the 2 percent of AGI limitation under §67 and was *not* one of the itemized deductions temporarily eliminated by TCJA in 2017.

The purpose of the IRD deduction is to prevent the double taxation of inherited property representing income that was accrued but untaxed at the time of the decedent's death. Examples of IRD include retirement plan assets, IRAs, unpaid interest and dividends, and accrued but unpaid salary. Most items of IRD are eventually distributed to beneficiaries, and the beneficiaries then include the IRD in their gross income. In the case of a traditional IRA or retirement plan where the assets have not yet been included in gross income, distributions are taxed to the beneficiary when the property is distributed from the IRA or retirement plan.

To understand the operation of an IRD deduction, suppose that Bob died with no lifetime gifts and an estate worth $20 million that includes an IRA worth $1 million. In 2022, the estate tax on this estate would total $3,176,000, and $400,000 of this tax would be attributable to the IRA. If the $1 million were immediately distributed to Nate, he would include $1 million in gross income and claim a $400,000 IRD as a miscellaneous itemized deduction. If Nate only received a distribution of $10,000 from the IRA, he would only include $10,000 in gross income and claim a deduction for $4,000 [(10,000/1,000,000) × $400,000].

Specific Inclusions Besides property in the probate estate, the gross estate also includes property transferred automatically at the decedent's death. These automatic transfers can occur without the help of a probate court because the ownership transfers by law at the time of death. For example, property can be transferred automatically through a living trust.

Certain automatic property transfers are specifically included in the gross estate because, while the decedent didn't own the property at death, they controlled the ultimate disposition of the property. That is, the decedent effectively determined who would receive the property at the time of death. Joint ownership of property is the most common form of automatic transfer, but the amounts included in the gross estate vary with the form of joint ownership. Property held in joint tenancy with right of survivorship legally transfers to the surviving tenant upon the joint tenant's death. For example, joint bank accounts are commonly owned in joint ownership with right of survivorship. In contrast, tenants in common hold divided rights to property and have the ability to transfer these rights during their life or upon death. Property held by tenants in common, such as real estate, does not automatically transfer at death and thus must be transferred via probate. Although the decedent's interest in jointly owned property (with the right of survivorship) ceases at death, the value of the interest the decedent held in this property is still included in the gross estate.[15]

Example 25-13

Nate and his father jointly own two parcels of real estate not included in the inventory above. One parcel is a vacation home in Colorado. Nate owns this property jointly with Bob and the title is held in joint ownership with the right of survivorship. Will this property be included in Bob's probate estate and/or gross estate?

Answer: The property will *not* be included in Bob's *probate* estate, but it will be included in Bob's *gross* estate. When Bob died, Nate automatically became the sole owner of the property without going through probate. However, the property will be included in Bob's gross estate because it is an automatic transfer that is specifically included in the gross estate by law.

The second parcel of land is real estate in west Texas that Nate and Bob hold as equal tenants in common. Will it be necessary to use probate to transfer ownership of Bob's share to the beneficiary named in Bob's will?

Answer: Yes, ownership must be transferred through probate. The value of Bob's one-half interest in the west Texas real estate is also included in his gross estate.

Another example of an automatic transfer is insurance on the life of the decedent. Proceeds of life insurance paid due to the death of the decedent are specifically included in the gross estate if either of two conditions is met. The proceeds are included in the gross estate if (1) the decedent owned the policy or had "incidents of ownership" such as the right to designate the beneficiary or (2) the decedent's estate or executor is the beneficiary of the insurance policy (that is, the executor must use the insurance proceeds to discharge the obligations of the estate).

Example 25-14

Bob owned and paid annual premiums on an insurance policy that, on his death, was to pay the beneficiary of his choice $500,000. Bob named Nate as the beneficiary, and the insurance company paid Nate $500,000 after receiving notification of Bob's death. Will Bob's gross estate include the value of the insurance proceeds paid to Nate?

(continued on page 25-20)

[15]§2040. There are a number of other transfers that are specifically included in the gross estate. For example, §§2036–2039 and §2041 address transfers with retained life estates, transfers taking place at death, revocable transfers, annuities, and powers of appointment. A discussion of these provisions is beyond the scope of this text.

Answer: Yes. The $500,000 of insurance proceeds is specifically included in Bob's estate despite the fact that it was paid directly to Nate and did not go through probate.

What if: Suppose Bob transferred ownership of the policy to Nate four years prior to his death. Nate had the power to designate the beneficiary of the policy, and he also paid the annual premiums. Will Bob's gross estate include the value of the insurance proceeds paid to Nate?

Answer: No. Bob had no incidents of ownership at his death (Nate controlled who would be paid the proceeds upon Bob's death), and the proceeds were not paid to his estate.

Value of jointly owned property included in the gross estate. The proportion of the value of jointly owned property included in the gross estate depends upon the type of ownership. When a decedent's interest is a tenancy in common (there is no right of survivorship), a proportion of the value of the property is included in the gross estate that matches the decedent's ownership interest. For example, consider a decedent who owned a one-third interest in property as a tenant in common. If the entire property is worth $120,000 at the decedent's death, then $40,000 is included in the gross estate.

The amount includable for property held as joint tenancy with the right of survivorship depends upon the marital status of the owners. When property is jointly owned by a married couple with the right of survivorship, *half the value* of the property is automatically included in the estate of the first spouse to die.[16] For *unmarried* co-owners, the value included in the decedent's gross estate is determined by the decedent's contribution to the total cost of the property. For example, consider a decedent who provided two-thirds of the total cost of property held as joint tenants with the right of survivorship. If the entire property is worth $240,000 at the decedent's death, then two-thirds ($160,000) is included in the gross estate.

Example 25-15

Bob and Nate originally purchased the Colorado vacation home seven years ago for $200,000 and held it as joint tenants with the right of survivorship. This property is not included in the list of property in Bob's probate estate because the title passes automatically to Nate upon Bob's death. Bob provided $150,000 of the purchase price, and Nate provided the remaining $50,000. The property was worth $400,000 at Bob's death. How much is included in his gross estate?

Answer: Bob's gross estate includes $300,000. For property held in joint tenancy with the right of survivorship, the amount included in the gross estate is equal to the proportion of the purchase price provided by the decedent. Bob provided 75 percent ($150,000 ÷ $200,000 = 75%). Hence, his gross estate will include $300,000 (75% × $400,000) of the value of the vacation home.

What if: Suppose Bob was married and owned the home with a spouse as joint tenants with the right of survivorship. What amount would be included in Bob's gross estate?

Answer: Bob's gross estate includes $200,000. For property held with a spouse in joint tenancy with the right of survivorship, the amount included in the gross estate is half the value of the property at death.

What if: The west Texas land Bob and Nate owned is valued at $500,200. They owned it as tenants in common, with Bob holding a one-quarter interest and Nate holding the rest. What amount is included in Bob's gross estate?

Answer: The amount included in the estate is $125,050 ($500,200 × 25%) because Bob owned a one-quarter interest in the property.

Exhibit 25-7 summarizes the rules for determining the value of jointly owned property included in a decedent's gross estate.

[16]In some states, joint tenancy with a right of survivorship between spouses is referred to as a *tenancy by the entirety*.

EXHIBIT 25-7 Amount of Jointly Owned Property Included in Gross Estate

Ownership Form	Marital Status of Co-owners	Amount in Gross Estate
Community property (discussed above)	Married	Half the fair market value
Joint tenancy with right of survivorship	Married	Half the fair market value
Joint tenancy with right of survivorship	Unmarried	Percentage of fair market value determined by decedent's contribution to total cost of the property
Tenancy in common	Married or unmarried	Percentage of fair market value determined by decedent's interest in the property

Transfers within three years of death. Certain transfers, such as transfers of life insurance policies, made within three years of the decedent's death are also included in the decedent's gross estate, valued as of the time of death. Without this provision, a simple but effective estate tax planning technique would be to transfer ownership in a life insurance policy just prior to the decedent's death. This strategy, called a *deathbed gift,* would reduce the decedent's transfer taxes on the life insurance by the difference between its proceeds from the policy (the value at death) and its value on the date transferred. Only certain transfers are specifically included under this provision, and they are often difficult to identify.

Gift taxes paid on transfers within three years of death. Gift taxes paid on any taxable gifts during the three-year period preceding the donor's death are also included in the decedent's gross estate. This inclusion provision prevents donors from escaping estate tax on the value of gift taxes paid within three years of death. In other words, the amount of gift taxes paid is included in the estate because it would have been included in the estate had the decedent kept the property until death.

Example 25-16

What if: Suppose Bob owned a life insurance policy and transferred all incidents of ownership in the policy to his son one year before dying from a fatal disease. Also suppose that Bob paid $40,000 of gift taxes on the transfer and the policy paid his son $3 million on Bob's death. What amount would be included in Bob's gross estate?

Answer: $3,040,000. Bob's estate would include proceeds of the policy ($3 million) because Bob transferred the incidents of ownership within three years of his death. The value of the transfer would also include the gift taxes paid ($40,000) when Bob transferred the policy.

Valuation Property is included in the gross estate at the *fair market value* on the date of the decedent's death. Virtually all the factors (and controversies) regarding valuation that we've already discussed for the gift tax also apply to the valuation of property for estate tax purposes. There are special use valuations that can apply to certain farming property and close businesses if this property constitutes a substantial portion of the gross estate, but a discussion of these rules is detailed beyond the scope of this text.

Example 25-17

At his death, Bob owned an original landscape painting made in the late 1800s by one of his ancestors, Tully Smith. Bob purchased the Smith painting for $25,000 in 1980, and last year an expert estimated it was worth $210,000. Nate has now had the painting appraised by another expert, who estimates its value at $250,000 based upon a painting by the same artist that sold at auction last month. What value should be placed on the painting for inclusion in the gross estate?

Answer: Nate should value the painting at $250,000, according to its specific characteristics and attributes (such as age, condition, history, authenticity, and so forth). Of course, the IRS might disagree with this value and seek to value the painting at a higher amount.

Future interests owned by the decedent at death, such as reversions and remainders, are also included in the gross estate. These interests are valued using the same techniques used to value future interests for gift tax purposes (explained previously).

Example 25-18

THE KEY FACTS

Valuation of Assets

- Property is included in the estate at its fair market value at the date of the decedent's death.
- The executor can elect to value the estate on an alternate valuation date, six months after death, if it reduces the gross estate and estate tax.

At the time of his death, Bob owned a reversion in a trust (a future interest in the property) he established for his favorite cousin, Becky. Under the terms of the trust, Becky is entitled to income for her life (a life estate), and Bob (or his heir) is entitled to the reversion. At the time of Bob's death, the trust assets were valued at $100,000, Becky was 35, and the §7520 interest rate was 6 percent. Should this reversion be included in Bob's gross estate, and, if so, what value is placed on the future interest?

Answer: Bob's reversion interest is included in his estate because this is a property right he owned at his death. Under Table S in the regulations (Exhibit 25-4), based upon Becky's age and the current interest rate at the time of Bob's death, the percentage of the property that represents the value of Bob's reversion is 11.217 percent. Thus, his reversion is valued at $11,217 ($100,000 × .11217).

What if: Suppose the trust was established for George, age 6. Would this influence the value of Bob's reversion interest?

Answer: Yes. Under Table S in the regulations and based upon George's age and the current interest rate, the portion of the property that represents the value of Bob's reversion is 2.749 percent. Thus, Bob's reversion is valued at $2,749 ($100,000 × .02749).

The executor of an estate, however, can elect—irrevocably—to have all the property in the gross estate valued on an **alternative valuation date.** The alternate date for valuing the estate is six months after the date of death or on the date of sale or distribution of the property (if this occurs before the end of the six-month period). This election is available only if it reduces the value of the gross estate and the combined estate and generation-skipping taxes.[17]

Example 25-19

What if: Bob's shares of FFP are included in his estate at a value of $19.5 million. Suppose the value of the shares plummet to $5 million several months after Bob's death. Further suppose that the drop in value causes the value of Bob's estate to drop from $28 million to $13.5 million and consequently reduces the tax on Bob's estate. Could Nate, as executor of Bob's estate, opt to value these shares at the lower value for estate tax purposes?

Answer: Yes. Nate could elect to value the shares on the alternative valuation date, six months after Bob's death. Bob's estate qualifies for this election because it reduces the value of the entire gross estate and the estate tax. Besides reducing the estate tax, the election would also reduce the tax basis of the property for beneficiaries.

Gross Estate Summary So far we've seen that the decedent's gross estate consists of the assets subject to probate as well as certain assets transferred outside probate. These latter assets include property owned by the decedent in joint tenancy with the right of survivorship as well as life insurance. The gross estate also includes certain property transferred by the decedent within three years of death and certain future interests owned by the decedent.

[17]Under §2032, the alternative valuation election is made on the estate tax return and is irrevocable on the due date. The election applies to all the property in the gross estate. The executor can also make a protective election to use the alternate valuation date in case it is later determined that the estate and estate tax would decrease under the election.

Example 25-20

Given previous examples, what is the value of Bob's gross estate?

Answer: The value of Bob's gross estate is $21,250,717, calculated as follows:

Property	Value	Explanation
Auto	$ 33,000	Example 25-12
Personal effects	48,000	Example 25-12
Smith painting	250,000	Example 25-17
Checking and savings accounts	75,250	Example 25-12
FFP shares	19,500,000	Example 25-12
Residence	400,000	Example 25-12
Other investments	8,200	Example 25-12
Life insurance proceeds	500,000	Example 25-14
Colorado vacation home	300,000	Examples 25-13 and 25-15
West Texas land	125,050	Examples 25-13 and 25-15
Reversion interest in Becky Trust	11,217	Example 25-18
Gross estate	**$21,250,717**	

The Taxable Estate

Referring to the federal estate tax formula in Exhibit 25-6, we calculate the **taxable estate** in two steps. The first step consists of subtracting from the gross estate the deductions allowed for administrative expenses, debts of the decedent, and losses incurred during the administration of the estate. These deductions are allowed because Congress intends to tax the amount transferred to beneficiaries. This step results in the **adjusted gross estate.** In the second step, the adjusted gross estate is reduced for transfers to a decedent's spouse (i.e., the marital deduction) and to charities (i.e., the charitable deduction). These deductions result in the taxable estate. We discuss each type of deduction next.

Administrative Expenses, Debts, Losses, and State Death Taxes Debts included in or incurred by the estate, such as mortgages and accrued taxes, are deductible. Expenses incurred in administering the estate, such as executor fees, attorney fees, and the like, are also deductible. Funeral expenses are deductible if reasonable in amount. Likewise, casualty and theft losses are deductible. These losses must be incurred during the administration of the estate; otherwise, any deductions belong to the new owner of the property. Finally, death taxes imposed by the state are also deductible.[18]

Example 25-21

Nate paid $6,685 in funeral expenses for his father's services, and during the administration of his father's estate, he paid executor fees of $4,032 and attorney fees of $9,500. In addition, Nate discovered Bob owed debts totaling $100,500. Because Michigan has no state death or inheritance taxes, no amounts were owed to the state. What is Bob's adjusted gross estate (gross estate minus expenses and debts)?

(continued on page 25-24)

[18]Sections 2053, 2054, and 2058 address expenses, losses, and state death taxes, respectively.

Answer: Bob's adjusted gross estate is $21,130,000, calculated as follows:

Gross estate (from Example 25-20)		$ 21,250,717
Funeral expenses	$ 6,685	
Executor fees and expenses	4,032	
Attorney fees	9,500	
Debts of the decedent	100,500	
Total expenses and debts		−120,717
Adjusted gross estate		**$21,130,000**

What if: Suppose that during the administration of Bob's estate a storm damaged the Colorado vacation home. Bob's share of the casualty loss to the home was $25,000. Would this be deductible in calculating Bob's taxable estate?

Answer: Yes, the executor can deduct this loss on the estate tax return. Note that personal (nonbusiness) casualty and theft losses are not deductible on income tax returns.

The estate may collect income earned during its administration and, therefore, the estate will need to file an estate *income* tax return. The executor has the option of deducting administration expenses (but not funeral expenses) on either the estate tax return or the estate's *income* tax return. While no double deduction is available, the choice is relatively simple. If the estate owes no estate taxes, then the executor should claim the deduction on the estate income tax return. If the estate owes estate taxes, the marginal estate tax rate is likely to be higher than the marginal income tax rate. Hence, it should probably claim the deduction on the estate tax return.

Marital and Charitable Deductions To avoid taxing a married couple's estate twice, Congress provides a deduction for bequests to a surviving spouse. To qualify for the marital deduction, the transferred property must be included in the estate of the deceased spouse. That is, the surviving spouse must receive the property from the decedent and control its ultimate disposition. For example, property that passes to the surviving spouse as a result of joint tenancy with the right of survivorship qualifies for the marital deduction, as would a direct bequest from the decedent. In contrast, transfers of property rights that are terminable do not generally qualify for the estate marital deduction (as discussed earlier, terminable interests are treated similarly for gift tax purposes). For example, suppose the decedent bequeaths the surviving spouse the right to occupy the decedent's residence until such time as the spouse remarries. The value of the right to possess the residence is a terminable interest and is not eligible for the marital deduction.[19] In general, the estate tax marital deduction is unlimited in amount. Hence, no tax would be imposed on a decedent who leaves their entire estate to a spouse.[20]

Charitable contributions of property are also deductible without any limitation. Charities are defined to include the usual public organizations (i.e., corporations organized exclusively for religious, charitable, scientific, literary, or educational purposes) but exclude certain nonprofit cemetery organizations. Interestingly, foreign charities qualify for the charitable deduction under the estate and gift tax but not under the income tax. No deduction is allowed unless the charitable bequest is specified under the last will and testament or

THE KEY FACTS

Estate Tax Deductions

- Estate tax deductions include the debts of the decedent, funeral expenses, and the costs of administering the estate, including casualty losses.
- The value of property interests bequeathed to a surviving spouse is deductible if the interest is not terminable.
- The value of property bequeathed to a qualified charity is deductible.

[19]The restriction on the estate tax deduction for terminable interests is drafted consistent with the gift tax deduction. As noted previously, *qualified terminable interest properties* (QTIPs for short) are an exception to the nondeductibility of terminable interest property. To qualify, the executor must agree to have qualifying terminable interests included in the estate of the surviving spouse. A detailed discussion of this exception is beyond the scope of this text.

[20]There are other credits that could also apply, but these are beyond the scope of this text. The credit for taxes on prior transfer is designed to adjust the tax for property that was subjected to estate tax within the last 10 years. There is also a credit for pre-1977 gift taxes paid on certain pre-1977 gifts that must be included in the gross estate. Both of these credits are equitable adjustments for potential multiple transfer taxes associated with sequential deaths and multiple inclusions, respectively. Prior to 2005, there was a credit for state death taxes.

is a transfer of property by the decedent before their death that is subsequently included in the decedent's estate. The amount of any bequest must be mandatory, although another person such as the executor can be given discretion to identify the charitable organization.

Example 25-22

Not long after Bob's death, Nate gathered the Smith family for a reading of Bob's will. The will was relatively simple because Bob was unmarried at the time of his death. Bob had an adjusted gross estate of $21,130,000 and left all of his property to Nate, with two exceptions. Bob bequeathed his reversion (future) interest in the trust (value of $11,217) to Becky, and he bequeathed the Smith painting (value of $250,000) to the Midwest Museum in Ann Arbor (a qualified charity). Are either of these bequests deductible in calculating Bob's taxable estate? What is Bob's taxable estate?

Answer: Bequests are not deductible unless made to spouses or charitable organizations. The bequest to the museum qualifies for the charitable deduction because the museum is a qualified charity. Because Bob was unmarried at his death, the other bequests do not qualify for the marital deduction. Bob's taxable estate is $20,880,000, calculated as follows:

Description	Amount
Adjusted gross estate	$ 21,130,000
Charitable deduction	−250,000
Taxable estate	**$20,880,000**

What if: Suppose Bob was married at the time of his death and left a portion of his FFP stock, valued at $4.5 million, to the surviving spouse. What amount of this transfer, if any, would qualify for the marital deduction?

Answer: Bob's estate would be entitled to a marital deduction of $4.5 million, the value of the entire spousal bequest. In the extreme, if Bob had left *all his property* to his spouse, the taxable estate would be reduced to zero.

Computation of the Estate Tax

Three additional steps are necessary to calculate the estate tax liability from the taxable estate. First, the taxable estate is increased by **adjusted taxable gifts** (defined below) to compute cumulative lifetime transfers (i.e., the estate tax base). The objective of adding previously taxed transfers to the taxable estate is to allow the estate tax base to reflect all transfers, both during life and at death. Second, a tentative tax is computed on cumulative lifetime transfers and reduced by the tax payable on adjusted taxable gifts (computed using the current tax rates). Finally, this tentative tax is then reduced by the applicable credit.

In contrast to the gift tax formula, the estate tax formula allows a reduction only for taxes *payable* on adjusted taxable gifts. Recall that the gift tax formula reduces the tax on cumulative transfers by the gift taxes on all prior transfers rather than the gift taxes payable. Taxes payable on adjusted taxable gifts are a hypothetical amount computed using the past amount of applicable credit but the current tax rate schedule. Another difference between the gift tax formula and the estate tax formula is that the entire applicable credit (not just the unused portion) reduces the tentative tax (because all prior transfers are included in the tax base). These differences are illustrated below.

Adjusted Taxable Gifts Adjusted taxable gifts are prior taxable gifts reduced by prior gifts that are already included in the gross estate. For example, the value of life insurance transferred within three years of death would not be included in adjusted taxable gifts, but the value of the life insurance proceeds paid at death would be included in the estate. Despite increasing cumulative transfers, adjusted taxable gifts are not subject to double tax because the tentative tax on cumulative transfers is reduced by taxes payable on adjusted taxable gifts calculated under the current tax rate schedule. It is important to note that although adjusted taxable gifts were made in prior years, all tax calculations are made using the *current* rate schedule.

Example 25-23

After reviewing all Bob's records, Nate determined that Bob's only taxable gift was his gift of FFP stock in 2009. This transfer resulted in a taxable gift of $1 million, the tax on which was entirely offset by the applicable credit. What is the amount of cumulative transfers subject to estate tax, and what is Bob's tentative estate tax?

Answer: Bob's estate includes $21,880,000 of cumulative taxable transfers, and Bob's tentative estate tax is $8,697,800, calculated as follows:

Description	Amount	Explanation
Adjusted taxable gifts	$ 1,000,000	Prior gift
Taxable estate	20,880,000	Taxable transfers in estate
Cumulative taxable transfers	**$21,880,000**	Total taxable transfers
Tentative tax	**$ 8,697,800**	Tax from current tax rate schedule

What if: Suppose Bob had not made any taxable gifts prior to his death. Without the prior gifts, what would be Bob's tentative estate tax?

Answer: Without the gift of stock, Bob's tentative tax would be $8,297,800, calculated as follows:

Description	Amount
Adjusted taxable gifts	$ 0
Taxable estate	20,880,000
Cumulative taxable transfers	$20,880,000
Tentative tax	**$ 8,297,800**

Note that Bob's tentative tax has decreased by $400,000. This is the amount of tax on the $1 million 2009 gift at the top marginal rate (40 percent).

What if: Suppose that Bob's 2009 taxable gift was $4 million and the gift tax exemption equivalent in 2009 was $1 million. What is the amount of the reduction of taxes payable on adjusted taxable gifts?

Answer: $1.2 million. The adjusted taxable gift of $4 million would result in a tax of $1,545,800 under the current rate schedule. However, because the transfer was made in 2009, the tax would be reduced by $345,800. This is the amount of the applicable credit for an exemption equivalent of $1 million calculated using the current tax rate schedule. The calculation would be made as follows:

Description	Amount
Current tax on adjusted taxable gifts	$ 1,545,800
Applicable credit ($1 million at current tax rate)	−345,800
Current taxes payable on adjusted taxable gifts	**$1,200,000**

Note that the credit is 40 percent of the gift in excess of the exemption equivalent ($4,000,000 − $1,000,000 = $3,000,000). The $4 million prior taxable transfer is included in the calculation of Bob's cumulative taxable transfers and the tentative estate tax is calculated as before.

Description	Amount
Adjusted taxable gifts	$ 4,000,000
Taxable estate	20,880,000
Cumulative taxable transfers	$24,880,000

Description	Amount
Tax on cumulative transfers	$ 9,897,800
Taxes payable on adjusted taxable gifts	−1,200,000
Tentative estate tax	$ 8,697,800

Hence, the adjusted taxable gift increases the amount of Bob's estate subject to the top estate tax rate. Adjusted taxable gifts are not subject to an additional transfer tax at the time of Bob's death for two reasons. First, the tax payable on adjusted taxable gifts is deducted when computing the tentative tax. Second, the estate tax on the $1 million of adjusted taxable gifts that is not offset by the taxes payable will be offset by the applicable credit when computing the gross estate tax.

THE KEY FACTS

Adjusted Taxable Gifts and the Applicable Credit

- Adjusted taxable gifts are added to the taxable estate to determine cumulative taxable transfers, and the tax is computed on cumulative taxable transfers.
- Adjusted taxable gifts are not subject to double tax because the tax on cumulative transfers is reduced for taxes payable on adjusted taxable gifts.
- Taxes payable on adjusted taxable gifts are a hypothetical tax computed using the current rate schedule applied to gifts not included in the gross estate.
- The applicable credit eliminates transfer taxes on estates with relatively small cumulative lifetime and testamentary transfers (total transfers under the exemption equivalent).

Applicable Credit Besides subtracting the credit for tax on adjusted taxable gifts, we reduce the gross estate tax by several other credits.[21] The most important is the applicable credit because it eliminates the estate tax on cumulative transfers up to the exemption equivalent ($12.06 million in 2022). Hence, estate taxes are imposed only on relatively large estates. The objective of the applicable credit is to prevent the application of transfer tax to taxpayers who either would not accumulate a relatively large amount of property transfers during their lifetime and/or would not have a relatively large value of assets to pass to heirs upon their death.

The shortcut to calculating the gift tax can also be used to calculate the estate tax if total taxable transfers exceed $1 million. Rather than compute the tax on the adjusted taxable gifts and the resulting tentative tax, instead compute the tax using 40 percent times the cumulative taxable transfers after subtracting the unused exemption equivalent and adjusted taxable gifts. This shortcut works if the taxable transfers exceed $1 million because the tax can be calculated by multiplying the taxable amount by the marginal tax rate, 40 percent.

Example 25-24

Bob died on February 7 of 2022. What amount of estate tax must be paid on his estate, given his prior taxable gift of $1 million? What is the due date for Bob's estate tax return?

Answer: Estate tax of $3,928,000 is due after applying the applicable credit, computed as follows:

Description	Amount
Tentative tax (from Example 25-23)	$ 8,697,800
Less: Applicable credit	4,769,800
Estate tax due	**$3,928,000**

Bob's executor must file the estate tax return (Form 706 in Exhibit 25-8) or request an extension of time within nine months of Bob's death (by November 7 of 2022).

Using the shortcut method, the estate tax is calculated as follows:

Shortcut to Estate Tax Calculation

Description	Exemption Equivalent
Cumulative taxable transfers ($1 million plus $20.88 million)	$ 21,880,000
Less total taxable gifts in prior periods	−1,000,000
Less unused exemption equivalent	−11,060,000
Taxable transfers in this period	$ 9,820,000
Times marginal tax rate (40%)	×40%
Estate tax on estate at the current tax rate	$ 3,928,000

What if: Suppose Bob did not make any taxable gifts during his life. What amount of estate tax would be owed upon his death?

Answer: Bob's estate would owe $3,528,000, computed as follows:

Description	Amount
Tentative tax (from Example 25-23)	$ 8,297,800
Less: Applicable credit	4,769,800
Estate tax due	**$3,528,000**

In this case, the absence of gifts prior to Bob's death (no adjusted taxable gifts) would result in a $400,000 savings. The reason is that over his lifetime, Bob made fewer taxable transfers ($1 million in fact).

What if: Suppose Bob's 2009 taxable gift was $4 million (instead of $1 million) and the gift tax exemption equivalent in 2009 was $1 million. What amount of estate tax would be owed upon Bob's death?

Answer: Bob's estate would owe $3,928,000, computed as follows:

Description	Amount
Tentative tax (from Example 25-23)	$ 8,697,800
Less: Applicable credit	4,769,800
Estate tax due	**$3,928,000**

(continued on page 25-28)

[21]Other transfers that are required to be included in the gross estate are described in §2035(a). A discussion of these transfers is beyond the scope of this text.

Bob's estate tax is not increased by the amount of the adjusted taxable gifts in excess of $1 million because these gifts were taxed in 2009. The taxes payable on adjusted taxable gifts eliminate the potential for double taxation. The portion of the 2009 gift that was not taxed in 2009 (recall that $1 million was offset by the applicable credit) is now subject to tax, however.

Using the shortcut method, Bob's estate tax could be calculated as follows:

Shortcut to Estate Tax Calculation

Description	Exemption Equivalent
Cumulative taxable transfers ($4 million plus $20.88 million)	$ 24,880,000
Less total taxable gifts in prior periods	−4,000,000
Less unused exemption equivalent	−11,060,000
Taxable transfers in this period	$ 9,820,000
Times marginal tax rate (40%)	×40%
Estate tax on estate at the current tax rate	$ 3,928,000

The applicable credit for a surviving spouse is based on the current exemption equivalent increased by the amount of the **deceased spousal unused exclusion (DSUE).** Under §2010(c)(5) the DSUE is irrevocably elected by the decedent's executor on a timely filed Form 706, and it is reduced to the extent that the deceased spouse used any of the applicable credit. For example, suppose a deceased spouse died in 2013 without using any of the $5.25 million applicable credit available in that year. If a DSUE election was made by the deceased spouse's executor, the surviving spouse's estate would be entitled to an exemption equivalent in 2022 of $17.31 million ($12.06 million plus $5.25 million). If the deceased spouse had used $2 million of the 2013 exemption equivalent prior to their death, then the surviving spouse would only be entitled to an exemption equivalent of $15.31 million ($12.06 million plus $3.25 million).

Besides eliminating transfer taxes for relatively small cumulative transfers, the exemption equivalent also acts as the transfer requirement for filing an estate return. That is, an estate tax return (Form 706) must be filed if the gross estate plus adjusted taxable gifts equals or exceeds the exemption equivalent. Exhibit 25-8 presents the first page of Form 706 for Bob Smith. The deadline for the estate tax return is nine months after the decedent's death.[22]

Example 25-25

What if: Using the facts in Example 25-24, suppose Bob's spouse died in 2015, at which time they left a gross estate of $5 million to Bob. Bob's spouse had never made a taxable gift, and the executor of the spouse's estate claimed a marital deduction for the $5 million transfer and made a portability election for the unused spousal exclusion of $5.43 million. What amount of estate tax would be owed upon Bob's death?

Answer: $1.756 million. Bob's estate would be entitled to claim an applicable credit based on the combination of the current exemption equivalent and the deceased spouse's unused 2015 exemption, or $17.49 million ($5.43 million + $12.06 million). Bob's estate would be entitled to an applicable credit equal to the current tax on $17.49 million of $6,941,800. Bob's estate tax would be computed as follows:

Description	Amount
Tentative tax	$ 8,697,800
Less: Applicable credit	6,941,800
Estate tax due	**$1,756,000**

[22]A six-month extension to file the estate tax return is automatically granted by the IRS. However, an estimate of the tax due must be paid on the due date of the return. In addition, an election for DSUE (called a portability election) must be made on a timely filed estate tax return regardless of whether the estate is otherwise required to file an estate tax return. Reg. §20.2010-2(a)(1) indicates that the IRS will not grant an extension of time to file an estate tax return merely to make a portability election.

EXHIBIT 25-8 Page 1 of Form 706 Estate Tax Return for Bob Smith

Form **706** (Rev. August 2019)
Department of the Treasury
Internal Revenue Service

United States Estate (and Generation-Skipping Transfer) Tax Return

▶ Estate of a citizen or resident of the United States (see instructions). To be filed for decedents dying after December 31, 2018.
▶ Go to *www.irs.gov/Form706* for instructions and the latest information.

OMB No. 1545-0015

Part 1—Decedent and Executor

1a Decedent's first name and middle initial (and maiden name, if any): **BOB**	1b Decedent's last name: **SMITH**			2 Decedent's social security no.: **000 00 0000**
3a City, town, or post office; county; state or province; country; and ZIP or foreign postal code: **ANN ARBOR WASHTENAW COUNTY MICHIGAN 48109**	3b Year domicile established: **1990**	4 Date of birth: **1940**		5 Date of death: **2022**
6a Name of executor (see instructions): **NATE SMITH**	6b Executor's address (number and street including apartment or suite no.; city, town, or post office; state or province; country; and ZIP or foreign postal code) and phone no.: **6500 TRAIL ROAD ANN ARBOR, MICHICAN 48109** Phone no. **(000) 000-0000**			
6c Executor's social security number (see instructions)				

6d If there are multiple executors, check here ☐ and attach a list showing the names, addresses, telephone numbers, and SSNs of the additional executors.

7a Name and location of court where will was probated or estate administered: **WASHTENAW COUNTY PROBATE COURT** — 7b Case number: **00-12345**

8 If decedent died testate, check here ▶ ☑ and attach a certified copy of the will. 9 If you extended the time to file this Form 706, check here ▶ ☐

10 If Schedule R-1 is attached, check here ▶ ☐ 11 If you are estimating the value of assets included in the gross estate on line 1 pursuant to the special rule of Reg. section 20.2010-2(a)(7)(ii), check here ▶ ☐

Part 2—Tax Computation

Line	Description	Sub-line	Sub-amount	Line	Amount
1	Total gross estate less exclusion (from Part 5—Recapitulation, item 13)			1	21,250,717
2	Tentative total allowable deductions (from Part 5—Recapitulation, item 24)			2	370,717
3a	Tentative taxable estate (subtract line 2 from line 1)			3a	20,880,000
b	State death tax deduction			3b	0
c	Taxable estate (subtract line 3b from line 3a)			3c	20,880,000
4	Adjusted taxable gifts (see instructions)			4	1,000,000
5	Add lines 3c and 4			5	21,880,000
6	Tentative tax on the amount on line 5 from Table A in the instructions			6	8,697,800
7	Total gift tax paid or payable (see instructions)			7	0
8	Gross estate tax (subtract line 7 from line 6)			8	8,697,800
9a	Basic exclusion amount	9a	12,060,000		
b	Deceased spousal unused exclusion (DSUE) amount from predeceased spouse(s), if any (from Section D, Part 6—Portability of Deceased Spousal Unused Exclusion)	9b	0		
c	Restored exclusion amount (see instructions)	9c	0		
d	Applicable exclusion amount (add lines 9a, 9b, and 9c)	9d	12,060,000		
e	Applicable credit amount (tentative tax on the amount in line 9d from Table A in the instructions)	9e	4,769,800		
10	Adjustment to applicable credit amount (May not exceed $6,000. See instructions.)	10	0		
11	Allowable applicable credit amount (subtract line 10 from line 9e)			11	4,769,800
12	Subtract line 11 from line 8 (but do not enter less than zero)			12	3,928,000
13	Credit for foreign death taxes (from Schedule P). (Attach Form(s) 706-CE.)	13			
14	Credit for tax on prior transfers (from Schedule Q)	14			
15	Total credits (add lines 13 and 14)			15	0
16	Net estate tax (subtract line 15 from line 12)			16	3,928,000
17	Generation-skipping transfer (GST) taxes payable (from Schedule R, Part 2, line 10)			17	0
18	Total transfer taxes (add lines 16 and 17)			18	3,928,000
19	Prior payments (explain in an attached statement)			19	0
20	Balance due (or overpayment) (subtract line 19 from line 18)			20	3,928,000

Under penalties of perjury, I declare that I have examined this return, including accompanying schedules and statements, and to the best of my knowledge and belief, it is true, correct, and complete. Declaration of preparer (other than the executor) is based on all information of which preparer has any knowledge.

Sign Here
▶ Signature of executor ▶ Date
▶ Signature of executor ▶ Date

Paid Preparer Use Only

Print/Type preparer's name	Preparer's signature	Date	Check ☐ if self-employed	PTIN
Firm's name ▶			Firm's EIN ▶	
Firm's address ▶			Phone no.	

For Privacy Act and Paperwork Reduction Act Notice, see instructions. Cat. No. 20548R Form **706** (Rev. 8-2019)

Source: irs.gov.

LO 25-4

WEALTH PLANNING CONCEPTS

Wealth planning coordinates both income and transfer tax strategies with nontax objectives. Before we explore transfer tax strategies, we briefly review the generation-skipping tax and outline income taxation of fiduciary entities. While these topics are certainly important, we note them only in passing because their complexity is beyond the scope of this text.

The Generation-Skipping Tax

The **generation-skipping tax (GST)** is a supplemental tax designed to prevent the avoidance of transfer taxes (both estate and gift tax) through transfers that skip a generation of recipients. For example, a grandparent could give a life estate in property to a child, with the remainder to a grandchild. When the child dies and the grandchild inherits the property, no transfer tax is imposed because nothing remains in the child's estate (the life estate terminates at death). In this way, the grandparent pays one transfer tax (on the initial gift) to transfer the property down two generations.

The GST is triggered by the transfer of property to someone more than one generation younger than the donor or decedent—a grandchild rather than a child. A transfer to a grandchild is not subject to GST, however, if the grandchild's parents are dead. The GST is very complex and can be triggered directly by transfers or indirectly by a termination of an interest. Fortunately, the GST is not widely applicable because it does not generally apply to transfers that qualify for an annual gift tax exclusion, and each donor/decedent is entitled to a relatively generous aggregate exemption ($12.06 million in 2022).

Income Tax Considerations

A **fiduciary** entity is a legal entity that takes possession of property for the benefit of a person. An **estate** is a legal entity, such as an estate or trust, that comes into existence upon a person's death to transfer the decedent's real and personal property. Likewise, a **trust** is also a legal entity whose purpose is to hold and administer the corpus for other persons (*beneficiaries*). While an estate exists only until the assets of the decedent are distributed, a trust may have a prolonged or even indefinite existence. Because these entities can exist for many years, special rules govern the taxation of income realized on property they hold. These rules are complex and relate to how fiduciaries account for income under state law. A detailed discussion is beyond the scope of this text, but we provide an overview below.

The trust or testamentary instrument (or, in the absence of an instrument, state law) determines how income and expenses are allocated between beneficiaries—under fiduciary accounting rules, income belongs to income beneficiaries and corpus (principal) belongs to the remainderman. For example, an instrument may allocate gains on the sale of assets to corpus and rental receipts to trust accounting income. Likewise, depreciation expense may be allocated to accounting income, whereas repairs may be allocated to corpus. Accounting income is important because it determines how much income can be (or must be) distributed. Trusts and estates may have discretion whether to accumulate income within the entity (for future distribution) or make current distributions.[23] Income retained by the entity is taxed as income to the entity, and consequently, the trust or estate must file an income tax return. In contrast, income distributed currently by the entity is taxed as income to the beneficiary. To accomplish this flow-through of income, trusts and estates are granted an income tax deduction for current distributions of income, and this deduction depends, in part, on accounting income.

To better understand how taxable income is divided between a trust or estate and its beneficiaries, it is helpful to first summarize the formula for determining taxable income.[24]

[23]Regulations under §§651–652 make a distinction between simple trusts and complex trusts. **Simple trusts** must distribute all trust accounting income currently (and cannot make charitable contributions), whereas **complex trusts** are not required by the trust instrument to distribute income currently.

[24]Subchapter J (§§641–692) contains the provisions governing income taxation of trusts and estates.

With few exceptions, the formula for calculating taxable income for a trust or an estate is analogous to the individual income tax formula. Gross income for the entity is determined in the same manner as gross income for an individual. For example, trusts are generally taxed on realized income, but they can exclude certain items from gross income, such as municipal interest, and make elections to defer certain items, such as installment gains.

Trusts and estates can also deduct expenses similar to an individual. For example, they may deduct trade or business expenses, interest, taxes, and charitable contributions. Lastly, trusts and estates are allowed a deduction for distributions of income to beneficiaries. It is this **distribution deduction** that operates to eliminate the potential for double taxation of income.

The maximum amount of the distribution deduction is the lesser of the amount actually distributed or **distributable net income (DNI).** DNI is calculated by adjusting taxable income before the distribution deduction for certain items of income and deduction. The calculation of DNI, and consequently taxable income, can be complicated by items such as net operating losses, net capital losses, charitable contributions, multiple beneficiaries, and discretionary (versus mandatory) distributions. Suffice it to say that the calculation of income tax for a trust or estate can be a very complicated matter.

While granting a trust or estate discretion over distributions complicates the calculation of taxable income, it might appear that this discretion also provides an opportunity to split income (by creating yet another taxpayer). However, the income tax rates applying to trusts and estates, provided in Appendix C in this text, are generally as high as or higher than the tax rates for individual beneficiaries. Hence, the potential income tax benefits from splitting income between these entities and beneficiaries are typically negligible.

Transfer Tax Planning Techniques

Transfer tax planning strategies are the same as those employed for income tax planning: timing, shifting, and conversion. Like income tax planning, wealth planning is primarily concerned with accomplishing the client's goals in the most efficient and effective manner after considering *both* tax and nontax costs. For the most part, wealth planning is directed to maximizing after-tax wealth to be transferred from an older generation to a younger generation. A critical constraint in this process, however, is determining how tax strategies can achieve the client's ultimate (tax and nontax) goals. Before attempting to integrate tax and nontax considerations, let's survey a few basic techniques for transfer tax planning.

THE KEY FACTS

Basic Wealth Planning Techniques

- A serial gift strategy saves gift taxes by converting a potentially large taxable transfer into multiple smaller transfers that qualify for the annual exclusion.
- Testamentary transfers allow a step-up in tax basis to fair market value, thereby eliminating income tax on unrealized appreciation.
- Lifetime gifts eliminate transfer taxes on post-gift appreciation.

Serial Gifts A **serial gift** strategy converts a large taxable transfer into a tax-exempt transfer by dividing it into multiple lifetime gifts. As long as the gifts qualify as present interests and do not exceed the annual exclusion, the transfers are exempt from all transfer taxes. Although serial gifts are an easy and low-cost planning strategy, this technique is limited in scope because only $16,000 per donee ($32,000 for married donors electing gift-splitting) can be transferred in 2022 (the amount is indexed for inflation) without any transfer tax. Hence, serial gifts can move significant amounts of wealth only if employed by multiple donors over multiple years and multiple donees.

Example 25-26

Suppose Harry and Wilma decide to begin transferring wealth to Dina and George. To what extent can serial gifts accomplish this goal without triggering gift taxes?

Answer: Harry and Wilma could each make annual gifts of $16,000 to Dina and George. These gifts would remove $64,000 per year from the Smiths' estate without triggering any transfer taxes (gift tax or generation-skipping tax). They could include any type of property as long as Dina and George can presently enjoy the property or income generated by it.

Step-Up in Tax Basis Timing is an important component in tax planning. Generally, a good tax planning strategy delays payment of tax, thereby reducing the present value of the tax paid. While deferral is important, transfer tax planning must also consider the potential appreciation of assets transferred and the effect of the income tax that could apply if and when the appreciation is realized. Gifted property generally retains the donor's basis in the property, meaning the donee takes a **carryover basis,** whereas inherited property takes a tax basis of fair market value. The advantage of gifting property is that the donor eliminates the transfer tax on any additional future appreciation on the gifted property. The disadvantage is that the unrealized appreciation of the gifted property will eventually be taxed (although at the donee's income tax rate). Thus, gifting appreciating property reduces future transfer taxes but at the cost of additional future income taxes imposed on the donee. In contrast, for inherited property, past appreciation (up to the date of death) will never be subject to income tax but instead is subject to transfer tax at the time of the transfer.

Example 25-27

What if: Suppose Harry currently owns 30 percent of the outstanding shares of FFP. These shares have a basis of $300,000 but are worth in excess of $2.7 million. Suppose Harry intends to transfer his FFP shares to his daughter Dina, who, in turn, intends to sell them after Harry's death (in three years). It is important to consider the extent to which income tax considerations influence whether Harry gifts these shares or holds them until his death.

Assume the transfer (whether by gift or inheritance) will be taxed at the top transfer rate of 40 percent, while when Dina sells the shares in three years, the gain will be taxed at a capital gains tax rate of 20 percent (ignoring the net investment income tax). Also assume the FFP shares will not appreciate and the prevailing interest rate is 6 percent. What is the total tax savings if Harry delays the transfer of the shares until his death three years hence?

Answer: The total tax savings is $686,280 if Harry delays the transfer until his death rather than gifting the shares to Dina immediately. See the following discussion and computations:

Description	Gift	Inheritance	Explanation
Gift tax paid	$1,080,000		40% × $2.7 million
Time value of gift tax	× 1.191		$(1.06)^3$
Future value of gift tax	$1,286,280		Value of gift tax paid
Estate tax paid		$1,080,000	40% × $2.7 million
Dina's capital gain tax of 20%	480,000	0	Gain of $2.4 million on gift due to carryover basis
Total taxes paid	$1,766,280	$1,080,000	$686,280 of tax savings

If a sale is planned, then the step-up in tax basis becomes critical to avoid being taxed on the accumulated appreciation. In this scenario, a testamentary transfer provides a step-up in tax basis and delays payment of the transfer tax for three years.

What if: Suppose Dina has no interest in selling the family business and intends to eventually transfer the shares to George. Moreover, suppose Harry believes the FFP shares will appreciate to $3.5 million within three years. To what extent should income tax considerations influence whether Harry transfers these shares immediately via gift or in three years via testamentary transfer? Estimate the total tax savings if Harry transfers the shares immediately rather than delaying the transfer until his death.

Answer: The tax savings is $113,720 if Harry transfers property immediately rather than delaying the transfer until his death. See the following discussion and computations:

Description	Gift	Inheritance	Explanation
Gift tax paid	$1,080,000		40% × $2.7 million
Time value of gift tax	× 1.191		$(1.06)^3$
Future value of gift tax	$1,286,280		Value of gift tax paid
Estate tax paid		$1,400,000	40% × $3.5 million
Total taxes paid	$1,286,280	$1,400,000	$113,720 of tax savings

If Dina plans to hold the shares indefinitely and the property is rapidly appreciating, then an inter vivos gift avoids having future appreciation taxed in Harry's estate. Although a gift of the shares would accelerate the imposition of transfer taxes, any unused applicable credit could minimize the amount of taxes due on the transfer. In this scenario, transfer via gift reduces total transfer taxes even though the gift tax is paid three years before an estate tax would be due.

Timing becomes critical in determining how to trade off income tax savings (step-up in tax basis) against transfer tax costs (paying gift tax now or paying estate taxes on additional appreciation later). Most tax advisers will suggest that elderly clients sell business assets or investments with unrealized losses because upon death the basis of these assets will be adjusted downward to fair market value. In other words, the adjustment to basis can be a step-down as well as a step-up, and a sale allows the loss to be deducted.

Integrated Wealth Plans

A client can have many nontax goals associated with the ultimate disposition of wealth, and some are very personal. It is often difficult to ascertain and prioritize them for planning purposes. However, an effective wealth plan must identify and integrate these personal objectives with tax costs. Often, the primary nontax objective of wealth planning is to preserve value during the transfer of control (management) of business assets. Thus, an essential nontax element of any effective wealth plan is to identify a safe mechanism to support the older generation in a specific lifestyle while transferring control to the younger generation.

Trusts are common vehicles for tax planning, in large part because these entities can be structured to achieve a great variety of tax and nontax objectives, including the support of specific beneficiaries.[25] The trustee is responsible for managing property in the trust, but the grantor can also give the trustee discretionary powers to provide flexibility. These powers can include the discretion to distribute income or corpus among beneficiaries. In addition, grantors can retain powers, including the ability to revoke the trust, select the trustee (original or successor), terminate beneficial interests, and add to the corpus. The most important aspect of an irrevocable trust is that the provisions (including powers and guidelines for the exercise of discretionary powers) cannot be changed once the trust instrument has been executed.

Specific types of trusts are common to many wealth transfer plans. For example, a **life insurance trust** is funded with an irrevocable transfer of a life insurance policy, and the trustee is given the power to name beneficiaries and redesignate them in case of divorce or death. Upon the death of the grantor, the amount of the policy is paid into the trust but not included in the grantor's estate. Moreover, an immediate cash distribution from the trust is not taxable income to the beneficiaries.

Example 25-28

Harry is planning to purchase a $2 million life insurance policy. He wants to use the proceeds to support Wilma after his death and have any remaining funds paid to his surviving children. How might Harry structure a trust to accomplish these goals?

Answer: Harry could transfer the policy to an irrevocable trust that directs the trustee to hold the policy and pay the premiums until Harry's death. At that time, the trustee could be directed to invest the $2 million proceeds and pay income to Wilma for the remainder of her life or until she remarries. At Wilma's death or remarriage, the trust terminates and pays the remaining funds to Harry's surviving children or their estates.

What if: Suppose Harry transfers the policy to an irrevocable trust and dies four years later. Will the use of this trust trigger any estate taxes at that time?

Answer: Harry's transfer of the policy to the trust will be a taxable gift at the time of the transfer to the extent of the value of the transfer. However, the $2 million proceeds from the policy will not be included in Harry's estate upon his death because the gift was not made within three years of Harry's death.

[25]Trusts are also popular because the trust property transfers outside probate, thereby avoiding both the costs and the publicity associated with probate.

Donors often use partnerships to transfer assets and for the control of a business in a systematic manner that also provides them with income and security. One specific form of partnership, the **family limited partnership,** divides a family business into various ownership interests, representing control of operations and future income and appreciation of the assets. Prior to restrictions enacted by Congress, these limited partnerships were sometimes used to transfer appreciation to members of a younger generation while allowing the older generation to effectively retain control of the business. Obviously, the intent of estate and gift taxes is to recognize transfers of assets that also represent control of the assets. Hence, it is not surprising that Congress revised the law to restrict the ability of family limited partnerships to effectively transfer appreciation in business assets and operations to younger generations without also transferring control.

CONCLUSION

In this chapter we learned to identify taxable transfers whether made during life (inter vivos transfers) or at death (testamentary transfers). We also learned how to calculate gift and estate taxes and described some fundamental transfer tax planning techniques. The simplest and most effective wealth planning technique is serial gifting. As long as the gifts are restricted to present interests under the annual exclusion, serial gifting avoids all transfer taxes. Other methods, such as family limited partnerships, can also be effective under the proper circumstances. In all cases, however, wealth planning should be carefully coordinated with other needs and objectives.

Summary

LO 25-1 Describe federal transfer taxes.

- Congress imposes a tax on transfers of property whether the transfer is a gift or occurs at death.
- The unified transfer tax scheme provides for a progressive tax rate schedule that applies to cumulative transfers. That is, transfers in all prior periods are taken into account when calculating the tax for a transfer in a current period.
- The applicable (unified) credit offsets transfer tax on cumulative lifetime transfers (the exemption equivalent) of $12.06 million for gifts and transfers at death made during 2022.
- Each transfer tax shares two common deductions: an unlimited deduction for charitable contributions and a marital deduction that allows almost unfettered transfers between spouses.
- Property transfers are valued at fair market value, defined as the value paid by a willing buyer to a willing seller. The determination of fair market value often depends upon the facts and circumstances surrounding the property.

LO 25-2 Calculate the federal gift tax.

- Lifetime transfers of property for no (or inadequate) consideration are taxed as gifts if the transfer is complete and irrevocable.
- Contributions to political parties or candidates, and medical and educational expenses paid on behalf of an unrelated individual, are excluded from gift taxation.
- Gifts are taxed at the fair market value of the donated property on the date the gift becomes complete, and small gifts are reduced by the annual exclusion ($16,000 in 2022) if they are present interests.

- With gift-splitting, married couples can elect to treat all gifts made in a year as if each spouse made one-half of each gift.
- Taxable gifts are calculated by adjusting current gifts for exclusions and gift-splitting, and then deducting the marital deduction (for qualifying gifts to a spouse) and the charitable deduction.
- Transfers of terminable interests in property, such as a life estate, will not generally qualify for the marital deduction.
- The gift tax on cumulative taxable gifts is computed by adding prior taxable gifts to current taxable gifts.
- The gift tax on cumulative gifts is reduced by the gift tax on prior taxable gifts and is calculated using the current rate schedule and ignoring any exemption equivalent used in prior years. The gift tax is then reduced by the *unused* portion of the exemption equivalent as converted into the applicable credit using the current tax rate schedule.

Compute the federal estate tax. **LO 25-3**

- The gross estate includes property owned by the decedent at death (the probate estate) and certain property transfers taking effect at death.
- Property the decedent owned jointly is included in the gross estate. The value of the decedent's interest is included when property is held in joint tenancy, whereas half the value of the property is included when held with a spouse in joint tenancy with the right of survivorship.
- Temporal interests begin or end with the passage of time. The value of a future interest, such as a remainder, can be determined from IRS tables, and the value of a present interest, such as a life estate, is calculated as the difference between the value of the future interest and the current value of the property.
- The gross estate is reduced by administrative expenses, debts of the decedent, and losses incurred during the administration of the estate, resulting in the adjusted gross estate.
- The adjusted gross estate is reduced for certain transfers to a surviving spouse (the marital deduction) and for transfers to charities (the charitable deduction), resulting in the taxable estate.
- The taxable estate is increased by adjusted taxable gifts to determine cumulative transfers.
- The tentative estate tax is calculated on cumulative transfers as reduced by the tax payable on adjusted taxable gifts calculated using the current rate schedule.
- The estate tax due is the tentative tax reduced by the full applicable credit.
- An estate is allowed to increase the exemption equivalent by the amount of a deceased spousal unused exclusion (DSUE) if an irrevocable election is made on the deceased spouse's timely filed estate tax return.

Understand how income and transfer taxation interact to affect wealth planning. **LO 25-4**

- The generation-skipping tax is a supplemental tax designed to prevent the avoidance of transfer taxes (both estate and gift taxes) through transfers that skip a generation of recipients.
- Trusts and estates are taxpayers taxed on accumulated (undistributed) income via a fiduciary income tax return.
- Because trust and estate income tax rates are generally as high as or higher than the tax rates for individual beneficiaries, the income tax benefits from splitting income between these entities and beneficiaries are typically negligible.
- A serial gift strategy saves gift taxes by converting a potentially large taxable transfer into a tax-exempt transfer of multiple smaller gifts that qualify for the annual exclusion of the donor.
- Testamentary transfers allow a step-up in tax basis to fair market value, thereby eliminating the income tax on unrealized appreciation. In contrast, appreciation of property transferred via inter vivos transfers may be eventually realized and taxed as income. However, a gift eliminates transfer taxes on expected future appreciation.

KEY TERMS

adequate consideration (25-5)
adjusted gross estate (25-23)
adjusted taxable gifts (25-25)
alternative valuation date (25-22)
annual exclusion (25-9)
applicable credit (25-2)
beneficiary (25-7)
carryover basis (25-32)
common-law states (25-10)
community-property states (25-10)
complex trust (25-30)
corpus (25-7)
current gifts (25-10)
deceased spousal unused exclusion (DSUE) (25-28)
distributable net income (DNI) (25-31)
distribution deduction (25-31)
donee (25-5)
donor (25-5)
estate (25-30)
executor (25-17)
exemption equivalent (25-3)
family limited partnership (25-34)
fiduciary (25-30)
fiduciary duty (25-7)
future interest (25-7)
generation-skipping tax (GST) (25-30)
grantor (25-7)
gross estate (25-17)
heirs (25-17)
inter vivos transfers (25-2)
joint tenancy (25-6)
joint tenancy with right of survivorship (25-6)
last will and testament (25-2)
life estate (25-7)
life insurance trust (25-33)
marital deduction (25-4)
nondeductible terminable interests (25-11)
present interest (25-7)
probate (25-17)
probate estate (25-17)
remainder (25-7)
remainderman (25-7)
reversion (25-7)
serial gift (25-31)
simple trust (25-30)
taxable estate (25-23)
taxable gifts (25-10)
tenancy in common (25-6)
terminable interest (25-7)
testamentary transfers (25-2)
trust (25-7, 25-30)
trustee (25-7)

DISCUSSION QUESTIONS

Discussion Questions are available in Connect®.

LO 25-1 1. Identify the features common to the gift tax formula and the estate tax formula.

LO 25-1 2. Explain why Congress felt it necessary to enact a gift tax to complement the estate tax.

LO 25-1 3. Describe the applicable credit and the purpose it serves in the gift and estate tax.

LO 25-1 4. Fredi is retired and living on a pension and has accumulated almost $1 million of property. Fredi would like to leave this property to her children. However, Fredi is afraid that the federal estate tax will appropriate much of her wealth. Explain whether this fear is well-founded.

LO 25-1 5. Define fair market value for transfer tax purposes.

LO 25-2 6. Describe the requirements for a complete gift, and contrast a gift of a present interest with a gift of a future interest.

LO 25-2 7. Describe the property transfers that qualify as gifts and define transfers that are not gifts for transfer tax purposes.

LO 25-2 8. Describe a situation in which a transfer of cash to a trust might be considered an incomplete gift.

LO 25-2 9. Identify two types of transfers for inadequate consideration that are specifically excluded from imposition of the gift tax.

LO 25-2 10. Under what circumstances will a deposit of cash to a bank account held in joint tenancy be considered a complete gift?

LO 25-2 11. Explain how a purchase of realty could result in a taxable gift.

LO 25-2 12. Describe the conditions for using the annual exclusion to offset an otherwise taxable transfer.

LO 25-2 13. List the conditions for making an election to split gifts.

LO 25-2 14. Describe the limitations on the deduction of transfers to charity.

15. Explain the purpose of adding prior taxable gifts to current taxable gifts and show whether these prior gifts could be taxed multiple times over the years. LO 25-2
16. Explain why the gross estate includes the value of certain property transferred by the decedent at death, such as property held in joint tenancy with the right of survivorship, even though this property is not subject to probate. LO 25-3
17. Identify the factors that determine the proportion of the value of property held in joint tenancy with the right of survivorship that will be included in a decedent's gross estate. LO 25-3
18. Ahmad owns a condo in Hawaii that he plans on using for the rest of his life. However, to ensure his sister Jana will own the property after his death, Ahmad deeded the remainder of the property to her. He signed the deed transferring the remainder in July 2009 when the condo was worth $250,000 and his life estate was worth $75,000. Ahmad died in January of this year, at which time the condo was worth $300,000. What amount, if any, is included in Ahmad's gross estate? Explain. LO 25-3 research
19. Paul is a widower with several grown children. He is considering transferring his residence into a trust for his children and retaining a life estate in it. Comment on whether this plan will prevent the value of the home from being included in Paul's gross estate when he dies. LO 25-3
20. Explain how a remainder and an income interest are valued for transfer tax purposes. LO 25-3
21. Explain why the fair market value of a life estate is more difficult to estimate than an income interest. LO 25-3
22. Describe a reason why transfers of terminable interests should not qualify for the marital deduction. LO 25-3
23. Adjusted taxable gifts are included in cumulative taxable transfers for calculating the estate tax. Explain whether including these gifts in the estate tax base will subject the gifts to double taxation. LO 25-3
24. People sometimes confuse the applicable credit with the exemption equivalent. Describe how these terms differ and how they are related. LO 25-3
25. Describe a reason why a generation-skipping tax was necessary to augment the estate and gift taxes. LO 25-4
26. Explain why an effective wealth transfer plan likely necessitates cooperation between lawyers, accountants, and investment advisers. LO 25-4
27. Describe how to initiate the construction of a comprehensive and effective wealth plan. LO 25-4
28. List two questions you might pose to a client to find out whether a program of serial gifts would be an advantageous wealth transfer plan. LO 25-4
29. A client in good health wants to support the college education of her teenage grandchild. The client holds various properties but proposes to make a gift of cash in the amount of the annual exclusion. Explain to the client why a direct gift of cash may not be advisable and what property might serve as a reasonable substitute. LO 25-4
30. An elderly client has a life insurance policy worth $40,000 that upon death pays $250,000 to a sole grandchild (or their estate). The client retains ownership of the policy. Outline the costs and benefits of transferring ownership of the policy to a life insurance trust. LO 25-4
31. Identify the sections in the Internal Revenue Code that authorize the use of qualified terminable interest property (QTIPs) for gift and estate tax purposes, respectively. LO 25-4 research
32. Under what conditions can an executor or trustee elect to claim a marital deduction for a transfer of a terminable interest to a spouse? LO 25-4 research
33. Explain how a transfer of property as a gift may have income tax implications to the donee. LO 25-4

PROBLEMS

Select problems are available in Connect®.

LO 25-2 34. Raquel transferred $100,000 of stock to a trust, with income to be paid to her nephew for 18 years and the remainder to her nephew's children (or their estates). Raquel named a bank as independent trustee but retained the power to determine how much income, if any, will be paid in any particular year. Is this transfer a complete gift? Explain.

LO 25-2 35. This year Gerry's friend, Dewey, was disabled. Gerry paid $15,000 to Dewey's doctor for medical expenses and paid $12,500 to State University for college tuition for Dewey's son. Has Gerry made taxable gifts and, if so, in what amounts?

LO 25-2 36. This year Omar and Mike purchased realty for $180,000 and took title as equal tenants in common. However, Mike was able to provide only $40,000 of the purchase price, and Omar provided the remaining $140,000. Has Omar made a complete gift to Mike and, if so, in what amount?

LO 25-2 37. Last year Nate opened a savings account with a deposit of $15,000. The account was in the name of Nate and Derrick, joint tenancy with the right of survivorship. Derrick did not contribute to the account, but this year he withdrew $5,000. Has Nate made a complete gift and, if so, what is the amount of the taxable gift and when was the gift made?

LO 25-2 38. Barry transfers $1,000,000 to an irrevocable trust with income to Robin for her life and the remainder to Maurice (or his estate). Calculate the value of the life estate and the remainder if Robin's age and the prevailing interest rate result in a Table S discount factor of .27 for the remainder.

LO 25-2 39. This year Jim created an irrevocable trust to provide for Ted, his 32-year-old nephew, and Ted's family. Jim transferred $70,000 to the trust and named a bank as the trustee. The trust was directed to pay income to Ted until he reaches age 35, and at that time the trust is to be terminated and the corpus is to be distributed to Ted's two children (or their estates). Determine the amount, if any, of the current gift and the taxable gift. If necessary, you may assume the relevant interest rate is 6 percent and Jim is unmarried.

LO 25-2 40. This year Colleen transferred $100,000 to an irrevocable trust that pays equal shares of income annually to three cousins (or their estates) for the next eight years. At that time, the trust is to be terminated and the corpus of the trust will revert to Colleen. Determine the amount, if any, of the current gifts and the taxable gifts. If necessary, you may assume the relevant interest rate is 6 percent and Colleen is unmarried. What is your answer if Colleen is married and elects to gift-split with the spouse?

LO 25-2 41. Sly is a widower and wants to make annual gifts of cash to each of his four children and six grandchildren. How much can Sly transfer to his children this year if he makes the maximum gifts eligible for the annual exclusion? What is the amount of the total transfer if Sly is married and elects gift-splitting, assuming his spouse makes no other gifts?

LO 25-2 42. Jack and Liz live in a community-property state and their vacation home is community property. This year they transferred the vacation home to an irrevocable trust that provides their son, Tom, a life estate in the home and the remainder to their daughter, Laura. Under the terms of the trust, Tom has the right to use the vacation home for the duration of his life, and Laura will automatically own the property after Tom's death. At the time of the gift, the home was valued at $500,000, Tom was 35 years old, and the §7520 rate was 5.4 percent. What is the amount, if any, of the taxable gifts? Would your answer be different if the home was not community property and Jack and Liz elected to gift-split?

43. David placed $80,000 in trust with income to Steve for his life and the remainder to Lil (or her estate). At the time of the gift, given the prevailing interest rate, Steve's life estate was valued at $65,000 and the remainder at $15,000. What is the amount, if any, of David's taxable gifts? LO 25-2

44. Stephen transferred $17,500 to an irrevocable trust for Graham. The trustee has the discretion to distribute income or corpus for Graham's benefit but is required to distribute all assets to Graham (or his estate) not later than Graham's 21st birthday. What is the amount, if any, of the taxable gift? LO 25-2

45. For the holidays, Marty gave a watch worth $25,000 to Sobia and jewelry worth $40,000 to Natalie. Has Marty made any taxable gifts this year and, if so, in what amounts? Does it matter if Marty is married and lives in a community-property state? LO 25-2

46. This year Jeff earned $850,000 and used it to purchase land in joint tenancy with a right of survivorship with Mary. Has Jeff made a taxable gift to Mary and, if so, in what amount? What is your answer if Jeff and Mary are married? LO 25-2

47. Laura is married to Willy. This year Laura transfers $500,000 into an irrevocable trust with the income to be paid annually to Willy for life (a life estate) and the remainder to Jenny. Calculate the amount of the taxable gifts from the transfers. LO 25-2

48. Red transferred $5,000,000 of cash to State University for a new sports complex. Calculate the amount of the taxable gift. LO 25-2

49. In 2010 Casey made a taxable gift of $5 million to both Stephanie and Linda (a total of $10 million in taxable gifts). Calculate the amount of gift tax due this year and Casey's unused exemption equivalent under the following alternatives. LO 25-2
   a) This year Casey made a *taxable gift* of $1 million to Stephanie. Casey is not married, and the 2010 gift was the only other taxable gift he has ever made.
   b) This year Casey made a *taxable gift* of $15 million to Stephanie. Casey is not married, and the 2010 gift was the only other taxable gift he has ever made.
   c) This year Casey made a *gift* worth $15 million to Stephanie. Casey married Helen last year, and they live in a common-law state. The 2010 gift was the only other taxable gift Casey or Helen has ever made. Casey and Helen elect to gift-split this year.

50. Tom Hruise was an entertainment executive who had a fatal accident on a film set. Tom's will directed his executor to distribute his cash and stock to his spouse, Kaffie, and the real estate to a church, The First Church of Methodology. The remainder of Tom's assets were to be placed in trust for three children. Tom's estate consisted of the following: LO 25-3 tax forms

Assets	
Personal assets	$ 800,000
Cash and stock	24,000,000
Intangible assets (film rights)	71,500,000
Real estate	15,000,000
	$111,300,000
Liabilities	
Mortgage	$ 3,200,000
Other liabilities	4,100,000
	$ 7,300,000

   a) Tom made a taxable gift of $8 million in 2011. Compute the estate tax for Tom's estate.
   b) Fill out lines 1 through 12 in part 2 of Form 706 for Tom's estate.

LO 25-3 51. Hal and Wendy are married, and they own a parcel of realty, Blackacre, as joint tenants with the right of survivorship. Hal owns an additional parcel of realty, Redacre, in his name alone. Suppose Hal should die when Blackacre is worth $800,000 and Redacre is worth $750,000. What value of realty would be included in Hal's probate estate, and what value would be included in Hal's gross estate?

LO 25-3 52. Walter owns a whole-life insurance policy worth $52,000 that directs the insurance company to pay the beneficiary $250,000 on Walter's death. Walter pays the annual premiums and has the power to designate the beneficiary of the policy (it is currently his son, James). What value of the policy, if any, will be included in Walter's estate upon his death?

LO 25-3 53. Many years ago James and Sergio purchased property for $450,000. Although they are listed as equal co-owners, Sergio was able to provide only $200,000 of the purchase price. James treated the additional $25,000 of his contribution to the purchase price as a gift to Sergio. If the property is worth $900,000 at Sergio's death, what amount would be included in Sergio's estate if the title to the property was tenants in common? What if the title was joint tenancy with right of survivorship?

LO 25-3 54. Terry transferred $500,000 of real estate into an irrevocable trust for her son, Lee. The trustee was directed to retain income until Lee's 21st birthday and then pay him the corpus of the trust. Terry retained the power to require the trustee to pay income to Lee at any time and the right to the assets if Lee predeceased her. What amount of the trust, if any, will be included in Terry's estate?

LO 25-3 55. Last year Robert transferred a life insurance policy worth $450,000 to an irrevocable trust with directions to distribute the corpus of the trust to a grandson, Danny, upon graduation from college, or to Danny's estate upon death. Robert paid $40,000 of gift tax on the transfer of the policy. Early this year, Robert died, and the insurance company paid $4 million to the trust. What amount, if any, is included in Robert's gross estate?

LO 25-3 research 56. Willie purchased a whole-life insurance policy on his brother, Benny. Under the policy, the insurance company will pay the named beneficiary $1 million upon the death of the insured, Benny. Willie names Tess the beneficiary, and upon Benny's death, Tess receives the proceeds of the policy, $1 million. Identify and discuss the transfer tax implications of this arrangement.

LO 25-3 57. Jimmy owns two parcels of real estate, Tara and Sundance. Tara is worth $240,000 and Sundance is worth $360,000. Jimmy plans to bequeath Tara directly to his spouse Lois and leave her a life estate in Sundance. What amount of value will be included in Jimmy's gross estate and taxable estate should he die now?

LO 25-3 58. Banele had a taxable estate of $15.5 million when they died this year. Calculate the amount of estate tax due (if any) under the following alternatives.

a) Banele's prior taxable gifts consist of a taxable gift of $1 million in 2005.
b) Banele's prior taxable gifts consist of a taxable gift of $1.5 million in 2005.
c) Explain how the tax calculation would change if Banele made a $1 million taxable gift in the year prior to their death.

LO 25-2 tax forms 59. Brad and Angelina are a married couple who have three children, Fred, Bridget, and Lisa. Two of the three children, Fred and Bridget, are from Brad's previous marriages. On Christmas this year, Brad gave each of the three children a cash gift of $10,000, and Angelina gave Lisa an additional cash gift of $40,000. Brad also gave stock worth $60,000 (adjusted basis of $10,000) to the Actors Guild (an "A" charity).

a) Brad and Angelina have chosen to split gifts. Calculate Brad's gift tax. Assume that Angelina has no previous taxable gifts, but Brad reported previous taxable gifts of $2 million in 2009 when he used $345,800 of applicable credit and paid $435,000 of gift taxes.
b) Fill out parts 1 and 4 of Form 709 for Brad.

60. Jones is seriously ill and has $6 million of property that he wants to leave to his four children. Jones is considering making a current gift of the property (rather than leaving the property to pass through a will). Assuming any taxable transfer will be subject to the highest transfer tax rate, determine how much gift tax Jones will owe if the transfers are made now. How much estate tax will be saved if Jones dies after three years, during which time the property appreciates to $6.8 million? Besides transfer taxes, what other tax and financial factors should Jones consider in making this choice? LO 25-4 planning

61. Oisha gave a parcel of realty to Julie valued at $210,000 (Oisha purchased the property five years ago for $88,000). Compute the amount of the taxable gift on the transfer, if any. Suppose several years later Julie sold the property for $216,000. What is the amount of her gain or loss, if any, on the sale? LO 25-4

62. Several years ago Doug invested $21,000 in stock. This year he gave his daughter Tina the stock on a day it was valued at $20,000. She promptly sold it for $19,500. Determine the amount of the taxable gift, if any, and calculate the amount of taxable income or gain, if any, for Tina. Assume Doug is not married and does not support Tina, who is 28. LO 25-4 research

63. Roberta is considering making annual gifts of $16,000 of stock to each of four children. Roberta expects to live another five years and to leave a taxable estate worth approximately $18 million. Roberta requests that you justify the gifts by estimating the estate tax savings from making the gifts. LO 25-4

64. Harold and Maude were married and lived in a common-law state. Maude died in 2018 with a taxable estate of $25 million and left it all to Harold. Maude's executor filed a timely estate tax return claiming the marital deduction for the property left to Harold including a valid portability election. Harold died this year, leaving the entire $25 million to their three children. Calculate how much estate tax is due from Harold's estate under the following two alternatives. LO 25-4
    a) Assume that neither Harold nor Maude had made any taxable gifts prior to this year.
    b) Assume that Harold and Maude each made a $1 million taxable gift in 2011 and offset the gift tax at that time with the applicable credit.

COMPREHENSIVE PROBLEMS

Select problems are available in Connect®.

65. Vince and Millie are married. Vince dies this year with a gross estate of $25 million and no adjusted prior gifts. Calculate the amount of estate tax due (if any) under the following *alternative* conditions: planning
    a) Vince leaves his entire estate to Millie.
    b) Vince leaves $10 million to Millie and the remainder to charity.
    c) Vince leaves $10 million to Millie and the remainder to his son, Paul.
    d) Vince leaves $10 million to Millie and the remainder to a trust whose trustee is required to pay income to Millie for her life and the remainder to Paul.

66. Diego is a single individual who owns a life insurance policy worth $1.5 million that will be worth $8 million upon his death. This year Diego transferred the policy and all incidents of ownership to an irrevocable trust that pays income annually to Diego's two children for 15 years and then distributes the corpus to the children in equal shares.
    a) Calculate the amount of gift tax due (if any) on the transfer of the insurance policy. Assume that Diego has made only one prior taxable gift of $12 million in January of 2018.

b) Diego died unexpectedly this year after transferring the policy. At the time of death, Diego's probate estate was $25 million, to be divided in equal shares between Diego's two children. Calculate the amount of cumulative taxable transfers for estate tax purposes.

67. Jack is single and made his first taxable gift of $1,000,000 in 2008. Jack made additional gifts in 2009, at which time he gave $1,750,000 to each of his three children and an additional $1,000,000 to State University (a charity). The annual exclusion in 2009 was $13,000. Recently Jack has been in poor health and would like you to estimate his estate tax should he die this year. Jack estimates his taxable estate (after deductions) will be worth $20.4 million at his death.

68. Montgomery has decided to engage in wealth planning and has listed the value of his assets below. The life insurance has a cash surrender value of $120,000, and the proceeds are payable to Montgomery's estate. The Walen Trust is an irrevocable trust created by Montgomery's brother 10 years ago and contains assets currently valued at $800,000. The income from the trust is payable to Montgomery's faithful butler, Walen, for his life, and the remainder is payable to Montgomery or his estate. Walen is currently 37 years old, and the §7520 interest rate is currently 5.4 percent. Montgomery is unmarried and plans to leave all his assets to his surviving relatives.

Property	Value	Adjusted Basis
Auto	$ 20,000	$ 55,000
Personal effects	75,000	110,000
Checking and savings accounts	250,000	250,000
Investments	2,500,000	770,000
Residence	1,400,000	980,000
Life insurance proceeds	1,000,000	50,000
Real estate investments	10,125,000	2,800,000
Walen Trust	800,000	80,000

a) Calculate the amount of the estate tax due (if any), assuming Montgomery dies this year and has never made any taxable gifts.

b) Calculate the amount of the estate tax due (if any), assuming Montgomery dies this year and made one taxable gift in 2006. The taxable gift was $1 million, and Montgomery used his 2006 applicable credit to avoid paying any gift tax.

c) Calculate the amount of the estate tax due (if any), assuming Montgomery dies this year and made one taxable gift in 2006. The taxable gift was $5 million, and Montgomery used his $1 million 2006 applicable credit to reduce the gift tax in 2006. Montgomery plans to bequeath his investments to charity and leave his remaining assets to his surviving relatives.

UWorld Roger CPA Review

Sample CPA Exam questions from Roger CPA Review are available in Connect as support for the topics in this text. These Multiple Choice Questions and Task-Based Simulations include expert-written explanations and solutions and provide a starting point for students to become familiar with the content and functionality of the actual CPA Exam.

Appendix A

Tax Forms

The tax forms can be found in the Instructor Resources and Additional Student Resources, as well as additional forms at www.irs.gov/forms-instructions. The Additional Student Resources can be accessed directly by students in the eBook Table of Contents. They can also be assigned by instructors within Connect.

Appendix B

Tax Terms Glossary

83(b) election a special tax election that employees who receive restricted stock or other property with ownership restrictions can make to accelerate income recognition from the normal date when restrictions lapse to the date when the restricted stock or other property is granted. The election also accelerates the employer's compensation deduction related to the restricted stock or other property.

§179 expense an incentive for small businesses that allows them to immediately expense a certain amount of tangible personal property placed in service during the year.

§197 intangibles intangible assets that are purchased that must be amortized over 180 months regardless of their actual useful lives.

§291 depreciation recapture the portion of a corporate taxpayer's gain on real property that is converted from §1231 gain to ordinary income.

§338(g) election an election by a corporate buyer of 80 percent or more of a corporation's stock to treat the acquisition as an asset acquisition and not a stock acquisition.

§338(h)(10) election a joint election by the corporate buyer and corporate seller of the stock of a subsidiary of the seller to treat the acquisition as a sale of the subsidiary's assets by the seller to the buyer.

§481 adjustment a change to taxable income associated with a change in accounting methods.

§704(b) capital accounts partners' capital accounts maintained using the accounting rules prescribed in the Section 704(b) regulations. Under these rules, capital accounts reflect the fair market value of property contributed to and distributed property from partnerships.

§1231 assets depreciable or real property used in a taxpayer's trade or business owned for more than one year.

§1231 look-back rule a tax rule requiring taxpayers to treat current year net §1231 gains as ordinary income when the taxpayer has deducted a §1231 loss as an ordinary loss in the five years preceding the current tax year.

§1245 property tangible personal property and intangible property subject to cost recovery deductions.

§1250 property real property subject to cost recovery deductions.

12-month rule regulation that allows prepaid business expenses to be currently deducted when the contract does not extend beyond 12 months and the contract period does not extend beyond the end of the tax year following the year of the payment.

30-day letter the IRS letter received after an audit that instructs the taxpayer that they have 30 days to either (1) request a conference with an appeals officer or (2) agree to the proposed adjustment.

90-day letter the IRS letter received after an audit and receipt of the 30-day letter that explains that the taxpayer has 90 days to either (1) pay the proposed deficiency or (2) file a petition in the U.S. Tax Court to hear the case. The 90-day letter is also known as the *statutory notice of deficiency.*

A

Abandoned spouse a married taxpayer who lives apart from their spouse for the last six months of the year (excluding temporary absences), who files a tax return separate from their spouse, and who maintains a household for a qualifying child.

Accelerated death benefits early receipt of life insurance proceeds that are not taxable under certain circumstances, such as the taxpayer is medically certified with an illness that is expected to cause death within 24 months.

Accountable plan an employer's reimbursement plan under which employees must submit documentation supporting expenses to receive reimbursement and reimbursements are limited to legitimate business expenses.

Accounting method the procedure for determining the taxable year in which a business recognizes a particular item of income or deduction, thereby dictating the timing of when a taxpayer reports income and deductions.

Accounting period a fixed period in which a business reports income and deductions.

Accrual method a method of accounting that generally recognizes income in the period earned and recognizes deductions in the period that liabilities are incurred.

Accrued market discount a ratable amount of the market discount at the time of purchase (based on the number of days the bond is held over the number of days until maturity when the bond is purchased) that is treated as interest income when a bond with market discount is sold before it matures.

Accumulated adjustments account (AAA) an account that reflects the cumulative income or loss for the time the corporation has been an S corporation.

Accumulated earnings and profits undistributed earnings and profits from years prior to the current year.

Accumulated earnings tax a tax assessed on C corporations that retain earnings without a business reason to do so.

Acquiescence issued after the IRS loses a trial-level or circuit court case when the IRS has decided to follow the court's adverse ruling in the future. It does not mean that the IRS agrees with the court's ruling. Instead, it simply means that the IRS will no longer litigate this issue.

Acquisition indebtedness debt secured by a qualified residence that is incurred in acquiring, constructing, or substantially improving the residence but only to the extent that the amount borrowed does not exceed certain borrowing limitations.

Action on decisions IRS pronouncement that explains the background reasoning behind an IRS acquiescence or nonacquiescence.

Active participant in a rental activity an individual who owns at least 10 percent of a rental property and participates in the process of making management decisions, such as approving new tenants, deciding on rental terms, and approving repairs and capital expenditures.

Ad valorem taxes taxes based on the value of property.

Additional Medicare tax a tax imposed at a rate of .9 percent for salary or wages or net self-employment earnings in excess of $200,000 ($125,000 for married filing separate; $250,000 of combined salary or wages or net self-employment earnings for married filing joint).

Adequate consideration a price paid that is equal in value to the service or property received.

Adjusted basis an asset's carrying value for tax purposes at a given point in time, measured as the initial basis (for example, cost) plus capital improvements less depreciation or amortization. Also called *adjusted tax basis.*

Adjusted gross estate gross estate reduced by administrative expenses, debts of the decedent, losses incurred during the administration of the estate, and state death taxes.

Adjusted gross income (AGI) gross income less deductions for AGI. AGI is an important reference point that is often used in other tax calculations.

Adjusted tax basis an asset's carrying value for tax purposes at a given point in time, measured as the initial basis (for example, cost) plus capital improvements less depreciation or amortization.

Adjusted taxable gifts cumulative taxable gifts from previous years other than gifts already included in the gross estate valued at date of gift values.

Affiliated group two or more "includible" corporations that are related through common stock ownership and eligible to file a U.S. consolidated tax return. An affiliated group consists of a parent corporation that owns directly 80 percent or more of the voting stock and value of another corporation and one or more subsidiary corporations that meet the 80 percent ownership requirement collectively. Includible corporations are taxable U.S. C corporations, excluding real estate investment trusts; regulated investment companies; and life insurance companies.

After-tax rate of return a taxpayer's before-tax rate of return on an investment minus the taxes paid on the income from the investment. The formula for an after-tax rate of return that is taxed annually is the before-tax rate of return × (1 − marginal tax rate) [i.e., $r = R \times (1 - t)$]. A taxpayer's after-tax rate of return on an investment held for more than one tax period is $r = (FV/I)^{1/n} - 1$, where r is the after-tax rate of return, FV is the after-tax future value of the investment, I is the original investment amount, and n is the number of periods the investment is held.

Aggregate approach a theory of taxing partnerships that ignores partnerships as entities and taxes partners as if they directly owned partnership net assets.

Alimony a support payment of cash made to a former spouse. The payment must be made under a written separation agreement or divorce decree that does not designate the payment as something other than alimony, the payment must be made when the spouses do not live together, and the payments must cease no later than when the recipient dies.

All-events test requires that income or expenses are recognized when (1) all events have occurred that determine or fix the right to receive the income or liability to make the payments and (2) the amount of the income or expense can be determined with reasonable accuracy.

All-inclusive income concept a definition of income that says that gross income means all income from whatever source derived.

Allocate as used in the sourcing rules, the process of associating a deduction with a specific item or items of gross income for purposes of computing foreign source taxable income.

Allocation the method of dividing or sourcing nonbusiness income to specific states.

Allowance method method used for financial reporting purposes; under this method, bad debt expense is based on an estimate of the amount of the bad debts in accounts receivable at year-end.

Alternative minimum tax (AMT) a tax on a broader tax base than the base for the "regular" tax; the additional tax paid when the tentative minimum tax (based on the alternative minimum tax base) exceeds the regular tax (based on the regular tax base). The alternative minimum tax is designed to require taxpayers to pay some minimum level of tax even when they have low or no regular taxable income as a result of certain tax breaks in the tax code.

Alternative minimum tax (AMT) base alternative minimum taxable income minus the alternative minimum tax exemption.

Alternative minimum tax (AMT) exemption a deduction to determine the alternative minimum tax base that is phased out based on alternative minimum taxable income.

Alternative minimum tax adjustments adjustments (positive or negative) to regular taxable income to arrive at the alternative minimum tax base.

Alternative minimum tax system a secondary or parallel tax system calculated on an *alternative* tax base that more closely reflects economic income than the regular income tax base. The system was designed to ensure that taxpayers generating economic income pay some *minimum* amount of income tax each year.

Alternative valuation date the date six months after the decedent's date of death.

Amortization the method of recovering the cost of intangible assets over a specific time period.

Amount realized the value of everything received by the seller in a transaction (cash, FMV of other property, and relief of liabilities) less selling costs.

Annotated tax services a tax service arranged by code section. For each code section, an annotated service includes the code section; a listing of the code section history; copies of congressional committee reports that explain changes to the code section; a copy of all the regulations issued for the specific code section; the service's unofficial explanation of the code section; and brief summaries (called annotations) of relevant court cases, revenue rulings, revenue procedures, and letter rulings that address issues specific to the code section.

Annual exclusion amount of gifts allowed to be made each year per donee (regardless of the number of donees) to prevent the taxation of relatively small gifts ($16,000 per donee per year currently).

Annualized income method a method for determining a corporation's required estimated tax payments when the taxpayer earns more income later in the year than earlier in the year. Requires corporations to base their first and second required estimated tax installments on their income from the first three months of the year, their third installment based on their taxable income from the first six months of the year, and the final installment based on their taxable income from the first nine months of the year.

Annuity a stream of equal payments over time.

Applicable credit also known as the *unified credit,* the amount of current tax on the exemption equivalent; designed to prevent transfer taxation of smaller cumulative transfers.

Apportion as used in the sourcing rules, the process of calculating the amount of a deduction that is associated with a specific item or items of gross income for purposes of computing foreign source taxable income.

Apportionment the method of dividing business income of an interstate business among the states where nexus exists.

Arm's-length amount price in transactions among unrelated taxpayers, where each transacting party negotiates for their own benefit.

Arm's-length transactions transactions among unrelated taxpayers, where each transacting party negotiates for their own benefit.

Articles of incorporation a document, filed by a corporation's founders with the state, describing the purpose, place of business, and other details of the corporation.

Articles of organization a document, filed by a limited liability company's founders with certain states, describing the purpose, place of business, and other details of the company.

Assignment of income doctrine the judicial doctrine holding that earned income is taxed to the taxpayer providing the service, and that income from property is taxed to the individual who owns the property when the income accrues.

At-risk amount an investor's risk of loss in a worst-case scenario. In a partnership, an amount generally equal to a partner's tax basis exclusive of the partner's share of nonrecourse debt.

At-risk rules tax rules limiting the losses flowing through to partners or S corporation shareholders to their amount "at risk" in the partnership.

Average tax rate a taxpayer's average level of taxation on each dollar of taxable income. Specifically,

$$\text{Average tax rate} = \frac{\text{Total tax}}{\text{Taxable income}}$$

B

Bargain element (of stock options) the difference between the fair market value of the employer's stock and the amount employees pay to acquire the employer's stock.

Barter clubs organizations that facilitate the exchange of rights to goods and services between members.

Base erosion and anti-abuse tax (BEAT) a 10 percent minimum tax imposed on a U.S. corporation's payments of interest and royalties to a related foreign party.

Basis a taxpayer's unrecovered investment in an asset that provides a reference point for measuring gain or loss when an asset is sold.

Before-tax rate of return a taxpayer's rate of return on an investment before paying taxes on the income from the investment.

Beneficiary person for whom trust property is held and administered.

Bonds debt instruments issued for a period of more than one year with the purpose of raising capital by borrowing.

Bond discount the result of issuing bonds for less than their maturity value.

Bond premium the result of issuing bonds for more than their maturity value.

Bonus depreciation additional depreciation allowed in the acquisition year for tangible personal property with a recovery period of 20 years or less.

Book (financial reporting) income the income or loss corporations report on their financial statements using applicable financial accounting standards.

Book equivalent of taxable income a company's pretax income from continuing operations adjusted for permanent differences.

Book–tax difference a difference in the amount of an income item or deduction item taken into account for book purposes compared to the amount taken into account for the same item for tax purposes.

Boot property given or received in an otherwise nontaxable transaction such as a like-kind exchange that may trigger gain to a party to the transaction. The term *boot* derives from a trading expression describing additional property a party to an exchange might throw in "to boot" to equalize the exchange.

Brackets a subset (or portion) of the tax base subject to a specific tax rate. Brackets are common to graduated taxes.

Bright-line test technical rules found in the tax law that provide the taxpayer with objective tests to determine the tax consequences of a transaction.

Built-in gain the difference between the fair market value and tax basis of property owned by an entity when the fair market value exceeds the tax basis.

Built-in gains tax a tax levied on S corporations that were formerly C corporations. The tax applies to net unrealized built-in gains at the time the corporation converted from a C corporation to the extent the gains are recognized during the built-in gains tax recognition period. The applicable tax rate is 21 percent.

Built-in gains tax recognition period the first five years a corporation operates as an S corporation after converting from a C corporation.

Built-in losses the difference between the fair market value and tax basis of property owned by an entity when the tax basis exceeds the fair market value.

Bunching itemized deductions a common planning strategy in which a taxpayer pays two years' worth of itemized expenses in one year to exceed the standard deduction in that year.

Business activity a profit-motivated activity that requires a relatively high level of involvement or effort from the taxpayer to generate income.

Business income income derived from business activities.

Business purpose doctrine the judicial doctrine that allows the IRS to challenge and disallow business expenses for transactions with no underlying business motivation.

Business tax credits nonrefundable credits designed to provide incentives for taxpayers to hire certain types of individuals or to participate in certain business activities.

C

C corporations a corporate taxpaying entity with income subject to taxation. Such a corporation is termed a "C" corporation because the corporation and its shareholders are subject to the provisions of Subchapter C of the Internal Revenue Code.

Cafeteria plan an employer plan that allows employees to choose benefits from a menu of nontaxable fringe benefits or receive cash compensation in lieu of the benefits.

Capital account an account reflecting a partner's share of the equity in a partnership. Capital accounts are maintained using tax accounting methods or other methods of accounting, including GAAP, at the discretion of the partnership.

Capital asset in general, an asset other than an asset used in a trade or business or an asset such as an account or note receivable acquired in a business from the sale of services or property.

Capital gain property any asset that would have generated a long-term capital gain if the taxpayer had sold the property for its fair market value.

Capital interest an economic right attached to a partnership interest giving a partner the right to receive cash or property in the event the partnership liquidates. A capital interest is synonymous with the liquidation value of a partnership interest.

Carryover basis the basis of an asset the transferee takes in property received in a nontaxable exchange. The basis of the asset carries over from the transferor to the transferee.

Cash method the method of accounting that recognizes income in the period in which cash, property, or services are received and recognizes deductions in the period paid.

Cash tax rate the tax rate computed by dividing a company's taxes paid during the year by its pretax income from continuing operations.

Cashless exercise a technique where options are exercised and at least a portion of the shares are sold in order to facilitate the purchase.

Ceiling limitation that is the maximum amount for adjustments to taxable income (or credits). The amounts in excess of the ceiling are either lost or carried to another tax year.

Certainty one of the criteria used to evaluate tax systems. Certainty means taxpayers should be able to determine when, where, and how much tax to pay.

Certificate of deposit (CD) an interest-bearing debt instrument offered by banks and savings and loans. Money removed from the CD before maturity is subject to a penalty.

Certificate of limited partnership a document limited partnerships must file with the state to be formally recognized by the state. The document is similar to articles of incorporation or articles or organization.

Certificate of organization a document, filed by a limited liability company's founders with certain states, describing the purpose, place of business, and other details of the company.

Character of income a type of income that is treated differently for tax purposes from other types of income. Common income characters (or types of income) include ordinary, capital, and qualified dividend.

Charitable contribution limit modified taxable income taxable income for purposes of determining the 10 percent of taxable income deduction limitation for corporate charitable contributions. Computed as taxable income before deducting (1) any charitable contributions, (2) the dividends-received deduction, and (3) capital loss carrybacks.

Child tax credit a $2,000 tax credit, subject to an AGI phase-out, for each qualifying child who is under age 17 at the end of the year and claimed as a dependent of the taxpayer, and a $500 credit, also subject to the AGI phase-out, for other qualified dependents claimed as dependents of the taxpayer.

Circular 230 regulations issued by the IRS that govern tax practice and apply to all persons practicing before the IRS. There are five parts of Circular 230: Subpart A describes who may practice before the IRS (e.g., CPAs, attorneys, enrolled agents) and what practicing before the IRS means (tax return preparation, representing clients before the IRS, etc.). Subpart B describes the duties and restrictions that apply to individuals governed by Circular 230. Subparts C and D explain sanctions and disciplinary proceedings for practitioners violating the Circular 230 provisions. Subpart E concludes with a few miscellaneous provisions (such as the Circular 230 effective date).

Citator a research tool that allows one to check the status of several types of tax authorities. A citator can be used to review the history of the case to find out, for example, whether it was subsequently appealed and overturned, and to identify subsequent cases that cite the case. Citators can also be used to check the status of revenue rulings, revenue procedures, and other IRS pronouncements.

Civil penalties monetary penalties imposed when tax practitioners or taxpayers violate tax statutes without reasonable cause—for example, as the result of negligence, intentional disregard of pertinent rules, willful disobedience, or outright fraud.

Claim of right doctrine judicial doctrine that states that income has been realized if a taxpayer receives income and there are no restrictions on the taxpayer's use of the income (for example, the taxpayer does not have an obligation to repay the amount).

Cliff vesting a qualified plan provision allowing for benefits to vest all at once after a specified period of time has passed.

Collectibles a type of capital asset that includes a work of art, a rug or antique, a metal or gem, a stamp or coin, an alcoholic beverage, or other similar items held for investment for more than one year.

Commercial domicile the state where a business is headquartered and directs operations; this location may be different from the place of incorporation.

Commercial traveler exception a statutory exception that exempts nonresidents from U.S. taxation of compensation from services if the individual is in the United States 90 days or less and earns compensation of $3,000 or less.

Common-law states the 41 states that have not adopted community property laws.

Community property states nine states (Arizona, California, Idaho, Louisiana, Nevada, New Mexico, Texas, Washington, and Wisconsin) that automatically equally divide the ownership of property acquired by either spouse during a marriage.

Community property systems systems in which state laws dictate how the income and property are legally shared between a husband and a wife.

Complex trust a trust that is not required by the trust instrument to distribute income currently.

Consolidated tax return a combined U.S. income tax return filed by an affiliated group of corporations.

Consolidations the combining of the assets and liabilities of two or more corporations into a new entity.

Constructive ownership rules that cause stock not owned by a taxpayer to be treated as beneficially owned by the taxpayer for purposes of meeting certain stock ownership tests.

Constructive receipt doctrine the judicial doctrine that provides that a taxpayer must recognize income when it is actually or constructively received. Constructive receipt is deemed to have occurred if the income has been credited to the taxpayer's account or if the income is unconditionally available to the taxpayer, the taxpayer is aware of the income's availability, and there are no restrictions on the taxpayer's control over the income.

Continuity of business enterprise (COBE) a judicial (now regulatory) requirement that the acquiring corporation continue the target corporation's historic business or continue to use a "significant" portion of the target corporation's historic business assets to be tax-deferred.

Continuity of interest (COI) a judicial (now regulatory) requirement that the transferors of stock in a reorganization collectively retain a continuing ownership (equity) interest in the target corporation's assets or historic business to be tax-deferred.

Contribution to capital a shareholder's or other person's contribution of cash or other property to a corporation without receipt of an additional equity interest in the corporation.

Controlled foreign corporation (CFC) a foreign corporation that is more than 50 percent owned by U.S. shareholders.

Convenience one of the criteria used to evaluate tax systems. Convenience means a tax system should be designed to facilitate the collection of tax revenues without undue hardship on the taxpayer or the government.

Corporation business entity recognized as a separate entity from its owners under state law.

Corpus the principal or property transferred to fund a trust or accumulated in the trust.

Correspondence examination an IRS audit conducted by mail and generally limited to one or two items on the taxpayer's return. Among the three types of audits, correspondence audits are generally the most common, the most narrow in scope, and the least complex. The IRS typically requests supporting documentation for one or more items on the taxpayer's return (e.g., documentation of charitable contributions deducted).

Cost depletion the method of recovering the cost of a natural resource that allows a taxpayer to estimate or determine the number of units that remain in the resource at the beginning of the year and allocate a pro rata share of the remaining basis to each unit of the resource that is extracted or sold during the year.

Cost recovery the method by which a company expenses the cost of acquiring capital assets. Cost recovery can take the form of depreciation, amortization, or depletion.

Covenants not to compete a contractual promise to refrain from conducting business or professional activities similar to those of another party.

Criminal penalties penalties commonly charged in tax evasion cases (i.e., willful intent to defraud the government). They are imposed only after normal due process, including a trial. Compared to civil cases, the standard of conviction is higher in a criminal trial (beyond a reasonable doubt). However, the penalties are also much higher, such as fines up to $100,000 for individuals plus a prison sentence.

Current earnings and profits a year-to-year calculation maintained by a corporation to determine if a distribution is a dividend. Earnings and profits are computed for the current year by adjusting taxable income to make it more closely resemble economic income.

Current gifts gifts completed during the calendar year that are not already exempted from the gift tax.

Current income tax expense (benefit) the amount of taxes paid or payable (refundable) in the current year.

Current tax liability (asset) the amount of taxes payable (refundable) in the current year.

D

***De minimis* fringe benefits** a nontaxable fringe benefit that allows employees to receive occasional or incidental benefits tax-free.

Debt basis the outstanding principal of direct loans from an S corporation shareholder to the S corporation. Once taxpayers deduct losses to the extent of their stock basis, they may deduct losses to the extent of their debt basis. When the debt basis has been reduced by losses, it is restored by income/gain allocations.

Deceased spousal unused exclusion (DSUE) amount of unused applicable credit from predeceased spouse.

Deductible temporary differences book–tax differences that will result in tax deductible amounts in future years when the related deferred tax asset is recovered.

Deduction for qualified business income subject to limitations, equal to 20 percent of the taxpayer's qualified business income.

Deductions amounts that are subtracted from gross income in calculating taxable income.

Deductions above the line for AGI deductions or deductions subtracted from gross income to determine AGI.

Deductions below the line from AGI deductions or deductions subtracted from AGI to calculate taxable income.

Deferral items, deferred income, or deferrals realized income that will be taxed as income in a subsequent year.

Deferred like-kind exchange a like-kind exchange where the taxpayer transfers like-kind property before receiving the like-kind property in exchange. The property to be received must be identified within 45 days and received within 180 days of the transfer of the property given up.

Deferred tax asset the expected future tax benefit attributable to deductible temporary differences and carryforwards.

Deferred tax liability the expected future tax cost attributable to taxable temporary differences.

Defined benefit plans employer-provided qualified plans that spell out the specific benefit employees will receive on retirement.

Defined contribution plans employer-provided qualified plans that specify the maximum annual contributions employers and/or employees may contribute to the plan.

Definitely related deductions deductions that are associated with the creation of a specific item or items of gross income.

Depletion the cost recovery method to allocate the cost of natural resources as they are removed.

Depreciation the cost recovery method to allocate the cost of tangible personal and real property over a specific time period.

Depreciation recapture the conversion of §1231 gain into ordinary income on a sale (or exchange) based on the amount of accumulated depreciation on the property at the time of sale or exchange.

Determination letters rulings requested by the taxpayer, issued by local IRS directors, and generally not controversial. An example of a determination letter is the request by an employer for the IRS to rule that the taxpayer's retirement plan is a "qualified plan."

DIF (Discriminant Function) system the DIF system assigns a score to each tax return that represents the probability that the tax liability on the return has been underreported (a higher score = a higher likelihood of underreporting). The IRS derives the weights assigned to specific tax return attributes from historical IRS audit adjustment data from the National Research Program. The DIF system then uses these (undisclosed) weights to score each tax return based on the tax return's characteristics. Returns with higher DIF scores are then reviewed to determine if an audit is the best course of action.

Direct conversions when a taxpayer receives noncash property rather than a cash payment as a replacement for property damaged or destroyed in an involuntary conversion.

Direct write-off method required method for deducting bad debts for tax purposes. Under this method, businesses deduct bad debt only when the debt becomes wholly or partially worthless.

Disability insurance sometimes called sick pay or wage replacement insurance. It pays the insured for wages lost due to injury or disability.

Discharge of indebtedness debt forgiveness.

Discount factor the factor based on the taxpayer's rate of return that is used to determine the present value of future cash inflows (e.g., tax savings) and outflows (taxes paid).

Disproportionate distributions partnership distributions that change the partners' relative ownership of hot assets.

Disqualifying disposition the sale of stock acquired using incentive stock options prior to satisfying certain holding period requirements. Failing to satisfy the holding period requirements converts the options into nonqualified stock options.

Disregarded entities unincorporated entity with one owner that is considered to be the same entity as the owner.

Disregarded entities (international tax) entities with one owner that are treated as flow-through entities for U.S. income tax purposes.

Distributable net income (DNI) the maximum amount of the distribution deduction by fiduciaries and the maximum aggregate amount of gross income reportable by beneficiaries.

Distribution deduction deduction by fiduciaries for distributions of income to beneficiaries that operates to eliminate the potential for double taxation of fiduciary income.

Dividend a distribution to shareholders of money or property from the corporation's earnings and profits.

Dividends-received deduction (DRD) a corporate deduction for part or all of a dividend received from another corporation.

Document perfection program a program under which all tax returns are checked for mathematical and tax calculation errors.

Donee person receiving a gift.

Donor person making a gift.

Double taxation the tax burden when an entity's income is subject to two levels of tax. Income of C corporations is subject to double taxation. The first level of tax is at the corporate level, and the second level of tax on corporate income occurs at the shareholder level.

DRD modified taxable income taxable income for purposes of applying the taxable income limitation for the dividends-received deduction. Computed as the dividend-receiving corporation's taxable income before deducting the dividends-received deduction, the net operating loss deduction, and capital loss carrybacks.

Dwelling unit property that provides a place suitable for people to occupy (live and sleep).

Dynamic forecasting the process of forecasting tax revenues that incorporates into the forecast how taxpayers may alter their activities in response to a tax law change.

E

Earmarked tax a tax assessed for a specific purpose (e.g., for education).

Earned income compensation and other forms of income received for providing goods or services in the ordinary course of business.

Earned income credit a refundable credit designed to help offset the effect of employment taxes on compensation paid to low-income taxpayers and to encourage lower-income taxpayers to seek employment.

Earnings and profits (E&P) a measure of a corporation's earnings that is similar to its economic earnings. Corporate dividends are taxable to shareholders to the extent they come from earnings and profits.

Economic income tax nexus the concept that businesses without a physical presence in the state may establish income tax nexus in the state through an economic presence there.

Economic performance test the requirement that must be met for an accrual method taxpayer to deduct an expense currently. The specific event that satisfies the economic performance test varies based on the type of expense.

Economic substance doctrine judicially based doctrine that requires transactions to meaningfully change a taxpayer's economic position *and* have a substantial purpose (apart from a federal income tax purpose) in order for a taxpayer to obtain tax benefits.

Economy one of the criteria used to evaluate tax systems. Economy means a tax system should minimize its compliance and administration costs.

Educational assistance benefits a nontaxable fringe benefit that allows an employer to provide a certain amount of education benefits on an annual basis.

Effective tax rate the taxpayer's average rate of taxation on each dollar of total income (taxable and nontaxable income). Specifically,

$$\text{Effective tax rate} = \frac{\text{Total tax}}{\text{Total income}}$$

Also (for income tax footnote purposes), the tax rate computed by dividing a company's income tax provision (expense or benefit) for the year by its pretax income from continuing operations.

Effectively connected income (ECI) net income that results from the conduct of a U.S. trade or business by a nonresident.

Employee a person who is hired to provide services to a company on a regular basis in exchange for compensation and who does not provide these services as part of an independent business.

Employment taxes taxes consisting of the Old Age, Survivors, and Disability Insurance (OASDI) tax, commonly called the Social Security tax, and the Medical Health Insurance (MHI) tax, known as the Medicare tax.

Enacted tax rate the statutory tax rate that will apply in the current or a future period.

Entity approach a theory of taxing partnerships that treats partnerships as entities separate from partners.

Equity one of the criteria used to evaluate a tax system. A tax system is considered fair or equitable if the tax is based on the taxpayer's ability to pay; taxpayers with a greater ability to pay tax pay more tax.

Escrow account (mortgage-related) a holding account with a taxpayer's mortgage lender. The taxpayer makes mortgage payments to the lender that include payment for the interest and principal and payments for property taxes. The lender maintains the payments for property taxes in the escrow account and uses the funds in the account to pay the property taxes when the taxes are due.

Estate fiduciary legal entity that comes into existence upon a person's death and is empowered by the probate court to gather and transfer the decedent's real and personal property.

Estimated tax payments quarterly tax payments that a taxpayer makes to the government if the tax withholding is insufficient to meet the taxpayer's tax liability.

Ex-dividend date the relevant date for determining who receives a dividend from a stock. Anyone purchasing stock before this date will receive current dividends. Otherwise, the purchaser must wait until subsequent dividends are declared before receiving them.

Excess business loss excess of aggregate business deductions for the year over aggregate business gross income or gain of an individual taxpayer plus a threshold amount depending on filing status.

Excess net passive income net passive investment income × passive investment income in excess of 25 percent of the S corporation's gross receipts divided by its passive investment income.

Excess net passive income tax a tax levied on an S corporation that has accumulated earnings and profits from years in which it operated as a C corporation if the corporation reports excess net passive income.

Exchange traded funds (ETF) diversified portfolios of securities owned and managed by a regulated investment company similar to mutual funds except they are traded on exchanges and the shares trade throughout the day like ordinary stock listings.

Excise taxes taxes levied on the retail sale of particular products. They differ from other taxes in that the tax base for an excise tax typically depends on the *quantity* purchased rather than a monetary amount.

Exclusions or excluded income realized income that is exempted from income taxation.

Executor the person who takes responsibility for collecting the assets of the decedent, paying the decedent's debts, and distributing the remaining assets to the rightful heirs.

Exemption equivalent the amount of cumulative taxable transfers a taxpayer can make without exceeding the applicable credit.

Exercise date the date employees use their stock options to acquire employer stock at a discounted price.

Exercise price the price at which holders of stock options may purchase stock in the corporation issuing the option.

Explicit taxes taxes directly imposed by a government.

F

Face value a specified final amount paid to the owner of a coupon bond on the date of maturity. The face value is also known as the *maturity value*.

Facts and circumstances test a test used to make a subjective determination such as whether the amount of salary paid to an employee is reasonable. The test requires the taxpayer and the IRS to consider all the relevant facts and circumstances surrounding the situation in order to make a decision. The relevant facts and circumstances are situation-specific.

Family limited partnership a partnership designed to save estate taxes by dividing a family business into various ownership interests representing control of operations and future income and appreciation of the assets.

Favorable book–tax difference a book–tax difference that requires a subtraction from book income in determining taxable income.

Federal short-term interest rate the quarterly interest rate used to determine the interest charged for tax underpayments (federal short-term rate plus 3 percent).

Federal/state adjustments amounts added to or subtracted from federal taxable income when firms compute taxable income for a particular state.

FICA taxes FICA (Federal Insurance Contributions Act) taxes is a term used to denote both the Social Security and Medicare taxes upon earned income. For self-employed taxpayers, the terms "FICA tax" and "self-employment tax" are synonymous.

Fiduciary a person or legal entity that takes possession of property for the benefit of beneficiaries.

Fiduciary duty a requirement that a fiduciary act in an objective and impartial manner and not favor one beneficiary over another.

Field examinations the least common audit. The IRS conducts these audits at the taxpayer's place of business or the location where the taxpayer's books, records, and source documents are maintained. Field examinations are generally the broadest in scope and most complex of the three audit types. They can last many months to multiple years and generally are limited to business returns and the most complex individual returns.

Filing status filing status places taxpayers into one of five categories (married filing jointly, married filing separately, qualifying widow or widower, head of household, and single) by marital status and family situation as of the end of the year. Filing status determines whether a taxpayer must file a tax return, appropriate tax rate schedules, standard deduction amounts, and certain deduction and credit limitation thresholds.

Final regulations regulations that have been issued in final form, and, thus, until revoked, they represent the Treasury's interpretation of the Code.

First-in, first-out (FIFO) method an accounting method that values the cost of assets sold under the assumption that the assets are sold in the same order in which they are purchased (i.e., first purchased, first sold).

Fiscal year a year that ends on the last day of a month other than December.

Fixed and determinable, annual or periodic (FDAP) income U.S. source passive income earned by a nonresident.

Flat tax a tax in which a single tax rate is applied throughout the tax base.

Flexible spending accounts (FSA) a plan that allows employees to contribute before-tax dollars that may be used for unreimbursed medical expenses or dependent care.

Flipping a term used to describe the real estate investment practice of acquiring a home, repairing or remodeling the home, and then immediately, or soon thereafter, selling it (presumably at a profit).

Floor limitation a minimum amount that an expenditure (or credit or other adjustment to taxable income) must meet before any amount is allowed.

Flow-through entities legal entities, like partnerships, limited liability companies, and S corporations, that do not pay income tax. Income and losses from flow-through entities are allocated to their owners.

For AGI deductions deductions that are subtracted from gross income to determine AGI.

For the convenience of the employer benefits nontaxable benefits employers provide to employees and employee spouses or dependents in the form of meals or lodging if provided on the employer's premises and provided for a purpose that is helpful or convenient for the employer.

Foreign base company income the sum of CFC's foreign personal holding company income, foreign base company sales income, and foreign base company services income.

Foreign base company sales income gross profit from the sale of personal property by (to) a U.S. corporation to (from) a CFC, where the product was manufactured outside the country of incorporation of the CFC and resold outside the country of incorporation of the CFC.

foreign branch an unincorporated division of a U.S. corporation located outside the United States.

Foreign personal holding company income a category of foreign source passive income that includes interest, dividends, rents, royalties, and gains from the sale of certain foreign property.

Foreign tax credit (FTC) a credit for income taxes paid to a foreign jurisdiction.

Foreign tax credit limitation the limit put on the use of creditable foreign taxes for the current year.

Foreign-derived intangible income (FDII) net income from certain export sales, services, and licensing of intangibles that is eligible for a 37.5 percent deduction by U.S. corporations.

Form 1065 the form partnerships file annually with the IRS to report partnership ordinary income (loss) and separately stated items for the year.

Form 1098 the form used by taxpayers to report the annual amount of interest and related expenses paid on a mortgage when the amount paid totals $600 or more.

Form 1120-S the form S corporations file annually with the IRS to report S corporation ordinary income (loss) and separately stated items for the year.

Form 2553 the form filed to elect S corporation status.

Form 7004 the form C corporations, partnerships, and S corporations file to receive an automatic extension to file their annual tax return.

Form W-2 a form filed by the employer for each employee detailing the income, Social Security, and Medicare wages and taxes withheld. Additionally, state income, state taxes withheld, dependent care benefits, and many other tax-related items are reported.

Form W-4 a form used by a taxpayer to supply their employer with the information necessary to determine the amount of tax to withhold from each paycheck.

Fringe benefits noncash benefits provided to an employee as a form of compensation. As a general rule, fringe benefits are taxable. However, certain fringe benefits are excluded from gross income.

From AGI deductions deductions subtracted from AGI to calculate taxable income.

FTC basket a category of income that requires a separate FTC limitation computation.

Full-month convention a convention that allows owners of intangibles to deduct an entire month's amortization in the month of purchase and month of disposition.

Future interest the right to receive property in the future.

G

GAAP capital accounts partners' capital accounts maintained using generally accepted accounting principles (GAAP).

General category income foreign source income that is not considered passive category income for foreign tax credit purposes (generally income from an active trade or business).

General partnership (GP) a partnership with partners who all have unlimited liability with respect to the liabilities of the entity.

Generation-skipping tax (GST) supplemental transfer tax designed to prevent the avoidance of estate and gift taxes through transfers that skip a generation of recipients.

Gift a transfer of property where no, or inadequate, consideration is paid for the property.

Gift tax the tax paid on a gift.

Global intangible low-taxed income (GILTI) a new category of income added by the Tax Cuts and Jobs Act that relates to "high return" income earned by a U.S. corporation's CFC and subject to a low foreign tax rate.

***Golsen* rule** the rule that states that the U.S. Tax Court will abide by the rulings of the circuit court that has appellate jurisdiction for a case.

Graded vesting a qualified plan rule that requires an increasing percentage of plan benefits to vest with each additional year of employment.

Graduated taxes taxes in which the tax base is divided into a series of monetary amounts, or brackets, where each successive bracket is taxed at a different (gradually higher or gradually lower) percentage rate.

Grant date the date on which employees receive stock options to acquire employer stock at a specified price.

Grantor person creating a trust.

Gross estate property owned by the decedent at death and certain property transfers taking effect at death.

Gross income realized income minus excluded and deferred income.

Gross receipts (for S corporations) the total amount of revenues (including passive investment income) received or accrued under the corporation's accounting method, not reduced by returns, allowances, cost of goods sold, or deductions. Gross receipts include net capital gains from the sales or exchanges of capital assets and gains from the sale or exchange of stock or securities (losses do not offset gains).

Gross receipts test determines if a business qualifies as a "small" business under an annual gross receipts test if its average annual gross receipts for the three prior taxable years does not exceed an indexed threshold set at $27 million for 2022. For purposes of the test, includes total sales (net of returns and allowances but not cost of goods sold), amounts received for services, and income from investments (including tax-exempt interest).

Group-term life insurance term life insurance provided by an employer to a group of employees.

Guaranteed payments payments made to partners or LLC members that are guaranteed because they are not contingent on partnership profits or losses. They are economically similar to shareholder salary payments.

H

Half-year convention a depreciation convention that allows owners of tangible personal property to take one-half of a year's worth of depreciation in the year of purchase and in the year of disposition regardless of when the asset was actually placed in service or sold.

Head of household one of five primary filing statuses. A taxpayer may file as head of household if they are unmarried as of the end of the year *and* pays more than half of the cost to maintain a household for a qualifying person who lives with the taxpayer for more than half of the year; or they pay more than half the costs to maintain a household for a parent who qualifies as the taxpayer's dependent.

Health and accident insurance fringe benefits often offered through employers, including health insurance, group-term life insurance, and accidental death and dismemberment policies.

Health savings accounts accounts that allow individuals covered by a high-deductible plan to set aside amounts to pay for qualified medical and dental expenses for the taxpayer, spouse, and dependents.

Heirs persons who inherit property from the deceased.

Home office deductions deductions relating to the use of an office in the home. A taxpayer must meet strict requirements to qualify for the deduction.

Horizontal equity one of the dimensions of equity. Horizontal equity is achieved if taxpayers in similar situations pay the same tax.

Hot assets unrealized receivables or inventory items defined in §751(a) that give rise to ordinary gains and losses. The exact definition of hot assets depends on whether it is in reference to dispositions of a partnership interest or distributions.

Hybrid entity an entity for which an election is available to choose the entity's tax status for U.S. tax purposes.

I

Impermissible accounting method an accounting method prohibited by tax laws.

Implicit taxes indirect taxes that result from a tax advantage the government grants to certain transactions to satisfy social, economic, or other objectives. They are defined as the reduced before-tax return that a tax-favored asset produces because of its tax-advantaged status.

Imputed income income from an economic benefit the taxpayer receives indirectly rather than directly. The amount of the income is based on comparable alternatives.

Inbound transaction a transaction conducted by a foreign person that is subject to U.S. taxation.

Incentive stock options (ISO) a type of stock option that allows employees to defer the bargain element for regular tax purposes until the stock acquired from option exercises is sold. The bargain element is taxed at capital gains rates provided the stock is retained long enough to satisfy certain holding period requirements. Employers cannot deduct the bargain element as compensation expense.

Income effect one of the two basic responses that a taxpayer may have when taxes increase. The income effect predicts that when taxpayers are taxed more (e.g., tax rate increases from 25 to 28 percent), they will work harder to generate the same after-tax dollars.

Income tax a tax in which the tax base is income. Income taxes are imposed by the federal government and by most states.

Income tax nexus the connection between a business and a tax jurisdiction sufficient to subject the business to the tax jurisdiction's income tax.

Income tax provision refers to the income tax expense or (benefit) reported on a company's financial statement and is composed of the current income tax expense or (benefit) and the deferred income tax expense or (benefit). These components may also be referred to as the current income tax provision and the deferred tax provision, respectively.

Independent contractor a person who provides services to another entity, usually under terms specified in a contract. The independent contractor has more control over how and when to do the work than does an employee.

Indirect conversions receipt of money or other property as a replacement for property that was destroyed or damaged in an involuntary conversion.

Individual retirement account (IRA) a tax-advantaged account in which individuals who have earned income can save for retirement.

Information matching program a program that compares the taxpayer's tax return to information submitted to the IRS from other taxpayers (e.g., banks, employers, mutual funds, brokerage companies, mortgage companies). Information matched includes items such as wages (e.g., Form W-2 submitted by employers), interest income (e.g., Form 1099-INT submitted by banks), dividend income (e.g., Form 1099-DIV submitted by brokerage companies), and so forth.

Inheritance a transfer of property when the owner is deceased (the transfer is made by the decedent's estate).

Initial public offering (IPO) the first sale of stock by a company to the public.

Inside basis the tax basis of an entity's assets and liabilities.

Installment sales sales for which taxpayers receive payment in more than one period.

Institutional shareholder an entity such as an investment company, mutual fund, brokerage, insurance company, pension fund, investment bank, and endowment fund, with large amounts to invest in corporate stock.

Intangible assets assets that do not have physical characteristics. Examples include goodwill, covenants not to compete, organizational expenditures, and research and experimentation expenses.

Inter vivos transfers gifts made by a donor during their lifetime.

Internal Revenue Code of 1986 the codified tax laws of the United States. Although the Code is frequently revised, there have been only three different codes since the Code was created in 1939 (i.e., the IRC of 1939, IRC of 1954, and IRC of 1986).

Interpretative regulations the most common regulations; they represent the Treasury's interpretation of the Code and are issued under the Treasury's general authority to interpret the Code.

Interstate commerce business conducted between parties in two or more states.

Inventory items (for sale of partnership interest purposes) classic inventory defined as property held for sale to customers in the ordinary course of business, but also assets that are not capital assets or §1231 assets, which would produce ordinary income if sold by the entity. There are actually two definitions of inventory items in §751. The §751(a) inventory items are defined in §751(d) to include all inventory items. The §751(b) definition includes only substantially appreciated inventory.

Investment activity a profit-seeking activity that is intermittent or occasional in frequency, including the production or collection of income or the management, conservation, or maintenance of property held for the production of income.

Investment income income received from portfolio-type investments. Portfolio income includes capital gains and losses, interest, dividend, annuity, and royalty income not derived in the ordinary course of a trade or business. When computing the deductibility of investment interest expense, however, capital gains and dividends subject to the preferential tax rate are not treated as investment income unless the taxpayer elects to have this income taxed at ordinary tax rates.

Investment interest expense interest paid on borrowings or loans that are used to fund portfolio investments. Individuals are allowed an itemized deduction for qualified investment interest paid during the year.

Involuntary conversions direct or indirect conversions of property through natural disaster, government condemnation, or accident that allows a taxpayer to defer realized gain if certain requirements are met.

IRS allocation method allocates expenses associated with rental use of the home between rental use and personal use. The percentage of total expenses allocated to rental use is the ratio of the number of rental use days for the property to the total days the property was used during the year.

Itemized deductions certain types of expenditures that Congress allows taxpayers to deduct as from AGI deductions.

J

Joint tenancy joint ownership of property by two or more people.

Joint tenancy with right of survivorship title to property that provides the co-owners with equal rights to it and that automatically transfers to the survivor(s) at the death of a co-owner.

K

Kiddie tax a tax imposed at parents' marginal tax rate on a child's unearned income.

L

Last will and testament the document that directs the transfer of ownership of the decedent's assets to the heirs.

Last-in, first-out (LIFO) method an accounting method that values the cost of assets sold under the assumption that assets are sold in the reverse order in which they are purchased (i.e., last purchased, first sold).

Late filing penalty a penalty assessed if a taxpayer does not file a tax return by the required date (the original due date plus extension).

Late payment penalty a tax penalty equal to .5 percent of the amount of tax owed for each month (or fraction thereof) that the tax is not paid.

Least aggregate deferral an approach to determine a partnership's required year-end if a majority of the partners don't have the same year-end and if the principal partners don't have the same year-end. As the name implies, this approach minimizes the combined tax deferral of the partners.

Legislative grace the concept that taxpayers receive certain tax benefits only because Congress writes laws that allow taxpayers to receive the tax benefits.

Legislative regulations the rarest type of regulation, issued when Congress specifically directs the Treasury Department to create regulations to address an issue in an area of law. In these instances, the Treasury is actually writing the law instead of interpreting the Code. Because legislative regulations actually represent tax law instead of an interpretation of tax law, legislative regulations have more authoritative weight than interpretative and procedural regulations.

Life estate the right to possess property and/or collect income from property for the duration of someone's life.

Life insurance trust a trust that is funded with an irrevocable transfer of a life insurance policy and that gives the trustee the power to redesignate beneficiaries.

LIFO recapture amount the excess of a C corporation's inventory basis under the FIFO method in excess of the inventory basis under the LIFO method in its final tax year as a C corporation before it becomes an S corporation.

LIFO recapture tax a tax levied on a C corporation that elects to be taxed as an S corporation when it is using the LIFO method for accounting for inventories.

Like-kind exchange a nontaxable (or partially taxable) trade or exchange of assets that are similar or related in use.

Limited liability company (LLC) a type of flow-through entity for federal income tax purposes. By state law, the owners of the LLC have limited liability with respect to the entity's debts or liabilities. Limited liability companies are generally taxed as partnerships for federal income tax purposes.

Limited partnership (LP) a partnership with at least one general partner with unlimited liability for the entity's debts and at least one limited partner with liability limited to the limited partner's investment in the partnership.

Liquidating distribution a distribution that terminates an owner's interest in the entity.

Liquidation value the amount a partner would receive if the partnership were to sell all its assets, pay its debts, and distribute its remaining assets to the partners in exchange for their partnership interests.

Listed property business assets that are often used for personal purposes. Depreciation on listed property is limited to the business-use portion of the asset.

Local taxes taxes imposed by local governments (cities, counties, school districts, etc.).

Long-term capital gains or losses gains or losses from the sale of capital assets held for more than 12 months.

Luxury automobiles automobiles on which the amount of annual depreciation expense is limited because the cost of the automobile exceeds a certain threshold. The definition excludes vehicles with gross vehicle weight exceeding 6,000 pounds.

M

M adjustments book–tax differences that corporations report on the Schedule M-1 or M-3 of Form 1120 as adjustments to book income to reconcile to taxable income.

Majority interest taxable year the common tax year of a group of partners who jointly hold greater than 50 percent of the profits and capital interests in the partnership.

Marginal tax rate the tax rate that applies to the *next additional increment* of a taxpayer's taxable income (or to deductions). Specifically,

$$\text{Marginal tax rate} = \frac{\Delta\ \text{Tax}}{\Delta\ \text{Taxable income}}$$

$$= \frac{(\text{New total tax} - \text{Old total tax})}{(\text{New taxable income} - \text{Old taxable income})}$$

where "old" refers to the current tax and "new" refers to the revised tax after incorporating the additional income (or deductions) in question.

Marital deduction the deduction for transfers of qualified property to a spouse.

Market discount the difference between the amount paid for a bond in a market purchase rather than at original issuance when the amount paid is less than the maturity value of the bond.

Market premium the difference between the amount paid for a bond in a market purchase rather than at original issuance when the amount paid is greater than the maturity value of the bond.

Marriage benefit the tax savings married couples receive by filing a joint return relative to the tax they would have paid had they each filed as single taxpayers. This typically occurs when one spouse is either not working or earns significantly less than the other spouse.

Marriage penalty the extra tax cost a married couple pays by filing a joint return relative to what they would have paid had they each filed as single taxpayers. This typically occurs when both spouses earn approximately the same amount of income.

Married filing jointly one of five primary filing statuses. A taxpayer may file jointly if they are legally married as of the end of the year (or one spouse died during the year and the surviving spouse did not remarry) and both spouses agree to jointly file. Married couples filing joint returns combine their income and deductions and share joint and several liability for the resulting tax.

Married filing separately one of five primary filing statuses. When married couples file separately, each spouse reports the income they received during the year and the deductions they paid on a tax return separate from the other spouse.

Maturity the amount of time to the expiration date, or maturity date, of a debt instrument. The maturity of a debt instrument is generally the life of the instrument, at which point a payment of the face value is due or the instrument terminates.

Maturity value the amount paid to a bondholder when the bond matures and the bondholder redeems the bond for cash.

Maximum 15 percent rate amount threshold for the 15 percent rate to apply to long-term capital gains. Any 0/15/20 percent capital gains included that result in taxable income above the maximum zero rate amount and up to the maximum 15 percent rate amount are taxed at 15 percent. The threshold is based on a taxpayer's filing status and income.

Maximum zero percent rate amount threshold for the zero percent rate to apply to long-term capital gains. Any 0/15/20 percent capital gains included in taxable income up to the maximum zero percent amount are taxed at 0 percent. It is based on a taxpayer's filing status and income level.

Medicare tax the Medical Health Insurance (MHI) tax. This tax helps pay medical costs for qualifying individuals. The Medicare tax rate for employees and employers is 1.45 percent on salary or wages. An additional Medicare tax of .9 percent is assessed on employees (not employers) on salary or wages in excess of $200,000 ($125,000 for married filing separate; $250,000 of combined salary or wages for married filing joint). Self-employed taxpayers pay both the employee and employer Medicare tax and additional Medicare tax.

Mergers the acquisition by one (acquiring) corporation of the assets and liabilities of another (target) corporation. No new entity is created in the transaction.

Mid-month convention a convention that allows owners of real property to take one-half of a month's depreciation during the month when the property was placed in service and in the month it was disposed of.

Mid-quarter convention a depreciation convention for tangible personal property that allows for one-half of a quarter's worth of depreciation in the quarter of purchase and in the quarter of disposition. This convention must be used when more than 40 percent of tangible personal property is placed into service in the fourth quarter of the tax year.

Minimum tax credit credit available in certain situations for the alternative minimum tax paid. The credit can be used only when the regular tax exceeds the tentative minimum tax.

Mixed-motive expenditures activities that involve a mixture of business and personal objectives.

Modified Accelerated Cost Recovery System (MACRS) the current tax depreciation system for tangible personal and real property. Depreciation under MACRS is calculated by finding the depreciation method, the recovery period, and the applicable convention.

Municipal bonds the common name for state and local government debt.

Mutual fund a diversified portfolio of securities owned and managed by a regulated investment company.

N

Negative basis adjustment (for special basis adjustment purposes) the sum of the recognized loss and the amount of the basis increase made by an owner receiving the distribution.

Net capital gain the excess of net long-term capital gain for the taxable year over net short-term capital loss for such year.

Net capital loss carryback the amount of a corporation's net capital loss from one year that it uses to offset net capital gains in any of the three preceding tax years.

Net capital loss carryover the amount of a corporation's or an individual's net capital loss from one year that it may use to offset net capital gains in future years.

Net earnings from self-employment the amount of earnings subject to self-employment income taxes. The amount is 92.35 percent of a taxpayer's self-employment income.

Net investment income (for determining deductibility of investment interest expense) gross investment income reduced by deductible investment expenses.

Net investment income tax a 3.8 percent tax on the lesser of (a) net investment income or (b) the excess of modified adjusted gross income over $250,000 for married-joint filers and surviving spouses, $125,000 for married-separate filers, and $200,000 for other taxpayers.

Net long-term capital gain the excess of long-term capital gains for the taxable year over the long-term capital losses for such year.

Net long-term capital loss the excess of long-term capital losses for the taxable year over the long-term capital gains for such year.

Net operating loss (NOL) the excess of allowable deductions over gross income.

Net operating loss carryback the amount of a pre-2018 net operating loss that a corporation elects to carry back to the two previous years to offset taxable income in those years.

Net operating loss carryover the amount of a current-year net operating loss that is carried forward for up to 20 years to offset taxable income in those years (20 years for pre-2018 losses; unlimited for post-2017 losses).

Net passive investment income passive investment income less any expenses connected with producing it.

Net short-term capital gain the excess of short-term capital gains for the taxable year over the short-term capital losses for such year.

Net short-term capital loss the excess of short-term capital losses for the taxable year over the short-term capital gains for such year.

Net unearned income unearned income in excess of a specified threshold amount of a child under the age of 19 or under the age of 24 if a full-time student.

Net unrealized built-in gain the net gain (if any) an S corporation that was formerly a C corporation would recognize if it sold each asset at its fair market value. It is measured on the first day of the corporation's first year as an S corporation.

Nexus the connection between a business and a tax jurisdiction sufficient to subject the business to the tax jurisdiction's tax system. Also, the connection that is required to exist between a jurisdiction and a potential taxpayer such that the jurisdiction asserts the right to impose a tax.

No-additional-cost services a nontaxable fringe benefit that provides employer services to employees with little cost to the employer (e.g., airline tickets or phone service).

Nonacquiescence issued after the IRS loses a trial-level or circuit court case when the IRS has decided to continue to litigate this issue.

Nonbusiness income all income except for business income—generally, investment income and rental income.

Nondeductible terminable interests transfers of property interests to a spouse that do not qualify for a marital deduction because the interest of the spouse terminates when some event occurs or after a specified amount of time and the property is then transferred to another person.

Nondomiciliary business a business operating in a state other than its commercial domicile.

Nonqualified deferred compensation compensation provided for under a nonqualified plan allowing employees to defer compensation to a future period.

Nonqualified stock options (NQO) a type of stock option requiring employees to treat the bargain element from options exercised as ordinary income in the tax year options are exercised. Correspondingly, employers may deduct the bargain element as compensation expense in the tax year options are exercised.

Nonrecaptured net §1231 loss a net §1231 loss that is deducted as an ordinary loss in one year and has not caused subsequent §1231 gain to be taxed as ordinary income.

Nonrecognition provisions tax laws that allow taxpayers to permanently exclude income from taxation or to defer recognizing realized income until a subsequent period.

Nonrecourse debt debt for which no partner bears any economic risk of loss. Mortgages on real property are a common form of nonrecourse debt.

Nonrefundable credits tax credits that reduce a taxpayer's gross tax liability but are limited to the amount of gross tax liability. Any credit not used in the current year is lost.

Nonresident alien a non-U.S. citizen who does not meet the criteria to be treated as a resident for U.S. tax purposes.

Nonservice partner a partner who receives a partnership interest in exchange for property rather than services.

Nontaxable fringe benefits an employer-provided benefit that may be excluded from an employee's income.

Not definitely related deductions deductions that are not associated with a specific item or items of gross income in computing the foreign tax credit limitation.

O

Office examinations the second most common audit. As the name suggests, the IRS conducts these audits at the local IRS office. These audits are typically broader in scope and more complex than correspondence examinations. Small businesses, taxpayers operating sole proprietorships, and middle- to high-income individual taxpayers are more likely, if audited, to have office examinations.

Operating distributions payments from an entity to its owners that represent a distribution of entity profits. Distributions generally fall into the category of operating distributions when the owners continue their interests in the entity after the distribution.

Operating income the annual income from a trade or business or rental activity.

Operating loss the annual loss from a trade or business or rental activity.

Option exercise the use of a stock option to acquire employer stock at a specified price.

Ordinary and necessary an expense that is normal or appropriate and that is helpful or conducive to the business activity.

Ordinary asset an asset created or used in a taxpayer's trade or business (e.g., accounts receivable or inventory) that generates ordinary income (or loss) on disposition.

Ordinary business income (loss) a partnership's or S corporation's remaining income or loss after separately stated items are removed. It is also referred to as nonseparately stated income (loss).

Ordinary income property property that if sold would generate income taxed at ordinary rates.

Organizational expenditures expenses that are (1) connected directly to the creation of a corporation or partnership, (2) chargeable to a capital account, and (3) generally amortized over 180 months (limited immediate expensing may be available).

Original issue discount (OID) a type of bond issued for less than the maturity or face value of the bond.

Outbound transaction a transaction conducted outside the United States by a U.S. person that is subject to U.S. taxation.

Outside basis an investor's tax basis in the stock of a corporation or the interest in a partnership or LLC.

P

Partial liquidation a distribution made by a corporation to shareholders that results from a contraction of the corporation's activities.

Partnership agreement an agreement among the partners in a partnership stipulating the partners' rights and responsibilities in the partnership.

Partnership interest an intangible asset reflecting the economic rights a partner has with respect to a partnership, including the right to receive assets in liquidation of the partnership (called a *capital interest*) and the right to be allocated profits and losses (called a *profits interest*).

Passive activity loss (PAL) rules tax rules designed to limit taxpayers' ability to deduct losses from activities in which they don't materially participate against income from other sources.

Passive category income foreign source personal holding company income, such as interest, dividends, rents, royalties, annuities, and gains from sale of certain assets, that is combined in computing the FTC limitation.

Passive investment income (PII) royalties, rents, dividends, interest (including tax-exempt interest), annuities, and gains from the sale or exchange of stock or securities.

Passive investments direct or indirect investments (other than through a C corporation) in a trade or business or rental activity in which the taxpayer does not materially participate.

Payment liabilities liabilities of accrual method businesses for which economic performance occurs when the business actually *pays* the liability for, among others, workers' compensation; tort; breach of contract or violation of law; rebates and refunds; awards, prizes, and jackpots; insurance, warranties, and service contracts provided *to* the business; and taxes.

Percentage depletion a method of recovering the cost of a natural resource that allows a taxpayer to recover or expense an amount based on a statutorily determined percentage.

Permanent book–tax differences items of income or deductions for either book purposes or tax purposes during the year but not both. Permanent differences do not reverse over time, so over the long run, the total amount of income or deduction for the item is different for book and tax purposes.

Permanent establishment generally, a fixed place of business through which an enterprise carries out its business. Examples include a place of management, a branch, an office, and a factory.

Permissible accounting method accounting method allowed under the tax law. Permissible accounting methods are adopted the first time a taxpayer uses the method on a tax return.

Person an individual, trust, estate, partnership, association, company, or corporation.

Personal expenses expenses incurred for personal motives. Personal expenses are not deductible for tax purposes.

Personal holding companies closely held corporations generating primarily investment income.

Personal holding company tax penalty tax on the undistributed income of a personal holding company.

Personal property all tangible property other than real property.

Personal property taxes a tax on the fair market value of all types of tangible and intangible property, except real property.

Point one percent of the principal amount of a loan. A home buyer might pay points to compensate the lender for services or for a lower interest rate.

Portfolio investments investments producing dividends, interest, royalties, annuities, or capital gains.

Positive basis adjustment (for special basis adjustment purposes) the sum of the gain recognized by the owners receiving distributed property and the amount of any required basis reduction.

Post-termination transition period (PTTP) the period that begins on the day after the last day of a corporation's last taxable year as an S corporation and generally ends on the later of (a) one year after the last S corporation day or (b) the due date for filing the return for the last year as an S corporation (including extensions).

Preferential tax rate a tax rate that is lower than the tax rate applied to ordinary income.

Present interest right to presently enjoy property or receive income from the property.

Present value the concept that $1 today is worth more than $1 in the future. For example, assuming an investor can earn a 5 percent after-tax return, $1 invested today should be worth $1.05 in one year. Hence, $1 today is equivalent to $1.05 in one year.

Primary authorities official sources of the tax law generated by the legislative branch (i.e., statutory authority issued by Congress), judicial branch (i.e., rulings by the U.S. district courts, U.S. Tax Court, U.S. Court of Federal Claims, U.S. circuit courts of appeals, or U.S. Supreme Court), or executive/administrative branch (i.e., Treasury or IRS pronouncements).

Principal partner a partner having a 5 percent or more interest in partnership capital or profits.

Principal residence the main place of residence for a taxpayer during the taxable year.

Private letter rulings IRS pronouncements issued in response to a taxpayer request for a ruling on specific issues for the taxpayer. They are common for proposed transactions with potentially large tax implications. For the requesting taxpayer, a private letter ruling has very high authority. For all other taxpayers, private letter rulings have little authoritative weight.

Private nonoperating foundations privately sponsored foundations that disburse funds to other charities.

Private operating foundations privately sponsored foundations that actually fund and conduct charitable activities.

Probate the process in the probate court of gathering property possessed by or titled in the name of a decedent at the time of death, paying the debts of the decedent, and transferring the ownership of any remaining property to the decedent's heirs.

Probate estate property possessed by or titled in the name of a decedent at the time of death.

Procedural regulations regulations that explain Treasury Department procedures as they relate to administering the Code.

Production of income a for-profit activity that doesn't rise to the level of a trade or business.

Profits interest an interest in a partnership giving a partner the right to share in future profits but not the right to share in the current value of a partnership's assets. Profits interests are generally not taxable in the year they are received.

Progressive tax rate structure a tax rate structure that imposes an increasing marginal tax rate as the tax base increases. As the tax base increases, both the marginal tax rate and the taxes paid increase.

Proportional tax rate structure also known as a *flat tax,* this tax rate structure imposes a constant tax rate throughout the tax base. As the tax base increases, the taxes paid increase proportionally.

Proposed regulations regulations issued in proposed form; they do not carry the same authoritative weight as temporary or final regulations. All regulations are issued in proposed form first to allow public comment on them.

Public Law 86-272 federal law passed by Congress that provides additional protection for sellers of tangible personal property against income tax nexus.

Q

Qualified business asset investment (QBAI) the tax basis of tangible personal property used in a trade or business that forms the basis for determining the deductions allowed for foreign-derived intangible income and global low-taxed intangible income.

Qualified business income (QBI) net business income from a qualified trade or business conducted in the United States. This is the tax base for the deduction for qualified business income.

Qualified dividends paid by domestic or certain qualified foreign corporations that are eligible for lower capital gains rates.

Qualified education expenses consist of tuition and related costs for enrolling the taxpayer, spouse, or a dependent at a postsecondary institution of higher education.

Qualified education loans loans whose proceeds are used to pay qualified education expenses.

Qualified employee discounts a nontaxable fringe benefit that provides a discount on employer goods (not to be discounted below the employer's cost) and services (up to a 20 percent discount) to employees.

Qualified equity grant a broad-based equity grant of either stock options or restricted stock units by a private corporation. Eligible employees may make an inclusion deferral election that may defer the income attributable to the qualified equity for up to five years.

Qualified nonrecourse financing nonrecourse debt secured by real property from a commercial lender unrelated to the borrower.

Qualified replacement property property acquired to replace property damaged or destroyed in an involuntary conversion. It must be of a similar or related use to the original property even if the replacement property is real property (e.g., rental real estate for rental real estate).

Qualified residence the taxpayer's principal residence and one other residence.

Qualified retirement accounts plans meeting certain requirements that allow compensation placed in the account to be tax-deferred until the taxpayer withdraws money from the account.

Qualified retirement plans employer-sponsored retirement plans that meet government-imposed funding and antidiscrimination requirements.

Qualified small business stock stock received at original issue from a corporation with a gross tax basis in its assets both before and after the issuance of no more than $50,000,000 and with 80 percent of the value of its assets used in the active conduct of certain qualified trades or businesses.

Qualified trade or business for purposes of the deduction for qualified business income, any trade or business other than a specified trade or business.

Qualified transportation fringe benefits a nontaxable fringe benefit provided by employers in the form of mass transit passes, parking, or company-owned carpool benefits.

Qualifying child an individual who qualifies as a dependent of a taxpayer by meeting a relationship, age, residence, and support test with respect to the taxpayer.

Qualifying relative an individual who is not a qualifying child of another taxpayer and who meets a relationship, support, and gross income test and thus qualifies to be a dependent of another taxpayer.

Qualifying widow or widower one of five primary filing statuses. Applies for up to two years after the year in which the taxpayer's spouse dies (the taxpayer files married filing jointly in the year of the spouse's death) as long as the taxpayer remains unmarried and maintains a household for a dependent child.

Question of fact a research question that hinges upon the facts and circumstances of the taxpayer's transaction.

Question of law a research question that hinges upon the interpretation of the law, such as interpreting a particular phrase in a code section.

R

Real property land and structures permanently attached to land.

Real property taxes a tax on the fair market value of land and structures permanently attached to land.

Realization gain or loss that results from an exchange of property rights in a transaction.

Realization principle the proposition that income only exists when there is a transaction with another party resulting in a measurable change in property rights.

Realized gain or loss the difference between the amount realized and the adjusted basis of an asset sold or otherwise disposed of.

Realized income income generated in a transaction with a second party in which there is a measurable change in property rights between parties.

Reasonable in amount an expenditure is reasonable when the amount paid is neither extravagant nor exorbitant.

Recognized gains or losses gains or losses included in gross income on a taxpayer's tax return. This is usually the realized gain or loss unless a nonrecognition provision applies.

Recourse debt liability held by a partnership for which at least one partner has economic risk of loss.

Recovery period a length of time prescribed by statute in which business property is depreciated or amortized.

Recurring item an election under economic performance to currently deduct an accrued liability if the liability is expected to persist in the future and either it is not material or a current deduction better matches revenue.

Refinance when a taxpayer pays off a current loan with the proceeds of a second loan.

Regressive tax rate structure a tax rate structure that imposes a decreasing marginal tax rate as the tax base increases. As the tax base increases, the taxes paid increase, but the marginal tax rate decreases.

Regulations the Treasury Department's official interpretation of the Internal Revenue Code. Regulations are the highest authority issued by the IRS.

Related-person transaction financial activities among family members, among owners and their businesses, or among businesses owned by the same owners.

Remainder the right to ownership of a property that transfers to a new owner, the remainderman, following a temporary interest.

Remainderman the person entitled to a remainder interest.

Reorganization a tax-deferred transaction (acquisition, disposition, recapitalization, or change of name or place of incorporation) that meets one of the seven statutory definitions found in §368(a)(1).

Requisite service period the period or periods during which an employee is required to provide service in exchange for an award under a share-based payment arrangement (ASC Topic 718, Glossary).

Research and experimentation (R&E) costs expenses for research including costs of research laboratories (salaries, materials, and other related expenses). Taxpayers amortize research and development costs over not less than 60 months from the time benefits are first derived from the research.

Residence-based jurisdiction taxation of income based on the taxpayer's residence.

Resident alien an individual who is not a U.S. citizen but is treated as a resident for U.S. tax purposes.

Restricted stock stock employees receive as compensation that may be sold only after the passage of time or after certain performance targets are achieved. Because employees are not entitled to immediately sell the restricted stock they receive, the value of the stock is generally not taxable to employees or deductible by employers until the selling restrictions lapse.

Return of capital the portion of proceeds from a sale (or distribution) representing a return of the original cost of the underlying property.

Revenue procedures second in administrative authoritative weight after regulations. Revenue procedures are much more detailed than regulations and explain in greater detail IRS practice and procedures in administering the tax law. Revenue procedures have the same authoritative weight as revenue rulings.

Revenue rulings second in administrative authoritative weight after regulations. Revenue rulings address the specific application of the Code and regulations to a specific factual situation. Revenue rulings have the same authoritative weight as revenue procedures.

Reverse hybrid entity a "check-the-box" entity owned by multiple persons for which corporation status is elected.

Reversion terms by which ownership of property returns to the original owner following a temporary interest.

Rollover a transfer of funds from a qualified retirement plan to another qualified retirement plan, from a qualified retirement plan to a Roth or traditional IRA, or from a traditional IRA to a Roth IRA.

Roth 401(k) a type of defined contribution plan that allows employees to contribute on an after-tax basis and receive distributions tax-free.

Roth IRA an individually managed retirement plan permitting individuals to contribute on an after-tax basis and receive distributions tax-free.

S

S corporation a corporation under state law that has elected to be taxed under the rules provided in Subchapter S of the Internal Revenue Code. Under Subchapter S, an S corporation is taxed as a flow-through entity.

Safe-harbor provision provision of the tax law that reduces or eliminates a taxpayer's liability under the law if the taxpayer meets certain requirements.

Salary a fixed regular payment by an employer to an employee in exchange for the employee's services; usually paid on a monthly basis, but typically expressed as an annual amount.

Sales tax a tax imposed on the retail price of goods (plus certain services). Retailers are responsible for collecting and remitting the tax; typically, sales tax is collected at the point of sale.

Sales tax nexus the connection between a business and a tax jurisdiction sufficient to subject the business to the tax jurisdiction's sales tax.

Same-day sale a phrase used to describe a situation where a taxpayer exercises stock options and then immediately sells the stock received through the option exercise.

Schedule C a schedule on which a taxpayer reports the income and deductions for a sole proprietorship.

Schedule K a schedule filed with a partnership's annual tax return listing its ordinary income (loss) and its separately stated items.

Schedule M adjustments book–tax differences that corporations report on the Schedule M-1 or M-3 of Form 1120 as adjustments to book income to reconcile to taxable income.

Secondary authorities unofficial tax authorities that interpret and explain the primary authorities, such as tax research services, tax articles, newsletters, and textbooks. Secondary authorities may be very helpful in understanding a tax issue, but they hold little weight in a tax dispute (hence, the term *unofficial* tax authorities).

Self-employment taxes Social Security and Medicare taxes paid by the self-employed on a taxpayer's net earnings from self-employment. For self-employed taxpayers, the terms "self-employment tax" and "FICA tax" are synonymous.

SEP IRA a simplified employee pension (SEP) that is administered through an individual retirement account (IRA). Available to self-employed taxpayers.

Separate tax return a state tax return methodology requiring that each related entity with nexus must file a separate tax return.

Separately stated items income, expenses, gains, losses, credits, and other items that are excluded from a partnership's or S corporation's operating income (loss) and disclosed to partners in a partnership or shareholders of an S corporation separately because their tax effects may be different for each partner or shareholder.

Serial gift transfer tax strategy that uses the annual exclusion to convert a potentially large taxable transfer into a tax-exempt transfer by dividing it into multiple inter vivos gifts spread over several periods or donees.

Service partner a partner who receives a partnership interest by contributing services rather than cash or property.

Settlement statement a statement that details the monies paid out and received by the buyer and seller in a real estate transaction.

Short-term capital gains or losses gains or losses from the sale of capital assets held for one year or less.

Simple trust a trust that must distribute all accounting income currently and cannot make charitable contributions.

Sin taxes taxes imposed on the purchase of goods (e.g., alcohol, tobacco products, etc.) that are considered socially less desirable.

Single one of five primary filing statuses. A taxpayer files as single if they are unmarried as of the end of the year and does not qualify for any of the other filing statuses. A taxpayer is considered single if they are unmarried or legally separated from their spouse under a divorce or separate maintenance decree.

Single-member LLC a limited liability company with only one member. Single-member LLCs with individual owners are taxed as sole proprietorships and as disregarded entities otherwise.

Social Security tax the Old Age, Survivors, and Disability Insurance (OASDI) tax. The tax is intended to provide basic pension coverage for the retired and disabled. Employees pay Social Security tax at a rate of 6.2 percent on the wage base (employers also pay 6.2 percent). Self-employed taxpayers are subject to a Social Security tax at a rate of 12.4 percent on their net earnings from self-employment. The base on which Social Security taxes are paid is limited to an annually determined amount of wages and/or net earnings from self-employment.

Social security wage base limitation limit on the amount of employee compensation and/or net earnings from self-employment subject to the social security tax. The amount is provided annually and is indexed for inflation.

Sole proprietorship a business entity that is not legally separate from the individual owner of the business. The income of a sole proprietorship is taxed and paid directly by the owner.

Solicitation selling activities or activities ancillary to selling that are protected under Public Law 86-272.

Source-based jurisdiction taxation of income based on where the income is earned.

Special allocations allocations of income, gain, expense, loss, etc., that are allocated to the owners of an entity in a manner out of proportion with the owners' interests in the entity. Special allocations can be made by entities treated as partnerships for federal income tax purposes.

Special basis adjustment an optional (sometimes mandatory) election to adjust the entity asset bases as a result of an owner's disposition of an interest in the entity or distributions from the entity to its owners.

Specific identification method an elective method for determining the cost of an asset sold. Under this method, the taxpayer specifically chooses the assets that are to be sold.

Specified service trade or business any trade or business involving the performance of services in the fields of health, law, consulting, athletics, financial services, brokerage services, or any trade or business where the principal asset of such trade or business is the reputation or skill of one or more of its employees or owners, or which involves the performance of services that consist of investing and investment management trading, or dealing in securities, partnership interests, or commodities. Architecture and engineering services (their services build things) are specifically excluded from the definition of specified service trade or business.

Spot rate the foreign currency exchange rate on a specific day.

Spousal IRA an IRA account for the spouse with the lesser amount of earned income. Contributions in this account belong to this spouse no matter where the funds for the contribution came from.

Standard deduction a fixed deduction offered in lieu of itemized deductions. The amount of the standard deduction depends on the taxpayer's filing status.

Stare decisis a doctrine meaning that a court will rule consistently with (a) its previous rulings (i.e., unless, due to evolving interpretations of the tax law over time, it decides to overturn an earlier decision) and (b) the rulings of higher courts with appellate jurisdiction (i.e., the courts to which its cases are appealed).

Start-up costs expenses that would be classified as business expenses except that the expenses are incurred before the business begins. These costs are generally capitalized and amortized over 180 months, but limited immediate expensing may be available.

State tax a tax imposed by one of the 50 U.S. states.

State tax base the federal taxable income plus or minus required state adjustments.

Statements on Standards for Tax Services (SSTS) standards of practice for tax professionals issued by the AICPA. Currently, there are seven SSTS that describe the tax professional standards when recommending a tax return position, answering questions on a tax return, preparing a tax return using data supplied by a client, using estimates on a tax return, taking a tax return position inconsistent with a previous year's tax return, discovering a tax return error, and giving tax advice to taxpayers.

Static forecasting the process of forecasting tax revenues based on the existing state of transactions while ignoring how taxpayers may alter their activities in response to a tax law change.

Statute of limitations defines the period in which the taxpayer can file an amended tax return or the IRS can assess a tax deficiency for a specific tax year. For both amended tax returns filed by a taxpayer and proposed tax assessments by the IRS, the statute of limitations generally ends three years from the *later* of (1) the date the tax return was actually filed or (2) the tax return's original due date.

Step-transaction doctrine judicial doctrine that allows the IRS to collapse a series of related transactions into one transaction to determine the tax consequences of the transaction.

Stock redemption a property distribution made to shareholders in return for some or all of their stock in the distributing corporation that is not in partial or complete liquidation of the corporation.

Stock split a stock redemption in which a corporation exchanges a ratio of shares of stock (e.g., 2 for 1) for each share held by the shareholder.

Stock-for-stock acquisitions an exchange of solely voting stock by the acquiring corporation in exchange for stock of the target corporation, after which the acquiring corporation controls (owns 80 percent or more of) the target corporation. Often referred to as a "Type B reorganization."

Strike price the price at which holders of stock options may purchase stock in the corporation issuing the option.

Structural tax rate the tax rate computed by dividing a company's income tax provision adjusted for nonrecurring permanent differences by its pretax income from continuing operations.

Subchapter K the portion of the Internal Revenue Code dealing with partnerships tax law.

Subchapter S the portion of the Internal Revenue Code containing tax rules for S corporations and their shareholders.

Subpart F income income earned by a controlled foreign corporation that is not eligible for deferral from U.S. taxation.

Substance-over-form doctrine judicial doctrine that allows the IRS to consider the transaction's substance regardless of its form and, where appropriate, reclassify the transaction according to its substance.

Substantial authority the standard used to determine whether a tax practitioner may recommend and a taxpayer may take a tax return position without being subject to IRS penalty under IRC §6694 and IRC §6662, respectively. A good CPA evaluates whether supporting authority is substantial or not based upon the supporting and opposing authorities' weight and relevance. Substantial authority suggests that the probability that the taxpayer's position will be sustained upon audit or litigation is in the 35 to 40 percent range or above.

Substantial basis reduction negative basis adjustment of more than $250,000 resulting from a distribution from an entity taxed as a partnership to its owners.

Substantial built-in loss exists when a partnership's adjusted basis in its property exceeds the property's fair market value by more than $250,000 when a transfer of an interest occurs or if the purchasing partner would be allocated a loss of more than $250,000 if the partnership assets were sold for fair market value immediately after the transfer.

Substantially appreciated inventory (for partnership disproportionate distributions purposes) inventory with a fair market value that exceeds its basis by more than 120 percent.

Substituted basis the transfer of the tax basis of stock or other property given up in an exchange to stock or other property received in return.

Substitution effect one of the two basic responses that a taxpayer may have when taxes increase. The substitution effect predicts that, when taxpayers are taxed more, rather than work more, they will substitute nontaxable activities (e.g., leisure pursuits) for taxable ones because the marginal value of taxable activities has decreased.

Sufficiency a standard for evaluating a good tax system. Sufficiency is defined as assessing the aggregate size of the tax revenues that must be generated and ensuring that the tax system provides these revenues.

Syndication costs costs partnerships incur to promote the sale of partnership interests to the public. Syndication expenses must be capitalized and are not amortizable.

T

Tax a payment required by a government that is unrelated to any specific benefit or service received from the government.

Tax accounting balance sheet a balance sheet that records a company's assets and liabilities at their tax bases instead of their financial accounting bases.

Tax avoidance the legal act of arranging one's transactions or affairs to reduce taxes paid.

Tax base the item that is being taxed (e.g., purchase price of a good, taxable income, etc.).

Tax basis the amount of a taxpayer's unrecovered cost of or investment in an asset; *see also* adjusted tax basis.

Tax benefit rule holds that a refund of an amount deducted in a previous period is only included in income to the extent that the deduction reduced taxable income.

Tax bracket a range of taxable income taxed at a specified rate.

Tax capital accounts partners' capital accounts initially determined using the tax basis of contributed property and maintained using tax accounting income and expense recognition principles.

Tax carryovers tax deductions or credits that cannot be used on the current-year tax return and that can be carried forward to reduce taxable income or taxes payable in a future year.

Tax Court allocation method allocates expenses associated with rental use of the home between rental use and personal use. Property taxes and mortgage interest are allocated to rental use of the home based on the ratio of the number of rental use days to the total days in the year. All other expenses are allocated to rental use based on the ratio of the number of rental use days to total days the property was used during the year.

Tax credits items that directly reduce a taxpayer's tax liability.

Tax evasion the willful attempt to defraud the government (i.e., by not paying taxes legally owed). Tax evasion falls outside the confines of legal tax avoidance.

Tax haven generally, a country offering very favorable tax laws for foreign businesses and individuals.

Tax rate the level of taxes imposed on the tax base, usually expressed as a percentage.

Tax rate schedule a schedule of progressive tax rates and the income ranges to which the rates apply that taxpayers may use to compute their gross tax liability.

Tax return preparers any person or entity who prepares for compensation, or who employs one or more persons to prepare for compensation, all or a substantial portion of any tax return or claim for refund.

Tax shelter an investment or other arrangement designed to produce tax benefits without any expectation of economic profits.

Tax tables IRS-provided tables that specify the federal income tax liability for individuals with taxable income within a specific range. The tables differ by filing status and reflect tax rates that increase with taxable income.

Tax treaties agreements negotiated between countries that describe the tax treatment of entities subject to tax in both countries (e.g., U.S. citizens earning investment income in Spain). The U.S. president has the authority to enter into a tax treaty with another country after receiving the Senate's advice.

Tax year a fixed period in which a business reports income and deductions, generally 12 months.

Tax-deferred transactions transactions where at least a portion of the realized gain or loss is not currently recognized.

Taxable estate adjusted gross estate reduced by the marital deduction and the charitable deduction.

Taxable fringe benefits a noncash fringe benefit provided by employers to an employee that is included in taxable income (e.g., auto allowance or group-term life over $50,000).

Taxable gifts the amount left after adjusting current gifts for gift splitting, annual exclusions, the marital deduction, and the charitable deduction.

Taxable income the tax base for the income tax.

Taxable temporary differences book–tax differences that will result in taxable amounts in future years when the related deferred tax liability is settled.

Technical advice memorandums rulings issued by the IRS national office, requested by an IRS agent, and generated for completed transactions.

Temporary book–tax differences book–tax differences that reverse over time such that, over the long term, corporations recognize the same amount of income or deductions for the items on their financial statements as they recognize on their tax returns.

Temporary regulations regulations issued with a limited life (three years for regulations issued after November 20, 1988). During their life, temporary regulations carry the same authoritative weight as final regulations.

Tenancy in common ownership in which owners hold divided rights to property and have the ability to transfer these rights during their life or upon their death.

Tentative minimum tax (TMT) the tax on the AMT tax base under the alternative minimum tax system.

Terminable interest a right to property that terminates at a specified time or upon the occurrence of a specified event, such as a life estate.

Testamentary transfers transfers that take place upon the death of the donor.

Third-party intermediaries people or organizations that facilitate the transfer of property between taxpayers in a like-kind exchange. Typically, the intermediary receives the cash from selling the property received from the taxpayer and uses it to acquire like-kind property identified by the taxpayer.

Throwback rule the rule that sales into a state without nexus are included with sales from the state the property was shipped from.

Topical tax services a tax service arranged by subject (i.e., topic). Topical services identify tax issues that relate to each topic and then explain and cite authorities relevant to the issue (code sections, regulations, court cases, revenue rulings, etc.).

Trade or business a profit-motivated activity characterized by a sustained, continuous, high level of individual involvement or effort.

Trade show rule a rule that permits businesses to have physical presence at conventions and trade shows, generally up to two weeks a year, without creating income tax nexus.

Traditional 401(k) a popular type of defined contribution plan with before-tax employee and employer contributions and taxable distributions.

Traditional IRA an individually managed retirement account with deductible contributions and taxable distributions.

Transfer taxes taxes on the transfer of wealth from one taxpayer to another. The estate and gift taxes are two examples of transfer taxes.

Travel expenses expenditures incurred while "away from home overnight," including the cost of transportation, meals, lodging, and incidental expenses.

Treasury bond a debt instrument issued by the U.S. Treasury at face value, at a discount, or at a premium, with a set interest rate and maturity date that pays interest semiannually. Treasury bonds have terms of 30 years.

Treasury note a debt instrument issued by the U.S. Treasury at face value, at a discount, or at a premium, with a set interest rate and maturity date that pays interest semiannually. Treasury notes have terms of 2, 5, or 10 years.

Trust fiduciary entity created to hold and administer the property for other persons according to the terms of a trust instrument.

Trustee the person responsible for administering a trust.

U

U.S. circuit courts of appeals the first level of appeals courts after the trial-level courts. There are 13 U.S. circuit courts of appeal: 1 for the Federal Circuit and 12 assigned to hear cases that originate from a specific circuit (e.g., the 11th Circuit Court of Appeals only hears cases originating within the 11th Circuit).

U.S. Constitution the founding law of the United States, ratified in 1789.

U.S. Court of Federal Claims one of the three trial-level courts. It is a national court that only hears monetary claims against the federal government.

U.S. district court one of three trial-level courts. It is the only court that allows a jury trial. There is at least one district court in each state.

U.S. savings bonds debt instruments issued by the U.S. Treasury at face value or at a discount, with a set maturity date. Interest earned from U.S. bonds is paid either at maturity or when the bonds are converted to cash before maturity.

U.S. Supreme Court the highest court in the United States. The Supreme Court hears only a few tax cases a year with great significance to a broad cross-section of taxpayers or cases litigating issues in which there has been disagreement among the circuit courts. For most tax cases, the Supreme Court refuses to hear the case (i.e., the *writ of certiorari* is denied) and, thus, litigation ends with the circuit court decision.

U.S. Tax Court a national court that only hears tax cases and where the judges are tax experts. The U.S. Tax Court is the only court that allows tax cases to be heard *before* the taxpayer pays the disputed liability and the only court with a small claims division (hearing claims involving disputed liabilities of $50,000 or less).

Uncertain tax position a tax return position for which a corporation does not have a high degree of certainty as to its tax consequences.

Underpayment penalty the penalty that applies when taxpayers fail to adequately prepay their tax liability. The underpayment penalty is determined by multiplying the federal short-term interest rate plus 3 percentage points by the amount of tax underpayment per quarter.

Unearned income income from property that accrues as time passes without effort on the part of the owner of the property.

Unemployment tax the tax that pays for temporary unemployment benefits for individuals terminated from their jobs without cause.

Unfavorable book–tax difference any book–tax difference that requires an add-back to book income in computing taxable income. This type of adjustment is unfavorable because it increases taxable income relative to book income.

Uniform cost capitalization (UNICAP) rules specify that inventories must be accounted for using full absorption rules to allocate the indirect costs of productive activities to inventory.

Unitary tax return a state tax return methodology requiring the activities of a group of related entities to be reported on a single tax return. The criteria for determining whether a group of entities must file a unitary tax return are functional integration, centralization of management, and economies of scale.

United States person a citizen or resident of the United States, a domestic corporation, a domestic partnership, or any U.S. estate or trust.

Unrealized receivables any rights to receive payment for (1) goods delivered, or to be delivered, or (2) services rendered, or to be rendered. Unrealized receivables also include other assets to the extent that they would produce ordinary income if sold for their fair market value.

Unrecaptured §1250 gain a type of §1231 gain derived from the sale of real estate held by a noncorporate taxpayer for more than one year in a trade or business or as rental property attributable to tax depreciation deducted at ordinary tax rates. This gain is taxable at a maximum 25 percent capital gains rate.

Unrelated business income income from a trade or business, regularly carried on, that is not substantially related to the charitable, educational, or other purpose that is the basis of the organization's exemption.

Use tax a tax imposed on the retail price of goods owned, possessed, or consumed within a state that were *not* purchased within the state.

V

Valuation allowance the portion of a deferred tax asset for which management determines it is more likely than not that a tax benefit will not be realized on a future tax return.

Value-added tax a tax imposed on the producer of goods (and services) based on the value added to the goods (services) at each stage of production. Value-added taxes are common in Europe.

Vertical equity one of the dimensions of equity. Vertical equity is achieved when taxpayers with greater ability to pay tax pay more tax relative to taxpayers with a lesser ability to pay tax.

Vesting the process of becoming legally entitled to receive a particular benefit without risk of forfeiture; gaining ownership.

Vesting date the date on which the taxpayer becomes legally entitled to receive a particular benefit without risk of forfeiture.

Vesting period period of employment over which employees earn the right to own and exercise stock options.

W

Wages a payment by an employer to an employee in exchange for the employee's services; typically expressed in an hourly, daily, or piecework rate.

Wash sale the sale of an investment if that same investment (or substantially identical investment) is purchased within 30 days before or after the sale date. Losses on wash sales are deferred.

Wherewithal to pay the ability or resources to pay taxes due from a particular transaction.

Withholdings taxes collected and remitted to the government by an employer from an employee's wages.

Working condition fringe benefits a nontaxable fringe benefit provided by employers that would be deductible as an ordinary and necessary business expense if paid by an employee (e.g., reimbursement for professional dues).

Writ of certiorari a document filed to request the U.S. Supreme Court to hear a case.

Z

Zero-coupon bond a type of bond issued at a discount that pays interest only at maturity.

Appendix C

Tax Rates

2022 Tax Rate Schedules

Individuals

Schedule X—Single

If taxable income is over:	But not over:	The tax is:
$ 0	$ 10,275	10% of taxable income
$ 10,275	$ 41,775	$1,027.5 plus 12% of the excess over $10,275
$ 41,775	$ 89,075	$4,807.5 plus 22% of the excess over $41,775
$ 89,075	$170,050	$15,213.5 plus 24% of the excess over $89,075
$175,050	$215,950	$34,647.5 plus 32% of the excess over $170,050
$215,950	$539,900	$49,335.50 plus 35% of the excess over $215,950
$539,900	—	$162,718 plus 37% of the excess over $539,900

Schedule Z—Head of Household

If taxable income is over:	But not over:	The tax is:
$ 0	$ 14,650	10% of taxable income
$ 14,650	$ 55,900	$1,465 plus 12% of the excess over $14,650
$ 55,900	$ 89,050	$6,415 plus 22% of the excess over $55,900
$ 89,050	$170,050	$13,708 plus 24% of the excess over $89,050
$170,050	$215,950	$33,148 plus 32% of the excess over $170,050
$215,950	$539,900	$47,836 plus 35% of the excess over $215,950
$539,900	—	$161,218.5 plus 37% of the excess over $539,900

Schedule Y-1—Married Filing Jointly or Qualifying Widow(er)

If taxable income is over:	But not over:	The tax is:
$ 0	$ 20,550	10% of taxable income
$ 20,550	$ 83,550	$2,055 plus 12% of the excess over $20,550
$ 83,550	$178,150	$9,615 plus 22% of the excess over $83,550
$178,150	$340,100	$30,427 plus 24% of the excess over $178,150
$340,100	$431,900	$69,295 plus 32% of the excess over $340,100
$431,900	$647,850	$98,671 plus 35% of the excess over $431,900
$647,850	—	$174,253.5 plus 37% of the excess over $647,850

Schedule Y-2—Married Filing Separately

If taxable income is over:	But not over:	The tax is:
$ 0	$ 10,275	10% of taxable income
$ 10,275	$ 41,775	$1,027.5 plus 12% of the excess over $10,275
$ 41,775	$ 89,075	$4,807.5 plus 22% of the excess over $41,775
$ 89,075	$170,050	$15,213.5 plus 24% of the excess over $89,075
$170,050	$215,950	$34,647.5 plus 32% of the excess over $170,050
$215,950	$323,925	$49,335.5 plus 35% of the excess over $215,950
$323,925	—	$87,126.75 plus 37% of the excess over $323,925

Estates and Trusts

If taxable income is over:	But not over:	The tax is:
$ 0	$ 2,750	10% of taxable income
$ 2,750	$ 9,850	$275 plus 24% of the excess over $2,750
$ 9,850	$13,450	$1,979 plus 35% of the excess over $9,850
$13,450		$3,239 plus 37% of the excess over $13,450

Tax Rates for Net Capital Gains and Qualified Dividends

	Taxable Income				
Rate*	Married Filing Jointly	Married Filing Separately	Single	Head of Household	Trusts and Estates
0%	$0–$83,350	$0–$41,675	$0–$41,675	$0–$55,800	$0–$2,800
15%	$83,351–$517,200	$41,676–$258,600	$41,676–$459,750	$55,801–$488,500	$2,801–$13,700
20%	$517,201+	$258,601+	$459,751+	$488,501+	$13,701+

*This rate applies to the net capital gains and qualified dividends that fall within the range of taxable income specified in the table (net capital gains and qualified dividends are included in taxable income last for this purpose).

Basic Standard Deduction Amounts*

Filing Status	2021 Amount	2022 Amount
Married Filing Jointly	$25,100	$25,900
Qualifying Widow or Widower	$25,100	$25,900
Married Filing Separately	$12,550	$12,950
Head of Household	$18,800	$19,400
Single	$12,550	$12,950

*For individuals claimed as a dependent on another return, the 2022 standard deduction is the greater of (1) $1,150 or (2) $400 plus earned income not to exceed the standard deduction amount of those who are not dependents.

Amount of Each Additional Standard Deduction for Taxpayers Who Are Age 65 or Blind

	2021 Amount	2022 Amount
Married taxpayers	$1,350	$1,400
Single taxpayer or head of household	$1,700	$1,750

Exemption Amount*

2021	2022
$4,300	$4,400

*Used for qualifying relative gross income test.

Corporations

Rate	Taxable Income
21%	All

Code Index

Page numbers followed by n refer to footnotes.

I.R.C. Sec.
1(g), **8**-6n
1(g)(2)(A), **8**-6n
1(g)(4), **8**-6n
1(h), **7**-21n, **20**-18n
1(h)(7), **7**-12n
2(a), **4**-22n
2(b), **4**-23n
21, **8**-34
21(e)(6), **8**-27n
22, **8**-34
23, **8**-34
24, **8**-34
24(a), **8**-24n
25A, **8**-34
25A(b), **8**-28n
25A(d), **8**-30n
25A(f)(1), **8**-29n
25A(f)(2), **8**-28n
25A(g)(3), **8**-28n
25A(i)(3), **8**-29n
25A(i)(4), **8**-29n
25A(i)(5), **8**-29n
25B, **8**-34
25D, **8**-34
26, **8**-35n
32, **8**-30n, **8**-34
32(i), **8**-31n
36B, **6**-7n, **6**-13n, **8**-34
38(c), **8**-35n
41, **8**-34
45F, **8**-34
45R, **8**-34
47, **8**-34
48, **8**-34
51, **8**-34
59A, **24**-31n
61(a), **4**-2n, **5**-2–3, **9**-2n, **12**-21
61(a)(12), **5**-20n
62, **6**-2n
66, **5**-9n
67, **25**-18
67(b)(10), **5**-12n
71(b), **5**-15n
71(c), **5**-15n
72(b)(3), **5**-12n
72(d), **5**-12n
72(t), **13**-23n
72(t)(2), **13**-10n, **13**-25n
72(t)(8)(D), **13**-23n
74, **22**-18
74(b), **5**-16n
74(c), **5**-17n
74(d), **5**-17n
79, **5**-24, **12**-22n, **12**-26, **12**-26n, **22**-18
83, **19**-5n
83(b), **12**-17–20, **19**-5n
83(i), **12**-20, **12**-20n
83(i)(2), **12**-20n
83(i)(3), **12**-20n
83(i)(4), **12**-20n
86(b)(2), **5**-18n
86(d), **5**-17n
101, **5**-23n, **5**-27n, **12**-25n
104, **5**-29n
105, **12**-26
105(b), **12**-27n
106, **5**-24, **12**-26, **12**-27n, **22**-18
108(a)(1)(B), **5**-21n
108(a)(1)(E), **5**-21n, **14**-8n
108(a)(1)(h), **14**-8n
108(a)(3), **5**-21n
108(f), **5**-21n
111, **5**-5n
117(b)(2), **5**-25n
118, **19**-18n
119, **5**-24, **12**-26, **22**-18
119(a)(1), **12**-27n
119(a)(2), **12**-28n
120, **22**-18
121, **5**-22n, **14**-4n
121(b)(5), **14**-6n
125, **5**-24, **12**-26, **12**-31n, **22**-18
127, **5**-24, **12**-26, **22**-18
127(a)(2), **12**-28n
127(b)(2), **12**-28n
129, **5**-24, **12**-26, **12**-28n, **22**-18
132, **5**-23n, **22**-18
132(a)(1), **5**-24, **12**-26, **12**-28n
132(a)(2), **5**-19n, **5**-24, **12**-26, **12**-29n
132(a)(3), **5**-24, **12**-26
132(a)(4), **5**-24, **12**-26, **12**-30n
132(a)(5), **5**-24, **12**-26, **12**-30n
132(f), **12**-30n
135(c)(4), **5**-26n
140, **5**-23n, **12**-25n
152, **4**-13n
152(b)(1), **4**-18n
152(c), **8**-24
152(c)(1)(E), **4**-13n
152(c)(3)(A), **4**-13n
152(c)(3)(B), **4**-13n
152(c)(4)(C), **4**-15n
152(d)(1)(B), **4**-16n
152(d)(3), **4**-16n
152(e), **4**-15n
152(f), **4**-21n
152(f)(1), **4**-14n, **4**-16n
152(f)(2), **4**-13n, **13**-34n
152(f)(5), **4**-14n, **4**-16n
162, **6**-2–3n, **9**-4, **9**-4n, **10**-25, **10**-35
162(a), **9**-4–5n
162(a)(1), **12**-2n
162(b)(4), **2**-13
162(c), **9**-6n
162(e), **9**-6n
162(e)(4)(B)(i), **2**-10
162(k), **18**-25n
162(l), **6**-7n, **22**-18n
162(l)(2)(B), **6**-8n
162(m), **12**-5n
163, **2**-16, **7**-27n
163(d), **6**-17n
163(h)(3)(E), **14**-13n
163(h)(3)(F), **14**-10n
163(j), **9**-12n, **16**-6, **20**-22n
163(j)(4), **20**-22n
163(j)(4)(A)(ii), **20**-22n
163(j)(4)(B)(iii), **20**-28n
163(j)(4)(C), **20**-22n
164, **6**-15n
164(d), **14**-16n
165, **6**-24n, **9**-13n
165(c), **14**-4n
165(d), **6**-24n
166(a), **9**-27n
167(f), **10**-36n, **10**-37n
168, **6**-31n
168(e)(6)(B), **10**-14n
168(g), **6**-31n
168(g)(2), **18**-6n
168(g)(3)(C), **10**-23n
168(i)(7)(B)(ii), **19**-17n
168(k)(1), **10**-21n
168(k)(2)(E)(ii), **10**-21n
168(k)(2)(F), **10**-25n
168(k)(2)(F)(i), **10**-25n
168(k)(6), **10**-21n
168(k)(7), **10**-21n
170(a), **16**-16n
170(a)(2), **16**-16n
170(c), **6**-18n
170(e)(5), **6**-21n
171, **7**-4n
174, **10**-35n
179, **10**-3–5n, **10**-6, **10**-7, **10**-10, **10**-11, **10**-14n, **10**-17–20n, **10**-17–21, **10**-23, **10**-24, **10**-26, **10**-27, **10**-29, **11**-12, **18**-6, **18**-7, **22**-10
179(b)(6), **10**-27n
179(f)(1), **10**-14n
179(f)(2), **10**-14n
183, **22**-14n
195, **9**-7n, **10**-35, **10**-35n
197, **9**-7n, **10**-31–32, **10**-31n, **10**-36, **10**-37, **10**-37n, **16**-9n, **19**-21n, **19**-23n
199A, **15**-9n, **22**-10, **22**-11
199A(a), **6**-29n
199A(b)(2)(B), **20**-23n
199A(b)(3), **20**-23n
199A(d)(2), **15**-9n, **20**-22n
199A(d)(3), **20**-22n
212, **6**-2n, **6**-5n, **7**-26n, **9**-4n
213(a), **6**-13n
213(d)(2), **6**-14n
213(d)(5), **6**-13n
213(d)(9)(A), **6**-14n
217, **6**-7n
219(c), **13**-21n
219(g)(3), **13**-20n
220, **22**-18
221, **6**-10n
221(d)(2), **5**-26n
223, **5**-24
243, **16**-19n
245A, **24**-16n
246(b)(1), **16**-20n
246(b)(2), **16**-20n
246(b)(3), **16**-20n
246(c), **16**-19n
248, **9**-7n, **10**-32n, **10**-35
248(a)(1), **10**-33n
250, **24**-17n
262(a), **9**-7n
263, **10**-4n
263A, **16**-6, **17**-9
263A(i), **9**-20n
263A(i)(3), **9**-30n
263(a), **9**-16n, **20**-10n
265, **7**-26n
267, **3**-12n, **11**-18, **11**-34
267(a), **7**-23n, **9**-27n, **11**-34, **11**-34n
267(a)(2), **3**-11n, **12**-5n
267(b), **9**-27n, **12**-5n, **19**-34n

267(c), **9**-27n, **11**-34n, **19**-34n
274, **9**-12n
274(c), **9**-10n
274(e)(20), **9**-9n
274(k), **9**-8n
274(n), **12**-27n
274(n)(2), **9**-9n
275(a)(1), **16**-5n
280A, **14**-26n
280A(c)(1), **14**-27n
280A(c)(5), **14**-20n, **14**-30n
280A(d)(1), **14**-2n
280A(d)(2), **14**-2n
280A(e), **14**-24n
280A(f)(1)(B), **14**-2n
280A(g), **14**-17n
280E, **9**-6n
280F(a)(1)(A), **10**-25n
280F(d)(4)(A), **9**-11n
280F(d)(5)(A), **10**-26n
291, **11**-14–15, **11**-18, **11**-33
301, **18**-2n, **19**-4n
301(b), **18**-12n
301(c), **18**-2n
301(d), **18**-12n
302, **18**-18n, **18**-26, **22**-19n
302(b)(1), **18**-19n, **18**-23n
302(b)(2), **18**-19, **18**-19n, **18**-23n
302(b)(3), **18**-19n, **18**-22n
302(b)(4), **18**-25n
302(c), **18**-22n
302(c)(2), **18**-22n
302(e), **18**-26, **18**-26n
303, **18**-18n
305, **18**-2n
305(a), **18**-16n
305(b), **18**-17n
307, **18**-16n
311, **18**-13n
311(a), **18**-25n
311(b), **18**-25n, **22**-22n
311(b)(2), **18**-13n
312, **18**-4n
312(a), **18**-14n, **18**-25n
312(b), **18**-14n, **18**-25n
312(n), **18**-5n
312(n)(7), **18**-25n
317(b), **18**-18n
318, **18**-20, **22**-18n, **24**-25
331, **19**-33n, **22**-23
332(a), **19**-34n
334(b)(1), **19**-34n
336, **22**-23
336(a), **19**-34n
336(b), **18**-13n
336(d)(1), **19**-34n
336(d)(2), **19**-36n
336(d)(3), **19**-37n
337(a), **19**-37n
338(g), **19**-24
338(h)(10), **19**-24
351, **11**-34, **11**-34n, **15**-31n, **19**-4–11, **19**-4n, **19**-13–15, **19**-18, **19**-25, **19**-26, **19**-28, **19**-34, **19**-36, **22**-2, **22**-12n
351(g), **19**-5n
355, **19**-31n
357(a), **19**-11n
357(b), **19**-11n
357(c), **19**-11–12
357(c)(3), **19**-13n
358, **19**-4n, **22**-12n
358(a), **19**-7n
358(a)(2), **19**-10n
362(a), **19**-14n
362(a)(2), **19**-18n
362(e)(2), **19**-15n
368(a), **11**-34n, **19**-32
368(a)(1), **19**-25n
368(a)(1)(A), **19**-26n
368(c), **19**-5n
382, **16**-14n
385, **18**-2n, **19**-4n, **22**-3n
401(a)(17), **13**-3n
401(k), **13**-3, **13**-6–8, **13**-7n, **13**-12–16, **13**-20, **13**-20n, **13**-29–31, **13**-33
402(g)(1), **13**-8n
402(g)(4), **13**-8n
403(b), **13**-6, **13**-7n
404(h), **13**-30n
408A(c)(3), **13**-27n
408A(c)(3)(B)(i), **13**-24n
408A(d)(2), **13**-25n
408A(d)(3)(F), **13**-27n
408(d)(3), **13**-27n
408(d)(8), **13**-23n
408(k), **13**-30n
408(m), **7**-12n
409A, **13**-18n
411(a), **13**-4n
411(c), **13**-8n
415(b)(1), **13**-3n
415(c)(1), **13**-8n
415(d)(1)(C), **13**-8n
422(a)(1), **12**-12n
443, **9**-14n
444, **20**-15n, **22**-9n
446(a), **9**-16n
446(b), **9**-16n
448, **16**-3n
448(a), **9**-16n
448(a)(2), **20**-16n
448(a)(3), **20**-16n
448(b)(3), **20**-16n
448(c), **9**-2n
448(d)(2), **15**-33n
448(d)(7), **9**-30n
451, **9**-23
451(b), **9**-18n
451(b)(3), **9**-18n
451(c), **9**-18n
453, **16**-6
453A, **11**-32n
453(b)(1), **11**-32n
453(d), **11**-32n
453(i), **11**-33n
454(a), **5**-26n, **7**-4n
457, **13**-6, **13**-7n
461, **9**-22n
461(1), **20**-35n
461(c), **9**-25n
461(g), **2**-20
461(g)(1), **2**-20
461(g)(2), **2**-20, **2**-21, **2**-23, **14**-13n
461(h), **9**-22n
461(h)(1), **9**-23
461(h)(3), **9**-26n
461(l), **7**-32n
465, **7**-29–30n, **20**-31, **22**-15
465(b)(2)(B), **22**-15n
465(b)(6), **20**-31n
469, **7**-30n, **15**-13n, **20**-23n, **20**-32n, **22**-16n
469(b)(7), **20**-33n
469(c), **7**-30n
469(c)(6), **20**-33
469(c)(7), **7**-33n
469(g), **7**-32n
469(g)(1)(A), **20**-34n
469(i), **14**-26n, **20**-33n
469(j), **14**-20n, **14**-25n
469(k), **20**-34n
471(c), **9**-19
471(c)(1), **22**-9n
471(c)(4), **9**-30n
472(c), **9**-22n
481, **9**-32, **9**-32n
501, **22**-2n
529(c)(3), **5**-26n
530(b), **5**-26n
531, **15**-22n
533, **15**-22n
541, **15**-22n
585, **22**-3n
612, **10**-38n
613, **10**-38n
613A(c)(1), **10**-38
613(b)(1), **10**-38
613(b)(2), **10**-38
613(b)(3), **10**-38
613(b)(6), **10**-38
641, **25**-30n
651, **25**-30n
652, **25**-30n
691(c), **25**-18
692, **25**-30n
701, **20**-17n
702, **20**-18n
702(b), **20**-8n, **20**-19n
703(b), **20**-14n
704(b), **20**-8–9, **20**-23n
704(c), **20**-23n
704(c)(1)(C), **21**-8n
704(d), **20**-30n
704(d)(3)(B), **20**-28n
705(a)(2), **20**-28n
706, **9**-15n
706(a), **20**-14n
706(b)(1)(B)(i), **20**-15n
706(b)(3), **20**-15n
706(d)(1), **20**-10n, **21**-8n
707(a)(2)(B), **20**-7n
707(b)(2), **11**-16n
707(c), **20**-19n
709, **10**-32–33n
721, **11**-34, **11**-34n, **20**-3n, **22**-2, **22**-31
722, **20**-4n
723, **20**-8n
724, **20**-8n
731, **20**-30n, **21**-3n, **21**-10n
731(a), **20**-7n
731(a)(1), **21**-10n
731(a)(2), **21**-13–14n
731(b), **21**-10n
731(c), **21**-11n
731(c)(1)(A), **21**-11n
732(a), **21**-11n
732(a)(2), **21**-11n
732(c), **21**-11n
732(c)(1), **21**-14n
732(c)(2), **21**-15n
732(c)(3), **21**-20n
733, **21**-10–11n
734(b), **21**-10n, **21**-27
734(d), **21**-27n
735(a), **21**-22n
735(b), **21**-22n
741, **21**-3n
742, **20**-13n
743, **21**-7n
743(b), **21**-27, **21**-27n
743(d), **21**-27n
751, **21**-3–4n
751(a), **21**-3–4n, **21**-25
751(b), **21**-3n, **21**-24–25, **21**-25n
751(c), **21**-3n, **21**-22
751(c)(1), **21**-3n
751(c)(2), **21**-3n
751(d), **21**-3n, **21**-22
751(d)(1), **21**-4n
752(a), **20**-4n
752(b), **20**-6n, **21**-12n
754, **21**-7n, **21**-10n, **21**-26–27, **21**-26n, **21**-28, **21**-29
755, **21**-10n, **21**-27, **21**-29
861, **24**-2, **24**-6n
861(a), **24**-7n
861(a)(3)(A), **24**-8n
861(a)(3)(B), **24**-8n
861(a)(3)(C), **24**-8n
862(a), **24**-7n
865, **24**-6n
871(i)(2)(A), **24**-7n
881(d), **24**-7n
901, **24**-21n
903, **24**-21n
904, **8**-33n, **8**-34
904(d), **24**-20n

911, **13**-33n, **24**-7, **24**-7n
911(b)(2), **5**-28n
911(c), **5**-29n
936, **22**-3n
951, **24**-25n
951A(a), **24**-16n
951(a), **24**-16n
951(b), **24**-25n
954(d), **24**-26n
957(a), **24**-25n
958(b), **24**-25n
960, **24**-27n
962, **24**-30n
965, **24**-25n
986(a)(1)(A), **24**-21n
999, **24**-2
1001(a), **5**-4n, **11**-5n, **19**-2n
1001(b), **19**-3n
1001(c), **19**-3n
1011, **10**-3n, **19**-3n
1012, **10**-3n, **21**-7n
1014, **10**-6n, **15**-21n
1014(a)(1), **11**-3n
1015, **10**-6n
1015(a), **11**-3n
1015(d), **10**-6n
1031, **11**-24, **11**-24n, **16**-6, **18**-5
1031(a), **11**-27n
1031(a)(2), **11**-25n
1031(a)(3), **11**-25n
1031(b), **11**-27n
1031(d), **11**-28
1032, **18**-18n, **19**-4n, **19**-13n
1033, **11**-29n
1033(a)(2)(B), **11**-30n
1059, **18**-26
1060, **19**-23n
1061(a), **20**-12n
1091, **7**-24n
1202, **7**-12, **7**-15, **11**-9
1202(b)(1), **7**-12n
1211, **11**-34n, **20**-18n
1211(a), **16**-13n
1211(b), **16**-13n
1212(a), **16**-13n
1212(a)(1)(A)(ii), **16**-13n
1221, **7**-7n, **11**-8n
1221(a), **4**-6n
1221(b)(3), **7**-9n
1223(1), **19**-14n
1223(2), **19**-14n, **20**-8n
1223(4), **18**-16n
1223(9), **11**-3n
1231, **4**-6n, **7**-13, **11**-7–20, **11**-11n, **11**-15n, **11**-17n, **11**-33, **19**-9, **19**-9n, **19**-14, **20**-7, **20**-18, **21**-2, **21**-4, **21**-25, **21**-25n, **22**-10, **22**-25
1231(b), **6**-19n
1239, **11**-16–17n, **11**-16–19
1239(a), **19**-9n
1244, **19**-19
1245, **11**-10–11n, **11**-10–15, **11**-18, **11**-20, **11**-33, **21**-3, **21**-25n
1250, **7**-11, **7**-13, **7**-15, **7**-17, **11**-9, **11**-10, **11**-14–17, **11**-14n, **11**-19, **11**-33, **11**-33n, **14**-8, **14**-31, **19**-9n, **21**-5n
1272, **7**-3n
1276(a), **7**-4n
1276(b), **7**-4n
1278(b)(1), **7**-4n
1341, **5**-8n
1361, **15**-5n, **22**-2n, **22**-3
1361(b), **15**-6n
1361(c)(5)(A), **22**-3n
1362(a), **15**-5n, **22**-3n, **22**-5
1362(b), **22**-4n
1362(b)(2), **22**-4n
1362(b)(5), **22**-4n
1362(d)(1)(B), **22**-5n
1362(d)(1)(D), **22**-5n
1362(e)(3)(A), **22**-7n
1362(e)(6)(D), **22**-7n
1362(f), **22**-6n
1362(g), **22**-8n
1363(d), **22**-28n
1366(a), **22**-9n
1366(d)(1)(B), **22**-14n
1366(d)(3), **22**-15
1366(f)(2), **22**-25n
1367(a)(2), **22**-13n
1368(d), **22**-19n
1368(e)(1)(C), **22**-20n
1371(e), **22**-22
1372(a), **22**-18n
1374, **22**-24n
1375, **22**-26n
1375(d), **22**-26n
1377(a), **22**-9n
1377(b), **22**-16n
1377(b)(1)(A), **22**-16n, **22**-23n
1377(b)(1)(B), **22**-23n
1377(b)(1)(C), **22**-23n
1378, **9**-15n
1378(b), **22**-9n
1402, **15**-14n
1411, **4**-7n, **7**-28n, **15**-13n, **20**-23n
1411(c)(2)(A), **20**-23n
1411(c)(3), **8**-13n
1441, **24**-7n
1502, **16**-26n
1504, **16**-19n
1504(a), **16**-26n
1504(a)(2), **19**-34n
2010(c)(5), **25**-28
2032, **25**-22n
2033, **25**-17n
2035(a), **25**-27n
2036, **25**-19n
2039, **25**-19n
2040, **25**-19n
2041, **25**-19n
2053, **25**-23n
2054, **25**-23n
2058, **25**-23n
2514, **25**-5n
2518, **25**-5n
5701(b), **1**-4n
6012, **2**-2n, **8**-38n
6501, **2**-16
6601, **8**-39n
6651, **8**-39n
6654, **8**-36n
6655, **16**-27n
6655(b)(2), **16**-30n
6655(c), **16**-27n
6655(d), **16**-27n, **16**-29n
6655(e), **16**-27n
6655(g)(2), **16**-29n
6662, **2**-16, **2**-17n, **2**-28n
6694, **2**-16, **2**-17n, **2**-24, **2**-25n, **2**-28
6695(g), **4**-23n, **8**-32
6698, **20**-24n, **22**-28n
7520, **25**-7, **25**-7n
7525, **2**-26n
7701(a)(1), **19**-4n, **24**-2n
7701(a)(9), **24**-2n
7701(a)(43), **19**-14n
7701(a)(44), **19**-8n
7701(b), **24**-4n
7701(o), **3**-19
7702B, **6**-14n
7704, **15**-5n, **20**-17n
7872, **5**-20n

Subject Index

Page numbers followed by n refer to footnotes.

AAA; *see* Accumulated adjustments account
Abandoned spouses, **4**-21, **B**-1
Above the line deductions; *see* For AGI deductions
Accelerated death benefits, **5**-28, **B**-1
Accelerated depreciation, **11**-10n, **11**-14, **11**-14n, **16**-7
Accelerated tax deductions, **3**-4–10
Accident insurance, **12**-27, **B**-8
Accountable plans, **5**-23, **5**-25, **B**-1
Accountants
  due diligence requirements for, **4**-23n
  penalties imposed on, **2**-24, **2**-26–28, **4**-23n
  registration requirements for, **2**-26
  responsibilities of, **2**-23–26
  unauthorized practice of law by, **2**-9n
Accounting errors, **17**-3
Accounting for income taxes, **17**-2–6
Accounting methods, **9**-15–32; *see also* Accrual method of accounting; Cash method of accounting
  for accrual deductions, **9**-22–28
  for accrual income, **9**-18
  adopting, **9**-29
  changing, **9**-30, **9**-30n, **9**-32, **10**-16n
  choosing, **16**-3
  for corporations, **16**-2–3, **16**-3n
  defined, **B**-1
  equity, **16**-8
  financial and tax, **9**-15–16
  hybrid, **5**-7n, **9**-16
  importance of, **9**-15
  income recognition and, **5**-7
  for inventory, **9**-19–22, **9**-19n
  overall methods, **9**-16–17
  for partnerships, **20**-16
  reserve, **22**-3n
  for S corporations, **22**-3n, **22**-8–9, **22**-9n
  stock options and, **12**-15–16
  tax consequences of changing, **9**-32
  for unearned income, **9**-18
Accounting periods, **9**-14–15, **16**-2–3, **20**-14–15, **22**-8–9, **B**-1
Accounting Standards Codification (ASC); *see specific ASC standards*
Accrual income, **9**-18
Accrual method of accounting
  accrual deductions and, **9**-22–28
  for advance payment for goods/services, **9**-18, **9**-29
  all-events test for deductions, **9**-22
  bad debt expense and, **9**-27, **9**-29
  for business expense deductions, **9**-22–28
  cash method vs., **9**-28–29
  compensation deduction and, **12**-3
  for corporations, **16**-3
  deduction recognition, **9**-29
  defined, **B**-1
  economic performance test and, **9**-22–26
  expenditures for tangible/intangible assets, **9**-29
  GAAP and, **9**-17, **17**-5
  income recognition and, **3**-11, **3**-11n, **5**-7, **9**-29
  for inventory, **9**-19
  limitations on accruals to related parties, **9**-27
  overview, **9**-17
  payment liabilities and, **9**-24–26
  prepaid business expenses, **9**-29
  prepaid interest expense, **9**-29
  revenue recognition and, **9**-18
  12-month rule in, **9**-16n
  for unearned income, **9**-18, **9**-29
Accrued market discount, **7**-4, **B**-1
Accumulated adjustments account (AAA), **22**-20–21, **22**-20–21n, **B**-1
Accumulated earnings and profits, **18**-3, **18**-14, **B**-1
Accumulated earnings tax, **15**-22, **B**-1
Acquiescence, **2**-17, **B**-1
Acquisition indebtedness, **6**-17, **14**-9–12, **14**-10–11n, **B**-1
Acquisitions; *see* Corporate acquisitions
Acquisition tax model, **19**-20–21
Actions on decisions, **2**-17, **2**-17n, **B**-2
Active business income, **7**-31, **20**-34
Active participant in a rental activity, **7**-33, **14**-26, **B**-2
Activities; *see* Business activities
Adams v. Commissioner (1999), **3**-20
Additional Medicare tax, **8**-14, **B**-2
Adequate consideration, **25**-5, **B**-2
Adjusted basis
  for cost recovery, **10**-3
  defined, **B**-2
  determination of, **11**-3–5
  for gain/loss on sale of assets, **11**-5
  gifts, **11**-3
  for inherited property, **11**-3
  for property converted from personal to business use, **11**-3–5
Adjusted gross estate, **25**-23, **B**-2
Adjusted gross income (AGI); *see also* For AGI deductions; From AGI deductions
  defined, **B**-2
  exceptions to, **8**-3–7
  on *IRS Form 1040,* **4**-2, **4**-9
  modified, **5**-17–18, **5**-27n, **6**-10, **20**-23n
  qualifying child and, **4**-15n
Adjusted taxable gifts, **25**-25–26, **B**-2
Adjusted tax basis, **19**-3, **19**-7–8, **B**-2
Administrative expenses, taxable estates and, **25**-23–24
Administrative sources of tax law
  citations, **2**-10
  letter rulings, **2**-10, **2**-16–17
  regulations, revenue rulings, and revenue procedures, **2**-15–16
  U.S. Treasury, **2**-15–17
Adobe's Proxy Statement (2021), **12**-8
Adoption expense credit, **8**-34
ADR (asset depreciation range), **10**-8n
ADS; *see* Alternative depreciation system
Ad valorem taxes, **1**-15, **B**-2
Advance payment, **9**-18, **9**-29
Affiliated groups, **16**-19n, **16**-26, **B**-2
After-tax cost of contributions, to defined contribution plans, **13**-9
After-tax cost of salary, **12**-4, **12**-7
After-tax rate of return, **1**-16–17, **3**-3, **3**-3n, **3**-16–17, **7**-2, **13**-12, **B**-2
Age, standard deduction and, **2**-2, **4**-10, **6**-26, **6**-26n, **C**-2
Age test for qualifying child, **4**-13, **4**-18, **4**-19
Aggregate approach, **20**-3, **B**-2
AGI; *see* Adjusted gross income
AgroFresh, **19**-24
AICPA (American Institute of CPAs), **2**-23–25
Alcohol, taxes on, **1**-4, **1**-4n, **1**-13, **1**-15
Alimony
  as for AGI deduction, **4**-9, **5**-15, **6**-10
  defined, **5**-14–15, **B**-2
  front loading restrictions, **5**-15n
  as gross income, **4**-6, **5**-14–15
  as nondeductible property transfers, **5**-15, **5**-15n
All-events test, **9**-18, **9**-22, **9**-23, **B**-2
All-inclusive income concept, **4**-2, **5**-2, **5**-14, **B**-2
Allocate, defined, **B**-2
Allocation
  defined, **B**-2
  general principles of, **24**-11–12
  IRS method for, **14**-18–20, **B**-9
  nonbusiness income and, **23**-4
  Tax Court method of, **14**-18–20, **B**-16
Allowance method, **9**-27, **B**-2
Alternative depreciation system (ADS), **10**-7n, **10**-23, **10**-23n
Alternative minimum tax (AMT), **8**-7–12
  adjustments, **8**-8–9, **B**-2
  AMT preference item, **7**-12n
  base, **8**-7, **B**-2
  computation, **8**-12
  defined, **B**-2
  depreciation for, **8**-9, **10**-29
  exemption, **8**-11, **8**-11n, **B**-2
  formula for, **8**-7–8
  itemized deductions and, **8**-8
  net investment income tax and, **8**-12n
  overview, **8**-7
  rate of, **8**-7n
  self-employment taxes and, **8**-12n
  standard deduction and, **8**-8
  system, **8**-7, **B**-2
  tax base for, **4**-11
Alternative minimum taxable income (AMTI), **8**-7–8
Alternative recovery period, **10**-8n, **10**-23n
Alternative tax systems, evaluation of, **1**-17–23
Alternative valuation date, **10**-6n, **25**-22, **25**-22n, **B**-2
Amended tax returns, **2**-3
American Families Plan, **3**-10
American Institute of CPAs (AICPA), **2**-23–25
American opportunity tax credit (AOTC), **4**-12, **5**-25n, **8**-28–30, **8**-29n, **8**-34
Amortization, **10**-31–37
  corporate and Treasury bonds, **7**-3–4, **7**-3–4n
  defined, **10**-2, **B**-2
  IRS Form 4562 for, **10**-36–37
  organizational expenditures, **10**-32–35, **10**-35n
  patents and copyrights, **10**-31, **10**-36, **10**-37n
  research and experimentation costs, **10**-31, **10**-35–36, **10**-35n
  Section 197 purchased intangibles, **10**-31–32, **10**-31n
  start-up costs, **10**-31, **10**-35
  summary of amortizable assets, **10**-36–37
Amount realized, **7**-8, **11**-2, **19**-3, **B**-2
AMT; *see* Alternative minimum tax
AMTI (alternative minimum taxable income), **8**-7–8
Angel investors, **22**-3
Annotated tax services, **2**-18, **B**-2
Annual basis adjustments, **22**-13
Annual exclusion, **25**-9, **25**-9n, **B**-2
Annualized income method, **16**-27–30, **B**-2
Annuities
  defined, **5**-11, **B**-2
  exclusion ratio, **5**-11
  expected return multiple for, **5**-12
  529 plans and, **5**-26n
  fixed, **5**-11–12
  as gross income, **4**-6
  income from, **5**-10–12
  joint-life, **5**-12
  portfolio investments and, **7**-2
  from qualified retirement plans, **5**-12n
  single-life, **5**-12
  as unearned income, **5**-10–12
  unrecovered costs of, **5**-12n
Anti-deferral rules, **24**-24–31
Anti-front loading rules, **5**-15n
AOTC; *see* American opportunity tax credit
Appeals process, **2**-6–9, **2**-7n
Apple Inc., **12**-19–20, **12**-27, **24**-2, **24**-28n, **24**-29, **24**-31
Applicable credit, **25**-2–4, **25**-14, **25**-27–28, **B**-2
Applicable exclusion amount, **25**-3, **25**-3n
Applicable tax rates, **7**-13
Apportion, defined, **B**-2

Apportionment
business income and, **23**-4
defined, **B**-3
general principles of, **24**-11–12
special rules for, **24**-12–13
state income taxes and, **23**-16n, **23**-23
Apportionment formula, **23**-19–23
Appraisals, **10**-4
Appreciation of assets, **11**-12
Arm's-length amount, **9**-5, **B**-3
Arm's-length transactions, **3**-12, **B**-3
Articles of incorporation/organization, **15**-2, **B**-3
ASC 230, *Statement of Cash Flows,* **17**-13n
ASC 450 contingencies, **23**-5n
ASC 718, *Stock Compensation,* **12**-15n, **16**-11
ASC 740, *Income Taxes*
balance sheet classification, **17**-29
calculation of total tax provision, **17**-18
complexity of, **17**-3
computation and disclosure of tax provisions, **17**-2
computation/reconciliation of income tax provision, **17**-31–32
on current income tax expense or benefit, **17**-10–11
deferred tax expense/liability, **17**-3–4, **17**-13, **17**-18
on disclosure of uncertain tax positions, **17**-28
on expected future taxable income, **17**-21
federal income tax expense, **16**-5
future reversals of temporary differences, **17**-20
on income tax footnote disclosure, **17**-29–33
on interest and penalties, **17**-28
objectives of, **17**-3–5
on potential future taxable income, **17**-20
on recognition and measurement, **17**-25
on subsequent events, **17**-27
on tax planning strategies, **17**-21
on temporary differences, **17**-9
on uncertain tax positions, **17**-24–26
valuation allowance for gross deferred tax assets, **17**-20
ASC 740-270, *Interim Reporting,* **17**-33
ASC 805, **19**-20n, **19**-23n
Asset and liability approach, **17**-3–4, **17**-13
Asset classes, **10**-8n
Asset depreciation range (ADR), **10**-8n
Asset dispositions, **5**-13, **11**-5–6
Assets; *see also* Business assets; Capital assets; Intangible assets; Personal-use assets
appreciation of, **11**-12
character of gain or loss on disposition, **11**-7–9
converted, **10**-5–6, **10**-5n
cost recovery and, **10**-2–3
deferred tax, **17**-2, **17**-20–23, **17**-29
depreciable, **11**-26n
digital, **7**-8, **7**-13
disposition of trade/business assets, **4**-6n, **4**-9
formula for calculating gain/loss from sale of, **5**-13
hot, **21**-3–7, **21**-3n, **B**-8
listed property, **9**-11n, **10**-22–24
losses on disposition of trade/business assets, **4**-9, **6**-6
ordinary, **11**-7–8, **B**-12
personal purposes/business use of, **10**-5–6
placed in service, **10**-7–10, **10**-14–21, **10**-25–26
property classes of, **10**-21n
property dispositions, **5**-13
recovery period (depreciable life), **10**-7–9
Section 1231 assets, **11**-7–10, **20**-7, **21**-4, **21**-25n, **B**-1
sold at loss, **11**-12–13
tangible, **9**-7, **9**-29, **10**-2
tax-favored, **1**-16
useful lives, **10**-8
Asset values, **10**-4
Assignment of income doctrine, **3**-12, **5**-8, **B**-3
At-risk amount, **7**-29–30, **7**-30n, **20**-31, **22**-15, **B**-3
At-risk limitation, **20**-31, **22**-15
At-risk rules, **7**-29, **7**-30n, **20**-31, **22**-15, **B**-3
Attribution from entities to owners or beneficiaries, **18**-21
Attribution from owners or beneficiaries to entities, **18**-22
Audits, **2**-4–9
appeals/litigation process, **2**-6–9, **2**-7n
corporate, **16**-7–8
correspondence examinations, **2**-6, **B**-4–5
ethical considerations and, **2**-5
field examinations, **2**-6, **B**-7
in income tax provision process, **17**-3, **17**-3n
office examinations, **2**-6, **B**-11
post-audit, **2**-6–9
selection of taxpayers for, **2**-4–5, **2**-4n
statute of limitations and, **2**-4, **17**-3n
types of, **2**-6
Automobiles, **9**-11, **10**-25–27n, **10**-25–29, **B**-10
Average tax rate, **1**-7–11, **B**-3
Avila, Adelaide, **10**-32
Awards, income from, **5**-16–17, **5**-16n, **5**-17n
Azar Nut Co. v. Commissioner (1991), **2**-10

Backdating stock options, **12**-15
Back-of-the-envelope method, **17**-18, **17**-22
Bad debt, **7**-10n
Bad debt expense, **9**-27, **9**-29
Balance sheet classification, **17**-29
Balance sheets, **17**-3, **17**-5, **17**-11–17, **17**-12n, **19**-22, **19**-32, **B**-16
Ballmer, Steve, **10**-32
Bandler, James, **13**-29
B&O (business and occupation) tax, **23**-25
Bargain element, **12**-9–14, **12**-11n, **12**-17, **16**-11, **B**-3
Barter clubs, **5**-4, **B**-3
Base erosion and anti-abuse tax (BEAT), **24**-31, **B**-3
Base erosion and profit sharing (BEPS), **24**-30–31
Basis (purchase price), **7**-4, **B**-3
Basket purchases, **10**-37n
Before-tax rate of return, **1**-16, **1**-17, **3**-16–17, **7**-2, **B**-3
Below the line deductions; *see* From AGI deductions
Beneficiaries, **25**-7, **25**-30, **B**-3
BEPS (base erosion and profit sharing), **24**-30–31
Berkshire Hathaway, **17**-22
Biden, Joe, **3**-10, **7**-9, **22**-17
Binomial option pricing model, **12**-15n
Bitcoin, **7**-8, **9**-3, **11**-7
Black-Scholes option pricing model, **12**-15n
Blackstone Group Inc., **15**-27–28
Blind taxpayers, **4**-10, **6**-26, **6**-26n, **C**-2
Blockchain networks, **9**-3
Bluescape, **9**-23
BNA Tax Management Portfolios, **2**-11, **2**-19
Bolton v. Commissioner (1982), **14**-18n
Bolton method, **14**-18n
Bond discounts, **7**-3–4, **7**-3–4n, **B**-3
Bond premiums, **7**-3–4, **7**-3–4n, **B**-3
Bonds
corporate, **7**-2, **7**-3–4, **7**-3n
defined, **B**-3
government, **7**-2
maturity of, **7**-3n, **7**-4
municipal, **1**-17, **3**-16, **3**-18, **3**-19, **4**-6, **5**-21–22, **B**-10
savings, **5**-26–27, **7**-3, **7**-4, **7**-4n, **7**-8n
timing of interest payments and taxes, **7**-6
Treasury, **1**-20, **7**-3–4, **7**-3n, **B**-17
zero-coupon, **7**-3, **B**-18
Bonus depreciation, **10**-6, **10**-21–22, **10**-21n, **10**-25–29, **B**-3
Bonuses, **3**-11, **5**-7–8, **5**-7n
Book equivalent of taxable income, **17**-9, **17**-18, **B**-3
Book expense, **16**-11
Book (financial reporting) income, **16**-3, **B**-3
Book–tax differences, **16**-3–21; *see also* Temporary book–tax differences
charitable contributions, **16**-16–18
corporate-specific deductions associated with, **16**-10–21
defined, **B**-3
dividends, **16**-8
dividends-received deduction, **16**-19–21
favorable, **16**-3, **16**-18, **16**-21, **17**-9, **17**-12, **17**-12n, **B**-7
federal income tax expense, **16**-5
goodwill acquired in asset acquisition, **16**-9, **16**-9n
net capital losses, **16**-13, **16**-13n
net operating losses, **16**-13n, **16**-14–16
overview, **16**-3–4
permanent, **16**-3–5, **16**-21, **17**-7–8, **17**-18, **B**-12
stock options, **16**-10–13
unfavorable, **16**-3, **16**-18, **17**-9, **17**-12, **17**-13, **B**-17
Boot (not-like-kind property), **11**-27–29, **19**-5, **19**-9–10, **B**-3
Brackets, tax, **1**-5–6, **8**-2, **B**-3, **B**-16
Branches; *see* Foreign branches
BRC Operating Co. LLC v. Commissioner (2021), **9**-23
Break-even analysis, **14**-14
Bribes, **9**-6
Bright-line tests, **18**-18, **18**-19, **19**-25, **B**-3
Brown v. Commissioner (2013), **10**-7n
Budget deficits, **1**-20
Buffett, Warren, **17**-22n
Built-in gains/losses, **20**-3–4, **B**-3
Built-in gains tax, **22**-24–25, **22**-25n, **B**-3
Built-in gains tax recognition period, **22**-24, **B**-3
Bunching itemized deductions, **6**-1, **6**-28, **B**-3
Burt Kroner v. Commissioner (2020), **25**-5
Bush, Jeb, **13**-6
Business activities; *see also* Trade or business activities
for AGI deductions and, **6**-2–9
deductions directly related to, **6**-2–6
deductions indirectly related to, **6**-7–9
deductions subsidizing specific activities, **6**-10
defined, **B**-3
level of involvement in, **9**-4n
profit-motivated, **6**-2
of self-employed individuals, **6**-2
Business and occupation (B&O) tax, **23**-25
Business assets
casualty losses, **9**-13–14
as charitable contributions, **6**-19
listed property, **9**-11n, **10**-22–24
losses on disposition of, **4**-9, **6**-6, **9**-13
for personal/business use, **9**-11–12
placed in service, **10**-8
recovery period for, **10**-8–9
Business casualty losses, **9**-13–14
Business deductions, **9**-4–14
accrual method for, **9**-22–28
all-events test for, **9**-22
bad debt expense, **9**-27, **9**-29
capital expenditures, **9**-7
casualty losses, **9**-13–14
expenditures against public policy, **9**-6
expenses for production of tax-exempt income, **9**-7
interest, **9**-12–13
limitations on, **9**-6–14
losses on disposition of business property, **9**-13
meals and entertainment, **9**-8–9, **9**-9n
mixed-motive expenditures, **9**-8–12, **B**-10
ordinary and necessary, **6**-3–4, **9**-4–5
overview, **9**-4
personal expenditures, **9**-7–8
political contributions and lobbying costs, **9**-6
property use, **9**-11–12
reasonable in amount, **9**-5–6
record keeping and other requirements, **9**-12
start-up costs and organizational expenditures, **9**-7
travel and transportation, **9**-9–10n, **9**-9–11, **9**-12n
Business entities, **15**-2–35; *see also* Entity tax characteristics; Flow-through entities
converting to other entity types, **15**-27–28, **15**-31
deductibility of losses, **15**-26–29
legal classification of, **15**-2
nondomiciliary, **23**-2, **23**-6, **23**-8, **23**-11, **B**-11
nontax characteristics of, **15**-2–4
responsibility for liabilities, **15**-3
rights, responsibilities, and legal arrangements among owners, **15**-3–4
summary of, **15**-4
tax classification of, **15**-5–7
unincorporated, **15**-5, **15**-5n, **20**-2, **20**-2n
Business expenses; *see also* Trade or business expenses
associated with production of tax-exempt income, **9**-7
deductions for, **4**-9, **6**-2–9, **9**-4
employee, **5**-23, **5**-25, **6**-3
employees vs. independent contractors, **8**-21–22
ethical considerations and, **9**-5
ordinary and necessary, **6**-3–4, **9**-4–5
prepaid, **9**-7, **9**-16, **9**-16n
reasonable in amount, **9**-5–6
tax deductions for, **3**-16
timing of, **10**-35
unreimbursed employee expenses, **6**-3
Business income
active, **7**-31, **20**-34
apportionment and, **23**-4
C corporations reporting of, **9**-2
deductions and, **6**-2
defined, **B**-3
as gross income, **4**-6, **5**-2
ordinary, **20**-17–23, **22**-10, **B**-12
partnerships reporting of, **9**-2
qualified, **4**-9, **6**-28–32, **6**-29–31n, **15**-9–13, **15**-9n, **15**-22, **20**-22–23, **B**-13
S corporations reporting of, **9**-2
sole proprietorships reporting of, **9**-2
state income taxes for, **23**-18–23
unrelated, **15**-21

Business interest limitation, **20**-22
Business mileage rate, **10**-26n
Business purpose doctrine, **3**-18, **3**-19, **B**-3
Business purpose test, **19**-25
Business tax credits, **8**-33–34, **B**-3
Business use of home, **14**-26–32
  direct vs. indirect expenses in, **14**-28–29
  home office deductions, **14**-26–32, **B**-8
  limitations on deductibility of expenses, **14**-29–32
Buy-and-hold strategies, **7**-8

Cafeteria plans, **5**-24, **12**-26, **12**-31, **B**-3
Calendar year, **9**-14, **9**-14n
Callahan, Patricia, **13**-29
Candy, sales tax on, **23**-5
Capital accounts, **20**-8–9, **B**-3
Capital assets; *see also* Personal residence
  as charitable contributions, **6**-19, **6**-20n
  defined, **4**-6, **7**-7, **7**-7n, **11**-8, **11**-8n, **B**-3
  gain or loss on disposition, **11**-8
  tax advantages of, **7**-8
  tax planning strategies for, **7**-25–26
Capital expenditures, **9**-7, **9**-7n
Capital gain property, **6**-19–20, **6**-20–21n, **16**-16, **B**-3
Capital gains and losses; *see also* Net capital gains and losses
  for AGI deductions and, **6**-6
  calculating tax liability on net capital gains, **7**-21–23
  classification by maximum applicable tax rates, **7**-13
  collectibles and, **7**-11–13, **7**-15
  deductions for, **4**-9
  defined, **4**-6
  limitations on capital losses, **7**-23–24
  long-term, **3**-15–16, **4**-7, **4**-7n, **6**-19, **7**-10–11, **7**-13–15, **7**-34–36, **B**-10
  netting process for, **4**-7, **7**-13–16, **7**-34–36
  personal-use assets and, **7**-23
  portfolio income and, **7**-2, **7**-7–26
  preferential tax rates for, **8**-4
  related party sales, **7**-23
  reporting of, **7**-16–20
  review of, **11**-9
  Section 1202 gain, **7**-12, **7**-12n
  short-term, **4**-7, **4**-7n, **7**-10, **7**-13–15, **7**-34–36, **B**-14
  tax planning strategies for, **7**-25–26
  25 percent gains, **7**-11, **7**-13–15, **7**-17, **7**-21, **7**-34–36
  28 percent gains, **7**-12–15, **7**-17, **7**-21, **7**-34–36
  types of, **7**-10–13
  unrecaptured Section 1250 gains, **7**-11
  wash sales, **7**-23–25
  0/15/20 percent category, **7**-12–15, **7**-21, **7**-34–36
Capital gains tax rates, **3**-8, **3**-10, **7**-9, **8**-4, **C**-2
Capital interest, **20**-3, **20**-10, **B**-3
Capitalized tangible assets, **9**-7
Capitalizing the expenditure, **9**-7n
Capital loss carryback/carryover, **16**-13, **16**-14, **16**-17, **16**-20, **22**-25n
Capone, Al, **2**-26
CARES (Coronavirus Aid, Relief, and Economic Security) Act of 2020, **22**-17n
Carried interests, **20**-12
Carryover basis
  of assets acquired by gift, **10**-6
  defined, **21**-11, **B**-3
  depreciation of, **19**-17
  gift tax and, **25**-7, **25**-7n, **25**-32
  for stock received, **19**-30
  of transferred property, **19**-14
Cars; *see* Automobiles
Cash contributions, **6**-18–19, **6**-18n
Cash distributions, **18**-11, **20**-30, **21**-9–10
Cash guaranteed payments, **20**-29n
Cash inflows, **3**-4
Cashless exercise, **12**-10, **B**-4
Cash method of accounting
  accrual method vs., **9**-28–29
  for advance payment for goods/services, **9**-29
  bad debt, **9**-29
  compensation deduction and, **12**-3
  for corporations, **16**-3, **16**-3n
  deduction recognition, **9**-29
  defined, **B**-4
  expenditures for tangible/intangible assets, **9**-29
  income recognition and, **3**-10–11, **5**-7, **9**-29
  for inventory, **9**-19
  prepaid business expenses, **9**-29
  prepaid interest expense, **9**-29
  12-month rule in, **9**-16, **9**-16n
  for unearned income, **9**-29
Cash outflows, **3**-4
Cash tax rate, **17**-33, **B**-4
Casualty and theft losses
  business casualty losses, **9**-13–14
  defined, **6**-24, **9**-13n
  as itemized deductions, **6**-24, **6**-24n
  on personal-use assets, **6**-24
Catch up contributions, **13**-20n, **13**-30n, **13**-31
CCH; *see* Commerce Clearing House
C corporations
  accounting period for, **9**-15
  after-tax profits of, **18**-2
  audits of, **16**-8
  business income reporting for, **9**-2
  corporate tax formulas for, **16**-2–3
  defined, **B**-3
  distributions from, **18**-2
  double taxation of, **15**-21–22
  due dates and extensions for, **2**-3, **2**-3n
  income earned by, **20**-2
  income shifting and, **3**-13
  limitations on accruals to related parties in, **9**-27
  net operating losses for, **15**-26, **22**-5
  overall tax rate of, **15**-18–22
  owner compensation in, **15**-22–23, **15**-26
  passive activity income and losses in, **7**-29
  as percentage of entity types, **15**-27–28
  as personal service corporations, **15**-33n
  S corporations and partnerships compared to, **22**-30–32
  as separate taxable entities, **9**-2n
  short tax years, **22**-7
  Subchapter C, **15**-5, **18**-2n, **19**-4, **19**-4n
  tax classification and characteristics, **15**-5, **15**-6, **15**-29–30, **15**-32–33, **16**-2, **18**-2n
CDs; *see* Certificates of deposit
Ceiling, for deductions, **6**-21–22, **B**-4
Cell phones, **5**-25, **9**-11, **9**-11n
CelticCapri Corp., **22**-17
CEOs, compensation for, **12**-5, **12**-7, **15**-26
Certainty in tax systems, **1**-22, **B**-4
Certificates of deposit (CDs), **6**-9, **7**-2, **7**-3, **7**-6, **B**-4
Certificates of limited partnership, **15**-2, **B**-4
Certificates of organization, **15**-2, **B**-4
Certified public accountants (CPAs), **2**-23–26
CESAs (Coverdell education savings accounts), **5**-26
CEX cryptocurrency exchange, **9**-3
CFCs (controlled foreign corporations), **24**-25–29, **B**-4
Chandrasekera, Shehan, **7**-13
Change-in-stock-ownership tests, **18**-19, **18**-20, **18**-26
Chapin v. Commissioner (1950), **11**-2n
Character of income, **4**-5–7, **B**-4
Charitable contributions
  alternative minimum tax and, **8**-8
  corporations and, **16**-16–18
  COVID-19 pandemic and, **6**-23
  deduction limitations, **6**-21–22, **6**-21n
  estate tax and, **25**-24–25
  ethical considerations and, **6**-23
  gift tax and, **25**-12
  as itemized deductions, **4**-10, **6**-16–23, **6**-18–21n
  limit modified taxable income, **16**-17, **B**-4
  money contributions, **6**-18–19, **6**-18n
  overview, **6**-18
  of property other than money, **6**-19–20, **6**-20n
  qualified charities, **6**-16–18, **6**-18n, **16**-16n
  of stock, **18**-24
  summary of limitation rules, **6**-21
  tax credits for, **6**-16–17
Check-the-box hybrid entities, **24**-22–23
Check-the-box regulations, **15**-5, **15**-6
Check the box rules, **20**-2n
Chevron, **19**-32
Child, qualifying, **4**-13–15, **4**-13n, **4**-15n, **4**-18, **4**-19, **4**-21n
Child and dependent care credit, **4**-12, **8**-26–28, **8**-27n, **8**-34; *see also* Qualifying child; Qualifying relative
Child support payments, **5**-15
Child tax credit, **4**-12, **8**-24–26, **8**-25n, **8**-34, **B**-4
Cigarette taxes; *see* Tobacco taxes
Circular 230 (IRS), **2**-23–26, **2**-25n, **B**-4
Citators, **2**-21, **B**-4
Civil penalties, **2**-26, **2**-27, **B**-4
Claim of right doctrine, **5**-7–8, **5**-8n, **B**-4
Class life of assets, **10**-8n
Class of stock, **19**-3n, **22**-3n
"Clawback" provision, **5**-7
Clayton Williams Energy Inc., **19**-32
Client letters, **2**-22–23
Clifford Crummey v. Commissioner (1968), **25**-9n
Cliff vesting, **13**-4, **B**-4
Closed facts, **2**-17
Closely held corporations, **15**-3n, **18**-2, **18**-18
Closer connection test, **24**-4, **24**-4n
Clothing for work, **9**-7
COBE (continuity of business enterprise), **19**-25, **B**-4
Coca-Cola Company, **13**-17–18
Code of Professional Conduct (AICPA), **2**-23, **2**-24
Cohan rule, **9**-12n
COI (continuity of interest), **19**-25, **B**-4
Collectibles, **7**-11–13, **7**-15, **B**-4
Combined qualified business income, **6**-29
Comcast's Proxy Statement (2021), **12**-25
Commerce Clause (U.S. Constitution), **23**-5
Commerce Clearing House (CCH)
  Master Tax Guide, **2**-9, **2**-11, **2**-18n
  Standard Federal Tax Reporter, **2**-11, **2**-18
  Tax Research Consultant, **2**-11, **2**-19
Commercial domiciles, **23**-2, **B**-4
Commercial traveler exception, **24**-8, **B**-4
Commissioner v. Duberstein (1960), **11**-3n
Commissioner v. Indianapolis Power & Light Co. (1990), **9**-18n
Commissioner v. Kowalski (1977), **2**-10
Commissioner v. Lincoln Electric Co. (1949), **9**-5n
Commissioner v. Newman (1947), **3**-19
Commissioner v. Sullivan (1958), **9**-6n
Committee reports, as source of tax law, **2**-10
Common ancestors, **22**-2, **22**-2n
Common carriers, **23**-12, **23**-12n
Common-law states, **25**-10–11, **B**-4
Community property states/systems, **4**-20n, **5**-8–9, **5**-8–9n, **25**-10–11, **25**-10n, **B**-4
Compensation, **12**-2–35; *see also* Deferred compensation; Nonqualified deferred compensation (NQDC)
  for employee–owners, **3**-13, **15**-23
  for employees, **12**-2
  for entity owners, **15**-22–25
  equity-based, **12**-7–21
  for executives, **12**-5, **12**-7, **15**-26
  fringe benefits, **12**-21–34
  as gross income, **4**-6, **5**-2
  multinational transactions and, **24**-8–9
  nontaxable compensation benefits, **3**-16
  reasonable, **6**-30n, **12**-2–3, **12**-2n, **15**-25
  salary and wages, **12**-2–7
  self-employment, **12**-2, **12**-2n
  for services, **4**-6, **5**-2, **5**-3, **24**-8–9
Compensation packages, **3**-2
Compensatory damages, **5**-29
Compensatory stock options, **12**-9–16, **12**-15n
Complete Auto Transit, Inc. v. Brady (1977), **23**-10, **23**-10n, **23**-18n
Complete liquidation, **19**-32–37
  liquidating corporation tax consequences of, **19**-34–37
  nontaxable liquidating distributions, **19**-37
  overview, **19**-32–33
  shareholder tax consequences of, **19**-33–34
  taxable liquidating distributions, **19**-34–36
Complex trusts, **25**-30n, **B**-4
Compliance, **16**-23–30
  consolidated tax returns and, **16**-26, **16**-26n
  corporate tax return due dates and extensions, **16**-26–30
  economy of tax systems and, **1**-22
  ethical considerations and, **16**-26
  IRS Form 1120, **16**-23–26, **16**-23n
  in partnership accounting, **20**-24–28
  Schedule M adjustments and, **16**-23, **16**-23n, **16**-25–26
  tax return due dates and extensions, **2**-3, **2**-3n
Computers, **9**-11, **9**-11n
Condemnation, **11**-30, **11**-30n
Congress, U.S., **1**-12, **1**-18, **1**-18n, **1**-22, **2**-12–13, **20**-3
Congressional Research Service, **20**-2
ConocoPhillips, **12**-23–24
Consolidated tax returns, **16**-8n, **16**-26, **16**-26n, **B**-4
Consolidations, **19**-26, **19**-32, **B**-4
Constant yield method, **7**-3–4n
Constitution, U.S.; *see* U.S. Constitution
Constructive ownership, **9**-27n, **18**-20, **19**-34n, **B**-4
Constructive receipt doctrine, **3**-10–11, **3**-11n, **5**-7, **B**-4

Continuity of business enterprise (COBE), **19**-25, **B**-4
Continuity of interest (COI), **19**-25, **B**-4
Contra accounts, **17**-20
Contributed property, **19**-4n, **20**-7–9, **21**-8n
Contribution limits, **13**-7–8, **13**-20n
Contributions, charitable; *see* Charitable contributions
Contributions to capital, **19**-18, **B**-4
Controlled foreign corporations (CFCs), **24**-25–29, **B**-4
Control test of property, **19**-5–7
Convenience of tax systems, **1**-22, **B**-4
Conversion strategies, **3**-2, **3**-15–18, **7**-9
Converted assets, **10**-5–6, **10**-5n
Copyrights, **10**-31, **10**-36, **10**-37n
Corliss v. Bowers (1930), **5**-7n
Coronavirus Aid, Relief, and Economic Security (CARES) Act of 2020, **22**-17n
Coronavirus pandemic; *see* COVID-19 pandemic
Corporate acquisitions, **19**-19–32
  acquisition tax model for, **19**-20–21
  goodwill acquired in, **16**-9, **16**-9n
  in oil and gas industry, **19**-32
  overview, **19**-20
  of partnership interest, **20**-13
  taxable, **19**-22–24
  tax consequences to, **19**-22–31
  tax-deferred, **19**-25–31
Corporate bonds, **7**-2, **7**-3–4, **7**-3n
Corporate formations
  assumption of shareholder liabilities and, **19**-11–13
  contributions to capital, **19**-18
  depreciable assets and, **19**-17–18
  liabilities in excess of basis and, **19**-11–13
  requirements for, **19**-4–7
  S corporations, **22**-2
  Section 351 and, **19**-4–10
  Section 1244 stock and, **19**-19
  tax-avoidance transactions and, **19**-11
  tax consequences to transferee corporation, **19**-13–16
  tax-deferred transfers of property in, **19**-3–19
  transactions subject to tax deferral, **19**-4
Corporate inversions, **24**-29
Corporate liquidation, **19**-32–37
  liquidating corporation tax consequences of, **19**-34–37
  nontaxable liquidating distributions, **19**-37
  overview, **19**-32–33
  shareholder tax consequences of, **19**-33–34
  taxable liquidating distributions, **19**-34–36
Corporate regular taxable income; *see also* Book–tax differences
  accounting periods and methods, **16**-2–3
  computation of, **16**-3–21
  corporate-specific deductions, **16**-10–21
  formula for, **16**-2–3
  summary of, **16**-22–23
Corporate Report of Nondividend Distributions, **18**-9
Corporate shareholders, **15**-20, **15**-21
Corporate takeovers, **21**-9
Corporations; *see also* C corporations; Foreign corporations; S corporations
  audit rates for, **16**-7–8
  closely held, **15**-3n, **18**-2, **18**-18
  compliance and, **16**-23–30
  defined, **B**-4
  due dates and extensions for, **2**-3, **2**-3n, **16**-26–30
  effective tax rate, importance of, **17**-32–33
  estimated taxes for, **1**-22, **16**-26–30, **22**-28
  filing requirements for, **2**-2
  income shifting and, **3**-13–14
  income tax rates, **1**-9, **C**-2
  legal classification of, **15**-2
  personal service, **15**-33n, **16**-3n
  professional, **15**-2–3n
  responsibility for liabilities, **15**-3
  shell, **19**-27
  small business, **19**-19
  state income taxes and, **23**-9–10
  tax breaks for, **16**-7
  venture capital firms and, **22**-3
Corpus, **25**-7, **B**-4
Correspondence examinations, **2**-6, **B**-4–5
Cost basis, **10**-3–6
Cost depletion, **10**-2, **10**-37–39, **B**-5
Cost-flow methods, **9**-21–22
Cost of goods sold, **9**-2, **9**-2n, **9**-6, **9**-6n, **9**-19, **9**-21–23
Cost recovery; *see also* Amortization; Depreciation
  assets and, **10**-2–3
  basis for, **10**-3–6
  defined, **10**-2n, **B**-5
  depletion and, **10**-2, **10**-37–39
  ethical considerations and, **10**-6
  gain created through cost recovery deductions, **11**-11–12
Cost segregation, **10**-14–15
"Coupon" rate, **7**-3
Covenants not to compete, **10**-31, **10**-31n, **B**-5
Coverdell education savings accounts (CESAs), **5**-26
Covered employees, **12**-4–7, **12**-14n
COVID-19 pandemic
  CARES Act and, **22**-17n
  charitable contribution deduction and, **6**-23
  executive compensation during, **12**-7
  individual recovery credit and, **8**-32
  oil and gas recession during, **19**-32
  stimulus packages during, **1**-18
  touring income for musicians during, **7**-9
  travel pattern changes due to, **14**-22
CPAs (certified public accountants), **2**-23-26
Creditable foreign taxes, **24**-21
Credit application sequence, **8**-35
Credits; *see* Tax credits
Criminal penalties, **2**-26, **2**-28, **B**-5
Crummey power, **25**-9n
Cryptocurrencies, **7**-8, **7**-13, **9**-3, **11**-7
Current earnings and profits, **18**-3–7, **18**-14, **B**-5; *see also* Earnings and profits (E&P)
Current gifts, **25**-10, **25**-13, **B**-5
Current income tax expense or benefit, **17**-10–11, **17**-19, **B**-5
Current tax liability or assets, **17**-3–4, **B**-5
Customer base, **10**-31, **10**-32n

Daily Tax Report, **2**-11
Damages, **5**-29–30
Date of grant; *see* Grant date
David E. Watson, P.C. v. United States (2012), **15**-25
Deathbed gifts, **25**-17n, **25**-21
Death tax; *see* Estate tax
Debt; *see also* Loans
  national, **1**-3, **1**-20
  nonrecourse, **20**-4–6, **20**-5n, **B**-11
  qualifying, **14**-8n, **14**-12
  recourse, **20**-4–5, **20**-5n, **B**-13
  secured by residence, **14**-9
  straight, **22**-3n
  taxable estate, **25**-23–24
Debt basis, **22**-14–15, **22**-15n, **B**-5
Debt forgiveness, **5**-21n, **14**-8, **14**-8n
Debt instruments, **1**-20
Deceased spousal unused exclusion (DSUE), **25**-28, **B**-5
Decedents, **25**-3n, **25**-17–25, **25**-28, **25**-30
Deductible temporary differences, **17**-12, **B**-5
Deductions; *see also* Business deductions; For AGI deductions; From AGI deductions; Itemized deductions; Standard deduction
  accelerated, **3**-4–10
  alimony paid, **5**-15
  ceiling for, **6**-21–22, **6**-21n, **B**-4
  charitable, **25**-12
  defined, **4**-8, **B**-5
  marital, **25**-4, **25**-10–11, **25**-11n, **25**-24, **B**-10
  mortgage interest, **6**-17, **6**-17n, **14**-8–15
  for qualified business income, **20**-22–23, **B**-5
  recovery of amounts previously deducted, **5**-5
  subsidizing specific activities, **6**-10
  timing strategies for, **3**-4–11
  U.S. source rules for, **24**-6, **24**-11–13
  wealth planning, **25**-31
Deemed asset purchase, **19**-24
Default provisions, **15**-3
Deferral period, **3**-7n
Deferral provisions, **5**-31
Deferrals from gross income, **4**-2, **4**-5, **4**-6
Deferral strategy limitations, **3**-10–11
Deferred compensation; *see also* Nonqualified deferred compensation (NQDC); Stock options
  defined benefit plans, **13**-3–6
  employer-qualified retirement plans, **13**-3
  individual retirement accounts, **13**-20–29
  qualified equity grants, **12**-20
  restricted stock, **12**-16–20
  self-employed retirement accounts, **13**-29–33
Deferred income, **3**-4–10, **4**-2, **4**-5, **4**-6, **5**-31, **B**-5
Deferred income tax expense or benefit, **17**-17–19
Deferred like-kind exchanges (Starker exchanges), **11**-25–26, **11**-25n, **B**-5
Deferred tax assets, **17**-2, **17**-20–23, **17**-29, **B**-5
Deferred tax liability, **17**-2, **17**-20–23, **17**-29, **B**-5
Deficits, budget, **1**-20
Defined benefit plans, **13**-3–6, **13**-13, **B**-5
Defined contribution plans, **13**-6–16
  after-tax cost of contributions to, **13**-9
  after-tax rates of return for, **13**-12
  contribution limits for, **13**-7–8
  defined, **13**-3, **B**-5
  defined benefit plans vs., **13**-13
  distributions from, **13**-10–12
  employer matching in, **13**-7
  overview, **13**-6–7
  Roth 401(k) plans, **13**-12–16
  traditional 401(k) plans, **13**-12, **13**-14–16
  vesting and, **13**-8–9
Definitely related deductions, **24**-11, **B**-5
De minimis fringe benefits, **5**-24, **12**-25, **12**-26, **12**-30, **B**-5
Democratic Party tax ideology, **1**-3
Dental expenses; *see* Medical and dental expenses
Dependent care benefits, **5**-24, **12**-26, **12**-28
Dependent care credit, **4**-12, **8**-26–28, **8**-27n, **8**-34
Dependents, **4**-13–19
  deductions for, **C**-2
  ethical considerations and, **4**-19
  flowchart for, **4**-29–30
  medical expenses of, **6**-13, **6**-13n
  qualifying child, **4**-13–15, **4**-13n, **4**-15n, **4**-18, **4**-19, **4**-21n
  qualifying relative, **4**-15–19
  requirements for, **4**-13–19
Depletion, **10**-2, **10**-37–39, **B**-5
Depreciable assets, **11**-26n, **19**-17–18
Depreciable basis, **10**-3n, **10**-7, **10**-10–11
Depreciation, **10**-6–30
  accelerated, **11**-10n, **11**-14, **11**-14n, **16**-7
  alternative minimum tax and, **8**-9, **10**-29
  bonus depreciation, **10**-6, **10**-21–22, **10**-21n, **10**-25–29, **B**-3
  conventions for, **10**-7, **10**-9–10
  cost recovery through, **9**-7
  defined, **10**-2, **B**-5
  half-year convention, **10**-9–12, **10**-40
  immediate expensing, **10**-17–20
  IRS Form 4562 for, **10**-29–30
  listed property, **10**-22–24
  of luxury automobiles, **10**-25–27n, **10**-25–29
  methods of, **10**-7–8
  mid-quarter convention, **10**-9, **10**-10, **10**-13, **10**-40–41
  of personal property, **10**-7–14
  of personal residence, **14**-6, **14**-8
  of placed in service assets, **10**-7–10, **10**-14–21, **10**-25–26
  of qualified property, **6**-31n
  of real property, **10**-7, **10**-14–16
  recovery period, **10**-7–9, **10**-8n
  summary, **10**-29–30
  timing strategies and, **3**-6
Depreciation recapture, **11**-10–15
  conversion strategies and, **3**-18
  defined, **B**-5
  Section 291 rules, **11**-14, **11**-15, **11**-33
  Section 1231 assets, **11**-10–13
  Section 1245 property, **11**-10–14, **11**-33
  Section 1250 for real property, **11**-14, **11**-33
Depreciation recovery period, **10**-7–9, **10**-8n
Depreciation tables, **10**-7, **10**-10–13, **10**-15–16
Determination letters, **2**-16, **B**-5
Dickinson, Jon, **18**-24
DIF system; *see* Discriminant Function system
Digital assets, **7**-8, **7**-13
Direct conversions, **11**-30, **B**-5
Direct foreign income taxes, **24**-21, **24**-21n
Direct vs. indirect expenses, **14**-28–29
Direct write-off method, **9**-27, **B**-5
Disability insurance, **5**-30, **B**-5
Disabled individuals, **8**-34
Discharge of indebtedness, **4**-6, **5**-20–21, **5**-20–21n, **B**-5
Disclosure Framework project (FASB), **17**-33

Disclosures
financial statement, **17**-29–33
income tax footnote disclosure, **17**-29–33
of uncertain tax positions, **17**-28
Discount factors, **3**-3–4, **25**-8, **B**-5
Discount points, **14**-13
Discounts, bond, **7**-3–4, **7**-3–4n, **B**-3
Discretionary medical expenses, **6**-14
Discriminant Function (DIF) system, **2**-4–5, **2**-4n, **B**-5
Disney Company's Proxy Statement (2021), **12**-33–34
Dispositions; *see also* Property dispositions
of assets used in trade or business, **4**-6n, **4**-9
special basis adjustments for, **21**-27–28
Disproportionate distributions, **21**-24–26, **B**-5
Disqualified property, **19**-34
Disqualifying disposition, **12**-12, **B**-5
Disregarded entities, **15**-5, **24**-22, **24**-24, **B**-5
Distributable net income (DNI), **25**-31, **B**-5
Distributed assets, character and holding period of, **21**-21–24
Distribution deduction, **25**-31, **B**-5
Distributions; *see also* Liquidating distributions; Property distributions
cash, **18**-11, **20**-30, **21**-9–10
defined benefit plans and, **13**-5
from defined contribution plans, **13**-10–12
disproportionate, **21**-24–26
lump-sum, **13**-20n
minimum, **13**-5, **13**-10n, **13**-15
noncash property to shareholders, **18**-12–14
operating, **21**-9–12, **22**-19–23, **B**-11
post-termination transition period, **22**-22–23, **22**-23n
Roth IRAs, **6**-8n, **13**-25–26
S corporations, **22**-19–23
to shareholders, **15**-7n, **18**-2
special basis adjustments for, **21**-29
traditional IRAs, **6**-8, **13**-23–24
Dividends
as after-tax profits, **18**-2
book–tax differences and, **16**-8
corporate tax consequences of noncash distributions, **18**-13
defined, **18**-2, **B**-6
determining amount from earnings and profits, **18**-2–15
as gross income, **4**-6, **5**-2
income shifting and, **3**-13, **3**-14n
interest vs., **7**-2–3
multinational transactions and, **24**-8
portfolio income and, **7**-2, **7**-3, **7**-6–7, **7**-6n
preferential tax rates for, **8**-4
qualified, **4**-7, **4**-7n, **7**-6, **7**-6n, **B**-13, **C**-2
stock, **7**-7n, **18**-2, **18**-16–17, **18**-16n
tax consequences to shareholders, **18**-16–17
as unearned income, **5**-10, **5**-14
Dividends-received deduction (DRD)
for corporations, **16**-8n, **16**-17, **16**-19–21, **18**-19
deduction limitation, **16**-20–21
defined, **15**-20, **B**-6
on foreign-source dividends, **24**-7, **24**-20
modified taxable income, **16**-20–21, **B**-6
for shareholders, **15**-20
DNI (distributable net income), **25**-31, **B**-5
Dock sales, **23**-20
Document perfection program, **2**-4, **2**-5, **B**-6
Domestic International Sales Corporation status, **22**-3n
Donors/donees, **25**-5–7, **25**-9, **25**-10, **25**-12, **B**-6
Double taxation
of C corporations, **15**-21–22
defined, **B**-6
of distributed corporate income, **18**-2
on dividend income, **7**-6n
exclusions that mitigate, **5**-27–29
of foreign-earned income, **5**-28–29
gifts and inheritances, **5**-27
income shifting and, **3**-13, **3**-14n
life insurance proceeds, **5**-27–28
Double-throwback rule, **23**-19n
Dow Chemical, **19**-24
Downstream acquisitions, **19**-26
Doyle v. Mitchell Brothers Co. (1918), **9**-4n
DRD; *see* Dividends-received deduction
Drucker, Jesse, **17**-28n
Drug dealers, **9**-6n
DSUE (deceased spousal unused exclusion), **25**-28, **B**-5
Dual basis rules, **10**-6n, **11**-3
Due diligence requirements, **4**-23n
Dwelling units, **14**-2–3, **14**-2n, **B**-6
Dynamic forecasting, **1**-18, **B**-6

Earmarked taxes, **1**-4, **B**-6
Earned income, **5**-10, **5**-14, **B**-6
Earned income credit, **4**-12, **8**-30–32, **8**-34, **B**-6
Earnings and profits (E&P)
accumulated, **18**-3, **18**-14, **B**-1
adjustments to, **18**-5–7
computing, **18**-4–7
current, **18**-3–7, **18**-14, **B**-5
deductible expenses that do not reduce, **18**-5
defined, **B**-6
determining dividend amount from, **18**-2–15
disallowance of certain expenses, **18**-5
negative current and negative accumulated, **18**-11
negative current and positive accumulated, **18**-10
noncash property distributions to shareholders, **18**-12–14
nondeductible expenses that reduce, **18**-5
nontaxable income included in, **18**-4
ordering of distributions, **18**-8, **18**-10–11
positive current and negative accumulated, **18**-10
positive current and positive accumulated, **18**-8
S corporations, **22**-19–21
summary of, **18**-11
template for computing, **18**-7
timing items requiring separate accounting methods, **18**-5–7
undistributed, **22**-2
Earnings per share, **12**-8
ECI; *see* Effectively connected income
E-commerce, **1**-15, **23**-5–8
Economic benefit, gross income and, **5**-2–4
Economic income, **1**-8
Economic income tax nexus, **23**-6–8, **23**-11, **B**-6
Economic performance test, **9**-22–26
cost of goods sold and, **9**-23
defined, **B**-6
overview, **9**-22, **9**-23–24
payment liabilities, **9**-24–26
providing goods/services to another party, **9**-25
receiving goods/services from another party, **9**-24
recurring item exceptions, **9**-26
renting/leasing property from another party, **9**-24–25
Economic substance doctrine, **3**-18–19, **B**-6
Economy of tax systems, **1**-22, **B**-6
Educational assistance benefits, **5**-24, **12**-26, **12**-28, **B**-6
Educational subsidies, **5**-26
Education credits, **8**-28–29n, **8**-28–30
Education expenses, **6**-10, **9**-8
Education loans, **6**-10
Education-related exclusions, **5**-25–27, **5**-25n
Effectively connected income (ECI), **24**-3, **24**-10, **24**-11, **B**-6
Effective tax rate
average tax rate vs., **1**-8
defined, **1**-8, **B**-6
foreign-derived intangible income and, **24**-17
global intangible low-taxed income and, **24**-30
high-tax subpart F income and, **24**-27
importance of, **17**-32–33
incidence of taxation captured by, **1**-11
interim period, **17**-33
permanent differences, **17**-8
regressive nature of, **1**-10–11, **1**-21
sales tax and, **1**-10n
EITF (Emerging Issues Task Force), **17**-2, **17**-2n
Elderly taxpayers, **4**-10, **6**-26, **6**-26n, **8**-34, **C**-2
Elliott, Justin, **10**-32, **13**-29
Emerging Issues Task Force (EITF), **17**-2, **17**-2n
Eminent domain, **11**-30n
Employees
business expenses of, **6**-3
cell phones of, **5**-25
compensation for, **12**-2
covered, **12**-4–7, **12**-14n
defined, **B**-6
disability policies purchased by, **5**-30
educational assistance for, **5**-24, **12**-26, **12**-28, **B**-6
expense reimbursements for, **5**-23, **5**-25
FICA taxes payable, **8**-14–16
nonqualified deferred compensation plans and, **13**-16–19
nontaxable fringe benefits and, **3**-2, **12**-31
qualified equity grants and, **12**-20
restricted stock considerations for, **12**-17–19
self-employed individuals vs., **8**-21–22
stock option considerations for, **12**-10–13
taxable fringe benefits and, **12**-22–24
Employer matching, **13**-7
Employer-provided child care credit, **8**-34
Employer-provided qualified plans, **13**-3
Employers
deductibility of salary payments by, **12**-2–7
defined contribution plan matching by, **13**-7
meals and lodging for convenience of, **12**-27–28
nonqualified deferred compensation plans and, **13**-17, **13**-19
nontaxable fringe benefits and, **3**-2, **12**-31
restricted stock considerations for, **12**-19–20
stock option considerations for, **12**-14–15
taxable fringe benefits and, **12**-24
Employment taxes, **8**-14–23
defined, **B**-6
FICA taxes, **8**-14–16, **12**-2
revenue generated from, **1**-12
tax base for, **1**-13
types of, **1**-12–13
withholding taxes, **12**-2
Enacted tax rate, **17**-15, **B**-6
Endorsement agreements, **24**-10
Energy credit, **8**-34
Enrolled agents, **2**-24n
Entertainment, deductions for, **9**-8
Entity approach, **20**-3, **B**-6
Entity tax characteristics, **15**-7–30
for C corporations, **15**-18–22
comparison across entities, **15**-29–30, **15**-32–33
converting to other entity types, **15**-27–28, **15**-31
deductibility of losses, **15**-26–29
for flow-through entities, **15**-7–18
overview, **15**-7
owner compensation, **15**-22–25
for shareholders, **15**-18–22
Entity tax classification, **15**-5–7
Equity-based compensation, **12**-7–21
overview, **12**-8
qualified equity grants, **12**-20, **B**-13
restricted stock, **12**-16–20
stock options and, **12**-9–16
summary of, **12**-20–21
Equity holders; *see* Shareholders
Equity in tax systems, **1**-20–21, **B**-6
Equity method of accounting, **16**-8
Escrow (holding) accounts, **14**-15, **B**-6
Estates
defined, **25**-30, **B**-6
filing requirements for, **2**-2, **2**-2n
gross, **25**-17–23
taxable, **25**-23–25, **B**-16
tax rates for, **C**-2
Estate tax, **25**-17–29
adjusted taxable gifts, **25**-25–26
administrative expenses, debts, losses, and state death taxes, **25**-23–24
applicable credit, **25**-2–3, **25**-27–28
charitable deductions and, **25**-24–25
computation of, **25**-25–29
for decedents, **25**-3n
defined, **B**-6
formula for, **25**-17
gross estate, **25**-17–23
jointly owned property, **25**-20–21
marital deduction, **25**-4, **25**-24
specific inclusions, **25**-19–21
taxable estate, **25**-23–25, **B**-16
transfers within three years of death, **25**-21
unified credit, **1**-13–14
valuation and, **25**-21–22
Estimated taxes
annualized income method for, **16**-26–30
for corporations, **1**-22, **16**-26–30, **22**-28
defined, **B**-6
in individual tax formula, **4**-12
payment of, **8**-36
penalties, **3**-7n
for self-employed individuals, **1**-22, **8**-20
ETFs; *see* Exchange traded funds
Ethical considerations
audits and, **2**-5
business expenses and, **9**-5
charitable contributions and, **6**-23

compliance and, **16**-26
cost recovery basis and, **10**-6
dependents and, **4**-19
e-commerce, **23**-8
in exchange of business assets, **19**-12
executive compensation and, **15**-26
FICA taxes and, **8**-22
gift tax and, **25**-6
gross income, **5**-17
income shifting and, **3**-14
look-back rule and, **11**-19
material participation and, **20**-34
in multinational transactions, **24**-11
partnership interests and, **21**-7
rental use of home and, **14**-17
retirement planning and, **13**-26
S corporations and, **22**-6
Section 351 and, **19**-6
stock options and, **12**-15
uncertain tax positions and, **17**-29
wash sales and, **7**-25
Eugene James v. United States (1961), **5**-3n
European Union (EU), **24**-31
Exact method for interest expenses, **14**-11n
Excess business loss, defined, **B**-6
Excess business loss limitation, **6**-6, **6**-6n, **15**-27, **20**-35, **22**-17, **22**-17n
Excess business loss rules, **7**-32, **7**-32n
Excess net passive income, **22**-26–27, **B**-6
Excess net passive income tax, **22**-24, **22**-26–27, **B**-6
Excess taxable income, **20**-22n
Exchanged basis, **11**-30, **B**-6
Exchanged basis property, **19**-8n
Exchange traded funds (ETFs), **7**-2, **7**-2n, **B**-6
Excise taxes, **1**-13, **1**-15, **1**-22, **B**-6
Exclusion ratio, **5**-11
Exclusions; *see also* Income exclusion provisions
defined, **B**-6
from gift taxes, **1**-13
from gross income, **4**-2, **4**-5, **4**-6
Ex-dividend date, **7**-6, **B**-6
Executive compensation, **12**-5, **12**-7, **15**-26
Executors, **25**-17, **25**-19, **25**-22–25, **25**-22n, **25**-28, **B**-6
Exemption equivalent, **25**-3, **B**-6
Exemptions, **8**-11, **8**-11n, **C**-2
Exercise date, **12**-9–12, **12**-15, **B**-7
Exercise price, **12**-8–14, **16**-10, **B**-7
Expected return multiple, **5**-12
Expenditures
capital, **9**-7, **9**-7n
mixed-motive, **9**-8–12, **B**-10
organizational, **9**-7, **10**-32–35, **10**-35n, **20**-12–13, **B**-12
personal, **9**-7–8
against public policy, **9**-6
research and experimentation, **10**-31, **10**-35–36, **10**-35n, **24**-13, **B**-14
Expenses; *see also* Business expenses; Interest expenses; Investment expenses; Medical and dental expenses; Rental expenses; Travel and transportation expenses
administrative, **25**-23–24
deductions for, **3**-16, **9**-4, **18**-5
education, **6**-10, **9**-8
excluded from taxable income, **18**-5
as itemized deductions, **4**-10
moving, **5**-23n, **6**-7
nondeductible expenses that reduce E&P, **18**-5
ordinary and necessary, **6**-3–4, **9**-4–5, **9**-4n, **B**-12
personal, **3**-16, **9**-7–8, **14**-30n, **B**-12
prepaid, **3**-6, **9**-7, **9**-16, **9**-16n, **9**-29
Explicit taxes, **1**-16, **B**-7
Extensions, **2**-3, **2**-3n, **8**-39

Facebook, **12**-27, **16**-12–13
Face value, **7**-2, **B**-7
Factor Presence Nexus Standard, **23**-11
Facts, open vs. closed, **2**-17
Facts and circumstances test, **12**-2–3, **B**-7
Failure-to-file penalty, **2**-3
Fair-market value (FMV)
of capital gain property, **6**-19
distributions of noncash property to shareholders and, **18**-12–14
monetary contributions and, **6**-19
of personal assets converted to business use, **10**-5, **10**-5n
of property in gross estate, **25**-21
real property taxes and, **14**-15, **14**-15n
of stock, **12**-17, **18**-16, **22**-12n
transferred property and, **25**-4
Fairness in tax systems, **1**-20–21
Family attribution, **18**-20–21
Family limited partnerships, **25**-34, **B**-7
Family members, transactions among, **3**-12, **3**-12n, **3**-14, **3**-14n
FAS 5, *Accounting for Contingencies,* **17**-24
FAS 109, *Accounting for Income Taxes,* **17**-24
FASB; *see* Financial Accounting Standards Board
FASB Concepts Statement No. 6, *Elements of Financial Statements,* **17**-4
FASB Interpretation (FIN) No. 48, *Accounting for Uncertainty in Income Taxes–An Interpretation of FASB Statement No. 109,* **17**-24–25, **17**-27–28
Faturechi, Robert, **10**-32
Favorable book–tax differences, **16**-3, **16**-18, **16**-21, **17**-9, **17**-12, **17**-12n, **B**-7
FDAP (fixed and determinable, annual or periodic) income, **24**-3, **B**-7
FDII; *see* Foreign-derived intangible income
Federal estate tax; *see* Estate tax
Federal gift tax; *see* Gift tax
Federal income tax computation, **8**-2–7
exceptions to basic computation, **8**-3–7
kiddie tax, **8**-5–6, **8**-11n
marriage penalty or benefit, **8**-3, **8**-4
net investment income tax, **8**-13, **8**-13n
preferential rate for capital gains and dividends, **4**-7, **8**-4, **8**-4n
tax rate schedules, **4**-11, **8**-2–3, **C**-1
Federal income taxes; *see also* Federal income tax computation
due date for, **1**-22
history of, **1**-12
progressive structure of, **1**-9
tax base for, **1**-5
Federal income tax expense (corporations), **16**-5
Federal Insurance Contributions Act (FICA) taxes, **8**-14–23, **8**-14n, **12**-2, **12**-2n, **12**-8n, **12**-24n, **15**-23, **B**-7
Federal judicial system, **2**-6–9
Federal short-term interest rate, **2**-3, **2**-3n, **8**-37–38, **B**-7
Federal/state adjustments, **23**-17, **B**-7
Federal student loan program, **8**-28n
Federal taxes; *see also* Federal income taxes
employment, **1**-12–13
estate and gift, **1**-13–14
excise, **1**-13
overview, **1**-11–12
revenue generated from, **1**-12
transfer, **1**-13–14, **5**-27
unemployment, **1**-10, **1**-10n, **1**-13, **1**-13n
Federal Tax Weekly Alert, **2**-11
Federal transfer taxes, **25**-2–4
Federal unemployment taxes, **1**-10, **1**-10n, **1**-13, **1**-13n
Federation of Tax Administrators, **23**-2n
FICA taxes; *see* Federal Insurance Contributions Act taxes
Fidelity Investments Charitable Gift Fund, **18**-24
Fiduciaries/fiduciary duties, **25**-7, **25**-30, **B**-7
Field examinations, **2**-6, **B**-7
FIFO method; *see* First-in, first-out method
52/53 week year, **9**-14, **9**-14n, **9**-15
Filing requirements
for corporations, **2**-2
due dates and extensions, **1**-22, **2**-3, **2**-3n
for estates, **2**-2, **2**-2n
gross income and, **2**-2, **8**-38
for individual taxpayers, **2**-2
late filing penalties, **2**-3, **8**-39, **B**-9
late payment penalties, **2**-3, **2**-3n, **8**-39
prepayments, **8**-36–38
for S corporations, **22**-28–30
statute of limitations, **2**-3–4
for trusts, **2**-2
Filing status, **4**-19–25; *see also* Head of household; Married filing jointly (MFJ); Married filing separately (MFS); Single filing status; Widows/widowers
for abandoned spouses, **4**-21, **B**-1
child tax credit and, **8**-24, **8**-25
defined, **B**-7
flowchart for determination of, **4**-32
gross income thresholds (2022), **2**-2
importance of, **4**-19
qualifying child and, **4**-13n
for same-sex married couples, **4**-20
standard deduction and, **2**-2, **4**-10, **4**-12, **6**-26, **C**-2
tax rate schedules and, **8**-2, **C**-1
FIN 48, **17**-24–25, **17**-27–28
Final regulations, **2**-10, **2**-15, **B**-7
Finance Committee (Senate), **2**-13
Financial Accounting Standards Board (FASB), **12**-15, **17**-2–4, **17**-33; *see also specific FAS standards*
Financial and tax accounting methods, **9**-15–16
Financial statement disclosure, **17**-29–33
Fines, **1**-4, **2**-28, **9**-6, **9**-6n
First Amendment, **3**-20
First-in, first-out (FIFO) method, **3**-6, **7**-9–10, **9**-19n, **9**-21–22, **B**-7
First-time homebuyers, **13**-23n
Fiscal year, **9**-14, **B**-7
529 plans, **5**-26, **5**-26n
Fixed and determinable, annual or periodic (FDAP) income, **24**-3, **B**-7
Fixed annuities, **5**-11–12
Flat taxes, **1**-5, **1**-9, **B**-7
Flexible spending accounts (FSAs), **5**-24, **5**-24n, **6**-13, **6**-13n, **12**-26, **12**-31, **B**-7
Flipping, **14**-5, **B**-7
Floor limitations, **6**-15, **6**-24, **B**-7
Flow-through entities
accounting period for, **9**-15
aggregate and entity concepts, **20**-3
for AGI deductions and, **6**-6, **6**-6n
business income taxation for, **15**-7–18
defined, **B**-7
hybrid entities treated as, **24**-23
income from, **5**-14
Medicare tax for, **15**-14n, **15**-15–16
net investment income tax for, **15**-13
overview, **20**-2–3
passive activity income and losses in, **7**-29
qualified business income deduction for, **15**-9–13, **15**-9n
S corporations as, **5**-14, **9**-2n
self-employment tax and, **15**-14–15, **15**-14n
tax classification of, **15**-5, **15**-6
tax requirements for, **23**-10
FMV; *see* Fair-market value
For AGI deductions, **6**-2–12
alimony paid, **4**-9, **5**-15, **6**-10
business expenses/activities, **4**-9, **6**-2–9
capital losses, **4**-9
common deductions, **4**-9
defined, **B**-5, **B**-7
excess business loss limitation, **6**-6, **6**-6n
flow-through entities, **6**-6, **6**-6n
health insurance for self-employed, **4**-9, **6**-7–8, **6**-7–8n
health savings accounts, **6**-8–9
on *IRS Form 1040,* **4**-9, **6**-2n, **6**-12
losses on dispositions of business assets, **4**-9, **6**-6
moving expenses, **6**-7
overview, **4**-8–9, **6**-2
penalty for early withdrawal of savings, **6**-9
qualified education expenses, **6**-10
qualified education loans, **6**-10
rent and royalty expenses, **4**-9, **6**-3, **6**-5–6, **6**-5–6n
retirement account contributions, **4**-9, **6**-8
self-employment tax deduction, **4**-9, **6**-8, **6**-8n, **8**-16–20, **15**-14
subsidizing specific activities, **6**-10
summary of, **6**-11–12
trade or business expenses, **6**-2n, **6**-3–4
Ford Motor Company, **12**-29, **17**-28
Forecasting, static vs. dynamic, **1**-18
Foreclosure of home, exclusion of gain from debt forgiveness on, **14**-8, **14**-8n
Foreign base company income, **24**-26–27, **B**-7
Foreign base company sales income, **24**-26, **B**-7
Foreign branches, **24**-2, **24**-20, **24**-23, **B**-7
Foreign branch income, **24**-5, **24**-20
Foreign corporations
compensation for services from, **24**-8
controlled, **24**-25–29
cross-border mergers with, **24**-29
dividends from, **24**-7, **24**-20, **24**-22
formation of, **24**-2
operating abroad through, **24**-16–17
qualified, **7**-6, **7**-6n
territorial approach for, **24**-3

Foreign Corrupt Practices Act of 1977, 24-11
Foreign-derived intangible income (FDII), 24-17, 24-18n, B-7
Foreign housing expenses, 24-7n
Foreign income taxes, 6-15, 6-16
Foreign personal holding company income, 24-26, B-7
Foreign shareholders, 15-21
Foreign source income
- anti-deferral rules and, 24-24–31
- double taxation of, 5-28–29, 24-5
- exclusions related to, 8-3n, 8-13
- FTC limitation categories of, 24-20
- intangible, 24-17, 24-18n
- tax credits and, 24-3
- TCJA changes to, 24-16, 24-17
- timing and scope of taxation, 24-22
- U.S. source rules for, 24-6–13

Foreign subsidiaries, 24-2, 24-22–25
Foreign tax credits (FTCs)
- creditable foreign taxes, 24-21
- defined, B-7
- direct taxes, 24-21, 24-21n
- foreign branch income, 24-20
- FTC basket, 24-20
- general category income, 24-20, B-8
- global intangible low-taxed income, 24-20, 24-25, 24-29–30, 24-30n
- "in lieu of" taxes, 24-21, 24-21n
- limitation categories of taxable income, 24-20
- limitation on, 24-5, B-7
- overview of system, 8-33–34, 24-5
- passive category income, 24-20
- summary of, 8-34

Foreign transportation expenses, 9-10, 9-10n
Forgiveness of debt, 5-21n, 14-8, 14-8n
Form of receipt, 5-4
"For profit" requirement, 9-4
For the convenience of the employer benefits, 12-27–28, B-7
Forward acquisitions, 19-26
Forward triangular type A mergers, 19-28–29, 19-31
401(k) plans
- individual, 13-31–33
- Roth, 13-12–16, B-14
- traditional, 13-12, 13-14–16, B-17

Fourteenth Amendment, 4-20
Fracking, 19-32
Franchise taxes, 23-2n, 23-9n
Fraudulent tax returns, 2-4
Fringe benefits, 12-21–34; *see also* Nontaxable fringe benefits
- defined, B-7
- *de minimis,* 5-24, 12-25, 12-26, 12-30, B-5
- employee considerations for, 12-22–24
- employee expense reimbursements, 5-23, 5-25
- employer considerations for, 12-24
- excluded from gross income, 5-23, 5-24
- income exclusion provisions for, 5-23, 5-23n, 5-25
- overview, 12-21
- for partners, 20-19n
- qualified, 5-23, 5-24, 6-7, 22-18n
- S corporations and, 22-18, 22-18n
- summary of, 12-33–34
- taxable, 12-21–24, 12-33–34, 22-18
- tax planning with, 12-31–33

From AGI deductions; *see also* Itemized deductions; Standard deduction
- defined, B-5, B-7
- overview, 4-8–10, 6-2
- for qualified business income, 4-9, 6-28–32, 6-29–31n, 15-9

Front loading restrictions, 5-15n
"Fruit and the tree" analogy, 3-12, 5-8n
FSAs; *see* Flexible spending accounts
FTC basket, 24-20, B-8
FTCs; *see* Foreign tax credits
Fuel taxes, 1-13, 1-15
"Full" depreciation recapture, 11-11n
Full-inclusion rule, 24-27
Full-month convention, 10-31, B-8
Future interest, 25-7, 25-8, B-8
Future value of money, 3-3

GAAP; *see* Generally accepted accounting principles
GAAP capital accounts, 20-8, B-8
Gain and loss recognition, 20-3–4
Gain or loss on disposition
- capital assets, 11-8
- character of assets, 11-7–9
- ordinary assets, 11-7–8
- property use and holding period, 11-7
- Section 1231 assets, 11-8–9
- summary of, 11-20

Gambling winnings/losses
- alternative minimum tax and, 8-8
- income from, 5-16–17, 5-17n
- as itemized deductions, 4-10, 6-24, 6-24n
- taxes on, 1-4n

Gardner, Matthew, 16-8
Gas industry, 19-32
Gasoline taxes, 1-13, 1-15
GCI (Geosyntec Consultants, Inc.), 18-24
General category income, 24-20, B-8
General depreciation system (GDS), 10-7n
General Electric, 19-4
Generally accepted accounting principles (GAAP)
- accrual method and, 9-17, 17-5
- balance sheet approach and, 17-13
- capital accounts, 20-8, B-8
- contributed property and, 19-4n
- financial statements and, 9-15, 17-2
- restricted stock expense and, 12-19
- stock option expense and, 12-15, 12-19
- uniform capitalization and, 9-20

General Motors Corporation, 17-28
General partnerships (GPs), 15-2, 20-2, B-8
Generation-skipping tax (GST), 25-2, 25-30, B-8
Geoffrey, Inc. v. South Carolina Tax Commission (1993), 23-11n
Geographic basis for compensation, 24-9
George Cohan v. Commissioner (1930), 9-12n
Geosyntec Consultants, Inc. (GCI), 18-24
Gift loans, 5-20n
Gifts
- adjusted basis, 11-3
- carryover basis of assets acquired as, 10-6
- completion of, 25-5, 25-5n
- in contemplation of death, 25-17n
- current, 25-10, 25-13, B-5
- deathbed, 25-17n, 25-21
- defined, 5-27, B-8
- dual basis rules for, 10-6n, 11-3
- income exclusion provisions for, 4-6, 5-27
- initial basis of, 11-3
- serial, 25-31, B-14
- taxable, 25-10–12, 25-25–26

Gift-splitting election, 25-4n, 25-10
Gift tax, 25-4–16
- applicable credit, 25-2–4, 25-14
- charitable deductions and, 25-12
- computation of, 25-12–16
- current taxable gifts, 25-13
- defined, B-8
- ethical considerations and, 25-6
- exclusions, 1-13, 5-27n, 25-9, 25-9n
- formula for, 25-4
- gift-splitting election, 25-4n, 25-10
- marital deduction, 25-4, 25-10–11, 25-11n
- nondeductible terminal interests, 25-11
- prior taxable gifts, 25-13
- rates for, 1-13
- taxable gifts, 25-10–12, 25-25–26, B-16
- transfers subject to, 25-5–9
- on transfers within three years of death, 25-21
- unified credit, 1-13–14
- valuation and, 25-7–8

Gillette Co. v. Franchise Tax Board (2015), 23-23
GILTI; *see* Global intangible low-taxed income
Global Business Alliance, 24-2n
Global intangible low-taxed income (GILTI), 24-16, 24-20, 24-25, 24-29–30, 24-30n, B-8
Golsen rule, 2-15, B-8
Goodwill, 9-7, 9-7n, 10-32n, 16-9, 16-9n, 19-22, 19-23n
Google, 2-11, 12-27, 24-2, 24-2n
Government bonds, 7-2
Government sales, 23-20
GPs; *see* General partnerships
Graded vesting, 13-4, B-8
Graduated taxes, 1-5–6, 1-12, B-8
Grant date, 12-10–12, 12-15–19, 12-21, 16-11, B-8
Grantors, 25-7, B-8
Grantor trusts, 22-2n
Green card test, 24-4
Gregory v. Helvering (1935), 19-25n
Gross estate, 25-17–23
- adjusted, 25-23, B-2
- defined, 25-17, B-8
- gift taxes paid on transfers within three years of death, 25-21
- jointly owned property in, 25-20–21
- specific inclusions, 25-19–21
- summary of, 25-22
- transfers within three years of death, 25-21
- valuation, 25-21–22

Gross income; *see also* Adjusted gross income (AGI)
- alimony, 4-6, 5-14–15
- from business, 4-6, 5-2, 6-2, 9-2
- calculation of, 9-23
- character of, 4-5–7
- defined, 2-2, 5-2, B-8
- from discharge of indebtedness, 4-6, 5-20–21, 5-20–21n
- economic benefit and, 5-2–4
- ethical considerations, 5-17
- exclusions and deferrals from, 4-2, 4-5, 4-6
- filing requirements and, 2-2, 8-38
- flow-through entities, 5-14
- form of receipt for, 5-4
- from imputed income, 5-19–20
- items included in, 4-2, 4-5, 5-2–4, 5-14–21
- prizes, awards, and gambling winnings, 5-16–17, 5-16n, 5-17n
- realization principle, 5-3
- recognition of, 5-2–4
- recovery of amounts previously deducted, 5-5
- return of capital principle, 5-4–5
- from Social Security benefits, 5-17–19, 5-17n
- summary (example), 5-31–32
- tax benefit rule and, 5-5
- thresholds by filing status (2022), 2-2
- U.S. source rules for, 24-6–13
- withholding tax and, 24-3

Gross income test, 4-16–19, 6-13n
Gross profit percentage, 11-32, 11-33
Gross receipts, 9-23, 22-6, 22-11n, 22-26, 23-12n, 23-25, B-8
Gross receipts test, 9-2, 9-28n, B-8
Gross-up, 12-23–24, 12-23–24n
Groupon, 23-9
Group-term life insurance, 12-22–23, 12-26–27, B-8
GST; *see* Generation-skipping tax
Guaranteed payments, 20-10n, 20-19, 20-19n, 20-21n, 20-29n, B-8

Half-year convention, 10-9–12, 10-40, B-8
Hand, Learned, 3-19
Hard fork, 9-3
Hazards of litigation, 2-6
Head of household
- defined, B-8
- gross income thresholds (2022), 2-2
- qualifying person for, 4-22–25, 4-23n, 4-31
- standard deduction for, 2-2, 4-10, 6-26, C-2
- tax rate schedule for, C-1

Health care reimbursement, 5-30
Health insurance
- deduction for self-employed taxpayers, 4-9, 6-7–8, 6-7–8n
- defined, B-8
- as nontaxable fringe benefit, 3-2, 12-26, 12-27
- premiums, 6-7, 6-7n, 6-13, 6-13n
- as qualifying fringe benefit, 5-24, 5-24n

Health savings accounts (HSAs), 5-24, 5-24n, 6-8–9, 6-9n, 6-13, 6-13n
Hedge funds, 20-2
Heirs, 25-17, B-8
Helvering v. Horst (1940), 5-8n
Hobbies, 6-24, 6-24n, 9-4
Hobby losses, 22-14n
Holding (escrow) accounts, 14-15, B-6
Holding period, 11-3, 11-7, 19-18, 20-7–9, 20-13, 21-21–24
Holmes, Oliver Wendell, Jr., 1-4, 5-7n
Holt, Stephen, 3-20
Home-equity indebtedness, 6-17, 6-17n, 14-10n
Home equity loans, 6-17, 14-9
Home mortgage interest deductions, 6-17, 6-17n, 14-8–15
Home mortgage interest expenses, 8-8, 14-10, 14-18–21, 14-20n, 14-29–30, 14-30n

- Home office deductions, 14-26–32, B-8; *see also* Business use of home
- Home ownership, 14-2–37; *see also* Personal residence; Rental use of home
  - business use of home, 14-26–32
  - depreciation and, 14-6, 14-8
  - home sale exclusion in unforeseen circumstances, 14-6–7, 14-7n
  - interest expense on home-related debt, 14-8–15
  - mortgage insurance and, 6-17n, 14-13
  - personal use of home, 14-4–16
  - points, 14-13–15
  - qualified residence, 14-9, B-13
  - real property taxes and, 14-15–16, 14-15–16n
  - tax and nontax consequences of, 14-3
- Home-related debt
  - acquisition indebtedness, 14-9–12, 14-10–11n
  - home-equity indebtedness, 6-17, 6-17n, 14-10n
  - interest deductions on, 14-13
  - interest expense on, 14-8–15
  - limitations on, 14-10–12
  - qualifying debt, 14-8n, 14-12
- Horizontal equity, 1-21, B-8
- Hospitals and long-term care facilities, 6-14, 6-14n
- Hot assets, 21-3–7, 21-3n, B-8
- House of Representatives, as source of tax law, 2-10, 2-12–13
- "How America Saves 2021" report (Vanguard), 13-7
- HSAs; *see* Health savings accounts
- Hybrid entities, 24-22–24, B-8
- Hybrid method of accounting, 5-7n, 9-16
- Hypothetical income tax expense, 17-31n
- Hypothetical tax provision, 17-31–32

- Immediate expensing, 10-17–20
  - bonus depreciation, 10-21–22, 10-21n
  - choice of assets for, 10-20
  - limits on, 10-18–19
  - overview, 10-17
- Impermissible accounting method, 9-29, 9-30, 9-32, B-8
- Implicit taxes, 1-16–17, 3-15, 3-18, B-8
- Imputed income, 5-19–20, B-8
- Imputed interest, 5-20
- Inbound transactions, 24-2, B-8
- Incentive stock options (ISOs), 12-10–15, 16-10–11, 16-10n, B-8
- Incidence of taxation, 1-11
- Income; *see also* Salary and wages
  - accrual, 9-18
  - alimony, 4-6, 5-14–15
  - all-events test for, 9-18
  - all-inclusive concept of, 4-2, 5-2, 5-14, B-2
  - from annuities, 5-10–12
  - assignment of income doctrine, 3-12, 5-8, B-3
  - business; *see* Business income
  - character of, 4-5–7, B-4
  - common income items, 4-6
  - compensation and fringe benefits, 4-6
  - deferred, 3-4–10, 4-2, 4-5, 4-6, 5-31, B-5
  - discharge of indebtedness, 4-6, 5-20–21, 5-20–21n
  - earned, 5-10, 5-14, B-6
  - economic, 1-8
  - effectively connected, 24-3, 24-10, 24-11, B-6
  - excess net passive, 22-26–27, B-6
  - excluded, 4-2, 4-5, 4-6
  - exclusion provisions; *see* Income exclusion provisions
  - fixed and determinable, annual or periodic, 24-3, B-7
  - from flow-through entities, 5-14
  - foreign source; *see* Foreign source income
  - gross; *see* Gross income
  - imputed, 5-19–20, B-8
  - interest and dividends, 4-6, 5-2, 7-3n
  - investment, 5-3, 7-2, 22-6, 22-6n, 22-26–27, B-9
  - nonbusiness, 23-4, 23-24, B-11
  - operating, 7-2, B-11
  - ordinary, 3-15, 4-6, 4-7, 20-17–23
  - passive investment, 22-6, 22-6n, B-12
  - portfolio; *see* Portfolio income
  - preferentially taxed, 4-7, 8-4, 8-4n, B-12
  - from prizes, awards, and gambling winnings, 5-16–17, 5-16n, 5-17n
  - production of, 11-8, B-13
  - from property, 5-10–13
  - property dispositions, 5-13
  - property sale gains, 4-6
  - realization and recognition of, 4-2, 4-5, 5-2–9
  - rents and royalties, 4-6, 5-2
  - retirement income, 4-6
  - from services, 5-10
  - from Social Security benefits, 5-17–19, 5-17n
  - subpart F, 24-16, 24-25–29, B-15
  - taxable; *see* Taxable income
  - taxpayer recognition of, 5-6–9
  - timing strategies and, 3-4–11
  - types of, 5-10–21
  - unearned; *see* Unearned income
- Income and loss allocations, for S corporations, 22-9
- Income and loss baskets, 20-33–34
- Income effect, 1-19, B-8
- Income exclusion provisions, 5-21–31
  - common exclusions, 4-6, 5-21–25
  - deferral provisions, 5-31
  - disability insurance, 5-30, B-5
  - education-related, 5-25-27, 5-25n
  - foreign-earned income, 5-28–29
  - fringe benefits, 5-23, 5-23n, 5-25
  - gifts and inheritances, 5-27
  - health care reimbursement, 5-30
  - life insurance proceeds, 5-27–28, 5-27n
  - municipal interest, 4-6, 5-21–22
  - personal injury payments, 5-29–30
  - sale of personal residence, 4-6, 5-22, 5-22n, 14-4–8
  - scholarships, 5-25, 5-25n
  - sickness and injury-related, 5-29–30
  - U.S. Series EE bonds, 5-26–27
  - workers' compensation, 5-29
- Income in respect of a decedent (IRD), 25-18
- Income recognition
  - accrual method and, 3-11, 3-11n, 5-7, 9-29
  - cash method and, 3-10–11, 5-7, 9-29
  - claim of right doctrine and, 5-7–8, 5-8n, B-4
  - constructive receipt doctrine and, 3-10–11, 3-11n, 5-7, B-4
  - deferral of, 3-6–7
  - of gross income, 5-2–4
  - by taxpayers, 5-6–9
  - unearned income and, 9-18
- Income-shifting strategies, 3-11–15
  - ethical considerations in, 3-14
  - family member transactions, 3-12, 3-12n, 3-14, 3-14n
  - jurisdictional considerations and limitations, 3-15
  - overview, 3-2, 3-11
  - owners and business transactions, 3-12–14
- Income statements, 17-3
- Income taxes; *see also* Federal income taxes; State income taxes
  - accounting for, 17-2–6
  - calculation of, 4-11, 8-2–7
  - complexity of, 1-22
  - defined, 17-3, B-8
  - foreign, 6-15, 6-16
  - tax base for, 1-5
  - wealth planning and, 25-30–31
- Income tax footnote disclosure, 17-29–33
- Income tax nexus, 23-2, 23-4, 23-10–14, 23-19, B-8
- Income tax planning; *see* Tax planning strategies
- Income tax positions, accounting for uncertainty in, 17-24–29
- Income tax provision process, 17-2–19
  - calculating deferred income tax expenses/benefits, 17-17–19
  - computing current income tax expenses/benefits, 17-10–11
  - current income tax expense or benefit, 17-10–11, 17-19
  - ending balances in balance sheet deferred tax asset/liability accounts, 17-11–17
  - overview, 17-2–6
  - permanent difference adjustments, 17-7–8
  - temporary differences and tax carryover amounts, 17-9
  - total income tax provision, 17-18
  - valuation allowance in, 17-20–24
- Income tax treaties, 2-14, 24-3, 24-3n, 24-17–18
- Independent contractors, 8-21–22, 8-21n, 23-13, B-8
- Indirect conversions, 11-30, B-9
- Indirect vs. direct expenses, 14-28–29
- Individual 401(k) plans, 13-31–33
- Individual income tax computation, 8-2–7; *see also* Alternative minimum tax (AMT)
  - exceptions to basic computation, 8-3–7
  - kiddie tax, 8-5–6, 8-11n
  - marriage penalty or benefit, 8-3, 8-4
  - net investment income tax, 8-13, 8-13n
  - preferential rate for capital gains and dividends, 4-7, 8-4, 8-4n
  - tax rate schedules, 4-11, 8-2–3, C-1
- Individual income tax formula, 4-2–32
  - for AGI deductions, 4-8–9
  - from AGI deductions, 4-8–10
  - alternative minimum tax, 4-11
  - common exclusions and deferrals, 4-6
  - comparison with corporate tax formula, 16-2
  - deductions, 4-8–11
  - dependents of taxpayer, 4-13–19, 4-29–30
  - filing status, 4-19–25, 4-31–32
  - for gross income, 4-2, 4-5–7
  - income tax calculation, 4-11, 8-2–7
  - self-employment taxes, 4-11
  - summary of, 4-25–28
  - tax credits, 4-12
  - tax prepayments, 4-12
- Individual recovery credit, 8-32
- Individual retirement accounts (IRAs), 13-20–29
  - contribution limits, 6-8n, 13-20n
  - defined, B-9
  - in gross estate, 25-18
  - overview, 13-20
  - Roth, 5-21n, 6-8n, 13-20, 13-24–29, 13-37, B-14
  - SEP, 13-29–31, B-14
  - SIMPLE, 13-30n
  - spousal, 13-21–22, B-15
  - traditional, 6-8, 13-20–24, 13-35–36, B-17
- Individual shareholders, 15-18
- Individual tax formula; *see* Individual income tax formula
- *Indopco v. Commissioner* (1992), 9-7n
- Information matching program, 2-4, 2-5, B-9
- Inheritances
  - defined, 5-27, B-9
  - income exclusion provisions for, 4-6, 5-27
  - property, 11-3
- Initial basis, 10-3–4, 10-3n, 11-3, 22-12
- Initial public offerings (IPOs), 15-3–4, 15-4n, 19-27–28, B-9
- Injury-related exclusions, 5-29–30
- "In lieu of" taxes, 24-21, 24-21n
- Inside basis, 20-4, 20-7–8, 21-7–8, 21-13–21, 21-27n, B-9
- Installment sales
  - deferral provisions for, 5-31
  - defined, B-9
  - exclusion from gross income, 4-6
  - gains ineligible for reporting, 11-33
  - gross profit percentage, 11-32, 11-33
  - principles of, 11-31–32, 11-32n
- Institute of Taxation and Economic Policy (ITEP), 16-7
- Institutional shareholders, 15-18, 15-21, B-9
- Insurance; *see also* Health insurance; Life insurance
  - accident, 12-27, B-8
  - disability, 5-30, B-5
  - mortgage, 6-17n, 14-13
- Intangible assets; *see also* Amortization
  - accrual method for, 9-29
  - amortizable intangible asset summary, 10-36–37
  - capital expenditures and, 9-7, 9-7n
  - cash method for, 9-29
  - cost recovery and, 10-2
  - defined, B-9
  - immediate expensing and, 10-17n
- Intangible personal property, 1-15
- Integrated transfer taxes, common features of, 25-2–4
- Integrated wealth plans, 25-33–34
- Interest; *see also* Partnership interests; Terminable interest
  - capital, 20-3, 20-10
  - carried, 20-12
  - continuity of, 19-25, B-4
  - from corporate and U.S. Treasury bonds, 7-3–4, 7-3n
  - deductions for, 9-12–13
  - dividends vs., 7-2–3
  - future, 25-7, 25-8, B-8
  - as gross income, 4-6, 5-2
  - imputed, 5-20
  - for late payments, 2-3, 2-3n
  - multinational transactions and, 24-7
  - from municipal bonds, 4-6, 5-21–22
  - portfolio income and, 7-2–6
  - present, 25-7, 25-8, B-12

Interest—*Cont.*
profits, **20**-3, **20**-3n, **20**-11
from qualified education loans, **6**-10
qualified residence interest, **14**-13
timing of payments and taxes, **7**-6
uncertain tax positions and, **17**-28
on underpayments, **8**-39n
as unearned income, **5**-10, **5**-14, **9**-18, **9**-29
Interest expense disallowance, **9**-12n
Interest expenses
home-related debt, **14**-8–15
investment, **6**-17, **6**-17n, **7**-26–29, **8**-8, **B**-9
as itemized deductions, **4**-10, **6**-17, **6**-17n
mortgage, **8**-8, **14**-10, **14**-18–21, **14**-20n, **14**-29–30, **14**-30n
multinational transactions and, **24**-13
prepaid, **9**-29
Interest income, **7**-3n
Interim period effective tax rates, **17**-33
Internal rate of return (IRR), **3**-17n
Internal Revenue Code (IRC)
citations, **2**-10
interpretations of, **2**-14, **2**-15
organization of, **2**-13–14
persons as defined by, **19**-4
as source of tax law, **2**-11–12
Subchapter C, **15**-5, **18**-2n, **19**-4, **19**-4n
Subchapter J, **25**-30n
Subchapter K, **20**-2, **20**-3, **21**-9, **B**-15
Subchapter N, **24**-2, **24**-25
Subchapter S, **15**-5, **20**-2, **22**-2n, **B**-15
as ultimate tax authority, **3**-19
Internal Revenue Code of 1939, **2**-12
Internal Revenue Code of 1954, **2**-12
Internal Revenue Code of 1986, **2**-11–13, **B**-9
Internal Revenue Service (IRS)
allocation method, **14**-18–20, **B**-9
appeals/litigation process, **2**-6–9, **2**-7n
assessment of tax deficiencies, **2**-3–4
audit process, **2**-4–9, **2**-4n, **17**-3
Circular 230, **2**-23–26, **2**-25n, **B**-4
corporate audit rate, **16**-7–8
filing extensions granted by, **2**-3
funding for, **2**-5
income tax filings with, **1**-22
judicial doctrines, **3**-18–19
rental expenses, method of allocating, **14**-18–20
Statistics of Income Tax report, **15**-27–28
Tax Exempt Organization Search, **6**-18n, **16**-16n
tax form errors made by, **7**-17
website of, **2**-18n, **5**-14n, **5**-25n
International Business Machines Corp. v. Department of Treasury (2016), **23**-23n
International operations, planning for, **24**-22–24
International supply chains, **24**-28
Internet sales; *see* E-commerce
Interpretative regulations, **2**-16, **B**-9
Interstate commerce, **23**-4, **B**-9
Inter vivos transfers, **25**-2, **B**-9
Inventory
accounting methods for, **9**-19–22, **9**-19n
cost-flow methods for, **9**-21–22
defined, **21**-4, **21**-4n
FIFO method for, **3**-6
gain or loss from sale of, **24**-11
LIFO method for, **3**-6
substantially appreciated, **21**-24–25, **B**-16
uniform capitalization and, **9**-19
valuation allowances, **9**-19n
Inventory items, **21**-3, **21**-3n, **B**-9
Investment activities, **6**-2–3, **6**-2n, **B**-9
Investment expenses
investment interest expense, **6**-17, **6**-17n, **7**-26–29, **8**-8, **B**-9
ordinary and necessary, **9**-4n
portfolio, **7**-26–29
tax deductions for, **3**-16, **6**-3
Investment income, **5**-3, **7**-2, **22**-6, **22**-6n, **22**-26–27, **B**-9; *see also* Net investment income
Investment interest expense, **6**-17, **6**-17n, **7**-26–29, **8**-8, **B**-9
Investment planning, **1**-16–17, **3**-7
Investments; *see also* Capital gains and losses; Investment expenses; Portfolio income
after-tax rate of return, **7**-2
before-tax rate of return, **7**-2
corporate and Treasury bonds, **7**-3–4, **7**-3n
dividends and, **7**-2, **7**-6–7, **7**-6n
interest and, **7**-2–6
overview, **7**-2
passive, **7**-2, **B**-12
portfolio, **7**-2, **7**-26–29, **B**-12
qualified business asset, **24**-17
savings bonds, **5**-26–27, **7**-3, **7**-4, **7**-4n
Involuntary conversions, **5**-31, **11**-29–31, **B**-9
Involuntary termination of S corporations, **22**-6
IPOs; *see* Initial public offerings
IRAs; *see* Individual retirement accounts
IRC; *see* Internal Revenue Code
IRD (income in respect of a decedent), **25**-18
IRR (internal rate of return), **3**-17n
IRS; *see* Internal Revenue Service
IRS Form 10-K, **17**-3, **17**-22, **17**-33, **24**-29
IRS Form 10-Q, **17**-33
IRS Form 656, **2**-6n
IRS Form 706, **25**-28–29
IRS Form 709, **25**-4, **25**-15–16
IRS Form 870, **2**-6
IRS Form 966, **19**-33
IRS Form 990, **15**-21
IRS Form 990-T, **15**-21
IRS Form 1040; see also Schedule C, Profit or Loss from Business
for AGI deductions on, **4**-9, **6**-2n, **6**-12
defined, **4**-2
examples of, **4**-3–5, **4**-26–28, **8**-40
Schedule A, Itemized Deductions, **4**-10, **6**-13, **6**-25, **14**-18
Schedule B, **7**-3n, **7**-6n, **20**-19n, **22**-12n
Schedule D, **7**-8, **7**-16–17, **7**-16n, **7**-20, **11**-23, **20**-19n
Schedule E, Rental or Royalty Income, **6**-5, **8**-16n, **14**-22–24, **20**-19n, **22**-12n
Schedule SE, Self-Employment Tax, **8**-16
Social Security Worksheet, **5**-33
IRS Form 1040NR, **24**-3
IRS Form 1065, **9**-2, **15**-5, **20**-24–27, **22**-30, **B**-7
IRS Form 1098, **14**-11, **14**-12
IRS Form 1099-B, **7**-9n, **7**-16–17, **7**-16n
IRS Form 1099-DIV, **2**-5, **7**-6
IRS Form 1099-INT, **2**-5
IRS Form 1099-NEC, **8**-21n, **12**-2
IRS Form 1099-OID, **7**-3
IRS Form 1099-R, **13**-5n
IRS Form 1116, **24**-13
IRS Form 1118, **24**-13–16
IRS Form 1120
balance sheets and, **17**-12n
for calendar-year corporations, **17**-3
complexity of, **17**-10–11
compliance with, **16**-23–26, **16**-23n
liquidation and, **19**-37
net operating losses and, **16**-16
taxable income on, **9**-2, **15**-5
IRS Form 1120-F, **24**-3
IRS Form 1120-S, **9**-2, **15**-5, **22**-10–11, **22**-10n, **22**-28–30, **B**-7
IRS Form 1120-X, **17**-11n
IRS Form 1139, **17**-11n
IRS Form 2120, **4**-16
IRS Form 2210, **8**-38, **8**-38n
IRS Form 2220, **16**-30
IRS Form 2553, **22**-4, **22**-4n, **B**-7
IRS Form 2555, **5**-28
IRS Form 3115, **9**-32, **10**-3n, **10**-16n, **20**-14, **22**-8
IRS Form 4562, **10**-29–30, **10**-36–37
IRS Form 4797, **11**-21–22
IRS Form 4952, **7**-26n
IRS Form 5471, **24**-27
IRS Form 5701, **17**-11n
IRS Form 6251, **8**-8, **8**-10
IRS Form 7004, **17**-3n, **20**-24, **22**-28, **B**-7
IRS Form 8283, **6**-23
IRS Form 8308, **21**-3n
IRS Form 8332, **4**-15n
IRS Form 8824, **11**-29
IRS Form 8829, **14**-32, **14**-33
IRS Form 8832, **15**-5, **24**-22
IRS Form 8867, **8**-32
IRS Form 8949, **7**-8, **7**-16, **7**-18–19
IRS Form 8959, **8**-16
IRS Form 8960, **7**-29, **8**-13n
IRS Form 8992, **24**-30
IRS Form 8993, **24**-30
IRS Form W-2
bonuses and, **5**-7n
defined, **B**-7
employee considerations and, **8**-21n, **12**-2, **12**-11n
example of, **12**-3
information matching program and, **2**-5
responsibilities for issuing, **5**-8n
withholdings and, **8**-36
IRS Form W-2G, **5**-17n
IRS Form W-4, **12**-2, **B**-7
IRS Publication 15-B, **12**-31
IRS Publication 17, **8**-38n
IRS Publication 514, **8**-34n
IRS Publication 526, **6**-18n
IRS Publication 527, **14**-20n
IRS Publication 946, **10**-7n
IRS Publication 970, **5**-25n, **12**-28
IRS Publication 972, **8**-25n
IRS Publication 1779, **8**-21n
IRS Uniform Lifetime Table, **13**-11
ISOs; *see* Incentive stock options
Itemized deductions, **6**-13–25; *see also* Business deductions
alternative minimum tax and, **8**-8
bunching, **6**-1, **6**-28
casualty and theft losses, **6**-24, **6**-24n
categories of, **4**-9–10
charitable contributions, **4**-10, **6**-16–23, **6**-18–21n
defined, **B**-9
gambling winnings/losses, **4**-10, **6**-24, **6**-24n
interest expenses, **4**-10, **6**-17, **6**-17n
medical and dental expenses, **4**-10, **6**-13–15
miscellaneous, **4**-10, **5**-17, **6**-24
not subject to AGI floor, **6**-24
summary of, **6**-24–25
taxes, **4**-10, **6**-15–17, **6**-16n
ITEP (Institute of Taxation and Economic Policy), **16**-7

Jakab, Spencer, **11**-7
James, LeBron, **10**-32
J.D. & Associates v. United States (2006), **15**-25
Joint Committee on Taxation, **1**-18n, **16**-8
Joint Conference Committee, **2**-13
Joint-life annuities, **5**-12
Jointly owned property, **25**-20–21
Joint tenancy, defined, **25**-6, **B**-9
Joint tenancy with right of survivorship, **25**-6, **25**-19, **25**-20, **25**-20n, **25**-22, **B**-9
Joint ventures, **21**-9
Jon Dickinson, et ux. vs. Commissioner (2020), **18**-24
Journal entries
for current and deferred income tax expense, **17**-19
for uncertain tax benefit reserve, **17**-26
for valuation allowance, **17**-21–22
Journal of Accountancy, **2**-11
Journal of Taxation, **2**-11
J.R. Cohen v. United States (1993), **2**-10
J.R. Huntsman v. Commissioner (1988 & 1990), **2**-20, **2**-23, **2**-28, **14**-13n
Judicial sources of tax law, **2**-10, **2**-14–15, **2**-15n
Judicial system, **2**-6–9
Jurisdictions
income shifting across, **3**-15
low-tax, **24**-22, **24**-28n
residence-based, **24**-2–3, **B**-14
source-based, **24**-2–3, **B**-15
variation of tax rates among, **3**-11

Keogh plans, **13**-29n
Keyword searches, **2**-19
Kickbacks, **9**-6
Kiddie tax, **3**-12n, **5**-8n, **8**-3n, **8**-5–6, **8**-11n, **8**-29n, **B**-9
Kroner, Burt, **25**-5

Lance, R. M., **12**-23–24
Lanco, Inc. v. Director, Division of Taxation (2006), **23**-11n
Last-in, first-out (LIFO) method, **3**-6, **9**-19n, **9**-21–22, **B**-9
Last-in, first-out (LIFO) recapture amount, **22**-28, **B**-9
Last-in, first-out (LIFO) recapture tax, **22**-24, **22**-27–28, **B**-9
Last will and testament, **25**-2, **B**-9
Late filing penalties, **2**-3, **8**-39, **20**-24n, **22**-28n, **B**-9
Late payment penalties, **2**-3, **2**-3n, **8**-39, **B**-9
Law reviews, **2**-11
Leasing property from another party, **9**-24–25

Least aggregate deferral, **20**-15, **B**-9
Legal classification of business entities, **15**-2
Legislative grace, **4**-8, **B**-9
Legislative regulations, **2**-16, **B**-9
Legislative sources of tax law
  citations, **2**-10
  Congress, **2**-12–13
  Internal Revenue Code, **2**-11–14
  process for, **2**-12–13, **3**-8
  tax treaties, **2**-14
  U.S. Constitution, **2**-11, **2**-12
Letter rulings, **2**-10, **2**-16–17
Levin, Carl, **24**-28n
Liabilities; *see also* Debt
  deferred tax, **17**-2, **17**-20–23, **17**-29
  noncash property distributions and, **18**-13
  payment, **9**-24–26, **19**-13, **B**-12
  payroll tax, **15**-3n
  responsibility for, **15**-3
  sales and use tax, **23**-3–4, **23**-3–4n, **23**-7–8
  shareholder, **19**-11–13
  state income taxes, **23**-24
Life estates, **25**-7, **25**-8, **B**-9
Life insurance
  coverage, **5**-24
  as gift, **25**-6
  in gross estate, **25**-19
  group-term, **12**-22–23, **12**-26–27, **B**-8
  premiums, **9**-7
  proceeds, **4**-6, **5**-27–28, **5**-27n
Life insurance trusts, **25**-33, **B**-9
Life tenants, **25**-7, **25**-8
Lifetime learning credits, **4**-12, **8**-28–30, **8**-29n, **8**-34
LIFO method; *see* Last-in, first-out method
LIFO (last-in, first-out) recapture amount, **22**-28, **B**-9
LIFO recapture tax; *see* Last-in, first-out recapture tax
Like-kind exchanges
  cost recovery basis for, **10**-6
  criteria for, **11**-24
  deferral provisions for, **5**-31, **18**-5
  deferred (Starker), **11**-25–26, **11**-25n
  defined, **B**-10
  exchanged basis, **11**-30
  exclusion from gross income, **4**-6
  non-like-kind property (boot), **11**-27–29
  overview, **11**-24
  personal property and, **11**-24
  property use and, **11**-25
  real property and, **11**-24–25
  reporting, **11**-29
  substituted basis, **11**-26
  tax consequences of, **11**-26–29
  timing requirements for, **11**-25–26
Like-kind property, **11**-24–25
Limited liability companies (LLCs)
  defined, **B**-10
  legal classification of, **15**-2, **20**-2
  loans made to, **20**-5n
  rights, responsibilities, and legal arrangement of owners, **15**-3–4, **15**-3n
  self-employment tax and, **20**-21, **20**-21n
  single-member, **15**-5
  venture capital firms and, **22**-3
Limited liability limited partnerships (LLLPs), **15**-2–3n
Limited liability partnerships (LLPs), **15**-2–3n
Limited partnerships (LPs), **15**-2, **15**-2–4n, **20**-2, **22**-3, **B**-10
Liquidating corporations, **19**-34–37
Liquidating distributions, **21**-12–24
  character and holding period of assets, **21**-21–24
  defined, **B**-10
  determining basis in distributed property, **21**-13–14
  gain or loss recognition in, **21**-13
  outside basis greater than inside basis, **21**-14–17
  outside basis less than inside basis, **21**-17–21
  overview, **21**-12–13
  in partnerships, **21**-9
  S corporations and, **22**-23
Liquidations
  corporate, **19**-32–37
  partial, **18**-2, **18**-25–26, **B**-12
Liquidation value, **20**-10, **B**-10
Listed property, **9**-11n, **10**-22–24, **B**-10
Litigation, hazards of, **2**-6
LLCs; *see* Limited liability companies
LLLPs (limited liability limited partnerships), **15**-2–3n
LLPs (limited liability partnerships), **15**-2–3n
Loans; *see also* Debt
  discount, **14**-13
  home equity, **6**-17, **14**-9
  origination charge, **14**-13
  secured by residence, **14**-9
Lobbying costs, **9**-6
Local taxes; *see* State and local taxes
Lodging
  deductions for, **6**-14, **6**-14n
  as nontaxable fringe benefit, **12**-27–28
  as qualifying fringe benefit, **5**-24
Long-term capital gains and losses, **3**-15–16, **4**-7, **4**-7n, **6**-19, **7**-10–11, **7**-13–15, **7**-34–36, **B**-10
Long-term care facilities, **6**-14, **6**-14n
Look-back rule, **11**-17–19, **B**-1
Look-through rules, **21**-5n
Losses; *see also* Capital gains and losses; Casualty and theft losses
  assets sold at, **11**-12–13
  deductibility for business entities, **15**-26–29
  on disposition of business assets, **4**-9, **6**-6, **9**-13
  excess business loss limitation, **6**-6, **6**-6n, **15**-27, **20**-35, **22**-17, **22**-17n
  net operating, **15**-26, **16**-13n, **16**-14–16, **17**-20, **22**-5, **B**-11
  operating, **7**-2, **B**-12
  on rental property, **14**-24–26
  on sale of capital assets, **4**-7
  substantial built-in, **21**-27, **B**-15–16
  taxable estate, **25**-23–24
Loss harvesting, **7**-26
Loss limitations, **20**-30–35
  at-risk, **20**-31
  income and loss baskets, **20**-33–34
  passive activity, **20**-32–34
  S corporations and, **22**-14–17
  tax-basis, **20**-30–31
Lower of cost or market method, **9**-19n
LPs; *see* Limited partnerships
Lucas v. Earl (1930), **3**-12, **5**-8n
Lump-sum distributions, **13**-20n
Luxury automobiles, **10**-25–27n, **10**-25–29, **B**-10

MACRS; *see* Modified Accelerated Cost Recovery System
M adjustments, **16**-23, **16**-23n, **16**-25–26, **B**-10
Magdalin, William, **6**-14
Majority interest taxable year, **20**-15, **B**-10
Manufactured inventory, gain or loss from sale of, **24**-11
Marginal tax rates, **1**-5–7, **1**-9–11, **3**-8, **3**-10, **8**-6, **8**-23, **B**-10
Margin tax, **23**-25
Marijuana producers, **9**-6n
Marital deductions, **25**-4, **25**-10–11, **25**-11n, **25**-24, **B**-10
Marketable securities, **21**-11n
Market discounts/premiums, **7**-4, **B**-10
Marriage benefit/penalty, **8**-3, **8**-4, **B**-10
Married filing jointly (MFJ)
  defined, **B**-10
  gross income thresholds (2022), **2**-2
  individual income tax formula and, **4**-19–20
  sale of personal residence and, **14**-5
  Social Security benefit taxability and, **5**-18
  standard deduction for, **2**-2, **4**-10, **6**-26, **C**-2
  tax rate schedule for, **C**-1
Married filing separately (MFS)
  defined, **B**-10
  gross income thresholds (2022), **2**-2
  individual income tax formula and, **4**-19–20
  Social Security benefit taxability and, **5**-18
  standard deduction for, **2**-2, **4**-10, **6**-26, **C**-2
  tax rate schedule for, **C**-1
Material participation, **7**-30, **7**-31, **20**-33, **20**-34
Mattel Inc., **17**-3
Maturity, defined, **B**-10
Maturity of bonds, **7**-3n, **7**-4
Maturity value, **7**-2, **B**-10
Maximum 15 percent rate amount, **7**-11, **7**-15n, **B**-10
Maximum zero percent rate amount, **7**-10–11, **7**-14–15, **7**-15n, **B**-10
Mayo Foundation for Medical Education & Research v. United States (2011), **2**-16
Mazur, Mark, **2**-5
Meals
  deductions for, **9**-8–9, **9**-9n
  as nontaxable fringe benefit, **12**-26–28
  as qualifying fringe benefit, **5**-24
Measurement, in uncertain tax positions, **17**-25
Medical and dental expenses
  common medical expenses, **6**-13
  deduction limitations, **6**-15
  discretionary, **6**-14
  health insurance coverage for, **5**-24, **5**-24n
  hospitals and long-term care facilities, **6**-14, **6**-14n
  as itemized deductions, **4**-10, **6**-13–15
  transportation and travel, **6**-14, **6**-14n
Medicare tax
  additional, **8**-14, **B**-2
  AGI and, **4**-12
  defined, **B**-10
  for employees, **6**-8, **8**-14–16
  for flow-through entities, **15**-14n, **15**-15–16
  objectives of, **1**-13, **8**-14
  proportional structure of, **1**-10n
  S corporations and, **22**-17, **22**-17n
  for self-employed individuals, **1**-13, **6**-8, **8**-16–20
  tax base for, **1**-13
Memorandum decisions (U.S. Tax Court), **2**-10, **2**-15n
Mergers, **19**-26–29, **19**-31, **B**-10
MFJ; *see* Married filing jointly
MFS; *see* Married filing separately
Microsoft Corporation, **17**-3, **17**-27, **17**-28
Mid-month convention, **10**-15, **10**-16, **10**-42–43, **B**-10
Mid-quarter convention, **10**-9, **10**-10, **10**-13, **10**-40–41, **B**-10
Mileage rate, **9**-9, **9**-9n, **10**-26n
Minimum distributions, **13**-5, **13**-10n, **13**-15
Minimum tax credit, **8**-12, **B**-10
Miscellaneous itemized deductions
  gambling losses, **5**-17
  gambling winnings/losses, **4**-10, **6**-24, **6**-24n
  not subject to AGI floor, **6**-24
  types of, **4**-10
  unrecovered costs of annuities, **5**-12n
Mixed-motive expenditures, **9**-8–12, **B**-10
Mobile phones; *see* Cell phones
Mobil Oil Corp. v. Vermont Tax Commissioner (1980), **23**-16, **23**-16n
Modified Accelerated Cost Recovery System (MACRS)
  defined, **B**-10
  depreciation and, **10**-7, **10**-7n
  half-year convention, **10**-9–12, **10**-40
  mid-quarter convention, **10**-9, **10**-10, **10**-13, **10**-40–41
  nonresidential real property mid-month convention, **10**-43
  recovery periods, **10**-7–9, **10**-23, **10**-26
  residential rental property mid-month convention, **10**-42
  tables, **10**-40–43
Modified AGI, **5**-17–18, **5**-27n, **6**-10, **20**-23n
Money donations, **6**-18–19, **6**-18n
Money market accounts, **7**-3, **7**-6
"More likely than not" standard, **2**-24n
Mortgage insurance, **6**-17n, **14**-13
Mortgage interest deductions, **6**-17, **6**-17n, **14**-8–15
Mortgage interest expenses, **8**-8, **14**-10, **14**-18–21, **14**-20n, **14**-29–30, **14**-30n
Mortgage payments, **5**-15n
Motor vehicles; *see* Automobiles
Moving expenses, **5**-23n, **6**-7
Ms, **16**-23, **16**-23n, **16**-25–26
MTC; *see* Multistate Tax Commission
Multinational transactions
  compensation and, **24**-8–9
  dividends and, **24**-8
  ethical considerations in, **24**-11
  interest and, **24**-7
  manufactured inventory sales, **24**-11
  nexus, **24**-2–3
  nonresident taxation, **24**-3
  real or purchased property sales, **24**-10
  rents and royalties, **24**-9
  resident as defined for tax purposes, **24**-4–5
  U.S. framework for taxing, **24**-2–5
  U.S. source rules for gross income and deductions, **24**-6–13
Multiple support declarations, **4**-16
Multistate Tax Commission (MTC), **23**-11, **23**-13, **23**-18n
Multistate Tax Compact, Article IV, Division of Income, **23**-24n
Municipal bonds, **1**-17, **3**-16, **3**-18, **3**-19, **4**-6, **5**-21–22, **B**-10
Music catalog sales, **7**-9

Musk, Elon, **11**-7, **12**-13–14
Mutual funds, **7**-2, **7**-2n, **7**-8n, **B**-11
Myers, Linda M., **6**-24n

National Bellas Hess, Inc. v. Department of Revenue of the State of Illinois (1967), **23**-6, **23**-6n
National debt, **1**-3, **1**-20
National Research Program (NRP), **2**-4, **2**-4n
Natural resources, **10**-2, **10**-37–39
Necessary expenses; *see* Ordinary and necessary expenses
Negative basis adjustment, **21**-29, **B**-11
Negative evidence, that valuation allowance is needed, **17**-21
Negative income tax, **8**-30
Net capital gains and losses
  book–tax differences and, **16**-13, **16**-13n
  calculating tax liability on, **7**-21–23
  long-term, **4**-7, **4**-7n, **7**-14–15, **7**-34–36, **B**-11
  short-term, **4**-7, **4**-7n, **7**-14–15, **7**-34–36, **B**-11
  tax rates by filing status, **C**-2
Net capital loss carryback/carryover, **16**-13, **16**-14, **16**-17, **16**-20, **B**-11
Net earnings from self-employment, **8**-16–18, **8**-18n, **15**-14, **B**-11
Net investment income, **6**-17, **6**-17n, **7**-26–28, **7**-28n, **B**-11
Net investment income tax
  AGI and, **4**-11–12
  alternative minimum tax and, **8**-12n
  calculation of, **7**-28–29
  computation of, **8**-13, **8**-13n
  defined, **B**-11
  on dividends, **4**-7n
  for flow-through entities, **15**-13
  partnerships and, **20**-23
  on passive income, **7**-33, **15**-13
  on S corporations, **22**-18, **22**-18n
  tax rate for, **1**-12
Net long-term capital gains and losses, **4**-7, **4**-7n, **7**-14–15, **7**-34–36, **B**-11
Net operating loss carryback/carryover, **16**-14–17, **17**-20, **B**-11
Net operating losses (NOLs), **15**-26, **16**-13n, **16**-14–16, **17**-20, **22**-5, **B**-11
Net passive income, **7**-33, **22**-26–27, **B**-6
Net passive investment income, **22**-26–27, **B**-11
Net short-term capital gains and losses, **4**-7, **4**-7n, **7**-14–15, **7**-34–36, **B**-11
Net taxation, **24**-3
Net unearned income, **8**-6, **B**-11
Net unrealized built-in gain, **22**-24, **B**-11
Newsletters, **2**-11
Nexus
  defined, **23**-2, **24**-2, **B**-11
  economic income tax, **23**-6–8, **23**-11, **B**-6
  income tax, **23**-2, **23**-4, **23**-10–14, **23**-19, **B**-8
  multinational transactions, **24**-2–3
  sales tax, **23**-2–4, **23**-5–7, **B**-14
NFTs (non-fungible tokens), **7**-13
90-day letters, **2**-6, **B**-1
No-additional-cost services, **5**-24, **12**-26, **12**-28, **B**-11
Noble Energy, **19**-32
"No business purpose" motives, **19**-11
NOLs; *see* Net operating losses
Nonacquiescence, **2**-17, **B**-11
Nonbusiness bad debt, **7**-10n
Nonbusiness income, **23**-4, **23**-24, **B**-11
Noncash payments, **9**-16
Noncash property distributions
  corporate tax consequences of, **18**-13
  effect on E&P, **18**-14
  fair market value of, **18**-12–14
  formula for, **18**-12
  liabilities, **18**-13
Noncorporate shareholders, **19**-33
Nondeductible personal expenses, **14**-30n
Nondeductible terminable interests, **25**-11, **B**-11
Nondomiciliary businesses, **23**-2, **23**-6, **23**-8, **23**-11, **B**-11
Non-fungible tokens (NFTs), **7**-13
Nonincome-based taxes, **23**-25
Non-like-kind property (boot), **11**-27–29
Nonmanaging LLC members, **20**-21n
Nonqualified deferred compensation (NQDC), **13**-16–19
  defined, **B**-11
  employee considerations, **13**-16–19
  employer considerations, **13**-17, **13**-19
  overview, **13**-2
  qualified defined contribution plans vs., **13**-16–17, **13**-19
Nonqualified preferred stock, **19**-5n
Nonqualified stock options (NQOs), **12**-10–15, **12**-17, **12**-20, **16**-10–13, **16**-10n, **17**-8, **B**-11
Nonqualified use provision, **14**-6
Nonrecaptured net Section 1231 losses, **11**-18–19, **B**-11
Nonrecognition provisions, **5**-21, **B**-11
Nonrecourse debt, **20**-4–6, **20**-5n, **B**-11
Nonrefundable credits, **8**-23–30, **8**-33–34, **8**-35n, **B**-11
Nonresidence (rental property), **14**-24–26
Nonresident aliens, **24**-4, **B**-11
Nonresidential property, **10**-14, **10**-14n, **10**-43, **11**-10n
Nonresidents, U.S. taxation of, **24**-3
Nonservice partners, **20**-10, **B**-11
Nontaxable compensation benefits, **3**-16
Nontaxable fringe benefits, **12**-25–31
  cafeteria plans and FSAs, **5**-24, **12**-26, **12**-31, **B**-3, **B**-7
  common forms of, **12**-26
  defined, **12**-25, **B**-11
  de minimis, **5**-24, **12**-25, **12**-26, **12**-30, **B**-5
  dependent care benefits, **5**-24, **12**-26, **12**-28
  discrimination among employees regarding, **5**-23n
  educational assistance, **5**-24, **12**-26, **12**-28, **B**-6
  employee/employer considerations for, **12**-31
  group-term life insurance, **12**-26–27
  health and accident insurance, **3**-2, **12**-26, **12**-27
  meals/lodging for convenience of employer, **12**-27–28
  no-additional-cost services, **5**-24, **12**-26, **12**-28
  qualified employee discounts, **5**-24, **12**-26, **12**-29, **B**-13
  qualified moving expense reimbursements, **5**-23n
  qualified transportation, **5**-24, **12**-26, **12**-30, **B**-13
  to S corporations, **22**-18
  summary of, **12**-33–34
  tax planning with, **12**-31–33
  working condition fringe benefits, **5**-24, **12**-26, **12**-30, **B**-18
Nontaxable liquidating distributions, **19**-37
Nontaxable stock distributions, **18**-16, **18**-16n
Nontax characteristics of business entities, **15**-2–4
Northwestern States Portland Cement Co. v. Minnesota (1959), **23**-10n
Not definitely related deductions, **24**-11, **B**-11
Not-for-profit activity, home rental as, **14**-24n
"Nowhere" income, **23**-19n
NQDC; *see* Nonqualified deferred compensation
NQOs; *see* Nonqualified stock options
NRP (National Research Program), **2**-4, **2**-4n

OAA (Other Adjustments Account), **22**-21n
OASDI (Old Age, Survivors, and Disability Insurance) tax; *see* Social Security tax
Obergefell v. Hodges (2015), **4**-20
OECD (Organization for Economic Cooperation and Development), **24**-30–31
Office examinations, **2**-6, **B**-11
OID; *see* Original issue discount
Oil industry, **19**-32
Old Age, Survivors, and Disability Insurance (OASDI) tax; *see* Social Security tax
150 percent declining balance, **10**-7, **10**-7n, **10**-10, **10**-29n
Online home rentals, **14**-22
Online sales; *see* E-commerce
Open facts, **2**-17
Operating distributions, **21**-9–12, **22**-19–23, **B**-11
Operating income, **7**-2, **B**-11
Operating losses, **7**-2, **B**-12; *see also* Net operating losses (NOLs)
Operating partnerships, cash distributions in, **20**-30
Option attribution, **18**-22
Option exercise, **12**-8, **12**-9, **12**-15, **B**-12
Ordinary and necessary expenses, **6**-3–4, **9**-4–5, **9**-4n, **B**-12
Ordinary assets, **11**-7–8, **B**-12
Ordinary business income (loss), **20**-17–23, **22**-10, **B**-12
Ordinary income, **3**-15, **4**-6, **4**-7, **20**-17–23
Ordinary income property, **6**-19, **6**-20, **11**-8n, **16**-16, **B**-12
Ordinary tax rates, **3**-8
Organizational expenditures, **9**-7, **10**-32–35, **10**-35n, **20**-12–13, **B**-12
Organizational form of businesses, **19**-2, **24**-24
Organization for Economic Cooperation and Development (OECD), **24**-30–31
Original basis, **10**-13
Original issue discount (OID), **7**-3, **7**-3n, **B**-12
Other Adjustments Account (OAA), **22**-21n
Outbound transactions, **24**-2, **B**-12
Outside basis
  allocation of, **21**-11, **21**-11n
  defined, **B**-12
  as greater than inside basis of distributed assets, **21**-14–17
  as less than inside basis of distributed assets, **21**-17–21
  partnerships and, **20**-4, **20**-6–8, **20**-13, **20**-30, **21**-7, **21**-7n, **21**-11–12
  for sellers, **21**-2, **21**-2n
Overpayments, **2**-3n, **2**-5, **4**-12
Ownership test, **14**-5

PAL (passive activity loss) limitation, **20**-32–34, **22**-16
PAL rules; *see* Passive activity loss rules
Pandemic; *see* COVID-19 pandemic
Partial depreciation recapture, **11**-14n
Partial liquidations, **18**-2, **18**-25–26, **B**-12
Participation exemption, **24**-16
Parties to the reorganization, **19**-25, **19**-30–31
Partnership accounting
  accounting methods for, **20**-16
  accounting periods in, **9**-15, **9**-15n, **20**-14–15
  allocating partners' shares of income and loss, **20**-23, **20**-23n
  business interest limitation, **20**-22
  compliance issues, **20**-24–28
  guaranteed payments and, **20**-19, **20**-19n
  net investment income tax and, **20**-23
  ordinary business income (loss) and, **20**-17–23
  overview, **20**-13–14
  qualified business income deduction, **20**-22–23
  reporting results of partnership operations, **20**-17–28
  required year-ends in, **20**-14–15
  self-employment taxes and, **20**-20–21, **20**-21n
  separately stated items and, **20**-17–23
  tax elections and, **20**-14
Partnership agreements, **15**-2, **B**-12
Partnership books, **20**-3n
Partnership compliance issues, **20**-24–28
Partnership distributions
  liquidating, **21**-12–24
  operating, **21**-9–12
Partnership formations, **20**-3–13
  capital interests and, **20**-3, **20**-10
  holding period in partnership interest, **20**-7
  initial tax basis and, **20**-4–7
  organization, start-up, and syndication costs, **20**-12–13, **20**-12n
  profits interests and, **20**-3, **20**-3n, **20**-11
  property contributions, **20**-3–9
  rules for allocating partnership debt to partners, **20**-5
  service contributions, **20**-3, **20**-9–11
  summary of outside basis and holding period, **20**-13
  tax basis and holding period in contributed property, **20**-7–9
Partnership interests
  acquisitions of, **20**-13
  allocating partners' shares of income and loss, **20**-23, **20**-23n
  basics of sales of, **21**-2–9
  business interest limitation, **20**-22
  buyer and partnership issues, **21**-7–8
  cash distributions in operating partnerships, **20**-30
  defined, **20**-3, **B**-12
  ethical considerations and, **21**-7
  holding period in, **20**-7
  partner's adjusted tax basis in, **20**-28–30
  seller issues, **21**-2–7
  varying interest rule, **21**-8
Partnerships
  accounting methods for, **20**-16
  accounting period for, **9**-15, **9**-15n, **20**-14–15
  business income reporting for, **9**-2

C and S corporations compared to, **22**-30–32
deduction of losses from, **5**-14n
due dates and extensions for, **2**-3
family limited, **25**-34, **B**-7
as flow-through entities, **5**-14
general, **15**-2, **20**-2, **B**-8
limitations on accruals to related parties in, **9**-27
limited, **15**-2, **15**-2–4n, **20**-2, **22**-3, **B**-10
limited liability, **15**-2–3n
limited liability limited, **15**-2–3n
owner compensation in, **15**-22, **15**-23
publicly traded, **20**-2n, **20**-17, **20**-34n
state income taxes and, **23**-9–10
tax classification and characteristics, **15**-5, **15**-6, **15**-29–30, **15**-32–33
Passive activity, defined, **7**-30, **20**-32–33
Passive activity income and losses, **7**-29–34
defined, **7**-31
income and loss baskets and, **20**-33
income and loss categories, **7**-31–32
loss limitations, **15**-27
net investment income tax on, **7**-33
overview, **7**-29–30
from publicly traded partnerships, **20**-34n
rental real estate rules, **7**-33, **7**-33n, **14**-20n, **14**-24–26
Passive activity loss (PAL) limitation, **20**-32–34, **22**-16
Passive activity loss (PAL) rules, **7**-30–31, **7**-30n, **7**-33, **20**-32, **20**-32n, **22**-16, **B**-12
Passive category income, **24**-20, **B**-12
Passive income, net investment income tax on, **7**-33, **15**-13
Passive investment companies (PICs), **23**-15
Passive investment income (PII), **22**-6, **22**-6n, **B**-12
Passive investments, **7**-2, **B**-12
Patents, **9**-7, **10**-31, **10**-36, **10**-37n
PATH (Protecting Americans from Tax Hikes) Act of 2015, **7**-12n
Pay-as-you-go basis, **8**-36
Payment liabilities, **9**-24–26, **19**-13, **B**-12
Payroll, **23**-21–23
Payroll tax liabilities, **15**-3n
PCAOB (Public Company Accounting Oversight Board), **17**-33
PCs (professional corporations), **15**-2–3n
Penalties
for accountants, **2**-24, **2**-26–28, **4**-23n
civil, **2**-26, **2**-27, **B**-4
criminal, **2**-26, **2**-28, **B**-5
for early withdrawal of savings, **6**-9
estimated tax payment, **3**-7n
failure-to-file, **2**-3
late filing, **2**-3, **8**-39, **20**-24n, **22**-28n, **B**-9
late payment, **2**-3, **2**-3n, **8**-39
marriage penalty, **8**-3, **8**-4
nondeductibility of, **9**-6, **9**-6n
taxes vs., **1**-4
uncertain tax positions and, **17**-28
underpayment, **2**-3, **2**-3n, **4**-12, **8**-14n, **8**-36–38, **8**-39n, **B**-17
Percentage depletion, **10**-38–39, **10**-39n, **B**-12
Permanent book–tax differences, **16**-3–5, **16**-21, **17**-7–8, **17**-18, **B**-12
Permanent establishments, **24**-18, **B**-12
Permissible accounting method, **9**-29, **9**-30, **9**-32, **B**-12
Personal credits, **8**-35n
Personal expenses, **3**-16, **9**-7–8, **14**-30n, **B**-12
Personal holding companies, **15**-22, **B**-12
Personal holding company tax, **15**-22, **B**-12
Personal injury payments, **5**-29–30
Personal property; *see also* Tangible personal property
calculating depreciation for, **10**-10–11
defined, **1**-15, **B**-12
depreciation conventions, **10**-7, **10**-9–13
depreciation method, **10**-7–8
depreciation recovery period, **10**-7–9, **10**-8n
half-year convention for, **10**-9–12, **10**-40
intangible, **1**-15
like-kind exchanges and, **11**-24
mid-quarter depreciation, **10**-9, **10**-10, **10**-13, **10**-40–41
purchased, gain or loss from, **24**-10
taxes on, **1**-5, **1**-15, **4**-10, **6**-15, **B**-12
Personal residence, **14**-4–16
basis rules for, **14**-4
business use of home, **14**-26–32
debt forgiveness on foreclosure, **14**-8, **14**-8n
depreciation of, **14**-6, **14**-8
exclusion of gain on sale of, **4**-6, **5**-22, **5**-22n, **14**-4–8
home sale exclusion in unforeseen circumstances, **14**-6–7, **14**-7n
interest expense on home-related debt, **14**-8–15
limitations on home-related debt, **14**-10–12
nonqualified use, **14**-6
ownership test, **14**-5
real property taxes on, **14**-15–16, **14**-15–16n
use test, **5**-22, **14**-2–3, **14**-5
Personal service corporations (PSCs), **15**-33n, **16**-3n
Personal tax credits, **8**-24–33
Personal-use assets
casualty and theft losses on, **6**-24
as charitable contributions, **6**-19
losses on sale of, **4**-7n, **7**-23
Personal-use property, **10**-7, **11**-3–5
Persons, defined, **19**-4, **24**-2n, **B**-12
Pet-related tax benefits, **4**-15
P.G. Cao v. Commissioner (1994 & 1996), **2**-20
Phones; *see* Cell phones
Physical presence, **23**-6–7, **24**-4
PICs (passive investment companies), **23**-15
PII; *see* Passive investment income
Placed in service assets, **10**-7–10, **10**-14–21, **10**-25–26
PLLCs (professional limited liability companies), **15**-2–3n
Points, **14**-13–15, **B**-12
Political contributions, **9**-6, **25**-6
Pollock v. Farmers' Loan and Trust Company (1895), **1**-12
Portfolio income, **7**-2–26
capital gains and losses, **7**-2, **7**-7–26
corporate and U.S. Treasury bonds, **7**-3–4, **7**-3n
defined, **7**-31, **20**-34
dividends, **7**-2, **7**-3, **7**-6–7, **7**-6n
interest, **7**-2–6
overview, **7**-2–3
savings bonds, **7**-3, **7**-4, **7**-4n
summary of, **7**-26
Portfolio investments, **7**-2, **7**-26–29, **B**-12
Positive basis adjustment, **21**-29, **B**-12
Postsecondary education, **6**-10n
Post-termination transition period (PTTP), **22**-15–16, **22**-16n, **22**-22–23, **22**-23n, **B**-12
Practical Tax Strategies (journal), **2**-11
Preferentially taxed income, **4**-7, **8**-4, **8**-4n, **B**-12
Preferential tax rate, **4**-7, **8**-4, **8**-4n, **B**-12
Premiums
bond, **7**-3–4, **7**-3–4n, **B**-3
health insurance, **6**-7, **6**-7n, **6**-13, **6**-13n
life insurance, **9**-7
mortgage insurance, **6**-17n
Premium tax credits, **6**-7n, **8**-34
Prepaid expenses, **3**-6, **9**-7, **9**-16, **9**-16n, **9**-29
Prepaid interest income, **9**-29
Preparer tax identification number (PTIN), **2**-26
Prepayments, **4**-12, **8**-36–38
Present interest, **25**-7, **25**-8, **B**-12
Present value of money, **3**-3–4, **B**-12
Previously taxable income (PTI), **22**-21n
Previously taxed capital, **21**-27n
Primary tax authorities, **2**-9, **2**-10, **B**-12
Principal partners, defined, **B**-12
Principal partners test, **20**-15
Principal residence, **14**-2–3, **B**-12
Private letter rulings, **2**-10, **2**-16, **B**-12
Private nonoperating foundations, **6**-21, **B**-12
Private operating foundations, **6**-21, **B**-12
Prizes, income from, **5**-16–17, **5**-16n, **5**-17n
Probate/probate estate, **25**-17, **B**-13
Procedural regulations, **2**-16, **B**-13
Production of income, **11**-8, **B**-13
Professional corporations (PCs), **15**-2–3n
Professional journals, **2**-11
Professional limited liability companies (PLLCs), **15**-2–3n
Professional sports team franchises, **10**-32, **21**-28–29
Profit-motivated activities, **6**-2
Profits interests, **20**-3, **20**-3n, **20**-11, **B**-13
Progressive tax rate structure, **1**-5, **1**-9–10, **1**-21, **B**-13
Prohibited interests, **18**-22–23
Property; *see also* Personal property; Real property
capital gain property, **6**-19–20, **6**-20–21n
as charitable contribution, **6**-19–20, **6**-20n
community property states/systems, **4**-20n, **5**-8–9, **5**-8–9n, **25**-10–11, **25**-10n, **B**-4
contributed, **19**-4n, **20**-7–9, **21**-8n
exchanged basis, **19**-8n
gains or losses from sale of, **4**-6, **5**-10
income from, **5**-10–13
like-kind exchanges and, **11**-24–25
nonresidential, **10**-14, **10**-14n, **10**-43, **11**-10n
ordinary income property, **6**-19, **6**-20
partnership formations and, **20**-3–9
qualified, **6**-31, **6**-31n, **10**-21, **10**-21n, **15**-11, **15**-11n
state income taxes on, **23**-21–23
transferred basis, **19**-14n
virtual currencies as, **7**-8, **11**-7
Property dispositions, **11**-2–6; *see also* Tax-deferred transactions
adjusted basis and, **11**-3–5
amount realized and, **11**-2
business property, **4**-9, **6**-6, **9**-13
income from, **5**-13
losses on, **4**-9, **6**-6, **9**-13
realized gain or loss, **11**-5–6
recognized gain or loss, **11**-6
review of taxation of, **19**-2–3
summary of formulas for gains/losses, **11**-6
Property distributions
as basis reductions, **20**-28n
corporate dividends, **18**-2
S corporations and, **22**-22
taxation of, **18**-2
Property factors, **23**-21–23
Property payments, **5**-15
Property taxes
personal, **1**-5, **1**-15, **4**-10, **6**-15, **B**-12
real, **1**-15, **14**-15–16, **14**-15–16n, **B**-13
tax base for, **1**-5, **1**-15, **1**-22
Property transactions, **3**-7, **19**-2–19
Property type, tax provisions by, **14**-3
Property use, **9**-11–12
Proportional tax rate structure, **1**-5, **1**-9–11, **1**-10n, **1**-21, **B**-13
Proposed regulations, **2**-10, **2**-15, **B**-13
ProPublica, **10**-32
Proration method, **21**-8, **21**-8n
Protecting Americans from Tax Hikes (PATH) Act of 2015, **7**-12n
PSCs (personal service corporations), **15**-33n, **16**-3n
PTI (previously taxable income), **22**-21n
PTIN (preparer tax identification number), **2**-26
PTTP; *see* Post-termination transition period
Public Company Accounting Oversight Board (PCAOB), **17**-33
Public Law 86-272, **23**-10–12, **23**-10n, **23**-25, **B**-13
Publicly traded partnerships, **20**-2n, **20**-17, **20**-34n
Public policy, expenditures against, **9**-6
Punitive damages, **5**-29–30
Purchased goodwill, **16**-9
Purchased personal property, gain or loss from sale of, **24**-10
Purchase method, **19**-20n

QTIPs (qualified terminable interest properties), **25**-11n, **25**-24n
Qualified business asset investment (QBAI), **24**-17, **B**-13
Qualified business income (QBI), **4**-9, **6**-28–32, **6**-29–31n, **15**-9–13, **15**-9n, **15**-22, **20**-22–23, **B**-13
Qualified charities, **6**-16–18, **6**-18n, **16**-16n
Qualified dividends, **4**-7, **4**-7n, **7**-6, **7**-6n, **B**-13, **C**-2
Qualified education expenses, **6**-10, **B**-13
Qualified education loans, **6**-10, **B**-13
Qualified employee discounts, **5**-24, **12**-26, **12**-29, **B**-13
Qualified equity grants, **12**-20, **B**-13
Qualified exchange intermediaries, **11**-25n
Qualified family farming corporations, **16**-3n
Qualified foreign corporations, **7**-6, **7**-6n
Qualified fringe benefits, **5**-23, **5**-24, **6**-7, **22**-18n
Qualified moving expense reimbursements, **5**-23n
Qualified nonrecourse financing, **20**-31, **B**-13
Qualified personal service corporations, **16**-3n
Qualified property, **6**-31, **6**-31n, **10**-21, **10**-21n, **15**-11, **15**-11n
Qualified replacement property, **11**-30, **B**-13
Qualified residence, **14**-9, **B**-13
Qualified residence interest, **14**-13
Qualified retirement accounts, **13**-19, **B**-13

Qualified retirement plans
  annuities from, **5**-12n
  classification of, **13**-3
  contributions as for AGI deduction, **4**-9
  deferral provisions for, **5**-31
  defined, **B**-13
  employer-provided, **13**-3
  individually managed, **13**-20–29
  nonqualified vs., **13**-19
  overview, **13**-2
  restrictions on, **13**-2
Qualified small business stock, **7**-11, **7**-12, **7**-12n, **B**-13
Qualified terminable interest properties (QTIPs), **25**-11n, **25**-24n
Qualified trade or business, **6**-29, **15**-9, **18**-26, **B**-13
Qualified transportation fringe benefits, **5**-24, **12**-26, **12**-30, **B**-13
Qualifying child
  age test for, **4**-13, **4**-18, **4**-19
  AGI and, **4**-15n
  custodial/noncustodial parent considerations, **4**-15, **4**-15n, **4**-21n
  defined, **B**-13
  divorced/separated parent considerations, **4**-15
  filing status and, **4**-13n
  relationship test for, **4**-13, **4**-18, **4**-19
  residence test for, **4**-13, **4**-18, **4**-19
  summary of dependency requirements, **4**-19
  support test for, **4**-14, **4**-18, **4**-19
  tiebreaking rules for, **4**-14–15
Qualifying debt, **14**-8n, **14**-12
Qualifying person, for head of household filing status, **4**-22–25, **4**-23n, **4**-31
Qualifying relative
  defined, **B**-13
  gross income test for, **4**-16–19, **6**-13n
  relationship test for, **4**-15–16, **4**-18, **4**-19
  summary of dependency requirements, **4**-19
  support test for, **4**-16, **4**-18, **4**-19
Qualifying widows or widowers; *see* Widows/widowers
Questions of fact, **2**-19, **2**-21, **B**-13
Questions of law, **2**-19, **2**-21, **B**-13
Quick reference sources, **2**-11
Quill Corporation, Petitioner v. North Dakota (1992), **23**-6, **23**-6n, **23**-11n

Railroad retirement benefits, **5**-17n
R&E costs; *see* Research and experimentation costs
Real estate exchanges, **11**-25n
Real estate taxes, **1**-5, **4**-10, **6**-15
Realization, defined, **B**-13
Realization principle, **5**-3, **19**-2, **B**-13
Realized gains or losses, **11**-5–6, **B**-13
Realized income, **4**-2, **4**-5, **B**-13
Real property
  applicable convention/method, **10**-15
  cost segregation and, **10**-14–15
  deductions for, **10**-2
  defined, **1**-15, **B**-13
  depreciation and, **10**-7, **10**-14–16
  depreciation tables, **10**-15–16
  gain or loss from sale of, **24**-10
  like-kind exchanges and, **11**-24–25
  mid-month convention for, **10**-15, **10**-16
  taxes on, **1**-15, **14**-15–16, **14**-15–16n, **B**-13
Reasonable basis, **2**-24, **2**-25n, **2**-28n
Reasonable compensation, **6**-30n, **12**-2–3, **12**-2n, **15**-25
Reasonable in amount, **9**-5–6, **B**-13
Recapture, **21**-4n; *see also* Depreciation recapture
Recognition; *see also* Income recognition
  ASC 740 on, **17**-25
  of deferred gain/loss, **19**-2–3
  gain and loss, **20**-3–4
Recognized gains or losses, **11**-6, **B**-13
Record keeping, **9**-12
Recourse debt, **20**-4–5, **20**-5n, **B**-13
Recovery of amounts previously deducted, **5**-5
Recovery periods (depreciable life), **10**-7–9, **10**-8n, **10**-23, **10**-26, **B**-13
Recurring item exceptions, **9**-26, **B**-13
Refinancing, **14**-9, **14**-10, **14**-13, **B**-14
Refundable credits, **8**-30–33
Registered tax return preparers, **2**-24n, **2**-26
Regressive tax rate structure, **1**-5, **1**-10–11, **1**-10n, **1**-21, **B**-14
Regular decisions (U.S. Tax Court), **2**-10, **2**-15n
Regular federal income tax computation; *see* Federal income tax computation
Regular tax rates, **8**-2–7
Regulations, administrative, **2**-15–16, **B**-14
Rehabilitation credit, **8**-34
Related parties
  capital losses on sales to, **7**-23
  compensation deduction restrictions, **12**-4–5
  defined, **19**-34, **19**-34n
  gains on sale of depreciable property to, **11**-16–17, **11**-17n
  limitations on accruals to, **9**-27
  loss disallowance rules, **11**-34–35, **11**-34n
  transactions among, **3**-12, **3**-12n, **3**-14n, **B**-14
Relationship tests, **4**-13, **4**-15–16, **4**-18, **4**-19
Relative, qualifying, **4**-15–19
Religious beliefs, refusal to pay taxes and, **3**-20
Remainder/remainderman, **25**-7–8, **B**-14
Renkemeyer, Campbell & Weaver, LLP v. Commissioner (2011), **20**-21n
Rental expenses
  deductions for, **4**-9, **6**-3, **6**-5–6, **6**-5n, **7**-26n
  Tax Court vs. IRS methods of allocating, **14**-18–20, **14**-18n
  by tier and deduction sequence, **14**-19–21
Rental real estate
  losses on, **14**-24–26
  nonresidence, **14**-24–26
  passive activity loss rules, **7**-33, **7**-33n, **14**-20n, **14**-24–26
  tier 1, 2, and 3 expenses, **14**-19–21, **14**-19n
Rental use of home, **14**-16–26
  ethical considerations and, **14**-17
  expenses by tier and deduction sequence, **14**-19–21
  flowchart of tax rules for, **14**-34–35
  losses on, **14**-24–26
  minimal rental use, **14**-17–18
  as not-for-profit activity, **14**-24n
  significant rental use, **14**-18–23, **14**-20n
  summary of tax rules, **14**-25
  Tax Court vs. IRS method of allocating expenses, **14**-18–20, **14**-18n
  use test, **14**-2–3
  as vacation home, **14**-18–23
Renting property from another party, **9**-24–25
Rents
  as gross income, **4**-6, **5**-2
  home office deduction for, **14**-26n
  source of income rules for, **24**-9
  as unearned income, **5**-10, **9**-18, **9**-29
Reorganizations, **19**-25–26n, **19**-25–32, **B**-14
Repatriation tax, **24**-29
Republican Party tax ideology, **1**-3
Requisite service period, **16**-10, **B**-14
Research activities, credits for increasing, **8**-34
Research and experimentation (R&E) costs, **10**-31, **10**-35–36, **10**-35n, **24**-13, **B**-14
Research Institute of America (RIA)
  Federal Tax Coordinator, **2**-11, **2**-19
  Federal Tax Handbook, **2**-9, **2**-11, **2**-18n
  United States Tax Reporter, **2**-11, **2**-18
Research memos, **2**-19–22
Research on taxes; *see* Tax research
Reserve accounting method, **22**-3n
Residence-based jurisdiction, **24**-2–3, **B**-14
Residence test for qualifying child, **4**-13, **4**-18, **4**-19
Resident, as defined for U.S. tax purposes, **24**-4–5
Resident aliens, **24**-4, **B**-14
Residential energy credit, **8**-34
Residential rental property, **10**-14, **10**-42
Restricted stock, **12**-16–20
  defined, **B**-14
  employee considerations for, **12**-17–19
  employer considerations for, **12**-19–20
  GAAP vs. tax expense, **12**-19
  qualified equity grants and, **12**-20
  sample timeline for, **12**-16
  Section 83(b) election and, **12**-17–19
Restricted stock units (RSUs), **12**-19–20
Reteif Goosen v. Commissioner (2011), **24**-10
Retirement income, **4**-6
Retirement planning; *see also* Defined contribution plans; Nonqualified deferred compensation (NQDC); Qualified retirement plans
  account contributions as for AGI deduction, **4**-9
  defined benefit plans, **13**-3–6, **13**-13
  employer-provided qualified plans, **13**-3
  ethical considerations and, **13**-26
  income deferral and, **3**-7
  individual retirement accounts, **13**-20–29
  qualified vs. nonqualified plan summary, **13**-19
  saver's credit, **13**-33–34
  for self-employed individuals, **6**-8n, **13**-29–33
Return of capital principle, **5**-4–5, **5**-11, **5**-13, **11**-6n, **18**-4, **B**-14
Revenue Act of 1913, **1**-12
Revenue forecasting, **1**-18
Revenue Procedure 87-56, **10**-8–9, **10**-8n, **10**-21n, **10**-23n
Revenue Procedure 87-57, **10**-10, **10**-14
Revenue procedures
  citations, **2**-10
  defined, **2**-16, **B**-14
  immediate expensing and, **10**-17n, **10**-19n
Revenue recognition; *see* Income recognition
Revenue rulings, **2**-10, **2**-16, **B**-14
Reverse acquisitions, **19**-26
Reverse hybrid entities, **24**-22, **24**-24, **B**-14
Reverse mergers, **19**-27–29, **19**-31
Reverse triangular Type A mergers, **19**-29, **19**-31
Reversion, **25**-7, **B**-14
RIA; *see* Research Institute of America
Riether v. United States (2012), **20**-21n
Rollovers, **13**-20n, **13**-27, **B**-14
Roth 401(k) plans, **13**-12–16, **B**-14
Roth IRAs, **13**-24–29
  contribution limits, **6**-8n, **13**-24–25, **13**-37
  defined, **B**-14
  distributions, **6**-8n, **13**-25–26
  exclusion of earnings on, **5**-21n
  overview, **13**-20
  rollover from traditional IRA, **13**-27
  traditional IRAs vs., **13**-28
Routine maintenance, **10**-5, **10**-5n
Royalties
  for AGI deductions and, **4**-9, **6**-3, **6**-5–6, **6**-6n
  conversion tax strategy and, **7**-9
  as gross income, **4**-6, **5**-2
  portfolio investments and, **7**-2
  source of income rules for, **24**-9
  as unearned income, **5**-10
RSUs (restricted stock units), **12**-19–20
Rubin, Richard, **7**-9

Safe-harbor provisions
  charitable contributions and, **6**-17
  debt obligations and, **22**-3
  defined, **B**-14
  de minimis, **10**-4
  qualified business income and, **6**-29n
  routine maintenance, **10**-5, **10**-5n
  tax prepayments and, **8**-36–38, **8**-37n
Salary and wages, **12**-2–7; *see also* Income
  after-tax cost of, **12**-4, **12**-7
  deductibility of salary payments, **12**-2–7
  defined, **B**-14, **B**-17
  employee considerations, **12**-2
  employer considerations, **12**-2–7
  facts and circumstances test for, **12**-2–3, **B**-7
  withholding taxes from, **12**-2
Sale of personal residence, **4**-6, **5**-22, **5**-22n, **14**-4–8
Sales tax
  defined, **B**-14
  for e-commerce sales, **1**-15, **23**-5–8
  as itemized deductions, **4**-10
  liability, **23**-3–4, **23**-3n, **23**-7–8
  nexus, **23**-2–4, **23**-5–7, **B**-14
  process for, **23**-3–4, **23**-3n
  proportional structure of, **1**-9–11, **1**-10n
  regressive structure of, **1**-10–11, **1**-10n
  tax base for, **1**-5, **1**-14, **1**-22
Same-day sales, **12**-10, **12**-12, **B**-14
Same-sex married couples, **4**-20
Sarbanes-Oxley Act of 2002, **17**-1
Saunders, Laura, **7**-9
Saver's credit, **8**-34, **13**-33–34
Savings, withdrawal of, **6**-9
Savings accounts, **7**-2, **7**-3, **7**-6
Savings bonds, **5**-26–27, **7**-3, **7**-4, **7**-4n, **7**-8n, **B**-17
Savings Incentive Match Plans for Employees (SIMPLE) IRAs, **13**-30n
Schedule A, Itemized Deductions, **4**-10, **6**-13, **6**-25, **14**-18

Schedule B, **7**-3n, **7**-6n, **20**-19n, **22**-12n
Schedule C, Profit or Loss from Business
business income and, **9**-2, **9**-31
defined, **B**-14
gambling winnings/losses and, **6**-24n
home office deductions and, **14**-29–30
rental income and, **6**-5n
retirement accounts for self-employed individuals and, **13**-30, **13**-31
self-employment tax and, **8**-16, **8**-16n
sole proprietorships and, **15**-5
trade or business expenses, **6**-3–4
Schedule D, **7**-8, **7**-16–17, **7**-16n, **7**-20, **11**-23, **20**-19n
Schedule E, Rental or Royalty Income, **6**-5, **8**-16n, **14**-22–24, **20**-19n, **22**-12n
Schedule K, **16**-16, **20**-24, **20**-26, **22**-28, **22**-29, **B**-14
Schedule K-1
example of, **20**-27, **22**-30
income from flow-through entities and, **5**-14
partnerships and, **20**-24, **20**-28
S corporations and, **22**-10–11, **22**-10n, **22**-28, **22**-30
Schedule K-2, **20**-28
Schedule K-3, **20**-28
Schedule L, **16**-26, **17**-12n
Schedule M-1, **9**-16n, **16**-23, **16**-23n, **16**-25–26
Schedule M-2, **16**-26
Schedule M-3, **9**-16n, **16**-23, **16**-23n, **16**-25–26
Schedule M adjustments, **16**-23, **16**-23n, **16**-25–26, **B**-14
Schedule SE, Self-Employment Tax, **8**-16
Schedule UTP, Uncertain Tax Position Statement, **17**-29
Scholarships, **5**-25, **5**-25n
S corporations, **22**-2–32
accounting methods for, **22**-3n, **22**-8–9, **22**-9n
accounting periods for, **9**-15, **9**-15n, **22**-8–9
benefits of, **22**-18
built-in gains tax, **22**-24–25, **22**-25n
business income reporting for, **9**-2
C corporations and partnerships compared to, **22**-30–32
debt basis and, **22**-14–15, **22**-15n
deduction of losses from, **5**-14n
defined, **22**-2, **B**-14
distributions, **22**-19–23
due dates and extensions for, **2**-3
elections, **22**-3–5, **22**-4n
estimated taxes and, **22**-28
ethical considerations and, **22**-6
excess net passive income tax and, **22**-24, **22**-26–27
excess of passive investment income, **22**-6
failure to meet requirements, **22**-6
filing requirements for, **22**-28–30
as flow-through entities, **5**-14, **9**-2n
formations, **22**-2
fringe benefits, **22**-18, **22**-18n
income and loss allocations, **22**-9
involuntary termination, **22**-6
LIFO recapture tax and, **22**-24, **22**-27–28
limitations on accruals to related parties in, **9**-27
liquidating distributions, **22**-23
loss limitations, **22**-14–17
net investment income tax, **22**-18, **22**-18n
operating issues, **22**-8–11
owner compensation in, **15**-22–23, **15**-25
as percentage of entity types, **15**-27–28
property distributions, **22**-22
qualification requirements, **22**-2
reelections, **22**-8
self-employment income and, **22**-17
separately stated items, **22**-10–11
shareholder's basis, **22**-12–18, **22**-12n
short tax years, **22**-7
specific identification method for, **22**-7, **22**-7n
state income taxes and, **23**-9–10
stock in, **22**-2n
Subchapter S, **15**-5, **20**-2, **22**-2n
tax classification and characteristics, **15**-5, **15**-5n, **15**-6, **15**-29–30, **15**-32–33, **20**-2
tax return for, **22**-28–30
termination of, **22**-5–8
voluntary terminations, **22**-5
Scripto, Inc. v. Carson, Sherriff, et al. (1960), **23**-6n
SEC; *see* Securities and Exchange Commission
Secondary tax authorities, **2**-9, **2**-11, **B**-14
Section 83(b) election, **12**-17–19, **B**-1
Section 179 expense, **10**-17–20
automobiles and, **10**-27
bonus depreciation, **10**-21–22, **10**-21n
choice of assets for, **10**-20
deductible expense, **10**-19
defined, **B**-1
limits on, **10**-18–19
TCJA expansion of, **10**-6
Section 197 intangibles, **10**-31–32, **10**-31n, **B**-1
Section 291 depreciation recapture, **11**-14, **11**-15, **11**-33, **B**-1
Section 338(g) election, **19**-24, **B**-1
Section 338(h)(10) election, **19**-24, **B**-1
Section 351 tax deferral
computing tax basis of stock received, **19**-8, **19**-10, **19**-14
control test of property and, **19**-5–7
disqualified property and, **19**-34
ethical considerations and, **19**-6
on property exchanged for stock, **19**-5
requirements of, **19**-4–7
shareholders, impact on, **19**-7–10
tax basis of property received, **19**-8, **19**-10, **19**-14
tax consequences of, **19**-7–10
transferee corporation and, **19**-13–16
on transfer of property to corporations, **19**-4–5
Section 481 adjustment, **9**-32, **B**-1
Section 704(b) capital accounts, **20**-8–9, **B**-1
Section 1031 exchange, **11**-24, **11**-24n
Section 1202 gain, **7**-12, **7**-12n
Section 1231 assets, **11**-7–10, **20**-7, **21**-4, **21**-25n, **B**-1
Section 1231(b) assets, **6**-19n
Section 1231 gains or losses
assets sold at losses, **11**-12–13
calculating net, **11**-17–20, **11**-17n
capital assets, **11**-8
character of, **11**-7–9
creation of gain through cost recovery deductions, **11**-11
defined, **4**-6n
depreciation recapture and, **11**-10–13
gain due to cost recovery deductions and asset appreciation, **11**-12
look-back rule, **11**-17–19, **B**-1
netting process, **11**-20
ordinary assets, **11**-7–8
partnerships and, **21**-25
recognition of, **11**-11n
unrecaptured gain for individuals, **11**-15, **11**-15n
Section 1231 look-back rule, **11**-17–19, **B**-1
Section 1239 recapture provision, **11**-16–17, **11**-17n
Section 1244 stock, **19**-19
Section 1245 property, **11**-10–14, **11**-10n, **11**-33, **B**-1
Section 1250 property
defined, **B**-1
depreciation recapture for real property, **11**-14
installment reporting and, **11**-33
unrecaptured gains, **7**-11, **11**-15, **11**-33n, **21**-5n
Section 7520 rate, **25**-7, **25**-7n
Secured loans, **14**-9
Securities and Exchange Commission (SEC), **9**-15, **17**-2, **17**-30, **17**-31, **17**-33
Security deposits, **9**-18n
Self-created goodwill, **16**-9n
Self-created patents, **10**-36
Self-employed business expenses, **6**-3
Self-employed individuals
business activities of, **6**-2
defined benefit plans and, **13**-6
employees vs., **8**-21–22
health insurance deductions for, **4**-9, **6**-7–8, **6**-7–8n
retirement planning for, **6**-8n, **13**-29–33
Self-employment compensation, **12**-2, **12**-2n
Self-employment income, S corporations and, **22**-17
Self-employment taxes, **8**-16–20
alternative minimum tax and, **8**-12n
calculating, **6**-8n
computation of, **8**-16–20
deductions for, **4**-9, **6**-8, **6**-8n, **15**-14
defined, **B**-14
estimated quarterly payments, **1**-22, **8**-20
filing requirements, **6**-27n, **8**-16n
for flow-through entities, **15**-14–15, **15**-14n
Medicare, **1**-13, **6**-8, **8**-16–20
partnership accounting and, **20**-20–21, **20**-21n
Social Security, **1**-13, **6**-8, **8**-16–20
tax base for, **4**-11
Senate, as source of tax law, **2**-10, **2**-12–13
Separately stated items, **20**-17–23, **22**-10–11, **B**-14
Separate taxpaying entities, **15**-5
Separate tax returns, **23**-15, **B**-14
SEP (simplified employee pension) IRAs, **13**-29–31, **B**-14
Serial gifts, **25**-31, **B**-14
Series EE bonds, **5**-26–27, **7**-4, **7**-4n, **7**-8n
Series I bonds, **7**-4, **7**-4n
Service partners, **20**-10–11, **20**-10–11n, **B**-14
Services
compensation for, **4**-6, **5**-2, **5**-3, **24**-8–9
income from, **5**-10
no-additional-cost, **5**-24, **12**-26, **12**-28, **B**-11
partnership formations, **20**-3, **20**-9–11
for tax research, **2**-11
topical tax, **2**-19, **B**-16
Settlement statement, **14**-13, **14**-36–37, **B**-14
Shareholder agreements, **22**-6n
Shareholders
complete liquidation, impact on, **19**-33–34
corporate, **15**-20, **15**-21
distributions to, **15**-7n, **18**-2
foreign, **15**-21
individual, **15**-18
institutional, **15**-18, **15**-21, **B**-9
liabilities, **19**-11–13
noncash property distributions to, **18**-12–14
noncorporate, **19**-33
rights, responsibilities, and legal arrangements among, **7**-3, **15**-3–4
Section 351 deferral and, **19**-7–10
tax consequences of receiving stock distributions, **18**-16–17
tax-exempt, **15**-21
U.S. shareholders, **24**-16
Shareholder's basis in S corporations, **22**-12–18, **22**-12n
Shell corporations, **19**-27
SHOP (small business health options program), **5**-24n
Short tax years, **22**-7
Short-term capital gains and losses, **4**-7, **4**-7n, **7**-10, **7**-13–15, **7**-34–36, **B**-14
Sickness and injury-related exclusions, **5**-29–30
Sideways attribution, **18**-22
Simani, Ellis, **10**-32
Similar and related-use test, **11**-30n
SIMPLE (Savings Incentive Match Plans for Employees) IRAs, **13**-30n
Simple trusts, **25**-30n, **B**-14
Simplified employee pension (SEP) IRAs, **13**-29–31, **B**-14
Simplified method for interest expenses, **14**-11n
Single filing status
defined, **B**-15
gross income thresholds (2022), **2**-2
individual income tax formula and, **4**-22
Social Security benefit taxability and, **5**-18
standard deduction for, **2**-2, **4**-10, **6**-26, **C**-2
tax rate schedule for, **C**-1
Single-life annuities, **5**-12
Single-member LLCs, **15**-5, **B**-15
Sin taxes, **1**-4, **1**-4n, **B**-14
Sixteenth Amendment, **1**-12, **2**-11
Small business corporations, **19**-19
Small businesses, gross receipts test for, **9**-2, **9**-28n
Small business health options program (SHOP), **5**-24n
Small Claims Division (U.S. Tax Court), **2**-7, **2**-7n, **2**-15n
Small employer health insurance credit, **8**-34
"Smell test," **3**-19
Smith, Adam, **1**-17n
Smoking; *see* Tobacco taxes
Social Security benefits, **5**-17–19, **5**-17n, **13**-2n
Social Security tax
caps for, **1**-10n, **1**-13
defined, **B**-15
for employees, **6**-8, **8**-14–16
objectives of, **1**-12–13, **8**-14
regressive structure of, **1**-10
S corporations and, **22**-17
for self-employed individuals, **1**-13, **6**-8, **8**-16–20
tax base for, **1**-13
withholdings in, **6**-13n
Social Security Trust fund, **13**-2n
Social Security wage base limitation, **15**-14
Social Security Worksheet, **5**-33
Software companies, **23**-8n

Sole proprietorships
  accounting period for, **9**-14
  business income reporting for, **9**-2
  defined, **B**-15
  income shifting and, **3**-12–13
  legal classification of, **15**-2
  organizational expenditures and, **10**-32n
  as percentage of entity types, **15**-27–28
  responsibility for liabilities, **15**-3
  with self-employment income, **13**-29n
  tax classification and characteristics, **15**-5, **15**-6, **15**-29–30, **15**-32–33
  unincorporated entities taxed as, **20**-2n
Solicitation, **23**-12–14, **B**-15
Source-based jurisdiction, **24**-2–3, **B**-15
Source of deduction rules, **24**-6, **24**-11–13
Source of income rules
  compensation for services and, **24**-8–9
  dividends and, **24**-8
  interest and, **24**-7
  manufactured inventory sales, **24**-11
  real or purchased property sales, **24**-10
  for rents and royalties, **24**-9
Sourcing receipts, **23**-20
South Dakota v. Wayfair Inc. (2018), **23**-6, **23**-6n
SPAC (special purpose acquisition company), **19**-27–28
Special allocations, **20**-23, **20**-23n, **B**-15
Special apportionment rules, **24**-12–13
Special basis adjustments, **21**-26–29
  defined, **B**-15
  for dispositions, **21**-27–28
  for distributions, **21**-29
  overview, **21**-26–27
  professional sports team franchises and, **21**-28–29
Special purpose acquisition company (SPAC), **19**-27–28
Special use valuation, **25**-21
Specific identification method, **7**-9–10, **9**-21, **22**-7, **22**-7n, **B**-15
Specified service trade or business, **6**-29, **15**-9–13, **15**-10n, **20**-22n, **B**-15
Split gifts, **25**-4n, **25**-10
Spot rate, **24**-21, **B**-15
Spousal IRA, **13**-21–22, **B**-15
SSTS (Statements on Standards for Tax Services), **2**-23–25, **B**-15
Standard deduction
  age and, **2**-2, **4**-10, **6**-26, **6**-26n, **C**-2
  as from AGI deduction, **4**-9, **4**-10
  alternative minimum tax, **8**-8
  blindness and, **4**-10, **6**-26, **6**-26n, **C**-2
  child's, **8**-6n
  defined, **6**-26, **B**-15
  filing status and, **2**-2, **4**-10, **4**-12, **6**-26, **C**-2
  purpose of, **6**-27
Standard mileage rate, **9**-9, **9**-9n
Stare decisis, **2**-15, **B**-15
Starker exchanges (deferred like-kind exchanges), **11**-25–26, **11**-25n, **B**-5
Starker v. United States (1979), **11**-25n
Start-up costs, **9**-7, **9**-7n, **10**-31, **10**-35, **20**-12–13, **B**-15
State and local taxes; *see also* State income taxes
  defined, **B**-10, **B**-15
  excise, **1**-15
  as itemized deductions, **4**-10, **6**-15–17, **6**-16n
  nonincome-based, **23**-25
  overview, **1**-14, **23**-2–4
  property, **1**-15
  revenue generated from, **1**-14
  sales and use, **1**-14–15, **23**-3–4, **23**-3–4n, **23**-5–9
  unemployment, **1**-10, **1**-10n, **1**-13, **1**-13n
State death taxes, **25**-23–24
State income taxes, **23**-9–25
  for business income, **23**-18–23
  dividing state tax base among states, **23**-18–24
  entities included, **23**-15–16
  exceptions and modifications to, **1**-14, **1**-14n
  flow-through entities and, **23**-10
  liability, **23**-24
  nexus, **23**-10–14, **23**-19
  on nonbusiness income, **23**-24
  process for, **23**-4
  progressive structure of, **1**-9
  on property, **23**-21–23
  Public Law 86-272 and, **23**-10–12, **23**-10n, **23**-25
  separate tax returns, **23**-15
  state taxable income, **23**-16–17
  tax base for, **1**-5
  unitary tax returns, **23**-15–16
Statements on Standards for Tax Services (SSTS), **2**-23–25, **B**-15
State taxable income, **23**-16–17
State tax base, **23**-4, **B**-15
State unemployment taxes, **1**-10, **1**-10n, **1**-13, **1**-13n
Static forecasting, **1**-18, **B**-15
Statute of limitations, **2**-3–4, **17**-3n, **B**-15
Statutory mergers, **19**-26, **19**-28, **19**-31
Statutory notice of deficiency, **2**-6
Statutory sources of tax law
  citations, **2**-10
  Congress, **2**-12–13
  Internal Revenue Code, **2**-11–14
  legislative process for, **2**-12–13
  tax treaties, **2**-14
  U.S. Constitution, **2**-11, **2**-12
Step-transaction doctrine, **3**-18, **3**-19, **B**-15
Step-up in tax basis, **25**-31–33
Stewardship expenses, **24**-12n
Stock
  charitable contribution of, **18**-24
  class of, **19**-3n, **22**-3n
  fair-market value of, **12**-17, **18**-16, **22**-12n
  holding period of, **19**-18
  nonqualified preferred, **19**-5n
  qualified small business, **7**-11, **7**-12, **7**-12n, **B**-13
  restricted, **12**-16–20
  in S corporations, **22**-2n
  tax basis in Section 351 transaction, **19**-8
Stock basis, **22**-12, **22**-12n, **22**-15n
Stock dividends
  annual returns from, **7**-7n
  distribution of, **18**-2, **18**-16–17
  nontaxable, **18**-16, **18**-16n
  taxable, **18**-17
Stock-for-stock acquisitions, **19**-29–30, **B**-15
Stock options, **12**-9–16
  accounting methods and, **12**-15–16
  ASC 718 and, **12**-15n, **16**-11
  backdating, **12**-15
  book–tax differences and, **16**-10–13
  characteristics of, **12**-9
  compensatory, **12**-9–16, **12**-15n
  economic value of, **12**-15n
  employee considerations for, **12**-10–13
  employer considerations for, **12**-14–15
  ethical considerations and, **12**-15
  GAAP vs. tax expense, **12**-15, **12**-19
  incentive, **12**-10–15, **16**-10–11, **16**-10n, **B**-8
  nonqualified, **12**-10–15, **12**-17, **12**-20, **16**-10–13, **16**-10n, **17**-8, **B**-11
  sample timeline for incentive and nonqualified options, **12**-10
Stock ownership tests, **18**-19
Stock redemptions, **18**-17–25
  as after-tax profits, **18**-2
  complete redemption, **18**-22–23
  defined, **B**-15
  form of, **18**-18–19
  not essentially equivalent to a dividend, **18**-23
  overview, **18**-18
  reduction of shareholder's ownership interest and, **18**-19–23
  substantially disproportionate, **18**-19–22
  tax consequences to distributing corporation, **18**-25
Stock split, **18**-16, **B**-15
Straight debt, **22**-3n
Straight-line method, **10**-7, **10**-7n, **10**-10, **10**-23, **10**-29n, **10**-34
Strike price, **12**-9, **12**-15, **B**-15
Structural tax rate, **17**-32, **B**-15
Student loans, **5**-21n
Subchapter C, **15**-5, **18**-2n, **19**-4, **19**-4n
Subchapter J, **25**-30n
Subchapter K, **20**-2, **20**-3, **21**-9, **B**-15
Subchapter N, **24**-2, **24**-25
Subchapter S, **15**-5, **20**-2, **22**-2n, **B**-15
Subpart F income, **24**-16, **24**-25–29, **B**-15
Subsequent events, in uncertain tax positions, **17**-27
Subsidiaries, **24**-2, **24**-22–25
Substance-over-form doctrine, **3**-18, **3**-19, **B**-15
Substantial authority standard, **2**-24, **2**-25n, **2**-28, **B**-15
Substantial basis reduction, **21**-10n, **21**-27, **B**-15
Substantial built-in loss, **21**-27, **B**-15–16
Substantially appreciated inventory, **21**-24–25, **B**-16
Substantially disproportionate stock redemptions, **18**-19–22
Substantially identical stocks and securities, **7**-24, **7**-24n
Substantial presence test, **24**-4
Substituted basis, **11**-26, **19**-7–8, **19**-26, **22**-12, **B**-16
Substitution effect, **1**-19, **B**-16
Sufficiency of tax systems, **1**-18–20, **B**-16
Supply chains, international, **24**-28
Support tests, **4**-14, **4**-16, **4**-18, **4**-19
Surviving spouses; *see* Widows/widowers
Syndication costs, **20**-12–13, **20**-12n, **B**-16

Tangible assets, **9**-7, **9**-29, **10**-2
Tangible personal property
  bonus depreciation, **10**-21–22, **10**-21n
  choice of assets for, **10**-20
  deductions for, **6**-20, **10**-2
  depreciation of, **10**-10
  examples of, **1**-15
  immediate expensing of, **10**-17–20, **10**-17n
  limits on immediate expensing, **10**-18–19
Taxable corporate acquisitions, **19**-22–24
Taxable estate, **25**-23–25, **B**-16
Taxable fringe benefits, **12**-21–24
  defined, **12**-21, **B**-16
  employee considerations for, **12**-22–24
  employer considerations for, **12**-24
  group-term life insurance, **12**-22–23
  to S corporations, **22**-18
  summary of, **12**-33–34
Taxable gifts, **25**-10–12, **25**-25–26, **B**-16
Taxable income; *see also* Corporate regular taxable income
  alternative minimum, **8**-7–8
  book equivalent of, **17**-9, **17**-18, **B**-3
  defined, **4**-2, **B**-16
  excess, **20**-22n
  expected future income exclusive of reversals/carryovers, **17**-21
  income excluded from, **18**-5
  in prior carryback years, **17**-21
  state, **23**-16–17
  summary of, **6**-32–33
  tax base for, **1**-5
  tax planning strategies for, **17**-21
  timing strategies for, **3**-4–11
Taxable liquidating distributions, **19**-34–36
Taxable stock distributions, **18**-17
Taxable temporary differences, **17**-12–17, **17**-20, **B**-16
Tax accounting balance sheets, **17**-11–17, **19**-32, **B**-16
Tax Adviser (journal), **2**-11
Tax-aligned international supply chains, **24**-28
Tax avoidance, **3**-19, **B**-16
Tax avoidance transactions, **19**-11
Tax base
  alternative minimum tax, **4**-11, **8**-7
  defined, **1**-5, **B**-16
  employment taxes, **1**-13
  excise taxes, **1**-13, **1**-15, **1**-22
  income taxes, **1**-5
  property taxes, **1**-5, **1**-15, **1**-22
  real estate taxes, **1**-5
  sales and use taxes, **1**-5, **1**-14–15, **1**-22
  self-employment taxes, **4**-11
  state tax, **23**-4, **B**-15
  transfer taxes, **1**-13
  unemployment taxes, **1**-13
Tax basis
  adjusted, **19**-3, **19**-7–8, **B**-2
  corporate acquisitions and, **19**-22
  for cost recovery, **10**-3–6
  defined, **10**-3n, **B**-16
  keeping track of, **18**-3–4
  loss limits, **7**-29
  of property received, **19**-14
  return of capital principle and, **5**-4, **5**-13, **18**-4
  sale proceeds from assets and, **5**-4, **7**-8–9
  in Section 351 transaction, **19**-8, **19**-10, **19**-14
  of shareholder's in stock, **19**-4
  step-up in, **25**-31–33
Tax-basis limitation, **20**-30–31, **22**-14–15
Tax benefit rule, **5**-5, **B**-16
Tax brackets, **1**-5–6, **8**-2, **B**-3, **B**-16
Tax capital accounts, **20**-8, **B**-16
Tax carryovers, **17**-4, **B**-16

Tax Commissioner of West Virginia v. MBNA America Bank, N.A. (2006), **23**-11n
Tax credits, **8**-23–35; *see also* Foreign tax credits (FTCs)
adoption expense, **8**-34
American opportunity, **4**-12, **5**-25n, **8**-28–30, **8**-29n, **8**-34
applicable, **25**-2–3
application sequence, **8**-35
business, **8**-33–34, **B**-3
for charitable contributions, **6**-16–17
child, **4**-12, **8**-24–26, **8**-25n, **8**-34, **B**-4
child and dependent care, **4**-12, **8**-26–28, **8**-27n, **8**-34
defined, **4**-12, **B**-16
earned income, **4**-12, **8**-30–32, **8**-34
education, **8**-28–29n, **8**-28–30
elderly and disabled, **8**-34
individual recovery, **8**-32
lifetime learning, **4**-12, **8**-28–30, **8**-29n, **8**-34
minimum, **8**-12, **B**-10
nonrefundable, **8**-23–30, **8**-33–34, **8**-35n
overview, **8**-23
partnerships and, **20**-17n
personal, **8**-24–33, **8**-35n
premium, **6**-7n, **8**-34
refundable, **8**-30–33
rehabilitation, **8**-34
for research activity, **8**-34
residential energy, **8**-34
sales tax credits, **1**-15
saver's, **8**-34
for S corporations, **22**-10n
summary of, **8**-34
unified, **1**-13–14
work opportunity, **8**-34
Tax Cuts and Jobs Act of 2017 (TCJA)
anti-deferral rules in, **24**-29
base erosion and anti-abuse tax in, **24**-31
corporate tax rate under, **17**-17
depreciation provisions in, **10**-2, **10**-6–7, **10**-9, **10**-10, **10**-21
foreign source income under, **24**-16, **24**-17
foreign tax credit categories in, **24**-20
investment expense deduction eliminated by, **7**-26n, **7**-27
ordinary tax rate under, **3**-8
personal property under, **10**-6, **10**-9, **10**-10
simplification of tax forms and, **7**-17
territorial approach to foreign-source income in, **24**-3, **24**-29
Tax deductions; *see* Deductions
Tax deferrals, **19**-4–7; *see also* Section 351 tax deferral
Tax-deferred corporate acquisitions, **19**-25–31
judicial principles underlying, **19**-25
summary of, **19**-31
type A asset, **19**-26–29
type B stock-for-stock, **19**-29–30
Tax deferred income, **4**-2, **4**-5, **4**-6
Tax-deferred transactions, **11**-24–35; *see also* Like-kind exchanges
installment sales, **4**-6, **5**-31, **11**-31–33, **11**-32n, **B**-9
involuntary conversions, **5**-31, **11**-29–31, **B**-9
overview, **11**-24
related-party loss disallowance rules, **11**-34–35, **11**-34n
Tax elections, **20**-14
Taxes; *see also* Filing requirements; Tax law; Tax planning strategies; *specific types of taxes*
ad valorem, **1**-15, **B**-2
built-in gains, **22**-24–25, **22**-25n, **B**-3
calculation of, **1**-5
defined, **1**-4, **B**-16
earmarked, **1**-4, **B**-6
employment; *see* Employment taxes
estimated; *see* Estimated taxes
excise, **1**-13, **1**-15, **1**-22, **B**-6
explicit, **1**-16, **B**-7
federal; *see* Federal taxes
FICA, **8**-14–23, **8**-14n, **12**-2, **12**-2n, **12**-8n, **12**-24n, **15**-23, **B**-7
financial decision making and, **1**-2–3
flat, **1**-5, **1**-9, **B**-7
franchise, **23**-2n, **23**-9n
graduated, **1**-5–6, **1**-12, **B**-8
implicit, **1**-16–17, **3**-15, **3**-18, **B**-8
investment decisions and, **1**-16–17
as itemized deductions, **4**-10, **6**-15–17, **6**-16n
Medicare; *see* Medicare tax
politics and, **1**-2–3
property; *see* Property taxes
real estate, **1**-5, **4**-10, **6**-15
role of, **1**-2–3
sales; *see* Sales tax
self-employment; *see* Self-employment taxes
sin, **1**-4, **1**-4n, **B**-14
Social Security; *see* Social Security tax
state and local; *see* State and local taxes
transfer, **1**-13–14, **5**-27, **25**-2–4, **B**-17
types of, **1**-11–17
unemployment, **1**-10, **1**-10n, **1**-13, **1**-13n, **B**-17
use; *see* Use tax
value-added, **1**-11–12, **B**-17
Taxes (journal), **2**-11
Tax evasion, **2**-28, **3**-19–20, **B**-16
Tax-exempt income, **4**-2, **4**-5, **9**-7
Tax Exempt Organization Search, **6**-18n, **16**-16n
Tax-exempt shareholders, **15**-21
Tax-favored assets, **1**-16
Tax Foundation, **16**-7
Tax gap, **2**-5, **3**-20
Tax havens, **24**-25, **24**-29, **B**-16
Tax home, **24**-4n
Tax law, **2**-9–17; *see also* Internal Revenue Code (IRC)
administrative sources of, **2**-10, **2**-15–17
judicial sources of, **2**-10, **2**-14–15, **2**-15n
legislative sources of, **2**-10, **2**-11–14, **3**-8
letter rulings, **2**-10, **2**-16–17
primary authorities on, **2**-9, **2**-10, **B**-12
secondary authorities on, **2**-9, **2**-11, **B**-14
tax treaties, **2**-14
Tax Law Review (New York University School of Law), **2**-11
Tax-loss harvesting, **7**-26
Tax Notes, **2**-11
Taxpayer Certainty and Disaster Relief Act of 2020, **9**-9n
Taxpayer Compliance Measurement Program, **2**-4n
Taxpayer filing requirements; *see* Filing requirements
Tax penalties; *see* Penalties
Tax planning strategies, **3**-1–21
ASC 740 on, **17**-21
capital assets and, **7**-25–26
conversion, **3**-2, **3**-15–18, **7**-9
for distributions, **18**-15
fringe benefits and, **12**-31–33
income-shifting, **3**-2, **3**-11–15
judicial doctrines impacting, **3**-18–19
limitations to, **3**-18–19
for maximizing after-tax wealth, **3**-2
overview, **3**-2
tax avoidance vs. tax evasion, **3**-19–20
timing, **3**-2–11
wealth planning and, **25**-31–33
Tax preferences, **1**-21
Tax prepayments, **4**-12
Tax professionals; *see* Accountants
Tax rates; *see also* Tax rate schedules; Tax rate structures
applicable, **7**-13
average, **1**-7–11, **B**-3
capital gains, **3**-8, **3**-10, **7**-9, **8**-4, **C**-2
cash, **17**-33, **B**-4
constant, **3**-4–7
corporate, **1**-9, **C**-2
decreasing, **3**-9–10
defined, **1**-5, **B**-16
effective, **1**-8, **1**-10–11, **1**-10n, **1**-21, **17**-8, **17**-33
enacted, **17**-15
estates and trusts, **C**-2
increasing, **3**-8–9
jurisdictional variation of, **3**-11
kiddie tax, **3**-12n, **5**-8n, **8**-3n, **8**-5–6, **8**-11n, **8**-29n, **B**-9
marginal, **1**-5–7, **1**-9–11, **3**-8, **3**-10, **8**-6, **8**-23, **B**-10
measuring, **1**-5–8
ordinary, **3**-8
preferential, **4**-7, **8**-4, **8**-4n, **B**-12
for qualified dividends, **C**-2
regular, **8**-2–7
structural, **17**-32, **B**-15
Tax rate schedules, **4**-11, **4**-11n, **8**-2–3, **B**-16, **C**-1
Tax rate structures
progressive, **1**-5, **1**-9–10, **1**-21, **B**-13
proportional, **1**-5, **1**-9–11, **1**-10n, **1**-21, **B**-13
regressive, **1**-5, **1**-10–11, **1**-10n, **1**-21, **B**-14
Tax refunds, **2**-2, **4**-12
Tax reporting, material weaknesses in, **17**-3
Tax research, **2**-17–23
analyzing tax authorities, **2**-19–21
client letters summarizing, **2**-22–23
documenting and communicating results, **2**-21–23
identifying issues in, **2**-17–18
keyword searches in, **2**-19
locating relevant authorities, **2**-18–19
research memos, **2**-19–22
services for, **2**-11
understanding facts in, **2**-17
Tax return preparers, **2**-24n, **2**-26
Tax shelters, **7**-30, **20**-16n, **B**-16
Tax summary, **8**-39–40
Tax systems, **1**-17–23
certainty in, **1**-22, **B**-4
convenience of, **1**-22, **B**-4
economy of, **1**-22, **B**-6
equity in, **1**-20–21, **B**-6
income vs. substitution effects, **1**-19
overview, **1**-17
static vs. dynamic forecasting, **1**-18
sufficiency of, **1**-18–20, **B**-16
trade-offs in, **1**-23
Tax tables, **4**-11, **4**-11n, **8**-3, **8**-3n, **B**-16
Tax treaties, **2**-14, **24**-3, **24**-3n, **24**-17–18, **B**-16
Tax violations; *see* Penalties
Tax withholdings, **4**-12, **8**-36, **12**-2, **24**-3, **24**-3n, **24**-18n, **B**-18
Tax year, **9**-14, **B**-16
TCJA; *see* Tax Cuts and Jobs Act of 2017
Technical advice memorandums, **2**-10, **2**-16, **B**-16
Telephones; *see* Cell phones
Temporary book–tax differences
charitable contributions and, **16**-18
common temporary differences, **16**-5–9, **17**-9
deductible, **17**-12, **B**-5
defined, **16**-3, **17**-12, **B**-16
dividends, **16**-8
expenses/losses that are deductible, **17**-12, **17**-13
future reversals of, **17**-20
goodwill acquired in asset acquisition, **16**-9
identification of, **17**-12
permanent book–tax differences vs., **16**-4
revenue/gains that are taxable, **17**-12, **17**-13
taxable, **17**-12–17, **17**-20, **B**-16
Temporary regulations, **2**-10, **2**-15, **B**-16
10-year look-forward rule, **18**-23
Tenancy by the entirety, **25**-20n
Tenancy in common, **25**-6, **25**-20, **B**-16
Tentative minimum tax (TMT), **8**-8, **8**-12, **B**-16
Terminable interest
defined, **B**-16
life estate and, **25**-7, **25**-8
nondeductible, **25**-11, **B**-11
qualified terminable interest properties, **25**-11n, **25**-24n
Termination of S corporations, **22**-5–8
Tesla, **11**-7, **12**-13–14
Testamentary transfers, **25**-2, **B**-16
Testamentary trusts, **22**-2n
Theft losses; *see* Casualty and theft losses
Thiel, Peter, **13**-29
Third-party intermediaries, **11**-25–26, **11**-25n, **B**-16
30-day letters, **2**-6, **B**-1
Throwback rule, **23**-19, **23**-19n, **B**-16
Tiebreaking rules, **4**-14–15, **24**-18
Time basis for compensation, **24**-9
Time value of money, **3**-3–4, **6**-28n
Timing requirements, for like-kind exchanges, **11**-25–26
Timing strategies, **3**-2–11
changing tax rates and, **3**-7–10
compensation deduction and, **12**-3–4
constant tax rates and, **3**-4–7
decreasing tax rates and, **3**-9–10
income and, **3**-4–11
for income deferral, **3**-4–10
increasing tax rates and, **3**-8–9
interest payments and taxes, **7**-6
limitations to, **3**-10–11
overview, **3**-2–3
present value of money and, **3**-3–4
separate accounting methods for E&P, **18**-5–7
for tax deductions, **3**-4–11
TMT; *see* Tentative minimum tax
Tobacco taxes, **1**-4, **1**-4n, **1**-13, **1**-15

Topical tax services, **2**-19, **B**-16
Total income tax provision, **17**-18
Trade or business activities, **6**-2, **9**-4, **20**-32, **20**-32n, **B**-17; *see also* Business activities
Trade or business expenses, **6**-2n, **6**-3; *see also* Business expenses
Trade show rule, **23**-13, **B**-17
Traditional 401(k) plans, **13**-12, **13**-14–16, **B**-17
Traditional IRAs, **13**-20–24
  deductible contributions, **6**-8, **13**-20–22
  deduction limitations, **13**-35–36
  defined, **B**-17
  distributions, **6**-8, **13**-23–24
  nondeductible contributions, **6**-8, **13**-23
  overview, **13**-20
  rollover to Roth IRA, **13**-27
  Roth IRAs vs., **13**-28
Transactions subject to tax deferral, **19**-4
Transferee corporation, tax consequences to, **19**-13–16
Transfer of property to corporations, **19**-4–5
Transferors, **5**-27
Transfer pricing, **3**-15, **24**-31
Transferred basis property, **19**-14n
Transfer taxes, **1**-13–14, **5**-27, **25**-2–4, **B**-17
Transfer tax planning techniques, **25**-31–33
Travel and transportation expenses
  deductions for, **9**-9–10n, **9**-9–11, **9**-12n
  defined, **B**-17
  for medical purposes, **6**-14, **6**-14n
Treasury bonds, **1**-20, **7**-3–4, **7**-3n, **B**-17
Treasury notes, **7**-3, **7**-3n, **B**-17
Treaties, tax, **2**-14, **24**-3, **24**-3n, **24**-17–18, **B**-16
Triangular mergers, **19**-28–29, **19**-31, **19**-32
Trump, Donald, **7**-17, **20**-33
Trustees, **25**-7, **B**-17
Trusts
  complex, **25**-30n, **B**-4
  defined, **25**-7, **25**-30, **B**-17
  filing requirements for, **2**-2
  grantor, **22**-2n
  life insurance, **25**-33, **B**-9
  simple, **25**-30n, **B**-14
  tax rates for, **C**-2
  testamentary, **22**-2n
  voting, **22**-2n
  in wealth planning, **25**-30, **25**-30n, **25**-33, **25**-33n
12-month rule, **9**-16, **9**-16n, **B**-1
20 percent deduction for qualified business income, **6**-29, **6**-30n
25 percent gains, **7**-11, **7**-13–15, **7**-17, **7**-21, **7**-34–36
28 percent gains, **7**-12–15, **7**-17, **7**-21, **7**-34–36
2 percent floor limit, **6**-24
200 percent (double) declining balance, **10**-7, **10**-7n, **10**-10
Type A reorganizations, **19**-26–29, **19**-26n, **19**-31
Type B stock-for-stock reorganizations, **19**-26n, **19**-29–31
Type C reorganizations, **19**-26n, **19**-31
Type D reorganizations, **19**-31
Type E reorganizations, **19**-31
Type F reorganizations, **19**-31
Type G reorganizations, **19**-31

UBIT (unrelated business income tax), **15**-21
ULCs (unlimited liability companies), **24**-23
Uncertain tax positions (UTPs)
  ASC 740 application to, **17**-24–26
  defined, **17**-11, **B**-17
  disclosures of, **17**-28
  ethical considerations and, **17**-29
  interest and penalties, **17**-28
  Microsoft Corporation disclosure of, **17**-27, **17**-28
  overview, **17**-24–25
  Schedule UTP, **17**-29
  subsequent events, **17**-27
Underpayment penalties, **2**-3, **2**-3n, **4**-12, **8**-14n, **8**-36–38, **8**-39n, **B**-17
Unearned income
  annuities as, **5**-10–12
  defined, **5**-10, **5**-10n, **B**-17
  dividends as, **5**-10, **5**-14
  interest as, **5**-10, **5**-14
  net, **8**-6, **B**-11
  property dispositions as, **5**-13
  rents and royalties as, **5**-10, **9**-18, **9**-29
Unemployment taxes, **1**-10, **1**-10n, **1**-13, **1**-13n, **B**-17
Unfavorable book–tax differences, **16**-3, **16**-18, **17**-9, **17**-12, **17**-13, **B**-17
Unforeseen circumstances, **14**-6–7, **14**-7n
Unified tax credit, **1**-13–14
Unified transfer tax rates, **25**-2
Uniform cost capitalization (UNICAP) rules, **9**-19, **9**-20, **B**-17
Uniform Division of Income Tax Purposes Act of 1957, **23**-18n
Uniforms and special clothing, **9**-7
Unincorporated entities, **15**-5, **15**-5n, **20**-2, **20**-2n
Unitary tax returns, **23**-15–16, **B**-17
United Airlines flight benefits, **12**-28, **12**-29
United States v. Davis (1970), **18**-23n
United States person, defined, **24**-25, **B**-17
Unlimited liability companies (ULCs), **24**-23
Unmarried taxpayers; *see* Single filing status
Unrealized receivables, **21**-3, **21**-3–4n, **21**-25n, **B**-17
Unrecaptured Section 1231 losses, **11**-19
Unrecaptured Section 1250 gains, **7**-11, **11**-15, **11**-33n, **21**-5n, **B**-17
Unrecognized tax benefits (UTBs), **17**-26, **17**-28
Unrecovered costs of annuities, **5**-12n
Unreimbursed employee business expenses, **6**-3
Unrelated business income, **15**-21
Unrelated business income tax (UBIT), **15**-21
Upstream acquisitions, **19**-26
U.S. Bureau of Economic Analysis, **24**-2, **24**-2n
U.S. Circuit Court of Appeals, **2**-7–10, **2**-15, **B**-17
U.S. Constitution, **1**-12, **2**-11, **2**-12, **4**-20, **23**-5, **B**-17
U.S. Court of Federal Claims, **2**-6–8, **2**-10, **2**-15, **B**-17
U.S. district court, **2**-6–8, **2**-10, **2**-15, **B**-17
U.S. President, tax law authority of, **2**-12–14
U.S. savings bonds, **5**-26–27, **7**-3, **7**-4, **7**-4n, **7**-8n, **B**-17
U.S. shareholders, **24**-16
U.S. Supreme Court
  in appeals process, **2**-8
  citations, **2**-10
  defined, **B**-17
  on income tax, **1**-12
  Internal Revenue Code and, **2**-14, **2**-14n
  stare decisis and, **2**-15
  on Treasury regulations, **2**-16
U.S. Tax Court
  allocation method, **14**-18–20, **B**-16
  in appeals process, **2**-6–8, **2**-7n
  citations, **2**-10
  defined, **B**-17
  memorandum decisions, **2**-10, **2**-15n
  regular decisions, **2**-10, **2**-15n
  rental expenses, method of allocating, **14**-18–20, **14**-18n
  Small Claims Division, **2**-7, **2**-7n, **2**-15n
  as source of tax law, **2**-15
U.S. Treasury bonds, **1**-20, **7**-3–4, **7**-3n
U.S. Treasury Department, **1**-2n, **2**-15–17; *see also* Internal Revenue Service (IRS)
Useful life, **10**-8
Use tax
  defined, **B**-17
  for e-commerce sales, **23**-8
  liability, **23**-4, **23**-4n, **23**-7
  process for, **23**-3–4, **23**-4n
  tax base for, **1**-14–15
Use test, **5**-22, **14**-2–3, **14**-5
UTBs (unrecognized tax benefits), **17**-26, **17**-28
UTPs; *see* Uncertain tax positions

Vacation homes, **14**-18–23
Valuation
  estate tax and, **25**-21–22
  gift tax and, **25**-7–8
  gross estate, **25**-21–22
  of remainders and other temporal interests, **25**-7–8
  special use, **25**-21
Valuation allowance
  defined, **B**-17
  determining need for, **17**-20–22
  expected future taxable income, **17**-21
  future reversals of temporary differences, **17**-20
  journal entries, **17**-21–22
  negative evidence that allowance is needed, **17**-21
  taxable income in prior carryback years, **17**-21
  tax planning strategies and, **17**-21
Value-added taxes, **1**-11–12, **B**-17
Value of remainder interest, **25**-7–8
Varying interest rule, **21**-8
Vehicles; *see* Automobiles
Venture capital firms, **22**-3
Vertical equity, **1**-21, **B**-17
Vesting
  cliff, **13**-4
  defined, **B**-17
  defined benefit plans and, **13**-4
  defined contribution plans and, **13**-8–9
  graded, **13**-4, **B**-8
  stock options and, **12**-9, **12**-10, **12**-15–17, **12**-19, **16**-10
Vesting dates, **12**-9, **12**-9n, **12**-10, **12**-16–17, **B**-17
Vesting period, **12**-15, **12**-19, **13**-4n, **16**-11, **B**-17
Vesting requirements, **13**-4n, **20**-10n
Virginia Tax Review (University of Virginia School of Law), **2**-11
Virtual currencies, **7**-8, **9**-3, **11**-7
Visteon Corporation, **18**-15
Voluntary revocations, **22**-5
Voluntary termination of S corporations, **22**-5
Voss v. Commissioner (2015), **14**-12
Voting power, **19**-5, **19**-5n, **19**-34, **19**-34n, **24**-16
Voting stock, **19**-5, **19**-29
Voting trusts, **22**-2n

Wage-based limits, **6**-31, **15**-9, **15**-11, **15**-13, **15**-14
Wage replacement insurance, **5**-30
Wages; *see* Salary and wages
Wainwright, John, **14**-9–10
Walmart's Proxy Statement (2021), **12**-24
Walt Disney Company's Proxy Statement (2021), **12**-33–34
Wamhoff, Steve, **16**-8
Warranties, **23**-13
Wash sales, **7**-23–25, **B**-17
Watson, David, **15**-25
Waxler Towing Co., Inc. v. United States (1981), **2**-10
Wayfair, **23**-5, **23**-6
Ways and Means Committee (House of Representatives), **2**-10, **2**-12, **2**-13
The Wealth of Nations (Smith), **1**-17n
Wealth planning, **25**-30–34
  generation-skipping tax, **25**-2, **25**-30
  income tax considerations, **25**-30–31
  integrated wealth plans, **25**-33–34
  serial gifts and, **25**-31
  step-up in tax basis and, **25**-31–33
  transfer tax planning techniques, **25**-31–33
Wealth tax proposal, **13**-29
Web sales; *see* E-commerce
Welch v. Helvering (1933), **9**-4n
Weyerhaeuser, **10**-2–3, **10**-22
Wherewithal to pay, **5**-3, **B**-18
Widows/widowers
  defined, **B**-13
  gross income thresholds (2022), **2**-2
  individual income tax formula and, **4**-22
  sale of personal residence and, **14**-5
  standard deduction for, **4**-10, **C**-2
  tax rate schedule for, **C**-1
William Wrigley Jr. Company, **23**-12–14, **23**-12n
Willing-buyer, willing-seller rule, **25**-4
Wisconsin Department of Revenue v. William Wrigley, Jr. Co. (1992), **23**-12–14, **23**-12n
Withholdings, **4**-12, **8**-36, **12**-2, **24**-3, **24**-3n, **24**-18n, **B**-18
Woodard v. Commissioner (2009), **2**-11
Workers' compensation, **5**-29
Working condition fringe benefits, **5**-24, **12**-26, **12**-30, **B**-18
Work opportunity credit, **8**-34
Writ of certiorari, **2**-8, **23**-11, **B**-18

XBiotech, **18**-26

Yauch, Eric, **22**-17

0/15/20 percent category, **7**-12–15, **7**-21, **7**-34–36, **11**-15
Zero-coupon bonds, **7**-3, **B**-18
Zuckerberg, Mark, **16**-12